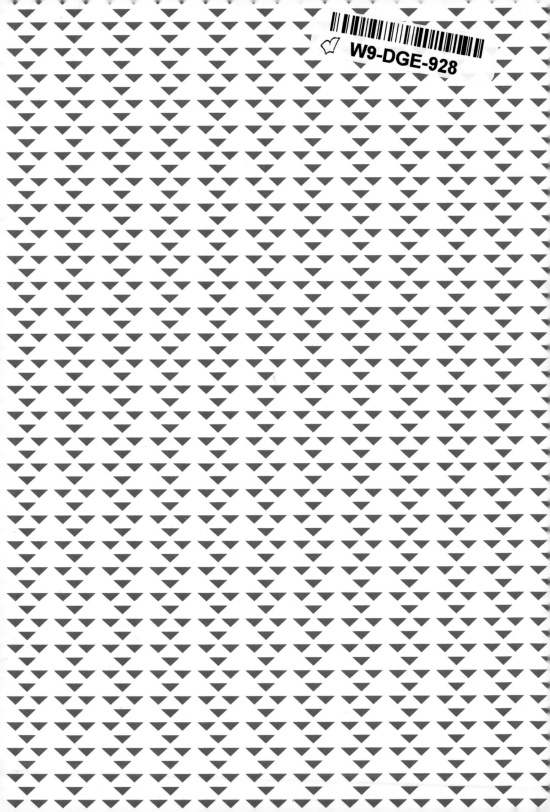

presented to

_____

by

_____

on

_____

She Reads Truth

BIBLE

RAECHEL MYERS - *General Editor*

AMANDA BIBLE WILLIAMS - *General Editor*

TREVIN WAX, PHD - *Publisher*

MELISSA FULLER - *Managing Editor*

HOLMAN®
BIBLES

NASHVILLE, TENNESSEE

The interior of the *She Reads Truth Bible* was designed and typeset using Bible Serif created by 2K/DENMARK, Højbjerg, Denmark. Proofreading of the CSB Scripture text was provided by Peachtree Editorial Services, Peachtree City, Georgia.

Author is represented by Alive Literary Agency, 7680 Goddard Street, Suite 200, Colorado Springs, Colorado, 80920, www.aliveliterary.com.

Binding	ISBN
Gray Linen Cloth	978-1-4336-4819-9
Gray Linen Cloth (Indexed)	978-1-4336-4820-5
Poppy Linen Cloth	978-1-4336-4821-2
Poppy Linen Cloth (Indexed)	978-1-4336-4822-9
Brown Genuine Cowhide	978-1-4336-4823-6
Brown Genuine Cowhide (Indexed)	978-1-4336-4825-0
Champagne Gold LeatherTouch	978-1-5359-7097-6
Champagne Gold LeatherTouch (Indexed)	978-1-5359-7098-3
Navy LeatherTouch	978-1-4336-1382-1
Navy LeatherTouch (Indexed)	978-1-4336-4824-3
Rose Gold LeatherTouch	978-1-5359-7099-0
Rose Gold LeatherTouch (Indexed)	978-1-5359-7100-3

Printed in China
10 11 12 13 14 15 16 — 26 25 24 23 22 21 20
RRD

*"The instruction of the LORD is perfect,
renewing one's life;
the testimony of the LORD is trustworthy,
making the inexperienced wise."*

PSALM 19:7

"Women in the Word of God every day" is our simple but significant mission. Even so, when the *She Reads Truth Bible* was a twinkle in our eyes, we trembled at the thought of interacting with God's Word in such an intimate way.

We believe there is nothing we or anyone else can add to Scripture to make it more relevant, more important, or more true. It is already all of those things. God's Word is living and active, and we confidently hold it higher than anything we do or say.

So why create a She Reads Truth Bible?

This Bible is our humble attempt to honor the inherently beautiful gospel with the aesthetic beauty it deserves. Scripture is a glorious collision of beauty, goodness, and truth, and we pray this book you hold in your hands represents that.

Our heart for the *She Reads Truth Bible* is not to add to or improve on the perfect and complete gift of Scripture God has given us. Rather, our heart is for everything we've included in this Bible to point back to God and His Word. Every human word and element in this book is an intentional invitation for you to both read Scripture and grow in your affection for it.

Each devotional seeks to show the gospel in every passage. We believe God is the main character of every story and it is our delight to find Him there.

The book introductions not only give cultural and geographical context, they place each book in context of the whole of Scripture. Each book also has its own reading plan with supplemental passages, intentionally making room for Scripture to interpret Scripture.

The Key Verse for each book was selected not simply as an artistic element, but as a tool to remember the theme of each individual book. Together, these 66 verses present the complete arc of Scripture, book by book.

Our earnest prayer is that our imperfect offerings on these pages highlight the perfection of Scripture, drawing you more deeply into the story of salvation. By the grace of God and the counsel of the Holy Spirit, may you become like the tree in Psalm 1, planted by streams of water, "that bears its fruit in its season and whose leaf does not wither" (v. 3). May you grow in affection for this beautiful, good, and true Book, and may you be a woman in the Word of God every day.

Grace and Peace to you,

Raechel Myers *Amanda Bible Williams*

Raechel Myers
Amanda Bible Williams
She Reads Truth, 2017

TABLE OF CONTENTS

BOOKS OF THE BIBLE

OLD TESTAMENT

NEW TESTAMENT

HOW TO READ THE BIBLE

We used to read our Bibles out of obligation. Perhaps you have too. Now we read our Bibles because it feels like coming home.

We used to read our Bibles out of fear. Maybe you know the feeling. Now we read our Bibles for a fresh breath of the truest freedom we've ever known.

We used to read our Bibles to find ourselves. Now we read our Bibles to find God.

We read our Bibles because God's Word is living and active, given to us for our salvation and sanctification, our instruction and correction, our comfort and joy.

We read our Bibles not just because we feel lost, but because without Him we are lost. We read our Bibles because we need the good news of the gospel every single day.

The Bible is God's Word. Every word of Scripture is living and active, breathed out by God, inspired by the Holy Spirit, and written and preserved by human writers (Heb 4:12; 2Tm 3:16-17; 2Pt 1:21).

The Bible is a historical record. The Old Testament records the creation of the world, the fall of man, the establishment of God's covenant with Israel, and the promise and anticipation of a Savior (Gn 2:4). The New Testament tells the true story of the birth, death and resurrection of that Savior, Jesus Christ, the birth of the Church, and the promise of Christ's return (Mt 1:1).

The Bible is meant to be read. Because God's Word is true, even the parts that are sad or scary or difficult to understand are good news. Every page, from cover to cover, is given that we might know God (Mt 4:4).

The Bible is for you. No amount of knowledge or wisdom makes you more or less qualified to meet God in His Word. Nothing you are doing, have done, or will do renders you ineligible for the good news of the gospel (1Tm 2:3-4).

The Bible is for right now. You can read the Bible right where you are, just as you are. It is the only living and active book in the world (Heb 4:12), and we can trust the Holy Spirit to illuminate the words He has already inspired (2Tm 3:16). The Bible exists for moments like this—the moment you lay it open and look for Him (Jn 20:31).

APPROACH GOD'S WORD

Approach it reverently. Because the Bible is living and active, given by God Himself, it is a profoundly powerful tool. God's Word must be approached with respect and reverence, even awe (Ps 111:10).

Approach it confidently. We are invited to read the inspired, complete, and sufficient Word of God with the Author Himself. You can approach the Bible, confident that it is for you and that you are not alone (Heb 4:16).

Approach it regularly. We can't approach God's Word only occasionally and expect our lives not to wither. God designed us to need Him, to be in an ongoing relationship with Him. One of the ways we grow in our relationship with Him is by spending regular time in His Word (Jms 4:8).

ENGAGE GOD'S WORD

Engage it expectantly. Each page of Scripture points to Jesus. Sometimes His presence is obvious (like in the Gospels) and other times it's perhaps more difficult to see (like in Leviticus). Keep looking, and expect to find Him there—the promised Rescuer, the healing Teacher, the suffering Messiah, and the returning Savior (Jn 1:1-4).

Engage it emotionally and intellectually. Engaging truth in only one way, whether with the most delicate emotions or the most advanced intellect, is to forfeit a full and true understanding of it (Ps 119:18). The gospel is a beautiful marriage of mind and spirit (Mt 22:37).

Engage it broadly. Reading God's Word as a complete work is an effective way to deepen our understanding of His story. We can learn much about Scripture by reading whole books at a time, even reading shorter books repeatedly. This is not the only way to read the Bible, but it is a powerful exercise, well worth the time and effort (Ps 119:105).

APPLY GOD'S WORD

Apply it appropriately. We would be foolish to approach God's Word looking only for how it applies to ourselves and others, forgetting to find what it says about Him. When we read our Bibles, we shouldn't first ask, "What does this mean to me?" but rather, "What does this mean?" (2Tm 2:15).

Apply it responsibly. Scripture is to be used for reproof (not injury), correction (not destruction), and training (not controlling) (2Tm 3:17).

Apply it permanently. When we memorize Scripture, we apply God's Word to our hearts and minds permanently, giving us tangible promises and clear direction. It's a way home for the home-sick (Jos 1:8).

READ PRAYERFULLY

Effective Bible reading can and should begin and end with prayer. Prayer affords us the privilege of approaching God the Father, allowing us to repent and intercede, petition and praise. Through the access granted us by Jesus, we can invite the Author Himself to be our companion as we read our Bibles (Mt 6:5-13).

BE DOERS OF THE WORD

James 1:22 instructs us to "be doers of the word, and not hearers only." Our lives are tangible reflections of the gospel we believe. Not because of who we are and what we do, but because of who He is and what He's done (Php 2:5-11).

We take God's Word with us, written on our hearts, with the Holy Spirit as our guide. When we abide in Christ, we are renewed by the power of His Word, even when we're not reading our Bibles (2Tm 2:7). Living out Truth is our job but it is our Father's work, and He is faithful to complete it (Php 1:6).

THE BIBLE IS GOD'S STORY

It is about His steadfast love for His people. It is about His sovereign plan, His grace, and His glory. You are meant to read it.

THIS IS THE GOSPEL

Do you know . . .

You were designed on purpose, with intention, love, and care.

You are broken—tragically broken. Not only by the sins you commit, but because of the sin nature in you.

You have hope—forgiveness and freedom for this moment and this season, for a lifetime and for eternity.

The gospel of Jesus Christ is every bit that simple, yet it is unfathomably profound. It is simple enough that a child can understand it, yet mysterious enough that the most educated theologians will always have more to learn. But don't misunderstand: the mystery of the gospel does nothing to negate its truth. As the Apostle Paul wrote, "now we see only a reflection as in a mirror, but then face to face. Now I know in part, but then I will know fully, as I am fully known " (1 Co 13:12).

For the word of the cross is foolishness to those who are perishing, but it is the power of God to us who are being saved. — 1 Corinthians 1:18

You bear God's image. The vastness of the ocean and the infinite reach of the sky, the delicate lines of snow-capped mountains and the majesty of God-carved canyons—none of these bears the image of the Creator Himself. The Bible tells us "the heavens declare the glory of God" (Ps 19:1), but when God created the world, He saved the best for last: *us.*

"So God created man in his own image;
he created him in the image of God;
he created them male and female" (Gn 1:27).

Glorifying God by bearing His image is our greatest calling. It is a call to humanness in its purest form, when God made us in His image and called us good.

God saw all that he had made, and it was very good indeed. — Genesis 1:31

We have all sinned. The perfection of creation was corrupted when Adam and Eve disobeyed God. God gave them one command: "you must not eat from the tree of the knowledge of good and evil" (Gn 2:17). We sin when we believe God is trying to keep the good stuff from us, when we become convinced that what we want is better than what God has for us. Adam and Eve believed that lie, and there was no undoing what had been done (Gn 3:4-5).

The consequence of that first sin was death (Gn 3:19), not only for Adam and Eve, but for all mankind. The human race is corporately guilty because of Adam's sin, and each one of us is individually guilty because of our own sin (Rm 3:23). Instead of paradise, we live in a broken, fallen world where the Enemy comes to kill, steal, and destroy (Jn 10:10).

For the wages of sin is death, but the gift of God is eternal life in Christ Jesus our Lord. — Romans 6:23

Death is not the whole story. Even before God gave Adam and Eve consequences for their sin, He promised redemption (Gn 3:15). God had a plan to make us new again, to give us life though we were dead in our sins (Eph 2:4).

In His steadfast love for His creation, God became man. Jesus was Immanuel, "God with us," walking among the people He came to save (Mt 1:23; Jn 1:1-3,14). Fully obedient to the Father and without sin, Jesus was the spotless Lamb. He was the only sacrifice that could pay the debt of our disobedience. In His immeasurable love for us, Jesus suffered a criminal's death on a cross (Rm 5:8). He took on our sins and took our place (Heb 10:10).

He humbled himself by becoming obedient to the point of death—even to death on a cross. — Philippians 2:8

Jesus is alive, and so is our hope. After three days in the grave, Jesus rose from the dead (Mt 28:6). He left the tomb and grave clothes behind and appeared to many, then ascended into heaven. Even now, He sits at the right hand of God the Father (Mk 16:19; Heb 10:12). Death has lost its power, swallowed up in the resurrection of Christ (1Co 15:55-56).

The everlasting life of Jesus is ours when we turn from our sin and trust in the love and perfection of Christ (Jn 3:16). God's Word promises "if we confess our sins, he is faithful and righteous to forgive us our sins and to cleanse us from all unrighteousness" (1Jn 1:9). Our sins are charged to Him. His righteousness is credited to us (Rm 8:3-5).

Because the penalty for our sin has been paid by Christ's death, we are no longer under a curse. We have victory in this lifetime, and we have the hope of eternity with Christ in the life to come. In Christ, we can stand before God blameless and beloved. Nothing and no one can ever separate us from His love (Rm 8:38-39).

This is good news! This is the gospel.

Since by the one man's trespass, death reigned through that one man, how much more will those who receive the overflow of grace and the gift of righteousness reign in life through the one man, Jesus Christ. — Romans 5:17

KEY FEATURES

GENRE INDICATOR

Because each literary style should be approached differently, we've color-coded the various genres to make them easy to locate and identify.

KEY VERSES

One theme verse was chosen for each individual book. Together, these 66 verses represent the complete arc of Scripture.

KEY VERSE ART: Each key verse has been beautifully hand-lettered by one of fifteen different artists. The key verse art serves to aid in memorization and celebrates the beauty of the gospel.

INTRODUCTION

CULTURAL CONTEXT: Each book introduction includes a brief overview of the approximate date of writing, authorship, historical context, and relevant geography.

MESSAGE & PURPOSE: Each introduction also identifies main themes of the writing.

BIBLICAL SIGNIFICANCE: This note identifies how we can give thanks for each book's unique contribution to the canon of Scripture.

MAPS Placing the book in its geographical context helps us understand its cultural context.

LAYOUT

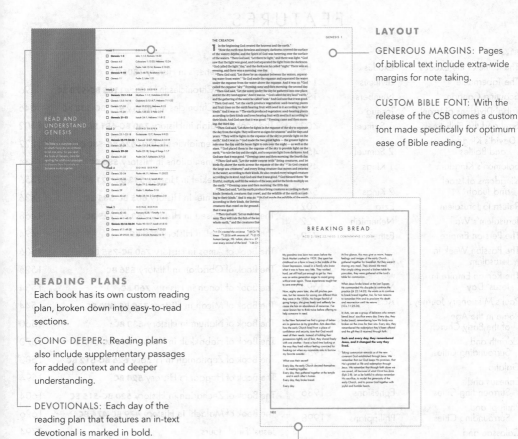

GENEROUS MARGINS: Pages of biblical text include extra-wide margins for note taking.

CUSTOM BIBLE FONT: With the release of the CSB comes a custom font made specifically for optimum ease of Bible reading.

READING PLANS

Each book has its own custom reading plan, broken down into easy-to-read sections.

GOING DEEPER: Reading plans also include supplementary passages for added context and deeper understanding.

DEVOTIONALS: Each day of the reading plan that features an in-text devotional is marked in bold.

DEVOTIONALS

Throughout the text, find 189 written responses to Scripture. Each devotional focuses on a particular passage and seeks to point solely to God and the gospel.

CHARTS

The charts provided illustrate how different passages of the Bible connect and relate to one another, highlighting themes of a particular book and the whole canon of Scripture.

TIMELINES

Including significant biblical and world events, the timelines provide historical context for the action of the book.

2091

2085

2066

2006

Destruction of Sodom and Gomorrah

Abraham moves to Canaan

Birth of Isaac

Birth of Jacob

FEATURES

INTRODUCTION TO THE CHRISTIAN STANDARD BIBLE®

The Bible is God's revelation to humanity. It is our only source for completely reliable information about God, what happens when we die, and where history is headed. The Bible does these things because it is God's inspired Word, inerrant in the original manuscripts. Bible translation brings God's Word from the ancient languages (Hebrew, Greek, and Aramaic) into today's world. In dependence on God's Spirit to accomplish this sacred task, the CSB Translation Oversight Committee and Holman Bible Publishers present the Christian Standard Bible.

Textual Base of the CSB

The textual base for the New Testament (NT) is the Nestle-Aland *Novum Testamentum Graece*, 28th edition, and the United Bible Societies' *Greek New Testament*, 5th corrected edition. The text for the Old Testament (OT) is the *Biblia Hebraica Stuttgartensia*, 5th edition.

Where there are significant differences among Hebrew, Aramaic, or Greek manuscripts, the translators follow what they believe is the original reading and indicate the main alternative(s) in footnotes. The CSB uses the traditional verse divisions found in most Protestant Bibles.

Goals of This Translation

- Provide English-speaking people worldwide with an accurate translation in contemporary English.
- Provide an accurate translation for personal study, sermon preparation, private devotions, and memorization.
- Provide a text that is clear and understandable, suitable for public reading, and shareable so that all may access its life-giving message.
- Affirm the authority of Scripture and champion its absolute truth against skeptical viewpoints.

Translation Philosophy of the CSB

Most discussions of Bible translations speak of two opposite approaches: formal equivalence and dynamic equivalence. This terminology is meaningful, but Bible translations cannot be neatly sorted into these two categories. There is room for another category of translation philosophy that capitalizes on the strengths of the other two.

1. Formal Equivalence:

Often called "word-for-word" (or "literal") translation, the principle of formal equivalence seeks as nearly as possible to preserve the structure of the original language. It seeks to represent each word of the original text with an exact equivalent word in the translation so that the reader can see word for word what the original human author wrote. The merits of this approach include its consistency with the conviction that the Holy Spirit did inspire the very words of Scripture in the original manuscripts. It also provides the English Bible student some access to the structure of the text in the original language. Formal equivalence can achieve accuracy to the degree that English has an exact equivalent for each word and that the grammatical patterns of the original language can be reproduced in understandable English. However, it can sometimes result in awkward, if not incomprehensible, English or in a misunderstanding of the author's intent. The literal rendering of ancient idioms is especially difficult.

2. Dynamic or Functional Equivalence:

Often called "thought-for-thought" translation, the principle of dynamic equivalence rejects as misguided the attempt to preserve the structure of the original language. It proceeds by extracting the meaning of a text from its form and then translating that meaning so that it makes the same impact on modern readers that the ancient text made on its original readers. Strengths of this approach include a high degree of clarity and readability, especially in places where the original is difficult to render word for word. It also acknowledges that accurate and effective translation may require interpretation. However, the meaning of a text cannot always be neatly separated from its form, nor can it always be precisely determined. A biblical author may have intended multiple meanings, but these may be lost with the elimination of normal structures. In striving for readability, dynamic equivalence also sometimes overlooks and loses some of the less prominent elements of meaning. Furthermore, lack of formal correspondence to the original makes it difficult to verify accuracy and thus can affect the usefulness of the translation for in-depth Bible study.

3. Optimal Equivalence:

In practice, translations are seldom if ever purely formal or dynamic but favor one theory of Bible translation or the other to varying degrees. Optimal equivalence as a translation philosophy recognizes that form cannot always be neatly separated from meaning and should not be changed unless comprehension demands it. The primary goal of translation is to convey the sense of the original with as much clarity as the original text and the translation language permit. Optimal equivalence appreciates the goals of formal equivalence but also recognizes its limitations. Optimal equivalence starts with an exhaustive analysis of the text at every level (word, phrase, clause, sentence, discourse) in the original language to determine its original meaning and intention (or purpose). Then, relying on the latest and best language tools and experts, the nearest corresponding semantic and linguistic equivalents are used to convey as much of the information and intention of the original text with as much clarity and readability as possible. This process assures the maximum transfer of both the words and the thoughts contained in the original.

The CSB uses optimal equivalence as its translation philosophy. In the many places throughout the Bible where a word-for-word rendering is understandable, a literal translation is used. When a word-for-word rendering might obscure the meaning for a modern audience, a more dynamic translation is used. The Christian Standard Bible places equal value on fidelity to the original and readability for a modern audience, resulting in a translation that achieves both goals.

The Gender Language Use in Bible Translation
The goal of the translators of the Christian Standard Bible has not been to promote a cultural ideology but to translate the Bible faithfully. Recognizing modern usage of English, the CSB regularly translates the plural of the Greek word ανθρωπος ("man") as "people" instead of "men," and occasionally the singular as "one," "someone," or "everyone," when the supporting pronouns in the original languages validate such a translation. While the CSB avoids using "he" or "him" unnecessarily, the translation does not restructure sentences to avoid them when they are in the text.

History of the CSB
After several years of preliminary development, Holman Bible Publishers, the oldest Bible publisher in North America, assembled an international, interdenominational team of one hundred scholars, editors, stylists, and proofreaders, all of whom were committed to biblical inerrancy. Outside consultants and reviewers contributed valuable suggestions from their areas of expertise. Working with the original languages, an executive team of translators edited, polished, and reviewed the final manuscript, which was first published as the Holman Christian Standard Bible (HCSB) in 2004.

A standing committee was also formed to maintain the HCSB translation and look for ways to improve readability without compromising accuracy. As with the original translation team, the committee that prepared this revision of the HCSB, renamed the Christian Standard Bible is international and interdenominational, comprising evangelical scholars who honor the inspiration and authority of God's written Word.

Traditional Features Found in the CSB
In keeping with a long line of Bible publications, the CSB has retained a number of features found in traditional Bibles:
1. Traditional theological vocabulary (for example, *justification, sanctification, redemption*) has been retained since such terms have no other translation equivalent that adequately communicates their exact meaning.
2. Traditional spellings of names and places found in most Bibles have been used to make the CSB compatible with most Bible study tools.
3. Some editions of the CSB will print the words of Christ in red letters to help readers easily locate the spoken words of the Lord Jesus Christ.
4. Descriptive headings, printed above each section of Scripture, help readers quickly identify the contents of that section.
5. OT passages quoted in the NT are indicated. In the CSB, they are set in boldface type.

Abbreviations in CSB Bibles

AD	In the year of our Lord
BC	before Christ
c.	century
ca	circa
chap(s).	chapter(s)
cp.	compare
DSS	Dead Sea Scrolls
e.g.	for example
Eng	English
etc.	et cetera
Gk	Greek
Hb	Hebrew
i.e.	that is
Lat	Latin
lit	literal(ly)
LXX	Septuagint—an ancient translation of the Old Testament into Greek
MT	Masoretic Text
NT	New Testament
ms(s)	manuscript(s)
OT	Old Testament
pl.	plural
Ps(s)	Psalm(s)
Sam	Samaritan Pentateuch
sg.	singular
Sym	Symmachus
Syr	Syriac
Tg	Targum
Theod	Theodotian
v./vv.	verse, verses
Vg	Vulgate—an ancient translation of the Bible into Latin
vol(s).	volume(s)

the
OLD TESTAMENT

genesis

 God saw all that he had made, and it was very good indeed. **1:31**

ON THE TIMELINE Authorship of the Torah (the first five books of the Old Testament) has consistently been attributed to Moses, an influential Israelite leader from the fifteenth century BC. Though Genesis is technically anonymous, both the Old and New Testaments recognize Moses as the Torah's author. Genesis was likely written during the forty years when the Israelites wandered in the desert (1446 BC–1406 BC). The events in Genesis begin at creation and conclude about 1800 BC with the circumstances leading up to the Israelites' time in the land of Egypt.

A LITTLE BACKGROUND The Torah (also a Hebrew term for "law") was seen as one unit until at least the second century BC. Some time before Christ was born it was divided into five separate books, later referred to as the Pentateuch. Genesis can be divided into two sections: the "primeval history," or the general history found in chapters 1–11, and the "patriarchal history," or the history focusing on God's covenant with Abraham and his descendants, found in chapters 12–50.

MESSAGE & PURPOSE Genesis is a book of new beginnings. It reveals the beginning of the heavens and the earth, of humanity and marriage, of sin and nations and languages, and the beginning of our need for a Savior. In Genesis we see that all God's creation was, in the beginning, thoroughly good; and in Genesis we see mankind's first sin and the consequences of that sin. All of our brokenness begins here, in the first book of the Bible, as does God's covenant to redeem His people.

Genesis provides both the universal history of humankind and the patriarchal history of the nation of Israel. It unfolds God's plan to bless and redeem humanity through Abraham's descendants, remaining faithful to His people despite their unfaithfulness to Him.

GIVE THANKS FOR THE BOOK OF GENESIS:

Genesis lays the groundwork for everything else we read and experience in Scripture. Through Genesis we understand where we came from, how we fell, and the beginning of God's gracious work on our behalf. Genesis establishes our foundational understanding of God's covenant with Israel through the giving of the Law. Without an understanding of the Law, we are unable to see our desperate need for our Savior, Jesus Christ.

THE BOOK OF GENESIS IN HISTORY

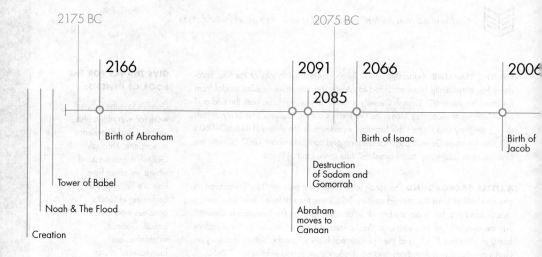

2175 BC

2166 — Birth of Abraham

Tower of Babel

Noah & The Flood

Creation

2075 BC

2091 — Abraham moves to Canaan

2085 — Destruction of Sodom and Gomorrah

2066 — Birth of Isaac

2006 — Birth of Jacob

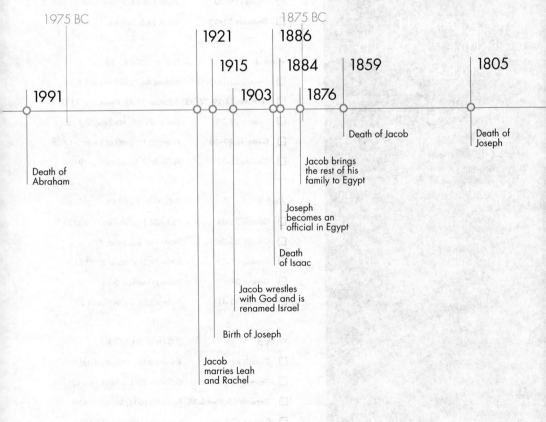

1975 BC

1921

1915

1875 BC

1886

1884

1859

1805

1991

1903

1876

Death of
Abraham

Death of Jacob

Death of
Joseph

Jacob brings
the rest of his
family to Egypt

Joseph
becomes an
official in Egypt

Death
of Isaac

Jacob wrestles
with God and is
renamed Israel

Birth of Joseph

Jacob
marries Leah
and Rachel

READ AND UNDERSTAND GENESIS

The Bible is a complete work in which many stories combine to tell one story. As you read the book of Genesis, consider reading the additional passages to discover how the whole of Scripture works together.

Week 1
GOING DEEPER

- [ ] **Genesis 1-3** — John 1:1-5; Romans 16:20
- [ ] Genesis 4-5 — Colossians 1:15-20; Hebrews 12:24
- [ ] Genesis 6-8 — Psalm 144:13-14; Romans 3:10-25
- [ ] **Genesis 9-10** — Luke 1:68-75; Revelation 10:1
- [ ] Genesis 11 — Psalm 2; Luke 1:51

Week 2
GOING DEEPER

- [ ] **Genesis 12:1–13:4** — Matthew 1:1-2; Galatians 3:10-14
- [ ] Genesis 13:5–16:16 — Galatians 3:15–4:7; Hebrews 7:11-22
- [ ] Genesis 17–18 — Mark 10:23-31; Hebrews 9:15
- [ ] Genesis 19–20 — Psalm 136:23; 2 Peter 2:7-9
- [ ] **Genesis 21–22** — Isaiah 54:1; Hebrews 11:8-12

Week 3
GOING DEEPER

- [ ] Genesis 23:1–25:18 — Ecclesiastes 12:7; Romans 9:9-23
- [ ] **Genesis 25:19–26:35** — 1 Samuel 14:47; Hebrews 6:13-18
- [ ] Genesis 27–28 — Psalm 121:5-8; Matthew 20:1-16
- [ ] **Genesis 29–30** — Psalm 25:18; Song of Songs 1:1-7
- [ ] Genesis 31–32 — Psalm 34:7; Ephesians 3:7-12

Week 4
GOING DEEPER

- [ ] Genesis 33–34 — Psalm 44:11; Hebrews 11:20-22
- [ ] Genesis 35–36 — Psalm 116:1-2; Isaiah 43:2
- [ ] Genesis 37–38 — Psalm 77:2; Matthew 27:27-31
- [ ] Genesis 39 — Psalm 1; Matthew 5:16
- [ ] Genesis 40–41 — Psalm 25:14; 2 Corinthians 3:5

Week 5
GOING DEEPER

- [ ] Genesis 42–43 — Romans 8:28; 1 Timothy 1:16
- [ ] Genesis 44:1–45:15 — Galatians 3:14; 1 Peter 1:10-12
- [ ] **Genesis 45:16–46:34** — Psalm 90:10-17; Isaiah 41:8-10
- [ ] Genesis 47:1–49:28 — Isaiah 63:9; Hebrews 7:23-25
- [ ] Genesis 49:29-33; 50 — Acts 2:22-24; Romans 12:19

THE CREATION

1 In the beginning God created the heavens and the earth.[A]

² Now the earth was formless and empty, darkness covered the surface of the watery depths, and the Spirit of God was hovering over the surface of the waters. ³ Then God said, "Let there be light," and there was light. ⁴ God saw that the light was good, and God separated the light from the darkness. ⁵ God called the light "day," and the darkness he called "night." There was an evening, and there was a morning: one day.

⁶ Then God said, "Let there be an expanse between the waters, separating water from water." ⁷ So God made the expanse and separated the water under the expanse from the water above the expanse. And it was so. ⁸ God called the expanse "sky."[B] Evening came and then morning: the second day.

⁹ Then God said, "Let the water under the sky be gathered into one place, and let the dry land appear." And it was so. ¹⁰ God called the dry land "earth," and the gathering of the water he called "seas." And God saw that it was good. ¹¹ Then God said, "Let the earth produce vegetation: seed-bearing plants and fruit trees on the earth bearing fruit with seed in it according to their kinds." And it was so. ¹² The earth produced vegetation: seed-bearing plants according to their kinds and trees bearing fruit with seed in it according to their kinds. And God saw that it was good. ¹³ Evening came and then morning: the third day.

¹⁴ Then God said, "Let there be lights in the expanse of the sky to separate the day from the night. They will serve as signs for seasons[C] and for days and years. ¹⁵ They will be lights in the expanse of the sky to provide light on the earth." And it was so. ¹⁶ God made the two great lights — the greater light to rule over the day and the lesser light to rule over the night — as well as the stars. ¹⁷ God placed them in the expanse of the sky to provide light on the earth, ¹⁸ to rule the day and the night, and to separate light from darkness. And God saw that it was good. ¹⁹ Evening came and then morning: the fourth day.

²⁰ Then God said, "Let the water swarm with[D] living creatures, and let birds fly above the earth across the expanse of the sky." ²¹ So God created the large sea-creatures[E] and every living creature that moves and swarms in the water, according to their kinds. He also created every winged creature according to its kind. And God saw that it was good. ²² God blessed them: "Be fruitful, multiply, and fill the waters of the seas, and let the birds multiply on the earth." ²³ Evening came and then morning: the fifth day.

²⁴ Then God said, "Let the earth produce living creatures according to their kinds: livestock, creatures that crawl, and the wildlife of the earth according to their kinds." And it was so. ²⁵ So God made the wildlife of the earth according to their kinds, the livestock according to their kinds, and all the creatures that crawl on the ground according to their kinds. And God saw that it was good.

²⁶ Then God said, "Let us make man[F] in[G] our image, according to our likeness. They will rule the fish of the sea, the birds of the sky, the livestock, the whole earth,[H] and the creatures that crawl[I] on the earth."

[A]1:1 Or *created the universe* [B]1:8 Or *"heavens."* [C]1:14 Or *for the appointed times* [D]1:20 Lit *with swarms of* [E]1:21 Or *created sea monsters* [F]1:26 Or *human beings*; Hb *'adam*, also in v. 27 [G]1:26 Or *as* [H]1:26 Syr reads *sky, and over every animal of the land* [I]1:26 Or *scurry*

²⁷ So God created man in his own image;
he created him in^A the image of God;
he created them male and female.

²⁸ God blessed them, and God said to them, "Be fruitful, multiply, fill the earth, and subdue it. Rule the fish of the sea, the birds of the sky, and every creature that crawls^B on the earth." ²⁹ God also said, "Look, I have given you every seed-bearing plant on the surface of the entire earth and every tree whose fruit contains seed. This will be food for you, ³⁰ for all the wildlife of the earth, for every bird of the sky, and for every creature that crawls on the earth — everything having the breath of life in it — I have given^C every green plant for food." And it was so. ³¹ God saw all that he had made, and it was very good indeed. Evening came and then morning: the sixth day.

2 So the heavens and the earth and everything in them were completed. ² On the seventh^D day God had completed his work that he had done, and he rested^E on the seventh day from all his work that he had done. ³ God blessed the seventh day and declared it holy, for on it he rested from all his work of creation.^F

MAN AND WOMAN IN THE GARDEN

⁴ These are the records of the heavens and the earth, concerning their creation. At the time^G that the Lord God made the earth and the heavens, ⁵ no shrub of the field had yet grown on the land,^H and no plant of the field had yet sprouted, for the Lord God had not made it rain on the land, and there was no man to work the ground. ⁶ But mist would come up from the earth and water all the ground. ⁷ Then the Lord God formed the man out of the dust from the ground and breathed the breath of life into his nostrils, and the man became a living being.

⁸ The Lord God planted a garden in Eden, in the east, and there he placed the man he had formed. ⁹ The Lord God caused to grow out of the ground every tree pleasing in appearance and good for food, including the tree of life in the middle of the garden, as well as the tree of the knowledge of good and evil.

¹⁰ A river went^I out from Eden to water the garden. From there it divided and became the source of four rivers.^J ¹¹ The name of the first is Pishon, which flows through the entire land of Havilah,^K where there is gold. ¹² Gold from that land is pure;^L bdellium^M and onyx^N are also there. ¹³ The name of the second river is Gihon, which flows through the entire land of Cush. ¹⁴ The name of the third river is Tigris, which runs east of Assyria. And the fourth river is the Euphrates.

¹⁵ The Lord God took the man and placed him in the garden of Eden to work it and watch over it. ¹⁶ And the Lord God commanded the man, "You are free to eat from any tree of the garden, ¹⁷ but you must not eat from the tree of the knowledge of good and evil, for on the day you eat from it, you will certainly die." ¹⁸ Then the Lord God said, "It is not good for the man to be

---

^A1:27 Or *man as his own image; he created him as*   ^B1:28 Or *and all scurrying animals*   ^C1:30 *I have given* added for clarity   ^D2:2 Sam, LXX, Syr read *sixth*   ^E2:2 Or *ceased*, also in v. 3   ^F2:3 Lit *work that God created to make*   ^G2:4 Lit *creation on the day*   ^H2:5 Or *earth*   ^I2:10 Or *goes*   ^J2:10 Lit *became four heads*   ^K2:11 Or *of the Havilah*   ^L2:12 Lit *good*   ^M2:12 A yellowish, transparent gum resin   ^N2:12 Identity of this precious stone uncertain

CLOSING THE DOOR ON SHAME

GENESIS 1–3; JOHN 1:1-5; ROMANS 16:20

When I read the chapters at the beginning of the Bible, where the world and all its inhabitants were as they were meant to be, a piece of me wants to pretend the story stops there.

God hung the stars, separated the waters, and created things so incredible and intricately beautiful our eyes can hardly make sense of them. "God saw all that he had made, and it was very good indeed" (Gn 1:31). The end.

I want to stay in that story—the story of untainted perfection, the story where God made Adam and Eve, and they "felt no shame" (Gn 2:25). Can you imagine?

Eve wasn't afraid to sing for fear someone might hear her. She wasn't ashamed of her teeth, her accent, or the shape of her toes. She could've been a size 2 or 22, with green eyes and curly hair, or brown eyes and straight hair. However Eve looked, she certainly wasn't ashamed of it! She walked around Eden with Adam, unashamed and at peace with her Maker.

Then along comes Genesis 3, and all the trombones in my head collectively "womp womp." In disobedience, Adam and Eve sought to become like God. They made the decision that who they were wasn't enough—they wanted more. With their sin came shame.

Genesis 3:7 says, "Then the eyes of both of them were opened, and they knew they were naked," so they made coverings to hide their nakedness. But all the fig leaves in Eden wouldn't hide the sin in their souls. Adam and Eve were ashamed to be seen by God—they were ashamed of their sin.

Shame is a powerful force. Like Satan himself, it tells us all kinds of lies. But isn't it interesting: Satan has a way of making us feel less ashamed of our sin (the thing that separates us from God), and more ashamed of ourselves (the thing that links us to Him).

When facing the world, we're ashamed of our image, God-given though it is. When facing God, we're ashamed of our sin. Shame is a double-headed monster from which there seems to be no escape. No wonder Eve wanted to hide!

But God has such good news for us today: there is a cure for shame of all kinds and for all time! "Therefore, there is now no condemnation for those in Christ Jesus" (Rm 8:1). We can call off the impossible search for a fig leaf large enough to hide our sin and shame from God. Adam and Eve let shame in the door, but Jesus bore the shame of the whole world on the cross, taking it to the grave with Him. He defeated sin and shame, and death itself, so we can be presented blameless and unashamed to the Father.

Jesus closed the door on shame and opened the door to repentance and freedom. Let us live in that freedom today.

alone. I will make a helper corresponding to him." ¹⁹ The LORD God formed out of the ground every wild animal and every bird of the sky, and brought each to the man to see what he would call it. And whatever the man called a living creature, that was its name. ²⁰ The man gave names to all the livestock, to the birds of the sky, and to every wild animal; but for the man[A] no helper was found corresponding to him. ²¹ So the LORD God caused a deep sleep to come over the man, and he slept. God took one of his ribs and closed the flesh at that place. ²² Then the LORD God made the rib he had taken from the man into a woman and brought her to the man. ²³ And the man said:

> This one, at last, is bone of my bone
> and flesh of my flesh;
> this one will be called "woman,"
> for she was taken from man.

²⁴ This is why a man leaves his father and mother and bonds with his wife, and they become one flesh. ²⁵ Both the man and his wife were naked, yet felt no shame.

THE TEMPTATION AND THE FALL

3 Now the serpent was the most cunning of all the wild animals that the LORD God had made. He said to the woman, "Did God really say, 'You can't eat from any tree in the garden'?"

² The woman said to the serpent, "We may eat the fruit from the trees in the garden. ³ But about the fruit of the tree in the middle of the garden, God said, 'You must not eat it or touch it, or you will die.'"

⁴ "No! You will not die," the serpent said to the woman. ⁵ "In fact, God knows that when[B] you eat it your eyes will be opened and you will be like God,[C] knowing good and evil." ⁶ The woman saw that the tree was good for food and delightful to look at, and that it was desirable for obtaining wisdom. So she took some of its fruit and ate it; she also gave some to her husband, who was with her, and he ate it. ⁷ Then the eyes of both of them were opened, and they knew they were naked; so they sewed fig leaves together and made coverings for themselves.

SIN'S CONSEQUENCES

⁸ Then the man and his wife heard the sound of the LORD God walking in the garden at the time of the evening breeze,[D] and they hid from the LORD God among the trees of the garden. ⁹ So the LORD God called out to the man and said to him, "Where are you?"

¹⁰ And he said, "I heard you[E] in the garden, and I was afraid because I was naked, so I hid."

¹¹ Then he asked, "Who told you that you were naked? Did you eat from the tree that I commanded you not to eat from?"

¹² The man replied, "The woman you gave to be with me — she gave me some fruit from the tree, and I ate."

¹³ So the LORD God asked the woman, "What is this you have done?"

And the woman said, "The serpent deceived me, and I ate."

ᴬ2:20 Or for Adam   ᴮ3:5 Lit on the day   ᶜ3:5 Or gods, or divine beings
ᴰ3:8 Lit at the wind of the day   ᴱ3:10 Lit the sound of you

LIES, SIN,
AND DEFLATED BALLOONS

GENESIS 3:1-24; ROMANS 3:23; ROMANS 6:23

The grocery store near our house has a thing about balloons.

Like clowns at a circus, the cashiers whimsically bestow one on each child who rolls past the register as a reward for their excellent (or terrible) behavior. The bad news? I have two children, and inevitably, one balloon always makes a break for it in the parking lot. Somewhere between the cart corral and the car seats, one balloon—only one—will seize its opportunity to slip free.

That's when they turn on each other. Greed overcomes my children, and all they can think about is the one thing they cannot have. By the time we pull into the driveway at home, whatever affection they once shared for each other is long-forgotten, discarded for the love of self.

One such scene occurred in our home last week. The very next day I came upon the coveted balloon, hovering hesitantly just above the dining room floor—forgotten, deflated, and worthless.

This is what sin does: it lies. It promises to be shiny and colorful and inflated with excitement forever. *It promises to be worth it.* Sin tells us that God wants to keep the good stuff from us, that what we want matters more than what He has for us (Gn 3:4-5).

In Eden God told Adam, "You are free to eat from any tree of the garden, but you must not eat from the tree of the knowledge of good and evil, for on the day you eat from it, you will certainly die" (Gn 2:16-17). Man had supremacy over all of the earth, but this exclusion, this one law, caused Adam to doubt God's motives.

Adam and Eve sinned the first sin (Gn 3:6-7), and for the first time in the history of the world, we felt shame. The lie of sin—that *this* will make us like God, and that we can live apart from Him—failed to deliver. And so the original glory of man and Eden was lost (Gn 3:8-21). God's tender warning that "you will certainly die" was true for them, and it's true for us.

The human race is guilty because of Adam's sin. Each one of us is also guilty because of our own sins. Daily, hourly, even moment-to-moment, we believe the lie that God's law is holding us back, that we know better. Just as we scramble to act (or think, or fail to act), the shimmer tarnishes, the balloon deflates, and what we thought we needed —the thing that caused us to act outside of God's law—is discarded by sunrise the next morning.

Sin wasn't worth it. It never is.

But friends, keep reading! There is more! (And if you can't possibly bear to wait, turn to Romans 5:17 for the most glorious hint!)

¹⁴ So the Lᴏʀᴅ God said to the serpent:

Because you have done this,
you are cursed more than any livestock
and more than any wild animal.
You will move on your belly
and eat dust all the days of your life.
¹⁵ I will put hostility between you and the woman,
and between your offspring and her offspring.
He will strike your head,
and you will strike his heel.

¹⁶ He said to the woman:

I will intensify your labor pains;
you will bear children with painful effort.
Your desire will be for your husband,
yet he will rule over you.

¹⁷ And he said to the man, "Because you listened to your wife and ate from the tree about which I commanded you, 'Do not eat from it':

The ground is cursed because of you.
You will eat from it by means of painful labor ᴬ
all the days of your life.
¹⁸ It will produce thorns and thistles for you,
and you will eat the plants of the field.
¹⁹ You will eat bread ᴮ by the sweat of your brow
until you return to the ground,
since you were taken from it.
For you are dust,
and you will return to dust."

²⁰ The man named his wife Eve ᶜ because she was the mother of all the living. ²¹ The Lᴏʀᴅ God made clothing from skins for the man and his wife, and he clothed them.

²² The Lᴏʀᴅ God said, "Since the man has become like one of us, knowing good and evil, he must not reach out, take from the tree of life, eat, and live forever." ²³ So the Lᴏʀᴅ God sent him away from the garden of Eden to work the ground from which he was taken. ²⁴ He drove the man out and stationed the cherubim and the flaming, whirling sword east of the garden of Eden to guard the way to the tree of life.

CAIN MURDERS ABEL

4 The man was intimate with his wife Eve, and she conceived and gave birth to Cain. She said, "I have had a male child with the Lᴏʀᴅ's help." ᴰ ² She also gave birth to his brother Abel. Now Abel became a shepherd of flocks, but Cain worked the ground. ³ In the course of time Cain presented some of the land's produce as an offering to the Lᴏʀᴅ. ⁴ And Abel also presented an offering — some of the firstborn of his flock and their fat portions.

ᴬ3:17 Lit *it through pain*   ᴮ3:19 Or *food*   ᶜ3:20 Lit *Living,* or *Life*   ᴰ4:1 Lit *the* Lᴏʀᴅ

The LORD had regard for Abel and his offering, ⁵ but he did not have regard for Cain and his offering. Cain was furious, and he looked despondent.ᴬ

⁶ Then the LORD said to Cain, "Why are you furious? And why do you look despondent?ᴮ ⁷ If you do what is right, won't you be accepted? But if you do not do what is right, sin is crouching at the door. Its desire is for you, but you must rule over it."

⁸ Cain said to his brother Abel, "Let's go out to the field."ᶜ And while they were in the field, Cain attacked his brother Abel and killed him.

⁹ Then the LORD said to Cain, "Where is your brother Abel?"

"I don't know," he replied. "Am I my brother's guardian?"

¹⁰ Then he said, "What have you done? Your brother's blood cries out to me from the ground! ¹¹ So now you are cursed, alienated from the ground that opened its mouth to receive your brother's blood you have shed.ᴰ ¹² If you work the ground, it will never again give you its yield. You will be a restless wanderer on the earth."

¹³ But Cain answered the LORD, "My punishmentᴱ is too great to bear! ¹⁴ Since you are banishing me today from the face of the earth, and I must hide from your presence and become a restless wanderer on the earth, whoever finds me will kill me."

¹⁵ Then the LORD replied to him, "In that case,ᶠ whoever kills Cain will suffer vengeance seven times over."ᴳ And he placed a mark on Cain so that whoever found him would not kill him. ¹⁶ Then Cain went out from the LORD's presence and lived in the land of Nod, east of Eden.

THE LINE OF CAIN

¹⁷ Cain was intimate with his wife, and she conceived and gave birth to Enoch. Then Cain became the builder of a city, and he named the city Enoch after his son. ¹⁸ Irad was born to Enoch, Irad fathered Mehujael, Mehujael fathered Methushael, and Methushael fathered Lamech. ¹⁹ Lamech took two wives for himself, one named Adah and the other named Zillah. ²⁰ Adah bore Jabal; he was the father of the nomadic herdsmen.ᴴ ²¹ His brother was named Jubal; he was the father of all who play the lyre and the flute. ²² Zillah bore Tubal-cain, who made all kinds of bronze and iron tools. Tubal-cain's sister was Naamah.

²³ Lamech said to his wives:

Adah and Zillah, hear my voice;
wives of Lamech, pay attention to my words.
For I killed a man for wounding me,
a young man for striking me.
²⁴ If Cain is to be avenged seven times over,
then for Lamech it will be seventy-seven times!

²⁵ Adam was intimate with his wife again, and she gave birth to a son and named him Seth, for she said, "God has givenᴵ me another childᴶ in place of

---

ᴬ4:5 Lit *and his face fell*   ᴮ4:6 Lit *why has your face fallen*   ᶜ4:8 Sam, LXX, Syr, Vg; MT omits *"Let's go out to the field."*   ᴰ4:11 Lit *blood from your hand* ᴱ4:13 Or *sin*   ᶠ4:15 LXX, Syr, Vg read *"Not so!"*   ᴳ4:15 Or *suffer severely* ᴴ4:20 Lit *the dweller of tent and livestock*   ᴵ4:25 The Hb word for *given* sounds like the name "Seth."   ᴶ4:25 Lit *seed*

Abel, since Cain killed him." ²⁶ A son was born to Seth also, and he named him Enosh. At that time people began to call on the name of the LORD.

THE LINE OF SETH

5 This is the document containing the family^A records of Adam.^B On the day that God created man,^C he made him in the likeness of God; ² he created them male and female. When they were created, he blessed them and called them mankind.^D

³ Adam was 130 years old when he fathered a son in his likeness, according to his image, and named him Seth. ⁴ Adam lived 800 years after he fathered Seth, and he fathered other sons and daughters. ⁵ So Adam's life lasted 930 years; then he died.

⁶ Seth was 105 years old when he fathered Enosh. ⁷ Seth lived 807 years after he fathered Enosh, and he fathered other sons and daughters. ⁸ So Seth's life lasted 912 years; then he died.

⁹ Enosh was 90 years old when he fathered Kenan. ¹⁰ Enosh lived 815 years after he fathered Kenan, and he fathered other sons and daughters. ¹¹ So Enosh's life lasted 905 years; then he died.

¹² Kenan was 70 years old when he fathered Mahalalel. ¹³ Kenan lived 840 years after he fathered Mahalalel, and he fathered other sons and daughters. ¹⁴ So Kenan's life lasted 910 years; then he died.

¹⁵ Mahalalel was 65 years old when he fathered Jared. ¹⁶ Mahalalel lived 830 years after he fathered Jared, and he fathered other sons and daughters. ¹⁷ So Mahalalel's life lasted 895 years; then he died.

¹⁸ Jared was 162 years old when he fathered Enoch. ¹⁹ Jared lived 800 years after he fathered Enoch, and he fathered other sons and daughters. ²⁰ So Jared's life lasted 962 years; then he died.

²¹ Enoch was 65 years old when he fathered Methuselah. ²² And after he fathered Methuselah, Enoch walked with God 300 years and fathered other sons and daughters. ²³ So Enoch's life lasted 365 years. ²⁴ Enoch walked with God; then he was not there because God took him.

²⁵ Methuselah was 187 years old when he fathered Lamech. ²⁶ Methuselah lived 782 years after he fathered Lamech, and he fathered other sons and daughters. ²⁷ So Methuselah's life lasted 969 years; then he died.

²⁸ Lamech was 182 years old when he fathered a son. ²⁹ And he named him Noah,^E saying, "This one will bring us relief from the agonizing labor of our hands, caused by the ground the LORD has cursed." ³⁰ Lamech lived 595 years after he fathered Noah, and he fathered other sons and daughters. ³¹ So Lamech's life lasted 777 years; then he died.

³² Noah was 500 years old, and he fathered Shem, Ham, and Japheth.

SONS OF GOD AND DAUGHTERS OF MANKIND

6 When mankind began to multiply on the earth and daughters were born to them, ² the sons of God saw that the daughters of mankind were beautiful, and they took any they chose as wives^F for themselves. ³ And the LORD said, "My Spirit will not remain^G with^H mankind forever, because

---

^A5:1 Lit *written family* ^B5:1 Or *mankind* ^C5:1 Or *Adam, human beings*
^D5:2 Hb *'adam* ^E5:29 In Hb, the name *Noah* sounds like "bring us relief."
^F6:2 Or *women* ^G6:3 Or *strive* ^H6:3 Or *in*

they are corrupt.^A Their days will be 120 years." ⁴ The Nephilim^B were on the earth both in those days and afterward, when the sons of God came to the daughters of mankind, who bore children to them. They were the powerful men of old, the famous men.

JUDGMENT DECREED

⁵ When the LORD saw that human wickedness was widespread on the earth and that every inclination of the human mind was nothing but evil all the time, ⁶ the LORD regretted that he had made man on the earth, and he was deeply grieved.^C ⁷ Then the LORD said, "I will wipe mankind, whom I created, off the face of the earth, together with the animals, creatures that crawl, and birds of the sky — for I regret that I made them." ⁸ Noah, however, found favor with the LORD.

GOD WARNS NOAH

⁹ These are the family records of Noah. Noah was a righteous man, blameless among his contemporaries; Noah walked with God. ¹⁰ And Noah fathered three sons: Shem, Ham, and Japheth.

¹¹ Now the earth was corrupt in God's sight, and the earth was filled with wickedness.^D ¹² God saw how corrupt the earth was, for every creature had corrupted its way on the earth. ¹³ Then God said to Noah, "I have decided to put an end to every creature, for the earth is filled with wickedness because of them; therefore I am going to destroy them along with the earth.

¹⁴ "Make yourself an ark of gopher^E wood. Make rooms in the ark, and cover it with pitch inside and outside. ¹⁵ This is how you are to make it: The ark will be 450 feet long, 75 feet wide, and 45 feet high.^F ¹⁶ You are to make a roof,^G finishing the sides of the ark to within eighteen inches^H of the roof. You are to put a door in the side of the ark. Make it with lower, middle, and upper decks.

¹⁷ "Understand that I am bringing a flood — floodwaters on the earth to destroy every creature under heaven with the breath of life in it. Everything on earth will perish. ¹⁸ But I will establish my covenant with you, and you will enter the ark with your sons, your wife, and your sons' wives. ¹⁹ You are also to bring into the ark two of all the living creatures, male and female, to keep them alive with you. ²⁰ Two of everything — from the birds according to their kinds, from the livestock according to their kinds, and from the animals that crawl on the ground according to their kinds — will come to you so that you can keep them alive. ²¹ Take with you every kind of food that is eaten; gather it as food for you and for them." ²² And Noah did this. He did everything that God had commanded him.

ENTERING THE ARK

7 Then the LORD said to Noah, "Enter the ark, you and all your household, for I have seen that you alone are righteous before me in this generation. ² You are to take with you seven pairs, a male and its female, of all the clean animals, and two of the animals that are not clean, a male and

---

^A 6:3 Lit *flesh*   ^B 6:4 Possibly means "fallen ones"; traditionally, "giants"; Nm 13:31-33   ^C 6:6 Lit *was grieved to his heart*   ^D 6:11 Or *injustice*, also in v. 13   ^E 6:14 Unknown species of tree; perhaps pine or cypress   ^F 6:15 Or *300 cubits long, 50 cubits wide, and 30 cubits high*   ^G 6:16 Or *window*, or *hatch*; Hb uncertain   ^H 6:16 Lit *to a cubit* its female, ³ and seven pairs, male and female, of the birds of the sky — in order to keep offspring alive throughout the earth. ⁴ Seven days from now I will make it rain on the earth forty days and forty nights, and every living thing I have made I will wipe off the face of the earth." ⁵ And Noah did everything that the LORD commanded him.

⁶ Noah was six hundred years old when the flood came and water covered the earth. ⁷ So Noah, his sons, his wife, and his sons' wives entered the ark because of the floodwaters. ⁸ From the clean animals, unclean animals, birds, and every creature that crawls on the ground, ⁹ two of each, male and female, came to Noah and entered the ark, just as God had commanded him. ¹⁰ Seven days later the floodwaters came on the earth.

THE FLOOD

¹¹ In the six hundredth year of Noah's life, in the second month, on the seventeenth day of the month, on that day all the sources of the vast watery depths burst open, the floodgates of the sky were opened, ¹² and the rain fell on the earth forty days and forty nights. ¹³ On that same day Noah and his three sons, Shem, Ham, and Japheth, entered the ark, along with Noah's wife and his three sons' wives. ¹⁴ They entered it with all the wildlife according to their kinds, all livestock according to their kinds, all the creatures that crawl on the earth according to their kinds, every flying creature — all the birds and every winged creature — according to their kinds. ¹⁵ Two of every creature that has the breath of life in it came to Noah and entered the ark. ¹⁶ Those that entered, male and female of every creature, entered just as God had commanded him. Then the LORD shut him in.

¹⁷ The flood continued for forty days on the earth; the water increased and lifted up the ark so that it rose above the earth. ¹⁸ The water surged and increased greatly on the earth, and the ark floated on the surface of the water. ¹⁹ Then the water surged even higher on the earth, and all the high mountains under the whole sky were covered. ²⁰ The mountains were covered as the water surged above them more than twenty feet.^A ²¹ Every creature perished — those that crawl on the earth, birds, livestock, wildlife, and those that swarm^B on the earth, as well as all mankind. ²² Everything with the breath of the spirit of life in its nostrils — everything on dry land died. ²³ He wiped out every living thing that was on the face of the earth, from mankind to livestock, to creatures that crawl, to the birds of the sky, and they were wiped off the earth. Only Noah was left, and those that were with him in the ark. ²⁴ And the water surged on the earth 150 days.

THE FLOOD RECEDES

8 God remembered Noah, as well as all the wildlife and all the livestock that were with him in the ark. God caused a wind^C to pass over the earth, and the water began to subside. ² The sources of the watery depths and the floodgates of the sky were closed, and the rain from the sky stopped. ³ The water steadily receded from the earth, and by the end of 150 days the water had decreased significantly. ⁴ The ark came to rest in the seventh month, on the seventeenth day of the month, on the mountains of Ararat.

---

^A7:20 Lit *surged 15 cubits*   ^B7:21 Lit *all the swarming swarms*   ^C8:1 Or *spirit;* Gn 1:2

⁵ The water continued to recede until the tenth month; in the tenth month, on the first day of the month, the tops of the mountains were visible. ⁶ After forty days Noah opened the window of the ark that he had made, ⁷ and he sent out a raven. It went back and forth until the water had dried up from the earth. ⁸ Then he sent out a dove to see whether the water on the earth's surface had gone down, ⁹ but the dove found no resting place for its foot. It returned to him in the ark because water covered the surface of the whole earth. He reached out and brought it into the ark to himself. ¹⁰ So Noah waited seven more days and sent out the dove from the ark again. ¹¹ When the dove came to him at evening, there was a plucked olive leaf in its beak. So Noah knew that the water on the earth's surface had gone down. ¹² After he had waited another seven days, he sent out the dove, but it did not return to him again. ¹³ In the six hundred and first year, [A] in the first month, on the first day of the month, the water that had covered the earth was dried up. Then Noah removed the ark's cover and saw that the surface of the ground was drying. ¹⁴ By the twenty-seventh day of the second month, the earth was dry.

THE LORD'S PROMISE

¹⁵ Then God spoke to Noah, ¹⁶ "Come out of the ark, you, your wife, your sons, and your sons' wives with you. ¹⁷ Bring out all the living creatures [B] that are with you — birds, livestock, those that crawl on the earth — and they will spread over the earth and be fruitful and multiply on the earth." ¹⁸ So Noah, along with his sons, his wife, and his sons' wives, came out. ¹⁹ All the animals, all the creatures that crawl, and all the flying creatures — everything that moves on the earth — came out of the ark by their families.

²⁰ Then Noah built an altar to the LORD. He took some of every kind of clean animal and every kind of clean bird and offered burnt offerings on the altar. ²¹ When the LORD smelled the pleasing aroma, he said to himself, "I will never again curse the ground because of human beings, even though the inclination of the human heart is evil from youth onward. And I will never again strike down every living thing as I have done.

²² As long as the earth endures,
seedtime and harvest, cold and heat,
summer and winter, and day and night
will not cease."

GOD'S COVENANT WITH NOAH

9 God blessed Noah and his sons and said to them, "Be fruitful and multiply and fill the earth. ² The fear and terror of you will be in every living creature on the earth, every bird of the sky, every creature that crawls on the ground, and all the fish of the sea. They are placed under your authority. [C] ³ Every creature that lives and moves will be food for you; as I gave the green plants, I have given you everything. ⁴ However, you must not eat meat with its lifeblood in it. ⁵ And I will require a penalty for your lifeblood; [D] I will require it from any animal and from any human; if someone murders a fellow human, I will require that person's life. [E]

[A] 8:13 = of Noah's life [B] 8:17 Lit *creatures of all flesh* [C] 9:2 Lit *are given in your hand* [D] 9:5 Lit *And your blood belonging to your life I will seek* [E] 9:5 Lit *any human; from the hand of a man his brother I will seek the life of the human.*

A LEGACY OF FAITH

GENESIS 9–10; LUKE 1:68-75

Every spiritual giant is standing on someone else's shoulders.

That is the unexpected sermon proclaimed through Noah's life after the flood. After the dramatic events found in Genesis 6–8, the narrative pivots past Noah to his family and a long list of names identifying Noah's children, grandchildren, and great-grandchildren.

Family. Generations. Descendants. Clans.

This is the drumbeat of generational language we hear in these chapters. The words father and son are mentioned nearly thirty times in just 61 verses. A chronic skimmer, I'm tempted to gloss over generational lists, but if I resist the urge and pay attention, I see the branches of Noah's family tree are loaded with significance.

Canaan was Noah's grandson (Gn 9:18). We will see that name again. (Check out the name of the place God promised Abraham in Gn 12:1-3 and the Israelites in Ex 3:17.) Egypt was another grandson of Noah. He would settle in the place where Joseph would later reign under Pharaoh (Gn 45:8) and where Jesus would flee with His parents, fulfilling an ancient prophecy (Mt 2:13-23). While it may seem like Jesus is far removed from this early story in Genesis, that isn't really the case. Noah's son Shem was a chosen branch on the family tree. From his line would come Abraham, the Israelites, King David, and ultimately Jesus, our Savior (Gn 11:10-32).

After the floodwaters receded, Noah went back to life as usual. He tended a vineyard and bounced grandbabies on his knee. For 350 years after the flood, life simply went on. Then something unremarkable happened: "So Noah's life lasted 950 years; then he died" (Gn 9:29). Despite his great triumph on the ark and his legacy of radical obedience, Noah's story ended with a funeral, just like mine will.

But the torch of faith was passed through the generations, and that flame can be traced back to this spark: "And Noah did everything that the LORD commanded him" (Gn 7:5).

Obedience to God was the gift Noah gave to the next generation. When we obey God, we are storing away treasure for those who will come behind us.

Noah's children and grandchildren made an impact we are still feeling today—but it didn't happen instantly. We can affect future generations, too, but we have to make peace with the marathon of life, refusing to settle for the sprint. Noah's life shows us that being serious about kingdom-building means being serious about delayed gratification. His story urges us to desire for the Lord to be glorified in His timing.

As God's people, we stand on the shoulders of those who have been faithful to obey before us. Their stories, like Noah's, remind us that when we obey, in time God builds a legacy through us.

⁶ Whoever sheds human blood,
by humans his blood will be shed,
for God made humans in his image.

⁷ But you, be fruitful and multiply; spread out over the earth and multiply on it."

⁸ Then God said to Noah and his sons with him, ⁹ "Understand that I am establishing my covenant with you and your descendants after you, ¹⁰ and with every living creature that is with you — birds, livestock, and all wildlife of the earth that are with you — all the animals of the earth that came out of the ark. ¹¹ I establish my covenant with you that never again will every creature be wiped out by floodwaters; there will never again be a flood to destroy the earth."

¹² And God said, "This is the sign of the covenant I am making between me and you and every living creature with you, a covenant for all future generations: ¹³ I have placed my bow in the clouds, and it will be a sign of the covenant between me and the earth. ¹⁴ Whenever I form clouds over the earth and the bow appears in the clouds, ¹⁵ I will remember my covenant between me and you and all the living creatures:ᴬ water will never again become a flood to destroy every creature. ¹⁶ The bow will be in the clouds, and I will look at it and remember the permanent covenant between God and all the living creaturesᴮ on earth." ¹⁷ God said to Noah, "This is the sign of the covenant that I have established between me and every creature on earth."

PROPHECIES ABOUT NOAH'S FAMILY

¹⁸ Noah's sons who came out of the ark were Shem, Ham, and Japheth. Ham was the father of Canaan. ¹⁹ These three were Noah's sons, and from them the whole earth was populated.

²⁰ Noah, as a man of the soil, began by plantingᶜ a vineyard. ²¹ He drank some of the wine, became drunk, and uncovered himself inside his tent. ²² Ham, the father of Canaan, saw his father naked and told his two brothers outside. ²³ Then Shem and Japheth took a cloak and placed it over both their shoulders, and walking backward, they covered their father's nakedness. Their faces were turned away, and they did not see their father naked.

²⁴ When Noah awoke from his drinking and learned what his youngest son had done to him, ²⁵ he said:

Canaan is cursed.
He will be the lowest of slaves to his brothers.

²⁶ He also said:

Blessed be the Lᴏʀᴅ, the God of Shem;
Let Canaan beᴰ Shem's slave.

²⁷ Let God extend Japheth;ᴱ
let Japheth dwell in the tents of Shem;
let Canaan be Shem's slave.

²⁸ Now Noah lived 350 years after the flood. ²⁹ So Noah's life lasted 950 years; then he died.

ᴬ9:15 Lit and creatures of all flesh   ᴮ9:16 Lit creatures of all flesh   ᶜ9:20 Or Noah began to be a farmer and planted   ᴰ9:26 As a wish or prayer; others interpret the verbs in vv. 26-27 as prophecy: Canaan will be . . .   ᴱ9:27 In Hb, the name Japheth sounds like the word "extend."

THE TABLE OF NATIONS

10 These are the family records of Noah's sons, Shem, Ham, and Japheth. They also had sons after the flood.

² Japheth's sons: Gomer, Magog, Madai, Javan, Tubal, Meshech, and Tiras. ³ Gomer's sons: Ashkenaz, Riphath, and Togarmah. ⁴ And Javan's sons: Elishah, Tarshish, Kittim, and Dodanim.ᴬ ⁵ From these descendants, the peoples of the coasts and islands spread out into their lands according to their clans in their nations, each with its own language.

⁶ Ham's sons: Cush, Mizraim, Put, and Canaan. ⁷ Cush's sons: Seba, Havilah, Sabtah, Raamah, and Sabteca. And Raamah's sons: Sheba and Dedan.

⁸ Cush fathered Nimrod, who began to be powerful in the land. ⁹ He was a powerful hunter in the sight of the Lᴏʀᴅ. That is why it is said, "Like Nimrod, a powerful hunter in the sight of the Lᴏʀᴅ." ¹⁰ His kingdom started with Babylon, Erech,ᴮ Accad,ᶜ and Calneh,ᴰ in the land of Shinar.ᴱ ¹¹ From that land he went to Assyria and built Nineveh, Rehoboth-ir, Calah, ¹² and Resen, between Nineveh and the great city Calah.

¹³ Mizraimᶠ fathered the people of Lud, Anam, Lehab, Naphtuh, ¹⁴ Pathrus, Casluh (the Philistines came from them), and Caphtor.

¹⁵ Canaan fathered Sidon his firstborn and Heth, ¹⁶ as well as the Jebusites, the Amorites, the Girgashites, ¹⁷ the Hivites, the Arkites, the Sinites, ¹⁸ the Arvadites, the Zemarites, and the Hamathites. Afterward the Canaanite clans scattered. ¹⁹ The Canaanite border went from Sidon going toward Gerar as far as Gaza, and going toward Sodom, Gomorrah, Admah, and Zeboiim as far as Lasha.

²⁰ These are Ham's sons by their clans, according to their languages, in their lands and their nations.

²¹ And Shem, Japheth's older brother, also had sons. Shem was the father of all the sons of Eber. ²² Shem's sons were Elam, Asshur, Arpachshad, Lud, and Aram.

²³ Aram's sons: Uz, Hul, Gether, and Mash.

²⁴ Arpachshad fatheredᴳ Shelah, and Shelah fathered Eber. ²⁵ Eber had two sons. One was named Peleg,ᴴ for during his days the earth was divided; his brother was named Joktan. ²⁶ And Joktan fathered Almodad, Sheleph, Hazarmaveth, Jerah, ²⁷ Hadoram, Uzal, Diklah, ²⁸ Obal, Abimael, Sheba, ²⁹ Ophir, Havilah, and Jobab. All these were Joktan's sons. ³⁰ Their settlements extended from Mesha to Sephar, the eastern hill country.

³¹ These are Shem's sons by their clans, according to their languages, in their lands and their nations.

³² These are the clans of Noah's sons, according to their family records, in their nations. The nations on earth spread out from these after the flood.

THE TOWER OF BABYLON

11 The whole earth had the same language and vocabulary.ᴵ ² As peopleᴶ migrated from the east,ᴷ they found a valley in the land of Shinar and settled there. ³ They said to each other, "Come, let us make oven-fired bricks." (They used brick for stone and asphalt for mortar.) ⁴ And they said, "Come,

---

ᴬ10:4 Some Hb mss, Sam, LXX read *Rodanim*; 1Ch 1:7   ᴮ10:10 Or *Uruk*
ᶜ10:10 Or *Akkad*   ᴰ10:10 Or *and all of them*   ᴱ10:10 Or *in Babylonia*
ᶠ10:13 = Egypt   ᴳ10:24 LXX reads *fathered Cainan, and Cainan fathered*; Gn
11:12-13; Lk 3:35-36   ᴴ10:25 = Division   ᴵ11:1 Lit *one lip and the same words*
ᴶ11:2 Lit *they*   ᴷ11:2 Or *migrated eastward*

let us build ourselves a city and a tower with its top in the sky. Let us make a name for ourselves; otherwise, we will be scattered throughout the earth."

⁵ Then the LORD came down to look over the city and the tower that the humans ^ were building. ⁶ The LORD said, "If they have begun to do this as one people all having the same language, then nothing they plan to do will be impossible for them. ⁷ Come, let's go down there and confuse their language so that they will not understand one another's speech." ⁸ So from there the LORD scattered them throughout the earth, and they stopped building the city. ⁹ Therefore it is called Babylon, ᴮ,ᶜ for there the LORD confused the language of the whole earth, and from there the LORD scattered them throughout the earth.

FROM SHEM TO ABRAM

¹⁰ These are the family records of Shem. Shem lived 100 years and fathered Arpachshad two years after the flood. ¹¹ After he fathered Arpachshad, Shem lived 500 years and fathered other sons and daughters. ¹² Arpachshad lived 35 years ᴰ and fathered Shelah. ¹³ After he fathered Shelah, Arpachshad lived 403 years and fathered other sons and daughters. ¹⁴ Shelah lived 30 years and fathered Eber. ¹⁵ After he fathered Eber, Shelah lived 403 years and fathered other sons and daughters. ¹⁶ Eber lived 34 years and fathered Peleg. ¹⁷ After he fathered Peleg, Eber lived 430 years and fathered other sons and daughters. ¹⁸ Peleg lived 30 years and fathered Reu. ¹⁹ After he fathered Reu, Peleg lived 209 years and fathered other sons and daughters. ²⁰ Reu lived 32 years and fathered Serug. ²¹ After he fathered Serug, Reu lived 207 years and fathered other sons and daughters. ²² Serug lived 30 years and fathered Nahor. ²³ After he fathered Nahor, Serug lived 200 years and fathered other sons and daughters. ²⁴ Nahor lived 29 years and fathered Terah. ²⁵ After he fathered Terah, Nahor lived 119 years and fathered other sons and daughters. ²⁶ Terah lived 70 years and fathered Abram, Nahor, and Haran.

²⁷ These are the family records of Terah. Terah fathered Abram, Nahor, and Haran, and Haran fathered Lot. ²⁸ Haran died in his native land, in Ur of the Chaldeans, during his father Terah's lifetime. ²⁹ Abram and Nahor took wives: Abram's wife was named Sarai, and Nahor's wife was named Milcah. She was the daughter of Haran, the father of both Milcah and Iscah. ³⁰ Sarai was unable to conceive; she did not have a child.

³¹ Terah took his son Abram, his grandson Lot (Haran's son), and his daughter-in-law Sarai, his son Abram's wife, and they set out together from Ur of the Chaldeans to go to the land of Canaan. But when they came to Haran, they settled there. ³² Terah lived 205 years and died in Haran.

THE CALL OF ABRAM

12

The LORD said to Abram:
Go out from your land,
    your relatives,
    and your father's house

---

^11:5 Or *the descendants of Adam*   ᴮ11:9 Hb *Babel*   ᶜ11:9 In Hb, the name for "Babylon," *babel* sounds like the word for "confuse," *balal.*   ᴰ11:12-13 LXX reads *years and fathered Cainan.* ¹³ *After he fathered Cainan, Arpachshad lived 430 years and fathered other sons and daughters, and he died. Cainan lived 130 years and fathered Shelah. After he fathered Shelah, Cainan lived 330 years and fathered other sons and daughters, and he died*; Gn 10:24; Lk 3:35-36

FAITH IN THE PROMISE MAKER

GENESIS 12:1–13:4; JOHN 8:56-58

We make promises all the time.

We make big promises, like, "I promise to love, honor, and obey, as long as we both shall live," and smaller promises, like, "I promise not to eat your leftover tortellini in the fridge." We make false promises: "I have read the terms and conditions." And we make casual promises: "I'll be right back!"

Promises are tools we use to navigate life together. However, we aren't always reliable in keeping these promises. This is true for all of us, in our own way. We're flesh-and-blood human, and the promises we willingly make are made of weakness.

But when God makes a promise, He keeps it. In fact, God keeps both sides of His promises.

When God promised to bless all the nations of the earth through Abram, the patriarch was so convinced God would make good on His Word that he left behind his home, his family, and his nation to follow the Lord (Gn 12:1-9).

What convinced Abram? In a world of promise-breakers, what made him so certain? Scripture tells us: it was his faith. By faith "he went out, although he did not know where he was going," clinging only to the promise God had given him (Heb 11:8-9).

Abram certainly faced times of questioning— times when he doubted God would fulfill His

promise, or at least suspected God might need a little help (Gn 12:10-20). But Abram's lack of faith couldn't—and didn't—thwart God's purposes.

No matter how much or how little we believe God's promises, they are still true. When we project our own human weakness and unbelief onto God's promises to us, we miss out on experiencing His peace—the peace that allows us to follow Him into unknown territory.

Abram didn't see the deliverance of his children, the inheritance of the Promised Land, or the Messiah coming to redeem the sins of the world. He died a man of faith, only seeing these promises from a distance, trusting God would fulfill each one to the fullest extent.

Jesus Christ is both the promise-making and promise-keeping God of Abraham. Before He went to the cross, Jesus declared that He is the God who promised to bless every nation through Abraham, and He, Himself, is also the fulfillment of that promise (Jn 8:30-59). Christ redeems sinners from sin and death and provides a way back to the Father (Jn 3:17).

Every one of God's promises is made perfect in Christ (2Co 1:20). He is the fulfillment of the law, He is the true Promised Land, and He is the realization of our every need, hope, and desire (Hg 2:7).

His promises are true.

to the land that I will show you.
2   I will make you into a great nation,
     I will bless you,
     I will make your name great,
     and you will be a blessing.
3   I will bless those who bless you,
     I will curse anyone who treats you with contempt,
     and all the peoples^A on earth
     will be blessed^B through you.^C

4 So Abram went, as the Lord had told him, and Lot went with him. Abram was seventy-five years old when he left Haran. 5 He took his wife Sarai, his nephew Lot, all the possessions they had accumulated, and the people they had acquired in Haran, and they set out for the land of Canaan. When they came to the land of Canaan, 6 Abram passed through the land to the site of Shechem, at the oak of Moreh. (At that time the Canaanites were in the land.) 7 The Lord appeared to Abram and said, "To your offspring I will give this land." So he built an altar there to the Lord who had appeared to him. 8 From there he moved on to the hill country east of Bethel and pitched his tent, with Bethel on the west and Ai on the east. He built an altar to the Lord there, and he called on the name of the Lord. 9 Then Abram journeyed by stages to the Negev.

ABRAM IN EGYPT

10 There was a famine in the land, so Abram went down to Egypt to stay there for a while because the famine in the land was severe. 11 When he was about to enter Egypt, he said to his wife Sarai, "Look, I know what a beautiful woman you are. 12 When the Egyptians see you, they will say, 'This is his wife.' They will kill me but let you live. 13 Please say you're my sister so it will go well for me because of you, and my life will be spared on your account." 14 When Abram entered Egypt, the Egyptians saw that the woman was very beautiful. 15 Pharaoh's officials saw her and praised her to Pharaoh, so the woman was taken to Pharaoh's household. 16 He treated Abram well because of her, and Abram acquired flocks and herds, male and female donkeys, male and female slaves, and camels.

17 But the Lord struck Pharaoh and his household with severe plagues because of Abram's wife Sarai. 18 So Pharaoh sent for Abram and said, "What have you done to me? Why didn't you tell me she was your wife? 19 Why did you say, 'She's my sister,' so that I took her as my wife? Now, here is your wife. Take her and go!" 20 Then Pharaoh gave his men orders about him, and they sent him away with his wife and all he had.

ABRAM AND LOT SEPARATE

13 Abram went up from Egypt to the Negev — he, his wife, and all he had, and Lot with him. 2 Abram was very rich in livestock, silver, and gold. 3 He went by stages from the Negev to Bethel, to the place between Bethel and Ai where his tent had formerly been, 4 to the site where he had built the altar. And Abram called on the name of the Lord there.

---

^A12:3 Lit clans   ^B12:3 Or will find blessing   ^C12:3 Or will bless themselves by you

⁵ Now Lot, who was traveling with Abram, also had flocks, herds, and tents. ⁶ But the land was unable to support them as long as they stayed together, for they had so many possessions that they could not stay together, ⁷ and there was quarreling between the herdsmen of Abram's livestock and the herdsmen of Lot's livestock. (At that time the Canaanites and the Perizzites were living in the land.)

⁸ So Abram said to Lot, "Please, let's not have quarreling between you and me, or between your herdsmen and my herdsmen, since we are relatives.ᴬ ⁹ Isn't the whole land before you? Separate from me: if you go to the left, I will go to the right; if you go to the right, I will go to the left."

¹⁰ Lot looked out and saw that the entire plainᴮ of the Jordan as far asᶜ Zoar was well watered everywhere like the LORD's garden and the land of Egypt. (This was before the LORD destroyed Sodom and Gomorrah.) ¹¹ So Lot chose the entire plain of the Jordan for himself. Then Lot journeyed eastward, and they separated from each other. ¹² Abram lived in the land of Canaan, but Lot lived in the cities on the plain and set up his tent near Sodom. ¹³ (Now the men of Sodom were evil, sinning immenselyᴰ against the LORD.)

¹⁴ After Lot had separated from him, the LORD said to Abram, "Look from the place where you are. Look north and south, east and west, ¹⁵ for I will give you and your offspring forever all the land that you see. ¹⁶ I will make your offspring like the dust of the earth, so that if anyone could count the dust of the earth, then your offspring could be counted. ¹⁷ Get up and walk around the land, through its length and width, for I will give it to you."

¹⁸ So Abram moved his tent and went to live near the oaks of Mamre at Hebron, where he built an altar to the LORD.

ABRAM RESCUES LOT

14 In those days King Amraphel of Shinar, King Arioch of Ellasar, King Chedorlaomer of Elam, and King Tidal of Goiimᴱ ² waged war against King Bera of Sodom, King Birsha of Gomorrah, King Shinab of Admah, and King Shemeber of Zeboiim, as well as the king of Bela (that is, Zoar). ³ All of these came as allies to the Siddim Valley (that is, the Dead Sea). ⁴ They were subject to Chedorlaomer for twelve years, but in the thirteenth year they rebelled. ⁵ In the fourteenth year Chedorlaomer and the kings who were with him came and defeated the Rephaim in Ashteroth-karnaim, the Zuzim in Ham, the Emim in Shaveh-kiriathaim, ⁶ and the Horites in the mountains of Seir, as far as El-paran by the wilderness. ⁷ Then they came back to invade En-mishpat (that is, Kadesh), and they defeated the whole territory of the Amalekites, as well as the Amorites who lived in Hazazon-tamar.

⁸ Then the king of Sodom, the king of Gomorrah, the king of Admah, the king of Zeboiim, and the king of Bela (that is, Zoar) went out and lined up for battle in the Siddim Valley ⁹ against King Chedorlaomer of Elam, King Tidal of Goiim, King Amraphel of Shinar, and King Arioch of Ellasar — four kings against five. ¹⁰ Now the Siddim Valley contained many asphalt pits, and as the kings of Sodom and Gomorrah fled, some fell into them,ᶠ but the rest fled to

---

ᴬ13:8 Lit brothers ᴮ13:10 Lit circle; i.e., probably the large round plain where the Jordan River empties into the Dead Sea, also in v. 11 ᶜ13:10 Lit Jordan as you go to ᴰ13:13 Lit evil and sinful ᴱ14:1 Or nations ᶠ14:10 Sam, LXX; MT reads fell there the mountains. ¹¹ The four kings took all the goods of Sodom and Gomorrah and all their food and went on. ¹² They also took Abram's nephew Lot and his possessions, for he was living in Sodom, and they went on.

¹³ One of the survivors came and told Abram the Hebrew, who lived near the oaks belonging to Mamre the Amorite, the brother of Eshcol and the brother of Aner. They were bound by a treaty with^A Abram. ¹⁴ When Abram heard that his relative had been taken prisoner, he assembled^B his 318 trained men, born in his household, and they went in pursuit as far as Dan. ¹⁵ And he and his servants deployed against them by night, defeated them, and pursued them as far as Hobah to the north of Damascus. ¹⁶ He brought back all the goods and also his relative Lot and his goods, as well as the women and the other people.

MELCHIZEDEK'S BLESSING

¹⁷ After Abram returned from defeating Chedorlaomer and the kings who were with him, the king of Sodom went out to meet him in the Shaveh Valley (that is, the King's Valley). ¹⁸ Melchizedek, king of Salem,^C brought out bread and wine; he was a priest to God Most High. ¹⁹ He blessed him and said:

Abram is blessed by God Most High,
Creator^D of heaven and earth,
²⁰ and blessed be God Most High
who has handed over your enemies to you.

And Abram gave him a tenth of everything.

²¹ Then the king of Sodom said to Abram, "Give me the people, but take the possessions for yourself."

²² But Abram said to the king of Sodom, "I have raised my hand in an oath to the LORD, God Most High, Creator of heaven and earth, ²³ that I will not take a thread or sandal strap or anything that belongs to you, so you can never say, 'I made Abram rich.' ²⁴ I will take nothing^E except what the servants have eaten. But as for the share of the men who came with me — Aner, Eshcol, and Mamre — they can take their share."

THE ABRAHAMIC COVENANT

15 After these events, the word of the LORD came to Abram in a vision:
Do not be afraid, Abram.
I am your shield;
your reward will be very great.

² But Abram said, "Lord GOD, what can you give me, since I am childless and the heir of my house is Eliezer of Damascus?"^F ³ Abram continued, "Look, you have given me no offspring, so a slave born in^G my house will be my heir."

⁴ Now the word of the LORD came to him: "This one will not be your heir; instead, one who comes from your own body^H will be your heir." ⁵ He took him outside and said, "Look at the sky and count the stars, if you are able to count them." Then he said to him, "Your offspring will be that numerous."

⁶ Abram believed the LORD, and he credited it to him as righteousness.

---

^A14:13 Lit were possessors of a covenant of   ^B14:14 Sam; MT reads poured out
^C14:18 = Jerusalem   ^D14:19 Or Possessor   ^E14:24 Lit nothing to me   ^F15:2 Hb
obscure   ^G15:3 Lit a son of   ^H15:4 Lit loins

⁷ He also said to him, "I am the LORD who brought you from Ur of the Chaldeans to give you this land to possess."

⁸ But he said, "Lord GOD, how can I know that I will possess it?"

⁹ He said to him, "Bring me a three-year-old cow, a three-year-old female goat, a three-year-old ram, a turtledove, and a young pigeon."

¹⁰ So he brought all these to him, cut them in half, and laid the pieces opposite each other, but he did not cut the birds in half. ¹¹ Birds of prey came down on the carcasses, but Abram drove them away. ¹² As the sun was setting, a deep sleep came over Abram, and suddenly great terror and darkness descended on him.

¹³ Then the LORD said to Abram, "Know this for certain: Your offspring will be resident aliens for four hundred years in a land that does not belong to them and will be enslaved and oppressed.ᴬ ¹⁴ However, I will judge the nation they serve, and afterward they will go out with many possessions. ¹⁵ But you will go to your fathers in peace and be buried at a good old age. ¹⁶ In the fourth generation they will return here, for the iniquity of the Amorites has not yet reached its full measure."ᴮ

¹⁷ When the sun had set and it was dark, a smoking fire pot and a flaming torch appeared and passed between the divided animals. ¹⁸ On that day the LORD made a covenant with Abram, saying, "I give this land to your offspring, from the Brook of Egypt to the great river, the Euphrates River: ¹⁹ the land of the Kenites, Kenizzites, Kadmonites, ²⁰ Hethites, Perizzites, Rephaim, ²¹ Amorites, Canaanites, Girgashites, and Jebusites."

HAGAR AND ISHMAEL

16 Abram's wife Sarai had not borne any children for him, but she owned an Egyptian slave named Hagar. ² Sarai said to Abram, "Since the LORD has prevented me from bearing children, go to my slave; perhaps through her I can build a family." And Abram agreed to what Sarai said.ᶜ ³ So Abram's wife Sarai took Hagar, her Egyptian slave, and gave her to her husband Abram as a wife for him. This happened after Abram had lived in the land of Canaan ten years. ⁴ He slept withᴰ Hagar, and she became pregnant. When she saw that she was pregnant, her mistress became contemptible to her. ⁵ Then Sarai said to Abram, "You are responsible for my suffering!ᴱ I put my slave in your arms,ᶠ and when she saw that she was pregnant, I became contemptible to her. May the LORD judge between me and you."

⁶ Abram replied to Sarai, "Here, your slave is in your hands; do whatever you want with her." Then Sarai mistreated her so much that she ran away from her.

⁷ The angel of the LORD found her by a spring in the wilderness, the spring on the way to Shur. ⁸ He said, "Hagar, slave of Sarai, where have you come from and where are you going?"

She replied, "I'm running away from my mistress Sarai."

⁹ The angel of the LORD said to her, "Go back to your mistress and submit to her authority." ¹⁰ The angel of the LORD said to her, "I will greatly multiply your offspring, and they will be too many to count."

ᴬ15:13 Lit *will serve them and they will oppress them*   ᴮ15:16 Lit *Amorites is not yet complete*   ᶜ16:2 Lit *Abram listened to the voice of Sarai*   ᴰ16:4 Lit *He came to*   ᴱ16:5 Or *"May my suffering be on you!*   ᶠ16:5 Lit *bosom*

¹¹ The angel of the LORD said to her, "You have conceived and will have a son. You will name him Ishmael,ᴬ for the LORD has heard your cry of affliction. ¹² This man will be like a wild donkey. His hand will be against everyone, and everyone's hand will be against him; he will settle near all his relatives."

¹³ So she named the LORD who spoke to her: "You are El-roi,"ᴮ for she said, "In this place, have I actually seen the one who sees me?"ᶜ ¹⁴ That is why the well is called Beer-lahai-roi.ᴰ It is between Kadesh and Bered.

¹⁵ So Hagar gave birth to Abram's son, and Abram named his son (whom Hagar bore) Ishmael. ¹⁶ Abram was eighty-six years old when Hagar bore Ishmael to him.

COVENANT CIRCUMCISION

17 When Abram was ninety-nine years old, the LORD appeared to him, saying, "I am God Almighty. Liveᴱ in my presence and be blameless. ² I will set up my covenant between me and you, and I will multiply you greatly."

³ Then Abram fell facedown and God spoke with him: ⁴ "As for me, here is my covenant with you: You will become the father of many nations. ⁵ Your name will no longer be Abram;ᶠ your name will be Abraham,ᴳ for I will make you the father of many nations. ⁶ I will make you extremely fruitful and will make nations and kings come from you. ⁷ I will confirm my covenant that is between me and you and your future offspring throughout their generations. It is a permanent covenant to be your God and the God of your offspring after you. ⁸ And to you and your future offspring I will give the land where you are residing — all the land of Canaan — as a permanent possession, and I will be their God."

⁹ God also said to Abraham, "As for you, you and your offspring after you throughout their generations are to keep my covenant. ¹⁰ This is my covenant between me and you and your offspring after you, which you are to keep: Every one of your males must be circumcised. ¹¹ You must circumcise the flesh of your foreskin to serve as a sign of the covenant between me and you.ᴴ ¹² Throughout your generations, every male among you is to be circumcised at eight days old — every male born in your household or purchased from any foreigner and not your offspring. ¹³ Whether born in your household or purchased, he must be circumcised. My covenant will be marked in your flesh as a permanent covenant. ¹⁴ If any male is not circumcised in the flesh of his foreskin, that man will be cut off from his people; he has broken my covenant."

¹⁵ God said to Abraham, "As for your wife Sarai, do not call her Sarai, for Sarahᴵ will be her name. ¹⁶ I will bless her; indeed, I will give you a son by her. I will bless her, and she will produce nations; kings of peoples will come from her."

¹⁷ Abraham fell facedown. Then he laughed and said to himself, "Can a child be born to a hundred-year-old man? Can Sarah, a ninety-year-old woman, give birth?" ¹⁸ So Abraham said to God, "If only Ishmael were acceptableᴶ to you!"

¹⁹ But God said, "No. Your wife Sarah will bear you a son, and you will name him Isaac.ᴷ I will confirm my covenant with him as a permanent covenant

---

ᴬ16:11 = God Hears ᴮ16:13 = God Sees Me ᶜ16:13 Hb obscure ᴰ16:14 = Well of the Living One Who Sees Me ᴱ17:1 Or *Walk* ᶠ17:5 = The Father Is Exalted ᴳ17:5 = Father of a Multitude ᴴ17:11 *You* in v. 11 is pl. ᴵ17:15 = Princess ᴶ17:18 Lit *alive* ᴷ17:19 = He Laughs for his future offspring. ²⁰ As for Ishmael, I have heard you. I will certainly bless him; I will make him fruitful and will multiply him greatly. He will father twelve tribal leaders, and I will make him into a great nation. ²¹ But I will confirm my covenant with Isaac, whom Sarah will bear to you at this time next year." ²² When he finished talking with him, God withdrew ᴬ from Abraham.

²³ So Abraham took his son Ishmael and those born in his household or purchased — every male among the members of Abraham's household — and he circumcised the flesh of their foreskin on that very day, just as God had said to him. ²⁴ Abraham was ninety-nine years old when the flesh of his foreskin was circumcised, ²⁵ and his son Ishmael was thirteen years old when the flesh of his foreskin was circumcised. ²⁶ On that same day Abraham and his son Ishmael were circumcised. ²⁷ And all the men of his household — whether born in his household or purchased from a foreigner — were circumcised with him.

ABRAHAM'S THREE VISITORS

18 The LORD appeared to Abraham at the oaks of Mamre while he was sitting at the entrance of his tent during the heat of the day. ² He looked up, and he saw three men standing near him. When he saw them, he ran from the entrance of the tent to meet them, bowed to the ground, ³ and said, "My lord, if I have found favor with you, please do not go on past your servant. ⁴ Let a little water be brought, that you may wash your feet and rest yourselves under the tree. ⁵ I will bring a bit of bread so that you may strengthen yourselves. ᴮ This is why you have passed your servant's way. Later, you can continue on."

"Yes," they replied, "do as you have said."

⁶ So Abraham hurried into the tent and said to Sarah, "Quick! Knead three measures ᶜ of fine flour and make bread." ᴰ ⁷ Abraham ran to the herd and got a tender, choice calf. He gave it to a young man, who hurried to prepare it. ⁸ Then Abraham took curds ᴱ and milk, as well as the calf that he had prepared, and set them before the men. He served ᶠ them as they ate under the tree.

SARAH LAUGHS

⁹ "Where is your wife Sarah?" they asked him.

"There, in the tent," he answered.

¹⁰ The LORD said, "I will certainly come back to you in about a year's time, and your wife Sarah will have a son!" Now Sarah was listening at the entrance of the tent behind him. ¹¹ Abraham and Sarah were old and getting on in years. ᴳ Sarah had passed the age of childbearing. ᴴ ¹² So she laughed to herself: "After I am worn out and my lord is old, will I have delight?"

¹³ But the LORD asked Abraham, "Why did Sarah laugh, saying, 'Can I really have a baby when I'm old?' ¹⁴ Is anything impossible for the LORD? At the appointed time I will come back to you, and in about a year she will have a son."

¹⁵ Sarah denied it. "I did not laugh," she said, because she was afraid.

But he replied, "No, you did laugh."

ᴬ17:22 Lit *went up*, or *ascended*   ᴮ18:5 Lit *may sustain your heart*   ᶜ18:6 Lit *three seahs*; about 21 quarts   ᴰ18:6 A round, thin, unleavened bread   ᴱ18:8 Or *butter*   ᶠ18:8 Lit *was standing by*   ᴳ18:11 Lit *days*   ᴴ18:11 Lit *The way of women had ceased for Sarah*

ABRAHAM'S PLEA FOR SODOM

¹⁶ The men got up from there and looked out over Sodom, and Abraham was walking with them to see them off. ¹⁷ Then the LORD said, "Should I hide what I am about to do from Abraham? ¹⁸ Abraham is to become a great and powerful nation, and all the nations of the earth will be blessed through him. ¹⁹ For I have chosen^A him so that he will command his children and his house after him to keep the way of the LORD by doing what is right and just. This is how the LORD will fulfill to Abraham what he promised him." ²⁰ Then the LORD said, "The outcry against Sodom and Gomorrah is immense, and their sin is extremely serious. ²¹ I will go down to see if what they have done justifies the cry that has come up to me. If not, I will find out."

²² The men turned from there and went toward Sodom while Abraham remained standing before the LORD.^B ²³ Abraham stepped forward and said, "Will you really sweep away the righteous with the wicked? ²⁴ What if there are fifty righteous people in the city? Will you really sweep it away instead of sparing the place for the sake of the fifty righteous people who are in it? ²⁵ You could not possibly do such a thing: to kill the righteous with the wicked, treating the righteous and the wicked alike. You could not possibly do that! Won't the Judge of the whole earth do what is just? "

²⁶ The LORD said, "If I find fifty righteous people in the city of Sodom, I will spare the whole place for their sake."

²⁷ Then Abraham answered, "Since I have ventured to speak to my lord — even though I am dust and ashes — ²⁸ suppose the fifty righteous lack five. Will you destroy the whole city for lack of five? "

He replied, "I will not destroy it if I find forty-five there."

²⁹ Then he spoke to him again, "Suppose forty are found there? "

He answered, "I will not do it on account of forty."

³⁰ Then he said, "Let my lord not be angry, and I will speak further. Suppose thirty are found there? "

He answered, "I will not do it if I find thirty there."

³¹ Then he said, "Since I have ventured to speak to my lord, suppose twenty are found there? "

He replied, "I will not destroy it on account of twenty."

³² Then he said, "Let my lord not be angry, and I will speak one more time. Suppose ten are found there? "

He answered, "I will not destroy it on account of ten." ³³ When the LORD had finished speaking with Abraham, he departed, and Abraham returned to his place.

THE DESTRUCTION OF SODOM AND GOMORRAH

19 The two angels entered Sodom in the evening as Lot was sitting in Sodom's gateway. When Lot saw them, he got up to meet them. He bowed with his face to the ground ² and said, "My lords, turn aside to your servant's house, wash your feet, and spend the night. Then you can get up early and go on your way."

---

^A 18:19 Lit *known*   ^B 18:22 Alt Hb tradition reads *while the LORD remained standing before Abraham*

"No," they said. "We would rather spend the night in the square." ³ But he urged them so strongly that they followed him and went into his house. He prepared a feast and baked unleavened bread for them, and they ate.

⁴ Before they went to bed, the men of the city of Sodom, both young and old, the whole population, surrounded the house. ⁵ They called out to Lot and said, "Where are the men who came to you tonight? Send them out to us so we can have sex with them!"

⁶ Lot went out to them at the entrance and shut the door behind him. ⁷ He said, "Don't do this evil, my brothers. ⁸ Look, I've got two daughters who haven't been intimate with a man. I'll bring them out to you, and you can do whatever you want ᴬ to them. However, don't do anything to these men, because they have come under the protection of my roof."

⁹ "Get out of the way!" they said, adding, "This one came here as an alien, but he's acting like a judge! Now we'll do more harm to you than to them." They put pressure on Lot and came up to break down the door. ¹⁰ But the angels ᴮ reached out, brought Lot into the house with them, and shut the door. ¹¹ They struck the men who were at the entrance of the house, both young and old, with blindness ᶜ so that they were unable to find the entrance.

¹² Then the angels said to Lot, "Do you have anyone else here: a son-in-law, your sons and daughters, or anyone else in the city who belongs to you? Get them out of this place, ¹³ for we are about to destroy this place because the outcry against its people is so great before the Lord, that the Lord has sent us to destroy it."

¹⁴ So Lot went out and spoke to his sons-in-law, who were going to marry ᴰ his daughters. "Get up," he said. "Get out of this place, for the Lord is about to destroy the city!" But his sons-in-law thought he was joking.

¹⁵ At daybreak the angels urged Lot on: "Get up! Take your wife and your two daughters who are here, or you will be swept away in the punishment ᴱ of the city." ¹⁶ But he hesitated. Because of the Lord's compassion for him, the men grabbed his hand, his wife's hand, and the hands of his two daughters. They brought him out and left him outside the city.

¹⁷ As soon as the angels got them outside, one of them ᶠ said, "Run for your lives! Don't look back and don't stop anywhere on the plain! Run to the mountains, or you will be swept away!"

¹⁸ But Lot said to them, "No, my lords ᴳ — please. ¹⁹ Your servant has indeed found favor with you, and you have shown me great kindness by saving my life. But I can't run to the mountains; the disaster will overtake me, and I will die. ²⁰ Look, this town is close enough for me to flee to. It is a small place. Please let me run to it — it's only a small place, isn't it? — so that I can survive."

²¹ And he said to him, "All right, ᴴ I'll grant your request ᴵ about this matter too and will not demolish the town you mentioned. ²² Hurry up! Run to it, for I cannot do anything until you get there." Therefore the name of the city is Zoar. ᴶ

ᴬ19:8 Lit *do what is good in your eyes*   ᴮ19:10 Lit *men*, also in v. 12   ᶜ19:11 Or *a blinding light*   ᴰ19:14 Lit *take*   ᴱ19:15 Or *iniquity*, or *guilt*   ᶠ19:17 LXX, Syr, Vg read *outside, they*   ᴳ19:18 Or *my Lord*, or *my lord*   ᴴ19:21 Or *"look!*   ᴵ19:21 Lit *I will lift up your face*   ᴶ19:22 In Hb, the name *Zoar* is related to "small" in v. 20; its previous name was "Bela"; Gn 14:2.

²³ The sun had risen over the land when Lot reached Zoar. ²⁴ Then out of the sky the LORD rained on Sodom and Gomorrah burning sulfur from the LORD. ²⁵ He demolished these cities, the entire plain, all the inhabitants of the cities, and whatever grew on the ground. ²⁶ But Lot's wife looked back and became a pillar of salt.

²⁷ Early in the morning Abraham went to the place where he had stood before the LORD. ²⁸ He looked down toward Sodom and Gomorrah and all the land of the plain, and he saw that smoke was going up from the land like the smoke of a furnace. ²⁹ So it was, when God destroyed the cities of the plain, he remembered Abraham and brought Lot out of the middle of the upheaval when he demolished the cities where Lot had lived.

THE ORIGIN OF MOAB AND AMMON

³⁰ Lot departed from Zoar and lived in the mountains along with his two daughters, because he was afraid to live in Zoar. Instead, he and his two daughters lived in a cave. ³¹ Then the firstborn said to the younger, "Our father is old, and there is no man in the land to sleep with us as is the custom of all the land. ³² Come, let's get our father to drink wine so that we can sleep with him and preserve our father's line." ³³ So they got their father to drink wine that night, and the firstborn came and slept with her father; he did not know when she lay down or when she got up.

³⁴ The next day the firstborn said to the younger, "Look, I slept with my father last night. Let's get him to drink wine again tonight so you can go sleep with him and we can preserve our father's line." ³⁵ That night they again got their father to drink wine, and the younger went and slept with him; he did not know when she lay down or when she got up.

³⁶ So both of Lot's daughters became pregnant by their father. ³⁷ The firstborn gave birth to a son and named him Moab.ᴬ He is the father of the Moabites of today. ³⁸ The younger also gave birth to a son, and she named him Ben-ammi.ᴮ He is the father of the Ammonites of today.

SARAH RESCUED FROM ABIMELECH

20 From there Abraham traveled to the region of the Negev and settled between Kadesh and Shur. While he was staying in Gerar, ² Abraham said about his wife Sarah, "She is my sister." So King Abimelech of Gerar had Sarah brought to him.

³ But God came to Abimelech in a dream by night and said to him, "You are about to die because of the woman you have taken, for she is a married woman."ᶜ

⁴ Now Abimelech had not approached her, so he said, "Lord, would you destroy a nation even though it is innocent? ⁵ Didn't he himself say to me, 'She is my sister'? And she herself said, 'He is my brother.' I did this with a clear conscienceᴰ and cleanᴱ hands."

⁶ Then God said to him in the dream, "Yes, I know that you did this with a clear conscience.ᶠ I have also kept you from sinning against me. Therefore I have not let you touch her. ⁷ Now return the man's wife, for he is a prophet,

---

ᴬ19:37 = From My Father   ᴮ19:38 = Son of My People   ᶜ20:3 Lit *is possessed by a husband*   ᴰ20:5 Lit *with integrity of my heart*   ᴱ20:5 Lit *cleanness of my*
ᶠ20:6 Lit *with integrity of your heart*

31

and he will pray for you and you will live. But if you do not return her, know that you will certainly die, you and all who are yours."

⁸ Early in the morning Abimelech got up, called all his servants together, and personally^A told them all these things, and the men were terrified.

⁹ Then Abimelech called Abraham in and said to him, "What have you done to us? How did I sin against you that you have brought such enormous guilt on me and on my kingdom? You have done things to me that should never be done." ¹⁰ Abimelech also asked Abraham, "What made you do this?"

¹¹ Abraham replied, "I thought, 'There is absolutely no fear of God in this place. They will kill me because of my wife.' ¹² Besides, she really is my sister, the daughter of my father though not the daughter of my mother, and she became my wife. ¹³ So when God had me wander from my father's house, I said to her: Show your loyalty to me wherever we go and say about me: 'He's my brother.'"

¹⁴ Then Abimelech took flocks and herds and male and female slaves, gave them to Abraham, and returned his wife Sarah to him. ¹⁵ Abimelech said, "Look, my land is before you. Settle wherever you want."^B ¹⁶ And he said to Sarah, "Look, I am giving your brother one thousand pieces of silver. It is a verification of your honor^C to all who are with you. You are fully vindicated."

¹⁷ Then Abraham prayed to God, and God healed Abimelech, his wife, and his female slaves so that they could bear children, ¹⁸ for the Lord had completely closed all the wombs in Abimelech's household on account of Sarah, Abraham's wife.

THE BIRTH OF ISAAC

21 The Lord came to Sarah as he had said, and the Lord did for Sarah what he had promised. ² Sarah became pregnant and bore a son to Abraham in his old age, at the appointed time God had told him. ³ Abraham named his son who was born to him — the one Sarah bore to him — Isaac. ⁴ When his son Isaac was eight days old, Abraham circumcised him, as God had commanded him. ⁵ Abraham was a hundred years old when his son Isaac was born to him.

⁶ Sarah said, "God has made me laugh, and everyone who hears will laugh with me."^D ⁷ She also said, "Who would have told Abraham that Sarah would nurse children? Yet I have borne a son for him^E in his old age."

HAGAR AND ISHMAEL SENT AWAY

⁸ The child grew and was weaned, and Abraham held a great feast on the day Isaac was weaned. ⁹ But Sarah saw the son mocking — the one Hagar the Egyptian had borne to Abraham. ¹⁰ So she said to Abraham, "Drive out this slave with her son, for the son of this slave will not be a coheir with my son Isaac!"

¹¹ This was very distressing to^F Abraham because of his son. ¹² But God said to Abraham, "Do not be distressed^G about the boy and about your slave. Whatever Sarah says to you, listen to her, because your offspring will be

---

^A 20:8 Lit *in their ears* ^B 20:15 Lit *Settle in the good in your eyes* ^C 20:16 Lit *a covering of the eyes* ^D 21:6 Isaac = He Laughs; Gn 17:19 ^E 21:7 Sam, Tg Jonathan; MT omits *him* ^F 21:11 Lit *was very bad in the eyes of* ^G 21:12 Lit *"Let it not be bad in your eyes*

THE GOD WHO SEES

GENESIS 16:4-6; 18:9-15; 21–22

Have you ever felt like Hagar? Trapped. Desperate for a break. Definitely not the one calling the shots. Wondering if God sees you?

Hagar was a servant, and because Sarai was in charge, Hagar one day found herself involuntarily married to Sarai's husband, Abram, and pregnant with his child.

I don't suppose Hagar had elaborate dreams for her humble life as a servant, but surely an unwanted marriage wasn't her first choice. In fact, the Bible tells us that when she learned she was pregnant, she looked on Sarai with contempt. Sarai wasn't particularly fond of Hagar, either (Gn 16:4-6).

Even in the Bible, lives are twisty and relationships are deeply flawed.

Fourteen years later, Sarai (now called Sarah) finally bore the child God had promised her (Gn 18:9-15). And by the time baby Isaac was weaned, Sarah was ready to eliminate, once and for all, the threat of Hagar's son to her own son's inheritance (Gn 21:7-10).

Just like that, Hagar and her son, Ishmael, were cast into the wilderness. Things had gone from good, to bad, to so bad that Hagar walked the distance of "about a bowshot" from her dehydrated and starving child because she couldn't bear to watch him die. "While she sat at a distance, she wept loudly" (Gn 21:16).

Have you been there? Completely out of options, not even sure where you went wrong in the first place? In desperate need of the Lord, but unsure if He even sees you?

Perhaps it's hard to look on Hagar's wilderness wanderings with anything but kind pity. Perhaps it's difficult to understand because your own circumstances have never been quite that dire.

The truth is, no matter our circumstances, Hagar's desperation for the Lord is exactly where each one of us ought to find ourselves every day. We ought to cry out, *Lord, I lift up my voice in desperate need of your mercy right now—this day! My only option is You. My life is a wilderness without You.*

Hagar's situation was rock-bottom awful with nowhere to go but up. But do you see what happened when she cried out?

God was right there. He saw her (Gn 21:17). Even in the driest desert, God saw Hagar.

This is the God of the Bible. He never takes His eyes off of His people. He never stops seeing them.

Whether we've been unjustly knocked down and drug out into the wilderness, or we're waking up in our warm beds with a thirst only He can satisfy—wherever we are, God sees us. He hears our pleas, and He meets our needs. Cry out to Him today.

traced through Isaac, ¹³ and I will also make a nation of the slave's son because he is your offspring."

¹⁴ Early in the morning Abraham got up, took bread and a waterskin, put them on Hagar's shoulders, and sent her and the boy away. She left and wandered in the Wilderness of Beer-sheba. ¹⁵ When the water in the skin was gone, she left the boy under one of the bushes ¹⁶ and went and sat at a distance, about a bowshot away, for she said, "I can't bear to watch the boy die!" While she sat at a distance, she ᴬ wept loudly.

¹⁷ God heard the boy crying, and the ᴮ angel of God called to Hagar from heaven and said to her, "What's wrong, Hagar? Don't be afraid, for God has heard the boy crying from the place where he is. ¹⁸ Get up, help the boy up, and grasp his hand, for I will make him a great nation." ¹⁹ Then God opened her eyes, and she saw a well. So she went and filled the waterskin and gave the boy a drink. ²⁰ God was with the boy, and he grew; he settled in the wilderness and became an archer. ²¹ He settled in the Wilderness of Paran, and his mother got a wife for him from the land of Egypt.

ABRAHAM'S COVENANT WITH ABIMELECH

²² At that time Abimelech, accompanied by Phicol the commander of his army, said to Abraham, "God is with you in everything you do. ²³ Swear to me by God here and now, that you will not break an agreement with me or with my children and descendants. As I have been loyal to you, so you will be loyal to me and to the country where you are a resident alien."

²⁴ And Abraham said, "I swear it." ²⁵ But Abraham complained to Abimelech because of the well that Abimelech's servants had seized.

²⁶ Abimelech replied, "I don't know who did this thing. You didn't report anything to me, so I hadn't heard about it until today."

²⁷ Abraham took flocks and herds and gave them to Abimelech, and the two of them made a covenant. ²⁸ Abraham separated seven ewe lambs from the flock. ²⁹ And Abimelech said to Abraham, "Why have you separated these seven ewe lambs?"

³⁰ He replied, "You are to accept the seven ewe lambs from me so that this act ᶜ will serve as my witness that I dug this well." ³¹ Therefore that place was called Beer-sheba ᴰ because it was there that the two of them swore an oath. ³² After they had made a covenant at Beer-sheba, Abimelech and Phicol, the commander of his army, left and returned to the land of the Philistines.

³³ Abraham planted a tamarisk tree in Beer-sheba, and there he called on the name of the LORD, the Everlasting God. ³⁴ And Abraham lived as an alien in the land of the Philistines for many days.

THE SACRIFICE OF ISAAC

22 After these things God tested Abraham and said to him, "Abraham!" "Here I am," he answered.

² "Take your son," he said, "your only son Isaac, whom you love, go to the land of Moriah, and offer him there as a burnt offering on one of the mountains I will tell you about."

ᴬ21:16 LXX reads *the boy*   ᴮ21:17 Or *an*   ᶜ21:30 Lit *that it*   ᴰ21:31 = Well of the Oath, or Seven Wells

³ So Abraham got up early in the morning, saddled his donkey, and took with him two of his young men and his son Isaac. He split wood for a burnt offering and set out to go to the place God had told him about. ⁴ On the third day Abraham looked up and saw the place in the distance. ⁵ Then Abraham said to his young men, "Stay here with the donkey. The boy and I will go over there to worship; then we'll come back to you." ⁶ Abraham took the wood for the burnt offering and laid it on his son Isaac. In his hand he took the fire and the knife, and the two of them walked on together.

⁷ Then Isaac spoke to his father Abraham and said, "My father."

And he replied, "Here I am, my son."

Isaac said, "The fire and the wood are here, but where is the lamb for the burnt offering?"

⁸ Abraham answered, "God himself will provide^A the lamb for the burnt offering, my son." Then the two of them walked on together.

⁹ When they arrived at the place that God had told him about, Abraham built the altar there and arranged the wood. He bound his son Isaac^B and placed him on the altar on top of the wood. ¹⁰ Then Abraham reached out and took the knife to slaughter his son.

¹¹ But the angel of the LORD called to him from heaven and said, "Abraham, Abraham!"

He replied, "Here I am."

¹² Then he said, "Do not lay a hand on the boy or do anything to him. For now I know that you fear God, since you have not withheld your only son from me." ¹³ Abraham looked up and saw a ram^C caught in the thicket by its horns. So Abraham went and took the ram and offered it as a burnt offering in place of his son. ¹⁴ And Abraham named that place The LORD Will Provide,^D so today it is said: "It will be provided^E on the LORD's mountain."

¹⁵ Then the angel of the LORD called to Abraham a second time from heaven ¹⁶ and said, "By myself I have sworn," this is the LORD's declaration: "Because you have done this thing and have not withheld your only son, ¹⁷ I will indeed bless you and make your offspring as numerous as the stars of the sky and the sand on the seashore. Your offspring will possess the city gates of their enemies. ¹⁸ And all the nations of the earth will be blessed^F by your offspring because you have obeyed my command."

¹⁹ Abraham went back to his young men, and they got up and went together to Beer-sheba. And Abraham settled in Beer-sheba.

REBEKAH'S FAMILY

²⁰ Now after these things Abraham was told, "Milcah also has borne sons to your brother Nahor: ²¹ Uz his firstborn, his brother Buz, Kemuel the father of Aram, ²² Chesed, Hazo, Pildash, Jidlaph, and Bethuel." ²³ And Bethuel fathered Rebekah. Milcah bore these eight to Nahor, Abraham's brother. ²⁴ His concubine, whose name was Reumah, also bore Tebah, Gaham, Tahash, and Maacah.

---

^A 22:8 Lit see   ^B 22:9 Or Isaac hand and foot   ^C 22:13 Some Hb mss, Sam, LXX, Syr, Tg; other Hb mss read saw behind him a ram   ^D 22:14 = Yahweh-yireh
^E 22:14 Or "He will be seen   ^F 22:18 Or will bless themselves, or will find blessing

SARAH'S BURIAL

23 Now Sarah lived 127 years; these were all the years of her life. ² Sarah died in Kiriath-arba (that is, Hebron) in the land of Canaan, and Abraham went to mourn for Sarah and to weep for her.

³ Then Abraham got up from beside his dead wife and spoke to the Hethites: ⁴ "I am an alien residing among you. Give me burial property among you so that I can bury my dead."ᴬ

⁵ The Hethites replied to Abraham, ᴮ ⁶ "Listen to us, my lord. You are a prince of Godᶜ among us. Bury your dead in our finest burial place.ᴰ None of us will withhold from you his burial place for burying your dead."

⁷ Then Abraham rose and bowed down to the Hethites, the people of the land. ⁸ He said to them, "If you are willing for me to bury my dead, listen to me and ask Ephron son of Zohar on my behalf ⁹ to give me the cave of Machpelah that belongs to him; it is at the end of his field. Let him give it to me in your presence, for the full price, as burial property."

¹⁰ Ephron was sitting among the Hethites. So in the hearingᴱ of all the Hethites who came to the gate of his city, Ephron the Hethite answered Abraham: ¹¹ "No, my lord. Listen to me. I give you the field, and I give you the cave that is in it. I give it to you in the sightᶠ of my people. Bury your dead."

¹² Abraham bowed down to the people of the land ¹³ and said to Ephron in the hearing of the people of the land, "Listen to me, if you please. Let me pay the price of the field. Accept it from me, and let me bury my dead there."

¹⁴ Ephron answered Abraham and said to him, ¹⁵ "My lord, listen to me. Land worth four hundred shekels of silver — what is that between you and me? Bury your dead." ¹⁶ Abraham agreed with Ephron, and Abraham weighed out to Ephron the silver that he had agreed to in the hearing of the Hethites: four hundred standard shekelsᴳ of silver. ¹⁷ So Ephron's field at Machpelah near Mamre — the field with its cave and all the trees anywhere within the boundaries of the field — became ¹⁸ Abraham's possession in the sight of all the Hethites who came to the gate of his city. ¹⁹ After this, Abraham buried his wife Sarah in the cave of the field at Machpelah near Mamre (that is, Hebron) in the land of Canaan. ²⁰ The field with its cave passed from the Hethites to Abraham as burial property.

A WIFE FOR ISAAC

24 Abraham was now old, getting on in years,ᴴ and the LORD had blessed him in everything. ² Abraham said to his servant, the elder of his household who managed all he owned, "Place your hand under my thigh, ³ and I will have you swear by the LORD, God of heaven and God of earth, that you will not take a wife for my son from the daughters of the Canaanites among whom I live, ⁴ but will go to my land and my family to take a wife for my son Isaac."

⁵ The servant said to him, "Suppose the woman is unwilling to follow me to this land? Should I have your son go back to the land you came from?"

ᴬ23:4 Lit dead from before me   ᴮ23:5 Lit Abraham, saying to him   ᶜ23:6 Or
a mighty prince   ᴰ23:6 Or finest graves   ᴱ23:10 Lit ears, also in vv. 13,16
ᶠ23:11 Lit in the eyes of the sons   ᴳ23:16 Lit 400 shekels passing to the merchant
ᴴ24:1 Lit days

⁶ Abraham answered him, "Make sure that you don't take my son back there. ⁷ The LORD, the God of heaven, who took me from my father's house and from my native land, who spoke to me and swore to me, 'I will give this land to your offspring' — he will send his angel before you, and you can take a wife for my son from there. ⁸ If the woman is unwilling to follow you, then you are free from this oath to me, but don't let my son go back there." ⁹ So the servant placed his hand under his master Abraham's thigh and swore an oath to him concerning this matter.

¹⁰ The servant took ten of his master's camels, and with all kinds of his master's goods in hand, he went to Aram-naharaim, to Nahor's town. ¹¹ At evening, the time when women went out to draw water, he made the camels kneel beside a well outside the town.

¹² "LORD, God of my master Abraham," he prayed, "make this happen for me today, and show kindness to my master Abraham. ¹³ I am standing here at the spring where the daughters of the men of the town are coming out to draw water. ¹⁴ Let the girl to whom I say, 'Please lower your water jug so that I may drink,' and who responds, 'Drink, and I'll water your camels also' — let her be the one you have appointed for your servant Isaac. By this I will know that you have shown kindness to my master."

¹⁵ Before he had finished speaking, there was Rebekah — daughter of Bethuel son of Milcah, the wife of Abraham's brother Nahor — coming with a jug on her shoulder. ¹⁶ Now the girl was very beautiful, a virgin — no man had been intimate with her. She went down to the spring, filled her jug, and came up. ¹⁷ Then the servant ran to meet her and said, "Please let me have a little water from your jug."

¹⁸ She replied, "Drink, my lord." She quickly lowered her jug to her hand and gave him a drink. ¹⁹ When she had finished giving him a drink, she said, "I'll also draw water for your camels until they have had enough to drink."ᴬ ²⁰ She quickly emptied her jug into the trough and hurried to the well again to draw water. She drew water for all his camels ²¹ while the man silently watched her to see whether or not the LORD had made his journey a success.

²² As the camels finished drinking, the man took a gold ring weighing half a shekel, and for her wrists two bracelets weighing ten shekels of gold. ²³ "Whose daughter are you?" he asked. "Please tell me, is there room in your father's house for us to spend the night?"

²⁴ She answered him, "I am the daughter of Bethuel son of Milcah, whom she bore to Nahor." ²⁵ She also said to him, "We have plenty of straw and feed and a place to spend the night."

²⁶ Then the man knelt low, worshiped the LORD, ²⁷ and said, "Blessed be the LORD, the God of my master Abraham, who has not withheld his kindness and faithfulness from my master. As for me, the LORD has led me on the journey to the house of my master's relatives."

²⁸ The girl ran and told her mother's household about these things. ²⁹ Now Rebekah had a brother named Laban, and Laban ran out to the man at the spring. ³⁰ As soon as he had seen the ring and the bracelets on his sister's wrists, and when he had heard his sister Rebekah's words — "The man said this to me!" — he went to the man. He was standing there by the camels at the spring.

ᴬ 24:19 Lit *they are finished drinking*

³¹ Laban said, "Come, you who are blessed by the LORD. Why are you standing out here? I have prepared the house and a place for the camels." ³² So the man came to the house, and the camels were unloaded. Straw and feed were given to the camels, and water was brought to wash his feet and the feet of the men with him.

³³ A meal was set before him, but he said, "I will not eat until I have said what I have to say."

So Laban said, "Please speak."

³⁴ "I am Abraham's servant," he said. ³⁵ "The LORD has greatly blessed my master, and he has become rich. He has given him flocks and herds, silver and gold, male and female slaves, and camels and donkeys. ³⁶ Sarah, my master's wife, bore a son to my master in her^A old age, and he has given him everything he owns. ³⁷ My master put me under this oath: 'You will not take a wife for my son from the daughters of the Canaanites in whose land I live ³⁸ but will go to my father's family and to my clan to take a wife for my son.' ³⁹ But I said to my master, 'Suppose the woman will not come back with me?' ⁴⁰ He said to me, 'The LORD before whom I have walked will send his angel with you and make your journey a success, and you will take a wife for my son from my clan and from my father's family. ⁴¹ Then you will be free from my oath if you go to my family and they do not give her to you — you will be free from my oath.'

⁴² "Today when I came to the spring, I prayed: LORD, God of my master Abraham, if only you will make my journey successful! ⁴³ I am standing here at a spring. Let the young woman^B who comes out to draw water, and I say to her, 'Please let me drink a little water from your jug,' ⁴⁴ and who responds to me, 'Drink, and I'll draw water for your camels also' — let her be the woman the LORD has appointed for my master's son.'

⁴⁵ "Before I had finished praying silently, there was Rebekah coming with her jug on her shoulder, and she went down to the spring and drew water. So I said to her, 'Please let me have a drink.' ⁴⁶ She quickly lowered her jug from her shoulder and said, 'Drink, and I'll water your camels also.' So I drank, and she also watered the camels. ⁴⁷ Then I asked her, 'Whose daughter are you?' She responded, 'The daughter of Bethuel son of Nahor, whom Milcah bore to him.' So I put the ring on her nose and the bracelets on her wrists. ⁴⁸ Then I knelt low, worshiped the LORD, and blessed the LORD, the God of my master Abraham, who guided me on the right way to take the granddaughter of my master's brother for his son. ⁴⁹ Now, if you are going to show kindness and faithfulness to my master, tell me; if not, tell me, and I will go elsewhere."^C

⁵⁰ Laban and Bethuel answered, "This is from the LORD; we have no choice in the matter.^D ⁵¹ Rebekah is here in front of you. Take her and go, and let her be a wife for your master's son, just as the LORD has spoken."

⁵² When Abraham's servant heard their words, he bowed to the ground before the LORD. ⁵³ Then he brought out objects of silver and gold, and garments, and gave them to Rebekah. He also gave precious gifts to her brother and her mother. ⁵⁴ Then he and the men with him ate and drank and spent the night.

When they got up in the morning, he said, "Send me to my master."

---

^A24:36 Sam, LXX read *his*   ^B24:43 Or *the virgin*   ^C24:49 Lit *go to the right or to the left*   ^D24:50 Lit *we cannot say to you anything bad or good*

⁵⁵ But her brother and mother said, "Let the girl stay with us for about ten days.ᴬ Then sheᴮ can go."

⁵⁶ But he responded to them, "Do not delay me, since the Lᴏʀᴅ has made my journey a success. Send me away so that I may go to my master."

⁵⁷ So they said, "Let's call the girl and ask her opinion."ᶜ

⁵⁸ They called Rebekah and said to her, "Will you go with this man?"

She replied, "I will go." ⁵⁹ So they sent away their sister Rebekah with the one who had nursed and raised her,ᴰ and Abraham's servant and his men.

⁶⁰ They blessed Rebekah, saying to her:

Our sister, may you become
thousands upon ten thousands.
May your offspring possess
the city gates of theirᴱ enemies.

⁶¹ Then Rebekah and her female servants got up, mounted the camels, and followed the man. So the servant took Rebekah and left.

⁶² Now Isaac was returning from Beer-lahai-roi,ᶠ for he was living in the Negev region. ⁶³ In the early evening Isaac went out to walkᴳ in the field, and looking up he saw camels coming. ⁶⁴ Rebekah looked up, and when she saw Isaac, she got down from her camel ⁶⁵ and asked the servant, "Who is that man in the field coming to meet us?"

The servant answered, "It is my master." So she took her veil and covered herself. ⁶⁶ Then the servant told Isaac everything he had done.

⁶⁷ And Isaac brought her into the tent of his mother Sarah and took Rebekah to be his wife. Isaac loved her, and he was comforted after his mother's death.

ABRAHAM'S OTHER WIFE AND SONS

25 Abraham had takenᴴ another wife, whose name was Keturah, ² and she bore him Zimran, Jokshan, Medan, Midian, Ishbak, and Shuah. ³ Jokshan fathered Sheba and Dedan. Dedan's sons were the Asshurim, Letushim, and Leummim. ⁴ And Midian's sons were Ephah, Epher, Hanoch, Abida, and Eldaah. All these were sons of Keturah. ⁵ Abraham gave everything he owned to Isaac. ⁶ But Abraham gave gifts to the sons of his concubines, and while he was still alive he sent them eastward, away from his son Isaac, to the land of the East.

ABRAHAM'S DEATH

⁷ This is the length of Abraham's life:ᴵ 175 years. ⁸ He took his last breath and died at a good old age, old and contented,ᴶ and he was gathered to his people. ⁹ His sons Isaac and Ishmael buried him in the cave of Machpelah near Mamre, in the field of Ephron son of Zohar the Hethite. ¹⁰ This was the field that Abraham bought from the Hethites. Abraham was buried there with his wife Sarah. ¹¹ After Abraham's death, God blessed his son Isaac, who lived near Beer-lahai-roi.

ᴬ24:55 Lit *us days or tenth* ᴮ24:55 Or *you* ᶜ24:57 Lit *mouth* ᴰ24:59 Lit *with her wet nurse*; Gn 35:8 ᴱ24:60 Lit *his* ᶠ24:62 = A Well of the Living One Who Sees Me ᴳ24:63 Or *pray, or meditate*; Hb obscure ᴴ25:1 Or *Abraham took* ᴵ25:7 Lit *And these are the days of the years of the life of Abraham that he lived* ᴶ25:8 Sam, LXX, Syr read *full of days*

ISHMAEL'S FAMILY RECORDS

¹²These are the family records of Abraham's son Ishmael, whom Hagar the Egyptian, Sarah's slave, bore to Abraham. ¹³These are the names of Ishmael's sons; their names according to the family records are Nebaioth, Ishmael's firstborn, then Kedar, Adbeel, Mibsam, ¹⁴Mishma, Dumah, Massa, ¹⁵Hadad, Tema, Jetur, Naphish, and Kedemah. ¹⁶These are Ishmael's sons, and these are their names by their settlements and encampments: twelve leaders^A of their clans.^B ¹⁷This is the length^C of Ishmael's life: 137 years. He took his last breath and died, and was gathered to his people. ¹⁸And they^D settled from Havilah to Shur, which is opposite Egypt as you go toward Asshur.^E He^F stayed near^G all his relatives.

THE BIRTH OF JACOB AND ESAU

¹⁹These are the family records of Isaac son of Abraham. Abraham fathered Isaac. ²⁰Isaac was forty years old when he took as his wife Rebekah daughter of Bethuel the Aramean from Paddan-aram and sister of Laban the Aramean. ²¹Isaac prayed to the LORD on behalf of his wife because she was childless. The LORD was receptive to his prayer, and his wife Rebekah conceived. ²²But the children inside her struggled with each other, and she said, "Why is this happening to me?"^H So she went to inquire of the LORD. ²³And the LORD said to her:

Two nations are in your womb;
two peoples will come from you and be separated.
One people will be stronger than the other,
and the older will serve the younger.

²⁴When her time came to give birth, there were indeed twins in her womb. ²⁵The first one came out red-looking,^I covered with hair^J like a fur coat, and they named him Esau. ²⁶After this, his brother came out grasping Esau's heel with his hand. So he was named Jacob.^K Isaac was sixty years old when they were born.

ESAU SELLS HIS BIRTHRIGHT

²⁷When the boys grew up, Esau became an expert hunter, an outdoorsman,^L but Jacob was a quiet man who stayed at home.^M ²⁸Isaac loved Esau because he had a taste for wild game, but Rebekah loved Jacob.

²⁹Once when Jacob was cooking a stew, Esau came in from the field exhausted. ³⁰He said to Jacob, "Let me eat some of that red stuff, because I'm exhausted." That is why he was also named Edom.^N

³¹Jacob replied, "First sell me your birthright."

³²"Look," said Esau, "I'm about to die, so what good is a birthright to me?"

³³Jacob said, "Swear to me first." So he swore to Jacob and sold his birthright to him. ³⁴Then Jacob gave bread and lentil stew to Esau; he ate, drank, got up, and went away. So Esau despised his birthright.

---

^A25:16 Or chieftains ^B25:16 Or peoples ^C25:17 Lit And these are the years
^D25:18 LXX, Vg read he ^E25:18 Or Assyria ^F25:18 = Ishmael and his descendants
^G25:18 Or He settled down alongside of ^H25:22 Lit said, "If thus, why this I?"
^I25:25 In Hb, red-looking sounds like "Edom"; Gn 32:3. ^J25:25 In Hb, hair
sounds like "Seir"; Gn 32:3. ^K25:26 = He Grasps the Heel ^L25:27 Lit a man of
the field ^M25:27 Lit man living in tents ^N25:30 = Red

THE PROMISE REAFFIRMED TO ISAAC

26 There was another famine in the land in addition to the one that had occurred in Abraham's time. And Isaac went to Abimelech, king of the Philistines, at Gerar. ²The LORD appeared to him and said, "Do not go down to Egypt. Live in the land that I tell you about; ³ stay in this land as an alien, and I will be with you and bless you. For I will give all these lands to you and your offspring, and I will confirm the oath that I swore to your father Abraham. ⁴ I will make your offspring as numerous as the stars of the sky, I will give your offspring all these lands, and all the nations of the earth will be blessed^A by your offspring, ⁵ because Abraham listened to me and kept my mandate, my commands, my statutes, and my instructions." ⁶ So Isaac settled in Gerar.

ISAAC'S DECEPTION

⁷ When the men of the place asked about his wife, he said, "She is my sister," for he was afraid to say "my wife," thinking, "The men of the place will kill me on account of Rebekah, for she is a beautiful woman." ⁸ When Isaac had been there for some time, Abimelech king of the Philistines looked down from the window and was surprised to see^B Isaac caressing his wife Rebekah.

⁹ Abimelech sent for Isaac and said, "So she is really your wife! How could you say, 'She is my sister'?"

Isaac answered him, "Because I thought I might die on account of her."

¹⁰ Then Abimelech said, "What is this you've done to us? One of the people could easily have slept with your wife, and you would have brought guilt on us." ¹¹ So Abimelech warned all the people, "Whoever harms this man or his wife will certainly be put to death."

CONFLICTS OVER WELLS

¹² Isaac sowed seed in that land, and in that year he reaped^C a hundred times what was sown. The LORD blessed him, ¹³ and the man became rich and kept getting richer until he was very wealthy. ¹⁴ He had flocks of sheep, herds of cattle, and many slaves, and the Philistines were envious of him. ¹⁵ Philistines stopped up all the wells that his father's servants had dug in the days of his father Abraham, filling them with dirt. ¹⁶ And Abimelech said to Isaac, "Leave us, for you are much too powerful for us."^D

¹⁷ So Isaac left there, camped in the Gerar Valley, and lived there. ¹⁸ Isaac reopened the wells that had been dug in the days of his father Abraham and that the Philistines had stopped up after Abraham died. He gave them the same names his father had given them. ¹⁹ Then Isaac's servants dug in the valley and found a well of spring^E water there. ²⁰ But the herdsmen of Gerar quarreled with Isaac's herdsmen and said, "The water is ours!" So he named the well Esek^F because they argued with him. ²¹ Then they dug another well and quarreled over that one also, so he named it Sitnah.^G ²² He moved from there and dug another, and they did not quarrel over it. He named it Rehoboth^H and said, "For now the LORD has made space for us, and we will be fruitful in the land."

---

^A 26:4 Or *will bless themselves*   ^B 26:8 Or *and he looked and behold* —
^C 26:12 Lit *found*   ^D 26:16 Or *are more numerous than we are*   ^E 26:19 Lit *living*
^F 26:20 = Argument   ^G 26:21 = Hostility   ^H 26:22 = Open Spaces

GRASPING GOD'S GRACE

GENESIS 25:19–26:35; GENESIS 49:8-12; 1 SAMUEL 14:47

Not many people can say they burst onto the scene like Jacob did. He made his entrance into the world holding onto the heel of his twin brother (Gn 25:26). So, naturally, that's what his parents named him: "He grasps the heel." (Aren't you glad you weren't named after some quirk in your birth story?)

Jacob's grasping didn't end at birth. His story reads like a laundry list of things he did to get what he wanted. He was determined and driven, willing to deceive and manipulate situations to get his way.

Jacob manipulated his brother, Esau, into handing over his birthright (Gn 25; 27:1-40), and then tricked his father, Isaac, into giving him Esau's rightful blessing. He worked fourteen years to make beautiful Rachel his wife, and then went outside God's design for marriage to get more sons (Gn 29:13-30). He entered a battle of wits with his uncle, Laban, and left with the lion's share of Laban's livestock (Gn 30:25-43). And in an over-the-top display of generosity, he tried to win his brother's forgiveness (Gn 33).

Jacob was a heel-grasper, alright. He was a man whose power-grabs seemed to live by the age-old adage, "The end justifies the means."

But this story isn't about a smooth-talking man. It's another instance of the ribbon of grace weaving its way through humanity—not only through Jacob's story, but through yours and mine.

See, we're heel-graspers, too. How often have we deceived ourselves or others to get what we wanted? How many ways have we manipulated situations, relying on our own cunning to succeed in life, rather than depending on God for all we need?

The good news for us is that God's promise to Jacob—the promise that the Lord would watch over and bless him—didn't depend on Jacob's report card (Gn 28:15). Again and again God reiterated His promise to bless the wayward go-getter, not because Jacob deserved it, but simply because it pleased God to do so. **It brings God immeasurable glory when He dumps buckets of blessing onto His unworthy children.**

Like a beautiful bookend to Jacob's story, God went on to change Jacob's name from "he grasps the heel" to Israel, meaning, "he struggles with God" (Gn 32:28). Jacob, the conniver and striver, became the father of a nation that birthed the Deliverer (Gn 49:8-12).

That's what God does for us, too—He doesn't leave us alone in our sin, but instead comes down to wrestle with us. He seeks us out face-to-face, so that by His touch we might be blessed (Gn 32:24-32).

THE LORD APPEARS TO ISAAC

²³ From there he went up to Beer-sheba, ²⁴ and the LORD appeared to him that night and said, "I am the God of your father Abraham. Do not be afraid, for I am with you. I will bless you and multiply your offspring because of my servant Abraham."

²⁵ So he built an altar there, called on the name of the LORD, and pitched his tent there. Isaac's servants also dug a well there.

COVENANT WITH ABIMELECH

²⁶ Now Abimelech came to him from Gerar with Ahuzzath his adviser and Phicol the commander of his army. ²⁷ Isaac said to them, "Why have you come to me? You hated me and sent me away from you."

²⁸ They replied, "We have clearly seen how the LORD has been with you. We think there should be an oath between two parties — between us and you. Let us make a covenant with you: ²⁹ You will not harm us, just as we have not harmed you but have done only what was good to you, sending you away in peace. You are now blessed by the LORD."

³⁰ So he prepared a banquet for them, and they ate and drank. ³¹ They got up early in the morning and swore an oath to each other.ᴬ Isaac sent them on their way, and they left him in peace. ³² On that same day Isaac's servants came to tell him about the well they had dug, saying to him, "We have found water!" ³³ He called it Sheba.ᴮ Therefore the name of the city is still Beer-sheba ᶜ today.

ESAU'S WIVES

³⁴ When Esau was forty years old, he took as his wives Judith daughter of Beeri the Hethite, and Basemath daughter of Elon the Hethite. ³⁵ They made life bitter ᴰ for Isaac and Rebekah.

THE STOLEN BLESSING

27 When Isaac was old and his eyes were so weak that he could not see, he called his older son Esau and said to him, "My son."

And he answered, "Here I am."

² He said, "Look, I am old and do not know the day of my death. ³ So now take your hunting gear, your quiver and bow, and go out in the field to hunt some game for me. ⁴ Then make me a delicious meal that I love and bring it to me to eat, so that I can bless you before I die."

⁵ Now Rebekah was listening to what Isaac said to his son Esau. So while Esau went to the field to hunt some game to bring in, ⁶ Rebekah said to her son Jacob, "Listen! I heard your father talking with your brother Esau. He said, ⁷ 'Bring me game and make a delicious meal for me to eat so that I can bless you in the LORD's presence before I die.' ⁸ Now, my son, listen to me and do what I tell you. ⁹ Go to the flock and bring me two choice young goats, and I will make them into a delicious meal for your father — the kind he loves. ¹⁰ Then take it to your father to eat so that he may bless you before he dies."

¹¹ Jacob answered Rebekah his mother, "Look, my brother Esau is a hairy man, but I am a man with smooth skin. ¹² Suppose my father touches me.

ᴬ26:31 Lit swore, each man to his brother   ᴮ26:33 Or Shibah   ᶜ26:33 = Well of the Oath   ᴰ26:35 Lit And they became bitterness of spirit

Then I will be revealed to him as a deceiver and bring a curse rather than a blessing on myself."

¹³ His mother said to him, "Your curse be on me, my son. Just obey me and go get them for me."

¹⁴ So he went and got the goats and brought them to his mother, and his mother made the delicious food his father loved. ¹⁵ Then Rebekah took the best clothes of her older son Esau, which were in the house, and had her younger son Jacob wear them. ¹⁶ She put the skins of the young goats on his hands and the smooth part of his neck. ¹⁷ Then she handed the delicious food and the bread she had made to her son Jacob.

¹⁸ When he came to his father, he said, "My father."

And he answered, "Here I am. Who are you, my son?"

¹⁹ Jacob replied to his father, "I am Esau, your firstborn. I have done as you told me. Please sit up and eat some of my game so that you may bless me."

²⁰ But Isaac said to his son, "How did you ever find it so quickly, my son?"

He replied, "Because the LORD your God made it happen for me."

²¹ Then Isaac said to Jacob, "Please come closer so I can touch you, my son. Are you really my son Esau or not?"

²² So Jacob came closer to his father Isaac. When he touched him, he said, "The voice is the voice of Jacob, but the hands are the hands of Esau." ²³ He did not recognize him, because his hands were hairy like those of his brother Esau; so he blessed him. ²⁴ Again he asked, "Are you really my son Esau?"

And he replied, "I am."

²⁵ Then he said, "Bring it closer to me, and let me eat some of my son's game so that I can bless you." Jacob brought it closer to him, and he ate; he brought him wine, and he drank.

²⁶ Then his father Isaac said to him, "Please come closer and kiss me, my son." ²⁷ So he came closer and kissed him. When Isaac smelledᴬ his clothes, he blessed him and said:

Ah, the smell of my son
is like the smell of a field
that the LORD has blessed.
²⁸ May God give to you —
from the dew of the sky
and from the richness of the land —
an abundance of grain and new wine.
²⁹ May peoples serve you
and nations bow in worship to you.
Be master over your relatives;
may your mother's sons bow in worship to you.
Those who curse you will be cursed,
and those who bless you will be blessed.

³⁰ As soon as Isaac had finished blessing Jacob and Jacob had left the presence of his father Isaac, his brother Esau arrived from his hunting. ³¹ He had also made some delicious food and brought it to his father. He said to his father, "Let my father get up and eat some of his son's game, so that you may bless me."

ᴬ27:27 Lit *smelled the smell of*

³² But his father Isaac said to him, "Who are you?"

He answered, "I am Esau your firstborn son."

³³ Isaac began to tremble uncontrollably. "Who was it then," he said, "who hunted game and brought it to me? I ate it all before you came in, and I blessed him. Indeed, he will be blessed!"

³⁴ When Esau heard his father's words, he cried out with a loud and bitter cry and said to his father, "Bless me too, my father!"

³⁵ But he replied, "Your brother came deceitfully and took your blessing."

³⁶ So he said, "Isn't he rightly named Jacob?ᴬ For he has cheated me twice now. He took my birthright, and look, now he has taken my blessing." Then he asked, "Haven't you saved a blessing for me?"

³⁷ But Isaac answered Esau, "Look, I have made him a master over you, have given him all of his relatives as his servants, and have sustained him with grain and new wine. What then can I do for you, my son?"

³⁸ Esau said to his father, "Do you have only one blessing, my father? Bless me too, my father!" And Esau wept loudly.ᴮ

³⁹ His father Isaac answered him,

Look, your dwelling place will be
away from the richness of the land,
away from the dew of the sky above.
⁴⁰   You will live by your sword,
and you will serve your brother.
But when you rebel,ᶜ
you will break his yoke from your neck.

ESAU'S ANGER

⁴¹ Esau held a grudge against Jacob because of the blessing his father had given him. And Esau determined in his heart: "The days of mourning for my father are approaching; then I will kill my brother Jacob."

⁴² When the words of her older son Esau were reported to Rebekah, she summoned her younger son Jacob and said to him, "Listen, your brother Esau is consoling himself by planning to kill you. ⁴³ So now, my son, listen to me. Flee at once to my brother Laban in Haran, ⁴⁴ and stay with him for a few days until your brother's anger subsides — ⁴⁵ until your brother's rage turns away from you and he forgets what you have done to him. Then I will send for you and bring you back from there. Why should I lose you both in one day?"

⁴⁶ So Rebekah said to Isaac, "I'm sick of my life because of these Hethite girls. If Jacob marries someone from around here,ᴰ like these Hethite girls, what good is my life?"

JACOB'S DEPARTURE

28 So Isaac summoned Jacob, blessed him, and commanded him, "Do not marry a Canaanite girl. ² Go at once to Paddan-aram, to the house of Bethuel, your mother's father. Marry one of the daughters of Laban, your mother's brother. ³ May God Almighty bless you and make you fruitful and multiply you so that you become an assembly of peoples. ⁴ May God give you and your offspring the blessing of Abraham so that you may

---

ᴬ27:36 = He Grasps the Heel   ᴮ27:38 Lit *Esau lifted up his voice and wept*
ᶜ27:40 Hb obscure   ᴰ27:46 Lit *someone like these daughters of the land*

possess the land where you live as a foreigner, the land God gave to Abraham." ⁵ So Isaac sent Jacob to Paddan-aram, to Laban son of Bethuel the Aramean, the brother of Rebekah, the mother of Jacob and Esau.

⁶ Esau noticed that Isaac blessed Jacob and sent him to Paddan-aram to get a wife there. When he blessed him, Isaac commanded Jacob, "Do not marry a Canaanite girl." ⁷ And Jacob listened to his father and mother and went to Paddan-aram. ⁸ Esau realized that his father Isaac disapproved of the Canaanite women, ⁹ so Esau went to Ishmael and married, in addition to his other wives, Mahalath daughter of Ishmael, Abraham's son. She was the sister of Nebaioth.

JACOB AT BETHEL

¹⁰ Jacob left Beer-sheba and went toward Haran. ¹¹ He reached a certain place and spent the night there because the sun had set. He took one of the stones from the place, put it there at his head, and lay down in that place. ¹² And he dreamed: A stairway was set on the ground with its top reaching the sky, and God's angels were going up and down on it. ¹³ The LORD was standing there beside him,ᴬ saying, "I am the LORD, the God of your father Abraham and the God of Isaac. I will give you and your offspring the land on which you are lying. ¹⁴ Your offspring will be like the dust of the earth, and you will spread out toward the west, the east, the north, and the south. All the peoples on earth will be blessed through you and your offspring. ¹⁵ Look, I am with you and will watch over you wherever you go. I will bring you back to this land, for I will not leave you until I have done what I have promised you."

¹⁶ When Jacob awoke from his sleep, he said, "Surely the LORD is in this place, and I did not know it." ¹⁷ He was afraid and said, "What an awesome place this is! This is none other than the house of God. This is the gate of heaven."

¹⁸ Early in the morning Jacob took the stone that was near his head and set it up as a marker. He poured oil on top of it ¹⁹ and named the place Bethel,ᴮ though previously the city was named Luz. ²⁰ Then Jacob made a vow: "If God will be with me and watch over me during this journey I'm making, if he provides me with food to eat and clothing to wear, ²¹ and if I return safely to my father's family, then the LORD will be my God. ²² This stone that I have set up as a marker will be God's house, and I will give to you a tenth of all that you give me."

JACOB MEETS RACHEL

29 Jacob resumed his journeyᶜ and went to the eastern country.ᴰ ² He looked and saw a well in a field. Three flocks of sheep were lying there beside it because the sheep were watered from this well. But a large stone covered the opening of the well. ³ The shepherds would roll the stone from the opening of the well and water the sheep when all the flocksᴱ were gathered there. Then they would return the stone to its place over the well's opening.

ᴬ28:13 Or *there above it* ᴮ28:19 = House of God ᶜ29:1 Lit *Jacob picked up his feet* ᴰ29:1 Lit *the land of the children of the east* ᴱ29:3 Sam, some LXX mss read *flocks and the shepherds*

⁴ Jacob asked the men at the well, "My brothers! Where are you from?"

"We're from Haran," they answered.

⁵ "Do you know Laban grandson of Nahor?" Jacob asked them.

They answered, "We know him."

⁶ "Is he well?" Jacob asked.

"Yes," they said, "and here is his daughter Rachel, coming with his sheep."

⁷ Then Jacob said, "Look, it is still broad daylight. It's not time for the animals to be gathered. Water the flock, then go out and let them graze."

⁸ But they replied, "We can't until all the flocks have been gathered and the stone is rolled from the well's opening. Then we will water the sheep."

⁹ While he was still speaking with them, Rachel came with her father's sheep, for she was a shepherdess. ¹⁰ As soon as Jacob saw his uncle Laban's daughter Rachel with his sheep,ᴬ he went up and rolled the stone from the opening and watered his uncle Laban's sheep. ¹¹ Then Jacob kissed Rachel and wept loudly.ᴮ ¹² He told Rachel that he was her father's relative, Rebekah's son. She ran and told her father.

JACOB DECEIVED

¹³ When Laban heard the news about his sister's son Jacob, he ran to meet him, hugged him, and kissed him. Then he took him to his house, and Jacob told him all that had happened. ¹⁴ Laban said to him, "Yes, you are my own flesh and blood."ᶜ

After Jacob had stayed with him a month, ¹⁵ Laban said to him, "Just because you're my relative, should you work for me for nothing? Tell me what your wages should be."

¹⁶ Now Laban had two daughters: the older was named Leah, and the younger was named Rachel. ¹⁷ Leah had tender eyes, but Rachel was shapely and beautiful. ¹⁸ Jacob loved Rachel, so he answered Laban, "I'll work for you seven years for your younger daughter Rachel."

¹⁹ Laban replied, "Better that I give her to you than to some other man. Stay with me." ²⁰ So Jacob worked seven years for Rachel, and they seemed like only a few days to him because of his love for her.

²¹ Then Jacob said to Laban, "Since my time is complete, give me my wife, so I can sleep withᴰ her." ²² So Laban invited all the men of the place and sponsored a feast. ²³ That evening, Laban took his daughter Leah and gave her to Jacob, and he slept with her. ²⁴ And Laban gave his slave Zilpah to his daughter Leah as her slave.

²⁵ When morning came, there was Leah! So he said to Laban, "What is this you have done to me? Wasn't it for Rachel that I worked for you? Why have you deceived me?"

²⁶ Laban answered, "It is not the custom in this place to give the younger daughter in marriage before the firstborn. ²⁷ Complete this week of wedding celebration, and we will also give you this younger one in return for working yet another seven years for me."

²⁸ And Jacob did just that. He finished the week of celebration, and Laban gave him his daughter Rachel as his wife. ²⁹ And Laban gave his slave Bilhah to his daughter Rachel as her slave. ³⁰ Jacob slept with Rachel also,

---

ᴬ29:10 Lit with the sheep of Laban his mother's brother ᴮ29:11 Lit and he lifted his voice and wept ᶜ29:14 Lit my bone and my flesh ᴰ29:21 Lit can go to and indeed, he loved Rachel more than Leah. And he worked for Laban another seven years.

JACOB'S SONS

[31] When the LORD saw that Leah was unloved, he opened her womb; but Rachel was unable to conceive. [32] Leah conceived, gave birth to a son, and named him Reuben,[A] for she said, "The LORD has seen my affliction; surely my husband will love me now."

[33] She conceived again, gave birth to a son, and said, "The LORD heard that I am unloved and has given me this son also." So she named him Simeon.[B]

[34] She conceived again, gave birth to a son, and said, "At last, my husband will become attached to me because I have borne three sons for him." Therefore he was named Levi.[C]

[35] And she conceived again, gave birth to a son, and said, "This time I will praise the LORD." Therefore she named him Judah.[D] Then Leah stopped having children.

30 When Rachel saw that she was not bearing Jacob any children, she envied her sister. "Give me sons, or I will die!" she said to Jacob.

[2] Jacob became angry with Rachel and said, "Am I in God's place, who has withheld offspring[E] from you?"

[3] Then she said, "Here is my maid Bilhah. Go sleep with her, and she'll bear children for me[F] so that through her I too can build a family." [4] So Rachel gave her slave Bilhah to Jacob as a wife, and he slept with her. [5] Bilhah conceived and bore Jacob a son. [6] Rachel said, "God has vindicated me; yes, he has heard me and given me a son," so she named him Dan.[G]

[7] Rachel's slave Bilhah conceived again and bore Jacob a second son. [8] Rachel said, "In my wrestlings with God,[H] I have wrestled with my sister and won," and she named him Naphtali.[I]

[9] When Leah saw that she had stopped having children, she took her slave Zilpah and gave her to Jacob as a wife. [10] Leah's slave Zilpah bore Jacob a son. [11] Then Leah said, "What good fortune!"[J] and she named him Gad.[K]

[12] When Leah's slave Zilpah bore Jacob a second son, [13] Leah said, "I am happy that the women call me happy," so she named him Asher.[L]

[14] Reuben went out during the wheat harvest and found some mandrakes in the field. When he brought them to his mother Leah, Rachel asked, "Please give me some of your son's mandrakes."

[15] But Leah replied to her, "Isn't it enough that you have taken my husband? Now you also want to take my son's mandrakes?"

"Well then," Rachel said, "he can sleep with you tonight in exchange for your son's mandrakes."

[A]29:32 = See, a Son; in Hb, the name *Reuben* sounds like "has seen my affliction." [B]29:33 In Hb, the name *Simeon* sounds like "has heard." [C]29:34 In Hb, the name *Levi* sounds like "attached to." [D]29:35 In Hb, the name *Judah* sounds like "praise." [E]30:2 Lit *the fruit of the womb* [F]30:3 Lit *bear on my knees* [G]30:6 In Hb, the name *Dan* sounds like "has vindicated," or "has judged." [H]30:8 Or *"With mighty wrestlings"* [I]30:8 In Hb, the name *Naphtali* sounds like "my wrestling." [J]30:11 Alt Hb tradition, LXX, Vg read *"Good fortune has come!"* [K]30:11 = Good Fortune [L]30:13 = Happy

GOD REMEMBERED RACHEL

GENESIS 29–30; GENESIS 35; PSALM 98:3; ISAIAH 49:16

If Leah was the "unloved wife," Rachel was the "beloved wife." Scripture says Rachel was "shapely and beautiful," and Jacob loved her from the moment he laid eyes on her (Gn 29:9-18). But while Leah was the fertile wife, Rachel was barren.

Unloved or childless, favored or fertile, Jacob's wives both walked through decades of hurt and resentment, comparison and competition. Rachel, desperate to conceive, even offered Leah a night with Jacob in exchange for a few mandrakes, a root thought to promote fertility. But God gave Leah another child, not Rachel. Three more, actually—two sons and a daughter. The mandrakes didn't have the power to give Rachel what she wanted, and so she felt forgotten, worthless.

We read this story and we want to hug Rachel and tell her, *Don't you see—Jacob loves you! God loves you! You aren't defined by the offspring you can or can't produce!*

Her response would be a sad one: *But in my world, children equal worth.*

And she'd be right. The world had all kinds of ideas about what gave people worth back then. While some of the definitions have changed, things aren't much different now, are they?

"Then God remembered Rachel. He listened to her and opened her womb."

GENESIS 30:22

This verse has always puzzled me. If "God remembered Rachel" in verse Genesis 30:22, had He forgotten her sometime before then? And if God had never opened her womb, would we believe He'd forgotten her entirely?

When reading Genesis, we discover this isn't the first time "God remembered" one of His children. He remembered Noah and His creation, saving them from the flood (Gn 8:1). He remembered Abraham and saved Lot from the destruction of Sodom and Gomorrah (Gn 19:29). It seems when God remembers someone it's always followed by a beneficial act.

On the flip side, when I search for a place in Scripture where God has forgotten someone, I come up short. Instead, I find verses like Psalm 98:3: "He has remembered his love and faithfulness to the house of Israel." And Isaiah 49:16: "Look, I have inscribed you on the palms of my hands; your walls are continually before me."

Had God ever forsaken Rachel? No, He'd treasured her all along. Her worth in His eyes had never come from her beauty or ability to bear children. **Rachel's worth may have fluctuated in the eyes of her world, but her true worth never changed in the eyes of her Creator.**

In this story of two sisters, each feeling forgotten in her own way, we see the God who remembers. He remembers His covenant promise to His people, graciously building up the nation of Israel in its homeland. He did not forget Leah in her rejection or Rachel in her desperation. And today, He has not forgotten you.

49

¹⁶ When Jacob came in from the field that evening, Leah went out to meet him and said, "You must come with me, for I have hired you with my son's mandrakes." So Jacob slept with her that night.

¹⁷ God listened to Leah, and she conceived and bore Jacob a fifth son. ¹⁸ Leah said, "God has rewarded me for giving my slave to my husband," and she named him Issachar.[A]

¹⁹ Then Leah conceived again and bore Jacob a sixth son. ²⁰ "God has given me a good gift," Leah said. "This time my husband will honor me because I have borne six sons for him," and she named him Zebulun.[B] ²¹ Later, Leah bore a daughter and named her Dinah.

²² Then God remembered Rachel. He listened to her and opened her womb. ²³ She conceived and bore a son, and she said, "God has taken away my disgrace." ²⁴ She named him Joseph[C] and said, "May the LORD add another son to me."

JACOB'S FLOCKS MULTIPLY

²⁵ After Rachel gave birth to Joseph, Jacob said to Laban, "Send me on my way so that I can return to my homeland. ²⁶ Give me my wives and my children that I have worked for, and let me go. You know how hard I have worked for you."

²⁷ But Laban said to him, "If I have found favor with you, stay. I have learned by divination that the LORD has blessed me because of you." ²⁸ Then Laban said, "Name your wages, and I will pay them."

²⁹ So Jacob said to him, "You know how I have served you and how your herds have fared with me. ³⁰ For you had very little before I came, but now your wealth has increased. The LORD has blessed you because of me. And now, when will I also do something for my own family?"

³¹ Laban asked, "What should I give you?"

And Jacob said, "You don't need to give me anything. If you do this one thing for me, I will continue to shepherd and keep your flock. ³² Let me go through all your sheep today and remove every sheep that is speckled or spotted, every dark-colored sheep among the lambs, and the spotted and speckled among the female goats. Such will be my wages. ³³ In the future when you come to check on my wages, my honesty will testify for me. If I have any female goats that are not speckled or spotted, or any lambs that are not black, they will be considered stolen."

³⁴ "Good," said Laban. "Let it be as you have said."

³⁵ That day Laban removed the streaked and spotted male goats and all the speckled and spotted female goats — every one that had any white on it — and every dark-colored one among the lambs, and he placed his sons in charge of them. ³⁶ He put a three-day journey between himself and Jacob. Jacob, meanwhile, was shepherding the rest of Laban's flock.

³⁷ Jacob then took branches of fresh poplar, almond, and plane wood, and peeled the bark, exposing white stripes on the branches. ³⁸ He set the peeled branches in the troughs in front of the sheep — in the water channels where the sheep came to drink. And the sheep bred when they came to drink. ³⁹ The flocks bred in front of the branches and bore streaked, speckled, and spotted young. ⁴⁰ Jacob separated the lambs and made the flocks face the streaked

---

[A]30:18 In Hb, the name *Issachar* sounds like "reward."   [B]30:20 In Hb, the name *Zebulun* sounds like "honored."   [C]30:24 = He Adds sheep and the completely dark sheep in Laban's flocks. Then he set his own stock apart and didn't put them with Laban's sheep. [41] Whenever the stronger of the flock were breeding, Jacob placed the branches in the troughs, in full view of the flocks, and they would breed in front of the branches. [42] As for the weaklings of the flocks, he did not put out the branches. So it turned out that the weak sheep belonged to Laban and the stronger ones to Jacob. [43] And the man became very rich.[A] He had many flocks, female and male slaves, and camels and donkeys.

JACOB SEPARATES FROM LABAN

31 Now Jacob heard what Laban's sons were saying: "Jacob has taken all that was our father's and has built this wealth from what belonged to our father." [2] And Jacob saw from Laban's face that his attitude toward him was not the same as before.

[3] The LORD said to him, "Go back to the land of your fathers and to your family, and I will be with you."

[4] Jacob had Rachel and Leah called to the field where his flocks were. [5] He said to them, "I can see from your father's face that his attitude toward me is not the same as before, but the God of my father has been with me. [6] You know that with all my strength I have served your father [7] and that he has cheated me and changed my wages ten times. But God has not let him harm me. [8] If he said, 'The spotted sheep will be your wages,' then all the sheep were born spotted. If he said, 'The streaked sheep will be your wages,' then all the sheep were born streaked. [9] God has taken away your father's herds and given them to me.

[10] "When the flocks were breeding, I saw in a dream that the streaked, spotted, and speckled males were mating with the females. [11] In that dream the angel of God said to me, 'Jacob!' and I said, 'Here I am.' [12] And he said, 'Look up and see: all the males that are mating with the flocks are streaked, spotted, and speckled, for I have seen all that Laban has been doing to you. [13] I am the God of Bethel, where you poured oil on the stone marker and made a solemn vow to me. Get up, leave this land, and return to your native land.'"

[14] Then Rachel and Leah answered him, "Do we have any portion or inheritance in our father's family? [15] Are we not regarded by him as outsiders? For he has sold us and has certainly spent our purchase price. [16] In fact, all the wealth that God has taken away from our father belongs to us and to our children. So do whatever God has said to you."

[17] So Jacob got up and put his children and wives on the camels. [18] He took all the livestock and possessions he had acquired in Paddan-aram, and he drove his herds to go to the land of Canaan, to his father Isaac. [19] When Laban had gone to shear his sheep, Rachel stole her father's household idols. [20] And Jacob deceived[B] Laban the Aramean, not telling him that he was fleeing. [21] He fled with all his possessions, crossed the Euphrates, and headed for[C] the hill country of Gilead.

LABAN OVERTAKES JACOB

[22] On the third day Laban was told that Jacob had fled. [23] So he took his relatives with him, pursued Jacob for seven days, and overtook him in the hill country of Gilead. [24] But God came to Laban the Aramean in a dream at

[A]30:43 Lit *The man spread out very much, very much*   [B]31:20 Lit *And he stole the heart of*   [C]31:21 Lit *and set his face to* night. "Watch yourself!" God warned him. "Don't say anything to Jacob, either good or bad."

²⁵ When Laban overtook Jacob, Jacob had pitched his tent in the hill country, and Laban and his relatives also pitched their tents in the hill country of Gilead. ²⁶ Laban said to Jacob, "What have you done? You have deceived me and taken my daughters away like prisoners of war! ²⁷ Why did you secretly flee from me, deceive me, and not tell me? I would have sent you away with joy and singing, with tambourines and lyres, ²⁸ but you didn't even let me kiss my grandchildren and my daughters. You have acted foolishly. ²⁹ I could do you great harm, but last night the God of your father said to me: 'Watch yourself! Don't say anything to Jacob, either good or bad.' ³⁰ Now you have gone off because you long for your father's family — but why have you stolen my gods?"

³¹ Jacob answered, "I was afraid, for I thought you would take your daughters from me by force. ³² If you find your gods with anyone here, he will not live! Before our relatives, point out anything that is yours and take it." Jacob did not know that Rachel had stolen the idols.

³³ So Laban went into Jacob's tent, Leah's tent, and the tents of the two concubines,ᴬ but he found nothing. When he left Leah's tent, he went into Rachel's tent. ³⁴ Now Rachel had taken Laban's household idols, put them in the saddlebag of the camel, and sat on them. Laban searched the whole tent but found nothing.

³⁵ She said to her father, "Don't be angry, my lord, that I cannot stand up in your presence; I am having my period." So Laban searched, but could not find the household idols.

JACOB'S COVENANT WITH LABAN

³⁶ Then Jacob became incensed and brought charges against Laban. "What is my crime?" he said to Laban. "What is my sin, that you have pursued me? ³⁷ You've searched all my possessions! Have you found anything of yours?ᴮ Put it here before my relatives and yours, and let them decide between the two of us. ³⁸ I've been with you these twenty years. Your ewes and female goats have not miscarried, and I have not eaten the rams from your flock. ³⁹ I did not bring you any of the flock torn by wild beasts; I myself bore the loss. You demanded payment from me for what was stolen by day or by night. ⁴⁰ There I was — the heat consumed me by day and the frost by night, and sleep fled from my eyes. ⁴¹ For twenty years in your household I served you — fourteen years for your two daughters and six years for your flocks — and you have changed my wages ten times! ⁴² If the God of my father, the God of Abraham, the Fear of Isaac, had not been with me, certainly now you would have sent me off empty-handed. But God has seen my affliction and my hard work,ᶜ and he issued his verdict last night."

⁴³ Then Laban answered Jacob, "The daughters are my daughters; the sons, my sons; and the flocks, my flocks! Everything you see is mine! But what can I do today for these daughters of mine or for the children they have borne? ⁴⁴ Come now, let's make a covenant, you and I. Let it be a witness between the two of us."

ᴬ31:33 Lit *servants*   ᴮ31:37 Lit *What have you found from all of the possessions of your house?*   ᶜ31:42 Lit *and the work of my hands*

⁴⁵ So Jacob picked out a stone and set it up as a marker. ⁴⁶ Then Jacob said to his relatives, "Gather stones." And they took stones and made a mound, then ate there by the mound. ⁴⁷ Laban named the mound Jegar-sahadutha, but Jacob named it Galeed.ᴬ

⁴⁸ Then Laban said, "This mound is a witness between you and me today." Therefore the place was called Galeed ⁴⁹ and also Mizpah,ᴮ for he said, "May the LORD watch between you and me when we are out of each other's sight. ⁵⁰ If you mistreat my daughters or take other wives, though no one is with us, understand that God will be a witness between you and me." ⁵¹ Laban also said to Jacob, "Look at this mound and the marker I have set up between you and me. ⁵² This mound is a witness and the marker is a witness that I will not pass beyond this mound to you, and you will not pass beyond this mound and this marker to do me harm. ⁵³ The God of Abraham, and the gods of Nahor — the gods of their fatherᶜ — will judge between us." And Jacob swore by the Fear of his father Isaac. ⁵⁴ Then Jacob offered a sacrifice on the mountain and invited his relatives to eat a meal. So they ate a meal and spent the night on the mountain. ⁵⁵ Laban got up early in the morning, kissed his grandchildren and daughters, and blessed them. Then Laban left to return home.

PREPARING TO MEET ESAU

32 Jacob went on his way, and God's angels met him. ² When he saw them, Jacob said, "This is God's camp." So he called that place Mahanaim.ᴰ

³ Jacob sent messengers ahead of him to his brother Esau in the land of Seir, the territory of Edom. ⁴ He commanded them, "You are to say to my lord Esau, 'This is what your servant Jacob says. I have been staying with Laban and have been delayed until now. ⁵ I have oxen, donkeys, flocks, and male and female slaves. I have sent this message to inform my lord, in order to seek your favor.'"

⁶ When the messengers returned to Jacob, they said, "We went to your brother Esau; he is coming to meet you — and he has four hundred men with him." ⁷ Jacob was greatly afraid and distressed; he divided the people with him into two camps, along with the flocks, herds, and camels. ⁸ He thought, "If Esau comes to one camp and attacks it, the remaining one can escape."

⁹ Then Jacob said, "God of my father Abraham and God of my father Isaac, the LORD who said to me, 'Go back to your land and to your family, and I will cause you to prosper,' ¹⁰ I am unworthy of all the kindness and faithfulness you have shown your servant. Indeed, I crossed over the Jordan with my staff, and now I have become two camps. ¹¹ Please rescue me from my brother Esau, for I am afraid of him; otherwise, he may come and attack me, the mothers, and their children. ¹² You have said, 'I will cause you to prosper, and I will make your offspring like the sand of the sea, too numerous to be counted.'"

¹³ He spent the night there and took part of what he had brought with him as a gift for his brother Esau: ¹⁴ two hundred female goats, twenty male goats, two hundred ewes, twenty rams, ¹⁵ thirty milk camels with their young, forty cows, ten bulls, twenty female donkeys, and ten male donkeys. ¹⁶ He entrusted

---

ᴬ31:47 *Jegar-sahadutha* is Aramaic, and *Galeed* is Hb; both names = Mound of Witness   ᴮ31:49 = Watchtower   ᶜ31:53 Two Hb mss, LXX omit *the gods of their father*   ᴰ32:2 = Two Camps them to his slaves as separate herds and said to them, "Go on ahead of me, and leave some distance between the herds."

[17] And he told the first one: "When my brother Esau meets you and asks, 'Who do you belong to? Where are you going? And whose animals are these ahead of you?' [18] then tell him, 'They belong to your servant Jacob. They are a gift sent to my lord Esau. And look, he is behind us.'"

[19] He also told the second one, the third, and everyone who was walking behind the animals, "Say the same thing to Esau when you find him. [20] You are also to say, 'Look, your servant Jacob is right behind us.'" For he thought, "I want to appease Esau with the gift that is going ahead of me. After that, I can face him, and perhaps he will forgive me."

[21] So the gift was sent on ahead of him while he remained in the camp that night. [22] During the night Jacob got up and took his two wives, his two slave women, and his eleven sons, and crossed the ford of Jabbok. [23] He took them and sent them across the stream, along with all his possessions.

JACOB WRESTLES WITH GOD

[24] Jacob was left alone, and a man wrestled with him until daybreak. [25] When the man saw that he could not defeat him, he struck Jacob's hip socket as they wrestled and dislocated his hip. [26] Then he said to Jacob, "Let me go, for it is daybreak."

But Jacob said, "I will not let you go unless you bless me."

[27] "What is your name?" the man asked.

"Jacob," he replied.

[28] "Your name will no longer be Jacob," he said. "It will be Israel[A] because you have struggled with God and with men and have prevailed."

[29] Then Jacob asked him, "Please tell me your name."

But he answered, "Why do you ask my name?" And he blessed him there.

[30] Jacob then named the place Peniel,[B] "For I have seen God face to face," he said, "yet my life has been spared." [31] The sun shone on him as he passed by Penuel[C] — limping because of his hip. [32] That is why, still today, the Israelites don't eat the thigh muscle that is at the hip socket: because he struck Jacob's hip socket at the thigh muscle.[D]

JACOB MEETS ESAU

33 Now Jacob looked up and saw Esau coming toward him with four hundred men. So he divided the children among Leah, Rachel, and the two slave women. [2] He put the slaves and their children first, Leah and her children next, and Rachel and Joseph last. [3] He himself went on ahead and bowed to the ground seven times until he approached his brother.

[4] But Esau ran to meet him, hugged him, threw his arms around him, and kissed him. Then they wept. [5] When Esau looked up and saw the women and children, he asked, "Who are these with you?"

He answered, "The children God has graciously given your servant." [6] Then the slaves and their children approached him and bowed down. [7] Leah and her children also approached and bowed down, and then Joseph and Rachel approached and bowed down.

[A]32:28 In Hb, the name *Israel* sounds like "he struggled (with) God."
[B]32:30 = Face of God   [C]32:31 Variant of *Peniel*   [D]32:32 Or *tendon*

⁸ So Esau said, "What do you mean by this whole procession^A I met?"

"To find favor with you, my lord," he answered.

⁹ "I have enough, my brother," Esau replied. "Keep what you have."

¹⁰ But Jacob said, "No, please! If I have found favor with you, take this gift from me. For indeed, I have seen your face, and it is like seeing God's face, since you have accepted me. ¹¹ Please take my present that was brought to you, because God has been gracious to me and I have everything I need." So Jacob urged him until he accepted.

¹² Then Esau said, "Let's move on, and I'll go ahead of you."

¹³ Jacob replied, "My lord knows that the children are weak, and I have nursing flocks and herds. If they are driven hard for one day, the whole herd will die. ¹⁴ Let my lord go ahead of his servant. I will continue on slowly, at a pace suited to the livestock and the children, until I come to my lord at Seir."

¹⁵ Esau said, "Let me leave some of my people with you."

But he replied, "Why do that? Please indulge me,^B my lord."

¹⁶ That day Esau started on his way back to Seir, ¹⁷ but Jacob went to Succoth. He built a house for himself and shelters for his livestock; that is why the place was called Succoth.^C

¹⁸ After Jacob came from Paddan-aram, he arrived safely at Shechem in the land of Canaan and camped in front of the city. ¹⁹ He purchased a section of the field where he had pitched his tent from the sons of Hamor, Shechem's father, for a hundred pieces of silver.^D ²⁰ And he set up an altar there and called it God, the God of Israel.^E

DINAH DEFILED

34 Leah's daughter Dinah, whom Leah bore to Jacob, went out to see some of the young women of the area. ² When Shechem — son of Hamor the Hivite, who was the region's chieftain — saw her, he took her and raped her. ³ He became infatuated with Jacob's daughter Dinah. He loved the young girl and spoke tenderly to her.^F ⁴ "Get me this girl as a wife," he told his father.

⁵ Jacob heard that Shechem had defiled his daughter Dinah, but since his sons were with his livestock in the field, he remained silent until they returned. ⁶ Meanwhile, Shechem's father Hamor came to speak with Jacob. ⁷ Jacob's sons returned from the field when they heard about the incident and were deeply grieved and very angry. For Shechem had committed an outrage against Israel by raping Jacob's daughter, and such a thing should not be done.

⁸ Hamor said to Jacob's sons, "My son Shechem has his heart set on your^G daughter. Please give her to him as a wife. ⁹ Intermarry with us; give your daughters to us, and take our daughters for yourselves. ¹⁰ Live with us. The land is before you. Settle here, move about, and acquire property in it."

¹¹ Then Shechem said to Dinah's father and brothers, "Grant me this favor,^H and I'll give you whatever you say. ¹² Demand of me a high compensation^I and gift; I'll give you whatever you ask me. Just give the girl to be my wife!"

---

^A33:8 Lit *camp*   ^B33:15 Lit *May I find favor in your eyes*   ^C33:17 = Stalls or Huts
^D33:19 Lit *100 qesitahs*; the value of this currency is unknown
^E33:20 = *El-Elohe-Israel*   ^F34:3 Lit *spoke to her heart*   ^G34:8 The Hb word for
your is pl, showing that Hamor is speaking to Jacob and his sons.   ^H34:11 Lit
"May I find favor in your eyes"   ^I34:12 Or *bride-price*, or *betrothal present*

¹³ But Jacob's sons answered Shechem and his father Hamor deceitfully because he had defiled their sister Dinah. ¹⁴ "We cannot do this thing," they said to them. "Giving our sister to an uncircumcised man is a disgrace to us. ¹⁵ We will agree with you only on this condition: if all your males are circumcised as we are. ¹⁶ Then we will give you our daughters, take your daughters for ourselves, live with you, and become one people. ¹⁷ But if you will not listen to us and be circumcised, then we will take our daughter and go."

¹⁸ Their words seemed good to Hamor and his son Shechem. ¹⁹ The young man did not delay doing this, because he was delighted with Jacob's daughter. Now he was the most important in all his father's family. ²⁰ So Hamor and his son Shechem went to the gate of their city and spoke to the men of their city.

²¹ "These men are peaceful toward us," they said. "Let them live in our land and move about in it, for indeed, the region is large enough for them. Let us take their daughters as our wives and give our daughters to them. ²² But the men will agree to live with us and be one people only on this condition: if all our men are circumcised as they are. ²³ Won't their livestock, their possessions, and all their animals become ours? Only let us agree with them, and they will live with us."

²⁴ All the men who had come to the city gates listened to Hamor and his son Shechem, and all those men were circumcised. ²⁵ On the third day, when they were still in pain, two of Jacob's sons, Simeon and Levi, Dinah's brothers, took their swords, went into the unsuspecting city, and killed every male. ²⁶ They killed Hamor and his son Shechem with their swords, took Dinah from Shechem's house, and went away. ²⁷ Jacob's sons came to the slaughter and plundered the city because their sister had been defiled. ²⁸ They took their flocks, herds, donkeys, and whatever was in the city and in the field. ²⁹ They captured all their possessions, dependents, and wives and plundered everything in the houses.

³⁰ Then Jacob said to Simeon and Levi, "You have brought trouble on me, making me odious to the inhabitants of the land, the Canaanites and the Perizzites. We are few in number; if they unite against me and attack me, I and my household will be destroyed."

³¹ But they answered, "Should he treat our sister like a prostitute?"

RETURN TO BETHEL

35 God said to Jacob, "Get up! Go to Bethel and settle there. Build an altar there to the God who appeared to you when you fled from your brother Esau."

² So Jacob said to his family and all who were with him, "Get rid of the foreign gods that are among you. Purify yourselves and change your clothes. ³ We must get up and go to Bethel. I will build an altar there to the God who answered me in my day of distress. He has been with me everywhere I have gone."

⁴ Then they gave Jacob all their foreign gods and their earrings, and Jacob hid them under the oak near Shechem. ⁵ When they set out, a terror from God came over the cities around them, and they did not pursue Jacob's sons. ⁶ So Jacob and all who were with him came to Luz (that is, Bethel) in the land of Canaan. ⁷ Jacob built an altar there and called the place El-bethel^A

^A35:7 = God of Bethel

because it was there that God had revealed himself to him when he was fleeing from his brother.

⁸ Deborah, the one who had nursed and raised Rebekah,ᴬ died and was buried under the oak south of Bethel. So Jacob named it Allon-bacuth.ᴮ

⁹ God appeared to Jacob again after he returned from Paddan-aram, and he blessed him. ¹⁰ God said to him, "Your name is Jacob; you will no longer be named Jacob, but your name will be Israel." So he named him Israel. ¹¹ God also said to him, "I am God Almighty. Be fruitful and multiply. A nation, indeed an assembly of nations, will come from you, and kings will descend from you.ᶜ ¹² I will give to you the land that I gave to Abraham and Isaac. And I will give the land to your future descendants." ¹³ Then God withdrewᴰ from him at the place where he had spoken to him.

¹⁴ Jacob set up a marker at the place where he had spoken to him — a stone marker. He poured a drink offering on it and anointed it with oil. ¹⁵ Jacob named the place where God had spoken with him Bethel.

RACHEL'S DEATH

¹⁶ They set out from Bethel. When they were still some distance from Ephrath, Rachel began to give birth, and her labor was difficult. ¹⁷ During her difficult labor, the midwife said to her, "Don't be afraid, for you have another son." ¹⁸ With her last breath — for she was dying — she named him Ben-oni,ᴱ but his father called him Benjamin.ᶠ ¹⁹ So Rachel died and was buried on the way to Ephrath (that is, Bethlehem). ²⁰ Jacob set up a marker on her grave; it is the marker at Rachel's grave still today.

ISRAEL'S SONS

²¹ Israel set out again and pitched his tent beyond the Tower of Eder.ᴳ ²² While Israel was living in that region, Reuben went in and slept with his father's concubine Bilhah, and Israel heard about it.

Jacob had twelve sons:
²³ Leah's sons were Reuben (Jacob's firstborn),
Simeon, Levi, Judah,
Issachar, and Zebulun.
²⁴ Rachel's sons were
Joseph and Benjamin.
²⁵ The sons of Rachel's slave Bilhah
were Dan and Naphtali.
²⁶ The sons of Leah's slave Zilpah
were Gad and Asher.
These are the sons of Jacob, who were born to him in Paddan-aram.

ISAAC'S DEATH

²⁷ Jacob came to his father Isaac at Mamre in Kiriath-arba (that is, Hebron), where Abraham and Isaac had stayed. ²⁸ Isaac lived 180 years. ²⁹ He took his last breath and died, and was gathered to his people, old and full of days. His sons Esau and Jacob buried him.

ᴬ35:8 Lit Deborah, Rebekah's wet nurse; Gn 24:59   ᴮ35:8 = Oak of Weeping
ᶜ35:11 Lit will come from your loins   ᴰ35:13 Lit went up   ᴱ35:18 = Son of My
Sorrow   ᶠ35:18 = Son of the Right Hand   ᴳ35:21 Or beyond Migdal-eder

ESAU'S FAMILY

36 These are the family records of Esau (that is, Edom). ² Esau took his wives from the Canaanite women: Adah daughter of Elon the Hethite, Oholibamah daughter of Anah and granddaughter^A of Zibeon the Hivite, ³ and Basemath daughter of Ishmael and sister of Nebaioth. ⁴ Adah bore Eliphaz to Esau, Basemath bore Reuel, ⁵ and Oholibamah bore Jeush, Jalam, and Korah. These were Esau's sons, who were born to him in the land of Canaan.

⁶ Esau took his wives, sons, daughters, and all the people of his household, as well as his herds, all his livestock, and all the property he had acquired in Canaan; he went to a land away from his brother Jacob. ⁷ For their possessions were too many for them to live together, and because of their herds, the land where they stayed could not support them. ⁸ So Esau (that is, Edom) lived in the mountains of Seir.

⁹ These are the family records of Esau, father of the Edomites in the mountains of Seir.

10 These are the names of Esau's sons:
Eliphaz son of Esau's wife Adah,
and Reuel son of Esau's wife Basemath.

11 The sons of Eliphaz were
Teman, Omar, Zepho, Gatam, and Kenaz.

12 Timna, a concubine of Esau's son Eliphaz,
bore Amalek to Eliphaz.
These are the sons of Esau's wife Adah.

13 These are Reuel's sons:
Nahath, Zerah, Shammah, and Mizzah.
These are the sons of Esau's wife Basemath.

14 These are the sons of Esau's wife Oholibamah
daughter of Anah and granddaughter^A of Zibeon:
She bore Jeush, Jalam, and Korah to Edom.

15 These are the chiefs among Esau's sons:
the sons of Eliphaz, Esau's firstborn:
chief Teman, chief Omar, chief Zepho, chief Kenaz,

16 chief Korah,^B chief Gatam, and chief Amalek.
These are the chiefs descended from Eliphaz
in the land of Edom.
These are the sons of Adah.

17 These are the sons of Reuel, Esau's son:
chief Nahath, chief Zerah, chief Shammah, and chief Mizzah.
These are the chiefs descended from Reuel
in the land of Edom.
These are the sons of Esau's wife Basemath.

---

^A36:2,14 Sam, LXX read *Anah son* ^B36:16 Sam omits *Korah*

18 These are the sons of Esau's wife Oholibamah:
    chief Jeush, chief Jalam, and chief Korah.
    These are the chiefs descended from Esau's wife Oholibamah
    daughter of Anah.
19 These are the sons of Esau (that is, Edom),
    and these are their chiefs.

SEIR'S FAMILY

20 These are the sons of Seir the Horite,
    the inhabitants of the land:
    Lotan, Shobal, Zibeon, Anah,
21 Dishon, Ezer, and Dishan.
    These are the chiefs among the Horites,
    the sons of Seir, in the land of Edom.
22 The sons of Lotan were Hori and Heman.
    Timna was Lotan's sister.
23 These are Shobal's sons:
    Alvan, Manahath, Ebal, Shepho, and Onam.
24 These are Zibeon's sons: Aiah and Anah.
    This was the Anah who found the hot springs^A in the wilderness
    while he was pasturing the donkeys of his father Zibeon.
25 These are the children of Anah:
    Dishon and Oholibamah daughter of Anah.
26 These are Dishon's sons:
    Hemdan, Eshban, Ithran, and Cheran.
27 These are Ezer's sons:
    Bilhan, Zaavan, and Akan.
28 These are Dishan's sons: Uz and Aran.

29 These are the chiefs among the Horites:
    chief Lotan, chief Shobal, chief Zibeon, chief Anah,
30 chief Dishon, chief Ezer, and chief Dishan.
    These are the chiefs among the Horites,
    clan by clan,^B in the land of Seir.

RULERS OF EDOM

31 These are the kings who reigned in the land of Edom
    before any king reigned over the Israelites:
32 Bela son of Beor reigned in Edom;
    the name of his city was Dinhabah.
33 When Bela died, Jobab son of Zerah from Bozrah reigned in his place.
34 When Jobab died, Husham from the land of the Temanites reigned
        in his place.
35 When Husham died, Hadad son of Bedad reigned in his place.
    He defeated Midian in the field of Moab;
    the name of his city was Avith.
36 When Hadad died, Samlah from Masrekah reigned in his place.

---

^A36:24 Syr, Vg; Tg reads the mules; Hb obscure   ^B36:30 Lit Horites, for their
chiefs

³⁷ When Samlah died, Shaul from Rehoboth on the Euphrates River
reigned in his place.
³⁸ When Shaul died, Baal-hanan son of Achbor reigned in his place.
³⁹ When Baal-hanan son of Achbor died, Hadar^A reigned in his place.
His city was Pau, and his wife's name was Mehetabel
daughter of Matred daughter of Me-zahab.

⁴⁰ These are the names of Esau's chiefs,
according to their families and their localities,
by their names:
chief Timna, chief Alvah, chief Jetheth,
⁴¹ chief Oholibamah, chief Elah, chief Pinon,
⁴² chief Kenaz, chief Teman, chief Mibzar,
⁴³ chief Magdiel, and chief Iram.
These are Edom's chiefs,
according to their settlements in the land they possessed.
Esau^B was father of the Edomites.

JOSEPH'S DREAMS

37

Jacob lived in the land where his father had stayed, the land of Canaan. ² These are the family records of Jacob.

At seventeen years of age, Joseph tended sheep with his brothers. The young man was working with the sons of Bilhah and Zilpah, his father's wives, and he brought a bad report about them to their father.

³ Now Israel loved Joseph more than his other sons because Joseph was a son born to him in his old age, and he made a robe of many colors^C for him. ⁴ When his brothers saw that their father loved him more than all his brothers, they hated him and could not bring themselves to speak peaceably to him.

⁵ Then Joseph had a dream. When he told it to his brothers, they hated him even more. ⁶ He said to them, "Listen to this dream I had: ⁷ There we were, binding sheaves of grain in the field. Suddenly my sheaf stood up, and your sheaves gathered around it and bowed down to my sheaf."

⁸ "Are you really going to reign over us?" his brothers asked him. "Are you really going to rule us?" So they hated him even more because of his dream and what he had said.

⁹ Then he had another dream and told it to his brothers. "Look," he said, "I had another dream, and this time the sun, moon, and eleven stars were bowing down to me."

¹⁰ He told his father and brothers, and his father rebuked him. "What kind of dream is this that you have had?" he said. "Am I and your mother and your brothers really going to come and bow down to the ground before you?" ¹¹ His brothers were jealous of him, but his father kept the matter in mind.

JOSEPH SOLD INTO SLAVERY

¹² His brothers had gone to pasture their father's flocks at Shechem. ¹³ Israel said to Joseph, "Your brothers, you know, are pasturing the flocks at Shechem. Get ready. I'm sending you to them."

---

^A36:39 Many Hb mss, Sam, Syr read *Hadad* ^B36:43 Lit *He Esau* ^C37:3 Or *robe with long sleeves*; see 2Sm 13:18,19

"I'm ready," Joseph replied.

¹⁴ Then Israel said to him, "Go and see how your brothers and the flocks are doing, and bring word back to me." So he sent him from the Hebron Valley, and he went to Shechem.

¹⁵ A man found him there, wandering in the field, and asked him, "What are you looking for?"

¹⁶ "I'm looking for my brothers," Joseph said. "Can you tell me where they are pasturing their flocks?"

¹⁷ "They've moved on from here," the man said. "I heard them say, 'Let's go to Dothan.'" So Joseph set out after his brothers and found them at Dothan.

¹⁸ They saw him in the distance, and before he had reached them, they plotted to kill him. ¹⁹ They said to one another, "Oh, look, here comes that dream expert!ᴬ ²⁰ So now, come on, let's kill him and throw him into one of the pits.ᴮ We can say that a vicious animal ate him. Then we'll see what becomes of his dreams!"

²¹ When Reuben heard this, he tried to save him from them.ᶜ He said, "Let's not take his life." ²² Reuben also said to them, "Don't shed blood. Throw him into this pit in the wilderness, but don't lay a hand on him" — intending to rescue him from them and return him to his father.

²³ When Joseph came to his brothers, they stripped off Joseph's robe, the robe of many colors that he had on. ²⁴ Then they took him and threw him into the pit. The pit was empty, without water.

²⁵ They sat down to eat a meal, and when they looked up, there was a caravan of Ishmaelites coming from Gilead. Their camels were carrying aromatic gum, balsam, and resin, going down to Egypt.

²⁶ Judah said to his brothers, "What do we gain if we kill our brother and cover up his blood? ²⁷ Come on, let's sell him to the Ishmaelites and not lay a hand on him, for he is our brother, our own flesh," and his brothers agreed. ²⁸ When Midianite traders passed by, his brothers pulled Joseph out of the pit and sold him for twenty pieces of silver to the Ishmaelites, who took Joseph to Egypt.

²⁹ When Reuben returned to the pit and saw that Joseph was not there, he tore his clothes. ³⁰ He went back to his brothers and said, "The boy is gone! What am I going to do?"ᴰ ³¹ So they took Joseph's robe, slaughtered a male goat, and dipped the robe in its blood. ³² They sent the robe of many colors to their father and said, "We found this. Examine it. Is it your son's robe or not?"

³³ His father recognized it. "It is my son's robe," he said. "A vicious animal has devoured him. Joseph has been torn to pieces!" ³⁴ Then Jacob tore his clothes, put sackcloth around his waist, and mourned for his son many days. ³⁵ All his sons and daughters tried to comfort him, but he refused to be comforted. "No," he said. "I will go down to Sheol to my son, mourning." And his father wept for him.

³⁶ Meanwhile, the Midianites sold Joseph in Egypt to Potiphar, an officer of Pharaoh and the captain of the guards.

ᴬ37:19 Lit *comes the lord of the dreams* ᴮ37:20 Or *cisterns* ᶜ37:21 Lit *their hands* ᴰ37:30 Lit *And I, where am I going?*

JUDAH AND TAMAR

38 At that time Judah left his brothers and settled near an Adullamite named Hirah. ² There Judah saw the daughter of a Canaanite named Shua; he took her as a wife and slept with her. ³ She conceived and gave birth to a son, and he named him Er. ⁴ She conceived again, gave birth to a son, and named him Onan. ⁵ She gave birth to another son and named him Shelah. It was at Chezib that ^(A,B) she gave birth to him.

⁶ Judah got a wife for Er, his firstborn, and her name was Tamar. ⁷ Now Er, Judah's firstborn, was evil in the Lord's sight, and the Lord put him to death. ⁸ Then Judah said to Onan, "Sleep with your brother's wife. Perform your duty as her brother-in-law and produce offspring for your brother." ⁹ But Onan knew that the offspring would not be his, so whenever he slept with his brother's wife, he released his semen on the ground so that he would not produce offspring for his brother. ¹⁰ What he did was evil in the Lord's sight, so he put him to death also.

¹¹ Then Judah said to his daughter-in-law Tamar, "Remain a widow in your father's house until my son Shelah grows up." For he thought, "He might die too, like his brothers." So Tamar went to live in her father's house.

¹² After a long time ^C Judah's wife, the daughter of Shua, died. When Judah had finished mourning, he and his friend Hirah the Adullamite went up to Timnah to his sheepshearers. ¹³ Tamar was told, "Your father-in-law is going up to Timnah to shear his sheep." ¹⁴ So she took off her widow's clothes, veiled her face, covered herself, and sat at the entrance to Enaim, ^D which is on the way to Timnah. For she saw that, though Shelah had grown up, she had not been given to him as a wife. ¹⁵ When Judah saw her, he thought she was a prostitute, for she had covered her face.

¹⁶ He went over to her and said, "Come, let me sleep with you," for he did not know that she was his daughter-in-law.

She said, "What will you give me for sleeping with me?"

¹⁷ "I will send you a young goat from my flock," he replied.

But she said, "Only if you leave something with me until you send it."

¹⁸ "What should I give you?" he asked.

She answered, "Your signet ring, your cord, and the staff in your hand." So he gave them to her and slept with her, and she became pregnant by him. ¹⁹ She got up and left, then removed her veil and put her widow's clothes back on.

²⁰ When Judah sent the young goat by his friend the Adullamite in order to get back the items he had left with the woman, he could not find her. ²¹ He asked the men of the place, "Where is the cult prostitute who was beside the road at Enaim?"

"There has been no cult prostitute here," they answered.

²² So the Adullamite returned to Judah, saying, "I couldn't find her, and besides, the men of the place said, 'There has been no cult prostitute here.'"

²³ Judah replied, "Let her keep the items for herself; otherwise we will become a laughingstock. After all, I did send this young goat, but you couldn't find her."

²⁴ About three months later Judah was told, "Your daughter-in-law, Tamar, has been acting like a prostitute, and now she is pregnant."

---

^A 38:5 LXX reads *She was at Chezib when*   ^B 38:5 Or *He was at Chezib when*
^C 38:12 Lit *And there were many days, and*   ^D 38:14 Or *sat by the mouth of the springs*

"Bring her out," Judah said, "and let her be burned to death!"

²⁵ As she was being brought out, she sent her father-in-law this message: "I am pregnant by the man to whom these items belong." And she added, "Examine them. Whose signet ring, cord, and staff are these?"

²⁶ Judah recognized them and said, "She is more in the right^A than I, since I did not give her to my son Shelah." And he did not know her intimately again.

²⁷ When the time came for her to give birth, there were twins in her womb. ²⁸ As she was giving birth, one of them put out his hand, and the midwife took it and tied a scarlet thread around it, announcing, "This one came out first." ²⁹ But then he pulled his hand back, out came his brother, and she said, "What a breakout you have made for yourself!" So he was named Perez.^B ³⁰ Then his brother, who had the scarlet thread tied to his hand, came out, and was named Zerah.^C

JOSEPH IN POTIPHAR'S HOUSE

39 Now Joseph had been taken to Egypt. An Egyptian named Potiphar, an officer of Pharaoh and the captain of the guards, bought him from the Ishmaelites who had brought him there. ² The LORD was with Joseph, and he became a successful man, serving^D in the household of his Egyptian master. ³ When his master saw that the LORD was with him and that the LORD made everything he did successful, ⁴ Joseph found favor with his master and became his personal attendant. Potiphar also put him in charge of his household and placed all that he owned under his authority.^E ⁵ From the time that he put him in charge of his household and of all that he owned, the LORD blessed the Egyptian's house because of Joseph. The LORD's blessing was on all that he owned, in his house and in his fields. ⁶ He left all that he owned under Joseph's authority;^F he did not concern himself with anything except the food he ate.

Now Joseph was well-built and handsome. ⁷ After some time^G his master's wife looked longingly at Joseph and said, "Sleep with me."

⁸ But he refused. "Look," he said to his master's wife, "with me here my master does not concern himself with anything in his house, and he has put all that he owns under my authority.^H ⁹ No one in this house is greater than I am. He has withheld nothing from me except you, because you are his wife. So how could I do this immense evil, and how could I sin against God?"

¹⁰ Although she spoke to Joseph day after day, he refused to go to bed with her.^I ¹¹ Now one day he went into the house to do his work, and none of the household servants were there.^J ¹² She grabbed him by his garment and said, "Sleep with me!" But leaving his garment in her hand, he escaped and ran outside. ¹³ When she saw that he had left his garment with her and had run outside, ¹⁴ she called her household servants. "Look," she said to them, "my husband brought a Hebrew man to make fools of us. He came to me so he could sleep with me, and I screamed as loud as I could. ¹⁵ When he heard me screaming for help,^K he left his garment beside me and ran outside."

---

^A 38:26 Or *more righteous*   ^B 38:29 = Breaking Out   ^C 38:30 = Brightness of Sunrise; perhaps related to the scarlet thread   ^D 39:2 Lit *and he was*   ^E 39:4 Lit *owned in his hand*   ^F 39:6 Lit *owned in Joseph's hand*   ^G 39:7 Lit *And after these things*   ^H 39:8 Lit *owns in my hand*   ^I 39:10 Lit *he did not listen to her to lie beside her, to be with her*   ^J 39:11 Lit *there in the house*   ^K 39:15 Lit *he heard that I raised my voice and I screamed*

¹⁶ She put Joseph's garment beside her until his master came home. ¹⁷ Then she told him the same story: "The Hebrew slave you brought to us came to make a fool of me, ¹⁸ but when I screamed for help,ᴬ he left his garment beside me and ran outside."

¹⁹ When his master heard the story his wife told him — "These are the things your slave did to me" — he was furious ²⁰ and had him thrown into prison, where the king's prisoners were confined. So Joseph was there in prison.

JOSEPH IN PRISON

²¹ But the LORD was with Joseph and extended kindness to him. He granted him favor with the prison warden. ²² The warden put all the prisoners who were in the prison under Joseph's authority,ᴮ and he was responsible for everything that was done there. ²³ The warden did not bother with anything under Joseph's authority,ᶜ because the LORD was with him, and the LORD made everything that he did successful.

JOSEPH INTERPRETS TWO PRISONERS' DREAMS

40 After this, the king of Egypt's cupbearer and baker offended their master, the king of Egypt. ² Pharaoh was angry with his two officers, the chief cupbearer and the chief baker, ³ and put them in custody in the house of the captain of the guards in the prison where Joseph was confined. ⁴ The captain of the guards assigned Joseph to them as their personal attendant, and they were in custody for some time.ᴰ

⁵ The king of Egypt's cupbearer and baker, who were confined in the prison, each had a dream. Both had a dream on the same night, and each dream had its own meaning. ⁶ When Joseph came to them in the morning, he saw that they looked distraught. ⁷ So he asked Pharaoh's officers who were in custody with him in his master's house, "Why do you look so sad today?"

⁸ "We had dreams," they said to him, "but there is no one to interpret them."

Then Joseph said to them, "Don't interpretations belong to God? Tell me your dreams."

⁹ So the chief cupbearer told his dream to Joseph: "In my dream there was a vine in front of me. ¹⁰ On the vine were three branches. As soon as it budded, its blossoms came out and its clusters ripened into grapes. ¹¹ Pharaoh's cup was in my hand, and I took the grapes, squeezed them into Pharaoh's cup, and placed the cup in Pharaoh's hand."

¹² "This is its interpretation," Joseph said to him. "The three branches are three days. ¹³ In just three days Pharaoh will lift up your head and restore you to your position. You will put Pharaoh's cup in his hand the way you used to when you were his cupbearer. ¹⁴ But when all goes well for you, remember that I was with you. Please show kindness to me by mentioning me to Pharaoh, and get me out of this prison. ¹⁵ For I was kidnapped from the land of the Hebrews, and even here I have done nothing that they should put me in the dungeon."ᴱ

¹⁶ When the chief baker saw that the interpretation was positive, he said to Joseph, "I also had a dream. Three baskets of white bread were on my head.

ᴬ39:18 Lit *I raised my voice and screamed*   ᴮ39:22 Lit *prison in the hand of Joseph*   ᶜ39:23 Lit *anything in his hand*   ᴰ40:4 Lit *custody days*
ᴱ40:15 Or *pit, or cistern*

[17] In the top basket were all sorts of baked goods for Pharaoh, but the birds were eating them out of the basket on my head."

[18] "This is its interpretation," Joseph replied. "The three baskets are three days. [19] In just three days Pharaoh will lift up your head — from off you — and hang you on a tree.[A] Then the birds will eat the flesh from your body."[B]

[20] On the third day, which was Pharaoh's birthday, he gave a feast for all his servants. He elevated[C] the chief cupbearer and the chief baker among his servants. [21] Pharaoh restored the chief cupbearer to his position as cupbearer, and he placed the cup in Pharaoh's hand. [22] But Pharaoh hanged[D] the chief baker, just as Joseph had explained to them. [23] Yet the chief cupbearer did not remember Joseph; he forgot him.

JOSEPH INTERPRETS PHARAOH'S DREAMS

41 At the end of two years Pharaoh had a dream: He was standing beside the Nile, [2] when seven healthy-looking, well-fed cows came up from the Nile and began to graze among the reeds. [3] After them, seven other cows, sickly and thin, came up from the Nile and stood beside those cows along the bank of the Nile. [4] The sickly, thin cows ate the healthy, well-fed cows. Then Pharaoh woke up. [5] He fell asleep and dreamed a second time: Seven heads of grain, plump and good, came up on one stalk. [6] After them, seven heads of grain, thin and scorched by the east wind, sprouted up. [7] The thin heads of grain swallowed up the seven plump, full ones. Then Pharaoh woke up, and it was only a dream.

[8] When morning came, he was troubled, so he summoned all the magicians of Egypt and all its wise men. Pharaoh told them his dreams, but no one could interpret them for him.

[9] Then the chief cupbearer said to Pharaoh, "Today I remember my faults. [10] Pharaoh was angry with his servants, and he put me and the chief baker in the custody of the captain of the guards. [11] He and I had dreams on the same night; each dream had its own meaning. [12] Now a young Hebrew, a slave of the captain of the guards, was with us there. We told him our dreams, he interpreted our dreams for us, and each had its own interpretation. [13] It turned out just the way he interpreted them to us: I was restored to my position, and the other man was hanged."

[14] Then Pharaoh sent for Joseph, and they quickly brought him from the dungeon.[E] He shaved, changed his clothes, and went to Pharaoh.

[15] Pharaoh said to Joseph, "I have had a dream, and no one can interpret it. But I have heard it said about you that you can hear a dream and interpret it."

[16] "I am not able to," Joseph answered Pharaoh. "It is God who will give Pharaoh a favorable answer."[F]

[17] So Pharaoh said to Joseph: "In my dream I was standing on the bank of the Nile, [18] when seven well-fed, healthy-looking cows came up from the Nile and grazed among the reeds. [19] After them, seven other cows — weak, very sickly, and thin — came up. I've never seen such sickly ones as these in all the land of Egypt. [20] Then the thin, sickly cows ate the first seven well-fed

---

[A] 40:19 Or *and impale you on a pole* [B] 40:19 Lit *eat your flesh from upon you*
[C] 40:20 Lit *He lifted up the head of* [D] 40:22 Or *impaled* [E] 41:14 Or *pit, or cistern*
[F] 41:16 Or *"God will answer Pharaoh with peace of mind."*

cows. [21] When they had devoured them, you could not tell that they had devoured them; their appearance was as bad as it had been before. Then I woke up. [22] In my dream I also saw seven heads of grain, full and good, coming up on one stalk. [23] After them, seven heads of grain — withered, thin, and scorched by the east wind — sprouted up. [24] The thin heads of grain swallowed the seven good ones. I told this to the magicians, but no one can tell me what it means."

[25] Then Joseph said to Pharaoh, "Pharaoh's dreams mean the same thing. God has revealed to Pharaoh what he is about to do. [26] The seven good cows are seven years, and the seven good heads are seven years. The dreams mean the same thing. [27] The seven thin, sickly cows that came up after them are seven years, and the seven worthless, scorched heads of grain are seven years of famine.

[28] "It is just as I told Pharaoh: God has shown Pharaoh what he is about to do. [29] Seven years of great abundance are coming throughout the land of Egypt. [30] After them, seven years of famine will take place, and all the abundance in the land of Egypt will be forgotten. The famine will devastate the land. [31] The abundance in the land will not be remembered because of the famine that follows it, for the famine will be very severe. [32] Since the dream was given twice to Pharaoh, it means that the matter has been determined by God, and he will carry it out soon.

[33] "So now, let Pharaoh look for a discerning and wise man and set him over the land of Egypt. [34] Let Pharaoh do this: Let him appoint overseers over the land and take a fifth of the harvest of the land of Egypt during the seven years of abundance. [35] Let them gather all the excess food during these good years that are coming. Under Pharaoh's authority, store the grain in the cities, so they may preserve it as food. [36] The food will be a reserve for the land during the seven years of famine that will take place in the land of Egypt. Then the country will not be wiped out by the famine."

JOSEPH EXALTED

[37] The proposal pleased Pharaoh and all his servants, [38] and he said to them, "Can we find anyone like this, a man who has God's spirit[A] in him?" [39] So Pharaoh said to Joseph, "Since God has made all this known to you, there is no one as discerning and wise as you are. [40] You will be over my house, and all my people will obey your commands.[B] Only I, as king,[C] will be greater than you." [41] Pharaoh also said to Joseph, "See, I am placing you over all the land of Egypt." [42] Pharaoh removed his signet ring from his hand and put it on Joseph's hand, clothed him with fine linen garments, and placed a gold chain around his neck. [43] He had Joseph ride in his second chariot, and servants called out before him, "Make way!"[D] So he placed him over all the land of Egypt. [44] Pharaoh said to Joseph, "I am Pharaoh and no one will be able to raise his hand or foot in all the land of Egypt without your permission." [45] Pharaoh gave Joseph the name Zaphenath-paneah and gave him a wife, Asenath daughter of Potiphera, priest at On.[E] And Joseph went throughout[F] the land of Egypt.

[A] 41:38 Or *the spirit of the gods,* or *a god's spirit*   [B] 41:40 Lit *will kiss your mouth*
[C] 41:40 Lit *Only the throne I*   [D] 41:43 Or *"Kneel!"*   [E] 41:45 Or *Heliopolis,* also in
v. 50   [F] 41:45 Or *Joseph gained authority over*

JOSEPH'S ADMINISTRATION

⁴⁶ Joseph was thirty years old when he entered the service of Pharaoh king of Egypt. Joseph left Pharaoh's presence and traveled throughout the land of Egypt.

⁴⁷ During the seven years of abundance the land produced outstanding harvests. ⁴⁸ Joseph gathered all the excess food in the land of Egypt during the seven years and put it in the cities. He put the food in every city from the fields around it. ⁴⁹ So Joseph stored up grain in such abundance — like the sand of the sea — that he stopped measuring it because it was beyond measure.

⁵⁰ Two sons were born to Joseph before the years of famine arrived. Asenath daughter of Potiphera, priest at On, bore them to him. ⁵¹ Joseph named the firstborn Manasseh ᴬ and said, "God has made me forget all my hardship and my whole family." ⁵² And the second son he named Ephraim ᴮ and said, "God has made me fruitful in the land of my affliction."

⁵³ Then the seven years of abundance in the land of Egypt came to an end, ⁵⁴ and the seven years of famine began, just as Joseph had said. There was famine in every land, but in the whole land of Egypt there was food. ⁵⁵ When the whole land of Egypt was stricken with famine, the people cried out to Pharaoh for food. Pharaoh told all Egypt, "Go to Joseph and do whatever he tells you." ⁵⁶ Now the famine had spread across the whole region, so Joseph opened all the storehouses and sold grain to the Egyptians, for the famine was severe in the land of Egypt. ⁵⁷ Every land came to Joseph in Egypt to buy grain, for the famine was severe in every land.

JOSEPH'S BROTHERS IN EGYPT

42 When Jacob learned that there was grain in Egypt, he said to his sons, "Why do you keep looking at each other? ² Listen," he went on, "I have heard there is grain in Egypt. Go down there and buy some for us so that we will live and not die." ³ So ten of Joseph's brothers went down to buy grain from Egypt. ⁴ But Jacob did not send Joseph's brother Benjamin with his brothers, for he thought, "Something might happen to him."

⁵ The sons of Israel were among those who came to buy grain, for the famine was in the land of Canaan. ⁶ Joseph was in charge of the country; he sold grain to all its people. His brothers came and bowed down before him with their faces to the ground. ⁷ When Joseph saw his brothers, he recognized them, but he treated them like strangers and spoke harshly to them.

"Where do you come from?" he asked.

"From the land of Canaan to buy food," they replied.

⁸ Although Joseph recognized his brothers, they did not recognize him. ⁹ Joseph remembered his dreams about them and said to them, "You are spies. You have come to see the weakness ᶜ of the land."

¹⁰ "No, my lord. Your servants have come to buy food," they said. ¹¹ "We are all sons of one man. We are honest; your servants are not spies."

¹² "No," he said to them. "You have come to see the weakness of the land."

¹³ But they replied, "We, your servants, were twelve brothers, the sons of one man in the land of Canaan. The youngest is now ᴰ with our father, and one is no longer living."

ᴬ41:51 In Hb, the name *Manasseh* sounds like the verb "forget."   ᴮ41:52 In Hb, the name *Ephraim* sounds like the word for "fruitful."   ᶜ42:9 Lit *nakedness*, also in v. 12   ᴰ42:13 Or *today*, also in v. 32

¹⁴ Then Joseph said to them, "I have spoken:ᴬ 'You are spies!' ¹⁵ This is how you will be tested: As surely as Pharaoh lives, you will not leave this place unless your youngest brother comes here. ¹⁶ Send one from among you to get your brother. The rest of you will be imprisoned so that your words can be tested to see if they are true. If they are not, then as surely as Pharaoh lives, you are spies!" ¹⁷ So Joseph imprisoned them together for three days.

¹⁸ On the third day Joseph said to them, "I fear God — do this and you will live. ¹⁹ If you are honest, let one of youᴮ be confined to the guardhouse, while the rest of you go and take grain to relieve the hunger of your households. ²⁰ Bring your youngest brother to me so that your words can be confirmed; then you won't die." And they consented to this.

²¹ Then they said to each other, "Obviously, we are being punished for what we did to our brother. We saw his deep distress when he pleaded with us, but we would not listen. That is why this trouble has come to us."

²² But Reuben replied: "Didn't I tell you not to harm the boy? But you wouldn't listen. Now we must account for his blood!"ᶜ

²³ They did not realize that Joseph understood them, since there was an interpreter between them. ²⁴ He turned away from them and wept. When he turned back and spoke to them, he took Simeon from them and had him bound before their eyes. ²⁵ Joseph then gave orders to fill their containers with grain, return each man's silver to his sack, and give them provisions for their journey. This order was carried out. ²⁶ They loaded the grain on their donkeys and left there.

THE BROTHERS RETURN HOME

²⁷ At the place where they lodged for the night, one of them opened his sack to get feed for his donkey, and he saw his silver there at the top of his bag. ²⁸ He said to his brothers, "My silver has been returned! It's here in my bag." Their hearts sank. Trembling, they turned to one another and said, "What is this that God has done to us?"

²⁹ When they reached their father Jacob in the land of Canaan, they told him all that had happened to them: ³⁰ "The man who is the lord of the country spoke harshly to us and accused us of spying on the country. ³¹ But we told him: We are honest and not spies. ³² We were twelve brothers, sons of the sameᴰ father. One is no longer living, and the youngest is now with our father in the land of Canaan. ³³ The man who is the lord of the country said to us, 'This is how I will know if you are honest: Leave one brother with me, take food to relieve the hunger of your households, and go. ³⁴ Bring back your youngest brother to me, and I will know that you are not spies but honest men. I will then give your brother back to you, and you can trade in the country.'"

³⁵ As they began emptying their sacks, there in each man's sack was his bag of silver! When they and their father saw their bags of silver, they were afraid. ³⁶ Their father Jacob said to them, "It's me that you make childless. Joseph is gone, and Simeon is gone. Now you want to take Benjamin. Everything happens to me!"

³⁷ Then Reuben said to his father, "You can kill my two sons if I don't bring him back to you. Put him in my care,ᴱ and I will return him to you."

ᴬ 42:14 Lit "That which I spoke to you saying: ᴮ 42:19 Lit your brothers   ᶜ 42:22 Lit
Even his blood is being sought! "   ᴰ 42:32 Lit of our   ᴱ 42:37 Lit hand

[38] But Jacob answered, "My son will not go down with you, for his brother is dead and he alone is left. If anything happens to him on your journey, you will bring my gray hairs down to Sheol in sorrow."

DECISION TO RETURN TO EGYPT

43 Now the famine in the land was severe. [2] When they had used up the grain they had brought back from Egypt, their father said to them, "Go back and buy us a little food."

[3] But Judah said to him, "The man specifically warned us: 'You will not see me again unless your brother is with you.' [4] If you will send our brother with us, we will go down and buy food for you. [5] But if you will not send him, we will not go, for the man said to us, 'You will not see me again unless your brother is with you.'"

[6] "Why have you caused me so much trouble?" Israel asked. "Why did you tell the man that you had another brother?"

[7] They answered, "The man kept asking about us and our family: 'Is your father still alive? Do you have another brother?' And we answered him accordingly. How could we know that he would say, 'Bring your brother here'?"

[8] Then Judah said to his father Israel, "Send the boy with me. We will be on our way so that we may live and not die — neither we, nor you, nor our dependents. [9] I will be responsible for him. You can hold me personally accountable![A] If I do not bring him back to you and set him before you, I will be guilty before you forever. [10] If we had not delayed, we could have come back twice by now."

[11] Then their father Israel said to them, "If it must be so, then do this: Put some of the best products of the land in your packs and take them down to the man as a gift — a little balsam and a little honey, aromatic gum and resin, pistachios and almonds. [12] Take twice as much silver with you. Return the silver that was returned to you in the top of your bags. Perhaps it was a mistake. [13] Take your brother also, and go back at once to the man. [14] May God Almighty cause the man to be merciful to you so that he will release your other brother and Benjamin to you. As for me, if I am deprived of my sons, then I am deprived."

THE RETURN TO EGYPT

[15] The men took this gift, double the amount of silver, and Benjamin. They immediately went down to Egypt and stood before Joseph.

[16] When Joseph saw Benjamin with them, he said to his steward, "Take the men to my house. Slaughter an animal and prepare it, for they will eat with me at noon." [17] The man did as Joseph had said and brought them to Joseph's house.

[18] But the men were afraid because they were taken to Joseph's house. They said, "We have been brought here because of the silver that was returned in our bags the first time. They intend to overpower us, seize us, make us slaves, and take our donkeys." [19] So they approached Joseph's steward[B] and spoke to him at the doorway of the house.

[20] They said, "My lord, we really did come down here the first time only to buy food. [21] When we came to the place where we lodged for the night

---

[A]43:9 Lit can seek him from my hand [B]43:19 Lit approached the one who was over the house and opened our bags of grain, each one's silver was at the top of his bag! It was the full amount of our silver, and we have brought it back with us. ²² We have brought additional silver with us to buy food. We don't know who put our silver in the bags."

²³ Then the steward said, "May you be well. Don't be afraid. Your God and the God of your father must have put treasure in your bags. I received your silver." Then he brought Simeon out to them. ²⁴ The steward brought the men into Joseph's house, gave them water to wash their feet, and got feed for their donkeys. ²⁵ Since the men had heard that they were going to eat a meal there, they prepared their gift for Joseph's arrival at noon. ²⁶ When Joseph came home, they brought him the gift they had carried into the house, and they bowed to the ground before him.

²⁷ He asked if they were well, and he said, "How is your elderly father that you told me about? Is he still alive?"

²⁸ They answered, "Your servant our father is well. He is still alive." And they knelt low and paid homage to him.

²⁹ When he looked up and saw his brother Benjamin, his mother's son, he asked, "Is this your youngest brother that you told me about?" Then he said, "May God be gracious to you, my son." ³⁰ Joseph hurried out because he was overcome with emotion for his brother, and he was about to weep. He went into an inner room and wept there. ³¹ Then he washed his face and came out. Regaining his composure, he said, "Serve the meal."

³² They served him by himself, his brothers by themselves, and the Egyptians who were eating with him by themselves, because Egyptians could not eat with Hebrews, since that is detestable to them. ³³ They were seated before him in order by age, from the firstborn to the youngest. The men looked at each other in astonishment. ³⁴ Portions were served to them from Joseph's table, and Benjamin's portion was five times larger than any of theirs. They drank and became drunk with Joseph.

JOSEPH'S FINAL TEST

44 Joseph commanded his steward, "Fill the men's bags with as much food as they can carry, and put each one's silver at the top of his bag. ² Put my cup, the silver one, at the top of the youngest one's bag, along with the silver for his grain." So he did as Joseph told him.

³ At morning light, the men were sent off with their donkeys. ⁴ They had not gone very far from the city when Joseph said to his steward, "Get up. Pursue the men, and when you overtake them, say to them, 'Why have you repaid evil for good? ⁵ Isn't this the cup that my master drinks from and uses for divination? What you have done is wrong!'"

⁶ When he overtook them, he said these words to them. ⁷ They said to him, "Why does my lord say these things? Your servants could not possibly do such a thing. ⁸ We even brought back to you from the land of Canaan the silver we found at the top of our bags. How could we steal silver or gold from your master's house? ⁹ If it is found with one of us, your servants, he must die, and the rest of us will become my lord's slaves."

¹⁰ The steward replied, "What you have said is right, but only the one who is found to have it will be my slave, and the rest of you will be blameless."

¹¹ So each one quickly lowered his sack to the ground and opened it. ¹² The steward searched, beginning with the oldest and ending with the youngest,

and the cup was found in Benjamin's sack. ¹³ Then they tore their clothes, and each one loaded his donkey and returned to the city.

¹⁴ When Judah and his brothers reached Joseph's house, he was still there. They fell to the ground before him. ¹⁵ "What is this you have done?" Joseph said to them. "Didn't you know that a man like me could uncover the truth by divination?"

¹⁶ "What can we say to my lord?" Judah replied. "How can we plead? How can we justify ourselves? God has exposed your servants' iniquity. We are now my lord's slaves — both we and the one in whose possession the cup was found."

¹⁷ Then Joseph said, "I swear that I will not do this. The man in whose possession the cup was found will be my slave. The rest of you can go in peace to your father."

JUDAH'S PLEA FOR BENJAMIN

¹⁸ But Judah approached him and said, "My lord, please let your servant speak personally to my lord.ᴬ Do not be angry with your servant, for you are like Pharaoh. ¹⁹ My lord asked his servants, 'Do you have a father or a brother?' ²⁰ and we answered my lord, 'We have an elderly father and a younger brother, the child of his old age. The boy's brother is dead. He is the only one of his mother's sons left, and his father loves him.' ²¹ Then you said to your servants, 'Bring him to me so that I can see him.' ²² But we said to my lord, 'The boy cannot leave his father. If he were to leave, his father would die.' ²³ Then you said to your servants, 'If your younger brother does not come down with you, you will not see me again.'

²⁴ "This is what happened when we went back to your servant my father: We reported to him the words of my lord. ²⁵ But our father said, 'Go again, and buy us a little food.' ²⁶ We told him, 'We cannot go down unless our younger brother goes with us. If our younger brother isn't with us, we cannot see the man.' ²⁷ Your servant my father said to us, 'You know that my wife bore me two sons. ²⁸ One is gone from me — I said he must have been torn to pieces — and I have never seen him again. ²⁹ If you also take this one from me and anything happens to him, you will bring my gray hairs down to Sheol in sorrow.'

³⁰ "So if I come to your servant my father and the boy is not with us — his life is wrapped up with the boy's life — ³¹ when he sees that the boy is not with us, he will die. Then your servants will have brought the gray hairs of your servant our father down to Sheol in sorrow. ³² Your servant became accountable to my father for the boy, saying, 'If I do not return him to you, I will always bear the guilt for sinning against you, my father.' ³³ Now please let your servant remain here as my lord's slave, in place of the boy. Let him go back with his brothers. ³⁴ For how can I go back to my father without the boy? I could not bear to see the grief that would overwhelm my father."

JOSEPH REVEALS HIS IDENTITY

45 Joseph could no longer keep his composure in front of all his attendants,ᴮ so he called out, "Send everyone away from me!" No one was with him when he revealed his identity to his brothers. ² But he wept so loudly that the Egyptians heard it, and also Pharaoh's household

---

ᴬ 44:18 Lit *speak a word in my lord's ears* ᴮ 45:1 Lit *all those standing about him*

BITTERNESS AND PULLING WEEDS

GENESIS 45:16–46:34; PSALM 121:5-8; MATTHEW 20:1-16; HEBREWS 12:15

Joseph's name is the one we put in the marquee when we read Genesis 37–50. From his coat of many colors, to his run-in with Potiphar's wife, to his abrupt rise to power—it's easy to see Joseph as the headliner of this story. But there is another player with a vital role in the text, a dark horse whose impact we often miss in our own stories.

Bitterness.

His brothers hated him. It was a hatred birthed out of sibling rivalry and fueled by their father, Jacob's, favoritism (Gn 37:2-4). Anyone with brothers or sisters can relate, but for Joseph's brothers, the bitterness was so strong it had them in a chokehold. "They hated him and could not bring themselves to speak peaceably to him" (Gn 37:3-4).

You've been there, right? You can't bear to be in the same room with someone who's offended you. Everything about them annoys you, and every word is a missile headed straight for your wounded heart.

So, what do we do when a bitter root shoots up? Scripture warns us, "Make sure that no one falls short of the grace of God and that no root of bitterness springs up, causing trouble and defiling many" (Heb 12:15).

This is God telling us to yank those roots out! Don't tend to them or coddle them like little seedlings. Show no mercy and get to chopping.

We're wise to ask why God's reaction to bitterness is so strong. Why does it matter when we're embittered? Surely, a little secret resentment couldn't hurt anyone, right?

Joseph's story has the answer. His brothers resented his every gift, hated his every vision, and were annoyed by his every word. At first they simply responded with sarcasm, but soon enough that bitter root grew into something much darker. They slid down the slippery slope from cutting remarks, to plotting Joseph's death, and eventually selling him to a band of enemy traders (Gn 37:18-36).

That's what bitterness does. Like a tiny weed that sprouts up one morning and covers everything by noonday, bitterness takes us further than we ever thought we'd go, nudging us to do and say things we never thought we would.

But bitterness isn't the star of Joseph's story. And it doesn't have to be the star of yours. (Be sure to read Genesis 45:21-24 to see how forgiveness and generosity smash the root of bitterness.)

It would have been easy for Joseph to become a bitter man. Instead, we see God's mercy at work in him in the form of the spiritual fruit of peace, patience, kindness, goodness, gentleness, self-control, and love. **It was by grace that Joseph was saved from bitterness, and the same grace has been extended to us in Christ.**

heard it. ³ Joseph said to his brothers, "I am Joseph! Is my father still living?" But they could not answer him because they were terrified in his presence.

⁴ Then Joseph said to his brothers, "Please, come near me," and they came near. "I am Joseph, your brother," he said, "the one you sold into Egypt. ⁵ And now don't be grieved or angry with yourselves for selling me here, because God sent me ahead of you to preserve life. ⁶ For the famine has been in the land these two years, and there will be five more years without plowing or harvesting. ⁷ God sent me ahead of you to establish you as a remnant within the land and to keep you alive by a great deliverance.^A ⁸ Therefore it was not you who sent me here, but God. He has made me a father to Pharaoh, lord of his entire household, and ruler over all the land of Egypt.

⁹ "Return quickly to my father and say to him, 'This is what your son Joseph says: "God has made me lord of all Egypt. Come down to me without delay. ¹⁰ You can settle in the land of Goshen and be near me — you, your children, and your grandchildren, your flocks, your herds, and all you have. ¹¹ There I will sustain you, for there will be five more years of famine. Otherwise, you, your household, and everything you have will become destitute." ' ¹² Look! Your eyes and the eyes of my brother Benjamin can see that I'm^B the one speaking to you. ¹³ Tell my father about all my glory in Egypt and about all you have seen. And bring my father here quickly."

¹⁴ Then Joseph threw his arms around his brother Benjamin and wept, and Benjamin wept on his shoulder. ¹⁵ Joseph kissed each of his brothers as he wept,^C and afterward his brothers talked with him.

THE RETURN FOR JACOB

¹⁶ When the news reached Pharaoh's palace, "Joseph's brothers have come," Pharaoh and his servants were pleased. ¹⁷ Pharaoh said to Joseph, "Tell your brothers, 'Do this: Load your animals and go on back to the land of Canaan. ¹⁸ Get your father and your families, and come back to me. I will give you the best of the land of Egypt, and you can eat from the richness of the land.' ¹⁹ You are also commanded to tell them, 'Do this: Take wagons from the land of Egypt for your dependents and your wives and bring your father here. ²⁰ Do not be concerned about your belongings, for the best of all the land of Egypt is yours.' "

²¹ The sons of Israel did this. Joseph gave them wagons as Pharaoh had commanded, and he gave them provisions for the journey. ²² He gave each of the brothers changes of clothes, but he gave Benjamin three hundred pieces of silver and five changes of clothes. ²³ He sent his father the following: ten donkeys carrying the best products of Egypt and ten female donkeys carrying grain, food, and provisions for his father on the journey. ²⁴ So Joseph sent his brothers on their way, and as they were leaving, he said to them, "Don't argue^D on the way."

²⁵ So they went up from Egypt and came to their father Jacob in the land of Canaan. ²⁶ They said, "Joseph is still alive, and he is ruler over all the land of Egypt!" Jacob was stunned,^E for he did not believe them. ²⁷ But

---

^A 45:7 Or keep alive for you many survivors   ^B 45:12 Lit that my mouth is
^C 45:15 Lit brothers, and he wept over them   ^D 45:24 Or be anxious   ^E 45:26 Lit
Jacob's heart was numb

when they told Jacob all that Joseph had said to them, and when he saw the wagons that Joseph had sent to transport him, the spirit of their father Jacob revived.

[28] Then Israel said, "Enough! My son Joseph is still alive. I will go to see him before I die."

JACOB LEAVES FOR EGYPT

46 Israel set out with all that he had and came to Beer-sheba, and he offered sacrifices to the God of his father Isaac. [2] That night God spoke to Israel in a vision: "Jacob, Jacob!" he said.

And Jacob replied, "Here I am."

[3] God said, "I am God, the God of your father. Do not be afraid to go down to Egypt, for I will make you into a great nation there. [4] I will go down with you to Egypt, and I will also bring you back. Joseph will close your eyes when you die."[A]

[5] Jacob left Beer-sheba. The sons of Israel took their father Jacob in the wagons Pharaoh had sent to carry him, along with their dependents and their wives. [6] They also took their cattle and possessions they had acquired in the land of Canaan. Then Jacob and all his offspring with him came to Egypt. [7] His sons and grandsons, his daughters and granddaughters, indeed all his offspring, he brought with him to Egypt.

JACOB'S FAMILY

[8] These are the names of the sons of Israel who came to Egypt — Jacob and his sons:

Jacob's firstborn: Reuben.

[9] Reuben's sons: Hanoch, Pallu, Hezron, and Carmi.

[10] Simeon's sons: Jemuel, Jamin, Ohad, Jachin, Zohar, and Shaul, the son of a Canaanite woman.

[11] Levi's sons: Gershon, Kohath, and Merari.

[12] Judah's sons: Er, Onan, Shelah, Perez, and Zerah; but Er and Onan died in the land of Canaan.

The sons of Perez were Hezron and Hamul.

[13] Issachar's sons: Tola, Puvah,[B] Jashub,[C] and Shimron.

[14] Zebulun's sons: Sered, Elon, and Jahleel.

[15] These were Leah's sons born to Jacob in Paddan-aram, as well as his daughter Dinah. The total number of persons:[D] thirty-three.

[16] Gad's sons: Ziphion, Haggi, Shuni, Ezbon, Eri, Arodi, and Areli.

[17] Asher's sons: Imnah, Ishvah, Ishvi, Beriah, and their sister Serah. Beriah's sons were Heber and Malchiel.

[18] These were the sons of Zilpah — whom Laban gave to his daughter Leah — that she bore to Jacob: sixteen persons.

[19] The sons of Jacob's wife Rachel: Joseph and Benjamin.

[20] Manasseh and Ephraim were born to Joseph in the land of Egypt. They were born to him by Asenath daughter of Potiphera, a priest at On.[E]

[A]46:4 Lit *will put his hand on your eyes*   [B]46:13 Sam, Syr read *Puah*; 1Ch 7:1
[C]46:13 Sam, LXX; MT reads *Iob*   [D]46:15 Lit *All persons his sons and his daughters:*
[E]46:20 Or *Heliopolis*

21 Benjamin's sons: Bela, Becher, Ashbel, Gera, Naaman, Ehi, Rosh, Muppim, Huppim, and Ard.

22 These were Rachel's sons who were born to Jacob: fourteen persons.

23 Dan's son:[A] Hushim.

24 Naphtali's sons: Jahzeel, Guni, Jezer, and Shillem.

25 These were the sons of Bilhah, whom Laban gave to his daughter Rachel. She bore to Jacob: seven persons.

26 The total number of persons belonging to Jacob — his direct descendants,[B] not including the wives of Jacob's sons — who came to Egypt: sixty-six.

27 And Joseph's sons who were born to him in Egypt: two persons. All those of Jacob's household who came to Egypt: seventy[C] persons.

JACOB ARRIVES IN EGYPT

28 Now Jacob had sent Judah ahead of him to Joseph to prepare for his arrival[D] at Goshen. When they came to the land of Goshen, 29 Joseph hitched the horses to his chariot and went up to Goshen to meet his father Israel. Joseph presented himself to him, threw his arms around him, and wept for a long time.

30 Then Israel said to Joseph, "I'm ready to die now because I have seen your face and you are still alive!"

31 Joseph said to his brothers and to his father's family, "I will go up and inform Pharaoh, telling him, 'My brothers and my father's family, who were in the land of Canaan, have come to me. 32 The men are shepherds; they also raise livestock. They have brought their flocks and herds and all that they have.' 33 When Pharaoh addresses you and asks, 'What is your occupation?' 34 you are to say, 'Your servants, both we and our fathers, have raised livestock[E] from our youth until now.' Then you will be allowed to settle in the land of Goshen, since all shepherds are detestable to Egyptians."

PHARAOH WELCOMES JACOB

47 So Joseph went and informed Pharaoh: "My father and my brothers, with their flocks and herds and all that they own, have come from the land of Canaan and are now in the land of Goshen."

2 He took five of his brothers and presented them to Pharaoh. 3 And Pharaoh asked his brothers, "What is your occupation?"

They said to Pharaoh, "Your servants, both we and our fathers, are shepherds." 4 And they said to Pharaoh, "We have come to stay in the land for a while because there is no grazing land for your servants' sheep, since the famine in the land of Canaan has been severe. So now, please let your servants settle in the land of Goshen."

5 Then Pharaoh said to Joseph, "Now that your father and brothers have come to you, 6 the land of Egypt is open before you; settle your father and brothers in the best part of the land. They can live in the land of Goshen. If you know of any capable men among them, put them in charge of my livestock."

7 Joseph then brought his father Jacob and presented him to Pharaoh, and Jacob blessed Pharaoh. 8 Pharaoh said to Jacob, "How many years have you lived?"

[A]46:23 Alt Hb tradition reads sons: [B]46:26 Lit Jacob who came out from his loins
[C]46:27 LXX reads 75; Ac 7:14   [D]46:28 Lit to give directions before him
[E]46:34 Lit fathers, are men of livestock

⁹ Jacob said to Pharaoh, "My pilgrimage has lasted 130 years. My years have been few and hard, and they have not reached the years of my fathers during their pilgrimages." ¹⁰ So Jacob blessed Pharaoh and departed from Pharaoh's presence.

¹¹ Then Joseph settled his father and brothers in the land of Egypt and gave them property in the best part of the land, the land of Rameses, as Pharaoh had commanded. ¹² And Joseph provided his father, his brothers, and all his father's family with food for their dependents.

THE LAND BECOMES PHARAOH'S

¹³ But there was no food in the entire region, for the famine was very severe. The land of Egypt and the land of Canaan were exhausted by the famine. ¹⁴ Joseph collected all the silver to be found in the land of Egypt and the land of Canaan in exchange for the grain they were purchasing, and he brought the silver to Pharaoh's palace. ¹⁵ When the silver from the land of Egypt and the land of Canaan was gone, all the Egyptians came to Joseph and said, "Give us food. Why should we die here in front of you? The silver is gone!"

¹⁶ But Joseph said, "Give me your livestock. Since the silver is gone, I will give you food in exchange for your livestock." ¹⁷ So they brought their livestock to Joseph, and he gave them food in exchange for the horses, the flocks of sheep, the herds of cattle, and the donkeys. That year he provided them with food in exchange for all their livestock.

¹⁸ When that year was over, they came the next year and said to him, "We cannot hide from our lord that the silver is gone and that all our livestock belongs to our lord. There is nothing left for our lord except our bodies and our land. ¹⁹ Why should we die here in front of you — both us and our land? Buy us and our land in exchange for food. Then we with our land will become Pharaoh's slaves. Give us seed so that we can live and not die, and so that the land won't become desolate."

²⁰ In this way, Joseph acquired all the land in Egypt for Pharaoh, because every Egyptian sold his field since the famine was so severe for them. The land became Pharaoh's, ²¹ and Joseph moved the people to the cities[A] from one end of Egypt to the other. ²² The only land he did not acquire belonged to the priests, for they had an allowance from Pharaoh. They ate from their allowance that Pharaoh gave them; therefore they did not sell their land.

²³ Joseph said to the people, "Understand today that I have acquired you and your land for Pharaoh. Here is seed for you. Sow it in the land. ²⁴ At harvest, you are to give a fifth of it to Pharaoh, and four-fifths will be yours as seed for the field and as food for yourselves, your households, and your dependents."

²⁵ "You have saved our lives," they said. "We have found favor with our lord and will be Pharaoh's slaves." ²⁶ So Joseph made it a law, still in effect today in the land of Egypt, that a fifth of the produce belongs to Pharaoh. Only the priests' land does not belong to Pharaoh.

ISRAEL SETTLES IN GOSHEN

²⁷ Israel settled in the land of Egypt, in the region of Goshen. They acquired property in it and became fruitful and very numerous. ²⁸ Now Jacob lived in the land of Egypt 17 years, and his life span was 147 years. ²⁹ When the time

ᴬ47:21 Sam, LXX, Vg read *and he made the people servants*

approached for him to die, he called his son Joseph and said to him, "If I have found favor with you, put your hand under my thigh and promise me that you will deal with me in kindness and faithfulness. Do not bury me in Egypt. ³⁰ When I rest with my fathers, carry me away from Egypt and bury me in their burial place."

Joseph answered, "I will do what you have asked."

³¹ And Jacob said, "Swear to me." So Joseph swore to him. Then Israel bowed in thanks at the head of his bed.ᴬ

JACOB BLESSES EPHRAIM AND MANASSEH

48 Some time after this, Joseph was told, "Your father is weaker." So he set out with his two sons, Manasseh and Ephraim. ² When Jacob was told, "Your son Joseph has come to you," Israel summoned his strength and sat up in bed.

³ Jacob said to Joseph, "God Almighty appeared to me at Luz in the land of Canaan and blessed me. ⁴ He said to me, 'I will make you fruitful and numerous; I will make many nations come from you, and I will give this land as a permanent possession to your future descendants.' ⁵ Your two sons born to you in the land of Egypt before I came to you in Egypt are now mine. Ephraim and Manasseh belong to me just as Reuben and Simeon do. ⁶ Children born to you after them will be yours and will be recorded under the names of their brothers with regard to their inheritance. ⁷ When I was returning from Paddan, to my sorrow Rachel died along the way, some distance from Ephrath in the land of Canaan. I buried her there along the way to Ephrath" (that is, Bethlehem).

⁸ When Israel saw Joseph's sons, he said, "Who are these?"

⁹ And Joseph said to his father, "They are my sons God has given me here."

So Israel said, "Bring them to me and I will bless them." ¹⁰ Now his eyesight was poor because of old age; he could hardlyᴮ see. Joseph brought them to him, and he kissed and embraced them. ¹¹ Israel said to Joseph, "I never expected to see your face again, but now God has even let me see your offspring." ¹² Then Joseph took them from his father's knees and bowed with his face to the ground.

EPHRAIM'S GREATER BLESSING

¹³ Then Joseph took them both — with his right hand Ephraim toward Israel's left, and with his left hand Manasseh toward Israel's right — and brought them to Israel. ¹⁴ But Israel stretched out his right hand and put it on the head of Ephraim, the younger, and crossing his hands, put his left on Manasseh's head, although Manasseh was the firstborn. ¹⁵ Then he blessed Joseph and said:

> The God before whom my fathers Abraham and Isaac walked,
> the God who has been my shepherd all my life to this day,
> ¹⁶ the angel who has redeemed me from all harm —
> may he bless these boys.
> And may they be called by my name
> and the names of my fathers Abraham and Isaac,
> and may they grow to be numerous within the land.

ᴬ 47:31 Or *Israel worshiped while leaning on the top of his staff* ᴮ 48:10 Lit *he was not able to*

¹⁷ When Joseph saw that his father had placed his right hand on Ephraim's head, he thought it was a mistake^A and took his father's hand to move it from Ephraim's head to Manasseh's. ¹⁸ Joseph said to his father, "Not that way, my father! This one is the firstborn. Put your right hand on his head."

¹⁹ But his father refused and said, "I know, my son, I know! He too will become a tribe,^B and he too will be great; nevertheless, his younger brother will be greater than he, and his offspring will become a populous nation."^C ²⁰ So he blessed them that day, putting Ephraim before Manasseh when he said, "The nation Israel will invoke blessings by you, saying, 'May God make you like Ephraim and Manasseh.'"

²¹ Israel said to Joseph, "Look, I am about to die, but God will be with you and will bring you back to the land of your fathers. ²² Over and above what I am giving your brothers, I am giving you the one mountain slope^D that I took from the Amorites with my sword and bow."

JACOB'S LAST WORDS

49 Then Jacob called his sons and said, "Gather around, and I will tell you what will happen to you in the days to come.^E

² Come together and listen, sons of Jacob;
   listen to your father Israel:

³ Reuben, you are my firstborn,
   my strength and the firstfruits of my virility,
   excelling in prominence, excelling in power.

⁴ Turbulent as water, you will not excel,
   because you got into your father's bed
   and you defiled it — he^F got into my bed.

⁵ Simeon and Levi are brothers;
   their knives are vicious weapons.

⁶ May I never enter their council;
   may I never join their assembly.
   For in their anger they kill men,
   and on a whim they hamstring oxen.

⁷ Their anger is cursed, for it is strong,
   and their fury, for it is cruel!
   I will disperse them throughout Jacob
   and scatter them throughout Israel.

⁸ Judah, your brothers will praise you.
   Your hand will be on the necks of your enemies;
   your father's sons will bow down to you.

⁹ Judah is a young lion —
   my son, you return from the kill.
   He crouches; he lies down like a lion

---

^A48:17 Or *he was displeased*; lit *head, it was bad in his eyes*   ^B48:19 Lit *people*
^C48:19 Or *a multitude of nations*; lit *a fullness of nations*   ^D48:22 Or *Shechem,*
Joseph's burial place; lit *one shoulder*   ^E49:1 Or *in the last days*   ^F49:4 LXX, Syr,
Tg read *you*

or a lioness — who dares to rouse him?

10 The scepter will not depart from Judah
or the staff from between his feet
until he whose right it is comes[A]
and the obedience of the peoples belongs to him.
11 He ties his donkey to a vine,
and the colt of his donkey to the choice vine.
He washes his clothes in wine
and his robes in the blood of grapes.
12 His eyes are darker than wine,
and his teeth are whiter than milk.

13 Zebulun will live by the seashore
and will be a harbor for ships,
and his territory will be next to Sidon.

14 Issachar is a strong donkey
lying down between the saddlebags.[B]
15 He saw that his resting place was good
and that the land was pleasant,
so he leaned his shoulder to bear a load
and became a forced laborer.

16 Dan will judge his people
as one of the tribes of Israel.
17 Dan will be a snake by the road,
a viper beside the path,
that bites the horse's heels
so that its rider falls backward.

18 I wait for your salvation, LORD.

19 Gad will be attacked by raiders,
but he will attack their heels.

20 Asher's[C] food will be rich,
and he will produce royal delicacies.

21 Naphtali is a doe set free
that bears beautiful fawns.

22 Joseph is a fruitful vine,
a fruitful vine beside a spring;
its branches[D] climb over the wall.[E]
23 The archers attacked him,
shot at him, and were hostile toward him.

[A]49:10 Or until tribute comes to him, or until Shiloh comes, or until he comes to
Shiloh [B]49:14 Or sheep pens [C]49:19-20 LXX, Syr, Vg; MT reads their heel.
[20]From Asher [D]49:22 Lit daughters [E]49:22 Hb obscure

24   Yet his bow remained steady,
        and his strong arms were made agile
        by the hands of the Mighty One of Jacob,
        by the name of^A the Shepherd, the Rock of Israel,
25   by the God of your father who helps you,
        and by the Almighty who blesses you
        with blessings of the heavens above,
        blessings of the deep that lies below,
        and blessings of the breasts and the womb.
26   The blessings of your father excel
        the blessings of my ancestors^B
        and^C the bounty of the ancient hills.^D
        May they rest on the head of Joseph,
        on the brow of the prince of his brothers.

27   Benjamin is a wolf; he tears his prey.
        In the morning he devours the prey,
        and in the evening he divides the plunder."

²⁸ These are the tribes of Israel, twelve in all, and this is what their father said to them. He blessed them, and he blessed each one with a suitable blessing.

JACOB'S BURIAL INSTRUCTIONS

²⁹ Then he commanded them: "I am about to be gathered to my people. Bury me with my fathers in the cave in the field of Ephron the Hethite. ³⁰ The cave is in the field of Machpelah near Mamre, in the land of Canaan. This is the field Abraham purchased from Ephron the Hethite as burial property. ³¹ Abraham and his wife Sarah are buried there, Isaac and his wife Rebekah are buried there, and I buried Leah there. ³² The field and the cave in it were purchased from the Hethites." ³³ When Jacob had finished giving charges to his sons, he drew his feet into the bed, took his last breath, and was gathered to his people.

JACOB'S BURIAL

50 Then Joseph, leaning over his father's face, wept and kissed him. ² He commanded his servants who were physicians to embalm his father. So they embalmed Israel. ³ They took forty days to complete this, for embalming takes that long, and the Egyptians mourned for him seventy days.

⁴ When the days of mourning were over, Joseph said to Pharaoh's household, "If I have found favor with you, please tell^E Pharaoh that ⁵ my father made me take an oath, saying, 'I am about to die. You must bury me there in the tomb that I made for myself in the land of Canaan.' Now let me go and bury my father. Then I will return."

⁶ So Pharaoh said, "Go and bury your father in keeping with your oath."

⁷ Then Joseph went to bury his father, and all Pharaoh's servants, the elders of his household, and all the elders of the land of Egypt went with him, ⁸ along with all Joseph's family, his brothers, and his father's family. Only

---

^A49:24 Syr, Tg; MT reads *Jacob, from there*   ^B49:26 Or *of the mountains*
^C49:26 Lit *to*   ^D49:26 Hb obscure   ^E50:4 Lit *please speak in the ears of*

their dependents, their flocks, and their herds were left in the land of Goshen. ⁹ Horses and chariots went up with him; it was a very impressive procession. ¹⁰ When they reached the threshing floor of Atad, which is across the Jordan, they lamented and wept loudly, and Joseph mourned seven days for his father. ¹¹ When the Canaanite inhabitants of the land saw the mourning at the threshing floor of Atad, they said, "This is a solemn mourning on the part of the Egyptians." Therefore the place is named Abel-mizraim.ᴬ It is across the Jordan.

¹² So Jacob's sons did for him what he had commanded them. ¹³ They carried him to the land of Canaan and buried him in the cave at Machpelah in the field near Mamre, which Abraham had purchased as burial property from Ephron the Hethite. ¹⁴ After Joseph buried his father, he returned to Egypt with his brothers and all who had gone with him to bury his father.

JOSEPH'S KINDNESS

¹⁵ When Joseph's brothers saw that their father was dead, they said to one another, "If Joseph is holding a grudge against us, he will certainly repay us for all the suffering we caused him."

¹⁶ So they sent this message to Joseph, "Before he died your father gave a command: ¹⁷ 'Say this to Joseph: Please forgive your brothers' transgression and their sin — the suffering they caused you.' Therefore, please forgive the transgression of the servants of the God of your father." Joseph wept when their message came to him. ¹⁸ His brothers also came to him, bowed down before him, and said, "We are your slaves!"

¹⁹ But Joseph said to them, "Don't be afraid. Am I in the place of God? ²⁰ You planned evil against me; God planned it for good to bring about the present result — the survival of many people. ²¹ Therefore don't be afraid. I will take care of you and your children." And he comforted them and spoke kindly to them.ᴮ

JOSEPH'S DEATH

²² Joseph and his father's family remained in Egypt. Joseph lived 110 years. ²³ He saw Ephraim's sons to the third generation; the sons of Manasseh's son Machir were recognized byᶜ,ᴰ Joseph.

²⁴ Joseph said to his brothers, "I am about to die, but God will certainly come to your aid and bring you up from this land to the land he swore to give to Abraham, Isaac, and Jacob." ²⁵ So Joseph made the sons of Israel take an oath: "When God comes to your aid, you are to carry my bones up from here."

²⁶ Joseph died at the age of 110. They embalmed him and placed him in a coffin in Egypt.

ᴬ 50:11 = Mourning of Egypt   ᴮ 50:21 Lit *spoke to their hearts*   ᶜ 50:23 Lit *were born on the knees of*   ᴰ 50:23 Referring to a ritual of adoption or of legitimation; Gn 30:3

exodus

 I am the LORD *your God, who brought you out of the land of Egypt, out of the place of slavery.* **20:2**

ON THE TIMELINE Along with the other four books of the Pentateuch, Exodus has long been considered the work of Moses. Moses could have written Exodus at any time during a forty-year span: after the Israelites finished constructing and dedicating the tabernacle at Mount Sinai (1445 BC) and before his death in the land of Moab (about 1406 BC). The events in Exodus pick up where Genesis ends, with the death of Joseph around 1805 BC, and conclude with the building of the tabernacle in 1445 BC.

A LITTLE BACKGROUND Our first hint about the book of Exodus comes from its title, derived from the Greek word meaning "departure." True to its name, Exodus is centered on the departure of God's people from Egypt, where they were held as slaves to Pharaoh. The date of the exodus itself is disputed, but biblical evidence favors 1446 BC. First Kings 6:1 tells us the exodus occurred 480 years before Solomon's fourth year as king, which was likely 966 BC. In Judges 11:26, Jephthah said Israel had been living in regions of Palestine for 300 years. Jephthah lived around 1100 BC, which dates the end of the wilderness journey around 1400 BC.

MESSAGE & PURPOSE The book of Exodus shows God at work for the people of Israel, so that He "might dwell among them" (Ex 29:46). God rescued the Israelites in order to make Himself known, not only by the exercise of His power but also through an ongoing covenant relationship based on His patience, grace, and forgiveness. The record of what the Lord did for the Israelites provided grounds for them to recognize Him as their God who deserved their complete loyalty and obedience, and made clear to them their identity as God's people.

GIVE THANKS FOR THE BOOK OF EXODUS:

Exodus is the high point of redemptive history in the Old Testament. Many patterns and concepts from Exodus are revisited elsewhere in Scripture, especially in the past, present, and future work of Jesus. From deliverance and provision to God's glory and presence, the themes of Exodus find their fulfillment in Christ.

MEDITERRANEAN SEA

CANAAN

MOA

LOWER
EGYPT

RAAMSES

PITHOM

GOSHEN

W. EL-ARISH

KADESH-
BARNEA

WILDERNESS
OF ZIN

EDOM

MEMPHIS

GREAT
BITTER LAKE

WILDERNESS
OF SHUR

LITTLE
BITTER LAKE

GULF OF SUEZ

SINAI

WILDERNESS
OF SIN

REPHIDIM

JEBEL MUSA
(MT. SINAI)

GULF OF AQABA

MIDIAN

ROUTE OF THE EXODUS

NORTHERN ROUTE

CENTRAL ROUTE

ALTERNATE CENTRAL ROUTE

SOUTHERN ROUTE

ALTERNATE ROUTE FROM
JEBEL MUSA TO KADESH-BARNEA

MAJOR HIGHWAY

READ AND UNDERSTAND EXODUS

The Bible is a complete work in which many stories combine to tell one story. As you read the book of Exodus, consider reading the additional passages to discover how the whole of Scripture works together.

ISRAEL OPPRESSED IN EGYPT

1 These are the names of the sons of Israel who came to Egypt with Jacob; each came with his family:
2 Reuben, Simeon, Levi, and Judah;
3 Issachar, Zebulun, and Benjamin;
4 Dan and Naphtali; Gad and Asher.

5 The total number of Jacob's descendants[A] was seventy;[B] Joseph was already in Egypt.

6 Joseph and all his brothers and all that generation eventually died. 7 But the Israelites were fruitful, increased rapidly, multiplied, and became extremely numerous so that the land was filled with them.

8 A new king, who did not know about Joseph, came to power in Egypt. 9 He said to his people, "Look, the Israelite people are more numerous and powerful than we are. 10 Come, let's deal shrewdly with them; otherwise they will multiply further, and when war breaks out, they will join our enemies, fight against us, and leave the country." 11 So the Egyptians assigned taskmasters over the Israelites to oppress them with forced labor. They built Pithom and Rameses as supply cities for Pharaoh. 12 But the more they oppressed them, the more they multiplied and spread so that the Egyptians came to dread[C] the Israelites. 13 They worked the Israelites ruthlessly 14 and made their lives bitter with difficult labor in brick and mortar and in all kinds of fieldwork. They ruthlessly imposed all this work on them.

15 The king of Egypt said to the Hebrew midwives — the first whose name was Shiphrah and the second whose name was Puah — 16 "When you help the Hebrew women give birth, observe them as they deliver. If the child is a son, kill him, but if it's a daughter, she may live." 17 The midwives, however, feared God and did not do as the king of Egypt had told them; they let the boys live. 18 So the king of Egypt summoned the midwives and asked them, "Why have you done this and let the boys live?"

19 The midwives said to Pharaoh, "The Hebrew women are not like the Egyptian women, for they are vigorous and give birth before the midwife can get to them."

20 So God was good to the midwives, and the people multiplied and became very numerous. 21 Since the midwives feared God, he gave them families. 22 Pharaoh then commanded all his people: "You must throw every son born to the Hebrews into the Nile, but let every daughter live."

MOSES'S BIRTH AND ADOPTION

2 Now a man from the family of Levi married a Levite woman. 2 The woman became pregnant and gave birth to a son; when she saw that he was beautiful,[D] she hid him for three months. 3 But when she could no longer hide him, she got a papyrus basket for him and coated it with asphalt and pitch. She placed the child in it and set it among the reeds by the bank of the Nile. 4 Then his sister stood at a distance in order to see what would happen to him.

5 Pharaoh's daughter went down to bathe at the Nile while her servant girls walked along the riverbank. She saw the basket among the reeds, sent her slave girl, took it, 6 opened it, and saw him, the child — and there he was, a little boy, crying. She felt sorry for him and said, "This is one of the Hebrew boys."

A 1:5 Lit *of people issuing from Jacob's loins*   B 1:5 LXX, DSS read *75*; Gn 46:27; Ac 7:14   C 1:12 Or *Egyptians loathed*   D 2:2 Or *healthy*

⁷ Then his sister said to Pharaoh's daughter, "Should I go and call a Hebrew woman who is nursing to nurse the boy for you?"

⁸ "Go," Pharaoh's daughter told her. So the girl went and called the boy's mother. ⁹ Then Pharaoh's daughter said to her, "Take this child and nurse him for me, and I will pay your wages." So the woman took the boy and nursed him. ¹⁰ When the child grew older, she brought him to Pharaoh's daughter, and he became her son. She named him Moses, ᴬ "Because," she said, "I drew him out of the water."

MOSES IN MIDIAN

¹¹ Years later, ᴮ after Moses had grown up, he went out to his own people ᶜ and observed their forced labor. He saw an Egyptian striking a Hebrew, one of his people. ¹² Looking all around and seeing no one, he struck the Egyptian dead and hid him in the sand. ¹³ The next day he went out and saw two Hebrews fighting. He asked the one in the wrong, "Why are you attacking your neighbor?" ᴰ

¹⁴ "Who made you a commander and judge over us?" the man replied. "Are you planning to kill me as you killed the Egyptian?"

Then Moses became afraid and thought, "What I did is certainly known."

¹⁵ When Pharaoh heard about this, he tried to kill Moses. But Moses fled from Pharaoh and went to live in the land of Midian, and sat down by a well.

¹⁶ Now the priest of Midian had seven daughters. They came to draw water and filled the troughs to water their father's flock. ¹⁷ Then some shepherds arrived and drove them away, but Moses came to their rescue and watered their flock. ¹⁸ When they returned to their father Reuel, ᴱ he asked, "Why have you come back so quickly today?"

¹⁹ They answered, "An Egyptian rescued us from the shepherds. He even drew water for us and watered the flock."

²⁰ "So where is he?" he asked his daughters. "Why then did you leave the man behind? Invite him to eat dinner."

²¹ Moses agreed to stay with the man, and he gave his daughter Zipporah to Moses in marriage. ²² She gave birth to a son whom he named Gershom, ᶠ for he said, "I have been a resident alien in a foreign land."

²³ After a long time, the king of Egypt died. The Israelites groaned because of their difficult labor; and they cried out; and their cry for help because of the difficult labor ascended to God. ²⁴ And God heard their groaning; and God remembered his covenant with Abraham, with Isaac, and with Jacob; ²⁵ and God saw the Israelites; and God knew.

MOSES AND THE BURNING BUSH

3 Meanwhile, Moses was shepherding the flock of his father-in-law Jethro, ᴳ the priest of Midian. He led the flock to the far side of the wilderness and came to Horeb, ᴴ the mountain of God. ² Then the angel of the LORD appeared to him in a flame of fire within a bush. As Moses looked, he saw

---

ᴬ2:10 The name *Moses* sounds like "drawing out" in Hb and "born" in Egyptian.
ᴮ2:11 Lit *And it was in those days*   ᶜ2:11 Lit *his brothers*   ᴰ2:13 Or *fellow Hebrew*   ᴱ2:18 Jethro's clan or last name was Reuel; Ex 3:1.   ᶠ2:22 In Hb the name *Gershom* sounds like the phrase "a stranger there."   ᴳ3:1 Moses's father-in-law's first name was *Jethro*; Ex 2:18.   ᴴ3:1 = Desolation; another name for Mount Sinai; Dt 4:10,15; 18:16; Mal 4:4

THE BURNING BUSH

EXODUS 3–4

They say the devil is in the details but more often than not, I find that God is there. It happens all the time in the Bible, when a small detail changes everything.

This particular story of Moses has one of those tiny details I've overlooked for years. I've known the story of the burning bush for as long as I can remember, and I can picture Moses there—shepherd stick in hand and shoes off to the side because, as it says in Exodus 3:5, he was standing on holy ground.

But go back to Exodus 3:4, just one little phrase before. There's this one detail that changed the whole story for me.

"When the LORD saw that he had gone over to look, God called out to him from the bush, 'Moses! Moses!'"

EXODUS 3:4

It wasn't until Moses noticed the bush on fire that God spoke out of it.

God wasn't calling him like you call kids in from the playground. The bush wasn't yelling out Moses' name like he was the next contestant on a game show. It was when Moses noticed—when he went over to look—that God spoke to him.

Look around you. What are the little moments, the details, the things God is waiting for you to notice?

There's this lake I walk around often. I walk the same path every time, the one that starts on the right and loops around the lake. About halfway through, there's a little sign with an arrow pointing to another path: Ganier Ridge. I've seen it lots of times, but I've always just kept on walking—even though it caught my eye each time I passed it.

One Saturday, I finally quit ignoring that little nudge and turned up that path. It was hard and steep, and it only got steeper as I climbed. *WHY AM I DOING THIS?* I thought, as a podcast about loving your city well played in my ears.

At the apex of the climb is a clearing, and when I reached it I paused by a bench to catch my breath. And then I saw it: the entire city skyline, right there in my view. *There's the city I love,* I thought, as the podcast reminded me that God places people in their cities on purpose.

He wanted me to hear it while I was seeing it. Once I noticed the "burning bush," and walked toward it, He spoke to me. It wasn't a huge deal, but it mattered to my heart.

Today, God uses His Word to speak to us. But He uses all sorts of things to get our attention and draw us deeper into His truth.

What is the thing God is using to get your attention? I bet it's different from the things He uses to grab mine—but that's okay, because it's meant for you, not me. Turn. Notice. Listen. God is not silent.

that the bush was on fire but was not consumed. ³ So Moses thought, "I must go over and look at this remarkable sight. Why isn't the bush burning up?"

⁴ When the Lord saw that he had gone over to look, God called out to him from the bush, "Moses, Moses!"

"Here I am," he answered.

⁵ "Do not come closer," he said. "Remove the sandals from your feet, for the place where you are standing is holy ground." ⁶ Then he continued, "I am the God of your father,ᴬ the God of Abraham, the God of Isaac, and the God of Jacob." Moses hid his face because he was afraid to look at God.

⁷ Then the Lord said, "I have observed the misery of my people in Egypt, and have heard them crying out because of their oppressors. I know about their sufferings, ⁸ and I have come down to rescue them from the power of the Egyptians and to bring them from that land to a good and spacious land, a land flowing with milk and honey — the territory of the Canaanites, Hethites, Amorites, Perizzites, Hivites, and Jebusites. ⁹ So because the Israelites' cry for help has come to me, and I have also seen the way the Egyptians are oppressing them, ¹⁰ therefore, go. I am sending you to Pharaoh so that you may lead my people, the Israelites, out of Egypt."

¹¹ But Moses asked God, "Who am I that I should go to Pharaoh and that I should bring the Israelites out of Egypt?"

¹² He answered, "I will certainly be with you, and this will be the sign to you that I am the one who sent you: when you bring the people out of Egypt, you will all worshipᴮ God at this mountain."

¹³ Then Moses asked God, "If I go to the Israelites and say to them, 'The God of your fathers has sent me to you,' and they ask me, 'What is his name?' what should I tell them?"

¹⁴ God replied to Moses, "I AM WHO I AM.ᶜ This is what you are to say to the Israelites: I AM has sent me to you." ¹⁵ God also said to Moses, "Say this to the Israelites: The Lord, the God of your fathers, the God of Abraham, the God of Isaac, and the God of Jacob, has sent me to you. This is my name forever; this is how I am to be remembered in every generation.

¹⁶ "Go and assemble the elders of Israel and say to them: The Lord, the God of your fathers, the God of Abraham, Isaac, and Jacob, has appeared to me and said: I have paid close attention to you and to what has been done to you in Egypt. ¹⁷ And I have promised you that I will bring you up from the misery of Egypt to the land of the Canaanites, Hethites, Amorites, Perizzites, Hivites, and Jebusites — a land flowing with milk and honey. ¹⁸ They will listen to what you say. Then you, along with the elders of Israel, must go to the king of Egypt and say to him: The Lord, the God of the Hebrews, has met with us. Now please let us go on a three-day trip into the wilderness so that we may sacrifice to the Lord our God.

¹⁹ "However, I know that the king of Egypt will not allow you to go, even under force from a strong hand. ²⁰ But when I stretch out my hand and strike Egypt with all my miracles that I will perform in it, after that, he will let you go. ²¹ And I will give these people such favor with the Egyptians that when you go, you will not go empty-handed. ²² Each woman will ask her neighbor and any woman staying in her house for silver and gold jewelry, and

---

ᴬ3:6 Sam, some LXX mss read *fathers*; Ac 7:32　ᴮ3:12 Or *serve*　ᶜ3:14 Or *I AM BECAUSE I AM*, or *I WILL BE WHO I WILL BE* clothing, and you will put them on your sons and daughters. So you will plunder the Egyptians."

MIRACULOUS SIGNS FOR MOSES

4 Moses answered, "What if they won't believe me and will not obey me but say, 'The LORD did not appear to you'?"

² The LORD asked him, "What is that in your hand?"

"A staff," he replied.

³ "Throw it on the ground," he said. So Moses threw it on the ground, it became a snake, and he ran from it. ⁴ The LORD told Moses, "Stretch out your hand and grab it by the tail." So he stretched out his hand and caught it, and it became a staff in his hand. ⁵ "This will take place," he continued, "so that they will believe that the LORD, the God of their fathers, the God of Abraham, the God of Isaac, and the God of Jacob, has appeared to you."

⁶ In addition the LORD said to him, "Put your hand inside your cloak." So he put his hand inside his cloak, and when he took it out, his hand was diseased, resembling snow.^A ⁷ "Put your hand back inside your cloak," he said. So he put his hand back inside his cloak, and when he took it out, it had again become like the rest of his skin. ⁸ "If they will not believe you and will not respond to the evidence of the first sign, they may believe the evidence of the second sign. ⁹ And if they don't believe even these two signs or listen to what you say, take some water from the Nile and pour it on the dry ground. The water you take from the Nile will become blood on the ground."

¹⁰ But Moses replied to the LORD, "Please, Lord, I have never been eloquent — either in the past or recently or since you have been speaking to your servant — because my mouth and my tongue are sluggish."^B

¹¹ The LORD said to him, "Who placed a mouth on humans? Who makes a person mute or deaf, seeing or blind? Is it not I, the LORD? ¹² Now go! I will help you speak^C and I will teach you what to say."

¹³ Moses said, "Please, Lord, send someone else."^D

¹⁴ Then the LORD's anger burned against Moses, and he said, "Isn't Aaron the Levite your brother? I know that he can speak well. And also, he is on his way now to meet you. He will rejoice when he sees you. ¹⁵ You will speak with him and tell him what to say. I will help both you and him to speak^E and will teach you both what to do. ¹⁶ He will speak to the people for you. He will serve as a mouth for you, and you will serve as God to him. ¹⁷ And take this staff in your hand that you will perform the signs with."

MOSES'S RETURN TO EGYPT

¹⁸ Then Moses went back to his father-in-law Jethro and said to him, "Please let me return to my relatives in Egypt and see if they are still living."

Jethro said to Moses, "Go in peace."

¹⁹ Now in Midian the LORD told Moses, "Return to Egypt, for all the men who wanted to kill you are dead." ²⁰ So Moses took his wife and sons, put them on a donkey, and returned to the land of Egypt. And Moses took God's staff in his hand.

---

^A 4:6 A reference to whiteness or flakiness of the skin   ^B 4:10 Lit heavy of mouth and heavy of tongue   ^C 4:12 Lit will be with your mouth   ^D 4:13 Lit send by the hand of whom you will send   ^E 4:15 Lit will be with your mouth and with his mouth

²¹ The LORD instructed Moses, "When you go back to Egypt, make sure you do before Pharaoh all the wonders that I have put within your power. But I will harden his heart^A so that he won't let the people go. ²² And you will say to Pharaoh: This is what the LORD says: Israel is my firstborn son. ²³ I told you: Let my son go so that he may worship me, but you refused to let him go. Look, I am about to kill your firstborn son!"

²⁴ On the trip, at an overnight campsite, it happened that the LORD confronted him and intended to put him to death. ²⁵ So Zipporah took a flint, cut off her son's foreskin, threw it at Moses's feet, and said, "You are a bridegroom of blood to me!" ²⁶ So he let him alone. At that time she said, "You are a bridegroom of blood," referring to the circumcision.

REUNION OF MOSES AND AARON

²⁷ Now the LORD had said to Aaron, "Go and meet Moses in the wilderness." So he went and met him at the mountain of God and kissed him. ²⁸ Moses told Aaron everything the LORD had sent him to say, and about all the signs he had commanded him to do. ²⁹ Then Moses and Aaron went and assembled all the elders of the Israelites. ³⁰ Aaron repeated everything the LORD had said to Moses and performed the signs before the people. ³¹ The people believed, and when they heard that the LORD had paid attention to them and that he had seen their misery, they knelt low and worshiped.

MOSES CONFRONTS PHARAOH

5 Later, Moses and Aaron went in and said to Pharaoh, "This is what the LORD, the God of Israel, says: Let my people go, so that they may hold a festival for me in the wilderness."

² But Pharaoh responded, "Who is the LORD that I should obey him by letting Israel go? I don't know^B the LORD, and besides, I will not let Israel go."

³ They answered, "The God of the Hebrews has met with us. Please let us go on a three-day trip into the wilderness so that we may sacrifice to the LORD our God, or else he may strike us with plague or sword."

⁴ The king of Egypt said to them, "Moses and Aaron, why are you causing the people to neglect their work? Get to your labor!" ⁵ Pharaoh also said, "Look, the people of the land are so numerous, and you would stop them from their labor."

FURTHER OPPRESSION OF ISRAEL

⁶ That day Pharaoh commanded the overseers of the people as well as their foremen: ⁷ "Don't continue to supply the people with straw for making bricks, as before. They must go and gather straw for themselves. ⁸ But require the same quota of bricks from them as they were making before; do not reduce it. For they are slackers — that is why they are crying out, 'Let us go and sacrifice to our God.' ⁹ Impose heavier work on the men. Then they will be occupied with it and not pay attention to deceptive words."

¹⁰ So the overseers and foremen of the people went out and said to them, "This is what Pharaoh says: 'I am not giving you straw. ¹¹ Go get straw yourselves wherever you can find it, but there will be no reduction at all in your workload.'" ¹² So the people scattered throughout the land of Egypt to gather

---

^A 4:21 Or *will make him stubborn* ^B 5:2 Or *recognize*

stubble for straw. [13] The overseers insisted, "Finish your assigned work each day, just as you did when straw was provided." [14] Then the Israelite foremen, whom Pharaoh's slave drivers had set over the people, were beaten and asked, "Why haven't you finished making your prescribed number of bricks yesterday or today, as you did before?"

[15] So the Israelite foremen went in and cried for help to Pharaoh: "Why are you treating your servants this way? [16] No straw has been given to your servants, yet they say to us, 'Make bricks!' Look, your servants are being beaten, but it is your own people who are at fault."

[17] But he said, "You are slackers. Slackers! That is why you are saying, 'Let us go sacrifice to the Lord.' [18] Now get to work. No straw will be given to you, but you must produce the same quantity of bricks."

[19] The Israelite foremen saw that they were in trouble when they were told, "You cannot reduce your daily quota of bricks." [20] When they left Pharaoh, they confronted Moses and Aaron, who stood waiting to meet them.

[21] "May the Lord take note of you and judge," they said to them, "because you have made us reek to Pharaoh and his officials — putting a sword in their hand to kill us!"

[22] So Moses went back to the Lord and asked, "Lord, why have you caused trouble for this people? And why did you ever send me? [23] Ever since I went in to Pharaoh to speak in your name he has caused trouble for this people, and you haven't rescued your people at all."

6 But the Lord replied to Moses, "Now you will see what I will do to Pharaoh: because of a strong hand he will let them go, and because of a strong hand he will drive them from his land."

GOD PROMISES FREEDOM

[2] Then God spoke to Moses, telling him, "I am the Lord. [3] I appeared to Abraham, Isaac, and Jacob as God Almighty, but I was not known to them by my name 'the Lord.' [A] [4] I also established my covenant with them to give them the land of Canaan, the land they lived in as aliens. [5] Furthermore, I have heard the groaning of the Israelites, whom the Egyptians are forcing to work as slaves, and I have remembered my covenant.

[6] "Therefore tell the Israelites: I am the Lord, and I will bring you out from the forced labor of the Egyptians and rescue you from slavery to them. I will redeem you with an outstretched arm and great acts of judgment. [7] I will take you as my people, and I will be your God. You will know that I am the Lord your God, who brought you out from the forced labor of the Egyptians. [8] I will bring you to the land that I swore [B] to give to Abraham, Isaac, and Jacob, and I will give it to you as a possession. I am the Lord." [9] Moses told this to the Israelites, but they did not listen to him because of their broken spirit and hard labor.

[10] Then the Lord spoke to Moses, [11] "Go and tell Pharaoh king of Egypt to let the Israelites go from his land."

[12] But Moses said in the Lord's presence: "If the Israelites will not listen to me, then how will Pharaoh listen to me, since I am such a poor speaker?" [C] [13] Then the Lord spoke to Moses and Aaron and gave them commands

---

[A] 6:3 Lord (in small capitals) stands for the personal name of God, which in Hb is Yahweh. There is a long tradition of substituting "Lord" for "Yahweh" out of reverence. [B] 6:8 Lit raised my hand [C] 6:12 Lit I have uncircumcised lips, also in v. 30

concerning both the Israelites and Pharaoh king of Egypt to bring the Israelites out of the land of Egypt.

GENEALOGY OF MOSES AND AARON

¹⁴ These are the heads of their fathers' families:

The sons of Reuben, the firstborn of Israel:
Hanoch and Pallu, Hezron and Carmi.
These are the clans of Reuben.

¹⁵ The sons of Simeon:
Jemuel, Jamin, Ohad, Jachin,
Zohar, and Shaul, the son of a Canaanite woman.
These are the clans of Simeon.

¹⁶ These are the names of the sons of Levi
according to their family records;
Gershon, Kohath, and Merari.
Levi lived 137 years.

¹⁷ The sons of Gershon:
Libni and Shimei, by their clans.

¹⁸ The sons of Kohath:
Amram, Izhar, Hebron, and Uzziel.
Kohath lived 133 years.

¹⁹ The sons of Merari:
Mahli and Mushi.
These are the clans of the Levites
according to their family records.

²⁰ Amram married his father's sister Jochebed,
and she bore him Aaron and Moses.
Amram lived 137 years.

²¹ The sons of Izhar:
Korah, Nepheg, and Zichri.

²² The sons of Uzziel:
Mishael, Elzaphan, and Sithri.

²³ Aaron married Elisheba,
daughter of Amminadab and sister of Nahshon.
She bore him Nadab and Abihu, Eleazar and Ithamar.

²⁴ The sons of Korah:
Assir, Elkanah, and Abiasaph.
These are the clans of the Korahites.

²⁵ Aaron's son Eleazar married
one of the daughters of Putiel,
and she bore him Phinehas.
These are the heads of the Levite families by their clans.

²⁶ It was this Aaron and Moses whom the LORD told, "Bring the Israelites
out of the land of Egypt according to their military divisions." ²⁷ Moses and
Aaron were the ones who spoke to Pharaoh king of Egypt in order to bring
the Israelites out of Egypt.

MOSES AND AARON BEFORE PHARAOH

[28] On the day the Lord spoke to Moses in the land of Egypt, [29] he said to him, "I am the Lord; tell Pharaoh king of Egypt everything I am telling you."

[30] But Moses replied in the Lord's presence, "Since I am such a poor speaker, how will Pharaoh listen to me?"

7 The Lord answered Moses, "See, I have made you like God to Pharaoh, and Aaron your brother will be your prophet. [2] You must say whatever I command you; then Aaron your brother must declare it to Pharaoh so that he will let the Israelites go from his land. [3] But I will harden Pharaoh's heart and multiply my signs and wonders in the land of Egypt. [4] Pharaoh will not listen to you, but I will put my hand into Egypt and bring the military divisions of my people the Israelites out of the land of Egypt by great acts of judgment. [5] The Egyptians will know that I am the Lord when I stretch out my hand against Egypt and bring out the Israelites from among them."

[6] So Moses and Aaron did this; they did just as the Lord commanded them. [7] Moses was eighty years old and Aaron eighty-three when they spoke to Pharaoh.

[8] The Lord said to Moses and Aaron, [9] "When Pharaoh tells you, 'Perform a miracle,' tell Aaron, 'Take your staff and throw it down before Pharaoh. It will become a serpent.'" [10] So Moses and Aaron went in to Pharaoh and did just as the Lord had commanded. Aaron threw down his staff before Pharaoh and his officials, and it became a serpent. [11] But then Pharaoh called the wise men and sorcerers — the magicians of Egypt, and they also did the same thing by their occult practices. [12] Each one threw down his staff, and it became a serpent. But Aaron's staff swallowed their staffs. [13] However, Pharaoh's heart was hard, and he did not listen to them, as the Lord had said.

THE FIRST PLAGUE: WATER TURNED TO BLOOD

[14] Then the Lord said to Moses, "Pharaoh's heart is hard: He refuses to let the people go. [15] Go to Pharaoh in the morning. When you see him walking out to the water, stand ready to meet him by the bank of the Nile. Take in your hand the staff that turned into a snake. [16] Tell him: The Lord, the God of the Hebrews, has sent me to tell you: Let my people go, so that they may worship[A] me in the wilderness, but so far you have not listened. [17] This is what the Lord says: Here is how you will know that I am the Lord. Watch. I am about to strike the water in the Nile with the staff in my hand, and it will turn to blood. [18] The fish in the Nile will die, the river will stink, and the Egyptians will be unable to drink water from it."

[19] So the Lord said to Moses, "Tell Aaron: Take your staff and stretch out your hand over the waters of Egypt — over their rivers, canals, ponds, and all their water reservoirs — and they will become blood. There will be blood throughout the land of Egypt, even in wooden and stone containers."

[20] Moses and Aaron did just as the Lord had commanded; in the sight of Pharaoh and his officials, he raised the staff and struck the water in the Nile, and all the water in the Nile was turned to blood. [21] The fish in the Nile died, and the river smelled so bad the Egyptians could not drink water from it. There was blood throughout the land of Egypt.

[A] 7:16 Or *serve*; Ex 4:23

²² But the magicians of Egypt did the same thing by their occult practices. So Pharaoh's heart was hard, and he would not listen to them, as the LORD had said. ²³ Pharaoh turned around, went into his palace, and didn't take even this to heart. ²⁴ All the Egyptians dug around the Nile for water to drink because they could not drink the water from the river. ²⁵ Seven days passed after the LORD struck the Nile.

THE SECOND PLAGUE: FROGS

8 Then the LORD said to Moses, "Go in to Pharaoh and tell him: This is what the LORD says: Let my people go, so that they may worship me. ² But if you refuse to let them go, then I will plague all your territory with frogs. ³ The Nile will swarm with frogs; they will come up and go into your palace, into your bedroom and on your bed, into the houses of your officials and your people, and into your ovens and kneading bowls. ⁴ The frogs will come up on you, your people, and all your officials."

⁵ The LORD then said to Moses, "Tell Aaron: Stretch out your hand with your staff over the rivers, canals, and ponds, and cause the frogs to come up onto the land of Egypt." ⁶ When Aaron stretched out his hand over the waters of Egypt, the frogs came up and covered the land of Egypt. ⁷ But the magicians did the same thing by their occult practices and brought frogs up onto the land of Egypt.

⁸ Pharaoh summoned Moses and Aaron and said, "Appeal to the LORD to remove the frogs from me and my people. Then I will let the people go and they can sacrifice to the LORD."

⁹ Moses said to Pharaoh, "You may have the honor of choosing. When should I appeal on behalf of you, your officials, and your people, that the frogs be taken away from you and your houses, and remain only in the Nile?"

¹⁰ "Tomorrow," he answered.

Moses replied, "As you have said, so that you may know there is no one like the LORD our God, ¹¹ the frogs will go away from you, your houses, your officials, and your people. The frogs will remain only in the Nile." ¹² After Moses and Aaron went out from Pharaoh, Moses cried out to the LORD for help concerning the frogs that he had brought against Pharaoh. ¹³ The LORD did as Moses had said: the frogs in the houses, courtyards, and fields died. ¹⁴ They piled them in countless heaps, and there was a terrible odor in the land. ¹⁵ But when Pharaoh saw there was relief, he hardened his heart and would not listen to them, as the LORD had said.

THE THIRD PLAGUE: GNATS

¹⁶ Then the LORD said to Moses, "Tell Aaron: Stretch out your staff and strike the dust of the land, and it will become gnats^A throughout the land of Egypt." ¹⁷ And they did this. Aaron stretched out his hand with his staff, and when he struck the dust of the land, gnats were on people and animals. All the dust of the land became gnats throughout the land of Egypt. ¹⁸ The magicians tried to produce gnats using their occult practices, but they could not. The gnats remained on people and animals.

¹⁹ "This is the finger of God," the magicians said to Pharaoh. But Pharaoh's heart was hard, and he would not listen to them, as the LORD had said.

---

^A8:16 Perhaps sand fleas or mosquitoes

THE FOURTH PLAGUE: SWARMS OF FLIES

[20] The Lord said to Moses, "Get up early in the morning and present yourself to Pharaoh when you see him going out to the water. Tell him: This is what the Lord says: Let my people go, so that they may worship[A] me. [21] But if you will not let my people go, then I will send swarms of flies[B] against you, your officials, your people, and your houses. The Egyptians' houses will swarm with flies, and so will the land where they live.[C] [22] But on that day I will give special treatment to the land of Goshen, where my people are living; no flies will be there. This way you will know that I, the Lord, am in the land. [23] I will make a distinction[D] between my people and your people. This sign will take place tomorrow."

[24] And the Lord did this. Thick swarms of flies went into Pharaoh's palace and his officials' houses. Throughout Egypt the land was ruined because of the swarms of flies. [25] Then Pharaoh summoned Moses and Aaron and said, "Go sacrifice to your God within the country."

[26] But Moses said, "It would not be right[E] to do that, because what we will sacrifice to the Lord our God is detestable to the Egyptians. If we sacrifice what the Egyptians detest in front of them, won't they stone us? [27] We must go a distance of three days into the wilderness and sacrifice to the Lord our God as he instructs us."

[28] Pharaoh responded, "I will let you go and sacrifice to the Lord your God in the wilderness, but don't go very far. Make an appeal for me."

[29] "As soon as I leave you," Moses said, "I will appeal to the Lord, and tomorrow the swarms of flies will depart from Pharaoh, his officials, and his people. But Pharaoh must not act deceptively again by refusing to let the people go and sacrifice to the Lord." [30] Then Moses left Pharaoh's presence and appealed to the Lord. [31] The Lord did as Moses had said: He removed the swarms of flies from Pharaoh, his officials, and his people; not one was left. [32] But Pharaoh hardened his heart this time also and did not let the people go.

THE FIFTH PLAGUE: DEATH OF LIVESTOCK

9 Then the Lord said to Moses, "Go in to Pharaoh and say to him: This is what the Lord, the God of the Hebrews, says: Let my people go, so that they may worship me. [2] But if you refuse to let them go and keep holding them, [3] then the Lord's hand will bring a severe plague against your livestock in the field — the horses, donkeys, camels, herds, and flocks. [4] But the Lord will make a distinction between the livestock of Israel and the livestock of Egypt, so that nothing of all that the Israelites own will die." [5] And the Lord set a time, saying, "Tomorrow the Lord will do this thing in the land." [6] The Lord did this the next day. All the Egyptian livestock died, but none among the Israelite livestock died. [7] Pharaoh sent messengers who saw that not a single one of the Israelite livestock was dead. But Pharaoh's heart was hard, and he did not let the people go.

THE SIXTH PLAGUE: BOILS

[8] Then the Lord said to Moses and Aaron, "Take handfuls of furnace soot, and Moses is to throw it toward heaven in the sight of Pharaoh. [9] It will become

---

[A]8:20 Or serve   [B]8:21 Or insects   [C]8:21 Lit are   [D]8:23 LXX, Syr, Vg; MT reads will place redemption   [E]8:26 Or allowable fine dust over the entire land of Egypt. It will become festering boils on people and animals throughout the land of Egypt." ¹⁰ So they took furnace soot and stood before Pharaoh. Moses threw it toward heaven, and it became festering boils on people and animals. ¹¹ The magicians could not stand before Moses because of the boils, for the boils were on the magicians as well as on all the Egyptians. ¹² But the LORD hardened Pharaoh's heart and he did not listen to them, as the LORD had told Moses.

THE SEVENTH PLAGUE: HAIL

¹³ Then the LORD said to Moses, "Get up early in the morning and present yourself to Pharaoh. Tell him: This is what the LORD, the God of the Hebrews says: Let my people go, so that they may worship me. ¹⁴ For this time I am about to send all my plagues against you,ᴬ your officials, and your people. Then you will know there is no one like me on the whole earth. ¹⁵ By now I could have stretched out my hand and struck you and your people with a plague, and you would have been obliterated from the earth. ¹⁶ However, I have let you live for this purpose: to show you my power and to make my name known on the whole earth. ¹⁷ You are still acting arrogantly againstᴮ my people by not letting them go. ¹⁸ Tomorrow at this time I will rain down the worst hail that has ever occurred in Egypt from the day it was founded until now. ¹⁹ Therefore give orders to bring your livestock and all that you have in the field into shelters. Every person and animal that is in the field and not brought inside will die when the hail falls on them." ²⁰ Those among Pharaoh's officials who feared the word of the LORD made their servants and livestock flee to shelters, ²¹ but those who didn't take to heart the LORD's word left their servants and livestock in the field.

²² Then the LORD said to Moses, "Stretch out your hand toward heaven and let there be hail throughout the land of Egypt — on people and animals and every plant of the field in the land of Egypt." ²³ So Moses stretched out his staff toward heaven, and the LORD sent thunder and hail. Lightning struck the land, and the LORD rained hail on the land of Egypt. ²⁴ The hail, with lightning flashing through it, was so severe that nothing like it had occurred in the land of Egypt since it had become a nation. ²⁵ Throughout the land of Egypt, the hail struck down everything in the field, both people and animals. The hail beat down every plant of the field and shattered every tree in the field. ²⁶ The only place it didn't hail was in the land of Goshen, where the Israelites were.

²⁷ Pharaoh sent for Moses and Aaron. "I have sinned this time," he said to them. "The LORD is the righteous one, and I and my people are the guilty ones. ²⁸ Make an appeal to the LORD. There has been enough of God's thunder and hail. I will let you go; you don't need to stay any longer."

²⁹ Moses said to him, "When I have left the city, I will spread out my hands to the LORD. The thunder will cease, and there will be no more hail, so that you may know the earthᶜ belongs to the LORD. ³⁰ But as for you and your officials, I know that you still do not fear the LORD God."

³¹ The flax and the barley were destroyed because the barley was ripeᴰ and the flax was budding, ³² but the wheat and the spelt were not destroyed since they are later crops.ᴱ

ᴬ9:14 Lit plagues to your heart   ᴮ9:17 Or still obstructing   ᶜ9:29 Or land
ᴰ9:31 Lit was ears of grain   ᴱ9:32 Lit are late

³³ Moses left Pharaoh and the city, and spread out his hands to the LORD. Then the thunder and hail ceased, and rain no longer poured down on the land. ³⁴ When Pharaoh saw that the rain, hail, and thunder had ceased, he sinned again and hardened his heart, he and his officials. ³⁵ So Pharaoh's heart was hard, and he did not let the Israelites go, as the LORD had said through Moses.

THE EIGHTH PLAGUE: LOCUSTS

10 Then the LORD said to Moses, "Go to Pharaoh, for I have hardened his heart and the hearts of his officials so that I may do these miraculous signs of mine among them,ᴬ ² and so that you may tellᴮ your son and grandson how severely I dealt with the Egyptians and performed miraculous signs among them, and you will know that I am the LORD."

³ So Moses and Aaron went in to Pharaoh and told him, "This is what the LORD, the God of the Hebrews, says: How long will you refuse to humble yourself before me? Let my people go, that they may worship me. ⁴ But if you refuse to let my people go, then tomorrow I will bring locusts into your territory. ⁵ They will cover the surface of the land so that no one will be able to see the land. They will eat the remainder left to you that escaped the hail; they will eat every tree you have growing in the fields. ⁶ They will fill your houses, all your officials' houses, and the houses of all the Egyptians — something your fathers and grandfathers never saw since the time they occupied the land until today." Then he turned and left Pharaoh's presence.

⁷ Pharaoh's officials asked him, "How long must this man be a snare to us? Let the men go, so that they may worship the LORD their God. Don't you realize yet that Egypt is devastated?"

⁸ So Moses and Aaron were brought back to Pharaoh. "Go, worship the LORD your God," Pharaoh said. "But exactly who will be going?"

⁹ Moses replied, "We will go with our young and with our old; we will go with our sons and with our daughters, with our flocks and with our herds because we must hold the LORD's festival."

¹⁰ He said to them, "The Lord would have to be with you if I would ever let you and your families go! Look out — you're heading for trouble. ¹¹ No, go — just able-bodied men — worship the LORD, since that's what you want." And they were driven from Pharaoh's presence.

¹² The LORD then said to Moses, "Stretch out your hand over the land of Egypt, and the locusts will come up over it and eat every plant in the land, everything that the hail left." ¹³ So Moses stretched out his staff over the land of Egypt, and the LORD sent an east wind over the land all that day and through the night. By morning the east wind had brought in the locusts. ¹⁴ The locusts went up over the entire land of Egypt and settled on the whole territory of Egypt. Never before had there been such a large number of locusts, and there never will be again. ¹⁵ They covered the surface of the whole land so that the land was black, and they consumed all the plants on the ground and all the fruit on the trees that the hail had left. Nothing green was left on the trees or the plants in the field throughout the land of Egypt.

¹⁶ Pharaoh urgently sent for Moses and Aaron and said, "I have sinned against the LORD your God and against you. ¹⁷ Please forgive my sin once

ᴬ10:1 Lit *mine in his midst*   ᴮ10:2 Lit *tell in the ears of* more and make an appeal to the Lord your God, so that he will just take this death away from me." ¹⁸ Moses left Pharaoh's presence and appealed to the Lord. ¹⁹ Then the Lord changed the wind to a strong west⁴ wind, and it carried off the locusts and blew them into the Red Sea. Not a single locust was left in all the territory of Egypt. ²⁰ But the Lord hardened Pharaoh's heart, and he did not let the Israelites go.

THE NINTH PLAGUE: DARKNESS

²¹ Then the Lord said to Moses, "Stretch out your hand toward heaven, and there will be darkness over the land of Egypt, a darkness that can be felt." ²² So Moses stretched out his hand toward heaven, and there was thick darkness throughout the land of Egypt for three days. ²³ One person could not see another, and for three days they did not move from where they were. Yet all the Israelites had light where they lived.

²⁴ Pharaoh summoned Moses and said, "Go, worship the Lord. Even your families may go with you; only your flocks and herds must stay behind."

²⁵ Moses responded, "You must also let us have ᴮ sacrifices and burnt offerings to prepare for the Lord our God. ²⁶ Even our livestock must go with us; not a hoof will be left behind because we will take some of them to worship the Lord our God. We will not know what we will use to worship the Lord until we get there."

²⁷ But the Lord hardened Pharaoh's heart, and he was unwilling to let them go. ²⁸ Pharaoh said to him, "Leave me! Make sure you never see my face again, for on the day you see my face, you will die."

²⁹ "As you have said," Moses replied, "I will never see your face again."

THE TENTH PLAGUE: DEATH OF THE FIRSTBORN

11 The Lord said ᶜ to Moses, "I will bring one more plague on Pharaoh and on Egypt. After that, he will let you go from here. When he lets you go, ᴰ he will drive you out of here. ² Now announce to the people that both men and women should ask their neighbors for silver and gold items." ³ The Lord gave ᴱ the people favor with the Egyptians. In addition, Moses himself was very highly regarded ᶠ in the land of Egypt by ᴳ Pharaoh's officials and the people.

⁴ So Moses said, "This is what the Lord says: About midnight I will go throughout Egypt, ⁵ and every firstborn male in the land of Egypt will die, from the firstborn of Pharaoh who sits on his throne to the firstborn of the servant girl who is at the grindstones, as well as every firstborn of the livestock. ⁶ Then there will be a great cry of anguish through all the land of Egypt such as never was before or ever will be again. ⁷ But against all the Israelites, whether people or animals, not even a dog will snarl, ᴴ so that you may know that the Lord makes a distinction between Egypt and Israel. ⁸ All these officials of yours will come down to me and bow before me, saying: Get out, you and all the people who follow you.ᴵ After that, I will get out." And he went out from Pharaoh's presence fiercely angry.

⁹ The Lord said to Moses, "Pharaoh will not listen to you, so that my wonders may be multiplied in the land of Egypt." ¹⁰ Moses and Aaron did all these

---

ᴬ10:19 Lit sea   ᴮ10:25 Lit also give in our hand   ᶜ11:1 Or had said   ᴰ11:1 Or go, it will be finished —   ᴱ11:3 Or had given   ᶠ11:3 Lit was very great   ᴳ11:3 Or in the eyes of   ᴴ11:7 Lit point its tongue   ᴵ11:8 Lit people at your feet wonders before Pharaoh, but the LORD hardened Pharaoh's heart, and he would not let the Israelites go out of his land.

INSTRUCTIONS FOR THE PASSOVER

12 The LORD said to Moses and Aaron in the land of Egypt: [2] "This month is to be the beginning of months for you; it is the first month of your year. [3] Tell the whole community of Israel that on the tenth day of this month they must each select an animal of the flock according to their fathers' families, one animal per family. [4] If the household is too small for a whole animal, that person and the neighbor nearest his house are to select one based on the combined number of people; you should apportion the animal according to what each will eat. [5] You must have an unblemished animal, a year-old male; you may take it from either the sheep or the goats. [6] You are to keep it until the fourteenth day of this month; then the whole assembly of the community of Israel will slaughter the animals at twilight. [7] They must take some of the blood and put it on the two doorposts and the lintel of the houses where they eat them. [8] They are to eat the meat that night; they should eat it, roasted over the fire along with unleavened bread and bitter herbs. [9] Do not eat any of it raw or cooked in boiling[A] water, but only roasted over fire — its head as well as its legs and inner organs. [10] You must not leave any of it until morning; any part of it left until morning you must burn. [11] Here is how you must eat it: You must be dressed for travel,[B] your sandals on your feet, and your staff in your hand. You are to eat it in a hurry; it is the LORD's Passover.

[12] "I will pass through the land of Egypt on that night and strike every firstborn male in the land of Egypt, both people and animals. I am the LORD; I will execute judgments against all the gods of Egypt. [13] The blood on the houses where you are staying will be a distinguishing mark for you; when I see the blood, I will pass over you. No plague will be among you to destroy you when I strike the land of Egypt.

[14] "This day is to be a memorial for you, and you must celebrate it as a festival to the LORD. You are to celebrate it throughout your generations as a permanent statute. [15] You must eat unleavened bread for seven days. On the first day you must remove yeast from your houses. Whoever eats what is leavened from the first day through the seventh day must be cut off from Israel. [16] You are to hold a sacred assembly on the first day and another sacred assembly on the seventh day. No work may be done on those days except for preparing what people need to eat — you may do only that.

[17] "You are to observe the Festival of Unleavened Bread because on this very day I brought your military divisions out of the land of Egypt. You must observe this day throughout your generations as a permanent statute. [18] You are to eat unleavened bread in the first month, from the evening of the fourteenth day of the month until the evening of the twenty-first day. [19] Yeast must not be found in your houses for seven days. If anyone eats something leavened, that person, whether a resident alien or native of the land, must be cut off from the community of Israel. [20] Do not eat anything leavened; eat unleavened bread in all your homes."[C]

[A] 12:9 Or or boiled at all in   [B] 12:11 Lit must have your waist girded   [C] 12:20 Or settlements

GOD OVER ALL THE EARTH

EXODUS 12:1–13:16

I thought about Egypt a lot as a kid—though, growing up on the Great Lakes, I was about as far from the Nile as you can get. Our house had an attic with a low ceiling and one dim light, and I was afraid to poke my head inside because I was sure I would see the Anubis. Have you ever seen a drawing of this creature? It's a man with the head of a jackal. For me, there's nothing so terrifying as a man's figure walking upright, wearing the head of a jackal.

The pantheon of false Egyptian gods was a terrifying mix of half-human, half-sacred animals. The Egyptians created supermen, but that's all they were: imagined concoctions of everyday things elevated to the rank of deity.

Each major aspect of Egyptian life was tied to a specific god. For example, Hapi was the god of the Nile River, and seasons of drought and flooding were linked to the vagaries of his changing moods. Moses would have known all about Egyptian gods. And Moses, like anyone raised in Egypt, would have seen the Nile's waters turning to blood as a blow struck specifically against the god of the Nile.

In fact, each of the ten plagues targeted one of the gods from the Egyptian pantheon. One by one, God chipped away at their false authority. This pattern fulfilled a specific promise that God made through Moses to Israel and Pharaoh:

In spite of this, Pharaoh's heart was hardened, and he waffled about whether he should let Israel go. In his indecision he ignored this truth

"I will pass through the land of Egypt on that night and strike every firstborn male in the land of Egypt, both people and animals. I am the LORD; I will execute judgments against all the gods of Egypt."

EXODUS 12:12

that Moses already knew: there is but one God, and He is God over all the earth (Ex 10:8). Pharaoh never learned this lesson, but the Egyptian people did. Their awe of the one true God inspired them to press their gold and jewels into the hands of their Hebrew slaves departing Egypt (Ex 12:35-36).

When reading about the plagues, it's easy to see them as an assault on the Egyptians and Pharaoh himself. While that's partly true, the central point was to destroy the idolatry of the false gods. The words "Let my people go!" not only meant freedom from slavery, but freedom from idolatry.

We don't have to live in fear of supermen with jackal heads or fertile women with frog faces. **There is only one God, and He is good.** In His great goodness, He not only frees us from bondage, but He also unmasks the gods and powers of this world.

²¹ Then Moses summoned all the elders of Israel and said to them, "Go, select an animal from the flock according to your families, and slaughter the Passover animal. ²² Take a cluster of hyssop, dip it in the blood that is in the basin, and brush the lintel and the two doorposts with some of the blood in the basin. None of you may go out the door of his house until morning. ²³ When the Lord passes through to strike Egypt and sees the blood on the lintel and the two doorposts, he will pass over the door and not let the destroyer enter your houses to strike you.

²⁴ "Keep this command permanently as a statute for you and your descendants. ²⁵ When you enter the land that the Lord will give you as he promised, you are to observe this ceremony. ²⁶ When your children ask you, 'What does this ceremony mean to you?' ²⁷ you are to reply, 'It is the Passover sacrifice to the Lord, for he passed over the houses of the Israelites in Egypt when he struck the Egyptians and spared our homes.'" So the people knelt low and worshiped. ²⁸ Then the Israelites went and did this; they did just as the Lord had commanded Moses and Aaron.

THE EXODUS

²⁹ Now at midnight the Lord struck every firstborn male in the land of Egypt, from the firstborn of Pharaoh who sat on his throne to the firstborn of the prisoner who was in the dungeon, and every firstborn of the livestock. ³⁰ During the night Pharaoh got up, he along with all his officials and all the Egyptians, and there was a loud wailing throughout Egypt because there wasn't a house without someone dead. ³¹ He summoned Moses and Aaron during the night and said, "Get out immediately from among my people, both you and the Israelites, and go, worship the Lord as you have said. ³² Take even your flocks and your herds as you asked and leave, and also bless me."

³³ Now the Egyptians pressured the people in order to send them quickly out of the country, for they said, "We're all going to die!" ³⁴ So the people took their dough before it was leavened, with their kneading bowls wrapped up in their clothes on their shoulders.

³⁵ The Israelites acted on Moses's word and asked the Egyptians for silver and gold items and for clothing. ³⁶ And the Lord gave the people such favor with the Egyptians that they gave them what they requested. In this way they plundered the Egyptians.

³⁷ The Israelites traveled from Rameses to Succoth, about six hundred thousand able-bodied men on foot, besides their families. ³⁸ A mixed crowd also went up with them, along with a huge number of livestock, both flocks and herds. ³⁹ The people baked the dough they had brought out of Egypt into unleavened loaves, since it had no yeast; for when they were driven out of Egypt, they could not delay and had not prepared provisions for themselves.

⁴⁰ The time that the Israelites lived in Egypt^A was 430 years. ⁴¹ At the end of 430 years, on that same day, all the Lord's military divisions went out from the land of Egypt. ⁴² It was a night of vigil in honor of the Lord, because he would bring them out of the land of Egypt. This same night is in honor of the Lord, a night vigil for all the Israelites throughout their generations.

^A 12:40 LXX, Sam add *and in Canaan*

PASSOVER INSTRUCTION

⁴³ The LORD said to Moses and Aaron, "This is the statute of the Passover: no foreigner may eat it. ⁴⁴ But any slave a man has purchased may eat it, after you have circumcised him. ⁴⁵ A temporary resident or hired worker may not eat the Passover. ⁴⁶ It is to be eaten in one house. You may not take any of the meat outside the house, and you may not break any of its bones. ⁴⁷ The whole community of Israel must celebrate[A] it. ⁴⁸ If an alien resides among you and wants to observe the LORD's Passover, every male in his household must be circumcised, and then he may participate;[B] he will become like a native of the land. But no uncircumcised person may eat it. ⁴⁹ The same law will apply to both the native and the alien who resides among you."

⁵⁰ Then all the Israelites did this; they did just as the LORD had commanded Moses and Aaron. ⁵¹ On that same day the LORD brought the Israelites out of the land of Egypt according to their military divisions.

13 The LORD spoke to Moses: ² "Consecrate every firstborn male to me, the firstborn from every womb among the Israelites, both man and domestic animal; it is mine."

³ Then Moses said to the people, "Remember this day when you came out of Egypt, out of the place of slavery, for the LORD brought you out of here by the strength of his hand. Nothing leavened may be eaten. ⁴ Today, in the month of Abib,[C] you are going out. ⁵ When the LORD brings you into the land of the Canaanites, Hethites, Amorites, Hivites, and Jebusites,[D] which he swore to your fathers that he would give you, a land flowing with milk and honey, you must carry out this ceremony in this month. ⁶ For seven days you must eat unleavened bread, and on the seventh day there is to be a festival to the LORD. ⁷ Unleavened bread is to be eaten for those seven days. Nothing leavened may be found among you, and no yeast may be found among you in all your territory. ⁸ On that day explain to your son, 'This is because of what the LORD did for me when I came out of Egypt.' ⁹ Let it serve as a sign for you on your hand and as a reminder on your forehead,[E] so that the LORD's instruction may be in your mouth; for the LORD brought you out of Egypt with a strong hand. ¹⁰ Keep this statute at its appointed time from year to year.

¹¹ "When the LORD brings you into the land of the Canaanites, as he swore to you and your fathers, and gives it to you, ¹² you are to present to the LORD every firstborn male of the womb. All firstborn offspring of the livestock you own that are males will be the LORD's. ¹³ You must redeem every firstborn of a donkey with a flock animal, but if you do not redeem it, break its neck. However, you must redeem every firstborn among your sons.

¹⁴ "In the future, when your son asks you, 'What does this mean?' say to him, 'By the strength of his hand the LORD brought us out of Egypt, out of the place of slavery. ¹⁵ When Pharaoh stubbornly refused to let us go, the LORD killed every firstborn male in the land of Egypt, both the firstborn of humans and the firstborn of livestock. That is why I sacrifice to the LORD all the firstborn of the womb that are males, but I redeem all the firstborn of

---

^A12:47 Lit do   ^B12:48 Lit *may come near to do it*   ^C13:4 March–April; called Nisan in the post-exilic period; Neh 2:1; Est 3:7   ^D13:5 DSS, Sam, LXX, Syr add *Girgashites* and *Perizzites*; Jos 3:10   ^E13:9 Lit *reminder between your eyes*

SING TO THE LORD

EXODUS 13:17–15:21; PSALM 34:18; PSALM 104:33, 35

I wanted to sob. I wanted to scream and curl into the fetal position. The last thing I wanted to do was sing.

Even so, I felt a song of praise welling up in my throat.

Our son had been born just 24 hours before. Prenatal tests showed major problems, so while God stitched him together in my womb, I prayed like I'd never prayed before. On the day of his birth, God spared him (and us) from the worst-case scenario we were expecting.

But then we found ourselves in a children's hospital for testing. There I saw children made bald by chemotherapy treatments and babies with feeding tubes. I saw their grieving and heartbroken parents.

And the song that kept welling up inside of me was "You Are Awesome In This Place." It felt unthinkable to hum it at the site of so much pain. But because I believe God is close to the broken-hearted, I knew He was with those facing times of trouble in the hospital rooms surrounding me (Ps 34:18).

And so I sang. I sang for the delivery of my healthy baby boy and for his deliverance from a scary diagnosis. I sang because Jesus is my Rescuer.

Miriam sang, too. After her people were (again) delivered from the hand of the Egyptians, she belted out her song of praise. No quiet humming for her, she whipped out a tambourine and danced, leading the women of Israel in the happiest conga line in history (Ex 15:19-21).

Miriam was with her people as they walked across a raging sea on dry land. Then with her own eyes, she watched Pharaoh and his army of more than 600 chariots drown in that very same sea (Ex 14:21-22,26-28).

God heard her prayers. His answer was so swift and spectacular that it drew from her a song of worship and praise.

Miriam's people could have moved on to the next problem that needed solving. They would need God's deliverance over and over again. But Miriam paused and worshiped God for what He had delivered her from, before moving on to where she wanted Him to take her next. She couldn't repay God for His rescue, but she could certainly take the time to praise Him for it.

Oftentimes, I'm so wrapped up in asking Him to be my Provider, I fail to see Him as my God and my Deliverer. He's rescued me from more than I can comprehend, and I want to learn to respond with a song of praise. I want to sing my heart out to Him in worship for all He has done, and for all He promises to do.

"I will sing to the LORD all my life;
I will sing praise to my God while
I live. . . .
My soul, bless the LORD!
Hallelujah!"

PSALM 104:33, 35

---

my sons.' ¹⁶ So let it be a sign on your hand and a symbol^A on your forehead, for the LORD brought us out of Egypt by the strength of his hand."

THE ROUTE OF THE EXODUS

¹⁷ When Pharaoh let the people go, God did not lead them along the road to the land of the Philistines, even though it was nearby; for God said, "The people will change their minds and return to Egypt if they face war." ¹⁸ So he led the people around toward the Red Sea along the road of the wilderness. And the Israelites left the land of Egypt in battle formation.

¹⁹ Moses took the bones of Joseph with him, because Joseph had made the Israelites swear a solemn oath, saying, "God will certainly come to your aid; then you must take my bones with you from this place."

²⁰ They set out from Succoth and camped at Etham on the edge of the wilderness. ²¹ The LORD went ahead of them in a pillar of cloud to lead them on their way during the day and in a pillar of fire to give them light at night, so that they could travel day or night. ²² The pillar of cloud by day and the pillar of fire by night never left its place in front of the people.

14 Then the LORD spoke to Moses: ² "Tell the Israelites to turn back and camp in front of Pi-hahiroth, between Migdol and the sea; you must camp in front of Baal-zephon, facing it by the sea. ³ Pharaoh will say of the Israelites: They are wandering around the land in confusion; the wilderness has boxed them in. ⁴ I will harden Pharaoh's heart so that he will pursue them. Then I will receive glory by means of Pharaoh and all his army, and the Egyptians will know that I am the LORD." So the Israelites did this.

THE EGYPTIAN PURSUIT

⁵ When the king of Egypt was told that the people had fled, Pharaoh and his officials changed their minds about the people and said: "What have we done? We have released Israel from serving us." ⁶ So he got his chariot ready and took his troops^B with him; ⁷ he took six hundred of the best chariots and all the rest of the chariots of Egypt, with officers in each one. ⁸ The LORD hardened the heart of Pharaoh king of Egypt, and he pursued the Israelites, who were going out defiantly.^C ⁹ The Egyptians — all Pharaoh's horses and chariots, his horsemen,^D and his army — chased after them and caught up with them as they camped by the sea beside Pi-hahiroth, in front of Baal-zephon.

¹⁰ As Pharaoh approached, the Israelites looked up and there were the Egyptians coming after them! The Israelites were terrified and cried out to the LORD for help. ¹¹ They said to Moses: "Is it because there are no graves in Egypt that you have taken us away to die in the wilderness? What have you done to us by bringing us out of Egypt? ¹² Isn't this what we told you in Egypt: Leave us alone so that we may serve the Egyptians? It would have been better for us to serve the Egyptians than to die in the wilderness."

¹³ But Moses said to the people, "Don't be afraid. Stand firm and see the LORD's salvation that he will accomplish for you today; for the Egyptians you see today, you will never see again. ¹⁴ The LORD will fight for you, and you must be quiet."

---

^A 13:16 Or *phylactery*   ^B 14:6 Lit *people*   ^C 14:8 Lit *with a raised hand*
^D 14:9 Or *chariot drivers*

ESCAPE THROUGH THE RED SEA

¹⁵ The LORD said to Moses, "Why are you crying out to me? Tell the Israelites to break camp. ¹⁶ As for you, lift up your staff, stretch out your hand over the sea, and divide it so that the Israelites can go through the sea on dry ground. ¹⁷ As for me, I am going to harden the hearts of the Egyptians so that they will go in after them, and I will receive glory by means of Pharaoh, all his army, and his chariots and horsemen. ¹⁸ The Egyptians will know that I am the LORD when I receive glory through Pharaoh, his chariots, and his horsemen."

¹⁹ Then the angel of God, who was going in front of the Israelite forces, moved and went behind them. The pillar of cloud moved from in front of them and stood behind them. ²⁰ It came between the Egyptian and Israelite forces. There was cloud and darkness, it lit up the night, and neither group came near the other all night long.

²¹ Then Moses stretched out his hand over the sea. The LORD drove the sea back with a powerful east wind all that night and turned the sea into dry land. So the waters were divided, ²² and the Israelites went through the sea on dry ground, with the waters like a wall to them on their right and their left.

²³ The Egyptians set out in pursuit — all Pharaoh's horses, his chariots, and his horsemen — and went into the sea after them. ²⁴ During the morning watch, the LORD looked down at the Egyptian forces from the pillar of fire and cloud, and threw the Egyptian forces into confusion. ²⁵ He caused their chariot wheels to swerve[A,B] and made them drive[C] with difficulty. "Let's get away from Israel," the Egyptians said, "because the LORD is fighting for them against Egypt!"

²⁶ Then the LORD said to Moses, "Stretch out your hand over the sea so that the water may come back on the Egyptians, on their chariots and horsemen." ²⁷ So Moses stretched out his hand over the sea, and at daybreak the sea returned to its normal depth. While the Egyptians were trying to escape from it, the LORD threw them into the sea. ²⁸ The water came back and covered the chariots and horsemen, plus the entire army of Pharaoh that had gone after them into the sea. Not even one of them survived.

²⁹ But the Israelites had walked through the sea on dry ground, with the waters like a wall to them on their right and their left. ³⁰ That day the LORD saved Israel from the power of the Egyptians, and Israel saw the Egyptians dead on the seashore. ³¹ When Israel saw the great power that the LORD used against the Egyptians, the people feared the LORD and believed in him and in his servant Moses.

ISRAEL'S SONG

15 Then Moses and the Israelites sang this song to the LORD. They said:
I will sing to the LORD,
    for he is highly exalted;
he has thrown the horse
    and its rider into the sea.
²   The LORD is my strength and my song;[D]
    he has become my salvation.
This is my God, and I will praise him,

---

^A14:25 Sam, LXX, Syr read *He bound their chariot wheels*   ^B14:25 Or *fall off*
^C14:25 Or *and they drove them*   ^D15:2 Or *might*

my father's God, and I will exalt him.

3 The Lord is a warrior;
the Lord is his name.

4 He threw Pharaoh's chariots
and his army into the sea;
the elite of his officers
were drowned in the Red Sea.

5 The floods covered them;
they sank to the depths like a stone.

6 Lord, your right hand is glorious in power.
Lord, your right hand shattered the enemy.

7 You overthrew your adversaries
by your great majesty.
You unleashed your burning wrath;
it consumed them like stubble.

8 The water heaped up at the blast from your nostrils;
the currents stood firm like a dam.
The watery depths congealed in the heart
of the sea.

9 The enemy said:
"I will pursue, I will overtake,
I will divide the spoil.
My desire will be gratified at their expense.
I will draw my sword;
my hand will destroy^A them."

10 But you blew with your breath,
and the sea covered them.
They sank like lead
in the mighty waters.

11 Lord, who is like you among the gods?
Who is like you, glorious in holiness,
revered with praises, performing wonders?

12 You stretched out your right hand,
and the earth swallowed them.

13 With your faithful love,
you will lead the people
you have redeemed;
you will guide them to your holy dwelling
with your strength.

14 When the peoples hear, they will shudder;
anguish will seize the inhabitants of Philistia.

15 Then the chiefs of Edom will be terrified;
trembling will seize the leaders of Moab;
all the inhabitants of Canaan will panic;

16 terror and dread will fall on them.

---

^A 15:9 Or conquer

They will be as still^A as a stone
because of your powerful arm
until your people pass by, Lord,
until the people whom you purchased^B pass by.

17 You will bring them in and plant them
on the mountain of your possession;
Lord, you have prepared the place
for your dwelling;
Lord,^c your hands have established the sanctuary.
18 The Lord will reign forever and ever!

19 When Pharaoh's horses with his chariots and horsemen went into the sea, the Lord brought the water of the sea back over them. But the Israelites walked through the sea on dry ground. 20 Then the prophetess Miriam, Aaron's sister, took a tambourine in her hand, and all the women came out following her with tambourines and dancing. 21 Miriam sang to them:

Sing to the Lord,
for he is highly exalted;
he has thrown the horse
and its rider into the sea.

WATER PROVIDED

22 Then Moses led Israel on from the Red Sea, and they went out to the Wilderness of Shur. They journeyed for three days in the wilderness without finding water. 23 They came to Marah, but they could not drink the water at Marah because it was bitter — that is why it was named Marah.^D 24 The people grumbled to Moses, "What are we going to drink?" 25 So he cried out to the Lord, and the Lord showed him a tree. When he threw it into the water, the water became drinkable.

The Lord made a statute and ordinance for them at Marah, and he tested them there. 26 He said, "If you will carefully obey the Lord your God, do what is right in his sight, pay attention to his commands, and keep all his statutes, I will not inflict any illnesses on you that I inflicted on the Egyptians. For I am the Lord who heals you."

27 Then they came to Elim, where there were twelve springs and seventy date palms, and they camped there by the water.

MANNA AND QUAIL PROVIDED

16 The entire Israelite community departed from Elim and came to the Wilderness of Sin, which is between Elim and Sinai, on the fifteenth day of the second month after they had left the land of Egypt. 2 The entire Israelite community grumbled against Moses and Aaron in the wilderness. 3 The Israelites said to them, "If only we had died by the Lord's hand in the land of Egypt, when we sat by pots of meat and ate all the bread we wanted. Instead, you brought us into this wilderness to make this whole assembly die of hunger!"

---

^A15:16 Or silent ^B15:16 Or created ^C15:17 Some Hb mss, DSS, Sam, Tg read
Lord ^D15:23 = Bitter or Bitterness

⁴ Then the Lᴏʀᴅ said to Moses, "I am going to rain bread from heaven for you. The people are to go out each day and gather enough for that day. This way I will test them to see whether or not they will follow my instructions. ⁵ On the sixth day, when they prepare what they bring in, it will be twice as much as they gather on other days."ᴬ

⁶ So Moses and Aaron said to all the Israelites: "This evening you will know that it was the Lᴏʀᴅ who brought you out of the land of Egypt, ⁷ and in the morning you will see the Lᴏʀᴅ's glory because he has heard your complaints about him. For who are we that you complain about us?" ⁸ Moses continued, "The Lᴏʀᴅ will give you meat to eat this evening and all the bread you want in the morning, for he has heard the complaints that you are raising against him. Who are we? Your complaints are not against us but against the Lᴏʀᴅ."

⁹ Then Moses told Aaron, "Say to the entire Israelite community, 'Come before the Lᴏʀᴅ, for he has heard your complaints.'" ¹⁰ As Aaron was speaking to the entire Israelite community, they turned toward the wilderness, and there in a cloud the Lᴏʀᴅ's glory appeared.

¹¹ The Lᴏʀᴅ spoke to Moses, ¹² "I have heard the complaints of the Israelites. Tell them: At twilight you will eat meat, and in the morning you will eat bread until you are full. Then you will know that I am the Lᴏʀᴅ your God."

¹³ So at evening quail came and covered the camp. In the morning there was a layer of dew all around the camp. ¹⁴ When the layer of dew evaporated, there were fine flakes on the desert surface, as fine as frost on the ground. ¹⁵ When the Israelites saw it, they asked one another, "What is it?" because they didn't know what it was.

Moses told them, "It is the bread the Lᴏʀᴅ has given you to eat. ¹⁶ This is what the Lᴏʀᴅ has commanded: 'Gather as much of it as each person needs to eat. You may take two quartsᴮ per individual, according to the number of people each of you has in his tent.'"

¹⁷ So the Israelites did this. Some gathered a lot, some a little. ¹⁸ When they measured it by quarts,ᶜ the person who gathered a lot had no surplus, and the person who gathered a little had no shortage. Each gathered as much as he needed to eat. ¹⁹ Moses said to them, "No one is to let any of it remain until morning." ²⁰ But they didn't listen to Moses; some people left part of it until morning, and it bred worms and stank. Therefore Moses was angry with them.

²¹ They gathered it every morning. Each gathered as much as he needed to eat, but when the sun grew hot, it melted. ²² On the sixth day they gathered twice as much food, four quartsᴰ apiece, and all the leaders of the community came and reported this to Moses. ²³ He told them, "This is what the Lᴏʀᴅ has said: 'Tomorrow is a day of complete rest, a holy Sabbath to the Lᴏʀᴅ. Bake what you want to bake, and boil what you want to boil, and set aside everything left over to be kept until morning.'"

²⁴ So they set it aside until morning as Moses commanded, and it didn't stink or have maggots in it. ²⁵ "Eat it today," Moses said, "because today is a Sabbath to the Lᴏʀᴅ. Today you won't find any in the field. ²⁶ For six days you will gather it, but on the seventh day, the Sabbath, there will be none."

ᴬ16:5 Lit as gathering day to day   ᴮ16:16 Lit an omer   ᶜ16:18 Lit by an omer
ᴰ16:22 Lit two omers

²⁷ Yet on the seventh day some of the people went out to gather, but they did not find any. ²⁸ Then the LORD said to Moses, "How long will you ᴬ refuse to keep my commands and instructions? ²⁹ Understand that the LORD has given you the Sabbath; therefore on the sixth day he will give you two days' worth of bread. Each of you stay where you are; no one is to leave his place on the seventh day." ³⁰ So the people rested on the seventh day.

³¹ The house of Israel named the substance manna. ᴮ It resembled coriander seed, was white, and tasted like wafers made with honey. ³² Moses said, "This is what the LORD has commanded: 'Two quarts ᶜ of it are to be preserved throughout your generations, so that they may see the bread I fed you in the wilderness when I brought you out of the land of Egypt.'"

³³ Moses told Aaron, "Take a container and put two quarts ᴰ of manna in it. Then place it before the LORD to be preserved throughout your generations." ³⁴ As the LORD commanded Moses, Aaron placed it before the testimony to be preserved.

³⁵ The Israelites ate manna for forty years, until they came to an inhabited land. They ate manna until they reached the border of the land of Canaan. ³⁶ (They used a measure called an omer, which held two quarts. ᴱ)

WATER FROM THE ROCK

17 The entire Israelite community left the Wilderness of Sin, moving from one place to the next according to the LORD's command. They camped at Rephidim, but there was no water for the people to drink. ² So the people complained to Moses, "Give us water to drink."

"Why are you complaining to me?" Moses replied to them. "Why are you testing the LORD?"

³ But the people thirsted there for water and grumbled against Moses. They said, "Why did you ever bring us up from Egypt to kill us and our children and our livestock with thirst?"

⁴ Then Moses cried out to the LORD, "What should I do with these people? In a little while they will stone me!"

⁵ The LORD answered Moses, "Go on ahead of the people and take some of the elders of Israel with you. Take the staff you struck the Nile with in your hand and go. ⁶ I am going to stand there in front of you on the rock at Horeb; when you hit the rock, water will come out of it and the people will drink." Moses did this in the sight of the elders of Israel. ⁷ He named the place Massah ᶠ and Meribah ᴳ because the Israelites complained, and because they tested the LORD, saying, "Is the LORD among us or not?"

THE AMALEKITES ATTACK

⁸ At Rephidim, Amalek ᴴ came and fought against Israel. ⁹ Moses said to Joshua, "Select some men for us and go fight against Amalek. Tomorrow I will stand on the hilltop with God's staff in my hand."

ᴬ16:28 The Hb word for *you* is pl, referring to the whole nation.
ᴮ16:31 = what?; Ex 16:15   ᶜ16:32 Lit *'A full omer*   ᴰ16:33 Lit *a full omer*
ᴱ16:36 Lit *(The omer is a tenth of an ephah.)*   ᶠ17:7 = Testing
ᴳ17:7 = Quarreling   ᴴ17:8 A seminomadic people descended from *Amalek*, a grandson of Esau; Gn 36:12

¹⁰ Joshua did as Moses had told him, and fought against Amalek, while Moses, Aaron, and Hur went up to the top of the hill. ¹¹ While Moses held up his hand,ᴬ Israel prevailed, but whenever he put his handᴬ down, Amalek prevailed. ¹² When Moses's hands grew heavy, they took a stone and put it under him, and he sat down on it. Then Aaron and Hur supported his hands, one on one side and one on the other so that his hands remained steady until the sun went down. ¹³ So Joshua defeated Amalek and his armyᴮ with the sword.

¹⁴ The LORD then said to Moses, "Write this down on a scroll as a reminder and recite it to Joshua: I will completely blot out the memory of Amalek under heaven."

¹⁵ And Moses built an altar and named it, "The LORD Is My Banner."ᶜ ¹⁶ He said, "Indeed, my hand is lifted up towardᴰ the LORD's throne. The LORD will be at war with Amalek from generation to generation."

JETHRO'S VISIT

18 Moses's father-in-law Jethro, the priest of Midian, heard about everything that God had done for Moses and for God's people Israel when the LORD brought Israel out of Egypt.

² Now Jethro, Moses's father-in-law, had taken in Zipporah, Moses's wife, after he had sent her back, ³ along with her two sons, one of whom was named Gershomᴱ (because Moses had said, "I have been a resident alien in a foreign land") ⁴ and the other Eliezer (because he had said, "The God of my father was my helper and rescued me from Pharaoh's sword").ꟳ

⁵ Moses's father-in-law Jethro, along with Moses's wife and sons, came to him in the wilderness where he was camped at the mountain of God. ⁶ He sent word to Moses, "I, your father-in-law Jethro, am coming to you with your wife and her two sons."

⁷ So Moses went out to meet his father-in-law, bowed down, and then kissed him. They asked each other how they had beenᴳ and went into the tent. ⁸ Moses recounted to his father-in-law all that the LORD had done to Pharaoh and the Egyptians for Israel's sake, all the hardships that confronted them on the way, and how the LORD rescued them.

⁹ Jethro rejoiced over all the good things the LORD had done for Israel when he rescued them from the power of the Egyptians. ¹⁰ "Blessed be the LORD," Jethro exclaimed, "who rescued you from the power of Egypt and from the power of Pharaoh. He has rescued the people from under the power of Egypt! ¹¹ Now I know that the LORD is greater than all gods, because he did wonders when the Egyptians acted arrogantly against Israel."ᴴ

¹² Then Jethro, Moses's father-in-law, brought a burnt offering and sacrifices to God, and Aaron came with all the elders of Israel to eat a meal with Moses's father-in-law in God's presence.

¹³ The next day Moses sat down to judge the people, and they stood around Moses from morning until evening. ¹⁴ When Moses's father-in-law saw everything he was doing for them he asked, "What is this thing you're doing

---

ᴬ17:11 Sam, LXX, Syr, Tg, Vg read *hands*   ᴮ17:13 Or *people*
ᶜ17:15 = *Yahweh-nissi*   ᴰ17:16 Or *hand was on,* or *hand was against;*
Hb obscure   ᴱ18:3 In Hb the name *Gershom* sounds like the phrase "a stranger
there."   ꟳ18:4 = *My God Is Help*   ᴳ18:7 Lit *other about well-being*
ᴴ18:11 Hb obscure

for the people? Why are you alone sitting as judge, while all the people stand around you from morning until evening?"

¹⁵ Moses replied to his father-in-law, "Because the people come to me to inquire of God. ¹⁶ Whenever they have a dispute, it comes to me, and I make a decision between one man and another. I teach them God's statutes and laws."

¹⁷ "What you're doing is not good," Moses's father-in-law said to him. ¹⁸ "You will certainly wear out both yourself and these people who are with you, because the task is too heavy for you. You can't do it alone. ¹⁹ Now listen to me; I will give you some advice, and God be with you. You be the one to represent the people before God and bring their cases to him. ²⁰ Instruct them about the statutes and laws, and teach them the way to live and what they must do. ²¹ But you should select from all the people able men, God-fearing, trustworthy, and hating dishonest profit. Place them over the people as commanders of thousands, hundreds, fifties, and tens. ²² They should judge the people at all times. Then they can bring you every major case but judge every minor case themselves. In this way you will lighten your load,ᴬ and they will bear it with you. ²³ If you do this, and God so directs you, you will be able to endure, and also all these people will be able to go home satisfied."ᴮ

²⁴ Moses listened to his father-in-law and did everything he said. ²⁵ So Moses chose able men from all Israel and made them leaders over the people as commanders of thousands, hundreds, fifties, and tens. ²⁶ They judged the people at all times; they would bring the hard cases to Moses, but they would judge every minor case themselves.

²⁷ Moses let his father-in-law go, and he journeyed to his own land.

ISRAEL AT SINAI

19 In the third month from the very day the Israelites left the land of Egypt, they came to the Sinai Wilderness. ² They traveled from Rephidim, came to the Sinai Wilderness, and camped in the wilderness. Israel camped there in front of the mountain.

³ Moses went up the mountain to God, and the LORD called to him from the mountain: "This is what you must say to the house of Jacob and explain to the Israelites: ⁴ 'You have seen what I did to the Egyptians and how I carried you on eagles' wings and brought you to myself. ⁵ Now if you will carefully listen to me and keep my covenant, you will be my own possession out of all the peoples, although the whole earth is mine, ⁶ and you will be my kingdom of priests and my holy nation.' These are the words that you are to say to the Israelites."

⁷ After Moses came back, he summoned the elders of the people and set before them all these words that the LORD had commanded him. ⁸ Then all the people responded together, "We will do all that the LORD has spoken." So Moses brought the people's words back to the LORD.

⁹ The LORD said to Moses, "I am going to come to you in a dense cloud, so that the people will hear when I speak with you and will always believe you." Moses reported the people's words to the LORD, ¹⁰ and the LORD told Moses, "Go to the people and consecrate them today and tomorrow. They must wash their clothes ¹¹ and be prepared by the third day, for on the third

ᴬ18:22 Lit *lighten from on you*   ᴮ18:23 Lit *go to their place in peace* day the LORD will come down on Mount Sinai in the sight of all the people. ¹²Put boundaries for the people all around the mountain and say: Be careful that you don't go up on the mountain or touch its base. Anyone who touches the mountain must be put to death. ¹³No hand may touch him;ᴬ instead he will be stoned or shot with arrows and not live, whether animal or human. When the ram's horn sounds a long blast, they may go up the mountain."

¹⁴Then Moses came down from the mountain to the people and consecrated them, and they washed their clothes. ¹⁵He said to the people, "Be prepared by the third day. Do not have sexual relations with women."

¹⁶On the third day, when morning came, there was thunder and lightning, a thick cloud on the mountain, and a very loud trumpet sound, so that all the people in the camp shuddered. ¹⁷Then Moses brought the people out of the camp to meet God, and they stood at the foot of the mountain. ¹⁸Mount Sinai was completely enveloped in smoke because the LORD came down on it in fire. Its smoke went up like the smoke of a furnace, and the whole mountain shook violently. ¹⁹As the sound of the trumpet grew louder and louder, Moses spoke and God answered him in the thunder.

²⁰The LORD came down on Mount Sinai at the top of the mountain. Then the LORD summoned Moses to the top of the mountain, and he went up. ²¹The LORD directed Moses, "Go down and warn the people not to break through to see the LORD; otherwise many of them will die. ²²Even the priests who come near the LORD must consecrate themselves, or the LORD will break out in anger against them."

²³Moses responded to the LORD, "The people cannot come up Mount Sinai, since you warned us: Put a boundary around the mountain and consecrate it." ²⁴And the LORD replied to him, "Go down and come back with Aaron. But the priests and the people must not break through to come up to the LORD, or he will break out in anger against them." ²⁵So Moses went down to the people and told them.

THE TEN COMMANDMENTS

20 Then God spoke all these words:

²I am the LORD your God, who brought you out of the land of Egypt, out of the place of slavery.

3 Do not have other gods besides me.

4 Do not make an idol for yourself, whether in the shape of anything in the heavens above or on the earth below or in the waters under the earth. ⁵Do not bow in worship to them, and do not serve them; for I, the LORD your God, am a jealous God, punishing the children for the fathers' iniquity, to the third and fourth generations of those who hate me, ⁶but showing faithful love to a thousand generations of those who love me and keep my commands.

7 Do not misuse the name of the LORD your God, because the LORD will not leave anyone unpunished who misuses his name.

8 Remember the Sabbath day, to keep it holy: ⁹You are to labor six days and do all your work, ¹⁰but the seventh day is a Sabbath to the LORD your God. You must not do any work — you, your son or daughter, your male or female servant, your livestock, or the resident alien

---

ᴬ19:13 Or *it*

GOOD NEWS

EXODUS 19:1–20:21; MATTHEW 5:17-19; HEBREWS 10:1-4, 12–14

"We will do all that the LORD has spoken" (Ex 19:8).

This was Israel's promise as they prepared to receive the Old Testament law.

Then came the smoke and fire, the sound of the trumpet and the thunder. The very apparent presence of the Lord was in their midst—they could see and feel Him there. And as the Israelites' declaration of promise still echoed across the peaks and valleys of Mount Sinai, God delivered the Law to Moses.

But while Moses was still on the mountain with the Lord, Aaron and the people forgot their promise to God. As the Law was being given, it was also being broken (Ex 32).

God's chosen people were fatally flawed, unfaithful from the moment the Law was carved onto the tablets by the very hand of the God who had rescued them. The blood of bulls and goats would be shed for generations in an attempt to atone for their unfaithfulness, only for them to be unfaithful again.

But friends, there is good news for you and me.

"Since the law has only a shadow of the good things to come, and not the reality itself of those things, it can never perfect the worshipers by the same sacrifices they continually offer year after year. Otherwise, wouldn't they have stopped being offered, since the worshipers, purified once and for all, would no longer have any consciousness of sins? But in the sacrifices there is a reminder of sins year after year. For it is

impossible for the blood of bulls and goats to take away sins" (Heb 10:1-4).

This is the Good News. No more bulls and goats—no more blood must be shed. Though it had once been that way due to mankind's sin, Jesus Christ, "after offering one sacrifice for sins forever . . . has perfected forever those who are sanctified" (Heb 10:12, 14).

Christ was the perfect sacrifice, but this doesn't make the law an obsolete relic. In Jesus' Sermon on the Mount—with the Pharisees in earshot—Christ made His purpose clear:

"I did not come to abolish but to fulfill. For truly I tell you, until heaven and earth pass away, not the smallest letter or one stroke of a letter will pass away from the law until all things are accomplished."

MATTHEW 5:17-18

The law remains and the debt has been paid. **The law reflects both God's perfection and our imperfection.** Like the Israelites at the base of Mount Sinai, we're an unfaithful people. We will promise to keep the law and we will fail. We are sure we can do better and we cannot. The law gives us order and shows us how we can please God.

We cannot keep our promise. But, "he who promised is faithful" (Heb 10:23). Thanks be to God.

who is within your city gates. ¹¹ For the LORD made the heavens and the earth, the sea, and everything in them in six days; then he rested on the seventh day. Therefore the LORD blessed the Sabbath day and declared it holy.

¹² Honor your father and your mother so that you may have a long life in the land that the LORD your God is giving you.

¹³ Do not murder.

¹⁴ Do not commit adultery.

¹⁵ Do not steal.

¹⁶ Do not give false testimony against your neighbor.

¹⁷ Do not covet your neighbor's house. Do not covet your neighbor's wife, his male or female servant, his ox or donkey, or anything that belongs to your neighbor.

THE PEOPLE'S REACTION

¹⁸ All the people witnessed^A the thunder and lightning, the sound of the trumpet, and the mountain surrounded by smoke. When the people saw it^B they trembled and stood at a distance. ¹⁹ "You speak to us, and we will listen," they said to Moses, "but don't let God speak to us, or we will die."

²⁰ Moses responded to the people, "Don't be afraid, for God has come to test you, so that you will fear him and will not^C sin." ²¹ And the people remained standing at a distance as Moses approached the total darkness where God was.

MOSES RECEIVES ADDITIONAL LAWS

²² Then the LORD told Moses, "This is what you are to say to the Israelites: You have seen that I have spoken to you from heaven. ²³ Do not make gods of silver to rival me; do not make gods of gold for yourselves.

²⁴ "Make an earthen altar for me, and sacrifice on it your burnt offerings and fellowship offerings, your flocks and herds. I will come to you and bless you in every place where I cause my name to be remembered. ²⁵ If you make a stone altar for me, do not build it out of cut stones. If you use your chisel on it, you will defile it. ²⁶ Do not go up to my altar on steps, so that your nakedness is not exposed on it.

21

"These are the ordinances that you are to set before them:

LAWS ABOUT SLAVES

² "When you buy a Hebrew slave, he is to serve for six years; then in the seventh he is to leave as a free man^D without paying anything. ³ If he arrives alone, he is to leave alone; if he arrives with^E a wife, his wife is to leave with him. ⁴ If his master gives him a wife and she bears him sons or daughters, the wife and her children belong to her master, and the man must leave alone.

⁵ "But if the slave declares, 'I love my master, my wife, and my children; I do not want to leave as a free man,' ⁶ his master is to bring him to the judges^F and then bring him to the door or doorpost. His master will pierce his ear with an awl, and he will serve his master for life.

---

^A20:18 Lit saw   ^B20:18 Sam, LXX, Syr, Tg, Vg read smoke. The people (or they) were afraid,   ^C20:20 Lit that the fear of him may be in you, and you do not
^D21:2 Lit to go forth   ^E21:3 Lit he is the husband of   ^F21:6 Or to God; that is, to his sanctuary or court

⁷ "When a man sells his daughter as a concubine,ᴬ she is not to leave as the male slaves do. ⁸ If she is displeasing to her master, who chose her for himself, then he must let her be redeemed. He has no right to sell her to foreigners because he has acted treacherously toward her. ⁹ Or if he chooses her for his son, he must deal with her according to the customary treatment of daughters. ¹⁰ If he takes an additional wife, he must not reduce the food, clothing, or marital rights of the first wife. ¹¹ And if he does not do these three things for her, she may leave free of charge, without any payment.ᴮ

LAWS ABOUT PERSONAL INJURY

¹² "Whoever strikes a person so that he dies must be put to death. ¹³ But if he did not intend any harm,ᶜ and yet God allowed it to happen, I will appoint a place for you where he may flee. ¹⁴ If a person schemes and willfullyᴰ acts against his neighbor to murder him, you must take him from my altar to be put to death.

¹⁵ "Whoever strikes his father or his mother must be put to death.

¹⁶ "Whoever kidnaps a person must be put to death, whether he sells him or the person is found in his possession.

¹⁷ "Whoever curses his father or his mother must be put to death.

¹⁸ "When men quarrel and one strikes the other with a stone or his fist, and the injured man does not die but is confined to bed, ¹⁹ if he can later get up and walk around outside leaning on his staff, then the one who struck him will be exempt from punishment. Nevertheless, he must pay for his lost work timeᴱ and provide for his complete recovery.

²⁰ "When a man strikes his male or female slave with a rod, and the slave dies under his abuse,ᶠ the owner must be punished.ᴳ ²¹ However, if the slave can stand up after a day or two, the owner should not be punishedᴴ because he is his owner's property.ᴵ

²² "When men get in a fight and hit a pregnant woman so that her children are born prematurely but there is no injury, the one who hit her must be fined as the woman's husband demands from him, and he must pay according to judicial assessment. ²³ If there is an injury, then you must give life for life, ²⁴ eye for eye, tooth for tooth, hand for hand, foot for foot, ²⁵ burn for burn, bruise for bruise, wound for wound.

²⁶ "When a man strikes the eye of his male or female slave and destroys it, he must let the slave go free in compensation for his eye. ²⁷ If he knocks out the tooth of his male or female slave, he must let the slave go free in compensation for his tooth.

²⁸ "When an oxᴶ gores a man or a woman to death, the ox must be stoned, and its meat may not be eaten, but the ox's owner is innocent. ²⁹ However, if the ox was in the habit of goring, and its owner has been warned yet does not restrain it, and it kills a man or a woman, the ox must be stoned, and its owner must also be put to death. ³⁰ If instead a ransom is demanded of him, he can pay a redemption price for his life in the full amount demanded from him. ³¹ If it gores a son or a daughter, he is to be dealt with according to this

---

ᴬ21:7 Or *servant* ᴮ21:11 She doesn't have to pay any redemption price.
ᶜ21:13 Lit *he was not lying in wait* ᴰ21:14 Or *maliciously* ᴱ21:19 Lit *his inactivity*
ᶠ21:20 Lit *hand* ᴳ21:20 Or *must suffer vengeance* ᴴ21:21 Or *not suffer*
vengeance ᴵ21:21 Lit *silver* ᴶ21:28 Or *a bull, or a steer*

same law. ³² If the ox gores a male or female slave, he must give thirty shekels of silver ᴬ to the slave's master, and the ox must be stoned.

³³ "When a man uncovers a pit or digs a pit, and does not cover it, and an ox or a donkey falls into it, ³⁴ the owner of the pit must give compensation; he must pay to its owner, but the dead animal will become his.

³⁵ "When a man's ox injures his neighbor's ox and it dies, they must sell the live ox and divide its proceeds; they must also divide the dead animal. ³⁶ If, however, it is known that the ox was in the habit of goring, yet its owner has not restrained it, he must compensate fully, ox for ox; the dead animal will become his.

LAWS ABOUT THEFT

22 "When a man steals an ox or a sheep and butchers it or sells it, he must repay five cattle for the ox or four sheep for the sheep. ² If a thief is caught in the act of breaking in, and he is beaten to death, no one is guilty of bloodshed. ³ But if this happens after sunrise, the householder is guilty of bloodshed. A thief must make full restitution. If he is unable, he is to be sold because of his theft. ⁴ If what was stolen — whether ox, donkey, or sheep — is actually found alive in his possession, he must repay double.

LAWS ABOUT CROP PROTECTION

⁵ "When a man lets a field or vineyard be grazed in, and then allows his animals to go and graze in someone else's field, he must repay ᴮ with the best of his own field or vineyard.

⁶ "When a fire gets out of control, spreads to thornbushes, and consumes stacks of cut grain, standing grain, or a field, the one who started the fire must make full restitution for what was burned.

LAWS ABOUT PERSONAL PROPERTY

⁷ "When a man gives his neighbor valuables ᶜ or goods to keep, but they are stolen from that person's house, the thief, if caught, must repay double. ⁸ If the thief is not caught, the owner of the house must present himself to the judges ᴰ to determine ᴱ whether or not he has taken his neighbor's property. ⁹ In any case of wrongdoing involving an ox, a donkey, a sheep, a garment, or anything else lost, and someone claims, 'That's mine,' ᶠ the case between the two parties is to come before the judges. ᴳ The one the judges condemn ᴴ must repay double to his neighbor.

¹⁰ "When a man gives his neighbor a donkey, an ox, a sheep, or any other animal to care for, but it dies, is injured, or is stolen, while no one is watching, ¹¹ there must be an oath before the Lᴏʀᴅ between the two of them to determine whether or not he has taken his neighbor's property. Its owner must accept the oath, and the other man does not have to make restitution. ¹² But if, in fact, the animal was stolen from his custody, he must make restitution to its owner. ¹³ If it was actually torn apart by a

---

ᴬ21:32 About one pound of silver   ᴮ22:5 LXX adds *from his field according to its produce. But if someone lets his animals graze an entire field, he must repay* ; DSS, Sam also support this reading.   ᶜ22:7 Lit *silver*   ᴰ22:8 Or *to God* ᴱ22:8 LXX, Tg, Vg read *swear*   ᶠ22:9 Lit *That is it*   ᴳ22:9 Or *before God* ᴴ22:9 Or *one whom God condemns* wild animal, he is to bring it as evidence; he does not have to make restitution for the torn carcass. ¹⁴ "When a man borrows an animal from his neighbor, and it is injured or dies while its owner is not there with it, the man must make full restitution. ¹⁵ If its owner is there with it, the man does not have to make restitution. If it was rented, the loss is covered by^A its rental price.

LAWS ABOUT SEDUCTION

¹⁶ "If a man seduces a virgin who is not engaged, and he sleeps with her, he must certainly pay the bridal price for her to be his wife. ¹⁷ If her father absolutely refuses to give her to him, he must pay an amount in silver equal to the bridal price for virgins.

CAPITAL OFFENSES

¹⁸ "Do not allow a sorceress to live.

¹⁹ "Whoever has sexual intercourse with an animal must be put to death.

²⁰ "Whoever sacrifices to any gods, except the LORD alone, is to be set apart for destruction.

LAWS PROTECTING THE VULNERABLE

²¹ "You must not exploit a resident alien or oppress him, since you were resident aliens in the land of Egypt.

²² "You must not mistreat any widow or fatherless child. ²³ If you do mistreat them, they will no doubt cry to me, and I will certainly hear their cry. ²⁴ My anger will burn, and I will kill you with the sword; then your wives will be widows and your children fatherless.

²⁵ "If you lend silver to my people, to the poor person among you, you must not be like a creditor to him; you must not charge him interest.

²⁶ "If you ever take your neighbor's cloak as collateral, return it to him before sunset. ²⁷ For it is his only covering; it is the clothing for his body.^B What will he sleep in? And if he cries out to me, I will listen because I am gracious.

RESPECT FOR GOD

²⁸ "You must not blaspheme God^C or curse a leader among your people.

²⁹ "You must not hold back offerings from your harvest or your vats. Give me the firstborn of your sons. ³⁰ Do the same with your cattle and your flock. Let them stay with their mothers for seven days, but on the eighth day you are to give them to me.

³¹ "Be my holy people. You must not eat the meat of a mauled animal found in the field; throw it to the dogs.

LAWS ABOUT HONESTY AND JUSTICE

23 "You must not spread a false report. Do not join^D the wicked to be a malicious witness.

² "You must not follow a crowd in wrongdoing. Do not testify in a lawsuit and go along with a crowd to pervert justice. ³ Do not show favoritism to a poor person in his lawsuit.

---

^A22:15 Lit rented, it comes with   ^B22:27 Lit skin   ^C22:28 Or judges   ^D23:1 Lit join hands with

⁴ "If you come across your enemy's stray ox or donkey, you must return it to him.

⁵ "If you see the donkey of someone who hates you lying helpless under its load, and you want to refrain from helping it, you must help with it.^A

⁶ "You must not deny justice to a poor person among you in his lawsuit. ⁷ Stay far away from a false accusation. Do not kill the innocent and the just, because I will not justify the guilty. ⁸ You must not take a bribe, for a bribe blinds the clear-sighted and corrupts the words^B of the righteous. ⁹ You must not oppress a resident alien; you yourselves know how it feels to be a resident alien because you were resident aliens in the land of Egypt.

SABBATHS AND FESTIVALS

¹⁰ "Sow your land for six years and gather its produce. ¹¹ But during the seventh year you are to let it rest and leave it uncultivated, so that the poor among your people may eat from it and the wild animals may consume what they leave. Do the same with your vineyard and your olive grove.

¹² "Do your work for six days but rest on the seventh day so that your ox and your donkey may rest, and the son of your female slave as well as the resident alien may be refreshed.

¹³ "Pay strict attention to everything I have said to you. You must not invoke the names of other gods; they must not be heard on your lips.^C

¹⁴ "Celebrate a festival in my honor three times a year. ¹⁵ Observe the Festival of Unleavened Bread. As I commanded you, you are to eat unleavened bread for seven days at the appointed time in the month of Abib,^D because you came out of Egypt in that month. No one is to appear before me empty-handed. ¹⁶ Also observe the Festival of Harvest^E with the firstfruits of your produce from what you sow in the field, and observe the Festival of Ingathering^F at the end of the year, when you gather your produce^G from the field. ¹⁷ Three times a year all your males are to appear before the Lord GOD.

¹⁸ "You must not offer the blood of my sacrifices with anything leavened. The fat of my festival offering must not remain until morning.

¹⁹ "Bring the best of the firstfruits of your land to the house of the LORD your God.

"You must not boil a young goat in its mother's milk.

PROMISES AND WARNINGS

²⁰ "I am going to send an angel before you to protect you on the way and bring you to the place I have prepared. ²¹ Be attentive to him and listen to him. Do not defy him, because he will not forgive your acts of rebellion, for my name is in him. ²² But if you will carefully obey him and do everything I say, then I will be an enemy to your enemies and a foe to your foes. ²³ For my angel will go before you and bring you to the land of the Amorites, Hethites, Perizzites, Canaanites, Hivites, and Jebusites, and I will wipe them out. ²⁴ Do

---

^A23:5 Or load, you must refrain from leaving it to him; you must set it free with him   ^B23:8 Or and subverts the cause   ^C23:13 Lit mouth   ^D23:15 March–April; called Nisan in the post-exilic period; Neh 2:1; Est 3:7   ^E23:16 The Festival of Harvest is called Festival of Weeks elsewhere; Ex 34:22. In the NT it is called Pentecost; Ac 2:1.   ^F23:16 The Festival of Ingathering is called Festival of Shelters elsewhere; Lv 23:34-36.   ^G23:16 Lit labors not bow in worship to their gods, and do not serve them. Do not imitate their practices. Instead, demolish them^A and smash their sacred pillars to pieces. ²⁵ Serve the Lᴏʀᴅ your God, and he^B will bless your bread and your water. I will remove illnesses from you. ²⁶ No woman will miscarry or be childless in your land. I will give you the full number of your days.

²⁷ "I will cause the people ahead of you to feel terror^C and will throw into confusion all the nations you come to. I will make all your enemies turn their backs to you in retreat. ^D ²⁸ I will send hornets^E in front of you, and they will drive the Hivites, Canaanites, and Hethites away from you. ²⁹ I will not drive them out ahead of you in a single year; otherwise, the land would become desolate, and wild animals would multiply against you. ³⁰ I will drive them out little by little ahead of you until you have become numerous^F and take possession of the land. ³¹ I will set your borders from the Red Sea to the Mediterranean Sea, ^G and from the wilderness to the Euphrates River. ^H For I will place the inhabitants of the land under your control, and you will drive them out ahead of you. ³² You must not make a covenant with them or their gods. ³³ They must not remain in your land, or else they will make you sin against me. If you serve their gods, it will be a snare for you."

THE COVENANT CEREMONY

24 Then he said to Moses, "Go up to the Lᴏʀᴅ, you and Aaron, Nadab, and Abihu, and seventy of Israel's elders, and bow in worship at a distance. ² Moses alone is to approach the Lᴏʀᴅ, but the others are not to approach, and the people are not to go up with him."

³ Moses came and told the people all the commands of the Lᴏʀᴅ and all the ordinances. Then all the people responded with a single voice, "We will do everything that the Lᴏʀᴅ has commanded." ⁴ And Moses wrote down all the words of the Lᴏʀᴅ. He rose early the next morning and set up an altar and twelve pillars for the twelve tribes of Israel at the base of the mountain. ⁵ Then he sent out young Israelite men, and they offered burnt offerings and sacrificed bulls as fellowship offerings to the Lᴏʀᴅ. ⁶ Moses took half the blood and set it in basins; the other half of the blood he splattered on the altar. ⁷ He then took the covenant scroll and read it aloud to the people. They responded, "We will do and obey all that the Lᴏʀᴅ has commanded."

⁸ Moses took the blood, splattered it on the people, and said, "This is the blood of the covenant that the Lᴏʀᴅ has made with you concerning all these words."

⁹ Then Moses went up with Aaron, Nadab, and Abihu, and seventy of Israel's elders, ¹⁰ and they saw the God of Israel. Beneath his feet was something like a pavement made of lapis lazuli, as clear as the sky itself. ¹¹ God did not harm^I the Israelite nobles; they saw him, and they ate and drank.

¹² The Lᴏʀᴅ said to Moses, "Come up to me on the mountain and stay there so that I may give you the stone tablets with the law and commandments I have written for their instruction."

¹³ So Moses arose with his assistant Joshua and went up the mountain of God. ¹⁴ He told the elders, "Wait here for us until we return to you. Aaron and Hur are

---

^A 23:24 Probably the idols   ^B 23:25 LXX, Vg read *I*   ^C 23:27 Lit *will send terror of me ahead of you*   ^D 23:27 Or *I will give your enemies to you by the neck*   ^E 23:28 Or *send panic*   ^F 23:30 Lit *fruitful*   ^G 23:31 Lit *the Sea of the Philistines* ^H 23:31 Lit *the River*   ^I 24:11 Lit *not stretch out his hand against* here with you. Whoever has a dispute should go to them." ¹⁵ When Moses went up the mountain, the cloud covered it. ¹⁶ The glory of the LORD settled on Mount Sinai, and the cloud covered it for six days. On the seventh day he called to Moses from the cloud. ¹⁷ The appearance of the LORD's glory to the Israelites was like a consuming fire on the mountaintop. ¹⁸ Moses entered the cloud as he went up the mountain, and he remained on the mountain forty days and forty nights.

OFFERINGS TO BUILD THE TABERNACLE

25 The LORD spoke to Moses: ² "Tell the Israelites to take an offering for me. You are to take my offering from everyone who is willing to give. ³ This is the offering you are to receive from them: gold, silver, and bronze; ⁴ blue, purple, and scarlet yarn; fine linen and goat hair; ⁵ ram skins dyed red and fine leather;ᴬ acacia wood; ⁶ oil for the light; spices for the anointing oil and for the fragrant incense; ⁷ and onyxᴮ along with other gemstones for mounting on the ephod and breastpiece.ᶜ

⁸ "They are to make a sanctuary for me so that I may dwell among them. ⁹ You must make it according to all that I show you — the pattern of the tabernacle as well as the pattern of all its furnishings.

THE ARK

¹⁰ "They are to make an ark of acacia wood, forty-five inches long, twenty-seven inches wide, and twenty-seven inches high.ᴰ ¹¹ Overlay it with pure gold; overlay it both inside and out. Also make a gold molding all around it. ¹² Cast four gold rings for it and place them on its four feet, two rings on one side and two rings on the other side. ¹³ Make poles of acacia wood and overlay them with gold. ¹⁴ Insert the poles into the rings on the sides of the ark in order to carry the ark with them. ¹⁵ The poles are to remain in the rings of the ark; they must not be removed from it. ¹⁶ Put the tablets ofᴱ the testimony that I will give you into the ark. ¹⁷ Make a mercy seat of pure gold, forty-five inches long and twenty-seven inches wide.ᶠ ¹⁸ Make two cherubim of gold; make them of hammered work at the two ends of the mercy seat. ¹⁹ Make one cherub at one end and one cherub at the other end. At its two ends, make the cherubim of one piece with the mercy seat. ²⁰ The cherubim are to have wings spread out above, covering the mercy seat with their wings, and are to face one another. The faces of the cherubim should be toward the mercy seat. ²¹ Set the mercy seat on top of the ark and put the tablets of the testimony that I will give you into the ark. ²² I will meet with you there above the mercy seat, between the two cherubim that are over the ark of the testimony; I will speak with you from there about all that I command you regarding the Israelites.

THE TABLE

²³ "You are to construct a table of acacia wood, thirty-six inches long, eighteen inches wide, and twenty-seven inches high.ᴳ ²⁴ Overlay it with pure

---

ᴬ25:5 Hb obscure   ᴮ25:7 Or *carnelian*   ᶜ25:7 Traditionally, *breastplate*
ᴰ25:10 Lit *two and a half cubits its length, one and a half cubits its width, and one and a half cubits its height*   ᴱ25:16 *the tablets of* supplied for clarity, also in v. 21   ᶠ25:17 Lit *two and a half cubits its length, one and a half cubits its width*
ᴳ25:23 Lit *two cubits its length, one cubit its width, and one and a half cubits its height*

gold and make a gold molding all around it. ²⁵ Make a three-inch ᴬ frame all around it and make a gold molding for it all around its frame. ²⁶ Make four gold rings for it, and attach the rings to the four corners at its four legs. ²⁷ The rings should be next to the frame as holders for the poles to carry the table. ²⁸ Make the poles of acacia wood and overlay them with gold, and the table can be carried by them. ²⁹ You are also to make its plates and cups, as well as its pitchers and bowls for pouring drink offerings. Make them out of pure gold. ³⁰ Put the Bread of the Presence on the table before me at all times.

THE LAMPSTAND

³¹ "You are to make a lampstand out of pure, hammered gold. It is to be made of one piece: its base and shaft, its ornamental cups, and its buds ᴮ and petals. ³² Six branches are to extend from its sides, three branches of the lampstand from one side and three branches of the lampstand from the other side. ³³ There are to be three cups shaped like almond blossoms, each with a bud and petals, on one branch, and three cups shaped like almond blossoms, each with a bud and petals, on the next branch. It is to be this way for the six branches that extend from the lampstand. ³⁴ There are to be four cups shaped like almond blossoms on the lampstand shaft along with its buds and petals. ³⁵ For the six branches that extend from the lampstand, a bud must be under the first pair of branches from it, a bud under the second pair of branches from it, and a bud under the third pair of branches from it. ³⁶ Their buds and branches are to be of one piece. ᶜ All of it is to be a single hammered piece of pure gold.

³⁷ "Make its seven lamps, and set them up so that they illuminate the area in front of it. ³⁸ Its snuffers and firepans must be of pure gold. ³⁹ The lampstand ᴰ with all these utensils is to be made from seventy-five pounds ᴱ of pure gold. ⁴⁰ Be careful to make them according to the pattern you have been shown on the mountain.

THE TABERNACLE

26 "You are to construct the tabernacle itself with ten curtains. You must make them of finely spun linen, and blue, purple, and scarlet yarn, with a design of cherubim worked into them. ² Each curtain should be forty-two feet ᶠ long and six feet ᴳ wide; all the curtains are to have the same measurements. ³ Five of the curtains should be joined together, and the other five curtains joined together. ⁴ Make loops of blue yarn on the edge of the last curtain in the first set, and do the same on the edge of the outermost curtain in the second set. ⁵ Make fifty loops on the one curtain and make fifty loops on the edge of the curtain in the second set, so that the loops line up together. ⁶ Also make fifty gold clasps and join the curtains together with the clasps, so that the tabernacle may be a single unit.

⁷ "You are to make curtains of goat hair for a tent over the tabernacle; make eleven of these curtains. ⁸ Each curtain should be forty-five feet ᴴ long and six feet wide. All eleven curtains are to have the same measurements. ⁹ Join five of the curtains by themselves, and the other six curtains by themselves. Then fold the sixth curtain double at the front of the tent. ¹⁰ Make fifty loops on the

---

ᴬ25:25 Lit Make it a handbreadth   ᴮ25:31 = the outer covering of a flower
ᶜ25:36 Lit piece with it   ᴰ25:39 Lit It   ᴱ25:39 Lit a talent   ᶠ26:2 Lit 28 cubits
ᴳ26:2 Lit four cubits, also in v. 8   ᴴ26:8 Lit 30 cubits

edge of one curtain, the outermost in the first set, and make fifty loops on the edge of the corresponding curtain of the second set. ¹¹ Make fifty bronze clasps; put the clasps through the loops and join the tent together so that it is a single unit. ¹² As for the flap that remains from the tent curtains, the leftover half curtain is to hang over the back of the tabernacle. ¹³ What remains along the length of the tent curtains — a half yard ᴬ on one side and a half yard on the other side — should hang over the sides of the tabernacle on either side to cover it. ¹⁴ Make a covering for the tent from ram skins dyed red and a covering of fine leather ᴮ on top of that.

¹⁵ "You are to make upright supports ᶜ of acacia wood for the tabernacle. ¹⁶ Each support is to be fifteen feet ᴰ long and twenty-seven ᴱ inches wide. ¹⁷ Each support will have two tenons for joining. Do the same for all the supports of the tabernacle. ¹⁸ Make the supports for the tabernacle as follows: twenty supports for the south side, ¹⁹ and make forty silver bases under the twenty supports, two bases under the first support for its two tenons, and two bases under the next support for its two tenons; ²⁰ twenty supports for the second side of the tabernacle, the north side, ²¹ along with their forty silver bases, two bases under the first support and two bases under each support; ²² and make six supports for the west side of the tabernacle. ²³ Make two additional supports for the two back corners of the tabernacle. ²⁴ They are to be paired at the bottom, and joined together ꜰ at the top in a single ring. So it should be for both of them; they will serve as the two corners. ²⁵ There are to be eight supports with their silver bases: sixteen bases; two bases under the first support and two bases under each support.

²⁶ "You are to make five crossbars of acacia wood for the supports on one side of the tabernacle, ²⁷ five crossbars for the supports on the other side of the tabernacle, and five crossbars for the supports of the back side of the tabernacle on the west. ²⁸ The central crossbar is to run through the middle of the supports from one end to the other. ²⁹ Then overlay the supports with gold, and make their rings of gold as the holders for the crossbars. Also overlay the crossbars with gold. ³⁰ You are to set up the tabernacle according to the plan for it that you have been shown on the mountain.

³¹ "You are to make a curtain of blue, purple, and scarlet yarn, and finely spun linen with a design of cherubim worked into it. ³² Hang it on four gold-plated pillars of acacia wood that have gold hooks and that stand on four silver bases. ³³ Hang the curtain under the clasps ᴳ and bring the ark of the testimony there behind the curtain, so the curtain will make a separation for you between the holy place and the most holy place. ³⁴ Put the mercy seat on the ark of the testimony in the most holy place. ³⁵ Place the table outside the curtain and the lampstand on the south side of the tabernacle, opposite the table; put the table on the north side.

³⁶ "For the entrance to the tent you are to make a screen embroidered ᴴ with blue, purple, and scarlet yarn, and finely spun linen. ³⁷ Make five pillars of acacia wood for the screen and overlay them with gold; their hooks are to be gold, and you are to cast five bronze bases for them.

ᴬ 26:13 Lit *the cubit*   ᴮ 26:14 Hb obscure   ᶜ 26:15 Or *frames, or beams*
ᴰ 26:16 Lit *10 cubits*   ᴱ 26:16 Lit *a cubit and a half*   ꜰ 26:24 Lit *and together they
are to be complete*   ᴳ 26:33 The *clasps* that join the ten curtains of the tabernacle;
Ex 26:6   ᴴ 26:36 Or *woven*

THE ALTAR OF BURNT OFFERING

27 ¹ "You are to construct the altar of acacia wood. The altar must be square, 7 ½ feet long, and 7 ½ feet wide;^A it must be 4 ½ feet high. ^B ² Make horns for it on its four corners; the horns are to be of one piece. ^C Overlay it with bronze. ³ Make its pots for removing ashes, and its shovels, basins, meat forks, and firepans; make all its utensils of bronze. ⁴ Construct a grate for it of bronze mesh, and make four bronze rings on the mesh at its four corners. ⁵ Set it below, under the altar's ledge, ^D so that the mesh comes halfway up^E the altar. ⁶ Then make poles for the altar, poles of acacia wood, and overlay them with bronze. ⁷ The poles are to be inserted into the rings so that the poles are on two sides of the altar when it is carried. ⁸ Construct the altar with boards so that it is hollow. They are to make it just as it was shown to you on the mountain.

THE COURTYARD

⁹ "You are to make the courtyard for the tabernacle. Make hangings for the south side of the courtyard out of finely spun linen, 150 feet^F long on that side ¹⁰ including twenty posts and twenty bronze bases, with silver hooks and silver bands^G for the posts. ¹¹ And so make hangings 150 feet long for the north side, including twenty posts and their twenty bronze bases, with silver hooks and silver bands for the posts. ¹² For the width of the courtyard, make hangings 75 feet^H long for the west side, including their ten posts and their ten bases. ¹³ And for the width of the courtyard on the east side toward the sunrise, 75 feet, ¹⁴ make hangings 22 ½ feet^I long for one side of the gate, including their three posts and their three bases. ¹⁵ And make hangings 22 ½ feet long for the other side, including their three posts and their three bases. ¹⁶ The gate of the courtyard is to have a 30-foot^J screen embroidered^K with blue, purple, and scarlet yarn, and finely spun linen. It is to have four posts and their four bases.

¹⁷ "All the posts around the courtyard are to be banded with silver and have silver hooks and bronze bases. ¹⁸ The courtyard is to be 150 feet long, 75 feet wide at each end, and 7 ½ feet high, ^L all of it made of finely spun linen. The bases of the posts are to be bronze. ¹⁹ All the utensils of the tabernacle for every use and all its tent pegs as well as all the tent pegs of the courtyard are to be made of bronze.

THE LAMPSTAND OIL

²⁰ "You are to command the Israelites to bring you pure oil from crushed olives for the light, in order to keep the lamp burning regularly. ²¹ In the tent of meeting outside the curtain that is in front of the testimony, Aaron and his sons are to tend the lamp from evening until morning before the LORD. This is to be a permanent statute for the Israelites throughout their generations.

---

^A27:1 Lit five cubits in length and five cubits in width   ^B27:1 Lit wide; and its height three cubits   ^C27:2 Lit piece with it   ^D27:5 Perhaps a ledge around the altar on which the priests could stand; Lv 9:22   ^E27:5 Or altar's rim, so that the grid comes halfway down   ^F27:9 Lit 100 cubits, also in v. 11   ^G27:10 Or connecting rods, also in v. 11   ^H27:12 Lit 50 cubits, also in v. 13   ^I27:14 Lit 15 cubits, also in v. 15   ^J27:16 Lit 20-cubit   ^K27:16 Or woven   ^L27:18 Lit be 100 by the cubit, and the width 50 by 50, and the height five cubits

COME, SIT WHERE MERCY IS

EXODUS 26–27; MATTHEW 27:50-51; HEBREWS 9:6-14

When I was growing up, my parents had two oversized comfy chairs in their bedroom. I call them "the prayer chairs" because I'd often find my mom or my dad there, reading their Bibles and praying. We had a lot of talks in those chairs—good talks where we laughed and told stories, and hard talks that were painful and involved tears. All kinds of talking was welcome in the prayer chairs. Grace and mercy were plentiful there.

On first read, Exodus 26–27 is a rather long list of architectural instructions for the building of the tabernacle: dimensions, materials, and many, many details. But if you let yourself step away a bit and rise above for an aerial view, what you see before you is a beautiful picture of God drawing near to His people.

"They are to make a sanctuary for me so that I may dwell among them."

EXODUS 25:8

The aerial view of these chapters reveals building plans for a room where grace and mercy dwell—like a set of prayer chairs for God and for you. A place where all kinds of talks are welcome and grace and mercy abound.

One of the most important pieces of the tabernacle is the mercy seat. That name alone is so inviting, isn't it? Come, sit where mercy is. In Exodus 25:22, God says, "I will meet with you

there above the mercy seat . . . I will speak with you from there . . ." How incredible for the God of the universe to set up a regular meeting spot for Him and Moses!

In the tabernacle layout, there is a barrier between the people and the mercy seat, something to divide the holy place from the most holy place: a curtain (Ex 26:33). This is the same curtain that was torn from top to bottom when Jesus' sacrifice was complete on the cross (Mt 27:51). Just as God commanded it to be hung, so He commanded it to come down when the final sacrifice was made—an invitation for us to step through and enter the mercy seat, no matter who we are.

The tabernacle points to Christ in every detail. As Hebrews explains, "he entered the most holy place once for all time, not by the blood of goats and calves, but by his own blood, having obtained eternal redemption" (Heb 9:12).

God's plan for the tabernacle was for the Israelites to build it, and for Jesus to tear it down and rebuild it in our hearts. **This was His plan all along, to dwell among us.** To draw us into the mercy seat where we can talk to Him, worship Him, and simply be with Him.

When we look at these chapters from 30,000 feet, we realize they aren't merely instructions. They are a blueprint for our own hearts—the place where God chose to dwell, and chooses to dwell still.

THE PRIESTLY GARMENTS

28

¹"Have your brother Aaron, with his sons, come to you from the Israelites to serve me as priest — Aaron, his sons Nadab and Abihu, Eleazar and Ithamar. ²Make holy garments for your brother Aaron, for glory and beauty. ³You are to instruct all the skilled artisans,ᴬ whom I have filled with a spirit of wisdom, to make Aaron's garments for consecrating him to serve me as priest. ⁴These are the garments that they must make: a breastpiece, an ephod, a robe, a specially woven tunic,ᴮ a turban, and a sash. They are to make holy garments for your brother Aaron and his sons so that they may serve me as priests. ⁵They should useᶜ gold; blue, purple, and scarlet yarn; and fine linen.

THE EPHOD

⁶"They are to make the ephod of finely spun linen embroideredᴰ with gold, and with blue, purple, and scarlet yarn. ⁷It must have two shoulder pieces attached to its two edges so that it can be joined together. ⁸The artistically woven waistband that is on the ephodᴱ must be of one piece,ᶠ according to the same workmanship of gold, of blue, purple, and scarlet yarn, and of finely spun linen.

⁹"Take two onyx stones and engrave on them the names of Israel's sons: ¹⁰six of their names on the first stone and the remaining six names on the second stone, in the order of their birth. ¹¹Engrave the two stones with the names of Israel's sons as a gem cutter engraves a seal. Mount them, surrounded with gold filigree settings. ¹²Fasten both stones on the shoulder pieces of the ephod as memorial stones for the Israelites. Aaron will carry their names on his two shoulders before the LORD as a reminder. ¹³Fashion gold filigree settings ¹⁴and two chains of pure gold; you will make them of braided cord work, and attach the cord chains to the settings.

THE BREASTPIECE

¹⁵"You are to make an embroidered breastpiece for making decisions.ᴳ Make it with the same workmanship as the ephod; make it of gold, of blue, purple, and scarlet yarn, and of finely spun linen. ¹⁶It must be square and folded double, nine inches long and nine inches wide.ᴴ ¹⁷Place a setting of gemstonesᴵ on it, four rows of stones:

The first row should be
a row of carnelian, topaz, and emerald;ᴶ
¹⁸ the second row,
a turquoise,ᴷ a lapis lazuli, and a diamond;ᴸ
¹⁹ the third row,
a jacinth,ᴮ an agate, and an amethyst;
²⁰ and the fourth row,
a beryl, an onyx, and a jasper.

ᴬ28:3 Lit *all wise of heart* ᴮ28:4,19 Hb obscure ᶜ28:5 Lit *receive* ᴰ28:6 Or *woven* ᴱ28:8 Lit *waistband of its ephod, which is on it* ᶠ28:8 Lit *piece with the ephod* ᴳ28:15 Used for determining God's will; Nm 27:21 ᴴ28:16 Lit *a span its length and a span its width* ᴵ28:17 Many of these stones cannot be identified with certainty. ᴶ28:17 Or *beryl* ᴷ28:18 Or *malachite, or garnet* ᴸ28:18 Hb obscure; LXX, Vg read *jasper*

They should be adorned with gold filigree in their settings. ²¹ The twelve stones are to correspond to the names of Israel's sons. Each stone must be engraved like a seal, with one of the names of the twelve tribes.

²² "You are to make braided chains ᴬ of pure gold cord work for the breastpiece. ²³ Fashion two gold rings for the breastpiece and attach them to its two corners. ²⁴ Then attach the two gold cords to the two gold rings at the corners of the breastpiece. ²⁵ Attach the other ends of the two cords to the two filigree settings, and in this way attach them to the ephod's shoulder pieces in the front. ²⁶ Make two other gold rings and put them at the two other corners of the breastpiece on the edge that is next to the inner border of the ephod. ²⁷ Make two more gold rings and attach them to the bottom of the ephod's two shoulder pieces on its front, close to its seam, ᴮ and above the ephod's woven waistband. ²⁸ The artisans are to tie the breastpiece from its rings to the rings of the ephod with a cord of blue yarn, so that the breastpiece is above the ephod's waistband and does not come loose from the ephod.

²⁹ "Whenever he enters the sanctuary, Aaron is to carry the names of Israel's sons over his heart on the breastpiece for decisions, as a continual reminder before the Lord. ³⁰ Place the Urim and Thummim in the breastpiece for decisions, so that they will also be over Aaron's heart whenever he comes before the Lord. Aaron will continually carry the means of decisions for the Israelites over his heart before the Lord.

THE ROBE

³¹ "You are to make the robe of the ephod entirely of blue yarn. ³² There should be an opening at its top in the center of it. Around the opening, there should be a woven collar with an opening like that of body armor ᶜ so that it does not tear. ³³ Make pomegranates of blue, purple, and scarlet yarn on its lower hem and all around it. Put gold bells between them all the way around, ³⁴ so that gold bells and pomegranates alternate around the lower hem of the robe. ³⁵ The robe will be worn by Aaron whenever he ministers, and its sound will be heard when he enters the sanctuary before the Lord and when he exits, so that he does not die.

THE TURBAN

³⁶ "You are to make a pure gold medallion and engrave it, like the engraving of a seal: HOLY TO THE LORD. ³⁷ Fasten it to a cord of blue yarn so it can be placed on the turban; the medallion is to be on the front of the turban. ³⁸ It will be on Aaron's forehead so that Aaron may bear the guilt connected with the holy offerings that the Israelites consecrate as all their holy gifts. It is always to be on his forehead, so that they may find acceptance with the Lord.

OTHER PRIESTLY GARMENTS

³⁹ "You are to weave the tunic from fine linen, make a turban of fine linen, and make an embroidered sash. ⁴⁰ Make tunics, sashes, and headbands for Aaron's sons to give them glory and beauty. ⁴¹ Put these on your brother Aaron and his sons; then anoint, ordain, ᴰ and consecrate them, so that

---

ᴬ28:22 The same *chains* mentioned in v. 14   ᴮ28:27 The place where the *shoulder pieces* join the front of the ephod   ᶜ28:32 Hb obscure   ᴰ28:41 Lit *anoint them, fill their hand* they may serve me as priests. [42] Make them linen undergarments to cover their naked bodies; they must extend from the waist to the thighs. [43] These must be worn by Aaron and his sons whenever they enter the tent of meeting or approach the altar to minister in the sanctuary area, so that they do not incur guilt and die. This is to be a permanent statute for Aaron and for his future descendants.

INSTRUCTIONS ABOUT CONSECRATION

29 "This is what you are to do for them to consecrate them to serve me as priests. Take a young bull and two unblemished rams, [2] with unleavened bread, unleavened cakes mixed with oil, and unleavened wafers coated with oil. Make them out of fine wheat flour, [3] put them in a basket, and bring them in the basket, along with the bull and two rams. [4] Bring Aaron and his sons to the entrance to the tent of meeting and wash them with water. [5] Then take the garments and clothe Aaron with the tunic, the robe for the ephod, the ephod itself, and the breastpiece; fasten the ephod on him with its woven waistband. [6] Put the turban on his head and place the holy diadem on the turban. [7] Take the anointing oil, pour it on his head, and anoint him. [8] You must also bring his sons and clothe them with tunics. [9] Tie the sashes on Aaron and his sons and fasten headbands on them. The priesthood is to be theirs by a permanent statute. This is the way you will ordain Aaron and[A] his sons.

[10] "You are to bring the bull to the front of the tent of meeting, and Aaron and his sons must lay their hands on the bull's head. [11] Slaughter the bull before the LORD at the entrance to the tent of meeting. [12] Take some of the bull's blood and apply it to the horns of the altar with your finger; then pour out all the rest of the blood at the base of the altar. [13] Take all the fat that covers the entrails, the fatty lobe of the liver, and the two kidneys with the fat on them, and burn them on the altar. [14] But burn the bull's flesh, its hide, and its waste outside the camp; it is a sin offering.

[15] "Take one ram, and Aaron and his sons are to lay their hands on the ram's head. [16] You are to slaughter the ram, take its blood, and splatter it on all sides of the altar. [17] Cut the ram into pieces. Wash its entrails and legs, and place them with its head and its pieces on the altar. [18] Then burn the whole ram on the altar; it is a burnt offering to the LORD. It is a pleasing aroma, a fire offering to the LORD.

[19] "You are to take the second ram, and Aaron and his sons must lay their hands on the ram's head. [20] Slaughter the ram, take some of its blood, and put it on Aaron's right earlobe, on his sons' right earlobes, on the thumbs of their right hands, and on the big toes of their right feet. Splatter the remaining blood on all sides of the altar. [21] Take some of the blood that is on the altar and some of the anointing oil, and sprinkle them on Aaron and his garments, as well as on his sons and their garments. So he and his garments will be holy, as well as his sons and their garments.

[22] "Take the fat from the ram, the fat tail, the fat covering the entrails, the fatty lobe of the liver, the two kidneys and the fat on them, and the right thigh (since this is a ram for ordination[B]); [23] take one loaf of bread,

---

[A]29:9 Lit you will fill the hand of Aaron and the hand of; Ex 29:23-24
[B]29:22 The priest would normally receive the right thigh to be eaten, but here it is burned; Lv 7:32-34.

one cake of bread made with oil, and one wafer from the basket of un-leavened bread that is before the LORD; ²⁴ and put all of them in the hands of Aaron and his ^A sons and present them as a presentation offering be-fore the LORD. ²⁵ Take them from their hands and burn them on the altar on top of the burnt offering, as a pleasing aroma before the LORD; it is a fire offering to the LORD.

²⁶ "Take the breast from the ram of Aaron's ordination and present it as a presentation offering before the LORD; it is to be your portion. ²⁷ Consecrate for Aaron and his sons the breast of the presentation offering that is present-ed and the thigh of the contribution that is lifted up from the ram of ordina-tion. ²⁸ This will belong to Aaron and his sons as a regular portion from the Israelites, for it is a contribution. It will be the Israelites' contribution from their fellowship sacrifices, their contribution to the LORD.

²⁹ "The holy garments that belong to Aaron are to belong to his sons after him, so that they can be anointed and ordained ^B in them. ³⁰ Any priest who is one of his sons and who succeeds him and enters the tent of meeting to minister in the sanctuary must wear them for seven days.

³¹ "You are to take the ram of ordination and boil its flesh in a holy place. ³² Aaron and his sons are to eat the meat of the ram and the bread that is in the basket at the entrance to the tent of meeting. ³³ They must eat those things by which atonement was made at the time of their ordi-nation ^C and consecration. An unauthorized person must not eat them, for these things are holy. ³⁴ If any of the meat of ordination or any of the bread is left until morning, burn what is left over. It must not be eaten because it is holy.

³⁵ "This is what you are to do for Aaron and his sons based on all I have commanded you. Take seven days to ordain them. ³⁶ Sacrifice a bull as a sin offering each day for atonement. Purify ^D the altar when you make atone-ment for it, and anoint it in order to consecrate it. ³⁷ For seven days you must make atonement for the altar and consecrate it. The altar will be especially holy. Whatever touches the altar will be consecrated.

³⁸ "This is what you are to offer regularly on the altar every day: two year-old lambs. ³⁹ In the morning offer one lamb, and at twilight offer the oth-er lamb. ⁴⁰ With the first lamb offer two quarts ^E of fine flour mixed with one quart ^F of oil from crushed olives, and a drink offering of one quart of wine. ⁴¹ You are to offer the second lamb at twilight. Offer a grain offer-ing and a drink offering with it, like the one in the morning, as a pleasing aroma, a fire offering to the LORD. ⁴² This will be a regular burnt offering throughout your generations at the entrance to the tent of meeting be-fore the LORD, where I will meet you ^G to speak with you. ⁴³ I will also meet with the Israelites there, and that place will be consecrated by my glory. ⁴⁴ I will consecrate the tent of meeting and the altar; I will also consecrate Aaron and his sons to serve me as priests. ⁴⁵ I will dwell among the Israel-ites and be their God. ⁴⁶ And they will know that I am the LORD their God, who brought them out of the land of Egypt, so that I might dwell among them. I am the LORD their God.

---

^A29:24 Lit in the hands of his   ^B29:29 Lit him for anointing in them and for filling their hand   ^C29:33 Lit made to fill their hand   ^D29:36 Or Make a sin offering on   ^E29:40 Lit offer a tenth   ^F29:40 Lit a fourth of a hin   ^G29:42 = Moses

THE INCENSE ALTAR

30 "You are to make an altar for the burning of incense; make it of acacia wood. ² It must be square, eighteen inches long and eighteen inches wide;[A] it must be thirty-six inches high.[B] Its horns must be of one piece with it. ³ Overlay its top, all around its sides, and its horns with pure gold; make a gold molding all around it. ⁴ Make two gold rings for it under the molding on two of its sides; put these on opposite sides of it to be holders for the poles to carry it with. ⁵ Make the poles of acacia wood and overlay them with gold.

⁶ "You are to place the altar in front of the curtain by the ark of the testimony — in front of the mercy seat that is over the testimony — where I will meet with you. ⁷ Aaron must burn fragrant incense on it; he must burn it every morning when he tends the lamps. ⁸ When Aaron sets up the lamps at twilight, he must burn incense. There is to be an incense offering before the LORD throughout your generations. ⁹ You must not offer unauthorized incense on it, or a burnt or grain offering; you are not to pour a drink offering on it.

¹⁰ "Once a year Aaron is to perform the atonement ceremony for the altar. Throughout your generations he is to perform the atonement ceremony for[C] it once a year, with the blood of the sin offering for atonement on the horns. The altar is especially holy to the LORD."

THE ATONEMENT MONEY

¹¹ The LORD spoke to Moses: ¹² "When you take a census of the Israelites to register them, each of the men must pay a ransom for his life to the LORD as they are registered. Then no plague will come on them as they are registered. ¹³ Everyone who is registered must pay half a shekel[D] according to the sanctuary shekel (twenty gerahs to the shekel). This half shekel is a contribution to the LORD. ¹⁴ Each man who is registered, twenty years old or more, must give this contribution to the LORD. ¹⁵ The wealthy may not give more and the poor may not give less than half a shekel when giving the contribution to the LORD to atone for[E] your lives. ¹⁶ Take the atonement price[F] from the Israelites and use it for the service of the tent of meeting. It will serve as a reminder for the Israelites before the LORD to atone for your lives."

THE BRONZE BASIN

¹⁷ The LORD spoke to Moses: ¹⁸ "Make a bronze basin for washing and a bronze stand for it. Set it between the tent of meeting and the altar, and put water in it. ¹⁹ Aaron and his sons must wash their hands and feet from the basin. ²⁰ Whenever they enter the tent of meeting or approach the altar to minister by burning an offering to the LORD, they must wash with water so that they will not die. ²¹ They must wash their hands and feet so that they will not die; this is to be a permanent statute for them, for Aaron and his descendants throughout their generations."

[A]30:2 Lit one cubit its length and one cubit its width [B]30:2 Lit wide; and two cubits its height [C]30:10 Or on [D]30:13 A shekel is about two-fifths of an ounce of silver [E]30:15 Or to ransom, also in v. 16 [F]30:16 Lit the silver of the atonement

THE ANOINTING OIL

[22] The LORD spoke to Moses: [23] "Take for yourself the finest spices: 12 ½ pounds[A] of liquid myrrh, half as much (6 ¼ pounds[B]) of fragrant cinnamon, 6 ¼ pounds of fragrant cane, [24] 12 ½ pounds of cassia (by the sanctuary shekel), and a gallon[C] of olive oil. [25] Prepare from these a holy anointing oil, a scented blend, the work of a perfumer; it will be holy anointing oil.

[26] "With it you are to anoint the tent of meeting, the ark of the testimony, [27] the table with all its utensils, the lampstand with its utensils, the altar of incense, [28] the altar of burnt offering with all its utensils, and the basin with its stand. [29] Consecrate them and they will be especially holy. Whatever touches them will be consecrated. [30] Anoint Aaron and his sons and consecrate them to serve me as priests.

[31] "Tell the Israelites: This will be my holy anointing oil throughout your generations. [32] It must not be used for ordinary anointing on a person's body, and you must not make anything like it using its formula. It is holy, and it must be holy to you. [33] Anyone who blends something like it or puts some of it on an unauthorized person must be cut off from his people."

THE SACRED INCENSE

[34] The LORD said to Moses: "Take fragrant spices: stacte, onycha, and galbanum; the spices and pure frankincense are to be in equal measures. [35] Prepare expertly blended incense from these; it is to be seasoned with salt, pure and holy. [36] Grind some of it into a fine powder and put some in front of the testimony in the tent of meeting, where I will meet with you. It must be especially holy to you. [37] As for the incense you are making, you must not make any for yourselves using its formula. It is to be regarded by you as holy — belonging to the LORD. [38] Anyone who makes something like it to smell its fragrance must be cut off from his people."

GOD'S PROVISION OF THE SKILLED WORKERS

31 The LORD also spoke to Moses: [2] "Look, I have appointed by name Bezalel son of Uri, son of Hur, of the tribe of Judah. [3] I have filled him with God's Spirit, with wisdom, understanding, and ability in every craft [4] to design artistic works in gold, silver, and bronze, [5] to cut gemstones for mounting, and to carve wood for work in every craft. [6] I have also selected Oholiab[D] son of Ahisamach, of the tribe of Dan, to be with him. I have put wisdom in the heart of every skilled artisan[E] in order to make all that I have commanded you: [7] the tent of meeting, the ark of the testimony, the mercy seat that is on top of it, and all the other furnishings of the tent — [8] the table with its utensils, the pure gold lampstand with all its utensils, the altar of incense, [9] the altar of burnt offering with all its utensils, the basin with its stand — [10] the specially woven[F] garments, both the holy garments for the priest Aaron and the garments for his sons to serve as priests, [11] the anointing oil, and the fragrant incense for the sanctuary. They must make them according to all that I have commanded you."

[A] 30:23 Lit *500* (shekels), also in v. 24   [B] 30:23 Lit *250* (shekels)   [C] 30:24 Lit *a hin*   [D] 31:6 LXX, Syr read *Eliab*   [E] 31:6 Lit *everyone wise of heart*   [F] 31:10 Hb obscure

OBSERVING THE SABBATH

[12] The LORD said to Moses: [13] "Tell the Israelites: You must observe my Sabbaths, for it is a sign between me and you throughout your generations, so that you will know that I am the LORD who consecrates you. [14] Observe the Sabbath, for it is holy to you. Whoever profanes it must be put to death. If anyone does work on it, that person must be cut off from his people. [15] Work may be done for six days, but on the seventh day there must be a Sabbath of complete rest, holy to the LORD. Anyone who does work on the Sabbath day must be put to death. [16] The Israelites must observe the Sabbath, celebrating it throughout their generations as a permanent covenant. [17] It is a sign forever between me and the Israelites, for in six days the LORD made the heavens and the earth, but on the seventh day he rested and was refreshed."

THE TWO STONE TABLETS

[18] When he finished speaking with Moses on Mount Sinai, he gave him the two tablets of the testimony, stone tablets inscribed by the finger of God.

THE GOLD CALF

32 When the people saw that Moses delayed in coming down from the mountain, they gathered around Aaron and said to him, "Come, make gods[A] for us who will go before us because this Moses, the man who brought us up from the land of Egypt — we don't know what has happened to him!"

[2] Aaron replied to them, "Take off the gold rings that are on the ears of your wives, your sons, and your daughters and bring them to me." [3] So all the people took off the gold rings that were on their ears and brought them to Aaron. [4] He took the gold from them, fashioned it with an engraving tool, and made it into an image of a calf.

Then they said, "Israel, these are your gods,[B] who brought you up from the land of Egypt!"

[5] When Aaron saw this, he built an altar in front of it and made an announcement: "There will be a festival to the LORD tomorrow." [6] Early the next morning they arose, offered burnt offerings, and presented fellowship offerings. The people sat down to eat and drink, and got up to party.

[7] The LORD spoke to Moses: "Go down at once! For your people you brought up from the land of Egypt have acted corruptly. [8] They have quickly turned from the way I commanded them; they have made for themselves an image of a calf. They have bowed down to it, sacrificed to it, and said, 'Israel, these are your gods, who brought you up from the land of Egypt.'" [9] The LORD also said to Moses: "I have seen this people, and they are indeed a stiff-necked people. [10] Now leave me alone, so that my anger can burn against them and I can destroy them. Then I will make you into a great nation."

[11] But Moses sought the favor of the LORD his God: "LORD, why does your anger burn against your people you brought out of the land of Egypt with great power and a strong hand? [12] Why should the Egyptians say, 'He brought them out with an evil intent to kill them in the mountains and eliminate them from the face of the earth'? Turn from your fierce anger and relent concerning this disaster planned for your people. [13] Remember your servants

---

[A] 32:1 Or *make a god,* also in v. 23   [B] 32:4 Or *"Israel, this is your god* or *"Israel, this is your God,* also in v. 8

Abraham, Isaac, and Israel — you swore to them by yourself and declared, 'I will make your offspring as numerous as the stars of the sky and will give your offspring all this land that I have promised, and they will inherit it forever.' " ¹⁴ So the LORD relented concerning the disaster he had said he would bring on his people.

¹⁵ Then Moses turned and went down the mountain with the two tablets of the testimony in his hands. They were inscribed on both sides — inscribed front and back. ¹⁶ The tablets were the work of God, and the writing was God's writing, engraved on the tablets.

¹⁷ When Joshua heard the sound of the people as they shouted, he said to Moses, "There is a sound of war in the camp."

¹⁸ But Moses replied:

It's not the sound of a victory cry
and not the sound of a cry of defeat;
I hear the sound of singing!

¹⁹ As he approached the camp and saw the calf and the dancing, Moses became enraged and threw the tablets out of his hands, smashing them at the base of the mountain. ²⁰ He took the calf they had made, burned it up, and ground it to powder. He scattered the powder over the surface of the water and forced the Israelites to drink the water.

²¹ Then Moses asked Aaron, "What did these people do to you that you have led them into such a grave sin?"

²² "Don't be enraged, my lord," Aaron replied. "You yourself know that the people are intent on evil. ²³ They said to me, 'Make gods for us who will go before us because this Moses, the man who brought us up from the land of Egypt — we don't know what has happened to him!' ²⁴ So I said to them, 'Whoever has gold, take it off,' and they gave it to me. When I threw it into the fire, out came this calf!"

²⁵ Moses saw that the people were out of control, for Aaron had let them get out of control, making them a laughingstock to their enemies.^A ²⁶ And Moses stood at the camp's entrance and said, "Whoever is for the LORD, come to me." And all the Levites gathered around him. ²⁷ He told them, "This is what the LORD, the God of Israel, says, 'Every man fasten his sword to his side; go back and forth through the camp from entrance to entrance, and each of you kill his brother, his friend, and his neighbor.' " ²⁸ The Levites did as Moses commanded, and about three thousand men fell dead that day among the people. ²⁹ Afterward Moses said, "Today you have been dedicated^B to the LORD, since each man went against his son and his brother. Therefore you have brought a blessing on yourselves today."

³⁰ The following day Moses said to the people, "You have committed a grave sin. Now I will go up to the LORD; perhaps I will be able to atone for your sin."

³¹ So Moses returned to the LORD and said, "Oh, these people have committed a grave sin; they have made a god of gold for themselves. ³² Now if you would only forgive their sin. But if not, please erase me from the book you have written."

³³ The LORD replied to Moses: "Whoever has sinned against me I will erase from my book. ³⁴ Now go, lead the people to the place I told you about; see,

---

^A 32:25 Hb obscure   ^B 32:29 Text emended; MT reads *"Today dedicate yourselves*; LXX, Vg read *"Today you have dedicated yourselves* my angel will go before you. But on the day I settle accounts, I will hold them accountable for their sin." [35] And the LORD inflicted a plague on the people for what they did with the calf Aaron had made.

THE TENT OUTSIDE THE CAMP

33 The LORD spoke to Moses: "Go up from here, you and the people you brought up from the land of Egypt, to the land I promised to Abraham, Isaac, and Jacob, saying: I will give it to your offspring. [2] I will send an angel ahead of you and will drive out the Canaanites, Amorites, Hethites, Perizzites,^A Hivites, and Jebusites. [3] Go up to a land flowing with milk and honey. But I will not go up with you because you are a stiff-necked people; otherwise, I might destroy you on the way." [4] When the people heard this bad news, they mourned and didn't put on their jewelry.

[5] For the LORD said to Moses: "Tell the Israelites: You are a stiff-necked people. If I went up with you for a single moment, I would destroy you. Now take off your jewelry, and I will decide what to do with you." [6] So the Israelites remained stripped of their jewelry from Mount Horeb onward.

[7] Now Moses took a tent and pitched it outside the camp, at a distance from the camp; he called it the tent of meeting. Anyone who wanted to consult the LORD would go to the tent of meeting that was outside the camp. [8] Whenever Moses went out to the tent, all the people would stand up, each one at the door of his tent, and they would watch Moses until he entered the tent. [9] When Moses entered the tent, the pillar of cloud would come down and remain at the entrance to the tent, and the LORD would speak with Moses. [10] As all the people saw the pillar of cloud remaining at the entrance to the tent, they would stand up, then bow in worship, each one at the door of his tent. [11] The LORD would speak with Moses face to face, just as a man speaks with his friend, then Moses would return to the camp. His assistant, the young man Joshua son of Nun, would not leave the inside of the tent.

THE LORD'S GLORY

[12] Moses said to the LORD, "Look, you have told me, 'Lead this people up,' but you have not let me know whom you will send with me. You said, 'I know you by name, and you have also found favor with me.' [13] Now if I have indeed found favor with you, please teach me your ways, and I will know you, so that I may find favor with you. Now consider that this nation is your people." [14] And he replied, "My presence will go with you, and I will give you rest."

[15] "If your presence does not go," Moses responded to him, "don't make us go up from here. [16] How will it be known that I and your people have found favor with you unless you go with us? I and your people will be distinguished by this from all the other people on the face of the earth."

[17] The LORD answered Moses, "I will do this very thing you have asked, for you have found favor with me, and I know you by name."

[18] Then Moses said, "Please, let me see your glory."

[19] He said, "I will cause all my goodness to pass in front of you, and I will proclaim the name 'the LORD' before you. I will be gracious to whom I will be gracious, and I will have compassion on whom I will have compassion."

^A33:2 Sam, LXX add *Girgashites*

²⁰ But he added, "You cannot see my face, for humans cannot see me and live." ²¹ The LORD said, "Here is a place near me. You are to stand on the rock, ²² and when my glory passes by, I will put you in the crevice of the rock and cover you with my hand until I have passed by. ²³ Then I will take my hand away, and you will see my back, but my face will not be seen."

NEW STONE TABLETS

34 The LORD said to Moses, "Cut two stone tablets like the first ones, and I will write on them the words that were on the first tablets, which you broke. ² Be prepared by morning. Come up Mount Sinai in the morning and stand before me on the mountaintop. ³ No one may go up with you; in fact, no one should be seen anywhere on the mountain. Even the flocks and herds are not to graze in front of that mountain."

⁴ Moses cut two stone tablets like the first ones. He got up early in the morning, and taking the two stone tablets in his hand, he climbed Mount Sinai, just as the LORD had commanded him.

⁵ The LORD came down in a cloud, stood with him there, and proclaimed his name, "the LORD." ⁶ The LORD passed in front of him and proclaimed:

The LORD — the LORD is a compassionate and gracious God, slow to anger and abounding in faithful love and truth, ⁷ maintaining faithful love to a thousand generations, forgiving iniquity, rebellion, and sin. But he will not leave the guilty unpunished, bringing the fathers' iniquity on the children and grandchildren to the third and fourth generation.

⁸ Moses immediately knelt low on the ground and worshiped. ⁹ Then he said, "My Lord, if I have indeed found favor with you, my Lord, please go with us (even though this is a stiff-necked people), forgive our iniquity and our sin, and accept us as your own possession."

COVENANT OBLIGATIONS

¹⁰ And the LORD responded: "Look, I am making a covenant. I will perform wonders in the presence of all your people that have never been done^A in the whole earth or in any nation. All the people you live among will see the LORD's work, for what I am doing with you is awe-inspiring. ¹¹ Observe what I command you today. I am going to drive out before you the Amorites, Canaanites, Hethites, Perizzites, Hivites, ^B and Jebusites. ¹² Be careful not to make a treaty with the inhabitants of the land that you are going to enter; otherwise, they will become a snare among you. ¹³ Instead, you must tear down their altars, smash their sacred pillars, and chop down their Asherah poles. ¹⁴ Because the LORD is jealous for his reputation, you are never to bow down to another god.^C He is a jealous God.

¹⁵ "Do not make a treaty with the inhabitants of the land, or else when they prostitute themselves with their gods and sacrifice to their gods, they will invite you, and you will eat their sacrifices. ¹⁶ Then you will take some of their daughters as brides for your sons. Their daughters will prostitute themselves with their gods and cause your sons to prostitute themselves with their gods.

---

^A 34:10 Lit created ^B 34:11 DSS, Sam, LXX add *Girgashites* ^C 34:14 Or *the LORD — his name is Jealous* or *the LORD, being jealous by nature*

¹⁷ "Do not make cast images of gods for yourselves.

¹⁸ "Observe the Festival of Unleavened Bread. You are to eat unleavened bread for seven days at the appointed time in the month of Abib,^ as I commanded you, for you came out of Egypt in the month of Abib.

¹⁹ "The firstborn male from every womb belongs to me, including all your male ᴮ,ᶜ livestock, the firstborn of cattle or sheep. ²⁰ You may redeem the firstborn of a donkey with a sheep, but if you do not redeem it, break its neck. You must redeem all the firstborn of your sons. No one is to appear before me empty-handed.

²¹ "You are to labor six days but you must rest on the seventh day; you must even rest during plowing and harvesting times.

²² "Observe the Festival of Weeks with the firstfruits of the wheat harvest, and the Festival of Ingathering ᴰ at the turn of the agricultural year. ²³ Three times a year all your males are to appear before the Lord Gᴏᴅ, the God of Israel. ²⁴ For I will drive out nations before you and enlarge your territory. No one will covet your land when you go up three times a year to appear before the Lᴏʀᴅ your God.

²⁵ "Do not present ᴱ the blood for my sacrifice with anything leavened. The sacrifice of the Passover Festival must not remain until morning.

²⁶ "Bring the best firstfruits of your land to the house of the Lᴏʀᴅ your God.

"You must not boil a young goat in its mother's milk."

²⁷ The Lᴏʀᴅ also said to Moses, "Write down these words, for I have made a covenant with you and with Israel based on these words."

²⁸ Moses was there with the Lᴏʀᴅ forty days and forty nights; he did not eat food or drink water. He wrote the Ten Commandments, the words of the covenant, on the tablets.

MOSES'S RADIANT FACE

²⁹ As Moses descended from Mount Sinai — with the two tablets of the testimony in his hands as he descended the mountain — he did not realize that the skin of his face shone as a result of his speaking with the Lᴏʀᴅ.ᶠ ³⁰ When Aaron and all the Israelites saw Moses, the skin of his face shone! They were afraid to come near him. ³¹ But Moses called out to them, so Aaron and all the leaders of the community returned to him, and Moses spoke to them. ³² Afterward all the Israelites came near, and he commanded them to do everything the Lᴏʀᴅ had told him on Mount Sinai. ³³ When Moses had finished speaking with them, he put a veil over his face. ³⁴ But whenever Moses went before the Lᴏʀᴅ to speak with him, he would remove the veil until he came out. After he came out, he would tell the Israelites what he had been commanded, ³⁵ and the Israelites would see that Moses's face ᴳ was radiant. Then Moses would put the veil over his face again until he went to speak with the Lᴏʀᴅ.

---

^34:18 March–April; called Nisan in the post-exilic period; Neh 2:1; Est 3:7
ᴮ34:19 LXX, Theod, Vg, Tg read *males*   ᶜ34:19 Hb obscure   ᴰ34:22 The Festival of Ingathering is called Festival of Shelters elsewhere; Lv 23:34-36.
ᴱ34:25 Lit *slaughter*   ᶠ34:29 Lit *with him*   ᴳ34:35 Lit *see Moses's face, that the skin of his face*

THE SABBATH COMMAND

35 Moses assembled the entire Israelite community and said to them, "These are the things that the LORD has commanded you to do: [2] For six days work is to be done, but on the seventh day you are to have a holy day, a Sabbath of complete rest to the LORD. Anyone who does work on it must be executed. [3] Do not light a fire in any of your homes on the Sabbath day."

BUILDING THE TABERNACLE

[4] Then Moses said to the entire Israelite community, "This is what the LORD has commanded: [5] Take up an offering among you for the LORD. Let everyone whose heart is willing bring this as the LORD's offering: gold, silver, and bronze; [6] blue, purple, and scarlet yarn; fine linen and goat hair; [7] ram skins dyed red and fine leather;[A] acacia wood; [8] oil for the light; spices for the anointing oil and for the fragrant incense; [9] and onyx with gemstones to mount on the ephod and breastpiece.

[10] "Let all the skilled artisans[B] among you come and make everything that the LORD has commanded: [11] the tabernacle — its tent and covering, its clasps and supports, its crossbars, its pillars and bases; [12] the ark with its poles, the mercy seat, and the curtain for the screen; [13] the table with its poles, all its utensils, and the Bread of the Presence; [14] the lampstand for light with its utensils and lamps as well as the oil for the light; [15] the altar of incense with its poles; the anointing oil and the fragrant incense; the entryway screen for the entrance to the tabernacle; [16] the altar of burnt offering with its bronze grate, its poles, and all its utensils; the basin with its stand; [17] the hangings of the courtyard, its posts and bases, and the screen for the gate of the courtyard; [18] the tent pegs for the tabernacle and the tent pegs for the courtyard, along with their ropes; [19] and the specially woven[A] garments for ministering in the sanctuary — the holy garments for the priest Aaron and the garments for his sons to serve as priests."

[20] Then the entire Israelite community left Moses's presence. [21] Everyone whose heart was moved and whose spirit prompted him came and brought an offering to the LORD for the work on the tent of meeting, for all its services, and for the holy garments. [22] Both men and women came; all who had willing hearts brought brooches, earrings, rings, necklaces, and all kinds of gold jewelry — everyone who presented a presentation offering of gold to the LORD. [23] Everyone who possessed blue, purple, or scarlet yarn, fine linen or goat hair, ram skins dyed red or fine leather,[A] brought them. [24] Everyone making an offering of silver or bronze brought it as a contribution to the LORD. Everyone who possessed acacia wood useful for any task in the work brought it. [25] Every skilled[C] woman spun yarn with her hands and brought it: blue, purple, and scarlet yarn, and fine linen. [26] And all the women whose hearts were moved spun the goat hair by virtue of their skill. [27] The leaders brought onyx and gemstones to mount on the ephod and breastpiece, [28] as well as the spice and oil for the light, for the anointing oil, and for the fragrant incense. [29] So the Israelites brought a freewill offering to the LORD, all the men and women whose hearts prompted them to bring something for all the work that the LORD, through Moses, had commanded to be done.

[A]35:7,19,23 Hb obscure [B]35:10 Lit *the wise of heart* [C]35:25 Lit *wise of heart*

BEZALEL AND OHOLIAB

[30] Moses then said to the Israelites: "Look, the LORD has appointed by name Bezalel son of Uri, son of Hur, of the tribe of Judah. [31] He has filled him with God's Spirit, with wisdom, understanding, and ability in every kind of craft [32] to design artistic works in gold, silver, and bronze, [33] to cut gemstones for mounting, and to carve wood for work in every kind of artistic craft. [34] He has also given[A] both him and Oholiab son of Ahisamach, of the tribe of Dan, the ability to teach others. [35] He has filled them with skill[B] to do all the work of a gem cutter; a designer; an embroiderer[C] in blue, purple, and scarlet yarn and fine linen; and a weaver. They can do every kind of craft

36

and design artistic designs. [1] Bezalel, Oholiab, and all the skilled[D] people are to work based on everything the LORD has commanded. The LORD has given them wisdom and understanding to know how to do all the work of constructing the sanctuary."

[2] So Moses summoned Bezalel, Oholiab, and every skilled person in whose heart the LORD had placed wisdom, all whose hearts moved them, to come to the work and do it. [3] They took from Moses's presence all the contributions that the Israelites had brought for the task of making the sanctuary. Meanwhile, the people continued to bring freewill offerings morning after morning.

[4] Then all the artisans who were doing all the work for the sanctuary came one by one from the work they were doing [5] and said to Moses, "The people are bringing more than is needed for the construction of the work the LORD commanded to be done."

[6] After Moses gave an order, they sent a proclamation throughout the camp: "Let no man or woman make anything else as an offering for the sanctuary." So the people stopped. [7] The materials were sufficient for them to do all the work. There was more than enough.

BUILDING THE TABERNACLE

[8] All the skilled artisans[E] among those doing the work made the tabernacle with ten curtains. Bezalel made them of finely spun linen, as well as blue, purple, and scarlet yarn, with a design of cherubim worked into them. [9] Each curtain was forty-two feet[F] long and six feet[G] wide; all the curtains had the same measurements. [10] He joined five of the curtains to each other, and the other five curtains he joined to each other. [11] He made loops of blue yarn on the edge of the last curtain in the first set and did the same on the edge of the outermost curtain in the second set. [12] He made fifty loops on the one curtain and fifty loops on the edge of the curtain in the second set, so that the loops lined up with each other. [13] He also made fifty gold clasps and joined the curtains to each other, so that the tabernacle became a single unit.

[14] He made curtains of goat hair for a tent over the tabernacle; he made eleven of them. [15] Each curtain was forty-five feet[H] long and six feet wide. All eleven curtains had the same measurements. [16] He joined five of the curtains together, and the other six together. [17] He made fifty loops on the

---

[A] 35:34 Lit *also put in his heart*   [B] 35:35 Lit *with wisdom of heart*   [C] 35:35 Or *weaver*   [D] 36:1 Lit *wise of heart, also in v. 2*   [E] 36:8 Lit *the wise of heart*   [F] 36:9 Lit *28 cubits*   [G] 36:9 Lit *four cubits, also in v. 15*   [H] 36:15 Lit *30 cubits* edge of the outermost curtain in the first set and fifty loops on the edge of the corresponding curtain in the second set. [18] He made fifty bronze clasps to join the tent together as a single unit. [19] He also made a covering for the tent from ram skins dyed red and a covering of fine leather[A] on top of it.

[20] He made upright supports[B] of acacia wood for the tabernacle. [21] Each support was fifteen feet[C] long and twenty-seven inches[D] wide. [22] Each support had two tenons for joining one to another. He did the same for all the supports of the tabernacle. [23] He made supports for the tabernacle as follows: twenty for the south side, [24] and he made forty silver bases to put under the twenty supports, two bases under the first support for its two tenons, and two bases under each of the following supports for their two tenons; [25] for the second side of the tabernacle, the north side, he made twenty supports, [26] with their forty silver bases, two bases under the first support and two bases under each of the following ones; [27] and for the back of the tabernacle, on the west side, he made six supports. [28] He also made two additional supports for the two back corners of the tabernacle. [29] They were paired at the bottom and joined together[E] at the[F] top in a single ring. This is what he did with both of them for the two corners. [30] So there were eight supports with their sixteen silver bases, two bases under each one.

[31] He made five crossbars of acacia wood for the supports on one side of the tabernacle, [32] five crossbars for the supports on the other side of the tabernacle, and five crossbars for those at the back of the tabernacle on the west. [33] He made the central crossbar run through the middle of the supports from one end to the other. [34] He overlaid them with gold and made their rings out of gold as holders for the crossbars. He also overlaid the crossbars with gold.

[35] Then he made the curtain with blue, purple, and scarlet yarn, and finely spun linen. He made it with a design of cherubim worked into it. [36] He made four pillars of acacia wood for it and overlaid them with gold; their hooks were of gold. And he cast four silver bases for the pillars.

[37] He made a screen embroidered[G] with blue, purple, and scarlet yarn, and finely spun linen for the entrance to the tent, [38] together with its five pillars and their hooks. He overlaid the tops of the pillars and their bands with gold, but their five bases were bronze.

MAKING THE ARK

37 Bezalel made the ark of acacia wood, forty-five inches long, twenty-seven inches wide, and twenty-seven inches high.[H] [2] He overlaid it with pure gold inside and out and made a gold molding all around it. [3] He cast four gold rings for it, for its four feet, two rings on one side and two rings on the other side. [4] He made poles of acacia wood and overlaid them with gold. [5] He inserted the poles into the rings on the sides of the ark for carrying the ark.

[6] He made a mercy seat of pure gold, forty-five inches long and twenty-seven inches wide.[I] [7] He made two cherubim of gold; he made them of

---

[A]36:19 Hb obscure   [B]36:20 Or made frames   [C]36:21 Lit 10 cubits
[D]36:21 Lit a cubit and a half   [E]36:29 Lit and together they are to be complete
[F]36:29 Lit its   [G]36:37 Or woven   [H]37:1 Lit two and a half cubits its length, one and a half cubits its width, and one and a half cubits its height   [I]37:6 Lit two and a half cubits its length and one and a half cubits its width

hammered work at the two ends of the mercy seat, [8] one cherub at one end and one cherub at the other end. At each end, he made a cherub of one piece with the mercy seat. [9] They had wings spread out. They faced each other and covered the mercy seat with their wings. The faces of the cherubim were looking toward the mercy seat.

MAKING THE TABLE

[10] He constructed the table of acacia wood, thirty-six inches long, eighteen inches wide, and twenty-seven inches high.[A] [11] He overlaid it with pure gold and made a gold molding all around it. [12] He made a three-inch[B] frame all around it and made a gold molding all around its frame. [13] He cast four gold rings for it and attached the rings to the four corners at its four legs. [14] The rings were next to the frame as holders for the poles to carry the table. [15] He made the poles for carrying the table from acacia wood and overlaid them with gold. [16] He also made the utensils that would be on the table out of pure gold: its plates and cups, as well as its bowls and pitchers for pouring drink offerings.

MAKING THE LAMPSTAND

[17] Then he made the lampstand out of pure hammered gold. He made it all of one piece: its base and shaft, its ornamental cups, and its buds and petals. [18] Six branches extended from its sides, three branches of the lampstand from one side and three branches of the lampstand from the other side. [19] There were three cups shaped like almond blossoms, each with a bud and petals, on one branch, and three cups shaped like almond blossoms, each with a bud and petals, on the next branch. It was this way for the six branches that extended from the lampstand. [20] There were four cups shaped like almond blossoms on the lampstand shaft along with its buds and petals. [21] For the six branches that extended from it, a bud was under the first pair of branches from it, a bud under the second pair of branches from it, and a bud under the third pair of branches from it. [22] Their buds and branches were of one piece with it. All of it was a single hammered piece of pure gold. [23] He also made its seven lamps, snuffers, and firepans of pure gold. [24] He made it and all its utensils of seventy-five pounds[C] of pure gold.

MAKING THE ALTAR OF INCENSE

[25] He made the altar of incense out of acacia wood. It was square, eighteen inches long and eighteen inches wide; it was thirty-six inches high.[D] Its horns were of one piece with it. [26] He overlaid it, its top, all around its sides, and its horns with pure gold. Then he made a gold molding all around it. [27] He made two gold rings for it under the molding on two of its sides; he put these on opposite sides of it to be holders for the poles to carry it with. [28] He made the poles of acacia wood and overlaid them with gold.

[29] He also made the holy anointing oil and the pure, fragrant, and expertly blended incense.

[A]37:10 Lit two cubits its length, one cubit its width, and one and a half cubits its height [B]37:12 Lit a handbreadth [C]37:24 Lit a talent [D]37:25 Lit a cubit its length, a cubit its width, and two cubits its height

MAKING THE ALTAR OF BURNT OFFERING

38

Bezalel constructed the altar of burnt offering from acacia wood. It was square, 7 ½ feet long and 7 ½ feet wide,^A and was 4 ½ feet^B high. ² He made horns for it on its four corners; the horns were of one piece with it. Then he overlaid it with bronze.

³ He made all the altar's utensils: the pots, shovels, basins, meat forks, and firepans; he made all its utensils of bronze. ⁴ He constructed for the altar a grate of bronze mesh under its ledge,^C halfway up from the bottom. ⁵ He cast four rings at the four corners of the bronze grate as holders for the poles. ⁶ He made the poles of acacia wood and overlaid them with bronze. ⁷ Then he inserted the poles into the rings on the sides of the altar in order to carry it with them. He constructed the altar with boards so that it was hollow.

MAKING THE BRONZE BASIN

⁸ He made the bronze basin and its stand from the bronze mirrors of the women who served at the entrance to the tent of meeting.

MAKING THE COURTYARD

⁹ Then he made the courtyard. The hangings on the south side of the courtyard were of finely spun linen, 150 feet^D long, ¹⁰ including their twenty posts and their twenty bronze bases, with silver hooks and silver bands^E for the posts. ¹¹ The hangings on the north side were also 150 feet long, including their twenty posts and twenty bronze bases. The hooks and bands of the posts were silver. ¹² The hangings on the west side were 75 feet^F long, including their ten posts and their ten bases, with silver hooks and silver bands for the posts. ¹³ And for the east side toward the sunrise, 75 feet long, ¹⁴ the hangings on one side of the gate were 22 ½ feet,^G including their three posts and their three bases. ¹⁵ It was the same for the other side of the courtyard gate. The hangings were 22 ½ feet, including their three posts and their three bases. ¹⁶ All the hangings around the courtyard were of finely spun linen. ¹⁷ The bases for the posts were bronze; the hooks and bands of the posts were silver; and the plating for the tops of the posts was silver. All the posts of the courtyard were banded with silver.

¹⁸ The screen for the gate of the courtyard was made of finely spun linen, expertly embroidered^H with blue, purple, and scarlet yarn. It was 30 feet^I long, and like the hangings of the courtyard, 7 ½ feet^J high.^K ¹⁹ It had four posts with their four bronze bases. Their hooks were silver, and their top plating and their bands were silver. ²⁰ All the tent pegs for the tabernacle and for the surrounding courtyard were bronze.

INVENTORY OF MATERIALS

²¹ This is the inventory for the tabernacle, the tabernacle of the testimony, that was recorded at Moses's command. It was the work of the Levites

---

^A38:1 Lit *five cubits its length and five cubits its width* ^B38:1 Lit *three cubits*
^C38:4 Or *rim* ^D38:9 Lit *100 cubits*, also in v. 11 ^E38:10 Or *connecting rods*,
also in vv. 11,17,19,28 ^F38:12 Lit *50 cubits*, also in v. 13 ^G38:14 Lit *15 cubits*,
also in v. 15 ^H38:18 Or *woven* ^I38:18 Lit *20 cubits* ^J38:18 Lit *five cubits*
^K38:18 Lit *high in width*

under the direction of[A] Ithamar son of Aaron the priest. [22] Bezalel son of Uri, son of Hur, of the tribe of Judah, made everything that the LORD commanded Moses. [23] With him was Oholiab son of Ahisamach, of the tribe of Dan, a gem cutter, a designer, and an embroiderer with blue, purple, and scarlet yarn, and fine linen.

[24] All the gold of the presentation offering that was used for the project in all the work on the sanctuary, was 2,193 pounds,[B] according to the sanctuary shekel. [25] The silver from those of the community who were registered was 7,544 pounds,[C] according to the sanctuary shekel — [26] one-fifth of an ounce[D] per man, that is, half a shekel according to the sanctuary shekel, from everyone twenty years old or more who had crossed over to the registered group, 603,550 men. [27] There were 7,500 pounds[E] of silver used to cast the bases of the sanctuary and the bases of the curtain — one hundred bases from 7,500 pounds, 75 pounds[F] for each base. [28] With the remaining 44 pounds[G] he made the hooks for the posts, overlaid their tops, and supplied bands for them.

[29] The bronze of the presentation offering totaled 5,310 pounds.[H] [30] He made with it the bases for the entrance to the tent of meeting, the bronze altar and its bronze grate, all the utensils for the altar, [31] the bases for the surrounding courtyard, the bases for the gate of the courtyard, all the tent pegs for the tabernacle, and all the tent pegs for the surrounding courtyard.

MAKING THE PRIESTLY GARMENTS

39 They made specially woven[I] garments for ministry in the sanctuary, and the holy garments for Aaron from the blue, purple, and scarlet yarn, just as the LORD had commanded Moses.

MAKING THE EPHOD

[2] Bezalel made the ephod of gold, of blue, purple, and scarlet yarn, and of finely spun linen. [3] They hammered out thin sheets of gold, and he[J] cut threads from them to interweave with the blue, purple, and scarlet yarn, and the fine linen in a skillful design. [4] They made shoulder pieces for attaching it; it was joined together at its two edges. [5] The artistically woven waistband that was on the ephod was of one piece with the ephod, according to the same workmanship of gold, of blue, purple, and scarlet yarn, and of finely spun linen, just as the LORD had commanded Moses.

[6] Then they mounted the onyx stones surrounded with gold filigree settings, engraved with the names of Israel's sons as a gem cutter engraves a seal. [7] He fastened them on the shoulder pieces of the ephod as memorial stones for the Israelites, just as the LORD had commanded Moses.

MAKING THE BREASTPIECE

[8] He also made the embroidered[K] breastpiece with the same workmanship as the ephod of gold, of blue, purple, and scarlet yarn, and of finely spun

---

[A]38:21 Lit Levites by the hand of [B]38:24 Lit 29 talents and 730 shekels
[C]38:25 Lit 100 talents and 1,775 shekels [D]38:26 Lit a beka [E]38:27 Lit 100 talents [F]38:27 Lit one talent [G]38:28 Lit 1,775 (shekels) [H]38:29 Lit 70 talents and 2,400 shekels [I]39:1 Hb obscure [J]39:3 Sam, Syr, Tg read they [K]39:8 Or woven

linen. [9] They made the breastpiece square and folded double, nine inches long and nine inches wide.[A] [10] They mounted four rows of gemstones[B] on it.

The first row was
a row of carnelian, topaz, and emerald;[C]

[11] the second row,
a turquoise,[D] a lapis lazuli, and a diamond;[E]

[12] the third row,
a jacinth,[F] an agate, and an amethyst;

[13] and the fourth row,
a beryl, an onyx, and a jasper.

They were surrounded with gold filigree in their settings.

[14] The twelve stones corresponded to the names of Israel's sons. Each stone was engraved like a seal with one of the names of the twelve tribes.

[15] They made braided chains of pure gold cord for the breastpiece. [16] They also fashioned two gold filigree settings and two gold rings and attached the two rings to its two corners. [17] Then they attached the two gold cords to the two gold rings on the corners of the breastpiece. [18] They attached the other ends of the two cords to the two filigree settings, and in this way they attached them to the ephod's shoulder pieces in front. [19] They made two other gold rings and put them at the two other corners of the breastpiece on the edge that is next to the inner border of the ephod. [20] They made two more gold rings and attached them to the bottom of the ephod's two shoulder pieces on its front, close to its seam,[G] above the ephod's woven waistband. [21] Then they tied the breastpiece from its rings to the rings of the ephod with a cord of blue yarn, so that the breastpiece was above the ephod's waistband and did not come loose from the ephod. They did just as the LORD had commanded Moses.

MAKING THE ROBE

[22] They made the woven robe of the ephod entirely of blue yarn. [23] There was an opening in the center of the robe like that of body armor[F] with a collar around the opening so that it would not tear. [24] They made pomegranates of finely spun blue, purple, and scarlet yarn[H] on the lower hem of the robe. [25] They made bells of pure gold and attached the bells between the pomegranates, all around the hem of the robe between the pomegranates, [26] a bell and a pomegranate alternating all around the lower hem of the robe[I] to be worn for ministry. They made it just as the LORD had commanded Moses.

THE OTHER PRIESTLY GARMENTS

[27] They made the tunics of fine woven linen for Aaron and his sons. [28] They made the turban and the ornate headbands[J] of fine linen, the linen undergarments of finely spun linen, [29] and the sash of finely spun linen expertly

---

[A]39:9 Lit *a span its length and a span its width*   [B]39:10 Many of these stones cannot be identified with certainty.   [C]39:10 Or *beryl*   [D]39:11 Or *malachite*, or *garnet*   [E]39:11 Hb uncertain; LXX, Vg read *jasper*   [F]39:12,23 Hb obscure   [G]39:20 The place where the *shoulder pieces* join the front of the ephod   [H]39:24 Sam, LXX, Vg add *and linen*   [I]39:26 Lit *bell and pomegranate, bell and pomegranate, on the hem of the robe around*   [J]39:28 Lit *and the headdresses of headbands* embroidered with blue, purple, and scarlet yarn. They did just as the LORD had commanded Moses.

MAKING THE HOLY DIADEM

[30] They made a medallion, the holy diadem, out of pure gold and wrote on it an inscription like the engraving on a seal: HOLY TO THE LORD. [31] They attached a cord of blue yarn to it in order to mount it on the turban, just as the LORD had commanded Moses.

MOSES'S INSPECTION OF THE TABERNACLE

[32] So all the work for the tabernacle, the tent of meeting, was finished. The Israelites did everything just as the LORD had commanded Moses. [33] They brought the tabernacle to Moses: the tent with all its furnishings, its clasps, its supports, its crossbars, and its pillars and bases; [34] the covering of ram skins dyed red and the covering of fine leather;[A] the curtain for the screen; [35] the ark of the testimony with its poles and the mercy seat; [36] the table, all its utensils, and the Bread of the Presence; [37] the pure gold lampstand, with its lamps arranged and all its utensils, as well as the oil for the light; [38] the gold altar; the anointing oil; the fragrant incense; the screen for the entrance to the tent; [39] the bronze altar with its bronze grate, its poles, and all its utensils; the basin with its stand; [40] the hangings of the courtyard, its posts and bases, the screen for the gate of the courtyard, its ropes and tent pegs, and all the furnishings for the service of the tabernacle, the tent of meeting; [41] and the specially woven[A] garments for ministering in the sanctuary, the holy garments for the priest Aaron and the garments for his sons to serve as priests. [42] The Israelites had done all the work according to everything the LORD had commanded Moses. [43] Moses inspected all the work they had accomplished. They had done just as the LORD commanded. Then Moses blessed them.

SETTING UP THE TABERNACLE

40 The LORD spoke to Moses: [2] "You are to set up the tabernacle, the tent of meeting, on the first day of the first month.[B] [3] Put the ark of the testimony there and screen off the ark with the curtain. [4] Then bring in the table and lay out its arrangement; also bring in the lampstand and set up its lamps. [5] Place the gold altar for incense in front of the ark of the testimony. Put up the screen for the entrance to the tabernacle. [6] Position the altar of burnt offering in front of the entrance to the tabernacle, the tent of meeting. [7] Place the basin between the tent of meeting and the altar, and put water in it. [8] Assemble the surrounding courtyard and hang the screen for the gate of the courtyard.

[9] "Take the anointing oil and anoint the tabernacle and everything in it; consecrate it along with all its furnishings so that it will be holy. [10] Anoint the altar of burnt offering and all its utensils; consecrate the altar so that it will be especially holy. [11] Anoint the basin and its stand and consecrate it.

[12] "Then bring Aaron and his sons to the entrance to the tent of meeting and wash them with water. [13] Clothe Aaron with the holy garments, anoint him,

---

[A]39:34,41 Hb obscure   [B]40:2 Lit on the day of the first month, on the first of the month and consecrate him, so that he can serve me as a priest. [14] Have his sons come forward and clothe them in tunics. [15] Anoint them just as you anointed their father, so that they may also serve me as priests. Their anointing will serve to inaugurate a permanent priesthood for them throughout their generations."

[16] Moses did everything just as the Lord had commanded him. [17] The tabernacle was set up in the first month of the second year, on the first day of the month.[A] [18] Moses set up the tabernacle: He laid its bases, positioned its supports, inserted its crossbars, and set up its pillars. [19] Then he spread the tent over the tabernacle and put the covering of the tent on top of it, just as the Lord had commanded Moses.

[20] Moses took the testimony and placed it in the ark, and attached the poles to the ark. He set the mercy seat on top of the ark. [21] He brought the ark into the tabernacle, put up the curtain for the screen, and screened off the ark of the testimony, just as the Lord had commanded him.

[22] Moses placed the table in the tent of meeting on the north side of the tabernacle, outside the curtain. [23] He arranged the bread on it before the Lord, just as the Lord had commanded him. [24] He put the lampstand in the tent of meeting opposite the table on the south side of the tabernacle [25] and set up the lamps before the Lord, just as the Lord had commanded him.

[26] Moses installed the gold altar in the tent of meeting, in front of the curtain, [27] and burned fragrant incense on it, just as the Lord had commanded him. [28] He put up the screen at the entrance to the tabernacle. [29] He placed the altar of burnt offering at the entrance to the tabernacle, the tent of meeting, and offered the burnt offering and the grain offering on it, just as the Lord had commanded him.

[30] He set the basin between the tent of meeting and the altar and put water in it for washing. [31] Moses, Aaron, and his sons washed their hands and feet from it. [32] They washed whenever they came to the tent of meeting and approached the altar, just as the Lord had commanded Moses.

[33] Next Moses set up the surrounding courtyard for the tabernacle and the altar and hung a screen for the gate of the courtyard. So Moses finished the work.

THE LORD'S GLORY

[34] The cloud covered the tent of meeting, and the glory of the Lord filled the tabernacle. [35] Moses was unable to enter the tent of meeting because the cloud rested on it, and the glory of the Lord filled the tabernacle.

[36] The Israelites set out whenever the cloud was taken up from the tabernacle throughout all the stages of their journey. [37] If the cloud was not taken up, they did not set out until the day it was taken up. [38] For the cloud of the Lord was over the tabernacle by day, and there was a fire inside the cloud by night, visible to the entire house of Israel throughout all the stages of their journey.

A 40:17 DSS, Sam, LXX add *of their coming out of Egypt*

I have Set you Apart from the nations TO BE Mine

leviticus

You are to be holy to me because I, the LORD, am holy, and I have set you apart from the nations to be mine. **20:26**

ON THE TIMELINE Leviticus was written between 1446 BC–1406 BC, after God established the covenant with Israel at Sinai (during the forty years Israel spent wandering in the wilderness). The events in the book occur between 1446 BC and 1445 BC, after God brought Israel out of Egypt when He established the Law and the covenant.

A LITTLE BACKGROUND About one year passed from the time Israel arrived at Sinai until they departed (Ex 19:1; Nm 10:11). During that time, Moses received the covenant from the Lord, built the tabernacle (Ex 40:17), and received all the instructions recorded in Leviticus and in the early chapters of Numbers. This block of material appears as a continuous narrative, extending from Exodus 19 through Leviticus and on to Numbers 10:11.

Leviticus is primarily a collection of laws, with a little historical narrative here and there. The laws can be divided into two groups: apodictic law, which includes both positive commands and negative commands, and casuistic law that is in the form of "if . . . then." For example, "if your offering is a grain offering prepared in a pan, it is to be made of fine flour with oil" (Lev 2:7).

MESSAGE & PURPOSE Moses wrote the book of Leviticus to the generation of Israelites entering the promised land. Leviticus provided regulations for worship, laws on ceremonial cleanness, moral laws, and instructions for holy days for the Israelites. The purpose of the book was to instruct Israel in holiness so that the Lord might abide among them and bless them. Key themes in Leviticus include holiness, sacrifice, atonement, priesthood, and redemption.

GIVE THANKS FOR THE BOOK OF LEVITICUS:

Studying Leviticus opens up a clearer picture of the sacrifice and redemption of Christ. The sacrificial system was established in order to provide atonement for the sins of Israel. The writer of Hebrews relied on the images of Leviticus in describing the person and role of Jesus Christ: the sacrifice, the priesthood, and the Day of Atonement (Heb 4:14–10:18). Studying Leviticus gives us a deeper devotion to Jesus Christ, a stronger worship of God, and a better understanding of daily Christian living.

THE TABERNACLE

READ AND UNDERSTAND LEVITICUS

The Bible is a complete work in which many stories combine to tell one story. As you read the book of Leviticus, consider reading the additional passages to discover how the whole of Scripture works together.

THE BURNT OFFERING

1 Then the LORD summoned Moses and spoke to him from the tent of meeting: ² "Speak to the Israelites and tell them: When any of you brings an offering to the LORD from the livestock, you may bring your offering from the herd or the flock.

³ "If his offering is a burnt offering from the herd, he is to bring an unblemished male. He will bring it to the entrance to the tent of meeting so that he ᴬ may be accepted by the LORD. ⁴ He is to lay his hand on the head of the burnt offering so it can be accepted on his behalf to make atonement for him. ⁵ He is to slaughter the bull before the LORD; Aaron's sons the priests are to present the blood and splatter it on all sides of the altar that is at the entrance to the tent of meeting. ⁶ Then he is to skin the burnt offering and cut it into pieces. ᴮ ⁷ The sons of Aaron the priest will prepare a fire on the altar and arrange wood on the fire. ⁸ Aaron's sons the priests are to arrange the pieces, the head, and the fat on top of the burning wood on the altar. ⁹ The offerer is to wash its entrails and legs with water. Then the priest will burn all of it on the altar as a burnt offering, a fire offering of a pleasing aroma to the LORD.

¹⁰ "But if his offering for a burnt offering is from the flock, from sheep or goats, he is to present an unblemished male. ¹¹ He will slaughter it on the north side of the altar before the LORD. Aaron's sons the priests will splatter its blood against the altar on all sides. ¹² He will cut the animal into pieces with its head and its fat, and the priest will arrange them on top of the burning wood on the altar. ¹³ But he is to wash the entrails and legs with water. The priest will then present all of it and burn it on the altar; it is a burnt offering, a fire offering of a pleasing aroma to the LORD.

¹⁴ "If his offering to the LORD is a burnt offering of birds, he is to present his offering from the turtledoves or young pigeons. ᶜ ¹⁵ Then the priest is to bring it to the altar, and will twist off its head and burn it on the altar; its blood should be drained at the side of the altar. ¹⁶ He will remove its digestive tract, ᴰ cutting off the tail feathers, and throw it on the east side of the altar at the place for ashes. ¹⁷ He will tear it open by its wings without dividing the bird. Then the priest is to burn it on the altar on top of the burning wood. It is a burnt offering, a fire offering of a pleasing aroma to the LORD.

THE GRAIN OFFERING

2 "When anyone presents a grain offering as an offering to the LORD, it is to consist of fine flour. He is to pour olive oil on it, put frankincense on it, ² and bring it to Aaron's sons the priests. The priest will take a handful of fine flour and oil from it, along with all its frankincense, and will burn this memorial portion of it on the altar, a fire offering of a pleasing aroma to the LORD. ³ But the rest of the grain offering will belong to Aaron and his sons; it is the holiest part of the fire offerings to the LORD.

⁴ "When you present a grain offering baked in an oven, it is to be made of fine flour, either unleavened cakes mixed with oil or unleavened wafers coated with oil. ⁵ If your offering is a grain offering prepared on a griddle, it is to be unleavened bread made of fine flour mixed with oil. ⁶ Break it into pieces and pour oil on it; it is a grain offering. ⁷ If your offering is a grain offering

---

ᴬ1:3 Or it   ᴮ1:6 Lit *its pieces,* also in v. 12   ᶜ1:14 Or *or pigeons*   ᴰ1:16 Or *its crop,* or *its crissum* prepared in a pan, it is to be made of fine flour with oil. ⁸ When you bring to the Lᴏʀᴅ the grain offering made in any of these ways, it is to be presented to the priest, and he will take it to the altar. ⁹ The priest will remove the memorial portionᴬ from the grain offering and burn it on the altar, a fire offering of a pleasing aroma to the Lᴏʀᴅ. ¹⁰ But the rest of the grain offering will belong to Aaron and his sons; it is the holiest part of the fire offerings to the Lᴏʀᴅ.

¹¹ "No grain offering that you present to the Lᴏʀᴅ is to be made with yeast, for you are not to burnᴮ any yeast or honey as a fire offering to the Lᴏʀᴅ. ¹² You may present them to the Lᴏʀᴅ as an offering of firstfruits, but they are not to be offered on the altar as a pleasing aroma. ¹³ You are to season each of your grain offerings with salt; you must not omit from your grain offering the salt of the covenant with your God. You are to present salt with each of your offerings.

¹⁴ "If you present a grain offering of firstfruits to the Lᴏʀᴅ, you are to present fresh heads of grain, crushed kernels, roasted on the fire, for your grain offering of firstfruits. ¹⁵ You are to put oil and frankincense on it; it is a grain offering. ¹⁶ The priest will then burn some of its crushed kernels and oil with all its frankincense as a fire offering to the Lᴏʀᴅ.

THE FELLOWSHIP OFFERING

3 "If his offering is a fellowship sacrifice, and he is presenting an animal from the herd, whether male or female, he is to present one without blemish before the Lᴏʀᴅ. ² He is to lay his hand on the head of his offering and slaughter it at the entrance to the tent of meeting. Then Aaron's sons the priests will splatter the blood on all sides of the altar. ³ He will present part of the fellowship sacrifice as a fire offering to the Lᴏʀᴅ: the fat surrounding the entrails, all the fat that is on the entrails, ⁴ and the two kidneys with the fat on them at the loins; he will also remove the fatty lobe of the liver with the kidneys. ⁵ Aaron's sons will burn it on the altar along with the burnt offering that is on the burning wood, a fire offering of a pleasing aroma to the Lᴏʀᴅ.

⁶ "If his offering as a fellowship sacrifice to the Lᴏʀᴅ is from the flock, he is to present a male or female without blemish. ⁷ If he is presenting a lamb for his offering, he is to present it before the Lᴏʀᴅ. ⁸ He must lay his hand on the head of his offering, then slaughter it before the tent of meeting. Aaron's sons will splatter its blood on all sides of the altar. ⁹ He will then present part of the fellowship sacrifice as a fire offering to the Lᴏʀᴅ consisting of its fat and the entire fat tail, which he is to remove close to the backbone. He will also remove the fat surrounding the entrails, all the fat on the entrails, ¹⁰ the two kidneys with the fat on them at the loins, and the fatty lobe of the liver above the kidneys. ¹¹ Then the priest will burn the food on the altar, as a fire offering to the Lᴏʀᴅ.

¹² "If his offering is a goat, he is to present it before the Lᴏʀᴅ. ¹³ He must lay his hand on its head and slaughter it before the tent of meeting. Aaron's sons will splatterᶜ its blood on all sides of the altar. ¹⁴ He will present part of his offering as a fire offering to the Lᴏʀᴅ: the fat surrounding the entrails, all the fat that is on the entrails, ¹⁵ and the two kidneys with the fat on them at the loins; he will also remove the fatty lobe of the liver with the

---

ᴬ2:9 Lit *portion of it*   ᴮ2:11 Some Hb mss, Sam, LXX, Tg read *present*
ᶜ3:13 Or *dash*

kidneys. [16] Then the priest will burn the food on the altar, as a fire offering for a pleasing aroma. [A]

"All fat belongs to the Lord. [17] This is a permanent statute throughout your generations, wherever you live: you must not eat any fat or any blood."

THE SIN OFFERING

4 Then the Lord spoke to Moses: [2] "Tell the Israelites: When someone sins unintentionally against any of the Lord's commands and does anything prohibited by them—

[3] "If the anointed priest sins, bringing guilt on the people, he is to present to the Lord a young, unblemished bull as a sin [B] offering for the sin he has committed. [4] He is to bring the bull to the entrance to the tent of meeting before the Lord, lay his hand on the bull's head, and slaughter it before the Lord. [5] The anointed priest will then take some of the bull's blood and bring it into the tent of meeting. [6] The priest is to dip his finger in the blood and sprinkle some of it seven times before the Lord in front of the curtain of the sanctuary. [7] The priest is to apply some of the blood to the horns of the altar of fragrant incense that is before the Lord in the tent of meeting. He must pour out the rest of the bull's blood at the base of the altar of burnt offering that is at the entrance to the tent of meeting. [8] He is to remove all the fat from the bull of the sin offering: the fat surrounding the entrails, all the fat that is on the entrails, [9] and the two kidneys with the fat on them at the loins. He will also remove the fatty lobe of the liver with the kidneys, [10] just as the fat is removed from the ox of the fellowship sacrifice. The priest is to burn them on the altar of burnt offering. [11] But the hide of the bull and all its flesh, with its head and legs, and its entrails and waste — [12] all the rest of the bull — he must bring to a ceremonially clean place outside the camp to the ash heap, and must burn it on a wood fire. It is to be burned at the ash heap.

[13] "Now if the whole community of Israel errs, and the matter escapes the notice of the assembly, so that they violate any of the Lord's commands and incur guilt by doing what is prohibited, [14] then the assembly must present a young bull as a sin offering. They are to bring it before the tent of meeting when the sin they have committed in regard to the command becomes known. [15] The elders of the community are to lay their hands on the bull's head before the Lord and it is to be slaughtered before the Lord. [16] The anointed priest will bring some of the bull's blood into the tent of meeting. [17] The priest is to dip his finger in the blood and sprinkle it seven times before the Lord in front of the curtain. [18] He is to apply some of the blood to the horns of the altar that is before the Lord in the tent of meeting. He will pour out the rest of the blood at the base of the altar of burnt offering that is at the entrance to the tent of meeting. [19] He is to remove all the fat from it and burn it on the altar. [20] He is to offer this bull just as he did with the bull in the sin offering; he will offer it the same way. So the priest will make atonement on their behalf, and they will be forgiven. [21] Then he will bring the bull outside the camp and burn it just as he burned the first bull. It is the sin offering for the assembly.

[22] "When a leader [C] sins and unintentionally violates any of the commands of the Lord his God by doing what is prohibited, and incurs guilt, [23] or someone

---

[A] 3:16 Sam, LXX add *to the Lord*   [B] 4:3 Or *purification*   [C] 4:22 Or *ruler* informs him about the sin he has committed, he is to bring an unblemished male goat as his offering. ²⁴ He is to lay his hand on the head of the goat and slaughter it at the place where the burnt offering is slaughtered before the Lᴏʀᴅ. It is a sin offering. ²⁵ Then the priest is to take some of the blood from the sin offering with his finger and apply it to the horns of the altar of burnt offering. The rest of its blood he is to pour out at the base of the altar of burnt offering. ²⁶ He must burn all its fat on the altar, like the fat of the fellowship sacrifice. In this way the priest will make atonement on his behalf for that person's sin, and he will be forgiven.

²⁷ "Now if any of the common people^A sins unintentionally by violating one of the Lᴏʀᴅ's commands, does what is prohibited, and incurs guilt, ²⁸ or if someone informs him about the sin he has committed, then he is to bring an unblemished female goat as his offering for the sin that he has committed. ²⁹ He is to lay his hand on the head of the sin offering and slaughter it at the place of the burnt offering. ³⁰ Then the priest is to take some of its blood with his finger and apply it to the horns of the altar of burnt offering. He is to pour out the rest of its blood at the base of the altar. ³¹ He is to remove all its fat just as the fat is removed from the fellowship sacrifice. The priest is to burn it on the altar as a pleasing aroma to the Lᴏʀᴅ. In this way the priest will make atonement on his behalf, and he will be forgiven.

³² "Or if the offering that he brings as a sin offering is a lamb, he is to bring an unblemished female. ³³ He is to lay his hand on the head of the sin offering and slaughter it as a sin offering at the place where the burnt offering is slaughtered. ³⁴ Then the priest is to take some of the blood of the sin offering with his finger and apply it to the horns of the altar of burnt offering. He is to pour out the rest of its blood at the base of the altar. ³⁵ He is to remove all its fat just as the fat of the lamb is removed from the fellowship sacrifice. The priest will burn it on the altar along with the fire offerings to the Lᴏʀᴅ. In this way the priest will make atonement on his behalf for the sin he has committed, and he will be forgiven.

CASES REQUIRING SIN OFFERINGS

5 "When someone sins in any of these ways: If he has seen, heard, or known about something he has witnessed, and did not respond to a public call to testify, he will bear his iniquity. ² Or if someone touches anything unclean — a carcass of an unclean wild animal, or unclean livestock, or an unclean swarming creature — without being aware of it, he is unclean and incurs guilt. ³ Or if he touches human uncleanness — any uncleanness by which one can become defiled — without being aware of it, but later recognizes it, he incurs guilt. ⁴ Or if someone swears rashly to do what is good or evil — concerning anything a person may speak rashly in an oath — without being aware of it, but later recognizes it, he incurs guilt in such an instance. ⁵ If someone incurs guilt in one of these cases, he is to confess he has committed that sin. ⁶ He must bring his penalty for guilt for the sin he has committed to the Lᴏʀᴅ: a female lamb or goat from the flock as a sin offering. In this way the priest will make atonement on his behalf for his sin.

---

^A 4:27 Lit *the people of the land*

⁷ "But if he cannot afford an animal from the flock, then he may bring to the LORD two turtledoves or two young pigeons as penalty for guilt for his sin — one as a sin offering and the other as a burnt offering. ⁸ He is to bring them to the priest, who will first present the one for the sin offering. He is to twist its head at the back of the neck without severing it. ⁹ Then he will sprinkle some of the blood of the sin offering on the side of the altar, while the rest of the blood is to be drained out at the base of the altar; it is a sin offering. ¹⁰ He will prepare the second bird as a burnt offering according to the regulation. In this way the priest will make atonement on his behalf for the sin he has committed, and he will be forgiven.

¹¹ "But if he cannot afford two turtledoves or two young pigeons, he may bring two quarts^A of fine flour^B as an offering for his sin. He must not put olive oil or frankincense on it, for it is a sin offering. ¹² He is to bring it to the priest, who will take a handful from it as its memorial portion and burn it on the altar along with the fire offerings to the LORD; it is a sin offering. ¹³ In this way the priest will make atonement on his behalf concerning the sin he has committed in any of these cases, and he will be forgiven. The rest will belong to the priest, like the grain offering."

THE GUILT OFFERING

¹⁴ Then the LORD spoke to Moses: ¹⁵ "If someone offends by sinning unintentionally in regard to any of the LORD's holy things,^C he must bring his penalty for guilt to the LORD: an unblemished ram from the flock (based on your assessment of its value in silver shekels, according to the sanctuary shekel) as a guilt offering. ¹⁶ He is to make restitution for his sin regarding any holy thing, adding a fifth of its value to it, and give it to the priest. Then the priest will make atonement on his behalf with the ram of the guilt offering, and he will be forgiven.

¹⁷ "If someone sins and without knowing it violates any of the LORD's commands concerning anything prohibited, he is guilty, and he will bear his iniquity. ¹⁸ He must bring an unblemished ram from the flock according to your assessment of its value as a guilt offering to the priest. Then the priest will make atonement on his behalf for the error he has committed unintentionally, and he will be forgiven. ¹⁹ It is a guilt offering; he is indeed guilty before the LORD."

6 The LORD spoke to Moses: ² "When someone sins and offends the LORD by deceiving his neighbor in regard to a deposit, a security,^D or a robbery; or defrauds his neighbor; ³ or finds something lost and lies about it; or swears falsely about any of the sinful things a person may do — ⁴ once he has sinned and acknowledged his guilt — he must return what he stole or defrauded, or the deposit entrusted to him, or the lost item he found, ⁵ or anything else about which he swore falsely. He will make full restitution for it and add a fifth of its value to it. He is to pay it to its owner on the day he acknowledges his guilt. ⁶ Then he is to bring his guilt offering to the LORD: an unblemished ram from the flock according to your assessment of its value as a guilt offering to the priest. ⁷ In this way the priest will make atonement on his behalf before the LORD, and he will be forgiven for anything he may have done to incur guilt."

---

^A5:11 Lit *one-tenth of an ephah*   ^B5:11 Lit *flour as a sin offering*   ^C5:15 Things dedicated to the LORD   ^D6:2 Or *an investment*

THE BURNT OFFERING

[8] The LORD spoke to Moses: [9] "Command Aaron and his sons: This is the law of the burnt offering; the burnt offering itself must remain on the altar's hearth all night until morning, while the fire of the altar is kept burning on it. [10] The priest is to put on his linen robe and linen undergarments.[A] He is to remove the ashes of the burnt offering the fire has consumed on the altar, and place them beside the altar. [11] Then he will take off his garments, put on other clothes, and bring the ashes outside the camp to a ceremonially clean place. [12] The fire on the altar is to be kept burning; it must not go out. Every morning the priest will burn wood on the fire. He is to arrange the burnt offering on the fire and burn the fat portions from the fellowship offerings on it. [13] Fire must be kept burning on the altar continually; it must not go out.

THE GRAIN OFFERING

[14] "Now this is the law of the grain offering: Aaron's sons will present it before the LORD in front of the altar. [15] The priest is to remove a handful of fine flour and olive oil from the grain offering, with all the frankincense that is on the offering, and burn its memorial portion on the altar as a pleasing aroma to the LORD. [16] Aaron and his sons may eat the rest of it. It is to be eaten in the form of unleavened bread in a holy place; they are to eat it in the courtyard of the tent of meeting. [17] It must not be baked with yeast; I have assigned it as their portion from my fire offerings. It is especially holy, like the sin offering and the guilt offering. [18] Any male among Aaron's descendants may eat it. It is a permanent portion[B] throughout your generations from the fire offerings to the LORD. Anything that touches the offerings will become holy."

[19] The LORD spoke to Moses: [20] "This is the offering that Aaron and his sons are to present to the LORD on the day that he is anointed: two quarts[C] of fine flour as a regular grain offering, half of it in the morning and half in the evening. [21] It is to be prepared with oil on a griddle; you are to bring it well-kneaded. You are to present it as a grain offering of baked pieces,[D] a pleasing aroma to the LORD. [22] The priest, who is one of Aaron's sons and will be anointed to take his place, is to prepare it. It must be completely burned as a permanent portion for the LORD. [23] Every grain offering for a priest will be a whole burnt offering; it is not to be eaten."

THE SIN OFFERING

[24] The LORD spoke to Moses: [25] "Tell Aaron and his sons: This is the law of the sin offering. The sin offering is most holy and must be slaughtered before the LORD at the place where the burnt offering is slaughtered. [26] The priest who offers it as a sin offering will eat it. It is to be eaten in a holy place, in the courtyard of the tent of meeting. [27] Anything that touches its flesh will become holy, and if any of its blood spatters on a garment, then you must wash that garment[E] in a holy place. [28] A clay pot in which the sin offering is boiled is to be broken; if it is boiled in a bronze vessel, it is to be scoured and rinsed with water. [29] Any male among the priests may eat it; it is especially holy. [30] But no sin offering may be eaten if its blood has been brought into the tent of meeting to make atonement in the holy place; it must be burned.

[A] 6:10 Lit undergarments on his flesh   [B] 6:18 Or statute   [C] 6:20 Lit a tenth of an ephah   [D] 6:21 Hb obscure   [E] 6:27 Lit wash what it spattered on

THE GUILT OFFERING

7 "Now this is the law of the guilt[A] offering; it is especially holy. [2] The guilt offering is to be slaughtered at the place where the burnt offering is slaughtered, and the priest is to splatter its blood on all sides of the altar. [3] The offerer is to present all the fat from it: the fat tail, the fat surrounding the entrails,[B] [4] and the two kidneys with the fat on them at the loins; he will also remove the fatty lobe of the liver with the kidneys. [5] The priest will burn them on the altar as a fire offering to the LORD; it is a guilt offering. [6] Any male among the priests may eat it. It is to be eaten in a holy place; it is especially holy.

[7] "The guilt offering is like the sin offering; the law is the same for both. It belongs to the priest who makes atonement with it. [8] As for the priest who presents someone's burnt offering, the hide of the burnt offering he has presented belongs to him; it is the priest's. [9] Any grain offering that is baked in an oven or prepared in a pan or on a griddle belongs to the priest who presents it; it is his. [10] But any grain offering, whether dry or mixed with oil, belongs equally to all of Aaron's sons.

THE FELLOWSHIP SACRIFICE

[11] "Now this is the law of the fellowship sacrifice that someone may present to the LORD: [12] If he presents it for thanksgiving, in addition to the thanksgiving sacrifice, he is to present unleavened cakes mixed with olive oil, unleavened wafers coated with oil, and well-kneaded cakes of fine flour mixed with oil. [13] He is to present as his offering cakes of leavened bread with his thanksgiving sacrifice of fellowship. [14] From the cakes he is to present one portion of each offering as a contribution to the LORD. It will belong to the priest who splatters the blood of the fellowship offering; it is his. [15] The meat of his thanksgiving sacrifice of fellowship must be eaten on the day he offers it; he may not leave any of it until morning.

[16] "If the sacrifice he offers is a vow or a freewill offering, it is to be eaten on the day he presents his sacrifice, and what is left over may be eaten on the next day. [17] But what remains of the sacrificial meat by the third day must be burned. [18] If any of the meat of his fellowship sacrifice is eaten on the third day, it will not be accepted. It will not be credited to the one who presents it; it is repulsive. The person who eats any of it will bear his iniquity.[C]

[19] "Meat that touches anything unclean must not be eaten; it is to be burned. Everyone who is clean may eat any other meat. [20] But the one who eats meat from the LORD's fellowship sacrifice while he is unclean, that person must be cut off from his people. [21] If someone touches anything unclean, whether human uncleanness, an unclean animal, or any unclean, abhorrent[D] creature, and eats meat from the LORD's fellowship sacrifice, that person is to be cut off from his people."

FAT AND BLOOD PROHIBITED

[22] The LORD spoke to Moses: [23] "Tell the Israelites: You are not to eat any fat of an ox, a sheep, or a goat. [24] The fat of an animal that dies naturally or is

---

[A]7:1 Or *restitution*   [B]7:3 LXX, Sam add *and all the fat that is on the entrails*; Lv 3:3,9,14; 4:8   [C]7:18 Or *will bear his guilt*   [D]7:21 Some Hb mss, Sam, Syr, Tg read *swarming* mauled by wild beasts^A may be used for any other purpose, but you must not eat it. [25] If anyone eats animal fat from a fire offering presented to the LORD, the person who eats it is to be cut off from his people. [26] Wherever you live, you must not eat the blood of any bird or animal. [27] Whoever eats any blood is to be cut off from his people."

THE PORTION FOR THE PRIESTS

[28] The LORD spoke to Moses: [29] "Tell the Israelites: The one who presents a fellowship sacrifice to the LORD is to bring an offering to the LORD from his sacrifice. [30] His own hands will bring the fire offerings to the LORD. He will bring the fat together with the breast. The breast is to be presented as a presentation offering before the LORD. [31] The priest is to burn the fat on the altar, but the breast belongs to Aaron and his sons. [32] You are to give the right thigh to the priest as a contribution from your fellowship sacrifices. [33] The son of Aaron who presents the blood of the fellowship offering and the fat will have the right thigh as a portion. [34] I have taken from the Israelites the breast of the presentation offering and the thigh of the contribution from their fellowship sacrifices, and have assigned them to the priest Aaron and to his sons as a permanent portion^B from the Israelites."

[35] This is the portion from the fire offerings to the LORD for Aaron and his sons since the day they were presented to serve the LORD as priests. [36] The LORD commanded this to be given to them by the Israelites on the day he anointed them. It is a permanent portion throughout their generations.

[37] This is the law for the burnt offering, the grain offering, the sin offering, the guilt offering, the ordination offering, and the fellowship sacrifice, [38] which the LORD commanded Moses on Mount Sinai on the day he commanded the Israelites to present their offerings to the LORD in the Wilderness of Sinai.

ORDINATION OF AARON AND HIS SONS

8 The LORD spoke to Moses: [2] "Take Aaron, his sons with him, the garments, the anointing oil, the bull of the sin^C offering, the two rams, and the basket of unleavened bread, [3] and assemble the whole community at the entrance to the tent of meeting." [4] So Moses did as the LORD commanded him, and the community assembled at the entrance to the tent of meeting. [5] Moses said to them, "This is what the LORD has commanded to be done."

[6] Then Moses presented Aaron and his sons and washed them with water. [7] He put the tunic on Aaron, wrapped the sash around him, clothed him with the robe, and put the ephod on him. He put the woven band of the ephod around him and fastened it to him. [8] Then he put the breastpiece on him and placed the Urim and Thummim into the breastpiece. [9] He also put the turban on his head and placed the gold medallion, the holy diadem, on the front of the turban, as the LORD had commanded Moses.

[10] Then Moses took the anointing oil and anointed the tabernacle and everything in it to consecrate them. [11] He sprinkled some of the oil on the altar seven times, anointing the altar with all its utensils, and the basin with its stand, to consecrate them. [12] He poured some of the anointing oil on Aaron's

---

^A7:24 Lit fat of a carcass or the fat of a mauled beast   ^B7:34 Or statute, also in v. 36   ^C8:2 Or purification head and anointed and consecrated him. [13] Then Moses presented Aaron's sons, clothed them with tunics, wrapped sashes around them, and fastened headbands on them, as the LORD had commanded Moses.

[14] Then he brought the bull near for the sin offering, and Aaron and his sons laid their hands on the head of the bull for the sin offering. [15] Then Moses slaughtered it,[A] took the blood, and applied it with his finger to the horns of the altar on all sides, purifying the altar. He poured out the blood at the base of the altar and consecrated it so that atonement can be made on it.[B] [16] Moses took all the fat that was on the entrails, the fatty lobe of the liver, and the two kidneys with their fat, and he burned them on the altar. [17] He burned the bull with its hide, flesh, and waste outside the camp, as the LORD had commanded Moses.

[18] Then he presented the ram for the burnt offering, and Aaron and his sons laid their hands on the head of the ram. [19] Moses slaughtered it and[C] splattered the blood on all sides of the altar. [20] Moses cut the ram into pieces and burned the head, the pieces, and the fat, [21] but he washed the entrails and legs with water. He then burned the entire ram on the altar. It was a burnt offering for a pleasing aroma, a fire offering to the LORD as he had commanded Moses.

[22] Next he presented the second ram, the ram of ordination, and Aaron and his sons laid their hands on the head of the ram. [23] Moses slaughtered it,[D] took some of its blood, and put it on Aaron's right earlobe, on the thumb of his right hand, and on the big toe of his right foot. [24] Moses also presented Aaron's sons and put some of the blood on their right earlobes, on the thumbs of their right hands, and on the big toes of their right feet. Then Moses splattered the blood on all sides of the altar. [25] He took the fat — the fat tail, all the fat that was on the entrails, the fatty lobe of the liver, and the two kidneys with their fat — as well as the right thigh. [26] From the basket of unleavened bread that was before the LORD he took one cake of unleavened bread, one cake of bread made with oil, and one wafer, and placed them on the fat portions and the right thigh. [27] He put all these in the hands of Aaron and his sons and presented them before the LORD as a presentation offering. [28] Then Moses took them from their hands and burned them on the altar with the burnt offering. This was an ordination offering for a pleasing aroma, a fire offering to the LORD. [29] He also took the breast and presented it before the LORD as a presentation offering; it was Moses's portion of the ordination ram as the LORD had commanded him.

[30] Then Moses took some of the anointing oil and some of the blood that was on the altar and sprinkled them on Aaron and his garments, as well as on his sons and their garments. In this way he consecrated Aaron and his garments, as well as his sons and their garments.

[31] Moses said to Aaron and his sons, "Boil the meat at the entrance to the tent of meeting and eat it there with the bread that is in the basket for the ordination offering as I commanded:[E] Aaron and his sons are to eat it. [32] Burn up what remains of the meat and bread. [33] Do not go outside the entrance

---

[A]8:14-15 Or offering, and he slaughtered it. [15]Then Moses   [B]8:15 Or it by making atonement for it   [C]8:18-19 Or ram, [19]and he slaughtered it. Moses   [D]8:22-23 Or ram, [23]and he slaughtered it. Moses   [E]8:31 LXX, Syr, Tg read was commanded; Ex 29:31-32 to the tent of meeting for seven days, until the time your days of ordination are completed, because it will take seven days to ordain you.[A] 34 The LORD commanded what has been done today in order to make atonement for you. 35 You must remain at the entrance to the tent of meeting day and night for seven days and keep the LORD's charge so that you will not die, for this is what I was commanded." 36 So Aaron and his sons did everything the LORD had commanded through Moses.

THE PRIESTLY MINISTRY INAUGURATED

9 On the eighth day Moses summoned Aaron, his sons, and the elders of Israel. 2 He said to Aaron, "Take a young bull for a sin[B] offering and a ram for a burnt offering, both without blemish, and present them before the LORD. 3 And tell the Israelites:[C] Take a male goat for a sin offering; a calf and a lamb, male yearlings without blemish, for a burnt offering; 4 an ox and a ram for a fellowship offering to sacrifice before the LORD; and a grain offering mixed with oil. For today the LORD is going to appear to you."

5 They brought what Moses had commanded to the front of the tent of meeting, and the whole community came forward and stood before the LORD. 6 Moses said, "This is what the LORD commanded you to do, that the glory of the LORD may appear to you." 7 Then Moses said to Aaron, "Approach the altar and sacrifice your sin offering and your burnt offering; make atonement for yourself and the people.[D] Sacrifice the people's offering and make atonement for them, as the LORD commanded."

8 So Aaron approached the altar and slaughtered the calf as a sin offering for himself. 9 Aaron's sons brought the blood to him, and he dipped his finger in the blood and applied it to the horns of the altar. He poured out the blood at the base of the altar. 10 He burned the fat, the kidneys, and the fatty lobe of the liver from the sin offering on the altar, as the LORD had commanded Moses. 11 He burned the flesh and the hide outside the camp.

12 Then he slaughtered the burnt offering. Aaron's sons brought him the blood, and he splattered it on all sides of the altar. 13 They brought him the burnt offering piece by piece, along with the head, and he burned them on the altar. 14 He washed the entrails and the legs and burned them with the burnt offering on the altar.

15 Aaron presented the people's offering. He took the male goat for the people's sin offering, slaughtered it, and made a sin offering with it as he did before. 16 He presented the burnt offering and sacrificed it according to the regulation. 17 Next he presented the grain offering, took a handful of it, and burned it on the altar in addition to the morning burnt offering.

18 Finally, he slaughtered the ox and the ram as the people's fellowship sacrifice. Aaron's sons brought him the blood, and he splattered it on all sides of the altar. 19 They also brought the fat portions from the ox and the ram — the fat tail, the fat surrounding the entrails, the kidneys, and the fatty lobe of the liver — 20 and placed these on the breasts. Aaron burned the fat portions on the altar, 21 but he presented the breasts and the right thigh as a presentation offering before the LORD, as Moses had commanded.[E]

A 8:33 Lit because he will fill your hands for seven days B 9:2 Or purification
C 9:3 Sam, LXX read elders of Israel D 9:7 LXX reads and your household
E 9:21 Some Hb mss, LXX, Sam read as the LORD commanded Moses

²² Aaron lifted up his hands toward the people and blessed them. He came down after sacrificing the sin offering, the burnt offering, and the fellowship offering. ²³ Moses and Aaron then entered the tent of meeting. When they came out, they blessed the people, and the glory of the LORD appeared to all the people. ²⁴ Fire came from the LORD and consumed the burnt offering and the fat portions on the altar. And when all the people saw it, they shouted and fell facedown.

NADAB AND ABIHU

10 Aaron's sons Nadab and Abihu each took his own firepan, put fire in it, placed incense on it, and presented unauthorized fire before the LORD, which he had not commanded them to do. ² Then fire came from the LORD and consumed them, and they died before the LORD. ³ Moses said to Aaron, "This is what the LORD has spoken:

I will demonstrate my holiness ᴬ
to those who are near me,
and I will reveal my glory ᴮ
before all the people."

And Aaron remained silent.

⁴ Moses summoned Mishael and Elzaphan, sons of Aaron's uncle Uzziel, and said to them, "Come here and carry your relatives away from the front of the sanctuary to a place outside the camp." ⁵ So they came forward and carried them in their tunics outside the camp, as Moses had said.

⁶ Then Moses said to Aaron and his sons Eleazar and Ithamar, "Do not let your hair hang loose and do not tear your clothes, or else you will die, and the LORD will become angry with the whole community. However, your brothers, the whole house of Israel, may weep over the conflagration the LORD ignited. ⁷ You must not go outside the entrance to the tent of meeting or you will die, for the LORD's anointing oil is on you." So they did as Moses said.

REGULATIONS FOR PRIESTS

⁸ The LORD spoke to Aaron: ⁹ "You and your sons are not to drink wine or beer when you enter the tent of meeting, or else you will die; this is a permanent statute throughout your generations. ¹⁰ You must distinguish between the holy and the common, and the clean and the unclean, ¹¹ and teach the Israelites all the statutes that the LORD has given to them through Moses."

¹² Moses spoke to Aaron and his remaining sons, Eleazar and Ithamar: "Take the grain offering that is left over from the fire offerings to the LORD, and eat it prepared without yeast beside the altar, because it is especially holy. ¹³ You must eat it in a holy place because it is your portion ᶜ and your sons' from the fire offerings to the LORD, for this is what I was commanded. ¹⁴ But you and your sons and your daughters may eat the breast of the presentation offering and the thigh of the contribution in any ceremonially clean place, because these portions have been assigned to you and your children from the Israelites' fellowship sacrifices. ¹⁵ They are to bring the thigh of the contribution and the breast of the presentation offering, together with the offerings of fat portions made by fire, to present as a presentation

ᴬ10:3 Or *will be treated as holy*   ᴮ10:3 Or *will be glorified*   ᶜ10:13 Or *statute* offering before the LORD. It will belong permanently to you and your children, as the LORD commanded."

¹⁶ Then Moses inquired carefully about the male goat of the sin offering, but it had already been burned up. He was angry with Eleazar and Ithamar, Aaron's surviving sons, and asked, ¹⁷ "Why didn't you eat the sin offering in the sanctuary area? For it is especially holy, and he has assigned it to you to take away the guilt of the community and make atonement for them before the LORD. ¹⁸ Since its blood was not brought inside the sanctuary, you should have eaten it in the sanctuary area, as I commanded."

¹⁹ But Aaron replied to Moses, "See, today they presented their sin offering and their burnt offering before the LORD. Since these things have happened to me, if I had eaten the sin offering today, would it have been acceptable in the LORD's sight?" ²⁰ When Moses heard this, it was acceptable to him. ᴬ

CLEAN AND UNCLEAN LAND ANIMALS

11 The LORD spoke to Moses and Aaron: ² "Tell the Israelites: You may eat all these kinds of land animals. ³ You may eat any animal with divided hooves and that chews the cud. ⁴ But among the ones that chew the cud or have divided hooves you are not to eat these:

camels, though they chew the cud,
do not have divided hooves — they are unclean for you;
⁵ hyraxes, though they chew the cud,
do not have hooves — they are unclean for you;
⁶ hares, though they chew the cud,
do not have hooves — they are unclean for you;
⁷ pigs, though they have divided hooves,
do not chew the cud — they are unclean for you.

⁸ Do not eat any of their meat or touch their carcasses — they are unclean for you.

CLEAN AND UNCLEAN AQUATIC ANIMALS

⁹ "This is what you may eat from all that is in the water: You may eat everything in the water that has fins and scales, whether in the seas or streams. ¹⁰ But these are to be abhorrent to you: everything in the seas or streams that does not have fins and scales among all the swarming things and other living creatures in the water. ¹¹ They are to remain abhorrent to you; you must not eat any of their meat, and you must abhor their carcasses. ¹² Everything in the water that does not have fins and scales will be abhorrent to you.

UNCLEAN BIRDS

¹³ "You are to abhor these birds. They must not be eaten because they are abhorrent:

eagles, ᴮ bearded vultures,
Egyptian vultures, ᶜ ¹⁴ kites, ᴰ
any kind of falcon, ᴱ

ᴬ10:20 Lit *acceptable in his sight*   ᴮ11:13 Or *griffon-vultures*   ᶜ11:13 Or *ospreys, or bearded vultures*   ᴰ11:14 Or *hawks*   ᴱ11:14 Or *buzzards, or hawks*

15 every kind of raven, 16 ostriches, A
short-eared owls, gulls, B
any kind of hawk,
17 little C owls, cormorants, D
long-eared owls, E
18 barn F owls, eagle owls, G
ospreys, 19 storks, H
any kind of heron, I
hoopoes, and bats.

CLEAN AND UNCLEAN FLYING INSECTS

20 "All winged insects that walk on all fours are to be abhorrent to you. 21 But you may eat these kinds of all the winged insects that walk on all fours: those that have jointed legs above their feet for hopping on the ground. 22 You may eat these:

any kind of locust, katydid, cricket, and grasshopper.

23 All other winged insects that have four feet are to be abhorrent to you.

PURIFICATION AFTER TOUCHING DEAD ANIMALS

24 "These will make you unclean. Whoever touches their carcasses will be unclean until evening, 25 and whoever carries any of their carcasses is to wash his clothes and will be unclean until evening. 26 All animals that have hooves but do not have a divided hoof and do not chew the cud are unclean for you. Whoever touches them becomes unclean. 27 All the four-footed animals that walk on their paws are unclean for you. Whoever touches their carcasses will be unclean until evening, 28 and anyone who carries their carcasses is to wash his clothes and will be unclean until evening. They are unclean for you.

29 "These creatures that swarm on the ground are unclean for you:

weasels, J mice,
any kind of large lizard, K
30 geckos, monitor lizards, L
common lizards, M skinks, N
and chameleons. O

31 These are unclean for you among all the swarming creatures. Whoever touches them when they are dead will be unclean until evening. 32 When any one of them dies and falls on anything it becomes unclean — any item of wood, clothing, leather, sackcloth, or any implement used for work. It is to be rinsed with water and will remain unclean until evening; then it will be clean. 33 If any of them falls into any clay pot, everything in it will become unclean; you are to break it. 34 Any edible food coming into contact with that unclean water will become unclean, and any drinkable liquid in any container will become unclean. 35 Anything one of their carcasses falls

---

A 11:16 Or eagle owls   B 11:16 Or long-eared owls   C 11:17 Or tawny   D 11:17 Or pelicans   E 11:17 Or ibis   F 11:18 Or little   G 11:18 Or pelicans, or horned owls   H 11:19 Or herons   I 11:19 Or cormorants, or hawks   J 11:29 Or mole rats, or rats   K 11:29 Or of thorn-tailed, or dabb lizard, or of crocodile   L 11:30 Or spotted lizards, or chameleons   M 11:30 Or geckos, or newts, or salamanders   N 11:30 Or sand lizards, or newts, or snails   O 11:30 Or salamanders, or moles on will become unclean. If it is an oven or stove, it is to be smashed; it is unclean and will remain unclean for you. ³⁶ A spring or cistern containing water will remain clean, but someone who touches a carcass in it will become unclean. ³⁷ If one of their carcasses falls on any seed that is to be sown, it is clean; ³⁸ but if water has been put on the seed and one of their carcasses falls on it, it is unclean for you.

³⁹ "If one of the animals that you use for food dies, anyone who touches its carcass will be unclean until evening. ⁴⁰ Anyone who eats some of its carcass is to wash his clothes and will be unclean until evening. Anyone who carries its carcass must wash his clothes and will be unclean until evening.

UNCLEAN SWARMING CREATURES

⁴¹ "All the creatures that swarm on the earth are abhorrent; they must not be eaten. ⁴² Do not eat any of the creatures that swarm on the earth, anything that moves on its belly or walks on all fours or on many feet,ᴬ for they are abhorrent. ⁴³ Do not become contaminated by any creature that swarms; do not become unclean or defiled by them. ⁴⁴ For I am the Lᴏʀᴅ your God, so you must consecrate yourselves and be holy because I am holy. Do not defile yourselves by any swarming creature that crawls on the ground. ⁴⁵ For I am the Lᴏʀᴅ, who brought you up from the land of Egypt to be your God, so you must be holy because I am holy.

⁴⁶ "This is the law concerning animals, birds, all living creatures that move in the water, and all creatures that swarm on the ground, ⁴⁷ in order to distinguish between the unclean and the clean, between the animals that may be eaten and those that may not be eaten."

PURIFICATION AFTER CHILDBIRTH

12 The Lᴏʀᴅ spoke to Moses: ² "Tell the Israelites: When a woman becomes pregnant and gives birth to a male child, she will be unclean seven days, as she is during the days of her menstrual impurity. ³ The flesh of his foreskin must be circumcised on the eighth day. ⁴ She will continue in purification from her bleeding for thirty-three days. She must not touch any holy thing or go into the sanctuary until completing her days of purification. ⁵ But if she gives birth to a female child, she will be unclean for two weeks as she is during her menstrual impurity. She will continue in purification from her bleeding for sixty-six days.

⁶ "When her days of purification are complete, whether for a son or daughter, she is to bring to the priest at the entrance to the tent of meeting a year-old male lamb for a burnt offering, and a young pigeon or a turtledove for a sinᴮ offering. ⁷ He will present them before the Lᴏʀᴅ and make atonement on her behalf; she will be clean from her discharge of blood. This is the law for a woman giving birth, whether to a male or female. ⁸ But if she doesn't have sufficient meansᶜ for a sheep, she may take two turtledoves or two young pigeons, one for a burnt offering and the other for a sin offering. Then the priest will make atonement on her behalf, and she will be clean."

ᴬ11:42 Lit *fours, to anything multiplying pairs of feet*   ᴮ12:6 Or *purification,* also in v. 8   ᶜ12:8 Lit *if her hand cannot obtain what is sufficient*

SKIN DISEASES

13 The LORD spoke to Moses and Aaron: [2] "When a person has a swelling,[A] scab,[B] or spot on the skin of his body, and it may be a serious disease on the skin of his body, he is to be brought to the priest Aaron or to one of his sons, the priests. [3] The priest will examine the sore on the skin of his body. If the hair in the sore has turned white and the sore appears to be deeper than the skin of his body, it is in fact a serious skin disease. After the priest examines him, he must pronounce him unclean. [4] But if the spot on the skin of his body is white and does not appear to be deeper than the skin, and the hair in it has not turned white, the priest will quarantine the stricken person for seven days. [5] The priest will then reexamine him on the seventh day. If he sees that the sore remains unchanged and has not spread on the skin, the priest will quarantine him for another seven days. [6] The priest will examine him again on the seventh day. If the sore has faded and has not spread on the skin, the priest is to pronounce him clean; it is a scab. The person is to wash his clothes and will become clean. [7] But if the scab spreads further on his skin after he has presented himself to the priest for his cleansing, he is to present himself again to the priest. [8] The priest will examine him, and if the scab has spread on the skin, then the priest must pronounce him unclean; he has a serious skin disease.

[9] "When a case of serious skin disease may have developed on a person, he is to be brought to the priest. [10] The priest will examine him. If there is a white swelling on the skin that has turned the hair white, and there is a patch of raw flesh in the swelling, [11] it is a chronic serious disease on the skin of his body, and the priest must pronounce him unclean. He need not quarantine him, for he is unclean. [12] But if the skin disease breaks out all over the skin so that it covers all the skin of the stricken person from his head to his feet so far as the priest can see, [13] the priest will look, and if the skin disease has covered his entire body, he is to pronounce the stricken person clean. Since he has turned totally white, he is clean. [14] But whenever raw flesh appears on him, he will be unclean. [15] When the priest examines the raw flesh, he must pronounce him unclean. Raw flesh is unclean; this is a serious skin disease. [16] But if the raw flesh changes[C] and[D] turns white, he is to go to the priest. [17] The priest will examine him, and if the sore has turned white, the priest must pronounce the stricken person clean; he is clean.

[18] "When a boil appears on the skin of someone's body and it heals, [19] and a white swelling or a reddish-white spot develops where the boil was, the person is to present himself to the priest. [20] The priest will make an examination, and if the spot seems to be beneath the skin and the hair in it has turned white, the priest must pronounce him unclean; it is a case of serious skin disease that has broken out in the boil. [21] But when the priest examines it, if there is no white hair in it, and it is not beneath the skin but is faded, the priest will quarantine him seven days. [22] If it spreads further on the skin, the priest must pronounce him unclean; it is in fact a disease. [23] But if the spot remains where it is and does not spread, it is only the scar from the boil. The priest is to pronounce him clean.

[A]13:2 Or *discoloration*   [B]13:2 Or *rash, or eruption*   [C]13:16 Or *recedes*
[D]13:16 Or *flesh again*

24 "When there is a burn on the skin of one's body produced by fire, and the patch made raw by the burn becomes reddish-white or white, 25 the priest is to examine it. If the hair in the spot has turned white and the spot appears to be deeper than the skin, it is a serious skin disease that has broken out in the burn. The priest must pronounce him unclean; it is a serious skin disease. 26 But when the priest examines it, if there is no white hair in the spot and it is not beneath the skin but is faded, the priest will quarantine him seven days. 27 The priest will reexamine him on the seventh day. If it has spread further on the skin, the priest must pronounce him unclean; it is in fact a case of serious skin disease. 28 But if the spot has remained where it was and has not spread on the skin but is faded, it is the swelling from the burn. The priest is to pronounce him clean, for it is only the scar from the burn.

29 "When a man or woman has a condition on the head or chin, 30 the priest is to examine the condition. If it appears to be deeper than the skin, and the hair in it is yellow and sparse, the priest must pronounce the person unclean. It is a scaly outbreak, a serious skin disease of the head or chin. 31 When the priest examines the scaly condition, if it does not appear to be deeper than the skin, and there is no black hair in it, the priest will quarantine the person with the scaly condition for seven days. 32 The priest will reexamine the condition on the seventh day. If the scaly outbreak has not spread and there is no yellow hair in it and it does not appear to be deeper than the skin, 33 the person is to shave himself but not shave the scaly area. Then the priest will quarantine the person who has the scaly outbreak for another seven days. 34 The priest will examine the scaly outbreak on the seventh day, and if it has not spread on the skin and does not appear to be deeper than the skin, the priest is to pronounce the person clean. He is to wash his clothes, and he will be clean. 35 But if the scaly outbreak spreads further on the skin after his cleansing, 36 the priest is to examine the person. If the scaly outbreak has spread on the skin, the priest does not need to look for yellow hair; the person is unclean. 37 But if as far as he can see, the scaly outbreak remains unchanged and black hair has grown in it, then it has healed; he is clean. The priest is to pronounce the person clean.

38 "When a man or a woman has white spots on the skin of the body, 39 the priest is to make an examination. If the spots on the skin of the body are dull white, it is only a rash^A that has broken out on the skin; the person is clean.

40 "If a man loses the hair of his head, he is bald, but he is clean. 41 Or if he loses the hair at his hairline, he is bald on his forehead, but he is clean. 42 But if there is a reddish-white condition on the bald head or forehead, it is a serious skin disease breaking out on his head or forehead. 43 The priest is to examine him, and if the swelling of the condition on his bald head or forehead is reddish-white, like the appearance of a serious skin disease on his body, 44 the man is afflicted with a serious skin disease; he is unclean. The priest must pronounce him unclean; the infection is on his head.

45 "The person who has a case of serious skin disease is to have his clothes torn and his hair hanging loose, and he must cover his mouth and cry out, 'Unclean, unclean!' 46 He will remain unclean as long as he has the disease; he is unclean. He must live alone in a place outside the camp.

---

^13:39 Hb obscure

CONTAMINATED FABRICS

47 "If a fabric is contaminated with mildew — in wool or linen fabric, 48 in the warp or weft of linen or wool, or in leather or anything made of leather — 49 and if the contamination is green or red in the fabric, the leather, the warp, the weft, or any leather article, it is a mildew contamination and is to be shown to the priest. 50 The priest is to examine the contamination and quarantine the contaminated fabric for seven days. 51 The priest is to reexamine the contamination on the seventh day. If it has spread in the fabric, the warp, the weft, or the leather, regardless of how it is used, the contamination is harmful mildew; it is unclean. 52 He is to burn the fabric, the warp or weft in wool or linen, or any leather article, which is contaminated. Since it is harmful mildew it must be burned.

53 "When the priest examines it, if the contamination has not spread in the fabric, the warp or weft, or any leather article, 54 the priest is to order whatever is contaminated to be washed and quarantined for another seven days. 55 After it has been washed, the priest is to reexamine the contamination. If the appearance of the contaminated article has not changed, it is unclean. Even though the contamination has not spread, you must burn the fabric. It is a fungus^A on the front or back of the fabric.

56 "If the priest examines it, and the contamination has faded after it has been washed, he is to cut the contaminated section out of the fabric, the leather, or the warp or weft. 57 But if it reappears in the fabric, the warp or weft, or any leather article, it has broken out again. You must burn whatever is contaminated. 58 But if the contamination disappears from the fabric, the warp or weft, or any leather article, which have been washed, it is to be washed again, and it will be clean.

59 "This is the law concerning a mildew contamination in wool or linen fabric, warp or weft, or any leather article, in order to pronounce it clean or unclean."

CLEANSING OF SKIN DISEASES

14 The LORD spoke to Moses: 2 "This is the law concerning the person afflicted with a skin disease on the day of his cleansing. He is to be brought to the priest, 3 who will go outside the camp and examine him. If the skin disease has disappeared from the afflicted person,^B 4 the priest will order that two live clean birds, cedar wood, scarlet yarn, and hyssop be brought for the one who is to be cleansed. 5 Then the priest will order that one of the birds be slaughtered over fresh water in a clay pot. 6 He is to take the live bird together with the cedar wood, scarlet yarn, and hyssop, and dip them all into the blood of the bird that was slaughtered over the fresh water. 7 He will then sprinkle the blood seven times on the one who is to be cleansed from the skin disease. He is to pronounce him clean and release the live bird over the open countryside. 8 The one who is to be cleansed must wash his clothes, shave off all his hair, and bathe with water; he is clean. Afterward he may enter the camp, but he must remain outside his tent for seven days. 9 He is to shave off all his hair again on the seventh day: his head, his beard, his eyebrows, and the rest of his hair. He is to wash his clothes and bathe himself with water; he is clean.

^A 13:55 Hb obscure ^B 14:3 Lit the person afflicted with skin disease

¹⁰ "On the eighth day he must take two unblemished male lambs, an un-blemished year-old ewe lamb, a grain offering of six quarts^A of fine flour mixed with olive oil, and one-third of a quart^B of olive oil. ¹¹ The priest who performs the cleansing will place the person who is to be cleansed, together with these offerings, before the LORD at the entrance to the tent of meeting. ¹² The priest is to take one male lamb and present it as a guilt offering, along with the one-third quart of olive oil, and he will present them as a presenta-tion offering before the LORD. ¹³ He is to slaughter the male lamb at the place in the sanctuary area where the sin offering and burnt offering are slaugh-tered, for like the sin offering, the guilt offering belongs to the priest; it is es-pecially holy. ¹⁴ The priest is to take some of the blood from the guilt offering and put it on the lobe of the right ear of the one to be cleansed, on the thumb of his right hand, and on the big toe of his right foot. ¹⁵ Then the priest will take some of the one-third quart of olive oil and pour it into his left palm. ¹⁶ The priest will dip his right finger into the oil in his left palm and sprinkle some of the oil with his finger seven times before the LORD. ¹⁷ From the oil remaining in his palm the priest will put some on the lobe of the right ear of the one to be cleansed, on the thumb of his right hand, and on the big toe of his right foot, on top of the blood of the guilt offering. ¹⁸ What is left of the oil in the priest's palm he is to put on the head of the one to be cleansed. In this way the priest will make atonement for him before the LORD. ¹⁹ The priest is to sacrifice the sin offering and make atonement for the one to be cleansed from his uncleanness. Afterward he will slaughter the burnt offering. ²⁰ The priest is to offer the burnt offering and the grain offering on the altar. The priest will make atonement for him, and he will be clean.

²¹ "But if he is poor and cannot afford these, he is to take one male lamb for a guilt offering to be presented in order to make atonement for him, along with two quarts^C of fine flour mixed with olive oil for a grain offering, one-third of a quart of olive oil, ²² and two turtledoves or two young pigeons, whatever he can afford, one to be a sin offering and the other a burnt offer-ing. ²³ On the eighth day he is to bring these things for his cleansing to the priest at the entrance to the tent of meeting before the LORD. ²⁴ The priest will take the male lamb for the guilt offering and the one-third quart of olive oil, and present them as a presentation offering before the LORD. ²⁵ After he slaughters the male lamb for the guilt offering, the priest is to take some of the blood of the guilt offering and put it on the right earlobe of the one to be cleansed, on the thumb of his right hand, and on the big toe of his right foot. ²⁶ Then the priest will pour some of the oil into his left palm. ²⁷ With his right finger the priest will sprinkle some of the oil in his left palm seven times before the LORD. ²⁸ The priest will also put some of the oil in his palm on the right earlobe of the one to be cleansed, on the thumb of his right hand, and on the big toe of his right foot, on the same place as the blood of the guilt offering. ²⁹ What is left of the oil in the priest's palm he is to put on the head of the one to be cleansed to make atonement for him before the LORD. ³⁰ He is to then sacrifice one type of what he can afford, either the turtledoves or young pigeons, ³¹ one as a sin offering and the other as a burnt offering,

---

^A 14:10 Lit *three-tenths*; probably three-tenths of an ephah   ^B 14:10 Lit *one log*, also in vv. 12,15,21,24   ^C 14:21 Lit *him, and one-tenth*; probably one-tenth of an ephah sacrificing what he can afford together with the grain offering. In this way the priest will make atonement before the LORD for the one to be cleansed. ³² This is the law for someone who has ᴬ a skin disease and cannot afford the cost of his cleansing."

CLEANSING OF CONTAMINATED OBJECTS

³³ The LORD spoke to Moses and Aaron: ³⁴ "When you enter the land of Canaan that I am giving you as a possession, and I place a mildew contamination in a house in the land you possess, ᴮ ³⁵ the owner of the house is to come and tell the priest: Something like mildew contamination has appeared ᶜ in my house. ³⁶ The priest must order them to clear the house before he enters to examine the contamination, so that nothing in the house becomes unclean. Afterward the priest will come to examine the house. ³⁷ He will examine it, and if the contamination in the walls of the house consists of green or red indentations ᴰ that appear to be beneath the surface of the wall, ³⁸ the priest is to go outside the house to its doorway and quarantine the house for seven days. ³⁹ The priest is to return on the seventh day and examine it. If the contamination has spread on the walls of the house, ⁴⁰ the priest must order that the stones with the contamination be pulled out and thrown into an unclean place outside the city. ⁴¹ He is to have the inside of the house completely scraped, and have the plaster ᴱ that is scraped off dumped in an unclean place outside the city. ⁴² Then they are to take different stones to replace the former ones and take additional plaster to replaster the house.

⁴³ "If the contamination reappears in the house after the stones have been pulled out, and after the house has been scraped and replastered, ⁴⁴ the priest is to come and examine it. If the contamination has spread in the house, it is harmful mildew; the house is unclean. ⁴⁵ It must be torn down with its stones, its beams, and all its plaster, and taken outside the city to an unclean place. ⁴⁶ Whoever enters the house during any of the days the priest quarantines it will be unclean until evening. ⁴⁷ Whoever lies down in the house is to wash his clothes, and whoever eats in it is to wash his clothes.

⁴⁸ "But when the priest comes and examines it, if the contamination has not spread in the house after it was replastered, he is to pronounce the house clean because the contamination has disappeared. ᶠ ⁴⁹ He is to take two birds, cedar wood, scarlet yarn, and hyssop to purify the house, ⁵⁰ and he is to slaughter one of the birds over a clay pot containing fresh water. ⁵¹ He will take the cedar wood, the hyssop, the scarlet yarn, and the live bird, dip them in the blood of the slaughtered bird and the fresh water, and sprinkle the house seven times. ⁵² He will purify the house with the blood of the bird, the fresh water, the live bird, the cedar wood, the hyssop, and the scarlet yarn. ⁵³ Then he is to release the live bird into the open countryside outside the city. In this way he will make atonement for the house, and it will be clean.

⁵⁴ "This is the law for any skin disease or mildew, for a scaly outbreak, ⁵⁵ for mildew in clothing or on a house, ⁵⁶ and for a swelling, scab, or spot, ⁵⁷ to determine when something is unclean or clean. This is the law regarding skin disease and mildew."

ᴬ14:32 Lit someone on whom there is   ᴮ14:34 Lit land of your possession
ᶜ14:35 Lit appeared to me   ᴰ14:37 Or eruptions; Hb obscure   ᴱ14:41 Lit dust, also in v. 42   ᶠ14:48 Lit healed

BODILY DISCHARGES

15 The Lord spoke to Moses and Aaron: ² "Speak to the Israelites and tell them: When any man has a discharge from his member, he is unclean. ³ This is uncleanness of his discharge: Whether his member secretes the discharge or retains it, he is unclean. All the days that his member secretes or retains anything because of his discharge,^A he is unclean. ⁴ Any bed the man with the discharge lies on will be unclean, and any furniture he sits on will be unclean. ⁵ Anyone who touches his bed is to wash his clothes and bathe with water, and he will remain unclean until evening. ⁶ Whoever sits on furniture that the man with the discharge was sitting on is to wash his clothes and bathe with water, and he will remain unclean until evening. ⁷ Whoever touches the body^B of the man with a discharge is to wash his clothes and bathe with water, and he will remain unclean until evening. ⁸ If the man with the discharge spits on anyone who is clean, he is to wash his clothes and bathe with water, and he will remain unclean until evening. ⁹ Any saddle the man with the discharge rides on will be unclean. ¹⁰ Whoever touches anything that was under him will be unclean until evening, and whoever carries such things is to wash his clothes and bathe with water, and he will remain unclean until evening. ¹¹ If the man with the discharge touches anyone without first rinsing his hands in water, the person who was touched is to wash his clothes and bathe with water, and he will remain unclean until evening. ¹² Any clay pot that the man with the discharge touches must be broken, while any wooden utensil is to be rinsed with water.

¹³ "When the man with the discharge has been cured of it, he is to count seven days for his cleansing, wash his clothes, and bathe his body in fresh water; he will be clean. ¹⁴ He must take two turtledoves or two young pigeons on the eighth day, come before the Lord at the entrance to the tent of meeting, and give them to the priest. ¹⁵ The priest is to sacrifice them, one as a sin offering and the other as a burnt offering. In this way the priest will make atonement for him before the Lord because of his discharge.

¹⁶ "When a man has an emission of semen, he is to bathe himself completely with water, and he will remain unclean until evening. ¹⁷ Any clothing or leather on which there is an emission of semen is to be washed with water, and it will remain unclean until evening. ¹⁸ If a man sleeps with a woman and has an emission of semen, both of them are to bathe with water, and they will remain unclean until evening.

¹⁹ "When a woman has a discharge, and it consists of blood from her body, she will be unclean because of her menstruation for seven days. Everyone who touches her will be unclean until evening. ²⁰ Anything she lies on during her menstruation will become unclean, and anything she sits on will become unclean. ²¹ Everyone who touches her bed is to wash his clothes and bathe with water, and he will remain unclean until evening. ²² Everyone who touches any furniture she was sitting on is to wash his clothes and bathe with water, and he will remain unclean until evening. ²³ If discharge is on the bed or the furniture she was sitting on, when he touches it he will be

---

^A 15:3 DSS, Sam, LXX; MT omits *he is unclean. All the days that his member secretes or retains anything because of his discharge*   ^B 15:7 Or *member, also* in v. 13

unclean until evening. ²⁴ If a man sleeps with her, and blood from her menstruation gets on him, he will be unclean for seven days, and every bed he lies on will become unclean.

²⁵ "When a woman has a discharge of her blood for many days, though it is not the time of her menstruation, or if she has a discharge beyond her period, she will be unclean all the days of her unclean discharge, as she is during the days of her menstruation. ²⁶ Any bed she lies on during the days of her discharge will be like her bed during menstrual impurity; any furniture she sits on will be unclean as in her menstrual period. ²⁷ Everyone who touches them will be unclean; he must wash his clothes and bathe with water, and he will remain unclean until evening. ²⁸ When she is cured of her discharge, she is to count seven days, and after that she will be clean. ²⁹ On the eighth day she must take two turtledoves or two young pigeons and bring them to the priest at the entrance to the tent of meeting. ³⁰ The priest is to sacrifice one as a sin offering and the other as a burnt offering. In this way the priest will make atonement for her before the Lord because of her unclean discharge.

³¹ "You must keep the Israelites from their uncleanness, so that they do not die by defiling my tabernacle that is among them. ³² This is the law for someone with a discharge: a man who has an emission of semen, becoming unclean by it; ³³ a woman who is in her menstrual period; anyone who has a discharge, whether male or female; and a man who sleeps with a woman who is unclean."

THE DAY OF ATONEMENT

16 The Lord spoke to Moses after the death of two of Aaron's sons when they approached the presence of^A the Lord and died. ² The Lord said to Moses: "Tell your brother Aaron that he may not come whenever he wants into the holy place behind the curtain in front of the mercy seat on the ark or else he will die, because I appear in the cloud above the mercy seat.

³ "Aaron is to enter the most holy place in this way: with a young bull for a sin offering and a ram for a burnt offering. ⁴ He is to wear a holy linen tunic, and linen undergarments are to be on his body. He is to tie a linen sash around him and wrap his head with a linen turban. These are holy garments; he must bathe his body with water before he wears them. ⁵ He is to take from the Israelite community two male goats for a sin offering and one ram for a burnt offering.

⁶ "Aaron will present the bull for his sin offering and make atonement for himself and his household. ⁷ Next he will take the two goats and place them before the Lord at the entrance to the tent of meeting. ⁸ After Aaron casts lots for the two goats, one lot for the Lord and the other for an uninhabitable place,^B,C ⁹ he is to present the goat chosen by lot for the Lord and sacrifice it as a sin offering. ¹⁰ But the goat chosen by lot for an uninhabitable place is to be presented alive before the Lord to make atonement with it by sending it into the wilderness for an uninhabitable place.

---

^A 16:1 LXX, Tg, Syr, Vg read *they brought strange fire before*; Nm 3:4
^B 16:8 Lit *for Azazel*, also in vv. 10 (2x),26   ^C 16:8 Perhaps a term that means "for the goat that departs," or "for removal," or "for a rough, difficult place," or "for a goat-demon"; Hb obscure, also in vv. 10,26

HITTING RESET ON OUR SIN

LEVITICUS 16; HEBREWS 10:1-18; HEBREWS 13:11-12; 1 PETER 2:24

Sometimes I wish for a reset button. A do-over. A fresh start, a clean slate. Like when the dirty laundry piles so high it has its own weather system. Or when you return to work from vacation to find 384 things requiring your immediate attention. Or when you've dug yourself a crater-sized hole with your words or actions and you're ashamed to ask for forgiveness for the umpteenth time.

Our messes can feel overwhelming.

I imagine that's how the Israelites felt. Their outright defiance outpaced the forgiveness that came through God's prescribed sin offerings at the tabernacle. After all, those sacrifices were never going to do the job (Heb 9:9). There was no way they could offer enough sacrifices to cover the laws they broke. Of course, God had a reason for every command He gave, but that must've been a small comfort to the people who were always breaking them.

They needed more than a sacrifice for every sin. They needed to be pardoned for the sinful nature that burned inside of each and every one of them. For this, as a precursor to the cross, the Lord gave them the Day of Atonement.

Once a year, the God who demanded their holiness would give them His. In so doing, He reminded the people of Israel that He alone was the giver of holiness. There was no way on earth they could reach perfection on their own (Heb 10:1-4).

That's the thing about our sin, isn't it? No matter how "good" we are, we can never be good enough. Not by a long shot. Just as our bills sometimes seem to outpace our income, our sin will always build faster than we can repent. The Day of Atonement was a taste of the reconciliation and forgiveness to come.

Some 1400 years after the first goat was led into the wilderness, symbolically carrying the sins of the Israelite people, Jesus "bore our sins in his body on the tree" (1Pt 2:24). **Christ became our ultimate, once-and-for-all reset.** His death and resurrection did what the atonement ceremony couldn't: He offered a permanent solution for our piles of sin. Because of His blood, shed for us, God sees believers as holy, as perfect (2Co 5:21).

If it weren't for Christ, we'd be playing eternal catch-up with our sin, striving for perfection we could never reach. After all, sin is a condition inside of us, not just a thing we do from time to time. Because Jesus became the atonement for our sins, we are granted God's holiness. Our slates—our very lives—have been wiped clean.

Thanks be to God.

¹¹ "When Aaron presents the bull for his sin offering and makes atonement for himself and his household, he will slaughter the bull for his sin offering. ¹² Then he is to take a firepan full of blazing coals from the altar before the LORD and two handfuls of finely ground fragrant incense, and bring them inside the curtain. ¹³ He is to put the incense on the fire before the LORD, so that the cloud of incense covers the mercy seat that is over the testimony, or else he will die. ¹⁴ He is to take some of the bull's blood and sprinkle it with his finger against the east side of the mercy seat; then he will sprinkle some of the blood with his finger before the mercy seat seven times.

¹⁵ "When he slaughters the male goat for the people's sin offering and brings its blood inside the curtain, he will do the same with its blood as he did with the bull's blood: He is to sprinkle it against the mercy seat and in front of it. ¹⁶ He will make atonement for the most holy place in this way for all their sins because of the Israelites' impurities and rebellious acts. He will do the same for the tent of meeting that remains among them, because it is surrounded by their impurities. ¹⁷ No one may be in the tent of meeting from the time he enters to make atonement in the most holy place until he leaves after he has made atonement for himself, his household, and the whole assembly of Israel. ¹⁸ Then he will go out to the altar that is before the LORD and make atonement for it. He is to take some of the bull's blood and some of the goat's blood and put it on the horns on all sides of the altar. ¹⁹ He is to sprinkle some of the blood on it with his finger seven times to cleanse and set it apart from the Israelites' impurities.

²⁰ "When he has finished making atonement for the most holy place, the tent of meeting, and the altar, he is to present the live male goat. ²¹ Aaron will lay both his hands on the head of the live goat and confess over it all the Israelites' iniquities and rebellious acts — all their sins. He is to put them on the goat's head and send it away into the wilderness by the man appointed for the task.ᴬ ²² The goat will carry all their iniquities into a desolate land, and the man will release it there.

²³ "Then Aaron is to enter the tent of meeting, take off the linen garments he wore when he entered the most holy place, and leave them there. ²⁴ He will bathe his body with water in a holy place and put on his clothes. Then he must go out and sacrifice his burnt offering and the people's burnt offering; he will make atonement for himself and for the people. ²⁵ He is to burn the fat of the sin offering on the altar. ²⁶ The man who released the goat for an uninhabitable place is to wash his clothes and bathe his body with water; afterward he may reenter the camp. ²⁷ The bull for the sin offering and the goat for the sin offering, whose blood was brought into the most holy place to make atonement, must be brought outside the camp and their hide, flesh, and waste burned. ²⁸ The one who burns them is to wash his clothes and bathe himself with water; afterward he may reenter the camp.

²⁹ "This is to be a permanent statute for you: In the seventh month, on the tenth day of the month you are to practice self-denial and do no work, both the native and the alien who resides among you. ³⁰ Atonement will be made for you on this day to cleanse you, and you will be clean from all your sins

ᴬ16:21 Lit *wilderness in the hand of a ready man*

before the LORD. [31] It is a Sabbath of complete rest for you, and you must practice self-denial; it is a permanent statute. [32] The priest who is anointed and ordained[A] to serve as high priest in place of his father will make atonement. He will put on the linen garments, the holy garments, [33] and make atonement for the most holy place. He will make atonement for the tent of meeting and the altar and will make atonement for the priests and all the people of the assembly. [34] This is to be a permanent statute for you, to make atonement for the Israelites once a year because of all their sins." And all this was done as the LORD commanded Moses.

FORBIDDEN SACRIFICES

17 The LORD spoke to Moses: [2] "Speak to Aaron, his sons, and all the Israelites and tell them: This is what the LORD has commanded: [3] Anyone from the house of Israel who slaughters an ox, sheep, or goat in the camp, or slaughters it outside the camp, [4] instead of bringing it to the entrance to the tent of meeting to present it as an offering to the LORD before his tabernacle — that person will be considered guilty.[B] He has shed blood and is to be cut off from his people. [5] This is so the Israelites will bring to the LORD the sacrifices they have been offering in the open country. They are to bring them to the priest at the entrance to the tent of meeting and offer them as fellowship sacrifices to the LORD. [6] The priest will then splatter the blood on the LORD's altar at the entrance to the tent of meeting and burn the fat as a pleasing aroma to the LORD. [7] They must no longer offer their sacrifices to the goat-demons that they have prostituted themselves with. This will be a permanent statute for them throughout their generations.

[8] "Say to them: Anyone from the house of Israel or from the aliens who reside among them who offers a burnt offering or a sacrifice [9] but does not bring it to the entrance to the tent of meeting to sacrifice it to the LORD, that person is to be cut off from his people.

EATING BLOOD AND CARCASSES PROHIBITED

[10] "Anyone from the house of Israel or from the aliens who reside among them who eats any blood, I will turn[C] against that person who eats blood and cut him off from his people. [11] For the life of a creature is in the blood, and I have appointed it to you to make atonement on the altar for[D] your lives, since it is the lifeblood that makes atonement. [12] Therefore I say to the Israelites: None of you and no alien who resides among you may eat blood.

[13] "Any Israelite or alien residing among them, who hunts down a wild animal or bird that may be eaten must drain its blood and cover it with dirt. [14] Since the life of every creature is its blood, I have told the Israelites: You are not to eat the blood of any creature, because the life of every creature is its blood; whoever eats it must be cut off.

[15] "Every person, whether the native or the resident alien, who eats an animal that died a natural death or was mauled by wild beasts is to wash his clothes and bathe with water, and he will remain unclean until evening; then he will be clean. [16] But if he does not wash his clothes and bathe himself, he will bear his iniquity."

[A]16:32 Lit and will fill his hand   [B]17:4 Lit tabernacle — blood will be charged against that person   [C]17:10 Lit will set my face   [D]17:11 Or to ransom

PROHIBITED PAGAN PRACTICES

18 The LORD spoke to Moses: [2] "Speak to the Israelites and tell them: I am the LORD your God. [3] Do not follow the practices of the land of Egypt, where you used to live, or follow the practices of the land of Canaan, where I am bringing you. You must not follow their customs. [4] You are to practice my ordinances and you are to keep my statutes by following them; I am the LORD your God. [5] Keep my statutes and ordinances; a person will live if he does them. I am the LORD.

[6] "You are not to come near any close relative[A] for sexual intercourse; I am the LORD. [7] You are not to violate the intimacy that belongs to your father and mother.[B] She is your mother; you must not have sexual intercourse with her. [8] You are not to have sex with your father's wife; she is your father's family. [9] You are not to have sexual intercourse with your sister, either your father's daughter or your mother's, whether born at home or born elsewhere. You are not to have sex with her. [10] You are not to have sexual intercourse with your son's daughter or your daughter's daughter, for they are your family.[C] [11] You are not to have sexual intercourse with your father's wife's daughter, who is adopted by[D] your father; she is your sister. [12] You are not to have sexual intercourse with your father's sister; she is your father's close relative. [13] You are not to have sexual intercourse with your mother's sister, for she is your mother's close relative. [14] You are not to violate the intimacy that belongs to[E] your father's brother by approaching his wife to have sexual intercourse; she is your aunt. [15] You are not to have sexual intercourse with your daughter-in-law. She is your son's wife; you are not to have sex with her. [16] You are not to have sexual intercourse with your brother's wife; she is your brother's family. [17] You are not to have sexual intercourse with a woman and her daughter. You are not to marry her son's daughter or her daughter's daughter and have sex with her. They are close relatives; it is depraved. [18] You are not to marry a woman as a rival to her sister and have sexual intercourse with her during her sister's lifetime.

[19] "You are not to approach a woman during her menstrual impurity to have sexual intercourse with her. [20] You are not to have sexual intercourse with[F] your neighbor's wife, defiling yourself with her.

[21] "You are not to sacrifice any of your children in the fire[G] to Molech. Do not profane the name of your God; I am the LORD. [22] You are not to sleep with a man as with a woman; it is detestable. [23] You are not to have sexual intercourse with[H] any animal, defiling yourself with it; a woman is not to present herself to an animal to mate with it; it is a perversion.

[24] "Do not defile yourselves by any of these practices, for the nations I am driving out before you have defiled themselves by all these things. [25] The land has become defiled, so I am punishing it for its iniquity, and the land will vomit out its inhabitants. [26] But you are to keep my statutes and ordinances. You must not commit any of these detestable acts — not

---

[A]18:6 Lit any flesh of his flesh   [B]18:7 Lit Do not uncover your father's nakedness and your mother's nakedness   [C]18:10 Lit because they are your nakedness   [D]18:11 Lit daughter, a relative of   [E]18:14 Lit Do not uncover the nakedness of   [F]18:20 Lit to give your emission of semen to   [G]18:21 Lit to make any of your children pass through the fire   [H]18:23 Lit to give your emission to the native or the alien who resides among you. ²⁷ For the people who were in the land prior to you have committed all these detestable acts, and the land has become defiled. ²⁸ If you defile the land, it will vomit you out as it has vomited out the nations that were before you. ²⁹ Any person who does any of these detestable practices is to be cut off from his people. ³⁰ You must keep my instruction to not do any of the detestable customs that were practiced before you, so that you do not defile yourselves by them; I am the LORD your God."

LAWS OF HOLINESS

19 The LORD spoke to Moses: ² "Speak to the entire Israelite community and tell them: Be holy because I, the LORD your God, am holy.

³ "Each of you is to respect his mother and father. You are to keep my Sabbaths; I am the LORD your God. ⁴ Do not turn to idols or make cast images of gods for yourselves; I am the LORD your God.

⁵ "When you offer a fellowship sacrifice to the LORD, sacrifice it so that you may be accepted. ⁶ It is to be eaten on the day you sacrifice it or on the next day, but what remains on the third day must be burned. ⁷ If any is eaten on the third day, it is a repulsive thing; it will not be accepted. ⁸ Anyone who eats it will bear his iniquity, for he has profaned what is holy to the LORD. That person is to be cut off from his people.

⁹ "When you reap the harvest of your land, you are not to reap to the very edge of your field or gather the gleanings of your harvest. ¹⁰ Do not strip your vineyard bare or gather its fallen grapes. Leave them for the poor and the resident alien; I am the LORD your God.

¹¹ "Do not steal. Do not act deceptively or lie to one another. ¹² Do not swear falsely by my name, profaning the name of your God; I am the LORD.

¹³ "Do not oppress your neighbor or rob him. The wages due a hired worker must not remain with you until morning. ¹⁴ Do not curse the deaf or put a stumbling block in front of the blind, but you are to fear your God; I am the LORD.

¹⁵ "Do not act unjustly when deciding a case. Do not be partial to the poor or give preference to the rich; judge your neighbor fairly. ¹⁶ Do not go about spreading slander among your people; do not jeopardize ᴬ your neighbor's life; I am the LORD.

¹⁷ "Do not harbor hatred against your brother. ᴮ Rebuke your neighbor directly, and you will not incur guilt because of him. ¹⁸ Do not take revenge or bear a grudge against members of your community, but love your neighbor as yourself; I am the LORD.

¹⁹ "You are to keep my statutes. Do not crossbreed two different kinds of your livestock, sow your fields with two kinds of seed, or put on a garment made of two kinds of material.

²⁰ "If a man has sexual intercourse with a woman who is a slave designated for another man, but she has not been redeemed or given her freedom, there must be punishment. ᶜ They are not to be put to death, because she had not been freed. ²¹ However, he must bring a ram as his guilt ᴰ offering to the LORD at the entrance to the tent of meeting. ²² The priest will

---

ᴬ19:16 Lit *not stand against*   ᴮ19:17 Or *your fellow Israelite*   ᶜ19:20 Or *compensation*   ᴰ19:21 Or *restitution* make atonement on his behalf before the LORD with the ram of the guilt offering for the sin he has committed, and he will be forgiven for the sin he committed.

²³ "When you come into the land and plant any kind of tree for food, you are to consider the fruit forbidden.ᴬ It will be forbidden to you for three years; it is not to be eaten. ²⁴ In the fourth year all its fruit is to be consecrated as a praise offering to the LORD. ²⁵ But in the fifth year you may eat its fruit. In this way its yield will increase for you; I am the LORD your God.

²⁶ "You are not to eat anything with blood in it.ᴮ You are not to practice divination or witchcraft. ²⁷ You are not to cut off the hair at the sides of your head or mar the edge of your beard. ²⁸ You are not to make gashes on your bodies for the dead or put tattoo marks on yourselves; I am the LORD.

²⁹ "Do not debaseᶜ your daughter by making her a prostitute, or the land will be prostituted and filled with depravity. ³⁰ Keep my Sabbaths and revere my sanctuary; I am the LORD.

³¹ "Do not turn to mediumsᴰ or consult spiritists,ᴱ or you will be defiled by them; I am the LORD your God.

³² "You are to rise in the presence of the elderly and honor the old. Fear your God; I am the LORD.

³³ "When an alien resides with you in your land, you must not oppress him. ³⁴ You will regard the alien who resides with you as the native-born among you. You are to love him as yourself, for you were aliens in the land of Egypt; I am the LORD your God.

³⁵ "Do not be unfair in measurements of length, weight, or volume. ³⁶ You are to have honest balances, honest weights, an honest dry measure,ᶠ and an honest liquid measure;ᴳ I am the LORD your God, who brought you out of the land of Egypt. ³⁷ Keep all my statutes and all my ordinances and do them; I am the LORD."

MOLECH WORSHIP AND SPIRITISM

20 The LORD spoke to Moses: ² "Say to the Israelites: Any Israelite or alien residing in Israel who gives any of his children to Molech must be put to death; the people of the country are to stone him. ³ I will turnᴴ against that man and cut him off from his people, because he gave his offspring to Molech, defiling my sanctuary and profaning my holy name. ⁴ But if the people of the country look the other way when that manᴵ gives any of his children to Molech, and do not put him to death, ⁵ then I will turn against that man and his family, and cut off from their people both him and all who followᴶ him in prostituting themselves with Molech.

⁶ "Whoever turns to mediumsᴰ or spiritistsᴱ and prostitutes himself with them, I will turn against that person and cut him off from his people. ⁷ Consecrate yourselves and be holy, for I am the LORD your God. ⁸ Keep my statutes and do them; I am the LORD who sets you apart.

ᴬ19:23 Lit *uncircumcised*   ᴮ19:26 Or *anything over its blood*   ᶜ19:29 Lit *profane*
ᴰ19:31; 20:6 Or *spirits of the dead*   ᴱ19:31; 20:6 Or *familiar spirits*   ᶠ19:36 Lit
honest ephah   ᴳ19:36 Lit *honest hin*   ᴴ20:3 Lit *will set my face, also in vv. 5,6*
ᴵ20:4 Lit *country ever close their eyes from that man when he*   ᴶ20:5 Lit *prostitute
themselves with*

YOU SHALL BE HOLY TO ME

LEVITICUS 19–20; EXODUS 25:8-9; 1 PETER 1:14-22; 1 JOHN 2:2

I've always liked rules. We firstborn high achievers are like that. We color inside the lines, go the speed limit, and wait to cross the street until a little light-up man tells us we can.

Whether you're a rebel who believes rules are made to be broken, or someone like me who loves to toe the line, your reaction to the book of Leviticus will likely be the same. In it, chapter after chapter, verse after verse, God outlines a long list of rules to the Israelites. Rules about what to eat. Rules about what to wear. Rules about relationships. Farming rules. Feasting rules. Fraternizing rules. So many rules!

We can get so caught up in what the rules are that we forget why they were given in the first place.

God Himself gave each instruction to Moses while the people of Israel camped at the base of Mount Sinai. It was necessary because the rules of engagement with God were about to change; no longer would God be speaking to one man from atop the mountain. He would dwell among the people (Ex 25:8-9). The rules were necessary because God is holy.

> *"You are to be holy to me because I, the LORD, am holy, and I have set you apart from the nations to be mine."*
>
> LEVITICUS 20:26

Isaiah 6:3 says God is perfectly and completely holy. He is holy, holy, holy. In His holiness, God cannot tolerate imperfection. In order for a holy God to dwell among the sinful people of Israel, they had to get rid of everything corrupt.

This is the reason Adam and Eve couldn't stay with God in the garden: He could not tolerate their sin. It's the reason Moses had to take off his sandals at the burning bush.

Our inability to keep the rules shines a spotlight on the holiness of God. Like the Israelites at the bottom of Mount Sinai, it's impossible for us to live lives pure enough to enter the presence of God. We desperately need Jesus' blood to cover our sins. The weight of all the rules we cannot follow is a beautiful reminder that His sacrifice exchanges our imperfection for His perfection (1Jn 2:2).

We're only counted as holy because Jesus made us so (1Pt 1:14-16).

FAMILY AND SEXUAL OFFENSES

⁹ "If anyone curses his father or mother, he must be put to death. He has cursed his father or mother; his death is his own fault.ᴬ

¹⁰ "If a man commits adultery with a married woman — if he commits adultery with his neighbor's wife — both the adulterer and the adulteress must be put to death. ¹¹ If a man sleeps with his father's wife, he has violated the intimacy that belongs to his father.ᴮ Both of them must be put to death; their death is their own fault.ᶜ ¹² If a man sleeps with his daughter-in-law, both of them must be put to death. They have acted perversely; their death is their own fault. ¹³ If a man sleeps with a man as with a woman, they have both committed a detestable act. They must be put to death; their death is their own fault. ¹⁴ If a man marriesᴰ a woman and her mother, it is depraved. Both he and they must be burned, so that there will be no depravity among you. ¹⁵ If a man has sexual intercourse withᴱ an animal, he must be put to death; you are also to kill the animal. ¹⁶ If a woman approaches any animal and mates with it, you are to kill the woman and the animal. They must be put to death; their death is their own fault. ¹⁷ If a man marries his sister, whether his father's daughter or his mother's daughter, and they have sexual relations,ᶠ it is a disgrace. They are to be cut off publicly from their people. He has had sexual intercourse with his sister; he will bear his iniquity. ¹⁸ If a man sleeps with a menstruating woman and has sexual intercourse with her, he has exposed the source of her flow, and she has uncovered the source of her blood. Both of them are to be cut off from their people. ¹⁹ You must not have sexual intercourse with your mother's sister or your father's sister, for it is exposing one's own blood relative; both people will bear their iniquity. ²⁰ If a man sleeps with his aunt, he has violated the intimacy that belongs to his uncle;ᴳ they will bear their guilt and die childless. ²¹ If a man marries his brother's wife, it is impurity. He has violated the intimacy that belongs to his brother;ᴴ they will be childless.

HOLINESS IN THE LAND

²² "You are to keep all my statutes and all my ordinances, and do them, so that the land where I am bringing you to live will not vomit you out. ²³ You must not follow the statutes of the nations I am driving out before you, for they did all these things, and I abhorred them. ²⁴ And I promised you: You will inherit their land, since I will give it to you to possess, a land flowing with milk and honey. I am the LORD your God who set you apart from the peoples. ²⁵ Therefore you are to distinguish the clean animal from the unclean one, and the unclean bird from the clean one. Do not become contaminated by any land animal, bird, or whatever crawls on the ground; I have set these apart as unclean for you. ²⁶ You are to be holy to me because I, the LORD, am holy, and I have set you apart from the nations to be mine.

²⁷ "A man or a woman who isᴵ a medium or a spiritist must be put to death. They are to be stoned; their death is their own fault."

ᴬ20:9 Lit *his blood on him*   ᴮ20:11 Lit *has uncovered his father's nakedness*
ᶜ20:11 Lit *their blood on them*, also in vv. 12,13,16,27   ᴰ20:14 Lit *takes*, also
in vv. 17,21   ᴱ20:15 Lit *man gives his emission to*   ᶠ20:17 Lit *and he sees her*
nakedness and she sees his nakedness   ᴳ20:20 Lit *has uncovered his uncle's*
nakedness   ᴴ20:21 Lit *has uncovered his brother's nakedness*   ᴵ20:27 Lit *is in them*

THE HOLINESS OF THE PRIESTS

21 The Lord said to Moses: "Speak to Aaron's sons, the priests, and tell them: A priest is not to make himself ceremonially unclean for a dead person among his relatives, ² except for his immediate family: his mother, father, son, daughter, or brother. ³ He may make himself unclean for his unmarried virgin sister in his immediate family. ⁴ He is not to make himself unclean for those related to him by marriage^A and so defile himself.

⁵ "Priests may not make bald spots on their heads, shave the edge of their beards, or make gashes on their bodies. ⁶ They are to be holy to their God and not profane the name of their God. For they present the fire offerings to the Lord, the food of their God, and they must be holy. ⁷ They are not to marry a woman defiled by prostitution.^B They are not to marry one divorced by her husband, for the priest is holy to his God. ⁸ You are to consider him holy since he presents the food of your God. He will be holy to you because I, the Lord who sets you apart, am holy. ⁹ If a priest's daughter defiles herself by promiscuity,^C she defiles her father; she must be burned to death.

¹⁰ "The priest who is highest among his brothers, who has had the anointing oil poured on his head and has been ordained^D to wear the clothes, must not dishevel his hair^E or tear his clothes. ¹¹ He must not go near any dead person or make himself unclean even for his father or mother. ¹² He must not leave the sanctuary or he will desecrate the sanctuary of his God, for the consecration of the anointing oil of his God is on him; I am the Lord.

¹³ "He is to marry a woman who is a virgin. ¹⁴ He is not to marry a widow, a divorced woman, or one defiled by prostitution. He is to marry a virgin from his own people, ¹⁵ so that he does not corrupt his bloodline^F among his people, for I am the Lord who sets him apart."

PHYSICAL DEFECTS AND PRIESTS

¹⁶ The Lord spoke to Moses: ¹⁷ "Tell Aaron: None of your descendants throughout your generations who has a physical defect is to come near to present the food of his God. ¹⁸ No man who has any defect is to come near: no man who is blind, lame, facially disfigured, or deformed; ¹⁹ no man who has a broken foot or hand, ²⁰ or who is a hunchback or a dwarf,^G or who has an eye defect, a festering rash, scabs, or a crushed testicle. ²¹ No descendant of the priest Aaron who has a defect is to come near to present the fire offerings to the Lord. He has a defect and is not to come near to present the food of his God. ²² He may eat the food of his God from what is especially holy as well as from what is holy. ²³ But because he has a defect, he must not go near the curtain or approach the altar. He is not to desecrate my holy places, for I am the Lord who sets them apart." ²⁴ Moses said this to Aaron and his sons and to all the Israelites.

PRIESTS AND THEIR FOOD

22 The Lord spoke to Moses: ² "Tell Aaron and his sons to deal respectfully with the holy offerings of the Israelites that they have consecrated to me, so they do not profane my holy name; I am the Lord. ³ Say to

---

^A 21:4 Lit *unclean a husband among his people*   ^B 21:7 Or *a prostitute, or a defiled woman*   ^C 21:9 Or *prostitution*   ^D 21:10 Lit *and one has filled his hand*   ^E 21:10 Or *not uncover his head*   ^F 21:15 Lit *not profane his seed*   ^G 21:20 Or *or emaciated* them: If any man from any of your descendants throughout your generations is in a state of uncleanness yet approaches the holy offerings that the Israelites consecrate to the LORD, that person will be cut off from my presence; I am the LORD. ⁴ No man of Aaron's descendants who has a skin disease^A or a discharge is to eat from the holy offerings until he is clean. Whoever touches anything made unclean by a dead person or by a man who has an emission of semen, ⁵ or whoever touches any swarming creature that makes him unclean or any person who makes him unclean — whatever his uncleanness — ⁶ the man who touches any of these will remain unclean until evening and is not to eat from the holy offerings unless he has bathed his body with water. ⁷ When the sun has set, he will become clean, and then he may eat from the holy offerings, for that is his food. ⁸ He must not eat an animal that died naturally or was mauled by wild beasts,^B making himself unclean by it; I am the LORD. ⁹ They must keep my instruction, or they will be guilty and die because they profane it; I am the LORD who sets them apart.

¹⁰ "No one outside a priest's family^C is to eat the holy offering. A foreigner staying with a priest or a hired worker is not to eat the holy offering. ¹¹ But if a priest purchases someone with his own silver, that person may eat it, and those born in his house may eat his food. ¹² If the priest's daughter is married to a man outside a priest's family,^D she is not to eat from the holy contributions.^E ¹³ But if the priest's daughter becomes widowed or divorced, has no children, and returns to her father's house as in her youth, she may share her father's food. But no outsider may share it. ¹⁴ If anyone eats a holy offering in error, he is to add a fifth to its value and give the holy offering to the priest. ¹⁵ The priests must not profane the holy offerings the Israelites give to the LORD ¹⁶ by letting the people eat their holy offerings and having them bear the penalty of restitution. For I am the LORD who sets them apart."

ACCEPTABLE SACRIFICES

¹⁷ The LORD spoke to Moses: ¹⁸ "Speak to Aaron, his sons, and all the Israelites and tell them: Any man of the house of Israel or of the resident aliens in Israel who presents his offering — whether they present payment of vows or freewill gifts to the LORD as burnt offerings — ¹⁹ must offer an unblemished male from the cattle, sheep, or goats in order for you to be accepted. ²⁰ You are not to present anything that has a defect, because it will not be accepted on your behalf.

²¹ "When a man presents a fellowship sacrifice to the LORD to fulfill a vow or as a freewill offering from the herd or flock, it has to be unblemished to be acceptable; there must be no defect in it. ²² You are not to present any animal to the LORD that is blind, injured, maimed, or has a running sore, festering rash, or scabs; you may not put any of them on the altar as a fire offering to the LORD. ²³ You may sacrifice as a freewill offering any animal from the herd or flock that has an elongated or stunted limb, but it is not acceptable as a vow offering. ²⁴ You are not to present to the LORD anything that has bruised, crushed, torn, or severed testicles; you must not sacrifice them in

---

^A 22:4 Or has leprosy or scale disease   ^B 22:8 Lit eat a carcass or a mauled beast   ^C 22:10 Lit "No stranger   ^D 22:12 Lit to a stranger   ^E 22:12 Lit the contribution of holy offerings your land. ²⁵ Neither you nor^A a foreigner are to present food to your God from any of these animals. They will not be accepted for you because they are deformed and have a defect."

²⁶ The LORD spoke to Moses: ²⁷ "When an ox, sheep, or goat is born, it is to remain with^B its mother for seven days; from the eighth day on, it will be acceptable as an offering, a fire offering to the LORD. ²⁸ But you are not to slaughter an animal from the herd or flock on the same day as its young. ²⁹ When you sacrifice a thank offering to the LORD, sacrifice it so that you may be accepted. ³⁰ It is to be eaten on the same day. Do not let any of it remain until morning; I am the LORD.

³¹ "You are to keep my commands and do them; I am the LORD. ³² You must not profane my holy name; I must be treated as holy among the Israelites. I am the LORD who sets you apart, ³³ the one who brought you out of the land of Egypt to be your God; I am the LORD."

HOLY DAYS

23 The LORD spoke to Moses: ² "Speak to the Israelites and tell them: These are my appointed times, the times of the LORD that you will proclaim as sacred assemblies.

³ "Work may be done for six days, but on the seventh day there is to be a Sabbath of complete rest, a sacred assembly. You are not to do any work; it is a Sabbath to the LORD wherever you live.

⁴ "These are the LORD's appointed times, the sacred assemblies you are to proclaim at their appointed times. ⁵ The Passover to the LORD comes in the first month, at twilight on the fourteenth day of the month. ⁶ The Festival of Unleavened Bread to the LORD is on the fifteenth day of the same month. For seven days you must eat unleavened bread. ⁷ On the first day you are to hold a sacred assembly; you are not to do any daily work. ⁸ You are to present a fire offering to the LORD for seven days. On the seventh day there will be a sacred assembly; do not do any daily work."

⁹ The LORD spoke to Moses: ¹⁰ "Speak to the Israelites and tell them: When you enter the land I am giving you and reap its harvest,^C you are to bring the first sheaf of your harvest to the priest. ¹¹ He will present the sheaf before the LORD so that you may be accepted; the priest is to present it on the day after the Sabbath. ¹² On the day you present the sheaf, you are to offer a year-old male lamb^D without blemish as a burnt offering to the LORD. ¹³ Its grain offering is to be four quarts^E of fine flour mixed with oil as a fire offering to the LORD, a pleasing aroma, and its drink offering will be one quart^F of wine. ¹⁴ You must not eat bread, roasted grain, or any new grain^G until this very day, and until you have brought the offering to your God. This is to be a permanent statute throughout your generations wherever you live.

¹⁵ "You are to count seven^H complete weeks^I starting from the day after the Sabbath, the day you brought the sheaf of the presentation offering. ¹⁶ You are to count fifty days until the day after the seventh Sabbath and then present an offering of new grain to the LORD. ¹⁷ Bring two loaves of bread from

---

^A22:25 Lit *nor from the hand of* ^B22:27 Lit *under* ^C23:10 = the barley harvest
^D23:12 Or *a male lamb in its first year* ^E23:13 Lit *two-tenths of an ephah*, also
in v. 17 ^F23:13 Lit *one-fourth of a hin* ^G23:14 Grain or bread from the new
harvest ^H23:15 Lit *count; they will be seven* ^I23:15 Or *Sabbaths*

your settlements as a presentation offering, each of them made from four quarts of fine flour, baked with yeast, as firstfruits to the Lord. [18] You are to present with the bread seven unblemished male lambs a year old, one young bull, and two rams. They will be a burnt offering to the Lord, with their grain offerings and drink offerings, a fire offering of a pleasing aroma to the Lord. [19] You are also to prepare one male goat as a sin offering, and two male lambs a year old as a fellowship sacrifice. [20] The priest will present the lambs with the bread of firstfruits as a presentation offering before the Lord; the bread and the two lambs will be holy to the Lord for the priest. [21] On that same day you are to make a proclamation and hold a sacred assembly. You are not to do any daily work. This is to be a permanent statute wherever you live throughout your generations. [22] When you reap the harvest of your land, you are not to reap all the way to the edge of your field or gather the gleanings of your harvest. Leave them for the poor and the resident alien; I am the Lord your God."

[23] The Lord spoke to Moses: [24] "Tell the Israelites: In the seventh month, on the first day of the month, you are to have a day of complete rest, commemoration, and trumpet blasts — a sacred assembly. [25] You must not do any daily work, but you must present a fire offering to the Lord."

[26] The Lord again spoke to Moses: [27] "The tenth day of this seventh month is the Day of Atonement. You are to hold a sacred assembly and practice self-denial; you are to present a fire offering to the Lord. [28] On this particular day you are not to do any work, for it is a Day of Atonement to make atonement for yourselves before the Lord your God. [29] If any person does not practice self-denial on this particular day, he is to be cut off from his people. [30] I will destroy among his people anyone who does any work on this same day. [31] You are not to do any work. This is a permanent statute throughout your generations wherever you live. [32] It will be a Sabbath of complete rest for you, and you must practice self-denial. You are to observe your Sabbath from the evening of the ninth day of the month until the following evening."

[33] The Lord spoke to Moses: [34] "Tell the Israelites: The Festival of Shelters [A] to the Lord begins on the fifteenth day of this seventh month and continues for seven days. [35] There is to be a sacred assembly on the first day; you are not to do any daily work. [36] You are to present a fire offering to the Lord for seven days. On the eighth day you are to hold a sacred assembly and present a fire offering to the Lord. It is a solemn gathering; you are not to do any daily work.

[37] "These are the Lord's appointed times that you are to proclaim as sacred assemblies for presenting fire offerings to the Lord, burnt offerings and grain offerings, sacrifices and drink offerings, each on its designated day. [38] These are in addition to the offerings for the Lord's Sabbaths, your gifts, all your vow offerings, and all your freewill offerings that you give to the Lord.

[39] "You are to celebrate the Lord's festival on the fifteenth day of the seventh month for seven days after you have gathered the produce of the land. There will be complete rest on the first day and complete rest on the eighth day. [40] On the first day you are to take the product of majestic trees — palm fronds, boughs of leafy trees, and willows of the brook — and rejoice before the Lord your God for seven days. [41] You are to celebrate it as a festival to the

[A] 23:34 Or *Tabernacles*, or *Booths*

LORD seven days each year. This is a permanent statute for you throughout your generations; celebrate it in the seventh month. ⁴² You are to live in shelters for seven days. All the native-born of Israel must live in shelters, ⁴³ so that your generations may know that I made the Israelites live in shelters when I brought them out of the land of Egypt; I am the LORD your God." ⁴⁴ So Moses declared the LORD's appointed times to the Israelites.

TABERNACLE OIL AND BREAD

24 The LORD spoke to Moses: ² "Command the Israelites to bring you pure oil from crushed olives for the light, in order to keep the lamp burning regularly. ³ Aaron is to tend it continually from evening until morning before the LORD outside the curtain of the testimony in the tent of meeting. This is a permanent statute throughout your generations. ⁴ He must continually tend the lamps on the pure gold lampstand in the LORD's presence.

⁵ "Take fine flour and bake it into twelve loaves; each loaf is to be made with four quarts.ᴬ ⁶ Arrange them in two rows, six to a row, on the pure gold table before the LORD. ⁷ Place pure frankincense near each row, so that it may serve as a memorial portion for the bread and a fire offering to the LORD. ⁸ The bread is to be set out before the LORD every Sabbath day as a permanent covenant obligation on the part of the Israelites. ⁹ It belongs to Aaron and his sons, who are to eat it in a holy place, for it is the holiest portion for him from the fire offerings to the LORD; this is a permanent rule."

A CASE OF BLASPHEMY

¹⁰ Now the son of an Israelite mother and an Egyptian father wasᴮ among the Israelites. A fight broke out in the camp between the Israelite woman's son and an Israelite man. ¹¹ Her son cursed and blasphemed the Name, and they brought him to Moses. (His mother's name was Shelomith, a daughter of Dibri of the tribe of Dan.) ¹² They put him in custody until the LORD's decision could be made clear to them.

¹³ Then the LORD spoke to Moses: ¹⁴ "Bring the one who has cursed to the outside of the camp and have all who heard him lay their hands on his head; then have the whole community stone him. ¹⁵ And tell the Israelites: If anyone curses his God, he will bear the consequences of his sin. ¹⁶ Whoever blasphemes the name of the LORD must be put to death; the whole community is to stone him. If he blasphemes the Name, he is to be put to death, whether the resident alien or the native.

¹⁷ "If a man kills anyone, he must be put to death. ¹⁸ Whoever kills an animal is to make restitution for it, life for life. ¹⁹ If any man inflicts a permanent injury on his neighbor, whatever he has done is to be done to him: ²⁰ fracture for fracture, eye for eye, tooth for tooth. Whatever injury he inflicted on the person, the same is to be inflicted on him. ²¹ Whoever kills an animal is to make restitution for it, but whoever kills a person is to be put to death. ²² You are to have the same law for the resident alien and the native, because I am the LORD your God."

²³ After Moses spoke to the Israelites, they brought the one who had cursed to the outside of the camp and stoned him. So the Israelites did as the LORD had commanded Moses.

ᴬ24:5 Lit *two-tenths of an ephah*   ᴮ24:10 Lit *went out*

SABBATH YEARS AND JUBILEE

25 The Lord spoke to Moses on Mount Sinai: ² "Speak to the Israelites and tell them: When you enter the land I am giving you, the land will observe a Sabbath to the Lord. ³ You may sow your field for six years, and you may prune your vineyard and gather its produce for six years. ⁴ But there will be a Sabbath of complete rest for the land in the seventh year, a Sabbath to the Lord: you are not to sow your field or prune your vineyard. ⁵ You are not to reap what grows by itself from your crop, or harvest the grapes of your untended vines. It is to be a year of complete rest for the land. ⁶ Whatever the land produces during the Sabbath year can be food for you — for yourself, your male or female slave, and the hired worker or alien who resides with you. ⁷ All of its growth may serve as food for your livestock and the wild animals in your land.

⁸ "You are to count seven sabbatical years, seven times seven years, so that the time period of the seven sabbatical years amounts to forty-nine. ⁹ Then you are to sound a trumpet loudly in the seventh month, on the tenth day of the month; you will sound it throughout your land on the Day of Atonement. ¹⁰ You are to consecrate the fiftieth year and proclaim freedom in the land for all its inhabitants. It will be your Jubilee, when each of you is to return to his property and each of you to his clan. ¹¹ The fiftieth year will be your Jubilee; you are not to sow, reap what grows by itself, or harvest its untended vines. ¹² It is to be holy to you because it is the Jubilee; you may only eat its produce directly from the field.

¹³ "In this Year of Jubilee, each of you will return to his property. ¹⁴ If you make a sale to your neighbor or a purchase from him, do not cheat one another. ¹⁵ You are to make the purchase from your neighbor based on the number of years since the last Jubilee. He is to sell to you based on the number of remaining harvest years. ¹⁶ You are to increase its price in proportion to a greater amount of years, and decrease its price in proportion to a lesser amount of years, because what he is selling to you is a number of harvests. ¹⁷ You are not to cheat one another, but fear your God, for I am the Lord your God.

¹⁸ "You are to keep my statutes and ordinances and carefully observe them, so that you may live securely in the land. ¹⁹ Then the land will yield its fruit, so that you can eat, be satisfied, and live securely in the land. ²⁰ If you wonder: 'What will we eat in the seventh year if we don't sow or gather our produce?' ²¹ I will appoint my blessing for you in the sixth year, so that it will produce a crop sufficient for three years. ²² When you sow in the eighth year, you will be eating from the previous harvest. You will be eating this until the ninth year when its harvest comes in.

²³ "The land is not to be permanently sold because it is mine, and you are only aliens and temporary residents on my land.ᴬ ²⁴ You are to allow the redemption of any land you occupy. ²⁵ If your brother becomes destitute and sells part of his property, his nearest relative may come and redeem what his brother has sold. ²⁶ If a man has no family redeemer, but he prospersᴮ and obtains enough to redeem his land, ²⁷ he may calculate the years since its sale, repay the balance to the man he sold it to, and return to his property. ²⁸ But if he cannot obtain enough to repay him, what he sold will remain in

ᴬ25:23 Lit *residents with me*   ᴮ25:26 Lit *but his hand reaches* the possession of its purchaser until the Year of Jubilee. It is to be released at the Jubilee, so that he may return to his property.

²⁹ "If a man sells a residence in a walled city, his right of redemption will last until a year has passed after its sale; his right of redemption will last a year. ³⁰ If it is not redeemed by the end of a full year, then the house in the walled city is permanently transferred to its purchaser throughout his generations. It is not to be released on the Jubilee. ³¹ But houses in settlements that have no walls around them are to be classified as open fields. The right to redeem such houses stays in effect, and they are to be released at the Jubilee.

³² "Concerning the Levitical cities, the Levites always have the right to redeem houses in the cities they possess. ³³ Whatever property one of the Levites can redeem^ — a house sold in a city they possess — is to be released at the Jubilee, because the houses in the Levitical cities are their possession among the Israelites. ³⁴ The open pastureland around their cities may not be sold, for it is their permanent possession.

³⁵ "If your brother becomes destitute and cannot sustain himself among ᴮ you, you are to support him as an alien or temporary resident, so that he can continue to live among you. ³⁶ Do not profit or take interest from him, but fear your God and let your brother live among you. ³⁷ You are not to lend him your silver with interest or sell him your food for profit. ³⁸ I am the Lᴏʀᴅ your God, who brought you out of the land of Egypt to give you the land of Canaan and to be your God.

³⁹ "If your brother among you becomes destitute and sells himself to you, you must not force him to do slave labor. ⁴⁰ Let him stay with you as a hired worker or temporary resident; he may work for you until the Year of Jubilee. ⁴¹ Then he and his children are to be released from you, and he may return to his clan and his ancestral property. ⁴² They are not to be sold as slaves, ᶜ because they are my servants ᴰ that I brought out of the land of Egypt. ⁴³ You are not to rule over them harshly but fear your God. ⁴⁴ Your male and female slaves are to be from the nations around you; you may purchase male and female slaves. ⁴⁵ You may also purchase them from the aliens residing with you, or from their families living among you — those born in your land. These may become your property. ⁴⁶ You may leave them to your sons after you to inherit as property; you can make them slaves for life. But concerning your brothers, the Israelites, you must not rule over one another harshly.

⁴⁷ "If an alien or temporary resident living among you prospers, but your brother living near him becomes destitute and sells himself to the alien living among you, or to a member of the resident alien's clan, ⁴⁸ he has the right of redemption after he has been sold. One of his brothers may redeem him. ⁴⁹ His uncle or cousin may redeem him, or any of his close relatives from his clan may redeem him. If he prospers, he may redeem himself. ⁵⁰ The one who purchased him is to calculate the time from the year he sold himself to him until the Year of Jubilee. The price of his sale will be determined by the number of years. It will be set for him like the daily wages of a hired worker. ⁵¹ If many years are still left, he must pay his redemption

---

^25:33 Hb obscure   ᴮ25:35 Lit and his hand falters with   ᶜ25:42 Lit sold with a sale of a slave   ᴰ25:42 Or slaves price in proportion to them based on his purchase price. ⁵² If only a few years remain until the Year of Jubilee, he will calculate and pay the price of his redemption in proportion to his remaining years. ⁵³ He will stay with him like a man hired year by year. A resident alien is not to rule over him harshly in your sight. ⁵⁴ If he is not redeemed in any of these ways, he and his children are to be released at the Year of Jubilee. ⁵⁵ For the Israelites are my servants. They are my servants that I brought out of the land of Egypt; I am the Lord your God.

COVENANT BLESSINGS AND DISCIPLINE

26 "Do not make idols for yourselves, set up a carved image or sacred pillar for yourselves, or place a sculpted stone in your land to bow down to it, for I am the Lord your God. ² Keep my Sabbaths and revere my sanctuary; I am the Lord.

³ "If you follow my statutes and faithfully observe my commands, ⁴ I will give you rain at the right time, and the land will yield its produce, and the trees of the field will bear their fruit. ⁵ Your threshing will continue until grape harvest, and the grape harvest will continue until sowing time; you will have plenty of food to eat and live securely in your land. ⁶ I will give peace to the land, and you will lie down with nothing to frighten you. I will remove dangerous animals from the land, and no sword will pass through your land. ⁷ You will pursue your enemies, and they will fall before you by the sword. ⁸ Five of you will pursue a hundred, and a hundred of you will pursue ten thousand; your enemies will fall before you by the sword.

⁹ "I will turn to you, make you fruitful and multiply you, and confirm my covenant with you. ¹⁰ You will eat the old grain of the previous year and will clear out the old to make room for the new. ¹¹ I will place my residence^A among you, and I will not reject you. ¹² I will walk among you and be your God, and you will be my people. ¹³ I am the Lord your God, who brought you out of the land of Egypt, so that you would no longer be their slaves. I broke the bars of your yoke and enabled you to live in freedom.^B

¹⁴ "But if you do not obey me and observe all these commands — ¹⁵ if you reject my statutes and despise my ordinances, and do not observe all my commands — and break my covenant, ¹⁶ then I will do this to you: I will bring terror on you — wasting disease and fever that will cause your eyes to fail and your life to ebb away. You will sow your seed in vain because your enemies will eat it. ¹⁷ I will turn^C against you, so that you will be defeated by your enemies. Those who hate you will rule over you, and you will flee even though no one is pursuing you.

¹⁸ "But if after these things you will not obey me, I will proceed to discipline you seven times for your sins. ¹⁹ I will break down your strong pride. I will make your sky like iron and your land like bronze, ²⁰ and your strength will be used up for nothing. Your land will not yield its produce, and the trees of the land will not bear their fruit.

²¹ "If you act with hostility toward me and are unwilling to obey me, I will multiply your plagues seven times for your sins. ²² I will send wild animals against you that will deprive you of your children, ravage your livestock, and reduce your numbers until your roads are deserted.

^A26:11 Or *tabernacle*   ^B26:13 Lit *to walk uprightly*   ^C26:17 Lit *will set my face*

²³ "If in spite of these things you do not accept my discipline, but act with hostility toward me, ²⁴ then I will act with hostility toward you; I also will strike you seven times for your sins. ²⁵ I will bring a sword against you to execute the vengeance of the covenant. Though you withdraw into your cities, I will send a pestilence among you, and you will be delivered into enemy hands. ²⁶ When I cut off your supply of bread, ten women will bake your bread in a single oven and ration out your bread by weight, so that you will eat but not be satisfied.

²⁷ "And if in spite of this you do not obey me but act with hostility toward me, ²⁸ I will act with furious hostility toward you; I will also discipline you seven times for your sins. ²⁹ You will eat the flesh of your sons; you will eat the flesh of your daughters. ³⁰ I will destroy your high places, cut down your shrines,ᴬ and heap your lifeless bodies on the lifeless bodies of your idols; I will reject you. ³¹ I will reduce your cities to ruins and devastate your sanctuaries. I will not smell the pleasing aroma of your sacrifices. ³² I also will devastate the land, so that your enemies who come to live there will be appalled by it. ³³ But I will scatter you among the nations, and I will draw a sword to chase after you. So your land will become desolate, and your cities will become ruins.

³⁴ "Then the land will make up for its Sabbath years during the time it lies desolate, while you are in the land of your enemies. At that time the land will rest and make up for its Sabbaths. ³⁵ As long as it lies desolate, it will have the rest it did not have during your Sabbaths when you lived there.

³⁶ "I will put anxiety in the hearts of those of you who survive in the lands of their enemies. The sound of a wind-driven leaf will put them to flight, and they will flee as one flees from a sword, and fall though no one is pursuing them. ³⁷ They will stumble over one another as if fleeing from a sword though no one is pursuing them. You will not be able to stand against your enemies. ³⁸ You will perish among the nations; the land of your enemies will devour you. ³⁹ Thoseᴮ who survive in the lands of your enemies will waste away because of their iniquity; they will also waste away because of their fathers' iniquities along with theirs.

⁴⁰ "But when they confess their iniquity and the iniquity of their fathers — their unfaithfulness that they practiced against me, and how they acted with hostility toward me, ⁴¹ and I acted with hostility toward them and brought them into the land of their enemies — and when their uncircumcised hearts are humbled and they make amends for their iniquity, ⁴² then I will remember my covenant with Jacob. I will also remember my covenant with Isaac and my covenant with Abraham, and I will remember the land. ⁴³ For the land abandoned by them will make up for its Sabbaths by lying desolate without the people, while they make amends for their iniquity, because they rejected my ordinances and abhorred my statutes. ⁴⁴ Yet in spite of this, while they are in the land of their enemies, I will not reject or abhor them so as to destroy them and break my covenant with them, since I am the Lord their God. ⁴⁵ For their sake I will remember the covenant with their fathers, whom I brought out of the land of Egypt in the sight of the nations to be their God; I am the Lord."

⁴⁶ These are the statutes, ordinances, and laws the Lord established between himself and the Israelites through Moses on Mount Sinai.

ᴬ 26:30 Or incense altars   ᴮ 26:39 Lit Those of you

FUNDING THE SANCTUARY

27 The LORD spoke to Moses: [2] "Speak to the Israelites and tell them: When someone makes a special vow to the LORD that involves the assessment of people, [3] if the assessment concerns a male from twenty to sixty years old, your assessment is fifty silver shekels measured by the standard sanctuary shekel. [4] If the person is a female, your assessment is thirty shekels. [5] If the person is from five to twenty years old, your assessment for a male is twenty shekels and for a female ten shekels. [6] If the person is from one month to five years old, your assessment for a male is five silver shekels, and for a female your assessment is three shekels of silver. [7] If the person is sixty years or more, your assessment is fifteen shekels for a male and ten shekels for a female. [8] But if one is too poor to pay the assessment, he is to present the person before the priest and the priest will set a value for him. The priest will set a value for him according to what the one making the vow can afford.

[9] "If the vow involves one of the animals that may be brought as an offering to the LORD, any of these he gives to the LORD will be holy. [10] He may not replace it or make a substitution for it, either good for bad, or bad for good. But if he does substitute one animal for another, both that animal and its substitute will be holy.

[11] "If the vow involves any of the unclean animals that may not be brought as an offering to the LORD, the animal must be presented before the priest. [12] The priest will set its value, whether high or low; the price will be set as the priest makes the assessment for you. [13] If the one who brought it decides to redeem it, he must add a fifth to the[A] assessed value.

[14] "When a man consecrates his house as holy to the LORD, the priest will assess its value, whether high or low. The price will stand just as the priest assesses it. [15] But if the one who consecrated his house redeems it, he must add a fifth to the assessed value, and it will be his.

[16] "If a man consecrates to the LORD any part of a field that he possesses, your assessment of value will be proportional to the seed needed to sow it, at the rate of fifty silver shekels for every five bushels[B] of barley seed.[C] [17] If he consecrates his field during the Year of Jubilee, the price will stand according to your assessment. [18] But if he consecrates his field after the Jubilee, the priest will calculate the price for him in proportion to the years left until the next Year of Jubilee, so that your assessment will be reduced. [19] If the one who consecrated the field decides to redeem it, he must add a fifth to the assessed value, and the field will transfer back to him. [20] But if he does not redeem the field or if he has sold it to another man, it is no longer redeemable. [21] When the field is released in the Jubilee, it will be holy to the LORD like a field permanently set apart; it becomes the priest's property.

[22] "If a person consecrates to the LORD a field he has purchased that is not part of his inherited landholding, [23] then the priest will calculate for him the amount of the assessment up to the Year of Jubilee, and the person will pay the assessed value on that day as a holy offering to the LORD. [24] In the Year of Jubilee the field will return to the one he bought it from, the original owner.

[A]27:13 Lit *your*, also in vv. 15,19,23   [B]27:16 Lit *for a homer*   [C]27:16 Or *grain*

²⁵ All your assessed values will be measured by the standard sanctuary shekel,ᴬ twenty gerahs to the shekel.

²⁶ "But no one can consecrate a firstborn of the livestock, whether an animal from the herd or flock, to the LORD, because a firstborn already belongs to the LORD. ²⁷ If it is one of the unclean livestock, it can be ransomed according to your assessment by adding a fifth of its value to it. If it is not redeemed, it can be sold according to your assessment.

²⁸ "Nothing that a man permanently sets apart to the LORD from all he owns, whether a person, an animal, or his inherited landholding, can be sold or redeemed; everything set apart is especially holy to the LORD. ²⁹ No person who has been set apart for destruction is to be ransomed; he must be put to death.

³⁰ "Every tenth of the land's produce, grain from the soil or fruit from the trees, belongs to the LORD; it is holy to the LORD. ³¹ If a man decides to redeem any part of this tenth, he must add a fifth to its value. ³² Every tenth animal from the herd or flock, which passes under the shepherd's rod, will be holy to the LORD. ³³ He is not to inspect whether it is good or bad, and he is not to make a substitution for it. But if he does make a substitution, both the animal and its substitute will be holy; they cannot be redeemed."

³⁴ These are the commands the LORD gave Moses for the Israelites on Mount Sinai.

ᴬ27:25 A *shekel* is about two-fifths of an ounce of silver

THE Lord IS Slow TO Anger AND Abounding IN Faithful Love

numbers

The Lord is slow to anger and abounding in faithful love, forgiving iniquity and rebellion. But he will not leave the guilty unpunished, bringing the consequences of the fathers' iniquity on the children to the third and fourth generation. **14:18**

ON THE TIMELINE Like the rest of the Pentateuch, the writing of Numbers is traditionally attributed to Moses. Moses likely wrote this book before the nation of Israel entered Canaan, about 1406 BC. Numbers continues the historical narrative begun in Exodus, picking up one month after the close of Exodus (Ex 40:2; Nm 1:1), which is about one year after the Israelites' departure from Egypt (1446 BC). Numbers covers the remaining thirty-nine years of the Israelites' stay in the wilderness, from Sinai to Kadesh, and finally to the plains on the eastern side of the Jordan River.

A LITTLE BACKGROUND The English title "Numbers" derives from the Septuagint name *Arithmoi*, based on the two military censuses in chapters 1 and 26. The Hebrew title, *Bemidbar*, "In the Wilderness," describes the geographical setting of much of the book—from the wilderness of Sinai to the arid plains of Moab, located east of the Dead Sea.

MESSAGE & PURPOSE Because of their rebellion, the first generation of Israelites was not permitted to enter the promised land, the land God had promised to Abraham and his descendants. However, God kept His promises to Abraham through the next generation of Israelites. The book of Numbers was written to the generation of Israelites entering the promised land.

Along with the other four books of the Pentateuch, Numbers provided reminders for Israel of all God had brought them through in the wilderness, as well as reminders of the consequences of disobedience. Numbers was written to teach the new generation of Israel that God is holy and pure and He required holiness and purity from those who claim Him as their God. The principal character in the book of Numbers is the Lord, the God of Israel. He is sovereign over the affairs of all people from all nations.

GIVE THANKS FOR THE BOOK OF NUMBERS:

By showing us how God responded to the unbelief of the Israelites, the book of Numbers emphasizes the importance of obedience in the life of a Christian. Numbers demonstrates that there are consequences for our disobedience, while also reminding us that God's grace remains and His redemptive plan will not be stopped.

SCOUTING CANAAN

BOUNDARY OF CANAAN

CONJECTURED BOUNDARY OF CANAAN

SPIES' ROUTE

CONTINUED ROUTE TO BORDER ▪▪▪

LEBO-HAMATH

DAMASCUS

LAISH

HAZOR

MEGIDDO

SHECHEM

JERUSALEM

HEBRON

ARAD

KADESH

MEDITERRANEAN SEA

JORDAN RIVER

DEAD SEA

WILDERNESS OF ZIN

EDOM

Week 1

Week 2

Week 3

Week 4

READ AND UNDERSTAND NUMBERS

The Bible is a complete work in which many stories combine to tell one story. As you read the book of Numbers, consider reading the additional passages to discover how the whole of Scripture works together.

THE CENSUS OF ISRAEL

1 The LORD spoke to Moses in the tent of meeting in the Wilderness of Sinai, on the first day of the second month of the second year after Israel's departure from the land of Egypt: ² "Take a census of the entire Israelite community by their clans and their fathers' families,^A counting the names of every male one by one. ³ You and Aaron are to register those who are twenty years old or more by their military divisions — everyone who can serve in Israel's army.^B ⁴ A man from each tribe is to be with you, each one the head of his ancestral family.^C ⁵ These are the names of the men who are to assist you:

Elizur son of Shedeur from Reuben;
⁶ Shelumiel son of Zurishaddai from Simeon;
⁷ Nahshon son of Amminadab from Judah;
⁸ Nethanel son of Zuar from Issachar;
⁹ Eliab son of Helon from Zebulun;
¹⁰ from the sons of Joseph:
Elishama son of Ammihud from Ephraim,
Gamaliel son of Pedahzur from Manasseh;
¹¹ Abidan son of Gideoni from Benjamin;
¹² Ahiezer son of Ammishaddai from Dan;
¹³ Pagiel son of Ochran from Asher;
¹⁴ Eliasaph son of Deuel^D from Gad;
¹⁵ Ahira son of Enan from Naphtali.

¹⁶ These are the men called from the community; they are leaders of their ancestral tribes, the heads of Israel's clans."

¹⁷ So Moses and Aaron took these men who had been designated by name, ¹⁸ and they assembled the whole community on the first day of the second month. They recorded their ancestry by their clans and their ancestral families, counting one by one the names of those twenty years old or more, ¹⁹ just as the LORD commanded Moses. He registered them in the Wilderness of Sinai:

²⁰ The descendants of Reuben, the firstborn of Israel: according to their family records by their clans and their ancestral families, counting one by one the names of every male twenty years old or more, everyone who could serve in the army, ²¹ those registered for the tribe of Reuben numbered 46,500.

²² The descendants of Simeon: according to their family records by their clans and their ancestral families, those registered counting one by one the names of every male twenty years old or more, everyone who could serve in the army, ²³ those registered for the tribe of Simeon numbered 59,300.

²⁴ The descendants of Gad: according to their family records by their clans and their ancestral families, counting the names of those twenty years old or more, everyone who could serve in the army, ²⁵ those registered for the tribe of Gad numbered 45,650.

---

^A 1:2 Lit *the house of their fathers*, also in vv. 18,20,22,24,26,28,30,32,34,36, 38,40,42,45   ^B 1:3 Lit *everyone going out to war in Israel*   ^C 1:4 Lit *the house of his fathers*, also in v. 44   ^D 1:14 LXX, Syr read *Reuel*

26 The descendants of Judah: according to their family records by their clans and their ancestral families, counting the names of those twenty years old or more, everyone who could serve in the army, 27 those registered for the tribe of Judah numbered 74,600.

28 The descendants of Issachar: according to their family records by their clans and their ancestral families, counting the names of those twenty years old or more, everyone who could serve in the army, 29 those registered for the tribe of Issachar numbered 54,400.

30 The descendants of Zebulun: according to their family records by their clans and their ancestral families, counting the names of those twenty years old or more, everyone who could serve in the army, 31 those registered for the tribe of Zebulun numbered 57,400.

32 The descendants of Joseph:

The descendants of Ephraim: according to their family records by their clans and their ancestral families, counting the names of those twenty years old or more, everyone who could serve in the army, 33 those registered for the tribe of Ephraim numbered 40,500.

34 The descendants of Manasseh: according to their family records by their clans and their ancestral families, counting the names of those twenty years old or more, everyone who could serve in the army, 35 those registered for the tribe of Manasseh numbered 32,200.

36 The descendants of Benjamin: according to their family records by their clans and their ancestral families, counting the names of those twenty years old or more, everyone who could serve in the army, 37 those registered for the tribe of Benjamin numbered 35,400.

38 The descendants of Dan: according to their family records by their clans and their ancestral families, counting the names of those twenty years old or more, everyone who could serve in the army, 39 those registered for the tribe of Dan numbered 62,700.

40 The descendants of Asher: according to their family records by their clans and their ancestral families, counting the names of those twenty years old or more, everyone who could serve in the army, 41 those registered for the tribe of Asher numbered 41,500.

42 The descendants of Naphtali: according to their family records by their clans and their ancestral families, counting the names of those twenty years old or more, everyone who could serve in the army, 43 those registered for the tribe of Naphtali numbered 53,400.

44 These are the men Moses and Aaron registered, with the assistance of the twelve leaders of Israel; each represented his ancestral family. 45 So all the Israelites twenty years old or more, everyone who could serve in

Israel's army, were registered by their ancestral families. ⁴⁶ All those registered numbered 603,550.

DUTIES OF THE LEVITES

⁴⁷ But the Levites were not registered with them by their ancestral tribe. ⁴⁸ For the LORD had told Moses: ⁴⁹ "Do not register or take a census of the tribe of Levi with the other Israelites. ⁵⁰ Appoint the Levites over the tabernacle of the testimony, all its furnishings, and everything in it. They are to transport the tabernacle and all its articles, take care of it, and camp around it. ⁵¹ Whenever the tabernacle is to move, the Levites are to take it down, and whenever it is to stop at a campsite, the Levites are to set it up. Any unauthorized person who comes near it is to be put to death.

⁵² "The Israelites are to camp by their military divisions, each man with his encampment and under his banner. ⁵³ The Levites are to camp around the tabernacle of the testimony and watch over it, so that no wrath will fall on the Israelite community." ⁵⁴ The Israelites did everything just as the LORD had commanded Moses.

ORGANIZATION OF THE CAMPS

2 The LORD spoke to Moses and Aaron: ² "The Israelites are to camp under their respective banners beside the flags of their ancestral families.ᴬ They are to camp around the tent of meeting at a distance from it:
³ Judah's military divisions will camp on the east side toward the sunrise under their banner. The leader of the descendants of Judah is Nahshon son of Amminadab. ⁴ His military division numbers 74,600. ⁵ The tribe of Issachar will camp next to it. The leader of the Issacharites is Nethanel son of Zuar. ⁶ His military division numbers 54,400. ⁷ The tribe of Zebulun will be next. The leader of the Zebulunites is Eliab son of Helon. ⁸ His military division numbers 57,400. ⁹ The total number in their military divisions who belong to Judah's encampment is 186,400; they will move out first.

¹⁰ Reuben's military divisions will camp on the south side under their banner. The leader of the Reubenites is Elizur son of Shedeur. ¹¹ His military division numbers 46,500. ¹² The tribe of Simeon will camp next to it. The leader of the Simeonites is Shelumiel son of Zurishaddai. ¹³ His military division numbers 59,300. ¹⁴ The tribe of Gad will be next. The leader of the Gadites is Eliasaph son of Deuel.ᴮ ¹⁵ His military division numbers 45,650. ¹⁶ The total number in their military divisions who belong to Reuben's encampment is 151,450; they will move out second.

¹⁷ The tent of meeting is to move out with the Levites' camp, which is in the middle of the camps. They are to move out just as they camp, each in his place,ᶜ with their banners.

¹⁸ Ephraim's military divisions will camp on the west side under their banner. The leader of the Ephraimites is Elishama son of Ammihud. ¹⁹ His

---

ᴬ2:2 Lit *the house of their fathers*, also in v. 32   ᴮ2:14 Some Hb mss, Sam, Vg; other Hb mss read *Reuel*   ᶜ2:17 Lit *each on his hand* military division numbers 40,500. [20] The tribe of Manasseh will be next to it. The leader of the Manassites is Gamaliel son of Pedahzur. [21] His military division numbers 32,200. [22] The tribe of Benjamin will be next. The leader of the Benjaminites is Abidan son of Gideoni. [23] His military division numbers 35,400. [24] The total in their military divisions who belong to Ephraim's encampment number 108,100; they will move out third.

[25] Dan's military divisions will camp on the north side under their banner. The leader of the Danites is Ahiezer son of Ammishaddai. [26] His military division numbers 62,700. [27] The tribe of Asher will camp next to it. The leader of the Asherites is Pagiel son of Ochran. [28] His military division numbers 41,500. [29] The tribe of Naphtali will be next. The leader of the Naphtalites is Ahira son of Enan. [30] His military division numbers 53,400. [31] The total number who belong to Dan's encampment is 157,600; they are to move out last, with their banners."

[32] These are the Israelites registered by their ancestral families. The total number in the camps by their military divisions is 603,550. [33] But the Levites were not registered among the Israelites, just as the LORD had commanded Moses. [34] The Israelites did everything the LORD commanded Moses; they camped by their banners in this way and moved out the same way, each man by his clan and by his ancestral family.[A]

AARON'S SONS AND THE LEVITES

3 These are the family records of Aaron and Moses at the time the LORD spoke with Moses on Mount Sinai. [2] These are the names of Aaron's sons: Nadab, the firstborn, and Abihu, Eleazar, and Ithamar. [3] These are the names of Aaron's sons, the anointed priests, who were ordained to serve as priests. [4] But Nadab and Abihu died in the LORD's presence when they presented unauthorized fire before the LORD in the Wilderness of Sinai, and they had no sons. So Eleazar and Ithamar served as priests under the direction of Aaron their father.

[5] The LORD spoke to Moses: [6] "Bring the tribe of Levi near and present them to the priest Aaron to assist him. [7] They are to perform duties for[B] him and the entire community before the tent of meeting by attending to the service of the tabernacle. [8] They are to take care of all the furnishings of the tent of meeting and perform duties for the Israelites by attending to the service of the tabernacle. [9] Assign the Levites to Aaron and his sons; they have been assigned exclusively to him[C] from the Israelites. [10] You are to appoint Aaron and his sons to carry out their priestly responsibilities, but any unauthorized person who comes near the sanctuary is to be put to death."

[11] The LORD spoke to Moses: [12] "See, I have taken the Levites from the Israelites in place of every firstborn Israelite from the womb. The Levites belong to me, [13] because every firstborn belongs to me. At the time I struck down every firstborn in the land of Egypt, I consecrated every firstborn in Israel to myself, both man and animal. They are mine; I am the LORD."

[A]2:34 Lit *the house of his fathers*   [B]3:7 Or *to guard*, also in v. 8   [C]3:9 Some Hb mss, LXX, Sam read *me*; Nm 8:16

THE LEVITICAL CENSUS

¹⁴ The LORD spoke to Moses in the Wilderness of Sinai: ¹⁵ "Register the Levites by their ancestral families^A and their clans. You are to register every male one month old or more." ¹⁶ So Moses registered them in obedience to the LORD as he had been commanded:

¹⁷ These were Levi's sons by name: Gershon, Kohath, and Merari.

¹⁸ These were the names of Gershon's sons by their clans: Libni and Shimei. ¹⁹ Kohath's sons by their clans were Amram, Izhar, Hebron, and Uzziel. ²⁰ Merari's sons by their clans were Mahli and Mushi. These were the Levite clans by their ancestral families.

²¹ The Libnite clan and the Shimeite clan came from Gershon; these were the Gershonite clans. ²² Those registered, counting every male one month old or more, numbered 7,500. ²³ The Gershonite clans camped behind the tabernacle on the west side, ²⁴ and the leader of the Gershonite families^B was Eliasaph son of Lael. ²⁵ The Gershonites' duties at the tent of meeting involved the tabernacle, the tent, its covering, the screen for the entrance to the tent of meeting, ²⁶ the hangings of the courtyard, the screen for the entrance to the courtyard that surrounds the tabernacle and the altar, and the tent ropes — all the work relating to these.

²⁷ The Amramite clan, the Izharite clan, the Hebronite clan, and the Uzzielite clan came from Kohath; these were the Kohathites. ²⁸ Counting every male one month old or more, there were 8,600^C responsible for the duties of^D the sanctuary. ²⁹ The clans of the Kohathites camped on the south side of the tabernacle, ³⁰ and the leader of the families of the Kohathite clans was Elizaphan son of Uzziel. ³¹ Their duties involved the ark, the table, the lampstand, the altars, the sanctuary utensils that were used with these, and the screen^E — and all the work relating to them. ³² The chief of the Levite leaders was Eleazar son of Aaron the priest; he had oversight of those responsible for the duties of the sanctuary.

³³ The Mahlite clan and the Mushite clan came from Merari; these were the Merarite clans. ³⁴ Those registered, counting every male one month old or more, numbered 6,200. ³⁵ The leader of the families of the Merarite clans was Zuriel son of Abihail; they camped on the north side of the tabernacle. ³⁶ The assigned duties of Merari's descendants involved the tabernacle's supports, crossbars, pillars, bases, all its equipment, and all the work related to these, ³⁷ in addition to the posts of the surrounding courtyard with their bases, tent pegs, and ropes.

³⁸ Moses, Aaron, and his sons, who performed the duties of^F the sanctuary as a service on behalf of the Israelites, camped in front of the

---

^A 3:15 Lit *the house of their fathers*, also in v. 20 ^B 3:24 Lit *a father's house*, also in vv. 30, 35 ^C 3:28 LXX reads *8,300* ^D 3:28 Or *for guarding*, also in v. 32 ^E 3:31 The screen between the most holy place and the holy place; Ex 35:12 ^F 3:38 Or *who guarded* tabernacle on the east, in front of the tent of meeting toward the sunrise. Any unauthorized person who came near it was to be put to death. ³⁹ The total number of all the Levite males one month old or more that Moses and Aaron^A registered by their clans at the LORD's command was 22,000.

REDEMPTION OF THE FIRSTBORN

⁴⁰ The LORD told Moses: "Register every firstborn male of the Israelites one month old or more, and list their names. ⁴¹ You are to take the Levites for me — I am the LORD — in place of every firstborn among the Israelites, and the Levites' cattle in place of every firstborn among the Israelites' cattle." ⁴² So Moses registered every firstborn among the Israelites, as the LORD commanded him. ⁴³ The total number of the firstborn males one month old or more listed by name was 22,273.

⁴⁴ The LORD spoke to Moses again: ⁴⁵ "Take the Levites in place of every firstborn among the Israelites, and the Levites' cattle in place of their cattle. The Levites belong to me; I am the LORD. ⁴⁶ As the redemption price for the 273 firstborn Israelites who outnumber the Levites, ⁴⁷ collect five shekels for each person, according to the standard sanctuary shekel — twenty gerahs to the shekel. ^B ⁴⁸ Give the silver to Aaron and his sons as the redemption price for those who are in excess among the Israelites."

⁴⁹ So Moses collected the redemption amount from those in excess of the ones redeemed by the Levites. ⁵⁰ He collected the silver from the firstborn Israelites: 1,365 shekels^C measured by the standard sanctuary shekel. ⁵¹ He gave the redemption silver to Aaron and his sons in obedience to the LORD, just as the LORD commanded Moses.

DUTIES OF THE KOHATHITES

4 The LORD spoke to Moses and Aaron: ² "Among the Levites, take a census of the Kohathites by their clans and their ancestral families, ^D ³ men from thirty years old to fifty years old — everyone who is qualified^E to do work at the tent of meeting.

⁴ "The service of the Kohathites at the tent of meeting concerns the most holy objects. ⁵ Whenever the camp is about to move on, Aaron and his sons are to go in, take down the screening curtain, and cover the ark of the testimony with it. ⁶ They are to place over this a covering made of fine leather,^F spread a solid blue cloth on top, and insert its poles.

⁷ "They are to spread a blue cloth over the table of the Presence and place the plates and cups on it, as well as the bowls and pitchers for the drink offering. The regular bread offering is to be on it. ⁸ They are to spread a scarlet cloth over them, cover them with a covering made of fine leather, and insert the poles in the table.

⁹ "They are to take a blue cloth and cover the lampstand used for light, with its lamps, snuffers, and firepans, as well as its jars of oil by which they service it. ¹⁰ Then they are to place it with all its utensils inside a covering made of fine leather and put them on the carrying frame.

---

^A 3:39 Some Hb mss, Sam, Syr omit and Aaron ^B 3:47 A shekel is about two-fifths of an ounce of silver ^C 3:50 Over 34 pounds of silver ^D 4:2 Lit the house of their fathers, also in vv. 22,29,34,38,40,42,46 ^E 4:3 Lit everyone entering the service ^F 4:6 Hb obscure, also in vv. 8,10,11,12,14,25

¹¹ "They are to spread a blue cloth over the gold altar, cover it with a covering made of fine leather, and insert its poles. ¹² They are to take all the serving utensils they use in the sanctuary, place them in a blue cloth, cover them with a covering made of fine leather, and put them on a carrying frame.

¹³ "They are to remove the ashes from the bronze altar, spread a purple cloth over it, ¹⁴ and place all the equipment on it that they use in serving: the fire-pans, meat forks, shovels, and basins — all the equipment of the altar. They are to spread a covering made of fine leather over it and insert its poles. ^A

¹⁵ "Aaron and his sons are to finish covering the holy objects and all their equipment whenever the camp is to move on. The Kohathites will come and carry them, but they are not to touch the holy objects or they will die. These are the transportation duties of the Kohathites regarding the tent of meeting.

¹⁶ "Eleazar, son of Aaron the priest, has oversight of the lamp oil, the fragrant incense, the daily grain offering, and the anointing oil. He has oversight of the entire tabernacle and everything in it, the holy objects and their utensils." ^B

¹⁷ Then the LORD spoke to Moses and Aaron: ¹⁸ "Do not allow the Kohathite tribal clans to be wiped out from the Levites. ¹⁹ Do this for them so that they may live and not die when they come near the most holy objects: Aaron and his sons are to go in and assign each man his task and transportation duty. ²⁰ The Kohathites are not to go in and look at the holy objects as they are covered ^C or they will die."

DUTIES OF THE GERSHONITES

²¹ The LORD spoke to Moses: ²² "Take a census of the Gershonites also, by their ancestral families and their clans. ²³ Register men from thirty years old to fifty years old, everyone who is qualified to perform service, to do work at the tent of meeting. ²⁴ This is the service of the Gershonite clans regarding work and transportation duties: ²⁵ They are to transport the tabernacle curtains, the tent of meeting with its covering and the covering made of fine leather on top of it, the screen for the entrance to the tent of meeting, ²⁶ the hangings of the courtyard, the screen for the entrance at the gate of the courtyard that surrounds the tabernacle and the altar, along with their ropes and all the equipment for their service. They will carry out everything that needs to be done with these items.

²⁷ "All the service of the Gershonites, all their transportation duties and all their other work, is to be done at the command of Aaron and his sons; you are to assign to them all that they are responsible to carry. ²⁸ This is the service of the Gershonite clans at the tent of meeting, and their duties will be under the direction of Ithamar son of Aaron the priest.

DUTIES OF THE MERARITES

²⁹ "As for the Merarites, you are to register them by their clans and their ancestral families. ³⁰ Register men from thirty years old to fifty years old, everyone who is qualified to do the work of the tent of meeting. ³¹ This is what they are responsible to carry as the whole of their service at the tent of meeting:

---

^A 4:14 Sam, LXX add *They are to take a purple cloth and cover the wash basin and its base. They are to place them in a covering made of fine leather and put them on the carrying frame.* ^B 4:16 Or *the sanctuary and its furnishings* ^C 4:20 Or *objects, even long enough to swallow,* the supports of the tabernacle, with its crossbars, pillars, and bases, [32] the posts of the surrounding courtyard with their bases, tent pegs, and ropes, including all their equipment and all the work related to them. You are to assign by name the items that they are responsible to carry. [33] This is the service of the Merarite clans regarding all their work at the tent of meeting, under the direction of Ithamar son of Aaron the priest."

CENSUS OF THE LEVITES

[34] So Moses, Aaron, and the leaders of the community registered the Kohathites by their clans and their ancestral families, [35] men from thirty years old to fifty years old, everyone who was qualified for work at the tent of meeting. [36] The men registered by their clans numbered 2,750. [37] These were the registered men of the Kohathite clans, everyone who could serve at the tent of meeting. Moses and Aaron registered them at the LORD's command through Moses.

[38] The Gershonites were registered by their clans and their ancestral families, [39] men from thirty years old to fifty years old, everyone who was qualified for work at the tent of meeting. [40] The men registered by their clans and their ancestral families numbered 2,630. [41] These were the registered men of the Gershonite clans. At the LORD's command Moses and Aaron registered everyone who could serve at the tent of meeting.

[42] The men of the Merarite clans were registered by their clans and their ancestral families, [43] those from thirty years old to fifty years old, everyone who was qualified for work at the tent of meeting. [44] The men registered by their clans numbered 3,200. [45] These were the registered men of the Merarite clans; Moses and Aaron registered them at the LORD's command through Moses.

[46] Moses, Aaron, and the leaders of Israel registered all the Levites by their clans and their ancestral families, [47] from thirty years old to fifty years old, everyone who was qualified to do the work of serving at the tent of meeting and transporting it. [48] Their registered men numbered 8,580. [49] At the LORD's command they were registered under the direction of Moses, each one according to his work and transportation duty, and his assignment was as the LORD commanded Moses.

ISOLATION OF THE UNCLEAN

5 The LORD instructed Moses: [2] "Command the Israelites to send away anyone from the camp who is afflicted with a skin disease, anyone who has a discharge, or anyone who is defiled because of a corpse. [3] Send away both male or female; send them outside the camp, so that they will not defile their camps where I dwell among them." [4] The Israelites did this, sending them outside the camp. The Israelites did as the LORD instructed Moses.

COMPENSATION FOR WRONGDOING

[5] The LORD spoke to Moses: [6] "Tell the Israelites: When a man or woman commits any sin against another, that person acts unfaithfully toward the LORD and is guilty. [7] The person is to confess the sin he has committed. He is to pay full compensation, add a fifth of its value to it, and give it to the individual he has wronged. [8] But if that individual has no relative to receive

compensation, the compensation goes to the LORD for the priest, along with the atonement ram by which the priest will make atonement for the guilty person. ⁹ Every holy contribution the Israelites present to the priest will be his. ¹⁰ Each one's holy contribution is his to give; what each one gives to the priest will be his."

THE JEALOUSY RITUAL

¹¹ The LORD spoke to Moses: ¹² "Speak to the Israelites and tell them: If any man's wife goes astray, is unfaithful to him, ¹³ and sleeps with another,^A but it is concealed from her husband, and she is undetected, even though she has defiled herself, since there is no witness against her, and she wasn't caught in the act; ¹⁴ and if a feeling of jealousy comes over the husband and he becomes jealous because of his wife who has defiled herself — or if a feeling of jealousy comes over him and he becomes jealous of her though she has not defiled herself — ¹⁵ then the man is to bring his wife to the priest. He is also to bring an offering for her of two quarts^B of barley flour. He is not to pour oil over it or put frankincense on it because it is a grain offering of jealousy, a grain offering for remembrance to draw attention to guilt.

¹⁶ "The priest is to bring her forward and have her stand before the LORD. ¹⁷ Then the priest is to take holy water in a clay bowl, take some of the dust from the tabernacle floor, and put it in the water. ¹⁸ After the priest has the woman stand before the LORD, he is to let down her hair^C and place in her hands the grain offering for remembrance, which is the grain offering of jealousy. The priest is to hold the bitter water that brings a curse. ¹⁹ The priest will require the woman to take an oath and will say to her, 'If no man has slept with you, if you have not gone astray and become defiled while under your husband's authority, be unaffected by this bitter water that brings a curse. ²⁰ But if you have gone astray while under your husband's authority, if you have defiled yourself and a man other than your husband has slept with you' — ²¹ at this point the priest will make the woman take the oath with the sworn curse, and he is to say to her — 'May the LORD make you into an object of your people's cursing and swearing when he makes your womb^D shrivel and your belly swell. ²² May this water that brings a curse enter your stomach, causing your belly to swell and your womb to shrivel.'

"And the woman will reply, 'Amen, Amen.'

²³ "Then the priest is to write these curses on a scroll and wash them off into the bitter water. ²⁴ He will require the woman to drink the bitter water that brings a curse, and it will enter her to cause bitter suffering. ²⁵ The priest is to take the grain offering of jealousy from the woman, present the offering before the LORD, and bring it to the altar. ²⁶ The priest is to take a handful of the grain offering as a memorial portion and burn it on the altar. Afterward, he will require the woman to drink the water.

²⁷ "When he makes her drink the water, if she has defiled herself and been unfaithful to her husband, the water that brings a curse will enter her to cause bitter suffering; her belly will swell, and her womb will shrivel. She will become a curse among her people. ²⁸ But if the woman has not

---

^A 5:13 Lit and man lies with her and has an emission of semen ^B 5:15 Lit a tenth of an ephah ^C 5:18 Or to uncover her head ^D 5:21 Lit thigh, also in vv. 22,27 defiled herself and is pure, she will be unaffected and will be able to conceive children.

²⁹ "This is the law regarding jealousy when a wife goes astray and defiles herself while under her husband's authority, ³⁰ or when a feeling of jealousy comes over a husband and he becomes jealous of his wife. He is to have the woman stand before the Lord, and the priest will carry out all these instructions for her. ³¹ The husband will be free of guilt, but that woman will bear her iniquity."

THE NAZIRITE VOW

6 The Lord instructed Moses: ² "Speak to the Israelites and tell them: When a man or woman makes a special vow, a Nazirite vow, to consecrate himself to the Lord, ³ he is to abstain from wine and beer. He must not drink vinegar made from wine or from beer. He must not drink any grape juice or eat fresh grapes or raisins. ⁴ He is not to eat anything produced by the grapevine, from seeds to skin, during the period of his consecration.

⁵ "You must not cut his hair^A throughout the time of his vow of consecration. He may be holy until the time is completed during which he consecrates himself to the Lord; he is to let the hair of his head grow long. ⁶ He must not go near a dead body during the time he consecrates himself to the Lord. ⁷ He is not to defile himself for his father or mother, or his brother or sister, when they die, while the mark of consecration to his God is on his head. ⁸ He is holy to the Lord during the time of consecration.

⁹ "If someone suddenly dies near him, defiling his consecrated head, he must shave his head on the day of his purification; he is to shave it on the seventh day. ¹⁰ On the eighth day he is to bring two turtledoves or two young pigeons to the priest at the entrance to the tent of meeting. ¹¹ The priest is to offer one as a sin offering and the other as a burnt offering to make atonement on behalf of the Nazirite, since he incurred guilt because of the corpse. On that day he is to consecrate his head again. ¹² He is to rededicate his time of consecration to the Lord and to bring a year-old male lamb as a guilt offering. But do not count the initial period of consecration because it became defiled.

¹³ "This is the law of the Nazirite: On the day his time of consecration is completed, he is to be brought to the entrance to the tent of meeting. ¹⁴ He is to present an offering to the Lord of one unblemished year-old male lamb as a burnt offering, one unblemished year-old female lamb as a sin offering, one unblemished ram as a fellowship offering, ¹⁵ along with their grain offerings and drink offerings, and a basket of unleavened cakes made from fine flour mixed with oil, and unleavened wafers coated with oil.

¹⁶ "The priest is to present these before the Lord and sacrifice the Nazirite's sin offering and burnt offering. ¹⁷ He will also offer the ram as a fellowship sacrifice to the Lord, together with the basket of unleavened bread. Then the priest will offer the accompanying grain offering and drink offering.

¹⁸ "The Nazirite is to shave his consecrated head at the entrance to the tent of meeting, take the hair from his head, and put it on the fire under

---

^A 6:5 Lit "A razor is not to pass over his head

the fellowship sacrifice. [19] The priest is to take the boiled shoulder from the ram, one unleavened cake from the basket, and one unleavened wafer, and put them into the hands of the Nazirite after he has shaved his consecrated head. [20] The priest is to present them as a presentation offering before the LORD. It is a holy portion for the priest, in addition to the breast of the presentation offering and the thigh of the contribution. After that, the Nazirite may drink wine.

[21] "These are the instructions about the Nazirite who vows his offering to the LORD for his consecration, in addition to whatever else he can afford; he must fulfill whatever vow he makes in keeping with the instructions for his consecration."

THE PRIESTLY BLESSING

[22] The LORD spoke to Moses: [23] "Tell Aaron and his sons, 'This is how you are to bless the Israelites. You should say to them,

[24]   "May the LORD bless you and protect you;
[25]   may the LORD make his face shine on you
       and be gracious to you;
[26]   may the LORD look with favor on you[A]
       and give you peace." '

[27] In this way they will pronounce my name over[B] the Israelites, and I will bless them."

OFFERINGS FROM THE LEADERS

7 On the day Moses finished setting up the tabernacle, he anointed and consecrated it and all its furnishings, along with the altar and all its utensils. After he anointed and consecrated these things, [2] the leaders of Israel, the heads of their ancestral families,[C] presented an offering. They were the tribal leaders who supervised the registration. [3] They brought as their offering before the LORD six covered carts and twelve oxen, a cart from every two leaders and an ox from each one, and presented them in front of the tabernacle.

[4] The LORD said to Moses, [5] "Accept these from them to be used in the work of the tent of meeting, and give this offering to the Levites, to each division according to their service."

[6] So Moses took the carts and oxen and gave them to the Levites. [7] He gave the Gershonites two carts and four oxen corresponding to their service, [8] and gave the Merarites four carts and eight oxen corresponding to their service, under the direction of Ithamar son of Aaron the priest. [9] But he did not give any to the Kohathites, since their responsibility was service related to the holy objects carried on their shoulders.

[10] The leaders also presented the dedication gift for the altar when it was anointed. The leaders presented their offerings in front of the altar. [11] The LORD told Moses, "Each day have one leader present his offering for the dedication of the altar."

[12] The one who presented his offering on the first day was Nahshon son of Amminadab from the tribe of Judah. [13] His offering was one silver

---

[A]6:26 Lit LORD lift his face to you   [B]6:27 Or put my name on   [C]7:2 Lit the house of their fathers dish weighing 3 ¼ pounds[A] and one silver basin weighing 1 ¾ pounds, [B] measured by the standard sanctuary shekel, both of them full of fine flour mixed with oil for a grain offering; [14] one gold bowl weighing four ounces, [C] full of incense; [15] one young bull, one ram, and one male lamb a year old, for a burnt offering; [16] one male goat for a sin offering; [17] and two bulls, five rams, five male goats, and five male lambs a year old, for the fellowship sacrifice. This was the offering of Nahshon son of Amminadab.

[18] On the second day Nethanel son of Zuar, leader of Issachar, presented an offering. [19] As his offering, he presented one silver dish weighing 3 ¼ pounds and one silver basin weighing 1 ¾ pounds, measured by the standard sanctuary shekel, both of them full of fine flour mixed with oil for a grain offering; [20] one gold bowl weighing four ounces, full of incense; [21] one young bull, one ram, and one male lamb a year old, for a burnt offering; [22] one male goat for a sin offering; [23] and two bulls, five rams, five male goats, and five male lambs a year old, for the fellowship sacrifice. This was the offering of Nethanel son of Zuar.

[24] On the third day Eliab son of Helon, leader of the Zebulunites, presented an offering. [25] His offering was one silver dish weighing 3 ¼ pounds and one silver basin weighing 1 ¾ pounds, measured by the standard sanctuary shekel, both of them full of fine flour mixed with oil for a grain offering; [26] one gold bowl weighing four ounces, full of incense; [27] one young bull, one ram, and one male lamb a year old, for a burnt offering; [28] one male goat for a sin offering; [29] and two bulls, five rams, five male goats, and five male lambs a year old, for the fellowship sacrifice. This was the offering of Eliab son of Helon.

[30] On the fourth day Elizur son of Shedeur, leader of the Reubenites, presented an offering. [31] His offering was one silver dish weighing 3 ¼ pounds and one silver basin weighing 1 ¾ pounds, measured by the standard sanctuary shekel, both of them full of fine flour mixed with oil for a grain offering; [32] one gold bowl weighing four ounces, full of incense; [33] one young bull, one ram, and one male lamb a year old, for a burnt offering; [34] one male goat for a sin offering; [35] and two bulls, five rams, five male goats, and five male lambs a year old, for the fellowship sacrifice. This was the offering of Elizur son of Shedeur.

[36] On the fifth day Shelumiel son of Zurishaddai, leader of the Simeonites, presented an offering. [37] His offering was one silver dish weighing 3 ¼ pounds and one silver basin weighing 1 ¾ pounds, measured by the standard sanctuary shekel, both of them full of fine flour mixed with oil for a grain offering; [38] one gold bowl weighing four ounces, full of incense; [39] one young bull, one ram, and one male lamb a year old, for a burnt offering; [40] one male goat for a sin offering; [41] and two bulls, five

---

[A] 7:13 Lit *dish, 130 its shekel-weight,* also in vv. 19,25,31,37,43,49,55,61,67, 73,79   [B] 7:13 Lit *70 shekels,* also in vv. 19,25,31,37,43,49,55,61,67,73,79
[C] 7:14 Lit *10* (shekels), also in vv. 20,26,32,38,44,50,56,62,68,74,80,86

rams, five male goats, and five male lambs a year old, for the fellowship sacrifice. This was the offering of Shelumiel son of Zurishaddai.

[42] On the sixth day Eliasaph son of Deuel,[A] leader of the Gadites, presented an offering. [43] His offering was one silver dish weighing 3¼ pounds and one silver basin weighing 1¾ pounds, measured by the standard sanctuary shekel, both of them full of fine flour mixed with oil for a grain offering; [44] one gold bowl weighing four ounces full of incense; [45] one young bull, one ram, and one male lamb a year old, for a burnt offering; [46] one male goat for a sin offering; [47] and two bulls, five rams, five male goats, and five male lambs a year old, for the fellowship sacrifice. This was the offering of Eliasaph son of Deuel.[A]

[48] On the seventh day Elishama son of Ammihud, leader of the Ephraimites, presented an offering. [49] His offering was one silver dish weighing 3¼ pounds and one silver basin weighing 1¾ pounds, measured by the standard sanctuary shekel, both of them full of fine flour mixed with oil for a grain offering; [50] one gold bowl weighing four ounces, full of incense; [51] one young bull, one ram, and one male lamb a year old, for a burnt offering; [52] one male goat for a sin offering; [53] and two bulls, five rams, five male goats, and five male lambs a year old, for the fellowship sacrifice. This was the offering of Elishama son of Ammihud.

[54] On the eighth day Gamaliel son of Pedahzur, leader of the Manassites, presented an offering. [55] His offering was one silver dish weighing 3¼ pounds and one silver basin weighing 1¾ pounds, measured by the standard sanctuary shekel, both of them full of fine flour mixed with oil for a grain offering; [56] one gold bowl weighing four ounces, full of incense; [57] one young bull, one ram, and one male lamb a year old, for a burnt offering; [58] one male goat for a sin offering; [59] and two bulls, five rams, five male goats, and five male lambs a year old, for the fellowship sacrifice. This was the offering of Gamaliel son of Pedahzur.

[60] On the ninth day Abidan son of Gideoni, leader of the Benjaminites, presented an offering. [61] His offering was one silver dish weighing 3¼ pounds and one silver basin weighing 1¾ pounds, measured by the standard sanctuary shekel, both of them full of fine flour mixed with oil for a grain offering; [62] one gold bowl weighing four ounces, full of incense; [63] one young bull, one ram, and one male lamb a year old, for a burnt offering; [64] one male goat for a sin offering; [65] and two bulls, five rams, five male goats, and five male lambs a year old, for the fellowship sacrifice. This was the offering of Abidan son of Gideoni.

[66] On the tenth day Ahiezer son of Ammishaddai, leader of the Danites, presented an offering. [67] His offering was one silver dish weighing 3¼ pounds and one silver basin weighing 1¾ pounds, measured by the standard sanctuary shekel, both of them full of fine flour mixed with oil for a grain offering; [68] one gold bowl weighing four ounces, full of

A7:42,47 LXX, Syr read *Reuel*

²⁵ The military divisions of the camp of Dan's descendants with their banner set out, serving as rear guard for all the camps, and Ahiezer son of Ammishaddai was over their divisions. ²⁶ Pagiel son of Ochran was over the division of the tribe of Asher's descendants, ²⁷ and Ahira son of Enan was over the division of the tribe of Naphtali's descendants. ²⁸ This was the order of march for the Israelites by their military divisions as they set out.

²⁹ Moses said to Hobab, descendant of Reuel the Midianite and Moses's relative by marriage: "We're setting out for the place the LORD promised: 'I will give it to you.' Come with us, and we will treat you well, for the LORD has promised good things to Israel."

³⁰ But he replied to him, "I don't want to go. Instead, I will go to my own land and my relatives."

³¹ "Please don't leave us," Moses said, "since you know where we should camp in the wilderness, and you can serve as our eyes. ³² If you come with us, whatever good the LORD does for us we will do for you."

³³ They set out from the mountain of the LORD on a three-day journey with the ark of the LORD's covenant traveling ahead of them for those three days to seek a resting place for them. ³⁴ Meanwhile, the cloud of the LORD was over them by day when they set out from the camp.

³⁵ Whenever the ark set out, Moses would say:

Arise, LORD!
Let your enemies be scattered,
and those who hate you flee from your presence.

³⁶ When it came to rest, he would say:

Return, LORD,
to the countless thousands of Israel.

COMPLAINTS ABOUT HARDSHIP

11 Now the people began complaining openly before^A the LORD about hardship. When the LORD heard, his anger burned, and fire from the LORD blazed among them and consumed the outskirts of the camp. ² Then the people cried out to Moses, and he prayed to the LORD, and the fire died down. ³ So that place was named Taberah,^B because the LORD's fire had blazed among them.

COMPLAINTS ABOUT FOOD

⁴ The riffraff^C among them had a strong craving for other food. The Israelites wept again and said, "Who will feed us meat? ⁵ We remember the free fish we ate in Egypt, along with the cucumbers, melons, leeks, onions, and garlic. ⁶ But now our appetite is gone;^D there's nothing to look at but this manna!"

⁷ The manna resembled coriander seed, and its appearance was like that of bdellium.^E ⁸ The people walked around and gathered it. They ground it on a pair of grinding stones or crushed it in a mortar, then boiled it in a cooking pot and shaped it into cakes. It tasted like a pastry cooked with the finest oil. ⁹ When the dew fell on the camp at night, the manna would fall with it.

---

^A 11:1 Lit *in the ears of*   ^B 11:3 = Blaze   ^C 11:4 Or *The mixed multitude*; Hb obscure
^D 11:6 Or *our lives are wasting away*, or *our throat is dry*   ^E 11:7 A yellowish, transparent gum resin

¹⁰ Moses heard the people, family after family, weeping at the entrance of their tents. The LORD was very angry; Moses was also provoked.^A ¹¹ So Moses asked the LORD, "Why have you brought such trouble on your servant? Why are you angry with me,^B and why do you burden me with all these people? ¹² Did I conceive all these people? Did I give them birth so you should tell me, 'Carry them at your breast, as a nanny carries a baby,' to the land that you swore to give their fathers? ¹³ Where can I get meat to give all these people? For they are weeping to me, 'Give us meat to eat!' ¹⁴ I can't carry all these people by myself. They are too much for me. ¹⁵ If you are going to treat me like this, please kill me right now if I have found favor with you, and don't let me see my misery^C anymore."

SEVENTY ELDERS ANOINTED

¹⁶ The LORD answered Moses, "Bring me seventy men from Israel known to you as elders and officers of the people. Take them to the tent of meeting and have them stand there with you. ¹⁷ Then I will come down and speak with you there. I will take some of the Spirit who is on you and put the Spirit on them. They will help you bear the burden of the people, so that you do not have to bear it by yourself.

¹⁸ "Tell the people: Consecrate yourselves in readiness for tomorrow, and you will eat meat because you wept in the LORD's hearing, 'Who will feed us meat? We were better off in Egypt.' The LORD will give you meat and you will eat. ¹⁹ You will eat, not for one day, or two days, or five days, or ten days, or twenty days, ²⁰ but for a whole month — until it comes out of your nostrils and becomes nauseating to you — because you have rejected the LORD who is among you, and wept before him: 'Why did we ever leave Egypt?' "

²¹ But Moses replied, "I'm in the middle of a people with six hundred thousand foot soldiers, yet you say, 'I will give them meat, and they will eat for a month.' ²² If flocks and herds were slaughtered for them, would they have enough? Or if all the fish in the sea were caught for them, would they have enough?"

²³ The LORD answered Moses, "Is the LORD's arm weak?^D Now you will see whether or not what I have promised will happen to you."

²⁴ Moses went out and told the people the words of the LORD. He brought seventy men from the elders of the people and had them stand around the tent. ²⁵ Then the LORD descended in the cloud and spoke to him. He took some of the Spirit that was on Moses and placed the Spirit on the seventy elders. As the Spirit rested on them, they prophesied, but they never did it again. ²⁶ Two men had remained in the camp, one named Eldad and the other Medad; the Spirit rested on them — they were among those listed, but had not gone out to the tent — and they prophesied in the camp. ²⁷ A young man ran and reported to Moses, "Eldad and Medad are prophesying in the camp." ²⁸ Joshua son of Nun, assistant to Moses since his youth,^E responded, "Moses, my lord, stop them!"

²⁹ But Moses asked him, "Are you jealous on my account? If only all the LORD's people were prophets and the LORD would place his Spirit on them!" ³⁰ Then Moses returned to the camp along with the elders of Israel.

---

^A 11:10 Lit and it was evil in the eyes of Moses   ^B 11:11 Lit Why have I not found favor in your eyes   ^C 11:15 Alt Hb tradition reads your misery   ^D 11:23 Lit the LORD's arm too short   ^E 11:28 Or Moses, from his elite young men

QUAIL IN THE CAMP

³¹ A wind sent by the LORD came up and blew quail in from the sea; it dropped them all around the camp. They were flying three feet ᴬ off ᴮ the ground for about a day's journey in every direction. ³² The people were up all that day and night and all the next day gathering the quail — the one who took the least gathered fifty bushels ᶜ — and they spread them out all around the camp. ᴰ

³³ While the meat was still between their teeth, before it was chewed, the LORD's anger burned against the people, and the LORD struck them with a very severe plague. ³⁴ So they named that place Kibroth-hattaavah, ᴱ because there they buried the people who had craved the meat.

³⁵ From Kibroth-hattaavah the people moved on to Hazeroth ᶠ and re-mained there.

MIRIAM AND AARON REBEL

12 Miriam and Aaron criticized Moses because of the Cushite wom-an he married (for he had married a Cushite woman). ² They said, "Does the LORD speak only through Moses? Does he not also speak through us?" And the LORD heard it. ³ Moses was a very humble man, more so than anyone on the face of the earth.

⁴ Suddenly the LORD said to Moses, Aaron, and Miriam, "You three come out to the tent of meeting." So the three of them went out. ⁵ Then the LORD descended in a pillar of cloud, stood at the entrance to the tent, and sum-moned Aaron and Miriam. When the two of them came forward, ⁶ he said:

"Listen to what I say:
If there is a prophet among you from the LORD,
I make myself known to him in a vision;
I speak with him in a dream.
⁷ Not so with my servant Moses;
he is faithful in ᴳ all my household.
⁸ I speak with him directly, ᴴ
openly, and not in riddles;
he sees the form of the LORD.

So why were you not afraid to speak against my servant Moses?" ⁹ The LORD's anger burned against them, and he left.

¹⁰ As the cloud moved away from the tent, Miriam's skin suddenly became diseased, resembling snow.ᴵ When Aaron turned toward her, he saw that she was diseased ¹¹ and said to Moses, "My lord, please don't hold against us this sin we have so foolishly committed. ¹² Please don't let her be like a dead baby ᴶ whose flesh is half eaten away when he comes out of his mother's womb."

¹³ Then Moses cried out to the LORD, "God, please heal her!"

¹⁴ The LORD answered Moses, "If her father had merely spit in her face, wouldn't she remain in disgrace for seven days? Let her be confined out-side the camp for seven days; after that she may be brought back in." ¹⁵ So

---

ᴬ11:31 Lit *two cubits*   ᴮ11:31 Or *They were three feet deep on*   ᶜ11:32 Lit *10 homers*   ᴰ11:32 To dry or cure the meat; 2Sm 17:19; Ezk 26:5,14
ᴱ11:34 = Graves of Craving   ᶠ11:35 = Settlements; Nm 12:16; 33:16-17
ᴳ12:7 Or *is entrusted with*   ᴴ12:8 Lit *mouth to mouth*   ᴵ12:10 A reference to whiteness or flakiness of the skin   ᴶ12:12 Alt Hb tradition reads *baby who comes out of our mother's womb and our flesh is half eaten away.*

Miriam was confined outside the camp for seven days, and the people did not move on until Miriam was brought back in. [16] After that, the people set out from Hazeroth and camped in the Wilderness of Paran.

SCOUTING OUT CANAAN

13 The LORD spoke to Moses: [2] "Send men to scout out the land of Canaan I am giving to the Israelites. Send one man who is a leader among them from each of their ancestral tribes." [3] Moses sent them from the Wilderness of Paran at the LORD's command. All the men were leaders in Israel. [4] These were their names:

Shammua son of Zaccur from the tribe of Reuben;
[5] Shaphat son of Hori from the tribe of Simeon;
[6] Caleb son of Jephunneh from the tribe of Judah;
[7] Igal son of Joseph from the tribe of Issachar;
[8] Hoshea son of Nun from the tribe of Ephraim;
[9] Palti son of Raphu from the tribe of Benjamin;
[10] Gaddiel son of Sodi from the tribe of Zebulun;
[11] Gaddi son of Susi from the tribe of Manasseh (from the tribe of Joseph);
[12] Ammiel son of Gemalli from the tribe of Dan;
[13] Sethur son of Michael from the tribe of Asher;
[14] Nahbi son of Vophsi from the tribe of Naphtali;
[15] Geuel son of Machi from the tribe of Gad.

[16] These were the names of the men Moses sent to scout out the land, and Moses renamed Hoshea son of Nun, Joshua.

[17] When Moses sent them to scout out the land of Canaan, he told them, "Go up this way to the Negev, then go up into the hill country. [18] See what the land is like, and whether the people who live there are strong or weak, few or many. [19] Is the land they live in good or bad? Are the cities they live in encampments or fortifications? [20] Is the land fertile or unproductive? Are there trees in it or not? Be courageous. Bring back some fruit from the land." It was the season for the first ripe grapes.

[21] So they went up and scouted out the land from the Wilderness of Zin[A] as far as Rehob near the entrance to Hamath. [B] [22] They went up through the Negev and came to Hebron, where Ahiman, Sheshai, and Talmai, the descendants of Anak, were living. Hebron was built seven years before Zoan in Egypt. [23] When they came to the Valley of Eshcol, they cut down a branch with a single cluster of grapes, which was carried on a pole by two men. They also took some pomegranates and figs. [24] That place was called the Valley of Eshcol[C] because of the cluster of grapes the Israelites cut there. [25] At the end of forty days they returned from scouting out the land.

REPORT ABOUT CANAAN

[26] The men went back to Moses, Aaron, and the entire Israelite community in the Wilderness of Paran at Kadesh. They brought back a report for them and the whole community, and they showed them the fruit of the land. [27] They reported to Moses: "We went into the land where you sent us. Indeed it is flowing with milk and honey, and here is some of its fruit. [28] However, the

---

[A]13:21 Southern border of the promised land   [B]13:21 Or *near Lebo-hamath*
[C]13:24 = Cluster

people living in the land are strong, and the cities are large and fortified. We also saw the descendants of Anak there. ²⁹ The Amalekites are living in the land of the Negev; the Hethites, Jebusites, and Amorites live in the hill country; and the Canaanites live by the sea and along the Jordan."

³⁰ Then Caleb quieted the people in the presence of Moses and said, "Let's go up now and take possession of the land because we can certainly conquer it! "

³¹ But the men who had gone up with him responded, "We can't attack the people because they are stronger than we are! " ³² So they gave a negative report to the Israelites about the land they had scouted: "The land we passed through to explore is one that devours its inhabitants, and all the people we saw in it are men of great size. ³³ We even saw the Nephilim there — the descendants of Anak come from the Nephilim! To ourselves we seemed like grasshoppers, and we must have seemed the same to them."

ISRAEL'S REFUSAL TO ENTER CANAAN

14 Then the whole community broke into loud cries, and the people wept that night. ² All the Israelites complained about Moses and Aaron, and the whole community told them, "If only we had died in the land of Egypt, or if only we had died in this wilderness! ³ Why is the LORD bringing us into this land to die by the sword? Our wives and children will become plunder. Wouldn't it be better for us to go back to Egypt? " ⁴ So they said to one another, "Let's appoint a leader and go back to Egypt."

⁵ Then Moses and Aaron fell facedown in front of the whole assembly of the Israelite community. ⁶ Joshua son of Nun and Caleb son of Jephunneh, who were among those who scouted out the land, tore their clothes ⁷ and said to the entire Israelite community: "The land we passed through and explored is an extremely good land. ⁸ If the LORD is pleased with us, he will bring us into this land, a land flowing with milk and honey, and give it to us. ⁹ Only don't rebel against the LORD, and don't be afraid of the people of the land, for we will devour them. Their protection has been removed from them, and the LORD is with us. Don't be afraid of them! "

¹⁰ While the whole community threatened to stone them, the glory of the LORD appeared to all the Israelites at the tent of meeting.

GOD'S JUDGMENT OF ISRAEL'S REBELLION

¹¹ The LORD said to Moses, "How long will these people despise me? How long will they not trust in me despite all the signs I have performed among them? ¹² I will strike them with a plague and destroy them. Then I will make you into a greater and mightier nation than they are."

¹³ But Moses replied to the LORD, "The Egyptians will hear about it, for by your strength you brought up this people from them. ¹⁴ They will tell it to the inhabitants of this land. They have heard that you, LORD, are among these people, how you, LORD, are seen face to face, how your cloud stands over them, and how you go before them in a pillar of cloud by day and in a pillar of fire by night. ¹⁵ If you kill this people with a single blow,ᴬ the nations that have heard of your fame will declare, ¹⁶ 'Since the LORD wasn't able to bring this people into the land he swore to give them, he has slaughtered them in the wilderness.'

ᴬ14:15 Lit *people as one man*

GRACE FOR THE GUILTY

NUMBERS 13–14; HEBREWS 3:1-6

There's a certain horror that comes with realizing the gravity of our mistakes. We've crossed a line, said something we can't take back, exposed the dark places inside us. We can't undo what's been done, and we can't avoid the consequences.

Numbers 14 contains a sobering story of rebellion that leads to gut-wrenching consequences. It's a story that should make us pause, even shrink back, at the powerful reality of discipline in the holy hands of God. He cannot ignore sin. To do so would undermine His righteousness and negate His justice.

It's a tragic unfolding of events. The nation of Israel chose to believe the faithless words of a few men over the faithful promises of God. Frustrated with the people and full of righteous fear, Moses approached the Lord on their behalf. He stood before God as Israel's advocate, having no case to argue, no excuses to offer for their rebellion. They were guilty. Undeniably, terrifyingly guilty. They'd questioned God's sovereignty, and Moses knew the people deserved to perish in the wake of their unbelief.

Moses didn't attempt to qualify their sin. Instead, he focused his faith on the flawless character of God and pointed to the glory at stake in the ultimate outcome. He recalled what he knew to be true about the One he served:

"The LORD is slow to anger and abounding in faithful love, forgiving iniquity and rebellion.

But he will not leave the guilty unpunished, bringing the consequences of the fathers' iniquity on the children to the third and fourth generation" (Nm 14:18).

Rebellion merits consequences. Moses knew God, in His holiness, would certainly discipline Israel, but he also believed that God was gracious and merciful.

What Moses believed about God was true on both counts. God was faithful to His character and His covenant. A remnant was spared, and the blessing of His presence continued with them into the promised land. The punishment for those who failed to believe was harsh, but ultimately grace prevailed on behalf of God's people.

We are born with the same sinful nature that plagued the Israelites. We stand before God undeniably, terrifyingly guilty. We are helpless in our defense and hopeless in our shame. **But the salvation the Israelites knew in part, we now know in full.** Israel had an advocate who could speak on their behalf. We have an Advocate who bore the weight of our sin and now speaks victory over our condemnation (Heb 3:1-6).

Jesus has paid our ransom and reconciled us back to God. Our reckless rebellion has been met with relentless love. He has offered us grace—infinite, life-giving grace. His truth has set us free and His blood has covered our sin. Thanks be to God.

¹⁷ "So now, may my Lord's power be magnified just as you have spoken: ¹⁸ The LORD is slow to anger and abounding in faithful love, forgiving iniquity and rebellion. But he will not leave the guilty unpunished, bringing the consequences of the fathers' iniquity on the children to the third and fourth generation. ¹⁹ Please pardon the iniquity of this people, in keeping with the greatness of your faithful love, just as you have forgiven them from Egypt until now."

²⁰ The LORD responded, "I have pardoned them as you requested. ²¹ Yet as surely as I live and as the whole earth is filled with the LORD's glory, ²² none of the men who have seen my glory and the signs I performed in Egypt and in the wilderness, and have tested me these ten times and did not obey me, ²³ will ever see the land I swore to give their fathers. None of those who have despised me will see it. ²⁴ But since my servant Caleb has a different spirit and has remained loyal to me, I will bring him into the land where he has gone, and his descendants will inherit it. ²⁵ Since the Amalekites and Canaanites are living in the lowlands,^A turn back tomorrow and head for the wilderness in the direction of the Red Sea."

²⁶ Then the LORD spoke to Moses and Aaron: ²⁷ "How long must I endure this evil community that keeps complaining about me? I have heard the Israelites' complaints that they make against me. ²⁸ Tell them: As surely as I live — this is the LORD's declaration — I will do to you exactly as I heard you say. ²⁹ Your corpses will fall in this wilderness — all of you who were registered in the census, the entire number of you twenty years old or more — because you have complained about me. ³⁰ I swear that none of you will enter the land I promised^B to settle you in, except Caleb son of Jephunneh and Joshua son of Nun. ³¹ I will bring your children whom you said would become plunder into the land you rejected, and they will enjoy it. ³² But as for you, your corpses will fall in this wilderness. ³³ Your children will be shepherds in the wilderness for forty years and bear the penalty for your acts of unfaithfulness until all your corpses lie scattered in the wilderness. ³⁴ You will bear the consequences of your iniquities forty years based on the number of the forty days that you scouted the land, a year for each day.^C You will know my displeasure.^D ³⁵ I, the LORD, have spoken. I swear that I will do this to the entire evil community that has conspired against me. They will come to an end in the wilderness, and there they will die."

³⁶ So the men Moses sent to scout out the land, and who returned and incited the entire community to complain about him by spreading a negative report about the land — ³⁷ those men who spread the negative report about the land were struck down by the LORD. ³⁸ Only Joshua son of Nun and Caleb son of Jephunneh remained alive of those men who went to scout out the land.

ISRAEL ROUTED

³⁹ When Moses reported these words to all the Israelites, the people were overcome with grief. ⁴⁰ They got up early the next morning and went up the ridge of the hill country, saying, "Let's go to the place the LORD promised, for we were wrong."

---

^A 14:25 Lit valley ^B 14:30 Lit I raised my hand ^C 14:34 Lit a day for the year, a day for the year ^D 14:34 Or my opposition

⁴¹ But Moses responded, "Why are you going against the LORD's command? It won't succeed. ⁴² Don't go, because the LORD is not among you and you will be defeated by your enemies. ⁴³ The Amalekites and Canaanites are right in front of you, and you will fall by the sword. The LORD won't be with you, since you have turned from following him."

⁴⁴ But they dared to go up the ridge of the hill country, even though the ark of the LORD's covenant and Moses did not leave the camp. ⁴⁵ Then the Amalekites and Canaanites who lived in that part of the hill country came down, attacked them, and routed them as far as Hormah.

LAWS ABOUT OFFERINGS

15 The LORD instructed Moses: ² "Speak to the Israelites and tell them: When you enter the land I am giving you to settle in, ³ and you make a fire offering to the LORD from the herd or flock — either a burnt offering or a sacrifice, to fulfill a vow, or as a freewill offering, or at your appointed festivals — to produce a pleasing aroma for the LORD, ⁴ the one presenting his offering to the LORD is also to present a grain offering of two quarts ᴬ of fine flour mixed with a quart ᴮ of oil. ⁵ Prepare a quart of wine as a drink offering with the burnt offering or sacrifice of each lamb.

⁶ "If you prepare a grain offering with a ram, it is to be four quarts ᶜ of fine flour mixed with a third of a gallon ᴰ of oil. ⁷ Also present a third of a gallon of wine for a drink offering as a pleasing aroma to the LORD.

⁸ "If you prepare a young bull as a burnt offering or as a sacrifice, to fulfill a vow, or as a fellowship offering to the LORD, ⁹ a grain offering of six quarts ᴱ of fine flour mixed with two quarts ᶠ of oil is to be presented with the bull. ¹⁰ Also present two quarts of wine as a drink offering. It is a fire offering of pleasing aroma to the LORD. ¹¹ This is to be done for each ox, ram, lamb, or goat. ¹² This is how you are to prepare each of them, no matter how many.

¹³ "Every Israelite is to prepare these things in this way when he presents a fire offering as a pleasing aroma to the LORD. ¹⁴ When an alien resides with you or someone else is among you and wants to prepare a fire offering as a pleasing aroma to the LORD, he is to do exactly as you do throughout your generations. ¹⁵ The assembly is to have the same statute for both you and the resident alien as a permanent statute throughout your generations. You and the alien will be alike before the LORD. ¹⁶ The same law and the same ordinance will apply to both you and the alien who resides with you."

¹⁷ The LORD instructed Moses: ¹⁸ "Speak to the Israelites and tell them: After you enter the land where I am bringing you, ¹⁹ you are to offer a contribution to the LORD when you eat from the food of the land. ²⁰ You are to offer a loaf from your first batch of dough as a contribution; offer it just like a contribution from the threshing floor. ²¹ Throughout your generations, you are to give the LORD a contribution from the first batch of your dough.

²² "When you sin unintentionally and do not obey all these commands that the LORD spoke to Moses — ²³ all that the LORD has commanded you through Moses, from the day the LORD issued the commands and onward throughout your generations — ²⁴ and if it was done unintentionally without

---

ᴬ15:4 Lit *a tenth* (of an ephah)   ᴮ15:4 Lit *a fourth hin,* also in v. 5   ᶜ15:6 Lit *two-tenths* (of an ephah)   ᴰ15:6 Lit *a third hin,* also in v. 7   ᴱ15:9 Lit *three-tenths* (of an ephah)   ᶠ15:9 Lit *a half hin,* also in v. 10

the community's awareness, the entire community is to prepare one young bull for a burnt offering as a pleasing aroma to the LORD, with its grain offering and drink offering according to the regulation, and one male goat as a sin offering. ²⁵ The priest will then make atonement for the entire Israelite community so that they may be forgiven, for the sin was unintentional. They are to bring their offering, one made by fire to the LORD, and their sin offering before the LORD for their unintentional sin. ²⁶ The entire Israelite community and the alien who resides among them will be forgiven, since it happened to all the people unintentionally.

²⁷ "If one person sins unintentionally, he is to present a year-old female goat as a sin offering. ²⁸ The priest will then make atonement before the LORD on behalf of the person who acts in error sinning unintentionally, and when he makes atonement for him, he will be forgiven. ²⁹ You are to have the same law for the person who acts in error, whether he is an Israelite or an alien who resides among you.

³⁰ "But the person who acts defiantly,ᴬ whether native or resident alien, blasphemes the LORD. That person is to be cut off from his people. ³¹ He will certainly be cut off, because he has despised the LORD's word and broken his command; his guilt remains on him."

SABBATH VIOLATION

³² While the Israelites were in the wilderness, they found a man gathering wood on the Sabbath day. ³³ Those who found him gathering wood brought him to Moses, Aaron, and the entire community. ³⁴ They placed him in custody because it had not been decided what should be done to him. ³⁵ Then the LORD told Moses, "The man is to be put to death. The entire community is to stone him outside the camp." ³⁶ So the entire community brought him outside the camp and stoned him to death, as the LORD had commanded Moses.

TASSELS FOR REMEMBRANCE

³⁷ The LORD said to Moses, ³⁸ "Speak to the Israelites and tell them that throughout their generations they are to make tassels for the corners of their garments, and put a blue cord on the tassel at each corner. ³⁹ These will serve as tassels for you to look at, so that you may remember all the LORD's commands and obey them and not prostitute yourselves by following your own heart and your own eyes. ⁴⁰ This way you will remember and obey all my commands and be holy to your God. ⁴¹ I am the LORD your God who brought you out of the land of Egypt to be your God; I am the LORD your God."

KORAH INCITES REBELLION

16 Now Korah son of Izhar, son of Kohath, son of Levi, with Dathan and Abiram, sons of Eliab, and On son of Peleth, sons of Reuben, took ² two hundred and fifty prominent Israelite men who were leaders of the community and representatives in the assembly, and they rebelled against Moses. ³ They came together against Moses and Aaron and told them, "You have gone too far! Everyone in the entire community is holy, and the LORD is among them. Why then do you exalt yourselves above the LORD's assembly?"

ᴬ15:30 Lit *with a high hand*

⁴ When Moses heard this, he fell facedown. ⁵ Then he said to Korah and all his followers, "Tomorrow morning the LORD will reveal who belongs to him, who is set apart, and the one he will let come near him. He will let the one he chooses come near him. ⁶ Korah, you and all your followers are to do this: take firepans, and tomorrow ⁷ place fire in them and put incense on them before the LORD. Then the man the LORD chooses will be the one who is set apart. It is you Levites who have gone too far!"

⁸ Moses also told Korah, "Now listen, Levites! ⁹ Isn't it enough for you that the God of Israel has separated you from the Israelite community to bring you near to himself, to perform the work at the LORD's tabernacle, and to stand before the community to minister to them? ¹⁰ He has brought you near, and all your fellow Levites who are with you, but you are pursuing the priesthood as well. ¹¹ Therefore, it is you and all your followers who have conspired against the LORD! As for Aaron, who is he ᴬ that you should complain about him?"

¹² Moses sent for Dathan and Abiram, the sons of Eliab, but they said, "We will not come! ¹³ Is it not enough that you brought us up from a land flowing with milk and honey to kill us in the wilderness? Do you also have to appoint yourself as ruler over us? ¹⁴ Furthermore, you didn't bring us to a land flowing with milk and honey or give us an inheritance of fields and vineyards. Will you gouge out the eyes of these men? We will not come!"

¹⁵ Then Moses became angry and said to the LORD, "Don't respect their offering. I have not taken one donkey from them or mistreated a single one of them." ¹⁶ So Moses told Korah, "You and all your followers are to appear before the LORD tomorrow — you, they, and Aaron. ¹⁷ Each of you is to take his firepan, place incense on it, and present his firepan before the LORD — 250 firepans. You and Aaron are each to present your firepan also."

¹⁸ Each man took his firepan, placed fire in it, put incense on it, and stood at the entrance to the tent of meeting along with Moses and Aaron. ¹⁹ After Korah assembled the whole community against them at the entrance to the tent of meeting, the glory of the LORD appeared to the whole community. ²⁰ The LORD spoke to Moses and Aaron, ²¹ "Separate yourselves from this community so I may consume them instantly."

²² But Moses and Aaron fell facedown and said, "God, God who gives breath to all, ᴮ when one man sins, will you vent your wrath on the whole community?"

²³ The LORD replied to Moses, ²⁴ "Tell the community: Get away from the dwellings of Korah, Dathan, and Abiram."

²⁵ Moses got up and went to Dathan and Abiram, and the elders of Israel followed him. ²⁶ He warned the community, "Get away now from the tents of these wicked men. Don't touch anything that belongs to them, or you will be swept away because of all their sins." ²⁷ So they got away from the dwellings of Korah, Dathan, and Abiram. Meanwhile, Dathan and Abiram came out and stood at the entrance of their tents with their wives, children, and infants.

²⁸ Then Moses said, "This is how you will know that the LORD sent me to do all these things and that it was not of my own will: ²⁹ If these men die naturally as all people would, and suffer the fate of all, then the LORD has not sent me. ³⁰ But if the LORD brings about something unprecedented, and the

ᴬ16:11 Or Aaron, what has he done ᴮ16:22 Or God of the spirits of all flesh ground opens its mouth and swallows them along with all that belongs to them so that they go down alive into Sheol, then you will know that these men have despised the LORD."

³¹ Just as he finished speaking all these words, the ground beneath them split open. ³² The earth opened its mouth and swallowed them and their households, all Korah's people, and all their possessions. ³³ They went down alive into Sheol with all that belonged to them. The earth closed over them, and they vanished from the assembly. ³⁴ At their cries, all the people of Israel who were around them fled because they thought, "The earth may swallow us too!" ³⁵ Fire also came out from the LORD and consumed the 250 men who were presenting the incense.

³⁶ Then the LORD spoke to Moses: ³⁷ "Tell Eleazar son of Aaron the priest to remove the firepans from the burning debris, because they are holy, and scatter the fire far away. ³⁸ As for the firepans of those who sinned at the cost of their own lives, make them into hammered sheets as plating for the altar, for they presented them before the LORD, and the firepans are holy. They will be a sign to the Israelites."

³⁹ So the priest Eleazar took the bronze firepans that those who were burned had presented, and they were hammered into plating for the altar, ⁴⁰ just as the LORD commanded him through Moses. It was to be a reminder for the Israelites that no unauthorized person outside the lineage of Aaron should approach to offer incense before the LORD and become like Korah and his followers.

⁴¹ The next day the entire Israelite community complained about Moses and Aaron, saying, "You have killed the LORD's people!" ⁴² When the community assembled against them, Moses and Aaron turned toward the tent of meeting, and suddenly the cloud covered it, and the LORD's glory appeared.

⁴³ Moses and Aaron went to the front of the tent of meeting, ⁴⁴ and the LORD said to Moses, ⁴⁵ "Get away from this community so that I may consume them instantly." But they fell facedown.

⁴⁶ Then Moses told Aaron, "Take your firepan, place fire from the altar in it, and add incense. Go quickly to the community and make atonement for them, because wrath has come from the LORD; the plague has begun." ⁴⁷ So Aaron took his firepan as Moses had ordered, ran into the middle of the assembly, and saw that the plague had begun among the people. After he added incense, he made atonement for the people. ⁴⁸ He stood between the dead and the living, and the plague was halted. ⁴⁹ But those who died from the plague numbered 14,700, in addition to those who died because of the Korah incident. ⁵⁰ Aaron then returned to Moses at the entrance to the tent of meeting, since the plague had been halted.

AARON'S STAFF CHOSEN

17 The LORD instructed Moses: ² "Speak to the Israelites and take one staff from them for each ancestral tribe,ᴬ twelve staffs from all the leaders of their tribes.ᴮ Write each man's name on his staff. ³ Write Aaron's name on Levi's staff, because there is to be one staff for the head of each tribe. ⁴ Then place them in the tent of meeting in front of the testimony

---

ᴬ 17:2 Lit *father's house*   ᴮ 17:2 Lit *the house of their fathers*, also in vv. 3,6 where I meet with you. ⁵ The staff of the man I choose will sprout, and I will rid myself of the Israelites' complaints that they have been making about you."

⁶ So Moses spoke to the Israelites, and each of their leaders gave him a staff, one for each of the leaders of their tribes, twelve staffs in all. Aaron's staff was among them. ⁷ Moses placed the staffs before the LORD in the tent of the testimony.

⁸ The next day Moses entered the tent of the testimony and saw that Aaron's staff, representing the house of Levi, had sprouted, formed buds, blossomed, and produced almonds! ⁹ Moses then brought out all the staffs from the LORD's presence to all the Israelites. They saw them, and each man took his own staff. ¹⁰ The LORD told Moses, "Put Aaron's staff back in front of the testimony to be kept as a sign for the rebels, so that you may put an end to their complaints before me, or else they will die." ¹¹ So Moses did as the LORD commanded him.

¹² Then the Israelites declared to Moses, "Look, we're perishing! We're lost; we're all lost! ¹³ Anyone who comes near the LORD's tabernacle will die. Will we all perish?"

PROVISION FOR THE PRIESTHOOD

18 The LORD said to Aaron, "You, your sons, and your ancestral family[A] will be responsible for iniquity against the sanctuary. You and your sons will be responsible for iniquity involving your priesthood. ² But also bring your relatives with you from the tribe of Levi, your ancestral tribe, so they may join you and assist you and your sons in front of the tent of the testimony. ³ They are to perform duties for you and for the whole tent. They must not come near the sanctuary equipment or the altar; otherwise, both they and you will die. ⁴ They are to join you and guard the tent of meeting, doing all the work at the tent, but no unauthorized person may come near you.

⁵ "You are to guard the sanctuary and the altar so that wrath may not fall on the Israelites again. ⁶ Look, I have selected your fellow Levites from the Israelites as a gift for you, assigned by the LORD to work at the tent of meeting. ⁷ But you and your sons will carry out your priestly responsibilities for everything concerning the altar and for what is inside the curtain, and you will do that work. I am giving you the work of the priesthood as a gift,[B] but an unauthorized person who comes near the sanctuary will be put to death."

SUPPORT FOR THE PRIESTS AND LEVITES

⁸ Then the LORD spoke to Aaron, "Look, I have put you in charge of the contributions brought to me. As for all the holy offerings of the Israelites, I have given them to you and your sons as a portion and a permanent statute. ⁹ A portion of the holiest offerings kept from the fire will be yours; every one of their offerings that they give me, whether the grain offering, sin offering, or guilt offering will be most holy for you and your sons. ¹⁰ You are to eat it as a most holy offering.[C] Every male may eat it; it is to be holy to you.

[A]18:1 Lit *the house of your father*   [B]18:7 Or *curtain. So you are to perform the service; a gift of your priesthood I grant*   [C]18:10 Or *it in a most holy place*

¹¹ "The contribution of their gifts also belongs to you. I have given all the Israelites' presentation offerings to you and to your sons and daughters as a permanent statute. Every ceremonially clean person in your house may eat it. ¹² I am giving you all the best of the fresh oil, new wine, and grain, which the Israelites give to the LORD as their firstfruits. ¹³ The firstfruits of all that is in their land, which they bring to the LORD, belong to you. Every clean person in your house may eat them.

¹⁴ "Everything in Israel that is permanently dedicated to the LORD belongs to you. ¹⁵ The firstborn of every living thing, human or animal, presented to the LORD belongs to you. But you must certainly redeem a human firstborn, and redeem the firstborn of an unclean animal. ¹⁶ You will pay the redemption price for a month-old male according to your assessment: five shekels^A of silver by the standard sanctuary shekel, which is twenty gerahs.

¹⁷ "However, you must not redeem the firstborn of an ox, a sheep, or a goat; they are holy. You are to splatter their blood on the altar and burn their fat as a fire offering for a pleasing aroma to the LORD. ¹⁸ But their meat belongs to you. It belongs to you like the breast of the presentation offering and the right thigh.

¹⁹ "I give to you and to your sons and daughters all the holy contributions that the Israelites present to the LORD as a permanent statute. It is a permanent covenant of salt before the LORD for you as well as your offspring."

²⁰ The LORD told Aaron, "You will not have an inheritance in their land; there will be no portion among them for you. I am your portion and your inheritance among the Israelites.

²¹ "Look, I have given the Levites every tenth in Israel as an inheritance in return for the work they do, the work of the tent of meeting. ²² The Israelites must never again come near the tent of meeting, or they will incur guilt and die. ²³ The Levites will do the work of the tent of meeting, and they will bear the consequences of their iniquity. The Levites will not receive an inheritance among the Israelites; this is a permanent statute throughout your generations. ²⁴ For I have given them the tenth that the Israelites present to the LORD as a contribution for their inheritance. That is why I told them that they would not receive an inheritance among the Israelites."

²⁵ The LORD instructed Moses, ²⁶ "Speak to the Levites and tell them: When you receive from the Israelites the tenth that I have given you as your inheritance, you are to present part of it as an offering to the LORD — a tenth of the tenth. ²⁷ Your offering will be credited to you as if it were your grain from the threshing floor or the full harvest from the winepress. ²⁸ You are to present an offering to the LORD from every tenth you receive from the Israelites. Give some of it to the priest Aaron as an offering to the LORD. ²⁹ You must present the entire offering due the LORD from all your gifts. The best part of the tenth is to be consecrated.

³⁰ "Tell them further: Once you have presented the best part of the tenth, and it is credited to you Levites as the produce of the threshing floor or the winepress, ³¹ then you and your household may eat it anywhere. It is your wage in return for your work at the tent of meeting. ³² You will not incur guilt because of it once you have presented the best part of it, but you must not defile the Israelites' holy offerings, so that you will not die."

---

^A18:16 A shekel is about two-fifths of an ounce

PURIFICATION RITUAL

19 The LORD spoke to Moses and Aaron, ² "This is the legal statute that the LORD has commanded: Instruct the Israelites to bring you an unblemished red cow that has no defect and has never been yoked. ³ Give it to the priest Eleazar, and he will have it brought outside the camp and slaughtered in his presence. ⁴ The priest Eleazar is to take some of its blood with his finger and sprinkle it seven times toward the front of the tent of meeting. ⁵ The cow is to be burned in his sight. Its hide, flesh, and blood, are to be burned along with its waste. ⁶ The priest is to take cedar wood, hyssop, and crimson yarn, and throw them onto the fire where the cow is burning. ⁷ Then the priest must wash his clothes and bathe his body in water; after that he may enter the camp, but he will remain ceremonially unclean until evening. ⁸ The one who burned the cow must also wash his clothes and bathe his body in water, and he will remain unclean until evening.

⁹ "A man who is clean is to gather up the cow's ashes and deposit them outside the camp in a ceremonially clean place. The ashes will be kept by the Israelite community for preparing the water to remove impurity; it is a sin offering. ¹⁰ Then the one who gathers up the cow's ashes must wash his clothes, and he will remain unclean until evening. This is a permanent statute for the Israelites and for the alien who resides among them.

¹¹ "The person who touches any human corpse will be unclean for seven days. ¹² He is to purify himself with the water[A] on the third day and the seventh day; then he will be clean. But if he does not purify himself on the third and seventh days, he will not be clean. ¹³ Anyone who touches a body of a person who has died, and does not purify himself, defiles the tabernacle of the LORD. That person will be cut off from Israel. He remains unclean because the water for impurity has not been sprinkled on him, and his uncleanness is still on him.

¹⁴ "This is the law when a person dies in a tent: everyone who enters the tent and everyone who is already in the tent will be unclean for seven days, ¹⁵ and any open container without a lid tied on it is unclean. ¹⁶ Anyone in the open field who touches a person who has been killed by the sword or has died, or who even touches a human bone, or a grave, will be unclean for seven days. ¹⁷ For the purification of the unclean person, they are to take some of the ashes of the burnt sin offering, put them in a jar, and add fresh water to them. ¹⁸ A person who is clean is to take hyssop, dip it in the water, and sprinkle the tent, all the furnishings, and the people who were there. He is also to sprinkle the one who touched a bone, a grave, a corpse, or a person who had been killed.

¹⁹ "The one who is clean is to sprinkle the unclean person on the third day and the seventh day. After he purifies the unclean person on the seventh day, the one being purified must wash his clothes and bathe in water, and he will be clean by evening. ²⁰ But a person who is unclean and does not purify himself, that person will be cut off from the assembly because he has defiled the sanctuary of the LORD. The water for impurity has not been sprinkled on him; he is unclean. ²¹ This is a permanent statute for them. The person who sprinkles the water for impurity is to wash his clothes, and whoever touches the water for impurity will be unclean until evening. ²² Anything

A19:12 Or *ashes*; lit *with it*

the unclean person touches will become unclean, and anyone who touches it will be unclean until evening."

WATER FROM THE ROCK

20 The entire Israelite community entered the Wilderness of Zin in the first month, and they[A] settled in Kadesh. Miriam died and was buried there.

² There was no water for the community, so they assembled against Moses and Aaron. ³ The people quarreled with Moses and said, "If only we had perished when our brothers perished before the Lord. ⁴ Why have you brought the Lord's assembly into this wilderness for us and our livestock to die here? ⁵ Why have you led us up from Egypt to bring us to this evil place? It's not a place of grain, figs, vines, and pomegranates, and there is no water to drink!"

⁶ Then Moses and Aaron went from the presence of the assembly to the doorway of the tent of meeting. They fell facedown, and the glory of the Lord appeared to them. ⁷ The Lord spoke to Moses, ⁸ "Take the staff and assemble the community. You and your brother Aaron are to speak to the rock while they watch, and it will yield its water. You will bring out water for them from the rock and provide drink for the community and their livestock."

⁹ So Moses took the staff from the Lord's presence just as he had commanded him. ¹⁰ Moses and Aaron summoned the assembly in front of the rock, and Moses said to them, "Listen, you rebels! Must we bring water out of this rock for you?" ¹¹ Then Moses raised his hand and struck the rock twice with his staff, so that abundant water gushed out, and the community and their livestock drank.

¹² But the Lord said to Moses and Aaron, "Because you did not trust me to demonstrate my holiness in the sight of the Israelites, you will not bring this assembly into the land I have given them." ¹³ These are the Waters of Meribah,[B] where the Israelites quarreled with the Lord, and he demonstrated his holiness to them.

EDOM DENIES PASSAGE

¹⁴ Moses sent messengers from Kadesh to the king of Edom, "This is what your brother Israel says, 'You know all the hardships that have overtaken us. ¹⁵ Our fathers went down to Egypt, and we lived in Egypt many years, but the Egyptians treated us and our fathers badly. ¹⁶ When we cried out to the Lord, he heard our plea,[C] and sent an angel,[D] and brought us out of Egypt. Now look, we are in Kadesh, a city on the border of your territory. ¹⁷ Please let us travel through your land. We won't travel through any field or vineyard, or drink any well water. We will travel the King's Highway; we won't turn to the right or the left until we have traveled through your territory.'"

¹⁸ But Edom answered him, "You will not travel through our land, or we will come out and confront you with the sword."

¹⁹ "We will go on the main road," the Israelites replied to them, "and if we or our herds drink your water, we will pay its price. There will be no problem; only let us travel through on foot."

[A]20:1 Lit the people [B]20:13 = Quarreling [C]20:16 Lit voice [D]20:16 Or a messenger

²⁰ Yet Edom insisted, "You may not travel through." And they came out to confront them with a large force of heavily-armed people.ᴬ ²¹ Edom refused to allow Israel to travel through their territory, and Israel turned away from them.

AARON'S DEATH

²² After they set out from Kadesh, the entire Israelite community came to Mount Hor. ²³ The LORD said to Moses and Aaron at Mount Hor on the border of the land of Edom, ²⁴ "Aaron will be gathered to his people; he will not enter the land I have given the Israelites, because you both rebelled against my command at the Waters of Meribah. ²⁵ Take Aaron and his son Eleazar and bring them up Mount Hor. ²⁶ Remove Aaron's garments and put them on his son Eleazar. Aaron will be gathered to his people and die there."

²⁷ So Moses did as the LORD commanded, and they climbed Mount Hor in the sight of the whole community. ²⁸ After Moses removed Aaron's garments and put them on his son Eleazar, Aaron died there on top of the mountain. Then Moses and Eleazar came down from the mountain. ²⁹ When the whole community saw that Aaron had passed away, the entire house of Israel mourned for him thirty days.

CANAANITE KING DEFEATED

21 When the Canaanite king of Arad, who lived in the Negev, heard that Israel was coming on the Atharim road, he fought against Israel and captured some prisoners. ² Then Israel made a vow to the LORD, "If you will hand this people over to us, we will completely destroy their cities." ³ The LORD listened to Israel's request and handed the Canaanites over to them, and Israel completely destroyed them and their cities. So they named the place Hormah.ᴮ

THE BRONZE SNAKE

⁴ Then they set out from Mount Hor by way of the Red Sea to bypass the land of Edom, but the people became impatient because of the journey. ⁵ The people spoke against God and Moses: "Why have you led us up from Egypt to die in the wilderness? There is no bread or water, and we detest this wretched food!" ⁶ Then the LORD sent poisonousᶜ snakes among the people, and they bit them so that many Israelites died.

⁷ The people then came to Moses and said, "We have sinned by speaking against the LORD and against you. Intercede with the LORD so that he will take the snakes away from us." And Moses interceded for the people.

⁸ Then the LORD said to Moses, "Make a snake image and mount it on a pole. When anyone who is bitten looks at it, he will recover." ⁹ So Moses made a bronze snake and mounted it on a pole. Whenever someone was bitten, and he looked at the bronze snake, he recovered.

JOURNEY AROUND MOAB

¹⁰ The Israelites set out and camped at Oboth. ¹¹ They set out from Oboth and camped at Iye-abarim in the wilderness that borders Moab on the east.

ᴬ20:20 Lit *with numerous people and a strong hand*   ᴮ21:3 = Destruction
ᶜ21:6 Lit *Burning*

¹² From there they went and camped at Zered Valley. ¹³ They set out from there and camped on the other side of the Arnon River, in the wilderness that extends from the Amorite border, because the Arnon was the Moabite border between Moab and the Amorites. ¹⁴ Therefore it is stated in the Book of the LORD's Wars:

> Waheb in Suphah
> and the ravines of the Arnon,
> ¹⁵ even the slopes of the ravines
> that extend to the site of Ar
> and lie along the border of Moab.

¹⁶ From there they went to Beer,ᴬ the well the LORD told Moses about, "Gather the people so I may give them water." ¹⁷ Then Israel sang this song:

> Spring up, well — sing to it!
> ¹⁸ The princes dug the well;
> the nobles of the people hollowed it out
> with a scepter and with their staffs.

They went from the wilderness to Mattanah, ¹⁹ from Mattanah to Nahaliel, from Nahaliel to Bamoth, ²⁰ from Bamoth to the valley in the territory of Moab near the Pisgah highlands that overlook the wasteland.ᴮ

AMORITE KINGS DEFEATED

²¹ Israel sent messengers to say to King Sihon of the Amorites: ²² "Let us travel through your land. We won't go into the fields or vineyards. We won't drink any well water. We will travel the King's Highway until we have traveled through your territory." ²³ But Sihon would not let Israel travel through his territory. Instead, he gathered his whole army and went out to confront Israel in the wilderness. When he came to Jahaz, he fought against Israel. ²⁴ Israel struck him with the sword and took possession of his land from the Arnon to the Jabbok, but only up to the Ammonite border, because it was fortified.ᶜ

²⁵ Israel took all the cities and lived in all these Amorite cities, including Heshbon and all its surrounding villages. ²⁶ Heshbon was the city of King Sihon of the Amorites, who had fought against the former king of Moab and had taken control of all his land as far as the Arnon. ²⁷ Therefore the poetsᴰ say:

> Come to Heshbon, let it be rebuilt;
> let the city of Sihon be restored.ᴱ
> ²⁸ For fire came out of Heshbon,
> a flame from the city of Sihon.
> It consumed Ar of Moab,
> the citizens of Arnon's heights.
> ²⁹ Woe to you, Moab!
> You have been destroyed, people of Chemosh!
> He gave up his sons as refugees,
> and his daughters into captivity
> to Sihon the Amorite king.

ᴬ21:16 = Well   ᴮ21:20 Or overlook Jeshimon   ᶜ21:24 LXX reads because the Ammonite border was Jazer   ᴰ21:27 Lit ones who speak proverbs   ᴱ21:27 Or firmly founded

³⁰ We threw them down;
Heshbon has been destroyed as far as Dibon.
We caused desolation as far as Nophah,
which reaches as far as Medeba.

³¹ So Israel lived in the Amorites' land. ³² After Moses sent spies to Jazer, Israel captured its surrounding villages and drove out the Amorites who were there.

³³ Then they turned and went up the road to Bashan, and King Og of Bashan came out against them with his whole army to do battle at Edrei. ³⁴ But the LORD said to Moses, "Do not fear him, for I have handed him over to you along with his whole army and his land. Do to him as you did to King Sihon of the Amorites, who lived in Heshbon." ³⁵ So they struck him, his sons, and his whole army until no one was left,^A and they took possession of his land.

BALAK HIRES BALAAM

22 The Israelites traveled on and camped in the plains of Moab near the Jordan across from Jericho. ² Now Balak son of Zippor saw all that Israel had done to the Amorites. ³ Moab was terrified of the people because they were numerous, and Moab dreaded the Israelites. ⁴ So the Moabites said to the elders of Midian, "This horde will devour everything around us like an ox eats up the green plants in the field."

Since Balak son of Zippor was Moab's king at that time, ⁵ he sent messengers to Balaam son of Beor at Pethor, which is by the Euphrates in the land of his people.^{B,C} Balak said to him: "Look, a people has come out of Egypt; they cover the surface of the land and are living right across from me. ⁶ Please come and put a curse on these people for me because they are more powerful than I am. I may be able to defeat them and drive them out of the land, for I know that those you bless are blessed and those you curse are cursed."

⁷ The elders of Moab and Midian departed with fees for divination in hand. They came to Balaam and reported Balak's words to him. ⁸ He said to them, "Spend the night here, and I will give you the answer the LORD tells me." So the officials of Moab stayed with Balaam.

⁹ Then God came to Balaam and asked, "Who are these men with you?"

¹⁰ Balaam replied to God, "Balak son of Zippor, king of Moab, sent this message to me: ¹¹ 'Look, a people has come out of Egypt, and they cover the surface of the land. Now come and put a curse on them for me. I may be able to fight against them and drive them away.'"

¹² Then God said to Balaam, "You are not to go with them. You are not to curse this people, for they are blessed."

¹³ So Balaam got up the next morning and said to Balak's officials, "Go back to your land, because the LORD has refused to let me go with you."

¹⁴ The officials of Moab arose, returned to Balak, and reported, "Balaam refused to come with us."

¹⁵ Balak sent officials again who were more numerous and higher in rank than the others. ¹⁶ They came to Balaam and said to him, "This is what Balak son of Zippor says: 'Let nothing keep you from coming to me, ¹⁷ for I will greatly honor you and do whatever you ask me. So please come and put a curse on these people for me!'"

---

^A21:35 Lit *left to him*   ^B22:5 Sam, Vg, Syr read *of the Ammonites*   ^C22:5 Or *of the Amawites*

¹⁸ But Balaam responded to the servants of Balak, "If Balak were to give me his house full of silver and gold, I could not go against the command of the LORD my God to do anything small or great. ¹⁹ Please stay here overnight as the others did, so that I may find out what else the LORD has to tell me."

²⁰ God came to Balaam at night and said to him, "Since these men have come to summon you, get up and go with them, but you must only do what I tell you." ²¹ When he got up in the morning, Balaam saddled his donkey and went with the officials of Moab.

BALAAM'S DONKEY AND THE ANGEL

²² But God was incensed that Balaam was going, and the angel of the LORD took his stand on the path to oppose him. Balaam was riding his donkey, and his two servants were with him. ²³ When the donkey saw the angel of the LORD standing on the path with a drawn sword in his hand, she turned off the path and went into the field. So Balaam hit her to return her to the path. ²⁴ Then the angel of the LORD stood in a narrow passage between the vineyards, with a stone wall on either side. ²⁵ The donkey saw the angel of the LORD and pressed herself against the wall, squeezing Balaam's foot against it. So he hit her once again. ²⁶ The angel of the LORD went ahead and stood in a narrow place where there was no room to turn to the right or the left. ²⁷ When the donkey saw the angel of the LORD, she crouched down under Balaam. So he became furious and beat the donkey with his stick.

²⁸ Then the LORD opened the donkey's mouth, and she asked Balaam, "What have I done to you that you have beaten me these three times?"

²⁹ Balaam answered the donkey, "You made me look like a fool. If I had a sword in my hand, I'd kill you now!"

³⁰ But the donkey said, "Am I not the donkey you've ridden all your life until today? Have I ever treated you this way before?"

"No," he replied.

³¹ Then the LORD opened Balaam's eyes, and he saw the angel of the LORD standing in the path with a drawn sword in his hand. Balaam knelt low and bowed in worship on his face. ³² The angel of the LORD asked him, "Why have you beaten your donkey these three times? Look, I came out to oppose you, because I consider what you are doing to be evil.^A ³³ The donkey saw me and turned away from me these three times. If she had not turned away from me, I would have killed you by now and let her live."

³⁴ Balaam said to the angel of the LORD, "I have sinned, for I did not know that you were standing in the path to confront me. And now, if it is evil in your sight, I will go back."

³⁵ Then the angel of the LORD said to Balaam, "Go with the men, but you are to say only what I tell you." So Balaam went with Balak's officials.

³⁶ When Balak heard that Balaam was coming, he went out to meet him at the Moabite city^B on the Arnon border at the edge of his territory. ³⁷ Balak asked Balaam, "Did I not send you an urgent summons? Why didn't you come to me? Am I really not able to reward you?"

³⁸ Balaam said to him, "Look, I have come to you, but can I say anything I want? I must speak only the message God puts in my mouth." ³⁹ So Balaam

---

^A22:32 Lit *because your way is perverse before me*   ^B22:36 Or *at Ir-moab,* or *at Ar of Moab* went with Balak, and they came to Kiriath-huzoth.[A] [40] Balak sacrificed cattle, sheep, and goats and sent for Balaam and the officials who were with him. [41] In the morning, Balak took Balaam and brought him to Bamoth-baal.[B] From there he saw the outskirts of the people's camp.

BALAAM'S ORACLES

23 Then Balaam said to Balak, "Build me seven altars here and prepare seven bulls and seven rams for me." [2] So Balak did as Balaam directed, and they offered a bull and a ram on each altar. [3] Balaam said to Balak, "Stay here by your burnt offering while I am gone. Maybe the LORD will meet with me. I will tell you whatever he reveals to me." So he went to a barren hill.

[4] God met with him and Balaam said to him, "I have arranged seven altars and offered a bull and a ram on each altar." [5] Then the LORD put a message in Balaam's mouth and said, "Return to Balak and say what I tell you."

[6] So he returned to Balak, who was standing there by his burnt offering with all the officials of Moab.

BALAAM'S FIRST ORACLE

[7] Balaam proclaimed his poem:

> Balak brought me from Aram;
> the king of Moab, from the eastern mountains:
> "Come, put a curse on Jacob for me;
> come, denounce Israel!"
> [8] How can I curse someone God has not cursed?
> How can I denounce someone the LORD has not denounced?
> [9] I see them from the top of rocky cliffs,
> and I watch them from the hills.
> There is a people living alone;
> it does not consider itself among the nations.
> [10] Who has counted the dust of Jacob
> or numbered even one-fourth of Israel?
> Let me die the death of the upright;
> let the end of my life be like theirs.

[11] "What have you done to me?" Balak asked Balaam. "I brought you to curse my enemies, but look, you have only blessed them!"

[12] He answered, "Shouldn't I say exactly what the LORD puts in my mouth?"

BALAAM'S SECOND ORACLE

[13] Then Balak said to him, "Please come with me to another place where you can see them. You will only see the outskirts of their camp; you won't see all of them. From there, put a curse on them for me." [14] So Balak took him to Lookout Field[C] on top of Pisgah, built seven altars, and offered a bull and a ram on each altar.

[15] Balaam said to Balak, "Stay here by your burnt offering while I seek the LORD over there."

[A] 22:39 = The City of Streets   [B] 22:41 = The High Places of Baal   [C] 23:14 Or to the field of Zophim

THE GOD WHO STOOPS TO CONQUER

NUMBERS 23–24; NUMBERS 11:1-15

In the summertime of my eighth year, the Toledo Zoo borrowed two giant pandas from a zoo in China. Mom braided our hair, tied our shoes, and drove over an hour to treat us to this wonder. But before we even made it to lunchtime, we complained of heat, hunger, boredom, and exhaustion. Instead of enjoying hippos and pandas, I griped and whined about stones in my jelly shoes and unacceptable PB&J sandwiches.

Mom valiantly steered us around the zoo, encouraging us to look up and take notice of the goodness at hand. I think she even treated us to ice cream on the way home. My eight-year-old brain assumed she was untroubled by the heat and the grievances of walking all day.

Now, I have five children of my own. I took them to the zoo by myself this summer. As a child, it never occurred to me that I wasn't the only one who was hot and tired. I'd never even considered that my mom might be subject to the same physical sensations of heat and exhaustion.

Why did my mom take me to the zoo? Why did she put herself through the torture of treating my sister and me to anything? Because she adored us.

This is a tiny picture of what God was doing for Israel when Balak asked Balaam to curse Israel for him. The people of Israel certainly deserved to be cursed. They were hot and tired in the wilderness, and in the ten chapters proceeding,

they whined and complained (Nm 11:1-15), rejected God's appointed leadership (Nm 12), and fell into outright rebellion (Nm 14; 16).

Yet, God repeatedly blessed the Israelites in spite of their sin. He adored them and He adores us, so much more than we deserve.

But, oh, aren't we just the same as those Israelites? I muster prayer time out of the last few seconds before I fall asleep, hoping God will be grateful for my efforts. I give Him the dregs of my day instead of my firstfruit.

In his book, *The Problem of Pain*, C.S. Lewis observes:

"If God were proud He would hardly have us on such terms: but He is not proud, He stoops to conquer, He will have us even though we have shown that we prefer everything else to Him, and come to Him because there is 'nothing better' now to be had."

How beautiful and humbling that God stoops to conquer us! **Despite our sin and ignorance of what it really cost Him to bless us, God regards us as righteous because of His covenant with us** (2Tm 1:9). We can't make ourselves more worthy of trips to the zoo or blessing from on high, because God has already met us and lovingly imputed His righteousness to us.

What grace!

¹⁶ The LORD met with Balaam and put a message in his mouth. Then he said, "Return to Balak and say what I tell you."

¹⁷ So he returned to Balak, who was standing there by his burnt offering with the officials of Moab. Balak asked him, "What did the LORD say?"

¹⁸ Balaam proclaimed his poem:

> Balak, get up and listen;
> son of Zippor, pay attention to what I say!
> ¹⁹ God is not a man, that he might lie,
> or a son of man, that he might change his mind.
> Does he speak and not act,
> or promise and not fulfill?
> ²⁰ I have indeed received a command to bless;
> since he has blessed,^A I cannot change it.
> ²¹ He considers no disaster for Jacob;
> he sees no trouble for Israel.^B
> The LORD their God is with them,
> and there is rejoicing over the King among them.
> ²² God brought them out of Egypt;
> he is like the horns of a wild ox for them.^C
> ²³ There is no magic curse against Jacob
> and no divination against Israel.
> It will now be said about Jacob and Israel,
> "What great things God has done!"
> ²⁴ A people rise up like a lioness;
> they rouse themselves like a lion.
> They will not lie down until they devour the prey
> and drink the blood of the slain.

²⁵ Then Balak told Balaam, "Don't curse them and don't bless them!"

²⁶ But Balaam answered him, "Didn't I tell you: Whatever the LORD says, I must do?"

BALAAM'S THIRD ORACLE

²⁷ Again Balak said to Balaam, "Please come. I will take you to another place. Maybe it will be agreeable to God that you can put a curse on them for me there." ²⁸ So Balak took Balaam to the top of Peor, which overlooks the wasteland.^D

²⁹ Balaam told Balak, "Build me seven altars here and prepare seven bulls and seven rams for me." ³⁰ So Balak did as Balaam said and offered a bull and a ram on each altar.

24 Since Balaam saw that it pleased the LORD to bless Israel, he did not go to seek omens as on previous occasions, but turned^E toward the wilderness. ² When Balaam looked up and saw Israel encamped tribe by tribe, the Spirit of God came on him, ³ and he proclaimed his poem:

> The oracle of Balaam son of Beor,
> the oracle of the man whose eyes are opened,

---

^A23:20 Sam, LXX read *since I will bless*   ^B23:21 Or *He does not observe sin in Jacob; he does not see wrongdoing in Israel*   ^C23:22 Or *Egypt; they have the horns of a wild ox*   ^D23:28 Or *overlooks Jeshimon*   ^E24:1 Lit *set his face*

⁴ the oracle of one who hears the sayings of God,
    who sees a vision from the Almighty,
    who falls into a trance with his eyes uncovered:
⁵ How beautiful are your tents, Jacob,
    your dwellings, Israel.
⁶ They stretch out like river valleys,ᴬ
    like gardens beside a stream,
    like aloes the Lord has planted,
    like cedars beside the water.
⁷ Water will flow from his buckets,
    and his seed will be by abundant water.
    His king will be greater than Agag,
    and his kingdom will be exalted.
⁸ God brought him out of Egypt;
    he is likeᴮ the horns of a wild ox for them.
    He will feed on enemy nations
    and gnaw their bones;
    he will strike them with his arrows.
⁹ He crouches, he lies down like a lion
    or a lioness — who dares to rouse him?
    Those who bless you will be blessed,
    and those who curse you will be cursed.

¹⁰ Then Balak became furious with Balaam, struck his hands together, and said to him, "I summoned you to put a curse on my enemies, but instead, you have blessed them these three times. ¹¹ Now go to your home! I said I would reward you richly, but look, the Lord has denied you a reward."

¹² Balaam answered Balak, "Didn't I previously tell the messengers you sent me: ¹³ If Balak were to give me his house full of silver and gold, I could not go against the Lord's command, to do anything good or bad of my own will? I will say whatever the Lord says. ¹⁴ Now I am going back to my people, but first, let me warn you what these people will do to your people in the future."

BALAAM'S FOURTH ORACLE

¹⁵ Then he proclaimed his poem:
    The oracle of Balaam son of Beor,
    the oracle of the man whose eyes are opened;
¹⁶ the oracle of one who hears the sayings of God
    and has knowledge from the Most High,
    who sees a vision from the Almighty,
    who falls into a trance with his eyes uncovered:
¹⁷ I see him, but not now;
    I perceive him, but not near.
    A star will come from Jacob,
    and a scepter will arise from Israel.
    He will smash the foreheadᶜ of Moab
    and strike downᴰ all the Shethites.ᴱ

ᴬ24:6 Or like date palms   ᴮ24:8 Or he has   ᶜ24:17 Or frontiers   ᴰ24:17 Sam reads and the skulls of; Jr 48:45   ᴱ24:17 Or Sethites

18   Edom will become a possession;
       Seir will become a possession of its enemies,
       but Israel will be triumphant.
19   One who comes from Jacob will rule;
       he will destroy the city's survivors.

20 Then Balaam saw Amalek and proclaimed his poem:
       Amalek was first among the nations,
       but his future is destruction.

21 Next he saw the Kenites and proclaimed his poem:
       Your dwelling place is enduring;
       your nest is set in the cliffs.
22   Kain will be destroyed
       when Asshur takes you captive.

23 Once more he proclaimed his poem:
       Ah, who can live when God does this?
24   Ships will come from the coast of Kittim;
       they will carry out raids against Asshur and Eber,
       but they too will come to destruction.
25 Balaam then arose and went back to his homeland, and Balak also went his way.

ISRAEL WORSHIPS BAAL

25 While Israel was staying in the Acacia Grove,^A the people began to prostitute themselves with the women of Moab. ² The women invited them to the sacrifices for their gods, and the people ate and bowed in worship to their gods. ³ So Israel aligned itself with Baal of Peor, and the LORD's anger burned against Israel. ⁴ The LORD said to Moses, "Take all the leaders of the people and execute^B them in broad daylight before the LORD so that his burning anger may turn away from Israel."

⁵ So Moses told Israel's judges, "Kill each of the men who aligned themselves with Baal of Peor."

PHINEHAS INTERVENES

⁶ An Israelite man came bringing a Midianite woman to his relatives in the sight of Moses and the whole Israelite community while they were weeping at the entrance to the tent of meeting. ⁷ When Phinehas son of Eleazar, son of Aaron the priest, saw this, he got up from the assembly, took a spear in his hand, ⁸ followed the Israelite man into the tent,^C and drove it through both the Israelite man and the woman — through her belly. Then the plague on the Israelites was stopped, ⁹ but those who died in the plague numbered twenty-four thousand.

¹⁰ The LORD spoke to Moses, ¹¹ "Phinehas son of Eleazar, son of Aaron the priest, has turned back my wrath from the Israelites because he was zealous among them with my zeal,^D so that I did not destroy the Israelites

---

^A25:1 Or in Shittim   ^B25:4 Or impale, or hang, or expose; Hb obscure
^C25:8 Perhaps a tent shrine or bridal tent   ^D25:11 Or jealousy

in my zeal. ¹² Therefore declare: I grant him my covenant of peace. ¹³ It will be a covenant of perpetual priesthood for him and his future descendants, because he was zealous for his God and made atonement for the Israelites."

¹⁴ The name of the slain Israelite man, who was struck dead with the Midianite woman, was Zimri son of Salu, the leader of a Simeonite family.^A ¹⁵ The name of the slain Midianite woman was Cozbi, the daughter of Zur, a tribal head of a family in Midian.

VENGEANCE AGAINST THE MIDIANITES

¹⁶ The Lord told Moses: ¹⁷ "Attack the Midianites and strike them dead. ¹⁸ For they attacked you with the treachery that they used against you in the Peor incident. They did the same in the case involving their sister Cozbi, daughter of the Midianite leader who was killed the day the plague came at Peor."

THE SECOND CENSUS

26 After the plague, the Lord said to Moses and Eleazar son of Aaron the priest, ² "Take a census of the entire Israelite community by their ancestral families^B of those twenty years old or more who can serve in Israel's army."

³ So Moses and the priest Eleazar said to them in the plains of Moab by the Jordan across from Jericho, ⁴ "Take a census of those twenty years old or more, as the Lord had commanded Moses and the Israelites who came out of the land of Egypt."

⁵ Reuben was the firstborn of Israel.
Reuben's descendants:
the Hanochite clan from Hanoch;
the Palluite clan from Pallu;
⁶ the Hezronite clan from Hezron;
the Carmite clan from Carmi.
⁷ These were the Reubenite clans,
and their registered men numbered 43,730.
⁸ The son of Pallu was Eliab.
⁹ The sons of Eliab were Nemuel, Dathan, and Abiram.
(It was Dathan and Abiram, chosen by the community, who fought against Moses and Aaron; they and Korah's followers fought against the Lord. ¹⁰ The earth opened its mouth and swallowed them with Korah, when his followers died and the fire consumed 250 men. They serve as a warning sign. ¹¹ The sons of Korah, however, did not die.)

¹² Simeon's descendants by their clans:
the Nemuelite clan from Nemuel;
the Jaminite clan from Jamin;
the Jachinite clan from Jachin;
¹³ the Zerahite clan from Zerah;
the Shaulite clan from Shaul.
¹⁴ These were the Simeonite clans, numbering 22,200 men.

---

^A 25:14 Lit *a father's house,* also in v. 15   ^B 26:2 Lit *the house of their fathers*

15 Gad's descendants by their clans:
the Zephonite clan from Zephon;
the Haggite clan from Haggi;
the Shunite clan from Shuni;
16 the Oznite clan from Ozni;
the Erite clan from Eri;
17 the Arodite clan from Arod;
the Arelite clan from Areli.
18 These were the Gadite clans numbered by their
registered men: 40,500.

19 Judah's sons included Er and Onan, but they died in the land of
Canaan. 20 Judah's descendants by their clans:
the Shelanite clan from Shelah;
the Perezite clan from Perez;
the Zerahite clan from Zerah.
21 The descendants of Perez:
the Hezronite clan from Hezron;
the Hamulite clan from Hamul.
22 These were Judah's clans numbered by their registered men: 76,500.

23 Issachar's descendants by their clans:
the Tolaite clan from Tola;
the Punite clan from Puvah;^A
24 the Jashubite clan from Jashub;
the Shimronite clan from Shimron.
25 These were Issachar's clans numbered by their
registered men: 64,300.

26 Zebulun's descendants by their clans:
the Seredite clan from Sered;
the Elonite clan from Elon;
the Jahleelite clan from Jahleel.
27 These were the Zebulunite clans numbered by their
registered men: 60,500.

28 Joseph's descendants by their clans from Manasseh and Ephraim:
29 Manasseh's descendants:
the Machirite clan from Machir.
Machir fathered Gilead;
the Gileadite clan from Gilead.
30 These were Gilead's descendants:
the Iezerite clan from Iezer;
the Helekite clan from Helek;
31 the Asrielite clan from Asriel;
the Shechemite clan from Shechem;
32 the Shemidaite clan from Shemida;
the Hepherite clan from Hepher;

---

^A26:23 Sam, LXX, Vg, Syr read *Puite clan from Puah*; 1Ch 7:1

33 Zelophehad son of Hepher had no sons — only daughters. The names of Zelophehad's daughters were Mahlah, Noah, Hoglah, Milcah, and Tirzah.

34 These were Manasseh's clans, numbered by their registered men: 52,700.

35 These were Ephraim's descendants by their clans:
the Shuthelahite clan from Shuthelah;
the Becherite clan from Becher;
the Tahanite clan from Tahan.

36 These were Shuthelah's descendants:
the Eranite clan from Eran.

37 These were the Ephraimite clans numbered by their registered men: 32,500.
These were Joseph's descendants by their clans.

38 Benjamin's descendants by their clans:
the Belaite clan from Bela;
the Ashbelite clan from Ashbel;
the Ahiramite clan from Ahiram;

39 the Shuphamite clan from Shupham; [A]
the Huphamite clan from Hupham.

40 Bela's descendants from Ard and Naaman:
the Ardite clan from Ard;
the Naamite clan from Naaman.

41 These were the Benjaminite clans numbered by their registered men: 45,600.

42 These were Dan's descendants by their clans:
the Shuhamite clan from Shuham.
These were the clans of Dan by their clans.

43 All the Shuhamite clans numbered by their registered men: 64,400.

44 Asher's descendants by their clans:
the Imnite clan from Imnah;
the Ishvite clan from Ishvi;
the Beriite clan from Beriah.

45 From Beriah's descendants:
the Heberite clan from Heber;
the Malchielite clan from Malchiel.

46 And the name of Asher's daughter was Serah.

47 These were the Asherite clans numbered by their registered men: 53,400.

48 Naphtali's descendants by their clans:
the Jahzeelite clan from Jahzeel;
the Gunite clan from Guni;

49 the Jezerite clan from Jezer;
the Shillemite clan from Shillem.

[A]26:39 Some Hb mss, Sam, LXX, Syr, Tg, Vg; other Hb mss read *Shephupham*

⁵⁰ These were the Naphtali clans numbered by their registered men: 45,400.

⁵¹ These registered Israelite men numbered 601,730.

⁵² The LORD spoke to Moses, ⁵³ "The land is to be divided among them as an inheritance based on the number of names. ⁵⁴ Increase the inheritance for a large tribe and decrease it for a small one. Each is to be given its inheritance according to those who were registered in it. ⁵⁵ The land is to be divided by lot; they will receive an inheritance according to the names of their ancestral tribes. ⁵⁶ Each inheritance will be divided by lot among the larger and smaller tribes."

⁵⁷ These were the Levites registered
by their clans:
the Gershonite clan from Gershon;
the Kohathite clan from Kohath;
the Merarite clan from Merari.
⁵⁸ These were the Levite family groups:
the Libnite clan,
the Hebronite clan,
the Mahlite clan,
the Mushite clan,
and the Korahite clan.

Kohath was the ancestor of Amram. ⁵⁹ The name of Amram's wife was Jochebed, a descendant of Levi, born to Levi in Egypt. She bore to Amram: Aaron, Moses, and their sister Miriam. ⁶⁰ Nadab, Abihu, Eleazar, and Ithamar were born to Aaron, ⁶¹ but Nadab and Abihu died when they presented unauthorized fire before the LORD. ⁶² Those registered were 23,000, every male one month old or more; they were not registered among the other Israelites, because no inheritance was given to them among the Israelites.

⁶³ These were the ones registered by Moses and the priest Eleazar when they registered the Israelites on the plains of Moab by the Jordan across from Jericho. ⁶⁴ But among them there was not one of those who had been registered by Moses and the priest Aaron when they registered the Israelites in the Wilderness of Sinai. ⁶⁵ For the LORD had said to them that they would all die in the wilderness. None of them was left except Caleb son of Jephunneh and Joshua son of Nun.

A CASE OF DAUGHTERS' INHERITANCE

27 The daughters of Zelophehad approached; Zelophehad was the son of Hepher, son of Gilead, son of Machir, son of Manasseh from the clans of Manasseh, the son of Joseph. These were the names of his daughters: Mahlah, Noah, Hoglah, Milcah, and Tirzah. ² They stood before Moses, the priest Eleazar, the leaders, and the entire community at the entrance to the tent of meeting and said, ³ "Our father died in the wilderness, but he was not among Korah's followers, who gathered together against the LORD. Instead, he died because of his own sin, and he had no sons. ⁴ Why should the name of our father be taken away from his clan? Since he had no son, give us property among our father's brothers."

[5] Moses brought their case before the LORD, [6] and the LORD answered him, [7] "What Zelophehad's daughters say is correct. You are to give them hereditary property among their father's brothers and transfer their father's inheritance to them. [8] Tell the Israelites: When a man dies without having a son, transfer his inheritance to his daughter. [9] If he has no daughter, give his inheritance to his brothers. [10] If he has no brothers, give his inheritance to his father's brothers. [11] If his father has no brothers, give his inheritance to the nearest relative of his clan, and he will take possession of it. This is to be a statutory ordinance for the Israelites as the LORD commanded Moses."

JOSHUA COMMISSIONED TO SUCCEED MOSES

[12] Then the LORD said to Moses, "Go up this mountain of the Abarim range[A] and see the land that I have given the Israelites. [13] After you have seen it, you will also be gathered to your people, as Aaron your brother was. [14] When the community quarreled in the Wilderness of Zin, both of you rebelled against my command to demonstrate my holiness in their sight at the waters." Those were the Waters of Meribah-kadesh[B] in the Wilderness of Zin.

[15] So Moses appealed to the LORD, [16] "May the LORD, the God who gives breath to all,[C] appoint a man over the community [17] who will go out before them and come back in before them, and who will bring them out and bring them in, so that the LORD's community won't be like sheep without a shepherd."

[18] The LORD replied to Moses, "Take Joshua son of Nun, a man who has the Spirit in him, and lay your hands on him. [19] Have him stand before the priest Eleazar and the whole community, and commission him in their sight. [20] Confer some of your authority on him so that the entire Israelite community will obey him. [21] He will stand before the priest Eleazar who will consult the LORD for him with the decision of the Urim. He and all the Israelites with him, even the entire community, will go out and come back in at his command."

[22] Moses did as the LORD commanded him. He took Joshua, had him stand before the priest Eleazar and the entire community, [23] laid his hands on him, and commissioned him, as the LORD had spoken through Moses.

PRESCRIBED OFFERINGS

28 The LORD spoke to Moses, [2] "Command the Israelites and say to them: Be sure to present to me at its appointed time my offering and my food as my fire offering, a pleasing aroma to me. [3] And say to them: This is the fire offering you are to present to the LORD:

DAILY OFFERINGS

"Each day present two unblemished year-old male lambs as a regular burnt offering. [4] Offer one lamb in the morning and the other lamb at twilight, [5] along with two quarts[D] of fine flour for a grain offering mixed with a quart[E] of olive oil from crushed olives. [6] It is a regular burnt offering established at Mount Sinai for a pleasing aroma, a fire offering to the LORD. [7] The drink offering is to be a quart with each lamb. Pour out the offering of beer to the LORD in the sanctuary area. [8] Offer the second lamb at twilight, along with

---

[A]27:12 = Mount Nebo; Nm 33:47-48; Dt 32:49; Jr 22:20   [B]27:14 = Quarreling
[C]27:16 Or *God of the spirits of all flesh*   [D]28:5 Lit *one-tenth of an ephah*
[E]28:5 Lit *a fourth of a hin*, also in v. 7

the same kind of grain offering and drink offering as in the morning. It is a fire offering, a pleasing aroma to the LORD.

SABBATH OFFERINGS

⁹ "On the Sabbath day present two unblemished year-old male lambs, four quarts⁴ of fine flour mixed with oil as a grain offering, and its drink offering. ¹⁰ It is the burnt offering for every Sabbath, in addition to the regular burnt offering and its drink offering.

MONTHLY OFFERINGS

¹¹ "At the beginning of each of your months present a burnt offering to the LORD: two young bulls, one ram, seven male lambs a year old — all unblemished — ¹² with six quarts⁸ of fine flour mixed with oil as a grain offering for each bull, four quarts of fine flour mixed with oil as a grain offering for the ram, ¹³ and two quarts⁶ of fine flour mixed with oil as a grain offering for each lamb. It is a burnt offering, a pleasing aroma, a fire offering to the LORD. ¹⁴ Their drink offerings are to be two quarts⁰ of wine with each bull, one and a third quarts⁶ with the ram, and one quart⁶ with each male lamb. This is the monthly burnt offering for all the months of the year. ¹⁵ And one male goat is to be offered as a sin offering to the LORD, in addition to the regular burnt offering with its drink offering.

OFFERINGS FOR PASSOVER

¹⁶ "The Passover to the LORD comes in the first month, on the fourteenth day of the month. ¹⁷ On the fifteenth day of this month there will be a festival; unleavened bread is to be eaten for seven days. ¹⁸ On the first day there is to be a sacred assembly; you are not to do any daily work. ¹⁹ Present a fire offering, a burnt offering to the LORD: two young bulls, one ram, and seven male lambs a year old. Your animals are to be unblemished. ²⁰ The grain offering with them is to be of fine flour mixed with oil; offer six quarts with each bull and four quarts with the ram. ²¹ Offer two quarts with each of the seven lambs ²² and one male goat for a sin offering to make atonement for yourselves. ²³ Offer these with the morning burnt offering that is part of the regular burnt offering. ²⁴ You are to offer the same food each day for seven days as a fire offering, a pleasing aroma to the LORD. It is to be offered with its drink offering and the regular burnt offering. ²⁵ On the seventh day you are to hold a sacred assembly; you are not to do any daily work.

OFFERINGS FOR THE FESTIVAL OF WEEKS

²⁶ "On the day of firstfruits, you are to hold a sacred assembly when you present an offering of new grain to the LORD at your Festival of Weeks; you are not to do any daily work. ²⁷ Present a burnt offering for a pleasing aroma to the LORD: two young bulls, one ram, and seven male lambs a year old, ²⁸ with their grain offering of fine flour mixed with oil, six quarts with each bull, four quarts with the ram, ²⁹ and two quarts with each of the seven lambs,

---

ᴬ28:9 Lit *two-tenths* (of an ephah), also in vv. 12,20,28   ᴮ28:12 Lit *three-tenths* (of an ephah), also in vv. 20,28   ᶜ28:13 Lit *one-tenth* (of an ephah), also in vv. 21,29   ᴰ28:14 Lit *a half hin*   ᴱ28:14 Lit *bull, a third hin*   ᶠ28:14 Lit *a fourth hin*

³⁰ and one male goat to make atonement for yourselves. ³¹ Offer them with their drink offerings in addition to the regular burnt offering and its grain offering. Your animals are to be unblemished.

FESTIVAL OF TRUMPETS OFFERINGS

29 "You are to hold a sacred assembly in the seventh month, on the first day of the month, and you are not to do any daily work. This will be a day of trumpet blasts for you. ² Offer a burnt offering as a pleasing aroma to the LORD: one young bull, one ram, seven male lambs a year old — all unblemished — ³ with their grain offering of fine flour mixed with oil, six quarts ᴬ with the bull, four quarts ᴮ with the ram, ⁴ and two quarts ᶜ with each of the seven male lambs. ⁵ Also offer one male goat as a sin offering to make atonement for yourselves. ⁶ These are in addition to the monthly and regular burnt offerings with their prescribed grain offerings and drink offerings. They are a pleasing aroma, a fire offering to the LORD.

OFFERINGS FOR THE DAY OF ATONEMENT

⁷ "You are to hold a sacred assembly on the tenth day of this seventh month and practice self-denial; do not do any work. ⁸ Present a burnt offering to the LORD, a pleasing aroma: one young bull, one ram, and seven male lambs a year old. All your animals are to be unblemished. ⁹ Their grain offering is to be of fine flour mixed with oil, six quarts with the bull, four quarts with the ram, ¹⁰ and two quarts with each of the seven lambs. ¹¹ Offer one male goat for a sin offering. The regular burnt offering with its grain offering and drink offerings are in addition to the sin offering of atonement.

OFFERINGS FOR THE FESTIVAL OF SHELTERS

¹² "You are to hold a sacred assembly on the fifteenth day of the seventh month; you do not do any daily work. You are to celebrate a seven-day festival for the LORD. ¹³ Present a burnt offering, a fire offering as a pleasing aroma to the LORD: thirteen young bulls, two rams, and fourteen male lambs a year old. They are to be unblemished. ¹⁴ Their grain offering is to be of fine flour mixed with oil, six quarts with each of the thirteen bulls, four quarts with each of the two rams, ¹⁵ and two quarts with each of the fourteen lambs. ¹⁶ Also offer one male goat as a sin offering. These are in addition to the regular burnt offering with its grain and drink offerings.

¹⁷ "On the second day present twelve young bulls, two rams, and fourteen male lambs a year old — all unblemished — ¹⁸ with their grain and drink offerings for the bulls, rams, and lambs, in proportion to their number. ¹⁹ Also offer one male goat as a sin offering. These are in addition to the regular burnt offering with its grain and drink and their drink offerings.

²⁰ "On the third day present eleven bulls, two rams, fourteen male lambs a year old — all unblemished — ²¹ with their grain and drink offerings for the bulls, rams, and lambs, in proportion to their number. ²² Also offer one male goat as a sin offering. These are in addition to the regular burnt offering with its grain and drink offerings.

ᴬ29:3 Lit *three-tenths* (of an ephah), also in vv. 9,14   ᴮ29:3 Lit *two-tenths* (of an ephah), also in vv. 9,14   ᶜ29:4 Lit *one-tenth* (of an ephah), also in vv. 10,15

²³ "On the fourth day present ten bulls, two rams, fourteen male lambs a year old — all unblemished — ²⁴ with their grain and drink offerings for the bulls, rams, and lambs, in proportion to their number. ²⁵ Also offer one male goat as a sin offering. These are in addition to the regular burnt offering with its grain and drink offerings.

²⁶ "On the fifth day present nine bulls, two rams, fourteen male lambs a year old — all unblemished — ²⁷ with their grain and drink offerings for the bulls, rams, and lambs, in proportion to their number. ²⁸ Also offer one male goat as a sin offering. These are in addition to the regular burnt offering with its grain and drink offerings.

²⁹ "On the sixth day present eight bulls, two rams, fourteen male lambs a year old — all unblemished — ³⁰ with their grain and drink offerings for the bulls, rams, and lambs, in proportion to their number. ³¹ Also offer one male goat as a sin offering. These are in addition to the regular burnt offering with its grain and drink offerings.

³² "On the seventh day present seven bulls, two rams, and fourteen male lambs a year old — all unblemished — ³³ with their grain and drink offerings for the bulls, rams, and lambs, in proportion to their number. ³⁴ Also offer one male goat as a sin offering. These are in addition to the regular burnt offering with its grain and drink offerings.

³⁵ "On the eighth day you are to hold a solemn assembly; you are not to do any daily work. ³⁶ Present a burnt offering, a fire offering as a pleasing aroma to the LORD: one bull, one ram, seven male lambs a year old — all unblemished — ³⁷ with their grain and drink offerings for the bulls, rams, and lambs, in proportion to their number. ³⁸ Also offer one male goat as a sin offering. These are in addition to the regular burnt offering with its grain and drink offerings.

³⁹ "Offer these to the LORD at your appointed times in addition to your vow and freewill offerings, whether burnt, grain, drink, or fellowship offerings." ⁴⁰ So Moses told the Israelites everything the LORD had commanded him.

REGULATIONS ABOUT VOWS

30 Moses told the leaders of the Israelite tribes, "This is what the LORD has commanded: ² When a man makes a vow to the LORD or swears an oath to put himself under an obligation, he must not break his word; he must do whatever he has promised.

³ "When a woman in her father's house during her youth makes a vow to the LORD or puts herself under an obligation, ⁴ and her father hears about her vow or the obligation she put herself under, and he says nothing to her, all her vows and every obligation she put herself under are binding. ⁵ But if her father prohibits her on the day he hears about it, none of her vows and none of the obligations she put herself under are binding. The LORD will release her because her father has prohibited her.

⁶ "If a woman marries while her vows or the rash commitment she herself made are binding, ⁷ and her husband hears about it and says nothing to her when he finds out, her vows are binding, and the obligations she put herself under are binding. ⁸ But if her husband prohibits her when he hears about it, he will cancel her vow that is binding or the rash commitment she herself made, and the LORD will release her.

⁹ "Every vow a widow or divorced woman puts herself under is binding on her.

¹⁰ "If a woman in her husband's house has made a vow or put herself under an obligation with an oath, ¹¹ and her husband hears about it, says nothing to her, and does not prohibit her, all her vows are binding, and every obligation she put herself under is binding. ¹² But if her husband cancels them on the day he hears about it, nothing that came from her lips, whether her vows or her obligation, is binding. Her husband has canceled them, and the LORD will release her. ¹³ Her husband may confirm or cancel any vow or any sworn obligation to deny herself. ¹⁴ If her husband says nothing at all to her from day to day, he confirms all her vows and obligations, which are binding. He has confirmed them because he said nothing to her when he heard about them. ¹⁵ But if he cancels them after he hears about them, he will be responsible for her commitment."[A]

¹⁶ These are the statutes that the LORD commanded Moses concerning the relationship between a man and his wife, or between a father and his daughter in his house during her youth.

WAR WITH MIDIAN

31 The LORD spoke to Moses, ² "Execute vengeance for the Israelites against the Midianites. After that, you will be gathered to your people."

³ So Moses spoke to the people, "Equip some of your men for war. They will go against Midian to inflict the LORD's vengeance on them. ⁴ Send one thousand men to war from each Israelite tribe." ⁵ So one thousand were recruited from each Israelite tribe out of the thousands[B] in Israel — twelve thousand equipped for war. ⁶ Moses sent one thousand from each tribe to war. They went with Phinehas son of Eleazar the priest, in whose care were the holy objects and signal trumpets.

⁷ They waged war against Midian, as the LORD had commanded Moses, and killed every male. ⁸ Along with the others slain by them, they killed the Midianite kings — Evi, Rekem, Zur, Hur, and Reba, the five kings of Midian. They also killed Balaam son of Beor with the sword. ⁹ The Israelites took the Midianite women and their dependents captive, and they plundered all their cattle, flocks, and property. ¹⁰ Then they burned all the cities where the Midianites lived, as well as all their encampments, ¹¹ and took away all the spoils of war and the captives, both people and animals. ¹² They brought the prisoners, animals, and spoils of war to Moses, the priest Eleazar, and the Israelite community at the camp on the plains of Moab by the Jordan across from Jericho.

¹³ Moses, the priest Eleazar, and all the leaders of the community went to meet them outside the camp. ¹⁴ But Moses became furious with the officers, the commanders of thousands and commanders of hundreds, who were returning from the military campaign. ¹⁵ "Have you let every female live?" he asked them. ¹⁶ "Yet they are the ones who, at Balaam's advice, incited the Israelites to unfaithfulness against the LORD in the Peor incident, so that the plague came against the LORD's community. ¹⁷ So now, kill every male among the dependents and kill every woman who has gone to bed with a man, ¹⁸ but keep alive for yourselves all the young females who have not gone to bed with a man.

[A]30:15 Or will bear her guilt [B]31:5 Or clans

¹⁹ "You are to remain outside the camp for seven days. All of you and your prisoners who have killed a person or touched the dead are to purify yourselves on the third day and the seventh day. ²⁰ Also purify everything: garments, leather goods, things made of goat hair, and every article of wood."

²¹ Then the priest Eleazar said to the soldiers who had gone to battle, "This is the legal statute the LORD commanded Moses: ²² The gold, silver, bronze, iron, tin, and lead — ²³ everything that can withstand fire — you are to pass through fire, and it will be clean. It must still be purified with the purification water. Anything that cannot withstand fire, pass through the water. ²⁴ On the seventh day wash your clothes, and you will be clean. After that you may enter the camp."

²⁵ The LORD told Moses, ²⁶ "You, the priest Eleazar, and the family heads of the community are to take a count of what was captured, people and animals. ²⁷ Then divide the captives between the troops who went out to war and the entire community. ²⁸ Set aside a tribute for the LORD from what belongs to the fighting men who went out to war: one out of every five hundred people, cattle, donkeys, sheep, and goats. ²⁹ Take the tribute from their half and give it to the priest Eleazar as a contribution to the LORD. ³⁰ From the Israelites' half, take one out of every fifty from the people, cattle, donkeys, sheep, and goats, all the livestock, and give them to the Levites who perform the duties of ᴬ the LORD's tabernacle."

³¹ So Moses and the priest Eleazar did as the LORD commanded Moses. ³² The captives remaining from the plunder the army had taken totaled:

675,000 sheep and goats,
³³   72,000 cattle,
³⁴   61,000 donkeys,
³⁵   and 32,000 people, all the females who had not gone to bed
       with a man.

³⁶ The half portion for those who went out to war numbered:
337,500 sheep and goats,
³⁷   and the tribute to the LORD was 675
       from the sheep and goats;
³⁸   from the 36,000 cattle,
       the tribute to the LORD was 72;
³⁹   from the 30,500 donkeys,
       the tribute to the LORD was 61;
⁴⁰   and from the 16,000 people,
       the tribute to the LORD was 32 people.

⁴¹ Moses gave the tribute to the priest Eleazar as a contribution for the LORD, as the LORD had commanded Moses.

⁴² From the Israelites' half, which Moses separated from the men who fought, ⁴³ the community's half was:
337,500 sheep and goats,
⁴⁴   36,000 cattle,
⁴⁵   30,500 donkeys,
⁴⁶   and 16,000 people.

ᴬ31:30 Or *who protect*

⁴⁷ Moses took one out of every fifty, selected from the people and the livestock of the Israelites' half. He gave them to the Levites who perform the duties of the Lord's tabernacle, as the Lord had commanded him.

⁴⁸ The officers who were over the thousands of the army, the commanders of thousands and of hundreds, approached Moses ⁴⁹ and told him, "Your servants have taken a census of the fighting men under our command, and not one of us is missing. ⁵⁰ So we have presented to the Lord an offering of the gold articles each man found — armlets, bracelets, rings, earrings, and necklaces — to make atonement for ourselves before the Lord."

⁵¹ Moses and the priest Eleazar received from them all the articles made out of gold. ⁵² All the gold of the contribution they offered to the Lord, from the commanders of thousands and of hundreds, was 420 pounds.ᴬ ⁵³ Each of the soldiers had taken plunder for himself. ⁵⁴ Moses and the priest Eleazar received the gold from the commanders of thousands and of hundreds and brought it into the tent of meeting as a memorial for the Israelites before the Lord.

TRANSJORDAN SETTLEMENTS

32 The Reubenites and Gadites had a very large number of livestock. When they surveyed the lands of Jazer and Gilead, they saw that the region was a good one for livestock. ² So the Gadites and Reubenites came to Moses, the priest Eleazar, and the leaders of the community and said: ³ "The territory of Ataroth, Dibon, Jazer, Nimrah, Heshbon, Elealeh, Sebam,ᴮ Nebo, and Beon, ⁴ which the Lord struck down before the community of Israel, is good land for livestock, and your servants own livestock." ⁵ They said, "If we have found favor with you, let this land be given to your servants as a possession. Don't make us cross the Jordan."

⁶ But Moses asked the Gadites and Reubenites, "Should your brothers go to war while you stay here? ⁷ Why are you discouraging the Israelites from crossing into the land the Lord has given them? ⁸ That's what your fathers did when I sent them from Kadesh-barnea to see the land. ⁹ After they went up as far as Eshcol Valley and saw the land, they discouraged the Israelites from entering the land the Lord had given them. ¹⁰ So the Lord's anger burned that day, and he swore an oath: ¹¹ 'Because they did not remain loyal to me, none of the men twenty years old or more who came up from Egypt will see the land I swore to give Abraham, Isaac, and Jacob — ¹² none except Caleb son of Jephunneh the Kenizzite and Joshua son of Nun, because they did remain loyal to the Lord.' ¹³ The Lord's anger burned against Israel, and he made them wander in the wilderness forty years until the whole generation that had done what was evil in the Lord's sight was gone. ¹⁴ And here you, a brood of sinners, stand in your fathers' place adding even more to the Lord's burning anger against Israel. ¹⁵ If you turn back from following him, he will once again leave this people in the wilderness, and you will destroy all of them."

¹⁶ Then they approached him and said, "We want to build sheep pens here for our livestock and cities for our dependents. ¹⁷ But we will arm ourselves and be ready to go ahead of the Israelites until we have brought them into their place. Meanwhile, our dependents will remain in the fortified cities

---

ᴬ31:52 Lit *16,750 shekels*   ᴮ32:3 Sam, LXX read *Sibmah* (v. 38); Syr reads *Sebah* because of the inhabitants of the land. [18] We will not return to our homes until each of the Israelites has taken possession of his inheritance. [19] Yet we will not have an inheritance with them across the Jordan and beyond, because our inheritance will be across the Jordan to the east."

[20] Moses replied to them, "If you do this — if you arm yourselves for battle before the LORD, [21] and every one of your armed men crosses the Jordan before the LORD until he has driven his enemies from his presence, [22] and the land is subdued before the LORD — afterward you may return and be free from obligation to the LORD and to Israel. And this land will belong to you as a possession before the LORD. [23] But if you don't do this, you will certainly sin against the LORD; be sure your sin will catch up with you. [24] Build cities for your dependents and pens for your flocks, but do what you have promised."

[25] The Gadites and Reubenites answered Moses, "Your servants will do just as my lord commands. [26] Our dependents, wives, livestock, and all our animals will remain here in the cities of Gilead, [27] but your servants are equipped for war before the LORD and will go across to the battle as my lord orders."

[28] So Moses gave orders about them to the priest Eleazar, Joshua son of Nun, and the family heads of the Israelite tribes. [29] Moses told them, "If the Gadites and Reubenites cross the Jordan with you, every man in battle formation before the LORD, and the land is subdued before you, you are to give them the land of Gilead as a possession. [30] But if they don't go across with you in battle formation, they must accept land in Canaan with you."

[31] The Gadites and Reubenites replied, "What the LORD has spoken to your servants is what we will do. [32] We will cross over in battle formation before the LORD into the land of Canaan, but we will keep our hereditary possession across the Jordan."

[33] So Moses gave them — the Gadites, Reubenites, and half the tribe of Manasseh son of Joseph — the kingdom of King Sihon of the Amorites and the kingdom of King Og of Bashan, the land including its cities with the territories surrounding them. [34] The Gadites rebuilt Dibon, Ataroth, Aroer, [35] Atroth-shophan, Jazer, Jogbehah, [36] Beth-nimrah, and Beth-haran as fortified cities, and built sheep pens. [37] The Reubenites rebuilt Heshbon, Elealeh, Kiriathaim, [38] as well as Nebo and Baal-meon (whose names were changed), and Sibmah. They gave names to the cities they rebuilt.

[39] The descendants of Machir son of Manasseh went to Gilead, captured it, and drove out the Amorites who were there. [40] So Moses gave Gilead to the clan of Machir son of Manasseh, and they settled in it. [41] Jair, a descendant of Manasseh, went and captured their villages, which he renamed Jair's Villages.[A] [42] Nobah went and captured Kenath with its surrounding villages and called it Nobah after his own name.

WILDERNESS TRAVELS REVIEWED

33 These were the stages of the Israelites' journey when they went out of the land of Egypt by their military divisions under the leadership of Moses and Aaron. [2] At the LORD's command, Moses wrote down the starting points for the stages of their journey; these are the stages listed by their starting points:

[A]32:41 Or renamed Havvoth-jair

³ They traveled from Rameses in the first month, on the fifteenth day of the month. On the day after the Passover the Israelites went out defiantly^A in the sight of all the Egyptians. ⁴ Meanwhile, the Egyptians were burying every firstborn male the LORD had struck down among them, for the LORD had executed judgment against their gods. ⁵ The Israelites traveled from Rameses and camped at Succoth.

⁶ They traveled from Succoth and camped at Etham, which is on the edge of the wilderness.

⁷ They traveled from Etham and turned back to Pi-hahiroth, which faces Baal-zephon, and they camped before Migdol.

⁸ They traveled from Pi-hahiroth^B and crossed through the middle of the sea into the wilderness. They took a three-day journey into the Wilderness of Etham and camped at Marah.

⁹ They traveled from Marah and came to Elim. There were twelve springs and seventy date palms at Elim, so they camped there.

¹⁰ They traveled from Elim and camped by the Red Sea.

¹¹ They traveled from the Red Sea and camped in the Wilderness of Sin.

¹² They traveled from the Wilderness of Sin and camped in Dophkah.

¹³ They traveled from Dophkah and camped at Alush.

¹⁴ They traveled from Alush and camped at Rephidim, where there was no water for the people to drink.

¹⁵ They traveled from Rephidim and camped in the Wilderness of Sinai.

¹⁶ They traveled from the Wilderness of Sinai and camped at Kibroth-hattaavah.

¹⁷ They traveled from Kibroth-hattaavah and camped at Hazeroth.

¹⁸ They traveled from Hazeroth and camped at Rithmah.

¹⁹ They traveled from Rithmah and camped at Rimmon-perez.

²⁰ They traveled from Rimmon-perez and camped at Libnah.

²¹ They traveled from Libnah and camped at Rissah.

²² They traveled from Rissah and camped at Kehelathah.

²³ They traveled from Kehelathah and camped at Mount Shepher.

²⁴ They traveled from Mount Shepher and camped at Haradah.

²⁵ They traveled from Haradah and camped at Makheloth.

²⁶ They traveled from Makheloth and camped at Tahath.

²⁷ They traveled from Tahath and camped at Terah.

²⁸ They traveled from Terah and camped at Mithkah.

²⁹ They traveled from Mithkah and camped at Hashmonah.

³⁰ They traveled from Hashmonah and camped at Moseroth.

³¹ They traveled from Moseroth and camped at Bene-jaakan.

³² They traveled from Bene-jaakan and camped at Hor-haggidgad.

³³ They traveled from Hor-haggidgad and camped at Jotbathah.

³⁴ They traveled from Jotbathah and camped at Abronah.

³⁵ They traveled from Abronah and camped at Ezion-geber.

³⁶ They traveled from Ezion-geber and camped in the Wilderness of Zin (that is, Kadesh).

³⁷ They traveled from Kadesh and camped at Mount Hor on the edge of the land of Edom. ³⁸ At the LORD's command, the priest Aaron climbed

---

^A 33:3 Lit *with a raised hand*; Ex 14:8   ^B 33:8 Some Hb mss, Sam, Syr, Vg; other Hb mss read *from before Hahiroth*

Mount Hor and died there on the first day of the fifth month in the fortieth year after the Israelites went out of the land of Egypt. [39] Aaron was 123 years old when he died on Mount Hor. [40] At that time the Canaanite king of Arad, who lived in the Negev in the land of Canaan, heard the Israelites were coming.

[41] They traveled from Mount Hor and camped at Zalmonah.

[42] They traveled from Zalmonah and camped at Punon.

[43] They traveled from Punon and camped at Oboth.

[44] They traveled from Oboth and camped at Iye-abarim on the border of Moab.

[45] They traveled from Iyim[A] and camped at Dibon-gad.

[46] They traveled from Dibon-gad and camped at Almon-diblathaim.

[47] They traveled from Almon-diblathaim and camped in the Abarim range facing Nebo.

[48] They traveled from the Abarim range and camped on the plains of Moab by the Jordan across from Jericho. [49] They camped by the Jordan from Beth-jeshimoth to the Acacia Meadow[B] on the plains of Moab.

INSTRUCTIONS FOR OCCUPYING CANAAN

[50] The LORD spoke to Moses in the plains of Moab by the Jordan across from Jericho, [51] "Tell the Israelites: When you cross the Jordan into the land of Canaan, [52] you must drive out all the inhabitants of the land before you, destroy all their stone images and cast images, and demolish all their high places. [53] You are to take possession of the land and settle in it because I have given you the land to possess. [54] You are to receive the land as an inheritance by lot according to your clans. Increase the inheritance for a large clan and decrease it for a small one. Whatever place the lot indicates for someone will be his. You will receive an inheritance according to your ancestral tribes. [55] But if you don't drive out the inhabitants of the land before you, those you allow to remain will become barbs for your eyes and thorns for your sides; they will harass you in the land where you will live. [56] And what I had planned to do to them, I will do to you."

BOUNDARIES OF THE PROMISED LAND

34 The LORD spoke to Moses, [2] "Command the Israelites and say to them: When you enter the land of Canaan, it will be allotted to you as an inheritance[C] with these borders:

[3] Your southern side will be from the Wilderness of Zin along the boundary of Edom. Your southern border on the east will begin at the east end of the Dead Sea. [4] Your border will turn south of the Scorpions' Ascent,[D] proceed to Zin, and end south of Kadesh-barnea. It will go to Hazar-addar and proceed to Azmon. [5] The border will turn from Azmon to the Brook of Egypt, where it will end at the Mediterranean Sea.

[6] Your western border will be the coastline of the Mediterranean Sea; this will be your western border.

[A]33:45 A shortened form of Iye-abarim   [B]33:49 Or to Abel-shittim
[C]34:2 Lit inheritance — the land of Canaan   [D]34:4 Lit of Scorpions; Jos 15:3; Jdg 1:36

⁷ This will be your northern border: From the Mediterranean Sea draw a line to Mount Hor; ⁸ from Mount Hor draw a line to the entrance of Hamath,ᴬ and the border will reach Zedad. ⁹ Then the border will go to Ziphron and end at Hazar-enan. This will be your northern border.

¹⁰ For your eastern border, draw a line from Hazar-enan to Shepham. ¹¹ The border will go down from Shepham to Riblah east of Ain. It will continue down and reach the eastern slope of the Sea of Chinnereth.ᴮ ¹² Then the border will go down to the Jordan and end at the Dead Sea. This will be your land defined by its borders on all sides."

¹³ So Moses commanded the Israelites, "This is the land you are to receive by lot as an inheritance, which the Lᴏʀᴅ commanded to be given to the nine and a half tribes. ¹⁴ For the tribe of Reuben's descendants and the tribe of Gad's descendants have received their inheritance according to their ancestral families,ᶜ and half the tribe of Manasseh has received its inheritance. ¹⁵ The two and a half tribes have received their inheritance across the Jordan east of Jericho, toward the sunrise."

LEADERS FOR DISTRIBUTING THE LAND

¹⁶ The Lᴏʀᴅ spoke to Moses, ¹⁷ "These are the names of the men who are to distribute the land as an inheritance for you: the priest Eleazar and Joshua son of Nun. ¹⁸ Take one leader from each tribe to distribute the land. ¹⁹ These are the names of the men:

Caleb son of Jephunneh from the tribe of Judah;
²⁰ Shemuel son of Ammihud from the tribe of Simeon's descendants;
²¹ Elidad son of Chislon from the tribe of Benjamin;
²² Bukki son of Jogli, a leader from the tribe of Dan's descendants;
²³ from the sons of Joseph:
Hanniel son of Ephod, a leader from the tribe of Manasseh's descendants,
²⁴ Kemuel son of Shiphtan, a leader from the tribe of Ephraim's descendants;
²⁵ Eli-zaphan son of Parnach, a leader from the tribe of Zebulun's descendants;
²⁶ Paltiel son of Azzan, a leader from the tribe of Issachar's descendants;
²⁷ Ahihud son of Shelomi, a leader from the tribe of Asher's descendants;
²⁸ Pedahel son of Ammihud, a leader from the tribe of Naphtali's descendants."

²⁹ These are the ones the Lᴏʀᴅ commanded to distribute the inheritance to the Israelites in the land of Canaan.

CITIES FOR THE LEVITES

35 The Lᴏʀᴅ again spoke to Moses in the plains of Moab by the Jordan across from Jericho: ² "Command the Israelites to give cities out of their hereditary property for the Levites to live in and pastureland around the cities. ³ The cities will be for them to live in, and their pasturelands will

---

ᴬ34:8 Or *to Lebo-hamath* ᴮ34:11 = the Sea of Galilee; Jos 12:3; 13:27; Lk 5:1
ᶜ34:14 Lit *the house of their fathers*

be for their herds, flocks, and all their other animals. ⁴ The pasturelands of the cities you are to give the Levites will extend from the city wall five hundred yards ᴬ on every side. ⁵ Measure a thousand yards ᴮ outside the city for the east side, a thousand yards for the south side, a thousand yards for the west side, and a thousand yards for the north side, with the city in the center. This will belong to them as pasturelands for the cities.

⁶ "The cities you give the Levites will include six cities of refuge, which you will provide so that the one who kills someone may flee there; in addition to these, give forty-two other cities. ⁷ The total number of cities you give the Levites will be forty-eight, along with their pasturelands. ⁸ Of the cities that you give from the Israelites' territory, you should take more from a larger tribe and less from a smaller one. Each tribe is to give some of its cities to the Levites in proportion to the inheritance it receives."

CITIES OF REFUGE

⁹ The LORD said to Moses, ¹⁰ "Speak to the Israelites and tell them: When you cross the Jordan into the land of Canaan, ¹¹ designate cities to serve as cities of refuge for you, so that a person who kills someone unintentionally may flee there. ¹² You will have the cities as a refuge from the avenger, so that the one who kills someone will not die until he stands trial before the assembly. ¹³ The cities you select will be your six cities of refuge. ¹⁴ Select three cities across the Jordan and three cities in the land of Canaan to be cities of refuge. ¹⁵ These six cities will serve as a refuge for the Israelites and for the alien or temporary resident among them, so that anyone who kills a person unintentionally may flee there.

¹⁶ "If anyone strikes a person with an iron object and death results, he is a murderer; the murderer must be put to death. ¹⁷ If anyone has in his hand a stone capable of causing death and strikes another person and he dies, the murderer must be put to death. ¹⁸ If anyone has in his hand a wooden object capable of causing death and strikes another person and he dies, the murderer must be put to death. ¹⁹ The avenger of blood himself is to kill the murderer; when he finds him, he is to kill him. ²⁰ Likewise, if anyone in hatred pushes a person or throws an object at him with malicious intent and he dies, ²¹ or if in hostility he strikes him with his hand and he dies, the one who struck him must be put to death; he is a murderer. The avenger of blood is to kill the murderer when he finds him.

²² "But if anyone suddenly pushes a person without hostility or throws any object at him without malicious intent ²³ or without looking drops a stone that could kill a person and he dies, but he was not his enemy and didn't intend to harm him, ²⁴ the assembly is to judge between the person who kills someone and the avenger of blood according to these ordinances. ²⁵ The assembly is to protect the one who kills someone from the avenger of blood. Then the assembly will return him to the city of refuge he fled to, and he must live there until the death of the high priest who was anointed with the holy oil.

²⁶ "If the one who kills someone ever goes outside the border of the city of refuge he fled to, ²⁷ and the avenger of blood finds him outside the border of his city of refuge and kills him, the avenger will not be guilty of bloodshed, ²⁸ for the one who killed a person was supposed to live in his city of refuge

ᴬ35:4 Lit *1,000 cubits*   ᴮ35:5 Lit *2,000 cubits*

until the death of the high priest. Only after the death of the high priest may the one who has killed a person return to the land he possesses. [29] These instructions will be a statutory ordinance for you throughout your generations wherever you live.

[30] "If anyone kills a person, the murderer is to be put to death based on the word of witnesses. But no one is to be put to death based on the testimony of one witness. [31] You are not to accept a ransom for the life of someone who is guilty of murder; he must be put to death. [32] Neither should you accept a ransom for the person who flees to his city of refuge, allowing him to return and live in the land before the death of the high priest.

[33] "Do not defile the land where you live, for bloodshed defiles the land, and there can be no atonement for the land because of the blood that is shed on it, except by the blood of the person who shed it. [34] Do not make the land unclean where you live and where I dwell; for I, the LORD, reside among the Israelites."

THE INHERITANCE OF ZELOPHEHAD'S DAUGHTERS

36 The family heads from the clan of the descendants of Gilead — the son of Machir, son of Manasseh — who were from the clans of the sons of Joseph, approached and addressed Moses and the leaders who were heads of the Israelite families. [2] They said, "The LORD commanded my lord to give the land as an inheritance by lot to the Israelites. My lord was further commanded by the LORD to give our brother Zelophehad's inheritance to his daughters. [3] If they marry any of the men from the other Israelite tribes, their inheritance will be taken away from our fathers' inheritance and added to that of the tribe into which they marry. Therefore, part of our allotted inheritance would be taken away. [4] When the Jubilee comes for the Israelites, their inheritance will be added to that of the tribe into which they marry, and their inheritance will be taken away from the inheritance of our ancestral tribe."

[5] So Moses commanded the Israelites at the word of the LORD, "What the tribe of Joseph's descendants says is right. [6] This is what the LORD has commanded concerning Zelophehad's daughters: They may marry anyone they like provided they marry within a clan of their ancestral tribe. [7] No inheritance belonging to the Israelites is to transfer from tribe to tribe, because each of the Israelites is to retain the inheritance of his ancestral tribe. [8] Any daughter who possesses an inheritance from an Israelite tribe must marry someone from the clan of her ancestral tribe, so that each of the Israelites will possess the inheritance of his fathers. [9] No inheritance is to transfer from one tribe to another, because each of the Israelite tribes is to retain its inheritance."

[10] The daughters of Zelophehad did as the LORD commanded Moses. [11] Mahlah, Tirzah, Hoglah, Milcah, and Noah, the daughters of Zelophehad, married cousins on their father's side. [12] They married men from the clans of the descendants of Manasseh son of Joseph, and their inheritance remained within the tribe of their father's clan.

[13] These are the commands and ordinances the LORD commanded the Israelites through Moses in the plains of Moab by the Jordan across from Jericho.

He keeps His gracious

— COVENANT —

loyalty for a

— THOUSAND —

generations

deuteronomy

 Know that the LORD your God is God, the faithful God who keeps his gracious covenant loyalty for a thousand generations with those who love him and keep his commands. **7:9**

ON THE TIMELINE Deuteronomy is the last installment of Moses' original writings to Israel. The events in Deuteronomy occurred over a relatively short time period as Israel prepared to enter Canaan in 1406 BC. The book was likely written right around that time, a message from Moses to the generation of Israelites that would enter the promised land.

A LITTLE BACKGROUND The title of this book of the Pentateuch, Deuteronomy, comes from the Septuagint (the Greek translation of the Old Testament) and means "second law" or "repetition of the law." The phrase is actually a mistranslation of Deuteronomy 17:18, which reads "a copy of this instruction." It's still a fitting title since much of the book contains repetitions of the laws found in Exodus, Leviticus, and Numbers.

MESSAGE & PURPOSE The purpose of Deuteronomy is to provide guidelines for the new covenant community—the generation of Israel entering the promised land—to enable them to live obediently before God and to carry out His intentions for them.

Three main themes appear regularly throughout the book:
1. *The nature and character of God* – There is no God but the Lord. His holiness and righteousness are reflected throughout the moral nature of His law.
2. *Covenant relationship* – God had entered into a covenant relationship with Israel out of love (Dt 7:8). In that covenant, as God's people, the Israelites were to honor their relationship with God by reflecting His character to the nations around them.
3. *The faithful response of God's people* – The Israelites' response to the covenant relationship with God was to live lives, both individually and as a nation, in total commitment to the Lord.

GIVE THANKS FOR THE BOOK OF DEUTERONOMY:

After the books of Psalms and Isaiah, the New Testament alludes to Deuteronomy more than any other book in the NT. Jesus and the apostles considered the book of Deuteronomy to be of paramount importance in their own teaching about God and His relationship with His chosen people and all of humanity. When Jesus was tempted in the wilderness, He quoted Deuteronomy to rebuke Satan (Mt 4:4-10).

THE TEN COMMANDMENTS

God is holy—not just in action but in essence. His law was given to articulate the requirements of the all-holy God to His people; but His people, being fallen and flawed, could not perfectly keep this law.

Jesus did not come to destroy the law, but to fulfill it—perfectly (Mt 5:17). What the law could not do because of the limits of the flesh, God did. Christ offered one sacrifice for sins forever, and those who are in Him are free from condemnation (Rm 8:1-3; Heb 10:12).

	GOD'S HOLINESS	ISRAEL'S BROKENNESS
1 Ex 20:3	"Do not have other gods besides me."	Solomon followed the gods of his many wives and turned his heart away from the Lord (1Kg 11).
2 Ex 20:4-6	"Do not make an idol for yourself . . . Do not bow in worship to them, and do not serve them."	The Israelites built and worshiped a gold calf in the desert (Ex 32), they worshiped the Baals instead of the Lord (Jdg 2:10-14), and Manasseh carved an image of Asherah and placed it in the temple of the Lord (2Kg 21:1-15).
3 Ex 20:7	"Do not misuse the name of the LORD your God."	Zedekiah made an oath in God's name and then he broke it (2Ch 36:11-14; Ezk 17:15-21).
4 Ex 20:8-11	"Remember the Sabbath day, to keep it holy."	Judah refused to observe Sabbath years (Lv 25:4).
5 Ex 20:12	"Honor your father and your mother."	Eli's sons Hophni and Phinehas did evil in the Lord's eyes and dishonored their father, who was a priest of the Lord (1Sm 2:12-17,23-25).
6 Ex 20:13	"Do not murder."	Absalom killed his brother Amnon (2Sm 13:28-29).
7 Ex 20:14	"Do not commit adultery."	David committed adultery with Bathsheba (2Sm 11).
8 Ex 20:15	"Do not steal."	Ahab murdered a man named Naboth in order to gain his vineyard (1Kg 21:1-19).
9 Ex 20:16	"Do not give false testimony against your neighbor."	King Saul lied to Samuel about the plunder he took from the Amalekites (1Sm 15:13-25).
10 Ex 20:17	"Do not covet your neighbor's house. Do not covet your neighbor's wife . . . or anything that belongs to your neighbor."	Achan coveted possessions and money from Jericho and took them for himself, after the Lord had commanded the Israelites to completely destroy everything (Jos 7:20-23).

**THE LAW WAS GIVEN THROUGH MOSES;
GRACE AND TRUTH CAME THROUGH JESUS CHRIST.**

JOHN 1:17

READ AND UNDERSTAND DEUTERONOMY

The Bible is a complete work in which many stories combine to tell one story. As you read the book of Deuteronomy, consider reading the additional passages to discover how the whole of Scripture works together.

INTRODUCTION

1 These are the words Moses spoke to all Israel across the Jordan in the wilderness, in the Arabah opposite Suph,[A] between Paran and Tophel, Laban, Hazeroth, and Di-zahab. ² It is an eleven-day journey from Horeb to Kadesh-barnea by way of Mount Seir. ³ In the fortieth year, in the eleventh month, on the first of the month, Moses told the Israelites everything the LORD had commanded him to say to them. ⁴ This was after he had defeated King Sihon of the Amorites, who lived in Heshbon, and King Og of Bashan, who lived in Ashtaroth, at Edrei. ⁵ Across the Jordan in the land of Moab, Moses began to explain this law, saying:

DEPARTURE FROM HOREB

⁶ "The LORD our God spoke to us at Horeb: 'You have stayed at this mountain long enough. ⁷ Resume your journey and go to the hill country of the Amorites and their neighbors in the Arabah, the hill country, the Judean foothills,[B] the Negev and the sea coast — to the land of the Canaanites and to Lebanon as far as the great river, the Euphrates River. ⁸ See, I have set the land before you. Enter and take possession of the land the LORD swore to give to your fathers Abraham, Isaac, and Jacob and their future descendants.'

LEADERS FOR THE TRIBES

⁹ "I said to you at that time: I can't bear the responsibility for you on my own. ¹⁰ The LORD your God has so multiplied you that today you are as numerous as the stars of the sky. ¹¹ May the LORD, the God of your fathers, increase you a thousand times more, and bless you as he promised you. ¹² But how can I bear your troubles, burdens, and disputes by myself? ¹³ Appoint for yourselves wise, understanding, and respected men from each of your tribes, and I will make them your leaders.

¹⁴ "You replied to me, 'What you propose to do is good.'

¹⁵ "So I took the leaders of your tribes, wise and respected men, and set them over you as leaders: commanders for thousands, hundreds, fifties, and tens, and officers for your tribes. ¹⁶ I commanded your judges at that time: Hear the cases between your brothers, and judge rightly between a man and his brother or his resident alien. ¹⁷ Do not show partiality when deciding a case; listen to small and great alike. Do not be intimidated by anyone, for judgment belongs to God. Bring me any case too difficult for you, and I will hear it. ¹⁸ At that time I commanded you about all the things you were to do.

ISRAEL'S DISOBEDIENCE AT KADESH–BARNEA

¹⁹ "We then set out from Horeb and went across all the great and terrible wilderness you saw on the way to the hill country of the Amorites, just as the LORD our God had commanded us. When we reached Kadesh-barnea, ²⁰ I said to you: You have reached the hill country of the Amorites, which the LORD our God is giving us. ²¹ See, the LORD your God has set the land before you. Go up and take possession of it as the LORD, the God of your fathers, has told you. Do not be afraid or discouraged.

²² "Then all of you approached me and said, 'Let's send men ahead of us, so that they may explore the land for us and bring us back a report about

A1:1 LXX, Tg, Vg read *the Red Sea*   B1:7 Or *the Shephelah*

CARRIED

DEUTERONOMY 1–2; ROMANS 8:15; HEBREWS 12:1-11

I'm not a sentimental person, but I well up almost every time I see my husband carry our boys. When we arrive home from a road trip late at night or they're too sick to trek upstairs, they can wrap their little boy arms and legs around his big, strong trunk, and relax into daddy love.

I don't get the same warm, fuzzy feelings when I watch my husband discipline our boys, but I know that both are necessary. Because discipline is tied to love, a dad who only dished out hugs wouldn't really be a loving father at all (Pr 3:12). On the flip side, a father who corrected without affection would be missing a critical half of the parenting equation. When my husband disciplines our children, he's being as loving as when he carries their sleepy selves to a warm bed. Parenting has taught me that law and love are not in conflict. They are both signs of deep love.

It can be tempting for us to divide God's Word into good cop/bad cop sections. We might see some of the Old Testament as the "bad cop" half, as we read through the laws, plagues, and judgments. The New Testament may feel a little better in our bones, as we read about God as our *Abba* Father, our Daddy (Rm 8:15).

But the Old Testament and New Testament are two parts of the same whole. They're telling the same story, pointing from every direction to a God who both disciplines us and sacrifices for us.

Deuteronomy 1 is proof of this parental paradox. Verse after verse, Moses reminds God's people about the painful consequences of their chronic rebellion. If we were among the Israelites listening to Moses teach, this would feel like a bit of a "squirmon" (that's what my pastor calls a sermon that makes you squirm in your pew). But when we start to feel like we've been ordered to the time-out chair, we find this tender gem:

"And you saw in the wilderness how the LORD your God carried you as a man carries his son all along the way you traveled until you reached this place."

DEUTERONOMY 1:31

Moses spoke these words forty years after the Exodus. God's people had learned plenty about His discipline during that time. The cycle of their rebellion, God's judgment, their repentance, and God's blessing had been repeated over and over as they wandered in the wilderness. But the picture God paints of that time isn't of a father ruling his family with an iron fist, but rather that of a father carrying his baby boys up the stairs.

Studying the whole Bible shows us there is no duality in the character of God. There is only our loving heavenly Father. May we never see ourselves as too big to be carried along by His love.

the route we should go up and the cities we will come to.' ²³ The plan seemed good to me, so I selected twelve men from among you, one man for each tribe. ²⁴ They left and went up into the hill country and came to the Valley of Eshcol, scouting the land. ²⁵ They took some of the fruit from the land in their hands, carried it down to us, and brought us back a report: 'The land the LORD our God is giving us is good.'

²⁶ "But you were not willing to go up. You rebelled against the command of the LORD your God. ²⁷ You grumbled in your tents and said, 'The LORD brought us out of the land of Egypt to hand us over to the Amorites in order to destroy us, because he hates us. ²⁸ Where can we go? Our brothers have made us lose heart,ᴬ saying: The people are larger and taller than we are; the cities are large, fortified to the heavens. We also saw the descendants of the Anakim there.'

²⁹ "So I said to you: Don't be terrified or afraid of them! ³⁰ The LORD your God who goes before you will fight for you, just as you saw him do for you in Egypt. ³¹ And you saw in the wilderness how the LORD your God carried you as a man carries his son all along the way you traveled until you reached this place. ³² But in spite of this you did not trust the LORD your God, ³³ who went before you on the journey to seek out a place for you to camp. He went in the fire by night and in the cloud by day to guide you on the road you were to travel.

³⁴ "When the LORD heard yourᴮ words, he grew angry and swore an oath: ³⁵ 'None of these men in this evil generation will see the good land I swore to give your fathers, ³⁶ except Caleb the son of Jephunneh. He will see it, and I will give him and his descendants the land on which he has set foot, because he remained loyal to the LORD.'

³⁷ "The LORD was angry with me also because of you and said: 'You will not enter there either. ³⁸ Joshua son of Nun, who attends you, will enter it. Encourage him, for he will enable Israel to inherit it. ³⁹ Your children, whom you said would be plunder, your sons whoᶜ don't yet know good from evil, will enter there. I will give them the land, and they will take possession of it. ⁴⁰ But you are to turn back and head for the wilderness by way of the Red Sea.'

⁴¹ "You answered me, 'We have sinned against the LORD. We will go up and fight just as the LORD our God commanded us.' Then each of you put on his weapons of war and thought it would be easy to go up into the hill country.

⁴² "But the LORD said to me, 'Tell them: Don't go up and fight, for I am not with you to keep you from being defeated by your enemies.' ⁴³ So I spoke to you, but you didn't listen. You rebelled against the LORD's command and defiantly went up into the hill country. ⁴⁴ Then the Amorites who lived there came out against you and chased you like a swarm of bees. They routed you from Seir as far as Hormah. ⁴⁵ When you returned, you wept before the LORD, but he didn't listen to your requests or pay attention to you. ⁴⁶ For this reason you stayed in Kadesh as long as you did.ᴰ

JOURNEY PAST SEIR

2 "Then we turned back and headed for the wilderness by way of the Red Sea, as the LORD had told me, and we traveled around the hill country of Seir for many days. ² The LORD then said to me, ³ 'You've been traveling around this hill country long enough; turn north. ⁴ Command the people: You

---

ᴬ1:28 Lit *have melted our hearts*   ᴮ1:34 Lit *the sound of your*   ᶜ1:39 Lit *who today*
ᴰ1:46 Lit *Kadesh for many days, according to the days you stayed*

are about to travel through the territory of your brothers, the descendants of Esau, who live in Seir. They will be afraid of you, so be very careful. ⁵ Don't provoke them, for I will not give you any of their land, not even a foot of it,^ because I have given Esau the hill country of Seir as his possession. ⁶ You may purchase food from them, so that you may eat, and buy water from them to drink. ⁷ For the LORD your God has blessed you in all the work of your hands. He has watched over your journey through this immense wilderness. The LORD your God has been with you this past forty years, and you have lacked nothing.'

JOURNEY PAST MOAB

⁸ "So we bypassed our brothers, the descendants of Esau, who live in Seir. We turned away from the Arabah road and from Elath and Ezion-geber. We traveled along the road to the Wilderness of Moab. ⁹ The LORD said to me, 'Show no hostility toward Moab, and do not provoke them to battle, for I will not give you any of their land as a possession, since I have given Ar as a possession to the descendants of Lot.' "

¹⁰ The Emim, a great and numerous people as tall as the Anakim, had previously lived there. ¹¹ They were also regarded as Rephaim, like the Anakim, though the Moabites called them Emim. ¹² The Horites had previously lived in Seir, but the descendants of Esau drove them out, destroying them completely^B and settling in their place, just as Israel did in the land of its possession the LORD gave them.

¹³ "The LORD said, 'Now get up and cross the Zered Valley.' So we crossed the Zered Valley. ¹⁴ The time we spent traveling from Kadesh-barnea until we crossed the Zered Valley was thirty-eight years until the entire generation of fighting men had perished from the camp, as the LORD had sworn to them. ¹⁵ Indeed, the LORD's hand was against them, to eliminate them from the camp until they had all perished.

JOURNEY PAST AMMON

¹⁶ "When all the fighting men had died among the people, ¹⁷ the LORD spoke to me, ¹⁸ 'Today you are going to cross the border of Moab at Ar. ¹⁹ When you get close to the Ammonites, don't show any hostility to them or provoke them, for I will not give you any of the Ammonites' land as a possession; I have given it as a possession to the descendants of Lot.' "

²⁰ This too used to be regarded as the land of the Rephaim. The Rephaim lived there previously, though the Ammonites called them Zamzummim, ²¹ a great and numerous people, tall as the Anakim. The LORD destroyed the Rephaim at the advance of the Ammonites, so that they drove them out and settled in their place. ²² This was just as he had done for the descendants of Esau who lived in Seir, when he destroyed the Horites before them; they drove them out and have lived in their place until now. ²³ The Caphtorim, who came from Caphtor,^C destroyed the Avvites, who lived in villages as far as Gaza, and settled in their place.

DEFEAT OF SIHON THE AMORITE

²⁴ "The LORD also said, 'Get up, move out, and cross the Arnon Valley. See, I have handed the Amorites' King Sihon of Heshbon and his land over to you.

---

^A 2:5 Lit *land as far as the width of a sole of a foot* ^B 2:12 Lit *them before them*
^C 2:23 Probably Crete

Begin to take possession of it; engage^A him in battle. ²⁵ Today I will begin to put the fear and dread of you on the peoples everywhere under heaven. They will hear the report about you, tremble, and be in anguish because of you.'

²⁶ "So I sent messengers with an offer of peace to King Sihon of Heshbon from the Wilderness of Kedemoth, saying, ²⁷ 'Let us travel through your land; we will keep strictly to the highway. We will not turn to the right or the left. ²⁸ You can sell us food in exchange for silver so we may eat, and give us water for silver so we may drink. Only let us travel through on foot, ²⁹ just as the descendants of Esau who live in Seir did for us, and the Moabites who live in Ar, until we cross the Jordan into the land the LORD our God is giving us.' ³⁰ But King Sihon of Heshbon would not let us travel through his land, for the LORD your God had made his spirit stubborn and his heart obstinate in order to hand him over to you, as has now taken place.

³¹ "Then the LORD said to me, 'See, I have begun to give Sihon and his land to you. Begin to take possession of it.' ³² So Sihon and his whole army came out against us for battle at Jahaz. ³³ The LORD our God handed him over to us, and we defeated him, his sons, and his whole army. ³⁴ At that time we captured all his cities and completely destroyed the people of every city, including the women and children. We left no survivors. ³⁵ We took only the livestock and the spoil from the cities we captured as plunder for ourselves. ³⁶ There was no city that was inaccessible to^B us, from Aroer on the rim of the Arnon Valley, along with the city in the valley, even as far as Gilead. The LORD our God gave everything to us. ³⁷ But you did not go near the Ammonites' land, all along the bank of the Jabbok River, the cities of the hill country, or any place that the LORD our God had forbidden.

DEFEAT OF OG OF BASHAN

3 "Then we turned and went up the road to Bashan, and King Og of Bashan came out against us with his whole army to do battle at Edrei. ² But the LORD said to me, 'Do not fear him, for I have handed him over to you along with his whole army and his land. Do to him as you did to King Sihon of the Amorites, who lived in Heshbon.' ³ So the LORD our God also handed over King Og of Bashan and his whole army to us. We struck him until there was no survivor left. ⁴ We captured all his cities at that time. There wasn't a city that we didn't take from them: sixty cities, the entire region of Argob, the kingdom of Og in Bashan. ⁵ All these were fortified with high walls, gates, and bars, besides a large number of rural villages. ⁶ We completely destroyed them, as we had done to King Sihon of Heshbon, destroying the men, women, and children of every city. ⁷ But we took all the livestock and the spoil from the cities as plunder for ourselves.

THE LAND OF THE TRANSJORDAN TRIBES

⁸ "At that time we took the land from the two Amorite kings across the Jordan, from the Arnon Valley as far as Mount Hermon, ⁹ which the Sidonians call Sirion, but the Amorites call Senir, ¹⁰ all the cities of the plateau, Gilead, and Bashan as far as Salecah and Edrei, cities of Og's kingdom in Bashan. ¹¹ (Only King Og of Bashan was left of the remnant of the Rephaim.

---

^A2:24 Or *provoke*   ^B2:36 Or *was too high for*

His bed^A was made of iron. Isn't it in Rabbah of the Ammonites? It is 13 ½ feet long and 6 feet wide by a standard measure.^{B})

¹² "At that time we took possession of this land. I gave to the Reubenites and Gadites the area extending from Aroer by the Arnon Valley, and half the hill country of Gilead along with its cities. ¹³ I gave to half the tribe of Manasseh the rest of Gilead and all Bashan, the kingdom of Og. The entire region of Argob, the whole territory of Bashan, used to be called the land of the Rephaim. ¹⁴ Jair, a descendant of Manasseh, took over the entire region of Argob as far as the border of the Geshurites and Maacathites. He called Bashan by his own name, Jair's Villages,^{C} as it is today. ¹⁵ I gave Gilead to Machir, ¹⁶ and I gave to the Reubenites and Gadites the area extending from Gilead to the Arnon Valley (the middle of the valley was the border) and up to the Jabbok River, the border of the Ammonites. ¹⁷ The Arabah and Jordan are also borders from Chinnereth^D as far as the Sea of the Arabah, the Dead Sea, under the slopes of Pisgah on the east.

¹⁸ "I commanded you at that time: The Lord your God has given you this land to possess. All your valiant men will cross over in battle formation ahead of your brothers the Israelites. ¹⁹ But your wives, dependents, and livestock — I know that you have a lot of livestock — will remain in the cities I have given you ²⁰ until the Lord gives rest to your brothers as he has to you, and they also take possession of the land the Lord your God is giving them across the Jordan. Then each of you may return to his possession that I have given you.

THE TRANSFER OF ISRAEL'S LEADERSHIP

²¹ "I commanded Joshua at that time: Your own eyes have seen everything the Lord your God has done to these two kings. The Lord will do the same to all the kingdoms you are about to enter. ²² Don't be afraid of them, for the Lord your God fights for you.

²³ "At that time I begged the Lord: ²⁴ Lord God, you have begun to show your greatness and your strong hand to your servant, for what god is there in heaven or on earth who can perform deeds and mighty acts like yours? ²⁵ Please let me cross over and see the beautiful land on the other side of the Jordan, that good hill country and Lebanon.

²⁶ "But the Lord was angry with me because of you^E and would not listen to me. The Lord said to me, 'That's enough! Do not speak to me again about this matter. ²⁷ Go to the top of Pisgah and look to the west, north, south, and east, and see it with your own eyes, for you will not cross the Jordan. ²⁸ But commission Joshua and encourage and strengthen him, for he will cross over ahead of the people and enable them to inherit this land that you will see.' ²⁹ So we stayed in the valley facing Beth-peor.

CALL TO OBEDIENCE

4 "Now, Israel, listen to the statutes and ordinances I am teaching you to follow, so that you may live, enter, and take possession of the land the Lord, the God of your fathers, is giving you. ² You must not add anything to what I command you or take anything away from it, so that you may keep

---

^{A}3:11 Or *sarcophagus* ^{B}3:11 Lit *nine cubits its length and four cubits its width, by a man's cubit* ^{C}3:14 Or *Havvoth-jair* ^{D}3:17 = the Sea of Galilee; Jos 12:3; 13:27; Lk 5:1 ^{E}3:26 Or *me for your sake* the commands of the LORD your God I am giving you. ³ Your eyes have seen what the LORD did at Baal-peor, for the LORD your God destroyed every one of you who followed Baal of Peor. ⁴ But you who have remained faithful^A to the LORD your God are all alive today. ⁵ Look, I have taught you statutes and ordinances as the LORD my God has commanded me, so that you may follow them in the land you are entering to possess. ⁶ Carefully follow them, for this will show your wisdom and understanding in the eyes of the peoples. When they hear about all these statutes, they will say, 'This great nation is indeed a wise and understanding people.' ⁷ For what great nation is there that has a god near to it as the LORD our God is to us whenever we call to him? ⁸ And what great nation has righteous statutes and ordinances like this entire law I set before you today?

⁹ "Only be on your guard and diligently watch yourselves, so that you don't forget the things your eyes have seen and so that they don't slip from your mind^B as long as you live. Teach them to your children and your grandchildren. ¹⁰ The day you stood before the LORD your God at Horeb, the LORD said to me, 'Assemble the people before me, and I will let them hear my words, so that they may learn to fear me all the days they live on the earth and may instruct their children.' ¹¹ You came near and stood at the base of the mountain, a mountain blazing with fire into the heavens and enveloped in a totally black cloud. ¹² Then the LORD spoke to you from the fire. You kept hearing the sound of the words, but didn't see a form; there was only a voice. ¹³ He declared his covenant to you. He commanded you to follow the Ten Commandments, which he wrote on two stone tablets. ¹⁴ At that time the LORD commanded me to teach you statutes and ordinances for you to follow in the land you are about to cross into and possess.

WORSHIPING THE TRUE GOD

¹⁵ "Diligently watch yourselves — because you did not see any form on the day the LORD spoke to you out of the fire at Horeb — ¹⁶ so you don't act corruptly and make an idol for yourselves in the shape of any figure: a male or female form, ¹⁷ or the form of any animal on the earth, any winged creature that flies in the sky, ¹⁸ any creature that crawls on the ground, or any fish in the waters under the earth. ¹⁹ When you look to the heavens and see the sun, moon, and stars — all the stars in the sky — do not be led astray to bow in worship to them and serve them. The LORD your God has provided them for all people everywhere under heaven. ²⁰ But the LORD selected you and brought you out of Egypt's iron furnace to be a people for his inheritance, as you are today.

²¹ "The LORD was angry with me on your account. He swore that I would not cross the Jordan and enter the good land the LORD your God is giving you as an inheritance. ²² I won't be crossing the Jordan because I am going to die in this land. But you are about to cross over and take possession of this good land. ²³ Be careful not to forget the covenant of the LORD your God that he made with you, and make an idol for yourselves in the shape of anything he has forbidden you. ²⁴ For the LORD your God is a consuming fire, a jealous God.

^A 4:4 Lit *have held on*   ^B 4:9 Or *don't depart from your heart*

²⁵ "When you have children and grandchildren and have been in the land a long time, and if you act corruptly, make an idol in the form of anything, and do what is evil in the sight of the LORD your God, angering him, ²⁶ I call heaven and earth as witnesses against you today that you will quickly perish from the land you are about to cross the Jordan to possess. You will not live long there, but you will certainly be destroyed. ²⁷ The LORD will scatter you among the peoples, and you will be reduced to a few survivors ᴬ among the nations where the LORD your God will drive you. ²⁸ There you will worship man-made gods of wood and stone, which cannot see, hear, eat, or smell. ²⁹ But from there, you will search for the LORD your God, and you will find him when you seek him with all your heart and all your soul. ³⁰ When you are in distress and all these things have happened to you, in the future you will return to the LORD your God and obey him. ³¹ He will not leave you, destroy you, or forget the covenant with your fathers that he swore to them by oath, because the LORD your God is a compassionate God.

³² "Indeed, ask about the earlier days that preceded you, from the day God created mankind ᴮ on the earth and from one end of the heavens to the other: Has anything like this great event ever happened, or has anything like it been heard of? ³³ Has a people heard God's voice speaking from the fire as you have, and lived? ³⁴ Or has a god attempted to go and take a nation as his own out of another nation, by trials, signs, wonders, and war, by a strong hand and an outstretched arm, by great terrors, as the LORD your God did for you in Egypt before your eyes? ³⁵ You were shown these things so that you would know that the LORD is God; there is no other besides him. ³⁶ He let you hear his voice from heaven to instruct you. He showed you his great fire on earth, and you heard his words from the fire. ³⁷ Because he loved your fathers, he chose their descendants after them and brought you out of Egypt by his presence and great power, ³⁸ to drive out before you nations greater and stronger than you and to bring you in and give you their land as an inheritance, as is now taking place. ³⁹ Today, recognize and keep in mind that the LORD is God in heaven above and on earth below; there is no other. ⁴⁰ Keep his statutes and commands, which I am giving you today, so that you and your children after you may prosper and so that you may live long in the land the LORD your God is giving you for all time."

CITIES OF REFUGE

⁴¹ Then Moses set apart three cities across the Jordan to the east. ⁴² Someone could flee there who committed manslaughter, killing his neighbor accidentally without previously hating him. He could flee to one of these cities and stay alive: ⁴³ Bezer in the wilderness on the plateau land, belonging to the Reubenites; Ramoth in Gilead, belonging to the Gadites; or Golan in Bashan, belonging to the Manassites.

INTRODUCTION TO THE LAW

⁴⁴ This is the law Moses gave the Israelites. ⁴⁵ These are the decrees, statutes, and ordinances Moses proclaimed to them after they came out of Egypt, ⁴⁶ across the Jordan in the valley facing Beth-peor in the land of King Sihon of the Amorites. He lived in Heshbon, and Moses and the Israelites defeated

---

ᴬ 4:27 Lit *be left few in number*   ᴮ 4:32 Or *Adam*

him after they came out of Egypt. [47] They took possession of his land and the land of Og king of Bashan, the two Amorite kings who were across the Jordan to the east, [48] from Aroer on the rim of the Arnon Valley as far as Mount Sion (that is, Hermon) [49] and all the Arabah on the east side of the Jordan as far as the Dead Sea below the slopes of Pisgah.

THE TEN COMMANDMENTS

5 Moses summoned all Israel and said to them, "Israel, listen to the statutes and ordinances I am proclaiming as you hear them today. Learn and follow them carefully. [2] The LORD our God made a covenant with us at Horeb. [3] He did not make this covenant with our fathers, but with all of us who are alive here today. [4] The LORD spoke to you face to face from the fire on the mountain. [5] At that time I was standing between the LORD and you to report the word[A] of the LORD to you, because you were afraid of the fire and did not go up the mountain. And he said:

[6] I am the LORD your God, who brought you out of the land of Egypt, out of the place of slavery.

[7] Do not have other gods besides me.

[8] Do not make an idol for yourself in the shape of anything in the heavens above or on the earth below or in the waters under the earth. [9] Do not bow in worship to them, and do not serve them, because I, the LORD your God, am a jealous God, punishing the children for the fathers' iniquity to the third and fourth generations of those who hate me, [10] but showing faithful love to a thousand generations of those who love me and keep my commands.

[11] Do not misuse the name of the LORD your God, because the LORD will not leave anyone unpunished who misuses his name.

[12] Be careful to remember the Sabbath day, to keep it holy as the LORD your God has commanded you. [13] You are to labor six days and do all your work, [14] but the seventh day is a Sabbath to the LORD your God. Do not do any work — you, your son or daughter, your male or female slave, your ox or donkey, any of your livestock, or the resident alien who lives within your city gates, so that your male and female slaves may rest as you do.

[15] Remember that you were a slave in the land of Egypt, and the LORD your God brought you out of there with a strong hand and an outstretched arm. That is why the LORD your God has commanded you to keep the Sabbath day.

[16] Honor your father and your mother, as the LORD your God has commanded you, so that you may live long and so that you may prosper in the land the LORD your God is giving you.

[17] Do not murder.

[18] Do not commit adultery.

[19] Do not steal.

[20] Do not give dishonest testimony against your neighbor.

[21] Do not covet your neighbor's wife or desire your neighbor's house, his field, his male or female slave, his ox or donkey, or anything that belongs to your neighbor.

[A]5:5 One Hb ms, DSS, Sam, LXX, Syr, Vg read *words*

THE PEOPLE'S RESPONSE

²² "The LORD spoke these commands in a loud voice to your entire assembly from the fire, cloud, and total darkness on the mountain; he added nothing more. He wrote them on two stone tablets and gave them to me. ²³ All of you approached me with your tribal leaders and elders when you heard the voice from the darkness and while the mountain was blazing with fire. ²⁴ You said, 'Look, the LORD our God has shown us his glory and greatness, and we have heard his voice from the fire. Today we have seen that God speaks with a person, yet he still lives. ²⁵ But now, why should we die? This great fire will consume us and we will die if we hear the voice of the LORD our God any longer. ²⁶ For who out of all mankind has heard the voice of the living God speaking from the fire, as we have, and lived? ²⁷ Go near and listen to everything the LORD our God says. Then you can tell us everything the LORD our God tells you; we will listen and obey.'

²⁸ "The LORD heard your^A words when you spoke to me. He said to me, 'I have heard the words that these people have spoken to you. Everything they have said is right. ²⁹ If only they had such a heart to fear me and keep all my commands always, so that they and their children would prosper forever. ³⁰ Go and tell them: Return to your tents. ³¹ But you stand here with me, and I will tell you every command — the statutes and ordinances — you are to teach them, so that they may follow them in the land I am giving them to possess.'

³² "Be careful to do as the LORD your God has commanded you; you are not to turn aside to the right or the left. ³³ Follow the whole instruction the LORD your God has commanded you, so that you may live, prosper, and have a long life in the land you will possess.

THE GREATEST COMMAND

6 "This is the command — the statutes and ordinances — the LORD your God has commanded me to teach you, so that you may follow them in the land you are about to enter and possess. ² Do this so that you may fear the LORD your God all the days of your life by keeping all his statutes and commands I am giving you, your son, and your grandson, and so that you may have a long life. ³ Listen, Israel, and be careful to follow them, so that you may prosper and multiply greatly, because the LORD, the God of your fathers, has promised you a land flowing with milk and honey.

⁴ "Listen, Israel: The LORD our God, the LORD is one.^B ⁵ Love the LORD your God with all your heart, with all your soul, and with all your strength. ⁶ These words that I am giving you today are to be in your heart. ⁷ Repeat them to your children. Talk about them when you sit in your house and when you walk along the road, when you lie down and when you get up. ⁸ Bind them as a sign on your hand and let them be a symbol^C on your forehead.^D ⁹ Write them on the doorposts of your house and on your city gates.

REMEMBERING GOD THROUGH OBEDIENCE

¹⁰ "When the LORD your God brings you into the land he swore to your fathers Abraham, Isaac, and Jacob that he would give you — a land with

---

^A5:28 Lit *the sound of your*   ^B6:4 Or *the LORD is our God; the LORD is one,* or *The LORD is our God, the LORD alone,* or *The LORD our God is one LORD*   ^C6:8 Or *phylactery;* Mt 23:5   ^D6:8 Lit *symbol between your eyes* large and beautiful cities that you did not build, [11] houses full of every good thing that you did not fill them with, cisterns that you did not dig, and vineyards and olive groves that you did not plant — and when you eat and are satisfied, [12] be careful not to forget the LORD who brought you out of the land of Egypt, out of the place of slavery. [13] Fear the LORD your God, worship him, and take your oaths in his name. [14] Do not follow other gods, the gods of the peoples around you, [15] for the LORD your God, who is among you, is a jealous God. Otherwise, the LORD your God will become angry with you and obliterate you from the face of the earth. [16] Do not test the LORD your God as you tested him at Massah. [17] Carefully observe the commands of the LORD your God, the decrees and statutes he has commanded you. [18] Do what is right and good in the LORD's sight, so that you may prosper and so that you may enter and possess the good land the LORD your God swore to give your fathers, [19] by driving out all your enemies before you, as the LORD has said.

[20] "When your son asks you in the future, 'What is the meaning of the decrees, statutes, and ordinances that the LORD our God has commanded you?' [21] tell him, 'We were slaves of Pharaoh in Egypt, but the LORD brought us out of Egypt with a strong hand. [22] Before our eyes the LORD inflicted great and devastating signs and wonders on Egypt, on Pharaoh, and on all his household, [23] but he brought us from there in order to lead us in and give us the land that he swore to our fathers. [24] The LORD commanded us to follow all these statutes and to fear the LORD our God for our prosperity always and for our preservation, as it is today. [25] Righteousness will be ours if we are careful to follow every one of these commands before the LORD our God, as he has commanded us.'

ISRAEL TO DESTROY IDOLATROUS NATIONS

7 "When the LORD your God brings you into the land you are entering to possess, and he drives out many nations before you — the Hethites, Girgashites, Amorites, Canaanites, Perizzites, Hivites and Jebusites, seven nations more numerous and powerful than you — [2] and when the LORD your God delivers them over to you and you defeat them, you must completely destroy them. Make no treaty with them and show them no mercy. [3] You must not intermarry with them, and you must not give your daughters to their sons or take their daughters for your sons, [4] because they will turn your sons away from me to worship other gods. Then the LORD's anger will burn against you, and he will swiftly destroy you. [5] Instead, this is what you are to do to them: tear down their altars, smash their sacred pillars, cut down their Asherah poles, and burn their carved images. [6] For you are a holy people belonging to the LORD your God. The LORD your God has chosen you to be his own possession out of all the peoples on the face of the earth.

[7] "The LORD had his heart set on you and chose you, not because you were more numerous than all peoples, for you were the fewest of all peoples. [8] But because the LORD loved you and kept the oath he swore to your fathers, he brought you out with a strong hand and redeemed you from the place of slavery, from the power of Pharaoh king of Egypt. [9] Know that the LORD your God is God, the faithful God who keeps his gracious covenant loyalty for a thousand generations with those who love him and keep his commands.

THE FAITHFUL GOD

DEUTERONOMY 6:10–7:26; HEBREWS 13:8

My family goes to the same beach every summer. We've gone since I was fifteen years old, and each time I go back, the beach looks exactly the same: same chairs, same tree, same rocky sand that hurts my bare feet. The same smells and sounds and sights.

But I've changed. Each year, I stand on the shore a different person than I was the year before. My life has been up and down, back and forth, as life always is: new friendships, painful loss, career success, embarrassing failures. But no matter where I've been or how different I look, my beach is constant. It's always the same. My beach, in a way, is faithful.

In Deuteronomy, God declared His faithfulness to the nation of Israel again and again. His people needed constant reminding that He wasn't going anywhere. They needed to know that no matter what they did or how far they strayed from Him, they were still chosen (Dt 7:7). And because God had chosen them, He would remain committed to them—not because they were perfect followers.

What sets the nation of Israel apart from all others in not Israel's faithfulness toward God, but God's faithfulness toward Israel.

In Deuteronomy 7:9, Moses said, "Know that the LORD your God is God, the faithful God who keeps his gracious covenant loyalty for a thousand generations with those who love him and keep his commands."

This one verse is chock-full of promises: The Lord is our God, and He is faithful to keep His covenant.

These are things Israel needed to hear at the tail end of forty years en route to the promised land. They'd fought battles, escaped slavery in Egypt, obeyed and disobeyed God—all while raising a new generation in a constant, nomadic state. If anyone ever needed to hear a sermon on God's faithfulness, it was them. I wonder if they whispered His promises to themselves. *"The LORD is my God. He is a faithful God. He keeps the covenant."*

You and I often approach the shore, weary and tired. With faint voices, we, too, whisper the promises of God to ourselves. And like Israel, we need them.

Year after year, I stand on that beach. I change but it does not. Since the beginning of time, people have stood on the promise of the unwavering faithfulness of God, and though we continue to change, mature, and grow, God remains as faithful and sure to us as He was to the people who read Deuteronomy for the first time ever. This is our God—the same, yesterday, today, and forever (Heb 13:8).

¹⁰ But he directly pays back ^A^ and destroys those who hate him. He will not hesitate to pay back directly ^B^ the one who hates him. ¹¹ So keep the command — the statutes and ordinances — that I am giving you to follow today.

¹² "If you listen to and are careful to keep these ordinances, the Lord your God will keep his covenant loyalty with you, as he swore to your fathers. ¹³ He will love you, bless you, and multiply you. He will bless your offspring, ^C^ and the produce of your land — your grain, new wine, and fresh oil — the young of your herds, and the newborn of your flocks, in the land he swore to your fathers that he would give you. ¹⁴ You will be blessed above all peoples; there will be no infertile male or female among you or your livestock. ¹⁵ The Lord will remove all sickness from you; he will not put on you all the terrible diseases of Egypt that you know about, but he will inflict them on all who hate you. ¹⁶ You must destroy all the peoples the Lord your God is delivering over to you and not look on them with pity. Do not worship their gods, for that will be a snare to you.

¹⁷ "If you say to yourself, 'These nations are greater than I; how can I drive them out?' ¹⁸ do not be afraid of them. Be sure to remember what the Lord your God did to Pharaoh and all Egypt: ¹⁹ the great trials that you saw, the signs and wonders, the strong hand and outstretched arm, by which the Lord your God brought you out. The Lord your God will do the same to all the peoples you fear. ²⁰ The Lord your God will also send hornets against them until all the survivors and those hiding from you perish. ²¹ Don't be terrified of them, for the Lord your God, a great and awesome God, is among you. ²² The Lord your God will drive out these nations before you little by little. You will not be able to destroy them all at once; otherwise, the wild animals will become too numerous for you. ²³ The Lord your God will give them over to you and throw them into great confusion until they are destroyed. ²⁴ He will hand their kings over to you, and you will wipe out their names under heaven. No one will be able to stand against you; you will annihilate them. ²⁵ Burn up the carved images of their gods. Don't covet the silver and gold on the images and take it for yourself, or else you will be ensnared by it, for it is detestable to the Lord your God. ²⁶ Do not bring any detestable thing into your house, or you will be set apart for destruction like it. You are to abhor and detest it utterly because it is set apart for destruction.

REMEMBER THE LORD

8 "Carefully follow every command I am giving you today, so that you may live and increase, and may enter and take possession of the land the Lord swore to your fathers. ² Remember that the Lord your God led you on the entire journey these forty years in the wilderness, so that he might humble you and test you to know what was in your heart, whether or not you would keep his commands. ³ He humbled you by letting you go hungry; then he gave you manna to eat, which you and your fathers had not known, so that you might learn that man does not live on bread alone but on every word that comes from the mouth of the Lord. ⁴ Your clothing did not wear out, and your feet did not swell these forty years. ⁵ Keep in mind that the Lord your God has been disciplining you just as a man disciplines his son.

---

^A^ 7:10 Lit *He pays back to their faces*   ^B^ 7:10 Lit *to pay back to their faces*
^C^ 7:13 Lit *bless the fruit of your womb*

⁶ So keep the commands of the LORD your God by walking in his ways and fearing him. ⁷ For the LORD your God is bringing you into a good land, a land with streams, springs, and deep water sources, flowing in both valleys and hills; ⁸ a land of wheat, barley, vines, figs, and pomegranates; a land of olive oil and honey; ⁹ a land where you will eat food without shortage, where you will lack nothing; a land whose rocks are iron and from whose hills you will mine copper. ¹⁰ When you eat and are full, you will bless the LORD your God for the good land he has given you.

¹¹ "Be careful that you don't forget the LORD your God by failing to keep his commands, ordinances, and statutes that I am giving you today. ¹² When you eat and are full, and build beautiful houses to live in, ¹³ and your herds and flocks grow large, and your silver and gold multiply, and everything else you have increases, ¹⁴ be careful that your heart doesn't become proud and you forget the LORD your God who brought you out of the land of Egypt, out of the place of slavery. ¹⁵ He led you through the great and terrible wilderness with its poisonous^A snakes and scorpions, a thirsty land where there was no water. He brought water out of the flint rock for you. ¹⁶ He fed you in the wilderness with manna, which your fathers had not known, in order to humble and test you, so that in the end he might cause you to prosper. ¹⁷ You may say to yourself, 'My power and my own ability have gained this wealth for me,' ¹⁸ but remember that the LORD your God gives you the power to gain wealth, in order to confirm his covenant he swore to your fathers, as it is today. ¹⁹ If you ever forget the LORD your God and follow other gods to serve them and bow in worship to them, I testify against you today that you will perish. ²⁰ Like the nations the LORD is about to destroy before you, you will perish if you do not obey the LORD your God.

WARNING AGAINST SELF-RIGHTEOUSNESS

9 "Listen, Israel: Today you are about to cross the Jordan to enter and drive out nations greater and stronger than you, with large cities fortified to the heavens. ² The people are strong and tall, the descendants of the Anakim. You know about them and you have heard it said about them, 'Who can stand up to the sons of Anak?' ³ But understand that today the LORD your God will cross over ahead of you as a consuming fire; he will devastate and subdue them before you. You will drive them out and destroy them swiftly, as the LORD has told you. ⁴ When the LORD your God drives them out before you, do not say to yourself, 'The LORD brought me in to take possession of this land because of my righteousness.' Instead, the LORD will drive out these nations before you because of their wickedness. ⁵ You are not going to take possession of their land because of your righteousness or your integrity. Instead, the LORD your God will drive out these nations before you because of their wickedness, in order to fulfill the promise he swore to your fathers, Abraham, Isaac, and Jacob. ⁶ Understand that the LORD your God is not giving you this good land to possess because of your righteousness, for you are a stiff-necked people.

ISRAEL'S REBELLION AND MOSES'S INTERCESSION

⁷ "Remember and do not forget how you provoked the LORD your God in the wilderness. You have been rebelling against the LORD from the day you left

the land of Egypt until you reached this place. ⁸ You provoked the LORD at Horeb, and he was angry enough with you to destroy you. ⁹ When I went up the mountain to receive the stone tablets, the tablets of the covenant the LORD made with you, I stayed on the mountain forty days and forty nights. I did not eat food or drink water. ¹⁰ On the day of the assembly the LORD gave me the two stone tablets, inscribed by God's finger. The exact words were on them, which the LORD spoke to you from the fire on the mountain. ¹¹ The LORD gave me the two stone tablets, the tablets of the covenant, at the end of the forty days and forty nights.

¹² "The LORD said to me, 'Get up and go down immediately from here. For your people whom you brought out of Egypt have acted corruptly. They have quickly turned from the way that I commanded them; they have made a cast image for themselves.' ¹³ The LORD also said to me, 'I have seen this people, and indeed, they are a stiff-necked people. ¹⁴ Leave me alone, and I will destroy them and blot out their name under heaven. Then I will make you into a nation stronger and more numerous than they.'

¹⁵ "So I went back down the mountain, while it was blazing with fire, and the two tablets of the covenant were in my hands. ¹⁶ I saw how you had sinned against the LORD your God; you had made a calf image for yourselves. You had quickly turned from the way the LORD had commanded for you. ¹⁷ So I took hold of the two tablets and threw them from my hands, shattering them before your eyes. ¹⁸ I fell down like the first time in the presence of the LORD for forty days and forty nights; I did not eat food or drink water because of all the sin you committed, doing what was evil in the LORD's sight and angering him. ¹⁹ I was afraid of the fierce anger the LORD had directed against you, because he was about to destroy you. But again the LORD listened to me on that occasion. ²⁰ The LORD was angry enough with Aaron to destroy him. But I prayed for Aaron at that time also. ²¹ I took the sinful calf you had made and burned it. I crushed it, thoroughly grinding it to powder as fine as dust, and threw its dust into the stream that came down from the mountain.

²² "You continued to provoke the LORD at Taberah, Massah, and Kibroth-hattaavah. ²³ When the LORD sent you from Kadesh-barnea, he said, 'Go up and possess the land I have given you'; you rebelled against the command of the LORD your God. You did not believe or obey him. ²⁴ You have been rebelling against the LORD ever since I haveᴬ known you.

²⁵ "I fell down in the presence of the LORD forty days and forty nights because the LORD had threatened to destroy you. ²⁶ I prayed to the LORD:

Lord GOD, do not annihilate your people, your inheritance, whom you redeemed through your greatness and brought out of Egypt with a strong hand. ²⁷ Remember your servants Abraham, Isaac, and Jacob. Disregard this people's stubbornness, and their wickedness and sin. ²⁸ Otherwise, those in the land you brought us from will say, 'Because the LORD wasn't able to bring them into the land he had promised them, and because he hated them, he brought them out to kill them in the wilderness.' ²⁹ But they are your people, your inheritance, whom you brought out by your great power and outstretched arm.

ᴬ9:24 Sam, LXX read *since he has*

to Lebanon and from the Euphrates River[A] to the Mediterranean Sea. [25] No one will be able to stand against you; the LORD your God will put fear and dread of you in all the land where you set foot, as he has promised you.

A BLESSING AND A CURSE

[26] "Look, today I set before you a blessing and a curse: [27] there will be a blessing, if you obey the commands of the LORD your God I am giving you today, [28] and a curse, if you do not obey the commands of the LORD your God and you turn aside from the path I command you today by following other gods you have not known. [29] When the LORD your God brings you into the land you are entering to possess, you are to proclaim the blessing at Mount Gerizim and the curse at Mount Ebal. [30] Aren't these mountains across the Jordan, beyond the western road in the land of the Canaanites, who live in the Arabah, opposite Gilgal, near the oaks[B] of Moreh? [31] For you are about to cross the Jordan to enter and take possession of the land the LORD your God is giving you. When you possess it and settle in it, [32] be careful to follow all the statutes and ordinances I set before you today.

THE CHOSEN PLACE OF WORSHIP

12 "Be careful to follow these statutes and ordinances in the land that the LORD, the God of your fathers, has given you to possess all the days you live on the earth. [2] Destroy completely all the places where the nations that you are driving out worship their gods — on the high mountains, on the hills, and under every green tree. [3] Tear down their altars, smash their sacred pillars, burn their Asherah poles, cut down the carved images of their gods, and wipe out their names from every[C] place. [4] Don't worship the LORD your God this way. [5] Instead, turn to the place the LORD your God chooses from all your tribes to put his name for his dwelling and go there. [6] You are to bring there your burnt offerings and sacrifices, your tenths and personal contributions,[D] your vow offerings and freewill offerings, and the firstborn of your herds and flocks. [7] You will eat there in the presence of the LORD your God and rejoice with your household in everything you do,[E] because the LORD your God has blessed you.

[8] "You are not to do as we are doing here today; everyone is doing whatever seems right in his own sight. [9] Indeed, you have not yet come into the resting place and the inheritance the LORD your God is giving you. [10] When you cross the Jordan and live in the land the LORD your God is giving you to inherit, and he gives you rest from all the enemies around you and you live in security, [11] then the LORD your God will choose the place to have his name dwell. Bring there everything I command you: your burnt offerings, sacrifices, offerings of the tenth, personal contributions,[F] and all your choice offerings you vow to the LORD. [12] You will rejoice before the LORD your God — you, your sons and daughters, your male and female slaves, and the Levite who is within your city gates, since he has no portion or inheritance among you. [13] Be careful not to offer your burnt offerings in all the sacred places you

---

[A] 11:24 Some Hb mss, LXX, Tg, Vg read *the great river, the river Euphrates*
[B] 11:30 Sam, LXX, Syr, Aq, Sym read *oak*; Gn 12:6   [C] 12:3 Lit *that*
[D] 12:6 Lit *and the contributions from your hands*   [E] 12:7 Lit *you put your hand to,*
also in v. 18   [F] 12:11 Lit *tenth, the contributions from your hands*

see. ¹⁴ You must offer your burnt offerings only in the place the LORD chooses in one of your tribes, and there you must do everything I command you.

SLAUGHTERING ANIMALS TO EAT

¹⁵ "But whenever you want, you may slaughter and eat meat within any of your city gates, according to the blessing the LORD your God has given you. Those who are clean or unclean may eat it, as they would a gazelle or deer, ¹⁶ but you must not eat the blood; pour it on the ground like water. ¹⁷ Within your city gates you may not eat the tenth of your grain, new wine, or fresh oil; the firstborn of your herd or flock; any of your vow offerings that you pledge; your freewill offerings; or your personal contributions.ᴬ ¹⁸ You are to eat them in the presence of the LORD your God at the place the LORD your God chooses — you, your son and daughter, your male and female slave, and the Levite who is within your city gates. Rejoice before the LORD your God in everything you do, ¹⁹ and be careful not to neglect the Levite, as long as you live in your land.

²⁰ "When the LORD your God enlarges your territory as he has promised you, and you say, 'I want to eat meat' because you have a strong desire to eat meat, you may eat it whenever you want. ²¹ If the place where the LORD your God chooses to put his name is too far from you, you may slaughter any of your herd or flock he has given you, as I have commanded you, and you may eat it within your city gates whenever you want. ²² Indeed, you may eat it as the gazelle and deer are eaten; both the clean and the unclean may eat it. ²³ But don't eat the blood, since the blood is the life, and you must not eat the life with the meat. ²⁴ Do not eat blood; pour it on the ground like water. ²⁵ Do not eat it, so that you and your children after you will prosper, because you will be doing what is right in the LORD's sight.

²⁶ "But you are to take the holy offerings you have and your vow offerings and go to the place the LORD chooses. ²⁷ Present the meat and blood of your burnt offerings on the altar of the LORD your God. The blood of your other sacrifices is to be poured out beside the altar of the LORD your God, but you may eat the meat. ²⁸ Be careful to obey all these things I command you, so that you and your children after you may prosper forever, because you will be doing what is good and right in the sight of the LORD your God.

²⁹ "When the LORD your God annihilates the nations before you, which you are entering to take possession of, and you drive them out and live in their land, ³⁰ be careful not to be ensnared by their ways after they have been destroyed before you. Do not inquire about their gods, asking, 'How did these nations worship their gods? I'll also do the same.' ³¹ You must not do the same to the LORD your God, because they practice every detestable act, which the LORD hates, for their gods. They even burn their sons and daughters in the fire to their gods. ³² Be careful to do everything I command you; do not add anything to it or take anything away from it.

THE FALSE PROPHET

13 "If a prophet or someone who has dreams arises among you and proclaims a sign or wonder to you, ² and that sign or wonder he has promised you comes about, but he says, 'Let us follow other gods,' which

---

ᴬ12:17 Lit *or the contributions from your hands*

you have not known, 'and let us worship them,' [3] do not listen to that prophet's words or to that dreamer. For the LORD your God is testing you to know whether you love the LORD your God with all your heart and all your soul. [4] You must follow the LORD your God and fear him. You must keep his commands and listen to him; you must worship him and remain faithful[A] to him. [5] That prophet or dreamer must be put to death, because he has urged rebellion against the LORD your God who brought you out of the land of Egypt and redeemed you from the place of slavery, to turn you from the way the LORD your God has commanded you to walk. You must purge the evil from you.

DON'T TOLERATE IDOLATRY

[6] "If your brother, the son of your mother,[B] or your son or daughter, or the wife you embrace, or your closest friend secretly entices you, saying, 'Let us go and worship other gods' — which neither you nor your fathers have known, [7] any of the gods of the peoples around you, near you or far from you, from one end of the earth to the other — [8] do not yield to him or listen to him. Show him no pity,[C] and do not spare him or shield him. [9] Instead, you must kill him. Your hand is to be the first against him to put him to death, and then the hands of all the people. [10] Stone him to death for trying to turn you away from the LORD your God who brought you out of the land of Egypt, out of the place of slavery. [11] All Israel will hear and be afraid, and they will no longer do anything evil like this among you.

[12] "If you hear it said about one of your cities the LORD your God is giving you to live in, [13] that wicked men have sprung up among you, led the inhabitants of their city astray, and said, 'Let us go and worship other gods,' which you have not known, [14] you are to inquire, investigate, and interrogate thoroughly. If the report turns out to be true that this detestable act has been done among you, [15] you must strike down the inhabitants of that city with the sword. Completely destroy everyone in it as well as its livestock with the sword. [16] You are to gather all its spoil in the middle of the city square and completely burn the city and all its spoil for the LORD your God. The city is to remain a mound of ruins forever; it is not to be rebuilt. [17] Nothing set apart for destruction is to remain in your hand, so that the LORD will turn from his burning anger and grant you mercy, show you compassion, and multiply you as he swore to your fathers. [18] This will occur if you obey the LORD your God, keeping all his commands I am giving you today, doing what is right in the sight of the LORD your God.

FORBIDDEN PRACTICES

14 "You are sons of the LORD your God; do not cut yourselves or make a bald spot on your head[D] on behalf of the dead, [2] for you are a holy people belonging to the LORD your God. The LORD has chosen you to be his own possession out of all the peoples on the face of the earth.

CLEAN AND UNCLEAN FOODS

[3] "You must not eat any detestable thing. [4] These are the animals you may eat:
oxen, sheep, goats,
[5] deer, gazelles, roe deer,

[A] 13:4 Lit *and hold on* [B] 13:6 DSS, Sam, LXX read *If the son of your father or the son of your mother* [C] 13:8 Lit *Your eye must not pity him* [D] 14:1 Or *forehead*

wild goats, ibexes, antelopes,
and mountain sheep.

[6] You may eat any animal that has hooves divided in two and chews the cud. [A]
[7] But among the ones that chew the cud or have divided hooves, you are not
to eat these:

camels, hares, and hyraxes,
though they chew the cud, they do not have hooves —
they are unclean for you;

[8] and pigs, though they have hooves, they do not chew the cud —
they are unclean for you.

Do not eat their meat or touch their carcasses.

[9] "You may eat everything from the water that has fins and scales, [10] but you
may not eat anything that does not have fins and scales — it is unclean for you.

[11] "You may eat every clean bird, [12] but these are the ones you may not eat:
eagles, bearded vultures,
black vultures, [13] the kites,
any kind of falcon, [B]

[14] every kind of raven, [15] ostriches,
short-eared owls, gulls,
any kind of hawk,

[16] little owls, long-eared owls,
barn owls, [17] eagle owls,
ospreys, cormorants, [18] storks,
any kind of heron,
hoopoes, and bats. [C]

[19] All winged insects are unclean for you; they may not be eaten. [20] But you
may eat every clean flying creature.

[21] "You are not to eat any carcass; you may give it to a resident alien within your city gates, and he may eat it, or you may sell it to a foreigner. For you
are a holy people belonging to the LORD your God. Do not boil a young goat
in its mother's milk.

A TENTH FOR THE LORD

[22] "Each year you are to set aside a tenth of all the produce grown in your
fields. [23] You are to eat a tenth of your grain, new wine, and fresh oil, and the
firstborn of your herd and flock, in the presence of the LORD your God at the
place where he chooses to have his name dwell, so that you will always learn
to fear the LORD your God. [24] But if the distance is too great for you to carry it,
since the place where the LORD your God chooses to put his name is too far
away from you and since the LORD your God has blessed you, [25] then exchange
it for silver, take the silver in your hand, and go to the place the LORD your God
chooses. [26] You may spend the silver on anything you want: cattle, sheep, goats,
wine, beer, or anything you desire. You are to feast there in the presence of
the LORD your God and rejoice with your family. [27] Do not neglect the Levite
within your city gates, since he has no portion or inheritance among you.

[A] 14:6 The Hb does not specify chewing the cud, but bringing up partially
digested food and swallowing it again.   [B] 14:13 Some Hb mss, Sam, LXX; other
Hb mss, Vg read *the falcon, the various kinds of kite*   [C] 14:5-18 The identification
of some of these animals is uncertain.

²⁸ "At the end of every three years, bring a tenth of all your produce for that year and store it within your city gates. ²⁹ Then the Levite, who has no portion or inheritance among you, the resident alien, the fatherless, and the widow within your city gates may come, eat, and be satisfied. And the LORD your God will bless you in all the work of your hands that you do.

DEBTS CANCELED

15 "At the end of every seven years you must cancel debts. ² This is how to cancel debt: Every creditorᴬ is to cancel what he has lent his neighbor. He is not to collect anything from his neighbor or brother, because the LORD's release of debts has been proclaimed. ³ You may collect something from a foreigner, but you must forgive whatever your brother owes you.

⁴ "There will be no poor among you, however, because the LORD is certain to bless you in the land the LORD your God is giving you to possess as an inheritance — ⁵ if only you obey the LORD your God and are careful to follow every one of these commands I am giving you today. ⁶ When the LORD your God blesses you as he has promised you, you will lend to many nations but not borrow; you will rule many nations, but they will not rule you.

LENDING TO THE POOR

⁷ "If there is a poor person among you, one of your brothers within any of your city gates in the land the LORD your God is giving you, do not be hardhearted or tightfisted toward your poor brother. ⁸ Instead, you are to open your hand to him and freely loan him enough for whatever need he has. ⁹ Be careful that there isn't this wicked thought in your heart, 'The seventh year, the year of canceling debts, is near,' and you are stingy toward your poor brother and give him nothing. He will cry out to the LORD against you, and you will be guilty. ¹⁰ Give to him, and don't have a stingy heartᴮ when you give, and because of this the LORD your God will bless you in all your work and in everything you do.ᶜ ¹¹ For there will never cease to be poor people in the land; that is why I am commanding you, 'Open your hand willingly to your poor and needy brother in your land.'

RELEASE OF SLAVES

¹² "If your fellow Hebrew, a man or woman, is sold to you and serves you six years, you must set him free in the seventh year. ¹³ When you set him free, do not send him away empty-handed. ¹⁴ Give generously to him from your flock, your threshing floor, and your winepress. You are to give him whatever the LORD your God has blessed you with. ¹⁵ Remember that you were a slave in the land of Egypt and the LORD your God redeemed you; that is why I am giving you this command today. ¹⁶ But if your slave says to you, 'I don't want to leave you,' because he loves you and your family, and is well off with you, ¹⁷ take an awl and pierce through his ear into the door, and he will become your slave for life. Also treat your female slave the same way. ¹⁸ Do not regard it as a hardshipᴰ when you set him free, because he worked for you six years — worth twice the wages of a hired worker. Then the LORD your God will bless you in everything you do.

ᴬ15:2 Lit *owner of a loan of his hand*   ᴮ15:10 Lit *and let not your heart be grudging*
ᶜ15:10 Lit *you put your hand to*   ᴰ15:18 Lit *Let it not be hard in your sight*

CONSECRATION OF FIRSTBORN ANIMALS

[19] "Consecrate to the LORD your God every firstborn male produced by your herd and flock. You are not to put the firstborn of your oxen to work or shear the firstborn of your flock. [20] Each year you and your family are to eat it before the LORD your God in the place the LORD chooses. [21] But if there is a defect in the animal, if it is lame or blind or has any serious defect, you may not sacrifice it to the LORD your God. [22] Eat it within your city gates; both the unclean person and the clean may eat it, as though it were a gazelle or deer. [23] But you must not eat its blood; pour it on the ground like water.

THE FESTIVAL OF PASSOVER

16 "Set aside the month of Abib[A] and observe the Passover to the LORD your God, because the LORD your God brought you out of Egypt by night in the month of Abib. [2] Sacrifice to the LORD your God a Passover animal from the herd or flock in the place where the LORD chooses to have his name dwell. [3] Do not eat leavened bread with it. For seven days you are to eat unleavened bread with it, the bread of hardship — because you left the land of Egypt in a hurry — so that you may remember for the rest of your life the day you left the land of Egypt. [4] No yeast is to be found anywhere in your territory for seven days, and none of the meat you sacrifice in the evening of the first day is to remain until morning. [5] You are not to sacrifice the Passover animal in any of the towns the LORD your God is giving you. [6] Sacrifice the Passover animal only at the place where the LORD your God chooses to have his name dwell. Do this in the evening as the sun sets at the same time of day you departed from Egypt. [7] You are to cook and eat it in the place the LORD your God chooses, and you are to return to your tents in the morning. [8] Eat unleavened bread for six days. On the seventh day there is to be a solemn assembly to the LORD your God; do not do any work.

THE FESTIVAL OF WEEKS

[9] "You are to count seven weeks, counting the weeks from the time the sickle is first put to the standing grain. [10] You are to celebrate the Festival of Weeks to the LORD your God with a freewill offering that you give in proportion to how the LORD your God has blessed you. [11] Rejoice before the LORD your God in the place where he chooses to have his name dwell — you, your son and daughter, your male and female slave, the Levite within your city gates, as well as the resident alien, the fatherless, and the widow among you. [12] Remember that you were slaves in Egypt; carefully follow these statutes.

THE FESTIVAL OF SHELTERS

[13] "You are to celebrate the Festival of Shelters for seven days when you have gathered in everything from your threshing floor and winepress. [14] Rejoice during your festival — you, your son and daughter, your male and female slave, as well as the Levite, the resident alien, the fatherless, and the widow within your city gates. [15] You are to hold a seven-day festival for the LORD your God

[A] 16:1 March–April; called Nisan in the post-exilic period; Neh 2:1; Est 3:7

in the place he chooses, because the LORD your God will bless you in all your produce and in all the work of your hands, and you will have abundant joy. ¹⁶ "All your males are to appear three times a year before the LORD your God in the place he chooses: at the Festival of Unleavened Bread, the Festival of Weeks, and the Festival of Shelters. No one is to appear before the LORD empty-handed. ¹⁷ Everyone must appear with a gift suited to his means, according to the blessing the LORD your God has given you.

APPOINTING JUDGES AND OFFICIALS

¹⁸ "Appoint judges and officials for your tribes in all your towns the LORD your God is giving you. They are to judge the people with righteous judgment. ¹⁹ Do not deny justice or show partiality to anyone. Do not accept a bribe, for it blinds the eyes of the wise and twists the words of the righteous. ²⁰ Pursue justice and justice alone, so that you will live and possess the land the LORD your God is giving you.

FORBIDDEN WORSHIP

²¹ "Do not set up an Asherah of any kind of wood next to the altar you will build for the LORD your God, ²² and do not set up a sacred pillar; the LORD your God hates them.

17 "Do not sacrifice to the LORD your God an ox or sheep with a defect or any serious flaw, for that is detestable to the LORD your God.

THE JUDICIAL PROCEDURE FOR IDOLATRY

² "If a man or woman among you in one of your towns that the LORD your God will give you is discovered doing evil in the sight of the LORD your God and violating his covenant ³ and has gone to serve other gods by bowing in worship to the sun, moon, or all the stars in the sky — which I have forbidden — ⁴ and if you are told or hear about it, then investigate it thoroughly. If the report turns out to be true that this detestable act has been done in Israel, ⁵ you are to bring out to your city gates that man or woman who has done this evil thing and stone them to death. ⁶ The one condemned to die is to be executed on the testimony of two or three witnesses. No one is to be executed on the testimony of a single witness. ⁷ The witnesses' hands are to be the first in putting him to death, and after that, the hands of all the people. You must purge the evil from you.

DIFFICULT CASES

⁸ "If a case is too difficult for you — concerning bloodshed, lawsuits, or assaults — cases disputed at your city gates, then go up to the place the LORD your God chooses. ⁹ You are to go to the Levitical priests and to the judge who presides at that time. Ask, and they will give you a verdict in the case. ¹⁰ You must abide by the verdict they give you at the place the LORD chooses. Be careful to do exactly as they instruct you. ¹¹ You must abide by the instruction they give you and the verdict they announce to you. Do not turn to the right or the left from the decision they declare to you. ¹² The person who acts arrogantly, refusing to listen either to the priest who stands there serving the LORD your God or to the judge, must die. You must purge the evil from Israel. ¹³ Then all the people will hear about it, be afraid, and no longer behave arrogantly.

APPOINTING A KING

14 "When you enter the land the LORD your God is giving you, take possession of it, live in it, and say, 'I will set a king over me like all the nations around me,' 15 you are to appoint over you the king the LORD your God chooses. Appoint a king from your brothers. You are not to set a foreigner over you, or one who is not of your people. 16 However, he must not acquire many horses for himself or send the people back to Egypt to acquire many horses, for the LORD has told you, 'You are never to go back that way again.' 17 He must not acquire many wives for himself so that his heart won't go astray. He must not acquire very large amounts of silver and gold for himself. 18 When he is seated on his royal throne, he is to write a copy of this instruction for himself on a scroll in the presence of the Levitical priests. 19 It is to remain with him, and he is to read from it all the days of his life, so that he may learn to fear the LORD his God, to observe all the words of this instruction, and to do these statutes. 20 Then his heart will not be exalted above his countrymen, he will not turn from this command to the right or the left, and he and his sons will continue reigning many years^A in Israel.

PROVISIONS FOR THE LEVITES

18 "The Levitical priests, the whole tribe of Levi, will have no portion or inheritance with Israel. They will eat the LORD's fire offerings; that is their^B,C inheritance. 2 Although Levi has no inheritance among his brothers, the LORD is his inheritance, as he promised him. 3 This is the priests' share from the people who offer a sacrifice, whether it is an ox, a sheep, or a goat; the priests are to be given the shoulder, jaws, and stomach. 4 You are to give him the firstfruits of your grain, new wine, and fresh oil, and the first sheared wool of your flock. 5 For the LORD your God has chosen him and his sons from all your tribes to stand and minister in his name from now on.^D 6 When a Levite leaves one of your towns in Israel where he was staying and wants to go to the place the LORD chooses, 7 he may serve in the name of the LORD his God like all his fellow Levites who minister there in the presence of the LORD. 8 They will eat equal portions besides what he has received from the sale of the family estate.^E

OCCULT PRACTICES VERSUS PROPHETIC REVELATION

9 "When you enter the land the LORD your God is giving you, do not imitate the detestable customs of those nations. 10 No one among you is to sacrifice his son or daughter in the fire,^F practice divination, tell fortunes, interpret omens, practice sorcery, 11 cast spells, consult a medium or a spiritist, or inquire of the dead. 12 Everyone who does these acts is detestable to the LORD, and the LORD your God is driving out the nations before you because of these detestable acts. 13 You must be blameless before the LORD your God. 14 Though these nations you are about to drive out listen to fortune-tellers and diviners, the LORD your God has not permitted you to do this.

15 "The LORD your God will raise up for you a prophet like me from among your own brothers. You must listen to him. 16 This is what you requested from

---

^A17:20 Lit *will lengthen days on his kingdom*   ^B18:1 LXX; MT reads *his*
^C18:1 Or *his*   ^D18:5 Lit *name all the days*   ^E18:8 Hb obscure   ^F18:10 Lit *to make his son or daughter pass through the fire*

the Lord your God at Horeb on the day of the assembly when you said, 'Let us not continue to hear the voice of the Lord our God or see this great fire any longer, so that we will not die!' ¹⁷ Then the Lord said to me, 'They have spoken well. ¹⁸ I will raise up for them a prophet like you from among their brothers. I will put my words in his mouth, and he will tell them everything I command him. ¹⁹ I will hold accountable whoever does not listen to my words that he speaks in my name. ²⁰ But the prophet who presumes to speak a message in my name that I have not commanded him to speak, or who speaks in the name of other gods — that prophet must die.' ²¹ You may say to yourself, 'How can we recognize a message the Lord has not spoken?' ²² When a prophet speaks in the Lord's name, and the message does not come true or is not fulfilled, that is a message the Lord has not spoken. The prophet has spoken it presumptuously. Do not be afraid of him.

CITIES OF REFUGE

19 "When the Lord your God annihilates the nations whose land he is giving you, so that you drive them out and live in their cities and houses, ² you are to set apart three cities for yourselves within the land the Lord your God is giving you to possess. ³ You are to determine the distances ᴬ and divide the land the Lord your God is granting you as an inheritance into three regions, so that anyone who commits manslaughter can flee to these cities. ᴮ

⁴ "Here is the law concerning a case of someone who kills a person and flees there to save his life, having killed his neighbor accidentally without previously hating him: ⁵ If, for example, he goes into the forest with his neighbor to cut timber, and his hand swings the ax to chop down a tree, but the blade flies off the handle and strikes his neighbor so that he dies, that person may flee to one of these cities and live. ⁶ Otherwise, the avenger of blood in the heat of his anger ᶜ might pursue the one who committed manslaughter, overtake him because the distance is great, and strike him dead. Yet he did not deserve to die, ᴰ since he did not previously hate his neighbor. ⁷ This is why I am commanding you to set apart three cities for yourselves. ⁸ If the Lord your God enlarges your territory as he swore to your fathers, and gives you all the land he promised to give them — ⁹ provided you keep every one of these commands I am giving you today and follow them, loving the Lord your God and walking in his ways at all times — you are to add three more cities to these three. ¹⁰ In this way, innocent blood will not be shed, and you will not become guilty of bloodshed in the land the Lord your God is giving you as an inheritance. ¹¹ But if someone hates his neighbor, lies in ambush for him, attacks him, and strikes him fatally, and flees to one of these cities, ¹² the elders of his city are to send for him, take him from there, and hand him over to the avenger of blood and he will die. ¹³ Do not look on him with pity but purge from Israel the guilt of shedding innocent blood, and you will prosper.

BOUNDARY MARKERS

¹⁴ "Do not move your neighbor's boundary marker, established at the start in the inheritance you will receive in the land the Lord your God is giving you to possess.

ᴬ 19:3 Or *to prepare the roads*   ᴮ 19:3 Lit *flee there*   ᶜ 19:6 Lit *heart*   ᴰ 19:6 Lit *did not have a judgment of death*

WITNESSES IN COURT

[15] "One witness cannot establish any iniquity or sin against a person, whatever that person has done. A fact must be established by the testimony of two or three witnesses.

[16] "If a malicious witness testifies against someone accusing him of a crime, [17] the two people in the dispute are to stand in the presence of the LORD before the priests and judges in authority at that time. [18] The judges are to make a careful investigation, and if the witness turns out to be a liar who has falsely accused his brother, [19] you must do to him as he intended to do to his brother. You must purge the evil from you. [20] Then everyone else will hear and be afraid, and they will never again do anything evil like this among you. [21] Do not show pity: life for life, eye for eye, tooth for tooth, hand for hand, and foot for foot.

RULES FOR WAR

20 "When you go out to war against your enemies and see horses, chariots, and an army larger than yours, do not be afraid of them, for the LORD your God, who brought you out of the land of Egypt, is with you. [2] When you are about to engage in battle, the priest is to come forward and address the army. [3] He is to say to them: 'Listen, Israel: Today you are about to engage in battle with your enemies. Do not be cowardly. Do not be afraid, alarmed, or terrified because of them. [4] For the LORD your God is the one who goes with you to fight for you against your enemies to give you victory.'

[5] "The officers are to address the army, 'Has any man built a new house and not dedicated it? Let him leave and return home. Otherwise, he may die in battle and another man dedicate it. [6] Has any man planted a vineyard and not begun to enjoy its fruit?[A] Let him leave and return home. Otherwise he may die in battle and another man enjoy its fruit.[B] [7] Has any man become engaged to a woman and not married her? Let him leave and return home. Otherwise he may die in battle and another man marry her.' [8] The officers will continue to address the army and say, 'Is there any man who is afraid or cowardly? Let him leave and return home, so that his brothers won't lose heart as he did.'[C] [9] When the officers have finished addressing the army, they will appoint military commanders to lead it.

[10] "When you approach a city to fight against it, make an offer of peace. [11] If it accepts your offer of peace and opens its gates to you, all the people found in it will become forced laborers for you and serve you. [12] However, if it does not make peace with you but wages war against you, lay siege to it. [13] When the LORD your God hands it over to you, strike down all its males with the sword. [14] But you may take the women, dependents, animals, and whatever else is in the city — all its spoil — as plunder. You may enjoy the spoil of your enemies that the LORD your God has given you. [15] This is how you are to treat all the cities that are far away from you and are not among the cities of these nations. [16] However, you must not let any living thing survive among the cities of these people the LORD your God is giving you as an inheritance. [17] You must completely destroy them — the Hethite, Amorite,

---

[A] 20:6 Lit *not put it to use*   [B] 20:6 Lit *man put it to use*   [C] 20:8 Lit *brothers' hearts won't melt like his own*

Canaanite, Perizzite, Hivite, and Jebusite — as the LORD your God has commanded you, [18] so that they won't teach you to do all the detestable acts they do for their gods, and you sin against the LORD your God.

[19] "When you lay siege to a city for a long time, fighting against it in order to capture it, do not destroy its trees by putting an ax to them, because you can get food from them. Do not cut them down. Are trees of the field human, to come under siege by you? [20] But you may destroy the trees that you know do not produce food. You may cut them down to build siege works against the city that is waging war against you, until it falls.

UNSOLVED MURDERS

21 "If a murder victim is found lying in a field in the land the LORD your God is giving you to possess, and it is not known who killed him, [2] your elders and judges are to come out and measure the distance from the victim to the nearby cities. [3] The elders of the city nearest to the victim are to get a young cow that has not been yoked or used for work. [4] The elders of that city will bring the cow down to a continually flowing stream, to a place not tilled or sown, and they will break its neck there by the stream. [5] Then the priests, the sons of Levi, will come forward, for the LORD your God has chosen them to serve him and pronounce blessings in his name, and they are to give a ruling in[A] every dispute and case of assault. [6] All the elders of the city nearest to the victim will wash their hands by the stream over the young cow whose neck has been broken. [7] They will declare, 'Our hands did not shed this blood; our eyes did not see it. [8] LORD, wipe away the guilt of your people Israel whom you redeemed, and do not hold the shedding of innocent blood against them.' Then the responsibility for bloodshed will be wiped away from them. [9] You must purge from yourselves the guilt of shedding innocent blood, for you will be doing what is right in the LORD's sight.

FAIR TREATMENT OF CAPTURED WOMEN

[10] "When you go to war against your enemies and the LORD your God hands them over to you and you take some of them prisoner, and [11] if you see a beautiful woman among the captives, desire her, and want to take her as your wife, [12] you are to bring her into your house. She is to shave her head, trim her nails, [13] remove the clothes she was wearing when she was taken prisoner, live in your house, and mourn for her father and mother a full month. After that, you may have sexual relations with her and be her husband, and she will be your wife. [14] Then if you are not satisfied with her, you are to let her go where she wants, but you must not sell her or treat her as merchandise,[B] because you have humiliated her.

THE RIGHT OF THE FIRSTBORN

[15] "If a man has two wives, one loved and the other unloved, and both the loved and the unloved bear him sons, and if the unloved wife has the firstborn son, [16] when that man gives what he has to his sons as an inheritance, he is not to show favoritism to the son of the loved wife as his firstborn over the firstborn of the unloved wife. [17] He must acknowledge the firstborn, the

---

A 21:5 Lit *and according to their mouth will be*   B 21:14 Hb obscure son of the unloved wife, by giving him two shares^A,B of his estate, for he is the firstfruits of his virility; he has the rights of the firstborn.

A REBELLIOUS SON

¹⁸ "If a man has a stubborn and rebellious son who does not obey his father or mother and doesn't listen to them even after they discipline him, ¹⁹ his father and mother are to take hold of him and bring him to the elders of his city, to the gate of his hometown. ²⁰ They will say to the elders of his city, 'This son of ours is stubborn and rebellious; he doesn't obey us. He's a glutton and a drunkard.' ²¹ Then all the men of his city will stone him to death. You must purge the evil from you, and all Israel will hear and be afraid.

DISPLAY OF EXECUTED PEOPLE

²² "If anyone is found guilty of an offense deserving the death penalty and is executed, and you hang his body on a tree, ²³ you are not to leave his corpse on the tree overnight but are to bury him that day, for anyone hung on a tree is under God's curse. You must not defile the land the LORD your God is giving you as an inheritance.

CARING FOR YOUR BROTHER'S PROPERTY

22 "If you see your brother Israelite's ox or sheep straying, do not ignore it; make sure you return it to your brother. ² If your brother does not live near you or you don't know him, you are to bring the animal to your home to remain with you until your brother comes looking for it; then you can return it to him. ³ Do the same for his donkey, his garment, or anything your brother has lost and you have found. You must not ignore it. ⁴ If you see your brother's donkey or ox fallen down on the road, do not ignore it; help him lift it up.

PRESERVING NATURAL DISTINCTIONS

⁵ "A woman is not to wear male clothing, and a man is not to put on a woman's garment, for everyone who does these things is detestable to the LORD your God.

⁶ "If you come across a bird's nest with chicks or eggs, either in a tree or on the ground along the road, and the mother is sitting on the chicks or eggs, do not take the mother along with the young. ⁷ You may take the young for yourself, but be sure to let the mother go free, so that you may prosper and live long. ⁸ If you build a new house, make a railing around your roof, so that you don't bring bloodguilt on your house if someone falls from it. ⁹ Do not plant your vineyard with two types of seed; otherwise, the entire harvest, both the crop you plant and the produce of the vineyard, will be defiled. ¹⁰ Do not plow with an ox and a donkey together. ¹¹ Do not wear clothes made of both wool and linen. ¹² Make tassels on the four corners of the outer garment you wear.

VIOLATIONS OF PROPER SEXUAL CONDUCT

¹³ "If a man marries a woman, has sexual relations with her, and comes to hate her, ¹⁴ and accuses her of shameful conduct, and gives her a bad name,

---

^A 21:17 Lit *him mouth of two, or two mouthfuls* ^B 21:17 Or *two-thirds* saying, 'I married this woman and was intimate with her, but I didn't find any evidence of her virginity,' ¹⁵ the young woman's father and mother will take the evidence of her virginity and bring it to the city elders at the city gate. ¹⁶ The young woman's father will say to the elders, 'I gave my daughter to this man as a wife, but he hates her. ¹⁷ He has accused her of shameful conduct, saying: "I didn't find any evidence of your daughter's virginity," but here is the evidence of my daughter's virginity.' They will spread out the cloth before the city elders. ¹⁸ Then the elders of that city will take the man and punish him. ¹⁹ They will also fine him a hundred silver shekels and give them to the young woman's father, because that man gave an Israelite virgin a bad name. She will remain his wife; he cannot divorce her as long as he lives. ²⁰ But if this accusation is true and no evidence of the young woman's virginity is found, ²¹ they will bring the woman to the door of her father's house, and the men of her city will stone her to death. For she has committed an outrage in Israel by being promiscuous while living in her father's house. You must purge the evil from you.

²² "If a man is discovered having sexual relations with another man's wife, both the man who had sex with the woman and the woman must die. You must purge the evil from Israel. ²³ If there is a young woman who is a virgin engaged to a man, and another man encounters her in the city and sleeps with her, ²⁴ take the two of them out to the gate of that city and stone them to death — the young woman because she did not cry out in the city and the man because he has violated his neighbor's fiancée. You must purge the evil from you. ²⁵ But if the man encounters an engaged woman in the open country, and he seizes and rapes her, only the man who raped her must die. ²⁶ Do nothing to the young woman, because she is not guilty of an offense deserving death. This case is just like one in which a man attacks his neighbor and murders him. ²⁷ When he found her in the field, the engaged woman cried out, but there was no one to rescue her. ²⁸ If a man encounters a young woman, a virgin who is not engaged, takes hold of her and rapes her, and they are discovered, ²⁹ the man who raped her is to give the young woman's father fifty silver shekels, and she will become his wife because he violated her. He cannot divorce her as long as he lives.

³⁰ "A man is not to marry his father's wife; he must not violate his father's marriage bed.ᴬ

EXCLUSION AND INCLUSION

23 "No man whose testicles have been crushedᴮ or whose penis has been cut off may enter the Lᴏʀᴅ's assembly. ² No one of illegitimate birth may enter the Lᴏʀᴅ's assembly; none of his descendants, even to the tenth generation, may enter the Lᴏʀᴅ's assembly. ³ No Ammonite or Moabite may enter the Lᴏʀᴅ's assembly; none of their descendants, even to the tenth generation, may ever enter the Lᴏʀᴅ's assembly. ⁴ This is because they did not meet you with food and water on the journey after you came out of Egypt, and because Balaam son of Beor from Pethor in Aram-naharaim was hired to curse you. ⁵ Yet the Lᴏʀᴅ your God would not listen to Balaam, but he turned the curse into a blessing for you because the Lᴏʀᴅ your God loves

---

ᴬ22:30 Lit *not uncover the edge of his father's garment*; Ru 3:9; Ezk 16:8
ᴮ23:1 Lit *man bruised by crushing*

you. ⁶ Never pursue their welfare or prosperity as long as you live. ⁷ Do not despise an Edomite, because he is your brother. Do not despise an Egyptian, because you were a resident alien in his land. ⁸ The children born to them in the third generation may enter the LORD's assembly.

CLEANLINESS OF THE CAMP

⁹ "When you are encamped against your enemies, be careful to avoid anything offensive. ¹⁰ If there is a man among you who is unclean because of a bodily emission during the night, he must go outside the camp; he may not come anywhere inside the camp. ¹¹ When evening approaches, he is to wash with water, and when the sun sets he may come inside the camp. ¹² You are to have a place outside the camp and go there to relieve yourself. ¹³ You are to have a digging tool in your equipment; when you relieve yourself, dig a hole with it and cover up your excrement. ¹⁴ For the LORD your God walks throughout your camp to protect you and deliver your enemies to you; so your encampments must be holy. He must not see anything indecent among you or he will turn away from you.

FUGITIVE SLAVES

¹⁵ "Do not return a slave to his master when he has escaped from his master to you. ¹⁶ Let him live among you wherever he wants within your city gates. Do not mistreat him.

CULT PROSTITUTION FORBIDDEN

¹⁷ "No Israelite woman is to be a cult prostitute, and no Israelite man is to be a cult prostitute. ¹⁸ Do not bring a female prostitute's wages or a male prostitute's ᴬ earnings into the house of the LORD your God to fulfill any vow, because both are detestable to the LORD your God.

INTEREST ON LOANS

¹⁹ "Do not charge your brother interest on silver, food, or anything that can earn interest. ²⁰ You may charge a foreigner interest, but you must not charge your brother Israelite interest, so that the LORD your God may bless you in everything you do ᴮ in the land you are entering to possess.

KEEPING VOWS

²¹ "If you make a vow to the LORD your God, do not be slow to keep it, because he will require it of you, and it will be counted against you as sin. ²² But if you refrain from making a vow, it will not be counted against you as sin. ²³ Be careful to do whatever comes from your lips, because you have freely vowed what you promised ᶜ to the LORD your God.

NEIGHBOR'S CROPS

²⁴ "When you enter your neighbor's vineyard, you may eat as many grapes as you want until you are full, but do not put any in your container. ²⁵ When you enter your neighbor's standing grain, you may pluck heads of grain with your hand, but do not put a sickle to your neighbor's grain.

ᴬ23:18 Lit a dog's   ᴮ23:20 Lit you put your hand to   ᶜ23:23 Lit promised with your mouth

MARRIAGE AND DIVORCE LAWS

24 "If a man marries a woman, but she becomes displeasing to him[A] because he finds something indecent about her, he may write her a divorce certificate, hand it to her, and send her away from his house. [2] If after leaving his house she goes and becomes another man's wife, [3] and the second man hates her, writes her a divorce certificate, hands it to her, and sends her away from his house or if he dies, [4] the first husband who sent her away may not marry her again after she has been defiled, because that would be detestable to the LORD. You must not bring guilt on the land the LORD your God is giving you as an inheritance.

[5] "When a man takes a bride, he must not go out with the army or be liable for any duty. He is free to stay at home for one year, so that he can bring joy to the wife he has married.

SAFEGUARDING LIFE

[6] "Do not take a pair of grindstones or even the upper millstone as security for a debt, because that is like taking a life as security.

[7] "If a man is discovered kidnapping one of his Israelite brothers, whether he treats him as a slave or sells him, the kidnapper must die. You must purge the evil from you.

[8] "Be careful with a person who has a case of serious skin disease, following carefully everything the Levitical priests instruct you to do. Be careful to do as I have commanded them. [9] Remember what the LORD your God did to Miriam on the journey after you left Egypt.

CONSIDERATION FOR PEOPLE IN NEED

[10] "When you make a loan of any kind to your neighbor, do not enter his house to collect what he offers as security. [11] Stand outside while the man you are making the loan to brings the security out to you. [12] If he is a poor man, do not sleep with the garment he has given as security. [13] Be sure to return it[B] to him at sunset. Then he will sleep in it and bless you, and this will be counted as righteousness to you before the LORD your God.

[14] "Do not oppress a hired worker who is poor and needy, whether one of your Israelite brothers or one of the resident aliens in a town[C] in your land. [15] You are to pay him his wages each day before the sun sets, because he is poor and depends on them. Otherwise he will cry out to the LORD against you, and you will be held guilty.

[16] "Fathers are not to be put to death for their children, and children are not to be put to death for their fathers; each person will be put to death for his own sin. [17] Do not deny justice to a resident alien or fatherless child, and do not take a widow's garment as security. [18] Remember that you were a slave in Egypt, and the LORD your God redeemed you from there. Therefore I am commanding you to do this.

[19] "When you reap the harvest in your field, and you forget a sheaf in the field, do not go back to get it. It is to be left for the resident alien, the fatherless, and the widow, so that the LORD your God may bless you in all the work of your hands. [20] When you knock down the fruit from your olive tree, do not

---

[A]24:1 Lit she does not find favor in his eyes   [B]24:13 Lit return what he has given as security   [C]24:14 Lit within the city gates go over the branches again. What remains will be for the resident alien, the fatherless, and the widow. ²¹ When you gather the grapes of your vineyard, do not glean what is left. What remains will be for the resident alien, the fatherless, and the widow. ²² Remember that you were a slave in the land of Egypt. Therefore I am commanding you to do this.

FAIRNESS AND MERCY

25 "If there is a dispute between men, they are to go to court, and the judges will hear their case. They will clear the innocent and condemn the guilty. ² If the guilty party deserves to be flogged, the judge will make him lie down and be flogged in his presence with the number of lashes appropriate for his crime. ³ He may be flogged with forty lashes, but no more. Otherwise, if he is flogged with more lashes than these, your brother will be degraded in your sight.

⁴ "Do not muzzle an ox while it treads out grain.

PRESERVING THE FAMILY LINE

⁵ "When brothers live on the same property ᴬ and one of them dies without a son, the wife of the dead man may not marry a stranger outside the family. Her brother-in-law is to take her as his wife, have sexual relations with her, and perform the duty of a brother-in-law for her. ⁶ The first son she bears will carry on the name of the dead brother, so his name will not be blotted out from Israel. ⁷ But if the man doesn't want to marry his sister-in-law, she is to go to the elders at the city gate and say, 'My brother-in-law refuses to preserve his brother's name in Israel. He isn't willing to perform the duty of a brother-in-law for me.' ⁸ The elders of his city will summon him and speak with him. If he persists and says, 'I don't want to marry her,' ⁹ then his sister-in-law will go up to him in the sight of the elders, remove his sandal from his foot, and spit in his face. Then she will declare, 'This is what is done to a man who will not build up his brother's house.' ¹⁰ And his family name in Israel will be 'The house of the man whose sandal was removed.'

¹¹ "If two men are fighting with each other, and the wife of one steps in to rescue her husband from the one striking him, and she puts out her hand and grabs his genitals, ¹² you are to cut off her hand. Do not show pity.

HONEST WEIGHTS AND MEASURES

¹³ "Do not have differing weights ᴮ in your bag, one heavy and one light. ¹⁴ Do not have differing dry measures in your house, a larger and a smaller. ¹⁵ You must have a full and honest weight, a full and honest dry measure, so that you may live long in the land the LORD your God is giving you. ¹⁶ For everyone who does such things and acts unfairly is detestable to the LORD your God.

REVENGE ON THE AMALEKITES

¹⁷ "Remember what the Amalekites did to you on the journey after you left Egypt. ¹⁸ They met you along the way and attacked all your stragglers from behind when you were tired and weary. They did not fear God. ¹⁹ When the LORD your God gives you rest from all the enemies around you in the land

---

ᴬ25:5 Lit *live together* ᴮ25:13 Lit *have a stone and a stone* the Lord your God is giving you to possess as an inheritance, blot out the memory of Amalek under heaven. Do not forget.

GIVING THE FIRSTFRUITS

26 "When you enter the land the Lord your God is giving you as an inheritance, and you take possession of it and live in it, ² take some of the first of all the land's produce that you harvest from the land the Lord your God is giving you and put it in a basket. Then go to the place where the Lord your God chooses to have his name dwell. ³ When you come before the priest who is serving at that time, say to him, 'Today I declare to the Lord your^A God that I have entered the land the Lord swore to our fathers to give us.'

⁴ "Then the priest will take the basket from you and place it before the altar of the Lord your God. ⁵ You are to respond by saying in the presence of the Lord your God:

My father was a wandering Aramean. He went down to Egypt with a few people and resided there as an alien. There he became a great, powerful, and populous nation. ⁶ But the Egyptians mistreated and oppressed us, and forced us to do hard labor. ⁷ So we called out to the Lord, the God of our fathers, and the Lord heard our cry and saw our misery, hardship, and oppression. ⁸ Then the Lord brought us out of Egypt with a strong hand and an outstretched arm, with terrifying power, and with signs and wonders. ⁹ He led us to this place and gave us this land, a land flowing with milk and honey. ¹⁰ I have now brought the first of the land's produce that you, Lord, have given me.

You will then place the container before the Lord your God and bow down to him. ¹¹ You, the Levites, and the resident aliens among you will rejoice in all the good things the Lord your God has given you and your household.

THE TENTH IN THE THIRD YEAR

¹² "When you have finished paying all the tenth of your produce in the third year, the year of the tenth, you are to give it to the Levites, resident aliens, fatherless children and widows, so that they may eat in your towns and be satisfied. ¹³ Then you will say in the presence of the Lord your God:

I have taken the consecrated portion out of my house; I have also given it to the Levites, resident aliens, fatherless children, and widows, according to all the commands you gave me. I have not violated or forgotten your commands. ¹⁴ I have not eaten any of it while in mourning, or removed any of it while unclean, or offered any of it for the dead. I have obeyed the Lord my God; I have done all you commanded me. ¹⁵ Look down from your holy dwelling, from heaven, and bless your people Israel and the land you have given us as you swore to our fathers, a land flowing with milk and honey.

COVENANT SUMMARY

¹⁶ "The Lord your God is commanding you this day to follow these statutes and ordinances. Follow them carefully with all your heart and all your soul. ¹⁷ Today you have affirmed that the Lord is your God and that you will walk

---

^A 26:3 LXX reads my

in his ways, keep his statutes, commands, and ordinances, and obey him. [18] And today the LORD has affirmed that you are his own possession as he promised you, that you are to keep all his commands, [19] that he will elevate you to praise, fame, and glory above all the nations he has made, and that you will be a holy people to the LORD your God as he promised."

THE LAW WRITTEN ON STONES

27 Moses and the elders of Israel commanded the people, "Keep every command I am giving you today. [2] When you cross the Jordan into the land the LORD your God is giving you, set up large stones and cover them with plaster. [3] Write all the words of this law on the stones after you cross to enter the land the LORD your God is giving you, a land flowing with milk and honey, as the LORD, the God of your fathers, has promised you. [4] When you have crossed the Jordan, you are to set up these stones on Mount Ebal, as I am commanding you today, and you are to cover them with plaster. [5] Build an altar of stones there to the LORD your God — do not use any iron tool on them. [6] Use uncut stones to build the altar of the LORD your God and offer burnt offerings to the LORD your God on it. [7] There you are to sacrifice fellowship offerings, eat, and rejoice in the presence of the LORD your God. [8] Write clearly all the words of this law on the plastered stones."

THE COVENANT CURSES

[9] Moses and the Levitical priests spoke to all Israel, "Be silent, Israel, and listen! This day you have become the people of the LORD your God. [10] Obey the LORD your God and follow his commands and statutes I am giving you today."

[11] On that day Moses commanded the people, [12] "When you have crossed the Jordan, these tribes will stand on Mount Gerizim to bless the people: Simeon, Levi, Judah, Issachar, Joseph, and Benjamin. [13] And these tribes will stand on Mount Ebal to deliver the curse: Reuben, Gad, Asher, Zebulun, Dan, and Naphtali. [14] The Levites will proclaim in a loud voice to every Israelite:

[15] 'The person who makes a carved idol or cast image, which is detestable to the LORD, the work of a craftsman, and sets it up in secret is cursed.'
And all the people will reply, 'Amen!'

[16] 'The one who dishonors his father or mother is cursed.'
And all the people will say, 'Amen!'

[17] 'The one who moves his neighbor's boundary marker is cursed.'
And all the people will say, 'Amen!'

[18] 'The one who leads a blind person astray on the road is cursed.'
And all the people will say, 'Amen!'

[19] 'The one who denies justice to a resident alien, a fatherless child, or a widow is cursed.'
And all the people will say, 'Amen!'

[20] 'The one who sleeps with his father's wife is cursed, for he has violated his father's marriage bed.'[A]
And all the people will say, 'Amen!'

[21] 'The one who has sexual intercourse with any animal is cursed.'
And all the people will say, 'Amen!'

[A]27:20 Lit *has uncovered the edge of his father's garment*; Ru 3:9; Ezk 16:8

²² 'The one who sleeps with his sister, whether his father's daughter or his mother's daughter is cursed.'
And all the people will say, 'Amen!'
²³ 'The one who sleeps with his mother-in-law is cursed.'
And all the people will say, 'Amen!'
²⁴ 'The one who secretly kills his neighbor is cursed.'
And all the people will say, 'Amen!'
²⁵ 'The one who accepts a bribe to kill an innocent person is cursed.'
And all the people will say, 'Amen!'
²⁶ 'Anyone who does not put the words of this law into practice is cursed.'
And all the people will say, 'Amen!'

BLESSINGS FOR OBEDIENCE

28 "Now if you faithfully obey the LORD your God and are careful to follow all his commands I am giving you today, the LORD your God will put you far above all the nations of the earth. ² All these blessings will come and overtake you, because you obey the LORD your God:

³   You will be blessed in the city
     and blessed in the country.
⁴   Your offspring[A] will be blessed,
     and your land's produce,
     and the offspring of your livestock,
     including the young of your herds
     and the newborn of your flocks.
⁵   Your basket and kneading bowl will be blessed.
⁶   You will be blessed when you come in
     and blessed when you go out.

⁷ "The LORD will cause the enemies who rise up against you to be defeated before you. They will march out against you from one direction but flee from you in seven directions. ⁸ The LORD will grant you a blessing on your barns and on everything you do;[B] he will bless you in the land the LORD your God is giving you. ⁹ The LORD will establish you as his holy people, as he swore to you, if you obey the commands of the LORD your God and walk in his ways. ¹⁰ Then all the peoples of the earth will see that you bear the LORD's name, and they will stand in awe of you. ¹¹ The LORD will make you prosper abundantly with offspring,[C] the offspring of your livestock, and your land's produce in the land the LORD swore to your fathers to give you. ¹² The LORD will open for you his abundant storehouse, the sky, to give your land rain in its season and to bless all the work of your hands. You will lend to many nations, but you will not borrow. ¹³ The LORD will make you the head and not the tail; you will only move upward and never downward if you listen to the LORD your God's commands I am giving you today and are careful to follow them. ¹⁴ Do not turn aside to the right or the left from all the things I am commanding you today, and do not follow other gods to worship them.

[A]28:4 Lit *The fruit of your womb,* also in v. 18   [B]28:8 Lit *you put your hand to,* also in v. 20   [C]28:11 Lit *abundantly in the fruit of your womb*

CURSES FOR DISOBEDIENCE

¹⁵ "But if you do not obey the LORD your God by carefully following all his commands and statutes I am giving you today, all these curses will come and overtake you:

¹⁶ You will be cursed in the city
and cursed in the country.
¹⁷ Your basket and kneading bowl will be cursed.
¹⁸ Your offspring will be cursed,
and your land's produce,
the young of your herds,
and the newborn of your flocks.
¹⁹ You will be cursed when you come in
and cursed when you go out.

²⁰ The LORD will send against you curses, confusion, and rebuke in everything you do until you are destroyed and quickly perish, because of the wickedness of your actions in abandoning me. ²¹ The LORD will make pestilence cling to you until he has exterminated you from the land you are entering to possess. ²² The LORD will afflict you with wasting disease, fever, inflammation, burning heat, drought,^A blight, and mildew; these will pursue you until you perish. ²³ The sky above you will be bronze, and the earth beneath you iron. ²⁴ The LORD will turn the rain of your land into falling^B dust; it will descend on you from the sky until you are destroyed. ²⁵ The LORD will cause you to be defeated before your enemies. You will march out against them from one direction but flee from them in seven directions. You will be an object of horror to all the kingdoms of the earth. ²⁶ Your corpses will be food for all the birds of the sky and the wild animals of the earth, with no one to scare them away.

²⁷ "The LORD will afflict you with the boils of Egypt, tumors, a festering rash, and scabies, from which you cannot be cured. ²⁸ The LORD will afflict you with madness, blindness, and mental confusion, ²⁹ so that at noon you will grope as a blind person gropes in the dark. You will not be successful in anything you do. You will only be oppressed and robbed continually, and no one will help you. ³⁰ You will become engaged to a woman, but another man will rape her. You will build a house but not live in it. You will plant a vineyard but not enjoy its fruit. ³¹ Your ox will be slaughtered before your eyes, but you will not eat any of it. Your donkey will be taken away from you and not returned to you. Your flock will be given to your enemies, and no one will help you. ³² Your sons and daughters will be given to another people, while your eyes grow weary looking for them every day. But you will be powerless to do anything.^C ³³ A people you don't know will eat your land's produce and everything you have labored for. You will only be oppressed and crushed continually. ³⁴ You will be driven mad by what you see. ³⁵ The LORD will afflict you with painful and incurable boils on your knees and thighs — from the sole of your foot to the top of your head.

³⁶ "The LORD will bring you and your king that you have appointed to a nation neither you nor your fathers have known, and there you will worship

---

^A 28:22 Or sword ^B 28:24 Lit powder and ^C 28:32 Lit day, and not for power
your hand

other gods, of wood and stone. ³⁷ You will become an object of horror, scorn, and ridicule among all the peoples where the LORD will drive you.

³⁸ "You will sow much seed in the field but harvest little, because locusts will devour it. ³⁹ You will plant and cultivate vineyards but not drink the wine or gather the grapes, because worms will eat them. ⁴⁰ You will have olive trees throughout your territory but not moisten your skin with oil, because your olives will drop off. ⁴¹ You will father sons and daughters, but they will not remain yours, because they will be taken prisoner. ⁴² Buzzing insects will take possession of all your trees and your land's produce. ⁴³ The resident alien among you will rise higher and higher above you, while you sink lower and lower. ⁴⁴ He will lend to you, but you won't lend to him. He will be the head, and you will be the tail.

⁴⁵ "All these curses will come, pursue, and overtake you until you are destroyed, since you did not obey the LORD your God and keep the commands and statutes he gave you. ⁴⁶ These curses will be a sign and a wonder against you and your descendants forever. ⁴⁷ Because you didn't serve the LORD your God with joy and a cheerful heart, even though you had an abundance of everything, ⁴⁸ you will serve your enemies the LORD will send against you, in famine, thirst, nakedness, and a lack of everything. He will place an iron yoke on your neck until he has destroyed you. ⁴⁹ The LORD will bring a nation from far away, from the ends of the earth, to swoop down on you like an eagle, a nation whose language you won't understand, ⁵⁰ a ruthless nation,ᴬ showing no respect for the old and not sparing the young. ⁵¹ They will eat the offspring of your livestock and your land's produce until you are destroyed. They will leave you no grain, new wine, fresh oil, young of your herds, or newborn of your flocks until they cause you to perish. ⁵² They will besiege you within all your city gates until your high and fortified walls, that you trust in, come down throughout your land. They will besiege you within all your city gates throughout the land the LORD your God has given you.

⁵³ "You will eat your offspring,ᴮ the flesh of your sons and daughters the LORD your God has given you during the siege and hardship your enemy imposes on you. ⁵⁴ The most sensitive and refined man among you will look grudginglyᶜ at his brother, the wife he embraces,ᴰ and the rest of his children, ⁵⁵ refusing to share with any of them his children's flesh that he will eat because he has nothing left during the siege and hardship your enemy imposes on you in all your towns. ⁵⁶ The most sensitive and refined woman among you, who would not venture to set the sole of her foot on the ground because of her refinement and sensitivity, will begrudge the husband she embraces, her son, and her daughter, ⁵⁷ the afterbirth that comes out from between her legs and the children she bears, because she will secretly eat them for lack of anything else during the siege and hardship your enemy imposes on you within your city gates.

⁵⁸ "If you are not careful to obey all the words of this law, which are written in this scroll, by fearing this glorious and awe-inspiring name — the LORD, your God — ⁵⁹ he will bring wondrous plagues on you and your descendants, severe and lasting plagues, and terrible and chronic sicknesses. ⁶⁰ He will afflict you again with all the diseases of Egypt, which you dreaded,

---

ᴬ28:50 Lit *a nation strong of face*   ᴮ28:53 Lit *eat the fruit of your womb*
ᶜ28:54 Lit *you his eye will be evil*   ᴰ28:54 Lit *wife of his bosom*

and they will cling to you. [61] The LORD will also afflict you with every sickness and plague not recorded in the book of this law, until you are destroyed. [62] Though you were as numerous as the stars of the sky, you will be left with only a few people, because you did not obey the LORD your God. [63] Just as the LORD was glad to cause you to prosper and to multiply you, so he will also be glad to cause you to perish and to destroy you. You will be ripped out of the land you are entering to possess. [64] Then the LORD will scatter you among all peoples from one end of the earth to the other, and there you will worship other gods, of wood and stone, which neither you nor your fathers have known. [65] You will find no peace among those nations, and there will be no resting place for the sole of your foot. There the LORD will give you a trembling heart, failing eyes, and a despondent spirit. [66] Your life will hang in doubt before you. You will be in dread night and day, never certain of survival. [67] In the morning you will say, 'If only it were evening!' and in the evening you will say, 'If only it were morning!' — because of the dread you will have in your heart and because of what you will see. [68] The LORD will take you back in ships to Egypt by a route that I said you would never see again. There you will sell yourselves to your enemies as male and female slaves, but no one will buy you."

RENEWING THE COVENANT

29 These are the words of the covenant the LORD commanded Moses to make with the Israelites in the land of Moab, in addition to the covenant he had made with them at Horeb. [2] Moses summoned all Israel and said to them, "You have seen with your own eyes everything the LORD did in Egypt to Pharaoh, to all his officials, and to his entire land. [3] You saw with your own eyes the great trials and those great signs and wonders. [4] Yet to this day the LORD has not given you a mind to understand, eyes to see, or ears to hear. [5] I led you forty years in the wilderness; your clothes and the sandals on your feet did not wear out; [6] you did not eat food or drink wine or beer — so that you might know that I am the LORD your God. [7] When you reached this place, King Sihon of Heshbon and King Og of Bashan came out against us in battle, but we defeated them. [8] We took their land and gave it as an inheritance to the Reubenites, the Gadites, and half the tribe of Manasseh. [9] Therefore, observe the words of this covenant and follow them, so that you will succeed in everything you do.

[10] "All of you are standing today before the LORD your God — your leaders, tribes, elders, officials, all the men of Israel, [11] your dependents, your wives, and the resident aliens in your camps who cut your wood and draw your water — [12] so that you may enter into the covenant of the LORD your God, which he is making with you today, so that you may enter into his oath [13] and so that he may establish you today as his people and he may be your God as he promised you and as he swore to your fathers Abraham, Isaac, and Jacob. [14] I am making this covenant and this oath not only with you, [15] but also with those who are standing here with us today in the presence of the LORD our God and with those who are not here today.

ABANDONING THE COVENANT

[16] "Indeed, you know how we lived in the land of Egypt and passed through the nations where you traveled. [17] You saw their abhorrent images and idols

made of wood, stone, silver, and gold, which were among them. [18] Be sure there is no man, woman, clan, or tribe among you today whose heart turns away from the LORD our God to go and worship the gods of those nations. Be sure there is no root among you bearing poisonous and bitter fruit. [19] When someone hears the words of this oath, he may consider himself exempt,[A] thinking, 'I will have peace even though I follow my own stubborn heart.' This will lead to the destruction of the well-watered land as well as the dry land. [20] The LORD will not be willing to forgive him. Instead, his anger and jealousy will burn against that person, and every curse written in this scroll will descend on him. The LORD will blot out his name under heaven, [21] and single him out for harm from all the tribes of Israel, according to all the curses of the covenant written in this book of the law.

[22] "Future generations of your children who follow you and the foreigner who comes from a distant country will see the plagues of that land and the sicknesses the LORD has inflicted on it. [23] All its soil will be a burning waste of sulfur and salt, unsown, producing nothing, with no plant growing on it, just like the fall of Sodom and Gomorrah, Admah and Zeboiim, which the LORD demolished in his fierce anger. [24] All the nations will ask, 'Why has the LORD done this to this land? Why this intense outburst of anger?' [25] Then people will answer, 'It is because they abandoned the covenant of the LORD, the God of their fathers, which he had made with them when he brought them out of the land of Egypt. [26] They began to serve other gods, bowing in worship to gods they had not known — gods that the LORD had not permitted them to worship. [27] Therefore the LORD's anger burned against this land, and he brought every curse written in this book on it. [28] The LORD uprooted them from their land in his anger, rage, and intense wrath, and threw them into another land where they are today.' [29] The hidden things belong to the LORD our God, but the revealed things belong to us and our children forever, so that we may follow all the words of this law.

RETURNING TO THE LORD

30 "When all these things happen to you — the blessings and curses I have set before you — and you come to your senses while you are in all the nations where the LORD your God has driven you, [2] and you and your children return to the LORD your God and obey him with all your heart and all your soul by doing[B] everything I am commanding you today, [3] then he will restore your fortunes,[C] have compassion on you, and gather you again from all the peoples where the LORD your God has scattered you. [4] Even if your exiles are at the farthest horizon,[D] he will gather you and bring you back from there. [5] The LORD your God will bring you into the land your fathers possessed, and you will take possession of it. He will cause you to prosper and multiply you more than he did your fathers. [6] The LORD your God will circumcise your heart and the hearts of your descendants, and you will love him with all your heart and all your soul so that you will live. [7] The LORD your God will put all these curses on your enemies who hate and persecute you. [8] Then you will again obey him and follow all his commands I am commanding you today. [9] The LORD your God will make you prosper abundantly

---

[A]29:19 Lit may bless himself in his heart   [B]30:2 Lit soul according to   [C]30:3 Or will end your captivity   [D]30:4 Lit skies in all the work of your hands, your offspring,^A the offspring of your livestock, and the produce of your land. Indeed, the LORD will again delight in your prosperity, as he delighted in that of your fathers, ¹⁰ when you obey the LORD your God by keeping his commands and statutes that are written in this book of the law and return to him with all your heart and all your soul.

CHOOSE LIFE

¹¹ "This command that I give you today is certainly not too difficult or beyond your reach. ¹² It is not in heaven so that you have to ask, 'Who will go up to heaven, get it for us, and proclaim it to us so that we may follow it?' ¹³ And it is not across the sea so that you have to ask, 'Who will cross the sea, get it for us, and proclaim it to us so that we may follow it?' ¹⁴ But the message is very near you, in your mouth and in your heart, so that you may follow it. ¹⁵ See, today I have set before you life and prosperity, death and adversity. ¹⁶ For^B I am commanding you today to love the LORD your God, to walk in his ways, and to keep his commands, statutes, and ordinances, so that you may live^C and multiply, and the LORD your God may bless you in the land you are entering to possess. ¹⁷ But if your heart turns away and you do not listen and you are led astray to bow in worship to other gods and serve them, ¹⁸ I tell you today that you will certainly perish and will not prolong your days in the land you are entering to possess across the Jordan. ¹⁹ I call heaven and earth as witnesses against you today that I have set before you life and death, blessing and curse. Choose life so that you and your descendants may live, ²⁰ love the LORD your God, obey him, and remain faithful^D to him. For he is your life, and he will prolong your days as you live in the land the LORD swore to give to your fathers Abraham, Isaac, and Jacob."

JOSHUA TAKES MOSES'S PLACE

31 Then Moses continued to speak these^E words to all Israel, ² saying, "I am now 120 years old; I can no longer act as your leader.^F The LORD has told me, 'You will not cross the Jordan.' ³ The LORD your God is the one who will cross ahead of you. He will destroy these nations before you, and you will drive them out. Joshua is the one who will cross ahead of you, as the LORD has said. ⁴ The LORD will deal with them as he did Sihon and Og, the kings of the Amorites, and their land when he destroyed them. ⁵ The LORD will deliver them over to you, and you must do to them exactly as I have commanded you. ⁶ Be strong and courageous; don't be terrified or afraid of them. For the LORD your God is the one who will go with you; he will not leave you or abandon you."

⁷ Moses then summoned Joshua and said to him in the sight of all Israel, "Be strong and courageous, for you will go with^G this people into the land the LORD swore to give to their fathers. You will enable them to take possession of it. ⁸ The LORD is the one who will go before you. He will be with you; he will not leave you or abandon you. Do not be afraid or discouraged."

---

^A 30:9 Lit hands in the fruit of your womb   ^B 30:16 LXX reads If you obey the commands of the LORD your God that   ^C 30:16 LXX reads ordinances, then you will live   ^D 30:20 Lit and hold on   ^E 31:1 Some Hb mss, DSS, LXX, Syr, Vg read all these   ^F 31:2 Lit no longer go out or come in   ^G 31:7 Some Hb mss, Sam, Syr, Vg read you will bring

⁹ Moses wrote down this law and gave it to the priests, the sons of Levi, who carried the ark of the LORD's covenant, and to all the elders of Israel. ¹⁰ Moses commanded them, "At the end of every seven years, at the appointed time in the year of debt cancellation, during the Festival of Shelters, ¹¹ when all Israel assembles ᴬ in the presence of the LORD your God at the place he chooses, you are to read this law aloud before all Israel. ¹² Gather the people — men, women, dependents, and the resident aliens within your city gates — so that they may listen and learn to fear the LORD your God and be careful to follow all the words of this law. ¹³ Then their children who do not know the law will listen and learn to fear the LORD your God as long as you live in the land you are crossing the Jordan to possess."

¹⁴ The LORD said to Moses, "The time of your death is now approaching. Call Joshua and present yourselves at the tent of meeting so that I may commission him." When Moses and Joshua went and presented themselves at the tent of meeting, ¹⁵ the LORD appeared at the tent in a pillar of cloud, and the cloud stood at the entrance to the tent.

¹⁶ The LORD said to Moses, "You are about to rest with your fathers, and these people will soon prostitute themselves with the foreign gods of the land they are entering. They will abandon me and break the covenant I have made with them. ¹⁷ My anger will burn against them on that day; I will abandon them and hide my face from them so that they will become easy prey. ᴮ Many troubles and afflictions will come to them. On that day they will say, 'Haven't these troubles come to us because our God is no longer with us?' ¹⁸ I will certainly hide my face on that day because of all the evil they have done by turning to other gods. ¹⁹ Therefore write down this song for yourselves and teach it to the Israelites; have them sing it, ᶜ so that this song may be a witness for me against the Israelites. ²⁰ When I bring them into the land I swore to give their fathers, a land flowing with milk and honey, they will eat their fill and prosper. ᴰ They will turn to other gods and worship them, despising me and breaking my covenant. ²¹ And when many troubles and afflictions come to them, this song will testify against them, because ᴱ their descendants will not have forgotten it. For I know what they are prone to do, ᶠ even before I bring them into the land I swore to give them." ²² So Moses wrote down this song on that day and taught it to the Israelites.

²³ The LORD commissioned Joshua son of Nun, "Be strong and courageous, for you will bring the Israelites into the land I swore to them, and I will be with you."

MOSES WARNS THE PEOPLE

²⁴ When Moses had finished writing down on a scroll every single word ᴳ of this law, ²⁵ he commanded the Levites who carried the ark of the LORD's covenant, ²⁶ "Take this book of the law and place it beside the ark of the covenant of the LORD your God so that it may remain there as a witness against you. ²⁷ For I know how rebellious and stiff-necked you are. If you are rebelling against the LORD now, while I am still alive, how much more

---

ᴬ31:11 Lit comes to appear   ᴮ31:17 Lit will be for devouring   ᶜ31:19 Lit Israelites; put it in their mouths   ᴰ31:20 Lit be fat   ᴱ31:21 Lit because the mouths of   ᶠ31:21 Or know the plans they are devising   ᴳ31:24 Lit scroll the words to their completion will you rebel after I am dead! [28] Assemble all your tribal elders and officers before me so that I may speak these words directly to them and call heaven and earth as witnesses against them. [29] For I know that after my death you will become completely corrupt and turn from the path I have commanded you. Disaster will come to you in the future, because you will do what is evil in the LORD's sight, angering him with what your hands have made." [30] Then Moses recited aloud every single word[A] of this song to the entire assembly of Israel:

SONG OF MOSES

32 Pay attention, heavens, and I will speak;
listen, earth, to the words from my mouth.

[2] Let my teaching fall like rain
and my word settle like dew,
like gentle rain on new grass
and showers on tender plants.

[3] For I will proclaim the LORD's name.
Declare the greatness of our God!

[4] The Rock — his work is perfect;
all his ways are just.
A faithful God, without bias,
he is righteous and true.

[5] His people have acted corruptly toward him;
this is their defect[B] — they are not his children
but a devious and crooked generation.

[6] Is this how you repay the LORD,
you foolish and senseless people?
Isn't he your Father and Creator?[C]
Didn't he make you and sustain you?

[7] Remember the days of old;
consider the years of past generations.
Ask your father, and he will tell you,
your elders, and they will teach you.

[8] When the Most High gave the nations their inheritance[D]
and divided the human race,
he set the boundaries of the peoples
according to the number of the people of Israel.[E]

[9] But the LORD's portion is his people,
Jacob, his own inheritance.

[10] He found him in a desolate land,
in a barren, howling wilderness;
he surrounded him, cared for him,
and protected him as the pupil of his eye.

[A]31:30 Lit *recited the words to their completion*   [B]32:5 Or *him; through their fault*; Hb obscure   [C]32:6 Or *Possessor*   [D]32:8 Or *Most High divided the nations*   [E]32:8 One DSS reads *number of the sons of God*; LXX reads *number of the angels of God*

11 He watches over^A his nest like an eagle
and hovers over his young;
he spreads his wings, catches him,
and carries him on his feathers.

12 The LORD alone led him,
with no help from a foreign god.^B

13 He made him ride on the heights of the land
and eat the produce of the field.
He nourished him with honey from the rock
and oil from flinty rock,

14 curds from the herd and milk from the flock,
with the fat of lambs,
rams from Bashan, and goats,
with the choicest grains of wheat;
you drank wine from the finest grapes.^C

15 Then^D Jeshurun^E became fat and rebelled —
you became fat, bloated, and gorged.
He abandoned the God who made him
and scorned the Rock of his salvation.

16 They provoked his jealousy with different gods;
they enraged him with detestable practices.

17 They sacrificed to demons, not God,
to gods they had not known,
new gods that had just arrived,
which your fathers did not fear.

18 You ignored the Rock who gave you birth;
you forgot the God who gave birth to you.

19 When the LORD saw this, he despised them,
angered by his sons and daughters.

20 He said: "I will hide my face from them;
I will see what will become of them,
for they are a perverse generation —
unfaithful children.

21 They have provoked my jealousy
with what is not a god;^F
they have enraged me with their worthless idols.
So I will provoke their jealousy
with what is not a people;^G
I will enrage them with a foolish nation.

22 For fire has been kindled because of my anger
and burns to the depths of Sheol;
it devours the land and its produce,
and scorches the foundations of the mountains.

---

^A32:11 Or *He stirs up* ^B32:12 Lit *him, and no foreign god with him*
^C32:14 Lit *drank the blood of grapes, fermenting wine* ^D32:15 DSS, Sam, LXX
add *Jacob ate his fill;* ^E32:15 = Upright One, referring to Israel ^F32:21 Lit *with
no gods* ^G32:21 Lit *with no people*

23 "I will pile disasters on them;
  I will use up my arrows against them.
24 They will be weak from hunger,
  ravaged by pestilence and bitter plague;
  I will unleash on them wild beasts with fangs,
  as well as venomous snakes that slither in the dust.
25 Outside, the sword will take their children,
  and inside, there will be terror;
  the young man and the young woman will be killed,
  the infant and the gray-haired man.

26 "I would have said: I will cut them to pieces[A]
  and blot out the memory of them from mankind,
27 if I had not feared provocation from the enemy,
  or feared that these foes might misunderstand
  and say: 'Our own hand has prevailed;
  it wasn't the LORD who did all this.'"

28 Israel is a nation lacking sense
  with no understanding at all.[B]
29 If only they were wise, they would comprehend this;
  they would understand their fate.
30 How could one pursue a thousand,
  or two put ten thousand to flight,
  unless their Rock had sold them,
  unless the LORD had given them up?
31 But their "rock" is not like our Rock,
  as even our enemies concede.
32 For their vine is from the vine of Sodom
  and from the fields of Gomorrah.
  Their grapes are poisonous;
  their clusters are bitter.
33 Their wine is serpents' venom,
  the deadly poison of cobras.

34 "Is it not stored up with me,
  sealed up in my vaults?
35 Vengeance[C] belongs to me; I will repay.[D]
  In time their foot will slip,
  for their day of disaster is near,
  and their doom is coming quickly."
36 The LORD will indeed vindicate his people
  and have compassion on his servants
  when he sees that their strength is gone
  and no one is left — slave or free.[E]

[A]32:26 LXX reads will scatter them   [B]32:28 Lit understanding in them
[C]32:35 Sam, LXX read On a day of vengeance   [D]32:35 LXX, Tg, Vg read
me; and recompense I will recompense   [E]32:36 Or left—even the weak and
impaired; Hb obscure

37 He will say: "Where are their gods,
the 'rock' they found refuge in?
38 Who ate the fat of their sacrifices
and drank the wine of their drink offerings?
Let them rise up and help you;
let it^A be a shelter for you.
39 See now that I alone am he;
there is no God but me.
I bring death and I give life;
I wound and I heal.
No one can rescue anyone from my power.
40 I raise my hand to heaven and declare:
As surely as I live forever,
41 when I sharpen my flashing sword,
and my hand takes hold of judgment,
I will take vengeance on my adversaries
and repay those who hate me.
42 I will make my arrows drunk with blood
while my sword devours flesh —
the blood of the slain and the captives,
the heads of the enemy leaders."^B

43 Rejoice, you nations, concerning his people,^C
for he will avenge the blood of his servants.^D
He will take vengeance on his adversaries;^E
he will purify his land and his people.^F

44 Moses came with Joshua^G son of Nun and recited all the words of this song in the presence of the people. 45 After Moses finished reciting all these words to all Israel, 46 he said to them, "Take to heart all these words I am giving as a warning to you today, so that you may command your children to follow all the words of this law carefully. 47 For they are not meaningless words to you but they are your life, and by them you will live long in the land you are crossing the Jordan to possess."

MOSES'S IMPENDING DEATH

48 On that same day the LORD spoke to Moses, 49 "Go up Mount Nebo in the Abarim range in the land of Moab, across from Jericho, and view the land of Canaan I am giving the Israelites as a possession. 50 Then you will die on the mountain that you go up, and you will be gathered to your people, just as your brother Aaron died on Mount Hor and was gathered to his people.

---

^A32:38 Sam, LXX, Tg, Vg read *them* ^B32:42 Or *the long-haired heads of the enemy* ^C32:43 LXX reads *Rejoice, you heavens, along with him, and let all the sons of God worship him; rejoice, you nations, with his people, and let all the angels of God strengthen themselves in him*; DSS read *Rejoice, you heavens, along with him, and let all the angels worship him*; Heb 1:6 ^D32:43 DSS, LXX read *sons* ^E32:43 DSS, LXX add *and he will recompense those who hate him*; v. 41 ^F32:43 Syr, Tg; DSS, Sam, LXX, Vg read *his people's land* ^G32:44 LXX, Syr, Vg; MT reads *Hoshea*; Nm 13:8,16

⁵¹ For both of you broke faith with me among the Israelites at the Waters of Meribath-kadesh in the Wilderness of Zin by failing to treat me as holy in their presence. ⁵² Although from a distance you will view the land that I am giving the Israelites, you will not go there."

MOSES'S BLESSINGS

33

¹ This is the blessing that Moses, the man of God, gave the Israelites before his death. ² He said:

The LORD came from Sinai
and appeared to them from Seir;
he shone on them from Mount Paran
and came with ten thousand holy ones,ᴬ
with lightningᴮ from his right handꟲ for them.

³   Indeed he loves the people.ᴰ
All yourᴱ holy ones are in your hand,
and they assembleꟳ at your feet.
Each receives your words.

⁴   Moses gave us instruction,
a possession for the assembly of Jacob.

⁵   So he became King in Jeshurunᴳ
when the leaders of the people gathered
with the tribes of Israel.

⁶   Let Reuben live and not die
though his people become few.

⁷ He said this about Judah:

LORD, hear Judah's cry and bring him to his people.
He fights for his causeᴴ with his own hands,
but may you be a help against his foes.

⁸ He said about Levi:

Your Thummim and Urim belong to
your faithful one;ᴵ
you tested him at Massah
and contended with him at the Waters of Meribah.

⁹   He said about his father and mother,
"I do not regard them."
He disregarded his brothers
and didn't acknowledge his sons,
for they kept your word
and maintained your covenant.

¹⁰ They will teach your ordinances to Jacob
and your instruction to Israel;
they will set incense before you
and whole burnt offerings on your altar.

ᴬ33:2 LXX reads *Mount Paran with ten thousands from Kadesh*   ᴮ33:2 Or *fiery law*; Hb obscure   ꟲ33:2 Or *ones, from his southland to the mountain slopes* ᴰ33:3 Or *peoples*   ᴱ33:3 Lit *his*, or *its*   ꟳ33:3 Hb obscure   ᴳ33:5 = *Upright One*, referring to Israel, also in v. 26   ᴴ33:7 Or *He contends for them* ᴵ33:8 DSS, LXX read *Give to Levi your Thummim, your Urim to your favored one*

GOD BURIES MOSES

DEUTERONOMY 33–34; NUMBERS 20:1-13; ACTS 7:20-22

Driving in the van, we talked about prosaic adult things in the front, while the children rattled around in the back. I was telling my husband about a memory-building chart I'd seen in college, and they were playing "touched you last." Later that morning, sitting next to my journal-obsessed nine-year-old, I looked over and saw a transcript of our conversation and a rendering of the chart I'd described.

Simultaneously surprised, delighted, and a little alarmed, I remembered how important we are to her. Right now, she is interested in everything we say and do. Objects, places, and ideas all hold special significance for my daughter if she hears that I love them.

It's a weighty thing to be so adored by someone, to be so intimately and lovingly observed. God invited Moses into intimacy. When Moses was born, "he was beautiful in God's sight" (Ac 7:20). God knew and watched Moses from the beginning, and He called Moses into a close and special journey with Him. Unlike my daughter, God wasn't simply eavesdropping on Moses; He was giving Moses the unimaginable gift of His loving attention.

God's attention seems so unfathomable to me. Why would the Almighty bother to attend to my nail-biting hesitations, or even my wedding day? **His is a love so big we cannot even fathom it.**

There are few places in history where we have such a beautiful record of God's tender and patient encounters with men. From the day of his birth, Moses enjoyed God's special favor and blessing, and this close relationship between God and Moses continued to Moses' final day.

Because of his sin at the waters of Meribah, Moses was not allowed to enter the promised land (Nm 20:11). But even in the midst of this heartbreaking judgment, God showed favor to Moses and allowed him a glimpse of His promised home for Israel.

God's favor doesn't look like what we'd expect it to. When I pray for His blessing and favor, in my heart, I'm often asking for things to go my way. **But the glory of God's blessing is not circumstantial at all—the blessing is intimacy with God Himself.**

Moses' life was a whirlwind of disappointments and triumphs, but regardless of what was going on in the tents and on the desert plain, God was with him. The final scene of Moses' life is private and tender: God buries him in a secret place. He was God's man.

May we long for this kind of intimacy with God. May "He who spoke to Moses" be our ever-present help in trouble, the shield that protects us. For "indeed he loves the people" (Dt 33:3), and He is our dwelling place; let us desire nothing more than to draw near to Him and see His face (Dt 33:27).

¹¹ Lᴏʀᴅ, bless his possessions,^A
and accept the work of his hands.
Break the back^B of his adversaries and enemies,
so that they cannot rise again.

¹² He said about Benjamin:
The Lᴏʀᴅ's beloved rests^C securely on him.
He^D shields him all day long,
and he rests on his shoulders.^E

¹³ He said about Joseph:
May his land be blessed by the Lᴏʀᴅ
with the dew of heaven's bounty
and the watery depths that lie beneath;

¹⁴ with the bountiful harvest from the sun
and the abundant yield of the seasons;

¹⁵ with the best products of the ancient mountains
and the bounty of the eternal hills;

¹⁶ with the choice gifts of the land
and everything in it;
and with the favor of him
who appeared^F in the burning bush.
May these rest on the head of Joseph,
on the brow of the prince of his brothers.

¹⁷ His firstborn bull has^G splendor,
and horns like^H those of a wild ox;
he gores all the peoples with them
to the ends of the earth.
Such are the ten thousands of Ephraim,
and such are the thousands of Manasseh.

¹⁸ He said about Zebulun:
Rejoice, Zebulun, in your journeys,
and Issachar, in your tents.

¹⁹ They summon the peoples to a mountain;
there they offer acceptable sacrifices.
For they draw from the wealth of the seas
and the hidden treasures of the sand.

²⁰ He said about Gad:
The one who enlarges Gad's territory
will be blessed.
He lies down like a lion
and tears off an arm or even a head.

²¹ He chose the best part for himself,
because a ruler's portion was assigned there for him.
He came with the leaders of the people;
he carried out the Lᴏʀᴅ's justice
and his ordinances for Israel.

---

^A33:11 Or abilities   ^B33:11 Or waist   ^C33:12 Or Let the Lᴏʀᴅ's beloved rest
^D33:12 LXX reads The Most High   ^E33:12 Or and he dwells among his mountain
slopes   ^F33:16 Lit dwelt   ^G33:17 Some DSS, Sam, LXX, Syr, Vg read A firstborn
bull — he has   ^H33:17 Lit and his horns are

²² He said about Dan:

> Dan is a young lion,
>> leaping out of Bashan.

²³ He said about Naphtali:

> Naphtali, enjoying approval,
>> full of the Lord's blessing,
>> take^A possession to the west and the south.

²⁴ He said about Asher:

> May Asher^B be the most blessed of the sons;
>> may he be the most favored among his brothers
>> and dip his foot in olive oil.
> ²⁵ May the bolts of your gate be iron and bronze,
>> and your strength last as long as you live.

> ²⁶ There is none like the God of Jeshurun,
>> who rides the heavens to your aid,
>> the clouds in his majesty.
> ²⁷ The God of old is your dwelling place,
>> and underneath are the everlasting arms.
>> He drives out the enemy before you
>> and commands, "Destroy!"
> ²⁸ So Israel dwells securely;
>> Jacob lives untroubled^C
>> in a land of grain and new wine;
>> even his skies drip with dew.
> ²⁹ How happy you are, Israel!
>> Who is like you,
>> a people saved by the Lord?
>> He is the shield that protects you,
>> the sword you boast in.
>> Your enemies will cringe before you,
>> and you will tread on their backs.^D

MOSES'S DEATH

34 Then Moses went up from the plains of Moab to Mount Nebo, to the top of Pisgah, which faces Jericho, and the Lord showed him all the land: Gilead as far as Dan, ² all of Naphtali, the land of Ephraim and Manasseh, all the land of Judah as far as the Mediterranean^E Sea, ³ the Negev, and the plain in the Valley of Jericho, the City of Palms, as far as Zoar. ⁴ The Lord then said to him, "This is the land I promised Abraham, Isaac, and Jacob, 'I will give it to your descendants.' I have let you see it with your own eyes, but you will not cross into it."

⁵ So Moses the servant of the Lord died there in the land of Moab, according to the Lord's word. ⁶ He buried him^F in the valley in the land of Moab facing Beth-peor, and no one to this day knows where his grave is. ⁷ Moses was one hundred twenty years old when he died; his eyes were not weak,

---

^A 33:23 Sam, LXX, Syr, Vg, Tg read *he will take* ^B 33:24 = Happy or Blessed;
Gn 30:13 ^C 33:28 Text emended; MT reads *Jacob's fountain is alone*
^D 33:29 Or *high places* ^E 34:2 Lit *Western* ^F 34:6 Or *he was buried*

and his vitality had not left him. [8] The Israelites wept for Moses in the plains of Moab thirty days. Then the days of weeping and mourning for Moses came to an end.

[9] Joshua son of Nun was filled with the spirit of wisdom because Moses had laid his hands on him. So the Israelites obeyed him and did as the LORD had commanded Moses. [10] No prophet has arisen again in Israel like Moses, whom the LORD knew face to face. [11] He was unparalleled for all the signs and wonders the LORD sent him to do against the land of Egypt — to Pharaoh, to all his officials, and to all his land, [12] and for all the mighty acts of power[A] and terrifying deeds that Moses performed in the sight of all Israel.

A34:12 Lit the strong hand

The LORD
YOUR GOD
IS WITH
YOU

joshua

Haven't I commanded you: be strong and courageous? Do not be afraid or discouraged, for the LORD your God is with you wherever you go. **1:9**

ON THE TIMELINE Joshua is the first of the historical books in the Old Testament. The events take place in the span between Moses' death and Joshua's, beginning with God telling Joshua to lead the people of Israel into the long-awaited promised land. Israel first appears in the land west of the Jordan River around 1406 BC, and Joshua dies after the tribal allotments of Israel, around 1380 BC.

A LITTLE BACKGROUND The author of the book of Joshua is not identified. If Joshua himself did not originally write the book that bears his name, someone who knew him well likely did. There are a number of references throughout Joshua that suggest final editing of the book after his lifetime. These include the death of Joshua and descriptions of memorials or names "still there today" (Jos 4:9; 10:27; 15:63; 23:8).

MESSAGE & PURPOSE Chapter 1 establishes Joshua as Israel's divinely appointed leader and successor to Moses. God addressed Joshua directly, promising both the land that He promised to Moses (Dt 34:4) and His divine presence (Jos 1:3-5). The commands to be strong and courageous (Jos 1:6-7,9) define the mission of Joshua.

The book of Joshua is a record of God's fulfillment of His part of the renewed covenant in Deuteronomy. God gave Israel victories, but each victory required a step of faith. God's provision for the people as their leader and guide was recorded in this book and recounted to later generations. God's divine leadership for Israel and His gracious gift of the promised land demonstrated how the people's faithful fulfillment of the covenant could result in abundant blessing.

GIVE THANKS FOR THE BOOK OF JOSHUA:

The book of Joshua describes the history of the generation of Israel who crossed the Jordan River and entered the promised land of Canaan. Joshua led God's people to defeat those who opposed them, and their battles have a place among the greatest stories of faith in the OT. God's holiness and saving acts are evident throughout the book, serving as a reminder of His faithfulness to His covenant and His people. By God's grace alone, the nation was able to occupy the land, receive their inheritance, and worship their God.

MEDITERRANEAN SEA

NAPHTALI

ASHER

SEA OF GALILEE

EAST
MANASSEH

ZEBULUN

ISSACHAR

WEST
MANASSEH

JORDAN RIVER

EPHRAIM

GAD

DAN

BENJAMIN

JERUSALEM

REUBEN

JUDAH

DEAD SEA

SIMEON

TRIBAL DIVISIONS

READ AND UNDERSTAND JOSHUA

The Bible is a complete work in which many stories combine to tell one story. As you read the book of Joshua, consider reading the additional passages to discover how the whole of Scripture works together.

ENCOURAGEMENT OF JOSHUA

1 After the death of Moses the Lord's servant, the Lord spoke to Joshua son of Nun, Moses's assistant: ² "Moses my servant is dead. Now you and all the people prepare to cross over the Jordan to the land I am giving the Israelites. ³ I have given you every place where the sole of your foot treads, just as I promised Moses. ⁴ Your territory will be from the wilderness and Lebanon to the great river, the Euphrates River — all the land of the Hittites — and west to the Mediterranean Sea.ᴬ ⁵ No one will be able to stand against you as long as you live. I will be with you, just as I was with Moses. I will not leave you or abandon you.

⁶ "Be strong and courageous, for you will distribute the land I swore to their fathers to give them as an inheritance. ⁷ Above all, be strong and very courageous to observe carefully the whole instruction my servant Moses commanded you. Do not turn from it to the right or the left, so that you will have success wherever you go. ⁸ This book of instruction must not depart from your mouth; you are to meditate onᴮ it day and night so that you may carefully observe everything written in it. For then you will prosper and succeed in whatever you do. ⁹ Haven't I commanded you: be strong and courageous? Do not be afraid or discouraged, for the Lord your God is with you wherever you go."

JOSHUA PREPARES THE PEOPLE

¹⁰ Then Joshua commanded the officers of the people: ¹¹ "Go through the camp and tell the people, 'Get provisions ready for yourselves, for within three days you will be crossing the Jordan to go in and take possession of the land the Lord your God is giving you to inherit.' "

¹² Joshua said to the Reubenites, the Gadites, and half the tribe of Manasseh: ¹³ "Remember what Moses the Lord's servant commanded you when he said, 'The Lord your God will give you rest, and he will give you this land.' ¹⁴ Your wives, dependents, and livestock may remain in the land Moses gave you on this side of the Jordan. But your best soldiers must cross over in battle formationᶜ ahead of your brothers and help them ¹⁵ until the Lord gives your brothers rest, as he has given you, and they too possess the land the Lord your God is giving them. You may then return to the land of your inheritance and take possession of what Moses the Lord's servant gave you on the east side of the Jordan."

¹⁶ They answered Joshua, "Everything you have commanded us we will do, and everywhere you send us we will go. ¹⁷ We will obey you, just as we obeyed Moses in everything. Certainly the Lord your God will be with you, as he was with Moses. ¹⁸ Anyone who rebels against your order and does not obey your words in all that you command him, will be put to death. Above all, be strong and courageous!"

SPIES SENT TO JERICHO

2 Joshua son of Nun secretly sent two men as spies from the Acacia Grove,ᴰ saying, "Go and scout the land, especially Jericho." So they left, and they came to the house of a prostitute named Rahab, and stayed there.

ᴬ 1:4 Lit and to the Great Sea, the going down of the sun   ᴮ 1:8 Or to recite
ᶜ 1:14 Or over armed   ᴰ 2:1 Or from Shittim

STRONG AND COURAGEOUS

JOSHUA 1; NUMBERS 13:30-33; DEUTERONOMY 31:1-6; PSALM 31:24

Who doesn't love the cowardly lion in *The Wizard of Oz*? We can't help but find a soft spot in our hearts for the neurotic, jittery "king of the jungle." The happiest of endings comes when the lion learns he doesn't need to borrow courage from the great wizard; he had what it takes all along.

The book of Joshua shows us this truth in reverse. After the death of Moses, God commissioned Joshua to lead His people into the promised land. As God passed the mantle of leadership to Joshua, He was crystal clear about what kind of commander Joshua should be.

"Be strong and courageous . . . Above all, be strong and very courageous . . . Haven't I commanded you: be strong and courageous?"

JOSHUA 1:6-7,9

Clearly, God was not looking for a weak leader to take His people into the promised land. But Joshua did not get the job because he was naturally bold and fearless. This ceremony wasn't like when the lion finally gets an audience with the wizard, only to find out he's always been brave.

The source of Joshua's strength did not lie within, but the courage he needed was available nevertheless. Let's finish reading Joshua 1:9 to see why:

"Do not be afraid or discouraged, for the Lord your God is with you wherever you go."

The Lord's presence was the reason for Joshua's courage.

Joshua was one of twelve spies sent into Canaan on the first approach to the promised land, and one of only two who believed God would keep His promise to give them the land (Nm 13:30-33).

He had heard Moses give an impassioned speech on his one hundred-twentieth birthday, begging the people of Israel to find their strength and courage in their strong God—not in what they saw or felt. Moses said to them, "Be strong and courageous; don't be terrified or afraid of them. For the Lord your God is the one who will go with you; he will not leave you or abandon you" (Dt 31:6).

Over and over again, Joshua had seen his people come to a hurdle they could not jump over on their own. But God had been strong enough to deliver them every single time.

I want God's words to Joshua to ring in my ears. I know I cannot do the things He has called me to on my own, but I can be strong and courageous because the God of the universe is with me. He will never leave me nor forsake me (Mt 28:20).

"Be strong, and let your heart be courageous, all you who put your hope in the Lord."

PSALM 31:24

---

² The king of Jericho was told, "Look, some of the Israelite men have come here tonight to investigate the land." ³ Then the king of Jericho sent word to Rahab and said, "Bring out the men who came to you and entered your house, for they came to investigate the entire land."

⁴ But the woman had taken the two men and hidden them. So she said, "Yes, the men did come to me, but I didn't know where they were from. ⁵ At nightfall, when the city gate was about to close, the men went out, and I don't know where they were going. Chase after them quickly, and you can catch up with them!" ⁶ But she had taken them up to the roof and hidden them among the stalks of flax that she had arranged on the roof. ⁷ The men pursued them along the road to the fords of the Jordan, and as soon as they left to pursue them, the city gate was shut.

THE PROMISE TO RAHAB

⁸ Before the men fell asleep, she went up on the roof ⁹ and said to them, "I know that the LORD has given you this land and that the terror of you has fallen on us, and everyone who lives in the land is panicking because of you.^A ¹⁰ For we have heard how the LORD dried up the water of the Red Sea before you when you came out of Egypt, and what you did to Sihon and Og, the two Amorite kings you completely destroyed across the Jordan. ¹¹ When we heard this, we lost heart, and everyone's courage failed^B because of you, for the LORD your God is God in heaven above and on earth below. ¹² Now please swear to me by the LORD that you will also show kindness to my father's family,^C because I showed kindness to you. Give me a sure sign^D ¹³ that you will spare the lives of my father, mother, brothers, sisters, and all who belong to them, and save us from death."

¹⁴ The men answered her, "We will give our lives for yours. If you don't report our mission, we will show kindness and faithfulness to you when the LORD gives us the land."

¹⁵ Then she let them down by a rope through the window, since she lived in a house that was built into the wall of the city. ¹⁶ "Go to the hill country so that the men pursuing you won't find you," she said to them. "Hide there for three days until they return; afterward, go on your way."

¹⁷ The men said to her, "We will be free from this oath you made us swear, ¹⁸ unless, when we enter the land, you tie this scarlet cord to the window through which you let us down. Bring your father, mother, brothers, and all your father's family into your house. ¹⁹ If anyone goes out the doors of your house, his death will be his own fault,^E and we will be innocent. But if anyone with you in the house should be harmed,^F his death will be our fault.^G ²⁰ And if you report our mission, we are free from the oath you made us swear."

²¹ "Let it be as you say," she replied, and she sent them away. After they had gone, she tied the scarlet cord to the window.

²² So the two men went into the hill country and stayed there three days until the pursuers had returned. They searched all along the way, but did

---

^A 2:9 Or *land panics at your approach*   ^B 2:11 Lit *and spirit no longer remained in anyone*   ^C 2:12 Lit *my father's house*   ^D 2:12 Or *a sign of truth*   ^E 2:19 Lit *his blood on his head*   ^F 2:19 Lit *if a hand should be on him*   ^G 2:19 Lit *his blood on our heads* not find them. ²³ Then the men returned, came down from the hill country, and crossed the Jordan. They went to Joshua son of Nun and reported everything that had happened to them. ²⁴ They told Joshua, "The LORD has handed over the entire land to us. Everyone who lives in the land is also panicking because of us."ᴬ

CROSSING THE JORDAN

3 Joshua started early the next morning and left the Acacia Groveᴮ with all the Israelites. They went as far as the Jordan and stayed there before crossing. ² After three days the officers went through the camp ³ and commanded the people: "When you see the ark of the covenant of the LORD your God carried by the Levitical priests, you are to break camp and follow it. ⁴ But keep a distance of about a thousand yardsᶜ between yourselves and the ark. Don't go near it, so that you can see the way to go, for you haven't traveled this way before."ᴰ

⁵ Joshua told the people, "Consecrate yourselves, because the LORD will do wonders among you tomorrow." ⁶ Then he said to the priests, "Carry the ark of the covenant and go on ahead of the people." So they carried the ark of the covenant and went ahead of them.

⁷ The LORD spoke to Joshua: "Today I will begin to exalt you in the sight of all Israel, so they will know that I will be with you just as I was with Moses. ⁸ Command the priests carrying the ark of the covenant: When you reach the edge of the water,ᴱ stand in the Jordan."

⁹ Then Joshua told the Israelites, "Come closer and listen to the words of the LORD your God." ¹⁰ He said: "You will know that the living God is among you and that he will certainly dispossess before you the Canaanites, Hethites, Hivites, Perizzites, Girgashites, Amorites, and Jebusites ¹¹ when the ark of the covenant of the Lord of the whole earth goes ahead of you into the Jordan. ¹² Now choose twelve men from the tribes of Israel, one man for each tribe. ¹³ When the feetᶠ of the priests who carry the ark of the LORD, the Lord of the whole earth, come to rest in the Jordan's water, its water will be cut off. The water flowing downstream will stand up in a mass."

¹⁴ When the people broke camp to cross the Jordan, the priests carried the ark of the covenant ahead of the people. ¹⁵ Now the Jordan overflows its banks throughout the harvest season. But as soon as the priests carrying the ark reached the Jordan, their feet touched the water at its edge ¹⁶ and the water flowing downstream stood still, rising up in a mass that extended as far asᴳ Adam, a city next to Zarethan. The water flowing downstream into the Sea of the Arabah — the Dead Sea — was completely cut off, and the people crossed opposite Jericho. ¹⁷ The priests carrying the ark of the LORD's covenant stood firmly on dry ground in the middle of the Jordan, while all Israel crossed on dry ground until the entire nation had finished crossing the Jordan.

ᴬ2:24 Or land also panics at our approach   ᴮ3:1 Or left Shittim   ᶜ3:4 Lit 2,000 cubits   ᴰ3:4 Lit yesterday and the day before   ᴱ3:8 Lit waters of the Jordan
ᶠ3:13 Lit soles of the feet   ᴳ3:16 Alt Hb tradition reads mass at

THE MEMORIAL STONES

4 After the entire nation had finished crossing the Jordan, the LORD spoke to Joshua: ²"Choose twelve men from the people, one man for each tribe, ³and command them: Take twelve stones from this place in the middle of the Jordan where the priests ᴬ are standing, carry them with you, and set them down at the place where you spend the night."

⁴So Joshua summoned the twelve men he had selected from the Israelites, one man for each tribe, ⁵and said to them, "Go across to the ark of the LORD your God in the middle of the Jordan. Each of you lift a stone onto his shoulder, one for each ᴮ of the Israelite tribes, ⁶so that this will be a sign among you. In the future, when your children ask you, 'What do these stones mean to you?' ⁷you should tell them, 'The water of the Jordan was cut off in front of the ark of the LORD's covenant. When it crossed the Jordan, the Jordan's water was cut off.' Therefore these stones will always be a memorial for the Israelites."

⁸The Israelites did just as Joshua had commanded them. The twelve men took stones from the middle of the Jordan, one for each ᶜ of the Israelite tribes, just as the LORD had told Joshua. They carried them to the camp and set them down there. ⁹Joshua also set up twelve stones in the middle ᴰ of the Jordan where the priests who carried the ark of the covenant were standing. The stones are still there today.

¹⁰The priests carrying the ark continued standing in the middle of the Jordan until everything was completed that the LORD had commanded Joshua to tell the people, in keeping with all that Moses had commanded Joshua. The people hurried across, ¹¹and after everyone had finished crossing, the priests with the ark of the LORD crossed in the sight of the people. ¹²The Reubenites, Gadites, and half the tribe of Manasseh went in battle formation in front of the Israelites, as Moses had instructed them. ¹³About forty thousand equipped for war crossed to the plains of Jericho in the LORD's presence.

¹⁴On that day the LORD exalted Joshua in the sight of all Israel, and they revered him throughout his life, as they had revered Moses. ¹⁵The LORD told Joshua, ¹⁶"Command the priests who carry the ark of the testimony to come up from the Jordan."

¹⁷So Joshua commanded the priests, "Come up from the Jordan." ¹⁸When the priests carrying the ark of the LORD's covenant came up from the middle of the Jordan, and their feet ᴱ stepped out on solid ground, the water of the Jordan resumed its course, flowing over all the banks as before.

¹⁹The people came up from the Jordan on the tenth day of the first month, and camped at Gilgal on the eastern limits of Jericho. ²⁰Then Joshua set up in Gilgal the twelve stones they had taken from the Jordan, ²¹and he said to the Israelites, "In the future, when your children ask their fathers, 'What is the meaning of these stones?' ²²you should tell your children, 'Israel crossed the Jordan on dry ground.' ²³For the LORD your God dried up the water of the Jordan before you until you had crossed over, just as the LORD your God did to the Red Sea, which he dried up before

---

ᴬ4:3 Lit feet of the priests, also in v. 9   ᴮ4:5 Lit shoulder according to the number
ᶜ4:8 Lit Jordan according to the number   ᴰ4:9 Or Now Joshua set up the twelve
stones that had been in the middle   ᴱ4:18 Lit and the soles of the feet of the priests

us until we had crossed over. [24] This is so that all the peoples of the earth may know that the LORD's hand is mighty, and so that you may always fear the LORD your God."

CIRCUMCISION OF THE ISRAELITES

5 When all the Amorite kings across the Jordan to the west and all the Canaanite kings near the sea heard how the LORD had dried up the water of the Jordan before the Israelites until they had crossed over, they lost heart and their courage failed[A] because of the Israelites.

[2] At that time the LORD said to Joshua, "Make flint knives and circumcise the Israelite men again." [3] So Joshua made flint knives and circumcised the Israelite men at Gibeath-haaraloth.[B] [4] This is the reason Joshua circumcised them: All the people who came out of Egypt who were males — all the men of war — had died in the wilderness along the way after they had come out of Egypt. [5] Though all the people who came out were circumcised, none of the people born in the wilderness along the way were circumcised after they had come out of Egypt. [6] For the Israelites wandered in the wilderness forty years until all the nation's men of war who came out of Egypt had died off because they did not obey the LORD. So the LORD vowed never to let them see the land he had sworn to their fathers to give us, a land flowing with milk and honey. [7] He raised up their sons in their place; it was these Joshua circumcised. They were still uncircumcised, since they had not been circumcised along the way. [8] After the entire nation had been circumcised, they stayed where they were in the camp until they recovered. [9] The LORD then said to Joshua, "Today I have rolled away the disgrace of Egypt from you." Therefore, that place is still called Gilgal today.

FOOD FROM THE LAND

[10] While the Israelites camped at Gilgal on the plains of Jericho, they observed the Passover on the evening of the fourteenth day of the month. [11] The day after Passover they ate unleavened bread and roasted grain from the produce of the land. [12] And the day after they ate from the produce of the land, the manna ceased. Since there was no more manna for the Israelites, they ate from the crops of the land of Canaan that year.

COMMANDER OF THE LORD'S ARMY

[13] When Joshua was near Jericho, he looked up and saw a man standing in front of him with a drawn sword in his hand. Joshua approached him and asked, "Are you for us or for our enemies?"

[14] "Neither," he replied. "I have now come as commander of the LORD's army."

Then Joshua bowed with his face to the ground in worship and asked him, "What does my lord want to say to his servant?"

[15] The commander of the LORD's army said to Joshua, "Remove the sandals from your feet, for the place where you are standing is holy." And Joshua did that.

[A]5:1 Lit *and they did not have spirit in them any more*   [B]5:3 Or *The Hill of Foreskins*

THE CONQUEST OF JERICHO

6 Now Jericho was strongly fortified because of the Israelites — no one leaving or entering. ² The Lord said to Joshua, "Look, I have handed Jericho, its king, and its best soldiers over to you. ³ March around the city with all the men of war, circling the city one time. Do this for six days. ⁴ Have seven priests carry seven ram's-horn trumpets in front of the ark. But on the seventh day, march around the city seven times, while the priests blow the trumpets. ⁵ When there is a prolonged blast of the horn and you hear its sound, have all the troops give a mighty shout. Then the city wall will collapse, and the troops will advance, each man straight ahead."

⁶ So Joshua son of Nun summoned the priests and said to them, "Take up the ark of the covenant and have seven priests carry seven trumpets in front of the ark of the Lord." ⁷ He said to the troops, "Move forward, march around the city, and have the armed men go ahead of the ark of the Lord."

⁸ After Joshua had spoken to the troops, seven priests carrying seven trumpets before the Lord moved forward and blew the trumpets; the ark of the Lord's covenant followed them. ⁹ While the trumpets were blowing, the armed men went in front of the priests who blew the trumpets, and the rear guard went behind the ark. ¹⁰ But Joshua had commanded the troops: "Do not shout or let your voice be heard. Don't let one word come out of your mouth until the time I say, 'Shout!' Then you are to shout." ¹¹ So the ark of the Lord was carried around the city, circling it once. They returned to the camp and spent the night there.ᴬ

¹² Joshua got up early the next morning. The priests took the ark of the Lord, ¹³ and the seven priests carrying seven trumpets marched in front of the ark of the Lord. While the trumpets were blowing, the armed men went in front of them, and the rear guard went behind the ark of the Lord. ¹⁴ On the second day they marched around the city once and returned to the camp. They did this for six days.

¹⁵ Early on the seventh day, they started at dawn and marched around the city seven times in the same way. That was the only day they marched around the city seven times. ¹⁶ After the seventh time, the priests blew the trumpets, and Joshua said to the troops, "Shout! For the Lord has given you the city. ¹⁷ But the city and everything in it are set apart to the Lord for destruction. Only Rahab the prostitute and everyone with her in the house will live, because she hid the messengers we sent. ¹⁸ But keep yourselves from the things set apart, or you will be set apart for destruction. If youᴮ take any of those things, you will set apart the camp of Israel for destruction and make trouble for it. ¹⁹ For all the silver and gold, and the articles of bronze and iron, are dedicated to the Lord and must go into the Lord's treasury."

²⁰ So the troops shouted, and the trumpets sounded. When they heard the blast of the trumpet, the troops gave a great shout, and the wall collapsed. The troops advanced into the city, each man straight ahead, and they captured the city. ²¹ They completely destroyed everything in the city with the sword — every man and woman, both young and old, and every ox, sheep, and donkey.

ᴬ6:11 Lit *at the camp* ᴮ6:18 LXX reads *you covet and;* Jos 7:21

REDEEMED

JOSHUA 2; 5–6; MATTHEW 1:1-6; HEBREWS 11:31; JAMES 2:25

Prostitute. Harlot.

Rahab is forever known by her most famous sin. When we meet her in Joshua 2, she is introduced simply as "a prostitute named Rahab." When her name appears later in Scripture—in Hebrews and in James—we see that word again.

It's how we know her.

Rahab met the one true God in a precarious time in the history of her homeland. She heard the stories of His faithfulness to His people, as the news traveled to Jericho. Her neighbors were deeply afraid because of all they had seen and heard. In Rahab's own words, they were panicked. But a different kind of fear was taking root in Rahab, one that would prompt her to forgo logic and act out of faith. Rahab was coming to fear the Lord.

Read again, in Joshua 2:11, how she described to the Israelite spies the reaction of her people to news of their victories. Rahab's statement of fear became her statement of faith! Her unassuming confession is even parallel to the charge Moses relates to the Israelites in Deuteronomy 4:39: "Today, recognize and keep in mind that the Lord is God in heaven above and on earth below; there is no other." She was beginning to believe in Him not only as the God of Israel, but as her God too.

Rahab knew the risk she was taking by hiding the spies and aligning herself with the enemy—

so much so, she made them promise to protect her and her family in return. Even in her brand-new faith, she trusted that the God who dried up the waters of the sea and brought the slaves out of Egypt could also rescue her. And He did.

The faith-filled actions of Rahab did more than save two Israelite spies; they began a new chapter of redemption in her story. That same powerful God who preserved His people in mighty ways is the God who saw Rahab and called her to Himself. He's the God who took a woman commonly labeled by her sin and made her a woman indelibly labeled by His grace (Rm 6:14).

Remember that passage in Hebrews? It lists Rahab among the heroes of the Faith (Heb 11:31).

That verse in James? It calls out Rahab as an example of those who are justified in Christ (Jms 2:25).

And in Matthew 1? We see Rahab—the prostitute—listed in the very lineage of Jesus Christ (Mt 1:5).

Do you see the exquisite thread of truth in Rahab's story? **No matter the label we give her, her true identity is given by the God who created and redeemed her.**

What labels do you give yourself today? As you read Rahab's story, remember: the only true name of a daughter of God is the one He Himself gives: Called. Faithful. Rescued. Redeemed.

RAHAB AND HER FAMILY SPARED

²² Joshua said to the two men who had scouted the land, "Go to the prostitute's house and bring the woman out of there, and all who are with her, just as you swore to her." ²³ So the young men who had scouted went in and brought out Rahab and her father, mother, brothers, and all who belonged to her. They brought out her whole family and settled them outside the camp of Israel.

²⁴ They burned the city and everything in it, but they put the silver and gold and the articles of bronze and iron into the treasury of the LORD's house. ²⁵ However, Joshua spared Rahab the prostitute, her father's family, and all who belonged to her, because she hid the messengers Joshua had sent to spy on Jericho, and she still lives in Israel today.

²⁶ At that time Joshua imposed this curse:

The man who undertakes
the rebuilding of this city, Jericho,
is cursed before the LORD.
He will lay its foundation
at the cost of his firstborn;
he will finish its gates
at the cost of his youngest.

²⁷ And the LORD was with Joshua, and his fame spread throughout the land.

DEFEAT AT AI

7 The Israelites, however, were unfaithful regarding the things set apart for destruction. Achan son of Carmi, son of Zabdi, son of Zerah, of the tribe of Judah, took some of what was set apart, and the LORD's anger burned against the Israelites.

² Joshua sent men from Jericho to Ai, which is near Beth-aven, east of Bethel, and told them, "Go up and scout the land." So the men went up and scouted Ai.

³ After returning to Joshua they reported to him, "Don't send all the people, but send about two thousand or three thousandᴬ men to attack Ai. Since the people of Ai are so few, don't wear out all our people there." ⁴ So about three thousand menᴮ went up there, but they fled from the men of Ai. ⁵ The men of Ai struck down about thirty-six of them and chased them from outside the city gate to the quarries,ᶜ striking them down on the descent. As a result, the people lost heart.ᴰ

⁶ Then Joshua tore his clothes and fell facedown to the ground before the ark of the LORD until evening, as did the elders of Israel; they all put dust on their heads. ⁷ "Oh, Lord GOD," Joshua said, "why did you ever bring these people across the Jordan to hand us over to the Amorites for our destruction? If only we had been content to remain on the other side of the Jordan! ⁸ What can I say, Lord, now that Israel has turned its back and run from its enemies? ⁹ When the Canaanites and all who live in the land hear about this, they will surround us and wipe out our name from the earth. Then what will you do about your great name?"

ᴬ7:3 Or send two or three military units of   ᴮ7:4 Lit men from the people
ᶜ7:5 Or to Shebarim   ᴰ7:5 Lit people's hearts melted and became like water

¹⁰ The LORD then said to Joshua, "Stand up! Why have you fallen facedown? ¹¹ Israel has sinned. They have violated my covenant that I appointed for them. They have taken some of what was set apart. They have stolen, deceived, and put those things with their own belongings. ¹² This is why the Israelites cannot stand against their enemies. They will turn their backs and run from their enemies, because they have been set apart for destruction. I will no longer be with you unless you remove from among you what is set apart.

¹³ "Go and consecrate the people. Tell them to consecrate themselves for tomorrow, for this is what the LORD, the God of Israel, says: There are things that are set apart among you, Israel. You will not be able to stand against your enemies until you remove what is set apart. ¹⁴ In the morning, present yourselves tribe by tribe. The tribe the LORD selects is to come forward clan by clan. The clan the LORD selects is to come forward family by family. The family the LORD selects is to come forward man by man. ¹⁵ The one who is caught with the things set apart must be burned, along with everything he has, because he has violated the LORD's covenant and committed an outrage in Israel."

ACHAN JUDGED

¹⁶ Joshua got up early the next morning. He had Israel come forward tribe by tribe, and the tribe of Judah was selected. ¹⁷ He had the clans of Judah come forward, and the Zerahite clan was selected. He had the Zerahite clan come forward by heads of families,ᴬ and Zabdi was selected. ¹⁸ He then had Zabdi's family come forward man by man, and Achan son of Carmi, son of Zabdi, son of Zerah, of the tribe of Judah, was selected. ¹⁹ So Joshua said to Achan, "My son, give glory to the LORD, the God of Israel, and make a confession to him.ᴮ I urge you, tell me what you have done. Don't hide anything from me."

²⁰ Achan replied to Joshua, "It is true. I have sinned against the LORD, the God of Israel. This is what I did: ²¹ When I saw among the spoils a beautiful cloak from Babylon,ᶜ five poundsᴰ of silver, and a bar of gold weighing a pound and a quarter,ᴱ I coveted them and took them. You can see for yourself. They are concealed in the ground inside my tent, with the silver under the cloak." ²² So Joshua sent messengers who ran to the tent, and there was the cloak, concealed in his tent, with the silver underneath. ²³ They took the things from inside the tent, brought them to Joshua and all the Israelites, and spread them out in the LORD's presence.

²⁴ Then Joshua and all Israel with him took Achan son of Zerah, the silver, the cloak, and the bar of gold, his sons and daughters, his ox, donkey, and sheep, his tent, and all that he had, and brought them up to the Valley of Achor. ²⁵ Joshua said, "Why have you brought us trouble? Today the LORD will bring you trouble!" So all Israel stoned themᶠ to death. They burned their bodies, threw stones on them, ²⁶ and raised over him a large pile of rocks that remains still today. Then the LORD turned from his burning anger. Therefore that place is called the Valley of Achorᴳ still today.

ᴬ7:17 Lit forward man by man ᴮ7:19 Or and praise him ᶜ7:21 Lit Shinar
ᴰ7:21 Lit 200 shekels ᴱ7:21 Lit 50 shekels ᶠ7:25 Lit him ᴳ7:26 Or of Trouble

CONQUEST OF AI

8 The LORD said to Joshua, "Do not be afraid or discouraged. Take all the troops with you and go attack Ai. Look, I have handed over to you the king of Ai, his people, city, and land. ² Treat Ai and its king as you did Jericho and its king, except that you may plunder its spoil and livestock for yourselves. Set an ambush behind the city."

³ So Joshua and all the troops set out to attack Ai. Joshua selected thirty thousand of his best soldiers and sent them out at night. ⁴ He commanded them: "Pay attention. Lie in ambush behind the city, not too far from it, and all of you be ready. ⁵ Then I and all the people who are with me will approach the city. When they come out against us as they did the first time, we will flee from them. ⁶ They will come after us until we have drawn them away from the city, for they will say, 'They are fleeing from us as before.' While we are fleeing from them, ⁷ you are to come out of your ambush and seize the city. The LORD your God will hand it over to you. ⁸ After taking the city, set it on fire. Follow the LORD's command — see that you do as I have ordered you." ⁹ So Joshua sent them out, and they went to the ambush site and waited between Bethel and Ai, to the west of Ai. But he spent that night with the troops.

¹⁰ Joshua started early the next morning and mobilized them. Then he and the elders of Israel led the troops up to Ai. ¹¹ All those[A] who were with him went up and approached the city, arriving opposite Ai, and camped to the north of it, with a valley between them and the city. ¹² Now Joshua had taken about five thousand men and set them in ambush between Bethel and Ai, to the west of the city. ¹³ The troops were stationed in this way: the main[B] camp to the north of the city and its rear guard to the west of the city. And that night Joshua went into the valley.

¹⁴ When the king of Ai saw the Israelites, the men of the city hurried and went out early in the morning so that he and all his people could engage Israel in battle at a suitable place facing the Arabah. But he did not know there was an ambush waiting for him behind the city. ¹⁵ Joshua and all Israel pretended to be beaten back by them and fled toward the wilderness. ¹⁶ Then all the troops of Ai were summoned to pursue them, and they pursued Joshua and were drawn away from the city. ¹⁷ Not a man was left in Ai or Bethel who did not go out after Israel, leaving the city exposed while they pursued Israel.

¹⁸ Then the LORD said to Joshua, "Hold out the javelin in your hand toward Ai, for I will hand the city over to you." So Joshua held out his javelin toward it. ¹⁹ When he held out his hand, the men in ambush rose quickly from their position. They ran, entered the city, captured it, and immediately set it on fire.

²⁰ The men of Ai turned and looked back, and smoke from the city was rising to the sky! They could not escape in any direction, and the troops who had fled to the wilderness now became the pursuers. ²¹ When Joshua and all Israel saw that the men in ambush had captured the city and that smoke was rising from it, they turned back and struck down the men of Ai. ²² Then men in ambush came out of the city against them, and the men of Ai were trapped between the Israelite forces, some on one side and some on the

---

[A]8:11 Lit *the people of war* [B]8:13 Lit *way: all the*

other. They struck them down until no survivor or fugitive remained, ²³ but they captured the king of Ai alive and brought him to Joshua.

²⁴ When Israel had finished killing everyone living in Ai who had pursued them into the open country, and when every last one of them had fallen by the sword, all Israel returned to Ai and struck it down with the sword. ²⁵ The total of those who fell that day, both men and women, was twelve thousand — all the people of Ai. ²⁶ Joshua did not draw back his hand that was holding the javelin until all the inhabitants of Ai were completely destroyed. ²⁷ Israel plundered only the cattle and spoil of that city for themselves, according to the LORD's command that he had given Joshua.

²⁸ Joshua burned Ai and left it a permanent ruin, still desolate today. ²⁹ He hungᴬ the body of the king of Ai on a treeᴮ until evening, and at sunset Joshua commanded that they take his body down from the tree. They threw it down at the entrance of the city gate and put a large pile of rocks over it, which still remains today.

RENEWED COMMITMENT TO THE LAW

³⁰ At that time Joshua built an altar on Mount Ebal to the LORD, the God of Israel, ³¹ just as Moses the LORD's servant had commanded the Israelites. He built it according to what is written in the book of the law of Moses: an altar of uncut stones on which no iron tool has been used. Then they offered burnt offerings to the LORD and sacrificed fellowship offerings on it. ³² There on the stones, Joshua copied the law of Moses, which he had written in the presence of the Israelites. ³³ All Israel — resident alien and citizen alike — with their elders, officers, and judges, stood on either side of the ark of the LORD's covenant facing the Levitical priests who carried it. Half of them were in front of Mount Gerizim and half in front of Mount Ebal, as Moses the LORD's servant had commanded earlier concerning blessing the people of Israel. ³⁴ Afterward, Joshua read aloud all the words of the law — the blessings as well as the curses — according to all that is written in the book of the law. ³⁵ There was not a word of all that Moses had commanded that Joshua did not read before the entire assembly of Israel, including the women, the dependents, and the resident aliens who livedᶜ among them.

DECEPTION BY GIBEON

9 When all the kings heard about Jericho and Ai, those who were west of the Jordan in the hill country, in the Judean foothills, ᴰ and all along the coast of the Mediterranean Sea toward Lebanon — the Hethites, Amorites, Canaanites, Perizzites, Hivites, and Jebusites — ² they formed a unified alliance to fight against Joshua and Israel.

³ When the inhabitants of Gibeon heard what Joshua had done to Jericho and Ai, ⁴ they acted deceptively. They gathered provisionsᴱ and took worn-out sacks on their donkeys and old wineskins, cracked and mended. ⁵ They wore old, patched sandals on their feet and threadbare clothing on their bodies. Their entire provision of bread was dry and crumbly. ⁶ They went to

---

ᴬ8:29 Or impaled   ᴮ8:29 Or wooden stake   ᶜ8:35 Lit walked   ᴰ9:1 Or the Shephelah   ᴱ9:4 Some Hb mss, LXX, Syr, Vg; other Hb mss read They went disguised as ambassadors

Joshua in the camp at Gilgal and said to him and the men of Israel, "We have come from a distant land. Please make a treaty with us."

7 The men of Israel replied to the Hivites, "Perhaps you live among us. How can we make a treaty with you?"

8 They said to Joshua, "We are your servants."

Then Joshua asked them, "Who are you and where do you come from?"

9 They replied to him, "Your servants have come from a faraway land because of the reputation of the LORD your God. For we have heard of his fame, and all that he did in Egypt, 10 and all that he did to the two Amorite kings beyond the Jordan — King Sihon of Heshbon and King Og of Bashan, who was in Ashtaroth. 11 So our elders and all the inhabitants of our land told us, 'Take provisions with you for the journey; go and meet them and say, "We are your servants. Please make a treaty with us." ' 12 This bread of ours was warm when we took it from our houses as food on the day we left to come to you; but see, it is now dry and crumbly. 13 These wineskins were new when we filled them; but see, they are cracked. And these clothes and sandals of ours are worn out from the extremely long journey." 14 Then the men of Israel took some of their provisions, but did not seek the LORD's decision. 15 So Joshua established peace with them and made a treaty to let them live, and the leaders of the community swore an oath to them.

GIBEON'S DECEPTION DISCOVERED

16 Three days after making the treaty with them, they heard that the Gibeonites were their neighbors, living among them. 17 So the Israelites set out and reached the Gibeonite cities on the third day. Now their cities were Gibeon, Chephirah, Beeroth, and Kiriath-jearim. 18 But the Israelites did not attack them, because the leaders of the community had sworn an oath to them by the LORD, the God of Israel. Then the whole community grumbled against the leaders.

19 All the leaders answered them, "We have sworn an oath to them by the LORD, the God of Israel, and now we cannot touch them. 20 This is how we will treat them: we will let them live, so that no wrath will fall on us because of the oath we swore to them." 21 They also said, "Let them live." So the Gibeonites became woodcutters and water carriers for the whole community, as the leaders had promised them.

22 Joshua summoned the Gibeonites and said to them, "Why did you deceive us by telling us you live far away from us, when in fact you live among us? 23 Therefore you are cursed and will always be slaves — woodcutters and water carriers for the house of my God."

24 The Gibeonites answered him, "It was clearly communicated to your servants that the LORD your God had commanded his servant Moses to give you all the land and to destroy all the inhabitants of the land before you. We greatly feared for our lives because of you, and that is why we did this. 25 Now we are in your hands. Do to us whatever you think is right."[A] 26 This is what Joshua did to them: he rescued them from the Israelites, and they did not kill them. 27 On that day he made them woodcutters and water carriers — as they are today — for the community and for the LORD's altar at the place he would choose.

A9:25 Lit *us as is good and as is right in your eyes do*

THE DAY THE SUN STOOD STILL

10 Now King Adoni-zedek of Jerusalem heard that Joshua had captured Ai and completely destroyed it, treating Ai and its king as he had Jericho and its king, and that the inhabitants of Gibeon had made peace with Israel and were living among them. ² So Adoni-zedek and his people were^A greatly alarmed because Gibeon was a large city like one of the royal cities; it was larger than Ai, and all its men were warriors. ³ Therefore King Adoni-zedek of Jerusalem sent word to King Hoham of Hebron, King Piram of Jarmuth, King Japhia of Lachish, and King Debir of Eglon, saying, ⁴ "Come up and help me. We will attack Gibeon, because they have made peace with Joshua and the Israelites." ⁵ So the five Amorite kings — the kings of Jerusalem, Hebron, Jarmuth, Lachish, and Eglon — joined forces, advanced with all their armies, besieged Gibeon, and fought against it.

⁶ Then the men of Gibeon sent word to Joshua in the camp at Gilgal: "Don't give up on^B your servants. Come quickly and save us! Help us, for all the Amorite kings living in the hill country have joined forces against us." ⁷ So Joshua and all his troops, including all his best soldiers, came from Gilgal.

⁸ The LORD said to Joshua, "Do not be afraid of them, for I have handed them over to you. Not one of them will be able to stand against you."

⁹ So Joshua caught them by surprise, after marching all night from Gilgal. ¹⁰ The LORD threw them into confusion before Israel. He defeated them in a great slaughter at Gibeon, chased them through the ascent of Beth-horon, and struck them down as far as Azekah and Makkedah. ¹¹ As they fled before Israel, the LORD threw large hailstones on them from the sky along the descent of Beth-horon all the way to Azekah, and they died. More of them died from the hail than the Israelites killed with the sword.

¹² On the day the LORD gave the Amorites over to the Israelites, Joshua spoke to the LORD in the presence of Israel:

"Sun, stand still over Gibeon,
and moon, over the Valley of Aijalon."
¹³ And the sun stood still
and the moon stopped
until the nation took vengeance on its enemies.

Isn't this written in the Book of Jashar?^C

So the sun stopped
in the middle of the sky
and delayed its setting
almost a full day.

¹⁴ There has been no day like it before or since, when the LORD listened to a man, because the LORD fought for Israel. ¹⁵ Then Joshua and all Israel with him returned to the camp at Gilgal.

EXECUTION OF THE FIVE KINGS

¹⁶ Now the five defeated kings had fled and hidden in the cave at Makkedah. ¹⁷ It was reported to Joshua: "The five kings have been found; they are hiding in the cave at Makkedah."

---

^A 10:2 One Hb ms, Syr, Vg read *So he was*   ^B 10:6 Lit *Don't withdraw your hands from*   ^C 10:13 Or *of the Upright*

THE SUN STANDS STILL

JOSHUA 9:1–10:15

Nothing makes me hustle like a deadline. Seriously, mention one in conversation and I'll be unable to hear you over the clock that starts ticking in my head.

In college, I worked for the school newspaper. The building was underground, beneath the university's basketball court, filled with the sounds of screeching sneakers and jammed printers. Sleep was replaced by a steady stream of caffeine and adrenaline, while stories forcefully flowed out of our fingers to be placed in the hands of our readers a few short hours later.

We basked in the knowledge that news couldn't become news without us. Everything was under our watch, from the latest rumors to the biggest announcements. The fluorescent hallway beams created a false sense of time, as we hibernated under the security of to-do lists and grammar rules. In the morning, we'd climb the stairs of reality, the latest issue in hand, to welcome the day. Before opening the door, we'd make bets on whether the sky would be dark or light, because we honestly couldn't tell the difference from our journalism bunker.

In Joshua 10, Joshua faces a firm deadline with a pretty serious agenda: save his people from the attack of five powerful kings. It's a bleak situation until the Lord says, "Do not be afraid of them, for I have handed them over to you. Not one of them will be able to stand against you" (Jos 10:8).

If God were to assign a project and a deadline to me, I imagine I'd descend the stairs to the newspaper office and begin strategizing my next move, emerging with a plan in the morning. But that's not what Joshua does.

Joshua asks God to make the sun stand still, giving him time to fulfill the mission at once. And God does it. The sun stops in the middle of the sky, delaying its setting almost a full day and giving Joshua the time needed to accomplish his task.

As I think about what a sight this must've been, I can't help but realize that, if it were I, I'd still be underground, oblivious to the stilled sun. Even worse than missing that newsworthy spectacle, I'd miss out on observing the intimate care of my Creator.

While I no longer work for the newspaper and now spend most of my time above ground, I haven't completely graduated from my own knee-deep ambition. I collect my cares and hide away from the very God who fought for Israel! But I don't want to spend my days strategizing. I want to get busy living like God has called me to live.

May we ask the Lord for a faith like Joshua's, boldly believing that God is in our corner. Let us stand and walk and live in the sunlight, knowing He is for us.

¹⁸ Joshua said, "Roll large stones against the mouth of the cave, and station men by it to guard the kings. ¹⁹ But as for the rest of you, don't stay there. Pursue your enemies and attack them from behind. Don't let them enter their cities, for the LORD your God has handed them over to you." ²⁰ So Joshua and the Israelites finished inflicting a terrible slaughter on them until they were destroyed, although a few survivors ran away to the fortified cities. ²¹ The people returned safely to Joshua in the camp at Makkedah. And no one dared to threaten^A the Israelites.

²² Then Joshua said, "Open the mouth of the cave, and bring those five kings to me out of there." ²³ That is what they did. They brought the five kings of Jerusalem, Hebron, Jarmuth, Lachish, and Eglon to Joshua out of the cave. ²⁴ When they had brought the kings to him, Joshua summoned all the men of Israel and said to the military commanders who had accompanied him, "Come here and put your feet on the necks of these kings." So the commanders came forward and put their feet on their necks. ²⁵ Joshua said to them, "Do not be afraid or discouraged. Be strong and courageous, for the LORD will do this to all the enemies you fight."

²⁶ After this, Joshua struck them down and executed them. He hung^B their bodies on five trees^C and they were there until evening. ²⁷ At sunset Joshua commanded that they be taken down from the trees and thrown into the cave where they had hidden. Then large stones were placed against the mouth of the cave, and the stones are still there today.

CONQUEST OF SOUTHERN CITIES

²⁸ On that day Joshua captured Makkedah and struck it down with the sword, including its king. He completely destroyed it^D and everyone in it, leaving no survivors. So he treated the king of Makkedah as he had the king of Jericho.

²⁹ Joshua and all Israel with him crossed from Makkedah to Libnah and fought against Libnah. ³⁰ The LORD also handed it and its king over to Israel. He struck it down, putting everyone in it to the sword, and left no survivors in it. He treated Libnah's king as he had the king of Jericho.

³¹ From Libnah, Joshua and all Israel with him crossed to Lachish. They laid siege to it and attacked it. ³² The LORD handed Lachish over to Israel, and Joshua captured it on the second day. He struck it down, putting everyone in it to the sword, just as he had done to Libnah. ³³ At that time King Horam of Gezer went to help Lachish, but Joshua struck him down along with his people, leaving no survivors.

³⁴ Then Joshua crossed from Lachish to Eglon and all Israel with him. They laid siege to it and attacked it. ³⁵ On that day they captured it and struck it down, putting everyone in it to the sword. He completely destroyed it that day, just as he had done to Lachish.

³⁶ Next, Joshua and all Israel with him went up from Eglon to Hebron and attacked it. ³⁷ They captured it and struck down its king, all its villages, and everyone in it with the sword. He left no survivors, just as he had done at Eglon. He completely destroyed Hebron and everyone in it.

³⁸ Finally, Joshua turned toward Debir and attacked it. And all Israel was with him. ³⁹ He captured it — its king and all its villages. They struck them

---

^A10:21 Lit No one sharpened his tongue against   ^B10:26 Or impaled
^C10:26 Or wooden stakes, also in v. 27   ^D10:28 Some Hb mss read them

down with the sword and completely destroyed everyone in it, leaving no survivors. He treated Debir and its king as he had treated Hebron and as he had treated Libnah and its king.

⁴⁰ So Joshua conquered the whole region — the hill country, the Negev, the Judean foothills,^A and the slopes — with all their kings, leaving no survivors. He completely destroyed every living being, as the Lord, the God of Israel, had commanded. ⁴¹ Joshua conquered everyone from Kadesh-barnea to Gaza, and all the land of Goshen as far as Gibeon. ⁴² Joshua captured all these kings and their land in one campaign,^B because the Lord, the God of Israel, fought for Israel. ⁴³ Then Joshua returned with all Israel to the camp at Gilgal.

CONQUEST OF NORTHERN CITIES

11 When King Jabin of Hazor heard this news, he sent a message to: King Jobab of Madon, the kings of Shimron and Achshaph, ² and the kings of the north in the hill country, the Arabah south of Chinnereth, the Judean foothills,^C and the Slopes of Dor^D to the west, ³ the Canaanites in the east and west, the Amorites, Hethites, Perizzites, and Jebusites in the hill country, and the Hivites at the foot of Hermon in the land of Mizpah. ⁴ They went out with all their armies — a multitude as numerous as the sand on the seashore — along with a vast number of horses and chariots. ⁵ All these kings joined forces; they came and camped together at the Waters of Merom to attack Israel.

⁶ The Lord said to Joshua, "Do not be afraid of them, for at this time tomorrow I will cause all of them to be killed before Israel. You are to hamstring their horses and burn their chariots." ⁷ So Joshua and all his troops surprised them at the Waters of Merom and attacked them. ⁸ The Lord handed them over to Israel, and they struck them down, pursuing them as far as greater Sidon and Misrephoth-maim, and to the east as far as the Valley of Mizpeh. They struck them down, leaving no survivors. ⁹ Joshua treated them as the Lord had told him; he hamstrung their horses and burned their chariots.

¹⁰ At that time Joshua turned back, captured Hazor, and struck down its king with the sword, because Hazor had formerly been the leader of all these kingdoms. ¹¹ They struck down everyone in it with the sword, completely destroying them; he left no one alive. Then he burned Hazor.

¹² Joshua captured all these kings and their cities and struck them down with the sword. He completely destroyed them, as Moses the Lord's servant had commanded. ¹³ However, Israel did not burn any of the cities that stood on their mounds except Hazor, which Joshua burned. ¹⁴ The Israelites plundered all the spoils and cattle of these cities for themselves. But they struck down every person with the sword until they had annihilated them, leaving no one alive. ¹⁵ Just as the Lord had commanded his servant Moses, Moses commanded Joshua. That is what Joshua did, leaving nothing undone of all that the Lord had commanded Moses.

SUMMARY OF CONQUESTS

¹⁶ So Joshua took all this land — the hill country, all the Negev, all the land of Goshen, the foothills, the Arabah, and the hill country of Israel with its

---

^A10:40 Or the Shephelah   ^B10:42 Lit land at one time   ^C11:2 Or Shephelah, also in v. 16   ^D11:2 Or and in Naphoth-dor foothills — [17] from Mount Halak, which ascends to Seir, as far as Baal-gad in the Valley of Lebanon at the foot of Mount Hermon. He captured all their kings and struck them down, putting them to death. [18] Joshua waged war with all these kings for a long time. [19] No city made peace with the Israelites except the Hivites who inhabited Gibeon; all of them were taken in battle. [20] For it was the LORD's intention to harden their hearts, so that they would engage Israel in battle, be completely destroyed without mercy, and be annihilated, just as the LORD had commanded Moses.

[21] At that time Joshua proceeded to exterminate the Anakim from the hill country — Hebron, Debir, Anab — all the hill country of Judah and of Israel. Joshua completely destroyed them with their cities. [22] No Anakim were left in the land of the Israelites, except for some remaining in Gaza, Gath, and Ashdod.

[23] So Joshua took the entire land, in keeping with all that the LORD had told Moses. Joshua then gave it as an inheritance to Israel according to their tribal allotments. After this, the land had rest from war.

TERRITORY EAST OF THE JORDAN

12 The Israelites struck down the following kings of the land and took possession of their land beyond the Jordan to the east and from the Arnon River to Mount Hermon, including all the Arabah eastward:

[2] King Sihon of the Amorites lived in Heshbon. He ruled from Aroer on the rim of the Arnon River, along the middle of the valley, and half of Gilead up to the Jabbok River (the border of the Ammonites), [3] the Arabah east of the Sea of Chinnereth to the Sea of Arabah (that is, the Dead Sea), eastward through Beth-jeshimoth and southward [A] below the slopes of Pisgah.

[4] King Og [B] of Bashan, of the remnant of the Rephaim, lived in Ashtaroth and Edrei. [5] He ruled over Mount Hermon, Salecah, all Bashan up to the Geshurite and Maacathite border, and half of Gilead to the border of King Sihon of Heshbon. [6] Moses the LORD's servant and the Israelites struck them down. And Moses the LORD's servant gave their land as an inheritance to the Reubenites, Gadites, and half the tribe of Manasseh.

TERRITORY WEST OF THE JORDAN

[7] Joshua and the Israelites struck down the following kings of the land beyond the Jordan to the west, from Baal-gad in the Valley of Lebanon to Mount Halak, which ascends toward Seir (Joshua gave their land as an inheritance to the tribes of Israel according to their allotments: [8] the hill country, the Judean foothills, [C] the Arabah, the slopes, the wilderness, and the Negev — the lands of the Hethites, Amorites, Canaanites, Perizzites, Hivites, and Jebusites):

[9]	the king of Jericho	one
	the king of Ai, which is next to Bethel	one
[10]	the king of Jerusalem	one
	the king of Hebron	one
[11]	the king of Jarmuth	one
	the king of Lachish	one
[12]	the king of Eglon	one

---

the king of Gezer	one
¹³ the king of Debir	one
the king of Geder	one
¹⁴ the king of Hormah	one
the king of Arad	one
¹⁵ the king of Libnah	one
the king of Adullam	one
¹⁶ the king of Makkedah	one
the king of Bethel	one
¹⁷ the king of Tappuah	one
the king of Hepher	one
¹⁸ the king of Aphek	one
the king of Lasharon	one
¹⁹ the king of Madon	one
the king of Hazor	one
²⁰ the king of Shimron-meron	one
the king of Achshaph	one
²¹ the king of Taanach	one
the king of Megiddo	one
²² the king of Kedesh	one
the king of Jokneam in Carmel	one
²³ the king of Dor in Naphath-dorᴬ	one
the king of Goiim in Gilgalᴮ	one
²⁴ the king of Tirzah	one
the total number of all kings:	thirty-one.

UNCONQUERED LANDS

13 Joshua was now old, advanced in age, and the LORD said to him, "You have become old, advanced in age, but a great deal of the land remains to be possessed. ² This is the land that remains:

All the districts of the Philistines and the Geshurites: ³ from the Shihor east of Egypt to the border of Ekron on the north (considered to be Canaanite territory) — the five Philistine rulers of Gaza, Ashdod, Ashkelon, Gath, and Ekron, as well as the Avvites ⁴ in the south; all the land of the Canaanites, from Arah of the Sidonians to Aphek and as far as the border of the Amorites; ⁵ the land of the Gebalites; and all Lebanon east from Baal-gad below Mount Hermon to the entrance of Hamathᶜ — ⁶ all the inhabitants of the hill country from Lebanon to Misrephoth-maim, all the Sidonians.

I will drive them out before the Israelites, only distribute the land as an inheritance for Israel, as I have commanded you. ⁷ Therefore, divide this land as an inheritance to the nine tribes and half the tribe of Manasseh."

THE INHERITANCE EAST OF THE JORDAN

⁸ With the other half of the tribe of Manasseh, the Reubenites and Gadites had received the inheritance Moses gave them beyond the Jordan to the east, just as Moses the LORD's servant had given them:

ᴬ12:23 Or *in the Slopes of Dor* ᴮ12:23 LXX reads *Galilee* ᶜ13:5 Or *to Lebo-hamath*

[9] From Aroer on the rim of the Arnon Valley, along with the city in the middle of the valley, all the Medeba plateau as far as Dibon, [10] and all the cities of King Sihon of the Amorites, who reigned in Heshbon, to the border of the Ammonites; [11] also Gilead and the territory of the Geshurites and Maacathites, all Mount Hermon, and all Bashan to Salecah — [12] the whole kingdom of Og in Bashan, who reigned in Ashtaroth and Edrei; he was one of the remaining Rephaim.

Moses struck them down and drove them out, [13] but the Israelites did not drive out the Geshurites and Maacathites. So Geshur and Maacath still live in Israel today.

[14] He did not, however, give any inheritance to the tribe of Levi. This was their inheritance, just as he had promised: the offerings made by fire to the LORD, the God of Israel.

REUBEN'S INHERITANCE

[15] To the tribe of Reuben's descendants by their clans, Moses gave [16] this as their territory:

From Aroer on the rim of the Arnon Valley, along with the city in the middle of the valley, the whole plateau as far as^ Medeba, [17] with Heshbon and all its cities on the plateau — Dibon, Bamoth-baal, Beth-baal-meon, [18] Jahaz, Kedemoth, Mephaath, [19] Kiriathaim, Sibmah, Zereth-shahar on the hill in the valley, [20] Beth-peor, the slopes of Pisgah, and Beth-jeshimoth — [21] all the cities of the plateau, and all the kingdom of King Sihon of the Amorites, who reigned in Heshbon. Moses had killed him and the chiefs of Midian — Evi, Rekem, Zur, Hur, and Reba — the princes of Sihon who lived in the land. [22] Along with those the Israelites put to death, they also killed the diviner, Balaam son of Beor, with the sword.

[23] The border of the Reubenites was the Jordan and its plain. This was the inheritance of the Reubenites by their clans, with the cities and their settlements.

GAD'S INHERITANCE

[24] To the tribe of the Gadites by their clans, Moses gave [25] this as their territory:

Jazer and all the cities of Gilead, and half the land of the Ammonites to Aroer, near Rabbah; [26] from Heshbon to Ramath-mizpeh and Betonim, and from Mahanaim to the border of Debir;^B [27] in the valley: Beth-haram, Beth-nimrah, Succoth, and Zaphon — the rest of the kingdom of King Sihon of Heshbon. Their land also included the Jordan and its territory as far as the edge of the Sea of Chinnereth on the east side of the Jordan.^C

[28] This was the inheritance of the Gadites by their clans, with the cities and their settlements.

EAST MANASSEH'S INHERITANCE

[29] And to half the tribe of Manasseh (that is, to half the tribe of Manasseh's descendants by their clans) Moses gave [30] this as their territory:

---

^A 13:16 Some Hb mss read *plateau near*   ^B 13:26 Or *Lidbir*, or *Lo-debar*
^C 13:27 Lit *Chinnereth beyond the Jordan to the east*

From Mahanaim through all Bashan — all the kingdom of King Og of Bashan, including all of Jair's Villages[A] that are in Bashan — sixty cities. [31] But half of Gilead, and Og's royal cities in Bashan — Ashtaroth and Edrei — are for the descendants of Machir son of Manasseh (that is, half the descendants of Machir by their clans).

[32] These were the portions Moses gave them on the plains of Moab beyond the Jordan east of Jericho. [33] But Moses did not give a portion to the tribe of Levi. The LORD, the God of Israel, was their inheritance, just as he had promised them.

ISRAEL'S INHERITANCE IN CANAAN

14 The Israelites received these portions that the priest Eleazar, Joshua son of Nun, and the family heads of the Israelite tribes gave them in the land of Canaan. [2] Their inheritance was by lot as the LORD commanded through Moses for the nine and a half tribes, [3] because Moses had given the inheritance to the two and a half tribes beyond the Jordan. But he gave no inheritance among them to the Levites. [4] The descendants of Joseph became two tribes, Manasseh and Ephraim. No portion of the land was given to the Levites except cities to live in, along with pasturelands for their cattle and livestock. [5] So the Israelites did as the LORD commanded Moses, and they divided the land.

CALEB'S INHERITANCE

[6] The descendants of Judah approached Joshua at Gilgal, and Caleb son of Jephunneh the Kenizzite said to him, "You know what the LORD promised Moses the man of God at Kadesh-barnea about you and me. [7] I was forty years old when Moses the LORD's servant sent me from Kadesh-barnea to scout the land, and I brought back an honest report. [8] My brothers who went with me caused the people to lose heart,[B] but I followed the LORD my God completely. [9] On that day Moses swore to me: 'The land where you have set foot will be an inheritance for you and your descendants forever, because you have followed the LORD my God completely.'

[10] "As you see, the LORD has kept me alive these forty-five years as he promised, since the LORD spoke this word to Moses while Israel was journeying in the wilderness. Here I am today, eighty-five years old. [11] I am still as strong today as I was the day Moses sent me out. My strength for battle and for daily tasks[C] is now as it was then. [12] Now give me this hill country the LORD promised me on that day, because you heard then that the Anakim are there, as well as large fortified cities. Perhaps the LORD will be with me and I will drive them out as the LORD promised."

[13] Then Joshua blessed Caleb son of Jephunneh and gave him Hebron as an inheritance. [14] Therefore, Hebron still belongs to Caleb son of Jephunneh the Kenizzite as an inheritance today because he followed the LORD, the God of Israel, completely. [15] Hebron's name used to be Kiriath-arba; Arba was the greatest man among the Anakim. After this, the land had rest from war.

[A] 13:30 Or all of Havvoth-jair   [B] 14:8 Lit people's hearts to melt with fear
[C] 14:11 Lit for going out and coming in

JUDAH'S INHERITANCE

15 Now the allotment for the tribe of the descendants of Judah by their clans was in the southernmost region, south to the Wilderness of Zin and over to the border of Edom.

² Their southern border began at the tip of the Dead Sea on the south bay.ᴬ ³ and went south of the Scorpions' Ascent,ᴮ proceeded to Zin, ascended to the south of Kadesh-barnea, passed Hezron, ascended to Addar, and turned to Karka. ⁴ It proceeded to Azmon and to the Brook of Egypt and so the border ended at the Mediterranean Sea. This is yourᶜ southern border.

⁵ Now the eastern border was along the Dead Sea to the mouth of the Jordan.

The border on the north side was from the bay of the sea at the mouth of the Jordan. ⁶ It ascended to Beth-hoglah, proceeded north of Beth-arabah, and ascended to the Stone of Bohan son of Reuben. ⁷ Then the border ascended to Debir from the Valley of Achor, turning north to the Gilgal that is opposite the Ascent of Adummim, which is south of the ravine. The border proceeded to the Waters of En-shemesh and ended at En-rogel. ⁸ From there the border ascended Ben Hinnom Valley to the southern Jebusite slope (that is, Jerusalem) and ascended to the top of the hill that faces Hinnom Valley on the west, at the northern end of Rephaim Valley. ⁹ From the top of the hill the border curved to the spring of the Waters of Nephtoah, went to the cities of Mount Ephron, and then curved to Baalah (that is, Kiriath-jearim). ¹⁰ The border turned westward from Baalah to Mount Seir, went to the northern slope of Mount Jearim (that is, Chesalon), descended to Beth-shemesh, and proceeded to Timnah. ¹¹ Then the border reached to the slope north of Ekron, curved to Shikkeron, proceeded to Mount Baalah, went to Jabneel, and ended at the Mediterranean Sea.

¹² Now the western border was the coastline of the Mediterranean Sea.

This was the boundary of the descendants of Judah around their clans.

CALEB AND OTHNIEL

¹³ He gave Caleb son of Jephunneh the following portion among the descendants of Judah based on the LORD's instruction to Joshua: Kiriath-arba (that is, Hebron; Arba was the father of Anak). ¹⁴ Caleb drove out from there the three sons of Anak: Sheshai, Ahiman, and Talmai, descendants of Anak. ¹⁵ From there he marched against the inhabitants of Debir, which used to be called Kiriath-sepher, ¹⁶ and Caleb said, "Whoever attacks and captures Kiriath-sepher, I will give my daughter Achsah to him as a wife." ¹⁷ So Othniel son of Caleb's brother, Kenaz, captured it, and Caleb gave his daughter Achsah to him as a wife. ¹⁸ When she arrived, she persuaded Othniel to ask her father for a field. As she got off her donkey, Caleb asked her, "What can I do for you?"

ᴬ15:2 Lit *Sea at the tongue that turns southward*   ᴮ15:3 Lit *of scorpions*
ᶜ15:4 LXX reads *their*

[19] She replied, "Give me a blessing. Since you have given me land in the Negev, give me the springs also." So he gave her the upper and lower springs.

JUDAH'S CITIES

[20] This was the inheritance of the tribe of the descendants of Judah by their clans.

[21] These were the outermost cities of the tribe of the descendants of Judah toward the border of Edom in the Negev: Kabzeel, Eder, Jagur, [22] Kinah, Dimonah, Adadah, [23] Kedesh, Hazor, Ithnan, [24] Ziph, Telem, Bealoth, [25] Hazor-hadattah, Kerioth-hezron (that is, Hazor), [26] Amam, Shema, Moladah, [27] Hazar-gaddah, Heshmon, Beth-pelet, [28] Hazar-shual, Beer-sheba, Biziothiah, [29] Baalah, Iim, Ezem, [30] Eltolad, Chesil, Hormah, [31] Ziklag, Madmannah, Sansannah, [32] Lebaoth, Shilhim, Ain, and Rimmon — twenty-nine cities in all, with their settlements.

[33] In the Judean foothills:[A] Eshtaol, Zorah, Ashnah, [34] Zanoah, En-gannim, Tappuah,[B] Enam, [35] Jarmuth, Adullam, Socoh,[C] Azekah, [36] Shaaraim, Adithaim, Gederah, and Gederothaim — fourteen cities, with their settlements; [37] Zenan, Hadashah, Migdal-gad, [38] Dilan, Mizpeh, Jokthe-el, [39] Lachish, Bozkath, Eglon, [40] Cabbon, Lahmam, Chitlish, [41] Gederoth, Beth-dagon, Naamah, and Makkedah — sixteen cities, with their settlements; [42] Libnah, Ether, Ashan, [43] Iphtah, Ashnah, Nezib, [44] Keilah, Achzib, and Mareshah — nine cities, with their settlements; [45] Ekron, with its surrounding villages and settlements; [46] from Ekron to the sea, all the cities near Ashdod, with their settlements; [47] Ashdod, with its surrounding villages and settlements; Gaza, with its surrounding villages and settlements, to the Brook of Egypt and the coastline of the Mediterranean Sea.

[48] In the hill country: Shamir, Jattir, Socoh, [49] Dannah, Kiriath-sannah (that is, Debir), [50] Anab, Eshtemoh, Anim, [51] Goshen, Holon, and Giloh — eleven cities, with their settlements; [52] Arab, Dumah,[D] Eshan, [53] Janim, Beth-tappuah, Aphekah, [54] Humtah, Kiriath-arba (that is, Hebron), and Zior — nine cities, with their settlements; [55] Maon, Carmel, Ziph, Juttah, [56] Jezreel, Jokdeam, Zanoah, [57] Kain, Gibeah, and Timnah — ten cities, with their settlements; [58] Halhul, Beth-zur, Gedor, [59] Maarath, Beth-anoth, and Eltekon — six cities, with their settlements;[E] [60] Kiriath-baal (that is, Kiriath-jearim), and Rabbah — two cities, with their settlements.

[61] In the wilderness: Beth-arabah, Middin, Secacah, [62] Nibshan, the City of Salt,[F] and En-gedi — six cities, with their settlements.

[63] But the descendants of Judah could not drive out the Jebusites who lived in Jerusalem. So the Jebusites still live in Jerusalem among the descendants of Judah today.

[A] 15:33 Or *the Shephelah* [B] 15:34 Or *En-gannim-tappuah* [C] 15:35 Or *Adullam-socoh* [D] 15:52 Some Hb mss read *Rumah* [E] 15:59 LXX adds *Tekoa, Ephrathah (that is, Bethlehem), Peor, Etam, Culom, Tatam, Sores, Carem, Gallim, Baither, and Manach — eleven cities, with their settlements* [F] 15:62 Or *Ir-hamelach*

JOSEPH'S INHERITANCE

16 The allotment for the descendants of Joseph went from the Jordan at Jericho to the Waters of Jericho on the east, through the wilderness ascending from Jericho into the hill country of Bethel. ² From Bethel it went to Luz and proceeded to the border of the Archites by Ataroth. ³ It then descended westward to the border of the Japhletites as far as the border of lower Beth-horon, then to Gezer, and ended at the Mediterranean Sea. ⁴ So Ephraim and Manasseh, the sons of Joseph, received their inheritance.

EPHRAIM'S INHERITANCE

⁵ This was the territory of the descendants of Ephraim by their clans: The border of their inheritance went from Ataroth-addar on the east to Upper Beth-horon. ⁶ In the north the border went westward from Michmethath; it turned eastward from Taanath-shiloh and passed it east of Janoah. ⁷ From Janoah it descended to Ataroth and Naarah, and then reached Jericho and went to the Jordan. ⁸ From Tappuah the border went westward along the Brook of Kanah and ended at the Mediterranean Sea.

This was the inheritance of the tribe of the descendants of Ephraim by their clans, together with ⁹ the cities set apart for the descendants of Ephraim within the inheritance of the descendants of Manasseh — all these cities with their settlements. ¹⁰ However, they did not drive out the Canaanites who lived in Gezer. So the Canaanites still live in Ephraim today, but they are forced laborers.

WEST MANASSEH'S INHERITANCE

17 This was the allotment for the tribe of Manasseh as Joseph's firstborn. Gilead and Bashan were given to Machir, the firstborn of Manasseh and the father of Gilead, because he was a man of war. ² So the allotment was for the rest of Manasseh's descendants by their clans, for the sons of Abiezer, Helek, Asriel, Shechem, Hepher, and Shemida. These are the male descendants of Manasseh son of Joseph, by their clans.

³ Now Zelophehad son of Hepher, son of Gilead, son of Machir, son of Manasseh, had no sons, only daughters. These are the names of his daughters: Mahlah, Noah, Hoglah, Milcah, and Tirzah. ⁴ They came before the priest Eleazar, Joshua son of Nun, and the leaders, saying, "The LORD commanded Moses to give us an inheritance among our male relatives." So they gave them an inheritance among their father's brothers, in keeping with the LORD's instruction. ⁵ As a result, ten tracts fell to Manasseh, besides the land of Gilead and Bashan, which are beyond the Jordan,^ ⁶ because Manasseh's daughters received an inheritance among his sons. The land of Gilead belonged to the rest of Manasseh's sons.

⁷ The border of Manasseh went from Asher to Michmethath near Shechem. It then went southward toward the inhabitants of En-tappuah. ⁸ The region of Tappuah belonged to Manasseh, but Tappuah itself on Manasseh's border belonged to the descendants of Ephraim.

---

^17:5 = east of the Jordan River

⁹ From there the border descended to the Brook of Kanah; south of the brook, cities belonged to Ephraim among Manasseh's cities. Manasseh's border was on the north side of the brook and ended at the Mediterranean Sea. ¹⁰ Ephraim's territory was to the south and Manasseh's to the north, with the Sea as its border. They reached Asher on the north and Issachar on the east. ¹¹ Within Issachar and Asher, Manasseh had Beth-shean, Ibleam, and the inhabitants of Dor with their surrounding villages; the inhabitants of En-dor, Taanach, and Megiddo — the three cities of ^A Naphath — with their surrounding villages.

¹² The descendants of Manasseh could not possess these cities, because the Canaanites were determined to stay in this land. ¹³ However, when the Israelites grew stronger, they imposed forced labor on the Canaanites but did not drive them out completely.

JOSEPH'S ADDITIONAL INHERITANCE

¹⁴ Joseph's descendants said to Joshua, "Why did you give us only one tribal allotment ^B as an inheritance? We have many people, because the LORD has been blessing us greatly."

¹⁵ "If you have so many people," Joshua replied to them, "go to the forest and clear an area for yourselves there in the land of the Perizzites and the Rephaim, because Ephraim's hill country is too small for you."

¹⁶ But the descendants of Joseph said, "The hill country is not enough for us, and all the Canaanites who inhabit the valley area have iron chariots, both at Beth-shean with its surrounding villages and in the Jezreel Valley."

¹⁷ So Joshua replied to Joseph's family (that is, Ephraim and Manasseh), "You have many people and great strength. You will not have just one allotment, ¹⁸ because the hill country will be yours also. It is a forest; clear it and its outlying areas will be yours. You can also drive out the Canaanites, even though they have iron chariots and are strong."

LAND DISTRIBUTION AT SHILOH

18 The entire Israelite community assembled at Shiloh and set up the tent of meeting there. The land had been subdued before them, ² but seven tribes among the Israelites were left who had not divided up their inheritance. ³ So Joshua asked the Israelites, "How long will you delay going out to take possession of the land that the LORD, the God of your fathers, gave you? ⁴ Appoint for yourselves three men from each tribe, and I will send them out. They are to go and survey the land, write a description of it for the purpose of their inheritance, and return to me. ⁵ Then they are to divide it into seven portions. Judah is to remain in its territory in the south and Joseph's family in their territory in the north. ⁶ When you have written a description of the seven portions of land and brought it to me, I will cast lots for you here in the presence of the LORD our God. ⁷ But the Levites among you do not get a portion, because their inheritance is the priesthood of the LORD. Gad, Reuben, and half the tribe of Manasseh have taken their inheritance beyond the Jordan to the east, which Moses the LORD's servant gave them."

^A 17:11 LXX, Vg read the third is   ^B 17:14 Lit one lot and one territory, also in v. 17

[8] As the men prepared to go, Joshua commanded them[A] to write down a description of the land, saying, "Go and survey the land, write a description of it, and return to me. I will then cast lots for you here in Shiloh in the presence of the LORD." [9] So the men left, went through the land, and described it by towns in a document of seven sections. They returned to Joshua at the camp in Shiloh. [10] Joshua cast lots for them at Shiloh in the presence of the LORD where he distributed the land to the Israelites according to their divisions.

BENJAMIN'S INHERITANCE

[11] The lot came up for the tribe of Benjamin's descendants by their clans, and their allotted territory lay between Judah's descendants and Joseph's descendants.

[12] Their border on the north side began at the Jordan, ascended to the slope of Jericho on the north, through the hill country westward, and ended at the wilderness around Beth-aven. [13] From there the border went toward Luz, to the southern slope of Luz (that is, Bethel); it then went down by Ataroth-addar, over the hill south of Lower Beth-horon.

[14] On the west side, from the hill facing Beth-horon on the south, the border curved, turning southward, and ended at Kiriath-baal (that is, Kiriath-jearim), a city of the descendants of Judah. This was the west side of their border.

[15] The south side began at the edge of Kiriath-jearim, and the border extended westward; it went to the spring at the Waters of Nephtoah. [16] The border descended to the foot of the hill that faces Ben Hinnom Valley at the northern end of Rephaim Valley. It ran down Hinnom Valley toward the south Jebusite slope and downward to En-rogel. [17] It curved northward and went to En-shemesh and on to Geliloth, which is opposite the Ascent of Adummim, and continued down to the Stone of Bohan son of Reuben. [18] Then it went north to the slope opposite the Arabah[B] and proceeded into the plains.[C] [19] The border continued to the north slope of Beth-hoglah and ended at the northern bay of the Dead Sea, at the southern end of the Jordan. This was the southern border.

[20] The Jordan formed the border on the east side.
This was the inheritance of Benjamin's descendants, by their clans, according to its surrounding borders.

BENJAMIN'S CITIES

[21] These were the cities of the tribe of Benjamin's descendants by their clans: Jericho, Beth-hoglah, Emek-keziz, [22] Beth-arabah, Zemaraim, Bethel, [23] Avvim, Parah, Ophrah, [24] Chephar-ammoni, Ophni, and Geba — twelve cities, with their settlements; [25] Gibeon, Ramah, Beeroth, [26] Mizpeh, Chephirah, Mozah, [27] Rekem, Irpeel, Taralah, [28] Zela, Haeleph, Jebus[D]

[A]18:8 Lit the ones going around [B]18:18 LXX reads went northward to Beth-arabah [C]18:18 Or the Arabah [D]18:28 Lit Jebusite (that is, Jerusalem), Gibeah, and Kiriath ᴬ — fourteen cities, with their settlements.

This was the inheritance for Benjamin's descendants by their clans.

SIMEON'S INHERITANCE

19 The second lot came out for Simeon, for the tribe of his descendants by their clans, but their inheritance was within the inheritance given to Judah's descendants. ² Their inheritance included

Beer-sheba (or Sheba), Moladah, ³ Hazar-shual, Balah, Ezem, ⁴ Eltolad, Bethul, Hormah, ⁵ Ziklag, Beth-marcaboth, Hazar-susah, ⁶ Beth-lebaoth, and Sharuhen — thirteen cities, with their settlements; ⁷ Ain, Rimmon, Ether, and Ashan — four cities, with their settlements; ⁸ and all the settlements surrounding these cities as far as Baalath-beer (Ramah in the south ᴮ).

This was the inheritance of the tribe of Simeon's descendants by their clans. ⁹ The inheritance of Simeon's descendants was within the territory of Judah's descendants, because the share for Judah's descendants was too large. So Simeon's descendants received an inheritance within Judah's portion.

ZEBULUN'S INHERITANCE

¹⁰ The third lot came up for Zebulun's descendants by their clans.

The territory of their inheritance stretched as far as Sarid; ¹¹ their border went up westward to Maralah, reached Dabbesheth, and met the brook east of Jokneam. ¹² From Sarid, it turned due east along the border of Chisloth-tabor, went to Daberath, and went up to Japhia. ¹³ From there, it went due east to Gath-hepher and to Eth-kazin; it extended to Rimmon, curving around to Neah. ¹⁴ The border then circled around Neah on the north to Hannathon and ended at Iphtah-el Valley, ¹⁵ along with Kattath, Nahalal, Shimron, Idalah, and Bethlehem — twelve cities, with their settlements.

¹⁶ This was the inheritance of Zebulun's descendants by their clans, these cities, with their settlements.

ISSACHAR'S INHERITANCE

¹⁷ The fourth lot came out for the tribe of Issachar's descendants by their clans.

¹⁸ Their territory went to Jezreel, and included Chesulloth, Shunem, ¹⁹ Hapharaim, Shion, Anaharath, ²⁰ Rabbith, Kishion, Ebez, ²¹ Remeth, En-gannim, En-haddah, and Beth-pazzez. ²² The border reached Tabor, Shahazumah, and Beth-shemesh, and ended at the Jordan — sixteen cities, with their settlements.

²³ This was the inheritance of the tribe of Issachar's descendants by their clans, the cities, with their settlements.

ASHER'S INHERITANCE

²⁴ The fifth lot came out for the tribe of Asher's descendants by their clans.

²⁵ Their boundary included Helkath, Hali, Beten, Achshaph, ²⁶ Allam-melech, Amad, and Mishal and reached westward to Carmel and Shihor-libnath. ²⁷ It turned eastward to Beth-dagon, reached Zebulun and Iphtah-el Valley, north toward Beth-emek and Neiel, and went north

ᴬ18:28 LXX, Syr read *Kiriath-jearim*   ᴮ19:8 Or *the Negev* to Cabul, ²⁸ Ebron, Rehob, Hammon, and Kanah, as far as greater Sidon. ²⁹ The boundary then turned to Ramah as far as the fortified city of Tyre; it turned back to Hosah and ended at the Mediterranean Sea, including Mahalab, Achzib,ᴬ ³⁰ Ummah, Aphek, and Rehob — twenty-two cities, with their settlements. ³¹ This was the inheritance of the tribe of Asher's descendants by their clans, these cities with their settlements.

NAPHTALI'S INHERITANCE

³² The sixth lot came out for Naphtali's descendants by their clans.

³³ Their boundary went from Heleph and from the oak in Zaanannim, including Adami-nekeb and Jabneel, as far as Lakkum, and ended at the Jordan. ³⁴ To the west, the boundary turned to Aznoth-tabor and went from there to Hukkok, reaching Zebulun on the south, Asher on the west, and Judahᴮ at the Jordan on the east. ³⁵ The fortified cities were Ziddim, Zer, Hammath, Rakkath, Chinnereth, ³⁶ Adamah, Ramah, Hazor, ³⁷ Kedesh, Edrei, En-hazor, ³⁸ Iron, Migdal-el, Horem, Beth-anath, and Beth-shemesh — nineteen cities, with their settlements. ³⁹ This was the inheritance of the tribe of Naphtali's descendants by their clans, the cities with their settlements.

DAN'S INHERITANCE

⁴⁰ The seventh lot came out for the tribe of Dan's descendants by their clans.

⁴¹ The territory of their inheritance included Zorah, Eshtaol, Ir-shemesh, ⁴² Shaalabbin, Aijalon, Ithlah, ⁴³ Elon, Timnah, Ekron, ⁴⁴ El-tekeh, Gibbethon, Baalath, ⁴⁵ Jehud, Bene-berak, Gath-rimmon, ⁴⁶ Me-jarkon, and Rakkon, with the territory facing Joppa.

⁴⁷ When the territory of the descendants of Dan slipped out of their control, they went up and fought against Leshem, captured it, and struck it down with the sword. So they took possession of it, lived there, and renamed Leshem after their ancestor Dan. ⁴⁸ This was the inheritance of the tribe of Dan's descendants by their clans, these cities with their settlements.

JOSHUA'S INHERITANCE

⁴⁹ When they had finished distributing the land into its territories, the Israelites gave Joshua son of Nun an inheritance among them. ⁵⁰ By the LORD's command, they gave him the city Timnath-serah in the hill country of Ephraim, which he requested. He rebuilt the city and lived in it.

⁵¹ These were the portions that the priest Eleazar, Joshua son of Nun, and the family heads distributed to the Israelite tribes by lot at Shiloh in the LORD's presence at the entrance to the tent of meeting. So they finished dividing up the land.

CITIES OF REFUGE

20 Then the LORD spoke to Joshua, ² "Tell the Israelites: Select your cities of refuge, as I instructed you through Moses, ³ so that a person who kills someone unintentionally or accidentally may flee there. These will be your refuge from the avenger of blood. ⁴ When someone flees to one

---

ᴬ19:29 Or *Sea, in the region of Achzib* ᴮ19:34 LXX omits *Judah* of these cities, stands at the entrance of the city gate, and states his case before[A] the elders of that city, they are to bring him into the city and give him a place to live among them. ⁵ And if the avenger of blood pursues him, they must not hand the one who committed manslaughter over to him, for he killed his neighbor accidentally and did not hate him beforehand. ⁶ He is to stay in that city until he stands trial before the assembly and until the death of the high priest serving at that time. Then the one who committed manslaughter may return home to his own city from which he fled."

⁷ So they designated Kedesh in the hill country of Naphtali in Galilee, Shechem in the hill country of Ephraim, and Kiriath-arba (that is, Hebron) in the hill country of Judah. ⁸ Across the Jordan east of Jericho, they selected Bezer on the wilderness plateau from Reuben's tribe, Ramoth in Gilead from Gad's tribe, and Golan in Bashan from Manasseh's tribe.

⁹ These are the cities appointed for all the Israelites and the aliens residing among them, so that anyone who kills a person unintentionally may flee there and not die at the hand of the avenger of blood until he stands before the assembly.

CITIES OF THE LEVITES

21 The Levite family heads approached the priest Eleazar, Joshua son of Nun, and the family heads of the Israelite tribes. ² At Shiloh, in the land of Canaan, they told them, "The Lord commanded through Moses that we be given cities to live in, with their pasturelands for our livestock." ³ So the Israelites, by the Lord's command, gave the Levites these cities with their pasturelands from their inheritance.

⁴ The lot came out for the Kohathite clans: The Levites who were the descendants of the priest Aaron received thirteen cities by lot from the tribes of Judah, Simeon, and Benjamin. ⁵ The remaining descendants of Kohath received ten cities by lot from the clans of the tribes of Ephraim, Dan, and half the tribe of Manasseh.

⁶ Gershon's descendants received thirteen cities by lot from the clans of the tribes of Issachar, Asher, Naphtali, and half the tribe of Manasseh in Bashan.

⁷ Merari's descendants received twelve cities for their clans from the tribes of Reuben, Gad, and Zebulun.

⁸ The Israelites gave these cities with their pasturelands around them to the Levites by lot, as the Lord had commanded through Moses.

CITIES OF AARON'S DESCENDANTS

⁹ The Israelites gave these cities by name from the tribes of the descendants of Judah and Simeon ¹⁰ to the descendants of Aaron from the Kohathite clans of the Levites, because they received the first lot. ¹¹ They gave them Kiriath-arba (that is, Hebron; Arba was the father of Anak) with its surrounding pasturelands in the hill country of Judah. ¹² But they gave the fields and settlements of the city to Caleb son of Jephunneh as his possession.

¹³ They gave to the descendants of the priest Aaron:

ᴬ20:4 Lit *in the ears of*

CLINGING TO GOD'S PROMISES

JOSHUA 20–21; GENESIS 12:1-3; 15:13-16

The nation of Israel had been through a lot.

They conquered the land of Canaan, driving out existing nations and taking over the land. They crossed the raging Jordan River. Before that, they wandered in the desert for forty years, waiting for God to signal when it was time to move. And before that, they were a nation of slaves, living in Egypt under hardship and oppression.

Yet God had His hand in all of it, like He does in our lives. In Genesis 15, God made a covenant promise to Abraham, spelling out exactly what would happen to his descendants.

God promised that Abraham would have numerous offspring. He kept that promise. The Israelites multiplied more and more the longer the Egyptians oppressed them (Ex 1:12).

God promised Abraham that his descendants would be enslaved for 400 years. And they were. The Egyptians worked the Israelites ruthlessly and made their lives bitter (Ex 1:13-14).

God also promised to judge the nation the Israelites served. Indeed, the Lord killed all the firstborn of Egypt and passed judgment against the gods of Egypt (Ex 12:12).

God promised that His people would leave the nation they served with overwhelming possessions. And they did. The Egyptians gave the Israelites silver, gold jewelry, and clothing as they left Egypt (Ex 12:35-36).

Finally, God promised to bring Abraham's descendants back to the promised land. In Joshua, we see God drive out the inhabitants of Canaan and give the land to Israel (Jos 21:43-44).

We serve the same God today. He makes promises to us as His children, just as He made promises to the house of Israel.

He will meet all our needs (Php 4:19).
He will provide for us (Mt 6:33).
He will never leave us or forsake us (Dt 31:8).
He has a purpose for us (Rm 8:28).

Remembering God's faithfulness in our past helps us cling to His promises in our present. When I struggle to believe that He will provide for my needs, I remember how He provided that check in the mail at exactly the right moment. When I'm overwhelmed with loneliness, I think of the friendships He's given me and how He Himself walked through dark moments with me. When I fear condemnation for my sin and mistakes, I recall the ways He's already redeemed my past.

God's promises are our foundation. He fulfills His every word. We can cling to His promises as we wander in the desert and fight the enemy. We can count on Him to come through.

"None of the good promises the LORD had made to the house of Israel failed. Everything was fulfilled."

JOSHUA 21:45

Hebron, the city of refuge for the one who commits manslaughter, with its pasturelands, Libnah with its pasturelands, ¹⁴ Jattir with its pasturelands, Eshtemoa with its pasturelands, ¹⁵ Holon with its pasturelands, Debir with its pasturelands, ¹⁶ Ain with its pasturelands, Juttah with its pasturelands, and Beth-shemesh with its pasturelands — nine cities from these two tribes.

¹⁷ From the tribe of Benjamin they gave:
Gibeon with its pasturelands, Geba with its pasturelands, ¹⁸ Anathoth with its pasturelands, and Almon with its pasturelands — four cities.
¹⁹ All thirteen cities with their pasturelands were for the priests, the descendants of Aaron.

CITIES OF KOHATH'S OTHER DESCENDANTS

²⁰ The allotted cities to the remaining clans of Kohath's descendants, who were Levites, came from the tribe of Ephraim. ²¹ The Israelites gave them:
Shechem, the city of refuge for the one who commits manslaughter, with its pasturelands in the hill country of Ephraim, Gezer with its pasturelands, ²² Kibzaim with its pasturelands, and Beth-horon with its pasturelands — four cities.

²³ From the tribe of Dan they gave:
Elteke with its pasturelands, Gibbethon with its pasturelands, ²⁴ Aijalon with its pasturelands, and Gath-rimmon with its pasturelands — four cities.

²⁵ From half the tribe of Manasseh they gave:
Taanach with its pasturelands and Gath-rimmon^A with its pasturelands — two cities.
²⁶ All ten cities with their pasturelands were for the clans of Kohath's other descendants.

CITIES OF GERSHON'S DESCENDANTS

²⁷ From half the tribe of Manasseh, they gave to the descendants of Gershon, who were one of the Levite clans:
Golan, the city of refuge for the one who commits manslaughter, with its pasturelands in Bashan, and Beeshterah with its pasturelands — two cities.

²⁸ From the tribe of Issachar they gave:
Kishion with its pasturelands, Daberath with its pasturelands, ²⁹ Jarmuth with its pasturelands, and En-gannim with its pasturelands — four cities.

³⁰ From the tribe of Asher they gave:
Mishal with its pasturelands, Abdon with its pasturelands, ³¹ Helkath with its pasturelands, and Rehob with its pasturelands — four cities.

^A 21:25 Or *Ibleam*

³² From the tribe of Naphtali they gave:
Kedesh in Galilee, the city of refuge for the one who commits manslaughter, with its pasturelands, Hammoth-dor with its pasturelands, and Kartan with its pasturelands — three cities.
³³ All thirteen cities with their pasturelands were for the Gershonites by their clans.

CITIES OF MERARI'S DESCENDANTS

³⁴ From the tribe of Zebulun, they gave to the clans of the descendants of Merari, who were the remaining Levites:
Jokneam with its pasturelands, Kartah with its pasturelands, ³⁵ Dimnah with its pasturelands, and Nahalal with its pasturelands — four cities.

³⁶ From the tribe of Reuben they gave:
Bezer with its pasturelands, Jahzah^A with its pasturelands, ³⁷ Kedemoth with its pasturelands, and Mephaath with its pasturelands — four cities.^B

³⁸ From the tribe of Gad they gave:
Ramoth in Gilead, the city of refuge for the one who commits manslaughter, with its pasturelands, Mahanaim with its pasturelands, ³⁹ Heshbon with its pasturelands, and Jazer with its pasturelands — four cities in all. ⁴⁰ All twelve cities were allotted to the clans of Merari's descendants, the remaining Levite clans.

⁴¹ Within the Israelite possession there were forty-eight cities in all with their pasturelands for the Levites. ⁴² Each of these cities had its own surrounding pasturelands; this was true for all the cities.

THE LORD'S PROMISES FULFILLED

⁴³ So the LORD gave Israel all the land he had sworn to give their fathers, and they took possession of it and settled there. ⁴⁴ The LORD gave them rest on every side according to all he had sworn to their fathers. None of their enemies were able to stand against them, for the LORD handed over all their enemies to them. ⁴⁵ None of the good promises the LORD had made to the house of Israel failed. Everything was fulfilled.

EASTERN TRIBES RETURN HOME

22 Joshua summoned the Reubenites, Gadites, and half the tribe of Manasseh ² and told them, "You have done everything Moses the LORD's servant commanded you and have obeyed me in everything I commanded you. ³ You have not deserted your brothers even once this whole time but have carried out the requirement of the command of the LORD your God. ⁴ Now that he has given your brothers rest, just as he promised them, return to your homes in your own land that Moses the LORD's servant gave you across the Jordan. ⁵ Only carefully obey the command and instruction that Moses the LORD's servant gave you: to love the LORD your God, walk in all his ways, keep his commands, be loyal to him, and serve him with all your heart and all your soul."

---

^A21:36 Or *Jahaz*   ^B21:36-37 Some Hb mss omit these vv.

⁶ Joshua blessed them and sent them on their way, and they went to their homes. ⁷ Moses had given territory to half the tribe of Manasseh in Bashan, but Joshua had given territory to the other half,ᴬ with their brothers, on the west side of the Jordan. When Joshua sent them to their homes and blessed them, ⁸ he said, "Return to your homes with great wealth: a huge number of cattle, and silver, gold, bronze, iron, and a large quantity of clothing. Share the spoil of your enemies with your brothers."

EASTERN TRIBES BUILD AN ALTAR

⁹ The Reubenites, Gadites, and half the tribe of Manasseh left the Israelites at Shiloh in the land of Canaan to return to their own land of Gilead, which they took possession of according to the LORD's command through Moses. ¹⁰ When they came to the region ofᴮ the Jordan in the land of Canaan, the Reubenites, Gadites, and half the tribe of Manasseh built a large, impressive altar there by the Jordan.

¹¹ Then the Israelites heard it said, "Look, the Reubenites, Gadites, and half the tribe of Manasseh have built an altar on the frontier of the land of Canaan at the region ofᶜ the Jordan, on the Israelite side." ¹² When the Israelites heard this, the entire Israelite community assembled at Shiloh to go to war against them.

EXPLANATION OF THE ALTAR

¹³ The Israelites sent Phinehas son of Eleazar the priest to the Reubenites, Gadites, and half the tribe of Manasseh, in the land of Gilead. ¹⁴ They sent ten leaders with him — one family leader for each tribe of Israel. All of them were heads of their ancestral familiesᴰ among the clans of Israel. ¹⁵ They went to the Reubenites, Gadites, and half the tribe of Manasseh, in the land of Gilead, and told them, ¹⁶ "This is what the LORD's entire community says: 'What is this treachery you have committed today against the God of Israel by turning away from the LORD and building an altar for yourselves, so that you are in rebellion against the LORD today? ¹⁷ Wasn't the iniquity of Peor, which brought a plague on the LORD's community, enough for us? We have not cleansed ourselves from it even to this day, ¹⁸ and now would you turn away from the LORD? If you rebel against the LORD today, tomorrow he will be angry with the entire community of Israel. ¹⁹ But if the land you possess is defiled, cross over to the land the LORD possesses where the LORD's tabernacle stands, and take possession of it among us. But don't rebel against the LORD or against us by building for yourselves an altar other than the altar of the LORD our God. ²⁰ Wasn't Achan son of Zerah unfaithful regarding what was set apart for destruction, bringing wrath on the entire community of Israel? He was not the only one who perished because of his iniquity.'"

²¹ The Reubenites, Gadites, and half the tribe of Manasseh answered the heads of the Israelite clans, ²² "The Mighty One, God, the LORD! The Mighty One, God, the LORD!ᴱ He knows, and may Israel also know. Do not spare us today, if it was in rebellion or treachery against the LORD ²³ that we have built for ourselves an altar to turn away from him. May the LORD himself hold us

---

ᴬ22:7 Lit to his half   ᴮ22:10 Or to Geliloth by   ᶜ22:11 Or at Geliloth by
ᴰ22:14 Lit the house of their fathers   ᴱ22:22 Or The LORD is the God of gods!
The LORD is the God of gods!

accountable if we intended to offer burnt offerings and grain offerings on it, or to sacrifice fellowship offerings on it. ²⁴ We actually did this from a specific concern that in the future your descendants might say to our descendants, 'What relationship do you have with the Lᴏʀᴅ, the God of Israel? ²⁵ For the Lᴏʀᴅ has made the Jordan a border between us and you descendants of Reuben and Gad. You have no share in the Lᴏʀᴅ!' So your descendants may cause our descendants to stop fearing the Lᴏʀᴅ.

²⁶ "Therefore we said: Let us take action and build an altar for ourselves, but not for burnt offering or sacrifice. ²⁷ Instead, it is to be a witness between us and you, and between the generations after us, so that we may carry out the worship of the Lᴏʀᴅ in his presence with our burnt offerings, sacrifices, and fellowship offerings. Then in the future, your descendants will not be able to say to our descendants, 'You have no share in the Lᴏʀᴅ!' ²⁸ We thought that if they said this to us or to our generations in the future, we would reply: Look at the replica of the Lᴏʀᴅ's altar that our fathers made, not for burnt offering or sacrifice, but as a witness between us and you. ²⁹ We would never ever rebel against the Lᴏʀᴅ or turn away from him today by building an altar for burnt offering, grain offering, or sacrifice, other than the altar of the Lᴏʀᴅ our God, which is in front of his tabernacle."

CONFLICT RESOLVED

³⁰ When the priest Phinehas and the community leaders, the heads of Israel's clans who were with him, heard what the descendants of Reuben, Gad, and Manasseh had to say, they were pleased. ³¹ Phinehas son of Eleazar the priest said to the descendants of Reuben, Gad, and Manasseh, "Today we know that the Lᴏʀᴅ is among us, because you have not committed this treachery against him. As a result, you have rescued the Israelites from the Lᴏʀᴅ's power."

³² Then the priest Phinehas son of Eleazar and the leaders returned from the Reubenites and Gadites in the land of Gilead to the Israelites in the land of Canaan and brought back a report to them. ³³ The Israelites were pleased with the report, and they blessed God. They spoke no more about going to war against them to ravage the land where the Reubenites and Gadites lived. ³⁴ So the Reubenites and Gadites named the altar: It^ is a witness between us that the Lᴏʀᴅ is God.

JOSHUA'S FAREWELL ADDRESS

23 A long time after the Lᴏʀᴅ had given Israel rest from all the enemies around them, Joshua was old, advanced in age. ² So Joshua summoned all Israel, including its elders, leaders, judges, and officers, and said to them, "I am old, advanced in age, ³ and you have seen for yourselves everything the Lᴏʀᴅ your God did to all these nations on your account, because it was the Lᴏʀᴅ your God who was fighting for you. ⁴ See, I have allotted these remaining nations to you as an inheritance for your tribes, including all the nations I have destroyed, from the Jordan westward to the Mediterranean Sea. ⁵ The Lᴏʀᴅ your God will force them back on your account and drive them out before you so that you can take possession of their land, as the Lᴏʀᴅ your God promised you.

^22:34 Some Hb mss, Syr, Tg read *altar Witness because it*

⁶ "Be very strong and continue obeying all that is written in the book of the law of Moses, so that you do not turn from it to the right or left ⁷ and so that you do not associate with these nations remaining among you. Do not call on the names of their gods or make an oath to them; do not serve them or bow in worship to them. ⁸ Instead, be loyal to the LORD your God, as you have been to this day.

⁹ "The LORD has driven out great and powerful nations before you, and no one is able to stand against you to this day. ¹⁰ One of you routed a thousand because the LORD your God was fighting for you, as he promised.ᴬ ¹¹ So diligently watch yourselves! Love the LORD your God! ¹² If you ever turn away and become loyal to the rest of these nations remaining among you, and if you intermarry or associate with them and they with you, ¹³ know for certain that the LORD your God will not continue to drive these nations out before you. They will become a snare and a trap for you, a sharp stickᴮ for your sides and thorns in your eyes, until you disappear from this good land the LORD your God has given you.

¹⁴ "I am now going the way of the whole earth, and you know with all your heart and all your soul that none of the good promises the LORD your God made to you has failed. Everything was fulfilled for you; not one promise has failed. ¹⁵ Since every good thing the LORD your God promised you has come about, so he will bring on you every bad thing until he has annihilated you from this good land the LORD your God has given you. ¹⁶ If you break the covenant of the LORD your God, which he commanded you, and go and serve other gods, and bow in worship to them, the LORD's anger will burn against you, and you will quickly disappear from this good land he has given you."

REVIEW OF ISRAEL'S HISTORY

24 Joshua assembled all the tribes of Israel at Shechem and summoned Israel's elders, leaders, judges, and officers, and they presented themselves before God. ² Joshua said to all the people, "This is what the LORD, the God of Israel, says: 'Long ago your ancestors, including Terah, the father of Abraham and Nahor, lived beyond the Euphrates River and worshiped other gods. ³ But I took your father Abraham from the region beyond the Euphrates River, led him throughout the land of Canaan, and multiplied his descendants. I gave him Isaac, ⁴ and to Isaac I gave Jacob and Esau. I gave the hill country of Seir to Esau as a possession.

" 'Jacob and his sons, however, went down to Egypt. ⁵ I sent Moses and Aaron, and I defeated Egypt by what I did within it, and afterward I brought you out. ⁶ When I brought your fathers out of Egypt and you reached the Red Sea, the Egyptians pursued your fathers with chariots and horsemen as far as the sea. ⁷ Your fathers cried out to the LORD, so he put darkness between you and the Egyptians, and brought the sea over them, engulfing them. Your own eyes saw what I did to Egypt. After that, you lived in the wilderness a long time.

⁸ " 'Later, I brought you to the land of the Amorites who lived beyond the Jordan. They fought against you, but I handed them over to you. You possessed their land, and I annihilated them before you. ⁹ Balak son of Zippor, king of Moab, set out to fight against Israel. He sent for Balaam son of Beor to

ᴬ23:10 Lit promised you   ᴮ23:13 Or a whip; Hb obscure

curse you, [10] but I would not listen to Balaam. Instead, he repeatedly blessed you, and I rescued you from him.

[11] " 'You then crossed the Jordan and came to Jericho. Jericho's citizens — as well as the Amorites, Perizzites, Canaanites, Hethites, Girgashites, Hivites, and Jebusites — fought against you, but I handed them over to you. [12] I sent hornets[A] ahead of you, and they drove out the two Amorite kings before you. It was not by your sword or bow. [13] I gave you a land you did not labor for, and cities you did not build, though you live in them; you are eating from vineyards and olive groves you did not plant.'

THE COVENANT RENEWAL

[14] "Therefore, fear the Lord and worship him in sincerity and truth. Get rid of the gods your fathers worshiped beyond the Euphrates River and in Egypt, and worship the Lord. [15] But if it doesn't please you to worship the Lord, choose for yourselves today: Which will you worship — the gods your fathers worshiped beyond the Euphrates River or the gods of the Amorites in whose land you are living? As for me and my family, we will worship the Lord."

[16] The people replied, "We will certainly not abandon the Lord to worship other gods! [17] For the Lord our God brought us and our fathers out of the land of Egypt, out of the place of slavery, and performed these great signs before our eyes. He also protected us all along the way we went and among all the peoples whose lands we traveled through. [18] The Lord drove out before us all the peoples, including the Amorites who lived in the land. We too will worship the Lord, because he is our God."

[19] But Joshua told the people, "You will not be able to worship the Lord, because he is a holy God. He is a jealous God; he will not forgive your transgressions and sins. [20] If you abandon the Lord and worship foreign gods, he will turn against you, harm you, and completely destroy you, after he has been good to you."

[21] "No!" the people answered Joshua. "We will worship the Lord."

[22] Joshua then told the people, "You are witnesses against yourselves that you yourselves have chosen to worship the Lord."

"We are witnesses," they said.

[23] "Then get rid of the foreign gods that are among you and turn your hearts to the Lord, the God of Israel."

[24] So the people said to Joshua, "We will worship the Lord our God and obey him."

[25] On that day Joshua made a covenant for the people at Shechem and established a statute and ordinance for them. [26] Joshua recorded these things in the book of the law of God; he also took a large stone and set it up there under the oak at the sanctuary of the Lord. [27] And Joshua said to all the people, "You see this stone — it will be a witness against us, for it has heard all the words the Lord said to us, and it will be a witness against you, so that you will not deny your God." [28] Then Joshua sent the people away, each to his own inheritance.

BURIAL OF THREE LEADERS

[29] After these things, the Lord's servant, Joshua son of Nun, died at the age of 110. [30] They buried him in his allotted territory at Timnath-serah, in the

---

A 24:12 Or sent terror

hill country of Ephraim north of Mount Gaash. [31] Israel worshiped the Lord throughout Joshua's lifetime and during the lifetimes of the elders who outlived Joshua and who had experienced all the works the Lord had done for Israel.

[32] Joseph's bones, which the Israelites had brought up from Egypt, were buried at Shechem in the parcel of land Jacob had purchased from the sons of Hamor, Shechem's father, for a hundred pieces of silver.[A] It was an inheritance for Joseph's descendants.

[33] And Eleazar son of Aaron died, and they buried him at Gibeah,[B] which had been given to his son Phinehas in the hill country of Ephraim.

[A]24:32 Lit a hundred qesitahs   [B]24:33 = the Hill

IN THOSE
DAYS THERE
WAS NO KING
IN ISRAEL
EVERYONE
DID WHATEVER
SEEMED RIGHT
TO HIM

judges

 In those days there was no king in Israel; everyone did whatever seemed right to him. **21:25**

ON THE TIMELINE The period of the Israelite judges took place between the conquest of the promised land under Joshua and the rise of the monarchy with Saul and David. The events can be safely dated from the beginning of the fourteenth century BC to the latter part of the eleventh century BC, a period of about 300 years (approximately 1380 BC to 1050 BC).

A LITTLE BACKGROUND When the book of Judges was written is not known with certainty. The Assyrian captivity of Israel is referenced in 18:30, which suggests a date of final editing after the exile of the northern kingdom in 722 BC. Meanwhile, the suggestion that readers could visit the site of Gideon's altar at Ophrah in 6:24 suggests a date prior to the exile of the southern kingdom, Judah, in 586 BC. The message of Judges would have resonated strongly at several points in Israel's history, and it has been argued that it fits well during the dark days of Manasseh (686–642 BC; 2Kg 21:1-18). Even so, it is still not possible to assign an exact date to the book.

MESSAGE & PURPOSE The book of Judges chronicles the moral and spiritual descent of Israel, from the relative high point at the beginning of the book through a series of downward spirals into the depths of degradation in chapters 17–21. Though God raised up a sequence of deliverers—the judges—they were unable to reverse this trend and some even became part of the problem themselves. By the end of the book, Israel had become as pagan and defiled as the Canaanites they had displaced.

GIVE THANKS FOR THE BOOK OF JUDGES:

The book of Judges shows us that the nation of Israel survived the dark days of the judges entirely by the grace of God. In mercy, He sent oppressors as re- minders of their rebellion. In mercy, He responded to their cries and raised up deliverers. Judges illustrates the fundamental problem of the human heart: when God's people forget His saving acts, they go after other gods. In the end, the book of Judges illustrates an eternal truth: the Lord will build His kingdom, in spite of our sin and rebellion.

THE JUDGES OF ISRAEL

LENGTH OF TERM AS JUDGE IN YEARS

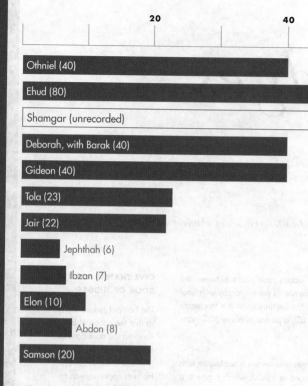

| | 20 | 40 | 60 | 80 Y |

Othniel (40)

Ehud (80)

Shamgar (unrecorded)

Deborah, with Barak (40)

Gideon (40)

Tola (23)

Jair (22)

Jephthah (6)

Ibzan (7)

Elon (10)

Abdon (8)

Samson (20)

Othniel JUDGES 3:7-11 Captured a powerful Canaanite city

Ehud JUDGES 3:12-30 Killed Eglon, king of Moab, and defeated the Moabites

Shamgar JUDGES 3:31 Killed 600 Philistines with an oxgoad

Deborah JUDGES 4–5 Defeated Sisera and the Canaanites and later sang a victory song with Barak

Gideon JUDGES 6–8 Destroyed his family idols, used a fleece to determine God's will, raised an army of 10,000, and defeated 135,000 Midianites with 300 soldiers

Tola JUDGES 10:1-2 Judged Israel for 23 years

Jair JUDGES 10:3-5 Had 30 sons

Jephthah JUDGES 10:6-12:7 Made a rash vow, defeated 20 Ammonite cities, and later battled jealous Ephraim

Ibzan JUDGES 12:8-10 Had 30 sons and 30 daughters

Elon JUDGES 12:11-12 Judged Israel for 10 years

Abdon JUDGES 12:13-15 Had 40 sons and 30 grandsons

Samson JUDGES 13–16 A Nazirite, killed a lion with his bare hands, burned the Philistine wheat fields, killed 1,000 Philistines with a donkey's jawbone, tore off an iron gate, was betrayed by Delilah, and destroyed thousands of Philistines in one last mighty act

READ AND UNDERSTAND JUDGES

The Bible is a complete work in which many stories combine to tell one story. As you read the book of Judges, consider reading the additional passages to discover how the whole of Scripture works together.

JUDAH'S LEADERSHIP AGAINST THE CANAANITES

1 After the death of Joshua, the Israelites inquired of the LORD, "Who will be the first to fight for us against the Canaanites?"

[2] The LORD answered, "Judah is to go. I have handed the land over to him."

[3] Judah said to his brother Simeon, "Come with me to my allotted territory, and let us fight against the Canaanites. I will also go with you to your allotted territory." So Simeon went with him.

[4] When Judah attacked, the LORD handed the Canaanites and Perizzites over to them. They struck down ten thousand men in Bezek. [5] They found Adoni-bezek in Bezek, fought against him, and struck down the Canaanites and Perizzites.

[6] When Adoni-bezek fled, they pursued him, caught him, and cut off his thumbs and big toes. [7] Adoni-bezek said, "Seventy kings with their thumbs and big toes cut off used to pick up scraps [A] under my table. God has repaid me for what I have done." They brought him to Jerusalem, and he died there.

[8] The men of Judah fought against Jerusalem, captured it, put it to the sword, and set the city on fire. [9] Afterward, the men of Judah marched down to fight against the Canaanites who were living in the hill country, the Negev, and the Judean foothills. [B] [10] Judah also marched against the Canaanites who were living in Hebron (Hebron was formerly named Kiriath-arba). They struck down Sheshai, Ahiman, and Talmai. [11] From there they marched against the residents of Debir (Debir was formerly named Kiriath-sepher).

[12] Caleb said, "Whoever attacks and captures Kiriath-sepher, I will give my daughter Achsah to him as a wife." [13] So Othniel son of Kenaz, Caleb's youngest brother, captured it, and Caleb gave his daughter Achsah to him as his wife.

[14] When she arrived, she persuaded Othniel to ask her father for a field. As she got off her donkey, Caleb asked her, "What do you want?" [15] She answered him, "Give me a blessing. Since you have given me land in the Negev, give me springs also." So Caleb gave her both the upper and lower springs.

[16] The descendants of the Kenite, Moses's father-in-law, had gone up with the men of Judah from the City of Palms [C] to the Wilderness of Judah, which was in the Negev of Arad. They went to live among the people.

[17] Judah went with his brother Simeon, struck the Canaanites who were living in Zephath, and completely destroyed the town. So they named the town Hormah. [18] Judah captured Gaza and its territory, Ashkelon and its territory, and Ekron and its territory. [19] The LORD was with Judah and enabled them to take possession of the hill country, but they could not drive out the people who were living in the valley because those people had iron chariots.

[20] Judah gave Hebron to Caleb, just as Moses had promised. Then Caleb drove out the three sons of Anak who lived there.

BENJAMIN'S FAILURE

[21] At the same time the Benjaminites did not drive out the Jebusites who were living in Jerusalem. The Jebusites have lived among the Benjaminites in Jerusalem to this day.

[A]1:7 Lit *toes cut off are gathering*   [B]1:9 Or *the Shephelah*   [C]1:16 = Jericho; Dt 34:3; Jdg 3:13; 2Ch 28:15

SUCCESS OF THE HOUSE OF JOSEPH

²² The house of Joseph also attacked Bethel, and the LORD was with them. ²³ They sent spies to Bethel (the town was formerly named Luz). ²⁴ The spies saw a man coming out of the town and said to him, "Please show us how to get into town, and we will show you kindness." ²⁵ When he showed them the way into the town, they put the town to the sword but released the man and his entire family. ²⁶ Then the man went to the land of the Hittites, built a town, and named it Luz. That is its name still today.

FAILURE OF THE OTHER TRIBES

²⁷ At that time Manasseh failed to take possession of Beth-shean and Taanach and their surrounding villages, or the residents of Dor, Ibleam, and Megiddo and their surrounding villages; the Canaanites were determined to stay in this land. ²⁸ When Israel became stronger, they made the Canaanites serve as forced labor but never drove them out completely.

²⁹ At that time Ephraim failed to drive out the Canaanites who were living in Gezer, so the Canaanites have lived among them in Gezer.

³⁰ Zebulun failed to drive out the residents of Kitron or the residents of Nahalol, so the Canaanites lived among them and served as forced labor.

³¹ Asher failed to drive out the residents of Acco or of Sidon, or Ahlab, Achzib, Helbah, Aphik, or Rehob. ³² The Asherites lived among the Canaanites who were living in the land, because they failed to drive them out.

³³ Naphtali did not drive out the residents of Beth-shemesh or the residents of Beth-anath. They lived among the Canaanites who were living in the land, but the residents of Beth-shemesh and Beth-anath served as their forced labor.

³⁴ The Amorites forced the Danites into the hill country and did not allow them to go down into the valley. ³⁵ The Amorites were determined to stay in ᴬ Har-heres, Aijalon, and Shaalbim. When the house of Joseph got the upper hand, ᴮ the Amorites ᶜ were made to serve as forced labor. ³⁶ The territory of the Amorites extended from the Scorpions' Ascent, that is from Sela upward.

PATTERN OF SIN AND JUDGMENT

2 The angel of the LORD went up from Gilgal to Bochim and said, "I brought you out of Egypt and led you into the land I had promised to your fathers. I also said: I will never break my covenant with you. ² You are not to make a covenant with the inhabitants of this land. You are to tear down their altars. But you have not obeyed me. What is this you have done? ³ Therefore, I now say: I will not drive out these people before you. They will be thorns ᴰ,ᴱ in your sides, and their gods will be a trap for you." ⁴ When the angel of the LORD had spoken these words to all the Israelites, the people wept loudly. ⁵ So they named that place Bochim ᶠ and offered sacrifices there to the LORD.

JOSHUA'S DEATH

⁶ Previously, when Joshua had sent the people away, the Israelites had gone to take possession of the land, each to his own inheritance. ⁷ The people

---

ᴬ1:35 Or *Amorites determined to live in*   ᴮ1:35 Lit *When the hand of the house of Joseph was heavy*   ᶜ1:35 LXX reads *Joseph became strong on the Amorites, they*   ᴰ2:3 LXX reads *affliction*   ᴱ2:3 Lit *traps*   ᶠ2:5 Or *Weeping* worshiped the Lord throughout Joshua's lifetime and during the lifetimes of the elders who outlived^A Joshua. They had seen all the Lord's great works he had done for Israel.

⁸ Joshua son of Nun, the servant of the Lord, died at the age of 110. ⁹ They buried him in the territory of his inheritance, in Timnath-heres, in the hill country of Ephraim, north of Mount Gaash. ¹⁰ That whole generation was also gathered to their ancestors. After them another generation rose up who did not know the Lord or the works he had done for Israel.

¹¹ The Israelites did what was evil in the Lord's sight. They worshiped the Baals ¹² and abandoned the Lord, the God of their fathers, who had brought them out of Egypt. They followed other gods from the surrounding peoples and bowed down to them. They angered the Lord, ¹³ for they abandoned him and worshiped Baal and the Ashtoreths.

¹⁴ The Lord's anger burned against Israel, and he handed them over to marauders who raided them. He sold them to^B the enemies around them, and they could no longer resist their enemies. ¹⁵ Whenever the Israelites went out, the Lord^C was against them and brought disaster on them, just as he had promised and sworn to them. So they suffered greatly.

¹⁶ The Lord raised up judges, who saved them from the power of their marauders, ¹⁷ but they did not listen to their judges. Instead, they prostituted themselves with other gods, bowing down to them. They quickly turned from the way of their fathers, who had walked in obedience to the Lord's commands. They did not do as their fathers did. ¹⁸ Whenever the Lord raised up a judge for the Israelites, the Lord was with him and saved the people from the power of their enemies while the judge was still alive.^D The Lord was moved to pity whenever they groaned because of those who were oppressing and afflicting them. ¹⁹ Whenever the judge died, the Israelites would act even more corruptly than their fathers, following other gods to serve them and bow in worship to them. They did not turn from their evil practices or their obstinate ways.

²⁰ The Lord's anger burned against Israel, and he declared, "Because this nation has violated my covenant that I made with their fathers and disobeyed me, ²¹ I will no longer drive out before them any of the nations Joshua left when he died. ²² I did this to test Israel and to see whether or not they would keep the Lord's way by walking in it, as their fathers had." ²³ The Lord left these nations and did not drive them out immediately. He did not hand them over to Joshua.

THE LORD TESTS ISRAEL

3 These are the nations the Lord left in order to test all those in Israel who had experienced^E none of the wars in Canaan. ² This was to teach the future generations of the Israelites how to fight in battle, especially those who had not fought before.^F ³ These nations included the five rulers of the Philistines and all of the Canaanites, the Sidonians, and the Hivites who lived in the Lebanese mountains from Mount Baal-hermon as far as the entrance to Hamath.^G ⁴ The Lord left them to test Israel, to determine if they would keep the Lord's commands he had given their fathers through^H Moses. ⁵ But

---

^A2:7 Lit *extended their days after* ^B2:14 Lit *into the hand of* ^C2:15 Lit *the hand of the Lord* ^D2:18 Lit *enemies all the days of the judge* ^E3:1 Lit *had known* ^F3:2 Lit *not known it* ^G3:3 Or *as Lebo-hamath* ^H3:4 Lit *by the hand of* they settled among the Canaanites, Hethites, Amorites, Perizzites, Hivites, and Jebusites. ⁶The Israelites took their daughters as wives for themselves, gave their own daughters to their sons, and worshiped their gods.

OTHNIEL, THE FIRST JUDGE

⁷The Israelites did what was evil in the LORD's sight; they forgot the LORD their God and worshiped the Baals and the Asherahs. ⁸The LORD's anger burned against Israel, and he sold them to ^A King Cushan-rishathaim ^B of Aram-na-haraim, ^C and the Israelites served him eight years.

⁹The Israelites cried out to the LORD. So the LORD raised up Othniel son of Kenaz, Caleb's youngest brother, as a deliverer to save the Israelites. ¹⁰The Spirit of the LORD came on him, and he judged Israel. Othniel went out to battle, and the LORD handed over King Cushan-rishathaim of Aram to him, so that Othniel overpowered him. ¹¹Then the land had peace for forty years, and Othniel son of Kenaz died.

EHUD

¹²The Israelites again did what was evil in the LORD's sight. He gave King Eglon of Moab power over Israel, because they had done what was evil in the LORD's sight. ¹³After Eglon convinced the Ammonites and the Amalekites to join forces with him, he attacked and defeated Israel and took possession of the City of Palms. ^D ¹⁴The Israelites served King Eglon of Moab eighteen years.

¹⁵Then the Israelites cried out to the LORD, and he raised up Ehud son of Gera, a left-handed Benjaminite, ^E as a deliverer for them. The Israelites sent him with the tribute for King Eglon of Moab.

¹⁶Ehud made himself a double-edged sword eighteen inches long. ^F He strapped it to his right thigh under his clothes ¹⁷and brought the tribute to King Eglon of Moab, who was an extremely fat man. ¹⁸When Ehud had finished presenting the tribute, he dismissed the people who had carried it. ¹⁹At the carved images near Gilgal he returned and said, "King Eglon, I have a secret message for you." The king said, "Silence!" and all his attendants left him. ²⁰Then Ehud approached him while he was sitting alone in his upstairs room where it was cool. Ehud said, "I have a message from God for you," and the king stood up from his throne. ²¹Ehud reached with his left hand, took the sword from his right thigh, and plunged it into Eglon's belly. ²²Even the handle went in after the blade, and Eglon's fat closed in over it, so that Ehud did not withdraw the sword from his belly. And the waste came out. ^G ²³Ehud escaped by way of the porch, closing and locking the doors of the upstairs room behind him.

²⁴Ehud was gone when Eglon's servants came in. They looked and found the doors of the upstairs room locked and thought he was relieving himself ^H in the cool room. ²⁵The servants waited until they became embarrassed and saw that he had still not opened the doors of the upstairs room. So they took the key and opened the doors — and there was their lord lying dead on the floor!

---

^A3:8 Lit into the hand of   ^B3:8 Lit Doubly-Evil   ^C3:8 = Mesopotamia
^D3:13 = Jericho; Dt 34:3; Jdg 1:16; 2Ch 28:15   ^E3:15 = son of the right hand
^F3:16 Lit sword a gomed in length   ^G3:22 Or And Eglon's bowels discharged
^H3:24 Lit was covering his feet

²⁶ Ehud escaped while the servants waited. He passed the Jordan near the carved images and reached Seirah. ²⁷ After he arrived, he sounded the ram's horn throughout the hill country of Ephraim. The Israelites came down with him from the hill country, and he became their leader. ²⁸ He told them, "Follow me, because the LORD has handed over your enemies, the Moabites, to you." So they followed him, captured the fords of the Jordan leading to Moab, and did not allow anyone to cross over. ²⁹ At that time they struck down about ten thousand Moabites, all stout and able-bodied men. Not one of them escaped. ³⁰ Moab became subject to Israel that day, and the land had peace for eighty years.

SHAMGAR

³¹ After Ehud, Shamgar son of Anath became judge. He also delivered Israel, striking down six hundred Philistines with a cattle prod.

DEBORAH AND BARAK

4 The Israelites again did what was evil in the sight of the LORD after Ehud had died. ² So the LORD sold them to King Jabin of Canaan, who reigned in Hazor. The commander of his army was Sisera who lived in Harosheth of the Nations.^A ³ Then the Israelites cried out to the LORD, because Jabin had nine hundred iron chariots, and he harshly oppressed them twenty years.

⁴ Deborah, a prophetess and the wife of Lappidoth, was judging Israel at that time. ⁵ She would sit under the palm tree of Deborah between Ramah and Bethel in the hill country of Ephraim, and the Israelites went up to her to settle disputes.

⁶ She summoned Barak son of Abinoam from Kedesh in Naphtali and said to him, "Hasn't the LORD, the God of Israel, commanded you: 'Go, deploy the troops on Mount Tabor, and take with you ten thousand men from the Naphtalites and Zebulunites? ⁷ Then I will lure Sisera commander of Jabin's army, his chariots, and his infantry at the Wadi Kishon to fight against you, and I will hand him over to you.' "

⁸ Barak said to her, "If you will go with me, I will go. But if you will not go with me, I will not go."

⁹ "I will gladly go with you," she said, "but you will receive no honor on the road you are about to take, because the LORD will sell Sisera to a woman." So Deborah got up and went with Barak to Kedesh. ¹⁰ Barak summoned Zebulun and Naphtali to Kedesh; ten thousand men followed him, and Deborah also went with him.

¹¹ Now Heber the Kenite had moved away from the Kenites, the sons of Hobab, Moses's father-in-law, and pitched his tent beside the oak tree of Zaanannim, which was near Kedesh.

¹² It was reported to Sisera that Barak son of Abinoam had gone up Mount Tabor. ¹³ Sisera summoned all his nine hundred iron chariots and all the troops who were with him from Harosheth of the Nations to the Wadi Kishon. ¹⁴ Then Deborah said to Barak, "Go! This is the day the LORD has handed Sisera over to you. Hasn't the LORD gone before you? " So Barak came down from Mount Tabor with ten thousand men following him.

^A 4:2 Or *Harosheth-ha-goiim*, also in vv. 13, 16

¹⁵ The LORD threw Sisera, all his charioteers, and all his army into a panic before Barak's assault. Sisera left his chariot and fled on foot. ¹⁶ Barak pursued the chariots and the army as far as Harosheth of the Nations, and the whole army of Sisera fell by the sword; not a single man was left.

¹⁷ Meanwhile, Sisera had fled on foot to the tent of Jael, the wife of Heber the Kenite, because there was peace between King Jabin of Hazor and the family of Heber the Kenite. ¹⁸ Jael went out to greet Sisera and said to him, "Come in, my lord. Come in with me. Don't be afraid." So he went into her tent, and she covered him with a blanket. ¹⁹ He said to her, "Please give me a little water to drink for I am thirsty." She opened a container of milk, gave him a drink, and covered him again. ²⁰ Then he said to her, "Stand at the entrance to the tent. If a man comes and asks you, 'Is there a man here?' say, 'No.'" ²¹ While he was sleeping from exhaustion, Heber's wife Jael took a tent peg, grabbed a hammer, and went silently to Sisera. She hammered the peg into his temple and drove it into the ground, and he died.

²² When Barak arrived in pursuit of Sisera, Jael went out to greet him and said to him, "Come and I will show you the man you are looking for." So he went in with her, and there was Sisera lying dead with a tent peg through his temple!

²³ That day God subdued King Jabin of Canaan before the Israelites. ²⁴ The power of the Israelites continued to increase against King Jabin of Canaan until they destroyed him.

DEBORAH'S SONG

5 On that day Deborah and Barak son of Abinoam sang:

² When the leaders lead[A] in Israel,
   when the people volunteer,
   blessed be the LORD.
³ Listen, kings! Pay attention, princes!
   I will sing to the LORD;
   I will sing praise to the LORD God of Israel.
⁴ LORD, when you came from Seir,
   when you marched from the fields of Edom,
   the earth trembled,
   the skies poured rain,
   and the clouds poured water.
⁵ The mountains melted before the LORD,
   even Sinai,[B] before the LORD, the God of Israel.

⁶ In the days of Shamgar son of Anath,
   in the days of Jael,
   the main roads were deserted
   because travelers kept to the side roads.
⁷ Villages were deserted,[C]
   they were deserted in Israel,
   until I,[D] Deborah, arose,
   a mother in Israel.

A 5:2 Or *the locks of hair are loose*   B 5:5 Or *LORD, this one of Sinai*   C 5:7 Hb obscure   D 5:7 Or *you*

⁸ Israel chose new gods,
then there was war in the city gates.
Not a shield or spear was seen
among forty thousand in Israel.

⁹ My heart is with the leaders of Israel,
with the volunteers of the people.
Blessed be the Lᴏʀᴅ!

¹⁰ You who ride on white ᴬ donkeys,
who sit on saddle blankets,
and who travel on the road, give praise!

¹¹ Let them tell the righteous acts of the Lᴏʀᴅ,
the righteous deeds of his warriors in Israel,
with the voices of the singers at the watering places. ᴬ

Then the Lᴏʀᴅ's people went down to the city gates.

¹² "Awake! Awake, Deborah!
Awake! Awake, sing a song!
Arise, Barak,
and take your prisoners,
son of Abinoam!"

¹³ Then the survivors came down to the nobles;
the Lᴏʀᴅ's people came down to me ᴮ
with the warriors.

¹⁴ Those with their roots in Amalek ᶜ came from Ephraim;
Benjamin came with your people after you.
The leaders came down from Machir,
and those who carry a marshal's staff came
from Zebulun.

¹⁵ The princes of Issachar were with Deborah;
Issachar was with Barak;
they were under his leadership ᴰ in the valley.
There was great searching ᴱ of heart
among the clans of Reuben.

¹⁶ Why did you sit among the sheep pens ᶠ
listening to the playing of pipes for the flocks?
There was great searching of heart
among the clans of Reuben.

¹⁷ Gilead remained beyond the Jordan.
Dan, why did you linger at the ships?
Asher remained at the seashore
and stayed in his harbors.

¹⁸ The people of Zebulun defied death,
Naphtali also, on the heights of the battlefield.

¹⁹ Kings came and fought.
Then the kings of Canaan fought

ᴬ5:10,11 Hb obscure   ᴮ5:13 LXX reads *down for him*   ᶜ5:14 LXX reads *in the valley*   ᴰ5:15 Lit *they set out as his feet*   ᴱ5:15 Some Hb mss, Syr read *There were great resolves*   ᶠ5:16 Or *the campfires*

at Taanach by the Waters of Megiddo,
but they did not plunder the silver.
20 The stars fought from the heavens;
the stars fought with Sisera from their paths.
21 The river Kishon swept them away,
the ancient river, the river Kishon.
March on, my soul, in strength!
22 The horses' hooves then hammered —
the galloping, galloping of his^A stallions.
23 "Curse Meroz," says the angel of the LORD,
"Bitterly curse her inhabitants,
for they did not come to help the LORD,
to help the LORD with the warriors."

24 Jael is most blessed of women,
the wife of Heber the Kenite;
she is most blessed among tent-dwelling women.
25 He asked for water; she gave him milk.
She brought him cream in a majestic bowl.
26 She reached for a tent peg,
her right hand, for a workman's hammer.
Then she hammered Sisera —
she crushed his head;
she shattered and pierced his temple.
27 He collapsed, he fell, he lay down
between her feet;
he collapsed, he fell between her feet;
where he collapsed, there he fell — dead.

28 Sisera's mother looked through the window;
she peered through the lattice, crying out:
"Why is his chariot so long in coming?
Why don't I hear the hoofbeats of his horses?"^B
29 Her wisest princesses answer her;
she even answers herself:^C
30 "Are they not finding and dividing the spoil —
a girl or two^D for each warrior,
the spoil of colored garments for Sisera,
the spoil of an embroidered garment or two
for my neck?"^E

31 LORD, may all your enemies perish as Sisera did.^F
But may those who love him
be like the rising of the sun in its strength.

And the land had peace for forty years.

---

^A 5:22 = Sisera's   ^B 5:28 Lit *Why have the hoofbeats of his chariots delayed*
^C 5:29 Lit *answers her words*   ^D 5:30 Lit *a womb or two wombs*   ^E 5:30 Hb
obscure   ^F 5:31 Lit *perish in this way*

MIDIAN OPPRESSES ISRAEL

6 The Israelites did what was evil in the sight of the LORD. So the LORD handed them over to Midian seven years, ² and they oppressed Israel. Because of Midian, the Israelites made hiding places for themselves in the mountains, caves, and strongholds. ³ Whenever the Israelites planted crops, the Midianites, Amalekites, and the Qedemites came and attacked them. ⁴ They encamped against them and destroyed the produce of the land, even as far as Gaza. They left nothing for Israel to eat, as well as no sheep, ox, or donkey. ⁵ For the Midianites came with their cattle and their tents like a great swarm of locusts. They and their camels were without number, and they entered the land to lay waste to it. ⁶ So Israel became poverty-stricken because of Midian, and the Israelites cried out to the LORD.

⁷ When the Israelites cried out to him because of Midian, ⁸ the LORD sent a prophet to them. He said to them, "This is what the LORD God of Israel says: 'I brought you out of Egypt and out of the place of slavery. ⁹ I rescued you from the power of Egypt and the power of all who oppressed you. I drove them out before you and gave you their land. ¹⁰ I said to you: I am the LORD your God. Do not fear the gods of the Amorites whose land you live in. But you did not obey me.'"

THE LORD CALLS GIDEON

¹¹ The angel of the LORD came, and he sat under the oak that was in Ophrah, which belonged to Joash, the Abiezrite. His son Gideon was threshing wheat in the winepress in order to hide it from the Midianites. ¹² Then the angel of the LORD appeared to him and said: "The LORD is with you, valiant warrior."

¹³ Gideon said to him, "Please, my lord, if the LORD is with us, why has all this happened? And where are all his wonders that our fathers told us about? They said, 'Hasn't the LORD brought us out of Egypt?' But now the LORD has abandoned us and handed us over to Midian."

¹⁴ The LORD turned to him and said, "Go in the strength you have and deliver Israel from the grasp of Midian. I am sending you!"

¹⁵ He said to him, "Please, Lord, how can I deliver Israel? Look, my family is the weakest in Manasseh, and I am the youngest in my father's family."

¹⁶ "But I will be with you," the LORD said to him. "You will strike Midian down as if it were one man."

¹⁷ Then he said to him, "If I have found favor with you, give me a sign that you are speaking with me. ¹⁸ Please do not leave this place until I return to you. Let me bring my gift and set it before you."

And he said, "I will stay until you return."

¹⁹ So Gideon went and prepared a young goat and unleavened bread from a half bushel^A of flour. He placed the meat in a basket and the broth in a pot. He brought them out and offered them to him under the oak.

²⁰ The angel of God said to him, "Take the meat with the unleavened bread, put it on this stone, and pour the broth on it." So he did that.

²¹ The angel of the LORD extended the tip of the staff that was in his hand and touched the meat and the unleavened bread. Fire came up from the rock and consumed the meat and the unleavened bread. Then the angel of the LORD vanished from his sight.

^A 6:19 Lit *an ephah*

²² When Gideon realized that he was the angel of the LORD, he said, "Oh no, Lord GOD! I have seen the angel of the LORD face to face!"

²³ But the LORD said to him, "Peace to you. Don't be afraid, for you will not die." ²⁴ So Gideon built an altar to the LORD there and called it The LORD Is Peace.ᴬ It is still in Ophrah of the Abiezrites today.

GIDEON TEARS DOWN A BAAL ALTAR

²⁵ On that very night the LORD said to him, "Take your father's young bull and a second bull seven years old. Then tear down the altar of Baal that belongs to your father and cut down the Asherah pole beside it. ²⁶ Build a well-constructed altar to the LORD your God on the top of this mound. Take the second bull and offer it as a burnt offering with the wood of the Asherah pole you cut down." ²⁷ So Gideon took ten of his male servants and did as the LORD had told him. But because he was too afraid of his father's family and the men of the city to do it in the daytime, he did it at night.

²⁸ When the men of the city got up in the morning, they found Baal's altar torn down, the Asherah pole beside it cut down, and the second bull offered up on the altar that had been built. ²⁹ They said to each other, "Who did this?" After they made a thorough investigation, they said, "Gideon son of Joash did it."

³⁰ Then the men of the city said to Joash, "Bring out your son. He must die, because he tore down Baal's altar and cut down the Asherah pole beside it."

³¹ But Joash said to all who stood against him, "Would you plead Baal's case for him? Would you save him? Whoever pleads his case will be put to death by morning! If he is a god, let him plead his own case because someone tore down his altar." ³² That day he was called Jerubbaal, since Joash said, "Let Baal contend with him," because he tore down his altar.

THE SIGN OF THE FLEECE

³³ All the Midianites, Amalekites, and Qedemites gathered together, crossed over the Jordan, and camped in the Jezreel Valley.

³⁴ The Spirit of the LORD envelopedᴮ Gideon, and he blew the ram's horn and the Abiezrites rallied behind him. ³⁵ He sent messengers throughout all of Manasseh, who rallied behind him. He also sent messengers throughout Asher, Zebulun, and Naphtali, who also came to meet him.

³⁶ Then Gideon said to God, "If you will deliver Israel by my hand, as you said, ³⁷ I will put a wool fleece here on the threshing floor. If dew is only on the fleece, and all the ground is dry, I will know that you will deliver Israel by my strength, as you said." ³⁸ And that is what happened. When he got up early in the morning, he squeezed the fleece and wrung dew out of it, filling a bowl with water.

³⁹ Gideon then said to God, "Don't be angry with me; let me speak one more time. Please allow me to make one more test with the fleece. Let it remain dry, and the dew be all over the ground." ⁴⁰ That night God did as Gideon requested: only the fleece was dry, and dew was all over the ground.

ᴬ6:24 = Yahweh-shalom   ᴮ6:34 Lit clothed; 1Ch 12:18; 2Ch 24:20

GOD SELECTS GIDEON'S ARMY

7 Jerubbaal (that is, Gideon) and all the troops who were with him, got up early and camped beside the spring of Harod. The camp of Midian was north of them, below the hill of Moreh, in the valley. ² The LORD said to Gideon, "You have too many troops for me to hand the Midianites over to them, or else Israel might elevate themselves over me and say,ᴬ 'My own strength saved me.' ³ Now announce to the troops: 'Whoever is fearful and trembling may turn back and leave Mount Gilead.' " So twenty-two thousand of the troops turned back, but ten thousand remained.

⁴ Then the LORD said to Gideon, "There are still too many troops. Take them down to the water, and I will test them for you there. If I say to you, 'This one can go with you,' he can go. But if I say about anyone, 'This one cannot go with you,' he cannot go." ⁵ So he brought the troops down to the water, and the LORD said to Gideon, "Separate everyone who laps water with his tongue like a dog. Do the same with everyone who kneels to drink." ⁶ The number of those who lapped with their hands to their mouths was three hundred men, and all the rest of the troops knelt to drink water. ⁷ The LORD said to Gideon, "I will deliver you with the three hundred men who lapped and hand the Midianites over to you. But everyone else is to go home." ⁸ So Gideon sent all the Israelites to their tents but kept the three hundred troops, who took the provisions and their trumpets. The camp of Midian was below him in the valley.

GIDEON SPIES ON THE MIDIANITE CAMP

⁹ That night the LORD said to him, "Get up and attack the camp, for I have handed it over to you. ¹⁰ But if you are afraid to attack the camp, go down with Purah your servant. ¹¹ Listen to what they say, and then you will be encouragedᴮ to attack the camp." So he went down with Purah his servant to the outpost of the troopsᶜ who were in the camp.

¹² Now the Midianites, Amalekites, and all the Qedemites had settled down in the valley like a swarm of locusts, and their camels were as innumerable as the sand on the seashore. ¹³ When Gideon arrived, there was a man telling his friend about a dream. He said, "Listen, I had a dream: a loaf of barley bread came tumbling into the Midianite camp, struck a tent, and it fell. The loaf turned the tent upside down so that it collapsed."

¹⁴ His friend answered: "This is nothing less than the sword of Gideon son of Joash, the Israelite. God has handed the entire Midianite camp over to him."

GIDEON ATTACKS THE MIDIANITES

¹⁵ When Gideon heard the account of the dream and its interpretation, he bowed in worship. He returned to Israel's camp and said, "Get up, for the LORD has handed the Midianite camp over to you." ¹⁶ Then he divided the three hundred men into three companies and gave each of the men a trumpet in one hand and an empty pitcher with a torch inside it in the other hand.

¹⁷ "Watch me," he said to them, "and do what I do. When I come to the outpost of the camp, do as I do. ¹⁸ When I and everyone with me blow our trumpets, you are also to blow your trumpets all around the camp. Then you will say, 'For the LORD and for Gideon!' "

ᴬ7:2 Lit brag against me ᴮ7:11 Lit then your hands will be strengthened
ᶜ7:11 Lit of those who were arranged in companies of 50

¹⁹ Gideon and the hundred men who were with him went to the outpost of the camp at the beginning of the middle watch after the sentries had been stationed. They blew their trumpets and broke the pitchers that were in their hands. ²⁰ The three companies blew their trumpets and shattered their pitchers. They held their torches in their left hands, their trumpets ᴬ in their right hands, and shouted, "A sword for the LORD and for Gideon!" ²¹ Each Israelite took his position around the camp, and the entire Midianite army began to run, and they cried out as they fled. ²² When Gideon's men blew their three hundred trumpets, the LORD caused the men in the whole army to turn on each other with their swords. They fled to Acacia House ᴮ in the direction of Zererah as far as the border of Abel-meholah near Tabbath. ²³ Then the men of Israel were called from Naphtali, Asher, and Manasseh, and they pursued the Midianites.

THE MEN OF EPHRAIM JOIN THE BATTLE

²⁴ Gideon sent messengers throughout the hill country of Ephraim with this message: "Come down to intercept the Midianites and take control of the watercourses ahead of them as far as Beth-barah and the Jordan." So all the men of Ephraim were called out, and they took control of the watercourses as far as Beth-barah and the Jordan. ²⁵ They captured Oreb and Zeeb, the two princes of Midian; they killed Oreb at the rock of Oreb and Zeeb at the winepress of Zeeb, while they were pursuing the Midianites. They brought the heads of Oreb and Zeeb to Gideon across the Jordan.

8 The men of Ephraim said to him, "Why have you done this to us, not calling us when you went to fight against the Midianites?" And they argued with him violently.

² So he said to them, "What have I done now compared to you? Is not the gleaning of Ephraim better than the grape harvest of Abiezer? ³ God handed over to you Oreb and Zeeb, the two princes of Midian. What was I able to do compared to you?" When he said this, their anger against him subsided.

GIDEON PURSUES THE KINGS OF MIDIAN

⁴ Gideon and the three hundred men came to the Jordan and crossed it. They were exhausted but still in pursuit. ⁵ He said to the men of Succoth, "Please give some loaves of bread to the troops under my command, ᶜ because they are exhausted, for I am pursuing Zebah and Zalmunna, the kings of Midian."

⁶ But the princes of Succoth asked, "Are ᴰ Zebah and Zalmunna now in your hands that we should give bread to your army?"

⁷ Gideon replied, "Very well, when the LORD has handed Zebah and Zalmunna over to me, I will tear ᴱ your flesh with thorns and briers from the wilderness!" ⁸ He went from there to Penuel and asked the same thing from them. The men of Penuel answered just as the men of Succoth had answered. ⁹ He also told the men of Penuel, "When I return safely, I will tear down this tower!"

¹⁰ Now Zebah and Zalmunna were in Karkor, and with them was their army of about fifteen thousand men, who were all those left of the entire army of the Qedemites. Those who had been killed were one hundred twenty

---

ᴬ7:20 Lit *trumpets to blow*   ᴮ7:22 Or *Beth-shittah*   ᶜ8:5 Lit *troops at my feet*
ᴰ8:6 Lit *Are the hands of*, also in v. 15   ᴱ8:7 Lit *thresh*

thousand armed men.^A ^11 Gideon traveled on the caravan route^B east of No-bah and Jogbehah and attacked their army while the army felt secure. ^12 Ze-bah and Zalmunna fled, and he pursued them. He captured these two kings of Midian and routed the entire army.

^13 Gideon son of Joash returned from the battle by the Ascent of Heres. ^14 He captured a youth from the men of Succoth and interrogated him. The youth wrote down for him the names of the seventy-seven leaders and elders of Succoth. ^15 Then he went to the men of Succoth and said, "Here are Zebah and Zalmunna. You taunted me about them, saying, 'Are Zebah and Zalmun-na now in your power that we should give bread to your exhausted men?'" ^16 So he took the elders of the city, and he took some thorns and briers from the wilderness, and he disciplined the men of Succoth with them. ^17 He also tore down the tower of Penuel and killed the men of the city.

^18 He asked Zebah and Zalmunna, "What kind of men did you kill at Tabor?"

"They were like you," they said. "Each resembled the son of a king."

^19 So he said, "They were my brothers, the sons of my mother! As the LORD lives, if you had let them live, I would not kill you." ^20 Then he said to Jether, his firstborn, "Get up and kill them." The youth did not draw his sword, for he was afraid because he was still a youth.

^21 Zebah and Zalmunna said, "Get up and strike us down yourself, for a man is judged by his strength." So Gideon got up, killed Zebah and Zalmun-na, and took the crescent ornaments that were on the necks of their camels.

GIDEON'S LEGACY

^22 Then the Israelites said to Gideon, "Rule over us, you as well as your sons and your grandsons, for you delivered us from the power of Midian."

^23 But Gideon said to them, "I will not rule over you, and my son will not rule over you; the LORD will rule over you." ^24 Then he said to them, "Let me make a request of you: Everyone give me an earring from his plunder." Now the enemy had gold earrings because they were Ishmaelites.

^25 They said, "We agree to give them." So they spread out a cloak, and every-one threw an earring from his plunder on it. ^26 The weight of the gold earrings he requested was forty-three pounds^C of gold, in addition to the crescent or-naments and ear pendants, the purple garments on the kings of Midian, and the chains on the necks of their camels. ^27 Gideon made an ephod from all this and put it in Ophrah, his hometown. Then all Israel prostituted themselves by worshiping it there, and it became a snare to Gideon and his household.

^28 So Midian was subdued before the Israelites, and they were no longer a threat.^D The land had peace for forty years during the days of Gideon. ^29 Jer-ubbaal (that is, Gideon) son of Joash went back to live at his house.

^30 Gideon had seventy sons, his own offspring, since he had many wives. ^31 His concubine who was in Shechem also bore him a son, and he named him Abimelech. ^32 Then Gideon son of Joash died at a good old age and was buried in the tomb of his father Joash in Ophrah of the Abiezrites.

^33 When Gideon died, the Israelites turned and prostituted themselves by worshiping the Baals and made Baal-berith^E their god. ^34 The Israelites did

---

^A 8:10 Lit *men who drew the sword* ^B 8:11 Lit *on the route of those who live in tents* ^C 8:26 Lit *1,700 shekels* ^D 8:28 Lit *they no longer raised their head* ^E 8:33 Lit *Baal of the Covenant,* or *Lord of the Covenant* not remember the LORD their God who had rescued them from the hand of the enemies around them. ³⁵ They did not show kindness to the house of Jerubbaal (that is, Gideon) for all the good he had done for Israel.

ABIMELECH BECOMES KING

9 Abimelech son of Jerubbaal went to Shechem and spoke to his uncles and to his mother's whole clan, saying, ² "Please speak in the hearing of all the citizens of Shechem, 'Is it better for you that seventy men, all the sons of Jerubbaal, rule over you or that one man rule over you?' Remember that I am your own flesh and blood." ^A

³ His mother's relatives spoke all these words about him in the hearing of all the citizens of Shechem, and they were favorable to Abimelech, for they said, "He is our brother." ⁴ So they gave him seventy pieces of silver from the temple of Baal-berith. ^B Abimelech used it to hire worthless and reckless men, and they followed him. ⁵ He went to his father's house in Ophrah and killed his seventy brothers, the sons of Jerubbaal, on top of a large stone. But Jotham, the youngest son of Jerubbaal, survived, because he hid. ⁶ Then all the citizens of Shechem and of Beth-millo gathered together and proceeded to make Abimelech king at the oak of the pillar in Shechem.

JOTHAM'S PARABLE

⁷ When they told Jotham, he climbed to the top of Mount Gerizim, raised his voice, and called to them:

Listen to me, citizens of Shechem,
and may God listen to you:

⁸ The trees decided
to anoint a king over themselves.
They said to the olive tree, "Reign over us."
⁹ But the olive tree said to them,
"Should I stop giving my oil
that people use to honor both God and men,
and rule ^C over the trees?"

¹⁰ Then the trees said to the fig tree,
"Come and reign over us."
¹¹ But the fig tree said to them,
"Should I stop giving
my sweetness and my good fruit,
and rule over trees?"

¹² Later, the trees said to the grapevine,
"Come and reign over us."
¹³ But the grapevine said to them,
"Should I stop giving my wine
that cheers both God and man,
and rule over trees?"

---

^A 9:2 Lit your bone and your flesh ^B 9:4 Lit Baal of the Covenant, or Lord of the Covenant ^C 9:9 Lit and go to sway, also in vv. 11,13

¹⁴ Finally, all the trees said to the bramble,
"Come and reign over us."
¹⁵ The bramble said to the trees,
"If you really are anointing me
as king over you,
come and find refuge in my shade.
But if not,
may fire come out from the bramble
and consume the cedars of Lebanon."

¹⁶ "Now if you have acted faithfully and honestly in making Abimelech king, if you have done well by Jerubbaal and his family, and if you have rewarded him appropriately for what he did — ¹⁷ for my father fought for you, risked his life, and rescued you from Midian, ¹⁸ and now you have attacked my father's family today, killed his seventy sons on top of a large stone, and made Abimelech, the son of his slave woman, king over the citizens of Shechem 'because he is your brother' — ¹⁹ so if you have acted faithfully and honestly with Jerubbaal and his house this day, rejoice in Abimelech and may he also rejoice in you. ²⁰ But if not, may fire come from Abimelech and consume the citizens of Shechem and Beth-millo, and may fire come from the citizens of Shechem and Beth-millo and consume Abimelech." ²¹ Then Jotham fled, escaping to Beer, and lived there because of his brother Abimelech.

ABIMELECH'S PUNISHMENT

²² When Abimelech had ruled over Israel three years, ²³ God sent an evil spirit between Abimelech and the citizens of Shechem. They treated Abimelech deceitfully, ²⁴ so that the crime against the seventy sons of Jerubbaal might come to justice and their blood would be avenged on their brother Abimelech, who killed them, and on the citizens of Shechem, who had helped him^A kill his brothers. ²⁵ The citizens of Shechem rebelled against him by putting men in ambush on the tops of the mountains, and they robbed everyone who passed by them on the road. So this was reported to Abimelech.

²⁶ Gaal son of Ebed came with his brothers and crossed into Shechem, and the citizens of Shechem trusted him. ²⁷ So they went out to the countryside and harvested grapes from their vineyards. They trampled the grapes and held a celebration. Then they went to the house of their god, and as they ate and drank, they cursed Abimelech. ²⁸ Gaal son of Ebed said, "Who is Abimelech and who is Shechem that we should serve him? Isn't he the son of Jerubbaal, and isn't Zebul his officer? You are to serve the men of Hamor, the father of Shechem. Why should we serve Abimelech? ²⁹ If only these people were in my power, I would remove Abimelech." So he said^B to Abimelech, "Gather your army and come out."

³⁰ When Zebul, the ruler of the city, heard the words of Gaal son of Ebed, he was angry. ³¹ So he secretly sent messengers to Abimelech, saying, "Beware! Gaal son of Ebed, with his brothers, have come to Shechem and are turning the city against you.^C ³² Now tonight, you and the troops with you, come and wait in ambush in the countryside. ³³ Then get up early, and at sunrise attack

---

^A9:24 Lit *had strengthened his hands*   ^B9:29 DSS read *They said*; LXX reads *I would say*   ^C9:31 Hb obscure

the city. When he and the troops who are with him come out against you, do to him whatever you can." ³⁴ So Abimelech and all the troops with him got up at night and waited in ambush for Shechem in four units.

³⁵ Gaal son of Ebed went out and stood at the entrance of the city gate. Then Abimelech and the troops who were with him got up from their ambush. ³⁶ When Gaal saw the troops, he said to Zebul, "Look, troops are coming down from the mountaintops!" But Zebul said to him, "The shadows of the mountains look like men to you."

³⁷ Then Gaal spoke again, "Look, troops are coming down from the central part of the land, and one unit is coming from the direction of the Diviners' Oak." ³⁸ Zebul replied, "What do you have to say now? You said, 'Who is Abimelech that we should serve him?' Aren't these the troops you despised? Now go and fight them!"

³⁹ So Gaal went out leading the citizens of Shechem and fought against Abimelech, ⁴⁰ but Abimelech pursued him, and Gaal fled before him. Numerous bodies were strewn as far as the entrance of the city gate. ⁴¹ Abimelech stayed in Arumah, and Zebul drove Gaal and his brothers from Shechem.

⁴² The next day when the people of Shechem ᴬ went into the countryside, this was reported to Abimelech. ⁴³ He took the troops, divided them into three companies, and waited in ambush in the countryside. He looked, and the people were coming out of the city, so he arose against them and struck them down. ⁴⁴ Then Abimelech and the units that were with him rushed forward and took their stand at the entrance of the city gate. The other two units rushed against all who were in the countryside and struck them down. ⁴⁵ So Abimelech fought against the city that entire day, captured it, and killed the people who were in it. Then he tore down the city and sowed it with salt.

⁴⁶ When all the citizens of the Tower of Shechem heard, they entered the inner chamber ᴮ of the temple of El-berith. ᶜ ⁴⁷ Then it was reported to Abimelech that all the citizens of the Tower of Shechem had gathered. ⁴⁸ So Abimelech and all the troops who were with him went up to Mount Zalmon. Abimelech took his ax in his hand and cut a branch from the trees. He picked up the branch, put it on his shoulder, and said to the troops who were with him, "Hurry and do what you have seen me do." ⁴⁹ Each of the troops also cut his own branch and followed Abimelech. They put the branches against the inner chamber and set it on fire; about a thousand men and women died, including all the men of the Tower of Shechem.

⁵⁰ Abimelech went to Thebez, camped against it, and captured it. ⁵¹ There was a strong tower inside the city, and all the men, women, and citizens of the city fled there. They locked themselves in and went up to the roof of the tower. ⁵² When Abimelech came to attack the tower, he approached its entrance to set it on fire. ⁵³ But a woman threw the upper portion of a millstone on Abimelech's head and fractured his skull. ⁵⁴ He quickly called his armor-bearer and said to him, "Draw your sword and kill me, or they'll say about me, 'A woman killed him.'" So his armor-bearer ran him through, and he died. ⁵⁵ When the Israelites saw that Abimelech was dead, they all went home.

⁵⁶ In this way, God brought back Abimelech's evil—the evil that Abimelech had done to his father when he killed his seventy brothers. ⁵⁷ God also

---

ᴬ9:42 *of Shechem* supplied for clarity   ᴮ9:46 Or *the crypt,* or *the vault*
ᶜ9:46 = God of the Covenant

brought back to the men of Shechem all their evil. So the curse of Jotham son of Jerubbaal came upon them.

TOLA AND JAIR

10 After Abimelech, Tola son of Puah, son of Dodo became judge and began to deliver Israel. He was from Issachar and lived in Shamir in the hill country of Ephraim. ² Tola judged Israel twenty-three years and when he died, was buried in Shamir.

³ After him came Jair the Gileadite, who judged Israel twenty-two years. ⁴ He had thirty sons who rode on thirty donkeys. They had thirty towns^A^ in Gilead, which are still called Jair's Villages^B^ today. ⁵ When Jair died, he was buried in Kamon.

ISRAEL'S REBELLION AND REPENTANCE

⁶ Then the Israelites again did what was evil in the sight of the LORD. They worshiped the Baals and the Ashtoreths, the gods of Aram, Sidon, and Moab, and the gods of the Ammonites and the Philistines. They abandoned the LORD and did not worship him. ⁷ So the LORD's anger burned against Israel, and he sold them to^C^ the Philistines and the Ammonites. ⁸ They shattered and crushed the Israelites that year, and for eighteen years they did the same to all the Israelites who were on the other side of the Jordan in the land of the Amorites in Gilead. ⁹ The Ammonites also crossed the Jordan to fight against Judah, Benjamin, and the house of Ephraim. Israel was greatly oppressed, ¹⁰ so they cried out to the LORD, saying, "We have sinned against you. We have abandoned our God and worshiped the Baals."

¹¹ The LORD said to the Israelites, "When the Egyptians, Amorites, Ammonites, Philistines, ¹² Sidonians, Amalekites, and Maonites^D^ oppressed you, and you cried out to me, did I not deliver you from them? ¹³ But you have abandoned me and worshiped other gods. Therefore, I will not deliver you again. ¹⁴ Go and cry out to the gods you have chosen. Let them deliver you whenever you are oppressed."

¹⁵ But the Israelites said, "We have sinned. Deal with us as you see fit;^E^ only rescue us today!" ¹⁶ So they got rid of the foreign gods among them and worshiped the LORD, and he became weary of Israel's misery.

¹⁷ The Ammonites were called together, and they camped in Gilead. So the Israelites assembled and camped at Mizpah. ¹⁸ The rulers^F^ of Gilead said to one another, "Which man will begin the fight against the Ammonites? He will be the leader of all the inhabitants of Gilead."

JEPHTHAH BECOMES ISRAEL'S LEADER

11 Jephthah the Gileadite was a valiant warrior, but he was the son of a prostitute, and Gilead was his father. ² Gilead's wife bore him sons, and when they grew up, they drove Jephthah out and said to him, "You will have no inheritance in our father's family, because you are the son of another woman." ³ So Jephthah fled from his brothers and lived in the land of Tob. Then some worthless men joined Jephthah and went on raids with him.

---

^A^10:4 LXX; MT reads *donkeys* ^B^10:4 Or *called Havvoth-jair* ^C^10:7 Lit *into the hand of* ^D^10:12 LXX reads *Midianites* ^E^10:15 Lit *Do to us what is good in your eyes* ^F^10:18 Lit *The people, rulers*

⁴ Some time later, the Ammonites fought against Israel. ⁵ When the Ammonites made war with Israel, the elders of Gilead went to get Jephthah from the land of Tob. ⁶ They said to him, "Come, be our commander, and let's fight the Ammonites."

⁷ Jephthah replied to the elders of Gilead, "Didn't you hate me and drive me out of my father's family? Why then have you come to me now when you're in trouble?"

⁸ They answered Jephthah, "That's true. But now we turn to you. Come with us, fight the Ammonites, and you will become leader of all the inhabitants of Gilead."

⁹ So Jephthah said to them, "If you are bringing me back to fight the Ammonites and the LORD gives them to me, I will be your leader."

¹⁰ The elders of Gilead said to Jephthah, "The LORD is our witness if we don't do as you say." ¹¹ So Jephthah went with the elders of Gilead. The people made him their leader and commander, and Jephthah repeated all his terms in the presence of the LORD at Mizpah.

JEPHTHAH REJECTS AMMONITE CLAIMS

¹² Jephthah sent messengers to the king of the Ammonites, asking, "What do you have against me that you have come to fight me in my land?"

¹³ The king of the Ammonites said to Jephthah's messengers, "When Israel came from Egypt, they seized my land from the Arnon to the Jabbok and the Jordan. Now restore it peaceably."

¹⁴ Jephthah again sent messengers to the king of the Ammonites ¹⁵ to tell him, "This is what Jephthah says: Israel did not take away the land of Moab or the land of the Ammonites. ¹⁶ But when they came from Egypt, Israel traveled through the wilderness to the Red Sea and came to Kadesh. ¹⁷ Israel sent messengers to the king of Edom, saying, 'Please let us travel through your land,' but the king of Edom would not listen. They also sent messengers to the king of Moab, but he refused. So Israel stayed in Kadesh.

¹⁸ "Then they traveled through the wilderness and around the lands of Edom and Moab. They came to the east side of the land of Moab and camped on the other side of the Arnon but did not enter into the territory of Moab, for the Arnon was the boundary of Moab.

¹⁹ "Then Israel sent messengers to Sihon king of the Amorites, king of Heshbon. Israel said to him, 'Please let us travel through your land to our country,' ²⁰ but Sihon would not trust Israel to pass through his territory. Instead, Sihon gathered all his troops, camped at Jahaz, and fought with Israel. ²¹ Then the LORD God of Israel handed over Sihon and all his troops to Israel, and they defeated them. So Israel took possession of the entire land of the Amorites who lived in that country. ²² They took possession of all the territory of the Amorites from the Arnon to the Jabbok and from the wilderness to the Jordan.

²³ "The LORD God of Israel has now driven out the Amorites before his people Israel, and will you now force us out? ²⁴ Isn't it true that you can have whatever your god Chemosh conquers for you, and we can have whatever the LORD our God conquers for us? ²⁵ Now are you any better than Balak son of Zippor, king of Moab? Did he ever contend with Israel or fight against them? ²⁶ While Israel lived three hundred years in Heshbon and Aroer and their surrounding villages, and in all the cities that are on the banks of the Arnon,

why didn't you take them back at that time? [27] I have not sinned against you, but you are doing me wrong by fighting against me. Let the LORD who is the judge decide today between the Israelites and the Ammonites." [28] But the king of the Ammonites would not listen to Jephthah's message that he sent him.

JEPHTHAH'S VOW AND SACRIFICE

[29] The Spirit of the LORD came on Jephthah, who traveled through Gilead and Manasseh, and then through Mizpah of Gilead. He crossed over to the Ammonites from Mizpah of Gilead. [30] Jephthah made this vow to the LORD: "If you in fact hand over the Ammonites to me, [31] whoever comes out the doors of my house to greet me when I return safely from the Ammonites will belong to the LORD, and I will offer that person as a burnt offering."

[32] Jephthah crossed over to the Ammonites to fight against them, and the LORD handed them over to him. [33] He defeated twenty of their cities with a great slaughter from Aroer all the way to the entrance of Minnith and to Abel-keramim. So the Ammonites were subdued before the Israelites.

[34] When Jephthah went to his home in Mizpah, there was his daughter, coming out to meet him with tambourines and dancing! She was his only child; he had no other son or daughter besides her. [35] When he saw her, he tore his clothes and said, "No! Not my daughter! You have devastated me! You have brought great misery on me.^A I have given my word to the LORD and cannot take it back."

[36] Then she said to him, "My father, you have given your word to the LORD. Do to me as you have said, for the LORD brought vengeance on your enemies, the Ammonites." [37] She also said to her father, "Let me do this one thing: Let me wander two months through the mountains with my friends and mourn my virginity."

[38] "Go," he said. And he sent her away two months. So she left with her friends and mourned her virginity as she wandered through the mountains. [39] At the end of two months, she returned to her father, and he kept the vow he had made about her. And she had never been intimate with a man. Now it became a custom in Israel [40] that four days each year the young women of Israel would commemorate the daughter of Jephthah the Gileadite.

CONFLICT WITH EPHRAIM

12 The men of Ephraim were called together and crossed the Jordan to Zaphon. They said to Jephthah, "Why have you crossed over to fight against the Ammonites but didn't call us to go with you? We will burn your house with you in it!"

[2] Then Jephthah said to them, "My people and I had a bitter conflict with the Ammonites. So I called for you, but you didn't deliver me from their power. [3] When I saw that you weren't going to deliver me, I took my life in my own hands and crossed over to the Ammonites, and the LORD handed them over to me. Why then have you come today to fight against me?"

[4] Then Jephthah gathered all of the men of Gilead. They fought and defeated Ephraim, because Ephraim had said, "You Gileadites are Ephraimite fugitives in the territories of Ephraim and Manasseh." [5] The Gileadites captured the fords of the Jordan leading to Ephraim. Whenever a fugitive

^A 11:35 Lit *have been among those who trouble me*

from Ephraim said, "Let me cross over," the Gileadites asked him, "Are you an Ephraimite?" If he answered, "No," ⁶ they told him, "Please say Shibboleth." If he said, "Sibboleth," because he could not pronounce it correctly, they seized him and executed him at the fords of the Jordan. At that time forty-two thousand from Ephraim died.

⁷ Jephthah judged Israel six years, and when he died, he was buried in one of the cities of Gilead.ᴬ

IBZAN, ELON, AND ABDON

⁸ Ibzan, who was from Bethlehem, judged Israel after Jephthah ⁹ and had thirty sons. He gave his thirty daughters in marriage to men outside the tribe and brought back thirty wives for his sons from outside the tribe. Ibzan judged Israel seven years, ¹⁰ and when he died, he was buried in Bethlehem.

¹¹ Elon, who was from Zebulun, judged Israel after Ibzan. He judged Israel ten years, ¹² and when he died, he was buried in Aijalon in the land of Zebulun.

¹³ After Elon, Abdon son of Hillel, who was from Pirathon, judged Israel. ¹⁴ He had forty sons and thirty grandsons, who rode on seventy donkeys. Abdon judged Israel eight years, ¹⁵ and when he died, he was buried in Pirathon in the land of Ephraim, in the hill country of the Amalekites.

BIRTH OF SAMSON

13 The Israelites again did what was evil in the LORD's sight, so the LORD handed them over to the Philistines forty years. ² There was a certain man from Zorah, from the family of Dan, whose name was Manoah; his wife was unable to conceive and had no children. ³ The angel of the LORD appeared to the woman and said to her, "It is true that you are unable to conceive and have no children, but you will conceive and give birth to a son. ⁴ Now please be careful not to drink wine or beer, or to eat anything unclean; ⁵ for indeed, you will conceive and give birth to a son. You must never cut his hair,ᴮ because the boy will be a Nazirite to God from birth, and he will begin to save Israel from the power of the Philistines."

⁶ Then the woman went and told her husband, "A man of God came to me. He looked like the awe-inspiring angel of God. I didn't ask him where he came from, and he didn't tell me his name. ⁷ He said to me, 'You will conceive and give birth to a son. Therefore, do not drink wine or beer, and do not eat anything unclean, because the boy will be a Nazirite to God from birth until the day of his death.'"

⁸ Manoah prayed to the LORD and said, "Please, Lord, let the man of God you sent come again to us and teach us what we should do for the boy who will be born."

⁹ God listened toᶜ Manoah, and the angel of God came again to the woman. She was sitting in the field, and her husband Manoah was not with her. ¹⁰ The woman ran quickly to her husband and told him, "The man who came to me the other day has just come back!"

¹¹ So Manoah got up and followed his wife. When he came to the man, he asked, "Are you the man who spoke to my wife?"

"I am," he said.

ᴬ12:7 LXX reads *in his city in Gilead*   ᴮ13:5 Lit *And a razor is not to go up on his head*   ᶜ13:9 Lit *to the voice of*

¹² Then Manoah asked, "When your words come true, what will be the boy's responsibilities and work?"

¹³ The angel of the LORD answered Manoah, "Your wife needs to do everything I told her. ¹⁴ She must not eat anything that comes from the grapevine or drink wine or beer. And she must not eat anything unclean. Your wife must do everything I have commanded her."

¹⁵ "Please stay here," Manoah told him, "and we will prepare a young goat for you."

¹⁶ The angel of the LORD said to him, "If I stay, I won't eat your food. But if you want to prepare a burnt offering, offer it to the LORD." (Manoah did not know he was the angel of the LORD.)

¹⁷ Then Manoah said to him, "What is your name, so that we may honor you when your words come true?"

¹⁸ "Why do you ask my name," the angel of the LORD asked him, "since it is beyond understanding."

¹⁹ Manoah took a young goat and a grain offering and offered them on a rock to the LORD, who did something miraculous^A while Manoah and his wife were watching. ²⁰ When the flame went up from the altar to the sky, the angel of the LORD went up in its flame. When Manoah and his wife saw this, they fell facedown on the ground. ²¹ The angel of the LORD did not appear again to Manoah and his wife. Then Manoah realized that it was the angel of the LORD.

²² "We're certainly going to die," he said to his wife, "because we have seen God!"

²³ But his wife said to him, "If the LORD had intended to kill us, he wouldn't have accepted the burnt offering and the grain offering from us, and he would not have shown us all these things or spoken to us like this."

²⁴ So the woman gave birth to a son and named him Samson. The boy grew, and the LORD blessed him. ²⁵ Then the Spirit of the LORD began to stir him in the Camp of Dan,^B between Zorah and Eshtaol.

SAMSON'S RIDDLE

14 Samson went down to Timnah and saw a young Philistine woman there. ² He went back and told his father and his mother: "I have seen a young Philistine woman in Timnah. Now get her for me as a wife."

³ But his father and mother said to him, "Can't you find a young woman among your relatives or among any of our people? Must you go to the uncircumcised Philistines for a wife?"

But Samson told his father, "Get her for me. She's the right one for me." ⁴ Now his father and mother did not know this was from the LORD, who wanted the Philistines to provide an opportunity for a confrontation.^C At that time, the Philistines were ruling Israel.

⁵ Samson went down to Timnah with his father and mother and came to the vineyards of Timnah. Suddenly a young lion came roaring at him, ⁶ the Spirit of the LORD came powerfully on him, and he tore the lion apart with his bare hands as he might have torn a young goat. But he did not tell his

---

^A13:19 LXX reads *to the LORD, to the one who works wonders*   ^B13:25 Or *in Mahaneh-dan*   ^C14:4 *for a confrontation* supplied for clarity father or mother what he had done. [7] Then he went and spoke to the woman, because she seemed right to Samson.

[8] After some time, when he returned to marry her, he left the road to see the lion's carcass, and there was a swarm of bees with honey in the carcass. [9] He scooped some honey into his hands and ate it as he went along. When he came to his father and mother, he gave some to them and they ate it. But he did not tell them that he had scooped the honey from the lion's carcass.

[10] His father went to visit the woman, and Samson prepared a feast there, as young men were accustomed to do. [11] When the Philistines saw him, they brought thirty men to accompany him.

[12] "Let me tell you a riddle," Samson said to them. "If you can explain it to me during the seven days of the feast and figure it out, I will give you thirty linen garments and thirty changes of clothes. [13] But if you can't explain it to me, you must give me thirty linen garments and thirty changes of clothes."

"Tell us your riddle," they replied.[A] "Let's hear it."

[14] So he said to them:

Out of the eater came something to eat,
and out of the strong came something sweet.

After three days, they were unable to explain the riddle. [15] On the fourth[B] day they said to Samson's wife, "Persuade your husband to explain the riddle to us, or we will burn you and your father's family to death. Did you invite us here to rob us?"

[16] So Samson's wife came to him, weeping, and said, "You hate me and don't love me! You told my people the riddle, but haven't explained it to me."

"Look," he said,[C] "I haven't even explained it to my father or mother, so why should I explain it to you?"

[17] She wept the whole seven days of the feast, and at last, on the seventh day, he explained it to her, because she had nagged him so much. Then she explained it to her people. [18] On the seventh day, before sunset, the men of the city said to him:

What is sweeter than honey?
What is stronger than a lion?

So he said to them:

If you hadn't plowed with my young cow,
you wouldn't know my riddle now!

[19] The Spirit of the LORD came powerfully on him, and he went down to Ashkelon and killed thirty of their men. He stripped them and gave their clothes to those who had explained the riddle. In a rage, Samson returned to his father's house, [20] and his wife was given to one of the men who had accompanied him.

SAMSON'S REVENGE

15 Later on, during the wheat harvest, Samson took a young goat as a gift and visited his wife. "I want to go to my wife in her room," he said. But her father would not let him enter.

[A] 14:13 Lit replied to him   [B] 14:15 LXX, Syr; MT reads seventh   [C] 14:16 Lit said to her

² "I was sure you hated her," her father said, "so I gave her to one of the men who accompanied you. Isn't her younger sister more beautiful than she is? Why not take her instead?"

³ Samson said to them, "This time I will be blameless when I harm the Philistines." ⁴ So he went out and caught three hundred foxes. He took torches, turned the foxes tail-to-tail, and put a torch between each pair of tails. ⁵ Then he ignited the torches and released the foxes into the standing grain of the Philistines. He burned the piles of grain and the standing grain as well as the vineyards and olive groves.

⁶ Then the Philistines asked, "Who did this?"

They were told, "It was Samson, the Timnite's son-in-law, because he took Samson's wife and gave her to his companion." So the Philistines went to her and her father and burned them to death.

⁷ Then Samson told them, "Because you did this, I swear that I won't rest until I have taken vengeance on you." ⁸ He tore them limb from limbᴬ and then went down and stayed in the cave at the rock of Etam.

⁹ The Philistines went up, camped in Judah, and raided Lehi. ¹⁰ So the men of Judah said, "Why have you attacked us?"

They replied, "We have come to tie Samson up and pay him back for what he did to us."

¹¹ Then three thousand men of Judah went to the cave at the rock of Etam, and they asked Samson, "Don't you realize that the Philistines rule us? What have you done to us?"

"I have done to them what they did to me," he answered.ᴮ

¹² They said to him, "We've come to tie you up and hand you over to the Philistines."

Then Samson told them, "Swear to me that you yourselves won't kill me."

¹³ "No," they said,ᶜ "we won't kill you, but we will tie you up securely and hand you over to them." So they tied him up with two new ropes and led him away from the rock.

¹⁴ When he came to Lehi, the Philistines came to meet him shouting. The Spirit of the LORD came powerfully on him, and the ropes that were on his arms and wrists became like burnt flax and fell off. ¹⁵ He found a fresh jawbone of a donkey, reached out his hand, took it, and killed a thousand men with it. ¹⁶ Then Samson said:

With the jawbone of a donkey
I have piled them in heaps.
With the jawbone of a donkey
I have killed a thousand men.

¹⁷ When he finished speaking, he threw away the jawbone and named that place Ramath-lehi.ᴰ ¹⁸ He became very thirsty and called out to the LORD: "You have accomplished this great victory through your servant. Must I now die of thirst and fall into the hands of the uncircumcised?" ¹⁹ So God split a hollow place in the ground at Lehi, and water came out of it. After Samson drank, his strength returned, and he revived. That is why he named it En-hakkore,ᴱ which is still in Lehi today. ²⁰ And he judged Israel twenty years in the days of the Philistines.

ᴬ15:8 Lit He struck them hip and thigh with a great slaughter   ᴮ15:11 Lit answered them   ᶜ15:13 Lit said to him   ᴰ15:17 = High Place of the Jawbone   ᴱ15:19 = Spring of the One Who Cried Out

SAMSON AND DELILAH

16 Samson went to Gaza, where he saw a prostitute and went to bed with her. ² When the Gazites heard that Samson was there, they surrounded the place and waited in ambush for him all that night at the city gate. They kept quiet all night, saying, "Let's wait until dawn; then we will kill him." ³ But Samson stayed in bed only until midnight. Then he got up, took hold of the doors of the city gate along with the two gateposts, and pulled them out, bar and all. He put them on his shoulders and took them to the top of the mountain overlooking Hebron.

⁴ Some time later, he fell in love with a woman named Delilah, who lived in the Sorek Valley. ⁵ The Philistine leaders went to her and said, "Persuade him to tell you ᴬ where his great strength comes from, so we can overpower him, tie him up, and make him helpless. Each of us will then give you 1,100 pieces of silver."

⁶ So Delilah said to Samson, "Please tell me, where does your great strength come from? How could someone tie you up and make you helpless?"

⁷ Samson told her, "If they tie me up with seven fresh bowstrings that have not been dried, I will become weak and be like any other man."

⁸ The Philistine leaders brought her seven fresh bowstrings that had not been dried, and she tied him up with them. ⁹ While the men in ambush were waiting in her room, she called out to him, "Samson, the Philistines are here!" ᴮ But he snapped the bowstrings as a strand of yarn snaps when it touches fire. The secret of his strength remained unknown.

¹⁰ Then Delilah said to Samson, "You have mocked me and told me lies! Won't you please tell me how you can be tied up?"

¹¹ He told her, "If they tie me up with new ropes that have never been used, I will become weak and be like any other man."

¹² Delilah took new ropes, tied him up with them, and shouted, "Samson, the Philistines are here!" But while the men in ambush were waiting in her room, he snapped the ropes off his arms like a thread.

¹³ Then Delilah said to Samson, "You have mocked me all along and told me lies! Tell me how you can be tied up."

He told her, "If you weave the seven braids on my head into the fabric on a loom — " ᶜ

¹⁴ She fastened the braids with a pin and called to him, "Samson, the Philistines are here!" He awoke from his sleep and pulled out the pin, with the loom and the web.

¹⁵ "How can you say, 'I love you,'" she told him, "when your heart is not with me? This is the third time you have mocked me and not told me what makes your strength so great!"

¹⁶ Because she nagged him day after day and pleaded with him until she wore him out, ᴰ ¹⁷ he told her the whole truth and said to her, "My hair has never been cut, ᴱ because I am a Nazirite to God from birth. If I am shaved, my strength will leave me, and I will become weak and be like any other man."

ᴬ16:5 Lit *him and see*   ᴮ16:9 Lit *are on you*, also in vv. 12,14,20   ᶜ16:13-14 LXX reads *loom and fasten them with a pin into the wall and I will become weak and be like any other man." *¹⁴*And while he was sleeping, Delilah wove the seven braids on his head into the loom.*   ᴰ16:16 Lit *him and he became short to death*
ᴱ16:17 Lit *A razor has not gone up on my head*

NAME YOUR PRICE

JUDGES 16; MATTHEW 27:3-10; ROMANS 12:21

Through the ages, plenty has been said about Delilah, and not much of it is nice. The Bible tells us she was loved by Samson—a judge of the nation of Israel and a man with an enormously impressive and depressive backstory. Born to a barren mother, Samson was the only judge to be called from the womb into judgeship. He was born under a Nazirite vow, forbidding him to drink strong drink, touch anything dead, or cut his hair—ever. (Read more about the Nazirite vow in Numbers 6:1-21.)

By the time Samson met Delilah, he'd already broken two-thirds of the Nazirite vow, making it evident he had no interest in delivering Israel. The Philistines saw Delilah as their opportunity to overcome Samson at last.

On Delilah's fourth attempt to find the source of his great strength, Samson finally trusts her—or cannot stand another moment of her nagging. Either way, he tells Delilah the truth behind his superhuman strength. That night, as she lulls him to sleep on her lap, a man shaves Samson's head entirely. The third portion of the Nazirite vow is broken, and the Spirit of the Lord leaves him. The Philistines gouge out his eyes and make him their slave.

Do you see yourself in Samson? Called to something great, maybe even given a position of influence, but using your privilege for your own gain, forsaking the reason you were sent to serve?

Maybe you see yourself in Delilah—like the nagging wife Proverbs 19:13 warns against?

Are you pursuing your own agenda, doing what it takes to get your way?

Perhaps we see a bit of ourselves in both of them. But when I read Judges 16, what I really want to know is, where do we see Jesus?

Look how much Delilah was paid to betray Samson: 1,100 pieces of silver, per person, from the lords of the Philistines who approached her. (Maybe there were two of them, maybe there were twenty; the Bible doesn't say. Either way, that's a lot of silver!)

Do you remember how many pieces of silver Judas was paid to betray Jesus? Thirty. Thirty pieces of silver (Mt 26:14-16).

Mercy.

I am quick to judge Delilah for her disloyalty —for what a deceitfully wicked woman she seemed to be. But when I remember that Jesus' own disciple betrayed Him for a fraction of her fee, my heart hardly knows what to think. *Judas, how could you sell Jesus for so little?*

And what is my price?

What lights my eyes and feels worth forsaking my Savior, even for a moment?

I'm praying no price is high enough for us to betray our Jesus. I'm praying, by God's grace, we would not be overcome by evil's nagging or bought with its shiny facade. I'm praying, in the way of Romans 12:21, we would "conquer evil with good."

[18] When Delilah realized that he had told her the whole truth, she sent this message to the Philistine leaders: "Come one more time, for he has told me the whole truth." The Philistine leaders came to her and brought the silver with them.

[19] Then she let him fall asleep on her lap and called a man to shave off the seven braids on his head. In this way, she made him helpless, and his strength left him. [20] Then she cried, "Samson, the Philistines are here!" When he awoke from his sleep, he said, "I will escape as I did before and shake myself free." But he did not know that the LORD had left him.

SAMSON'S DEFEAT AND DEATH

[21] The Philistines seized him and gouged out his eyes. They brought him down to Gaza and bound him with bronze shackles, and he was forced to grind grain in the prison. [22] But his hair began to grow back after it had been shaved.

[23] Now the Philistine leaders gathered together to offer a great sacrifice to their god Dagon. They rejoiced and said:

Our god has handed over
our enemy Samson to us.

[24] When the people saw him, they praised their god and said:

Our god has handed over to us
our enemy who destroyed our land
and who multiplied our dead.

[25] When they were in good spirits,[A] they said, "Bring Samson here to entertain us." So they brought Samson from prison, and he entertained them. They had him stand between the pillars.

[26] Samson said to the young man who was leading him by the hand, "Lead me where I can feel the pillars supporting the temple, so I can lean against them." [27] The temple was full of men and women; all the leaders of the Philistines were there, and about three thousand men and women were on the roof watching Samson entertain them. [28] He called out to the LORD: "Lord GOD, please remember me. Strengthen me, God, just once more. With one act of vengeance, let me pay back the Philistines for my two eyes." [29] Samson took hold of the two middle pillars supporting the temple and leaned against them, one on his right hand and the other on his left. [30] Samson said, "Let me die with the Philistines." He pushed with all his might, and the temple fell on the leaders and all the people in it. And those he killed at his death were more than those he had killed in his life.

[31] Then his brothers and all his father's family came down, carried him back, and buried him between Zorah and Eshtaol in the tomb of his father Manoah. So he judged Israel twenty years.

MICAH'S PRIEST

17 There was a man from the hill country of Ephraim named Micah. [2] He said to his mother, "The 1,100 pieces of silver taken from you, and that I heard you place a curse on — here's the silver. I took it."

Then his mother said, "My son, may you be blessed by the LORD!"

[3] He returned the 1,100 pieces of silver to his mother, and his mother said, "I personally consecrate the silver to the LORD for my son's benefit to make

---

[A] 16:25 Or *When they were feeling good*

a carved image and a silver idol.^A I will give it back to you." ⁴ So he returned the silver to his mother, and she took five pounds of silver and gave it to a silversmith. He made it into a carved image and a silver idol, and it was in Micah's house.

⁵ This man Micah had a shrine, and he made an ephod and household idols, and installed one of his sons to be his priest. ⁶ In those days there was no king in Israel; everyone did whatever seemed right to him.

⁷ There was a young man, a Levite from Bethlehem in Judah, who was staying within the clan of Judah. ⁸ The man left the town of Bethlehem in Judah to stay wherever he could find a place. On his way he came to Micah's home in the hill country of Ephraim.

⁹ "Where do you come from?" Micah asked him.

He answered him, "I am a Levite from Bethlehem in Judah, and I'm going to stay wherever I can find a place."

¹⁰ Micah replied,^B "Stay with me and be my father and priest, and I will give you four ounces of silver a year, along with your clothing and provisions." So the Levite went in ¹¹ and agreed to stay with the man, and the young man became like one of his sons. ¹² Micah consecrated the Levite, and the young man became his priest and lived in Micah's house. ¹³ Then Micah said, "Now I know that the LORD will be good to me, because a Levite has become my priest."

DAN'S INVASION AND IDOLATRY

18 In those days, there was no king in Israel, and the Danite tribe was looking for territory to occupy. Up to that time no territory had been captured by them among the tribes of Israel. ² So the Danites sent out five brave men from all their clans, from Zorah and Eshtaol, to scout out the land and explore it. They told them, "Go and explore the land."

They came to the hill country of Ephraim as far as the home of Micah and spent the night there. ³ While they were near Micah's home, they recognized the accent of the young Levite. So they went over to him and asked, "Who brought you here? What are you doing in this place? What is keeping you here?" ⁴ He told them, "This is what Micah has done for me: He has hired me, and I became his priest."

⁵ Then they said to him, "Please inquire of God for us to determine if we will have a successful journey."

⁶ The priest told them, "Go in peace. The LORD is watching over the journey you are going on."

⁷ The five men left and came to Laish. They saw that the people who were there were living securely, in the same way as the Sidonians, quiet and unsuspecting. There was nothing lacking^C in the land and no oppressive ruler. They were far from the Sidonians, having no alliance with anyone.^D

⁸ When the men went back to their relatives at Zorah and Eshtaol, their relatives asked them, "What did you find out?"

⁹ They answered, "Come on, let's attack them, for we have seen the land, and it is very good. Why wait? Don't hesitate to go and invade and take possession of the land! ¹⁰ When you get there, you will come to an unsuspecting people and a spacious land, for God has handed it over to you. It is a place

---

^A 17:3 Or *image and a cast image*, also in v. 4   ^B 17:10 Lit *replied to him*
^C 18:7 Hb obscure   ^D 18:7 MT; some LXX mss, Sym, Old Lat, Syr read *Aram*

where nothing on earth is lacking." ¹¹ Six hundred Danites departed from Zorah and Eshtaol armed with weapons of war. ¹² They went up and camped at Kiriath-jearim in Judah. This is why the place is still called the Camp of Dan^A today; it is west of Kiriath-jearim. ¹³ From there they traveled to the hill country of Ephraim and arrived at Micah's house.

¹⁴ The five men who had gone to scout out the land of Laish told their brothers, "Did you know that there are an ephod, household gods, and a carved image and a silver idol^B in these houses? Now think about what you should do." ¹⁵ So they detoured there and went to the house of the young Levite at the home of Micah and greeted him. ¹⁶ The six hundred Danite men were standing by the entrance of the city gate, armed with their weapons of war. ¹⁷ Then the five men who had gone to scout out the land went in and took the carved image, the ephod, the household idols, and the silver idol, ^C while the priest was standing by the entrance of the city gate with the six hundred men armed with weapons of war.

¹⁸ When they entered Micah's house and took the carved image, the ephod, the household idols, and the silver idol, the priest said to them, "What are you doing?"

¹⁹ They told him, "Be quiet. Keep your mouth shut.^D Come with us and be a father and a priest to us. Is it better for you to be a priest for the house of one person or for you to be a priest for a tribe and family in Israel?" ²⁰ So the priest was pleased and took his ephod, household idols, and carved image, and went with the people. ²¹ They prepared to leave, putting their dependents, livestock, and possessions in front of them.

²² After they were some distance from Micah's house, the men who were in the houses near it were mustered and caught up with the Danites. ²³ They called to the Danites, who turned to face them, and said to Micah, "What's the matter with you that you mustered the men?"

²⁴ He said, "You took the gods I had made and the priest, and went away. What do I have left? How can you say to me, 'What's the matter with you?'"

²⁵ The Danites said to him, "Don't raise your voice against us, or angry men will attack you, and you and your family will lose your lives." ²⁶ The Danites went on their way, and Micah turned to go back home, because he saw that they were stronger than he was.

²⁷ After they had taken the gods Micah had made and the priest that belonged to him, they went to Laish, to a quiet and unsuspecting people. They killed them with their swords and burned the city. ²⁸ There was no one to rescue them because it was far from Sidon and they had no alliance with anyone. It was in a valley that belonged to Beth-rehob. They rebuilt the city and lived in it. ²⁹ They named the city Dan, after the name of their ancestor Dan, who was born to Israel. The city was formerly named Laish.

³⁰ The Danites set up the carved image for themselves. Jonathan son of Gershom, son of Moses,^E and his sons were priests for the Danite tribe until the time of the exile from the land. ³¹ So they set up for themselves Micah's carved image that he had made, and it was there as long as the house of God was in Shiloh.

---

^A 18:12 Or called Mahaneh-dan   ^B 18:14 Or image, the cast image
^C 18:17 Or the cast image, also in v. 18   ^D 18:19 Lit Put your hand on your mouth
^E 18:30 Some Hb mss, LXX, Vg; other Hb mss read Manasseh

OUTRAGE IN BENJAMIN

19 In those days, when there was no king in Israel, a Levite staying in a remote part of the hill country of Ephraim acquired a woman from Bethlehem in Judah as his concubine. ² But she was unfaithful to ᴬ him and left him for her father's house in Bethlehem in Judah. She was there for four months. ³ Then her husband got up and followed her to speak kindly to her ᴮ and bring her back. He had his servant with him and a pair of donkeys. So she brought him to her father's house, and when the girl's father saw him, he gladly welcomed him. ⁴ His father-in-law, the girl's father, detained him, and he stayed with him for three days. They ate, drank, and spent the nights there.

⁵ On the fourth day, they got up early in the morning and prepared to go, but the girl's father said to his son-in-law, "Have something to eat to keep up your strength and then you can go." ⁶ So they sat down and the two of them ate and drank together. Then the girl's father said to the man, "Please agree to stay overnight and enjoy yourself." ⁷ The man got up to go, but his father-in-law persuaded him, so he stayed and spent the night there again. ⁸ He got up early in the morning of the fifth day to leave, but the girl's father said to him, "Please keep up your strength." So they waited until late afternoon and the two of them ate. ⁹ The man got up to go with his concubine and his servant, when his father-in-law, the girl's father, said to him, "Look, night is coming. Please spend the night. See, the day is almost over. Spend the night here, enjoy yourself, then you can get up early tomorrow for your journey and go home."

¹⁰ But the man was unwilling to spend the night. He got up, departed, and arrived opposite Jebus (that is, Jerusalem). The man had his two saddled donkeys and his concubine with him. ¹¹ When they were near Jebus and the day was almost gone, the servant said to his master, "Please, why not let us stop at this Jebusite city and spend the night here?"

¹² But his master replied to him, "We will not stop at a foreign city where there are no Israelites. Let's move on to Gibeah." ¹³ "Come on," he said, ᶜ "let's try to reach one of these places and spend the night in Gibeah or Ramah." ¹⁴ So they continued on their journey, and the sun set as they neared Gibeah in Benjamin. ¹⁵ They stopped ᴰ to go in and spend the night in Gibeah. The Levite went in and sat down in the city square, but no one took them into their home to spend the night.

¹⁶ In the evening, an old man came in from his work in the field. He was from the hill country of Ephraim, but he was residing in Gibeah where the people were Benjaminites. ¹⁷ When he looked up and saw the traveler in the city square, the old man asked, "Where are you going, and where do you come from?"

¹⁸ He answered him, "We're traveling from Bethlehem in Judah to the remote hill country of Ephraim, where I am from. I went to Bethlehem in Judah, and now I'm going to the house of the LORD. ᴱ No one has taken me into his home, ¹⁹ although there's straw and feed for the donkeys, and I have bread and wine for me, my concubine, and the servant ᶠ with us. There is nothing we lack."

ᴬ19:2 LXX reads *was angry with* ᴮ19:3 Lit *speak to her heart* ᶜ19:13 Lit *said to his servant* ᴰ19:15 Lit *stopped there* ᴱ19:18 LXX reads *to my house* ᶠ19:19 Some Hb mss, Syr, Tg, Vg; other Hb mss read *servants*

²⁰ "Welcome!" said the old man. "I'll take care of everything you need. Only don't spend the night in the square." ²¹ So he brought him to his house and fed the donkeys. Then they washed their feet and ate and drank. ²² While they were enjoying themselves, all of a sudden, wicked men of the city surrounded the house and beat on the door. They said to the old man who was the owner of the house, "Bring out the man who came to your house so we can have sex with him!"

²³ The owner of the house went out and said to them, "Please don't do this evil, my brothers. After all, this man has come into my house. Don't commit this horrible outrage. ²⁴ Here, let me bring out my virgin daughter and the man's concubine now. Abuse them and do whatever you want^A to them. But don't commit this outrageous thing against this man."

²⁵ But the men would not listen to him, so the man seized his concubine and took her outside to them. They raped^B her and abused her all night until morning. At daybreak they let her go. ²⁶ Early that morning, the woman made her way back, and as it was getting light, she collapsed at the doorway of the man's house where her master was.

²⁷ When her master got up in the morning, opened the doors of the house, and went out to leave on his journey, there was the woman, his concubine, collapsed near the doorway of the house with her hands on the threshold. ²⁸ "Get up," he told her. "Let's go." But there was no response. So the man put her on his donkey and set out for home.

²⁹ When he entered his house, he picked up a knife, took hold of his concubine, cut her into twelve pieces, limb by limb, and then sent her throughout the territory of Israel. ³⁰ Everyone who saw it said, "Nothing like this has ever happened or has been seen since the day the Israelites came out of the land of Egypt until now.^C Think it over, discuss it, and speak up!"

WAR AGAINST BENJAMIN

20 All the Israelites from Dan to Beer-sheba and from the land of Gilead came out, and the community assembled as one body before the LORD at Mizpah. ² The leaders of all the people and of all the tribes of Israel presented themselves in the assembly of God's people: four hundred thousand armed^D foot soldiers. ³ The Benjaminites heard that the Israelites had gone up to Mizpah.

The Israelites asked, "Tell us, how did this evil act happen?"

⁴ The Levite, the husband of the murdered woman, answered: "I went to Gibeah in Benjamin with my concubine to spend the night. ⁵ Citizens of Gibeah came to attack me and surrounded the house at night. They intended to kill me, but they raped my concubine, and she died. ⁶ Then I took my concubine and cut her in pieces, and sent her throughout Israel's territory, because they have committed a wicked outrage in Israel. ⁷ Look, all of you are Israelites. Give your judgment and verdict here and now."

⁸ Then all the people stood united and said, "None of us will go to his tent or return to his house. ⁹ Now this is what we will do to Gibeah: we will attack

---

^A19:24 Lit do what is good in your eyes   ^B19:25 Lit knew   ^C19:30 LXX reads until now." He commanded the men he sent out, saying, "You will say this to all the men of Israel: Has anything like this happened since the day the Israelites came out of Egypt until this day?   ^D20:2 Lit drawing the sword it. By lot [10] we will take ten men out of every hundred from all the tribes of Israel, and one hundred out of every thousand, and one thousand out of every ten thousand to get provisions for the troops when they go to Gibeah in Benjamin to punish them for all the outrage they committed in Israel."

[11] So all the men of Israel gathered united against the city. [12] Then the tribes of Israel sent men throughout the tribe of Benjamin, saying, "What is this evil act that has happened among you? [13] Hand over the wicked men in Gibeah so we can put them to death and eradicate evil from Israel." But the Benjaminites would not listen to their fellow Israelites. [14] Instead, the Benjaminites gathered together from their cities to Gibeah to go out and fight against the Israelites. [15] On that day the Benjaminites mobilized twenty-six thousand armed men[A] from their cities, besides seven hundred fit young men rallied by the inhabitants of Gibeah. [16] There were seven hundred fit young men who were left-handed among all these troops; all could sling a stone at a hair and not miss.

[17] The Israelites, apart from Benjamin, mobilized four hundred thousand armed men, every one an experienced warrior. [18] They set out, went to Bethel, and inquired of God. The Israelites asked, "Who is to go first to fight for us against the Benjaminites?"

And the LORD answered, "Judah will be first."

[19] In the morning, the Israelites set out and camped near Gibeah. [20] The men of Israel went out to fight against Benjamin and took their battle positions against Gibeah. [21] The Benjaminites came out of Gibeah and slaughtered twenty-two thousand men of Israel on the field that day. [22] But the Israelite troops rallied and again took their battle positions in the same place where they positioned themselves on the first day. [23] They went up, wept before the LORD until evening, and inquired of him: "Should we again attack our brothers the Benjaminites?"

And the LORD answered: "Fight against them."

[24] On the second day the Israelites advanced against the Benjaminites. [25] That same day the Benjaminites came out from Gibeah to meet them and slaughtered an additional eighteen thousand Israelites on the field; all were armed.[B]

[26] The whole Israelite army went to Bethel where they wept and sat before the LORD. They fasted that day until evening and offered burnt offerings and fellowship offerings to the LORD. [27] Then the Israelites inquired of the LORD. In those days, the ark of the covenant of God was there, [28] and Phinehas son of Eleazar, son of Aaron, was serving before it. The Israelites asked: "Should we again fight against our brothers the Benjaminites or should we stop?"

The LORD answered: "Fight, because I will hand them over to you tomorrow." [29] So Israel set up an ambush around Gibeah. [30] On the third day the Israelites fought against the Benjaminites and took their battle positions against Gibeah as before. [31] Then the Benjaminites came out against the troops and were drawn away from the city. They began to attack the troops as before, killing about thirty men of Israel on the highways, one of which goes up to Bethel and the other to Gibeah through the open country. [32] The Benjaminites said, "We are defeating them as before."

[A]20:15 Lit men drawing the sword, also in vv. 17,46   [B]20:25 Lit were drawing the sword, also in v. 35

But the Israelites said, "Let's flee and draw them away from the city to the highways." ³³ So all the men of Israel got up from their places and took their battle positions at Baal-tamar, while the Israelites in ambush charged out of their places west of ^A Geba. ³⁴ Then ten thousand fit young men from all Israel made a frontal assault against Gibeah, and the battle was fierce, but the Benjaminites did not know that disaster was about to strike them. ³⁵ The LORD defeated Benjamin in the presence of Israel, and on that day the Israelites slaughtered 25,100 men of Benjamin; all were armed. ³⁶ Then the Benjaminites realized they had been defeated.

The men of Israel had retreated before Benjamin, because they were confident in the ambush they had set against Gibeah. ³⁷ The men in ambush had rushed quickly against Gibeah; they advanced and put the whole city to the sword. ³⁸ The men of Israel had a prearranged signal with the men in ambush: when they sent up a great cloud of smoke from the city, ³⁹ the men of Israel would return to the battle. When Benjamin had begun to strike them down, killing about thirty men of Israel, they said, "They're defeated before us, just as they were in the first battle." ⁴⁰ But when the column of smoke began to go up from the city, Benjamin looked behind them, and the whole city was going up in smoke. ^B ⁴¹ Then the men of Israel returned, and the men of Benjamin were terrified when they realized that disaster had struck them. ⁴² They retreated before the men of Israel toward the wilderness, but the battle overtook them, and those who came out of the cities ^C slaughtered those between them. ⁴³ They surrounded the Benjaminites, pursued them, and easily overtook them near Gibeah toward the east. ⁴⁴ There were eighteen thousand men who died from Benjamin; all were warriors. ⁴⁵ Then Benjamin turned and fled toward the wilderness to Rimmon Rock, and Israel killed five thousand men on the highways. They overtook them at Gidom and struck two thousand more dead.

⁴⁶ All the Benjaminites who died that day were twenty-five thousand armed men; all were warriors. ⁴⁷ But six hundred men escaped into the wilderness to Rimmon Rock and stayed there four months. ⁴⁸ The men of Israel turned back against the other Benjaminites and killed them with their swords — the entire city, the animals, and everything that remained. They also burned all the cities that remained.

BRIDES FOR BENJAMIN

21 The men of Israel had sworn an oath at Mizpah: "None of us will give his daughter to a Benjaminite in marriage." ² So the people went to Bethel and sat there before God until evening. They wept loudly and bitterly, ³ and cried out, "Why, LORD God of Israel, has it occurred ^D that one tribe is missing in Israel today?" ⁴ The next day the people got up early, built an altar there, and offered burnt offerings and fellowship offerings. ⁵ The Israelites asked, "Who of all the tribes of Israel didn't come to the LORD with the assembly?" For a great oath had been taken that anyone who had not come to the LORD at Mizpah would certainly be put to death.

⁶ But the Israelites had compassion on their brothers, the Benjaminites, and said, "Today a tribe has been cut off from Israel. ⁷ What should we do

---

^A 20:33 LXX, Syr, Vg; MT reads *places in the plain of*, or *places in the cave of*
^B 20:40 Lit *up to the sky*   ^C 20:42 LXX, Vg read *city*   ^D 21:3 Lit *has this occurred in Israel*

A LONG HISTORY OF SHORTSIGHTEDNESS

JUDGES 21; DEUTERONOMY 12:8-14

As a kid, I remember thinking how great it would be to do whatever I wanted. No rules, no curfew, nothing between me and my freedom. I couldn't understand why all the dos and don'ts were necessary, so I danced around the edges of rebellion in those early years. I was a preacher's kid, after all, and naturally, I felt compelled to help my pastor expand his credibility on the topics of long-suffering and grace.

I'd ever so slightly tiptoe over the line, convinced those boundaries were cramping my style. Today, I'm thankful my parents' boundaries wouldn't budge. Looking back, I realize my view of freedom was severely shortsighted.

Scripture tells this story over and over again. Since the fall of humanity, our sin-stained hearts have fought restlessly within the boundaries of God's commands, pining after a woefully shallow definition of freedom.

The law of the Lord was etched deep into Israel's heritage, permeating every aspect of their daily lives. Yet their hearts remained restless, their vision shortsighted. They tested their God-given boundaries time after time, and with each taste of "freedom" grew more fascinated with the darkness beyond.

So God gave them over to their depravity. Judges 21:25 is the kind of verse that sends chills down my spine:

"In those days there was no king in Israel; everyone did whatever seemed right to him."

It's sobering to realize the end result of getting what we want. The Israelites chose worldly pleasures over eternal rewards, selfish ambition over godly purpose, powerless idols over the one true God. Freedom was defined as everyone doing whatever seemed right to them. No rules. No consequences. No king.

The root of their rebellion is found in the first part of this verse: "there was no king in Israel." Joshua was dead. Moses, a distant memory. The judges appointed by God couldn't seem to get organized. In the absence of strong spiritual leadership, the people floundered. In their arrogance, they refused to recognize the authority of the King of kings. In the midst of self-inflicted chaos, they forgot Who had been leading them all along.

This chapter of Israel's story ends in a tangle of blind ambitions and worthless pursuits. **Everyone acted freely, yet none of them experienced the true freedom they longed for.**

We dare not read this narrative with any sense of superiority or pride. Left to our own devices we, too, are bent toward willful rebellion. Laws and boundaries were never intended to save us, but they do serve an important role in our salvation. They reveal the shortsighted nature of our humanity and point to our desperate need for a Savior. Even now, the King of kings offers true freedom to anyone who embraces His mercy and bows to His lordship.

about wives for the survivors? We've sworn to the Lord not to give them any of our daughters as wives." 8 They asked, "Which city among the tribes of Israel didn't come to the Lord at Mizpah?" It turned out that no one from Jabesh-gilead had come to the camp and the assembly. 9 For when the roll was called, no men were there from the inhabitants of Jabesh-gilead.

10 The congregation sent twelve thousand brave warriors^ there and commanded them: "Go and kill the inhabitants of Jabesh-gilead with the sword, including women and dependents. 11 This is what you should do: Completely destroy every male, as well as every woman who has gone to bed with a man." 12 They found among the inhabitants of Jabesh-gilead four hundred young virgins, who had not gone to bed with a man, and they brought them to the camp at Shiloh in the land of Canaan.

13 The whole congregation sent a message of peace to the Benjaminites who were at Rimmon Rock. 14 Benjamin returned at that time, and Israel gave them the women they had kept alive from Jabesh-gilead. But there were not enough for them.

15 The people had compassion on Benjamin, because the Lord had made this gap in the tribes of Israel. 16 The elders of the congregation said, "What should we do about wives for those who are left, since the women of Benjamin have been destroyed?" 17 They said, "There must be heirs for the survivors of Benjamin, so that a tribe of Israel will not be wiped out. 18 But we can't give them our daughters as wives." For the Israelites had sworn, "Anyone who gives a wife to a Benjaminite is cursed." 19 They also said, "Look, there's an annual festival to the Lord in Shiloh, which is north of Bethel, east of the highway that goes up from Bethel to Shechem, and south of Lebonah."

20 Then they commanded the Benjaminites: "Go and hide in the vineyards. 21 Watch, and when you see the young women of Shiloh come out to perform the dances, each of you leave the vineyards and catch a wife for yourself from the young women of Shiloh, and go to the land of Benjamin. 22 When their fathers or brothers come to us and protest, we will tell them, 'Show favor to them, since we did not get enough wives for each of them in the battle. You didn't actually give the women to them, so ᴮ you are not guilty of breaking your oath.'"

23 The Benjaminites did this and took the number of women they needed from the dancers they caught. They went back to their own inheritance, rebuilt their cities, and lived in them. 24 At that time, each of the Israelites returned from there to his own tribe and family. Each returned from there to his own inheritance.

25 In those days there was no king in Israel; everyone did whatever seemed right to him.

---

^21:10 Lit twelve thousand of their sons of valor   ᴮ21:22 Lit at this time

May His Name Become Well Known in Israel.

ruth

 The women said to Naomi, "Blessed be the LORD, who has not left you without a family redeemer today. May his name become well known in Israel." **4:14**

ON THE TIMELINE The book of Ruth is set "during the time of the judges" (Ru 1:1), a period of social and religious disorder when "everyone did whatever seemed right to him" (Jdg 17:6). Historically, this era bridged the time between the conquest of the land under Joshua and the rise of King David, whose genealogy forms the conclusion of the book. The book of Ruth opens with a famine in the land and ends with the birth of Obed, the grandfather of King David (likely around 1150 BC to 1100 BC).

A LITTLE BACKGROUND The book of Ruth gets its name from one of its principal characters, a Moabite woman named Ruth who was the ancestor of David and Jesus. After reading the book of Judges, which paints a dark and depressing picture of Israel, the story of Ruth comes as a welcome relief. Although the book is relatively short, it is rich in examples of kindness, faith, and patience. Ruth is one of the five scrolls that were to be read during the Jewish festivals, in particular the Festival of Weeks.

MESSAGE & PURPOSE The book of Ruth demonstrates how the Lord shows His covenant faithfulness to His undeserving people, often in surprising ways. The genealogy of David at the end of the book shows that the Lord worked through this story to provide for His people's need of a king.

A correlation is sometimes made between the redemption of Ruth by Boaz and the redemption of sinners by Christ. Because of God's covenant faithfulness, He has provided, in Jesus, the Redeemer we all need.

GIVE THANKS FOR THE BOOK OF RUTH:

Ruth's covenantal faithfulness to Naomi and to God showed those who were not ethnic Israelites that they, too, could be incorporated into the people of God through faith. If Moabites who joined themselves to the Lord could be accepted, there was hope for other Gentiles as well (Is 56:3-7). The book of Ruth effectively answered questions that may have been raised over the legitimacy of the Davidic line, given his Moabite roots, and it also serves as a demonstration of Paul's later statement that there is "no distinction between Jew and Greek" when it comes to the gospel (Rm 10:12).

SALMON

RAHAB

ELIMELECH

NAOMI

MAHLON   CHILION

BOAZ   RUTH   ORPAH

OBED

JESSE

DAVID

JESUS

= MARRIED

READ AND UNDERSTAND RUTH

The Bible is a complete work in which many stories combine to tell one story. As you read the book of Ruth, consider reading the additional passages to discover how the whole of Scripture works together.

NAOMI'S FAMILY IN MOAB

1 During the time[A] of the judges, there was a famine in the land. A man left Bethlehem[B] in Judah with his wife and two sons to stay in the territory of Moab for a while. [2] The man's name was Elimelech,[C] and his wife's name was Naomi.[D] The names of his two sons were Mahlon[E] and Chilion.[F] They were Ephrathites from Bethlehem in Judah. They entered the fields of Moab and settled there. [3] Naomi's husband Elimelech died, and she was left with her two sons. [4] Her sons took Moabite women as their wives: one was named Orpah and the second was named Ruth. After they lived in Moab about ten years, [5] both Mahlon and Chilion also died, and Naomi was left without her two children and without her husband.

RUTH'S LOYALTY TO NAOMI

[6] She and her daughters-in-law set out to return from the territory of Moab, because she had heard in Moab that the LORD had paid attention to his people's need by providing them food. [7] She left the place where she had been living, accompanied by her two daughters-in-law, and traveled along the road leading back to the land of Judah.

[8] Naomi said to them, "Each of you go back to your mother's home. May the LORD show kindness to you as you have shown to the dead and to me. [9] May the LORD grant each of you rest in the house of a new husband." She kissed them, and they wept loudly.

[10] They said to her, "We insist on returning with you to your people."

[11] But Naomi replied, "Return home, my daughters. Why do you want to go with me? Am I able to have any more sons who could become your husbands? [12] Return home, my daughters. Go on, for I am too old to have another husband. Even if I thought there was still hope for me to have a husband tonight and to bear sons, [13] would you be willing to wait for them to grow up? Would you restrain yourselves from remarrying?[G] No, my daughters, my life is much too bitter for you to share,[H] because the LORD's hand has turned against me." [14] Again they wept loudly, and Orpah kissed her mother-in-law, but Ruth clung to her. [15] Naomi said, "Look, your sister-in-law has gone back to her people and to her gods. Follow your sister-in-law."

[16] But Ruth replied:

Don't plead with me to abandon you
or to return and not follow you.
For wherever you go, I will go,
and wherever you live, I will live;
your people will be my people,
and your God will be my God.
[17] Where you die, I will die,
and there I will be buried.
May the LORD punish me,[I]
and do so severely,
if anything but death separates you and me.

[A]1:1 Lit *In the days of the judging* [B]1:1 = House of Bread [C]1:2 = My God Is King [D]1:2 = Pleasant [E]1:2 = Sickly [F]1:2 = Weak or Failing [G]1:13 Lit *marrying a man* [H]1:13 Lit *daughters, for more bitter to me than you* [I]1:17 A solemn oath formula; 1Sm 3:17; 2Sm 3:9,35; 1Kg 2:23; 2Kg 6:31

SHE STAYED

RUTH 1:6-18; HOSEA 2:23; TITUS 2:1-5

Whether you've met one, have one, or are one, you know—a relationship with a mother-in-law isn't always one that comes easily. Even in the best of family dynamics, the delicate relationship between mother-in-law and daughter-in-law does not feel like home right away.

The relationship between Ruth and Naomi is realistic but remarkable. It involves the expected dose of awkward, but it also illustrates a profound truth: when God calls us to Himself, even relational discomfort cannot keep us away.

Naomi's husband had died, and so had her sons. I imagine Ruth, Orpah, and Naomi sitting around the metaphorical kitchen table, staring at their hands. Together, but alone, the bonds that held them seemingly gone. Each wilting under her own personal loss. *What happens next? How do we pick up the pieces from this?*

Ruth chooses Naomi—that's her next step. She binds herself to her mother-in-law. It's so unexpected. She could've stayed in her hometown, with her people. But no. She said, "your people will be my people!" (Ru 1:16). Imagine giving up your people and moving across the country to live with your mother-in-law. I'm just saying, it's unexpected.

Ruth vows to do six things with Naomi: travel with her, dwell with her, claim her people, worship her God, die where she dies, and be buried where she is buried. Ruth isn't messing around.

She could've said, "Okay, let's go, I'll check it out and see if it's for me." Nope, Ruth was all in.

This decision to stay with Naomi was so all-encompassing because it was a decision to follow the God of Israel. God used this mother-in-law relationship to woo Ruth to Himself and, quite unexpectedly, plant her in the genealogy of Christ. It wasn't Naomi's beauty, riches, or liveliness that drew Ruth to her; it was her wisdom, virtue, and grace—fruit God had graciously grown and preserved in her, despite her enormous loss.

Ruth saw the mighty work God was doing in Naomi, and didn't want her brush with the God of Israel to end. So there she stayed, clinging to the one person who linked her to Him.

Ruth's faithfulness to Naomi was not of her own strength. But in the midst of Naomi's doubt and sorrow, God revealed Himself as faithful and compassionate. Naomi believed God was afflicting her, yet Ruth was able to see that despite their misfortune, God was still for them.

What kind of God is this who could draw us—against all odds—into what seems like the least comforting of circumstances? A loving God. One who offers good news in a time of trouble, bread in a time of famine, blessing in a season of barrenness, and joy that overcomes all sorrow. This is what Ruth saw in Naomi's God. This is why she could conclude with certainty, "your God will be my God" (Ru 1:16).

¹⁸ When Naomi saw that Ruth was determined to go with her, she stopped talking to her.

¹⁹ The two of them traveled until they came to Bethlehem. When they entered Bethlehem, the whole town was excited about their arrival^A and the local women exclaimed, "Can this be Naomi?"

²⁰ "Don't call me Naomi. Call me Mara,"^B she answered, "for the Almighty has made me very bitter. ²¹ I went away full, but the LORD has brought me back empty. Why do you call me Naomi, since the LORD has opposed^C me, and the Almighty has afflicted me?"

²² So Naomi came back from the territory of Moab with her daughter-in-law Ruth the Moabitess. They arrived in Bethlehem at the beginning of the barley harvest.

RUTH AND BOAZ MEET

2 Now Naomi had a relative on her husband's side. He was a prominent man of noble character from Elimelech's family. His name was Boaz.

² Ruth the Moabitess asked Naomi, "Will you let me go into the fields and gather fallen grain behind someone with whom I find favor?"

Naomi answered her, "Go ahead, my daughter." ³ So Ruth left and entered the field to gather grain behind the harvesters. She happened to be in the portion of the field belonging to Boaz, who was from Elimelech's family.

⁴ Later, when Boaz arrived from Bethlehem, he said to the harvesters, "The LORD be with you."

"The LORD bless you," they replied.

⁵ Boaz asked his servant who was in charge of the harvesters, "Whose young woman is this?"

⁶ The servant answered, "She is the young Moabite woman who returned with Naomi from the territory of Moab. ⁷ She asked, 'Will you let me gather fallen grain among the bundles behind the harvesters?' She came and has been on her feet since early morning, except that she rested a little in the shelter."^D

⁸ Then Boaz said to Ruth, "Listen, my daughter.^E Don't go and gather grain in another field, and don't leave this one, but stay here close to my female servants. ⁹ See which field they are harvesting, and follow them. Haven't I ordered the young men not to touch you?^F When you are thirsty, go and drink from the jars the young men have filled."

¹⁰ She fell facedown, bowed to the ground, and said to him, "Why have I found favor with you, so that you notice me, although I am a foreigner?"

¹¹ Boaz answered her, "Everything you have done for your mother-in-law since your husband's death has been fully reported to me: how you left your father and mother and your native land, and how you came to a people you didn't previously know. ¹² May the LORD reward you for what you have done, and may you receive a full reward from the LORD God of Israel, under whose wings you have come for refuge."

---

^A1:19 Lit excited because of them ^B1:20 = Bitter ^C 1:21 LXX, Syr, Vg read has humiliated ^D2:7 LXX reads morning, and until evening she has not rested in the field a little; Vg reads morning until now and she did not return to the house; Hb uncertain ^E2:8 Lit "Haven't you heard, my daughter? ^F2:9 Either sexual or physical harassment

A PAPA BEAR KIND OF LOVE

RUTH 2:4-17; DEUTERONOMY 28:8-9; PSALM 36:7-9

My older sister recently had her first child, a girl named Rosie. Let me tell you, I'm more obsessed with this little person than I ever imagined I could be. And it's no surprise that my sister's a natural in her new role as a mom. She's always been a nurturer.

Because I'm not a mom and was curious, when Rosie was a few weeks old I asked my sister, "What's it like to love your own child?"

"It's different from loving anyone else, even my husband," she told me. "My love for her involves this fierce need and desire to protect her. It's a mama bear kind of love."

I imagine Boaz felt a similar type of love toward Ruth—a papa bear, protective kind of love. Their story displays protection and provision more than romance and fireworks.

From the moment he first meets her, Boaz protects and provides for Ruth, telling the others to watch out for her, making sure she has plenty of grain, inviting her to eat with him. His actions prove his feelings for her are deeper than a crush; they are rooted in a deep need to protect her, to cover her.

As a widow, and even worse in their culture, a foreigner, Ruth is surprised and a little confused by Boaz's attention. So she flat out asks him, "Why have I found favor with you, so that you notice, although I am a foreigner?" (Ru 2:10).

Boaz tells Ruth her reputation has preceded her, and then gives her this beautiful blessing:

"May you receive a full reward from the Lord God of Israel, under whose wings you have come for refuge" (Ru 2:12).

Under whose wings you have come for refuge. I love the picture Boaz paints of God's protection —God as our refuge. Like a mama bird in the nest, He puts His wings around us. He provides for us.

Boaz is kind to the most lowly. He didn't owe Ruth anything, and she didn't deserve anything, but he gave her everything. Security. A covering. A home. And soon, a son who would continue the bloodline of Jesus (Mt 1:1-17).

Before the cross of Jesus, we echo Ruth's question: *"Why are you so kind to notice me? Look at me. I'm nobody, a foreigner. My hands are empty, and I'm undeserving."*

But Christ's love lifts our head and tells us who we are in Him. We are His. We're not empty, and we're certainly not foreigners. We're covered by the blood of Christ and adopted into the family of God. Like Ruth, we're now blood relatives of Jesus, and nothing can undo that.

Boaz was God's provision for Ruth. Jesus is God's provision for us.

So we take in Ruth's blessing from Boaz as our own: May we receive a full reward from the Lord God of Israel, under whose wings we have come for refuge. Amen.

[13] "My lord," she said, "I have found favor with you, for you have comforted and encouraged[A] your servant, although I am not like one of your female servants."

[14] At mealtime Boaz told her, "Come over here and have some bread and dip it in the vinegar sauce." So she sat beside the harvesters, and he offered her roasted grain. She ate and was satisfied and had some left over.

[15] When she got up to gather grain, Boaz ordered his young men, "Let her even gather grain among the bundles, and don't humiliate her. [16] Pull out some stalks from the bundles for her and leave them for her to gather. Don't rebuke her." [17] So Ruth gathered grain in the field until evening. She beat out what she had gathered, and it was about twenty-six quarts[B] of barley. [18] She picked up the grain and went into the town, where her mother-in-law saw what she had gleaned. She brought out what she had left over from her meal and gave it to her.

[19] Her mother-in-law said to her, "Where did you gather barley today, and where did you work? May the LORD bless the man who noticed you."

Ruth told her mother-in-law whom she had worked with and said, "The name of the man I worked with today is Boaz."

[20] Then Naomi said to her daughter-in-law, "May the LORD bless him because he has not abandoned his kindness to the living or the dead." Naomi continued, "The man is a close relative. He is one of our family redeemers."

[21] Ruth the Moabitess said, "He also told me, 'Stay with my young men until they have finished all of my harvest.'"

[22] So Naomi said to her daughter-in-law Ruth, "My daughter, it is good for you to work[C] with his female servants, so that nothing will happen to you in another field." [23] Ruth stayed close to Boaz's female servants and gathered grain until the barley and the wheat harvests were finished. And she lived with[D] her mother-in-law.

RUTH'S APPEAL TO BOAZ

3 Ruth's mother-in-law Naomi said to her, "My daughter, shouldn't I find rest for you, so that you will be taken care of? [2] Now isn't Boaz our relative? Haven't you been working with his female servants? This evening he will be winnowing barley on the threshing floor. [3] Wash, put on perfumed oil, and wear your best clothes. Go down to the threshing floor, but don't let the man know you are there until he has finished eating and drinking. [4] When he lies down, notice the place where he's lying, go in and uncover his feet, and lie down. Then he will explain to you what you should do."

[5] So Ruth said to her, "I will do everything you say."[E] [6] She went down to the threshing floor and did everything her mother-in-law had charged her to do. [7] After Boaz ate, drank, and was in good spirits,[F] he went to lie down at the end of the pile of barley, and she came secretly, uncovered his feet, and lay down.

[8] At midnight, Boaz was startled, turned over, and there lying at his feet was a woman! [9] So he asked, "Who are you?"

"I am Ruth, your servant," she replied. "Take me under your wing,[G] for you are a family redeemer."

[A]2:13 Lit *and spoken to the heart of*   [B]2:17 Lit *about an ephah*   [C]2:22 Lit *go out*   [D]2:23 Some Hb mss, Vg read *she returned to*   [E]3:5 Alt Hb tradition reads *say to me*   [F]3:7 Lit *and his heart was glad*   [G]3:9 Or *"Spread the edge of your garment;* lit *"Spread the wing of your garment; Ru 2:12*

¹⁰ Then he said, "May the LORD bless you, my daughter. You have shown more kindness now than before,ᴬ because you have not pursued younger men, whether rich or poor. ¹¹ Now don't be afraid, my daughter. I will do for you whatever you say,ᴮ since all the people in my townᶜ know that you are a woman of noble character. ¹² Yes, it is true that I am a family redeemer, but there is a redeemer closer than I am. ¹³ Stay here tonight, and in the morning, if he wants to redeem you, that's good. Let him redeem you. But if he doesn't want to redeem you, as the LORD lives, I will. Now lie down until morning."

¹⁴ So she lay down at his feet until morning but got up while it was still dark.ᴰ Then Boaz said, "Don't let it be known that aᴱ woman came to the threshing floor." ¹⁵ And he told Ruth, "Bring the shawl you're wearing and hold it out." When she held it out, he shoveled six measures of barley into her shawl, and sheᶠ went into the town.

¹⁶ She went to her mother-in-law, Naomi, who asked her, "What happened,ᴳ my daughter?"

Then Ruth told her everything the man had done for her. ¹⁷ She said, "He gave me these six measures of barley, because he said,ᴴ 'Don't go back to your mother-in-law empty-handed.'"

¹⁸ Naomi said, "My daughter, wait until you find out how things go, for he won't rest unless he resolves this today."

RUTH AND BOAZ MARRY

4 Boaz went to the gate of the town and sat down there. Soon the family redeemer Boaz had spoken about came by. Boaz said, "Come over hereᴵ and sit down." So he went over and sat down. ² Then Boaz took ten men of the town's elders and said, "Sit here." And they sat down. ³ He said to the redeemer, "Naomi, who has returned from the territory of Moab, is selling the portion of the field that belonged to our brother Elimelech. ⁴ I thought I should inform you:ᴶ Buy it back in the presence of those seated here and in the presence of the elders of my people. If you want to redeem it, do it. But if you doᴷ not want to redeem it, tell me so that I will know, because there isn't anyone other than you to redeem it, and I am next after you."

"I want to redeem it," he answered.

⁵ Then Boaz said, "On the day you buy the field from Naomi, you will acquireᴸ Ruth the Moabitess, the wife of the deceased man, to perpetuate the man's name on his property."ᴹ

⁶ The redeemer replied, "I can't redeem it myself, or I will ruin my own inheritance. Take my right of redemption, because I can't redeem it."

ᴬ3:10 Lit *kindness at the last than at the first* ᴮ3:11 Some Hb mss, Orig, Syr, Tg, Vg read *say to me* ᶜ3:11 Lit *all the gate of my people* ᴰ3:14 Lit *up before a man could recognize his companion* ᴱ3:14 LXX; MT reads *the* ᶠ3:15 Some Hb mss, Aramaic, Syr, Vg; other Hb mss read *he* ᴳ3:16 Lit *"Who are you* ᴴ3:17 Alt Hb tradition, LXX, Syr, Tg read *said to me* ᴵ4:1 Or *said, "Come here Mr. So-and-so* ᴶ4:4 Lit *should uncover your ear, saying* ᴷ4:4 Some Hb mss, LXX, Syr, Vg; other Hb mss read *if he does* ᴸ4:5 Lit *Naomi and from* ᴹ4:5 Alt Hb tradition reads *Naomi, I will have already acquired from Ruth the Moabitess, the wife of the dead man, the privilege of raising up the name of the dead man on his property*

[7] At an earlier period in Israel, a man removed his sandal and gave it to the other party in order to make any matter legally binding concerning the right of redemption or the exchange of property. This was the method of legally binding a transaction in Israel.

[8] So the redeemer removed his sandal and said to Boaz, "Buy back the property yourself."

[9] Boaz said to the elders and all the people, "You are witnesses today that I am buying from Naomi everything that belonged to Elimelech, Chilion, and Mahlon. [10] I have also acquired Ruth the Moabitess, Mahlon's widow, as my wife, to perpetuate the deceased man's name on his property, so that his name will not disappear among his relatives or from the gate of his hometown. You are witnesses today."

[11] All the people who were at the city gate, including the elders, said, "We are witnesses. May the LORD make the woman who is entering your house like Rachel and Leah, who together built the house of Israel. May you be powerful in Ephrathah and your name well known in Bethlehem. [12] May your house become like the house of Perez, the son Tamar bore to Judah, because of the offspring the LORD will give you by this young woman."

[13] Boaz took Ruth and she became his wife. He slept with her, and the LORD granted conception to her, and she gave birth to a son. [14] The women said to Naomi, "Blessed be the LORD, who has not left you without a family redeemer today. May his name become well known in Israel. [15] He will renew your life and sustain you in your old age. Indeed, your daughter-in-law, who loves you and is better to you than seven sons, has given birth to him." [16] Naomi took the child, placed him on her lap, and became his nanny. [17] The neighbor women said, "A son has been born to Naomi," and they named him Obed.^A He was the father of Jesse, the father of David.

DAVID'S GENEALOGY FROM JUDAH'S SON

[18] Now these are the family records of Perez:
Perez fathered Hezron,
[19] Hezron fathered Ram,^B
Ram fathered Amminadab,
[20] Amminadab fathered Nahshon,
Nahshon fathered Salmon,
[21] Salmon fathered Boaz,
Boaz fathered Obed,
[22] Obed fathered Jesse,
and Jesse fathered David.

---

^A4:17 = Servant   ^B4:19 LXX reads *Aram*; Mt 1:3-4

BENEATH THE TAPESTRY

RUTH 4:13-22; MATTHEW 1:2-6; ROMANS 15:12

Have you ever seen the Bayeux Tapestry? I haven't seen it in person. It lives in Normandy, France—*ooh la la!* The tapestry narrates William the Conqueror's victory at the Battle of Hastings. It's very famous, very big, and sometimes very beautiful. The top side of it makes sense and tells a story. The underside is a hot mess and looks like the weaver didn't have a plan.

God's will throughout history is like a tapestry. We are underneath looking up, and all the random threads tied in knots and snarls don't make sense to us. We can't see the tapestry of history like God sees it. From His perspective it tells the story of His love and plan for mankind from the beginning of time.

Our earthly perspective is limited. So, when God weaves together the family line of Christ, He uses people we would never expect. We assume the line of ancestry for the Son of God would be filled with "respectable" leaders. But God used women, foreigners, illegitimate children, and a prostitute. (Sidebar: We live in a great world where women can be leaders, but Ruth lived in a world where leaders only looked like serious-faced, respectable men.)

Ruth was not only a foreigner; she was from an enemy country, Moab. The Israelites despised the Moabites. So when Ruth walked into town, that's likely what they saw—a woman with the invisible label of "Moabite" hovering over her head. She herself wasn't guilty, but she was an easy target for prejudice. And God chose

to weave her into His Kingly line. See how the tapestry looks crazy from underneath?

God makes Ruth an ancestor of David and the Messiah. It is the greatest of honors. This is the story God was penning all along, from the beginning of the book.

Look at some of the names in Christ's genealogy:
Perez
Hezron
Ram
Amminadab
Nahshon
Salmon
Boaz
Obed
Jesse
David

Do you know all the people on that list? I don't.

The story of Ruth shows us there are no insignificant people in God's plan, even if we only know them as a name on a list. He takes the despised and the rejected, the lowly and the insignificant, even His enemies, and He binds them to Christ.

What looks messy and meaningless to us is, from God's perspective, an intentional and precise way He is working to establish His kingdom. He takes what appear to be loose, broken, and unrelated threads and reveals how He was weaving something eternally beautiful all along.

THEY HAVE
NOT
REJECTED
YOU
THEY HAVE REJECTED
ME

1 samuel

 But the LORD told him, "Listen to the people and everything they say to you. They have not rejected you; they have rejected me as their king." **8:7**

ON THE TIMELINE The events in 1 Samuel occur at the end of the period of the judges. The narrative begins with the birth of Samuel (around 1105 BC), the last judge in Israel, and concludes with the death of Israel's first king, Saul (1011 BC). 1 Samuel 27:6 suggests the book was not written until a few generations after the division of the kingdom of Israel, around 930 BC.

A LITTLE BACKGROUND Originally written as one book, 1 and 2 Samuel highlight a significant time of transition in Israel's history. As 1 Samuel begins, Israel is a loosely organized tribal people living under poor spiritual leadership. Even still, God's plan for His people continued as He raised up Samuel to guide Israel's transition from a theocracy to a monarchy. Saul's kingship constitutes the remainder of 1 Samuel, while David's kingship is largely the focus of 2 Samuel.

MESSAGE & PURPOSE
The books of 1 and 2 Samuel focus on four major themes:
1. *Leadership* – Examples of both good and bad leadership are shown through-out 1 and 2 Samuel. When leaders focused their attention on the Lord and saw their leadership roles as instruments for His glory, they flourished. When they abandoned the Lord and used their offices for their own gain, they failed.
2. *God's sovereignty* – God's provision for Israel is apparent at every turn. God provided spiritual leadership through Samuel, a king for Israel through Saul and later David, and the leaders and resources needed for Israel to defeat their enemies and live out their purpose in the land.
3. *Sin's consequences* – God takes sin seriously, and the awful consequences of sin are displayed throughout 1 and 2 Samuel.
4. *Covenant* – 1 and 2 Samuel describe God's relationship with His covenant people and His faithful response to the terms of that covenant.

GIVE THANKS FOR THE BOOK OF 1 SAMUEL:

As God established a king in Israel, He also established a new covenant with David, one that would ultimately find its fulfillment in the Lord Jesus Christ. Though 1 and 2 Samuel display plenty of examples of leadership failures in Israel, the mercy and grace of God is displayed through His promise to use this broken nation to bring about the Savior of the world.

SAUL AND THE PHILISTINES

AMMONITE ROUTES — ·—·—· →
SAUL'S ROUTES ——————→
JONATHAN'S ROUTES — — — →
ISRAEL'S ROUTES — ·· — ·· — →
PHILISTINES' ROUTES ·········→

PHOENICIA

ARAM

GESHUR

GILEAD

SEA of GALILEE

MEDITERRANEAN SEA

MT. CARMEL

MEGIDDO

SHUNEM

JEZREEL

R. Yarmuk

RAMOTH-GILEAD

IBLEAM

MT. GILBOA

R. Jordan

Saul defeats
Nahash

DOTHAN

SOCOH

MT. EBAL

SHECHEM

JABESH-GILEAD

MAHANAIM

R. Jabbok

MT. GERIZIM

APHEK

JOGBEHAH

BETH-HORON

GEZER

MIZPAH

RABBAH

AIJALON

MICHMASH

GIBEAH

EKRON

JERUSALEM

MT. NEBO

AMMON

GATH

HEBRON

R. Arnon

GAZA

DEAD SEA

BEERSHEBA

MOAB

R. Zered

EDOM

AMALEK

PHILISTIA

SAUL'S REBELLION AGAINST THE PHILISTINES

UPPER
BETH-HORON

MIZPAH

MICHMASH

Jonathan's
victory prompts
the Philistines
to assemble a
large army at
Michmash

GEBA

W. Suweinet

RAMAH

GIBEAH

BATTLE OF MICHMASH

MICHMASH

Jonathan kills
twenty men and
causes panic

GEBA

Pass at rocks
of Bozes & Senah

W. Suweinet

READ AND UNDERSTAND 1 SAMUEL

The Bible is a complete work in which many stories combine to tell one story. As you read the book of 1 Samuel, consider reading the additional passages to discover how the whole of Scripture works together.

HANNAH'S VOW

1 There was a man from Ramathaim-zophim in^A the hill country of Ephraim. His name was Elkanah son of Jeroham, son of Elihu, son of Tohu, son of Zuph, an Ephraimite. ² He had two wives, the first named Hannah and the second Peninnah. Peninnah had children, but Hannah was childless. ³ This man would go up from his town every year to worship and to sacrifice to the Lord of Armies at Shiloh, where Eli's two sons, Hophni and Phinehas, were the Lord's priests.

⁴ Whenever Elkanah offered a sacrifice, he always gave portions of the meat to his wife Peninnah and to each of her sons and daughters. ⁵ But he gave a double^B portion to Hannah, for he loved her even though the Lord had kept her from conceiving. ⁶ Her rival would taunt her severely just to provoke her, because the Lord had kept Hannah from conceiving. ⁷ Year after year, when she went up to the Lord's house, her rival taunted her in this way. Hannah would weep and would not eat. ⁸ "Hannah, why are you crying?" her husband Elkanah would ask. "Why won't you eat? Why are you troubled? Am I not better to you than ten sons?"

⁹ On one occasion, Hannah got up after they ate and drank at Shiloh.^C The priest Eli was sitting on a chair by the doorpost of the Lord's temple. ¹⁰ Deeply hurt, Hannah prayed to the Lord and wept with many tears. ¹¹ Making a vow, she pleaded, "Lord of Armies, if you will take notice of your servant's affliction, remember and not forget me, and give your servant a son,^D I will give him to the Lord all the days of his life, and his hair will never be cut."^E

¹² While she continued praying in the Lord's presence, Eli watched her mouth. ¹³ Hannah was praying silently,^F and though her lips were moving, her voice could not be heard. Eli thought she was drunk ¹⁴ and said to her, "How long are you going to be drunk? Get rid of your wine!"

¹⁵ "No, my lord," Hannah replied. "I am a woman with a broken heart. I haven't had any wine or beer; I've been pouring out my heart before the Lord. ¹⁶ Don't think of me as a wicked woman; I've been praying from the depth of my anguish and resentment."

¹⁷ Eli responded, "Go in peace, and may the God of Israel grant the request you've made of him."

¹⁸ "May your servant find favor with you," she replied. Then Hannah went on her way; she ate and no longer looked despondent.^G

SAMUEL'S BIRTH AND DEDICATION

¹⁹ The next morning Elkanah and Hannah got up early to worship before the Lord. Afterward, they returned home to Ramah. Then Elkanah was intimate with his wife Hannah, and the Lord remembered her. ²⁰ After some time,^H Hannah conceived and gave birth to a son. She named him Samuel,^I because she said, "I requested him from the Lord."

²¹ When Elkanah and all his household went up to make the annual sacrifice and his vow offering to the Lord, ²² Hannah did not go and explained to

---

^A 1:1 Or *from Ramathaim, a Zuphite from*   ^B 1:5 Or *gave only one* ; Hb obscure
^C 1:9 LXX adds *and presented herself before the Lord*   ^D 1:11 Lit *a seed of men*
^E 1:11 Lit *and no razor will go up on his head*   ^F 1:13 Lit *praying to her heart*
^G 1:18 Lit *and her face was not to her again*   ^H 1:20 Lit *In the turning of the days*
^I 1:20 In Hb, the name *Samuel* sounds like the phrase "requested from God."

BOWED IN WORSHIP

1 SAMUEL 1:1–2:11

I bow in worship every morning when I wake up, but sometimes I bow to the wrong thing.

I slap the alarm notification on my phone for the third time, silently and sleepily vowing to get to bed earlier than the night before, then I put the phone down and get up. But first, I do a quick scan through the usual suspects—email, texts, social media. *It'll only take a minute!* I think to myself, as one minute becomes many. Before stepping out of bed, I've set my heart and mind at the world's feet, consuming whatever it happens to send my way at 6:05 a.m.

Maybe it's my penchant for distraction that makes my heart so drawn to Hannah's faithfulness. Scripture describes her praying again and again to the Lord, pouring out her heart, bowing in worship to God. I'm sure she wasn't perfect—but, oh, how she prayed!

Hannah's prayers were not obligatory, half-hearted, or empty. She prayed honestly and openly; she prayed as if her life depended on it. "Deeply hurt, Hannah prayed to the LORD and wept with many tears," we read in 1 Samuel 1:10. "I've been praying from the depth of my anguish and resentment" (1Sm 1:16), she said. The good, the bad, and the painful—Hannah brought it all to God as an act of worship.

What was it about Hannah that created in her the worshiping heart I long to have? Why was prayer Hannah's first resort instead of her last? The Bible doesn't tell us outright, but we're given some solid clues.

She believed in God's power. Hannah approached God with reverence, asking boldly for His blessing.

She trusted in God's goodness. Hannah offered her beloved son Samuel as God's servant before he was even conceived. What trusting resolve!

She rested in God's presence. We get a glimpse of how Hannah responded in sorrow and even how she began her day in the midst of hard times of waiting.

Hannah's habit of prayer was less about her goodness and more about God's greatness.

After Samuel's birth, Hannah carried her son up to the tabernacle, dedicating him to the Lord. It's here that we see her back where she started in 1 Samuel 1—presenting her whole self in prayer before God. Though her prayers of anguish had become a song of thanksgiving, Hannah's posture was still the same. In supplication and in praise, she bowed in worship before the Lord.

We serve a powerful, loving, and good God—the God who is like no other. May we give our worshipful glances and prayerful pleas to Him and Him alone. When our lives ache with need, may we bring them to the throne. When our hearts break, may we pour them out to God. When we rise in the morning, may we rise in worship.

her husband, "After the child is weaned, I'll take him to appear in the Lord's presence and to stay there permanently."

²³ Her husband Elkanah replied, "Do what you think is best,ᴬ and stay here until you've weaned him. May the Lord confirm yourᴮ word." So Hannah stayed there and nursed her son until she weaned him. ²⁴ When she had weaned him, she took him with her to Shiloh, as well as a three-year-old bull,ᶜ half a bushelᴰ of flour, and a clay jar of wine. Though the boy was still young,ᴱ she took him to the Lord's house at Shiloh. ²⁵ Then they slaughtered the bull and brought the boy to Eli.

²⁶ "Please, my lord," she said, "as surely as you live, my lord, I am the woman who stood here beside you praying to the Lord. ²⁷ I prayed for this boy, and since the Lord gave me what I asked him for, ²⁸ I now give the boy to the Lord. For as long as he lives, he is given to the Lord." Then heᶠ worshiped the Lord there.ᴳ

HANNAH'S TRIUMPHANT PRAYER

2 Hannah prayed:
My heart rejoices in the Lord;
my horn is lifted up by the Lord.
My mouth boasts over my enemies,
because I rejoice in your salvation.

² There is no one holy like the Lord.
There is no one besides you!
And there is no rock like our God.

³ Do not boast so proudly,
or let arrogant words come out of your mouth,
for the Lord is a God of knowledge,
and actions are weighed by him.

⁴ The bows of the warriors are broken,
but the feeble are clothed with strength.

⁵ Those who are full hire themselves out for food,
but those who are starving hunger no more.
The woman who is childless gives birth to seven,
but the woman with many sons pines away.

⁶ The Lord brings death and gives life;
he sends some down to Sheol, and he raises others up.

⁷ The Lord brings poverty and gives wealth;
he humbles and he exalts.

⁸ He raises the poor from the dust
and lifts the needy from the trash heap.
He seats them with noblemen
and gives them a throne of honor.ᴴ
For the foundations of the earth are the Lord's;
he has set the world on them.

ᴬ1:23 Lit *what is good in your eyes* ᴮ1:23 DSS, LXX, Syr; MT reads *his* ᶜ1:24 DSS, LXX, Syr; MT reads *Shiloh with three bulls* ᴰ1:24 Lit *bull and an ephah* ᴱ1:24 Lit *And the youth was a youth* ᶠ1:28 DSS read *she*; some Hb mss, Syr, Vg read *they* ᴳ1:28 LXX reads *Then she left him there before the Lord* ᴴ2:8 DSS, LXX add *He gives the vow of the one who makes a vow and he blesses the years of the just.*

⁹ He guards the steps^ of his faithful ones,
  but the wicked perish in darkness,
  for a person does not prevail by his own strength.
¹⁰ Those who oppose the LORD will be shattered;^B
  he will thunder in the heavens against them.
  The LORD will judge the ends of the earth.
  He will give power to his king;
  he will lift up the horn of his anointed.^C

¹¹ Elkanah went home to Ramah, but the boy served the LORD in the presence of the priest Eli.

ELI'S FAMILY JUDGED

¹² Eli's sons were wicked men; they did not respect the LORD ¹³ or the priests' share of the sacrifices from the people. When anyone offered a sacrifice, the priest's servant would come with a three-pronged meat fork while the meat was boiling ¹⁴ and plunge it into the container, kettle, cauldron, or cooking pot. The priest would claim for himself whatever the meat fork brought up. This is the way they treated all the Israelites who came there to Shiloh. ¹⁵ Even before the fat was burned, the priest's servant would come and say to the one who was sacrificing, "Give the priest some meat to roast, because he won't accept boiled meat from you — only raw." ¹⁶ If that person said to him, "The fat must be burned first; then you can take whatever you want for yourself," the servant would reply, "No, I insist that you hand it over right now. If you don't, I'll take it by force!" ¹⁷ So the servants' sin was very severe in the presence of the LORD, because the men treated the LORD's offering with contempt.

¹⁸ Samuel served in the LORD's presence—this mere boy was dressed in the linen ephod. ¹⁹ Each year his mother made him a little robe and took it to him when she went with her husband to offer the annual sacrifice. ²⁰ Eli would bless Elkanah and his wife: "May the LORD give you children by this woman in place of the one she^D has given to the LORD." Then they would go home.

²¹ The LORD paid attention to Hannah's need, and she conceived and gave birth to three sons and two daughters. Meanwhile, the boy Samuel grew up in the presence of the LORD.

²² Now Eli was very old. He heard about everything his sons were doing to all Israel and how they were sleeping with the women who served at the entrance to the tent of meeting. ²³ He said to them, "Why are you doing these things? I have heard about your evil actions from all these people. ²⁴ No, my sons, the news I hear the LORD's people spreading is not good. ²⁵ If one person sins against another, God can intercede for him, but if a person sins against the LORD, who can intercede for him?" But they would not listen to their father, since the LORD intended to kill them. ²⁶ By contrast, the boy Samuel grew in stature and in favor with the LORD and with people.

²⁷ A man of God came to Eli and said to him, "This is what the LORD says: 'Didn't I reveal myself to your forefather's family^E when they were in Egypt and belonged to Pharaoh's palace? ²⁸ Out of all the tribes of Israel, I chose

^2:9 Lit feet ^B2:10 DSS, LXX read The LORD shatters those who dispute with him ^C2:10 Or Messiah ^D2:20 DSS; MT reads he ^E2:27 Lit the palace of your father

407

your house[A] to be my priests, to offer sacrifices on my altar, to burn incense, and to wear an ephod in my presence. I also gave your forefather's family all the Israelite fire offerings. 29 Why, then, do all of you despise my sacrifices and offerings that I require at the place of worship? You have honored your sons more than me, by making yourselves fat with the best part of all of the offerings of my people Israel.'

30 "Therefore, this is the declaration of the LORD, the God of Israel: 'I did say that your family and your forefather's family would walk before me forever. But now,' this is the LORD's declaration, 'no longer! For those who honor me I will honor, but those who despise me will be disgraced. 31 Look, the days are coming when I will cut off your strength and the strength of your forefather's house, so that none in your family will reach old age. 32 You will see distress in the place of worship, in spite of all that is good in Israel, and no one in your family will ever again reach old age. 33 Any man from your family I do not cut off from my altar will bring grief[B] and sadness to you. All your descendants will die violently.[C,D] 34 This will be the sign that will come to you concerning your two sons Hophni and Phinehas: both of them will die on the same day.

35 " 'Then I will raise up a faithful priest for myself. He will do whatever is in my heart and mind. I will establish a lasting dynasty for him, and he will walk before my anointed one for all time. 36 Anyone who is left in your family will come and bow down to him for a piece of silver or a loaf of bread. He will say: Please appoint me to some priestly office so I can have a piece of bread to eat.'"

SAMUEL'S CALL

3 The boy Samuel served the LORD in Eli's presence. In those days the word of the LORD was rare and prophetic visions were not widespread. 2 One day Eli, whose eyesight was failing, was lying in his usual place. 3 Before the lamp of God had gone out, Samuel was lying down in the temple of the LORD, where the ark of God was located.

4 Then the LORD called Samuel,[E] and he answered, "Here I am." 5 He ran to Eli and said, "Here I am; you called me."

"I didn't call," Eli replied. "Go back and lie down." So he went and lay down.

6 Once again the LORD called, "Samuel!"

Samuel got up, went to Eli, and said, "Here I am; you called me."

"I didn't call, my son," he replied. "Go back and lie down."

7 Now Samuel did not yet know the LORD, because the word of the LORD had not yet been revealed to him. 8 Once again, for the third time, the LORD called Samuel. He got up, went to Eli, and said, "Here I am; you called me."

Then Eli understood that the LORD was calling the boy. 9 He told Samuel, "Go and lie down. If he calls you, say, 'Speak, LORD, for your servant is listening.'" So Samuel went and lay down in his place.

10 The LORD came, stood there, and called as before, "Samuel, Samuel!"

Samuel responded, "Speak, for your servant is listening."

11 The LORD said to Samuel, "I am about to do something in Israel that everyone who hears about it will shudder.[F] 12 On that day I will carry out against

---

[A]2:28 Lit *selected him* [B]2:33 Lit *grief to your eyes* [C]2:33 DSS, LXX read *die by the sword of men* [D]2:33 Lit *die men* [E]3:4 DSS, LXX read *called, "Samuel! Samuel!"* [F]3:11 Lit *about it, his two ears will tingle*; Hb obscure

Eli everything I said about his family, from beginning to end. ¹³ I told him that I am going to judge his family forever because of the iniquity he knows about: his sons are cursing God, ᴬ and he has not stopped them. ¹⁴ Therefore, I have sworn to Eli's family: The iniquity of Eli's family will never be wiped out by either sacrifice or offering."

¹⁵ Samuel lay down until the morning; then he opened the doors of the LORD's house. He was afraid to tell Eli the vision, ¹⁶ but Eli called him and said, "Samuel, my son."

"Here I am," answered Samuel.

¹⁷ "What was the message he gave you?" Eli asked. "Don't hide it from me. May God punish you and do so severely if you hide anything from me that he told you." ¹⁸ So Samuel told him everything and did not hide anything from him. Eli responded, "He is the LORD. Let him do what he thinks is good." ᴮ

¹⁹ Samuel grew, and the LORD was with him, and he fulfilled everything Samuel prophesied. ᶜ ²⁰ All Israel from Dan to Beer-sheba knew that Samuel was a confirmed prophet of the LORD. ²¹ The LORD continued to appear in

4 Shiloh, because there he revealed himself to Samuel by his word. ¹ And Samuel's words came to all Israel.

THE ARK CAPTURED BY THE PHILISTINES

Israel went out to meet the Philistines in battle and ᴰ camped at Ebenezer while the Philistines camped at Aphek. ² The Philistines lined up in battle formation against Israel, and as the battle intensified, Israel was defeated by the Philistines, who struck down about four thousand men on the battlefield.

³ When the troops returned to the camp, the elders of Israel asked, "Why did the LORD defeat us today before the Philistines? Let's bring the ark of the LORD's covenant from Shiloh. Then it ᴱ will go with us and save us from our enemies." ⁴ So the people sent men to Shiloh to bring back the ark of the covenant of the LORD of Armies, who is enthroned between the cherubim. Eli's two sons, Hophni and Phinehas, were there with the ark of the covenant of God. ⁵ When the ark of the covenant of the LORD entered the camp, all the Israelites raised such a loud shout that the ground shook.

⁶ The Philistines heard the sound of the war cry and asked, "What's this loud shout in the Hebrews' camp?" When the Philistines discovered that the ark of the LORD had entered the camp, ⁷ they panicked. "A god has entered their camp!" they said. "Woe to us, nothing like this has happened before. ᶠ ⁸ Woe to us, who will rescue us from these magnificent gods? These are the gods that slaughtered the Egyptians with all kinds of plagues in the wilderness. ⁹ Show some courage and be men, Philistines! Otherwise, you'll serve the Hebrews just as they served you. Now be men and fight!"

¹⁰ So the Philistines fought, and Israel was defeated, and each man fled to his tent. The slaughter was severe — thirty thousand of the Israelite foot soldiers fell. ¹¹ The ark of God was captured, and Eli's two sons, Hophni and Phinehas, died.

ᴬ3:13 LXX, Old Lat; MT reads them   ᴮ3:18 Lit *what is good in his eyes*
ᶜ3:19 Lit *he let none of his words fall to the ground*   ᴰ4:1 LXX reads *In those days the Philistines gathered together to fight against Israel, and Israel went out to engage them in battle. They*   ᴱ4:3 Or *he*   ᶠ4:7 Lit *yesterday or the day before*

ELI'S DEATH AND ICHABOD'S BIRTH

¹² That same day, a Benjaminite man ran from the battle and came to Shiloh. His clothes were torn, and there was dirt on his head. ¹³ When he arrived, there was Eli sitting on his chair beside the road watching, because he was anxious about the ark of God. When the man entered the city to give a report, the entire city cried out.

¹⁴ Eli heard the outcry and asked, "Why this commotion?" The man quickly came and reported to Eli. ¹⁵ At that time Eli was ninety-eight years old, and his eyes didn't move^A because he couldn't see.

¹⁶ The man said to Eli, "I'm the one who came from the battle.^B I fled from there today."

"What happened, my son?" Eli asked.

¹⁷ The messenger answered, "Israel has fled from the Philistines, and also there was a great slaughter among the people. Your two sons, Hophni and Phinehas, are both dead, and the ark of God has been captured." ¹⁸ When he mentioned the ark of God, Eli fell backward off the chair by the city gate, and since he was old and heavy, his neck broke and he died. Eli had judged Israel forty years.

¹⁹ Eli's daughter-in-law, the wife of Phinehas, was pregnant and about to give birth. When she heard the news about the capture of God's ark and the deaths of her father-in-law and her husband, she collapsed and gave birth because her labor pains came on her. ²⁰ As she was dying,^C the women taking care of her said, "Don't be afraid. You've given birth to a son!" But she did not respond or pay attention. ²¹ She named the boy Ichabod,^D saying, "The glory has departed from Israel," referring to the capture of the ark of God and to the deaths of her father-in-law and her husband. ²² "The glory has departed from Israel," she said, "because the ark of God has been captured."

THE ARK IN PHILISTINE HANDS

5 After the Philistines had captured the ark of God, they took it from Ebenezer to Ashdod, ² brought it into the temple of Dagon^E and placed it next to his statue.^F ³ When the people of Ashdod got up early the next morning, there was Dagon, fallen with his face to the ground before the ark of the LORD. So they took Dagon and returned him to his place. ⁴ But when they got up early the next morning, there was Dagon, fallen with his face to the ground before the ark of the LORD. This time, Dagon's head and both of his hands were broken off and lying on the threshold. Only Dagon's torso remained.^G ⁵ That is why, still today, the priests of Dagon and everyone who enters the temple of Dagon in Ashdod do not step on Dagon's threshold.

⁶ The LORD's hand was heavy on the people of Ashdod. He terrified the people of Ashdod and its territory and afflicted them with tumors.^H,I ⁷ When the people of Ashdod saw what was happening, they said, "The ark of Israel's God must not stay here with us, because his hand is strongly against us and

---

^A 4:15 Lit *his eyes stood*; 1Kg 14:4   ^B 4:16 LXX reads *camp*   ^C 4:20 LXX reads *And in her time of delivery, she was about to die*   ^D 4:21 = Where Is Glory?   ^E 5:2 A Philistine god of the sea, grain, or storm   ^F 5:2 Lit *to Dagon*   ^G 5:4 LXX; Hb reads *Only Dagon remained on it*   ^H 5:6 LXX adds *He brought up mice against them, and they swarmed in their ships. Then mice went up into the land and there was a mortal panic in the city.*   ^I 5:6 Perhaps bubonic plague our god Dagon." [8] So they called all the Philistine rulers together and asked, "What should we do with the ark of Israel's God?"

"The ark of Israel's God should be moved to Gath," they replied. So they moved the ark of Israel's God. [9] After they had moved it, the LORD's hand was against the city of Gath, causing a great panic. He afflicted the people of the city, from the youngest to the oldest, with an outbreak of tumors.

[10] The people of Gath then sent the ark of God to Ekron, but when it got there, the Ekronites cried out, "They've moved the ark of Israel's God to us to kill us and our people!"[A]

[11] The Ekronites called all the Philistine rulers together. They said, "Send the ark of Israel's God away. Let it return to its place so it won't kill us and our people!"[B] For the fear of death pervaded the city; God's hand was oppressing them. [12] Those who did not die were afflicted with tumors, and the outcry of the city went up to heaven.

THE RETURN OF THE ARK

6 When the ark of the LORD had been in Philistine territory for seven months, [2] the Philistines summoned the priests and the diviners and pleaded, "What should we do with the ark of the LORD? Tell us how we can send it back to its place."

[3] They replied, "If you send the ark of Israel's God away, do not send it without an offering. Send back a guilt offering to him, and you will be healed. Then the reason his hand hasn't been removed from you will be revealed."[C]

[4] They asked, "What guilt offering should we send back to him?"

And they answered, "Five gold tumors and five gold mice corresponding to the number of Philistine rulers, since there was one plague for both you[D] and your rulers. [5] Make images of your tumors and of your mice that are destroying the land. Give glory to Israel's God, and perhaps he will stop oppressing you,[E] your gods, and your land. [6] Why harden your hearts as the Egyptians and Pharaoh hardened theirs? When he afflicted them, didn't they send Israel away, and Israel left?

[7] "Now then, prepare one new cart and two milk cows that have never been yoked. Hitch the cows to the cart, but take their calves away and pen them up. [8] Take the ark of the LORD, place it on the cart, and put the gold objects that you're sending him as a guilt offering in a box beside the ark. Send it off and let it go its way. [9] Then watch: If it goes up the road to its homeland toward Beth-shemesh, it is the LORD who has made this terrible trouble for us. However, if it doesn't, we will know that it was not his hand that punished us — it was just something that happened to us by chance."

[10] The men did this: They took two milk cows, hitched them to the cart, and confined their calves in the pen. [11] Then they put the ark of the LORD on the cart, along with the box containing the gold mice and the images of their tumors. [12] The cows went straight up the road to Beth-shemesh. They stayed on that one highway, lowing as they went; they never strayed to the

---

[A] 5:10 DSS, LXX read *"Why have you moved . . . people?"*   [B] 5:11 DSS, LXX read *"Why don't you return it to . . . people?"*   [C] 6:3 DSS, LXX read *healed, and an atonement shall be made for you. Shouldn't his hand be removed from you?"*   [D] 6:4 Some Hb mss, LXX; other Hb mss read *them*   [E] 6:5 Lit *will lighten the heaviness of his hand from you* right or to the left. The Philistine rulers were walking behind them to the territory of Beth-shemesh.

¹³ The people of Beth-shemesh were harvesting wheat in the valley, and when they looked up and saw the ark, they were overjoyed to see it. ¹⁴ The cart came to the field of Joshua of Beth-shemesh and stopped there near a large rock. The people of the city chopped up the cart and offered the cows as a burnt offering to the LORD. ¹⁵ The Levites removed the ark of the LORD, along with the box containing the gold objects, and placed them on the large rock. That day the people of Beth-shemesh offered burnt offerings and made sacrifices to the LORD. ¹⁶ When the five Philistine rulers observed this, they returned to Ekron that same day.

¹⁷ As a guilt offering to the LORD, the Philistines had sent back one gold tumor for each city: Ashdod, Gaza, Ashkelon, Gath, and Ekron. ¹⁸ The number of gold mice also corresponded to the number of Philistine cities of the five rulers, the fortified cities and the outlying villages. The large rock ᴬ on which the ark of the LORD was placed is still in the field of Joshua of Beth-shemesh today.

¹⁹ God struck down the people of Beth-shemesh because they looked inside the ark of the LORD. ᴮ He struck down seventy persons. ᶜ The people mourned because the LORD struck them with a great slaughter. ²⁰ The people of Beth-shemesh asked, "Who is able to stand in the presence of the LORD this holy God? To whom should the ark go from here?"

²¹ They sent messengers to the residents of Kiriath-jearim, saying, "The Philistines have returned the ark of the LORD. Come down and get it." ᴰ

7 So the people of Kiriath-jearim came for the ark of the LORD and took it to Abinadab's house on the hill. They consecrated his son Eleazar to take care of it.

VICTORY AT MIZPAH

² Time went by until twenty years had passed since the ark had been taken to Kiriath-jearim. Then the whole house of Israel longed for the LORD. ³ Samuel told them, "If you are returning to the LORD with all your heart, get rid of the foreign gods and the Ashtoreths that are among you, dedicate yourselves to ᴱ the LORD, and worship only him. Then he will rescue you from the Philistines." ⁴ So the Israelites removed the Baals and the Ashtoreths and only worshiped the LORD.

⁵ Samuel said, "Gather all Israel at Mizpah, and I will pray to the LORD on your behalf." ⁶ When they gathered at Mizpah, they drew water and poured it out in the LORD's presence. They fasted that day, and there they confessed, "We have sinned against the LORD." And Samuel judged the Israelites at Mizpah.

⁷ When the Philistines heard that the Israelites had gathered at Mizpah, their rulers marched up toward Israel. When the Israelites heard about it, they were afraid because of the Philistines. ⁸ The Israelites said to Samuel,

---

ᴬ 6:18 Some Hb mss, DSS, LXX, Tg; other Hb mss read *meadow*   ᴮ 6:19 LXX reads *But the sons of Jeconiah did not rejoice with the men of Beth-shemesh when they saw the ark of the LORD.*   ᶜ 6:19 Some Hb mss, Josephus; other Hb mss read *70 men, 50,000 men*   ᴰ 6:21 Lit *and bring it up to you*   ᴱ 7:3 Lit *you and set your hearts on*

"Don't stop crying out to the LORD our God for us, so that he will save us from the Philistines."

⁹ Then Samuel took a young lamb and offered it as a whole burnt offering to the LORD. He cried out to the LORD on behalf of Israel, and the LORD answered him. ¹⁰ Samuel was offering the burnt offering as the Philistines approached to fight against Israel. The LORD thundered loudly against the Philistines that day and threw them into such confusion that they were defeated by Israel. ¹¹ Then the men of Israel charged out of Mizpah and pursued the Philistines striking them down all the way to a place below Beth-car.

¹² Afterward, Samuel took a stone and set it upright between Mizpah and Shen. He named it Ebenezer,^A explaining, "The LORD has helped us to this point." ¹³ So the Philistines were subdued and^B did not invade Israel's territory again. The LORD's hand was against the Philistines all of Samuel's life. ¹⁴ The cities from Ekron to Gath, which they had taken from Israel, were restored; Israel even rescued their surrounding territories from Philistine control. There was also peace between Israel and the Amorites.

¹⁵ Samuel judged Israel throughout his life. ¹⁶ Every year he would go on a circuit to Bethel, Gilgal, and Mizpah and would judge Israel at all these locations. ¹⁷ Then he would return to Ramah because his home was there, he judged Israel there, and he built an altar to the LORD there.

ISRAEL'S DEMAND FOR A KING

8 When Samuel grew old, he appointed his sons as judges over Israel. ² His firstborn son's name was Joel and his second was Abijah. They were judges in Beer-sheba. ³ However, his sons did not walk in his ways — they turned toward dishonest profit, took bribes, and perverted justice.

⁴ So all the elders of Israel gathered together and went to Samuel at Ramah. ⁵ They said to him, "Look, you are old, and your sons do not walk in your ways. Therefore, appoint a king to judge us the same as all the other nations have."

⁶ When they said, "Give us a king to judge us," Samuel considered their demand wrong, so he prayed to the LORD. ⁷ But the LORD told him, "Listen to the people and everything they say to you. They have not rejected you; they have rejected me as their king. ⁸ They are doing the same thing to you that they have done to me,^C since the day I brought them out of Egypt until this day, abandoning me and worshiping other gods. ⁹ Listen to them, but solemnly warn them and tell them about the customary rights of the king who will reign over them."

¹⁰ Samuel told all the LORD's words to the people who were asking him for a king. ¹¹ He said, "These are the rights of the king who will reign over you: He will take your sons and put them to his use in his chariots, on his horses, or running in front of his chariots. ¹² He can appoint them for his use as commanders of thousands or commanders of fifties, to plow his ground and reap his harvest, or to make his weapons of war and the equipment for his chariots. ¹³ He can take your daughters to become perfumers, cooks, and bakers. ¹⁴ He can take your best fields, vineyards, and olive orchards and give them to his servants. ¹⁵ He can take a tenth of your grain and your vineyards and give them to his officials and servants. ¹⁶ He can take your

---

^A 7:12 = Stone of Help   ^B 7:13 LXX reads *The LORD humbled the Philistines and they*
^C 8:8 LXX; MT omits *to me*

REJECTING THE KING

1 SAMUEL 8; PSALM 72; PROVERBS 1:29-33; 2 PETER 2:19

Here we go again. In 1 Samuel 8, we find Israel rejecting their God, the One who rescued them from slavery, provided for them in the desert, and gave them victory over their enemies.

Israel instead demanded a king who would judge them, go before them, and fight their battles (1Sm 8:20). Ironically, the King they rejected was the only king to fulfill this request. God had already been their Judge (Dt 32:36), gone out before them (Ex 13:21), and fought their battles (Ex 13:21; 14:14).

But they wanted a king "the same as all the other nations" (1Sm 8:5). So they rejected their true King, the God of heaven and earth. God granted their request and gave them over to their desires, but not without a warning. He promised to give them a king like all the other nations—but He would give them one who was selfish, oppressive, and ruthless. They didn't heed His warning.

I want to be like everyone else, too. I want to look like everyone else, to be both beautiful and adorable, and so I make my appearance king. Then I find myself overcome by my obsessive eating habits and exercise routine. Turns out that king won't provide what I need.

I want to have what everyone else has, to feel important and sophisticated, and so I make my possessions king. I spend my time, money, and energy filling my closet with pretty new dresses. But I'll never have enough because this king demands more and more and more.

I could go on, and I'm sure you could, too. Our individual kings demand more from us than we'd ever be willing to give. They lie and tell us that if we could have what the world has, we would have freedom. Second Peter 2:19 warns against this:

> *"They promise them freedom, but they themselves are slaves of corruption, since people are enslaved to whatever defeats them."*

This is what happens when we, like Israel, fall prey to the desire of being like everyone else. Instead of gaining freedom, we become slaves of corruption. **In our efforts to be like the world, we miss out on what we truly need—freedom that can only come from submitting ourselves to the true King, Jesus Christ.**

Through Israel's rebellion God provided what they really needed. He would later appoint David as king over Israel, and through his family, provide the true King in Jesus Christ. He is the One who ultimately goes before us and fights our battles (Rv 19:11-16). He is all we need, and only in submitting to Him as King will we find freedom instead of slavery (Lk 4:18).

male servants, your female servants, your best young men,[A] and your donkeys and use them for his work. [17] He can take a tenth of your flocks, and you yourselves can become his servants. [18] When that day comes, you will cry out because of the king you've chosen for yourselves, but the LORD won't answer you on that day."

[19] The people refused to listen to Samuel. "No!" they said. "We must have a king over us. [20] Then we'll be like all the other nations: our king will judge us, go out before us, and fight our battles."

[21] Samuel listened to all the people's words and then repeated them to the LORD.[B] [22] "Listen to them," the LORD told Samuel. "Appoint a king for them."

Then Samuel told the men of Israel, "Each of you, go back to your city."

SAUL ANOINTED KING

9 There was a prominent man of Benjamin named Kish son of Abiel, son of Zeror, son of Becorath, son of Aphiah, son of a Benjaminite. [2] He had a son named Saul, an impressive young man. There was no one more impressive among the Israelites than he. He stood a head taller than anyone else.[C]

[3] One day the donkeys of Saul's father Kish wandered off. Kish said to his son Saul, "Take one of the servants with you and go look for the donkeys." [4] Saul and his servant went through the hill country of Ephraim and then through the region of Shalishah, but they didn't find them. They went through the region of Shaalim — nothing. Then they went through the Benjaminite region but still didn't find them.

[5] When they came to the land of Zuph, Saul said to the servant who was with him, "Come on, let's go back, or my father will stop worrying about the donkeys and start worrying about us."

[6] "Look," the servant said, "there's a man of God in this city who is highly respected; everything he says is sure to come true. Let's go there now. Maybe he'll tell us which way we should go."

[7] "Suppose we do go," Saul said to his servant, "what do we take the man? The food from our packs is gone, and there's no gift to take to the man of God. What do we have?"

[8] The servant answered Saul: "Here, I have a little[D] silver. I'll give it to the man of God, and he will tell us which way we should go."

[9] Formerly in Israel, a man who was going to inquire of God would say, "Come, let's go to the seer," for the prophet of today was formerly called the seer.

[10] "Good," Saul replied to his servant. "Come on, let's go." So they went to the city where the man of God was. [11] As they were climbing the hill to the city, they found some young women coming out to draw water and asked, "Is the seer here?"

[12] The women answered, "Yes, he is ahead of you. Hurry, he just now entered the city, because there's a sacrifice for the people at the high place today. [13] As soon as you enter the city, you will find him before he goes to the high place to eat. The people won't eat until he comes because he must bless the sacrifice; after that, the guests can eat. Go up immediately — you can find him now." [14] So they went up toward the city.

Saul and his servant were entering the city when they saw Samuel coming toward them on his way to the high place. ¹⁵ Now the day before Saul's arrival, the Lᴏʀᴅ had informed Samuel,ᴬ ¹⁶ "At this time tomorrow I will send you a man from the land of Benjamin. Anoint him ruler over my people Israel. He will save them from the Philistines because I have seen the affliction of my people, for their cry has come to me." ¹⁷ When Samuel saw Saul, the Lᴏʀᴅ told him, "Here is the man I told you about; he will govern my people."

¹⁸ Saul approached Samuel in the city gate and asked, "Would you please tell me where the seer's house is?"

¹⁹ "I am the seer," Samuel answered.ᴮ "Go up ahead of me to the high place and eat with me today. When I send you off in the morning, I'll tell you everything that's in your heart. ²⁰ As for the donkeys that wandered away from you three days ago, don't worry about them because they've been found. And who does all Israel desire but you and all your father's family?"

²¹ Saul responded, "Am I not a Benjaminite from the smallest of Israel's tribes and isn't my clan the least important of all the clans of the Benjaminite tribe? So why have you said something like this to me?"

²² Samuel took Saul and his servant, brought them to the banquet hall, and gave them a place at the head of the thirtyᶜ or so men who had been invited. ²³ Then Samuel said to the cook, "Get the portion of meat that I gave you and told you to set aside."

²⁴ The cook picked up the thigh and what was attached to it and set it before Saul. Then Samuel said, "Notice that the reserved piece is set before you. Eat it because it was saved for you for this solemn event at the time I said, 'I've invited the people.'" So Saul ate with Samuel that day. ²⁵ Afterward, they went down from the high place to the city, and Samuel spoke with Saul on the roof.ᴰ

²⁶ They got up early, and just before dawn, Samuel called to Saul on the roof, "Get up, and I'll send you on your way!" Saul got up, and both he and Samuel went outside. ²⁷ As they were going down to the edge of the city, Samuel said to Saul, "Tell the servant to go on ahead of us, but you stay for a while, and I'll reveal the word of God to you." So the servant went on.

10 Samuel took the flask of oil, poured it out on Saul's head, kissed him, and said, "Hasn't the Lᴏʀᴅ anointed you ruler over his inheritance?ᴱ ² Today when you leave me, you'll find two men at Rachel's Grave at Zelzah in the territory of Benjamin. They will say to you, 'The donkeys you went looking for have been found, and now your father has stopped being concerned about the donkeys and is worried about you, asking: What should I do about my son?'

³ "You will proceed from there until you come to the oak of Tabor. Three men going up to God at Bethel will meet you there, one bringing three goats, one bringing three loaves of bread, and one bringing a clay jar of wine. ⁴ They will ask how you are and give you two loavesᶠ of bread, which you will accept from them.

ᴬ9:15 Lit had uncovered Samuel's ear, saying   ᴮ9:19 Lit answered Saul
ᶜ9:22 LXX reads 70   ᴰ9:25 LXX reads city. They prepared a bed for Saul on the
roof, and he slept.   ᴱ10:1 LXX adds And you will reign over the Lᴏʀᴅ's people,
and you will save them from the hand of their enemies all around. And this is
the sign to you that the Lᴏʀᴅ has anointed you ruler over his inheritance.
ᶠ10:4 DSS, LXX read wave offerings

⁵ "After that you will come to Gibeah of God where there are Philistine garrisons. ᴬ When you arrive at the city, you will meet a group of prophets coming down from the high place prophesying. They will be preceded by harps,
tambourines, flutes, and lyres. ⁶ The Spirit of the LORD will come powerfully
on you, you will prophesy with them, and you will be transformed. ⁷ When
these signs have happened to you, do whatever your circumstances require ᴮ
because God is with you. ⁸ Afterward, go ahead of me to Gilgal. I will come
to you to offer burnt offerings and to sacrifice fellowship offerings. Wait
seven days until I come to you and show you what to do."

⁹ When Saul turned around ᶜ to leave Samuel, God changed his heart, ᴰ
and all the signs came about that day. ¹⁰ When Saul and his servant arrived
at Gibeah, a group of prophets met him. Then the Spirit of God came powerfully on him, and he prophesied along with them.

¹¹ Everyone who knew him previously and saw him prophesy with the
prophets asked each other, "What has happened to the son of Kish? Is Saul
also among the prophets?"

¹² Then a man who was from there asked, "And who is their father?"

As a result, "Is Saul also among the prophets?" became a popular saying.
¹³ Then Saul finished prophesying and went to the high place.

¹⁴ Saul's uncle asked him and his servant, "Where did you go?"

"To look for the donkeys," Saul answered. "When we saw they weren't
there, we went to Samuel."

¹⁵ "Tell me," Saul's uncle asked, "what did Samuel say to you?"

¹⁶ Saul told him, "He assured us the donkeys had been found." However,
Saul did not tell him what Samuel had said about the matter of kingship.

SAUL RECEIVED AS KING

¹⁷ Samuel summoned the people to the LORD at Mizpah ¹⁸ and said to the Israelites, "This is what the LORD, the God of Israel, says: 'I brought Israel out of
Egypt, and I rescued you from the power of the Egyptians and all the kingdoms that were oppressing you.' ¹⁹ But today you have rejected your God,
who saves you from all your troubles and afflictions. You said to him, 'You ᴱ
must set a king over us.' Now therefore present yourselves before the LORD
by your tribes and clans."

²⁰ Samuel had all the tribes of Israel come forward, and the tribe of Benjamin was selected. ²¹ Then he had the tribe of Benjamin come forward by
its clans, and the Matrite clan was selected. ᶠ Finally, Saul son of Kish was
selected. But when they searched for him, they could not find him. ²² They
again inquired of the LORD, "Has the man come here yet?"

The LORD replied, "There he is, hidden among the supplies."

²³ They ran and got him from there. When he stood among the people, he
stood a head taller than anyone else. ᴳ ²⁴ Samuel said to all the people, "Do
you see the one the LORD has chosen? There is no one like him among the
entire population."

ᴬ10:5 Or *governors* ᴮ10:7 Lit *do for yourself whatever your hand finds*
ᶜ10:9 Lit *turned his shoulder* ᴰ10:9 Lit *God turned to him another heart*
ᴱ10:19 Some Hb mss, LXX, Syr, Vg read *You said, 'No, you* ᶠ10:21 LXX adds
And he had the Matrite clan come forward, man by man. ᴳ10:23 Lit *people,*
and he was higher than any of the people from his shoulder and up

And all the people shouted,[A] "Long live the king!"

²⁵ Samuel proclaimed to the people the rights of kingship. He wrote them on a scroll, which he placed in the presence of the LORD. Then Samuel sent all the people home.

²⁶ Saul also went to his home in Gibeah, and brave men whose hearts God had touched went with him. ²⁷ But some wicked men said, "How can this guy save us?" They despised him and did not bring him a gift, but Saul said nothing.[B,C]

SAUL'S DELIVERANCE OF JABESH-GILEAD

11 Nahash[D] the Ammonite came up and laid siege to Jabesh-gilead. All the men of Jabesh said to him, "Make a treaty with us, and we will serve you."

² Nahash the Ammonite replied, "I'll make one with you on this condition: that I gouge out everyone's right eye and humiliate all Israel."

³ "Don't do anything to us for seven days," the elders of Jabesh said to him, "and let us send messengers throughout the territory of Israel. If no one saves us, we will surrender to you."

⁴ When the messengers came to Gibeah, Saul's hometown, and told the terms to[E] the people, all wept aloud. ⁵ Just then Saul was coming in from the field behind his oxen. "What's the matter with the people? Why are they weeping?" Saul inquired, and they repeated to him the words of the men from Jabesh.

⁶ When Saul heard these words, the Spirit of God suddenly came powerfully on him, and his anger burned furiously. ⁷ He took a team of oxen, cut them in pieces, and sent them throughout the territory of Israel by messengers who said, "This is what will be done to the ox of anyone who doesn't march behind Saul and Samuel." As a result, the terror of the LORD fell on the people, and they went out united.

⁸ Saul counted them at Bezek. There were three hundred thousand[F] Israelites and thirty thousand[G] men from Judah. ⁹ He told the messengers who had come, "Tell this to the men of Jabesh-gilead: 'Deliverance will be yours tomorrow by the time the sun is hot.'" So the messengers told the men of Jabesh, and they rejoiced.

¹⁰ Then the men of Jabesh said to Nahash, "Tomorrow we will come out, and you can do whatever you want[H] to us."

¹¹ The next day Saul organized the troops into three divisions. During the morning watch, they invaded the Ammonite camp and slaughtered them until the heat of the day. There were survivors, but they were so scattered that no two of them were left together.

[A] 10:24 LXX reads *acknowledged and said*   [B] 10:27 DSS add *Nahash king of the Ammonites had been severely oppressing the Gadites and Reubenites. He gouged out the right eye of each of them and brought fear and trembling on Israel. Of the Israelites beyond the Jordan none remained whose right eye Nahash, king of the Ammonites, had not gouged out. But there were seven thousand men who had escaped from the Ammonites and entered Jabesh-gilead.*   [C] 10:27 Lit *gift, and he was like a mute person*   [D] 11:1 DSS, LXX read *About a month later, Nahash*   [E] 11:4 Lit *in the ears of*   [F] 11:8 LXX reads *600,000*   [G] 11:8 DSS, LXX read *70,000*   [H] 11:10 Lit *do what is good in your eyes*

SAUL'S CONFIRMATION AS KING

[12] Afterward, the people said to Samuel, "Who said that Saul should not[A] reign over us? Give us those men so we can kill them!"

[13] But Saul ordered, "No one will be executed this day, for today the LORD has provided deliverance in Israel."

[14] Then Samuel said to the people, "Come, let's go to Gilgal, so we can renew the kingship there." [15] So all the people went to Gilgal, and there in the LORD's presence they made Saul king. There they sacrificed fellowship offerings in the LORD's presence, and Saul and all the men of Israel rejoiced greatly.

SAMUEL'S FINAL PUBLIC SPEECH

12 Then Samuel said to all Israel, "I have carefully listened to everything you said to me and placed a king over you. [2] Now you can see that the king is leading you. As for me, I'm old and gray, and my sons are here with you. I have led you from my youth until now. [3] Here I am. Bring charges against me before the LORD and his anointed: Whose ox or donkey have I taken? Whom have I wronged or mistreated? From whom have I accepted a bribe to overlook something?[B,C] I will return it to you."

[4] "You haven't wronged us, you haven't mistreated us, and you haven't taken anything from anyone," they responded.

[5] He said to them, "The LORD is a witness against you, and his anointed is a witness today that you haven't found anything in my hand."

"He is a witness," they said.

[6] Then Samuel said to the people, "The LORD, who appointed Moses and Aaron and who brought your ancestors up from the land of Egypt, is a witness.[D] [7] Now present yourselves, so I may confront you before the LORD about all the righteous acts he has done for you and your ancestors.

[8] "When Jacob went to Egypt,[E] your ancestors cried out to the LORD, and he sent them Moses and Aaron, who led your ancestors out of Egypt and settled them in this place. [9] But they forgot the LORD their God, so he handed them over to Sisera commander of the army of Hazor, to the Philistines, and to the king of Moab. These enemies fought against them. [10] Then they cried out to the LORD and said, 'We have sinned, for we abandoned the LORD and worshiped the Baals and the Ashtoreths. Now rescue us from the power of our enemies, and we will serve you.' [11] So the LORD sent Jerubbaal, Barak,[F] Jephthah, and Samuel. He rescued you from the power of the enemies around you, and you lived securely. [12] But when you saw that Nahash king of the Ammonites was coming against you, you said to me, 'No, we must have a king reign over us' — even though the LORD your God is your king.

[13] "Now here is the king you've chosen, the one you requested. Look, this is the king the LORD has placed over you. [14] If you fear the LORD, worship and obey him, and if you don't rebel against the LORD's command, then both you and the king who reigns over you will follow the LORD your God. [15] However,

---

[A]11:12 Some Hb mss, LXX; other Hb mss omit *not*   [B]12:3 LXX reads *bribe or a pair of shoes? Testify against me.*   [C]12:3 Lit *bribe and will hide my eyes with it?*   [D]12:6 LXX; MT omits *is a witness*   [E]12:8 LXX reads *"When Jacob and his sons went to Egypt and Egypt humbled them*   [F]12:11 LXX, Syr; MT reads *Bedan* ; Jdg 4:6; Heb 11:32

if you disobey the LORD and rebel against his command, the LORD's hand will be against you as it was against your ancestors.^A

[16] "Now, therefore, present yourselves and see this great thing that the LORD will do before your eyes. [17] Isn't the wheat harvest today? I will call on the LORD, and he will send thunder and rain so that you will recognize^B what an immense evil you committed in the LORD's sight by requesting a king for yourselves." [18] Samuel called on the LORD, and on that day the LORD sent thunder and rain. As a result, all the people greatly feared the LORD and Samuel.

[19] They pleaded with Samuel, "Pray to the LORD your God for your servants so we won't die! For we have added to all our sins the evil of requesting a king for ourselves."

[20] Samuel replied, "Don't be afraid. Even though you have committed all this evil, don't turn away from following the LORD. Instead, worship the LORD with all your heart. [21] Don't turn away to follow worthless^C things that can't profit or rescue you; they are worthless. [22] The LORD will not abandon his people, because of his great name and because he has determined to make you his own people.

[23] "As for me, I vow that I will not sin against the LORD by ceasing to pray for you. I will teach you the good and right way. [24] Above all, fear the LORD and worship him faithfully with all your heart; consider the great things he has done for you. [25] However, if you continue to do what is evil, both you and your king will be swept away."

SAUL'S FAILURE

13 Saul was thirty years^D old when he became king, and he reigned forty-two years^E over Israel.^F [2] He chose three thousand men from Israel for himself: two thousand were with Saul at Michmash and in Bethel's hill country, and one thousand were with Jonathan in Gibeah of Benjamin. He sent the rest of the troops away, each to his own tent.

[3] Jonathan attacked the Philistine garrison^G that was in Geba, and the Philistines heard about it. So Saul blew the ram's horn throughout the land saying, "Let the Hebrews hear!"^H [4] And all Israel heard the news, "Saul has attacked the Philistine garrison, and Israel is now repulsive to the Philistines." Then the troops were summoned to join Saul at Gilgal.

[5] The Philistines also gathered to fight against Israel: three thousand^I chariots, six thousand horsemen, and troops as numerous as the sand on the seashore. They went up and camped at Michmash, east of Beth-aven.^J

[6] The men of Israel saw that they were in trouble because the troops were in a difficult situation. They hid in caves, in thickets, among rocks, and in holes and cisterns. [7] Some Hebrews even crossed the Jordan to the land of Gad and Gilead.

Saul, however, was still at Gilgal, and all his troops were gripped with fear. [8] He waited seven days for the appointed time that Samuel had set, but

---

^A 12:15 LXX *against you and against your king*   ^B 12:17 Lit *know and see*
^C 12:21 LXX reads *away after empty*   ^D 13:1 Some LXX mss; MT reads *was one year*   ^E 13:1 Text emended; MT reads *two years*   ^F 13:1 Some LXX mss omit v. 1
^G 13:3 Or *governor*, also in v. 4   ^H 13:3 LXX reads *"The slaves have revolted"*
^I 13:5 One LXX ms, Syr; MT reads *30,000*   ^J 13:5 LXX reads *Michmash, opposite Beth-horon to the south*

Samuel didn't come to Gilgal, and the troops were deserting him. ⁹ So Saul said, "Bring me the burnt offering and the fellowship offerings." Then he offered the burnt offering.

¹⁰ Just as he finished offering the burnt offering, Samuel arrived. So Saul went out to greet him, ¹¹ and Samuel asked, "What have you done?"

Saul answered, "When I saw that the troops were deserting me and you didn't come within the appointed days and the Philistines were gathering at Michmash, ¹² I thought, 'The Philistines will now descend on me at Gilgal, and I haven't sought the LORD's favor.' So I forced myself to offer the burnt offering."

¹³ Samuel said to Saul, "You have been foolish. You have not kept the command the LORD your God gave you. It was at this time that the LORD would have permanently established your reign over Israel, ¹⁴ but now your reign will not endure. The LORD has found a man after his own heart,ᴬ and the LORD has appointed him as ruler over his people, because you have not done what the LORD commanded." ¹⁵ Then Samuel wentᴮ from Gilgal to Gibeah in Benjamin. Saul registered the troops who were with him, about six hundred men.

¹⁶ Saul, his son Jonathan, and the troops who were with them were staying in Geba of Benjamin, and the Philistines were camped at Michmash. ¹⁷ Raiding parties went out from the Philistine camp in three divisions. One division headed toward the Ophrah road leading to the land of Shual. ¹⁸ The next division headed toward the Beth-horon road, and the last division headed down the border road that looks out over the Zeboim Valley toward the wilderness.

¹⁹ No blacksmith could be found in all the land of Israel because the Philistines had said, "Otherwise, the Hebrews will make swords or spears." ²⁰ So all the Israelites went to the Philistines to sharpen their plows, mattocks, axes, and sickles.ᶜ ²¹ The price was two-thirds of a shekelᴰ for plows and mattocks, and one-third of a shekel for pitchforks and axes, and for putting a point on a cattle prod. ²² So on the day of battle not a sword or spear could be found in the hand of any of the troops who were with Saul and Jonathan; only Saul and his son Jonathan had weapons.

JONATHAN'S VICTORY OVER THE PHILISTINES

14 ²³ Now a Philistine garrison took control of the pass at Michmash. ¹ That same day Saul's son Jonathan said to the attendant who carried his weapons, "Come on, let's cross over to the Philistine garrison on the other side." However, he did not tell his father.

² Saul was staying under the pomegranate tree in Migron on the outskirts of Gibeah.ᴱ The troops with him numbered about six hundred. ³ Ahijah, who was wearing an ephod, was also there. He was the son of Ahitub, the brother of Ichabod son of Phinehas, son of Eli the LORD's priest at Shiloh. But the troops did not know that Jonathan had left.

⁴ There were sharp columnsᶠ of rock on both sides of the pass that Jonathan intended to cross to reach the Philistine garrison. One was named

---

ᴬ13:14 Lit *man according to his heart* ᴮ13:15 LXX reads *Samuel left Gilgal and went on his way, and the rest of the people followed Saul to join the people in his army. They went* ᶜ13:20 LXX; MT reads *plowshares* ᴰ13:21 Lit *of a pim;* about one-fourth ounce of silver ᴱ14:2 LXX reads *on top of the hill* ᶠ14:4 Lit *There was a tooth*

Bozez and the other Seneh; ⁵ one stood to the north in front of Michmash and the other to the south in front of Geba. ⁶ Jonathan said to the attendant who carried his weapons, "Come on, let's cross over to the garrison of these uncircumcised men. Perhaps the LORD will help us. Nothing can keep the LORD from saving, whether by many or by few."

⁷ His armor-bearer responded, "Do what is in your heart. You choose. I'm right here with you whatever you decide."

⁸ "All right," Jonathan replied, "we'll cross over to the men and then let them see us. ⁹ If they say, 'Wait until we reach you,' then we will stay where we are and not go up to them. ¹⁰ But if they say, 'Come on up,' then we'll go up, because the LORD has handed them over to us — that will be our sign."

¹¹ They let themselves be seen by the Philistine garrison, and the Philistines said, "Look, the Hebrews are coming out of the holes where they've been hiding!" ¹² The men of the garrison called to Jonathan and his armor-bearer. "Come on up, and we'll teach you a lesson!" they said.

"Follow me," Jonathan told his armor-bearer, "for the LORD has handed them over to Israel." ¹³ Jonathan climbed up using his hands and feet, with his armor-bearer behind him. Jonathan cut them down, and his armor-bearer followed and finished them off. ¹⁴ In that first assault Jonathan and his armor-bearer struck down about twenty men in a half-acre field.

A DEFEAT FOR THE PHILISTINES

¹⁵ Terror spread through the Philistine camp and the open fields to all the troops. Even the garrison and the raiding parties were terrified. The earth shook, and terror spread from God.ᴬ ¹⁶ When Saul's watchmen in Gibeah of Benjamin looked, they saw the panicking troops scattering in every direction. ¹⁷ So Saul said to the troops with him, "Call the roll and determine who has left us." They called the roll and saw that Jonathan and his armor-bearer were gone.

¹⁸ Saul told Ahijah, "Bring the ark of God," for it was with the Israelitesᴮ at that time. ¹⁹ While Saul spoke to the priest, the panic in the Philistine camp increased in intensity. So Saul said to the priest, "Stop what you're doing."ᶜ

²⁰ Saul and all the troops with him assembled and marched to the battle, and there the Philistines were, fighting against each other in great confusion! ²¹ There were Hebrews from the area who had gone earlier into the camp to join the Philistines, but even they joined the Israelites who were with Saul and Jonathan. ²² When all the Israelite men who had been hiding in the hill country of Ephraim heard that the Philistines were fleeing, they also joined Saul and Jonathan in the battle. ²³ So the LORD saved Israel that day.

SAUL'S RASH OATH

The battle extended beyond Beth-aven, ²⁴ and the men of Israel were worn out that day, for Saul hadᴰ placed the troops under an oath: "The man who eats food before evening, before I have taken vengeance on my enemies is cursed." So none of the troops tasted any food.

ᴬ14:15 Or and a great terror spread   ᴮ14:18 LXX reads "Bring the ephod."
For he wore the ephod before Israel   ᶜ14:19 Lit "Withdraw your hand"
ᴰ14:24 LXX adds committed a great act of ignorance and

²⁵ Everyone^A went into the forest, and there was honey on the ground. ²⁶ When the troops entered the forest, they saw the flow of honey, but none of them ate any of it^B because they feared the oath. ²⁷ However, Jonathan had not heard his father make the troops swear the oath. He reached out with the end of the staff he was carrying and dipped it into the honeycomb. When he ate the honey,^C he had renewed energy.^D ²⁸ Then one of the troops said, "Your father made the troops solemnly swear, 'The man who eats food today is cursed,' and the troops are exhausted."

²⁹ Jonathan replied, "My father has brought trouble to the land. Just look at how I have renewed energy^E because I tasted a little of this honey. ³⁰ How much better if the troops had eaten freely today from the plunder they took from their enemies! Then the slaughter of the Philistines would have been much greater."

³¹ The Israelites struck down the Philistines that day from Michmash all the way to Aijalon. Since the Israelites were completely exhausted, ³² they rushed to the plunder, took sheep, goats, cattle, and calves, slaughtered them on the ground, and ate meat with the blood still in it. ³³ Some reported to Saul: "Look, the troops are sinning against the Lᴏʀᴅ by eating meat with the blood still in it."

Saul said, "You have been unfaithful. Roll a large stone over here at once." ³⁴ He then said, "Go among the troops and say to them, 'Let each man bring me his ox or his sheep. Do the slaughtering here and then you can eat. Don't sin against the Lᴏʀᴅ by eating meat with the blood in it.'" So every one of the troops brought his ox that night and slaughtered it there. ³⁵ Then Saul built an altar to the Lᴏʀᴅ; it was the first time he had built an altar to the Lᴏʀᴅ.

³⁶ Saul said, "Let's go down after the Philistines tonight and plunder them until morning. Don't let even one remain!"

"Do whatever you want,"^F the troops replied.

But the priest said, "Let's approach God here."

³⁷ So Saul inquired of God, "Should I go after the Philistines? Will you hand them over to Israel?" But God did not answer him that day.

³⁸ Saul said, "All you leaders of the troops, come here. Let us investigate^G how this sin has occurred today. ³⁹ As surely as the Lᴏʀᴅ lives who saves Israel, even if it is because of my son Jonathan, he must die!" Not one of the troops answered him.

⁴⁰ So he said to all Israel, "You will be on one side, and I and my son Jonathan will be on the other side."

And the troops replied, "Do whatever you want."

⁴¹ So Saul said to the Lᴏʀᴅ, "God of Israel, why have you not answered your servant today? If the unrighteousness is in me or in my son Jonathan, Lᴏʀᴅ God of Israel, give Urim; but if the fault is in your people Israel, give Thummim."^H Jonathan and Saul were selected, and the troops were cleared of the charge.

⁴² Then Saul said, "Cast the lot between me and my son Jonathan," and Jonathan was selected. ⁴³ Saul commanded him, "Tell me what you did."

---

^A14:25 Lit *All the land*   ^B14:26 Lit *but there was none who raised his hand to his mouth*   ^C14:27 Lit *he returned his hand to his mouth*   ^D14:27 Lit *his eyes became bright*   ^E14:29 Lit *how my eyes became bright*   ^F14:36 Lit *Do what is good in your eyes,* also in v. 40   ^G14:38 Lit *know and see*   ^H14:41 LXX; MT reads *said to the* Lᴏʀᴅ, *"God of Israel, give us the right decision."*

Jonathan told him, "I tasted a little honey with the end of the staff I was carrying. I am ready to die!"

⁴⁴ Saul declared to him, "May God punish me and do so severely if you do not die, Jonathan!"

⁴⁵ But the people said to Saul, "Must Jonathan die, who accomplished such a great deliverance for Israel? No, as the LORD lives, not a hair of his head will fall to the ground, for he worked with God's help today." So the people redeemed Jonathan, and he did not die. ⁴⁶ Then Saul gave up the pursuit of the Philistines, and the Philistines returned to their own territory.

SUMMARY OF SAUL'S KINGSHIP

⁴⁷ When Saul assumed the kingship over Israel, he fought against all his enemies in every direction: against Moab, the Ammonites, Edom, the kings of Zobah, and the Philistines. Wherever he turned, he caused havoc.ᴬ ⁴⁸ He fought bravely, defeated the Amalekites, and rescued Israel from those who plundered them.

⁴⁹ Saul's sons were Jonathan, Ishvi, and Malchishua. The names of his two daughters were Merab, his firstborn, and Michal, the younger. ⁵⁰ The name of Saul's wife was Ahinoam daughter of Ahimaaz. The name of the commander of his army was Abner son of Saul's uncle Ner. ⁵¹ Saul's father was Kish. Abner's father was Ner son of Abiel.

⁵² The conflict with the Philistines was fierce all of Saul's days, so whenever Saul noticed any strong or valiant man, he enlisted him.

SAUL REJECTED AS KING

15 Samuel told Saul, "The LORD sent me to anoint you as king over his people Israel. Now, listen to the words of the LORD. ² This is what the LORD of Armies says: 'I witnessedᴮ what the Amalekites did to the Israelites when they opposed them along the way as they were coming out of Egypt. ³ Now go and attack the Amalekites and completely destroy everything they have. Do not spare them. Kill men and women, infants and nursing babies, oxen and sheep, camels and donkeys.'"

⁴ Then Saul summoned the troops and counted them at Telaim: two hundred thousand foot soldiers and ten thousand men from Judah. ⁵ Saul came to the city of Amalek and set up an ambush in the wadi. ⁶ He warned the Kenites, "Since you showed kindness to all the Israelites when they came out of Egypt, go on and leave! Get away from the Amalekites, or I'll sweep you away with them." So the Kenites withdrew from the Amalekites.

⁷ Then Saul struck down the Amalekites from Havilah all the way to Shur, which is next to Egypt. ⁸ He captured King Agag of Amalek alive, but he completely destroyed all the rest of the people with the sword. ⁹ Saul and the troops spared Agag, and the best of the sheep, goats, cattle, and choice animals,ᶜ as well as the young rams and the best of everything else. They were not willing to destroy them, but they did destroy all the worthless and unwanted things.

¹⁰ Then the word of the LORD came to Samuel, ¹¹ "I regret that I made Saul king, for he has turned away from following me and has not carried out my instructions." So Samuel became angry and cried out to the LORD all night.

ᴬ14:47 LXX reads *he was victorious*   ᴮ15:2 LXX reads *I will avenge*   ᶜ15:9 Lit *and the second ones*

¹²Early in the morning Samuel got up to confront Saul, but it was reported to Samuel, "Saul went to Carmel where he set up a monument for himself. Then he turned around and went down to Gilgal." ¹³When Samuel came to him, Saul said, "May the LORD bless you. I have carried out the LORD's instructions."

¹⁴Samuel replied, "Then what is this sound of sheep, goats,ᴬ and cattle I hear?"

¹⁵Saul answered, "The troops brought them from the Amalekites and spared the best sheep, goats, and cattle in order to offer a sacrifice to the LORD your God, but the rest we destroyed."

¹⁶"Stop!" exclaimed Samuel. "Let me tell you what the LORD said to me last night."

"Tell me," he replied.

¹⁷Samuel continued, "Although you once considered yourself unimportant, have you not become the leader of the tribes of Israel? The LORD anointed you king over Israel ¹⁸and then sent you on a mission and said: 'Go and completely destroy the sinful Amalekites. Fight against them until you have annihilated them.' ¹⁹So why didn't you obey the LORD? Why did you rush on the plunder and do what was evil in the LORD's sight?"

²⁰"But I did obey the LORD!" Saul answered.ᴮ "I went on the mission the LORD gave me: I brought back King Agag of Amalek, and I completely destroyed the Amalekites. ²¹The troops took sheep, goats, and cattle from the plunder — the best of what was set apart for destruction — to sacrifice to the LORD your God at Gilgal."

²²Then Samuel said:

Does the LORD take pleasure in burnt offerings and sacrifices
    as much as in obeying the LORD?
Look: to obey is better than sacrifice,
    to pay attention is better than the fat of rams.
23 For rebellion is like the sin of divination,
    and defiance is like wickedness and idolatry.
Because you have rejected the word of the LORD,
    he has rejected you as king.

²⁴Saul answered Samuel, "I have sinned. I have transgressed the LORD's command and your words. Because I was afraid of the people, I obeyed them. ²⁵Now therefore, please forgive my sin and return with me so I can worship the LORD."

²⁶Samuel replied to Saul, "I will not return with you. Because you rejected the word of the LORD, the LORD has rejected you from being king over Israel." ²⁷When Samuel turned to go, Saul grabbed the corner of his robe, and it tore. ²⁸Samuel said to him, "The LORD has torn the kingship of Israel away from you today and has given it to your neighbor who is better than you. ²⁹Furthermore, the Eternal One of Israel does not lie or change his mind, for he is not man who changes his mind."

³⁰Saul said, "I have sinned. Please honor me now before the elders of my people and before Israel. Come back with me so I can bow in worship to the

---

ᴬ15:14 Lit sheep in my ears ᴮ15:20 Lit answered Samuel

Lord your God." ³¹ Then Samuel went back, following Saul, and Saul bowed down to the Lord.

³² Samuel said, "Bring me King Agag of Amalek."

Agag came to him trembling,ᴬ for he thought, "Certainly the bitterness of death has come."ᴮ,ᶜ

³³ Samuel declared:

As your sword has made women childless,

so your mother will be childless among women.

Then he hacked Agag to pieces before the Lord at Gilgal.

³⁴ Samuel went to Ramah, and Saul went up to his home in Gibeah of Saul. ³⁵ Even to the day of his death, Samuel never saw Saul again. Samuel mourned for Saul, and the Lord regretted he had made Saul king over Israel.

SAMUEL ANOINTS DAVID

16 The Lord said to Samuel, "How long are you going to mourn for Saul, since I have rejected him as king over Israel? Fill your horn with oil and go. I am sending you to Jesse of Bethlehem because I have selected a king from his sons."

² Samuel asked, "How can I go? Saul will hear about it and kill me!"

The Lord answered, "Take a young cow with you and say, 'I have come to sacrifice to the Lord.' ³ Then invite Jesse to the sacrifice, and I will let you know what you are to do. You are to anoint for me the one I indicate to you."

⁴ Samuel did what the Lord directed and went to Bethlehem. When the elders of the town met him, they trembledᴰ and asked, "Doᴱ you come in peace?"

⁵ "In peace," he replied. "I've come to sacrifice to the Lord. Consecrate yourselves and come with me to the sacrifice."ᶠ Then he consecrated Jesse and his sons and invited them to the sacrifice. ⁶ When they arrived, Samuel saw Eliab and said, "Certainly the Lord's anointed one is here before him."

⁷ But the Lord said to Samuel, "Do not look at his appearance or his stature because I have rejected him. Humans do not see what the Lord sees,ᴳ for humans see what is visible,ᴴ but the Lord sees the heart."

⁸ Jesse called Abinadab and presented him to Samuel. "The Lord hasn't chosen this one either," Samuel said. ⁹ Then Jesse presented Shammah, but Samuel said, "The Lord hasn't chosen this one either." ¹⁰ After Jesse presented seven of his sons to him, Samuel told Jesse, "The Lord hasn't chosen any of these." ¹¹ Samuel asked him, "Are these all the sons you have?"

"There is still the youngest," he answered, "but right now he's tending the sheep." Samuel told Jesse, "Send for him. We won't sit down to eat until he gets here." ¹² So Jesse sent for him. He had beautiful eyes and a healthy,ᴵ handsome appearance.

Then the Lord said, "Anoint him, for he is the one." ¹³ So Samuel took the horn of oil and anointed him in the presence of his brothers, and the Spirit of the Lord came powerfully on David from that day forward. Then Samuel set out and went to Ramah.

ᴬ15:32 Hb obscure ᴮ15:32 LXX reads *Is death bitter in this way?*
ᶜ15:32 Lit *turned* ᴰ16:4 LXX reads *were astonished* ᴱ16:4 DSS, LXX read
"Seer, do ᶠ16:5 LXX reads *and rejoice with me today* ᴳ16:7 LXX reads *God
does not see as a man sees* ᴴ16:7 Lit *for the man sees according to the eyes*
ᴵ16:12 Or *ruddy*

A DIAMOND IN THE ROUGH

1 SAMUEL 16; RUTH 4:18-22; LUKE 6:45

About the time my future groom and I started looking at rings, a story circulated through my college dorm that put many of us hopeful brides-to-be on high alert. Whether true or simply an urban legend, I can't say. But long after my now-husband popped the question, the story has stuck with me. It goes like this . . .

A handsome young man decided to propose to a beautiful girl. He told her that since they were poor college kids, he could not afford much of a ring. He proposed with a small cubic zirconia, a manufactured replacement for a real diamond. But secretly, he purchased a beautiful, expensive, whopper of a diamond and planned to have it put in the setting for their wedding day. But when the blushing bride-to-be discovered her ring was a fake, she demanded the real thing. The groom was so turned off by her shallow behavior that he broke off the engagement. Only then did the girl learn that he'd planned all along to take her breath away with a real diamond.

In 1 Samuel, we find a similar tale of fake worth and diamonds in the rough. Saul had been anointed as the first king of Israel. He seemed to have it all, but it didn't take long for his façade to crack. Saul was deeply flawed. His dependence on the Lord turned out to be counterfeit, and in 1 Samuel 15, the Lord rejected Saul as king of Israel.

Israel's prophet, Samuel, was grieved by Saul's failings. I imagine he might have felt like that bride-to-be, who thought her boyfriend bought her a diamond only to discover she'd been

given a chunk of glass. But God was like the groom with something better tucked away. Despite Israel's long history of bratty behavior, He planned to replace Saul with a king so good he'd become the measuring stick for all other kings to come.

At the Lord's prompting, Samuel went to the house of Jesse looking for a new king. Jesse had eight sons and he paraded all but the youngest in front of Samuel. Each time, the Lord said "no." Samuel was baffled by God's rejection of such strong, capable men. God's explanation put a magnifying glass over Samuel's heart.

"But the LORD said to Samuel, 'Do not look at his appearance or his stature because I have rejected him. Humans do not see what the LORD sees, for humans see what is visible, but the LORD sees the heart.'"

1 SAMUEL 16:7

David didn't look like a king. His father thought so little of him that he didn't even bring him in from the field. But God chose him. **Beneath an unimpressive exterior, God saw treasures in David's heart.**

We can't polish ourselves pretty enough to create our own worth. But God mines for value in each of our hearts.

DAVID IN SAUL'S COURT

[14] Now the Spirit of the LORD had left Saul, and an evil spirit sent from the LORD began to torment him, [15] so Saul's servants said to him, "You see that an evil spirit from God is tormenting you. [16] Let our lord command your servants here in your presence to look for someone who knows how to play the lyre. Whenever the evil spirit from God comes on you, that person can play the lyre, and you will feel better."

[17] Then Saul commanded his servants, "Find me someone who plays well and bring him to me."

[18] One of the young men answered, "I have seen a son of Jesse of Bethlehem who knows how to play the lyre. He is also a valiant man, a warrior, eloquent, handsome, and the LORD is with him."

[19] Then Saul dispatched messengers to Jesse and said, "Send me your son David, who is with the sheep." [20] So Jesse took a donkey loaded with bread, a wineskin, and one young goat and sent them by his son David to Saul. [21] When David came to Saul and entered his service, Saul loved him very much, and David became his armor-bearer. [22] Then Saul sent word to Jesse: "Let David remain in my service, for he has found favor with me." [23] Whenever the spirit from God came on Saul, David would pick up his lyre and play, and Saul would then be relieved, feel better, and the evil spirit would leave him.

DAVID VERSUS GOLIATH

17 The Philistines gathered their forces for war at Socoh in Judah and camped between Socoh and Azekah in Ephes-dammim. [2] Saul and the men of Israel gathered and camped in the Valley of Elah; then they lined up in battle formation to face the Philistines.

[3] The Philistines were standing on one hill, and the Israelites were standing on another hill with a ravine between them. [4] Then a champion named Goliath, from Gath, came out from the Philistine camp. He was nine feet, nine inches[A,B] tall [5] and wore a bronze helmet[C] and bronze scale armor that weighed one hundred twenty-five pounds. [D] [6] There was bronze armor on his shins, and a bronze javelin was slung between his shoulders. [7] His spear shaft was like a weaver's beam, and the iron point of his spear weighed fifteen pounds. [E] In addition, a shield-bearer was walking in front of him.

[8] He stood and shouted to the Israelite battle formations: "Why do you come out to line up in battle formation?" He asked them, "Am I not a Philistine and are you not servants of Saul? Choose one of your men and have him come down against me. [9] If he wins in a fight against me and kills me, we will be your servants. But if I win against him and kill him, then you will be our servants and serve us." [10] Then the Philistine said, "I defy the ranks of Israel today. Send me a man so we can fight each other!" [11] When Saul and all Israel heard these words from the Philistine, they lost their courage and were terrified.

[12] Now David was the son of the Ephrathite from Bethlehem of Judah named Jesse. Jesse had eight sons and during Saul's reign was already an old man. [13] Jesse's three oldest sons had followed Saul to the war, and their names

---

[A]17:4 DSS, LXX read *four cubits and a span* [B]17:4 Lit *was six cubits and a span*
[C]17:5 Lit *helmet on his head* [D]17:5 Lit *5,000 shekels* [E]17:7 Lit *600 shekels*

were Eliab, the firstborn, Abinadab, the next, and Shammah, the third, ¹⁴ and David was the youngest. The three oldest had followed Saul, ¹⁵ but David kept going back and forth from Saul to tend his father's flock in Bethlehem.

¹⁶ Every morning and evening for forty days the Philistine came forward and took his stand. ¹⁷ One day Jesse had told his son David: "Take this half-bushel^A of roasted grain along with these ten loaves of bread for your brothers and hurry to their camp. ¹⁸ Also take these ten portions of cheese to the field commander.^B Check on the well-being of your brothers and bring a confirmation from them. ¹⁹ They are with Saul and all the men of Israel in the Valley of Elah fighting with the Philistines."

²⁰ So David got up early in the morning, left the flock with someone to keep it, loaded up, and set out as Jesse had charged him.

He arrived at the perimeter of the camp as the army was marching out to its battle formation shouting their battle cry. ²¹ Israel and the Philistines lined up in battle formation facing each other. ²² David left his supplies in the care of the quartermaster and ran to the battle line. When he arrived, he asked his brothers how they were. ²³ While he was speaking with them, suddenly the champion named Goliath, the Philistine from Gath, came forward from the Philistine battle line and shouted his usual words, which David heard. ²⁴ When all the Israelite men saw Goliath, they retreated from him terrified.

²⁵ Previously, an Israelite man had declared: "Do you see this man who keeps coming out? He comes to defy Israel. The king will make the man who kills him very rich and will give him his daughter. The king will also make the family of that man's father exempt from paying taxes in Israel."

²⁶ David spoke to the men who were standing with him: "What will be done for the man who kills that Philistine and removes this disgrace from Israel? Just who is this uncircumcised Philistine that he should defy the armies of the living God?"

²⁷ The troops told him about the offer, concluding, "That is what will be done for the man who kills him."

²⁸ David's oldest brother Eliab listened as he spoke to the men, and he became angry with him. "Why did you come down here?" he asked. "Who did you leave those few sheep with in the wilderness? I know your arrogance and your evil heart — you came down to see the battle!"

²⁹ "What have I done now?" protested David. "It was just a question." ³⁰ Then he turned from those beside him to others in front of him and asked about the offer. The people gave him the same answer as before.

³¹ What David said was overheard and reported to Saul, so he had David brought to him. ³² David said to Saul, "Don't let anyone be discouraged by^C him; your servant will go and fight this Philistine!"

³³ But Saul replied, "You can't go fight this Philistine. You're just a youth, and he's been a warrior since he was young."

³⁴ David answered Saul: "Your servant has been tending his father's sheep. Whenever a lion or a bear came and carried off a lamb from the flock, ³⁵ I went after it, struck it down, and rescued the lamb from its mouth. If it reared up against me, I would grab it by its fur,^D strike it down, and kill it. ³⁶ Your

---

servant has killed lions and bears; this uncircumcised Philistine will be like one of them, for he has defied the armies of the living God." ³⁷ Then David said, "The LORD who rescued me from the paw of the lion and the paw of the bear will rescue me from the hand of this Philistine."

Saul said to David, "Go, and may the LORD be with you."

³⁸ Then Saul had his own military clothes put on David. He put a bronze helmet on David's head and had him put on armor. ³⁹ David strapped his sword on over the military clothes and tried to walk, but he was not used to them. "I can't walk in these," David said to Saul, "I'm not used to them." So David took them off. ⁴⁰ Instead, he took his staff in his hand and chose five smooth stones from the wadi and put them in the pouch, in his shepherd's bag. Then, with his sling in his hand, he approached the Philistine.

⁴¹ The Philistine came closer and closer to David, with the shield-bearer in front of him. ⁴² When the Philistine looked and saw David, he despised him because he was just a youth, healthy^A and handsome. ⁴³ He said to David, "Am I a dog that you come against me with sticks?"^B Then he cursed David by his gods. ⁴⁴ "Come here," the Philistine called to David, "and I'll give your flesh to the birds of the sky and the wild beasts!"

⁴⁵ David said to the Philistine: "You come against me with a sword, spear, and javelin, but I come against you in the name of the LORD of Armies, the God of the ranks of Israel — you have defied him. ⁴⁶ Today, the LORD will hand you over to me. Today, I'll strike you down, remove your head, and give the corpses^C of the Philistine camp to the birds of the sky and the wild creatures of the earth. Then all the world will know that Israel has a God, ⁴⁷ and this whole assembly will know that it is not by sword or by spear that the LORD saves, for the battle is the LORD's. He will hand you over to us."

⁴⁸ When the Philistine started forward to attack him, David ran quickly to the battle line to meet the Philistine. ⁴⁹ David put his hand in the bag, took out a stone, slung it, and hit the Philistine on his forehead. The stone sank into his forehead, and he fell facedown to the ground. ⁵⁰ David defeated the Philistine with a sling and a stone. David overpowered the Philistine and killed him without having a sword. ⁵¹ David ran and stood over him. He grabbed the Philistine's sword, pulled it from its sheath, and used it to kill him. Then he cut off his head. When the Philistines saw that their hero was dead, they fled. ⁵² The men of Israel and Judah rallied, shouting their battle cry, and chased the Philistines to the entrance of the valley and to the gates of Ekron.^D Philistine bodies were strewn all along the Shaaraim road to Gath and Ekron.

⁵³ When the Israelites returned from the pursuit of the Philistines, they plundered their camps. ⁵⁴ David took Goliath's^E head and brought it to Jerusalem, but he put Goliath's weapons in his own tent.

⁵⁵ ^F When Saul had seen David going out to confront the Philistine, he asked Abner the commander of the army, "Whose son is this youth, Abner?"

"Your Majesty, as surely as you live, I don't know," Abner replied.

⁵⁶ The king said, "Find out whose son this young man is!"

---

^A17:42 Or ruddy   ^B17:43 Some LXX mss add and stones?" And David said, "No! Worse than a dog!"   ^C17:46 LXX reads give your limbs and the limbs
^D17:52 LXX reads Ashkelon   ^E17:54 Lit the Philistine's   ^F17:55 LXX omits 1Sm 17:55–18:5

⁵⁷ When David returned from killing the Philistine, Abner took him and brought him before Saul with the Philistine's head still in his hand. ⁵⁸ Saul said to him, "Whose son are you, young man?"

"The son of your servant Jesse of Bethlehem," David answered.

DAVID'S SUCCESS

18 When David had finished speaking with Saul, Jonathan was bound to David in close friendship,^ and loved him as much as he loved himself. ² Saul kept David with him from that day on and did not let him return to his father's house.

³ Jonathan made a covenant with David because he loved him as much as himself. ⁴ Then Jonathan removed the robe he was wearing and gave it to David, along with his military tunic, his sword, his bow, and his belt.

⁵ David marched out with the army and was successful in everything Saul sent him to do. Saul put him in command of the fighting men, which pleased all the people and Saul's servants as well.

⁶ As the troops were coming back, when David was returning from killing the Philistine, the women came out from all the cities of Israel to meet King Saul, singing and dancing with tambourines, with shouts of joy, and with three-stringed instruments. ⁷ As they danced, the women sang:

> Saul has killed his thousands,
>> but David his tens of thousands.

⁸ Saul was furious and resented this song.^B "They credited tens of thousands to David," he complained, "but they only credited me with thousands. What more can he have but the kingdom?" ⁹ So Saul watched David jealously from that day forward.

SAUL ATTEMPTS TO KILL DAVID

¹⁰ The next day an evil spirit sent from God came powerfully on Saul, and he began to rave^C inside the palace. David was playing the lyre as usual, but Saul was holding a spear, ¹¹ and he threw it, thinking, "I'll pin David to the wall." But David got away from him twice.

¹² Saul was afraid of David, because the Lord was with David but had left Saul. ¹³ Therefore, Saul sent David away from him and made him commander over a thousand men. David led the troops ¹⁴ and continued to be successful in all his activities because the Lord was with him. ¹⁵ When Saul observed that David was very successful, he dreaded him. ¹⁶ But all Israel and Judah loved David because he was leading their troops. ¹⁷ Saul told David, "Here is my oldest daughter Merab. I'll give her to you as a wife, if you will be a warrior for me and fight the Lord's battles." But Saul was thinking, "I don't need to raise a hand against him; let the hand of the Philistines be against him."

¹⁸ Then David responded, "Who am I, and what is my family or my father's clan in Israel that I should become the king's son-in-law?" ¹⁹ When it was time to give Saul's daughter Merab to David, she was given to Adriel the Meholathite as a wife.

---

^18:1 Lit *the life of Jonathan was bound to the life of David*   ^B 18:8 Lit *furious; this saying was evil in his eyes*   ^C 18:10 Or *prophesy*

DAVID'S MARRIAGE TO MICHAL

[20] Now Saul's daughter Michal loved David, and when it was reported to Saul, it pleased him. [A] [21] "I'll give her to him," Saul thought. "She'll be a trap for him, and the hand of the Philistines will be against him." So Saul said to David a second time, "You can now be my son-in-law."

[22] Saul then ordered his servants, "Speak to David in private and tell him, 'Look, the king is pleased with you, and all his servants love you. Therefore, you should become the king's son-in-law.'"

[23] Saul's servants reported these words directly to David, [B] but he replied, "Is it trivial in your sight to become the king's son-in-law? I am a poor commoner."

[24] The servants reported back to Saul, "These are the words David spoke."

[25] Then Saul replied, "Say this to David: 'The king desires no other bride-price except a hundred Philistine foreskins, to take revenge on his enemies.'" Actually, Saul intended to cause David's death at the hands of the Philistines.

[26] When the servants reported these terms to David, he was pleased [C] to become the king's son-in-law. Before the wedding day arrived, [D] [27] David and his men went out and killed two hundred [E] Philistines. He brought their foreskins and presented them as full payment to the king to become his son-in-law. Then Saul gave his daughter Michal to David as his wife. [28] Saul realized [F] that the LORD was with David and that his daughter Michal loved him, [29] and he became even more afraid of David. As a result, Saul was David's enemy from then on.

[30] Every time the Philistine commanders came out to fight, David was more successful than all of Saul's officers. So his name became well known.

DAVID DELIVERED FROM SAUL

19

Saul ordered his son Jonathan and all his servants to kill David. But Saul's son Jonathan liked David very much, [2] so he told him: "My father Saul intends to kill you. Be on your guard in the morning and hide in a secret place and stay there. [3] I'll go out and stand beside my father in the field where you are and talk to him about you. When I see what he says, I'll tell you."

[4] Jonathan spoke well of David to his father Saul. He said to him: "The king should not sin against his servant David. He hasn't sinned against you; in fact, his actions have been a great advantage to you. [5] He took his life in his hands when he struck down the Philistine, and the LORD brought about a great victory for all Israel. You saw it and rejoiced, so why would you sin against innocent blood by killing David for no reason?"

[6] Saul listened to Jonathan's advice and swore an oath: "As surely as the LORD lives, David will not be killed." [7] So Jonathan summoned David and told him all these words. Then Jonathan brought David to Saul, and he served him as he did before.

[8] When war broke out again, David went out and fought against the Philistines. He defeated them with such great force that they fled from him.

[9] Now an evil spirit sent from the LORD came on Saul as he was sitting in his palace holding a spear. David was playing the lyre, [10] and Saul tried to pin David to the wall with the spear. As the spear struck the wall, David eluded

---

[A] 18:20 Lit *Saul, the thing was right in his eyes* [B] 18:23 Lit *words in David's ears*
[C] 18:26 Lit *David, it was right in David's eyes* [D] 18:26 Lit *And the days were not full* [E] 18:27 LXX reads *100* [F] 18:28 Lit *saw and knew*

Saul, ran away, and escaped that night. ¹¹ Saul sent agents to David's house to watch for him and kill him in the morning. But his wife Michal warned David, "If you don't escape tonight, you will be dead tomorrow!" ¹² So she lowered David from the window, and he fled and escaped. ¹³ Then Michal took the household idol and put it on the bed, placed some goat hair on its head, and covered it with a garment. ¹⁴ When Saul sent agents to seize David, Michal said, "He's sick."

¹⁵ Saul sent the agents back to see David and said, "Bring him on his bed so I can kill him." ¹⁶ When the agents arrived, to their surprise, the household idol was on the bed with some goat hair on its head.

¹⁷ Saul asked Michal, "Why did you deceive me like this? You sent my enemy away, and he has escaped!"

She answered him, "He said to me, 'Let me go! Why should I kill you?'"

¹⁸ So David fled and escaped and went to Samuel at Ramah and told him everything Saul had done to him. Then he and Samuel left and stayed at Naioth.

¹⁹ When it was reported to Saul that David was at Naioth in Ramah, ²⁰ he sent agents to seize David. However, when they saw the group of prophets prophesying with Samuel leading them, the Spirit of God came on Saul's agents, and they also started prophesying. ²¹ When they reported to Saul, he sent other agents, and they also began prophesying. So Saul tried again and sent a third group of agents, and even they began prophesying. ²² Then Saul himself went to Ramah. He came to the large cistern at Secu and asked, "Where are Samuel and David?"

"At Naioth in Ramah," someone said.

²³ So he went to Naioth in Ramah. The Spirit of God also came on him, and as he walked along, he prophesied until he entered Naioth in Ramah. ²⁴ Saul then removed his clothes and also prophesied before Samuel; he collapsed and lay naked all that day and all that night. That is why they say, "Is Saul also among the prophets?"

JONATHAN PROTECTS DAVID

20 David fled from Naioth in Ramah and came to Jonathan and asked, "What have I done? What did I do wrong? How have I sinned against your father so that he wants to take my life?"

² Jonathan said to him, "No, you won't die. Listen, my father doesn't do anything, great or small, without telling me.ᴬ So why would he hide this matter from me? This can't be true."

³ But David said, "Your father certainly knows that I have found favor with you. He has said, 'Jonathan must not know of this, or else he will be grieved.'" David also swore, "As surely as the LORD lives and as you yourself live, there is but a step between me and death."

⁴ Jonathan said to David, "Whatever you say, I will do for you."

⁵ So David told him, "Look, tomorrow is the New Moon, and I'm supposed to sit down and eat with the king. Instead, let me go, and I'll hide in the countryside for the next two nights.ᴮ ⁶ If your father misses me at all, say, 'David urgently requested my permission to go quickly to his hometown Bethlehem for an annual sacrifice there involving the whole clan.' ⁷ If he says, 'Good,' then your servant is safe, but if he becomes angry, you will know he has evil

---

ᴬ20:2 Lit without uncovering my ear ᴮ20:5 Lit countryside until the third night intentions. [8] Deal kindly with[A] your servant, for you have brought me into a covenant with you before the LORD. If I have done anything wrong, then kill me yourself; why take me to your father?"

[9] "No!" Jonathan responded. "If I ever find out my father has evil intentions against you, wouldn't I tell you about it?"

[10] So David asked Jonathan, "Who will tell me if your father answers you harshly?"

[11] He answered David, "Come on, let's go out to the countryside." So both of them went out to the countryside. [12] "By the LORD, the God of Israel, I will sound out my father by this time tomorrow or the next day. If I find out that he is favorable toward you, will I not send for you and tell you?[B] [13] If my father intends to bring evil on you, may the LORD punish Jonathan and do so severely if I do not tell you[C] and send you away so you may leave safely. May the LORD be with you, just as he was with my father. [14] If I continue to live, show me kindness[D] from the LORD, but if I die, [15] don't ever withdraw your kindness from my household — not even when the LORD cuts off every one of David's enemies from the face of the earth." [16] Then Jonathan made a covenant with the house of David, saying, "May the LORD hold David's enemies accountable."[E] [17] Jonathan once again swore to David[F] in his love for him, because he loved him as he loved himself.

[18] Then Jonathan said to him, "Tomorrow is the New Moon; you'll be missed because your seat will be empty. [19] The following day hurry down and go to the place where you hid on the day this incident began and stay beside the rock Ezel. [20] I will shoot three arrows beside it as if I'm aiming at a target. [21] Then I will send a servant and say, 'Go and find the arrows!' Now, if I expressly say to the servant, 'Look, the arrows are on this side of you — get them,' then come, because as the LORD lives, it is safe for you and there is no problem. [22] But if I say this to the youth, 'Look, the arrows are beyond you!' then go, for the LORD is sending you away. [23] As for the matter you and I have spoken about, the LORD will be a witness[G] between you and me forever." [24] So David hid in the countryside.

At the New Moon, the king sat down to eat the meal. [25] He sat at his usual place on the seat by the wall. Jonathan sat facing him[H] and Abner took his place beside Saul, but David's place was empty. [26] Saul did not say anything that day because he thought, "Something unexpected has happened; he must be ceremonially unclean — yes, that's it, he is unclean."

[27] However, the day after the New Moon, the second day, David's place was still empty, and Saul asked his son Jonathan, "Why didn't Jesse's son come to the meal either yesterday or today?"

[28] Jonathan answered, "David asked for my permission to go to Bethlehem. [29] He said, 'Please let me go because our clan is holding a sacrifice in the town, and my brother has told me to be there. So now, if I have found favor with you, let me go so I can see my brothers.' That's why he didn't come to the king's table."

[A]20:8 Or *Show loyalty to*   [B]20:12 Lit *and uncover your ear*   [C]20:13 Lit *severely — I will uncover your ear*   [D]20:14 Or *loyalty,* also in v. 15   [E]20:16 Lit LORD *require it from the hand of David's enemies*   [F]20:17 LXX; MT reads *Jonathan once again made David swear*   [G]20:23 LXX; MT omits *a witness*   [H]20:25 Text emended; MT reads *Jonathan got up*

³⁰ Then Saul became angry with Jonathan and shouted, "You son of a perverse and rebellious woman! Don't I know that you are siding with Jesse's son to your own shame and to the disgrace of your mother?^A ³¹ Every day Jesse's son lives on earth you and your kingship are not secure. Now send for him and bring him to me — he must die!"

³² Jonathan answered his father back: "Why is he to be killed? What has he done?"

³³ Then Saul threw his spear at Jonathan to kill him, so he knew that his father was determined to kill David. ³⁴ He got up from the table fiercely angry and did not eat any food that second day of the New Moon, for he was grieved because of his father's shameful behavior toward David.

³⁵ In the morning Jonathan went out to the countryside for the appointed meeting with David. A young servant was with him. ³⁶ He said to the servant, "Run and find the arrows I'm shooting." As the servant ran, Jonathan shot an arrow beyond him. ³⁷ He came to the location of the arrow that Jonathan had shot, but Jonathan called to him and said, "The arrow is beyond you, isn't it?" ³⁸ Then Jonathan called to him, "Hurry up and don't stop!" Jonathan's servant picked up the arrow and returned to his master. ³⁹ He did not know anything; only Jonathan and David knew the arrangement. ⁴⁰ Then Jonathan gave his equipment to the servant who was with him and said, "Go, take it back to the city."

⁴¹ When the servant had gone, David got up from the south side of the stone Ezel, fell facedown to the ground, and paid homage three times. Then he and Jonathan kissed each other and wept with each other, though David wept more.

⁴² Jonathan then said to David, "Go in the assurance the two of us pledged in the name of the LORD when we said: The LORD will be a witness between you and me and between my offspring and your offspring forever." Then David left, and Jonathan went into the city.

DAVID FLEES TO NOB

21 David went to the priest Ahimelech at Nob. Ahimelech was afraid to meet David, so he said to him, "Why are you alone and no one is with you?"

² David answered the priest Ahimelech, "The king gave me a mission, but he told me, 'Don't let anyone know anything about the mission I'm sending you on or what I have ordered you to do.' I have stationed my young men at a certain place. ³ Now what do you have on hand? Give me five loaves of bread or whatever can be found."

⁴ The priest told him, "There is no ordinary bread on hand. However, there is consecrated bread, but the young men may eat it^B only if they have kept themselves from women."

⁵ David answered him, "I swear that women are being kept from us, as always when I go out to battle. The young men's bodies^C are consecrated even on an ordinary mission, so of course their bodies are consecrated today." ⁶ So the priest gave him the consecrated bread, for there was no bread there except the Bread of the Presence that had been removed from the

---

^A 20:30 Lit *your mother's nakedness*   ^B 21:4 DSS; MT omits *may eat it*
^C 21:5 Lit *vessels*

presence of the LORD. When the bread was removed, it had been replaced with warm bread.

[7] One of Saul's servants, detained before the LORD, was there that day. His name was Doeg the Edomite, chief of Saul's shepherds.

[8] David said to Ahimelech, "Do you have a spear or sword on hand? I didn't even bring my sword or my weapons since the king's mission was urgent."

[9] The priest replied, "The sword of Goliath the Philistine, whom you killed in the Valley of Elah, is here, wrapped in a cloth behind the ephod. If you want to take it for yourself, then take it, for there isn't another one here."

"There's none like it!" David said. "Give it to me."

DAVID FLEES TO GATH

[10] David fled that day from Saul's presence and went to King Achish of Gath. [11] But Achish's servants said to him, "Isn't this David, the king of the land? Don't they sing about him during their dances:

Saul has killed his thousands,

but David his tens of thousands?"

[12] David took this to heart[A] and became very afraid of King Achish of Gath, [13] so he pretended to be insane in their presence. He acted like a madman around them,[B] scribbling[C] on the doors of the city gate and letting saliva run down his beard.

[14] "Look! You can see the man is crazy," Achish said to his servants. "Why did you bring him to me? [15] Do I have such a shortage of crazy people that you brought this one to act crazy around me? Is this one going to come into my house?"

SAUL'S INCREASING PARANOIA

22 So David left Gath and took refuge in the cave of Adullam. When David's brothers and his father's whole family heard, they went down and joined him there. [2] In addition, every man who was desperate, in debt, or discontented rallied around him, and he became their leader. About four hundred men were with him.

[3] From there David went to Mizpeh of Moab where he said to the king of Moab, "Please let my father and mother stay with you until I know what God will do for me." [4] So he left them in the care of the king of Moab, and they stayed with him the whole time David was in the stronghold.

[5] Then the prophet Gad said to David, "Don't stay in the stronghold. Leave and return to the land of Judah." So David left and went to the forest of Hereth.

[6] Saul heard that David and his men had been discovered. At that time Saul was in Gibeah, sitting under the tamarisk tree at the high place. His spear was in his hand, and all his servants were standing around him. [7] Saul said to his servants, "Listen, men of Benjamin: Is Jesse's son going to give all of you fields and vineyards? Do you think he'll make all of you commanders of thousands and commanders of hundreds? [8] That's why all of you have conspired against me! Nobody tells me[D] when my own son makes a covenant

---

[A]21:12 Lit David placed these words in his heart   [B]21:13 Lit madman in their hand   [C]21:13 LXX reads drumming   [D]22:8 Lit No one uncovers my ear with Jesse's son. None of you cares about me or tells me[A] that my son has stirred up my own servant to wait in ambush for me, as is the case today."

⁹ Then Doeg the Edomite, who was in charge of Saul's servants, answered: "I saw Jesse's son come to Ahimelech son of Ahitub at Nob. ¹⁰ Ahimelech inquired of the LORD for him and gave him provisions. He also gave him the sword of Goliath the Philistine."

SLAUGHTER OF THE PRIESTS

¹¹ The king sent messengers to summon the priest Ahimelech son of Ahitub, and his father's whole family, who were priests in Nob. All of them came to the king. ¹² Then Saul said, "Listen, son of Ahitub!"

"I'm at your service, my lord," he said.

¹³ Saul asked him, "Why did you and Jesse's son conspire against me? You gave him bread and a sword and inquired of God for him, so he could rise up against me and wait in ambush, as is the case today."

¹⁴ Ahimelech replied to the king: "Who among all your servants is as faithful as David? He is the king's son-in-law, captain of your bodyguard, and honored in your house. ¹⁵ Was today the first time I inquired of God for him? Of course not! Please don't let the king make an accusation against your servant or any of my father's family, for your servant didn't have any idea[B] about all this."

¹⁶ But the king said, "You will die, Ahimelech — you and your father's whole family!"

¹⁷ Then the king ordered the guards standing by him, "Turn and kill the priests of the LORD because they sided with David. For they knew he was fleeing, but they didn't tell me."[C] But the king's servants would not lift a hand to execute the priests of the LORD.

¹⁸ So the king said to Doeg, "Go and execute the priests!" So Doeg the Edomite went and executed the priests himself. On that day, he killed eighty-five men who wore linen ephods. ¹⁹ He also struck down Nob, the city of the priests, with the sword — both men and women, infants and nursing babies, oxen, donkeys, and sheep.

²⁰ However, one of the sons of Ahimelech son of Ahitub escaped. His name was Abiathar, and he fled to David. ²¹ Abiathar told David that Saul had killed the priests of the LORD. ²² Then David said to Abiathar, "I knew that Doeg the Edomite was there that day and that he was sure to report to Saul. I myself am responsible for[D] the lives of everyone in your father's family. ²³ Stay with me. Don't be afraid, for the one who wants to take my life wants to take your life. You will be safe with me."

DELIVERANCE AT KEILAH

23 It was reported to David: "Look, the Philistines are fighting against Keilah and raiding the threshing floors."

² So David inquired of the LORD: "Should I launch an attack against these Philistines?"

The LORD answered David, "Launch an attack against the Philistines and rescue Keilah."

[A]22:8 Lit or uncovers my ear   [B]22:15 Lit didn't know a thing, small or large
[C]22:17 Lit didn't uncover my ear   [D]22:22 LXX, Syr, Vg; MT reads I myself turn in

³ But David's men said to him, "Look, we're afraid here in Judah; how much more if we go to Keilah against the Philistine forces!"

⁴ Once again, David inquired of the LORD, and the LORD answered him: "Go at once to Keilah, for I will hand the Philistines over to you." ⁵ Then David and his men went to Keilah, fought against the Philistines, drove their livestock away, and inflicted heavy losses on them. So David rescued the inhabitants of Keilah. ⁶ Abiathar son of Ahimelech fled to David at Keilah, and he brought an ephod with him.

⁷ When it was reported to Saul that David had gone to Keilah, he said, "God has handed him over to me, for he has trapped himself by entering a town with barred gates." ⁸ Then Saul summoned all the troops to go to war at Keilah and besiege David and his men.

⁹ When David learned that Saul was plotting evil against him, he said to the priest Abiathar, "Bring the ephod." ¹⁰ Then David said, "LORD God of Israel, your servant has reliable information that Saul intends to come to Keilah and destroy the town because of me. ¹¹ Will the citizens of Keilah hand me over to him? Will Saul come down as your servant has heard? LORD God of Israel, please tell your servant."

The LORD answered, "He will come down."

¹² Then David asked, "Will the citizens of Keilah hand me and my men over to Saul?"

"They will," the LORD responded.

¹³ So David and his men, numbering about six hundred, left Keilah at once and moved from place to place. When it was reported to Saul that David had escaped from Keilah, he called off the expedition. ¹⁴ David then stayed in the wilderness strongholds and in the hill country of the Wilderness of Ziph. Saul searched for him every day, but God did not hand David over to him.

A RENEWED COVENANT

¹⁵ David was in the Wilderness of Ziph in Horesh when he saw that Saul had come out to take his life. ¹⁶ Then Saul's son Jonathan came to David in Horesh and encouraged him in his faith^A in God, ¹⁷ saying, "Don't be afraid, for my father Saul will never lay a hand on you. You yourself will be king over Israel, and I'll be your second-in-command. Even my father Saul knows it is true." ¹⁸ Then the two of them made a covenant in the LORD's presence. Afterward, David remained in Horesh, while Jonathan went home.

DAVID'S NARROW ESCAPE

¹⁹ Some Ziphites came up to Saul at Gibeah and said, "David is^B hiding among us in the strongholds in Horesh on the hill of Hachilah south of Jeshimon. ²⁰ Now, whenever the king wants to come down, let him come down. Our part will be to hand him over to the king."

²¹ "May you be blessed by the LORD," replied Saul, "for you have shown concern for me. ²² Go and check again. Investigate^C where he goes^D and who has seen him there; they tell me he is extremely cunning. ²³ Investigate^E all the places where he hides. Then come back to me with accurate information,

---

^A 23:16 Lit and strengthened his hand   ^B 23:19 Lit "Is David not . . . Jeshimon?"
^C 23:22 Lit Know and see   ^D 23:22 Lit watch his place where his foot will be
^E 23:23 Lit See and know

438

and I'll go with you. If it turns out he really is in the region, I'll search for him among all the clans^A of Judah." ²⁴ So they went to Ziph ahead of Saul.

Now David and his men were in the wilderness near Maon in the Arabah south of Jeshimon, ²⁵ and Saul and his men went to look for him. When David was told about it, he went down to the rock and stayed in the Wilderness of Maon. Saul heard of this and pursued David there.

²⁶ Saul went along one side of the mountain and David and his men went along the other side. Even though David was hurrying to get away from Saul, Saul and his men were closing in on David and his men to capture them. ²⁷ Then a messenger came to Saul saying, "Come quickly, because the Philistines have raided the land!" ²⁸ So Saul broke off his pursuit of David and went to engage the Philistines. Therefore, that place was named the Rock of Separation. ²⁹ From there David went up and stayed in the strongholds of En-gedi.

DAVID SPARES SAUL

24 When Saul returned from pursuing the Philistines, he was told, "David is in the wilderness near En-gedi." ² So Saul took three thousand of Israel's fit young men and went to look for David and his men in front of the Rocks of the Wild Goats. ³ When Saul came to the sheep pens along the road, a cave was there, and he went in to relieve himself.^B David and his men were staying in the recesses of the cave, ⁴ so they said to him, "Look, this is the day the LORD told you about: 'I will hand your enemy over to you so you can do to him whatever you desire.'" Then David got up and secretly cut off the corner of Saul's robe.

⁵ Afterward, David's conscience bothered^C him because he had cut off the corner of Saul's robe.^D ⁶ He said to his men, "I swear before the LORD: I would never do such a thing to my lord, the LORD's anointed. I will never lift my hand against him, since he is the LORD's anointed." ⁷ With these words David persuaded^E his men, and he did not let them rise up against Saul.

Then Saul left the cave and went on his way. ⁸ After that, David got up, went out of the cave, and called to Saul, "My lord the king!" When Saul looked behind him, David knelt low with his face to the ground and paid homage. ⁹ David said to Saul, "Why do you listen to the words of people who say, 'Look, David intends to harm you'? ¹⁰ You can see with your own eyes that the LORD handed you over to me today in the cave. Someone advised me to kill you, but I^F,G took pity on you and said: I won't lift my hand against my lord, since he is the LORD's anointed. ¹¹ Look, my father! Look at the corner of your robe in my hand, for I cut it off, but I didn't kill you. Recognize^H that I've committed no crime or rebellion. I haven't sinned against you even though you are hunting me down to take my life.

¹² "May the LORD judge between me and you, and may the LORD take vengeance on you for me, but my hand will never be against you. ¹³ As the old proverb says, 'Wickedness comes from wicked people.' My hand will never be against you. ¹⁴ Who has the king of Israel come after? What are you

---

^A 23:23 Or *thousands* ^B 24:3 Lit *to cover his feet* ^C 24:5 Lit *David's heart struck*
^D 24:5 Some Hb mss, LXX, Syr, Vg; other Hb mss omit *robe* ^E 24:7 Or *restrained*
^F 24:10 LXX, Syr, Tg; MT reads *she or it* ^G 24:10 Or *my eye* ^H 24:11 Lit *Know and see*

DAVID'S DEFENDER

1 SAMUEL 23:15–24:22; PROVERBS 25:21-22

When righteous young David has the chance to take out paranoid, egotistical, narcissistic Saul twice and doesn't do it, part of me wants to throw my hands up in frustration. That's not how the story should go! The hero is supposed to seize his opportunity to conquer his enemy, then ride off into the sunset as the credits roll.

Instead, David's anti-climactic showdown with Saul reminds us who the real Hero is. In 1 Samuel 24, David and a small army of followers are on the run. Saul and an army of three thousand soldiers are hunting David with the goal to kill him.

In an ironic, almost comical twist, the paranoid king decides to relieve himself in the very cave where David and his men were hiding. If I'd been in David's squad, I would've joined their rallying cry.

"Look, this is the day the LORD told you about: 'I will hand your enemy over to you so you can do to him whatever you desire.'"

1 SAMUEL 24:4

Take your shot! He's got it coming! Eliminate the threat! Instead, David sneaks up behind his archenemy and cuts off the corner of his robe.

Wait. What?

David had already been anointed king, and clearly, Saul was no good for God's people—

his thirst for David's blood was insatiable. So why then, does David opt to take a piece of Saul's robe, as opposed to a piece of the man himself?

How could David be so bridled in the face of an enemy so bent on his destruction? It wasn't that David didn't crave relief from his enemy. He hadn't assumed a position of defeat. **He knew the battle ultimately belonged to the Lord.**

At the mouth of the cave, David said these words to Saul:

"May the LORD judge between me and you, and may the LORD take vengeance on you for me, but my hand will never be against you."

1 SAMUEL 24:12

We don't have to seek revenge or take out our enemies. David's defender is our defender. When we find ourselves face-to-face with a threat, our Father's advice is to respond with kindness and let Him do what He will (Pr 25:21-22).

David's restraint helps us grasp the big picture. If we widen the lens, we can see that the Lord has disarmed our ultimate enemy, Satan. We don't have to head into every fight with fists clenched. We don't have to be the judge and jury in our search for justice. David's defender is fighting for us. The battle belongs to the Lord!

chasing after? A dead dog? A single flea? [15] May the LORD be judge and decide between you and me. May he take notice and plead my case and deliver[A] me from you."

[16] When David finished saying these things to him, Saul replied, "Is that your voice, David my son?" Then Saul wept aloud [17] and said to David, "You are more righteous than I, for you have done what is good to me though I have done what is evil to you. [18] You yourself have told me today what good you did for me: when the LORD handed me over to you, you didn't kill me. [19] When a man finds his enemy, does he let him go unharmed?[B] May the LORD repay you with good for what you've done for me today.

[20] "Now I know for certain you will be king, and the kingdom of Israel will be established[C] in your hand. [21] Therefore swear to me by the LORD that you will not cut off my descendants or wipe out my name from my father's family." [22] So David swore to Saul. Then Saul went back home, and David and his men went up to the stronghold.

DAVID, NABAL, AND ABIGAIL

25 Samuel died, and all Israel assembled to mourn for him, and they buried him by his home in Ramah. David then went down to the Wilderness of Paran.[D]

[2] A man in Maon had a business in Carmel; he was a very rich man with three thousand sheep and one thousand goats and was shearing his sheep in Carmel. [3] The man's name was Nabal, and his wife's name, Abigail. The woman was intelligent and beautiful, but the man, a Calebite, was harsh and evil in his dealings.

[4] While David was in the wilderness, he heard that Nabal was shearing sheep, [5] so David sent ten young men instructing them, "Go up to Carmel, and when you come to Nabal, greet him[E] in my name. [6] Then say this: 'Long life to you,[F] and peace to you, peace to your family, and peace to all that is yours. [7] I hear that you are shearing.[G] When your shepherds were with us, we did not harass them, and nothing of theirs was missing the whole time they were in Carmel. [8] Ask your young men, and they will tell you. So let my young men find favor with you, for we have come on a feast[H] day. Please give whatever you have on hand to your servants and to your son David.'"

[9] David's young men went and said all these things to Nabal on David's behalf,[I] and they waited.[J] [10] Nabal asked them, "Who is David? Who is Jesse's son? Many slaves these days are running away from their masters. [11] Am I supposed to take my bread, my water, and my meat that I butchered for my shearers and give them to these men? I don't know where they are from."

[12] David's young men retraced their steps. When they returned to him, they reported all these words. [13] He said to his men, "All of you, put on your swords!" So each man put on his sword, and David also put on his sword. About four hundred men followed David while two hundred stayed with the supplies.

[14] One of Nabal's young men informed Abigail, Nabal's wife: "Look, David sent messengers from the wilderness to greet our master, but he screamed at

---

[A] 24:15 Lit render a verdict for   [B] 24:19 Lit go on a good way   [C] 24:20 Or will flourish   [D] 25:1 LXX reads to Maon   [E] 25:5 Or Nabal, ask him for peace   [F] 25:6 Lit 'To life'   [G] 25:7 Lit you have shearers   [H] 25:8 Lit good   [I] 25:9 Lit name   [J] 25:9 LXX reads and he became arrogant them. [15] The men treated us very well. When we were in the field, we weren't harassed and nothing of ours was missing the whole time we were living among them. [16] They were a wall around us, both day and night, the entire time we were with them herding the sheep. [17] Now consider carefully[A] what you should do, because there is certain to be trouble for our master and his entire family. He is such a worthless fool nobody can talk to him!"

[18] Abigail hurried, taking two hundred loaves of bread, two clay jars of wine, five butchered sheep, a bushel[B] of roasted grain, one hundred clusters of raisins, and two hundred cakes of pressed figs, and loaded them on donkeys. [19] Then she said to her male servants, "Go ahead of me. I will be right behind you." But she did not tell her husband Nabal.

[20] As she rode the donkey down a mountain pass hidden from view, she saw David and his men coming toward her and met them. [21] David had just said, "I guarded everything that belonged to this man in the wilderness for nothing. He was not missing anything, yet he paid me back evil for good. [22] May God punish me[C] and do so severely if I let any of his males[D] survive until morning."

[23] When Abigail saw David, she quickly got off the donkey and knelt down with her face to the ground and paid homage to David. [24] She knelt at his feet and said, "The guilt is mine, my lord, but please let your servant speak to you directly. Listen to the words of your servant. [25] My lord should pay no attention to this worthless fool Nabal, for he lives up to his name:[E] His name means 'stupid,' and stupidity is all he knows.[F] I, your servant, didn't see my lord's young men whom you sent. [26] Now my lord, as surely as the LORD lives and as you yourself live— it is the LORD who kept you from participating in bloodshed and avenging yourself by your own hand—may your enemies and those who intend to harm my lord be like Nabal. [27] Let this gift your servant has brought to my lord be given to the young men who follow my lord. [28] Please forgive your servant's offense, for the LORD is certain to make a lasting dynasty for my lord because he fights the LORD's battles. Throughout your life, may evil[G] not be found in you.

[29] "Someone is pursuing you and intends to take your life. My lord's life is tucked safely in the place[H] where the LORD your God protects the living, but he is flinging away your enemies' lives like stones from a sling. [30] When the LORD does for my lord all the good he promised you and appoints you ruler over Israel, [31] there will not be remorse or a troubled conscience for my lord because of needless bloodshed or my lord's revenge. And when the LORD does good things for my lord, may you remember me your servant."

[32] Then David said to Abigail, "Blessed be the LORD God of Israel, who sent you to meet me today! [33] May your discernment be blessed, and may you be blessed. Today you kept me from participating in bloodshed and avenging myself by my own hand. [34] Otherwise, as surely as the LORD God of Israel lives, who prevented me from harming you, if you had not come quickly to meet me, Nabal wouldn't have had any males[I] left by morning light." [35] Then

---

[A]25:17 Lit Now know and see   [B]25:18 Lit sheep, five seahs   [C]25:22 LXX; MT reads David's enemies   [D]25:22 Lit of those of his who are urinating against the wall   [E]25:25 Lit for as is his name is, so he is   [F]25:25 Lit and foolishness is with him   [G]25:28 Or trouble   [H]25:29 Lit bundle   [I]25:34 Lit had anyone urinating against a wall

David accepted what she had brought him and said, "Go home in peace. See, I have heard what you said and have granted your request."

³⁶ Then Abigail went to Nabal, and there he was in his house, holding a feast fit for a king. Nabal's heart was cheerful,ᴬ and he was very drunk, so she didn't say anythingᴮ to him until morning light.

³⁷ In the morning when Nabal sobered up,ᶜ his wife told him about these events. His heart diedᴰ and he became a stone. ³⁸ About ten days later, the LORD struck Nabal dead.

³⁹ When David heard that Nabal was dead, he said, "Blessed be the LORD who championed my cause against Nabal's insults and restrained his servant from doing evil. The LORD brought Nabal's evil deeds back on his own head."

Then David sent messengers to speak to Abigail about marrying him. ⁴⁰ When David's servants came to Abigail at Carmel, they said to her, "David sent us to bring you to him as a wife."

⁴¹ She stood up, paid homage with her face to the ground, and said, "Here I am, your servant, a slave to wash the feet of my lord's servants." ⁴² Then Abigail got up quickly, and with her five female servants accompanying her, rode on the donkey following David's messengers. And so she became his wife.

⁴³ David also married Ahinoam of Jezreel, and the two of them became his wives. ⁴⁴ But Saul gave his daughter Michal, David's wife, to Palti son of Laish, who was from Gallim.

DAVID AGAIN SPARES SAUL

26 Then the Ziphites came to Saul at Gibeah saying, "David is hiding on the hill of Hachilah opposite Jeshimon." ² So Saul, accompanied by three thousand of the fit young men of Israel, went immediately to the Wilderness of Ziph to search for David there. ³ Saul camped beside the road at the hill of Hachilah opposite Jeshimon. David was living in the wilderness and discovered Saul had come there after him. ⁴ So David sent out spies and knew for certain that Saul had come. ⁵ Immediately, David went to the place where Saul had camped. He saw the place where Saul and Abner son of Ner, the commander of his army, were lying down. Saul was lying inside the inner circle of the camp with the troops camped around him. ⁶ Then David asked Ahimelech the Hethite and Joab's brother Abishai son of Zeruiah, "Who will go with me into the camp to Saul?"

"I'll go with you," answered Abishai.

⁷ That night, David and Abishai came to the troops, and Saul was lying there asleep in the inner circle of the camp with his spear stuck in the ground by his head. Abner and the troops were lying around him. ⁸ Then Abishai said to David, "Today God has delivered your enemy to you. Let me thrust the spear through him into the ground just once. I won't have to strike him twice!"

⁹ But David said to Abishai, "Don't destroy him, for who can lift a hand against the LORD's anointed and be innocent?" ¹⁰ David added, "As the LORD lives, the LORD will certainly strike him down: either his day will come and he will die, or he will go into battle and perish. ¹¹ However, because of the

---

ᴬ 25:36 Lit Nabal's heart was good on him   ᴮ 25:36 Lit anything at all
ᶜ 25:37 Lit when the wine had gone out of Nabal   ᴰ 25:37 Lit Then his heart died within him

LORD, I will never lift my hand against the LORD's anointed. Instead, take the spear and the water jug by his head, and let's go."

¹² So David took the spear and the water jug by Saul's head, and they went their way. No one saw them, no one knew, and no one woke up; they all remained asleep because a deep sleep from the LORD came over them. ¹³ David crossed to the other side and stood on top of the mountain at a distance; there was a considerable space between them. ¹⁴ Then David shouted to the troops and to Abner son of Ner: "Aren't you going to answer, Abner?"

"Who are you who calls to the king?" Abner asked.

¹⁵ David called to Abner, "You're a man, aren't you? Who in Israel is your equal? So why didn't you protect your lord the king when one of the people came to destroy him? ¹⁶ What you have done is not good. As the LORD lives, all of you deserve to dieᴬ since you didn't protect your lord, the LORD's anointed. Now look around; where are the king's spear and water jug that were by his head?"

¹⁷ Saul recognized David's voice and asked, "Is that your voice, my son David?"

"It is my voice, my lord and king," David said. ¹⁸ Then he continued, "Why is my lord pursuing his servant? What have I done? What crime have I committed? ¹⁹ Now, may my lord the king please hear the words of his servant: If it is the LORD who has incited you against me, then may he accept an offering. But if it is people, may they be cursed in the presence of the LORD, for today they have banished me from sharing in the inheritance of the LORD saying, 'Go and worship other gods.' ²⁰ So don't let my blood fall to the ground far from the LORD's presence, for the king of Israel has come out to search for a single flea, like one who pursues a partridge in the mountains."

²¹ Saul responded, "I have sinned. Come back, my son David, I will never harm you again because today you considered my life precious. I have been a fool! I've committed a grave error."

²² David answered, "Here is the king's spear; have one of the young men come over and get it. ²³ The LORD will repay every man for his righteousness and his loyalty. I wasn't willing to lift my hand against the LORD's anointed, even though the LORD handed you over to me today. ²⁴ Just as I considered your life valuable today, so may the LORD consider my life valuable and rescue me from all trouble."

²⁵ Saul said to him, "You are blessed, my son David. You will certainly do great things and will also prevail." Then David went on his way, and Saul returned home.

DAVID FLEES TO ZIKLAG

27 David said to himself, "One of these days I'll be swept away by Saul. There is nothing better for me than to escape immediately to the land of the Philistines. Then Saul will give up searching for me everywhere in Israel, and I'll escape from him." ² So David set out with his six hundred men and went over to Achish son of Maoch, the king of Gath. ³ David and his men stayed with Achish in Gath. Each man had his family with him, and David had his two wives: Ahinoam of Jezreel and Abigail of Carmel, Nabal's widow. ⁴ When it was reported to Saul that David had fled to Gath, he no longer searched for him.

ᴬ26:16 Lit *you are sons of death*

⁵ Now David said to Achish, "If I have found favor with you, let me be given a place in one of the outlying towns, so I can live there. Why should your servant live in the royal city with you?" ⁶ That day Achish gave Ziklag to him, and it still belongs to the kings of Judah today. ⁷ The length of time that David stayed in Philistine territory amounted to a year and four months.

⁸ David and his men went up and raided the Geshurites, the Girzites,ᴬ and the Amalekites. From ancient times they had been the inhabitants of the region through Shur as far as the land of Egypt. ⁹ Whenever David attacked the land, he did not leave a single person alive, either man or woman, but he took flocks, herds, donkeys, camels, and clothing. Then he came back to Achish, ¹⁰ who inquired, "Where did you raid today?"ᴮ

David replied, "The south country of Judah," "The south country of the Jerahmeelites," or "The south country of the Kenites."

¹¹ David did not let a man or woman live to be brought to Gath, for he said, "Or they will inform on us and say, 'This is what David did.'" This was David's custom during the whole time he stayed in the Philistine territory. ¹² So Achish trusted David, thinking, "Since he has made himself repulsive to his people Israel, he will be my servant forever."

SAUL AND THE MEDIUM

28 At that time, the Philistines gathered their military units into one army to fight against Israel. So Achish said to David, "You know, of course, that you and your men must march out in the armyᶜ with me."

² David replied to Achish, "Good, you will find out what your servant can do."

So Achish said to David, "Very well, I will appoint you as my permanent bodyguard."

³ By this time Samuel had died, all Israel had mourned for him and buried him in Ramah, his city, and Saul had removed the mediums and spiritists from the land. ⁴ The Philistines gathered and camped at Shunem. So Saul gathered all Israel, and they camped at Gilboa. ⁵ When Saul saw the Philistine camp, he was afraid and his heart pounded. ⁶ He inquired of the LORD, but the LORD did not answer him in dreams or by the Urim or by the prophets. ⁷ Saul then said to his servants, "Find me a woman who is a medium, so I can go and consult her."

His servants replied, "There is a woman at En-dor who is a medium."

⁸ Saul disguised himself by putting on different clothes and set out with two of his men. They came to the woman at night, and Saul said, "Consult a spirit for me. Bring up for me the one I tell you."

⁹ But the woman said to him, "You surely know what Saul has done, how he has cut off the mediums and spiritists from the land. Why are you setting a trap for me to get me killed?"

¹⁰ Then Saul swore to her by the LORD: "As surely as the LORD lives, no punishment will come to youᴰ from this."

¹¹ "Who is it that you want me to bring up for you?" the woman asked.

"Bring up Samuel for me," he answered.

¹² When the woman saw Samuel, she screamed, and then she asked Saul, "Why did you deceive me? You are Saul!"

ᴬ27:8 Alt Hb tradition reads *Gezerites*   ᴮ27:10 Some Hb mss, Syr, Tg; LXX, Vg, DSS read *"Against whom did you raid today?"*   ᶜ28:1 DSS, LXX read *battle*
ᴰ28:10 Or *lives, you will not incur guilt*

¹³ But the king said to her, "Don't be afraid. What do you see?"

"I see a spirit form^A coming up out of the earth," the woman answered.

¹⁴ Then Saul asked her, "What does he look like?"

"An old man is coming up," she replied. "He's wearing a robe." Then Saul knew that it was Samuel, and he knelt low with his face to the ground and paid homage.

¹⁵ "Why have you disturbed me by bringing me up?" Samuel asked Saul.

"I'm in serious trouble," replied Saul. "The Philistines are fighting against me and God has turned away from me. He doesn't answer me anymore, either through the prophets or in dreams. So I've called on you to tell me what I should do."

¹⁶ Samuel answered, "Since the LORD has turned away from you and has become your enemy, why are you asking me? ¹⁷ The LORD has done^B exactly what he said through me: The LORD has torn the kingship out of your hand and given it to your neighbor David. ¹⁸ You did not obey the LORD and did not carry out his burning anger against Amalek; therefore the LORD has done this to you today. ¹⁹ The LORD will also hand Israel over to the Philistines along with you. Tomorrow you and your sons will be with me,^C and the LORD will hand Israel's army over to the Philistines."

²⁰ Immediately, Saul fell flat on the ground. He was terrified by Samuel's words and was also weak because he had not eaten anything all day and all night. ²¹ The woman came over to Saul, and she saw that he was terrified and said to him, "Look, your servant has obeyed you. I took my life in my hands and did what you told me to do. ²² Now please listen to your servant. Let me set some food in front of you. Eat and it will give you strength so you can go on your way."

²³ He refused, saying, "I won't eat," but when his servants and the woman urged him, he listened to them. He got up off the ground and sat on the bed.

²⁴ The woman had a fattened calf at her house, and she quickly slaughtered it. She also took flour, kneaded it, and baked unleavened bread. ²⁵ She served it to Saul and his servants, and they ate. Afterward, they got up and left that night.

PHILISTINES REJECT DAVID

29 The Philistines brought all their military units together at Aphek while Israel was camped by the spring in Jezreel. ² As the Philistine leaders were passing in review with their units of hundreds and thousands, David and his men were passing in review behind them with Achish. ³ Then the Philistine commanders asked, "What are these Hebrews doing here?"

Achish answered the Philistine commanders, "That is David, servant of King Saul of Israel. He has been with me a considerable period of time.^D From the day he defected until today, I've found no fault with him."

⁴ The Philistine commanders, however, were enraged with Achish and told him, "Send that man back and let him return to the place you assigned him. He must not go down with us into battle only to become our adversary during the battle. What better way could he ingratiate himself with his master than with the heads of our men? ⁵ Isn't this the David they sing about during their dances:

---

^A28:13 Or *a god, or a divine being*   ^B28:17 Some Hb, some LXX mss, Vg read *done to you*   ^C28:19 LXX reads *sons will fall*   ^D29:3 Hb obscure

Saul has killed his thousands,
but David his tens of thousands?"

⁶ So Achish summoned David and told him, "As the Lord lives, you are an honorable man. I think it is good^A to have you fighting^B in this unit with me, because I have found no fault in you from the day you came to me until today. But the leaders don't think you are reliable. ⁷ Now go back quietly and you won't be doing anything the Philistine leaders think is wrong."

⁸ "But what have I done?" David replied to Achish. "From the first day I entered your service until today, what have you found against your servant to keep me from going to fight against the enemies of my lord the king?"

⁹ Achish answered David, "I'm convinced that you are as reliable as an angel of God. But the Philistine commanders have said, 'He must not go into battle with us.' ¹⁰ So get up early in the morning, you and your masters' servants who came with you.^C When you've all gotten up early, go as soon as it's light." ¹¹ So David and his men got up early in the morning to return to the land of the Philistines. And the Philistines went up to Jezreel.

DAVID'S DEFEAT OF THE AMALEKITES

30 David and his men arrived in Ziklag on the third day. The Amalekites had raided the Negev and attacked and burned Ziklag. ² They also had kidnapped the women and everyone^D in it from youngest to oldest. They had killed no one but had carried them off as they went on their way.

³ When David and his men arrived at the town, they found it burned. Their wives, sons, and daughters had been kidnapped. ⁴ David and the troops with him wept loudly until they had no strength left to weep. ⁵ David's two wives, Ahinoam the Jezreelite and Abigail the widow of Nabal the Carmelite, had also been kidnapped. ⁶ David was in an extremely difficult position because the troops talked about stoning him, for they were all very bitter over the loss of their sons and daughters. But David found strength in the Lord his God.

⁷ David said to the priest Abiathar son of Ahimelech, "Bring me the ephod." So Abiathar brought it to him, ⁸ and David asked the Lord: "Should I pursue these raiders? Will I overtake them?"

The Lord replied to him, "Pursue them, for you will certainly overtake them and rescue the people."

⁹ So David and the six hundred men with him went. They came to the Wadi Besor, where some stayed behind. ¹⁰ David and four hundred of the men continued the pursuit, while two hundred stopped because they were too exhausted to cross the Wadi Besor.

¹¹ David's men found an Egyptian in the open country and brought him to David. They gave him some bread to eat and water to drink. ¹² Then they gave him some pressed figs and two clusters of raisins. After he ate he revived, for he hadn't eaten food or drunk water for three days and three nights.

¹³ Then David said to him, "Who do you belong to? Where are you from?"

"I'm an Egyptian, the slave of an Amalekite man," he said. "My master abandoned me when I got sick three days ago. ¹⁴ We raided the south country of

---

^A 29:6 Lit It was good in my eyes   ^B 29:6 Lit you going out and coming in
^C 29:10 LXX adds and go to the place I appointed you to. Don't take this evil matter to heart, for you are good before me.   ^D 30:2 LXX; MT omits and everyone

the Cherethites, the territory of Judah, and the south country of Caleb, and we burned Ziklag."

¹⁵ David then asked him, "Will you lead me to these raiders?"

He said, "Swear to me by God that you won't kill me or turn me over to my master, and I will lead you to them."

¹⁶ So he led him, and there were the Amalekites, spread out over the entire area, eating, drinking, and celebrating because of the great amount of plunder they had taken from the land of the Philistines and the land of Judah. ¹⁷ David slaughtered them from twilight until the evening of the next day. None of them escaped, except four hundred young men who got on camels and fled.

¹⁸ David recovered everything the Amalekites had taken; he also rescued his two wives. ¹⁹ Nothing of theirs was missing from the youngest to the oldest, including the sons and daughters, and all the plunder the Amalekites had taken. David got everything back. ²⁰ He took all the flocks and herds, which were driven ahead of the other livestock, and the people shouted, "This is David's plunder!"

²¹ When David came to the two hundred men who had been too exhausted to go with him and had been left at the Wadi Besor, they came out to meet him and to meet the troops with him. When David approached the men, he greeted them, ²² but all the corrupt and worthless men among those who had gone with David argued, "Because they didn't go with us, we will not give any of the plunder we recovered to them except for each man's wife and children. They may take them and go."

²³ But David said, "My brothers, you must not do this with what the LORD has given us. He protected us and handed over to us the raiders who came against us. ²⁴ Who can agree to your proposal? The share of the one who goes into battle is to be the same as the share of the one who remains with the supplies. They will share equally." ²⁵ And it has been so from that day forward. David established this policy ᴬ as a law and an ordinance for Israel and it still continues today.

²⁶ When David came to Ziklag, he sent some of the plunder to his friends, the elders of Judah, saying, "Here is a gift for you from the plunder of the LORD's enemies." ²⁷ He sent gifts ᴮ to those in Bethel, in Ramoth of the Negev, and in Jattir; ²⁸ to those in Aroer, in Siphmoth, and in Eshtemoa; ²⁹ to those in Racal, in the towns of the Jerahmeelites, and in the towns of the Kenites; ³⁰ to those in Hormah, in Bor-ashan, and in Athach; ³¹ to those in Hebron, and to those in all the places where David and his men had roamed.

THE DEATH OF SAUL AND HIS SONS

31 The Philistines fought against Israel, and Israel's men fled from them and were killed on Mount Gilboa. ² The Philistines pursued Saul and his sons and killed his sons, Jonathan, Abinadab, and Malchishua. ³ When the battle intensified against Saul, the archers found him and severely wounded him. ᶜ ⁴ Then Saul said to his armor-bearer, "Draw your sword and run me through with it, or these uncircumcised men will come and run me through and torture me!" But his armor-bearer would not do it because he

---

ᴬ30:25 *this policy* supplied for clarity   ᴮ30:27 *He sent gifts* supplied for clarity
ᶜ31:3 LXX reads *and he was wounded under the ribs*

was terrified. Then Saul took his sword and fell on it. [5] When his armor-bearer saw that Saul was dead, he also fell on his own sword and died with him. [6] So on that day, Saul died together with his three sons, his armor-bearer, and all his men.

[7] When the men of Israel on the other side of the valley and on the other side of the Jordan saw that Israel's men had fled and that Saul and his sons were dead, they abandoned the cities and fled. So the Philistines came and settled in them.

[8] The next day when the Philistines came to strip the slain, they found Saul and his three sons dead on Mount Gilboa. [9] They cut off Saul's head, stripped off his armor, and sent messengers throughout the land of the Philistines to spread the good news in the temples of their idols and among the people. [10] Then they put his armor in the temple of the Ashtoreths and hung his body on the wall of Beth-shan.

[11] When the residents of Jabesh-gilead heard what the Philistines had done to Saul, [12] all their brave men set out, journeyed all night, and retrieved the body of Saul and the bodies of his sons from the wall of Beth-shan. When they arrived at Jabesh, they burned the bodies there. [13] Afterward, they took their bones and buried them under the tamarisk tree in Jabesh and fasted seven days.

THE LORD
Himself
WILL MAKE A
House
FOR YOU

2 samuel

 The Lord declares to you: The Lord himself will make a house for you. **7:11**

ON THE TIMELINE The events in 2 Samuel occur directly after Saul's death (1011 BC), as David was established as king of Israel. The book closes at the end of David's reign, just before 971 BC, after God established the location where the temple was to be built. First Samuel 27:6 suggests this book was not completed until a few generations after the division of the kingdom of Israel, around 930 BC.

A LITTLE BACKGROUND Originally written as one book, 1 and 2 Samuel highlight a significant time of transition in Israel's history. As 1 Samuel begins, Israel is a loosely organized tribal people living under poor spiritual leadership. Even still, God's plan for His people continued as He raised up Samuel to guide Israel's transition from a theocracy to a monarchy. Saul's kingship constitutes the remainder of 1 Samuel, while David's kingship is largely the focus of 2 Samuel.

MESSAGE & PURPOSE
The books of 1 and 2 Samuel focus on four major themes:

1. *Leadership* – Examples of both good and bad leadership are shown throughout 1 and 2 Samuel. When leaders focused their attention on the Lord and saw their leadership roles as instruments for His glory, they flourished. When they abandoned the Lord and used their offices for their own gain, they failed.

2. *God's sovereignty* – God's provision for Israel is apparent at every turn. God provided spiritual leadership through Samuel, a king for Israel, and the leaders and resources needed for Israel to defeat their enemies and live out their purpose in the land.

3. *Sin's consequences* – God takes sin seriously, and the awful consequences of sin are displayed throughout 1 and 2 Samuel.

4. *Covenant* – 1 and 2 Samuel describe God's relationship with His covenant people and His faithful response to the terms of that covenant.

GIVE THANKS FOR THE BOOK OF 2 SAMUEL:

As God established a king in Israel, He also established a new covenant with David, one that would ultimately find its fulfillment in the Lord Jesus Christ. Though 1 and 2 Samuel display plenty of examples of leadership failures in Israel, the mercy and grace of God is displayed through His promise to use this broken nation to bring about the Savior of the world.

DAVID'S KINGDOM AND BATTLES

DAVID'S ROUTES ——————
ARAMEAN FORCES ————————
PHILISTINE THREAT ·····················
EDOMITE THREAT & RETREAT —·—·—·—·

10 David takes bronze from Tibhath, Cun, and Berothai to make bronze sea in Solomon's temple

3 David strikes Hadadezer, king of Zobah

6 Hadadezer ass a large Aramea

7 David pursues Hadadezer a se and inflicts serious defeat at He

9 David defeats the Amme

8 David sends Joab in retaliation of public humiliation

1 David defeats Philistine advance, gains control of Shephelah

2 David defeats the Moabites

4 David defeats the Edomites

5 David's triumph in the Valley of Salt forces the Edomite king to flee to Egypt

TIBHATH
CUN
BEROTHAI
ZOBAH
DAMASCUS
MAACAH
ARAM
SEA of GALILEE
ASHTAROTH
HELAM
RAMOTH-GILEAD
R. Jordan
BETH-SHAN
JABESH-GILEAD
MT. EBAL
R. Jabbok
SHECHEM
RABBAH
BETHEL
MICHMASH
GIBEAH
JERUSALEM
MT. NEBO
GATH
VALLEY OF REPHAIM
PHILISTIA
HEBRON
DEAD SEA
ARAD
MOAB
AMM
VALLEY of SALT
BOZRAH
EDOM
MT. CARMEL
PHOENICIA
MEDITERRANEAN SEA

READ AND UNDERSTAND 2 SAMUEL

The Bible is a complete work in which many stories combine to tell one story. As you read the book of 2 Samuel, consider reading the additional passages to discover how the whole of Scripture works together.

RESPONSES TO SAUL'S DEATH

1 After the death of Saul, David returned from defeating the Amalekites and stayed at Ziklag two days. ² On the third day a man with torn clothes and dust on his head came from Saul's camp. When he came to David, he fell to the ground and paid homage. ³ David asked him, "Where have you come from?"

He replied to him, "I've escaped from the Israelite camp."

⁴ "What was the outcome? Tell me," David asked him.

"The troops fled from the battle," he answered. "Many of the troops have fallen and are dead. Also, Saul and his son Jonathan are dead."

⁵ David asked the young man who had brought him the report, "How do you know Saul and his son Jonathan are dead?"

⁶ "I happened to be on Mount Gilboa," he replied, "and there was Saul, leaning on his spear. At that very moment the chariots and the cavalry were closing in on him. ⁷ When he turned around and saw me, he called out to me, so I answered: I'm at your service. ⁸ He asked me, 'Who are you?' I told him: I'm an Amalekite. ⁹ Then he begged me, 'Stand over me and kill me, for I'm mortally wounded,ᴬ but my life still lingers.' ¹⁰ So I stood over him and killed him because I knew that after he had fallen he couldn't survive. I took the crown that was on his head and the armband that was on his arm, and I've brought them here to my lord."

¹¹ Then David took hold of his clothes and tore them, and all the men with him did the same. ¹² They mourned, wept, and fasted until the evening for those who died by the sword — for Saul, his son Jonathan, the Lᴏʀᴅ's people, and the house of Israel.

¹³ David inquired of the young man who had brought him the report, "Where are you from?"

"I'm the son of a resident alien," he said. "I'm an Amalekite."

¹⁴ David questioned him, "How is it that you were not afraid to lift your hand to destroy the Lᴏʀᴅ's anointed?" ¹⁵ Then David summoned one of his servants and said, "Come here and kill him!" The servant struck him, and he died. ¹⁶ For David had said to the Amalekite, "Your blood is on your own head because your own mouth testified against you by saying, 'I killed the Lᴏʀᴅ's anointed.'"

¹⁷ David sang the following lament for Saul and his son Jonathan, ¹⁸ and he ordered that the Judahites be taught The Song of the Bow. It is written in the Book of Jashar:ᴮ

¹⁹ The splendor of Israel lies slain on your heights.
How the mighty have fallen!

²⁰ Do not tell it in Gath,
don't announce it in the marketplaces of Ashkelon,
or the daughters of the Philistines will rejoice,
and the daughters of the uncircumcised will celebrate.

²¹ Mountains of Gilboa,
let no dew or rain be on you,
or fields of offerings,ᶜ
for there the shield of the mighty was defiled —
the shield of Saul, no longer anointed with oil.

²² Jonathan's bow never retreated,

ᴬ1:9 LXX reads *for terrible darkness has taken hold of me*   ᴮ1:18 Or *of the Upright*
ᶜ1:21 LXX reads *firstfruits*

454

Saul's sword never returned unstained,^A
from the blood of the slain,
from the flesh^B of the mighty.

23 Saul and Jonathan,
loved and delightful,
they were not parted in life or in death.
They were swifter than eagles, stronger than lions.

24 Daughters of Israel, weep for Saul,
who clothed you in scarlet, with luxurious things,
who decked your garments with gold ornaments.

25 How the mighty have fallen in the thick of battle!
Jonathan lies slain on your heights.

26 I grieve for you, Jonathan, my brother.
You were such a friend to me.
Your love for me was more wondrous
than the love of women.

27 How the mighty have fallen
and the weapons of war have perished!

DAVID, KING OF JUDAH

2 Some time later, David inquired of the LORD: "Should I go to one of the towns of Judah?"

The LORD answered him, "Go."

Then David asked, "Where should I go?"

"To Hebron," the LORD replied.

² So David went there with his two wives, Ahinoam the Jezreelite and Abigail, the widow of Nabal the Carmelite. ³ In addition, David brought the men who were with him, each one with his family, and they settled in the towns near Hebron. ⁴ Then the men of Judah came, and there they anointed David king over the house of Judah. They told David: "It was the men of Jabesh-gilead who buried Saul."

⁵ David sent messengers to the men of Jabesh-gilead and said to them, "The LORD bless you, because you have shown this kindness to Saul your lord when you buried him. ⁶ Now, may the LORD show kindness and faithfulness to you, and I will also show the same goodness to you because you have done this deed. ⁷ Therefore, be strong^C and valiant, for though Saul your lord is dead, the house of Judah has anointed me king over them."

⁸ Abner son of Ner, commander of Saul's army, took Saul's son Ish-bosheth^{D,E} and moved him to Mahanaim. ⁹ He made him king over Gilead, Asher, Jezreel, Ephraim, Benjamin — over all Israel. ¹⁰ Saul's son Ish-bosheth was forty years old when he became king over Israel; he reigned for two years. The house of Judah, however, followed David. ¹¹ The length of time that David was king in Hebron over the house of Judah was seven years and six months.

¹² Abner son of Ner and soldiers of Ish-bosheth son of Saul marched out from Mahanaim to Gibeon. ¹³ So Joab son of Zeruiah and David's soldiers marched out and met them by the pool of Gibeon. The two groups took up positions on opposite sides of the pool.

---

^A1:22 Lit empty ^B1:22 Lit fat ^C2:7 Lit Therefore, strengthen your hands
^D2:8 Some LXX mss read Ishbaal; 1Ch 8:33; 9:39 ^E2:8 = Man of Shame

EVERYTHING IS UNDER CONTROL

2 SAMUEL 2; 1 SAMUEL 16

Have you ever watched the 1950s movie, *Sunset Boulevard*? Norma, an aging Hollywood starlet, longs for a comeback. She's deluded enough to think that by sheer force of will, she can break back into the business with a new movie. It goes horribly wrong for her, and the movie ends as she descends a staircase, guilty of murder, smiling and waving to the flashes of reporters' cameras as she's taken into police custody. Norma couldn't loosen her vulture-grip on her own fame enough to see reality.

Now, I'm not usually a wide-eyed crazy lady clawing at the scraps of my imagined life. Or am I? *Do I try to hold on to things that are gone and out of my control? Do I secretly attempt to force God to do my bidding?* I suspect that because of our sin nature, we all try to control our own circumstances, instead of trusting God to go to bat for us.

The aging starlet reminds me of King Saul. While Saul was still in power, Samuel anointed David as God's choice for king (1Sm 16:1). Instead of gracefully stepping down, Saul raged, fighting for years against both David and the will of God.

Look at the story from David's perspective. He was the youngest and the least impressive of all his brothers. Although Samuel did have a small family ceremony after he anointed him, not much changed right away for David. He was still the little brother who had to tend the sheep.

But one very significant thing did change immediately: the Spirit of the Lord came upon David and departed from Saul, who was then plagued by an evil spirit (1Sm 16:14). Although David didn't actually assume the throne for years after he was anointed, the Spirit of the Lord was with him. That was more valuable than ten thousand thrones (1Sm 18:28). While Saul scraped and grasped to keep control of his kingdom, David waited on God's timing and spent the years learning to listen to the Lord.

Despite the Lord's clear choice of David as king over Israel, Saul was unwilling to give up the kingdom. He knew David would be king, but he was unable to let go of his delusion of power before his death (1Sm 24:22).

David didn't have to scramble and fight for the crown. The Lord chose him, and He gave David his throne (2Sm 2). **David didn't have to take matters into his own hands. God had everything under control. And He still does.**

We don't have to claw, hustle, and scratch to make things happen in our lives. God is sovereign. In spite of all Saul's labors, his day was over as David's was ready to begin.

Let's join with David and wait patiently for the Lord. He will defend and protect us.

[14] Then Abner said to Joab, "Let's have the young men get up and compete in front of us."

"Let them get up," Joab replied.

[15] So they got up and were counted off — twelve for Benjamin and Ishbosheth son of Saul, and twelve from David's soldiers. [16] Then each man grabbed his opponent by the head and thrust his sword into his opponent's side so that they all died together. So this place, which is in Gibeon, is named Field of Blades.[A]

[17] The battle that day was extremely fierce, and Abner and the men of Israel were defeated by David's soldiers. [18] The three sons of Zeruiah were there: Joab, Abishai, and Asahel. Asahel was a fast runner, like one of the wild gazelles. [19] He chased Abner and did not turn to the right or the left in his pursuit of him. [20] Abner glanced back and said, "Is that you, Asahel?"

"Yes it is," Asahel replied.

[21] Abner said to him, "Turn to your right or left, seize one of the young soldiers, and take whatever you can get from him." But Asahel would not stop chasing him. [22] Once again, Abner warned Asahel, "Stop chasing me. Why should I strike you to the ground? How could I ever look your brother Joab in the face?"

[23] But Asahel refused to turn away, so Abner hit him in the stomach with the butt of his spear. The spear went through his body, and he fell and died right there. As they all came to the place where Asahel had fallen and died, they stopped, [24] but Joab and Abishai pursued Abner. By sunset, they had gone as far as the hill of Ammah, which is opposite Giah on the way to the wilderness of Gibeon.

[25] The Benjaminites rallied to Abner; they formed a unit and took their stand on top of a hill. [26] Then Abner called out to Joab: "Must the sword devour forever? Don't you realize this will only end in bitterness? How long before you tell the troops to stop pursuing their brothers?"

[27] "As God lives," Joab replied, "if you had not spoken up, the troops wouldn't have stopped pursuing their brothers until morning." [28] Then Joab blew the ram's horn, and all the troops stopped; they no longer pursued Israel or continued to fight. [29] So Abner and his men marched through the Arabah all that night. They crossed the Jordan, marched all morning,[B] and arrived at Mahanaim.

[30] When Joab had turned back from pursuing Abner, he gathered all the troops. In addition to Asahel, nineteen of David's soldiers were missing, [31] but they had killed 360 of the Benjaminites and Abner's men. [32] Afterward, they carried Asahel to his father's tomb in Bethlehem and buried him. Then Joab and his men marched all night and reached Hebron at dawn.

CIVIL WAR

3 During the long war between the house of Saul and the house of David, David was growing stronger and the house of Saul was becoming weaker.

[2] Sons were born to David in Hebron:

His firstborn was Amnon,
by Ahinoam the Jezreelite;

[3] his second was Chileab,
by Abigail, the widow of Nabal the Carmelite;

> the third was Absalom,
> son of Maacah the daughter of King Talmai of Geshur;
⁴ the fourth was Adonijah,
> son of Haggith;
> the fifth was Shephatiah,
> son of Abital;
⁵ the sixth was Ithream,
> by David's wife Eglah.

These were born to David in Hebron.

⁶ During the war between the house of Saul and the house of David, Abner kept acquiring more power in the house of Saul. ⁷ Now Saul had a concubine whose name was Rizpah daughter of Aiah, and Ish-bosheth questioned Abner, "Why did you sleep with my father's concubine?"

⁸ Abner was very angry about Ish-bosheth's accusation. "Am I a dog's head^A who belongs to Judah?" he asked. "All this time I've been loyal to the family of your father Saul, to his brothers, and to his friends and haven't betrayed you to David, but now you accuse me of wrongdoing with this woman! ⁹ May God punish Abner and do so severely if I don't do for David what the Lᴏʀᴅ swore to him: ¹⁰ to transfer the kingdom from the house of Saul and establish the throne of David over Israel and Judah from Dan to Beer-sheba." ¹¹ Ish-bosheth did not dare respond to Abner because he was afraid of him.

¹² Abner sent messengers as his representatives to say to David, "Whose land is it? Make your covenant with me, and you can be certain I am on your side to turn all Israel over to you."

¹³ David replied, "Good, I will make a covenant with you. However, there's one thing I require of you: You will not see my face unless you first bring Saul's daughter Michal when you come to see me."

¹⁴ Then David sent messengers to say to Ish-bosheth son of Saul, "Give me back my wife, Michal. I was engaged to her for the price of a hundred Philistine foreskins."

¹⁵ So Ish-bosheth sent someone to take her away from her husband, Paltiel son of Laish. ¹⁶ Her husband followed her, weeping all the way to Bahurim. Abner said to him, "Go back." So he went back.

THE ASSASSINATION OF ABNER

¹⁷ Abner conferred with the elders of Israel: "In the past you wanted David to be king over you. ¹⁸ Now take action, because the Lᴏʀᴅ has spoken concerning David: 'Through my servant David I will save my people Israel from the power of the Philistines and the power of all Israel's enemies.'"

¹⁹ Abner also informed the Benjaminites and went to Hebron to inform David about all that was agreed on by Israel and the whole house of Benjamin. ²⁰ When Abner and twenty men came to David at Hebron, David held a banquet for him and his men.

²¹ Abner said to David, "Let me now go and I will gather all Israel to my lord the king. They will make a covenant with you, and you will reign over all you desire." So David dismissed Abner, and he went in peace.

²² Just then David's soldiers and Joab returned from a raid and brought a large amount of plundered goods with them. Abner was not with David in

---

^A 3:8 = a despised person

Hebron because David had dismissed him, and he had gone in peace. [23] When Joab and his whole army arrived, Joab was informed, "Abner son of Ner came to see the king, the king dismissed him, and he went in peace."

[24] Joab went to the king and said, "What have you done? Look here, Abner came to you. Why did you dismiss him? Now he's getting away. [25] You know that Abner son of Ner came to deceive you and to find out about your military activities[A] and everything you're doing." [26] Then Joab left David and sent messengers after Abner. They brought him back from the well[B] of Sirah, but David was unaware of it. [27] When Abner returned to Hebron, Joab pulled him aside to the middle of the city gate, as if to speak to him privately, and there Joab stabbed him in the stomach. So Abner died in revenge for the death of Asahel,[C] Joab's brother.

[28] David heard about it later and said: "I and my kingdom are forever innocent before the LORD concerning the blood of Abner son of Ner. [29] May it hang over Joab's head and his father's whole family, and may the house of Joab never be without someone who has a discharge or a skin disease, or a man who can only work a spindle,[D] or someone who falls by the sword or starves." [30] Joab and his brother Abishai killed Abner because he had put their brother Asahel to death in the battle at Gibeon.

[31] David then ordered Joab and all the people who were with him, "Tear your clothes, put on sackcloth, and mourn over Abner." And King David walked behind the coffin.[E]

[32] When they buried Abner in Hebron, the king wept aloud at Abner's tomb. All the people wept, [33] and the king sang a lament for Abner:

Should Abner die as a fool dies?
[34]   Your hands were not bound,
        your feet not placed in bronze shackles.
        You fell like one who falls victim to criminals.
And all the people wept over him even more.

[35] Then they came to urge David to eat food while it was still day, but David took an oath: "May God punish me and do so severely if I taste bread or anything else before sunset!" [36] All the people took note of this, and it pleased them. In fact, everything the king did pleased them. [37] On that day all the troops and all Israel were convinced that the king had no part in the killing of Abner son of Ner.

[38] Then the king said to his soldiers, "You must know that a great leader has fallen in Israel today. [39] As for me, even though I am the anointed king, I have little power today. These men, the sons of Zeruiah, are too fierce for me. May the LORD repay the evildoer according to his evil!"

THE ASSASSINATION OF ISH-BOSHETH

4 When Saul's son Ish-bosheth heard that Abner had died in Hebron, he gave up,[F] and all Israel was dismayed. [2] Saul's son had two men who were leaders of raiding parties: one named Baanah and the other Rechab, sons of Rimmon the Beerothite of the Benjaminites. Beeroth is also considered part of Benjamin, [3] and the Beerothites fled to Gittaim and still reside there as aliens today.

[A]3:25 Lit your going out and your coming in   [B]3:26 Or cistern   [C]3:27 Lit And he died for the blood of Asahel   [D]3:29 LXX reads who uses a crutch   [E]3:31 Or the bier; lit the bed   [F]4:1 Lit his hands dropped

⁴ Saul's son Jonathan had a son whose feet were crippled. He was five years old when the report about Saul and Jonathan came from Jezreel. His nanny ᴬ picked him up and fled, but as she was hurrying to flee, he fell and became lame. His name was Mephibosheth.

⁵ Rechab and Baanah, the sons of Rimmon the Beerothite, set out and arrived at Ish-bosheth's house during the heat of the day while the king was taking his midday nap. ⁶ They entered the interior of the house as if to get wheat and stabbed him in the stomach. Then Rechab and his brother Baanah escaped. ⁷ They had entered the house while Ish-bosheth was lying on his bed in his bedroom and stabbed and killed him. They removed his head, took it, and traveled by way of the Arabah all night. ⁸ They brought Ish-bosheth's head to David at Hebron and said to the king, "Here's the head of Ish-bosheth son of Saul, your enemy who intended to take your life. Today the LORD has granted vengeance to my lord the king against Saul and his offspring."

⁹ But David answered Rechab and his brother Baanah, sons of Rimmon the Beerothite, "As the LORD lives, the one who has redeemed my life from every distress, ¹⁰ when the person told me, 'Look, Saul is dead,' he thought he was a bearer of good news, but I seized him and put him to death at Ziklag. That was my reward to him for his news! ¹¹ How much more when wicked men kill a righteous man in his own house on his own bed! So now, should I not require his blood from you and purge you from the earth?"

¹² So David gave orders to the young men, and they killed Rechab and Baanah. They cut off their hands and feet and hung their bodies by the pool in Hebron, but they took Ish-bosheth's head and buried it in Abner's tomb in Hebron.

DAVID, KING OF ISRAEL

5 All the tribes of Israel came to David at Hebron and said, "Here we are, your own flesh and blood. ᴮ ² Even while Saul was king over us, you were the one who led us out to battle and brought us back. The LORD also said to you, 'You will shepherd my people Israel, and you will be ruler over Israel.' "

³ So all the elders of Israel came to the king at Hebron. King David made a covenant with them at Hebron in the LORD's presence, and they anointed David king over Israel.

⁴ David was thirty years old when he began his reign; he reigned forty years. ⁵ In Hebron he reigned over Judah seven years and six months, and in Jerusalem he reigned thirty-three years over all Israel and Judah.

⁶ The king and his men marched to Jerusalem against the Jebusites who inhabited the land. The Jebusites had said to David: "You will never get in here. Even the blind and lame can repel you" thinking, "David can't get in here."

⁷ Yet David did capture the stronghold of Zion, that is, the city of David. ⁸ He said that day, "Whoever attacks the Jebusites must go through the water shaft to reach the lame and the blind who are despised by David." ᶜ For this reason it is said, "The blind and the lame will never enter the house." ᴰ

⁹ David took up residence in the stronghold, which he named the city of David. He built it up all the way around from the supporting terraces inward.

ᴬ 4:4 Lit *His nurse*   ᴮ 5:1 Lit *your bone and your flesh*   ᶜ 5:8 Alt Hb tradition, LXX, Tg, Syr read *who despise David*   ᴰ 5:8 Or *temple*, or *palace*

[10] David became more and more powerful, and the LORD God of Armies was with him. [11] King Hiram of Tyre sent envoys to David; he also sent cedar logs, carpenters, and stonemasons, and they built a palace for David. [12] Then David knew that the LORD had established him as king over Israel and had exalted his kingdom for the sake of his people Israel.

[13] After he arrived from Hebron, David took more concubines and wives from Jerusalem, and more sons and daughters were born to him. [14] These are the names of those born to him in Jerusalem: Shammua, Shobab, Nathan, Solomon, [15] Ibhar, Elishua, Nepheg, Japhia, [16] Elishama, Eliada, and Eliphelet.

[17] When the Philistines heard that David had been anointed king over Israel, they all went in search of David, but he heard about it and went down to the stronghold. [18] So the Philistines came and spread out in the Valley of Rephaim.

[19] Then David inquired of the LORD: "Should I attack the Philistines? Will you hand them over to me?"

The LORD replied to David, "Attack, for I will certainly hand the Philistines over to you."

[20] So David went to Baal-perazim and defeated them there and said, "Like a bursting flood, the LORD has burst out against my enemies before me." Therefore, he named that place The Lord Bursts Out. [A] [21] The Philistines abandoned their idols there, and David and his men carried them off.

[22] The Philistines came up again and spread out in the Valley of Rephaim. [23] So David inquired of the LORD, and he answered, "Do not attack directly, but circle around behind them and come at them opposite the balsam trees. [24] When you hear the sound of marching in the tops of the balsam trees, act decisively, for then the LORD will have gone out ahead of you to strike down the army of the Philistines." [25] So David did exactly as the LORD commanded him, and he struck down the Philistines all the way from Geba to Gezer.

DAVID MOVES THE ARK

6 David again assembled all the fit young men in Israel: thirty thousand. [2] He and all his troops set out to bring the ark of God from Baale-judah. [B] The ark bears the Name, the name of the LORD of Armies who is enthroned between the cherubim. [3] They set the ark of God on a new cart and transported it from Abinadab's house, which was on the hill. Uzzah and Ahio, [C] sons of Abinadab, were guiding the cart [4] and brought it with the ark of God from Abinadab's house on the hill. Ahio walked in front of the ark. [5] David and the whole house of Israel were dancing before the LORD with all kinds of fir wood instruments, [D] lyres, harps, tambourines, sistrums, [E] and cymbals.

[6] When they came to Nacon's threshing floor, Uzzah reached out to the ark of God and took hold of it because the oxen had stumbled. [7] Then the LORD's anger burned against Uzzah, and God struck him dead on the spot for his irreverence, and he died there next to the ark of God. [8] David was angry because of the LORD's outburst against Uzzah, so he named that

---

[A] 5:20 Or *Baal-perazim*; 2Sm 6:8; 1Ch 13:11   [B] 6:2 = Kiriath-jearim in 1Sm 7:1; 1Ch 13:6; 2Ch 1:4   [C] 6:3 Or *And his brothers*   [D] 6:5 DSS, LXX read *with tuned instruments with strength, with songs*; 1Ch 13:8   [E] 6:5 = an Egyptian percussion instrument place Outburst Against Uzzah,[A] as it is today. [9] David feared the LORD that day and said, "How can the ark of the LORD ever come to me?" [10] So he was not willing to bring the ark of the LORD to the city of David; instead, he diverted it to the house of Obed-edom of Gath. [11] The ark of the LORD remained in his house three months, and the LORD blessed Obed-edom and his whole family.

[12] It was reported to King David: "The LORD has blessed Obed-edom's family and all that belongs to him because of the ark of God." So David went and had the ark of God brought up from Obed-edom's house to the city of David with rejoicing. [13] When those carrying the ark of the LORD advanced six steps, he sacrificed an ox and a fattened calf. [14] David was dancing[B] with all his might before the LORD wearing a linen ephod. [15] He and the whole house of Israel were bringing up the ark of the LORD with shouts and the sound of the ram's horn. [16] As the ark of the LORD was entering the city of David, Saul's daughter Michal looked down from the window and saw King David leaping and dancing before the LORD, and she despised him in her heart.

[17] They brought the ark of the LORD and set it in its place inside the tent David had pitched for it. Then David offered burnt offerings and fellowship offerings in the LORD's presence. [18] When David had finished offering the burnt offering and the fellowship offerings, he blessed the people in the name of the LORD of Armies. [19] Then he distributed a loaf of bread, a date cake, and a raisin cake to each one in the entire Israelite community, both men and women. Then all the people went home.

[20] When David returned home to bless his household, Saul's daughter Michal came out to meet him. "How the king of Israel honored himself today!" she said. "He exposed himself today in the sight of the slave girls of his subjects like a vulgar person would expose himself."

[21] David replied to Michal, "It was before the LORD who chose me over your father and his whole family to appoint me ruler over the LORD's people Israel. I will dance before the LORD, [22] and I will dishonor myself and humble myself even more.[C,D] However, by the slave girls you spoke about, I will be honored." [23] And Saul's daughter Michal had no child to the day of her death.

THE LORD'S COVENANT WITH DAVID

7 When the king had settled into his palace and the LORD had given him rest on every side from all his enemies, [2] the king said to the prophet Nathan, "Look, I am living in a cedar house while the ark of God sits inside tent curtains."

[3] So Nathan told the king, "Go and do all that is on your mind, for the LORD is with you."

[4] But that night the word of the LORD came to Nathan: [5] "Go to my servant David and say, 'This is what the LORD says: Are you to build me a house to dwell in? [6] From the time I brought the Israelites out of Egypt until today I have not dwelt in a house; instead, I have been moving around with a tent as my dwelling. [7] In all my journeys with all the Israelites, have I ever spoken a word to one of the tribes of Israel, whom I commanded to shepherd my people Israel, asking: Why haven't you built me a house of cedar?'

[A]6:8 Or *Perez-uzzah*; 2Sm 5:20   [B]6:14 Or *whirling*   [C]6:22 LXX reads *more and I will be humble in your eyes*   [D]6:22 Lit *more and I will be humble in my own eyes*

THE GENEROSITY OF GOD

2 SAMUEL 6–7; GENESIS 9; GENESIS 12; EXODUS 19; LUKE 22:20

I've always assumed that a covenant is an if/then agreement. If you do x, then I'll do y. If you fail to do x, then I'm entitled to y. Since dissecting legal mumbo-jumbo isn't really my thing, the idea of a covenant always felt a little sterile to me.

Maybe that's why I typically paid little attention to the Old Testament covenants. God's covenant promises are mentioned in many places, so I did plenty of glossing over them. The biggies include the Noahic Covenant found in Genesis 9, the Abrahamic Covenant in Genesis 12, and the Mosaic Covenant in Exodus 19.

Because I only skimmed these passages, I thought the covenants were cut-and-dried versions of this: If God's people obey the law, they get blessed; if they fail to obey the law, they get cursed. Certainly, there are blessings that come with obedience and consequences that come with rebellion—but that isn't the bottom line. It's not how God does business.

God's covenants are not equal partnerships. God gives infinitely more than He ever plans to receive. We see this clearly in God's covenant with David (2Sm 7). God had been blessing David since childhood, but here, He makes it official. God promises David these things: fame and prestige, deep roots, safety and security, legacy, and a bright future.

God promised big! This is the "then" portion of God's covenant with David. But what was the "if"? What did David have to do to earn these lavish gifts? Well, for starters he had to....

[Crickets]

Nothing. There is no "if" to qualify God's "then." David doesn't have do his part for this covenant agreement to stand. God gives generously out

of extravagant love, not legal obligation. And David's response is awestruck worship.

"This is why you are great, Lord GOD. There is no one like you, and there is no God besides you, as all we have heard confirms."

2 SAMUEL 7:22

David enjoyed what I missed when I zoomed past the previous covenants: God doesn't love us out of obligation. There is no way for the scales to be equal when man enters into a covenant with the God who created him.

The covenants of the Old Testament are like neon signs pointing to something bigger and better. They set the table for the fulfillment of God's covenant of grace, perfected in the finished work of Christ on our behalf.

"In the same way he also took the cup after the supper and said, 'This cup is the new covenant in my blood, which is poured out for you.'"

LUKE 22:20

The covenant Jesus offers us is this: we bring our nothing, and He gives us everything. The scales are forever tipped in our favor. May we learn to stop glossing over the goodness of our God. Instead, let us respond in worship to the God who gives extravagantly.

8 "So now this is what you are to say to my servant David: 'This is what the LORD of Armies says: I took you from the pasture, from tending the flock, to be ruler over my people Israel. 9 I have been with you wherever you have gone, and I have destroyed all your enemies before you. I will make a great name for you like that of the greatest on the earth. 10 I will designate a place for my people Israel and plant them, so that they may live there and not be disturbed again. Evildoers will not continue to oppress them as they have done 11 ever since the day I ordered judges to be over my people Israel. I will give you rest from all your enemies.

" 'The LORD declares to you: The LORD himself will make a house for you. 12 When your time comes and you rest with your fathers, I will raise up after you your descendant, who will come from your body, and I will establish his kingdom. 13 He is the one who will build a house for my name, and I will establish the throne of his kingdom forever. 14 I will be his father, and he will be my son. When he does wrong, I will discipline him with a rod of men and blows from mortals. 15 But my faithful love will never leave him as it did when I removed it from Saul, whom I removed from before you. 16 Your house and kingdom will endure before me^A forever, and your throne will be established forever.' "

17 Nathan reported all these words and this entire vision to David.

DAVID'S PRAYER OF THANKSGIVING

18 Then King David went in, sat in the LORD's presence, and said,

Who am I, Lord GOD, and what is my house that you have brought me this far? 19 What you have done so far^B was a little thing to you, Lord GOD, for you have also spoken about your servant's house in the distant future. And this is a revelation^C for mankind, Lord GOD. 20 What more can David say to you? You know your servant, Lord GOD. 21 Because of your word and according to your will, you have revealed all these great things to your servant.

22 This is why you are great, Lord GOD. There is no one like you, and there is no God besides you, as all we have heard confirms. 23 And who is like your people Israel? God came to one nation on earth in order to redeem a people for himself, to make a name for himself, and to perform for them^D great and awesome acts,^E driving out nations and their gods before your people you redeemed for yourself from Egypt. 24 You established your people Israel to be your own people forever, and you, LORD, have become their God.

25 Now, LORD God, fulfill the promise forever that you have made to your servant and his house. Do as you have promised, 26 so that your name will be exalted forever, when it is said, "The LORD of Armies is God over Israel." The house of your servant David will be established before you 27 since you, LORD of Armies, God of Israel, have revealed this to your servant when you said, "I will build a house for you." Therefore, your servant has found the courage to pray this prayer to you. 28 Lord GOD,

---

^A 7:16 Some Hb mss, LXX, Syr; other Hb mss read *you*   ^B 7:19 Lit *Yet this*
^C 7:19 Or *custom*, or *instruction*   ^D 7:23 Some Hb mss, Tg, Vg, Syr; other Hb mss read *you*   ^E 7:23 LXX; MT reads *acts for your land*

you are God; your words are true, and you have promised this good thing to your servant. ²⁹ Now, please bless your servant's house so that it will continue before you forever. For you, Lord God, have spoken, and with your blessing your servant's house will be blessed forever.

DAVID'S VICTORIES

8 After this, David defeated the Philistines, subdued them, and took Metheg-ammah^A from Philistine control.^B ² He also defeated the Moabites, and after making them lie down on the ground, he measured them off with a cord. He measured every two cord lengths of those to be put to death and one full length of those to be kept alive. So the Moabites became David's subjects and brought tribute.

³ David also defeated Hadadezer son of Rehob, king of Zobah, when he went to restore his control at the Euphrates River. ⁴ David captured seventeen hundred horsemen^C and twenty thousand foot soldiers from him, and he hamstrung all the horses and kept a hundred chariots.^D

⁵ When the Arameans of Damascus came to assist King Hadadezer of Zobah, David struck down twenty-two thousand Aramean men. ⁶ Then he placed garrisons in Aram of Damascus, and the Arameans became David's subjects and brought tribute. The Lord made David victorious wherever he went.

⁷ David took the gold shields of Hadadezer's officers and brought them to Jerusalem. ⁸ King David also took huge quantities of bronze from Betah^E and Berothai, Hadadezer's cities.

⁹ When King Toi of Hamath heard that David had defeated the entire army of Hadadezer, ¹⁰ he sent his son Joram to King David to greet him and to congratulate him because David had fought against Hadadezer and defeated him, for Toi and Hadadezer had fought many wars. Joram had items of silver, gold, and bronze with him. ¹¹ King David also dedicated these to the Lord, along with the silver and gold he had dedicated from all the nations he had subdued — ¹² from Edom,^F Moab, the Ammonites, the Philistines, the Amalekites, and the spoil of Hadadezer son of Rehob, king of Zobah.

¹³ David made a reputation for himself when he returned from striking down eighteen thousand Edomites^G in Salt Valley.^H ¹⁴ He placed garrisons throughout Edom, and all the Edomites were subject to David. The Lord made David victorious wherever he went.

¹⁵ So David reigned over all Israel, administering justice and righteousness for all his people.

¹⁶ Joab son of Zeruiah was over the army;
Jehoshaphat son of Ahilud was court historian;

¹⁷ Zadok son of Ahitub and Ahimelech son of Abiathar were priests;
Seraiah was court secretary;

¹⁸ Benaiah son of Jehoiada was over the Cherethites and the Pelethites;
and David's sons were chief officials.^I

---

^A8:1 Or *took control of the mother city*; Hb obscure   ^B8:1 LXX reads *them, and David took tribute out of the hand of the Philistines*   ^C8:4 LXX, DSS read *1,000 chariots and 7,000 horsemen*   ^D8:4 Or *chariot horses*   ^E8:8 Some LXX mss, Syr read *Tebah*   ^F8:12 Some Hb mss, LXX, Syr; other Hb mss read *Aram*; 1Ch 18:11
^G8:13 Some Hb mss, LXX, Syr; other Hb mss read *Arameans*; 1Ch 18:12
^H8:13 = the Dead Sea region   ^I8:18 LXX; MT reads *were priests*; 1Ch 18:17

DAVID'S KINDNESS TO MEPHIBOSHETH

9 David asked, "Is there anyone remaining from the family of Saul I can show kindness to for Jonathan's sake?" ² There was a servant of Saul's family named Ziba. They summoned him to David, and the king said to him, "Are you Ziba?"

"I am your servant," he replied.

³ So the king asked, "Is there anyone left of Saul's family that I can show the kindness of God to?"

Ziba said to the king, "There is still Jonathan's son who was injured in both feet."

⁴ The king asked him, "Where is he?"

Ziba answered the king, "You'll find him in Lo-debar at the house of Machir son of Ammiel." ⁵ So King David had him brought from the house of Machir son of Ammiel in Lo-debar.

⁶ Mephibosheth son of Jonathan son of Saul came to David, fell facedown, and paid homage. David said, "Mephibosheth!"

"I am your servant," he replied.

⁷ "Don't be afraid," David said to him, "since I intend to show you kindness for the sake of your father Jonathan. I will restore to you all your grandfather Saul's fields, and you will always eat meals at my table."

⁸ Mephibosheth paid homage and said, "What is your servant that you take an interest in a dead dog like me?"

⁹ Then the king summoned Saul's attendant Ziba and said to him, "I have given to your master's grandson all that belonged to Saul and his family. ¹⁰ You, your sons, and your servants are to work the ground for him, and you are to bring in the crops so your master's grandson will have food to eat. But Mephibosheth, your master's grandson, is always to eat at my table." Now Ziba had fifteen sons and twenty servants.

¹¹ Ziba said to the king, "Your servant will do all my lord the king commands."

So Mephibosheth ate at David's^A table just like one of the king's sons. ¹² Mephibosheth had a young son whose name was Mica. All those living in Ziba's house were Mephibosheth's servants. ¹³ However, Mephibosheth lived in Jerusalem because he always ate at the king's table. His feet had been injured.

WAR WITH THE AMMONITES

10 Some time later, the king of the Ammonites died, and his son Hanun became king in his place. ² Then David said, "I'll show kindness to Hanun son of Nahash, just as his father showed kindness to me."

So David sent his emissaries to console Hanun concerning his father. However, when they arrived in the land of the Ammonites, ³ the Ammonite leaders said to Hanun their lord, "Just because David has sent men with condolences for you, do you really believe he's showing respect for your father? Instead, hasn't David sent his emissaries in order to scout out the city, spy on it, and demolish it?" ⁴ So Hanun took David's emissaries, shaved off half their beards, cut their clothes in half at the hips, and sent them away.

⁵ When this was reported to David, he sent someone to meet them, since they were deeply humiliated. The king said, "Stay in Jericho until your beards grow back; then return."

^A9:11 LXX; Syr reads *the king's*; Vg reads *your*; MT reads *my*

⁶ When the Ammonites realized they had become repulsive to David, they hired twenty thousand foot soldiers from the Arameans of Beth-rehob and Zobah, one thousand men from the king of Maacah, and twelve thousand men from Tob.

⁷ David heard about it and sent Joab and all the elite troops. ⁸ The Ammonites marched out and lined up in battle formation at the entrance to the city gate while the Arameans of Zobah and Rehob and the men of Tob and Maacah were in the field by themselves. ⁹ When Joab saw that there was a battle line in front of him and another behind him, he chose some of Israel's finest young men and lined up in formation to engage the Arameans. ¹⁰ He placed the rest of the forces under the command of his brother Abishai. They lined up in formation to engage the Ammonites.

¹¹ "If the Arameans are too strong for me," Joab said, "then you will be my help. However, if the Ammonites are too strong for you, I'll come to help you. ¹² Be strong! Let's prove ourselves strong for our people and for the cities of our God. May the LORD's will be done." ᴬ

¹³ Joab and his troops advanced to fight against the Arameans, and they fled before him. ¹⁴ When the Ammonites saw that the Arameans had fled, they too fled before Abishai and entered the city. So Joab withdrew from the attack against the Ammonites and went to Jerusalem.

¹⁵ When the Arameans saw that they had been defeated by Israel, they regrouped. ¹⁶ Hadadezer sent messengers to bring the Arameans who were beyond the Euphrates River, and they came to Helam with Shobach, commander of Hadadezer's army, leading them.

¹⁷ When this was reported to David, he gathered all Israel, crossed the Jordan, and went to Helam. Then the Arameans lined up to engage David in battle and fought against him. ¹⁸ But the Arameans fled before Israel, and David killed seven hundred of their charioteers and forty thousand foot soldiers. ᴮ He also struck down Shobach commander of their army, who died there. ¹⁹ When all the kings who were Hadadezer's subjects saw that they had been defeated by Israel, they made peace with Israel and became their subjects. After this, the Arameans were afraid to ever help the Ammonites again.

DAVID'S ADULTERY WITH BATHSHEBA

11 In the spring when kings march out to war, David sent Joab with his officers and all Israel. They destroyed the Ammonites and besieged Rabbah, but David remained in Jerusalem.

² One evening David got up from his bed and strolled around on the roof of the palace. From the roof he saw a woman bathing — a very beautiful woman. ³ So David sent someone to inquire about her, and he said, "Isn't this Bathsheba, daughter of Eliam and wife of Uriah the Hethite? " ᶜ

⁴ David sent messengers to get her, and when she came to him, he slept with her. Now she had just been purifying herself from her uncleanness. Afterward, she returned home. ⁵ The woman conceived and sent word to inform David: "I am pregnant."

⁶ David sent orders to Joab: "Send me Uriah the Hethite." So Joab sent Uriah to David. ⁷ When Uriah came to him, David asked how Joab and the troops

---

ᴬ10:12 Lit the LORD do what is good in his eyes   ᴮ10:18 Some LXX mss; MT reads horsemen; 1Ch 19:18   ᶜ11:3 DSS add Joab's armor-bearer were doing and how the war was going. [8] Then he said to Uriah, "Go down to your house and wash your feet." So Uriah left the palace, and a gift from the king followed him. [9] But Uriah slept at the door of the palace with all his master's servants; he did not go down to his house.

[10] When it was reported to David, "Uriah didn't go home," David questioned Uriah, "Haven't you just come from a journey? Why didn't you go home?"

[11] Uriah answered David, "The ark, Israel, and Judah are dwelling in tents, and my master Joab and his soldiers[A] are camping in the open field. How can I enter my house to eat and drink and sleep with my wife? As surely as you live and by your life, I will not do this!"

[12] "Stay here today also," David said to Uriah, "and tomorrow I will send you back." So Uriah stayed in Jerusalem that day and the next. [13] Then David invited Uriah to eat and drink with him, and David got him drunk. He went out in the evening to lie down on his cot with his master's servants, but he did not go home.

URIAH'S DEATH ARRANGED

[14] The next morning David wrote a letter to Joab and sent it with Uriah. [15] In the letter he wrote:

Put Uriah at the front of the fiercest fighting, then withdraw from him so that he is struck down and dies.

[16] When Joab was besieging the city, he put Uriah in the place where he knew the best enemy soldiers were. [17] Then the men of the city came out and attacked Joab, and some of the men from David's soldiers fell in battle; Uriah the Hethite also died.

[18] Joab sent someone to report to David all the details of the battle. [19] He commanded the messenger, "When you've finished telling the king all the details of the battle — [20] if the king's anger gets stirred up and he asks you, 'Why did you get so close to the city to fight? Didn't you realize they would shoot from the top of the wall? [21] At Thebez, who struck Abimelech son of Jerubbesheth?[B,C] Didn't a woman drop an upper millstone on him from the top of the wall so that he died? Why did you get so close to the wall?' — then say, 'Your servant Uriah the Hethite is dead also.'" [22] Then the messenger left.

When he arrived, he reported to David all that Joab had sent him to tell. [23] The messenger reported to David, "The men gained the advantage over us and came out against us in the field, but we counterattacked right up to the entrance of the city gate. [24] However, the archers shot down on your servants from the top of the wall, and some of the king's servants died. Your servant Uriah the Hethite is also dead."

[25] David told the messenger, "Say this to Joab: 'Don't let this matter upset you because the sword devours all alike. Intensify your fight against the city and demolish it.' Encourage him."

[26] When Uriah's wife heard that her husband Uriah had died, she mourned for him.[D] [27] When the time of mourning ended, David had her brought to his house. She became his wife and bore him a son. However, the Lord considered what David had done to be evil.

[A] 11:11 Lit servants   [B] 11:21 LXX reads Jerubbaal   [C] 11:21 = Gideon   [D] 11:26 Lit her husband

NATHAN'S PARABLE AND DAVID'S REPENTANCE

12 So the Lord sent Nathan to David. When he arrived, he said to him: There were two men in a certain city, one rich and the other poor. ² The rich man had very large flocks and herds, ³ but the poor man had nothing except one small ewe lamb that he had bought. He raised her, and she grew up with him and with his children. From his meager food she would eat, from his cup she would drink, and in his arms she would sleep. She was like a daughter to him. ⁴ Now a traveler came to the rich man, but the rich man could not bring himself to take one of his own sheep or cattle to prepare for the traveler who had come to him. Instead, he took the poor man's lamb and prepared it for his guest.ᴬ

⁵ David was infuriated with the man and said to Nathan: "As the Lord lives, the man who did this deserves to die! ⁶ Because he has done this thing and shown no pity, he must pay four lambs for that lamb."

⁷ Nathan replied to David, "You are the man! This is what the Lord God of Israel says: 'I anointed you king over Israel, and I rescued you from Saul. ⁸ I gave your master's house to you and your master's wives into your arms,ᴮ and I gave you the house of Israel and Judah, and if that was not enough, I would have given you even more. ⁹ Why then have you despised the Lord's command by doing what I considerᶜ evil? You struck down Uriah the Hethite with the sword and took his wife as your own wife — you murdered him with the Ammonite's sword. ¹⁰ Now therefore, the sword will never leave your house because you despised me and took the wife of Uriah the Hethite to be your own wife.'

¹¹ "This is what the Lord says, 'I am going to bring disaster on you from your own family: I will take your wives and give them to anotherᴰ before your very eyes, and he will sleep with them in broad daylight.ᴱ ¹² You acted in secret, but I will do this before all Israel and in broad daylight.'"ᶠ

¹³ David responded to Nathan, "I have sinned against the Lord."

Then Nathan replied to David, "And the Lord has taken away your sin; you will not die. ¹⁴ However, because you treatedᴳ the Lord with such contempt in this matter, the son born to you will die." ¹⁵ Then Nathan went home.

THE DEATH OF BATHSHEBA'S SON

The Lord struck the baby that Uriah's wife had borne to David, and he became deathly ill. ¹⁶ David pleaded with God for the boy. He fasted, went home, and spent the night lying on the ground. ¹⁷ The elders of his house stood beside him to get him up from the ground, but he was unwilling and would not eat anything with them.

¹⁸ On the seventh day the baby died. But David's servants were afraid to tell him the baby was dead. They said, "Look, while the baby was alive, we spoke to him, and he wouldn't listen to us. So how can we tell him the baby is dead? He may do something desperate."

ᴬ12:4 Lit for the man who had come to him   ᴮ12:8 Lit bosom   ᶜ12:9 Alt Hb tradition reads what he considers   ᴰ12:11 Or to your neighbor   ᴱ12:11 Lit in the eyes of this sun   ᶠ12:12 Lit and before the sun   ᴳ12:14 Alt Hb tradition, one LXX ms; MT reads treated the enemies of; DSS read treated the word of

¹⁹ When David saw that his servants were whispering to each other, he guessed that the baby was dead. So he asked his servants, "Is the baby dead?"

"He is dead," they replied.

²⁰ Then David got up from the ground. He washed, anointed himself, changed his clothes, went to the Lord's house, and worshiped. Then he went home and requested something to eat. So they served him food, and he ate.

²¹ His servants asked him, "Why have you done this? While the baby was alive, you fasted and wept, but when he died, you got up and ate food."

²² He answered, "While the baby was alive, I fasted and wept because I thought, 'Who knows? The Lord may be gracious to me and let him live.' ²³ But now that he is dead, why should I fast? Can I bring him back again? I'll go to him, but he will never return to me."

THE BIRTH OF SOLOMON

²⁴ Then David comforted his wife Bathsheba; he went to her and slept with her. She gave birth to a son and named ᴬ him Solomon. ᴮ The Lord loved him, ²⁵ and he sent a message through the prophet Nathan, who named ᶜ him Jedidiah, ᴰ because of the Lord.

CAPTURE OF THE CITY OF RABBAH

²⁶ Joab fought against Rabbah of the Ammonites and captured the royal fortress. ²⁷ Then Joab sent messengers to David to say, "I have fought against Rabbah and have also captured its water supply. ²⁸ Now therefore, assemble the rest of the troops, lay siege to the city, and capture it. Otherwise I will be the one to capture the city, and it will be named after me." ²⁹ So David assembled all the troops and went to Rabbah; he fought against it and captured it. ³⁰ He took the crown from the head of their king, ᴱ and it was placed on David's head. The crown weighed seventy-five pounds ᶠ of gold, and it had a precious stone in it. In addition, David took away a large quantity of plunder from the city. ³¹ He removed the people who were in the city and put them to work with saws, iron picks, and iron axes, and to labor at brickmaking. He did the same to all the Ammonite cities. Then he and all his troops returned to Jerusalem.

AMNON RAPES TAMAR

13 Some time passed. David's son Absalom had a beautiful sister named Tamar, and David's son Amnon was infatuated with her. ² Amnon was frustrated to the point of making himself sick over his sister Tamar because she was a virgin, but it seemed impossible to do anything to her. ³ Amnon had a friend named Jonadab, a son of David's brother Shimeah. Jonadab was a very shrewd man, ⁴ and he asked Amnon, "Why are you, the king's son, so miserable every morning? Won't you tell me?"

Amnon replied, "I'm in love with Tamar, my brother Absalom's sister."

⁵ Jonadab said to him, "Lie down on your bed and pretend you're sick. When your father comes to see you, say to him, 'Please let my sister Tamar

---

ᴬ12:24 Alt Hb tradition reads he named   ᴮ12:24 In Hb, the name Solomon sounds like "peace."   ᶜ12:25 Or prophet to name   ᴰ12:25 = Beloved of the Lord   ᴱ12:30 LXX reads of Milcom; some emend to Molech; 1Kg 11:5,33   ᶠ12:30 Lit a talent come and give me something to eat. Let her prepare a meal in my presence so I can watch and eat from her hand.'"

⁶ So Amnon lay down and pretended to be sick. When the king came to see him, Amnon said to him, "Please let my sister Tamar come and make a couple of cakes in my presence so I can eat from her hand."

⁷ David sent word to Tamar at the palace: "Please go to your brother Amnon's house and prepare a meal for him."

⁸ Then Tamar went to his house while Amnon was lying down. She took dough, kneaded it, made cakes in his presence, and baked them. ⁹ She brought the pan and set it down in front of him, but he refused to eat. Amnon said, "Everyone leave me!" And everyone left him. ¹⁰ "Bring the meal to the bedroom," Amnon told Tamar, "so I can eat from your hand." Tamar took the cakes she had made and went to her brother Amnon's bedroom. ¹¹ When she brought them to him to eat, he grabbed her and said, ᴬ "Come sleep with me, my sister!"

¹² "Don't, my brother!" she cried. "Don't disgrace me, for such a thing should never be done in Israel. Don't commit this outrage! ¹³ Where could I ever go with my humiliation? And you — you would be like one of the outrageous fools in Israel! Please, speak to the king, for he won't keep me from you." ¹⁴ But he refused to listen to her, and because he was stronger than she was, he disgraced her by raping her.

¹⁵ So Amnon hated Tamar with such intensity that the hatred he hated her with was greater than the love he had loved her with. "Get out of here!" he said.

¹⁶ "No," she cried, ᴮ "sending me away is much worse than the great wrong you've already done to me!"

But he refused to listen to her. ¹⁷ Instead, he called to the servant who waited on him: "Get this away from me, throw her out, and bolt the door behind her!" ¹⁸ Amnon's servant threw her out and bolted the door behind her. Now Tamar was wearing a long-sleeved ᶜ garment, because this is what the king's virgin daughters wore. ¹⁹ Tamar put ashes on her head and tore the long-sleeved garment she was wearing. She put her hand on her head and went away crying out.

²⁰ Her brother Absalom said to her: "Has your brother Amnon been with you? Be quiet for now, my sister. He is your brother. Don't take this thing to heart." So Tamar lived as a desolate woman in the house of her brother Absalom.

ABSALOM MURDERS AMNON

²¹ When King David heard about all these things, he was furious. ᴰ ²² Absalom didn't say anything to Amnon, either good or bad, because he hated Amnon since he disgraced his sister Tamar.

²³ Two years later, Absalom's sheepshearers were at Baal-hazor near Ephraim, and Absalom invited all the king's sons. ²⁴ Then he went to the king and said, "Your servant has just hired sheepshearers. Will the king and his servants please come with your servant?"

ᴬ13:11 Lit *said to her*   ᴮ13:16 Lit *she said to him*   ᶜ13:18 Or *an ornamented*;
Gn 37:3   ᴰ13:21 LXX, DSS add *but he did not grieve the spirit of Amnon his son,
for he loved him because he was his firstborn*; 1Kg 1:6

²⁵ The king replied to Absalom, "No, my son, we should not all go, or we would be a burden to you." Although Absalom urged him, he wasn't willing to go, though he did bless him.

²⁶ "If not," Absalom said, "please let my brother Amnon go with us."

The king asked him, "Why should he go with you?" ²⁷ But Absalom urged him, so he sent Amnon and all the king's sons.ᴬ

²⁸ Now Absalom commanded his young men, "Watch Amnon until he is in a good mood from the wine. When I order you to strike Amnon, then kill him. Don't be afraid. Am I not the one who has commanded you? Be strong and valiant!" ²⁹ So Absalom's young men did to Amnon just as Absalom had commanded. Then all the rest of the king's sons got up, and each fled on his mule.

³⁰ While they were on the way, a report reached David: "Absalom struck down all the king's sons; not even one of them survived!" ³¹ In response the king stood up, tore his clothes, and lay down on the ground, and all his servants stood by with their clothes torn.

³² But Jonadab, son of David's brother Shimeah, spoke up: "My lord must not think they have killed all the young men, the king's sons, because only Amnon is dead. In fact, Absalom has planned thisᴮ ever since the day Amnon disgraced his sister Tamar. ³³ So now, my lord the king, don't take seriously the report that says all the king's sons are dead. Only Amnon is dead."

³⁴ Meanwhile, Absalom had fled. When the young man who was standing watch looked up, there were many people coming from the road west of him from the side of the mountain.ᶜ ³⁵ Jonadab said to the king, "Look, the king's sons have come! It's exactly like your servant said." ³⁶ Just as he finished speaking, the king's sons entered and wept loudly. Then the king and all his servants also wept very bitterly. ³⁷ But Absalom fled and went to Talmai son of Ammihud, king of Geshur. And David mourned for his sonᴰ every day.

³⁸ After Absalom had fled to Geshur and had been there three years, ³⁹ King Davidᴱ longed to go to Absalom, for David had finished grieving over Amnon's death.

ABSALOM RESTORED TO DAVID

14 Joab son of Zeruiah realized that the king's mind was on Absalom. ² So Joab sent someone to Tekoa to bring a wise woman from there. He told her, "Pretend to be in mourning: dress in mourning clothes and don't put on any oil. Act like a woman who has been mourning for the dead for a long time. ³ Go to the king and speak these words to him." Then Joab told her exactly what to say.ᶠ

⁴ When the woman from Tekoa cameᴳ to the king, she fell facedown to the ground, paid homage, and said, "Help me, Your Majesty!"

⁵ "What's the matter?" the king asked her.

"Sadly, I am a widow; my husband died," she said. ⁶ "Your servant had two sons. They were fighting in the field with no one to separate them, and one

---

ᴬ13:27 LXX adds *And Absalom prepared a feast like a royal feast.* ᴮ13:32 Lit *In fact, it was established on the mouth of Absalom* ᶜ13:34 LXX adds *And the watchman came and reported to the king saying, "I see men on the Horonaim road on the side of the mountain."* ᴰ13:37 Probably Amnon ᴱ13:39 DSS, LXX, Tg read *David's spirit* ᶠ14:3 Lit *Joab put the words into her mouth* ᴳ14:4 Some Hb mss, LXX, Syr, Tg, Vg; other Hb mss read *spoke* struck the other and killed him. ⁷ Now the whole clan has risen up against your servant and said, 'Hand over the one who killed his brother so we may put him to death for the life of the brother he murdered. We will eliminate the heir!' They would extinguish my one remaining ember by not preserving my husband's name or posterity on earth."

⁸ The king told the woman, "Go home. I will issue a command on your behalf."

⁹ Then the woman of Tekoa said to the king, "My lord the king, may any blame be on me and my father's family, and may the king and his throne be innocent."

¹⁰ "Whoever speaks to you," the king said, "bring him to me. He will not trouble you again!"

¹¹ She replied, "Please, may the king invoke the Lord your God, so that the avenger of blood will not increase the loss, and they will not eliminate my son!"

"As the Lord lives," he vowed, "not a hair of your son will fall to the ground."

¹² Then the woman said, "Please, may your servant speak a word to my lord the king?"

"Speak," he replied.

¹³ The woman asked, "Why have you devised something similar against the people of God? When the king spoke as he did about this matter, he has pronounced his own guilt. The king has not brought back his own banished one. ¹⁴ We will certainly die and be like water poured out on the ground, which can't be recovered. But God would not take away a life; he would devise plans so that the one banished from him does not remain banished.

¹⁵ "Now therefore, I've come to present this matter to my lord the king because the people have made me afraid. Your servant thought: I must speak to the king. Perhaps the king will grant his servant's request. ¹⁶ The king will surely listen in order to keep his servant from the grasp of this man who would eliminate both me and my son from God's inheritance. ¹⁷ Your servant thought: May the word of my lord the king bring relief, for my lord the king is able to discern the good and the bad like the angel of God. May the Lord your God be with you."

¹⁸ Then the king answered the woman, "I'm going to ask you something; don't conceal it from me!"

"Let my lord the king speak," the woman replied.

¹⁹ The king asked, "Did Joab put you up to^A all this?"

The woman answered. "As you live, my lord the king, no one can turn to the right or left from all my lord the king says. Yes, your servant Joab is the one who gave orders to me; he told your servant exactly what to say.^B ²⁰ Joab your servant has done this to address the issue indirectly,^C but my lord has wisdom like the wisdom of the angel of God, knowing everything on earth."

²¹ Then the king said to Joab, "I hereby grant this request. Go, bring back the young man Absalom."

²² Joab fell with his face to the ground in homage and blessed the king. "Today," Joab said, "your servant knows I have found favor with you, my lord the king, because the king has granted the request of your servant."

---

^A 14:19 Lit "Is the hand of Joab in   ^B 14:19 Lit he put all these words into the mouth of your servant   ^C 14:20 Lit to go around the face of the matter

²³ So Joab got up, went to Geshur, and brought Absalom to Jerusalem. ²⁴ However, the king added, "He may return to his house, but he may not see my face." So Absalom returned to his house, but he did not see the king.^A

²⁵ No man in all Israel was as handsome and highly praised as Absalom. From the sole of his foot to the top of his head, he did not have a single flaw. ²⁶ When he shaved his head — he shaved it at the end of every year because his hair got so heavy for him that he had to shave it off — he would weigh the hair from his head and it would be five pounds^B according to the royal standard.

²⁷ Three sons were born to Absalom, and a daughter named Tamar, who was a beautiful woman. ²⁸ Absalom resided in Jerusalem two years but never saw the king. ²⁹ Then Absalom sent for Joab in order to send him to the king, but Joab was unwilling to come to him. So he sent again, a second time, but he still would not come. ³⁰ Then Absalom said to his servants, "See, Joab has a field right next to mine, and he has barley there. Go and set fire to it!" So Absalom's servants set the field on fire.^C

³¹ Then Joab came to Absalom's house and demanded, "Why did your servants set my field on fire?"

³² "Look," Absalom explained to Joab, "I sent for you and said, 'Come here. I want to send you to the king to ask: Why have I come back from Geshur? I'd be better off if I were still there.' So now, let me see the king. If I am guilty, let him kill me."

³³ Joab went to the king and told him. So David summoned Absalom, who came to the king and paid homage with his face to the ground before him. Then the king kissed Absalom.

ABSALOM'S REVOLT

15 After this, Absalom got himself a chariot, horses, and fifty men to run before him. ² He would get up early and stand beside the road leading to the city gate. Whenever anyone had a grievance to bring before the king for settlement, Absalom called out to him and asked, "What city are you from?" If he replied, "Your servant is from one of the tribes of Israel," ³ Absalom said to him, "Look, your claims are good and right, but the king does not have anyone to listen to you." ⁴ He added, "If only someone would appoint me judge in the land. Then anyone who had a grievance or dispute could come to me, and I would make sure he received justice." ⁵ When a person approached to pay homage to him, Absalom reached out his hand, took hold of him, and kissed him. ⁶ Absalom did this to all the Israelites who came to the king for a settlement. So Absalom stole the hearts of the men of Israel.

⁷ When four^D years had passed, Absalom said to the king, "Please let me go to Hebron to fulfill a vow I made to the LORD. ⁸ For your servant made a vow when I lived in Geshur of Aram, saying: If the LORD really brings me back to Jerusalem, I will worship the LORD in Hebron."^E

⁹ "Go in peace," the king said to him. So he went to Hebron.

---

^A14:24 Lit *king's face*   ^B14:26 Lit *200 shekels*   ^C14:30 DSS, LXX add *So Joab's servants came to him with their clothes torn and said, "Absalom's servants have set the field on fire!"*   ^D15:7 Some LXX mss, Syr, Vg; other LXX mss, MT read *40*
^E15:8 Some LXX mss; MT omits *in Hebron*

¹⁰ Then Absalom sent agents throughout the tribes of Israel with this message: "When you hear the sound of the ram's horn, you are to say, 'Absalom has become king in Hebron!'"

¹¹ Two hundred men from Jerusalem went with Absalom. They had been invited and were going innocently, for they did not know the whole situation. ¹² While he was offering the sacrifices, Absalom sent for David's adviser Ahithophel the Gilonite, from his city of Giloh. So the conspiracy grew strong, and the people supporting Absalom continued to increase.

¹³ Then an informer came to David and reported, "The hearts of the men of Israel are with Absalom."

¹⁴ David said to all the servants with him in Jerusalem, "Get up. We have to flee, or we will not escape from Absalom! Leave quickly, or he will overtake us quickly, heap disaster on us, and strike the city with the edge of the sword."

¹⁵ The king's servants said to the king, "Whatever my lord the king decides, we are your servants." ¹⁶ Then the king set out, and his entire household followed him. But he left behind ten concubines to take care of the palace. ¹⁷ So the king set out, and all the people followed him. They stopped at the last house ¹⁸ while all his servants marched past him. Then all the Cherethites, the Pelethites, and the people of Gath— six hundred men who came with him from there — marched past the king.

¹⁹ The king said to Ittai of Gath, "Why are you also going with us? Go back and stay with the new king since you're both a foreigner and an exile from your homeland. ²⁰ Besides, you only arrived yesterday; should I make you wander around with us today while I go wherever I can? Go back and take your brothers with you. May the LORD show you^A kindness and faithfulness."

²¹ But in response, Ittai vowed to the king, "As the LORD lives and as my lord the king lives, wherever my lord the king is, whether it means life or death, your servant will be there!"

²² "March on," David replied to Ittai. So Ittai of Gath marched past with all his men and the dependents who were with him. ²³ Everyone in the countryside was weeping loudly while all the people were marching out of the city. As the king was crossing the Kidron Valley, all the people were marching past on the road that leads to the wilderness.

²⁴ Zadok was also there, and all the Levites with him were carrying the ark of the covenant of God. They set the ark of God down, and Abiathar offered sacrifices^B until the people had finished marching past. ²⁵ Then the king instructed Zadok, "Return the ark of God to the city. If I find favor with the LORD, he will bring me back and allow me to see both it and its^C dwelling place. ²⁶ However, if he should say, 'I do not delight in you,' then here I am — he can do with me whatever pleases him."^D

²⁷ The king also said to the priest Zadok, "Look,^E return to the city in peace and your two sons with you: your son Ahimaaz and Abiathar's son Jonathan. ²⁸ Remember, I'll wait at the fords^F of the wilderness until word comes from you to inform me." ²⁹ So Zadok and Abiathar returned the ark of God to Jerusalem and stayed there.

---

^A15:20 LXX; MT omits Lit *May the LORD show you*   ^B15:24 Or *Abiathar went up*
^C15:25 Or *his*   ^D15:26 Lit *me what is good in his eyes*   ^E15:27 LXX; MT reads
"Are you a seer?   ^F15:28 Alt Hb tradition reads *plains*

³⁰ David was climbing the slope of the Mount of Olives, weeping as he ascended. His head was covered, and he was walking barefoot. All of the people with him covered their heads and went up, weeping as they ascended.

³¹ Then someone reported to David: "Ahithophel is among the conspirators with Absalom."

"Lord," David pleaded, "please turn the counsel of Ahithophel into foolishness!"

³² When David came to the summit where he used to worship God, Hushai the Archite was there to meet him with his robe torn and dust on his head. ³³ David said to him, "If you go away with me, you'll be a burden to me, ³⁴ but if you return to the city and tell Absalom, 'I will be your servant, Your Majesty! Previously, I was your father's servant, but now I will be your servant,' then you can counteract Ahithophel's counsel for me. ³⁵ Won't the priests Zadok and Abiathar be there with you? Report everything you hear from the palace to the priests Zadok and Abiathar. ³⁶ Take note: their two sons are there with them—Zadok's son Ahimaaz and Abiathar's son Jonathan. Send them to tell me everything you hear." ³⁷ So Hushai, David's personal adviser, entered Jerusalem just as Absalom was entering the city.

ZIBA HELPS DAVID

16 When David had gone a little beyond the summit,ᴬ Ziba, Mephibosheth's servant, was right there to meet him. He had a pair of saddled donkeys loaded with two hundred loaves of bread, one hundred clusters of raisins, one hundred bunches of summer fruit, and a clay jar of wine. ² The king said to Ziba, "Why do you have these?"

Ziba answered, "The donkeys are for the king's household to ride, the bread and summer fruit are for the young men to eat, and the wine is for those to drink who become exhausted in the wilderness."

³ "Where is your master's grandson?" the king asked.

"Why, he's staying in Jerusalem," Ziba replied to the king, "for he said, 'Today, the house of Israel will restore my grandfather's kingdom to me.'"

⁴ The king said to Ziba, "All that belongs to Mephibosheth is now yours!"

"I bow before you," Ziba said. "May I find favor with you, my lord the king!"

SHIMEI CURSES DAVID

⁵ When King David got to Bahurim, a man belonging to the family of the house of Saul was just coming out. His name was Shimei son of Gera, and he was yelling curses as he approached. ⁶ He threw stones at David and at all the royalᴮ servants, the people and the warriors on David's right and left. ⁷ Shimei said as he cursed: "Get out, get out, you man of bloodshed, you wicked man! ⁸ The Lord has paid you back for all the blood of the house of Saul in whose place you became king, and the Lord has handed the kingdom over to your son Absalom. Look, you are in trouble because you're a man of bloodshed!"

⁹ Then Abishai son of Zeruiah said to the king, "Why should this dead dog curse my lord the king? Let me go over and remove his head!"

¹⁰ The king replied, "Sons of Zeruiah, do we agree on anything? He curses me this way because the Lord ᶜ told him, 'Curse David!' Therefore, who can

---

ᴬ 16:1 = Mount of Olives   ᴮ 16:6 Lit all King David's   ᶜ 16:10 Alt Hb tradition reads If he curses, and if the Lord say, 'Why did you do that?' " [11] Then David said to Abishai and all his servants, "Look, my own son, my own flesh and blood,[A] intends to take my life — how much more now this Benjaminite! Leave him alone and let him curse me; the LORD has told him to. [12] Perhaps the LORD will see my affliction[B] and restore goodness to me instead of Shimei's curses today." [13] So David and his men proceeded along the road as Shimei was going along the ridge of the hill opposite him. As Shimei went, he cursed David, threw stones at him, and kicked up dust. [14] Finally, the king and all the people with him arrived[C] exhausted, so they rested there.

ABSALOM'S ADVISERS

[15] Now Absalom and all the Israelites came to Jerusalem. Ahithophel was also with him. [16] When David's friend Hushai the Archite came to Absalom, Hushai said to Absalom, "Long live the king! Long live the king!"

[17] "Is this your loyalty to your friend?" Absalom asked Hushai. "Why didn't you go with your friend?"

[18] "Not at all," Hushai answered Absalom. "I am on the side of the one that the LORD, this people, and all the men of Israel have chosen. I will stay with him. [19] Furthermore, whom will I serve if not his son? As I served in your father's presence, I will also serve in yours."

[20] Then Absalom said to Ahithophel, "Give me your advice. What should we do?"

[21] Ahithophel replied to Absalom, "Sleep with your father's concubines whom he left to take care of the palace. When all Israel hears that you have become repulsive to your father, everyone with you will be encouraged."[D] [22] So they pitched a tent for Absalom on the roof, and he slept with his father's concubines in the sight of all Israel.

[23] Now the advice Ahithophel gave in those days was like someone asking about a word from God — such was the regard that both David and Absalom had for Ahithophel's advice. **17** [1] Ahithophel said to Absalom, "Let me choose twelve thousand men, and I will set out in pursuit of David tonight. [2] I will attack him while he is weary and discouraged,[E] throw him into a panic, and all the people with him will scatter. I will strike down only the king [3] and bring all the people back to you. When everyone returns except the man you're looking for, all[F] the people will be at peace." [4] This proposal seemed right to Absalom and all the elders of Israel.

[5] Then Absalom said, "Summon Hushai the Archite also. Let's hear what he has to say as well."

[6] So Hushai came to Absalom, and Absalom told him: "Ahithophel offered this proposal. Should we carry out his proposal? If not, what do you say?"

[7] Hushai replied to Absalom, "The advice Ahithophel has given this time is not good." [8] Hushai continued, "You know your father and his men. They are warriors and are desperate like a wild bear robbed of her cubs. Your

---

[A] 16:11 Lit son who came from my belly   [B] 16:12 Some Hb mss, LXX, Syr, Vg; one Hb tradition reads iniquity; alt Hb tradition reads eyes; another Hb tradition reads will look with his eye   [C] 16:14 LXX adds at the Jordan   [D] 16:21 Lit father, the hands of everyone with you will be strong   [E] 17:2 Lit and weak of hands   [F] 17:3 LXX reads to you as a bride returns to her husband. You seek the life of only one man, and all father is an experienced soldier who won't spend the night with the people. [9] He's probably already hiding in one of the caves[A] or some other place. If some of our troops fall[B] first, someone is sure to hear and say, 'There's been a slaughter among the people who follow Absalom.' [10] Then, even a brave man with the heart of a lion will lose heart[C] because all Israel knows that your father and the valiant men with him are warriors. [11] Instead, I advise that all Israel from Dan to Beer-sheba — as numerous as the sand by the sea — be gathered to you and that you personally go into battle. [12] Then we will attack David wherever we find him, and we will descend on him like dew on the ground. Not even one will be left—neither he nor any of the men with him. [13] If he retreats to some city, all Israel will bring ropes to that city, and we will drag its stones[D] into the valley until not even a pebble can be found there." [14] Since the LORD had decreed that Ahithophel's good advice be undermined in order to bring about Absalom's ruin, Absalom and all the men of Israel said, "The advice of Hushai the Archite is better than Ahithophel's advice."

DAVID INFORMED OF ABSALOM'S PLANS

[15] Hushai then told the priests Zadok and Abiathar, "This is what[E] Ahithophel advised Absalom and the elders of Israel, and this is what[F] I advised. [16] Now send someone quickly and tell David, 'Don't spend the night at the wilderness ford,[G] but be sure to cross over the Jordan,[H] or the king and all the people with him will be devoured.'"

[17] Jonathan and Ahimaaz were staying at En-rogel, where a servant girl would come and pass along information to them. They in turn would go and inform King David, because they dared not be seen entering the city. [18] However, a young man did see them and informed Absalom. So the two left quickly and came to the house of a man in Bahurim. He had a well in his courtyard, and they climbed down into it. [19] Then his wife took the cover, placed it over the mouth of the well, and scattered grain on it so nobody would know anything.

[20] Absalom's servants came to the woman at the house and asked, "Where are Ahimaaz and Jonathan?"

"They passed by toward the water,"[I] the woman replied to them. The men searched but did not find them, so they returned to Jerusalem.

[21] After they had gone, Ahimaaz and Jonathan climbed out of the well and went and informed King David. They told him, "Get up and immediately ford the river, for Ahithophel has given this advice against you." [22] So David and all the people with him got up and crossed the Jordan. By daybreak, there was no one who had not crossed the Jordan. [23] When Ahithophel realized that his advice had not been followed, he saddled his donkey and set out for his house in his hometown. He set his house in order and hanged himself. So he died and was buried in his father's tomb.

[24] David had arrived at Mahanaim by the time Absalom crossed the Jordan with all the men of Israel. [25] Now Absalom had appointed Amasa over

---

[A] 17:9 Or pits, or ravines   [B] 17:9 Lit And it will be when a falling on them at
[C] 17:10 Lit melt   [D] 17:13 Lit drag it   [E] 17:15 Lit "Like this and like this   [F] 17:15 Lit
and like this and like this   [G] 17:16 Some Hb mss; MT reads plains   [H] 17:16 the
Jordan supplied for clarity   [I] 17:20 Or brook; Hb obscure

the army in Joab's place. Amasa was the son of a man named Ithra^A the Isra-elite;^B Ithra had married Abigail daughter of Nahash.^C Abigail was a sister to Zeruiah, Joab's mother. ²⁶ And Israel and Absalom camped in the land of Gilead. ²⁷ When David came to Mahanaim, Shobi son of Nahash from Rab-bah of the Ammonites, Machir son of Ammiel from Lo-debar, and Barzil-lai the Gileadite from Rogelim ²⁸ brought beds, basins,^D and pottery items. They also brought wheat, barley, flour, roasted grain, beans, lentils,^E ²⁹ hon-ey, curds, sheep, goats, and cheese^F from the herd for David and the people with him to eat. They had reasoned, "The people must be hungry, exhaust-ed, and thirsty in the wilderness."

ABSALOM'S DEFEAT

18 David reviewed his troops and appointed commanders of thou-sands and of hundreds over them. ² He then sent out the troops, a third under Joab, a third under Joab's brother Abishai son of Zeruiah, and a third under Ittai of Gath. The king said to the troops, "I must also march out with you."

³ "You must not go!" the people pleaded. "If we have to flee, they will not pay any attention to us. Even if half of us die, they will not pay any atten-tion to us because you are worth^G ten thousand of us. Therefore, it is better if you support us from the city."

⁴ "I will do whatever you think is best," the king replied to them. So he stood beside the city gate while all the troops marched out by hundreds and thousands. ⁵ The king commanded Joab, Abishai, and Ittai, "Treat the young man Absalom gently for my sake." All the people heard the king's orders to all the commanders about Absalom.

⁶ Then David's forces marched into the field to engage Israel in battle, which took place in the forest of Ephraim. ⁷ Israel's army was defeated by David's soldiers, and the slaughter there was vast that day — twenty thou-sand dead. ⁸ The battle spread over the entire area, and that day the forest claimed more people than the sword.

ABSALOM'S DEATH

⁹ Absalom was riding on his mule when he happened to meet David's sol-diers. When the mule went under the tangled branches of a large oak tree, Absalom's head was caught fast in the tree. The mule under him kept going, so he was suspended in midair.^H ¹⁰ One of the men saw him and informed Joab. He said, "I just saw Absalom hanging in an oak tree!"

¹¹ "You just saw him!" Joab exclaimed.^I "Why didn't you strike him to the ground right there? I would have given you ten silver pieces^J and a belt!"

¹² The man replied to Joab, "Even if I had the weight of a thousand pieces of silver^K in my hand, I would not raise my hand against the king's son. For

---

^A 17:25 Or *Jether*   ^B 17:25 Some LXX mss read *Ishmaelite*   ^C 17:25 Some LXX mss read *Jesse*   ^D 17:28 LXX reads *brought 10 embroidered beds with double coverings, 10 vessels*   ^E 17:28 LXX, Syr; MT adds *roasted grain*   ^F 17:29 Hb obscure   ^G 18:3 Some Hb mss, LXX, Vg; other Hb mss read *because there would now be about*   ^H 18:9 Lit *was between heaven and earth*   ^I 18:11 Lit *Joab said to the man who told him*   ^J 18:11 About four ounces of silver   ^K 18:12 About 25 pounds of silver we heard the king command you, Abishai, and Ittai, 'Protect the young man Absalom for me.'[A] [13] If I had jeopardized my own [B] life — and nothing is hidden from the king — you would have abandoned me."

[14] Joab said, "I'm not going to waste time with you!" He then took three spears in his hand and thrust them into Absalom's chest. While Absalom was still alive in the oak tree, [15] ten young men who were Joab's armor-bearers surrounded Absalom, struck him, and killed him. [16] Joab blew the ram's horn, and the troops broke off their pursuit of Israel because Joab restrained them. [17] They took Absalom, threw him into a large pit in the forest, and raised up a huge mound of stones over him. And all Israel fled, each to his tent.

[18] When he was alive, Absalom had taken a pillar and raised it up for himself in the King's Valley, since he thought, "I have no son to preserve the memory of my name." So he named the pillar after himself. It is still called Absalom's Monument today.

[19] Ahimaaz son of Zadok said, "Please let me run and tell the king the good news that the Lord has vindicated him by freeing him from his enemies."

[20] Joab replied to him, "You are not the man to take good news today. You may do it another day, but today you aren't taking good news, because the king's son is dead." [21] Joab then said to a Cushite, "Go tell the king what you have seen." The Cushite bowed to Joab and took off running.

[22] However, Ahimaaz son of Zadok persisted and said to Joab, "No matter what, please let me also run behind the Cushite!"

Joab replied, "My son, why do you want to run since you won't get a reward?"[C]

[23] "No matter what, I want to run!"

"Then run!" Joab said to him. So Ahimaaz ran by way of the plain and outran the Cushite.

[24] David was sitting between the city gates when the watchman went up to the roof of the city gate and over to the wall. The watchman looked out and saw a man running alone. [25] He called out and told the king.

The king said, "If he's alone, he bears good news."

As the first runner came closer, [26] the watchman saw another man running. He called out to the gatekeeper, "Look! Another man is running alone!"

"This one is also bringing good news," said the king.

[27] The watchman said, "The way the first man runs looks to me like the way Ahimaaz son of Zadok runs."

"This is a good man; he comes with good news," the king commented.

[28] Ahimaaz called out to the king, "All is well," and paid homage to the king with his face to the ground. He continued, "Blessed be the Lord your God! He delivered up the men who rebelled against my lord the king."

[29] The king asked, "Is the young man Absalom all right?"

Ahimaaz replied, "When Joab sent the king's servant and your servant, I saw a big disturbance, but I don't know what it was."

[30] The king said, "Move aside and stand here." So he stood to one side.

[31] Just then the Cushite came and said, "May my lord the king hear the good news: The Lord has vindicated you today by freeing you from all who rise against you!"

[A]18:12 Some Hb mss, LXX, Tg, Vg; other Hb mss read 'Protect, whoever, the young man Absalom'; Hb obscure   [B]18:13 Alt Hb tradition reads jeopardized his   [C]18:22 Or you have no good news?

³² The king asked the Cushite, "Is the young man Absalom all right?"

The Cushite replied, "I wish that the enemies of my lord the king, along with all who rise up against you with evil intent, would become like that young man."

³³ The king was deeply moved and went up to the chamber above the city gate and wept. As he walked, he cried, "My son Absalom! My son, my son Absalom! If only I had died instead of you, Absalom, my son, my son!"

DAVID'S KINGDOM RESTORED

19

It was reported to Joab, "The king is weeping. He's mourning over Absalom." ² That day's victory was turned into mourning for all the troops because on that day the troops heard, "The king is grieving over his son." ³ So they returned to the city quietly that day like troops come in when they are humiliated after fleeing in battle. ⁴ But the king covered his face and cried loudly, "My son Absalom! Absalom, my son, my son!"

⁵ Then Joab went into the house to the king and said, "Today you have shamed all your soldiers — those who saved your life as well as your sons, your wives, and your concubines — ⁶ by loving your enemies and hating those who love you! Today you have made it clear that the commanders and soldiers mean nothing to you. In fact, today I know that if Absalom were alive and all of us were dead, it would be fine with you!ᴬ

⁷ "Now get up! Go out and encourageᴮ your soldiers, for I swear by the Lᴏʀᴅ that if you don't go out, not a man will remain with you tonight. This will be worse for you than all the trouble that has come to you from your youth until now!"

⁸ So the king got up and sat in the city gate, and all the people were told: "Look, the king is sitting in the city gate." Then they all came into the king's presence.

Meanwhile, each Israelite had fled to his tent. ⁹ People throughout all the tribes of Israel were arguing among themselves, saying, "The king rescued us from the grasp of our enemies, and he saved us from the grasp of the Philistines, but now he has fled from the land because of Absalom. ¹⁰ But Absalom, the man we anointed over us, has died in battle. So why do you say nothing about restoring the king?"

¹¹ King David sent word to the priests Zadok and Abiathar: "Say to the elders of Judah, 'Why should you be the last to restore the king to his palace? The talk of all Israel has reached the king at his house. ¹² You are my brothers, my flesh and blood.ᶜ So why should you be the last to restore the king?' ¹³ And tell Amasa, 'Aren't you my flesh and blood?ᴰ May God punish me and do so severely if you don't become commander of my army from now on instead of Joab!'"

¹⁴ So he won overᴱ all the men of Judah, and they unanimously sent word to the king: "Come back, you and all your servants." ¹⁵ Then the king returned. When he arrived at the Jordan, Judah came to Gilgal to meet the king and escort him across the Jordan.

¹⁶ Shimei son of Gera, the Benjaminite from Bahurim, hurried down with the men of Judah to meet King David. ¹⁷ There were a thousand men from

---

ᴬ19:6 Lit be right in your eyes   ᴮ19:7 Lit speak to the heart of   ᶜ19:12 Lit my bone and my flesh   ᴰ19:13 Lit my bone and my flesh?   ᴱ19:14 Lit he turned the heart of

Benjamin with him. Ziba, an attendant from the house of Saul, with his fifteen sons and twenty servants also rushed down to the Jordan ahead of the king. [18] They forded the Jordan to bring the king's household across and do whatever the king desired.[A]

When Shimei son of Gera crossed the Jordan, he fell facedown before the king [19] and said to him, "My lord, don't hold me guilty, and don't remember your servant's wrongdoing on the day my lord the king left Jerusalem. May the king not take it to heart. [20] For your servant knows that I have sinned. But look! Today I am the first one of the entire house of Joseph to come down to meet my lord the king."

[21] Abishai son of Zeruiah asked, "Shouldn't Shimei be put to death for this, because he cursed the LORD's anointed?"

[22] David answered, "Sons of Zeruiah, do we agree on anything? Have you become my adversary today? Should any man be killed in Israel today? Am I not aware that today I'm king over Israel?" [23] So the king said to Shimei, "You will not die." Then the king gave him his oath.

[24] Mephibosheth, Saul's grandson, also went down to meet the king. He had not taken care of his feet, trimmed his mustache, or washed his clothes from the day the king left until the day he returned safely. [25] When he came from Jerusalem to meet the king, the king asked him, "Mephibosheth, why didn't you come with me?"

[26] "My lord the king," he replied, "my servant Ziba betrayed me. Actually your servant said: 'I'll saddle the donkey for myself[B] so that I may ride it and go with the king' — for your servant is lame. [27] Ziba slandered your servant to my lord the king. But my lord the king is like the angel of God, so do whatever you think best.[C] [28] For my grandfather's entire family deserves death from my lord the king, but you set your servant among those who eat at your table. So what further right do I have to keep on making appeals to the king?"

[29] The king said to him, "Why keep on speaking about these matters of yours? I hereby declare: you and Ziba are to divide the land."

[30] Mephibosheth said to the king, "Instead, since my lord the king has come to his palace safely, let Ziba take it all!"

[31] Barzillai the Gileadite had come down from Rogelim and accompanied the king to the Jordan River to see him off at the Jordan. [32] Barzillai was a very old man — eighty years old — and since he was a very wealthy man, he had provided for the needs of the king while he stayed in Mahanaim.

[33] The king said to Barzillai, "Cross over with me, and I'll provide for you[D] at my side in Jerusalem."

[34] Barzillai replied to the king, "How many years of my life are left that I should go up to Jerusalem with the king? [35] I'm now eighty years old. Can I discern what is pleasant and what is not? Can your servant taste what he eats or drinks? Can I still hear the voice of male and female singers? Why should your servant be an added burden to my lord the king? [36] Since your servant is only going with the king a little way across the Jordan, why should the king repay me with such a reward? [37] Please let your servant return so that I may die in my own city near the tomb of my father and mother. But here

---

[A]19:18 Lit do what is good in his eyes   [B]19:26 LXX, Syr, Vg read said to him, 'Saddle the donkey for me   [C]19:27 Lit do what is good in your eyes
[D]19:33 LXX reads for your old age; Ru 4:15

is your servant Chimham: let him cross over with my lord the king. Do for him what seems good to you."[A]

³⁸ The king replied, "Chimham will cross over with me, and I will do for him what seems good to you, and whatever you desire from me I will do for you." ³⁹ So all the people crossed the Jordan, and then the king crossed. The king kissed Barzillai and blessed him, and Barzillai returned to his home.

⁴⁰ The king went on to Gilgal, and Chimham went with him. All the troops of Judah and half of Israel's escorted the king. ⁴¹ Suddenly, all the men of Israel came to the king. They asked him, "Why did our brothers, the men of Judah, take you away secretly and transport the king and his household across the Jordan, along with all of David's men?"

⁴² All the men of Judah responded to the men of Israel, "Because the king is our relative. Why does this make you angry? Have we ever eaten anything of the king's or been honored at all?"[B]

⁴³ The men of Israel answered the men of Judah: "We have ten shares in the king, so we have a greater claim to David than you. Why then do you despise us? Weren't we the first to speak of restoring our king?" But the words of the men of Judah were harsher than those of the men of Israel.

SHEBA'S REVOLT

20 Now a wicked man, a Benjaminite named Sheba son of Bichri, happened to be there. He blew the ram's horn and shouted:

We have no portion in David,
no inheritance in Jesse's son.
Each man to his tent,[C] Israel!

² So all the men of Israel deserted David and followed Sheba son of Bichri, but the men of Judah from the Jordan all the way to Jerusalem remained loyal to their king.

³ When David came to his palace in Jerusalem, he took the ten concubines he had left to take care of the palace and placed them under guard. He provided for them, but he was not intimate with them. They were confined until the day of their death, living as widows.

⁴ The king said to Amasa, "Summon the men of Judah to me within three days and be here yourself." ⁵ Amasa went to summon Judah, but he took longer than the time allotted him. ⁶ So David said to Abishai, "Sheba son of Bichri will do more harm to us than Absalom. Take your lord's soldiers and pursue him, or he will find fortified cities and elude us."[D]

⁷ So Joab's men, the Cherethites, the Pelethites, and all the warriors marched out under Abishai's command;[E] they left Jerusalem to pursue Sheba son of Bichri. ⁸ They were at the great stone in Gibeon when Amasa joined them. Joab was wearing his uniform and over it was a belt around his waist with a sword in its sheath. As he approached, the sword fell out. ⁹ Joab asked Amasa, "Are you well, my brother?" Then with his right hand Joab grabbed Amasa by the beard to kiss him. ¹⁰ Amasa was not on guard against the sword in Joab's hand, and Joab stabbed him in the stomach with it and spilled his intestines out on the ground. Joab did not stab him again, and Amasa died.

[A]19:37 Lit what is good in your eyes, also in v. 38   [B]19:42 LXX reads king's or has he given us a gift or granted us a portion   [C]20:1 Alt Hb tradition reads gods   [D]20:6 Lit and snatch away our eyes   [E]20:7 Lit out following him

Joab and his brother Abishai pursued Sheba son of Bichri. ¹¹ One of Joab's young men had stood over Amasa saying, "Whoever favors Joab and whoever is for David, follow Joab!" ¹² Now Amasa had been writhing in his blood in the middle of the highway, and the man had seen that all the troops stopped. So he moved Amasa from the highway to the field and threw a garment over him because he realized that all those who encountered Amasa were stopping. ¹³ When he was removed from the highway, all the men passed by and followed Joab to pursue Sheba son of Bichri.

¹⁴ Sheba passed through all the tribes of Israel to Abel of Beth-maacah. All the Berites ^A^ came together and followed him. ¹⁵ Joab's troops came and besieged Sheba in Abel of Beth-maacah. They built a siege ramp against the outer wall of the city. While all the troops with Joab were battering the wall to make it collapse, ¹⁶ a wise woman called out from the city, "Listen! Listen! Please tell Joab to come here and let me speak with him."

¹⁷ When he had come near her, the woman asked, "Are you Joab?"

"I am," he replied.

"Listen to the words of your servant," she said to him.

He answered, "I'm listening."

¹⁸ She said, "In the past they used to say, 'Seek counsel in Abel,' and that's how they settled disputes. ¹⁹ I am one of the peaceful and faithful in Israel, but you're trying to destroy a city that is like a mother in Israel. Why would you devour the LORD's inheritance?"

²⁰ Joab protested: "Never! I would never devour or demolish! ²¹ That is not the case. There is a man named Sheba son of Bichri, from the hill country of Ephraim, who has rebelled against King David. Deliver this one man, and I will withdraw from the city."

The woman replied to Joab, "Watch! His head will be thrown over the wall to you." ²² The woman went to all the people with her wise counsel, and they cut off the head of Sheba son of Bichri and threw it to Joab. So he blew the ram's horn, and they dispersed from the city, each to his own tent. Joab returned to the king in Jerusalem.

²³ Joab commanded the whole army of Israel;

 Benaiah son of Jehoiada was over the Cherethites and Pelethites;

²⁴ Adoram ^B^ was over forced labor;

 Jehoshaphat son of Ahilud was court historian;

²⁵ Sheva was court secretary;

 Zadok and Abiathar were priests;

²⁶ and in addition, Ira the Jairite was David's priest.

JUSTICE FOR THE GIBEONITES

21 During David's reign there was a famine for three successive years, so David inquired ^C^ of the LORD. The LORD answered, "It is due to Saul and to his bloody family, because he killed the Gibeonites."

² The Gibeonites were not Israelites but rather a remnant of the Amorites. The Israelites had taken an oath concerning them, but Saul had tried to kill them in his zeal for the Israelites and Judah. So David summoned the Gibeonites and spoke to them. ³ He asked the Gibeonites, "What should I do for

---

^A^20:14 LXX, Vg read *Bichrites*   ^B^20:24 Some Hb mss, LXX, Syr read *Adoniram* ; 1Kg 4:6; 5:14   ^C^21:1 Lit *sought the face of* you? How can I make atonement so that you will bring a blessing on[A] the LORD's inheritance?"

[4] The Gibeonites said to him, "We are not asking for silver and gold from Saul or his family, and we cannot put anyone to death in Israel."

"Whatever you say, I will do for you," he said.

[5] They replied to the king, "As for the man who annihilated us and plotted to destroy us so we would not exist within the whole territory of Israel, [6] let seven of his male descendants be handed over to us so we may hang[B] them in the presence of the LORD at Gibeah of Saul, the LORD's chosen."

The king answered, "I will hand them over."

[7] David spared Mephibosheth, the son of Saul's son Jonathan, because of the oath of the LORD that was between David and Jonathan, Saul's son. [8] But the king took Armoni and Mephibosheth, who were the two sons whom Rizpah daughter of Aiah had borne to Saul, and the five sons whom Merab[C] daughter of Saul had borne to Adriel son of Barzillai the Meholathite [9] and handed them over to the Gibeonites. They hanged[D] them on the hill in the presence of the LORD; the seven of them died together. They were executed in the first days of the harvest at the beginning of the barley harvest.[E]

THE BURIAL OF SAUL'S FAMILY

[10] Rizpah, Aiah's daughter, took sackcloth and spread it out for herself on the rock from the beginning of the harvest[F] until the rain poured down from heaven on the bodies. She kept the birds of the sky from them by day and the wild animals by night.

[11] When it was reported to David what Saul's concubine Rizpah daughter of Aiah had done, [12] he went and got the bones of Saul and his son Jonathan from the citizens of Jabesh-gilead. They had stolen them from the public square of Beth-shan where the Philistines had hung the bodies the day the Philistines killed Saul at Gilboa. [13] David had the bones brought from there. They gathered up the bones of Saul's family who had been hanged [14] and buried the bones of Saul and his son Jonathan at Zela in the land of Benjamin in the tomb of Saul's father Kish. They did everything the king commanded. After this, God was receptive to prayer for the land.

THE PHILISTINE GIANTS

[15] The Philistines again waged war against Israel. David went down with his soldiers, and they fought the Philistines, but David became exhausted. [16] Then Ishbi-benob, one of the descendants of the giant,[G] whose bronze spear weighed about eight pounds[H] and who wore new armor, intended to kill David. [17] But Abishai son of Zeruiah came to his aid, struck the Philistine, and killed him. Then David's men swore to him: "You must never again go out with us to battle. You must not extinguish the lamp of Israel."

[18] After this, there was another battle with the Philistines at Gob. At that time Sibbecai the Hushathite killed Saph, who was one of the descendants of the giant.

[A] 21:3 Lit *will bless*   [B] 21:6 Or *impale*, or *expose*   [C] 21:8 Some Hb mss, LXX, Syr, Tg; other Hb mss read *Michal*   [D] 21:9 Or *impaled*, or *exposed*, also in v. 13   [E] 21:9 = March–April   [F] 21:10 = April to October   [G] 21:16 Or *Raphah*, also in vv. 18,20,22   [H] 21:16 Lit *300* (shekels)

¹⁹ Once again there was a battle with the Philistines at Gob, and Elhanan son of Jaare-oregim the Bethlehemite killed^A Goliath of Gath. The shaft of his spear was like a weaver's beam.

²⁰ At Gath there was still another battle. A huge man was there with six fingers on each hand and six toes on each foot — twenty-four in all. He, too, was descended from the giant. ²¹ When he taunted Israel, Jonathan, son of David's brother Shimei, killed him.

²² These four were descended from the giant in Gath and were killed by David and his soldiers.

DAVID'S SONG OF THANKSGIVING

22 David spoke the words of this song to the LORD on the day the LORD rescued him from the grasp of all his enemies and from the grasp of Saul. ² He said:

The LORD is my rock, my fortress, and my deliverer,
³   my God,^B my rock where I seek refuge.
My shield, the horn of my salvation, my stronghold, my refuge,
   and my Savior, you save me from violence.
⁴   I called to the LORD, who is worthy of praise,
   and I was saved from my enemies.
⁵   For the waves of death engulfed me;
   the torrents of destruction terrified me.
⁶   The ropes of Sheol entangled me;
   the snares of death confronted me.

⁷   I called to the LORD in my distress;
I called to my God.
From his temple he heard my voice,
   and my cry for help reached his ears.
⁸   Then the earth shook and quaked;
the foundations of the heavens^C trembled;
they shook because he burned with anger.
⁹   Smoke rose from his nostrils,
and consuming fire came from his mouth;
coals were set ablaze by it.^D
¹⁰   He bent the heavens and came down,
total darkness beneath his feet.
¹¹   He rode on a cherub and flew,
soaring^E on the wings of the wind.
¹²   He made darkness a canopy around him,
a gathering^F of water and thick clouds.
¹³   From the radiance of his presence,
blazing coals were ignited.
¹⁴   The LORD thundered from heaven;
the Most High made his voice heard.

---

^A21:19 1Ch 20:5 adds *the brother of* ^B22:3 LXX, Ps 18:2 read *my God*;
MT reads *God of* ^C22:8 Some Hb mss, Syr, Vg read *mountains*; Ps 18:7
^D22:9 Or *him* ^E22:11 Some Hb mss; other Hb mss, Syr, Tg read *he was seen*
^F22:12 Or *sieve*, or *mass*; Hb obscure

15 He shot arrows and scattered them;
   he hurled lightning bolts and routed them.
16 The depths of the sea became visible,
   the foundations of the world were exposed
   at the rebuke of the LORD,
   at the blast of the breath of his nostrils.

17 He reached down from on high
   and took hold of me;
   he pulled me out of deep water.
18 He rescued me from my powerful enemy
   and from those who hated me,
   for they were too strong for me.
19 They confronted me in the day of my calamity,
   but the LORD was my support.
20 He brought me out to a spacious place;
   he rescued me because he delighted in me.

21 The LORD rewarded me
   according to my righteousness;
   he repaid me
   according to the cleanness of my hands.
22 For I have kept the ways of the LORD
   and have not turned from my God to wickedness.
23 Indeed, I let all his ordinances guide me[A]
   and have not disregarded his statutes.
24 I was blameless before him
   and kept myself from my iniquity.
25 So the LORD repaid me
   according to my righteousness,
   according to my cleanness[B] in his sight.

26 With the faithful
   you prove yourself faithful,
   with the blameless
   you prove yourself blameless,
27 with the pure
   you prove yourself pure;
   but with the crooked
   you prove yourself shrewd.
28 You rescue an oppressed people,
   but your eyes are set against the proud —
   you humble them.
29 LORD, you are my lamp;
   the LORD illuminates my darkness.
30 With you I can attack a barricade,[C]
   and with my God I can leap over a wall.

[A]22:23 Lit *Indeed, all his ordinances have been in front of me*   [B]22:25 LXX, Syr,
Vg read *to the cleanness of my hands*; Ps 18:24   [C]22:30 Or *a ridge*, or *raiders*

³¹ God — his way is perfect;
the word of the LORD is pure.
He is a shield to all who take refuge in him.

³² For who is God besides the LORD?
And who is a rock? Only our God.
³³ God is my strong refuge;^A
he makes my way perfect.^B
³⁴ He makes my feet like the feet of a deer
and sets me securely on the^C heights.^D
³⁵ He trains my hands for war;
my arms can bend a bow of bronze.
³⁶ You have given me the shield of your salvation;
your help^E exalts me.
³⁷ You make a spacious place beneath me for my steps,
and my ankles do not give way.
³⁸ I pursue my enemies and destroy them;
I do not turn back until they are wiped out.
³⁹ I wipe them out and crush them,
and they do not rise;
they fall beneath my feet.
⁴⁰ You have clothed me with strength for battle;
you subdue my adversaries beneath me.
⁴¹ You have made my enemies retreat before me;^F
I annihilate those who hate me.
⁴² They look, but there is no one to save them —
they look to the LORD, but he does not answer them.
⁴³ I pulverize them like dust of the earth;
I crush them and trample them like mud
in the streets.

⁴⁴ You have freed me from the feuds among my people;
you have preserved me as head of nations;
a people I had not known serve me.
⁴⁵ Foreigners submit to me cringing;
as soon as they hear, they obey me.
⁴⁶ Foreigners lose heart
and come trembling from their fortifications.

⁴⁷ The LORD lives — blessed be my rock!
God, the rock of my salvation, is exalted.
⁴⁸ God — he grants me vengeance
and casts down peoples under me.
⁴⁹ He frees me from my enemies.

---

^A22:33 DSS, some LXX mss, Syr, Vg read *God clothes me with strength*; Ps
18:32 ^B22:33 Some LXX mss, Syr; MT reads *he sets free the blameless his
way*; Hb obscure ^C22:34 LXX; some Hb mss read *my*; other Hb mss read *his*
^D22:34 Or *on my high places* ^E22:36 LXX reads *humility*; Ps 18:35 ^F22:41 Lit
you gave me the neck of my enemies

You exalt me above my adversaries;
you rescue me from violent men.

⁵⁰ Therefore I will give thanks to you among the nations, Lᴏʀᴅ;
I will sing praises about your name.

⁵¹ He is a tower of salvation forᴬ his king;
he shows loyalty to his anointed,
to David and his descendants forever.

DAVID'S LAST WORDS

23 These are the last words of David:
The declaration of David son of Jesse,
the declaration of the man raised on high,ᴮ
the one anointed by the God of Jacob.
This is the most delightful of Israel's songs.

² The Spirit of the Lᴏʀᴅ spoke through me,
his word was on my tongue.

³ The God of Israel spoke;
the Rock of Israel said to me,
"The one who rules the people with justice,
who rules in the fear of God,

⁴ is like the morning light when the sun rises
on a cloudless morning,
the glisten of rain on sprouting grass."

⁵ Is it not true my house is with God?
For he has established a permanent covenant with me,
ordered and secured in every detail.
Will he not bring about
my whole salvation and my every desire?

⁶ But all the wicked are like thorns raked aside;
they can never be picked up by hand.

⁷ The man who touches them
must be armed with iron and the shaft of a spear.
They will be completely burned up on the spot.

EXPLOITS OF DAVID'S WARRIORS

⁸ These are the names of David's warriors:

Josheb-basshebeth the Tahchemonite was chief of the officers.ᶜ He wielded his spearᴰ against eight hundred men that he killed at one time.

⁹ After him, Eleazar son of Dodo son of an Ahohite was among the three warriors with David when they defied the Philistines. The men of Israel retreated in the place they had gathered for battle, ¹⁰ but Eleazar stood his ground and attacked the Philistines until his hand was tired and stuck to his sword. The Lᴏʀᴅ brought about a great victory that day. Then the troops came back to him, but only to plunder the dead.

ᴬ22:51 DSS read *he gives great victory to*   ᴮ23:1 Or *raised up by the high God*
ᶜ23:8 Some Hb mss, LXX read *Three*   ᴰ23:8 Some Hb mss; other Hb mss, LXX
read *He was Adino the Eznite*

¹¹ After him was Shammah son of Agee the Hararite. The Philistines had assembled in formation where there was a field full of lentils. The troops fled from the Philistines, ¹² but Shammah took his stand in the middle of the field, defended it, and struck down the Philistines. So the LORD brought about a great victory.

¹³ Three of the thirty leading warriors went down at harvest time and came to David at the cave of Adullam, while a company of Philistines was camping in the Valley of Rephaim. ¹⁴ At that time David was in the stronghold, and a Philistine garrison was at Bethlehem. ¹⁵ David was extremely thirsty^A and said, "If only someone would bring me water to drink from the well at the city gate of Bethlehem!" ¹⁶ So three of the warriors broke through the Philistine camp and drew water from the well at the gate of Bethlehem. They brought it back to David, but he refused to drink it. Instead, he poured it out to the LORD. ¹⁷ David said, "LORD, I would never do such a thing! Is this not the blood of men who risked their lives?" So he refused to drink it. Such were the exploits of the three warriors.

¹⁸ Abishai, Joab's brother and son of Zeruiah, was leader of the Three.^B He wielded his spear against three hundred men and killed them, gaining a reputation among the Three. ¹⁹ Was he not more honored than the Three? He became their commander even though he did not become one of the Three.

²⁰ Benaiah son of Jehoiada was the son of a brave man from Kabzeel, a man of many exploits. Benaiah killed two sons^C of Ariel^D of Moab, and he went down into a pit on a snowy day and killed a lion. ²¹ He also killed an Egyptian, an impressive man. Even though the Egyptian had a spear in his hand, Benaiah went down to him with a club, snatched the spear out of the Egyptian's hand, and then killed him with his own spear. ²² These were the exploits of Benaiah son of Jehoiada, who had a reputation among the three warriors. ²³ He was the most honored of the Thirty, but he did not become one of the Three. David put him in charge of his bodyguard.

²⁴ Among the Thirty were
    Joab's brother Asahel,
    Elhanan son of Dodo of Bethlehem,
²⁵   Shammah the Harodite,
    Elika the Harodite,
²⁶   Helez the Paltite,
    Ira son of Ikkesh the Tekoite,
²⁷   Abiezer the Anathothite,
    Mebunnai the Hushathite,
²⁸   Zalmon the Ahohite,
    Maharai the Netophathite,
²⁹   Heleb son of Baanah the Netophathite,
    Ittai son of Ribai from Gibeah of the Benjaminites,
³⁰   Benaiah the Pirathonite,
    Hiddai from the wadis of Gaash,^E
³¹   Abi-albon the Arbathite,
    Azmaveth the Barhumite,

---

^A 23:15 Lit *And David craved*   ^B 23:18 Some Hb mss, Syr read *the Thirty*
^C 23:20 LXX; MT omits *sons*   ^D 23:20 Or *two warriors*   ^E 23:30 Or *from Nahale-gaash*

32 Eliahba the Shaalbonite,
    the sons of Jashen,
    Jonathan son of[A] 33 Shammah the Hararite,
    Ahiam son of Sharar the Hararite,
34 Eliphelet son of Ahasbai son of the Maacathite,
    Eliam son of Ahithophel the Gilonite,
35 Hezro the Carmelite,
    Paarai the Arbite,
36 Igal son of Nathan from Zobah,
    Bani the Gadite,
37 Zelek the Ammonite,
    Naharai the Beerothite, the armor-bearer for Joab son of Zeruiah,
38 Ira the Ithrite,
    Gareb the Ithrite,
39 and Uriah the Hethite.

There were thirty-seven in all.

DAVID'S MILITARY CENSUS

24 The Lord's anger burned against Israel again, and he stirred up David against them to say: "Go, count the people of Israel and Judah." ² So the king said to Joab, the commander of his army, "Go through all the tribes of Israel from Dan to Beer-sheba and register the troops so I can know their number."

³ Joab replied to the king, "May the Lord your God multiply the troops a hundred times more than they are — while my lord the king looks on! But why does my lord the king want to do this?"

⁴ Yet the king's order prevailed over Joab and the commanders of the army. So Joab and the commanders of the army left the king's presence to register the troops of Israel.

⁵ They crossed the Jordan and camped in Aroer, south of the town in the middle of the valley, and then proceeded toward Gad and Jazer. ⁶ They went to Gilead and to the land of the Hittites[B] and continued on to Dan-jaan and around to Sidon. ⁷ They went to the fortress of Tyre and all the cities of the Hivites and Canaanites. Afterward, they went to the Negev of Judah at Beer-sheba.

⁸ When they had gone through the whole land, they returned to Jerusalem at the end of nine months and twenty days. ⁹ Joab gave the king the total of the registration of the troops. There were eight hundred thousand valiant armed men[C] from Israel and five hundred thousand men from Judah.

¹⁰ David's conscience troubled him after he had taken a census of the troops. He said to the Lord, "I have sinned greatly in what I've done. Now, Lord, because I've been very foolish, please take away your servant's guilt."

DAVID'S PUNISHMENT

¹¹ When David got up in the morning, the word of the Lord had come to the prophet Gad, David's seer: ¹² "Go and say to David, 'This is what the Lord says: I am offering you three choices. Choose one of them, and I will do it to you.'"

[A]23:32 Some LXX mss; MT omits *son of*; 1Ch 11:34 [B]24:6 LXX; MT reads *of Tahtim-hodshi*; Hb obscure [C]24:9 Lit *men of valor drawing the sword*

¹³ So Gad went to David, told him the choices, and asked him, "Do you want three^A years of famine to come on your land, to flee from your foes three months while they pursue you, or to have a plague in your land three days? Now, consider carefully^B what answer I should take back to the one who sent me."

¹⁴ David answered Gad, "I have great anxiety. Please, let us fall into the Lord's hands because his mercies are great, but don't let me fall into human hands."

¹⁵ So the Lord sent a plague on Israel from that morning until the appointed time, and from Dan to Beer-sheba seventy thousand men died. ¹⁶ Then the angel extended his hand toward Jerusalem to destroy it, but the Lord relented concerning the destruction and said to the angel who was destroying the people, "Enough, withdraw your hand now!" The angel of the Lord was then at the threshing floor of Araunah^C the Jebusite.

¹⁷ When David saw the angel striking the people, he said to the Lord, "Look, I am the one who has sinned; I am the one^D who has done wrong. But these sheep, what have they done? Please, let your hand be against me and my father's family."

DAVID'S ALTAR

¹⁸ Gad came to David that day and said to him, "Go up and set up an altar to the Lord on the threshing floor of Araunah the Jebusite." ¹⁹ David went up in obedience to Gad's command, just as the Lord had commanded. ²⁰ Araunah looked down and saw the king and his servants coming toward him, so he went out and paid homage to the king with his face to the ground.

²¹ Araunah said, "Why has my lord the king come to his servant?"

David replied, "To buy the threshing floor from you in order to build an altar to the Lord, so the plague on the people may be halted."

²² Araunah said to David, "My lord the king may take whatever he wants^E and offer it. Here are the oxen for a burnt offering and the threshing sledges and ox yokes for the wood. ²³ Your Majesty, Araunah gives everything here to the king." Then he said to the king, "May the Lord your God accept you."

²⁴ The king answered Araunah, "No, I insist on buying it from you for a price, for I will not offer to the Lord my God burnt offerings that cost me nothing." David bought the threshing floor and the oxen for twenty ounces^F of silver. ²⁵ He built an altar to the Lord there and offered burnt offerings and fellowship offerings. Then the Lord was receptive to prayer for the land, and the plague on Israel ended.

---

^A24:13 LXX; MT reads *seven*; 1Ch 21:12   ^B24:13 Lit *Now, know and see*
^C24:16 = Ornan in 1Ch 21:15-28; 2Ch 3:1   ^D24:17 LXX reads *shepherd*
^E24:22 Lit *take what is good in his eyes*   ^F24:24 Lit *50 shekels*

the Lord He is God

1 kings

When all the people saw it, they fell facedown and said, "The LORD, he is God! The LORD, he is God!" **18:39**

ON THE TIMELINE The history recorded in 1 Kings covers approximately 120 years. It begins around 970 BC, with the death of King David, and ends around 850 BC, with the death of King Ahab and his son Ahaziah's rise as king in Israel. During this time, in 931 BC, the nation of Israel split into two kingdoms.

A LITTLE BACKGROUND First and 2 Kings are the history of the kings and kingdoms of Israel and Judah. Originally, the two were one book, but they were later divided by the translators of the Septuagint (the Greek translation of the Old Testament).

The Davidic covenant (first introduced in 2 Samuel) established the king as the moral representative of the people for covenant purposes. Therefore, up through kings Azariah (also known as Uzziah) and Jotham, the moral state of the king was treated as representative of the moral state of the people. Covenant blessings were given or withheld on the basis of the king's behavior, making the behavior of the king the basis of covenant faithfulness for any given reign.

MESSAGE & PURPOSE
The theological perspective of 1 and 2 Kings is expressed in a number of themes:
1. The sinfulness of the kings and the nation
2. The conflict between the demands of practical politics and the demands of faith
3. The glory God gave to the obedient covenant kings
4. God's harshness in judgment on some occasions and leniency on others
5. The conflict between the worship of the Lord and the worship of other gods.

GIVE THANKS FOR THE BOOK OF 1 KINGS:

For the Bible writers, history could not have existed without God's purposes, thereby making all history theological. The Babylonian exiles wanted an explanation for what they saw as the failure of the religious system in Israel, so they looked to historical apologetics to find their answers. The books of 1 and 2 Kings interpreted Hebrew history in light of OT covenant theology, finding the "failure" was due not to God but to God's people who did not uphold their part of the covenant. God is faithful to His covenant with us, even when we are not.

SOLOMON'S KINGDOM

BOUNDARY OF SOLOMON'S KINGDOM

AREA OF SOLOMON'S INFLUENCE

TERRITORY CONQUERED BY DAVID

SAUL'S KINGDOM

MAJOR HIGHWAY

MEDITERRANEAN SEA

PHOENICIA

KING'S HIGHWAY

SIDON

TYRE

DAN

DAMASCUS

MEGIDDO

RAMOTH-
GILEAD

JOPPA

SHECHEM

AMMON

GAZA

JERUSALEM

INT'L COASTAL HIGHWAY

MOAB

TAMAR

KADESH-
BARNEA

EDOM

EGYPT

EASTERN DESERT

READ AND UNDERSTAND 1 KINGS

The Bible is a complete work in which many stories combine to tell one story. As you read the book of 1 Kings, consider reading the additional passages to discover how the whole of Scripture works together.

DAVID'S LAST DAYS

1 Now King David was old and advanced in age. Although they covered him with bedclothes, he could not get warm. ² So his servants said to him: "Let us[A] search for a young virgin for my lord the king. She is to attend the king and be his caregiver. She is to lie by your side so that my lord the king will get warm." ³ They searched for a beautiful girl throughout the territory of Israel; they found Abishag the Shunammite[B] and brought her to the king. ⁴ The girl was of unsurpassed beauty, and she became the king's caregiver. She attended to him, but he was not intimate with[C] her.

ADONIJAH'S BID FOR POWER

⁵ Adonijah son of Haggith kept exalting himself, saying, "I will be king!" He prepared chariots, cavalry, and fifty men to run ahead of him.[D] ⁶ But his father had never once infuriated him by asking, "Why did you do that?" In addition, he was quite handsome and was born after Absalom. ⁷ He conspired[E] with Joab son of Zeruiah and with the priest Abiathar. They supported Adonijah, ⁸ but the priest Zadok, Benaiah son of Jehoiada, the prophet Nathan, Shimei, Rei, and David's royal guard[F] did not side with Adonijah.

⁹ Adonijah sacrificed sheep, goats, cattle, and fattened cattle near the stone of Zoheleth, which is next to En-rogel. He invited all his royal brothers and all the men of Judah, the servants of the king, ¹⁰ but he did not invite the prophet Nathan, Benaiah, the royal guard, or his brother Solomon.

NATHAN'S AND BATHSHEBA'S APPEALS

¹¹ Then Nathan said to Bathsheba, Solomon's mother, "Have you not heard that Adonijah son of Haggith has become king and our lord David does not know it? ¹² Now please come and let me advise you. Save your life and the life of your son Solomon. ¹³ Go, approach King David and say to him, 'My lord the king, did you not swear to your servant: Your son Solomon is to become king after me, and he is the one who is to sit on my throne? So why has Adonijah become king?' ¹⁴ At that moment, while you are still there speaking with the king, I'll come in after you and confirm your words."

¹⁵ So Bathsheba went to the king in his bedroom. Since the king was very old, Abishag the Shunammite was attending to him. ¹⁶ Bathsheba knelt low and paid homage to the king, and he asked, "What do you want?"

¹⁷ She replied, "My lord, you swore to your servant by the Lord your God, 'Your son Solomon is to become king after me, and he is the one who is to sit on my throne.' ¹⁸ Now look, Adonijah has become king. And,[G] my lord the king, you didn't know it. ¹⁹ He has lavishly sacrificed oxen, fattened cattle, and sheep. He invited all the king's sons, the priest Abiathar, and Joab the commander of the army, but he did not invite your servant Solomon. ²⁰ Now, my lord the king, the eyes of all Israel are on you to tell them who will sit on the throne of my lord the king after him. ²¹ Otherwise, when my lord the king rests with his fathers, I and my son Solomon will be regarded as criminals."

[A]1:2 Lit *them*   [B]1:3 Shunem was a town in the hill country of Issachar at the foot of Mt. Moreh; Jos 19:17-18.   [C]1:4 Lit *he did not know*   [D]1:5 Heralds announcing his procession   [E]1:7 Lit *His words were*   [F]1:8 Lit *David's warriors*   [G]1:18 Some Hb mss, LXX, Vg, Syr; other Hb mss read *And now*

²² At that moment, while she was still speaking with the king, the prophet Nathan arrived, ²³ and it was announced to the king, "The prophet Nathan is here." He came into the king's presence and paid homage to him with his face to the ground.

²⁴ "My lord the king," Nathan said, "did you say, 'Adonijah is to become king after me, and he is the one who is to sit on my throne'? ²⁵ For today he went down and lavishly sacrificed oxen, fattened cattle, and sheep. He invited all the sons of the king, the commanders of the army, and the priest Abiathar. And look! They're eating and drinking in his presence, and they're saying, 'Long live King Adonijah!' ²⁶ But he did not invite me — me, your servant — or the priest Zadok or Benaiah son of Jehoiada or your servant Solomon. ²⁷ I'm certain my lord the king would not have let this happen without letting your servant A know who will sit on my lord the king's throne after him."

SOLOMON CONFIRMED KING

²⁸ King David responded by saying, "Call in Bathsheba for me." So she came into the king's presence and stood before him. ²⁹ The king swore an oath and said, "As the LORD lives, who has redeemed my life from every difficulty, ³⁰ just as I swore to you by the LORD God of Israel: Your son Solomon is to become king after me, and he is the one who is to sit on my throne in my place, that is exactly what I will do this very day."

³¹ Bathsheba knelt low with her face to the ground, paying homage to the king, and said, "May my lord King David live forever!"

³² King David then said, "Call in the priest Zadok, the prophet Nathan, and Benaiah son of Jehoiada for me." So they came into the king's presence. ³³ The king said to them, "Take my servants with you, have my son Solomon ride on my own mule, and take him down to Gihon. ³⁴ There, the priest Zadok and the prophet Nathan are to anoint him as king over Israel. You are to blow the ram's horn and say, 'Long live King Solomon!' ³⁵ You are to come up after him, and he is to come in and sit on my throne. He is the one who is to become king in my place; he is the one I have commanded to be ruler over Israel and Judah."

³⁶ "Amen," Benaiah son of Jehoiada replied to the king. "May the LORD, the God of my lord the king, so affirm it. ³⁷ Just as the LORD was with my lord the king, so may he B be with Solomon and make his throne greater than the throne of my lord King David."

³⁸ Then the priest Zadok, the prophet Nathan, Benaiah son of Jehoiada, the Cherethites, and the Pelethites went down, had Solomon ride on King David's mule, and took him to Gihon. ³⁹ The priest Zadok took the horn of oil from the tabernacle and anointed Solomon. Then they blew the ram's horn, and all the people proclaimed, "Long live King Solomon!" ⁴⁰ All the people went up after him, playing flutes and rejoicing with such a great joy that the earth split open from the sound. C

ADONIJAH HEARS OF SOLOMON'S CORONATION

⁴¹ Adonijah and all the invited guests who were with him heard the noise as they finished eating. Joab heard the sound of the ram's horn and said, "Why

---

A 1:27 Some Hb mss, LXX; alt Hb tradition reads *servants* B 1:37 Alt Hb tradition reads *so he will* C 1:40 LXX reads *the land resounded with their noise* is the town in such an uproar?" ⁴²He was still speaking when Jonathan son of Abiathar the priest, suddenly arrived. Adonijah said, "Come in, for you are an important man, and you must be bringing good news."

⁴³"Unfortunately not," Jonathan answered him. "Our lord King David has made Solomon king. ⁴⁴And with Solomon, the king has sent the priest Zadok, the prophet Nathan, Benaiah son of Jehoiada, the Cherethites, and the Pelethites, and they have had him ride on the king's mule. ⁴⁵The priest Zadok and the prophet Nathan have anointed him king in Gihon. They have gone up from there rejoicing. The town has been in an uproar; that's the noise you heard. ⁴⁶Solomon has even taken his seat on the royal throne.

⁴⁷"The king's servants have also gone to congratulate our lord King David, saying, 'May your God make the name of Solomon more well known than your name, and may he make his throne greater than your throne.' Then the king bowed in worship on his bed. ⁴⁸And the king went on to say this: 'Blessed be the LORD God of Israel! Today he has provided one to sit on my throne, and I am a witness.'"ᴬ

⁴⁹Then all of Adonijah's guests got up trembling and went their separate ways. ⁵⁰Adonijah was afraid of Solomon, so he got up and went to take hold of the horns of the altar.

⁵¹It was reported to Solomon: "Look, Adonijah fears King Solomon, and he has taken hold of the horns of the altar, saying, 'Let King Solomon firstᴮ swear to me that he will not kill his servant with the sword.'"

⁵²Then Solomon said, "If he is a man of character, not a single hair of his will fall to the ground, but if evil is found in him, he dies." ⁵³So King Solomon sent for him, and they took him down from the altar. He came and paid homage to King Solomon, and Solomon said to him, "Go to your home."

DAVID'S DYING INSTRUCTIONS TO SOLOMON

2 As the time approached for David to die, he ordered his son Solomon, ²"As for me, I am going the way of all of the earth. Be strong and be a man, ³and keep your obligation to the LORD your God to walk in his ways and to keep his statutes, commands, ordinances, and decrees. This is written in the law of Moses, so that you will have success in everything you do and wherever you turn, ⁴and so that the LORD will fulfill his promise that he made to me: 'If your sons guard their way to walk faithfully before me with all their heart and all their soul, you will never fail to have a man on the throne of Israel.'

⁵"You also know what Joab son of Zeruiah did to me and what he did to the two commanders of Israel's army, Abner son of Ner and Amasa son of Jether. He murdered them in a time of peace to avenge blood shed in war. He spilled that blood on his own waistband and on the sandals of his feet.ᶜ ⁶Act according to your wisdom, and do not let his gray head descend to Sheol in peace.

⁷"Show kindness to the sons of Barzillai the Gileadite and let them be among those who eat at your table because they supported me when I fled from your brother Absalom.

⁸"Keep an eye on Shimei son of Gera, the Benjaminite from Bahurim who is with you. He uttered malicious curses against me the day I went to Mahanaim.

ᴬ1:48 Lit *and my eyes are seeing*   ᴮ1:51 Some Hb mss, LXX, Syr, Vg read *today*
ᶜ2:5 LXX, Old Lat read *on my waistband and . . . my feet;* v. 31

But he came down to meet me at the Jordan River, and I swore to him by the LORD: 'I will never kill you with the sword.' ⁹ So don't let him go unpunished, for you are a wise man. You know how to deal with him to bring his gray head down to Sheol with blood."

¹⁰ Then David rested with his fathers and was buried in the city of David. ¹¹ The length of time David reigned over Israel was forty years: he reigned seven years in Hebron and thirty-three years in Jerusalem. ¹² Solomon sat on the throne of his father David, and his kingship was firmly established.

ADONIJAH'S FOOLISH REQUEST

¹³ Now Adonijah son of Haggith came to Bathsheba, Solomon's mother. She asked, "Do you come peacefully?"

"Peacefully," he replied, ¹⁴ and then asked, "May I talk with you?" ᴬ

"Go ahead," she answered.

¹⁵ "You know the kingship was mine," he said. "All Israel expected me to be king, but then the kingship was turned over to my brother, for the LORD gave it to him. ¹⁶ So now I have just one request of you; don't turn me down." ᴮ

She said to him, "Go on."

¹⁷ He replied, "Please speak to King Solomon since he won't turn you down. Let him give me Abishag the Shunammite as a wife."

¹⁸ "Very well," Bathsheba replied. "I will speak to the king for you."

¹⁹ So Bathsheba went to King Solomon to speak to him about Adonijah. The king stood up to greet her, bowed to her, sat down on his throne, and had a throne placed for the king's mother. So she sat down at his right hand.

²⁰ Then she said, "I have just one small request of you. Don't turn me down."

"Go ahead and ask, mother," the king replied, "for I won't turn you down."

²¹ So she said, "Let Abishag the Shunammite be given to your brother Adonijah as a wife."

²² King Solomon answered his mother, "Why are you requesting Abishag the Shunammite for Adonijah? Since he is my elder brother, you might as well ask the kingship for him, for the priest Abiathar, and for Joab son of Zeruiah." ᶜ ²³ Then King Solomon took an oath by the LORD: "May God punish me and do so severely if Adonijah has not made this request at the cost of his life. ²⁴ And now, as the LORD lives — the one who established me, seated me on the throne of my father David, and made me a dynasty as he promised — I swear Adonijah will be put to death today!" ²⁵ Then King Solomon dispatched Benaiah son of Jehoiada, who struck down Adonijah, and he died.

ABIATHAR'S BANISHMENT

²⁶ The king said to the priest Abiathar, "Go to your fields in Anathoth. Even though you deserve to die, I will not put you to death today, since you carried the ark of the Lord GOD in the presence of my father David and you suffered through all that my father suffered." ²⁷ So Solomon banished Abiathar from being the LORD's priest, and it fulfilled the LORD's prophecy he had spoken at Shiloh against Eli's family.

ᴬ2:14 Lit *then said, "I have a word for you."*   ᴮ2:16 Lit *don't make me turn my face*   ᶜ2:22 LXX, Vg, Syr read *kingship for him, and on his side are Abiathar the priest and Joab son of Zeruiah*

JOAB'S EXECUTION

[28] The news reached Joab. Since he had supported Adonijah but not Absalom, Joab fled to the LORD's tabernacle and took hold of the horns of the altar.

[29] It was reported to King Solomon: "Joab has fled to the LORD's tabernacle and is now beside the altar." Then Solomon sent[A] Benaiah son of Jehoiada and told him, "Go and strike him down!"

[30] So Benaiah went to the tabernacle and said to Joab, "This is what the king says: 'Come out!'"

But Joab said, "No, for I will die here."

So Benaiah took a message back to the king, "This is what Joab said, and this is how he answered me."

[31] The king said to him, "Do just as he says. Strike him down and bury him in order to remove from me and from my father's family the blood that Joab shed without just cause. [32] The LORD will bring back his own blood on his head because he struck down two men more righteous and better than he, without my father David's knowledge. With his sword, Joab murdered Abner son of Ner, commander of Israel's army, and Amasa son of Jether, commander of Judah's army. [33] The responsibility for their deaths will come back to Joab and to his descendants[B] forever, but for David, his descendants, his dynasty, and his throne, there will be peace from the LORD forever."

[34] Benaiah son of Jehoiada went up, struck down Joab, and put him to death. He was buried at his house in the wilderness. [35] Then the king appointed Benaiah son of Jehoiada in Joab's place over the army, and he appointed the priest Zadok in Abiathar's place.

SHIMEI'S BANISHMENT AND EXECUTION

[36] Then the king summoned Shimei and said to him, "Build a house for yourself in Jerusalem and live there, but don't leave there and go anywhere else. [37] On the day you do leave and cross the Kidron Valley, know for sure that you will certainly die. Your blood will be on your own head."

[38] Shimei said to the king, "The sentence is fair; your servant will do as my lord the king has spoken." And Shimei lived in Jerusalem for a long time.

[39] But then, at the end of three years, two of Shimei's slaves ran away to Achish son of Maacah, king of Gath. Shimei was informed, "Look, your slaves are in Gath." [40] So Shimei saddled his donkey and set out to Achish at Gath to search for his slaves. He went and brought them back from Gath.

[41] It was reported to Solomon that Shimei had gone from Jerusalem to Gath and had returned. [42] So the king summoned Shimei and said to him, "Didn't I make you swear by the LORD and warn you, saying, 'On the day you leave and go anywhere else, know for sure that you will certainly die'? And you said to me, 'The sentence is fair; I will obey.' [43] So why have you not kept the LORD's oath and the command that I gave you?" [44] The king also said, "You yourself know all the evil that you did to my father David. Therefore, the LORD has brought back your evil on your head, [45] but King Solomon will be blessed, and David's throne will remain established before the LORD forever."

[A]2:29 LXX adds Joab a message: "What is the matter with you, that you have fled to the altar?" And Joab replied, "Because I feared you, I have fled to the Lord." And Solomon the king sent   [B]2:33 Lit Their blood will return on the head of Joab and on the head of his seed

⁴⁶ Then the king commanded Benaiah son of Jehoiada, and he went out and struck Shimei down, and he died. So the kingdom was established in Solomon's hand.

THE LORD APPEARS TO SOLOMON

3 Solomon made an alliance^A with Pharaoh king of Egypt by marrying Pharaoh's daughter. Solomon brought her to the city of David until he finished building his palace, the LORD's temple, and the wall surrounding Jerusalem. ² However, the people were sacrificing on the high places, because until that time a temple for the LORD's name had not been built. ³ Solomon loved the LORD by walking in the statutes of his father David, but he also sacrificed and burned incense on the high places.

⁴ The king went to Gibeon to sacrifice there because it was the most famous high place. He offered a thousand burnt offerings on that altar. ⁵ At Gibeon the LORD appeared to Solomon in a dream at night. God said, "Ask. What should I give you?"

⁶ And Solomon replied, "You have shown great and faithful love to your servant, my father David, because he walked before you in faithfulness, righteousness, and integrity.^B You have continued this great and faithful love for him by giving him a son to sit on his throne, as it is today.

⁷ "LORD my God, you have now made your servant king in my father David's place. Yet I am just a youth with no experience in leadership.^C ⁸ Your servant is among your people you have chosen, a people too many to be numbered or counted. ⁹ So give your servant a receptive heart to judge your people and to discern between good and evil. For who is able to judge this great people of yours?"

¹⁰ Now it pleased the Lord that Solomon had requested this. ¹¹ So God said to him, "Because you have requested this and did not ask for long life^D or riches for yourself, or the death^E of your enemies, but you asked discernment for yourself to administer justice, ¹² I will therefore do what you have asked. I will give you a wise and understanding heart, so that there has never been anyone like you before and never will be again. ¹³ In addition, I will give you what you did not ask for: both riches and honor, so that no king will be your equal during your entire life. ¹⁴ If you walk in my ways and keep my statutes and commands just as your father David did, I will give you a long life."

¹⁵ Then Solomon woke up and realized it had been a dream. He went to Jerusalem, stood before the ark of the Lord's covenant, and offered burnt offerings and fellowship offerings. Then he held a feast for all his servants.

SOLOMON'S WISDOM

¹⁶ Then two women who were prostitutes came to the king and stood before him. ¹⁷ One woman said, "Please, my lord, this woman and I live in the same house, and I had a baby while she was in the house. ¹⁸ On the third day after I gave birth, she also had a baby and we were alone. No one else^F was with us in the house; just the two of us were there. ¹⁹ During the night this woman's son died because she lay on him. ²⁰ She got up in the middle of the night

---

^A 3:1 Lit Solomon made himself a son-in-law   ^B 3:6 Lit and uprightness of heart with you   ^C 3:7 Lit am a little youth and do not know to go out or come in   ^D 3:11 Lit for many days   ^E 3:11 Lit life   ^F 3:18 Lit No stranger

PRACTICAL WISDOM

1 KINGS 3; JAMES 1:5

After reading 1 Kings 3 aloud to my children, I asked them, "If you could ask God for anything, what would it be?"

My eight-year-old quickly offered a smug, "Peace for all the world," while her younger brother added, "To be a dinosaur with wings." The boy's answer is so much more honest, isn't it? My poor children live with parents who both read and study Scripture as part of our jobs, so it's like they're perpetually enrolled in an "Intro to Bible" course they can't drop. Sometimes the easy, moralistic answer comes first to our minds.

You've got a problem? Well, have I got the answer for you: it's Jesus!

Fortunately, God didn't give Solomon "world peace" and easy answers. God gave Solomon wisdom and a heart of discernment. Wisdom is more than quick knowledge and general hopes for peace; it is the ability to discern what to do in complex situations. Real life can be complicated and sad and confusing and weird. Easy answers and simple judgments just don't cut it.

When I read the story of the two women with newborn babies in 1 Kings, I feel the angry terror of the mother who rolled over and crushed her baby in the night. Can't you hear her stifled howl of desperation when she realizes the horror of what has happened? Fueled by desperation and sorrow, she does the unimaginable (1Kg 3:20).

We know the woman is wrong for taking the living child as her own, but we also know her

pain. We've all tasted unbearable sorrow; we've all been shocked by our own bent to sin. "There is no one righteous, not even one" (Rm 3:10).

When these women bring their complicated crises to Solomon, his response is fascinating. An abstract answer wasn't going to suffice. **Wisdom is intensely practical. It puts into action what is true and good.** Solomon wasn't cunning and clever; he was careful, discerning, and judicious. He gave two simple instructions:

"Bring me a sword."

"Cut the living boy in two."

And at once, what was murky became crystal clear.

Clear discernment does not come naturally to us. But "God's wisdom was in [Solomon]" (1Kg 3:28). Israel saw God's truth in Solomon's wisdom.

Our human answers of world peace and dinosaurs can't solve the issues because real wisdom comes from God (Pr 9:10). And He invites us to ask for it.

"Now if any of you lacks wisdom, he should ask God—who gives to all generously and ungrudgingly—and it will be given to him."

JAMES 1:5

---

and took my son from my side while your servant was asleep. She laid him in her arms, and she put her dead son in my arms. ²¹ When I got up in the morning to nurse my son, I discovered he was dead. That morning, when I looked closely at him I realized that he was not the son I gave birth to."

²² "No," the other woman said. "My son is the living one; your son is the dead one."

The first woman said, "No, your son is the dead one; my son is the living one." So they argued before the king.

²³ The king replied, "This woman says, 'This is my son who is alive, and your son is dead,' but that woman says, 'No, your son is dead, and my son is alive.'" ²⁴ The king continued, "Bring me a sword." So they brought the sword to the king. ²⁵ And the king said, "Cut the living boy in two and give half to one and half to the other."

²⁶ The woman whose son was alive spoke to the king because she felt great compassion[A] for her son. "My lord, give her the living baby," she said, "but please don't have him killed!"

But the other one said, "He will not be mine or yours. Cut him in two!"

²⁷ The king responded, "Give the living baby to the first woman, and don't kill him. She is his mother." ²⁸ All Israel heard about the judgment the king had given, and they stood in awe of the king because they saw that God's wisdom was in him to carry out justice.

SOLOMON'S OFFICIALS

4 King Solomon reigned over all Israel, ² and these were his officials:
Azariah son of Zadok, priest;
³ Elihoreph and Ahijah the sons of Shisha, secretaries;
Jehoshaphat son of Ahilud, court historian;
⁴ Benaiah son of Jehoiada, in charge of the army;
Zadok and Abiathar, priests;
⁵ Azariah son of Nathan, in charge of the deputies;
Zabud son of Nathan, a priest and adviser to the king;
⁶ Ahishar, in charge of the palace;
and Adoniram son of Abda, in charge of forced labor.

⁷ Solomon had twelve deputies for all Israel. They provided food for the king and his household; each one made provision for one month out of the year. ⁸ These were their names:
Ben-hur, in the hill country of Ephraim;
⁹ Ben-deker, in Makaz, Shaalbim, Beth-shemesh, and Elon-beth-hanan;
¹⁰ Ben-hesed, in Arubboth (he had Socoh and the whole land of Hepher);
¹¹ Ben-abinadab, in all Naphath-dor (Taphath daughter of Solomon was his wife);
¹² Baana son of Ahilud, in Taanach, Megiddo, and all Beth-shean which is beside Zarethan below Jezreel, from Beth-shean to Abel-meholah, as far as the other side of Jokmeam;
¹³ Ben-geber, in Ramoth-gilead (he had the villages of Jair son of Manasseh, which are in Gilead, and he had the region of Argob, which is in Bashan, sixty great cities with walls and bronze bars);

A3:26 Lit *because her compassion grew hot*

¹⁴ Ahinadab son of Iddo, in Mahanaim;

¹⁵ Ahimaaz, in Naphtali (he also had married a daughter of Solomon — Basemath);

¹⁶ Baana son of Hushai, in Asher and Bealoth;

¹⁷ Jehoshaphat son of Paruah, in Issachar;

¹⁸ Shimei son of Ela, in Benjamin;

¹⁹ Geber son of Uri, in the land of Gilead, the country of King Sihon of the Amorites and of King Og of Bashan.

There was one deputy in the land of Judah.ᴬ

SOLOMON'S PROVISIONS

²⁰ Judah and Israel were as numerous as the sand by the sea; they were eating, drinking, and rejoicing. ²¹ Solomon ruled all the kingdoms from the Euphrates River to the land of the Philistines and as far as the border of Egypt. They offered tribute and served Solomon all the days of his life.

²² Solomon's provisions for one day were 150 bushelsᴮ of fine flour and 300 bushelsᶜ of meal, ²³ ten fattened cattle, twenty range cattle, and a hundred sheep and goats, besides deer, gazelles, roebucks, and pen-fed poultry,ᴰ ²⁴ for he had dominion over everything west of the Euphrates from Tiphsah to Gaza and over all the kings west of the Euphrates. He had peace on all his surrounding borders. ²⁵ Throughout Solomon's reign, Judah and Israel lived in safety from Dan to Beer-sheba, each person under his own vine and his own fig tree. ²⁶ Solomon had forty thousandᴱ stalls of horses for his chariots, and twelve thousand horsemen. ²⁷ Each of those deputies for a month in turn provided food for King Solomon and for everyone who came to King Solomon's table. They neglected nothing. ²⁸ Each man brought the barley and the straw for the chariot teams and the other horses to the required place according to his assignment.ᶠ

SOLOMON'S WISDOM AND LITERARY GIFTS

²⁹ God gave Solomon wisdom, very great insight, and understanding as vast as the sand on the seashore. ³⁰ Solomon's wisdom was greater than the wisdom of all the people of the East, greater than all the wisdom of Egypt. ³¹ He was wiser than anyone — wiser than Ethan the Ezrahite, and Heman, Calcol, and Darda, sons of Mahol. His reputation extended to all the surrounding nations.

³² Solomon spoke 3,000 proverbs, and his songs numbered 1,005. ³³ He spoke about trees, from the cedar in Lebanon to the hyssop growing out of the wall. He also spoke about animals, birds, reptiles, and fish. ³⁴ Emissaries of all peoples, sent by every king on earth who had heard of his wisdom, came to listen to Solomon's wisdom.

HIRAM'S BUILDING MATERIALS

5 King Hiram of Tyre sent his emissaries to Solomon when he heard that he had been anointed king in his father's place, for Hiram had always been friends with David.

² Solomon sent this message to Hiram: ³ "You know my father David was not able to build a temple for the name of the Lᴏʀᴅ his God. This was because

---

ᴬ4:19 LXX; MT omits *of Judah* ᴮ4:22 Lit *30 cors* ᶜ4:22 Lit *60 cors* ᴰ4:23 Hb obscure ᴱ4:26 2Ch 9:25 reads *4,000 stalls* ᶠ4:28 Lit *judgment* of the warfare all around him until the LORD put his enemies under his feet. ⁴ The LORD my God has now given me rest on every side; there is no enemy or crisis. ⁵ So I plan to build a temple for the name of the LORD my God, according to what the LORD promised my father David: 'I will put your son on your throne in your place, and he will build the temple for my name.'

⁶ "Therefore, command that cedars from Lebanon be cut down for me. My servants will be with your servants, and I will pay your servants' wages according to whatever you say, for you know that not a man among us knows how to cut timber like the Sidonians."

⁷ When Hiram heard Solomon's words, he rejoiced greatly and said, "Blessed be the LORD today! He has given David a wise son to be over this great people!" ⁸ Then Hiram sent a reply to Solomon, saying, "I have heard your message; I will do everything you want regarding the cedar and cypress timber. ⁹ My servants will bring the logs down from Lebanon to the sea, and I will make them into rafts to go by sea to the place you indicate. I will break them apart there, and you can take them away. You then can meet my needs by providing my household with food."

¹⁰ So Hiram provided Solomon with all the cedar and cypress timber he wanted, ¹¹ and Solomon provided Hiram with one hundred thousand bushels^A of wheat as food for his household and one hundred ten thousand gallons^B of oil from crushed olives. Solomon did this for Hiram year after year.

¹² The LORD gave Solomon wisdom, as he had promised him. There was peace between Hiram and Solomon, and the two of them made a treaty.

SOLOMON'S WORKFORCE

¹³ Then King Solomon drafted forced laborers from all Israel; the labor force numbered thirty thousand men. ¹⁴ He sent ten thousand to Lebanon each month in shifts; one month they were in Lebanon, two months they were at home. Adoniram was in charge of the forced labor. ¹⁵ Solomon had seventy thousand porters and eighty thousand stonecutters in the mountains, ¹⁶ not including his thirty-three hundred^C deputies in charge of the work. They supervised the people doing the work. ¹⁷ The king commanded them to quarry large, costly stones to lay the foundation of the temple with dressed stones. ¹⁸ So Solomon's builders and Hiram's builders, along with the Gebalites, quarried the stone and prepared the timber and stone for the temple's construction.

BUILDING THE TEMPLE

6 Solomon began to build the temple for the LORD in the four hundred eightieth year after the Israelites came out of the land of Egypt, in the fourth year of his reign over Israel, in the month of Ziv, which is the second month.^D ² The temple that King Solomon built for the LORD was ninety feet^E long, thirty feet^F wide, and forty-five feet^G high. ³ The portico in front of the temple sanctuary was thirty feet long extending across the temple's width, and fifteen feet deep^H in front of the temple. ⁴ He also made windows with beveled frames^I for the temple.

---

^A5:11 Lit *20,000 cors*   ^B5:11 LXX reads *20,000 baths*; MT reads *20 cors*
^C5:16 Some LXX mss read *3,600*; 2Ch 2:2,18   ^D6:1 April–May   ^E6:2 Lit *60 cubits*   ^F6:2 Lit *20 cubits*, also in vv. 3,16,20   ^G6:2 Lit *30 cubits*   ^H6:3 Lit *10 cubits wide*   ^I6:4 Hb obscure

⁵ He then built a chambered structure ᴬ along the temple wall, encircling the walls of the temple, that is, the sanctuary and the inner sanctuary. And he made side chambers ᴮ all around. ⁶ The lowest chamber was 7 ½ feet ᶜ wide, the middle was 9 feet ᴰ wide, and the third was 10 ½ feet ᴱ wide. He also provided offset ledges for the temple all around the outside so that nothing would be inserted into the temple walls. ⁷ The temple's construction used finished stones cut at the quarry so that no hammer, chisel, or any iron tool was heard in the temple while it was being built.

⁸ The door for the lowest ᶠ side chamber was on the right side of the temple. They ᴳ went up a stairway ᴴ to the middle chamber, and from the middle to the third. ⁹ When he finished building the temple, he paneled it with boards and planks of cedar. ¹⁰ He built the chambers along the entire temple, joined to the temple with cedar beams; each story was 7 ½ feet high.

¹¹ The word of the Lᴏʀᴅ came to Solomon: ¹² "As for this temple you are building — if you walk in my statutes, observe my ordinances, and keep all my commands by walking in them, I will fulfill my promise to you, which I made to your father David. ¹³ I will dwell among the Israelites and not abandon my people Israel."

¹⁴ When Solomon finished building the temple,ᴵ ¹⁵ he paneled the interior temple walls with cedar boards; from the temple floor to the surface of the ceiling he overlaid the interior with wood. He also overlaid the floor with cypress boards. ¹⁶ Then he lined thirty feet of the rear of the temple with cedar boards from the floor to the surface of the ceiling,ᴶ and he built the interior as an inner sanctuary, the most holy place. ¹⁷ The temple, that is, the sanctuary in front of the most holy place,ᴷ was sixty feet ᴸ long. ¹⁸ The cedar paneling inside the temple was carved with ornamental gourds and flower blossoms. Everything was cedar; not a stone could be seen.

¹⁹ He prepared the inner sanctuary inside the temple to put the ark of the Lᴏʀᴅ's covenant there. ²⁰ The interior of the sanctuary was thirty feet long, thirty feet wide, and thirty feet high; he overlaid it with pure gold. He also overlaid the cedar altar. ²¹ Next, Solomon overlaid the interior of the temple with pure gold, and he hung ᴹ gold chains across the front of the inner sanctuary and overlaid it with gold. ²² So he added the gold overlay to the entire temple until everything was completely finished, including the entire altar that belongs to the inner sanctuary.

²³ In the inner sanctuary he made two cherubim 15 feet ᴺ high out of olive wood. ²⁴ One wing of the first cherub was 7 ½ feet long, and the other wing was 7 ½ feet long. The wingspan was 15 feet from tip to tip. ²⁵ The second cherub also was 15 feet; both cherubim had the same size and shape. ²⁶ The first cherub's height was 15 feet and so was the second cherub's. ²⁷ Then he put the cherubim inside the inner temple. Since their wings were spread out, the first one's wing touched one wall while the second cherub's wing touched

---

ᴬ6:5 Lit *built the temple of chamber*   ᴮ6:5 Lit *made ribs or sides*   ᶜ6:6 Lit *five cubits*, also in vv. 10,24   ᴰ6:6 Lit *six cubits*   ᴱ6:6 Lit *seven cubits*   ᶠ6:8 LXX, Tg; MT reads *middle*   ᴳ6:8 = People   ᴴ6:8 Hb obscure   ᴵ6:11-14 LXX omits these vv.   ᴶ6:16 LXX; MT omits *of the ceiling*; 1Kg 6:15   ᴷ6:17 Lit *front of me*; Hb obscure   ᴸ6:17 Lit *40 cubits*   ᴹ6:21 Lit *he caused to pass across*   ᴺ6:23 Lit *10 cubits*, also in vv. 24,25,26 the other[A] wall, and in the middle of the temple their wings were touching wing to wing. 28 He also overlaid the cherubim with gold.

29 He carved all the surrounding temple walls with carved engravings — cherubim, palm trees, and flower blossoms — in the inner and outer sanctuaries. 30 He overlaid the temple floor with gold in both the inner and the outer sanctuaries.

31 For the entrance of the inner sanctuary, he made olive wood doors. The pillars of the doorposts were five-sided.[B] 32 The two doors were made of olive wood. He carved cherubim, palm trees, and flower blossoms on them and overlaid them with gold, hammering gold over the cherubim and palm trees. 33 In the same way, he made four-sided[B] olive wood doorposts for the sanctuary entrance. 34 The two doors were made of cypress wood; the first door had two folding sides, and the second door had two folding panels. 35 He carved cherubim, palm trees, and flower blossoms on them and overlaid them with gold applied evenly over the carving. 36 He built the inner courtyard with three rows of dressed stone and a row of trimmed cedar beams.

37 The foundation of the LORD's temple was laid in Solomon's fourth year in the month of Ziv. 38 In his eleventh year in the month of Bul, which is the eighth month,[C] the temple was completed in every detail and according to every specification. So he built it in seven years.

SOLOMON'S PALACE COMPLEX

7 Solomon completed his entire palace complex after thirteen years of construction. 2 He built the House of the Forest of Lebanon. It was one hundred fifty feet[D] long, seventy-five feet[E] wide, and forty-five feet[F] high on four rows of cedar pillars, with cedar beams on top of the pillars. 3 It was paneled above with cedar at the top of the chambers that rested on forty-five pillars, fifteen per row. 4 There were three rows of window frames, facing each other[G] in three tiers.[H] 5 All the doors and doorposts had rectangular frames, the openings facing each other[I] in three tiers. 6 He made the hall of pillars seventy-five feet long and forty-five feet wide. A portico was in front of the pillars, and a canopy with pillars[B] was in front of them. 7 He made the Hall of the Throne where he would judge — the Hall of Judgment. It was paneled with cedar from the floor to the rafters.[J] 8 Solomon's own palace where he would live, in the other courtyard behind the hall, was of similar construction. And he made a house like this hall for Pharaoh's daughter, his wife.[K]

9 All of these buildings were of costly stones, cut to size and sawed with saws on the inner and outer surfaces, from foundation to coping and from the outside to the great courtyard. 10 The foundation was made of large, costly stones twelve and fifteen feet[L] long. 11 Above were also costly stones, cut to size, as well as cedar wood. 12 Around the great courtyard, as well as the inner courtyard of the LORD's temple and the portico of the temple, were three rows of dressed stone and a row of trimmed cedar beams.

[A]6:27 Lit the second   [B]6:31,33; 7:6 Hb obscure   [C]6:38 = October–November
[D]7:2 Lit 100 cubits   [E]7:2 Lit 50 cubits, also in v. 6   [F]7:2 Lit 30 cubits, also
in vv. 6,23   [G]7:4 Lit frames, window to window   [H]7:4 Lit three times; = at 3
different places, also in v. 5   [I]7:5 Lit frames, opposing window to window
[J]7:7 Syr, Vg; MT reads floor   [K]7:8 Lit daughter he had taken   [L]7:10 Lit ten cubits
and eight cubits

¹³ King Solomon had Hiram[A] brought from Tyre. ¹⁴ He was a widow's son from the tribe of Naphtali, and his father was a man of Tyre, a bronze craftsman. Hiram had great skill, understanding, and knowledge to do every kind of bronze work. So he came to King Solomon and carried out all his work.

THE BRONZE PILLARS

¹⁵ He cast two bronze pillars, each 27 feet[B] high and 18 feet[C] in circumference.[D] ¹⁶ He also made two capitals of cast bronze to set on top of the pillars; 7½ feet[E] was the height of the first capital, and 7½ feet was also the height of the second capital. ¹⁷ The capitals on top of the pillars had gratings of latticework, wreaths[F] made of chainwork — seven for the first capital and seven for the second.

¹⁸ He made the pillars with two encircling rows of pomegranates on the one grating to cover the capital on top; he did the same for the second capital. ¹⁹ And the capitals on top of the pillars in the portico were shaped like lilies, six feet[G] high. ²⁰ The capitals on the two pillars were also immediately above the rounded surface next to the grating, and two hundred pomegranates were in rows encircling each[H] capital. ²¹ He set up the pillars at the portico of the sanctuary: he set up the right pillar and named it Jachin;[I] then he set up the left pillar and named it Boaz.[J] ²² The tops of the pillars were shaped like lilies. Then the work of the pillars was completed.

THE BASIN

²³ He made the cast metal basin,[K] 15 feet[L] from brim to brim, perfectly round. It was 7½ feet high and 45 feet in circumference. ²⁴ Ornamental gourds encircled it below the brim, ten every half yard,[M] completely encircling the basin. The gourds were cast in two rows when the basin was cast. ²⁵ It stood on twelve oxen, three facing north, three facing west, three facing south, and three facing east. The basin was on top of them and all their hindquarters were toward the center. ²⁶ The basin was three inches[N] thick, and its rim was fashioned like the brim of a cup or of a lily blossom. It held eleven thousand gallons.[O]

THE BRONZE WATER CARTS

²⁷ Then he made ten bronze water carts.[P] Each water cart was 6 feet long, 6 feet wide, and 4½ feet[Q] high. ²⁸ This was the design of the carts: They had frames; the frames were between the cross-pieces, ²⁹ and on the frames between the cross-pieces were lions, oxen, and cherubim. On the cross-pieces there was a pedestal above, and below the lions and oxen were wreaths of hanging[R] work. ³⁰ Each cart had four bronze wheels with bronze axles. Underneath the four corners of the basin were cast supports, each next

to a wreath. ³¹ And the water cart's opening inside the crown on top was eighteen inches^A wide. The opening was round, made as a pedestal twenty-seven inches^B wide. On it were carvings, but their frames were square, not round. ³² There were four wheels under the frames, and the wheel axles were part of the water cart; each wheel was twenty-seven inches^C tall. ³³ The wheels' design was similar to that of chariot wheels: their axles, rims, spokes, and hubs were all of cast metal. ³⁴ Four supports were at the four corners of each water cart; each support was one piece with the water cart. ³⁵ At the top of the cart was a band nine inches^D high encircling it; also, at the top of the cart, its braces and its frames were one piece with it. ³⁶ He engraved cherubim, lions, and palm trees on the plates of its braces and on its frames, wherever each had space, with encircling wreaths. ³⁷ In this way he made the ten water carts using the same casting, dimensions, and shape for all of them.

BRONZE BASINS AND OTHER UTENSILS

³⁸ Then he made ten bronze basins — each basin held 220 gallons^E and each was six feet wide — one basin for each of the ten water carts. ³⁹ He set five water carts on the right side of the temple and five on the left side. He put the basin near the right side of the temple toward the southeast. ⁴⁰ Then Hiram made the basins, the shovels, and the sprinkling basins.

COMPLETION OF THE BRONZE WORKS

So Hiram finished all the work that he was doing for King Solomon on the Lord's temple: ⁴¹ two pillars; bowls for the capitals that were on top of the two pillars; the two gratings for covering both bowls of the capitals that were on top of the pillars; ⁴² the four hundred pomegranates for the two gratings (two rows of pomegranates for each grating covering both capitals' bowls on top of the pillars); ⁴³ the ten water carts; the ten basins on the water carts; ⁴⁴ the basin; the twelve oxen underneath the basin; ⁴⁵ and the pots, shovels, and sprinkling basins. All the utensils that Hiram made for King Solomon at the Lord's temple were made of burnished bronze. ⁴⁶ The king had them cast in clay molds in the Jordan Valley between Succoth and Zarethan. ⁴⁷ Solomon left all the utensils unweighed because there were so many; the weight of the bronze was not determined.

COMPLETION OF THE GOLD FURNISHINGS

⁴⁸ Solomon also made all the equipment in the Lord's temple: the gold altar; the gold table that the Bread of the Presence was placed on; ⁴⁹ the pure gold lampstands in front of the inner sanctuary, five on the right and five on the left; the gold flowers, lamps, and tongs; ⁵⁰ the pure gold ceremonial bowls, wick trimmers, sprinkling basins, ladles,^F and firepans; and the gold hinges for the doors of the inner temple (that is, the most holy place) and for the doors of the temple sanctuary.

⁵¹ So all the work King Solomon did in the Lord's temple was completed. Then Solomon brought in the consecrated things of his father David — the

---

^A 7:31 Lit a cubit   ^B 7:31 Lit one and a half cubits   ^C 7:32 Lit was one and a half cubits   ^D 7:35 Lit half a cubit   ^E 7:38 Lit 40 baths   ^F 7:50 Or dishes, or spoons; lit palms silver, the gold, and the utensils — and put them in the treasuries of the Lord's temple.

SOLOMON'S DEDICATION OF THE TEMPLE

8 At that time Solomon assembled the elders of Israel, all the tribal heads and the ancestral leaders of the Israelites before him at Jerusalem in order to bring the ark of the Lord's covenant from the city of David, that is Zion. ² So all the men of Israel were assembled in the presence of King Solomon in the month of Ethanim, which is the seventh month, ᴬ at the festival.

³ All the elders of Israel came, and the priests picked up the ark. ⁴ The priests and the Levites brought the ark of the Lord, the tent of meeting, and the holy utensils that were in the tent. ⁵ King Solomon and the entire congregation of Israel, who had gathered around him and were with him in front of the ark, were sacrificing sheep, goats, and cattle that could not be counted or numbered, because there were so many. ⁶ The priests brought the ark of the Lord's covenant to its place, into the inner sanctuary of the temple, to the most holy place beneath the wings of the cherubim. ⁷ For the cherubim were spreading their wings over ᴮ the place of the ark, so that the cherubim covered the ark and its poles from above. ⁸ The poles were so long that their ends were seen from the holy place in front of the inner sanctuary, but they were not seen from outside the sanctuary; they are still there today. ⁹ Nothing was in the ark except the two stone tablets that Moses had put there at Horeb, ᶜ where the Lord made a covenant with the Israelites when they came out of the land of Egypt.

¹⁰ When the priests came out of the holy place, the cloud filled the Lord's temple, ¹¹ and because of the cloud, the priests were not able to continue ministering, for the glory of the Lord filled the temple.

¹² Then Solomon said:

The Lord said that he would dwell in total darkness.
¹³ I have indeed built an exalted temple for you,
a place for your dwelling forever.

¹⁴ The king turned around and blessed the entire congregation of Israel while they were standing. ¹⁵ He said:

Blessed be the Lord God of Israel!
He spoke directly to my father David,
and he has fulfilled the promise by his power.
He said,
¹⁶ "Since the day I brought my people Israel out of Egypt,
I have not chosen a city to build a temple in
among any of the tribes of Israel,
so that my name would be there.
But I have chosen David to rule my people Israel."
¹⁷ My father David had his heart set
on building a temple for the name of the Lord, the God of Israel.
¹⁸ But the Lord said to my father David,
"Since your heart was set on building a temple for my name,
you have done well to have this desire. ᴰ

ᴬ8:2 = September–October ᴮ8:7 LXX; MT reads *toward* ᶜ8:9 = Sinai
ᴰ8:18 Lit *well because it was with your heart*

19 Yet you are not the one to build it;
instead, your son, your own offspring,
will build it for my name."
20 The LORD has fulfilled what he promised.
I have taken the place of my father David,
and I sit on the throne of Israel, as the LORD promised.
I have built the temple for the name of the LORD, the God of Israel.
21 I have provided a place there for the ark,
where the LORD's covenant is
that he made with our ancestors
when he brought them out of the land of Egypt.

SOLOMON'S PRAYER

22 Then Solomon stood before the altar of the LORD in front of the entire
congregation of Israel and spread out his hands toward heaven. 23 He said:
LORD God of Israel,
there is no God like you
in heaven above or on earth below,
who keeps the gracious covenant
with your servants who walk before you
with all their heart.
24 You have kept what you promised
to your servant, my father David.
You spoke directly to him
and you fulfilled your promise by your power
as it is today.
25 Therefore, LORD God of Israel,
keep what you promised
to your servant, my father David:
You will never fail to have a man
to sit before me on the throne of Israel,
if only your sons take care to walk before me
as you have walked before me.
26 Now LORD^A God of Israel,
please confirm what you promised
to your servant, my father David.

27 But will God indeed live on earth?
Even heaven, the highest heaven, cannot contain you,
much less this temple I have built.
28 Listen^B to your servant's prayer and his petition,
LORD my God,
so that you may hear the cry and the prayer
that your servant prays before you today,
29 so that your eyes may watch over this temple night and day,
toward the place where you said,
"My name will be there,"

---

^A 8:26 Some Hb mss, LXX, Syr, Tg, Vg, 2Ch 6:16; other Hb mss omit LORD
^B 8:28 Lit Turn

and so that you may hear the prayer
that your servant prays toward this place.
³⁰ Hear the petition of your servant
and your people Israel,
which they pray toward this place.
May you hear in your dwelling place in heaven.
May you hear and forgive.

³¹ When a man sins against his neighbor
and is forced to take an oath,^A
and he comes to take an oath
before your altar in this temple,
³² may you hear in heaven and act.
May you judge your servants,
condemning the wicked man by bringing
what he has done on his own head
and providing justice for the righteous
by rewarding him according to his righteousness.

³³ When your people Israel are defeated before an enemy,
because they have sinned against you,
and they return to you and praise your name,
and they pray and plead with you
for mercy in this temple,
³⁴ may you hear in heaven
and forgive the sin of your people Israel.
May you restore them to the land
you gave their ancestors.

³⁵ When the skies are shut and there is no rain,
because they have sinned against you,
and they pray toward this place
and praise your name,
and they turn from their sins
because you are afflicting them,
³⁶ may you hear in heaven
and forgive the sin of your servants
and your people Israel,
so that you may teach them the good way
they should walk in.
May you send rain on your land
that you gave your people for an inheritance.

³⁷ When there is famine in the land,
when there is pestilence,
when there is blight or mildew, locust or grasshopper,
when their enemy besieges them
in the land and its cities,^B

---

^A8:31 Lit *and he lifts a curse against him to curse him*   ^B8:37 Lit *land of its gates*

when there is any plague or illness,
38 every prayer or petition
that any person or that all your people Israel may have —
they each know their own affliction[A] —
as they spread out their hands toward this temple,
39 may you hear in heaven, your dwelling place,
and may you forgive, act, and give to everyone
according to all their ways, since you know each heart,
for you alone know every human heart,
40 so that they may fear you
all the days they live on the land
you gave our ancestors.

41 Even for the foreigner who is not of your people Israel
but has come from a distant land
because of your name —
42 for they will hear of your great name,
strong hand, and outstretched arm,
and will come and pray toward this temple —
43 may you hear in heaven, your dwelling place,
and do according to all the foreigner asks.
Then all peoples of earth will know your name,
to fear you as your people Israel do
and to know that this temple I have built
bears your name.

44 When your people go out to fight against their enemies,[B]
wherever you send them,
and they pray to the Lord
in the direction of the city you have chosen
and the temple I have built for your name,
45 may you hear their prayer and petition in heaven
and uphold their cause.

46 When they sin against you —
for there is no one who does not sin —
and you are angry with them
and hand them over to the enemy,
and their captors deport them to the enemy's country —
whether distant or nearby —
47 and when they come to their senses[C]
in the land where they were deported
and repent and petition you in their captors' land:
"We have sinned and done wrong;
we have been wicked,"
48 and when they return to you with all their heart and all their soul
in the land of their enemies who took them captive,

[A]8:38 Lit *know in his heart of a plague* [B]8:44 Some Hb mss, some ancient versions,
2Ch 6:34; other Hb mss read *enemy* [C]8:47 Lit *they return to their heart*

and when they pray to you in the direction of their land
that you gave their ancestors,
the city you have chosen,
and the temple I have built for your name,
⁴⁹ may you hear in heaven, your dwelling place,
their prayer and petition and uphold their cause.
⁵⁰ May you forgive your people
who sinned against you
and all their rebellions ᴬ against you,
and may you grant them compassion
before their captors,
so that they may treat them compassionately.
⁵¹ For they are your people and your inheritance;
you brought them out of Egypt,
out of the middle of an iron furnace.
⁵² May your eyes be open to your servant's petition
and to the petition of your people Israel,
listening to them whenever they call to you.
⁵³ For you, Lord GOD, have set them apart as your inheritance
from all peoples of the earth,
as you spoke through your servant Moses
when you brought our ancestors out of Egypt.

SOLOMON'S BLESSING

⁵⁴ When Solomon finished praying this entire prayer and petition to the LORD, he got up from kneeling before the altar of the LORD, with his hands spread out toward heaven, ⁵⁵ and he stood and blessed the whole congregation of Israel with a loud voice: ⁵⁶ "Blessed be the LORD! He has given rest to his people Israel according to all he has said. Not one of all the good promises he made through his servant Moses has failed. ⁵⁷ May the LORD our God be with us as he was with our ancestors. May he not abandon us or leave us ⁵⁸ so that he causes us to be devoted ᴮ to him, to walk in all his ways, and to keep his commands, statutes, and ordinances, which he commanded our ancestors. ⁵⁹ May my words with which I have made my petition before the LORD be near the LORD our God day and night. May he uphold his servant's cause and the cause of his people Israel, as each day requires. ⁶⁰ May all the peoples of the earth know that the LORD is God. There is no other! ⁶¹ Be wholeheartedly devoted to the LORD our God to walk in his statutes and to keep his commands, as it is today."

⁶² The king and all Israel with him were offering sacrifices in the LORD's presence. ⁶³ Solomon offered a sacrifice of fellowship offerings to the LORD: twenty-two thousand cattle and one hundred twenty thousand sheep and goats. In this manner the king and all the Israelites dedicated the LORD's temple.

⁶⁴ On the same day, the king consecrated the middle of the courtyard that was in front of the LORD's temple because that was where he offered the burnt offering, the grain offering, and the fat of the fellowship offerings

---

ᴬ8:50 Lit *rebellions that they have rebelled*   ᴮ8:58 Lit *causes our hearts to be inclined* since the bronze altar before the LORD was too small to accommodate the burnt offerings, the grain offerings, and the fat of the fellowship offerings.

⁶⁵ Solomon and all Israel with him — a great assembly, from the entrance of Hamath ᴬ to the Brook of Egypt — observed the festival at that time in the presence of the LORD our God, seven days, and seven more days — fourteen days. ᴮ ⁶⁶ On the fifteenth day ᶜ he sent the people away. So they blessed the king and went to their homes ᴰ rejoicing and with happy hearts for all the goodness that the LORD had done for his servant David and for his people Israel.

THE LORD'S RESPONSE

9 When Solomon finished building the temple of the LORD, the royal palace, and all that Solomon desired to do, ² the LORD appeared to Solomon a second time just as he had appeared to him at Gibeon. ³ The LORD said to him: I have heard your prayer and petition you have made before me. I have consecrated this temple you have built, to put ᴱ my name there forever; my eyes and my heart will be there at all times.

⁴ As for you, if you walk before me as your father David walked, with a heart of integrity and in what is right, doing everything I have commanded you, and if you keep my statutes and ordinances, ⁵ I will establish your royal throne over Israel forever, as I promised your father David: You will never fail to have a man on the throne of Israel.

⁶ If you or your sons turn away from following me and do not keep my commands — my statutes that I have set before you — and if you go and serve other gods and bow in worship to them, ⁷ I will cut off Israel from the land I gave them, and I will reject ᶠ the temple I have sanctified for my name. Israel will become an object of scorn and ridicule among all the peoples. ⁸ Though this temple is now exalted, ᴳ everyone who passes by will be appalled and will scoff. ᴴ They will say: Why did the LORD do this to this land and this temple? ⁹ Then they will say: Because they abandoned the LORD their God who brought their ancestors out of the land of Egypt. They held on to other gods and bowed in worship to them and served them. Because of this, the LORD brought all this ruin on them.

KING HIRAM'S TWENTY TOWNS

¹⁰ At the end of twenty years during which Solomon had built the two houses, the LORD's temple and the royal palace — ¹¹ King Hiram of Tyre having supplied him with cedar and cypress logs and gold for his every wish — King Solomon gave Hiram twenty towns in the land of Galilee. ¹² So Hiram went out from Tyre to look over the towns that Solomon had given him, but he was not pleased with them. ¹³ So he said, "What are these towns you've given me, my brother?" So he called them the Land of Cabul, ᴵ as they are still called today. ¹⁴ Now Hiram had sent the king nine thousand pounds ᴶ of gold.

ᴬ8:65 Or *from Lebo-hamath* ᴮ8:65 Temple dedication lasted seven days, and the Festival of Shelters lasted seven days. ᶜ8:66 Lit *the eighth day* ᴰ8:66 Lit *tents* ᴱ9:3 Or *by putting* ᶠ9:7 Lit *send from my presence* ᴳ9:8 Some ancient versions read *temple will become a ruin* ᴴ9:8 Lit *hiss* ᴵ9:13 = Like Nothing ᴶ9:14 Lit *120 talents*

SOLOMON'S FORCED LABOR

¹⁵ This is the account of the forced labor that King Solomon had imposed to build the Lord's temple, his own palace, the supporting terraces, the wall of Jerusalem, and Hazor, Megiddo, and Gezer. ¹⁶ Pharaoh king of Egypt had attacked and captured Gezer. He then burned it, killed the Canaanites who lived in the city, and gave it as a dowry to his daughter, Solomon's wife. ¹⁷ Then Solomon rebuilt Gezer, Lower Beth-horon, ¹⁸ Baalath, Tamar^A,B in the Wilderness of Judah, ¹⁹ all the storage cities that belonged to Solomon, the chariot cities, the cavalry cities, and whatever Solomon desired to build in Jerusalem, Lebanon, or anywhere else in the land of his dominion.

²⁰ As for all the peoples who remained of the Amorites, Hethites, Perizzites, Hivites, and Jebusites, who were not Israelites — ²¹ their descendants who remained in the land after them, those whom the Israelites were unable to destroy completely — Solomon imposed forced labor on them; it is still this way today. ²² But Solomon did not consign the Israelites to slavery; they were soldiers, his servants, his commanders, his captains, and commanders of his chariots and his cavalry. ²³ These were the deputies who were over Solomon's work: 550 who supervised the people doing the work.

SOLOMON'S OTHER ACTIVITIES

²⁴ Pharaoh's daughter moved from the city of David to the house that Solomon had built for her; he then built the terraces.

²⁵ Three times a year Solomon offered burnt offerings and fellowship offerings on the altar he had built for the Lord, and he burned incense with them in the Lord's presence. So he completed the temple.

²⁶ King Solomon put together a fleet of ships at Ezion-geber, which is near Eloth on the shore of the Red Sea in the land of Edom. ²⁷ With the fleet, Hiram sent his servants, experienced seamen, along with Solomon's servants. ²⁸ They went to Ophir and acquired gold there — sixteen tons^C — and delivered it to Solomon.

THE QUEEN OF SHEBA

10 The queen of Sheba heard about Solomon's fame connected with the name of the Lord and came to test him with riddles. ² She came to Jerusalem with a very large entourage, with camels bearing spices, gold in great abundance, and precious stones. She came to Solomon and spoke to him about everything that was on her mind. ³ So Solomon answered all her questions; nothing was too difficult for the king to explain to her. ⁴ When the queen of Sheba observed all of Solomon's wisdom, the palace he had built, ⁵ the food at his table, his servants' residence, his attendants' service and their attire, his cupbearers, and the burnt offerings he offered at the Lord's temple, it took her breath away.

⁶ She said to the king, "The report I heard in my own country about your words and about your wisdom is true. ⁷ But I didn't believe the reports until I came and saw with my own eyes. Indeed, I was not even told half. Your wisdom and prosperity far exceed the report I heard. ⁸ How happy

---

^A 9:18 Alt Hb traditions, LXX, Syr, Tg, Vg read *Tadmor*; 2Ch 8:4   ^B 9:18 Tamar was a city in southern Judah; Ezk 47:19; 48:28.   ^C 9:28 Lit *420 talents* are your men.^A How happy are these servants of yours, who always stand in your presence hearing your wisdom. ⁹Blessed be the LORD your God! He delighted in you and put you on the throne of Israel, because of the LORD's eternal love for Israel. He has made you king to carry out justice and righteousness."

¹⁰Then she gave the king four and a half tons^B of gold, a great quantity of spices, and precious stones. Never again did such a quantity of spices arrive as those the queen of Sheba gave to King Solomon.

¹¹In addition, Hiram's fleet that carried gold from Ophir brought from Ophir a large quantity of almug^C wood and precious stones. ¹²The king made the almug wood into steps for the LORD's temple and the king's palace and into lyres and harps for the singers. Never before did such almug wood arrive, and the like has not been seen again.

¹³King Solomon gave the queen of Sheba her every desire — whatever she asked — besides what he had given her out of his royal bounty. Then she, along with her servants, returned to her own country.

SOLOMON'S WEALTH

¹⁴The weight of gold that came to Solomon annually was twenty-five tons,^D ¹⁵besides what came from merchants, traders' merchandise, and all the Arabian kings and governors of the land.

¹⁶King Solomon made two hundred large shields of hammered gold; fifteen pounds^E of gold went into each shield. ¹⁷He made three hundred small shields of hammered gold; nearly four pounds^F of gold went into each shield. The king put them in the House of the Forest of Lebanon.

¹⁸The king also made a large ivory throne and overlaid it with fine gold. ¹⁹The throne had six steps; there was a rounded top at the back of the throne, armrests on either side of the seat, and two lions standing beside the armrests. ²⁰Twelve lions were standing there on the six steps, one at each end. Nothing like it had ever been made in any other kingdom.

²¹All of King Solomon's drinking cups were gold, and all the utensils of the House of the Forest of Lebanon were pure gold. There was no silver, since it was considered as nothing in Solomon's time, ²²for the king had ships of Tarshish at sea with Hiram's fleet, and once every three years the ships of Tarshish would arrive bearing gold, silver, ivory, apes, and peacocks.^G

²³King Solomon surpassed all the kings of the world in riches and in wisdom. ²⁴The whole world wanted an audience with Solomon to hear the wisdom that God had put in his heart. ²⁵Every man would bring his annual tribute: items^H of silver and gold, clothing, weapons,^I spices, and horses and mules.

²⁶Solomon accumulated 1,400 chariots and 12,000 horsemen and stationed them in the chariot cities and with the king in Jerusalem. ²⁷The king made silver as common in Jerusalem as stones, and he made cedar as abundant as sycamore in the Judean foothills. ²⁸Solomon's horses were imported from Egypt and Kue.^J The king's traders bought them from Kue at the going price.

---

^A10:8 LXX, Syr read *your wives*   ^B10:10 Lit *120 talents*   ^C10:11 = algum in 2Ch 2:8; 9:10-11   ^D10:14 Lit *666 talents*   ^E10:16 Lit *600* (shekels)   ^F10:17 Lit *three minas*   ^G10:22 Or *baboons*   ^H10:25 Or *vessels, or weapons*   ^I10:25 Or *fragrant balsam*   ^J10:28 = Cilicia

²⁹ A chariot was imported from Egypt for fifteen pounds ᴬ of silver, and a horse for nearly four pounds. ᴮ In the same way, they exported them to all the kings of the Hittites and to the kings of Aram through their agents.

SOLOMON'S UNFAITHFULNESS TO GOD

11 King Solomon loved many foreign women in addition to Pharaoh's daughter: Moabite, Ammonite, Edomite, Sidonian, and Hittite women ² from the nations about which the LORD had told the Israelites, "You must not intermarry with them, and they must not intermarry with you, because they will turn your heart away to follow their gods." To these women Solomon was deeply attached ᶜ in love. ³ He had seven hundred wives who were princesses and three hundred who were concubines, and they turned his heart away.

⁴ When Solomon was old, his wives turned his heart away to follow other gods. He was not wholeheartedly devoted to the LORD his God, as his father David had been. ⁵ Solomon followed Ashtoreth, the goddess of the Sidonians, and Milcom, the abhorrent idol of the Ammonites. ⁶ Solomon did what was evil in the LORD's sight, and unlike his father David, he did not remain loyal to the LORD.

⁷ At that time, Solomon built a high place for Chemosh, the abhorrent idol of Moab, and for Milcom, ᴰ the abhorrent idol of the Ammonites, on the hill across from Jerusalem. ⁸ He did the same for all his foreign wives, who were burning incense and offering sacrifices to their gods.

⁹ The LORD was angry with Solomon, because his heart had turned away from the LORD, the God of Israel, who had appeared to him twice. ¹⁰ He had commanded him about this, so that he would not follow other gods, but Solomon did not do what the LORD had commanded.

¹¹ Then the LORD said to Solomon, "Since you have done this ᴱ and did not keep my covenant and my statutes, which I commanded you, I will tear the kingdom away from you and give it to your servant. ¹² However, I will not do it during your lifetime for the sake of your father David; I will tear it out of your son's hand. ¹³ Yet I will not tear the entire kingdom away from him. I will give one tribe to your son for the sake of my servant David and for the sake of Jerusalem that I chose."

SOLOMON'S ENEMIES

¹⁴ So the LORD raised up Hadad the Edomite as an enemy against Solomon. He was of the royal family in Edom. ¹⁵ Earlier, when David was in Edom, Joab, the commander of the army, had gone to bury the dead and had struck down every male in Edom. ¹⁶ For Joab and all Israel had remained there six months, until he had killed every male in Edom. ¹⁷ Hadad fled to Egypt, along with some Edomites from his father's servants. At the time Hadad was a small boy. ¹⁸ Hadad and his men set out from Midian and went to Paran. They took men with them from Paran and went to Egypt, to Pharaoh king of Egypt, who gave Hadad a house, ordered that he be given food, and gave him land. ¹⁹ Pharaoh liked Hadad so much ᶠ that he gave him a wife, the sister of his own wife, Queen Tahpenes. ²⁰ Tahpenes's sister gave birth to Hadad's son

---

ᴬ10:29 Lit 600 shekels   ᴮ10:29 Lit 150 shekels   ᶜ11:2 Lit Solomon clung
ᴰ11:7 Lit Molech   ᴱ11:11 Lit "Since this was with you   ᶠ11:19 Lit Hadad found much favor in Pharaoh's eyes

Genubath. Tahpenes herself weaned him in Pharaoh's palace, and Genubath lived there along with Pharaoh's sons.

²¹ When Hadad heard in Egypt that David rested with his fathers and that Joab, the commander of the army, was dead, Hadad said to Pharaoh, "Let me leave, so I may go to my own country."

²² But Pharaoh asked him, "What do you lack here with me for you to want to go back to your own country?"

"Nothing," he replied, "but please let me leave."

²³ God raised up Rezon son of Eliada as an enemy against Solomon. Rezon had fled from his master King Hadadezer of Zobah ²⁴ and gathered men to himself. He became leader of a raiding party when David killed the Zobaites. He ᴬ went to Damascus, lived there, and became king in Damascus. ²⁵ Rezon was Israel's enemy throughout Solomon's reign, adding to the trouble Hadad had caused. He reigned over Aram ᴮ and loathed Israel.

²⁶ Now Solomon's servant, Jeroboam son of Nebat, was an Ephraimite from Zeredah. His widowed mother's name was Zeruah. Jeroboam rebelled against Solomon, ²⁷ and this is the reason he rebelled against the king: Solomon had built the supporting terraces and repaired the opening in the wall of the city of his father David. ²⁸ Now the man Jeroboam was capable, and Solomon noticed the young man because he was getting things done. So he appointed him over the entire labor force of the house of Joseph.

²⁹ During that time, the prophet Ahijah the Shilonite met Jeroboam on the road as Jeroboam came out of Jerusalem. Now Ahijah had wrapped himself with a new cloak, and the two of them were alone in the open field. ³⁰ Then Ahijah took hold of the new cloak he had on, tore it into twelve pieces, ³¹ and said to Jeroboam, "Take ten pieces for yourself, for this is what the LORD God of Israel says: 'I am about to tear the kingdom out of Solomon's hand. I will give you ten tribes, ³² but one tribe will remain his for the sake of my servant David and for the sake of Jerusalem, the city I chose out of all the tribes of Israel. ³³ For they have abandoned me; they have bowed down to Ashtoreth, the goddess of the Sidonians, to Chemosh, the god of Moab, and to Milcom, the god of the Ammonites. They have not walked in my ways to do what is right in my sight and to carry out my statutes and my judgments as his father David did.

³⁴ " 'However, I will not take the whole kingdom from him but will let him be ruler all the days of his life for the sake of my servant David, whom I chose and who kept my commands and my statutes. ³⁵ I will take ten tribes of the kingdom from his son and give them to you. ³⁶ I will give one tribe to his son, so that my servant David will always have a lamp before me in Jerusalem, the city I chose for myself to put my name there. ³⁷ I will appoint you, and you will reign as king over all you want, and you will be king over Israel.

³⁸ " 'After that, if you obey all I command you, walk in my ways, and do what is right in my sight in order to keep my statutes and my commands as my servant David did, I will be with you. I will build you a lasting dynasty just as I built for David, and I will give you Israel. ³⁹ I will humble David's descendants, because of their unfaithfulness, but not forever.' " ᶜ

ᴬ11:24 LXX; Hb reads *They*   ᴮ11:25 Some Hb mss, LXX, Syr read *Edom*
ᶜ11:38-39 LXX omits *and I will give . . . but not forever*

⁴⁰ Therefore, Solomon tried to kill Jeroboam, but he fled to Egypt, to King Shishak of Egypt, where he remained until Solomon's death.

SOLOMON'S DEATH

⁴¹ The rest of the events of Solomon's reign, along with all his accomplishments and his wisdom, are written in the Book of Solomon's Events. ⁴² The length of Solomon's reign in Jerusalem over all Israel totaled forty years. ⁴³ Solomon rested with his fathers and was buried in the city of his father David. His son Rehoboam became king in his place.

THE KINGDOM DIVIDED

12 Then Rehoboam went to Shechem, for all Israel had gone to Shechem to make him king. ² When Jeroboam son of Nebat heard about it, he stayed in Egypt, where he had fled from King Solomon's presence. Jeroboam stayed in Egypt.ᴬ ³ But they summoned him, and Jeroboam and the whole assembly of Israel came and spoke to Rehoboam: ⁴ "Your father made our yoke harsh. You, therefore, lighten your father's harsh service and the heavy yoke he put on us, and we will serve you."

⁵ Rehoboam replied, "Go away for three days and then return to me." So the people left. ⁶ Then King Rehoboam consulted with the elders who had served his father Solomon when he was alive, asking, "How do you advise me to respond to this people?"

⁷ They replied, "Today if you will be a servant to this people and serve them, and if you respond to them by speaking kind words to them, they will be your servants forever."

⁸ But he rejected the advice of the elders who had advised him and consulted with the young men who had grown up with him and attended him. ⁹ He asked them, "What message do you advise that we send back to this people who said to me, 'Lighten the yoke your father put on us'?"

¹⁰ Then the young men who had grown up with him told him, "This is what you should say to this people who said to you, 'Your father made our yoke heavy, but you, make it lighter on us!' This is what you should tell them: 'My little finger is thicker than my father's waist! ¹¹ Although my father burdened you with a heavy yoke, I will add to your yoke; my father disciplined you with whips, but I will discipline you with barbed whips.'"ᴮ

¹² So Jeroboam and all the people came to Rehoboam on the third day, as the king had ordered: "Return to me on the third day." ¹³ Then the king answered the people harshly. He rejected the advice the elders had given him ¹⁴ and spoke to them according to the young men's advice: "My father made your yoke heavy, but I will add to your yoke; my father disciplined you with whips, but I will discipline you with barbed whips."

¹⁵ The king did not listen to the people, because this turn of events came from the LORD to carry out his word, which the LORD had spoken through Ahijah the Shilonite to Jeroboam son of Nebat. ¹⁶ When all Israel saw that the king had not listened to them, the people answered him:

> What portion do we have in David?
> We have no inheritance in the son of Jesse.

ᴬ 12:2 LXX, Vg read *Jeroboam returned from Egypt;* 2Ch 10:2   ᴮ 12:11 Lit *with scorpions,* also in v. 14

Israel, return to your tents;

David, now look after your own house!

So Israel went to their tents, [17] but Rehoboam reigned over the Israelites living in the cities of Judah.

[18] Then King Rehoboam sent Adoram, [A] who was in charge of forced labor, but all Israel stoned him to death. King Rehoboam managed to get into the chariot and flee to Jerusalem. [19] Israel is still in rebellion against the house of David today.

REHOBOAM IN JERUSALEM

[20] When all Israel heard that Jeroboam had come back, they summoned him to the assembly and made him king over all Israel. No one followed the house of David except the tribe of Judah alone. [21] When Rehoboam arrived in Jerusalem, he mobilized one hundred eighty thousand fit young soldiers from the entire house of Judah and the tribe of Benjamin to fight against the house of Israel to restore the kingdom to Rehoboam son of Solomon. [22] But the word of God came to Shemaiah, the man of God: [23] "Say to Rehoboam son of Solomon, king of Judah, to the whole house of Judah and Benjamin, and to the rest of the people, [24] 'This is what the LORD says: You are not to march up and fight against your brothers, the Israelites. Each of you return home, for this situation is from me.'"

So they listened to the word of the LORD and went back according to the word of the LORD.

JEROBOAM'S IDOLATRY

[25] Jeroboam built Shechem in the hill country of Ephraim and lived there. From there he went out and built Penuel. [26] Jeroboam said to himself, "The kingdom might now return to the house of David. [27] If these people regularly go to offer sacrifices in the LORD's temple in Jerusalem, the heart of these people will return to their lord, King Rehoboam of Judah. They will kill me and go back to the king of Judah." [28] So the king sought advice.

Then he made two golden calves, and he said to the people, "Going to Jerusalem is too difficult for you. Israel, here are your gods [B] who brought you up from the land of Egypt." [29] He set up one in Bethel, and put the other in Dan. [30] This led to sin; the people walked in procession before one of the calves all the way to Dan. [C]

[31] Jeroboam also made shrines [D] on the high places and made priests from the ranks of the people who were not Levites. [32] Jeroboam made a festival in the eighth month on the fifteenth day of the month, like the festival in Judah. He offered sacrifices on the altar; he made this offering in Bethel to sacrifice to the calves he had made. He also stationed the priests in Bethel for the high places he had made. [33] He offered sacrifices on [E] the altar he had set up in Bethel on the fifteenth day of the eighth month. He chose this month on his own. He made a festival for the Israelites, offered sacrifices on the altar, and burned incense.

[A] 12:18 LXX reads *Adoniram*; 1Kg 4:6; 5:14   [B] 12:28 Or *here is your God*, or *here is your god*   [C] 12:30 Some LXX mss read *calves to Bethel and the other to Dan*   [D] 12:31 Lit *a house*   [E] 12:33 Or *He went up to*

JUDGMENT ON JEROBOAM

13 A man of God came, however, from Judah to Bethel by the word of the LORD while Jeroboam was standing beside the altar to burn incense. ² The man of God cried out against the altar by the word of the LORD: "Altar, altar, this is what the LORD says, 'A son will be born to the house of David, named Josiah, and he will sacrifice on you the priests of the high places who are burning incense on you. Human bones will be burned on you.'" ³ He gave a sign that day. He said, "This is the sign that the LORD has spoken: 'The altar will now be ripped apart, and the ashes that are on it will be poured out.'"

⁴ When the king heard the message that the man of God had cried out against the altar at Bethel, Jeroboam stretched out his hand from the altar and said, "Arrest him!" But the hand he stretched out against him withered, and he could not pull it back to himself. ⁵ The altar was ripped apart, and the ashes poured from the altar, according to the sign that the man of God had given by the word of the LORD.

⁶ Then the king responded to the man of God, "Plead for the favor of the LORD your God and pray for me so that my hand may be restored to me." So the man of God pleaded for the favor of the LORD, and the king's hand was restored to him and became as it had been at first.

⁷ Then the king declared to the man of God, "Come home with me, refresh yourself, and I'll give you a reward."

⁸ But the man of God replied, "If you were to give me half your house, I still wouldn't go with you, and I wouldn't eat food or drink water in this place, ⁹ for this is what I was commanded by the word of the LORD: 'You must not eat food or drink water or go back the way you came.'" ¹⁰ So he went another way; he did not go back by the way he had come to Bethel.

THE OLD PROPHET AND THE MAN OF GOD

¹¹ Now a certain old prophet was living in Bethel. His son^A came and told him all the deeds that the man of God had done that day in Bethel. His sons also told their father the words that he had spoken to the king. ¹² Then their father asked them, "Which way did he go?" His sons had seen^B the way taken by the man of God who had come from Judah. ¹³ Then he said to his sons, "Saddle the donkey for me." So they saddled the donkey for him, and he got on it. ¹⁴ He followed the man of God and found him sitting under an oak tree. He asked him, "Are you the man of God who came from Judah?"

"I am," he said.

¹⁵ Then he said to him, "Come home with me and eat some food."

¹⁶ But he answered, "I cannot go back with you or accompany you; I will not eat food or drink water with you in this place. ¹⁷ For a message came to me by the word of the LORD: 'You must not eat food or drink water there or go back by the way you came.'"

¹⁸ He said to him, "I am also a prophet like you. An angel spoke to me by the word of the LORD: 'Bring him back with you to your house so that he may eat food and drink water.'" The old prophet deceived him, ¹⁹ and the man of God went back with him, ate food in his house, and drank water.

---

^A13:11 Some Hb mss, LXX, Syr, Vg read *sons*   ^B13:12 LXX, Syr, Tg, Vg read *sons showed him*

²⁰ While they were sitting at the table, the word of the LORD came to the prophet who had brought him back, ²¹ and the prophet cried out to the man of God who had come from Judah, "This is what the LORD says: 'Because you rebelled against the LORD's command and did not keep the command that the LORD your God commanded you — ²² but you went back and ate food and drank water in the place that he said to you, "Do not eat food and do not drink water" — your corpse will never reach the grave of your fathers.'"

²³ So after he had eaten food and after he had drunk, the old prophet saddled the donkey for the prophet he had brought back. ²⁴ When he left,ᴬ a lion attackedᴮ him along the way and killed him. His corpse was thrown on the road, and the donkey was standing beside it; the lion was standing beside the corpse too.

²⁵ There were men passing by who saw the corpse thrown on the road and the lion standing beside it, and they went and spoke about it in the city where the old prophet lived. ²⁶ When the prophet who had brought him back from his way heard about it, he said, "He is the man of God who disobeyed the LORD's command. The LORD has given him to the lion, and it has mauled and killed him, according to the word of the LORD that he spoke to him."

²⁷ Then the old prophet instructed his sons, "Saddle the donkey for me." They saddled it, ²⁸ and he went and found the corpse thrown on the road with the donkey and the lion standing beside the corpse. The lion had not eaten the corpse or mauled the donkey. ²⁹ So the prophet lifted the corpse of the man of God and laid it on the donkey and brought it back. The old prophet came into the city to mourn and to bury him. ³⁰ Then he laid the corpse in his own grave, and they mourned over him: "Oh, my brother!"

³¹ After he had buried him, he said to his sons, "When I die, bury me in the grave where the man of God is buried; lay my bones beside his bones, ³² for the message that he cried out by the word of the LORD against the altar in Bethel and against all the shrines of the high places in the cities of Samaria is certain to happen."

³³ Even after this, Jeroboam did not repent of his evil way but again made priests for the high places from the ranks of the people. He ordained whoever so desired it, and they became priests of the high places. ³⁴ This was the sin that caused the house of Jeroboam to be cut off and obliterated from the face of the earth.

DISASTER ON THE HOUSE OF JEROBOAM

14 At that time Abijah son of Jeroboam became sick. ² Jeroboam said to his wife, "Go disguise yourself, so they won't know that you're Jeroboam's wife, and go to Shiloh. The prophet Ahijah is there; it was he who told about me becoming king over this people. ³ Take with you ten loaves of bread, some cakes, and a jar of honey, and go to him. He will tell you what will happen to the boy."

⁴ Jeroboam's wife did that: she went to Shiloh and arrived at Ahijah's house. Ahijah could not see; he was blindᶜ due to his age. ⁵ But the LORD had said to Ahijah, "Jeroboam's wife is coming soon to ask you about her son, for he is sick. You are to say such and such to her. When she arrives, she will be disguised."

ᴬ13:23-24 LXX reads *donkey, and he turned* ²⁴*and left, and*   ᴮ13:24 Lit *met*
ᶜ14:4 Lit *see, for his eyes stood*; 1Sm 4:15

⁶ When Ahijah heard the sound of her feet entering the door, he said, "Come in, wife of Jeroboam! Why are you disguised? I have bad news for you. ⁷ Go tell Jeroboam, 'This is what the LORD God of Israel says: I raised you up from among the people, appointed you ruler over my people Israel, ⁸ tore the kingdom away from the house of David, and gave it to you. But you were not like my servant David, who kept my commands and followed me with all his heart, doing only what is right in my sight. ⁹ You behaved more wickedly than all who were before you. In order to anger me, you have proceeded to make for yourself other gods and cast images, but you have flung me behind your back. ¹⁰ Because of all this, I am about to bring disaster on the house of Jeroboam:

I will wipe out all of Jeroboam's males,ᴬ
both slave and free,ᴮ in Israel;
I will sweep away the house of Jeroboam
as one sweeps away dung until it is all gone!
¹¹ Anyone who belongs to Jeroboam and dies in the city,
the dogs will eat,
and anyone who dies in the field,
the birdsᶜ will eat,
for the LORD has spoken!'

¹² "As for you, get up and go to your house. When your feet enter the city, the boy will die. ¹³ All Israel will mourn for him and bury him. He alone out of Jeroboam's house will be given a proper burial because out of the house of Jeroboam something favorable to the LORD God of Israel was found in him. ¹⁴ The LORD will raise up for himself a king over Israel, who will wipe out the house of Jeroboam. This is the day, yes,ᴰ even today! ¹⁵ For the LORD will strike Israel so that they willᴱ shake as a reed shakes in water. He will uproot Israel from this good soil that he gave to their ancestors. He will scatter them beyond the Euphrates because they made their Asherah poles, angering the LORD. ¹⁶ He will give up Israel because of Jeroboam's sins that he committed and caused Israel to commit."

¹⁷ Then Jeroboam's wife got up and left and went to Tirzah. As she was crossing the threshold of the house, the boy died. ¹⁸ He was buried, and all Israel mourned for him, according to the word of the LORD he had spoken through his servant the prophet Ahijah.

¹⁹ As for the rest of the events of Jeroboam's reign, how he waged war and how he reigned, note that they are written in the Historical Record of Israel's Kings. ²⁰ The length of Jeroboam's reign was twenty-two years. He rested with his fathers, and his son Nadab became king in his place.

JUDAH'S KING REHOBOAM

²¹ Now Rehoboam, Solomon's son, reigned in Judah. Rehoboam was forty-one years old when he became king; he reigned seventeen years in Jerusalem, the city where the LORD had chosen from all the tribes of Israel to put his name. Rehoboam's mother's name was Naamah the Ammonite.

ᴬ14:10 Lit *eliminate Jeroboam's one who urinates against the wall*   ᴮ14:10 Or *males, even the weak and impaired*; Hb obscure   ᶜ14:11 Lit *birds of the sky*
ᴰ14:14 Hb obscure   ᴱ14:15 *so that they will* supplied for clarity

²² Judah did what was evil in the LORD's sight. They provoked him to jealous anger more than all that their ancestors had done with the sins they committed. ²³ They also built for themselves high places, sacred pillars, and Asherah poles on every high hill and under every green tree; ²⁴ there were even male cult prostitutes in the land. They imitated all the detestable practices of the nations the LORD had dispossessed before the Israelites.

²⁵ In the fifth year of King Rehoboam, King Shishak of Egypt went to war against Jerusalem. ²⁶ He seized the treasuries of the LORD's temple and the treasuries of the royal palace. He took everything. He took all the gold shields that Solomon had made. ²⁷ King Rehoboam made bronze shields to replace them and committed them into the care of the captains of the guards^A who protected the entrance to the king's palace. ²⁸ Whenever the king entered the LORD's temple, the guards would carry the shields, then they would take them back to the armory.^B

²⁹ The rest of the events of Rehoboam's reign, along with all his accomplishments, are written about in the Historical Record of Judah's Kings. ³⁰ There was war between Rehoboam and Jeroboam throughout their reigns. ³¹ Rehoboam rested with his fathers and was buried with his fathers in the city of David. His mother's name was Naamah the Ammonite. His son Abijam^C became king in his place.

JUDAH'S KING ABIJAM

15 In the eighteenth year of Israel's King Jeroboam son of Nebat, Abijam became king over Judah, ² and he reigned three years in Jerusalem. His mother's name was Maacah daughter^D of Abishalom.

³ Abijam walked in all the sins his father before him had committed, and he was not wholeheartedly devoted to the LORD his God as his ancestor David had been. ⁴ But for the sake of David, the LORD his God gave him a lamp in Jerusalem by raising up his son after him and by preserving Jerusalem. ⁵ For David did what was right in the LORD's sight, and he did not turn aside from anything he had commanded him all the days of his life, except in the matter of Uriah the Hethite.

⁶ There had been war between Rehoboam and Jeroboam all the days of Rehoboam's life. ⁷ The rest of the events of Abijam's reign, along with all his accomplishments, are written in the Historical Record of Judah's Kings. There was also war between Abijam and Jeroboam. ⁸ Abijam rested with his fathers and was buried in the city of David. His son Asa became king in his place.

JUDAH'S KING ASA

⁹ In the twentieth year of Israel's King Jeroboam, Asa became king of Judah, ¹⁰ and he reigned forty-one years in Jerusalem. His grandmother's^E name was Maacah daughter of Abishalom.

¹¹ Asa did what was right in the LORD's sight, as his ancestor David had done. ¹² He banished the male cult prostitutes from the land and removed all of the idols that his fathers had made. ¹³ He also removed his grandmother^F

---

^A14:27 Lit *the runners*   ^B14:28 Lit *the chamber of the runners*   ^C14:31 = Abijah in 2Ch 13   ^D15:2 Possibly granddaughter, also in v. 10; 2Ch 13:2   ^E15:10 Lit *mother's*   ^F15:13 Lit *mother*

527

Maacah from being queen mother because she had made an obscene image of Asherah. Asa chopped down her obscene image and burned it in the Kidron Valley. ¹⁴ The high places were not taken away, but Asa was wholeheartedly devoted to the LORD his entire life. ¹⁵ He brought his father's consecrated gifts and his own consecrated gifts into the LORD's temple: silver, gold, and utensils.

¹⁶ There was war between Asa and King Baasha of Israel throughout their reigns. ¹⁷ Israel's King Baasha went to war against Judah. He built Ramah in order to keep anyone from leaving or coming to King Asa of Judah. ¹⁸ So Asa withdrew all the silver and gold that remained in the treasuries of the LORD's temple and the treasuries of the royal palace and gave it to his servants. Then King Asa sent them to Ben-hadad son of Tabrimmon son of Hezion king of Aram who lived in Damascus, saying, ¹⁹ "There is a treaty between me and you, between my father and your father. Look, I have sent you a gift of silver and gold. Go and break your treaty with King Baasha of Israel so that he will withdraw from me."

²⁰ Ben-hadad listened to King Asa and sent the commanders of his armies against the cities of Israel. He attacked Ijon, Dan, Abel-beth-maacah, all Chinnereth, and the whole land of Naphtali. ²¹ When Baasha heard about it, he quit building Ramah and stayed in Tirzah. ²² Then King Asa gave a command to everyone without exception in Judah, and they carried away the stones of Ramah and the timbers Baasha had built it with. Then King Asa built Geba of Benjamin and Mizpah with them.

²³ The rest of all the events of Asa's reign, along with all his might, all his accomplishments, and the cities he built, are written in the Historical Record of Judah's Kings. But in his old age he developed a disease in his feet. ²⁴ Then Asa rested with his fathers and was buried in the city of his ancestor David. His son Jehoshaphat became king in his place.

ISRAEL'S KING NADAB

²⁵ Nadab son of Jeroboam became king over Israel in the second year of Judah's King Asa; he reigned over Israel two years. ²⁶ Nadab did what was evil in the LORD's sight and walked in the ways of his father and the sin he had caused Israel to commit.

²⁷ Then Baasha son of Ahijah of the house of Issachar conspired against Nadab, and Baasha struck him down at Gibbethon of the Philistines while Nadab and all Israel were besieging Gibbethon. ²⁸ In the third year of Judah's King Asa, Baasha killed Nadab and reigned in his place.

²⁹ When Baasha became king, he struck down the entire house of Jeroboam. He did not leave Jeroboam any survivors butᴬ destroyed his family according to the word of the LORD he had spoken through his servant Ahijah the Shilonite. ³⁰ This was because Jeroboam had angeredᴮ the LORD God of Israel by the sins he had committed and had caused Israel to commit.

³¹ The rest of the events of Nadab's reign, along with all his accomplishments, are written in the Historical Record of Israel's Kings. ³² There was war between Asa and King Baasha of Israel throughout their reigns.

ᴬ15:29 Lit Jeroboam anyone breathing until he   ᴮ15:30 Lit provoked in the provocation of

ISRAEL'S KING BAASHA

³³ In the third year of Judah's King Asa, Baasha son of Ahijah became king over all Israel, and he reigned in Tirzah twenty-four years. ³⁴ He did what was evil in the LORD's sight and walked in the ways of Jeroboam and the sin he had caused Israel to commit.

16 Now the word of the LORD came to Jehu son of Hanani against Baasha: ² "Because I raised you up from the dust and made you ruler over my people Israel, but you have walked in the ways of Jeroboam and have caused my people Israel to sin, angering me with their sins, ³ take note: I will eradicate Baasha and his house, and I will make your house like the house of Jeroboam son of Nebat:

⁴   Anyone who belongs to Baasha and dies in the city,
     the dogs will eat,
     and anyone who is his and dies in the field,
     the birds ᴬ will eat."

⁵ The rest of the events of Baasha's reign, along with all his accomplishments and might, are written in the Historical Record of Israel's Kings. ⁶ Baasha rested with his fathers and was buried in Tirzah. His son Elah became king in his place. ⁷ But through the prophet Jehu son of Hanani the word of the LORD also had come against Baasha and against his house because of all the evil he had done in the LORD's sight. His actions angered the LORD, and Baasha's house became like the house of Jeroboam, because he had struck it down.

ISRAEL'S KING ELAH

⁸ In the twenty-sixth year of Judah's King Asa, Elah son of Baasha became king over Israel, and he reigned in Tirzah two years.

⁹ His servant Zimri, commander of half his chariots, conspired against him while Elah was in Tirzah getting drunk in the house of Arza, who was in charge of the household at Tirzah. ¹⁰ In the twenty-seventh year of Judah's King Asa, Zimri went in, struck Elah down, killing him. Then Zimri became king in his place.

¹¹ When he became king, as soon as he was seated on his throne, Zimri struck down the entire house of Baasha. He did not leave a single male, ᴮ including his kinsmen and his friends. ¹² So Zimri destroyed the entire house of Baasha, according to the word of the LORD he had spoken against Baasha through the prophet Jehu. ¹³ This happened because of all the sins of Baasha and those of his son Elah, which they committed and caused Israel to commit, angering the LORD God of Israel with their worthless idols.

¹⁴ The rest of the events of Elah's reign, along with all his accomplishments, are written in the Historical Record of Israel's Kings.

ISRAEL'S KING ZIMRI

¹⁵ In the twenty-seventh year of Judah's King Asa, Zimri became king for seven days in Tirzah. Now the troops were encamped against Gibbethon of the Philistines. ¹⁶ When these troops heard that Zimri had not only conspired but had also struck down the king, then all Israel made Omri, the army

---

ᴬ 16:4 Lit birds of the sky   ᴮ 16:11 Lit leave him one who urinates against the wall

PUSHY BROADS AND
REDEEMING LOVE

1 KINGS 16:29–17:24; 1 KINGS 18:1-6; 1 KINGS 19:1-5; 1 KINGS 21;
PSALM 86:5; PROVERBS 6:16-19

When I was a kid, my mother cautioned me, "Whatever you do, don't turn into a pushy broad." I assured her she had nothing to worry about. No way did I want to become the kind of woman who shoved people around, barked out orders, or made demands.

Then I grew up and became a pushy broad. Not in public, of course. Just at home with my darling husband. "Clean that up." "Move that over." "Carry that out." Reading the words Jezebel said to her husband, Ahab—"Now, exercise your royal power over Israel" (1Kg 21:7)—I have to admit, I'm hearing my voice.

Way too much like Jezebel. Not at all like Jesus.

It's a good thing God doesn't give up on us. When we open His Word, He opens our hearts, washes us clean, and makes us new. Even pushy broads like me can experience the power of God's loving-kindness, which recreates us in the image of His Son and brings forth fruit worthy of His name.

Jezebel, though, never sought God's love. She was all about Baal, the false god her father worshiped. A bad branch on a bad tree bears bad fruit, guaranteed. When the Bible tells us, "The LORD hates six things; in fact, seven are de-testable to him," Jezebel had them all: "arrogant eyes, a lying tongue, hands that shed innocent blood, a heart that plots wicked schemes, feet eager to run to evil, a lying witness who gives false testimony, and one who stirs up trouble among brothers" (Pr 6:16-19).

Can we find a glimmer of light in this sordid story? Some shimmering truth that shows us God is still at work in the lives of His people, then and now?

Take a look at Jezebel's husband, who tore his clothes and put on sackcloth and ashes. We definitely see some repentance going on there, even after this man did more to make God angry than all the kings of Israel who came before him (1Kg 16:33; 21:27).

When the Lord saw the changed attitude of Ahab's heart, demonstrated by his actions, He said to the prophet Elijah, "Have you seen how Ahab has humbled himself before me?" (1Kg 21:29). God was merciful to Ahab and postponed His wrath, all because Ahab sought His forgiveness. Despite the king's many sins, his humility bore healthy fruit.

God stands ready to shower His mercy on us. Not because of our goodness, but because of His goodness. Not because of our on-again, off-again obedience, but because of His never-ending, ever-redeeming love.

"For you, Lord, are kind and ready to forgive, abounding in faithful love to all who call on you."

PSALM 86:5

---

commander, king over Israel that very day in the camp. [17] Omri along with all Israel marched up from Gibbethon and besieged Tirzah. [18] When Zimri saw that the city was captured, he entered the citadel of the royal palace and burned it down over himself. He died [19] because of the sin he committed by doing what was evil in the LORD's sight and by walking in the ways of Jeroboam and the sin he caused Israel to commit.

[20] The rest of the events of Zimri's reign, along with the conspiracy that he instigated, are written in the Historical Record of Israel's Kings. [21] At that time the people of Israel were divided: half the people followed Tibni son of Ginath, to make him king, and half followed Omri. [22] However, the people who followed Omri proved stronger than those who followed Tibni son of Ginath. So Tibni died and Omri became king.

ISRAEL'S KING OMRI

[23] In the thirty-first year of Judah's King Asa, Omri became king over Israel, and he reigned twelve years. He reigned six years in Tirzah, [24] then he bought the hill of Samaria from Shemer for 150 pounds[A] of silver, and he built up the hill. He named the city he built Samaria[B] based on the name Shemer, the owner of the hill.

[25] Omri did what was evil in the LORD's sight; he did more evil than all who were before him. [26] He walked in all the ways of Jeroboam son of Nebat in every respect and continued in his sins that he caused Israel to commit, angering the LORD God of Israel with their worthless idols. [27] The rest of the events of Omri's reign, along with his accomplishments and the might he exercised, are written in the Historical Record of Israel's Kings. [28] Omri rested with his fathers and was buried in Samaria. His son Ahab became king in his place.

ISRAEL'S KING AHAB

[29] Ahab son of Omri became king over Israel in the thirty-eighth year of Judah's King Asa; Ahab son of Omri reigned over Israel in Samaria twenty-two years. [30] But Ahab son of Omri did what was evil in the LORD's sight more than all who were before him. [31] Then, as if following the sin of Jeroboam son of Nebat were not enough, he married Jezebel, the daughter of Ethbaal king of the Sidonians, and then proceeded to serve Baal and bow in worship to him. [32] He set up an altar for Baal in the temple of Baal that he had built in Samaria. [33] Ahab also made an Asherah pole. Ahab did more to anger the LORD God of Israel than all the kings of Israel who were before him.

[34] During his reign, Hiel the Bethelite built Jericho. At the cost of Abiram his firstborn, he laid its foundation, and at the cost of Segub his youngest, he finished its gates, according to the word of the LORD he had spoken through Joshua son of Nun.

ELIJAH ANNOUNCES FAMINE

17 Now Elijah the Tishbite, from the Gilead settlers,[C] said to Ahab, "As the LORD God of Israel lives, in whose presence I stand, there will be no dew or rain during these years except by my command!"

A 16:24 Lit for two talents   B 16:24 = Belonging to Shemer's Clan   C 17:1 LXX reads from Tishbe of Gilead

² Then the word of the LORD came to him: ³ "Leave here, turn eastward, and hide at the Wadi Cherith where it enters the Jordan. ⁴ You are to drink from the wadi. I have commanded the ravens to provide for you there."

⁵ So he proceeded to do what the LORD commanded. Elijah left and lived at the Wadi Cherith where it enters the Jordan. ⁶ The ravens kept bringing him bread and meat in the morning and in the evening, and he would drink from the wadi. ⁷ After a while, the wadi dried up because there had been no rain in the land.

ELIJAH AND THE WIDOW

⁸ Then the word of the LORD came to him: ⁹ "Get up, go to Zarephath that belongs to Sidon and stay there. Look, I have commanded a woman who is a widow to provide for you there." ¹⁰ So Elijah got up and went to Zarephath. When he arrived at the city gate, there was a widow gathering wood. Elijah called to her and said, "Please bring me a little water in a cup and let me drink." ¹¹ As she went to get it, he called to her and said, "Please bring me a piece of bread in your hand."

¹² But she said, "As the LORD your God lives, I don't have anything baked — only a handful of flour in the jar and a bit of oil in the jug. Just now, I am gathering a couple of sticks in order to go prepare it for myself and my son so we can eat it and die."

¹³ Then Elijah said to her, "Don't be afraid; go and do as you have said. But first make me a small loaf from it and bring it out to me. Afterward, you may make some for yourself and your son, ¹⁴ for this is what the LORD God of Israel says, 'The flour jar will not become empty and the oil jug will not run dry until the day the LORD sends rain on the surface of the land.'"

¹⁵ So she proceeded to do according to the word of Elijah. Then the woman, Elijah, and her household ate for many days. ¹⁶ The flour jar did not become empty, and the oil jug did not run dry, according to the word of the LORD he had spoken through^A Elijah.

THE WIDOW'S SON RAISED

¹⁷ After this, the son of the woman who owned the house became ill. His illness got worse until he stopped breathing. ¹⁸ She said to Elijah, "Man of God, why are you here? Have you come to call attention to my iniquity so that my son is put to death?"

¹⁹ But Elijah said to her, "Give me your son." So he took him from her arms, brought him up to the upstairs room where he was staying, and laid him on his own bed. ²⁰ Then he cried out to the LORD and said, "LORD my God, have you also brought tragedy on the widow I am staying with by killing her son?" ²¹ Then he stretched himself out over the boy three times. He cried out to the LORD and said, "LORD my God, please let this boy's life come into him again!"

²² So the LORD listened to Elijah, and the boy's life came into him again, and he lived. ²³ Then Elijah took the boy, brought him down from the upstairs room into the house, and gave him to his mother. Elijah said, "Look, your son is alive."

²⁴ Then the woman said to Elijah, "Now I know you are a man of God and the LORD's word from your mouth is true."

^A 17:16 Lit by the hand of

ELIJAH'S MESSAGE TO AHAB

18

After a long time, the word of the LORD came to Elijah in the third year: "Go and present yourself to Ahab. I will send rain on the surface of the land." ² So Elijah went to present himself to Ahab.

The famine was severe in Samaria. ³ Ahab called for Obadiah, who was in charge of the palace. Obadiah was a man who greatly feared the LORD ⁴ and took a hundred prophets and hid them, fifty men to a cave, and provided them with food and water when Jezebel slaughtered the LORD's prophets. ⁵ Ahab said to Obadiah, "Go throughout the land to every spring and to every wadi. Perhaps we'll find grass so we can keep the horses and mules alive and not have to destroy any cattle." ⁶ They divided the land between them in order to cover it. Ahab went one way by himself, and Obadiah went the other way by himself.

⁷ While Obadiah was walking along the road, Elijah suddenly met him. When Obadiah recognized him, he fell facedown and said, "Is it you, my lord Elijah?"

⁸ "It is I," he replied. "Go tell your lord, 'Elijah is here!'"ᴬ

⁹ But Obadiah said, "What sin have I committed, that you are handing your servant over to Ahab to put me to death? ¹⁰ As the LORD your God lives, there is no nation or kingdom where my lord has not sent someone to search for you. When they said, 'He is not here,' he made that kingdom or nation swear they had not found you.

¹¹ "Now you say, 'Go tell your lord, "Elijah is here!"' ¹² But when I leave you, the Spirit of the LORD may carry you off to some place I don't know. Then when I go report to Ahab and he doesn't find you, he will kill me. But I, your servant, have feared the LORD from my youth. ¹³ Wasn't it reported to my lord what I did when Jezebel slaughtered the LORD's prophets? I hid a hundred of the prophets of the LORD, fifty men to a cave, and I provided them with food and water. ¹⁴ Now you say, 'Go tell your lord, "Elijah is here!"' He will kill me!"

¹⁵ Then Elijah said, "As the LORD of Armies lives, in whose presence I stand, today I will present myself to Ahab."

¹⁶ Obadiah went to meet Ahab and told him. Then Ahab went to meet Elijah. ¹⁷ When Ahab saw Elijah, Ahab said to him, "Is that you, the one ruining Israel?"

¹⁸ He replied, "I have not ruined Israel, but you and your father's family have, because you have abandoned the LORD's commands and followed the Baals. ¹⁹ Now summon all Israel to meet me at Mount Carmel, along with the 450 prophets of Baal and the 400 prophets of Asherah who eat at Jezebel's table."

ELIJAH AT MOUNT CARMEL

²⁰ So Ahab summoned all the Israelites and gathered the prophets at Mount Carmel. ²¹ Then Elijah approached all the people and said, "How long will you waver between two opinions?ᴮ If the LORD is God, follow him. But if Baal, follow him." But the people didn't answer him a word.

²² Then Elijah said to the people, "I am the only remaining prophet of the LORD, but Baal's prophets are 450 men. ²³ Let two bulls be given to us. They are to choose one bull for themselves, cut it in pieces, and place it on the wood but not light the fire. I will prepare the other bull and place it on the

---

ᴬ18:8 The Hb words translated 'Elijah is here' also mean 'Look, my God is the LORD' ᴮ18:21 Lit you hobble on two crutches?

FIRE FROM HEAVEN

1 KINGS 18–19; MATTHEW 5:16

I was in high school enjoying a back-to-school BBQ when I almost got arrested for disturbing the peace.

The trouble started when someone discovered a leftover firework in the garage. This was not some wimpy roman candle. This was a monster —one of those fireworks designed to make people say "ooh" and "ahh," or in our case, "Whoops. Sorry, Officer."

We took our contraband out into the street and lit it up. There were a few "oohs" and "ahhs" and maybe a couple of "hit the decks!" as the firework erupted slightly above the roofs of the neighborhood.

The excitement fizzled about as fast as the pyrotechnics when a police cruiser showed up. Some smooth talking kept us out of serious trouble, but I learned my lesson: if you're going to light the sky on fire, secure the proper permits.

Elijah didn't need a permit for the show God put on in 1 Kings 18. He was a prophet chosen by God to speak truth at a time of spiritual crisis. The wicked king Ahab had introduced the false god, Baal, to Israel, ushering in a fifty-year strain on the spiritual condition of God's people. In an attempt at a cosmic showdown, Ahab assembled 450 of his prophets, Elijah, and the Israelites at Mount Carmel.

Though seriously outnumbered, Elijah didn't back down. Instead, he drew this hard line in the sand:

"Then Elijah approached all the people and said, 'How long will you waver between two opinions?' If the LORD is God, follow him. But if Baal, follow him'" (1Kg 18:21).

What happened next answered Elijah's question.

The prophets of Baal built an altar, placed a sacrifice on it and called for fire from heaven. They worked themselves into a tizzy all day, but not so much as a spark fell from Baal.

Next, Elijah prepared a sacrifice, built an altar, and dug a trench around it. He asked for a bucket of water to be poured on the sacrifice, then a second and a third (to show off). He asked God to send fire so that everyone would know that the Lord is God. And God did. God sent a fire so hot it burned up the altar, the wood, the sacrifice, the dust, and the water in the trench. (Who's showing off now?)

"When all the people saw it, they fell facedown and said, "The LORD, he is God! The LORD, he is God!"

1 KINGS 18:39

God still uses flashes of bright light to point others to Him. **Like Elijah called down fire to show that the Lord is God, our lives bear the light of our heavenly Father.**

May our lives point directly to the one true God:

"In the same way, let your light shine before others, so that they may see your good works and give glory to your Father in heaven."

MATTHEW 5:16

---

wood but not light the fire. [24] Then you call on the name of your god, and I will call on the name of the LORD. The God who answers with fire, he is God."

All the people answered, "That's fine."

[25] Then Elijah said to the prophets of Baal, "Since you are so numerous, choose for yourselves one bull and prepare it first. Then call on the name of your god but don't light the fire."

[26] So they took the bull that he gave them, prepared it, and called on the name of Baal from morning until noon, saying, "Baal, answer us!" But there was no sound; no one answered. Then they danced[A] around the altar they had made.

[27] At noon Elijah mocked them. He said, "Shout loudly, for he's a god! Maybe he's thinking it over; maybe he has wandered away;[B] or maybe he's on the road. Perhaps he's sleeping and will wake up!" [28] They shouted loudly, and cut themselves with knives and spears, according to their custom, until blood gushed over them. [29] All afternoon they kept on raving until the offering of the evening sacrifice, but there was no sound; no one answered, no one paid attention.

[30] Then Elijah said to all the people, "Come near me." So all the people approached him. Then he repaired the LORD's altar that had been torn down: [31] Elijah took twelve stones — according to the number of the tribes of the sons of Jacob, to whom the word of the LORD had come, saying, "Israel will be your name" — [32] and he built an altar with the stones in the name of the LORD. Then he made a trench around the altar large enough to hold about four gallons.[C,D] [33] Next, he arranged the wood, cut up the bull, and placed it on the wood. He said, "Fill four water pots with water and pour it on the offering to be burned and on the wood." [34] Then he said, "A second time!" and they did it a second time. And then he said, "A third time!" and they did it a third time. [35] So the water ran all around the altar; he even filled the trench with water.

[36] At the time for offering the evening sacrifice, the prophet Elijah approached the altar and said, "LORD, the God of Abraham, Isaac, and Israel, today let it be known that you are God in Israel and I am your servant, and that at your word I have done all these things. [37] Answer me, LORD! Answer me so that this people will know that you, the LORD, are God and that you have turned their hearts back."

[38] Then the LORD's fire fell and consumed the burnt offering, the wood, the stones, and the dust, and it licked up the water that was in the trench. [39] When all the people saw it, they fell facedown and said, "The LORD, he is God! The LORD, he is God!"

[40] Then Elijah ordered them, "Seize the prophets of Baal! Do not let even one of them escape." So they seized them, and Elijah brought them down to the Wadi Kishon and slaughtered them there. [41] Elijah said to Ahab, "Go up, eat and drink, for there is the sound of a rainstorm."

[42] So Ahab went to eat and drink, but Elijah went up to the summit of Carmel. He bent down on the ground and put his face between his knees. [43] Then he said to his servant, "Go up and look toward the sea."

So he went up, looked, and said, "There's nothing."

Seven times Elijah said, "Go back."

[A]18:26 Or hobbled   [B]18:27 Or has turned aside; possibly to relieve himself
[C]18:32 LXX reads trench containing two measures of seed   [D]18:32 Lit altar
corresponding to a house of two seahs of seed

⁴⁴ On the seventh time, he reported, "There's a cloud as small as a man's hand coming up from the sea."

Then Elijah said, "Go and tell Ahab, 'Get your chariot ready and go down so the rain doesn't stop you.' "

⁴⁵ In a little while, the sky grew dark with clouds and wind, and there was a downpour. So Ahab got in his chariot and went to Jezreel. ⁴⁶ The power of the LORD was on Elijah, and he tucked his mantle under his belt and ran ahead of Ahab to the entrance of Jezreel.

ELIJAH'S JOURNEY TO HOREB

19 Ahab told Jezebel everything that Elijah had done and how he had killed all the prophets with the sword. ² So Jezebel sent a messenger to Elijah, saying, "May the gods punish me and do so severely if I don't make your life like the life of one of them by this time tomorrow!"

³ Then Elijah became afraid^A and immediately ran for his life. When he came to Beer-sheba that belonged to Judah, he left his servant there, ⁴ but he went on a day's journey into the wilderness. He sat down under a broom tree and prayed that he might die. He said, "I have had enough! LORD, take my life, for I'm no better than my fathers." ⁵ Then he lay down and slept under the broom tree.

Suddenly, an angel touched him. The angel told him, "Get up and eat." ⁶ Then he looked, and there at his head was a loaf of bread baked over hot stones, and a jug of water. So he ate and drank and lay down again. ⁷ Then the angel of the LORD returned for a second time and touched him. He said, "Get up and eat, or the journey will be too much for you." ⁸ So he got up, ate, and drank. Then on the strength from that food, he walked forty days and forty nights to Horeb, the mountain of God. ⁹ He entered a cave there and spent the night.

ELIJAH'S ENCOUNTER WITH THE LORD

Suddenly, the word of the LORD came to him, and he said to him, "What are you doing here, Elijah?"

¹⁰ He replied, "I have been very zealous for the LORD God of Armies, but the Israelites have abandoned your covenant, torn down your altars, and killed your prophets with the sword. I alone am left, and they are looking for me to take my life."

¹¹ Then he said, "Go out and stand on the mountain in the LORD's presence."

At that moment, the LORD passed by. A great and mighty wind was tearing at the mountains and was shattering cliffs before the LORD, but the LORD was not in the wind. After the wind there was an earthquake, but the LORD was not in the earthquake. ¹² After the earthquake there was a fire, but the LORD was not in the fire. And after the fire there was a voice, a soft whisper. ¹³ When Elijah heard it, he wrapped his face in his mantle and went out and stood at the entrance of the cave.

Suddenly, a voice came to him and said, "What are you doing here, Elijah?"

¹⁴ "I have been very zealous for the LORD God of Armies," he replied, "but the Israelites have abandoned your covenant, torn down your altars, and killed your prophets with the sword. I alone am left, and they're looking for me to take my life."

^A 19:3 Some Hb mss, LXX, Syr, Vg; other Hb mss read *He saw*

¹⁵ Then the LORD said to him, "Go and return by the way you came to the Wilderness of Damascus. When you arrive, you are to anoint Hazael as king over Aram. ¹⁶ You are to anoint Jehu son of Nimshi as king over Israel and Elisha son of Shaphat from Abel-meholah as prophet in your place. ¹⁷ Then Jehu will put to death whoever escapes the sword of Hazael, and Elisha will put to death whoever escapes the sword of Jehu. ¹⁸ But I will leave seven thousand in Israel — every knee that has not bowed to Baal and every mouth that has not kissed him."

ELISHA'S APPOINTMENT AS ELIJAH'S SUCCESSOR

¹⁹ Elijah left there and found Elisha son of Shaphat as he was plowing. Twelve teams of oxen were in front of him, and he was with the twelfth team. Elijah walked by him and threw his mantle over him. ²⁰ Elisha left the oxen, ran to follow Elijah, and said, "Please let me kiss my father and mother, and then I will follow you."

"Go on back," he replied, "for what have I done to you?"

²¹ So he turned back from following him, took the team of oxen, and slaughtered^A them. With the oxen's wooden yoke and plow, he cooked the meat and gave it to the people, and they ate. Then he left, followed Elijah, and served him.

VICTORY OVER BEN-HADAD

20 Now King Ben-hadad of Aram assembled his entire army. Thirty-two kings, along with horses and chariots, were with him. He marched up, besieged Samaria, and fought against it. ² He sent messengers into the city to King Ahab of Israel and said to him, "This is what Ben-hadad says: ³ 'Your silver and your gold are mine! And your best wives and children are mine as well!'"

⁴ Then the king of Israel answered, "Just as you say, my lord the king: I am yours, along with all that I have."

⁵ The messengers then returned and said, "This is what Ben-hadad says: 'I have sent messengers to you, saying: You are to give me your silver, your gold, your wives, and your children. ⁶ But at this time tomorrow I will send my servants to you,^B and they will search your palace and your servants' houses. They will lay their hands on and take away whatever is precious to you.'"

⁷ Then the king of Israel called for all the elders of the land and said, "Recognize^C that this one is only looking for trouble, for he demanded my wives, my children, my silver, and my gold, and I didn't turn him down."

⁸ All the elders and all the people said to him, "Don't listen or agree."

⁹ So he said to Ben-hadad's messengers, "Say to my lord the king, 'Everything you demanded of your servant the first time, I will do, but this thing I cannot do.'" So the messengers left and took word back to him.

¹⁰ Then Ben-hadad sent messengers to him and said, "May the gods punish me and do so severely if Samaria's dust amounts to a handful for each of the people who follow me."

¹¹ The king of Israel answered, "Say this: 'Don't let the one who puts on his armor boast like the one who takes it off.'"

---

^A 19:21 Or sacrificed   ^B 20:6 Lit take all the delight of your eyes   ^C 20:7 Lit "Know and see

¹²When Ben-hadad heard this response, while he and the kings were drinking in their quarters,^A he said to his servants, "Take your positions." So they took their positions against the city.

¹³A prophet approached King Ahab of Israel and said, "This is what the Lord says: 'Do you see this whole huge army? Watch, I am handing it over to you today so that you may know that I am the Lord.'"

¹⁴Ahab asked, "By whom?"

And the prophet said, "This is what the Lord says: 'By the young men of the provincial leaders.'"

Then he asked, "Who is to start the battle?"

He said, "You."

¹⁵So Ahab mobilized the young men of the provincial leaders, and there were 232. After them he mobilized all the Israelite troops: 7,000. ¹⁶They marched out at noon while Ben-hadad and the thirty-two kings who were helping him were getting drunk in their quarters. ¹⁷The young men of the provincial leaders marched out first. Then Ben-hadad sent out scouts, and they reported to him, saying, "Men are marching out of Samaria."

¹⁸So he said, "If they have marched out in peace, take them alive, and if they have marched out for battle, take them alive."

¹⁹The young men of the provincial leaders and the army behind them marched out from the city, ²⁰and each one struck down his opponent. So the Arameans fled and Israel pursued them, but King Ben-hadad of Aram escaped on a horse with the cavalry. ²¹Then the king of Israel marched out and attacked the cavalry and the chariots. He inflicted a severe slaughter on Aram.

²²The prophet approached the king of Israel and said to him, "Go and strengthen yourself, then consider carefully^B what you should do, for in the spring the king of Aram will attack you."

²³Now the king of Aram's servants said to him, "Their gods are gods of the hill country. That's why they were stronger than we were. Instead, we should fight with them on the plain; then we will certainly be stronger than they are. ²⁴Also do this: remove each king from his position and appoint captains in their place. ²⁵Raise another army for yourself like the army you lost — horse for horse, chariot for chariot — and let's fight with them on the plain; and we will certainly be stronger than they are." The king listened to them and did it.

²⁶In the spring, Ben-hadad mobilized the Arameans and went up to Aphek to battle Israel. ²⁷The Israelites mobilized, gathered supplies, and went to fight them. The Israelites camped in front of them like two little flocks of goats, while the Arameans filled the landscape.

²⁸Then the man of God approached and said to the king of Israel, "This is what the Lord says: 'Because the Arameans have said: The Lord is a god of the mountains and not a god of the valleys, I will hand over all this whole huge army to you. Then you will know that I am the Lord.'"

²⁹They camped opposite each other for seven days. On the seventh day, the battle took place, and the Israelites struck down the Arameans — one hundred thousand foot soldiers in one day. ³⁰The ones who remained fled into the city of Aphek, and the wall fell on those twenty-seven thousand remaining men.

^A20:12 Lit *booths*, also in v. 16 ^B20:22 Lit *then know and see*

Ben-hadad also fled and went into an inner room in the city. ³¹ His servants said to him, "Consider this: we have heard that the kings of the house of Israel are merciful kings. So let's put sackcloth around our waists and ropes around our heads, and let's go out to the king of Israel. Perhaps he will spare your life."

³² So they dressed with sackcloth around their waists and ropes around their heads, went to the king of Israel, and said, "Your servant Ben-hadad says, 'Please spare my life.'"

So he said, "Is he still alive? He is my brother."

³³ Now the men were looking for a sign of hope, so they quickly picked up on this ᴬ and responded, "Yes, it is your brother Ben-hadad."

Then he said, "Go and bring him."

So Ben-hadad came out to him, and Ahab had him come up into the chariot. ³⁴ Then Ben-hadad said to him, "I restore to you the cities that my father took from your father, and you may set up marketplaces for yourself in Damascus, like my father set up in Samaria."

Ahab responded, "On the basis of this treaty, I release you." So he made a treaty with him and released him.

AHAB REBUKED BY THE LORD

³⁵ One of the sons of the prophets said to his fellow prophet by the word of the LORD, "Strike me!" But the man refused to strike him.

³⁶ He told him, "Because you did not listen to the LORD, mark my words: When you leave me, a lion will kill you." When he left him, a lion attacked and killed him.

³⁷ The prophet found another man and said to him, "Strike me!" So the man struck him, inflicting a wound. ³⁸ Then the prophet went and waited for the king on the road. He disguised himself with a bandage over his eyes. ³⁹ As the king was passing by, he cried out to the king and said, "Your servant marched out into the middle of the battle. Suddenly, a man turned aside and brought someone to me and said, 'Guard this man! If he is ever missing, it will be your life in place of his life, or you will weigh out seventy-five pounds ᴮ of silver.' ⁴⁰ But while your servant was busy here and there, he disappeared."

The king of Israel said to him, "That will be your sentence; you yourself have decided it."

⁴¹ He quickly removed the bandage from his eyes. The king of Israel recognized that he was one of the prophets. ⁴² The prophet said to him, "This is what the LORD says: 'Because you released from your hand the man I had set apart for destruction, it will be your life in place of his life and your people in place of his people.'" ⁴³ The king of Israel left for home resentful and angry, and he entered Samaria.

AHAB AND NABOTH'S VINEYARD

21 Some time passed after these events. Naboth the Jezreelite had a vineyard; it was in Jezreel next to the palace of King Ahab of Samaria. ² So Ahab spoke to Naboth, saying, "Give me your vineyard so I can have it for a vegetable garden, since it is right next to my palace. I will

---

ᴬ20:33 Some Hb mss, alt Hb tradition, LXX; other Hb mss read *they hastened and caught hold; "Is this it?"* ᴮ20:39 Lit *a talent* give you a better vineyard in its place, or if you prefer, I will give you its value in silver."

³ But Naboth said to Ahab, "I will never give my fathers' inheritance to you." ⁴ So Ahab went to his palace resentful and angry because of what Naboth the Jezreelite had told him. He had said, "I will not give you my fathers' inheritance." He lay down on his bed, turned his face away, and didn't eat any food.

⁵ Then his wife Jezebel came to him and said to him, "Why are you so upset that you refuse to eat?"

⁶ "Because I spoke to Naboth the Jezreelite," he replied. "I told him: Give me your vineyard for silver, or if you wish, I will give you a vineyard in its place. But he said, 'I won't give you my vineyard!'"

⁷ Then his wife Jezebel said to him, "Now, exercise your royal power over Israel. Get up, eat some food, and be happy. For I will give you the vineyard of Naboth the Jezreelite." ⁸ So she wrote letters in Ahab's name and sealed them with his seal. She sent the letters to the elders and nobles who lived with Naboth in his city. ⁹ In the letters, she wrote:

Proclaim a fast and seat Naboth at the head of the people. ¹⁰ Then seat two wicked men opposite him and have them testify against him, saying, "You have cursed God and the king!" Then take him out and stone him to death.

¹¹ The men of his city, the elders and nobles who lived in his city, did as Jezebel had sent word to them, just as it was written in the letters she had sent them. ¹² They proclaimed a fast and seated Naboth at the head of the people. ¹³ The two wicked men came in and sat opposite him. Then the wicked men testified against Naboth in the presence of the people, saying, "Naboth has cursed God and the king!" So they took him outside the city and stoned him to death with stones. ¹⁴ Then they sent word to Jezebel: "Naboth has been stoned to death."

¹⁵ When Jezebel heard that Naboth had been stoned to death, she said to Ahab, "Get up and take possession of the vineyard of Naboth the Jezreelite who refused to give it to you for silver, since Naboth isn't alive, but dead." ¹⁶ When Ahab heard that Naboth was dead, he got up to go down to the vineyard of Naboth the Jezreelite to take possession of it.

THE LORD'S JUDGMENT ON AHAB

¹⁷ Then the word of the LORD came to Elijah the Tishbite: ¹⁸ "Get up and go to meet King Ahab of Israel, who is in Samaria. He's in Naboth's vineyard, where he has gone to take possession of it. ¹⁹ Tell him, 'This is what the LORD says: Have you murdered and also taken possession?' Then tell him, 'This is what the LORD says: In the place where the dogs licked up Naboth's blood, the dogs will also lick up your blood!'"

²⁰ Ahab said to Elijah, "So, my enemy, you've found me, have you?"

He replied, "I have found you because you devoted yourself to do what is evil in the LORD's sight. ²¹ This is what the LORD says:ᴬ 'I am about to bring disaster on you and will eradicate your descendants:

I will wipe out all of Ahab's males,ᴮ
both slave and free,ᶜ in Israel;

ᴬ21:21 LXX; MT omits *This is what the LORD says*   ᴮ21:21 Lit *eliminate Ahab's one who urinates against the wall*   ᶜ21:21 Or *males, even the weak and impaired*; Hb obscure

WHEN JUDGMENT MEETS COMPASSION

1 KINGS 20–21; PSALM 136:1; ISAIAH 55

In a long line of wicked kings who disregarded God's law, Ahab was the worst (1Kg 16:30). Ahab and his pagan wife, Jezebel, repeatedly raised a rebel fist at God.

Ahab deserved to be punished. For proof, we don't have to look any further than Naboth's vineyard.

Ahab knew of God, but he did not fear God. And even though his kingdom was vast, he found himself obsessed over a small vineyard owned by a man named Naboth. Ahab wanted the vineyard and Naboth refused to hand it over. In a show of sneaky support for her man, Jezebel ordered that Naboth be killed, and Ahab got his vineyard. But, the murder of an innocent man for a few rows of grapes did not go unnoticed by God.

God sent the prophet Elijah to announce His coming judgment: God would wipe Ahab and his wife from the face of the earth, along with their male children. God described, in gory detail, what would become of the royal family.

As I track the story of Ahab, my first reaction to this judgment is, "Yes! Finally!" Ahab's rebellion wreaked havoc on the nation of Israel for two decades. He was the catalyst for a fifty-year spiritual crisis. If anyone deserved God's judgment, it was Ahab.

But then, Ahab did the unthinkable. He repented. And God responded with an equally unthinkable reaction. He relented.

Ahab was more wicked and rebellious than any other king in Israel's history. Yet, because he repented, God delayed His judgment.

"Have you seen how Ahab has humbled himself before me? I will not bring the disaster during his lifetime, because he has humbled himself before me. I will bring the disaster on his house during his son's lifetime."

1 KINGS 21:29

You'll notice God did not remove His judgment altogether; he delayed it a generation. It's a tough concept to swallow—the idea that mercy for a father meant judgment on his sons. This is one of those tough lines in Scripture where we have to lean into the truth of Isaiah 55:8: "'For my thoughts are not your thoughts, and your ways are not my ways.' This is the LORD's declaration."

And that verse, Isaiah 55:8? Read in context, it is about repentance. God is a just God— He must be. He will not let our sins go unpunished. But He is also compassionate. He is good (Ps 136:1).

God is willing to forgive those who repent, even when their sins stack as high as Ahab's did. This dimension of God's character may not always make sense to me, but I am so grateful for it.

Lord, thank You for offering grace to sinners. Teach me to repent. Amen.

²² I will make your house like the house of Jeroboam son of Nebat and like the house of Baasha son of Ahijah, because you have angered me and caused Israel to sin.' ²³ The LORD also speaks of Jezebel: 'The dogs will eat Jezebel in the plot of land^A at Jezreel:

²⁴   Anyone who belongs to Ahab and dies in the city, the dogs will eat,
        and anyone who dies in the field, the birds^B will eat.' "

²⁵ Still, there was no one like Ahab, who devoted himself to do what was evil in the LORD's sight, because his wife Jezebel incited him. ²⁶ He committed the most detestable acts by following idols as the Amorites had, whom the LORD had dispossessed before the Israelites.

²⁷ When Ahab heard these words, he tore his clothes, put sackcloth over his body, and fasted. He lay down in sackcloth and walked around subdued. ²⁸ Then the word of the LORD came to Elijah the Tishbite: ²⁹ "Have you seen how Ahab has humbled himself before me? I will not bring the disaster during his lifetime, because he has humbled himself before me. I will bring the disaster on his house during his son's lifetime."

JEHOSHAPHAT'S ALLIANCE WITH AHAB

22 There was a lull of three years without war between Aram and Israel. ² However, in the third year, King Jehoshaphat of Judah went to visit the king of Israel. ³ The king of Israel had said to his servants, "Don't you know that Ramoth-gilead is ours, but we're doing nothing to take it from the king of Aram?" ⁴ So he asked Jehoshaphat, "Will you go with me to fight Ramoth-gilead?"

Jehoshaphat replied to the king of Israel, "I am as you are, my people as your people, my horses as your horses." ⁵ But Jehoshaphat said to the king of Israel, "First, please ask what the LORD's will is."

⁶ So the king of Israel gathered the prophets, about four hundred men, and asked them, "Should I go against Ramoth-gilead for war or should I refrain?"

They replied, "March up, and the Lord will hand it over to the king."

⁷ But Jehoshaphat asked, "Isn't there a prophet of the LORD here anymore? Let's ask him."

⁸ The king of Israel said to Jehoshaphat, "There is still one man who can inquire of the LORD, but I hate him because he never prophesies good about me, but only disaster. He is Micaiah son of Imlah."

"The king shouldn't say that!" Jehoshaphat replied.

⁹ So the king of Israel called an officer and said, "Hurry and get Micaiah son of Imlah!"

¹⁰ Now the king of Israel and King Jehoshaphat of Judah, clothed in royal attire, were each sitting on his own throne. They were on the threshing floor at the entrance to the gate of Samaria, and all the prophets were prophesying in front of them. ¹¹ Then Zedekiah son of Chenaanah made iron horns and said, "This is what the LORD says: 'You will gore the Arameans with these until they are finished off.'" ¹² And all the prophets were prophesying the same: "March up to Ramoth-gilead and succeed, for the LORD will hand it over to the king."

---

^A 21:23 Some Hb mss, Syr, Tg, Vg, 2Kg 9:36; other Hb mss, LXX read *the rampart*
^B 21:24 Lit *birds of the sky*

MICAIAH'S MESSAGE OF DEFEAT

[13] The messenger who went to call Micaiah instructed him, "Look, the words of the prophets are unanimously favorable for the king. So let your words be like theirs, and speak favorably."

[14] But Micaiah said, "As the LORD lives, I will say whatever the LORD says to me."

[15] So he went to the king, and the king asked him, "Micaiah, should we go to Ramoth-gilead for war, or should we refrain?"

Micaiah told him, "March up and succeed. The LORD will hand it over to the king."

[16] But the king said to him, "How many times must I make you swear not to tell me anything but the truth in the name of the LORD?"

[17] So Micaiah said:

I saw all Israel scattered on the hills
like sheep without a shepherd.
And the LORD said,
"They have no master;
let everyone return home in peace."

[18] So the king of Israel said to Jehoshaphat, "Didn't I tell you he never prophesies good about me, but only disaster?"

[19] Then Micaiah said, "Therefore, hear the word of the LORD: I saw the LORD sitting on his throne, and the whole heavenly army was standing by him at his right hand and at his left hand. [20] And the LORD said, 'Who will entice Ahab to march up and fall at Ramoth-gilead?' So one was saying this and another was saying that.

[21] "Then a spirit came forward, stood in the LORD's presence, and said, 'I will entice him.'

[22] "The LORD asked him, 'How?'

"He said, 'I will go and become a lying spirit in the mouth of all his prophets.'

"Then he said, 'You will certainly entice him and prevail. Go and do that.'

[23] "You see, the LORD has put a lying spirit into the mouth of all these prophets of yours, and the LORD has pronounced disaster against you."

[24] Then Zedekiah son of Chenaanah came up, hit Micaiah on the cheek, and demanded, "Did[A] the Spirit of the LORD leave me to speak to you?"

[25] Micaiah replied, "You will soon see when you go to hide in an inner chamber on that day."

[26] Then the king of Israel ordered, "Take Micaiah and return him to Amon, the governor of the city, and to Joash, the king's son, [27] and say, 'This is what the king says: Put this guy in prison and feed him only a little bread and water[B] until I come back safely.'"

[28] But Micaiah said, "If you ever return safely, the LORD has not spoken through me." Then he said, "Listen, all you people!"[C]

AHAB'S DEATH

[29] Then the king of Israel and Judah's King Jehoshaphat went up to Ramoth-gilead. [30] But the king of Israel said to Jehoshaphat, "I will disguise myself

---

[A]22:24 Lit "Which way did   [B]22:27 Lit him on bread of oppression and water of oppression   [C]22:28 LXX omits Then he said, "Listen, all you people!"

and go into battle, but you wear your royal attire." So the king of Israel disguised himself and went into battle.

³¹ Now the king of Aram had ordered his thirty-two chariot commanders, "Do not fight with anyone at all^A except the king of Israel."

³² When the chariot commanders saw Jehoshaphat, they shouted, "He must be the king of Israel!" So they turned to fight against him, but Jehoshaphat cried out. ³³ When the chariot commanders saw that he was not the king of Israel, they turned back from pursuing him.

³⁴ But a man drew his bow without taking special aim and struck the king of Israel through the joints of his armor. So he said to his charioteer, "Turn around and take me out of the battle,^B for I am badly wounded!" ³⁵ The battle raged throughout that day, and the king was propped up in his chariot facing the Arameans. He died that evening, and blood from his wound flowed into the bottom of the chariot. ³⁶ Then the cry rang out in the army as the sun set, declaring:

> Each man to his own city,
> and each man to his own land!

³⁷ So the king died and was brought to Samaria. They buried the king in Samaria. ³⁸ Then someone washed the chariot at the pool of Samaria. The dogs licked up his blood, and the prostitutes bathed in it, according to the word of the Lord that he had spoken.

³⁹ The rest of the events of Ahab's reign, along with all his accomplishments, including the ivory palace he built, and all the cities he built, are written in the Historical Record of Israel's Kings. ⁴⁰ Ahab rested with his fathers, and his son Ahaziah became king in his place.

JUDAH'S KING JEHOSHAPHAT

⁴¹ Jehoshaphat son of Asa became king over Judah in the fourth year of Israel's King Ahab. ⁴² Jehoshaphat was thirty-five years old when he became king; he reigned twenty-five years in Jerusalem. His mother's name was Azubah daughter of Shilhi. ⁴³ He walked in all the ways of his father Asa; he did not turn away from them but did what was right in the Lord's sight. However, the high places were not taken away;^C the people still sacrificed and burned incense on the high places. ⁴⁴ Jehoshaphat also made peace with the king of Israel.

⁴⁵ The rest of the events of Jehoshaphat's reign, along with the might he exercised and how he waged war, are written in the Historical Record of Judah's Kings. ⁴⁶ He eradicated from the land the rest of the male cult prostitutes who were left from the days of his father Asa. ⁴⁷ There was no king in Edom; a deputy served as king. ⁴⁸ Jehoshaphat made ships of Tarshish to go to Ophir for gold, but they did not go because the ships were wrecked at Ezion-geber. ⁴⁹ At that time, Ahaziah son of Ahab said to Jehoshaphat, "Let my servants go with your servants in the ships," but Jehoshaphat was not willing. ⁵⁰ Jehoshaphat rested with his fathers and was buried with them in the city of his ancestor David. His son Jehoram became king in his place.

---

^A22:31 Lit with small or with great ^B22:34 LXX; MT reads camp ^C22:43 LXX, Syr, Vg read he did not remove the high places

ISRAEL'S KING AHAZIAH

[51] Ahaziah son of Ahab became king over Israel in Samaria in the seventeenth year of Judah's King Jehoshaphat, and he reigned over Israel two years. [52] He did what was evil in the LORD's sight. He walked in the ways of his father, in the ways of his mother, and in the ways of Jeroboam son of Nebat, who had caused Israel to sin. [53] He served Baal and bowed in worship to him. He angered the LORD God of Israel just as his father had done.

for the Sake of His servant David, the Lord was unwilling to destroy Judah

2 kings

 For the sake of his servant David, the LORD was unwilling to destroy Judah. **8:19**

ON THE TIMELINE The history recorded in 2 Kings covers approximately 300 years. The book begins around 850 BC with the death of King Ahab and ends around 560 BC with the release of King Jehoiachin from prison in Babylon. During this time, both kingdoms went into exile (Israel in 722 BC and Judah in 586 BC).

A LITTLE BACKGROUND First and 2 Kings are the history of the kings and kingdoms of Israel and Judah. Originally, the two were one book, but they were later divided by the translators of the Septuagint (the Greek translation of the Old Testament).

The Davidic covenant (first introduced in 2 Samuel) established the king as the moral representative of the people for covenant purposes. Therefore, up through kings Azariah (also known as Uzziah) and Jotham, the moral state of the king was treated as representative of the moral state of the people. Covenant blessings were given or withheld on the basis of the king's behavior, making the behavior of the king the basis of covenant faithfulness for any given reign.

MESSAGE & PURPOSE

The theological perspective of 1 and 2 Kings is expressed in a number of themes:

1. The sinfulness of the kings and the nation
2. The conflict between the demands of practical politics and the demands of faith
3. The glory God gave to the obedient covenant kings
4. God's harshness in judgment on some occasions and leniency on others
5. The conflict between the worship of the Lord and the worship of other gods.

GIVE THANKS FOR THE BOOK OF 2 KINGS:

For the Bible writers, history could not have existed without God's purposes, thereby making all history theological. The Babylonian exiles wanted an explanation for what they saw as the failure of the religious system in Israel, so they looked to historical apologetics to find their answers. The books of 1 and 2 Kings interpreted Hebrew history in light of OT covenant theology, finding the "failure" was due not to God but to God's people who did not uphold their part of the covenant. God is faithful to His covenant with us, even when we are not.

MEDITERRANEAN SEA

DAN

ARAM

JEZREEL

JABESH-GILEAD

SAMARIA

TIRZAH

SHECHEM

ISRAEL

BETHEL

JERICHO

AMMON

JERUSALEM

BETHLEHEM

HEBRON

DEAD SEA

BEER-SHEBA

JUDAH

MOAB

PHILISTIA

INT'L COASTAL HIGHWAY

KING'S HIGHWAY

TAMAR

EDOM

KINGDOMS OF ISRA
AND JUDA

READ AND UNDERSTAND 2 KINGS

The Bible is a complete work in which many stories combine to tell one story. As you read the book of 2 Kings, consider reading the additional passages to discover how the whole of Scripture works together.

AHAZIAH'S SICKNESS AND DEATH

1 After Ahab's death, Moab rebelled against Israel. ² Ahaziah had fallen through the latticed window of his upstairs room in Samaria and was injured. So he sent messengers, instructing them, "Go inquire of Baal-zebub,^A the god of Ekron, whether I will recover from this injury."

³ But the angel of the LORD said to Elijah the Tishbite, "Go and meet the messengers of the king of Samaria and say to them, 'Is it because there is no God in Israel that you are going to inquire of Baal-zebub, the god of Ekron? ⁴ Therefore, this is what the LORD says: You will not get up from your sickbed; you will certainly die.'" Then Elijah left.

⁵ The messengers returned to the king, who asked them, "Why have you come back?"

⁶ They replied, "A man came to meet us and said, 'Go back to the king who sent you and declare to him: This is what the LORD says: Is it because there is no God in Israel that you're sending these men to inquire of Baal-zebub, the god of Ekron? Therefore, you will not get up from your sickbed; you will certainly die.'"

⁷ The king asked them, "What sort of man came up to meet you and spoke those words to you?"

⁸ They replied, "A hairy man with a leather belt around his waist."

He said, "It's Elijah the Tishbite."

⁹ So King Ahaziah sent a captain with his fifty men to Elijah. When the captain went up to him, he was sitting on top of the hill. He announced, "Man of God, the king declares, 'Come down!'"

¹⁰ Elijah responded to the captain, "If I am a man of God, may fire come down from heaven and consume you and your fifty men." Then fire came down from heaven and consumed him and his fifty men.

¹¹ So the king sent another captain with his fifty men to Elijah. He took in the situation^B and announced, "Man of God, this is what the king says: 'Come down immediately!'"

¹² Elijah responded, "If I am a man of God, may fire come down from heaven and consume you and your fifty men." So a divine fire^C came down from heaven and consumed him and his fifty men.

¹³ Then the king sent a third captain with his fifty men. The third captain went up and fell on his knees in front of Elijah and begged him, "Man of God, please let my life and the lives of these fifty servants of yours be precious to you. ¹⁴ Already fire has come down from heaven and consumed the first two captains with their companies, but this time let my life be precious to you."

¹⁵ The angel of the LORD said to Elijah, "Go down with him. Don't be afraid of him." So he got up and went down with him to the king.

¹⁶ Then Elijah said to King Ahaziah, "This is what the LORD says: 'Because you have sent messengers to inquire of Baal-zebub, the god of Ekron — is it because there is no God in Israel for you to inquire of his will? — you will not get up from your sickbed; you will certainly die.'"

¹⁷ Ahaziah died according to the word of the LORD that Elijah had spoken. Since he had no son, Joram^D became king in his place. This happened in the second year of Judah's King Jehoram son of Jehoshaphat.^E ¹⁸ The rest of the

---

^A 1:2 = Lord of the Flies   ^B 1:11 Lit *He answered*   ^C 1:12 Lit *a fire of God*
^D 1:17 Lit *Jehoram*; 2Kg 8:16   ^E 1:17 LXX omits *in the second year . . . Jehoshaphat*

events of Ahaziah's reign, along with his accomplishments, are written in the Historical Record of Israel's Kings.[A]

ELIJAH IN THE WHIRLWIND

2 The time had come for the LORD to take Elijah up to heaven in a whirlwind. Elijah and Elisha were traveling from Gilgal, [2] and Elijah said to Elisha, "Stay here; the LORD is sending me on to Bethel."

But Elisha replied, "As the LORD lives and as you yourself live, I will not leave you." So they went down to Bethel.

[3] Then the sons of the prophets who were at Bethel came out to Elisha and said, "Do you know that the LORD will take your master away from you today?"

He said, "Yes, I know. Be quiet."

[4] Elijah said to him, "Elisha, stay here; the LORD is sending me to Jericho."

But Elisha said, "As the LORD lives and as you yourself live, I will not leave you." So they went to Jericho.

[5] Then the sons of the prophets who were in Jericho came up to Elisha and said, "Do you know that the LORD will take your master away from you today?"

He said, "Yes, I know. Be quiet."

[6] Elijah said to him, "Stay here; the LORD is sending me to the Jordan."

But Elisha said, "As the LORD lives and as you yourself live, I will not leave you." So the two of them went on.

[7] Fifty men from the sons of the prophets came and stood observing them at a distance while the two of them stood by the Jordan. [8] Elijah took his mantle, rolled it up, and struck the water, which parted to the right and left. Then the two of them crossed over on dry ground. [9] When they had crossed over, Elijah said to Elisha, "Tell me what I can do for you before I am taken from you."

So Elisha answered, "Please, let me inherit two shares of your spirit."

[10] Elijah replied, "You have asked for something difficult. If you see me being taken from you, you will have it. If not, you won't."

[11] As they continued walking and talking, a chariot of fire with horses of fire suddenly appeared and separated the two of them. Then Elijah went up into heaven in the whirlwind. [12] As Elisha watched, he kept crying out, "My father, my father, the chariots and horsemen of Israel!"

ELISHA SUCCEEDS ELIJAH

When he could see him no longer, he took hold of his own clothes, tore them in two, [13] picked up the mantle that had fallen off Elijah, and went back and stood on the bank of the Jordan. [14] He took the mantle Elijah had dropped, and he struck the water. "Where is the LORD God of Elijah?" he asked. He struck the water himself, and it parted to the right and the left, and Elisha crossed over.

[15] When the sons of the prophets from Jericho who were observing saw him, they said, "The spirit of Elijah rests on Elisha." They came to meet him and bowed down to the ground in front of him.

[16] Then the sons of the prophets said to Elisha, "Since there are fifty strong men here with your servants, please let them go and search for your master. Maybe the Spirit of the LORD has carried him away and put him on one of the mountains or into one of the valleys."

[A]1:18 LXX adds 4 more vv. here similar to 2Kg 3:1-3.

He answered, "Don't send them."

[17] However, they urged him to the point of embarrassment, so he said, "Send them." They sent fifty men, who looked for three days but did not find him. [18] When they returned to him in Jericho where he was staying, he said to them, "Didn't I tell you not to go?"

[19] The men of the city said to Elisha, "My lord can see that even though the city's location is good, the water is bad and the land unfruitful."

[20] He replied, "Bring me a new bowl and put salt in it."

After they had brought him one, [21] Elisha went out to the spring, threw salt in it, and said, "This is what the LORD says: 'I have healed this water. No longer will death or unfruitfulness result from it.'" [22] Therefore, the water still remains healthy today according to the word that Elisha spoke.

[23] From there Elisha went up to Bethel. As he was walking up the path, some small boys came out of the city and jeered at him, chanting, "Go up, baldy! Go up, baldy!" [24] He turned around, looked at them, and cursed them in the name of the LORD. Then two female bears came out of the woods and mauled forty-two of the children. [25] From there Elisha went to Mount Carmel, and then he returned to Samaria.

ISRAEL'S KING JORAM

3 Joram son of Ahab became king over Israel in Samaria during the eighteenth year of Judah's King Jehoshaphat, and he reigned twelve years. [2] He did what was evil in the LORD's sight, but not like his father and mother, for he removed the sacred pillar of Baal his father had made. [3] Nevertheless, Joram clung to the sins that Jeroboam son of Nebat had caused Israel to commit. He did not turn away from them.

MOAB'S REBELLION AGAINST ISRAEL

[4] King Mesha of Moab was a sheep breeder. He used to pay the king of Israel one hundred thousand lambs and the wool of one hundred thousand rams, [5] but when Ahab died, the king of Moab rebelled against the king of Israel. [6] So King Joram marched out from Samaria at that time and mobilized all Israel. [7] Then he sent a message to King Jehoshaphat of Judah: "The king of Moab has rebelled against me. Will you go with me to fight against Moab?"

Jehoshaphat said, "I will go. I am as you are, my people as your people, my horses as your horses."

[8] He asked, "Which route should we take?"

He replied, "The route of the Wilderness of Edom."

[9] So the king of Israel, the king of Judah, and the king of Edom set out. After they had traveled their indirect route for seven days, they had no water for the army or the animals with them.

[10] Then the king of Israel said, "Oh no, the LORD has summoned these three kings, only to hand them over to Moab."

[11] But Jehoshaphat said, "Isn't there a prophet of the LORD here? Let's inquire of the LORD through him."

One of the servants of the king of Israel answered, "Elisha son of Shaphat, who used to pour water on Elijah's hands, is here."

[12] Jehoshaphat affirmed, "The word of the LORD is with him." So the king of Israel and Jehoshaphat and the king of Edom went to him.

¹³ However, Elisha said to King Joram of Israel, "What do we have in common? Go to the prophets of your father and your mother!"

But the king of Israel replied, "No, because it is the LORD who has summoned these three kings to hand them over to Moab."

¹⁴ Elisha responded, "By the life of the LORD of Armies, before whom I stand: If I did not have respect for King Jehoshaphat of Judah, I wouldn't look at you; I would not take notice of you. ¹⁵ Now, bring me a musician."

While the musician played, the LORD's hand came on Elisha. ¹⁶ Then he said, "This is what the LORD says: 'Dig ditch after ditch in this wadi.' ¹⁷ For the LORD says, 'You will not see wind or rain, but the wadi will be filled with water, and you will drink — you and your cattle and your animals.' ¹⁸ This is easy in the LORD's sight. He will also hand Moab over to you. ¹⁹ Then you will attack every fortified city and every choice city. You will cut down every good tree and stop up every spring. You will ruin every good piece of land with stones."

²⁰ About the time for the grain offering the next morning, water suddenly came from the direction of Edom and filled the land.

²¹ All Moab had heard that the kings had come up to fight against them. So all who could bear arms, from the youngest to the oldest, were summoned and took their stand at the border. ²² When they got up early in the morning, the sun was shining on the water, and the Moabites saw that the water across from them was red like blood. ²³ "This is blood!" they exclaimed. "The kings have crossed swords^A and their men have killed one another. So, to the spoil, Moab!"

²⁴ However, when the Moabites came to Israel's camp, the Israelites attacked them, and they fled from them. So Israel went into the land attacking the Moabites. ²⁵ They would destroy the cities, and each of them would throw a stone to cover every good piece of land. They would stop up every spring and cut down every good tree. This went on until only the buildings of Kir-hareseth were left. Then men with slings surrounded the city and attacked it.

²⁶ When the king of Moab saw that the battle was too fierce for him, he took seven hundred swordsmen with him to try to break through to the king of Edom, but they could not do it. ²⁷ So he took his firstborn son, who was to become king in his place, and offered him as a burnt offering on the city wall. Great wrath was on the Israelites, and they withdrew from him and returned to their land.

THE WIDOW'S OIL MULTIPLIED

4 One of the wives of the sons of the prophets cried out to Elisha, "Your servant, my husband, has died. You know that your servant feared the LORD. Now the creditor is coming to take my two children as his slaves."

² Elisha asked her, "What can I do for you? Tell me, what do you have in the house?"

She said, "Your servant has nothing in the house except a jar of oil."

³ Then he said, "Go out and borrow empty containers from all your neighbors. Do not get just a few. ⁴ Then go in and shut the door behind you and your sons, and pour oil into all these containers. Set the full ones to one side." ⁵ So she left.

---

^A 3:23 Or *have been laid waste*

FAITH AND PROVISION

2 KINGS 4:1–5:19

I learned the art of chips and salsa from my best friend Ashley. I know some of you may think you're experienced at consuming this savory snack (I did, too). But say "adios" to your old ways because I'm here to change them.

You see, when Ashley spies piñatas and sombreros in the window of her favorite Mexican restaurant, it's game time. As soon as we're seated, I'm immediately abandoned in the brightly colored booth as the artist approaches her salsa bar canvas. A little while later, she'll return, carrying plastic cups overflowing with mild, medium, hot, and tomatillo salsas. Placing them on the table, the mild on my side and the medium on hers, she begins sprinkling salt in each cup. The first time I watched this ritual, I knew I'd found my best friend.

Ashley is determined to always maintain equal portions of chips and salsa. She may bug the server for more chips or make several trips to the salsa bar, but the cups and basket never know what it's like to be empty as long as Ashley is around.

Unlike my friend's chip basket and salsa cups, the widow in 2 Kings 4 knew emptiness. She had lost her husband, which meant she had also lost her income. The tragedy left her with two hungry children and a tiny bit of oil.

When the widow asked the prophet Elisha for help, he sent her on a mission to gather containers from all her neighbors, then fill them up, one by one, with her small reserve of oil. And though it must have seemed ludicrous, she did exactly as he said.

> "After she had shut the door behind her and her sons, they kept bringing her containers, and she kept pouring. When they were full, she said to her son, 'Bring me another container.' But he replied, 'There aren't any more.' Then the oil stopped."
>
> 2 KINGS 4:5-6

With the diligence of Ashley refilling her salsa cups, the widow faithfully filled each container to the brim.

But why was the widow doing the pouring? Why didn't the prophet Elisha simply hand over what she needed to support her family? Why didn't the containers magically fill themselves?

The widow received more than oil that day; she received the gift of a tangible faith. She got to hold her faith not only in her heart but also in her hands, watching in awe as her simple act of obedience revealed God's already-planned provision. We, too, must sink our sinful hands in the promises of God to experience His abundance. **His supply is all we need.**

Are you staring at the tiny bit of oil you have left today? Reach out in faith, expecting our heavenly Father's provision. May we praise Him for pouring out promises and keeping every single one.

After she had shut the door behind her and her sons, they kept bringing her containers, and she kept pouring. [6] When they were full, she said to her son, "Bring me another container."

But he replied, "There aren't any more." Then the oil stopped.

[7] She went and told the man of God, and he said, "Go sell the oil and pay your debt; you and your sons can live on the rest."

THE SHUNAMMITE WOMAN'S HOSPITALITY

[8] One day Elisha went to Shunem. A prominent woman who lived there persuaded him to eat some food. So whenever he passed by, he stopped there to eat. [9] Then she said to her husband, "I know that the one who often passes by here is a holy man of God, [10] so let's make a small, walled-in upper room and put a bed, a table, a chair, and a lamp there for him. Whenever he comes, he can stay there."

THE SHUNAMMITE WOMAN'S SON

[11] One day he came there and stopped at the upstairs room to lie down. [12] He ordered his attendant Gehazi, "Call this Shunammite woman." So he called her and she stood before him.

[13] Then he said to Gehazi, "Say to her, 'Look, you've gone to all this trouble for us. What can we do for you? Can we speak on your behalf to the king or to the commander of the army?'"

She answered, "I am living among my own people."

[14] So he asked, "Then what should be done for her?"

Gehazi answered, "Well, she has no son, and her husband is old."

[15] "Call her," Elisha said. So Gehazi called her, and she stood in the doorway. [16] Elisha said, "At this time next year you will have a son in your arms."

Then she said, "No, my lord. Man of God, do not lie to your servant."

[17] The woman conceived and gave birth to a son at the same time the following year, as Elisha had promised her.

THE SHUNAMMITE'S SON RAISED

[18] The child grew and one day went out to his father and the harvesters. [19] Suddenly he complained to his father, "My head! My head!"

His father told his servant, "Carry him to his mother." [20] So he picked him up and took him to his mother. The child sat on her lap until noon and then died. [21] She went up and laid him on the bed of the man of God, shut him in, and left.

[22] She summoned her husband and said, "Please send me one of the servants and one of the donkeys, so I can hurry to the man of God and come back again."

[23] But he said, "Why go to him today? It's not a New Moon or a Sabbath."

She replied, "Everything is all right."

[24] Then she saddled the donkey and said to her servant, "Go fast; don't slow the pace for me unless I tell you." [25] So she came to the man of God at Mount Carmel.

When the man of God saw her at a distance, he said to his attendant Gehazi, "Look, there's the Shunammite woman. [26] Run out to meet her and ask, 'Are you all right? Is your husband all right? Is your son all right?'"

And she answered, "Everything's all right."

²⁷ When she came up to the man of God at the mountain, she clung to his feet. Gehazi came to push her away, but the man of God said, "Leave her alone — she is in severe anguish, and the LORD has hidden it from me. He hasn't told me."

²⁸ Then she said, "Did I ask my lord for a son? Didn't I say, 'Do not lie to me?'"

²⁹ So Elisha said to Gehazi, "Tuck your mantle under your belt, take my staff with you, and go. If you meet anyone, don't stop to greet him, and if a man greets you, don't answer him. Then place my staff on the boy's face."

³⁰ The boy's mother said to Elisha, "As the LORD lives and as you yourself live, I will not leave you." So he got up and followed her.

³¹ Gehazi went ahead of them and placed the staff on the boy's face, but there was no sound or sign of life, so he went back to meet Elisha and told him, "The boy didn't wake up."

³² When Elisha got to the house, he discovered the boy lying dead on his bed. ³³ So he went in, closed the door behind the two of them, and prayed to the LORD. ³⁴ Then he went up and lay on the boy: he put mouth to mouth, eye to eye, hand to hand. While he bent down over him, the boy's flesh became warm. ³⁵ Elisha got up, went into the house, and paced back and forth. Then he went up and bent down over him again. The boy sneezed seven times and opened his eyes.

³⁶ Elisha called Gehazi and said, "Call the Shunammite woman." He called her and she came. Then Elisha said, "Pick up your son." ³⁷ She came, fell at his feet, and bowed to the ground; she picked up her son and left.

THE DEADLY STEW

³⁸ When Elisha returned to Gilgal, there was a famine in the land. The sons of the prophets were sitting before him. He said to his attendant, "Put on the large pot and make stew for the sons of the prophets."

³⁹ One went out to the field to gather herbs and found a wild vine from which he gathered as many wild gourds as his garment would hold. Then he came back and cut them up into the pot of stew, but they were unaware of what they were.ᴬ

⁴⁰ They served some for the men to eat, but when they ate the stew they cried out, "There's death in the pot, man of God!" And they were unable to eat it.

⁴¹ Then Elisha said, "Get some flour." He threw it into the pot and said, "Serve it for the people to eat." And there was nothing bad in the pot.

THE MULTIPLIED BREAD

⁴² A man from Baal-shalishah came to the man of God with his sack full ofᴮ twenty loaves of barley bread from the first bread of the harvest. Elisha said, "Give it to the people to eat."

⁴³ But Elisha's attendant asked, "What? Am I to set this before a hundred men?"

"Give it to the people to eat," Elisha said, "for this is what the LORD says: 'They will eat, and they will have some left over.'" ⁴⁴ So he set it before them, and as the LORD had promised, they ate and had some left over.

ᴬ4:39 *of what they were added for clarity*   ᴮ4:42 *Or with some heads of fresh grain and*

NAAMAN'S DISEASE HEALED

5 Naaman, commander of the army for the king of Aram, was a man important to his master and highly regarded because through him, the LORD had given victory to Aram. The man was a valiant warrior, but he had a skin disease.

² Aram had gone on raids and brought back from the land of Israel a young girl who served Naaman's wife. ³ She said to her mistress, "If only my master were with the prophet who is in Samaria, he would cure him of his skin disease."

⁴ So Naaman went and told his master what the girl from the land of Israel had said. ⁵ Therefore, the king of Aram said, "Go, and I will send a letter with you to the king of Israel."

So he went and took with him 750 pounds[A] of silver, 150 pounds[B] of gold, and ten sets of clothing. ⁶ He brought the letter to the king of Israel, and it read:

When this letter comes to you, note that I have sent you my servant Naaman for you to cure him of his skin disease.

⁷ When the king of Israel read the letter, he tore his clothes and asked, "Am I God, killing and giving life that this man expects me to cure a man of his skin disease? Recognize[C] that he is only picking a fight with me."

⁸ When Elisha the man of God heard that the king of Israel had torn his clothes, he sent a message to the king, "Why have you torn your clothes? Have him come to me, and he will know there is a prophet in Israel." ⁹ So Naaman came with his horses and chariots and stood at the door of Elisha's house.

¹⁰ Then Elisha sent him a messenger, who said, "Go wash seven times in the Jordan and your skin will be restored and you will be clean."

¹¹ But Naaman got angry and left, saying, "I was telling myself: He will surely come out, stand and call on the name of the LORD his God, and wave his hand over the place and cure the skin disease. ¹² Aren't Abana and Pharpar, the rivers of Damascus, better than all the waters of Israel? Couldn't I wash in them and be clean?" So he turned and left in a rage.

¹³ But his servants approached and said to him, "My father, if the prophet had told you to do some great thing, would you not have done it? How much more should you do it when he only tells you, 'Wash and be clean'?" ¹⁴ So Naaman went down and dipped himself in the Jordan seven times, according to the command of the man of God. Then his skin was restored and became like the skin of a small boy, and he was clean.

¹⁵ Then Naaman and his whole company went back to the man of God, stood before him, and declared, "I know there's no God in the whole world except in Israel. Therefore, please accept a gift from your servant."

¹⁶ But Elisha said, "As the LORD lives, in whose presence I stand, I will not accept it." Naaman urged him to accept it, but he refused.

¹⁷ Naaman responded, "If not, please let your servant be given as much soil as a pair of mules can carry, for your servant will no longer offer a burnt offering or a sacrifice to any other god but the LORD. ¹⁸ However, in a particular matter may the LORD pardon your servant: When my master, the king of Aram, goes into the temple of Rimmon to bow in worship

---

[A]5:5 Lit 10 talents   [B]5:5 Lit 6,000 shekels   [C]5:7 Lit Know and see while he is leaning on my arm,^A and I have to bow in the temple of Rimmon — when I bow^B in the temple of Rimmon, may the LORD pardon your servant in this matter."

¹⁹ So he said to him, "Go in peace."

GEHAZI'S GREED PUNISHED

After Naaman had traveled a short distance from Elisha, ²⁰ Gehazi, the attendant of Elisha the man of God, thought, "My master has let this Aramean Naaman off lightly by not accepting from him what he brought. As the LORD lives, I will run after him and get something from him."

²¹ So Gehazi pursued Naaman. When Naaman saw someone running after him, he got down from the chariot to meet him and asked, "Is everything all right?"

²² Gehazi said, "It's all right. My master has sent me to say, 'I have just now discovered that two young men from the sons of the prophets have come to me from the hill country of Ephraim. Please give them seventy-five pounds^C of silver and two sets of clothing.'"

²³ But Naaman insisted, "Please, accept one hundred fifty pounds."^D He urged Gehazi and then packed one hundred fifty pounds of silver in two bags with two sets of clothing. Naaman gave them to two of his attendants who carried them ahead of Gehazi. ²⁴ When Gehazi came to the hill,^E he took the gifts from them and deposited them in the house. Then he dismissed the men, and they left.

²⁵ Gehazi came and stood by his master. "Where did you go, Gehazi?" Elisha asked him.

He replied, "Your servant didn't go anywhere."

²⁶ "And my heart didn't go^F when the man got down from his chariot to meet you," Elisha said. "Is this a time to accept silver and clothing, olive orchards and vineyards, flocks and herds, and male and female slaves? ²⁷ Therefore, Naaman's skin disease will cling to you and your descendants forever." So Gehazi went out from his presence diseased, resembling snow.^G

THE FLOATING AX HEAD

6 The sons of the prophets said to Elisha, "Please notice that the place where we live under your supervision^H is too small for us. ² Please let us go to the Jordan where we can each get a log and can build ourselves a place to live there."

"Go," he said.

³ Then one said, "Please come with your servants."

"I'll come," he answered.

⁴ So he went with them, and when they came to the Jordan, they cut down trees. ⁵ As one of them was cutting down a tree, the iron ax head fell into the water, and he cried out, "Oh, my master, it was borrowed!"

⁶ Then the man of God asked, "Where did it fall?"

---

^A5:18 Lit worship, and he leans on my hand   ^B5:18 LXX, Vg read when he bows himself   ^C5:22 Lit a talent   ^D5:23 Lit two talents   ^E5:24 Or citadel   ^F5:26 Or "Did not my heart go   ^G5:27 A reference to whiteness or flakiness of the skin   ^H6:1 Lit we are living before you

When he showed him the place, the man of God cut a piece of wood, threw it there, and made the iron float. ⁷ Then he said, "Pick it up." So he reached out and took it.

THE ARAMEAN WAR

⁸ When the king of Aram was waging war against Israel, he conferred with his servants, "My camp will be at such and such a place."

⁹ But the man of God sent word to the king of Israel: "Be careful passing by this place, for the Arameans are going down there." ¹⁰ Consequently, the king of Israel sent word to the place the man of God had told him about. The man of God repeatedly^A warned the king, so the king would be on his guard.

¹¹ The king of Aram was enraged because of this matter, and he called his servants and demanded of them, "Tell me, which one of us is for the king of Israel?"

¹² One of his servants said, "No one, my lord the king. Elisha, the prophet in Israel, tells the king of Israel even the words you speak in your bedroom."

¹³ So the king said, "Go and see where he is, so I can send men to capture him." When he was told, "Elisha is in Dothan," ¹⁴ he sent horses, chariots, and a massive army there. They went by night and surrounded the city.

¹⁵ When the servant of the man of God got up early and went out, he discovered an army with horses and chariots surrounding the city. So he asked Elisha, "Oh, my master, what are we to do?"

¹⁶ Elisha said, "Don't be afraid, for those who are with us outnumber those who are with them."

¹⁷ Then Elisha prayed, "LORD, please open his eyes and let him see." So the LORD opened the servant's eyes, and he saw that the mountain was covered with horses and chariots of fire all around Elisha.

¹⁸ When the Arameans came against him, Elisha prayed to the LORD, "Please strike this nation with blindness."^B So he struck them with blindness, according to Elisha's word. ¹⁹ Then Elisha said to them, "This is not the way, and this is not the city. Follow me, and I will take you to the man you're looking for." And he led them to Samaria. ²⁰ When they entered Samaria, Elisha said, "LORD, open these men's eyes and let them see." So the LORD opened their eyes, and they saw that they were in the middle of Samaria.

²¹ When the king of Israel saw them, he said to Elisha, "Should I kill them, should I kill them, my father?"

²² Elisha replied, "Don't kill them. Do you kill those you have captured with your sword or your bow? Set food and water in front of them so they can eat and drink and go to their master."

²³ So he prepared a big feast for them. When they had eaten and drunk, he sent them away, and they went to their master. The Aramean raiders did not come into Israel's land again.

THE SIEGE OF SAMARIA

²⁴ Some time later, King Ben-hadad of Aram brought all his military units together and marched up and laid siege to Samaria. ²⁵ So there was a severe famine in Samaria, and they continued the siege against it until a donkey's

---

^A 6:10 Lit *not once and not twice*   ^B 6:18 Or *a blinding light* head sold for thirty-four ounces^A of silver, and a cup^B of dove's dung^C sold for two ounces^D of silver.

^26 As the king of Israel was passing by on the wall, a woman cried out to him, "My lord the king, help!"

^27 He answered, "If the LORD doesn't help you, where can I get help for you? From the threshing floor or the winepress?" ^28 Then the king asked her, "What's the matter?"

She said, "This woman said to me, 'Give up your son, and we will eat him today. Then we will eat my son tomorrow.' ^29 So we boiled my son and ate him, and I said to her the next day, 'Give up your son, and we will eat him,' but she has hidden her son."

^30 When the king heard the woman's words, he tore his clothes. Then, as he was passing by on the wall, the people saw that there was sackcloth under his clothes next to his skin. ^31 He announced, "May God punish me and do so severely if the head of Elisha son of Shaphat remains on his shoulders today."

^32 Elisha was sitting in his house, and the elders were sitting with him. The king sent a man ahead of him, but before the messenger got to him, Elisha said to the elders, "Do you see how this murderer has sent someone to remove my head? Look, when the messenger comes, shut the door to keep him out. Isn't the sound of his master's feet behind him?"

^33 While Elisha was still speaking with them, the messenger^E came down to him. Then he said, "This disaster is from the LORD. Why should I wait for the LORD any longer?"

7 Elisha replied, "Hear the word of the LORD! This is what the LORD says: 'About this time tomorrow at Samaria's gate, six quarts^F of fine flour will sell for a half ounce of silver^G and twelve quarts^H of barley will sell for a half ounce of silver.'"

^2 Then the captain, the king's right-hand man,^I responded to the man of God, "Look, even if the LORD were to make windows in heaven, could this really happen?"

Elisha announced, "You will in fact see it with your own eyes, but you won't eat any of it."

^3 Now four men with a skin disease were at the entrance to the city gate. They said to each other, "Why just sit here until we die? ^4 If we say, 'Let's go into the city,' we will die there because the famine is in the city, but if we sit here, we will also die. So now, come on. Let's surrender to the Arameans' camp. If they let us live, we will live; if they kill us, we will die."

^5 So the diseased men got up at twilight to go to the Arameans' camp. When they came to the camp's edge, they discovered that no one was there, ^6 for the Lord^J had caused the Aramean camp to hear the sound of chariots, horses, and a large army. The Arameans had said to each other, "The king of Israel must have hired the kings of the Hittites and the kings of Egypt to attack us." ^7 So they had gotten up and fled at twilight, abandoning their tents, horses, and donkeys. The camp was intact, and they had fled for their lives.

---

^A 6:25 Lit for 80; "shekels" is assumed ^B 6:25 Lit a fourth of a kab ^C 6:25 Or seedpods, or wild onions ^D 6:25 Lit for five; "shekels" is assumed ^E 6:33 Some emend to king ^F 7:1 Lit a seah, also in vv. 16,18 ^G 7:1 Lit for a shekel, also in vv. 16,18 ^H 7:1 Lit two seahs, also in vv. 16,18 ^I 7:2 Lit captain, upon whose hand the king leaned, also in v. 17 ^J 7:6 Some Hb mss read LORD

[8] When these diseased men came to the edge of the camp, they went into a tent to eat and drink. Then they picked up the silver, gold, and clothing and went off and hid them. They came back and entered another tent, picked things up, and hid them. [9] Then they said to each other, "We're not doing what is right. Today is a day of good news. If we are silent and wait until morning light, our punishment will catch up with us. So let's go tell the king's household."

[10] The diseased men came and called to the city's gatekeepers and told them, "We went to the Aramean camp and no one was there — no human sounds. There was nothing but tethered horses and donkeys, and the tents were intact." [11] The gatekeepers called out, and the news was reported to the king's household.

[12] So the king got up in the night and said to his servants, "Let me tell you what the Arameans have done to us. They know we are starving, so they have left the camp to hide in the open country, thinking, 'When they come out of the city, we will take them alive and go into the city.'"

[13] But one of his servants responded, "Please, let messengers take five of the horses that are left in the city. Their fate is like the entire Israelite community who will die,[A] so let's send them and see."

[14] The messengers took two chariots with horses, and the king sent them after the Aramean army, saying, "Go and see." [15] So they followed them as far as the Jordan. They saw that the whole way was littered with clothes and equipment the Arameans had thrown off in their haste. The messengers returned and told the king.

[16] Then the people went out and plundered the Aramean camp. It was then that six quarts of fine flour sold for a half ounce of silver and twelve quarts of barley sold for a half ounce of silver, according to the word of the LORD. [17] The king had appointed the captain, his right-hand man, to be in charge of the city gate, but the people trampled him in the gate. He died, just as the man of God had predicted when the king had come to him. [18] When the man of God had said to the king, "About this time tomorrow twelve quarts of barley will sell for a half ounce of silver and six quarts of fine flour will sell for a half ounce of silver at Samaria's gate," [19] this captain had answered the man of God, "Look, even if the LORD were to make windows in heaven, could this really happen?" Elisha had said, "You will in fact see it with your own eyes, but you won't eat any of it." [20] This is what happened to him: the people trampled him in the city gate, and he died.

THE SHUNAMMITE'S LAND RESTORED

8 Elisha said to the woman whose son he had restored to life, "Get ready, you and your household, and go live as a resident alien wherever you can. For the LORD has announced a seven-year famine, and it has already come to the land."

[2] So the woman got ready and did what the man of God said. She and her household lived as resident aliens in the land of the Philistines for seven years. [3] When the woman returned from the land of the Philistines at the end of seven years, she went to appeal to the king for her house and field.

[A]7:13 Some Hb mss, LXX, Syr, Vg; other Hb mss read *left in it. Indeed, they are like the whole multitude of Israel that are left in it; indeed, they are like the whole multitude of Israel who will die.*

HE IS THE LIGHT

2 KINGS 8:16-29; 2 SAMUEL 7:15-16; ROMANS 8:28

In 2 Kings, Israel is split into two kingdoms: the northern kingdom of Israel (ten tribes) and the southern kingdom of Judah (Judah and Benjamin). For the most part, Israel's kings rejected God while Judah remained faithful to the Lord.

Until Jehoram.

Jehoram married the daughter of Ahab, a king who went down in history for straying further away from God's law than any other king. Jehoram followed in his father-in-law's rebellious footsteps and did what was evil in the sight of the Lord.

God had reason to destroy Jehoram and the entire kingdom of Judah. But He refrained.

Sometimes God allows evil and sin to continue because He has a greater purpose in mind. In this case, it was our redemption.

"For the sake of his servant David, the LORD was unwilling to destroy Judah, since he had promised to give a lamp to David and his sons forever."

2 KINGS 8:19

Our incredibly faithful God honored a promise He made to Jehoram's great, great, great, great grandfather, King David. God promised to establish David's line and throne forever. Through David's line, God would bring Jesus Christ, the Messiah, into the world.

As a direct descendant of King David, Jesus—who was, is, and always will be the true King of the nation of Israel—called Himself "the light of the world" (Jn 8:12).

He is the light that fulfills God's promise to King David.

He is the light that brings us out of darkness and corruption.

He is the light that provides a way to redemption.

God did not destroy Jehoram for his wickedness because, in doing so, He would have terminated the line of David and the ancestry of the Messiah. By allowing the people of Judah to continue in their wickedness, God's greater purpose of redemption remained intact.

I've walked through seasons of blatant sin, trial, and darkness. Each time I've wondered when God was going to step in and pull me out. And each time I've cried out for help, feeling as though God had left me alone in my sin, or left me in the midst of a difficult season because of past sin. When I look back, I can clearly see God's faithfulness. He does not treat us as our sins deserve (Ps 103:10).

In times when He seems absent, God is still working for our good and for His glory. Sometimes He reveals His purposes for hard seasons right away, and sometimes He takes years. We can be confident He is always working to redeem us, always bringing us back to the light of the world, Jesus Christ.

⁴ The king had been speaking to Gehazi, the attendant of the man of God, saying, "Tell me all the great things Elisha has done."

⁵ While he was telling the king how Elisha restored the dead son to life, the woman whose son he had restored to life came to appeal to the king for her house and field. So Gehazi said, "My lord the king, this is the woman and this is the son Elisha restored to life."

⁶ When the king asked the woman, she told him the story. So the king appointed a court official for her, saying, "Restore all that was hers, along with all the income from the field from the day she left the country until now."

ARAM'S KING HAZAEL

⁷ Elisha came to Damascus while King Ben-hadad of Aram was sick, and the king was told, "The man of God has come here." ⁸ So the king said to Hazael, "Take a gift with you and go meet the man of God. Inquire of the Lord through him, 'Will I recover from this sickness?'"

⁹ Hazael went to meet Elisha, taking with him a gift: forty camel-loads of all the finest products of Damascus. When he came and stood before him, he said, "Your son, King Ben-hadad of Aram, has sent me to ask you, 'Will I recover from this sickness?'"

¹⁰ Elisha told him, "Go say to him, 'You are sure toᴬ recover.' But the Lord has shown me that he is sure to die." ¹¹ Then he stared steadily at him until he was ashamed.

The man of God wept, ¹² and Hazael asked, "Why is my lord weeping?"

He replied, "Because I know the evil you will do to the people of Israel. You will set their fortresses on fire. You will kill their young men with the sword. You will dash their children to pieces. You will rip open their pregnant women."

¹³ Hazael said, "How could your servant, a mere dog, do such a mighty deed?"

Elisha answered, "The Lord has shown me that you will be king over Aram."

¹⁴ Hazael left Elisha and went to his master, who asked him, "What did Elisha say to you?"

He responded, "He told me you are sure to recover." ¹⁵ The next day Hazael took a heavy cloth, dipped it in water, and spread it over the king's face. Ben-hadad died, and Hazael reigned in his place.

JUDAH'S KING JEHORAM

¹⁶ In the fifth year of Israel's King Joram son of Ahab, Jehoramᴮ son of Jehoshaphat became king of Judah, replacing his father.ᶜ ¹⁷ He was thirty-two years old when he became king, and he reigned eight years in Jerusalem. ¹⁸ He walked in the ways of the kings of Israel, as the house of Ahab had done, for Ahab's daughter was his wife. He did what was evil in the Lord's sight. ¹⁹ For the sake of his servant David, the Lord was unwilling to destroy Judah, since he had promised to give a lamp to David and his sons forever.

²⁰ During Jehoram's reign, Edom rebelled against Judah's control and appointed their own king. ²¹ So Jehoram crossed over to Zair with all his chariots. Then at night he set out to attack the Edomites who had surrounded him and the chariot commanders, but his troops fled to their tents. ²² So Edom is still in rebellion against Judah's control today. Libnah also rebelled at that time.

ᴬ8:10 Alt Hb tradition reads You will not   ᴮ8:16 = The Lord is Exalted   ᶜ8:16 Lit Judah; Jehoshaphat had been king of Judah

²³ The rest of the events of Jehoram's reign, along with all his accomplishments, are written in the Historical Record of Judah's Kings. ²⁴ Jehoram rested with his fathers and was buried with his fathers in the city of David, and his son Ahaziah became king in his place.

JUDAH'S KING AHAZIAH

²⁵ In the twelfth year of Israel's King Joram son of Ahab, Ahaziah son of Jehoram became king of Judah. ²⁶ Ahaziah was twenty-two years old when he became king, and he reigned one year in Jerusalem. His mother's name was Athaliah, granddaughter of Israel's King Omri. ²⁷ He walked in the ways of the house of Ahab and did what was evil in the LORD's sight like the house of Ahab, for his father had married into^A the house of Ahab.

²⁸ Ahaziah went with Joram son of Ahab to fight against King Hazael of Aram in Ramoth-gilead, and the Arameans wounded Joram. ²⁹ So King Joram returned to Jezreel to recover from the wounds that the Arameans had inflicted on him in Ramoth-gilead^B when he fought against Aram's King Hazael. Then Judah's King Ahaziah son of Jehoram went down to Jezreel to visit Joram son of Ahab since Joram was ill.

JEHU ANOINTED AS ISRAEL'S KING

9 The prophet Elisha called one of the sons of the prophets and said, "Tuck your mantle under your belt, take this flask of oil with you, and go to Ramoth-gilead. ² When you get there, look for Jehu son of Jehoshaphat, son of Nimshi. Go in, get him away from his colleagues, and take him to an inner room. ³ Then take the flask of oil, pour it on his head, and say, 'This is what the LORD says: "I anoint you king over Israel."' Open the door and escape. Don't wait." ⁴ So the young prophet^C went to Ramoth-gilead.

⁵ When he arrived, the army commanders were sitting there, so he said, "I have a message for you, commander."

Jehu asked, "For which one of us?"

He answered, "For you, commander."

⁶ So Jehu got up and went into the house. The young prophet poured the oil on his head and said, "This is what the LORD God of Israel says: 'I anoint you king over the LORD's people, Israel. ⁷ You are to strike down the house of your master Ahab so that I may avenge the blood shed by the hand of Jezebel — the blood of my servants the prophets and of all the servants of the LORD. ⁸ The whole house of Ahab will perish, and I will wipe out all of Ahab's males,^D both slave and free,^E in Israel. ⁹ I will make the house of Ahab like the house of Jeroboam son of Nebat and like the house of Baasha son of Ahijah. ¹⁰ The dogs will eat Jezebel in the plot of land at Jezreel — no one will bury her.'" Then the young prophet opened the door and escaped.

¹¹ When Jehu came out to his master's servants, they asked, "Is everything all right? Why did this crazy person come to you?"

Then he said to them, "You know the sort and their ranting."

¹² But they replied, "That's a lie! Tell us!"

---

^A 8:27 Lit for he was related by marriage to ^B 8:29 Lit Ramah ^C 9:4 Or the young man, the attendant of the prophet ^D 9:8 Lit wipe out Ahab's one who urinates against a wall ^E 9:8 Or males, even the weak and impaired; Hb obscure

So Jehu said, "He talked to me about this and that and said, 'This is what the LORD says: I anoint you king over Israel.' "

¹³ Each man quickly took his garment and put it under Jehu on the bare steps.ᴬ They blew the ram's horn and proclaimed, "Jehu is king!"

¹⁴ Then Jehu son of Jehoshaphat, son of Nimshi, conspired against Joram. Joram and all Israel had been at Ramoth-gilead on guard against King Hazael of Aram. ¹⁵ But King Joram had returned to Jezreel to recover from the wounds that the Arameans had inflicted on him when he fought against Aram's King Hazael. Jehu said, "If you commanders wish to make me king,ᴮ then don't let anyone escape from the city to go tell about it in Jezreel."

JEHU KILLS JORAM AND AHAZIAH

¹⁶ Jehu got into his chariot and went to Jezreel since Joram was laid up there and King Ahaziah of Judah had gone down to visit Joram. ¹⁷ Now the watchman was standing on the tower in Jezreel. He saw Jehu's mob approaching and shouted, "I see a mob!"

Joram responded, "Choose a rider and send him to meet them and have him ask, 'Do you come in peace?' "

¹⁸ So a horseman went to meet Jehu and said, "This is what the king asks: 'Do you come in peace?' "

Jehu replied, "What do you have to do with peace?ᶜ Fall in behind me."

The watchman reported, "The messenger reached them but hasn't started back."

¹⁹ So he sent out a second horseman, who went to them and said, "This is what the king asks: 'Do you come in peace?' "

Jehu answered, "What do you have to do with peace? Fall in behind me."

²⁰ Again the watchman reported, "He reached them but hasn't started back. Also, the driving is like that of Jehu son of Nimshi — he drives like a madman."

²¹ "Get the chariot ready!" Joram shouted, and they got it ready. Then King Joram of Israel and King Ahaziah of Judah set out, each in his own chariot, and met Jehu at the plot of land of Naboth the Jezreelite. ²² When Joram saw Jehu he asked, "Do you come in peace, Jehu?"

He answered, "What peace can there be as long as there is so much prostitution and sorcery from your mother Jezebel?"

²³ Joram turned around and fled, shouting to Ahaziah, "It's treachery, Ahaziah!"

²⁴ Then Jehu drew his bow and shot Joram between the shoulders. The arrow went through his heart, and he slumped down in his chariot. ²⁵ Jehu said to Bidkar his aide, "Pick him up and throw him on the plot of ground belonging to Naboth the Jezreelite. For remember when you and I were riding side by side behind his father Ahab, and the LORD uttered this pronouncement against him: ²⁶ 'As surely as I saw the blood of Naboth and the blood of his sons yesterday' — this is the LORD's declaration — 'so will I repay you on this plot of land' — this is the LORD's declaration. So now, according to the word of the LORD, pick him up and throw him on the plot of land."

²⁷ When King Ahaziah of Judah saw what was happening, he fled up the road toward Beth-haggan. Jehu pursued him, shouting, "Shoot him too!" So

ᴬ9:13 Lit on the bones of the steps   ᴮ9:15 Lit "If your desire exists   ᶜ9:18 Lit What to you and to peace, also in v. 19

they shot him in his chariot^A at Gur Pass near Ibleam, but he fled to Megiddo and died there. ²⁸ Then his servants carried him to Jerusalem in a chariot and buried him in his fathers' tomb in the city of David. ²⁹ It was in the eleventh year of Joram son of Ahab that Ahaziah had become king over Judah.

JEHU KILLS JEZEBEL

³⁰ When Jehu came to Jezreel, Jezebel heard about it, so she painted her eyes, fixed her hair,^B and looked down from the window. ³¹ As Jehu entered the city gate, she said, "Do you come in peace, Zimri, killer of your master?"

³² He looked up toward the window and said, "Who is on my side? Who?" Two or three eunuchs looked down at him, ³³ and he said, "Throw her down!" So they threw her down, and some of her blood splattered on the wall and on the horses, and Jehu rode over her.

³⁴ Then he went in, ate and drank, and said, "Take care of this cursed woman and bury her, since she's a king's daughter." ³⁵ But when they went out to bury her, they did not find anything but the skull, the feet, and the hands. ³⁶ So they went back and told him, and he said, "This fulfills the LORD's word that he spoke through his servant Elijah the Tishbite: 'In the plot of land at Jezreel, the dogs will eat Jezebel's flesh. ³⁷ Jezebel's corpse will be like manure on the surface of the ground in the plot of land at Jezreel so that no one will be able to say: This is Jezebel.'"

JEHU KILLS THE HOUSE OF AHAB

10 Since Ahab had seventy sons in Samaria, Jehu wrote letters and sent them to Samaria to the rulers of Jezreel, to the elders, and to the guardians of Ahab's sons,^C saying:

² Your master's sons are with you, and you have chariots, horses, a fortified city, and weaponry, so when this letter arrives ³ select the most qualified^D of your master's sons, set him on his father's throne, and fight for your master's house.

⁴ However, they were terrified and reasoned, "Look, two kings couldn't stand against him; how can we?"

⁵ So the overseer of the palace, the overseer of the city, the elders, and the guardians sent a message to Jehu: "We are your servants, and we will do whatever you tell us. We will not make anyone king. Do whatever you think is right."^E

⁶ Then Jehu wrote them a second letter, saying:

If you are on my side, and if you will obey me, bring me the heads of your master's sons^F at this time tomorrow at Jezreel.

All seventy of the king's sons were being cared for by the city's prominent men. ⁷ When the letter came to them, they took the king's sons and slaughtered all seventy, put their heads in baskets, and sent them to Jehu at Jezreel. ⁸ When the messenger came and told him, "They have brought the heads of the king's sons," the king said, "Pile them in two heaps at the entrance of the city gate until morning."

---

^A9:27 LXX, Syr, Vg; MT omits *So they shot him*   ^B9:30 Lit *made her head pleasing*   ^C10:1 LXX; MT reads *of Ahab*   ^D10:3 Lit *the good and the upright*   ^E10:5 Lit *Do what is good in your eyes*   ^F10:6 Lit *heads of the men of the sons of your master*

⁹ The next morning when he went out and stood at the gate, he said to all the people, "You are innocent. It was I who conspired against my master and killed him. But who struck down all these? ¹⁰ Know, then, that not a word the LORD spoke against the house of Ahab will fail, for the LORD has done what he promised through his servant Elijah." ¹¹ So Jehu killed all who remained of the house of Ahab in Jezreel — all his great men, close friends, and priests — leaving him no survivors.

¹² Then he set out and went to Samaria. On the way, while he was at Beth-eked of the Shepherds, ¹³ Jehu met the relatives of King Ahaziah of Judah and asked, "Who are you?"

They answered, "We're Ahaziah's relatives. We've come down to greet the king's sons and the queen mother's sons."

¹⁴ Then Jehu ordered, "Take them alive." So they took them alive and then slaughtered them at the pit of Beth-eked — forty-two men. He didn't spare any of them.

¹⁵ When he left there, he found Jehonadab son of Rechab coming to meet him. He greeted him and then asked, "Is your heart one with mine?"ᴬ

"It is," Jehonadab replied.

Jehu said, "If it is,ᴮ give me your hand."

So he gave him his hand, and Jehu pulled him up into the chariot with him. ¹⁶ Then he said, "Come with me and see my zeal for the LORD!" So he let him ride with him in his chariot. ¹⁷ When Jehu came to Samaria, he struck down all who remained from the house of Ahab in Samaria until he had annihilated his house, according to the word of the LORD spoken to Elijah.

JEHU KILLS THE BAAL WORSHIPERS

¹⁸ Then Jehu brought all the people together and said to them, "Ahab served Baal a little, but Jehu will serve him a lot. ¹⁹ Now, therefore, summon to me all the prophets of Baal, all his servants, and all his priests. None must be missing, for I have a great sacrifice for Baal. Whoever is missing will not live." However, Jehu was acting deceptively in order to destroy the servants of Baal. ²⁰ Jehu commanded, "Consecrate a solemn assembly for Baal." So they called one.

²¹ Then Jehu sent messengers throughout all Israel, and all the servants of Baalᶜ came; no one failed to come. They entered the temple of Baal, and it was filled from one end to the other. ²² Then he said to the custodian of the wardrobe, "Bring out the garments for all the servants of Baal." So he brought out their garments.

²³ Then Jehu and Jehonadab son of Rechab entered the temple of Baal, and Jehu said to the servants of Baal, "Look carefully to see that there are no servants of the LORD here among you — only servants of Baal." ²⁴ Then they went in to offer sacrifices and burnt offerings.

Now Jehu had stationed eighty men outside, and he warned them, "Whoever allows any of the men I am placing in your hands to escape will forfeit his life for theirs." ²⁵ When he finished offering the burnt offering, Jehu said to the guards and officers, "Go in and kill them. Don't let anyone out." So they struck them down with the sword. Then the guards and officers threw

---

ᴬ10:15 Lit *heart upright like my heart is with your heart*   ᴮ10:15 LXX, Syr, Vg; MT reads *mine?" Jehonadab said, "It is and it is*   ᶜ10:21 LXX adds —*all his priests and all his prophets*—

the bodies out and went into the inner room of the temple of Baal. [26] They brought out the pillar of the temple of Baal and burned it, [27] and they tore down the pillar of Baal. Then they tore down the temple of Baal and made it a latrine — which it still is today.

EVALUATION OF JEHU'S REIGN

[28] Jehu eliminated Baal worship from Israel, [29] but he did not turn away from the sins that Jeroboam son of Nebat had caused Israel to commit — worshiping the gold calves that were in Bethel and Dan. [30] Nevertheless, the LORD said to Jehu, "Because you have done well in carrying out what is right in my sight and have done to the house of Ahab all that was in my heart, four generations of your sons will sit on the throne of Israel."

[31] Yet Jehu was not careful to follow the instruction of the LORD God of Israel with all his heart. He did not turn from the sins that Jeroboam had caused Israel to commit.

[32] In those days the LORD began to reduce the size of Israel. Hazael defeated the Israelites throughout their territory [33] from the Jordan eastward: the whole land of Gilead — the Gadites, the Reubenites, and the Manassites — from Aroer which is by the Arnon Valley through Gilead to Bashan.[A]

[34] The rest of the events of Jehu's reign, along with all his accomplishments and all his might, are written in the Historical Record of Israel's Kings. [35] Jehu rested with his fathers and was buried in Samaria. His son Jehoahaz became king in his place. [36] The length of Jehu's reign over Israel in Samaria was twenty-eight years.

ATHALIAH USURPS THE THRONE

11 When Athaliah, Ahaziah's mother, saw that her son was dead, she proceeded to annihilate all the royal heirs. [2] Jehosheba, who was King Jehoram's daughter and Ahaziah's sister, secretly rescued Joash son of Ahaziah from among the king's sons who were being killed and put him and the one who nursed him in a bedroom. So he was hidden from Athaliah and was not killed. [3] Joash was in hiding with her in the LORD's temple six years while Athaliah reigned over the land.

ATHALIAH OVERTHROWN

[4] In the seventh year, Jehoiada sent for the commanders of hundreds, the Carites, and the guards. He had them come to him in the LORD's temple, where he made a covenant with them and put them under oath. He showed them the king's son [5] and commanded them, "This is what you are to do: A third of you who come on duty on the Sabbath are to provide protection for the king's palace. [6] A third are to be at the Foundation[B] Gate and a third at the gate behind the guards. You are to take turns providing protection for the palace.[C]

[7] "Your two divisions that go off duty on the Sabbath are to provide the king protection at the LORD's temple. [8] Completely surround the king with weapons in hand. Anyone who approaches the ranks is to be put to death. Be with the king in all his daily tasks."[D]

[A]10:33 Lit *Arnon Valley and Gilead and Bashan* [B]11:6 See 2Ch 23:5; MT here reads *Sur* [C]11:6 Hb obscure [D]11:8 Lit *king when he goes out and when he comes in*

⁹ So the commanders of hundreds did everything the priest Jehoiada commanded. They each brought their men — those coming on duty on the Sabbath and those going off duty — and came to the priest Jehoiada. ¹⁰ The priest gave to the commanders of hundreds King David's spears and shields that were in the Lord's temple. ¹¹ Then the guards stood with their weapons in hand surrounding the king — from the right side of the temple to the left side, by the altar and by the temple.

¹² Jehoiada brought out the king's son, put the crown on him, gave him the testimony,ᴬ and made him king. They anointed him and clapped their hands and cried, "Long live the king!"

¹³ When Athaliah heard the noise from the guard and the crowd, she went out to the people at the Lord's temple. ¹⁴ She looked, and there was the king standing by the pillar according to the custom. The commanders and the trumpeters were by the king, and all the people of the land were rejoicing and blowing trumpets. Athaliah tore her clothes and screamed "Treason! Treason!"

¹⁵ Then the priest Jehoiada ordered the commanders of hundreds in charge of the army, "Take her out between the ranks, and put to death by the sword anyone who follows her," for the priest had said, "She is not to be put to death in the Lord's temple." ¹⁶ So they arrested her, and she went through the horse entrance to the king's palace, where she was put to death.

JEHOIADA'S REFORMS

¹⁷ Then Jehoiada made a covenant between the Lord, the king, and the people that they would be the Lord's people and another covenant between the king and the people.ᴮ ¹⁸ So all the people of the land went to the temple of Baal and tore it down. They smashed its altars and images to pieces, and they killed Mattan, the priest of Baal, at the altars.

Then Jehoiada the priest appointed guards for the Lord's temple. ¹⁹ He took the commanders of hundreds, the Carites, the guards, and all the people of the land, and they brought the king from the Lord's temple. They entered the king's palace by way of the guards' gate. Then Joash sat on the throne of the kings. ²⁰ All the people of the land rejoiced, and the city was quiet, for they had put Athaliah to death by the sword in the king's palace.

JUDAH'S KING JOASH

12 ²¹ Joashᶜ was seven years old when he became king. ¹ In the seventh year of Jehu, Joash became king, and he reigned forty years in Jerusalem. His mother's name was Zibiah; she was from Beer-sheba. ² Throughout the time the priest Jehoiada instructed him, Joash did what was right in the Lord's sight. ³ Yet the high places were not taken away; the people continued sacrificing and burning incense on the high places.

REPAIRING THE TEMPLE

⁴ Then Joash said to the priests, "All the dedicated silver brought to the Lord's temple, census silver, silver from vows, and all silver voluntarily given for

---

ᴬ11:12 Or *him the copy of the covenant,* or *him a diadem,* or *him jewels*
ᴮ11:17 Some Gk versions, 2Ch 23:16 omit *and another covenant between the king and the people*   ᶜ11:21 = The Lord Has Bestowed

the LORD's temple — ⁵each priest is to take it from his assessor^A and repair whatever damage is found in the temple."^B

⁶But by the twenty-third year of the reign of King Joash, the priests had not repaired the damage^C to the temple. ⁷So King Joash called the priest Jehoiada and the other priests and asked, "Why haven't you repaired the temple's damage? Since you haven't, don't take any silver from your assessors; instead, hand it over for the repair of the temple." ⁸So the priests agreed that they would receive no silver from the people and would not be the ones to repair the temple's damage.

⁹Then the priest Jehoiada took a chest, bored a hole in its lid, and set it beside the altar on the right side as one enters the LORD's temple; the priests who guarded the threshold put into the chest all the silver that was brought to the LORD's temple. ¹⁰Whenever they saw there was a large amount of silver in the chest, the king's secretary and the high priest would go bag up and tally the silver found in the LORD's temple. ¹¹Then they would give the weighed silver to those doing the work — those who oversaw the LORD's temple. They in turn would pay it out to those working on the LORD's temple — the carpenters, the builders, ¹²the masons, and the stonecutters — and would use it to buy timber and quarried stone to repair the damage to the LORD's temple and for all expenses for temple repairs.

¹³However, no silver bowls, wick trimmers, sprinkling basins, trumpets, or any articles of gold or silver were made for the LORD's temple from the contributions^D brought to the LORD's temple. ¹⁴Instead, it was given to those doing the work, and they repaired the LORD's temple with it. ¹⁵No accounting was required from the men who received the silver to pay those doing the work, since they worked with integrity. ¹⁶The silver from the guilt offering and the sin offering was not brought to the LORD's temple since it belonged to the priests.

ARAMEAN INVASION OF JUDAH

¹⁷At that time King Hazael of Aram marched up and fought against Gath and captured it. Then he planned to attack Jerusalem. ¹⁸So King Joash of Judah took all the items consecrated by himself and by his ancestors — Judah's kings Jehoshaphat, Jehoram, and Ahaziah — as well as all the gold found in the treasuries of the LORD's temple and in the king's palace, and he sent them to King Hazael of Aram. Then Hazael withdrew from Jerusalem.

JOASH ASSASSINATED

¹⁹The rest of the events of Joash's reign, along with all his accomplishments, are written in the Historical Record of Judah's Kings. ²⁰Joash's servants conspired against him and attacked him at Beth-millo on the road that goes down to Silla. ²¹It was his servants Jozabad^E son of Shimeath and Jehozabad son of Shomer who attacked him. He died and they buried him with his fathers in the city of David, and his son Amaziah became king in his place.

---

^A12:5 Hb obscure   ^B12:5 Lit *repair the breach of the temple wherever there is found a breach*   ^C12:6 Lit *breach* in 2Kg 12:5-12   ^D12:13 Lit *silver*
^E12:21 Some Hb mss, LXX read *Jozacar*; 2Ch 24:26 reads *Zabad*

ISRAEL'S KING JEHOAHAZ

13 In the twenty-third year of Judah's King Joash son of Ahaziah, Jehoahaz son of Jehu became king over Israel in Samaria, and he reigned seventeen years. ² He did what was evil in the LORD's sight and followed the sins that Jeroboam son of Nebat had caused Israel to commit; he did not turn away from them. ³ So the LORD's anger burned against Israel, and he handed them over to King Hazael of Aram and to his son Ben-hadad during their reigns.

⁴ Then Jehoahaz sought the LORD's favor, and the LORD heard him, for he saw the oppression the king of Aram inflicted on Israel. ⁵ Therefore, the LORD gave Israel a deliverer, and they escaped from the power of the Arameans. Then the people of Israel returned to their former way of life, ^ ⁶ but they didn't turn away from the sins that the house of Jeroboam had caused Israel to commit. Jehoahaz continued them, and the Asherah pole also remained standing in Samaria. ⁷ Jehoahaz did not have an army left, except for fifty horsemen, ten chariots, and ten thousand foot soldiers, because the king of Aram had destroyed them, making them like dust at threshing.

⁸ The rest of the events of Jehoahaz's reign, along with all his accomplishments and his might, are written in the Historical Record of Israel's Kings. ⁹ Jehoahaz rested with his fathers, and he was buried in Samaria. His son Jehoash ᴮ became king in his place.

ISRAEL'S KING JEHOASH

¹⁰ In the thirty-seventh year of Judah's King Joash, Jehoash son of Jehoahaz became king over Israel in Samaria, and he reigned sixteen years. ¹¹ He did what was evil in the LORD's sight. He did not turn away from all the sins that Jeroboam son of Nebat had caused Israel to commit, but he continued them.

¹² The rest of the events of Jehoash's reign, along with all his accomplishments and the power he had to wage war against Judah's King Amaziah, are written in the Historical Record of Israel's Kings. ¹³ Jehoash rested with his fathers, and Jeroboam sat on his throne. Jehoash was buried in Samaria with the kings of Israel.

ELISHA'S DEATH

¹⁴ When Elisha became sick with the illness from which he died, King Jehoash of Israel went down and wept over him and said, "My father, my father, the chariots and horsemen of Israel!"

¹⁵ Elisha responded, "Get a bow and arrows." So he got a bow and arrows. ¹⁶ Then Elisha said to the king of Israel, "Grasp the bow." So the king grasped it, and Elisha put his hands on the king's hands. ¹⁷ Elisha said, "Open the east window." So he opened it. Elisha said, "Shoot!" So he shot. Then Elisha said, "The LORD's arrow of victory, yes, the arrow of victory over Aram. You are to strike down the Arameans in Aphek until you have put an end to them."

¹⁸ Then Elisha said, "Take the arrows!" So he took them. Then Elisha said to the king of Israel, "Strike the ground!" So he struck the ground three times and stopped. ¹⁹ The man of God was angry with him and said, "You should have struck the ground five or six times. Then you would have struck down

---

^13:5 Lit *Israel dwelt in their tents as formerly*   ᴮ13:9 Lit *Joash*

Aram until you had put an end to them, but now you will strike down Aram only three times." ²⁰ Then Elisha died and was buried.

Now Moabite raiders used to come into the land in the spring of the year. ²¹ Once, as the Israelites were burying a man, suddenly they saw a raiding party, so they threw the man into Elisha's tomb. When he touched Elisha's bones, the man revived and stood up!

GOD'S MERCY ON ISRAEL

²² King Hazael of Aram oppressed Israel throughout the reign of Jehoahaz, ²³ but the LORD was gracious to them, had compassion on them, and turned toward them because of his covenant with Abraham, Isaac, and Jacob. He was not willing to destroy them. Even now he has not banished them from his presence.

²⁴ King Hazael of Aram died, and his son Ben-hadad became king in his place. ²⁵ Then Jehoash son of Jehoahaz took back from Ben-hadad son of Hazael the cities that Hazael had taken in war from Jehoash's father Jehoahaz. Jehoash defeated Ben-hadad three times and recovered the cities of Israel.

JUDAH'S KING AMAZIAH

14 In the second year of Israel's King Jehoash^A son of Jehoahaz, ^B Amaziah son of Joash became king of Judah. ² He was twenty-five years old when he became king, and he reigned twenty-nine years in Jerusalem. His mother's name was Jehoaddan; ^C she was from Jerusalem. ³ He did what was right in the LORD's sight, but not like his ancestor David. He did everything his father Joash had done. ⁴ Yet the high places were not taken away, and the people continued sacrificing and burning incense on the high places.

⁵ As soon as the kingdom was firmly in his grasp, Amaziah killed his servants who had killed his father the king. ⁶ However, he did not put the children of the killers to death, as it is written in the book of the law of Moses where the LORD commanded, "Fathers are not to be put to death because of children, and children are not to be put to death because of fathers; instead, each one will be put to death for his own sin."

⁷ Amaziah killed ten thousand Edomites in Salt Valley. He took Sela in battle and called it Joktheel, which is still its name today. ⁸ Amaziah then sent messengers to Jehoash son of Jehoahaz, son of Jehu, king of Israel, and challenged him: "Come, let's meet face to face."

⁹ King Jehoash of Israel sent word to King Amaziah of Judah, saying, "The thistle in Lebanon once sent a message to the cedar in Lebanon, saying, 'Give your daughter to my son as a wife.' Then a wild animal in Lebanon passed by and trampled the thistle. ¹⁰ You have indeed defeated Edom, and you have become overconfident. ^D Enjoy your glory and stay at home. Why should you stir up such trouble that you fall — you and Judah with you?"

¹¹ But Amaziah would not listen, so King Jehoash of Israel advanced. He and King Amaziah of Judah met face to face at Beth-shemesh that belonged to Judah. ¹² Judah was routed before Israel, and each man fled to his own tent. ¹³ King Jehoash of Israel captured Judah's King Amaziah son of Joash, ^E son of Ahaziah, at Beth-shemesh. Then Jehoash went to Jerusalem and broke

^A14:1 Lit *Joash*, also in vv. 23,27   ^B14:1 Lit *Joahaz*   ^C14:2 Alt Hb tradition, some Hb mss, Syr, Tg, Vg, 2Ch 25:1; other Hb mss, LXX read *Jehoaddin*   ^D14:10 Lit *and your heart has lifted you*   ^E14:13 Lit *Jehoash* down two hundred yards^A of Jerusalem's wall from the Ephraim Gate to the Corner Gate. ¹⁴ He took all the gold and silver, all the articles found in the LORD's temple and in the treasuries of the king's palace, and some hostages. Then he returned to Samaria.

JEHOASH'S DEATH

¹⁵ The rest of the events of Jehoash's reign, along with his accomplishments, his might, and how he waged war against King Amaziah of Judah, are written in the Historical Record of Israel's Kings. ¹⁶ Jehoash rested with his fathers, and he was buried in Samaria with the kings of Israel. His son Jeroboam became king in his place.

AMAZIAH'S DEATH

¹⁷ Judah's King Amaziah son of Joash lived fifteen years after the death of Israel's King Jehoash son of Jehoahaz. ¹⁸ The rest of the events of Amaziah's reign are written in the Historical Record of Judah's Kings. ¹⁹ A conspiracy was formed against him in Jerusalem, and he fled to Lachish. However, men were sent after him to Lachish, and they put him to death there. ²⁰ They carried him back on horses, and he was buried in Jerusalem with his fathers in the city of David.

²¹ Then all the people of Judah took Azariah,^B who was sixteen years old, and made him king in place of his father Amaziah. ²² After Amaziah the king rested with his fathers, Azariah rebuilt Elath^C and restored it to Judah.

ISRAEL'S KING JEROBOAM

²³ In the fifteenth year of Judah's King Amaziah son of Joash, Jeroboam son of Jehoash became king of Israel in Samaria, and he reigned forty-one years. ²⁴ He did what was evil in the LORD's sight. He did not turn away from all the sins Jeroboam son of Nebat had caused Israel to commit.

²⁵ He restored Israel's border from Lebo-hamath as far as the Sea of the Arabah, according to the word the LORD, the God of Israel, had spoken through his servant, the prophet Jonah son of Amittai from Gath-hepher. ²⁶ For the LORD saw that the affliction of Israel was very bitter for both slaves and free people.^D There was no one to help Israel. ²⁷ The LORD had not said he would blot out the name of Israel under heaven, so he delivered them by the hand of Jeroboam son of Jehoash.

²⁸ The rest of the events of Jeroboam's reign — along with all his accomplishments, the power he had to wage war, and how he recovered for Israel Damascus and Hamath, which had belonged to Judah^E — are written in the Historical Record of Israel's Kings. ²⁹ Jeroboam rested with his fathers, the kings of Israel. His son Zechariah became king in his place.

JUDAH'S KING AZARIAH

15 In the twenty-seventh year of Israel's King Jeroboam, Azariah^F son of Amaziah became king of Judah. ² He was sixteen years old when he became king, and he reigned fifty-two years in Jerusalem. His mother's name was Jecoliah; she was from Jerusalem. ³ Azariah did what was right

---

^A 14:13 Lit *400 cubits*   ^B 14:21 = Uzziah in 2Ch 26:1   ^C 14:22 = Eloth in 2Ch 26:2   ^D 14:26 Hb obscure   ^E 14:28 Lit *recovered Damascus and for Judah in Israel*; Hb obscure   ^F 15:1 = Uzziah in 2Ch 26:3

in the LORD's sight just as his father Amaziah had done. ⁴ Yet the high plac-es were not taken away; the people continued sacrificing and burning in-cense on the high places.

⁵ The LORD afflicted the king, and he had a serious skin disease until the day of his death. He lived in quarantine,^ while Jotham, the king's son, was over the household governing the people of the land.

⁶ The rest of the events of Azariah's reign, along with all his accomplish-ments, are written in the Historical Record of Judah's Kings. ⁷ Azariah rest-ed with his fathers and was buried with his fathers in the city of David. His son Jotham became king in his place.

ISRAEL'S KING ZECHARIAH

⁸ In the thirty-eighth year of Judah's King Azariah, Zechariah son of Jerobo-am reigned over Israel in Samaria for six months. ⁹ He did what was evil in the LORD's sight as his fathers had done. He did not turn away from the sins Jeroboam son of Nebat had caused Israel to commit.

¹⁰ Shallum son of Jabesh conspired against Zechariah. He struck him down publicly,^B killed him, and became king in his place. ¹¹ As for the rest of the events of Zechariah's reign, they are written in the Historical Record of Is-rael's Kings. ¹² The word of the LORD that he spoke to Jehu was, "Four gener-ations of your sons will sit on the throne of Israel," and it was so.

ISRAEL'S KING SHALLUM

¹³ In the thirty-ninth year of Judah's King Uzziah,^C Shallum son of Jabesh became king; he reigned in Samaria a full month. ¹⁴ Then Menahem son of Gadi came up from Tirzah to Samaria and struck down Shallum son of Ja-besh there. He killed him and became king in his place. ¹⁵ As for the rest of the events of Shallum's reign, along with the conspiracy that he formed, they are written in the Historical Record of Israel's Kings.

ISRAEL'S KING MENAHEM

¹⁶ At that time, starting from Tirzah, Menahem attacked Tiphsah, all who were in it, and its territory because they wouldn't surrender. He ripped open all the pregnant women.

¹⁷ In the thirty-ninth year of Judah's King Azariah, Menahem son of Gadi became king over Israel, and he reigned ten years in Samaria. ¹⁸ He did what was evil in the LORD's sight. Throughout his reign, he did not turn away from the sins Jeroboam son of Nebat had caused Israel to commit.

¹⁹ King Pul^D of Assyria invaded the land, so Menahem gave Pul seventy-five thousand pounds^E of silver so that Pul would support him to strengthen his grasp on the kingdom. ²⁰ Then Menahem exacted twenty ounces^F of silver from each of the prominent men of Israel to give to the king of Assyria. So the king of Assyria withdrew and did not stay there in the land.

²¹ The rest of the events of Menahem's reign, along with all his accom-plishments, are written in the Historical Record of Israel's Kings. ²² Mena-hem rested with his fathers, and his son Pekahiah became king in his place.

---

^A15:5 Lit *in a house of exemption from duty*   ^B15:10 Some LXX mss read *down at Ibleam*; Hb uncertain   ^C15:13 = Azariah, also in vv. 30,32,34   ^D15:19 = Tiglath-pileser   ^E15:19 Lit *1,000 talents*   ^F15:20 Lit *50 shekels*

ISRAEL'S KING PEKAHIAH

23 In the fiftieth year of Judah's King Azariah, Pekahiah son of Menahem became king over Israel in Samaria, and he reigned two years. 24 He did what was evil in the LORD's sight and did not turn away from the sins Jeroboam son of Nebat had caused Israel to commit.

25 Then his officer, Pekah son of Remaliah, conspired against him and struck him down in Samaria at the citadel of the king's palace — with Argob and Arieh.ᴬ There were fifty Gileadite men with Pekah. He killed Pekahiah and became king in his place.

26 As for the rest of the events of Pekahiah's reign, along with all his accomplishments, they are written in the Historical Record of Israel's Kings.

ISRAEL'S KING PEKAH

27 In the fifty-second year of Judah's King Azariah, Pekah son of Remaliah became king over Israel in Samaria, and he reigned twenty years. 28 He did what was evil in the LORD's sight. He did not turn away from the sins Jeroboam son of Nebat had caused Israel to commit.

29 In the days of King Pekah of Israel, King Tiglath-pileser of Assyria came and captured Ijon, Abel-beth-maacah, Janoah, Kedesh, Hazor, Gilead, and Galilee — all the land of Naphtali — and deported the people to Assyria.

30 Then Hoshea son of Elah organized a conspiracy against Pekah son of Remaliah. He attacked him, killed him, and became king in his place in the twentieth year of Jotham son of Uzziah.

31 As for the rest of the events of Pekah's reign, along with all his accomplishments, they are written in the Historical Record of Israel's Kings.

JUDAH'S KING JOTHAM

32 In the second year of Israel's King Pekah son of Remaliah, Jotham son of Uzziah became king of Judah. 33 He was twenty-five years old when he became king, and he reigned sixteen years in Jerusalem. His mother's name was Jerusha daughter of Zadok. 34 He did what was right in the LORD's sight just as his father Uzziah had done. 35 Yet the high places were not taken away; the people continued sacrificing and burning incense on the high places.

Jotham built the Upper Gate of the LORD's temple. 36 The rest of the events of Jotham's reign, along with all his accomplishments, are written in the Historical Record of Judah's Kings. 37 In those days the LORD began sending Aram's King Rezin and Pekah son of Remaliah against Judah. 38 Jotham rested with his fathers and was buried with his fathers in the city of his ancestor David. His son Ahaz became king in his place.

JUDAH'S KING AHAZ

16 In the seventeenth year of Pekah son of Remaliah, Ahaz son of Jotham became king of Judah. 2 Ahaz was twenty years old when he became king, and he reigned sixteen years in Jerusalem. He did not do what was right in the sight of the LORD his God like his ancestor David 3 but walked in the ways of the kings of Israel. He even sacrificed his son in the fire,ᴮ

ᴬ15:25 Hb obscure   ᴮ16:3 Lit *even made his son pass through the fire* imitating the detestable practices of the nations the LORD had dispossessed before the Israelites. ⁴He sacrificed and burned incense on the high places, on the hills, and under every green tree.

⁵Then Aram's King Rezin and Israel's King Pekah son of Remaliah came to wage war against Jerusalem. They besieged Ahaz but were not able to conquer him. ⁶At that time Aram's King Rezin recovered Elath for Aram and expelled the Judahites from Elath. Then the Arameans came to Elath, and they still live there today.

⁷So Ahaz sent messengers to King Tiglath-pileser of Assyria, saying, "I am your servant and your son. March up and save me from the grasp of the king of Aram and of the king of Israel, who are rising up against me." ⁸Ahaz also took the silver and gold found in the LORD's temple and in the treasuries of the king's palace and sent them to the king of Assyria as a bribe. ⁹So the king of Assyria listened to him and marched up to Damascus and captured it. He deported its people to Kir but put Rezin to death.

AHAZ'S IDOLATRY

¹⁰King Ahaz went to Damascus to meet King Tiglath-pileser of Assyria. When he saw the altar that was in Damascus, King Ahaz sent a model of the altar and complete plans for its construction to the priest Uriah. ¹¹Uriah built the altar according to all the instructions King Ahaz sent from Damascus. Therefore, by the time King Ahaz came back from Damascus, the priest Uriah had completed it. ¹²When the king came back from Damascus, he saw the altar. Then he approached the altar and ascended it.ᴬ ¹³He offered his burnt offering and his grain offering, poured out his drink offering, and splattered the blood of his fellowship offerings on the altar. ¹⁴He took the bronze altar that was before the LORD in front of the temple between his altar and the LORD's temple, and put it on the north side of his altar.

¹⁵Then King Ahaz commanded the priest Uriah, "Offer on the great altar the morning burnt offering, the evening grain offering, and the king's burnt offering and his grain offering. Also offer the burnt offering of all the people of the land, their grain offering, and their drink offerings. Splatter on the altar all the blood of the burnt offering and all the blood of sacrifice. The bronze altar will be for me to seek guidance."ᴮ ¹⁶The priest Uriah did everything King Ahaz commanded.

¹⁷Then King Ahaz cut off the frames of the water cartsᶜ and removed the bronze basin from each of them. He took the basinᴰ from the bronze oxen that were under it and put it on a stone pavement. ¹⁸To satisfy the king of Assyria, he removed from the LORD's temple the Sabbath canopy they had built in the palace, and he closed the outer entrance for the king.

AHAZ'S DEATH

¹⁹The rest of the events of Ahaz's reign, along with his accomplishments, are written in the Historical Record of Judah's Kings. ²⁰Ahaz rested with his fathers and was buried with his fathers in the city of David, and his son Hezekiah became king in his place.

ᴬ16:12 Or and offered on it: ᴮ16:15 Hb obscure   ᶜ16:17 Lit the stands
ᴰ16:17 Lit sea

ISRAEL'S KING HOSHEA

17 In the twelfth year of Judah's King Ahaz, Hoshea son of Elah became king over Israel in Samaria, and he reigned nine years. ² He did what was evil in the LORD's sight, but not like the kings of Israel who preceded him.

³ King Shalmaneser of Assyria attacked him, and Hoshea became his vassal and paid him tribute. ⁴ But the king of Assyria caught Hoshea in a conspiracy: He had sent envoys to So king of Egypt and had not paid tribute to the king of Assyria as in previous years.ᴬ Therefore the king of Assyria arrested him and put him in prison. ⁵ The king of Assyria invaded the whole land, marched up to Samaria, and besieged it for three years.

THE FALL OF SAMARIA

⁶ In the ninth year of Hoshea, the king of Assyria captured Samaria. He deported the Israelites to Assyria and settled them in Halah, along the Habor (Gozan's river), and in the cities of the Medes.

WHY ISRAEL FELL

⁷ This disaster happened because the people of Israel sinned against the LORD their God who had brought them out of the land of Egypt from the power of Pharaoh king of Egypt and because they worshipedᴮ other gods. ⁸ They lived according to the customs of the nations that the LORD had dispossessed before the Israelites and according to what the kings of Israel did. ⁹ The Israelites secretly did thingsᶜ against the LORD their God that were not right. They built high places in all their towns from watchtower to fortified city. ¹⁰ They set up for themselves sacred pillars and Asherah poles on every high hill and under every green tree. ¹¹ They burned incense there on all the high places just like the nations that the LORD had driven out before them had done. They did evil things, angering the LORD. ¹² They served idols, although the LORD had told them, "You must not do this." ¹³ Still, the LORD warned Israel and Judah through every prophet and every seer, saying, "Turn from your evil ways and keep my commands and statutes according to the whole law I commanded your ancestors and sent to you through my servants the prophets."

¹⁴ But they would not listen. Instead they became obstinate likeᴰ their ancestors who did not believe the LORD their God. ¹⁵ They rejected his statutes and his covenant he had made with their ancestors and the warnings he had given them. They followed worthless idols and became worthless themselves, following the surrounding nations the LORD had commanded them not to imitate. ¹⁶ They abandoned all the commands of the LORD their God. They made cast images for themselves, two calves, and an Asherah pole. They bowed in worship to all the stars in the sky and served Baal. ¹⁷ They sacrificed their sons and daughters in the fireᴱ and practiced divination and interpreted omens. They devoted themselves to do what was evil in the LORD's sight and angered him.

¹⁸ Therefore, the LORD was very angry with Israel, and he removed them from his presence. Only the tribe of Judah remained. ¹⁹ Even Judah did not

---

ᴬ17:4 Lit as year by year   ᴮ17:7 Lit feared   ᶜ17:9 Or Israelites spoke words
ᴰ17:14 Lit they stiffened their neck like the neck of   ᴱ17:17 Lit They made their
sons and daughters pass through the fire

keep the commands of the Lord their God but lived according to the customs Israel had practiced. [20] So the Lord rejected all the descendants of Israel, punished them, and handed them over to plunderers until he had banished them from his presence.

SUMMARY OF ISRAEL'S HISTORY

[21] When the Lord tore Israel from the house of David, Israel made Jeroboam son of Nebat king. Then Jeroboam led Israel away from following the Lord and caused them to commit immense sin. [22] The Israelites persisted in all the sins that Jeroboam committed and did not turn away from them. [23] Finally, the Lord removed Israel from his presence just as he had declared through all his servants the prophets. So Israel has been exiled to Assyria from their homeland to this very day.

FOREIGN REFUGEES IN ISRAEL

[24] Then the king of Assyria brought people from Babylon, Cuthah, Avva, Hamath, and Sepharvaim and settled them in place of the Israelites in the cities of Samaria. The settlers took possession of Samaria and lived in its cities. [25] When they first lived there, they did not fear the Lord. So the Lord sent lions among them, which killed some of them. [26] The settlers said to the king of Assyria, "The nations that you have deported and placed in the cities of Samaria do not know the requirements of the god of the land. Therefore he has sent lions among them that are killing them because the people don't know the requirements of the god of the land."

[27] Then the king of Assyria issued a command: "Send back one of the priests you deported. Have him go and live there so he can teach them the requirements of the god of the land." [28] So one of the priests they had deported came and lived in Bethel, and he began to teach them how they should fear the Lord.

[29] But the people of each nation were still making their own gods in the cities where they lived and putting them in the shrines of the high places that the people of Samaria had made. [30] The men of Babylon made Succoth-benoth, the men of Cuth made Nergal, the men of Hamath made Ashima, [31] the Avvites made Nibhaz and Tartak, and the Sepharvites burned their children in the fire to Adrammelech and Anammelech, the gods of Sepharvaim. [32] They feared the Lord, but they also made from their ranks priests for the high places, who were working for them at the shrines of the high places. [33] They feared the Lord, but they also worshiped their own gods according to the practice of the nations from which they had been deported.

[34] They are still observing the former practices to this day. None of them fear the Lord or observe the statutes and ordinances, the law and commandments that the Lord had commanded the descendants of Jacob, whom he had given the name Israel. [35] The Lord made a covenant with Jacob's descendants and commanded them, "Do not fear other gods; do not bow in worship to them; do not serve them; do not sacrifice to them. [36] Instead fear the Lord, who brought you up from the land of Egypt with great power and an outstretched arm. You are to bow down to him, and you are to sacrifice to him. [37] You are to be careful always to observe the statutes, the ordinances, the law, and the commandments he wrote for you; do not fear other gods. [38] Do not forget the covenant that I have made with you. Do not fear other gods, [39] but fear the Lord your God, and he will rescue you from all your enemies."

⁴⁰ However, these nations would not listen but continued observing their former practices. ⁴¹ They feared the LORD but also served their idols. Still today, their children and grandchildren continue doing as their fathers did.

JUDAH'S KING HEZEKIAH

18 In the third year of Israel's King Hoshea son of Elah, Hezekiah son of Ahaz became king of Judah. ² He was twenty-five years old when he became king, and he reigned twenty-nine years in Jerusalem. His mother's name was Abiᴬ daughter of Zechariah. ³ He did what was right in the LORD's sight just as his ancestor David had done. ⁴ He removed the high places, shattered the sacred pillars, and cut down the Asherah poles. He broke into pieces the bronze snake that Moses made, for until then the Israelites were burning incense to it. It was called Nehushtan. ᴮ

⁵ Hezekiah relied on the LORD God of Israel; not one of the kings of Judah was like him, either before him or after him. ⁶ He remained faithful to the LORD and did not turn from following him but kept the commands the LORD had commanded Moses.

⁷ The LORD was with him, and wherever he went he prospered. He rebelled against the king of Assyria and did not serve him. ⁸ He defeated the Philistines as far as Gaza and its borders, from watchtower to fortified city.

REVIEW OF ISRAEL'S FALL

⁹ In the fourth year of King Hezekiah, which was the seventh year of Israel's King Hoshea son of Elah, Assyria's King Shalmaneser marched against Samaria and besieged it. ¹⁰ The Assyrians captured it at the end of three years. In the sixth year of Hezekiah, which was the ninth year of Israel's King Hoshea, Samaria was captured. ¹¹ The king of Assyria deported the Israelites to Assyria and put them in Halah, along the Habor (Gozan's river), and in the cities of the Medes, ¹² because they did not listen to the LORD their God but violated his covenant — all he had commanded Moses the servant of the LORD. They did not listen, and they did not obey.

SENNACHERIB'S INVASION

¹³ In the fourteenth year of King Hezekiah, Assyria's King Sennacherib attacked all the fortified cities of Judah and captured them. ¹⁴ So King Hezekiah of Judah sent word to the king of Assyria at Lachish: "I have done wrong; withdraw from me. Whatever you demand from me, I will pay." The king of Assyria demanded eleven tonsᶜ of silver and one tonᴰ of gold from King Hezekiah of Judah. ¹⁵ So Hezekiah gave him all the silver found in the LORD's temple and in the treasuries of the king's palace.

¹⁶ At that time Hezekiah stripped the gold from the doors of the LORD's sanctuary and from the doorposts he had overlaid and gave it to the king of Assyria.

¹⁷ Then the king of Assyria sent the field marshal, the chief of staff, and his royal spokesman, along with a massive army, from Lachish to King Hezekiah at Jerusalem. They advanced and came to Jerusalem, andᴱ they took their position by the aqueduct of the upper pool, by the road to the Launderer's

---

ᴬ18:2 = Abijah in 2Ch 29:1   ᴮ18:4 = A Bronze Thing   ᶜ18:14 Lit *300 talents*
ᴰ18:14 Lit *30 talents*   ᴱ18:17 LXX, Syr, Vg; MT reads *and came and*

Field. [18] They called for the king, but Eliakim son of Hilkiah, who was in charge of the palace, Shebnah the court secretary, and Joah son of Asaph, the court historian, came out to them.

THE ROYAL SPOKESMAN'S SPEECH

[19] Then the royal spokesman said to them, "Tell Hezekiah this is what the great king, the king of Assyria, says: 'What are you relying on?[A] [20] You think mere words are strategy and strength for war. Who are you now relying on so that you have rebelled against me? [21] Now look, you are relying on Egypt, that splintered reed of a staff that will pierce the hand of anyone who grabs it and leans on it. This is what Pharaoh king of Egypt is to all who rely on him. [22] Suppose you say to me, "We rely on the LORD our God." Isn't he the one whose high places and altars Hezekiah has removed, saying to Judah and to Jerusalem, "You must worship at this altar in Jerusalem"?'

[23] "So now, make a bargain with my master the king of Assyria. I'll give you two thousand horses if you're able to supply riders for them! [24] How then can you drive back a single officer among the least of my master's servants? How can you rely on Egypt for chariots and for horsemen? [25] Now, have I attacked this place to destroy it without the LORD's approval? The LORD said to me, 'Attack this land and destroy it.'"

[26] Then Eliakim son of Hilkiah, Shebnah, and Joah said to the royal spokesman, "Please speak to your servants in Aramaic, since we understand it. Don't speak with us in Hebrew[B] within earshot of the people on the wall."

[27] But the royal spokesman said to them, "Has my master sent me to speak these words only to your master and to you? Hasn't he also sent me to the men who sit on the wall, destined with you to eat their own excrement and drink their own urine?"

[28] The royal spokesman stood and called out loudly in Hebrew: "Hear the word of the great king, the king of Assyria. [29] This is what the king says: 'Don't let Hezekiah deceive you; he can't rescue you from my power. [30] Don't let Hezekiah persuade you to rely on the LORD by saying, "Certainly the LORD will rescue us! This city will not be handed over to the king of Assyria."'

[31] "Don't listen to Hezekiah, for this is what the king of Assyria says: 'Make peace[C] with me and surrender to me. Then each of you may eat from his own vine and his own fig tree, and each may drink water from his own cistern [32] until I come and take you away to a land like your own land — a land of grain and new wine, a land of bread and vineyards, a land of olive trees and honey — so that you may live and not die. But don't listen to Hezekiah when he misleads you, saying, "The LORD will rescue us." [33] Has any of the gods of the nations ever rescued his land from the power of the king of Assyria? [34] Where are the gods of Hamath and Arpad? Where are the gods of Sepharvaim, Hena, and Ivvah?[D] Have they rescued Samaria from my power? [35] Who among all the gods of the lands has rescued his land from my power? So will the LORD rescue Jerusalem from my power?'"

[36] But the people kept silent; they did not answer him at all, for the king's command was, "Don't answer him." [37] Then Eliakim son of Hilkiah, who was

---

[A] 18:19 Lit 'What is this trust which you trust   [B] 18:26 Lit Judahite, also in v. 28
[C] 18:31 Lit a blessing   [D] 18:34 Some LXX mss, Old Lat read Sepharvaim? Where are the gods of the land of Samaria?

in charge of the palace, Shebna the court secretary, and Joah son of Asaph, the court historian, came to Hezekiah with their clothes torn and reported to him the words of the royal spokesman.

HEZEKIAH SEEKS ISAIAH'S COUNSEL

19 When King Hezekiah heard their report, he tore his clothes, covered himself with sackcloth, and went into the LORD's temple. ² He sent Eliakim, who was in charge of the palace, Shebna the court secretary, and the leading priests, who were wearing sackcloth, to the prophet Isaiah son of Amoz. ³ They said to him, "This is what Hezekiah says: 'Today is a day of distress, rebuke, and disgrace, for children have come to the point of birth, but there is no strength to deliver them. ⁴ Perhaps the LORD your God will hear all the words of the royal spokesman, whom his master the king of Assyria sent to mock the living God, and will rebuke him for the words that the LORD your God has heard. Therefore, offer a prayer for the surviving remnant.'"

⁵ So the servants of King Hezekiah went to Isaiah, ⁶ who said to them, "Tell your master, 'The LORD says this: Don't be afraid because of the words you have heard, with which the king of Assyria's attendants have blasphemed me. ⁷ I am about to put a spirit in him, and he will hear a rumor and return to his own land, where I will cause him to fall by the sword.'"

SENNACHERIB'S DEPARTING THREAT

⁸ When the royal spokesman heard that the king of Assyria had pulled out of Lachish, he left and found him fighting against Libnah. ⁹ The king had heard concerning King Tirhakah of Cush, "Look, he has set out to fight against you." So he again sent messengers to Hezekiah, saying, ¹⁰ "Say this to King Hezekiah of Judah: 'Don't let your God, on whom you rely, deceive you by promising that Jerusalem will not be handed over to the king of Assyria. ¹¹ Look, you have heard what the kings of Assyria have done to all the countries: They completely destroyed them. Will you be rescued? ¹² Did the gods of the nations that my predecessors destroyed rescue them — nations such as Gozan, Haran, Rezeph, and the Edenites in Telassar? ¹³ Where is the king of Hamath, the king of Arpad, the king of the city of^A Sepharvaim, Hena, or Ivvah?'"

HEZEKIAH'S PRAYER

¹⁴ Hezekiah took the letter from the messengers' hands, read it, then went up to the LORD's temple, and spread it out before the LORD. ¹⁵ Then Hezekiah prayed before the LORD:

LORD God of Israel, enthroned between the cherubim, you are God — you alone — of all the kingdoms of the earth. You made the heavens and the earth. ¹⁶ Listen closely, LORD, and hear; open your eyes, LORD, and see. Hear the words that Sennacherib has sent to mock the living God. ¹⁷ LORD, it is true that the kings of Assyria have devastated the nations and their lands. ¹⁸ They have thrown their gods into the fire, for they were not gods but made by human hands — wood and stone. So they have destroyed them. ¹⁹ Now, LORD our God, please save us from his power so that all the kingdoms of the earth may know that you, LORD, are God — you alone.

---

^A19:13 Or *king of Lair,*

GOD'S ANSWER THROUGH ISAIAH

[20] Then Isaiah son of Amoz sent a message to Hezekiah: "The LORD, the God of Israel says, 'I have heard your prayer to me about King Sennacherib of Assyria.' [21] This is the word the LORD has spoken against him:

Virgin Daughter Zion
despises you and scorns you;
Daughter Jerusalem
shakes her head behind your back.
[22] Who is it you mocked and blasphemed?
Against whom have you raised your voice
and lifted your eyes in pride?
Against the Holy One of Israel!
[23] You have mocked the Lord[A] through[B] your messengers.
You have said, 'With my many chariots
I have gone up to the heights of the mountains,
to the far recesses of Lebanon.
I cut down its tallest cedars,
its choice cypress trees.
I came to its farthest outpost,
its densest forest.
[24] I dug wells
and drank water in foreign lands.
I dried up all the streams of Egypt
with the soles of my feet.'

[25] Have you not heard?
I designed it long ago;
I planned it in days gone by.
I have now brought it to pass,
and you have crushed fortified cities
into piles of rubble.
[26] Their inhabitants have become powerless,
dismayed, and ashamed.
They are plants of the field,
tender grass,
grass on the rooftops,
blasted by the east wind.[C]

[27] But I know your sitting down,
your going out and your coming in,
and your raging against me.
[28] Because your raging against me
and your arrogance have reached my ears,
I will put my hook in your nose
and my bit in your mouth;
I will make you go back
the way you came.

[A] 19:23 Many mss read LORD   [B] 19:23 Lit by the hand of   [C] 19:26 DSS; MT reads *blasted before standing grain*; Is 37:27

²⁹ "This will be the sign for you: This year you will eat what grows on its own, and in the second year what grows from that. But in the third year sow and reap, plant vineyards and eat their fruit. ³⁰ The surviving remnant of the house of Judah will again take root downward and bear fruit upward. ³¹ For a remnant will go out from Jerusalem, and survivors, from Mount Zion. The zeal of the LORD of Armies will accomplish this.

³²   Therefore, this is what the LORD says about the king of Assyria:
He will not enter this city,
shoot an arrow here,
come before it with a shield,
or build up a siege ramp against it.
³³   He will go back
the way he came,
and he will not enter this city.
    This is the LORD's declaration.
³⁴   I will defend this city and rescue it
for my sake and for the sake of my servant David."

DEFEAT AND DEATH OF SENNACHERIB

³⁵ That night the angel of the LORD went out and struck down one hundred eighty-five thousand in the camp of the Assyrians. When the people got up the next morning — there were all the dead bodies! ³⁶ So King Sennacherib of Assyria broke camp and left. He returned home and lived in Nineveh.

³⁷ One day, while he was worshiping in the temple of his god Nisroch, his sons Adrammelech and Sharezer struck him down with the sword and escaped to the land of Ararat. Then his son Esar-haddon became king in his place.

HEZEKIAH'S ILLNESS AND RECOVERY

20 In those days Hezekiah became terminally ill. The prophet Isaiah son of Amoz came and said to him, "This is what the LORD says: 'Set your house in order, for you are about to die; you will not recover.'"

² Then Hezekiah turned his face to the wall and prayed to the LORD, ³ "Please, LORD, remember how I have walked before you faithfully and wholeheartedly and have done what pleases you."ᴬ And Hezekiah wept bitterly.

⁴ Isaiah had not yet gone out of the inner courtyard when the word of the LORD came to him: ⁵ "Go back and tell Hezekiah, the leader of my people, 'This is what the LORD God of your ancestor David says: I have heard your prayer; I have seen your tears. Look, I will heal you. On the third day from now you will go up to the LORD's temple. ⁶ I will add fifteen years to your life. I will rescue you and this city from the grasp of the king of Assyria. I will defend this city for my sake and for the sake of my servant David.'"

⁷ Then Isaiah said, "Bring a lump of pressed figs." So they brought it and applied it to his infected skin, and he recovered.

⁸ Hezekiah had asked Isaiah, "What is the sign that the LORD will heal me and that I will go up to the LORD's temple on the third day?"

⁹ Isaiah said, "This is the sign to you from the LORD that he will do what he has promised: Should the shadow go ahead ten steps or go back ten steps?"

ᴬ20:3 Lit *what is good in your eyes*

¹⁰ Then Hezekiah answered, "It's easy for the shadow to lengthen ten steps. No, let the shadow go back ten steps." ¹¹ So the prophet Isaiah called out to the LORD, and he brought the shadow^A back the ten steps it had descended on the stairway of Ahaz.^B

HEZEKIAH'S FOLLY

¹² At that time Merodach-baladan^C son of Baladan, king of Babylon, sent letters and a gift to Hezekiah since he heard that he had been sick. ¹³ Hezekiah listened to the letters and showed the envoys his whole treasure house — the silver, the gold, the spices, and the precious oil — and his armory, and everything that was found in his treasuries. There was nothing in his palace and in all his realm that Hezekiah did not show them.

¹⁴ Then the prophet Isaiah came to King Hezekiah and asked him, "Where did these men come from and what did they say to you?"

Hezekiah replied, "They came from a distant country, from Babylon."

¹⁵ Isaiah asked, "What have they seen in your palace?"

Hezekiah answered, "They have seen everything in my palace. There isn't anything in my treasuries that I didn't show them."

¹⁶ Then Isaiah said to Hezekiah, "Hear the word of the LORD: ¹⁷ 'Look, the days are coming when everything in your palace and all that your fathers have stored up until today will be carried off to Babylon; nothing will be left,' says the LORD. ¹⁸ 'Some of your descendants — who come from you, whom you father — will be taken away, and they will become eunuchs^D in the palace of the king of Babylon.'"

¹⁹ Then Hezekiah said to Isaiah, "The word of the LORD that you have spoken is good," for he thought: Why not, if there will be peace and security during my lifetime?

HEZEKIAH'S DEATH

²⁰ The rest of the events of Hezekiah's reign, along with all his might and how he made the pool and the tunnel and brought water into the city, are written in the Historical Record of Judah's Kings. ²¹ Hezekiah rested with his fathers, and his son Manasseh became king in his place.

JUDAH'S KING MANASSEH

21 Manasseh was twelve years old when he became king, and he reigned fifty-five years in Jerusalem. His mother's name was Hephzibah. ² He did what was evil in the LORD's sight, imitating the detestable practices of the nations that the LORD had dispossessed before the Israelites. ³ He rebuilt the high places that his father Hezekiah had destroyed and reestablished the altars for Baal. He made an Asherah, as King Ahab of Israel had done; he also bowed in worship to all the stars in the sky and served them. ⁴ He built altars in the LORD's temple, where the LORD had said, "Jerusalem is where I will put my name." ⁵ He built altars to all the stars in the sky in both courtyards of the LORD's temple. ⁶ He sacrificed his son in the fire,^E practiced

---

^A 20:11 Lit *shadow on the steps*   ^B 20:11 Tg, Vg; DSS read *on the steps of Ahaz's roof chamber*; Is 38:8   ^C 20:12 Some Hb mss, LXX, Syr, Tg, some Vg mss, Is 39:1; other Hb mss read *Berodach-baladan*   ^D 20:18 Or *court officials*   ^E 21:6 Lit *He made his son pass through the fire* witchcraft and divination, and consulted mediums and spiritists. He did a huge amount of evil in the LORD's sight, angering him.

⁷ Manasseh set up the carved image of Asherah, which he made, in the temple that the LORD had spoken about to David and his son Solomon: "I will establish my name forever in this temple and in Jerusalem, which I have chosen out of all the tribes of Israel. ⁸ I will never again cause the feet of the Israelites to wander from the land I gave to their ancestors if only they will be careful to do all I have commanded them — the whole law that my servant Moses commanded them." ⁹ But they did not listen; Manasseh caused them to stray so that they did worse evil than the nations the LORD had destroyed before the Israelites.

¹⁰ The LORD said through his servants the prophets, ¹¹ "Since King Manasseh of Judah has committed all these detestable acts — worse evil than the Amorites who preceded him had done — and by means of his idols has also caused Judah to sin, ¹² this is what the LORD God of Israel says: 'I am about to bring such disaster on Jerusalem and Judah that everyone who hears about it will shudder.ᴬ ¹³ I will stretch over Jerusalem the measuring line used on Samaria and the mason's level used on the house of Ahab, and I will wipe Jerusalem clean as one wipes a bowl — wiping it and turning it upside down. ¹⁴ I will abandon the remnant of my inheritance and hand them over to their enemies. They will become plunder and spoil to all their enemies, ¹⁵ because they have done what is evil in my sight and have angered me from the day their ancestors came out of Egypt until today.' "

¹⁶ Manasseh also shed so much innocent blood that he filled Jerusalem with it from one end to another. This was in addition to his sin that he caused Judah to commit, so that they did what was evil in the LORD's sight.

MANASSEH'S DEATH

¹⁷ The rest of the events of Manasseh's reign, along with all his accomplishments and the sin that he committed, are written in the Historical Record of Judah's Kings. ¹⁸ Manasseh rested with his fathers and was buried in the garden of his own house, the garden of Uzza. His son Amon became king in his place.

JUDAH'S KING AMON

¹⁹ Amon was twenty-two years old when he became king, and he reigned two years in Jerusalem. His mother's name was Meshullemeth daughter of Haruz; she was from Jotbah. ²⁰ He did what was evil in the LORD's sight, just as his father Manasseh had done. ²¹ He walked in all the ways his father had walked; he served the idols his father had served, and he bowed in worship to them. ²² He abandoned the LORD God of his ancestors and did not walk in the ways of the LORD.

²³ Amon's servants conspired against him and put the king to death in his own house. ²⁴ The common peopleᴮ killed all who had conspired against King Amon, and they made his son Josiah king in his place.

²⁵ The rest of the events of Amon's reign, along with his accomplishments, are written in the Historical Record of Judah's Kings. ²⁶ He was buried in his tomb in the garden of Uzza, and his son Josiah became king in his place.

ᴬ21:12 Lit about it, his two ears will tingle; Hb obscure   ᴮ21:24 Lit The people of the land

JUDAH'S KING JOSIAH

22 Josiah was eight years old when he became king, and he reigned thirty-one years in Jerusalem. His mother's name was Jedidah the daughter of Adaiah; she was from Bozkath. ² He did what was right in the LORD's sight and walked in all the ways of his ancestor David; he did not turn to the right or the left.

JOSIAH REPAIRS THE TEMPLE

³ In the eighteenth year of King Josiah, the king sent the court secretary Shaphan son of Azaliah, son of Meshullam, to the LORD's temple, saying, ⁴ "Go up to the high priest Hilkiah so that he may total up the silver brought into the LORD's temple — the silver the doorkeepers have collected from the people. ⁵ It is to be given to those doing the work — those who oversee the LORD's temple. They in turn are to give it to the workmen in the LORD's temple to repair the damage. ⁶ They are to give it to the carpenters, builders, and masons to buy timber and quarried stone to repair the temple. ⁷ But no accounting is to be required from them for the silver given to them since they work with integrity."

THE BOOK OF THE LAW FOUND

⁸ The high priest Hilkiah told the court secretary Shaphan, "I have found the book of the law in the LORD's temple," and he gave the book to Shaphan, who read it.

⁹ Then the court secretary Shaphan went to the king and reported,ᴬ "Your servants have emptied out the silver that was found in the temple and have given it to those doing the work — those who oversee the LORD's temple." ¹⁰ Then the court secretary Shaphan told the king, "The priest Hilkiah has given me a book," and Shaphan read it in the presence of the king.

¹¹ When the king heard the words of the book of the law, he tore his clothes. ¹² Then he commanded the priest Hilkiah, Ahikam son of Shaphan, Achbor son of Micaiah, the court secretary Shaphan, and the king's servant Asaiah: ¹³ "Go and inquire of the LORD for me, the people, and all Judah about the words in this book that has been found. For great is the LORD's wrath that is kindled against us because our ancestors have not obeyed the words of this book in order to do everything written about us."

HULDAH'S PROPHECY OF JUDGMENT

¹⁴ So the priest Hilkiah, Ahikam, Achbor, Shaphan, and Asaiah went to the prophetess Huldah, wife of Shallum son of Tikvah, son of Harhas, keeper of the wardrobe. She lived in Jerusalem in the Second District. They spoke with her.

¹⁵ She said to them, "This is what the LORD God of Israel says: Say to the man who sent you to me, ¹⁶ 'This is what the LORD says: I am about to bring disaster on this place and on its inhabitants, fulfillingᴮ all the words of the book that the king of Judah has read, ¹⁷ because they have abandoned me and burned incense to other gods in order to anger me with all the work of their hands. My wrath will be kindled against this place, and it will not be quenched.' ¹⁸ Say this to the king of Judah who sent you to inquire of the LORD:

ᴬ22:9 Lit *and returned a word to the king and said*   ᴮ22:16 *fulfilling* supplied for clarity

'This is what the LORD God of Israel says: As for the words that you heard, ¹⁹ because your heart was tender and you humbled yourself before the LORD when you heard what I spoke against this place and against its inhabitants, that they would become a desolation and a curse, and because you have torn your clothes and wept before me, I myself have heard' — this is the LORD's declaration. ²⁰ 'Therefore, I will indeed gather you to your fathers, and you will be gathered to your grave in peace. Your eyes will not see all the disaster that I am bringing on this place.'"

Then they reported^A to the king.

COVENANT RENEWAL

23 So the king sent messengers, and they gathered all the elders of Judah and Jerusalem to him. ² Then the king went to the LORD's temple with all the men of Judah and all the inhabitants of Jerusalem, as well as the priests and the prophets — all the people from the youngest to the oldest. He read in their hearing all the words of the book of the covenant that had been found in the LORD's temple. ³ Next, the king stood by the pillar^B and made a covenant in the LORD's presence to follow the LORD and to keep his commands, his decrees, and his statutes with all his heart and with all his soul in order to carry out the words of this covenant that were written in this book; all the people agreed to^C the covenant.

JOSIAH'S REFORMS

⁴ Then the king commanded the high priest Hilkiah and the priests of the second rank and the doorkeepers to bring out of the LORD's sanctuary all the articles made for Baal, Asherah, and all the stars in the sky. He burned them outside Jerusalem in the fields of the Kidron and carried their ashes to Bethel. ⁵ Then he did away with the idolatrous priests the kings of Judah had appointed to burn incense at the high places in the cities of Judah and in the areas surrounding Jerusalem. They had burned incense to Baal, and to the sun, moon, constellations, and all the stars in the sky. ⁶ He brought out the Asherah pole from the LORD's temple to the Kidron Valley outside Jerusalem. He burned it at the Kidron Valley, beat it to dust, and threw its dust on the graves of the common people.^D ⁷ He also tore down the houses of the male cult prostitutes that were in the LORD's temple, in which the women were weaving tapestries^E for Asherah.

⁸ Then Josiah brought all the priests from the cities of Judah, and he defiled the high places from Geba to Beer-sheba, where the priests had burned incense. He tore down the high places of the city gates at the entrance of the gate of Joshua the governor of the city (on the left at the city gate). ⁹ The priests of the high places, however, did not come up to the altar of the LORD in Jerusalem; instead, they ate unleavened bread with their fellow priests.

¹⁰ He defiled Topheth, which is in Ben Hinnom Valley, so that no one could sacrifice his son or daughter in the fire^F to Molech. ¹¹ He did away with the horses that the kings of Judah had dedicated to the sun. They had been at

---

^A 22:20 Lit *returned a word*   ^B 23:3 2Ch 34:31 reads *platform*   ^C 23:3 Lit *people took a stand in*   ^D 23:6 Lit *the sons of the people*   ^E 23:7 Or *clothing*   ^F 23:10 Lit *could make his son or daughter pass through the fire* the entrance of the Lord's temple in the precincts by the chamber of Na-than-melech, the eunuch. He also burned the chariots of the sun.

¹² The king tore down the altars that the kings of Judah had made on the roof of Ahaz's upper chamber. He also tore down the altars that Manasseh had made in the two courtyards of the Lord's temple. Then he smashed themᴬ there and threw their dust into the Kidron Valley. ¹³ The king also de-filed the high places that were across from Jerusalem, to the south of the Mount of Destruction, which King Solomon of Israel had built for Ashto-reth, the abhorrent idol of the Sidonians; for Chemosh, the abhorrent idol of Moab; and for Milcom, the detestable idol of the Ammonites. ¹⁴ He broke the sacred pillars into pieces, cut down the Asherah poles, then filled their places with human bones.

¹⁵ He even tore down the altar at Bethel and the high place that had been made by Jeroboam son of Nebat, who caused Israel to sin. He burned the high place, crushed it to dust, and burned the Asherah. ¹⁶ As Josiah turned, he saw the tombs there on the mountain. He sent someone to take the bones out of the tombs, and he burned them on the altar. He defiled it according to the word of the Lord proclaimed by the man of Godᴮ who proclaimed these things. ¹⁷ Then he said, "What is this monument I see?"

The men of the city told him, "It is the tomb of the man of God who came from Judah and proclaimed these things that you have done to the altar at Bethel."

¹⁸ So he said, "Let him rest. Don't let anyone disturb his bones." So they left his bones undisturbed with the bones of the prophet who came from Samaria.

¹⁹ Josiah also removed all the shrines of the high places that were in the cities of Samaria, which the kings of Israel had made to anger the Lord. Jo-siah did the same things to them that he had done at Bethel. ²⁰ He slaugh-tered on the altars all the priests of those high places, and he burned human bones on the altars. Then he returned to Jerusalem.

PASSOVER OBSERVED

²¹ The king commanded all the people, "Observe the Passover of the Lord your God as written in the book of the covenant." ²² No such Passover had ever been observed from the time of the judges who judged Israel through the entire time of the kings of Israel and Judah. ²³ But in the eighteenth year of King Josiah, the Lord's Passover was observed in Jerusalem.

FURTHER ZEAL FOR THE LORD

²⁴ In addition, Josiah eradicated the mediums, the spiritists, household idols, images, and all the abhorrent things that were seen in the land of Judah and in Jerusalem. He did this in order to carry out the words of the law that were written in the book that the priest Hilkiah found in the Lord's temple. ²⁵ Before him there was no king like him who turned to the Lord with all his heart and with all his soul and with all his strength according to all the law of Moses, and no one like him arose after him.

²⁶ In spite of all that, the Lord did not turn from the fury of his intense burning anger, which burned against Judah because of all the affronts with

---

ᴬ23:12 Text emended; MT reads *he ran from*   ᴮ23:16 LXX adds *when Jeroboam stood by the altar of the feast. And he turned and raised his eyes to the tomb of the man of God* which Manasseh had angered him. ²⁷ For the LORD had said, "I will also remove Judah from my presence just as I have removed Israel. I will reject this city Jerusalem, that I have chosen, and the temple about which I said, 'My name will be there.'"

JOSIAH'S DEATH

²⁸ The rest of the events of Josiah's reign, along with all his accomplishments, are written in the Historical Record of Judah's Kings. ²⁹ During his reign, Pharaoh Neco king of Egypt marched up to help the king of Assyria at the Euphrates River. King Josiah went to confront him, and at Megiddo when Neco saw him he killed him. ³⁰ From Megiddo his servants carried his dead body in a chariot, brought him into Jerusalem, and buried him in his own tomb. Then the common people^A took Jehoahaz son of Josiah, anointed him, and made him king in place of his father.

JUDAH'S KING JEHOAHAZ

³¹ Jehoahaz was twenty-three years old when he became king, and he reigned three months in Jerusalem. His mother's name was Hamutal daughter of Jeremiah; she was from Libnah. ³² He did what was evil in the LORD's sight just as his ancestors had done. ³³ Pharaoh Neco imprisoned him at Riblah in the land of Hamath to keep him from reigning in Jerusalem, and he imposed on the land a fine of seventy-five hundred pounds^B of silver and seventy-five pounds^C of gold.

JUDAH'S KING JEHOIAKIM

³⁴ Then Pharaoh Neco made Eliakim son of Josiah king in place of his father Josiah and changed Eliakim's name to Jehoiakim. But Neco took Jehoahaz and went to Egypt, and he died there. ³⁵ So Jehoiakim gave the silver and the gold to Pharaoh, but at Pharaoh's command he taxed the land to give it. He exacted the silver and the gold from the common people, each according to his assessment, to give it to Pharaoh Neco.

³⁶ Jehoiakim was twenty-five years old when he became king, and he reigned eleven years in Jerusalem. His mother's name was Zebidah daughter of Pedaiah; she was from Rumah. ³⁷ He did what was evil in the LORD's sight just as his ancestors had done.

JEHOIAKIM'S REBELLION AND DEATH

24 During Jehoiakim's reign, King Nebuchadnezzar of Babylon attacked. Jehoiakim became his vassal for three years, and then he turned and rebelled against him. ² The LORD sent Chaldean, Aramean, Moabite, and Ammonite raiders against Jehoiakim. He sent them against Judah to destroy it, according to the word of the LORD he had spoken through his servants the prophets. ³ Indeed, this happened to Judah at the LORD's command to remove them from his presence. It was because of the sins of Manasseh, according to all he had done, ⁴ and also because of all the innocent blood he had shed. He had filled Jerusalem with innocent blood, and the LORD was not willing to forgive.

---

^A23:30 Lit *the people of the land*, also in v. 35   ^B23:33 Lit *100 talents*
^C23:33 Lit *one talent*

⁵ The rest of the events of Jehoiakim's reign, along with all his accomplishments, are written in the Historical Record of Judah's Kings. ⁶ Jehoiakim rested with his fathers, and his son Jehoiachin became king in his place.

⁷ Now the king of Egypt did not march out of his land again, for the king of Babylon took everything that had belonged to the king of Egypt, from the Brook of Egypt to the Euphrates River.

JUDAH'S KING JEHOIACHIN

⁸ Jehoiachin was eighteen years old when he became king, and he reigned three months in Jerusalem. His mother's name was Nehushta daughter of Elnathan; she was from Jerusalem. ⁹ He did what was evil in the Lord's sight just as his father had done.

DEPORTATIONS TO BABYLON

¹⁰ At that time the servants of King Nebuchadnezzar of Babylon marched up to Jerusalem, and the city came under siege. ¹¹ King Nebuchadnezzar of Babylon came to the city while his servants were besieging it. ¹² King Jehoiachin of Judah, along with his mother, his servants, his commanders, and his officials,ᴬ surrendered to the king of Babylon.

So the king of Babylon took him captive in the eighth year of his reign. ¹³ He also carried off from there all the treasures of the Lord's temple and the treasures of the king's palace, and he cut into pieces all the gold articles that King Solomon of Israel had made for the Lord's sanctuary, just as the Lord had predicted. ¹⁴ He deported all Jerusalem and all the commanders and all the best soldiers — ten thousand captives including all the craftsmen and metalsmiths. Except for the poorest people of the land, no one remained.

¹⁵ Nebuchadnezzar deported Jehoiachin to Babylon. He took the king's mother, the king's wives, his officials, and the leading men of the land into exile from Jerusalem to Babylon. ¹⁶ The king of Babylon brought captive into Babylon all seven thousand of the best soldiers and one thousand craftsmen and metalsmiths — all strong and fit for war. ¹⁷ And the king of Babylon made Mattaniah, Jehoiachin'sᴮ uncle, king in his place and changed his name to Zedekiah.

JUDAH'S KING ZEDEKIAH

¹⁸ Zedekiah was twenty-one years old when he became king, and he reigned eleven years in Jerusalem. His mother's name was Hamutal daughter of Jeremiah; she was from Libnah. ¹⁹ Zedekiah did what was evil in the Lord's sight just as Jehoiakim had done. ²⁰ Because of the Lord's anger, it came to the point in Jerusalem and Judah that he finally banished them from his presence. Then Zedekiah rebelled against the king of Babylon.

NEBUCHADNEZZAR'S SIEGE OF JERUSALEM

25 In the ninth year of Zedekiah's reign, on the tenth day of the tenth month, King Nebuchadnezzar of Babylon advanced against Jerusalem with his entire army. They laid siege to the city and built a siege wall against it all around. ² The city was under siege until King Zedekiah's eleventh year.

ᴬ24:12 Or eunuchs ᴮ24:17 Lit his

YOURS, LORD, IS THE Kingdom

1 chronicles

 Yours, LORD, is the greatness and the power and the glory and the splendor and the majesty, for everything in the heavens and on earth belongs to you. Yours, LORD, is the kingdom, and you are exalted as head over all. **29:11**

ON THE TIMELINE The book of 1 Chronicles includes extensive genealogies from the time of Adam, focusing on the reign of King David. The events in 1 Chronicles, excluding the genealogies, begin with the deaths of Saul and his sons and King David's rise to the throne in Israel, around 1011 BC. The book concludes with the death of King David and the enthronement of Solomon in 971 BC.

A LITTLE BACKGROUND First and 2 Chronicles are the first and second books of a four-book series that includes Ezra and Nehemiah. Together, these four books provide a priestly history of Israel from the time of Adam to the rebuilding of the house of God and the walls of Jerusalem. It is likely that the two Chronicles were, at one time, a single scroll.

An ancient tradition ascribes the authorship of Chronicles to Ezra. Among other criteria, this identification is supported by the fact that the last verses of Chronicles are the first verses of the book of Ezra.

MESSAGE & PURPOSE Having resettled in Jerusalem after the exile, the Israelites needed to reconnect with their identity as the people of God. Chronicles met this purpose by reminding them of their heritage and by directing them back to God's presence in their midst as symbolized by the temple.

The important ideas emphasized in 1 and 2 Chronicles are:
1. A direct connection to God's people in the past
2. The continuity of the line of David on the throne of Judah
3. The centrality of the temple and its rituals in focusing on God
4. The importance of music in worshiping God
5. The invincibility of God's people when they obey Him
6. The inevitability of punishment when God's people disobey Him.

GIVE THANKS FOR THE BOOK OF 1 CHRONICLES:

Chronicles brings together many dimensions of biblical revelation, such as historical events (as recounted in Genesis through Kings), temple ritual (as prescribed in Leviticus), sin and judgment (as preached by the prophets), and even some psalms. The books of 1 and 2 Chronicles give us the big picture of Old Testament history, capturing the Davidic covenant in light of Israel's history back to Adam and pointing to the eternal continuation of that covenant through the reign of the Messiah.

THE BOOK OF 1 CHRONICLES IN HISTORY

1110 BC   1085 BC   1060 BC   1035 BC

1105

1080

1051

1050

Birth of
Samuel

Birth
of Saul

Birth of
David

Saul anointed king of Israel

1010 BC   985 BC   960 BC

975

1003

971

1025   1000   970

○   ○   ○ ○   ○ ○ ○

David moves the ark of   King David dies
the covenant to Jerusalem

Death of
Samuel   David becomes   Solomon becomes
king of Israel   king of Israel

Death of Saul

David becomes   Absalom's revolt
king of Judah

READ AND UNDERSTAND 1 CHRONICLES

The Bible is a complete work in which many stories combine to tell one story. As you read the book of 1 Chronicles, consider reading the additional passages to discover how the whole of Scripture works together.

Week 1	GOING DEEPER
☐ 1 Chronicles 1–2	Luke 3:23-38; Galatians 3:16
☐ 1 Chronicles 3–4	Galatians 3:13-14; Hebrews 11:16
☐ **1 Chronicles 5–6**	Ephesians 1:13-14; Hebrews 10:19-22
☐ 1 Chronicles 7–8	Isaiah 9:6-7; Matthew 1:6-16
☐ 1 Chronicles 9:1-34	Numbers 25:6-13; Galatians 3:28-29

Week 2	GOING DEEPER
☐ 1 Chronicles 9:35–11:9	1 Samuel 5:1-4; Psalm 78:70-72
☐ 1 Chronicles 11:10–12:40	2 Samuel 23:8-39; Ephesians 4:4-6
☐ 1 Chronicles 13–14	Psalm 21; Romans 3:20-26
☐ 1 Chronicles 15–16	Psalm 96; Hebrews 13:15
☐ 1 Chronicles 17–18	2 Samuel 7:5-16; Romans 1:1-6

Week 3	GOING DEEPER
☐ 1 Chronicles 19–20	Psalm 24:1-10; Luke 10:18-20
☐ **1 Chronicles 21–22**	Psalm 6; John 14:6
☐ 1 Chronicles 23–25	Numbers 4:5-15; Romans 12:1
☐ 1 Chronicles 26–27	Psalm 33:13-22; John 10:7-10
☐ **1 Chronicles 28–29**	Psalm 132; Genesis 2:1-3

FROM ADAM TO ABRAHAM

1 Adam, Seth, Enosh,
² Kenan, Mahalalel, Jared,
³ Enoch, Methuselah, Lamech,
⁴ Noah, Noah's sons:ᴬ
Shem, Ham, and Japheth.

⁵ Japheth's sons: Gomer, Magog, Madai, Javan, Tubal, Meshech, and Tiras.
⁶ Gomer's sons: Ashkenaz, Riphath,ᴮ and Togarmah.
⁷ Javan's sons: Elishah, Tarshish, Kittim, and Rodanim.ᶜ

⁸ Ham's sons: Cush, Mizraim,ᴰ Put, and Canaan.
⁹ Cush's sons: Seba, Havilah, Sabta, Raama, and Sabteca.
Raama's sons: Sheba and Dedan.
¹⁰ Cush fathered Nimrod, who was the first to become a great warrior on earth.
¹¹ Mizraim fathered the people of Lud, Anam, Lehab, Naphtuh,
¹² Pathrus, Casluh (the Philistines came from them), and Caphtor.
¹³ Canaan fathered Sidon as his firstborn and Heth, ¹⁴ as well as the Jebusites, Amorites, Girgashites, ¹⁵ Hivites, Arkites, Sinites,
¹⁶ Arvadites, Zemarites, and Hamathites.

¹⁷ Shem's sons: Elam, Asshur, Arpachshad, Lud, Aram, Uz, Hul, Gether, and Meshech.
¹⁸ Arpachshad fathered Shelah, and Shelah fathered Eber. ¹⁹ Two sons were born to Eber. One of them was named Pelegᴱ because the earth was divided during his lifetime, and the name of his brother was Joktan. ²⁰ Joktan fathered Almodad, Sheleph, Hazarmaveth, Jerah,
²¹ Hadoram, Uzal, Diklah, ²² Ebal, Abimael, Sheba, ²³ Ophir, Havilah, and Jobab. All of these were Joktan's sons.

²⁴ Shem, Arpachshad, Shelah,
²⁵ Eber, Peleg, Reu,
²⁶ Serug, Nahor, Terah,
²⁷ and Abram (that is, Abraham).

ABRAHAM'S DESCENDANTS

²⁸ Abraham's sons: Isaac and Ishmael.

²⁹ These are their family records: Nebaioth, Ishmael's firstborn, Kedar, Adbeel, Mibsam, ³⁰ Mishma, Dumah, Massa, Hadad, Tema, ³¹ Jetur, Naphish, and Kedemah.
These were Ishmael's sons.

ᴬ1:4 LXX; MT omits *Noah's sons* ᴮ1:6 Some Hb mss, LXX, Vg; other Hb mss read *Diphath*; Gn 10:3 ᶜ1:7 Some Hb mss, Syr read *Dodanim*; Gn 10:4
ᴰ1:8 = Egypt ᴱ1:19 = Division

³² The sons born to Keturah, Abraham's concubine: Zimran, Jokshan, Medan, Midian, Ishbak, and Shuah.

Jokshan's sons: Sheba and Dedan.

³³ Midian's sons: Ephah, Epher, Hanoch, Abida, and Eldaah.

All of these were Keturah's descendants.

³⁴ Abraham fathered Isaac.

Isaac's sons: Esau and Israel.

³⁵ Esau's sons: Eliphaz, Reuel, Jeush, Jalam, and Korah.

³⁶ Eliphaz's sons: Teman, Omar, Zephi, Gatam, and Kenaz; and by Timna, Amalek.ᴬ

³⁷ Reuel's sons: Nahath, Zerah, Shammah, and Mizzah.

THE EDOMITES

³⁸ Seir's sons: Lotan, Shobal, Zibeon, Anah, Dishon, Ezer, and Dishan.

³⁹ Lotan's sons: Hori and Homam. Timna was Lotan's sister.

⁴⁰ Shobal's sons: Alian, Manahath, Ebal, Shephi, and Onam.

Zibeon's sons: Aiah and Anah.

⁴¹ Anah's son: Dishon.

Dishon's sons: Hamran, Eshban, Ithran, and Cheran.

⁴² Ezer's sons: Bilhan, Zaavan, and Jaakan.

Dishan's sons: Uz and Aran.

⁴³ These were the kings who reigned in the land of Edom before any king reigned over the Israelites:

Bela son of Beor.

Bela's town was named Dinhabah.

⁴⁴ When Bela died, Jobab son of Zerah from Bozrah reigned in his place.

⁴⁵ When Jobab died, Husham from the land of the Temanites reigned in his place.

⁴⁶ When Husham died, Hadad son of Bedad, who defeated Midian in the territory of Moab, reigned in his place.

Hadad's town was named Avith.

⁴⁷ When Hadad died, Samlah from Masrekah reigned in his place.

⁴⁸ When Samlah died, Shaul from Rehoboth on the Euphrates River reigned in his place.

⁴⁹ When Shaul died, Baal-hanan son of Achbor reigned in his place.

⁵⁰ When Baal-hanan died, Hadad reigned in his place.

Hadad's city was named Pai, and his wife's name was Mehetabel daughter of Matred, daughter of Me-zahab.

⁵¹ Then Hadad died.

Edom's chiefs: Timna, Alvah,ᴮ Jetheth, ⁵² Oholibamah, Elah, Pinon, ⁵³ Kenaz, Teman, Mibzar, ⁵⁴ Magdiel, and Iram.

These were Edom's chiefs.

ᴬ1:36 LXX; MT reads *and Timna and Amalek*; Gn 36:12   ᴮ1:51 Alt Hb tradition reads *Aliah*

ISRAEL'S SONS

2 These were Israel's sons:
Reuben, Simeon, Levi,
Judah, Issachar, Zebulun,
² Dan, Joseph, Benjamin,
Naphtali, Gad, and Asher.

JUDAH'S DESCENDANTS

³ Judah's sons: Er, Onan, and Shelah. These three were born to him by Bath-shua the Canaanite woman. Er, Judah's firstborn, was evil in the LORD's sight, so he put him to death. ⁴ Judah's daughter-in-law Tamar bore Perez and Zerah to him. Judah had five sons in all.

⁵ Perez's sons: Hezron and Hamul.
⁶ Zerah's sons: Zimri, Ethan, Heman, Calcol, and Dara ^A — five in all.
⁷ Carmi's son: Achar, ^B who brought trouble on Israel when he was unfaithful by taking the things set apart for destruction.
⁸ Ethan's son: Azariah.
⁹ Hezron's sons, who were born to him: Jerahmeel, Ram, and Chelubai. ^C

¹⁰ Ram fathered Amminadab, and Amminadab fathered Nahshon, a leader of Judah's descendants.
¹¹ Nahshon fathered Salma, and Salma fathered Boaz.
¹² Boaz fathered Obed, and Obed fathered Jesse.
¹³ Jesse fathered Eliab, his firstborn; Abinadab was born second, Shimea third, ¹⁴ Nethanel fourth, Raddai fifth, ¹⁵ Ozem sixth, and David seventh.
¹⁶ Their sisters were Zeruiah and Abigail. Zeruiah's three sons: Abishai, Joab, and Asahel. ¹⁷ Amasa's mother was Abigail, and his father was Jether the Ishmaelite.

¹⁸ Caleb son of Hezron had children by his wife Azubah and by Jerioth. These were Azubah's sons: Jesher, Shobab, and Ardon. ¹⁹ When Azubah died, Caleb married Ephrath, and she bore Hur to him. ²⁰ Hur fathered Uri, and Uri fathered Bezalel. ²¹ After this, Hezron slept with the daughter of Machir the father of Gilead. Hezron had married her when he was sixty years old, and she bore Segub to him. ²² Segub fathered Jair, who possessed twenty-three towns in the land of Gilead. ²³ But Geshur and Aram captured ^D Jair's Villages ^E along with Kenath and its surrounding villages — sixty towns. All these were the descendants of Machir father of Gilead. ²⁴ After Hezron's death in Caleb-ephrathah, his wife Abijah bore ^F Ashhur to him. He was the father of Tekoa.

²⁵ The sons of Jerahmeel, Hezron's firstborn: Ram, his firstborn, Bunah, Oren, Ozem, and Ahijah. ²⁶ Jerahmeel had another wife named Atarah, who was the mother of Onam.

---

^A 2:6 Some Hb mss, LXX, Syr, Tg, Vg read *Darda*; 1Kg 4:31   ^B 2:7 = Trouble; Achan in Jos 7:1,16-26   ^C 2:9 = Caleb   ^D 2:23 Lit *took from them*   ^E 2:23 Or *captured Havvoth-jair*   ^F 2:24 LXX, Vg read *death, Caleb slept with Ephrath (Hezron's wife was Abijah) and she bore*

²⁷ The sons of Ram, Jerahmeel's firstborn: Maaz, Jamin, and Eker.

²⁸ Onam's sons: Shammai and Jada.

Shammai's sons: Nadab and Abishur. ²⁹ Abishur's wife was named Abihail, who bore Ahban and Molid to him.

³⁰ Nadab's sons: Seled and Appaim. Seled died without children.

³¹ Appaim's son: Ishi.

Ishi's son: Sheshan.

Sheshan's descendant: Ahlai.

³² The sons of Jada, brother of Shammai: Jether and Jonathan. Jether died without children.

³³ Jonathan's sons: Peleth and Zaza. These were the descendants of Jerahmeel.

³⁴ Sheshan had no sons, only daughters, but he did have an Egyptian servant whose name was Jarha. ³⁵ Sheshan gave his daughter in marriage to his servant Jarha, and she bore Attai to him.

³⁶ Attai fathered Nathan, and Nathan fathered Zabad.

³⁷ Zabad fathered Ephlal, and Ephlal fathered Obed.

³⁸ Obed fathered Jehu, and Jehu fathered Azariah.

³⁹ Azariah fathered Helez, and Helez fathered Elasah.

⁴⁰ Elasah fathered Sismai, and Sismai fathered Shallum.

⁴¹ Shallum fathered Jekamiah, and Jekamiah fathered Elishama.

⁴² The sons of Caleb brother of Jerahmeel: Mesha, his firstborn, fathered Ziph, and Mareshah, his second son,ᴬ fathered Hebron.

⁴³ Hebron's sons: Korah, Tappuah, Rekem, and Shema.

⁴⁴ Shema fathered Raham, who fathered Jorkeam, and Rekem fathered Shammai.

⁴⁵ Shammai's son was Maon, and Maon fathered Beth-zur.

⁴⁶ Caleb's concubine Ephah was the mother of Haran, Moza, and Gazez. Haran fathered Gazez.

⁴⁷ Jahdai's sons: Regem, Jotham, Geshan, Pelet, Ephah, and Shaaph.

⁴⁸ Caleb's concubine Maacah was the mother of Sheber and Tirhanah.

⁴⁹ She was also the mother of Shaaph, Madmannah's father, and of Sheva, the father of Machbenah and Gibea. Caleb's daughter was Achsah.

⁵⁰ These were Caleb's descendants.

The sons of Hur, Ephrathah's firstborn:

Shobal fathered Kiriath-jearim;

⁵¹ Salma fathered Bethlehem,

and Hareph fathered Beth-gader.

⁵² These were the descendants of Shobal the father of Kiriath-jearim: Haroeh, half of the Manahathites,ᴮ ⁵³ and the families of Kiriath-jearim — the Ithrites, Puthites, Shumathites, and Mishraites. The Zorathites and Eshtaolites descended from these.

ᴬ 2:42 Lit and the sons of Mareshah   ᴮ 2:52 Lit Manuhoth

⁵⁴ Salma's descendants: Bethlehem, the Netophathites, Atroth-beth-joab, and half of the Manahathites, the Zorites, ⁵⁵ and the families of scribes who lived in Jabez — the Tirathites, Shimeathites, and Sucathites. These are the Kenites who came from Hammath, the father of Rechab's family.

DAVID'S DESCENDANTS

3 These were David's sons who were born to him in Hebron:
Amnon was the firstborn, by Ahinoam of Jezreel;
Daniel was born second, by Abigail of Carmel;
² Absalom son of Maacah, daughter of King Talmai of Geshur, was third;
Adonijah son of Haggith was fourth;
³ Shephatiah, by Abital, was fifth;
and Ithream, by David's wife Eglah, was sixth.
⁴ Six sons were born to David in Hebron, where he reigned seven years and six months, and he reigned in Jerusalem thirty-three years.
⁵ These sons were born to him in Jerusalem:
Shimea, Shobab, Nathan, and Solomon. These four were born to him by Bath-shua daughter of Ammiel.
⁶ David's other sons: Ibhar, Elishua,ᴬ Eliphelet, ⁷ Nogah, Nepheg, Japhia,
⁸ Elishama, Eliada, and Eliphelet — nine sons.
⁹ These were all David's sons, with their sister Tamar, in addition to the sons by his concubines.

JUDAH'S KINGS

¹⁰ Solomon's son was Rehoboam;
his son was Abijah, his son Asa,
his son Jehoshaphat, ¹¹ his son Jehoram,ᴮ,ᶜ
his son Ahaziah, his son Joash,
¹² his son Amaziah, his son Azariah,
his son Jotham, ¹³ his son Ahaz,
his son Hezekiah, his son Manasseh,
¹⁴ his son Amon, and his son Josiah.
¹⁵ Josiah's sons:
Johanan was the firstborn, Jehoiakim second,
Zedekiah third, and Shallum fourth.
¹⁶ Jehoiakim's sons:
his sons Jeconiah and Zedekiah.

DAVID'S LINE AFTER THE EXILE

¹⁷ The sons of Jeconiah the captive:
his sons Shealtiel, ¹⁸ Malchiram, Pedaiah, Shenazzar, Jekamiah, Hoshama, and Nedabiah.
¹⁹ Pedaiah's sons: Zerubbabel and Shimei.
Zerubbabel's sons: Meshullam and Hananiah, with their sister Shelomith; ²⁰ and five others — Hashubah, Ohel, Berechiah, Hasadiah, and Jushab-hesed.

ᴬ3:6 Lit Elishama; 2Sm 5:15; 1Ch 14:5 ᴮ3:11 Lit Joram ᶜ3:11 = The Lord is Exalted

²¹ Hananiah's descendants: Pelatiah, Jeshaiah, and the sons of Rephaiah, Arnan, Obadiah, and Shecaniah.ᴬ

²² The sonᴮ of Shecaniah: Shemaiah.

Shemaiah's sons: Hattush, Igal, Bariah, Neariah, and Shaphat — six.

²³ Neariah's sons: Elioenai, Hizkiah, and Azrikam — three.

²⁴ Elioenai's sons: Hodaviah, Eliashib, Pelaiah, Akkub, Johanan, Delaiah, and Anani — seven.

JUDAH'S DESCENDANTS

4 Judah's sons: Perez, Hezron, Carmi, Hur, and Shobal.
² Reaiah son of Shobal fathered Jahath, and Jahath fathered Ahumai and Lahad.

These were the families of the Zorathites.

³ These were Etam's sons:ᶜ Jezreel, Ishma, and Idbash, and their sister was named Hazzelelponi.

⁴ Penuel fathered Gedor, and Ezer fathered Hushah.

These were the sons of Hur, Ephrathah's firstborn and the father of Bethlehem:

⁵ Ashhur fathered Tekoa and had two wives, Helah and Naarah.

⁶ Naarah bore Ahuzzam, Hepher, Temeni, and Haahashtari to him. These were Naarah's sons.

⁷ Helah's sons: Zereth, Zohar,ᴰ and Ethnan. ⁸ Koz fathered Anub, Zobebah,ᴱ and the families of Aharhel son of Harum.

⁹ Jabezᶠ was more honored than his brothers. His mother named him Jabez and said, "I gave birth to him in pain."

¹⁰ Jabez called out to the God of Israel: "If only you would bless me, extend my border, let your hand be with me, and keep me from harm, so that I will not experience pain."ᴳ And God granted his request.

¹¹ Chelub brother of Shuhah fathered Mehir, who was the father of Eshton. ¹² Eshton fathered Beth-rapha, Paseah, and Tehinnah the father of Irnahash. These were the men of Recah.

¹³ Kenaz's sons: Othniel and Seraiah.

Othniel's sons: Hathath and Meonothai.ᴴ

¹⁴ Meonothai fathered Ophrah,

and Seraiah fathered Joab, the ancestor of those in the Craftsmen's Valley,ᴵ for they were craftsmen.

¹⁵ The sons of Caleb son of Jephunneh: Iru, Elah, and Naam.

Elah's son: Kenaz.

¹⁶ Jehallelel's sons: Ziph, Ziphah, Tiria, and Asarel.

¹⁷ Ezrah's sons: Jether, Mered, Epher, and Jalon. Mered's wife Bithiah gave birth to Miriam, Shammai, and Ishbah the father of Eshtemoa.

¹⁸ These were the sons of Pharaoh's daughter Bithiah; Mered had married her. His Judean wife gave birth to Jered the father of Gedor,

---

ᴬ3:21 LXX reads *Jeshaiah, his son Rephaiah, his son Arnan, his son Obadiah, and his son Shecaniah* ᴮ3:22 LXX; MT reads *sons* ᶜ4:3 LXX; MT reads *father* ᴰ4:7 Alt Hb tradition reads *Izhar* ᴱ4:8 Or *Hazzobebah* ᶠ4:9 In Hb, the name *Jabez* sounds like "he causes pain." ᴳ4:10 Or *not cause any pain* ᴴ4:13 LXX, Vg; MT omits *and Meonothai* ᴵ4:14 Or *the Ge-harashim*

Heber the father of Soco, and Jekuthiel the father of Zanoah. ¹⁹ The sons of Hodiah's wife, the sister of Naham: the father of Keilah the Garmite and the father of Eshtemoa the Maacathite.
²⁰ Shimon's sons: Amnon, Rinnah, Ben-hanan, and Tilon.
Ishi's sons: Zoheth and Ben-zoheth.

²¹ The sons of Shelah son of Judah: Er the father of Lecah, Laadah the father of Mareshah, the families of the guild ᴬ of linen workers at Beth-ashbea, ²² Jokim, the men of Cozeba; and Joash and Saraph, who married Moabites ᴮ and returned to Lehem. ᶜ These names are from ancient records. ²³ They were the potters and residents of Netaim and Gederah. They lived there in the service of the king.

SIMEON'S DESCENDANTS

²⁴ Simeon's sons: Nemuel, Jamin, Jarib, Zerah, and Shaul;
²⁵ Shaul's sons: his son Shallum, his son Mibsam, and his son Mishma.
²⁶ Mishma's sons: his son Hammuel, his son Zaccur, and his son Shimei.

²⁷ Shimei had sixteen sons and six daughters, but his brothers did not have many children, so their whole family did not become as numerous as the Judeans. ²⁸ They lived in Beer-sheba, Moladah, Hazar-shual, ²⁹ Bilhah, Ezem, Tolad, ³⁰ Bethuel, Hormah, Ziklag, ³¹ Beth-marcaboth, Hazar-susim, Beth-biri, and Shaaraim. These were their cities until David became king. ³² Their villages were Etam, Ain, Rimmon, Tochen, and Ashan — five cities, ³³ and all their surrounding villages as far as Baal. These were their settlements, and they kept a genealogical record for themselves.

³⁴ Meshobab, Jamlech, Joshah son of Amaziah,
³⁵ Joel, Jehu son of Joshibiah, son of Seraiah, son of Asiel,
³⁶ Elioenai, Jaakobah, Jeshohaiah, Asaiah, Adiel, Jesimiel, Benaiah,
³⁷ and Ziza son of Shiphi, son of Allon, son of Jedaiah, son of Shimri, son of Shemaiah —

³⁸ these mentioned by name were leaders in their families. Their ancestral houses increased greatly. ³⁹ They went to the entrance of Gedor, to the east side of the valley to seek pasture for their flocks. ⁴⁰ They found rich, good pasture, and the land was broad, peaceful, and quiet, for some Hamites had lived there previously.

⁴¹ These who were recorded by name came in the days of King Hezekiah of Judah, attacked the Hamites' tents and the Meunites who were found there, and set them apart for destruction, as they are today. Then they settled in their place because there was pasture for their flocks. ⁴² Now five hundred men from these sons of Simeon went with Pelatiah, Neariah, Rephaiah, and Uzziel, the descendants of Ishi, as their leaders to Mount Seir. ⁴³ They struck down the remnant of the Amalekites who had escaped, and they still live there today.

ᴬ 4:21 Lit *house*   ᴮ 4:22 Or *who ruled over Moab*   ᶜ 4:22 Tg, Vg; MT reads *and Jashubi Lehem*

REUBEN'S DESCENDANTS

5 These were the sons of Reuben the firstborn of Israel. He was the first-born, but his birthright was given to the sons of Joseph son of Israel, because Reuben defiled his father's bed. He is not listed in the genealogy according to birthright. ² Although Judah became strong among his brothers and a ruler came from him, the birthright was given to Joseph.

³ The sons of Reuben, Israel's firstborn:
Hanoch, Pallu, Hezron, and Carmi.

⁴ Joel's sons: his son Shemaiah,
his son Gog, his son Shimei,

⁵ his son Micah, his son Reaiah,
his son Baal, ⁶ and his son Beerah.

Beerah was a leader of the Reubenites, and King Tiglath-pileser^A of Assyria took him into exile. ⁷ His relatives by their families as they are recorded in their family records:
Jeiel the chief, Zechariah,

⁸ and Bela son of Azaz,
son of Shema, son of Joel.

They settled in Aroer as far as Nebo and Baal-meon. ⁹ They also settled in the east as far as the edge of the desert that extends to the Euphrates River, because their herds had increased in the land of Gilead. ¹⁰ During Saul's reign they waged war against the Hagrites, who were defeated by their power. And they lived in their tents throughout the region east of Gilead.

GAD'S DESCENDANTS

¹¹ The sons of Gad lived next to them in the land of Bashan as far as Salecah:

¹² Joel the chief, Shapham the second in command, Janai, and Shaphat in Bashan.

¹³ Their relatives according to their ancestral houses: Michael, Meshullam, Sheba, Jorai, Jacan, Zia, and Eber — seven.

¹⁴ These were the sons of Abihail son of Huri,
son of Jaroah, son of Gilead,
son of Michael, son of Jeshishai,
son of Jahdo, son of Buz.

¹⁵ Ahi son of Abdiel, son of Guni, was head of their ancestral family.^B

¹⁶ They lived in Gilead, in Bashan and its surrounding villages, and throughout the pasturelands of Sharon. ¹⁷ All of them were registered in the genealogies during the reigns of Judah's King Jotham and Israel's King Jeroboam.

¹⁸ The descendants of Reuben and Gad and half the tribe of Manasseh had 44,760 warriors who could serve in the army — men who carried shield and sword, drew the bow, and were trained for war. ¹⁹ They waged war against the Hagrites, Jetur, Naphish, and Nodab. ²⁰ They received help against these enemies because they cried out to God in battle, and the Hagrites and all their allies were

---

^A 5:6 LXX; MT reads *Tilgath-pilneser*   ^B 5:15 Lit *the house of their fathers*, also in v. 24

WHY SO MANY GENEALOGIES?

1 CHRONICLES 5–6

It's embarrassing to read biblical genealogies out loud—so many names, so hard to pronounce. But it's also hard to read them silently. I get lost in all the lists. We even tried to use them as a baby name book when naming our firstborn, but what little girl can pull off "Hazzelelponi" (1Ch 4:3)?

What is the purpose of so many genealogies in the Bible? Like the rest of the Bible, the genealogies are "inspired by God" (2Tm 3:16). They are there to teach us the gospel.

The genealogies in Scripture remind us that **the gospel is personal.** Think how your fingers trace names of fallen soldiers carved in the black marble of the Vietnam War monument in Washington DC. Each name belongs to an actual person. In the same way, the men and women of these genealogies were ordinary, real people.

For example, in 1 Chronicles 2:34, you can read about Sheshan who "had no sons, only daughters." I wonder if there was an empty place in his heart that longed for a son. But his family was included, and the line of Hezron was continued through his grandsons. We are getting a peek into the personal lives of the particular people God chose to bear His name.

Beyond noticing the freckles on the faces of individual people, the genealogies also help us step way back and see how **the gospel is historical.** The stories in the Bible happened in real time and space. We have a real record of family lines from Adam to Abraham to David to Jacob to the twelve tribes of Israel in exile.

Finally, the genealogies teach us that **the gospel makes everything matter.** Our comings and goings count in the economy of eternity:

- The quality of our work matters, "for they were craftsmen" (1Ch 4:14).
- Our gifts count. "They were the potters and residents of Netaim and Gederah. They lived there in the service of the king" (1Ch 4:23).
- Faithfulness is paramount in our engagement with culture. "But they were unfaithful to the God of their ancestors" (1Ch 5:25).
- Our patterns of worship have lasting significance. "They ministered with song ... they performed their task according to the regulations given to them" (1Ch 6:32).
- Our griefs and struggles carry eternal weight. "Their father Ephraim mourned a long time, and his relatives came to comfort him" (1Ch 7:22).

The genealogies of the Old Testament may seem distant, but they are a reminder that we, too, are numbered in God's record. If we are in Christ, our names are written in the Lamb's Book of Life (Mal 3:16; Rv 20:12). Let us be grateful for genealogies to remind of us this gospel truth, and rejoice in a God who cares for His people both personally and historically.

handed over to them. He was receptive to their prayer because they trusted in him. ²¹ They captured the Hagrites' livestock — fifty thousand of their camels, two hundred fifty thousand sheep, and two thousand donkeys — as well as one hundred thousand people. ²² Many of the Hagrites were killed because it was God's battle. And they lived there in the Hagrites' place until the exile.

HALF THE TRIBE OF MANASSEH

²³ The descendants of half the tribe of Manasseh settled in the land from Bashan to Baal-hermon (that is, Senir or Mount Hermon); they were numerous. ²⁴ These were the heads of their ancestral families: Epher, Ishi, Eliel, Azriel, Jeremiah, Hodaviah, and Jahdiel. They were valiant warriors, famous men, and heads of their ancestral houses. ²⁵ But they were unfaithful to the God of their ancestors. They prostituted themselves with the gods of the nations^A God had destroyed before them. ²⁶ So the God of Israel roused the spirit of King Pul (that is, Tiglath-pileser^B) of Assyria, and he took the Reubenites, Gadites, and half the tribe of Manasseh into exile. He took them to Halah, Habor, Hara, and Gozan's river, where they are until today.

THE LEVITES

6 Levi's sons: Gershom,^C Kohath, and Merari.
² Kohath's sons: Amram, Izhar, Hebron, and Uzziel.
³ Amram's children: Aaron, Moses, and Miriam.
  Aaron's sons: Nadab, Abihu, Eleazar, and Ithamar.
⁴ Eleazar fathered Phinehas;
  Phinehas fathered Abishua;
⁵ Abishua fathered Bukki;
  Bukki fathered Uzzi;
⁶ Uzzi fathered Zerahiah;
  Zerahiah fathered Meraioth;
⁷ Meraioth fathered Amariah;
  Amariah fathered Ahitub;
⁸ Ahitub fathered Zadok;
  Zadok fathered Ahimaaz;
⁹ Ahimaaz fathered Azariah;
  Azariah fathered Johanan;
¹⁰ Johanan fathered Azariah, who served as priest in the temple that
    Solomon built in Jerusalem;
¹¹ Azariah fathered Amariah;
  Amariah fathered Ahitub;
¹² Ahitub fathered Zadok;
  Zadok fathered Shallum;
¹³ Shallum fathered Hilkiah;
  Hilkiah fathered Azariah;
¹⁴ Azariah fathered Seraiah;
  and Seraiah fathered Jehozadak.
¹⁵ Jehozadak went into exile when the LORD sent Judah and Jerusalem
    into exile at the hands of Nebuchadnezzar.

---

^A 5:25 Lit *the peoples of the land*   ^B 5:26 LXX; MT reads *Tilgath-pilneser*
^C 6:1 In Hb Levi's son's name is spelled "Gershon" here and many other places

16 Levi's sons: Gershom, Kohath, and Merari.
17 These are the names of Gershom's sons: Libni and Shimei.
18 Kohath's sons: Amram, Izhar, Hebron and Uzziel.
19 Merari's sons: Mahli and Mushi.
   These are the Levites' families according to their fathers:
20 Of Gershom: his son Libni,
   his son Jahath, his son Zimmah,
21 his son Joah, his son Iddo,
   his son Zerah, and his son Jeatherai.
22 Kohath's sons: his son Amminadab,
   his son Korah, his son Assir,
23 his son Elkanah, his son Ebiasaph,
   his son Assir, 24 his son Tahath,
   his son Uriel, his son Uzziah,
   and his son Shaul.
25 Elkanah's sons: Amasai and Ahimoth,
26 his son Elkanah, his son Zophai,
   his son Nahath, 27 his son Eliab,
   his son Jeroham, and his son Elkanah.
28 Samuel's sons: his firstborn Joel,^A
   and his second son Abijah.
29 Merari's sons: Mahli, his son Libni,
   his son Shimei, his son Uzzah,
30 his son Shimea, his son Haggiah,
   and his son Asaiah.

THE MUSICIANS

31 These are the men David put in charge of the music in the LORD's temple after the ark came to rest there. 32 They ministered with song in front of the tabernacle, the tent of meeting, until Solomon built the LORD's temple in Jerusalem, and they performed their task according to the regulations given to them. 33 These are the men who served with their sons.

From the Kohathites: Heman the singer,
son of Joel, son of Samuel,
34 son of Elkanah, son of Jeroham,
son of Eliel, son of Toah,
35 son of Zuph, son of Elkanah,
son of Mahath, son of Amasai,
36 son of Elkanah, son of Joel,
son of Azariah, son of Zephaniah,
37 son of Tahath, son of Assir,
son of Ebiasaph, son of Korah,
38 son of Izhar, son of Kohath,
son of Levi, son of Israel.

39 Heman's relative was Asaph, who stood at his right hand:
Asaph son of Berechiah, son of Shimea,
40 son of Michael, son of Baaseiah,

---

^A 6:28 Some LXX mss, Syr, Arabic; other Hb mss omit *Joel*; 1Sm 8:2

son of Malchijah, ⁴¹ son of Ethni,
son of Zerah, son of Adaiah,
⁴² son of Ethan, son of Zimmah,
son of Shimei, ⁴³ son of Jahath,
son of Gershom, son of Levi.

⁴⁴ On the left, their relatives were Merari's sons:
Ethan son of Kishi, son of Abdi,
son of Malluch, ⁴⁵ son of Hashabiah,
son of Amaziah, son of Hilkiah,
⁴⁶ son of Amzi, son of Bani,
son of Shemer, ⁴⁷ son of Mahli,
son of Mushi, son of Merari,
son of Levi.

AARON'S DESCENDANTS

⁴⁸ Their relatives, the Levites, were assigned to all the service of the tabernacle, God's temple. ⁴⁹ But Aaron and his sons did all the work of the most holy place. They presented the offerings on the altar of burnt offerings and on the altar of incense to make atonement for Israel according to all that Moses the servant of God had commanded.

⁵⁰ These are Aaron's sons: his son Eleazar,
his son Phinehas, his son Abishua,
⁵¹ his son Bukki, his son Uzzi,
his son Zerahiah, ⁵² his son Meraioth,
his son Amariah, his son Ahitub,
⁵³ his son Zadok, and his son Ahimaaz.

THE SETTLEMENTS OF THE LEVITES

⁵⁴ These were the places assigned to Aaron's descendants from the Kohathite family for their settlements in their territory, because the first lot was for them. ⁵⁵ They were given Hebron in the land of Judah and its surrounding pasturelands, ⁵⁶ but the fields and settlements around the city were given to Caleb son of Jephunneh. ⁵⁷ Aaron's descendants were given:

Hebron (a city of refuge), Libnah and its pasturelands, Jattir, Eshtemoa and its pasturelands, ⁵⁸ Hilenᴬ and its pasturelands, Debir and its pasturelands, ⁵⁹ Ashan and its pasturelands, and Beth-shemesh and its pasturelands. ⁶⁰ From the tribe of Benjamin they were given Geba and its pasturelands, Alemeth and its pasturelands, and Anathoth and its pasturelands. They had thirteen towns in all among their families.

⁶¹ To the rest of the Kohathites, ten towns from half the tribe of Manasseh were assigned by lot.

⁶² The Gershomites were assigned thirteen towns from the tribes of Issachar, Asher, Naphtali, and Manasseh in Bashan according to their families.

⁶³ The Merarites were assigned by lot twelve towns from the tribes of Reuben, Gad, and Zebulun according to their families. ⁶⁴ So the Israelites gave

ᴬ6:58 Some Hb mss, LXX; other Hb mss read *Hilez*

these towns and their pasturelands to the Levites. ⁶⁵ They assigned by lot the towns named above from the tribes of the descendants of Judah, Simeon, and Benjamin.

⁶⁶ Some of the families of the Kohathites were given towns from the tribe of Ephraim for their territory:

⁶⁷ Shechem (a city of refuge) with its pasturelands in the hill country of Ephraim, Gezer and its pasturelands, ⁶⁸ Jokmeam and its pasturelands, Beth-horon and its pasturelands, ⁶⁹ Aijalon and its pasturelands, and Gath-rimmon and its pasturelands. ⁷⁰ From half the tribe of Manasseh, Aner and its pasturelands, and Bileam and its pasturelands were given to the rest of the families of the Kohathites.

⁷¹ The Gershomites received:

Golan in Bashan and its pasturelands, and Ashtaroth and its pasturelands from the families of half the tribe of Manasseh. ⁷² From the tribe of Issachar they received Kedesh and its pasturelands, Daberath and its pasturelands, ⁷³ Ramoth and its pasturelands, and Anem and its pasturelands. ⁷⁴ From the tribe of Asher they received Mashal and its pasturelands, Abdon and its pasturelands, ⁷⁵ Hukok and its pasturelands, and Rehob and its pasturelands. ⁷⁶ From the tribe of Naphtali they received Kedesh in Galilee and its pasturelands, Hammon and its pasturelands, and Kiriathaim and its pasturelands.

⁷⁷ The rest of the Merarites received:

From the tribe of Zebulun they received Rimmono and its pasturelands and Tabor and its pasturelands. ⁷⁸ From the tribe of Reuben across the Jordan at Jericho, to the east of the Jordan, they received Bezer in the desert and its pasturelands, Jahzah and its pasturelands, ⁷⁹ Kedemoth and its pasturelands, and Mephaath and its pasturelands. ⁸⁰ From the tribe of Gad they received Ramoth in Gilead and its pasturelands, Mahanaim and its pasturelands, ⁸¹ Heshbon and its pasturelands, and Jazer and its pasturelands.

ISSACHAR'S DESCENDANTS

7 Issachar's sons: Tola, Puah, Jashub, and Shimron — four.
² Tola's sons: Uzzi, Rephaiah, Jeriel, Jahmai, Ibsam, and Shemuel, the heads of their ancestral families.ᴬ During David's reign, 22,600 descendants of Tola were recorded as valiant warriors in their family records.
³ Uzzi's son: Izrahiah.
Izrahiah's sons: Michael, Obadiah, Joel, Isshiah. All five of them were chiefs. ⁴ Along with them, they had 36,000 troops for battle according to the family records of their ancestral families, for they had many wives and children. ⁵ Their tribesmen who were valiant warriors belonging to all the families of Issachar totaled 87,000 in their genealogies.

BENJAMIN'S DESCENDANTS

⁶ Three of Benjamin's sons: Bela, Becher, and Jediael.

ᴬ7:2 Lit *the house of their fathers,* also in vv. 4,7,9,40

[7] Bela's sons: Ezbon, Uzzi, Uzziel, Jerimoth, and Iri — five. They were valiant warriors and heads of their ancestral families; 22,034 were listed in their genealogies.

[8] Becher's sons: Zemirah, Joash, Eliezer, Elioenai, Omri, Jeremoth, Abijah, Anathoth, and Alemeth; all these were Becher's sons. [9] Their family records were recorded according to the heads of their ancestral families — 20,200 valiant warriors.

[10] Jediael's son: Bilhan.

Bilhan's sons: Jeush, Benjamin, Ehud, Chenaanah, Zethan, Tarshish, and Ahishahar. [11] All these sons of Jediael listed by family heads were valiant warriors; there were 17,200 who could serve in the army. [12] Shuppim and Huppim were sons of Ir, and the Hushim were the sons of Aher.

NAPHTALI'S DESCENDANTS

[13] Naphtali's sons: Jahziel, Guni, Jezer, and Shallum — Bilhah's sons.

MANASSEH'S DESCENDANTS

[14] Manasseh's sons through his Aramean concubine: Asriel and Machir the father of Gilead. [15] Machir took wives from Huppim and Shuppim. The name of his sister was Maacah. Another descendant was named Zelophehad, but he had only daughters.

[16] Machir's wife Maacah gave birth to a son, and she named him Peresh. His brother was named Sheresh, and his sons were Ulam and Rekem. [17] Ulam's son: Bedan. These were the sons of Gilead son of Machir, son of Manasseh. [18] His sister Hammolecheth gave birth to Ishhod, Abiezer, and Mahlah.

[19] Shemida's sons: Ahian, Shechem, Likhi, and Aniam.

EPHRAIM'S DESCENDANTS

[20] Ephraim's sons: Shuthelah, and his son Bered,
his son Tahath, his son Eleadah,
his son Tahath, [21] his son Zabad,
his son Shuthelah, also Ezer, and Elead.

The men of Gath, born in the land, killed them because they went down to raid their cattle. [22] Their father Ephraim mourned a long time, and his relatives[A] came to comfort him. [23] He slept with his wife, and she conceived and gave birth to a son. So he named him Beriah, because there had been misfortune in his home.[B] [24] His daughter was Sheerah, who built Lower and Upper Beth-horon and Uzzen-sheerah,

[25] his son Rephah,[C] his son Resheph,
his son Telah, his son Tahan,
[26] his son Ladan, his son Ammihud,
his son Elishama, [27] his son Nun,
and his son Joshua.

[A] 7:22 Or *his brothers* [B] 7:23 In Hb, the name *Beriah* sounds like "in misfortune."
[C] 7:25 Probably Ephraim's son

²⁸ Their holdings and settlements were Bethel and its surrounding villages; Naaran to the east, Gezer and its villages to the west, and Shechem and its villages as far as Ayyah and its villages, ²⁹ and along the borders of the descendants of Manasseh, Beth-shean, Taanach, Megiddo, and Dor with their surrounding villages. The sons of Joseph son of Israel lived in these towns.

ASHER'S DESCENDANTS

³⁰ Asher's sons: Imnah, Ishvah, Ishvi, and Beriah, with their sister Serah.
³¹ Beriah's sons: Heber, and Malchiel, who fathered Birzaith.
³² Heber fathered Japhlet, Shomer, and Hotham, with their sister Shua.
³³ Japhlet's sons: Pasach, Bimhal, and Ashvath. These were Japhlet's sons.
³⁴ Shemer's sons: Ahi, Rohgah, Hubbah, and Aram.
³⁵ His brother Helem's sons: Zophah, Imna, Shelesh, and Amal.
³⁶ Zophah's sons: Suah, Harnepher, Shual, Beri, Imrah, ³⁷ Bezer, Hod, Shamma, Shilshah, Ithran, and Beera.
³⁸ Jether's sons: Jephunneh, Pispa, and Ara.
³⁹ Ulla's sons: Arah, Hanniel, and Rizia.
⁴⁰ All these were Asher's descendants. They were the heads of their ancestral families, chosen men, valiant warriors, and chiefs among the leaders. The number of men listed in their genealogies for military service was 26,000.

BENJAMIN'S DESCENDANTS

8 Benjamin fathered Bela, his firstborn; Ashbel was born second, Aharah third, ² Nohah fourth, and Rapha fifth.
³ Bela's sons: Addar, Gera, Abihud, ᴬ ⁴ Abishua, Naaman, Ahoah, ⁵ Gera, Shephuphan, and Huram.
⁶ These were Ehud's sons, who were the heads of the families living in Geba and who were deported to Manahath: ⁷ Naaman, Ahijah, and Gera. Gera deported them and was the father of Uzza and Ahihud.
⁸ Shaharaim had sons in the territory of Moab after he had divorced his wives Hushim and Baara. ⁹ His sons by his wife Hodesh: Jobab, Zibia, Mesha, Malcam, ¹⁰ Jeuz, Sachia, and Mirmah. These were his sons, family heads. ¹¹ He also had sons by Hushim: Abitub and Elpaal.
¹² Elpaal's sons: Eber, Misham, and Shemed who built Ono and Lod and its surrounding villages, ¹³ Beriah and Shema, who were the family heads of Aijalon's residents and who drove out the residents of Gath, ¹⁴ Ahio, ᴮ Shashak, and Jeremoth.
¹⁵ Zebadiah, Arad, Eder, ¹⁶ Michael, Ishpah, and Joha were Beriah's sons.
¹⁷ Zebadiah, Meshullam, Hizki, Heber, ¹⁸ Ishmerai, Izliah, and Jobab were Elpaal's sons.
¹⁹ Jakim, Zichri, Zabdi, ²⁰ Elienai, Zillethai, Eliel, ²¹ Adaiah, Beraiah, and Shimrath were Shimei's sons.
²² Ishpan, Eber, Eliel, ²³ Abdon, Zichri, Hanan, ²⁴ Hananiah, Elam, Anthothijah, ²⁵ Iphdeiah, and Penuel were Shashak's sons.

ᴬ8:3 Or *Gera father of Ehud*; Jdg 3:15   ᴮ8:13-14 LXX reads *Gath* ¹⁴*and their brother*

²⁶ Shamsherai, Shehariah, Athaliah, ²⁷ Jareshiah, Elijah, and Zichri were Jeroham's sons.

²⁸ These were family heads, chiefs according to their family records; they lived in Jerusalem.

²⁹ Jeiel^A fathered Gibeon and lived in Gibeon. His wife's name was Maacah. ³⁰ Abdon was his firstborn son, then Zur, Kish, Baal, Nadab, ³¹ Gedor, Ahio, Zecher, ³² and Mikloth who fathered Shimeah. These also lived opposite their relatives in Jerusalem, with their other relatives.

³³ Ner fathered Kish, Kish fathered Saul, and Saul fathered Jonathan, Malchishua, Abinadab, and Esh-baal.^B

³⁴ Jonathan's son was Merib-baal,^C and Merib-baal fathered Micah.

³⁵ Micah's sons: Pithon, Melech, Tarea, and Ahaz.

³⁶ Ahaz fathered Jehoaddah, Jehoaddah fathered Alemeth, Azmaveth, and Zimri, and Zimri fathered Moza.

³⁷ Moza fathered Binea. His son was Raphah, his son Elasah, and his son Azel.

³⁸ Azel had six sons, and these were their names: Azrikam, Bocheru, Ishmael, Sheariah, Obadiah, and Hanan. All these were Azel's sons.

³⁹ His brother Eshek's sons: Ulam was his firstborn, Jeush second, and Eliphelet third.

⁴⁰ Ulam's sons were valiant warriors and archers.^D They had many sons and grandsons — 150 of them.

All these were among Benjamin's sons.

AFTER THE EXILE

9 All Israel was registered in the genealogies that are written in the Book of the Kings of Israel. But Judah was exiled to Babylon because of their unfaithfulness. ² The first to live in their towns on their own property again were Israelites, priests, Levites, and temple servants.

³ These people from the descendants of Judah, Benjamin, Ephraim, and Manasseh settled in Jerusalem:

⁴ Uthai son of Ammihud, son of Omri, son of Imri, son of Bani, a descendant^E of Perez son of Judah;

⁵ from the Shilonites:
Asaiah the firstborn and his sons;

⁶ and from the descendants of Zerah:
Jeuel and their relatives — 690 in all.

⁷ The Benjaminites: Sallu son of Meshullam, son of Hodaviah, son of Hassenuah;

⁸ Ibneiah son of Jeroham;

Elah son of Uzzi, son of Michri;

Meshullam son of Shephatiah, son of Reuel, son of Ibnijah;

⁹ and their relatives according to their family records — 956 in all. All these men were heads of their ancestral families.^F

---

^A 8:29 LXX; MT omits *Jeiel*; 1Ch 9:35   ^B 8:33 = Man of Baal   ^C 8:34 = Baal Contends   ^D 8:40 Lit *valiant ones who string the bow*   ^E 9:4 Lit *Bani, from the sons*   ^F 9:9 Lit *the house of their fathers,* also in v. 13

¹⁰ The priests: Jedaiah; Jehoiarib; Jachin;
¹¹ Azariah son of Hilkiah, son of Meshullam, son of Zadok, son of
Meraioth, son of Ahitub, the chief official of God's temple;
¹² Adaiah son of Jeroham, son of Pashhur, son of Malchijah;
Maasai son of Adiel, son of Jahzerah, son of Meshullam, son of
Meshillemith, son of Immer;
¹³ and their relatives, the heads of their ancestral families — 1,760 in all.
They were capable men employed in the ministry of God's temple.

¹⁴ The Levites: Shemaiah son of Hasshub, son of Azrikam, son of
Hashabiah of the Merarites;
¹⁵ Bakbakkar, Heresh, Galal, and Mattaniah, son of Mica, son of Zichri,
son of Asaph;
¹⁶ Obadiah son of Shemaiah, son of Galal, son of Jeduthun;
and Berechiah son of Asa, son of Elkanah who lived in the settlements
of the Netophathites.

¹⁷ The gatekeepers: Shallum, Akkub, Talmon, Ahiman, and their relatives.
Shallum was their chief; ¹⁸ he was previously stationed at the King's
Gate on the east side. These were the gatekeepers from the camp of the
Levites.
¹⁹ Shallum son of Kore, son of Ebiasaph, son of Korah and his relatives
from his father's family,^A the Korahites, were assigned to guard the
thresholds of the tent.^B Their ancestors had been assigned to the LORD's
camp as guardians of the entrance. ²⁰ In earlier times Phinehas son of
Eleazar had been their leader, and the LORD was with him. ²¹ Zechariah
son of Meshelemiah was the gatekeeper at the entrance to the tent of
meeting.

²² The total number of those chosen to be gatekeepers at the thresholds
was 212. They were registered by genealogy in their settlements. David and
the seer Samuel had appointed them to their trusted positions. ²³ So they
and their sons were assigned as guards to the gates of the LORD's temple,
which had been the tent-temple. ²⁴ The gatekeepers were on the four sides:
east, west, north, and south. ²⁵ Their relatives came from their settlements
at fixed times to be with them seven days, ²⁶ but the four chief gatekeepers,
who were Levites, were entrusted with the rooms and the treasuries of God's
temple. ²⁷ They spent the night in the vicinity of God's temple, because they
had guard duty and were in charge of opening it every morning.

²⁸ Some of them were in charge of the utensils used in worship. They would
count them when they brought them in and when they took them out. ²⁹ Others
were put in charge of the furnishings and all the utensils of the sanctuary, as well as the fine flour, wine, oil, incense, and spices. ³⁰ Some of the
priests' sons mixed the spices. ³¹ A Levite called Mattithiah, the firstborn of
Shallum the Korahite, was entrusted with baking the bread.^C ³² Some of the
Kohathites' relatives were responsible for preparing the rows of the Bread
of the Presence every Sabbath.

---

^A9:19 Lit *the house of his father* ^B9:19 = the temple ^C 9:31 Lit *with things
prepared in pans*

³³ The singers, the heads of the Levite families, stayed in the temple chambers and were exempt from other tasks because they were on duty day and night. ³⁴ These were the heads of the Levite families, chiefs according to their family records; they lived in Jerusalem.

SAUL'S FAMILY

³⁵ Jeiel fathered Gibeon and lived in Gibeon. His wife's name was Maacah. ³⁶ Abdon was his firstborn son, then Zur, Kish, Baal, Ner, Nadab, ³⁷ Gedor, Ahio, Zechariah, and Mikloth. ³⁸ Mikloth fathered Shimeam. These also lived opposite their relatives in Jerusalem with their other relatives.

³⁹ Ner fathered Kish, Kish fathered Saul, and Saul fathered Jonathan, Malchishua, Abinadab, and Esh-baal.

⁴⁰ Jonathan's son was Merib-baal, and Merib-baal fathered Micah.

⁴¹ Micah's sons: Pithon, Melech, Tahrea, and Ahaz.ᴬ

⁴² Ahaz fathered Jarah;

Jarah fathered Alemeth, Azmaveth, and Zimri;

Zimri fathered Moza.

⁴³ Moza fathered Binea.

His son was Rephaiah, his son Elasah, and his son Azel.

⁴⁴ Azel had six sons, and these were their names: Azrikam, Bocheru, Ishmael, Sheariah, Obadiah, and Hanan. These were Azel's sons.

THE DEATH OF SAUL AND HIS SONS

10 The Philistines fought against Israel, and Israel's men fled from them. Many were killed on Mount Gilboa. ² The Philistines pursued Saul and his sons and killed his sons Jonathan, Abinadab, and Malchishua. ³ When the battle intensified against Saul, the archers spotted him and severely wounded him. ⁴ Then Saul said to his armor-bearer, "Draw your sword and run me through with it, or these uncircumcised men will come and torture me." But his armor-bearer would not do it because he was terrified. Then Saul took his sword and fell on it. ⁵ When his armor-bearer saw that Saul was dead, he also fell on his own sword and died. ⁶ So Saul and his three sons died — his whole house died together.

⁷ When all the men of Israel in the valley saw that the army had fled and that Saul and his sons were dead, they abandoned their cities and fled. So the Philistines came and settled in them.

⁸ The next day when the Philistines came to strip the slain, they found Saul and his sons dead on Mount Gilboa. ⁹ They stripped Saul, cut off his head, took his armor, and sent messengers throughout the land of the Philistines to spread the good news to their idols and the people. ¹⁰ Then they put his armor in the temple of their gods and hung his skull in the temple of Dagon.

¹¹ When all Jabesh-gilead heard of everything the Philistines had done to Saul, ¹² all their brave men set out and retrieved the body of Saul and the bodies of his sons and brought them to Jabesh. They buried their bones under the oakᴮ in Jabesh and fasted seven days.

ᴬ9:41 LXX, Syr, Tg, Vg, Arabic; MT omits *and Ahaz*; 1Ch 8:35 ᴮ10:12 Or *terebinth, or large tree*

¹³ Saul died for his unfaithfulness to the Lord because he did not keep the Lord's word. He even consulted a medium for guidance, ¹⁴ but he did not inquire of the Lord. So the Lord put him to death and turned the kingdom over to David son of Jesse.

DAVID'S ANOINTING AS KING

11 All Israel came together to David at Hebron and said, "Here we are, your own flesh and blood.ᴬ ² Even previously when Saul was king, you were leading Israel out to battle and bringing us back. The Lord your God also said to you, 'You will shepherd my people Israel, and you will be ruler over my people Israel.'"

³ So all the elders of Israel came to the king at Hebron. David made a covenant with them at Hebron in the Lord's presence, and they anointed David king over Israel, in keeping with the Lord's word through Samuel.

DAVID'S CAPTURE OF JERUSALEM

⁴ David and all Israel marched to Jerusalem (that is, Jebus); the Jebusites who inhabited the land were there. ⁵ The inhabitants of Jebus said to David, "You will never get in here." Yet David did capture the stronghold of Zion, that is, the city of David.

⁶ David said, "Whoever is the first to kill a Jebusite will become chief commander." Joab son of Zeruiah went up first, so he became the chief.

⁷ Then David took up residence in the stronghold; therefore, it was called the city of David. ⁸ He built up the city all the way around, from the supporting terraces to the surrounding parts, and Joab restored the rest of the city. ⁹ David steadily grew more powerful, and the Lord of Armies was with him.

EXPLOITS OF DAVID'S WARRIORS

¹⁰ The following were the chiefs of David's warriors who, together with all Israel, strongly supported him in his reign to make him king according to the Lord's word about Israel. ¹¹ This is the list of David's warriors:

Jashobeam son of Hachmoni was chief of the Thirty;ᴮ he wielded his spear against three hundred and killed them at one time.

¹² After him, Eleazar son of Dodo the Ahohite was one of the three warriors. ¹³ He was with David at Pas-dammim when the Philistines had gathered there for battle. There was a portion of a field full of barley, where the troops had fled from the Philistines. ¹⁴ But Eleazar and Davidᶜ took their stand in the middle of the field and defended it. They killed the Philistines, and the Lord gave them a great victory.

¹⁵ Three of the thirty chief men went down to David, to the rock at the cave of Adullam, while the Philistine army was encamped in the Valley of Rephaim. ¹⁶ At that time David was in the stronghold, and a Philistine garrison was at Bethlehem. ¹⁷ David was extremely thirstyᴰ and said, "If only someone would bring me water to drink from the well at the city gate of Bethlehem!" ¹⁸ So the Three broke through the Philistine camp and drew water from the well at the gate of Bethlehem. They brought it back to David, but he refused to drink it. Instead, he poured it out to the Lord. ¹⁹ David said, "I would

---

ᴬ 11:1 Lit *your bone and your flesh*   ᴮ 11:11 Alt Hb tradition reads *Three*
ᶜ 11:14 Lit *But they*   ᴰ 11:17 Lit *And David craved*

never do such a thing in the presence of my God! How can I drink the blood of these men who risked their lives?" For they brought it at the risk of their lives. So he would not drink it. Such were the exploits of the three warriors.

²⁰ Abishai, Joab's brother, was the leader of the Three.ᴬ He raised his spear against three hundred men and killed them, gaining a reputation among the Three. ²¹ He was more honored than the Three and became their commander even though he did not become one of the Three.

²² Benaiah son of Jehoiada was the son of a brave manᴮ from Kabzeel, a man of many exploits. Benaiah killed two sons of Ariel of Moab,ᶜ and he went down into a pit on a snowy day and killed a lion. ²³ He also killed an Egyptian who was seven and a half feet tall.ᴰ Even though the Egyptian had a spear in his hand like a weaver's beam, Benaiah went down to him with a club, snatched the spear out of the Egyptian's hand, and then killed him with his own spear. ²⁴ These were the exploits of Benaiah son of Jehoiada, who had a reputation among the three warriors. ²⁵ He was the most honored of the Thirty, but he did not become one of the Three. David put him in charge of his bodyguard.

²⁶ The best soldiers were
> Joab's brother Asahel,
> Elhanan son of Dodo of Bethlehem,
²⁷   Shammoth the Harorite,
> Helez the Pelonite,
²⁸   Ira son of Ikkesh the Tekoite,
> Abiezer the Anathothite,
²⁹   Sibbecai the Hushathite,
> Ilai the Ahohite,
³⁰   Maharai the Netophathite,
> Heled son of Baanah the Netophathite,
³¹   Ithai son of Ribai from Gibeah of the Benjaminites,
> Benaiah the Pirathonite,
³²   Hurai from the wadis of Gaash,
> Abiel the Arbathite,
³³   Azmaveth the Baharumite,
> Eliahba the Shaalbonite,
³⁴   the sons ofᴱ Hashem the Gizonite,
> Jonathan son of Shagee the Hararite,
³⁵   Ahiam son of Sachar the Hararite,
> Eliphal son of Ur,
³⁶   Hepher the Mecherathite,
> Ahijah the Pelonite,
³⁷   Hezro the Carmelite,
> Naarai son of Ezbai,
³⁸   Joel the brother of Nathan,
> Mibhar son of Hagri,
³⁹   Zelek the Ammonite,
> Naharai the Beerothite, the armor-bearer for Joab son of Zeruiah,

---

⁴⁰ Ira the Ithrite,
    Gareb the Ithrite,
⁴¹ Uriah the Hethite,
    Zabad son of Ahlai,
⁴² Adina son of Shiza the Reubenite, chief of the Reubenites, and thirty
    with him,
⁴³ Hanan son of Maacah,
    Joshaphat the Mithnite,
⁴⁴ Uzzia the Ashterathite,
    Shama and Jeiel the sons of Hotham the Aroerite,
⁴⁵ Jediael son of Shimri and his brother Joha the Tizite,
⁴⁶ Eliel the Mahavite,
    Jeribai and Joshaviah, the sons of Elnaam,
    Ithmah the Moabite,
⁴⁷ Eliel, Obed, and Jaasiel the Mezobaite.

DAVID'S FIRST SUPPORTERS

12 The following were the men who came to David at Ziklag while he
was still banned from the presence of Saul son of Kish. They were
among the warriors who helped him in battle. ² They were archers who could
use either the right or left hand, both to sling stones and shoot arrows from
a bow. They were Saul's relatives from Benjamin:

³ Their chief was Ahiezer son of Shemaah the Gibeathite.
Then there was his brother Joash;
Jeziel and Pelet sons of Azmaveth;
Beracah, Jehu the Anathothite;
⁴ Ishmaiah the Gibeonite, a warrior among the Thirty and a leader over
the Thirty;
Jeremiah, Jahaziel, Johanan, Jozabad the Gederathite;
⁵ Eluzai, Jerimoth, Bealiah, Shemariah, Shephatiah the Haruphite;
⁶ Elkanah, Isshiah, Azarel, Joezer, and Jashobeam, the Korahites;
⁷ and Joelah and Zebadiah, the sons of Jeroham from Gedor.

⁸ Some Gadites defected to David at his stronghold in the desert. They were
valiant warriors, trained for battle, expert with shield and spear. Their faces
were like the faces of lions, and they were as swift as gazelles on the mountains.

⁹   Ezer was the chief, Obadiah second, Eliab third,
¹⁰ Mishmannah fourth, Jeremiah fifth,
¹¹ Attai sixth, Eliel seventh,
¹² Johanan eighth, Elzabad ninth,
¹³ Jeremiah tenth, and Machbannai eleventh.

¹⁴ These Gadites were army commanders; the least of them was a match for
a hundred, and the greatest of them for a thousand. ¹⁵ These are the men
who crossed the Jordan in the first month ᴬ when it was overflowing all its
banks, and put to flight all those in the valleys to the east and to the west.

¹⁶ Other Benjaminites and men from Judah also went to David at the stronghold. ¹⁷ David went out to meet them and said to them, "If you have come in
peace to help me, my heart will be united with you, but if you have come to

---

ᴬ12:15 = Nisan (March–April)

betray me to my enemies even though my hands have done no wrong, may the God of our ancestors look on it and judge."

18 Then the Spirit enveloped[A] Amasai, chief of the Thirty, and he said:

We are yours, David,
we are with you, son of Jesse!
Peace, peace to you,
and peace to him who helps you,
for your God helps you.

So David received them and made them leaders of his troops.

19 Some Manassites defected to David when he went with the Philistines to fight against Saul. However, they did not help the Philistines because the Philistine rulers sent David away after a discussion. They said, "It will be our heads if he defects to his master Saul." 20 When David went to Ziklag, some men from Manasseh defected to him: Adnah, Jozabad, Jediael, Michael, Jozabad, Elihu, and Zillethai, chiefs of thousands in Manasseh. 21 They helped David against the raiders, for they were all valiant warriors and commanders in the army. 22 At that time, men came day after day to help David until there was a great army, like an army of God.[B]

DAVID'S SOLDIERS IN HEBRON

23 The numbers of the armed troops who came to David at Hebron to turn Saul's kingdom over to him, according to the LORD's word, were as follows:

24 From the Judahites: 6,800 armed troops bearing shields and spears.

25 From the Simeonites: 7,100 valiant warriors ready for war.

26 From the Levites: 4,600 27 in addition to Jehoiada, leader of the house of Aaron, with 3,700 men; 28 and Zadok, a young valiant warrior, with 22 commanders from his father's family.[C]

29 From the Benjaminites, the relatives of Saul: 3,000 (up to that time the majority of the Benjaminites maintained their allegiance to the house of Saul).

30 From the Ephraimites: 20,800 valiant warriors who were famous men in their ancestral families.[D]

31 From half the tribe of Manasseh: 18,000 designated by name to come and make David king.

32 From the Issacharites, who understood the times and knew what Israel should do: 200 chiefs with all their relatives under their command.

33 From Zebulun: 50,000 who could serve in the army, trained for battle with all kinds of weapons of war, with one purpose to help David.[E]

34 From Naphtali: 1,000 commanders accompanied by 37,000 men with shield and spear.

35 From the Danites: 28,600 trained for battle.

36 From Asher: 40,000 who could serve in the army, trained for battle.

37 From across the Jordan — from the Reubenites, Gadites, and half the tribe of Manasseh: 120,000 men equipped with all the military weapons of war.

A 12:18 Lit clothed; Jdg 6:34; 2Ch 24:20   B 12:22 Or like the ultimate army
C 12:28 Lit the house of his father   D 12:30 Lit the house of their fathers
E 12:33 LXX; MT omits David

³⁸ All these warriors, lined up in battle formation, came to Hebron whole-heartedly determined to make David king over all Israel. All the rest of Israel was also of one mind to make David king. ³⁹ They spent three days there eating and drinking with David, for their relatives had provided for them. ⁴⁰ In addition, their neighbors from as far away as Issachar, Zebulun, and Naphtali came and brought food on donkeys, camels, mules, and oxen — abundant provisions of flour, fig cakes, raisins, wine and oil, herds, and flocks. Indeed, there was joy in Israel.

DAVID AND THE ARK

13 David consulted with all his leaders, the commanders of hundreds and of thousands. ² Then he said to the whole assembly of Israel, "If it seems good to you, and if this is from the LORD our God, let us spread out and send the message to the rest of our relatives in all the districts of Israel, including the priests and Levites in their cities with pasturelands, that they should gather together with us. ³ Then let us bring back the ark of our God, for we did not inquire of him^A in Saul's days." ⁴ Since the proposal seemed right to all the people, the whole assembly agreed to do it.

⁵ So David assembled all Israel, from the Shihor of Egypt to the entrance of Hamath,^B to bring the ark of God from Kiriath-jearim. ⁶ David and all Israel went to Baalah (that is, Kiriath-jearim that belongs to Judah) to take from there the ark of God, which bears the name of the LORD who is enthroned between the cherubim. ⁷ At Abinadab's house they set the ark of God on a new cart. Uzzah and Ahio^C were guiding the cart.

⁸ David and all Israel were dancing with all their might before God with songs and with lyres, harps, tambourines, cymbals, and trumpets. ⁹ When they came to Chidon's threshing floor, Uzzah reached out to hold the ark because the oxen had stumbled. ¹⁰ Then the LORD's anger burned against Uzzah, and he struck him dead because he had reached out to the ark. So he died there in the presence of God.

¹¹ David was angry because of the LORD's outburst against Uzzah, so he named that place Outburst Against Uzzah,^D as it is still named today. ¹² David feared God that day and said, "How can I ever bring the ark of God to me?" ¹³ So David did not bring the ark of God home^E to the city of David; instead, he diverted it to the house of Obed-edom of Gath. ¹⁴ The ark of God remained with Obed-edom's family in his house for three months, and the LORD blessed his family and all that he had.

GOD'S BLESSING ON DAVID

14 King Hiram of Tyre sent envoys to David, along with cedar logs, stonemasons, and carpenters to build a palace for him. ² Then David knew that the LORD had established him as king over Israel and that his kingdom had been exalted for the sake of his people Israel.

³ David took more wives in Jerusalem, and he became the father of more sons and daughters. ⁴ These are the names of the children born to him in Jerusalem: Shammua, Shobab, Nathan, Solomon, ⁵ Ibhar, Elishua, Elpelet, ⁶ Nogah, Nepheg, Japhia, ⁷ Elishama, Beeliada, and Eliphelet.

---

^A 13:3 Or did not seek it   ^B 13:5 Or to Lebo-hamath   ^C 13:7 Or And his brothers
^D 13:11 Or Perez-uzzah   ^E 13:13 Lit to himself

⁸ When the Philistines heard that David had been anointed king over all Israel, they all went in search of David; when David heard of this, he went out to face them. ⁹ Now the Philistines had come and raided in the Valley of Rephaim, ¹⁰ so David inquired of God, "Should I attack the Philistines? Will you hand them over to me?"

The LORD replied, "Attack, and I will hand them over to you."

¹¹ So the Israelites went up to Baal-perazim, and David defeated the Philistines there. Then David said, "Like a bursting flood, God has used me to burst out against my enemies." Therefore, they named that place The Lord Bursts Out.ᴬ ¹² The Philistines abandoned their idols there, and David ordered that they be burned in the fire.

¹³ Once again the Philistines raided in the valley. ¹⁴ So David again inquired of God, and God answered him, "Do not pursue them directly. Circle around them and attack them opposite the balsam trees. ¹⁵ When you hear the sound of marching in the tops of the balsam trees, then go out to battle, for God will have gone out ahead of you to strike down the army of the Philistines." ¹⁶ So David did as God commanded him, and they struck down the Philistine army from Gibeon to Gezer. ¹⁷ Then David's fame spread throughout the lands, and the LORD caused all the nations to be terrified of him.

THE ARK COMES TO JERUSALEM

15 David built houses for himself in the city of David, and he prepared a place for the ark of God and pitched a tent for it. ² Then David said, "No one but the Levites may carry the ark of God, because the LORD has chosen them to carry the ark of the LORD and to minister before him forever."

³ David assembled all Israel at Jerusalem to bring the ark of the LORD to the place he had prepared for it. ⁴ Then he gathered together the descendants of Aaron and the Levites:

⁵ From the Kohathites, Uriel the leader and 120 of his relatives; ⁶ from the Merarites, Asaiah the leader and 220 of his relatives; ⁷ from the Gershomites,ᴮ Joel the leader and 130 of his relatives; ⁸ from the Elizaphanites, Shemaiah the leader and 200 of his relatives; ⁹ from the Hebronites, Eliel the leader and 80 of his relatives; ¹⁰ from the Uzzielites, Amminadab the leader and 112 of his relatives.

¹¹ David summoned the priests Zadok and Abiathar and the Levites Uriel, Asaiah, Joel, Shemaiah, Eliel, and Amminadab. ¹² He said to them, "You are the heads of the Levite families. You and your relatives must consecrate yourselves so that you may bring the ark of the LORD God of Israel to the place I have prepared for it. ¹³ For the LORD our God burst out in anger against us because you Levites were not with us the first time, for we didn't inquire of him about the proper procedures." ¹⁴ So the priests and the Levites consecrated themselves to bring up the ark of the LORD God of Israel. ¹⁵ Then the Levites carried the ark of God the way Moses had commanded according to the word of the LORD: on their shoulders with the poles.

¹⁶ Then David told the leaders of the Levites to appoint their relatives as singers and to have them raise their voices with joy accompanied by musical instruments — harps, lyres, and cymbals. ¹⁷ So the Levites appointed Heman son of Joel; from his relatives, Asaph son of Berechiah; and from their

ᴬ14:11 Or *Baal-perazim*   ᴮ15:7 = Gershonites

relatives the Merarites, Ethan son of Kushaiah. ¹⁸ With them were their relatives second in rank: Zechariah, Jaaziel,ᴬ Shemiramoth, Jehiel, Unni, Eliab, Benaiah, Maaseiah, Mattithiah, Eliphelehu, Mikneiah, and the gatekeepers Obed-edom and Jeiel. ¹⁹ The singers Heman, Asaph, and Ethan were to sound the bronze cymbals; ²⁰ Zechariah, Aziel, Shemiramoth, Jehiel, Unni, Eliab, Maaseiah, and Benaiah were to play harps according to *Alamoth*ᴮ ²¹ and Mattithiah, Eliphelehu, Mikneiah, Obed-edom, Jeiel, and Azaziah were to lead the music with lyres according to the *Sheminith*. ²² Chenaniah, the leader of the Levites in music, was to direct the music because he was skillful. ²³ Berechiah and Elkanah were to be gatekeepers for the ark. ²⁴ The priests, Shebaniah, Joshaphat, Nethanel, Amasai, Zechariah, Benaiah, and Eliezer, were to blow trumpets before the ark of God. Obed-edom and Jehiah were also to be gatekeepers for the ark.

²⁵ David, the elders of Israel, and the commanders of thousands went with rejoicing to bring the ark of the covenant of the LORD from the house of Obed-edom. ²⁶ Because God helped the Levites who were carrying the ark of the covenant of the LORD, with God's help, they sacrificed seven bulls and seven rams.

²⁷ Now David was dressed in a robe of fine linen, as were all the Levites who were carrying the ark, as well as the singers and Chenaniah, the music leader of the singers. David also wore a linen ephod. ²⁸ So all Israel brought up the ark of the covenant of the LORD with shouts, the sound of the ram's horn, trumpets, and cymbals, and the playing of harps and lyres. ²⁹ As the ark of the covenant of the LORD was entering the city of David, Saul's daughter Michal looked down from the window and saw King David leapingᶜ and dancing, and she despised him in her heart.

16 They brought the ark of God and placed it inside the tent David had pitched for it. Then they offered burnt offerings and fellowship offerings in God's presence. ² When David had finished offering the burnt offerings and the fellowship offerings, he blessed the people in the name of the LORD. ³ Then he distributed to each and every Israelite, both men and women, a loaf of bread, a date cake, and a raisin cake.

⁴ David appointed some of the Levites to be ministers before the ark of the LORD, to celebrate the LORD God of Israel, and to give thanks and praise to him. ⁵ Asaph was the chief and Zechariah was second to him. Jeiel, Shemiramoth, Jehiel, Mattithiah, Eliab, Benaiah, Obed-edom, and Jeiel played the harps and lyres, while Asaph sounded the cymbals ⁶ and the priests Benaiah and Jahaziel blew the trumpets regularly before the ark of the covenant of God.

DAVID'S PSALM OF THANKSGIVING

⁷ On that day David decreed for the first time that thanks be given to the LORD by Asaph and his relatives:

⁸ Give thanks to the LORD; call on his name;
  proclaim his deeds among the peoples.
⁹ Sing to him; sing praise to him;

ᴬ15:18 Some Hb mss, LXX; other Hb mss read *Zechariah son and Jaaziel*
ᴮ15:20 This may refer to a high pitch, perhaps a tune sung by soprano voices; the Hb word means "young women"; Ps 46 title ᶜ15:29 Or *whirling*

tell about all his wondrous works!

¹⁰ Honor his holy name;
let the hearts of those who seek the LORD rejoice.
¹¹ Seek the LORD and his strength;
seek his face always.
¹² Remember the wondrous works he has done,
his wonders, and the judgments he has pronounced,ᴬ
¹³ you offspring of Israel his servant,
Jacob's descendants — his chosen ones.

¹⁴ He is the LORD our God;
his judgments govern the whole earth.
¹⁵ Remember his covenant forever —
the promise he ordained for a thousand generations,
¹⁶ the covenant he made with Abraham,
sworeᴮ to Isaac,
¹⁷ and confirmed to Jacob as a decree,
and to Israel as a permanent covenant:
¹⁸ "I will give the land of Canaan to you
as your inherited portion."

¹⁹ When theyᶜ were few in number,
very few indeed, and resident aliens in Canaan
²⁰ wandering from nation to nation
and from one kingdom to another,
²¹ he allowed no one to oppress them;
he rebuked kings on their behalf:
²² "Do not touch my anointed ones
or harm my prophets."

²³ Let the whole earth sing to the LORD.
Proclaim his salvation from day to day.
²⁴ Declare his glory among the nations,
his wondrous works among all peoples.

²⁵ For the LORD is great and highly praised;
he is feared above all gods.
²⁶ For all the gods of the peoples are idols,
but the LORD made the heavens.
²⁷ Splendor and majesty are before him;
strength and joy are in his place.
²⁸ Ascribe to the LORD, families of the peoples,
ascribe to the LORD glory and strength.
²⁹ Ascribe to the LORD the glory of his name;
bring an offering and come before him.
Worship the LORD in the splendor of his holiness;
³⁰ let the whole earth tremble before him.

ᴬ16:12 Lit *judgments of his mouth*   ᴮ16:16 Lit *and his oath*   ᶜ16:19 One Hb ms,
LXX, Vg; other Hb mss read *you*

The world is firmly established;
it cannot be shaken.
31 Let the heavens be glad and the earth rejoice,
and let them say among the nations, "The LORD reigns!"
32 Let the sea and all that fills it resound;
let the fields and everything in them exult.
33 Then the trees of the forest will shout for joy before the LORD,
for he is coming to judge the earth.

34 Give thanks to the LORD, for he is good;
his faithful love endures forever.
35 And say: "Save us, God of our salvation;
gather us and rescue us from the nations
so that we may give thanks to your holy name
and rejoice in your praise.
36 Blessed be the LORD God of Israel
from everlasting to everlasting."

Then all the people said, "Amen" and "Praise the LORD."

37 So David left Asaph and his relatives there before the ark of the LORD's covenant to minister regularly before the ark according to the daily requirements. 38 He assigned Obed-edom and his^A sixty-eight relatives. Obed-edom son of Jeduthun and Hosah were to be gatekeepers. 39 David left the priest Zadok and his fellow priests before the tabernacle of the LORD at the high place in Gibeon 40 to offer burnt offerings regularly, morning and evening, to the LORD on the altar of burnt offerings and to do everything that was written in the law of the LORD, which he had commanded Israel to keep. 41 With them were Heman, Jeduthun, and the rest who were chosen and designated by name to give thanks to the LORD — for his faithful love endures forever. 42 Heman and Jeduthun had with them trumpets and cymbals to play and musical instruments of God. Jeduthun's sons were at the city gate.

43 Then all the people went home, and David returned home to bless his household.

THE LORD'S COVENANT WITH DAVID

17 When David had settled into his palace, he said to the prophet Nathan, "Look! I am living in a cedar house while the ark of the LORD's covenant is under tent curtains."

2 So Nathan told David, "Do all that is on your mind, for God is with you."

3 But that night the word of God came to Nathan: 4 "Go to David my servant and say, 'This is what the LORD says: You are not the one to build me a house to dwell in. 5 From the time I brought Israel out of Egypt until today I have not dwelt in a house; instead, I have moved from one tent site to another, and from one tabernacle location to another.^B 6 In all my journeys throughout Israel, have I ever spoken a word to even one of the judges of Israel, whom I commanded to shepherd my people, asking: Why haven't you built me a house of cedar?'

---

^A 16:38 LXX, Syr, Vg; Hb reads their   ^B 17:5 Lit I was from tent to tent and from tabernacle

⁷ "So now this is what you are to say to my servant David: 'This is what the LORD of Armies says: I took you from the pasture, from tending the flock, to be ruler over my people Israel. ⁸ I have been with you wherever you have gone, and I have destroyed all your enemies before you. I will make a name for you like that of the greatest on the earth. ⁹ I will designate a place for my people Israel and plant them, so that they may live there and not be disturbed again. Evildoers will not continue to oppress them as they have done ¹⁰ ever since the day I ordered judges to be over my people Israel. I will also subdue all your enemies.

"'Furthermore, I declare to you that the LORD himself will build a house for you. ¹¹ When your time comes to be with your fathers, I will raise up after you your descendant, who is one of your own sons, and I will establish his kingdom. ¹² He is the one who will build a house for me, and I will establish his throne forever. ¹³ I will be his father, and he will be my son. I will not remove my faithful love from him as I removed it from the one who was before you. ¹⁴ I will appoint him over my house and my kingdom forever, and his throne will be established forever.'"

¹⁵ Nathan reported all these words and this entire vision to David.

DAVID'S PRAYER OF THANKSGIVING

¹⁶ Then King David went in, sat in the LORD's presence, and said,
Who am I, LORD God, and what is my house that you have brought me this far? ¹⁷ This was a little thing to you,ᴬ God, for you have spoken about your servant's house in the distant future. You regard me as a man of distinction,ᴮ LORD God. ¹⁸ What more can David say to you for honoring your servant? You know your servant. ¹⁹ LORD, you have done this whole great thing, making known all these great promises for the sake of your servant and according to your will. ²⁰ LORD, there is no one like you, and there is no God besides you, as all we have heard confirms. ²¹ And who is like your people Israel? God, you came to one nation on earth to redeem a people for yourself, to make a name for yourself through great and awesome works by driving out nations before your people you redeemed from Egypt. ²² You made your people Israel your own people forever, and you, LORD, have become their God.

²³ Now, LORD, let the word that you have spoken concerning your servant and his house be confirmed forever, and do as you have promised. ²⁴ Let your name be confirmed and magnified forever in the saying, "The LORD of Armies, the God of Israel, is God over Israel." May the house of your servant David be established before you. ²⁵ Since you, my God, have revealed toᶜ your servant that you will build him a house, your servant has found courage to pray in your presence. ²⁶ LORD, you indeed are God, and you have promised this good thing to your servant. ²⁷ So now, you have been pleased to bless your servant's house that it may continue before you forever. For you, LORD, have blessed it, and it is blessed forever.

ᴬ17:17 Lit *thing in your eyes*   ᴮ17:17 Hb obscure   ᶜ17:25 Lit *have uncovered the ear of*

DAVID'S MILITARY CAMPAIGNS

18 After this, David defeated the Philistines, subdued them, and took Gath and its surrounding villages from Philistine control. ²He also defeated the Moabites, and they became David's subjects and brought tribute.

³David also defeated King Hadadezer of Zobah at Hamath when he went to establish his control at the Euphrates River. ⁴David captured one thousand chariots, seven thousand horsemen, and twenty thousand foot soldiers from him, hamstrung all the horses, and kept a hundred chariots.ᴬ

⁵When the Arameans of Damascus came to assist King Hadadezer of Zobah, David struck down twenty-two thousand Aramean men. ⁶Then he placed garrisonsᴮ in Aram of Damascus, and the Arameans became David's subjects and brought tribute. The Lᴏʀᴅ made David victorious wherever he went.

⁷David took the gold shields carried by Hadadezer's officers and brought them to Jerusalem. ⁸From Tibhath and Cun, Hadadezer's cities, David also took huge quantities of bronze, from which Solomon made the bronze basin,ᶜ the pillars, and the bronze articles.

⁹When King Tou of Hamath heard that David had defeated the entire army of King Hadadezer of Zobah, ¹⁰he sent his son Hadoram to King David to greet him and to congratulate him because David had fought against Hadadezer and defeated him, for Tou and Hadadezer had fought many wars. Hadoram brought all kinds of gold, silver, and bronze items. ¹¹King David also dedicated these to the Lᴏʀᴅ, along with the silver and gold he had carried off from all the nations — from Edom, Moab, the Ammonites, the Philistines, and the Amalekites.

¹²Abishai son of Zeruiah struck down eighteen thousand Edomites in the Salt Valley. ¹³He put garrisons in Edom, and all the Edomites were subject to David. The Lᴏʀᴅ made David victorious wherever he went.

¹⁴So David reigned over all Israel, administering justice and righteousness for all his people.

15 Joab son of Zeruiah was over the army;
      Jehoshaphat son of Ahilud was court historian;
16 Zadok son of Ahitub and Ahimelechᴰ son of Abiathar were priests;
      Shavsha was court secretary;
17 Benaiah son of Jehoiada was over the Cherethites and the Pelethites;
      and David's sons were the chief officials at the king's side.

WAR WITH THE AMMONITES

19 Some time later, King Nahash of the Ammonites died, and his son became king in his place. ²Then David said, "I'll show kindness to Hanun son of Nahash, because his father showed kindness to me."

So David sent messengers to console him concerning his father. However, when David's emissaries arrived in the land of the Ammonites to console him, ³the Ammonite leaders said to Hanun, "Just because David has sent men with condolences for you, do you really believe he's showing respect for your father? Instead, haven't his emissaries come in order to scout out,

---

ᴬ18:4 Or *chariot horses* ᴮ18:6 Some Hb mss, LXX, Vg; other Hb mss omit *garrisons*; 2Sm 8:6 ᶜ18:8 Lit *sea* ᴰ18:16 Some Hb mss, LXX, Syr, Vg; other Hb mss read *Abimelech*; 2Sm 8:17

overthrow, and spy on the land?" ⁴ So Hanun took David's emissaries, shaved them, cut their clothes in half at the hips, and sent them away.

⁵ It was reported to David about his men, so he sent messengers to meet them, since the men were deeply humiliated. The king said, "Stay in Jericho until your beards grow back; then return."

⁶ When the Ammonites realized they had made themselves repulsive to David, Hanun and the Ammonites sent thirty-eight tons ᴬ of silver to hire chariots and horsemen from Aram-naharaim, Aram-maacah, and Zobah. ⁷ They hired thirty-two thousand chariots and the king of Maacah with his army, who came and camped near Medeba. The Ammonites also came together from their cities for the battle.

⁸ David heard about this and sent Joab and all the elite troops. ⁹ The Ammonites marched out and lined up in battle formation at the entrance of the city while the kings who had come were in the field by themselves. ¹⁰ When Joab saw that there was a battle line in front of him and another behind him, he chose some of Israel's finest young men ᴮ and lined up in formation to engage the Arameans. ¹¹ He placed the rest of the forces under the command of his brother Abishai. They lined up in formation to engage the Ammonites.

¹² "If the Arameans are too strong for me," Joab said, "then you'll be my help. However, if the Ammonites are too strong for you, I'll help you. ¹³ Be strong! Let's prove ourselves strong for our people and for the cities of our God. May the LORD's will be done." ᶜ

¹⁴ Joab and the people with him approached the Arameans for battle, and they fled before him. ¹⁵ When the Ammonites saw that the Arameans had fled, they likewise fled before Joab's brother Abishai and entered the city. Then Joab went to Jerusalem.

¹⁶ When the Arameans realized that they had been defeated by Israel, they sent messengers to summon the Arameans who were beyond the Euphrates River. They were led by Shophach, the commander of Hadadezer's army.

¹⁷ When this was reported to David, he gathered all Israel and crossed the Jordan. He came up to the Arameans and lined up against them. When David lined up to engage them, they fought against him. ¹⁸ But the Arameans fled before Israel, and David killed seven thousand of their charioteers and forty thousand foot soldiers. He also killed Shophach, commander of the army. ¹⁹ When Hadadezer's subjects saw that they had been defeated by Israel, they made peace with David and became his subjects. After this, the Arameans were never willing to help the Ammonites again.

CAPTURE OF THE CITY OF RABBAH

20 In the spring ᴰ when kings march out to war, Joab led the army and destroyed the Ammonites' land. He came to Rabbah and besieged it, but David remained in Jerusalem. Joab attacked Rabbah and demolished it. ² Then David took the crown from the head of their king, ᴱ,ᶠ and it was placed on David's head. He found that the crown weighed seventy-five pounds ᴳ of gold, and there was a precious stone in it. In addition, David took away a large quantity of plunder from the city. ³ He brought out the people who were in it

---

ᴬ19:6 Lit *1,000 talents*   ᴮ19:10 Lit *Israel's choice ones*   ᶜ19:13 Lit *the LORD do what is good in his eyes*   ᴰ20:1 Lit *At the time of the return of the year*
ᴱ20:2 LXX, Vg read *of Milcom*   ᶠ20:2 = Molech; 1Kg 11:5,7   ᴳ20:2 Lit *a talent*

and put them to work with saws,^A iron picks, and axes.^B David did the same to all the Ammonite cities. Then he and all his troops returned to Jerusalem.

THE PHILISTINE GIANTS

⁴ After this, a war broke out with the Philistines at Gezer. At that time Sibbecai the Hushathite killed Sippai, a descendant of the Rephaim,^C and the Philistines were subdued.

⁵ Once again there was a battle with the Philistines, and Elhanan son of Jair killed Lahmi the brother of Goliath of Gath. The shaft of his spear was like a weaver's beam.

⁶ There was still another battle at Gath where there was a man of extraordinary stature with six fingers on each hand and six toes on each foot — twenty-four in all. He, too, was descended from the giant.^D ⁷ When he taunted Israel, Jonathan son of David's brother Shimei killed him.

⁸ These were the descendants of the giant in Gath killed by David and his soldiers.

DAVID'S MILITARY CENSUS

21 Satan^E rose up against Israel and incited David to count the people of Israel. ² So David said to Joab and the commanders of the troops, "Go and count Israel from Beer-sheba to Dan and bring a report to me so I can know their number."

³ Joab replied, "May the Lᴏʀᴅ multiply the number of his people a hundred times over! My lord the king, aren't they all my lord's servants? Why does my lord want to do this? Why should he bring guilt on Israel?"

⁴ Yet the king's order prevailed over Joab. So Joab left and traveled throughout Israel and then returned to Jerusalem. ⁵ Joab gave the total troop registration to David. In all Israel there were one million one hundred thousand armed men^F and in Judah itself four hundred seventy thousand armed men. ⁶ But he did not include Levi and Benjamin in the count because the king's command was detestable to him. ⁷ This command was also evil in God's sight, so he afflicted Israel.

⁸ David said to God, "I have sinned greatly because I have done this thing. Now, please take away your servant's guilt, for I've been very foolish."

DAVID'S PUNISHMENT

⁹ Then the Lᴏʀᴅ instructed Gad, David's seer, ¹⁰ "Go and say to David, 'This is what the Lᴏʀᴅ says: I am offering you three choices. Choose one of them for yourself, and I will do it to you.'"

¹¹ So Gad went to David and said to him, "This is what the Lᴏʀᴅ says: 'Take your choice: ¹² three years of famine, or three months of devastation by your foes with the sword of your enemy overtaking you, or three days of the sword of the Lᴏʀᴅ — a plague on the land, the angel of the Lᴏʀᴅ bringing destruction to the whole territory of Israel.' Now decide what answer I should take back to the one who sent me."

---

^A 20:3 Text emended; MT reads *and sawed them with the saw*; 2Sm 12:31
^B 20:3 Text emended; MT reads *saws*; 2Sm 12:31   ^C 20:4 Or *the Rephaites*
^D 20:6 Or *Raphah*, also in v. 8   ^E 21:1 Or *An adversary*; Jb 1:6; Zch 3:1-2
^F 21:5 Lit *men drawing the sword*

KNOW YOUR BIBLE, KNOW YOUR GOD

1 CHRONICLES 21–22

Garlic heals ailments and makes food taste good. I figure if some garlic is good for flavor and good for health, why not use all the garlic? I love it so much; I can't help but add a little more. My husband makes good-natured jokes about keeping away vampires, but I think what he really means is, *"please don't add garlic to every soup, roast, and casserole I eat."*

I'm working on garlic moderation, but I keep forgetting and leaning toward garlic excess. It's hard to remember the lessons we learn from history. From figuring out how to cook for the folks we love, to remembering how much we are cherished, we have to learn about our people to really know them.

We also have to learn about God to really know Him. In 1 Chronicles 21, David forgets, but then he remembers.

David decided to take a census. Seems innocent and civic-minded, but it's not. David wanted a census of his military might so he could, as they say, count his chickens. He wanted to rest easy in the knowledge that his army was the mightiest. But the only reason his army ever had any success was the grace of God, so there was no need to count and rely on human power.

After David learned the nitty, gritty details of his military power, he knew that he had sinned. God rebuked him and gave him three choices:

- Three years of famine
- Three months of military devastation
- Three days of the sword of the Lord

And this is the best part of the story. Watch how David responded: "Please, let me fall into the Lord's hands because his mercies are very great, but don't let me fall into human hands" (1Ch 21:13).

David knew the Lord! He knew His promises. And because of that, David chose punishment by God's hand. You see, he knew of God's great mercy. **We can know God's character, too, by knowing His Word.**

David knew of God's mercy both personally and historically. He had learned to trust the hand of God above all others because God had made a covenant with David and his children (1Ch 17:1-14). David knew "the Lord is a compassionate and gracious God" (Ex 34:6), and "his anger lasts only a moment, but his favor, a lifetime!" (Ps 30:5).

If we know God's promises, we will know our God. When we remember how God has been merciful and provided for His people, we can hold tight to that truth ourselves.

I may not remember how to season food for my husband, but I pray that we can remember that God is "gracious and compassionate, slow to anger, abounding in faithful love, and he relents from sending disaster" (Jl 2:13).

May we know our Bibles and know our God!

¹³ David answered Gad, "I'm in anguish. Please, let me fall into the LORD's hands because his mercies are very great, but don't let me fall into human hands."

¹⁴ So the LORD sent a plague on Israel, and seventy thousand Israelite men died. ¹⁵ Then God sent an angel to Jerusalem to destroy it, but when the angel was about to destroy the city,ᴬ the LORD looked, relented concerning the destruction, and said to the angel who was destroying the people, "Enough, withdraw your hand now!" The angel of the LORD was then standing at the threshing floor of Ornanᴮ the Jebusite.

¹⁶ When David looked up and saw the angel of the LORD standing between earth and heaven, with his drawn sword in his hand stretched out over Jerusalem, David and the elders, clothed in sackcloth, fell facedown. ¹⁷ David said to God, "Wasn't I the one who gave the order to count the people? I am the one who has sinned and acted very wickedly. But these sheep, what have they done? LORD my God, please let your hand be against me and against my father's family, but don't let the plague be against your people."

DAVID'S ALTAR

¹⁸ So the angel of the LORD ordered Gad to tell David to go and set up an altar to the LORD on the threshing floor of Ornan the Jebusite. ¹⁹ David went up at Gad's command spoken in the name of the LORD.

²⁰ Ornan was threshing wheat when he turned and saw the angel. His four sons, who were with him, hid. ²¹ David came to Ornan, and when Ornan looked and saw David, he left the threshing floor and bowed to David with his face to the ground.

²² Then David said to Ornan, "Give me this threshing-floor plot so that I may build an altar to the LORD on it. Give it to me for the full price, so the plague on the people may be stopped."

²³ Ornan said to David, "Take it! My lord the king may do whatever he wants.ᶜ See, I give the oxen for the burnt offerings, the threshing sledges for the wood, and the wheat for the grain offering — I give it all."

²⁴ King David answered Ornan, "No, I insist on paying the full price, for I will not take for the LORD what belongs to you or offer burnt offerings that cost me nothing."

²⁵ So David gave Ornan fifteen pounds of goldᴰ for the plot. ²⁶ He built an altar to the LORD there and offered burnt offerings and fellowship offerings. He called on the LORD, and he answered him with fire from heaven on the altar of burnt offering.

²⁷ Then the LORD spoke to the angel, and he put his sword back into its sheath. ²⁸ At that time, David offered sacrifices there when he saw that the LORD answered him at the threshing floor of Ornan the Jebusite. ²⁹ The tabernacle of the LORD, which Moses made in the wilderness, and the altar of burnt offering were at the high place in Gibeon, ³⁰ but David could not go before it to inquire of God, because he was terrified of the sword of the

22 LORD's angel. ¹ Then David said, "This is the house of the LORD God, and this is the altar of burnt offering for Israel."

ᴬ 21:15 Lit *but as he was destroying*   ᴮ 21:15-28 = Araunah in 2Sm 24:16-24
ᶜ 21:23 Lit *do what is good in his eyes*   ᴰ 21:25 Lit *600 shekels of gold by weight*

DAVID'S PREPARATIONS FOR THE TEMPLE

² So David gave orders to gather the resident aliens that were in the land of Israel, and he appointed stonecutters to cut finished stones for building God's house. ³ David supplied a great deal of iron to make the nails for the doors of the gates and for the fittings, together with an immeasurable quantity of bronze, ⁴ and innumerable cedar logs because the Sidonians and Tyrians had brought a large quantity of cedar logs to David. ⁵ David said, "My son Solomon is young and inexperienced, and the house that is to be built for the LORD must be exceedingly great and famous and glorious in all the lands. Therefore, I will make provision for it." So David made lavish preparations for it before his death.

⁶ Then he summoned his son Solomon and charged him to build a house for the LORD God of Israel. ⁷ "My son," David said to Solomon, "It was in my heart to build a house for the name of the LORD my God, ⁸ but the word of the LORD came to me: 'You have shed much blood and waged great wars. You are not to build a house for my name because you have shed so much blood on the ground before me. ⁹ But a son will be born to you; he will be a man of rest. I will give him rest from all his surrounding enemies, for his name will be Solomon,ᴬ and I will give peace and quiet to Israel during his reign. ¹⁰ He is the one who will build a house for my name. He will be my son, and I will be his father. I will establish the throne of his kingdom over Israel forever.'

¹¹ "Now, my son, may the LORD be with you, and may you succeed in building the house of the LORD your God, as he said about you. ¹² Above all, may the LORD give you insight and understanding when he puts you in charge of Israel so that you may keep the law of the LORD your God. ¹³ Then you will succeed if you carefully follow the statutes and ordinances the LORD commanded Moses for Israel. Be strong and courageous. Don't be afraid or discouraged.

¹⁴ "Notice I have taken great pains to provide for the house of the LORD — 3,775 tons of gold, 37,750 tons of silver,ᴮ and bronze and iron that can't be weighed because there is so much of it. I have also provided timber and stone, but you will need to add more to them. ¹⁵ You also have many workers: stonecutters, masons, carpenters, and people skilled in every kind of work ¹⁶ in gold, silver, bronze, and iron — beyond number. Now begin the work, and may the LORD be with you."

¹⁷ Then David ordered all the leaders of Israel to help his son Solomon: ¹⁸ "The LORD your God is with you, isn't he? And hasn't he given you rest on every side? For he has handed the land's inhabitants over to me, and the land has been subdued before the LORD and his people. ¹⁹ Now determine in your mind and heart to seek the LORD your God. Get started building the LORD God's sanctuary so that you may bring the ark of the LORD's covenant and the holy articles of God to the temple that is to be built for the name of the LORD."

THE DIVISIONS OF THE LEVITES

23 When David was old and full of days, he installed his son Solomon as king over Israel. ² Then he gathered all the leaders of Israel, the priests, and the Levites. ³ The Levites thirty years old or more were counted; the total number of men was thirty-eight thousand by headcount. ⁴ "Of

---

ᴬ22:9 In Hb, the name *Solomon* sounds like "peace."   ᴮ22:14 Lit *100,000 talents of gold and 1,000,000 talents of silver* these," David said, "twenty-four thousand are to be in charge of the work on the Lord's temple, six thousand are to be officers and judges, ⁵ four thousand are to be gatekeepers, and four thousand are to praise the Lord with the instruments that I have made for worship."

⁶ Then David divided them into divisions according to Levi's sons: Gershom,ᴬ Kohath, and Merari.

⁷ The Gershonites: Ladan and Shimei.

⁸ Ladan's sons: Jehiel was the first, then Zetham, and Joel — three.

⁹ Shimei's sons: Shelomoth, Haziel, and Haran — three. Those were the heads of the families of Ladan.

¹⁰ Shimei's sons: Jahath, Zizah,ᴮ Jeush, and Beriah. Those were Shimei's sons — four. ¹¹ Jahath was the first and Zizah was the second; however, Jeush and Beriah did not have many sons, so they became one familyᶜ and received a single assignment.

¹² Kohath's sons: Amram, Izhar, Hebron, and Uzziel — four.

¹³ Amram's sons: Aaron and Moses.

Aaron, along with his descendants, was set apart forever to consecrate the most holy things, to burn incense in the presence of the Lord, to minister to him, and to pronounce blessings in his name forever. ¹⁴ As for Moses the man of God, his sons were named among the tribe of Levi.

¹⁵ Moses's sons: Gershom and Eliezer.

¹⁶ Gershom's sons: Shebuel was first.

¹⁷ Eliezer's sons were Rehabiah, first; Eliezer did not have any other sons, but Rehabiah's sons were very numerous.

¹⁸ Izhar's sons: Shelomith was first.

¹⁹ Hebron's sons: Jeriah was first, Amariah second, Jahaziel third, and Jekameam fourth.

²⁰ Uzziel's sons: Micah was first, and Isshiah second.

²¹ Merari's sons: Mahli and Mushi.

Mahli's sons: Eleazar and Kish.

²² Eleazar died having no sons, only daughters. Their cousins, the sons of Kish, married them.

²³ Mushi's sons: Mahli, Eder, and Jeremoth — three.

²⁴ These were the descendants of Levi by their ancestral familiesᴰ — the family heads, according to their registration by name in the headcount — twenty years old or more, who worked in the service of the Lord's temple. ²⁵ For David said, "The Lord God of Israel has given rest to his people, and he has come to stay in Jerusalem forever. ²⁶ Also, the Levites no longer need to carry the tabernacle or any of the equipment for its service" — ²⁷ for according to the last words of David, the Levites twenty years old or more were to be counted — ²⁸ "but their duty will be to assist the descendants of Aaron with the service of the Lord's temple, being responsible for the courts and the chambers, the purification of all the holy things, and the work of the service of God's temple — ²⁹ as well as the rows of the Bread of the Presence, the fine flour for the grain offering, the wafers of unleavened bread, the baking,ᴱ the mixing, and all measurements of volume and length. ³⁰ They

---

ᴬ23:6 Lit *Gershon*   ᴮ23:10 LXX, Vg; MT reads *Zina*   ᶜ23:11 Lit *a father's house*
ᴰ23:24 Lit *the house of their fathers*   ᴱ23:29 Lit *the griddle*

are also to stand every morning to give thanks and praise to the LORD, and likewise in the evening. ³¹ Whenever burnt offerings are offered to the LORD on the Sabbaths, New Moons, and appointed festivals, they are to offer them regularly in the LORD's presence according to the number prescribed for them. ³² They are to carry out their responsibilities for the tent of meeting, for the holy place, and for their relatives, the descendants of Aaron, in the service of the LORD's temple."

THE DIVISIONS OF THE PRIESTS

24 The divisions of the descendants of Aaron were as follows: Aaron's sons were Nadab, Abihu, Eleazar, and Ithamar. ² But Nadab and Abihu died before their father, and they had no sons, so Eleazar and Ithamar served as priests. ³ Together with Zadok from the descendants of Eleazar and Ahimelech from the descendants of Ithamar, David divided them according to the assigned duties of their service. ⁴ Since more leaders were found among Eleazar's descendants than Ithamar's, they were divided accordingly: sixteen heads of ancestral families ᴬ were from Eleazar's descendants, and eight heads of ancestral families were from Ithamar's. ⁵ They were assigned by lot, for there were officers of the sanctuary and officers of God among both Eleazar's and Ithamar's descendants.

⁶ The secretary, Shemaiah son of Nethanel, a Levite, recorded them in the presence of the king and the officers, the priest Zadok, Ahimelech son of Abiathar, and the heads of families of the priests and the Levites. One ancestral family ᴮ was taken for Eleazar, and then one for Ithamar.

⁷ The first lot fell to Jehoiarib, the second to Jedaiah,
⁸ the third to Harim, the fourth to Seorim,
⁹ the fifth to Malchijah, the sixth to Mijamin,
¹⁰ the seventh to Hakkoz, the eighth to Abijah,
¹¹ the ninth to Jeshua, the tenth to Shecaniah,
¹² the eleventh to Eliashib, the twelfth to Jakim,
¹³ the thirteenth to Huppah, the fourteenth to Jeshebeab,
¹⁴ the fifteenth to Bilgah, the sixteenth to Immer,
¹⁵ the seventeenth to Hezir, the eighteenth to Happizzez,
¹⁶ the nineteenth to Pethahiah, the twentieth to Jehezkel,
¹⁷ the twenty-first to Jachin, the twenty-second to Gamul,
¹⁸ the twenty-third to Delaiah, and the twenty-fourth to Maaziah.

¹⁹ These had their assigned duties for service when they entered the LORD's temple, according to their regulations, which they received from their ancestor Aaron, as the LORD God of Israel had commanded him.

THE REST OF THE LEVITES

²⁰ As for the rest of Levi's sons:
from Amram's sons: Shubael;
from Shubael's sons: Jehdeiah.
²¹ From Rehabiah:
from Rehabiah's sons: Isshiah was the first.
²² From the Izharites: Shelomoth;

ᴬ24:4 Lit *house of fathers*   ᴮ24:6 Lit *father's house*

from Shelomoth's sons: Jahath.
²³ Hebron's^ sons:
Jeriah the first, Amariah the second,
Jahaziel the third, and Jekameam the fourth.
²⁴ From Uzziel's sons: Micah;
from Micah's sons: Shamir.
²⁵ Micah's brother: Isshiah;
from Isshiah's sons: Zechariah.
²⁶ Merari's sons: Mahli and Mushi,
and from his sons, Jaaziah his son.^B
²⁷ Merari's sons, by his son Jaaziah:^C
Shoham, Zaccur, and Ibri.
²⁸ From Mahli: Eleazar, who had no sons.
²⁹ From Kish, from Kish's sons: Jerahmeel.
³⁰ Mushi's sons: Mahli, Eder, and Jerimoth.

Those were the descendants of the Levites according to their ancestral families.^D ³¹ They also cast lots the same way as their relatives the descendants of Aaron did in the presence of King David, Zadok, Ahimelech, and the heads of the families of the priests and Levites — the family heads and their younger brothers alike.

THE LEVITICAL MUSICIANS

25 David and the officers of the army also set apart some of the sons of Asaph, Heman, and Jeduthun, who were to prophesy accompanied by lyres, harps, and cymbals. This is the list of the men who performed their service:
² From Asaph's sons:
Zaccur, Joseph, Nethaniah, and Asarelah, sons of Asaph, under Asaph's authority, who prophesied under the authority of the king.
³ From Jeduthun: Jeduthun's sons:
Gedaliah, Zeri, Jeshaiah, Shimei,^E Hashabiah, and Mattithiah — six — under the authority of their father Jeduthun, prophesying to the accompaniment of lyres, giving thanks and praise to the Lord.
⁴ From Heman: Heman's sons:
Bukkiah, Mattaniah, Uzziel, Shebuel, Jerimoth, Hananiah, Hanani, Eliathah, Giddalti, Romamti-ezer, Joshbekashah, Mallothi, Hothir, and Mahazioth. ⁵ All these sons of Heman, the king's seer, were given by the promises of God to exalt him,^F for God had given Heman fourteen sons and three daughters.

⁶ All these men were under their own fathers' authority for the music in the Lord's temple, with cymbals, harps, and lyres for the service of God's temple. Asaph, Jeduthun, and Heman were under the king's authority. ⁷ They numbered 288 together with their relatives who were all trained and skillful

---

^A24:23 Some Hb mss, some LXX mss; other Hb mss omit *Hebron's*; 1Ch 23:19
^B24:26 Or *Mushi; Jaaziah's sons: Beno.* ^C24:27 Or *sons, Jaaziah: Beno,*
^D24:30 Lit *the house of their fathers* ^E25:3 One Hb ms, LXX; other Hb mss omit
Shimei ^F25:5 Lit *by the words of God to lift a horn*

in music for the LORD. [8] They cast lots for their duties, young and old alike, teacher as well as pupil.

[9] The first lot for Asaph fell to Joseph, his sons, and his relatives —   12 [A]
to Gedaliah the second: him, his relatives, and his sons —   12

[10] the third to Zaccur, his sons, and his relatives —   12

[11] the fourth to Izri, [B] his sons, and his relatives —   12

[12] the fifth to Nethaniah, his sons, and his relatives —   12

[13] the sixth to Bukkiah, his sons, and his relatives —   12

[14] the seventh to Jesarelah, his sons, and his relatives —   12

[15] the eighth to Jeshaiah, his sons, and his relatives —   12

[16] the ninth to Mattaniah, his sons, and his relatives —   12

[17] the tenth to Shimei, his sons, and his relatives —   12

[18] the eleventh to Azarel, [C] his sons, and his relatives —   12

[19] the twelfth to Hashabiah, his sons, and his relatives —   12

[20] the thirteenth to Shubael, his sons, and his relatives —   12

[21] the fourteenth to Mattithiah, his sons, and his relatives —   12

[22] the fifteenth to Jeremoth, his sons, and his relatives —   12

[23] the sixteenth to Hananiah, his sons, and his relatives —   12

[24] the seventeenth to Joshbekashah, his sons, and his relatives —   12

[25] the eighteenth to Hanani, his sons, and his relatives —   12

[26] the nineteenth to Mallothi, his sons, and his relatives —   12

[27] the twentieth to Eliathah, his sons, and his relatives —   12

[28] the twenty-first to Hothir, his sons, and his relatives —   12

[29] the twenty-second to Giddalti, his sons, and his relatives —   12

[30] the twenty-third to Mahazioth, his sons, and his relatives —   12

[31] and the twenty-fourth to Romamti-ezer, his sons,
and his relatives —   12.

THE LEVITICAL GATEKEEPERS

26 The following were the divisions of the gatekeepers:
From the Korahites: Meshelemiah son of Kore, one of the sons of Asaph.

[2] Meshelemiah had sons:
Zechariah the firstborn, Jediael the second,
Zebadiah the third, Jathniel the fourth,
[3] Elam the fifth, Jehohanan the sixth,
and Eliehoenai the seventh.
[4] Obed-edom also had sons:
Shemaiah the firstborn, Jehozabad the second,
Joah the third, Sachar the fourth,
Nethanel the fifth, [5] Ammiel the sixth,
Issachar the seventh, and Peullethai the eighth,
for God blessed him.
[6] Also, to his son Shemaiah were born sons who ruled their ancestral families [D] because they were strong, capable men.
[7] Shemaiah's sons: Othni, Rephael, Obed, and Elzabad; his relatives Elihu and Semachiah were also capable men. [8] All of these were among the

---

[A] 25:9 LXX; MT lacks *his sons, and his relatives—12*   [B] 25:11 Variant of Zeri
[C] 25:18 Variant of Uzziel   [D] 26:6 Lit *the house of their fathers,* also in v. 13

sons of Obed-edom with their sons and relatives; they were capable men with strength for the work — sixty-two from Obed-edom. ⁹ Meshelemiah also had sons and relatives who were capable men — eighteen.

¹⁰ Hosah, from the Merarites, also had sons: Shimri the first (although he was not the firstborn, his father had appointed him as the first), ¹¹ Hilkiah the second, Tebaliah the third, and Zechariah the fourth. The sons and relatives of Hosah were thirteen in all.

¹² These divisions of the gatekeepers, under their leading men, had duties for ministering in the LORD's temple, just as their relatives did. ¹³ They cast lots for each temple gate according to their ancestral families, young and old alike.

¹⁴ The lot for the east gate fell to Shelemiah.ᴬ They also cast lots for his son Zechariah, an insightful counselor, and his lot came out for the north gate. ¹⁵ Obed-edom's was the south gate, and his sons' lot was for the storehouses; ¹⁶ it was the west gate and the gate of Shallecheth on the ascending highway for Shuppim and Hosah.

There were guards stationed at every watch. ¹⁷ There were six Levites each dayᴮ on the east, four each day on the north, four each day on the south, and two pair at the storehouses. ¹⁸ As for the court on the west, there were four at the highway and two at the court. ¹⁹ Those were the divisions of the gatekeepers from the descendants of the Korahites and Merarites.

THE LEVITICAL TREASURERS AND OTHER OFFICIALS

²⁰ From the Levites, Ahijah was in charge of the treasuries of God's temple and the treasuries of what had been dedicated. ²¹ From the sons of Ladan, who were the descendants of the Gershonites through Ladan and were the family heads belonging to Ladan the Gershonite: Jehieli. ²² The sons of Jehieli, Zetham and his brother Joel, were in charge of the treasuries of the LORD's temple.

²³ From the Amramites, the Izharites, the Hebronites, and the Uzzielites: ²⁴ Shebuel, a descendant of Moses's son Gershom, was the officer in charge of the treasuries. ²⁵ His relatives through Eliezer: his son Rehabiah, his son Jeshaiah, his son Joram, his son Zichri, and his son Shelomith.ᶜ ²⁶ This Shelomith and his relatives were in charge of all the treasuries of what had been dedicated by King David, by the family heads who were the commanders of thousands and of hundreds, and by the army commanders. ²⁷ They dedicated part of the plunder from their battles for the repair of the LORD's temple. ²⁸ All that the seer Samuel, Saul son of Kish, Abner son of Ner, and Joab son of Zeruiah had dedicated, along with everything else that had been dedicated, were in the care of Shelomith and his relatives.

²⁹ From the Izrahites: Chenaniah and his sons had duties outside the templeᴰ as officers and judges over Israel. ³⁰ From the Hebronites: Hashabiah and his relatives, 1,700 capable men, had assigned duties in Israel west of the Jordan for all the work of the LORD and for the service of the king. ³¹ From the Hebronites: Jerijah was the head of the Hebronites, according to the family

---

ᴬ26:14 Variant of Meshelemiah   ᴮ26:17 LXX; MT omits *each day*   ᶜ26:25 Or *Shelomoth*, also in vv. 26,28   ᴰ26:29 *the temple* added for clarity records of his ancestors. A search was made in the fortieth year of David's reign and strong, capable men were found among them at Jazer in Gilead. [32] There were among Jerijah's relatives 2,700 capable men who were family heads. King David appointed them over the Reubenites, the Gadites, and half the tribe of Manasseh as overseers in every matter relating to God and the king.

DAVID'S SECULAR OFFICIALS

27 This is the list of the Israelites, the family heads, the commanders of thousands and the commanders of hundreds, and their officers who served the king in every matter to do with the divisions that were on rotated military duty each month throughout[A] the year. There were 24,000 in each division:

[2] Jashobeam son of Zabdiel was in charge of the first division, for the first month; 24,000 were in his division. [3] He was a descendant of Perez and chief of all the army commanders for the first month.

[4] Dodai the Ahohite was in charge of the division for the second month, and Mikloth was the leader; 24,000 were in his division.

[5] The third army commander, as chief for the third month, was Benaiah son of the priest Jehoiada; 24,000 were in his division. [6] This Benaiah was a mighty man among the Thirty and over the Thirty, and his son Ammizabad was in charge[B] of his division.

[7] The fourth commander, for the fourth month, was Joab's brother Asahel, and his son Zebadiah was commander after him; 24,000 were in his division.

[8] The fifth, for the fifth month, was the commander Shamhuth the Izrahite; 24,000 were in his division.

[9] The sixth, for the sixth month, was Ira son of Ikkesh the Tekoite; 24,000 were in his division.

[10] The seventh, for the seventh month, was Helez the Pelonite from the descendants of Ephraim; 24,000 were in his division.

[11] The eighth, for the eighth month, was Sibbecai the Hushathite, a Zerahite; 24,000 were in his division.

[12] The ninth, for the ninth month, was Abiezer the Anathothite, a Benjaminite; 24,000 were in his division.

[13] The tenth, for the tenth month, was Maharai the Netophathite, a Zerahite; 24,000 were in his division.

[14] The eleventh, for the eleventh month, was Benaiah the Pirathonite from the descendants of Ephraim; 24,000 were in his division.

[15] The twelfth, for the twelfth month, was Heldai the Netophathite, of Othniel's family;[C] 24,000 were in his division.

[16] The following were in charge of the tribes of Israel:
For the Reubenites, Eliezer son of Zichri was the chief official;
for the Simeonites, Shephatiah son of Maacah;
[17] for the Levites, Hashabiah son of Kemuel; for Aaron, Zadok;
[18] for Judah, Elihu, one of David's brothers; for Issachar, Omri son of Michael;

A27:1 Lit *that came in and went out month by month for all months of*   B27:6 LXX; MT omits *in charge*   C27:15 Lit *belonging to Othniel*

¹⁹ for Zebulun, Ishmaiah son of Obadiah;
for Naphtali, Jerimoth son of Azriel;
²⁰ for the Ephraimites, Hoshea son of Azaziah;
for half the tribe of Manasseh, Joel son of Pedaiah;
²¹ for half the tribe of Manasseh in Gilead, Iddo son of Zechariah;
for Benjamin, Jaasiel son of Abner;
²² for Dan, Azarel son of Jeroham.
Those were the leaders of the tribes of Israel.

²³ David didn't count the men aged twenty or under, for the LORD had said he would make Israel as numerous as the stars of the sky. ²⁴ Joab son of Zeruiah began to count them, but he didn't complete it. There was wrath against Israel because of this census, and the number was not entered in the Historical Record^A of King David.

²⁵ Azmaveth son of Adiel was in charge of the king's storehouses.
Jonathan son of Uzziah was in charge of the storehouses in the country, in the cities, in the villages, and in the fortresses.
²⁶ Ezri son of Chelub was in charge of those who worked in the fields tilling the soil.
²⁷ Shimei the Ramathite was in charge of the vineyards.
Zabdi the Shiphmite was in charge of the produce of the vineyards for the wine cellars.
²⁸ Baal-hanan the Gederite was in charge of the olive and sycamore trees in the Judean foothills.^B
Joash was in charge of the stores of olive oil.
²⁹ Shitrai the Sharonite was in charge of the herds that grazed in Sharon, while Shaphat son of Adlai was in charge of the herds in the valleys.
³⁰ Obil the Ishmaelite was in charge of the camels.
Jehdeiah the Meronothite was in charge of the donkeys.
³¹ Jaziz the Hagrite was in charge of the flocks.
All these were officials in charge of King David's property.

³² David's uncle Jonathan was a counselor; he was a man of understanding and a scribe. Jehiel son of Hachmoni attended^C the king's sons. ³³ Ahithophel was the king's counselor. Hushai the Archite was the king's friend. ³⁴ After Ahithophel came Jehoiada son of Benaiah, then Abiathar. Joab was the commander of the king's army.

DAVID COMMISSIONS SOLOMON TO BUILD THE TEMPLE

28 David assembled all the leaders of Israel in Jerusalem: the leaders of the tribes, the leaders of the divisions in the king's service, the commanders of thousands and the commanders of hundreds, and the officials in charge of all the property and cattle of the king and his sons, along with the court officials, the fighting men, and all the best soldiers. ² Then King David rose to his feet and said, "Listen to me, my brothers and my people. It was in my heart to build a house as a resting place for the ark of the LORD's covenant and as a footstool for our God. I had made preparations to build,

---

^A27:24 LXX; MT reads *the number of the Historical Record*   ^B27:28 Or *the Shephelah*   ^C27:32 Lit *was with*

³ but God said to me, 'You are not to build a house for my name because you are a man of war and have shed blood.'

⁴ "Yet the LORD God of Israel chose me out of all my father's family to be king over Israel forever. For he chose Judah as leader, and from the house of Judah, my father's family, and from my father's sons, he was pleased to make me king over all Israel. ⁵ And out of all my sons — for the LORD has given me many sons — he has chosen my son Solomon to sit on the throne of the LORD's kingdom over Israel. ⁶ He said to me, 'Your son Solomon is the one who is to build my house and my courts, for I have chosen him to be my son, and I will be his father. ⁷ I will establish his kingdom forever if he perseveres in keeping my commands and my ordinances as he is doing today.'

⁸ "So now in the sight of all Israel, the assembly of the LORD, and in the hearing of our God, observe and follow all the commands of the LORD your God so that you may possess this good land and leave it as an inheritance to your descendants forever.

⁹ "As for you, Solomon my son, know the God of your father, and serve him wholeheartedly and with a willing mind, for the LORD searches every heart and understands the intention of every thought. If you seek him, he will be found by you, but if you abandon him, he will reject you forever. ¹⁰ Realize now that the LORD has chosen you to build a house for the sanctuary. Be strong, and do it."

¹¹ Then David gave his son Solomon the plans for the portico of the temple and its buildings, treasuries, upstairs rooms, inner rooms, and a room for the mercy seat. ¹² The plans contained everything he had in mind ᴬ for the courts of the LORD's house, all the surrounding chambers, the treasuries of God's house, and the treasuries for what is dedicated. ¹³ Also included were plans for the divisions of the priests and the Levites; all the work of service in the LORD's house; all the articles of service of the LORD's house; ¹⁴ the weight of gold for all the articles for every kind of service; the weight of all the silver articles for every kind of service; ¹⁵ the weight of the gold lampstands and their gold lamps, including the weight of each lampstand and its lamps; the weight of each silver lampstand and its lamps, according to the service of each lampstand; ¹⁶ the weight of gold for each table for the rows of the Bread of the Presence and the silver for the silver tables; ¹⁷ the pure gold for the forks, sprinkling basins, and pitchers; the weight of each gold dish; the weight of each silver bowl; ¹⁸ the weight of refined gold for the altar of incense; and the plans for the chariot of ᴮ the gold cherubim that spread out their wings and cover the ark of the LORD's covenant.

¹⁹ David concluded, "By the LORD's hand on me, he enabled me to understand everything in writing, all the details of the plan." ᶜ

²⁰ Then David said to his son Solomon, "Be strong and courageous, and do the work. Don't be afraid or discouraged, for the LORD God, my God, is with you. He won't leave you or abandon you until all the work for the service of the LORD's house is finished. ²¹ Here are the divisions of the priests and the Levites for all the service of God's house. Every willing person of any skill will be at your disposal for the work, and the leaders and all the people are at your every command."

ᴬ 28:12 Or *he received from the Spirit*   ᴮ 28:18 Or *chariot, that is*; Ps 18:10; Ezk 1:5,15   ᶜ 28:19 Hb obscure

CONTRIBUTIONS FOR BUILDING THE TEMPLE

29 Then King David said to all the assembly, "My son Solomon — God has chosen him alone — is young and inexperienced. The task is great because the building will not be built for a human but for the LORD God. ² So to the best of my ability I've made provision for the house of my God: gold for the gold articles, silver for the silver, bronze for the bronze, iron for the iron, and wood for the wood, as well as onyx, stones for mounting, ᴬ antimony, ᴮ stones of various colors, all kinds of precious stones, and a great quantity of marble. ³ Moreover, because of my delight in the house of my God, I now give my personal treasures of gold and silver for the house of my God over and above all that I've provided for the holy house: ⁴ 100 tons ᶜ of gold (gold of Ophir) and 250 tons ᴰ of refined silver for overlaying the walls of the buildings, ⁵ the gold for the gold work and the silver for the silver, for all the work to be done by the craftsmen. Now who will volunteer to consecrate himself to the LORD today?"

⁶ Then the leaders of the households, the leaders of the tribes of Israel, the commanders of thousands and of hundreds, and the officials in charge of the king's work gave willingly. ⁷ For the service of God's house they gave 185 tons ᴱ of gold and 10,000 gold coins, ᶠ 375 tons ᴳ of silver, 675 tons ᴴ of bronze, and 4,000 tons ᴵ of iron. ⁸ Whoever had precious stones gave them to the treasury of the LORD's house under the care of Jehiel the Gershonite. ⁹ Then the people rejoiced because of their leaders' willingness to give, for they had given to the LORD wholeheartedly. King David also rejoiced greatly.

DAVID'S PRAYER

¹⁰ Then David blessed the LORD in the sight of all the assembly. David said,
May you be blessed, LORD God of our father Israel, from eternity to eternity. ¹¹ Yours, LORD, is the greatness and the power and the glory and the splendor and the majesty, for everything in the heavens and on earth belongs to you. Yours, LORD, is the kingdom, and you are exalted as head over all. ¹² Riches and honor come from you, and you are the ruler of everything. Power and might are in your hand, and it is in your hand to make great and to give strength to all. ¹³ Now therefore, our God, we give you thanks and praise your glorious name.

¹⁴ But who am I, and who are my people, that we should be able to give as generously as this? For everything comes from you, and we have given you only what comes from your own hand. ᴶ ¹⁵ For we are aliens and temporary residents in your presence as were all our ancestors. Our days on earth are like a shadow, without hope. ¹⁶ LORD our God, all this wealth that we've provided for building you a house for your holy name comes from your hand; everything belongs to you. ¹⁷ I know, my God, that you test the heart and that you are pleased with what is right. I have willingly given all these things with an upright heart, and now I have

---

ᴬ29:2 Or *mosaic*   ᴮ29:2 In Hb, the word *antimony* is similar to "turquoise"; Ex 28:18.   ᶜ 29:4 Lit *3,000 talents*   ᴰ29:4 Lit *7,000 talents*   ᴱ29:7 Lit *5,000 talents*   ᶠ29:7 Or *drachmas, or darics*   ᴳ29:7 Lit *10,000 talents*   ᴴ29:7 Lit *18,000 talents*   ᴵ29:7 Lit *100,000 talents*   ᴶ29:14 Lit *and from your hand we have given to you*

THE REAL TREASURE

1 CHRONICLES 28–29; 1 CHRONICLES 17:10-14; MATTHEW 6:19-24

God chose Solomon to build the temple, but Solomon was young and inexperienced. So David, at the end of his life, used his knowledge and resources to gather together all the materials young Solomon would need to build a house for the Lord.

In 1 Chronicles 29, King David gives his all to make preparations for the temple because he took "delight" in the house of God (1Ch 29:3). The temple would be home to the very presence of God for generations to come, and David gathered the finest materials to honor Him.

The leaders of the community contributed their treasure, too, offering up gold and silver by the ton, their precious stones, and the work of their hands. Then they gathered their voices and praised the Lord as David lead them, praying:

"Yours, LORD, is the greatness and the power and the glory and the splendor and the majesty, for everything in the heavens and on earth belongs to you. Yours, LORD, is the kingdom, and you are exalted as head over all."

1 CHRONICLES 29:11

The people gave all they had because they knew it all belonged to the Lord. And though they would forget like the generations before and after them, for this moment in time they remembered: the true treasure was not their wealth; it was the presence of the living God.

Jesus taught the same truth to the crowds gathered at the Sermon on the Mount:

"Don't store up for yourselves treasures on earth, where moth and rust destroy and where thieves break in and steal. But store up for yourselves treasures in heaven, where neither moth nor rust destroys, and where thieves don't break in and steal. For where your treasure is, there your heart will be also."

MATTHEW 6:19-21

There are times when, by God's grace, I have sacrificed earthly treasure to the Lord "wholeheartedly" like those worshipers in chapter 29 (v. 9). There are also times—so many—when I give out of guilt, out of obligation, or not at all. But the point of my giving is not for the whole-heart instances to outweigh the others. The purpose is to worship the Lord—with all my heart, with all my mind, and with all my strength (Dt 6:4).

For Christians, **our heart is the temple of the Lord.** David and Solomon built a beautiful temple where the Spirit of the Lord would reside, but Jesus reminds us that we ourselves have become that temple—creations even more glorious than Solomon's temple.

seen your people who are present[A] here giving joyfully and[B] willingly to you. [18] LORD God of Abraham, Isaac, and Israel, our ancestors, keep this desire forever in the thoughts of the hearts of your people, and confirm their hearts toward you. [19] Give my son Solomon an undivided heart to keep and to carry out all your commands, your decrees, and your statutes, and to build the building for which I have made provision.

[20] Then David said to the whole assembly, "Blessed be the LORD your God." So the whole assembly praised the LORD God of their ancestors. They knelt low and paid homage to the LORD and the king.

[21] The following day they offered sacrifices to the LORD and burnt offerings to the LORD: a thousand bulls, a thousand rams, and a thousand lambs, along with their drink offerings, and sacrifices in abundance for all Israel. [22] They ate and drank with great joy in the LORD's presence that day.

THE ENTHRONEMENT OF SOLOMON

Then, for a second time, they made David's son Solomon king; they anointed him[C] as the LORD's ruler, and Zadok as the priest. [23] Solomon sat on the LORD's throne as king in place of his father David. He prospered, and all Israel obeyed him. [24] All the leaders and the mighty men, and all of King David's sons as well, pledged their allegiance to King Solomon. [25] The LORD highly exalted Solomon in the sight of all Israel and bestowed on him such royal majesty as had not been bestowed on any king over Israel before him.

A SUMMARY OF DAVID'S LIFE

[26] David son of Jesse was king over all Israel. [27] The length of his reign over Israel was forty years; he reigned in Hebron for seven years and in Jerusalem for thirty-three. [28] He died at a good old age, full of days, riches, and honor, and his son Solomon became king in his place. [29] As for the events of King David's reign, from beginning to end, note that they are written in the Events of the Seer Samuel, the Events of the Prophet Nathan, and the Events of the Seer Gad, [30] along with all his reign, his might, and the incidents that affected him and Israel and all the kingdoms of the surrounding lands.

[A] 29:17 Lit found   [B] 29:17 Or now with joy I've seen your people who are present here giving   [C] 29:22 LXX, Tg, Vg; MT omits him

IF MY PEOPLE

HUMBLE

THEMSELVES,
I WILL HEAR FROM

HEAVEN

&

HEAL

THEIR LAND

2 chronicles

 If I shut the sky so there is no rain, or if I command the grasshopper to consume the land, or if I send pestilence on my people, and my people, who bear my name, humble themselves, pray and seek my face, and turn from their evil ways, then I will hear from heaven, forgive their sin, and heal their land. **7:13-14**

ON THE TIMELINE The book of 2 Chronicles focuses on all the kings who followed David up to the exile and reinstatement of Jerusalem (971 BC to 538 BC). It covers the same time period as 1 and 2 Kings, but 2 Chronicles focuses primarily on the kings of Judah. The content of 1 and 2 Chronicles implies that they were written sometime after the return from the exile, perhaps the middle of the fifth century BC.

A LITTLE BACKGROUND First and 2 Chronicles are the first and second books of a four-book series that includes Ezra and Nehemiah. Together, these four books provide a priestly history of Israel from the time of Adam to the rebuilding of the house of God and the walls of Jerusalem. It is likely that the two Chronicles were, at one time, a single scroll.

An ancient tradition ascribes the authorship of Chronicles to Ezra. Among other criteria, this identification is supported by the fact that the last verses of Chronicles are the first verses of the book of Ezra.

MESSAGE & PURPOSE Having resettled in Jerusalem after the exile, the people needed to reconnect with their identity as the people of God. Chronicles met this purpose by reminding them of their heritage and by directing them back to God's presence in their midst as symbolized by the temple.

The important ideas that 1 and 2 Chronicles emphasize are:
1. A direct connection to God's people in the past
2. The continuity of the line of David on the throne of Judah
3. The centrality of the temple and its rituals in focusing on God
4. The importance of music in worshiping God
5. The invincibility of God's people when they obey Him
6. The inevitability of punishment when God's people disobey Him.

GIVE THANKS FOR THE BOOK OF 2 CHRONICLES:

Chronicles brings together many dimensions of biblical revelation, such as historical events (as recounted in Genesis through Kings), temple ritual (as prescribed in Leviticus), sin and judgment (as preached by the prophets), and even some psalms. The books of 1 and 2 Chronicles give us the big picture of Old Testament history, capturing the Davidic covenant in light of Israel's history back to Adam and pointing to the eternal continuation of that covenant through the reign of the Messiah.

THE BOOK OF 2 CHRONICLES IN HISTORY

950 BC

850 BC

750 BC

971

967

Temple
construction
begins

Solomon
made king
of Israel

931

911

Kingdom
splits

911-870 BC
King Asa
in Judah

874

870

863

853

863-850 BC
Elijah the
prophet
ministers
to Israel

874-853 BC
King Ahab
in Israel

835

835-796 BC
King Joash
in Judah

796

793

793-753 BC
King Jeroboam II
in Israel

75

650 BC

550 BC

722

609

605

701

642

597

538

696

640

586

696-642 BC
King Manasseh
in Judah

640-609 BC
King Josiah
in Judah

586-538 BC
Babylonian Exile

Temple destroyed

People of Judah
taken captive

Decree
of Cyrus

Assyria invades Judah

First Babylonian siege
of Judah — royal family
and nobility taken captive

Israel invaded by Assyria

Assyrian captivity begins

End of Northern Kingdom

End of Assyrian Empire

READ AND UNDERSTAND 2 CHRONICLES

The Bible is a complete work in which many stories combine to tell one story. As you read the book of 2 Chronicles, consider reading the additional passages to discover how the whole of Scripture works together.

Week 1	GOING DEEPER
☐ 2 Chronicles 1:1–2:16	Exodus 31:1-11; John 15:7
☐ 2 Chronicles 2:17–5:1	Exodus 26:31-35; Hebrews 9:11-14
☐ 2 Chronicles 5:2–6:42	John 1:14; Hebrews 9:1-5
☐ **2 Chronicles 7–8**	Psalm 136; John 2:18-22
☐ 2 Chronicles 9	1 Kings 10:1-13; Psalm 72

Week 2	GOING DEEPER
☐ 2 Chronicles 10–11	Proverbs 15:1; Matthew 11:29-30
☐ 2 Chronicles 12:1–14:1	Psalm 22:1-5; John 14:21
☐ 2 Chronicles 14:2–15:19	Matthew 21:12-16; Ephesians 1:3-14
☐ 2 Chronicles 16–17	Psalm 33:16-22; Philippians 2:9-11
☐ 2 Chronicles 18–19	Isaiah 42:1-4; Romans 2:9-11

Week 3	GOING DEEPER
☐ 2 Chronicles 20	Ezra 8:21-23; Psalm 44
☐ **2 Chronicles 21–22**	Deuteronomy 10:12-14; Matthew 2:13-18
☐ 2 Chronicles 23–24	Psalm 2; Jeremiah 7:21-26
☐ 2 Chronicles 25–26	Proverbs 16:18; Isaiah 6:1-8
☐ 2 Chronicles 27–28	John 13:34-35; 1 John 3:16

Week 4	GOING DEEPER
☐ **2 Chronicles 29:1–31:1**	Micah 6:6-8; Galatians 3:13-14
☐ 2 Chronicles 31:2–32:23	Deuteronomy 31:6; Hebrews 2:14-18
☐ 2 Chronicles 32:24–33:25	Ezekiel 13:21; 1 Timothy 1:15
☐ 2 Chronicles 34–35	Ezra 6:19-22; Proverbs 26:17
☐ 2 Chronicles 36	Jeremiah 25:1-7; Romans 11:1-2

SOLOMON'S REQUEST FOR WISDOM

1 Solomon son of David strengthened his hold on his kingdom. The LORD his God was with him and highly exalted him. ² Then Solomon spoke to all Israel, to the commanders of thousands and of hundreds, to the judges, and to every leader in all Israel — the family heads. ³ Solomon and the whole assembly with him went to the high place that was in Gibeon because God's tent of meeting, which the LORD's servant Moses had made in the wilderness, was there. ⁴ Now David had brought the ark of God from Kiriath-jearim to the place^A he had set up for it, because he had pitched a tent for it in Jerusalem, ⁵ but he put^B the bronze altar, which Bezalel son of Uri, son of Hur, had made, in front of the LORD's tabernacle. Solomon and the assembly inquired of him^C there. ⁶ Solomon offered sacrifices there in the LORD's presence on the bronze altar at the tent of meeting; he offered a thousand burnt offerings on it.

⁷ That night God appeared to Solomon and said to him: "Ask. What should I give you?"

⁸ And Solomon said to God: "You have shown great and faithful love to my father David, and you have made me king in his place. ⁹ LORD God, let your promise to my father David now come true. For you have made me king over a people as numerous as the dust of the earth. ¹⁰ Now grant me wisdom and knowledge so that I may lead these people, for who can judge this great people of yours?"

¹¹ God said to Solomon, "Since this was in your heart, and you have not requested riches, wealth, or glory, or for the life of those who hate you, and you have not even requested long life, but you have requested for yourself wisdom and knowledge that you may judge my people over whom I have made you king, ¹² wisdom and knowledge are given to you. I will also give you riches, wealth, and glory, unlike what was given to the kings who were before you, or will be given to those after you." ¹³ So Solomon went to Jerusalem from^D the high place that was in Gibeon in front of the tent of meeting, and he reigned over Israel.

SOLOMON'S HORSES AND WEALTH

¹⁴ Solomon accumulated 1,400 chariots and 12,000 horsemen, which he stationed in the chariot cities and with the king in Jerusalem. ¹⁵ The king made silver and gold as common in Jerusalem as stones, and he made cedar as abundant as sycamore in the Judean foothills. ¹⁶ Solomon's horses came from Egypt and Kue.^E The king's traders would get them from Kue at the going price. ¹⁷ A chariot could be imported from Egypt for fifteen pounds^F of silver and a horse for nearly four pounds.^G In the same way, they exported them to all the kings of the Hittites and to the kings of Aram through their agents.

SOLOMON'S LETTER TO HIRAM

2 Solomon decided to build a temple for the name of the LORD and a royal palace for himself, ² so he assigned 70,000 men as porters, 80,000 men as stonecutters in the mountains, and 3,600 as supervisors over them.

---

^A1:4 Vg; MT omits *the place*   ^B1:5 Some Hb mss, Tg, Syr; other Hb mss, LXX, Vg read *but there was*   ^C1:5 Or *it*   ^D1:13 LXX, Vg; MT reads *to*   ^E1:16 = Cilicia   ^F1:17 Lit *600 shekels*   ^G1:17 Lit *150 shekels*

[3] Then Solomon sent word to King Hiram[A] of Tyre:

Do for me what you did for my father David. You sent him cedars to build him a house to live in. [4] Now I am building a temple for the name of the Lord my God in order to dedicate it to him for burning fragrant incense before him, for displaying the rows of the Bread of the Presence continuously, and for sacrificing burnt offerings for the morning and the evening, the Sabbaths and the New Moons, and the appointed festivals of the Lord our God. This is ordained for Israel permanently. [5] The temple that I am building will be great, for our God is greater than any of the gods. [6] But who is able to build a temple for him, since even heaven and the highest heaven cannot contain him? Who am I then that I should build a temple for him except as a place to burn incense before him? [7] Therefore, send me an artisan who is skilled in engraving to work with gold, silver, bronze, and iron, and with purple, crimson, and blue yarn. He will work with the artisans who are with me in Judah and Jerusalem, appointed by my father David. [8] Also, send me cedar, cypress, and algum[B] logs from Lebanon, for I know that your servants know how to cut the trees of Lebanon. Note that my servants will be with your servants [9] to prepare logs for me in abundance because the temple I am building will be great and wondrous. [10] I will give your servants, the woodcutters who cut the trees, one hundred thousand bushels[C] of wheat flour, one hundred thousand bushels of barley, one hundred ten thousand gallons[D] of wine, and one hundred ten thousand gallons of oil.

HIRAM'S REPLY

[11] Then King Hiram of Tyre wrote a letter[E] and sent it to Solomon:

Because the Lord loves his people, he set you over them as king. [12] Hiram also said:

Blessed be the Lord God of Israel, who made the heavens and the earth! He gave King David a wise son with insight and understanding, who will build a temple for the Lord and a royal palace for himself. [13] I have now sent Huram-abi,[F] a skillful man who has understanding. [14] He is the son of a woman from the daughters of Dan. His father is a man of Tyre. He knows how to work with gold, silver, bronze, iron, stone, and wood, with purple, blue, crimson yarn, and fine linen. He knows how to do all kinds of engraving and to execute any design that may be given him. I have sent him to be with your artisans and the artisans of my lord, your father David. [15] Now, let my lord send the wheat, barley, oil, and wine to his servants as promised. [16] We will cut logs from Lebanon, as many as you need, and bring them to you as rafts by sea to Joppa. You can then take them up to Jerusalem.

SOLOMON'S WORKFORCE

[17] Solomon took a census of all the resident alien men in the land of Israel, after the census that his father David had conducted, and the total was

---

[A] 2:3 Some Hb mss, LXX, Syr, Vg; other Hb mss read *Huram*; 2Sm 5:11; 1Kg 5:1-2
[B] 2:8 = almug in 1Kg 10:11-12 [C] 2:10 Lit *20,000 cors* [D] 2:10 Lit *20,000 baths*
[E] 2:11 Lit *Tyre said in writing* [F] 2:13 Lit *Huram my father*

153,600. [18] Solomon made 70,000 of them porters, 80,000 stonecutters in the mountains, and 3,600 supervisors to make the people work.

BUILDING THE TEMPLE

3 Then Solomon began to build the LORD's temple in Jerusalem on Mount Moriah where the LORD[A] had appeared to his father David, at the site David had prepared on the threshing floor of Ornan[B] the Jebusite. [2] He began to build on the second day of the second month in the fourth year of his reign. [3] These are Solomon's foundations[C] for building God's temple: the length[D] was ninety feet,[E] and the width thirty feet.[F] [4] The portico, which was across the front extending across the width of the temple, was thirty feet wide; its height was thirty feet;[G] he overlaid its inner surface with pure gold. [5] The larger room[H] he paneled with cypress wood, overlaid with fine gold, and decorated with palm trees and chains. [6] He adorned the temple with precious stones for beauty, and the gold was the gold of Parvaim. [7] He overlaid the temple — the beams, the thresholds, its walls and doors — with gold, and he carved cherubim on the walls.

THE MOST HOLY PLACE

[8] Then he made the most holy place; its length corresponded to the width of the temple, 30 feet, and its width was 30 feet. He overlaid it with forty-five thousand pounds[I] of fine gold. [9] The weight of the nails was twenty ounces[J] of gold, and he overlaid the ceiling with gold.

[10] He made two cherubim of sculptured work, for the most holy place, and he overlaid them with gold. [11] The overall length of the wings of the cherubim was 30 feet: the wing of one was 7 ½ feet,[K] touching the wall of the room; its other wing was 7 ½ feet, touching the wing of the other cherub. [12] The wing of the other[L] cherub was 7 ½ feet, touching the wall of the room; its other wing was 7 ½ feet, reaching the wing of the other cherub. [13] The wingspan of these cherubim was 30 feet. They stood on their feet and faced the larger room.[M]

[14] He made the curtain of blue, purple, and crimson yarn and fine linen, and he wove cherubim into it.

THE BRONZE PILLARS

[15] In front of the temple he made two pillars, each 27 feet[N] high. The capital on top of each was 7 ½ feet high. [16] He had made chainwork in the inner sanctuary and also put it on top of the pillars. He made a hundred pomegranates and fastened them into the chainwork. [17] Then he set up the pillars in front of the sanctuary, one on the right and one on the left. He named the one on the right Jachin[O] and the one on the left Boaz.[P]

[A]3:1 LXX; Tg reads *the angel of the LORD*; MT reads *he*   [B]3:1 = Araunah in 2Sm 24:16-24   [C]3:3 Tg reads *The measurements which Solomon decreed*   [D]3:3 Lit *length — cubits in the former measure —*   [E]3:3 Lit *60 cubits*   [F]3:3 Lit *20 cubits*, also in vv. 4,8,11,13   [G]3:4 LXX, Syr; MT reads *120 cubits*   [H]3:5 Lit *The house*   [I]3:8 Lit *600 talents*   [J]3:9 Lit *50 shekels*   [K]3:11 Lit *five cubits*, also in vv. 12,15   [L]3:12 Syr, Vg; MT reads *the one*   [M]3:13 Lit *the house*   [N]3:15 Syr reads *18 cubits* (27 feet); Hb reads *35 cubits* (52 ½ feet)   [O]3:17 = He Will Establish   [P]3:17 = Strength Is in Him

THE ALTAR, RESERVOIR, AND BASINS

4 He made a bronze altar 30 feet[A] long, 30 feet wide, and 15 feet[B] high. ² Then he made the cast metal basin,[C] 15 feet from brim to brim, perfectly round. It was 7½ feet[D] high and 45 feet[E] in circumference. ³ The likeness of oxen[F] was below it, completely encircling it, ten every half yard,[G] completely surrounding the basin. The oxen were cast in two rows when the basin was cast. ⁴ It stood on twelve oxen, three facing north, three facing west, three facing south, and three facing east. The basin was on top of them and all their hindquarters were toward the center. ⁵ The basin was three inches[H] thick, and its rim was fashioned like the brim of a cup or a lily blossom. It could hold eleven thousand gallons.[I]

⁶ He made ten basins for washing and he put five on the right and five on the left. The parts of the burnt offering were rinsed in them, but the basin was used by the priests for washing.

THE LAMPSTANDS, TABLES, AND COURTS

⁷ He made the ten gold lampstands according to their specifications and put them in the sanctuary, five on the right and five on the left. ⁸ He made ten tables and placed them in the sanctuary, five on the right and five on the left. He also made a hundred gold bowls.

⁹ He made the courtyard of the priests and the large court, and doors for the court. He overlaid the doors with bronze. ¹⁰ He put the basin on the right side, toward the southeast. ¹¹ Then Huram[J] made the pots, the shovels, and the bowls.

COMPLETION OF THE BRONZE FURNISHINGS

So Huram finished doing the work that he was doing for King Solomon in God's temple: ¹² two pillars; the bowls and the capitals on top of the two pillars; the two gratings for covering both bowls of the capitals that were on top of the pillars; ¹³ the four hundred pomegranates for the two gratings (two rows of pomegranates for each grating covering both capitals' bowls on top of the pillars). ¹⁴ He also made the water carts[K] and the basins on the water carts. ¹⁵ The one basin and the twelve oxen underneath it, ¹⁶ the pots, the shovels, the forks, and all their utensils — Huram-abi[L] made them for King Solomon for the LORD's temple. All these were made of polished bronze. ¹⁷ The king had them cast in clay molds in the Jordan Valley between Succoth and Zeredah. ¹⁸ Solomon made all these utensils in such great abundance that the weight of the bronze was not determined.

COMPLETION OF THE GOLD FURNISHINGS

¹⁹ Solomon also made all the equipment in God's temple: the gold altar; the tables on which to put the Bread of the Presence; ²⁰ the lampstands and their lamps of pure gold to burn in front of the inner sanctuary according to specifications; ²¹ the flowers, lamps, and gold tongs — of purest gold; ²² the wick

---

[A] 4:1 Lit *20 cubits* [B] 4:1 Lit *10 cubits*, also in v. 2 [C] 4:2 Lit *sea* [D] 4:2 Lit *five cubits* [E] 4:2 Lit *30 cubits* [F] 4:3 = gourds in 1Kg 7:24 [G] 4:3 Lit *10 per cubit* [H] 4:5 Lit *a handbreadth* [I] 4:5 Text emended; MT reads *3,000 baths* in 1Kg 7:26 [J] 4:11 = Hiram in 1Kg 7:13,40,45 [K] 4:14 Lit *the stands* [L] 4:16 Lit *Huram my father* trimmers, sprinkling basins, ladles, ^A^ and firepans — of purest gold; and the entryway to the temple, its inner doors to the most holy place, and the doors of the temple sanctuary — of gold.

5 So all the work Solomon did for the LORD's temple was completed. Then Solomon brought the consecrated things of his father David — the silver, the gold, and all the utensils — and put them in the treasuries of God's temple.

PREPARATIONS FOR THE TEMPLE DEDICATION

² At that time Solomon assembled at Jerusalem the elders of Israel — all the tribal heads, the ancestral chiefs of the Israelites — in order to bring the ark of the covenant of the LORD up from the city of David, that is, Zion. ³ So all the men of Israel were assembled in the king's presence at the festival; this was in the seventh month. ^B^

⁴ All the elders of Israel came, and the Levites picked up the ark. ⁵ They brought up the ark, the tent of meeting, and the holy utensils that were in the tent. The priests and the Levites brought them up. ⁶ King Solomon and the entire congregation of Israel who had gathered around him were in front of the ark sacrificing sheep, goats, and cattle that could not be counted or numbered because there were so many. ⁷ The priests brought the ark of the LORD's covenant to its place, into the inner sanctuary of the temple, to the most holy place, beneath the wings of the cherubim. ⁸ And the cherubim spread their wings over the place of the ark so that the cherubim formed a cover above the ark and its poles. ⁹ The poles were so long that their ends were seen from the holy place ^C^ in front of the inner sanctuary, but they were not seen from outside; they are still there today. ¹⁰ Nothing was in the ark except the two tablets that Moses had put in it at Horeb, ^D^ where the LORD had made a covenant with the Israelites when they came out of Egypt.

¹¹ Now all the priests who were present had consecrated themselves regardless of their divisions. When the priests came out of the holy place, ¹² the Levitical singers dressed in fine linen and carrying cymbals, harps, and lyres were standing east of the altar, and with them were 120 priests blowing trumpets. The Levitical singers were descendants of Asaph, Heman, and Jeduthun and their sons and relatives. ¹³ The trumpeters and singers joined together to praise and thank the LORD with one voice. They raised their voices, accompanied by trumpets, cymbals, and musical instruments, in praise to the LORD:

> For he is good;
> his faithful love endures forever.

The temple, the LORD's temple, was filled with a cloud. ¹⁴ And because of the cloud, the priests were not able to continue ministering, for the glory of the LORD filled God's temple.

SOLOMON'S DEDICATION OF THE TEMPLE

6 Then Solomon said:
The LORD said he would dwell in total darkness,
² but I have built an exalted temple for you,
a place for your residence forever.

---

^A^4:22 Or *dishes,* or *spoons;* lit *palms*   ^B^5:3 = Tishri (September–October)
^C^5:9 Some Hb mss, LXX; other Hb mss read *the ark;* 1Kg 8:8   ^D^5:10 = Sinai

³ Then the king turned and blessed the entire congregation of Israel while they were standing. ⁴ He said:

Blessed be the Lᴏʀᴅ God of Israel!
He spoke directly to my father David,
and he has fulfilled the promise
by his power.
He said,

⁵ "Since the day I brought my people Israel
out of the land of Egypt,
I have not chosen a city to build a temple in
among any of the tribes of Israel,
so that my name would be there,
and I have not chosen a man
to be ruler over my people Israel.

⁶ But I have chosen Jerusalem
so that my name will be there,
and I have chosen David
to be over my people Israel."

⁷ My father David had his heart set
on building a temple for the name of the Lᴏʀᴅ, the God of Israel.

⁸ However, the Lᴏʀᴅ said to my father David,
"Since it was your desire to build a temple for my name,
you have done well to have this desire.

⁹ Yet, you are not the one to build the temple,
but your son, your own offspring,
will build the temple for my name."

¹⁰ So the Lᴏʀᴅ has fulfilled what he promised.
I have taken the place of my father David
and I sit on the throne of Israel, as the Lᴏʀᴅ promised.
I have built the temple for the name of the Lᴏʀᴅ, the God of Israel.

¹¹ I have put the ark there,
where the Lᴏʀᴅ's covenant is
that he made with the Israelites.

SOLOMON'S PRAYER

¹² Then Solomon stood before the altar of the Lᴏʀᴅ in front of the entire congregation of Israel and spread out his hands. ¹³ For Solomon had made a bronze platform 7 ½ feet ᴬ long, 7 ½ feet wide, and 4 ½ feet ᴮ high and put it in the court. He stood on it, knelt down in front of the entire congregation of Israel, and spread out his hands toward heaven. ¹⁴ He said:

Lᴏʀᴅ God of Israel,
there is no God like you
in heaven or on earth,
who keeps his gracious covenant
with your servants who walk before you
with all their heart.

¹⁵ You have kept what you promised

ᴬ6:13 Lit *five cubits* ᴮ6:13 Lit *three cubits*

to your servant, my father David.
You spoke directly to him,
and you fulfilled your promise by your power,
as it is today.

¹⁶ Therefore, Lord God of Israel,
keep what you promised
to your servant, my father David:
"You will never fail to have a man
to sit before me on the throne of Israel,
if only your sons guard their way to walk in my Law
as you have walked before me."

¹⁷ Now, Lord God of Israel, please confirm
what you promised to your servant David.

¹⁸ But will God indeed live on earth with humans?
Even heaven, the highest heaven, cannot contain you,
much less this temple I have built.

¹⁹ Listen^A to your servant's prayer and his petition,
Lord my God,
so that you may hear the cry and the prayer
that your servant prays before you,

²⁰ so that your eyes watch over this temple
day and night,
toward the place where you said
you would put your name;
and so that you may hear the prayer
your servant prays toward this place.

²¹ Hear the petitions of your servant
and your people Israel,
which they pray toward this place.
May you hear in your dwelling place in heaven.
May you hear and forgive.

²² If a man sins against his neighbor
and is forced to take an oath^B
and he comes to take an oath
before your altar in this temple,

²³ may you hear in heaven and act.
May you judge your servants,
condemning the wicked man by bringing
what he has done on his own head
and providing justice for the righteous
by rewarding him according to his righteousness.

²⁴ If your people Israel are defeated before an enemy,
because they have sinned against you,
and they return to you and praise your name,
and they pray and plead for mercy

---

^A 6:19 Lit Turn   ^B 6:22 Lit and he lifts a curse against him to curse him before you in this temple,

25 may you hear in heaven
and forgive the sin of your people Israel.
May you restore them to the land
you gave them and their ancestors.

26 When the skies are shut and there is no rain
because they have sinned against you,
and they pray toward this place
and praise your name,
and they turn from their sins
because you are afflicting[A] them,

27 may you hear in heaven
and forgive the sin of your servants
and your people Israel,
so that you may teach them the good way
they should walk in.
May you send rain on your land
that you gave your people for an inheritance.

28 When there is famine in the land,
when there is pestilence,
when there is blight or mildew, locust or grasshopper,
when their enemies besiege them
in the land and its cities,[B,C]
when there is any plague or illness,

29 every prayer or petition
that any person or that all your people Israel may have —
they each know their own affliction[D] and suffering —
as they spread out their hands toward this temple,

30 may you hear in heaven, your dwelling place,
and may you forgive and give to everyone[E]
according to all their ways, since you know each heart,
for you alone know the human heart,

31 so that they may fear you
and walk in your ways
all the days they live on the land
you gave our ancestors.

32 Even for the foreigner who is not of your people Israel
but has come from a distant land
because of your great name
and your strong hand and outstretched arm:
when he comes and prays toward this temple,

33 may you hear in heaven in your dwelling place,
and do all the foreigner asks you.

A 6:26 LXX, Vg; MT reads *answering*; 1 Kg 8:35   B 6:28 Lit *land of its gates*
C 6:28 Lit *if his (Israel's) enemies besiege him in the land of his gates*; Jos 2:7;
Jdg 16:2-3   D 6:29 Lit *plague*   E 6:30 Lit *give for the man*

Then all the peoples of the earth will know your name,
to fear you as your people Israel do
and know that this temple I have built
bears your name.

³⁴ When your people go out to fight against their enemies,
wherever you send them,
and they pray to you
in the direction of this city you have chosen
and the temple that I have built for your name,
³⁵ may you hear their prayer and petition in heaven
and uphold their cause.

³⁶ When they sin against you —
for there is no one who does not sin —
and you are angry with them
and hand them over to the enemy,
and their captors deport them
to a distant or nearby country,
³⁷ and when they come to their senses
in the land where they were deported
and repent and petition you in their captors' land,
saying: "We have sinned and done wrong;
we have been wicked,"
³⁸ and when they return to you with all their mind
and all their heart
in the land of their captivity
where they were taken captive,
and when they pray in the direction of their land
that you gave their ancestors,
and the city you have chosen,
and toward the temple I have built for your name,
³⁹ may you hear their prayer and petitions in heaven,
your dwelling place,
and uphold their cause.ᴬ
May you forgive your people
who sinned against you.

⁴⁰ Now, my God,
please let your eyes be open
and your ears attentive
to the prayer of this place.
⁴¹ Now therefore:

Arise, LORD God, come to your resting place,
you and your powerful ark.
May your priests, LORD God, be clothed with salvation,
and may your faithful people rejoice in goodness.

ᴬ6:39 Lit and do their judgment, or justice

⁴² LORD God, do not reject your anointed one;ᴬ
remember the promises to your servant David.

THE DEDICATION CEREMONIES

7 When Solomon finished praying, fire descended from heaven and consumed the burnt offering and the sacrifices, and the glory of the LORD filled the temple. ² The priests were not able to enter the LORD's temple because the glory of the LORD filled the temple of the LORD. ³ All the Israelites were watching when the fire descended and the glory of the LORD came on the temple. They bowed down on the pavement with their faces to the ground. They worshiped and praised the LORD:

For he is good,
for his faithful love endures forever.

⁴ The king and all the people were offering sacrifices in the LORD's presence. ⁵ King Solomon offered a sacrifice of twenty-two thousand cattle and one hundred twenty thousand sheep and goats. In this manner the king and all the people dedicated God's temple. ⁶ The priests and the Levites were standing at their stations. The Levites had the musical instruments of the LORD, which King David had made to give thanks to the LORD — "for his faithful love endures forever" — when he offered praise with them. Across from the Levites, the priests were blowing trumpets, and all the people were standing. ⁷ Since the bronze altar that Solomon had made could not accommodate the burnt offering, the grain offering, and the fat of the fellowship offerings, Solomon first consecrated the middle of the courtyard that was in front of the LORD's temple and then offered the burnt offerings and the fat of the fellowship offerings there.

⁸ So Solomon and all Israel with him — a very great assembly, from the entrance to Hamathᴮ to the Brook of Egypt — observed the festival at that time for seven days. ⁹ On the eighth dayᶜ they held a sacred assembly, for the dedication of the altar lasted seven days and the festival seven days. ¹⁰ On the twenty-third day of the seventh month he sent the people home,ᴰ rejoicing and with happy hearts for the goodness the LORD had done for David, for Solomon, and for his people Israel.

¹¹ So Solomon finished the LORD's temple and the royal palace. Everything that had entered Solomon's heart to do for the LORD's temple and for his own palace succeeded.

THE LORD'S RESPONSE

¹² Then the LORD appeared to Solomon at night and said to him:
I have heard your prayer and have chosen this place for myself as a temple of sacrifice. ¹³ If I shut the sky so there is no rain, or if I command the grasshopper to consume the land, or if I send pestilence on my people, ¹⁴ and my people, who bear my name, humble themselves, pray and seek my face, and turn from their evil ways, then I will hear from heaven, forgive their sin, and heal their land. ¹⁵ My eyes will now

---

ᴬ6:42 Some Hb mss, LXX; other Hb mss read *ones*; Ps 132:10   ᴮ7:8 Or *from Lebo-hamath*   ᶜ7:9 = the day after the festival, or the 15th day   ᴰ7:10 Lit *people to their tents*

RESTORATION THROUGH REPENTANCE

2 CHRONICLES 7–8; ROMANS 8:38-39

Valentine's Day was always a big deal in our house. My mom made heart-shaped blueberry muffins. My dad got us flowers. We went to school with our backpacks stuffed with treats for our friends. With three daughters in the house, it was impossible to over-celebrate the day of love.

One year, instead of the usual flowers, my dad got my sisters and me a framed piece of paper. On it, he had written a simple promise: that he would always be faithful to our mom and to us. That we would never have to worry about coming home and finding him gone. He would always be there.

In 2 Chronicles 7, another Father makes a promise to His children. It is the covenant God made with Solomon after Solomon finished building the temple.

"If . . . my people, who bear my name, humble themselves, pray and seek my face, and turn from their evil ways, then I will hear from heaven, forgive their sin, and heal their land."

2 CHRONICLES 7:13-14

The people of Israel had turned their backs on God many times. Even so, God made Solomon this promise—a covenant focused on the practice of repentance and God's merciful response.

I sometimes hear the word *repentance* and associate it with punishment. *I did something wrong, I have to tell God, He'll be mad at me for a while, then things will blow over.* But God's words to Solomon in this passage describe an act of restoration: "I will hear from heaven, forgive their sin, and heal their land." These phrases point to a relationship restored because **repentance is vital to a restored relationship with God.**

My dad made a promise to me, a covenant, which I have never forgotten. But that did not mean parenting was easy for him and my mom. I am a sinner, and I have sinned against them often. But I am a sinner who knew that when I came home, my dad would still be there. Our relationship was priority for him, and it was important to him that I knew that.

The covenant with Solomon shows us a God who desires to be restored to His people, and it points to Christ, who would restore that relationship once and for all.

We don't all have dads who write promises to us and frame them for Valentine's Day, but as believers we all live under Christ's covenant—one that says "neither death nor life, nor angels nor rulers, nor things present nor things to come, nor powers, nor height nor depth, nor any other created thing will be able to separate us from the love of God that is in Christ Jesus our Lord!" (Rm 8:38-39).

Those are words worth framing.

be open and my ears attentive to prayer from this place. [16] And I have now chosen and consecrated this temple so that my name may be there forever; my eyes and my heart will be there at all times.

[17] As for you, if you walk before me as your father David walked, doing everything I have commanded you, and if you keep my statutes and ordinances, [18] I will establish your royal throne, as I promised your father David: You will never fail to have a man ruling in Israel.

[19] However, if you turn away and abandon my statutes and my commands that I have set before you and if you go and serve other gods and bow in worship to them, [20] then I will uproot Israel from the soil that I gave them, and this temple that I have sanctified for my name I will banish from my presence; I will make it an object of scorn and ridicule among all the peoples. [21] As for this temple, which was exalted, everyone who passes by will be appalled and will say: Why did the LORD do this to this land and this temple? [22] Then they will say: Because they abandoned the LORD God of their ancestors who brought them out of the land of Egypt. They clung to other gods and bowed in worship to them and served them. Because of this, he brought all this ruin on them.

SOLOMON'S LATER BUILDING PROJECTS

8 At the end of twenty years during which Solomon had built the LORD's temple and his own palace — [2] Solomon had rebuilt the cities Hiram[A] gave him and settled Israelites there — [3] Solomon went to Hamath-zobah and seized it. [4] He built Tadmor in the wilderness along with all the storage cities that he built in Hamath. [5] He built Upper Beth-horon and Lower Beth-horon — fortified cities with walls, gates, and bars — [6] Baalath, all the storage cities that belonged to Solomon, all the chariot cities, the cavalry cities, and everything Solomon desired to build in Jerusalem, Lebanon, or anywhere else in the land of his dominion.

[7] As for all the peoples who remained of the Hethites, Amorites, Perizzites, Hivites, and Jebusites, who were not from Israel — [8] their descendants who remained in the land after them, those the Israelites had not completely destroyed — Solomon imposed forced labor on them; it is this way today. [9] But Solomon did not consign the Israelites to be slaves for his work; they were soldiers, commanders of his captains, and commanders of his chariots and his cavalry. [10] These were King Solomon's deputies: 250 who supervised the people.

[11] Solomon brought the daughter of Pharaoh from the city of David to the house he had built for her, for he said, "My wife must not live in the house[B] of King David of Israel because the places the ark of the LORD has come into are holy."

PUBLIC WORSHIP ESTABLISHED AT THE TEMPLE

[12] At that time Solomon offered burnt offerings to the LORD on the LORD's altar he had made in front of the portico. [13] He followed the daily requirement for offerings according to the commandment of Moses for Sabbaths, New

A 8:2 = the king of Tyre   B 8:11 LXX reads *city*

Moons, and the three annual appointed festivals: the Festival of Unleavened Bread, the Festival of Weeks, and the Festival of Shelters. ¹⁴ According to the ordinances of his father David, he appointed the divisions of the priests over their service, of the Levites over their responsibilities to offer praise and to minister before the priests following the daily requirement, and of the gatekeepers by their divisions with respect to each temple gate, for this had been the command of David, the man of God. ¹⁵ They did not turn aside from the king's command regarding the priests and the Levites concerning any matter or concerning the treasuries. ¹⁶ All of Solomon's work was carried out from the day the foundation was laid for the LORD's temple until it was finished. So the LORD's temple was completed.

SOLOMON'S FLEET

¹⁷ At that time Solomon went to Ezion-geber and to Eloth on the seashore in the land of Edom. ¹⁸ So Hiram ᴬ sent ships to him by his servants along with crews of experienced seamen. They went with Solomon's servants to Ophir, took from there seventeen tons ᴮ of gold, and delivered it to King Solomon.

THE QUEEN OF SHEBA

9 The queen of Sheba heard of Solomon's fame, so she came to test Solomon with difficult questions at Jerusalem with a very large entourage, with camels bearing spices, gold in abundance, and precious stones. She came to Solomon and spoke with him about everything that was on her mind. ² So Solomon answered all her questions; nothing was too difficult for Solomon to explain to her. ³ When the queen of Sheba observed Solomon's wisdom, the palace he had built, ⁴ the food at his table, his servants' residence, his attendants' service and their attire, his cupbearers and their attire, and the burnt offerings he offered at the LORD's temple, it took her breath away.

⁵ She said to the king, "The report I heard in my own country about your words and about your wisdom is true. ⁶ But I didn't believe their reports until I came and saw with my own eyes. Indeed, I was not even told half of your great wisdom! You far exceed the report I heard. ⁷ How happy are your men. ᶜ How happy are these servants of yours, who always stand in your presence hearing your wisdom. ⁸ Blessed be the LORD your God! He delighted in you and put you on his throne as king for the LORD your God. Because your God loved Israel enough to establish them forever, he has set you over them as king to carry out justice and righteousness."

⁹ Then she gave the king four and a half tons ᴰ of gold, a great quantity of spices, and precious stones. There never were such spices as those the queen of Sheba gave to King Solomon. ¹⁰ In addition, Hiram's servants and Solomon's servants who brought gold from Ophir also brought algum wood and precious stones. ¹¹ The king made the algum wood into walkways for the LORD's temple and for the king's palace and into lyres and harps for the singers. Never before had anything like them been seen in the land of Judah.

¹² King Solomon gave the queen of Sheba her every desire, whatever she asked — far more than she had brought the king. Then she, along with her servants, returned to her own country.

ᴬ 8:18 Lit *Huram*   ᴮ 8:18 Lit *450 talents*   ᶜ 9:7 LXX, Old Lat read *wives*; 1Kg 10:8
ᴰ 9:9 Lit *120 talents*

SOLOMON'S WEALTH

[13] The weight of gold that came to Solomon annually was twenty-five tons,[A] [14] besides what was brought by the merchants and traders. All the Arabian kings and governors of the land also brought gold and silver to Solomon.

[15] King Solomon made two hundred large shields of hammered gold; 15 pounds[B] of hammered gold went into each shield. [16] He made three hundred small shields of hammered gold; 7 ½ pounds[C] of gold went into each shield. The king put them in the House of the Forest of Lebanon.

[17] The king also made a large ivory throne and overlaid it with pure gold. [18] The throne had six steps; there was a footstool covered in gold for the throne, armrests on either side of the seat, and two lions standing beside the armrests. [19] Twelve lions were standing there on the six steps, one at each end. Nothing like it had ever been made in any other kingdom.

[20] All of King Solomon's drinking cups were gold, and all the utensils of the House of the Forest of Lebanon were pure gold. There was no silver, since it was considered as nothing in Solomon's time, [21] for the king's ships kept going to Tarshish with Hiram's servants, and once every three years the ships of Tarshish would arrive bearing gold, silver, ivory, apes, and peacocks.[D]

[22] King Solomon surpassed all the kings of the world in riches and wisdom. [23] All the kings of the world wanted an audience with Solomon to hear the wisdom God had put in his heart. [24] Each of them would bring his own gift — items[E] of silver and gold, clothing, weapons,[F,G] spices, and horses and mules — as an annual tribute.

[25] Solomon had four thousand stalls for horses and chariots, and twelve thousand horsemen. He stationed them in the chariot cities and with the king in Jerusalem. [26] He ruled over all the kings from the Euphrates River to the land of the Philistines and as far as the border of Egypt. [27] The king made silver as common in Jerusalem as stones, and he made cedar as abundant as sycamore in the Judean foothills. [28] They were bringing horses for Solomon from Egypt and from all the countries.

SOLOMON'S DEATH

[29] The remaining events of Solomon's reign, from beginning to end, are written in the Events of the Prophet Nathan, the Prophecy of Ahijah the Shilonite, and the Visions of the Seer Iddo concerning Jeroboam son of Nebat. [30] Solomon reigned in Jerusalem over all Israel for forty years. [31] Solomon rested with his fathers and was buried in the city of his father David. His son Rehoboam became king in his place.

THE KINGDOM DIVIDED

10 Then Rehoboam went to Shechem, for all Israel had gone to Shechem to make him king. [2] When Jeroboam son of Nebat heard about it — for he was in Egypt where he had fled from King Solomon's presence — Jeroboam returned from Egypt. [3] So they summoned him. Then Jeroboam and all Israel came and spoke to Rehoboam: [4] "Your father made our yoke

---

[A] 9:13 Lit 666 talents   [B] 9:15 Lit 600 (shekels)   [C] 9:16 Lit 300 (shekels)
[D] 9:21 Or baboons   [E] 9:24 Or vessels, or weapons   [F] 9:24 LXX reads resin
[G] 9:24 Or fragrant balsam

harsh. Therefore, lighten your father's harsh service and the heavy yoke he put on us, and we will serve you."

⁵ Rehoboam replied, "Return to me in three days." So the people left.

⁶ Then King Rehoboam consulted with the elders who had attended his father Solomon when he was alive, asking, "How do you advise me to respond to this people?"

⁷ They replied, "If you will be kind to this people and please them by speaking kind words to them, they will be your servants forever."

⁸ But he rejected the advice of the elders who had advised him, and he consulted with the young men who had grown up with him, the ones attending him. ⁹ He asked them, "What message do you advise we send back to this people who said to me, 'Lighten the yoke your father put on us'?"

¹⁰ Then the young men who had grown up with him told him, "This is what you should say to the people who said to you, 'Your father made our yoke heavy, but you, make it lighter on us!' This is what you should say to them: 'My little finger is thicker than my father's waist! ¹¹ Now therefore, my father burdened you with a heavy yoke, but I will add to your yoke; my father disciplined you with whips, but I, with barbed whips.' "ᴬ

¹² So Jeroboam and all the people came to Rehoboam on the third day, just as the king had ordered, saying, "Return to me on the third day." ¹³ Then the king answered them harshly. King Rehoboam rejected the elders' advice ¹⁴ and spoke to them according to the young men's advice, saying, "My father made your yoke heavy,ᴮ but I will add to it; my father disciplined you with whips, but I, with barbed whips."

¹⁵ The king did not listen to the people because the turn of events came from God, in order that the Lᴏʀᴅ might carry out his word that he had spoken through Ahijah the Shilonite to Jeroboam son of Nebat.

¹⁶ When all Israel sawᶜ that the king had not listened to them, the people answered the king:

> What portion do we have in David?
> We have no inheritance in the son of Jesse.
> Israel, each to your tent;
> David, look after your own house now!

So all Israel went to their tents. ¹⁷ But as for the Israelites living in the cities of Judah, Rehoboam reigned over them.

¹⁸ Then King Rehoboam sent Hadoram,ᴰ who was in charge of the forced labor, but the Israelites stoned him to death. However, King Rehoboam managed to get into his chariot to flee to Jerusalem. ¹⁹ Israel is in rebellion against the house of David until today.

REHOBOAM IN JERUSALEM

11 When Rehoboam arrived in Jerusalem, he mobilized the house of Judah and Benjamin — one hundred eighty thousand fit young soldiers — to fight against Israel to restore the reign to Rehoboam. ² But the word of the Lᴏʀᴅ came to Shemaiah, the man of God: ³ "Say to Rehoboam son of Solomon, king of Judah, to all Israel in Judah and Benjamin, and to

---

ᴬ10:11 Lit *with scorpions*, also in v. 14 ᴮ10:14 Some Hb mss, LXX; other Hb mss read *I will make your yoke heavy*; 1Kg 12:14 ᶜ10:16 Some Hb mss, LXX; other Hb mss omit *saw*; 1Kg 12:16 ᴰ10:18 = Adoram in 1Kg 12:18

the rest of the people: ⁴ 'This is what the LORD says: You are not to march up and fight against your brothers. Each of you return home, for this incident has come from me.' "

So they listened to what the LORD said and turned back from going against Jeroboam.

JUDAH'S KING REHOBOAM

⁵ Rehoboam stayed in Jerusalem, and he fortified cities^ in Judah. ⁶ He built up Bethlehem, Etam, Tekoa, ⁷ Beth-zur, Soco, Adullam, ⁸ Gath, Mareshah, Ziph, ⁹ Adoraim, Lachish, Azekah, ¹⁰ Zorah, Aijalon, and Hebron, which are fortified cities in Judah and in Benjamin. ¹¹ He strengthened their fortifications and put leaders in them with supplies of food, oil, and wine. ¹² He also put large shields and spears in each and every city to make them very strong. So Judah and Benjamin were his.

¹³ The priests and Levites from all their regions throughout Israel took their stand with Rehoboam, ¹⁴ for the Levites left their pasturelands and their possessions and went to Judah and Jerusalem, because Jeroboam and his sons refused to let them serve as priests of the LORD. ¹⁵ Jeroboam appointed his own priests for the high places, the goat-demons, and the golden calves he had made. ¹⁶ Those from every tribe of Israel who had determined in their hearts to seek the LORD their God followed the Levites to Jerusalem to sacrifice to the LORD, the God of their ancestors. ¹⁷ So they strengthened the kingdom of Judah and supported Rehoboam son of Solomon for three years, because they walked in the ways of David and Solomon for three years.

¹⁸ Rehoboam married Mahalath, daughter of David's son Jerimoth and of Abihail daughter of Jesse's son Eliab. ¹⁹ She bore sons to him: Jeush, Shemariah, and Zaham. ²⁰ After her, he married Maacah daughter^B of Absalom. She bore Abijah, Attai, Ziza, and Shelomith to him. ²¹ Rehoboam loved Maacah daughter of Absalom more than all his wives and concubines. He acquired eighteen wives and sixty concubines and was the father of twenty-eight sons and sixty daughters.

²² Rehoboam appointed Abijah son of Maacah as chief, leader among his brothers, intending to make him king. ²³ Rehoboam also showed discernment by dispersing some of his sons to all the regions of Judah and Benjamin and to all the fortified cities. He gave them plenty of provisions and sought many wives for them.

SHISHAK'S INVASION

12 When Rehoboam had established his sovereignty and royal power, he abandoned the law of the LORD — he and all Israel with him. ² Because they were unfaithful to the LORD, in the fifth year of King Rehoboam, King Shishak of Egypt went to war against Jerusalem ³ with 1,200 chariots, 60,000 cavalrymen, and countless people who came with him from Egypt — Libyans, Sukkiim, and Cushites. ⁴ He captured the fortified cities of Judah and came as far as Jerusalem.

⁵ Then the prophet Shemaiah went to Rehoboam and the leaders of Judah who were gathered at Jerusalem because of Shishak. He said to them:

"This is what the LORD says: 'You have abandoned me; therefore, I have abandoned you to Shishak.'"

⁶ So the leaders of Israel and the king humbled themselves and said, "The LORD is righteous."

⁷ When the LORD saw that they had humbled themselves, the LORD's message came to Shemaiah: "They have humbled themselves; I will not destroy them but will grant them a little deliverance. My wrath will not be poured out on Jerusalem through Shishak. ⁸ However, they will become his servants so that they may recognize the difference between serving me and serving the kingdoms of other lands."

⁹ So King Shishak of Egypt went to war against Jerusalem. He seized the treasuries of the LORD's temple and the treasuries of the royal palace. He took everything. He took the gold shields that Solomon had made. ¹⁰ King Rehoboam made bronze shields to replace them and committed them into the care of the captains of the guards ᴬ who protected the entrance to the king's palace. ¹¹ Whenever the king entered the LORD's temple, the guards would carry the shields and take them back to the armory. ᴮ ¹² When Rehoboam humbled himself, the LORD's anger turned away from him, and he did not destroy him completely. Besides that, conditions were good in Judah.

REHOBOAM'S LAST DAYS

¹³ King Rehoboam established his royal power in Jerusalem. Rehoboam was forty-one years old when he became king, and he reigned seventeen years in Jerusalem, the city the LORD had chosen from all the tribes of Israel to put his name. Rehoboam's mother's name was Naamah the Ammonite. ¹⁴ Rehoboam did what was evil, because he did not determine in his heart to seek the LORD.

¹⁵ The events of Rehoboam's reign, from beginning to end, are written in the Events of the Prophet Shemaiah and of the Seer Iddo concerning genealogies. There was war between Rehoboam and Jeroboam throughout their reigns. ¹⁶ Rehoboam rested with his fathers and was buried in the city of David. His son Abijah ᶜ became king in his place.

JUDAH'S KING ABIJAH

13 In the eighteenth year of Israel's King Jeroboam, Abijah ᶜ became king over Judah, ² and he reigned three years in Jerusalem. His mother's name was Micaiah ᴰ daughter of Uriel; she was from Gibeah.

There was war between Abijah and Jeroboam. ³ Abijah set his army of warriors in order with four hundred thousand fit young men. Jeroboam arranged his mighty army of eight hundred thousand fit young men in battle formation against him. ⁴ Then Abijah stood on Mount Zemaraim, which is in the hill country of Ephraim, and said, "Jeroboam and all Israel, hear me. ⁵ Don't you know that the LORD God of Israel gave the kingship over Israel to David and his descendants forever by a covenant of salt? ⁶ But Jeroboam son of Nebat, a servant of Solomon son of David, rose up and rebelled against his lord. ⁷ Then worthless and wicked men gathered around him to

---

ᴬ 12:10 Lit *the runners* ᴮ 12:11 Lit *the chamber of the runners*
ᶜ 12:16; 13:1 = Abijam in 1Kg 14:31–15:8 ᴰ 13:2 LXX, Syr, Arabic read
Maacah; 1Kg 15:2; 2Ch 11:22

resist Rehoboam son of Solomon when Rehoboam was young, inexperienced, and unable to assert himself against them.

⁸ "And now you are saying you can assert yourselves against the Lord's kingdom, which is in the hand of one of David's sons. You are a vast number and have with you the golden calves that Jeroboam made for you as gods. ᴬ ⁹ Didn't you banish the priests of the Lord, the descendants of Aaron and the Levites, and make your own priests like the peoples of other lands do? Whoever comes to ordain himself with a young bull and seven rams may become a priest of what are not gods.

¹⁰ "But as for us, the Lord is our God. We have not abandoned him; the priests ministering to the Lord are descendants of Aaron, and the Levites serve at their tasks. ¹¹ They offer a burnt offering and fragrant incense to the Lord every morning and every evening, and they set the rows of the Bread of the Presence on the ceremonially clean table. They light the lamps of the gold lampstand every evening. We are carrying out the requirements of the Lord our God, while you have abandoned him. ¹² Look, God and his priests are with us at our head. The trumpets are ready to sound the charge against you. Israelites, don't fight against the Lord God of your ancestors, for you will not succeed."

¹³ Now Jeroboam had sent an ambush around to advance from behind them. So they were in front of Judah, and the ambush was behind them. ¹⁴ Judah turned and discovered that the battle was in front of them and behind them, so they cried out to the Lord. Then the priests blew the trumpets, ¹⁵ and the men of Judah raised the battle cry. When the men of Judah raised the battle cry, God routed Jeroboam and all Israel before Abijah and Judah. ¹⁶ So the Israelites fled before Judah, and God handed them over to them. ¹⁷ Then Abijah and his people struck them with a mighty blow, and five hundred thousand fit young men of Israel were killed. ¹⁸ The Israelites were subdued at that time. The Judahites succeeded because they depended on the Lord, the God of their ancestors.

¹⁹ Abijah pursued Jeroboam and captured some cities from him: Bethel, Jeshanah, and Ephron, ᴮ along with their surrounding villages. ²⁰ Jeroboam no longer retained his power ᶜ during Abijah's reign; ultimately, the Lord struck him and he died.

²¹ However, Abijah grew strong, acquired fourteen wives, and fathered twenty-two sons and sixteen daughters. ²² The rest of the events of Abijah's reign, along with his ways and his sayings, are written in the Writing of the

14 Prophet Iddo. ¹ Abijah rested with his fathers and was buried in the city of David. His son Asa became king in his place. During his reign the land experienced peace for ten years.

JUDAH'S KING ASA

² Asa did what was good and right in the sight of the Lord his God. ³ He removed the pagan altars and the high places. He shattered their sacred pillars and chopped down their Asherah poles. ⁴ He told the people of Judah to seek the Lord God of their ancestors and to carry out the instruction and the commands. ⁵ He also removed the high places and the shrines ᴰ from all the cities of Judah, and the kingdom experienced peace under him.

ᴬ13:8 Or *God*; 1Kg 12:28   ᴮ13:19 Alt Hb tradition reads *Ephrain*   ᶜ13:20 Lit *He did not restrain the power of Jeroboam*   ᴰ14:5 Or *incense altars*

⁶ Because the land experienced peace, Asa built fortified cities in Judah. No one made war with him in those days because the LORD gave him rest. ⁷ So he said to the people of Judah, "Let's build these cities and surround them with walls and towers, with doors and bars. The land is still ours because we sought the LORD our God. We sought him and he gave us rest on every side." So they built and succeeded.

THE CUSHITE INVASION

⁸ Asa had an army of three hundred thousand from Judah bearing large shields and spears, and two hundred eighty thousand from Benjamin bearing regular shields and drawing the bow. All these were valiant warriors. ⁹ Then Zerah the Cushite came against them with an army of one million men and three hundredᴬ chariots. They came as far as Mareshah. ¹⁰ So Asa marched out against him and lined up in battle formation in Zephathah Valley at Mareshah.

¹¹ Then Asa cried out to the LORD his God: "LORD, there is no one besides you to help the mighty and those without strength. Help us, LORD our God, for we depend on you, and in your name we have come against this large army. LORD, you are our God. Do not let a mere mortal hinder you."

¹² So the LORD routed the Cushites before Asa and before Judah, and the Cushites fled. ¹³ Then Asa and the people who were with him pursued them as far as Gerar. The Cushites fell until they had no survivors, for they were crushed before the LORD and his army. So the people of Judah carried off a great supply of loot. ¹⁴ Then they attacked all the cities around Gerar because the terror of the LORD was on them. They also plundered all the cities, since there was a great deal of plunder in them. ¹⁵ They also attacked the tents of the herdsmen and captured many sheep and camels. Then they returned to Jerusalem.

REVIVAL UNDER ASA

15 The Spirit of God came on Azariah son of Oded. ² So he went out to meet Asa and said to him, "Asa and all Judah and Benjamin, hear me. The LORD is with you when you are with him. If you seek him, he will be found by you, but if you abandon him, he will abandon you. ³ For many years Israel has been without the true God, without a teaching priest, and without instruction, ⁴ but when they turned to the LORD God of Israel in their distress and sought him, he was found by them. ⁵ In those times there was no peace for those who went about their daily activities because the residents of the lands had many conflicts. ⁶ Nation was crushed by nation and city by city, for God troubled them with every possible distress. ⁷ But as for you, be strong; don't give up,ᴮ for your work has a reward."

⁸ When Asa heard these words and the prophecy of Azariah son of Oded the prophet, he took courage and removed the abhorrent idols from the whole land of Judah and Benjamin and from the cities he had captured in the hill country of Ephraim. He renovated the altar of the LORD that was in front of the portico of the LORD's temple. ⁹ Then he gathered all Judah and Benjamin, as well as those from the tribes of Ephraim, Manasseh, and Simeon who were residing among them, for they had defected

---

ᴬ14:9 Syr, Arabic read *30,000*   ᴮ15:7 Lit *don't let your hands drop* to him from Israel in great numbers when they saw that the LORD his God was with him.

¹⁰ They were gathered in Jerusalem in the third month of the fifteenth year of Asa's reign. ¹¹ At that time they sacrificed to the LORD seven hundred cattle and seven thousand sheep and goats from all the plunder they had brought. ¹² Then they entered into a covenant to seek the LORD God of their ancestors with all their heart and all their soul. ¹³ Whoever would not seek the LORD God of Israel would be put to death, young or old,ᴬ man or woman. ¹⁴ They took an oath to the LORD in a loud voice, with shouting, with trumpets, and with rams' horns. ¹⁵ All Judah rejoiced over the oath, for they had sworn it with all their mind. They had sought him with all their heart, and he was found by them. So the LORD gave them rest on every side.

¹⁶ King Asa also removed Maacah, his grandmother,ᴮ from being queen mother because she had made an obscene image of Asherah. Asa chopped down her obscene image, then crushed it and burned it in the Kidron Valley. ¹⁷ The high places were not taken away from Israel; nevertheless, Asa was wholeheartedly devoted his entire life.ᶜ ¹⁸ He brought his father's consecrated gifts and his own consecrated gifts into God's temple: silver, gold, and utensils.

¹⁹ There was no war until the thirty-fifth year of Asa's reign.

ASA'S TREATY WITH ARAM

16 In the thirty-sixth year of Asa, Israel's King Baasha went to war against Judah. He built Ramah in order to keep anyone from leaving or coming to King Asa of Judah. ² So Asa brought out the silver and gold from the treasuries of the LORD's temple and the royal palace and sent it to Aram's King Ben-hadad, who lived in Damascus, saying, ³ "There's a treaty between me and you, between my father and your father. Look, I have sent you silver and gold. Go break your treaty with Israel's King Baasha so that he will withdraw from me."

⁴ Ben-hadad listened to King Asa and sent the commanders of his armies to the cities of Israel. They attacked Ijon, Dan, Abel-maim,ᴰ and all the storage citiesᴱ of Naphtali. ⁵ When Baasha heard about it, he quit building Ramah and stopped his work. ⁶ Then King Asa brought all Judah, and they carried away the stones of Ramah and the timbers Baasha had built it with. Then he built Geba and Mizpah with them.

HANANI'S REBUKE OF ASA

⁷ At that time, the seer Hanani came to King Asa of Judah and said to him, "Because you depended on the king of Aram and have not depended on the LORD your God, the army of the king of Aram has escaped from you. ⁸ Were not the Cushites and Libyans a vast army with many chariots and horsemen? When you depended on the LORD, he handed them over to you. ⁹ For the eyes of the LORD roam throughout the earth to show himself strong for those who are wholeheartedly devoted to him. You have been foolish in this matter. Therefore, you will have wars from now on." ¹⁰ Asa was enraged with

---

ᴬ15:13 Or insignificant or great   ᴮ15:16 Lit mother; 1Kg 15:2; 2Ch 11:22
ᶜ15:17 Lit wholehearted all his days   ᴰ16:4 Abel-beth-maacah in 1Kg 15:20
ᴱ16:4 = all Chinnereth in 1Kg 15:20

the seer and put him in prison^A because of his anger over this. And Asa mistreated some of the people at that time.

ASA'S DEATH

[11] Note that the events of Asa's reign, from beginning to end, are written in the Book of the Kings of Judah and Israel. [12] In the thirty-ninth year of his reign, Asa developed a disease in his feet, and his disease became increasingly severe. Yet even in his disease he didn't seek the LORD but only the physicians. [13] Asa rested with his fathers; he died in the forty-first year of his reign. [14] He was buried in his own tomb that he had made for himself in the city of David. They laid him out in a coffin that was full of spices and various mixtures of prepared ointments; then they made a great fire in his honor.

JUDAH'S KING JEHOSHAPHAT

17 His son Jehoshaphat became king in his place and strengthened himself against Israel. [2] He stationed troops in every fortified city of Judah and set garrisons in the land of Judah and in the cities of Ephraim that his father Asa had captured.

[3] Now the LORD was with Jehoshaphat because he walked in the former ways of his father David.^B He did not seek the Baals [4] but sought the God of his father and walked by his commands, not according to the practices of Israel. [5] So the LORD established the kingdom in his hand. Then all Judah brought him tribute, and he had riches and honor in abundance. [6] His mind rejoiced in the LORD's ways, and he again removed the high places and Asherah poles from Judah.

JEHOSHAPHAT'S EDUCATIONAL PLAN

[7] In the third year of his reign, Jehoshaphat sent his officials — Ben-hail,^C Obadiah, Zechariah, Nethanel, and Micaiah — to teach in the cities of Judah. [8] The Levites with them were Shemaiah, Nethaniah, Zebadiah,^D Asahel, Shemiramoth, Jehonathan, Adonijah, Tobijah, and Tob-adonijah; the priests, Elishama and Jehoram, were with these Levites. [9] They taught throughout Judah, having the book of the LORD's instruction with them. They went throughout the towns of Judah and taught the people.

[10] The terror of the LORD was on all the kingdoms of the lands that surrounded Judah, so they didn't fight against Jehoshaphat. [11] Some of the Philistines also brought gifts and silver as tribute to Jehoshaphat, and the Arabs brought him flocks: 7,700 rams and 7,700 male goats.

JEHOSHAPHAT'S MILITARY MIGHT

[12] Jehoshaphat grew stronger and stronger. He built fortresses and storage cities in Judah [13] and carried out great works in the towns of Judah. He had fighting men, valiant warriors, in Jerusalem. [14] These are their numbers according to their ancestral families.^E For Judah, the commanders of thousands:

Adnah the commander and three hundred thousand valiant warriors with him;

---

^A 16:10 Lit *the house of stocks*   ^B 17:3 Some Hb mss, LXX omit *David*
^C 17:7 = Son of Power   ^D 17:8 Some Hb mss, Syr, Tg, Arabic read *Zechariah*
^E 17:14 Lit *the house of their fathers*

15 next to him, Jehohanan the commander and two hundred eighty thousand with him;

16 next to him, Amasiah son of Zichri, the volunteer of the LORD, and two hundred thousand valiant warriors with him;

17 from Benjamin, Eliada, a valiant warrior, and two hundred thousand with him armed with bow and shield;

18 next to him, Jehozabad and one hundred eighty thousand with him equipped for war.

19 These were the ones who served the king, besides those he stationed in the fortified cities throughout all Judah.

JEHOSHAPHAT'S ALLIANCE WITH AHAB

18 Now Jehoshaphat had riches and honor in abundance, and he made an alliance with Ahab through marriage.[A] 2 Then after some years, he went down to visit Ahab in Samaria. Ahab sacrificed many sheep, goats, and cattle for him and for the people who were with him. Then he persuaded him to attack Ramoth-gilead, 3 for Israel's King Ahab asked Judah's King Jehoshaphat, "Will you go with me to Ramoth-gilead?"

He replied to him, "I am as you are, my people as your people; we will be with you in the battle." 4 But Jehoshaphat said to the king of Israel, "First, please ask what the LORD's will is."

5 So the king of Israel gathered the prophets, four hundred men, and asked them, "Should we go to Ramoth-gilead for war or should I refrain?"

They replied, "March up, and God will hand it over to the king."

6 But Jehoshaphat asked, "Isn't there a prophet of the LORD here anymore? Let's ask him."

7 The king of Israel said to Jehoshaphat, "There is still one man who can inquire of the LORD, but I hate him because he never prophesies good about me, but only disaster. He is Micaiah son of Imlah."

"The king shouldn't say that," Jehoshaphat replied.

8 So the king of Israel called an officer and said, "Hurry and get Micaiah son of Imlah!"

9 Now the king of Israel and King Jehoshaphat of Judah, clothed in royal attire, were each sitting on his own throne. They were sitting on the threshing floor at the entrance to Samaria's gate, and all the prophets were prophesying in front of them. 10 Then Zedekiah son of Chenaanah made iron horns and said, "This is what the LORD says: 'You will gore the Arameans with these until they are finished off.'" 11 And all the prophets were prophesying the same, saying, "March up to Ramoth-gilead and succeed, for the LORD will hand it over to the king."

MICAIAH'S MESSAGE OF DEFEAT

12 The messenger who went to call Micaiah instructed him, "Look, the words of the prophets are unanimously favorable for the king. So let your words be like theirs, and speak favorably."

13 But Micaiah said, "As the LORD lives, I will say whatever my God says."[B]

A 18:1 Lit made himself a son-in-law to Ahab; 1Kg 3:1; Ezr 9:14   B 18:13 LXX, Vg add to me; 1Kg 22:14

¹⁴ So he went to the king, and the king asked him, "Micaiah, should we go to Ramoth-gilead for war, or should I^A refrain?"

Micaiah said, "March up and succeed, for they will be handed over to you."

¹⁵ But the king said to him, "How many times must I make you swear not to tell me anything but the truth in the name of the LORD?"

¹⁶ So Micaiah said:

I saw all Israel scattered on the hills
like sheep without a shepherd.
And the LORD said,
"They have no master;
let each return home in peace."

¹⁷ So the king of Israel said to Jehoshaphat, "Didn't I tell you he never prophesies good about me, but only disaster?"

¹⁸ Then Micaiah said, "Therefore, hear the word of the LORD. I saw the LORD sitting on his throne, and the whole heavenly army was standing at his right hand and at his left hand. ¹⁹ And the LORD said, 'Who will entice King Ahab of Israel to march up and fall at Ramoth-gilead?' So one was saying this and another was saying that.

²⁰ "Then a spirit came forward, stood before the LORD, and said, 'I will entice him.'

"The LORD asked him, 'How?'

²¹ "So he said, 'I will go and become a lying spirit in the mouth of all his prophets.'

"Then he said, 'You will entice him and also prevail. Go and do that.'

²² "Now, you see, the LORD has put a lying spirit into the mouth of^B these prophets of yours, and the LORD has pronounced disaster against you."

²³ Then Zedekiah son of Chenaanah came up, hit Micaiah on the cheek, and demanded, "Which way did the spirit from the LORD leave me to speak to you?"

²⁴ Micaiah replied, "You will soon see when you go to hide in an inner chamber on that day."

²⁵ Then the king of Israel ordered, "Take Micaiah and return him to Amon, the governor of the city, and to Joash, the king's son, ²⁶ and say, 'This is what the king says: Put this guy in prison and feed him only a little bread and water^C until I come back safely.' "

²⁷ But Micaiah said, "If you ever return safely, the LORD has not spoken through me." Then he said, "Listen, all you people!"

AHAB'S DEATH

²⁸ Then the king of Israel and Judah's King Jehoshaphat went up to Ramoth-gilead. ²⁹ But the king of Israel said to Jehoshaphat, "I will disguise myself and go into battle, but you wear your royal attire." So the king of Israel disguised himself, and they went into battle.

³⁰ Now the king of Aram had ordered his chariot commanders, "Do not fight with anyone at all^D except the king of Israel."

³¹ When the chariot commanders saw Jehoshaphat, they shouted, "He must be the king of Israel!" So they turned to attack him, but Jehoshaphat

---

^A 18:14 LXX reads we; 1Kg 22:15   ^B 18:22 Some Hb mss, LXX, Syr, Vg add all;
1Kg 22:23   ^C 18:26 Lit him on bread of oppression and water of oppression
^D 18:30 Lit with small or with great

cried out and the LORD helped him. God drew them away from him. ³² When the chariot commanders saw that he was not the king of Israel, they turned back from pursuing him.

³³ But a man drew his bow without taking special aim and struck the king of Israel through the joints of his armor. So he said to the charioteer, "Turn around and take me out of the battle,^A for I am badly wounded!" ³⁴ The battle raged throughout that day, and the king of Israel propped himself up in his chariot facing the Arameans until evening. Then he died at sunset.

JEHU'S REBUKE OF JEHOSHAPHAT

19 King Jehoshaphat of Judah returned to his home in Jerusalem in peace. ² Then Jehu son of the seer Hanani went out to confront him^B and said to King Jehoshaphat, "Do you help the wicked and love those who hate the LORD? Because of this, the LORD's wrath is on you. ³ However, some good is found in you, for you have eradicated the Asherah poles from the land and have decided to seek God."

JEHOSHAPHAT'S REFORMS

⁴ Jehoshaphat lived in Jerusalem, and once again he went out among the people from Beer-sheba to the hill country of Ephraim and brought them back to the LORD, the God of their ancestors. ⁵ He appointed judges in all the fortified cities of the land of Judah, city by city. ⁶ Then he said to the judges, "Consider what you are doing, for you do not judge for a mere mortal, but for the LORD, who is with you in the matter of judgment. ⁷ And now, may the terror of the LORD be on you. Watch what you do, for there is no injustice or partiality or taking bribes with the LORD our God."

⁸ Jehoshaphat also appointed in Jerusalem some of the Levites and priests and some of the Israelite family heads for deciding the LORD's will and for settling disputes of the residents of^C Jerusalem. ⁹ He commanded them, saying, "In the fear of the LORD, with integrity, and wholeheartedly, you are to do the following: ¹⁰ For every dispute that comes to you from your brothers who dwell in their cities — whether it regards differences of bloodguilt, law, commandment, statutes, or judgments — you are to warn them, so they will not incur guilt before the LORD and wrath will not come on you and your brothers. Do this, and you will not incur guilt.

¹¹ "Note that Amariah, the chief priest, is over you in all matters related to the LORD, and Zebadiah son of Ishmael, the ruler of the house of Judah, in all matters related to the king, and the Levites are officers in your presence. Be strong; may the LORD be with those who do what is good."

WAR AGAINST EASTERN ENEMIES

20 After this, the Moabites and Ammonites, together with some of the Meunites,^D came to fight against Jehoshaphat. ² People came and told Jehoshaphat, "A vast number from beyond the Dead Sea and from Edom^E has come to fight against you; they are already in Hazazon-tamar" (that is, En-gedi). ³ Jehoshaphat was afraid, and he resolved to seek the LORD.

---

^A18:33 LXX, Vg; MT reads *camp*   ^B19:2 Lit *to his face*   ^C19:8 LXX, Vg; MT reads *disputes and they returned to*   ^D20:1 LXX; MT reads *Ammonites*; 2Ch 26:7
^E20:2 Some Hb mss, Old Lat; other Hb mss read *Aram*

Then he proclaimed a fast for all Judah, ⁴who gathered to seek the Lord. They even came from all the cities of Judah to seek him.

JEHOSHAPHAT'S PRAYER

⁵Then Jehoshaphat stood in the assembly of Judah and Jerusalem in the Lord's temple before the new courtyard. ⁶He said:

Lord, God of our ancestors, are you not the God who is in heaven, and do you not rule over all the kingdoms of the nations? Power and might are in your hand, and no one can stand against you. ⁷Are you not our God who drove out the inhabitants of this land before your people Israel and who gave it forever to the descendants of Abraham your friend? ⁸They have lived in the land and have built you a sanctuary in it for your name and have said, ⁹"If disaster comes on us — sword or judgment, pestilence or famine — we will stand before this temple and before you, for your name is in this temple. We will cry out to you because of our distress, and you will hear and deliver."

¹⁰Now here are the Ammonites, Moabites, and the inhabitants of Mount Seir. You did not let Israel invade them when Israel came out of the land of Egypt, but Israel turned away from them and did not destroy them. ¹¹Look how they repay us by coming to drive us out of your possession that you gave us as an inheritance. ¹²Our God, will you not judge them? For we are powerless before this vast number that comes to fight against us. We do not know what to do, but we look to you.ᴬ

GOD'S ANSWER

¹³All Judah was standing before the Lord with their dependents, their wives, and their children. ¹⁴In the middle of the congregation, the Spirit of the Lord came on Jahaziel (son of Zechariah, son of Benaiah, son of Jeiel, son of Mattaniah, a Levite from Asaph's descendants), ¹⁵and he said, "Listen carefully, all Judah and you inhabitants of Jerusalem, and King Jehoshaphat. This is what the Lord says: 'Do not be afraid or discouraged because of this vast number, for the battle is not yours, but God's. ¹⁶Tomorrow, go down against them. You will see them coming up the Ascent of Ziz, and you will find them at the end of the valley facing the Wilderness of Jeruel. ¹⁷You do not have to fight this battle. Position yourselves, stand still, and see the salvation of the Lord. He is with you, Judah and Jerusalem. Do not be afraid or discouraged. Tomorrow, go out to face them, for the Lord is with you.'"

¹⁸Then Jehoshaphat knelt low with his face to the ground, and all Judah and the inhabitants of Jerusalem fell down before the Lord to worship him. ¹⁹Then the Levites from the sons of the Kohathites and the Korahites stood up to praise the Lord God of Israel shouting loudly.

VICTORY AND PLUNDER

²⁰In the morning they got up early and went out to the wilderness of Tekoa. As they were about to go out, Jehoshaphat stood and said, "Hear me, Judah and you inhabitants of Jerusalem. Believe in the Lord your God, and you will be established; believe in his prophets, and you will succeed." ²¹Then

---

ᴬ20:12 Lit *but on you our eyes*

he consulted with the people and appointed some to sing for the LORD and some to praise the splendor of his holiness. When they went out in front of the armed forces, they kept singing:^A

Give thanks to the LORD,
for his faithful love endures forever.

²² The moment they began their shouts and praises, the LORD set an ambush against the Ammonites, Moabites, and the inhabitants of Mount Seir who came to fight against Judah, and they were defeated. ²³ The Ammonites and Moabites turned against the inhabitants of Mount Seir and completely annihilated them. When they had finished with the inhabitants of Seir, they helped destroy each other.

²⁴ When Judah came to a place overlooking the wilderness, they looked for the large army, but there were only corpses lying on the ground; nobody had escaped. ²⁵ Then Jehoshaphat and his people went to gather the plunder. They found among them^B an abundance of goods on the bodies^C and valuable items. So they stripped them until nobody could carry any more. They were gathering the plunder for three days because there was so much. ²⁶ They assembled in the Valley of Beracah^D on the fourth day, for there they blessed the LORD. Therefore, that place is still called the Valley of Beracah today.

²⁷ Then all the men of Judah and Jerusalem turned back with Jehoshaphat their leader, returning joyfully to Jerusalem, for the LORD enabled them to rejoice over their enemies. ²⁸ So they came into Jerusalem to the LORD's temple with harps, lyres, and trumpets.

²⁹ The terror of God was on all the kingdoms of the lands when they heard that the LORD had fought against the enemies of Israel. ³⁰ Then Jehoshaphat's kingdom was quiet, for his God gave him rest on every side.

SUMMARY OF JEHOSHAPHAT'S REIGN

³¹ Jehoshaphat became king over Judah. He was thirty-five years old when he became king, and he reigned twenty-five years in Jerusalem. His mother's name was Azubah daughter of Shilhi. ³² He walked in the ways of Asa his father; he did not turn away from it but did what was right in the LORD's sight. ³³ However, the high places were not taken away; the people had not yet set their hearts on the God of their ancestors.

³⁴ The rest of the events of Jehoshaphat's reign from beginning to end are written in the Events of Jehu son of Hanani, which is recorded in the Book of Israel's Kings.

JEHOSHAPHAT'S FLEET OF SHIPS

³⁵ After this, Judah's King Jehoshaphat made an alliance with Israel's King Ahaziah, who was guilty of wrongdoing. ³⁶ Jehoshaphat formed an alliance with him to make ships to go to Tarshish, and they made the ships in Ezion-geber. ³⁷ Then Eliezer son of Dodavahu of Mareshah prophesied against Jehoshaphat, saying, "Because you formed an alliance with Ahaziah, the LORD has broken up what you have made." So the ships were wrecked and were not able to go to Tarshish.

---

^A 20:21 Lit *saying* ^B 20:25 LXX reads *found cattle* ^C 20:25 Some Hb mss, Old Lat, Vg read *goods, garments* ^D 20:26 = Blessing

JEHORAM BECOMES KING OVER JUDAH

21 Jehoshaphat rested with his fathers and was buried with his fathers in the city of David. His son Jehoram^A became king in his place. ² He had brothers, sons of Jehoshaphat: Azariah, Jehiel, Zechariah, Azariah, Michael, and Shephatiah; all these were the sons of King Jehoshaphat of Judah.^B ³ Their father had given them many gifts of silver, gold, and valuable things, along with fortified cities in Judah, but he gave the kingdom to Jehoram because he was the firstborn. ⁴ When Jehoram had established himself over his father's kingdom, he strengthened his position by killing with the sword all his brothers as well as some of the princes of Israel.

JUDAH'S KING JEHORAM

⁵ Jehoram was thirty-two years old when he became king, and he reigned eight years in Jerusalem. ⁶ He walked in the ways of the kings of Israel, as the house of Ahab had done, for Ahab's daughter was his wife. He did what was evil in the LORD's sight, ⁷ but for the sake of the covenant the LORD had made with David, he was unwilling to destroy the house of David since the LORD had promised to give a lamp to David and to his sons forever.

⁸ During Jehoram's reign, Edom rebelled against Judah's control and appointed their own king. ⁹ So Jehoram crossed into Edom with his commanders and all his chariots. Then at night he set out to attack the Edomites who had surrounded him and the chariot commanders. ¹⁰ And now Edom is still in rebellion against Judah's control today. Libnah also rebelled at that time against his control because he had abandoned the LORD, the God of his ancestors. ¹¹ Jehoram also built high places in the hills^C of Judah, and he caused the inhabitants of Jerusalem to prostitute themselves, and he led Judah astray.

ELIJAH'S LETTER TO JEHORAM

¹² Then a letter came to Jehoram from the prophet Elijah, saying:
This is what the LORD, the God of your ancestor David says: "Because you have not walked in the ways of your father Jehoshaphat or in the ways of King Asa of Judah ¹³ but have walked in the ways of the kings of Israel, have caused Judah and the inhabitants of Jerusalem to prostitute themselves like the house of Ahab prostituted itself, and also have killed your brothers, your father's family, who were better than you, ¹⁴ the LORD is now about to strike your people, your sons, your wives, and all your possessions with a horrible affliction. ¹⁵ You yourself will be struck with many illnesses, including a disease of the intestines, until your intestines come out day after day because of the disease."

JEHORAM'S LAST DAYS

¹⁶ The LORD roused the spirit of the Philistines and the Arabs who lived near the Cushites to attack Jehoram. ¹⁷ So they went to war against Judah and invaded it. They carried off all the possessions found in the king's palace and also his sons and wives; not a son was left to him except Jehoahaz,^D his youngest son.

---

^A21:1 = Joram ^B21:2 Some Hb mss, LXX, Syr, Vg, Arabic; other Hb mss read *Israel* ^C21:11 Some Hb mss, LXX, Vg read *cities* ^D21:17 LXX, Syr, Tg read *Ahaziah*

¹⁸ After all these things, the LORD afflicted him in his intestines with an incurable disease. ¹⁹ This continued day after day until two full years passed. Then his intestines came out because of his disease, and he died from severe^A illnesses. But his people did not hold a fire in his honor like the fire in honor of his fathers.

²⁰ Jehoram was thirty-two years old when he became king; he reigned eight years in Jerusalem. He died to no one's regret^B and was buried in the city of David but not in the tombs of the kings.

JUDAH'S KING AHAZIAH

22 Then the inhabitants of Jerusalem made Ahaziah, his youngest son, king in his place, because the troops that had come with the Arabs to the camp had killed all the older sons.^C So Ahaziah son of Jehoram became king of Judah. ² Ahaziah was twenty-two^D years old when he became king, and he reigned one year in Jerusalem. His mother's name was Athaliah, granddaughter^E of Omri.

³ He walked in the ways of the house of Ahab, for his mother gave him evil advice. ⁴ So he did what was evil in the LORD's sight like the house of Ahab, for they were his advisers after the death of his father, to his destruction. ⁵ He also followed their advice and went with Joram^F son of Israel's King Ahab to fight against King Hazael of Aram, in Ramoth-gilead. The Arameans^G wounded Joram, ⁶ so he returned to Jezreel to recover from the wounds they inflicted on him in Ramoth-gilead^H when he fought against King Hazael of Aram. Then Judah's King Ahaziah^I son of Jehoram went down to Jezreel to visit Joram son of Ahab since Joram was ill.

⁷ Ahaziah's downfall came from God when he went to Joram. When Ahaziah arrived, he went out with Joram to meet Jehu son of Nimshi, whom the LORD had anointed to destroy the house of Ahab. ⁸ So when Jehu executed judgment on the house of Ahab, he found the rulers of Judah and the sons of Ahaziah's brothers who were serving Ahaziah, and he killed them. ⁹ Then Jehu looked for Ahaziah, and Jehu's soldiers captured him (he was hiding in Samaria). So they brought Ahaziah to Jehu, and they killed him. The soldiers buried him, for they said, "He is the grandson of Jehoshaphat who sought the LORD with all his heart." So no one from the house of Ahaziah had the strength to rule the kingdom.

ATHALIAH USURPS THE THRONE

¹⁰ When Athaliah, Ahaziah's mother, saw that her son was dead, she proceeded to annihilate all the royal heirs^J of the house of Judah. ¹¹ Jehoshabeath,^K the king's daughter, rescued Joash son of Ahaziah from the king's sons who were being killed and put him and the one who nursed him in a bedroom. Now Jehoshabeath was the daughter of King Jehoram and the wife of the priest Jehoiada. Since she was Ahaziah's sister, she hid Joash from Athaliah so that she did not kill him. ¹² While Athaliah reigned over the land, he was hiding with them in God's temple six years.

---

^A 21:19 Lit evil ^B 21:20 Lit He walked in no desirability ^C 22:1 Lit the former ones
^D 22:2 Some LXX mss, Syr; MT reads 42; 2Kg 8:26 ^E 22:2 Lit daughter
^F 22:5 = Jehoram ^G 22:5 Lit Rammites ^H 22:6 Lit in Ramah ^I 22:6 Some Hb mss,
LXX, Syr, Vg; other Hb mss read Azariah ^J 22:10 Lit seed ^K 22:11 = Jehosheba;
2Kg 11:2

BAD BULBS

2 CHRONICLES 21–22

I grew up in a town where the elevation is high, the roads are steep, and it's normal to get carsick on the way to the grocery store. Since moving to a bigger, flatter city, I'm homesick for the mountain views, snow days, and lack of rush hour traffic. However, there are some aspects of big city life that are ridiculously magical. Take string lights, for example.

In my mountain town, I knew string lights as *The Most Frustrating Christmas Decoration Ever*. I'd painstakingly untangle them and plug them in, only to discover that one belligerent bulb had burned out, rendering the entire strand useless.

But in big cities, I've learned, string lights are not stored in basements for once-a-year displays. They are welcome anytime, anywhere—summer barbecues, farmers markets in the fall, and restaurant patios all year round. Based on my holiday experiences gone awry, my immediate thought upon noticing this trend was how expensive it must be, replacing strand after strand due to a single bad bulb.

Then one day I noticed someone replacing a dead bulb with a new one, allowing the strand to continue shining. Clearly, the string lights I was used to were old news. This was a different kind altogether! I went to the store that same day and joined the Year Round Lights Club.

I don't think Athaliah would agree with my "ridiculously magical" stance on string lights. She'd probably even toss a perfectly good strand—which is what she attempted to do in Jerusalem. After losing her son, Ahaziah, King of Judah, she decided to destroy all other possible heirs to ensure her reign in the kingdom. While she did gain a throne in Jerusalem, she ruled for six years without knowing that an heir to the throne had escaped her clutches and was indeed still alive.

"When Athaliah, Ahaziah's mother, saw that her son was dead, she proceeded to annihilate all the royal heirs of the house of Judah. Jehoshabeath, the king's daughter, rescued Joash son of Ahaziah from the king's sons who were being killed and put him and the one who nursed him in a bedroom" (2Ch 22:10-11).

Rescued by a faith-filled woman named Jehoshabeath, Joash and his nurse were safely tucked away in God's temple, far away from Athaliah.

But the story gets even better. You see, Joash was the last living heir of David's lineage, which would later become Christ's lineage. Jehoshabeath's faith—which was uncommon in her own family—made way for the Savior's birth in the line of Judah! Not to mention, her name in Hebrew literally means, "The Lord is an oath," marking God's kept promise.

God destroys our dark with His light and life. He does not let a single sinner ruin an entire lineage, and His redemptive hand never tires. May we confidently hang over us His string of promises kept, knowing His goodness will always glow.

ATHALIAH OVERTHROWN

23 Then, in the seventh year, Jehoiada summoned his courage and took the commanders of hundreds into a covenant with him: Azariah son of Jeroham, Ishmael son of Jehohanan, Azariah son of Obed, Maaseiah son of Adaiah, and Elishaphat son of Zichri. ² They made a circuit throughout Judah. They gathered the Levites from all the cities of Judah and the family heads of Israel, and they came to Jerusalem.

³ Then the whole assembly made a covenant with the king in God's temple. Jehoiada said to them, "Here is the king's son! He will reign, just as the LORD promised concerning David's sons. ⁴ This is what you are to do: a third of you, priests and Levites who are coming on duty on the Sabbath, are to be gatekeepers. ⁵ A third are to be at the king's palace, and a third are to be at the Foundation Gate, and all the troops will be in the courtyards of the LORD's temple. ⁶ No one is to enter the LORD's temple but the priests and those Levites who serve; they may enter because they are holy, but all the people are to obey the requirement of the LORD. ⁷ Completely surround the king with weapons in hand. Anyone who enters the temple is to be put to death. Be with the king in all his daily tasks."ᴬ

⁸ So the commanders of hundreds did everything the priest Jehoiada commanded. They each brought their men — those coming on duty on the Sabbath and those going off duty on the Sabbath — for the priest Jehoiada did not release the divisions. ⁹ The priest Jehoiada gave to the commanders of hundreds King David's spears, shields, and quiversᴮ that were in God's temple. ¹⁰ Then he stationed all the troops with their weapons in hand surrounding the king — from the right side of the temple to the left side, by the altar and by the temple.

¹¹ They brought out the king's son, put the crown on him, gave him the testimony, and made him king. Jehoiada and his sons anointed him and cried, "Long live the king!"

¹² When Athaliah heard the noise from the troops, the guards, and those praising the king, she went to the troops in the LORD's temple. ¹³ As she looked, there was the king standing by his pillarᶜ at the entrance. The commanders and the trumpeters were by the king, and all the people of the land were rejoicing and blowing trumpets while the singers with musical instruments were leading the praise. Athaliah tore her clothes and screamed, "Treason! Treason!"

¹⁴ Then the priest Jehoiada sent out the commanders of hundreds, those in charge of the army, saying, "Take her out between the ranks, and put anyone who follows her to death by the sword," for the priest had said, "Don't put her to death in the LORD's temple." ¹⁵ So they arrested her, and she went by the entrance of the Horse Gate to the king's palace, where they put her to death.

JEHOIADA'S REFORMS

¹⁶ Then Jehoiada made a covenant between himself, the king, and the people that they would be the LORD's people. ¹⁷ So all the people went to the temple of Baal and tore it down. They smashed its altars and images and killed Mattan, the priest of Baal, at the altars.

ᴬ23:7 Lit *king when he comes in and when he goes out*   ᴮ23:9 Or *spears and large and small shields*   ᶜ23:13 LXX reads *post*

¹⁸ Then Jehoiada put the oversight of the LORD's temple into the hands of the Levitical priests, whom David had appointed over the LORD's temple, to offer burnt offerings to the LORD as it is written in the law of Moses, with rejoicing and song ordained by⁴ David. ¹⁹ He stationed gatekeepers at the gates of the LORD's temple so that nothing unclean could enter for any reason. ²⁰ Then he took with him the commanders of hundreds, the nobles, the governors of the people, and all the people of the land and brought the king down from the LORD's temple. They entered the king's palace through the Upper Gate and seated the king on the throne of the kingdom. ²¹ All the people of the land rejoiced, and the city was quiet, for they had put Athaliah to death by the sword.

JUDAH'S KING JOASH

24 Joash was seven years old when he became king, and he reigned forty years in Jerusalem. His mother's name was Zibiah; she was from Beer-sheba. ² Throughout the time of the priest Jehoiada, Joash did what was right in the LORD's sight. ³ Jehoiada acquired two wives for him, and he was the father of sons and daughters.

REPAIRING THE TEMPLE

⁴ Afterward, Joash took it to heart to renovate the LORD's temple. ⁵ So he gathered the priests and Levites and said, "Go out to the cities of Judah and collect silver from all Israel to repair the temple of your God as needed year by year, and do it quickly."

However, the Levites did not hurry. ⁶ So the king called Jehoiada the high priest and said, "Why haven't you required the Levites to bring from Judah and Jerusalem the tax imposed by the LORD's servant Moses and the assembly of Israel for the tent of the testimony? ⁷ For the sons of that wicked Athaliah broke into the LORD's temple and even used the sacred things of the LORD's temple for the Baals."

⁸ At the king's command a chest was made and placed outside the gate of the LORD's temple. ⁹ Then a proclamation was issued in Judah and Jerusalem that the tax God's servant Moses imposed on Israel in the wilderness be brought to the LORD. ¹⁰ All the leaders and all the people rejoiced, brought the tax, and put it in the chest until it was full. ¹¹ Whenever the chest was brought by the Levites to the king's overseers, and when they saw that there was a large amount of silver, the king's secretary and the high priest's deputy came and emptied the chest, picked it up, and returned it to its place. They did this daily and gathered the silver in abundance. ¹² Then the king and Jehoiada gave it to those in charge of the labor on the LORD's temple, who were hiring stonecutters and carpenters to renovate the LORD's temple, also blacksmiths and coppersmiths to repair the LORD's temple.

¹³ The workmen did their work, and through them the repairs progressed. They restored God's temple to its specifications and reinforced it. ¹⁴ When they finished, they presented the rest of the silver to the king and Jehoiada, who made articles for the LORD's temple with it — articles for ministry and for making burnt offerings, and ladles ᴮ and articles of gold and silver. They regularly offered burnt offerings in the LORD's temple throughout Jehoiada's life.

---

⁴23:18 Lit *song on the hands of*   ᴮ24:14 Or *dishes*, or *spoons*; lit *palms*

JOASH'S APOSTASY

¹⁵ Jehoiada died when he was old and full of days; he was 130 years old at his death. ¹⁶ He was buried in the city of David with the kings because he had done what was good in Israel with respect to God and his temple.

¹⁷ However, after Jehoiada died, the rulers of Judah came and paid homage to the king. Then the king listened to them, ¹⁸ and they abandoned the temple of the LORD, the God of their ancestors, and served the Asherah poles and the idols. So there was wrath against Judah and Jerusalem for this guilt of theirs. ¹⁹ Nevertheless, he sent them prophets to bring them back to the LORD; they admonished them, but the people would not listen.

²⁰ The Spirit of God enveloped^A Zechariah son of Jehoiada the priest. He stood above the people and said to them, "This is what God says, 'Why are you transgressing the LORD's commands so that you do not prosper? Because you have abandoned the LORD, he has abandoned you.'" ²¹ But they conspired against him and stoned him at the king's command in the courtyard of the LORD's temple. ²² King Joash didn't remember the kindness that Zechariah's father Jehoiada had extended to him, but killed his son. While he was dying, he said, "May the LORD see and demand an account."

ARAMEAN INVASION OF JUDAH

²³ At the turn of the year, an Aramean army attacked Joash. They entered Judah and Jerusalem and destroyed all the leaders of the people among them and sent all the plunder to the king of Damascus. ²⁴ Although the Aramean army came with only a few men, the LORD handed over a vast army to them because the people of Judah had abandoned the LORD, the God of their ancestors. So they executed judgment on Joash.

JOASH ASSASSINATED

²⁵ When the Arameans saw that Joash had many wounds, they left him. His servants conspired against him, and killed him on his bed, because he had shed the blood of the sons of the priest Jehoiada. So he died, and they buried him in the city of David, but they did not bury him in the tombs of the kings.

²⁶ Those who conspired against him were Zabad, son of the Ammonite woman Shimeath, and Jehozabad, son of the Moabite woman Shimrith.^B ²⁷ The accounts concerning his sons, the many divine pronouncements about him, and the restoration of God's temple are recorded in the Writing of the Book of the Kings. His son Amaziah became king in his place.

JUDAH'S KING AMAZIAH

25 Amaziah became king when he was twenty-five years old, and he reigned twenty-nine years in Jerusalem. His mother's name was Jehoaddan; she was from Jerusalem. ² He did what was right in the LORD's sight but not wholeheartedly.

³ As soon as the kingdom was firmly in his grasp,^C he executed his servants who had killed his father the king. ⁴ However, he did not put their children to death, because — as it is written in the Law, in the book of Moses, where the

---

^A24:20 Lit clothed   ^B24:26 = Shomer in 2Kg 12:21   ^C25:3 LXX, Syr; MT reads was strong on him; 1Kg 14:4

LORD commanded — "Fathers are not to die because of children, and children are not to die because of fathers, but each one will die for his own sin."

AMAZIAH'S CAMPAIGN AGAINST EDOM

⁵ Then Amaziah gathered Judah and assembled them according to ancestral families,ᴬ according to commanders of thousands, and according to commanders of hundreds. He numbered those twenty years old or more for all Judah and Benjamin. He found there to be three hundred thousand fit young men who could serve in the army, bearing spear and shield. ⁶ Then for 7,500 poundsᴮ of silver he hired one hundred thousand valiant warriors from Israel.

⁷ However, a man of God came to him and said, "King, do not let Israel's army go with you, for the LORD is not with Israel — all the Ephraimites. ⁸ But if you go with them, do it! Be strong for battle! But God will make you stumble before the enemy, for God has the power to help or to make one stumble."

⁹ Then Amaziah said to the man of God, "What should I do about the 7,500 pounds of silver I gave to Israel's division?"

The man of God replied, "The LORD is able to give you much more than this."

¹⁰ So Amaziah released the division that came to him from Ephraim to go home. But they got very angry with Judah and returned home in a fierce rage.

¹¹ Amaziah strengthened his position and led his people to the Salt Valley. He struck down ten thousand Seirites,ᶜ ¹² and the Judahites captured ten thousand alive. They took them to the top of a cliff where they threw them off, and all of them were dashed to pieces.

¹³ As for the men of the division that Amaziah sent back so they would not go with him into battle, they raided the cities of Judah from Samaria to Beth-horon, struck down three thousand of their people, and took a great deal of plunder.

¹⁴ After Amaziah came from the attack on the Edomites, he brought the gods of the Seirites and set them up as his gods. He worshiped before them and burned incense to them. ¹⁵ So the LORD's anger was against Amaziah, and he sent a prophet to him, who said, "Why have you sought a people's gods that could not rescue their own people from you?"

¹⁶ While he was still speaking to him, the king asked, "Have we made you the king's counselor? Stop, why should you lose your life?"

So the prophet stopped, but he said, "I know that God intends to destroy you, because you have done this and have not listened to my advice."

AMAZIAH'S WAR WITH ISRAEL'S KING JEHOASH

¹⁷ King Amaziah of Judah took counsel and sent word to Jehoashᴰ son of Jehoahaz, son of Jehu, king of Israel, and challenged him: "Come, let's meet face to face."

¹⁸ King Jehoash of Israel sent word to King Amaziah of Judah, saying, "The thistle in Lebanon sent a message to the cedar in Lebanon, saying, 'Give your daughter to my son as a wife.' Then a wild animal in Lebanon passed by and trampled the thistle. ¹⁹ You have said, 'Look, Iᴱ have defeated Edom,' and you have become overconfidentᶠ that you will get glory. Now stay at home. Why stir up such trouble so that you fall and Judah with you?"

ᴬ25:5 Lit *house of fathers*   ᴮ25:6 Lit *100 talents*, also in v. 9   ᶜ25:11 = Edomites, also in v. 14   ᴰ25:17 Lit *Joash*   ᴱ25:19 Some LXX mss, Old Lat, Tg, Vg; MT reads *you*   ᶠ25:19 Lit *and your heart has lifted you*

²⁰ But Amaziah would not listen, for this turn of events was from God in order to hand them over to their enemies because they went after the gods of Edom. ²¹ So King Jehoash of Israel advanced. He and King Amaziah of Judah met face to face at Beth-shemesh that belonged to Judah. ²² Judah was routed before Israel, and each man fled to his own tent. ²³ King Jehoash of Israel captured Judah's King Amaziah son of Joash, son of Jehoahaz,^ at Beth-shemesh. Then Jehoash took him to Jerusalem and broke down two hundred yards^B of Jerusalem's wall from the Ephraim Gate to the Corner Gate.^C ²⁴ He took all the gold, silver, all the utensils that were found with Obed-edom in God's temple, the treasures of the king's palace, and the hostages. Then he returned to Samaria.

AMAZIAH'S DEATH

²⁵ Judah's King Amaziah son of Joash lived fifteen years after the death of Israel's King Jehoash son of Jehoahaz. ²⁶ The rest of the events of Amaziah's reign, from beginning to end, are written in the Book of the Kings of Judah and Israel.

²⁷ From the time Amaziah turned from following the LORD, a conspiracy was formed against him in Jerusalem, and he fled to Lachish. However, men were sent after him to Lachish, and they put him to death there. ²⁸ They carried him back on horses and buried him with his fathers in the city of Judah.^D

JUDAH'S KING UZZIAH

26 All the people of Judah took Uzziah,^E who was sixteen years old, and made him king in place of his father Amaziah. ² After Amaziah the king rested with his fathers, Uzziah rebuilt Eloth^F and restored it to Judah.

³ Uzziah was sixteen years old when he became king, and he reigned fifty-two years in Jerusalem. His mother's name was Jecoliah; she was from Jerusalem. ⁴ He did what was right in the LORD's sight just as his father Amaziah had done. ⁵ He sought God throughout the lifetime of Zechariah, the teacher of the fear^G of God. During the time that he sought the LORD, God gave him success.

UZZIAH'S EXPLOITS

⁶ Uzziah went out to wage war against the Philistines, and he tore down the wall of Gath, the wall of Jabneh, and the wall of Ashdod. Then he built cities in the vicinity of Ashdod and among the Philistines. ⁷ God helped him against the Philistines, the Arabs that live in Gur-baal, and the Meunites. ⁸ The Ammonites^H paid tribute to Uzziah, and his fame spread as far as the entrance of Egypt, for God made him very powerful. ⁹ Uzziah built towers in Jerusalem at the Corner Gate, the Valley Gate, and the corner buttress, and he fortified them. ¹⁰ Since he had many cattle both in the Judean foothills^I and the plain, he built towers in the desert and dug many wells. And since

---

^A 25:23 = Ahaziah in 2Kg 14:13   ^B 25:23 Lit *400 cubits*   ^C 25:23 Some Hb mss; other Hb mss read *to Happoneh*   ^D 25:28 Some Hb mss read *city of David*   ^E 26:1 = Azariah in 2Kg 14:21   ^F 26:2 LXX, Syr, Vg read *Elath*   ^G 26:5 Some Hb mss, LXX, Syr, Tg, Arabic; other Hb mss, Vg read *visions*   ^H 26:8 LXX reads *Meunites*   ^I 26:10 Or *the Shephelah* he was a lover of the soil, he had farmers and vinedressers in the hills and in the fertile lands.^A

¹¹ Uzziah had an army equipped for combat that went out to war by division according to their assignments, as recorded by Jeiel the court secretary and Maaseiah the officer under the authority of Hananiah, one of the king's commanders. ¹² The total number of family heads was 2,600 valiant warriors. ¹³ Under their authority was an army of 307,500 equipped for combat, a powerful force to help the king against the enemy. ¹⁴ Uzziah provided the entire army with shields, spears, helmets, armor, bows, and slingstones. ¹⁵ He made skillfully designed devices in Jerusalem to shoot arrows and catapult large stones for use on the towers and on the corners. So his fame spread even to distant places, for he was wondrously helped until he became strong.

UZZIAH'S DISEASE

¹⁶ But when he became strong, he grew arrogant, and it led to his own destruction. He acted unfaithfully against the Lord his God by going into the Lord's sanctuary to burn incense on the incense altar. ¹⁷ The priest Azariah, along with eighty brave priests of the Lord, went in after him. ¹⁸ They took their stand against King Uzziah and said, "Uzziah, you have no right to offer incense to the Lord — only the consecrated priests, the descendants of Aaron, have the right to offer incense. Leave the sanctuary, for you have acted unfaithfully! You will not receive honor from the Lord God."

¹⁹ Uzziah, with a firepan in his hand to offer incense, was enraged. But when he became enraged with the priests, in the presence of the priests in the Lord's temple beside the altar of incense, a skin disease broke out on his forehead. ²⁰ Then Azariah the chief priest and all the priests turned to him and saw that he was diseased on his forehead. They rushed him out of there. He himself also hurried to get out because the Lord had afflicted him. ²¹ So King Uzziah was diseased to the time of his death. He lived in quarantine^B with a serious skin disease and was excluded from access to the Lord's temple, while his son Jotham was over the king's household governing the people of the land.

²² Now the prophet Isaiah son of Amoz wrote about the rest of the events of Uzziah's reign, from beginning to end. ²³ Uzziah rested with his fathers, and he was buried with his fathers in the burial ground of the kings' cemetery, for they said, "He has a skin disease." His son Jotham became king in his place.

JUDAH'S KING JOTHAM

27 Jotham was twenty-five years old when he became king, and he reigned sixteen years in Jerusalem. His mother's name was Jerushah daughter of Zadok. ² He did what was right in the Lord's sight just as his father Uzziah had done. In addition, he didn't enter the Lord's sanctuary, but the people still behaved corruptly.

³ Jotham built the Upper Gate of the Lord's temple, and he built extensively on the wall of Ophel. ⁴ He also built cities in the hill country of Judah and fortresses and towers in the forests. ⁵ He waged war against the king of the Ammonites. He overpowered the Ammonites, and that year they gave him

---

^A 26:10 Or *in Carmel*   ^B 26:21 Lit *in a house of exemption from duty*

7,500 pounds[A] of silver, 50,000 bushels[B] of wheat, and 50,000 bushels of barley. They paid him the same in the second and third years. ⁶ So Jotham strengthened his position because he did not waver in obeying[C] the LORD his God.

⁷ As for the rest of the events of Jotham's reign, along with all his wars and his ways, note that they are written in the Book of the Kings of Israel and Judah. ⁸ He was twenty-five years old when he became king, and he reigned sixteen years in Jerusalem. ⁹ Jotham rested with his fathers and was buried in the city of David. His son Ahaz became king in his place.

JUDAH'S KING AHAZ

28 Ahaz was twenty years old when he became king, and he reigned sixteen years in Jerusalem. He did not do what was right in the LORD's sight like his ancestor David, ² for he walked in the ways of the kings of Israel and made cast images of the Baals. ³ He burned incense in Ben Hinnom Valley and burned his children in[D] the fire, imitating the detestable practices of the nations the LORD had dispossessed before the Israelites. ⁴ He sacrificed and burned incense on the high places, on the hills, and under every green tree.

⁵ So the LORD his God handed Ahaz over to the king of Aram. He attacked him and took many captives to Damascus.

Ahaz was also handed over to the king of Israel, who struck him with great force: ⁶ Pekah son of Remaliah killed one hundred twenty thousand in Judah in one day — all brave men — because they had abandoned the LORD God of their ancestors. ⁷ An Ephraimite warrior named Zichri killed the king's son Maaseiah, Azrikam governor of the palace, and Elkanah who was second to the king. ⁸ Then the Israelites took two hundred thousand captives from their brothers — women, sons, and daughters. They also took a great deal of plunder from them and brought it to Samaria.

⁹ A prophet of the LORD named Oded was there. He went out to meet the army that came to Samaria and said to them, "Look, the LORD God of your ancestors handed them over to you because of his wrath against Judah, but you slaughtered them in a rage that has reached heaven. ¹⁰ Now you plan to reduce the people of Judah and Jerusalem, male and female, to slavery. Are you not also guilty before the LORD your God? ¹¹ Listen to me and return the captives you took from your brothers, for the LORD's burning anger is on you."

¹² So some men who were leaders of the Ephraimites — Azariah son of Jehohanan, Berechiah son of Meshillemoth, Jehizkiah son of Shallum, and Amasa son of Hadlai — stood in opposition to those coming from the war. ¹³ They said to them, "You must not bring the captives here, for you plan to bring guilt on us from the LORD to add to our sins and our guilt. For we have much guilt, and burning anger is on Israel."

¹⁴ The army left the captives and the plunder in the presence of the officers and the congregation. ¹⁵ Then the men who were designated by name took charge of the captives and provided clothes for their naked ones from the plunder. They clothed them, gave them sandals, food and drink, dressed their wounds, and provided donkeys for all the feeble. The Israelites brought them to Jericho, the City of Palms, among their brothers. Then they returned to Samaria.

[A]27:5 Lit *100 talents* [B]27:5 Lit *10,000 cors* [C]27:6 Lit *he established his ways before* [D]28:3 LXX, Syr, Tg read *and passed his children through*

¹⁶ At that time King Ahaz asked the king of Assyria for help. ¹⁷ The Edomites came again, attacked Judah, and took captives. ¹⁸ The Philistines also raided the cities of the Judean foothills ᴬ and the Negev of Judah. They captured and occupied Beth-shemesh, Aijalon, and Gederoth, as well as Soco, Timnah, and Gimzo with their surrounding villages. ¹⁹ For the LORD humbled Judah because of King Ahaz of Judah, ᴮ who threw off restraint in Judah and was unfaithful to the LORD. ²⁰ Then King Tiglath-pileser ᶜ of Assyria came against Ahaz; he oppressed him and did not give him support. ²¹ Although Ahaz plundered the LORD's temple and the palace of the king and of the rulers and gave the plunder to the king of Assyria, it did not help him.

²² At the time of his distress, King Ahaz himself became more unfaithful to the LORD. ²³ He sacrificed to the gods of Damascus which had defeated him; he said, "Since the gods of the kings of Aram are helping them, I will sacrifice to them so that they will help me." But they were the downfall of him and of all Israel.

²⁴ Then Ahaz gathered up the utensils of God's temple, cut them into pieces, shut the doors of the LORD's temple, and made himself altars on every street corner in Jerusalem. ²⁵ He made high places in every city of Judah to offer incense to other gods, and he angered the LORD, the God of his ancestors.

AHAZ'S DEATH

²⁶ As for the rest of his deeds and all his ways, from beginning to end, they are written in the Book of the Kings of Judah and Israel. ²⁷ Ahaz rested with his fathers and was buried in the city, in Jerusalem, but they did not bring him into the tombs of the kings of Israel. His son Hezekiah became king in his place.

JUDAH'S KING HEZEKIAH

29 Hezekiah was twenty-five years old when he became king, and he reigned twenty-nine years in Jerusalem. His mother's name was Abijah ᴰ daughter of Zechariah. ² He did what was right in the LORD's sight just as his ancestor David had done.

³ In the first year of his reign, in the first month, he opened the doors of the LORD's temple and repaired them. ⁴ Then he brought in the priests and Levites and gathered them in the eastern public square. ⁵ He said to them, "Hear me, Levites. Consecrate yourselves now and consecrate the temple of the LORD, the God of your ancestors. Remove everything impure from the holy place. ⁶ For our fathers were unfaithful and did what is evil in the sight of the LORD our God. They abandoned him, turned their faces away from the LORD's dwelling place, and turned their backs on him. ᴱ ⁷ They also closed the doors of the portico, extinguished the lamps, did not burn incense, and did not offer burnt offerings in the holy place of the God of Israel. ⁸ Therefore, the wrath of the LORD was on Judah and Jerusalem, and he made them an object of terror, horror, and mockery, ᶠ as you see with your own eyes. ⁹ Our fathers fell by the sword, and our sons, our daughters, and our wives are in captivity because of this. ¹⁰ It is in my heart now to make a covenant with the LORD, the God of Israel so that his burning anger may turn away from us.

ᴬ28:18 Or *the Shephelah*   ᴮ28:19 Some Hb mss; other Hb mss read *Israel*
ᶜ28:20 Text emended; MT reads *Tilgath-pilneser*; 1Ch 5:6,26   ᴰ29:1 = Abi in
2Kg 18:2   ᴱ29:6 Lit *and they gave the back of the neck*   ᶠ29:8 Lit *hissing*

THIS IS NOT WHO YOU ARE

2 CHRONICLES 29–31:1; MICAH 6:6-8; GALATIANS 3:13-14

I once heard the story of a small African village that uses corporate discipline for wrongdoing. Instead of punishment, the tribe circles the offender and reminds him of their identity.

> You are not a thief. You're a hard worker.
> You are not violent. You're gentle.
> You are not a liar. You tell the truth.

Instead of calling out the offense, they look the offender in the eye and say, "This is not who you are."

As God's people, sometimes we need to be reminded who we are.

Hezekiah plays this role for the people of Israel in 2 Chronicles 29–30.

In the first month of his reign, Hezekiah called the Levites together and gave a passionate speech. Though they had abandoned the temple and stopped consecrating themselves or making sacrifices, Hezekiah wouldn't let their new identity stick. After all, these were the families who had been set apart for the ministry in the temple since the days of Moses. He reminded them what their jobs were and who their fathers were and what God had called them to do (2Ch 29:4-10).

I can almost picture Hezekiah tenderly saying, "Look at me," before he said these next words: "My sons, don't be negligent now, for the LORD has chosen you to stand in his presence, to serve him, and to be his ministers and burners of incense" (2Ch 29:11).

Hezekiah reminded the people of their God-given identity. Life had lowered the collective bar, and they had settled for a less-than-spectacular identity as a nation. Hezekiah circled them up and said, "This is not who you are."

Suddenly, a group of men who had been hypnotized by bad rulers and ruthless enemies snapped out of it. They rolled up their sleeves and got to work. Because Hezekiah reminded them who they were, they acted like the priests they'd always been.

When they saw their identity and their God through a new frame, they burst out in spontaneous worship that lasted for 14 days (2 Ch 30:23).

I forget who I am all the time.

> I think I'm an orphan, when really I'm adopted.
> I think I'm abandoned, when really I'm adored.
> I think I'm a troublemaker, when really I'm forgiven.

God's Word lifts my eyes. It reminds me who I am. It reminds me who God is. It shakes me out of the trance of thinking I am "less than."

Is your identity murky as you read these words? Hear Hezekiah's reminder to his people: "This is not who you are." Raise your head, lift your eyes, square your shoulders, and walk in the new identity Christ died to give you.

¹¹ My sons, don't be negligent now, for the LORD has chosen you to stand in his presence, to serve him, and to be his ministers and burners of incense."

CLEANSING THE TEMPLE

¹² Then the Levites stood up:

Mahath son of Amasai and Joel son of Azariah from the Kohathites;
Kish son of Abdi and Azariah son of Jehallelel from the Merarites;
Joah son of Zimmah and Eden son of Joah from the Gershonites;

¹³ Shimri and Jeuel from the Elizaphanites;
Zechariah and Mattaniah from the Asaphites;

¹⁴ Jehiel^A and Shimei from the Hemanites;
Shemaiah and Uzziel from the Jeduthunites.

¹⁵ They gathered their brothers together, consecrated themselves, and went according to the king's command by the words of the LORD to cleanse the LORD's temple.

¹⁶ The priests went to the entrance of the LORD's temple to cleanse it. They took all the unclean things they found in the LORD's sanctuary to the courtyard of the LORD's temple. Then the Levites received them and took them outside to the Kidron Valley. ¹⁷ They began the consecration on the first day of the first month, and on the eighth day of the month they came to the portico of the LORD's temple. They consecrated the LORD's temple for eight days, and on the sixteenth day of the first month they finished.

¹⁸ Then they went inside to King Hezekiah and said, "We have cleansed the whole temple of the LORD, the altar of burnt offering and all its utensils, and the table for the rows of the Bread of the Presence and all its utensils. ¹⁹ We have set up and consecrated all the utensils that King Ahaz rejected during his reign when he became unfaithful. They are in front of the altar of the LORD."

RENEWAL OF TEMPLE WORSHIP

²⁰ King Hezekiah got up early, gathered the city officials, and went to the LORD's temple. ²¹ They brought seven bulls, seven rams, seven lambs, and seven male goats as a sin offering for the kingdom, for the sanctuary, and for Judah. Then he told the descendants of Aaron, the priests, to offer them on the altar of the LORD. ²² So they slaughtered the bulls, and the priests received the blood and splattered it on the altar. They slaughtered the rams and splattered the blood on the altar. They slaughtered the lambs and splattered the blood on the altar. ²³ Then they brought the goats for the sin offering right into the presence of the king and the congregation, who laid their hands on them. ²⁴ The priests slaughtered the goats and put their blood on the altar for a sin offering, to make atonement for all Israel, for the king said that the burnt offering and sin offering were for all Israel.

²⁵ Hezekiah stationed the Levites in the LORD's temple with cymbals, harps, and lyres according to the command of David, Gad the king's seer, and the prophet Nathan. For the command was from the LORD through his prophets. ²⁶ The Levites stood with the instruments of David, and the priests with the trumpets.

²⁷ Then Hezekiah ordered that the burnt offering be offered on the altar. When the burnt offerings began, the song of the LORD and the trumpets began,

---

^A29:14 Alt Hb tradition reads *Jehuel*

accompanied by the instruments of King David of Israel. [28] The whole assembly was worshiping, singing the song, and blowing the trumpets — all this continued until the burnt offering was completed. [29] When the burnt offerings were completed, the king and all those present with him bowed down and worshiped. [30] Then King Hezekiah and the officials told the Levites to sing praise to the LORD in the words of David and of the seer Asaph. So they sang praises with rejoicing and knelt low and worshiped.

[31] Hezekiah concluded, "Now you are consecrated[A] to the LORD. Come near and bring sacrifices and thank offerings to the LORD's temple." So the congregation brought sacrifices and thank offerings, and all those with willing hearts brought burnt offerings. [32] The number of burnt offerings the congregation brought was seventy bulls, one hundred rams, and two hundred lambs; all these were for a burnt offering to the LORD. [33] Six hundred bulls and three thousand sheep and goats were consecrated.

[34] However, since there were not enough priests, they weren't able to skin all the burnt offerings, so their Levite brothers helped them until the work was finished and until the priests consecrated themselves. For the Levites were more conscientious[B] to consecrate themselves than the priests were. [35] Furthermore, the burnt offerings were abundant, along with the fat of the fellowship offerings and with the drink offerings for the burnt offering.

So the service of the LORD's temple was established. [36] Then Hezekiah and all the people rejoiced over how God had prepared the people, for it had come about suddenly.

CELEBRATION OF THE PASSOVER

30 Then Hezekiah sent word throughout all Israel and Judah, and he also wrote letters to Ephraim and Manasseh to come to the LORD's temple in Jerusalem to observe the Passover of the LORD, the God of Israel. [2] For the king and his officials and the entire congregation in Jerusalem decided to observe the Passover of the LORD in the second month, [3] because they were not able to observe it at the appropriate time. Not enough of the priests had consecrated themselves, and the people hadn't been gathered together in Jerusalem. [4] The proposal pleased the king and the congregation, [5] so they affirmed the proposal and spread the message throughout all Israel, from Beer-sheba to Dan, to come to observe the Passover of the LORD, the God of Israel in Jerusalem, for they hadn't observed it often,[C] as prescribed.[D]

[6] So the couriers went throughout Israel and Judah with letters from the hand of the king and his officials, and according to the king's command, saying, "Israelites, return to the LORD, the God of Abraham, Isaac, and Israel so that he may return to those of you who remain, who have escaped the grasp of the kings of Assyria. [7] Don't be like your fathers and your brothers who were unfaithful to the LORD, the God of their ancestors so that he made them an object of horror as you yourselves see. [8] Don't become obstinate[E] now like your fathers did. Give your allegiance[F] to the LORD, and come to his sanctuary that he has consecrated forever. Serve the LORD your God so that he may turn his burning anger away from you, [9] for when you

---

[A]29:31 Lit Now you have filled your hands   [B]29:34 Lit upright of heart; Ps 32:11; 64:10   [C]30:5 Or in great numbers   [D]30:5 Lit often, according to what is written   [E]30:8 Lit Don't stiffen your neck   [F]30:8 Lit hand return to the LORD, your brothers and your sons will receive mercy in the presence of their captors and will return to this land. For the LORD your God is gracious and merciful; he will not turn his face away from you if you return to him."

¹⁰ The couriers traveled from city to city in the land of Ephraim and Manasseh as far as Zebulun, but the inhabitants^A laughed at them and mocked them. ¹¹ But some from Asher, Manasseh, and Zebulun humbled themselves and came to Jerusalem. ¹² Also, the power of God was at work in Judah to unite them^B to carry out the command of the king and his officials by the word of the LORD.

¹³ A very large assembly of people was gathered in Jerusalem to observe the Festival of Unleavened Bread in the second month. ¹⁴ They proceeded to take away the altars that were in Jerusalem, and they took away the incense altars and threw them into the Kidron Valley. ¹⁵ They slaughtered the Passover lamb on the fourteenth day of the second month. The priests and Levites were ashamed, and they consecrated themselves and brought burnt offerings to the LORD's temple. ¹⁶ They stood at their prescribed posts, according to the law of Moses, the man of God. The priests splattered the blood received from the Levites, ¹⁷ for there were many in the assembly who had not consecrated themselves, and so the Levites were in charge of slaughtering the Passover lambs for every unclean person to consecrate the lambs to the LORD. ¹⁸ A large number of the people — many from Ephraim, Manasseh, Issachar, and Zebulun — were ritually unclean, yet they had eaten the Passover contrary to what was written. But Hezekiah had interceded for them, saying, "May the good LORD provide atonement on behalf of ¹⁹ whoever sets his whole heart on seeking God, the LORD, the God of his ancestors, even though not according to the purification rules of the sanctuary." ²⁰ So the LORD heard Hezekiah and healed the people. ²¹ The Israelites who were present in Jerusalem observed the Festival of Unleavened Bread seven days with great joy, and the Levites and the priests praised the LORD day after day with loud instruments. ²² Then Hezekiah encouraged^C all the Levites who performed skillfully before the LORD. They ate at the appointed festival for seven days, sacrificing fellowship offerings and giving thanks to the LORD, the God of their ancestors.

²³ The whole congregation decided to observe seven more days, so they observed seven days with joy, ²⁴ for King Hezekiah of Judah contributed one thousand bulls and seven thousand sheep for the congregation. Also, the officials contributed one thousand bulls and ten thousand sheep for the congregation, and many priests consecrated themselves. ²⁵ Then the whole assembly of Judah with the priests and Levites, the whole assembly that came from Israel, the resident aliens who came from the land of Israel, and those who were living in Judah, rejoiced. ²⁶ There was great rejoicing in Jerusalem, for nothing like this was known since the days of Solomon son of David, the king of Israel.

²⁷ Then the priests and the Levites stood to bless the people, and God heard them, and their prayer came into his holy dwelling place in heaven.

---

^A 30:10 Lit but they ^B 30:12 Lit to give them one heart ^C 30:22 Lit spoke to the heart of

REMOVAL OF IDOLATRY

31 When all this was completed, all Israel who had attended went out to the cities of Judah and broke up the sacred pillars, chopped down the Asherah poles, and tore down the high places and altars throughout Judah and Benjamin, as well as in Ephraim and Manasseh, to the last one.^A Then all the Israelites returned to their cities, each to his own possession.

OFFERINGS FOR LEVITES

^2 Hezekiah reestablished the divisions of the priests and Levites for the burnt offerings and fellowship offerings, for ministry, for giving thanks, and for praise in the gates of the camp of the LORD, each division corresponding to his service among the priests and Levites. ^3 The king contributed^B from his own possessions for the regular morning and evening burnt offerings, the burnt offerings of the Sabbaths, of the New Moons, and of the appointed feasts, as written in the law of the LORD. ^4 He told the people who lived in Jerusalem to give a contribution for the priests and Levites so that they could devote their energy to the law of the LORD. ^5 When the word spread, the Israelites gave liberally of the best of the grain, new wine, fresh oil, honey, and of all the produce of the field, and they brought in an abundance, a tenth of everything. ^6 As for the Israelites and Judahites who lived in the cities of Judah, they also brought a tenth of the herds and flocks, and a tenth of the dedicated things that were consecrated to the LORD their God. They gathered them into large piles. ^7 In the third month they began building up the piles, and they finished in the seventh month. ^8 When Hezekiah and his officials came and viewed the piles, they blessed the LORD and his people Israel.

^9 Hezekiah asked the priests and Levites about the piles. ^10 The chief priest Azariah, of the household of Zadok, answered him, "Since they began bringing the offering to the LORD's temple, we eat and are satisfied and there is plenty left over because the LORD has blessed his people; this abundance is what is left over."

^11 Hezekiah told them to prepare chambers in the LORD's temple, and they prepared them. ^12 The offering, the tenth, and the dedicated things were brought faithfully. Conaniah the Levite was the officer in charge of them, and his brother Shimei was second. ^13 Jehiel, Azaziah, Nahath, Asahel, Jerimoth, Jozabad, Eliel, Ismachiah, Mahath, and Benaiah were deputies under the authority of Conaniah and his brother Shimei by appointment of King Hezekiah and of Azariah the chief official of God's temple.

^14 Kore son of Imnah the Levite, the keeper of the East Gate, was over the freewill offerings to God to distribute the contribution to the LORD and the consecrated things. ^15 Eden, Miniamin, Jeshua, Shemaiah, Amariah, and Shecaniah in the cities of the priests were to distribute it faithfully under his authority to their brothers by divisions, whether large or small. ^16 In addition, they distributed it to males registered by genealogy three^C years old and above; to all who would enter the LORD's temple for their daily duty, for their service in their responsibilities according to their divisions. ^17 They distributed also to those recorded by genealogy of the priests by their ancestral families and the Levites twenty years old and above, by their responsibilities

---

^A31:1 Lit *Manasseh, until finishing*   ^B31:3 Lit *The king's portion*   ^C31:16 Or *30;* 1Ch 23:3

in their divisions; [18] to those registered by genealogy — with all their dependents, wives, sons, and daughters — of the whole assembly (for they had faithfully consecrated themselves as holy); [19] and to the descendants of Aaron, the priests, in the common fields of their cities, in each and every city. There were men who were registered by name to distribute a portion to every male among the priests and to every Levite recorded by genealogy.

[20] Hezekiah did this throughout all Judah. He did what was good and upright and true before the LORD his God. [21] He was diligent in every deed that he began in the service of God's temple, in the instruction and the commands, in order to seek his God, and he prospered.

SENNACHERIB'S INVASION

32 After these faithful deeds, King Sennacherib of Assyria came and entered Judah. He laid siege to the fortified cities and intended[A] to break into them. [2] Hezekiah saw that Sennacherib had come and that he planned[B] war on Jerusalem, [3] so he consulted with his officials and his warriors about stopping up the water of the springs that were outside the city, and they helped him. [4] Many people gathered and stopped up all the springs and the stream that flowed through the land; they said, "Why should the kings of Assyria come and find abundant water?" [5] Then Hezekiah strengthened his position by rebuilding the entire broken-down wall and heightening the towers and the other outside wall. He repaired the supporting terraces of the city of David, and made an abundance of weapons and shields.

[6] He set military commanders over the people and gathered the people in the square of the city gate. Then he encouraged them,[C] saying, [7] "Be strong and courageous! Don't be afraid or discouraged before the king of Assyria or before the large army that is with him, for there are more with us than with him. [8] He has only human strength,[D] but we have the LORD our God to help us and to fight our battles." So the people relied on the words of King Hezekiah of Judah.

SENNACHERIB'S SERVANT'S SPEECH

[9] After this, while King Sennacherib of Assyria with all his armed forces besieged[E] Lachish, he sent his servants to Jerusalem against King Hezekiah of Judah and against all those of Judah who were in Jerusalem, saying, [10] "This is what King Sennacherib of Assyria says: 'What are you relying on that you remain in Jerusalem under siege? [11] Isn't Hezekiah misleading you to give you over to death by famine and thirst when he says, "The LORD our God will keep us from the grasp of the king of Assyria"? [12] Didn't Hezekiah himself remove his high places and his altars and say to Judah and Jerusalem, "You must worship before one altar, and you must burn incense on it"?

[13] "'Don't you know what I and my fathers have done to all the peoples of the lands? Have any of the national gods of the lands been able to rescue their land from my power? [14] Who among all the gods of these nations that my predecessors completely destroyed was able to rescue his people from my power, that your God should be able to deliver you from my power? [15] So

---

[A]32:1 Lit *said to himself* [B]32:2 Lit *that his face was for* [C]32:6 Lit *he spoke to their hearts* [D]32:8 Lit *With him an arm of flesh* [E]32:9 Lit *with his dominion was against* now, don't let Hezekiah deceive you, and don't let him mislead you like this. Don't believe him, for no god of any nation or kingdom has been able to rescue his people from my power or the power of my fathers. How much less will your God rescue you from my power!'"

[16] His servants said more against the LORD God and against his servant Hezekiah. [17] He also wrote letters to mock the LORD, the God of Israel, saying against him:

Just like the national gods of the lands that did not rescue their people from my power, so Hezekiah's God will not rescue his people from my power.

[18] Then they called out loudly in Hebrew[A] to the people of Jerusalem, who were on the wall, to frighten and discourage them in order that he might capture the city. [19] They spoke against the God of Jerusalem like they had spoken against the gods of the peoples of the earth, which were made by human hands.

DELIVERANCE FROM SENNACHERIB

[20] King Hezekiah and the prophet Isaiah son of Amoz prayed about this and cried out to heaven, [21] and the LORD sent an angel who annihilated every valiant warrior, leader, and commander in the camp of the king of Assyria. So the king of Assyria returned in disgrace to his land. He went to the temple of his god, and there some of his own children struck him down with the sword. [22] So the LORD saved Hezekiah and the inhabitants of Jerusalem from the power of King Sennacherib of Assyria and from the power of all others. He gave them rest[B] on every side. [23] Many were bringing an offering to the LORD to Jerusalem and valuable gifts to King Hezekiah of Judah, and he was exalted in the eyes of all the nations after that.

HEZEKIAH'S ILLNESS AND PRIDE

[24] In those days Hezekiah became sick to the point of death, so he prayed to the LORD, and he spoke to him and gave him a miraculous sign. [25] However, because his heart was proud, Hezekiah didn't respond according to the benefit that had come to him. So there was wrath on him, Judah, and Jerusalem. [26] Then Hezekiah humbled himself for the pride of his heart — he and the inhabitants of Jerusalem — so the LORD's wrath didn't come on them during Hezekiah's lifetime.

HEZEKIAH'S WEALTH AND WORKS

[27] Hezekiah had abundant riches and glory, and he made himself treasuries for silver, gold, precious stones, spices, shields, and every desirable item. [28] He made warehouses for the harvest of grain, new wine, and fresh oil, and stalls for all kinds of cattle, and pens for flocks. [29] He made cities for himself, and he acquired vast numbers of flocks and herds, for God gave him abundant possessions.

[30] This same Hezekiah blocked the outlet of the water of the Upper Gihon and channeled it smoothly downward and westward to the city of David. Hezekiah succeeded in everything he did. [31] When the ambassadors of Babylon's

[A]32:18 Lit Judahite [B]32:22 Lit He led them; Ps 23:2

rulers were sent^ to him to inquire about the miraculous sign that happened in the land, God left him to test him and discover what was in his heart.

HEZEKIAH'S DEATH

³² As for the rest of the events of Hezekiah's reign and his deeds of faithful love, note that they are written in the Visions of the Prophet Isaiah son of Amoz, and in the Book of the Kings of Judah and Israel. ³³ Hezekiah rested with his fathers and was buried on the ascent to the tombs of David's descendants. All Judah and the inhabitants of Jerusalem paid him honor at his death. His son Manasseh became king in his place.

JUDAH'S KING MANASSEH

33 Manasseh was twelve years old when he became king, and he reigned fifty-five years in Jerusalem. ² He did what was evil in the LORD's sight, imitating the detestable practices of the nations that the LORD had dispossessed before the Israelites. ³ He rebuilt the high places that his father Hezekiah had torn down and reestablished the altars for the Baals. He made Asherah poles, and he bowed in worship to all the stars in the sky and served them. ⁴ He built altars in the LORD's temple, where the LORD had said, "Jerusalem is where my name will remain forever." ⁵ He built altars to all the stars in the sky in both courtyards of the LORD's temple. ⁶ He passed his sons through the fire in Ben Hinnom Valley. He practiced witchcraft, divination, and sorcery, and consulted mediums and spiritists. He did a huge amount of evil in the LORD's sight, angering him.

⁷ Manasseh set up a carved image of the idol, which he had made, in God's temple that God had spoken about to David and his son Solomon: "I will establish my name forever^B in this temple and in Jerusalem, which I have chosen out of all the tribes of Israel. ⁸ I will never again remove the feet of the Israelites from the land where I stationed your^C ancestors, if only they will be careful to do all I have commanded them through Moses — all the law, statutes, and judgments." ⁹ So Manasseh caused Judah and the inhabitants of Jerusalem to stray so that they did worse evil than the nations the LORD had destroyed before the Israelites.

MANASSEH'S REPENTANCE

¹⁰ The LORD spoke to Manasseh and his people, but they didn't listen. ¹¹ So he brought against them the military commanders of the king of Assyria. They captured Manasseh with hooks, bound him with bronze shackles, and took him to Babylon. ¹² When he was in distress, he sought the favor of the LORD his God and earnestly humbled himself before the God of his ancestors. ¹³ He prayed to him, and the LORD was receptive to his prayer. He granted his request and brought him back to Jerusalem, to his kingdom. So Manasseh came to know that the LORD is God.

¹⁴ After this, he built the outer wall of the city of David from west of Gihon in the valley to the entrance of the Fish Gate; he brought it around the Ophel, and he heightened it considerably. He also placed military commanders in all the fortified cities of Judah.

---

^32:31 LXX, Tg, Vg; MT reads *of Babylon sent* ^33:7 LXX, Syr, Tg, Vg; 2Kg 21:7;
MT reads *name for Elom* ^33:8 LXX, Syr, Vg read *land I gave to their*; 2Kg 21:8

¹⁵ He removed the foreign gods and the idol from the LORD's temple, along with all the altars that he had built on the mountain of the LORD's temple and in Jerusalem, and he threw them outside the city. ¹⁶ He built ᴬ the altar of the LORD and offered fellowship and thank offerings on it. Then he told Judah to serve the LORD, the God of Israel. ¹⁷ However, the people still sacrificed at the high places, but only to the LORD their God.

MANASSEH'S DEATH

¹⁸ The rest of the events of Manasseh's reign, along with his prayer to his God and the words of the seers who spoke to him in the name of the LORD, the God of Israel, are written in the Events of Israel's Kings. ¹⁹ His prayer and how God was receptive to his prayer, and all his sin and unfaithfulness and the sites where he built high places and set up Asherah poles and carved images before he humbled himself, they are written in the Events of Hozai. ²⁰ Manasseh rested with his fathers, and he was buried in his own house. His son Amon became king in his place.

JUDAH'S KING AMON

²¹ Amon was twenty-two years old when he became king, and he reigned two years in Jerusalem. ²² He did what was evil in the LORD's sight, just as his father Manasseh had done. Amon sacrificed to all the carved images that his father Manasseh had made, and he served them. ²³ But he did not humble himself before the LORD like his father Manasseh humbled himself; instead, Amon increased his guilt.

²⁴ So his servants conspired against him and put him to death in his own house. ²⁵ The common people ᴮ killed all who had conspired against King Amon, and they made his son Josiah king in his place.

JUDAH'S KING JOSIAH

34 Josiah was eight years old when he became king, and he reigned thirty-one years in Jerusalem. ² He did what was right in the LORD's sight and walked in the ways of his ancestor David; he did not turn aside to the right or the left.

JOSIAH'S REFORM

³ In the eighth year of his reign, while he was still a youth, Josiah began to seek the God of his ancestor David, and in the twelfth year he began to cleanse Judah and Jerusalem of the high places, the Asherah poles, the carved images, and the cast images. ⁴ Then in his presence the altars of the Baals were torn down, and he chopped down the shrines ᶜ that were above them. He shattered the Asherah poles, the carved images, and the cast images, crushed them to dust, and scattered them over the graves of those who had sacrificed to them. ⁵ He burned the bones of the priests on their altars. So he cleansed Judah and Jerusalem. ⁶ He did the same in the cities of Manasseh, Ephraim, and Simeon, and as far as Naphtali and on their surrounding mountain shrines. ᴰ

ᴬ33:16 Some Hb mss, Syr, Tg, Arabic; other Hb mss, LXX, Vg read *restored*
ᴮ33:25 Lit *The people of the land*   ᶜ34:4 Lit *incense altars*, also in v. 7
ᴰ34:6 One Hb tradition reads *Naphtali with their swords*; alt Hb tradition, Syr, Vg read *Naphtali, the ruins all around*; Hb obscure

[7] He tore down the altars, and he smashed the Asherah poles and the carved images to powder. He chopped down all the shrines throughout the land of Israel and returned to Jerusalem.

JOSIAH'S REPAIR OF THE TEMPLE

[8] In the eighteenth year of his reign, in order to cleanse the land and the temple, Josiah sent Shaphan son of Azaliah, along with Maaseiah the governor of the city and the court historian Joah son of Joahaz, to repair the temple of the LORD his God.

[9] So they went to the high priest Hilkiah and gave him the silver brought into God's temple. The Levites and the doorkeepers had collected it from Manasseh, Ephraim, and from the entire remnant of Israel, and from all Judah, Benjamin, and the inhabitants of Jerusalem. [10] They gave it to those doing the work — those who oversaw the LORD's temple. They gave it to the workmen who were working in the LORD's temple, to repair and restore the temple; [11] they gave it to the carpenters and builders and also used it to buy quarried stone and timbers — for joining and making beams — for the buildings that Judah's kings had destroyed.

[12] The men were doing the work with integrity. Their overseers were Jahath and Obadiah, Levites from the Merarites, and Zechariah and Meshullam from the Kohathites as supervisors. The Levites were all skilled with musical instruments. [13] They were also over the porters and were supervising all those doing the work task by task. Some of the Levites were secretaries, officers, and gatekeepers.

THE RECOVERY OF THE BOOK OF THE LAW

[14] When they brought out the silver that had been deposited in the LORD's temple, the priest Hilkiah found the book of the law of the LORD written by the hand of Moses. [15] Consequently, Hilkiah told the court secretary Shaphan, "I have found the book of the law in the LORD's temple," and he gave the book to Shaphan.

[16] Shaphan took the book to the king, and also reported, "Your servants are doing all that was placed in their hands. [17] They have emptied out the silver that was found in the LORD's temple and have given it to the overseers and to those doing the work." [18] Then the court secretary Shaphan told the king, "The priest Hilkiah gave me a book," and Shaphan read from it in the presence of the king.

[19] When the king heard the words of the law, he tore his clothes. [20] Then he commanded Hilkiah, Ahikam son of Shaphan, Abdon son of Micah, the court secretary Shaphan, and the king's servant Asaiah, [21] "Go and inquire of the LORD for me and for those remaining in Israel and Judah, concerning the words of the book that was found. For great is the LORD's wrath that is poured out on us because our ancestors have not kept the word of the LORD in order to do everything written in this book."

HULDAH'S PROPHECY OF JUDGMENT

[22] So Hilkiah and those the king had designated[A] went to the prophetess Huldah, the wife of Shallum son of Tokhath, son of Hasrah, keeper of the

---

A34:22 LXX; MT omits *designated*

wardrobe. She lived in Jerusalem in the Second District. They spoke with her about this.

²³ She said to them, "This is what the LORD God of Israel says: Say to the man who sent you to me, ²⁴ 'This is what the LORD says: I am about to bring disaster on this place and on its inhabitants, fulfilling^A all the curses written in the book that they read in the presence of the king of Judah, ²⁵ because they have abandoned me and burned incense to other gods so as to anger me with all the works of their hands. My wrath will be poured out on this place, and it will not be quenched.' ²⁶ Say this to the king of Judah who sent you to inquire of the LORD: 'This is what the LORD God of Israel says: As for the words that you heard, ²⁷ because your heart was tender and you humbled yourself before God when you heard his words against this place and against its inhabitants, and because you humbled yourself before me, and you tore your clothes and wept before me, I myself have heard' — this is the LORD's declaration. ²⁸ 'I will indeed gather you to your fathers, and you will be gathered to your grave in peace. Your eyes will not see all the disaster that I am bringing on this place and on its inhabitants.' "

Then they reported to the king.

AFFIRMATION OF THE COVENANT BY JOSIAH AND THE PEOPLE

²⁹ So the king sent messengers and gathered all the elders of Judah and Jerusalem. ³⁰ The king went up to the LORD's temple with all the men of Judah and the inhabitants of Jerusalem, as well as the priests and the Levites — all the people from the oldest to the youngest. He read in their hearing all the words of the book of the covenant that had been found in the LORD's temple. ³¹ Then the king stood at his post and made a covenant in the LORD's presence to follow the LORD and to keep his commands, his decrees, and his statutes with all his heart and with all his soul in order to carry out the words of the covenant written in this book.

³² He had all those present in Jerusalem and Benjamin agree^B to it. So all the inhabitants of Jerusalem carried out the covenant of God, the God of their ancestors.

³³ So Josiah removed everything that was detestable from all the lands belonging to the Israelites, and he required all who were present in Israel to serve the LORD their God. Throughout his reign they did not turn aside from following the LORD, the God of their ancestors.

JOSIAH'S PASSOVER OBSERVANCE

35 Josiah observed the LORD's Passover and slaughtered the Passover lambs on the fourteenth day of the first month. ² He appointed the priests to their responsibilities and encouraged them to serve in the LORD's temple. ³ He said to the Levites who taught all Israel the holy things of the LORD, "Put the holy ark in the temple built by Solomon son of David king of Israel. Since you do not have to carry it on your shoulders, now serve the LORD your God and his people Israel.

⁴ "Organize your ancestral families^C by your divisions according to the written instruction of King David of Israel and that of his son Solomon. ⁵ Serve

---

^A34:24 *fulfilling* supplied for clarity   ^B34:32 Lit *take a stand.*   ^C35:4 Lit *the house of your fathers* in the holy place by the groupings of the ancestral families^A for your brothers, the lay people,^B and according to the division of the Levites by family. ⁶ Slaughter the Passover lambs, consecrate yourselves, and make preparations for your brothers to carry out the word of the LORD through Moses."

⁷ Then Josiah donated thirty thousand sheep, lambs, and young goats, plus three thousand cattle from his own possessions, for the Passover sacrifices for all the lay people who were present.

⁸ His officials also donated willingly for the people, the priests, and the Levites. Hilkiah, Zechariah, and Jehiel, chief officials of God's temple, gave twenty-six hundred Passover sacrifices and three hundred cattle for the priests. ⁹ Conaniah and his brothers Shemaiah and Nethanel, and Hashabiah, Jeiel, and Jozabad, officers of the Levites, donated five thousand Passover sacrifices for the Levites, plus five hundred cattle.

¹⁰ So the service was established; the priests stood at their posts and the Levites in their divisions according to the king's command. ¹¹ Then they slaughtered the Passover lambs, and while the Levites were skinning the animals, the priests splattered the blood^C they had been given.^D ¹² They removed the burnt offerings so that they might be given to the groupings of the ancestral families^E of the lay people to offer to the LORD, according to what is written in the book of Moses; they did the same with the cattle. ¹³ They roasted the Passover lambs with fire according to regulation. They boiled the holy sacrifices in pots, kettles, and bowls; and they quickly brought them to the lay people. ¹⁴ Afterward, they made preparations for themselves and for the priests, since the priests, the descendants of Aaron, were busy offering up burnt offerings and fat until night. So the Levites made preparations for themselves and for the priests, the descendants of Aaron.

¹⁵ The singers, the descendants of Asaph, were at their stations according to the command of David, Asaph, Heman, and Jeduthun the king's seer. Also, the gatekeepers were at each temple gate. None of them left their tasks because their Levite brothers had made preparations for them.

¹⁶ So all the service of the LORD was established that day for observing the Passover and for offering burnt offerings on the altar of the LORD, according to the command of King Josiah. ¹⁷ The Israelites who were present in Judah also observed the Passover at that time and the Festival of Unleavened Bread for seven days. ¹⁸ No Passover had been observed like it in Israel since the days of the prophet Samuel. None of the kings of Israel ever observed a Passover like the one that Josiah observed with the priests, the Levites, all Judah, the Israelites who were present in Judah, and the inhabitants of Jerusalem. ¹⁹ In the eighteenth year of Josiah's reign, this Passover was observed.

JOSIAH'S LAST DEEDS AND DEATH

²⁰ After all this that Josiah had prepared for the temple, King Neco of Egypt marched up to fight at Carchemish by the Euphrates, and Josiah went out to confront him. ²¹ But Neco sent messengers to him, saying, "What is the issue between you and me, king of Judah? I have not come against you today^F

---

^A35:5 Lit the house of the fathers   ^B35:5 Lit the sons of the people, also in vv. 7,12,13   ^C35:11 LXX, Vg, Tg; MT omits blood   ^D35:11 Lit splattered from their hand   ^E35:12 Lit house of fathers   ^F35:21 LXX, Syr, Tg, Vg; MT reads Not against you, you today but I am fighting another dynasty.^A God told me to hurry. Stop opposing God who is with me; don't make him destroy you!"

²² But Josiah did not turn away from him; instead, in order to fight with him he disguised himself.^B He did not listen to Neco's words from the mouth of God, but went to the Valley of Megiddo to fight. ²³ The archers shot King Josiah, and he said to his servants, "Take me away, for I am severely wounded!" ²⁴ So his servants took him out of the war chariot, carried him in his second chariot, and brought him to Jerusalem. Then he died, and they buried him in the tomb of his fathers. All Judah and Jerusalem mourned for Josiah. ²⁵ Jeremiah chanted a dirge over Josiah, and all the male and female singers still speak of Josiah in their dirges today. They established them as a statute for Israel, and indeed they are written in the Dirges.

²⁶ The rest of the events of Josiah's reign, along with his deeds of faithful love according to what is written in the law of the LORD, ²⁷ and his words, from beginning to end, are written in the Book of the Kings of Israel and Judah.

JUDAH'S KING JEHOAHAZ

36 Then the common people^C took Jehoahaz son of Josiah and made him king in Jerusalem in place of his father.

² Jehoahaz^D was twenty-three years old when he became king, and he reigned three months in Jerusalem. ³ The king of Egypt deposed him in Jerusalem and fined the land seventy-five hundred pounds^E of silver and seventy-five pounds^F of gold.

JUDAH'S KING JEHOIAKIM

⁴ Then King Neco of Egypt made Jehoahaz's brother Eliakim king over Judah and Jerusalem and changed Eliakim's name to Jehoiakim. But Neco took his brother Jehoahaz and brought him to Egypt.

⁵ Jehoiakim was twenty-five years old when he became king, and he reigned eleven years in Jerusalem. He did what was evil in the sight of the LORD his God. ⁶ Now King Nebuchadnezzar of Babylon attacked him and bound him in bronze shackles to take him to Babylon. ⁷ Also Nebuchadnezzar took some of the articles of the LORD's temple to Babylon and put them in his temple in Babylon.

⁸ The rest of the deeds of Jehoiakim, the detestable actions he committed, and what was found against him, are written in the Book of Israel's Kings. His son Jehoiachin became king in his place.

JUDAH'S KING JEHOIACHIN

⁹ Jehoiachin was eighteen^G years old when he became king, and he reigned three months and ten days in Jerusalem. He did what was evil in the LORD's sight. ¹⁰ In the spring^H Nebuchadnezzar sent for him and brought him to Babylon along with the valuable articles of the LORD's temple. Then he made Jehoiachin's brother Zedekiah king over Judah and Jerusalem.

---

^A35:21 Lit house   ^B35:22 LXX reads *he was determined*   ^C36:1 Lit *the people of the land*   ^D36:2 = *Joahaz,* also in v. 4   ^E36:3 Lit *100 talents*   ^F36:3 Lit *one talent*   ^G36:9 Some Hb mss, LXX; 2Kg 24:8; other Hb mss read *eight*
^H36:10 Lit *At the return of the year*

JUDAH'S KING ZEDEKIAH

[11] Zedekiah was twenty-one years old when he became king, and he reigned eleven years in Jerusalem. [12] He did what was evil in the sight of the LORD his God and did not humble himself before the prophet Jeremiah at the LORD's command. [13] He also rebelled against King Nebuchadnezzar who had made him swear allegiance by God. He became obstinate[A] and hardened his heart against returning to the LORD, the God of Israel. [14] All the leaders of the priests and the people multiplied their unfaithful deeds, imitating all the detestable practices of the nations, and they defiled the LORD's temple that he had consecrated in Jerusalem.

THE DESTRUCTION OF JERUSALEM

[15] But the LORD, the God of their ancestors sent word against them by the hand of his messengers, sending them time and time again, for he had compassion on his people and on his dwelling place. [16] But they kept ridiculing God's messengers, despising his words, and scoffing at his prophets, until the LORD's wrath was so stirred up against his people that there was no remedy. [17] So he brought up against them the king of the Chaldeans, who killed their fit young men with the sword in the house of their sanctuary. He had no pity on young men or young women, elderly or aged; he handed them all over to him. [18] He took everything to Babylon — all the articles of God's temple, large and small, the treasures of the LORD's temple, and the treasures of the king and his officials. [19] Then the Chaldeans burned God's temple. They tore down Jerusalem's wall, burned all its palaces, and destroyed all its valuable articles.

[20] He deported those who escaped from the sword to Babylon, and they became servants to him and his sons until the rise of the Persian[B] kingdom. [21] This fulfilled the word of the LORD through Jeremiah, and the land enjoyed its Sabbath rest all the days of the desolation until seventy years were fulfilled.

THE DECREE OF CYRUS

[22] In the first year of King Cyrus of Persia, in order to fulfill the word of the LORD spoken through[C] Jeremiah, the LORD roused the spirit of King Cyrus of Persia to issue a proclamation throughout his entire kingdom and also to put it in writing:

[23] This is what King Cyrus of Persia says: The LORD, the God of the heavens, has given me all the kingdoms of the earth and has appointed me to build him a temple at Jerusalem in Judah. Any of his people among you may go up, and may the LORD his God be with him.

THE FOUNDATION OF THE Lord's House HAD BEEN LAID

ezra

They sang with praise and thanksgiving to the LORD: "For he is good; his faithful love to Israel endures forever." Then all the people gave a great shout of praise to the LORD because the foundation of the LORD's house had been laid. **3:11**

ON THE TIMELINE It is commonly believed that Ezra was written shortly after the events of Nehemiah's ministry, no later than 400 BC. The events in Ezra take place between 538 BC and 457 BC. While the author of Ezra is anonymous, it is widely accepted that Ezra wrote the book that bears his name.

A LITTLE BACKGROUND The book of Ezra begins when Cyrus the Great (king of Persia) conquered Babylon in 538 BC and issued a decree, which allowed the Jews to return to Jerusalem from exile and rebuild the temple, fulfilling Jeremiah's prophecy (Ezr 1:1-4; Jr 25:12). However, opposition halted the progress of the temple project. In 515 BC, Darius the Mede issued another decree, which allowed the Jews to finish rebuilding the temple without interruption. The reconstruction continued under the leadership of Zerubbabel (the governor of Jerusalem), Joshua (the high priest), and the prophets Haggai and Zechariah.

Ezra's mission was to realign the hearts of the people to their God and reestablish the system of worship in Jerusalem. His ministry also focused on the adornment of the temple once its construction was complete.

MESSAGE & PURPOSE Ezra continues where 2 Chronicles leaves off. While it provides us with key historical insights, it is also rich with instruction for God's people. A few key themes include:

1. *The continuity of God's people* – The returning exiles experienced a new exodus and remained a part of God's redemptive plan.
2. *Holiness* – For the people to continue the covenant relationship with God, it was important for them to remain separate and pure in matters of doctrine, ethics, and customs.
3. *Scripture* – Ezra and Nehemiah are both noteworthy examples of the power of God at work through the written Word.
4. *Worship* – Only after the place of worship was finished did the people rebuild the walls.
5. *Prayer* – The whole rebuilding of the wall was covered in prayer.

GIVE THANKS FOR THE BOOK OF EZRA:

The events in the book of Ezra—the rebuilding of the temple, the stabilizing of Jerusalem, and the Jewish community that developed—all played key roles leading to the life and ministry of Jesus recorded in the Gospels. The rebuilt temple may have paled in comparison to Solomon's temple, but it would serve as a place of worship for the Jews for centuries until Christ removed the need for a physical temple.

CAS

MEDITERRANEAN
SEA

First Sheshbazzar,
then Zerubbabel, led
groups of Jewish
exiles back to Judah
between approx. 537
and 522 BC

Nehemiah
of the dire
conditions
Judah and
to Jerusale
royal appo

BABYLON

JERUSALEM

SUSA

Under the leadership
of Sheshbazzar and
Zerubbabel, the Jews
began rebuilding the
temple in Jerusalem

Ezra leads a group of
Jews back to Jerusalem.
He is appointed minister
of religious affairs
by Artaxerxes

PER

SYRO-ARABIAN
DESERT

RED
SEA

RETURN TO JERUSALEM

CYRUS' PERSIAN EMPIRE

SHESHBAZZAR'S & ZERUBBABEL'S ROUTE

EZRA'S & NEHEMIAH'S ROUTE

READ AND UNDERSTAND EZRA

The Bible is a complete work in which many stories combine to tell one story. As you read the book of Ezra, consider reading the additional passages to discover how the whole of Scripture works together.

THE DECREE OF CYRUS

1 In the first year of King Cyrus of Persia, in order to fulfill the word of the Lord spoken through Jeremiah, the Lord roused the spirit of King Cyrus to issue a proclamation throughout his entire kingdom and to put it in writing:

² This is what King Cyrus of Persia says: "The Lord, the God of the heavens, has given me all the kingdoms of the earth and has appointed me to build him a house at Jerusalem in Judah. ³ Any of his people among you, may his God be with him, and may he go to Jerusalem in Judah and build the house of the Lord, the God of Israel, the God who is in Jerusalem. ⁴ Let every survivor, wherever he resides, be assisted by the men of that region with silver, gold, goods, and livestock, along with a freewill offering for the house of God in Jerusalem."

RETURN FROM EXILE

⁵ So the family heads of Judah and Benjamin, along with the priests and Levites — everyone whose spirit God had roused — prepared to go up and rebuild the Lord's house in Jerusalem. ⁶ All their neighbors supported them [A] with silver articles, gold, goods, livestock, and valuables, in addition to all that was given as a freewill offering. ⁷ King Cyrus also brought out the articles of the Lord's house that Nebuchadnezzar had taken from Jerusalem and had placed in the house of his gods. ⁸ King Cyrus of Persia had them brought out under the supervision of Mithredath the treasurer, who counted them out to Sheshbazzar the prince of Judah. ⁹ This was the inventory:

30 gold basins, 1,000 silver basins,

29 silver knives, ¹⁰ 30 gold bowls,

410 various [B] silver bowls, and 1,000 other articles.

¹¹ The gold and silver articles totaled 5,400. Sheshbazzar brought all of them when the exiles went up from Babylon to Jerusalem.

THE EXILES WHO RETURNED

2 These now are the people of the province who came from those captive exiles King Nebuchadnezzar of Babylon [C] had deported to Babylon. They returned to Jerusalem and Judah, each to his own town. ² They came with Zerubbabel, Jeshua, Nehemiah, Seraiah, Reelaiah, Mordecai, Bilshan, Mispar, Bigvai, Rehum, and Baanah.

The number of the Israelite men included [D]

³	Parosh's descendants	2,172
⁴	Shephatiah's descendants	372
⁵	Arah's descendants	775
⁶	Pahath-moab's descendants:	
	Jeshua's and Joab's descendants	2,812
⁷	Elam's descendants	1,254
⁸	Zattu's descendants	945
⁹	Zaccai's descendants	760
¹⁰	Bani's descendants	642

[A] 1:6 Lit *strengthened their hands* [B] 1:10 Or *similar* [C] 2:1 Nebuchadnezzar reigned 605–562 BC [D] 2:2 Lit *the men of the people of Israel*

11	Bebai's descendants	623
12	Azgad's descendants	1,222
13	Adonikam's descendants	666
14	Bigvai's descendants	2,056
15	Adin's descendants	454
16	Ater's descendants: of Hezekiah	98
17	Bezai's descendants	323
18	Jorah's descendants	112
19	Hashum's descendants	223
20	Gibbar's descendants	95
21	Bethlehem's people	123
22	Netophah's men	56
23	Anathoth's men	128
24	Azmaveth's people	42
25	Kiriatharim's, Chephirah's, and Beeroth's people	743
26	Ramah's and Geba's people	621
27	Michmas's men	122
28	Bethel's and Ai's men	223
29	Nebo's people	52
30	Magbish's people	156
31	the other Elam's people	1,254
32	Harim's people	320
33	Lod's, Hadid's, and Ono's people	725
34	Jericho's people	345
35	Senaah's people	3,630

³⁶ The priests included
Jedaiah's descendants of the house of Jeshua 973
³⁷ Immer's descendants 1,052
³⁸ Pashhur's descendants 1,247
³⁹ and Harim's descendants 1,017

⁴⁰ The Levites included
Jeshua's and Kadmiel's descendants
from Hodaviah's descendants 74

⁴¹ The singers included
Asaph's descendants 128

⁴² The gatekeepers' descendants included
Shallum's descendants, Ater's descendants,
Talmon's descendants, Akkub's descendants,
Hatita's descendants, Shobai's descendants, in all 139

⁴³ The temple servants included
Ziha's descendants, Hasupha's descendants,
Tabbaoth's descendants, ⁴⁴ Keros's descendants,
Siaha's descendants, Padon's descendants,
⁴⁵ Lebanah's descendants, Hagabah's descendants,
Akkub's descendants, ⁴⁶ Hagab's descendants,

Shalmai's[A] descendants, Hanan's descendants,
47 Giddel's descendants, Gahar's descendants,
Reaiah's descendants, 48 Rezin's descendants,
Nekoda's descendants, Gazzam's descendants,
49 Uzza's descendants, Paseah's descendants,
Besai's descendants, 50 Asnah's descendants,
Meunim's[B] descendants, Nephusim's[C] descendants,
51 Bakbuk's descendants, Hakupha's descendants,
Harhur's descendants, 52 Bazluth's descendants,
Mehida's descendants, Harsha's descendants,
53 Barkos's descendants, Sisera's descendants,
Temah's descendants, 54 Neziah's descendants,
and Hatipha's descendants.

55 The descendants of Solomon's servants included
Sotai's descendants, Hassophereth's descendants,
Peruda's descendants, 56 Jaalah's descendants,
Darkon's descendants, Giddel's descendants,
57 Shephatiah's descendants, Hattil's descendants,
Pochereth-hazzebaim's descendants,
    and Ami's descendants.
58 All the temple servants
and the descendants of Solomon's servants   392.

59 The following are those who came from Tel-melah, Tel-harsha, Cherub, Addan, and Immer but were unable to prove that their ancestral families[D] and their lineage were Israelite:
60 Delaiah's descendants,
Tobiah's descendants,
Nekoda's descendants   652

61 and from the descendants of the priests: the descendants of Hobaiah, the descendants of Hakkoz, the descendants of Barzillai — who had taken a wife from the daughters of Barzillai the Gileadite and who bore their name. 62 These searched for their entries in the genealogical records, but they could not be found, so they were disqualified from the priesthood. 63 The governor ordered them not to eat the most holy things until there was a priest who could consult the Urim and Thummim.

64 The whole combined assembly numbered   42,360
65 not including their 7,337 male and female servants,
and their 200 male and female singers.
66 They had 736 horses, 245 mules,
67 435 camels, and 6,720 donkeys.

GIFTS FOR THE WORK

68 After they arrived at the LORD's house in Jerusalem, some of the family heads gave freewill offerings for the house of God in order to have it rebuilt on its original site. 69 Based on what they could give, they gave 61,000

A 2:46 Alt Hb tradition reads *Shamlai's*   B 2:50 Alt Hb tradition reads *Meinim's*
C 2:50 Alt Hb tradition reads *Nephisim's*   D 2:59 Lit *that the house of their fathers*

gold coins,^ 6,250 pounds^B of silver, and 100 priestly garments to the treasury for the project. ^70^ The priests, Levites, singers, gatekeepers, temple servants, and some of the people settled in their towns, and the rest of Israel settled in their towns.

SACRIFICE RESTORED

3 When the seventh month arrived, and the Israelites were in their towns, the people gathered as one in Jerusalem. ^2^ Jeshua son of Jozadak and his brothers the priests along with Zerubbabel son of Shealtiel and his brothers began to build the altar of Israel's God in order to offer burnt offerings on it, as it is written in the law of Moses, the man of God. ^3^ They set up the altar on its foundation and offered burnt offerings for the morning and evening on it to the Lord even though they feared the surrounding peoples. ^4^ They celebrated the Festival of Shelters as prescribed, and offered burnt offerings each day, based on the number specified by ordinance for each festival day. ^5^ After that, they offered the regular burnt offering and the offerings for the beginning of each month^C and for all the Lord's appointed holy occasions, as well as the freewill offerings brought to^D the Lord.

^6^ On the first day of the seventh month they began to offer burnt offerings to the Lord, even though the foundation of the Lord's temple had not yet been laid. ^7^ They gave money to the stonecutters and artisans, and gave food, drink, and oil to the people of Sidon and Tyre, so they would bring cedar wood from Lebanon to Joppa by sea, according to the authorization given them by King Cyrus of Persia.

REBUILDING THE TEMPLE

^8^ In the second month of the second year after they arrived at God's house in Jerusalem, Zerubbabel son of Shealtiel, Jeshua son of Jozadak, and the rest of their brothers, including the priests, the Levites, and all who had returned to Jerusalem from the captivity, began to build. They appointed the Levites who were twenty years old or more to supervise the work on the Lord's house. ^9^ Jeshua with his sons and brothers, Kadmiel with his sons, and the sons of Judah^E and of Henadad, with their sons and brothers, the Levites, joined together to supervise those working on the house of God.

TEMPLE FOUNDATION COMPLETED

^10^ When the builders had laid the foundation of the Lord's temple, the priests, dressed in their robes and holding trumpets, and the Levites descended from Asaph, holding cymbals, took their positions to praise the Lord, as King David of Israel had instructed. ^11^ They sang with praise and thanksgiving to the Lord: "For he is good; his faithful love to Israel endures forever." Then all the people gave a great shout of praise to the Lord because the foundation of the Lord's house had been laid.

^12^ But many of the older priests, Levites, and family heads, who had seen the first temple, wept loudly when they saw the foundation of this temple, but many others shouted joyfully. ^13^ The people could not distinguish the

---

^A^2:69 Or drachmas, or darics   ^B^2:69 Lit *5,000 minas*   ^C^3:5 Lit *for the new moons*   ^D^3:5 Lit *well as those of everyone making a freewill offering to*
^E^3:9 Or *Hodaviah*; Neh 7:43; 1 Esdras 5:58

PEACE IN UNEXPECTED PLACES

EZRA 2:68–3:13; HAGGAI 2:9

I love the delicate crinkle I hear when I turn a page in my Bible. With each turn I feel like I'm pulling back a little of the curtain and seeing more of who God is. I'm humbled, inspired, enthralled.

In the pages of my Bible, I've discovered that God is our comforter. God is our hope. God is our redeemer.

These knock-your-socks-off statements about God are absolutely true, but I've also realized these qualities are often most clearly seen through the lens of pain.

The Bible tells us God is our comforter, and life has pain. God is our hope, and life is disappointing. God is our redeemer, and our world is broken. God is our savior, and we are sinners.

Ezra 3 tells the story of people who returned from exile with the mission to rebuild the temple that had been destroyed. When the builders finished the foundation, the people came together to celebrate. Ezra 3:11 talks about their joy: "Then all the people gave a great shout of praise to the LORD because the foundation of the LORD's house had been laid." The next verse reveals the disappointment: "But many of the older priests, Levites, and family heads, who had seen the first temple, wept loudly when they saw the foundation of this temple" (Ezr 3:12).

The people weeping had seen the golden walls, smelled the cedar planks, and experienced the overwhelming grandeur of Solomon's temple (1Kg 6). Compared to it, this new one would have seemed like it was an off-brand temple, purchased at a discount store with a coupon.

The difference between "what could have been" and "what is" pierced their hearts with disappointment. I've felt that sting before, too.

We all experience the pain of living in a fallen world. Sometimes it's just dealing with irritating facts of life: houses get messy, workdays drag, cars break, savings accounts shrink. Other times, it's much bigger. It's loss and pain that leave scars never fully healed until heaven. Babies die. Cancer spreads. Loneliness aches.

But if we follow the story of the people rebuilding the temple, we pull back more of the curtain to once again see God's power and grace shining brightly.

This is the Lord's declaration over the new temple in Haggai 2:9: "The final glory of this house will be greater than the first," says the LORD of Armies. "I will provide peace in this place."

"I will provide peace..." What powerful words!

God invites us to bring our pain and disappointment into His presence. And then He declares a mighty statement over our broken places: He will make the glory of our future great, even if it looks different from what we expected or ever wanted. He will provide peace.

sound of the joyful shouting from that of the[A] weeping, because the people were shouting so loudly. And the sound was heard far away.

OPPOSITION TO REBUILDING THE TEMPLE

4 When the enemies of Judah and Benjamin heard that the returned exiles[B] were building a temple for the Lord, the God of Israel, ² they approached Zerubbabel and the family heads and said to them, "Let us build with you, for we also worship your God and have been sacrificing to him[C] since the time King Esar-haddon of Assyria brought us here."

³ But Zerubbabel, Jeshua, and the other heads of Israel's families answered them, "You may have no part with us in building a house for our God, since we alone will build it for the Lord, the God of Israel, as King Cyrus, the king of Persia has commanded us." ⁴ Then the people who were already in the land[D] discouraged[E] the people of Judah and made them afraid to build. ⁵ They also bribed officials to act against them to frustrate their plans throughout the reign of King Cyrus of Persia and until the reign of King Darius of Persia.

OPPOSITION TO REBUILDING THE CITY

⁶ At the beginning of the reign of Ahasuerus, the people who were already in the land wrote an accusation against the residents of Judah and Jerusalem. ⁷ During the time of King Artaxerxes of Persia, Bishlam, Mithredath, Tabeel and the rest of his colleagues wrote to King Artaxerxes. The letter was written in Aramaic and translated.[F]

⁸ Rehum the chief deputy and Shimshai the scribe wrote a letter to King Artaxerxes concerning Jerusalem as follows:

⁹ From Rehum[G] the chief deputy, Shimshai the scribe, and the rest of their colleagues — the judges and magistrates[H] from Tripolis, Persia, Erech, Babylon, Susa (that is, the people of Elam),[I] ¹⁰ and the rest of the peoples whom the great and illustrious Ashurbanipal[J] deported and settled in the cities of Samaria and the region west of the Euphrates River.

¹¹ This is the text of the letter they sent to him:

To King Artaxerxes from your servants, the men from the region west of the Euphrates River:

¹² Let it be known to the king that the Jews who came from you have returned to us at Jerusalem. They are rebuilding that rebellious and evil city, finishing its walls, and repairing its foundations. ¹³ Let it now be known to the king that if that city is rebuilt and its walls are finished, they will not pay tribute, duty, or land tax, and the royal revenue[I] will suffer. ¹⁴ Since we have taken an oath of loyalty to the king,[K] and it is not right for us to witness his dishonor, we have sent to inform the king ¹⁵ that a search should be made in your fathers' record books. In these record books you will discover and verify that the city is a rebellious city, harmful to kings and provinces. There have been revolts in it since

---

[A]3:13 Lit *the people*   [B]4:1 Lit *the sons of the exile*   [C]4:2 Alt Hb tradition reads *have not been sacrificing*   [D]4:4 Lit *people of the land,* also in v. 6   [E]4:4 Lit *weakened the hands of*   [F]4:7 Ezr 4:8–6:18 is written in Aramaic.   [G]4:9 Lit *Then Rehum*   [H]4:9 Or *ambassadors*   [I]4:9,13 Aramaic obscure   [J]4:10 Lit *Osnappar*   [K]4:14 Lit *have eaten the salt of the palace* ancient times. That is why this city was destroyed. ¹⁶ We advise the king that if this city is rebuilt and its walls are finished, you will not have any possession west of the Euphrates.

ARTAXERXES'S REPLY

¹⁷ The king sent a reply to his chief deputy Rehum, Shimshai the scribe, and the rest of their colleagues living in Samaria and elsewhere in the region west of the Euphrates River:

Greetings.

¹⁸ The letter you sent us has been translated and read ᴬ in my presence. ¹⁹ I issued a decree and a search was conducted. It was discovered that this city has had uprisings against kings since ancient times, and there have been rebellions and revolts in it. ²⁰ Powerful kings have also ruled over Jerusalem and exercised authority over the whole region west of the Euphrates River, and tribute, duty, and land tax were paid to them. ²¹ Therefore, issue an order for these men to stop, so that this city will not be rebuilt until a further decree has been pronounced by me. ²² See that you not neglect this matter. Otherwise, the damage will increase and the royal interests ᴮ will suffer.

²³ As soon as the text of King Artaxerxes's letter was read to Rehum, Shimshai the scribe, and their colleagues, they immediately went to the Jews in Jerusalem and forcibly stopped them.

REBUILDING OF THE TEMPLE RESUMED

²⁴ Now the construction of God's house in Jerusalem had stopped and remained at a standstill until the second year of the reign of King Darius of Persia. ¹ But when the prophets Haggai and Zechariah son of Iddo prophesied to the Jews who were in Judah and Jerusalem, in the name of the God of Israel who was over them, ² Zerubbabel son of Shealtiel and Jeshua son of Jozadak began to rebuild God's house in Jerusalem. The prophets of God were with them, helping them.

³ At that time Tattenai the governor of the region west of the Euphrates River, Shethar-bozenai, and their colleagues came to the Jews and asked, "Who gave you the order to rebuild this temple and finish this structure?" ᶜ ⁴ They also asked them, "What are the names of the workers ᴰ who are constructing this building?" ⁵ But God was watching ᴱ over the Jewish elders. These men wouldn't stop them until a report was sent to Darius, so that they could receive written instructions about this matter.

THE LETTER TO DARIUS

⁶ This is the text of the letter that Tattenai the governor of the region west of the Euphrates River, Shethar-bozenai, and their colleagues, the officials in the region, sent to King Darius. ⁷ They sent him a report, written as follows:

To King Darius:

ᴬ4:18 Or *been read clearly*   ᴮ4:22 Lit *the kings*   ᶜ5:3 Or *finish its furnishings,* also in v. 9   ᴰ5:4 One Aramaic ms, LXX, Syr; MT reads *Then we told them exactly what the names of the men were*   ᴱ5:5 Lit *But the eye of their God was*

All greetings.

[8] Let it be known to the king that we went to the house of the great God in the province of Judah. It is being built with cut[A] stones, and its beams are being set in the walls. This work is being done diligently and succeeding through the people's efforts. [9] So we questioned the elders and asked, "Who gave you the order to rebuild this temple and finish this structure?" [10] We also asked them for their names, so that we could write down the names of their leaders for your information.

[11] This is the reply they gave us:

We are the servants of the God of the heavens and earth, and we are rebuilding the temple that was built many years ago, which a great king of Israel built and finished. [12] But since our fathers angered the God of the heavens, he handed them over to King Nebuchadnezzar of Babylon, the Chaldean, who destroyed this temple and deported the people to Babylon. [13] However, in the first year of King Cyrus of Babylon, he issued a decree to rebuild the house of God. [14] He also took from the temple in Babylon the gold and silver articles of God's house that Nebuchadnezzar had taken from the temple in Jerusalem and carried them to the temple in Babylon. He released them from the temple in Babylon to a man named Sheshbazzar, the governor by the appointment of King Cyrus. [15] Cyrus told him, "Take these articles, put them in the temple in Jerusalem, and let the house of God be rebuilt on its original site." [16] Then this same Sheshbazzar came and laid the foundation of God's house in Jerusalem. It has been under construction from that time until now, but it has not been completed.

[17] So if it pleases the king, let a search of the royal archives[B] in Babylon be conducted to see if it is true that a decree was issued by King Cyrus to rebuild the house of God in Jerusalem. Let the king's decision regarding this matter be sent to us.

DARIUS'S SEARCH

6 King Darius gave the order, and they searched in the library of Babylon in the archives.[C] [2] But it was in the fortress of Ecbatana in the province of Media that a scroll was found with this record written on it:
[3] In the first year of King Cyrus, he issued a decree concerning the house of God in Jerusalem:

Let the house be rebuilt as a place for offering sacrifices, and let its original foundations be retained.[D] Its height is to be ninety feet[E] and its width ninety feet, [4] with three layers of cut[A] stones and one of timber. The cost is to be paid from the royal treasury.[F] [5] The gold and silver articles of God's house that Nebuchadnezzar took from the temple in

---

[A]5:8; 6:4 Or *huge*   [B]5:17 Lit *treasure house*   [C]6:1 Lit *Babylon where the treasures were stored*   [D]6:3 Lit *be brought forth*   [E]6:3 Lit *60 cubits*   [F]6:4 Lit *the king's house*

Jerusalem and carried to Babylon must also be returned. They are to be brought to the temple in Jerusalem where they belong^A and put into the house of God.

DARIUS'S DECREE

⁶ Therefore, you must stay away from that place, Tattenai governor of the region west of the Euphrates River, Shethar-bozenai, and your^B colleagues, the officials in the region. ⁷ Leave the construction of the house of God alone. Let the governor and elders of the Jews rebuild this house of God on its original site.

⁸ I hereby issue a decree concerning what you are to do, so that the elders of the Jews can rebuild the house of God:

The cost is to be paid in full to these men out of the royal revenues from the taxes of the region west of the Euphrates River, so that the work will not stop. ⁹ Whatever is needed — young bulls, rams, and lambs for burnt offerings to the God of the heavens, or wheat, salt, wine, and oil, as requested by the priests in Jerusalem — let it be given to them every day without fail, ¹⁰ so that they can offer sacrifices of pleasing aroma to the God of the heavens and pray for the life of the king and his sons.

¹¹ I also issue a decree concerning any man who interferes with this directive:

Let a beam be torn from his house and raised up; he will be impaled on it, and his house will be made into a garbage dump because of this offense. ¹² May the God who caused his name to dwell there overthrow any king or people who dares^C to harm or interfere with this house of God in Jerusalem. I, Darius, have issued the decree. Let it be carried out diligently.

¹³ Then Tattenai governor of the region west of the Euphrates River, Shethar-bozenai, and their colleagues diligently carried out what King Darius had decreed. ¹⁴ So the Jewish elders continued successfully with the building under the prophesying of Haggai the prophet and Zechariah son of Iddo. They finished the building according to the command of the God of Israel and the decrees of Cyrus, Darius, and King Artaxerxes of Persia. ¹⁵ This house was completed on the third day of the month of Adar in the sixth year of the reign of King Darius.

TEMPLE DEDICATION AND THE PASSOVER

¹⁶ Then the Israelites, including the priests, the Levites, and the rest of the exiles, celebrated the dedication of the house of God with joy. ¹⁷ For the dedication of God's house they offered one hundred bulls, two hundred rams, and four hundred lambs, as well as twelve male goats as a sin offering for all Israel — one for each Israelite tribe. ¹⁸ They also appointed the priests by

---

^A 6:5 Lit Jerusalem, to its place,   ^B 6:6 Lit their   ^C 6:12 Lit who stretches out its hand their divisions and the Levites by their groups to the service of God in Jerusalem, according to what is written in the book of Moses.

¹⁹ The exiles observed the Passover on the fourteenth day of the first month. ²⁰ All of the priests and Levites were ceremonially clean, because they had purified themselves. They killed the Passover lamb for themselves, their priestly brothers, and all the exiles. ²¹ The Israelites who had returned from exile ate it, together with all who had separated themselves from the uncleanness of the Gentiles of the land ᴬ in order to worship the Lᴏʀᴅ, the God of Israel. ²² They observed the Festival of Unleavened Bread for seven days with joy, because the Lᴏʀᴅ had made them joyful, having changed the Assyrian king's attitude toward them, so that he supported them ᴮ in the work on the house of the God of Israel.

EZRA'S ARRIVAL

7 After these events, during the reign of King Artaxerxes of Persia, Ezra — Seraiah's son, Azariah's son,
Hilkiah's son, ² Shallum's son,
Zadok's son, Ahitub's son,
³ Amariah's son, Azariah's son,
Meraioth's son, ⁴ Zerahiah's son,
Uzzi's son, Bukki's son,
⁵ Abishua's son, Phinehas's son,
Eleazar's son, the chief priest Aaron's son
⁶ — came up from Babylon. He was a scribe skilled in the law of Moses, which the Lᴏʀᴅ, the God of Israel, had given. The king had granted him everything he requested because the hand of the Lᴏʀᴅ his God was on him. ⁷ Some of the Israelites, priests, Levites, singers, gatekeepers, and temple servants accompanied him to Jerusalem in the seventh year of King Artaxerxes.

⁸ Ezra ᶜ came to Jerusalem in the fifth month, during the seventh year of the king. ⁹ He began the journey from Babylon on the first day of the first month and arrived in Jerusalem on the first day of the fifth month since the gracious hand of his God was on him. ¹⁰ Now Ezra had determined in his heart to study the law of the Lᴏʀᴅ, obey it, and teach its statutes and ordinances in Israel.

LETTER FROM ARTAXERXES

¹¹ This is the text of the letter King Artaxerxes gave to Ezra the priest and scribe, an expert in matters of the Lᴏʀᴅ's commands and statutes for Israel: ᴰ

¹² Artaxerxes, king of kings, to Ezra the priest, an expert in the law of the God of the heavens:

Greetings.

¹³ I issue a decree that any of the Israelites in my kingdom, including their priests and Levites, who want to go to Jerusalem, may go with you. ¹⁴ You are sent by the king and his seven counselors to evaluate Judah and Jerusalem according to the law of your God, which is in your

---

ᴬ6:21 Lit *land to them*   ᴮ6:22 Lit *strengthened their hands*   ᶜ7:8 LXX, Syr, Vg read *They*   ᴰ7:11 Ezr 7:12-26 is written in Aramaic.

possession. ¹⁵ You are also to bring the silver and gold the king and his counselors have willingly given to the God of Israel, whose dwelling is in Jerusalem, ¹⁶ and all the silver and gold you receive throughout the province of Babylon, together with the freewill offerings given by the people and the priests to the house of their God in Jerusalem. ¹⁷ Then you are to be diligent to buy with this money bulls, rams, and lambs, along with their grain and drink offerings, and offer them on the altar at the house of your God in Jerusalem. ¹⁸ You may do whatever seems best to you and your brothers with the rest of the silver and gold, according to the will of your God. ¹⁹ Deliver to the God of Jerusalem all the articles given to you for the service of the house of your God. ²⁰ You may use the royal treasury^A to pay for anything else needed for the house of your God.

²¹ I, King Artaxerxes, issue a decree to all the treasurers in the region west of the Euphrates River:

Whatever Ezra the priest, an expert in the law of the God of the heavens, asks of you must be provided in full, ²² up to 7,500 pounds^B of silver, 500 bushels^C of wheat, 550 gallons^D of wine, 550 gallons of oil, and salt without limit.^{E} ²³ Whatever is commanded by the God of heaven must be done diligently for the house of the God of the heavens, so that wrath will not fall on the realm of the king and his sons. ²⁴ Be advised that you do not have authority to impose tribute, duty, and land tax on any priests, Levites, singers, doorkeepers, temple servants, or other servants of this house of God.

²⁵ And you, Ezra, according to^F God's wisdom that you possess, appoint magistrates and judges to judge all the people in the region west of the Euphrates who know the laws of your God and to teach anyone who does not know them. ²⁶ Anyone who does not keep the law of your God and the law of the king, let the appropriate judgment be executed against him, whether death, banishment, confiscation of property, or imprisonment.

²⁷ Blessed be the Lᴏʀᴅ, the God of our fathers, who has put it into the king's mind to glorify the house of the Lᴏʀᴅ in Jerusalem, ²⁸ and who has shown favor to me before the king, his counselors, and all his powerful officers. So I took courage because I was strengthened by the hand of the Lᴏʀᴅ my God,^{G} and I gathered Israelite leaders to return with me.

THOSE RETURNING WITH EZRA

8 These are the family heads and the genealogical records of those who returned with me from Babylon during the reign of King Artaxerxes:
² Gershom, from Phinehas's descendants;
Daniel, from Ithamar's descendants;
Hattush, from David's descendants,

---

^{A}7:20 Lit the king's house ^{B}7:22 Lit 100 talents ^{C}7:22 Lit 100 cors ^{D}7:22 Lit 100 baths ^{E}7:22 Lit without instruction ^{F}7:25 Lit to your ^{G}7:28 Lit because the hand of the Lᴏʀᴅ my God was on me

3   who was of Shecaniah's descendants;
    Zechariah, from Parosh's descendants,
    and 150 men^A with him who were registered by genealogy;
4   Eliehoenai son of Zerahiah
    from Pahath-moab's descendants,
    and 200 men with him;
5   Shecaniah^B son of Jahaziel
    from Zattu's descendants,
    and 300 men with him;
6   Ebed son of Jonathan
    from Adin's descendants,
    and 50 men with him;
7   Jeshaiah son of Athaliah
    from Elam's descendants,
    and 70 men with him;
8   Zebadiah son of Michael
    from Shephatiah's descendants,
    and 80 men with him;
9   Obadiah son of Jehiel
    from Joab's descendants,
    and 218 men with him;
10 Shelomith^C son of Josiphiah
    from Bani's descendants,
    and 160 men with him;
11 Zechariah son of Bebai
    from Bebai's descendants,
    and 28 men with him;
12 Johanan son of Hakkatan
    from Azgad's descendants,
    and 110 men with him;
13 these are the last ones, from Adonikam's descendants,
    and their names are
    Eliphelet, Jeuel, and Shemaiah,
    and 60 men with them;
14 Uthai and Zaccur^D
    from Bigvai's descendants,
    and 70 men with them.

¹⁵ I gathered them at the river^E that flows to Ahava, and we camped there for three days. I searched among the people and priests, but found no Levites there. ¹⁶ Then I summoned the leaders: Eliezer, Ariel, Shemaiah, Elnathan, Jarib, Elnathan, Nathan, Zechariah, and Meshullam, as well as the teachers Joiarib and Elnathan. ¹⁷ I sent them to Iddo, the leader at Casiphia, with a message for^F him and his brothers, the temple servants at Casiphia, that they should bring us ministers for the house of our God. ¹⁸ Since the gracious

---

^A8:3 Or *males*; also in vv. 4-14   ^B8:5 LXX, 1 Esdras 8:32; MT reads *the descendants of Shecaniah*   ^C8:10 Some LXX mss, 1 Esdras 8:36; MT reads *the descendants of Shelomith*   ^D8:14 Alt Hb tradition, some LXX mss read *Zabud*   ^E8:15 Or *canal*
^F8:17 Lit *Casiphia, and I put in their mouth the words to speak to*

hand of our God was on us, they brought us Sherebiah — a man of insight from the descendants of Mahli, a descendant of Levi son of Israel — along with his sons and brothers, 18 men, ¹⁹ plus Hashabiah, along with Jeshaiah, from the descendants of Merari, and his brothers and their sons, 20 men. ²⁰ There were also 220 of the temple servants, who had been appointed by David and the leaders for the work of the Levites. All were identified by name.

PREPARING TO RETURN

²¹ I proclaimed a fast by the Ahava River,ᴬ so that we might humble ourselves before our God and ask him for a safe journey for us, our dependents, and all our possessions. ²² I did this because I was ashamed to ask the king for infantry and cavalry to protect us from enemies during the journey, since we had told him, "The hand of our God is gracious to all who seek him, but his fierce anger is against all who abandon him." ²³ So we fasted and pleaded with our God about this, and he was receptive to our prayer.

²⁴ I selected twelve of the leading priests, along with Sherebiah, Hashabiah, and ten of their brothers. ²⁵ I weighed out to them the silver, the gold, and the articles — the contribution for the house of our God that the king, his counselors, his leaders, and all the Israelites who were present had offered. ²⁶ I weighed out to them 24 tonsᴮ of silver, silver articles weighing 7,500 pounds,ᶜ 7,500 pounds of gold, ²⁷ twenty gold bowls worth a thousand gold coins,ᴰ and two articles of fine gleaming bronze, as valuable as gold. ²⁸ Then I said to them, "You are holy to the LORD, and the articles are holy. The silver and gold are a freewill offering to the LORD God of your fathers. ²⁹ Guard them carefully until you weigh them out in the chambers of the LORD's house before the leading priests, Levites, and heads of the Israelite families in Jerusalem." ³⁰ So the priests and Levites took charge of the silver, the gold, and the articles that had been weighed out, to bring them to the house of our God in Jerusalem.

ARRIVAL IN JERUSALEM

³¹ We set out from the Ahava River on the twelfth day of the first month to go to Jerusalem. We were strengthened by our God,ᴱ and he kept us from the grasp of the enemy and from ambush along the way. ³² So we arrived at Jerusalem and rested there for three days. ³³ On the fourth day the silver, the gold, and the articles were weighed out in the house of our God into the care of the priest Meremoth son of Uriah. Eleazar son of Phinehas was with him. The Levites Jozabad son of Jeshua and Noadiah son of Binnui were also with them. ³⁴ Everything was verified by number and weight, and the total weight was recorded at that time.

³⁵ The exiles who had returned from the captivity offered burnt offerings to the God of Israel: twelve bulls for all Israel, ninety-six rams, and seventy-seven lambs, along with twelve male goats as a sin offering. All this was a burnt offering for the LORD. ³⁶ They also delivered the king's edicts to the royal satraps and governors of the region west of the Euphrates, so that they would support the people and the house of God.

ᴬ8:21 Or *Canal*, also in v. 31   ᴮ8:26 Lit *650 talents*   ᶜ8:26 Lit *100 talents*
ᴰ8:27 Or *1,000 drachmas*, or *1,000 darics*   ᴱ8:31 Lit *The hand of our God was on us*

ISRAEL'S INTERMARRIAGE

9 After these things had been done, the leaders approached me and said: "The people of Israel, the priests, and the Levites have not separated themselves from the surrounding peoples whose detestable practices are like those of the Canaanites, Hethites, Perizzites, Jebusites, Ammonites, Moabites, Egyptians, and Amorites. ² Indeed, the Israelite men[A] have taken some of their daughters as wives for themselves and their sons, so that the holy seed has become mixed with the surrounding peoples. The leaders[B] and officials have taken the lead in this unfaithfulness!" ³ When I heard this report, I tore my tunic and robe, pulled out some of the hair from my head and beard, and sat down devastated.

EZRA'S CONFESSION

⁴ Everyone who trembled at the words of the God of Israel gathered around me, because of the unfaithfulness of the exiles, while I sat devastated until the evening offering. ⁵ At the evening offering, I got up from my time of humiliation, with my tunic and robe torn. Then I fell on my knees and spread out my hands to the LORD my God. ⁶ And I said:

My God, I am ashamed and embarrassed to lift my face toward you, my God, because our iniquities are higher than our heads and our guilt is as high as the heavens. ⁷ Our guilt has been terrible from the days of our fathers until the present. Because of our iniquities we have been handed over, along with our kings and priests, to the surrounding kings, and to the sword, captivity, plundering, and open shame, as it is today. ⁸ But now, for a brief moment, grace has come from the LORD our God to preserve a remnant for us and give us a stake in his holy place. Even in our slavery, God has given us a little relief and light to our eyes. ⁹ Though we are slaves, our God has not abandoned us in our slavery. He has extended grace to us in the presence of the Persian kings, giving us relief, so that we can rebuild the house of our God and repair its ruins, to give us a wall in Judah and Jerusalem.

¹⁰ Now, our God, what can we say in light of[C] this? For we have abandoned the commands ¹¹ you gave through your servants the prophets, saying: "The land you are entering to possess is an impure land. The surrounding peoples have filled it from end to end with their uncleanness by their impurity and detestable practices. ¹² So do not give your daughters to their sons in marriage or take their daughters for your sons. Never pursue their welfare or prosperity, so that you will be strong, eat the good things of the land, and leave it as an inheritance to your sons forever." ¹³ After all that has happened to us because of our evil deeds and terrible guilt — though you, our God, have punished us less than our iniquities deserve and have allowed us to survive[D] — ¹⁴ should we break your commands again and intermarry with the peoples who commit these detestable practices? Wouldn't you become so angry with us that you would destroy us, leaving neither remnant nor survivor? ¹⁵ LORD God of Israel, you are righteous, for we survive as a

---

^A 9:2 Lit *they*   ^B 9:2 Lit *hand of the leaders*   ^C 9:10 Lit *say after*   ^D 9:13 Lit *and gave us a remnant like this* remnant today. Here we are before you with our guilt, though no one can stand in your presence because of this.

SENDING AWAY FOREIGN WIVES

10 While Ezra prayed and confessed, weeping and falling facedown before the house of God, an extremely large assembly of Israelite men, women, and children gathered around him. The people also wept bitterly. ² Then Shecaniah son of Jehiel, an Elamite, responded to Ezra: "We have been unfaithful to our God by marrying foreign women from the surrounding peoples, but there is still hope for Israel in spite of this. ³ Let us therefore make a covenant before our God to send away all the foreign wives and their children, according to the counsel of my lord and of those who tremble at the command of our God. Let it be done according to the law. ⁴ Get up, for this matter is your responsibility, and we support you. Be strong and take action!"

⁵ Then Ezra got up and made the leading priests, Levites, and all Israel take an oath to do what had been said; so they took the oath. ⁶ Ezra then went from the house of God and walked to the chamber of Jehohanan son of Eliashib, where he spent the night.ᴬ He did not eat food or drink water, because he was mourning over the unfaithfulness of the exiles.

⁷ They circulated a proclamation throughout Judah and Jerusalem that all the exiles should gather at Jerusalem. ⁸ Whoever did not come within three days would forfeit all his possessions,ᴮ according to the decision of the leaders and elders, and would be excluded from the assembly of the exiles.

⁹ So all the men of Judah and Benjamin gathered in Jerusalem within the three days. On the twentieth day of the ninth month, all the people sat in the square at the house of God, trembling because of this matter and because of the heavy rain. ¹⁰ Then the priest Ezra stood up and said to them, "You have been unfaithful by marrying foreign women, adding to Israel's guilt. ¹¹ Therefore, make a confession to the LORD, the God of your fathers, and do his will. Separate yourselves from the surrounding peoples and your foreign wives."

¹² Then all the assembly responded loudly: "Yes, we will do as you say! ¹³ But there are many people, and it is the rainy season. We don't have the stamina to stay out in the open. This isn't something that can be done in a day or two, for we have rebelled terribly in this matter. ¹⁴ Let our leaders represent the entire assembly. Then let all those in our towns who have married foreign women come at appointed times, together with the elders and judges of each town, in order to avert the fierce anger of our God concerningᶜ this matter." ¹⁵ Only Jonathan son of Asahel and Jahzeiah son of Tikvah opposed this, with Meshullam and Shabbethai the Levite supporting them.

¹⁶ The exiles did what had been proposed. The priest Ezra selected menᴰ who were family heads, all identified by name, to representᴱ their ancestral families.ᶠ They convened on the first day of the tenth month to investigate the matter, ¹⁷ and by the first day of the first month they had dealt with all the men who had married foreign women.

ᴬ10:6 1 Esdras 9:2, Syr; MT, Vg read *he went*   ᴮ10:8 Lit *would set apart all his possessions for destruction*   ᶜ10:14 Some Hb mss, LXX, Vg; other Hb mss read *until*   ᴰ10:16 1 Esdras 9:16, Syr; MT, Vg read *priest and men were selected*   ᴱ10:16 Lit *name, for*   ᶠ10:16 Lit *the house of their fathers*

THOSE MARRIED TO FOREIGN WIVES

¹⁸ The following were found to have married foreign women from the descendants of the priests:

from the descendants of Jeshua son of Jozadak and his brothers:
Maaseiah, Eliezer, Jarib, and Gedaliah. ¹⁹ They pledged[A] to send their wives away, and being guilty, they offered a ram from the flock for their guilt;

20 Hanani and Zebadiah from Immer's descendants;
21 Maaseiah, Elijah, Shemaiah, Jehiel, and Uzziah
        from Harim's descendants;
22 Elioenai, Maaseiah, Ishmael, Nethanel, Jozabad, and Elasah
        from Pashhur's descendants.

²³ The Levites:
Jozabad, Shimei, Kelaiah (that is Kelita), Pethahiah, Judah, and Eliezer.

²⁴ The singers:
Eliashib.

The gatekeepers:
Shallum, Telem, and Uri.

²⁵ The Israelites:
Parosh's descendants: Ramiah, Izziah, Malchijah, Mijamin, Eleazar,
    Malchijah,[B] and Benaiah;
26 Elam's descendants: Mattaniah, Zechariah, Jehiel, Abdi, Jeremoth,
        and Elijah;
27 Zattu's descendants: Elioenai, Eliashib, Mattaniah, Jeremoth, Zabad,
        and Aziza;
28 Bebai's descendants: Jehohanan, Hananiah, Zabbai, and Athlai;
29 Bani's descendants: Meshullam, Malluch, Adaiah, Jashub, Sheal,
        and Jeremoth;
30 Pahath-moab's descendants: Adna, Chelal, Benaiah, Maaseiah,
        Mattaniah, Bezalel, Binnui, and Manasseh;
31 Harim's descendants: Eliezer, Isshijah, Malchijah, Shemaiah,
        Shimeon, ³² Benjamin, Malluch, and Shemariah;
33 Hashum's descendants: Mattenai, Mattattah, Zabad, Eliphelet,
        Jeremai, Manasseh, and Shimei;

³⁴ Bani's descendants: Maadai, Amram, Uel, ³⁵ Benaiah, Bedeiah, Cheluhi, ³⁶ Vaniah, Meremoth, Eliashib, ³⁷ Mattaniah, Mattenai, Jaasu, ³⁸ Bani, Binnui, Shimei, ³⁹ Shelemiah, Nathan, Adaiah, ⁴⁰ Machnadebai, Shashai, Sharai, ⁴¹ Azarel, Shelemiah, Shemariah, ⁴² Shallum, Amariah, and Joseph;

43 Nebo's descendants: Jeiel, Mattithiah, Zabad, Zebina, Jaddai, Joel,
        and Benaiah.

⁴⁴ All of these had married foreign women, and some of the wives had given birth to children.

[A]10:19 Lit gave their hand   [B]10:25 Some LXX mss, 1 Esdras 9:26 read Hashabiah

Come, Let's Rebuild Jerusalem's Wall

nehemiah

 So I said to them, "You see the trouble we are in. Jerusalem lies in ruins and its gates have been burned. Come, let's rebuild Jerusalem's wall, so that we will no longer be a disgrace." **2:17**

ON THE TIMELINE Nehemiah was written in the late fifth century BC. Nehemiah's ministry in Jerusalem occurred in 444 BC, after he led the third major group of exiles back to Jerusalem. The Jews had been released by the decree of Cyrus in 538 BC and were allowed to return to Jerusalem at that time, though many of them remained in Babylon and Persia.

A LITTLE BACKGROUND Nehemiah was the cupbearer to Persia's Artaxerxes I. Nehemiah returned to Jerusalem under a special leave of absence from the king and led the returned exiles in rebuilding the walls of Jerusalem, resettling Jerusalem, and reestablishing the Law in Israel. While the author of Nehemiah is anonymous, ancient Jewish sources usually credit Ezra as the author of both Ezra and Nehemiah.

Until the third century AD, the books of Ezra and Nehemiah were regarded as a single book. Both books contain material found in the other, and in many ways they complete each other. In the Jewish community, Ezra and Nehemiah were not separated into two distinct books until the fifteenth-century printing of the Hebrew Bible.

MESSAGE & PURPOSE The book of Nehemiah records the rebuilding of the walls in Jerusalem despite opposition and difficulty. Nehemiah exhorts the people to remain faithful to the Lord and return to Him in the restored capital of Israel. It is written to the people of Israel to remind them of God's redemptive plan; to encourage them to remain separate and pure in matters of doctrine, ethics, and customs; and to remain steadfast in their covenant with God.

GIVE THANKS FOR THE BOOK OF NEHEMIAH:

The events that occurred in Nehemiah—the rebuilding of the wall, the stabilizing of Jerusalem, and the Jewish community that developed—all played key roles leading to the life and ministry of Jesus recorded in the Gospels. The rebuilt temple may have paled in comparison to Solomon's temple, but it would serve as a place of worship for the Jews for centuries until Christ removed the need for a physical temple.

TOWER OF
HANANEL

TOWER OF
THE HUNDRED

FISH GATE

SHEEP GATE

MUSTER GATE

TEMPLE

EAST GATE

HORSE GATE

GREAT
PROJECTING
TOWER

WESTERN HILLTOP

VALLEY GATE

WATER GATE

NEHEMIAH'S
NIGHT WALK

OLDER WALL

KIDRON VALLEY

POOL OF SILOAM

FOUNTAIN GATE

STAIRS
DESCENDING
FROM THE CITY
OF DAVID

JERUSALEM'S WALL

READ AND UNDERSTAND NEHEMIAH

The Bible is a complete work in which many stories combine to tell one story. As you read the book of Nehemiah, consider reading the additional passages to discover how the whole of Scripture works together.

1

The words of Nehemiah son of Hacaliah:

NEWS FROM JERUSALEM

During the month of Chislev in the twentieth year, when I was in the fortress city of Susa, [2] Hanani, one of my brothers, arrived with men from Judah, and I questioned them about Jerusalem and the Jewish remnant that had survived the exile. [3] They said to me, "The remnant in the province, who survived the exile, are in great trouble and disgrace. Jerusalem's wall has been broken down, and its gates have been burned."

NEHEMIAH'S PRAYER

[4] When I heard these words, I sat down and wept. I mourned for a number of days, fasting and praying before the God of the heavens. [5] I said,

LORD, the God of the heavens, the great and awe-inspiring God who keeps his gracious covenant with those who love him and keep his commands, [6] let your eyes be open and your ears be attentive to hear your servant's prayer that I now pray to you day and night for your servants, the Israelites. I confess the sins[A] we have committed against you. Both I and my father's family have sinned. [7] We have acted corruptly toward you and have not kept the commands, statutes, and ordinances you gave your servant Moses. [8] Please remember what you commanded your servant Moses: "If you are unfaithful, I will scatter you among the peoples. [9] But if you return to me and carefully observe my commands, even though your exiles were banished to the farthest horizon,[B] I will gather them from there and bring them to the place where I chose to have my name dwell." [10] They are your servants and your people. You redeemed them by your great power and strong hand. [11] Please, Lord, let your ear be attentive to the prayer of your servant and to that of your servants who delight to revere your name. Give your servant success today, and grant him compassion in the presence of this man.[C]

At the time, I was the king's cupbearer.

NEHEMIAH SENT TO JERUSALEM

2

During the month of Nisan in the twentieth year of King Artaxerxes, when wine was set before him, I took the wine and gave it to the king. I had never been sad in his presence, [2] so the king said to me, "Why are you[D] sad, when you aren't sick? This is nothing but sadness of heart."

I was overwhelmed with fear [3] and replied to the king, "May the king live forever! Why should I[E] not be sad when the city where my ancestors are buried lies in ruins and its gates have been destroyed by fire?"

[4] Then the king asked me, "What is your request?"

So I prayed to the God of the heavens [5] and answered the king, "If it pleases the king, and if your servant has found favor with you, send me to Judah and to the city where my ancestors are buried,[F] so that I may rebuild it."

[6] The king, with the queen seated beside him, asked me, "How long will your journey take, and when will you return?" So I gave him a definite time, and it pleased the king to send me.

[A] 1:6 Lit sins of the Israelites [B] 1:9 Lit skies [C] 1:11 = the king [D] 2:2 Lit "Why is your face [E] 2:3 Lit my face [F] 2:5 Lit city, the house of the graves of my fathers,

HE IS LISTENING

NEHEMIAH 1; PSALM 35:13; MARK 2:1-12

Do you remember the story in Mark 2 of the four men who wanted desperately to get their paralyzed friend to Jesus? They heard Jesus was in town, and they carried their buddy on a stretcher to where He was. The house was so crowded with people that the door was completely blocked, but they were not deterred. The men wanted healing for their friend, so they carried him up onto the roof, cut a hole, and lowered him into the center of the room.

First of all, I want friends like these guys! And second, their persistence paid off. Jesus forgave the man's sins right away, because no matter how sick we are, our sin is always more profound. Then Jesus told the man, "get up, take your mat, and go home" (Mk 2:11).

The four men were willing to put aside all earthly sensibilities because their friend needed Jesus. And what could be more urgent than that?

Roughly 400 years earlier, Nehemiah was a similar friend with a similar faith. He lived a solid 800+ miles from home, selecting wines for the king of Babylon. Although he was in exile, Nehemiah enjoyed a life of prestige and influence until he received word that his people and his city had suffered a great devastation.

Like the four men in Jerusalem some 400 years later, Nehemiah's compassion compelled him to seek the Lord on behalf of his people at any cost:

"When I heard these words, I sat down and wept. I mourned for a number of days, fasting and praying before the God of the heavens. I said, 'LORD, the God of the heavens . . . let your eyes be open and your ears be attentive to hear your servant's prayer that I now pray to you day and night for your servants, the Israelites . . .'"

NEHEMIAH 1:4-6

When I think about the men who pursued Jesus tirelessly on behalf of their sick friend, and Nehemiah who petitioned and fasted and repented before the Lord on behalf of his people, I remember this: however compassionate those men were, God's compassion is greater still. Because we serve a God of compassion who answers the persistent petitions of His people (Neh 2:1-9) we can approach the throne as boldly, as reverently, and with the same persistence, and be heard by the Almighty God upon whom no prayers are wasted.

Your God hears you. Let's seek Him more every day. Let's petition Him through persistent prayer for good things for ourselves and others! Like Edith Schaeffer said, let's "reverence the amazing opportunity to ask help from the everlasting God, the Creator of the Universe."

[7] I also said to the king: "If it pleases the king, let me have letters written to the governors of the region west of the Euphrates River, so that they will grant me safe passage until I reach Judah. [8] And let me have a letter written to Asaph, keeper of the king's forest, so that he will give me timber to rebuild the gates of the temple's fortress, the city wall, and the home where I will live."[A] The king granted my requests, for the gracious hand of my God was on me.

[9] I went to the governors of the region west of the Euphrates and gave them the king's letters. The king had also sent officers of the infantry and cavalry with me. [10] When Sanballat the Horonite and Tobiah the Ammonite official heard that someone had come to pursue the prosperity of the Israelites, they were greatly displeased.

PREPARING TO REBUILD THE WALLS

[11] After I arrived in Jerusalem and had been there three days, [12] I got up at night and took a few men with me. I didn't tell anyone what my God had laid on my heart to do for Jerusalem. The only animal I took[B] was the one I was riding. [13] I went out at night through the Valley Gate toward the Serpent's[C] Well and the Dung Gate, and I inspected the walls of Jerusalem that had been broken down and its gates that had been destroyed by fire. [14] I went on to the Fountain Gate and the King's Pool, but farther down it became too narrow for my animal to go through. [15] So I went up at night by way of the valley and inspected the wall. Then heading back, I entered through the Valley Gate and returned. [16] The officials did not know where I had gone or what I was doing, for I had not yet told the Jews, priests, nobles, officials, or the rest of those who would be doing the work. [17] So I said to them, "You see the trouble we are in. Jerusalem lies in ruins and its gates have been burned. Come, let's rebuild Jerusalem's wall, so that we will no longer be a disgrace." [18] I told them how the gracious hand of my God had been on me, and what the king had said to me.

They said, "Let's start rebuilding," and their hands were strengthened[D] to do this good work.

[19] When Sanballat the Horonite, Tobiah the Ammonite official, and Geshem the Arab heard about this, they mocked and despised us, and said, "What is this you're doing? Are you rebelling against the king?"

[20] I gave them this reply, "The God of the heavens is the one who will grant us success. We, his servants, will start building, but you have no share, right, or historic claim in Jerusalem."

REBUILDING THE WALLS

3 The high priest Eliashib and his fellow priests began rebuilding the Sheep Gate. They dedicated it and installed its doors. After building the wall to the Tower of the Hundred and the Tower of Hananel, they dedicated it. [2] The men of Jericho built next to Eliashib, and next to them Zaccur son of Imri built.

FISH GATE

[3] The sons of Hassenaah built the Fish Gate. They built it with beams and installed its doors, bolts, and bars. [4] Next to them Meremoth son of Uriah, son

---

[A] 2:8 Lit enter [B] 2:12 Lit animal with me [C] 2:13 Or Dragon's [D] 2:18 Lit they put their hands

SHREDDED SECURITY BLANKETS

NEHEMIAH 2:11-20; GALATIANS 4:26; EPHESIANS 2:19-22

All of my children were blankie babies. My oldest attached to a blue quilt with yellow ducks. He's a big boy now, but he still sleeps with its frayed and tattered remains.

The book of Nehemiah tells the story of the mending of one of Israel's security blankets, the wall that surrounded their treasured city of Jerusalem. If we trace the history of the wall, we find it was built under the leadership of Solomon at a time when Israel's future seemed bright (1Kg 3:1). God's people were "too many to be numbered or counted" (1Kg 3:8). His temple was under construction (1Kg 6:1). There was peace from border to border (1Kg 4:25).

Fast-forward to Nehemiah's day and all of this had reversed. Many of his countrymen were beginning to forget their home. Jerusalem was abandoned. The temple was destroyed. God's people were both scattered and enslaved.

My babies' blankets don't actually keep them safe. That's my job as their parent. But they cling to them as a symbol of my protection. In the same way, the wall was never the ultimate source of security for Israel, but the broken wall was symbolic of the fact that something was broken in their relationship with God.

When Nehemiah heard that the wall around Jerusalem had been destroyed, he grieved deeply. This news was the straw that broke the proverbial camel's back. If you've experienced deep grief, you know it can happen this way. One look, or smell, or sentence can force all the agony to erupt at once. Nehemiah was weeping for all the loss, all the sorrow, all the shame. He longed for the wall to be restored, yes, but he was really dreaming of the day his people would be restored to their home.

But why rebuild a wall around a broken city?

Because you have to start somewhere. Nehemiah led his people in rebuilding the wall so that they would remember that God's anger would not burn forever, that He would restore His people, that He would keep His covenant.

Brick by brick, Nehemiah and the people of Israel rebuilt Jerusalem on the foundation of God's promises, not their own experiences. They were learning to see beyond a broken wall, trusting God and looking to a time when all would be set right.

Sometimes, faith means looking past the landscape of destruction around us to the restoration God has promised on the horizon. Whether our security blankets are shredded or intact, let's find comfort in the firm foundation of our faithful God.

of Hakkoz, made repairs. Beside them Meshullam son of Berechiah, son of Meshezabel, made repairs. Next to them Zadok son of Baana made repairs. [5] Beside them the Tekoites made repairs, but their nobles did not lift a finger to help[A] their supervisors.

OLD GATE, BROAD WALL, AND TOWER OF THE OVENS

[6] Joiada son of Paseah and Meshullam son of Besodeiah repaired the Old[B] Gate. They built it with beams and installed its doors, bolts, and bars. [7] Next to them the repairs were done by Melatiah the Gibeonite, Jadon the Meronothite, and the men of Gibeon and Mizpah, who were under the authority[C] of the governor of the region west of the Euphrates River. [8] After him Uzziel son of Harhaiah, the goldsmith, made repairs, and next to him Hananiah son of the perfumer made repairs. They restored Jerusalem as far as the Broad Wall.

[9] Next to them Rephaiah son of Hur, ruler of half the district of Jerusalem, made repairs. [10] After them Jedaiah son of Harumaph made repairs across from his house. Next to him Hattush the son of Hashabneiah made repairs. [11] Malchijah son of Harim and Hasshub son of Pahath-moab made repairs to another section, as well as to the Tower of the Ovens. [12] Beside him Shallum son of Hallohesh, ruler of half the district of Jerusalem, made repairs — he and his daughters.

VALLEY GATE, DUNG GATE, AND FOUNTAIN GATE

[13] Hanun and the inhabitants of Zanoah repaired the Valley Gate. They rebuilt it and installed its doors, bolts, and bars, and repaired five hundred yards[D] of the wall to the Dung Gate. [14] Malchijah son of Rechab, ruler of the district of Beth-haccherem, repaired the Dung Gate. He rebuilt it and installed its doors, bolts, and bars.

[15] Shallun[E] son of Col-hozeh, ruler of the district of Mizpah, repaired the Fountain Gate. He rebuilt it and roofed it. Then he installed its doors, bolts, and bars. He also made repairs to the wall of the Pool of Shelah near the king's garden, as far as the stairs that descend from the city of David.

[16] After him Nehemiah son of Azbuk, ruler of half the district of Beth-zur, made repairs up to a point opposite the tombs of David, as far as the artificial pool and the House of the Warriors. [17] Next to him the Levites made repairs under Rehum son of Bani. Beside him Hashabiah, ruler of half the district of Keilah, made repairs for his district. [18] After him their fellow Levites made repairs under Binnui[F] son of Henadad, ruler of half the district of Keilah. [19] Next to him Ezer son of Jeshua, ruler of Mizpah, made repairs to another section opposite the ascent to the armory at the Angle.

THE ANGLE, WATER GATE, AND TOWER ON THE OPHEL

[20] After him Baruch son of Zabbai[G] diligently repaired another section, from the Angle to the door of the house of the high priest Eliashib. [21] Beside him Meremoth son of Uriah, son of Hakkoz, made repairs to another section,

[A] 3:5 Lit not bring their neck to the work of   [B] 3:6 Or Jeshanah   [C] 3:7 Or Mizpah, the seat   [D] 3:13 Lit 1,000 cubits   [E] 3:15 Some Hb mss, Syr read Shallum
[F] 3:18 Some Hb mss, Syr, LXX; Neh 3:24; other Hb mss, Vg read Bavvai
[G] 3:20 Alt Hb tradition, Vg read Zaccai; Ezr 2:9

YOU AND YOUR WALL

NEHEMIAH 3; JOHN 9; ACTS 3

This is the good part. Don't glaze over it.

If you've spent any length of time in the Old Testament, you know that sometimes there are chunks of names and names and names. We can skim right past Nehemiah 3, or we can dig in to find what God has for us here.

Every great and powerful move of God— from the rebuilding of walls, to the planting of churches, to the leading of a children's Bible study—comes down to a section like this. The people have to get up, stop talking and vision casting, and start putting beams down. They have to walk over to their neighbor's house. They have to move to that city where they know God is calling them. Have the conversation. Do the work.

It isn't always beautiful or glamorous or filled with spiritual fervor and fluffy feelings, but it is so very good and necessary if we want to get the wall built. Ephesians 4:16 reminds us that "the whole body, fitted and knit together by every supporting ligament, promotes the growth of the body for building up itself in love by the proper working of each individual part."

Can I tell you a little secret about one of these builders that may shed some light for us? Did you notice Shallum, in Nehemiah 3:15? He's one of the dozens listed, but he repaired the wall of the Pool of Shelah. No biggie, right? Well, it is actually a huge deal. It's one man, offering his time and effort to rebuild his community. But there's more to the story.

In John 9, they're calling this pool "Siloam," but don't be confused—it's the same pool. Hundreds of years later, Jesus stood at the very pool Shallum repaired, and gave sight to a man who was blind from birth. As Shallum was laying stone after stone in that very spot, he couldn't possibly have known that all those years later, the Messiah would reveal His deity to a blind man in that very spot. This is an important place.

It is easy for us to get caught up in the daunting or mundane tasks that fill our days and miss the significance God is manufacturing through our labor. Could it be that the section of the wall God has given you is important for your sanctification and His glory today, but that He might also have an eternal plan for the work you're doing? **What if your simple job is the setting for miraculous, kingdom-size work for generations to come?**

I'm willing to bet, in one way or another, it absolutely is.

729

from the door of Eliashib's house to the end of his house. ²² And next to him the priests from the surrounding area made repairs.

²³ After them Benjamin and Hasshub made repairs opposite their house. Beside them Azariah son of Maaseiah, son of Ananiah, made repairs beside his house. ²⁴ After him Binnui son of Henadad made repairs to another section, from the house of Azariah to the Angle and the corner. ²⁵ Palal son of Uzai made repairs opposite the Angle and tower that juts out from the king's upper palace,^ by the courtyard of the guard. Beside him Pedaiah son of Parosh ²⁶ and the temple servants living on Ophel made repairs opposite the Water Gate toward the east and the tower that juts out. ²⁷ Next to him the Tekoites made repairs to another section from a point opposite the great tower that juts out, as far as the wall of Ophel.

HORSE GATE, INSPECTION GATE, AND SHEEP GATE

²⁸ Each of the priests made repairs above the Horse Gate, each opposite his own house. ²⁹ After them Zadok son of Immer made repairs opposite his house. And beside him Shemaiah son of Shecaniah, guard of the East Gate, made repairs. ³⁰ Next to him Hananiah son of Shelemiah and Hanun the sixth son of Zalaph made repairs to another section.

After them Meshullam son of Berechiah made repairs opposite his room. ³¹ Next to him Malchijah, one of the goldsmiths, made repairs to the house of the temple servants and the merchants, opposite the Inspection ᴮ Gate, and as far as the upstairs room on the corner. ³² The goldsmiths and merchants made repairs between the upstairs room on the corner and the Sheep Gate.

PROGRESS IN SPITE OF OPPOSITION

4 When Sanballat heard that we were rebuilding the wall, he became furious. He mocked the Jews ² before his colleagues and the powerful men ᶜ of Samaria, and said, "What are these pathetic Jews doing? Can they restore it by themselves? Will they offer sacrifices? Will they ever finish it? Can they bring these burnt stones back to life from the mounds of rubble?" ³ Then Tobiah the Ammonite, who was beside him, said, "Indeed, even if a fox climbed up what they are building, he would break down their stone wall!"

⁴ Listen, our God, for we are despised. Make their insults return on their own heads and let them be taken as plunder to a land of captivity. ⁵ Do not cover their guilt or let their sin be erased from your sight, because they have angered ᴰ the builders.

⁶ So we rebuilt the wall until the entire wall was joined together up to half its height, for the people had the will to keep working.

⁷ When Sanballat, Tobiah, and the Arabs, Ammonites, and Ashdodites heard that the repair to the walls of Jerusalem was progressing and that the gaps were being closed, they became furious. ⁸ They all plotted together to come and fight against Jerusalem and throw it into confusion. ⁹ So we prayed to our God and stationed a guard because of them day and night.

¹⁰ In Judah, it was said: ᴱ

The strength of the laborer fails,
since there is so much rubble.

---

^3:25 Or and the upper tower that juts out from the palace   ᴮ3:31 Or Muster   ᶜ4:2 Or the army   ᴰ4:5 Or provoked you in front of   ᴱ4:10 Lit Judah said

> We will never be able
> to rebuild the wall.

¹¹ And our enemies said, "They won't realize it^A until we're among them and can kill them and stop the work." ¹² When the Jews who lived nearby arrived, they said to us time and again, ^B "Everywhere you turn, they attack^C us." ¹³ So I stationed people behind the lowest sections of the wall, at the vulnerable areas. I stationed them by families with their swords, spears, and bows. ¹⁴ After I made an inspection, I stood up and said to the nobles, the officials, and the rest of the people, "Don't be afraid of them. Remember the great and awe-inspiring Lord, and fight for your countrymen, your sons and daughters, your wives and homes."

SWORD AND TROWEL

¹⁵ When our enemies heard that we knew their scheme and that God had frustrated it, every one of us returned to his own work on the wall. ¹⁶ From that day on, half of my men did the work while the other half held spears, shields, bows, and armor. The officers supported all the people of Judah, ¹⁷ who were rebuilding the wall. The laborers who carried the loads worked with one hand and held a weapon with the other. ¹⁸ Each of the builders had his sword strapped around his waist while he was building, and the trumpeter was beside me. ¹⁹ Then I said to the nobles, the officials, and the rest of the people: "The work is enormous and spread out, and we are separated far from one another along the wall. ²⁰ Wherever you hear the trumpet sound, rally to us there. Our God will fight for us!" ²¹ So we continued the work, while half of the men were holding spears from daybreak until the stars came out. ²² At that time, I also said to the people, "Let everyone and his servant spend the night inside Jerusalem, so that they can stand guard by night and work by day." ²³ And I, my brothers, my servants, and the men of the guard with me never took off our clothes. Each carried his weapon, even when washing.^D

SOCIAL INJUSTICE

5 There was a widespread outcry from the people and their wives against their Jewish countrymen. ² Some were saying, "We, our sons, and our daughters are numerous. Let us get grain so that we can eat and live." ³ Others were saying, "We are mortgaging our fields, vineyards, and homes to get grain during the famine." ⁴ Still others were saying, "We have borrowed money to pay the king's tax on our fields and vineyards. ⁵ We and our children are just like our countrymen and their children, yet we are subjecting our sons and daughters to slavery. Some of our daughters are already enslaved, but we are powerless^E because our fields and vineyards belong to others."

⁶ I became extremely angry when I heard their outcry and these complaints. ⁷ After seriously considering the matter, I accused the nobles and officials, saying to them, "Each of you is charging his countrymen interest." So

---

^A 4:11 Lit won't know or see   ^B 4:12 Lit us 10 times   ^C 4:12 Or again from every place, "You must return to   ^D 4:23 Lit Each his weapon the water   ^E 5:5 Lit but there is not the power in our hand

I called a large assembly against them [8] and said, "We have done our best to buy back our Jewish countrymen who were sold to foreigners, but now you sell your own countrymen, and we have to buy them back." They remained silent and could not say a word. [9] Then I said, "What you are doing isn't right. Shouldn't you walk in the fear of our God and not invite the reproach of our foreign enemies? [10] Even I, as well as my brothers and my servants, have been lending them money and grain. Please, let us stop charging this interest. [A] [11] Return their fields, vineyards, olive groves, and houses to them immediately, along with the percentage [B] of the money, grain, new wine, and fresh oil that you have been assessing them."

[12] They responded: "We will return these things and require nothing more from them. We will do as you say."

So I summoned the priests and made everyone take an oath to do this. [13] I also shook the folds of my robe and said, "May God likewise shake from his house and property everyone who doesn't keep this promise. May he be shaken out and have nothing!"

The whole assembly said, "Amen," and they praised the LORD. Then the people did as they had promised.

GOOD AND BAD GOVERNORS

[14] Furthermore, from the day King Artaxerxes appointed me to be their governor in the land of Judah — from the twentieth year until his thirty-second year, twelve years — I and my associates never ate from the food allotted to the governor. [15] The governors who preceded me had heavily burdened the people, taking from them food and wine as well as a pound [C] of silver. Their subordinates also oppressed the people, but because of the fear of God, I didn't do this. [16] Instead, I devoted myself to the construction of this wall, and all my subordinates were gathered there for the work. We didn't buy any land.

[17] There were 150 Jews and officials, as well as guests from the surrounding nations at my table. [18] Each [D] day, one ox, six choice sheep, and some fowl were prepared for me. An abundance of all kinds of wine was provided every ten days. But I didn't demand the food allotted to the governor, because the burden on the people was so heavy.

[19] Remember me favorably, my God, for all that I have done for this people.

ATTEMPTS TO DISCOURAGE THE BUILDERS

6 When Sanballat, Tobiah, Geshem the Arab, and the rest of our enemies heard that I had rebuilt the wall and that no gap was left in it — though at that time I had not installed the doors in the city gates — [2] Sanballat and Geshem sent me a message: "Come, let's meet together in the villages of [E] the Ono Valley." They were planning to harm me.

[3] So I sent messengers to them, saying, "I am doing important work and cannot come down. Why should the work cease while I leave it and go down to you?" [4] Four times they sent me the same proposal, and I gave them the same reply.

[5] Sanballat sent me this same message a fifth time by his aide, who had an open letter in his hand. [6] In it was written:

[A] 5:10 Or *us forgive these debts*   [B] 5:11 Lit *hundred*   [C] 5:15 Lit *40 shekels*
[D] 5:18 Lit *And that which was prepared each*   [E] 6:2 Or *together at Kephirim in*

It is reported among the nations — and Geshem[A] agrees — that you and the Jews plan to rebel. This is the reason you are building the wall. According to these reports, you are to become their king ⁷ and have even set up the prophets in Jerusalem to proclaim on your behalf: "There is a king in Judah." These rumors will be heard by the king. So come, let's confer together.

⁸ Then I replied to him, "There is nothing to these rumors you are spreading; you are inventing them in your own mind." ⁹ For they were all trying to intimidate us, saying, "They will drop their hands from[B] the work, and it will never be finished."

But now, my God, strengthen my hands.

ATTEMPTS TO INTIMIDATE NEHEMIAH

¹⁰ I went to the house of Shemaiah son of Delaiah, son of Mehetabel, who was restricted to his house. He said:

Let's meet at the house of God,
inside the temple.
Let's shut the temple doors
because they're coming to kill you.
They're coming to kill you tonight![C]

¹¹ But I said, "Should a man like me run away? How can someone like me enter the temple and live? I will not go." ¹² I realized that God had not sent him, because of the prophecy he spoke against me. Tobiah and Sanballat had hired him. ¹³ He was hired, so that I would be intimidated, do as he suggested, sin, and get a bad reputation, in order that they could discredit me.

¹⁴ My God, remember Tobiah and Sanballat for what they have done, and also the prophetess Noadiah and the other prophets who wanted to intimidate me.

THE WALL COMPLETED

¹⁵ The wall was completed in fifty-two days, on the twenty-fifth day of the month Elul. ¹⁶ When all our enemies heard this, all the surrounding nations were intimidated and lost their confidence,[D] for they realized that this task had been accomplished by our God.

¹⁷ During those days, the nobles of Judah sent many letters to Tobiah, and Tobiah's letters came to them. ¹⁸ For many in Judah were bound by oath to him, since he was a son-in-law of Shecaniah son of Arah, and his son Jehohanan had married the daughter of Meshullam son of Berechiah. ¹⁹ These nobles kept mentioning Tobiah's good deeds to me, and they reported my words to him. And Tobiah sent letters to intimidate me.

THE EXILES RETURN

7 When the wall had been rebuilt and I had the doors installed, the gatekeepers, singers, and Levites were appointed. ² Then I put my brother Hanani in charge of Jerusalem, along with Hananiah, commander of the fortress, because he was a faithful man who feared God more than most. ³ I said to them, "Do not open the gates of Jerusalem until the sun is hot, and let the

---

[A]6:6 Lit Gashmu   [B]6:9 Or will give up on   [C]6:10 Or by night   [D]6:16 Lit and fell greatly in their eyes doors be shut and securely fastened while the guards are on duty. Station the citizens of Jerusalem as guards, some at their posts and some at their homes."

⁴ The city was large and spacious, but there were few people in it, and no houses had been built yet. ⁵ Then my God put it into my mind to assemble the nobles, the officials, and the people to be registered by genealogy. I found the genealogical record of those who came back first, and I found the following written in it:

⁶ These are the people of the province who went up among the captive exiles deported by King Nebuchadnezzar of Babylon. Each of them returned to Jerusalem and Judah, to his own town. ⁷ They came with Zerubbabel, Jeshua, Nehemiah, Azariah, Raamiah, Nahamani, Mordecai, Bilshan, Mispereth, Bigvai, Nehum, and Baanah.

The number of the Israelite men included^A

⁸	Parosh's descendants	2,172
⁹	Shephatiah's descendants	372
¹⁰	Arah's descendants	652
¹¹	Pahath-moab's descendants:	
	Jeshua's and Joab's descendants	2,818
¹²	Elam's descendants	1,254
¹³	Zattu's descendants	845
¹⁴	Zaccai's descendants	760
¹⁵	Binnui's descendants	648
¹⁶	Bebai's descendants	628
¹⁷	Azgad's descendants	2,322
¹⁸	Adonikam's descendants	667
¹⁹	Bigvai's descendants	2,067
²⁰	Adin's descendants	655
²¹	Ater's descendants: of Hezekiah	98
²²	Hashum's descendants	328
²³	Bezai's descendants	324
²⁴	Hariph's descendants	112
²⁵	Gibeon's^B descendants	95
²⁶	Bethlehem's and Netophah's men	188
²⁷	Anathoth's men	128
²⁸	Beth-azmaveth's men	42
²⁹	Kiriath-jearim's, Chephirah's, and Beeroth's men	743
³⁰	Ramah's and Geba's men	621
³¹	Michmas's men	122
³²	Bethel's and Ai's men	123
³³	the other Nebo's men	52
³⁴	the other Elam's people	1,254
³⁵	Harim's people	320
³⁶	Jericho's people	345
³⁷	Lod's, Hadid's, and Ono's people	721
³⁸	Senaah's people	3,930.

³⁹ The priests included
Jedaiah's descendants of the house of Jeshua   973

^A7:7 Lit *the men of the people of Israel*   ^B7:25 = Gibbar's in Ezr 2:20

[40]	Immer's descendants	1,052
[41]	Pashhur's descendants	1,247
[42]	Harim's descendants	1,017.

[43] The Levites included
Jeshua's descendants: of Kadmiel
Hodevah's descendants 74.

[44] The singers included
Asaph's descendants 148.

[45] The gatekeepers included
Shallum's descendants, Ater's descendants,
Talmon's descendants, Akkub's descendants,
Hatita's descendants, Shobai's descendants 138.

[46] The temple servants included
Ziha's descendants, Hasupha's descendants,
Tabbaoth's descendants, [47] Keros's descendants,
Sia's descendants, Padon's descendants,
[48] Lebanah's descendants, Hagabah's descendants,
Shalmai's descendants, [49] Hanan's descendants,
Giddel's descendants, Gahar's descendants,
[50] Reaiah's descendants, Rezin's descendants,
Nekoda's descendants, [51] Gazzam's descendants,
Uzza's descendants, Paseah's descendants,
[52] Besai's descendants, Meunim's descendants,
Nephishesim's[A] descendants, [53] Bakbuk's descendants,
Hakupha's descendants, Harhur's descendants,
[54] Bazlith's descendants, Mehida's descendants,
Harsha's descendants, [55] Barkos's descendants,
Sisera's descendants, Temah's descendants,
[56] Neziah's descendants, Hatipha's descendants.

[57] The descendants of Solomon's servants included
Sotai's descendants, Sophereth's descendants,
Perida's descendants, [58] Jaala's descendants,
Darkon's descendants, Giddel's descendants,
[59] Shephatiah's descendants, Hattil's descendants,
Pochereth-hazzebaim's descendants, Amon's descendants.

[60] All the temple servants
and the descendants of Solomon's servants 392.

[61] The following are those who came from Tel-melah, Tel-harsha, Cherub, Addon, and Immer, but were unable to prove that their ancestral families[B] and their lineage were Israelite:
[62] Delaiah's descendants,

[A]7:52 Alt Hb tradition reads *Nephushesim's* [B]7:61 Lit *the house of their fathers*

Tobiah's descendants,
and Nekoda's descendants

642

[63] and from the priests: the descendants of Hobaiah, the descendants of Hak-koz, and the descendants of Barzillai — who had taken a wife from the daughters of Barzillai the Gileadite and who bore their name. [64] These searched for their entries in the genealogical records, but they could not be found, so they were disqualified from the priesthood. [65] The governor ordered them not to eat the most holy things until there was a priest who could consult the Urim and Thummim.

[66] The whole combined assembly numbered   42,360

[67] not including their 7,337 male and female servants,
as well as their 245 male and female singers.

[68] They had 736 horses, 245 mules,[A]

[69] 435 camels, and 6,720 donkeys.

[70] Some of the family heads contributed to the project. The governor gave 1,000 gold coins,[B] 50 bowls, and 530 priestly garments to the treasury. [71] Some of the family heads gave 20,000 gold coins and 2,200 silver minas to the treasury for the project. [72] The rest of the people gave 20,000 gold coins, 2,000 silver minas, and 67 priestly garments. [73] The priests, Levites, gatekeepers, temple singers, some of the people, temple servants, and all Israel settled in their towns.

PUBLIC READING OF THE LAW

When the seventh month came and the Israelites had settled in their towns, **8** [1] all the people gathered together at the square in front of the Water Gate. They asked the scribe Ezra to bring the book of the law of Moses that the LORD had given Israel. [2] On the first day of the seventh month, the priest Ezra brought the law before the assembly of men, women, and all who could listen with understanding. [3] While he was facing the square in front of the Water Gate, he read out of it from daybreak until noon before the men, the women, and those who could understand. All the people listened attentively[C] to the book of the law. [4] The scribe Ezra stood on a high wooden platform made for this purpose. Mattithiah, Shema, Anaiah, Uriah, Hilkiah, and Maaseiah stood beside him on his right; to his left were Pedaiah, Mishael, Malchijah, Hashum, Hash-baddanah, Zechariah, and Meshullam. [5] Ezra opened the book in full view of all the people, since he was elevated above everyone. As he opened it, all the people stood up. [6] Ezra blessed the LORD, the great God, and with their hands uplifted all the people said, "Amen, Amen!" Then they knelt low and worshiped the LORD with their faces to the ground.

[7] Jeshua, Bani, Sherebiah, Jamin, Akkub, Shabbethai, Hodiah, Maaseiah, Kelita, Azariah, Jozabad, Hanan, and Pelaiah, who were Levites,[D] explained the law to the people as they stood in their places. [8] They read out of the book of the law of God, translating and giving the meaning so that the people could understand what was read. [9] Nehemiah the governor, Ezra the priest and scribe, and the Levites who were instructing the people said to all of

---

[A]7:68 Some Hb mss, LXX; Ezr 2:66; other Hb mss omit v. 68   [B]7:70 Or *drachmas,* or *darics;* also in vv. 71,72   [C]8:3 Lit *The ears of all the people listened*   [D]8:7 Vg, 1 Esdras 9:48; MT reads *Pelaiah and the Levites* them, "This day is holy to the LORD your God. Do not mourn or weep." For all the people were weeping as they heard the words of the law. [10] Then he said to them, "Go and eat what is rich, drink what is sweet, and send portions to those who have nothing prepared, since today is holy to our Lord. Do not grieve, because the joy of the LORD is your strength."[A] [11] And the Levites quieted all the people, saying, "Be still, since today is holy. Don't grieve." [12] Then all the people began to eat and drink, send portions, and have a great celebration, because they had understood the words that were explained to them.

FESTIVAL OF SHELTERS OBSERVED

[13] On the second day, the family heads of all the people, along with the priests and Levites, assembled before the scribe Ezra to study the words of the law. [14] They found written in the law how the LORD had commanded through Moses that the Israelites should dwell in shelters during the festival of the seventh month. [15] So they proclaimed and spread this news throughout their towns and in Jerusalem, saying, "Go out to the hill country and bring back branches of olive, wild olive, myrtle, palm, and other leafy trees to make shelters, just as it is written." [16] The people went out, brought back branches, and made shelters for themselves on each of their rooftops and courtyards, the court of the house of God, the square by the Water Gate, and the square by the Ephraim Gate. [17] The whole community that had returned from exile made shelters and lived in them. The Israelites had not celebrated like this from the days of Joshua son of Nun until that day. And there was tremendous joy. [18] Ezra[B] read out of the book of the law of God every day, from the first day to the last. The Israelites celebrated the festival for seven days, and on the eighth day there was an assembly, according to the ordinance.

NATIONAL CONFESSION OF SIN

9 On the twenty-fourth day of this month the Israelites assembled; they were fasting, wearing sackcloth, and had put dust on their heads. [2] Those of Israelite descent separated themselves from all foreigners, and they stood and confessed their sins and the iniquities of their fathers. [3] While they stood in their places, they read from the book of the law of the LORD their God for a fourth of the day and spent another fourth of the day in confession and worship of the LORD their God. [4] Jeshua, Bani, Kadmiel, Shebaniah, Bunni, Sherebiah, Bani, and Chenani stood on the raised platform built for the Levites and cried out loudly to the LORD their God. [5] Then the Levites — Jeshua, Kadmiel, Bani, Hashabneiah, Sherebiah, Hodiah, Shebaniah, and Pethahiah — said, "Stand up. Blessed be the LORD your God from everlasting to everlasting."

Blessed be your glorious name,
and may it be exalted above all blessing and praise.
[6] You,[C] LORD, are the only God.[D]
You created the heavens,
the highest heavens with all their stars,
the earth and all that is on it,
the seas and all that is in them.
You give life to all of them,

[A]8:10 Or *stronghold*   [B]8:18 Some Hb mss, Syr read *They*   [C]9:6 LXX reads *And Ezra said: You*   [D]9:6 Lit *are alone* and all the stars of heaven worship you.

7 You, the LORD,
   are the God who chose Abram
   and brought him out of Ur of the Chaldeans,
   and changed his name to Abraham.

8 You found his heart faithful in your sight,
   and made a covenant with him
   to give the land of the Canaanites,
   Hethites, Amorites, Perizzites,
   Jebusites, and Girgashites —
   to give it to his descendants.
   You have fulfilled your promise,
   for you are righteous.

9 You saw the oppression of our ancestors in Egypt
   and heard their cry at the Red Sea.

10 You performed signs and wonders against Pharaoh,
   all his officials, and all the people of his land,
   for you knew how arrogantly they treated our ancestors.
   You made a name for yourself
   that endures to this day.

11 You divided the sea before them,
   and they crossed through it on dry ground.
   You hurled their pursuers into the depths
   like a stone into raging water.

12 You led them with a pillar of cloud by day,
   and with a pillar of fire by night,
   to illuminate the way they should go.

13 You came down on Mount Sinai,
   and spoke to them from heaven.
   You gave them impartial ordinances, reliable instructions,
   and good statutes and commands.

14 You revealed your holy Sabbath to them,
   and gave them commands, statutes, and instruction
   through your servant Moses.

15 You provided bread from heaven for their hunger;
   you brought them water from the rock for their thirst.
   You told them to go in and possess the land
   you had sworn^A to give them.

16 But our ancestors acted arrogantly;
   they became stiff-necked and did not listen to your commands.

17 They refused to listen
   and did not remember your wonders
   you performed among them.
   They became stiff-necked and appointed a leader
   to return to their slavery in Egypt.^B

---

^A9:15 Lit *lifted your hand* ^B9:17 Some Hb mss, LXX; other Hb mss read *in their rebellion*

But you are a forgiving God,
gracious and compassionate,
slow to anger and abounding in faithful love,
and you did not abandon them.
¹⁸ Even after they had cast an image of a calf
for themselves and said,
"This is your god who brought you out of Egypt,"
and they had committed terrible blasphemies,
¹⁹ you did not abandon them in the wilderness
because of your great compassion.
During the day the pillar of cloud
never turned away from them,
guiding them on their journey.
And during the night the pillar of fire
illuminated the way they should go.
²⁰ You sent your good Spirit to instruct them.
You did not withhold your manna from their mouths,
and you gave them water for their thirst.
²¹ You provided for them in the wilderness forty years,
and they lacked nothing.
Their clothes did not wear out,
and their feet did not swell.

²² You gave them kingdoms and peoples
and established boundaries for them.
They took possession
of the land of King Sihon^A of Heshbon
and of the land of King Og of Bashan.
²³ You multiplied their descendants
like the stars of the sky
and brought them to the land
you told their ancestors to go in and possess.
²⁴ So their descendants went in and possessed the land:
You subdued the Canaanites who inhabited the land before them
and handed their kings and the surrounding peoples over to them,
to do as they pleased with them.
²⁵ They captured fortified cities and fertile land
and took possession of well-supplied houses,
cisterns cut out of rock, vineyards,
olive groves, and fruit trees in abundance.
They ate, were filled,
became prosperous, and delighted in your great goodness.

²⁶ But they were disobedient and rebelled against you.
They flung your law behind their backs
and killed your prophets
who warned them
in order to turn them back to you.

---

^A 9:22 One Hb ms, LXX; other Hb mss, Vg read *of Sihon, even the land of the king*

They committed terrible blasphemies.

²⁷ So you handed them over to their enemies,
who oppressed them.
In their time of distress, they cried out to you,
and you heard from heaven.
In your abundant compassion
you gave them deliverers, who rescued them
from the power of their enemies.

²⁸ But as soon as they had relief,
they again did what was evil in your sight.
So you abandoned them to the power of their enemies,
who dominated them.
When they cried out to you again,
you heard from heaven and rescued them
many times in your compassion.

²⁹ You warned them to turn back to your law,
but they acted arrogantly
and would not obey your commands.
They sinned against your ordinances,
which a person will live by if he does them.
They stubbornly resisted,ᴬ
stiffened their necks, and would not obey.

³⁰ You were patient with them for many years,
and your Spirit warned them through your prophets,
but they would not listen.
Therefore, you handed them over to the surrounding peoples.

³¹ However, in your abundant compassion,
you did not destroy them or abandon them,
for you are a gracious and compassionate God.

³² So now, our God — the great, mighty,
and awe-inspiring God who keeps his gracious covenant —
do not view lightly all the hardships that have afflicted us,
our kings and leaders,
our priests and prophets,
our ancestors and all your people,
from the days of the Assyrian kings until today.

³³ You are righteous concerning all that has happened to us,
because you have acted faithfully,
while we have acted wickedly.

³⁴ Our kings, leaders, priests, and ancestors
did not obey your law
or listen to your commands
and warnings you gave them.

³⁵ When they were in their kingdom,
with your abundant goodness that you gave them,
and in the spacious and fertile land you set before them,
they would not serve you or turn from their wicked ways.

ᴬ9:29 Lit *They gave a stubborn shoulder*

³⁶ Here we are today,
 slaves in the land you gave our ancestors
 so that they could enjoy its fruit
  and its goodness.
 Here we are — slaves in it!
³⁷ Its abundant harvest goes to the kings
 you have set over us,
 because of our sins.
 They rule over our bodies
 and our livestock as they please.
 We are in great distress.

ISRAEL'S VOW OF FAITHFULNESS

³⁸ In view of all this, we are making a binding agreement in writing on a sealed document containing the names of our leaders, Levites, and priests.

10 Those whose seals were on the document were
 the governor Nehemiah son of Hacaliah, and Zedekiah,

² Seraiah, Azariah, Jeremiah,
³ Pashhur, Amariah, Malchijah,
⁴ Hattush, Shebaniah, Malluch,
⁵ Harim, Meremoth, Obadiah,
⁶ Daniel, Ginnethon, Baruch,
⁷ Meshullam, Abijah, Mijamin,
⁸ Maaziah, Bilgai, and Shemaiah.
 These were the priests.

⁹ The Levites were
 Jeshua son of Azaniah,
 Binnui of the sons of Henadad, Kadmiel,
¹⁰ and their brothers
 Shebaniah, Hodiah, Kelita, Pelaiah, Hanan,
¹¹ Mica, Rehob, Hashabiah,
¹² Zaccur, Sherebiah, Shebaniah,
¹³ Hodiah, Bani, and Beninu.

¹⁴ The heads of the people were
 Parosh, Pahath-moab, Elam, Zattu, Bani,
¹⁵ Bunni, Azgad, Bebai,
¹⁶ Adonijah, Bigvai, Adin,
¹⁷ Ater, Hezekiah, Azzur,
¹⁸ Hodiah, Hashum, Bezai,
¹⁹ Hariph, Anathoth, Nebai,
²⁰ Magpiash, Meshullam, Hezir,
²¹ Meshezabel, Zadok, Jaddua,
²² Pelatiah, Hanan, Anaiah,
²³ Hoshea, Hananiah, Hasshub,
²⁴ Hallohesh, Pilha, Shobek,
²⁵ Rehum, Hashabnah, Maaseiah,
²⁶ Ahijah, Hanan, Anan,
²⁷ Malluch, Harim, Baanah.

²⁸ The rest of the people — the priests, Levites, gatekeepers, singers, and temple servants, along with their wives, sons, and daughters, everyone who is able to understand and who has separated themselves from the surrounding peoples to obey the law of God — ²⁹ join with their noble brothers and commit themselves with a sworn oath^A to follow the law of God given through God's servant Moses and to obey carefully all the commands, ordinances, and statutes of the LORD our Lord.

DETAILS OF THE VOW

³⁰ We will not give our daughters in marriage to the surrounding peoples and will not take their daughters as wives for our sons.

³¹ When the surrounding peoples bring merchandise or any kind of grain to sell on the Sabbath day, we will not buy from them on the Sabbath or a holy day. We will also leave the land uncultivated in the seventh year and will cancel every debt.

³² We will impose the following commands on ourselves:

To give an eighth of an ounce of silver^B yearly for the service of the house of our God: ³³ the bread displayed before the LORD,^C the daily grain offering, the regular burnt offering, the Sabbath and New Moon offerings, the appointed festivals, the holy things, the sin offerings to atone for Israel, and for all the work of the house of our God.

³⁴ We have cast lots among the priests, Levites, and people for the donation of wood by our ancestral families^D at the appointed times each year. They are to bring the wood to our God's house to burn on the altar of the LORD our God, as it is written in the law.

³⁵ We will bring the firstfruits of our land and of every fruit tree to the LORD's house year by year. ³⁶ We will also bring the firstborn of our sons and our livestock, as prescribed by the law, and will bring the firstborn of our herds and flocks to the house of our God, to the priests who serve in our God's house. ³⁷ We will bring a loaf from our first batch of dough to the priests at the storerooms of the house of our God. We will also bring the firstfruits of our grain offerings, of every fruit tree, and of the new wine and fresh oil. A tenth of our land's produce belongs to the Levites, for the Levites are to collect the one-tenth offering in all our agricultural towns. ³⁸ A priest from Aaron's descendants is to accompany the Levites when they collect the tenth, and the Levites are to take a tenth of this offering to the storerooms of the treasury in the house of our God. ³⁹ For the Israelites and the Levites are to bring the contributions of grain, new wine, and fresh oil to the storerooms where the articles of the sanctuary are kept and where the priests who minister are, along with the gatekeepers and singers. We will not neglect the house of our God.

---

^A 10:29 Lit *and enter in a curse and in an oath*   ^B 10:32 Lit *give one-third of a shekel*   ^C 10:33 Lit *rows of bread*   ^D 10:34 Lit *the house of our fathers*

RESETTLING JERUSALEM

11

Now the leaders of the people stayed in Jerusalem, and the rest of the people cast lots for one out of ten to come and live in Jerusalem, the holy city, while the other nine-tenths remained in their towns. ² The people blessed all the men who volunteered to live in Jerusalem.

³ These are the heads of the province who stayed in Jerusalem (but in the villages of Judah each lived on his own property in their towns — the Israelites, priests, Levites, temple servants, and descendants of Solomon's servants — ⁴ while some of the descendants of Judah and Benjamin settled in Jerusalem): Judah's descendants:

Athaiah son of Uzziah, son of Zechariah, son of Amariah, son of Shephatiah, son of Mahalalel, of Perez's descendants; ⁵ and Maaseiah son of Baruch, son of Col-hozeh, son of Hazaiah, son of Adaiah, son of Joiarib, son of Zechariah, a descendant of the Shilonite. ⁶ The total number of Perez's descendants, who settled in Jerusalem, was 468 capable men.

⁷ These were Benjamin's descendants:

Sallu son of Meshullam, son of Joed, son of Pedaiah, son of Kolaiah, son of Maaseiah, son of Ithiel, son of Jeshaiah, ⁸ and after him Gabbai and Sallai: 928. ⁹ Joel son of Zichri was the officer over them, and Judah son of Hassenuah was second in command over the city.

¹⁰ The priests:

Jedaiah son of Joiarib, Jachin, and ¹¹ Seraiah son of Hilkiah, son of Meshullam, son of Zadok, son of Meraioth, son of Ahitub, the chief official of God's temple, ¹² and their relatives who did the work at the temple: 822. Adaiah son of Jeroham, son of Pelaliah, son of Amzi, son of Zechariah, son of Pashhur, son of Malchijah ¹³ and his relatives, the heads of families: 242. Amashsai son of Azarel, son of Ahzai, son of Meshillemoth, son of Immer, ¹⁴ and their relatives, capable men: 128. Zabdiel son of Haggedolim, was their chief.

¹⁵ The Levites:

Shemaiah son of Hasshub, son of Azrikam, son of Hashabiah, son of Bunni; ¹⁶ and Shabbethai and Jozabad, from the heads of the Levites, who supervised the work outside the house of God; ¹⁷ Mattaniah son of Mica, son of Zabdi, son of Asaph, the one^A who began the thanksgiving in prayer; Bakbukiah, second among his relatives; and Abda son of Shammua, son of Galal, son of Jeduthun. ¹⁸ All the Levites in the holy city: 284.

¹⁹ The gatekeepers:

Akkub, Talmon, and their relatives, who guarded the city gates: 172.

---

^A11:17 Lit *the head*

²⁰ The rest of Israel, the priests, and the Levites were in all the villages of Judah, each on his own inherited property. ²¹ The temple servants lived on Ophel; Ziha and Gishpa supervised the temple servants.

THE LEVITES AND PRIESTS

²² The leader of the Levites in Jerusalem was Uzzi son of Bani, son of Hashabiah, son of Mattaniah, son of Mica, of the descendants of Asaph, who were singers for the service of God's house. ²³ There was, in fact, a command of the king regarding them, and an ordinance regulating the singers' daily tasks. ²⁴ Pethahiah son of Meshezabel, of the descendants of Zerah son of Judah, was the king's agent^A in every matter concerning the people.

²⁵ As for the farming settlements with their fields:
Some of Judah's descendants lived in Kiriath-arba
and Dibon and their surrounding villages, and Jekabzeel and
its settlements;
²⁶ in Jeshua, Moladah, Beth-pelet,
²⁷ Hazar-shual, and Beer-sheba and its surrounding villages;
²⁸ in Ziklag and Meconah and its surrounding villages;
²⁹ in En-rimmon, Zorah, Jarmuth, and
³⁰ Zanoah and Adullam with their settlements;
in Lachish with its fields and Azekah
and its surrounding villages.
So they settled from Beer-sheba to Hinnom Valley.

³¹ Benjamin's descendants:
from Geba,^B Michmash, Aija,
and Bethel and its surrounding villages,
³² Anathoth, Nob, Ananiah,
³³ Hazor, Ramah, Gittaim,
³⁴ Hadid, Zeboim, Neballat,
³⁵ Lod, and Ono, in Craftsmen's Valley.
³⁶ Some of the Judean divisions of Levites were in Benjamin.

12

These are the priests and Levites who went up with Zerubbabel son of Shealtiel and with Jeshua:
Seraiah, Jeremiah, Ezra,
² Amariah, Malluch, Hattush,
³ Shecaniah, Rehum, Meremoth,
⁴ Iddo, Ginnethoi, Abijah,
⁵ Mijamin, Maadiah, Bilgah,
⁶ Shemaiah, Joiarib, Jedaiah,
⁷ Sallu, Amok, Hilkiah, Jedaiah.
These were the heads of the priests and their relatives in the days of Jeshua.
⁸ The Levites:
Jeshua, Binnui, Kadmiel,
Sherebiah, Judah, and Mattaniah —
he and his relatives were in charge of the songs of praise.

---

^A11:24 Lit *was at the king's hand* ^B11:31 Or *descendants from Geba lived in*

9 Bakbukiah, Unni,^A and their relatives stood opposite them in the services.
10 Jeshua fathered Joiakim,
Joiakim fathered Eliashib,
Eliashib fathered Joiada,
11 Joiada fathered Jonathan,
and Jonathan fathered Jaddua.^B

12 In the days of Joiakim, the heads of the priestly families were

Meraiah	of Seraiah,
Hananiah	of Jeremiah,
13 Meshullam	of Ezra,
Jehohanan	of Amariah,
14 Jonathan	of Malluchi,
Joseph	of Shebaniah,
15 Adna	of Harim,
Helkai	of Meraioth,
16 Zechariah	of Iddo,
Meshullam	of Ginnethon,
17 Zichri	of Abijah,
Piltai	of Moadiah, of Miniamin,
18 Shammua	of Bilgah,
Jehonathan	of Shemaiah,
19 Mattenai	of Joiarib,
Uzzi	of Jedaiah,
20 Kallai	of Sallai,
Eber	of Amok,
21 Hashabiah	of Hilkiah,
and Nethanel	of Jedaiah.

22 In the days of Eliashib, Joiada, Johanan, and Jaddua, the heads of the families of the Levites and priests were recorded while Darius the Persian ruled. 23 Levi's descendants, the family heads, were recorded in the Book of the Historical Events during the days of Johanan son of Eliashib. 24 The heads of the Levites — Hashabiah, Sherebiah, and Jeshua son of Kadmiel, along with their relatives opposite them — gave praise and thanks, division by division, as David the man of God had prescribed. 25 This included Mattaniah, Bakbukiah, and Obadiah. Meshullam, Talmon, and Akkub were gatekeepers who guarded the storerooms at the city gates. 26 These served in the days of Joiakim son of Jeshua, son of Jozadak, and in the days of Nehemiah the governor and Ezra the priest and scribe.

DEDICATION OF THE WALL

27 At the dedication of the wall of Jerusalem, they sent for the Levites wherever they lived and brought them to Jerusalem to celebrate the joyous dedication with thanksgiving and singing accompanied by cymbals, harps, and lyres. 28 The singers gathered from the region around Jerusalem, from the settlements of the Netophathites, 29 from Beth-gilgal, and from the fields of

---

^A12:9 Alt Hb tradition reads *Unno*   ^B12:10-11 These men were high priests.

Geba and Azmaveth, for they had built settlements for themselves around Jerusalem. ³⁰ After the priests and Levites had purified themselves, they purified the people, the city gates, and the wall.

³¹ Then I brought the leaders of Judah up on top of the wall, and I appointed two large processions that gave thanks. One went to the right on the wall, toward the Dung Gate. ³² Hoshaiah and half the leaders of Judah followed, ³³ along with Azariah, Ezra, Meshullam, ³⁴ Judah, Benjamin, Shemaiah, Jeremiah, ³⁵ and some of the priests' sons with trumpets, and Zechariah son of Jonathan, son of Shemaiah, son of Mattaniah, son of Micaiah, son of Zaccur, son of Asaph followed ³⁶ as well as his relatives — Shemaiah, Azarel, Milalai, Gilalai, Maai, Nethanel, Judah, and Hanani, with the musical instruments of David, the man of God. Ezra the scribe went in front of them. ³⁷ At the Fountain Gate they climbed the steps of the city of David on the ascent of the wall and went above the house of David to the Water Gate on the east.

³⁸ The second thanksgiving procession went to the left, and I followed it with half the people along the top of the wall, past the Tower of the Ovens to the Broad Wall, ³⁹ above the Ephraim Gate, and by the Old Gate, the Fish Gate, the Tower of Hananel, and the Tower of the Hundred, to the Sheep Gate. They stopped at the Gate of the Guard. ⁴⁰ The two thanksgiving processions stood in the house of God. So did I and half of the officials accompanying me, ⁴¹ as well as the priests:

Eliakim, Maaseiah, Miniamin,
Micaiah, Elioenai, Zechariah,
and Hananiah, with trumpets;
⁴² and Maaseiah, Shemaiah, Eleazar,
Uzzi, Jehohanan, Malchijah, Elam, and Ezer.

Then the singers sang, with Jezrahiah as the leader. ⁴³ On that day they offered great sacrifices and rejoiced because God had given them great joy. The women and children also celebrated, and Jerusalem's rejoicing was heard far away.

SUPPORT OF THE LEVITES' MINISTRY

⁴⁴ On that same day men were placed in charge of the rooms that housed the supplies, contributions, firstfruits, and tenths. The legally required portions for the priests and Levites were gathered from the village fields, because Judah was grateful to the priests and Levites who were serving. ⁴⁵ They performed the service of their God and the service of purification, along with the singers and gatekeepers, as David and his son Solomon had prescribed. ⁴⁶ For long ago, in the days of David and Asaph, there were heads ᴬ of the singers and songs of praise and thanksgiving to God. ⁴⁷ So in the days of Zerubbabel and Nehemiah, all Israel contributed the daily portions for the singers and gatekeepers. They also set aside daily portions for the Levites, and the Levites set aside daily portions for Aaron's descendants.

NEHEMIAH'S FURTHER REFORMS

13 At that time the book of Moses was read publicly to ᴮ the people. The command was found written in it that no Ammonite or Moabite should ever enter the assembly of God, ² because they did not meet the Israelites with food and water. Instead, they hired Balaam against them to

---

ᴬ12:46 Alt Hb tradition reads *there was a head* ᴮ13:1 Lit *read in the ears of* curse them, but our God turned the curse into a blessing. ³ When they heard the law, they separated all those of mixed descent from Israel.

⁴ Now before this, the priest Eliashib had been put in charge of the storerooms of the house of our God. He was a relative ᴬ of Tobiah ⁵ and had prepared a large room for him where they had previously stored the grain offerings, the frankincense, the articles, and the tenths of grain, new wine, and fresh oil prescribed for the Levites, singers, and gatekeepers, along with the contributions for the priests.

⁶ While all this was happening, I was not in Jerusalem, because I had returned to King Artaxerxes of Babylon in the thirty-second year of his reign. It was only later that I asked the king for a leave of absence ⁷ so I could return to Jerusalem. Then I discovered the evil that Eliashib had done on behalf of Tobiah by providing him a room in the courts of God's house. ⁸ I was greatly displeased and threw all of Tobiah's household possessions out of the room. ⁹ I ordered that the rooms be purified, and I had the articles of the house of God restored there, along with the grain offering and frankincense. ¹⁰ I also found out that because the portions for the Levites had not been given, each of the Levites and the singers performing the service had gone back to his own field. ¹¹ Therefore, I rebuked the officials, asking, "Why has the house of God been neglected?" I gathered the Levites and singers together and stationed them at their posts. ¹² Then all Judah brought a tenth of the grain, new wine, and fresh oil into the storehouses. ¹³ I appointed as treasurers over the storehouses the priest Shelemiah, the scribe Zadok, and Pedaiah of the Levites, with Hanan son of Zaccur, son of Mattaniah to assist them, because they were considered trustworthy. They were responsible for the distribution to their colleagues.

¹⁴ Remember me for this, my God, and don't erase the deeds of faithful love I have done for the house of my God and for its services.

¹⁵ At that time I saw people in Judah treading winepresses on the Sabbath. They were also bringing in stores of grain and loading them on donkeys, along with wine, grapes, and figs. All kinds of goods were being brought to Jerusalem on the Sabbath day. So I warned them against selling food on that day. ¹⁶ The Tyrians living there were importing fish and all kinds of merchandise and selling them on the Sabbath to the people of Judah in Jerusalem.

¹⁷ I rebuked the nobles of Judah and said to them: "What is this evil you are doing — profaning the Sabbath day? ¹⁸ Didn't your ancestors do the same, so that our God brought all this disaster on us and on this city? And now you are rekindling his anger against Israel by profaning the Sabbath!"

¹⁹ When shadows began to fall on the city gates of Jerusalem just before the Sabbath, I gave orders that the city gates be closed and not opened until after the Sabbath. I posted some of my men at the gates, so that no goods could enter during the Sabbath day. ²⁰ Once or twice the merchants and those who sell all kinds of goods camped outside Jerusalem, ²¹ but I warned them, "Why are you camping in front of the wall? If you do it again, I'll use force ᴮ against you." After that they did not come again on the Sabbath. ²² Then I instructed the Levites to purify themselves and guard the city gates in order to keep the Sabbath day holy.

ᴬ 13:4 Or *an associate*   ᴮ 13:21 Lit *again, I will send a hand*

BACK TO THE START

NEHEMIAH 13; PHILIPPIANS 1:6

Sometimes the ancient Israelites remind me of a group of middle schoolers at church camp. God shows them their sin and a new passion is lit within. All sweaty and sunburned, they commit and recommit their lives to obedience and Christian music.

Of course, it doesn't take long before that church-camp high wears off. They no longer have chapel services twice a day, the songs they sing back at their home church aren't nearly as hip, they aren't eating lunch across the table from their youth pastor, and, doggone it, their parents just don't understand.

It's a little humorous when we think of the Israelites as middle school campers, but it's a lot less pretty when we see these patterns of disobedience at work in church members, leaders, and ourselves.

God had done an awesome thing for Israel—He rebuilt their wall and restored their gates; but not only that, the Israelites were also restored spiritually. They were a city again, brought back from exile and thriving in every way. Many of them must have wondered if they'd ever see this day again. And so, they re-covenanted with God (Neh 10:37-39). And this time, they really did mean it.

But when Nehemiah went back to Babylon to serve the king, all Israel's confessing and camp-fire songs became a distant memory. And they forgot their covenant—forgot their God—again.

Why do you think the book of Nehemiah ends the way it does—with failure and backsliding instead of a permanently changed people? What does God want us to see here about Himself and the Church?

Like Israel, we fail over and over, again and again. Like them, we are weak. We quickly fall back into the enticing ways of sin and forget our heavenly Father and all He has done for us.

But when we focus on our inability to remain faithful, we forget the other side: "while we were still sinners, Christ died for us" (Rm 5:8). Regardless of the number of times we have and will fall back into sin, Jesus' sacrifice still covers us. He will not leave us in darkness. He will continue to do His good work in us.

This is our Savior. He never gives up on us. He continues to pursue our hearts and mold them more and more into His image, even when it feels like we've slid back to the start. Praise the Lord that sanctification is a process!

"I am sure of this, that he who started a good work in you will carry it on to completion until the day of Christ Jesus."

PHILIPPIANS 1:6

Remember me for this also, my God, and look on me with compassion according to the abundance of your faithful love.

²³ In those days I also saw Jews who had married women from Ashdod, Ammon, and Moab. ²⁴ Half of their children spoke the language of Ashdod or the language of one of the other peoples but could not speak Hebrew.^A ²⁵ I rebuked them, cursed them, beat some of their men, and pulled out their hair. I forced them to take an oath before God and said, "You must not give your daughters in marriage to their sons or take their daughters as wives for your sons or yourselves! ²⁶ Didn't King Solomon of Israel sin in matters like this? There was not a king like him among many nations. He was loved by his God, and God made him king over all Israel, yet foreign women drew him into sin. ²⁷ Why then should we hear about you doing all this terrible evil and acting unfaithfully against our God by marrying foreign women?" ²⁸ Even one of the sons of Jehoiada, son of the high priest Eliashib, had become a son-in-law to Sanballat the Horonite. So I drove him away from me.

²⁹ Remember them, my God, for defiling the priesthood as well as the covenant of the priesthood and the Levites.

³⁰ So I purified them from everything foreign and assigned specific duties to each of the priests and Levites. ³¹ I also arranged for the donation of wood at the appointed times and for the firstfruits.

Remember me, my God, with favor.

---

^A 13:24 Lit *Judahite*

For Such A Time As This

esther

 If you keep silent at this time, relief and deliverance will come to the Jewish people from another place, but you and your father's family will be destroyed. Who knows, perhaps you have come to your royal position for such a time as this. **4:14**

ON THE TIMELINE The story of Esther is rooted in the historical account of King Ahasuerus, who ruled as king of Persia from 486–465 BC. Esther is made queen of Persia in approximately 479 BC, Haman's plot to destroy the Jews occurs in 474 BC, and the first celebration of Purim occurs in 473 BC. The events in Esther occur before the events of Nehemiah, but after the Decree of Cyrus had allowed the Jews in exile to return to Jerusalem. Most likely the book was written in the fourth century BC with Mordecai as its author.

A LITTLE BACKGROUND The book of Esther never mentions God by name, although His presence is implied in Mordecai's allusion to divine providence (Est 4:14). The book of Esther is tightly connected with specific historical events, yet it is also a piece of literature, a narrative with all of the literary features necessary to make a great story. Esther is also unique in that its purposes are not always explicitly stated but are derived from the story as a whole.

MESSAGE & PURPOSE For the Jewish people scattered around the Persian Empire, the book of Esther was a story that gave encouragement and hope. It provided a model of how Jewish people could not just survive, but thrive in a Gentile environment. It displayed the work of God, evident but unseen, in the unfolding story of deliverance and redemption—making an orphan girl the queen and using her courage and influence to save the Jews from annihilation.

GIVE THANKS FOR THE BOOK OF ESTHER:

Without ever mentioning God directly, the book of Esther underscores the providence of God. God's promise to give the Jews an eternal ruler remained in place, even in the face of threatened annihilation. Esther shows us that many Jews remained faithful to their God even in exile. Some scholars believe they kept their identity as God's people through the synagogues that developed as centers of the Jewish community wherever Jews were dispersed. The synagogues would later play a significant role as the gospel spread throughout the Roman Empire.

BLACK SEA

MACEDONIA

TROAS

THERMOPYLAE

CAPPADOCIA

MALATYA

NINEVAH

The Persian advance is stopped
in 486 BC by Greek warriors.
Darius retreats in defeat

The Battle
of Thermopylae

BABYLON

MEDITERRANEAN SEA

JERUSALEM

ARABIA

Ahasueru
sacks Babylo
in 480 BC

Southern Palestine is valuable
due to its control of the major
routes leading to Egypt

EGYPT

SAHARA DESERT

SYRO-ARABIA
DESERT

RED SEA

PERSIAN EMPIRE

PERSIAN EMPIRE
ROYAL ROAD
OTHER ROADS

CASPIAN SEA

Site where Darius
began building a
new royal residence

Ahasuerus dies in
coup in 465 BC

ONIA

PERSIS

PERSIAN GULF

INDUS VALLEY

READ AND UNDERSTAND ESTHER

The Bible is a complete work in which many stories combine to tell one story. As you read the book of Esther, consider reading the additional passages to discover how the whole of Scripture works together.

Week 1	GOING DEEPER
☐ **Esther 1**	Psalm 32:7; Proverbs 27:15-16
☐ Esther 2	Proverbs 31:10-31; John 10:27-29
☐ Esther 3	Psalm 68:20; Proverbs 16:33
☐ **Esther 4**	Isaiah 15:1-3; Romans 5:6-11
☐ Esther 5	Proverbs 16:18; Mark 6:14-29

Week 2	GOING DEEPER
☐ Esther 6	Proverbs 26:27; Isaiah 52:1-2
☐ **Esther 7**	Psalm 91:2-3; Revelation 20:11-15
☐ Esther 8	Romans 8:10-11; Colossians 3:1-4
☐ Esther 9:1-22	Nehemiah 8:10; Luke 1:46-55
☐ **Esther 9:23–10:3**	Leviticus 16:29-31; Ephesians 1:3-14

VASHTI ANGERS THE KING

1 These events took place during the days of Ahasuerus, who ruled 127 provinces from India to Cush. ² In those days King Ahasuerus reigned from his royal throne in the fortress at Susa. ³ He held a feast in the third year of his reign for all his officials and staff, the army of Persia and Media, the nobles, and the officials from the provinces. ⁴ He displayed the glorious wealth of his kingdom and the magnificent splendor of his greatness for a total of 180 days.

⁵ At the end of this time, the king held a week-long banquet in the garden courtyard of the royal palace for all the people, from the greatest to the least, who were present in the fortress of Susa. ⁶ White and violet linen hangings were fastened with fine white and purple linen cords to silver rods on marble^A columns. Gold and silver couches were arranged on a mosaic pavement of red feldspar, ^B marble, mother-of-pearl, and precious stones.

⁷ Drinks were served in an array of gold goblets, each with a different design. Royal wine flowed freely, according to the king's bounty. ⁸ The drinking was according to royal decree: "There are no restrictions." The king had ordered every wine steward in his household to serve whatever each person wanted. ⁹ Queen Vashti also gave a feast for the women of King Ahasuerus's palace.

¹⁰ On the seventh day, when the king was feeling good from the wine, Ahasuerus commanded Mehuman, Biztha, Harbona, Bigtha, Abagtha, Zethar, and Carkas — the seven eunuchs who personally served him — ¹¹ to bring Queen Vashti before him with her royal crown. He wanted to show off her beauty to the people and the officials, because she was very beautiful. ¹² But Queen Vashti refused to come at the king's command that was delivered by his eunuchs. The king became furious and his anger burned within him.

THE KING'S DECREE

¹³ The king consulted the wise men who understood the times, ^C for it was his normal procedure to confer with experts in law and justice. ¹⁴ The most trusted ones ^D were Carshena, Shethar, Admatha, Tarshish, Meres, Marsena, and Memucan. They were the seven officials of Persia and Media who had personal access to the king and occupied the highest positions in the kingdom. ¹⁵ The king asked, "According to the law, what should be done with Queen Vashti, since she refused to obey King Ahasuerus's command that was delivered by the eunuchs?"

¹⁶ Memucan said in the presence of the king and his officials, "Queen Vashti has wronged not only the king, but all the officials and the peoples who are in every one of King Ahasuerus's provinces. ¹⁷ For the queen's action will become public knowledge to all the women and cause them to despise their husbands and say, 'King Ahasuerus ordered Queen Vashti brought before him, but she did not come.' ¹⁸ Before this day is over, the noble women of Persia and Media who hear about the queen's act will say the same thing to all the king's officials, resulting in more contempt and fury.

¹⁹ "If it meets the king's approval, he should personally issue a royal decree. Let it be recorded in the laws of Persia and Media, so that it cannot be revoked: Vashti is not to enter King Ahasuerus's presence, and her royal position is to be given to another woman who is more worthy than she. ²⁰ The

---

^A 1:6 Or *alabaster*   ^B 1:6 Or *of porphyry*   ^C 1:13 Or *understood propitious times*
^D 1:14 Lit *Those near him*

THE AUTHOR AND THE LEAD

ESTHER 1; 2 PETER 1:19

Everyone has a strong response to this passage.

There are two main camps: Vashti the brave and Vashti the bad.

Vashti the brave: Some smart people think Ahasuerus (also called Xerxes) was a drunken voyeur who wanted to show off his gorgeous queen to his party guests. She refused. I call this the "Vashti, you go girl" response.

Vashti the bad: On the other hand, some scholars argue Ahasuerus was calling his queen to perform a normal state function: show up at the party. Ahasuerus was planning to go to war with Greece, and he needed Vashti to show up to underscore to all the visiting dignitaries that he was powerful and magnificent enough to be the guy who could defeat the Greeks. It was embarrassing when she refused him. Ahasuerus and his wise men make an example of her to keep other women from undercutting their husbands as well.

Whether we interpret Vashti's actions as brave or bad, this story is about God and His providential care for His chosen people in exile. Vashti is a side note in the book of Esther, but **God is the main character of every story.**

The easy response to this passage is to fall into the same trap as Ahasuerus and think the story is about him, or Vashti, or even Esther. Our temptation is to draw an easy moral here: if Vashti did

right, it's "stand up for your dignity," and if she was wrong, it's "submit to authority."

But let's push past those easy responses and consider wisdom rather than moralism. It's hard to decipher what the people in this story are up to, and Scripture doesn't give us a final verdict on Vashti's actions. What we do know is Queen Vashti had to come and go so Queen Esther could take her place. God would use Esther to save Israel from genocide in the Babylonian exile.

God doesn't necessarily call us to understand everything that's happening in Vashti's story, or even in our own story! But He does call us to be faithful in the everyday things. He calls us to wisdom. When we look at Vashti, we aren't going to find it. We have to look to the main character in every story: God.

Wisdom is a lamp shining in a dark place (2Pt 1:19). It is looking to God for our guidance rather than to the ways or expectations of man. Wisdom isn't knowing all the answers—it's knowing what's important, and walking in light of that.

We don't get all the details about the stories we read, and we don't even get all the details about the stories we're in. We do, however, get the bullet points from the author and star Himself: Do justice. Love mercy. Walk humbly (Mc 6:8).

Don't be afraid of what you don't know. God knows. Walk in His wisdom.

decree the king issues will be heard throughout his vast kingdom, so all women will honor their husbands, from the greatest to the least."

²¹ The king and his counselors approved the proposal, and he followed Memucan's advice. ²² He sent letters to all the royal provinces, to each province in its own script and to each ethnic group in its own language, that every man should be master of his own house and speak in the language of his own people.

THE SEARCH FOR A NEW QUEEN

2 Some time later, when King Ahasuerus's rage had cooled down, he remembered Vashti, what she had done, and what was decided against her. ² The king's personal attendants suggested, "Let a search be made for beautiful young virgins for the king. ³ Let the king appoint commissioners in each province of his kingdom, so that they may gather all the beautiful young virgins to the harem at the fortress of Susa. Put them under the supervision of Hegai, the king's eunuch, keeper of the women, and give them the required beauty treatments. ⁴ Then the young woman who pleases the king will become queen instead of Vashti." This suggestion pleased the king, and he did accordingly.

⁵ In the fortress of Susa, there was a Jewish man named Mordecai son of Jair, son of Shimei, son of Kish, a Benjaminite. ⁶ He had been taken into exile from Jerusalem with the other captives when King Nebuchadnezzar of Babylon took King Jeconiah of Judah into exile. ⁷ Mordecai was the legal guardian of his cousinᴬ Hadassah (that is, Esther), because she had no father or mother. The young woman had a beautiful figure and was extremely good-looking. When her father and mother died, Mordecai had adopted her as his own daughter.

⁸ When the king's command and edict became public knowledge and when many young women were gathered at the fortress of Susa under Hegai's supervision, Esther was taken to the palace, into the supervision of Hegai, keeper of the women. ⁹ The young woman pleased him and gained his favor so that he accelerated the process of the beauty treatments and the special diet that she received. He assigned seven hand-picked female servants to her from the palace and transferred her and her servants to the harem's best quarters.

¹⁰ Esther did not reveal her ethnicity or her family background, because Mordecai had ordered her not to make them known. ¹¹ Every day Mordecai took a walk in front of the harem's courtyard to learn how Esther was doing and to see what was happening to her.

¹² During the year before each young woman's turn to go to King Ahasuerus, the harem regulation required her to receive beauty treatments with oil of myrrh for six months and then with perfumes and cosmetics for another six months. ¹³ When the young woman would go to the king, she was given whatever she requested to take with her from the harem to the palace. ¹⁴ She would go in the evening, and in the morning she would return to a second harem under the supervision of the king's eunuch Shaashgaz, keeper of the concubines. She never went to the king again, unless he desired her and summoned her by name.

ᴬ2:7 Lit uncle's daughter

ESTHER BECOMES QUEEN

¹⁵ Esther was the daughter of Abihail, the uncle of Mordecai who had adopted her as his own daughter. When her turn came to go to the king, she did not ask for anything except what Hegai, the king's eunuch, keeper of the women, suggested. Esther gained favor in the eyes of everyone who saw her. ¹⁶ She was taken to King Ahasuerus in the palace in the tenth month, the month Tebeth, in the seventh year of his reign. ¹⁷ The king loved Esther more than all the other women. She won more favor and approval from him than did any of the other virgins. He placed the royal crown on her head and made her queen in place of Vashti. ¹⁸ The king held a great banquet for all his officials and staff. It was Esther's banquet. He freed his provinces from tax payments and gave gifts worthy of the king's bounty.

MORDECAI SAVES THE KING

¹⁹ When the virgins were gathered a second time, Mordecai was sitting at the King's Gate. ²⁰ (Esther had not revealed her family background or her ethnicity, as Mordecai had directed. She obeyed Mordecai's orders, as she always had while he raised her.)

²¹ During those days while Mordecai was sitting at the King's Gate, Bigthan and Teresh, two of the king's eunuchs who guarded the entrance, became infuriated and planned to assassinate ᴬ King Ahasuerus. ²² When Mordecai learned of the plot, he reported it to Queen Esther, and she told the king on Mordecai's behalf. ²³ When the report was investigated and verified, both men were hanged on the gallows. This event was recorded in the Historical Record in the king's presence.

HAMAN'S PLAN TO KILL THE JEWS

3 After all this took place, King Ahasuerus honored Haman, son of Hammedatha the Agagite. He promoted him in rank and gave him a higher position than all the other officials. ² The entire royal staff at the King's Gate bowed down and paid homage to Haman, because the king had commanded this to be done for him. But Mordecai would not bow down or pay homage. ³ The members of the royal staff at the King's Gate asked Mordecai, "Why are you disobeying the king's command?" ⁴ When they had warned him day after day and he still would not listen to them, they told Haman in order to see if Mordecai's actions would be tolerated, since he had told them he was a Jew.

⁵ When Haman saw that Mordecai was not bowing down or paying him homage, he was filled with rage. ⁶ And when he learned of Mordecai's ethnic identity, it seemed repugnant to Haman to do away with ᴮ Mordecai alone. He planned to destroy all of Mordecai's people, the Jews, throughout Ahasuerus's kingdom.

⁷ In the first month, the month of Nisan, in King Ahasuerus's twelfth year, the Pur — that is, the lot — was cast before Haman for each day in each month, and it fell on the twelfth month, the month Adar. ⁸ Then Haman informed King Ahasuerus, "There is one ethnic group, scattered throughout the peoples in every province of your kingdom, keeping themselves separate. Their laws are different from everyone else's and they do not obey

---

ᴬ2:21 Lit *and they sought to stretch out a hand against*   ᴮ3:6 Lit *to stretch out a hand against*

TAKING PART IN GOD'S WORK

ESTHER 4; LUKE 19:37-40

Rachel is a scourge to the devil in Vienna.

Every time I saw her she was flushed with excitement over a recent chance to share the gospel. Any encounter on the subway, any phone call, and every relationship irresistibly impelled her to tell people the good news. Although she was a gifted linguist with a degree from Cambridge, she carried Bible tracts in her pockets and she wasn't afraid to use them.

No amount of poor or sad or weird was enough to keep Rachel from befriending strangers and reaching out to them with hope and love. She is inspiring and a little overwhelming.

One afternoon Rachel invited me to a street music event she was staging on Kärntner Straße. She is a classical violinist and had gathered other string musicians to play a concert and share the gospel on that ancient, black stone street.

Feeling both shy and peckish, I got a gelato and went antique shopping instead.

I missed an opportunity. God didn't need me to help share His gospel; His gospel will go forth whether I stand up and speak His name or not. In fact, if I can't muster a good word about the Lord, the very stones will cry out in my place (Lk 19:40).

God invites us to join His work, not for His sake, but for ours. God invited Esther to join Him in saving the Jewish nation. If Esther had refused to go to the king, God still would have saved His people, but she would have missed an opportunity. As Esther's cousin Mordecai said:

> "If you keep silent at this time, relief and deliverance will come to the Jewish people from another place, but you and your father's family will be destroyed. Who knows, perhaps you have come to your royal position for such a time as this."
>
> ESTHER 4:14

Our refusal to take part in God's work doesn't thwart God. It limits our privilege to take part in what He is doing. God can even use unrepentant sinners to achieve His good purposes. Consider Pharaoh, Caiaphas the high priest, and Pontius Pilate (Ex 9:12; Jn 18:14; 19:5-16).

God's providence is comprehensive, wise, and holy. His timing and calling are no mistake, and He has placed us, like Esther, here, now, and for such a time as this.

We, like Esther, can have courage, comfort, and peace. From a human perspective, our lives and circumstances can seem totally out of control and scary. But we can rest in God's providence, knowing that He is working.

Look for God's invitation to join Him in His work. Have courage, comfort, and peace—you can join Him! You can get a gelato later.

the king's laws. It is not in the king's best interest to tolerate them. ⁹ If the king approves, let an order be drawn up authorizing their destruction, and I will pay 375 tons of silver to ᴬ the officials for deposit in the royal treasury."

¹⁰ The king removed his signet ring from his finger and gave it to Haman son of Hammedatha the Agagite, the enemy of the Jewish people. ¹¹ Then the king told Haman, "The money and people are given to you to do with as you see fit."

¹² The royal scribes were summoned on the thirteenth day of the first month, and the order was written exactly as Haman commanded. It was intended for the royal satraps, the governors of each of the provinces, and the officials of each ethnic group and written for each province in its own script and to each ethnic group in its own language. It was written in the name of King Ahasuerus and sealed with the royal signet ring. ¹³ Letters were sent by couriers to each of the royal provinces telling the officials to destroy, kill, and annihilate all the Jewish people — young and old, women and children — and plunder their possessions on a single day, the thirteenth day of Adar, the twelfth month. ᴮ

¹⁴ A copy of the text, issued as law throughout every province, was distributed to all the peoples so that they might get ready for that day. ¹⁵ The couriers left, spurred on by royal command, and the law was issued in the fortress of Susa. The king and Haman sat down to drink, while the city of Susa was in confusion.

MORDECAI APPEALS TO ESTHER

4 When Mordecai learned all that had occurred, he tore his clothes, put on sackcloth and ashes, went into the middle of the city, and cried loudly and bitterly. ² He went only as far as the King's Gate, since the law prohibited anyone wearing sackcloth from entering the King's Gate. ³ There was great mourning among the Jewish people in every province where the king's command and edict came. They fasted, wept, and lamented, and many lay in sackcloth and ashes.

⁴ Esther's female servants and her eunuchs came and reported the news to her, and the queen was overcome with fear. She sent clothes for Mordecai to wear so that he would take off his sackcloth, but he did not accept them. ⁵ Esther summoned Hathach, one of the king's eunuchs who attended her, and dispatched him to Mordecai to learn what he was doing and why. ᶜ ⁶ So Hathach went out to Mordecai in the city square in front of the King's Gate. ⁷ Mordecai told him everything that had happened as well as the exact amount of money Haman had promised to pay the royal treasury for the slaughter of the Jews.

⁸ Mordecai also gave him a copy of the written decree issued in Susa ordering their destruction, so that Hathach might show it to Esther, explain it to her, and command her to approach the king, implore his favor, and plead with him personally for her people. ⁹ Hathach came and repeated Mordecai's response to Esther.

¹⁰ Esther spoke to Hathach and commanded him to tell Mordecai, ¹¹ "All the royal officials and the people of the royal provinces know that one law

---

ᴬ 3:9 Lit *will weigh 10,000 silver talents on the hands of*   ᴮ 3:13 LXX adds the text of Ahasuerus's letter here.   ᶜ 4:5 Lit *what is this and why is this* officials of the 127 provinces from India to Cush. The edict was written for each province in its own script, for each ethnic group in its own language, and to the Jews in their own script and language.

¹⁰ Mordecai wrote in King Ahasuerus's name and sealed the edicts with the royal signet ring. He sent the documents by mounted couriers, who rode fast horses bred in the royal stables.

¹¹ The king's edict gave the Jews in each and every city the right to assemble and defend themselves, to destroy, kill, and annihilate every ethnic and provincial army hostile to them, including women and children, and to take their possessions as spoils of war. ¹² This would take place on a single day throughout all the provinces of King Ahasuerus, on the thirteenth day of the twelfth month, the month Adar.

¹³ A copy of the text, issued as law throughout every province, was distributed to all the peoples so the Jews could be ready to avenge themselves against their enemies on that day. ¹⁴ The couriers rode out in haste on their royal horses at the king's urgent command. The law was also issued in the fortress of Susa.

¹⁵ Mordecai went from the king's presence clothed in royal purple and white, with a great gold crown and a purple robe of fine linen. The city of Susa shouted and rejoiced, ¹⁶ and the Jews celebrated ᴬ with gladness, joy, and honor. ¹⁷ In every province and every city, wherever the king's command and his law reached, joy and rejoicing took place among the Jews. There was a celebration and a holiday. ᴮ And many of the ethnic groups of the land professed themselves to be Jews because fear of the Jews had overcome them.

VICTORIES OF THE JEWS

9 The king's command and law went into effect on the thirteenth day of the twelfth month, the month Adar. On the day when the Jews' enemies had hoped to overpower them, just the opposite happened. The Jews overpowered those who hated them. ² In each of King Ahasuerus's provinces the Jews assembled in their cities to attack those who intended to harm them. ᶜ Not a single person could withstand them; fear of them fell on every nationality.

³ All the officials of the provinces, the satraps, the governors, and the royal civil administrators ᴰ aided the Jews because they feared Mordecai. ⁴ For Mordecai exercised great power in the palace, and his fame spread throughout the provinces as he became more and more powerful.

⁵ The Jews put all their enemies to the sword, killing and destroying them. They did what they pleased to those who hated them. ⁶ In the fortress of Susa the Jews killed and destroyed five hundred men, ⁷ including Parshandatha, Dalphon, Aspatha, ⁸ Poratha, Adalia, Aridatha, ⁹ Parmashta, Arisai, Aridai, and Vaizatha. ¹⁰ They killed these ten sons of Haman son of Hammedatha, the enemy of the Jews. However, they did not seize ᴱ any plunder.

¹¹ On that day the number of people killed in the fortress of Susa was reported to the king. ¹² The king said to Queen Esther, "In the fortress of Susa the Jews have killed and destroyed five hundred men, including Haman's

---

ᴬ8:16 Lit had light   ᴮ8:17 Lit good day   ᶜ9:2 Lit cities to send out a hand against the seekers of their evil   ᴰ9:3 Lit and those who do the king's work ; Est 3:9
ᴱ9:10 Lit not put their hands on, also in vv. 15,16

ten sons. What have they done in the rest of the royal provinces? Whatever you ask will be given to you. Whatever you seek will also be done."

[13] Esther answered, "If it pleases the king, may the Jews who are in Susa also have tomorrow to carry out today's law, and may the bodies of Haman's ten sons be hung on the gallows." [14] The king gave the orders for this to be done, so a law was announced in Susa, and they hung the bodies of Haman's ten sons. [15] The Jews in Susa assembled again on the fourteenth day of the month of Adar and killed three hundred men in Susa, but they did not seize any plunder.

[16] The rest of the Jews in the royal provinces assembled, defended themselves, and gained relief from their enemies. They killed seventy-five thousand[A] of those who hated them, but they did not seize any plunder. [17] They fought on the thirteenth day of the month of Adar and rested on the fourteenth, and it became a day of feasting and rejoicing.

[18] But the Jews in Susa had assembled on the thirteenth and the fourteenth days of the month. They rested on the fifteenth day of the month, and it became a day of feasting and rejoicing. [19] This explains why the rural Jews who live in villages observe the fourteenth day of the month of Adar as a time of rejoicing and feasting. It is a holiday when they send gifts to one another.

[20] Mordecai recorded these events and sent letters to all the Jews in all of King Ahasuerus's provinces, both near and far. [21] He ordered them to celebrate the fourteenth and fifteenth days of the month of Adar every year [22] because during those days the Jews gained relief from their enemies. That was the month when their sorrow was turned into rejoicing and their mourning into a holiday. They were to be days of feasting, rejoicing, and of sending gifts to one another and to the poor.

[23] So the Jews agreed to continue the practice they had begun, as Mordecai had written them to do. [24] For Haman son of Hammedatha the Agagite, the enemy of all the Jews, had plotted against the Jews to destroy them. He cast the Pur — that is, the lot — to crush and destroy them. [25] But when the matter was brought before the king, he commanded by letter that the evil plan Haman had devised against the Jews return on his own head and that he should be hanged with his sons on the gallows. [26] For this reason these days are called Purim, from the word Pur. Because of all the instructions in this letter as well as what they had witnessed and what had happened to them, [27] the Jews bound themselves, their descendants, and all who joined with them to a commitment that they would not fail to celebrate these two days each and every year according to the written instructions and according to the time appointed. [28] These days are remembered and celebrated by every generation, family, province, and city, so that these days of Purim will not lose their significance in Jewish life[B] and their memory will not fade from their descendants.

[29] Queen Esther, daughter of Abihail, along with Mordecai the Jew, wrote this second letter with full authority to confirm the letter about Purim. [30] He sent letters with assurances of peace and security[C] to all the Jews who were in the 127 provinces of the kingdom of Ahasuerus, [31] in order to confirm these days of Purim at their proper time just as Mordecai the Jew and Esther the

---

[A] 9:16 Some LXX mss read *10,107*; other LXX mss read *15,000*   [B] 9:28 LXX reads *will be celebrated into all times*   [C] 9:30 Or *of peace and faithfulness*

REMEMBERING OUR RESCUE

ESTHER 9:23–10:3; PSALM 78:1-8

When I helped my parents move into their home a few years ago, I ran across a box of my mom's prayer journals. I spread them out on the floor, not to read them but to take in the sheer number of them. They were a legacy of faith, Ebenezer's chronicling God's faithfulness through time—days and years and seasons of prayer and praise to God from His precious daughter (1Sm 7:12). I snuck a picture so I could remember.

As the book of Esther draws to a close, I'm struck by the care and determination with which Mordecai preserves the story—their story. The days of Purim would be observed from that time forward, on the same days each year, for all generations. The Lord delivered His people from their enemies; He turned their sorrow into gladness and their mourning into a holiday. And they vow, joyfully yet solemnly, to remember.

What a vivid picture of the restoration we experience in the gospel of Jesus. We were weeping and sorrowful, but now we're throwing a party! Is this not the mix of reverence and joy with which we should view our salvation? We have been rescued from our enemy, even from ourselves. We have been preserved and restored in the midst of threats to our very souls.

In these last chapters of Esther, we learn that remembering involves more than whimsical, fleeting thoughts. **Remembering is a spiritual discipline that reorients our hearts and minds to the gospel of Jesus.**

Memories are powerful. Regularly and intentionally recalling the goodness of our God is an act of faithfulness that restores the fullness and joy of our salvation. They connect us to the legacy of God's people. It is the legacy of Mordecai and Esther, Abraham and Mary and Paul—a legacy that, by God's grace, will stretch far beyond us.

Remembering the past also gives us a new lens through which to view the future. How have you seen God's faithfulness in your life in the past week? The last year? What about in the lives of the generations that came before you? Like the prayers and praise that fill the pages of my mom's journals, remembering God's faithfulness in the past gives us courage to believe in His faithfulness for the future.

Our sovereign God is active in our lives today like He was active in the story of Queen Esther. Let's regularly remember and rejoice in God's rescue of His people, for ourselves and those who come after us, "so that they might put their confidence in God" (Ps 78:7).

"We will not hide them from their children, but will tell a future generation the praiseworthy acts of the LORD, his might, and the wondrous works he has performed."

PSALM 78:4

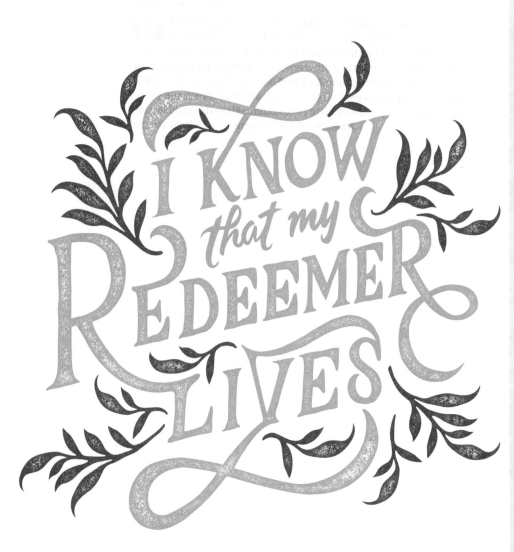

I KNOW that my REDEEMER LIVES

job

 But I know that my Redeemer lives, and at the end he will stand on the dust. **19:25**

ON THE TIMELINE Although Job is set in the patriarchal period, its date of writing and author are unknown. Jewish tradition places the authorship of Job in the time of Moses, approximately 1440 BC.

A LITTLE BACKGROUND In Job's era, wealth was measured in possession of cattle and servants. Like other Old Testament patriarchal family heads, Job performed priestly duties, including offering sacrifices for his family. And like the patriarchs, Job lived to be more than one hundred years old. Geographically, the events took place in the northern Arabian Peninsula, in the land of Uz (Jb 1:1), often associated with Edom.

MESSAGE & PURPOSE The book of Job demonstrates that a sovereign, righteous God is sufficient and trustworthy for every situation in life, even in the most difficult circumstances. Along with this truth, Job portrays other additional themes:

1. *Character* – Job is introduced as a man of character (Jb 1:1), and God testified to his consistently blameless character (Jb 1:8; 2:3). As Job saw it, in God's dealings with man, God does not appear always to reward a blameless and pure life (Jb 9:23; 10:14).
2. *Righteousness* – Job stated that his righteousness was the central issue in his situation (Jb 6:29), yet he wondered how he could convince God of this (Jb 9:2; 15,20; 10:15). All three of Job's friends condemned Job's attitude as self-righteous (Jb 32:1).
3. *Justice* – Job wanted to receive justice in his situation (Jb 19:7; 23:4). He renounced injustice (Jb 27:4) and modeled justice in his dealings with others (Jb 29:14; 31:13-15). Job felt that God had not always dealt justly with him (Jb 14:3; 23:10-16; 34:5-6). Rather than championing his own righteousness, Job is called to understand God's essential righteousness by which He justly governs the universe (Jb 40:7-14).

GIVE THANKS FOR THE BOOK OF JOB:

In the book of Job we are reminded that suffering comes to everyone, the righteous and unrighteous alike. God does not always keep the righteous from danger or suffering. Ultimately, God controls all of life's situations, including limiting the power of Satan. The book of Job demonstrates poignantly that God's comfort and strength are always available to the trusting soul.

JOB & JESUS

The Old Testament book of Job shares an intimate connection with the New Testament. Job's weightiest questions are perfectly answered in the person of Jesus Christ.

JOB ASKED	JESUS ANSWERED

JOB 9:32-33

Who can help us approach God?

1 TIMOTHY 2:5

"For there is one God and one mediator between God and humanity, the man Christ Jesus."

JOB 14:14

Is there life after death?

JOHN 11:25

"I am the resurrection and the life. The one who believes in me, even if he dies, will live."

JOB 16:19-21

Is there anyone in heaven working on our behalf?

HEBREWS 9:24

"For Christ did not enter a sanctuary made with hands ... but into heaven itself, so that he might now appear in the presence of God for us."

JOB 21:7-15

What is of eternal importance in life?

JOHN 3:16

"For God loved the world in this way: He gave his one and only Son, so that everyone who believes in him will not perish but have eternal life."

JOB 23:3-5

Where do we find God?

JOHN 14:19

"The one who has seen me has seen the Father."

ONE THING JOB KNEW:
"BUT I KNOW THAT MY REDEEMER LIVES, AND AT THE END HE WILL STAND ON THE DUST."

JOB 19:25

READ AND UNDERSTAND JOB

The Bible is a complete work in which many stories combine to tell one story. As you read the book of Job, consider reading the additional passages to discover how the whole of Scripture works together.

JOB AND HIS FAMILY

1 There was a man in the country of Uz named Job. He was a man of complete integrity, who feared God and turned away from evil. ² He had seven sons and three daughters. ³ His estate included seven thousand sheep and goats, three thousand camels, five hundred yoke of oxen, five hundred female donkeys, and a very large number of servants. Job was the greatest man among all the people of the east.

⁴ His sons used to take turns having banquets at their homes. They would send an invitation to their three sisters to eat and drink with them. ⁵ Whenever a round of banqueting was over, Job would send for his children and purify them, rising early in the morning to offer burnt offerings for ^A all of them. For Job thought, "Perhaps my children have sinned, having cursed God in their hearts." This was Job's regular practice.

SATAN'S FIRST TEST OF JOB

⁶ One day the sons of God came to present themselves before the Lᴏʀᴅ, and Satan ^B also came with them. ⁷ The Lᴏʀᴅ asked Satan, "Where have you come from?"

"From roaming through the earth," Satan answered him, "and walking around on it."

⁸ Then the Lᴏʀᴅ said to Satan, "Have you considered my servant Job? No one else on earth is like him, a man of perfect integrity, who fears God and turns away from evil."

⁹ Satan answered the Lᴏʀᴅ, "Does Job fear God for nothing? ¹⁰ Haven't you placed a hedge around him, his household, and everything he owns? You have blessed the work of his hands, and his possessions have increased in the land. ¹¹ But stretch out your hand and strike everything he owns, and he will surely curse you to your face."

¹² "Very well," the Lᴏʀᴅ told Satan, "everything he owns is in your power. However, do not lay a hand on Job himself." So Satan left the Lᴏʀᴅ's presence.

¹³ One day when Job's sons and daughters were eating and drinking wine in their oldest brother's house, ¹⁴ a messenger came to Job and reported: "While the oxen were plowing and the donkeys grazing nearby, ¹⁵ the Sabeans swooped down and took them away. They struck down the servants with the sword, and I alone have escaped to tell you!"

¹⁶ He was still speaking when another messenger came and reported: "God's fire fell from heaven. It burned the sheep and the servants and devoured them, and I alone have escaped to tell you!"

¹⁷ That messenger was still speaking when yet another came and reported: "The Chaldeans formed three bands, made a raid on the camels, and took them away. They struck down the servants with the sword, and I alone have escaped to tell you!"

¹⁸ He was still speaking when another messenger came and reported: "Your sons and daughters were eating and drinking wine in their oldest brother's house. ¹⁹ Suddenly a powerful wind swept in from the desert and struck the four corners of the house. It collapsed on the young people so that they died, and I alone have escaped to tell you!"

²⁰ Then Job stood up, tore his robe, and shaved his head. He fell to the ground and worshiped, ²¹ saying:

^A 1:5 Lit *for the number of*   ^B 1:6 Or *the adversary*

WHAT GOD ALLOWS
FOR HIS GLORY

JOB 1–2

When I was a kid, the tooth fairy was not a welcomed visitor.

I had friends who would wiggle free a not-ready tooth in exchange for a couple of quarters, but I was not one of them. I wanted my teeth to stay right where I had them, thank you very much. The whole thing seemed bloody, painful, and totally not worth the coins I would find under my pillow the next morning. So, I resolved against all teeth-pulling activities. If my pearly whites were going to come out of my mouth, they would have to fall out on their own.

Inevitably, I came of tooth-losing age, and as my baby teeth began to say their goodbyes, I'd do my best to barricade their exit. One morning, I woke up to a gaping hole where my tooth once was, gifts from the tooth fairy slipped under my pillow. My tongue furiously circled the empty gap. *How dare someone open my mouth and steal my teeth while I was asleep!*

When I read Job's story of tremendous grief, I can feel the air whistle through my own familiar voids. In the night, suffering comes to us, stealing what we once claimed as our own —joy, control, love, possessions, people.

Suffering stole all of those things from Job, following a rarely recorded conversation between God and Satan. When Satan threatened to strike down everything Job owned, God's response was a little confusing.

> "'Very well,' the LORD told Satan, 'everything he owns is in your power. However, do not lay a hand on Job himself.'"
>
> JOB 1:12

The passage does not say that God was over-ruled or overthrown by Satan. He is always in complete control of what's happening. So, what made God allow Job's suffering?

Like most of us in our own trials, Job never knew why. But his words at the end of chapter 1 give us something to consider. Gripped with grief, Job falls to the ground in worship, proclaiming, "The LORD gives, and the LORD takes away. Blessed be the name of the LORD" (Jb 1:21).

God's glory has the final word.

When we compare Job to Christ—the ultimate sufferer—we find a similar outcome: God allows Christ to be crucified. But just as Jesus identifies with and understands our suffering, He also provides an end to it, proclaiming, "It is finished!" (Jn 19:30).

God's glory has the final word.

Years later, I no longer have gaping holes in my mouth from the tooth fairy's extractions. Suffering, too, is merely an interim chapter, a gap that will be filled fully and finally in glory. Praise the name of the Lord.

Naked I came from my mother's womb,
and naked I will leave this life. ^A
The LORD gives, and the LORD takes away.
Blessed be the name of the LORD.

²² Throughout all this Job did not sin or blame God for anything. ^B

SATAN'S SECOND TEST OF JOB

2 One day the sons of God came again to present themselves before the LORD, and Satan also came with them to present himself before the LORD. ² The LORD asked Satan, "Where have you come from?"

"From roaming through the earth," Satan answered him, "and walking around on it."

³ Then the LORD said to Satan, "Have you considered my servant Job? No one else on earth is like him, a man of perfect integrity, who fears God and turns away from evil. He still retains his integrity, even though you incited me against him, to destroy him for no good reason."

⁴ "Skin for skin!" Satan answered the LORD. "A man will give up everything he owns in exchange for his life. ⁵ But stretch out your hand and strike his flesh and bones, and he will surely curse you to your face."

⁶ "Very well," the LORD told Satan, "he is in your power; only spare his life."
⁷ So Satan left the LORD's presence and infected Job with terrible boils from the soles of his feet to the top of his head. ⁸ Then Job took a piece of broken pottery to scrape himself while he sat among the ashes.

⁹ His wife said to him, "Are you still holding on to your integrity? Curse God and die!"

¹⁰ "You speak as a foolish woman speaks," he told her. "Should we accept only good from God and not adversity?" Throughout all this Job did not sin in what he said. ^C

JOB'S THREE FRIENDS

¹¹ Now when Job's three friends — Eliphaz the Temanite, Bildad the Shuhite, and Zophar the Naamathite — heard about all this adversity that had happened to him, each of them came from his home. They met together to go and sympathize with him and comfort him. ¹² When they looked from a distance, they could barely recognize him. They wept aloud, and each man tore his robe and threw dust into the air and on his head. ¹³ Then they sat on the ground with him seven days and nights, but no one spoke a word to him because they saw that his suffering was very intense.

JOB'S OPENING SPEECH

3 After this, Job began to speak and cursed the day he was born. ² He said:
³ May the day I was born perish,
and the night that said,
"A boy is conceived."
⁴ If only that day had turned to darkness!
May God above not care about it,

---

^A1:21 Lit *will return there*; Ps 139:13,15   ^B1:22 Lit *or ascribe blame to God*
^C2:10 Lit *sin with his lips*

or light shine on it.

5 May darkness and gloom reclaim it,
and a cloud settle over it.
May what darkens the day terrify it.

6 If only darkness had taken that night away!
May it not appear^A among the days of the year
or be listed in the calendar.^B

7 Yes, may that night be barren;
may no joyful shout be heard in it.

8 Let those who curse days
condemn it,
those who are ready to rouse Leviathan.

9 May its morning stars grow dark.
May it wait for daylight but have none;
may it not see the breaking^C of dawn.

10 For that night did not shut
the doors of my mother's womb,
and hide sorrow from my eyes.

11 Why was I not stillborn;
why didn't I die as I came from the womb?

12 Why did the knees receive me,
and why were there breasts for me to nurse?

13 Now I would certainly be lying down in peace;
I would be asleep.
Then I would be at rest

14 with the kings and counselors of the earth,
who rebuilt ruined cities for themselves,

15 or with princes who had gold,
who filled their houses with silver.

16 Or why was I not hidden like a miscarried child,
like infants who never see daylight?

17 There the wicked cease to make trouble,
and there the weary find rest.

18 The captives are completely at rest;
they do not hear a taskmaster's voice.

19 Both small and great are there,
and the slave is set free from his master.

20 Why is light given to one burdened with grief,
and life to those whose existence is bitter,

21 who wait for death, but it does not come,
and search for it more than for hidden treasure,

22 who are filled with much joy
and are glad when they reach the grave?

23 Why is life given to a man whose path is hidden,
whom God has hedged in?

---

^A3:6 LXX, Syr, Tg, Vg; MT reads *rejoice*   ^B3:6 Lit *or enter the number of months*
^C3:9 Lit *the eyelids*

²⁴ I sigh when food is put before me,^A
and my groans pour out like water.
²⁵ For the thing I feared has overtaken me,
and what I dreaded has happened to me.
²⁶ I cannot relax or be calm;
I have no rest, for turmoil has come.

FIRST SERIES OF SPEECHES

ELIPHAZ SPEAKS

4 Then Eliphaz the Temanite replied:
² Should anyone try to speak with you
when you are exhausted?
Yet who can keep from speaking?
³ Indeed, you have instructed many
and have strengthened weak hands.
⁴ Your words have steadied the one who was stumbling
and braced the knees that were buckling.
⁵ But now that this has happened to you,
you have become exhausted.
It strikes you, and you are dismayed.
⁶ Isn't your piety your confidence,
and the integrity of your life^B your hope?
⁷ Consider: Who has perished when he was innocent?
Where have the honest^C been destroyed?
⁸ In my experience, those who plow injustice
and those who sow trouble reap the same.
⁹ They perish at a single blast from God
and come to an end by the breath of his nostrils.
¹⁰ The lion may roar and the fierce lion growl,
but the teeth of young lions are broken.
¹¹ The strong lion dies if it catches no prey,
and the cubs of the lioness are scattered.

¹² A word was brought to me in secret;
my ears caught a whisper of it.
¹³ Among unsettling thoughts from visions in the night,
when deep sleep comes over men,
¹⁴ fear and trembling came over me
and made all my bones shake.
¹⁵ I felt a draft^D on my face,
and the hair on my body stood up.
¹⁶ A figure stood there,
but I could not recognize its appearance;
a form loomed before my eyes.
I heard a whispering voice:
¹⁷ "Can a mortal be righteous before God?

---

^A3:24 Or *My sighing serves as my food*   ^B4:6 Lit *ways*   ^C4:7 Or *the upright, or those with integrity*   ^D4:15 Or *a spirit*

Can a man be more pure than his Maker?"

¹⁸ If God puts no trust in his servants
and he charges his angels with foolishness,ᴬ

¹⁹ how much more those who dwell in clay houses,
whose foundation is in the dust,
who are crushed like a moth!

²⁰ They are smashed to pieces from dawn to dusk;
they perish forever while no one notices.

²¹ Are their tent cords not pulled up?
They die without wisdom.

5 Call out! Will anyone answer you?
Which of the holy ones will you turn to?

² For anger kills a fool,
and jealousy slays the gullible.

³ I have seen a fool taking root,
but I immediately pronounced a curse on his home.

⁴ His children are far from safety.
They are crushed at the city gate,
with no one to rescue them.

⁵ The hungry consume his harvest,
even taking it out of the thorns.ᴮ
The thirstyᶜ pant for his children's wealth.

⁶ For distress does not grow out of the soil,
and trouble does not sprout from the ground.

⁷ But humans are born for trouble
as surely as sparks fly upward.

⁸ However, if I were you, I would appeal to God
and would present my case to him.

⁹ He does great and unsearchable things,
wonders without number.

¹⁰ He gives rain to the earth
and sends water to the fields.

¹¹ He sets the lowly on high,
and mourners are lifted to safety.

¹² He frustrates the schemes of the crafty
so that theyᴰ achieve no success.

¹³ He traps the wise in their craftiness
so that the plans of the deceptive
are quickly brought to an end.

¹⁴ They encounter darkness by day,
and they grope at noon
as if it were night.

¹⁵ He saves the needy from their sharp wordsᴱ
and from the clutches of the powerful.

ᴬ4:18 Or *error*; Hb obscure   ᴮ5:5 Hb obscure   ᶜ5:5 Aq, Sym, Syr, Vg; MT
reads *snares*   ᴰ5:12 Lit *their hands*   ᴱ5:15 Lit *from the sword of their mouth*;
Ps 55:21; 59:7

¹⁶ So the poor have hope,
and injustice shuts its mouth.

¹⁷ See how happy is the person whom God corrects;
so do not reject the discipline of the Almighty.

¹⁸ For he wounds but he also bandages;
he strikes, but his hands also heal.

¹⁹ He will rescue you from six calamities;
no harm will touch you in seven.

²⁰ In famine he will redeem you from death,
and in battle, from the power of the sword.

²¹ You will be safe from slander^A
and not fear destruction when it comes.

²² You will laugh at destruction and hunger
and not fear the land's wild creatures.

²³ For you will have a covenant with the stones of the field,
and the wild animals will be at peace with you.

²⁴ You will know that your tent is secure,
and nothing will be missing when you inspect your home.

²⁵ You will also know that your offspring will be many
and your descendants like the grass of the earth.

²⁶ You will approach the grave in full vigor,
as a stack of sheaves is gathered in its season.

²⁷ We have investigated this, and it is true!
Hear it and understand it for yourself.

JOB'S REPLY TO ELIPHAZ

6 Then Job answered:
² If only my grief could be weighed
and my devastation placed with it on the scales.

³ For then it would outweigh the sand of the seas!
That is why my words are rash.

⁴ Surely the arrows of the Almighty have pierced^B me;
my spirit drinks their poison.
God's terrors are arrayed against me.

⁵ Does a wild donkey bray over fresh grass
or an ox low over its fodder?

⁶ Is bland food eaten without salt?
Is there flavor in an egg white?^C

⁷ I refuse to touch them;
they are like contaminated food.

⁸ If only my request would be granted
and God would provide what I hope for:

⁹ that he would decide to crush me,
to unleash his power and cut me off!

¹⁰ It would still bring me comfort,

---

^A5:21 Lit be hidden from the whip of the tongue ^B6:4 Lit Almighty are in
^C6:6 Hb obscure

and I would leap for joy in unrelenting pain
that I have not denied^A the words of the Holy One.

11 What strength do I have, that I should continue to hope?
What is my future, that I should be patient?
12 Is my strength that of stone,
or my flesh made of bronze?
13 Since I cannot help myself,
the hope for success has been banished from me.

14 A despairing man should receive loyalty from his friends,^B
even if he abandons the fear of the Almighty.
15 My brothers are as treacherous as a wadi,
as seasonal streams that overflow
16 and become darkened^C because of ice,
and the snow melts into them.
17 The wadis evaporate in warm weather;
they disappear from their channels in hot weather.
18 Caravans turn away from their routes,
go up into the desert, and perish.
19 The caravans of Tema look for these streams.
The traveling merchants of Sheba hope for them.
20 They are ashamed because they had been confident
of finding water.
When they arrive there, they are disappointed.
21 So this is what you have now become to me.^D
When you see something dreadful, you are afraid.
22 Have I ever said: "Give me something"
or "Pay a bribe for me from your wealth"
23 or "Deliver me from the enemy's hand"
or "Redeem me from the hand of the ruthless"?

24 Teach me, and I will be silent.
Help me understand what I did wrong.
25 How painful honest words can be!
But what does your rebuke prove?
26 Do you think that you can disprove my words
or that a despairing man's words are mere wind?
27 No doubt you would cast lots for a fatherless child
and negotiate a price to sell your friend.

28 But now, please look at me;
I will not lie to your face.
29 Reconsider; don't be unjust.
Reconsider; my righteousness is still the issue.
30 Is there injustice on my tongue
or can my palate not taste disaster?

---

^A 6:10 Lit *hidden*   ^B 6:14 Lit *To the despairing his friend loyalty*   ^C 6:16 Or *turbid*
^D 6:21 Alt Hb tradition reads *So you have now become nothing*

7 Isn't each person consigned to forced labor on earth?
Are not his days like those of a hired worker?

² Like a slave he longs for shade;
like a hired worker he waits for his pay.

³ So I have been made to inherit months of futility,
and troubled nights have been assigned to me.

⁴ When I lie down I think,
"When will I get up?"
But the evening drags on endlessly,
and I toss and turn until dawn.

⁵ My flesh is clothed with maggots and encrusted
with dirt.ᴬ
My skin forms scabsᴮ and then oozes.

⁶ My days pass more swiftly than a weaver's shuttle;
they come to an end without hope.

⁷ Remember that my life is but a breath.
My eye will never again see anything good.

⁸ The eye of anyone who looks on me
will no longer see me.
Your eyes will look for me, but I will be gone.

⁹ As a cloud fades away and vanishes,
so the one who goes down to Sheol will never rise again.

¹⁰ He will never return to his house;
his hometown will no longer rememberᶜ him.

¹¹ Therefore I will not restrain my mouth.
I will speak in the anguish of my spirit;
I will complain in the bitterness of my soul.

¹² Am I the seaᴰ or a sea monster,
that you keep me under guard?

¹³ When I say, "My bed will comfort me,
and my couch will ease my complaint,"

¹⁴ then you frighten me with dreams,
and terrify me with visions,

¹⁵ so that I prefer stranglingᴱ —
death rather than life in this body.ᶠ

¹⁶ I give up! I will not live forever.
Leave me alone, for my days are a breath.ᴳ

¹⁷ What is a mere human, that you think so highly of him
and pay so much attention to him?

¹⁸ You inspect him every morning,
and put him to the test every moment.

¹⁹ Will you ever look away from me,
or leave me alone long enough to swallow?ᴴ

ᴬ7:5 Or and dirty scabs   ᴮ7:5 Lit skin hardens   ᶜ7:10 Lit know   ᴰ7:12 Or the
sea god   ᴱ7:15 Or suffocation   ᶠ7:15 Lit than my bones   ᴳ7:16 Or are futile
ᴴ7:19 Lit swallow my saliva?

20 If I have sinned, what have I done to you,
    Watcher of humanity?
    Why have you made me your target,
    so that I have become a burden to you?[A]
21 Why not forgive my sin
    and pardon my iniquity?
    For soon I will lie down in the grave.
    You will eagerly seek me, but I will be gone.

BILDAD SPEAKS

8 Then Bildad the Shuhite replied:
    [2] How long will you go on saying these things?
    Your words are a blast of wind.
3   Does God pervert justice?
    Does the Almighty pervert what is right?
4   Since your children sinned against him,
    he gave them over to their rebellion.
5   But if you earnestly seek God
    and ask the Almighty for mercy,
6   if you are pure and upright,
    then he will move even now on your behalf
    and restore the home where your righteousness dwells.
7   Then, even if your beginnings were modest,
    your final days will be full of prosperity.

8   For ask the previous generation,
    and pay attention to what their fathers discovered,
9   since we were born only yesterday and know nothing.
    Our days on earth are but a shadow.
10 Will they not teach you and tell you
    and speak from their understanding?
11 Does papyrus grow where there is no marsh?
    Do reeds flourish without water?
12 While still uncut shoots,
    they would dry up quicker than any other plant.
13 Such is the destiny[B] of all who forget God;
    the hope of the godless will perish.
14 His source of confidence is fragile;[C]
    what he trusts in is a spider's web.
15 He leans on his web, but it doesn't stand firm.
    He grabs it, but it does not hold up.
16 He is a well-watered plant in the sunshine;
    his shoots spread out over his garden.
17 His roots are intertwined around a pile of rocks.
    He looks for a home among the stones.
18 If he is uprooted[D] from his place,
    it will deny knowing him, saying, "I never saw you."

[A]7:20 Alt Hb tradition, LXX; MT, Vg read *myself*   [B]8:13 Lit *Such are the ways*
[C]8:14 Or *cut off*; Hb obscure   [D]8:18 Or *destroyed*

¹⁹ Surely this is the joy of his way of life;
yet others will sprout from the dust.
²⁰ Look, God does not reject a person of integrity,
and he will not support^A evildoers.
²¹ He will yet fill your mouth with laughter
and your lips with a shout of joy.
²² Your enemies will be clothed with shame;
the tent of the wicked will no longer exist.

JOB'S REPLY TO BILDAD

9 Then Job answered:
² Yes, I know what you've said is true,
but how can a person be justified before God?
³ If one wanted to take him to court,
he could not answer God^B once in a thousand times.
⁴ God is wise and all-powerful.
Who has opposed him and come out unharmed?
⁵ He removes mountains without their knowledge,
overturning them in his anger.
⁶ He shakes the earth from its place
so that its pillars tremble.
⁷ He commands the sun not to shine
and seals off the stars.
⁸ He alone stretches out the heavens
and treads on the waves of the sea.^C
⁹ He makes the stars: the Bear,^D Orion,
the Pleiades, and the constellations^E of the southern sky.
¹⁰ He does great and unsearchable things,
wonders without number.
¹¹ If he passed by me, I wouldn't see him;
if he went by, I wouldn't recognize him.
¹² If he snatches something, who can stop^F him?
Who can ask him, "What are you doing?"
¹³ God does not hold back his anger;
Rahab's assistants cringe in fear beneath him!

¹⁴ How then can I answer him
or choose my arguments against him?
¹⁵ Even if I were in the right, I could not answer.
I could only beg my Judge for mercy.
¹⁶ If I summoned him and he answered me,
I do not believe he would pay attention to what I said.
¹⁷ He batters me with a whirlwind
and multiplies my wounds without cause.
¹⁸ He doesn't let me catch my breath
but fills me with bitter experiences.

---

^A8:20 Lit *grasp the hand of*   ^B9:3 Or *court, God would not answer him*   ^C9:8 Or
and walks on the back of the sea god   ^D9:9 Or *Aldebaran*   ^E9:9 Or *chambers*
^F9:12 Or *dissuade*

never to return.

22 It is a land of blackness like the deepest darkness,
gloomy and chaotic,
where even the light is like^A the darkness."

ZOPHAR SPEAKS

11 Then Zophar the Naamathite replied:
2 Should this abundance of words go unanswered
and such a talker^B be acquitted?

3 Should your babbling put others to silence,
so that you can keep on ridiculing
with no one to humiliate you?

4 You have said, "My teaching is sound,
and I am pure in your sight."

5 But if only God would speak
and open his lips against you!

6 He would show you the secrets of wisdom,
for true wisdom has two sides.
Know then that God has chosen to overlook
some of your iniquity.

7 Can you fathom the depths of God
or discover the limits of the Almighty?

8 They are higher than the heavens — what can you do?
They are deeper than Sheol — what can you know?

9 Their measure is longer than the earth
and wider than the sea.

10 If he passes by and throws someone in prison
or convenes a court, who can stop him?

11 Surely he knows which people are worthless.
If he sees iniquity, will he not take note of it?

12 But a stupid person will gain understanding
as soon as a wild donkey is born a human!

13 As for you, if you redirect your heart
and spread out your hands to him in prayer —

14 if there is iniquity in your hand, remove it,
and don't allow injustice to dwell in your tents —

15 then you will hold your head high, free from fault.
You will be firmly established and unafraid.

16 For you will forget your suffering,
recalling it only as water that has flowed by.

17 Your life will be brighter than noonday;
its darkness^C will be like the morning.

18 You will be confident, because there is hope.
You will look carefully about and lie down in safety.

---

^A 10:22 Lit *chaotic, and shines as*   ^B 11:2 Lit *a man of lips*   ^C 11:17 Text emended;
MT reads *noonday; you are dark, you*

¹⁹ You will lie down with no one to frighten you,
and many will seek your favor.
²⁰ But the sight of the wicked will fail.
Their way of escape will be cut off,
and their only hope is their last breath.

JOB'S REPLY TO ZOPHAR

12 Then Job answered:
²No doubt you are the people,
and wisdom will die with you!
³ But I also have a mind like you;
I am not inferior to you.
Who doesn't know the things you are talking about?ᴬ

⁴ I am a laughingstock to myᴮ friends,
by calling on God, who answers me.ᶜ
The righteous and upright man is a laughingstock.
⁵ The one who is at ease holds calamity in contempt
and thinks it is prepared for those
whose feet are slipping.
⁶ The tents of robbers are safe,
and those who trouble God are secure;
God holds them in his hands.ᴰ

⁷ But ask the animals, and they will instruct you;
ask the birds of the sky, and they will tell you.
⁸ Or speak to the earth, and it will instruct you;
let the fish of the sea inform you.
⁹ Which of all these does not know
that the hand of the LORD has done this?
¹⁰ The life of every living thing is in his hand,
as well as the breath of all mankind.
¹¹ Doesn't the ear test words
as the palate tastes food?
¹² Wisdom is found with the elderly,
and understanding comes with long life.

¹³ Wisdom and strength belong to God;
counsel and understanding are his.
¹⁴ Whatever he tears down cannot be rebuilt;
whoever he imprisons cannot be released.
¹⁵ When he withholds water, everything dries up,
and when he releases it, it destroys the land.
¹⁶ True wisdom and power belong to him.
The deceived and the deceiver are his.
¹⁷ He leads counselors away barefoot
and makes judges go mad.

ᴬ12:3 Lit *With whom are not such things as these?* ᴮ12:4 Lit *his* ᶜ12:4 Lit *him*
ᴰ12:6 Or *secure; to those who bring their god in their hands*

18 He releases the bonds^A put on by kings
and fastens a belt around their waists.
19 He leads priests away barefoot
and overthrows established leaders.
20 He deprives trusted advisers of speech
and takes away the elders' good judgment.
21 He pours out contempt on nobles
and disarms^B the strong.
22 He reveals mysteries from the darkness
and brings the deepest darkness into the light.
23 He makes nations great, then destroys them;
he enlarges nations, then leads them away.
24 He deprives the world's leaders of reason,
and makes them wander in a trackless wasteland.
25 They grope around in darkness without light;
he makes them stagger like a drunkard.

13 Look, my eyes have seen all this;
my ears have heard and understood it.
2 Everything you know, I also know;
I am not inferior to you.
3 Yet I prefer to speak to the Almighty
and argue my case before God.
4 You use lies like plaster;
you are all worthless healers.
5 If only you would shut up
and let that be your wisdom!

6 Hear now my argument,
and listen to my defense.^C
7 Would you testify unjustly on God's behalf
or speak deceitfully for him?
8 Would you show partiality to him
or argue the case in his defense?
9 Would it go well if he examined you?
Could you deceive him as you would deceive a man?
10 Surely he would rebuke you
if you secretly showed partiality.
11 Would God's majesty not terrify you?
Would his dread not fall on you?
12 Your memorable sayings are proverbs of ash;
your defenses are made of clay.

13 Be quiet,^D and I will speak.
Let whatever comes happen to me.
14 I will put^E myself at risk^F

---

^A12:18 Text emended; MT reads *discipline*   ^B12:21 Lit *and loosens the belt of*
^C13:6 Lit *to the claims of my lips*   ^D13:13 Lit *quiet before me*   ^E13:14 LXX; MT
reads *Why do I put*   ^F13:14 Lit *I take my flesh in my teeth*

and take my life in my own hands.

¹⁵ Even if he kills me, I will hope in him.ᴬ
I will still defend my ways before him.

¹⁶ Yes, this will result in my deliverance,
for no godless person can appear before him.

¹⁷ Pay close attention to my words;
let my declaration ring in your ears.

¹⁸ Now then, I have prepared my case;
I know that I am right.

¹⁹ Can anyone indict me?
If so, I will be silent and die.

²⁰ Only grant these two things to me, God,
so that I will not have to hide from your presence:

²¹ remove your hand from me,
and do not let your terror frighten me.

²² Then call, and I will answer,
or I will speak, and you can respond to me.

²³ How many iniquities and sins have I committed?ᴮ
Reveal to me my transgression and sin.

²⁴ Why do you hide your face
and consider me your enemy?

²⁵ Will you frighten a wind-driven leaf?
Will you chase after dry straw?

²⁶ For you record bitter accusations against me
and make me inherit the iniquities of my youth.

²⁷ You put my feet in the stocks
and stand watch over all my paths,
setting a limit for the solesᶜ of my feet.

²⁸ A person wears out like something rotten,
like a moth-eaten garment.

14 Anyone born of woman
is short of days and full of trouble.

² He blossoms like a flower, then withers;
he flees like a shadow and does not last.

³ Do you really take notice of one like this?
Will you bring me into judgment against you?ᴰ

⁴ Who can produce something pure from what is impure?
No one!

⁵ Since a person's days are determined
and the number of his months depends on you,
and since you have setᴱ limits he cannot pass,

⁶ look away from him and let him rest
so that he can enjoy his day like a hired worker.

ᴬ13:15 Some Hb mss read *I will be without hope*   ᴮ13:23 Lit *sins are to me*
ᶜ13:27 Lit *paths. You mark a line around the roots*   ᴰ14:3 LXX, Syr, Vg read *him*
ᴱ14:5 Lit *set his*

7   There is hope for a tree:
    If it is cut down, it will sprout again,
    and its shoots will not die.

8   If its roots grow old in the ground
    and its stump starts to die in the soil,

9   the scent of water makes it thrive
    and produce twigs like a sapling.

10 But a person dies and fades away;
    he breathes his last — where is he?

11 As water disappears from a lake
    and a river becomes parched and dry,

12 so people lie down never to rise again.
    They will not wake up until the heavens are no more;
    they will not stir from their sleep.

13 If only you would hide me in Sheol
    and conceal me until your anger passes.
    If only you would appoint a time for me
    and then remember me.

14 When a person dies, will he come back to life?
    If so, I would wait all the days of my struggle
    until my relief comes.

15 You would call, and I would answer you.
    You would long for the work of your hands.

16 For then you would count my steps
    but would not take note of my sin.

17 My rebellion would be sealed up in a bag,
    and you would cover over my iniquity.

18 But as a mountain collapses and crumbles
    and a rock is dislodged from its place,

19 as water wears away stones
    and torrents wash away the soil from the land,
    so you destroy a man's hope.

20 You completely overpower him, and he passes on;
    you change his appearance and send him away.

21 If his sons receive honor, he does not know it;
    if they become insignificant, he is unaware of it.

22 He feels only the pain of his own body
    and mourns only for himself.

SECOND SERIES OF SPEECHES
ELIPHAZ SPEAKS

15 Then Eliphaz the Temanite replied:
²Does a wise man answer with empty^A counsel
or fill himself^B with the hot east wind?

3   Should he argue with useless talk

---

^A 15:2 Lit *windy*; Jb 16:3   ^B 15:2 Lit *his belly*

or with words that serve no good purpose?

⁴ But you even undermine the fear of God
and hinder meditation before him.

⁵ Your iniquity teaches you what to say,
and you choose the language of the crafty.

⁶ Your own mouth condemns you, not I;
your own lips testify against you.

⁷ Were you the first human ever born,
or were you brought forth before the hills?

⁸ Do you listen in on the council of God,
or have a monopoly on wisdom?

⁹ What do you know that we don't?
What do you understand that is not clear to us?

¹⁰ Both the gray-haired and the elderly are with us—
older than your father.

¹¹ Are God's consolations not enough for you,
even the words that deal gently with you?

¹² Why has your heart misled you,
and why do your eyes flash

¹³ as you turn your anger^A against God
and allow such words to leave your mouth?

¹⁴ What is a mere human, that he should be pure,
or one born of a woman, that he should be righteous?

¹⁵ If God puts no trust in his holy ones
and the heavens are not pure in his sight,

¹⁶ how much less one who is revolting and corrupt,
who drinks injustice like water?

¹⁷ Listen to me and I will inform you.
I will describe what I have seen,

¹⁸ what the wise have declared and not concealed,
that came from their ancestors,

¹⁹ to whom alone the land was given
when no foreigner passed among them.

²⁰ A wicked person writhes in pain all his days,
throughout the number of years reserved for the ruthless.

²¹ Dreadful sounds fill his ears;
when he is at peace, a robber attacks him.

²² He doesn't believe he will return from darkness;
he is destined for the sword.

²³ He wanders about for food, asking, "Where is it?"
He knows the day of darkness is at hand.

²⁴ Trouble and distress terrify him,
overwhelming him like a king prepared for battle.

²⁵ For he has stretched out his hand against God
and has arrogantly opposed the Almighty.

---

^A15:13 Or *spirit*

7 My eyes have grown dim from grief,
and my whole body has become but a shadow.
8 The upright are appalled at this,
and the innocent are roused against the godless.
9 Yet the righteous person will hold to his way,
and the one whose hands are clean will grow stronger.
10 But come back and try again, all of you.ᴬ
I will not find a wise man among you.

11 My days have slipped by;
my plans have been ruined,
even the things dear to my heart.
12 They turned night into day
and made light seem near in the face of darkness.
13 If I await Sheol as my home,
spread out my bed in darkness,
14 and say to corruption, "You are my father,"
and to the maggot, "My mother" or "My sister,"
15 where then is my hope?
Who can see any hope for me?
16 Will it go down to the gates of Sheol,
or will we descend together to the dust?

BILDAD SPEAKS

18 Then Bildad the Shuhite replied:
² How long until you stop talking?
Show some sense, and then we can talk.
3 Why are we regarded as cattle,
as stupid in your sight?
4 You who tear yourself in angerᴮ —
should the earth be abandoned on your account,
or a rock be removed from its place?

5 Yes, the light of the wicked is extinguished;
the flame of his fire does not glow.
6 The light in his tent grows dark,
and the lamp beside him is put out.
7 His powerful stride is shortened,
and his own schemes trip him up.
8 For his own feet lead him into a net,
and he strays into its mesh.
9 A trap catches him by the heel;
a noose seizes him.
10 A rope lies hidden for him on the ground,
and a snare waits for him along the path.
11 Terrors frighten him on every side
and harass him at every step.

ᴬ17:10 Some Hb mss, LXX, Vg; other Hb mss read *them* ᴮ18:4 Lit *He who tears himself in his anger*

12 His strength is depleted;
12 His strength is depleted;
   disaster lies ready for him to stumble.[A]

13 Parts of his skin are eaten away;
   death's firstborn consumes his limbs.

14 He is ripped from the security of his tent
   and marched away to the king of terrors.

15 Nothing he owned remains in his tent.
   Burning sulfur is scattered over his home.

16 His roots below dry up,
   and his branches above wither away.

17 All memory of him perishes from the earth;
   he has no name anywhere.[B]

18 He is driven from light to darkness
   and chased from the inhabited world.

19 He has no children or descendants
      among his people,
   no survivor where he used to live.

20 Those in the west are appalled at his fate,
   while those in the east tremble in horror.

21 Indeed, such is the dwelling of the unjust man,
   and this is the place of the one who does not
      know God.

JOB'S REPLY TO BILDAD

19 Then Job answered:
   ² How long will you torment me
   and crush me with words?

3 You have humiliated me ten times now,
   and you mistreat[C] me without shame.

4 Even if it is true that I have sinned,
   my mistake concerns only[D] me.

5 If you really want to appear superior to me
   and would use my disgrace as evidence against me,

6 then understand that it is God who has wronged me
   and caught me in his net.

7 I cry out: "Violence!" but get no response;
   I call for help, but there is no justice.

8 He has blocked my way so that I cannot pass through;
   he has veiled my paths with darkness.

9 He has stripped me of my honor
   and removed the crown from my head.

10 He tears me down on every side so that I am ruined.[E]
   He uproots my hope like a tree.

11 His anger burns against me,
   and he regards me as one of his enemies.

12 His troops advance together;

[A]18:12 Or *disaster hungers for him*   [B]18:17 Or *name in the streets*   [C]19:3 Hb obscure   [D]19:4 Lit *mistake lives with*   [E]19:10 Lit *gone*

MY REDEEMER LIVES

JOB 18–19; JAMES 5:10-11

The last few years had been pretty terrible for the man. He and his wife, Anna, had four beautiful children—three girls and a boy—when scarlet fever stole the life of their only son. The boy was just four years old.

The family was wealthy; he was a successful lawyer with influential friends. The year after his little boy died, the man invested a sizeable portion of their money in northern Chicago's growing real estate market. Several months later, it was gone—the property and the family fortune destroyed by the Great Chicago Fire of 1871.

But it's what came next that undid him.

The year was 1873, two years after the fire. He sent Anna and their children (there were four girls now, one born since the loss of their son) ahead to England for a family holiday. He stayed back on business with the plan of following shortly after. Only, something went terribly wrong. The ship collided with another in the Atlantic, and the girls perished at sea. A grieved Anna reached shore and sent her husband a telegram: "Survived alone."

Have you ever felt that depth of sorrow? Have you ever found yourself standing, lost and suddenly alone, in the wreckage of what was or what might have been?

We know our Redeemer lives. We believe it, even when we cannot feel it.

Yet grief is thick and tangible and our bodies strain under its weight. Whatever and whomever we grieve, the emotions consume and toss us like ragdolls in the waves till we have no energy left to swim. So we do the only thing we know to do: we give the grief back to God.

James 5:10-11 promises God counts us blessed when we endure. Job, a sad but shining example of patience in suffering, endured the worst and God replenished the life that was taken from him (Jb 42). But regardless of the outcome of our circumstances, whether the Lord physically restores us on this earth or restores us fully in glory, our God is still full of compassion and mercy. We must remain convinced of this. *Our living Redeemer will stand on the dust at last, and we will see Him* (Jb 19:25-26).

When a broken Chicago businessman named Horatio Spafford sailed past the very spot on the Atlantic where his baby girls sank into the depths, he offered up these words of worship to the God who presides over all the sorrows and the seas, to the One who has borne the whole of our grief and our sin:

*"Whatever my lot, Thou has taught me to say,
It is well, it is well with my soul."*

Whatever your lot, worship the Lord today. He is your living Redeemer, and "at the end he will stand on the dust" (Jb 19:25).

they construct a ramp^A against me
and camp around my tent.

¹³ He has removed my brothers from me;
my acquaintances have abandoned me.
¹⁴ My relatives stop coming by,
and my close friends have forgotten me.
¹⁵ My house guests^B and female servants regard me
as a stranger;
I am a foreigner in their sight.
¹⁶ I call for my servant, but he does not answer,
even if I beg him with my own mouth.
¹⁷ My breath is offensive to my wife,
and my own family^C finds me repulsive.
¹⁸ Even young boys scorn me.
When I stand up, they mock me.
¹⁹ All of my best friends^D despise me,
and those I love have turned against me.
²⁰ My skin and my flesh cling to my bones;
I have escaped with only the skin of my teeth.

²¹ Have mercy on me, my friends, have mercy,
for God's hand has struck me.
²² Why do you persecute me as God does?
Will you never get enough of my flesh?

²³ I wish that my words were written down,
that they were recorded on a scroll
²⁴ or were inscribed in stone forever
by an iron stylus and lead!
²⁵ But I know that my Redeemer lives,^E
and at the end he will stand on the dust.
²⁶ Even after my skin has been destroyed,^F
yet I will see God in^G my flesh.
²⁷ I will see him myself;
my eyes will look at him, and not as a stranger.^H
My heart longs^I within me.

²⁸ If you say, "How will we pursue him,
since the root of the problem lies with him?"^J
²⁹ then be afraid of the sword,
because wrath brings punishment by the sword,
so that you may know there is a judgment.

---

^A19:12 Lit *they raise up their way*   ^B19:15 Or *The resident aliens in my household*
^C19:17 Lit *and the sons of my belly*   ^D19:19 Lit *of the men of my council*
^E19:25 Or *know my living Redeemer*   ^F19:26 Lit *skin which they destroyed,* or
skin they destroyed in this way   ^G19:26 Or *apart from*   ^H19:27 Or *not a stranger*
^I19:27 Lit *My kidneys grow faint*   ^J19:28 Some Hb mss, LXX, Vg; other Hb mss
read *me*

ZOPHAR SPEAKS

20 Then Zophar the Naamathite replied:
² This is why my unsettling thoughts compel me to answer,
because I am upset!ᴬ

³ I have heard a rebuke that insults me,
and my understandingᴮ makes me reply.

⁴ Don't you know that ever since antiquity,
from the time a human was placed on earth,
⁵ the joy of the wicked has been brief
and the happiness of the godless has lasted
only a moment?
⁶ Though his arrogance reaches heaven,
and his head touches the clouds,
⁷ he will vanish forever like his own dung.
Those who knowᶜ him will ask, "Where is he?"
⁸ He will fly away like a dream and never be found;
he will be chased away like a vision in the night.
⁹ The eye that saw him will see him no more,
and his household will no longer see him.
¹⁰ His children will beg fromᴰ the poor,
for his own hands must give back his wealth.
¹¹ His frame may be full of youthful vigor,
but it will lie down with him in dust.

¹² Though evil tastes sweet in his mouth
and he conceals it under his tongue,
¹³ though he cherishes it and will not let it go
but keeps it in his mouth,
¹⁴ yet the food in his stomach turns
into cobras' venom inside him.
¹⁵ He swallows wealth but must vomit it up;
God will force it from his stomach.
¹⁶ He will suck the poison of cobras;
a viper's fangsᴱ will kill him.
¹⁷ He will not enjoy the streams,
the rivers flowing with honey and curds.
¹⁸ He must return the fruit of his labor without consuming it;
he doesn't enjoy the profits from his trading.
¹⁹ For he oppressed and abandoned the poor;
he seized a house he did not build.

²⁰ Because his appetite is never satisfied,ᶠ
he does not let anything he desires escape.
²¹ Nothing is left for him to consume;
therefore, his prosperity will not last.

ᴬ20:2 Lit because of my feeling within me   ᴮ20:3 Lit and a spirit from my
understanding   ᶜ20:7 Lit have seen   ᴰ20:10 Or children must compensate
ᴱ20:16 Lit tongue   ᶠ20:20 Lit Because he does not know ease in his stomach

22 At the height of his success^A distress will come to him;
the full weight of misery^B will crush him.

23 When he fills his stomach,
God will send his burning anger against him,
raining it down on him while he is eating.^C

24 If he flees from an iron weapon,
an arrow from a bronze bow will pierce him.

25 He pulls it out of his back,
the flashing tip out of his liver.^D
Terrors come over him.

26 Total darkness is reserved for his treasures.
A fire unfanned by human hands will consume him;
it will feed on what is left in his tent.

27 The heavens will expose his iniquity,
and the earth will rise up against him.

28 The possessions in his house will be removed,
flowing away on the day of God's anger.

29 This is the wicked person's lot from God,
the inheritance God ordained for him.

JOB'S REPLY TO ZOPHAR

21 Then Job answered:
2 Pay close attention to my words;
let this be the consolation you offer.

3 Bear with me while I speak;
then after I have spoken, you may continue mocking.

4 As for me, is my complaint against a human being?
Then why shouldn't I be impatient?

5 Look at me and shudder;
put your hand over your mouth.

6 When I think about it, I am terrified
and my body trembles in horror.

7 Why do the wicked continue to live,
growing old and becoming powerful?

8 Their children are established while they are still alive,^E
and their descendants, before their eyes.

9 Their homes are secure and free of fear;
no rod from God strikes them.

10 Their bulls breed without fail;
their cows calve and do not miscarry.

11 They let their little ones run around like lambs;
their children skip about,

12 singing to the tambourine and lyre
and rejoicing at the sound of the flute.

---

^A20:22 Lit *In the fullness of his excess*   ^B20:22 Some Hb mss, LXX, Vg; other Hb
mss read *the hand of everyone in misery*   ^C20:23 Text emended; MT reads *him,
against his flesh*   ^D20:25 Or *gallbladder*   ^E21:8 Lit *established before them with
them*

13 They spend^A their days in prosperity
  and go down to Sheol in peace.
14 Yet they say to God, "Leave us alone!
  We don't want to know your ways.
15 Who is the Almighty, that we should serve him,
  and what will we gain by pleading with him?"
16 But their prosperity is not of their own doing.
  The counsel of the wicked is far from me!

17 How often is the lamp of the wicked put out?
  Does disaster^B come on them?
  Does he apportion destruction in his anger?
18 Are they like straw before the wind,
  like chaff a storm sweeps away?
19 God reserves a person's punishment for his children.
  Let God repay the person himself, so that he may know it.
20 Let his own eyes see his demise;
  let him drink from the Almighty's wrath!
21 For what does he care about his family once he is dead,
  when the number of his months has run out?

22 Can anyone teach God knowledge,
  since he judges the exalted ones?^C
23 One person dies in excellent health,^D
  completely secure^E and at ease.
24 His body is^F well fed,^G
  and his bones are full of marrow.^H
25 Yet another person dies with a bitter soul,
  having never tasted prosperity.
26 But they both lie in the dust,
  and worms cover them.

27 I know your thoughts very well,
  the schemes by which you would wrong me.
28 For you say, "Where now is the nobleman's house?"
  and "Where are the tents the wicked lived in?"
29 Have you never consulted those who travel the roads?
  Don't you accept their reports?^I
30 Indeed, the evil person is spared from the day of disaster,
  rescued from the day of wrath.
31 Who would denounce his behavior to his face?
  Who would repay him for what he has done?
32 He is carried to the grave,
  and someone keeps watch over his tomb.

---

^A21:13 Alt Hb tradition reads *fully enjoy* ^B21:17 Lit *their disaster*
^C21:22 Probably angels ^D21:23 Lit *in bone of his perfection* ^E21:23 Text
emended; MT reads *health, all at ease* ^F21:24 Or *His sides are*; Hb obscure
^G21:24 Lit *is full of milk* ^H21:24 Lit *and the marrow of his bones is watered*
^I21:29 Lit *signs*

33 The dirt on his grave is ^A^ sweet to him.
Everyone follows behind him,
and those who go before him are without number.

34 So how can you offer me such futile comfort?
Your answers are deceptive.

THIRD SERIES OF SPEECHES

ELIPHAZ SPEAKS

22 Then Eliphaz the Temanite replied:
² Can a man be of any use to God?
Can even a wise man be of use to him?

3 Does it delight the Almighty if you are righteous?
Does he profit if you perfect your behavior?

4 Does he correct you and take you to court
because of your piety?

5 Isn't your wickedness abundant
and aren't your iniquities endless?

6 For you took collateral from your brothers without cause,
stripping off their clothes and leaving them naked.

7 You gave no water to the thirsty
and withheld food from the famished,

8 while the land belonged to a powerful man
and an influential man lived on it.

9 You sent widows away empty-handed,
and the strength of the fatherless was ^B^ crushed.

10 Therefore snares surround you,
and sudden dread terrifies you,

11 or darkness, so you cannot see,
and a flood of water covers you.

12 Isn't God as high as the heavens?
And look at the highest stars — how lofty they are!

13 Yet you say, "What does God know?
Can he judge through total darkness?

14 Clouds veil him so that he cannot see,
as he walks on the circle of the sky."

15 Will you continue on the ancient path
that wicked men have walked?

16 They were snatched away before their time,
and their foundations were washed away by a river.

17 They were the ones who said to God, "Leave us alone!"
and "What can the Almighty do to us?" ^C^

18 But it was he who filled their houses with good things.
The counsel of the wicked is far from me!

---

^A^21:33 Lit *The clods of the wadi are*   ^B^22:9 LXX, Syr, Vg, Tg read *you have*
^C^22:17 LXX, Syr; MT reads *them*

¹⁹ The righteous see this and rejoice;
   the innocent mock them, saying,

²⁰ "Surely our opponents are destroyed,
   and fire has consumed what they left behind."

²¹ Come to terms with God and be at peace;
   in this way^A good will come to you.

²² Receive instruction from his mouth,
   and place his sayings in your heart.

²³ If you return to the Almighty, you will be renewed.
   If you banish injustice from your tent

²⁴ and consign your gold to the dust,
   the gold of Ophir to the stones in the wadis,

²⁵ the Almighty will be your gold
   and your finest silver.

²⁶ Then you will delight in the Almighty
   and lift up your face to God.

²⁷ You will pray to him, and he will hear you,
   and you will fulfill your vows.

²⁸ When you make a decision, it will be carried out,^B
   and light will shine on your ways.

²⁹ When others are humiliated and you say,
       "Lift them up,"
   God will save the humble.^C

³⁰ He will even rescue the guilty one,
   who will be rescued by the purity of your hands.

JOB'S REPLY TO ELIPHAZ

23 Then Job answered:
   ² Today also my complaint is bitter.^D
   His^E hand is heavy despite my groaning.

³ If only I knew how to find him,
   so that I could go to his throne.

⁴ I would plead my case before him
   and fill my mouth with arguments.

⁵ I would learn how^F he would answer me;
   and understand what he would say to me.

⁶ Would he prosecute me forcefully?
   No, he would certainly pay attention to me.

⁷ Then an upright man could reason with him,
   and I would escape from my Judge^G forever.

⁸ If I go east, he is not there,
   and if I go west, I cannot perceive him.

⁹ When he is at work to the north, I cannot see him;
   when he turns south, I cannot find him.

---

^A22:21 Lit peace; by them   ^B22:28 Lit out for you   ^C22:29 Lit bowed of eyes
^D23:2 Syr, Tg, Vg; MT reads rebellion   ^E23:2 LXX, Syr; MT reads My   ^F23:5 Lit
the words   ^G23:7 Or judgment

¹⁰ Yet he knows the way I have taken;ᴬ
when he has tested me, I will emerge as pure gold.
¹¹ My feet have followed in his tracks;
I have kept to his way and not turned aside.
¹² I have not departed from the commands from his lips;
I have treasuredᴮ the words from his mouth
more than my daily food.

¹³ But he is unchangeable; who can oppose him?
He does what he desires.
¹⁴ He will certainly accomplish what he has decreed for me,
and he has many more things like these in mind.ᶜ
¹⁵ Therefore I am terrified in his presence;
when I consider this, I am afraid of him.
¹⁶ God has made my heart faint;
the Almighty has terrified me.
¹⁷ Yet I am not destroyedᴰ by the darkness,
by the thick darkness that covers my face.

24 Why does the Almighty not reserve times for judgment?
Why do those who know him never see his days?
² The wicked displace boundary markers.
They steal a flock and provide pasture for it.
³ They drive away the donkeys owned by the fatherless
and take the widow's ox as collateral.
⁴ They push the needy off the road;
the poor of the land are forced into hiding.
⁵ Like wild donkeys in the wilderness,
the poor go out to their task of foraging for food;
the desert provides nourishment for their children.
⁶ They gather their fodder in the field
and glean the vineyards of the wicked.
⁷ Without clothing, they spend the night naked,
having no covering against the cold.
⁸ Drenched by mountain rains,
they huddle againstᴱ the rocks, shelterless.
⁹ The fatherless infant is snatched from the breast;
the nursing child of the poor is seized as collateral.ᶠ
¹⁰ Without clothing, they wander about naked.
They carry sheaves but go hungry.
¹¹ They crush olives in their presses;ᴳ
they tread the winepresses, but go thirsty.
¹² From the city, menᴴ groan;
the mortally wounded cry for help,
yet God pays no attention to this crime.

ᴬ23:10 Lit *way with me*   ᴮ23:12 LXX, Vg read *treasured in my bosom*
ᶜ23:14 Lit *these with him*   ᴰ23:17 Or *silenced*   ᴱ24:8 Lit *they embrace*
ᶠ24:9 Text emended; MT reads *breast; they seize collateral against the poor*
ᴳ24:11 Lit *olives between their rows*   ᴴ24:12 One Hb ms, Syr read *the dying*

13 The wicked are those who rebel against the light.
  They do not recognize its ways
  or stay on its paths.
14 The murderer rises at dawn
  to kill the poor and needy,
  and by night he becomes a thief.
15 The adulterer's eye watches for twilight,
  thinking, "No eye will see me,"
  and he covers his face.
16 In the dark they break^A into houses;
  by day they lock themselves in,^B
  never experiencing the light.
17 For the morning is like darkness to them.
  Surely they are familiar with the terrors of darkness!

18 They float^C on the surface of the water.
  Their section of the land is cursed,
  so that they never go to their vineyards.
19 As dry ground and heat snatch away the melted snow,
  so Sheol steals those who have sinned.
20 The womb forgets them;
  worms feed on them;
  they are remembered no more.
  So injustice is broken like a tree.
21 They prey on^D the childless woman who is unable
      to conceive,
  and do not deal kindly with the widow.
22 Yet God drags away^E the mighty by his power;
  when he rises up, they have no assurance of life.
23 He gives them a sense of security, so they can rely on it,
  but his eyes watch over their ways.
24 They are exalted for a moment, then gone;
  they are brought low and shrivel up like everything else.^F
  They wither like heads of grain.

25 If this is not true, then who can prove me a liar
  and show that my speech is worthless?

BILDAD SPEAKS

25

Then Bildad the Shuhite replied:
  ² Dominion and dread belong to him,
  the one who establishes harmony in his heights.
3 Can his troops be numbered?
  Does his light not shine on everyone?
4 How can a human be justified before God?
  How can one born of woman be pure?

---

^A24:16 Lit *dig* ^B24:16 Lit *they seal for themselves* ^C24:18 Lit *are insignificant*
^D24:21 LXX, Tg read *They harm* ^E24:22 Or *God prolongs the life of*
^F24:24 LXX reads *like a mallow plant in the heat*

⁵ If even the moon does not shine
and the stars are not pure in his sight,
⁶ how much less a human, who is a maggot,
a son of man,^A who is a worm!

JOB'S REPLY TO BILDAD

26 Then Job answered:
² How you have helped the powerless
and delivered the arm that is weak!
³ How you have counseled the unwise
and abundantly provided insight!
⁴ With whom did you speak these words?
Whose breath came out of your mouth?

⁵ The departed spirits tremble
beneath the waters and all that inhabit them.
⁶ Sheol is naked before God,
and Abaddon has no covering.
⁷ He stretches the northern skies over empty space;
he hangs the earth on nothing.
⁸ He wraps up the water in his clouds,
yet the clouds do not burst beneath its weight.
⁹ He obscures the view of his throne,
spreading his cloud over it.
¹⁰ He laid out the horizon on the surface of the waters
at the boundary between light and darkness.
¹¹ The pillars that hold up the sky tremble,
astounded at his rebuke.
¹² By his power he stirred the sea,
and by his understanding he crushed Rahab.
¹³ By his breath the heavens gained their beauty;
his hand pierced the fleeing serpent.^B
¹⁴ These are but the fringes of his ways;
how faint is the word we hear of him!
Who can understand his mighty thunder?

27 Job continued his discourse, saying:
² As God lives, who has deprived me of justice,
and the Almighty who has made me bitter,
³ as long as my breath is still in me
and the breath from God remains in my nostrils,
⁴ my lips will not speak unjustly,
and my tongue will not utter deceit.
⁵ I will never affirm that you are right.
I will maintain my integrity^C until I die.
⁶ I will cling to my righteousness and never let it go.
My conscience will not accuse me as long as I live!

---

^A25:6 Or *a mere mortal* ^B26:13 = Leviathan ^C27:5 Lit *will not remove my integrity from me*

⁷ May my enemy be like the wicked
and my opponent like the unjust.
⁸ For what hope does the godless person have when he is cut off,
when God takes away his life?
⁹ Will God hear his cry
when distress comes on him?
¹⁰ Will he delight in the Almighty?
Will he call on God at all times?
¹¹ I will teach you about God's power.
I will not conceal what the Almighty has planned.ᴬ
¹² All of you have seen this for yourselves,
why do you keep up this empty talk?

¹³ This is a wicked man's lot from God,
the inheritance the ruthless receive from the Almighty.
¹⁴ Even if his children increase, they are destined for the sword;
his descendants will never have enough food.
¹⁵ Those who survive him will be buried by the plague,
yet their widows will not weep for them.
¹⁶ Though he piles up silver like dust
and heaps up fine clothing like clay —
¹⁷ he may heap it up, but the righteous will wear it,
and the innocent will divide up his silver.
¹⁸ The house he built is like a moth's cocoon
or a shelter set up by a watchman.
¹⁹ He lies down wealthy, but will do so no more;
when he opens his eyes, it is gone.
²⁰ Terrors overtake him like a flood;
a storm wind sweeps him away at night.
²¹ An east wind picks him up, and he is gone;
it carries him away from his place.
²² It blasts at him without mercy,
while he flees desperately from its force.
²³ It claps its hands at him
and scoffs at him from its place.

A HYMN TO WISDOM

28 Surely there is a mine for silver
and a place where gold is refined.
² Iron is taken from the ground,
and copper is smelted from ore.
³ A miner puts an end to the darkness;
he probesᴮ the deepest recesses
for ore in the gloomy darkness.
⁴ He cuts a shaft far from human habitation,
in places unknown to those who walk above ground.
Suspended far away from people,
the miners swing back and forth.

ᴬ27:11 Lit what is with the Almighty   ᴮ28:3 Lit probes all

⁵ Food may come from the earth,
but below the surface the earth is transformed as by fire.

⁶ Its rocks are a source of lapis lazuli,
containing flecks of gold.

⁷ No bird of prey knows that path;
no falcon's eye has seen it.

⁸ Proud beasts have never walked on it;
no lion has ever prowled over it.

⁹ The miner uses a flint tool
and turns up ore from the root of the mountains.

¹⁰ He cuts out channels in the rocks,
and his eyes spot every treasure.

¹¹ He dams up the streams from flowing[A]
so that he may bring to light what is hidden.

¹² But where can wisdom be found,
and where is understanding located?

¹³ No one can know its value,[B]
since it cannot be found in the land of the living.

¹⁴ The ocean depths say, "It's not in me,"
while the sea declares, "I don't have it."

¹⁵ Gold cannot be exchanged for it,
and silver cannot be weighed out for its price.

¹⁶ Wisdom cannot be valued in the gold of Ophir,
in precious onyx or lapis lazuli.

¹⁷ Gold and glass do not compare with it,
and articles of fine gold cannot be exchanged for it.

¹⁸ Coral and quartz are not worth mentioning.
The price of wisdom is beyond pearls.

¹⁹ Topaz from Cush cannot compare with it,
and it cannot be valued in pure gold.

²⁰ Where then does wisdom come from,
and where is understanding located?

²¹ It is hidden from the eyes of every living thing
and concealed from the birds of the sky.

²² Abaddon and Death say,
"We have heard news of it with our ears."

²³ But God understands the way to wisdom,
and he knows its location.

²⁴ For he looks to the ends of the earth
and sees everything under the heavens.

²⁵ When God fixed the weight of the wind
and distributed the water by measure,

²⁶ when he established a limit[C] for the rain
and a path for the lightning,

²⁷ he considered wisdom and evaluated it;

[A]28:11 LXX, Vg read *He explores the sources of the streams*   [B]28:13 LXX reads *way*   [C]28:26 Or *decree*

he established it and examined it.
28 He said to mankind,
"The fear of the Lord—that is wisdom.
And to turn from evil is understanding."

JOB'S FINAL CLAIM OF INNOCENCE

29 Job continued his discourse, saying:
2 If only I could be as in months gone by,
in the days when God watched over me,
3 when his lamp shone above my head,
and I walked through darkness by his light!
4 I would be as I was in the days of my youth
when God's friendship rested on my tent,
5 when the Almighty was still with me
and my children were around me,
6 when my feet were bathed in curds
and the rock poured out streams of oil for me!

7 When I went out to the city gate
and took my seat in the town square,
8 the young men saw me and withdrew,
while older men stood to their feet.
9 City officials stopped talking
and covered their mouths with their hands.
10 The noblemen's voices were hushed,
and their tongues stuck to the roof of their mouths.
11 When they heard me, they blessed me,
and when they saw me, they spoke well of me.[A]
12 For I rescued the poor who cried out for help,
and the fatherless child who had no one
to support him.
13 The dying blessed me,
and I made the widow's heart rejoice.
14 I clothed myself in righteousness,
and it enveloped me;
my just decisions were like a robe and a turban.
15 I was eyes to the blind
and feet to the lame.
16 I was a father to the needy,
and I examined the case of the stranger.
17 I shattered the fangs of the unjust
and snatched the prey from his teeth.

18 So I thought, "I will die in my own nest
and multiply my days as the sand.[B]
19 My roots will have access to water,
and the dew will rest on my branches all night.

[A] 29:11 Lit When an ear heard, it called me blessed, and when an eye saw,
it testified for me   [B] 29:18 Or as the phoenix

²⁰ My whole being will be refreshed within me,
and my bow will be renewed in my hand."

²¹ Men listened to me with expectation,
waiting silently for my advice.
²² After a word from me they did not speak again;
my speech settled on them like dew.
²³ They waited for me as for the rain
and opened their mouths as for spring showers.
²⁴ If I smiled at them, they couldn't believe it;
they were thrilled at^A the light of my countenance.
²⁵ I directed their course and presided as chief.
I lived as a king among his troops,
like one who comforts those who mourn.

30 But now they mock me,
men younger than I am,
whose fathers I would have refused to put
with my sheep dogs.
² What use to me was the strength of their hands?
Their vigor had left them.
³ Emaciated from poverty and hunger,
they gnawed the dry land,
the desolate wasteland by night.
⁴ They plucked mallow^B among the shrubs,
and the roots of the broom tree were their food.
⁵ They were banished from human society;
people shouted at them as if they were thieves.
⁶ They are living on the slopes of the wadis,
among the rocks and in holes in the ground.
⁷ They bray among the shrubs;
they huddle beneath the thistles.
⁸ Foolish men, without even a name.
They were forced to leave the land.

⁹ Now I am mocked by their songs;
I have become an object of scorn to them.
¹⁰ They despise me and keep their distance from me;
they do not hesitate to spit in my face.
¹¹ Because God has loosened my^C bowstring
and oppressed me,
they have cast off restraint in my presence.
¹² The rabble^D rise up at my right;
they trap^E my feet
and construct their siege ramp^F against me.
¹³ They tear up my path;

---

^A29:24 Lit *they did not cast down*   ^B30:4 Or *saltwort*   ^C30:11 Alt Hb tradition, LXX, Vg read *his*   ^D30:12 Hb obscure   ^E30:12 Lit *stretch out*   ^F30:12 Lit *and raise up their destructive paths*

they contribute to my destruction,
without anyone to help them.

14 They advance as through a gaping breach;
they keep rolling in through the ruins.

15 Terrors are turned loose against me;
they chase my dignity away like the wind,
and my prosperity has passed by like a cloud.

16 Now my life is poured out before me,
and days of suffering have seized me.

17 Night pierces my bones,
but my gnawing pains never rest.

18 My clothing is distorted with great force;
he chokes me by the neck of my garment.^A

19 He throws me into the mud,
and I have become like dust and ashes.

20 I cry out to you for help, but you
do not answer me;
when I stand up, you merely look at me.

21 You have turned against me with cruelty;
you harass me with your strong hand.

22 You lift me up on the wind and make me ride it;
you scatter me in the storm.

23 Yes, I know that you will lead me to death —
the place appointed for all who live.

24 Yet no one would stretch out his hand
against a ruined person^B
when he cries out to him for help
because of his distress.

25 Have I not wept for those who have fallen
on hard times?
Has my soul not grieved for the needy?

26 But when I hoped for good, evil came;
when I looked for light, darkness came.

27 I am churning within^C and cannot rest;
days of suffering confront me.

28 I walk about blackened, but not by the sun.^D
I stood in the assembly and cried out for help.

29 I have become a brother to jackals
and a companion of ostriches.

30 My skin blackens and flakes off,^E
and my bones burn with fever.

31 My lyre is used for mourning
and my flute for the sound of weeping.

---

^A30:18 Hb obscure   ^B30:24 Lit *a heap of ruins*   ^C30:27 Lit *My bowels boil*
^D30:28 Or *walk in sunless gloom*   ^E30:30 Lit *blackens away from me*

31 I have made a covenant with my eyes.
How then could I look at a young woman?[A]

2 For what portion would I have from God above,
or what inheritance from the Almighty on high?
3 Doesn't disaster come to the unjust
and misfortune to evildoers?
4 Does he not see my ways
and number all my steps?

5 If I have walked in falsehood
or my foot has rushed to deceit,
6 let God weigh me on accurate scales,
and he will recognize my integrity.

7 If my step has turned from the way,
my heart has followed my eyes,
or impurity has stained my hands,
8 let someone else eat what I have sown,
and let my crops be uprooted.

9 If my heart has gone astray over a woman
or I have lurked at my neighbor's door,
10 let my own wife grind grain for another man,
and let other men sleep with[B] her.
11 For that would be a disgrace;
it would be an iniquity deserving punishment.
12 For it is a fire that consumes down to Abaddon;
it would destroy my entire harvest.

13 If I have dismissed the case of my male or female servants
when they made a complaint against me,
14 what could I do when God stands up to judge?
How should I answer him when he calls me to account?
15 Did not the one who made me in the womb also make them?
Did not the same God form us both in the womb?

16 If I have refused the wishes of the poor
or let the widow's eyes go blind,
17 if I have eaten my few crumbs alone
without letting the fatherless eat any of it —
18 for from my youth, I raised him as his father,
and since the day I was born[C] I guided the widow —
19 if I have seen anyone dying for lack of clothing
or a needy person without a cloak,
20 if he[D] did not bless me
while warming himself with the fleece from my sheep,
21 if I ever cast my vote[E] against a fatherless child

[A]31:1 Or a virgin [B]31:10 Lit men kneel down over [C]31:18 Lit and from my mother's womb [D]31:20 Lit his loins [E]31:21 Lit I raise my hand

when I saw that I had support in the city gate,
22 then let my shoulder blade fall from my back,
and my arm be pulled from its socket.
23 For disaster from God terrifies me,
and because of his majesty I could not do these things.

24 If I placed my confidence in gold
or called fine gold my trust,
25 if I have rejoiced because my wealth is great
or because my own hand has acquired so much,
26 if I have gazed at the sun when it was shining
or at the moon moving in splendor,
27 so that my heart was secretly enticed
and I threw them a kiss, A
28 this would also be an iniquity deserving punishment,
for I would have denied God above.

29 Have I rejoiced over my enemy's distress,
or become excited when trouble came his way?
30 I have not allowed my mouth to sin
by asking for his life with a curse.
31 Haven't the members of my household said,
"Who is there who has not had enough to eat at Job's table?"
32 No stranger had to spend the night on the street,
for I opened my door to the traveler.
33 Have I covered my transgressions as others do B
by hiding my iniquity in my heart
34 because I greatly feared the crowds
and because the contempt of the clans terrified me,
so I grew silent and would not go outside?

35 If only I had someone to hear my case!
Here is my signature; let the Almighty answer me.
Let my Opponent compose his indictment.
36 I would surely carry it on my shoulder
and wear it like a crown.
37 I would give him an account of all my steps;
I would approach him like a prince.

38 If my land cries out against me
and its furrows join in weeping,
39 if I have consumed its produce without payment
or shown contempt for its tenants, C
40 then let thorns grow instead of wheat
and stinkweed instead of barley.

The words of Job are concluded.

A31:27 Lit and my hand kissed my mouth   B31:33 Or as Adam   C31:39 Lit or
caused the breath of its tenants to breathe out

ELIHU'S ANGRY RESPONSE

32 So these three men quit answering Job, because he was righteous in his own eyes. ² Then Elihu son of Barachel the Buzite from the family of Ram became angry. He was angry at Job because he had justified himself rather than God. ³ He was also angry at Job's three friends because they had failed to refute him and yet had condemned him. ^A

⁴ Now Elihu had waited to speak to Job because they were all older than he. ⁵ But when he saw that the three men could not answer Job, he became angry.

⁶ So Elihu son of Barachel the Buzite replied:

I am young in years,
while you are old;
therefore I was timid and afraid
to tell you what I know.
⁷ I thought that age should speak
and maturity should teach wisdom.
⁸ But it is the spirit in a person—
the breath from the Almighty—
that gives anyone understanding.
⁹ It is not only the old who are wise
or the elderly who understand how to judge.
¹⁰ Therefore I say, "Listen to me.
I too will declare what I know."
¹¹ Look, I waited for your conclusions;
I listened to your insights
as you sought for words.
¹² I paid close attention to you.
Yet no one proved Job wrong;
not one of you refuted his arguments.
¹³ So do not claim, "We have found wisdom;
let God deal with him, not man."
¹⁴ But Job has not directed his argument to me,
and I will not respond to him with your arguments.

¹⁵ Job's friends are dismayed and can no longer answer;
words have left them.
¹⁶ Should I continue to wait now that they are silent,
now that they stand there and no longer answer?
¹⁷ I too will answer; ^B
yes, I will tell what I know.
¹⁸ For I am full of words,
and my spirit ^C compels me to speak.
¹⁹ My heart ^D is like unvented wine;
it is about to burst like new wineskins.
²⁰ I must speak so that I can find relief;
I must open my lips and respond.
²¹ I will be partial to no one,
and I will not give anyone an undeserved title.

---

^A32:3 Alt Hb tradition reads condemned God   ^B32:17 Lit answer my part
^C32:18 Lit and the spirit of my belly   ^D32:19 Lit belly

²² For I do not know how to give such titles;
otherwise, my Maker would remove me in an instant.

ELIHU CONFRONTS JOB

33

But now, Job, pay attention to my speech,
and listen to all my words.
² I am going to open my mouth;
my tongue will form words on my palate.
³ My words come from my upright heart,
and my lips speak with sincerity what they know.
⁴ The Spirit of God has made me,
and the breath of the Almighty gives me life.
⁵ Refute me if you can.
Prepare your case against me; take your stand.
⁶ I am just like you before God;
I was also pinched off from a piece of clay.
⁷ Fear of me should not terrify you;
no pressure from me should weigh you down.

⁸ Surely you have spoken in my hearing,
and I have heard these very^A words:
⁹ "I am pure, without transgression;
I am clean and have no iniquity.
¹⁰ But he finds reasons to oppose me;
he regards me as his enemy.
¹¹ He puts my feet in the stocks;
he stands watch over all my paths."

¹² But I tell you that you are wrong in this matter,
since God is greater than man.
¹³ Why do you take him to court
for not answering anything a person asks?^B
¹⁴ For God speaks time and again,
but a person may not notice it.
¹⁵ In a dream, a vision in the night,
when deep sleep comes over people
as they slumber on their beds,
¹⁶ he uncovers their ears
and terrifies them^C with warnings,
¹⁷ in order to turn a person from his actions
and suppress the pride of a person.
¹⁸ God spares his soul from the Pit,
his life from crossing the river of death.^D
¹⁹ A person may be disciplined on his bed with pain
and constant distress in his bones,
²⁰ so that he detests bread,
and his soul despises his favorite food.

---

^A33:8 Lit *heard a sound of*   ^B33:13 Lit *court, for he does not answer all his words*
^C33:16 LXX; MT reads *and seals*   ^D33:18 Or *from perishing by the sword*

²¹ His flesh wastes away to nothing,ᴬ
and his unseen bones stick out.
²² He draws near to the Pit,
and his life to the executioners.
²³ If there is an angel on his side,
one mediator out of a thousand,
to tell a person what is right for himᴮ
²⁴ and to be gracious to him and say,
"Spare him from going down to the Pit;
I have found a ransom,"
²⁵ then his flesh will be healthierᶜ than in his youth,
and he will return to the days of his youthful vigor.
²⁶ He will pray to God, and God will delight in him.
That person will see his face with a shout of joy,
and God will restore his righteousness to him.
²⁷ He will look at men and say,
"I have sinned and perverted what was right;
yet I did not get what I deserved.ᴰ
²⁸ He redeemed my soul from going down to the Pit,
and I will continue to see the light."
²⁹ God certainly does all these things
two or three times to a person
³⁰ in order to turn him back from the Pit,
so he may shine with the light of life.
³¹ Pay attention, Job, and listen to me.
Be quiet, and I will speak.
³² But if you have something to say,ᴱ answer me;
speak, for I would like to justify you.
³³ If not, then listen to me;
be quiet, and I will teach you wisdom.

34

Then Elihu continued,ᶠ saying:
² Hear my words, you wise ones,
and listen to me, you knowledgeable ones.
³ Doesn't the ear test words
as the palate tastes food?
⁴ Let us judge for ourselves what is right;
let us decide together what is good.
⁵ For Job has declared, "I am righteous,
yet God has deprived me of justice.
⁶ Would I lie about my case?
My woundᴳ is incurable,
though I am without transgression."
⁷ What man is like Job?
He drinks derision like water.
⁸ He keeps company with evildoers

ᴬ33:21 Lit *away from sight* ᴮ33:23 Or *to vouch for a person's uprightness*
ᶜ33:25 Hb obscure ᴰ33:27 Lit *and the same was not to me* ᴱ33:32 Lit *If there are words* ᶠ34:1 Lit *answered* ᴳ34:6 Lit *arrow*

and walks with wicked men.
9 For he has said, "A man gains nothing
when he becomes God's friend."

10 Therefore listen to me, you men of understanding.
It is impossible for God to do wrong,
and for the Almighty to act unjustly.
11 For he repays a person according to his deeds,
and he gives him what his conduct deserves. ^A
12 Indeed, it is true that God does not act wickedly
and the Almighty does not pervert justice.
13 Who gave him authority over the earth?
Who put him in charge of the entire world?
14 If he put his mind to it
and withdrew the spirit and breath he gave,
15 every living thing would perish together
and mankind would return to the dust.

16 If you have understanding, hear this;
listen to what I have to say.
17 Could one who hates justice govern the world?
Will you condemn the mighty Righteous One,
18 who says to a king, "Worthless man!"
and to nobles, "Wicked men!"?
19 God is not partial to princes
and does not favor the rich over the poor,
for they are all the work of his hands.
20 They die suddenly in the middle of the night;
people shudder, then pass away.
Even the mighty are removed without effort.

21 For his eyes watch over a man's ways,
and he observes all his steps.
22 There is no darkness, no deep darkness,
where evildoers can hide.
23 God does not need to examine a person further,
that one should ^B approach him in court.
24 He shatters the mighty without an investigation
and sets others in their place.
25 Therefore, he recognizes their deeds
and overthrows them by night, and they are crushed.
26 In full view of the public, ^C
he strikes them for their wickedness,
27 because they turned aside from following him
and did not understand any of his ways
28 but caused the poor to cry out to him,
and he heard the outcry of the needy.

---

^A 34:11 Lit and like a path of a man, he causes him to find   ^B 34:23 Some emend
to God has not appointed a time for man to   ^C 34:26 Lit In a place of spectators

29 But when God is silent, who can declare him guilty?
   When he hides his face, who can see him?
   Yet he watches over both individuals and nations,
30 so that godless men should not rule
   or ensnare the people.

31 Suppose someone says to God,
   "I have endured my punishment;
   I will no longer act wickedly.
32 Teach me what I cannot see;
   if I have done wrong, I won't do it again."
33 Should God repay you on your terms
   when you have rejected his?
   You must choose, not I!
   So declare what you know.
34 Reasonable men will say to me,
   along with the wise men who hear me,
35 "Job speaks without knowledge;
   his words are without insight."
36 If only Job were tested to the limit,
   because his answers are like those of wicked men.
37 For he adds rebellion to his sin;
   he scornfully claps in our presence,
   while multiplying his words against God.

35 Then Elihu continued, saying:
² Do you think it is just when you say,
   "I am righteous before God"?
³ For you ask, "What does it profit you,^A
   and what benefit comes to me, if I do not sin?"
⁴ I will answer you
   and your friends with you.
⁵ Look at the heavens and see;
   gaze at the clouds high above you.
⁶ If you sin, how does it affect God?
   If you multiply your transgressions, what does it do to him?
⁷ If you are righteous, what do you give him,
   or what does he receive from your hand?
⁸ Your wickedness affects a person like yourself,
   and your righteousness, a son of man.^B
⁹ People cry out because of severe oppression;
   they shout for help because of the power of the mighty.
¹⁰ But no one asks, "Where is God my Maker,
   who provides us with songs in the night,
¹¹ who gives us more understanding than the animals of the earth
   and makes us wiser than the birds of the sky?"
¹² There they cry out, but he does not answer,
   because of the pride of evil people.

^A35:3 Some emend to *me* ^B35:8 Or *a mere mortal*

¹³ Indeed, God does not listen to empty cries,
and the Almighty does not take note of it —
¹⁴ how much less when ᴬ you complain ᴮ
that you do not see him,
that your case is before him
and you are waiting for him.
¹⁵ But now, because God's anger does not punish
and he does not pay attention to transgression, ᶜ
¹⁶ Job opens his mouth in vain
and multiplies words without knowledge.

36 Then Elihu continued, saying:
²Be patient with me a little longer, and I will inform you,
for there is still more to be said on God's behalf.
³ I will get my knowledge from a distant place
and ascribe justice to my Maker.
⁴ Indeed, my words are not false;
one who has complete knowledge is with you.

⁵ Yes, God is mighty, but he despises no one;
he understands all things. ᴰ
⁶ He does not keep the wicked alive,
but he gives justice to the oppressed.
⁷ He does not withdraw his gaze from the righteous,
but he seats them forever with enthroned kings,
and they are exalted.

⁸ If people are bound with chains
and trapped by the cords of affliction,
⁹ God tells them what they have done
and how arrogantly they have transgressed.
¹⁰ He opens their ears to correction
and tells them to repent from iniquity.
¹¹ If they listen and serve him,
they will end their days in prosperity
and their years in happiness.
¹² But if they do not listen,
they will cross the river of death ᴱ
and die without knowledge.

¹³ Those who have a godless heart harbor anger;
even when God binds them, they do not cry for help.
¹⁴ They die in their youth;
their life ends among male cult prostitutes.
¹⁵ God rescues the afflicted by their affliction;
he instructs them by their torment.

ᴬ35:14 Or *how then can*   ᴮ35:14 Lit *say*   ᶜ35:15 LXX, Vg; MT reads *folly,*
or *arrogance*; Hb obscure   ᴰ36:5 Lit *he is mighty in strength of heart*
ᴱ36:12 Or *will perish by the sword*

16 Indeed, he lured you from the jaws^A of distress
to a spacious and unconfined place.
Your table was spread with choice food.
17 Yet now you are obsessed with the judgment due the wicked;
judgment and justice have seized you.
18 Be careful that no one lures you with riches;^B
do not let a large ransom^C lead you astray.
19 Can your wealth^D or all your physical exertion
keep you from distress?
20 Do not long for the night
when nations will disappear from their places.
21 Be careful that you do not turn to iniquity,
for that is why you have been tested by^E affliction.

22 Look, God shows himself exalted by his power.
Who is a teacher like him?
23 Who has appointed his way for him,
and who has declared, "You have done wrong"?
24 Remember that you should praise his work,
which people have sung about.
25 All mankind has seen it;
people have looked at it from a distance.
26 Yes, God is exalted beyond our knowledge;
the number of his years cannot be counted.
27 For he makes waterdrops evaporate;^F
they distill the rain into its^G mist,
28 which the clouds pour out
and shower abundantly on mankind.
29 Can anyone understand how the clouds spread out
or how the thunder roars from God's pavilion?
30 See how he spreads his lightning around him
and covers the depths of the sea.
31 For he judges the nations with these;
he gives food in abundance.
32 He covers his hands with lightning
and commands it to hit its mark.
33 The^H thunder declares his presence;^I
the cattle also, the approaching storm.

37 My heart pounds at this
and leaps from my chest.^J
2 Just listen to his thunderous voice
and the rumbling that comes from his mouth.
3 He lets it loose beneath the entire sky;
his lightning to the ends of the earth.

---

^A36:16 Lit *from a mouth of narrowness* ^B36:18 Or *you into mockery*
^C36:18 Or *bribe* ^D36:19 Or *cry for help* ^E36:21 Or *for you have preferred this*
to ^F36:27 Lit *he draws in waterdrops* ^G36:27 Or *his* ^H36:33 Lit *His,* or *Its*
^I36:33 Lit *thunder announces concerning him* or *it* ^J37:1 Lit *from its place*

4 Then there comes a roaring sound;
God thunders with his majestic voice.
He does not restrain the lightning
when his rumbling voice is heard.

5 God thunders wondrously with his voice;
he does great things that we cannot comprehend.

6 For he says to the snow, "Fall to the earth,"
and the torrential rains, his mighty torrential rains,

7 serve as his sign to all mankind,
so that all men may know his work.

8 The wild animals enter their lairs
and stay in their dens.

9 The windstorm comes from its chamber,
and the cold from the driving north winds.

10 Ice is formed by the breath of God,
and watery expanses are frozen.

11 He saturates clouds with moisture;
he scatters his lightning through them.

12 They swirl about,
turning round and round at his direction,
accomplishing everything he commands them
over the surface of the inhabited world.

13 He causes this to happen for punishment,
for his land, or for his faithful love.

14 Listen to this, Job.
Stop and consider God's wonders.

15 Do you know how God directs his clouds
or makes their lightning flash?

16 Do you understand how the clouds float,
those wonderful works of him who has
perfect knowledge?

17 You whose clothes get hot
when the south wind brings calm to the land,

18 can you help God spread out the skies
as hard as a cast metal mirror?

19 Teach us what we should say to him;
we cannot prepare our case because of our darkness.

20 Should he be told that I want to speak?
Can a man speak when he is confused?

21 Now no one can even look at the sun
when it is in the skies,
after a wind has swept through and cleared
the clouds away.^

22 Yet out of the north he comes, shrouded in a golden glow;
awesome majesty surrounds him.

23 The Almighty — we cannot reach him —
he is exalted in power!

---

^37:21 Lit *and cleaned them*

He will not violate justice and abundant righteousness,
²⁴ therefore, men fear him.
He does not look favorably on any who are wise in heart.

THE LORD SPEAKS

38

Then the LORD answered Job from the whirlwind. He said:
² Who is this who obscures my counsel
with ignorant words?
³ Get ready to answer me like a man;
when I question you, you will inform me.
⁴ Where were you when I established the earth?
Tell me, if you have^A understanding.
⁵ Who fixed its dimensions? Certainly you know!
Who stretched a measuring line across it?
⁶ What supports its foundations?
Or who laid its cornerstone
⁷ while the morning stars sang together
and all the sons of God shouted for joy?

⁸ Who enclosed the sea behind doors
when it burst from the womb,
⁹ when I made the clouds its garment
and total darkness its blanket,^B
¹⁰ when I determined its boundaries^C
and put its bars and doors in place,
¹¹ when I declared: "You may come this far, but no farther;
your proud waves stop here"?

¹² Have you ever in your life commanded the morning
or assigned the dawn its place,
¹³ so it may seize the edges of the earth
and shake the wicked out of it?
¹⁴ The earth is changed as clay is by a seal;
its hills stand out like the folds of a garment.
¹⁵ Light^D is withheld from the wicked,
and the arm raised in violence is broken.

¹⁶ Have you traveled to the sources of the sea
or walked in the depths of the oceans?
¹⁷ Have the gates of death been revealed to you?
Have you seen the gates of deep darkness?
¹⁸ Have you comprehended the extent of the earth?
Tell me, if you know all this.

¹⁹ Where is the road to the home of light?
Do you know where darkness lives,
²⁰ so you can lead it back to its border?

---

^A38:4 Lit know   ^B38:9 Lit swaddling clothes   ^C38:10 Lit I broke my statute on it
^D38:15 Lit Their light

Are you familiar with the paths to its home?
²¹ Don't you know? You were already born;
you have lived so long!ᴬ
²² Have you entered the place where the snow is stored?
Or have you seen the storehouses of hail,
²³ which I hold in reserve for times of trouble,
for the day of warfare and battle?
²⁴ What road leads to the place where light is dispersed?ᴮ
Where is the source of the east wind that spreads across the earth?

²⁵ Who cuts a channel for the flooding rain
or clears the way for lightning,
²⁶ to bring rain on an uninhabited land,
on a desert with no human life,ᶜ
²⁷ to satisfy the parched wasteland
and cause the grass to sprout?
²⁸ Does the rain have a father?
Who fathered the drops of dew?
²⁹ Whose womb did the ice come from?
Who gave birth to the frost of heaven
³⁰ when water becomes as hard as stone,ᴰ
and the surface of the watery depths is frozen?

³¹ Can you fasten the chains of the Pleiades
or loosen the belt of Orion?
³² Can you bring out the constellationsᴱ in their season
and lead the Bearᶠ and her cubs?
³³ Do you know the laws of heaven?
Can you impose itsᴳ authority on earth?
³⁴ Can you commandᴴ the clouds
so that a flood of water covers you?
³⁵ Can you send out lightning bolts, and they go?
Do they report to you: "Here we are"?

³⁶ Who put wisdom in the heartᴵ
or gave the mind understanding?
³⁷ Who has the wisdom to number the clouds?
Or who can tilt the water jars of heaven
³⁸ when the dust hardens like cast metal
and the clods of dirt stick together?

³⁹ Can you hunt prey for a lioness
or satisfy the appetite of young lions
⁴⁰ when they crouch in their dens
and lie in wait within their lairs?

ᴬ38:21 Lit born; the number of your days is great   ᴮ38:24 Or where lightning
is distributed   ᶜ38:26 Lit no man in it   ᴰ38:30 Lit water hides itself as the stone
ᴱ38:32 Or Mazzaroth; Hb obscure   ᶠ38:32 Or lead Aldebaran   ᴳ38:33 Or
God's   ᴴ38:34 Lit lift up your voice to   ᴵ38:36 Or the inner self; Ps 51:6

⁴¹ Who provides the raven's food
when its young cry out to God
and wander about for lack of food?

39 Do you know when mountain goats give birth?
Have you watched the deer in labor?
² Can you count the months they are pregnant ᴬ
so you can know the time they give birth?
³ They crouch down to give birth to their young;
they deliver their newborn. ᴮ
⁴ Their offspring are healthy and grow up in the open field.
They leave and do not return. ᶜ

⁵ Who set the wild donkey free?
Who released the swift donkey from its harness?
⁶ I made the desert its home,
and the salty wasteland its dwelling.
⁷ It scoffs at the noise of the village
and never hears the shouts of a driver.
⁸ It roams the mountains for its pastureland,
searching for anything green.
⁹ Would the wild ox be willing to serve you?
Would it spend the night by your feeding trough?
¹⁰ Can you hold the wild ox to a furrow by its harness?
Will it plow the valleys behind you?
¹¹ Can you depend on it because its strength is great?
Would you leave it to do your hard work?
¹² Can you trust the wild ox to harvest your grain
and bring it to your threshing floor?

¹³ The wings of the ostrich flap joyfully,
but are her feathers and plumage like the stork's? ᴰ
¹⁴ She abandons her eggs on the ground
and lets them be warmed in the sand.
¹⁵ She forgets that a foot may crush them
or that some wild animal may trample them.
¹⁶ She treats her young harshly, as if they were not her own,
with no fear that her labor may have been in vain.
¹⁷ For God has deprived her of wisdom;
he has not endowed her with understanding.
¹⁸ When she proudly ᴰ spreads her wings,
she laughs at the horse and its rider.

¹⁹ Do you give strength to the horse?
Do you adorn his neck with a mane? ᴰ
²⁰ Do you make him leap like a locust?
His proud snorting fills one with terror.

ᴬ39:2 Lit *months they fulfill*   ᴮ39:3 Or *they send away their labor pains*
ᶜ39:4 Lit *return to them*   ᴰ39:13,18,19 Hb obscure

21 He paws[A] in the valley and rejoices in his strength;
 he charges into battle.[B]
22 He laughs at fear, since he is afraid of nothing;
 he does not run from the sword.
23 A quiver rattles at his side,
 along with a flashing spear and a javelin.
24 He charges ahead[C] with trembling rage;
 he cannot stand still at the trumpet's sound.
25 When the trumpet blasts, he snorts defiantly.[D]
 He smells the battle from a distance;
 he hears the officers' shouts and the battle cry.

26 Does the hawk take flight by your understanding
 and spread its wings to the south?
27 Does the eagle soar at your command
 and make its nest on high?
28 It lives on a cliff where it spends the night;
 its stronghold is on a rocky crag.
29 From there it searches for prey;
 its eyes penetrate the distance.
30 Its brood gulps down blood,
 and where the slain are, it is there.

40

The LORD answered Job:
2 Will the one who contends with the Almighty correct him?
Let him who argues with God give an answer.[E]

3 Then Job answered the LORD:
4 I am so insignificant. How can I answer you?
 I place my hand over my mouth.
5 I have spoken once, and I will not reply;
 twice, but now I can add nothing.

6 Then the LORD answered Job from the whirlwind:
7 Get ready to answer me like a man;
 When I question you, you will inform me.
8 Would you really challenge my justice?
 Would you declare me guilty to justify yourself?
9 Do you have an arm like God's?
 Can you thunder with a voice like his?

10 Adorn yourself with majesty and splendor,
 and clothe yourself with honor and glory.
11 Pour out your raging anger;
 look on every proud person and humiliate him.
12 Look on every proud person and humble him;

[A]39:21 LXX, Syr; MT reads They dig   [B]39:21 Lit he goes out to meet the
weaponry   [C]39:24 Lit He swallows the ground   [D]39:25 Lit he says, "Aha!"
[E]40:2 Lit God respond to it

trample the wicked where they stand.^A

13 Hide them together in the dust;
imprison them in the grave.^B

14 Then I will confess to you
that your own right hand can deliver you.

15 Look at Behemoth,
which I made along with you.
He eats grass like cattle.

16 Look at the strength of his back^C
and the power in the muscles of his belly.

17 He stiffens his tail like a cedar tree;
the tendons of his thighs are woven firmly together.

18 His bones are bronze tubes;
his limbs are like iron rods.

19 He is the foremost of God's works;
only his Maker can draw the sword against him.

20 The hills yield food for him,
while all sorts of wild animals play there.

21 He lies under the lotus plants,
hiding in the protection^D of marshy reeds.

22 Lotus plants cover him with their shade;
the willows by the brook surround him.

23 Though the river rages, Behemoth is unafraid;
he remains confident, even if the Jordan surges up to his mouth.

24 Can anyone capture him while he looks on,^E
or pierce his nose with snares?

41 Can you pull in Leviathan with a hook
or tie his tongue down with a rope?

2 Can you put a cord^F through his nose
or pierce his jaw with a hook?

3 Will he beg you for mercy
or speak softly to you?

4 Will he make a covenant with you
so that you can take him as a slave forever?

5 Can you play with him like a bird
or put him on a leash^G for your girls?

6 Will traders bargain for him
or divide him among the merchants?

7 Can you fill his hide with harpoons
or his head with fishing spears?

8 Lay a^H hand on him.
You will remember the battle
and never repeat it!

9 Any hope of capturing him proves false.

---

^A40:12 Lit wicked in their place ^B40:13 Lit together; bind their faces in the
hidden place ^C40:16 Or waist ^D40:21 Lit plants, in the hiding place ^E40:24
Lit capture it in its eyes ^F41:2 Lit reed ^G41:5 Lit or bind him ^H41:8 Lit your

Does a person not collapse at the very sight of him?
10 No one is ferocious enough to rouse Leviathan;
who then can stand against me?
11 Who confronted me, that I should repay him?
Everything under heaven belongs to me.

12 I cannot be silent about his limbs,
his power, and his graceful proportions.
13 Who can strip off his outer covering?
Who can penetrate his double layer of armor?^A
14 Who can open his jaws,^B
surrounded by those terrifying teeth?
15 His pride is in his rows of scales,
closely sealed together.
16 One scale is so close to another^C
that no air can pass between them.
17 They are joined to one another,
so closely connected^D they cannot be separated.
18 His snorting^E flashes with light,
while his eyes are like the rays^F of dawn.
19 Flaming torches shoot from his mouth;
fiery sparks fly out!
20 Smoke billows from his nostrils
as from a boiling pot or burning reeds.
21 His breath sets coals ablaze,
and flames pour out of his mouth.
22 Strength resides in his neck,
and dismay dances before him.
23 The folds of his flesh are joined together,
solid as metal^G and immovable.
24 His heart is as hard as a rock,
as hard as a lower millstone!
25 When Leviathan rises, the mighty^H are terrified;
they withdraw because of his thrashing.
26 The sword that reaches him will have no effect,
nor will a spear, dart, or arrow.
27 He regards iron as straw,
and bronze as rotten wood.
28 No arrow can make him flee;
slingstones become like stubble to him.
29 A club is regarded as stubble,
and he laughs at the sound of a javelin.
30 His undersides are jagged potsherds,
spreading the mud like a threshing sledge.
31 He makes the depths seethe like a cauldron;

---

^A41:13 LXX; MT reads *double bridle*   ^B41:14 Lit *open the doors of his face*
^C41:16 Lit *One by one they approach*   ^D41:17 Lit *another; they cling together
and*   ^E41:18 Or *sneezing*   ^F41:18 Lit *eyelids*   ^G41:23 Lit *together, hard on him*
^H41:25 Or *the divine beings*

he makes the sea like an ointment jar.
32 He leaves a shining wake behind him;[A]
one would think the deep had gray hair!
33 He has no equal on earth —
a creature devoid of fear!
34 He surveys everything that is haughty;
he is king over all the proud beasts.[B]

JOB REPLIES TO THE LORD

42 Then Job replied to the LORD:
2 I[C] know that you can do anything
and no plan of yours can be thwarted.
3 You asked, "Who is this who conceals my counsel with ignorance?"
Surely I spoke about things I did not understand,
things too wondrous for me to[D] know.
4 You said, "Listen now, and I will speak.
When I question you, you will inform me."
5 I had heard reports about you,
but now my eyes have seen you.
6 Therefore, I reject my words and am sorry for them;
I am dust and ashes.[E,F]

7 After the LORD had finished speaking[G] to Job, he said to Eliphaz the Temanite: "I am angry with you and your two friends, for you have not spoken the truth about me, as my servant Job has. 8 Now take seven bulls and seven rams, go to my servant Job, and offer a burnt offering for yourselves. Then my servant Job will pray for you. I will surely accept his prayer and not deal with you as your folly deserves. For you have not spoken the truth about me, as my servant Job has." 9 Then Eliphaz the Temanite, Bildad the Shuhite, and Zophar the Naamathite went and did as the LORD had told them, and the LORD accepted Job's prayer.

GOD RESTORES JOB

10 After Job had prayed for his friends, the LORD restored his fortunes and doubled his previous possessions. 11 All his brothers, sisters, and former acquaintances came to him and dined with him in his house. They sympathized with him and comforted him concerning all the adversity the LORD had brought on him. Each one gave him a piece of silver[H] and a gold earring.

12 So the LORD blessed the last part of Job's life more than the first. He owned fourteen thousand sheep and goats, six thousand camels, one thousand yoke of oxen, and one thousand female donkeys. 13 He also had seven sons and three daughters. 14 He named his first daughter Jemimah, his second Keziah, and his third Keren-happuch. 15 No women as beautiful as Job's daughters could be found in all the land, and their father granted them an inheritance with their brothers.

16 Job lived 140 years after this and saw his children and their children to the fourth generation. 17 Then Job died, old and full of days.

[A]41:32 Lit *a path* [B]41:34 Lit *the children of pride* [C]42:2 Alt Hb tradition reads *You*
[D]42:3 Lit *me, and I did not* [E]42:6 LXX reads *I despise myself and melt; I consider myself dust and ashes* [F]42:6 Lit *I reject and I relent, concerning dust and ashes* [G]42:7 Lit *speaking these words* [H]42:11 Lit *a qesitah*; the value of this currency is unknown

RESTORED

JOB 42; ISAIAH 61:1-3; JOHN 16:33

Restoration.

It's a beautiful word because it represents the process of fixing brokenness, of replacing something that was lost. We long for restoration because we're broken people who face suffering and pain. A devastating diagnosis, an unexpected job loss, a difficult relationship—so many experiences in life leave us longing for relief. In those moments, we ache for healing and wholeness. We ache for restoration.

The ache inside us serves its greatest purpose when it drives us to our knees in desperation, compelling us to seek comfort in the strong and healing presence of our Savior. This is God's glorious intent for every hardship we face. As difficult as it is to understand, God is at work even in our pain.

Job is the proverbial poster-child for suffering. In one of the most well-known yet least understood stories in Scripture, Job lost everything dear to him—quickly and through no apparent fault of his own. A righteous man who honored the Lord suddenly became part of a cosmic negotiation between God and Satan. God allowed Satan to inflict pain on Job's life in different forms, knowing that Job's heart would remain steadfast. And it did.

As the story unfolds, we see Job suffer in ways most of us can't even fathom. Yet he remained determined to trust God's goodness and sovereignty in the midst of his deep pain.

Job believed in God's faithfulness even as he ached for restoration.

Notice how that restoration eventually unfolds. God didn't erase Job's painful memories. He didn't turn back the clock to the way things were. What He did instead was much more glorious. He redeemed all Job had endured. On a canvas of suffering, God painted a radiant picture of grace and redemption. After the dust settled and the darkness faded, something beautiful was left standing: a life restored.

The final chapter of Job's story is one of the most profound passages in Scripture. Job 42 gives us the ending we've longed for. We find tangible evidence of restoration and discover that our great God is indeed willing and able to bring beauty from ashes (Is 61:3).

Our God is in the business of restoring our brokenness and redeeming our pain. And that God-ordained restoration and redemption looks different in each of our lives.

For Job it unfolded like this: "So the LORD blessed the last part of Job's life more than the first" (Jb 42:12). He died, old and "full of days." Job's story comes to a close as the Great Redeemer takes center stage, restoring and reconciling all things for His glory.

This is the ending our hearts ache for: not to have our earthly bodies or possessions restored, but to be fully restored by the God who made us and fully reconciled to Him in Glory.

I was helpless and He saved me.

psalms

 The LORD is gracious and righteous; our God is compassionate. The LORD guards the inexperienced; I was helpless, and he saved me. **116:5-6**

ON THE TIMELINE The book of Psalms consists of many different hymns and prayers composed by individuals and used by the community. If one were to take the names in the titles as authors, the date of composition ranges from the time of Moses (fifteenth century BC) to a time following the exiles (sixth century BC or later). Some of the titles contain historical information that might indicate the setting of the composition, although even this, like the authorship, is subject to interpretation.

A LITTLE BACKGROUND Since the book is a collection of many different psalms written over a long time, there is not one author for this collection. By far the most common designation in the titles is "of David" which may refer to David. David's role as a musician in Saul's court (1Sm 16:14-23) as well as his many experiences as a shepherd, a soldier, and a king make him a likely candidate for writing many of these psalms. Other titles include the designations of Solomon (Pss 72; 127), Asaph (Pss 50; 73–83), the sons of Korah (Pss 42; 44–49; 84–85; 87–88), Ethan (Ps 89), Heman son of Korah (Ps 88), and Moses (Ps 90).

MESSAGE & PURPOSE The whole range of human emotions is mirrored in this rich collection of 150 psalms. This record of the responses of God's people in worship and prayer serves the purpose of teaching us how to relate to God in various circumstances of life. The Psalms also demonstrate God's sovereignty and goodness to His people in order to instill confidence in those who trust in Him.

GIVE THANKS FOR THE BOOK OF PSALMS:

The Psalms are deeply relational. They give us a beautiful look into who God is, how He acts, and how His people respond. The struggle to understand how God's attributes, particularly His sovereignty and goodness, relate to life experiences is a major theme in the collection. These words are from people who had not lost their faith in God, although they might have been tempted to at times (Ps 73). Like us, they wrestled with how God was dealing with them personally and as a community.

CHRIST IN THE PSALMS

Though written long before His birth, the Psalms are filled with references to Jesus Christ.

Both the Jewish and Christian faiths have long believed that many Psalms referred as much to the promised Messiah as they did to current events of the time. The Messiah was to be a descendant of David, so it was expected that many of the royal psalms, or songs, would apply to Him.

Jesus Himself frequently quoted the Psalms, and Christ followers point to many passages in Psalms which describe in detail events of His life and death. Almost everything that happened at the crucifixion, including many of Jesus' words during His final hours, were prophesied in Psalms.

PSALM	REFERENCE TO CHRIST	FULFILLMENT IN THE NEW TESTAMENT
2:7	The Messiah will be God's Son.	HEBREWS 1:5-6
16:8-10	He will rise from the dead.	LUKE 24:5-7
22:1-21	He will experience agony on the cross.	MATTHEW 27:32-56
22:15	He will thirst while on the cross.	JOHN 19:28
22:18	Evil men will throw dice for His clothing.	MATTHEW 27:35; JOHN 19:23-24
22:22	He will declare God's name.	HEBREWS 2:12
34:20	His bones will not be broken.	JOHN 19:36-37
40:6-8	He will do God's will.	HEBREWS 10:5-7
41:9	His close friend will betray Him.	LUKE 22:48
45:6-7	His throne will last forever.	HEBREWS 1:8-9
68:18	He will ascend into heaven.	EPHESIANS 4:8-10
69:9	He will be zealous for God.	JOHN 2:17
69:21	He will be offered vinegar for His thirst on the cross.	MATTHEW 27:48
89:3-4,35-36	He will be a descendant of David.	LUKE 1:31-33
96:13	He will return to judge the world.	1 THESSALONIANS 1:10
110:1	He is David's son and David's Lord.	MATTHEW 22:44
110:4	He is the eternal priest-king.	HEBREWS 6:20
118:22	He will be rejected by many but accepted by God.	1 PETER 2:7-8

Week 1

		GOING DEEPER
☐	**Psalms 1–2**	Matthew 5:3-11; Hebrews 1:5
☐	Psalms 3–4	Ephesians 4:26; 1 Thessalonians 4:13-18
☐	Psalms 5–6	Isaiah 38:18-20; Hebrews 10:19-22
☐	**Psalms 7–8**	Romans 3:23-26; Hebrews 2:5-9
☐	**Psalms 9–10**	Isaiah 2:1-5; Romans 15:8-13

Week 2

		GOING DEEPER
☐	Psalms 11–12	John 14:6; James 1:12
☐	Psalms 13–14	Colossians 1:13-14; Hebrews 5:7-10
☐	Psalms 15–16	Isaiah 33:13-16; Acts 2:25-34
☐	Psalm 17	Matthew 26:51-56; Revelation 22:4
☐	Psalm 18	2 Samuel 7:4-17; Romans 15:8-13

Week 3

		GOING DEEPER
☐	**Psalm 19**	Proverbs 24:13-14; Romans 10:16-21
☐	Psalms 20–21	John 11:25-26; 1 Corinthians 15:17-22
☐	Psalm 22	Matthew 27:32-44; Hebrews 2:10-13
☐	**Psalms 23–24**	John 10:11-18; Acts 1:9-11
☐	Psalm 25	Exodus 34:6-7; John 5:36

Week 4

		GOING DEEPER
☐	Psalms 26–27	Exodus 40:34-35; John 8:12
☐	**Psalms 28–30**	John 5:24; 2 Corinthians 2:15-17
☐	**Psalm 31**	Luke 23:44-46; 1 Peter 3:10-13
☐	Psalm 32	Romans 4:1-12; 2 Corinthians 5:17-19
☐	Psalm 33	Isaiah 42:10-13; John 1:14

Week 5

		GOING DEEPER
☐	**Psalm 34**	Ephesians 1:3; 1 Peter 3:8-13
☐	Psalms 35–36	Romans 3:9-20; Colossians 1:13-14
☐	Psalm 37	Proverbs 2:21-22; Colossians 2:15
☐	Psalms 38–39	John 3:36; Romans 5:1
☐	Psalms 40–41	John 13:13-19; Hebrews 10:1-10

READ AND UNDERSTAND PSALMS

The Bible is a complete work in which many stories combine to tell one story. As you read the book of Psalms, consider reading the additional passages to discover how the whole of Scripture works together.

Week 6

		GOING DEEPER
☐	Psalms 42–43	Jonah 2:1-9; Romans 8:35-39
☐	Psalm 44	Deuteronomy 7:6-8; Job 13:20-24
☐	Psalms 45–47	Isaiah 2:1-5; Ephesians 2:19-22
☐	Psalms 48–49	Romans 10:8-10; Galatians 4:2
☐	**Psalms 50–52**	2 Samuel 12:1-14; Romans 12:1

Week 7

		GOING DEEPER
☐	Psalms 53–54	Acts 4:11-12; Colossians 3:1-4
☐	**Psalms 55–56**	John 13:16-20; 1 Peter 5:6-7
☐	Psalms 57–58	Luke 24:45-47; Ephesians 1:3-4
☐	Psalms 59–60	1 Samuel 19:11-18; Acts 13:32-37
☐	Psalms 61–63	Proverbs 20:28; John 10:30

Week 8

		GOING DEEPER
☐	**Psalms 64–66**	Luke 9:35; Hebrews 10:19-22
☐	Psalms 67–68	Numbers 6:24-26; Isaiah 45:22
☐	Psalms 69–70	John 15:21-27; Romans 15:1-4
☐	Psalms 71–72	Isaiah 2:1-5; Romans 1:1-6
☐	Psalm 73	Matthew 5:8; John 1:14

Week 9

		GOING DEEPER
☐	Psalms 74–75	1 Corinthians 1:20; Ephesians 3:8-11
☐	Psalms 76–77	Isaiah 38:20; John 16:33
☐	Psalm 78	Deuteronomy 6:6-9; Matthew 13:34-35
☐	Psalms 79–80	John 13:31-32; 15:1
☐	Psalms 81–83	Hebrews 1:3; 1 Peter 2:13-17

Week 10

		GOING DEEPER
☐	Psalms 84–86	John 2:19-21; Revelation 15:3-4
☐	Psalms 87–88	Ephesians 3:4-6; Revelation 21:24-26
☐	Psalm 89	2 Samuel 7:8-16; Isaiah 48:12-13
☐	Psalms 90–91	Isaiah 40:6-8; James 1:11
☐	Psalms 92–94	Exodus 34:5-7; Isaiah 53:10

READ AND UNDERSTAND PSALMS

BOOK I (Psalms 1–41)

THE TWO WAYS

1 How happy is the one who does not
walk in the advice of the wicked
or stand in the pathway with sinners
or sit in the company of mockers!
² Instead, his delight is in the LORD's instruction,
and he meditates on it day and night.
³ He is like a tree planted beside flowing streams^A
that bears its fruit in its season
and whose leaf does not wither.
Whatever he does prospers.

⁴ The wicked are not like this;
instead, they are like chaff that the wind blows away.
⁵ Therefore the wicked will not stand up
in the judgment,
nor sinners in the assembly of the righteous.

⁶ For the LORD watches over the way of the righteous,
but the way of the wicked leads to ruin.

CORONATION OF THE SON

2 Why do the nations rage
and the peoples plot in vain?
² The kings of the earth take their stand,
and the rulers conspire together
against the LORD and his Anointed One:^B
³ "Let's tear off their chains
and throw their ropes off of us."

⁴ The one enthroned^C in heaven laughs;
the Lord ridicules them.
⁵ Then he speaks to them in his anger
and terrifies them in his wrath:
⁶ "I have installed my king
on Zion, my holy mountain."

⁷ I will declare the LORD's decree.
He said to me, "You are my Son;^D
today I have become your Father.
⁸ Ask of me,
and I will make the nations your inheritance
and the ends of the earth your possession.
⁹ You will break them with an iron scepter;
you will shatter them like pottery."

---

^A1:3 Or *beside irrigation channels*   ^B2:2 Or *anointed one*   ^C2:4 Lit *who sits*
^D2:7 Or *son, also in v. 12*

PLANTED

PSALMS 1–2; COLOSSIANS 2:6-7

I love this imagery of the tree in Psalm 1.

I want to be that tree, strong and rooted in my faith, bearing fruit. But when I read this psalm, I can't help but notice how I fall short.

I don't always meditate on God's Word day and night. I don't always take delight in it. And I have chosen the way of the wicked too many times to count. When it comes down to it, my behavior and heart more closely resemble the chaff than the tree—a flimsy weed tossed here and there, following my selfish desires, loving God's Word one day and disregarding it the next.

But isn't this what Scripture does? It not only teaches us how to walk with the Lord, but it also highlights our inevitable failure to do so. **Psalm 1 does not merely call us to the fruitful behavior of avoiding sin's path and delighting in the Lord's law. It points to the One who did those things on our behalf.**

Jesus did not know sin (2Co 5:21). There was no deceit in Him (1Pt 2:22). He was tempted in every way yet resisted every time (Heb 4:15). Jesus fully embodies the "tree planted beside flowing streams that bears its fruit in season and whose leaf does not wither" (Ps 1:3). He exemplified it each day He walked this earth in human flesh, and He exemplifies it even now as He sits at the Father's right hand in heaven.

Knowing we could not walk perfectly, Jesus paved the way to redemption for us.

We don't have to read Psalm 1 and feel shame about falling short. Because of Jesus, we can read Psalm 1 and worship our Savior whose death and resurrection represent the grace that allows us to walk with our Lord, even when our walks are not perfect. Even when our paths are crooked and our detours are long. That is a part of the journey.

As we pursue Christ, our roots deepen and strengthen. By grace through faith, we begin to desire God and His Word in a deep and real way until one day we look up and notice how our branches, by no power of our own, are bearing fruit that brings glory to our God and to our Savior.

May we seek to be planted in His righteousness and perfection alone, looking to His Word and resting in His presence, that we might grow in His likeness.

"So then, just as you have received Christ Jesus as Lord, continue to live in him, being rooted and built up in him and established in the faith, just as you were taught, and overflowing with gratitude."

COLOSSIANS 2:6-7

---

¹⁰ So now, kings, be wise;
receive instruction, you judges of the earth.
¹¹ Serve the LORD with reverential awe
and rejoice with trembling.
¹² Pay homage to ^A the Son or he will be angry
and you will perish in your rebellion, ^B
for his anger may ignite at any moment.
All who take refuge in him are happy.

CONFIDENCE IN TROUBLED TIMES

3 *A psalm of David when he fled from his son Absalom.*
LORD, how my foes increase!
There are many who attack me.
² Many say about me,
"There is no help for him in God." *Selah*

³ But you, LORD, are a shield around me,
my glory, and the one who lifts up my head.
⁴ I cry aloud to the LORD,
and he answers me from his holy mountain. *Selah*

⁵ I lie down and sleep;
I wake again because the LORD sustains me.
⁶ I will not be afraid of thousands of people
who have taken their stand against me on every side.

⁷ Rise up, LORD!
Save me, my God!
You strike all my enemies on the cheek;
you break the teeth of the wicked.
⁸ Salvation belongs to the LORD;
may your blessing be on your people. *Selah*

A NIGHT PRAYER

4 *For the choir director: with stringed instruments.*
A psalm of David.
¹ Answer me when I call,
God, who vindicates me. ^C
You freed me from affliction;
be gracious to me and hear my prayer.

² How long, exalted ones, ^D will my honor be insulted?
How long will you love what is worthless
and pursue a lie? *Selah*
³ Know that the LORD has set apart
the faithful for himself;
the LORD will hear when I call to him.

---

^A 2:12 Lit *Kiss* ^B 2:12 Lit *perish in the way* ^C 4:1 Or *God of my righteousness*
^D 4:2 Lit *long, sons of a man*

4 Be angry[A] and do not sin;
on your bed, reflect in your heart and be still. *Selah*

5 Offer sacrifices in righteousness[B]
and trust in the LORD.

6 Many are asking, "Who can show us anything good?"
Let the light of your face shine on us, LORD.

7 You have put more joy in my heart
than they have when their grain and new wine abound.

8 I will both lie down and sleep in peace,
for you alone, LORD, make me live in safety.

THE REFUGE OF THE RIGHTEOUS

5 *For the choir director: with the flutes. A psalm of David.*

Listen to my words, LORD;
consider my sighing.

2 Pay attention to the sound of my cry,
my King and my God,
for I pray to you.

3 In the morning, LORD, you hear my voice;
in the morning I plead my case to you
and watch expectantly.

4 For you are not a God who delights in wickedness;
evil cannot dwell with you.

5 The boastful cannot stand in your sight;
you hate all evildoers.

6 You destroy those who tell lies;
the LORD abhors violent and treacherous people.

7 But I enter your house
by the abundance of your faithful love;
I bow down toward your holy temple
in reverential awe of you.

8 LORD, lead me in your righteousness
because of my adversaries;
make your way straight before me.

9 For there is nothing reliable in what they say;
destruction is within them;
their throat is an open grave;
they flatter with their tongues.

10 Punish them, God;
let them fall by their own schemes.
Drive them out because of their many crimes,
for they rebel against you.

[A]4:4 Or *Tremble*   [B]4:5 Or *Offer right sacrifices*

¹¹ But let all who take refuge in you rejoice;
let them shout for joy forever.
May you shelter them,
and may those who love your name boast about you.
¹² For you, LORD, bless the righteous one;
you surround him with favor like a shield.

A PRAYER FOR MERCY

6 For the choir director: with stringed instruments, according to Sheminith. A psalm of David.

¹ LORD, do not rebuke me in your anger;
do not discipline me in your wrath.
² Be gracious to me, LORD, for I am weak;ᴬ
heal me, LORD, for my bones are shaking;
³ my whole being is shaken with terror.
And you, LORD — how long?

⁴ Turn, LORD! Rescue me;
save me because of your faithful love.
⁵ For there is no remembrance of you in death;
who can thank you in Sheol?

⁶ I am weary from my groaning;
with my tears I dampen my bed
and drench my couch every night.
⁷ My eyes are swollen from grief;
they grow old because of all my enemies.

⁸ Depart from me, all evildoers,
for the LORD has heard the sound of my weeping.
⁹ The LORD has heard my plea for help;
the LORD accepts my prayer.
¹⁰ All my enemies will be ashamed and shake with terror;
they will turn back and suddenly be disgraced.

PRAYER FOR JUSTICE

7 A Shiggaion of David, which he sang to the LORD concerning the words of Cush, a Benjaminite.

¹ LORD my God, I seek refuge in you;
save me from all my pursuers and rescue me
² or theyᴮ will tear me like a lion,
ripping me apart with no one to rescue me.

³ LORD my God, if I have done this,
if there is injustice on my hands,
⁴ if I have done harm to one at peace with me
or have plunderedᶜ my adversary without cause,
⁵ may an enemy pursue and overtake me;

ᴬ6:2 Or sick   ᴮ7:2 Lit he   ᶜ7:4 Or me and have spared

may he trample me to the ground
and leave my honor in the dust.   *Selah*

6 Rise up, Lord, in your anger;
lift yourself up against the fury of my adversaries;
awake for me;[A]
you have ordained a judgment.
7 Let the assembly of peoples gather around you;
take your seat on high over it.
8 The Lord judges the peoples;
vindicate me, Lord,
according to my righteousness and my integrity.

9 Let the evil of the wicked come to an end,
but establish the righteous.
The one who examines the thoughts and emotions[B]
is a righteous God.
10 My shield is with God,
who saves the upright in heart.
11 God is a righteous judge
and a God who shows his wrath every day.

12 If anyone does not repent,
he will sharpen his sword;
he has strung his bow and made it ready.
13 He has prepared his deadly weapons;
he tips his arrows with fire.

14 See, the wicked one is pregnant with evil,
conceives trouble, and gives birth to deceit.
15 He dug a pit and hollowed it out
but fell into the hole he had made.
16 His trouble comes back on his own head;
his own violence comes down on top of his head.

17 I will thank the Lord for his righteousness;
I will sing about the name of the Lord Most High.

GOD'S GLORY, HUMAN DIGNITY

8 *For the choir director: on the* Gittith. *A psalm of David.*
Lord, our Lord,
how magnificent is your name throughout the earth!

You have covered the heavens with your majesty.[C]
2 From the mouths of infants and nursing babies,
you have established a stronghold[D]

[A]7:6 LXX reads *awake, Lord my God*   [B]7:9 Lit *examines hearts and kidneys*
[C]8:1 Lit *earth, which has set your splendor upon the heavens*   [D]8:2 LXX reads
established praise

WHY WE MATTER

PSALMS 7–8; ROMANS 3:23-26; HEBREWS 2:5-9

I love my life: my work, my coffee, my books, my family. But every so often, I look around and suddenly feel small and insignificant. Other women seem to be conquering mountains for the kingdom, while I'm standing in front of my dishwasher in sweatpants. Some women travel the country or even the world, speaking to and influencing thousands of people, while my own circle of influence seems rather trivial. I start to wonder if I really matter.

It can become a bad habit, weighing our worth and viewing our value through the lens of accomplishment. Even worse, we measure our significance by what other people think of us. Fearing man's opinion above God's is a perpetual trap (Pr 29:25). It's a horrible way to live, always evaluating our importance by the world's standards.

Even King David considered his place in all of creation, but in doing so, he remembered his Creator.

"When I observe your heavens, the work of your fingers, the moon and the stars, which you set in place, what is a human being that you remember him, a son of man that you look after him?"

PSALM 8:3-4

There is a divine order to things—one that our Creator alone determines.

David, conqueror of kingdoms, sometimes searched for significance, and we are certainly prone to do the same. So our hearts repeat the king's question: Who are we in light of a vast and wondrous universe?

"You made him little less than God and crowned him with glory and honor. You made him ruler over the works of your hands; you put everything under his feet . . ."

PSALM 8:5-6

If God's Word is true, then we are hardly insignificant to our Father. We are His creation—created in His own image "for good works, which God prepared ahead of time" (Eph 2:10).

We bear the image of God. We matter because we matter to Him. So no matter how small or unimportant we may feel, we must remember who we are in Christ Jesus. In an impossibly vast universe, we are His treasured possession and He delights in us (Dt 14:2; Zph 3:17).

For every day we walk on this earth, our existence reveals God's glory. Who we are in Him can help point others to the Creator and their own significance in His eyes. He created us and came to redeem us, we belong to Him, and He calls us by name (Is 43:1). May His voice ring louder than all the others.

on account of your adversaries
in order to silence the enemy and the avenger.

3 When I observe your heavens,
   the work of your fingers,
   the moon and the stars,
   which you set in place,
4 what is a human being that you remember him,
   a son of man[A] that you look after him?
5 You made him little less than God[B,C]
   and crowned him with glory and honor.
6 You made him ruler over the works of your hands;
   you put everything under his feet:
7 all the sheep and oxen,
   as well as the animals in the wild,
8 the birds of the sky,
   and the fish of the sea
   that pass through the currents of the seas.

9 Lord, our Lord,
   how magnificent is your name throughout the earth!

CELEBRATION OF GOD'S JUSTICE

9 *For the choir director: according to* Muth-labben. *A psalm of David.*
   I will thank the Lord with all my heart;
   I will declare all your wondrous works.
2 I will rejoice and boast about you;
   I will sing about your name, Most High.

3 When my enemies retreat,
   they stumble and perish before you.
4 For you have upheld my just cause;
   you are seated on your throne as a righteous judge.
5 You have rebuked the nations:
   You have destroyed the wicked;
   you have erased their name forever and ever.
6 The enemy has come to eternal ruin.
   You have uprooted the cities,
   and the very memory of them has perished.

7 But the Lord sits enthroned forever;
   he has established his throne for judgment.
8 And he judges the world with righteousness;
   he executes judgment on the nations with fairness.
9 The Lord is a refuge for the persecuted,
   a refuge in times of trouble.
10 Those who know your name trust in you

A8:4 Or *a mere mortal*   B8:5 LXX reads *angels*   C8:5 Or *heavenly beings;* Hb
Elohim

because you have not abandoned
those who seek you, LORD.

11 Sing to the LORD, who dwells in Zion;
proclaim his deeds among the nations.
12 For the one who seeks an accounting
for bloodshed remembers them;
he does not forget the cry of the oppressed.

13 Be gracious to me, LORD;
consider my affliction at the hands of those
who hate me.
Lift me up from the gates of death,
14 so that I may declare all your praises.
I will rejoice in your salvation
within the gates of Daughter Zion.

15 The nations have fallen into the pit they made;
their foot is caught in the net they have concealed.
16 The LORD has made himself known;
he has executed justice,
snaring the wicked
by the work of their hands. *Higgaion. Selah*

17 The wicked will return to Sheol —
all the nations that forget God.
18 For the needy will not always be forgotten;
the hope of the oppressed^A will not perish forever.

19 Rise up, LORD! Do not let mere humans prevail;
let the nations be judged in your presence.
20 Put terror in them, LORD;
let the nations know they are only humans. *Selah*

NEED FOR GOD'S JUSTICE

10 LORD,^B,C why do you stand so far away?
Why do you hide in times of trouble?
2 In arrogance the wicked relentlessly pursue their victims;
let them be caught in the schemes they have devised.

3 For the wicked one boasts about his own cravings;
the one who is greedy curses^D and despises the LORD.
4 In all his scheming,
the wicked person arrogantly thinks,^E
"There's no accountability,
since there's no God."

---

^A9:18 Alt Hb tradition reads *humble*   ^B10:1 Some Hb mss, LXX connect Pss 9–10.
^C10:1 Together Pss 9–10 form a partial acrostic.   ^D10:3 Or *he blesses the greedy*
^E10:4 Lit *wicked according to the height of his nose*

HE REMEMBERS THE AFFLICTED

PSALMS 9–10; ESTHER 3:1–4:3; MATTHEW 27:46

"Rise up, LORD God! Lift up your hand. Do not forget the oppressed."

PSALM 10:12

Mordecai's knees hit the cold, hard ground. He tore his clothes, crying out in anguish. The wicked Haman had issued a law declaring that Mordecai's people, the Jews, would be destroyed (Est 3:13).

As Haman and King Ahasuerus sat down to drink, Mordecai put on sackcloth and ashes, mourning loudly and bitterly throughout a city thrown into chaos by the king's edict (Est 4:1).

While Mordecai isn't the author of Psalm 10, I can't help but wonder if his thoughts were similar to the words of this psalm when he heard this news in Susa. Great affliction had come upon the Jews—a people already oppressed and scattered throughout the Persian Empire. The people mourned and cried out while the wicked boasted about their scheme, arrogantly defying God.

"LORD, why do you stand so far away? Why do you hide in times of trouble?" (Ps 10:1).

Centuries later, the Son of God let out a similar cry as He willingly hung on the cross, offering Himself on behalf of sinners.

"My God, my God, why have you abandoned me?" (Ps 22:1; Mt 27:46).

In the darkest moment in history, when the only righteous man to ever live was brutally murdered, when it looked like God had forgotten His only Son in His anguish, God's thoughts were on the afflicted.

God, in His infinite power, had the ability to reach down from heaven in that moment and

save Jesus from suffering. But He remembered the afflicted.

By allowing Jesus to complete His work on the cross, God prepared the way of hope for mankind, facing eternal affliction because of sin.

"LORD, you have heard the desire of the humble; you will strengthen their hearts. You will listen carefully, doing justice for the fatherless and the oppressed so that mere humans from the earth may terrify them no more."

PSALM 10:17-18

He heard our desire for a Savior, and He sent His only Son (Jn 3:16).

He strengthened the hearts of the humble, giving them the gift of salvation through Jesus (Rm 6:23).

He brought justice for the fatherless, adopting us as His children (Rm 8:15).

He offered freedom to those afflicted and enslaved by sin (Rm 8:1-2).

He removed our reason to fear, because the powers of darkness have no authority over us in Christ (Rm 8:38-39).

God is always at work for His glory and for the good of His people.

God wasn't absent in Susa when Haman attempted to destroy the Jews and Mordecai tore his robe. God wasn't absent at Calvary when His Son suffered for sinners. And He isn't absent in your story.

Find courage in His promises, and wait expectantly for His deliverance.

⁵ His ways are always secure;ᴬ
your lofty judgments have no effect on him;ᴮ
he scoffs at all his adversaries.
⁶ He says to himself, "I will never be moved —
from generation to generation without calamity."
⁷ Cursing, deceit, and violence fill his mouth;
trouble and malice are under his tongue.
⁸ He waits in ambush near settlements;
he kills the innocent in secret places.
His eyes are on the lookout for the helpless;
⁹ he lurks in secret like a lion in a thicket.
He lurks in order to seize a victim;
he seizes a victim and drags him in his net.
¹⁰ So he is oppressed and beaten down;
helpless people fall because of the wicked one's strength.
¹¹ He says to himself, "God has forgotten;
he hides his face and will never see."

¹² Rise up, LORD God! Lift up your hand.
Do not forget the oppressed.
¹³ Why has the wicked person despised God?
He says to himself, "You will not demand an account."
¹⁴ But you yourself have seen trouble and grief,
observing it in order to take the matter into your hands.
The helpless one entrusts himself to you;
you are a helper of the fatherless.
¹⁵ Break the arm of the wicked, evil person,
until you look for his wickedness,
but it can't be found.

¹⁶ The LORD is King forever and ever;
the nations will perish from his land.
¹⁷ LORD, you have heard the desire of the humble;
you will strengthen their hearts.
You will listen carefully,
¹⁸ doing justice for the fatherless and the oppressed
so that mere humans from the earth may terrify them
no more.

REFUGE IN THE LORD

11 *For the choir director. Of David.*
I have taken refuge in the LORD.
How can you say to me,
"Escape to the mountainsᶜ like a bird!
² For look, the wicked string bows;
they put their arrows on bowstrings
to shoot from the shadows at the upright in heart.

ᴬ10:5 Or *prosperous* ᴮ10:5 Lit *judgments are away from in front of him*
ᶜ11:1 Lit *your mountain*

3 When the foundations are destroyed,
what can the righteous do?"

4 The Lord is in his holy temple;
the Lord—his throne is in heaven.
His eyes watch;
his gaze[A] examines everyone.[B]
5 The Lord examines the righteous,
but he hates the wicked
and[C] those who love violence.
6 Let him rain burning coals[D] and sulfur on the wicked;
let a scorching wind be the portion in their cup.
7 For the Lord is righteous; he loves righteous deeds.
The upright will see his face.

OPPRESSION BY THE WICKED

12 *For the choir director: according to* Sheminith. *A psalm of David.*

Help, Lord, for no faithful one remains;
the loyal have disappeared from the human race.[E]
2 They lie to one another;
they speak with flattering lips and deceptive hearts.
3 May the Lord cut off all flattering lips
and the tongue that speaks boastfully.
4 They say, "Through our tongues we have power;
our lips are our own — who can be our master?"

5 "Because of the devastation of the needy
and the groaning of the poor,
I will now rise up," says the Lord.
"I will provide safety for the one who longs for it."

6 The words of the Lord are pure words,
like silver refined in an earthen furnace,
purified seven times.

7 You, Lord, will guard us;[F]
you will protect us[G] from this generation forever.
8 The wicked prowl[H] all around,
and what is worthless is exalted by the human race.

A PLEA FOR DELIVERANCE

13 *For the choir director. A psalm of David.*

How long, Lord? Will you forget me forever?
How long will you hide your face from me?

[A]11:4 Lit *eyelids* [B]11:4 Or *examines the descendants of Adam* [C]11:5 Or *righteous and the wicked, and he hates* [D]11:6 Sym; MT reads *rain snares, fire* [E]12:1 Or *the descendants of Adam*, also in v. 8 [F]12:7 Some Hb mss, LXX, Jer; other Hb mss read *them* [G]12:7 Some Hb mss, LXX; other Hb mss read *him* [H]12:8 Lit *walk about*

2 How long will I store up anxious concerns[A] within me,
agony in my mind every day?
How long will my enemy dominate me?

3 Consider me and answer, LORD my God.
Restore brightness to my eyes;
otherwise, I will sleep in death.
4 My enemy will say, "I have triumphed over him,"
and my foes will rejoice because I am shaken.

5 But I have trusted in your faithful love;
my heart will rejoice in your deliverance.
6 I will sing to the LORD
because he has treated me generously.

A PORTRAIT OF SINNERS

14 *For the choir director. Of David.*
The fool says in his heart, "There's no God."
They are corrupt; they do vile deeds.
There is no one who does good.
2 The LORD looks down from heaven
on the human race[B]
to see if there is one who is wise,
one who seeks God.
3 All have turned away;
all alike have become corrupt.
There is no one who does good,
not even one.

4 Will evildoers never understand?
They consume my people as they consume bread;
they do not call on the LORD.

5 Then[C] they will be filled with dread,
for God is with those who are[D] righteous.
6 You sinners frustrate the plans of the oppressed,
but the LORD is his refuge.

7 Oh, that Israel's deliverance would come
from Zion!
When the LORD restores the fortunes of his people,[E]
let Jacob rejoice, let Israel be glad.

A DESCRIPTION OF THE GODLY

15 *A psalm of David.*
LORD, who can dwell in your tent?
Who can live on your holy mountain?

[A]13:2 Or *up counsels*   [B]14:2 Or *the descendants of Adam*   [C]14:5 Or *There*
[D]14:5 Lit *with the generation of the*   [E]14:7 Or *restores his captive people*

2 The one who lives blamelessly,
 practices righteousness,
and acknowledges the truth in his heart —
3 who does not slander with his tongue,
who does not harm his friend
or discredit his neighbor,
4 who despises the one rejected by the LORD[A]
but honors those who fear the LORD,
who keeps his word whatever the cost,
5 who does not lend his silver at interest
or take a bribe against the innocent —
the one who does these things will never be shaken.

CONFIDENCE IN THE LORD

16

A Miktam of David.

Protect me, God, for I take refuge in you.
2 I[B] said to the LORD, "You are my Lord;
I have nothing good besides you."[C]
3 As for the holy people who are in the land,
they are the noble ones.
All my delight is in them.
4 The sorrows of those who take another god
for themselves will multiply;
I will not pour out their drink offerings of blood,
and I will not speak their names with my lips.

5 LORD, you are my portion[D]
and my cup of blessing;
you hold my future.
6 The boundary lines have fallen for me
in pleasant places;
indeed, I have a beautiful inheritance.

7 I will bless the LORD who counsels me —
even at night when my thoughts trouble me.[E]
8 I always let the LORD guide me.[F]
Because he is at my right hand,
I will not be shaken.

9 Therefore my heart is glad
and my whole being rejoices;
my body also rests securely.
10 For you will not abandon me to Sheol;
you will not allow your faithful one to see decay.
11 You reveal the path of life to me;

[A]15:4 Lit *in his eyes the rejected is despised* [B]16:2 Some Hb mss, LXX, Syr, Jer;
other Hb mss read *You* [C]16:2 Or *"Lord, my good; there is none besides you."*
[D]16:5 Or *allotted portion* [E]16:7 Or *at night my heart instructs me* [F]16:8 Lit
I place the LORD in front of me always

in your presence is abundant joy;
at your right hand are eternal pleasures.

A PRAYER FOR PROTECTION

17 *A prayer of David.*

LORD, hear a just cause;
pay attention to my cry;
listen to my prayer —
from lips free of deceit.
2 Let my vindication come from you,
for you see what is right.
3 You have tested my heart;
you have examined me at night.
You have tried me and found nothing evil;
I have determined that my mouth will not sin.^A
4 Concerning what people do:
by the words from your lips
I have avoided the ways of the violent.
5 My steps are on your paths;
my feet have not slipped.

6 I call on you, God,
because you will answer me;
listen closely to me; hear what I say.
7 Display the wonders of your faithful love,
Savior of all who seek refuge
from those who rebel
against your right hand.^B
8 Protect me as the pupil of your eye;
hide me in the shadow of your wings
9 from^C the wicked who treat me violently,^D
my deadly enemies who surround me.

10 They are uncaring;^E
their mouths speak arrogantly.
11 They advance against me;^F
now they surround me.
They are determined^G
to throw me to the ground.
12 They are^H like a lion eager to tear,
like a young lion lurking in ambush.

13 Rise up, LORD!
Confront him; bring him down.
With your sword, save me from the wicked.

---

^A17:3 Or *evil; my mouth will not sin*   ^B17:7 Or *love, you who save with your right hand those seeking refuge from adversaries*   ^C17:9 Lit *from the presence of*   ^D17:9 Or *who plunder me*   ^E17:10 Lit *have closed up their fat*   ^F17:11 Vg; MT reads *Our steps*   ^G17:11 Lit *They set their eyes*   ^H17:12 Lit *He is*

¹⁴ With your hand, LORD, save me from men,
from men of the world
whose portion is in this life:
You fill their bellies with what you have in store;
their sons are satisfied,
and they leave their surplus to their children.

¹⁵ But I will see your face in righteousness;
when I awake, I will be satisfied
with your presence. ^A

PRAISE FOR DELIVERANCE

18 *For the choir director. Of the servant of the LORD, David, who spoke the words of this song to the LORD on the day the LORD rescued him from the grasp of all his enemies and from the power of Saul. He said:*

¹ I love you, LORD, my strength.
² The LORD is my rock,
my fortress, and my deliverer,
my God, my rock where I seek refuge,
my shield and the horn of my salvation,
my stronghold.
³ I called to the LORD, who is worthy of praise,
and I was saved from my enemies.

⁴ The ropes of death were wrapped around me;
the torrents of destruction terrified me.
⁵ The ropes of Sheol entangled me;
the snares of death confronted me.
⁶ I called to the LORD in my distress,
and I cried to my God for help.
From his temple he heard my voice,
and my cry to him reached his ears.

⁷ Then the earth shook and quaked;
the foundations of the mountains trembled;
they shook because he burned with anger.
⁸ Smoke rose from his nostrils,
and consuming fire came from his mouth;
coals were set ablaze by it. ^B
⁹ He bent the heavens and came down,
total darkness beneath his feet.
¹⁰ He rode on a cherub and flew,
soaring on the wings of the wind.
¹¹ He made darkness his hiding place,
dark storm clouds his canopy around him.
¹² From the radiance of his presence,
his clouds swept onward with hail
and blazing coals.

---

^A17:15 Lit *form* ^B18:8 Or *him*

13 The Lord thundered from^A heaven;
   the Most High made his voice heard.^B
14 He shot his arrows and scattered them;
   he hurled^C lightning bolts and routed them.
15 The depths of the sea became visible,
   the foundations of the world were exposed,
   at your rebuke, Lord,
   at the blast of the breath of your nostrils.

16 He reached down from on high
   and took hold of me;
   he pulled me out of deep water.
17 He rescued me from my powerful enemy
   and from those who hated me,
   for they were too strong for me.
18 They confronted me in the day of my calamity,
   but the Lord was my support.
19 He brought me out to a spacious place;
   he rescued me because he delighted in me.

20 The Lord rewarded me
   according to my righteousness;
   he repaid me
   according to the cleanness of my hands.
21 For I have kept the ways of the Lord
   and have not turned from my God to wickedness.
22 Indeed, I let all his ordinances guide me^D
   and have not disregarded his statutes.
23 I was blameless toward him
   and kept myself from my iniquity.
24 So the Lord repaid me
   according to my righteousness,
   according to the cleanness of my hands in his sight.

25 With the faithful
   you prove yourself faithful,
   with the blameless
   you prove yourself blameless,
26 with the pure
   you prove yourself pure;
   but with the crooked
   you prove yourself shrewd.
27 For you rescue an oppressed people,
   but you humble those with haughty eyes.
28 Lord, you light my lamp;
   my God illuminates my darkness.

---

^A18:13 Some Hb mss, LXX, Tg, Jer; other Hb mss read *in*   ^B18:13 Some Hb
mss read *voice, with hail and blazing coals*   ^C18:14 Or *multiplied*   ^D18:22 Lit
Indeed, all his ordinances have been in front of me

29 With you I can attack a barricade,[A]
  and with my God I can leap over a wall.

30 God — his way is perfect;
  the word of the Lord is pure.
  He is a shield to all who take refuge in him.
31 For who is God besides the Lord?
  And who is a rock? Only our God.
32 God — he clothes me with strength
  and makes my way perfect.
33 He makes my feet like the feet of a deer
  and sets me securely on the heights.[B]
34 He trains my hands for war;
  my arms can bend a bow of bronze.
35 You have given me the shield of your salvation;
  your right hand upholds me,
  and your humility exalts me.
36 You make a spacious place beneath me for my steps,
  and my ankles do not give way.

37 I pursue my enemies and overtake them;
  I do not turn back until they are wiped out.
38 I crush them, and they cannot get up;
  they fall beneath my feet.
39 You have clothed me with strength for battle;
  you subdue my adversaries beneath me.
40 You have made my enemies retreat before me;[C]
  I annihilate those who hate me.
41 They cry for help, but there is no one to save them —
  they cry to the Lord, but he does not answer them.
42 I pulverize them like dust before the wind;
  I trample them[D] like mud in the streets.

43 You have freed me from the feuds among the people;
  you have appointed me the head of nations;
  a people I had not known serve me.
44 Foreigners submit to me cringing;
  as soon as they hear they obey me.
45 Foreigners lose heart
  and come trembling from their fortifications.

46 The Lord lives — blessed be my rock!
  The God of my salvation is exalted.
47 God — he grants me vengeance
  and subdues peoples under me.
48 He frees me from my enemies.

[A]18:29 Or a ridge, or raiders   [B]18:33 Or on my high places   [C]18:40 Or You
gave me the necks of my enemies   [D]18:42 Some Hb mss, LXX, Syr, Tg; other Hb
mss read I poured them out

You exalt me above my adversaries;
you rescue me from violent men.
49 Therefore I will give thanks to you among the nations, LORD;
I will sing praises about your name.
50 He gives great victories to his king;
he shows loyalty to his anointed,
to David and his descendants forever.

THE WITNESS OF CREATION AND SCRIPTURE

19 *For the choir director. A psalm of David.*
The heavens declare the glory of God,
and the expanse proclaims the work of his hands.
2 Day after day they pour out speech;
night after night they communicate knowledge. [A]
3 There is no speech; there are no words;
their voice is not heard.
4 Their message [B] has gone out to the whole earth,
and their words to the ends of the world.

In the heavens he has pitched a tent for the sun.
5 It is like a bridegroom coming from his home;
it rejoices like an athlete running a course.
6 It rises from one end of the heavens
and circles to their other end;
nothing is hidden from its heat.

7 The instruction of the LORD is perfect,
renewing one's life;
the testimony of the LORD is trustworthy,
making the inexperienced wise.
8 The precepts of the LORD are right,
making the heart glad;
the command of the LORD is radiant,
making the eyes light up.
9 The fear of the LORD is pure,
enduring forever;
the ordinances of the LORD are reliable
and altogether righteous.
10 They are more desirable than gold —
than an abundance of pure gold;
and sweeter than honey
dripping from a honeycomb.
11 In addition, your servant is warned by them,
and in keeping them there is an abundant reward.

12 Who perceives his unintentional sins?
Cleanse me from my hidden faults.

[A]19:2 Or *Day to day pours out speech, and night to night communicates knowledge*   [B]19:4 LXX, Sym, Syr, Vg; MT reads *line*

WHAT THE HEAVENS DECLARE

PSALM 19; ROMANS 1:20

"Look at the stars! look, look up at the skies!
O look at all the fire-folk sitting in the air!
The bright boroughs, the circle-citadels there!
Down in dim woods the diamond delves! the
elves'-eyes! The grey lawns cold where gold,
where quickgold lies!"
GERARD MANLEY HOPKINS, "THE STARLIGHT
NIGHT"

Gerard Manley Hopkins penned these gorgeous lines in nineteenth-century England, but men and women have been exclaiming over the beauty of creation in every land since the beginning of time.

We can't stop our jaws from dropping when we see God's creation. The power in the stinging, salty ocean waves can knock you off your feet, and the sweetness of a hummingbird can break your heart. Even after a lifetime of hearing it, thunder is still a surprise every time, and the leaves of a beech tree turning in a big wind to show their white underside always make me sigh with joy.

I think God means for creation to stop us in our tracks. Creation is God's first missionary. In other words, the beauty of nature is busy drawing us to Christ.

"For his invisible attributes, that is, his eternal power and divine nature, have been clearly seen since the creation of the world, being understood through what he has made. As a result, people are without excuse."

ROMANS 1:20

Creation is beautiful because it is saying something about God. It's saying, "God made me!" The heavens declare the glory of God because God bestowed some of His glory on them. He invites us to learn about Him through the things He created.

Writers do not rejoice in the beauty of God's law as often. But the law and instruction of God's Word give light to creation. In fact, the psalmist compares the brilliance of Scripture to that of the heavens. The Word of God is even greater, more magnificent, more beautiful, and more explicit a witness of Him.

The psalmist explains that the instruction of the Lord is perfect, and renews the soul (Ps 19:7). In the same way that nature overwhelms and enlivens us with its beauty, so God's Word gladdens our hearts, and makes our eyes light up (Ps 19:8).

In the face of God's glorious creation and His perfect law, we are called both to revel and to repent. God's glory and perfection, like the majestic sun, call us to Himself.

The Lord is our rock, and He alone is sure. All of creation declares that He is good.

¹³ Moreover, keep your servant from willful sins;
do not let them rule me.
Then I will be blameless
and cleansed from blatant rebellion.
¹⁴ May the words of my mouth
and the meditation of my heart
be acceptable to you,
Lord, my rock and my Redeemer.

DELIVERANCE IN BATTLE

20 For the choir director. A psalm of David.
May the Lord answer you in a day of trouble;
may the name of Jacob's God protect you.
² May he send you help from the sanctuary
and sustain you from Zion.
³ May he remember all your offerings
and accept your burnt offering. *Selah*

⁴ May he give you what your heart desires
and fulfill your whole purpose.
⁵ Let us shout for joy at your victory
and lift the banner in the name of our God.
May the Lord fulfill all your requests.

⁶ Now I know that the Lord gives victory to his anointed;
he will answer him from his holy heaven
with mighty victories from his right hand.
⁷ Some take pride in chariots, and others in horses,
but we take pride in the name of the Lord our God.
⁸ They collapse and fall,
but we rise and stand firm.
⁹ Lord, give victory to the king!
May heᴬ answer us on the day that we call.

THE KING'S VICTORY

21 For the choir director. A psalm of David.
Lord, the king finds joy in your strength.
How greatly he rejoices in your victory!
² You have given him his heart's desire
and have not denied the request of his lips. *Selah*
³ For you meet him with rich blessings;
you place a crown of pure gold on his head.
⁴ He asked you for life, and you gave it to him —
length of days forever and ever.
⁵ His glory is great through your victory;
you confer majesty and splendor on him.
⁶ You give him blessings forever;
you cheer him with joy in your presence.

ᴬ20:9 Or Lord, save. May the king

7   For the king relies on the LORD;
    through the faithful love of the Most High
    he is not shaken.

8   Your hand will capture all your enemies;
    your right hand will seize those who hate you.
9   You will make them burn
    like a fiery furnace when you appear;
    the LORD will engulf them in his wrath,
    and fire will devour them.
10 You will wipe their progeny from the earth
    and their offspring from the human race.^A
11 Though they intend to harm^B you
    and devise a wicked plan, they will not prevail.
12 Instead, you will put them to flight
    when you ready your bowstrings
        to shoot at them.

13 Be exalted, LORD, in your strength;
    we will sing and praise your might.

FROM SUFFERING TO PRAISE

22 *For the choir director: according to "The Deer of the Dawn."
A psalm of David.*

1   My God, my God, why have you abandoned me?
    Why are you so far from my deliverance
    and from my words of groaning?
2   My God, I cry by day, but you do not answer,
    by night, yet I have no rest.
3   But you are holy,
    enthroned on the praises of Israel.
4   Our fathers trusted in you;
    they trusted, and you rescued them.
5   They cried to you and were set free;
    they trusted in you and were not disgraced.

6   But I am a worm and not a man,
    scorned by mankind and despised by people.
7   Everyone who sees me mocks me;
    they sneer^C and shake their heads:
8   "He relies on^D the LORD;
    let him save him;
    let the LORD^E rescue him,
    since he takes pleasure in him."

9   It was you who brought me out of the womb,
    making me secure at my mother's breast.

---

^A21:10 Or *the descendants of Adam*   ^B21:11 Lit *they stretch out harm against*
^C22:7 Lit *separate with the lip*   ^D22:8 Or *Rely on*   ^E22:8 Lit *let him*

¹⁰ I was given over to you at birth;^A
    you have been my God from my mother's womb.

¹¹ Don't be far from me, because distress is near
    and there's no one to help.

¹² Many bulls surround me;
    strong ones of Bashan encircle me.
¹³ They open their mouths against me —
    lions, mauling and roaring.
¹⁴ I am poured out like water,
    and all my bones are disjointed;
    my heart is like wax,
    melting within me.
¹⁵ My strength is dried up like baked clay;
    my tongue sticks to the roof of my mouth.
    You put me into the dust of death.
¹⁶ For dogs have surrounded me;
    a gang of evildoers has closed in on me;
    they pierced^B my hands and my feet.
¹⁷ I can count all my bones;
    people^C look and stare at me.
¹⁸ They divided my garments among themselves,
    and they cast lots for my clothing.

¹⁹ But you, LORD, don't be far away.
    My strength, come quickly to help me.
²⁰ Rescue my life from the sword,
    my only life^D from the power of these dogs.
²¹ Save me from the lion's mouth,
    from the horns of wild oxen.

    You answered me!^E
²² I will proclaim your name to my brothers and sisters;
    I will praise you in the assembly.
²³ You who fear the LORD, praise him!
    All you descendants of Jacob, honor him!
    All you descendants of Israel, revere him!
²⁴ For he has not despised or abhorred
    the torment of the oppressed.
    He did not hide his face from him
    but listened when he cried to him for help.

²⁵ I will give praise in the great assembly
    because of you;
    I will fulfill my vows

---

^A22:10 Lit was cast on you from the womb   ^B22:16 Some Hb mss, LXX, Syr;
other Hb mss read me; like a lion   ^C22:17 Lit they   ^D22:20 Lit my only one
^E22:21 Or oxen you rescued me

before those who fear you.[A]
26 The humble will eat and be satisfied;
those who seek the LORD will praise him.
May your hearts live forever!

27 All the ends of the earth will remember
and turn to the LORD.
All the families of the nations
will bow down before you,
28 for kingship belongs to the LORD;
he rules the nations.
29 All who prosper on earth will eat
and bow down;
all those who go down to the dust
will kneel before him —
even the one who cannot preserve his life.
30 Their descendants will serve him;
the next generation will be told
about the Lord.
31 They will come and declare his righteousness;
to a people yet to be born
they will declare what he has done.

THE GOOD SHEPHERD

23 *A psalm of David.*
The LORD is my shepherd;
I have what I need.
2 He lets me lie down in green pastures;
he leads me beside quiet waters.
3 He renews my life;
he leads me along the right paths[B]
for his name's sake.
4 Even when I go through the darkest valley,[C]
I fear no danger,
for you are with me;
your rod and your staff — they comfort me.

5 You prepare a table before me
in the presence of my enemies;
you anoint my head with oil;
my cup overflows.
6 Only goodness and faithful love
will pursue me
all the days of my life,
and I will dwell in[D] the house of the LORD
as long as I live.[E]

[A]22:25 Lit *him*   [B]23:3 Or *me in paths of righteousness*   [C]23:4 Or *the valley of the shadow of death*   [D]23:6 LXX, Sym, Syr, Tg, Vg, Jer; MT reads *will return to*
[E]23:6 Lit LORD *for length of days*; traditionally LORD *forever*

GIVE THANKS IN PLENTY

PSALMS 23–24; JOHN 10:11-18; ACTS 1:9-11

It seems so simple: give thanks in plenty. That's what those cornucopia centerpieces adorning our tables at Thanksgiving are all about, right?

I'm relatively well versed in bowing my head when times are good. I return thanks at mealtime for the food set before me and for the hands that prepared it. I have lived my life thanking the Lord when my needs were supplied—when college acceptance letters arrived and job offers were received, when the harvest was good and the report card was favorable, when the touchdown pass was completed, and that time I made it to the gas station just before the remaining fumes in my gas tank were exhausted.

"You anoint my head with oil; my cup overflows."

PSALM 23:5

Literal plenty makes a whole lot of sense to me—to all of us. We know it when we see it. We slap a "blessed" on the gifts we've been given, knowing full well who the Giver is.

But I can't imagine that's where we ought to land. I don't think that's it.

The truth is, plenty is oh-so-much more than moments and mail and meatloaf. "Plenty" does not equal prosperity, just as "want" does not equal poverty. Our circumstances are not situated on a sliding scale from famine to abundance, and we would be sorely mistaken to allow our thanks to take a ride on that hypothetical scale.

For the believer in Christ, plenty and want are both constant states of being.

Yes, we all have real, felt needs. And we have noticeable, tangible blessings. But beyond the surface—in light of eternity—our constant state is a want of grace, and God is our constant and plentiful supplier.

He is our plenty. Our overflowing cups have absolutely nothing to do with bank accounts, or people, or horn-shaped centerpieces. They do not overflow with success and they do not empty with failure. Our cups overflow with the grace and mercy of an everlasting God—they overflow because there is always more than we can ask or imagine. This is our plenty.

Wherever we find ourselves on the worldly poverty-to-prosperity scale, let us see ourselves in constant want of His grace and ever in possession of an overflowing cup of mercy from an all-sufficient God. And let us give thanks.

"Think how much grace one saint requires, so much that nothing but the Infinite could supply him for one day; and yet the Lord spreads his table, not for one, but many saints, not for one day, but for many years; not for many years only, but for generation after generation."
C.H. SPURGEON, "MORNING AND EVENING"

THE KING OF GLORY

24 *A psalm of David.*

The earth and everything in it,
the world and its inhabitants,
belong to the LORD;
2 for he laid its foundation on the seas
and established it on the rivers.

3 Who may ascend the mountain of the LORD?
Who may stand in his holy place?
4 The one who has clean hands and a pure heart,
who has not appealed to[A] what is false,
and who has not sworn deceitfully.
5 He will receive blessing from the LORD,
and righteousness[B] from the God of his salvation.
6 Such is the generation of those who inquire of him,
who seek the face of the God of Jacob.[C]   *Selah*

7 Lift up your heads, you gates!
Rise up, ancient doors!
Then the King of glory will come in.
8 Who is this King of glory?
The LORD, strong and mighty,
the LORD, mighty in battle.
9 Lift up your heads, you gates!
Rise up, ancient doors!
Then the King of glory will come in.
10 Who is he, this King of glory?
The LORD of Armies,
he is the King of glory.   *Selah*

DEPENDENCE ON THE LORD

25 *Of David.*

LORD, I appeal to you.[D]
2 My God, I trust in you.
Do not let me be disgraced;
do not let my enemies gloat over me.
3 No one who waits for you
will be disgraced;
those who act treacherously without cause
will be disgraced.

4 Make your ways known to me, LORD;
teach me your paths.
5 Guide me in your truth and teach me,
for you are the God of my salvation;

[A]24:4 Lit *not lifted up his soul to*   [B]24:5 Or *vindication*   [C]24:6 LXX; some Hb
mss, Syr read *seek your face, God of Jacob*; some Hb mss read *seek your face,
Jacob*   [D]25:1 Or *To you, LORD, I lift up my soul*

I wait for you all day long.
6 Remember, LORD, your compassion
and your faithful love,
for they have existed from antiquity.[A]
7 Do not remember the sins of my youth
or my acts of rebellion;
in keeping with your faithful love,
remember me
because of your goodness, LORD.

8 The LORD is good and upright;
therefore he shows sinners the way.
9 He leads the humble in what is right
and teaches them his way.
10 All the LORD's ways show faithful love
and truth
to those who keep his covenant and decrees.
11 LORD, for the sake of your name,
forgive my iniquity, for it is immense.

12 Who is this person who fears the LORD?
He will show him the way he should choose.
13 He will live a good life,
and his descendants will inherit the land.[B]
14 The secret counsel of the LORD
is for those who fear him,
and he reveals his covenant to them.
15 My eyes are always on the LORD,
for he will pull my feet out of the net.

16 Turn to me and be gracious to me,
for I am alone and afflicted.
17 The distresses of my heart increase;[C]
bring me out of my sufferings.
18 Consider my affliction and trouble,
and forgive all my sins.
19 Consider my enemies;
they are numerous,
and they hate me violently.
20 Guard me and rescue me;
do not let me be put to shame,
for I take refuge in you.
21 May integrity and what is right
watch over me,
for I wait for you.

22 God, redeem Israel, from all its distresses.

[A]25:6 Or everlasting [B]25:13 Or earth [C]25:17 Or Relieve the distresses of my heart

PRAYER FOR VINDICATION

26 *Of David.*

Vindicate me, Lord,
because I have lived with integrity
and have trusted in the Lord without wavering.
2 Test me, Lord, and try me;
examine my heart and mind.
3 For your faithful love guides me,^A
and I live by your truth.

4 I do not sit with the worthless
or associate with hypocrites.
5 I hate a crowd of evildoers,
and I do not sit with the wicked.
6 I wash my hands in innocence
and go around your altar, Lord,
7 raising my voice in thanksgiving
and telling about your wondrous works.

8 Lord, I love the house where you dwell,
the place where your glory resides.
9 Do not destroy me along with sinners,
or my life along with men of bloodshed
10 in whose hands are evil schemes
and whose right hands are filled with bribes.

11 But I live with integrity;
redeem me and be gracious to me.
12 My foot stands on level ground;
I will bless the Lord in the assemblies.

MY STRONGHOLD

27 *Of David.*

The Lord is my light and my salvation —
whom should I fear?
The Lord is the stronghold of my life —
whom should I dread?
2 When evildoers came against me to devour my flesh,
my foes and my enemies stumbled and fell.
3 Though an army deploys against me,
my heart will not be afraid;
though a war breaks out against me,
I will still be confident.

4 I have asked one thing from the Lord;
it is what I desire:
to dwell in the house of the Lord
all the days of my life,

---

^A26:3 Lit *love is in front of my eyes*

gazing on the beauty of the LORD
and seeking him in his temple.
⁵ For he will conceal me in his shelter
in the day of adversity;
he will hide me under the cover of his tent;
he will set me high on a rock.
⁶ Then my head will be high
above my enemies around me;
I will offer sacrifices in his tent
with shouts of joy.
I will sing and make music to the LORD.

⁷ LORD, hear my voice when I call;
be gracious to me and answer me.
⁸ My heart says this about you:
"Seek^A his face."
LORD, I will seek your face.
⁹ Do not hide your face from me;
do not turn your servant away in anger.
You have been my helper;
do not leave me or abandon me,
God of my salvation.
¹⁰ Even if my father and mother abandon me,
the LORD cares for me.

¹¹ Because of my adversaries,
show me your way, LORD,
and lead me on a level path.
¹² Do not give me over to the will of my foes,
for false witnesses rise up against me,
breathing violence.

¹³ I am certain that I will see the LORD's goodness
in the land of the living.
¹⁴ Wait for the LORD;
be strong, and let your heart be courageous.
Wait for the LORD.

MY STRENGTH

28

Of David.

LORD, I call to you;
my rock, do not be deaf to me.
If you remain silent to me,
I will be like those going down to the Pit.
² Listen to the sound of my pleading
when I cry to you for help,
when I lift up my hands
toward your holy sanctuary.

^A 27:8 The command is pl in Hb

³ Do not drag me away with the wicked,
  with the evildoers,
  who speak in friendly ways with their neighbors
  while malice is in their hearts.
⁴ Repay them according to what they have done —
  according to the evil of their deeds.
  Repay them according to the work
    of their hands;
  give them back what they deserve.
⁵ Because they do not consider
  what the Lord has done
  or the work of his hands,
  he will tear them down and not rebuild them.

⁶ Blessed be the Lord,
  for he has heard the sound of my pleading.
⁷ The Lord is my strength and my shield;
  my heart trusts in him, and I am helped.
  Therefore my heart celebrates,
  and I give thanks to him with my song.

⁸ The Lord is the strength of his people;^A
  he is a stronghold of salvation for his anointed.
⁹ Save your people, bless your possession,
  shepherd them, and carry them forever.

THE VOICE OF THE LORD

29 *A psalm of David.*
  Ascribe to the Lord, you heavenly beings,^B
  ascribe to the Lord glory and strength.
² Ascribe to the Lord the glory due his name;
  worship the Lord
  in the splendor of his holiness.^C

³ The voice of the Lord is above the waters.
  The God of glory thunders —
  the Lord, above the vast water,
⁴ the voice of the Lord in power,
  the voice of the Lord in splendor.
⁵ The voice of the Lord breaks the cedars;
  the Lord shatters the cedars of Lebanon.
⁶ He makes Lebanon skip like a calf,
  and Sirion, like a young wild ox.
⁷ The voice of the Lord flashes flames of fire.
⁸ The voice of the Lord shakes the wilderness;
  the Lord shakes the wilderness of Kadesh.

---

^A28:8 Some Hb mss, LXX, Syr; other Hb mss read *strength for them*   ^B29:1 Or
you sons of gods, or *you sons of mighty ones*   ^C29:2 Or *in holy attire,* or *in holy*
appearance

THE LORD SITS ENTHRONED

PSALMS 28–30; GENESIS 6–7

On a warm, spring day when the sky is blue and the temperature just right, fair weather makes me want to sing along with the birds. But in my neck of the woods, blue skies can be replaced with ominous clouds without warning. Sure, every year brings days of pure weather perfection, but there are also thunderstorms, tornadoes, heat waves, and blizzards.

Even with Doppler radar, first alert forecasts, and climate-controlled homes, weather remains unpredictable. Fair and pleasant one season, misery-making the next, it cannot be pigeonholed or forced to cooperate. We can't make weather patterns bend to our whims or operate on our schedule, even if we have a meticulously planned day that depends on sunshine or we've been dreaming of a white Christmas since October.

Weather does what weather is going to do. Life can be like that, too.

You might want to grab a raincoat and an umbrella before you read Psalm 29. From thunder and lightning, to earthquakes, wildfires, and floods, David describes almost every meteorological symbol we might see on a weather map in this short psalm (Ps 29:3,7-10).

Since we can assume David didn't moonlight as a weatherman, what was the point of all that weather talk? Why string our worst weather fears together in a single psalm? David tells us the answer upfront:

> "Ascribe to the LORD, you heavenly beings, ascribe to the LORD glory and strength. Ascribe to the LORD the glory due his name; worship the LORD in the splendor of his holiness."
>
> PSALM 29:1-2

David wants to give God His due. God is glorious! More glorious than a beautiful sunset or a perfect, cloudless afternoon. God is strong! Stronger than straight-line winds or the blaze of a raging forest fire.

"The LORD sits enthroned over the flood; the LORD sits enthroned, King forever" (Ps 29:10).

Even as creation was ushered in with an expanse of waters, God was there, seated on His throne and speaking Word into life (Gn 1:7). And later, when humanity's rebellion was so offensive He needed to wipe the slate clean with a flood (Gn 6–7), God was still seated on His throne.

No matter what happens in our own lives, whether the proverbial sun is shining or we're hunkered down praying for a storm to pass, God remains in control and on His throne. **The universe He created is still firmly in His hands** (Heb 1:3). We can declare His goodness and rest in His care, whatever the weather.

9 The voice of the LORD makes the deer
    give birth^A
and strips the woodlands bare.

In his temple all cry, "Glory!"

10 The LORD sits enthroned over the flood;
    the LORD sits enthroned, King forever.
11 The LORD gives his people strength;
    the LORD blesses his people with peace.

JOY IN THE MORNING

30 *A psalm; a dedication song for the house. Of David.*
    I will exalt you, LORD,
because you have lifted me up
and have not allowed my enemies
    to triumph over me.
2 LORD my God,
    I cried to you for help, and you healed me.
3 LORD, you brought me up from Sheol;
    you spared me from among those
going down^B to the Pit.

4 Sing to the LORD, you his faithful ones,
    and praise his holy name.
5 For his anger lasts only a moment,
    but his favor, a lifetime.
Weeping may stay overnight,
    but there is joy in the morning.

6 When I was secure, I said,
    "I will never be shaken."
7 LORD, when you showed your favor,
    you made me stand like a strong mountain;
when you hid your face, I was terrified.
8 LORD, I called to you;
    I sought favor from my Lord:
9 "What gain is there in my death,
    if I go down to the Pit?
Will the dust praise you?
    Will it proclaim your truth?
10 LORD, listen and be gracious to me;
    LORD, be my helper."

11 You turned my lament into dancing;
    you removed my sackcloth
    and clothed me with gladness,

---

^A29:9 Or *the oaks shake*   ^B30:3 Some Hb mss, LXX, Theod, Orig, Syr; other Hb
mss, Aq, Sym, Tg, Jer read *from going down*

¹² so that I can sing to you and not be silent.
Lᴏʀᴅ my God, I will praise you forever.

A PLEA FOR PROTECTION

31

For the choir director. A psalm of David.

Lᴏʀᴅ, I seek refuge in you;
let me never be disgraced.
Save me by your righteousness.
² Listen closely to me; rescue me quickly.
Be a rock of refuge for me,
a mountain fortress to save me.
³ For you are my rock and my fortress;
you lead and guide me
for your name's sake.
⁴ You will free me from the net
that is secretly set for me,
for you are my refuge.
⁵ Into your hand I entrust my spirit;
you have redeemed me,^A Lᴏʀᴅ, God of truth.

⁶ I^B hate those who are devoted to worthless idols,
but I trust in the Lᴏʀᴅ.
⁷ I will rejoice and be glad in your faithful love
because you have seen my affliction.
You know the troubles of my soul
⁸ and have not handed me over to the enemy.
You have set my feet in a spacious place.

⁹ Be gracious to me, Lᴏʀᴅ,
because I am in distress;
my eyes are worn out from frustration —
my whole being^C as well.
¹⁰ Indeed, my life is consumed with grief
and my years with groaning;
my strength has failed
because of my iniquity,^D
and my bones waste away.
¹¹ I am ridiculed by all my adversaries
and even by my neighbors.
I am dreaded by my acquaintances;
those who see me in the street run from me.
¹² I am forgotten: gone from memory
like a dead person — like broken pottery.
¹³ I have heard the gossip of many;
terror is on every side.
When they conspired against me,
they plotted to take my life.

---

^A31:5 Or *spirit. Redeem me* ^B31:6 One Hb ms, LXX, Syr, Vg, Jer read *You*
^C31:9 Lit *my soul and my belly* ^D31:10 LXX, Syr, Sym read *affliction*

GIVE THANKS IN SORROW

PSALM 31

Growing up, my younger brother played every instrument he could get his hands on—the trumpet, guitar, piano, ukulele, and unfortunately, the bagpipes. I loved being part of a musical family. I didn't love being part of a we're-learning-to-be-musical family.

One day, my brother came home with a new piece of music in hand. The composer's note at the top read, "Play muted, with sorrow."

He began playing the song on his trumpet, and I braced myself for sweet relief as he transitioned into the "sorrow" section. Much to my dismay and delight, I learned that the mute didn't silence the sound; it changed it. The piercing, shrill signature of the instrument was replaced by a deliciously pleasing sound. The sound emerging from the horn was unlike anything that could be produced by the trumpet alone.

Sometimes, I feel like God is asking me to put a mute on my feelings. When His Word says to be thankful in every situation, I find myself thinking, *Even in this? In grief, in fear, in sorrow? You can't possibly mean in this.*

It's easy to forget that all songs of thanksgiving don't have the same sound. I don't know exactly what musical directions were given when the Psalms were played aloud as songs, but I can guess that many of them were instructed to be played "with sorrow."

God doesn't ask us to silence our sorrow in favor of thanksgiving. Rather, He uses our sorrow to proclaim a type of thanksgiving we wouldn't be able to express otherwise. Just as the trumpet's song isn't any less a melody when it changes in pitch, your sorrow isn't any less a sound of thanksgiving than your highest shouts of joy. Sorrow is a connection to Christ and our need for Him in its purest form.

Maybe you've avoided playing a thanksgiving song because it won't sound the same as it did during a happier season in your life. But it doesn't need to. **True thanksgiving doesn't remove our sorrows. It acknowledges the coming glory that will.**

The thanks belong to Him, who says our sorrows will someday be dealt with, once and for all. The giving of our souls says that, even if our earthly hopes have been deferred, our eternal hope will never be lost.

When you think you'll never again be able to sing a song of thanksgiving, try it anyway. The tune of worship in sorrow is one of the most precious sounds the world can ever hear—and we need to hear it.

Our hearts will never be fully at home in this fallen world of tragedy and loss, but we were created to praise the Hope of Glory (Col 1:27). Give Him thanks in your sorrow, even—especially—if it's muted.

¹⁴ But I trust in you, LORD;
I say, "You are my God."
¹⁵ The course of my life is in your power;
rescue me from the power of my enemies
and from my persecutors.
¹⁶ Make your face shine on your servant;
save me by your faithful love.
¹⁷ LORD, do not let me be disgraced when I call on you.
Let the wicked be disgraced;
let them be quiet^A,B in Sheol.
¹⁸ Let lying lips
that arrogantly speak against the righteous
in proud contempt be silenced.

¹⁹ How great is your goodness
that you have stored up for those who fear you
and accomplished in the sight of everyone^C
for those who take refuge in you.
²⁰ You hide them in the protection of your presence;
you conceal them in a shelter
from human schemes,
from quarrelsome tongues.
²¹ Blessed be the LORD,
for he has wondrously shown his faithful love to me
in a city under siege.
²² In my alarm I said,
"I am cut off from your sight."
But you heard the sound of my pleading
when I cried to you for help.

²³ Love the LORD, all his faithful ones.
The LORD protects the loyal,
but fully repays the arrogant.
²⁴ Be strong, and let your heart be courageous,
all you who put your hope in the LORD.

THE JOY OF FORGIVENESS

32 Of David. A Maskil.
How joyful is the one
whose transgression is forgiven,
whose sin is covered!
² How joyful is a person whom
the LORD does not charge with iniquity
and in whose spirit is no deceit!

³ When I kept silent, my bones became brittle
from my groaning all day long.

---

^A31:17 LXX reads brought down   ^B31:17 Or them wail   ^C31:19 Or of the descendants of Adam

⁴ For day and night your hand was heavy on me;
my strength was drained^A
as in the summer's heat. *Selah*

⁵ Then I acknowledged my sin to you
and did not conceal my iniquity.
I said, "I will confess my transgressions
to the Lᴏʀᴅ,"
and you forgave the guilt of my sin. *Selah*

⁶ Therefore let everyone who is faithful
pray to you immediately.^B
When great floodwaters come,
they will not reach him.

⁷ You are my hiding place;
you protect me from trouble.
You surround me with joyful shouts
of deliverance. *Selah*

⁸ I will instruct you and show you the way to go;
with my eye on you, I will give counsel.

⁹ Do not be like a horse or mule,
without understanding,
that must be controlled with bit and bridle
or else it will not come near you.

¹⁰ Many pains come to the wicked,
but the one who trusts in the Lᴏʀᴅ
will have faithful love surrounding him.

¹¹ Be glad in the Lᴏʀᴅ and rejoice,
you righteous ones;
shout for joy,
all you upright in heart.

PRAISE TO THE CREATOR

33 Rejoice in the Lᴏʀᴅ, you righteous ones;
praise from the upright is beautiful.

² Praise the Lᴏʀᴅ with the lyre;
make music to him with a ten-stringed harp.

³ Sing a new song to him;
play skillfully on the strings, with a joyful shout.

⁴ For the word of the Lᴏʀᴅ is right,
and all his work is trustworthy.

⁵ He loves righteousness and justice;
the earth is full of the Lᴏʀᴅ's unfailing love.

⁶ The heavens were made by the word of the Lᴏʀᴅ,
and all the stars, by the breath of his mouth.

---

^A 32:4 Hb obscure   ^B 32:6 Lit *you at a time of finding*

⁷ He gathers the water of the sea into a heap;^A
he puts the depths into storehouses.

⁸ Let the whole earth fear the LORD;
let all the inhabitants of the world
stand in awe of him.

⁹ For he spoke, and it came into being;
he commanded, and it came into existence.

¹⁰ The LORD frustrates the counsel of the nations;
he thwarts the plans of the peoples.

¹¹ The counsel of the LORD stands forever,
the plans of his heart from generation to generation.

¹² Happy is the nation whose God is the LORD —
the people he has chosen to be his own possession!

¹³ The LORD looks down from heaven;
he observes everyone.

¹⁴ He gazes on all the inhabitants of the earth
from his dwelling place.

¹⁵ He forms the hearts of them all;
he considers all their works.

¹⁶ A king is not saved by a large army;
a warrior will not be rescued by great strength.

¹⁷ The horse is a false hope for safety;
it provides no escape by its great power.

¹⁸ But look, the LORD keeps his eye on those
who fear him —
those who depend on his faithful love

¹⁹ to rescue them from death
and to keep them alive in famine.

²⁰ We wait for the LORD;
he is our help and shield.

²¹ For our hearts rejoice in him
because we trust in his holy name.

²² May your faithful love rest on us, LORD,
for we put our hope in you.

THE LORD DELIVERS THE RIGHTEOUS

34 *Concerning David, when he pretended to be insane in the presence
of Abimelech, who drove him out, and he departed.*

¹ I will bless the LORD at all times;
his praise will always be on my lips.

² I will boast in the LORD;
the humble will hear and be glad.

³ Proclaim the LORD's greatness with me;
let us exalt his name together.

^A33:7 LXX, Tg, Syr, Vg, Jer read *sea as in a bottle*

NEVER OUT OF SIGHT

PSALM 34

I once spent several months in New York City writing for a small church plant. Every weekday I took the express train from my apartment to our office in lower Manhattan. While my daily routine remained the same, the commute was never predictable.

One morning, I boarded the subway during rush hour and miraculously managed to get a seat on the train. Triumphantly, I sat back and began reading the paper. At the next stop, a little girl and her mother got on and stood together in the aisle. Packed like sardines, people passed in and out as quickly as they could. When a seat opened up, the little girl sat down directly in front of her mom and seemed content to rest for a few minutes.

Pretty soon, a seat across the aisle opened up and the mom seized the opportunity to catch her breath. As people filled the few feet between them, the girl lost sight of her mother. Above the noise of the train and the chaos of rush hour, I heard a sweet little voice (with a hint of panic) say, "Mom, I can't see you. Are you still there?"

Her mom answered quickly and confidently, "I know you can't see me right now, sweetheart, but I can still see you. I promise I won't let you out of my sight."

I watched as the girl relaxed at the sound of her mother's voice. All she needed was reassurance that the one she trusted most in this world had her safely in sight.

The beauty of that moment wasn't lost on me. I saw my own reflection in the panicked eyes of the little girl. We've all experienced times when fear has gripped us, even paralyzed us, because we couldn't see God in our circumstances. We've stood in unfamiliar territory, unsure of the future and desperate to hear the voice of the One who can calm our fears. A patient and loving Father, God offers assurance through His Word.

"The eyes of the LORD are on the righteous, and his ears are open to their cry for help."

PSALM 34:15

It's a simple truth that steadies my pulse: God sees me. Even when we cannot see Him, He knows right where we are. This promise gives me sweet peace.

Perhaps you're in a season right now when life seems confusing or crowded with uncertainty. Maybe you need to be reminded today of this truth: you are never out of His sight.

Even when circumstances cloud our view, God's sovereignty is strong enough to hold us. No matter how loud the noise of the chaos around us seems, He always hears our cry for help.

Look past the noisy crowd, friend. Trust His faithfulness. Stand on His promises. Lean in and let the nearness of His presence steady your heart.

4 I sought the LORD, and he answered me
and rescued me from all my fears.
5 Those who look to him are[A] radiant with joy;
their faces will never be ashamed.
6 This poor man cried, and the LORD heard him
and saved him from all his troubles.
7 The angel of the LORD encamps
around those who fear him, and rescues them.

8 Taste and see that the LORD is good.
How happy is the person who
takes refuge in him!
9 You who are his holy ones, fear the LORD,
for those who fear him lack nothing.
10 Young lions[B] lack food and go hungry,
but those who seek the LORD
will not lack any good thing.

11 Come, children, listen to me;
I will teach you the fear of the LORD.
12 Who is someone who desires life,
loving a long life to enjoy what is good?
13 Keep your tongue from evil
and your lips from deceitful speech.
14 Turn away from evil and do what is good;
seek peace and pursue it.

15 The eyes of the LORD are on the righteous,
and his ears are open to their cry for help.
16 The face of the LORD is set
against those who do what is evil,
to remove[C] all memory of them from the earth.
17 The righteous[D] cry out, and the LORD hears,
and rescues them from all their troubles.
18 The LORD is near the brokenhearted;
he saves those crushed in spirit.

19 One who is righteous has many adversities,
but the LORD rescues him from them all.
20 He protects all his bones;
not one of them is broken.
21 Evil brings death to the wicked,
and those who hate the righteous
will be punished.
22 The LORD redeems the life of his servants,
and all who take refuge in him
will not be punished.

[A]34:5 Some Hb mss, LXX, Aq, Syr, Jer read *Look to him and be*   [B]34:10 LXX, Syr,
Vg read *The rich*   [C]34:16 Or *cut off*   [D]34:17 Lit *They*

PRAYER FOR VICTORY

35 *Of David.*

Oppose my opponents, LORD;
fight those who fight me.
2 Take your shields — large and small —
and come to my aid.
3 Draw the spear and javelin against my pursuers,
and assure me: "I am your deliverance."

4 Let those who intend to take my life
be disgraced and humiliated;
let those who plan to harm me
be turned back and ashamed.
5 Let them be like chaff in the wind,
with the angel of the LORD driving them away.
6 Let their way be dark and slippery,
with the angel of the LORD pursuing them.
7 They hid their net for me without cause;
they dug a pit for me without cause.
8 Let ruin come on him unexpectedly,
and let the net that he hid ensnare him;
let him fall into it — to his ruin.

9 Then I will rejoice in the LORD;
I will delight in his deliverance.
10 All my bones will say,
"LORD, who is like you,
rescuing the poor from one too strong for him,
the poor or the needy from one who robs him?"

11 Malicious witnesses come forward;
they question me about things I do not know.
12 They repay me evil for good,
making me desolate.
13 Yet when they were sick,
my clothing was sackcloth;
I humbled myself with fasting,
and my prayer was genuine.[A]
14 I went about mourning as if for my friend
or brother;
I was bowed down with grief,
like one mourning for a mother.
15 But when I stumbled, they gathered in glee;
they gathered against me.
Assailants I did not know
tore at me and did not stop.
16 With godless mockery[B]
they gnashed their teeth at me.

[A] 35:13 Lit *prayer returned to my chest* [B] 35:16 Hb obscure

¹⁷ Lord, how long will you look on?
Rescue me from their ravages;
rescue my precious life from the young lions.

¹⁸ I will praise you in the great assembly;
I will exalt you among many people.

¹⁹ Do not let my deceitful enemies rejoice over me;
do not let those who hate me without cause
wink at me maliciously.

²⁰ For they do not speak in friendly ways,
but contrive fraudulent schemes[A]
against those who live peacefully in the land.

²¹ They open their mouths wide against me and say,
"Aha, aha! We saw it!"[B]

²² You saw it, Lord; do not be silent.
Lord, do not be far from me.

²³ Wake up and rise to my defense,
to my cause, my God and my Lord!

²⁴ Vindicate me, Lord my God,
in keeping with your righteousness,
and do not let them rejoice over me.

²⁵ Do not let them say in their hearts,
"Aha! Just what we wanted."
Do not let them say,
"We have swallowed him up!"

²⁶ Let those who rejoice at my misfortune
be disgraced and humiliated;
let those who exalt themselves over me
be clothed with shame and reproach.

²⁷ Let those who want my vindication
shout for joy and be glad;
let them continually say,
"The Lord be exalted.
He takes pleasure in his servant's well-being."

²⁸ And my tongue will proclaim your righteousness,
your praise all day long.

HUMAN WICKEDNESS AND GOD'S LOVE

36 *For the choir director. Of David, the Lord's servant.*

An oracle within my heart
concerning the transgression of the wicked person:
Dread of God has no effect on him.[C]

² For with his flattering opinion of himself,
he does not discover and hate his iniquity.

³ The words from his mouth are malicious and deceptive;
he has stopped acting wisely and doing good.

[A]35:20 Lit *but devise fraudulent words*   [B]35:21 Lit *Our eyes saw!*   [C]36:1 Lit
There is no dread of God in front of his eyes

4   Even on his bed he makes malicious plans.
    He sets himself on a path that is not good,
    and he does not reject evil.

5   LORD, your faithful love reaches to heaven,
    your faithfulness to the clouds.
6   Your righteousness is like the highest mountains,
    your judgments like the deepest sea.
    LORD, you preserve people and animals.
7   How priceless your faithful love is, God!
    People take refuge in the shadow of your wings.
8   They are filled from the abundance of your house.
    You let them drink from your refreshing stream.
9   For the wellspring of life is with you.
    By means of your light we see light.

10 Spread your faithful love over those
        who know you,
    and your righteousness over the upright in heart.
11 Do not let the foot of the arrogant come near me
    or the hand of the wicked drive me away.
12 There! The evildoers have fallen.
    They have been thrown down and cannot rise.

INSTRUCTION IN WISDOM

37 *Of David.*
    Do not be agitated by evildoers;
    do not envy those who do wrong.
2   For they wither quickly like grass
    and wilt like tender green plants.

3   Trust in the LORD and do what is good;
    dwell in the land and live securely.^A
4   Take delight in the LORD,
    and he will give you your heart's desires.

5   Commit your way to the LORD;
    trust in him, and he will act,
6   making your righteousness shine like the dawn,
    your justice like the noonday.

7   Be silent before the LORD and wait expectantly for him;
    do not be agitated by one who prospers in his way,
    by the person who carries out evil plans.

8   Refrain from anger and give up your rage;
    do not be agitated — it can only bring harm.
9   For evildoers will be destroyed,

---

^A37:3 Or *and cultivate faithfulness,* or *and befriend faithfulness*

but those who put their hope in the LORD
will inherit the land.

10 A little while, and the wicked person will be no more;
though you look for him, he will not be there.
11 But the humble will inherit the land
and will enjoy abundant prosperity.

12 The wicked person schemes against the righteous
and gnashes his teeth at him.
13 The Lord laughs at him
because he sees that his day is coming.

14 The wicked have drawn the sword and strung the^A bow
to bring down the poor and needy
and to slaughter those whose way is upright.
15 Their swords will enter their own hearts,
and their bows will be broken.

16 The little that the righteous person has is better
than the abundance of many wicked people.
17 For the arms of the wicked will be broken,
but the LORD supports the righteous.

18 The LORD watches over the blameless all their days,
and their inheritance will last forever.
19 They will not be disgraced in times of adversity;
they will be satisfied in days of hunger.

20 But the wicked will perish;
the LORD's enemies, like the glory of the pastures,
will fade away —
they will fade away like smoke.

21 The wicked person borrows and does not repay,
but the righteous one is gracious and giving.
22 Those who are blessed by the LORD
will inherit the land,
but those cursed by him will be destroyed.

23 A person's steps are established by the LORD,
and he takes pleasure in his way.
24 Though he falls, he will not be overwhelmed,
because the LORD supports him with his hand.

25 I have been young and now I am old,
yet I have not seen the righteous abandoned
or his children begging for bread.

^A 37:14 Lit *their*

26 He is always generous, always lending,
and his children are a blessing.

27 Turn away from evil, do what is good,
and settle permanently.
28 For the LORD loves justice
and will not abandon his faithful ones.
They are kept safe forever,
but the children of the wicked will be destroyed.
29 The righteous will inherit the land
and dwell in it permanently.

30 The mouth of the righteous utters wisdom;
his tongue speaks what is just.
31 The instruction of his God is in his heart;
his steps do not falter.

32 The wicked one lies in wait for the righteous
and intends to kill him;
33 the LORD will not leave him
in the power of the wicked one
or allow him to be condemned when he is judged.

34 Wait for the LORD and keep his way,
and he will exalt you to inherit the land.
You will watch when the wicked are destroyed.

35 I have seen a wicked, violent person
well-rooted,[A] like a flourishing native tree.
36 Then I[B] passed by and noticed he was gone;
I searched for him, but he could not be found.

37 Watch the blameless and observe the upright,
for the person of peace will have a future.[C]
38 But transgressors will all be eliminated;
the future of the wicked will be destroyed.

39 The salvation of the righteous is from the LORD,
their refuge in a time of distress.
40 The LORD helps and delivers them;
he will deliver them from the wicked and will save them
because they take refuge in him.

PRAYER OF A SUFFERING SINNER

38 *A psalm of David to bring remembrance.*
LORD, do not punish me in your anger
or discipline me in your wrath.

[A] 37:35 Hb obscure [B] 37:36 LXX, Syr, Vg, Jer; MT reads *he* [C] 37:37 Or *posterity*, also in v. 38

² For your arrows have sunk into me,
and your hand has pressed down on me.

³ There is no soundness in my body
because of your indignation;
there is no health^A in my bones
because of my sin.
⁴ For my iniquities have flooded over my head;
they are a burden too heavy for me to bear.
⁵ My wounds are foul and festering
because of my foolishness.
⁶ I am bent over and brought very low;
all day long I go around in mourning.
⁷ For my insides are full of burning pain,
and there is no soundness in my body.
⁸ I am faint and severely crushed;
I groan because of the anguish of my heart.

⁹ Lord, my every desire is in front of you;
my sighing is not hidden from you.
¹⁰ My heart races, my strength leaves me,
and even the light of my eyes has faded.^B
¹¹ My loved ones and friends stand back
from my affliction,
and my relatives stand at a distance.
¹² Those who intend to kill me set traps,
and those who want to harm me threaten
to destroy me;
they plot treachery all day long.

¹³ I am like a deaf person; I do not hear.
I am like a speechless person
who does not open his mouth.
¹⁴ I am like a man who does not hear
and has no arguments in his mouth.
¹⁵ For I put my hope in you, LORD;
you will answer me, my Lord, my God.
¹⁶ For I said, "Don't let them rejoice over me —
those who are arrogant toward me when I stumble."
¹⁷ For I am about to fall,
and my pain is constantly with me.
¹⁸ So I confess my iniquity;
I am anxious because of my sin.
¹⁹ But my enemies are vigorous and powerful;^C
many hate me for no reason.
²⁰ Those who repay evil for good
attack me for pursuing good.

---

^A38:3 Hb *shalom*   ^B38:10 Or *and the light of my eyes — even that is not with me*
^C38:19 Or *numerous*

²¹ LORD, do not abandon me;
my God, do not be far from me.
²² Hurry to help me,
my Lord, my salvation.

THE FLEETING NATURE OF LIFE

39 *For the choir director, for Jeduthun.*
A psalm of David.

¹ I said, "I will guard my ways
so that I may not sin with my tongue;
I will guard my mouth with a muzzle
as long as the wicked are in my presence."
² I was speechless and quiet;
I kept silent, even from speaking good,
and my pain intensified.
³ My heart grew hot within me;
as I mused, a fire burned.
I spoke with my tongue:
⁴ "LORD, make me aware of my end
and the number of my days
so that I will know how short-lived I am.
⁵ In fact, you have made my days just inches long,
and my life span is as nothing to you.
Yes, every human being stands as only a vapor.   *Selah*
⁶ Yes, a person goes about like a mere shadow.
Indeed, they rush around in vain,
gathering possessions
without knowing who will get them.

⁷ "Now, Lord, what do I wait for?
My hope is in you.
⁸ Rescue me from all my transgressions;
do not make me the taunt of fools.
⁹ I am speechless; I do not open my mouth
because of what you have done.
¹⁰ Remove your torment from me.
Because of the force of your hand I am finished.
¹¹ You discipline a person with punishment
for iniquity,
consuming like a moth what is precious to him;
yes, every human being is only a vapor.   *Selah*

¹² "Hear my prayer, LORD,
and listen to my cry for help;
do not be silent at my tears.
For I am here with you as an alien,
a temporary resident like all my ancestors.
¹³ Turn your angry gaze from me
so that I may be cheered up
before I die and am gone."

THANKSGIVING AND A CRY FOR HELP

40 *For the choir director. A psalm of David.*
I waited patiently for the LORD,
and he turned to me and heard my cry for help.
2 He brought me up from a desolate^A pit,
out of the muddy clay,
and set my feet on a rock,
making my steps secure.
3 He put a new song in my mouth,
a hymn of praise to our God.
Many will see and fear,
and they will trust in the LORD.

4 How happy is anyone
who has put his trust in the LORD
and has not turned to the proud
or to those who run after lies!
5 LORD my God, you have done many things —
your wondrous works and your plans for us;
none can compare with you.
If I were to report and speak of them,
they are more than can be told.

6 You do not delight in sacrifice and offering;
you open my ears to listen.^B
You do not ask for a whole burnt offering or a sin offering.
7 Then I said, "See, I have come;
in the scroll it is written about me.
8 I delight to do your will, my God,
and your instruction is deep within me."

9 I proclaim righteousness in the great assembly;
see, I do not keep my mouth closed^C —
as you know, LORD.
10 I did not hide your righteousness in my heart;
I spoke about your faithfulness and salvation;
I did not conceal your constant love and truth
from the great assembly.

11 LORD, you do not^D withhold your compassion from me.
Your constant love and truth will always guard me.
12 For troubles without number have surrounded me;
my iniquities have overtaken me; I am unable to see.
They are more than the hairs of my head,
and my courage leaves me.
13 LORD, be pleased to rescue me;
hurry to help me, LORD.

---

^A40:2 Or *watery* ^B40:6 Lit *you hollow out ears for me* ^C40:9 Lit *not restrain my lips* ^D40:11 Or *LORD, do not*

14 Let those who intend to take my life
  be disgraced and confounded.
  Let those who wish me harm
  be turned back and humiliated.
15 Let those who say to me, "Aha, aha!"
  be appalled because of their shame.

16 Let all who seek you rejoice and be glad in you;
  let those who love your salvation continually say,
  "The Lord is great!"
17 I am oppressed and needy;
  may the Lord think of me.
  You are my helper and my deliverer;
  my God, do not delay.

VICTORY IN SPITE OF BETRAYAL

41

For the choir director. A psalm of David.

Happy is one who is considerate of the poor;
  the Lord will save him in a day of adversity.
2 The Lord will keep him and preserve him;
  he will be blessed in the land.
  You will not give him over to the desire of his enemies.
3 The Lord will sustain him on his sickbed;
  you will heal him on the bed where he lies.

4 I said, "Lord, be gracious to me;
  heal me, for I have sinned against you."
5 My enemies speak maliciously about me:
  "When will he die and be forgotten?"
6 When one of them comes to visit,
    he speaks deceitfully;
  he stores up evil in his heart;
  he goes out and talks.
7 All who hate me whisper together about me;
  they plan to harm me.
8 "Something awful has overwhelmed him,[A]
  and he won't rise again from where he lies!"
9 Even my friend[B] in whom I trusted,
  one who ate my bread,
  has raised his heel against me.

10 But you, Lord, be gracious to me and raise me up;
  then I will repay them.
11 By this I know that you delight in me:
  my enemy does not shout in triumph over me.
12 You supported me because of my integrity
  and set me in your presence forever.

[A] 41:8 Lit "A thing of worthlessness has been poured into him   [B] 41:9 Lit Even a
man of my peace

883

¹³ Blessed be the L ord God of Israel,
from everlasting to everlasting.
Amen and amen.

BOOK II (Psalms 42–72)

LONGING FOR GOD

42 *For the choir director. A Maskil of the sons of Korah.*
As a deer longs for flowing streams,
so I long for you, God.
² I thirst for God, the living God.
When can I come and appear before God?
³ My tears have been my food day and night,
while all day long people say to me,
"Where is your God?"
⁴ I remember this as I pour out my heart:
how I walked with many,
leading the festive procession
to the house of God,
with joyful and thankful shouts.

⁵ Why, my soul, are you so dejected?
Why are you in such turmoil?
Put your hope in God, for I will still praise him,
my Savior and my God.
⁶ I^A am deeply depressed;
therefore I remember you from the land of Jordan
and the peaks of Hermon, from Mount Mizar.
⁷ Deep calls to deep in the roar of your waterfalls;
all your breakers and your billows
have swept over me.
⁸ The L ord will send his faithful love by day;
his song will be with me in the night —
a prayer to the God of my life.

⁹ I will say to God, my rock,
"Why have you forgotten me?
Why must I go about in sorrow
because of the enemy's oppression?"
¹⁰ My adversaries taunt me,
as if crushing my bones,
while all day long they say to me,
"Where is your God?"
¹¹ Why, my soul, are you so dejected?
Why are you in such turmoil?
Put your hope in God, for I will still praise him,
my Savior and my God.

---

^A42:5-6 Some Hb mss, LXX, Syr; other Hb mss read *him, the salvation of his
presence.* ⁶*My God, I*

43 [A] Vindicate me, God, and champion my cause
against an unfaithful nation;
rescue me from the deceitful and unjust person.

2 For you are the God of my refuge.
Why have you rejected me?
Why must I go about in sorrow
because of the enemy's oppression?

3 Send your light and your truth; let them lead me.
Let them bring me to your holy mountain,
to your dwelling place.

4 Then I will come to the altar of God,
to God, my greatest joy.
I will praise you with the lyre,
God, my God.

5 Why, my soul, are you so dejected?
Why are you in such turmoil?
Put your hope in God, for I will still praise him,
my Savior and my God.

ISRAEL'S COMPLAINT

44 *For the choir director. A Maskil of the sons of Korah.*
God, we have heard with our ears —
our ancestors have told us —
the work you accomplished in their days,
in days long ago:

2 In order to plant them,
you displaced the nations by your hand;
in order to settle them,
you brought disaster on the peoples.

3 For they did not take the land by their sword —
their arm did not bring them victory —
but by your right hand, your arm,
and the light of your face,
because you were favorable toward them.

4 You are my King, my God,
who ordains [B] victories for Jacob.

5 Through you we drive back our foes;
through your name we trample our enemies.

6 For I do not trust in my bow,
and my sword does not bring me victory.

7 But you give us victory over our foes
and let those who hate us be disgraced.

8 We boast in God all day long;
we will praise your name forever. *Selah*

[A] Ps 43 Many Hb mss connect Pss 42 and 43   [B] 44:4 LXX, Syr, Aq; MT reads
King, God; ordain

⁹ But you have rejected and humiliated us;
you do not march out with our armies.
¹⁰ You make us retreat from the foe,
and those who hate us
have taken plunder for themselves.
¹¹ You hand us over to be eaten like sheep
and scatter us among the nations.
¹² You sell your people for nothing;
you make no profit from selling them.
¹³ You make us an object of reproach to our neighbors,
a source of mockery and ridicule to those around us.
¹⁴ You make us a joke among the nations,
a laughingstock^A among the peoples.
¹⁵ My disgrace is before me all day long,
and shame has covered my face,
¹⁶ because of the taunts^B of the scorner and reviler,
because of the enemy and avenger.

¹⁷ All this has happened to us,
but we have not forgotten you
or betrayed your covenant.
¹⁸ Our hearts have not turned back;
our steps have not strayed from your path.
¹⁹ But you have crushed us in a haunt of jackals
and have covered us with deepest darkness.
²⁰ If we had forgotten the name of our God
and spread out our hands to a foreign god,
²¹ wouldn't God have found this out,
since he knows the secrets of the heart?
²² Because of you we are being put
to death all day long;
we are counted as sheep to be slaughtered.

²³ Wake up, Lord! Why are you sleeping?
Get up! Don't reject us forever!
²⁴ Why do you hide
and forget our affliction and oppression?
²⁵ For we have sunk down to the dust;
our bodies cling to the ground.
²⁶ Rise up! Help us!
Redeem us because of your faithful love.

A ROYAL WEDDING SONG

45 *For the choir director: according to "The Lilies."*
A Maskil of the sons of Korah. A love song.

¹ My heart is moved by a noble theme
as I recite my verses to the king;
my tongue is the pen of a skillful writer.

---

^A44:14 Lit *shaking of the head* ^B44:16 Lit *voice*

2 You are the most handsome of men;[A]
  grace flows from your lips.
  Therefore God has blessed you forever.

3 Mighty warrior, strap your sword at your side.
  In your majesty and splendor —
4 in your splendor ride triumphantly
  in the cause of truth, humility, and justice.
  May your right hand show your awe-inspiring acts.
5 Your sharpened arrows pierce the hearts of the king's enemies;
  the peoples fall under you.

6 Your throne, God, is[B] forever and ever;
  the scepter of your kingdom is a scepter of justice.
7 You love righteousness and hate wickedness;
  therefore God, your God, has anointed you with the oil of joy
  more than your companions.
8 Myrrh, aloes, and cassia perfume all your garments;
  from ivory palaces harps bring you joy.
9 Kings' daughters are among your honored women;
  the queen, adorned with gold from Ophir,
  stands at your right hand.

10 Listen, daughter, pay attention and consider:
   forget your people and your father's house,
11 and the king will desire your beauty.
   Bow down to him, for he is your lord.
12 The daughter of Tyre, the wealthy people,
   will seek your favor with gifts.

13 In her chamber, the royal daughter is all glorious,
   her clothing embroidered with gold.
14 In colorful garments she is led to the king;
   after her, the virgins, her companions, are brought to you.
15 They are led in with gladness and rejoicing;
   they enter the king's palace.

16 Your sons will succeed your ancestors;
   you will make them princes throughout the land.
17 I will cause your name to be remembered for all generations;
   therefore the peoples will praise you forever and ever.

GOD OUR REFUGE

46

*For the choir director. A song of the sons of Korah.
According to* Alamoth.

1 God is our refuge and strength,
  a helper who is always found

[A]45:2 Or *of the descendants of Adam*   [B]45:6 Or *Your divine throne is,* or *Your throne is God's*

in times of trouble.
2 Therefore we will not be afraid,
  though the earth trembles
  and the mountains topple
  into the depths of the seas,
3 though its water roars and foams
  and the mountains quake with its turmoil.   *Selah*

4 There is a river —
  its streams delight the city of God,
  the holy dwelling place of the Most High.
5 God is within her; she will not be toppled.
  God will help her when the morning dawns.
6 Nations rage, kingdoms topple;
  the earth melts when he lifts his voice.
7 The LORD of Armies is with us;
  the God of Jacob is our stronghold.   *Selah*

8 Come, see the works of the LORD,
  who brings devastation on the earth.
9 He makes wars cease throughout the earth.
  He shatters bows and cuts spears to pieces;
  he sets wagons ablaze.
10 "Stop your fighting, and know that I am God,
  exalted among the nations,
      exalted on the earth."
11 The LORD of Armies is with us;
  the God of Jacob is our stronghold.   *Selah*

GOD OUR KING

47 *For the choir director.*
A psalm of the sons of Korah.

1 Clap your hands, all you peoples;
  shout to God with a jubilant cry.
2 For the LORD, the Most High,
  is awe-inspiring,
  a great King over the whole earth.
3 He subdues peoples under us
  and nations under our feet.
4 He chooses for us our inheritance —
  the pride of Jacob, whom he loves.   *Selah*

5 God ascends among shouts of joy,
  the LORD, with the sound of trumpets.
6 Sing praise to God, sing praise;
  sing praise to our King, sing praise!
7 Sing a song of wisdom,^A
  for God is King of the whole earth.

---

^A 47:7 Or *Sing a maskil*

8 God reigns over the nations;
 God is seated on his holy throne.
9 The nobles of the peoples have assembled
 with the people of the God of Abraham.
 For the leaders^A of the earth belong to God;
 he is greatly exalted.

ZION EXALTED

48 A song. A psalm of the sons of Korah.
 The LORD is great and highly praised
 in the city of our God.
 His holy mountain, ² rising splendidly,
 is the joy of the whole earth.
 Mount Zion — the summit of Zaphon —
 is the city of the great King.
3 God is known as a stronghold
 in its citadels.

4 Look! The kings assembled;
 they advanced together.
5 They looked and froze with fear;
 they fled in terror.
6 Trembling seized them there,
 agony like that of a woman in labor,
7 as you wrecked the ships of Tarshish
 with the east wind.

8 Just as we heard, so we have seen
 in the city of the LORD of Armies,
 in the city of our God;
 God will establish it forever. *Selah*

9 God, within your temple,
 we contemplate your faithful love.
10 Like your name, God, so your praise
 reaches to the ends of the earth;
 your right hand is filled with justice.
11 Mount Zion is glad.
 Judah's villages^B rejoice
 because of your judgments.

12 Go around Zion, encircle it;
 count its towers,
13 note its ramparts; tour its citadels
 so that you can tell a future generation:
14 "This God, our God forever and ever —
 he will always lead us."^C

---

^A 47:9 Lit shields ^B 48:11 Lit daughters ^C 48:14 Some Hb mss, LXX; other Hb mss
read over death

MISPLACED TRUST IN WEALTH

49 *For the choir director. A psalm of the sons of Korah.*

Hear this, all you peoples;
listen, all who inhabit the world,

2 both low and high,
rich and poor together.

3 My mouth speaks wisdom;
my heart's meditation
brings understanding.

4 I turn my ear to a proverb;
I explain my riddle with a lyre.

5 Why should I fear in times of trouble?
The iniquity of my foes surrounds me.

6 They trust in their wealth
and boast of their abundant riches.

7 Yet these cannot redeem a person[A]
or pay his ransom to God —

8 since the price of redeeming him is too costly,
one should forever stop trying[B] —

9 so that he may live forever
and not see the Pit.

10 For one can see that the wise die;
the foolish and stupid also pass away.
Then they leave their wealth to others.

11 Their graves are their permanent homes,[C]
their dwellings from generation to generation,
though they have named estates
after themselves.

12 But despite his assets,[D] mankind will not last;
he is like the animals that perish.

13 This is the way of those who are arrogant,
and of their followers,
who approve of their words.[E]   *Selah*

14 Like sheep they are headed for Sheol;
Death will shepherd them.
The upright will rule over them
in the morning,
and their form will waste away in Sheol,[F]
far from their lofty abode.

15 But God will redeem me
from the power of Sheol,
for he will take me.   *Selah*

[A]49:7 Or *Certainly he cannot redeem himself,* or *Yet he cannot redeem a brother*
[B]49:8 Or *costly, it will cease forever*   [C]49:11 LXX, Syr, Tg; MT reads *Their inner
thought is that their houses are eternal*   [D]49:12 Or *honor*   [E]49:13 Lit *and after
them with their mouth they were pleased*   [F]49:14 Hb obscure

16 Do not be afraid when a person gets rich,
  when the wealth^A of his house increases.
17 For when he dies, he will take nothing at all;
  his wealth will not follow him down.
18 Though he blesses himself during his lifetime —
  and you are acclaimed when you do well for yourself —
19 he will go to the generation of his fathers;
  they will never see the light.
20 Mankind, with his assets
  but without understanding,
  is like the animals that perish.

GOD AS JUDGE

50 *A psalm of Asaph.*
  The Mighty One, God,^B the LORD, speaks;
  he summons the earth
  from the rising of the sun to its setting.
2 From Zion, the perfection of beauty,
  God appears in radiance.^C
3 Our God is coming; he will not be silent!
  Devouring fire precedes him,
  and a storm rages around him.
4 On high, he summons heaven and earth
  in order to judge his people:
5 "Gather my faithful ones to me,
  those who made a covenant with me by sacrifice."
6 The heavens proclaim his righteousness,
  for God is the Judge.   *Selah*

7 "Listen, my people, and I will speak;
  I will testify against you, Israel.
  I am God, your God.
8 I do not rebuke you for your sacrifices
  or for your burnt offerings,
  which are continually before me.
9 I will not take a bull from your household
  or male goats from your pens,
10 for every animal of the forest is mine,
  the cattle on a thousand hills.
11 I know every bird of the mountains,
  and the creatures of the field are mine.
12 If I were hungry, I would not tell you,
  for the world and everything in it is mine.
13 Do I eat the flesh of bulls
  or drink the blood of goats?
14 Sacrifice a thank offering to God,
  and pay your vows to the Most High.

---

^A49:16 Or *glory,* also in v. 17   ^B50:1 Or *The God of gods*   ^C50:2 Or *God shines forth*

¹⁵ Call on me in a day of trouble;
I will rescue you, and you will honor me."

¹⁶ But God says to the wicked:
"What right do you have to recite my statutes
and to take my covenant on your lips?
¹⁷ You hate instruction
and fling my words behind you.
¹⁸ When you see a thief,
you make friends with him,
and you associate with adulterers.
¹⁹ You unleash your mouth for evil
and harness your tongue for deceit.
²⁰ You sit, maligning your brother,
slandering your mother's son.
²¹ You have done these things, and I kept silent;
you thought I was just like you.
But I will rebuke you
and lay out the case before you.^A

²² "Understand this, you who forget God,
or I will tear you apart,
and there will be no one to rescue you.
²³ Whoever sacrifices a thank offering honors me,
and whoever orders his conduct,
I will show him the salvation of God."

A PRAYER FOR RESTORATION

51 *For the choir director. A psalm of David, when the prophet Nathan came to him after he had gone to Bathsheba.*

¹ Be gracious to me, God,
according to your faithful love;
according to your abundant compassion,
blot out my rebellion.
² Completely wash away my guilt
and cleanse me from my sin.
³ For I am conscious of my rebellion,
and my sin is always before me.
⁴ Against you — you alone — I have sinned
and done this evil in your sight.
So you are right when you pass sentence;
you are blameless when you judge.
⁵ Indeed, I was guilty when I was born;
I was sinful when my mother conceived me.

⁶ Surely you desire integrity in the inner self,
and you teach me wisdom deep within.
⁷ Purify me with hyssop, and I will be clean;

^A50:21 Lit *lay it out before your eyes*

SHOW ME MY SIN

PSALMS 50–52; HOSEA 9:1-17

Once upon a time I was tasked by a mentor to pray every day for two weeks that God would show me my sin, and to ask two people close to me to do the same for me. It was one of the most shocking and enlightening exercises of my spiritual life to date. You guys, that prayer is no joke.

David's words in Psalm 51 echo what I learned those few weeks. My flesh is weak and my sin is frightening.

"For I am conscious of my rebellion, and my sin is always before me. Against you—you alone—I have sinned and done this evil in your sight."

PSALM 51:3-4

Although what I learned was, well, appalling, that simple prayer taught me a priceless truth of the gospel: **the larger my view of my sin, the larger my view of the cross.**

Seeing more of what should separate me from a holy God means seeing more of Christ. Understanding the vastness of my sin means understanding the vastness of Jesus' love and sacrifice for me.

The cross covers it all.

Why the cross? Why such a sacrifice? Because we are Israel-caliber sinners. Our holy God cannot be near sin and He could not be near us were it not for Jesus.

In Hosea 9, we read a portrayal of what should be the consequence of Israel's sin, and ours.

"Woe to them when I depart from them! . . . I will drive them from my house because of their evil, wicked actions. I will no longer love them . . ."

HOSEA 9:12,15

It is painful to see our sin for what it is—an offense to the heart of our holy God. But it is important, too. When we look on our sin without flinching, we begin to grasp the lengths to which the Holy One has gone to draw us to Him.

As David grieves his sin in Psalm 51, so should we grieve the sin in our own life. As he cries out for mercy, saying, "Save me from the guilt of bloodshed, God—God of my salvation" (Ps 51:14), so should we cry out for mercy. But friend, do not despair! Look up to see the cross of Jesus Christ, big enough to cover every ounce of your sin and shame.

Have you ever prayed that God would reveal your sin to you? Consider praying that prayer every day for two weeks, and ask another believer whom you trust to do the same on your behalf.

Be ready—God will hear your prayer. As the Holy Spirit pulls back the veil to reveal the corners of your sinful heart, look to the Savior. Repent and rejoice in His steadfast love.

Yes, our God hates sin, as should we. But, oh, how He loves us.

wash me, and I will be whiter than snow.
8 Let me hear joy and gladness;
let the bones you have crushed rejoice.
9 Turn your face away^A from my sins
and blot out all my guilt.

10 God, create a clean heart for me
and renew a steadfast^B spirit within me.
11 Do not banish me from your presence
or take your Holy Spirit from me.
12 Restore the joy of your salvation to me,
and sustain me by giving me a willing spirit.
13 Then I will teach the rebellious your ways,
and sinners will return to you.

14 Save me from the guilt of bloodshed, God —
God of my salvation —
and my tongue will sing of your righteousness.
15 Lord, open my lips,
and my mouth will declare your praise.
16 You do not want a sacrifice, or I would give it;
you are not pleased with a burnt offering.
17 The sacrifice pleasing to God is^C a broken spirit.
You will not despise a broken and humbled heart, God.

18 In your good pleasure, cause Zion to prosper;
build the walls of Jerusalem.
19 Then you will delight in righteous sacrifices,
whole burnt offerings;
then bulls will be offered on your altar.

GOD JUDGES THE PROUD

52 *For the choir director. A Maskil of David. When Doeg the Edomite went and reported to Saul, telling him, "David went to Ahimelech's house."*

1 Why boast about evil, you hero!
God's faithful love is constant.
2 Like a sharpened razor,
your tongue devises destruction,
working treachery.
3 You love evil instead of good,
lying instead of speaking truthfully. *Selah*
4 You love any words that destroy,
you treacherous tongue!

5 This is why God will bring you down forever.
He will take you, ripping you out of your tent;
he will uproot you from the land of the living. *Selah*
6 The righteous will see and fear,

---

^A 51:9 Lit *Hide your face*   ^B 51:10 Or *right*   ^C 51:17 Lit *The sacrifices of God are* and they will derisively say about that hero,[A]

7 "Here is the man
who would not make God his refuge,
but trusted in the abundance of his riches,
taking refuge in his destructive behavior."

8 But I am like a flourishing olive tree
in the house of God;
I trust in God's faithful love forever and ever.

9 I will praise you forever for what you have done.
In the presence of your faithful people,
I will put my hope in your name, for it is good.

A PORTRAIT OF SINNERS

53 *For the choir director: on Mahalath. A Maskil of David.*
The fool says in his heart, "There's no God."
They are corrupt, and they do vile deeds.
There is no one who does good.

2 God looks down from heaven on the human race[B]
to see if there is one who is wise,
one who seeks God.

3 All have turned away;
all alike have become corrupt.
There is no one who does good,
not even one.

4 Will evildoers never understand?
They consume my people as they consume bread;
they do not call on God.

5 Then they will be filled with dread —
dread like no other —
because God will scatter
the bones of those who besiege you.
You will put them to shame,
for God has rejected them.

6 Oh, that Israel's deliverance would come from Zion!
When God restores the fortunes of his people,[C]
let Jacob rejoice, let Israel be glad.

PRAYER FOR DELIVERANCE

54 *For the choir director: with stringed instruments. A Maskil of David. When
the Ziphites went and said to Saul, "Is David not hiding among us?"*

1 God, save me by your name,
and vindicate me by your might!

2 God, hear my prayer;
listen to the words from my mouth.

[A] 52:6 Lit *about him* [B] 53:2 Or *the descendants of Adam* [C] 53:6 Or *restores his
captive people*

3 For strangers rise up against me,
and violent men intend to kill me.
They do not let God guide them.^A   *Selah*

4 God is my helper;
the Lord is the sustainer of my life.^B
5 He will repay my adversaries for their evil.
Because of your faithfulness, annihilate them.

6 I will sacrifice a freewill offering to you.
I will praise your name, LORD,
because it is good.
7 For he has rescued me from every trouble,
and my eye has looked down on my enemies.

BETRAYAL BY A FRIEND

55 *For the choir director: with stringed instruments. A Maskil of David.*
God, listen to my prayer
and do not hide from my plea for help.
2 Pay attention to me and answer me.
I am restless and in turmoil with my complaint,
3 because of the enemy's words,^C
because of the pressure^D of the wicked.
For they bring down disaster on me
and harass me in anger.

4 My heart shudders within me;
terrors of death sweep over me.
5 Fear and trembling grip me;
horror has overwhelmed me.
6 I said, "If only I had wings like a dove!
I would fly away and find rest.
7 How far away I would flee;
I would stay in the wilderness.   *Selah*
8 I would hurry to my shelter
from the raging wind and the storm."

9 Lord, confuse^E and confound their speech,^F
for I see violence and strife in the city;
10 day and night they make the rounds on its walls.
Crime and trouble are within it;
11 destruction is inside it;
oppression and deceit never leave its marketplace.

12 Now it is not an enemy who insults me —
otherwise I could bear it;

---

^A54:3 Lit They do not set God in front of them   ^B54:4 Or is with those who sustain
my life   ^C55:3 Lit voice   ^D55:3 Or threat, or oppression   ^E55:9 Or destroy
^F55:9 Lit and divide their tongue

it is not a foe who rises up against me —
   otherwise I could hide from him.
13 But it is you, a man who is my peer,
   my companion and good friend!
14 We used to have close fellowship;
   we walked with the crowd
      into the house of God.

15 Let death take them by surprise;
   let them go down to Sheol alive,
   because evil is in their homes and within them.
16 But I call to God,
   and the Lord will save me.
17 I complain and groan morning, noon, and night,
   and he hears my voice.
18 Though many are against me,
   he will redeem me from my battle unharmed.
19 God, the one enthroned from long ago,   *Selah*
   will hear and will humiliate them
   because they do not change
   and do not fear God.

20 My friend acts violently
   against those at peace with him;
   he violates his covenant.
21 His buttery words are smooth,
   but war is in his heart.
   His words are softer than oil,
   but they are drawn swords.

22 Cast your burden on the Lord,
   and he will sustain you;
   he will never allow the righteous to be shaken.

23 God, you will bring them down
   to the Pit of destruction;
   men of bloodshed and treachery
   will not live out half their days.
   But I will trust in you.

A CALL FOR GOD'S PROTECTION

56
For the choir director: according to "A Silent Dove Far Away."
A Miktam of David. When the Philistines seized him in Gath.

1 Be gracious to me, God, for a man is trampling me;
   he fights and oppresses me all day long.
2 My adversaries trample me all day,
   for many arrogantly fight against me.[A]

[A]56:2 Or *many fight against me, O exalted one,* or *many fight against me from the heights*

THE PRIVILEGE OF BOLD ASKING

PSALMS 55–56; MATTHEW 26:36-46; LUKE 18:1-8

"You yourself have recorded my wanderings. Put my tears in your bottle. Are they not in your book? Then my enemies will retreat on the day when I call. This I know: God is for me."

PSALM 56:8-9

If there was ever a picture of intimate prayer, it is found in the gut-wrenching psalms of David.

In Psalm 56, we find David seized by the Philistines, in danger for his life. His prayer alternates between cries for help and affirmation of his ultimate trust in God. But then he asks, "Will they escape in spite of such sin?" (Ps 56:7). The breathless desperation is almost audible.

I hear honesty and familiarity in David's words. Not formality or formula.

In Jesus' prayer in Gethsemane we hear an even deeper intimacy with the Father—a balance of the heart's deepest longing with surrender to the complete sovereignty of God.

"My Father, if it is possible, let this cup pass from me. Yet not as I will, but as you will" (Mt 26:39).

Jesus' cry is the ultimate collision of remarkable boldness and astounding trust—trust in the God who holds it all in His loving, omnipotent hands. He is the One in whose name we pray, whose perfect sacrifice grants us access to the very throne of God.

Then comes the parable of the persistent widow in Luke 18, and again our minds go reeling.

"Will not God grant justice to his elect who cry out to him day and night? Will he delay helping them?" (Lk 18:7).

It's tempting to think this is how prayer works, that the squeaky wheel gets the grease. We wonder if God's answers to prayer are subject to His emotional whim. But we know better.

We know Christ speaks of us as beloved children, and tells us our Father delights in giving us all we need (Mt 7:11). We know the God who hears our prayers is the same God who cares for the birds of the air. "Aren't you worth more than they?" (Mt 6:26). So when we read of the widow who asks relentlessly and unapologetically for mercy, we long to do the same. When we dare to imagine asking for what we need, like children do, we begin to understand: this **bold asking is our privilege as His daughters.**

The pleas of an honest heart following hard after God are music to His ears. May we bring a chorus of trust and adoration and boldness to His throne today.

3 When I am afraid,
   I will trust in you.
4 In God, whose word I praise,
   in God I trust; I will not be afraid.
   What can mere mortals do to me?

5 They twist my words all day long;
   all their thoughts against me are evil.
6 They stir up strife,[A] they lurk;
   they watch my steps
   while they wait to take my life.
7 Will they escape in spite of such sin?
   God, bring down the nations in wrath.

8 You yourself have recorded my wanderings.[B]
   Put my tears in your bottle.
   Are they not in your book?
9 Then my enemies will retreat
      on the day when I call.
   This I know: God is for me.

10 In God, whose word I praise,
   in the Lord, whose word I praise,
11 in God I trust; I will not be afraid.
   What can mere humans do to me?

12 I am obligated by vows[C] to you, God;
   I will make my thank offerings to you.
13 For you rescued me from death,
   even my feet from stumbling,
   to walk before God in the light of life.

PRAISE FOR GOD'S PROTECTION

57 *For the choir director: "Do Not Destroy." A Miktam of David.
When he fled before Saul into the cave.*

1 Be gracious to me, God, be gracious to me,
   for I take refuge in you.
   I will seek refuge in the shadow of your wings
   until danger passes.
2 I call to God Most High,
   to God who fulfills his purpose for me.[D]
3 He reaches down from heaven and saves me,
   challenging the one who tramples me.   *Selah*
   God sends his faithful love and truth.
4 I am surrounded by lions;
   I lie down among devouring lions —
   people whose teeth are spears and arrows,

---

whose tongues are sharp swords.
⁵ God, be exalted above the heavens;
let your glory be over the whole earth.
⁶ They prepared a net for my steps;
I was despondent.
They dug a pit ahead of me,
but they fell into it!

Selah

⁷ My heart is confident, God, my heart is confident.
I will sing; I will sing praises.
⁸ Wake up, my soul!
Wake up, harp and lyre!
I will wake up the dawn.
⁹ I will praise you, Lord, among the peoples;
I will sing praises to you among the nations.
¹⁰ For your faithful love is as high as the heavens;
your faithfulness reaches the clouds.
¹¹ God, be exalted above the heavens;
let your glory be over the whole earth.

A CRY AGAINST INJUSTICE

58 For the choir director: "Do Not Destroy."
A Miktam of David.

¹ Do you really speak righteously, you mighty ones?ᴬ
Do you judge people fairly?
² No, you practice injustice in your hearts;
with your hands you weigh out violence
in the land.

³ The wicked go astray from the womb;
liars wander about from birth.
⁴ They have venom like the venom of a snake,
like the deaf cobra that stops up its ears,
⁵ that does not listen to the sound of the charmers
who skillfully weave spells.

⁶ God, knock the teeth out of their mouths;
LORD, tear out the young lions' fangs.
⁷ May they vanish like water that flows by;
may they aim their blunted arrows.ᴮ
⁸ Like a slug that moves along in slime,
like a woman's miscarried child,
may they not see the sun.

⁹ Before your pots can feel the heat of the thorns —
whether green or burning —
he will sweep them away.ᶜ

ᴬ58:1 Or *Can you really speak righteousness in silence?* ᴮ58:7 Hb obscure
ᶜ58:9 Or *thorns, he will sweep it away, whether raw or cooking*

¹⁰ The righteous one will rejoice
    when he sees the retribution;
    he will wash his feet in the blood of the wicked.
¹¹ Then people will say,
    "Yes, there is a reward for the righteous!
    There is a God who judges on earth!"

GOD OUR STRONGHOLD

59 *For the choir director: "Do Not Destroy." A Miktam of David.
When Saul sent agents to watch the house and kill him.*

¹ Rescue me from my enemies, my God;
    protect me from those who rise up against me.
² Rescue me from those who practice sin,
    and save me from men of bloodshed.
³ Because look, LORD, they set an ambush for me.
    Powerful men attack me,
    but not because of any sin or rebellion of mine.
⁴ For no fault of mine,
    they run and take up a position.
    Awake to help me, and take notice.
⁵ LORD God of Armies, you are the God of Israel.
    Rise up to punish all the nations;
    do not show favor to any wicked traitors.   *Selah*

⁶ They return at evening, snarling like dogs
    and prowling around the city.
⁷ Look, they spew from their mouths —
    sharp words from^A their lips.
    "For who," they say, "will hear?"
⁸ But you laugh at them, LORD;
    you ridicule all the nations.
⁹ I will keep watch for you, my^B strength,
    because God is my stronghold.
¹⁰ My faithful God^C will come to meet me;
    God will let me look down on
        my adversaries.

¹¹ Do not kill them; otherwise, my people will forget.
    By your power, make them homeless wanderers
    and bring them down,
    Lord, our shield.
¹² For the sin of their mouths and the words
        of their lips,
    let them be caught in their pride.
    They utter curses and lies.
¹³ Consume them in rage;
    consume them until they are gone.

---

^A59:7 Lit *swords are on*   ^B59:9 Some Hb mss, LXX, Vg, Tg; other Hb mss read *his*
^C59:10 Alt Hb tradition reads *My God in his faithful love*

Then people will know throughout[A] the earth
that God rules over Jacob. *Selah*

14 And they return at evening, snarling like dogs
and prowling around the city.
15 They scavenge for food;
they growl if they are not satisfied.

16 But I will sing of your strength
and will joyfully proclaim
your faithful love in the morning.
For you have been a stronghold for me,
a refuge in my day of trouble.
17 To you, my strength, I sing praises,
because God is my stronghold —
my faithful God.

PRAYER IN DIFFICULT TIMES

60 *For the choir director: according to "The Lily of Testimony."*
A Miktam of David for teaching. When he fought with
Aram-naharaim and Aram-zobah, and Joab returned and struck Edom
in Salt Valley, killing twelve thousand.

1 God, you have rejected us;
you have broken us down;
you have been angry. Restore us![B]
2 You have shaken the land and split it open.
Heal its fissures, for it shudders.
3 You have made your people suffer hardship;
you have given us wine to drink
that made us stagger.
4 You have given a signal flag to those
who fear you,
so that they can flee before the archers.[C] *Selah*
5 Save with your right hand, and answer me,
so that those you love may be rescued.

6 God has spoken in his sanctuary:[D]
"I will celebrate!
I will divide up Shechem.
I will apportion the Valley of Succoth.
7 Gilead is mine, Manasseh is mine,
and Ephraim is my helmet;
Judah is my scepter.
8 Moab is my washbasin.
I throw my sandal on Edom;
I shout in triumph over Philistia."

[A]59:13 Lit *know to the ends of* [B]60:1 Or *Turn back to us* [C]60:4 Or *can rally*
before the archers, or can rally because of the truth [D]60:6 Or *has promised by*
his holy nature

9 Who will bring me to the fortified city?
Who will lead me to Edom?
10 God, haven't you rejected us?
God, you do not march out with our armies.
11 Give us aid against the foe,
for human help is worthless.
12 With God we will perform valiantly;
he will trample our foes.

SECURITY IN GOD

61 For the choir director: on stringed instruments. Of David.

God, hear my cry;
pay attention to my prayer.
2 I call to you from the ends of the earth
when my heart is without strength.
Lead me to a rock that is high above me,
3 for you have been a refuge for me,
a strong tower in the face of the enemy.
4 I will dwell in your tent forever
and take refuge under the shelter of your wings. *Selah*

5 God, you have heard my vows;
you have given a heritage
to those who fear your name.
6 Add days to the king's life;
may his years span many generations.
7 May he sit enthroned before God forever.
Appoint faithful love and truth to guard him.
8 Then I will continually sing of your name,
fulfilling my vows day by day.

TRUST IN GOD ALONE

62 For the choir director: according to Jeduthun.
A psalm of David.

1 I am at rest in God alone;
my salvation comes from him.
2 He alone is my rock and my salvation,
my stronghold; I will never be shaken.

3 How long will you threaten a man?
Will all of you attack[A]
as if he were a leaning wall
or a tottering fence?
4 They only plan to bring him down
from his high position.
They take pleasure in lying;
they bless with their mouths,
but they curse inwardly. *Selah*

[A]62:3 Some Hb mss read *you be struck down*

⁵ Rest in God alone, my soul,
  for my hope comes from him.
⁶ He alone is my rock and my salvation,
  my stronghold; I will not be shaken.
⁷ My salvation and glory depend on God,
  my strong rock.
  My refuge is in God.
⁸ Trust in him at all times, you people;
  pour out your hearts before him.
  God is our refuge.

Selah

⁹ Common people are only a vapor;
  important people, an illusion.
  Together on a scale,
  they weigh less than^A a vapor.
¹⁰ Place no trust in oppression,
   or false hope in robbery.
   If wealth increases,
   don't set your heart on it.

¹¹ God has spoken once;
   I have heard this twice:
   strength belongs to God,
¹² and faithful love belongs to you, Lord.
   For you repay each according to his works.

PRAISE GOD WHO SATISFIES

63 *A psalm of David. When he was in the Wilderness of Judah.*
   God, you are my God; I eagerly seek you.
   I thirst for you;
   my body faints for you
   in a land that is dry, desolate, and without water.
² So I gaze on you in the sanctuary
  to see your strength and your glory.

³ My lips will glorify you
  because your faithful love is better than life.
⁴ So I will bless you as long as I live;
  at your name, I will lift up my hands.
⁵ You satisfy me as with rich food;^B
  my mouth will praise you with joyful lips.

⁶ When I think of you as I lie on my bed,
  I meditate on you during the night watches
⁷ because you are my helper;
  I will rejoice in the shadow of your wings.
⁸ I follow close to you;
  your right hand holds on to me.

---

^A62:9 Lit *they go up more than* ^B63:5 Lit *with fat and fatness*

9 But those who intend to destroy my life
will go into the depths of the earth.

10 They will be given over to the power of the sword;
they will become a meal for jackals.

11 But the king will rejoice in God;
all who swear by him will boast,
for the mouths of liars will be shut.

PROTECTION FROM EVILDOERS

64 For the choir director. A psalm of David.

God, hear my voice when I am in anguish.
Protect my life from the terror of the enemy.

2 Hide me from the scheming of wicked people,
from the mob of evildoers,

3 who sharpen their tongues like swords
and aim bitter words like arrows,

4 shooting from concealed places at the blameless.
They shoot at him suddenly and are not afraid.

5 They adopt[A] an evil plan;
they talk about hiding traps and say,
"Who will see them?"[B]

6 They devise crimes and say,
"We have perfected a secret plan."
The inner man and the heart are mysterious.

7 But God will shoot them with arrows;
suddenly, they will be wounded.

8 They will be made to stumble;
their own tongues work against them.
All who see them will shake their heads.

9 Then everyone will fear
and will tell about God's work,
for they will understand what he has done.

10 The righteous one rejoices in the LORD
and takes refuge in him;
all those who are upright in heart
will offer praise.

GOD'S CARE FOR THE EARTH

65 For the choir director.
A psalm of David. A song.

1 Praise is rightfully yours,[C]
God, in Zion;
vows to you will be fulfilled.

2 All humanity will come to you,
the one who hears prayer.

[A]64:5 Or They strengthen themselves with   [B]64:5 Or it   [C]65:1 Or Praise is
silence to you, or Praise awaits you

³ Iniquities overwhelm me;
only you can atone for our rebellions.
⁴ How happy is the one you choose
and bring near to live in your courts!
We will be satisfied with the goodness
of your house,
the holiness of your temple.ᴬ

⁵ You answer us in righteousness,
with awe-inspiring works,
God of our salvation,
the hope of all the ends of the earth
and of the distant seas.
⁶ You establish the mountains by your power;
you are robed with strength.
⁷ You silence the roar of the seas,
the roar of their waves,
and the tumult of the nations.
⁸ Those who live far away are awed by your signs;
you make east and west shout for joy.

⁹ You visit the earth and water it abundantly,
enriching it greatly.
God's stream is filled with water,
for you prepare the earth in this way,
providing people with grain.
¹⁰ You soften it with showers and bless its growth,
soaking its furrows and leveling its ridges.
¹¹ You crown the year with your goodness;
your carts overflow with plenty.ᴮ
¹² The wilderness pastures overflow,
and the hills are robed with joy.
¹³ The pastures are clothed with flocks
and the valleys covered with grain.
They shout in triumph; indeed, they sing.

PRAISE FOR GOD'S MIGHTY ACTS

66 *For the choir director. A song. A psalm.*
Let the whole earth shout joyfully to God!
² Sing about the glory of his name;
make his praise glorious.
³ Say to God, "How awe-inspiring
are your works!
Your enemies will cringe before you
because of your great strength.
⁴ The whole earth will worship you
and sing praise to you.
They will sing praise to your name."

Selah

ᴬ65:4 Or *house, your holy temple* ᴮ65:11 Lit *your paths drip with fat*

FINDING THE MISSING PIECES

PSALMS 64–66

Growing up, our Easter tradition involved my grandparents enthusiastically stuffing plastic eggs with jellybeans, toys, coins, and the occasional dollar bill. Then, the adults teamed up to hide the eggs, while the kids waited inside, covering our eyes until it was time to begin the hunt.

First, we'd go to all of the usual spots—Papa's shed, under the garden hose, in the carport. Eventually and without fail, we'd end up circled in the yard, counting our loot and realizing how many eggs were still hidden. Despite the practice afforded by this annual ritual, we could never manage to find all the eggs.

As the seasons changed from spring to summer, my grandparents would uncover eggs while doing yard work. They'd bubble wrap them and mail them off to their grandchildren states away. Long after our baskets full of green and yellow grass had been tucked away, we'd gladly receive these Easter treasures via parcel post.

In Greek traditions, Psalm 66 is known as the Psalm of the Resurrection and is often recited on Easter Sunday. As I read the psalmist's words, I can't help but remember popping open a plastic egg and experiencing the joy of finding a treat inside.

The book of Psalms is one of my favorites. Conveniently plopped in the middle of God's story, its writers do not hesitate to say what they're really thinking. It reminds me of the commentary given by my cousins and me as we gathered around our Easter haul.

"Ooh, a quarter!"
"Sweet! Chocolate!"
"Does anybody want my black licorice jelly beans?"

Instead of giggling over coins and candies, the psalmists express a range of reactions to serving an unseen God. Leave it to them to crack open pieces of God's character over and over again, a highlight reel of all He's done and will continue to do.

"Come and see the wonders of God; his acts for humanity are awe-inspiring."

PSALM 66:5

It's the best treasure possible, remembering that the God who parted the Red Sea is the same God who hears our prayers. The God who rules forever by His might will also never turn His faithful love from us.

We, too, get to find the pieces we've been missing, opening God's Word to find that the God who rescues on Easter Sunday is still on the throne Monday morning. May we revel in His faithfulness and proclaim the sweetness of His mercy.

"Come and listen, all who fear God, and I will tell what he has done for me . . . He has not turned away my prayer or turned his faithful love from me."

PSALM 66:16,20

---

⁵ Come and see the wonders of God;
    his acts for humanity[A] are awe-inspiring.
⁶ He turned the sea into dry land,
    and they crossed the river on foot.
    There we rejoiced in him.
⁷ He rules forever by his might;
    he keeps his eye on the nations.
    The rebellious should not exalt themselves.   *Selah*
⁸ Bless our God, you peoples;
    let the sound of his praise be heard.
⁹ He keeps us alive[B]
    and does not allow our feet to slip.

¹⁰ For you, God, tested us;
    you refined us as silver is refined.
¹¹ You lured us into a trap;
    you placed burdens on our backs.
¹² You let men ride over our heads;
    we went through fire and water,
    but you brought us out to abundance.[C]

¹³ I will enter your house with burnt offerings;
    I will pay you my vows
¹⁴ that my lips promised
    and my mouth spoke during my distress.
¹⁵ I will offer you fattened sheep as burnt offerings,
    with the fragrant smoke of rams;
    I will sacrifice bulls with goats.   *Selah*

¹⁶ Come and listen, all who fear God,
    and I will tell what he has done for me.
¹⁷ I cried out to him with my mouth,
    and praise was on my tongue.
¹⁸ If I had been aware of malice in my heart,
    the Lord would not have listened.
¹⁹ However, God has listened;
    he has paid attention to the sound of my prayer.
²⁰ Blessed be God!
    He has not turned away my prayer
    or turned his faithful love from me.

ALL WILL PRAISE GOD

67 *For the choir director: with stringed instruments. A psalm. A song.*
    May God be gracious to us and bless us;
    may he make his face shine upon us   *Selah*
² so that your way may be known on earth,
    your salvation among all nations.

[A]66:5 Or *for the descendants of Adam*   [B]66:9 Lit *He sets our soul in life*
[C]66:12 Or *a place of satisfaction*

3 Let the peoples praise you, God;
  let all the peoples praise you.
4 Let the nations rejoice and shout for joy,
  for you judge the peoples with fairness
  and lead the nations on earth.   *Selah*
5 Let the peoples praise you, God,
  let all the peoples praise you.

6 The earth has produced its harvest;
  God, our God, blesses us.
7 God will bless us,
  and all the ends of the earth will fear him.

GOD'S MAJESTIC POWER

68 For the choir director. A psalm of David. A song.
God arises. His enemies scatter,
  and those who hate him flee from his presence.
2 As smoke is blown away,
  so you blow them away.
  As wax melts before the fire,
  so the wicked are destroyed before God.
3 But the righteous are glad;
  they rejoice before God and celebrate with joy.

4 Sing to God! Sing praises to his name.
  Exalt him who rides on the clouds[A] —
  his name is the LORD[B] — and celebrate before him.
5 God in his holy dwelling is
  a father of the fatherless
  and a champion of widows.
6 God provides homes for those who are deserted.
  He leads out the prisoners to prosperity,[C]
  but the rebellious live in a scorched land.

7 God, when you went out before your people,
  when you marched through the desert,   *Selah*
8 the earth trembled and the skies poured rain
  before God, the God of Sinai,[D]
  before God, the God of Israel.
9 You, God, showered abundant rain;
  you revived your inheritance when it languished.
10 Your people settled in it;
  God, you provided for the poor by your goodness.

11 The Lord gave the command;
  a great company of women brought the good news:
12 "The kings of the armies flee — they flee!"

[A]68:4 Or *rides through the desert* [B]68:4 Hb *Yah* [C]68:6 Or *prisoners with joyous music*; Hb uncertain [D]68:8 Or *God, this one of Sinai*

She who stays at home divides the spoil.

13 While[A] you lie among the sheep pens,[B]
the wings of a dove are covered with silver,
and its feathers with glistening gold.

14 When the Almighty scattered kings in the land,
it snowed on Zalmon.[C]

15 Mount Bashan is God's towering mountain;
Mount Bashan is a mountain of many peaks.

16 Why gaze with envy, you mountain peaks,
at the mountain God desired for his abode?
The Lord will dwell there forever!

17 God's chariots are tens of thousands,
thousands and thousands;
the Lord is among them in the sanctuary[D]
as he was at Sinai.

18 You ascended to the heights, taking away captives;
you received gifts from[E] people,
even from the rebellious,
so that the Lord God might dwell there.[F]

19 Blessed be the Lord!
Day after day he bears our burdens;
God is our salvation.   *Selah*

20 Our God is a God of salvation,
and escape from death belongs to the Lord my Lord.

21 Surely God crushes the heads of his enemies,
the hairy brow of one who goes on in his guilty acts.

22 The Lord said, "I will bring them back from Bashan;
I will bring them back from the depths of the sea

23 so that your foot may wade[G] in blood
and your dogs' tongues may have their share
from the enemies."

24 People have seen your procession, God,
the procession of my God,
my King, in the sanctuary.

25 Singers lead the way,
with musicians following;
among them are young women
playing tambourines.

26 Bless God in the assemblies;
bless the Lord from the fountain of Israel.

27 There is Benjamin, the youngest, leading them,
the rulers of Judah in their assembly,[H]
the rulers of Zebulun, the rulers of Naphtali.

[A]68:13 Or *If*   [B]68:13 Or *the campfires*, or *the saddlebags*; Hb obscure
[C]68:14 Or *Black Mountain*   [D]68:17 Or *in holiness*, also in v. 24   [E]68:18 Lit *among*
[F]68:18 Or *even those rebelling against the Lord God's living there*; Hb obscure
[G]68:23 LXX, Syr read *dip*   [H]68:27 Hb obscure

28 Your God has decreed your strength.
Show your strength, God,
you who have acted on our behalf.
29 Because of your temple at Jerusalem,
kings will bring tribute to you.
30 Rebuke the beast in the reeds,
the herd of bulls with the calves of the peoples.
Trample underfoot those with bars of silver.[A]
Scatter the peoples who take pleasure in war.
31 Ambassadors will come[B] from Egypt;
Cush will stretch out its hands to God.

32 Sing to God, you kingdoms of the earth;
sing praise to the Lord,   *Selah*
33 to him who rides in the ancient, highest heavens.
Look, he thunders with his powerful voice!
34 Ascribe power to God.
His majesty is over Israel,
his power is among the clouds.
35 God, you are awe-inspiring in your sanctuaries.
The God of Israel gives power and strength to his people.
Blessed be God!

A PLEA FOR RESCUE

69

*For the choir director: according to "The Lilies."
Of David.*

1 Save me, God,
for the water has risen to my neck.
2 I have sunk in deep mud, and there is no footing;
I have come into deep water,
and a flood sweeps over me.
3 I am weary from my crying;
my throat is parched.
My eyes fail, looking for my God.
4 Those who hate me without cause
are more numerous than the hairs of my head;
my deceitful enemies, who would destroy me,
are powerful.
Though I did not steal, I must repay.

5 God, you know my foolishness,
and my guilty acts are not hidden from you.
6 Do not let those who put their hope in you
be disgraced because of me,
Lord GOD of Armies;
do not let those who seek you

[A]68:30 Or *peoples, trampling on those who take pleasure in silver, or peoples, trampling on the bars of silver, or peoples, who trample each other for bars of silver*   [B]68:31 Or *They bring red cloth, or They bring bronze*

be humiliated because of me,
God of Israel.
7 For I have endured insults because of you,
and shame has covered my face.
8 I have become a stranger to my brothers
and a foreigner to my mother's sons
9 because zeal for your house has consumed me,
and the insults of those who insult you
have fallen on me.
10 I mourned and fasted,
but it brought me insults.
11 I wore sackcloth as my clothing,
and I was a joke to them.
12 Those who sit at the city gate talk about me,
and drunkards make up songs about me.

13 But as for me, LORD,
my prayer to you is for a time of favor.
In your abundant, faithful love, God,
answer me with your sure salvation.
14 Rescue me from the miry mud; don't let me sink.
Let me be rescued from those who hate me
and from the deep water.
15 Don't let the floodwaters sweep over me
or the deep swallow me up;
don't let the Pit close its mouth over me.
16 Answer me, LORD,
for your faithful love is good.
In keeping with your abundant compassion,
turn to me.
17 Don't hide your face from your servant,
for I am in distress.
Answer me quickly!
18 Come near to me and redeem me;
ransom me because of my enemies.

19 You know the insults I endure —
my shame and disgrace.
You are aware of all my adversaries.
20 Insults have broken my heart,
and I am in despair.
I waited for sympathy,
but there was none;
for comforters, but found no one.
21 Instead, they gave me gall for my food,
and for my thirst
they gave me vinegar to drink.

22 Let their table set before them be a snare,
and let it be a trap for their allies.

23 Let their eyes grow too dim to see,
   and let their hips continually quake.
24 Pour out your rage on them,
   and let your burning anger overtake them.
25 Make their fortification desolate;
   may no one live in their tents.
26 For they persecute the one you struck
   and talk about the pain of those you wounded.
27 Charge them with crime on top of crime;
   do not let them share in your righteousness.
28 Let them be erased from the book of life
   and not be recorded with the righteous.

29 But as for me — poor and in pain —
   let your salvation protect me, God.
30 I will praise God's name with song
   and exalt him with thanksgiving.
31 That will please the LORD more than an ox,
   more than a bull with horns and hooves.
32 The humble will see it and rejoice.
   You who seek God, take heart!
33 For the LORD listens to the needy
   and does not despise
   his own who are prisoners.

34 Let heaven and earth praise him,
   the seas and everything that moves in them,
35 for God will save Zion
   and build up^A the cities of Judah.
   They will live there and possess it.
36 The descendants of his servants will inherit it,
   and those who love his name will live in it.

A CALL FOR DELIVERANCE

70 For the choir director. Of David. To bring remembrance.
God, hurry to rescue me.
LORD, hurry to help me!

2 Let those who seek to kill me
   be disgraced and confounded;
   let those who wish me harm
   be turned back and humiliated.
3 Let those who say, "Aha, aha!"
   retreat because of their shame.

4 Let all who seek you rejoice and be glad in you;
   let those who love your salvation
   continually say, "God is great!"

---

^A69:35 Or and rebuild

⁵ I am oppressed and needy;
hurry to me, God.
You are my help and my deliverer;
LORD, do not delay.

GOD'S HELP IN OLD AGE

71 LORD, I seek refuge in you;
let me never be disgraced.

² In your justice, rescue and deliver me;
listen closely to me and save me.

³ Be a rock of refuge for me,
where I can always go.
Give the command to save me,
for you are my rock and fortress.

⁴ Deliver me, my God, from the power of the wicked,
from the grasp of the unjust and oppressive.

⁵ For you are my hope, Lord GOD,
my confidence from my youth.

⁶ I have leaned on you from birth;
you took me from my mother's womb.
My praise is always about you.

⁷ I am like a miraculous sign to many,
and you are my strong refuge.

⁸ My mouth is full of praise
and honor to you all day long.

⁹ Don't discard me in my old age.
As my strength fails, do not abandon me.

¹⁰ For my enemies talk about me,
and those who spy on me plot together,

¹¹ saying, "God has abandoned him;
chase him and catch him,
for there is no one to rescue him."

¹² God, do not be far from me;
my God, hurry to help me.

¹³ May my adversaries be disgraced and destroyed;
may those who intend to harm me
be covered with disgrace and humiliation.

¹⁴ But I will hope continually
and will praise you more and more.

¹⁵ My mouth will tell about your righteousness
and your salvation all day long,
though I cannot sum them up.

¹⁶ I come because of the mighty acts of the Lord GOD;
I will proclaim your righteousness, yours alone.

¹⁷ God, you have taught me from my youth,
and I still proclaim your wondrous works.

¹⁸ Even while I am old and gray,
God, do not abandon me,

while I proclaim your power
to another generation,
your strength to all who are to come.

19 Your righteousness reaches the heights, God,
you who have done great things;
God, who is like you?

20 You caused me to experience
many troubles and misfortunes,
but you will revive me again.
You will bring me up again,
even from the depths of the earth.

21 You will increase my honor
and comfort me once again.

22 Therefore, I will praise you with a harp
for your faithfulness, my God;
I will sing to you with a lyre,
Holy One of Israel.

23 My lips will shout for joy
when I sing praise to you
because you have redeemed me.

24 Therefore, my tongue will proclaim
your righteousness all day long,
for those who intend to harm me
will be disgraced and confounded.

A PRAYER FOR THE KING

72

Of Solomon.

God, give your justice to the king
and your righteousness to the king's son.

2 He will judge your people with righteousness
and your afflicted ones with justice.

3 May the mountains bring well-being^A to the people
and the hills, righteousness.

4 May he vindicate the afflicted among the people,
help the poor,
and crush the oppressor.

5 May they fear you^B while the sun endures
and as long as the moon, throughout all generations.

6 May the king be like rain that falls on the cut grass,
like spring showers that water the earth.

7 May the righteous^C flourish in his days
and well-being abound
until the moon is no more.

8 May he rule from sea to sea
and from the Euphrates

---

^A 72:3 Or peace, also in v. 7   ^B 72:5 LXX reads May he continue   ^C 72:7 Some
Hb mss, LXX, Syr, Jer read May righteousness

to the ends of the earth.
⁹ May desert tribes kneel before him
and his enemies lick the dust.
¹⁰ May the kings of Tarshish
and the coasts and islands bring tribute,
the kings of Sheba and Seba offer gifts.
¹¹ Let all kings bow in homage to him,
all nations serve him.

¹² For he will rescue the poor who cry out
and the afflicted who have no helper.
¹³ He will have pity on the poor and helpless
and save the lives of the poor.
¹⁴ He will redeem them from oppression and violence,
for their lives are ᴬ precious ᴮ in his sight.

¹⁵ May he live long!
May gold from Sheba be given to him.
May prayer be offered for him continually,
and may he be blessed all day long.
¹⁶ May there be plenty of grain in the land;
may it wave on the tops of the mountains.
May its crops be like Lebanon.
May people flourish in the cities
like the grass of the field.
¹⁷ May his name endure forever;
as long as the sun shines,
may his fame increase.
May all nations be blessed by him
and call him blessed.

¹⁸ Blessed be the LORD God, the God of Israel,
who alone does wonders.
¹⁹ Blessed be his glorious name forever;
the whole earth is filled with his glory.
Amen and amen.
²⁰ The prayers of David son of Jesse are concluded.

BOOK III (Psalms 73–89)

GOD'S WAYS VINDICATED

73 *A psalm of Asaph.*
God is indeed good to Israel,
to the pure in heart.
² But as for me, my feet almost slipped;
my steps nearly went astray.
³ For I envied the arrogant;
I saw the prosperity of the wicked.

ᴬ72:14 Lit *their blood is*   ᴮ72:14 Or *valuable*

4 They have an easy time until they die,[A]
and their bodies are well fed.[B]

5 They are not in trouble like others;
they are not afflicted like most people.

6 Therefore, pride is their necklace,
and violence covers them like a garment.

7 Their eyes bulge out from fatness;
the imaginations of their hearts run wild.

8 They mock, and they speak maliciously;
they arrogantly threaten oppression.

9 They set their mouths against heaven,
and their tongues strut across the earth.

10 Therefore his people turn to them[C]
and drink in their overflowing words.[D]

11 The wicked say, "How can God know?
Does the Most High know everything?"

12 Look at them — the wicked!
They are always at ease,
and they increase their wealth.

13 Did I purify my heart
and wash my hands in innocence for nothing?

14 For I am afflicted all day long
and punished every morning.

15 If I had decided to say these things aloud,
I would have betrayed your people.[E]

16 When I tried to understand all this,
it seemed hopeless[F]

17 until I entered God's sanctuary.
Then I understood their destiny.

18 Indeed, you put them in slippery places;
you make them fall into ruin.

19 How suddenly they become a desolation!
They come to an end, swept away by terrors.

20 Like one waking from a dream,
Lord, when arising, you will despise their image.

21 When I became embittered
and my innermost being[G] was wounded,

22 I was stupid and didn't understand;
I was an unthinking animal toward you.

23 Yet I am always with you;
you hold my right hand.

24 You guide me with your counsel,
and afterward you will take me up in glory.[H]

[A]73:4 Lit For there are no pangs to their death [B]73:4 Lit fat [C]73:10 Lit turn here [D]73:10 Lit and waters of fullness are drained by them [E]73:15 Lit betrayed the generation of your sons [F]73:16 Lit it was trouble in my eyes [G]73:21 Lit my kidneys [H]73:24 Or will receive me with honor

²⁵ Who do I have in heaven but you?
   And I desire nothing on earth but you.
²⁶ My flesh and my heart may fail,
   but God is the strength^A of my heart,
   my portion forever.
²⁷ Those far from you will certainly perish;
   you destroy all who are unfaithful to you.
²⁸ But as for me, God's presence is my good.
   I have made the Lord GOD my refuge,
   so I can tell about all you do.

PRAYER FOR ISRAEL

74

A Maskil *of Asaph.*

Why have you rejected us forever, God?
Why does your anger burn
   against the sheep of your pasture?
² Remember your congregation,
   which you purchased long ago
   and redeemed as the tribe for your own possession.
   Remember Mount Zion where you dwell.
³ Make your way^B to the perpetual ruins,
   to all that the enemy has destroyed in the sanctuary.
⁴ Your adversaries roared in the meeting place
   where you met with us.^C
   They set up their emblems as signs.
⁵ It was like men in a thicket of trees,
   wielding axes,
⁶ then smashing all the carvings
   with hatchets and picks.
⁷ They set your sanctuary on fire;
   they utterly^D desecrated
   the dwelling place of your name.
⁸ They said in their hearts,
   "Let us oppress them relentlessly."
   They burned every place throughout the land
   where God met with us.^E
⁹ There are no signs for us to see.
   There is no longer a prophet.
   And none of us knows how long this will last.
¹⁰ God, how long will the enemy mock?
   Will the foe insult your name forever?
¹¹ Why do you hold back your hand?
   Stretch out^F your right hand and destroy them!

¹² God my King is from ancient times,
   performing saving acts on the earth.

---

^A73:26 Lit rock   ^B74:3 Lit *Lift up your steps*   ^C74:4 Lit *in your meeting place*
^D74:7 Lit *they to the ground*   ^E74:8 Lit *every meeting place of God in the land*
^F74:11 Lit *From your bosom*

13 You divided the sea with your strength;
   you smashed the heads of the sea monsters in the water;
14 you crushed the heads of Leviathan;
   you fed him to the creatures of the desert.
15 You opened up springs and streams;
   you dried up ever-flowing rivers.
16 The day is yours, also the night;
   you established the moon and the sun.
17 You set all the boundaries of the earth;
   you made summer and winter.

18 Remember this: the enemy has mocked the LORD,
   and a foolish people has insulted your name.
19 Do not give to beasts the life of your dove;[A]
   do not forget the lives of your poor people forever.
20 Consider the covenant,
   for the dark places of the land are full of violence.
21 Do not let the oppressed turn away in shame;
   let the poor and needy praise your name.
22 Rise up, God, champion your cause!
   Remember the insults
   that fools bring against you all day long.
23 Do not forget the clamor of your adversaries,
   the tumult of your opponents that goes up
      constantly.

GOD JUDGES THE WICKED

75

For the choir director: "Do Not Destroy."
A psalm of Asaph. A song.

1 We give thanks to you, God;
   we give thanks to you, for your name is near.
   People tell about your wondrous works.

2 "When I choose a time,
   I will judge fairly.
3 When the earth and all its inhabitants shake,
   I am the one who steadies its pillars.   *Selah*
4 I say to the boastful, 'Do not boast,'
   and to the wicked, 'Do not lift up your horn.
5 Do not lift up your horn against heaven[B]
   or speak arrogantly.'"

6 Exaltation does not come
   from the east, the west, or the desert,
7 for God is the Judge:
   He brings down one and exalts another.
8 For there is a cup in the LORD's hand,

[A]74:19 One Hb ms, LXX, Syr read *life that praises you*   [B]75:5 Lit *horn to the height*

full of wine blended with spices,
and he pours from it.
All the wicked of the earth will drink,
draining it to the dregs.

⁹ As for me, I will tell about him forever;
I will sing praise to the God of Jacob.

¹⁰ "I will cut off all the horns of the wicked,
but the horns of the righteous
will be lifted up."

GOD, THE POWERFUL JUDGE

76 *For the choir director: with stringed instruments.
A psalm of Asaph. A song.*

¹ God is known in Judah;
his name is great in Israel.
² His tent is in Salem,
his dwelling place in Zion.
³ There he shatters the bow's flaming arrows,
the shield, the sword,
and the weapons of war. *Selah*

⁴ You are resplendent and majestic
coming down from the mountains of prey.
⁵ The brave-hearted have been plundered;
they have slipped into their final sleep.
None of the warriors was able to lift a hand.
⁶ At your rebuke, God of Jacob,
both chariot and horse lay still.

⁷ And you — you are to be feared.ᴬ
When you are angry,
who can stand before you?
⁸ From heaven you pronounced judgment.
The earth feared and grew quiet
⁹ when God rose up to judge
and to save all the lowly of the earth. *Selah*
¹⁰ Even human wrath will praise you;
you will clothe yourself
with the wrath that remains.ᴮ

¹¹ Make and keep your vows
to the LORD your God;
let all who are around him bring tribute
to the awe-inspiring one.ᶜ
¹² He humbles the spirit of leaders;
he is feared by the kings of the earth.

ᴬ76:7 Or *are awe-inspiring* ᴮ76:10 Hb obscure ᶜ76:11 Or *tribute with awe*

CONFIDENCE IN A TIME OF CRISIS

77 *For the choir director: according to Jeduthun. Of Asaph. A psalm.*
    I cry aloud to God,
    aloud to God, and he will hear me.

2   I sought the Lord in my day of trouble.
    My hands were continually lifted up
    all night long;
    I refused to be comforted.
3   I think of God; I groan;
    I meditate; my spirit becomes weak.   *Selah*

4   You have kept me from closing my eyes;
    I am troubled and cannot speak.
5   I consider days of old,
    years long past.
6   At night I remember my music;
    I meditate in my heart, and my spirit ponders.

7   "Will the Lord reject forever
    and never again show favor?
8   Has his faithful love ceased forever?
    Is his promise at an end for all generations?
9   Has God forgotten to be gracious?
    Has he in anger withheld his compassion?"   *Selah*

10 So I say, "I am grieved
    that the right hand of the Most High has changed."ᴬ
11 I will remember the LORD's works;
    yes, I will remember your ancient wonders.
12 I will reflect on all you have done
    and meditate on your actions.

13 God, your way is holy.
    What god is great like God?
14 You are the God who works wonders;
    you revealed your strength among the peoples.
15 With power you redeemed your people,
    the descendants of Jacob and Joseph.   *Selah*

16 The water saw you, God.
    The water saw you; it trembled.
    Even the depths shook.
17 The clouds poured down water.
    The storm clouds thundered;
    your arrows flashed back and forth.
18 The sound of your thunder was in the whirlwind;
    lightning lit up the world.
    The earth shook and quaked.

ᴬ77:10 Hb obscure

19 Your way went through the sea
and your path through the vast water,
but your footprints were unseen.
20 You led your people like a flock
by the hand of Moses and Aaron.

LESSONS FROM ISRAEL'S PAST

78 A Maskil of Asaph.

My people, hear my instruction;
listen to the words from my mouth.
2 I will declare wise sayings;
I will speak mysteries from the past —
3 things we have heard and known
and that our fathers have passed down to us.
4 We will not hide them from their children,
but will tell a future generation
the praiseworthy acts of the Lord,
his might, and the wondrous works
he has performed.
5 He established a testimony in Jacob
and set up a law in Israel,
which he commanded our fathers
to teach to their children
6 so that a future generation —
children yet to be born — might know.
They were to rise and tell their children
7 so that they might put their confidence in God
and not forget God's works,
but keep his commands.
8 Then they would not be like their fathers,
a stubborn and rebellious generation,
a generation whose heart was not loyal
and whose spirit was not faithful to God.

9 The Ephraimite archers turned back
on the day of battle.
10 They did not keep God's covenant
and refused to live by his law.
11 They forgot what he had done,
the wondrous works he had shown them.
12 He worked wonders in the sight of their fathers
in the land of Egypt, the territory of Zoan.
13 He split the sea and brought them across;
the water stood firm like a wall.
14 He led them with a cloud by day
and with a fiery light throughout the night.
15 He split rocks in the wilderness
and gave them drink as abundant as the depths.
16 He brought streams out of the stone
and made water flow down like rivers.

17 But they continued to sin against him,
   rebelling in the desert against the Most High.
18 They deliberately[A] tested God,
   demanding the food they craved.
19 They spoke against God, saying,
   "Is God able to provide food in the wilderness?
20 Look! He struck the rock and water gushed out;
   torrents overflowed.
   But can he also provide bread
   or furnish meat for his people?"
21 Therefore, the LORD heard and became furious;
   then fire broke out against Jacob,
   and anger flared up against Israel
22 because they did not believe God
   or rely on his salvation.
23 He gave a command to the clouds above
   and opened the doors of heaven.
24 He rained manna for them to eat;
   he gave them grain from heaven.
25 People[B] ate the bread of angels.[C]
   He sent them an abundant supply of food.
26 He made the east wind blow in the skies
   and drove the south wind by his might.
27 He rained meat on them like dust,
   and winged birds like the sand of the seas.
28 He made them fall in the camp,
   all around the tents.
29 The people ate and were completely satisfied,
   for he gave them what they craved.
30 Before they had turned from what they craved,
   while the food was still in their mouths,
31 God's anger flared up against them,
   and he killed some of their best men.
   He struck down Israel's fit young men.

32 Despite all this, they kept sinning
   and did not believe his wondrous works.
33 He made their days end in futility,
   their years in sudden disaster.
34 When he killed some of them,
   the rest began to seek him;
   they repented and searched for God.
35 They remembered that God was their rock,
   the Most High God, their Redeemer.
36 But they deceived him with their mouths,
   they lied to him with their tongues,
37 their hearts were insincere toward him,
   and they were unfaithful to his covenant.

[A]78:18 Lit *in their heart* [B]78:25 Lit *Man* [C]78:25 Lit *mighty ones*

³⁸ Yet he was compassionate;
he atoned for their iniquity
and did not destroy them.
He often turned his anger aside
and did not unleash^A all his wrath.

³⁹ He remembered that they were only flesh,
a wind that passes and does not return.

⁴⁰ How often they rebelled against him
in the wilderness
and grieved him in the desert.

⁴¹ They constantly tested God
and provoked the Holy One of Israel.

⁴² They did not remember his power shown
on the day he redeemed them from the foe,

⁴³ when he performed his miraculous signs in Egypt
and his wonders in the territory of Zoan.

⁴⁴ He turned their rivers into blood,
and they could not drink from their streams.

⁴⁵ He sent among them swarms of flies,
which fed on them,
and frogs, which devastated them.

⁴⁶ He gave their crops to the caterpillar
and the fruit of their labor to the locust.

⁴⁷ He killed their vines with hail
and their sycamore fig trees with a flood.

⁴⁸ He handed over their livestock to hail
and their cattle to lightning bolts.

⁴⁹ He sent his burning anger against them:
fury, indignation, and calamity —
a band of deadly messengers.^B

⁵⁰ He cleared a path for his anger.
He did not spare them from death
but delivered their lives to the plague.

⁵¹ He struck all the firstborn in Egypt,
the first progeny of the tents of Ham.

⁵² He led his people out like sheep
and guided them like a flock in the wilderness.

⁵³ He led them safely, and they were not afraid;
but the sea covered their enemies.

⁵⁴ He brought them to his holy territory,
to the mountain his right hand acquired.

⁵⁵ He drove out nations before them.
He apportioned their inheritance by lot
and settled the tribes of Israel in their tents.

⁵⁶ But they rebelliously tested the Most High God,
for they did not keep his decrees.

---

^A78:38 Or *stir up*   ^B78:49 Or *angels*

57 They treacherously turned away like their fathers;
   they became warped like a faulty bow.
58 They enraged him with their high places
   and provoked his jealousy
      with their carved images.
59 God heard and became furious;
   he completely rejected Israel.
60 He abandoned the tabernacle at Shiloh,
   the tent where he resided among mankind.
61 He gave up his strength to captivity
   and his splendor to the hand of a foe.
62 He surrendered his people to the sword
   because he was enraged with his heritage.
63 Fire consumed his chosen young men,
   and his young women had no wedding songs. [A]
64 His priests fell by the sword,
   and the widows could not lament.

65 The Lord awoke as if from sleep,
   like a warrior from the effects of wine.
66 He beat back his foes;
   he gave them lasting disgrace.
67 He rejected the tent of Joseph
   and did not choose the tribe of Ephraim.
68 He chose instead the tribe of Judah,
   Mount Zion, which he loved.
69 He built his sanctuary like the heights,
   like the earth that he established forever.
70 He chose David his servant
   and took him from the sheep pens;
71 he brought him from tending ewes
   to be shepherd over his people Jacob —
   over Israel, his inheritance.
72 He shepherded them with a pure heart
   and guided them with his skillful hands.

FAITH AMID CONFUSION

79

A psalm of Asaph.

God, the nations have invaded your inheritance,
   desecrated your holy temple,
   and turned Jerusalem into ruins.
2 They gave the corpses of your servants
   to the birds of the sky for food,
   the flesh of your faithful ones
   to the beasts of the earth.
3 They poured out their blood
   like water all around Jerusalem,
   and there was no one to bury them.

[A] 78:63 Lit *virgins were not praised*

⁴ We have become an object of reproach
   to our neighbors,
   a source of mockery and ridicule
   to those around us.

⁵ How long, LORD? Will you be angry forever?
   Will your jealousy keep burning like fire?
⁶ Pour out your wrath on the nations
   that don't acknowledge you,
   on the kingdoms that don't call on your name,
⁷ for they have devoured Jacob
   and devastated his homeland.
⁸ Do not hold past iniquities ᴬ against us;
   let your compassion come to us quickly,
   for we have become very weak.

⁹ God of our salvation, help us —
   for the glory of your name.
   Rescue us and atone for our sins,
   for your name's sake.
¹⁰ Why should the nations ask,
   "Where is their God?"
   Before our eyes,
   let vengeance for the shed blood of your servants
   be known among the nations.
¹¹ Let the groans of the prisoners reach you;
   according to your great power,
   preserve those condemned to die.

¹² Pay back sevenfold to our neighbors
   the reproach they have hurled at you, Lord.
¹³ Then we, your people, the sheep of your pasture,
   will thank you forever;
   we will declare your praise
   to generation after generation.

A PRAYER FOR RESTORATION

80 *For the choir director: according to "The Lilies."*
A testimony of Asaph. A psalm.

¹ Listen, Shepherd of Israel,
   who leads Joseph like a flock;
   you who sit enthroned between the cherubim,
   shine ² on Ephraim,
   Benjamin, and Manasseh.
   Rally your power and come to save us.
³ Restore us, God;
   make your face shine on us,
   so that we may be saved.

ᴬ79:8 Or *hold the sins of past generations*

4 Lord God of Armies,
   how long will you be angry
   with your people's prayers?
5 You fed them the bread of tears
   and gave them a full measure^A
   of tears to drink.
6 You put us at odds with our neighbors;
   our enemies mock us.
7 Restore us, God of Armies;
   make your face shine on us, so that we may be saved.

8 You dug up a vine from Egypt;
   you drove out the nations and planted it.
9 You cleared a place for it;
   it took root and filled the land.
10 The mountains were covered by its shade,
   and the mighty cedars^B with its branches.
11 It sent out sprouts toward the Sea^C
   and shoots toward the River.^D

12 Why have you broken down its walls
   so that all who pass by pick its fruit?
13 Boars from the forest tear at it
   and creatures of the field feed on it.
14 Return, God of Armies.
   Look down from heaven and see;
   take care of this vine,
15 the root^E your right hand planted,
   the son^F that you made strong for yourself.
16 It was cut down and burned;
   they^G perish at the rebuke of your countenance.
17 Let your hand be with the man at your right hand,
   with the son of man
   you have made strong for yourself.
18 Then we will not turn away from you;
   revive us, and we will call on your name.
19 Restore us, Lord, God of Armies;
   make your face shine on us,
      so that we may be saved.

A CALL TO OBEDIENCE

81 *For the choir director: on the* Gittith. *Of Asaph.*

   Sing for joy to God our strength;
   shout in triumph to the God of Jacob.
2 Lift up a song — play the tambourine,
   the melodious lyre, and the harp.

---

^A80:5 Lit *a one-third measure*   ^B80:10 Lit *the cedars of God*   ^C80:11 = the
Mediterranean   ^D80:11 = the Euphrates   ^E80:15 Hb obscure   ^F80:15 Or *shoot*
^G80:16 Or *may they*

³ Blow the horn on the day of our feasts^A
during the new moon
and during the full moon.
⁴ For this is a statute for Israel,
an ordinance of the God of Jacob.
⁵ He set it up as a decree for Joseph
when he went throughout^B the land of Egypt.

I heard an unfamiliar language:
⁶ "I relieved his shoulder from the burden;
his hands were freed from carrying the basket.
⁷ You called out in distress, and I rescued you;
I answered you from the thundercloud.
I tested you at the Waters of Meribah.   *Selah*
⁸ Listen, my people, and I will admonish you.
Israel, if you would only listen to me!
⁹ There must not be a strange god among you;
you must not bow down to a foreign god.
¹⁰ I am the LORD your God,
who brought you up from the land of Egypt.
Open your mouth wide, and I will fill it.

¹¹ "But my people did not listen to my voice;
Israel did not obey me.
¹² So I gave them over to their stubborn hearts
to follow their own plans.
¹³ If only my people would listen to me
and Israel would follow my ways,
¹⁴ I would quickly subdue their enemies
and turn my hand against their foes."
¹⁵ Those who hate the LORD
would cower to him;
their doom would last forever.
¹⁶ But he would feed Israel^C with the best wheat.
"I would satisfy you with honey from the rock."

A PLEA FOR RIGHTEOUS JUDGMENT

82 *A psalm of Asaph.*
God stands in the divine assembly;
he pronounces judgment among the gods:^D
² "How long will you judge unjustly
and show partiality to the wicked?   *Selah*
³ Provide justice for the needy and the fatherless;
uphold the rights of the oppressed
and the destitute.
⁴ Rescue the poor and needy;
save them from the power of the wicked."

---

^A81:3 Lit *feast*   ^B81:5 Or *went out against*   ^C81:16 Lit *him*   ^D82:1 Or *the heavenly beings,* or *the earthly rulers;* Hb *elohim*

5 They do not know or understand;
they wander in darkness.
All the foundations of the earth are shaken.

6 I said, "You are gods;
you are all sons of the Most High.
7 However, you will die like humans
and fall like any other ruler."

8 Rise up, God, judge the earth,
for all the nations belong to you.

PRAYER AGAINST ENEMIES

83
A song. A psalm of Asaph.
God, do not keep silent.
Do not be deaf, God; do not be quiet.
2 See how your enemies make an uproar;
those who hate you have acted arrogantly.^A
3 They devise clever schemes against your people;
they conspire against your treasured ones.
4 They say, "Come, let us wipe them out as a nation
so that Israel's name will no longer be remembered."
5 For they have conspired with one mind;
they form an alliance^B against you —
6 the tents of Edom and the Ishmaelites,
Moab and the Hagrites,
7 Gebal, Ammon, and Amalek,
Philistia with the inhabitants of Tyre.
8 Even Assyria has joined them;
they lend support^C to the sons of Lot.^D   *Selah*

9 Deal with them as you did with Midian,
as you did with Sisera
and Jabin at the Kishon River.
10 They were destroyed at En-dor;
they became manure for the ground.
11 Make their nobles like Oreb and Zeeb,
and all their tribal leaders like Zebah and Zalmunna,
12 who said, "Let us seize God's pastures for ourselves."

13 Make them like tumbleweed, my God,
like straw before the wind.
14 As fire burns a forest,
as a flame blazes through mountains,
15 so pursue them with your tempest
and terrify them with your storm.
16 Cover their faces with shame

---

^A 83:2 Lit *have lifted their head*   ^B 83:5 Lit *they cut a covenant*   ^C 83:8 Lit *they are an arm*   ^D 83:8 = Moab and Ammon so that they will seek your name, LORD.

17 Let them be put to shame and terrified forever;
   let them perish in disgrace.
18 May they know that you alone —
   whose name is the LORD —
   are the Most High over the whole earth.

LONGING FOR GOD'S HOUSE

84 *For the choir director: on the* Gittith.
A psalm of the sons of Korah.

1 How lovely is your dwelling place,
   LORD of Armies.
2 I long and yearn
   for the courts of the LORD;
   my heart and flesh cry out for[A] the living God.

3 Even a sparrow finds a home,
   and a swallow, a nest for herself
   where she places her young —
   near your altars, LORD of Armies,
   my King and my God.
4 How happy are those who reside in your house,
   who praise you continually.   *Selah*

5 Happy are the people whose strength is in you,
   whose hearts are set on pilgrimage.
6 As they pass through the Valley of Baca,[B]
   they make it a source of spring water;
   even the autumn rain will cover it with blessings.[C]
7 They go from strength to strength;
   each appears before God in Zion.

8 LORD God of Armies, hear my prayer;
   listen, God of Jacob.   *Selah*
9 Consider our shield,[D] God;
   look on the face of your anointed one.

10 Better a day in your courts
   than a thousand anywhere else.
   I would rather stand at the threshold of the house of my God
   than live in the tents of wicked people.
11 For the LORD God is a sun and shield.
   The LORD grants favor and honor;
   he does not withhold the good
   from those who live with integrity.
12 Happy is the person who trusts in you,
   LORD of Armies!

A 84:2 Or *flesh shout for joy to*   B 84:6 Or *Valley of Tears*   C 84:6 Or *pools*
D 84:9 = the king

RESTORATION OF FAVOR

85

For the choir director. A psalm of the sons of Korah.

LORD, you showed favor to your land;
you restored the fortunes of Jacob.^A

2   You forgave your people's guilt;
you covered all their sin.   *Selah*

3   You withdrew all your fury;
you turned from your burning anger.

4   Return to us, God of our salvation,
and abandon your displeasure with us.

5   Will you be angry with us forever?
Will you prolong your anger for all generations?

6   Will you not revive us again
so that your people may rejoice in you?

7   Show us your faithful love, LORD,
and give us your salvation.

8   I will listen to what God will say;
surely the LORD will declare peace
to his people, his faithful ones,
and not let them go back to foolish ways.

9   His salvation is very near those who fear him,
so that glory may dwell in our land.

10 Faithful love and truth will join together;
righteousness and peace will embrace.

11 Truth will spring up from the earth,
and righteousness will look down from heaven.

12 Also, the LORD will provide what is good,
and our land will yield its crops.

13 Righteousness will go before him
to prepare the way for his steps.

LAMENT AND PETITION

86

A prayer of David.

Listen, LORD, and answer me,
for I am poor and needy.

2   Protect my life, for I am faithful.
You are my God; save your servant who trusts in you.

3   Be gracious to me, Lord,
for I call to you all day long.

4   Bring joy to your servant's life,
because I appeal to you, Lord.

5   For you, Lord, are kind and ready to forgive,
abounding in faithful love to all who call on you.

6   LORD, hear my prayer;

---

^A 85:1 Or *restored Jacob from captivity*

listen to my plea for mercy.
⁷ I call on you in the day of my distress,
for you will answer me.

⁸ Lord, there is no one like you among the gods,
and there are no works like yours.
⁹ All the nations you have made
will come and bow down before you, Lord,
and will honor your name.
¹⁰ For you are great and perform wonders;
you alone are God.

¹¹ Teach me your way, LORD,
and I will live by your truth.
Give me an undivided mind to fear your name.
¹² I will praise you with all my heart, Lord my God,
and will honor your name forever.
¹³ For your faithful love for me is great,
and you rescue my life from the depths of Sheol.

¹⁴ God, arrogant people have attacked me;
a gang of ruthless men intends to kill me.
They do not let you guide them.ᴬ
¹⁵ But you, Lord, are a compassionate and gracious God,
slow to anger and abounding in faithful love and truth.
¹⁶ Turn to me and be gracious to me.
Give your strength to your servant;
save the son of your female servant.
¹⁷ Show me a sign of your goodness;
my enemies will see and be put to shame
because you, LORD, have helped and comforted me.

ZION, THE CITY OF GOD

87 *A psalm of the sons of Korah. A song.*
The city he foundedᴮ is on the holy mountains.
² The LORD loves Zion's city gates
more than all the dwellings of Jacob.
³ Glorious things are said about you,
city of God. *Selah*

⁴ "I will make a record of those who know me:
Rahab, Babylon, Philistia, Tyre, and Cush —
each one was born there."
⁵ And it will be said of Zion,
"This one and that one were born in her."
The Most High himself will establish her.
⁶ When he registers the peoples,
the LORD will record,

ᴬ86:14 Lit *They do not set you in front of them* ᴮ87:1 Lit *His foundation*

"This one was born there." *Selah*

7 Singers and dancers[A] alike will say,[B]
"My whole source of joy is[C] in you."

A CRY OF DESPERATION

88 *A song. A psalm of the sons of Korah. For the choir director: according to Mahalath Leannoth. A Maskil of Heman the Ezrahite.*

1 LORD, God of my salvation,
I cry out before you day and night.
2 May my prayer reach your presence;
listen to my cry.

3 For I have had enough troubles,
and my life is near Sheol.
4 I am counted among those going down to the Pit.
I am like a man without strength,
5 abandoned[D] among the dead.
I am like the slain lying in the grave,
whom you no longer remember,
and who are cut off from your care.[E]

6 You have put me in the lowest part of the Pit,
in the darkest places, in the depths.
7 Your wrath weighs heavily on me;
you have overwhelmed me with all your waves. *Selah*
8 You have distanced my friends from me;
you have made me repulsive to them.
I am shut in and cannot go out.
9 My eyes are worn out from crying.
LORD, I cry out to you all day long;
I spread out my hands to you.

10 Do you work wonders for the dead?
Do departed spirits rise up to praise you? *Selah*
11 Will your faithful love be declared in the grave,
your faithfulness in Abaddon?
12 Will your wonders be known in the darkness
or your righteousness in the land of oblivion?

13 But I call to you for help, LORD;
in the morning my prayer meets you.
14 LORD, why do you reject me?
Why do you hide your face from me?
15 From my youth,
I have been suffering and near death.
I suffer your horrors; I am desperate.
16 Your wrath sweeps over me;

[A]87:7 Or *musicians* [B]87:7 Or *As they dance they will sing* [C]87:7 Lit *"All my springs, are* [D]88:5 Or *set free* [E]88:5 Or *hand*

your terrors destroy me.
17 They surround me like water all day long;
they close in on me from every side.
18 You have distanced loved one and neighbor from me;
darkness is my only friend.^A

PERPLEXITY ABOUT GOD'S PROMISES

89 A Maskil *of Ethan the Ezrahite.*

I will sing about the LORD's faithful love forever;
I will proclaim your faithfulness to all generations
with my mouth.
2 For I will declare,
"Faithful love is built up forever;
you establish your faithfulness in the heavens."

3 The LORD said,
"I have made a covenant with my chosen one;
I have sworn an oath to David my servant:
4 'I will establish your offspring forever
and build up your throne for all generations.'" *Selah*

5 LORD, the heavens praise your wonders —
your faithfulness also —
in the assembly of the holy ones.
6 For who in the skies can compare with the LORD?
Who among the heavenly beings^B is like the LORD?
7 God is greatly feared in the council of the holy ones,
more awe-inspiring than^C all who surround him.
8 LORD God of Armies,
who is strong like you, LORD?
Your faithfulness surrounds you.
9 You rule the raging sea;
when its waves surge, you still them.
10 You crushed Rahab like one who is slain;
you scattered your enemies with your powerful arm.
11 The heavens are yours; the earth also is yours.
The world and everything in it — you founded them.
12 North and south — you created them.
Tabor and Hermon shout for joy at your name.
13 You have a mighty arm;
your hand is powerful;
your right hand is lifted high.
14 Righteousness and justice are the foundation
of your throne;
faithful love and truth go before you.
15 Happy are the people who know the joyful shout;
LORD, they walk in the light from your face.

---

^A88:18 Or *from me, my friends. Oh darkness!*   ^B89:6 Or *the angels,* or *the sons of the mighty*   ^C89:7 Or *ones, revered by*

16 They rejoice in your name all day long,
   and they are exalted by your righteousness.
17 For you are their magnificent strength;
   by your favor our horn is exalted.
18 Surely our shield^A belongs to the LORD,
   our king to the Holy One of Israel.

19 You once spoke in a vision to your faithful ones
   and said: "I have granted help to a warrior;
   I have exalted one chosen^B from the people.
20 I have found David my servant;
   I have anointed him with my sacred oil.
21 My hand will always be with him,
   and my arm will strengthen him.
22 The enemy will not oppress^C him;
   the wicked will not afflict him.
23 I will crush his foes before him
   and strike those who hate him.
24 My faithfulness and love will be with him,
   and through my name
   his horn will be exalted.
25 I will extend his power to the sea
   and his right hand to the rivers.
26 He will call to me, 'You are my Father,
   my God, the rock of my salvation.'
27 I will also make him my firstborn,
   greatest of the kings of the earth.
28 I will always preserve my faithful love for him,
   and my covenant with him will endure.
29 I will establish his line forever,
   his throne as long as heaven lasts.^D
30 If his sons abandon my instruction
   and do not live by my ordinances,
31 if they dishonor my statutes
   and do not keep my commands,
32 then I will call their rebellion
   to account with the rod,
   their iniquity with blows.
33 But I will not withdraw
   my faithful love from him
   or betray my faithfulness.
34 I will not violate my covenant
   or change what my lips have said.
35 Once and for all
   I have sworn an oath by my holiness;
   I will not lie to David.
36 His offspring will continue forever,

---

^A 89:18 = the king   ^B 89:19 Or exalted a young man   ^C 89:22 Or not exact tribute
from   ^D 89:29 Lit as days of heaven

his throne like the sun before me,
37 like the moon, established forever,
a faithful witness in the sky." *Selah*

38 But you have spurned and rejected him;
you have become enraged with your anointed.
39 You have repudiated the covenant with your servant;
you have completely dishonored his crown.[A]
40 You have broken down all his walls;
you have reduced his fortified cities to ruins.
41 All who pass by plunder him;
he has become an object of ridicule
to his neighbors.
42 You have lifted high the right hand of his foes;
you have made all his enemies rejoice.
43 You have also turned back his sharp sword
and have not let him stand in battle.
44 You have made his splendor[B] cease
and have overturned his throne.
45 You have shortened the days of his youth;
you have covered him with shame. *Selah*

46 How long, LORD? Will you hide forever?
Will your anger keep burning like fire?
47 Remember how short my life is.
Have you created everyone for nothing?
48 What courageous person can live and never see death?
Who can save himself from the power of Sheol? *Selah*
49 Lord, where are the former acts of your faithful love
that you swore to David in your faithfulness?
50 Remember, Lord, the ridicule against your servants —
in my heart I carry abuse from all the peoples —
51 how your enemies have ridiculed, LORD,
how they have ridiculed every step of your anointed.

52 Blessed be the LORD forever.
Amen and amen.

BOOK IV (Psalms 90–106)

ETERNAL GOD AND MORTAL MAN

90 A prayer of Moses, the man of God.
Lord, you have been our refuge[C]
in every generation.
2 Before the mountains were born,
before you gave birth to the earth and the world,
from eternity to eternity, you are God.

[A]89:39 Lit *have dishonored his crown to the ground* [B]89:44 Hb obscure
[C]90:1 Some Hb mss, LXX; other Hb mss read *dwelling place*

3   You return mankind to the dust,
    saying, "Return, descendants of Adam."
4   For in your sight a thousand years
    are like yesterday that passes by,
    like a few hours of the night.
5   You end their lives;[A] they sleep.
    They are like grass that grows in the morning —
6   in the morning it sprouts and grows;
    by evening it withers and dries up.

7   For we are consumed by your anger;
    we are terrified by your wrath.
8   You have set our iniquities before you,
    our secret sins in the light of your presence.
9   For all our days ebb away under your wrath;
    we end our years like a sigh.
10 Our lives last[B] seventy years
    or, if we are strong, eighty years.
    Even the best of them are[C] struggle and sorrow;
    indeed, they pass quickly and we fly away.
11 Who understands the power of your anger?
    Your wrath matches the fear that is due you.
12 Teach us to number our days carefully
    so that we may develop wisdom in our hearts.[D]

13 LORD — how long?
    Turn and have compassion on your servants.
14 Satisfy us in the morning with your faithful love
    so that we may shout with joy and be glad all our days.
15 Make us rejoice for as many days
        as you have humbled us,
    for as many years as we have seen adversity.
16 Let your work be seen by your servants,
    and your splendor by their children.
17 Let the favor of the Lord our God be on us;
    establish for us the work of our hands —
    establish the work of our hands!

THE PROTECTION OF THE MOST HIGH

91   The one who lives under the protection of the Most High
       dwells in the shadow of the Almighty.

2   I will say[E] concerning the LORD, who is
        my refuge and my fortress,
    my God in whom I trust:

[A]90:5 Or *You overwhelm them*; Hb obscure   [B]90:10 Lit *The days of our years in them*   [C]90:10 LXX, Tg, Syr, Vg read *Even their span is*; Hb obscure   [D]90:12 Or *develop a heart of wisdom*   [E]91:1-2 LXX, Syr, Jer read *2Almighty, saying*, or *2Almighty, he will say*

³ He himself will rescue you from the bird trap,
from the destructive plague.
⁴ He will cover you with his feathers;
you will take refuge under his wings.
His faithfulness will be a protective shield.
⁵ You will not fear the terror of the night,
the arrow that flies by day,
⁶ the plague that stalks in darkness,
or the pestilence that ravages at noon.
⁷ Though a thousand fall at your side
and ten thousand at your right hand,
the pestilence will not reach you.
⁸ You will only see it with your eyes
and witness the punishment of the wicked.

⁹ Because you have made the LORD — my refuge,
the Most High — your dwelling place,
¹⁰ no harm will come to you;
no plague will come near your tent.
¹¹ For he will give his angels orders concerning you,
to protect you in all your ways.
¹² They will support you with their hands
so that you will not strike your foot
against a stone.
¹³ You will tread on the lion and the cobra;
you will trample the young lion
and the serpent.

¹⁴ Because he has his heart set on me,
I will deliver him;
I will protect him because he knows my name.
¹⁵ When he calls out to me, I will answer him;
I will be with him in trouble.
I will rescue him and give him honor.
¹⁶ I will satisfy him with a long life
and show him my salvation.

GOD'S LOVE AND FAITHFULNESS

92 A psalm. A song for the Sabbath day.

It is good to give thanks to the LORD,
to sing praise to your name, Most High,
² to declare your faithful love in the morning
and your faithfulness at night,
³ with a ten-stringed harpᴬ
and the music of a lyre.

⁴ For you have made me rejoice, LORD,
by what you have done;

ᴬ92:3 Or ten-stringed instrument and a harp

I will shout for joy
because of the works of your hands.
5 How magnificent are your works, LORD,
how profound your thoughts!
6 A stupid person does not know,
a fool does not understand this:
7 though the wicked sprout like grass
and all evildoers flourish,
they will be eternally destroyed.
8 But you, LORD, are exalted forever.
9 For indeed, LORD, your enemies —
indeed, your enemies will perish;
all evildoers will be scattered.
10 You have lifted up my horn
like that of a wild ox;
I have been anointed[A] with the finest oil.
11 My eyes look at my enemies;
when evildoers rise against me,
my ears hear them.

12 The righteous thrive like a palm tree
and grow like a cedar tree in Lebanon.
13 Planted in the house of the LORD,
they thrive in the courts of our God.
14 They will still bear fruit in old age,
healthy and green,
15 to declare: "The LORD is just;
he is my rock,
and there is no unrighteousness in him."

GOD'S ETERNAL REIGN

93 The LORD reigns! He is robed in majesty;
the LORD is robed, enveloped in strength.
The world is firmly established;
it cannot be shaken.
2 Your throne has been established
from the beginning;[B]
you are from eternity.
3 The floods have lifted up, LORD,
the floods have lifted up their voice;
the floods lift up their pounding waves.
4 Greater than the roar of a huge torrent —
the mighty breakers of the sea —
the LORD on high is majestic.

5 LORD, your testimonies are completely reliable;
holiness adorns your house
for all the days to come.

---

^A92:10 Syr reads *you have anointed me* ^B93:2 Lit *from then*

THE JUST JUDGE

94 ¹ LORD, God of vengeance —
God of vengeance, shine!
² Rise up, Judge of the earth;
repay the proud what they deserve.
³ LORD, how long will the wicked —
how long will the wicked celebrate?

⁴ They pour out arrogant words;
all the evildoers boast.
⁵ LORD, they crush your people;
they oppress your heritage.
⁶ They kill the widow and the resident alien
and murder the fatherless.
⁷ They say, "The LORD doesn't see it.
The God of Jacob doesn't pay attention."

⁸ Pay attention, you stupid people!
Fools, when will you be wise?
⁹ Can the one who shaped the ear not hear,
the one who formed the eye not see?
¹⁰ The one who instructs nations,
the one who teaches mankind knowledge —
does he not discipline?
¹¹ The LORD knows the thoughts of mankind;
they are futile.

¹² LORD, how happy is anyone you discipline
and teach from your law
¹³ to give him relief from troubled times
until a pit is dug for the wicked.
¹⁴ The LORD will not leave his people
or abandon his heritage,
¹⁵ for the administration of justice will again be righteous,
and all the upright in heart will follow^A it.

¹⁶ Who stands up for me against the wicked?
Who takes a stand for me against evildoers?
¹⁷ If the LORD had not been my helper,
I would soon rest in the silence of death.
¹⁸ If I say, "My foot is slipping,"
your faithful love will support me, LORD.
¹⁹ When I am filled with cares,
your comfort brings me joy.

²⁰ Can a corrupt throne be your ally,
a throne that makes evil laws?
²¹ They band together against the life of the righteous

^A94:15 Or *heart will support*; lit *heart after*

and condemn the innocent to death.
22 But the LORD is my refuge;
my God is the rock of my protection.
23 He will pay them back for their sins
and destroy them for their evil.
The LORD our God will destroy them.

WORSHIP AND WARNING

95

Come, let us shout joyfully to the LORD,
shout triumphantly to the rock of our salvation!
2 Let us enter his presence with thanksgiving;
let us shout triumphantly to him in song.

3 For the LORD is a great God,
a great King above all gods.
4 The depths of the earth are in his hand,
and the mountain peaks are his.
5 The sea is his; he made it.
His hands formed the dry land.

6 Come, let us worship and bow down;
let us kneel before the LORD our Maker.
7 For he is our God,
and we are the people of his pasture,
the sheep under his care.^A

Today, if you hear his voice:
8 Do not harden your hearts as at Meribah,
as on that day at Massah in the wilderness
9 where your fathers tested me;
they tried me, though they had seen what I did.
10 For forty years I was disgusted with that generation;
I said, "They are a people whose hearts go astray;
they do not know my ways."
11 So I swore in my anger,
"They will not enter my rest."

KING OF THE EARTH

96

Sing a new song to the LORD;
let the whole earth sing to the LORD.
2 Sing to the LORD, bless his name;
proclaim his salvation from day to day.
3 Declare his glory among the nations,
his wondrous works among all peoples.

4 For the LORD is great and is highly praised;
he is feared above all gods.
5 For all the gods of the peoples are idols,

---

^A95:7 Lit sheep of his hand

THE SECRET TO SOFT HEARTS

PSALMS 95–97

In those rare moments when I complain, it's because there is a perfectly legitimate horror that needs to be catalogued. Certainly my companions need to know if the food, play, conversation, or temperature is not up to my standards. I assume my friends and family are glad to have me there to notate the error.

In reality, it's sometimes difficult to be objective about how much we criticize, and how our bellyaching can affect those around us. Why do we think of our own grumbling as small, but are exhausted by the grumbling of others? It's possible that I complain more about my kids' complaining than they actually complain in the first place.

Grumbling and complaining seem innocuous enough, but they were actually a big problem for Israel in the Old Testament. The Israelites had to wander for forty years in the desert because they complained and refused to trust the Lord (Nm 14).

God knew we, too, would be prone to grumble. In His goodness, He gave us instruction in Scripture for how to worship Him. Such is the lyrical Psalm 95, which begins with an invitation to come before the Lord, offering up two different kinds of worship.

First, the psalmist cries out, "Come, let us shout joyfully to the LORD" (Ps 95:1), prompting us to worship with great joy and exuberance. This is the "go tell it on the mountain" kind of worship,

urging us to shout and sing and consider God's great works.

The second type of worship is slightly different: "Come, let us worship and bow down" (Ps 95:6). This is a reminder to worship in silent reverence, at times even kneeling before the Lord, and contemplating His shepherding care for us.

In both manifestations of worship, God promises He will give us rest. The rest He offers is not only the promised land of Canaan, but also heaven.

I am dog-tired, so I am excited about this promised rest—especially considering that the alternatives to rest are a hardened heart, judgment, and wrath (Ps 95:8-11). I don't want any of the things on that list!

I don't believe the psalmist is saying "worship or die!" Rather, he is showing the natural conclusion to a life lived looking up in worship, versus a life spent looking down in complaint. Grumbling slowly hardens our hearts, and worship slowly aligns our hearts with God and His promises. **Hard hearts lead to judgment and unrest, but worship leads us to joy and eternal rest.**

Let us worship our God with both joy and holy reverence. Let us praise Him for His steadfast character, as well as His provision, both daily and eternally. And as we thank Him for His goodness toward us, may we learn to listen for His voice, even as we worship Him.

but the LORD made the heavens.
6   Splendor and majesty are before him;
strength and beauty are in his sanctuary.

7   Ascribe to the LORD, you families of the peoples,
ascribe to the LORD glory and strength.
8   Ascribe to the LORD the glory of his name;
bring an offering and enter his courts.
9   Worship the LORD in the splendor of his holiness;
let the whole earth tremble before him.

10 Say among the nations: "The LORD reigns.
The world is firmly established; it cannot be shaken.
He judges the peoples fairly."
11 Let the heavens be glad and the earth rejoice;
let the sea and all that fills it resound.
12 Let the fields and everything in them celebrate.
Then all the trees of the forest will shout for joy
13 before the LORD, for he is coming —
for he is coming to judge the earth.
He will judge the world with righteousness
and the peoples with his faithfulness.

THE MAJESTIC KING

97

The LORD reigns! Let the earth rejoice;
let the many coasts and islands be glad.

2   Clouds and total darkness surround him;
righteousness and justice are the foundation of his throne.
3   Fire goes before him
and burns up his foes on every side.
4   His lightning lights up the world;
the earth sees and trembles.
5   The mountains melt like wax
at the presence of the LORD —
at the presence of the Lord of the whole earth.

6   The heavens proclaim his righteousness;
all the peoples see his glory.

7   All who serve carved images,
those who boast in idols, will be put to shame.
All the gods[A] must worship him.

8   Zion hears and is glad,
Judah's villages[B] rejoice
because of your judgments, LORD.
9   For you, LORD,

A 97:7 LXX, Syr read *All his angels*; Heb 1:6   B 97:8 Lit *daughters*

are the Most High over the whole earth;
you are exalted above all the gods.

¹⁰ You who love the Lord, hate evil!
He protects the lives of his faithful ones;
he rescues them from the power of the wicked.
¹¹ Light dawns^{A,B} for the righteous,
gladness for the upright in heart.
¹² Be glad in the Lord, you righteous ones,
and give thanks to his holy name.^C

PRAISE THE KING

98 *A psalm.*

Sing a new song to the Lord,
for he has performed wonders;
his right hand and holy arm
have won him victory.
² The Lord has made his victory known;
he has revealed his righteousness
in the sight of the nations.
³ He has remembered his love
and faithfulness to the house of Israel;
all the ends of the earth
have seen our God's victory.

⁴ Let the whole earth shout to the Lord;
be jubilant, shout for joy, and sing.
⁵ Sing to the Lord with the lyre,
with the lyre and melodious song.
⁶ With trumpets and the blast of the ram's horn
shout triumphantly
in the presence of the Lord, our King.

⁷ Let the sea and all that fills it,
the world and those who live in it, resound.
⁸ Let the rivers clap their hands;
let the mountains shout together for joy
⁹ before the Lord,
for he is coming to judge the earth.
He will judge the world righteously
and the peoples fairly.

THE KING IS HOLY

99 The Lord reigns! Let the peoples tremble.
He is enthroned between the cherubim.
Let the earth quake.
² The Lord is great in Zion;

---

^A97:11 One Hb ms, LXX, some ancient versions read *rises to shine*; Ps 112:4
^B97:11 Lit *Light is sown*   ^C97:12 Lit *to the memory of his holiness*

he is exalted above all the peoples.
3 Let them praise your great
and awe-inspiring name.
He is holy.

4 The mighty King loves justice.
You have established fairness;
you have administered justice
and righteousness in Jacob.
5 Exalt the LORD our God;
bow in worship at his footstool.
He is holy.

6 Moses and Aaron were among his priests;
Samuel also was among those calling on his name.
They called to the LORD and he answered them.
7 He spoke to them in a pillar of cloud;
they kept his decrees and the statutes he gave them.
8 LORD our God, you answered them.
You were a forgiving God to them,
but an avenger of their sinful actions.

9 Exalt the LORD our God;
bow in worship at his holy mountain,
for the LORD our God is holy.

BE THANKFUL

100 *A psalm of thanksgiving.*
Let the whole earth shout triumphantly to the LORD!
2 Serve the LORD with gladness;
come before him with joyful songs.
3 Acknowledge that the LORD is God.
He made us, and we are his^A—
his people, the sheep of his pasture.
4 Enter his gates with thanksgiving
and his courts with praise.
Give thanks to him and bless his name.
5 For the LORD is good, and his faithful love
endures forever;
his faithfulness, through all generations.

A VOW OF INTEGRITY

101 *A psalm of David.*
I will sing of faithful love and justice;
I will sing praise to you, LORD.
2 I will pay attention to the way of integrity.
When will you come to me?
I will live with a heart of integrity in my house.

---

^A100:3 Alt Hb tradition, some Hb mss, LXX, Syr, Vg read *and not we ourselves*

³ I will not let anything worthless guide me.ᴬ
I hate the practice of transgression;
it will not cling to me.
⁴ A devious heart will be far from me;
I will not be involved withᴮ evil.

⁵ I will destroy anyone
who secretly slanders his neighbor;
I cannot tolerate anyone
with haughty eyes or an arrogant heart.
⁶ My eyes favor the faithful of the land
so that they may sit down with me.
The one who follows the way of integrity
may serve me.
⁷ No one who acts deceitfully
will live in my palace;
the one who tells lies
will not be retained here to guide me.ᶜ
⁸ Every morning I will destroy
all the wicked of the land,
wiping out all evildoers from the LORD's city.

AFFLICTION IN LIGHT OF ETERNITY

102

A prayer of a suffering person who is weak and pours out his lament before the LORD.

¹ LORD, hear my prayer;
let my cry for help come before you.
² Do not hide your face from me in my day of trouble.
Listen closely to me;
answer me quickly when I call.

³ For my days vanish like smoke,
and my bones burn like a furnace.
⁴ My heart is suffering, withered like grass;
I even forget to eat my food.
⁵ Because of the sound of my groaning,
my flesh sticks to my bones.
⁶ I am like an eagle owl,
like a little owl among the ruins.
⁷ I stay awake;
I am like a solitary bird on a roof.
⁸ My enemies taunt me all day long;
they ridicule and use my name as a curse.
⁹ I eat ashes like bread
and mingle my drinks with tears
¹⁰ because of your indignation and wrath;
for you have picked me up and thrown me aside.

ᴬ101:3 Lit *I will not put a worthless thing in front of my eyes*   ᴮ101:4 Lit *not know*
ᶜ101:7 Lit *be established in front of my eyes*

11 My days are like a lengthening shadow,
and I wither away like grass.

12 But you, LORD, are enthroned forever;
your fame endures to all generations.
13 You will rise up and have compassion on Zion,
for it is time to show favor to her —
the appointed time has come.
14 For your servants take delight in its stones
and favor its dust.

15 Then the nations will fear the name of the LORD,
and all the kings of the earth your glory,
16 for the LORD will rebuild Zion;
he will appear in his glory.
17 He will pay attention to the prayer of the destitute
and will not despise their prayer.

18 This will be written for a later generation,
and a people who have not yet been created
will praise the LORD:
19 He looked down from his holy heights —
the LORD gazed out from heaven to earth —
20 to hear a prisoner's groaning,
to set free those condemned to die, ^A
21 so that they might declare
the name of the LORD in Zion
and his praise in Jerusalem,
22 when peoples and kingdoms are assembled
to serve the LORD.

23 He has broken my ^B strength in midcourse;
he has shortened my days.
24 I say: "My God, do not take me
in the middle of my life! ^C
Your years continue through all generations.
25 Long ago you established the earth,
and the heavens are the work of your hands.
26 They will perish, but you will endure;
all of them will wear out like clothing.
You will change them like a garment,
and they will pass away.
27 But you are the same,
and your years will never end.
28 Your servants' children will dwell securely,
and their offspring will be established
before you."

---

^A 102:20 Lit *free sons of death*   ^B 102:23 Some Hb mss, LXX read *his*
^C 102:24 Lit *my days*

THE FORGIVING GOD

103 *Of David.*
My soul, bless the LORD,
and all that is within me, bless his holy name.
² My soul, bless the LORD,
and do not forget all his benefits.

³ He forgives all your iniquity;
he heals all your diseases.
⁴ He redeems your life from the Pit;
he crowns you with faithful love and compassion.
⁵ He satisfies you ^A with good things;
your youth is renewed like the eagle.

⁶ The LORD executes acts of righteousness
and justice for all the oppressed.
⁷ He revealed his ways to Moses,
his deeds to the people of Israel.
⁸ The LORD is compassionate and gracious,
slow to anger and abounding in faithful love.
⁹ He will not always accuse us
or be angry forever.
¹⁰ He has not dealt with us as our sins deserve
or repaid us according to our iniquities.

¹¹ For as high as the heavens are above the earth,
so great is his faithful love
toward those who fear him.
¹² As far as the east is from the west,
so far has he removed
our transgressions from us.
¹³ As a father has compassion on his children,
so the LORD has compassion on those who fear him.
¹⁴ For he knows what we are made of,
remembering that we are dust.

¹⁵ As for man, his days are like grass —
he blooms like a flower of the field;
¹⁶ when the wind passes over it, it vanishes,
and its place is no longer known. ^B
¹⁷ But from eternity to eternity
the LORD's faithful love is toward those who fear him,
and his righteousness toward the grandchildren
¹⁸ of those who keep his covenant,
who remember to observe his precepts.
¹⁹ The LORD has established his throne in heaven,
and his kingdom rules over all.

---

^A 103:5 Lit *satisfies your ornament*; Hb obscure   ^B 103:16 Lit *place no longer knows it*

20 Bless the LORD,
all his angels of great strength,
who do his word,
obedient to his command.
21 Bless the LORD, all his armies,
his servants who do his will.
22 Bless the LORD, all his works
in all the places where he rules.
My soul, bless the LORD!

GOD THE CREATOR

104
My soul, bless the LORD!
LORD my God, you are very great;
you are clothed with majesty and splendor.
2 He wraps himself in light as if it were a robe,
spreading out the sky like a canopy,
3 laying the beams of his palace
on the waters above,
making the clouds his chariot,
walking on the wings of the wind,
4 and making the winds his messengers,[A]
flames of fire his servants.

5 He established the earth on its foundations;
it will never be shaken.
6 You covered it with the deep
as if it were a garment;
the water stood above the mountains.
7 At your rebuke the water fled;
at the sound of your thunder they hurried away —
8 mountains rose and valleys sank[B] —
to the place you established for them.
9 You set a boundary they cannot cross;
they will never cover the earth again.

10 He causes the springs to gush into the valleys;
they flow between the mountains.
11 They supply water for every wild beast;
the wild donkeys quench their thirst.
12 The birds of the sky live beside the springs;
they make their voices heard among the foliage.
13 He waters the mountains from his palace;
the earth is satisfied by the fruit of your labor.

14 He causes grass to grow for the livestock
and provides crops for man to cultivate,
producing food from the earth,

[A] 104:4 Or angels [B] 104:7-8 Or away. They flowed over the mountains and went down valleys

¹⁵ wine that makes human hearts glad —
making his face shine with oil —
and bread that sustains human hearts.

¹⁶ The trees of the LORD flourish, ^A
the cedars of Lebanon that he planted.
¹⁷ There the birds make their nests;
storks make their homes in the pine trees.
¹⁸ The high mountains are for the wild goats;
the cliffs are a refuge for hyraxes.

¹⁹ He made the moon to mark the ^B festivals; ^C
the sun knows when to set.
²⁰ You bring darkness, and it becomes night,
when all the forest animals stir.
²¹ The young lions roar for their prey
and seek their food from God.
²² The sun rises; they go back
and lie down in their dens.
²³ Man goes out to his work
and to his labor until evening.

²⁴ How countless are your works, LORD!
In wisdom you have made them all;
the earth is full of your creatures. ^D
²⁵ Here is the sea, vast and wide,
teeming with creatures beyond number —
living things both large and small.
²⁶ There the ships move about,
and Leviathan, which you formed to play there.

²⁷ All of them wait for you
to give them their food at the right time.
²⁸ When you give it to them,
they gather it;
when you open your hand,
they are satisfied with good things.
²⁹ When you hide your face,
they are terrified;
when you take away their breath,
they die and return to the dust.
³⁰ When you send your breath, ^E
they are created,
and you renew the surface of the ground.

³¹ May the glory of the LORD endure forever;
may the LORD rejoice in his works.

---

^A104:16 Lit are satisfied   ^B104:19 Lit moon for   ^C104:19 Or the appointed times
^D104:24 Lit possessions   ^E104:30 Or Spirit

32 He looks at the earth, and it trembles;
he touches the mountains,
and they pour out smoke.

33 I will sing to the LORD all my life;
I will sing praise to my God while I live.

34 May my meditation be pleasing to him;
I will rejoice in the LORD.

35 May sinners vanish from the earth
and wicked people be no more.
My soul, bless the LORD!
Hallelujah!

GOD'S FAITHFULNESS TO HIS PEOPLE

105 Give thanks to the LORD, call on his name;
proclaim his deeds among the peoples.

2 Sing to him, sing praise to him;
tell about all his wondrous works!

3 Honor his holy name;
let the hearts of those who seek the LORD rejoice.

4 Seek the LORD and his strength;
seek his face always.

5 Remember the wondrous works he has done,
his wonders, and the judgments
he has pronounced,[A]

6 you offspring of Abraham his servant,
Jacob's descendants — his chosen ones.

7 He is the LORD our God;
his judgments govern the whole earth.

8 He remembers his covenant forever,
the promise he ordained
for a thousand generations —

9 the covenant he made with Abraham,
swore[B] to Isaac,

10 and confirmed to Jacob as a decree
and to Israel as a permanent covenant:

11 "I will give the land of Canaan to you
as your inherited portion."

12 When they were few in number,
very few indeed,
and resident aliens in Canaan,

13 wandering from nation to nation
and from one kingdom to another,

14 he allowed no one to oppress them;
he rebuked kings on their behalf:

15 "Do not touch my anointed ones,
or harm my prophets."

[A]105:5 Lit judgments of his mouth   [B]105:9 Lit and his oath

¹⁶ He called down famine against the land
and destroyed the entire food supply.
¹⁷ He had sent a man ahead of them —
Joseph, who was sold as a slave.
¹⁸ They hurt his feet with shackles;
his neck was put in an iron collar.
¹⁹ Until the time his prediction came true,
the word of the LORD tested him.
²⁰ The king sent for him and released him;
the ruler of peoples set him free.
²¹ He made him master of his household,
ruler over all his possessions —
²² binding^A his officials at will
and instructing his elders.

²³ Then Israel went to Egypt;
Jacob lived as an alien in the land of Ham.^B
²⁴ The LORD^C made his people very fruitful;
he made them more numerous than their foes,
²⁵ whose hearts he turned to hate his people
and to deal deceptively with his servants.
²⁶ He sent Moses his servant,
and Aaron, whom he had chosen.
²⁷ They performed his miraculous signs among them,
and wonders in the land of Ham.
²⁸ He sent darkness, and it became dark —
for did they not defy his commands?
²⁹ He turned their water into blood
and caused their fish to die.
³⁰ Their land was overrun with frogs,
even in their royal chambers.
³¹ He spoke, and insects came —
gnats throughout their country.
³² He gave them hail for rain,
and lightning throughout their land.
³³ He struck their vines and fig trees
and shattered the trees of their territory.
³⁴ He spoke, and locusts came —
young locusts without number.
³⁵ They devoured all the vegetation in their land
and consumed the produce of their land.
³⁶ He struck all the firstborn in their land,
all their first progeny.

³⁷ Then he brought Israel out with silver and gold,
and no one among his tribes stumbled.
³⁸ Egypt was glad when they left,

---

^A105:22 LXX, Syr, Vg read *teaching*   ^B105:23 = Egypt, also in v. 27
^C105:24 Lit *He*

for the dread of Israel[A] had fallen on them.

39 He spread a cloud as a covering
and gave a fire to light up the night.

40 They asked, and he brought quail
and satisfied them with bread from heaven.

41 He opened a rock, and water gushed out;
it flowed like a stream in the desert.

42 For he remembered his holy promise
to Abraham his servant.

43 He brought his people out with rejoicing,
his chosen ones with shouts of joy.

44 He gave them the lands of the nations,
and they inherited
what other peoples had worked for.

45 All this happened
so that they might keep his statutes
and obey his instructions.
Hallelujah!

ISRAEL'S UNFAITHFULNESS TO GOD

106 Hallelujah!
Give thanks to the LORD, for he is good;
his faithful love endures forever.

2 Who can declare the LORD's mighty acts
or proclaim all the praise due him?

3 How happy are those who uphold justice,
who practice righteousness at all times.

4 Remember me, LORD,
when you show favor to your people.
Come to me with your salvation

5 so that I may enjoy the prosperity
of your chosen ones,
rejoice in the joy of your nation,
and boast about your heritage.

6 Both we and our fathers have sinned;
we have done wrong and have acted wickedly.

7 Our fathers in Egypt did not grasp
the significance of your wondrous works
or remember your many acts of faithful love;
instead, they rebelled by the sea — the Red Sea.

8 Yet he saved them for his name's sake,
to make his power known.

9 He rebuked the Red Sea, and it dried up;
he led them through the depths as through a desert.

10 He saved them from the power of the adversary;

A105:38 Lit *them*

he redeemed them from the power of the enemy.
¹¹ Water covered their foes;
not one of them remained.
¹² Then they believed his promises
and sang his praise.

¹³ They soon forgot his works
and would not wait for his counsel.
¹⁴ They were seized with craving in the wilderness
and tested God in the desert.
¹⁵ He gave them what they asked for,
but sent a wasting disease among them.

¹⁶ In the camp they were envious of Moses
and of Aaron, the LORD's holy one.
¹⁷ The earth opened up and swallowed Dathan;
it covered the assembly of Abiram.
¹⁸ Fire blazed throughout their assembly;
flames consumed the wicked.

¹⁹ At Horeb they made a calf
and worshiped the cast metal image.
²⁰ They exchanged their glory^A,B
for the image of a grass-eating ox.
²¹ They forgot God their Savior,
who did great things in Egypt,
²² wondrous works in the land of Ham,^C
awe-inspiring acts at the Red Sea.
²³ So he said he would have destroyed them —
if Moses his chosen one
had not stood before him in the breach
to turn his wrath away from destroying them.

²⁴ They despised the pleasant land
and did not believe his promise.
²⁵ They grumbled in their tents
and did not listen to the LORD.
²⁶ So he raised his hand against them with an oath
that he would make them fall in the desert
²⁷ and would disperse their descendants^D
among the nations,
scattering them throughout the lands.

²⁸ They aligned themselves with Baal of Peor
and ate sacrifices offered to lifeless gods.^E
²⁹ They angered the LORD with their deeds,

---

^A 106:20 Alt Hb tradition reads *his glory*, or *my glory*   ^B 106:20 = God
^C 106:22 = Egypt   ^D 106:27 Syr; MT reads *would make their descendants fall*
^E 106:28 Lit *sacrifices for dead ones*

and a plague broke out against them.

30 But Phinehas stood up and intervened,
and the plague was stopped.

31 It was credited to him as righteousness
throughout all generations to come.

32 They angered the LORD at the Waters of Meribah,
and Moses suffered[A] because of them;

33 for they embittered his spirit,[B]
and he spoke rashly with his lips.

34 They did not destroy the peoples
as the LORD had commanded them

35 but mingled with the nations
and adopted their ways.

36 They served their idols,
which became a snare to them.

37 They sacrificed their sons and daughters to demons.

38 They shed innocent blood —
the blood of their sons and daughters
whom they sacrificed to the idols of Canaan;
so the land became polluted with blood.

39 They defiled themselves by their actions
and prostituted themselves by their deeds.

40 Therefore the LORD's anger burned against his people,
and he abhorred his own inheritance.

41 He handed them over to the nations;
those who hated them ruled over them.

42 Their enemies oppressed them,
and they were subdued under their power.

43 He rescued them many times,
but they continued to rebel deliberately
and were beaten down by their iniquity.

44 When he heard their cry,
he took note of their distress,

45 remembered his covenant with them,
and relented according to the abundance
of his faithful love.

46 He caused them to be pitied
before all their captors.

47 Save us, LORD our God,
and gather us from the nations,
so that we may give thanks to your holy name
and rejoice in your praise.

[A]106:32 Lit and it was evil for Moses   [B]106:33 Some Hb mss, LXX, Syr, Jer; other
Hb mss read they rebelled against his Spirit

⁴⁸ Blessed be the LORD God of Israel,
from everlasting to everlasting.
Let all the people say, "Amen!"
Hallelujah!

BOOK V (Psalms 107–150)

THANKSGIVING FOR GOD'S DELIVERANCE

107 Give thanks to the LORD,
for he is good;
his faithful love endures forever.

² Let the redeemed of the LORD proclaim
that he has redeemed them
from the power of the foe

³ and has gathered them from the lands —
from the east and the west,
from the north and the south.

⁴ Some^A wandered in the desolate wilderness,
finding no way to a city where they could live.

⁵ They were hungry and thirsty;
their spirits failed^B within them.

⁶ Then they cried out to the LORD in their trouble;
he rescued them from their distress.

⁷ He led them by the right path
to go to a city where they could live.

⁸ Let them give thanks to the LORD
for his faithful love
and his wondrous works for all humanity.

⁹ For he has satisfied the thirsty
and filled the hungry with good things.

¹⁰ Others sat in darkness and gloom^C —
prisoners in cruel chains —

¹¹ because they rebelled against God's commands
and despised the counsel of the Most High.

¹² He broke their spirits^D with hard labor;
they stumbled, and there was no one to help.

¹³ Then they cried out to the LORD in their trouble;
he saved them from their distress.

¹⁴ He brought them out of darkness and gloom
and broke their chains apart.

¹⁵ Let them give thanks to the LORD
for his faithful love
and his wondrous works for all humanity.

¹⁶ For he has broken down the bronze gates
and cut through the iron bars.

---

^A107:4 Lit They, also in vv. 10,23   ^B107:5 Lit their soul fainted   ^C107:10 Or the
shadow of death, also in v. 14   ^D107:12 Lit hearts

17 Fools suffered affliction
because of their rebellious ways and their iniquities.
18 They loathed all food
and came near the gates of death.
19 Then they cried out to the LORD in their trouble;
he saved them from their distress.
20 He sent his word and healed them;
he rescued them from the Pit.
21 Let them give thanks to the LORD
for his faithful love
and his wondrous works for all humanity.
22 Let them offer sacrifices of thanksgiving
and announce his works with shouts of joy.

23 Others went to sea in ships,
conducting trade on the vast water.
24 They saw the LORD's works,
his wondrous works in the deep.
25 He spoke and raised a stormy wind
that stirred up the waves of the sea.[A]
26 Rising up to the sky, sinking down to the depths,
their courage[B] melting away in anguish,
27 they reeled and staggered like a drunkard,
and all their skill was useless.
28 Then they cried out to the LORD in their trouble,
and he brought them out of their distress.
29 He stilled the storm to a whisper,
and the waves of the sea[C] were hushed.
30 They rejoiced when the waves[D] grew quiet.
Then he guided them to the harbor they longed for.
31 Let them give thanks to the LORD
for his faithful love
and his wondrous works for all humanity.
32 Let them exalt him in the assembly of the people
and praise him in the council of the elders.

33 He turns rivers into desert,
springs into thirsty ground,
34 and fruitful land into salty wasteland,
because of the wickedness of its inhabitants.
35 He turns a desert into a pool,
dry land into springs.
36 He causes the hungry to settle there,
and they establish a city where they can live.
37 They sow fields and plant vineyards
that yield a fruitful harvest.
38 He blesses them, and they multiply greatly;
he does not let their livestock decrease.

[A]107:25 Lit of it   [B]107:26 Lit souls   [C]107:29 Lit of them   [D]107:30 Lit when they

957

³⁹ When they are diminished and are humbled
by cruel oppression and sorrow,
⁴⁰ he pours contempt on nobles
and makes them wander in a trackless wasteland.
⁴¹ But he lifts the needy out of their suffering
and makes their families multiply like flocks.
⁴² The upright see it and rejoice,
and all injustice shuts its mouth.

⁴³ Let whoever is wise pay attention to these things
and consider the LORD's acts of faithful love.

A PLEA FOR VICTORY

108
A song. A psalm of David.

My heart is confident, God;
I will sing; I will sing praises
with the whole of my being.^A
² Wake up, harp and lyre!
I will wake up the dawn.
³ I will praise you, LORD, among the peoples;
I will sing praises to you among the nations.
⁴ For your faithful love is higher
than the heavens,
and your faithfulness reaches to the clouds.
⁵ God, be exalted above the heavens,
and let your glory be over the whole earth.
⁶ Save with your right hand and answer me
so that those you love may be rescued.

⁷ God has spoken in his sanctuary:^B
"I will celebrate!
I will divide up Shechem.
I will apportion the Valley of Succoth.
⁸ Gilead is mine, Manasseh is mine,
and Ephraim is my helmet;
Judah is my scepter.
⁹ Moab is my washbasin;
I throw my sandal on Edom.
I shout in triumph over Philistia."

¹⁰ Who will bring me to the fortified city?
Who will lead me to Edom?
¹¹ God, haven't you rejected us?
God, you do not march out with our armies.
¹² Give us aid against the foe,
for human help is worthless.
¹³ With God we will perform valiantly;
he will trample our foes.

^A108:1 Lit *praises, even my glory*   ^B108:7 Or *has promised by his holy nature*

PRAYER AGAINST AN ENEMY

109
For the choir director. A psalm of David.
God of my praise, do not be silent.

2 For wicked and deceitful mouths open against me;
   they speak against me with lying tongues.
3 They surround me with hateful words
   and attack me without cause.
4 In return for my love they accuse me,
   but I continue to pray.[A]
5 They repay me evil for good,
   and hatred for my love.

6 Set a wicked person over him;
   let an accuser[B] stand at his right hand.
7 When he is judged, let him be found guilty,
   and let his prayer be counted as sin.
8 Let his days be few;
   let another take over his position.
9 Let his children be fatherless
   and his wife a widow.
10 Let his children wander as beggars,
   searching for food far[C] from their demolished homes.
11 Let a creditor seize all he has;
   let strangers plunder what he has worked for.
12 Let no one show him kindness,
   and let no one be gracious to his fatherless children.
13 Let the line of his descendants be cut off;
   let their name be blotted out in the next generation.
14 Let the iniquity of his fathers
   be remembered before the LORD,
   and do not let his mother's sin be blotted out.
15 Let their sins[D] always remain before the LORD,
   and let him remove[E] all memory of them from the earth.

16 For he did not think to show kindness,
   but pursued the suffering, needy, and brokenhearted
   in order to put them to death.
17 He loved cursing — let it fall on him;
   he took no delight in blessing — let it be far from him.
18 He wore cursing like his coat —
   let it enter his body like water
   and go into his bones like oil.
19 Let it be like a robe he wraps around himself,
   like a belt he always wears.
20 Let this be the LORD's payment to my accusers,
   to those who speak evil against me.

[A]109:4 Lit *but I, prayer* [B]109:6 Or *adversary* [C]109:10 LXX reads *beggars, driven far* [D]109:15 Lit *Let them* [E]109:15 Or *cut off*

²¹ But you, LORD, my Lord,
deal kindly with me for your name's sake;
because your faithful love is good, rescue me.
²² For I am suffering and needy;
my heart is wounded within me.
²³ I fade away like a lengthening shadow;
I am shaken off like a locust.
²⁴ My knees are weak from fasting,
and my body is emaciated.ᴬ
²⁵ I have become an object of ridicule to my accusers;ᴮ
when they see me, they shake their heads in scorn.

²⁶ Help me, LORD my God;
save me according to your faithful love
²⁷ so they may know that this is your hand
and that you, LORD, have done it.
²⁸ Though they curse, you will bless.
When they rise up, they will be put to shame,
but your servant will rejoice.
²⁹ My accusers will be clothed with disgrace;
they will wear their shame like a cloak.
³⁰ I will fervently thank the LORD with my mouth;
I will praise him in the presence of many.
³¹ For he stands at the right hand of the needy
to save him from those who would condemn him.

THE PRIESTLY KING

110

A psalm of David.

This is the declaration of the LORD
to my Lord:
"Sit at my right hand
until I make your enemies your footstool."
² The LORD will extend your mighty scepter from Zion.
Ruleᶜ over your surroundingᴰ enemies.
³ Your people will volunteer
on your day of battle.ᴱ
In holy splendor, from the womb of the dawn,
the dew of your youth belongs to you.ᶠ
⁴ The LORD has sworn an oath and will not take it back:
"You are a priest forever
according to the pattern of Melchizedek."

⁵ The Lord is at your right hand;
he will crush kings on the day of his anger.
⁶ He will judge the nations, heaping up corpses;
he will crush leaders over the entire world.

ᴬ109:24 Lit *denied from fat* ᴮ109:25 Lit *to them* ᶜ110:2 One Hb ms, LXX,
Tg read *You will rule* ᴰ110:2 Lit *Rule in the midst of your* ᴱ110:3 Lit *power*
ᶠ110:3 Hb obscure

7   He will drink from the brook by the road;
    therefore, he will lift up his head.

PRAISE FOR THE LORD'S WORKS

111

Hallelujah!^A
I will praise the LORD with all my heart
in the assembly of the upright
        and in the congregation.

2   The LORD's works are great,
    studied by all who delight in them.
3   All that he does is splendid and majestic;
    his righteousness endures forever.
4   He has caused his wondrous works
        to be remembered.
    The LORD is gracious and compassionate.
5   He has provided food for those who fear him;
    he remembers his covenant forever.
6   He has shown his people the power of his works
    by giving them the inheritance of the nations.
7   The works of his hands are truth and justice;
    all his instructions are trustworthy.
8   They are established forever and ever,
    enacted in truth and in uprightness.
9   He has sent redemption to his people.
    He has ordained his covenant forever.
    His name is holy and awe-inspiring.

10 The fear of the LORD is the beginning of wisdom;
    all who follow his instructions^B
        have good insight.
    His praise endures forever.

THE TRAITS OF THE RIGHTEOUS

112

Hallelujah!^A
Happy is the person who fears the LORD,
taking great delight in his commands.

2   His descendants will be powerful in the land;
    the generation of the upright will be blessed.
3   Wealth and riches are in his house,
    and his righteousness endures forever.
4   Light shines in the darkness for the upright.
    He is gracious, compassionate, and righteous.
5   Good will come to the one who lends generously
    and conducts his business fairly.
6   He will never be shaken.
    The righteous one will be remembered forever.

^A111:1; 112:1 The lines of this poem form an acrostic.   ^B111:10 Lit follow them

961

⁷ He will not fear bad news;
his heart is confident, trusting in the LORD.
⁸ His heart is assured; he will not fear.
In the end he will look in triumph on his foes.
⁹ He distributes freely to the poor;
his righteousness endures forever.
His horn will be exalted in honor.

¹⁰ The wicked one will see it and be angry;
he will gnash his teeth in despair.
The desire of the wicked leads to ruin.

PRAISE TO THE MERCIFUL GOD

113 Hallelujah!
Give praise, servants of the LORD;
praise the name of the LORD.
² Let the name of the LORD be blessed
both now and forever.
³ From the rising of the sun to its setting,
let the name of the LORD be praised.

⁴ The LORD is exalted above all the nations,
his glory above the heavens.
⁵ Who is like the LORD our God —
the one enthroned on high,
⁶ who stoops down to look
on the heavens and the earth?
⁷ He raises the poor from the dust
and lifts the needy from the trash heap
⁸ in order to seat them with nobles —
with the nobles of his people.
⁹ He gives the childless woman a household,
making her the joyful mother of children.
Hallelujah!

GOD'S DELIVERANCE OF ISRAEL

114 When Israel came out of Egypt —
the house of Jacob from a people
who spoke a foreign language —
² Judah became his sanctuary,
Israel, his dominion.

³ The sea looked and fled;
the Jordan turned back.
⁴ The mountains skipped like rams,
the hills, like lambs.
⁵ Why was it, sea, that you fled?
Jordan, that you turned back?
⁶ Mountains, that you skipped like rams?
Hills, like lambs?

7 Tremble, earth, at the presence of the Lord,
  at the presence of the God of Jacob,

8 who turned the rock into a pool,
  the flint into a spring.

GLORY TO GOD ALONE

115

Not to us, LORD, not to us,
but to your name give glory
because of your faithful love, because of your truth.

2 Why should the nations say,
  "Where is their God?"

3 Our God is in heaven
  and does whatever he pleases.

4 Their idols are silver and gold,
  made by human hands.

5 They have mouths but cannot speak,
  eyes, but cannot see.

6 They have ears but cannot hear,
  noses, but cannot smell.

7 They have hands but cannot feel,
  feet, but cannot walk.
  They cannot make a sound with their throats.

8 Those who make them are[A] just like them,
  as are all who trust in them.

9 Israel,[B] trust in the LORD!
  He is their help and shield.

10 House of Aaron, trust in the LORD!
   He is their help and shield.

11 You who fear the LORD, trust in the LORD!
   He is their help and shield.

12 The LORD remembers us and will bless us.
   He will bless the house of Israel;
   he will bless the house of Aaron;

13 he will bless those who fear the LORD —
   small and great alike.

14 May the LORD add to your numbers,
   both yours and your children's.

15 May you be blessed by the LORD,
   the Maker of heaven and earth.

16 The heavens are the LORD's,[C]
   but the earth he has given to the human race.

17 It is not the dead who praise the LORD,
   nor any of those descending
     into the silence of death.

[A]115:8 Or *May those who make them become* [B]115:9 Some Hb mss, LXX, Syr
read *House of Israel* [C]115:16 Lit *the LORD's heavens*

¹⁸ But we will bless the LORD,
both now and forever.
Hallelujah!

THANKS TO GOD FOR DELIVERANCE

116 I love the LORD because he has heard
my appeal for mercy.
² Because he has turned his ear to me,
I will call out to him as long as I live.

³ The ropes of death were wrapped around me,
and the torments of Sheol overcame me;
I encountered trouble and sorrow.
⁴ Then I called on the name of the LORD:
"LORD, save me! "

⁵ The LORD is gracious and righteous;
our God is compassionate.
⁶ The LORD guards the inexperienced;
I was helpless, and he saved me.
⁷ Return to your rest, my soul,
for the LORD has been good to you.
⁸ For you, LORD, rescued me from death,
my eyes from tears,
my feet from stumbling.
⁹ I will walk before the LORD
in the land of the living.
¹⁰ I believed, even when I said,
"I am severely oppressed."
¹¹ In my alarm I said,
"Everyone is a liar."

¹² How can I repay the LORD
for all the good he has done for me?
¹³ I will take the cup of salvation
and call on the name of the LORD.
¹⁴ I will fulfill my vows to the LORD
in the presence of all his people.

¹⁵ The death of his faithful ones
is valuable in the LORD's sight.
¹⁶ LORD, I am indeed your servant;
I am your servant, the son of your female servant.
You have loosened my bonds.

¹⁷ I will offer you a sacrifice of thanksgiving
and call on the name of the LORD.
¹⁸ I will fulfill my vows to the LORD
in the presence of all his people,
¹⁹ in the courts of the LORD's house —

HELPLESS BUT HOPEFUL

PSALMS 116–118

When was the last time you felt helpless?

Maybe you were stranded in an unfamiliar place, or struggling in a relationship that felt hopelessly distant. For me, it was suffering through an illness that caught me completely off guard. When something is beyond our control it can be uncomfortable and frustrating. No one wants to admit their inability to help themselves.

Sin seems to have hardwired the desire for self-reliance into our DNA. We want to be in control. We want to believe we're self-sustaining. But ironically, recognizing our helplessness is the first step to true hopefulness.

This counterintuitive reality is woven throughout the verses of Psalm 116, giving us a glimpse of a man desperate for God's grace, a soul utterly powerless to produce the peace and salvation he longs for. The psalmist fears death, persecution, isolation, and affliction. He is physically, emotionally, and spiritually at the end of himself.

In his helplessness, the psalmist runs to God. And in God's presence, he finds hope.

"The LORD is gracious and righteous; our God is compassionate.
The LORD guards the inexperienced; I was helpless, and he saved me."

PSALM 116:5-6

What a beautiful picture of God's character! The Lord is both gracious and righteous. His compassion spans the width of eternity. His forgiveness stretches as far as the east is from the west. He is the protector of the weak. He guards the simple and saves the helpless.

Read through Psalm 116 again. Do you see it? Over and over again, the psalmist's praise of the Lord is intimately tied to the admission of his own weakness.

"The ropes of death were wrapped around me, and the torments of Sheol overcame me; I encountered trouble and sorrow. Then I called on the name of the LORD: 'LORD, save me!'" (Ps 116:3-4).

Our weakness and need make God's grace such good news.

Scripture is full of hope for those who acknowledge their own weakness and trust in God's unfailing strength. This is the heartbeat of the gospel.

"For while we were still helpless, at the right time, Christ died for the ungodly" (Rm 5:6).

Jesus offers grace that saves and sustains us, strengthens and comforts us. He calls us, cleanses us, equips us, and ultimately gives us life everlasting. Being weak is our greatest strength when it leads to desperate dependence on God. Being helpless is never hopeless when it leads us to the cross.

"So I take pleasure in weaknesses, insults, hardships, persecutions, and in difficulties, for the sake of Christ. For when I am weak, then I am strong."

2 CORINTHIANS 12:10

---

within you, Jerusalem.
Hallelujah!

UNIVERSAL CALL TO PRAISE

117 Praise the LORD, all nations!
Glorify him, all peoples!
2 For his faithful love to us is great;
the LORD's faithfulness endures forever.
Hallelujah!

THANKSGIVING FOR VICTORY

118 Give thanks to the LORD, for he is good;
his faithful love endures forever.
2 Let Israel say,
"His faithful love endures forever."
3 Let the house of Aaron say,
"His faithful love endures forever."
4 Let those who fear the LORD say,
"His faithful love endures forever."

5 I called to the LORD in distress;
the LORD answered me
and put me in a spacious place. [A]
6 The LORD is for me; I will not be afraid.
What can a mere mortal do to me?
7 The LORD is my helper,
Therefore, I will look in triumph on those who hate me.

8 It is better to take refuge in the LORD
than to trust in humanity.
9 It is better to take refuge in the LORD
than to trust in nobles.

10 All the nations surrounded me;
in the name of the LORD I destroyed them.
11 They surrounded me, yes, they surrounded me;
in the name of the LORD I destroyed them.
12 They surrounded me like bees;
they were extinguished like a fire among thorns;
in the name of the LORD I destroyed them.
13 They [B] pushed me hard to make me fall,
but the LORD helped me.
14 The LORD is my strength and my song;
he has become my salvation.

15 There are shouts of joy and victory
in the tents of the righteous:
"The LORD's right hand performs valiantly!

[A] 118:5 Or answered me with freedom   [B] 118:13 Lit You

16   The LORD's right hand is raised.
     The LORD's right hand performs valiantly!"

17   I will not die, but I will live
     and proclaim what the LORD has done.

18   The LORD disciplined me severely
     but did not give me over to death.

19   Open the gates of righteousness for me;
     I will enter through them
     and give thanks to the LORD.

20   This is the LORD's gate;
     the righteous will enter through it.

21   I will give thanks to you
     because you have answered me
     and have become my salvation.

22   The stone that the builders rejected
     has become the cornerstone.

23   This came from the LORD;
     it is wondrous in our sight.

24   This is the day the LORD has made;
     let us rejoice and be glad in it.

25   LORD, save us!
     LORD, please grant us success!

26   He who comes in the name
     of the LORD is blessed.
     From the house of the LORD we bless you.

27   The LORD is God and has given us light.
     Bind the festival sacrifice with cords
     to the horns of the altar.

28   You are my God, and I will give you thanks.
     You are my God; I will exalt you.

29   Give thanks to the LORD, for he is good;
     his faithful love endures forever.

DELIGHT IN GOD'S WORD

א Aleph

119 How^A happy are those whose way is blameless,
     who walk according to the LORD's instruction!

2   Happy are those who keep his decrees
     and seek him with all their heart.

3   They do nothing wrong;
     they walk in his ways.

4   You have commanded that your precepts
     be diligently kept.

5   If only my ways were committed
     to keeping your statutes!

6   Then I would not be ashamed

---

^A119:1 The stanzas of this poem form an acrostic.

when I think about all your commands.
⁷ I will praise you with an upright heart
when I learn your righteous judgments.
⁸ I will keep your statutes;
never abandon me.

ב Beth

⁹ How can a young man keep his way pure?
By keeping your^A word.
¹⁰ I have sought you with all my heart;
don't let me wander from your commands.
¹¹ I have treasured your word in my heart
so that I may not sin against you.
¹² Lord, may you be blessed;
teach me your statutes.
¹³ With my lips I proclaim
all the judgments from your mouth.
¹⁴ I rejoice in the way revealed by your decrees
as much as in all riches.
¹⁵ I will meditate on your precepts
and think about your ways.
¹⁶ I will delight in your statutes;
I will not forget your word.

ג Gimel

¹⁷ Deal generously with your servant
so that I might live;
then I will keep your word.
¹⁸ Open my eyes so that I may contemplate
wondrous things from your instruction.
¹⁹ I am a resident alien on earth;
do not hide your commands from me.
²⁰ I am continually overcome
with longing for your judgments.
²¹ You rebuke the arrogant,
the ones under a curse,
who wander from your commands.
²² Take insult and contempt away from me,
for I have kept your decrees.
²³ Though princes sit together speaking against me,
your servant will think about your statutes;
²⁴ your decrees are my delight
and my counselors.

ד Daleth

²⁵ My life is down in the dust;
give me life through your word.
²⁶ I told you about my life,

---

^A 119:9 Or *keeping it according to your*

and you answered me;
teach me your statutes.

27 Help me understand
the meaning of your precepts
so that I can meditate on your wonders.

28 I am weary[A] from grief;
strengthen me through your word.

29 Keep me from the way of deceit
and graciously give me your instruction.

30 I have chosen the way of truth;
I have set your ordinances before me.

31 I cling to your decrees;
LORD, do not put me to shame.

32 I pursue the way of your commands,
for you broaden my understanding.[B]

ה He

33 Teach me, LORD, the meaning[C] of your statutes,
and I will always keep them.[D]

34 Help me understand your instruction,
and I will obey it
and follow it with all my heart.

35 Help me stay on the path of your commands,
for I take pleasure in it.

36 Turn my heart to your decrees
and not to dishonest profit.

37 Turn my eyes
from looking at what is worthless;
give me life in your ways.[E]

38 Confirm what you said to your servant,
for it produces reverence for you.

39 Turn away the disgrace I dread;
indeed, your judgments are good.

40 How I long for your precepts!
Give me life through your righteousness.

ו Waw

41 Let your faithful love come to me, LORD,
your salvation, as you promised.

42 Then I can answer the one who taunts me,
for I trust in your word.

43 Never take the word of truth from my mouth,
for I hope in your judgments.

44 I will always obey your instruction,
forever and ever.

45 I will walk freely in an open place
because I study your precepts.

[A]119:28 Or I weep [B]119:32 Lit you enlarge my heart [C]119:33 Lit way
[D]119:33 Or will keep it as my reward [E]119:37 Some Hb mss, Tg read word

⁴⁶ I will speak of your decrees before kings
and not be ashamed.
⁴⁷ I delight in your commands,
which I love.
⁴⁸ I will lift up my hands to your commands,
which I love,
and will meditate on your statutes.

ז Zayin

⁴⁹ Remember your word to your servant;
you have given me hope through it.
⁵⁰ This is my comfort in my affliction:
Your promise has given me life.
⁵¹ The arrogant constantly ridicule me,
but I do not turn away from your instruction.
⁵² Lᴏʀᴅ, I remember your judgments from long ago
and find comfort.
⁵³ Rage seizes me because of the wicked
who reject your instruction.
⁵⁴ Your statutes are the theme of my song
during my earthly life.ᴬ
⁵⁵ Lᴏʀᴅ, I remember your name in the night,
and I obey your instruction.
⁵⁶ This is my practice:
I obey your precepts.

ח Cheth

⁵⁷ The Lᴏʀᴅ is my portion;ᴮ
I have promised to keep your words.
⁵⁸ I have sought your favor with all my heart;
be gracious to me according to your promise.
⁵⁹ I thought about my ways
and turned my steps back to your decrees.
⁶⁰ I hurried, not hesitating
to keep your commands.
⁶¹ Though the ropes of the wicked
were wrapped around me,
I did not forget your instruction.
⁶² I rise at midnight to thank you
for your righteous judgments.
⁶³ I am a friend to all who fear you,
to those who keep your precepts.
⁶⁴ Lᴏʀᴅ, the earth is filled with your faithful love;
teach me your statutes.

ט Teth

⁶⁵ Lᴏʀᴅ, you have treated your servant well,
just as you promised.

ᴬ119:54 Lit song in the house of my sojourning ᴮ119:57 Lit You are my portion, Lᴏʀᴅ

66 Teach me good judgment and discernment,
for I rely on your commands.
67 Before I was afflicted I went astray,
but now I keep your word.
68 You are good, and you do what is good;
teach me your statutes.
69 The arrogant have smeared me with lies,
but I obey your precepts with all my heart.
70 Their hearts are hard and insensitive,
but I delight in your instruction.
71 It was good for me to be afflicted
so that I could learn your statutes.
72 Instruction from your lips is better for me
than thousands of gold and silver pieces.

י Yod

73 Your hands made me and formed me;
give me understanding
so that I can learn your commands.
74 Those who fear you will see me and rejoice,
for I put my hope in your word.
75 I know, LORD, that your judgments are just
and that you have afflicted me fairly.
76 May your faithful love comfort me
as you promised your servant.
77 May your compassion come to me
so that I may live,
for your instruction is my delight.
78 Let the arrogant be put to shame
for slandering me with lies;
I will meditate on your precepts.
79 Let those who fear you,
those who know your decrees, turn to me.
80 May my heart be blameless regarding your statutes
so that I will not be put to shame.

כ Kaph

81 I long for your salvation;
I put my hope in your word.
82 My eyes grow weary
looking for what you have promised;
I ask, "When will you comfort me?"
83 Though I have become like a wineskin dried by smoke,
I do not forget your statutes.
84 How many days must your servant wait?
When will you execute judgment on my persecutors?
85 The arrogant have dug pits for me;
they violate your instruction.
86 All your commands are true;
people persecute me with lies — help me!

971

87 They almost ended my life on earth,
but I did not abandon your precepts.
88 Give me life in accordance with your faithful love,
and I will obey the decree you have spoken.

ל Lamed

89 LORD, your word is forever;
it is firmly fixed in heaven.
90 Your faithfulness is for all generations;
you established the earth, and it stands firm.
91 Your judgments stand firm today,
for all things are your servants.
92 If your instruction had not been my delight,
I would have died in my affliction.
93 I will never forget your precepts,
for you have given me life through them.
94 I am yours; save me,
for I have studied your precepts.
95 The wicked hope to destroy me,
but I contemplate your decrees.
96 I have seen a limit to all perfection,
but your command is without limit.

מ Mem

97 How I love your instruction!
It is my meditation all day long.
98 Your commands make me wiser than my enemies,
for they are always with me.
99 I have more insight than all my teachers
because your decrees are my meditation.
100 I understand more than the elders
because I obey your precepts.
101 I have kept my feet from every evil path
to follow your word.
102 I have not turned from your judgments,
for you yourself have instructed me.
103 How sweet your word is to my taste —
sweeter than honey in my mouth.
104 I gain understanding from your precepts;
therefore I hate every false way.

נ Nun

105 Your word is a lamp for my feet
and a light on my path.
106 I have solemnly sworn
to keep your righteous judgments.
107 I am severely afflicted;
LORD, give me life according to your word.
108 LORD, please accept my freewill offerings of praise,
and teach me your judgments.

109 My life is constantly in danger,[A]
   yet I do not forget your instruction.
110 The wicked have set a trap for me,
   but I have not wandered from your precepts.
111 I have your decrees as a heritage forever;
   indeed, they are the joy of my heart.
112 I am resolved to obey your statutes
   to the very end.[B]

‏ס‎ Samek

113 I hate those who are double-minded,
   but I love your instruction.
114 You are my shelter and my shield;
   I put my hope in your word.
115 Depart from me, you evil ones,
   so that I may obey my God's commands.
116 Sustain me as you promised, and I will live;
   do not let me be ashamed of my hope.
117 Sustain me so that I can be safe
   and always be concerned about your statutes.
118 You reject all who stray from your statutes,
   for their deceit is a lie.
119 You remove all the wicked on earth
   as if they were[C] dross from metal;
   therefore, I love your decrees.
120 I tremble[D] in awe of you;
   I fear your judgments.

‏ע‎ Ayin

121 I have done what is just and right;
   do not leave me to my oppressors.
122 Guarantee your servant's well-being;
   do not let the arrogant oppress me.
123 My eyes grow weary looking for your salvation
   and for your righteous promise.
124 Deal with your servant based on
      your faithful love;
   teach me your statutes.
125 I am your servant; give me understanding
   so that I may know your decrees.
126 It is time for the LORD to act,
   for they have violated your instruction.
127 Since I love your commands
   more than gold, even the purest gold,
128 I carefully follow all your precepts
   and hate every false way.

[A]119:109 Lit *in my hand*   [B]119:112 Or *statutes; the reward is eternal*
[C]119:119 Some Hb mss, DSS, LXX, Aq, Sym, Jer read *All the wicked of the earth you count as*   [D]119:120 Lit *My flesh shudders*

פ Pe

129 Your decrees are wondrous;
therefore I obey them.
130 The revelation of your words brings light
and gives understanding to the inexperienced.
131 I open my mouth and pant
because I long for your commands.
132 Turn to me and be gracious to me,
as is your practice toward those who love your name.
133 Make my steps steady through your promise;
don't let any sin dominate me.
134 Redeem me from human oppression,
and I will keep your precepts.
135 Make your face shine on your servant,
and teach me your statutes.
136 My eyes pour out streams of tears
because people do not follow your instruction.

צ Tsade

137 You are righteous, LORD,
and your judgments are just.
138 The decrees you issue are righteous
and altogether trustworthy.
139 My anger overwhelms me
because my foes forget your words.
140 Your word is completely pure,
and your servant loves it.
141 I am insignificant and despised,
but I do not forget your precepts.
142 Your righteousness is an everlasting righteousness,
and your instruction is true.
143 Trouble and distress have overtaken me,
but your commands are my delight.
144 Your decrees are righteous forever.
Give me understanding, and I will live.

ק Qoph

145 I call with all my heart; answer me, LORD.
I will obey your statutes.
146 I call to you; save me,
and I will keep your decrees.
147 I rise before dawn and cry out for help;
I put my hope in your word.
148 I am awake through each watch of the night
to meditate on your promise.
149 In keeping with your faithful love, hear my voice.
LORD, give me life in keeping with your justice.
150 Those who pursue evil plans^A come near;

---

^A119:150 Some Hb mss, LXX, Sym, Jer read *who maliciously persecute me*

CAUSE FOR CELEBRATION

PSALMS 120–123; ROMANS 5:3-4

Psalms 120 through 134 are known as the Songs of Ascent. Like the hymns you hum as you drive to church on Sunday morning, these psalms were traditionally sung by pilgrims as they made their way to Jerusalem. Only, unlike a Sunday drive, the journey these pilgrims were on involved leaving their familiar places and people, and passing through dangerous, often unwelcoming, lands.

Maybe you know what it's like to feel out of place, alone in your convictions. The psalmist did, and it caused him to cry out, "LORD, rescue me from lying lips and a deceitful tongue" (Ps 120:2). As the travelers sang about persecution on their pilgrimage to Zion (the mountain of God), we, too, often find ourselves alone or under attack as we seek to honor Him.

God's Word never tells us our troubles will go away because we follow Christ, or that our enemies will eventually see things from our perspective. The Bible doesn't promise the "warrior's sharp arrows" won't sting and the "burning charcoal" won't burn (Ps 120:4).

But do you know what Scripture does say about persecution? God tells us that it's a cause for celebration.

Whoa.

Instead of promising that our suffering will soon be over, or that our enemies will one day be miserable, God's Word promises something better, something eternal:

> ". . . But we also rejoice in our afflictions, because we know that affliction produces endurance, endurance produces proven character, and proven character produces hope."
>
> ROMANS 5:3-4

It all makes sense on paper. But it's hard to think in terms of eternity when the liar is prospering, when your loved ones are hurting, and your integrity seems to be running you into the ground. It's a real struggle to think in terms of celebration when this temporary world is a particularly painful place to live.

But the Holy Spirit—ever faithful, ever gentle—realigns my heart and reminds me of that four-letter word: *hope*.

It's what the Israelites had as they began their journey to the mountain of God.

It's what I had when I woke up this morning, and what I'll have when I climb into bed tonight.

Hope is our good gift, our reward, from our great and loving God. And it comes out of suffering.

Not only does the Bible give us this promise—it gives us proof. The greatest hope of all was produced and purchased by the suffering of our Savior, Jesus Christ. **His resurrection is the reason we can hope today, no matter the road we're traveling.**

We can suffer with a skip in our step, we can rejoice in our suffering, because hope is real. It is promised. It is proven, and it is ours in Christ Jesus. Thanks be to God.

6 The sun will not strike you by day
or the moon by night.

7 The Lord will protect you from all harm;
he will protect your life.
8 The Lord will protect your coming
and going
both now and forever.

A PRAYER FOR JERUSALEM

122

A song of ascents. Of David.
I rejoiced with those who said to me,
"Let us go to the house of the Lord."
2 Our feet were standing
within your gates, Jerusalem —

3 Jerusalem, built as a city should be,
solidly united,
4 where the tribes, the Lord's tribes, go up
to give thanks to the name of the Lord.
(This is an ordinance for Israel.)
5 There, thrones for judgment are placed,
thrones of the house of David.

6 Pray for the well-being[A] of Jerusalem:
"May those who love you be secure;
7 may there be peace within your walls,
security within your fortresses."
8 Because of my brothers and friends,
I will say, "May peace be in you."[B]
9 Because of the house of the Lord our God,
I will pursue your prosperity.

LOOKING FOR GOD'S FAVOR

123

A song of ascents.
I lift my eyes to you,
the one enthroned in heaven.
2 Like a servant's eyes
on his master's hand,
like a servant girl's eyes on her mistress's hand,
so our eyes are on the Lord our God
until he shows us favor.

3 Show us favor, Lord, show us favor,
for we've had more than enough contempt.
4 We've had more than enough
scorn from the arrogant
and contempt from the proud.

[A]122:6 Or *peace* [B]122:8 = Jerusalem

THE LORD IS ON OUR SIDE

124
A song of ascents. Of David.

If the Lord had not been on our side —
let Israel say —

2 If the Lord had not been on our side
when people attacked us,

3 then they would have swallowed us alive
in their burning anger against us.

4 Then the water would have engulfed us;
the torrent would have swept over us;

5 the raging water would have swept over us.

6 Blessed be the Lord,
who has not let us be ripped apart by their teeth.

7 We have escaped like a bird from the hunter's net;
the net is torn, and we have escaped.

8 Our help is in the name of the Lord,
the Maker of heaven and earth.

ISRAEL'S STABILITY

125
A song of ascents.

Those who trust in the Lord are like Mount Zion.
It cannot be shaken; it remains forever.

2 The mountains surround Jerusalem
and the Lord surrounds his people,
both now and forever.

3 The scepter of the wicked will not remain
over the land allotted to the righteous,
so that the righteous will not apply
their hands to injustice.

4 Do what is good, Lord, to the good,
to those whose hearts are upright.

5 But as for those who turn aside to crooked ways,
the Lord will banish them with the evildoers.

Peace be with Israel.

ZION'S RESTORATION

126
A song of ascents.

When the Lord restored the fortunes of Zion,[A]
we were like those who dream.

2 Our mouths were filled with laughter then,
and our tongues with shouts of joy.
Then they said among the nations,
"The Lord has done great things for them."

3 The Lord had done great things for us;
we were joyful.

[A]126:1 Or *Lord returned those of Zion who had been captives*

⁴ Restore our fortunes,ᴬ Lᴏʀᴅ,
   like watercourses in the Negev.
⁵ Those who sow in tears
   will reap with shouts of joy.
⁶ Though one goes along weeping,
   carrying the bag of seed,
   he will surely come back with shouts of joy,
   carrying his sheaves.

THE BLESSING OF THE LORD

127

A song of ascents. Of Solomon.
Unless the Lᴏʀᴅ builds a house,
its builders labor over it in vain;
unless the Lᴏʀᴅ watches over a city,
the watchman stays alert in vain.

² In vain you get up early and stay up late,
   working hard to have enough food —
   yes, he gives sleep to the one he loves.ᴮ

³ Sons are indeed a heritage from the Lᴏʀᴅ,
   offspring, a reward.
⁴ Like arrows in the hand of a warrior
   are the sons born in one's youth.
⁵ Happy is the man who has filled
      his quiver with them.
   They will never be put to shame
   when they speak with their enemies at the city gate.

BLESSINGS FOR THOSE WHO FEAR GOD

128

A song of ascents.
How happy is everyone
   who fears the Lᴏʀᴅ,
   who walks in his ways!
² You will surely eat
   what your hands have worked for.
   You will be happy,
   and it will go well for you.
³ Your wife will be like a fruitful vine
   within your house,
   your children, like young olive trees
   around your table.
⁴ In this very way
   the man who fears the Lᴏʀᴅ
   will be blessed.

⁵ May the Lᴏʀᴅ bless you from Zion,
   so that you will see the prosperity of Jerusalem

ᴬ126:4 Or *Return our captives*   ᴮ127:2 Or *yes, he gives such things to his loved ones while they sleep*

all the days of your life
⁶ and will see your children's children!

Peace be with Israel.

PROTECTION OF THE OPPRESSED

129

A song of ascents.
Since my youth they have often attacked me —
let Israel say —
² Since my youth they have often attacked me,
but they have not prevailed against me.
³ Plowmen plowed over my back;
they made their furrows long.
⁴ The LORD is righteous;
he has cut the ropes of the wicked.

⁵ Let all who hate Zion
be driven back in disgrace.
⁶ Let them be like grass on the rooftops,
which withers before it grows up^A
⁷ and can't even fill the hands of the reaper
or the arms of the one who binds sheaves.
⁸ Then none who pass by will say,
"May the LORD's blessing be on you.
We bless you in the name of the LORD."

AWAITING REDEMPTION

130

A song of ascents.
Out of the depths I call to you, LORD!
² Lord, listen to my voice;
let your ears be attentive
to my cry for help.

³ LORD, if you kept an account of iniquities,
Lord, who could stand?
⁴ But with you there is forgiveness,
so that you may be revered.

⁵ I wait for the LORD; I wait
and put my hope in his word.
⁶ I wait for the Lord
more than watchmen for the morning —
more than watchmen for the morning.

⁷ Israel, put your hope in the LORD.
For there is faithful love with the LORD,
and with him is redemption
in abundance.

---

^A129:6 Or *it can be pulled out*

8 And he will redeem Israel
from all its iniquities.

A CHILDLIKE SPIRIT

131

A song of ascents. Of David.

Lord, my heart is not proud;
my eyes are not haughty.
I do not get involved with things
too great or too wondrous for me.

2 Instead, I have calmed and quieted my soul
like a weaned child with its mother;
my soul is like a weaned child.

3 Israel, put your hope in the Lord,
both now and forever.

DAVID AND ZION CHOSEN

132

A song of ascents.

Lord, remember David
and all the hardships he endured,

2 and how he swore an oath to the Lord,
making a vow to the Mighty One of Jacob:

3 "I will not enter my house
or get into my bed,

4 I will not allow my eyes to sleep
or my eyelids to slumber

5 until I find a place for the Lord,
a dwelling for the Mighty One of Jacob."

6 We heard of the ark in Ephrathah;[A]
we found it in the fields of Jaar.[B]

7 Let us go to his dwelling place;
let us worship at his footstool.

8 Rise up, Lord, come to your resting place,
you and your powerful ark.

9 May your priests be clothed with righteousness,
and may your faithful people shout for joy.

10 For the sake of your servant David,
do not reject your anointed one.[C]

11 The Lord swore an oath to David,
a promise he will not abandon:
"I will set one of your offspring[D]
on your throne.

12 If your sons keep my covenant
and my decrees that I will teach them,
their sons will also sit on your throne forever."

[A]132:6 = Bethlehem [B]132:6 = Kiriath-jearim [C]132:10 = the king [D]132:11 Lit
set the fruit of your belly

HE KEEPS HIS PROMISES

PSALMS 128–132

"The LORD swore an oath to David,
a promise he will not abandon:
'I will set one of your offspring on
your throne.'"

PSALM 132:11

I don't know about you, but I struggle to make plans one month, one week, sometimes even one day out. Life is unpredictable; my emotions, my body, the state of my house are unpredictable. When I read in Scripture that our God makes promises—grand promises!—to nations, to generations, even to us today and keeps them all, I have two distinct reactions: I am relieved. And then, I doubt.

Isn't it too good to be true?

Psalm 132 is a song about promises. It is about a promise David made to God, a vow not to rest until he found "a place for the LORD, a dwelling for the Mighty One of Jacob" (Ps 132:5). What David is searching for is the ark of the covenant, a wooden box containing reminders of God's promises and provisions for the people of Israel. The ark was a symbol of God's presence. David vowed to find it, to keep it near, and he did just that (2Sm 6:12-17).

But more than this, Psalm 132 is about God's promise to David. God made a covenant with David that his future generations would inherit the throne and that God's presence and provision would be with them.

If we learn one thing in Scripture, it's that our God delights in keeping His promises (2Pt 3:9). He delights in redeeming us and in exceeding our expectations.

It's true that David's son Solomon inherited the throne, but the larger story is one even David could not have imagined. God fulfilled His covenant with David through Christ, God's own Son. God not only gave David's line the throne; God gave them—and us—Himself.

"This is my resting place forever;
I will make my home here because
I have desired it."

PSALM 132:14

Friends, this means us. **God dwells with us, forever.**

He dwells within us (1Co 3:16)—not because of our goodness, accomplishments, or faithfulness, but because He desires us. He has chosen us.

He chose you yesterday. He chooses you today. He will choose you tomorrow (Jn 6:37-39; Rm 8:38-39).

But the promise does not end there. He vows to bless us. He promises salvation and joy, physical and spiritual provision. We can expect His faithfulness. We can expect His blessing.

Our God may not be predictable, but He is faithful. He is trustworthy. We can expect Him to do what He says He will do.

¹³ For the LORD has chosen Zion;
he has desired it for his home:
¹⁴ "This is my resting place forever;
I will make my home here
because I have desired it.
¹⁵ I will abundantly bless its food;
I will satisfy its needy with bread.
¹⁶ I will clothe its priests with salvation,
and its faithful people will shout for joy.
¹⁷ There I will make a horn grow for David;
I have prepared a lamp for my anointed one.
¹⁸ I will clothe his enemies with shame,
but the crown he wears^A will be glorious."

LIVING IN HARMONY

133 *A song of ascents. Of David.*
How good and pleasant it is
when brothers live together in harmony!
² It is like fine oil on the head,
running down on the beard,
running down Aaron's beard
onto his robes.
³ It is like the dew of Hermon^B
falling on the mountains of Zion.
For there the LORD has appointed the blessing —
life forevermore.

CALL TO EVENING WORSHIP

134 *A song of ascents.*
Now bless the LORD,
all you servants of the LORD
who stand in the LORD's house at night!
² Lift up your hands in the holy place
and bless the LORD!

³ May the LORD,
Maker of heaven and earth,
bless you from Zion.

THE LORD IS GREAT

135 Hallelujah!
Praise the name of the LORD.
Give praise, you servants of the LORD
² who stand in the house of the LORD,
in the courts of the house of our God.
³ Praise the LORD, for the LORD is good;
sing praise to his name, for it is delightful.

---

^A132:18 Lit but on him his crown ^B133:3 The tallest mountain in the region, noted for its abundant precipitation

4 For the LORD has chosen Jacob
    for himself,
  Israel as his treasured possession.

5 For I know that the LORD is great;
  our Lord is greater than all gods.
6 The LORD does whatever he pleases
  in heaven and on earth,
  in the seas and all the depths.
7 He causes the clouds to rise from the ends
    of the earth.
  He makes lightning for the rain
  and brings the wind from his storehouses.

8 He struck down the firstborn of Egypt,
  both people and animals.
9 He sent signs and wonders
    against you, Egypt,
  against Pharaoh and all his officials.
10 He struck down many nations
  and slaughtered mighty kings:
11 Sihon king of the Amorites,
  Og king of Bashan,
  and all the kings of Canaan.
12 He gave their land as an inheritance,
  an inheritance to his people Israel.

13 LORD, your name endures forever,
  your reputation, LORD,
  through all generations.
14 For the LORD will vindicate his people
  and have compassion on his servants.

15 The idols of the nations are
    of silver and gold,
  made by human hands.
16 They have mouths but cannot speak,
  eyes, but cannot see.
17 They have ears but cannot hear;
  indeed, there is no breath in their mouths.
18 Those who make them are just like them,
  as are all who trust in them.

19 House of Israel, bless the LORD!
  House of Aaron, bless the LORD!
20 House of Levi, bless the LORD!
  You who revere the LORD, bless the LORD!
21 Blessed be the LORD from Zion;
  he dwells in Jerusalem.
  Hallelujah!

GOD'S LOVE IS ETERNAL

136 Give thanks to the LORD, for he is good.
His faithful love endures forever.

2 Give thanks to the God of gods.
His faithful love endures forever.

3 Give thanks to the Lord of lords.
His faithful love endures forever.

4 He alone does great wonders.
His faithful love endures forever.

5 He made the heavens skillfully.
His faithful love endures forever.

6 He spread the land on the waters.
His faithful love endures forever.

7 He made the great lights:
His faithful love endures forever.

8 the sun to rule by day,
His faithful love endures forever.

9 the moon and stars to rule by night.
His faithful love endures forever.

10 He struck the firstborn of the Egyptians
His faithful love endures forever.

11 and brought Israel out from among them
His faithful love endures forever.

12 with a strong hand and outstretched arm.
His faithful love endures forever.

13 He divided the Red Sea
His faithful love endures forever.

14 and led Israel through,
His faithful love endures forever.

15 but hurled Pharaoh
and his army into the Red Sea.
His faithful love endures forever.

16 He led his people in the wilderness.
His faithful love endures forever.

17 He struck down great kings
His faithful love endures forever.

18 and slaughtered famous kings —
His faithful love endures forever.

19 Sihon king of the Amorites
His faithful love endures forever.

20 and Og king of Bashan —
His faithful love endures forever.

21 and gave their land as an inheritance,
His faithful love endures forever.

22 an inheritance to Israel his servant.
His faithful love endures forever.

23 He remembered us in our humiliation
His faithful love endures forever.

24 and rescued us from our foes.
His faithful love endures forever.

25 He gives food to every creature.
   His faithful love endures forever.
26 Give thanks to the God of heaven!
   His faithful love endures forever.

LAMENT OF THE EXILES

137
By the rivers of Babylon —
   there we sat down and wept
when we remembered Zion.
2 There we hung up our lyres
   on the poplar trees,
3 for our captors there asked us for songs,
   and our tormentors, for rejoicing:
   "Sing us one of the songs of Zion."

4 How can we sing the LORD's song
   on foreign soil?
5 If I forget you, Jerusalem,
   may my right hand forget its skill.
6 May my tongue stick to the roof of my mouth
   if I do not remember you,
   if I do not exalt Jerusalem as my greatest joy!

7 Remember, LORD, what the Edomites said
   that day[A] at Jerusalem:
   "Destroy it! Destroy it
   down to its foundations!"
8 Daughter Babylon, doomed to destruction,
   happy is the one who pays you back
   what you have done to us.
9 Happy is he who takes your little ones
   and dashes them against the rocks.

A THANKFUL HEART

138
Of David.
I will give you thanks with all my heart;
   I will sing your praise before the heavenly beings.[B]
2 I will bow down toward your holy temple
   and give thanks to your name
   for your constant love and truth.
   You have exalted your name
   and your promise above everything else.[C]
3 On the day I called, you answered me;
   you increased strength within me.[D]

4 All the kings on earth will give you thanks, LORD,

[A]137:7 The day Jerusalem fell to the Babylonians in 586 BC [B]138:1 Or *before the gods,* or *before judges,* or *before kings*; Hb *elohim* [C]138:2 Or *You have exalted your promise above all your name* [D]138:3 Hb obscure

when they hear what you have promised.[A]
5 They will sing of the LORD's ways,
for the LORD's glory is great.
6 Though the LORD is exalted,
he takes note of the humble;
but he knows the haughty from a distance.

7 If I walk into the thick of danger,
you will preserve my life
from the anger of my enemies.
You will extend your hand;
your right hand will save me.
8 The LORD will fulfill his purpose for me.
LORD, your faithful love endures forever;
do not abandon the work of your hands.

THE ALL-KNOWING, EVER-PRESENT GOD

139

For the choir director. A psalm of David.

LORD, you have searched me and known me.
2 You know when I sit down and when I stand up;
you understand my thoughts from far away.
3 You observe my travels and my rest;
you are aware of all my ways.
4 Before a word is on my tongue,
you know all about it, LORD.
5 You have encircled me;
you have placed your hand on me.
6 This wondrous knowledge is beyond me.
It is lofty; I am unable to reach it.

7 Where can I go to escape your Spirit?
Where can I flee from your presence?
8 If I go up to heaven, you are there;
if I make my bed in Sheol, you are there.
9 If I live at the eastern horizon
or settle at the western limits,[B]
10 even there your hand will lead me;
your right hand will hold on to me.
11 If I say, "Surely the darkness will hide me,
and the light around me will be night" —
12 even the darkness is not dark to you.
The night shines like the day;
darkness and light are alike to you.

13 For it was you who created my inward parts;[C]
you knit me together in my mother's womb.
14 I will praise you

[A]138:4 Lit *hear the words of your mouth* [B]139:9 Lit *I take up the wings of the dawn; I dwell at the end of the sea* [C]139:13 Lit *my kidneys*

FULLY KNOWN

PSALMS 138–139; JOHN 10:14-16

Last year, I wrote a book—a spiritual memoir of sorts. It was a gift to pursue this dream, but toward the end of the writing process, the time came for me to send that book to the people I had written about. I wanted them to be able to see what I had written about them before my words went out to the rest of the world.

I had been dreading this for weeks. I hadn't written bad things about anyone, but I knew sending them my book meant exposing a part of myself they had not seen before. They would know what I really thought about them, what I was thinking when we had certain conversations, and the lessons they had taught me, both good and bad.

After I hit "send" on those emails, I wanted to crawl into a hole. Exposing our true selves can have this effect on us.

In Psalm 139, David describes our God with beautiful imagery, how He creates us, encircles us, places His hand over us, leads us, and sees us. Then, David ends with this prayer:

"Search me, God, and know my heart; test me and know my concerns. See if there is any offensive way in me; lead me in the everlasting way."

PSALM 139:23-24

My sinful heart wants to add a quick caveat to that. "Search me, but don't search too hard. Know me, but don't know this part of me."

As much as we desire to be fully known, the thought of someone actually knowing everything about us is a little bit terrifying. Even though we know the characteristics of God described in Psalm 139 are true—He creates us, encircles us, and leads us—we have this ancient, knee-jerk reaction to hide ourselves from Him when we sin, to hide our shame from Him (Gn 3:8).

It can be difficult for us to understand that God sees us differently than we see ourselves (1Sm 16:7). Scripture says those who have been baptized in Christ "have been clothed with Christ" (Gl 3:27). I like this metaphor because it explains two things: Christ covers us, and we look different in Christ.

Because of Jesus, we have new clothes; so when God sees us, He sees the new us, not the old us. It's in these new garments that we approach the throne, and it's there that we receive the opposite of what we deserve: mercy and grace (Heb 4:16).

When we are confident in our covering in Christ, there is no reason to cringe or run into a hole when we ask Him to search us and to know us. He is the God who creates you, leads you, and encircles you. There is nothing He doesn't already know, and there is nothing that can keep you from Him when you are in Christ Jesus (Rm 8:38-39).

because I have been remarkably
and wondrously made.[A,B]
Your works are wondrous,
and I know this very well.
15 My bones were not hidden from you
when I was made in secret,
when I was formed in the depths of the earth.
16 Your eyes saw me when I was formless;
all my days were written in your book and planned
before a single one of them began.

17 God, how precious[C] your thoughts are to me;
how vast their sum is!
18 If I counted them,
they would outnumber the grains of sand;
when I wake up,[D] I am still with you.

19 God, if only you would kill the wicked —
you bloodthirsty men, stay away from me —
20 who invoke you deceitfully.
Your enemies swear by you falsely.
21 LORD, don't I hate those who hate you,
and detest those who rebel against you?
22 I hate them with extreme hatred;
I consider them my enemies.

23 Search me, God, and know my heart;
test me and know my concerns.
24 See if there is any offensive[E] way in me;
lead me in the everlasting way.

PRAYER FOR RESCUE

140

For the choir director. A psalm of David.
Rescue me, LORD, from evil men.
Keep me safe from violent men
2 who plan evil in their hearts.
They stir up wars all day long.
3 They make their tongues
as sharp as a snake's bite;
viper's venom is under their lips.

Selah

4 Protect me, LORD,
from the power of the wicked.
Keep me safe from violent men
who plan to make me stumble.[F]

[A]139:14 DSS, some LXX mss, Syr, Jer read *because you are remarkable and wonderful* [B]139:14 Hb obscure [C]139:17 Or *difficult* [D]139:18 Some Hb mss read
I come to an end [E]139:24 Or *idolatrous* [F]140:4 Lit *to trip up my steps*

⁵ The proud hide a trap with ropes for me;
  they spread a net along the path
  and set snares for me. *Selah*

⁶ I say to the LORD, "You are my God."
  Listen, LORD, to my cry for help.
⁷ LORD, my Lord, my strong Savior,
  you shield my head on the day of battle.
⁸ LORD, do not grant the desires of the wicked;
  do not let them achieve their goals.
  Otherwise, they will become proud. *Selah*

⁹ When those who surround me rise up,ᴬ
  may the trouble their lips cause
    overwhelm them.
¹⁰ Let hot coals fall on them.
  Let them be thrown into the fire,
  into the abyss, never again to rise.
¹¹ Do not let a slanderer stay in the land.
  Let evil relentlesslyᴮ hunt down a violent man.

¹² Iᶜ know that the LORD upholds
  the just cause of the poor,
  justice for the needy.
¹³ Surely the righteous will praise your name;
  the upright will live in your presence.

PROTECTION FROM SIN AND SINNERS

141
A psalm of David.
LORD, I call on you; hurry to help me.
  Listen to my voice when I call on you.
² May my prayer be set before you as incense,
  the raising of my hands as the evening offering.

³ LORD, set up a guard for my mouth;
  keep watch at the door of my lips.
⁴ Do not let my heart turn to any evil thing
  or perform wicked acts
  with men who commit sin.
  Do not let me feast on their delicacies.
⁵ Let the righteous one strike me —
  it is an act of faithful love;
  let him rebuke me —
  it is oil for my head;
  let meᴰ not refuse it.
  Even now my prayer is against
  the evil acts of the wicked.ᴱ

ᴬ140:9 Lit *Head of those who surround me*   ᴮ140:11 Hb obscure   ᶜ140:12 Alt
Hb tradition reads *You*   ᴰ141:5 Lit *my head*   ᴱ141:5 Lit *of them*

6 When their rulers[A] will be thrown off
   the sides of a cliff,
   the people[B] will listen to my words,
   for they are pleasing.

7 As when one plows and breaks up the soil,
   turning up rocks,
   so our[C] bones have been scattered
   at the mouth of Sheol.

8 But my eyes look to you, LORD, my Lord.
   I seek refuge in you; do not let me die.[D]
9 Protect me from the trap they have set for me,
   and from the snares of evildoers.
10 Let the wicked fall into their own nets,
   while I pass by safely.

A CRY OF DISTRESS

142 *A Maskil of David. When he was in the cave. A prayer.*

1 I cry aloud to the LORD;
   I plead aloud to the LORD for mercy.
2 I pour out my complaint before him;
   I reveal my trouble to him.
3 Although my spirit is weak within me,
   you know my way.

   Along this path I travel
   they have hidden a trap for me.
4 Look to the right and see:[E]
   no one stands up for me;
   there is no refuge for me;
   no one cares about me.

5 I cry to you, LORD;
   I say, "You are my shelter,
   my portion in the land of the living."
6 Listen to my cry,
   for I am very weak.
   Rescue me from those who pursue me,
   for they are too strong for me.
7 Free me from prison
   so that I can praise your name.
   The righteous will gather around me
   because you deal generously with me.

[A]141:6 Or judges [B]141:6 Lit cliff, and they [C]141:7 DSS reads my; some LXX mss, Syr read their [D]141:8 Or not pour out my life [E]142:4 DSS, LXX, Syr, Vg, Tg read I look to the right and I see

A CRY FOR HELP

143
A psalm of David.
LORD, hear my prayer.
In your faithfulness listen to my plea,
and in your righteousness answer me.

2 Do not bring your servant
into judgment,
for no one alive is righteous
in your sight.

3 For the enemy has pursued me,
crushing me to the ground,
making me live in darkness
like those long dead.

4 My spirit is weak within me;
my heart is overcome with dismay.

5 I remember the days of old;
I meditate on all you have done;
I reflect on the work of your hands.

6 I spread out my hands to you;
I am like parched land before you. *Selah*

7 Answer me quickly, LORD;
my spirit fails.
Don't hide your face from me,
or I will be like those
going down to the Pit.

8 Let me experience
your faithful love in the morning,
for I trust in you.
Reveal to me the way I should go
because I appeal to you.

9 Rescue me from my enemies, LORD;
I come to you for protection.[A]

10 Teach me to do your will,
for you are my God.
May your gracious Spirit
lead me on level ground.

11 For your name's sake, LORD,
let me live.
In your righteousness deliver me
from trouble,

12 and in your faithful love
destroy my enemies.
Wipe out all those who attack me,
for I am your servant.

[A]143:9 One Hb ms, LXX; some Hb mss read *I cover myself to you*

A KING'S PRAYER

144 *Of David.*

Blessed be the Lord, my rock
who trains my hands for battle
and my fingers for warfare.
2 He is my faithful love and my fortress,
my stronghold and my deliverer.
He is my shield, and I take refuge in him;
he subdues my people^A under me.

3 Lord, what is a human that you care for him,
a son of man^B that you think of him?
4 A human is like a breath;
his days are like a passing shadow.

5 Lord, part your heavens and come down.
Touch the mountains, and they will smoke.
6 Flash your lightning and scatter the foe;^C
shoot your arrows and rout them.
7 Reach down^D from on high;
rescue me from deep water,
and set me free
from the grasp of foreigners
8 whose mouths speak lies,
whose right hands are deceptive.

9 God, I will sing a new song to you;
I will play on a ten-stringed harp for you —
10 the one who gives victory to kings,
who frees his servant David
from the deadly sword.
11 Set me free and rescue me
from foreigners
whose mouths speak lies,
whose right hands are deceptive.

12 Then our sons will be like plants
nurtured in their youth,
our daughters, like corner pillars
that are carved in the palace style.
13 Our storehouses will be full,
supplying all kinds of produce;
our flocks will increase by thousands
and tens of thousands in our open fields.
14 Our cattle will be well fed.^E
There will be no breach in the walls,

---

^A144:2 Some Hb mss, DSS, Aq, Syr, Tg, Jer read *subdues peoples*; 2Sm 22:48;
Ps 18:47   ^B144:3 Or *a mere mortal*   ^C144:6 Lit *scatter them*   ^D144:7 Lit *down
your hands*   ^E144:14 Or *will bear heavy loads,* or *will be pregnant*

no going into captivity,[A]
and no cry of lament in our public squares.
15 Happy are the people with such blessings.
Happy are the people whose God is the LORD.

PRAISING GOD'S GREATNESS

145

A hymn of David.

I[B] exalt you, my God the King,
and bless your name forever and ever.
2 I will bless you every day;
I will praise your name forever and ever.

3 The LORD is great and is highly praised;
his greatness is unsearchable.
4 One generation will declare your works to the next
and will proclaim your mighty acts.
5 I[C] will speak of your splendor and glorious majesty
and[D] your wondrous works.
6 They will proclaim the power
of your awe-inspiring acts,
and I will declare your greatness.[E]
7 They will give a testimony of your great goodness
and will joyfully sing of your righteousness.

8 The LORD is gracious and compassionate,
slow to anger and great in faithful love.
9 The LORD is good to everyone;
his compassion rests on all he has made.
10 All you have made will thank you, LORD;
the[F] faithful will bless you.
11 They will speak of the glory of your kingdom
and will declare your might,
12 informing all people of your mighty acts
and of the glorious splendor of your[G] kingdom.
13 Your kingdom is an everlasting kingdom;
your rule is for all generations.
The LORD is faithful in all his words
and gracious in all his actions.[H]

14 The LORD helps all who fall;
he raises up all who are oppressed.[I]
15 All eyes look to you,
and you give them their food at the proper time.

[A]144:14 Or *be no plague, no miscarriage*   [B]145:1 The lines of this poem form
an acrostic.   [C]145:5 LXX, Syr read *They*   [D]145:5 LXX, Syr read *and they will
tell of*   [E]145:6 Alt Hb tradition, Jer read *great deeds*   [F]145:10 Lit *your*
[G]145:12 LXX, Syr, Jer; MT reads *his*   [H]145:13 One Hb ms, DSS, LXX, Syr; some
Hb mss omit *The LORD is faithful in all his words and gracious in all his actions.*
[I]145:14 Lit *bowed down*

16 You open your hand
and satisfy the desire
of every living thing.

17 The LORD is righteous in all his ways
and faithful in all his acts.
18 The LORD is near all who call out to him,
all who call out to him with integrity.
19 He fulfills the desires of those who fear him;
he hears their cry for help and saves them.
20 The LORD guards all those who love him,
but he destroys all the wicked.
21 My mouth will declare the LORD's praise;
let every living thing
bless his holy name forever and ever.

THE GOD OF COMPASSION

146 Hallelujah!
My soul, praise the LORD.
2 I will praise the LORD all my life;
I will sing to my God as long as I live.

3 Do not trust in nobles,
in a son of man,^A who cannot save.
4 When his breath^B leaves him,
he returns to the ground;
on that day his plans die.

5 Happy is the one whose help is
the God of Jacob,
whose hope is in the LORD his God,
6 the Maker of heaven and earth,
the sea and everything in them.
He remains faithful forever,
7 executing justice for the exploited
and giving food to the hungry.
The LORD frees prisoners.
8 The LORD opens the eyes of the blind.
The LORD raises up those
who are oppressed.^C
The LORD loves the righteous.
9 The LORD protects resident aliens
and helps the fatherless and the widow,
but he frustrates the ways of the wicked.

10 The LORD reigns forever;
Zion, your God reigns for all generations.
Hallelujah!

^A146:3 Or *a mere mortal* ^B146:4 Or *spirit* ^C146:8 Lit *bowed down*

GOD RESTORES JERUSALEM

147

Hallelujah!
How good it is to sing to our God,
for praise is pleasant and lovely.

2   The LORD rebuilds Jerusalem;
he gathers Israel's exiled people.
3   He heals the brokenhearted
and bandages their wounds.
4   He counts the number of the stars;
he gives names to all of them.
5   Our Lord is great, vast in power;
his understanding is infinite.[A]
6   The LORD helps the oppressed
but brings the wicked to the ground.

7   Sing to the LORD with thanksgiving;
play the lyre to our God,
8   who covers the sky with clouds,
prepares rain for the earth,
and causes grass to grow on the hills.
9   He provides the animals with their food,
and the young ravens, what they cry for.

10   He is not impressed by the strength of a horse;
he does not value the power of a warrior.[B]
11   The LORD values those who fear him,
those who put their hope in his faithful love.

12   Exalt the LORD, Jerusalem;
praise your God, Zion!
13   For he strengthens the bars of your city gates
and blesses your children within you.
14   He endows your territory with prosperity;[C]
he satisfies you with the finest wheat.

15   He sends his command throughout the earth;
his word runs swiftly.
16   He spreads snow like wool;
he scatters frost like ashes;
17   he throws his hailstones like crumbs.
Who can withstand his cold?
18   He sends his word and melts them;
he unleashes his winds,[D] and the water flows.

19   He declares his word to Jacob,
his statutes and judgments to Israel.

[A]147:5 Lit *understanding has no number*   [B]147:10 Lit *the legs of the man*
[C]147:14 Or *peace*   [D]147:18 Or *breath*

20 He has not done this for every nation;
   they do not know his judgments.
   Hallelujah!

CREATION'S PRAISE OF THE LORD

148 Hallelujah!
   Praise the LORD from the heavens;
   praise him in the heights.
2 Praise him, all his angels;
   praise him, all his heavenly armies.
3 Praise him, sun and moon;
   praise him, all you shining stars.
4 Praise him, highest heavens,
   and you waters above the heavens.
5 Let them praise the name of the LORD,
   for he commanded, and they were created.
6 He set them in position forever and ever;
   he gave an order that will never pass away.

7 Praise the LORD from the earth,
   all sea monsters and ocean depths,
8 lightning^A and hail, snow and cloud,
   stormy wind that executes his command,
9 mountains and all hills,
   fruit trees and all cedars,
10 wild animals and all cattle,
   creatures that crawl and flying birds,
11 kings of the earth and all peoples,
   princes and all judges of the earth,
12 young men as well as young women,
   old and young together.
13 Let them praise the name of the LORD,
   for his name alone is exalted.
   His majesty covers heaven and earth.
14 He has raised up a horn for his people,
   resulting in praise to all his faithful ones,
   to the Israelites, the people close to him.
   Hallelujah!

PRAISE FOR GOD'S TRIUMPH

149 Hallelujah!
   Sing to the LORD a new song,
   his praise in the assembly of the faithful.
2 Let Israel celebrate its Maker;
   let the children of Zion rejoice in their King.
3 Let them praise his name with dancing
   and make music to him with tambourine and lyre.
4 For the LORD takes pleasure in his people;

^A148:8 Or *fire*

he adorns the humble with salvation.
5 Let the faithful celebrate in triumphal glory;
let them shout for joy on their beds.

6 Let the exaltation of God be in their mouths[A]
and a double-edged sword in their hands,
7 inflicting vengeance on the nations
and punishment on the peoples,
8 binding their kings with chains
and their dignitaries with iron shackles,
9 carrying out the judgment decreed against them.
This honor is for all his faithful people.
Hallelujah!

PRAISE THE LORD

150
Hallelujah!
Praise God in his sanctuary.
Praise him in his mighty expanse.
2 Praise him for his powerful acts;
praise him for his abundant greatness.

3 Praise him with trumpet blast;
praise him with harp and lyre.
4 Praise him with tambourine and dance;
praise him with strings and flute.
5 Praise him with resounding cymbals;
praise him with clashing cymbals.

6 Let everything that breathes praise the LORD.
Hallelujah!

A 149:6 Lit throat

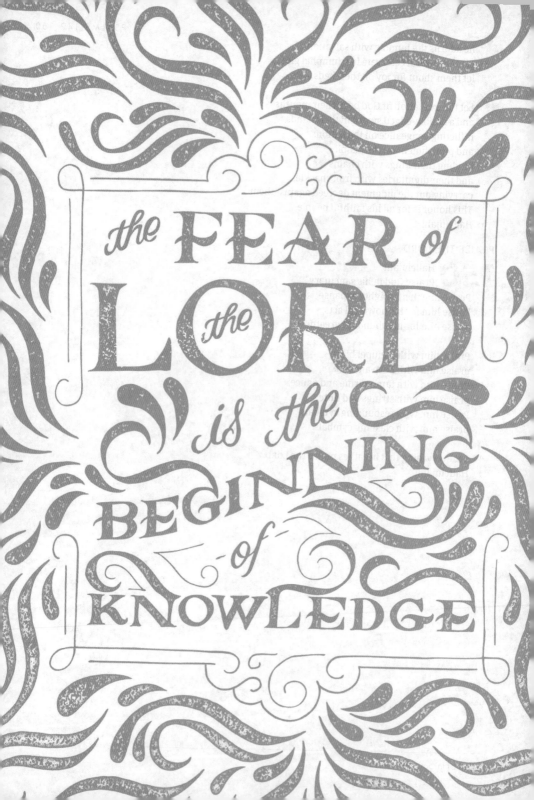

the FEAR of the LORD is the BEGINNING of KNOWLEDGE

proverbs

The fear of the LORD is the beginning of knowledge; fools despise wisdom and discipline. **1:7**

ON THE TIMELINE Solomon is credited with the proverbs in chapters 1–29 of the book of Proverbs (Pr 1:1; 10:1). There is biblical evidence that Solomon was wise and a collector of wise sayings (1Kg 3:5-14). Chapters 1–24 may have been written during his reign (971–931 BC), while chapters 25–29 were Solomon's proverbs collected by King Hezekiah during his reign, from 716–687/6 BC (Pr 25:1). The last two chapters are credited to Agur and Lemuel (Pr 30:1; 31:1), though nothing more is known about them.

A LITTLE BACKGROUND The reign of Solomon represented the peak of prosperity for the nation of Israel. The period saw the greatest extent of the territory, and there was peace and international trade (1Kg 4:20-25; 10:21-29). It is likely Solomon knew about the ancient tradition of wisdom in Egypt (1Kg 3:1), but through inspiration and God's gift, he composed even better sayings (1Kg 3:12; 10:6-7,23).

Solomon addressed his teaching to his son or sons, but these inspired, wise sayings are applicable to all people.

MESSAGE & PURPOSE Because these proverbs are a part of the whole of God's Word, they are not simply for entertainment; they exhort, encourage, and offer hope. Solomon called readers, especially youth, to pursue wisdom rather than foolishness. He encouraged the inexperienced to become wise rather than mockers, to be teachable rather than incorrigible, to live rather than to die. He predicted that people who pursued wisdom would generally find success and happiness in this life, but he promised they would absolutely find joy and blessing in eternity.

GIVE THANKS FOR THE BOOK OF PROVERBS:

The book of Proverbs demands humility. It presumes we have much to learn, and rightly so. If we are looking to crack the code to a successful, easy life, searching for the key in these proverbs will only yield an unassailable to-do list. However, if we want to search for wisdom in an effort to know and enjoy God, then we can approach Proverbs vulnerably, ready to examine our own hearts. We can trust our loving heavenly Father and believe that His scrutiny is for our good.

A GUIDE TO THEMES IN PROVERBS

THE BOOK OF PROVERBS IS RICH WITH WISDOM FOR ALL AREAS OF LIFE

GOD

MAN

BLESSINGS AND CURSES	3:33 27:14 28:20 28:27	
THE COMMANDS OF GOD	4:1-4 6:20-23 29:18 30:5	
THE FEAR OF GOD	3:7-8 8:13 19:23 31:30	
HOW GOD SEES MAN	5:21 16:2 16:7 20:24	
THE WAY OF WISDOM	1:7-9 2:1-12 10:8 28:26	
WHAT GOD HATES	6:16-19 17:15 21:27 28:9	
WHAT GOD LOVES	11:1 15:9 16:11 14:31	

ADVERSITY	3:25-26 17:17 18:14 24:16
DRUNKENNESS	20:1 21:17 26:9 31:4-7
HAPPINESS	3:13 15:23 24:17 29:18
THE HEART	12:25 13:12 14:10 15:13
HUMILITY VS. PRIDE	11:2 15:33 22:4 27:1-2
PATIENCE VS. ANGER	14:29 15:1 19:11 25:8
SEDUCTION AND ENVY	3:31-32 12:26 24:1-2 24:19-20
SPIRITUAL AND PHYSICAL HEALTH	4:20-22 14:30 18:14 25:25
STRENGTH	10:29 14:26 18:10 20:29
THE WAY OF FOLLY	3:35 9:13-18 17:12 18:2

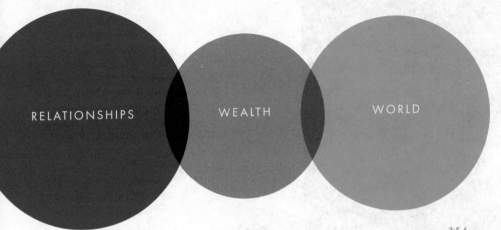

RELATIONSHIPS

ADULTERY	2:11-19 5:1-17 7:4-27 9:13-18
CORRECTION	3:11-12 6:23 12:1 19:20
COUNSEL AND INSTRUCTION	8:10-11 12:15 15:22 17:10
FRIENDSHIP	17:9 18:24 19:6 27:6
NEIGHBORS	14:21 25:17 27:10 29:5
PARENTS AND CHILDREN	14:26 19:18 22:6 22:15
QUARRELS	3:30-31 10:12 17:14 25:8-9
THE TONGUE	10:11 15:1-2 26:4-5 31:8-9
A VIRTUOUS WOMAN	12:4 14:1 18:22 31:10-31

WEALTH

ENVY	6:34 14:30 21:25-26 28:16
DEBT	6:1-5 11:15 22:7 22:26-27
GENEROSITY VS. GREED	3:9 3:27-28 19:17 21:26
GLUTTONY	23:1-8 23:19-21 25:16 28:7
SECURITY	1:33 3:9-10 4:13 13:6
WEALTH VS. POVERTY	6:10-11 11:4 20:21 22:1-2, 4

WORLD

CALLING	3:5-6 15:22 16:9 19:21
DILIGENCE	4:23 12:27 13:11 22:29
FAITHFULNESS	11:13 20:6 25:13,19 28:20
GOOD VS. EVIL	1:10-19 11:3-5 14:14 25:21-22
RIGHTEOUSNESS VS. WICKEDNESS	3:3-4 10:28 14:32 28:13
HOPE AND MERCY	13:23 18:13, 17 21:15 22:28
LAZINESS AND SLOTH	6:6-11 12:14 15:9 19:15
JUSTICE	12:17-22 13:5 16:6 20:17

READ AND UNDERSTAND PROVERBS

The Bible is a complete work in which many stories combine to tell one story. As you read the book of Proverbs, consider reading the additional passages to discover how the whole of Scripture works together.

Week 1

GOING DEEPER

- [ ] **Proverbs 1–2** — John 1:14; 1 Corinthians 1:30
- [ ] Proverbs 3–4 — Deuteronomy 18:1-5; John 14:6
- [ ] Proverbs 5:1–7:5 — John 11:25-26; 1 Corinthians 15:58
- [ ] **Proverbs 7:6–8:36** — John 8:44-47; James 1:5
- [ ] Proverbs 9 — Psalm 141; Revelation 19:9

Week 2

GOING DEEPER

- [ ] Proverbs 10:1–11:15 — James 5:19-20; 1 Peter 4:8
- [ ] Proverbs 11:16–12:28 — Ephesians 4:29; 1 Peter 4:14-19
- [ ] Proverbs 13:1–14:20 — John 6:68-69; Hebrews 12:5-11
- [ ] Proverbs 14:21–15:33 — Deuteronomy 5:7-11; James 1:19-20
- [ ] Proverbs 16:1–17:15 — Romans 3:21-26; Hebrews 4:12-13

Week 3

GOING DEEPER

- [ ] Proverbs 17:16–18:24 — 1 Peter 2:13-17; Revelation 20:11-15
- [ ] Proverbs 19:1–20:15 — Matthew 6:33; Colossians 3:12-14
- [ ] Proverbs 20:16–21:31 — Romans 12:17-21; 1 Peter 2:21-23
- [ ] Proverbs 22:1–23:21 — Deuteronomy 24:10-13; Psalm 19:14
- [ ] Proverbs 23:22–24:34 — Matthew 16:18; Ephesians 5:17-21

Week 4

GOING DEEPER

- [ ] Proverbs 25:1–26:16 — Luke 14:7-11; Colossians 2:1-3
- [ ] Proverbs 26:17–27:27 — Matthew 6:34; Colossians 3:15-17
- [ ] **Proverbs 28–29** — John 15:18-20; 2 Corinthians 3:12-14
- [ ] Proverbs 30 — Psalm 12:6; John 3:12-15
- [ ] **Proverbs 31** — Ephesians 5:22-33; Revelation 19:6-8

THE PURPOSE OF PROVERBS

1 The proverbs of Solomon son of David, king of Israel:
² For learning wisdom and discipline;
for understanding insightful sayings;
³ for receiving prudent instruction
in righteousness, justice, and integrity;
⁴ for teaching shrewdness
to the inexperienced,ᴬ
knowledge and discretion to a young man —
⁵ let a wise person listen and increase learning,
and let a discerning person obtain guidance —
⁶ for understanding a proverb or a parable,ᴮ
the words of the wise, and their riddles.

⁷ The fear of the LORD
is the beginning of knowledge;
fools despise wisdom and discipline.

AVOID THE PATH OF THE VIOLENT

⁸ Listen, my son, to your father's instruction,
and don't reject your mother's teaching,
⁹ for they will be a garland of favor on your head
and pendantsᶜ around your neck.
¹⁰ My son, if sinners entice you,
don't be persuaded.
¹¹ If they say — "Come with us!
Let's set an ambush and kill someone.ᴰ
Let's attack some innocent person just for fun!ᴱ
¹² Let's swallow them alive, like Sheol,
whole, like those who go down to the Pit.
¹³ We'll find all kinds of valuable property
and fill our houses with plunder.
¹⁴ Throw in your lot with us,
and we'll all share the loot"ᶠ —
¹⁵ my son, don't travel that road with them
or set foot on their path,
¹⁶ because their feet run toward evil
and they hurry to shed blood.
¹⁷ It is useless to spread a net
where any bird can see it,
¹⁸ but they set an ambush to kill themselves;ᴳ
they attack their own lives.
¹⁹ Such are the paths of all
who make profit dishonestly;
it takes the lives of those who receive it.ᴴ

ᴬ1:4 Or *simple*, or *gullible*   ᴮ1:6 Or *an enigma*   ᶜ1:9 Lit *chains*   ᴰ1:11 Lit *Let's ambush for blood*   ᴱ1:11 Lit *person for no reason*   ᶠ1:14 Lit *us; one bag will be for all of us*   ᴳ1:18 Lit *they ambush for their blood*   ᴴ1:19 Lit *takes the life of its masters*

THE FEAR OF THE LORD

As a kid, I would sit next to my mom in church with my legs swinging from the pew. (I sometimes needed to rest my eyes, and fortunately for me, this was the wonderful era when moms wore shoulder pads.) As I observed the peaceful look on my mom's face every week during worship, I formed my first understanding of what it looked like to love the Lord.

You can imagine my confusion when one Sunday evening the preacher read this from the pulpit:

"The fear of the LORD is the beginning of knowledge; fools despise wisdom and discipline."

PROVERBS 1:7

Pardon me? Did the Bible just say God wants me to be scared of Him the way I'm scared of spiders in my bed? My mom's face never showed any sign of that kind of fear as she worshiped Him.

I was relieved to learn that the sort of fear we're called to have toward God is a "holy reverence." It is more a posture than a feeling—a position of awe, wonder, and worship before the Lord. Wrestling with God's magnificence stirs up a holy fear in my heart because He is more powerful and wild than I can truly understand.

As children, it was easy to think of wisdom as something contained in textbooks and

conversations with grownups. But that peaceful look on my mother's face wasn't because she was older and smarter than me; it came from knowing and fearing—revering as holy— the One who holds all wisdom. It came from knowing Jesus.

I'm an adult now, but wisdom still seems like something we set out to gain: get this level of education and that amount of experience, learn from your mistakes and do better next time around. Scripture, however, tells us true wisdom is something more—something not measured in degrees or accomplishments. **True wisdom comes from God.**

The true and timeless wisdom we long for will never come from a formula we create, but only from the One who created us. It does not begin with us or our efforts, our discipline, or even our good intentions. It begins with God. Wisdom is a gift only He can give.

As you read through the book of Proverbs, remember this call from the writer of Hebrews: *keep your eyes on Jesus,* "the source and perfecter of our faith. For the joy that lay before him, he endured the cross, despising the shame, and sat down at the right hand of the throne of God" (Heb 12:2).

May your reverent fear of the Savior keep your eyes stayed on Him. The God who knew and loved you long before your young feet dangled from too-tall chairs is the source of all wisdom, and invites us to know Him in His Word. Thanks be to God!

WISDOM'S PLEA

20 Wisdom calls out in the street;
    she makes her voice heard in the public squares.
21 She cries out above^A the commotion;
    she speaks at the entrance of the city gates:
22 "How long, inexperienced ones,
        will you love ignorance?
    How long will you mockers enjoy mocking
    and you fools hate knowledge?
23 If you respond to my warning,^B
    then I will pour out my spirit on you
    and teach you my words.
24 Since I called out and you refused,
    extended my hand and no one paid attention,
25 since you neglected all my counsel
    and did not accept my correction,
26 I, in turn, will laugh at your calamity.
    I will mock when terror strikes you,
27 when terror strikes you like a storm
    and your calamity comes like a whirlwind,
    when trouble and stress overcome you.
28 Then they will call me, but I won't answer;
    they will search for me, but won't find me.
29 Because they hated knowledge,
    didn't choose to fear the Lord,
30 were not interested in my counsel,
    and rejected all my correction,
31 they will eat the fruit of their way
    and be glutted with their own schemes.
32 For the apostasy of the inexperienced will kill them,
    and the complacency of fools will destroy them.
33 But whoever listens to me will live securely
    and be undisturbed by the dread of danger."

WISDOM'S WORTH

2 My son, if you accept my words
    and store up my commands within you,
2 listening closely^C to wisdom
    and directing your heart to understanding;
3 furthermore, if you call out to insight
    and lift your voice to understanding,
4 if you seek it like silver
    and search for it like hidden treasure,
5 then you will understand the fear of the Lord
    and discover the knowledge of God.
6 For the Lord gives wisdom;
    from his mouth come knowledge and understanding.

---

^A1:21 Lit *at the head of*   ^B1:23 Lit *you turn back to my reprimand*   ^C2:2 Lit *you,*
stretching out your ear

⁷ He stores up success[A] for the upright;
He is a shield for those who live with integrity
⁸ so that he may guard the paths of justice
and protect the way of his faithful followers.
⁹ Then you will understand righteousness, justice,
and integrity — every good path.
¹⁰ For wisdom will enter your heart,
and knowledge will delight you.
¹¹ Discretion will watch over you,
and understanding will guard you.
¹² It will rescue you from the way of evil —
from anyone who says perverse things,
¹³ from those who abandon the right paths
to walk in ways of darkness,
¹⁴ from those who enjoy doing evil
and celebrate perversion,
¹⁵ whose paths are crooked,
and whose ways are devious.
¹⁶ It will rescue you from a forbidden woman,
from a wayward woman with her flattering talk,
¹⁷ who abandons the companion of her youth
and forgets the covenant of her God;
¹⁸ for her house sinks down to death
and her ways to the land of the departed spirits.
¹⁹ None return who go to her;
none reach the paths of life.
²⁰ So follow the way of the good,
and keep to the paths of the righteous.
²¹ For the upright will inhabit the land,
and those of integrity will remain in it;
²² but the wicked will be cut off from the land,
and the treacherous ripped out of it.

TRUST THE LORD

3 My son, don't forget my teaching,
but let your heart keep my commands;
² for they will bring you
many days, a full life,[B] and well-being.
³ Never let loyalty and faithfulness leave you.
Tie them around your neck;
write them on the tablet of your heart.
⁴ Then you will find favor and high regard
with God and people.

⁵ Trust in the LORD with all your heart,
and do not rely on your own understanding;
⁶ in all your ways know him,
and he will make your paths straight.

[A]2:7 Or *resourcefulness* [B]3:2 Lit *days, years of life*

7 Don't be wise in your own eyes;
  fear the LORD and turn away from evil.
8 This will be healing for your body[A]
  and strengthening for your bones.
9 Honor the LORD with your possessions
  and with the first produce
    of your entire harvest;
10 then your barns will be completely filled,
  and your vats will overflow with new wine.
11 Do not despise the LORD's instruction, my son,
  and do not loathe his discipline;
12 for the LORD disciplines the one he loves,
  just as a father disciplines the son in whom
    he delights.

WISDOM BRINGS HAPPINESS

13 Happy is a man who finds wisdom
  and who acquires understanding,
14 for she is more profitable than silver,
  and her revenue is better than gold.
15 She is more precious than jewels;
  nothing you desire can equal her.
16 Long life[B] is in her right hand;
  in her left, riches and honor.
17 Her ways are pleasant,
  and all her paths, peaceful.
18 She is a tree of life to those who embrace her,
  and those who hold on to her are happy.

19 The LORD founded the earth by wisdom
  and established the heavens by understanding.
20 By his knowledge the watery depths broke open,
  and the clouds dripped with dew.

21 Maintain sound wisdom and discretion.
  My son, don't lose sight of them.
22 They will be life for you[C]
  and adornment[D] for your neck.
23 Then you will go safely on your way;
  your foot will not stumble.
24 When you lie[E] down, you will not be afraid;
  you will lie down, and your sleep
    will be pleasant.
25 Don't fear sudden danger
  or the ruin of the wicked when it comes,
26 for the LORD will be your confidence[F]
  and will keep your foot from a snare.

[A]3:8 Lit navel [B]3:16 Lit Length of days [C]3:22 Or be your throat [D]3:22 Or grace
[E]3:24 LXX reads sit [F]3:26 Or be at your side

TREAT OTHERS FAIRLY

27 When it is in your power,[A]
don't withhold good from the one to whom it belongs.

28 Don't say to your neighbor, "Go away! Come back later.
I'll give it tomorrow" — when it is there with you.

29 Don't plan any harm against your neighbor,
for he trusts you and lives near you.

30 Don't accuse anyone without cause,
when he has done you no harm.

31 Don't envy a violent man
or choose any of his ways;

32 for the devious are detestable to the LORD,
but he is a friend[B] to the upright.

33 The LORD's curse is on the household of the wicked,
but he blesses the home of the righteous;

34 He mocks those who mock,
but gives grace to the humble.

35 The wise will inherit honor,
but he holds up fools to dishonor.[C]

A FATHER'S EXAMPLE

4 Listen, sons, to a father's discipline,
and pay attention so that you may gain understanding,

2 for I am giving you good instruction.
Don't abandon my teaching.

3 When I was a son with my father,
tender and precious to my mother,

4 he taught me and said:
"Your heart must hold on to my words.
Keep my commands and live.

5 Get wisdom, get understanding;
don't forget or turn away from the words from my mouth.

6 Don't abandon wisdom, and she will watch over you;
love her, and she will guard you.

7 Wisdom is supreme — so get wisdom.
And whatever else you get, get understanding.

8 Cherish her, and she will exalt you;
if you embrace her, she will honor you.

9 She will place a garland of favor on your head;
she will give you a crown of beauty."

TWO WAYS OF LIFE

10 Listen, my son. Accept my words,
and you will live many years.

11 I am teaching you the way of wisdom;
I am guiding you on straight paths.

12 When you walk, your steps will not be hindered;

[A]3:27 Lit *in the power of your hands*   [B]3:32 Or *confidential counsel*
[C]3:35 Or *but haughty fools dishonor*, or *but fools exalt dishonor*

when you run, you will not stumble.
13 Hold on to instruction; don't let go.
Guard it, for it is your life.
14 Keep off the path of the wicked;
don't proceed on the way of evil ones.
15 Avoid it; don't travel on it.
Turn away from it, and pass it by.
16 For they can't sleep
unless they have done what is evil;
they are robbed of sleep
unless they make someone stumble.
17 They eat the bread of wickedness
and drink the wine of violence.
18 The path of the righteous is like the light of dawn,
shining brighter and brighter until midday.
19 But the way of the wicked is like the darkest gloom;
they don't know what makes them stumble.

THE STRAIGHT PATH

20 My son, pay attention to my words;
listen closely to my sayings.
21 Don't lose sight of them;
keep them within your heart.
22 For they are life to those who find them,
and health to one's whole body.
23 Guard your heart above all else,^A
for it is the source of life.
24 Don't let your mouth speak dishonestly,
and don't let your lips talk deviously.
25 Let your eyes look forward;
fix your gaze^B straight ahead.
26 Carefully consider the path^C for your feet,
and all your ways will be established.
27 Don't turn to the right or to the left;
keep your feet away from evil.

AVOID SEDUCTION

5 My son, pay attention to my wisdom;
listen closely^D to my understanding
2 so that you may maintain discretion
and your lips safeguard knowledge.
3 Though the lips of the forbidden woman drip honey
and her words are^E smoother than oil,
4 in the end she's as bitter as wormwood
and as sharp as a double-edged sword.
5 Her feet go down to death;
her steps head straight for Sheol.

---

^A4:23 Or *heart with all diligence*   ^B4:25 Lit *eyelids*   ^C4:26 Or *Clear a path*
^D5:1 Lit *wisdom; stretch out your ear*   ^E5:3 Lit *her palate is*

⁶ She doesn't consider the path of life;
  she doesn't know that her ways are unstable.

⁷ So now, sons, listen to me,
  and don't turn away from the words from my mouth.
⁸ Keep your way far from her.
  Don't go near the door of her house.
⁹ Otherwise, you will give up your vitality to others
  and your years to someone cruel;
¹⁰ strangers will drain your resources,
  and your hard-earned pay will end up in a foreigner's house.
¹¹ At the end of your life, you will lament
  when your physical body has been consumed,
¹² and you will say, "How I hated discipline,
  and how my heart despised correction.
¹³ I didn't obey my teachers
  or listen closely^A to my instructors.
¹⁴ I am on the verge of complete ruin
  before the entire community."

ENJOY MARRIAGE

¹⁵ Drink water from your own cistern,
  water flowing from your own well.
¹⁶ Should your springs flow in the streets,
  streams in the public squares?
¹⁷ They should be for you alone
  and not for you to share with strangers.
¹⁸ Let your fountain be blessed,
  and take pleasure in the wife of your youth.
¹⁹ A loving deer, a graceful doe^B —
  let her breasts always satisfy you;
  be lost in her love forever.
²⁰ Why, my son, would you lose yourself
  with a forbidden woman
  or embrace a wayward woman?
²¹ For a man's ways are before the Lord's eyes,
  and he considers all his paths.
²² A wicked man's iniquities will trap him;
  he will become tangled in the ropes of his own sin.
²³ He will die because there is no discipline,
  and be lost because of his great stupidity.

FINANCIAL ENTANGLEMENTS

6 My son, if you have put up security for your neighbor^C
  or entered into an agreement with^D a stranger,
² you have been snared by the words of your mouth,
  trapped by the words from your mouth.

---

^A 5:13 Lit *or turn my ear* ^B 5:19 Or *graceful mountain goat* ^C 6:1 Or *friend*
^D 6:1 Lit *or slapped hands for*

3   Do this, then, my son, and free yourself,
    for you have put yourself in your neighbor's power:
    Go, humble yourself, and plead with your neighbor.
4   Don't give sleep to your eyes
    or slumber to your eyelids.
5   Escape like a gazelle from a hunter,^A
    like a bird from a hunter's trap.^A

LAZINESS

6   Go to the ant, you slacker!
    Observe its ways and become wise.
7   Without leader, administrator, or ruler,
8   it prepares its provisions in summer;
    it gathers its food during harvest.
9   How long will you stay in bed, you slacker?
    When will you get up from your sleep?
10 A little sleep, a little slumber,
    a little folding of the arms to rest,
11 and your poverty will come like a robber,
    your need, like a bandit.

THE MALICIOUS MAN

12 A worthless person, a wicked man
    goes around speaking dishonestly,
13 winking his eyes, signaling with his feet,
    and gesturing with his fingers.
14 He always plots evil with perversity in his heart;
    he stirs up trouble.
15 Therefore calamity will strike him suddenly;
    he will be shattered instantly, beyond recovery.

WHAT THE LORD HATES

16 The LORD hates six things;
    in fact, seven are detestable to him:
17 arrogant eyes, a lying tongue,
    hands that shed innocent blood,
18 a heart that plots wicked schemes,
    feet eager to run to evil,
19 a lying witness who gives false testimony,
    and one who stirs up trouble among brothers.

WARNING AGAINST ADULTERY

20 My son, keep your father's command,
    and don't reject your mother's teaching.
21 Always bind them to your heart;
    tie them around your neck.
22 When you walk here and there, they will guide you;
    when you lie down, they will watch over you;

---

^A6:5 Lit hand

when you wake up, they will talk to you.
23 For a command is a lamp, teaching is a light,
    and corrective discipline is the way to life.
24 They will protect you from an evil woman,[A]
    from the flattering[B] tongue of a wayward woman.
25 Don't lust in your heart for her beauty
    or let her captivate you with her eyelashes.
26 For a prostitute's fee is only a loaf of bread,[C]
    but the wife of another man[D] goes after
        a precious life.
27 Can a man embrace fire
    and his clothes not be burned?
28 Can a man walk on burning coals
    without scorching his feet?
29 So it is with the one who sleeps with
        another man's wife;
    no one who touches her will go unpunished.
30 People don't despise the thief if he steals
    to satisfy himself when he is hungry.
31 Still, if caught, he must pay seven times as much;
    he must give up all the wealth in his house.
32 The one who commits adultery[E] lacks sense;
    whoever does so destroys himself.
33 He will get a beating[F] and dishonor,
    and his disgrace will never be removed.
34 For jealousy enrages a husband,
    and he will show no mercy
        when he takes revenge.
35 He will not be appeased by anything
    or be persuaded by lavish bribes.

7 My son, obey my words,
    and treasure my commands.
2 Keep my commands and live,
    and guard my instructions
        as you would the pupil of your eye.
3 Tie them to your fingers;
    write them on the tablet of your heart.
4 Say to wisdom, "You are my sister,"
    and call understanding your relative.
5 She will keep you from a forbidden woman,
    a wayward woman with her flattering talk.

A STORY OF SEDUCTION

6 At the window of my house
    I looked through my lattice.

[A]6:24 LXX reads from a married woman   [B]6:24 Lit smooth   [C]6:26 Or On
account of a prostitute, one is left with only a loaf of bread   [D]6:26 Lit but a wife
of a man   [E]6:32 Lit commits adultery with a woman   [F]6:33 Or plague

7 I saw among the inexperienced,^A
I noticed among the youths,
a young man lacking sense.

8 Crossing the street near her corner,
he strolled down the road to her house

9 at twilight, in the evening,
in the dark of the night.

10 A woman came to meet him
dressed like a prostitute,
having a hidden agenda.^B

11 She is loud and defiant;
her feet do not stay at home.

12 Now in the street, now in the squares,
she lurks at every corner.

13 She grabs him and kisses him;
she brazenly says^C to him,

14 "I've made fellowship offerings;
today I've fulfilled my vows.

15 So I came out to meet you,
to search for you, and I've found you.

16 I've spread coverings on my bed —
richly colored linen from Egypt.

17 I've perfumed my bed
with myrrh, aloes, and cinnamon.

18 Come, let's drink deeply of lovemaking until morning.
Let's feast on each other's love!

19 My husband isn't home;
he went on a long journey.

20 He took a bag of silver with him
and will come home at the time of the full moon."

21 She seduces him with her persistent pleading;
she lures with her flattering^D talk.

22 He follows her impulsively
like an ox going to the slaughter,
like a deer bounding toward a trap^E

23 until an arrow pierces its^F liver,
like a bird darting into a snare —
he doesn't know it will cost him his life.

24 Now, sons, listen to me,
and pay attention to the words from my mouth.

25 Don't let your heart turn aside to her ways;
don't stray onto her paths.

26 For she has brought many down to death;
her victims are countless.^G

---

^A7:7 Or simple, or gullible, or naive   ^B7:10 Or prostitute with a guarded heart
^C7:13 Lit she makes her face strong and says   ^D7:21 Lit smooth   ^E7:22 Text
emended; MT reads like a shackle to the discipline of a fool; Hb obscure
^F7:23 Or his   ^G7:26 Or and powerful men are all her victims

²⁷ Her house is the road to Sheol,
descending to the chambers of death.

WISDOM'S APPEAL

8 Doesn't wisdom call out?
Doesn't understanding make her voice heard?
² At the heights overlooking the road,
at the crossroads, she takes her stand.
³ Beside the gates leading into the city,
at the main entrance, she cries out:
⁴ "People, I call out to you;
my cry is to the children of Adam.
⁵ Learn to be shrewd, you who are inexperienced;
develop common sense, you who are foolish.
⁶ Listen, for I speak of noble things,
and what my lips say is right.
⁷ For my mouth tells the truth,
and wickedness is detestable to my lips.
⁸ All the words from my mouth are righteous;
none of them are deceptive or perverse.
⁹ All of them are clear to the perceptive,
and right to those who discover knowledge.
¹⁰ Accept my instruction instead of silver,
and knowledge rather than pure gold.
¹¹ For wisdom is better than jewels,
and nothing desirable can equal it.
¹² I, wisdom, share a home with shrewdness
and have knowledge and discretion.
¹³ To fear the LORD is to hate evil.
I hate arrogant pride, evil conduct,
and perverse speech.
¹⁴ I possess good advice and sound wisdom;ᴬ
I have understanding and strength.
¹⁵ It is by me that kings reign
and rulers enact just law;
¹⁶ by me, princes lead,
as do nobles and all righteous judges.ᴮ
¹⁷ I love those who love me,
and those who search for me find me.
¹⁸ With me are riches and honor,
lasting wealth and righteousness.
¹⁹ My fruit is better than solid gold,
and my harvest than pure silver.
²⁰ I walk in the ways of righteousness,
along the paths of justice,
²¹ giving wealth as an inheritance to those who love me,
and filling their treasuries.

ᴬ8:14 Or resourcefulness   ᴮ8:16 Some Hb mss, LXX read nobles who judge the earth

NO SHORTCUT TO THE GOOD STUFF

PROVERBS 7:6–8:36; 1 KINGS 3:7-14

Were I the newly appointed young ruler of God's favored nation, with direct access to the God of the universe, I'm not sure my first big "ask" would be for wisdom. I'd want something a little flashier—something I could tell my friends about or snap a photo of for my mom's fridge. King Solomon's first big "ask," however, demonstrated a hint of the very thing he sought (1Kg 3:9).

The Lord said to Solomon, "I will therefore do what you have asked. I will give you a wise and understanding heart, so that there has never been anyone like you before and never will be again. In addition, I will give you what you did not ask for: both riches and honor, so that no king will be your equal during your entire life" (1Kg 3:12-13).

Solomon got power. He got riches. He got popularity and legacy. But the path to all of those things started with wisdom. No shortcut could have delivered him to the same destination.

This is the very lesson that Proverbs 8 teaches us. Where Proverbs 7 personifies sin's seduction as a forbidden woman, Proverbs 8 personifies wisdom as a patient, ever-present, and generous teacher.

Lest we convince ourselves that wisdom is unattainable or undesirable, Solomon writes, "Doesn't wisdom call out? Doesn't understanding make her voice heard?" (Pr 8:1). And "those who search for me find me" (Pr 8:17).

Proverbs 8 gives us lenses to see that everywhere we look, wisdom is calling us to live lives anchored in God's Truth. There are no shortcuts to wisdom, but Solomon reminds us that the pursuit of God's Truth has rich rewards:

- "For wisdom is better than jewels, and nothing desirable can equal it" (Pr 8:11).
- Wisdom's roommate is shrewdness. Her neighbors are knowledge and discretion (Pr 8:12). If you find one, you find the others.
- Wisdom is what you'll see behind the curtain of all great leaders. It's how courageous kings reign, righteous rulers enact the law, judges judge fairly (Pr 8:15).
- Wisdom is a skilled craftsman (Pr 8:30). It's what we all need to master the trades God has given us.
- Those who find wisdom find life (Pr 8:35), happiness (Pr 8:34), wealth (Pr 8:18), and God's favor (Pr 8:35).

Overachievers like me want to add "get wisdom" to our to-do lists, but ultimately **my pursuit of wisdom is an outflow of my craving to know God.** It is an act of worship, and the rewards are gifts from Him, not achievements of mine.

May God give us eyes to see wisdom as the priceless treasure she is. May we look for her around every corner, praying like Solomon that we would find her. And in finding her, may we more deeply know the heart of our wise God.

22 "The Lord acquired[A] me
   at the beginning of his creation,[B]
   before his works of long ago.
23 I was formed[C] before ancient times,
   from the beginning, before the earth began.
24 I was born
   when there were no watery depths
   and no springs filled with water.
25 Before the mountains were established,
   prior to the hills, I was given birth —
26 before he made the land, the fields,
   or the first soil on earth.
27 I was there when he established the heavens,
   when he laid out the horizon on the surface of the ocean,
28 when he placed the skies above,
   when the fountains of the ocean gushed out,
29 when he set a limit for the sea
   so that the waters would not violate his command,
   when he laid out the foundations of the earth.
30 I was a skilled craftsman[D] beside him.
   I was his[E] delight every day,
   always rejoicing before him.
31 I was rejoicing in his inhabited world,
   delighting in the children of Adam.

32 "And now, sons, listen to me;
   those who keep my ways are happy.
33 Listen to instruction and be wise;
   don't ignore it.
34 Anyone who listens to me is happy,
   watching at my doors every day,
   waiting by the posts of my doorway.
35 For the one who finds me finds life
   and obtains favor from the Lord,
36 but the one who misses me[F] harms himself;
   all who hate me love death."

WISDOM VERSUS FOOLISHNESS

9 Wisdom has built her house;
   she has carved out her seven pillars.
2 She has prepared her meat; she has mixed her wine;
   she has also set her table.
3 She has sent out her female servants;
   she calls out from the highest points of the city:
4 "Whoever is inexperienced, enter here!"
   To the one who lacks sense, she says,

[A]8:22 Or possessed, or made   [B]8:22 Lit way   [C]8:23 Or consecrated
[D]8:30 Or a confidant, or a child, or was constantly   [E]8:30 LXX; MT omits his
[F]8:36 Or who sins against me

⁵ "Come, eat my bread,
and drink the wine I have mixed.
⁶ Leave inexperience behind, and you will live;
pursue the way of understanding.
⁷ The one who corrects a mocker
will bring abuse on himself;
the one who rebukes the wicked will get hurt.^A
⁸ Don't rebuke a mocker, or he will hate you;
rebuke the wise, and he will love you.
⁹ Instruct the wise, and he will be wiser still;
teach the righteous, and he will learn more.

¹⁰ "The fear of the LORD is the beginning of wisdom,
and the knowledge of the Holy One is understanding.
¹¹ For by me your days will be many,
and years will be added to your life.
¹² If you are wise, you are wise for your own benefit;
if you mock, you alone will bear the consequences."

¹³ Folly is a rowdy woman;
she is gullible and knows nothing.
¹⁴ She sits by the doorway of her house,
on a seat at the highest point of the city,
¹⁵ calling to those who pass by,
who go straight ahead on their paths:
¹⁶ "Whoever is inexperienced, enter here!"
To the one who lacks sense, she says,
¹⁷ "Stolen water is sweet,
and bread eaten secretly is tasty!"
¹⁸ But he doesn't know that the departed spirits are there,
that her guests are in the depths of Sheol.

A COLLECTION OF SOLOMON'S PROVERBS

10

Solomon's proverbs:
A wise son brings joy to his father,
but a foolish son, heartache to his mother.

² Ill-gotten gains do not profit anyone,
but righteousness rescues from death.

³ The LORD will not let the righteous go hungry,
but he denies the wicked what they crave.

⁴ Idle hands make one poor,
but diligent hands bring riches.

⁵ The son who gathers during summer is prudent;
the son who sleeps during harvest is disgraceful.

---

^A 9:7 Lit man: his blemish

⁶ Blessings are on the head of the righteous,
but the mouth of the wicked conceals violence.

⁷ The remembrance of the righteous is a blessing,
but the name of the wicked will rot.

⁸ A wise heart accepts commands,
but foolish lips will be destroyed.

⁹ The one who lives with integrity lives securely,
but whoever perverts his ways will be found out.

¹⁰ A sly wink of the eye causes grief,
and foolish lips will be destroyed.

¹¹ The mouth of the righteous is a fountain of life,
but the mouth of the wicked conceals violence.

¹² Hatred stirs up conflicts,
but love covers all offenses.

¹³ Wisdom is found on the lips of the discerning,
but a rod is for the back of the one
who lacks sense.

¹⁴ The wise store up knowledge,
but the mouth of the fool hastens destruction.

¹⁵ The wealth of the rich is his fortified city;
the poverty of the poor is their destruction.

¹⁶ The reward of the righteous is life;
the wages of the wicked is punishment.

¹⁷ The one who follows instruction is
on the path to life,
but the one who rejects correction goes astray.

¹⁸ The one who conceals hatred has lying lips,
and whoever spreads slander is a fool.

¹⁹ When there are many words,
sin is unavoidable,
but the one who controls his lips is prudent.

²⁰ The tongue of the righteous is pure silver;
the heart of the wicked is of little value.

²¹ The lips of the righteous feed many,
but fools die for lack of sense.

22 The LORD's blessing enriches,
and he adds no painful effort to it.ᴬ

23 As shameful conduct is pleasure for a fool,
so wisdom is for a person of understanding.

24 What the wicked dreads will come to him,
but what the righteous desire will be given to them.

25 When the whirlwind passes,
the wicked are no more,
but the righteous are secure forever.

26 Like vinegar to the teeth and smoke to the eyes,
so the slacker is to the one who sends him on an errand.

27 The fear of the LORD prolongs life,ᴮ
but the years of the wicked are cut short.

28 The hope of the righteous is joy,
but the expectation of the wicked will perish.

29 The way of the LORD is a stronghold for the honorable,
but destruction awaits the malicious.

30 The righteous will never be shaken,
but the wicked will not remain on the earth.

31 The mouth of the righteous produces wisdom,
but a perverse tongue will be cut out.

32 The lips of the righteous know what is appropriate,
but the mouth of the wicked, only what is perverse.

11 Dishonest scales are detestable to the LORD,
but an accurate weight is his delight.

2 When arrogance comes, disgrace follows,
but with humility comes wisdom.

3 The integrity of the upright guides them,
but the perversity of the treacherous destroys them.

4 Wealth is not profitable on a day of wrath,
but righteousness rescues from death.

5 The righteousness of the blameless clears his path,
but the wicked person will fall because of his wickedness.

ᴬ10:22 Or and painful effort adds nothing to it   ᴮ10:27 Lit LORD adds to days

⁶ The righteousness of the upright rescues them,
but the treacherous are trapped by their own desires.

⁷ When the wicked person dies,
his expectation comes to nothing,
and hope placed in wealth^{A,B} vanishes.

⁸ The righteous one is rescued from trouble;
in his place, the wicked one goes in.

⁹ With his mouth the ungodly destroys his neighbor,
but through knowledge the righteous are rescued.

¹⁰ When the righteous thrive, a city rejoices;
when the wicked die, there is joyful shouting.

¹¹ A city is built up by the blessing of the upright,
but it is torn down by the mouth of the wicked.

¹² Whoever shows contempt for his neighbor
lacks sense,
but a person with understanding keeps silent.

¹³ A gossip goes around revealing a secret,
but a trustworthy person keeps a confidence.

¹⁴ Without guidance, a people will fall,
but with many counselors there is deliverance.

¹⁵ If someone puts up security for a stranger,
he will suffer for it,
but the one who hates such agreements is protected.

¹⁶ A gracious woman gains honor,
but violent^C people gain only riches.

¹⁷ A kind man benefits himself,
but a cruel person brings ruin on himself.

¹⁸ The wicked person earns an empty wage,
but the one who sows righteousness, a true reward.

¹⁹ Genuine righteousness leads to life,
but pursuing evil leads to death.

²⁰ Those with twisted minds are detestable
to the LORD,
but those with blameless conduct are his delight.

---

^A11:7 LXX reads *hope of the ungodly* ^B11:7 Or *strength* ^C11:16 Or *ruthless*

21 Be assured^ that a wicked person
will not go unpunished,
but the offspring of the righteous will escape.

22 A beautiful woman who rejects good sense
is like a gold ring in a pig's snout.

23 The desire of the righteous turns out well,
but the hope of the wicked leads to wrath.

24 One person gives freely,
yet gains more;
another withholds what is right,
only to become poor.

25 A generous person will be enriched,
and the one who gives a drink of water
will receive water.

26 People will curse anyone who hoards grain,
but a blessing will come to the one who sells it.

27 The one who searches for what is good seeks favor,
but if someone looks for trouble,
it will come to him.

28 Anyone trusting in his riches will fall,
but the righteous will flourish like foliage.

29 The one who brings ruin on his household
will inherit the wind,
and a fool will be a slave
to someone whose heart is wise.

30 The fruit of the righteous is a tree of life,
and a wise person captivates people.

31 If the righteous will be repaid on earth,
how much more the wicked and sinful.

12 Whoever loves discipline loves knowledge,
but one who hates correction is stupid.

2 One who is good obtains favor from the LORD,
but he condemns a person who schemes.

3 No one can be made secure by wickedness,
but the root of the righteous is immovable.

---

^11:21 Lit Hand to hand

⁴ A wife of noble character^A is her husband's crown,
but a wife who causes shame
is like rottenness in his bones.

⁵ The thoughts of the righteous are just,
but guidance from the wicked is deceitful.

⁶ The words of the wicked are a deadly ambush,
but the speech of the upright rescues them.

⁷ The wicked are overthrown and perish,
but the house of the righteous will stand.

⁸ A man is praised for his insight,
but a twisted mind is despised.

⁹ Better to be disregarded, yet have a servant,
than to act important but have no food.

¹⁰ The righteous cares about his animal's health,
but even the merciful acts of the wicked are cruel.

¹¹ The one who works his land will have plenty of food,
but whoever chases fantasies lacks sense.

¹² The wicked desire what evil people have caught,^B
but the root of the righteous is productive.

¹³ By rebellious speech an evil person is trapped,
but a righteous person escapes from trouble.

¹⁴ A person will be satisfied with good
by the fruit of his mouth,
and the work of a person's hands will reward him.

¹⁵ A fool's way is right in his own eyes,
but whoever listens to counsel is wise.

¹⁶ A fool's displeasure is known at once,
but whoever ignores an insult is sensible.

¹⁷ Whoever speaks the truth declares what is right,
but a false witness speaks deceit.

¹⁸ There is one who speaks rashly,
like a piercing sword;
but the tongue of the wise brings healing.

---

^A 12:4 Or A wife of quality, or A wife of good character   ^B 12:12 Or desire a
stronghold of evil

19   Truthful lips endure forever,
       but a lying tongue, only a moment.

20   Deceit is in the hearts of those who plot evil,
       but those who promote peace have joy.

21   No disaster overcomes the righteous,
       but the wicked are full of misery.

22   Lying lips are detestable to the LORD,
       but faithful people are his delight.

23   A shrewd person conceals knowledge,
       but a foolish heart publicizes stupidity.

24   The diligent hand will rule,
       but laziness will lead to forced labor.

25   Anxiety in a person's heart weighs it down,
       but a good word cheers it up.

26   A righteous person is careful in dealing
         with his neighbor,[A]
       but the ways of the wicked lead them astray.

27   A lazy hunter doesn't roast his game,
       but to a diligent person, his wealth is precious.

28   There is life in the path of righteousness,
       and in its path there is no death.[B]

13

   A wise son responds to his father's discipline,
       but a mocker doesn't listen to rebuke.

2   From the fruit of his mouth,
       a person will enjoy good things,
       but treacherous people have
         an appetite for violence.

3   The one who guards his mouth protects his life;
       the one who opens his lips invites his own ruin.

4   The slacker craves, yet has nothing,
       but the diligent is fully satisfied.

5   The righteous hate lying,
       but the wicked bring disgust and shame.

[A]12:26 Or person guides his neighbor   [B]12:28 Or righteousness, but the crooked way leads to death

6   Righteousness guards people of integrity,[A]
    but wickedness undermines the sinner.

7   One person pretends to be rich but has nothing;
    another pretends to be poor but has abundant wealth.

8   Riches are a ransom for a person's life,
    but a poor person hears no threat.

9   The light of the righteous shines brightly,
    but the lamp of the wicked is put out.

10 Arrogance leads to nothing but strife,
    but wisdom is gained by those who take advice.

11 Wealth obtained by fraud will dwindle,
    but whoever earns it through labor[B] will multiply it.

12 Hope delayed makes the heart sick,
    but desire fulfilled is a tree of life.

13 The one who has contempt for instruction
        will pay the penalty,
    but the one who respects a command
        will be rewarded.

14 A wise person's instruction is a fountain of life,
    turning people away from the snares of death.

15 Good sense wins favor,
    but the way of the treacherous never changes.[C]

16 Every sensible person acts knowledgeably,
    but a fool displays his stupidity.

17 A wicked envoy falls into trouble,
    but a trustworthy courier brings healing.

18 Poverty and disgrace come to those
    who ignore discipline,
    but the one who accepts correction will be honored.

19 Desire fulfilled is sweet to the taste,
    but to turn from evil is detestable to fools.

20 The one who walks with the wise will become wise,
    but a companion of fools will suffer harm.

[A]13:6 Lit guards integrity of way   [B]13:11 Lit whoever gathers upon his hand
[C]13:15 LXX, Syr, Tg read treacherous will perish

21 Disaster pursues sinners,
but good rewards the righteous.

22 A good man leaves an inheritance to his^A grandchildren,
but the sinner's wealth is stored up for the righteous.

23 The uncultivated field of the poor yields abundant food,
but without justice, it is swept away.

24 The one who will not use the rod hates his son,
but the one who loves him disciplines him diligently.

25 A righteous person eats until he is satisfied,
but the stomach of the wicked is empty.

14 Every wise woman builds her house,
but a foolish one tears it down with her own hands.

2 Whoever lives with integrity fears the LORD,
but the one who is devious in his ways despises him.

3 The proud speech of a fool brings a rod of discipline,^B
but the lips of the wise protect them.

4 Where there are no oxen, the feeding trough is empty,^C
but an abundant harvest comes through the strength of an ox.

5 An honest witness does not deceive,
but a dishonest witness utters lies.

6 A mocker seeks wisdom and doesn't find it,
but knowledge comes easily to the perceptive.

7 Stay away from a foolish person;
you will gain no knowledge from his speech.

8 The sensible person's wisdom is to consider his way,
but the stupidity of fools deceives them.

9 Fools mock at making reparation,^D
but there is goodwill among the upright.

10 The heart knows its own bitterness,
and no outsider shares in its joy.

11 The house of the wicked will be destroyed,
but the tent of the upright will flourish.

¹² There is a way that seems right to a person,
but its end is the way to death.

¹³ Even in laughter a heart may be sad,
and joy may end in grief.

¹⁴ The disloyal one will get what his conduct deserves,
and a good one, what his deeds deserve.

¹⁵ The inexperienced one believes anything,
but the sensible one watches[A] his steps.

¹⁶ A wise person is cautious and turns from evil,
but a fool is easily angered and is careless.[B]

¹⁷ A quick-tempered person acts foolishly,
and one who schemes is hated.

¹⁸ The inexperienced inherit foolishness,
but the sensible are crowned with knowledge.

¹⁹ The evil bow before those who are good,
and the wicked, at the gates of the righteous.

²⁰ A poor person is hated even by his neighbor,
but there are many who love the rich.

²¹ The one who despises his neighbor sins,
but whoever shows kindness to the poor will be happy.

²² Don't those who plan evil go astray?
But those who plan good find loyalty and faithfulness.

²³ There is profit in all hard work,
but endless talk[C] leads only to poverty.

²⁴ The crown of the wise is their wealth,
but the foolishness of fools produces foolishness.

²⁵ A truthful witness rescues lives,
but one who utters lies is deceitful.

²⁶ In the fear of the LORD one has strong confidence
and his children have a refuge.

²⁷ The fear of the LORD is a fountain of life,
turning people away from the snares of death.

[A]14:15 Lit the prudent understands   [B]14:16 Or and falls   [C]14:23 Lit but word of lips

28 A large population is a king's splendor,
   but a shortage of people is a ruler's devastation.

29 A patient person shows great understanding,
   but a quick-tempered one promotes foolishness.

30 A tranquil heart is life to the body,
   but jealousy is rottenness to the bones.

31 The one who oppresses the poor person insults
      his Maker,
   but one who is kind to the needy honors him.

32 The wicked one is thrown down by his own sin,
   but the righteous one has a refuge in his death.

33 Wisdom resides in the heart of the discerning;
   she is known^A even among fools.

34 Righteousness exalts a nation,
   but sin is a disgrace to any people.

35 A king favors a prudent servant,
   but his anger falls on a disgraceful one.

15 A gentle answer turns away anger,
   but a harsh word stirs up wrath.

2 The tongue of the wise makes knowledge attractive,
   but the mouth of fools blurts out foolishness.

3 The eyes of the LORD are everywhere,
   observing the wicked and the good.

4 The tongue that heals is a tree of life,
   but a devious tongue^B breaks the spirit.

5 A fool despises his father's discipline,
   but a person who accepts correction is sensible.

6 The house of the righteous has great wealth,
   but trouble accompanies the income of the wicked.

7 The lips of the wise broadcast knowledge,
   but not so the heart of fools.

8 The sacrifice of the wicked is detestable to the LORD,
   but the prayer of the upright is his delight.

---

^A 14:33 LXX reads *unknown*   ^B 15:4 Lit *but crookedness in it*

⁹ The LORD detests the way of the wicked,
   but he loves the one who pursues righteousness.

¹⁰ Discipline is harsh for the one who leaves the path;
   the one who hates correction will die.

¹¹ Sheol and Abaddon lie open before the LORD —
   how much more, human hearts.

¹² A mocker doesn't love one who corrects him;
   he will not consult the wise.

¹³ A joyful heart makes a face cheerful,
   but a sad heart produces a broken spirit.

¹⁴ A discerning mind seeks knowledge,
   but the mouth of fools feeds on foolishness.

¹⁵ All the days of the oppressed are miserable,
   but a cheerful heart has a continual feast.

¹⁶ Better a little with the fear of the LORD
   than great treasure with turmoil.

¹⁷ Better a meal of vegetables where there is love
   than a fattened ox with hatred.

¹⁸ A hot-tempered person stirs up conflict,
   but one slow to anger calms strife.

¹⁹ A slacker's way is like a thorny hedge,
   but the path of the upright is a highway.

²⁰ A wise son brings joy to his father,
   but a foolish man despises his mother.

²¹ Foolishness brings joy to one without sense,
   but a person with understanding walks
      a straight path.

²² Plans fail when there is no counsel,
   but with many advisers they succeed.

²³ A person takes joy in giving an answer;^A
   and a timely word — how good that is!

²⁴ For the prudent the path of life leads upward,
   so that he may avoid going down to Sheol.

^A 15:23 Lit *in an answer of his mouth*

25 The LORD tears apart the house of the proud,
but he protects the widow's territory.

26 The LORD detests the plans of the one who is evil,
but pleasant words are pure.

27 The one who profits dishonestly troubles his household,
but the one who hates bribes will live.

28 The mind of the righteous person thinks before answering,
but the mouth of the wicked blurts out evil things.

29 The LORD is far from the wicked,
but he hears the prayer of the righteous.

30 Bright eyes cheer the heart;
good news strengthens[A] the bones.

31 One who[B] listens to life-giving rebukes
will be at home among the wise.

32 Anyone who ignores discipline despises himself,
but whoever listens to correction acquires good sense.[C]

33 The fear of the LORD is what wisdom teaches,
and humility comes before honor.

16 The reflections of the heart belong to mankind,
but the answer of the tongue is from the LORD.

2 All a person's ways seem right to him,
but the LORD weighs motives.[D]

3 Commit your activities to the LORD,
and your plans will be established.

4 The LORD has prepared everything for his purpose —
even the wicked for the day of disaster.

5 Everyone with a proud heart is detestable to the LORD;
be assured,[E] he will not go unpunished.

6 Iniquity is atoned for by loyalty and faithfulness,
and one turns from evil by the fear of the LORD.

7 When a person's ways please the LORD,
he makes even his enemies to be at peace with him.

[A]15:30 Lit makes fat   [B]15:31 Lit An ear that   [C]15:32 Lit acquires a heart
[D]16:2 Lit spirits   [E]16:5 Lit hand to hand

8   Better a little with righteousness
    than great income with injustice.

9   A person's heart plans his way,
    but the LORD determines his steps.

10 God's verdict is on the lips of a king;^A
    his mouth should not give an unfair judgment.

11 Honest balances and scales are the LORD's;
    all the weights in the bag are his concern.

12 Wicked behavior is detestable to kings,
    since a throne is established
        through righteousness.

13 Righteous lips are a king's delight,
    and he loves one who speaks honestly.

14 A king's fury is a messenger of death,
    but a wise person appeases it.

15 When a king's face lights up, there is life;
    his favor is like a cloud with spring rain.

16 Get wisdom —
    how much better it is than gold!
    And get understanding —
    it is preferable to silver.

17 The highway of the upright avoids evil;
    the one who guards his way protects his life.

18 Pride comes before destruction,
    and an arrogant spirit before a fall.

19 Better to be lowly of spirit with the humble^B
    than to divide plunder with the proud.

20 The one who understands a matter finds success,
    and the one who trusts in the LORD will be happy.

21 Anyone with a wise heart is called discerning,
    and pleasant speech^C increases learning.

22 Insight is a fountain of life for its possessor,
    but the discipline of fools is folly.

---

^A16:10 Or A divination is on the lips of a king   ^B16:19 Alt Hb tradition reads
afflicted   ^C16:21 Lit and sweetness of lips

23 The heart of a wise person instructs his mouth;
   it adds learning to his speech.^A

24 Pleasant words are a honeycomb:
   sweet to the taste^B and health to the body.^C

25 There is a way that seems right to a person,
   but its end is the way to death.

26 A worker's appetite works for him
   because his hunger^D urges him on.

27 A worthless person digs up evil,
   and his speech is like a scorching fire.

28 A contrary person spreads conflict,
   and a gossip separates close friends.

29 A violent person lures his neighbor,
   leading him on a path that is not good.

30 The one who narrows his eyes
      is planning deceptions;
   the one who compresses his lips brings about evil.

31 Gray hair is a glorious crown;
   it is found in the ways of righteousness.

32 Patience is better than power,
   and controlling one's emotions,^E
      than capturing a city.

33 The lot is cast into the lap,
   but its every decision is from the LORD.

17 Better a dry crust with peace
   than a house full of feasting with strife.

2 A prudent servant will rule over a disgraceful son
   and share an inheritance among brothers.

3 A crucible for silver, and a smelter for gold,
   and the LORD is the tester of hearts.

4 A wicked person listens to malicious talk;^F
   a liar pays attention to a destructive tongue.

---

^A 16:23 Lit *learning upon his lips*   ^B 16:24 Lit *throat*   ^C 16:24 Lit *bones*
^D 16:26 Lit *mouth*   ^E 16:32 Lit *and ruling over one's spirit*   ^F 17:4 Lit *to lips of iniquity*

⁵ The one who mocks the poor insults his Maker,
   and one who rejoices over calamity
   will not go unpunished.

⁶ Grandchildren are the crown of the elderly,
   and the pride of children is their fathers.

⁷ Eloquent words are not appropriate on a fool's lips;
   how much worse are lies for a ruler.

⁸ A bribe seems like a magic stone to its owner;
   wherever he turns, he succeeds.

⁹ Whoever conceals an offense promotes love,
   but whoever gossips about it separates friends.

¹⁰ A rebuke cuts into a perceptive person
   more than a hundred lashes into a fool.

¹¹ An evil person desires only rebellion;
   a cruel messenger^A will be sent against him.

¹² Better for a person to meet a bear robbed of her cubs
   than a fool in his foolishness.

¹³ If anyone returns evil for good,
   evil will never depart from his house.

¹⁴ To start a conflict is to release a flood;
   stop the dispute before it breaks out.

¹⁵ Acquitting the guilty and condemning the just —
   both are detestable to the Lord.

¹⁶ Why does a fool have money in his hand
   with no intention of buying wisdom?

¹⁷ A friend loves at all times,
   and a brother is born for a difficult time.

¹⁸ One without sense enters an agreement^B
   and puts up security for his friend.

¹⁹ One who loves to offend loves strife;
   one who builds a high threshold invites injury.

²⁰ One with a twisted mind will not succeed,
   and one with deceitful speech will fall into ruin.

---

^A 17:11 Or a merciless angel   ^B 17:18 Lit sense slaps hands

21 A man fathers a fool to his own sorrow;
the father of a fool has no joy.

22 A joyful heart is good medicine,
but a broken spirit dries up the bones.

23 A wicked person secretly takes a bribe
to subvert the course of justice.

24 Wisdom is the focus of the perceptive,
but a fool's eyes roam to the ends of the earth.

25 A foolish son is grief to his father
and bitterness to the one who bore him.

26 It is certainly not good to fine an innocent person
or to beat a noble for his honesty.[A]

27 The one who has knowledge restrains his words,
and one who keeps a cool head[B]
is a person of understanding.

28 Even a fool is considered wise when he keeps silent —
discerning, when he seals his lips.

18 One who isolates himself pursues selfish desires;
he rebels against all sound wisdom.

2 A fool does not delight in understanding,
but only wants to show off his opinions.[C]

3 When a wicked person comes,
contempt also comes,
and along with dishonor, derision.

4 The words of a person's mouth
are deep waters,
a flowing river, a fountain of wisdom.[D]

5 It is not good to show partiality to the guilty,
denying an innocent person justice.

6 A fool's lips lead to strife,
and his mouth provokes a beating.

7 A fool's mouth is his devastation,
and his lips are a trap for his life.

[A] 17:26 Or noble unfairly [B] 17:27 Lit spirit [C] 18:2 Lit to uncover his heart
[D] 18:4 Or waters; a fountain of wisdom is a flowing river

⁸ A gossip's words are like choice food
   that goes down to one's innermost being.ᴬ

⁹ The one who is lazy in his work
   is brother to a vandal.ᴮ

¹⁰ The name of the LORD is a strong tower;
   the righteous run to it and are protected.ᶜ

¹¹ The wealth of the rich is his fortified city;
   in his imagination it is like a high wall.

¹² Before his downfall a person's heart is proud,
   but humility comes before honor.

¹³ The one who gives an answer before he listens—
   this is foolishness and disgrace for him.

¹⁴ A person's spirit can endure sickness,
   but who can survive a broken spirit?

¹⁵ The mind of the discerning acquires knowledge,
   and the ear of the wise seeks it.

¹⁶ A person's gift opens doorsᴰ for him
   and brings him before the great.

¹⁷ The first to state his case seems right
   until another comes and cross-examines him.

¹⁸ Casting the lot ends quarrels
   and separates powerful opponents.

¹⁹ An offended brother is harder to reachᴱ
   than a fortified city,
   and quarrels are like the bars of a fortress.

²⁰ From the fruit of a person's mouth his stomach
     is satisfied;
   he is filled with the product of his lips.

²¹ Death and life are in the power of the tongue,
   and those who love it will eat its fruit.

²² A man who finds a wife finds a good thing
   and obtains favor from the LORD.

ᴬ18:8 Lit to the chambers of the belly   ᴮ18:9 Lit master of destruction
ᶜ18:10 Lit raised high   ᴰ18:16 Lit gift makes room   ᴱ18:19 LXX, Syr, Tg, Vg read
is stronger

23 The poor person pleads,
    but the rich one answers roughly.

24 One with many friends may be harmed, [A]
    but there is a friend who stays closer than a brother.

19 Better a poor person who lives with integrity
    than someone who has deceitful lips and is a fool.

2   Even zeal is not good without knowledge,
    and the one who acts hastily [B] sins.

3   A person's own foolishness leads him astray,
    yet his heart rages against the LORD.

4   Wealth attracts many friends,
    but a poor person is separated from his friend.

5   A false witness will not go unpunished,
    and one who utters lies will not escape.

6   Many seek a ruler's favor,
    and everyone is a friend of one who gives gifts.

7   All the brothers of a poor person hate him;
    how much more do his friends
    keep their distance from him!
    He may pursue them with words,
    but they are not there. [C]

8   The one who acquires good sense [D] loves himself;
    one who safeguards understanding finds success.

9   A false witness will not go unpunished,
    and one who utters lies perishes.

10 Luxury is not appropriate for a fool —
    how much less for a slave to rule over princes!

11 A person's insight gives him patience,
    and his virtue is to overlook an offense.

12 A king's rage is like the roaring of a lion,
    but his favor is like dew on the grass.

13 A foolish son is his father's ruin,
    and a wife's nagging is an endless dripping.

[A] 18:24 Some LXX mss, Syr, Tg, Vg read *friends must be friendly*   [B] 19:2 Lit *who is hasty with feet*   [C] 19:7 Hb uncertain   [D] 19:8 Lit *acquires a heart*

¹⁴ A house and wealth are inherited from fathers,
but a prudent wife is from the LORD.

¹⁵ Laziness induces deep sleep,
and a lazy person will go hungry.

¹⁶ The one who keeps commands preserves himself;
one who disregards^A his ways will die.

¹⁷ Kindness to the poor is a loan to the LORD,
and he will give a reward to the lender.^B

¹⁸ Discipline your son while there is hope;
don't set your heart on being the cause
of his death.^C

¹⁹ A person with intense anger bears the penalty;
if you rescue him, you'll have to do it again.

²⁰ Listen to counsel and receive instruction
so that you may be wise later in life.^D

²¹ Many plans are in a person's heart,
but the LORD's decree will prevail.

²² What is desirable in a person is his fidelity;
better to be a poor person than a liar.

²³ The fear of the LORD leads to life;
one will sleep at night^E without danger.

²⁴ The slacker buries his hand in the bowl;
he doesn't even bring it back to his mouth!

²⁵ Strike a mocker, and the inexperienced
learn a lesson;
rebuke the discerning, and he gains knowledge.

²⁶ The one who plunders his father and evicts his mother
is a disgraceful and shameful son.

²⁷ If you stop listening to correction, my son,
you will stray from the words of knowledge.

²⁸ A worthless witness mocks justice,
and a wicked mouth swallows iniquity.

---

^A19:16 Or despises, or treats lightly   ^B19:17 Lit to him   ^C19:18 Lit don't lift up
your soul to his death   ^D19:20 Lit in your end   ^E19:23 Lit will spend the night
satisfied

²⁹ Judgments are prepared for mockers,
and beatings for the backs of fools.

20

Wine is a mocker, beer is a brawler;
whoever goes astray^A because of them is not wise.

² A king's terrible wrath is like the roaring of a lion;
anyone who provokes him endangers himself.

³ Honor belongs to the person who ends a dispute,
but any fool can get himself into a quarrel.

⁴ The slacker does not plow during planting season;^B
at harvest time he looks,^C and there is nothing.

⁵ Counsel in a person's heart is deep water;
but a person of understanding draws it out.

⁶ Many a person proclaims his own loyalty,
but who can find a trustworthy person?

⁷ A righteous person acts with integrity;
his children who come after him will be happy.

⁸ A king sitting on a throne to judge
separates out all evil with his eyes.

⁹ Who can say, "I have kept my heart pure;
I am cleansed from my sin"?

¹⁰ Differing weights and varying measures^D —
both are detestable to the Lord.

¹¹ Even a young man is known by his actions —
by whether his behavior is pure and upright.

¹² The hearing ear and the seeing eye —
the Lord made them both.

¹³ Don't love sleep, or you will become poor;
open your eyes, and you'll have enough to eat.

¹⁴ "It's worthless, it's worthless!" the buyer says,
but after he is on his way, he gloats.

¹⁵ There is gold and a multitude of jewels,
but knowledgeable lips are a rare treasure.

---

^A20:1 Or *whoever staggers*   ^B20:4 Lit *plow in winter*   ^C20:4 Lit *inquires*
^D20:10 Lit *Stone and stone, measure and measure*

¹⁶ Take his garment,
for he has put up security for a stranger;
get collateral if it is for foreigners.

¹⁷ Food gained by fraud is sweet to a person,
but afterward his mouth is full of gravel.

¹⁸ Finalize plans with counsel,
and wage war with sound guidance.

¹⁹ The one who reveals secrets is a constant gossip;
avoid someone with a big mouth.

²⁰ Whoever curses his father or mother —
his lamp will go out in deep darkness.

²¹ An inheritance gained prematurely
will not be blessed ultimately.

²² Don't say, "I will avenge this evil!"
Wait on the LORD, and he will rescue you.

²³ Differing weightsᴬ are detestable to the LORD,
and dishonest scales are unfair.

²⁴ Even a courageous person's steps are determined
by the LORD,
so how can anyone understand his own way?

²⁵ It is a trap for anyone to dedicate
something rashly
and later to reconsider his vows.

²⁶ A wise king separates out the wicked
and drives the threshing wheel over them.

²⁷ The LORD's lamp sheds light on a person's life,ᴮ
searching the innermost parts.ᶜ

²⁸ Loyalty and faithfulness guard a king;
through loyalty he maintains his throne.

²⁹ The glory of young men is their strength,
and the splendor of old men is gray hair.

³⁰ Lashes and wounds purge away evil,
and beatings cleanse the innermost parts.ᴰ

ᴬ20:23 Lit *A stone and a stone* ᴮ20:27 Lit *breath* ᶜ20:27 Lit *the chambers of the belly* ᴰ20:30 Lit *beatings the chambers of the belly*

21
A king's heart is like channeled water in the LORD's hand:
He directs it wherever he chooses.

2 All a person's ways seem right to him,
but the LORD weighs hearts.

3 Doing what is righteous and just
is more acceptable to the LORD than sacrifice.

4 The lamp that guides the wicked —
haughty eyes and an arrogant heart — is sin.

5 The plans of the diligent certainly lead to profit,
but anyone who is reckless certainly becomes poor.

6 Making a fortune through a lying tongue
is a vanishing mist,[A] a pursuit of death.[B,C]

7 The violence of the wicked sweeps them away
because they refuse to act justly.

8 A guilty one's conduct is crooked,
but the behavior of the innocent is upright.

9 Better to live on the corner of a roof
than to share a house with a nagging wife.

10 A wicked person desires evil;
he has no consideration[D] for his neighbor.

11 When a mocker is punished,
the inexperienced become wiser;
when one teaches a wise man,
he acquires knowledge.

12 The Righteous One[E] considers the house of the wicked;
he brings the wicked to ruin.

13 The one who shuts his ears to the cry of the poor
will himself also call out and not be answered.

14 A secret gift soothes anger,
and a covert bribe, fierce rage.

15 Justice executed is a joy to the righteous
but a terror to those who practice iniquity.

A21:6 Or a breath blown away   B21:6 Some Hb mss, LXX, Vg read a snare of
death   C21:6 Lit is vanity, ones seeking death   D21:10 Or favor   E21:12 Or
righteous one

¹⁶ The person who strays from the way of prudence
will come to rest in the assembly of the departed spirits.

¹⁷ The one who loves pleasure will become poor;
whoever loves wine and oil will not get rich.

¹⁸ The wicked are a ransom for the righteous,
and the treacherous, forᴬ the upright.

¹⁹ Better to live in a wilderness
than with a nagging and hot-tempered wife.

²⁰ Precious treasure and oil are in the dwelling of
a wise person,
but a fool consumes them. ᴮ

²¹ The one who pursues righteousness and faithful love
will find life, righteousness, and honor.

²² A wise person went up against a city of warriors
and brought down its secure fortress.

²³ The one who guards his mouth and tongue
keeps himself out of trouble.

²⁴ The arrogant and proud person, named "Mocker,"
acts with excessive arrogance.

²⁵ A slacker's craving will kill him
because his hands refuse to work.
²⁶ He is filled with cravingᶜ all day long,
but the righteous give and don't hold back.

²⁷ The sacrifice of a wicked person is detestable —
how much more so
when he brings it with ulterior motives!

²⁸ A lying witness will perish,
but the one who listens will speak successfully.

²⁹ A wicked person puts on a bold face,
but the upright one considers his way.

³⁰ No wisdom, no understanding, and no counsel
will prevail against the LORD.

³¹ A horse is prepared for the day of battle,
but victory comes from the LORD.

ᴬ21:18 Or *in place of*   ᴮ21:20 Lit *it*   ᶜ21:26 Lit *He craves a craving*

22 A good name is to be chosen over great wealth;
favor is better than silver and gold.

2 Rich and poor have this in common:[A]
the LORD makes them all.

3 A sensible person sees danger and takes cover,
but the inexperienced keep going and are punished.

4 Humility, the fear of the LORD,
results in wealth, honor, and life.

5 There are thorns and snares on the way
of the crooked;
the one who guards himself stays far from them.

6 Start a youth out on his way;
even when he grows old he will not depart from it.

7 The rich rule over the poor,
and the borrower is a slave to the lender.

8 The one who sows injustice will reap disaster,
and the rod of his fury will be destroyed.

9 A generous person[B] will be blessed,
for he shares his food with the poor.

10 Drive out a mocker, and conflict goes too;
then quarreling and dishonor will cease.

11 The one who loves a pure heart
and gracious lips — the king is his friend.

12 The LORD's eyes keep watch over knowledge,
but he overthrows the words of the treacherous.

13 The slacker says, "There's a lion outside!
I'll be killed in the public square!"

14 The mouth of the forbidden woman is a deep pit;
a man cursed by the LORD will fall into it.

15 Foolishness is bound to the heart of a youth;
a rod of discipline will separate it from him.

16 Oppressing the poor to enrich oneself,
and giving to the rich — both lead only to poverty.

[A] 22:2 Lit poor meet [B] 22:9 Lit Good of eye

WORDS OF THE WISE

¹⁷ Listen closely,ᴬ pay attention to the words of the wise,
and apply your mind to my knowledge.
¹⁸ For it is pleasing if you keep them within you
and if they areᴮ constantly on your lips.
¹⁹ I have instructed you today — even you —
so that your confidence may be in the Lᴏʀᴅ.
²⁰ Haven't I written for you thirty sayingsᶜ
about counsel and knowledge,
²¹ in order to teach you true and reliable words,
so that you may give a dependable reportᴰ
to those who sent you?

²² Don't rob a poor person because he is poor,
and don't crush the oppressed at the city gate,
²³ for the Lᴏʀᴅ will champion their cause
and will plunder those who plunder them.

²⁴ Don't make friends with an angry person,ᴱ
and don't be a companion of a hot-tempered one,
²⁵ or you will learn his ways
and entangle yourself in a snare.

²⁶ Don't be one of those who enter agreements,ᶠ
who put up security for loans.
²⁷ If you have nothing with which to pay,
even your bed will be taken from under you.

²⁸ Don't move an ancient boundary marker
that your fathers set up.

²⁹ Do you see a person skilled in his work?
He will stand in the presence of kings.
He will not stand in the presence of the unknown.

23 When you sit down to dine with a ruler,
consider carefully whatᴳ is before you,
² and put a knife to your throat
if you have a bigᴴ appetite;
³ don't desire his choice food,
for that food is deceptive.

⁴ Don't wear yourself out to get rich;
because you know better, stop!

ᴬ22:17 Lit *Stretch out your ear*   ᴮ22:18 Or *you; let them be*, or *you, so that they are*
ᶜ22:20 Text emended; one Hb tradition reads *you previously*; alt Hb tradition
reads *you excellent things*; LXX, Syr, Vg read *you three times*   ᴰ22:21 Lit *give
dependable words*   ᴱ22:24 Lit *with a master of anger*   ᶠ22:26 Lit *Don't be
among hand slappers*   ᴳ23:1 Or *who*   ᴴ23:2 Lit *you are the master of an*

5   As soon as your eyes fly to it, it disappears,
for it makes wings for itself
and flies like an eagle to the sky.

6   Don't eat a stingy person's bread,[A]
and don't desire his choice food,
7   for it's like someone calculating inwardly.[B]
"Eat and drink," he says to you,
but his heart is not with you.
8   You will vomit the little you've eaten
and waste your pleasant words.

9   Don't speak to[C] a fool,
for he will despise the insight of your words.

10   Don't move an ancient boundary marker,
and don't encroach on the fields of the fatherless,
11   for their Redeemer is strong,
and he will champion their cause against you.

12   Apply yourself to discipline
and listen to words of knowledge.

13   Don't withhold discipline from a youth;
if you punish him with a rod, he will not die.
14   Punish him with a rod,
and you will rescue his life from Sheol.

15   My son, if your heart is wise,
my heart will indeed rejoice.
16   My innermost being will celebrate
when your lips say what is right.

17   Don't let your heart envy sinners;
instead, always fear the LORD.
18   For then you will have a future,
and your hope will not be dashed.

19   Listen, my son, and be wise;
keep your mind on the right course.
20   Don't associate with those who drink too much wine
or with those who gorge themselves on meat.
21   For the drunkard and the glutton will become poor,
and grogginess will clothe them in rags.

22   Listen to your father who gave you life,
and don't despise your mother when[D] she is old.

[A]23:6 Lit eat bread of an evil eye   [B]23:7 LXX reads it is like someone swallowing a hair in the throat   [C]23:9 Lit in the ears of   [D]23:22 Or because

23 Buy — and do not sell — truth,
wisdom, instruction, and understanding.

24 The father of a righteous son will rejoice greatly,
and one who fathers a wise son will delight in him.

25 Let your father and mother have joy,
and let her who gave birth to you rejoice.

26 My son, give me your heart,
and let your eyes observe my ways.

27 For a prostitute is a deep pit,
and a wayward woman is a narrow well;

28 indeed, she sets an ambush like a robber
and increases the number of unfaithful people.

29 Who has woe? Who has sorrow?
Who has conflicts? Who has complaints?
Who has wounds for no reason?
Who has red eyes?

30 Those who linger over wine;
those who go looking for mixed wine.

31 Don't gaze at wine because it is red,
because it gleams in the cup
and goes down smoothly.

32 In the end it bites like a snake
and stings like a viper.

33 Your eyes will see strange things,
and you will say absurd things.[A]

34 You'll be like someone sleeping out at sea
or lying down on the top of a ship's mast.

35 "They struck me, but[B] I feel no pain!
They beat me, but I didn't know it!
When will I wake up?
I'll look for another drink."

24 Don't envy the evil
or desire to be with them,

2 for their hearts plan violence,
and their words stir up trouble.

3 A house is built by wisdom,
and it is established by understanding;

4 by knowledge the rooms are filled
with every precious and beautiful treasure.

5 A wise warrior is better than a strong one,[C]
and a man of knowledge than one of strength;[D]

[A]23:33 Or will speak perversities, or inverted things   [B]23:35 LXX, Syr, Tg, Vg
read me," you will say, "but   [C]24:5 LXX, Syr; MT reads is in strength
[D]24:5 LXX, Syr, Tg; MT reads knowledge exerts strength

6 for you should wage war with sound guidance —
 victory comes with many counselors.

7 Wisdom is inaccessible to[A] a fool;
 he does not open his mouth at the city gate.

8 The one who plots evil
 will be called a schemer.
9 A foolish scheme is sin,
 and a mocker is detestable to people.

10 If you do nothing in a difficult time,
 your strength is limited.
11 Rescue those being taken off to death,
 and save those stumbling toward slaughter.
12 If you say, "But we didn't know about this,"
 won't he who weighs hearts consider it?
 Won't he who protects your life know?
 Won't he repay a person according to his work?

13 Eat honey, my son, for it is good,
 and the honeycomb is sweet to your palate;
14 realize that wisdom is the same for you.
 If you find it, you will have a future,
 and your hope will never fade.

15 Don't set an ambush, you wicked one,
 at the camp of the righteous man;
 don't destroy his dwelling.
16 Though a righteous person falls seven times,
 he will get up,
 but the wicked will stumble into ruin.

17 Don't gloat when your enemy falls,
 and don't let your heart rejoice
 when he stumbles,
18 or the LORD will see, be displeased,
 and turn his wrath away from him.

19 Don't be agitated by evildoers,
 and don't envy the wicked.
20 For the evil have no future;
 the lamp of the wicked will be put out.

21 My son, fear the LORD, as well as the king,
 and don't associate with rebels,[B]
22 for destruction will come suddenly from them;
 who knows what distress these two can bring?

[A] 24:7 Lit *is too high for*   [B] 24:21 Or *those given to change*

23 These sayings also belong to the wise:

It is not good to show partiality in judgment.
24 Whoever says to the guilty, "You are innocent" —
peoples will curse him, and nations will denounce him;
25 but it will go well with those who convict the guilty,
and a generous blessing will come to them.

26 He who gives an honest answer
gives a kiss on the lips.

27 Complete your outdoor work, and prepare your field;
afterward, build your house.

28 Don't testify against your neighbor without cause.
Don't deceive with your lips.
29 Don't say, "I'll do to him what he did to me;
I'll repay the man for what he has done."

30 I went by the field of a slacker
and by the vineyard of one lacking sense.
31 Thistles had come up everywhere,
weeds covered the ground,
and the stone wall was ruined.
32 I saw, and took it to heart;
I looked, and received instruction:
33 a little sleep, a little slumber,
a little folding of the arms to rest,
34 and your poverty will come like a robber,
and your need, like a bandit.

HEZEKIAH'S COLLECTION

25

These too are proverbs of Solomon,
which the men of King Hezekiah of Judah copied.

2 It is the glory of God to conceal a matter
and the glory of kings to investigate a matter.
3 As the heavens are high and the earth is deep,
so the hearts of kings cannot be investigated.

4 Remove impurities from silver,
and material will be produced[A] for a silversmith.[B]
5 Remove the wicked from the king's presence,
and his throne will be established in righteousness.

6 Don't boast about yourself before the king,
and don't stand in the place of the great;

[A]25:4 Lit will come out; Ex 32:24 [B]25:4 Or and a vessel will be produced by a silversmith

7 for it is better for him to say to you, "Come up here!"
than to demote you in plain view of a noble.[A]

8 Don't take a matter to court hastily.
Otherwise, what will you do afterward
if your opponent[B] humiliates you?
9 Make your case with your opponent
without revealing another's secret;
10 otherwise, the one who hears will disgrace you,
and you'll never live it down.[C]

11 A word spoken at the right time
is like gold apples in silver settings.
12 A wise correction to a receptive ear
is like a gold ring or an ornament of gold.

13 To those who send him, a trustworthy envoy
is like the coolness of snow on a harvest day;
he refreshes the life of his masters.

14 The one who boasts about a gift that does not exist
is like clouds and wind without rain.
15 A ruler can be persuaded through patience,
and a gentle tongue can break a bone.
16 If you find honey, eat only what you need;
otherwise, you'll get sick from it and vomit.
17 Seldom set foot in your neighbor's house;
otherwise, he'll get sick of you and hate you.

18 A person giving false testimony against his neighbor
is like a club, a sword, or a sharp arrow.
19 Trusting an unreliable person in a difficult time
is like a rotten tooth or a faltering foot.

20 Singing songs to a troubled heart
is like taking off clothing on a cold day
or like pouring vinegar on soda.[D]

21 If your enemy is hungry, give him food to eat,
and if he is thirsty, give him water to drink;
22 for you will heap burning coals on his head,
and the LORD will reward you.

23 The north wind produces rain,
and a backbiting tongue, angry looks.
24 Better to live on the corner of a roof

[A]25:7 Lit you before a noble whom your eyes see   [B]25:8 Or neighbor, also in
v. 9   [C]25:10 Lit and your evil report will not turn back   [D]25:20 Lit natron, or
sodium carbonate

than to share a house with a nagging wife.

25 Good news from a distant land
is like cold water to a parched throat. [A]

26 A righteous person who yields to the wicked
is like a muddied spring or a polluted well.

27 It is not good to eat too much honey
or to seek glory after glory. [B]

28 A person who does not control his temper
is like a city whose wall is broken down.

26

Like snow in summer and rain at harvest,
honor is inappropriate for a fool.

2 Like a flitting sparrow or a fluttering swallow,
an undeserved curse goes nowhere.

3 A whip for the horse, a bridle for the donkey,
and a rod for the backs of fools.

4 Don't answer a fool according to his foolishness
or you'll be like him yourself.

5 Answer a fool according to his foolishness
or he'll become wise in his own eyes.

6 The one who sends a message by a fool's hand
cuts off his own feet and drinks violence.

7 A proverb in the mouth of a fool
is like lame legs that hang limp.

8 Giving honor to a fool
is like binding a stone in a sling.

9 A proverb in the mouth of a fool
is like a stick with thorns,
brandished by [C] the hand of a drunkard.

10 The one who hires a fool or who hires those passing by
is like an archer who wounds everyone.

11 As a dog returns to its vomit,
so also a fool repeats his foolishness.

12 Do you see a person who is wise in his own eyes?
There is more hope for a fool than for him.

13 The slacker says, "There's a lion in the road —
a lion in the public square!"

14 A door turns on its hinges,
and a slacker, on his bed.

15 The slacker buries his hand in the bowl;
he is too weary to bring it to his mouth!

16 In his own eyes, a slacker is wiser
than seven who can answer sensibly.

17 A person who is passing by and meddles in a quarrel that's not his
is like one who grabs a dog by the ears.

[A]25:25 Or a weary person [B]25:27 Lit seek their glory, glory [C]26:9 Lit thorn
that goes up into

¹⁸ Like a madman who throws flaming darts and deadly arrows,
¹⁹ so is the person who deceives his neighbor
   and says, "I was only joking!"

²⁰ Without wood, fire goes out;
   without a gossip, conflict dies down.
²¹ As charcoal for embers and wood for fire,
   so is a quarrelsome person for kindling strife.
²² A gossip's words are like choice food
   that goes down to one's innermost being.^A

²³ Smooth^B lips with an evil heart
   are like glaze on an earthen vessel.
²⁴ A hateful person disguises himself with his speech
   and harbors deceit within.
²⁵ When he speaks graciously, don't believe him,
   for there are seven detestable things in his heart.
²⁶ Though his hatred is concealed by deception,
   his evil will be revealed in the assembly.
²⁷ The one who digs a pit will fall into it,
   and whoever rolls a stone —
   it will come back on him.
²⁸ A lying tongue hates those it crushes,
   and a flattering mouth causes ruin.

27

Don't boast about tomorrow,
for you don't know what a day might bring.

² Let another praise you, and not your own mouth —
   a stranger, and not your own lips.

³ A stone is heavy and sand, a burden,
   but aggravation from a fool outweighs them both.

⁴ Fury is cruel, and anger a flood,
   but who can withstand jealousy?

⁵ Better an open reprimand
   than concealed love.

⁶ The wounds of a friend are trustworthy,
   but the kisses of an enemy are excessive.

⁷ A person who is full tramples on a honeycomb,
   but to a hungry person, any bitter thing is sweet.

⁸ Anyone wandering from his home
   is like a bird wandering from its nest.

---

^A26:22 Lit *to the chambers of the belly*   ^B26:23 LXX; MT reads *Burning*

⁹ Oil and incense bring joy to the heart,
and the sweetness of a friend is better
than self-counsel. ᴬ

¹⁰ Don't abandon your friend or your father's friend,
and don't go to your brother's house
in your time of calamity;
better a neighbor nearby than a brother far away.

¹¹ Be wise, my son, and bring my heart joy,
so that I can answer anyone who taunts me.

¹² A sensible person sees danger and takes cover;
the inexperienced keep going and are punished.

¹³ Take his garment,
for he has put up security for a stranger;
get collateral if it is for foreigners. ᴮ

¹⁴ If one blesses his neighbor
with a loud voice early in the morning,
it will be counted as a curse to him.

¹⁵ An endless dripping on a rainy day
and a nagging wife are alike;
¹⁶ the one who controls her controls the wind
and grasps oil with his right hand.

¹⁷ Iron sharpens iron,
and one person sharpens another. ᶜ

¹⁸ Whoever tends a fig tree will eat its fruit,
and whoever looks after his master
will be honored.

¹⁹ As water reflects the face,
so the heart reflects the person.

²⁰ Sheol and Abaddon are never satisfied,
and people's eyes are never satisfied.

²¹ A crucible refines silver, a smelter refines gold,
and a person refines his praise.

²² Though you grind a fool
in a mortar with a pestle along with grain,
you will not separate his foolishness from him.

ᴬ27:9 LXX reads *heart, but the soul is torn up by affliction*   ᴮ27:13 Lit *a foreign woman*   ᶜ27:17 Lit *and a man sharpens his friend's face*

23 Know well the condition of your flock,
  and pay attention to your herds,
24 for wealth is not forever;
  not even a crown lasts for all time.
25 When hay is removed and new growth appears
  and the grain from the hills is gathered in,
26 lambs will provide your clothing,
  and goats, the price of a field;
27 there will be enough goat's milk for your food —
  food for your household
  and nourishment for your female servants.

28

The wicked flee when no one is pursuing them,
  but the righteous are as bold as a lion.

2 When a land is in rebellion, it has many rulers,
  but with a discerning and knowledgeable person, it endures.

3 A destitute leader^A who oppresses the poor
  is like a driving rain that leaves no food.

4 Those who reject the law praise the wicked,
  but those who keep the law pit themselves against them.

5 The evil do not understand justice,
  but those who seek the LORD understand everything.

6 Better the poor person who lives with integrity
  than the rich one who distorts right and wrong.^B

7 A discerning son keeps the law,
  but a companion of gluttons humiliates his father.

8 Whoever increases his wealth through excessive interest
  collects it for one who is kind to the poor.

9 Anyone who turns his ear away from hearing the law —
  even his prayer is detestable.

10 The one who leads the upright into an evil way
  will fall into his own pit,
  but the blameless will inherit what is good.

11 A rich person is wise in his own eyes,
  but a poor one who has discernment sees through him.

12 When the righteous triumph,
  there is great rejoicing,^C

---

^A28:3 LXX reads *A wicked man* ^B28:6 Lit *who twists two ways* ^C28:12 Lit *glory*

but when the wicked come to power,
people hide.

13 The one who conceals his sins
will not prosper,
but whoever confesses and renounces them
will find mercy.

14 Happy is the one who is always reverent,
but one who hardens his heart falls
into trouble.

15 A wicked ruler over a helpless people
is like a roaring lion or a charging bear.

16 A leader who lacks understanding
is very oppressive,
but one who hates dishonest profit
prolongs his life.

17 Someone burdened by bloodguilt[A]
will be a fugitive until death.
Let no one help him.

18 The one who lives with integrity will be helped,
but one who distorts right and wrong[B]
will suddenly fall.

19 The one who works his land
will have plenty of food,
but whoever chases fantasies
will have his fill of poverty.

20 A faithful person will have many blessings,
but one in a hurry to get rich
will not go unpunished.

21 It is not good to show partiality —
yet even a courageous person may sin
for a piece of bread.

22 A greedy one[C] is in a hurry for wealth;
he doesn't know that poverty will come to him.

23 One who rebukes a person will later find
more favor
than one who flatters[D] with his tongue.

[A]28:17 Lit the blood of a person   [B]28:18 Lit who is twisted regarding two ways
[C]28:22 Lit A man with an evil eye   [D]28:23 Lit is smooth

24 The one who robs his father or mother
and says, "That's no sin,"
is a companion to a person who destroys.

25 A greedy person stirs up conflict,
but whoever trusts in the LORD will prosper.

26 The one who trusts in himself[A] is a fool,
but one who walks in wisdom will be safe.

27 The one who gives to the poor
will not be in need,
but one who turns his eyes away[B]
will receive many curses.

28 When the wicked come to power,
people hide,
but when they are destroyed,
the righteous flourish.

29

One who becomes stiff-necked,
after many reprimands
will be shattered instantly —
beyond recovery.

2 When the righteous flourish, the people rejoice,
but when the wicked rule, people groan.

3 A man who loves wisdom brings joy to his father,
but one who consorts with prostitutes destroys his wealth.

4 By justice a king brings stability to a land,
but a person who demands "contributions"[C]
demolishes it.

5 A person who flatters[D] his neighbor
spreads a net for his feet.

6 An evil person is caught by sin,
but the righteous one sings and rejoices.

7 The righteous person knows the rights[E] of the poor,
but the wicked one does not understand these concerns.

8 Mockers inflame a city,
but the wise turn away anger.

[A]28:26 Lit his heart [B]28:27 Lit who shuts his eyes [C]29:4 The Hb word for contributions usually refers to offerings in worship. [D]29:5 Lit is smooth on [E]29:7 Lit justice

BE THOU MY VISION

PROVERBS 28–29; PHILIPPIANS 3:7-11; HEBREWS 12:1-2

"Protect your bishops!"

My high school chess and algebra teacher was known for his catchphrases. In pre-calculus he'd remind us every morning, "You go from what you know, to where you've got to go!" And whether he was wearing his chess hat (he actually sometimes wore a chess-teaching hat) or his algebra hat, he could often be seen through the glass door of the classroom, scrawling the words "WITHOUT A VISION, THE PEOPLE WILL PERISH!" across the top of the chalkboard with his tiny piece of chalk.

It wasn't until much later that I realized this was not just a way to get us to show our work or win a chess match. He was teaching the Bible to us.

"Without revelation people run wild, but one who follows divine instruction will be happy."

PROVERBS 29:18

That kernel of truth stuck with me. You can't wildly move your pawns around the chessboard without a plan and hope it works out. And definitely don't start working a math problem without knowing where you're headed.

We all need a vision. **But true vision, as it turns out, is less strategy and more heartbeat.**

I don't pretend to think my heart has fully matured in this area since my high school days, but I do see the Lord faithfully teaching me to delight in the law of God in my inner being (Rm 7:22). And when I set my heart on earthly things, the Holy Spirit reminds me of the lasting richness that comes from setting my mind on things above (Col 3:2).

I think this is why I love the hymn "Be Thou My Vision" so much. The author isn't interested in anything short of Jesus. There's no glancing to the right or to the left, no weaving from side to side. And when we sing this song-prayer ourselves, we call on the Lord to be our Vision, our Wisdom, our true Word, our battle Shield, our Dignity and Delight—our One Thing and All Things.

When we ask God to be our "best thought," "great Father," "soul's Shelter" and "high Tower"—that's when strategy falls quickly to the wayside and we march to the beat of a heart that longs for heaven.

Proverbs 29:18 is absolutely right (and, I suppose, so was my chess teacher). We can laugh about the reality that we could lose a chess match, but the truth outlasts all earthly things, and the risk is much greater: without a vision, we will most certainly perish.

As believers, let our vision be simply this: "to know him and the power of his resurrection and the fellowship of his sufferings, being conformed to his death, assuming that I will somehow reach the resurrection from among the dead" (Php 3:10-11).

9 If a wise person goes to court with a fool,
   there will be ranting and raving but no resolution. [A]

10 Bloodthirsty men hate an honest person,
   but the upright care about him. [B]

11 A fool gives full vent to his anger, [C]
   but a wise person holds it in check.

12 If a ruler listens to lies,
   all his officials will be wicked.

13 The poor and the oppressor have this in common: [D]
   the LORD gives light to the eyes of both.

14 A king who judges the poor with fairness —
   his throne will be established forever.

15 A rod of correction imparts wisdom,
   but a youth left to himself [E]
   is a disgrace to his mother.

16 When the wicked increase, rebellion increases,
   but the righteous will see their downfall.

17 Discipline your child, and it will bring you
        peace of mind
   and give you delight.

18 Without revelation [F] people run wild,
   but one who follows divine instruction will be happy.

19 A servant cannot be disciplined by words;
   though he understands, he doesn't respond.

20 Do you see someone who speaks too soon?
   There is more hope for a fool than for him.

21 A servant pampered from his youth
   will become arrogant [G] later on.

22 An angry person stirs up conflict,
   and a hot-tempered one [H] increases rebellion.

23 A person's pride will humble him,
   but a humble spirit will gain honor.

[A]29:9 Lit rest   [B]29:10 Or person, and seek the life of the upright   [C]29:11 Lit spirit   [D]29:13 Lit oppressor meet   [E]29:15 Lit youth sent away   [F]29:18 Lit vision   [G]29:21 Hb obscure   [H]29:22 Lit a master of rage

24 To be a thief's partner is to hate oneself;
   he hears the curse but will not testify.

25 The fear of mankind is a snare,
   but the one who trusts in the LORD is protected.^A

26 Many desire a ruler's favor,
   but a person receives justice from the LORD.

27 An unjust person is detestable to the righteous,
   and one whose way is upright
   is detestable to the wicked.

THE WORDS OF AGUR

30 The words of Agur son of Jakeh.
   The pronouncement.^B

The man's oration to Ithiel, to Ithiel and Ucal:^C

2 I am more stupid than any other person,^D
   and I lack a human's ability to understand.

3 I have not gained wisdom,
   and I have no knowledge of the Holy One.

4 Who has gone up to heaven and come down?
   Who has gathered the wind in his hands?
   Who has bound up the waters in a cloak?
   Who has established all the ends of the earth?
   What is his name,
   and what is the name of his son —
   if you know?

5 Every word of God is pure;^E
   he is a shield to those who take refuge in him.

6 Don't add to his words,
   or he will rebuke you, and you will be proved
      a liar.

7 Two things I ask of you;
   don't deny them to me before I die:

8 Keep falsehood and deceitful words far from me.
   Give me neither poverty nor wealth;
   feed me with the food I need.

9 Otherwise, I might have too much
   and deny you, saying, "Who is the LORD?"

---

^A29:25 Lit *raised high*   ^B30:1 Or *son of Jakeh from Massa*; Pr 31:1   ^C30:1 Hb
uncertain. Sometimes read with different word division as *oration: I am weary,
God, I am weary, God, and I am exhausted*, or *oration: I am not God,
I am not God, that I should prevail*. LXX reads *My son, fear my words and when
you have received them repent. The man says these things to the believers in
God, and I pause*.   ^D30:2 Lit *I am more stupid than a man*   ^E30:5 Lit *refined*

or I might have nothing and steal,
profaning[A] the name of my God.

10 Don't slander a servant to his master
or he will curse you, and you will
become guilty.

11 There is a generation that curses its father
and does not bless its mother.
12 There is a generation that is pure in its own eyes,
yet is not washed from its filth.
13 There is a generation — how haughty its eyes
and pretentious its looks.[B]
14 There is a generation whose teeth are swords,
whose fangs are knives,
devouring the oppressed from the land
and the needy from among mankind.

15 The leech has two daughters: "Give, Give!"
Three things are never satisfied;
four never say, "Enough!":
16 Sheol; a childless womb;
earth, which is never satisfied with water;
and fire, which never says, "Enough!"

17 As for the eye that ridicules a father
and despises obedience to a mother,
may ravens of the valley pluck it out
and young vultures eat it.

18 Three things are too wondrous for me;
four I can't understand:
19 the way of an eagle in the sky,
the way of a snake on a rock,
the way of a ship at sea,
and the way of a man
with a young woman.

20 This is the way of an adulteress:
she eats and wipes her mouth
and says, "I've done nothing wrong."

21 The earth trembles under three things;
it cannot bear up under four:
22 a servant when he becomes king,
a fool when he is stuffed with food,
23 an unloved woman when she marries,
and a servant girl when she ousts her queen.

[A]30:9 Lit *grabbing* [B]30:13 Lit *and its eyelids lifted up*

24 Four things on earth are small,
yet they are extremely wise:
25 ants are not a strong people,
yet they store up their food in the summer;
26 hyraxes are not a mighty people,
yet they make their homes in the cliffs;
27 locusts have no king,
yet all of them march in ranks;
28 a lizard^A can be caught in your hands,
yet it lives in kings' palaces.

29 Three things are stately in their stride;
four are stately in their walk:
30 a lion, which is mightiest among beasts
and doesn't retreat before anything;
31 a strutting rooster;^B a goat;
and a king at the head of his army.^C

32 If you have been foolish by exalting yourself
or if you've been scheming,
put your hand over your mouth.
33 For the churning of milk produces butter,
and twisting a nose draws blood,
and stirring up anger produces strife.

THE WORDS OF LEMUEL

31

The words of King Lemuel,
a pronouncement^D that his mother taught him:

2 What should I say, my son?
What, son of my womb?
What, son of my vows?
3 Don't spend your energy on women
or your efforts on those who destroy kings.
4 It is not for kings, Lemuel,
it is not for kings to drink wine
or for rulers to desire beer.
5 Otherwise, he will drink,
forget what is decreed,
and pervert justice for all the oppressed.^E
6 Give beer to one who is dying
and wine to one whose life is bitter.
7 Let him drink so that he can forget his poverty
and remember his trouble no more.
8 Speak up^F for those who have no voice,^G

---

^A30:28 Or *spider*   ^B30:31 Or *a greyhound*   ^C30:31 LXX reads *king addressing his people*   ^D31:1 Or *of Lemuel, king of Massa, or of King Lemuel, a burden*   ^E31:5 Lit *sons of affliction*   ^F31:8 Lit *Open your mouth, also in v. 9*   ^G31:8 Lit *who are mute*

SHE FEARS THE LORD

PROVERBS 31

The virtues of the "capable wife" are impressive. Each time I read them I begin with bright eyes and a lively heart to celebrate the virtuous woman. But by the end of the list I am slumped in my chair, hunched and furrowed with disappointment over my profound shortcomings in the field of "good wifery."

With my bowed and tired head resting on my forearm, I exhale and lament the pathetic distance between me and the woman from Proverbs 31.

Where does all this glorious elaborate goodness come from? I can rise early sometimes, but that combined with the field buying, feeding the family, speaking pious words of wisdom, giving to the poor, never having idle hands, and anticipating the needs of a husband—it sounds like a marathon of unachievable daily goodness. But the passage ends with the key: "A woman who fears the LORD will be praised" (Pr 31:30).

So, let's start there: the fear of the LORD. This is the beginning of wisdom. And the fruit of that God-fearing will begin to bloom in our lives.

As a young wife, an estimable woman from my church taught me a few things about homemaking, and I remember feeling absolutely staggered that she cleaned her baseboards once a week. *Baseboards, Florentine quiche, garden planting . . . and I have to look good doing it?* I remember feeling panic grip me as I clutched my brand new pleated apron.

I still have to breathe deeply when I survey the breadth of my responsibilities. But my tiny domestic empire doesn't depend on mastery of crème brûlée or stain removal; it hinges on the fear of the Lord. **Whatever virtue we have will grow naturally out of our dependence on Christ.** The lofty virtues of wisdom, thrift, and faithfulness that are so valued in this passage become an extension of Christ in us, when we are pursuing Him.

Rather than be overawed by this extraordinary list, we can submit ourselves to Christ and begin faithfully with the small things. For indeed, as G. K. Chesterton explains, "the most extraordinary thing in the world is an ordinary man and an ordinary woman and their ordinary children" (G. K. Chersterton, *Orthodoxy*). Every day, average obedience in the same direction is the simple thing that changes the world.

Keep this list close. It's such a good list. If we begin with the fear of the Lord, He will make us brave, trustworthy, industrious, strong, and good. Some women adorn themselves with gems, but the rare woman who adorns herself in Christ is the gem. Walk in His way, and He will reveal His gorgeous, shining goodness in you.

for the justice of all who are dispossessed.^A

⁹ Speak up, judge righteously,
and defend the cause of the oppressed and needy.

IN PRAISE OF A WIFE OF NOBLE CHARACTER

¹⁰ Who can find a wife of noble character?^B
She is far more precious than jewels.^C

¹¹ The heart of her husband trusts in her,
and he will not lack anything good.

¹² She rewards him with good, not evil,
all the days of her life.

¹³ She selects wool and flax
and works with willing hands.

¹⁴ She is like the merchant ships,
bringing her food from far away.

¹⁵ She rises while it is still night
and provides food for her household
and portions^D for her female servants.

¹⁶ She evaluates a field and buys it;
she plants a vineyard with her earnings.^E

¹⁷ She draws on her strength^F
and reveals that her arms are strong.

¹⁸ She sees that her profits are good,
and her lamp never goes out at night.

¹⁹ She extends her hands to the spinning staff,
and her hands hold the spindle.

²⁰ Her hands reach^G out to the poor,
and she extends her hands to the needy.

²¹ She is not afraid for her household when it snows,
for all in her household are doubly clothed.^H

²² She makes her own bed coverings;
her clothing is fine linen and purple.

²³ Her husband is known at the city gates,
where he sits among the elders of the land.

²⁴ She makes and sells linen garments;
she delivers belts^I to the merchants.

²⁵ Strength and honor are her clothing,
and she can laugh at the time to come.

²⁶ Her mouth speaks wisdom,
and loving instruction^J is on her tongue.

²⁷ She watches over the activities of her household
and is never idle.^K

²⁸ Her children rise up and call her blessed;

---

^A31:8 Lit *all the sons of passing away*   ^B31:10 Or *a wife of quality*, or *a capable wife*   ^C31:10 Vv. 10-31 form an acrostic.   ^D31:15 Or *tasks*   ^E31:16 Or *vineyard by her own labors*   ^F31:17 Lit *She wraps strength around her like a belt*
^G31:20 Lit *Her hand reaches*   ^H31:21 LXX, Vg; MT reads *are dressed in scarlet*
^I31:24 Or *sashes*   ^J31:26 Or *and the teaching of kindness*   ^K31:27 Lit *and does not eat the bread of idleness*

her husband also praises her:

29   "Many women[A] have done noble deeds,
        but you surpass them all!"

30   Charm is deceptive and beauty is fleeting,
        but a woman who fears the LORD will be praised.

31   Give her the reward of her labor,[B]
        and let her works praise her at the city gates.

Fear God & keep His commands

ecclesiastes

 When all has been heard, the conclusion of the matter is this: fear God and keep his commands, because this is for all humanity. **12:13**

ON THE TIMELINE Strong evidence attests that Ecclesiastes comes from the age of Solomon—971 BC through 931 BC—and Solomon is traditionally credited as the author. According to Ecclesiastes 1:1 and 12, the author was David's son and a king over Israel from Jerusalem. Ecclesiastes 12:9 speaks of the author as a writer of Proverbs, another book credited to Solomon.

A LITTLE BACKGROUND Ecclesiastes is wisdom literature, meaning it is in the part of the Bible that is especially concerned with helping readers cope with the practical and philosophical issues of life. Books like Proverbs and Ecclesiastes are, in essence, the biblical answer to the search for truths to live by. Proverbs is basic wisdom, giving the reader fundamental principles to live by, while Ecclesiastes is a heavier read. Ecclesiastes engages the weighty but necessary question: Does death nullify all purpose and meaning in life?

MESSAGE & PURPOSE Ecclesiastes examines major endeavors of life in light of the reality of death. It shows us that we and our works are futile—that is, destined to perish—and we must not waste our lives trying to justify our existence with pursuits that ultimately mean nothing. The book warns specifically about the pursuit of intellectual accomplishments, wealth and luxury, politics and religion. Instead of pursuing these purposes, which will not last, Ecclesiastes prompts us to do two simple but profound things: enjoy life and fear God.

GIVE THANKS FOR THE BOOK OF ECCLESIASTES:

Ecclesiastes is a book that awakens us to our own mortality, begging us to seriously consider how we should live. It knocks away all the façades we use to disguise the fact that life is short and all our accomplishments will pass away. In this way, Ecclesiastes anticipates the New Testament teaching that only God's grace, and not our zeal, saves us.

THEMES IN ECCLESIASTES

Solomon's candid words in the book of Ecclesiastes offer practical perspectives on the situations we all face, while pointing us back to the wisdom and sovereignty of God.

THEME	EXPLANATION
SEARCHING	Solomon was on the hunt for happiness, but his search was futile so long as it depended on his circumstances. Solomon's search, like ours, could only be satisfied by finding fulfillment in the God who gives wisdom, knowledge, and joy. Circumstances change, but God remains the same.
EMPTINESS	Solomon felt a void in his life—one he could not fill with pleasure, wealth, or success. When our sinful appetites feed on desires of the flesh, we remain hungry. God alone can supply the nourishment our hearts need.
WORK	It hurt Solomon to see others trying to build success for their own glory. Work done for and in response to God is a gift, but work done apart from God yields no lasting reward or benefit.
DEATH	The gospel is a banner of eternal hope over our temporary human lives. Death is certain and human works are ultimately futile, but God and His Word will last forever. Believers can give thanks at the end of their lives, knowing the certainty of death will be overcome by the certainty of life in Christ.
WISDOM	Education fills our minds with knowledge, but true wisdom is given only by God. To increase in wisdom and understanding means growing in the knowledge, fear, and love of God, and resting in the truth and promises of His Word.

READ AND UNDERSTAND ECCLESIASTES

The Bible is a complete work in which many stories combine to tell one story. As you read the book of Ecclesiastes, consider reading the additional passages to discover how the whole of Scripture works together.

EVERYTHING IS FUTILE

1 The words of the Teacher,^A son of David, king in Jerusalem. ² "Absolute futility," says the Teacher.
"Absolute futility. Everything is futile."

³ What does a person gain for all his efforts
that he labors at under the sun?

⁴ A generation goes and a generation comes,
but the earth remains forever.

⁵ The sun rises and the sun sets;
panting, it returns to the place
where it rises.

⁶ Gusting to the south,
turning to the north,
turning, turning, goes the wind,
and the wind returns in its cycles.

⁷ All the streams flow to the sea,
yet the sea is never full;
to the place where the streams flow,
there they flow again.

⁸ All things^B are wearisome,
more than anyone can say.
The eye is not satisfied by seeing
or the ear filled with hearing.

⁹ What has been is what will be,
and what has been done is what will be done;
there is nothing new under the sun.

¹⁰ Can one say about anything,
"Look, this is new"?
It has already existed in the ages before us.

¹¹ There is no remembrance of those who^C came before;
and of those who will come after
there will also be no remembrance
by those who follow them.

THE LIMITATIONS OF WISDOM

¹² I, the Teacher, have been^D king over Israel in Jerusalem. ¹³ I applied my mind to examine and explore through wisdom all that is done under heaven. God has given people^E this miserable task to keep them occupied. ¹⁴ I have seen all the things that are done under the sun and have found everything to be futile, a pursuit of the wind.^F

¹⁵ What is crooked cannot be straightened;
what is lacking cannot be counted.

¹⁶ I said to myself, "See, I have amassed wisdom far beyond all those who were over Jerusalem before me, and my mind has thoroughly grasped^G

---

^A 1:1 Or of Qoheleth, or of the Leader of the Assembly ^B 1:8 Or words
^C 1:11 Or of the things that ^D 1:12 Or Teacher, was ^E 1:13 Or given the descendants of Adam ^F 1:14 Or a feeding on wind, or an affliction of spirit; also in v. 17 ^G 1:16 Or discerned

wisdom and knowledge." [17] I applied my mind to know wisdom and knowledge, madness and folly; I learned that this too is a pursuit of the wind.

[18] For with much wisdom is much sorrow;
as knowledge increases, grief increases.

THE EMPTINESS OF PLEASURE

2 I said to myself, "Go ahead, I will test you with pleasure; enjoy what is good." But it turned out to be futile. [2] I said about laughter, "It is madness," and about pleasure, "What does this accomplish?" [3] I explored with my mind the pull of wine on my body — my mind still guiding me with wisdom — and how to grasp folly, until I could see what is good for people to do under heaven[A] during the few days of their lives.

THE EMPTINESS OF POSSESSIONS

[4] I increased my achievements. I built houses and planted vineyards for myself. [5] I made gardens and parks for myself and planted every kind of fruit tree in them. [6] I constructed reservoirs for myself from which to irrigate a grove of flourishing trees. [7] I acquired male and female servants and had slaves who were born in my house. I also owned livestock — large herds and flocks — more than all who were before me in Jerusalem. [8] I also amassed silver and gold for myself, and the treasure of kings and provinces. I gathered male and female singers for myself, and many concubines, the delights of men.[B,C] [9] So I became great and surpassed all who were before me in Jerusalem; my wisdom also remained with me. [10] All that my eyes desired, I did not deny them. I did not refuse myself any pleasure, for I took pleasure in all my struggles. This was my reward for all my struggles. [11] When I considered all that I had accomplished[D] and what I had labored to achieve, I found everything to be futile and a pursuit of the wind.[E] There was nothing to be gained under the sun.

THE RELATIVE VALUE OF WISDOM

[12] Then I turned to consider wisdom, madness, and folly, for what will the king's successor[F] be like? He[G] will do what has already been done. [13] And I realized that there is an advantage to wisdom over folly, like the advantage of light over darkness.

[14] The wise person has eyes in his head,
but the fool walks in darkness.

Yet I also knew that one fate comes to them both. [15] So I said to myself, "What happens to the fool will also happen to me. Why then have I been overly wise?" And I said to myself that this is also futile. [16] For, just like the fool, there is no lasting remembrance of the wise, since in the days to come both will be forgotten. How is it that the wise person dies just like the fool? [17] Therefore, I hated life because the work that was done under the sun was distressing to me. For everything is futile and a pursuit of the wind.

[A]2:3 Two Hb mss, LXX, Syr read *the sun*   [B]2:8 LXX, Theod, Syr read *and male cupbearers and female cupbearers*; Aq, Tg, Vg read *a cup and cups*; Hb obscure   [C]2:8 Or *many treasures that people delight in*   [D]2:11 Lit *all my works that my hands had done*   [E]2:11 Or *a feeding on wind*, or *an affliction of spirit*; also in vv. 17,26   [F]2:12 Lit *the man who comes after the king*   [G]2:12 Some Hb mss read *They*

THE EMPTINESS OF WORK

[18] I hated all my work that I labored at under the sun because I must leave it to the one who comes after me. [19] And who knows whether he will be wise or a fool? Yet he will take over all my work that I labored at skillfully under the sun. This too is futile. [20] So I began to give myself over[A] to despair concerning all my work that I had labored at under the sun. [21] When there is a person whose work was done with wisdom, knowledge, and skill, and he must give his portion to a person who has not worked for it, this too is futile and a great wrong. [22] For what does a person get with all his work and all his efforts that he labors at under the sun? [23] For all his days are filled with grief, and his occupation is sorrowful; even at night, his mind does not rest. This too is futile.

[24] There is nothing better for a person than to eat, drink, and enjoy[B,C] his work. I have seen that even this is from God's hand, [25] because who can eat and who can enjoy life[D] apart from him?[E] [26] For to the person who is pleasing in his sight, he gives wisdom, knowledge, and joy; but to the sinner he gives the task of gathering and accumulating in order to give to the one who is pleasing in God's sight. This too is futile and a pursuit of the wind.

THE MYSTERY OF TIME

3 There is an occasion for everything,
and a time for every activity under heaven:

[2] a time to give birth and a time to die;
a time to plant and a time to uproot;[F]
[3] a time to kill and a time to heal;
a time to tear down and a time to build;
[4] a time to weep and a time to laugh;
a time to mourn and a time to dance;
[5] a time to throw stones and a time to gather stones;
a time to embrace and a time to avoid embracing;
[6] a time to search and a time to count as lost;
a time to keep and a time to throw away;
[7] a time to tear and a time to sew;
a time to be silent and a time to speak;
[8] a time to love and a time to hate;
a time for war and a time for peace.

[9] What does the worker gain from his struggles? [10] I have seen the task that God has given the children of Adam to keep them occupied. [11] He has made everything appropriate[G] in its time. He has also put eternity in their hearts,[H] but no one can discover the work God has done from beginning to end. [12] I know that there is nothing better for them than to rejoice and enjoy the[I] good life. [13] It is also the gift of God whenever anyone eats, drinks,

---

[A]2:20 Lit *And I turned to cause my heart* [B]2:24 Syr, Tg; MT reads *There is no good in a person who eats and drinks and enjoys* [C]2:24 Lit *and his soul sees good* [D]2:25 LXX, Theod, Syr read *can drink* [E]2:25 Some Hb mss, LXX, Syr read *me* [F]3:2 Lit *uproot what is planted* [G]3:11 Or *beautiful* [H]3:11 Or *has put a sense of past and future into their minds, or has placed ignorance in their hearts* [I]3:12 Lit *his*

TIME WELL SPENT

ECCLESIASTES 3; JOHN 12:20-36

*"Truly I tell you, unless a grain
of wheat falls to the ground
and dies, it remains by itself.
But if it dies, it produces much
fruit."*

JOHN 12:24

Every fruit-bearing harvest—whether literal or metaphorical—involves a time to live and a time to die. Life is a turning carousel of seasons, some for scattering and some for gathering, some for sowing and some for reaping, some for mourning and some for dancing.

There's something both comforting and unsettling about this reality. We long for the beauty that comes with growth, yet we struggle in the process of change. Ecclesiastes 3 tells us there's a time for everything (v.1). Every season has a purpose and a part to play in the bigger story of our lives.

Throughout the book of Ecclesiastes, King Solomon reminds us that time is fleeting and no earthly authority can stop it, manipulate it, negotiate with it, or reset it. We cannot undo what's been done. We can't force time to unfold at the pace of our choosing or buy it back once it's been used up. We live within its boundaries but they don't have to hold us captive. We can welcome each new season, knowing that in time we discover more about the One who is sovereign over every moment—past, present, and future.

Chances are, if we got to map out the seasons of our lives, we'd probably handpick the experiences that make us feel the most alive and at ease. It's natural to long for moments where we find ourselves on the more comfortable side of Solomon's equations—healing, building, laughing, dancing, and loving.

But to completely bypass times of restlessness, loss, and sorrow would ultimately rob us of the necessary and beautiful process of growth. No one welcomes pain, but we can learn to embrace what it stirs inside us: a deep, desperate longing for the presence of our Savior.

Time is sacred because it is God's gift to us. There is a rhythm to it that invites us to walk with purpose and grace through all the twists and turns of life. For those who linger in the presence of Jesus, every season and every circumstance becomes an opportunity to know Him more fully.

That doesn't mean we won't still wrestle with change or unexpected challenges in the days to come. We will always struggle to make sense of time because we were created for more than momentary experiences, temporary pleasures, and short-lived victories. Forever is written on our souls; a desire for something permanent is woven into our DNA. The result is a desperate longing for the One who has remained the same for all eternity.

We can navigate these ever-changing seasons by holding fast to our never-changing God. And we can rest assured that every moment in His hands is time well spent.

and enjoys all his efforts. [14] I know that everything God does will last forever; there is no adding to it or taking from it. God works so that people will be in awe of him. [15] Whatever is, has already been, and whatever will be, already is. However, God seeks justice for the persecuted.[A]

THE MYSTERY OF INJUSTICE AND DEATH

[16] I also observed under the sun: there is wickedness at the place of judgment and there is wickedness at the place of righteousness. [17] I said to myself, "God will judge the righteous and the wicked, since there is a time for every activity and every work." [18] I said to myself, "This happens so that God may test the children of Adam and they may see for themselves that they are like animals." [19] For the fate of the children of Adam and the fate of animals is the same. As one dies, so dies the other; they all have the same breath. People have no advantage over animals since everything is futile. [20] All are going to the same place; all come from dust, and all return to dust. [21] Who knows if the spirits of the children of Adam go upward and the spirits of animals go downward to the earth? [22] I have seen that there is nothing better than for a person to enjoy his activities because that is his reward. For who can enable him to see what will happen after he dies?[B]

4 Again, I observed all the acts of oppression being done under the sun. Look at the tears of those who are oppressed; they have no one to comfort them. Power is with those who oppress them; they have no one to comfort them. [2] So I commended the dead, who have already died, more than the living, who are still alive. [3] But better than either of them is the one who has not yet existed, who has not seen the evil activity that is done under the sun.

THE LONELINESS OF WEALTH

[4] I saw that all labor and all skillful work is due to one person's jealousy of another. This too is futile and a pursuit of the wind.[C]

> [5] The fool folds his arms
> and consumes his own flesh.
> [6] Better one handful with rest
> than two handfuls with effort and a pursuit of the wind.

[7] Again, I saw futility under the sun: [8] There is a person without a companion,[D] without even a son or brother, and though there is no end to all his struggles, his eyes are still not content with riches. "Who am I struggling for," he asks, "and depriving myself of good things?" This too is futile and a miserable task.

[9] Two are better than one because they have a good reward for their efforts. [10] For if either falls, his companion can lift him up; but pity the one who falls without another to lift him up. [11] Also, if two lie down together, they can keep warm; but how can one person alone keep warm? [12] And if someone overpowers one person, two can resist him. A cord of three strands is not easily broken.

[A]3:15 Lit God seeks what is pursued   [B]3:22 Lit after him   [C]4:4 Or a feeding on wind, or an affliction of spirit; also in vv. 6,16   [D]4:8 Lit person, but there is not a second,

¹³ Better is a poor but wise youth than an old but foolish king who no longer pays attention to warnings. ¹⁴ For he came from prison to be king, even though he was born poor in his kingdom. ¹⁵ I saw all the living, who move about under the sun, follow^A a second youth who succeeds him. ¹⁶ There is no limit to all the people who were before them, yet those who come later will not rejoice in him. This too is futile and a pursuit of the wind.

CAUTION IN GOD'S PRESENCE

5 Guard your steps when you go to the house of God. Better to approach in obedience than to offer the sacrifice as fools do, for they ignorantly do wrong. ² Do not be hasty to speak, and do not be impulsive to make a speech before God. God is in heaven and you are on earth, so let your words be few. ³ Just as dreams accompany much labor, so also a fool's voice comes with many words. ⁴ When you make a vow to God, don't delay fulfilling it, because he does not delight in fools. Fulfill what you vow. ⁵ Better that you do not vow than that you vow and not fulfill it. ⁶ Do not let your mouth bring guilt on you, and do not say in the presence of the messenger that it was a mistake. Why should God be angry with your words and destroy the work of your hands? ⁷ For many dreams bring futility, so do many words. Therefore, fear God.

THE REALITIES OF WEALTH

⁸ If you see oppression of the poor and perversion of justice and righteousness in the province, don't be astonished at the situation, because one official protects another official, and higher officials protect them. ⁹ The profit from the land is taken by all; the king is served by the field.^B

¹⁰ The one who loves silver is never satisfied with silver, and whoever loves wealth is never satisfied with income. This too is futile. ¹¹ When good things increase, the ones who consume them multiply; what, then, is the profit to the owner, except to gaze at them with his eyes? ¹² The sleep of the worker is sweet, whether he eats little or much, but the abundance of the rich permits him no sleep.

¹³ There is a sickening tragedy I have seen under the sun: wealth kept by its owner to his harm. ¹⁴ That wealth was lost in a bad venture, so when he fathered a son, he was empty-handed. ¹⁵ As he came from his mother's womb, so he will go again, naked as he came; he will take nothing for his efforts that he can carry in his hands. ¹⁶ This too is a sickening tragedy: exactly as he comes, so he will go. What does the one gain who struggles for the wind? ¹⁷ What is more, he eats in darkness all his days, with much frustration, sickness, and anger.

¹⁸ Here is what I have seen to be good: It is appropriate to eat, drink, and experience good in all the labor one does under the sun during the few days of his life God has given him, because that is his reward. ¹⁹ Furthermore, everyone to whom God has given riches and wealth, he has also allowed him to enjoy them, take his reward, and rejoice in his labor. This is a gift of God, ²⁰ for he does not often consider the days of his life because God keeps him occupied with the joy of his heart.

---

^A 4:15 Lit *with*   ^B 5:9 Hb obscure

6 Here is a tragedy I have observed under the sun, and it weighs heavily on humanity:[A] [2] God gives a person riches, wealth, and honor so that he lacks nothing of all he desires for himself, but God does not allow him to enjoy them. Instead, a stranger will enjoy them. This is futile and a sickening tragedy. [3] A man may father a hundred children and live many years. No matter how long he lives,[B] if he is not satisfied by good things and does not even have a proper burial, I say that a stillborn child is better off than he. [4] For he comes in futility and he goes in darkness, and his name is shrouded in darkness. [5] Though a stillborn child does not see the sun and is not conscious, it has more rest than he. [6] And if a person lives a thousand years twice, but does not experience happiness, do not both go to the same place?

[7] All of a person's labor is for his stomach,[C]
yet the appetite is never satisfied.

[8] What advantage then does the wise person have over the fool? What advantage is there for the poor person who knows how to conduct himself before others? [9] Better what the eyes see than wandering desire. This too is futile and a pursuit of the wind.[D]

[10] Whatever exists was given its name long ago,[E] and it is known what mankind is. But he is not able to contend with the one stronger than he. [11] For when there are many words, they increase futility. What is the advantage for mankind? [12] For who knows what is good for anyone in life, in the few days of his futile life that he spends like a shadow? Who can tell anyone what will happen after him under the sun?

WISE SAYINGS

7 A good name is better than fine perfume,
and the day of one's death is better than the day
of one's birth.
[2] It is better to go to a house of mourning
than to go to a house of feasting,
since that is the end of all mankind,
and the living should take it to heart.
[3] Grief is better than laughter,
for when a face is sad, a heart may be glad.
[4] The heart of the wise is in a house of mourning,
but the heart of fools is in a house of pleasure.
[5] It is better to listen to rebuke from a wise person
than to listen to the song of fools,
[6] for like the crackling of burning thorns under the pot,
so is the laughter of the fool.
This too is futile.
[7] Surely, the practice of extortion turns a wise person
into a fool,
and a bribe corrupts the mind.
[8] The end of a matter is better than its beginning;

[A] 6:1 Or *it is common among men*   [B] 6:3 Lit *how many years*   [C] 6:7 Lit *mouth*
[D] 6:9 Or *a feeding on wind,* or *an affliction of spirit*   [E] 6:10 Lit *name already*

a patient spirit is better than a proud spirit.
⁹ Don't let your spirit rush to be angry,
for anger abides in the heart of fools.
¹⁰ Don't say, "Why were the former days better than these?"
since it is not wise of you to ask this.
¹¹ Wisdom is as good as an inheritance
and an advantage to those who see the sun,
¹² because wisdom is protection as silver is protection;
but the advantage of knowledge
is that wisdom preserves the life of its owner.
¹³ Consider the work of God,
for who can straighten out
what he has made crooked?

¹⁴ In the day of prosperity be joyful, but in the day of adversity, consider: God has made the one as well as the other, so that no one can discover anything that will come after him.

AVOIDING EXTREMES

¹⁵ In my futile life^A I have seen everything: someone righteous perishes in spite of his righteousness, and someone wicked lives long in spite of his evil. ¹⁶ Don't be excessively righteous, and don't be overly wise. Why should you destroy yourself? ¹⁷ Don't be excessively wicked, and don't be foolish. Why should you die before your time? ¹⁸ It is good that you grasp the one and do not let the other slip from your hand. For the one who fears God will end up with both of them.
¹⁹ Wisdom makes the wise person stronger
than ten rulers of a city.
²⁰ There is certainly no one righteous on the earth
who does good and never sins.

²¹ Don't pay attention^B to everything people say, or you may hear your servant cursing you, ²² for in your heart you know that many times you yourself have cursed others.

WHAT THE TEACHER FOUND

²³ I have tested all this by wisdom. I resolved, "I will be wise," but it was beyond me. ²⁴ What exists is beyond reach and very deep. Who can discover it? ²⁵ I turned my thoughts to know, explore, and examine wisdom and an explanation for things, and to know that wickedness is stupidity and folly is madness. ²⁶ And I find more bitter than death the woman who is a trap: her heart a net and her hands chains. The one who pleases God will escape her, but the sinner will be captured by her. ²⁷ "Look," says the Teacher, "I have discovered this by adding one thing to another to find out the explanation, ²⁸ which my soul continually searches for but does not find: I found one person in a thousand, but none of those was a woman. ²⁹ Only see this: I have discovered that God made people upright, but they pursued many schemes."

---

^A7:15 Lit days   ^B7:21 Lit Don't give your heart

WISDOM, AUTHORITIES, AND INEQUITIES

8 Who is like the wise person, and who knows the interpretation of a matter? A person's wisdom brightens his face, and the sternness of his face is changed.

[2] Keep[A] the king's command because of your oath made before God. [3] Do not be in a hurry; leave his presence, and don't persist in a bad cause, since he will do whatever he wants. [4] For the king's word is authoritative, and who can say to him, "What are you doing?" [5] The one who keeps a command will not experience anything harmful, and a wise heart knows the right time and procedure. [6] For every activity there is a right time and procedure, even though a person's troubles are heavy on him. [7] Yet no one knows what will happen because who can tell him what will happen? [8] No one has authority over the wind[B] to restrain it, and there is no authority over the day of death; no one is discharged during battle, and wickedness will not allow those who practice it to escape. [9] All this I have seen, applying my mind to all the work that is done under the sun, at a time when one person has authority over another to his harm.

[10] In such circumstances, I saw the wicked buried. They came and went from the holy place, and they were praised[C] in the city where they did those things. This too is futile. [11] Because the sentence against an evil act is not carried out quickly, the heart of people is filled with the desire to commit evil. [12] Although a sinner does evil a hundred times and prolongs his life, I also know that it will go well with God-fearing people, for they are reverent before him. [13] However, it will not go well with the wicked, and they will not lengthen their days like a shadow, for they are not reverent before God.

[14] There is a futility that is done on the earth: there are righteous people who get what the actions of the wicked deserve, and there are wicked people who get what the actions of the righteous deserve. I say that this too is futile. [15] So I commended enjoyment because there is nothing better for a person under the sun than to eat, drink, and enjoy himself, for this will accompany him in his labor during the days of his life that God gives him under the sun.

[16] When I applied my mind to know wisdom and to observe the activity that is done on the earth (even though one's eyes do not close in sleep day or night), [17] I observed all the work of God and concluded that a person is unable to discover the work that is done under the sun. Even though a person labors hard to explore it, he cannot find it; even if a wise person claims to know it, he is unable to discover it.

ENJOY LIFE DESPITE DEATH

9 Indeed, I took all this to heart and explained it all: The righteous, the wise, and their works are in God's hands. People don't know whether to expect love or hate. Everything lies ahead of them. [2] Everything is the same for everyone: There is one fate for the righteous and the wicked, for the good and the bad,[D] for the clean and the unclean, for the one who sacrifices and the one who does not sacrifice. As it is for the good, so also it is for the sinner; as it is for the one who takes an oath, so also for the one who fears

---

[A]8:2 Some Hb mss, LXX, Vg, Tg, Syr; other Hb mss read *I, keep*   [B]8:8 Or *life-breath*
[C]8:10 Some Hb mss, LXX, Aq, Theod, Sym; other Hb mss read *forgotten*
[D]9:2 LXX, Aq, Syr, Vg; MT omits *and the bad*

an oath. ³ This is an evil in all that is done under the sun: there is one fate for everyone. In addition, the hearts of people are full of evil, and madness is in their hearts while they live; after that they go to the dead. ⁴ But there is hope for whoever is joined^ with all the living, since a live dog is better than a dead lion. ⁵ For the living know that they will die, but the dead don't know anything. There is no longer a reward for them because the memory of them is forgotten. ⁶ Their love, their hate, and their envy have already disappeared, and there is no longer a portion for them in all that is done under the sun.

⁷ Go, eat your bread with pleasure, and drink your wine with a cheerful heart, for God has already accepted your works. ⁸ Let your clothes be white all the time, and never let oil be lacking on your head. ⁹ Enjoy life with the wife you love all the days of your fleeting^B life, which has been given to you under the sun, all your fleeting days. For that is your portion in life and in your struggle under the sun. ¹⁰ Whatever your hands find to do, do with all your strength, because there is no work, planning, knowledge, or wisdom in Sheol where you are going.

THE LIMITATIONS OF WISDOM

¹¹ Again I saw under the sun that the race is not to the swift, or the battle to the strong, or bread to the wise, or riches to the discerning, or favor to the skillful; rather, time and chance happen to all of them. ¹² For certainly no one knows his time: like fish caught in a cruel net or like birds caught in a trap, so people are trapped in an evil time as it suddenly falls on them.

¹³ I have observed that this also is wisdom under the sun, and it is significant to me: ¹⁴ There was a small city with few men in it. A great king came against it, surrounded it, and built large siege works against it. ¹⁵ Now a poor wise man was found in the city, and he delivered the city by his wisdom. Yet no one remembered that poor man. ¹⁶ And I said, "Wisdom is better than strength, but the wisdom of the poor man is despised, and his words are not heeded."

¹⁷   The calm words of the wise are heeded
        more than the shouts of a ruler over fools.
¹⁸   Wisdom is better than weapons of war,
        but one sinner can destroy much good.

THE BURDEN OF FOLLY

10   Dead flies make a perfumer's oil ferment and stink;
         so a little folly outweighs wisdom and honor.
²   A wise person's heart goes to the^C right,
        but a fool's heart to the left.
³   Even when the fool walks along the road, his heart lacks sense,
        and he shows everyone he is a fool.
⁴   If the ruler's anger rises against you, don't leave your post,
        for calmness puts great offenses to rest.

⁵ There is an evil I have seen under the sun, an error proceeding from the presence of the ruler:
⁶   The fool is appointed to great heights,
        but the rich remain in lowly positions.

---

^9:4 Alt Hb tradition reads *chosen*   ^B9:9 Or *futile*   ^C10:2 Lit *his*

⁷ I have seen slaves on horses,
    but princes walking on the ground like slaves.

⁸ The one who digs a pit may fall into it,
    and the one who breaks through a wall may be bitten
      by a snake.
⁹ The one who quarries stones may be hurt by them;
    the one who splits logs may be endangered by them.
¹⁰ If the ax is dull, and one does not sharpen its edge,
    then one must exert more strength;
    however, the advantage of wisdom is that it brings success.
¹¹ If the snake bites before it is charmed,
    then there is no advantage for the charmer.[A]
¹² The words from the mouth of a wise person are gracious,
    but the lips of a fool consume him.
¹³ The beginning of the words from his mouth is folly,
    but the end of his speaking is evil madness;
¹⁴ yet the fool multiplies words.
    No one knows what will happen,
    and who can tell anyone what will happen after him?
¹⁵ The struggles of fools weary them,
    for they don't know how to go to the city.
¹⁶ Woe to you, land, when your king is a youth
    and your princes feast in the morning.
¹⁷ Blessed are you, land, when your king is a son of nobles
    and your princes feast at the proper time —
    for strength and not for drunkenness.
¹⁸ Because of laziness the roof caves in,
    and because of negligent hands the house leaks.
¹⁹ A feast is prepared for laughter,
    and wine makes life happy,
    and money[B] is the answer for everything.
²⁰ Do not curse the king even in your thoughts,
    and do not curse a rich person even in your bedroom,
    for a bird of the sky may carry the message,
    and a winged creature may report the matter.

INVEST IN LIFE

11 Send your bread on the surface of the water,
    for after many days you may find it.
² Give a portion to seven or even to eight,
    for you don't know what disaster may happen on earth.
³ If the clouds are full, they will pour out rain on the earth;
    whether a tree falls to the south or the north,
    the place where the tree falls, there it will lie.
⁴ One who watches the wind will not sow,
    and the one who looks at the clouds will not reap.
⁵ Just as you don't know the path of the wind,

ᴬ10:11 Lit *master of the tongue*   ᴮ10:19 Lit *silver*

or how bones develop in[A] the womb of a pregnant woman,
so also you don't know the work of God who makes everything.

⁶ In the morning sow your seed,
and at evening do not let your hand rest,
because you don't know which will succeed,
whether one or the other,
or if both of them will be equally good.

⁷ Light is sweet,
and it is pleasing for the eyes to see the sun.

⁸ Indeed, if someone lives many years,
let him rejoice in them all,
and let him remember the days of darkness, since they will be many.
All that comes is futile.

⁹ Rejoice, young person, while you are young,
and let your heart be glad in the days of your youth.
And walk in the ways of your heart
and in the desire of your eyes;
but know that for all of these things God will bring you to judgment.

¹⁰ Remove sorrow from your heart,
and put away pain from your flesh,
because youth and the prime of life are fleeting.

THE TWILIGHT OF LIFE

12 So remember your Creator in the days of your youth:
Before the days of adversity come,
and the years approach when you will say,
"I have no delight in them";

² before the sun and the light are darkened,
and the moon and the stars,
and the clouds return after[B] the rain;

³ on the day when the guardians of the house tremble,
and the strong men stoop,
the women who grind grain cease because they are few,
and the ones who watch through the windows see dimly,

⁴ the doors at the street are shut
while the sound of the mill fades;
when one rises at the sound of a bird,
and all the daughters of song grow faint.

⁵ Also, they are afraid of heights and dangers on the road;
the almond tree blossoms,
the grasshopper loses its spring,[C]
and the caper berry has no effect;
for the mere mortal is headed to his eternal home,
and mourners will walk around in the street;

⁶ before the silver cord is snapped,[D]
and the gold bowl is broken,

[A]11:5 Or *know how the life-breath comes to the bones in*   [B]12:2 Or *with*
[C]12:5 Or *grasshopper is weighed down, or grasshopper drags itself along*
[D]12:6 Alt Hb tradition reads *removed*

THE CONCLUSION OF THE MATTER

I recently stood at the grave of my favorite grandparent. As I mourned the loss of my "Pop" I felt the sting of Solomon's famous words in the book of Ecclesiastes:

"'Absolute futility,' says the Teacher. 'Everything is futile.'"
ECCLESIASTES 12:8

Pop lived a good life but when he died at the age of 92, he was left with nothing much.

My grandma died several years earlier, after sixty years of marriage. Dementia clouded Pop's brain so much that he didn't remember her at all in the end. Upon retirement he received a pension and a plaque and was promptly replaced. He sold his home and watched his life savings dwindle from the cost of long-term care. Though his life was fuller than most, his marriage, wealth, and achievements did not carry him through to the end.

I missed my grandfather terribly, but I also grieved the implications of this truth for my own life: so much of what I've spent my life building will just make a good bonfire in the end.

The book of Ecclesiastes takes a hard look at how to find meaning in life, despite the seemingly futile nature of everything. It's a book that dares to ask deep questions and refuses to accept pat answers. Where Proverbs is highly practical, Ecclesiastes is highly philosophical. King Solomon knew how it felt to have it all, but he had to face the fact that his life was a vapor compared to eternity (Ps 39:5). Once Solomon crossed that great threshold from life to death, not a single possession or moment of power would amount to a hill of beans.

Then what?

"When all has been heard, the conclusion of the matter is this: fear God and keep his commands, because this is for all humanity."
ECCLESIASTES 12:13

Jesus taught this in Matthew 22:36-38 when an expert in the law asked Him, "Teacher, which command in the law is the greatest?"

Like Solomon, Jesus used the opportunity to point past the temporal toward the eternal. He responded, "Love the Lord your God with all your heart, with all your soul, and with all your mind. This is the greatest and most important command."

Life is short. Most of what we've spent our lives building won't last forever. This is good news!

God invites us into a relationship with Him that will continue through the ages. When we love and serve Him, we are doing the same thing today that we will be doing ten million years from now. We can focus on the futile or fix our eyes on eternity. I want to choose the latter, and repeat the prayer of the great revivalist, Jonathan Edwards, "Lord, stamp eternity on my eyeballs."

and the jar is shattered at the spring,
and the wheel is broken into the well;
7 and the dust returns to the earth as it once was,
and the spirit returns to God who gave it.
8 "Absolute futility," says the Teacher. "Everything is futile."

THE TEACHER'S OBJECTIVES AND CONCLUSION

9 In addition to the Teacher being a wise man, he constantly taught the people knowledge; he weighed, explored, and arranged many proverbs. 10 The Teacher sought to find delightful sayings and write words of truth accurately. 11 The sayings of the wise are like cattle prods, and those from masters of collections are like firmly embedded nails. The sayings are given by one Shepherd.[A]

12 But beyond these, my son, be warned: there is no end to the making of many books, and much study wearies the body. 13 When all has been heard, the conclusion of the matter is this: fear God and keep his commands, because this is for all[B] humanity. 14 For God will bring every act to judgment, including every hidden thing, whether good or evil.

A 12:11 Or by a shepherd   B 12:13 Or is the whole duty of

A huge **TORRENT** CANNOT **EXTINGUISH** LOVE; RIVERS CANNOT SWEEP *it away*

song of songs

 A huge torrent cannot extinguish love; rivers cannot sweep it away. If a man were to give all his wealth for love, it would be utterly scorned. **8:7**

ON THE TIMELINE Song of Songs is commonly dated to the time of King Solomon, about 971 BC to 931 BC.

A LITTLE BACKGROUND The Song claims authorship by Solomon in its title, "The Song of Songs which is Solomon's." Though the church has long accepted this at face value, modern critics question Solomon's authorship. A common objection is the king's well-known possession of 700 wives and 300 concubines (1Kg 11:3). How could a man who lived like that write a song about devotion to one woman, if not for the effect of God's grace on his heart? In this way, Solomon foreshadowed other biblical writers who, except for God's grace and calling, were the least qualified for their roles.

MESSAGE & PURPOSE The central theme of the Song of Songs is a celebration of the goodness and beauty of romantic love. The Song's romantic ideals are as captivating as its imagery: emotional intimacy and sensitive communication, delightful sexuality and profound companionship, common perspective and willing forgiveness. The book illustrates respect, integrity, and security; love's devotion through bleak seasons of winter; and love's renewal in new seasons of spring.

Since the Song portrays a perfect love, it is natural for the songwriter to compare it to God's love for Israel. Solomon's love is like God's love for His people, and Shulammite's love is like a response from those people to God. The New Testament tells us a man's love for his wife should emulate Christ's love for His bride (Eph 5:22-33), and Solomon's Song shows such a marriage patterned after divine love.

GIVE THANKS FOR SONG OF SONGS:

Solomon's Song inspires a pursuit of the love it so beautifully describes. This romance is not a modern fairytale or a fantasy; it reflects God's desire to form within us a pure and devoted love. The Song shows there is bliss in married love that is reflective of the greater love the Church experiences as the bride of Christ. Greater than its celebration of romantic love, Song of Songs helps us anticipate the full consummation of our relationship with Christ when He returns for His bride.

THEMES IN SONG OF SONGS

Song of Songs is a timeless love story. Its themes call us into deeper relationships on earth as we look forward to the ultimate wedding celebration of the Lord Jesus Christ and His Church (Rv 19).

THEME	EXPLANATION
LOVE	Over time, Solomon's relationship with his bride turned into a love story full of romantic beauty and wonder. The intensity of their love colored their lives, affecting them physically, spiritually, and emotionally. Solomon's story is a vivid illustration of the power of love—it is not to be regarded casually or used to manipulate others, but upheld with commitment and honor.
COMMITMENT	Christ's love for His bride, the Church, is the ultimate example of committed love. As God protects His love for us, we must also do the same for others. Marriage is the daily celebration and remembrance of our commitment to our spouses, made possible by God's commitment to us.
SEX	Sex is a good and purposeful gift from God. Because He loves us, God calls us to steward this good gift by enjoying it within the covenant of marriage. Sex should be motivated by love, not lust; it is meant to express mutual love, not seek selfish gain.
BEAUTY	Solomon and his bride list what they admire about one another in romantic language, showing us the spontaneity and mystery of love, as well as a picture of true beauty. Beauty in its fullest sense is not just a physical attribute—it encompasses personality, purity of heart, strength of character, and so much more.
PERSEVERANCE	Over time, loneliness, isolation, and indifference crept into Solomon's marriage. Their intoxicating love grew cold and walls rose between them. This drastic change serves as a sobering reminder that we must be quick to defend and renew our love and commitment to one another, addressing problems before they become barriers.
WISDOM	Human wisdom doesn't contain all the answers. Knowledge and education have their limits. To understand life and make right choices, we need the wisdom that can be found only in God's Word.

READ AND UNDERSTAND SONG OF SONGS

The Bible is a complete work in which many stories combine to tell one story. As you read the Song of Songs, consider reading the additional passages to discover how the whole of Scripture works together.

1 The Song of Songs, which is Solomon's.

Woman

2 Oh, that he would kiss me with the kisses of his mouth!
For your caresses[A] are more delightful than wine.
3 The fragrance of your perfume is intoxicating;
your name is perfume poured out.
No wonder young women[B] adore you.
4 Take me with you — let's hurry.
Oh, that the king would bring[C] me to his chambers.

Young Women

We will rejoice and be glad in you;
we will celebrate your caresses more than wine.

Woman

It is only right that they adore you.

5 Daughters of Jerusalem,
I am dark like the tents of Kedar,
yet lovely like the curtains of Solomon.
6 Do not stare at me because I am dark,
for the sun has gazed on me.
My mother's sons were angry with me;
they made me take care of the vineyards.
I have not taken care of my own vineyard.

7 Tell me, you whom I love:
Where do you pasture your sheep?
Where do you let them rest at noon?
Why should I be like one who veils herself[D]
beside the flocks of your companions?

Man[E]

8 If you do not know,
most beautiful of women,
follow[F] the tracks of the flock,
and pasture your young goats
near the shepherds' tents.

9 I compare you, my darling,
to a[G] mare among Pharaoh's chariots.
10 Your cheeks are beautiful with jewelry,
your neck with its necklace.
11 We will make gold jewelry for you,
accented with silver.

[A] 1:2 Or *acts of love* [B] 1:3 Or *wonder virgins* [C] 1:4 Or *The king has brought*
[D] 1:7 Or *who wanders* [E] 1:8 Some understand the young women to be the
speakers in this verse. [F] 1:8 Lit *go out for yourself into* [G] 1:9 Lit *my*

Woman

12 While the king is on his couch,^A
   my perfume^B releases its fragrance.
13 The one I love is a sachet of myrrh to me,
   spending the night between my breasts.
14 The one I love is a cluster of henna blossoms to me,
   in the vineyards of En-gedi.

Man

15 How beautiful you are, my darling.
   How very beautiful!
   Your eyes are doves.

Woman

16 How handsome you are, my love.
   How delightful!
   Our bed is verdant;
17 the beams of our house are cedars,
   and our rafters are cypresses.^C

2 I am a wildflower^D of Sharon,
   a lily^E of the valleys.

Man

2 Like a lily among thorns,
   so is my darling among the young women.

Woman

3 Like an apricot^F tree among the trees of the forest,
   so is my love among the young men.
   I delight to sit in his shade,
   and his fruit is sweet to my taste.
4 He brought me to the banquet hall,^G
   and he looked on me with love.^H
5 Sustain me with raisins;
   refresh me with apricots,^I
   for I am lovesick.
6 May his left hand be under my head,
   and his right arm embrace me.
7 Young women of Jerusalem, I charge you
   by the gazelles and the wild does of the field,
   do not stir up or awaken love
   until the appropriate time.^J

8 Listen! My love is approaching.
   Look! Here he comes,
   leaping over the mountains,

---

^A1:12 Or *is at his table* ^B1:12 Lit *nard* ^C1:17 Or *firs*, or *pines* ^D2:1 Traditionally
rose ^E2:1 Or *lotus* ^F2:3 Or *apple* ^G2:4 Lit *the house of wine* ^H2:4 Or *and
his banner over me is love* ^I2:5 Or *apples* ^J2:7 Lit *until it pleases*

I AM HIS

SONG OF SONGS 2:8–3:11; 6:3; 7:10

I had a death grip on my husband for the first decade of our marriage. So desperate was my craving to see us through "till death do us part" that I white-knuckled it through our relationship. I was determined to hold on tight enough for both of us.

But I could never fully grasp the security I craved so deeply. Holding on that tightly squeezed the love and fun out of our relationship.

Since marriage is ultimately a picture of Christ and the Church, this approach to covenant love has also caused strain in my relationship with Jesus. Always secretly fearful that He would change His mind about me, I have tried to keep us glued together with works well done and duties faithfully fulfilled.

But as desperation and anxiety couldn't bolt the door on my marriage, striving couldn't make Jesus love me more. Through years of tender care and collisions with His Word, I am learning that security flows out of devoted love, not anxious control.

In Song of Songs, Shulammite is the soon-to-be bride of wise King Solomon, and she has her own need for security. Right before the wedding, she says these words:

"My love is mine and I am his."

SONG OF SONGS 2:16

But, as the Shulammite and Solomon's love story unfolds, her tone begins to shift. After the wedding she says, "I am my love's, and my love is mine" (Sg 6:3). Then, as the Shulammite and Solomon mature into an old, married couple, she says, "I am my love's and his desire is for me" (Sg 7:10).

Let's drag a magnifying glass over this subtle progression.

At first, the Shulammite's security is found in knowing that her man belongs to her. Her possession of him is primary; his possession of her is secondary. (As I've already mentioned, I've seen what this looks like in real life. It's not pretty.) Then, after the wedding, the Shulammite's possession of Solomon was secondary: "I am my love's and my love is mine." And finally, it's gone altogether: "his desire is for me."

It took decades for the bride in this story to understand that her security did not come from her possession of her groom, but from his devoted love to her.

Song of Songs is much more than a human love story. As is the case throughout Scripture, God uses marriage as an illustration for the love between Himself and His people. God is always represented by the groom and we are always the bride. **His love hinges on His faithfulness, not ours.**

bounding over the hills.
⁹ My love is like a gazelle
or a young stag.
See, he is standing behind our wall,
gazing through the windows,
peering through the lattice.
¹⁰ My love calls to me:

Man

Arise, my darling.
Come away, my beautiful one.
¹¹ For now the winter is past;
the rain has ended and gone away.
¹² The blossoms appear in the countryside.
The time of singing ᴬ has come,
and the turtledove's cooing is heard in our land.
¹³ The fig tree ripens its figs;
the blossoming vines give off their fragrance.
Arise, my darling.
Come away, my beautiful one.

¹⁴ My dove, in the clefts of the rock,
in the crevices of the cliff,
let me see your face, ᴮ
let me hear your voice;
for your voice is sweet,
and your face is lovely.

Woman ᶜ

¹⁵ Catch the foxes for us —
the little foxes that ruin the vineyards —
for our vineyards are in bloom.

Woman

¹⁶ My love is mine and I am his;
he feeds among the lilies.
¹⁷ Until the day breaks ᴰ
and the shadows flee,
turn around, my love, and be like a gazelle
or a young stag on the divided mountains. ᴱ

3 In my bed at night ᶠ
I sought the one I love;
I sought him, but did not find him. ᴳ
² I will arise now and go about the city,

ᴬ2:12 Or *pruning*   ᴮ2:14 Or *form*   ᶜ2:15 The speaker could be the woman,
the man, or both.   ᴰ2:17 Lit *breathes*   ᴱ2:17 Or *the Bether mountains, or the
mountains of spices*; Hb obscure   ᶠ3:1 Or *bed night after night*   ᴳ3:1 LXX adds
I called him, but he did not answer me

through the streets and the plazas.
I will seek the one I love.
I sought him, but did not find him.
³ The guards who go about the city found me.
I asked them, "Have you seen the one I love?"
⁴ I had just passed them
when I found the one I love.
I held on to him and would not let him go
until I brought him to my mother's house —
to the chamber of the one who conceived me.
⁵ Young women of Jerusalem, I charge you
by the gazelles and the wild does of the field,
do not stir up or awaken love
until the appropriate time.ᴬ

Narrator

⁶ Who is this coming up from the wilderness
like columns of smoke,
scented with myrrh and frankincense
from every fragrant powder of the merchant?

⁷ Look! Solomon's bed
surrounded by sixty warriors
from the mighty men of Israel.
⁸ All of them are skilled with swords
and trained in warfare.
Each has his sword at his side
to guard against the terror of the night.

⁹ King Solomon made a carriage for himself
with wood from Lebanon.
¹⁰ He made its posts of silver,
its backᴮ of gold,
and its seat of purple.
Its interior is inlaid with loveᶜ
by the young women of Jerusalem.
¹¹ Go out, young women of Zion,
and gaze at King Solomon,
wearing the crown his mother placed on him
on the day of his wedding —
the day of his heart's rejoicing.

Man

4 How beautiful you are, my darling.
How very beautiful!
Behind your veil,
your eyes are doves.
Your hair is like a flock of goats

ᴬ3:5 Lit *until it pleases* ᴮ3:10 Or *base,* or *canopy* ᶜ3:10 Or *leather* streaming down Mount Gilead.

2 Your teeth are like a flock of newly shorn sheep
coming up from washing,
each one bearing twins,
and none has lost its young.^A

3 Your lips are like a scarlet cord,
and your mouth^B is lovely.
Behind your veil,
your brow^C is like a slice of pomegranate.

4 Your neck is like the tower of David,
constructed in layers.
A thousand shields are hung on it —
all of them shields of warriors.

5 Your breasts are like two fawns,
twins of a gazelle, that feed among the lilies.

6 Until the day breaks^D
and the shadows flee,
I will make my way to the mountain of myrrh
and the hill of frankincense.

7 You are absolutely beautiful, my darling;
there is no imperfection in you.

8 Come with me from Lebanon,^E my bride;
come with me from Lebanon!
Descend from the peak of Amana,
from the summit of Senir and Hermon,
from the dens of the lions,
from the mountains of the leopards.

9 You have captured my heart, my sister, my bride.
You have captured my heart with one glance of your eyes,
with one jewel of your necklace.

10 How delightful your caresses are, my sister, my bride.
Your caresses are much better than wine,
and the fragrance of your perfume than any balsam.

11 Your lips drip sweetness like the honeycomb, my bride.
Honey and milk are under your tongue.
The fragrance of your garments is like the fragrance
    of Lebanon.

12 My sister, my bride, you are a locked garden —
a locked garden^F and a sealed spring.

13 Your branches are a paradise^G of pomegranates
with choicest fruits;
henna with nard,

14 nard and saffron, calamus and cinnamon,

---

^A 4:2 Lit *and no one bereaved among them*   ^B 4:3 Or *speech*   ^C 4:3 Or *temple*,
or *cheek*, or *lips*   ^D 4:6 Lit *breathes*   ^E 4:8 In Hb, the word for *Lebanon* is similar
to "frankincense" in Sg 4:6,14,15.   ^F 4:12 Some Hb mss read *locked fountain*
^G 4:13 Or *park*, or *orchard*

with all the trees of frankincense,
myrrh and aloes,
with all the best spices.
¹⁵ You are a garden spring,
a well of flowing water
streaming from Lebanon.

Woman

¹⁶ Awaken, north wind;
come, south wind.
Blow on my garden,
and spread the fragrance of its spices.
Let my love come to his garden
and eat its choicest fruits.

Man

5 I have come to my garden — my sister, my bride.
I gather^A my myrrh with my spices.
I eat my honeycomb with my honey.
I drink my wine with my milk.

Narrator

Eat, friends!
Drink, be intoxicated with caresses!^B

Woman

² I was sleeping, but my heart was awake.
A sound! My love was knocking!

Man

Open to me, my sister, my darling,
my dove, my perfect one.
For my head is drenched with dew,
my hair with droplets of the night.

Woman

³ I have taken off my clothing.
How can I put it back on?
I have washed my feet.
How can I get them dirty?
⁴ My love thrust his hand through the opening,
and my feelings were stirred for him.
⁵ I rose to open for my love.
My hands dripped with myrrh,
my fingers with flowing myrrh
on the handles of the bolt.
⁶ I opened to my love,
but my love had turned and gone away.

^A 5:1 Lit *pluck*   ^B 5:1 Or *Drink your fill, lovers*

My heart sank[A] because he had left.[B]
I sought him, but did not find him.
I called him, but he did not answer.

7 The guards who go about the city found me.
They beat and wounded me;
they took my cloak[C] from me —
the guardians of the walls.

8 Young women of Jerusalem,
    I charge you,
if you find my love,
tell him that I am lovesick.

Young Women

9 What makes the one you love better
    than another,
most beautiful of women?
What makes him better than another,
that you would give us this charge?

Woman

10 My love is fit and strong,[D]
notable among ten thousand.

11 His head is purest gold.
His hair is wavy[E]
and black as a raven.

12 His eyes are like doves
beside flowing streams,
washed in milk
and set like jewels.[F]

13 His cheeks are like beds of spice,
mounds of[G] perfume.
His lips are lilies,
dripping with flowing myrrh.

14 His arms[H] are rods of gold
set[I] with beryl.
His body[J] is an ivory panel
covered with lapis lazuli.

15 His legs are alabaster pillars
set on pedestals of pure gold.
His presence is like Lebanon,
as majestic as the cedars.

16 His mouth is sweetness.
He is absolutely desirable.
This is my love, and this is my friend,
young women of Jerusalem.

[A]5:6 Lit *My soul went out*   [B]5:6 Or *spoken*   [C]5:7 Or *veil, or shawl*   [D]5:10 Or *is radiant and ruddy*   [E]5:11 Or *is like palm leaves*; Hb obscure   [F]5:12 Lit *milk sitting in fullness*   [G]5:13 LXX, Vg read *spice, yielding*   [H]5:14 Lit *hands*   [I]5:14 Lit *filled*; Sg 5:2,12   [J]5:14 Lit *abdomen*

Young Women

6 Where has your love gone,
most beautiful of women?
Which way has he^A turned?
We will seek him with you.

Woman

2 My love has gone down to his garden,
to beds of spice,
to feed in the gardens
and gather lilies.
3 I am my love's and my love is mine;
he feeds among the lilies.

Man

4 You are as beautiful as Tirzah, my darling,
lovely as Jerusalem,
awe-inspiring as an army with banners.
5 Turn your eyes away from me,
for they captivate me.
Your hair is like a flock of goats
streaming down from Gilead.
6 Your teeth are like a flock of ewes
coming up from washing,
each one having a twin,
and not one missing.^B
7 Behind your veil,
your brow^C is like a slice of pomegranate.
8 There are sixty queens
and eighty concubines
and young women^D without number.
9 But my dove, my virtuous one, is unique;
she is the favorite of her mother,
perfect to the one who gave her birth.
Women see her and declare her fortunate;
queens and concubines also, and they sing her praises:

10 Who is this who shines like the dawn,
as beautiful as the moon,
bright as the sun,
awe-inspiring as an army with banners?

Woman

11 I came down to the walnut grove
to see the blossoms of the valley,
to see if the vines were budding
and the pomegranates blooming.

---

^A6:1 Lit *your love*   ^B6:6 Lit *and no one bereaved among them*   ^C6:7 Or *temple,*
or cheek, or lips   ^D6:8 Or *and virgins*; Sg 1:3

¹² I didn't know what was happening to me.
I felt like I was
in a chariot with a nobleman.^A

Young Women

¹³ Come back, come back, Shulammite!^B
Come back, come back,
   that we may look at you!

Man

How you gaze at the Shulammite,
as you look at the dance of the two camps!^C

7 How beautiful are your sandaled feet, princess!^D
The curves of your thighs are like jewelry,
the handiwork of a master.
² Your navel is a rounded bowl;
it never lacks mixed wine.
Your belly is a mound of wheat
surrounded by lilies.
³ Your breasts are like two fawns,
twins of a gazelle.
⁴ Your neck is like a tower of ivory,
your eyes like pools in Heshbon
by Bath-rabbim's gate.
Your nose is like the tower of Lebanon
looking toward Damascus.
⁵ Your head crowns you^E like Mount Carmel,
the hair of your head like purple cloth —
a king could be held captive in your tresses.
⁶ How beautiful you are and how pleasant,
my love, with such delights!
⁷ Your stature is like a palm tree;
your breasts are clusters of fruit.
⁸ I said, "I will climb the palm tree
and take hold of its fruit."
May your breasts be like clusters of grapes,
and the fragrance of your breath like apricots.
⁹ Your mouth^F is like fine wine —

Woman

flowing smoothly for my love,
gliding past my lips and teeth!^G
¹⁰ I am my love's,
and his desire is for me.

---

^A6:12 Hb obscure   ^B6:13 Or *the perfect one*, or *the peaceable one*   ^C6:13 Or *dance of Mahanaim*   ^D7:1 Lit *daughter of a nobleman*, or *prince*   ^E7:5 Lit *head upon you is*   ^F7:9 Lit *palate*   ^G7:9 LXX, Syr, Vg; MT reads *past lips of sleepers*

11 Come, my love,
let's go to the field;
let's spend the night
among the henna blossoms. A
12 Let's go early to the vineyards;
let's see if the vine has budded,
if the blossom has opened,
if the pomegranates are in bloom.
There I will give you my caresses.
13 The mandrakes give off a fragrance,
and at our doors is every delicacy,
both new and old.
I have treasured them up for you, my love.

8 If only I could treat you like my brother, B
one who nursed at my mother's breasts,
I would find you in public and kiss you,
and no one would scorn me.
2 I would lead you, I would take you,
to the house of my mother who taught me. C
I would give you spiced wine to drink
from the juice of my pomegranate.
3 May his left hand be under my head,
and his right arm embrace me.
4 Young women of Jerusalem, I charge you,
do not stir up or awaken love
until the appropriate time.

Young Women

5 Who is this coming up from the wilderness,
leaning on the one she loves?

Woman

I awakened you under the apricot tree.
There your mother conceived you;
there she conceived and gave you birth.
6 Set me as a seal on your heart,
as a seal on your arm.
For love is as strong as death;
jealousy is as unrelenting as Sheol.
Love's flames are fiery flames —
an almighty flame! D
7 A huge torrent cannot extinguish love;
rivers cannot sweep it away.
If a man were to give all his wealth E
for love,
it would be utterly scorned.

A 7:11 Or the villages   B 8:1 Lit Would that you were like a brother to me
C 8:2 LXX adds and into the chamber of the one who bore me   D 8:6 Or the blaze
of the LORD   E 8:7 Lit all the wealth of his house

MADE FOR LOVE

SONG OF SONGS 8; DEUTERONOMY 4:24

What makes you blush?

We don't always blush from embarrassment; we sometimes blush in surprise and delight. Can you remember a time you blushed with delighted surprise? Sometimes I blush over gifts and sometimes I blush about compliments, but my cheeks were at their rosiest when I first met my love. There's a certain look he used to give me that told me he was utterly slain by me—and, oh, how it made my cheeks burn. The surprises of love, the power of love, and love's delights are the sweetest things I have ever experienced.

God didn't have to allow us to fall in love with each other. I imagine that we could theoretically procreate, carry on the species, and get our jobs done without love. But God is love, and He gave us the subtle delights of love to hold all of life's pieces together. Love elevates the mundane to magical. I remember us sitting in a car together; we talked and he touched my fingers—that was all. But when the car door opened for me to get out, I was so incapacitated I literally fell on the ground.

God didn't have to let us fall ridiculously in love with each other. But He made us for love!

Song of Songs makes me blush. In fact, it makes me blush like a wedding night makes us blush— at the surprise and joy of intimacy.

Two beautiful parallels between Christ as the bridegroom to the Church and the husband as bridegroom to his bride stand out. People who love each other desire time together, and they pursue it in spite of obstacles.

"A huge torrent cannot extinguish love." Have you ever longed to be with your beloved? We desire that Christ will write our name on His heart and in His book. He has done this, saying, "Look, I have inscribed you on the palms of my hands" (Is 49:16). He invites us to write His name as a seal on our own hearts (Sg 8:6-7).

"Rivers cannot sweep it away." Have you ever loved in spite of obstacles? Just as the pains of disappointed love are like a death, the love of Christ for the Church is as strong as death. Our love for Christ makes us dead to everything else. Indeed, we cannot be separated from the love of Christ even by death (Sg 8:6-7; Rm 8:38).

Without love we have nothing (1Co 13:1). God's intimate adoration cannot be bought or traded; we can't earn it. It is impossible, inexplicable, and overwhelming. Just like falling in love.

Brothers

8 Our sister is young;
she has no breasts.
What will we do for our sister
on the day she is spoken for?

9 If she is a wall,
we will build a silver barricade on her.
If she is a door,
we will enclose her with cedar planks.

Woman

10 I am^A a wall
and my breasts like towers.
So in his eyes I have become
like one who finds^B peace.^C

11 Solomon owned a vineyard in Baal-hamon.
He leased the vineyard to tenants.
Each was to bring for his fruit
one thousand pieces of silver.

12 I have my own vineyard.^D
The one thousand are for you, Solomon,
but two hundred for those who take care of its fruits.

Man

13 You^E who dwell in the gardens,
companions are listening for your voice;
let me hear you!

Woman

14 Run away with me,^F my love,
and be like a gazelle
or a young stag
on the mountains of spices.

---

^A8:10 Or *was* ^B8:10 Or *brings* ^C8:10 In Hb, the word for *peace* sounds similar
to Solomon and Shulammite. ^D8:12 Lit *My vineyard, which is mine, is before me*;
Sg 1:6 ^E8:13 In Hb, the word for *You* is feminine. ^F8:14 Lit *Flee*

isaiah

Now this is what the Lord says — the one who created you, Jacob, and the one who formed you, Israel — "Do not fear, for I have redeemed you; I have called you by your name; you are mine." **43:1**

ON THE TIMELINE Isaiah 6:1 records that Isaiah received his prophetic call in the last year of Uzziah's reign over Judah (about 742 BC), and 37:38 suggests that he lived until the death of Sennacherib (681 BC). The events in Isaiah occur between those dates, around the time when the kingdom of Israel was taken into captivity by Assyria (722 BC).

A LITTLE BACKGROUND The book of Isaiah presents itself as the writing of Isaiah, son of Amoz. Not much is known about Isaiah apart from his prophecy. The superscription (an introductory element common to books of prophecy) in 1:1 dates Isaiah's prophetic activity as covering all or part of the reigns of four kings of Judah: Uzziah (783–742 BC), Jotham (742–735 BC), Ahaz (735–716 BC), and Hezekiah (716–686 BC).

The events prophesied extended beyond the eighth century BC, through the rest of the Old Testament period and beyond. The New Testament authors cited prophecies from Isaiah as finding fulfillment in the events surrounding Jesus Christ.

MESSAGE & PURPOSE

Isaiah's message to the nation of Judah is a straightforward one:

1. Isaiah accused God's people of sin and rebellion against the One who made and redeemed them.

2. He instructed them to turn from sin to obedience.

3. He announced God's just judgment on them because of their sin.

4. God revealed His future restoration of the people—the faithful remnant that survived the judgment. This restoration included both judgment on the nations (Is 13–23) and a future turning of the nations to God (Is 2:1-4).

The first part of the book of Isaiah (chaps. 1–39) emphasizes sin, the call to repentance, and judgment. The second part (chaps. 40–66) emphasizes the hope of restoration as revealed by God and foretold by the prophet.

GIVE THANKS FOR THE BOOK OF ISAIAH

Many readers are drawn to Isaiah for the passages describing a future anointed king, or Messiah (Is 9:1-7; 11:1-9), and those describing the Servant (Is 42:1-9; 49:1-6; 50:4-6; 52:13–53:12). But a full reading of Isaiah truly enriches our understanding of how these prophecies and more are indeed fulfilled in Jesus Christ. He is the Messiah; He is the Suffering Servant.

THE BOOK OF ISAIAH IN HISTORY

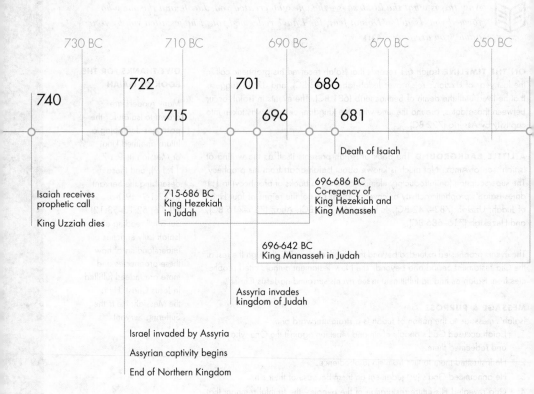

730 BC   710 BC   690 BC   670 BC   650 BC

740

722   701   686

715   696   681

Death of Isaiah

696-686 BC
Co-regency of
King Hezekiah and
King Manasseh

Isaiah receives
prophetic call

715-686 BC
King Hezekiah
in Judah

King Uzziah dies

696-642 BC
King Manasseh in Judah

Assyria invades
kingdom of Judah

Israel invaded by Assyria

Assyrian captivity begins

End of Northern Kingdom

READ AND UNDERSTAND ISAIAH

The Bible is a complete work in which many stories combine to tell one story. As you read the book of Isaiah, consider reading the additional passages to discover how the whole of Scripture works together.

READ AND UNDERSTAND ISAIAH

1 The vision concerning Judah and Jerusalem that Isaiah son of Amoz saw during the reigns [A,B] of Kings Uzziah, Jotham, Ahaz, and Hezekiah of Judah.

JUDAH ON TRIAL

2 Listen, heavens, and pay attention, earth,
for the LORD has spoken:
"I have raised children [C] and brought them up,
but they have rebelled against me.
3 The ox knows its owner,
and the donkey its master's feeding trough,
but Israel does not know;
my people do not understand."

4 Oh sinful nation,
people weighed down with iniquity,
brood of evildoers,
depraved children!
They have abandoned the LORD;
they have despised the Holy One of Israel;
they have turned their backs on him.

5 Why do you want more beatings?
Why do you keep on rebelling?
The whole head is hurt,
and the whole heart is sick.
6 From the sole of the foot even to the head,
no spot is uninjured —
wounds, welts, and festering sores
not cleansed, bandaged,
or soothed with oil.

7 Your land is desolate,
your cities burned down;
foreigners devour your fields
right in front of you —
a desolation, like a place demolished by foreigners.
8 Daughter Zion is abandoned
like a shelter in a vineyard,
like a shack in a cucumber field,
like a besieged city.
9 If the LORD of Armies
had not left us a few survivors,
we would be like Sodom,
we would resemble Gomorrah.

10 Hear the word of the LORD,
you rulers of Sodom!
Listen to the instruction of our God,

THE PERFECT PARENT

ISAIAH 1–2; PSALM 30:5

My fuse is about an inch long and highly combustible. This is the painful truth parenthood has exposed in me. The Lord is graciously refining me in this area. But, more often than I'd like, this is how things go down at my house:

Child disobeys. *I warn.*

Child ignores. *I warn again.*

Child ignores again. *I lose my temper and say words like "always" and "never" way more than any parenting book would ever excuse. (As in, "You always leave your LEGOS all over the house. I am never buying you another set!")*

Child cries and retreats to his room. *Guilt gives me a gut punch.*

In the calm after the storm, I usually tiptoe into my child's room, pull him into my lap, and we talk calmly about what happened. Once I've blown my top, they know I mean business and they listen with attentive ears. I'm so breathless from the gut punch that I'm forced to speak calmly and quietly. Together, we make slow (and sometimes painful) progress toward a healthy, happy home.

God is a perfect Father, never sinful in His response toward us. But we are like children, frustratingly disobedient. In Isaiah 1:2, the prophet says, "the LORD has spoken: 'I have raised children and brought them up, but they have rebelled against me.'"

For 15 verses, God speaks through Isaiah to His wayward children. Repeatedly asking them why they keep rebelling (Is 1:5). Expressing how fed up He is (Is 1:13-14). Vowing to ignore their prayers because of their sin (Is 1:15). Laying down a list of rules (Is 1:16-17).

And then, the pivot happens. True to His character, His anger doesn't last long (Ps 30:5). Though our holy God cannot tolerate **His children's sin, His love compels Him to keep showing us the right path. Even His wrath is rooted in love.**

"'Come, let us settle this,' says the LORD. 'Though your sins are scarlet, they will be as white as snow; though they are crimson red, they will be like wool.'"

ISAIAH 1:18

The God of the universe, the one by whom and for whom all things were made, stoops down, looks His children in the eyes and says, "Let's talk about this." That blows this mama's mind!

The book of Isaiah helps me walk a mile in my children's Velcro® shoes. Like Israel, I am a rebellious child. I ignore my Father's instructions. I'm also a beloved daughter, prone to doubt her Father's love. But in every story about God and His people, I see a Perfect Parent, willing to pull His children onto His lap and say, "Let's talk about this." And there, from within His embrace, He reminds us that He's already done all of the hard work to bring us home to Him forever.

you people of Gomorrah!

11 "What are all your sacrifices to me?"
asks the LORD.
"I have had enough of burnt offerings and rams
and the fat of well-fed cattle;
I have no desire for the blood of bulls,
lambs, or male goats.

12 When you come to appear before me,
who requires this from you —
this trampling of my courts?

13 Stop bringing useless offerings.
Your incense is detestable to me.
New Moons and Sabbaths,
and the calling of solemn assemblies —
I cannot stand iniquity with a festival.

14 I hate your New Moons and prescribed festivals.
They have become a burden to me;
I am tired of putting up with them.

15 When you spread out your hands in prayer,
I will refuse to look at you;
even if you offer countless prayers,
I will not listen.
Your hands are covered with blood.

PURIFICATION OF JERUSALEM

16 "Wash yourselves. Cleanse yourselves.
Remove your evil deeds from my sight.
Stop doing evil.

17 Learn to do what is good.
Pursue justice.
Correct the oppressor.[A]
Defend the rights of the fatherless.
Plead the widow's cause.

18 "Come, let us settle this,"
says the LORD.
"Though your sins are scarlet,
they will be as white as snow;
though they are crimson red,
they will be like wool.

19 If you are willing and obedient,
you will eat the good things of the land.

20 But if you refuse and rebel,
you will be devoured by the sword."
For the mouth of the LORD has spoken.

21 The faithful town —
what an adulteress[B] she has become!

[A]1:17 Or *Aid the oppressed*   [B]1:21 Or *prostitute*

She was once full of justice.
Righteousness once dwelt in her,
but now, murderers!

²² Your silver has become dross to be discarded,
your beer^A is diluted with water.

²³ Your rulers are rebels,
friends of thieves.
They all love graft
and chase after bribes.
They do not defend the rights of the fatherless,
and the widow's case never comes before them.

²⁴ Therefore the Lord God of Armies,
the Mighty One of Israel, declares:
"Ah, I will get even with my foes;
I will take revenge against my enemies.

²⁵ I will turn my hand against you
and will burn away your dross completely;^B
I will remove all your impurities.

²⁶ I will restore your judges to what they were at first,^C
and your advisers to what they were at the start.^D
Afterward you will be called the Righteous City,
a Faithful Town."

²⁷ Zion will be redeemed by justice,
those who repent, by righteousness.

²⁸ At the same time both rebels and sinners will be broken,
and those who abandon the Lord will perish.

²⁹ Indeed, they^E will be ashamed of the sacred trees
you desired,
and you will be embarrassed because of the garden shrines
you have chosen.

³⁰ For you will become like an oak
whose leaves are withered,
and like a garden without water.

³¹ The strong one will become tinder,
and his work a spark;
both will burn together,
with no one to extinguish the flames.

THE CITY OF PEACE

2 The vision that Isaiah son of Amoz saw concerning Judah and Jerusalem:
² In the last days
the mountain of the Lord's house will be established
at the top of the mountains
and will be raised above the hills.

---

^A 1:22 Or *wine*   ^B 1:25 Lit *dross as with lye*   ^C 1:26 Lit *judges as at the first*   ^D 1:26 Lit *advisers as at the beginning*   ^E 1:29 Some Hb mss; other Hb mss, Tg read *you*

All nations will stream to it,
3 and many peoples will come and say,
"Come, let us go up to the mountain of the LORD,
to the house of the God of Jacob.
He will teach us about his ways
so that we may walk in his paths."
For instruction will go out of Zion
and the word of the LORD from Jerusalem.
4 He will settle disputes among the nations
and provide arbitration for many peoples.
They will beat their swords into plows
and their spears into pruning knives.
Nation will not take up the sword against nation,
and they will never again train for war.

THE DAY OF THE LORD

5 House of Jacob,
come and let us walk in the LORD's light.
6 For you have abandoned your people,
the house of Jacob,
because they are full of divination from the East
and of fortune-tellers like the Philistines.
They are in league^A with foreigners.
7 Their^B,C land is full of silver and gold,
and there is no limit to their treasures;
their land is full of horses,
and there is no limit to their chariots.
8 Their land is full of idols;
they worship the work of their hands,
what their fingers have made.
9 So humanity is brought low,
and each person is humbled.
Do not forgive them!
10 Go into the rocks
and hide in the dust
from the terror of the LORD
and from his majestic splendor.
11 The pride of mankind^D will be humbled,
and human loftiness will be brought low;
the LORD alone will be exalted on that day.

12 For a day belonging to the LORD of Armies is coming
against all that is proud and lofty,
against all that is lifted up — it will be humbled —
13 against all the cedars of Lebanon,
lofty and lifted up,
against all the oaks of Bashan,

---

^A2:6 Or They teem, or They partner; Hb obscure ^B2:7 Lit Its ^C2:7 = the house of Jacob ^D2:11 Lit Mankind's proud eyes

¹⁴ against all the high mountains,
against all the lofty hills,
¹⁵ against every high tower,
against every fortified wall,
¹⁶ against every ship of Tarshish,
and against every splendid sea vessel.
¹⁷ The pride of mankind will be brought low,
and human loftiness will be humbled;
the LORD alone will be exalted on that day.
¹⁸ The idols will vanish completely.

¹⁹ People will go into caves in the rocks
and holes in the ground,
away from the terror of the LORD
and from his majestic splendor,
when he rises to terrify the earth.
²⁰ On that day people will throw
their silver and gold idols,
which they made to worship,
to the moles and the bats.
²¹ They will go into the caves of the rocks
and the crevices in the cliffs,
away from the terror of the LORD
and from his majestic splendor,
when he rises to terrify the earth.
²² Put no more trust in a mere human,
who has only the breath in his nostrils.
What is he really worth?

JUDAH'S LEADERS JUDGED

3 Note this: The Lord GOD of Armies
is about to remove from Jerusalem and from Judah
every kind of security:
the entire supply of bread and water,
² heroes and warriors,
judges and prophets,
fortune-tellers and elders,
³ commanders of fifty and dignitaries,
counselors, cunning magicians,ᴬ and necromancers.ᴮ
⁴ "I will make youths their leaders,
and unstable rulersᶜ will govern them."
⁵ The people will oppress one another,
man against man, neighbor against neighbor;
the young will act arrogantly toward the old,
and the worthless toward the honorable.
⁶ A man will even seize his brother
in his father's house, saying:
"You have a cloak — you be our leader!

ᴬ3:3 Or *skilled craftsmen*   ᴮ3:3 Or *mediums*   ᶜ3:4 Or *mischief-makers*

This heap of rubble will be under your control."
7   On that day he will cry out, saying:
    "I'm not a healer.
    I don't even have food or clothing in my house.
    Don't make me the leader of the people!"
8   For Jerusalem has stumbled
    and Judah has fallen
    because they have spoken and acted against the LORD,
    defying his glorious presence.
9   The look on their faces testifies against them,
    and like Sodom, they flaunt their sin;
    they do not conceal it.
    Woe to them,
    for they have brought disaster on themselves.
10   Tell the righteous that it will go well for them,
    for they will eat the fruit of their labor.
11   Woe to the wicked — it will go badly for them,
    for what they have done will be done to them.
12   Youths oppress my people,
    and women rule over them.
    My people, your leaders mislead you;
    they confuse the direction of your paths.

13   The LORD rises to argue the case
    and stands to judge the people.
14   The LORD brings this charge
    against the elders and leaders of his people:
    "You have devastated the vineyard.
    The plunder from the poor is in your houses.
15   Why do you crush my people
    and grind the faces of the poor?"
        This is the declaration
        of the Lord GOD of Armies.

JERUSALEM'S WOMEN JUDGED

16 The LORD also says:
        Because the daughters of Zion are haughty,
        walking with heads held high
        and seductive eyes,
        prancing along,
        jingling their ankle bracelets,
17   the Lord will put scabs on the heads
        of the daughters of Zion,
        and the LORD will shave their foreheads bare.

18 On that day the Lord will strip their finery: ankle bracelets, headbands, crescents, 19 pendants, bracelets, veils, 20 headdresses, ankle jewelry, sashes, perfume bottles, amulets, 21 signet rings, nose rings, 22 festive robes, capes, cloaks, purses, 23 garments, linen clothes, turbans, and shawls.
24   Instead of perfume there will be a stench;

instead of a belt, a rope;
instead of beautifully styled hair, baldness;
instead of fine clothes, sackcloth;
instead of beauty, branding.^A
25 Your men will fall by the sword,
your warriors in battle.
26 Then her gates will lament and mourn;
deserted, she will sit on the ground.

4 On that day seven women
will seize one man, saying,
"We will eat our own bread
and provide our own clothing.
Just let us bear your name.
Take away our disgrace."

ZION'S FUTURE GLORY

² On that day the Branch^B of the Lord will be beautiful and glorious, and the fruit of the land will be the pride and glory of Israel's survivors. ³ Whoever remains in Zion and whoever is left in Jerusalem will be called holy — all in Jerusalem written in the book of life^C — ⁴ when the Lord has washed away the filth of the daughters of Zion and cleansed the bloodguilt from the heart of Jerusalem by a spirit of judgment and a spirit of burning. ⁵ Then the Lord will create a cloud of smoke by day and a glowing flame of fire by night over the entire site of Mount Zion and over its assemblies. For there will be a canopy over all the glory,^D ⁶ and there will be a shelter for shade from heat by day, and a refuge and shelter from storm and rain.

SONG OF THE VINEYARD

5 I will sing about the one I love,
a song about my loved one's vineyard:
The one I love had a vineyard
on a very fertile hill.
² He broke up the soil, cleared it of stones,
and planted it with the finest vines.
He built a tower in the middle of it
and even dug out a winepress there.
He expected it to yield good grapes,
but it yielded worthless grapes.

³ So now, residents of Jerusalem
and men of Judah,
please judge between me
and my vineyard.
⁴ What more could I have done for my vineyard
than I did?
Why, when I expected a yield of good grapes,
did it yield worthless grapes?

---

^A 3:24 DSS read *shame*   ^B 4:2 Or *plant*   ^C 4:3 Lit *Jerusalem recorded for life*
^D 4:5 Or *For glory will be a canopy over all*

5 Now I will tell you
what I am about to do to my vineyard:
I will remove its hedge,
and it will be consumed;
I will tear down its wall,
and it will be trampled.

6 I will make it a wasteland.
It will not be pruned or weeded;
thorns and briers will grow up.
I will also give orders to the clouds
that rain should not fall on it.

7 For the vineyard of the LORD of Armies
is the house of Israel,
and the men^A of Judah,
the plant he delighted in.
He expected justice
but saw injustice;
he expected righteousness,
but heard cries of despair.

JUDAH'S SINS DENOUNCED

8 Woe to those who add house to house
and join field to field
until there is no more room
and you alone are left in the land.

9 I heard the LORD of Armies say:
Indeed, many houses will become desolate,
grand and lovely ones without inhabitants.

10 For a ten-acre^B vineyard will yield
only six gallons of wine,^C
and ten bushels^D of seed will yield
only one bushel of grain.^E

11 Woe to those who rise early in the morning
in pursuit of beer,
who linger into the evening,
inflamed by wine.

12 At their feasts they have lyre, harp,
tambourine, flute, and wine.
They do not perceive the LORD's actions,
and they do not see the work of his hands.

13 Therefore my people will go into exile
because they lack knowledge;
her^F dignitaries are starving,
and her masses are parched with thirst.

---

^A 5:7 Lit man   ^B 5:10 Lit ten-yoke   ^C 5:10 Lit one bath   ^D 5:10 Lit one homer
^E 5:10 Lit yield an ephah   ^F 5:13 Lit its

¹⁴ Therefore Sheol enlarges its throat
and opens wide its enormous jaws,
and down go Zion's dignitaries, her masses,
her crowds, and those who celebrate in her!
¹⁵ Humanity is brought low, each person is humbled,
and haughty eyes are humbled.
¹⁶ But the LORD of Armies is exalted by his justice,
and the holy God shows that he is holy through
his righteousness.
¹⁷ Lambs will graze
as if in^A their own pastures,
and resident aliens^B will eat
among the ruins of the rich.

¹⁸ Woe to those who drag iniquity
with cords of deceit
and pull sin along with cart ropes,
¹⁹ to those who say:
"Let him hurry up and do his work quickly
so that we can see it!
Let the plan of the Holy One of Israel take place
so that we can know it!"
²⁰ Woe to those who call evil good
and good evil,
who substitute darkness for light
and light for darkness,
who substitute bitter for sweet
and sweet for bitter.
²¹ Woe to those who consider themselves wise
and judge themselves clever.^C
²² Woe to those who are heroes at drinking wine,
who are champions at pouring beer,
²³ who acquit the guilty for a bribe
and deprive the innocent of justice.

²⁴ Therefore, as a tongue of fire consumes straw
and as dry grass shrivels in the flame,
so their roots will become like something rotten
and their blossoms will blow away like dust,
for they have rejected
the instruction of the LORD of Armies,
and they have despised
the word of the Holy One of Israel.
²⁵ Therefore the LORD's anger burned against his people.
He raised his hand against them and struck them;
the mountains quaked,
and their corpses were like garbage in the streets.

---

^A 5:17 Syr reads graze in   ^B 5:17 LXX reads sheep   ^C 5:21 Lit and clever before
their face

In all this, his anger has not turned away,
and his hand is still raised to strike.

²⁶ He raises a signal flag for the distant nations
and whistles for them from the ends of the earth.
Look — how quickly and swiftly they come!
²⁷ None of them grows weary or stumbles;
no one slumbers or sleeps.
No belt is loose
and no sandal strap broken.
²⁸ Their arrows are sharpened,
and all their bows strung.
Their horses' hooves are like flint;
their chariot wheels are like a whirlwind.
²⁹ Their roaring is like a lion's;
they roar like young lions;
they growl and seize their prey
and carry it off,
and no one can rescue it.
³⁰ On that day they will roar over it,
like the roaring of the sea.
When one looks at the land,
there will be darkness and distress;
light will be obscured by clouds.ᴬ

ISAIAH'S CALL AND MISSION

6 In the year that King Uzziah died, I saw the Lord seated on a high and lofty throne, and the hem of his robe filled the temple. ² Seraphimᴮ were standing above him; they each had six wings: with two they covered their faces, with two they covered their feet, and with two they flew. ³ And one called to another:

Holy, holy, holy is the LORD of Armies;
his glory fills the whole earth.

⁴ The foundations of the doorways shook at the sound of their voices, and the temple was filled with smoke.
⁵ Then I said:

Woe is me for I am ruinedᶜ
because I am a man of unclean lips
and live among a people of unclean lips,
and because my eyes have seen the King,
the LORD of Armies.

⁶ Then one of the seraphim flew to me, and in his hand was a glowing coal that he had taken from the altar with tongs. ⁷ He touched my mouth with it and said:

Now that this has touched your lips,
your iniquity is removed
and your sin is atoned for.

ᴬ5:30 Lit *its clouds* ᴮ6:2 = heavenly beings ᶜ6:5 Or *I must be silent*

⁸ Then I heard the voice of the Lord asking:

Who should I send?
Who will go for us?

I said:

Here I am. Send me.

⁹ And he replied:

Go! Say to these people:
Keep listening, but do not understand;
keep looking, but do not perceive.
¹⁰ Make the minds^A of these people dull;
deafen their ears and blind their eyes;
otherwise they might see with their eyes
and hear with their ears,
understand with their minds,
turn back, and be healed.

¹¹ Then I said, "Until when, Lord?" And he replied:

Until cities lie in ruins without inhabitants,
houses are without people,
the land is ruined and desolate,
¹² and the LORD drives the people far away,
leaving great emptiness in the land.
¹³ Though a tenth will remain in the land,
it will be burned again.
Like the terebinth or the oak
that leaves a stump when felled,
the holy seed is the stump.

THE MESSAGE TO AHAZ

7 This took place during the reign of Ahaz, son of Jotham, son of Uzziah king of Judah: Aram's King Rezin and Israel's King Pekah son of Remaliah went to fight against Jerusalem, but they were not able to conquer it.
² When it became known to the house of David that Aram had occupied Ephraim, the heart of Ahaz^B and the hearts of his people trembled like trees of a forest shaking in the wind.
³ The LORD said to Isaiah, "Go out with your son Shear-jashub^C to meet Ahaz at the end of the conduit of the upper pool, by the road to the Launderer's Field. ⁴ Say to him: Calm down and be quiet. Don't be afraid or cowardly because of these two smoldering sticks, the fierce anger of Rezin and Aram, and the son of Remaliah. ⁵ For Aram, along with Ephraim and the son of Remaliah, has plotted harm against you. They say, ⁶ 'Let us go up against Judah, terrorize it, and conquer it for ourselves. Then we can install Tabeel's son as king in it.'"
⁷ This is what the Lord GOD says:

It will not happen; it will not occur.

---

^A6:10 Lit heart   ^B7:2 Lit Aram has rested upon Ephraim, his heart
^C7:3 = A Remnant Will Return

8   The^A chief city of Aram is Damascus,
      the chief of Damascus is Rezin
      (within sixty-five years
      Ephraim will be too shattered to be a people),
9   the chief city of Ephraim is Samaria,
      and the chief of Samaria is the son of Remaliah.
      If you do not stand firm in your faith,
      then you will not stand at all.

THE IMMANUEL PROPHECY

¹⁰ Then the LORD spoke again to Ahaz: ¹¹ "Ask for a sign from the LORD your God — it can be as deep as Sheol or as high as heaven."

¹² But Ahaz replied, "I will not ask. I will not test the LORD."

¹³ Isaiah said, "Listen, house of David! Is it not enough for you to try the patience of men? Will you also try the patience of my God? ¹⁴ Therefore, the Lord himself will give you^B a sign: See, the virgin will conceive,^C have a son, and name him Immanuel.^D ¹⁵ By the time he learns to reject what is bad and choose what is good, he will be eating curds^E and honey. ¹⁶ For before the boy knows to reject what is bad and choose what is good, the land of the two kings you dread will be abandoned. ¹⁷ The LORD will bring on you, your people, and your father's house such a time as has never been since Ephraim separated from Judah: He will bring the king of Assyria."

18   On that day
      the LORD will whistle to flies
      at the farthest streams of the Nile
      and to bees in the land of Assyria.
19   All of them will come and settle
      in the steep ravines, in the clefts of the rocks,
      in all the thornbushes, and in all the water holes.

²⁰ On that day the Lord will use a razor hired from beyond the Euphrates River — the king of Assyria — to shave the hair on your heads, the hair on your legs, and even your beards.

21   On that day
      a man will raise a young cow and two sheep,
22   and from the abundant milk they give
      he will eat curds,
      for every survivor in the land will eat curds and honey.

23   And on that day
      every place where there were a thousand vines,
      worth a thousand pieces of silver,
      will become thorns and briers.
24   A man will go there with bow and arrows
      because the whole land will be thorns and briers.
25   You will not go to all the hills
      that were once tilled with a hoe,

---

^A 7:8 Lit For the   ^B 7:14 In Hb, the word you is pl   ^C 7:14 Or virgin is pregnant, will
^D 7:14 = God With Us   ^E 7:15 Or sour milk

for fear of the thorns and briers.
Those hills will be places for oxen to graze
and for sheep to trample.

THE COMING ASSYRIAN INVASION

8 Then the LORD said to me, "Take a large piece of parchment[A] and write on it with an ordinary pen:[B] Maher-shalal-hash-baz.[C] 2 I have appointed[D] trustworthy witnesses — the priest Uriah and Zechariah son of Jeberechiah."

3 I was then intimate with the prophetess, and she conceived and gave birth to a son. The LORD said to me, "Name him Maher-shalal-hash-baz, 4 for before the boy knows how to call 'Father,' or 'Mother,' the wealth of Damascus and the spoils of Samaria will be carried off to the king of Assyria."

5 The LORD spoke to me again:

6 Because these people rejected
the slowly flowing water of Shiloah
and rejoiced with[E] Rezin
and the son of Remaliah,
7 the Lord will certainly bring against them
the mighty rushing water of the Euphrates River —
the king of Assyria and all his glory.
It will overflow its channels
and spill over all its banks.
8 It will pour into Judah,
flood over it, and sweep through,
reaching up to the neck;
and its flooded banks[F]
will fill your entire land, Immanuel!

9 Band together,[G] peoples, and be broken;
pay attention, all you distant lands;
prepare for war, and be broken;
prepare for war, and be broken.
10 Devise a plan; it will fail.
Make a prediction; it will not happen.
For God is with us.[H]

THE LORD OF ARMIES, THE ONLY REFUGE

11 For this is what the LORD said to me with great power, to keep[I] me from going the way of this people:

12 Do not call everything a conspiracy
these people say is a conspiracy.
Do not fear what they fear;
do not be terrified.
13 You are to regard only the LORD of Armies as holy.

[A]8:1 Hb obscure [B]8:1 Lit *with the pen of a man* [C]8:1 = Speeding to the Plunder, Hurrying to the Spoil [D]8:2 Vg; MT, one DSS ms read *I will appoint*; one DSS ms, LXX, Syr, Tg read *Appoint* [E]8:6 Or *and rejoiced over* [F]8:8 Lit *its outspread wings* [G]8:9 Or *Raise the war cry*, or *Be shattered* [H]8:10 Hb *Immanuel* [I]8:11 DSS; MT reads *instruct*

Only he should be feared;
only he should be held in awe.
14 He will be a sanctuary;
but for the two houses of Israel,
he will be a stone to stumble over
and a rock to trip over,
and a trap and a snare to the inhabitants of Jerusalem.
15 Many will stumble over these;
they will fall and be broken;
they will be snared and captured.

16 Bind up the testimony.
Seal up the instruction among my disciples.
17 I will wait for the LORD,
who is hiding his face from the house of Jacob.
I will wait for him.

18 Here I am with the children the LORD has given me to be signs and wonders in Israel from the LORD of Armies who dwells on Mount Zion. 19 When they say to you, "Inquire of the mediums and the spiritists who chirp and mutter," shouldn't a people inquire of their God?ᴬ Should they inquire of the dead on behalf of the living? 20 Go to God's instruction and testimony! If they do not speak according to this word, there will be no dawn for them.
21 They will wander through the land, dejected and hungry. When they are famished, they will become enraged, and, looking upward, will curse their king and their God. 22 They will look toward the earth and see only distress, darkness, and the gloom of affliction, and they will be driven into thick darkness.

BIRTH OF THE PRINCE OF PEACE

9 Nevertheless, the gloom of the distressed land will not be like that of the former times when he humbled the land of Zebulun and the land of Naphtali. But in the future he will bring honor to the way of the sea, to the land east of the Jordan, and to Galilee of the nations.
2 The people walking in darkness
have seen a great light;
a light has dawned
on those living in the land of darkness.
3 You have enlarged the nation
and increased its joy.ᴮ
The people have rejoiced before you
as they rejoice at harvest time
and as they rejoice when dividing spoils.
4 For you have shattered their oppressive yoke
and the rod on their shoulders,
the staff of their oppressor,
just as you did on the day of Midian.

ᴬ8:19 Or gods   ᴮ9:3 Alt Hb tradition reads *have not increased joy*

⁵ For every trampling boot of battle
and the bloodied garments of war
will be burned as fuel for the fire.
⁶ For a child will be born for us,
a son will be given to us,
and the government will be on his shoulders.
He will be named
Wonderful Counselor, Mighty God,
Eternal Father, Prince of Peace.
⁷ The dominion will be vast,
and its prosperity will never end.
He will reign on the throne of David
and over his kingdom,
to establish and sustain it
with justice and righteousness from now on and forever.
The zeal of the LORD of Armies will accomplish this.

THE HAND RAISED AGAINST ISRAEL

⁸ The Lord sent a message against Jacob;
it came against Israel.
⁹ All the people —
Ephraim and the inhabitants of Samaria — will know it.
They will say with pride and arrogance:
¹⁰ "The bricks have fallen,
but we will rebuild with cut stones;
the sycamores have been cut down,
but we will replace them with cedars."
¹¹ The LORD has raised up Rezin's adversaries against him
and stirred up his enemies.
¹² Aram from the east and Philistia from the west
have consumed Israel with open mouths.
In all this, his anger has not turned away,
and his hand is still raised to strike.

¹³ The people did not turn to him who struck them;
they did not seek the LORD of Armies.
¹⁴ So the LORD cut off Israel's head and tail,
palm branch and reed in a single day.
¹⁵ The head is the elder, the honored one;
the tail is the prophet, the one teaching lies.
¹⁶ The leaders of the people mislead them,
and those they mislead are swallowed up.ᴬ
¹⁷ Therefore the Lord does not rejoice
overᴮ Israel's young men
and has no compassion
on its fatherless and widows,
for everyone is a godless evildoer,
and every mouth speaks folly.

ᴬ9:16 Or *are confused*   ᴮ9:17 DSS read *not spare*

THE REMNANT WILL RETURN

²⁰ On that day the remnant of Israel and the survivors of the house of Jacob will no longer depend on the one who struck them, but they will faithfully depend on the LORD, the Holy One of Israel.

²¹ The remnant will return, the remnant of Jacob,
   to the Mighty God.
²² Israel, even if your people were as numerous
   as the sand of the sea,
   only a remnant of them will return.
   Destruction has been decreed;
   justice overflows.
²³ For throughout the land
   the Lord GOD of Armies
   is carrying out a destruction that was decreed.

²⁴ Therefore, the Lord GOD of Armies says this: "My people who dwell in Zion, do not fear Assyria, though they strike you with a rod and raise their staff over you as the Egyptians did. ²⁵ In just a little while my wrath will be spent and my anger will turn to their destruction." ²⁶ And the LORD of Armies will brandish a whip against him as he did when he struck Midian at the rock of Oreb; and he will raise his staff over the sea as he did in Egypt.

GOD WILL JUDGE ASSYRIA

²⁷ On that day
   his burden will fall from your shoulders,
   and his yoke from your neck.
   The yoke will be broken because your neck will be too large.ᴬ
²⁸ Assyria has come to Aiath
   and has gone through Migron,
   storing their equipment at Michmash.
²⁹ They crossed over at the ford, saying,
   "We will spend the night at Geba."
   The people of Ramah are trembling;
   those at Gibeah of Saul have fled.
³⁰ Cry aloud, daughter of Gallim!
   Listen, Laishah!
   Anathoth is miserable.
³¹ Madmenah has fled.
   The inhabitants of Gebim have sought refuge.
³² Today the Assyrians will stand at Nob,
   shaking their fists at the mountain of Daughter Zion,
   the hill of Jerusalem.
³³ Look, the Lord GOD of Armies
   will chop off the branches with terrifying power,
   and the tall trees will be cut down,
   the high trees felled.
³⁴ He is clearing the thickets of the forest with an ax,
   and Lebanon with its majesty will fall.

ᴬ10:27 Lit *because of fatness*; Hb obscure

REIGN OF THE DAVIDIC KING

11 Then a shoot will grow from the stump of Jesse,
and a branch from his roots will bear fruit.
2 The Spirit of the LORD will rest on him —
a Spirit of wisdom and understanding,
a Spirit of counsel and strength,
a Spirit of knowledge and of the fear of the LORD.
3 His delight will be in the fear of the LORD.
He will not judge
by what he sees with his eyes,
he will not execute justice
by what he hears with his ears,
4 but he will judge the poor righteously
and execute justice for the oppressed of the land.
He will strike the land
with a scepter[A] from his mouth,
and he will kill the wicked
with a command[B] from his lips.
5 Righteousness will be a belt around his hips;
faithfulness will be a belt around his waist.
6 The wolf will dwell with the lamb,
and the leopard will lie down with the goat.
The calf, the young lion, and the fattened calf will be together,
and a child will lead them.
7 The cow and the bear will graze,
their young ones will lie down together,
and the lion will eat straw like cattle.
8 An infant will play beside the cobra's pit,
and a toddler will put his hand into a snake's den.
9 They will not harm or destroy each other
on my entire holy mountain,
for the land will be as full
of the knowledge of the LORD
as the sea is filled with water.

ISRAEL REGATHERED

10 On that day the root of Jesse
will stand as a banner for the peoples.
The nations will look to him for guidance,
and his resting place will be glorious.

11 On that day the Lord will extend his hand a second time to recover the remnant of his people who survive — from Assyria, Egypt, Pathros, Cush, Elam, Shinar, Hamath, and the coasts and islands of the west.
12 He will lift up a banner for the nations
and gather the dispersed of Israel;
he will collect the scattered of Judah
from the four corners of the earth.

A11:4 Lit *the rod*   B11:4 Lit *with the breath*

THE TRUE VINE

ISAIAH 10:5–12:6; JOHN 15:1-8

It is a barren landscape we stumble upon in Isaiah 11.

In the previous chapter, God has struck down every kingdom that comes against Judah, using the imagery of an axe taken to all the trees in the forest. It is stumps and dryness as far as the eye can see, with the exception of one small sign of life:

"Then a shoot will grow from the stump of Jesse, and a branch from his roots will bear fruit."

ISAIAH 11:1

Jesus, born of the bloodline of Jesse, David's father, is the only surviving hope in an otherwise hopeless world. He is a shoot, or branch, that will come back, bear fruit, and establish a kingdom of peace.

Were I an Israelite in the southern kingdom of Judah, oh, how I would have clung to those words. And, oh, how I want to cling to them today as I look around at the forest I've grown.

The trees in my forest are shaped like idols and they grow to stifle the work Christ is doing in me. I water these trees and trim their branches, in search of the life they promise to give. But every time—every single time—I find they bring emptiness instead. I know what it's like to grow a forest, and I know what it's like to see every tree cut down, for my idols to be stripped away, one by one, by the gracious hand of my Father. When the painful work is done, I look up and see the true Source of the garden, the only remnant of life.

When the things of our lives are torn down, a visual path is cleared that reveals Jesus in a way we couldn't see Him before the trees fell. This stripping gives us the strength to cling to the True Vine.

Jesus said it Himself. "I am the vine; you are the branches. The one who remains in me and I in him produces much fruit, because you can do nothing without me" (Jn 15:5).

Sometimes everything must be torn down in order for us to see that Christ truly is at the center of it all, the reason for everything, the source of our life and all life. **Even in a seemingly barren land, He rises up. The root and the branch, the Alpha and the Omega.** He was never absent. He has always been here. Through every story and circumstance, a vine running throughout all of history. Christ is in every last inch.

One day this will all be so evident. We will gather together under one banner and the entire world will know. "The nations will look to him for guidance, and his resting place will be glorious" (Is 11:10). Until then, we wait, knowing that no matter how bleak or despairing the landscape appears, the one True Vine grows still.

13 Ephraim's envy will cease;
Judah's harassing will end.
Ephraim will no longer be envious of Judah,
and Judah will not harass Ephraim.

14 But they will swoop down
on the Philistine flank to the west.
Together they will plunder the people of the east.
They will extend their power over Edom and Moab,
and the Ammonites will be their subjects.

15 The LORD will divide[A,B] the Gulf of Suez.[C]
He will wave his hand over the Euphrates
with his mighty wind
and will split it into seven streams,
letting people walk through on foot.

16 There will be a highway for the remnant of his people
who will survive from Assyria,
as there was for Israel
when they came up from the land of Egypt.

A SONG OF PRAISE

12 On that day you will say:
"I will give thanks to you, LORD,
although you were angry with me.
Your anger has turned away,
and you have comforted me.

2 Indeed, God is my salvation;
I will trust him and not be afraid,
for the LORD, the LORD himself,
is my strength and my song.
He has become my salvation."

3 You will joyfully draw water
from the springs of salvation,

4 and on that day you will say:
"Give thanks to the LORD; proclaim his name!
Make his works known among the peoples.
Declare that his name is exalted.

5 Sing to the LORD, for he has done glorious things.
Let this be known throughout the earth.

6 Cry out and sing, citizen of Zion,
for the Holy One of Israel is among you
in his greatness."

A PRONOUNCEMENT AGAINST BABYLON

13 A pronouncement concerning Babylon that Isaiah son of Amoz saw:
2 Lift up a banner on a barren mountain.
Call out to them.
Signal with your hand, and they will go

A 11:15 Text emended; MT reads *destroy*   B 11:15 Or *dry up*   C 11:15 Lit *the Sea of Egypt*

through the gates of the nobles.
3 I have commanded my consecrated ones;
yes, I have called my warriors,
who celebrate my triumph,
to execute my wrath.
4 Listen, a commotion on the mountains,
like that of a mighty people!
Listen, an uproar among the kingdoms,
like nations being gathered together!
The LORD of Armies is mobilizing an army for war.
5 They are coming from a distant land,
from the farthest horizon —
the LORD and the weapons of his wrath —
to destroy the whole country.ᴬ

6 Wail! For the day of the LORD is near.
It will come as destruction from the Almighty.
7 Therefore everyone's hands will become weak,
and every man will lose heart.ᴮ
8 They will be horrified;
pain and agony will seize them;
they will be in anguish like a woman in labor.
They will look at each other,
their faces flushed with fear.
9 Look, the day of the LORD is coming —
cruel, with rage and burning anger —
to make the earth a desolation
and to destroy its sinners.
10 Indeed, the stars of the sky and its constellationsᶜ
will not give their light.
The sun will be dark when it rises,
and the moon will not shine.
11 I will punish the world for its evil,
and wicked people for their iniquities.
I will put an end to the pride of the arrogant
and humiliate the insolence of tyrants.
12 I will make a human more scarce than fine gold,
and mankind more rare than the gold of Ophir.
13 Therefore I will make the heavens tremble,
and the earth will shake from its foundations
at the wrath of the LORD of Armies,
on the day of his burning anger.
14 Like wandering gazelles
and like sheep without a shepherd,
each one will turn to his own people,
each one will flee to his own land.
15 Whoever is found will be stabbed,
and whoever is caught will die by the sword.

ᴬ13:5 Or earth   ᴮ13:7 Lit every man's heart will melt   ᶜ13:10 Or Orions

16 Their children will be dashed to pieces before their eyes;
their houses will be looted,
and their wives raped.

17 Look! I am stirring up the Medes against them,
who cannot be bought off with^A silver
and who have no desire for gold.

18 Their bows will cut young men to pieces.
They will have no compassion on offspring;
they will not look with pity on children.

19 And Babylon, the jewel of the kingdoms,
the glory of the pride of the Chaldeans,
will be like Sodom and Gomorrah
when God overthrew them.

20 It will never be inhabited
or lived in from generation to generation;
a nomad will not pitch his tent there,
and shepherds will not let their flocks rest there.

21 But desert creatures will lie down there,
and owls will fill the houses.
Ostriches will dwell there,
and wild goats will leap about.

22 Hyenas will howl in the fortresses,
and jackals, in the luxurious palaces.
Babylon's time is almost up;
her days are almost over.

ISRAEL'S RETURN

14 For the LORD will have compassion on Jacob and will choose Israel again. He will settle them on their own land. The resident alien will join them and be united with the house of Jacob. ² The nations will escort Israel and bring it to its homeland. Then the house of Israel will possess them as male and female slaves in the LORD's land. They will make captives of their captors and will rule over their oppressors.

DOWNFALL OF THE KING OF BABYLON

³ When the LORD gives you rest from your pain, torment, and the hard labor you were forced to do, ⁴ you will sing this song of contempt about the king of Babylon and say:
How the oppressor has quieted down,
and how the raging^B has become quiet!

5 The LORD has broken the staff of the wicked,
the scepter of the rulers.

6 It struck the peoples in anger
with unceasing blows.
It subdued the nations in rage
with relentless persecution.

7 The whole earth is calm and at rest;

^A13:17 Lit *who have no regard for*   ^B14:4 DSS; Hb uncertain

people shout with a ringing cry.
8 Even the cypresses and the cedars of Lebanon
   rejoice over you:
   "Since you have been laid low,
   no lumberjack has come against us."

9 Sheol below is eager to greet your coming,
   stirring up the spirits of the departed for you —
   all the rulers[A] of the earth —
   making all the kings of the nations
   rise from their thrones.
10 They all respond to you, saying,
   "You too have become as weak as we are;
   you have become like us!
11 Your splendor has been brought down to Sheol,
   along with the music of your harps.
   Maggots are spread out under you,
   and worms cover you."

12 Shining morning star,[B]
   how you have fallen from the heavens!
   You destroyer of nations,
   you have been cut down to the ground.
13 You said to yourself,
   "I will ascend to the heavens;
   I will set up my throne
   above the stars of God.
   I will sit on the mount of the gods' assembly,
   in the remotest parts of the North.[C]
14 I will ascend above the highest clouds;
   I will make myself like the Most High."
15 But you will be brought down to Sheol
   into the deepest regions of the Pit.

16 Those who see you will stare at you;
   they will look closely at you:
   "Is this the man who caused the earth to tremble,
   who shook the kingdoms,
17 who turned the world into a wilderness,
   who destroyed its cities
   and would not release the prisoners to return home?"
18 All the kings of the nations
   lie in splendor, each in his own tomb.
19 But you are thrown out without a grave,
   like a worthless branch,
   covered by those slain with the sword
   and dumped into a rocky pit like a trampled corpse.
20 You will not join them in burial,

[A]14:9 Lit rams   [B]14:12 Or *Day Star, son of the dawn*   [C]14:13 Or *of Zaphon*

because you destroyed your land
and slaughtered your own people.
The offspring of evildoers
will never be mentioned again.
²¹ Prepare a place of slaughter for his sons,
because of the iniquity of their fathers.
They will never rise up to possess a land
or fill the surface of the earth with cities.

²² "I will rise up against them" — this is the declaration of the LORD of Armies — "and I will cut off from Babylon her reputation, remnant, offspring, and posterity" — this is the LORD's declaration. ²³ "I will make her a swampland and a region for herons,^A and I will sweep her away with the broom of destruction."

This is the declaration of the LORD of Armies.

ASSYRIA WILL BE DESTROYED

²⁴ The LORD of Armies has sworn:
As I have purposed, so it will be;
as I have planned it, so it will happen.
²⁵ I will break Assyria in my land;
I will tread him down on my mountain.
Then his yoke will be taken from them,
and his burden will be removed from their shoulders.
²⁶ This is the plan prepared
for the whole earth,
and this is the hand stretched out
against all the nations.
²⁷ The LORD of Armies himself has planned it;
therefore, who can stand in its way?
It is his hand that is outstretched,
so who can turn it back?

A PRONOUNCEMENT AGAINST PHILISTIA

²⁸ In the year that King Ahaz died, this pronouncement came:
²⁹ Don't rejoice, all of you in Philistia,
because the rod of the one who struck you is broken.
For a viper will come from the root^B of a snake,
and from its egg comes a flying serpent.
³⁰ Then the firstborn of the poor will be well fed,
and the impoverished will lie down in safety,
but I will kill your root with hunger,
and your remnant will be slain.
³¹ Wail, you gates! Cry out, city!
Tremble with fear, all Philistia!
For a cloud of dust is coming from the north,
and there is no one missing from the invader's ranks.
³² What answer will be given to the messengers from that nation?

^A 14:23 Or *hedgehogs*; Hb obscure   ^B 14:29 Or *stock*

The LORD has founded Zion,
and his oppressed people find refuge in her.

A PRONOUNCEMENT AGAINST MOAB

15 A pronouncement concerning Moab:
Ar in Moab is devastated,
destroyed in a night.
Kir in Moab is devastated,
destroyed in a night.

² Dibon went up to its temple
to weep at its high places.
Moab wails on Nebo and at ^A Medeba.
Every head is shaved;
every beard is chopped short.

³ In its streets they wear sackcloth;
on its rooftops and in its public squares
everyone wails,
falling down and weeping.

⁴ Heshbon and Elealeh cry out;
their voices are heard as far away as Jahaz.
Therefore the soldiers of Moab cry out,
and they tremble. ^B

⁵ My heart cries out over Moab,
whose fugitives flee as far as Zoar,
to Eglath-shelishiyah;
they go up the Ascent of Luhith weeping;
they raise a cry of destruction
on the road to Horonaim.

⁶ The Waters of Nimrim are desolate;
the grass is withered, the foliage is gone,
and the vegetation has vanished.

⁷ So they carry their wealth and belongings
over the Wadi of the Willows.

⁸ For their cry echoes
throughout the territory of Moab.
Their wailing reaches Eglaim;
their wailing reaches Beer-elim.

⁹ The Waters of Dibon ^C are full of blood,
but I will bring on Dibon ^C even more than this —
a lion for those who escape from Moab,
and for the survivors in the land.

16 Send lambs to the ruler of the land,
from Sela in the desert
to the mountain of Daughter Zion.

² Like a bird fleeing,
forced from the nest,

---

^A 15:2 Or *wails over Nebo and over*   ^B 15:4 Lit *out, he trembles within himself*
^C 15:9 DSS, some LXX mss, Vg; MT reads *Dimon*

the daughters of Moab
will be at the fords of the Arnon.

3 Give us counsel and make a decision.
Shelter us at noonday
with shade that is as dark as night.
Hide the refugees;
do not betray the one who flees.
4 Let my refugees stay with you;
be a refuge for Moab ^A from the aggressor.

When the oppressor has gone,
destruction has ended,
and marauders have vanished from the land,
5 a throne will be established in love,
and one will sit on it faithfully ^B
in the tent of David,
judging and pursuing what is right,
quick to execute justice.

6 We have heard of Moab's pride —
how very proud he is —
his haughtiness, his pride, his arrogance,
and his empty boasting.
7 Therefore let Moab wail;
let every one of them wail for Moab.
You who are completely devastated, mourn
for the raisin cakes of Kir-hareseth.
8 For Heshbon's terraced vineyards
and the grapevines of Sibmah have withered.
The rulers of the nations
have trampled its choice vines
that reached as far as Jazer
and spread to the desert.
Their shoots spread out
and reached the sea.
9 So I join with Jazer
to weep for the vines of Sibmah;
I drench Heshbon and Elealeh with my tears.
Triumphant shouts have fallen silent ^C
over your summer fruit and your harvest.
10 Joy and rejoicing have been removed from the orchard;
no one is singing or shouting for joy in the vineyards.
No one tramples grapes ^D in the winepresses.
I have put an end to the shouting.
11 Therefore I moan like the sound of a lyre for Moab,
as does my innermost being for Kir-heres.

---

^A 16:4 Or you; Moab — be a refuge for him   ^B 16:5 Or continually   ^C 16:9 Or
Battle cries have fallen   ^D 16:10 Lit wine

12 When Moab appears
    and tires himself out on the high place
    and comes to his sanctuary to pray,
    it will do him no good.

13 This is the message that the LORD previously announced about Moab.
14 And now the LORD says, "In three years, as a hired worker counts years,
Moab's splendor will become an object of contempt, in spite of a very large
population. And those who are left will be few and weak."

A PRONOUNCEMENT AGAINST DAMASCUS

17 A pronouncement concerning Damascus:
    Look, Damascus is no longer a city.
    It has become a ruined heap.
2   The cities of Aroer are abandoned;
    they will be places for flocks.
    They will lie down without fear.
3   The fortress disappears from Ephraim,
    and a kingdom from Damascus.
    The remnant of Aram will be
    like the splendor of the Israelites.
        This is the declaration of the LORD of Armies.

JUDGMENT AGAINST ISRAEL

4   On that day
    the splendor of Jacob will fade,
    and his healthy body^A will become emaciated.
5   It will be as if a reaper had gathered standing grain —
    his arm harvesting the heads of grain —
    and as if one had gleaned heads of grain
    in the Valley of Rephaim.
6   Only gleanings will be left in Israel,
    as if an olive tree had been beaten —
    two or three olives at the very top of the tree,
    four or five on its fruitful branches.
        This is the declaration of the LORD,
        the God of Israel.

7 On that day people will look to their Maker and will turn their eyes to
the Holy One of Israel. 8 They will not look to the altars they made with their
hands or to the Asherahs and shrines^B they made with their fingers.

9   On that day their strong cities will be
    like the abandoned woods and mountaintops
    that were abandoned because of the Israelites;
    there will be desolation.
10 For you have forgotten the God of your salvation,
    and you have failed to remember
    the rock of your strength;

---

^A 17:4 Lit and the fat of his flesh   ^B 17:8 Or incense altars

therefore you will plant beautiful plants
and set out cuttings from exotic vines.
¹¹ On the day that you plant,
you will help them to grow,
and in the morning
you will help your seed to sprout,
but the harvest will vanish
on the day of disease and incurable pain.

JUDGMENT AGAINST THE NATIONS

¹² Ah! The roar of many peoples —
they roar like the roaring of the seas.
The raging of the nations —
they rage like the rumble of rushing water.
¹³ The nations rage like the rumble of a huge torrent.
He rebukes them, and they flee far away,
driven before the wind like chaff on the hills
and like tumbleweeds before a gale.
¹⁴ In the evening — sudden terror!
Before morning — it is gone!
This is the fate of those who plunder us
and the lot of those who ravage us.

THE LORD'S MESSAGE TO CUSH

18 Woe to the land of buzzing insect wings^A
beyond the rivers of Cush,
² which sends envoys by sea,
in reed vessels over the water.

Go, swift messengers,
to a nation tall and smooth-skinned,
to a people feared far and near,
a powerful nation with a strange language,^B
whose land is divided by rivers.
³ All you inhabitants of the world
and you who live on the earth,
when a banner is raised on the mountains, look!
When a trumpet sounds, listen!

⁴ For the LORD said to me:
I will quietly look out from my place,
like shimmering heat in sunshine,
like a rain cloud in harvest heat.
⁵ For before the harvest, when the blossoming
is over
and the blossom becomes a ripening grape,
he will cut off the shoots with a pruning knife,
and tear away and remove the branches.

---

^A18:1 Or *of sailing ships* ^B18:2 Hb obscure

⁶ They will all be left for the birds of prey on the hills
and for the wild animals of the land.
The birds of prey will spend the summer feeding on them,
and all the wild animals the winter.

⁷ At that time a gift will be brought to the LORD of Armies from^A a people tall and smooth-skinned, a people feared far and near, a powerful nation with a strange language, whose land is divided by rivers — to Mount Zion, the place of the name of the LORD of Armies.

A PRONOUNCEMENT AGAINST EGYPT

19 A pronouncement concerning Egypt:
Look, the LORD rides on a swift cloud
and is coming to Egypt.
Egypt's idols will tremble before him,
and Egypt will lose heart.^B

² I will provoke Egyptians against Egyptians;
each will fight against his brother
and each against his friend,
city against city, kingdom against kingdom.
³ Egypt's spirit will be disturbed within it,
and I will frustrate its plans.
Then they will inquire of idols, ghosts,
mediums, and spiritists.
⁴ I will hand over Egypt to harsh masters,
and a strong king will rule it.
This is the declaration of the Lord GOD of Armies.

⁵ The water of the sea will dry up,
and the river will be parched and dry.
⁶ The channels will stink;
they will dwindle, and Egypt's canals will be parched.
Reed and rush will wilt.
⁷ The reeds by the Nile, by the mouth of the river,
and all the cultivated areas of the Nile
will wither, blow away, and vanish.
⁸ Then the fishermen will mourn.
All those who cast hooks into the Nile will lament,
and those who spread nets on the water will give up.
⁹ Those who work with flax will be dismayed;
those combing it and weaving linen will turn pale.^C
¹⁰ Egypt's weavers^D will be dejected;
all her wage earners will be demoralized.

¹¹ The princes of Zoan are complete fools;
Pharaoh's wisest advisers give stupid advice!
How can you say to Pharaoh,

---

^A18:7 DSS, LXX, Vg; MT omits *from*   ^B19:1 Lit *Egypt's heart will melt within it*
^C19:9 DSS, Tg; MT reads *weavers of white cloth*   ^D19:10 Or *foundations*

"I am oneᴬ of the wise,
    a student of easternᴮ kings"?
12   Where then are your wise men?
    Let them tell you and reveal
    what the LORD of Armies has planned against Egypt.
13   The princes of Zoan have been fools;
    the princes of Memphis are deceived.
    Her tribal chieftains have led Egypt astray.
14   The LORD has mixed within her a spirit of confusion.
    The leaders have made Egypt stagger in all she does,
    as a drunkard staggers in his vomit.
15   No head or tail, palm or reed,
    will be able to do anything for Egypt.

EGYPT WILL KNOW THE LORD

¹⁶ On that day Egypt will be like women and will tremble with fear because of the threatening hand of the LORD of Armies when he raises it against them. ¹⁷ The land of Judah will terrify Egypt; whenever Judah is mentioned, Egypt will tremble because of what the LORD of Armies has planned against it.

¹⁸ On that day five cities in the land of Egypt will speak the language of Canaan and swear loyalty to the LORD of Armies. One of the cities will be called the City of the Sun.ᶜ,ᴰ

¹⁹ On that day there will be an altar to the LORD in the center of the land of Egypt and a pillar to the LORD near her border. ²⁰ It will be a sign and witness to the LORD of Armies in the land of Egypt. When they cry out to the LORD because of their oppressors, he will send them a savior and leader, and he will rescue them. ²¹ The LORD will make himself known to Egypt, and Egypt will know the LORD on that day. They will offer sacrifices and offerings; they will make vows to the LORD and fulfill them. ²² The LORD will strike Egypt, striking and healing. Then they will turn to the LORD and he will be receptive to their prayers and heal them.

²³ On that day there will be a highway from Egypt to Assyria. Assyria will go to Egypt, Egypt to Assyria, and Egypt will worship with Assyria.

²⁴ On that day Israel will form a triple alliance with Egypt and Assyria — a blessing within the land. ²⁵ The LORD of Armies will bless them, saying, "Egypt my people, Assyria my handiwork, and Israel my inheritance are blessed."

NO HELP FROM CUSH OR EGYPT

20 In the year that the chief commander, sent by King Sargon of Assyria, came to Ashdod and attacked and captured it — ² during that time the LORD had spoken through Isaiah son of Amoz, saying, "Go, take off your sackclothᴱ and remove the sandals from your feet," and he did that, going stripped and barefoot — ³ the LORD said, "As my servant Isaiah has gone stripped and barefoot three years as a sign and omen against Egypt and Cush, ⁴ so the king of Assyria will lead the captives of Egypt and the exiles of

---

ᴬ19:11 Lit *a son* ᴮ19:11 Lit *a son of ancient* ᶜ19:18 Some Hb mss, DSS, Sym, Tg, Vg, Arabic; other Hb mss read *of Destruction*; LXX reads *of Righteousness* ᴰ19:18 = the ancient Egyptian city Heliopolis ᴱ20:2 Lit *off the sackcloth from your waist*

Cush, young and old alike, stripped and barefoot, with bared buttocks — to Egypt's shame. ⁵ Those who made Cush their hope and Egypt their boast will be dismayed and ashamed. ⁶ And the inhabitants of this coastland will say on that day, 'Look, this is what has happened to those we relied on and fled to for help to rescue us from the king of Assyria! Now, how will we escape?'"

A JUDGMENT ON BABYLON

21 A pronouncement concerning the desert by the sea:
Like storms that pass over the Negev,
it comes from the desert, from the land of terror.

² A troubling vision is declared to me:
"The treacherous one acts treacherously,
and the destroyer destroys.
Advance, Elam! Lay siege, you Medes!
I will put an end to all the groaning."

³ Therefore I amᴬ filled with anguish.
Pain grips me, like the pain of a woman in labor.
I am too perplexed to hear,
too dismayed to see.
⁴ My heart staggers;
horror terrifies me.
He has turned my last glimmer of hopeᴮ
into sheer terror.
⁵ Prepare a table, and spread out a carpet!
Eat and drink!
Rise up, you princes, and oil the shields!

⁶ For the Lord has said to me,
"Go, post a lookout;
let him report what he sees.
⁷ When he sees riders —
pairs of horsemen,
riders on donkeys,
riders on camels —
he must pay close attention."
⁸ Then the lookoutᶜ reported,
"Lord, I stand on the watchtower all day,
and I stay at my post all night.
⁹ Look, riders come —
horsemen in pairs."
And he answered, saying,
"Babylon has fallen, has fallen.
All the images of her gods
have been shattered on the ground."

¹⁰ My people who have been crushed

ᴬ21:3 Lit *my waist is*, or *my insides are*   ᴮ21:4 Lit *my twilight*   ᶜ21:8 DSS, Syr; MT reads *Then a lion*

on the threshing floor,
I have declared to you
what I have heard from the LORD of Armies,
the God of Israel.

A PRONOUNCEMENT AGAINST DUMAH

[11] A pronouncement concerning Dumah:[A]
One calls to me from Seir,
"Watchman, what is left of the night?
Watchman, what is left of the night?"
[12]   The watchman said,
"Morning has come, and also night.
If you want to ask, ask!
Come back again."

A PRONOUNCEMENT AGAINST ARABIA

[13] A pronouncement concerning Arabia:
In the desert[B] brush
you will camp for the night,
you caravans of Dedanites.
[14]   Bring water for the thirsty.
The inhabitants of the land of Tema
meet[C] the refugees with food.
[15]   For they have fled from swords,
from the drawn sword,
from the bow that is strung,
and from the stress of battle.

[16] For the Lord said this to me: "Within one year, as a hired worker counts years, all the glory of Kedar will be gone. [17] The remaining Kedarite archers will be few in number." For the LORD, the God of Israel, has spoken.

A PRONOUNCEMENT AGAINST JERUSALEM

22
A pronouncement concerning the Valley of Vision:
What's the matter with you?
Why have all of you gone up to the rooftops?
[2]   The noisy city, the jubilant town,
is filled with celebration.
Your dead did not die by the sword;
they were not killed in battle.
[3]   All your rulers have fled together,
captured without a bow.
All your fugitives were captured together;
they had fled far away.
[4]   Therefore I said,
"Look away from me! Let me weep bitterly!
Do not try to comfort me

[A] 21:11 Some Hb mss, LXX read *Edom*   [B] 21:13 LXX, Syr, Tg, Vg read *desert at evening*   [C] 21:14 LXX, Syr, Tg, Vg read *meet* as a command about the destruction of my dear[A] people."

5 For the Lord God of Armies
   had a day of tumult, trampling, and confusion
   in the Valley of Vision —
   people shouting[B] and crying to the mountains;
6 Elam took up a quiver
   with chariots and horsemen,[C]
   and Kir uncovered the shield.
7 Your best valleys were full of chariots,
   and horsemen were positioned at the city gates.
8 He removed the defenses of Judah.

On that day you looked to the weapons in the House of the Forest. ⁹ You saw that there were many breaches in the walls of the city of David. You collected water from the lower pool. ¹⁰ You counted the houses of Jerusalem so that you could tear them down to fortify the wall. ¹¹ You made a reservoir between the walls for the water of the ancient pool, but you did not look to the one who made it, or consider the one who created it long ago.

12 On that day the Lord God of Armies
   called for weeping, for wailing, for shaven heads,
   and for the wearing of sackcloth.
13 But look: joy and gladness,
   butchering of cattle, slaughtering of sheep and goats,
   eating of meat, and drinking of wine —
   "Let us eat and drink, for tomorrow we die!"
14 The Lord of Armies has directly revealed to me:
   "This iniquity will not be wiped out for you people as long as you
      live."[D]
   The Lord God of Armies has spoken.

A PRONOUNCEMENT AGAINST SHEBNA

¹⁵ The Lord God of Armies said: "Go to Shebna, that steward who is in charge of the palace, and say to him: ¹⁶ What are you doing here? Who authorized you to carve out a tomb for yourself here, carving your tomb on the height and cutting a resting place for yourself out of rock? ¹⁷ Look, you strong man! The Lord is about to shake you violently. He will take hold of you, ¹⁸ wind you up into a ball, and sling you into a wide land.[E] There you will die, and there your glorious chariots will be — a disgrace to the house of your lord. ¹⁹ I will remove you from your office; you will be ousted from your position.

²⁰ "On that day I will call for my servant, Eliakim son of Hilkiah. ²¹ I will clothe him with your robe and tie your sash around him. I will hand your authority over to him, and he will be like a father to the inhabitants of Jerusalem and to the house of Judah. ²² I will place the key of the house of David on his shoulder; what he opens, no one can close; what he closes, no one can open. ²³ I will drive him, like a peg, into a firm place. He will be a throne of honor for his father's family. ²⁴ They will hang on him all the glory of his

---

A22:4 Lit of the daughter of my   B22:5 Or Vision — a tearing down of a wall, or
Vision — Kir raged; Hb obscure   C22:6 Lit chariots of man   D22:14 Lit for you
until you die   E22:17-18 Hb obscure

1139

father's family: the descendants and the offshoots — all the small vessels, from bowls to every kind of jar. [25] On that day" — the declaration of the LORD of Armies — "the peg that was driven into a firm place will give way, be cut off, and fall, and the load on it will be destroyed." Indeed, the LORD has spoken.

A PRONOUNCEMENT AGAINST TYRE

23 A pronouncement concerning Tyre:
Wail, ships of Tarshish,
for your haven has been destroyed.
Word has reached them from the land of Cyprus. [A]

[2] Mourn, inhabitants of the coastland,
you merchants of Sidon;
your agents have crossed the sea [B]

[3] over deep water.
Tyre's revenue was the grain from Shihor —
the harvest of the Nile.
She was the merchant among the nations.

[4] Be ashamed, Sidon, the stronghold of the sea,
for the sea has spoken:
"I have not been in labor or given birth.
I have not raised young men
or brought up young women."

[5] When the news reaches Egypt,
they will be in anguish over the news about Tyre.

[6] Cross over to Tarshish;
wail, inhabitants of the coastland!

[7] Is this your jubilant city,
whose origin was in ancient times,
whose feet have taken her
to reside far away?

[8] Who planned this against Tyre,
the bestower of crowns,
whose traders are princes,
whose merchants are the honored ones of the earth?

[9] The LORD of Armies planned it,
to desecrate all its glorious beauty,
to disgrace all the honored ones of the earth.

[10] Overflow [C] your land like the Nile, daughter of Tarshish;
there is no longer anything to restrain you. [D]

[11] He stretched out his hand over the sea;
he made kingdoms tremble.
The LORD has commanded
that the Canaanite fortresses be destroyed.

[12] He said,
"You will not celebrate anymore,
ravished young woman, daughter of Sidon.
Get up and cross over to Cyprus —

[A] 23:1 Hb *Kittim* [B] 23:2 DSS; MT reads *Sidon, whom the seafarers have filled*
[C] 23:10 DSS, LXX read *Work* [D] 23:10 Or *longer any harbor*

even there you will have no rest!"
13 Look at the land of the Chaldeans —
a people who no longer exist.
Assyria destined it for desert creatures.
They set up their siege towers
and stripped its palaces.
They made it a ruin.
14 Wail, ships of Tarshish,
because your fortress is destroyed!

15 On that day Tyre will be forgotten for seventy years — the life span of one king. At the end of seventy years, what the song says about the prostitute will happen to Tyre:
16 Pick up your lyre,
stroll through the city,
you forgotten prostitute.
Play skillfully,
sing many a song
so that you will be remembered.

17 And at the end of the seventy years, the LORD will restore Tyre and she will go back into business, prostituting herself with all the kingdoms of the world throughout the earth. 18 But her profits and wages will be dedicated to the LORD. They will not be stored or saved, for her profit will go to those who live in the LORD's presence, to provide them with ample food and sacred clothing.

THE EARTH JUDGED

24 Look, the LORD is stripping the earth bare
and making it desolate.
He will twist its surface and scatter its inhabitants:
2 people and priest alike,
servant and master,
female servant and mistress,
buyer and seller,
lender and borrower,
creditor and debtor.
3 The earth will be stripped completely bare
and will be totally plundered,
for the LORD has spoken this message.

4 The earth mourns and withers;
the world wastes away and withers;
the exalted people of the earth waste away.
5 The earth is polluted by its inhabitants,
for they have transgressed teachings,
overstepped decrees,
and broken the permanent covenant.
6 Therefore a curse has consumed the earth,
and its inhabitants have become guilty;

the earth's inhabitants have been burned,
and only a few survive.
7 The new wine mourns;
the vine withers.
All the carousers now groan.
8 The joyful tambourines have ceased.
The noise of the jubilant has stopped.
The joyful lyre has ceased.
9 They no longer sing and drink wine;
beer is bitter to those who drink it.
10 The city of chaos is shattered;
every house is closed to entry.
11 In the streets they cry^A for wine.
All joy grows dark;
earth's rejoicing goes into exile.
12 Only desolation remains in the city;
its gate has collapsed in ruins.
13 For this is how it will be on earth
among the nations:
like a harvested olive tree,
like a gleaning after a grape harvest.

14 They raise their voices, they sing out;
they proclaim in the west
the majesty of the LORD.
15 Therefore, in the east honor the LORD!
In the coasts and islands of the west
honor the name of the LORD,
the God of Israel.
16 From the ends of the earth we hear songs:
The Splendor of the Righteous One.

But I said, "I waste away! I waste away!^B
Woe is me."
The treacherous act treacherously;
the treacherous deal very treacherously.

17 Panic, pit, and trap await you
who dwell on the earth.
18 Whoever flees at the sound of panic
will fall into a pit,
and whoever escapes from the pit
will be caught in a trap.
For the windows on high are opened,
and the foundations of the earth are shaken.
19 The earth is completely devastated;
the earth is split open;
the earth is violently shaken.

^A 24:11 Lit *streets she cries* ^B 24:16 Hb obscure

20 The earth staggers like a drunkard
and sways like a hut.
Earth's rebellion weighs it down,
and it falls, never to rise again.

21 On that day the LORD will punish
the army of the heights in the heights
and the kings of the ground on the ground.

22 They will be gathered together
like prisoners in a pit.
They will be confined to a dungeon;
after many days they will be punished.

23 The moon will be put to shame
and the sun disgraced,
because the LORD of Armies will reign as king
on Mount Zion in Jerusalem,
and he will display his glory
in the presence of his elders.

SALVATION AND JUDGMENT ON THAT DAY

25 LORD, you are my God;
I will exalt you. I will praise your name,
for you have accomplished wonders,
plans formed long ago, with perfect faithfulness.

2 For you have turned the city into a pile of rocks,
a fortified city, into ruins;
the fortress of barbarians is no longer a city;
it will never be rebuilt.

3 Therefore, a strong people will honor you.
The cities of violent nations will fear you.

4 For you have been a stronghold for the poor person,
a stronghold for the needy in his distress,
a refuge from storms and a shade from heat.
When the breath of the violent
is like a storm against a wall,

5 like heat in a dry land,
you will subdue the uproar of barbarians.
As the shade of a cloud cools the heat of the day,
so he will silence the song of the violent.

6 On this mountain, ^A
the LORD of Armies will prepare for all the peoples a feast of choice
meat,
a feast with aged wine, prime cuts of choice meat, ^B fine vintage wine.

7 On this mountain
he will destroy the burial shroud,
the shroud over all the peoples,
the sheet covering all the nations;

---

^A 25:6 = Mount Zion   ^B 25:6 Lit wine, fat full of marrow

⁸ he will destroy death forever.
The Lord GOD will wipe away the tears
from every face
and remove his people's disgrace
from the whole earth,
for the LORD has spoken.

⁹ On that day it will be said,
"Look, this is our God;
we have waited for him, and he has saved us.
This is the LORD; we have waited for him.
Let us rejoice and be glad in his salvation."

¹⁰ For the LORD's power will rest on this mountain.

But Moab will be trampled in his place^A
as straw is trampled in a dung pile.

¹¹ He will spread out his arms in the middle of it,
as a swimmer spreads out his arms to swim.
His pride will be brought low,
along with the trickery of his hands.

¹² The high-walled fortress will be brought down,
thrown to the ground, to the dust.

THE SONG OF JUDAH

26 On that day this song will be sung in the land of Judah:
We have a strong city.
Salvation is established as walls and ramparts.

² Open the gates
so a righteous nation can come in —
one that remains faithful.

³ You will keep the mind that is dependent on you
in perfect peace,
for it is trusting in you.

⁴ Trust in the LORD forever,
because in the LORD, the LORD himself, is an everlasting rock!

⁵ For he has humbled those who live in lofty places —
an inaccessible city.
He brings it down; he brings it down to the ground;
he throws it to the dust.

⁶ Feet trample it,
the feet of the humble,
the steps of the poor.

GOD'S PEOPLE VINDICATED

⁷ The path of the righteous is level;
you clear a straight path for the righteous.

⁸ Yes, LORD, we wait for you
in the path of your judgments.

---

^A25:10 Or *trampled under him*

Our desire is for your name and renown.
9 I long for you in the night;
   yes, my spirit within me diligently seeks you,
   for when your judgments are in the land,
   the inhabitants of the world will learn righteousness.
10 But if the wicked man is shown favor,
   he does not learn righteousness.
   In a righteous land he acts unjustly
   and does not see the majesty of the LORD.

11 LORD, your hand is lifted up to take action,
   but they do not see it.
   Let them see your zeal for your people
   and be put to shame.
   Let fire consume your adversaries.
12 LORD, you will establish peace for us,
   for you have also done all our work for us.
13 LORD our God, lords other than you have owned^A us,
   but we remember your name alone.

14 The dead do not live;
   departed spirits do not rise up.
   Indeed, you have punished and destroyed them;
   you have wiped out all memory of them.
15 You have added to the nation, LORD.
   You have added to the nation; you are honored.
   You have expanded all the borders of the land.
16 LORD, they went to you in their distress;
   they poured out whispered prayers
   because your discipline fell on them.^B
17 As a pregnant woman about to give birth
   writhes and cries out in her pains,
   so we were before you, LORD.
18 We became pregnant, we writhed in pain;
   we gave birth to wind.
   We have won no victories on earth,
   and the earth's inhabitants have not fallen.

19 Your dead will live; their bodies^C will rise.
   Awake and sing, you who dwell in the dust!
   For you will be covered with the morning dew,^D
   and the earth will bring out the departed spirits.

20 Go, my people, enter your rooms
   and close your doors behind you.
   Hide for a little while until the wrath has passed.
21 For look, the LORD is coming from his place

---

^A 26:13 Or married   ^B 26:16 Hb obscure   ^C 26:19 Lit live; my body they
^D 26:19 Lit For your dew is a dew of lights

to punish the inhabitants of the earth for their iniquity.
The earth will reveal the blood shed on it
and will no longer conceal her slain.

LEVIATHAN SLAIN

27 On that day the LORD with his relentless, large, strong sword will bring judgment on Leviathan, the fleeing serpent — Leviathan, the twisting serpent. He will slay the monster that is in the sea.

THE LORD'S VINEYARD

2   On that day
sing about a desirable vineyard:
3   I am the LORD, who watches over it
to water it regularly.
So that no one disturbs it,
I watch over it night and day.
4   I am not angry.
If only there were thorns and briers for me to battle,
I would trample them
and burn them to the ground.
5   Or let it take hold of my strength;
let it make peace with me —
make peace with me.
6   In days to come, Jacob will take root.
Israel will blossom and bloom
and fill the whole world with fruit.

7   Did the LORD strike Israel
as he struck the one who struck Israel?
Was Israel killed like those killed by the LORD?
8   You disputed with Israel
by banishing and driving her away.^A
He removed her with his severe storm
on the day of the east wind.
9   Therefore Jacob's iniquity will be atoned for in this way,
and the result of the removal of his sin will be this:
when he makes all the altar stones
like crushed bits of chalk,
no Asherah poles or incense altars will remain standing.
10   For the fortified city will be desolate,
pastures deserted and abandoned like a wilderness.
Calves will graze there,
and there they will spread out and strip its branches.
11   When its branches dry out, they will be broken off.
Women will come and make fires with them,
for they are not a people with understanding.
Therefore their Maker will not have compassion on them,
and their Creator will not be gracious to them.

^A 27:8 Hb obscure

12 On that day
the LORD will thresh grain from the Euphrates River
as far as the Wadi of Egypt,
and you Israelites will be gathered one by one.
13 On that day
a great trumpet will be blown,
and those lost in the land of Assyria will come,
as well as those dispersed in the land of Egypt;
and they will worship the LORD
at Jerusalem on the holy mountain.

WOE TO SAMARIA

28 Woe to the majestic crown of Ephraim's drunkards,
and to the fading flower of its beautiful splendor,
which is on the summit above the rich valley.
Woe to those overcome with wine.
2 Look, the Lord has a strong and mighty one —
like a devastating hail storm,
like a storm with strong flooding water.
He will bring it across the land with his hand.
3 The majestic crown of Ephraim's drunkards
will be trampled underfoot.
4 The fading flower of his beautiful splendor,
which is on the summit above the rich valley,
will be like a ripe fig before the summer harvest.
Whoever sees it will swallow it
while it is still in his hand.
5 On that day
the LORD of Armies will become a crown of beauty
and a diadem of splendor
to the remnant of his people,
6 a spirit of justice
to the one who sits in judgment,
and strength
to those who repel attacks at the city gate.

7 Even these stagger because of wine
and stumble under the influence of beer:
priest and prophet stagger because of beer,
they are confused by wine.
They stumble because of beer,
they are muddled in their visions,
they stumble in their judgments.
8 Indeed, all their tables are covered with vomit;
there is no place without a stench.
9 Who is he trying to teach?
Who is he trying to instruct?
Infants^A just weaned from milk?

^A 28:9 Lit Those

Babies[A] removed from the breast?

10 "Law after law, law after law,
line after line, line after line,
a little here, a little there."[B]

11 For he will speak to this people
with stammering speech
and in a foreign language.

12 He had said to them:
"This is the place of rest;
let the weary rest;
this is the place of repose."
But they would not listen.

13 The word of the LORD will come to them:
"Law after law, law after law,
line after line, line after line,
a little here, a little there,"
so they go stumbling backward,
to be broken, trapped, and captured.

A DEAL WITH DEATH

14 Therefore hear the word of the LORD, you scoffers
who rule this people in Jerusalem.

15 For you said, "We have made a covenant with Death,
and we have an agreement with Sheol;
when the overwhelming catastrophe[C] passes through,
it will not touch us,
because we have made falsehood our refuge
and have hidden behind treachery."

16 Therefore the Lord GOD said:
"Look, I have laid a stone in Zion,
a tested stone,
a precious cornerstone, a sure foundation;
the one who believes will be unshakable.[D]

17 And I will make justice the measuring line
and righteousness the mason's level."
Hail will sweep away the false refuge,
and water will flood your hiding place.

18 Your covenant with Death will be dissolved,
and your agreement with Sheol will not last.
When the overwhelming catastrophe passes through,
you will be trampled.

19 Every time it passes through,
it will carry you away;
it will pass through every morning —
every day and every night.
Only terror will cause you

[A]28:9 Lit *Those*   [B]28:10 Hb obscure, also in v. 13   [C]28:15 Or *whip*; Hb obscure, also in v. 18   [D]28:16 Lit *will not hurry* to understand the message.[A]

20 Indeed, the bed is too short to stretch out on,
and its cover too small to wrap up in.

21 For the LORD will rise up as he did at Mount Perazim.
He will rise in wrath, as at the Valley of Gibeon,
to do his work, his unexpected work,
and to perform his task, his unfamiliar task.

22 So now, do not scoff,
or your shackles will become stronger.
Indeed, I have heard from the Lord GOD of Armies
a decree of destruction for the whole land.

GOD'S WONDERFUL ADVICE

23 Listen and hear my voice.
Pay attention and hear what I say.

24 Does the plowman plow every day to plant seed?
Does he continuously break up
and cultivate the soil?

25 When he has leveled its surface,
does he not then scatter black cumin
and sow cumin?
He plants wheat in rows and barley in plots,
with spelt as their border.

26 His God teaches him order;
he instructs him.

27 Certainly black cumin is not threshed
with a threshing board,
and a cart wheel is not rolled over the cumin.
But black cumin is beaten out with a stick,
and cumin with a rod.

28 Bread grain is crushed,
but is not threshed endlessly.
Though the wheel of the farmer's cart rumbles,
his horses do not crush it.

29 This also comes from the LORD of Armies.
He gives wondrous advice;
he gives great wisdom.

WOE TO JERUSALEM

29
Woe to Ariel,[B] Ariel,
the city where David camped!
Continue year after year;
let the festivals recur.

2 I will oppress Ariel,
and there will be mourning and crying,
and she will be to me like an Ariel.

3 I will camp in a circle around you;

[A]28:19 Or *The understanding of the message will cause sheer terror*   [B]29:1 Or *Altar Hearth*, or *Lion of God*; Hb obscure, also in v. 2

I will besiege you with earth ramps,
and I will set up my siege towers against you.
⁴ You will be brought down;
you will speak from the ground,
and your words will come from low in the dust.
Your voice will be like that of a spirit
from the ground;
your speech will whisper from the dust.

⁵ Your many foes^A will be like fine dust,
and many of the ruthless, like blowing chaff.
Then suddenly, in an instant,
⁶ you will be punished by the Lord of Armies
with thunder, earthquake, and loud noise,
storm, tempest, and a flame of consuming fire.
⁷ All the many nations
going out to battle against Ariel —
all the attackers, the siege works against her,
and those who oppress her —
will then be like a dream, a vision in the night.
⁸ It will be like a hungry one who dreams he is eating,
then wakes and is still hungry;
and like a thirsty one who dreams he is drinking,
then wakes and is still thirsty, longing for water.
So it will be for all the many nations
who go to battle against Mount Zion.

⁹ Stop and be astonished;
blind yourselves and be blind!
They are drunk,^B but not with wine;
they stagger,^C but not with beer.
¹⁰ For the Lord has poured out on you
an overwhelming urge to^D sleep;
he has shut your eyes (the prophets)
and covered your heads (the seers).

¹¹ For you the entire vision will be like the words of a sealed document. If it is given to one who can read and he is asked to read it,^E he will say, "I can't read it, because it is sealed." ¹² And if the document is given to one who cannot read and he is asked to read it,^F he will say, "I can't read."
¹³ The Lord said:
These people approach me with their speeches
to honor me with lip-service^G —
yet their hearts are far from me,
and human rules direct their worship of me.^H

---

^A29:5 Lit *foreigners* ^B29:9 LXX, Tg, Vg read *Be drunk* ^C29:9 Tg, Vg read *wine; stagger* ^D29:10 Lit *you a spirit of* ^E29:11 Lit *If one gives it to one who knows the document, saying, "Read this, please"* ^F29:12 Lit *who does not know the document, saying, "Read this, please"* ^G29:13 Lit *their mouth and honor me with its lips* ^H29:13 Lit *their fearing of me is a taught command of men*

14 Therefore, I will again confound these people
with wonder after wonder.
The wisdom of their wise will vanish,
and the perception of their perceptive
will be hidden.

15 Woe to those who go to great lengths
to hide their plans from the LORD.
They do their works in the dark,
and say, "Who sees us? Who knows us?"

16 You have turned things around,
as if the potter were the same as the clay.
How can what is made say about its maker,
"He didn't make me"?
How can what is formed
say about the one who formed it,
"He doesn't understand what he's doing"?

17 Isn't it true that in just a little while
Lebanon will become an orchard,
and the orchard will seem like a forest?

18 On that day the deaf will hear
the words of a document,
and out of a deep darkness
the eyes of the blind will see.

19 The humble will have joy
after joy in the LORD,
and the poor people will rejoice
in the Holy One of Israel.

20 For the ruthless one will vanish,
the scorner will disappear,
and all those who lie in wait with evil intent
will be killed —

21 those who, with their speech,
accuse a person of wrongdoing,
who set a trap for the one mediating at
the city gate
and without cause deprive the righteous of justice.

22 Therefore, the LORD who redeemed Abraham says this about the house
of Jacob:
Jacob will no longer be ashamed,
and his face will no longer be pale.

23 For when he sees his children,
the work of my hands within his nation,
they will honor my name,
they will honor the Holy One of Jacob
and stand in awe of the God of Israel.

24 Those who are confused will gain understanding,
and those who grumble will accept instruction.

CONDEMNATION OF THE EGYPTIAN ALLIANCE

30 Woe to the rebellious children!
This is the LORD's declaration.
They carry out a plan, but not mine;
they make an alliance,
but against my will,
piling sin on top of sin.

2 Without asking my advice
they set out to go down to Egypt
in order to seek shelter under Pharaoh's protection
and take refuge in Egypt's shadow.

3 But Pharaoh's protection will become your shame,
and refuge in Egypt's shadow your humiliation.

4 For though his^A princes are at Zoan
and his messengers reach as far as Hanes,

5 everyone will be ashamed
because of a people who can't help.
They are of no benefit, they are no help;
they are good for nothing but shame and disgrace.

6 A pronouncement concerning the animals of the Negev:^B
Through a land of trouble and distress,
of lioness and lion,
of viper and flying serpent,
they carry their wealth on the backs of donkeys
and their treasures on the humps of camels,
to a people who will not help them.

7 Egypt's help is completely worthless;
therefore, I call her:
Rahab Who Just Sits.

8 Go now, write it on a tablet in their presence
and inscribe it on a scroll;
it will be for the future,
forever and ever.

9 They are a rebellious people,
deceptive children,
children who do not want to listen to the LORD's instruction.

10 They say to the seers, "Do not see,"
and to the prophets,
"Do not prophesy the truth to us.
Tell us flattering things.
Prophesy illusions.

11 Get out of the way!
Leave the pathway.
Rid us of the Holy One of Israel."

12 Therefore the Holy One of Israel says:
"Because you have rejected this message

^A30:4 Or *Judah's* ^B30:6 Or *Southland*

and have trusted in oppression and deceit,
and have depended on them,

13 this iniquity of yours will be
like a crumbling gap,
a bulge in a high wall
whose collapse will come in an instant — suddenly!

14 Its collapse will be like the shattering
of a potter's jar, crushed to pieces,
so that not even a fragment of pottery
will be found among its shattered remains —
no fragment large enough to take fire from a hearth
or scoop water from a cistern."

15 For the Lord GOD, the Holy One of Israel, has said:
"You will be delivered by returning and resting;
your strength will lie in quiet confidence.
But you are not willing."

16 You say, "No!
We will escape on horses" —
therefore you will escape! —
and, "We will ride on fast horses" —
but those who pursue you will be faster.

17 One thousand will flee at the threat of one,
at the threat of five you will flee,
until you remain
like a solitary pole on a mountaintop
or a banner on a hill.

THE LORD'S MERCY TO ISRAEL

18 Therefore the LORD is waiting to show you mercy,
and is rising up to show you compassion,
for the LORD is a just God.
All who wait patiently for him are happy.

¹⁹ For people will live on Zion in Jerusalem. You will never weep again; he will show favor to you at the sound of your outcry; as soon as he hears, he will answer you. ²⁰ The Lord will give you meager bread and water during oppression, but your Teacher^A will not hide any longer. Your eyes will see your Teacher, ²¹ and whenever you turn to the right or to the left, your ears will hear this command behind you: "This is the way. Walk in it." ²² Then you will defile your silver-plated idols and your gold-plated images. You will throw them away like menstrual cloths, and call them filth.

²³ Then he will send rain for your seed that you have sown in the ground, and the food, the produce of the ground, will be rich and plentiful. On that day your cattle will graze in open pastures. ²⁴ The oxen and donkeys that work the ground will eat salted fodder scattered with winnowing shovel and fork. ²⁵ Streams flowing with water will be on every high mountain and every raised hill on the day of great slaughter when the towers fall. ²⁶ The moonlight will be as bright as the sunlight, and the sunlight will be seven

^A30:20 Or *teachers*

times brighter — like the light of seven days — on the day that the LORD bandages his people's injuries and heals the wounds he inflicted.

ANNIHILATION OF THE ASSYRIANS

27 Look there! The LORD [A] is coming from far away,
    his anger burning and heavy with smoke. [B]
    His lips are full of fury,
    and his tongue is like a consuming fire.

28 His breath is like an overflowing torrent
    that rises to the neck.
    He comes to sift the nations in a sieve of destruction
    and to put a bridle on the jaws of the peoples
    to lead them astray.

29 Your singing will be like that
    on the night of a holy festival,
    and your heart will rejoice
    like one who walks to the music of a flute,
    going up to the mountain of the LORD,
    to the Rock of Israel.

30 And the LORD will make the splendor of his voice heard
    and reveal his arm striking in angry wrath
    and a flame of consuming fire,
    in driving rain, a torrent, and hailstones.

31 Assyria will be shattered by the voice of the LORD.
    He will strike with a rod.

32 And every stroke of the appointed [C] staff
    that the LORD brings down on him
    will be to the sound of tambourines and lyres;
    he will fight against him with brandished weapons.

33 Indeed! Topheth has been ready
    for the king for a long time.
    Its funeral pyre is deep and wide,
    with plenty of fire and wood.
    The breath of the LORD, like a torrent of burning sulfur,
    kindles it.

THE LORD, THE ONLY HELP

31 Woe to those who go down to Egypt for help
    and who depend on horses!
    They trust in the abundance of chariots
    and in the large number of horsemen.
    They do not look to the Holy One of Israel
    and they do not seek the LORD.

2   But he also is wise and brings disaster.
    He does not go back on what he says;
    he will rise up against the house of the wicked
    and against the allies of evildoers.

[A] 30:27 Or *Look, the name of the LORD*   [B] 30:27 Hb obscure   [C] 30:32 Some Hb mss read *punishing*

³ Egyptians are men, not God;
    their horses are flesh, not spirit.
When the LORD raises his hand to strike,
    the helper will stumble
and the one who is helped will fall;
    both will perish together.

⁴ For this is what the LORD said to me:
As a lion or young lion growls over its prey
    when a band of shepherds is called out against it,
and is not terrified by their shouting
    or subdued by their noise,
so the LORD of Armies will come down
    to fight on Mount Zion
    and on its hill.

⁵ Like hovering birds,
    so the LORD of Armies will protect Jerusalem —
by protecting it, he will rescue it,
    by sparing it, he will deliver it.

⁶ Return to the one the Israelites have greatly rebelled against. ⁷ For on that day, every one of you will reject the silver and gold idols that your own hands have sinfully made.

⁸ Then Assyria will fall,
    but not by human sword;
a sword will devour him,
    but not one made by man.
He will flee from the sword;
    his young men will be put to forced labor.
⁹ His rock^A will pass away because of fear,
    and his officers will be afraid because of the signal flag.
This is the LORD's declaration — whose fire is in Zion and whose furnace is in Jerusalem.

THE RIGHTEOUS KINGDOM ANNOUNCED

32 Indeed, a king will reign righteously,
    and rulers will rule justly.
² Each will be like a shelter from the wind,
    a refuge from the rain,
like flowing streams in a dry land
    and the shade of a massive rock in an arid land.
³ Then the eyes of those who see will not be closed,
    and the ears of those who hear will listen.
⁴ The reckless mind will gain knowledge,
    and the stammering tongue will speak clearly and fluently.
⁵ A fool will no longer be called a noble,
    nor a scoundrel said to be important.

---

^A 31:9 Perhaps the Assyrian king

⁶ For a fool speaks foolishness
  and his mind plots iniquity.
  He lives in a godless way
  and speaks falsely about the LORD.
  He leaves the hungry empty
  and deprives the thirsty of drink.
⁷ The scoundrel's weapons are destructive;
  he hatches plots to destroy the needy with lies,
  even when the poor person says what is right.
⁸ But a noble person plans noble things;
  he stands up for noble causes.

⁹ Stand up, you complacent women;
  listen to me.
  Pay attention to what I say,
  you overconfident daughters.
¹⁰ In a little more than a year
  you overconfident ones will shudder,
  for the grapes will fail
  and the harvest will not come.
¹¹ Shudder, you complacent ones;
  tremble, you overconfident ones!
  Strip yourselves bare
  and put sackcloth around your waists.
¹² Beat your breasts in mourning
  for the delightful fields and the fruitful vines,
¹³ for the ground of my people
  growing thorns and briers,
  indeed, for every joyous house in the jubilant city.
¹⁴ For the palace will be deserted,
  the busy city abandoned.
  The hill and the watchtower will become
  barren places forever,
  the joy of wild donkeys,
  and a pasture for flocks,
¹⁵ until the Spirit^A from on high is poured out on us.
  Then the desert will become an orchard,
  and the orchard will seem like a forest.
¹⁶ Then justice will inhabit the wilderness,
  and righteousness will dwell in the orchard.
¹⁷ The result of righteousness will be peace;
  the effect of righteousness
  will be quiet confidence forever.
¹⁸ Then my people will dwell in a peaceful place,
  in safe and secure dwellings.
¹⁹ But hail will level the forest,^B
  and the city will sink into the depths.
²⁰ You will be happy as you sow seed

^A32:15 Or *a wind*   ^B32:19 Hb obscure

beside abundant water,
and as you let oxen and donkeys range freely.

THE LORD RISES UP

33 Woe, you destroyer never destroyed,
you traitor never betrayed!
When you have finished destroying,
you will be destroyed.
When you have finished betraying,
they will betray you.

² LORD, be gracious to us! We wait for you.
Be our strength every morning
and our salvation in time of trouble.
³ The peoples flee at the thunderous noise;
the nations scatter when you rise in your majesty.
⁴ Your spoil will be gathered as locusts are gathered;
people will swarm over it like an infestation of locusts.
⁵ The LORD is exalted, for he dwells on high;
he has filled Zion with justice and righteousness.
⁶ There will be times of security for you —
a storehouse of salvation, wisdom, and knowledge.
The fear of the LORD is Zion's treasure.

⁷ Listen! Their warriors cry loudly in the streets;
the messengers of peace weep bitterly.
⁸ The highways are deserted;
travel has ceased.
An agreement has been broken,
citiesᴬ despised,
and human life disregarded.
⁹ The land mourns and withers;
Lebanon is ashamed and wilted.
Sharon is like a desert;
Bashan and Carmel shake off their leaves.
¹⁰ "Now I will rise up," says the LORD.
"Now I will lift myself up.
Now I will be exalted.
¹¹ You will conceive chaff;
you will give birth to stubble.
Your breath is fire that will consume you.
¹² The peoples will be burned to ashes,
like thorns cut down and burned in a fire.
¹³ You who are far off, hear what I have done;
you who are near, know my strength."

¹⁴ The sinners in Zion are afraid;
trembling seizes the ungodly:

ᴬ33:8 DSS read *witnesses*

"Who among us can dwell with a consuming fire?
Who among us can dwell with ever-burning flames?"

¹⁵ The one who lives righteously
and speaks rightly,
who refuses profit from extortion,
whose hand never takes a bribe,
who stops his ears from listening to murderous plots
and shuts his eyes against evil schemes —

¹⁶ he will dwell on the heights;
his refuge will be the rocky fortresses,
his food provided, his water assured.

¹⁷ Your eyes will see the King in his beauty;
you will see a vast land.

¹⁸ Your mind will meditate on the past terror:
"Where is the accountant?ᴬ
Where is the tribute collector?ᴮ
Where is the one who spied out our defenses?"ᶜ

¹⁹ You will no longer see the barbarians,
a people whose speech is difficult to comprehend —
who stammer in a language that is not understood.

²⁰ Look at Zion, the city of our festival times.
Your eyes will see Jerusalem,
a peaceful pasture, a tent that does not wander;
its tent pegs will not be pulled up
nor will any of its cords be loosened.

²¹ For the majestic one, our LORD, will be there,
a place of rivers and broad streams
where ships that are rowed will not go,
and majestic vessels will not pass.

²² For the LORD is our Judge,
the LORD is our Lawgiver,
the LORD is our King.
He will save us.

²³ Your ropes are slack;
they cannot hold the base of the mast
or spread out the flag.
Then abundant spoil will be divided,
the lame will plunder it,

²⁴ and none there will say, "I am sick."
The people who dwell there
will be forgiven their iniquity.

THE JUDGMENT OF THE NATIONS

34 You nations, come here and listen;
you peoples, pay attention!
Let the earth and all that fills it hear,
the world and all that comes from it.

ᴬ33:18 Lit *counter*   ᴮ33:18 Lit *weigher*   ᶜ33:18 Lit *who counts towers*

2 The LORD is angry with all the nations,
 furious with all their armies.
 He will set them apart for destruction,
 giving them over to slaughter.
3 Their slain will be thrown out,
 and the stench of their corpses will rise;
 the mountains will flow^A with their blood.
4 All^B the stars in the sky will dissolve.
 The sky will roll up like a scroll,
 and its stars will all wither
 as leaves wither on the vine,
 and foliage on the fig tree.

THE JUDGMENT OF EDOM

5 When my sword has drunk its fill^C in the heavens,
 it will then come down on Edom
 and on the people I have set apart for destruction.
6 The LORD's sword is covered with blood.
 It drips with fat,
 with the blood of lambs and goats,
 with the fat of the kidneys of rams.
 For the LORD has a sacrifice in Bozrah,
 a great slaughter in the land of Edom.
7 The wild oxen will be struck^D down with them,
 and young bulls with the mighty bulls.
 Their land will be soaked with^E blood,
 and their soil will be saturated with fat.

8 For the LORD has a day of vengeance,
 a time of paying back Edom
 for its hostility against Zion.
9 Edom's streams will be turned into pitch,
 her soil into sulfur;
 her land will become burning pitch.
10 It will never go out — day or night.
 Its smoke will go up forever.
 It will be desolate, from generation to generation;
 no one will pass through it forever and ever.
11 Eagle owls^F and herons^G will possess it,
 and long-eared owls and ravens will dwell there.
 The LORD will stretch out a measuring line
 and a plumb line over her
 for her destruction and chaos.
12 No nobles will be left to proclaim a king,
 and all her princes will come to nothing.
13 Her palaces will be overgrown with thorns;

---

^A34:3 Or melt, or dissolve ^B34:4 DSS read And the valleys will be split, and all
^C34:5 DSS read sword will appear ^D34:7 Or will go ^E34:7 Or will drink its
fill of ^F34:11 Or Pelicans ^G34:11 Or hedgehogs

her fortified cities, with thistles and briers.
She will become a dwelling for jackals,
an abode[A] for ostriches.

14 The desert creatures will meet hyenas,
and one wild goat will call to another.
Indeed, the night birds will stay there
and will find a resting place.

15 Sand partridges[B] will make their nests there;
they will lay and hatch their eggs
and will gather their broods under their shadows.
Indeed, the birds of prey will gather there,
each with its mate.

16 Search and read the scroll of the LORD:
Not one of them will be missing,
none will be lacking its mate,
because he has ordered it by my[C] mouth,
and he will gather them by his Spirit.

17 He has cast the lot for them;
his hand allotted their portion with a measuring line.
They will possess it forever;
they will dwell in it from generation to generation.

THE RANSOMED RETURN TO ZION

35 The wilderness and the dry land will be glad;
the desert will rejoice and blossom like a wildflower.[D]

2 It will blossom abundantly
and will also rejoice with joy and singing.
The glory of Lebanon will be given to it,
the splendor of Carmel and Sharon.
They will see the glory of the LORD,
the splendor of our God.

3 Strengthen the weak hands,
steady the shaking knees!

4 Say to the cowardly:
"Be strong; do not fear!
Here is your God; vengeance is coming.
God's retribution is coming; he will save you."

5 Then the eyes of the blind will be opened,
and the ears of the deaf unstopped.

6 Then the lame will leap like a deer,
and the tongue of the mute will sing for joy,
for water will gush in the wilderness,
and streams in the desert;

7 the parched ground will become a pool,
and the thirsty land springs.
In the haunt of jackals, in their lairs,

A34:13 DSS, LXX, Syr, Tg; MT reads *jackals, grass*   B34:15 Or *Arrow snakes,*
or *Owls*   C34:16 Some Hb mss; other Hb mss, DSS, Syr, Tg read *his*   D35:1 Or
meadow saffron ; traditionally *rose*

there will be grass, reeds, and papyrus.
8   A road will be there and a way;
     it will be called the Holy Way.
     The unclean will not travel on it,
     but it will be for the one who walks the path.
     Fools will not wander on it.
9   There will be no lion there,
     and no vicious beast will go up on it;
     they will not be found there.
     But the redeemed will walk on it,
10   and the ransomed of the LORD will return
     and come to Zion with singing,
     crowned with unending joy.
     Joy and gladness will overtake them,
     and sorrow and sighing will flee.

SENNACHERIB'S INVASION

36 In the fourteenth year of King Hezekiah, King Sennacherib of Assyria attacked all the fortified cities of Judah and captured them. ² Then the king of Assyria sent his royal spokesman, along with a massive army, from Lachish to King Hezekiah at Jerusalem. The Assyrian stood near the conduit of the upper pool, by the road to the Launderer's Field. ³ Eliakim son of Hilkiah, who was in charge of the palace, Shebna the court secretary, and Joah son of Asaph, the court historian, came out to him.

⁴ The royal spokesman said to them, "Tell Hezekiah:

The great king, the king of Assyria, says this: What are you relying on?ᴬ ⁵ Youᴮ think mere words are strategy and strength for war. Who are you now relying on that you have rebelled against me? ⁶ Look, you are relying on Egypt, that splintered reed of a staff that will pierce the hand of anyone who grabs it and leans on it. This is how Pharaoh king of Egypt is to all who rely on him. ⁷ Suppose you say to me, 'We rely on the LORD our God.' Isn't he the one whose high places and altars Hezekiah has removed, saying to Judah and Jerusalem, 'You are to worship at this altar'?

⁸ "Now make a deal with my master, the king of Assyria. I'll give you two thousand horses if you're able to supply riders for them! ⁹ How then can you drive back a single officer among the least of my master's servants? How can you rely on Egypt for chariots and horsemen? ¹⁰ Have I attacked this land to destroy it without the LORD's approval? The LORD said to me, 'Attack this land and destroy it.'"

¹¹ Then Eliakim, Shebna, and Joah said to the royal spokesman, "Please speak to your servants in Aramaic, since we understand it. Don't speak to us in Hebrewᶜ within earshot of the people who are on the wall."

¹² But the royal spokesman replied, "Has my master sent me to speak these words to your master and to you, and not to the men who are sitting on the

---

ᴬ36:4 Lit *What is this trust that you trust*   ᴮ36:5 Many Hb mss, DSS, 2Kg 18:20; MT reads *I*   ᶜ36:11 Lit *Judahite*, also in v. 13

wall, who are destined with you to eat their own excrement and drink their own urine?"

¹³ Then the royal spokesman stood and called out loudly in Hebrew: Listen to the words of the great king, the king of Assyria! ¹⁴ This is what the king says: "Don't let Hezekiah deceive you, for he cannot rescue you. ¹⁵ Don't let Hezekiah persuade you to rely on the Lord, saying, 'The Lord will certainly rescue us! This city will not be handed over to the king of Assyria.'"

¹⁶ Don't listen to Hezekiah, for this is what the king of Assyria says: "Make peaceᴬ with me and surrender to me. Then every one of you may eat from his own vine and his own fig tree and drink water from his own cistern ¹⁷ until I come and take you away to a land like your own land — a land of grain and new wine, a land of bread and vineyards. ¹⁸ Beware that Hezekiah does not mislead you by saying, 'The Lord will rescue us.' Has any one of the gods of the nations rescued his land from the power of the king of Assyria? ¹⁹ Where are the gods of Hamath and Arpad? Where are the gods of Sepharvaim? Have they rescued Samaria from my power? ²⁰ Who among all the gods of these lands ever rescued his land from my power? So will the Lord rescue Jerusalem from my power?"

²¹ But they kept silent; they didn't say anything, for the king's command was, "Don't answer him." ²² Then Eliakim son of Hilkiah, who was in charge of the palace, Shebna the court secretary, and Joah son of Asaph, the court historian, came to Hezekiah with their clothes torn and reported to him the words of the royal spokesman.

HEZEKIAH SEEKS ISAIAH'S COUNSEL

37 When King Hezekiah heard their report, he tore his clothes, put on sackcloth, and went to the Lord's temple. ² He sent Eliakim, who was in charge of the palace, Shebna the court secretary, and the leading priests, who were wearing sackcloth, to the prophet Isaiah son of Amoz. ³ They said to him, "This is what Hezekiah says: 'Today is a day of distress, rebuke, and disgrace. It is as if children have come to the point of birth, and there is no strength to deliver them. ⁴ Perhaps the Lord your God will hear all the words of the royal spokesman, whom his master the king of Assyria sent to mock the living God, and will rebuke him for the words that the Lord your God has heard. Therefore offer a prayer for the surviving remnant.'"

⁵ So the servants of King Hezekiah went to Isaiah, ⁶ who said to them, "Tell your master, 'The Lord says this: Don't be afraid because of the words you have heard, with which the king of Assyria's attendants have blasphemed me. ⁷ I am about to put a spirit in him and he will hear a rumor and return to his own land, where I will cause him to fall by the sword.'"

SENNACHERIB'S LETTER

⁸ When the royal spokesman heard that the king of Assyria had pulled out of Lachish, he left and found him fighting against Libnah. ⁹ The king had heard concerning King Tirhakah of Cush, "He has set out to fight against you." So

ᴬ36:16 Lit a blessing

when he heard this, he sent messengers to Hezekiah, saying, ¹⁰ "Say this to King Hezekiah of Judah: 'Don't let your God, on whom you rely, deceive you by promising that Jerusalem won't be handed over to the king of Assyria. ¹¹ Look, you have heard what the kings of Assyria have done to all the countries: they completely destroyed them. Will you be rescued? ¹² Did the gods of the nations that my predecessors destroyed rescue them — Gozan, Haran, Rezeph, and the Edenites in Telassar? ¹³ Where is the king of Hamath, the king of Arpad, the king of the city of ᴬ Sepharvaim, Hena, or Ivvah?' "

HEZEKIAH'S PRAYER

¹⁴ Hezekiah took the letter from the messengers' hands, read it, then went up to the Lord's temple and spread it out before the Lord. ¹⁵ Then Hezekiah prayed to the Lord:

¹⁶ Lord of Armies, God of Israel, enthroned between the cherubim, you are God — you alone — of all the kingdoms of the earth. You made the heavens and the earth. ¹⁷ Listen closely, Lord, and hear; open your eyes, Lord, and see. Hear all the words that Sennacherib has sent to mock the living God. ¹⁸ Lord, it is true that the kings of Assyria have devastated all these countries and their lands. ¹⁹ They have thrown their gods into the fire, for they were not gods but made from wood and stone by human hands. So they have destroyed them. ²⁰ Now, Lord our God, save us from his power so that all the kingdoms of the earth may know that you, Lord, are God ᴮ — you alone.

GOD'S ANSWER THROUGH ISAIAH

²¹ Then Isaiah son of Amoz sent a message to Hezekiah: "The Lord, the God of Israel, says, 'Because you prayed to me about King Sennacherib of Assyria, ²² this is the word the Lord has spoken against him:

Virgin Daughter Zion
despises you and scorns you;
Daughter Jerusalem shakes her head
behind your back.
23 Who is it you have mocked and blasphemed?
Against whom have you raised your voice
and lifted your eyes in pride?
Against the Holy One of Israel!
24 You have mocked the Lord through ᶜ your servants.
You have said, "With my many chariots
I have gone up to the heights of the mountains,
to the far recesses of Lebanon.
I cut down its tallest cedars,
its choice cypress trees.
I came to its distant heights,
its densest forest.
25 I dug wells and drank water in foreign lands. ᴰ
I dried up all the streams of Egypt
with the soles of my feet."

ᴬ 37:13 Or king of Lair, ᴮ 37:20 are God supplied for clarity; see v. 16
ᶜ 37:24 Lit by the hand of ᴰ 37:25 DSS, 2Kg 19:24; MT omits in foreign lands

26   Have you not heard?
      I designed it long ago;
      I planned it in days gone by.
      I have now brought it to pass,
      and you have crushed fortified cities
      into piles of rubble.
27   Their inhabitants have become powerless,
      dismayed, and ashamed.
      They are plants of the field,
      tender grass,
      grass on the rooftops,
      blasted by the east wind.^A

28   But I know your sitting down,
      your going out and your coming in,
      and your raging against me.
29   Because your raging against me
      and your arrogance have reached
            my ears,
      I will put my hook in your nose
      and my bit in your mouth;
      I will make you go back
      the way you came.

30 " 'This will be the sign for you: This year you will eat what grows on its own, and in the second year what grows from that. But in the third year sow and reap, plant vineyards and eat their fruit. 31 The surviving remnant of the house of Judah will again take root downward and bear fruit upward. 32 For a remnant will go out from Jerusalem, and survivors from Mount Zion. The zeal of the LORD of Armies will accomplish this.'

33 "Therefore, this is what the LORD says about the king of Assyria:
      He will not enter this city,
      shoot an arrow here,
      come before it with a shield,
      or build up a siege ramp against it.
34   He will go back
      the way he came,
      and he will not enter this city.
            This is the LORD's declaration.
35   I will defend this city and rescue it
      for my sake
      and for the sake of my servant David."

DEFEAT AND DEATH OF SENNACHERIB

36 Then the angel of the LORD went out and struck down one hundred eighty-five thousand in the camp of the Assyrians. When the people got up the next morning — there were all the dead bodies! 37 So King Sennacherib of Assyria broke camp and left. He returned home and lived in Nineveh.

^A37:27 DSS; MT reads rooftops, field before standing grain

38 One day, while he was worshiping in the temple of his god Nisroch, his sons Adrammelech and Sharezer struck him down with the sword and escaped to the land of Ararat. Then his son Esar-haddon became king in his place.

HEZEKIAH'S ILLNESS AND RECOVERY

38

In those days Hezekiah became terminally ill. The prophet Isaiah son of Amoz came and said to him, "This is what the LORD says: 'Set your house in order, for you are about to die; you will not recover.' "[A]

2 Then Hezekiah turned his face to the wall and prayed to the LORD. 3 He said, "Please, LORD, remember how I have walked before you faithfully and whole-heartedly, and have done what pleases you."[B] And Hezekiah wept bitterly.

4 Then the word of the LORD came to Isaiah: 5 "Go and tell Hezekiah, 'This is what the LORD God of your ancestor David says: I have heard your prayer; I have seen your tears. Look, I am going to add fifteen years to your life.[C] 6 And I will rescue you and this city from the grasp of the king of Assyria; I will defend this city. 7 This is the sign to you from the LORD that he will do what[D] he has promised:[E] 8 I am going to make the sun's shadow that goes down on the stairway of Ahaz go back by ten steps.' " So the sun's shadow[F] went back the ten steps it had descended.

9 A poem by King Hezekiah of Judah after he had been sick and had recovered from his illness:

10   I said: In the prime[G] of my life
     I must go to the gates of Sheol;
     I am deprived of the rest of my years.
11   I said: I will never see the LORD,
     the LORD in the land of the living;
     I will not look on humanity any longer
     with the inhabitants of what is passing away.[H]
12   My dwelling is plucked up and removed from me
     like a shepherd's tent.
     I have rolled up my life like a weaver;
     he cuts me off from the loom.
     By nightfall[I] you make an end of me.
13   I thought until the morning:
     He will break all my bones like a lion.
     By nightfall you make an end of me.
14   I chirp like a swallow or a crane;
     I moan like a dove.
     My eyes grow weak looking upward.
     Lord, I am oppressed; support me.

15   What can I say?
     He has spoken to me,
     and he himself has done it.

[A]38:1 Lit *live*   [B]38:3 Lit *what is good in your eyes*   [C]38:5 Lit *days*, also in v. 10
[D]38:7 Lit *this thing*   [E]38:7 Lit *said*   [F]38:8 Lit *And the sun*   [G]38:10 Lit *quiet*
[H]38:11 Some Hb mss, Tg read *of the world*   [I]38:12 Lit *From day until night*, also in v. 13

I walk along slowly all my years
because of the bitterness of my soul.
¹⁶ Lord, by such things people live,
and in every one of them my spirit finds life;
you have restored me to health
and let me live.
¹⁷ Indeed, it was for my own well-being
that I had such intense bitterness;
but your love has delivered me
from the Pit of destruction,
for you have thrown all my sins behind your back.
¹⁸ For Sheol cannot thank you;
Death cannot praise you.
Those who go down to the Pit
cannot hope for your faithfulness.
¹⁹ The living, only the living can thank you,
as I do today;
a father will make your faithfulness known to children.
²⁰ The Lord is ready to save me;
we will play stringed instruments
all the days of our lives
at the house of the Lord.

²¹ Now Isaiah had said, "Let them take a lump of pressed figs and apply it to his infected skin, so that he may recover." ²² And Hezekiah had asked, "What is the sign that I will go up to the Lord's temple?"

HEZEKIAH'S FOLLY

39 At that time Merodach-baladan son of Baladan, king of Babylon, sent letters and a gift to Hezekiah since he heard that he had been sick and had recovered. ² Hezekiah was pleased with the letters, and he showed the envoys his treasure house — the silver, the gold, the spices, and the precious oil — and all his armory, and everything that was found in his treasuries. There was nothing in his palace and in all his realm that Hezekiah did not show them.

³ Then the prophet Isaiah came to King Hezekiah and asked him, "What did these men say, and where did they come to you from?"

Hezekiah replied, "They came to me from a distant country, from Babylon."

⁴ Isaiah asked, "What have they seen in your palace?"

Hezekiah answered, "They have seen everything in my palace. There isn't anything in my treasuries that I didn't show them."

⁵ Then Isaiah said to Hezekiah, "Hear the word of the Lord of Armies: ⁶ 'Look, the days are coming when everything in your palace and all that your fathers have stored up until today will be carried off to Babylon; nothing will be left,' says the Lord. ⁷ 'Some of your descendants — who come from you, whom you father — will be taken away, and they will become eunuchs in the palace of the king of Babylon.'"

⁸ Then Hezekiah said to Isaiah, "The word of the Lord that you have spoken is good," for he thought: There will be peace and security during my lifetime.

GOD'S PEOPLE COMFORTED

40 "Comfort, comfort my people,"
says your God.

2 "Speak tenderly to^A Jerusalem,
and announce to her
that her time of forced labor is over,
her iniquity has been pardoned,
and she has received from the LORD's hand
double for all her sins."

3 A voice of one crying out:
Prepare the way of the LORD in the wilderness;
make a straight highway for our God
in the desert.

4 Every valley will be lifted up,
and every mountain and hill will be leveled;
the uneven ground will become smooth
and the rough places, a plain.

5 And the glory of the LORD will appear,
and all humanity^B together will see it,
for the mouth of the LORD has spoken.

6 A voice was saying, "Cry out!"
Another said,^C "What should I cry out?"
"All humanity is grass,
and all its goodness is like the flower of the field.

7 The grass withers, the flowers fade
when the breath^D of the LORD blows on them;^E
indeed, the people are grass.

8 The grass withers, the flowers fade,
but the word of our God remains forever."

9 Zion, herald of good news,
go up on a high mountain.
Jerusalem, herald of good news,
raise your voice loudly.
Raise it, do not be afraid!
Say to the cities of Judah,
"Here is your God!"

10 See, the Lord GOD comes with strength,
and his power establishes his rule.
His wages are with him,
and his reward accompanies him.

11 He protects his flock like a shepherd;
he gathers the lambs in his arms
and carries them in the fold of his garment.
He gently leads those that are nursing.

---

^A40:2 Lit *Speak to the heart of* ^B40:5 Lit *flesh* ^C40:6 DSS, LXX, Vg read *I said*
^D40:7 Or *wind*, or *Spirit* ^E40:7 Lit *it*

¹² Who has measured the waters in the hollow of his hand
or marked off the heavens with the span of his hand?
Who has gathered the dust of the earth in a measure
or weighed the mountains on a balance
and the hills on the scales?
¹³ Who has directed^A the Spirit of the LORD,
or who gave him counsel?
¹⁴ Who did he consult?
Who gave him understanding
and taught him the paths of justice?
Who taught him knowledge
and showed him the way of understanding?
¹⁵ Look, the nations are like a drop in a bucket;
they are considered as a speck of dust on the scales;
he lifts up the islands like fine dust.
¹⁶ Lebanon's cedars are not enough for fuel,
or its animals enough for a burnt offering.
¹⁷ All the nations are as nothing before him;
they are considered by him
as empty nothingness.

¹⁸ With whom will you compare God?
What likeness will you set up for comparison with him?
¹⁹ An idol? — something that a smelter casts
and a metalworker plates with gold
and makes silver chains for?
²⁰ A poor person contributes wood for a pedestal
that will not rot.^B
He looks for a skilled craftsman
to set up an idol that will not fall over.

²¹ Do you not know?
Have you not heard?
Has it not been declared to you
from the beginning?
Have you not considered
the foundations of the earth?
²² God is enthroned above the circle of the earth;
its inhabitants are like grasshoppers.
He stretches out the heavens like thin cloth
and spreads them out like a tent to live in.
²³ He reduces princes to nothing
and makes judges of the earth like a wasteland.
²⁴ They are barely planted, barely sown,
their stem hardly takes root in the ground
when he blows on them and they wither,
and a whirlwind carries them away like stubble.

---

^A40:13 Or *measured,* or *comprehended*   ^B40:20 Or *who is too poor for such an offering,* or *who chooses mulberry wood as a votive gift;* Hb obscure

25 "To whom will you compare me,
   or who is my equal?" asks the Holy One.
26 Look up^A and see!
   Who created these?
   He brings out the stars by number;
   he calls all of them by name.
   Because of his great power and strength,
   not one of them is missing.

27 Jacob, why do you say,
   and, Israel, why do you assert:
   "My way is hidden from the LORD,
   and my claim is ignored by my God"?
28 Do you not know?
   Have you not heard?
   The LORD is the everlasting God,
   the Creator of the whole earth.
   He never becomes faint or weary;
   there is no limit to his understanding.
29 He gives strength to the faint
   and strengthens the powerless.
30 Youths may become faint and weary,
   and young men stumble and fall,
31 but those who trust in the LORD
   will renew their strength;
   they will soar on wings like eagles;
   they will run and not become weary,
   they will walk and not faint.

THE LORD VERSUS THE NATIONS' GODS

41 "Be silent before me, coasts and islands!
   And let peoples renew their strength.
   Let them approach; let them testify;
   let's come together for the trial.
2 Who has stirred up someone from the east?
   In righteousness he calls him to serve.^B,C
   The LORD hands nations over to him,
   and he subdues kings.
   He makes them like dust with his sword,
   like wind-driven stubble with his bow.
3 He pursues them, going on safely,
   hardly touching the path with his feet.
4 Who has performed and done this,
   calling the generations
      from the beginning?
   I am the LORD, the first
   and with the last — I am he."

---

^A 40:26 Lit *Lift up your eyes on high*   ^B 41:2 Or *Righteousness calls him to serve*
^C 41:2 Lit *to his foot*

⁵ The coasts and islands see and are afraid,
  the whole earth trembles.
  They approach and arrive.
⁶ Each one helps the other,
  and says to another, "Take courage!"
⁷ The craftsman encourages the metalworker;
  the one who flattens with the hammer
  encourages the one who strikes the anvil,
  saying of the soldering, "It is good."
  He fastens it with nails so that it will not fall over.

⁸ But you, Israel, my servant,
  Jacob, whom I have chosen,
  descendant of Abraham, my friend —
⁹ I brought^A you from the ends of the earth
  and called you from its farthest corners.
  I said to you: You are my servant;
  I have chosen you; I haven't rejected you.
¹⁰ Do not fear, for I am with you;
  do not be afraid, for I am your God.
  I will strengthen you; I will help you;
  I will hold on to you with my righteous
    right hand.

¹¹ Be sure that all who are enraged against you
  will be ashamed and disgraced;
  those who contend with you
  will become as nothing and will perish.
¹² You will look for those who contend with you,
  but you will not find them.
  Those who war against you
  will become absolutely nothing.
¹³ For I am the LORD your God,
  who holds your right hand,
  who says to you, 'Do not fear,
  I will help you.
¹⁴ Do not fear, you worm Jacob,
  you men^B of Israel.
  I will help you' —
    this is the LORD's declaration.
  Your Redeemer is the Holy One of Israel.
¹⁵ See, I will make you into a sharp threshing board,
  new, with many teeth.
  You will thresh mountains and pulverize them
  and make hills into chaff.
¹⁶ You will winnow them
  and a wind will carry them away,
  a whirlwind will scatter them.

^A 41:9 Or seized ^B 41:14 LXX reads small number; DSS read dead ones

But you will rejoice in the LORD;
you will boast in the Holy One of Israel.

17 The poor and the needy seek water, but there is none;
their tongues are parched with thirst.
I will answer them.
I am the LORD, the God of Israel.
I will not abandon them.
18 I will open rivers on the barren heights,
and springs in the middle of the plains.
I will turn the desert into a pool
and dry land into springs.
19 I will plant cedars,
acacias, myrtles, and olive trees in the wilderness.
I will put juniper trees,
elms, and cypress trees together in the desert,
20 so that all may see and know,
consider and understand,
that the hand of the LORD has done this,
the Holy One of Israel has created it.

21 "Submit your case," says the LORD.
"Present your arguments," says Jacob's King.
22 "Let them come and tell us
what will happen.
Tell us the past events,
so that we may reflect on them
and know the outcome,
or tell us the future.
23 Tell us the coming events,
then we will know that you are gods.
Indeed, do something good or bad,
then we will be in awe^A when we see it.
24 Look, you are nothing
and your work is worthless.
Anyone who chooses you is detestable.

25 "I have stirred up one from the north, and he has come,
one from the east who invokes my^B name.
He will march over rulers as if they were mud,
like a potter who treads the clay.
26 Who told about this from the beginning,
so that we might know,
and from times past,
so that we might say, 'He is right'?
No one announced it,
no one told it,
no one heard your words.

---

^A 41:23 DSS read *we may hear*   ^B 41:25 DSS read *his*

27 I was the first to say to Zion,[A]
'Look! Here they are!'
And I gave Jerusalem a herald with good news.
28 When I look, there is no one;
there is no counselor among them;
when I ask them, they have nothing to say.
29 Look, all of them are a delusion;[B]
their works are nonexistent;
their images are wind and emptiness.

THE SERVANT'S MISSION

42 "This is my servant; I strengthen him,
this is my chosen one; I delight in him.
I have put my Spirit on him;
he will bring justice[C] to the nations.
2 He will not cry out or shout
or make his voice heard in the streets.
3 He will not break a bruised reed,
and he will not put out a smoldering wick;
he will faithfully bring justice.
4 He will not grow weak or be discouraged
until he has established justice on earth.
The coasts and islands will wait for his instruction."

5 This is what God, the LORD, says —
who created the heavens and stretched them out,
who spread out the earth and what comes from it,
who gives breath to the people on it
and spirit to those who walk on it —
6 "I am the LORD. I have called you
for a righteous purpose,[D]
and I will hold you by your hand.
I will watch over you, and I will appoint you
to be a covenant for the people
and a light to the nations,
7 in order to open blind eyes,
to bring out prisoners from the dungeon,
and those sitting in darkness from the prison house.
8 I am the LORD. That is my name,
and I will not give my glory to another
or my praise to idols.
9 The past events have indeed happened.
Now I declare new events;
I announce them to you before they occur."

A SONG OF PRAISE

10 Sing a new song to the LORD;

[A] 41:27 Lit First to Zion [B] 41:29 DSS, Syr read are nothing [C] 42:1 DSS read his justice [D] 42:6 Or you by my righteousness; lit you in righteousness

sing his praise from the ends of the earth,
you who go down to the sea with all that fills it,
you coasts and islands with your^A inhabitants.

11 Let the desert and its cities shout,
the settlements where Kedar dwells cry aloud.
Let the inhabitants of Sela sing for joy;
let them cry out from the mountaintops.

12 Let them give glory to the LORD
and declare his praise in the coasts and islands.

13 The LORD advances like a warrior;
he stirs up his zeal like a soldier.
He shouts, he roars aloud,
he prevails over his enemies.

14 "I have kept silent from ages past;
I have been quiet and restrained myself.
But now, I will groan like a woman in labor,
gasping breathlessly.

15 I will lay waste mountains and hills
and dry up all their vegetation.
I will turn rivers into islands
and dry up marshes.

16 I will lead the blind by a way they did not know;
I will guide them on paths they have not known.
I will turn darkness to light in front of them
and rough places into level ground.
This is what I will do for them,
and I will not abandon them.

17 They will be turned back and utterly ashamed —
those who trust in an idol
and say to a cast image,
'You are our gods!'

ISRAEL'S BLINDNESS AND DEAFNESS

18 "Listen, you deaf!
Look, you blind, so that you may see.

19 Who is blind but my servant,
or deaf like my messenger I am sending?
Who is blind like my dedicated one,^B
or blind like the servant of the LORD?

20 Though seeing many things,^C you pay no attention.
Though his ears are open, he does not listen."

21 Because of his righteousness, the LORD was pleased
to magnify his instruction and make it glorious.

22 But this is a people plundered and looted,
all of them trapped in holes

---

^A 42:10 Lit *their*   ^B 42:19 Hb obscure   ^C 42:20 Alt Hb tradition reads *You see many things;*

or imprisoned in dungeons.
They have become plunder
with no one to rescue them
and loot, with no one saying, "Give it back!"

23 Who among you will hear this?
Let him listen and obey in the future.
24 Who gave Jacob to the robber,^A
and Israel to the plunderers?
Was it not the LORD?
Have we not sinned against him?
They were not willing to walk in his ways,
and they would not listen to his instruction.
25 So he poured out his furious anger
and the power of war on Jacob.
It surrounded him with fire, but he did not know it;
it burned him, but he didn't take it to heart.

RESTORATION OF ISRAEL

43 Now this is what the LORD says —
the one who created you, Jacob,
and the one who formed you, Israel —
"Do not fear, for I have redeemed you;
I have called you by your name; you are mine.
2 I will be with you
when you pass through the waters,
and when you pass through the rivers,
they will not overwhelm you.
You will not be scorched
when you walk through the fire,
and the flame will not burn you.
3 For I am the LORD your God,
the Holy One of Israel, and your Savior.
I have given Egypt as a ransom for you,
Cush and Seba in your place.
4 Because you are precious in my sight
and honored, and I love you,
I will give people in exchange for you
and nations instead of your life.
5 Do not fear, for I am with you;
I will bring your descendants from the east,
and gather you from the west.
6 I will say to the north, 'Give them up!'
and to the south, 'Do not hold them back!'
Bring my sons from far away,
and my daughters from the ends of the earth —
7 everyone who bears my name
and is created for my glory.
I have formed them; indeed, I have made them."

^A 42:24 Lit to loot

YOU ARE MINE

ISAIAH 42–43

I miss Pluto.

When I was a kid, there were nine planets in our solar system. But somewhere between getting my college degree and buying our first house, Pluto got bumped from planet status on a technicality. I've never gotten used to rattling off the names of the heavenly bodies and stopping short at Neptune.

Recently I was bemoaning Pluto's tragic and seemingly unstable galactic status when my husband laughed and reasoned with me, "Honey. Pluto hasn't changed. Nothing has changed about what it's made of—it's just that the people who have never actually been to Pluto don't call it a planet anymore."

I bet you feel a lot like Pluto sometimes. I do. For better or worse, we allow someone who doesn't know us—someone trillions of miles away— define us. We receive the world's labels and live at the mercy of everyone else's "technicalities." We trade the truth we know about ourselves for a lie, and go on living misunderstood, mislabeled, or plain forgotten.

But how can we halt this orbit of lies? How can we respond when we're pretty sure some of the unfortunate (or downright awful) labels the world sticks to our chests are technically true about us?

Let's turn to God's Word together. Let's let the One who made us tell us what we're made of and what we're made for. **Only God has the ability to define you,** so let's see how He defines you.

He calls you beloved (Rm 9:25).
You are his treasured possession (Dt 7:6).

You are His child (Jn 1:12; Rm 8:17).
You are free (Gl 5:1).
You have been redeemed (Eph 1:7).
You have been and will be restored (Col 1:13-14; 1Pt 5:10).
You have been and can be forgiven (Heb 10:17; 1Jn 1:9).

That's not all. Your God—the One Hebrews 13:8 tells us is forever unchanging—He not only names you, He pursues you and cares for you personally.

He knew each of your days before you were conceived (Ps 139:16).
He has your name written on the palm of His hands (Is 49:16).
It is your name—yours!—which He has called "mine" (Is 43:1).
It is your head on which He numbers each strand of hair, and your tears of which He keeps count (Mt 10:29-31; Ps 56:8).
It was for you He died while you were yet a sinner (Rm 5:8).

The world will label you all your life. Tall, short, smart, bossy, ugly, pretty, worth it, and not. But here is the only label that truly matters:

"Now this is what the LORD says— the one who created you, Jacob, and the one who formed you, Israel— 'Do not fear, for I have redeemed you; I have called you by your name; you are mine.'"

ISAIAH 43:1

8 Bring out a people who are blind, yet have eyes,
and are deaf, yet have ears.
9 All the nations are gathered together,
and the peoples are assembled.
Who among them can declare this,
and tell us the former things?
Let them present their witnesses
to vindicate themselves,
so that people may hear and say, "It is true."
10 "You are my witnesses" —
this is the LORD's declaration —
"and my servant whom I have chosen,
so that you may know and believe me
and understand that I am he.
No god was formed before me,
and there will be none after me.
11 I — I am the LORD.
Besides me, there is no Savior.
12 I alone declared, saved, and proclaimed —
and not some foreign god[A] among you.
So you are my witnesses" —
this is the LORD's declaration —
"and[B] I am God.
13 Also, from today on I am he alone,
and none can rescue from my power.
I act, and who can reverse it?"

GOD'S DELIVERANCE OF REBELLIOUS ISRAEL

14 This is what the LORD, your Redeemer, the Holy One of Israel says:
Because of you, I will send an army[C] to Babylon
and bring all of them as fugitives,[D]
even the Chaldeans in the ships in which
they rejoice.[E]
15 I am the LORD, your Holy One,
the Creator of Israel, your King.

16 This is what the LORD says —
who makes a way in the sea,
and a path through raging water,
17 who brings out the chariot and horse,
the army and the mighty one together
(they lie down, they do not rise again;
they are extinguished, put out like a wick) —
18 "Do not remember the past events,
pay no attention to things of old.
19 Look, I am about to do something new;
even now it is coming. Do you not see it?

A 43:12 Lit not a foreigner   B 43:12 Or that   C 43:14 an army supplied for clarity
D 43:14 Or will break down all their bars   E 43:14 Hb obscure

Indeed, I will make a way in the wilderness,
rivers[A] in the desert.

20 Wild animals —
jackals and ostriches — will honor me,
because I provide water in the wilderness,
and rivers in the desert,
to give drink to my chosen people.

21 The people I formed for myself
will declare my praise.

22 "But, Jacob, you have not called on me,
because, Israel, you have become weary of me.

23 You have not brought me your sheep for burnt offerings
or honored me with your sacrifices.
I have not burdened you with offerings
or wearied you with incense.[B]

24 You have not bought me aromatic cane with silver,
or satisfied me with the fat of your sacrifices.
But you have burdened me with your sins;
you have wearied me with your iniquities.

25 "I — I sweep away your transgressions
for my own sake
and remember your sins no more.

26 Remind me. Let's argue the case together.
Recount the facts, so that you may be vindicated.

27 Your first father sinned,
and your mediators have rebelled against me.

28 So I defiled the officers of the sanctuary,
and set Jacob apart for destruction
and Israel for scorn.

SPIRITUAL BLESSING

44 "And now listen, Jacob my servant,
Israel whom I have chosen.

2 This is the word of the LORD
your Maker, the one who formed you from the womb:
He will help you.
Do not fear, Jacob my servant,
Jeshurun[C] whom I have chosen.

3 For I will pour water on the thirsty land
and streams on the dry ground;
I will pour out my Spirit on your descendants
and my blessing on your offspring.

4 They will sprout among[D] the grass
like poplars by flowing streams.

5 This one will say, 'I am the LORD's';

[A]43:19 DSS read *paths*   [B]43:23 I.e., with demands for offerings and incense
[C]44:2 = Upright One   [D]44:4 Some Hb mss, DSS, LXX read *as among*

another will use the name of Jacob;
still another will write on his hand, 'The LORD's,'
and take on the name of Israel."

NO GOD OTHER THAN THE LORD

⁶ This is what the LORD, the King of Israel and its Redeemer, the LORD of Armies, says:

I am the first and I am the last.
There is no God but me.
⁷ Who, like me, can announce the future?
Let him say so and make a case before me,
since I have established an ancient people.
Let these gods declare^ the coming things,
and what will take place.
⁸ Do not be startled or afraid.
Have I not told you and declared it long ago?
You are my witnesses!
Is there any God but me?
There is no other Rock; I do not know any.

⁹ All who make idols are nothing,
and what they treasure benefits no one.
Their witnesses do not see or know anything,
so they will be put to shame.
¹⁰ Who makes a god or casts a metal image
that benefits no one?
¹¹ Look, all its worshipers will be put to shame,
and the craftsmen are humans.
They all will assemble and stand;
they all will be startled and put to shame.

¹² The ironworker labors over the coals,
shapes the idol with hammers,
and works it with his strong arm.
Also he grows hungry and his strength fails;
he doesn't drink water and is faint.
¹³ The woodworker stretches out a measuring line,
he outlines it with a stylus;
he shapes it with chisels
and outlines it with a compass.
He makes it according to a human form,
like a beautiful person,
to dwell in a temple.
¹⁴ He cuts down^ cedars for his use,
or he takes a cypress or an oak.
He lets it grow strong among the trees of the forest.
He plants a laurel, and the rain makes it grow.
¹⁵ A person can use it for fuel.

^44:7 Lit declare them — ^B 44:14 Lit To cut down for himself

He takes some of it and warms himself;
also he kindles a fire and bakes bread;
he even makes it into a god and worships it;
he makes an idol from it and bows down to it.

16 He burns half of it in a fire,
and he roasts meat on that half.
He eats the roast and is satisfied.
He warms himself and says, "Ah!
I am warm, I see the blaze."

17 He makes a god or his idol with the rest of it.
He bows down to it and worships;
he prays to it, "Save me, for you are my god."

18 Such people ᴬ do not comprehend
and cannot understand,
for he has shut their eyes ᴮ so they cannot see,
and their minds so they cannot understand.

19 No one comes to his senses; ᶜ
no one has the perception or insight to say,
"I burned half of it in the fire,
I also baked bread on its coals,
I roasted meat and ate.
Should I make something detestable with the rest of it?
Should I bow down to a block of wood?"

20 He feeds on ᴰ ashes.
His deceived mind has led him astray,
and he cannot rescue himself,
or say, "Isn't there a lie in my right hand?"

21 Remember these things, Jacob,
and Israel, for you are my servant;
I formed you, you are my servant;
Israel, you will never be forgotten by me. ᴱ

22 I have swept away your transgressions like a cloud,
and your sins like a mist.
Return to me,
for I have redeemed you.

23 Rejoice, heavens, for the LORD has acted;
shout, depths of the earth.
Break out into singing, mountains,
forest, and every tree in it.
For the LORD has redeemed Jacob,
and glorifies himself through Israel.

RESTORATION OF ISRAEL THROUGH CYRUS

24 This is what the LORD, your Redeemer who formed you from the womb, says:
I am the LORD, who made everything;

ᴬ44:18 Lit They ᴮ44:18 Or for their eyes are shut ᶜ44:19 Lit No one returns to
his heart ᴰ44:20 Or He shepherds ᴱ44:21 DSS, LXX, Tg read Israel, do not
forget me

who stretched out the heavens by myself;
who alone spread out the earth;
²⁵ who destroys the omens of the false prophets
and makes fools of diviners;
who confounds the wise
and makes their knowledge foolishness;
²⁶ who confirms the message of his servant
and fulfills the counsel of his messengers;
who says to Jerusalem, "She will be inhabited,"
and to the cities of Judah, "They will be rebuilt,"
and I will restore her ruins;
²⁷ who says to the depths of the sea, "Be dry,"
and I will dry up your rivers;
²⁸ who says to Cyrus, "My shepherd,
he will fulfill all my pleasure"
and says to Jerusalem, "She will be rebuilt,"
and of the temple, "Its foundation will be laid."

45

The LORD says this to Cyrus, his anointed,
whose right hand I have grasped
to subdue nations before him
and disarm^A kings,
to open doors before him,
and even city gates will not be shut:
² "I will go before you
and level the uneven places;^B
I will shatter the bronze doors
and cut the iron bars in two.
³ I will give you the treasures of darkness
and riches from secret places,
so that you may know that I am the LORD.
I am the God of Israel, who calls you by your name.
⁴ I call you by your name,
for the sake of my servant Jacob
and Israel my chosen one.
I give a name to you,
though you do not know me.
⁵ I am the LORD, and there is no other;
there is no God but me.
I will strengthen^C you,
though you do not know me,
⁶ so that all may know from the rising of the sun to its setting
that there is no one but me.
I am the LORD, and there is no other.
⁷ I form light and create darkness,
I make success and create disaster;
I am the LORD, who does all these things.

---

^A45:1 Lit *unloosen the waist of*   ^B45:2 DSS, LXX read *the mountains*
^C45:5 Lit *gird*

8   "Heavens, sprinkle from above,
    and let the skies shower righteousness.
    Let the earth open up
    so that salvation will sprout
    and righteousness will spring up with it.
    I, the LORD, have created it.

9   "Woe to the one who argues
        with his Maker —
    one clay pot among many.[A]
    Does clay say to the one forming it,
    'What are you making?'
    Or does your work say,
    'He has no hands'?[B]
10 Woe to the one who says to his father,
    'What are you fathering?'
    or to his mother,[C]
    'What are you giving birth to?'"
11 This is what the LORD,
    the Holy One of Israel and its Maker, says:
    "Ask me what is to happen to[D] my sons,
    and instruct me about the work of my hands.
12 I made the earth,
    and created humans on it.
    It was my hands that stretched out the heavens,
    and I commanded everything in them.
13 I have stirred him up in righteousness,
    and will level all roads for him.
    He will rebuild my city,
    and set my exiles free,
    not for a price or a bribe,"
    says the LORD of Armies.

GOD ALONE IS THE SAVIOR

14 This is what the LORD says:
    "The products of Egypt
        and the merchandise of Cush
    and the Sabeans, men of stature,
    will come over to you
    and will be yours;
    they will follow you,
    they will come over in chains
    and bow down to you.
    They will confess[E] to you,
    'God is indeed with you, and there is no other;
    there is no other God.'"

[A]45:9 Lit a clay pot with clay pots of the ground   [B]45:9 Or making? Your work
has no hands.   [C]45:10 Lit to a woman   [D]45:11 Or me the coming things about
[E]45:14 Lit pray

¹⁵ Yes, you are a God who hides,
God of Israel, Savior.
¹⁶ All of them are put to shame, even humiliated;
the makers of idols go in humiliation together.
¹⁷ Israel will be saved by the LORD
with an everlasting salvation;
you will not be put to shame or humiliated
for all eternity.

¹⁸ For this is what the LORD says —
the Creator of the heavens,
the God who formed the earth and made it,
the one who established it
(he did not create it to be a wasteland,
but formed it to be inhabited) —
he says, "I am the LORD,
and there is no other.
¹⁹ I have not spoken in secret,
somewhere in a land of darkness.
I did not say to the descendants of Jacob:
Seek me in a wasteland.
I am the LORD, who speaks righteously,
who declares what is right.

²⁰ "Come, gather together,
and approach, you fugitives of the nations.
Those who carry their wooden idols
and pray to a god who cannot save
have no knowledge.
²¹ Speak up and present your case ᴬ —
yes, let them consult each other.
Who predicted this long ago?
Who announced it from ancient times?
Was it not I, the LORD?
There is no other God but me,
a righteous God and Savior;
there is no one except me.
²² Turn to me and be saved,
all the ends of the earth.
For I am God,
and there is no other.
²³ By myself I have sworn;
truth has gone from my mouth,
a word that will not be revoked:
Every knee will bow to me,
every tongue will swear allegiance.
²⁴ It will be said about me, 'Righteousness and strength
are found only in the LORD.'"

ᴬ45:21 Lit *and approach*

All who are enraged against him
will come to him and be put to shame.
25 All the descendants of Israel
will be justified and find glory through the LORD.

THERE IS NO ONE LIKE GOD

46 Bel crouches; Nebo cowers.
Idols depicting them are consigned to beasts and cattle.
The images you carry are loaded,
as a burden for the weary animal.
2 The gods cower; they crouch together;
they are not able to rescue the burden,
but they themselves go into captivity.

3 "Listen to me, house of Jacob,
all the remnant of the house of Israel,
who have been sustained from the womb,
carried along since birth.
4 I will be the same until your old age,
and I will bear you up when you turn gray.
I have made you, and I will carry you;
I will bear and rescue you.

5 "Who will you compare me or make me equal to?
Who will you measure me with,
so that we should be like each other?
6 Those who pour out their bags of gold
and weigh out silver on scales —
they hire a goldsmith and he makes it into a god.
Then they kneel and bow down to it.
7 They lift it to their shoulder and bear it along;
they set it in its place, and there it stands;
it does not budge from its place.
They cry out to it but it doesn't answer;
it saves no one from his trouble.

8 "Remember this and be brave;[A]
take it to heart, you transgressors!
9 Remember what happened long ago,
for I am God, and there is no other;
I am God, and no one is like me.
10 I declare the end from the beginning,
and from long ago what is not yet done,
saying: my plan will take place,
and I will do all my will.
11 I call a bird of prey[B] from the east,
a man for my purpose from a far country.
Yes, I have spoken; so I will also bring it about.

[A] 46:8 Hb obscure   [B] 46:11 = Cyrus

I have planned it; I will also do it.
12 Listen to me, you hardhearted,
  far removed from justice:
13 I am bringing my justice near;
  it is not far away,
  and my salvation will not delay.
  I will put salvation in Zion,
  my splendor in Israel.

THE FALL OF BABYLON

47 "Go down and sit in the dust,
  Virgin Daughter Babylon.
Sit on the ground without a throne,
  Daughter Chaldea!
For you will no longer be called pampered and spoiled.
2 Take millstones and grind flour;
  remove your veil,
  strip off your skirt, bare your thigh,
  wade through the streams.
3 Your nakedness will be uncovered,
  and your disgrace will be exposed.
  I will take vengeance;
  I will spare no one."^A
4 The Holy One of Israel is our Redeemer;
  The Lord of Armies is his name.

5 "Daughter Chaldea,
  sit in silence and go into darkness.
  For you will no longer be called mistress of kingdoms.
6 I was angry with my people;
  I profaned my possession,
  and I handed them over to you.
  You showed them no mercy;
  you made your yoke very heavy on the elderly.
7 You said, 'I will be the queen forever.'
  You did not take these things to heart
  or think about their outcome.

8 "So now hear this, lover of luxury,
  who sits securely,
  who says to herself,
  'I am, and there is no one else.
  I will never be a widow
  or know the loss of children.'
9 These two things will happen to you
  suddenly, in one day:
  loss of children and widowhood.
  They will happen to you in their entirety,

^A47:3 Hb obscure

in spite of your many sorceries
and the potency of your spells.
10 You were secure in your wickedness;
you said, 'No one sees me.'
Your wisdom and knowledge
led you astray.
You said to yourself,
'I am, and there is no one else.'
11 But disaster will happen to you;
you will not know how to avert it.
And it will fall on you,
but you will be unable to ward it off.[A]
Devastation will happen to you suddenly
and unexpectedly.
12 So take your stand with your spells
and your many sorceries,
which you have wearied yourself with
    from your youth.
Perhaps you will be able to succeed;
perhaps you will inspire terror!
13 You are worn out with your many consultations.
So let the astrologers stand and save you —
those who observe the stars,
those who predict monthly
what will happen to you.
14 Look, they are like stubble;
fire burns them.
They cannot rescue themselves
from the power[B] of the flame.
This is not a coal for warming themselves,
or a fire to sit beside!
15 This is what they are to you —
those who have wearied you
and have traded with you from your youth —
each wanders on his own way;
no one can save you.

ISRAEL MUST LEAVE BABYLON

48 "Listen to this, house of Jacob —
those who are called by the name Israel
and have descended from[C] Judah,
who swear by the name of the LORD
and declare the God of Israel,
but not in truth or righteousness.
2 For they are named after the Holy City,
and lean on the God of Israel;
his name is the LORD of Armies.
3 I declared the past events long ago;

[A]47:11 Or to atone for it   [B]47:14 Lit hand   [C]48:1 Lit have come from the waters of

they came out of my mouth; I proclaimed them.
Suddenly I acted, and they occurred.
4 Because I know that you are stubborn,
and your neck is iron[A]
and your forehead bronze,
5 therefore I declared to you long ago.
I announced it to you before it occurred,
so you could not claim, 'My idol caused them;
my carved image and cast idol control them.'
6 You have heard it. Observe it all.
Will you not acknowledge it?
From now on I will announce new things to you,
hidden things that you have not known.
7 They have been created now, and not long ago;
you have not heard of them before today,
so you could not claim, 'I already knew them!'
8 You have never heard; you have never known;
for a long time your ears have not been open.
For I knew that you were very treacherous,
and were known as a rebel from birth.
9 I will delay my anger for the sake of my name,
and I will restrain myself for your benefit and for my praise,
so that you will not be destroyed.
10 Look, I have refined you, but not as silver;
I have tested[B] you in the furnace of affliction.
11 I will act for my own sake, indeed, my own,
for how can I[C] be defiled?
I will not give my glory to another.

12 "Listen to me, Jacob,
and Israel, the one called by me:
I am he; I am the first,
I am also the last.
13 My own hand founded the earth,
and my right hand spread out the heavens;
when I summoned them,
they stood up together.
14 All of you, assemble and listen!
Who among the idols[D] has declared these things?
The LORD loves him;[E]
he will accomplish his will against Babylon,
and his arm will be against the Chaldeans.
15 I — I have spoken;
yes, I have called him;
I have brought him,
and he will succeed in his mission.
16 Approach me and listen to this.

[A]48:4 Lit is an iron sinew   [B]48:10 DSS; MT reads chosen   [C]48:11 DSS, Syr; MT reads it   [D]48:14 Lit among them   [E]48:14 = Cyrus

From the beginning I have not spoken in secret;
from the time anything existed, I was there."
And now the Lord GOD
    has sent me and his Spirit.

17 This is what the LORD, your Redeemer, the Holy One of Israel says:
I am the LORD your God,
who teaches you for your benefit,
who leads you in the way you should go.

18 If only you had paid attention to my commands.
Then your peace would have been like a river,
and your righteousness like the waves of the sea.

19 Your descendants would have been as countless
        as the sand,
and the offspring of your body like its grains;
their name would not be cut off
or eliminated from my presence.

20 Leave Babylon,
    flee from the Chaldeans!
Declare with a shout of joy,
    proclaim this,
let it go out to the end of the earth;
    announce,
    "The LORD has redeemed his servant Jacob!"

21 They did not thirst
when he led them through the deserts;
he made water flow from the rock for them;
he split the rock, and water gushed out.

22 "There is no peace for the wicked," says the LORD.

THE SERVANT BRINGS SALVATION

49 Coasts and islands,^A listen to me;
    distant peoples, pay attention.
The LORD called me before I was born.
He named me while I was in my mother's womb.

2 He made my words like a sharp sword;
he hid me in the shadow of his hand.
He made me like a sharpened arrow;
he hid me in his quiver.

3 He said to me, "You are my servant,
Israel, in whom I will be glorified."

4 But I myself said: I have labored in vain,
I have spent my strength for nothing and futility;
yet my vindication is with the LORD,
and my reward is with my God.

5 And now, says the LORD,
who formed me from the womb to be his servant,

A 49:1 Or *Islands*

to bring Jacob back to him
so that Israel might be gathered to him;
for I am honored in the sight of the Lord,
and my God is my strength —

6 he says,
"It is not enough for you to be my servant
raising up the tribes of Jacob
and restoring the protected ones of Israel.
I will also make you a light for the nations,
to be my salvation to the ends of the earth."

7 This is what the Lord,
the Redeemer of Israel, his Holy One, says
to one who is despised,
to one abhorred by people, A
to a servant of rulers:
"Kings will see, princes will stand up,
and they B will all bow down
because of the Lord, who is faithful,
the Holy One of Israel — and he has chosen you."

8 This is what the Lord says:
I will answer you in a time of favor,
and I will help you in the day of salvation.
I will keep you, and I will appoint you
to be a covenant for the people,
to restore the land,
to make them possess the desolate inheritances,

9 saying to the prisoners: Come out,
and to those who are in darkness: Show yourselves.
They will feed along the pathways,
and their pastures will be on all the barren heights.

10 They will not hunger or thirst,
the scorching heat or sun will not strike them;
for their compassionate one will guide them,
and lead them to springs.

11 I will make all my mountains into a road,
and my highways will be raised up.

12 See, these will come from far away,
from the north and from the west, C
and from the land of Sinim. D,E

13 Shout for joy, you heavens!
Earth, rejoice!
Mountains break into joyful shouts!
For the Lord has comforted his people,
and will have compassion on his afflicted ones.

A 49:7 Or by the nation   B 49:7 Lit princes and they   C 49:12 Lit sea
D 49:12 DSS read of the Syenites   E 49:12 Perhaps modern Aswan in southern Egypt

ZION REMEMBERED

14 Zion says, "The LORD has abandoned me;
the Lord has forgotten me!"

15 "Can a woman forget her nursing child,
or lack compassion for the child of her womb?
Even if these forget,
yet I will not forget you.

16 Look, I have inscribed you on the palms of my hands;
your walls are continually before me.

17 Your builders^A hurry;
those who destroy and devastate you will leave you.

18 Look up, and look around.
They all gather together; they come to you.
As I live" —
this is the LORD's declaration —
"you will wear all your children^B as jewelry,
and put them on as a bride does.

19 For your waste and desolate places
and your land marked by ruins —
will now be indeed too small for the inhabitants,
and those who swallowed you up will be far away.

20 Yet as you listen, the children
that you have been deprived of will say,
'This place is too small for me;
make room for me so that I may settle.'

21 Then you will say within yourself,
'Who fathered these for me?
I was deprived of my children and unable
to conceive,
exiled and wandering —
but who brought them up?
See, I was left by myself —
but these, where did they come from?'"^C

22 This is what the Lord GOD says:
Look, I will lift up my hand to the nations,
and raise my banner to the peoples.
They will bring your sons in their arms,
and your daughters will be carried on their shoulders.

23 Kings will be your guardians
and their queens^D your nursing mothers.
They will bow down to you
with their faces to the ground
and lick the dust at your feet.
Then you will know that I am the LORD;
those who put their hope in me
will not be put to shame.

---

^A 49:17 DSS, Aq, Theod, Vg; MT, Syr, Sym read sons   ^B 49:18 Lit all of them
^C 49:21 Lit where are they   ^D 49:23 Lit princesses

²⁴ Can the prey be taken from a mighty man,
or the captives of a tyrant^A be delivered?
²⁵ For this is what the LORD says:
"Even the captives of a mighty man will be taken,
and the prey of a tyrant will be delivered;
I will contend with the one who contends with you,
and I will save your children.
²⁶ I will make your oppressors eat their own flesh,
and they will be drunk with their own blood
as with sweet wine.
Then all people will know
that I, the LORD, am your Savior,
and your Redeemer, the Mighty One of Jacob."

50

This is what the LORD says:
Where is your mother's divorce certificate
that I used to send her away?
Or to which of my creditors did I sell you?
Look, you were sold for your iniquities,
and your mother was sent away
because of your transgressions.
² Why was no one there when I came?
Why was there no one to answer when I called?
Is my arm too weak to redeem?
Or do I have no power to rescue?
Look, I dry up the sea by my rebuke;
I turn the rivers into a wilderness;
their fish rot because of lack of water
and die of thirst.
³ I dress the heavens in black
and make sackcloth their clothing.

THE OBEDIENT SERVANT

⁴ The Lord GOD has given me
the tongue of those who are instructed
to know how to sustain the weary with a word.
He awakens me each morning;
he awakens my ear to listen like those being instructed.
⁵ The Lord GOD has opened my ear,
and I was not rebellious;
I did not turn back.
⁶ I gave my back to those who beat me,
and my cheeks to those who tore out my beard.
I did not hide my face from scorn and spitting.
⁷ The Lord GOD will help me;
therefore I have not been humiliated;
therefore I have set my face like flint,
and I know I will not be put to shame.

^49:24 DSS, Syr, Vg; MT reads *a righteous man*

8 The one who vindicates me is near;
  who will contend with me?
  Let us confront each other.[A]
  Who has a case against me?[B]
  Let him come near me!
9 In truth, the Lord God will help me;
  who will condemn me?
  Indeed, all of them will wear out like a garment;
  a moth will devour them.
10 Who among you fears the Lord
  and listens to his servant?
  Who among you walks in darkness,
  and has no light?
  Let him trust in the name of the Lord;
  let him lean on his God.
11 Look, all you who kindle a fire,
  who encircle yourselves with[C] torches;
  walk in the light of your fire
  and of the torches you have lit!
  This is what you'll get from my hand:
  you will lie down in a place of torment.

SALVATION FOR ZION

51 Listen to me, you who pursue righteousness,
  you who seek the Lord:
  Look to the rock from which you were cut,
  and to the quarry from which you were dug.
2 Look to Abraham your father,
  and to Sarah who gave birth to you.
  When I called him, he was only one;
  I blessed him and made him many.
3 For the Lord will comfort Zion;
  he will comfort all her waste places,
  and he will make her wilderness like Eden,
  and her desert like the garden of the Lord.
  Joy and gladness will be found in her,
  thanksgiving and melodious song.

4 Pay attention to me, my people,
  and listen to me, my nation;
  for instruction will come from me,
  and my justice for a light to the nations.
  I will bring it about quickly.
5 My righteousness is near,
  my salvation appears,
  and my arms will bring justice to the nations.
  The coasts and islands will put their hope in me,

[A] 50:8 Lit us stand [B] 50:8 Lit Who is lord of my judgment [C] 50:11 Syr reads who set ablaze and they will look to my strength.[A]

6 Look up to the heavens,
and look at the earth beneath;
for the heavens will vanish like smoke,
the earth will wear out like a garment,
and its inhabitants will die like gnats.[B]
But my salvation will last forever,
and my righteousness will never be shattered.

7 Listen to me, you who know righteousness,
the people in whose heart is my instruction:
do not fear disgrace by men,
and do not be shattered by their taunts.
8 For moths will devour them like a garment,
and worms will eat them like wool.
But my righteousness will last forever,
and my salvation for all generations.

9 Wake up, wake up!
Arm of the LORD, clothe yourself with strength.
Wake up as in days past,
as in generations long ago.
Wasn't it you who hacked Rahab to pieces,
who pierced the sea monster?
10 Wasn't it you who dried up the sea,
the waters of the great deep,
who made the sea-bed into a road
for the redeemed to pass over?
11 And the ransomed of the LORD will return
and come to Zion with singing,
crowned with unending joy.
Joy and gladness will overtake them,
and sorrow and sighing will flee.

12 I — I am the one who comforts you.
Who are you that you should fear humans who die,
or a son of man who is given up like grass?
13 But you have forgotten the LORD, your Maker,
who stretched out the heavens
and laid the foundations of the earth.
You are in constant dread all day long
because of the fury of the oppressor,
who has set himself to destroy.
But where is the fury of the oppressor?
14 The prisoner[C] is soon to be set free;
he will not die and go to the Pit,
and his food will not be lacking.
15 For I am the LORD your God

[A]51:5 Lit arm   [B]51:6 Or die in like manner   [C]51:14 Hb obscure

who stirs up the sea so that its waves roar —
his name is the LORD of Armies.

16 I have put my words in your mouth,
and covered you in the shadow of my hand,
in order to plant^A the heavens,
to found the earth,
and to say to Zion, "You are my people."

17 Wake yourself, wake yourself up!
Stand up, Jerusalem,
you who have drunk the cup of his fury
from the LORD's hand;
you who have drunk the goblet to the dregs —
the cup that causes people to stagger.

18 There is no one to guide her
among all the children she has raised;
there is no one to take hold of her hand
among all the offspring she has brought up.

19 These two things have happened to you:
devastation and destruction,
famine and sword.
Who will grieve for you?
How can I^B comfort you?

20 Your children have fainted;
they lie at the head of every street
like an antelope in a net.
They are full of the LORD's fury,
the rebuke of your God.

21 So listen to this, suffering
and drunken one — but not with wine.

22 This is what your Lord says —
the LORD, even your God,
who defends his people —
"Look, I have removed from your hand
the cup that causes staggering;
that goblet, the cup of my fury.
You will never drink it again.

23 I will put it into the hands of your tormentors,
who said to you:
Lie down, so we can walk over you.
You made your back like the ground,
and like a street for those who walk on it."

52 "Wake up, wake up;
put on your strength, Zion!
Put on your beautiful garments,
Jerusalem, the Holy City!

---

^A51:16 Syr reads *to stretch out* ^B51:19 DSS, LXX, Syr, Vg read *you? Who can*

For the uncircumcised and the unclean
will no longer enter you.

2 Stand up, shake the dust off yourself!
Take your seat, Jerusalem.
Remove the bonds^A from your neck,
captive Daughter Zion."

3 For this is what the LORD says:
"You were sold for nothing,
and you will be redeemed without silver."

4 For this is what the Lord GOD says:
"At first my people went down to Egypt to reside there,
then Assyria oppressed them without cause.^B

5 So now what have I here" —
this is the LORD's declaration —
"that my people are taken away for nothing?
Its rulers wail" —
this is the LORD's declaration —
"and my name is continually blasphemed all day long.

6 Therefore my people will know my name;
therefore they will know on that day
that I am he who says:
Here I am."

7 How beautiful on the mountains
are the feet of the herald,
who proclaims peace,
who brings news of good things,
who proclaims salvation,
who says to Zion, "Your God reigns!"

8 The voices of your watchmen —
they lift up their voices,
shouting for joy together;
for every eye will see
when the LORD returns to Zion.

9 Be joyful, rejoice together,
you ruins of Jerusalem!
For the LORD has comforted his people;
he has redeemed Jerusalem.

10 The LORD has displayed his holy arm
in the sight of all the nations;
all the ends of the earth will see
the salvation of our God.

11 Leave, leave, go out from there!
Do not touch anything unclean;
go out from her, purify yourselves,
you who carry the vessels of the LORD.

---

^A 52:2 Alt Hb tradition reads *The bonds are removed*   ^B 52:4 Or *them at last*, or *them for nothing*

12 For you will not leave in a hurry,
and you will not have to take flight;
because the Lord is going before you,
and the God of Israel is your rear guard.

THE SERVANT'S SUFFERING AND EXALTATION

13 See, my servant[A] will be successful;[B]
he will be raised and lifted up and greatly exalted.

14 Just as many were appalled at you[C] —
his appearance was so disfigured
that he did not look like a man,
and his form did not resemble a human being —

15 so he will sprinkle many nations.[D]
Kings will shut their mouths because of him,
for they will see what had not been told them,
and they will understand what they had not heard.

53 Who has believed what we have heard?[E]
And to whom has the arm of the Lord been revealed?

2 He grew up before him like a young plant
and like a root out of dry ground.
He didn't have an impressive form
or majesty that we should look at him,
no appearance that we should desire him.

3 He was despised and rejected by men,
a man of suffering who knew what sickness was.
He was like someone people turned away from;[F]
he was despised, and we didn't value him.

4 Yet he himself bore our sicknesses,
and he carried our pains;
but we in turn regarded him stricken,
struck down by God, and afflicted.

5 But he was pierced because of our rebellion,
crushed because of our iniquities;
punishment for our peace was on him,
and we are healed by his wounds.

6 We all went astray like sheep;
we all have turned to our own way;
and the Lord has punished him
for[G] the iniquity of us all.

7 He was oppressed and afflicted,
yet he did not open his mouth.
Like a lamb led to the slaughter

[A]52:13 Tg adds *the Messiah*   [B]52:13 Or *will act wisely*   [C]52:14 Some Hb mss,
Syr, Tg read *him*   [D]52:15 LXX reads *so many nations will marvel at him*
[E]53:1 Or *believed our report*   [F]53:3 Lit *And like a hiding of faces from him*
[G]53:6 Or *has placed on him*; lit *with*

THE SUFFERING SERVANT

ISAIAH 52:13–54:17; ROMANS 3:21-26; 2 CORINTHIANS 8:9

"The Son of God became a man to enable men to become the sons of God."
C. S. LEWIS, *MERE CHRISTIANITY*

Sometimes, life can be exhausting. We run around trying to accomplish the things, maintain the relationships, and solve all the problems. We rarely look up to consider anything but our own present circumstances.

It's a struggle to connect the physical life with the spiritual. Why would I bother thinking of others, or looking to Christ?

God knew this about us. He knows we are a bunch of selfish, hungry stinkers with tunnel vision. He connected the physical and spiritual for us in the person of Christ. Christ became low to make His dwelling among us.

What does it mean to become low? C. S. Lewis once said, "If you want to get the hang of it, think how you would like to become a slug or a crab." And that's the flavor of it. Imagine becoming a slug and trying to convince the other slugs that redemption is at hand. *Prepare ye the way of the Lord, you slugs!* They'd probably just sigh and slime away.

That is what Christ did for us. He became low for our sakes. He gave up His glory and endured all manner of earthly suffering. Because of this, we gain everything.

Why do I let the details of the physical world obscure this most important spiritual fact? Because I'm like a slug trying to understand geometry. It's hard. This is why I need reminders. I need to read these dear words:

"But he was pierced because of our rebellion, crushed because of our iniquities; punishment for our peace was on him, and we are healed by his wounds."

ISAIAH 53:5

Jesus knew we needed redemption. From the beginning of our existence He had our redemption planned out.

He endured sickness for our healing.
He suffered loneliness for our redemption.
He withstood wounds for our comfort.
He braved pain for our peace. And if that wasn't enough, He experienced separation from His Holy Father in order to bring us, wretched slugs, back into His presence. Thanks be to the One who left everything so we could become one with Him.

and like a sheep silent before her shearers,
he did not open his mouth.

8 He was taken away because of oppression and judgment;
and who considered his fate?[A]
For he was cut off from the land of the living;
he was struck because of my people's rebellion.

9 He was assigned a grave with the wicked,
but he was with a rich man at his death,
because he had done no violence
and had not spoken deceitfully.

10 Yet the LORD was pleased to crush him severely.[B]
When[C] you make him a guilt offering,
he will see his seed, he will prolong his days,
and by his hand, the LORD's pleasure will be accomplished.

11 After his anguish,
he will see light[D] and be satisfied.
By his knowledge,
my righteous servant will justify many,
and he will carry their iniquities.

12 Therefore I will give him[E] the many as a portion,
and he will receive[F] the mighty as spoil,
because he willingly submitted to death,
and was counted among the rebels;
yet he bore the sin of many
and interceded for the rebels.

FUTURE GLORY FOR ISRAEL

54 "Rejoice, childless one, who did not give birth;
burst into song and shout,
you who have not been in labor!
For the children of the desolate one will be more
than the children of the married woman,"
says the LORD.

2 "Enlarge the site of your tent,
and let your tent curtains be stretched out;
do not hold back;
lengthen your ropes,
and drive your pegs deep.

3 For you will spread out to the right and to the left,
and your descendants will dispossess nations
and inhabit the desolate cities.

4 "Do not be afraid, for you will not be put to shame;
don't be humiliated, for you will not be disgraced.
For you will forget the shame of your youth,

[A]53:8 Or and as for his generation, who considered him? [B]53:10 Or him; he
made him sick. [C]53:10 Or If [D]53:11 DSS, LXX; MT omits light [E]53:12 Or him
with [F]53:12 Or receive with

and you will no longer remember
the disgrace of your widowhood.
5 Indeed, your husband is your Maker —
his name is the LORD of Armies —
and the Holy One of Israel is your Redeemer;
he is called the God of the whole earth.
6 For the LORD has called you,
like a wife deserted and wounded in spirit,
a wife of one's youth when she is rejected,"
says your God.
7 "I deserted you for a brief moment,
but I will take you back with abundant compassion.
8 In a surge of anger
I hid my face from you for a moment,
but I will have compassion on you
with everlasting love,"
says the LORD your Redeemer.
9 "For this is like the days^A of Noah to me:
when I swore that the water of Noah
would never flood the earth again,
so I have sworn that I will not be angry with you
or rebuke you.
10 Though the mountains move
and the hills shake,
my love will not be removed from you
and my covenant of peace will not be shaken,"
says your compassionate LORD.

11 "Poor Jerusalem, storm-tossed, and not comforted,
I will set your stones in black mortar,^B
and lay your foundations in lapis lazuli.
12 I will make your fortifications^C out of rubies,
your gates out of sparkling stones,
and all your walls out of precious stones.
13 Then all your children will be taught by the LORD,
their prosperity will be great,
14 and you will be established
on a foundation of righteousness.
You will be far from oppression,
you will certainly not be afraid;
you will be far from terror,
it will certainly not come near you.
15 If anyone attacks you,
it is not from me;
whoever attacks you
will fall before you.
16 Look, I have created the craftsman

---

^A 54:9 DSS, Cairo Geniza; MT, LXX read *waters*   ^B 54:11 Lit *in antimony*
^C 54:12 Lit *suns*; perhaps *shields*; Ps 84:11

who blows on the charcoal fire
and produces a weapon suitable for its task;
and I have created the destroyer to cause havoc.
¹⁷ No weapon formed against you will succeed,
and you will refute any accusation^A
raised against you in court.
This is the heritage of the LORD's servants,
and their vindication is from me."
This is the LORD's declaration.

COME TO THE LORD

55 "Come, everyone who is thirsty,
come to the water;
and you without silver,
come, buy, and eat!
Come, buy wine and milk
without silver and without cost!
² Why do you spend silver on what is not food,
and your wages on what does not satisfy?
Listen carefully to me, and eat what is good,
and you will enjoy the choicest of foods.^B
³ Pay attention and come to me;
listen, so that you will live.
I will make a permanent covenant with you
on the basis of the faithful kindnesses of David.^C
⁴ Since I have made him a witness to the peoples,
a leader and commander for the peoples,
⁵ so you will summon a nation you do not know,
and nations who do not know you will run to you.
For the LORD your God,
even the Holy One of Israel,
has glorified you."

⁶ Seek the LORD while he may be found;
call to him while he is near.
⁷ Let the wicked one abandon his way
and the sinful one his thoughts;
let him return to the LORD,
so he may have compassion on him,
and to our God, for he will freely forgive.

⁸ "For my thoughts are not your thoughts,
and your ways are not my ways."
This is the LORD's declaration.
⁹ "For as heaven is higher than earth,
so my ways are higher than your ways,
and my thoughts than your thoughts.

---

^A54:17 Lit refute every tongue   ^B55:2 Lit enjoy fatness   ^C55:3 Or with you,
the faithful acts of kindness shown to David

¹⁰ For just as rain and snow fall from heaven
and do not return there
without saturating the earth
and making it germinate and sprout,
and providing seed to sow
and food to eat,

¹¹ so my word that comes from my mouth
will not return to me empty,
but it will accomplish what I please
and will prosper in what I send it to do."

¹² You will indeed go out with joy
and be peacefully guided;
the mountains and the hills will break into singing
before you,
and all the trees of the field will clap their hands.

¹³ Instead of the thornbush, a cypress will come up,
and instead of the brier, a myrtle will come up;
this will stand as a monument for the Lord,
an everlasting sign that will not be destroyed.

A HOUSE OF PRAYER FOR ALL

56 This is what the Lord says:
Preserve justice and do what is right,
for my salvation is coming soon,
and my righteousness will be revealed.

² Happy is the person who does this,
the son of man who holds it fast,
who keeps the Sabbath without desecrating it,
and keeps his hand from doing any evil.

³ No foreigner who has joined himself to the Lord
should say,
"The Lord will exclude me from his people,"
and the eunuch should not say,
"Look, I am a dried-up tree."

⁴ For the Lord says this:
"For the eunuchs who keep my Sabbaths,
and choose what pleases me,
and hold firmly to my covenant,

⁵ I will give them, in my house and within my walls,
a memorial and a name
better than sons and daughters.
I will give each of them an everlasting name
that will never be cut off.

⁶ As for the foreigners who join themselves
to the Lord
to minister to him, to love the name of the Lord,
and to become his servants —
all who keep the Sabbath without desecrating it

and who hold firmly to my covenant —
7 I will bring them to my holy mountain
and let them rejoice in my house of prayer.
Their burnt offerings and sacrifices
will be acceptable on my altar,
for my house will be called a house of prayer
for all nations."
8   This is the declaration of the Lord GOD,
who gathers the dispersed of Israel:
"I will gather to them still others
besides those already gathered."

UNRIGHTEOUS LEADERS CONDEMNED

9   All you animals of the field and forest,
come and eat!
10   Israel's[A] watchmen are blind, all of them,
they know nothing;
all of them are mute dogs,
they cannot bark;
they dream, lie down,
and love to sleep.
11   These dogs have fierce appetites;
they never have enough.
And they are shepherds
who have no discernment;
all of them turn to their own way,
every last one for his own profit.
12   "Come, let me get some wine,
let's guzzle some beer;
and tomorrow will be like today,
only far better!"

57 The righteous person perishes,
and no one takes it to heart;
the faithful are taken away,
with no one realizing
that the righteous person is taken away
because of[B] evil.
2   He will enter into peace —
they will rest on their beds[C] —
everyone who lives uprightly.

PAGAN RELIGION DENOUNCED

3   But come here,
you witch's sons,
offspring of an adulterer and a prostitute![D]
4   Who are you mocking?

[A]56:10 Or *His*, or *Its*   [B]57:1 Or *taken away from the presence of*   [C]57:2 Either
their deathbeds or their graves   [D]57:3 Lit *and she acted as a prostitute*

Who are you opening your mouth
and sticking out your tongue at?
Isn't it you, you rebellious children,
you offspring of liars,
5 who burn with lust among the oaks,
under every green tree,
who slaughter children in the wadis
below the clefts of the rocks?
6 Your portion is among the smooth stones
of the wadi;
indeed, they are your lot.
You have even poured out a drink offering to them;
you have offered a grain offering;
should I be satisfied with these?
7 You have placed your bed
on a high and lofty mountain;
you also went up there to offer sacrifice.
8 You have set up your memorial
behind the door and doorpost.
For away from me, you stripped,
went up, and made your bed wide,
and you have made a bargain^A for yourself with them.
You have loved their bed;
you have gazed on their genitals.^B,^C
9 You went to the king with oil
and multiplied your perfumes;
you sent your envoys far away
and sent them down even to Sheol.
10 You became weary on your many journeys,
but you did not say, "It's hopeless!"
You found a renewal of your strength;^D
therefore you did not grow weak.
11 Who was it you dreaded and feared,
so that you lied and didn't remember me
or take it to heart?
I have kept silent for a long time, haven't I?^E
So you do not fear me.
12 I will announce your righteousness,
and your works — they will not profit you.
13 When you cry out,
let your collection of idols rescue you!
The wind will carry all of them off,
a breath will take them away.
But whoever takes refuge in me
will inherit the land
and possess my holy mountain.

---

^A57:8 Lit you cut   ^B57:8 Lit hand   ^C57:8 In Hb, the word "hand" is probably a euphemism for genitals.   ^D57:10 Lit found life of your hand   ^E57:11 LXX reads And I, when I see you, I pass by

HEALING AND PEACE

14 He said,
"Build it up, build it up, prepare the way,
remove every obstacle from my people's way."

15 For the High and Exalted One,
who lives forever, whose name is holy, says this:
"I live in a high and holy place,
and with the oppressed and lowly of spirit,
to revive the spirit of the lowly
and revive the heart of the oppressed.

16 For I will not accuse you forever,
and I will not always be angry;
for then the spirit would grow weak before me,
even the breath, which I have made.

17 Because of his sinful greed I was angry,
so I struck him; I was angry and hid;
but he went on turning back to the desires of his heart.

18 I have seen his ways, but I will heal him;
I will lead him and restore comfort
to him and his mourners,

19 creating words of praise."[A]
The LORD says,
"Peace, peace to the one who is far or near,
and I will heal him.

20 But the wicked are like the storm-tossed sea,
for it cannot be still,
and its water churns up mire and muck.

21 There is no peace for the wicked,"
says my God.

TRUE FASTING

58 "Cry out loudly,[B] don't hold back!
Raise your voice like a trumpet.
Tell my people their transgression
and the house of Jacob their sins.

2 They seek me day after day
and delight to know my ways,
like a nation that does what is right
and does not abandon the justice of their God.
They ask me for righteous judgments;
they delight in the nearness of God."

3 "Why have we fasted, but you have not seen?
We have denied ourselves, but you haven't noticed!"[C]
"Look, you do as you please on the day of your fast,
and oppress all your workers.

4 You fast with contention and strife
to strike viciously with your fist.

[A] 57:19 Lit creating fruit of the lips   [B] 58:1 Lit with throat   [C] 58:3 These are Israel's
words to God.

You cannot fast as you do today,
hoping to make your voice heard on high.
⁵ Will the fast I choose be like this:
A day for a person to deny himself,
to bow his head like a reed,
and to spread out sackcloth and ashes?
Will you call this a fast
and a day acceptable to the LORD?
⁶ Isn't this the fast I choose:
To break the chains of wickedness,
to untie the ropes of the yoke,
to set the oppressed free,
and to tear off every yoke?
⁷ Is it not to share your bread with the hungry,
to bring the poor and homeless into your house,
to clothe the naked when you see him,
and not to ignore your own flesh and blood?ᴬ
⁸ Then your light will appear like the dawn,
and your recovery will come quickly.
Your righteousness will go before you,
and the LORD's glory will be your rear guard.
⁹ At that time, when you call, the LORD will answer;
when you cry out, he will say, 'Here I am.'
If you get rid of the yoke among you,
the finger-pointing and malicious speaking,
¹⁰ and if you offer yourselfᴮ to the hungry,
and satisfy the afflicted one,
then your light will shine in the darkness,
and your night will be like noonday.
¹¹ The LORD will always lead you,
satisfy you in a parched land,
and strengthen your bones.
You will be like a watered garden
and like a spring whose water never runs dry.
¹² Some of you will rebuild the ancient ruins;
you will restore the foundations laid long ago;
you will be called the repairer of broken walls,
the restorer of streets where people live.

¹³ "If you keep from desecratingᶜ the Sabbath,
from doing whatever you want on my holy day;
if you call the Sabbath a delight,
and the holy day of the LORD honorable;
if you honor it, not going your own ways,
seeking your own pleasure, or talking business;ᴰ,ᴱ
¹⁴ then you will delight in the LORD,

ᴬ58:7 Lit *not hide yourself from your flesh* ᴮ58:10 Some Hb mss, LXX, Syr read *offer your bread* ᶜ58:13 Lit *keep your foot from* ᴰ58:13 Or *idly* ᴱ58:13 Lit *or speak a word*

and I will make you ride over the heights of the land,
and let you enjoy the heritage of your father Jacob."
For the mouth of the LORD has spoken.

SIN AND REDEMPTION

59 Indeed, the LORD's arm is not too weak to save,
and his ear is not too deaf to hear.
2 But your iniquities are separating you
from your God,
and your sins have hidden his face from you
so that he does not listen.
3 For your hands are defiled with blood
and your fingers, with iniquity;
your lips have spoken lies,
and your tongues mutter injustice.
4 No one makes claims justly;
no one pleads honestly.
They trust in empty and worthless words;
they conceive trouble and give birth to iniquity.
5 They hatch viper's eggs
and weave spider's webs.
Whoever eats their eggs will die;
crack one open, and a viper is hatched.
6 Their webs cannot become clothing,
and they cannot cover themselves with their works.
Their works are sinful works,
and violent acts are in their hands.
7 Their feet run after evil,
and they rush to shed innocent blood.
Their thoughts are sinful thoughts;
ruin and wretchedness are in their paths.
8 They have not known the path of peace,
and there is no justice in their ways.
They have made their roads crooked;
no one who walks on them will know peace.

9 Therefore justice is far from us,
and righteousness does not reach us.
We hope for light, but there is darkness;
for brightness, but we live in the night.
10 We grope along a wall like the blind;
we grope like those without eyes.
We stumble at noon as though it were twilight;
we are like the dead among those who are healthy.
11 We all growl like bears
and moan like doves.
We hope for justice, but there is none;
for salvation, but it is far from us.
12 For our transgressions have multiplied before you,
and our sins testify against us.

For our transgressions are with us,
and we know our iniquities:
13 transgression and deception against the Lord,
turning away from following our God,
speaking oppression and revolt,
conceiving and uttering lying words from the heart.
14 Justice is turned back,
and righteousness stands far off.
For truth has stumbled in the public square,
and honesty cannot enter.
15 Truth is missing,
and whoever turns from evil is plundered.

The Lord saw that there was no justice,
and he was offended.
16 He saw that there was no man —
he was amazed that there was no one interceding;
so his own arm brought salvation,
and his own righteousness supported him.
17 He put on righteousness as body armor,
and a helmet of salvation on his head;
he put on garments of vengeance for clothing,
and he wrapped himself in zeal as in a cloak.
18 So he will repay according to their deeds:
fury to his enemies,
retribution to his foes,
and he will repay the coasts and islands.
19 They will fear the name of the Lord in the west
and his glory in the east;[A]
for he will come like a rushing stream
driven by the wind of the Lord.
20 "The Redeemer will come to Zion,
and to those in Jacob who turn from transgression."
This is the Lord's declaration.

21 "As for me, this is my covenant with them," says the Lord: "My Spirit who is on you, and my words that I have put in your mouth, will not depart from your mouth, or from the mouths of your children, or from the mouths of your children's children, from now on and forever," says the Lord.

THE LORD'S GLORY IN ZION

60 Arise, shine, for your light has come,
and the glory of the Lord shines over you.[B]
2 For look, darkness will cover the earth,
and total darkness the peoples;
but the Lord will shine over you,
and his glory will appear over you.
3 Nations will come to your light,

A 59:19 Lit sunrise   B 60:1 = Jerusalem

and kings to your shining brightness.

4 Raise your eyes and look around:
   they all gather and come to you;
   your sons will come from far away,
   and your daughters on the hips of nannies.

5 Then you will see and be radiant,
   and your heart will tremble and rejoice,[A]
   because the riches of the sea will become yours
   and the wealth of the nations will come to you.

6 Caravans of camels will cover your land[B] —
   young camels of Midian and Ephah —
   all of them will come from Sheba.
   They will carry gold and frankincense
   and proclaim the praises of the LORD.

7 All the flocks of Kedar will be gathered to you;
   the rams of Nebaioth will serve you
   and go up on my altar as an acceptable sacrifice.
   I will glorify my beautiful house.

8 Who are these who fly like a cloud,
   like doves to their shelters?

9 Yes, the coasts and islands will wait for me
   with the ships of Tarshish in the lead,
   to bring your children from far away,
   their silver and gold with them,
   for the honor of the LORD your God,
   the Holy One of Israel,
   who has glorified you.

10 Foreigners will rebuild your walls,
   and their kings will serve you.
   Although I struck you in my wrath,
   yet I will show mercy to you with my favor.

11 Your city gates will always be open;
   they will never be shut day or night
   so that the wealth of the nations
   may be brought into you,
   with their kings being led in procession.

12 For the nation and the kingdom
   that will not serve you will perish;
   those nations will be annihilated.

13 The glory of Lebanon will come to you —
   its pine, elm, and cypress together —
   to beautify the place of my sanctuary,
   and I will glorify my dwelling place.[C]

14 The sons of your oppressors
   will come and bow down to you;
   all who reviled you
   will fall facedown at your feet.

[A] 60:5 Lit expand   [B] 60:6 Lit cover you   [C] 60:13 Lit glorify the place of my feet

They will call you the City of the LORD,
Zion of the Holy One of Israel.
¹⁵ Instead of your being deserted and hated,
with no one passing through,
I will make you an object of eternal pride,
a joy from age to age.
¹⁶ You will nurse on the milk of nations,
and nurse at the breast of kings;
you will know that I, the LORD, am your Savior
and Redeemer, the Mighty One of Jacob.

¹⁷ I will bring gold instead of bronze;
I will bring silver instead of iron,
bronze instead of wood,
and iron instead of stones.
I will appoint peace as your government
and righteousness as your overseers.
¹⁸ Violence will never again be heard of
in your land;
devastation and destruction
will be gone from your borders.
You will call your walls Salvation
and your city gates Praise.
¹⁹ The sun will no longer be your light by day,
and the brightness of the moon
will not shine on you.
The LORD will be your everlasting light,
and your God will be your splendor.
²⁰ Your sun will no longer set,
and your moon will not fade;
for the LORD will be your everlasting light,
and the days of your sorrow will be over.
²¹ All your people will be righteous;
they will possess the land forever;
they are the branch I planted,
the work of my^A hands,
so that I may be glorified.
²² The least will become a thousand,
the smallest a mighty nation.
I am the LORD;
I will accomplish it quickly in its time.

MESSIAH'S JUBILEE

61 The Spirit of the Lord GOD is on me,
because the LORD has anointed me
to bring good news to the poor.
He has sent me to heal^B the brokenhearted,
to proclaim liberty to the captives

---

^A 60:21 LXX, DSS read *his* ^B 61:1 Lit *bind up*

and freedom to the prisoners;
2 to proclaim the year of the LORD's favor,
and the day of our God's vengeance;
to comfort all who mourn,
3 to provide for those who mourn in Zion;
to give them a crown of beauty instead of ashes,
festive oil instead of mourning,
and splendid clothes instead of despair. [A]
And they will be called righteous trees,
planted by the LORD
to glorify him.

4 They will rebuild the ancient ruins;
they will restore the former devastations;
they will renew the ruined cities,
the devastations of many generations.
5 Strangers will stand and feed your flocks,
and foreigners will be your plowmen and vinedressers.
6 But you will be called the LORD's priests;
they will speak of you as ministers of our God;
you will eat the wealth of the nations,
and you will boast in their riches.
7 In place of your shame, you will have
a double portion;
in place of disgrace, they will rejoice over their share.
So they will possess double in their land,
and eternal joy will be theirs.

8 For I the LORD love justice;
I hate robbery and injustice; [B]
I will faithfully reward my people
and make a permanent covenant with them.
9 Their descendants will be known among the nations,
and their posterity among the peoples.
All who see them will recognize
that they are a people the LORD has blessed.

10 I rejoice greatly in the LORD,
I exult in my God;
for he has clothed me with the garments of salvation
and wrapped me in a robe of righteousness,
as a groom wears a turban
and as a bride adorns herself with her jewels.
11 For as the earth produces its growth,
and as a garden enables what is sown to spring up,
so the Lord GOD will cause righteousness and praise
to spring up before all the nations.

[A] 61:3 Lit a dim spirit [B] 61:8 Some Hb mss, DSS, LXX, Syr, Tg, Vg; other Hb mss
read robbery with a burnt offering

ZION'S RESTORATION

62 I will not keep silent because of Zion,
and I will not keep still because of Jerusalem,
until her righteousness shines like a bright light
and her salvation, like a flaming torch.

2 Nations will see your righteousness
and all kings, your glory.
You will be given a new name
that the Lord's mouth will announce.

3 You will be a glorious crown in the Lord's hand,
and a royal diadem in the palm of your God's hand.

4 You will no longer be called Deserted,
and your land will not be called Desolate;
instead, you will be called My Delight Is in Her, A
and your land Married; B
for the Lord delights in you,
and your land will be married.

5 For as a young man marries a young woman,
so your sons will marry you;
and as a groom rejoices over his bride,
so your God will rejoice over you.

6 Jerusalem,
I have appointed watchmen on your walls;
they will never be silent, day or night.
There is no rest for you,
who remind the Lord.

7 Do not give him rest
until he establishes and makes Jerusalem
the praise of the earth.

8 The Lord has sworn with his right hand
and his strong arm:
I will no longer give your grain
to your enemies for food,
and foreigners will not drink the new wine
for which you have labored.

9 For those who gather grain will eat it
and praise the Lord,
and those who harvest the grapes will drink the wine
in my holy courts.

10 Go out, go out through the city gates;
prepare a way for the people!
Build it up, build up the highway;
clear away the stones!
Raise a banner for the peoples.

11 Look, the Lord has proclaimed

A 62:4 Or *Hephzibah*   B 62:4 Or *Beulah*

to the ends of the earth,
"Say to Daughter Zion:
Look, your salvation is coming,
his wages are with him,
and his reward accompanies him."
12 And they will be called[A] the Holy People,
the LORD's Redeemed;
and you will be called Cared For,
A City Not Deserted.

THE LORD'S DAY OF VENGEANCE

63 Who is this coming from Edom
in crimson-stained garments from Bozrah —
this one who is splendid in his apparel,
striding in his formidable[B] might?

It is I, proclaiming vindication,[C]
powerful to save.

2 Why are your clothes red,
and your garments like one who treads a winepress?

3 I trampled the winepress alone,
and no one from the nations was with me.
I trampled them in my anger
and ground them underfoot in my fury;
their blood spattered my garments,
and all my clothes were stained.
4 For I planned the day of vengeance,
and the year of my redemption[D] came.
5 I looked, but there was no one to help,
and I was amazed that no one assisted;
so my arm accomplished victory for me,
and my wrath assisted me.
6 I crushed nations in my anger;
I made them drunk with my wrath
and poured out their blood on the ground.

REMEMBRANCE OF GRACE

7 I will make known the LORD's faithful love
and the LORD's praiseworthy acts,
because of all the LORD has done for us —
even the many good things
he has done for the house of Israel,
which he did for them based on his compassion
and the abundance of his faithful love.
8 He said, "They are indeed my people,

[A]62:12 Lit will call them [B]63:1 Syr, Vg read apparel, striding forward in
[C]63:1 Or righteousness [D]63:4 Or blood retribution

children who will not be disloyal,"
and he became their Savior.

9 In all their suffering, he suffered,[A]
and the angel of his presence saved them.
He redeemed them
because of his love and compassion;
he lifted them up and carried them
all the days of the past.

10 But they rebelled
and grieved his Holy Spirit.
So he became their enemy
and fought against them.

11 Then he[B] remembered the days of the past,
the days of Moses and his people.
Where is he who brought them out of the sea
with the shepherds[C] of his flock?
Where is he who put his Holy Spirit
among the flock?

12 He made his glorious strength
available at the right hand of Moses,
divided the water before them
to make an eternal name for himself,

13 and led them through the depths
like a horse in the wilderness,
so that they did not stumble.

14 Like cattle that go down into the valley,
the Spirit of the LORD gave them[D] rest.
You led your people this way
to make a glorious name for yourself.

ISRAEL'S PRAYER

15 Look down from heaven and see
from your lofty home — holy and beautiful.
Where is your zeal and your might?
Your yearning[E] and your compassion
are withheld from me.

16 Yet you are our Father,
even though Abraham does not know us
and Israel doesn't recognize us.
You, LORD, are our Father;
your name is Our Redeemer
from Ancient Times.

17 Why, LORD, do you make us stray from your ways?
You harden our hearts so we do not fear[F] you.
Return, because of your servants,
the tribes of your heritage.

[A]63:9 Alt Hb tradition reads *did not suffer*   [B]63:11 Or *they*   [C]63:11 LXX, Tg, Syr
read *shepherd*   [D]63:14 Lit *him*   [E]63:15 Lit *The agitation of your inward parts*
[F]63:17 Lit *our heart from fearing*

18 Your holy people had a possession[A]
for a little while,
but our enemies have trampled down
your sanctuary.

19 We have become like those you never ruled,
like those who did not bear your name.

64 If only you would tear the heavens open
and come down,
so that mountains would quake at your presence —

2 just as fire kindles brushwood,
and fire boils water —
to make your name known to your enemies,
so that nations will tremble at your presence!

3 When you did awesome works
that we did not expect,
you came down,
and the mountains quaked at your presence.

4 From ancient times no one has heard,
no one has listened to,
no eye has seen any God except you
who acts on behalf of the one who waits for him.

5 You welcome the one who joyfully does what is right;
they remember you in your ways.
But we have sinned, and you were angry.
How can we be saved if we remain in our sins?[B]

6 All of us have become like something unclean,
and all our righteous acts are like a polluted[C] garment;
all of us wither like a leaf,
and our iniquities carry us away like the wind.

7 No one calls on your name,
striving to take hold of you.
For you have hidden your face from us
and made us melt because of[D,E] our iniquity.

8 Yet LORD, you are our Father;
we are the clay, and you are our potter;
we all are the work of your hands.

9 LORD, do not be terribly angry
or remember our iniquity forever.
Please look — all of us are your people!

10 Your holy cities have become a wilderness;
Zion has become a wilderness,
Jerusalem a desolation.

11 Our holy and beautiful[F] temple,
where our fathers praised you,

[A]63:18 Or *Your people possessed your holy place*   [B]64:5 Lit *angry; in them*
continually and we will be saved; Hb obscure   [C]64:6 Lit *menstrual*   [D]64:7 LXX,
Syr, Vg, Tg read *and delivered us into the hand of*   [E]64:7 Lit *melt by the hand of*
[F]64:11 Or *glorious;* Is 60:7

has been burned down,
and all that was dear to us lies in ruins.

¹² LORD, after all this, will you restrain yourself?
Will you keep silent and afflict us severely?

THE LORD'S RESPONSE

65 "I was sought by those who did not ask;
I was found by those who did not seek me.
I said, 'Here I am, here I am,'
to a nation that did not call on ^A my name.

² I spread out my hands all day long
to a rebellious people
who walk in the path that is not good,
following their own thoughts.

³ These people continually anger me
to my face,
sacrificing in gardens,
burning incense on bricks,

⁴ sitting among the graves,
spending nights in secret places,
eating the meat of pigs,
and putting polluted broth in their bowls. ᴮ

⁵ They say, 'Keep to yourself,
don't come near me, for I am too holy for you!'
These practices are smoke in my nostrils,
a fire that burns all day long.

⁶ Look, it is written in front of me:
I will not keep silent, but I will repay;
I will repay them fully ᶜ

⁷ for your iniquities and the iniquities
of your ᴰ fathers together,"
says the LORD.
"Because they burned incense on the mountains
and reproached me on the hills,
I will reward them fully ᴱ
for their former deeds."

⁸ The LORD says this:

"As the new wine is found in a bunch of grapes,
and one says, 'Don't destroy it,
for there's some good ᶠ in it,'
so I will act because of my servants
and not destroy them all.

⁹ I will produce descendants from Jacob,
and heirs to my mountains from Judah;
my chosen ones will possess it,

---

^A65:1 Or that was not called by ᴮ65:3-4 These vv. describe pagan worship.
ᶜ65:6 Lit repay into their lap ᴰ65:7 LXX, Syr read for their iniquities and the
iniquities of their ᴱ65:7 Lit reward into their lap ᶠ65:8 Or there's a blessing

and my servants will dwell there.
10 Sharon will be a pasture for flocks,
and the Valley of Achor a place for herds to lie down,
for my people who have sought me.
11 But you who abandon the LORD,
who forget my holy mountain,
who prepare a table for Fortune
and fill bowls of mixed wine for Destiny,^A
12 I will destine you for the sword,
and all of you will kneel down to be slaughtered,
because I called and you did not answer,
I spoke and you did not hear;
you did what was evil in my sight
and chose what I did not delight in."

13 Therefore, this is what the Lord GOD says:
"My servants will eat,
but you will be hungry;
my servants will drink,
but you will be thirsty;
my servants will rejoice,
but you will be put to shame.
14 My servants will shout for joy from a glad heart,
but you will cry out from an anguished heart,
and you will lament out of a broken spirit.
15 You will leave your name behind
as a curse for my chosen ones,
and the Lord GOD will kill you;
but he will give his servants another name.
16 Whoever asks for a blessing in the land
will ask for a blessing by the God of truth,
and whoever swears in the land
will swear by the God of truth.
For the former troubles will be forgotten
and hidden from my sight.

A NEW CREATION

17 "For I will create a new heaven and a new earth;
the past events will not be remembered or come to mind.
18 Then be glad and rejoice forever
in what I am creating;
for I will create Jerusalem to be a joy
and its people to be a delight.
19 I will rejoice in Jerusalem
and be glad in my people.
The sound of weeping and crying
will no longer be heard in her.
20 In her, a nursing infant will no longer live

---

^A 65:11 Pagan gods

only a few days, [A]
or an old man not live out his days.
Indeed, the one who dies at a hundred years old
will be mourned as a young man, [B]
and the one who misses a hundred years
will be considered cursed.

21 People will build houses and live in them;
they will plant vineyards and eat their fruit.

22 They will not build and others live in them;
they will not plant and others eat.
For my people's lives will be
like the lifetime of a tree.
My chosen ones will fully enjoy
the work of their hands.

23 They will not labor without success
or bear children destined for disaster,
for they will be a people blessed by the LORD
along with their descendants.

24 Even before they call, I will answer;
while they are still speaking, I will hear.

25 The wolf and the lamb will feed together, [C]
and the lion will eat straw like cattle,
but the serpent's food will be dust!
They will not do what is evil or destroy
on my entire holy mountain,"
says the LORD.

FINAL JUDGMENT AND JOYOUS RESTORATION

66 This is what the LORD says:
Heaven is my throne,
and earth is my footstool.
Where could you possibly build a house for me?
And where would my resting place be?

2 My hand made all these things,
and so they all came into being.
This is the LORD's declaration.
I will look favorably on this kind of person:
one who is humble, submissive [D] in spirit,
and trembles at my word.

3 One person slaughters an ox, another kills a person;
one person sacrifices a lamb, another breaks a dog's neck;
one person offers a grain offering, another offers pig's blood;
one person offers incense, another praises an idol —
all these have chosen their ways
and delight in their abhorrent practices.

4 So I will choose their punishment,
and I will bring on them what they dread

[A] 65:20 Lit *her, no longer infant of days* [B] 65:20 Lit *the youth of a hundred years will die* [C] 65:25 Lit *as one* [D] 66:2 Lit *broken*

because I called and no one answered;
  I spoke and they did not listen;
they did what was evil in my sight
  and chose what I did not delight in.

⁵ You who tremble at his word,
  hear the word of the LORD:
"Your brothers who hate and exclude you
  for my name's sake have said,
'Let the LORD be glorified
  so that we can see your joy!'
But they will be put to shame."

⁶ A sound of uproar from the city!
  A voice from the temple —
the voice of the LORD,
  paying back his enemies what they deserve!

⁷ Before Zion was in labor, she gave birth;
  before she was in pain, she delivered a boy.
⁸ Who has heard of such a thing?
  Who has seen such things?
Can a land be born in one day
  or a nation be delivered in an instant?
Yet as soon as Zion was in labor,
  she gave birth to her sons.
⁹ "Will I bring a baby to the point of birth
  and not deliver it?"
says the LORD;
  "or will I who deliver, close the womb?"
says your God.
¹⁰ Be glad for Jerusalem and rejoice over her,
  all who love her.
Rejoice greatly with her,
  all who mourn over her —
¹¹ so that you may nurse and be satisfied
  from her comforting breast
and drink deeply and delight yourselves
  from her glorious breasts.

¹² For this is what the LORD says:
  I will make peace flow to her like a river,
and the wealthᴬ of nations like a flood;
  you will nurse and be carried on her hip
and bounced on her lap.
¹³ As a mother comforts her son,
  so I will comfort you,
and you will be comforted in Jerusalem.

---

14 You will see, you will rejoice,
and you[A] will flourish like grass;
then the LORD's power will be revealed to his servants,
but he will show his wrath against his enemies.
15 Look, the LORD will come with fire —
his chariots are like the whirlwind —
to execute his anger with fury
and his rebuke with flames of fire.
16 For the LORD will execute judgment
on all people with his fiery sword,
and many will be slain by the LORD.

17 "Those who dedicate and purify themselves to enter the groves following their leader,[B] eating meat from pigs, vermin,[C] and rats, will perish together." This is the LORD's declaration.

18 "Knowing[D] their works and their thoughts, I have come to gather all nations and languages; they will come and see my glory. 19 I will establish a sign among them, and I will send survivors from them to the nations — to Tarshish, Put,[E] Lud (who are archers), Tubal, Javan, and the coasts and islands far away — who have not heard about me or seen my glory. And they will proclaim my glory among the nations. 20 They will bring all your brothers from all the nations as a gift to the LORD on horses and chariots, in litters, and on mules and camels, to my holy mountain Jerusalem," says the LORD, "just as the Israelites bring an offering in a clean vessel to the house of the LORD. 21 I will also take some of them as priests and Levites," says the LORD.

22 "For just as the new heavens and the new earth,
which I will make,
will remain before me" —
this is the LORD's declaration —
"so your offspring and your name will remain.
23 All mankind will come to worship me
from one New Moon to another
and from one Sabbath to another,"
says the LORD.

24 "As they leave, they will see the dead bodies of those who have rebelled against me; for their worm will never die, their fire will never go out, and they will be a horror to all mankind."

[A]66:14 Lit your bones   [B]66:17 Hb obscure   [C]66:17 Lit abhorrent things
[D]66:18 LXX, Syr; MT omits Knowing   [E]66:19 LXX; MT reads Pul

jeremiah

 "Instead, this is the covenant I will make with the house of Israel after those days" —the LORD's declaration. "I will put my teaching within them and write it on their hearts. I will be their God, and they will be my people." **31:33**

ON THE TIMELINE The book of Jeremiah discusses the last days of Judah, spanning roughly 640 BC to 580 BC. While the nation of Israel had already been captured by Assyria (722 BC), Jeremiah's message comes before Judah's exile to Babylon. Portions of his message were written after the first exile to Babylon (Jr 29) and during the two deportations that followed (605 BC, 597 BC, and 586 BC).

A LITTLE BACKGROUND Jeremiah was a priest from the town of Anathoth (Jr 1:1), near Jerusalem. At the Lord's command, he neither married nor had children because of the impending judgment that would come upon the next generation. A contemporary of Habakkuk and possibly Obadiah, Jeremiah's ministry as a prophet began in 626 BC and ended after 586 BC.

The book and prophet Jeremiah hold at least two great distinctions among all the Old Testament prophets: at 1,364 verses, it is the longest prophetic book in the Bible; and we are told more about Jeremiah's life than any of the other 15 writing prophets.

MESSAGE & PURPOSE During the tumultuous times of the end of the seventh century and beginning of the sixth century BC, Jeremiah came bearing a word from God for the stubborn people of Judah (Jr 1:2). Of the 349 times the OT uses the phrase "thus says the LORD," Jeremiah accounts for 157 of them. The people of Judah felt immune to any threat of divine judgment, but Jeremiah repeatedly warned them about the vanity of their reliance on rituals and other means of external, formal religion. The prophetic word of God was to make the people see their meaningless outward piety and turn to the Lord.

GIVE THANKS FOR THE BOOK OF JEREMIAH

The best known passage in Jeremiah is the new covenant text in Jeremiah 31:31-34, which is also the largest OT text quoted in the New Testament (Heb 8:8-12; 10:16-17). Arguably better than any other, this passage links God's ancient promises to Eve (Gn 3:15), Abraham (Gn 12:1-3), and David (2Sm 7:16-19) with NT assurances that God in Christ grants believers new hearts, salvation, and fellowship with Him.

THE BOOK OF JEREMIAH IN HISTORY

630 BC

600 BC

612

640   626   609   586

605   597

580

Beginning of
King Josiah's
reign in Judah

Birth of
Jeremiah

Jeremiah receives
prophetic call

Second
Babylonian
invasion of
Judah — people
taken into
captivity

End of
Jeremiah's
ministry

First Babylonian siege of
Judah — Daniel and other
princes taken to Babylon

Temple and wall of
Jerusalem destroyed

Babylonian
exile begins

Pharaoh Necho
invades Judah

End of Assyrian
Empire

Fall of Nineveh

Week 1

		GOING DEEPER
☐	Jeremiah 1	Isaiah 6:4-7; 1 Peter 1:21
☐	Jeremiah 2:1–3:5	Judges 2:11-15; John 4:10-14
☐	Jeremiah 3:6–5:13	2 Kings 23:15-20; Ephesians 1:3-14
☐	Jeremiah 5:14–6:30	Psalm 95; Micah 6:6-8
☐	Jeremiah 7–9	1 Kings 8:41-43; Luke 19:41-44

Week 2

		GOING DEEPER
☐	Jeremiah 10–11	Proverbs 1:1-7; Hebrews 12:5-11
☐	Jeremiah 12	Hosea 11:1-9; Matthew 15:1-9
☐	Jeremiah 13–14	Psalm 25:7; 2 Peter 2:1-3
☐	Jeremiah 15–16	Exodus 15:2-3; Luke 11:45-52
☐	Jeremiah 17	Exodus 20:8-11; Hebrews 10:22

Week 3

		GOING DEEPER
☐	**Jeremiah 18–19**	2 Kings 21:10-12; Romans 9:20-21
☐	Jeremiah 20–22	Isaiah 9:6-7; John 11:25-26
☐	**Jeremiah 23–24**	Exodus 12:33-38; Colossians 1:13-14
☐	Jeremiah 25	2 Kings 17:13-14; 1 Peter 4:17-19
☐	Jeremiah 26	Micah 3:12; Matthew 21:33-46

READ AND UNDERSTAND JEREMIAH

The Bible is a complete work in which many stories combine to tell one story. As you read the book of Jeremiah, consider reading the additional passages to discover how the whole of Scripture works together.

READ AND UNDERSTAND JEREMIAH

1 The words of Jeremiah, the son of Hilkiah, one of the priests living in Anathoth in the territory of Benjamin. ² The word of the Lord came to him in the thirteenth year of the reign of Josiah son of Amon, king of Judah. ³ It also came throughout the days of Jehoiakim son of Josiah, king of Judah, until the fifth month of the eleventh year of Zedekiah son of Josiah, king of Judah, when the people of Jerusalem went into exile.

THE CALL OF JEREMIAH

⁴ The word of the Lord came to me:

5   I chose you before I formed you in the womb;
       I set you apart before you were born.
       I appointed you a prophet to the nations.

⁶ But I protested, "Oh no, Lord God! Look, I don't know how to speak since I am only a youth."

⁷ Then the Lord said to me:

       Do not say, "I am only a youth,"
       for you will go to everyone I send you to
       and speak whatever I tell you.
8   Do not be afraid of anyone,
       for I will be with you to rescue you.
           This is the Lord's declaration.

⁹ Then the Lord reached out his hand, touched my mouth, and told me:

       I have now filled your mouth with my words.
10   See, I have appointed you today
       over nations and kingdoms
       to uproot and tear down,
       to destroy and demolish,
       to build and plant.

TWO VISIONS

¹¹ Then the word of the Lord came to me, asking, "What do you see, Jeremiah?"

I replied, "I see a branch of an almond tree."

¹² The Lord said to me, "You have seen correctly, for I watch over^A my word to accomplish it." ¹³ Again the word of the Lord came to me asking, "What do you see?"

And I replied, "I see a boiling pot, its lip tilted from the north to the south."

¹⁴ Then the Lord said to me, "Disaster will be poured out^B from the north on all who live in the land. ¹⁵ Indeed, I am about to summon all the clans and kingdoms of the north."

           This is the Lord's declaration.
       They will come, and each king will set up
         his throne
       at the entrance to Jerusalem's gates.
       They will attack all her surrounding walls
       and all the other cities of Judah.

---

^A 1:12 In Hb, the word for *almond tree* sounds like the word for *watch over*
^B 1:14 LXX reads *will boil*

¹⁶ "I will pronounce my judgments against them for all the evil they did when they abandoned me to burn incense to other gods and to worship the works of their own hands.

¹⁷ "Now, get ready. Stand up and tell them everything that I command you. Do not be intimidated by them or I will cause you to cower before them. ¹⁸ Today, I am the one who has made you a fortified city, an iron pillar, and bronze walls against the whole land — against the kings of Judah, its officials, its priests, and the population. ¹⁹ They will fight against you but never prevail over you, since I am with you to rescue you."

This is the LORD's declaration.

ISRAEL ACCUSED OF APOSTASY

2 The word of the LORD came to me: ² "Go and announce directly to Jerusalem that this is what the LORD says:

I remember the loyalty of your youth,
your love as a bride —
how you followed me in the wilderness,
in a land not sown.
³ Israel was holy to the LORD,
the firstfruits of his harvest.
All who ate of it found themselves guilty;
disaster came on them."

This is the LORD's declaration.

⁴ Hear the word of the LORD, house of Jacob
and all families of the house of Israel.
⁵ This is what the LORD says:

What fault did your fathers find in me
that they went so far from me,
followed worthless idols,
and became worthless themselves?
⁶ They stopped asking, "Where is the LORD
who brought us from the land of Egypt,
who led us through the wilderness,
through a land of deserts and ravines,
through a land of drought and darkness,ᴬ
a land no one traveled through
and where no one lived?"
⁷ I brought you to a fertile land
to eat its fruit and bounty,
but after you entered, you defiled my land;
you made my inheritance detestable.
⁸ The priests quit asking, "Where is the LORD?"
The experts in the law no longer knew me,
and the rulers rebelled against me.
The prophets prophesied byᴮ Baal
and followed useless idols.

ᴬ2:6 Or shadow of death ᴮ2:8 = in the name of

9 Therefore, I will bring a case against you again.
    This is the LORD's declaration.
I will bring a case against your children's children.
10 Cross over to the coasts of Cyprus^A
    and take a look.
Send someone to Kedar and consider carefully;
see if there has ever been anything like this:
11 Has a nation ever exchanged its gods?
(But they were not gods!)
Yet my people have exchanged their^B Glory
for useless idols.
12 Be appalled at this, heavens;
be shocked and utterly desolated!
    This is the LORD's declaration.

13 For my people have committed a double evil:
They have abandoned me,
the fountain of living water,
and dug cisterns for themselves —
cracked cisterns that cannot hold water.

CONSEQUENCES OF APOSTASY

14 Is Israel a slave?
Was he born into slavery?^C
Why else has he become a prey?
15 The young lions have roared at him;
they have roared loudly.
They have laid waste his land.
His cities are in ruins, without inhabitants.
16 The men of Memphis and Tahpanhes
have also broken your skull.
17 Have you not brought this on yourself
by abandoning the LORD your God
while he was leading you along the way?
18 Now what will you gain
by traveling along the way to Egypt
to drink the water of the Nile?^D
What will you gain
by traveling along the way to Assyria
to drink the water of the Euphrates?
19 Your own evil will discipline you;
your own apostasies will reprimand you.
Recognize^E how evil and bitter it is
for you to abandon the LORD your God
and to have no fear of me.
    This is the declaration
    of the Lord GOD of Armies.

---

^A2:10 Lit to the islands of Kittim   ^B2:11 Alt Hb tradition reads my   ^C2:14 Lit born of a house   ^D2:18 Lit of Shihor   ^E2:19 Lit Know and see

20 For long ago I^A broke your yoke;
I^A tore off your chains.
You insisted, "I will not serve!"
On every high hill
and under every green tree
you lay down like a prostitute.

21 I planted you, a choice vine
from the very best seed.
How then could you turn into
a degenerate, foreign vine?

22 Even if you wash with lye
and use a great amount of bleach,^B
the stain of your iniquity is still in front of me.
This is the Lord GOD's declaration.

23 How can you protest, "I am not defiled;
I have not followed the Baals"?
Look at your behavior in the valley;
acknowledge what you have done.
You are a swift young camel
twisting and turning on her way,

24 a wild donkey at home^C in the wilderness.
She sniffs the wind in the heat of her desire.
Who can control her passion?
All who look for her will not become weary;
they will find her in her mating season.^D

25 Keep your feet from going bare
and your throat from thirst.
But you say, "It's hopeless;
I love strangers,
and I will continue to follow them."

26 Like the shame of a thief when he is caught,
so the house of Israel has been put to shame.
They, their kings, their officials,
their priests, and their prophets

27 say to a tree, "You are my father,"
and to a stone, "You gave birth to me."
For they have turned their back to me
and not their face,
yet in their time of disaster they beg,
"Rise up and save us!"

28 But where are your gods you made for yourself?
Let them rise up and save you
in your time of disaster if they can,
for your gods are as numerous as your cities, Judah.

---

^A2:20 LXX reads *you* ^B2:22 Lit *cleansing agent* ^C2:24 Lit *donkey taught*
^D2:24 Lit *her month*

JUDGMENT DESERVED

29 Why do you bring a case against me?
All of you have rebelled against me.
    This is the LORD's declaration.

30 I have struck down your children in vain;
they would not accept discipline.
Your own sword has devoured your prophets
like a ravaging lion.

31 Evil generation,
pay attention to the word of the LORD!
Have I been a wilderness to Israel
or a land of dense darkness?
Why do my people claim,
"We will go where we want;"[A]
we will no longer come to you"?

32 Can a young woman forget her jewelry
or a bride her wedding sash?
Yet my people have forgotten me
for countless days.

33 How skillfully you pursue love;
you also teach evil women your ways.

34 Moreover, your skirts are stained
with the blood of the innocent poor.
You did not catch them breaking and entering.
But in spite of all these things

35 you claim, "I am innocent.
His anger is sure to turn away from me."
But I will certainly judge you
because you have said, "I have not sinned."

36 How unstable you are,
constantly changing your ways!
You will be put to shame by Egypt
just as you were put to shame by Assyria.

37 Moreover, you will be led out from here
with your hands on your head
since the LORD has rejected those you trust;
you will not succeed even with their help.[B]

WAGES OF APOSTASY

3 If[C] a man divorces his wife
and she leaves him to marry another,
can he ever return to her?
Wouldn't such a land[D] become totally defiled?
But you!
You have prostituted yourself with many partners —
can you return to me?
    This is the LORD's declaration.

[A]2:31 Or "We have taken control, or "We can roam   [B]2:37 Lit with them
[C]3:1 One Hb ms, LXX, Syr; other Hb mss read Saying: If   [D]3:1 LXX reads woman

2 Look to the barren heights and see.
Where have you not been immoral?
You sat waiting for them beside the highways
like a nomad in the desert.
You have defiled the land
with your prostitution and wickedness.

3 This is why the showers haven't come —
why there has been no spring rain.
You have the brazen look of a prostitute[A]
and refuse to be ashamed.

4 Haven't you recently called to me,
    "My Father.
You were my friend in my youth.

5 Will he bear a grudge forever?
Will he be endlessly infuriated?"
This is what you have said,
but you have done the evil things
you are capable of.

UNFAITHFUL ISRAEL, TREACHEROUS JUDAH

6 In the days of King Josiah the LORD asked me, "Have you seen what unfaithful Israel has done? She has ascended every high hill and gone under every green tree to prostitute herself there. 7 I thought, 'After she has done all these things, she will return to me.' But she didn't return, and her treacherous sister Judah saw it. 8 I[B] observed that it was because unfaithful Israel had committed adultery that I had sent her away and had given her a certificate of divorce. Nevertheless, her treacherous sister Judah was not afraid but also went and prostituted herself. 9 Indifferent to[C] her prostitution, she defiled the land and committed adultery with stones and trees. 10 Yet in spite of all this, her treacherous sister Judah didn't return to me with all her heart — only in pretense."

This is the LORD's declaration.

11 The LORD announced to me, "Unfaithful Israel has shown herself more righteous than treacherous Judah. 12 Go, proclaim these words to the north, and say,

'Return, unfaithful Israel.
    This is the LORD's declaration.
I will not look on you with anger,[D]
for I am unfailing in my love.
    This is the LORD's declaration.
I will not be angry forever.

13 Only acknowledge your guilt —
you have rebelled against the LORD your God.
You have scattered your favors to strangers
under every green tree
and have not obeyed me.
    This is the LORD's declaration.

A3:3 Lit have a prostitute's forehead   B3:8 One Hb ms, Syr read She   C3:9 Lit From the lightness of   D3:12 Lit not cause my face to fall on you

¹⁴ "'Return, you faithless children — this is the LORD's declaration — for I am your master,ᴬ and I will take you, one from a city and two from a family, and I will bring you to Zion. ¹⁵ I will give you shepherds who are loyal to me,ᴮ and they will shepherd you with knowledge and skill. ¹⁶ When you multiply and increase in the land, in those days — this is the LORD's declaration — no one will say again, "The ark of the LORD's covenant." It will never come to mind, and no one will remember or miss it. Another one will not be made.ᶜ ¹⁷ At that time Jerusalem will be called The LORD's Throne, and all the nations will be gathered to it, to the name of the LORD in Jerusalem. They will cease to follow the stubbornness of their evil hearts. ¹⁸ In those days the house of Judah will join with the house of Israel, and they will come together from the land of the north to the land I have given your ancestors to inherit.'"

TRUE REPENTANCE

¹⁹ I thought, "How I long to make you my sons
    and give you a desirable land,
    the most beautiful inheritance of all the nations."
I thought, "You will call me 'My Father'
    and never turn away from me."

²⁰ However, as a woman may betray her lover,ᴰ
    so you have betrayed me, house of Israel.
        This is the LORD's declaration.

²¹ A sound is heard on the barren heights:
    the children of Israel weeping and begging for mercy,
    for they have perverted their way;
    they have forgotten the LORD their God.

²² Return, you faithless children.
    I will heal your unfaithfulness.
"Here we are, coming to you,
    for you are the LORD our God.

²³ Surely, falsehood comes from the hills,
    commotion from the mountains,
    but the salvation of Israel
    is only in the LORD our God.

²⁴ From the time of our youth
    the shameful oneᴱ has consumed
    what our fathers have worked for —
    their flocks and their herds,
    their sons and their daughters.

²⁵ Let us lie down in our shame;
    let our disgrace cover us.
We have sinned against the LORD our God,
    both we and our fathers,
    from the time of our youth even to this day.
    We have not obeyed the LORD our God."

ᴬ3:14 Or husband   ᴮ3:15 Lit shepherds according to my heart   ᶜ3:16 Or It will no longer be done   ᴰ3:20 Lit friend   ᴱ3:24 = Baal

BLESSING OR CURSE

4 If you return,[A] Israel —
    this is the LORD's declaration —
you will return to me,
if you remove your abhorrent idols
from my presence
and do not waver,
² then you can swear, "As the LORD lives,"
in truth, in justice, and in righteousness,
then the nations will be blessed[B] by him
and will pride themselves in him.

³ For this is what the LORD says to the men of Judah and Jerusalem:
    Break up the unplowed ground;
    do not sow among the thorns.
⁴ Circumcise yourselves to the LORD;
    remove the foreskin of your hearts,
    men of Judah and residents of Jerusalem.
    Otherwise, my wrath will break out like fire
    and burn with no one to extinguish it
    because of your evil deeds.

JUDGMENT FROM THE NORTH

⁵ Declare in Judah, proclaim in Jerusalem, and say:
    Blow the ram's horn throughout the land.
    Cry out loudly and say:
    Assemble yourselves,
    and let's flee to the fortified cities.
⁶ Lift up a signal flag toward Zion.
    Run for cover! Don't stand still!
    For I am bringing disaster from the north —
    a crushing blow.
⁷ A lion has gone up from his thicket;
    a destroyer of nations has set out.
    He has left his lair
    to make your land a waste.
    Your cities will be reduced to uninhabited ruins.
⁸ Because of this, put on sackcloth;
    mourn and wail,
    for the LORD's burning anger
    has not turned away from us.

⁹ "On that day" — this is the LORD's declaration — "the king and the officials will lose their courage. The priests will tremble in fear, and the prophets will be scared speechless."

¹⁰ I said, "Oh no, Lord GOD, you have certainly deceived this people and Jerusalem, by announcing, 'You will have peace,' while a sword is at[C] our throats."

[A] 4:1 Or *Repent*   [B] 4:2 Or *will bless themselves*   [C] 4:10 Lit *sword touches*

¹¹ "At that time it will be said to this people and to Jerusalem, 'A searing wind blows from the barren heights in the wilderness on the way to my dear^A people. It comes not to winnow or to sift; ¹² a wind too strong for this comes at my call.^B Now I will also pronounce judgments against them.' "

13   Look, he advances like clouds;
        his chariots are like a storm.
        His horses are swifter than eagles.
        Woe to us, for we are ruined!
14   Wash the evil from your heart, Jerusalem,
        so that you will be delivered.
        How long will you harbor
        malicious thoughts?
15   For a voice announces from Dan,
        proclaiming malice
            from Mount Ephraim.
16   Warn the nations: Look!
        Proclaim to Jerusalem:
        Those who besiege are coming
        from a distant land;
        they raise their voices
        against the cities of Judah.
17   They have her surrounded
        like those who guard a field,
        because she has rebelled against me.
            This is the LORD's declaration.
18   Your way and your actions
        have brought this on you.
        This is your punishment. It is very bitter,
        because it has reached your heart!

JEREMIAH'S LAMENT

19   My anguish, my anguish!^C I writhe in agony!
        Oh, the pain in^D my heart!
        My heart pounds;
        I cannot be silent.
        For you, my soul,
        have heard the sound of the ram's horn —
        the shout of battle.
20   Disaster after disaster is reported
        because the whole land is destroyed.
        Suddenly my tents are destroyed,
        my tent curtains, in a moment.
21   How long must I see the signal flag
        and hear the sound of the ram's horn?

22   "For my people are fools;
        they do not know me.

---

^A4:11 Lit to the daughter of my   ^B4:12 Lit comes for me   ^C4:19 Lit My inner parts,
my inner parts   ^D4:19 Lit the walls of

They are foolish children,
without understanding.
They are skilled in doing what is evil,
but they do not know how to do what is good."

23 I looked at the earth,
and it was formless and empty.
I looked to the heavens,
and their light was gone.
24 I looked at the mountains,
and they were quaking;
all the hills shook.
25 I looked, and there was no human being,
and all the birds of the sky had fled.
26 I looked, and the fertile field was
a wilderness.
All its cities were torn down
because of the LORD
and his burning anger.

27 For this is what the LORD says:
The whole land will be a desolation,
but I will not finish it off.
28 Because of this, the earth will mourn;
the skies above will grow dark.
I have spoken; I have planned,
and I will not relent or turn back from it.

29 Every city flees
at the sound of the horseman
and the archer.
They enter the thickets
and climb among the rocks.
Every city is abandoned;
no inhabitant is left.
30 And you, devastated one,
what are you doing
that you dress yourself in scarlet,
that you adorn yourself with gold jewelry,
that you enhance your eyes with makeup?
You beautify yourself for nothing.
Your lovers reject you;
they intend to take your life.
31 I hear a cry like a woman in labor,
a cry of anguish like one bearing
her first child.
The cry of Daughter Zion gasping for breath,
stretching out her hands:
"Woe is me, for my life is weary
because of the murderers!"

THE DEPRAVITY OF JERUSALEM

5 Roam through the streets of Jerusalem.
Investigate;^A
search in her squares.
If you find one person,
any who acts justly,
who pursues faithfulness,
then I will forgive her.
2 When they say, "As the LORD lives,"
they are swearing falsely.
3 LORD, don't your eyes look for faithfulness?
You have struck them, but they felt no pain.
You finished them off,
but they refused to accept discipline.
They made their faces harder than rock,
and they refused to return.

4 Then I thought:
They are just the poor;
they have been foolish.
For they don't understand the way of the LORD,
the justice of their God.
5 I will go to the powerful
and speak to them.
Surely they know the way of the LORD,
the justice of their God.
However, these also had broken the yoke
and torn off the chains.
6 Therefore, a lion from the forest will strike them down.
A wolf from arid plains will ravage them.
A leopard stalks their cities.
Anyone who leaves them will be torn to pieces
because their rebellious acts are many,
their unfaithful deeds numerous.

7 Why should I forgive you?
Your children have abandoned me
and sworn by those who are not gods.
I satisfied their needs, yet they committed adultery;
they gashed themselves at the ^B prostitute's house.
8 They are well-fed,^C eager^D stallions,
each neighing after someone else's wife.
9 Should I not punish them for these things?
This is the LORD's declaration.
Should I not avenge myself
on such a nation as this?

¹⁰ Go up among her vineyard terraces and destroy them,
but do not finish them off.
Prune away her shoots,
for they do not belong to the LORD.
¹¹ They, the house of Israel and the house of Judah,
have dealt very treacherously with me.
This is the LORD's declaration.
¹² They have contradicted the LORD
and insisted, "It won't happen.ᴬ
Harm won't come to us;
we won't see sword or famine."
¹³ The prophets become only wind,
for the LORD's word is not in them.
This will in fact happen to them.

COMING JUDGMENT

¹⁴ Therefore, this is what the Lord GOD of Armies says:
Because you have spoken this word,
I am going to make my words
become fire in your mouth.
These people are the wood,
and the fire will consume them.
¹⁵ I am about to bring a nation
from far away against you,
house of Israel.
This is the LORD's declaration.
It is an established nation,
an ancient nation,
a nation whose language you do not know
and whose speech you do not understand.
¹⁶ Their quiver is like an open grave;
they are all warriors.
¹⁷ They will consume your harvest and your food.
They will consume your sons and your daughters.
They will consume your flocks and your herds.
They will consume your vines and your fig trees.
With the sword they will destroy
your fortified cities in which you trust.

¹⁸ "But even in those days" — this is the LORD's declaration — "I will not finish you off. ¹⁹ When people ask, 'For what offense has the LORD our God done all these things to us?' You will respond to them, 'Just as you abandoned me and served foreign gods in your land, so will you serve strangers in a land that is not yours.'

²⁰ "Declare this in the house of Jacob; proclaim it in Judah, saying:
²¹ Hear this,
you foolish and senselessᴮ people.
They have eyes, but they don't see.

ᴬ5:12 Lit *"He does not exist* ᴮ5:21 Lit *without heart*

They have ears, but they don't hear.

22 Do you not fear me?
　　This is the LORD's declaration.
Do you not tremble before me,
the one who set the sand as the boundary of the sea,
an enduring barrier that it cannot cross?
The waves surge, but they cannot prevail.
They roar but cannot pass over it.

23 But these people have stubborn and rebellious hearts.
They have turned aside and have gone away.

24 They have not said to themselves,
'Let's fear the LORD our God,
who gives the seasonal rains, both autumn and spring,
who guarantees to us the fixed weeks of the harvest.'

25 Your guilty acts have diverted these things from you.
Your sins have withheld my bounty from you,

26 for wicked men live among my people.
They watch like hunters[A] lying in wait.[B]
They set a trap;
they catch men.

27 Like a cage full of birds,
so their houses are full of deceit.
Therefore they have grown powerful and rich.

28 They have become fat and sleek.
They have also excelled in evil matters.
They have not taken up cases,
such as the case of the fatherless, so they might prosper,
and they have not defended the rights of the needy.

29 Should I not punish them for these things?
　　This is the LORD's declaration.
Should I not avenge myself
on such a nation as this?

30 An appalling, horrible thing
has taken place in the land.

31 The prophets prophesy falsely,
and the priests rule by their own authority.
My people love it like this.
But what will you do at the end of it?

THREATENED SIEGE OF JERUSALEM

6 "Run for cover
out of Jerusalem, Benjaminites.
Sound the ram's horn in Tekoa;
raise a smoke signal over Beth-haccherem,[C]
for disaster threatens from the north,
even a crushing blow.

2 Though she is beautiful and delicate,

A 5:26 Lit *hunters of birds*　　B 5:26 Hb obscure　　C 6:1 = House of the Vineyard

I will destroy[A] Daughter Zion.
3 Shepherds and their flocks will come against her;
they will pitch their tents all around her.
Each will pasture his own portion.
4 Set them apart for war against her;
rise up, let's attack at noon.
Woe to us, for the day is passing;
the evening shadows grow long.
5 Rise up, let's attack by night.
Let us destroy her fortresses."

6 For this is what the LORD of Armies says:
Cut down the trees;
raise a siege ramp against Jerusalem.
This city must be punished.
There is nothing but oppression within her.
7 As a well gushes out its water,
so she pours out her evil.[B]
Violence and destruction resound in her.
Sickness and wounds keep coming to my attention.
8 Be warned, Jerusalem,
or I will turn away from you;
I will make you a desolation,
a land without inhabitants.

WRATH ON ISRAEL

9 This is what the LORD of Armies says:
Glean the remnant of Israel
as thoroughly as a vine.
Pass your hand once more like a grape gatherer
over the branches.

10 Who can I speak to and give such a warning[C]
that they will listen?
Look, their ear is uncircumcised,[D]
so they cannot pay attention.
See, the word of the LORD has become contemptible to them —
they find no pleasure in it.
11 But I am full of the LORD's wrath;
I am tired of holding it back.
Pour it out on the children in the street,
on the gathering of young men as well.
For both husband and wife will be captured,
the old with the very old.[E]
12 Their houses will be turned over to others,
their fields and wives as well,

[A]6:2 Or silence [B]6:7 Or well keeps its water fresh, so she keeps her evil fresh
[C]6:10 Or and bear witness [D]6:10 They are unresponsive to God. [E]6:11 Lit with fullness of days

for I will stretch out my hand
against the inhabitants of the land.
This is the Lord's declaration.

13 For from the least to the greatest of them,
everyone is making profit dishonestly.
From prophet to priest,
everyone deals falsely.

14 They have treated my people's brokenness superficially,
claiming, "Peace, peace,"
when there is no peace.

15 Were they ashamed when they acted so detestably?
They weren't at all ashamed.
They can no longer feel humiliation.
Therefore, they will fall among the fallen.
When I punish them, they will collapse,
says the Lord.

DISASTER BECAUSE OF DISOBEDIENCE

16 This is what the Lord says:
Stand by the roadways and look.
Ask about the ancient paths,
"Which is the way to what is good?"
Then take it
and find rest for yourselves.
But they protested, "We won't!"

17 I appointed watchmen over you
and said, "Listen for the sound of the ram's horn."
But they protested, "We won't listen!"

18 Therefore listen, you nations
and you witnesses,
learn what the charge is against them.

19 Listen, earth!
I am about to bring disaster on these people,
the fruit of their own plotting,
for they have paid no attention to my words.
They have rejected my instruction.

20 What use to me is frankincense from Sheba
or sweet cane from a distant land?
Your burnt offerings are not acceptable;
your sacrifices do not please me.

21 Therefore, this is what the Lord says:
I am going to place stumbling blocks before these people;
fathers and sons together will stumble over them;
friends and neighbors will also perish.

A CRUEL NATION FROM THE NORTH

22 This is what the Lord says:
Look, an army is coming from a northern land;

a great nation will be stirred up
from the remote regions of the earth.
23 They grasp bow and javelin.
They are cruel and show no mercy.
Their voice roars like the sea,
and they ride on horses,
lined up like men in battle formation
against you, Daughter Zion.

24 We have heard about it,
and our hands have become weak.
Distress has seized us —
pain, like a woman in labor.
25 Don't go out to the fields;
don't walk on the road.
For the enemy has a sword;
terror is on every side.

26 My dear[A] people, dress yourselves in sackcloth
and roll in the dust.
Mourn as you would for an only son,
a bitter lament,
for suddenly the destroyer will come on us.

JEREMIAH APPOINTED AS AN EXAMINER

27 I have appointed you to be an assayer among my people —
a refiner[B] —
so you may know and assay their way of life.
28 All are stubborn rebels
spreading slander.
They are bronze and iron;
all of them are corrupt.
29 The bellows blow,
blasting the lead with fire.
The refining is completely in vain;
the evil ones are not separated out.
30 They are called rejected silver,
for the LORD has rejected them.

FALSE TRUST IN THE TEMPLE

7 This is the word that came to Jeremiah from the LORD: 2 "Stand in the gate of the house of the LORD and there call out this word: 'Hear the word of the LORD, all you people of Judah who enter through these gates to worship the LORD.

3 "'This is what the LORD of Armies, the God of Israel, says: Correct your ways and your actions, and I will allow you to live in this place. 4 Do not trust deceitful words, chanting, "This is the temple of the LORD, the temple of the LORD, the temple of the LORD." 5 Instead, if you really correct your ways and

---

[A]6:26 Lit *Daughter of my* [B]6:27 Text emended; MT reads *fortress* your actions, if you act justly toward one another,[A] 6 if you no longer oppress the resident alien, the fatherless, and the widow and no longer shed innocent blood in this place or follow other gods, bringing harm on yourselves, 7 I will allow you to live in this place, the land I gave to your ancestors long ago and forever. 8 But look, you keep trusting in deceitful words that cannot help.

9 " 'Do you steal, murder, commit adultery, swear falsely, burn incense to Baal, and follow other gods that you have not known? 10 Then do you come and stand before me in this house that bears my name and say, "We are rescued, so we can continue doing all these detestable acts"? 11 Has this house, which bears my name, become a den of robbers in your view? Yes, I too have seen it. This is the LORD's declaration.

SHILOH AS A WARNING

12 " 'But return to my place that was at Shiloh, where I made my name dwell at first. See what I did to it because of the evil of my people Israel. 13 Now, because you have done all these things — this is the LORD's declaration — and because I have spoken to you time and time again[B] but you wouldn't listen, and I have called to you, but you wouldn't answer, 14 what I did to Shiloh I will do to the house that bears my name — the house in which you trust — the place that I gave you and your ancestors. 15 I will banish you from my presence, just as I banished all of your brothers, all the descendants of Ephraim.'

DO NOT PRAY FOR JUDAH

16 "As for you, do not pray for these people. Do not offer a cry or a prayer on their behalf, and do not beg me, for I will not listen to you. 17 Don't you see how they behave in the cities of Judah and in the streets of Jerusalem? 18 The sons gather wood, the fathers light the fire, and the women knead dough to make cakes for the queen of heaven,[C] and they pour out drink offerings to other gods so that they provoke me to anger. 19 But are they really provoking me?" This is the LORD's declaration. "Isn't it they themselves being provoked to disgrace?"

20 Therefore, this is what the Lord GOD says: "Look, my anger — my burning wrath — is about to be poured out on this place, on people and animals, on the tree of the field, and on the produce of the land. My wrath will burn and not be quenched."

OBEDIENCE OVER SACRIFICE

21 This is what the LORD of Armies, the God of Israel, says: "Add your burnt offerings to your other sacrifices, and eat the meat yourselves, 22 for when I brought your ancestors out of the land of Egypt, I did not speak with them or command them concerning burnt offering and sacrifice. 23 However, I did give them this command: 'Obey me, and then I will be your God, and you will be my people. Follow every way I command you so that it may go well with you.' 24 Yet they didn't listen or pay attention but followed their own advice and their own stubborn, evil heart. They went backward and not forward. 25 Since the day your ancestors came out of the land of Egypt until today, I

A7:5 Lit justly between a man and his neighbor   B7:13 Lit you rising early and speaking   C7:18 = a pagan goddess have sent all my servants the prophets to you time and time again.[A] ²⁶ However, my people wouldn't listen to me or pay attention but became obstinate;[B] they did more evil than their ancestors.

A LAMENT FOR DISOBEDIENT JUDAH

²⁷ "When you speak all these things to them, they will not listen to you. When you call to them, they will not answer you. ²⁸ Therefore, declare to them, 'This is the nation that would not listen to the LORD their God and would not accept discipline. Truth[C] has perished — it has disappeared from their mouths. ²⁹ Cut off the hair of your sacred vow[D] and throw it away. Raise up a dirge on the barren heights, for the LORD has rejected and abandoned the generation under his wrath.'

³⁰ "For the Judeans have done what is evil in my sight." This is the LORD's declaration. "They have set up their abhorrent things in the house that bears my name in order to defile it. ³¹ They have built the high places of Topheth[E] in Ben Hinnom Valley[F] in order to burn their sons and daughters in the fire, a thing I did not command; I never entertained the thought.[G]

³² "Therefore, look, the days are coming" — the LORD's declaration — "when this place will no longer be called Topheth and Ben Hinnom Valley, but the Valley of Slaughter. Topheth will become a cemetery,[H] because there will be no other burial place. ³³ The corpses of these people will become food for the birds of the sky and for the wild animals of the land, with no one to scare them away. ³⁴ I will remove from the cities of Judah and the streets of Jerusalem the sound of joy and gladness and the voices of the groom and the bride, for the land will become a desolate waste.

DEATH OVER LIFE

8 "At that time" — this is the LORD's declaration — "the bones of the kings of Judah, the bones of her officials, the bones of the priests, the bones of the prophets, and the bones of the residents of Jerusalem will be brought out of their graves. ² They will be exposed to the sun, the moon, and all the stars in the sky, which they have loved, served, followed, consulted, and worshiped. Their bones will not be collected and buried but will become like manure on the soil's surface. ³ Death will be chosen over life by all the survivors of this evil family, those who remain wherever I have banished them." This is the declaration of the LORD of Armies.

⁴ "You are to say to them: This is what the LORD says:

Do people fall and not get up again?
If they turn away, do they not return?
⁵ Why have these people turned away?
Why is Jerusalem always turning away?
They take hold of deceit;
they refuse to return.
⁶ I have paid careful attention.
They do not speak what is right.

[A]7:25 Lit you, each day rising early and sending   [B]7:26 Lit but stiffened their neck   [C]7:28 Or Faithfulness   [D]7:29 Lit off your consecration   [E]7:31 Lit of the fireplace   [F]7:31 A valley south of Jerusalem   [G]7:31 Lit command, and it did not arise on my heart   [H]7:32 Lit They will bury in Topheth

No one regrets his evil,
asking, 'What have I done?'
Everyone has stayed his course
like a horse rushing into battle.
7 Even storks in the sky
know their seasons.
Turtledoves, swallows, and cranes[A]
are aware of their migration,
but my people do not know
the requirements of the LORD.

PUNISHMENT FOR JUDAH'S LEADERS

8 "How can you claim, 'We are wise;
the law of the LORD is with us'?
In fact, the lying pen of scribes
has produced falsehood.
9 The wise will be put to shame;
they will be dismayed and snared.
They have rejected the word of the LORD,
so what wisdom do they really have?
10 Therefore, I will give their wives to other men,
their fields to new occupants,
for from the least to the greatest,
everyone is making profit dishonestly.
From prophet to priest,
everyone deals falsely.
11 They have treated the brokenness
of my dear[B] people superficially,
claiming, 'Peace, peace,'
when there is no peace.
12 Were they ashamed when they acted so detestably?
They weren't at all ashamed.
They can no longer feel humiliation.
Therefore, they will fall among the fallen.
When I punish them, they will collapse,"
says the LORD.

13 I will gather them and bring them to an end.[C]
This is the LORD's declaration.
There will be no grapes on the vine,
no figs on the fig tree,
and even the leaf will wither.
Whatever I have given them will be lost to them.

GOD'S PEOPLE UNREPENTANT

14 Why are we just sitting here?
Gather together; let us enter the fortified cities

[A]8:7 Hb obscure [B]8:11 Lit of the daughter of my, also in vv. 19,21,22
[C]8:13 Lit Gathering I will end them

and perish there,[A]
for the LORD our God has destroyed[B] us.
He has given us poisoned water to drink,
because we have sinned against the LORD.

15 We hoped for peace, but there was nothing good;
for a time of healing, but there was only terror.

16 From Dan, the snorting of horses is heard.
At the sound of the neighing of mighty steeds,
the whole land quakes.
They come to devour the land
and everything in it,
the city and all its residents.

17 Indeed, I am about to send snakes among you,
poisonous vipers that cannot be charmed.
They will bite you.
This is the LORD's declaration.

LAMENT OVER JUDAH

18 My joy has flown away;
grief has settled on me.
My heart is sick.

19 Listen — the cry of my dear people
from a faraway land,
"Is the LORD no longer in Zion,
her King not within her?"
Why have they angered me
with their carved images,
with their worthless foreign idols?

20 Harvest has passed, summer has ended,
but we have not been saved.

21 I am broken by the brokenness
of my dear people.
I mourn; horror has taken hold of me.

22 Is there no balm in Gilead?
Is there no physician there?
So why has the healing of my dear people
not come about?

9 If my head were a flowing spring,
my eyes a fountain of tears,
I would weep day and night
over the slain of my dear[C] people.

2 If only I had a traveler's lodging place
in the wilderness,
I would abandon my people
and depart from them,

[A]8:14 Or there be silenced   [B]8:14 Or silenced   [C]9:1 Lit slain among the
daughter of my

for they are all adulterers,
a solemn assembly of treacherous people.

3 They bent their tongues like their bows;
lies and not faithfulness prevail in the land,
for they proceed from one evil to another,
and they do not take me into account.
This is the LORD's declaration.

IMMINENT RUIN AND EXILE

4 Everyone has to be on guard against his friend.
Don't trust any brother,
for every brother will certainly deceive,
and every friend spread slander.
5 Each one betrays his friend;
no one tells the truth.
They have taught their tongues to speak lies;
they wear themselves out doing wrong.
6 You live in a world of deception.^A
In their deception they refuse to know me.
This is the LORD's declaration.

7 Therefore, this is what the LORD of Armies says:
I am about to refine them and test them,
for what else can I do
because of my dear^B people?^C
8 Their tongues are deadly arrows —
they speak deception.
With his mouth
one speaks peaceably with his friend,
but inwardly he sets up an ambush.
9 Should I not punish them for these things?
This is the LORD's declaration.
Should I not avenge myself
on such a nation as this?

10 I will raise weeping and a lament
over the mountains,
a dirge over the wilderness grazing land,
for they have been so scorched
that no one passes through.
The sound of cattle is no longer heard.
From the birds of the sky to the animals,
everything has fled — they have
gone away.
11 I will make Jerusalem a heap of rubble,
a jackals' den.

---

^A9:6 LXX reads *Oppression on oppression, deceit on deceit*   ^B9:7 Lit *of the
daughter of my*   ^C9:7 LXX, Tg read *because of their evils*

I will make the cities of Judah a desolation,
an uninhabited place.

¹²Who is the person wise enough to understand this? Who has the LORD spoken to, that he may explain it? Why is the land destroyed and scorched like a wilderness, so no one can pass through?

¹³The LORD said, "It is because they abandoned my instruction, which I set before them, and did not obey my voice or walk according to it. ¹⁴Instead, they followed the stubbornness of their hearts and followed the Baals as their fathers taught them." ¹⁵Therefore, this is what the LORD of Armies, the God of Israel, says: "I am about to feed this people wormwood and give them poisonous water to drink. ¹⁶I will scatter them among the nations that they and their fathers have not known. I will send a sword after them until I have finished them off."

MOURNING OVER JUDAH

¹⁷This is what the LORD of Armies says:
Consider, and summon the women who mourn;
send for the skillful women.

¹⁸ Let them come quickly to raise a lament over us
so that our eyes may overflow with tears,
our eyelids be soaked with weeping.

¹⁹ For a sound of lamentation is heard from Zion:
How devastated we are.
We are greatly ashamed,
for we have abandoned the land;
our dwellings have been torn down.

²⁰ Now hear the word of the LORD, you women.
Pay attention toᴬ the words from his mouth.
Teach your daughters a lament
and one another a dirge,

²¹ for Death has climbed through our windows;
it has entered our fortresses,
cutting off children from the streets,
young men from the squares.

²²"Speak as follows: 'This is what the LORD declares: Human corpses will fall like manure on the surface of the field, like newly cut grain after the reaper with no one to gather it.

BOAST IN THE LORD

²³"'This is what the LORD says:
The wise person should not boast in his wisdom;
the strong should not boast in his strength;
the wealthy should not boast in his wealth.

²⁴ But the one who boasts should boast in this:
that he understands and knows me —

ᴬ9:20 Lit *Your ears must receive*

that I am the LORD, showing faithful love,
justice, and righteousness on the earth,
for I delight in these things.
This is the LORD's declaration.

25 " 'Look, the days are coming — this is the LORD's declaration — when I will punish all the circumcised yet uncircumcised: 26 Egypt, Judah, Edom, the Ammonites, Moab, and all the inhabitants of the desert who clip the hair on their temples.A All these nations are uncircumcised, and the whole house of Israel is uncircumcised in heart.' "

FALSE GODS CONTRASTED WITH THE CREATOR

10 Hear the word that the LORD has spoken toB you, house of Israel. 2 This is what the LORD says:
Do not learn the way of the nations
or be terrified by signs in the heavens,
although the nations are terrified by them,
3 for the customs of the peoples are worthless.
Someone cuts down a tree from the forest;
it is worked by the hands of a craftsman
with a chisel.
4 He decorates it with silver and gold.
It is fastened with hammer and nails,
so it won't totter.
5 Like scarecrows in a cucumber patch,
their idols cannot speak.
They must be carried because they cannot walk.
Do not fear them for they can do no harm —
and they cannot do any good.

6 LORD, there is no one like you.
You are great;
your name is great in power.
7 Who should not fear you,
King of the nations?
It is what you deserve.
For among all the wise people of the nations
and among all their kingdoms,
there is no one like you.
8 They are both stupid and foolish,
instructed by worthless idols
made of wood!
9 Beaten silver is brought from Tarshish
and gold from Uphaz.C
The work of a craftsman
and of a goldsmith's hands
is clothed in blue and purple,
all the work of skilled artisans.

A9:26 Or who live in distant places B10:1 Or against C10:9 Or Ophir

¹⁰ But the Lᴏʀᴅ is the true God;
he is the living God and eternal King.
The earth quakes at his wrath,
and the nations cannot endure his rage.

¹¹ You are to say this to them: "The gods that did not make the heavens and the earth will perish from the earth and from under these heavens."[A]

¹² He made the earth by his power,
established the world by his wisdom,
and spread out the heavens by his understanding.

¹³ When he thunders,[B]
the waters in the heavens are in turmoil,
and he causes the clouds to rise
from the ends of the earth.
He makes lightning for the rain
and brings the wind from his storehouses.

¹⁴ Everyone is stupid and ignorant.
Every goldsmith is put to shame
by his carved image,
for his cast images are a lie;
there is no breath in them.

¹⁵ They are worthless, a work to be mocked.
At the time of their punishment
they will be destroyed.

¹⁶ Jacob's Portion[C] is not like these
because he is the one who formed all things.
Israel is the tribe of his inheritance;
the Lᴏʀᴅ of Armies is his name.

EXILE AFTER THE SIEGE

¹⁷ Gather up your belongings[D] from the ground,
you who live under siege.

¹⁸ For this is what the Lᴏʀᴅ says:
Look, I am flinging away
the land's residents at this time
and bringing them such distress
that they will feel it.

JEREMIAH GRIEVES

¹⁹ Woe to me because of my brokenness —
I am severely wounded!
I exclaimed, "This is my intense suffering,
but I must bear it."

²⁰ My tent is destroyed;
all my tent cords are snapped.
My sons have departed from me and are no more.

[A]10:11 This is the only Aramaic v. in Jr. [B]10:13 Lit *At his giving of the voice*
[C]10:16 = the Lᴏʀᴅ [D]10:17 Lit *bundle*

I have no one to pitch my tent again
or to hang up my curtains.
21 For the shepherds are stupid:
They don't seek the LORD.
Therefore they have not prospered,
and their whole flock is scattered.
22 Listen! A noise — it is coming —
a great commotion from the land to the north.
The cities of Judah will be made desolate,
a jackals' den.

23 I know, LORD,
that a person's way of life is not his own;
no one who walks determines his own steps.
24 Discipline me, LORD, but with justice —
not in your anger,
or you will reduce me to nothing.
25 Pour out your wrath on the nations
that don't recognize you
and on the families
that don't call on your name,
for they have consumed Jacob;
they have consumed him and finished him off
and made his homeland desolate.

REMINDER OF THE COVENANT

11 This is the word that came to Jeremiah from the LORD: ² "Listen to the words of this covenant and tell them to the men of Judah and the residents of Jerusalem. ³ Tell them, 'This is what the LORD, the God of Israel, says: "Let a curse be on the man who does not obey the words of this covenant, ⁴ which I commanded your ancestors when I brought them out of the land of Egypt, out of the iron furnace." I declared, "Obey me, and do everything that I command you, and you will be my people, and I will be your God," ⁵ in order to establish the oath I swore to your ancestors, to give them a land flowing with milk and honey, as it is today.' "

I answered, "Amen, LORD."

⁶ The LORD said to me, "Proclaim all these words in the cities of Judah and in the streets of Jerusalem: 'Obey the words of this covenant and carry them out.' ⁷ For I strongly warned your ancestors when I brought them out of the land of Egypt until today, warning them time and time again,^A 'Obey me.' ⁸ Yet they would not obey or pay attention; each one followed the stubbornness of his evil heart. So I brought on them all the curses of this covenant, because they had not done what I commanded them to do."

⁹ The LORD said to me, "A conspiracy has been discovered among the men of Judah and the residents of Jerusalem. ¹⁰ They have returned to the iniquities of their fathers who refused to obey my words and have followed other gods to worship them. The house of Israel and the house of Judah broke my covenant I made with their ancestors.

---

^A 11:7 Lit *today, rising early and warning*

¹¹ "Therefore, this is what the LORD says: I am about to bring on them disaster that they cannot escape. They will cry out to me, but I will not hear them. ¹² Then the cities of Judah and the residents of Jerusalem will go and cry out to the gods they have been burning incense to, but they certainly will not save them in their time of disaster. ¹³ Your gods are indeed as numerous as your cities, Judah, and the altars you have set up to Shame^A — altars to burn incense to Baal — as numerous as the streets of Jerusalem.

¹⁴ "As for you, do not pray for these people. Do not raise up a cry or a prayer on their behalf, for I will not be listening when they call out to me at the time of their disaster.

¹⁵   What right does my beloved have
        to be in my house,
        having carried out so many evil schemes?
        Can holy meat^B prevent your disaster^C
        so you can celebrate?
¹⁶   The LORD named you
        a flourishing olive tree,
        beautiful with well-formed fruit.
        He has set fire to it,
        and its branches are consumed^D
        with the sound of a mighty tumult.

¹⁷ "The LORD of Armies who planted you has decreed disaster against you, because of the disaster^E the house of Israel and the house of Judah brought on themselves when they angered me by burning incense to Baal."

¹⁸   The LORD informed me, so I knew.
        Then you helped me to see their deeds,
¹⁹   for I was like a docile^F lamb led to slaughter.
        I didn't know that they had devised plots
            against me:
        "Let's destroy the tree with its fruit;^G
        let's cut him off from the land of the living
        so that his name will no longer
            be remembered."
²⁰   But, LORD of Armies, who judges righteously,
        who tests heart^H and mind,
        let me see your vengeance on them,
        for I have presented my case to you.

²¹ Therefore, here is what the LORD says concerning the people of Anathoth who intend to take your life. They warn, "Do not prophesy in the name of the LORD, or you will certainly die at our hand." ²² Therefore, this is what the LORD of Armies says: "I am about to punish them. The young men will die by the sword; their sons and daughters will die by famine. ²³ They will have no remnant, for I will bring disaster on the people of Anathoth in the year of their punishment."

---

^A11:13 = Baal   ^B11:15 = sacrificial meat   ^C11:15 LXX; MT reads *meat pass from you*   ^D11:16 Vg; MT reads *broken*   ^E11:17 Or *evil*   ^F11:19 Or *pet*   ^G11:19 Lit *bread*   ^H11:20 Lit *kidneys*

JEREMIAH'S COMPLAINT

12 You will be righteous, LORD,
even if I bring a case against you.
Yet, I wish to contend with you:
Why does the way of the wicked prosper?
Why do all the treacherous live at ease?

2 You planted them, and they have taken root.
They have grown and produced fruit.
You are ever on their lips,[A]
but far from their conscience.[B]

3 As for you, LORD, you know me; you see me.
You test whether my heart is with you.
Drag the wicked away like sheep to slaughter
and set them apart for the day of killing.

4 How long will the land mourn
and the grass of every field wither?
Because of the evil of its residents,
animals and birds have been swept away,
for the people have said,
"He cannot see what our end will be."[C]

THE LORD'S RESPONSE

5 If you have raced with runners
and they have worn you out,
how can you compete with horses?
If you stumble[D] in a peaceful land,
what will you do in the thickets of the Jordan?

6 Even your brothers — your own father's family —
even they were treacherous to you;
even they have cried out loudly after you.
Do not have confidence in them,
though they speak well of you.

7 I have abandoned my house;
I have deserted my inheritance.
I have handed the love of my life
over to her enemies.

8 My inheritance has behaved toward me
like a lion in the forest.
She has roared against me.
Therefore, I hate her.

9 Is my inheritance like a hyena[E] to me?
Are birds of prey circling her?
Go, gather all the wild animals;
bring them to devour her.

10 Many shepherds have destroyed my vineyard;
they have trampled my plot of land.

[A]12:2 Lit *are near in their mouth*   [B]12:2 Lit *kidneys*   [C]12:4 LXX reads *see our ways*   [D]12:5 Or *you are secure*   [E]12:9 Hb obscure

They have turned my desirable plot
into a desolate wasteland.
11   They have made it a desolation.
It mourns, desolate, before me.
All the land is desolate,
but no one takes it to heart.
12   Over all the barren heights in the wilderness
the destroyers have come,
for the LORD has a sword that devours
from one end of the earth to the other.
No one has peace.
13   They have sown wheat but harvested thorns.
They have exhausted themselves but have no profit.
Be put to shame by your harvests
because of the LORD's burning anger.

14 This is what the LORD says: "Concerning all my evil neighbors who attack the inheritance that I bequeathed to my people, Israel, I am about to uproot them from their land, and I will uproot the house of Judah from them. 15 After I have uprooted them, I will once again have compassion on them and return each one to his inheritance and to his land. 16 If they will diligently learn the ways of my people — to swear by my name, 'As the LORD lives,' just as they taught my people to swear by Baal — they will be built up among my people. 17 However, if they will not obey, then I will uproot and destroy that nation."

This is the LORD's declaration.

LINEN UNDERWEAR

13 This is what the LORD said to me: "Go and buy yourself a linen undergarment and put it on.^A But do not put it in water." 2 So I bought underwear as the LORD instructed me and put it on.

3 Then the word of the LORD came to me a second time: 4 "Take the underwear that you bought and are wearing,^B and go at once to the Euphrates^C and hide it in a rocky crevice." 5 So I went and hid it by the Euphrates, as the LORD commanded me.

6 A long time later the LORD said to me, "Go at once to the Euphrates and get the underwear that I commanded you to hide there." 7 So I went to the Euphrates and dug up the underwear and got it from the place where I had hidden it, but it was ruined — of no use at all.

8 Then the word of the LORD came to me: 9 "This is what the LORD says: Just like this I will ruin the great pride of both Judah and Jerusalem. 10 These evil people, who refuse to listen to me, who follow the stubbornness of their own hearts, and who have followed other gods to serve and bow in worship — they will be like this underwear, of no use at all. 11 Just as underwear clings to one's waist, so I fastened the whole house of Israel and of Judah to me" — this is the LORD's declaration — "so that they might be my people for my fame, praise, and glory, but they would not obey.

---

^A13:1 Lit *around your waist*   ^B13:4 Lit *wearing around your waist*
^C13:4-7 Perhaps a place near Anathoth with the same spelling as the river

THE WINE JARS

¹² "Say this to them: 'This is what the LORD, the God of Israel, says: Every jar should be filled with wine.' Then they will respond to you, 'Don't we know that every jar should be filled with wine?' ¹³ And you will say to them, 'This is what the LORD says: I am about to fill all who live in this land — the kings who reign for David on his throne, the priests, the prophets, and all the residents of Jerusalem — with drunkenness. ¹⁴ I will smash them against each other, fathers and sons alike — this is the LORD's declaration. I will allow no mercy, pity, or compassion to keep me from destroying them.' "

THE LORD'S WARNING

15 Listen and pay attention. Do not be proud,
for the LORD has spoken.

16 Give glory to the LORD your God
before he brings darkness,
before your feet stumble
on the mountains at dusk.
You wait for light,
but he brings darkest gloom^A
and makes total darkness.

17 But if you will not listen,
my innermost being will weep in secret
because of your pride.
My eyes will overflow with tears,
for the LORD's flock has been taken captive.

18 Say to the king and the queen mother:
Take a humble seat,
for your glorious crowns
have fallen from your heads.

19 The cities of the Negev are under siege;
no one can help them.
All of Judah has been taken into exile,
taken completely into exile.

20 Look up and see
those coming from the north.
Where is the flock entrusted to you,
the sheep that were your pride?

THE DESTINY OF JERUSALEM

21 What will you say when he appoints
close friends as leaders over you,
ones you yourself trained?
Won't labor pains seize you,
as they do a woman in labor?

22 And when you ask yourself,
"Why have these things happened to me?"

---

^A13:16 Or brings a shadow of death

it is because of your great guilt
that your skirts have been stripped off,
your body exposed. ^A

23 Can the Cushite change his skin,
or a leopard his spots?
If so, you might be able to do what is good,
you who are instructed in evil.

24 I will scatter you ^B like drifting chaff
before the desert wind.

25 This is your lot,
what I have decreed for you —
this is the Lord's declaration —
because you have forgotten me
and trusted in lies.

26 I will pull your skirts up over your face
so that your shame might be seen.

27 Your adulteries and your lustful neighing,
your depraved prostitution
on the hills, in the fields —
I have seen your abhorrent acts.
Woe to you, Jerusalem!
You are unclean —
for how long yet?

THE DROUGHT

14 This is the word of the Lord that came to Jeremiah concerning the drought:

2 Judah mourns;
her city gates languish.
Her people are on the ground in mourning;
Jerusalem's cry rises up.

3 Their nobles send their servants ^C for water.
They go to the cisterns;
they find no water;
their containers return empty.
They are ashamed and humiliated;
they cover their heads.

4 The ground is cracked
since no rain has fallen on the land.
The farmers are ashamed;
they cover their heads.

5 Even the doe in the field
gives birth and abandons her fawn
since there is no grass.

6 Wild donkeys stand on the barren heights
panting for air like jackals.
Their eyes fail
because there are no green plants.

---

^A 13:22 Lit *your heels have suffered violence*   ^B 13:24 Lit *them*   ^C 14:3 Lit *little ones*

7 Though our iniquities testify against us,
   Lord, act for your name's sake.
   Indeed, our rebellions are many;
   we have sinned against you.
8 Hope of Israel,
   its Savior in time of distress,
   why are you like a resident alien in the land,
   like a traveler stopping only for the night?
9 Why are you like a helpless man,
   like a warrior unable to save?
   Yet you are among us, Lord,
   and we bear your name.
   Don't leave us!

10 This is what the Lord says concerning these people:
   Truly they love to wander;
   they never rest their feet.
   So the Lord does not accept them.
   Now he will remember their iniquity
   and punish their sins.

FALSE PROPHETS TO BE PUNISHED

11 Then the Lord said to me, "Do not pray for the well-being of these people. 12 If they fast, I will not hear their cry of despair. If they offer burnt offering and grain offering, I will not accept them. Rather, I will finish them off by sword, famine, and plague."

13 And I replied, "Oh no, Lord God! The prophets are telling them, 'You won't see sword or suffer famine. I will certainly give you lasting peace in this place.' "

14 But the Lord said to me, "These prophets are prophesying a lie in my name. I did not send them, nor did I command them or speak to them. They are prophesying to you a false vision, worthless divination, the deceit of their own minds.

15 "Therefore, this is what the Lord says concerning the prophets who prophesy in my name, though I did not send them, and who say, 'There will never be sword or famine in this land.' By sword and famine these prophets will meet their end. 16 The people they are prophesying to will be thrown into the streets of Jerusalem because of the famine and the sword. There will be no one to bury them — they, their wives, their sons, and their daughters. I will pour out their own evil on them."

JEREMIAH'S REQUEST

17 You are to speak this word to them:
   Let my eyes overflow with tears;
   day and night may they not stop,
   for the virgin daughter of my people
   has been destroyed by a crushing blow,
   an extremely severe wound.
18 If I go out to the field,
   look — those slain by the sword!
   If I enter the city,
   look — those ill from famine!

For both prophet and priest
travel to a land they do not know.

¹⁹ Have you completely rejected Judah?
Do you detest Zion?
Why do you strike us
with no hope of healing for us?
We hoped for peace,
but there was nothing good;
for a time of healing,
but there was only terror.
²⁰ We acknowledge our wickedness, LORD,
the iniquity of our fathers;
indeed, we have sinned against you.
²¹ For your name's sake, don't despise us.
Don't disdain your glorious throne.
Remember your covenant with us;
do not break it.
²² Can any of the worthless idols of the nations bring rain?
Or can the skies alone give showers?
Are you not the LORD our God?
We therefore put our hope in you,
for you have done all these things.

THE LORD'S NEGATIVE RESPONSE

15 Then the LORD said to me: "Even if Moses and Samuel should stand before me, my compassions would not reach out to these people. Send them from my presence, and let them go. ² If they ask you, 'Where will we go?' tell them: This is what the LORD says:

Those destined for death, to death;
those destined for the sword, to the sword.
Those destined for famine, to famine;
those destined for captivity, to captivity.

³ "I will ordain four kinds^A of judgment for them" — this is the LORD's declaration — "the sword to kill, the dogs to drag away, and the birds of the sky and the wild animals of the land to devour and destroy. ⁴ I will make them a horror to all the kingdoms of the earth because of Manasseh son of Hezekiah, the king of Judah, for what he did in Jerusalem.

⁵ Who will have pity on you, Jerusalem?
Who will show sympathy toward you?
Who will turn aside
to ask about your well-being?
⁶ You have left me."
This is the LORD's declaration.
"You have turned your back,
so I have stretched out my hand against you
and destroyed you.

---

^A15:3 Lit *families*

I am tired of showing compassion.

7 I scattered them with a winnowing fork
at the city gates of the land.
I made them childless; I destroyed my people.
They would not turn from their ways.

8 I made their widows more numerous
than the sand of the seas.
I brought a destroyer at noon
against the mother of young men.
I suddenly released on her
agitation and terrors.

9 The mother of seven grew faint;
she breathed her last breath.
Her sun set while it was still day;
she was ashamed and humiliated.
The rest of them I will give over to the sword
in the presence of their enemies."
This is the LORD's declaration.

JEREMIAH'S COMPLAINT

10 Woe is me, my mother,
that you gave birth to me,
a man who incites dispute and conflict
in all the land.
I did not lend or borrow,
yet everyone curses me.

THE LORD'S RESPONSE

11 The LORD said:
Haven't I set you loose for your good?
Haven't I punished you
in a time of trouble,
in a time of distress with the enemy?[A]

12 Can anyone smash iron,
iron from the north, or bronze?

13 I will give up your wealth
and your treasures as plunder,
without cost, for all your sins
in all your borders.

14 Then I will make you serve your enemies[B]
in a land you do not know,
for my anger will kindle a fire
that will burn against you.

JEREMIAH'S PRAYER FOR VENGEANCE

15 You know, LORD;
remember me and take note of me.

[A]15:11 Hb obscure [B]15:14 Some Hb mss, LXX, Syr, Tg; other Hb mss read *you pass through*

Avenge me against my persecutors.
In your patience,^A don't take me away.
Know that I suffer disgrace for your honor.
16 Your words were found, and I ate them.
Your words became a delight to me
and the joy of my heart,
for I bear your name,
LORD God of Armies.
17 I never sat with the band of revelers,
and I did not celebrate with them.
Because your hand was on me, I sat alone,
for you filled me with indignation.
18 Why has my pain become unending,
my wound incurable,
refusing to be healed?
You truly have become
like a mirage to me —
water that is not reliable.

JEREMIAH TOLD TO REPENT

19 Therefore, this is what the LORD says:
If you return, I will take you back;
you will stand in my presence.
And if you speak noble words,
rather than worthless ones,
you will be my spokesman.
It is they who must return to you;
you must not return to them.
20 Then I will make you a fortified wall
of bronze
to this people.
They will fight against you
but will not overcome you,
for I am with you
to save you and rescue you.
This is the LORD's declaration.
21 I will rescue you from the power of evil people
and redeem you from the grasp of the ruthless.

NO MARRIAGE FOR JEREMIAH

16 The word of the LORD came to me: 2 "Do not marry or have sons or daughters in this place. 3 For this is what the LORD says concerning sons and daughters born in this place as well as concerning the mothers who bear them and the fathers who father them in this land: 4 They will die from deadly diseases. They will not be mourned or buried but will be like manure on the soil's surface. They will be finished off by sword and famine. Their corpses will become food for the birds of the sky and for the wild animals of the land.

---

^A15:15 Lit In the slowness of your anger

[5] "For this is what the LORD says: Don't enter a house where a mourning feast is taking place.[A] Don't go to lament or sympathize with them, for I have removed my peace from these people as well as my faithful love and compassion." This is the LORD's declaration. [6] "Both great and small will die in this land without burial. No lament will be made for them, nor will anyone cut himself or shave his head for them.[B] [7] Food won't be provided for the mourner to comfort him because of the dead. A consoling drink won't be given him for the loss of his father or mother. [8] Do not enter the house where feasting is taking place to sit with them to eat and drink. [9] For this is what the LORD of Armies, the God of Israel, says: I am about to eliminate from this place, before your very eyes and in your time, the sound of joy and gladness, the voice of the groom and the bride.

ABANDONING THE LORD AND HIS LAW

[10] "When you tell these people all these things, they will say to you, 'Why has the LORD declared all this terrible disaster against us? What is our iniquity? What is our sin that we have committed against the LORD our God?' [11] Then you will answer them, 'Because your fathers abandoned me — this is the LORD's declaration — and followed other gods, served them, and bowed in worship to them. Indeed, they abandoned me and did not keep my instruction. [12] You did more evil than your fathers. Look, each one of you was following the stubbornness of his evil heart, not obeying me. [13] So I will hurl you from this land into a land that you and your fathers are not familiar with. There you will worship other gods both day and night, for I will not grant you grace.'[C]

[14] "However, look, the days are coming" — the LORD's declaration — "when it will no longer be said, 'As the LORD lives who brought the Israelites from the land of Egypt,' [15] but rather, 'As the LORD lives who brought the Israelites from the land of the north and from all the other lands where he had banished them.' For I will return them to their land that I gave to their ancestors.

PUNISHMENT OF EXILE

[16] "I am about to send for many fishermen" — this is the LORD's declaration — "and they will fish for them. Then I will send for many hunters, and they will hunt them down on every mountain and hill and out of the clefts of the rocks, [17] for my gaze takes in all their ways. They are not concealed from me, and their iniquity is not hidden from my sight. [18] I will first repay them double for their iniquity and sin because they have polluted my land. They have filled my inheritance with the carcasses of their abhorrent and detestable idols."

[19] LORD, my strength and my stronghold,
  my refuge in a time of distress,
  the nations will come to you
  from the ends of the earth, and they will say,
  "Our fathers inherited only lies,
  worthless idols of no benefit at all."
[20] Can one make gods for himself?
  But they are not gods.
[21] "Therefore, I am about to inform them,

[A]16:5 Lit house of mourning   [B]16:6 This custom demonstrated pagan mourning rituals.   [C]16:13 Or compassion

and this time I will make them know
my power and my might;
then they will know that my name is the LORD."

THE PERSISTENT SIN OF JUDAH

17 The sin of Judah is inscribed
with an iron stylus.
With a diamond point
it is engraved on the tablet of their hearts
and on the horns of their^A altars,
2 while their children remember their altars
and their Asherah poles, by the green trees
on the high hills —
3 my mountains in the countryside.
I will give up your wealth
and all your treasures as plunder
because of the sin of your high places^B
in all your borders.
4 You will, on your own, relinquish your inheritance
that I gave you.
I will make you serve your enemies
in a land you do not know,
for you have set my anger on fire;
it will burn forever.

CURSE AND BLESSING

5 This is what the LORD says:
Cursed is the person who trusts in mankind.
He makes human flesh his strength,
and his heart turns from the LORD.
6 He will be like a juniper in the Arabah;
he cannot see when good comes
but dwells in the parched places in the wilderness,
in a salt land where no one lives.
7 The person who trusts in the LORD,
whose confidence indeed is the LORD, is blessed.
8 He will be like a tree planted by water:
it sends its roots out toward a stream,
it doesn't fear when heat comes,
and its foliage remains green.
It will not worry in a year of drought
or cease producing fruit.

THE DECEITFUL HEART

9 The heart is more deceitful than anything else,
and incurable — who can understand it?
10 I, the LORD, examine the mind,

---

^A 17:1 Some Hb mss, Syr, Vg; other Hb mss read *your* ^B 17:3 Lit *plunder, your high places because of sin*

I test the heart[A]
to give to each according to his way,
according to what his actions deserve.

11 He who makes a fortune unjustly
is like a partridge that hatches eggs it didn't lay.
In the middle of his life
his riches will abandon him,
so in the end he will be a fool.

12 A glorious throne
on high from the beginning
is the place of our sanctuary.

13 LORD, the hope of Israel,
all who abandon you
will be put to shame.
All who turn away from me
will be written in the dirt,
for they have abandoned
the LORD, the fountain of living water.

JEREMIAH'S PLEA

14 Heal me, LORD, and I will be healed;
save me, and I will be saved,
for you are my praise.

15 Hear how they keep challenging me,
"Where is the word of the LORD?
Let it come!"

16 But I have not run away from being your shepherd,
and I have not longed for the fatal day.
You know my words were spoken in your presence.

17 Don't become a terror to me.
You are my refuge in the day of disaster.

18 Let my persecutors be put to shame,
but don't let me be put to shame.
Let them be terrified, but don't let me be terrified.
Bring on them the day of disaster;
shatter them with total[B] destruction.

OBSERVING THE SABBATH

19 This is what the LORD said to me, "Go and stand at the People's Gate, through which the kings of Judah enter and leave, as well as at all the gates of Jerusalem. 20 Announce to them, 'Hear the word of the LORD, kings of Judah, all Judah, and all the residents of Jerusalem who enter through these gates. 21 This is what the LORD says: Watch yourselves; do not pick up a load and bring it in through Jerusalem's gates on the Sabbath day. 22 Do not carry a load out of your houses on the Sabbath day or do any work, but keep the Sabbath day holy, just as I commanded your ancestors. 23 They wouldn't listen or pay attention but became obstinate, not listening or accepting discipline.

[A]17:10 Lit kidneys [B]17:18 Lit double

²⁴ " 'However, if you listen to me — this is the Lᴏʀᴅ's declaration — and do not bring loads through the gates of this city on the Sabbath day, but keep the Sabbath day holy and do no work on it, ²⁵ kings and princes will enter through the gates of this city. They will sit on the throne of David; they will ride in chariots and on horses with their officials, the men of Judah, and the residents of Jerusalem. This city will be inhabited forever. ²⁶ Then people will come from the cities of Judah and from the area around Jerusalem, from the land of Benjamin and from the Judean foothills, from the hill country and from the Negev bringing burnt offerings and sacrifices, grain offerings and frankincense, and thank offerings to the house of the Lᴏʀᴅ. ²⁷ But if you do not listen to me to keep the Sabbath day holy by not carrying a load while entering the gates of Jerusalem on the Sabbath day, I will set fire to its gates, and it will consume the citadels of Jerusalem and not be extinguished.' "

PARABLE OF THE POTTER

18 This is the word that came to Jeremiah from the Lᴏʀᴅ: ² "Go down at once to the potter's house; there I will reveal my words to you." ³ So I went down to the potter's house, and there he was, working away at the wheel.ᴬ ⁴ But the jar that he was making from the clay became flawed in the potter's hand, so he made it into another jar, as it seemed right for him to do.

⁵ The word of the Lᴏʀᴅ came to me: ⁶ "House of Israel, can I not treat you as this potter treats his clay? " — this is the Lᴏʀᴅ's declaration. "Just like clay in the potter's hand, so are you in my hand, house of Israel. ⁷ At one moment I might announce concerning a nation or a kingdom that I will uproot, tear down, and destroy it. ⁸ However, if that nation about which I have made the announcement turns from its evil, I will relent concerning the disaster I had planned to do to it. ⁹ At another time I might announce concerning a nation or a kingdom that I will build and plant it. ¹⁰ However, if it does what is evil in my sight by not listening to me, I will relent concerning the good I had said I would do to it. ¹¹ So now, say to the men of Judah and to the residents of Jerusalem, 'This is what the Lᴏʀᴅ says: Look, I am about to bring harm to you and make plans against you. Turn now, each from your evil way, and correct your ways and your deeds.' ¹² But they will say, 'It's hopeless. We will continue to follow our plans, and each of us will continue to act according to the stubbornness of his evil heart.' "

DELUDED ISRAEL

¹³ Therefore, this is what the Lᴏʀᴅ says:

Ask among the nations,
who has heard things like these?
Virgin Israel has done a most horrible thing.
¹⁴ Does the snow of Lebanon ever leave the highland crags?
Or does cold water flowing from a distance ever fail?
¹⁵ Yet my people have forgotten me.
They burn incense to worthless idols
that make them stumble in their ways
on the ancient roads,
and make them walk on new paths, not the highway.

ᴬ18:3 Lit *pair of stones*

THE POTTER AND THE CLAY

JEREMIAH 18–19; ROMANS 9:20-21

I would make a truly terrible stunt double. Sure, you could call me athletic and a true daredevil. But only if by "daredevil" you mean drinking coffee after noon, and by "athletic" you mean stretching to hit the snooze button for the fourteenth time.

However, there is one thing I get crazy for, and it's the tilt-a-whirl at the state fair. Ever since I stood on my tippy-toes as a little girl to pass the height requirement, it's been my annual supplier of adrenaline. The moment I step on the magenta platform full of freely spinning circular cars, I untie the elastic holding my ponytail and let my Type A tendencies fall away. Sitting in the sacred seat of all the daredevils who have come before me, I grip the metal bar in my lap and prepare for a stomach-churning good time. This is living on the edge.

I'll admit that when I read the potter and the clay illustration in Jeremiah 18, I'm not as eager to jump on the wheel and start spinning.

"'House of Israel, can I not treat you as this potter treats his clay?' —this is the LORD's declaration. 'Just like clay in the potters hand, so are you in my hand, house of Israel.'"

JEREMIAH 18:6

It's a beautiful illustration, yes, but it's also terrifying and makes me want to tighten my ponytail elastic. When I realize the lack of control given to the clay, I notice that maybe my definition of risk-taking isn't so accurate after all.

Jeremiah may have felt the same reluctance toward this analogy. He'd seen nations fall and people flee. A mere piece of clay himself, he wanted to get a few answers from the Potter before jumping on the wheel. *Will you do the same thing to us? Will you destroy us, or will you make us into art?*

Daredevils and chickens alike, we're all calculating the risk of our next move. Fear tells us we're one car crash, text message, doctor's visit, or break-up away from despair. *If we're the clay, can the Potter be trusted?*

In this passage, God actually underscores His power to create destruction (Jr 18:7), and I'm not so sure I want to be subject to His hand. **But as His children, we remember that the mold was perfect before sin, and because of Christ, He still works to shape us back into His original plan of perfection.**

Yes, we may be one turn of the wheel away from suffering, but we are always within arm's reach of redemption. As His clay, spinning in the tension of grief and grace, we can fix our eyes on the still, patient Potter. He can be trusted to make each of us into a beautiful masterpiece.

16 They have made their land a horror,
a perpetual object of scorn;^A
all who pass by it will be appalled
and shake their heads.

17 I will scatter them before the enemy like the east wind.
I will show them^B my back and not my face
on the day of their calamity.

PLOT AGAINST JEREMIAH

18 Then certain ones said, "Come, let's make plans against Jeremiah, for instruction will never be lost from the priest, or counsel from the wise, or a word from the prophet. Come, let's denounce him^C and pay no attention to all his words."

19 Pay attention to me, LORD.
Hear what my opponents are saying!

20 Should good be repaid with evil?
Yet they have dug a pit for me.
Remember how I stood before you
to speak good on their behalf,
to turn your anger from them.

21 Therefore, hand their children over to famine,
and give them over to the power of the sword.
Let their wives become childless and widowed,
their husbands slain by deadly disease,^D
their young men struck down by the sword in battle.

22 Let a cry be heard from their houses
when you suddenly bring raiders against them,
for they have dug a pit to capture me
and have hidden snares for my feet.

23 But you, LORD, know
all their deadly plots against me.
Do not wipe out their iniquity;
do not blot out their sin before you.
Let them be forced to stumble before you;
deal with them in the time of your anger.

THE CLAY JAR

19 This is what the LORD says: "Go, buy a potter's clay jar. Take^E some of the elders of the people and some of the leading priests 2 and go out to Ben Hinnom Valley near the entrance of the Potsherd Gate. Proclaim there the words I speak to you. 3 Say, 'Hear the word of the LORD, kings of Judah and residents of Jerusalem. This is what the LORD of Armies, the God of Israel, says: I am going to bring such disaster on this place that everyone who hears about it will shudder^F 4 because they have abandoned me and made this a foreign place. They have burned incense in it to other gods that they, their fathers, and the kings of Judah have never known.

---

^A18:16 Lit *hissing* ^B18:17 LXX, Lat, Syr, Tg; MT reads *will look at them*
^C18:18 Lit *let's strike him with the tongue* ^D18:21 Lit *by death* ^E19:1 Syr, Tg; MT omits *Take* ^F19:3 Lit *about it, his ears will tingle*; Hb obscure

They have filled this place with the blood of the innocent. ⁵ They have built high places to Baal on which to burn their children in the fire as burnt offerings to Baal, something I have never commanded or mentioned; I never entertained the thought.ᴬ

⁶ " 'Therefore, look, the days are coming — this is the Lᴏʀᴅ's declaration — when this place will no longer be called Topheth and Ben Hinnom Valley, but Slaughter Valley. ⁷ I will spoil the plans of Judah and Jerusalem in this place. I will make them fall by the sword before their enemies, by the hand of those who intend to take their life. I will provide their corpses as food for the birds of the sky and for the wild animals of the land. ⁸ I will make this city desolate, an object of scorn. Everyone who passes by it will be appalled and scoff because of all its wounds. ⁹ I will make them eat the flesh of their sons and their daughters, and they will eat each other's flesh in the distressing siege inflicted on them by their enemies who intend to take their life.'

¹⁰ "Then you are to shatter the jar in the presence of the people going with you, ¹¹ and you are to proclaim to them, 'This is what the Lᴏʀᴅ of Armies says: I will shatter these people and this city, like one shatters a potter's jar that can never again be mended. They will bury the dead in Topheth because there is no other place for burials. ¹² That is what I will do to this place — this is the declaration of the Lᴏʀᴅ — and to its residents, making this city like Topheth. ¹³ The houses of Jerusalem and the houses of the kings of Judah will become impure like that place Topheth — all the houses on whose rooftops they have burned incense to all the stars in the sky and poured out drink offerings to other gods.' "

¹⁴ Jeremiah returned from Topheth, where the Lᴏʀᴅ had sent him to prophesy, stood in the courtyard of the Lᴏʀᴅ's temple, and proclaimed to all the people, ¹⁵ "This is what the Lᴏʀᴅ of Armies, the God of Israel, says: 'I am about to bring on this city — and on all its cities — every disaster that I spoke against it, for they have become obstinate, not obeying my words.' "

JEREMIAH BEATEN BY PASSHUR

20 Pashhur the priest, the son of Immer and chief official in the temple of the Lᴏʀᴅ, heard Jeremiah prophesying these things. ² So Pashhur had the prophet Jeremiah beaten and put him in the stocks at the Upper Benjamin Gate in the Lᴏʀᴅ's temple. ³ The next day, when Pashhur released Jeremiah from the stocks, Jeremiah said to him, "The Lᴏʀᴅ does not call you Pashhur, but Terror Is on Every Side,ᴮ ⁴ for this is what the Lᴏʀᴅ says, 'I am about to make you a terror to both yourself and those you love. They will fall by the sword of their enemies before your very eyes. I will hand Judah over to the king of Babylon, and he will deport them to Babylon and put them to the sword. ⁵ I will give away all the wealth of this city, all its products and valuables. Indeed, I will hand all the treasures of the kings of Judah over to their enemies. They will plunder them, seize them, and carry them off to Babylon. ⁶ As for you, Pashhur, and all who live in your house, you will go into captivity. You will go to Babylon. There you will die, and there you will be buried, you and all your friends to whom you prophesied lies.' "

ᴬ19:5 Lit *mentioned, and it did not arise on my heart*   ᴮ20:3 = *Magor-missabib*

JEREMIAH COMPELLED TO PREACH

7 You deceived me, LORD, and I was deceived.
You seized me and prevailed.
I am a laughingstock all the time;
everyone ridicules me.
8 For whenever I speak, I cry out,
I proclaim, "Violence and destruction!"
so the word of the LORD has become my
constant disgrace and derision.
9 I say, "I won't mention him
or speak any longer in his name."
But his message becomes a fire burning in my heart,
shut up in my bones.
I become tired of holding it in,
and I cannot prevail.
10 For I have heard the gossip of many people,
"Terror is on every side!
Report him; let's report him!"
Everyone I trusted^A watches for my fall.
"Perhaps he will be deceived
so that we might prevail against him
and take our vengeance on him."
11 But the LORD is with me like a violent warrior.
Therefore, my persecutors will stumble and not prevail.
Since they have not succeeded, they will be utterly shamed,
an everlasting humiliation that will never be forgotten.
12 LORD of Armies, testing the righteous
and seeing the heart^B and mind,
let me see your vengeance on them,
for I have presented my case to you.
13 Sing to the LORD!
Praise the LORD,
for he rescues the life of the needy
from evil people.

JEREMIAH'S LAMENT

14 May the day I was born
be cursed.
May the day my mother bore me
never be blessed.
15 May the man be cursed
who brought the news to my father, saying,
"A male child is born to you,"
bringing him great joy.
16 Let that man be like the cities
the LORD demolished without compassion.
Let him hear an outcry in the morning
and a war cry at noontime

1266

^A 20:10 Lit Every man of my peace ^B 20:12 Lit kidneys

17 because he didn't kill me in the womb
so that my mother might have been my grave,
her womb eternally pregnant.
18 Why did I come out of the womb
to see only struggle and sorrow,
to end my life in shame?

ZEDEKIAH'S REQUEST DENIED

21 This is the word that came to Jeremiah from the LORD when King Zedekiah sent Pashhur son of Malchijah and the priest Zephaniah son of Maaseiah to Jeremiah, asking, ² "Inquire of the LORD on our behalf, since King Nebuchadnezzar^A of Babylon is making war against us. Perhaps the LORD will perform for us something like all his past wondrous works so that Nebuchadnezzar will withdraw from us."

³ But Jeremiah answered, "This is what you are to say to Zedekiah: ⁴ 'This is what the LORD, the God of Israel, says: I am about to repel the weapons of war in your hands, those you are using to fight the king of Babylon and the Chaldeans^B who are besieging you outside the wall, and I will bring them into the center of this city. ⁵ I myself will fight against you with an outstretched hand and a strong arm, with anger, rage, and intense wrath. ⁶ I will strike the residents of this city, both people and animals. They will die in a severe plague. ⁷ Afterward — this is the LORD's declaration — King Zedekiah of Judah, his officers, and the people — those in this city who survive the plague, the sword, and the famine — I will hand over to King Nebuchadnezzar of Babylon, to their enemies, yes, to those who intend to take their lives. He will put them to the sword; he won't spare them or show pity or compassion.'

A WARNING FOR THE PEOPLE

⁸ "But tell this people, 'This is what the LORD says: Look, I am setting before you the way of life and the way of death. ⁹ Whoever stays in this city will die by the sword, famine, and plague, but whoever goes out and surrenders to the Chaldeans who are besieging you will live and will retain his life like the spoils of war. ¹⁰ For I have set my face against this city to bring disaster and not good — this is the LORD's declaration. It will be handed over to the king of Babylon, who will burn it.'

¹¹ "And to the house of the king of Judah say this: 'Hear the word of the LORD! ¹² House of David, this is what the LORD says:

Administer justice every morning,
and rescue the victim of robbery
from his oppressor,
or my anger will flare up like fire
and burn unquenchably
because of your evil deeds.
13 Beware! I am against you,
you who sit above the valley,
you atop the rocky plateau —
this is the LORD's declaration —

---

^A 21:2 Lit *Nebuchadrezzar*   ^B 21:4 = Babylonians

you who say, "Who can come down against us?
Who can enter our hiding places?"
14 I will punish you according to what you have done —
this is the Lord's declaration.
I will kindle a fire in your forest
that will consume everything around it.'"

JUDGMENT AGAINST SINFUL KINGS

22 This is what the Lord says: "Go down to the palace of the king of Judah and announce this word there. ² You are to say, 'Hear the word of the Lord, king of Judah, you who sit on the throne of David — you, your officers, and your people who enter these gates. ³ This is what the Lord says: Administer justice and righteousness. Rescue the victim of robbery from his oppressor. Don't exploit or brutalize the resident alien, the fatherless, or the widow. Don't shed innocent blood in this place. ⁴ For if you conscientiously carry out this word, then kings sitting on David's throne will enter through the gates of this palace riding on chariots and horses — they, their officers, and their people. ⁵ But if you do not obey these words, then I swear by myself — this is the Lord's declaration — that this house will become a ruin.'"

⁶ For this is what the Lord says concerning the house of the king of Judah:

"You are like Gilead to me,
or the summit of Lebanon,
but I will certainly turn you into a wilderness,
uninhabited cities.
7 I will set apart destroyers against you,
each with his weapons.
They will cut down the choicest of your cedars
and throw them into the fire.

⁸ "Many nations will pass by this city and ask one another, 'Why did the Lord do such a thing to this great city?' ⁹ They will answer, 'Because they abandoned the covenant of the Lord their God and bowed in worship to other gods and served them.'"

A MESSAGE CONCERNING SHALLUM

10 Do not weep for the dead;
do not mourn for him.
Weep bitterly for the one who has gone away,
for he will never return again
and see his native land.

¹¹ For this is what the Lord says concerning Shallum son of Josiah, king of Judah, who became king in place of his father Josiah, and who has left this place: "He will never return here again, ¹² but he will die in the place where they deported him, never seeing this land again."

A MESSAGE CONCERNING JEHOIAKIM

13 Woe for the one who builds his palace
through unrighteousness,

his upstairs rooms through injustice,
who makes his neighbor serve without pay
and will not give him his wages,
14 who says, "I will build myself a massive palace,
with spacious upstairs rooms."
He will cut windows^A in it,
and it will be paneled with cedar
and painted bright red.
15 Are you a king because you excel in cedar?
Didn't your father eat and drink
and administer justice and righteousness?
Then it went well with him.
16 He took up the case of the poor and needy;
then it went well.
Is this not what it means to know me?
This is the LORD's declaration.
17 But you have eyes and a heart for nothing
except your own dishonest profit,
shedding innocent blood
and committing extortion and oppression.

18 Therefore, this is what the LORD says concerning Jehoiakim son of Josiah, king of Judah:

They will not mourn for him, saying,
"Woe, my brother!" or "Woe, my sister!"
They will not mourn for him, saying,
"Woe, lord! Woe, his majesty!"
19 He will be buried like a donkey,
dragged off and thrown
outside Jerusalem's gates.
20 Go up to Lebanon and cry out;
raise your voice in Bashan;
cry out from Abarim,
for all your lovers^B have been crushed.
21 I spoke to you when you were secure.
You said, "I will not listen."
This has been your way since youth;
indeed, you have never listened to me.
22 The wind will take charge of^C all
your shepherds,
and your lovers will go into captivity.
Then you will be ashamed and humiliated
because of all your evil.
23 You residents of Lebanon,
nestled among the cedars,
how you will groan^D when pains come on you,
agony like a woman in labor.

A MESSAGE CONCERNING CONIAH

[24] "As I live" — this is the LORD's declaration — "though you, Coniah[A] son of Jehoiakim, the king of Judah, were a signet ring on my right hand, I would tear you from it. [25] In fact, I will hand you over to those you dread, who intend to take your life, to Nebuchadnezzar king of Babylon and the Chaldeans. [26] I will hurl you and the mother who gave birth to you into another land, where neither of you were born, and there you will both die. [27] They will never return to the land they long to return to."

[28] Is this man Coniah a despised, shattered pot,
a jar no one wants?
Why are he and his descendants hurled out
and cast into a land they have not known?

[29] Earth, earth, earth,
hear the word of the LORD!

[30] This is what the LORD says:
Record this man as childless,
a man who will not be successful in his lifetime.
None of his descendants will succeed
in sitting on the throne of David
or ruling again in Judah.

THE LORD AND HIS SHEEP

23 "Woe to the shepherds who destroy and scatter the sheep of my pasture!" This is the LORD's declaration. [2] "Therefore, this is what the LORD, the God of Israel, says about the shepherds who tend my people: You have scattered my flock, banished them, and have not attended to them. I am about to attend to you because of your evil acts" — this is the LORD's declaration. [3] "I will gather the remnant of my flock from all the lands where I have banished them, and I will return them to their grazing land. They will become fruitful and numerous. [4] I will raise up shepherds over them who will tend them. They will no longer be afraid or discouraged, nor will any be missing." This is the LORD's declaration.

THE RIGHTEOUS BRANCH OF DAVID

[5] "Look, the days are coming" — this is the LORD's declaration —
"when I will raise up a Righteous Branch for David.
He will reign wisely as king
and administer justice and righteousness in the land.
[6] In his days Judah will be saved,
and Israel will dwell securely.
This is the name he will be called:
The LORD Is Our Righteousness.[B]

[7] "Look, the days are coming" — the LORD's declaration — "when it will no longer be said, 'As the LORD lives who brought the Israelites from the land of Egypt,' [8] but, 'As the LORD lives, who brought and led the descendants of the house of Israel from the land of the north and from all the

[A]22:24 = Jehoiachin [B]23:6 = Yahweh-zidkenu

TURN AND RETURN

JEREMIAH 23–24; JOEL 2:12-27

"Lord, even my repentance is broken. Help me."

Those are the words I scrawled in my notebook one morning as I tried desperately to lay my heart bare before God, frustrated that the process did not make me "feel" better. I am a sinner, and I know that, too. He is the one true God, and I know this. The lines of communication were open and I was trying to get there emotionally—wherever "there" is—but the warm fuzzies weren't coming.

I went back to Scripture and looked for the words "turn" and "return." Maybe the answer was there. Maybe I could learn how to come to Jesus all over again.

The first "return" I found was in Jeremiah 24:7: "They will be my people, and I will be their God because they will return to me with all their heart."

Then in Joel 2:12, God says through the prophet, "turn to me with all your heart" and again one verse later—"return to the LORD your God."

Much to my dismay, the call to return to God is not part of a long list of to-dos, a checklist that would give me confidence I was returning correctly. No, there is one qualification: to return with all my heart.

Evidently the cleaned up, feel-good part of my heart is not all God is looking for. He doesn't want only the parts of my heart I'm willing to

let others see—He wants the whole messy, confused, narcissistic, achy thing. You and I and our whole unholy selves are called to turn fully, openly, and sans-covering to the holy, almighty God of all the universe.

"I will give them a heart to know me," God says through the prophet Jeremiah, "that I am the LORD" (Jr 24:7). But as we come to know our God's compassion and mercy, we also come to know His incomparable holiness. It's no wonder we try to come to Him with layers of lies and pride and every other self-preservation instinct intact. It would make sense . . . were it not for Jesus.

The cross of Jesus is the path by which we return to our holy, gracious God. We need not fashion our own defense or disguise to shield our brokenness from His eyes. The blood of Jesus is our covering.

Our actions do not give us the right to return. Our emotions do not grant us access to God. We return because—and only because—Jesus Christ goes before us, His cross as our banner and His grace as our plea.

Friends, when you doubt that your whole, achy self is welcome in the presence of our God, look to the cross. When you fear your return is lacking, that your repentance itself falls short, look to the cross.

The cross of Jesus is our only way to the Father—not just the first time, but every time.

other countries where I^A had banished them.' They will dwell once more in their own land."

FALSE PROPHETS CONDEMNED

^9 Concerning the prophets:

My heart is broken within me,
and all my bones tremble.
I have become like a drunkard,
like a man overcome by wine,
because of the LORD,
because of his holy words.

^10 For the land is full of adulterers;
the land mourns because of the curse,
and the grazing lands in the wilderness have dried up.
Their way of life^B has become evil,
and their power is not rightly used

^11 because both prophet and priest are ungodly,
even in my house I have found their evil.
This is the LORD's declaration.

^12 Therefore, their way will seem
like slippery paths in the gloom.
They will be driven away and fall down there,
for I will bring disaster on them,
the year of their punishment.
This is the LORD's declaration.

^13 Among the prophets of Samaria
I saw something disgusting:
They prophesied by Baal
and led my people Israel astray.

^14 Among the prophets of Jerusalem also
I saw a horrible thing:
They commit adultery and walk in lies.
They strengthen the hands of evildoers,
and none turns his back on evil.
They are all like Sodom to me;
Jerusalem's residents are like Gomorrah.

^15 Therefore, this is what the LORD of Armies says concerning the prophets:
I am about to feed them wormwood
and give them poisoned water to drink,
for from the prophets of Jerusalem
ungodliness^C has spread throughout the land.

^16 This is what the LORD of Armies says: "Do not listen to the words of the prophets who prophesy to you. They are deluding you. They speak visions from their own minds, not from the LORD's mouth. ^17 They keep on saying to those who despise me, 'The LORD has spoken: You will have peace.' They

^A 23:8 LXX reads *he*   ^B 23:10 Lit *Their manner of running*   ^C 23:15 Or *pollution* have said to everyone who follows the stubbornness of his heart, 'No harm will come to you.'"

18 For who has stood in the council of the LORD
to see and hear his word?
Who has paid attention to his word and obeyed?

19 Look, a storm from the LORD!
Wrath has gone out,
a whirling storm.
It will whirl about the heads of the wicked.

20 The LORD's anger will not turn away
until he has completely fulfilled the purposes of his heart.
In time to come you will understand it clearly.

21 I did not send out these prophets,
yet they ran.
I did not speak to them,
yet they prophesied.

22 If they had really stood in my council,
they would have enabled my people to hear my words
and would have turned them from their evil ways
and their evil deeds.

23 "Am I a God who is only near" — this is the LORD's declaration — "and not a God who is far away? 24 Can a person hide in secret places where I cannot see him?" — the LORD's declaration. "Do I not fill the heavens and the earth?" — the LORD's declaration.

25 "I have heard what the prophets who prophesy a lie in my name have said: 'I had a dream! I had a dream!' 26 How long will this continue in the minds of the prophets prophesying lies, prophets of the deceit of their own minds? 27 Through their dreams that they tell one another, they plan to cause my people to forget my name as their fathers forgot my name through Baal worship. 28 The prophet who has only a dream should recount the dream, but the one who has my word should speak my word truthfully, for what is straw compared to grain?" — this is the LORD's declaration. 29 "Is not my word like fire" — this is the LORD's declaration — "and like a hammer that pulverizes rock? 30 Therefore, take note! I am against the prophets" — the LORD's declaration — "who steal my words from each other. 31 I am against the prophets" — the LORD's declaration — "who use their own tongues to make a declaration. 32 I am against those who prophesy false dreams" — the LORD's declaration — "telling them and leading my people astray with their reckless lies. It was not I who sent or commanded them, and they are of no benefit at all to these people" — this is the LORD's declaration.

THE BURDEN OF THE LORD

33 "Now when these people or a prophet or a priest asks you, 'What is the burden^ of the LORD?' you will respond to them, 'What is the burden? I will throw you away! This is the LORD's declaration.' 34 As for the prophet, priest,

---

^23:33 The Hb word for *burden* (Ex 23:5; 2Sm 15:33) can also mean "oracle" (Is 13:1; Nah 1:10).

or people who say, 'The burden of the LORD,' I will punish that man and his household. [35] This is what each man is to say to his friend and to his brother: 'What has the LORD answered?' or 'What has the LORD spoken?' [36] But no longer refer to[A] the burden of the LORD, for each man's word becomes his burden and you pervert the words of the living God, the LORD of Armies, our God. [37] Say to the prophet, 'What has the LORD answered you?' or 'What has the LORD spoken?' [38] But if you say, 'The burden of the LORD,' then this is what the LORD says: Because you have said, 'The burden of the LORD,' and I specifically told you not to say, 'The burden of the LORD,' [39] I will surely forget you.[B] I will throw you away from my presence — both you and the city that I gave you and your fathers. [40] I will bring on you everlasting disgrace and humiliation that will never be forgotten."

THE GOOD AND THE BAD FIGS

24 After King Nebuchadnezzar of Babylon had deported Jeconiah[C] son of Jehoiakim king of Judah, the officials of Judah, and the craftsmen and metalsmiths from Jerusalem and had brought them to Babylon, the LORD showed me two baskets of figs placed in front of the temple of the LORD. [2] One basket contained very good figs, like early figs, but the other basket contained very bad figs, so bad they were inedible. [3] The LORD said to me, "What do you see, Jeremiah?"

I said, "Figs! The good figs are very good, but the bad figs are extremely bad, so bad they are inedible."

[4] The word of the LORD came to me: [5] "This is what the LORD, the God of Israel, says: Like these good figs, so I regard as good the exiles from Judah I sent away from this place to the land of the Chaldeans. [6] I will keep my eyes on them for their good and will return them to this land. I will build them up and not demolish them; I will plant them and not uproot them. [7] I will give them a heart to know me, that I am the LORD. They will be my people, and I will be their God because they will return to me with all their heart.

[8] "But as for the bad figs, so bad they are inedible, this is what the LORD says: In this way I will deal with King Zedekiah of Judah, his officials, and the remnant of Jerusalem — those remaining in this land or living in the land of Egypt. [9] I will make them an object of horror and a disaster to all the kingdoms of the earth, an example for disgrace, scorn, ridicule, and cursing, wherever I have banished them. [10] I will send the sword, famine, and plague against them until they have perished from the land I gave to them and their ancestors."

THE SEVENTY-YEAR EXILE

25 This is the word that came to Jeremiah concerning all the people of Judah in the fourth year of Jehoiakim son of Josiah, king of Judah (which was the first year of King Nebuchadnezzar of Babylon). [2] The prophet Jeremiah spoke concerning all the people of Judah and all the residents of Jerusalem as follows: [3] "From the thirteenth year of Josiah son of Amon, king of Judah, until this very day — twenty-three years — the word of the LORD has come to me, and I have spoken to you time and time

---

[A]23:36 Or longer remember   [B]23:39 Some Hb mss; other Hb mss, LXX, Syr, Vg read surely lift you up   [C]24:1 = Jehoiachin again,^A but you have not obeyed. ^4 The LORD sent all his servants the prophets to you time and time again,^B but you have not obeyed or even paid attention.^C ^5 He announced, 'Turn, each of you, from your evil way of life and from your evil deeds. Live in the land the LORD gave to you and your ancestors long ago and forever. ^6 Do not follow other gods to serve them and to bow in worship to them, and do not anger me by the work of your hands. Then I will do you no harm.

^7 "'But you have not obeyed me' — this is the LORD's declaration — 'with the result that you have angered me by the work of your hands and brought disaster on yourselves.'

^8 "Therefore, this is what the LORD of Armies says: 'Because you have not obeyed my words, ^9 I am going to send for all the families of the north' — this is the LORD's declaration — 'and send for my servant Nebuchadnezzar king of Babylon, and I will bring them against this land, against its residents, and against all these surrounding nations, and I will completely destroy them and make them an example of horror and scorn, and ruins forever. ^10 I will eliminate the sound of joy and gladness from them — the voice of the groom and the bride, the sound of the millstones and the light of the lamp. ^11 This whole land will become a desolate ruin, and these nations will serve the king of Babylon for seventy years. ^12 When the seventy years are completed, I will punish the king of Babylon and that nation' — this is the LORD's declaration — 'the land of the Chaldeans, for their iniquity, and I will make it a ruin forever. ^13 I will bring on that land all my words I have spoken against it, all that is written in this book that Jeremiah prophesied against all the nations. ^14 For many nations and great kings will enslave them, and I will repay them according to their deeds and the work of their hands.'"

THE CUP OF GOD'S WRATH

^15 This is what the LORD, the God of Israel, said to me: "Take this cup of the wine of wrath from my hand and make all the nations to whom I am sending you drink from it. ^16 They will drink, stagger,^D and go out of their minds because of the sword I am sending among them."

^17 So I took the cup from the LORD's hand and made all the nations to whom the LORD sent me drink from it.

^18 Jerusalem and the other cities of Judah, its kings and its officials, to make them a desolate ruin, an example for scorn and cursing — as it is today;

^19 Pharaoh king of Egypt, his officers, his leaders, all his people,

^20 and all the mixed peoples;

all the kings of the land of Uz;

all the kings of the land of the Philistines — Ashkelon, Gaza, Ekron, and the remnant of Ashdod;

^21 Edom, Moab, and the Ammonites;

^22 all the kings of Tyre,

all the kings of Sidon,

and the kings of the coasts and islands;

---

^A25:3 Lit you; rising early and speaking ^B25:4 Lit to you, rising early and sending ^C25:4 Lit even inclined your ear to hear ^D25:16 Or vomit

²³ Dedan, Tema, Buz, and all those who clip the hair on their temples;ᴬ
²⁴ all the kings of Arabia,
and all the kings of the mixed peoples who have settled in the desert;
²⁵ all the kings of Zimri,
all the kings of Elam,
and all the kings of Media;
²⁶ all the kings of the north, both near and far from one another;
that is, all the kingdoms of the world throughout the earth.
Finally, the king of Sheshachᴮ will drink after them.

²⁷ "Then you are to say to them, 'This is what the Lord of Armies, the God of Israel, says: Drink, get drunk, and vomit. Fall down and never get up again, as a result of the sword I am sending among you.' ²⁸ Ifᶜ they refuse to accept the cup from your hand and drink, you are to say to them, 'This is what the Lord of Armies says: You must drink! ²⁹ For I am already bringing disaster on the city that bears my name, so how could you possibly go unpunished? You will not go unpunished, for I am summoning a sword against all the inhabitants of the earth. This is the declaration of the Lord of Armies.'

JUDGMENT ON THE WHOLE WORLD

³⁰ "As for you, you are to prophesy all these things to them, and say to them:
The Lord roars from on high;
he makes his voice heard from his holy dwelling.
He roars loudly over his grazing land;
he calls out with a shout, like those who tread grapes,
against all the inhabitants of the earth.
³¹ The tumult reaches to the ends of the earth
because the Lord brings a case against the nations.
He enters into judgment with all people.
As for the wicked, he hands them over to the sword —
this is the Lord's declaration.

³² "This is what the Lord of Armies says:
Pay attention! Disaster spreads
from nation to nation.
A huge storm is stirred up
from the ends of the earth."

³³ Those slain by the Lord on that day will be scattered from one end of the earth to the other. They will not be mourned, gathered, or buried. They will be like manure on the soil's surface.
³⁴ Wail, you shepherds, and cry out.
Roll in the dust, you leaders of the flock.
Because the days of your slaughter have come,
you will fall and become shattered like a precious vase.
³⁵ Flight will be impossible for the shepherds,
and escape, for the leaders of the flock.
³⁶ Hear the sound of the shepherds' cry,

ᴬ25:23 Or who live in distant places   ᴮ25:26 = Babylon   ᶜ25:28 Or When

the wail of the leaders of the flock,
for the LORD is destroying their pasture.
37 Peaceful grazing land will become lifeless
because of the LORD's burning anger.
38 He has left his den like a lion,
for their land has become a desolation
because of the sword[A] of the oppressor,
because of his burning anger.

JEREMIAH'S SPEECH IN THE TEMPLE

26 At the beginning of the reign of Jehoiakim son of Josiah, king of Judah, this word came from the LORD: ² "This is what the LORD says: Stand in the courtyard of the LORD's temple and speak all the words I have commanded you to speak to all Judah's cities that are coming to worship there. Do not hold back a word. ³ Perhaps they will listen and turn — each from his evil way of life — so that I might relent concerning the disaster that I plan to do to them because of the evil of their deeds. ⁴ You are to say to them, 'This is what the LORD says: If you do not listen to me by living according to my instruction that I set before you ⁵ and by listening to the words of my servants the prophets — whom I have been sending to you time and time again,[B] though you did not listen — ⁶ I will make this temple like Shiloh. I will make this city an example for cursing for all the nations of the earth.'"

JEREMIAH SEIZED

⁷ The priests, the prophets, and all the people heard Jeremiah speaking these words in the temple of the LORD. ⁸ When he finished the address the LORD had commanded him to deliver to all the people, immediately the priests, the prophets, and all the people took hold of him, yelling, "You must surely die! ⁹ How dare you prophesy in the name of the LORD, 'This temple will become like Shiloh and this city will become an uninhabited ruin'!" Then all the people crowded around Jeremiah at the LORD's temple.

¹⁰ When the officials of Judah heard about these things, they went from the king's palace to the LORD's temple and sat at the entrance of the New Gate of the LORD's temple.[C] ¹¹ Then the priests and prophets said to the officials and all the people, "This man deserves the death sentence because he has prophesied against this city, as you have heard with your own ears."

JEREMIAH'S DEFENSE

¹² Then Jeremiah said to all the officials and all the people, "The LORD sent me to prophesy all the words that you have heard against this temple and city. ¹³ So now, correct your ways and deeds, and obey the LORD your God so that he might relent concerning the disaster he had pronounced against you. ¹⁴ As for me, here I am in your hands; do to me what you think is good and right. ¹⁵ But know for certain that if you put me to death, you will bring innocent blood on yourselves, on this city, and on its residents, for it is certain the LORD has sent me to speak all these things directly to you."

[A]25:38 Some Hb mss, LXX, Tg; other Hb mss read *burning*   [B]26:5 Lit *you, rising early and sending*   [C]26:10 Many Hb mss, Syr, Tg, Vg; other Hb mss read *the New Gate of the LORD*

JEREMIAH RELEASED

[16] Then the officials and all the people told the priests and prophets, "This man doesn't deserve the death sentence, for he has spoken to us in the name of the LORD our God!"

[17] Some of the elders of the land stood up and said to all the assembled people, [18] "Micah the Moreshite prophesied in the days of King Hezekiah of Judah and said to all the people of Judah, 'This is what the LORD of Armies says:

Zion will be plowed like a field,
Jerusalem will become ruins,
and the temple's mountain will be a high thicket.'

[19] Did King Hezekiah of Judah and all the people of Judah put him to death? Did not the king fear the LORD and plead for the LORD's favor,[A] and did not the LORD relent concerning the disaster he had pronounced against them? We are about to bring a terrible disaster on ourselves!"

THE PROPHET URIAH

[20] Another man was also prophesying in the name of the LORD — Uriah son of Shemaiah from Kiriath-jearim. He prophesied against this city and against this land in words like all those of Jeremiah. [21] King Jehoiakim, all his warriors, and all the officials heard his words, and the king tried to put him to death. When Uriah heard, he fled in fear and went to Egypt. [22] But King Jehoiakim sent men to Egypt: Elnathan son of Achbor and certain other men with him went to Egypt. [23] They brought Uriah out of Egypt and took him to King Jehoiakim, who executed him with the sword and threw his corpse into the burial place of the common people.[B]

[24] But Ahikam son of Shaphan supported Jeremiah, so he was not handed over to the people to be put to death.

THE YOKE OF BABYLON

27 At the beginning of the reign of Zedekiah[C] son of Josiah, king of Judah, this word came to Jeremiah from the LORD:[D] [2] This is what the LORD said to me: "Make chains and yoke bars for yourself and put them on your neck. [3] Send word to the king of Edom, the king of Moab, the king of the Ammonites, the king of Tyre, and the king of Sidon through messengers who are coming to King Zedekiah of Judah in Jerusalem. [4] Command them to go to their masters, saying, 'This is what the LORD of Armies, the God of Israel, says: Tell this to your masters: [5] "By my great strength and outstretched arm, I made the earth, and the people, and animals on the face of the earth. I give it to anyone I please.[E] [6] So now I have placed all these lands under the authority of my servant Nebuchadnezzar, king of Babylon. I have even given him the wild animals to serve him. [7] All nations will serve him, his son, and his grandson until the time for his own land comes, and then many nations and great kings will enslave him.

[8] "'"As for the nation or kingdom that does not serve King Nebuchadnezzar of Babylon and does not place its neck under the yoke of the king of Babylon, that nation I will punish by sword, famine, and plague — this is the

---

[A]26:19 Or and appease the LORD [B]26:23 Lit the sons of the people
[C]27:1 Some Hb mss, Syr, Arabic; other Hb mss, DSS read Jehoiakim [D]27:1 LXX omits this v. [E]27:5 Lit to whomever is upright in my eyes

LORD's declaration — until through him I have destroyed it. ⁹ So you should not listen to your prophets, diviners, dreamers, fortune-tellers, or sorcerers who say to you, 'Don't serve the king of Babylon!' ¹⁰ They are prophesying a lie to you so that you will be removed from your land. I will banish you, and you will perish. ¹¹ But as for the nation that will put its neck under the yoke of the king of Babylon and serve him, I will leave it in its own land, and that nation will cultivate^A it and reside in it. This is the LORD's declaration."'"

WARNING TO ZEDEKIAH

¹² I spoke to King Zedekiah of Judah in the same way: "Put your necks under the yoke of the king of Babylon, serve him and his people, and live! ¹³ Why should you and your people die by the sword, famine, and plague as the LORD has threatened against any nation that does not serve the king of Babylon? ¹⁴ Do not listen to the words of the prophets who are telling you, 'Don't serve the king of Babylon,' for they are prophesying a lie to you. ¹⁵ 'I have not sent them' — this is the LORD's declaration — 'and they are prophesying falsely in my name; therefore, I will banish you, and you will perish — you and the prophets who are prophesying to you.'"

¹⁶ Then I spoke to the priests and all these people, saying, "This is what the LORD says: 'Do not listen to the words of your prophets. They are prophesying to you, claiming, "Look, very soon now the articles of the LORD's temple will be brought back from Babylon." They are prophesying a lie to you. ¹⁷ Do not listen to them. Serve the king of Babylon and live! Why should this city become a ruin? ¹⁸ If they are indeed prophets and if the word of the LORD is with them, let them intercede with the LORD of Armies not to let the articles that remain in the LORD's temple, in the palace of the king of Judah, and in Jerusalem go to Babylon.' ¹⁹ For this is what the LORD of Armies says about the pillars, the basin,^B the water carts, and the rest of the articles that still remain in this city, ²⁰ those King Nebuchadnezzar of Babylon did not take when he deported Jeconiah^C son of Jehoiakim, king of Judah, from Jerusalem to Babylon along with all the nobles of Judah and Jerusalem. ²¹ Yes, this is what the LORD of Armies, the God of Israel, says about the articles that remain in the temple of the LORD, in the palace of the king of Judah, and in Jerusalem: ²² 'They will be taken to Babylon and will remain there until I attend to them again.' This is the LORD's declaration. 'Then I will bring them up and restore them to this place.'"

HANANIAH'S FALSE PROPHECY

28 In that same year, at the beginning of the reign of King Zedekiah of Judah, in the fifth month of the fourth year, the prophet Hananiah son of Azzur from Gibeon said to me in the temple of the LORD in the presence of the priests and all the people, ² "This is what the LORD of Armies, the God of Israel, says: 'I have broken the yoke of the king of Babylon. ³ Within two years I will restore to this place all the articles of the LORD's temple that King Nebuchadnezzar of Babylon took from here and transported to Babylon. ⁴ And I will restore to this place Jeconiah^C son of Jehoiakim, king of Judah, and all the exiles from Judah who went to Babylon' — this is the LORD's declaration — 'for I will break the yoke of the king of Babylon.'"

---

^A 27:11 Lit work   ^B 27:19 Lit sea   ^C 27:20; 28:4 = Jehoiachin

JEREMIAH'S RESPONSE TO HANANIAH

⁵ The prophet Jeremiah replied to the prophet Hananiah in the presence of the priests and all the people who were standing in the temple of the LORD. ⁶ The prophet Jeremiah said, "Amen! May the LORD do that. May the LORD make the words you have prophesied come true and may he restore the articles of the LORD's temple and all the exiles from Babylon to this place! ⁷ Only listen to this message I am speaking in your hearing and in the hearing of all the people. ⁸ The prophets who preceded you and me from ancient times prophesied war, disaster,ᴬ and plague against many lands and great kingdoms. ⁹ As for the prophet who prophesies peace — only when the word of the prophet comes true will the prophet be recognized as one the LORD has truly sent."

HANANIAH BREAKS JEREMIAH'S YOKE

¹⁰ The prophet Hananiah then took the yoke bar from the neck of the prophet Jeremiah and broke it. ¹¹ In the presence of all the people Hananiah proclaimed, "This is what the LORD says: 'In this way, within two years I will break the yoke of King Nebuchadnezzar of Babylon from the neck of all the nations.'" The prophet Jeremiah then went on his way.

THE LORD'S WORD AGAINST HANANIAH

¹² After the prophet Hananiah had broken the yoke bar from the neck of the prophet Jeremiah, the word of the LORD came to Jeremiah: ¹³ "Go say to Hananiah, 'This is what the LORD says: You broke a wooden yoke bar, but in its place you will make an iron yoke bar. ¹⁴ For this is what the LORD of Armies, the God of Israel, says: I have put an iron yoke on the neck of all these nations that they might serve King Nebuchadnezzar of Babylon, and they will serve him. I have even put the wild animals under him.'"

¹⁵ The prophet Jeremiah said to the prophet Hananiah, "Listen, Hananiah! The LORD did not send you, but you have led these people to trust in a lie. ¹⁶ Therefore, this is what the LORD says: 'I am about to send you off the face of the earth. You will die this year because you have preached rebellion against the LORD.'" ¹⁷ And the prophet Hananiah died that year in the seventh month.

JEREMIAH'S LETTER TO THE EXILES

29 This is the text of the letter that the prophet Jeremiah sent from Jerusalem to the remaining exiled elders, the priests, the prophets, and all the people Nebuchadnezzar had deported from Jerusalem to Babylon. ² This was after King Jeconiah,ᴮ the queen mother, the court officials, the officials of Judah and Jerusalem, the craftsmen, and the metalsmiths had left Jerusalem. ³ He sent the letter with Elasah son of Shaphan and Gemariah son of Hilkiah, whom Zedekiah king of Judah sent to Babylon to King Nebuchadnezzar of Babylon. The letter stated:

⁴ This is what the LORD of Armies, the God of Israel, says to all the exiles I deported from Jerusalem to Babylon: ⁵ "Build houses and live in them. Plant gardens and eat their produce. ⁶ Find wives for yourselves, and have sons and daughters. Find wives for your sons and give your daughters to men in marriage so that they may bear sons and daughters. Multiply there; do not decrease. ⁷ Pursue the well-beingᶜ of the

ᴬ28:8 Some Hb mss, Vg read *famine*   ᴮ29:2 = Jehoiachin   ᶜ29:7 Or *peace* city I have deported you to. Pray to the LORD on its behalf, for when it thrives, you will thrive."

⁸ For this is what the LORD of Armies, the God of Israel, says: "Don't let your prophets who are among you and your diviners deceive you, and don't listen to the dreams you elicit from them, ⁹ for they are prophesying falsely to you in my name. I have not sent them." This is the LORD's declaration.

¹⁰ For this is what the LORD says: "When seventy years for Babylon are complete, I will attend to you and will confirm my promise concerning you to restore you to this place. ¹¹ For I know the plans I have for you" — this is the LORD's declaration — "plans for your well-being, not for disaster, to give you a future and a hope. ¹² You will call to me and come and pray to me, and I will listen to you. ¹³ You will seek me and find me when you search for me with all your heart. ¹⁴ I will be found by you" — this is the LORD's declaration — "and I will restore your fortunesᴬ and gather you from all the nations and places where I banished you" — this is the LORD's declaration. "I will restore you to the place from which I deported you."

¹⁵ You have said, "The LORD has raised up prophets for us in Babylon!" ¹⁶ But this is what the LORD says concerning the king sitting on David's throne and concerning all the people living in this city — that is, concerning your brothers who did not go with you into exile. ¹⁷ This is what the LORD of Armies says: "I am about to send sword, famine, and plague against them, and I will make them like rotten figs that are inedible because they are so bad. ¹⁸ I will pursue them with sword, famine, and plague. I will make them a horror to all the kingdoms of the earth — a curse and a desolation, an object of scorn and a disgrace among all the nations where I have banished them. ¹⁹ I will do this because they have not listened to my words" — this is the LORD's declaration — "the words that I sent to them with my servants the prophets time and time again.ᴮ And you too have not listened." This is the LORD's declaration.

²⁰ Hear the word of the LORD, all you exiles I have sent from Jerusalem to Babylon. ²¹ This is what the LORD of Armies, the God of Israel, says about Ahab son of Kolaiah and concerning Zedekiah son of Maaseiah, the ones prophesying a lie to you in my name: "I am about to hand them over to King Nebuchadnezzar of Babylon, and he will kill them before your very eyes. ²² Based on what happens to them, all the exiles of Judah who are in Babylon will create a curse that says, 'May the LORD make you like Zedekiah and Ahab, whom the king of Babylon roasted in the fire!' ²³ because they have committed an outrage in Israel by committing adultery with their neighbors' wives and have spoken in my name a lie, which I did not command them. I am he who knows, and I am a witness." This is the LORD's declaration.

ᴬ29:14 Or will end your captivity   ᴮ29:19 Lit prophets, rising up early and sending

KNOWING GOD THROUGH HIS PROMISES

JEREMIAH 29; DEUTERONOMY 4:29; ROMANS 8:28

I once promised my sister she could borrow my car for a weekend while I was out of town. A couple weeks later, a friend asked to do the same, assuming the offer extended to her also. Surprised at her assumption, I tried to explain that the promise was specifically for that situation. All promises are given in context, and that context matters.

Every promise we come upon in Scripture helps us know God better. But when we assume every promise in the Old Testament translates directly into our context, we forget they were made to a specific person or group, in a specific political climate, under unique circumstances.

Jeremiah 29 is written to the people of Judah who had been taken into captivity by Nebuchadnezzar, the king of Babylon. God sends a specific message through Jeremiah to this specific group of people.

He gives them commands for how they are to live while in exile, and He tells them the exile will last seventy years. I wonder if the exiles, upon hearing this, thought of the forty years their ancestors spent wandering in the wilderness. Those forty years were meant to be enough time to naturally kill off a rebellious generation. Seventy years in exile would almost double the wilderness timeframe; not only would the current generation die off, but so would many of their children.

You can almost feel the people's discouragement. Yet God promises to restore them. His very next statement is this:

> "For I know the plans I have for you . . . plans for your well-being, not for disaster, to give you a future and a hope."
>
> JEREMIAH 29:11

God tells the people of Judah His plans for their future. When they call out to God, when their hearts have repented and turned from the evil that sent them into exile, He will hear them and be found by them (Jr 29:12-14). God's plans for Judah's future included seventy years of exile, but they also included restoration.

So, what does this specific promise, made at a specific time, to a specific group of people, tell us specifically about the character of God?

Jeremiah's words tell us **we serve a God who cares about the future of His people.** Through the promises He made to the exiles in Judah, we see a God who makes a habit of restoring us, even when our hearts rebel over and over again.

God's character and heart are displayed on every page of the Old Testament. The way He pursues, cares for, and restores Israel tells us about the God we serve, One who is gracious and full of compassion and mercy.

More than promises made under certain circumstances to specific people in the Old Testament, we must cling to Him and His proven character. In the midst of uncertainty, we can be confident of one thing: God remains the same.

²⁴ To Shemaiah the Nehelamite you are to say, ²⁵ "This is what the LORD of Armies, the God of Israel, says: You^A in your own name have sent out letters to all the people of Jerusalem, to the priest Zephaniah son of Maaseiah, and to all the priests, saying, ²⁶ 'The LORD has appointed you priest in place of the priest Jehoiada to be the chief officer in the temple of the LORD, responsible for every madman who acts like a prophet. You must confine him in the stocks and an iron collar. ²⁷ So now, why have you not rebuked Jeremiah of Anathoth who has been acting like a prophet among you? ²⁸ For he has sent word to us in Babylon, claiming, "The exile will be long. Build houses and settle down. Plant gardens and eat their produce." ' "
²⁹ The priest Zephaniah read this letter in the hearing of the prophet Jeremiah.

A MESSAGE ABOUT SHEMAIAH

³⁰ Then the word of the LORD came to Jeremiah: ³¹ "Send a message to all the exiles, saying, 'This is what the LORD says concerning Shemaiah the Nehelamite. Because Shemaiah prophesied to you, though I did not send him, and made you trust a lie, ³² this is what the LORD says: I am about to punish Shemaiah the Nehelamite and his descendants. There will not be even one of his descendants living among these people, nor will any ever see the good that I will bring to my people — this is the LORD's declaration — for he has preached rebellion against the LORD.' "

RESTORATION FROM CAPTIVITY

30 This is the word that came to Jeremiah from the LORD. ² "This is what the LORD, the God of Israel, says: Write on a scroll all the words that I have spoken to you, ³ for look, the days are coming" — this is the LORD's declaration — "when I will restore the fortunes^B of my people Israel and Judah," says the LORD. "I will restore them to the land I gave to their ancestors and they will possess it."

⁴ These are the words the LORD spoke to Israel and Judah. ⁵ This is what the LORD says:

We have heard a cry of terror,
of dread — there is no peace.
⁶ Ask and see
whether a male can give birth.
Why then do I see every man
with his hands on his stomach like a woman in labor
and every face turned pale?
⁷ How awful that day will be!
There will be no other like it!
It will be a time of trouble for Jacob,
but he will be saved out of it.

⁸ On that day —
this is the declaration of the LORD of Armies —
I will break his yoke from your neck
and tear off your chains,
and strangers will never again enslave him.

---

^A 29:25 Lit *Because you*   ^B 30:3 Or *will end the captivity*

⁹ They will serve the LORD their God
and David their king,
whom I will raise up for them.

¹⁰ As for you, my servant Jacob,
do not be afraid —
this is the LORD's declaration —
and do not be discouraged, Israel,
for without fail I will save you out of a distant place,
your descendants, from the land of their captivity!
Jacob will return and have calm and quiet
with no one to frighten him.
¹¹ For I will be with you —
this is the LORD's declaration —
to save you!
I will bring destruction on all the nations
where I have scattered you;
however, I will not bring destruction on you.
I will discipline you justly,
and I will by no means leave you unpunished.

HEALING ZION'S WOUNDS

¹² For this is what the LORD says:
Your injury is incurable;
your wound most severe.
¹³ You have no defender for your case.
There is no remedy for your sores,
and no healing for you.^A
¹⁴ All your lovers have forgotten you;
they no longer look for you,
for I have struck you as an enemy would,
with the discipline of someone cruel,
because of your enormous guilt
and your innumerable sins.
¹⁵ Why do you cry out about your injury?
Your pain has no cure!
I have done these things to you
because of your enormous guilt
and your innumerable sins.
¹⁶ Nevertheless, all who devoured you will be devoured,
and all your adversaries — all of them —
will go off into exile.
Those who plunder you will be plundered,
and all who raid you will be raided.
¹⁷ But I will bring you health
and will heal you of your wounds —
this is the LORD's declaration —

---

^A30:13 Or *No one pleads that your sores should be healed. There is no remedy for you.*

for they call you Outcast,
Zion whom no one cares about.

RESTORATION OF THE LAND

¹⁸ This is what the LORD says:
I will certainly restore the fortunes^A of Jacob's tents
and show compassion on his dwellings.
Every city will be rebuilt on its mound;
every citadel will stand on its proper site.
¹⁹ Thanksgiving will come out of them,
a sound of rejoicing.
I will multiply them, and they will not decrease;
I will honor them, and they will not be insignificant.
²⁰ His children will be as in past days;
his congregation will be established in my presence.
I will punish all his oppressors.
²¹ Jacob's leader will be one of them;
his ruler will issue from him.
I will invite him to me, and he will approach me,
for who would otherwise risk his life to approach me?
This is the LORD's declaration.
²² You will be my people,
and I will be your God.

THE WRATH OF GOD

²³ Look, a storm from the LORD!
Wrath has gone out,
a churning storm.
It will whirl about the heads of the wicked.
²⁴ The LORD's burning anger will not turn back
until he has completely fulfilled the purposes of his heart.
In time to come you will understand it.

GOD'S RELATIONSHIP WITH HIS PEOPLE

31

"At that time" — this is the LORD's declaration — "I will be the God
of all the families of Israel, and they will be my people."
² This is what the LORD says:
The people who survived the sword
found favor in the wilderness.
When Israel went to find rest,
³ the LORD appeared to him^B from far away.
I have loved you with an everlasting love;
therefore, I have continued to extend faithful love to you.
⁴ Again I will build you so that you will be rebuilt,
Virgin Israel.
You will take up your tambourines again
and go out in joyful dancing.
⁵ You will plant vineyards again

---

^A30:18 Or *certainly end the captivity*   ^B31:3 LXX; MT reads *me*

on the mountains of Samaria;
the planters will plant and will enjoy the fruit.
⁶ For there will be a day when watchmen will call out
in the hill country of Ephraim,
"Come, let's go up to Zion,
to the LORD our God!"

GOD'S PEOPLE BROUGHT HOME

⁷ For this is what the LORD says:
Sing with joy for Jacob;
shout for the foremost of the nations!
Proclaim, praise, and say,
"LORD, save your people,
the remnant of Israel!"
⁸ Watch! I am going to bring them from the northern land.
I will gather them from remote regions of the earth —
the blind and the lame will be with them,
along with those who are pregnant and those
about to give birth.
They will return here as a great assembly!
⁹ They will come weeping,
but I will bring them back with consolation.ᴬ
I will lead them to wadis filled with water,
by a smooth way where they will not stumble,
for I am Israel's Father,
and Ephraim is my firstborn.
¹⁰ Nations, hear the word of the LORD,
and tell it among the far off coasts and islands!
Say, "The one who scattered Israel will gather him.
He will watch over him as a shepherd guards his flock,
¹¹ for the LORD has ransomed Jacob
and redeemed him from the power of one
stronger than he."
¹² They will come and shout for joy on the heights of Zion;
they will be radiant with joy
because of the LORD's goodness,
because of the grain, the new wine, the fresh oil,
and because of the young of the flocks and herds.
Their life will be like an irrigated garden,
and they will no longer grow weak from hunger.
¹³ Then the young women will rejoice with dancing,
while young and old men rejoice together.
I will turn their mourning into joy,
give them consolation,
and bring happiness out of grief.
¹⁴ I will refresh the priests with an abundance,ᴮ
and my people will be satisfied with my goodness.
This is the LORD's declaration.

ᴬ31:9 LXX; MT reads *supplications* ᴮ31:14 Lit *fatness*

MINE

I'd just fallen asleep; the sky outside the cabin was not quite fully dark. Then I felt it again, the sense that a small face breathed close to mine— our third son and favorite four-year-old. He does this almost every night.

I listened to his small lungs breathe in and out while I drew up the energy to roll over and make room for him in our wide bed. His feet and elbows and knees and fingers were all cold. I love the passive heat transfer from my sleepy warm body to his.

This boy is my very own. Too young for school, he spends most days at home with me. He has learned to love what I love. Through the magic of genetics and our years of quiet afternoons together, he has become like me.

Our children learn how to be people by watching us. They study how we put away silverware and how we drive a car. In the same way, God is making us His very own. Over the mornings and afternoons and birthdays and Sundays, He is writing His Law on our hearts (Heb 8:10). He is making us like Him (2Co 5:17).

In Jeremiah 31:33, God makes this bold declaration:

"'Instead, this is the covenant I will make with the house of Israel after those days'—the LORD's declaration. 'I will put my teaching within them and write it on their hearts. I will be their God, and they will be my people.'"

He is laying claim to us: "I will be their God, and they will be my people." A beloved friend of mine likes to quote Abraham Kuyper, who once said, "There is not a square inch in the whole domain of our human existence over which Christ, who is Sovereign over all, does not cry, mine!" (Abraham Kuyper, "Sphere Sovereignty").

God is pointing to you and to me and saying, "Mine!" **He claims us and makes us His own by the power of His grace, not by the resolve of our own souls.** It is God who makes covenants with us. We don't keep covenants—we smash them. He both makes the covenant and keeps it.

God writes His teaching on our hearts so it's close to us. It's within reach. It's ours. Remember when the Law is written in cold hard stone? The new covenant isn't in a museum. It's written somewhere handy and nearby: our hearts.

Our God invites us to know Him with the sweetness of a parent to a child. He hasn't made His covenant a puzzle for us—He writes it simply and clearly. There's no secret to it. He invites us to clarity and understanding so we can know Him and follow Him with delight.

He has written His covenant on our hearts, thereby making us fully His. We are so dear to Him.

LAMENT TURNED TO JOY

¹⁵ This is what the LORD says:

A voice was heard in Ramah,
a lament with bitter weeping —
Rachel weeping for her children,
refusing to be comforted for her children
because they are no more.

¹⁶ This is what the LORD says:

Keep your voice from weeping
and your eyes from tears,
for the reward for your work will come —
this is the LORD's declaration —
and your children will return from the enemy's land.
¹⁷ There is hope for your future —
this is the LORD's declaration —
and your children will return
to their own territory.
¹⁸ I have surely heard Ephraim moaning,
"You disciplined me, and I have been disciplined
like an untrained calf.
Take me back, so that I can return,
for you, LORD, are my God.
¹⁹ After my return, I felt regret;
After I was instructed, I struck my thigh in grief.
I was ashamed and humiliated
because I bore the disgrace of my youth."
²⁰ Isn't Ephraim a precious son to me,
a delightful child?
Whenever I speak against him,
I certainly still think about him.
Therefore, my inner being yearns for him;
I will truly have compassion on him.
This is the LORD's declaration.

REPENTANCE AND RESTORATION

²¹ Set up road markers for yourself;
establish signposts!
Keep the highway in mind,
the way you have traveled.
Return, Virgin Israel!
Return to these cities of yours.
²² How long will you turn here and there,
faithless daughter?
For the LORD creates something new
in the land^A —
a female^B will shelter^C a man.

---

^A31:22 Or *new on earth*   ^B31:22 Or *woman*   ^C31:22 Or *female surrounds,* or *female courts;* Hb obscure

²³ This is what the LORD of Armies, the God of Israel, says: "When I restore their fortunes,ᴬ they will once again speak this word in the land of Judah and in its cities: 'May the LORD bless you, righteous settlement, holy mountain.' ²⁴ Judah and all its cities will live in it together — also farmers and those who moveᴮ with the flocks — ²⁵ for I satisfy the thirsty person and feed all those who are weak."

²⁶ At this I awoke and looked around. My sleep had been most pleasant to me.

²⁷ "Look, the days are coming" — this is the LORD's declaration — "when I will sow the house of Israel and the house of Judah with the seed of people and the seed of animals. ²⁸ Just as I watched over them to uproot and to tear them down, to demolish and to destroy, and to cause disaster, so will I watch over them to build and to plant them" — this is the LORD's declaration. ²⁹ "In those days, it will never again be said,

'The fathers have eaten sour grapes,
    and the children's teeth are set on edge.'

³⁰ Rather, each will die for his own iniquity. Anyone who eats sour grapes — his own teeth will be set on edge.

THE NEW COVENANT

³¹ "Look, the days are coming" — this is the LORD's declaration — "when I will make a new covenant with the house of Israel and with the house of Judah. ³² This one will not be like the covenant I made with their ancestors on the day I took them by the hand to lead them out of the land of Egypt — my covenant that they broke even though I am their master"ᶜ — the LORD's declaration. ³³ "Instead, this is the covenant I will make with the house of Israel after those days" — the LORD's declaration. "I will put my teaching within them and write it on their hearts. I will be their God, and they will be my people. ³⁴ No longer will one teach his neighbor or his brother, saying, 'Know the LORD,' for they will all know me, from the least to the greatest of them" — this is the LORD's declaration. "For I will forgive their iniquity and never again remember their sin.

³⁵ "This is what the LORD says:
    The one who gives the sun for light by day,
        the fixed order of moon and stars for light by night,
    who stirs up the sea and makes its waves roar —
        the LORD of Armies is his name:
³⁶   If this fixed order departs from before me —
        this is the LORD's declaration —
    only then will Israel's descendants cease
        to be a nation before me forever.

³⁷ "This is what the LORD says:
    Only if the heavens above can be measured
        and the foundations of the earth below explored,
    will I reject all of Israel's descendants
        because of all they have done —
            this is the LORD's declaration.

ᴬ31:23 Or I end their captivity ᴮ31:24 Tg, Vg, Aq, Sym; MT reads and they will move ᶜ31:32 Or husband

³⁸ "Look, the days are coming" — the LORD's declaration — "when the city^A from the Tower of Hananel to the Corner Gate will be rebuilt for the LORD. ³⁹ A measuring line will once again stretch out straight to the hill of Gareb and then turn toward Goah. ⁴⁰ The whole valley — the corpses, the ashes, and all the fields as far as the Kidron Valley to the corner of the Horse Gate to the east — will be holy to the LORD. It will never be uprooted or demolished again."

JEREMIAH'S LAND PURCHASE

32 This is the word that came to Jeremiah from the LORD in the tenth year of King Zedekiah of Judah, which was the eighteenth year of Nebuchadnezzar. ² At that time, the army of the king of Babylon was besieging Jerusalem, and the prophet Jeremiah was imprisoned in the guard's courtyard in the palace of the king of Judah. ³ King Zedekiah of Judah had imprisoned him, saying, "Why are you prophesying as you do? You say, 'This is what the LORD says: Look, I am about to hand this city over to Babylon's king, and he will capture it. ⁴ King Zedekiah of Judah will not escape from the Chaldeans; indeed, he will certainly be handed over to Babylon's king. They will speak face to face^B and meet eye to eye. ⁵ He will take Zedekiah to Babylon, where he will stay until I attend to him — this is the LORD's declaration. For you will fight the Chaldeans, but you will not succeed.' "

⁶ Jeremiah replied, "The word of the LORD came to me: ⁷ Watch! Hanamel, the son of your uncle Shallum, is coming to you to say, 'Buy my field in Anathoth for yourself, for you own the right of redemption to buy it.'

⁸ "Then, as the LORD had said, my cousin Hanamel came to the guard's courtyard and urged me, 'Please buy my field in Anathoth in the land of Benjamin, for you own the right of inheritance and redemption. Buy it for yourself.' Then I knew that this was the word of the LORD. ⁹ So I bought the field in Anathoth from my cousin Hanamel, and I weighed out the silver to him — seventeen shekels^C of silver. ¹⁰ I recorded it on a scroll, sealed it, called in witnesses, and weighed out the silver on the scales. ¹¹ I took the purchase agreement — the sealed copy with its terms and conditions and the open copy — ¹² and gave the purchase agreement to Baruch son of Neriah, son of Mahseiah. I did this in the sight of my cousin^D Hanamel, the witnesses who had signed the purchase agreement, and all the Judeans sitting in the guard's courtyard.

¹³ "I charged Baruch in their sight, ¹⁴ 'This is what the LORD of Armies, the God of Israel, says: Take these scrolls — this purchase agreement with the sealed copy and this open copy — and put them in an earthen storage jar so they will last a long time. ¹⁵ For this is what the LORD of Armies, the God of Israel, says: Houses, fields, and vineyards will again be bought in this land.'

¹⁶ "After I had given the purchase agreement to Baruch, son of Neriah, I prayed to the LORD: ¹⁷ Oh, Lord GOD! You yourself made the heavens and earth by your great power and with your outstretched arm. Nothing is too difficult for you! ¹⁸ You show faithful love to thousands but lay the fathers' iniquity on their sons' laps after them, great and mighty God whose name is the LORD of Armies, ¹⁹ the one great in counsel and powerful in action. Your eyes are on

---

^A31:38 = Jerusalem   ^B32:4 Lit *His mouth will speak with his mouth*
^C32:9 About seven ounces   ^D32:12 Some Hb mss, LXX, Syr; other Hb mss read *uncle*

all the ways of the children of men^A in order to reward each person according to his ways and as the result of his actions. ²⁰ You performed signs and wonders in the land of Egypt and still do today, both in Israel and among all mankind. You made a name for yourself, as is the case today. ²¹ You brought your people Israel out of Egypt with signs and wonders, with a strong hand and an outstretched arm, and with great terror. ²² You gave them this land you swore to give to their ancestors, a land flowing with milk and honey. ²³ They entered and possessed it, but they did not obey you or live according to your instructions. They failed to perform all you commanded them to do, and so you have brought all this disaster on them. ²⁴ Look! Siege ramps have come against the city to capture it, and the city, as a result of the sword, famine, and plague, has been handed over to the Chaldeans who are fighting against it. What you have spoken has happened. Look, you can see it! ²⁵ Yet you, Lord God, have said to me, 'Purchase the field and call in witnesses' — even though the city has been handed over to the Chaldeans!"

²⁶ The word of the Lord came to Jeremiah: ²⁷ "Look, I am the Lord, the God over every creature. Is anything too difficult for me? ²⁸ Therefore, this is what the Lord says: I am about to hand this city over to the Chaldeans, to Babylon's king Nebuchadnezzar, and he will capture it. ²⁹ The Chaldeans who are fighting against this city will come and set this city on fire. They will burn it, including the houses where incense has been burned to Baal on their rooftops and where drink offerings have been poured out to other gods to anger me. ³⁰ From their youth, the Israelites and Judeans have done nothing but what is evil in my sight! They have done nothing but anger me by the work of their hands" — this is the Lord's declaration — ³¹ "for this city has caused my wrath and fury from the day it was built until now. I will therefore remove it from my presence ³² because of all the evil the Israelites and Judeans have done to anger me — they, their kings, their officials, their priests, and their prophets, the men of Judah, and the residents of Jerusalem. ³³ They have turned their backs to me and not their faces. Though I taught them time and time again,^B they do not listen and receive discipline. ³⁴ They have placed their abhorrent things in the house that bears my name and have defiled it. ³⁵ They have built the high places of Baal in Ben Hinnom Valley to sacrifice their sons and daughters in the fire^C to Molech — something I had not commanded them. I had never entertained the thought^D that they do this detestable act causing Judah to sin!

³⁶ "Now therefore, this is what the Lord, the God of Israel, says to this city about which you said, 'It has been handed over to Babylon's king through sword, famine, and plague': ³⁷ I will certainly gather them from all the lands where I have banished them in my anger, rage and intense wrath, and I will return them to this place and make them live in safety. ³⁸ They will be my people, and I will be their God. ³⁹ I will give them integrity of heart and action^E so that they will fear me always, for their good and for the good of their descendants after them.

⁴⁰ "I will make a permanent covenant with them: I will never turn away from doing good to them, and I will put fear of me in their hearts so they will never

---

^A32:19 Or Adam   ^B32:33 Lit them, rising up early and teaching   ^C32:35 Lit to make their sons and daughters pass through the fire   ^D32:35 Lit them, and it did not arise on my heart   ^E32:39 Lit give them one heart and one way again turn away from me. ⁴¹ I will take delight in them to do what is good for them, and with all my heart and mind I will faithfully plant them in this land.

⁴² "For this is what the LORD says: Just as I have brought all this terrible disaster on these people, so am I about to bring on them all the good I am promising them. ⁴³ Fields will be bought in this land about which you are saying, 'It's a desolation without people or animals; it has been handed over to the Chaldeans!' ⁴⁴ Fields will be purchased, the transaction written on a scroll and sealed, and witnesses will be called on in the land of Benjamin, in the areas surrounding Jerusalem, and in Judah's cities — the cities of the hill country, the cities of the Judean foothills, and the cities of the Negev — because I will restore their fortunes."ᴬ

This is the LORD's declaration.

ISRAEL'S RESTORATION

33 While he was still confined in the guard's courtyard, the word of the LORD came to Jeremiah a second time: ² "The LORD who made the earth, ᴮ the LORD who forms it to establish it, the LORD is his name, says this: ³ Call to me and I will answer you and tell you great and incomprehensible things you do not know. ⁴ For this is what the LORD, the God of Israel, says concerning the houses of this city and the palaces of Judah's kings, the ones torn down for defense against the assault ramps and the sword: ⁵ The people coming to fight the Chaldeans will fill the houses with the corpses of their own men that I strike down in my wrath and rage. I have hidden my face from this city because of all their evil. ⁶ Yet I will certainly bring health and healing to it and will indeed heal them. I will let them experience the abundanceᶜ of true peace. ⁷ I will restore the fortunesᴰ of Judah and of Israel and will rebuild them as in former times. ⁸ I will purify them from all the iniquity they have committed against me, and I will forgive all the iniquities they have committed against me, rebelling against me. ⁹ This city will bear on my behalf a name of joy, praise, and glory before all the nations of the earth, who will hear of all the prosperity I will give them. They will tremble with awe because of all the good and all the peace I will bring about for them.

¹⁰ "This is what the LORD says: In this place, which you say is a ruin, without people or animals — that is, in Judah's cities and Jerusalem's streets that are a desolation without people, without inhabitants, and without animals — there will be heard again ¹¹ a sound of joy and gladness, the voice of the groom and the bride, and the voice of those saying,

Give thanks to the LORD of Armies,

for the LORD is good;

his faithful love endures forever

as they bring thank offerings to the temple of the LORD. For I will restore the fortunes of the land as in former times, says the LORD.

¹² "This is what the LORD of Armies says: In this desolate place — without people or animals — and in all its cities there will once more be a grazing land where shepherds may rest flocks. ¹³ The flocks will again pass under the hands of the one who counts them in the cities of the hill country, the cities

ᴬ32:44 Or will end their captivity   ᴮ33:2 LXX; MT reads made it   ᶜ33:6 Or fragrance; Hb obscure   ᴰ33:7 Or will end the captivity, also in v. 11

of the Judean foothills, the cities of the Negev, the land of Benjamin — the areas around Jerusalem and in Judah's cities, says the LORD.

GOD'S COVENANT WITH DAVID

14 "Look, the days are coming" —
    this is the LORD's declaration —
    "when I will fulfill the good promise
    that I have spoken
    concerning the house of Israel
    and the house of Judah.

15 In those days and at that time
    I will cause a Righteous Branch
    to sprout up for David,
    and he will administer justice
    and righteousness in the land.

16 In those days Judah will be saved,
    and Jerusalem will dwell securely,
    and this is what she will be named:
    The LORD Is Our Righteousness. [A]

17 "For this is what the LORD says: David will never fail to have a man sitting on the throne of the house of Israel. 18 The Levitical priests will never fail to have a man always before me to offer burnt offerings, to burn grain offerings, and to make sacrifices."

19 The word of the LORD came to Jeremiah: 20 "This is what the LORD says: If you can break my covenant with the day and my covenant with the night so that day and night cease to come at their regular time, 21 then also my covenant with my servant David may be broken. If that could happen, then he would not have a son reigning on his throne and the Levitical priests would not be my ministers. 22 Even as the stars of heaven cannot be counted, and the sand of the sea cannot be measured, so too I will make innumerable the descendants of my servant David and the Levites who minister to me."

23 The word of the LORD came to Jeremiah: 24 "Have you not noticed what these people have said? They say, 'The LORD has rejected the two families he had chosen.' My people are treated with contempt and no longer regarded as a nation among them. 25 This is what the LORD says: If I do not keep my covenant with the day and with the night, and if I fail to establish the fixed order of heaven and earth, 26 then I might also reject the descendants of Jacob and of my servant David. That is, I would not take rulers from his descendants to rule over the descendants of Abraham, Isaac, and Jacob. But in fact, I will restore their fortunes [B] and have compassion on them."

JEREMIAH'S WORD TO KING ZEDEKIAH

34 This is the word that came to Jeremiah from the LORD when King Nebuchadnezzar of Babylon, his whole army, all the kingdoms of the lands under his control, and all other peoples were fighting against Jerusalem and all its surrounding cities: 2 "This is what the LORD, the God of Israel, says: Go, speak to King Zedekiah of Judah, and tell him, 'This is what

---

A33:16 = Yahweh-zidkenu   B33:26 Or I will end their captivity the LORD says: I am about to hand this city over to the king of Babylon, and he will burn it. ³ As for you, you will not escape from him but are certain to be captured and handed over to him. You will meet the king of Babylon eye to eye and speak face to face;ᴬ you will go to Babylon.

⁴ " 'Yet hear the LORD's word, King Zedekiah of Judah. This is what the LORD says concerning you: You will not die by the sword; ⁵ you will die peacefully. There will be a burning ceremony for you just like the burning ceremonies for your ancestors, the kings of old who came before you. "Oh, master!" will be the lament for you, for I have spoken this word. This is the LORD's declaration.' "

⁶ So the prophet Jeremiah related all these words to King Zedekiah of Judah in Jerusalem ⁷ while the king of Babylon's army was attacking Jerusalem and all of Judah's remaining cities — that is, Lachish and Azekah, for they were the only ones left of Judah's fortified cities.

THE PEOPLE AND THEIR SLAVES

⁸ This is the word that came to Jeremiah from the LORD after King Zedekiah made a covenant with all the people who were in Jerusalem to proclaim freedom to them. ⁹ As a result, each was to let his male and female Hebrew slaves go free, and no one was to enslave his fellow Judean. ¹⁰ All the officials and people who entered into covenant to let their male and female slaves go free — in order not to enslave them any longer — obeyed and let them go free. ¹¹ Afterward, however, they changed their minds and took back their male and female slaves they had let go free and forced them to become slaves again.

¹² Then the word of the LORD came to Jeremiah from the LORD: ¹³ "This is what the LORD, the God of Israel, says: I made a covenant with your ancestors when I brought them out of the land of Egypt, out of the place of slavery, saying, ¹⁴ 'At the end of seven years, each of you must let his fellow Hebrew who sold himselfᴮ to you go. He may serve you six years, but then you must let him go free from your service.' But your ancestors did not obey me or pay any attention. ¹⁵ Today you repented and did what pleased me, each of you proclaiming freedom for his neighbor. You made a covenant before me at the house that bears my name. ¹⁶ But you have changed your minds and profaned my name. Each has taken back his male and female slaves who had been let go free to go wherever they wanted, and you have again forced them to be your slaves.

¹⁷ "Therefore, this is what the LORD says: You have not obeyed me by proclaiming freedom, each for his fellow Hebrew and for his neighbor. I hereby proclaim freedom for you — this is the LORD's declaration — to the sword, to plague, and to famine! I will make you a horror to all the earth's kingdoms. ¹⁸ As for those who disobeyed my covenant, not keeping the terms of the covenant they made before me, I will treat them like the calf they cut in two in order to pass between its pieces. ¹⁹ The officials of Judah and Jerusalem, the court officials, the priests, and all the people of the land who passed between the pieces of the calf — ²⁰ all these I will hand over to their enemies, to those who intend to take their life. Their corpses will become food for the birds of the sky and for the wild animals

---

ᴬ34:3 Lit *and his mouth will speak to your mouth*   ᴮ34:14 Or *who was sold* of the land. ²¹ I will hand King Zedekiah of Judah and his officials over to their enemies, to those who intend to take their lives, to the king of Babylon's army that is withdrawing. ²² I am about to give the command — this is the LORD's declaration — and I will bring them back to this city. They will fight against it, capture it, and burn it. I will make Judah's cities a desolation, without inhabitant."

THE RECHABITES' EXAMPLE

35 This is the word that came to Jeremiah from the LORD in the days of Jehoiakim son of Josiah, king of Judah: ² "Go to the house of the Rechabites, speak to them, and bring them to one of the chambers of the temple of the LORD to offer them a drink of wine."

³ So I took Jaazaniah son of Jeremiah, son of Habazziniah, and his brothers and all his sons — the entire house of the Rechabites — ⁴ and I brought them into the temple of the LORD to a chamber occupied by the sons of Hanan son of Igdaliah, a man of God, who had a chamber near the officials' chamber, which was above the chamber of Maaseiah son of Shallum the doorkeeper. ⁵ I set jars filled with wine and some cups before the sons of the house of the Rechabites and said to them, "Drink wine!"

⁶ But they replied, "We do not drink wine, for Jonadab, son of our ancestor Rechab, commanded: 'You and your descendants must never drink wine. ⁷ You must not build a house or sow seed or plant a vineyard. Those things are not for you. Rather, you must live in tents your whole life, so you may live a long time on the soil where you stay as a resident alien.' ⁸ We have obeyed Jonadab, son of our ancestor Rechab, in all he commanded us. So we haven't drunk wine our whole life — we, our wives, our sons, and our daughters. ⁹ We also have not built houses to live in and do not have vineyard, field, or seed. ¹⁰ But we have lived in tents and have obeyed and done everything our ancestor Jonadab commanded us. ¹¹ However, when King Nebuchadnezzar of Babylon marched into the land, we said, 'Come, let's go into Jerusalem to get away from the Chaldean and Aramean armies.' So we have been living in Jerusalem."

¹² Then the word of the LORD came to Jeremiah: ¹³ "This is what the LORD of Armies, the God of Israel, says: Go, say to the men of Judah and the residents of Jerusalem, 'Will you not accept discipline by listening to my words? — this is the LORD's declaration. ¹⁴ The words of Jonadab, son of Rechab, have been carried out. He commanded his descendants not to drink wine, and they have not drunk to this day because they have obeyed their ancestor's command. But I have spoken to you time and time again, ᴬ and you have not obeyed me! ¹⁵ Time and time again ᴮ I have sent you all my servants the prophets, proclaiming, "Turn, each one from his evil way, and correct your actions. Stop following other gods to serve them. Live in the land that I gave you and your ancestors." But you did not pay attention or obey me. ¹⁶ Yes, the sons of Jonadab son of Rechab carried out their ancestor's command he gave them, but these people have not obeyed me. ¹⁷ Therefore, this is what the LORD, the God of Armies, the God of Israel, says: I will certainly bring on Judah and on all the residents of Jerusalem all the disaster I have pronounced against

---

ᴬ35:14 Lit *you, rising up early and speaking* ᴮ35:15 Lit *Rising up early and sending* them because I have spoken to them, but they have not obeyed, and I have called to them, but they did not answer.'"

¹⁸ But to the house of the Rechabites Jeremiah said, "This is what the LORD of Armies, the God of Israel, says: 'Because you have obeyed the command of your ancestor Jonadab and have kept all his commands and have done everything he commanded you, ¹⁹ this is what the LORD of Armies, the God of Israel, says: Jonadab son of Rechab will never fail to have a man to stand before me always.'"

JEREMIAH DICTATES A SCROLL

36 In the fourth year of Jehoiakim son of Josiah, king of Judah, this word came to Jeremiah from the LORD: ² "Take a scroll, and write on it all the words I have spoken to you concerning Israel, Judah, and all the nations from the time I first spoke to you during Josiah's reign until today. ³ Perhaps when the house of Judah hears about all the disaster I am planning to bring on them, each one of them will turn from his evil way. Then I will forgive their iniquity and their sin."

⁴ So Jeremiah summoned Baruch son of Neriah. At Jeremiah's dictation,ᴬ Baruch wrote on a scroll all the words the LORD had spoken to Jeremiah. ⁵ Then Jeremiah commanded Baruch, "I am restricted; I cannot enter the temple of the LORD, ⁶ so you must go and read from the scroll — which you wrote at my dictationᴮ — the words of the LORD in the hearing of the people at the temple of the LORD on a day of fasting. Read his words in the hearing of all the Judeans who are coming from their cities. ⁷ Perhaps their petition will come before the LORD, and each one will turn from his evil way, for the anger and fury that the LORD has pronounced against this people are intense." ⁸ So Baruch son of Neriah did everything the prophet Jeremiah had commanded him. At the LORD's temple he read the LORD's words from the scroll.

BARUCH READS THE SCROLL

⁹ In the fifth year of Jehoiakim son of Josiah, king of Judah, in the ninth month, all the people of Jerusalem and all those coming in from Judah's cities into Jerusalem proclaimed a fast before the LORD. ¹⁰ Then at the LORD's temple, in the chamber of Gemariah son of Shaphan the scribe, in the upper courtyard at the opening of the New Gate of the LORD's temple, in the hearing of all the people, Baruch read Jeremiah's words from the scroll.

¹¹ When Micaiah son of Gemariah, son of Shaphan, heard all the words of the LORD from the scroll, ¹² he went down to the scribe's chamber in the king's palace. All the officials were sitting there — Elishama the scribe, Delaiah son of Shemaiah, Elnathan son of Achbor, Gemariah son of Shaphan, Zedekiah son of Hananiah, and all the other officials. ¹³ Micaiah reported to them all the words he had heard when Baruch read from the scroll in the hearing of the people. ¹⁴ Then all the officials sent word to Baruch through Jehudi son of Nethaniah, son of Shelemiah, son of Cushi, saying, "Bring the scroll that you read in the hearing of the people, and come." So Baruch son of Neriah took the scroll and went to them. ¹⁵ They said to him, "Sit down and read it in our hearing." So Baruch read it in their hearing.

ᴬ36:4 Lit From Jeremiah's mouth   ᴮ36:6 Lit wrote from my mouth

¹⁶ When they had heard all the words, they turned to each other in fear and said to Baruch, "We must surely tell the king all these things." ¹⁷ Then they asked Baruch, "Tell us, how did you write all these words? At his dictation?"ᴬ

¹⁸ Baruch said to them, "At his dictation. He recited all these words to me while I was writing on the scroll in ink."

JEHOIAKIM BURNS THE SCROLL

¹⁹ The officials said to Baruch, "You and Jeremiah must hide and tell no one where you are." ²⁰ Then, after depositing the scroll in the chamber of Elishama the scribe, the officials came to the king at the courtyard and reported everything in the hearing of the king. ²¹ The king sent Jehudi to get the scroll, and he took it from the chamber of Elishama the scribe. Jehudi then read it in the hearing of the king and all the officials who were standing by the king. ²² Since it was the ninth month, the king was sitting in his winter quarters with a fire burning in front of him. ²³ As soon as Jehudi would read three or four columns, Jehoiakim would cut the scrollᴮ with a scribe's knife and throw the columns into the fire in the hearth until the entire scroll was consumed by the fire in the hearth. ²⁴ As they heard all these words, the king and all of his servants did not become terrified or tear their clothes. ²⁵ Even though Elnathan, Delaiah, and Gemariah had urged the king not to burn the scroll, he did not listen to them. ²⁶ Then the king commanded Jerahmeel the king's son, Seraiah son of Azriel, and Shelemiah son of Abdeel to seize the scribe Baruch and the prophet Jeremiah, but the LORD hid them.

JEREMIAH DICTATES ANOTHER SCROLL

²⁷ After the king had burned the scroll and the words Baruch had written at Jeremiah's dictation,ᶜ the word of the LORD came to Jeremiah: ²⁸ "Take another scroll, and once again write on it the original words that were on the original scroll that King Jehoiakim of Judah burned. ²⁹ You are to proclaim concerning King Jehoiakim of Judah, 'This is what the LORD says: You have burned the scroll, asking, "Why have you written on it that the king of Babylon will certainly come and destroy this land and cause it to be without people or animals?" ³⁰ Therefore, this is what the LORD says concerning King Jehoiakim of Judah: He will have no one to sit on David's throne, and his corpse will be thrown out to be exposed to the heat of day and the frost of night. ³¹ I will punish him, his descendants, and his officers for their iniquity. I will bring on them, on the residents of Jerusalem, and on the people of Judah all the disaster, which I warned them about but they did not listen.' "

³² Then Jeremiah took another scroll and gave it to Baruch son of Neriah, the scribe, and he wrote on it at Jeremiah's dictationᴰ all the words of the scroll that Jehoiakim, Judah's king, had burned in the fire. And many other words like them were added.

ᴬ36:17 Lit *From his mouth*, also in v. 18   ᴮ36:23 Lit *columns, he would tear it*
ᶜ36:27 Lit *written from Jeremiah's mouth*   ᴰ36:32 Lit *it from Jeremiah's mouth*

JERUSALEM'S LAST DAYS

37

Zedekiah son of Josiah reigned as king in the land of Judah in place of Coniah[A] son of Jehoiakim, for King Nebuchadnezzar of Babylon made him king. [2] He and his officers and the people of the land did not obey the words of the LORD that he spoke through the prophet Jeremiah.

[3] Nevertheless, King Zedekiah sent Jehucal son of Shelemiah and Zephaniah son of Maaseiah, the priest, to the prophet Jeremiah, requesting, "Please pray to the LORD our God for us!" [4] Jeremiah was going about his daily tasks[B] among the people, for he had not yet been put into the prison. [5] Pharaoh's army had left Egypt, and when the Chaldeans, who were besieging Jerusalem, heard the report, they withdrew from Jerusalem.

[6] The word of the LORD came to the prophet Jeremiah: [7] "This is what the LORD, the God of Israel, says: This is what you will say to Judah's king, who is sending you to inquire of me: 'Watch: Pharaoh's army, which has come out to help you, is going to return to its own land of Egypt. [8] The Chaldeans will then return and fight against this city. They will capture it and burn it. [9] This is what the LORD says: Don't deceive yourselves by saying, "The Chaldeans will leave us for good," for they will not leave. [10] Indeed, if you were to strike down the entire Chaldean army that is fighting with you, and there remained among them only the badly wounded[C] men, each in his tent, they would get up and burn this city.'"

JEREMIAH'S IMPRISONMENT

[11] When the Chaldean army withdrew from Jerusalem because of Pharaoh's army, [12] Jeremiah started to leave Jerusalem to go to the land of Benjamin to claim his portion there among the people. [13] But when he was at the Benjamin Gate, an officer of the guard was there, whose name was Irijah son of Shelemiah, son of Hananiah, and he apprehended the prophet Jeremiah, saying, "You are defecting to the Chaldeans."

[14] "That's a lie," Jeremiah replied. "I am not defecting to the Chaldeans!" Irijah would not listen to him but apprehended Jeremiah and took him to the officials. [15] The officials were angry at Jeremiah and beat him and placed him in jail in the house of Jonathan the scribe, for it had been made into a prison. [16] So Jeremiah went into a cell in the dungeon and stayed there many days.

JEREMIAH SUMMONED BY ZEDEKIAH

[17] King Zedekiah later sent for him and received him, and in his house privately asked him, "Is there a word from the LORD?"

"There is," Jeremiah responded. He continued, "You will be handed over to the king of Babylon." [18] Then Jeremiah said to King Zedekiah, "How have I sinned against you or your servants or these people that you have put me in prison? [19] Where are your prophets who prophesied to you, claiming, 'The king of Babylon will not come against you and this land'? [20] So now please listen, my lord the king. May my petition come before you. Don't send me back to the house of Jonathan the scribe, or I will die there."

[21] So King Zedekiah gave orders, and Jeremiah was placed in the guard's courtyard. He was given a loaf of bread each day from the bakers' street until

---

[A]37:1 = Jehoiachin [B]37:4 Lit *was coming in and going out* [C]37:10 Lit *the pierced* all the bread was gone from the city. So Jeremiah remained in the guard's courtyard.

JEREMIAH THROWN INTO A CISTERN

38 Now Shephatiah son of Mattan, Gedaliah son of Pashhur, Ju-cal[A] son of Shelemiah, and Pashhur son of Malchijah heard the words Jeremiah was speaking to all the people: ² "This is what the LORD says: 'Whoever stays in this city will die by the sword, famine, and plague, but whoever surrenders to the Chaldeans will live. He will retain his life like the spoils of war and will live.' ³ This is what the LORD says: 'This city will most certainly be handed over to the king of Babylon's army, and he will capture it.'"

⁴ The officials then said to the king, "This man ought to die, because he is weakening the morale[B] of the warriors who remain in this city and of all the people by speaking to them in this way. This man is not pursuing the welfare of this people, but their harm."

⁵ King Zedekiah said, "Here he is; he's in your hands since the king can't do anything against you." ⁶ So they took Jeremiah and dropped him into the cistern of Malchiah the king's son, which was in the guard's courtyard, lowering Jeremiah with ropes. There was no water in the cistern, only mud, and Jeremiah sank in the mud.

⁷ But Ebed-melech, a Cushite court official in the king's palace, heard Jeremiah had been put into the cistern. While the king was sitting at the Benjamin Gate, ⁸ Ebed-melech went from the king's palace and spoke to the king: ⁹ "My lord the king, these men have been evil in all they have done to the prophet Jeremiah. They have dropped him into the cistern where he will die from hunger, because there is no more bread in the city."

¹⁰ So the king commanded Ebed-melech, the Cushite, "Take from here thirty men under your authority[C] and pull the prophet Jeremiah up from the cistern before he dies."

¹¹ So Ebed-melech took the men under his authority[D] and went to the king's palace to a place below the storehouse.[E] From there he took old rags and worn-out clothes and lowered them by ropes to Jeremiah in the cistern. ¹² Ebed-melech the Cushite called down to Jeremiah, "Place these old rags and clothes between your armpits and the ropes." Jeremiah did this. ¹³ They pulled him up with the ropes and lifted him out of the cistern, but he remained in the guard's courtyard.

ZEDEKIAH'S FINAL MEETING WITH JEREMIAH

¹⁴ King Zedekiah sent for the prophet Jeremiah and received him at the third entrance of the LORD's temple. The king said to Jeremiah, "I am going to ask you something; don't hide anything from me."

¹⁵ Jeremiah replied to Zedekiah, "If I tell you, you will kill me, won't you? Besides, if I give you advice, you won't listen to me anyway."

¹⁶ King Zedekiah swore to Jeremiah in private, "As the LORD lives, who has given us this life, I will not kill you or hand you over to these men who intend to take your life."

A38:1 = Jehucal in Jr 37:3 B38:4 Lit hands C38:10 Lit men in your hand
D38:11 Lit men in his hand E38:11 Or treasury

[17] Jeremiah therefore said to Zedekiah, "This is what the LORD, the God of Armies, the God of Israel, says: 'If indeed you surrender to the officials of the king of Babylon, then you will live, this city will not be burned, and you and your household will survive. [18] But if you do not surrender to the officials of the king of Babylon, then this city will be handed over to the Chaldeans. They will burn it, and you yourself will not escape from them.'"

[19] But King Zedekiah said to Jeremiah, "I am worried about the Judeans who have defected to the Chaldeans. They may hand me over to the Judeans to abuse me."

[20] "They will not hand you over," Jeremiah replied. "Obey the LORD in what I am telling you, so it may go well for you and you can live. [21] But if you refuse to surrender, this is the verdict[A] that the LORD has shown me: [22] 'All the women[B] who remain in the palace of Judah's king will be brought out to the officials of the king of Babylon and will say to you,[C]

"Your trusted friends[D] misled[E] you
and overcame you.
Your feet sank into the mire,
and they deserted you."

[23] All your wives and children will be brought out to the Chaldeans. You yourself will not escape from them, for you will be seized by the king of Babylon and this city will burn.'"

[24] Then Zedekiah warned Jeremiah, "Don't let anyone know about this conversation[F] or you will die. [25] The officials may hear that I have spoken with you and come and demand of you, 'Tell us what you said to the king; don't hide anything from us and we won't kill you. Also, what did the king say to you?' [26] If they do, tell them, 'I was bringing before the king my petition that he not return me to the house of Jonathan to die there.'" [27] All the officials did come to Jeremiah, and they questioned him. He reported the exact words to them the king had commanded, and they quit speaking with him because the conversation[G] had not been overheard. [28] Jeremiah remained in the guard's courtyard until the day Jerusalem was captured, and he was there when it happened.[H]

THE FALL OF JERUSALEM TO BABYLON

39 In the ninth year of King Zedekiah of Judah, in the tenth month, King Nebuchadnezzar of Babylon advanced against Jerusalem with his entire army and laid siege to it. [2] In the fourth month of Zedekiah's eleventh year, on the ninth day of the month, the city was broken into. [3] All the officials of the king of Babylon entered and sat at the Middle Gate: Nergal-sharezer, Samgar, Nebusarsechim[I] the chief of staff, Nergal-sharezer the chief soothsayer, and all the rest of the officials of Babylon's king.

[4] When King Zedekiah of Judah and all the fighting men saw them, they fled. They left the city at night by way of the king's garden through the city gate between the two walls. They left along the route to the Arabah. [5] However, the Chaldean army pursued them and overtook Zedekiah in the

---

[A]38:21 Or *promise*; lit *word*   [B]38:22 Or *wives*   [C]38:22 *to you* supplied for clarity   [D]38:22 Lit *"The men of your peace"*   [E]38:22 Or *incited*   [F]38:24 Lit *about these words*   [G]38:27 Lit *word*   [H]38:28 Or *captured. This is what happened when Jerusalem was captured:*   [I]39:3 LXX; MT reads *Samgar-nebu, Sarsechim* plains of Jericho. They arrested him and brought him up to Nebuchadnez-zar, Babylon's king, at Riblah in the land of Hamath. The king passed sentence on him there.

⁶ At Riblah the king of Babylon slaughtered Zedekiah's sons before his eyes, and he also slaughtered all Judah's nobles. ⁷ Then he blinded Zedekiah and put him in bronze chains to take him to Babylon. ⁸ The Chaldeans next burned down the king's palace and the people's houses and tore down the walls of Jerusalem. ⁹ Nebuzaradan, the captain of the guards, deported the rest of the people to Babylon — those who had remained in the city and those deserters who had defected to him along with the rest of the people who remained. ¹⁰ However, Nebuzaradan, the captain of the guards, left in the land of Judah some of the poor people who owned nothing, and he gave them vineyards and fields at that time.

JEREMIAH FREED BY NEBUCHADNEZZAR

¹¹ Speaking through Nebuzaradan, captain of the guards, King Nebuchadnez-zar of Babylon gave orders concerning Jeremiah: ¹² "Take him and look after him. Don't do him any harm, but do for him whatever he says." ¹³ Nebuzara-dan, captain of the guards, Nebushazban the chief of staff, Nergal-sharezer the chief soothsayer, and all the captains of Babylon's king ¹⁴ had Jeremi-ah brought from the guard's courtyard and turned him over to Gedaliah son of Ahikam, son of Shaphan, to take him home. So he settled among his own people.

¹⁵ Now the word of the LORD had come to Jeremiah when he was confined in the guard's courtyard: ¹⁶ "Go tell Ebed-melech the Cushite, 'This is what the LORD of Armies, the God of Israel, says: I am about to fulfill my words for disaster and not for good against this city. They will take place before your eyes on that day. ¹⁷ But I will rescue you on that day — this is the LORD's declaration — and you will not be handed over to the men you dread. ¹⁸ Indeed, I will certainly deliver you so that you do not fall by the sword. Because you have trusted in me, you will retain your life like the spoils of war. This is the LORD's declaration.'"

JEREMIAH STAYS IN JUDAH

40 This is the word that came to Jeremiah from the LORD after Neb-uzaradan, captain of the guards, released him at Ramah. When he found him, he was bound in chains with all the exiles of Jerusalem and Judah who were being exiled to Babylon. ² The captain of the guards took Jeremiah and said to him, "The LORD your God decreed this disaster on this place, ³ and the LORD has fulfilled it. He has done just what he decreed. Because you people have sinned against the LORD and have not obeyed him, this thing has happened. ⁴ Now pay attention: Today I am setting you free from the chains that were on your hands. If it pleases you to come with me to Babylon, come, and I will take care of you. But if it seems wrong to you to come with me to Babylon, go no farther.ᴬ Look — the whole land is in front of you. Wherever it seems good and right for you to go, go there." ⁵ When Jeremiah had not yet turned to go, Nebuzaradan said to him,ᴮ "Returnᶜ to

---

ᴬ 40:4 Lit Babylon, stop   ᴮ 40:5 Nebuzaradan said to him supplied for clarity
ᶜ 40:5 LXX reads "But if not, run, return ; Hb obscure

Gedaliah son of Ahikam, son of Shaphan, whom the king of Babylon has appointed over the cities of Judah, and stay with him among the people or go wherever it seems right for you to go." So the captain of the guards gave him a ration and a gift and released him. ⁶ Jeremiah therefore went to Gedaliah son of Ahikam at Mizpah, and he stayed with him among the people who remained in the land.

GEDALIAH ADVISES PEACE

⁷ All the commanders of the armies that were in the countryside — they and their men — heard that the king of Babylon had appointed Gedaliah son of Ahikam over the land. He had been put in charge of the men, women, and children from among the poorest of the land, who had not been deported to Babylon. ⁸ So they came to Gedaliah at Mizpah. The commanders included Ishmael son of Nethaniah, Johanan and Jonathan the sons of Kareah, Seraiah son of Tanhumeth, the sons of Ephai the Netophathite, and Jezaniah son of the Maacathite — they and their men.

⁹ Gedaliah son of Ahikam, son of Shaphan, swore an oath to them and their men, assuring them, "Don't be afraid to serve the Chaldeans. Live in the land and serve the king of Babylon, and it will go well for you. ¹⁰ As for me, I am going to live in Mizpah to represent you^A before the Chaldeans who come to us. As for you, gather wine, summer fruit, and oil, place them in your storage jars, and live in the cities you have captured."

¹¹ When all the Judeans in Moab and among the Ammonites and in Edom and in all the other lands also heard that the king of Babylon had left a remnant in Judah and had appointed Gedaliah son of Ahikam, son of Shaphan, over them, ¹² they all returned from all the places where they had been banished and came to the land of Judah, to Gedaliah at Mizpah, and harvested a great amount of wine and summer fruit.

¹³ Meanwhile, Johanan son of Kareah and all the commanders of the armies in the countryside came to Gedaliah at Mizpah ¹⁴ and warned him, "Don't you realize that Baalis, king of the Ammonites, has sent Ishmael son of Nethaniah to kill you?" But Gedaliah son of Ahikam would not believe them. ¹⁵ Then Johanan son of Kareah suggested to Gedaliah in private at Mizpah, "Let me go kill Ishmael son of Nethaniah. No one will know it. Why should he kill you and allow all of Judah that has gathered around you to scatter and the remnant of Judah to perish?"

¹⁶ But Gedaliah son of Ahikam responded to Johanan son of Kareah, "Don't do that! What you're saying about Ishmael is a lie."

GEDALIAH ASSASSINATED BY ISHMAEL

41 In the seventh month, Ishmael son of Nethaniah, son of Elishama, of the royal family and one of the king's chief officers, came with ten men to Gedaliah son of Ahikam at Mizpah. They ate a meal together there in Mizpah, ² but then Ishmael son of Nethaniah and the ten men who were with him got up and struck down Gedaliah son of Ahikam, son of Shaphan, with the sword; he killed the one the king of Babylon had appointed in the land. ³ Ishmael also struck down all the Judeans who were with Gedaliah at Mizpah, as well as the Chaldean soldiers who were there.

^A40:10 Lit *to stand*

⁴ On the day after he had killed Gedaliah, when no one knew yet, ⁵ eighty men came from Shechem, Shiloh, and Samaria who had shaved their beards, torn their clothes, and gashed themselves, and who were carrying grain and incense offerings to bring to the temple of the LORD. ⁶ Ishmael son of Nethaniah came out of Mizpah to meet them, weeping as he came. When he encountered them, he said, "Come to Gedaliah son of Ahikam!"⁷ But when they came into the city, Ishmael son of Nethaniah and the men with him slaughtered them and threw them into ᴬ a cistern.

⁸ However, there were ten men among them who said to Ishmael, "Don't kill us, for we have hidden treasure in the field — wheat, barley, oil, and honey!" So he stopped and did not kill them along with their companions. ⁹ Now the cistern where Ishmael had thrown all the corpses of the men he had struck down was a large one ᴮ that King Asa had made in the encounter with King Baasha of Israel. Ishmael son of Nethaniah filled it with the slain.

¹⁰ Then Ishmael took captive all the rest of the people of Mizpah including the daughters of the king — all those who remained in Mizpah over whom Nebuzaradan, captain of the guards, had appointed Gedaliah son of Ahikam. Ishmael son of Nethaniah took them captive and set off to cross over to the Ammonites.

THE CAPTIVES RESCUED BY JOHANAN

¹¹ When Johanan son of Kareah and all the commanders of the armies with him heard of all the evil that Ishmael son of Nethaniah had done, ¹² they took all their men and went to fight with Ishmael son of Nethaniah. They found him by the great pool in Gibeon. ¹³ When all the people held by Ishmael saw Johanan son of Kareah and all the commanders of the army with him, they rejoiced. ¹⁴ All the people whom Ishmael had taken captive from Mizpah turned around and rejoined Johanan son of Kareah. ¹⁵ But Ishmael son of Nethaniah escaped from Johanan with eight men and went to the Ammonites. ¹⁶ Johanan son of Kareah and all the commanders of the armies with him then took from Mizpah all the remnant of the people whom he had recovered from Ishmael son of Nethaniah after Ishmael had killed Gedaliah son of Ahikam — men, soldiers, women, children, and court officials whom he brought back from Gibeon. ¹⁷ They left, stopping in Geruth Chimham, which is near Bethlehem, in order to make their way into Egypt, ¹⁸ away from the Chaldeans. For they feared them because Ishmael son of Nethaniah had struck down Gedaliah son of Ahikam, whom the king of Babylon had appointed over the land.

THE PEOPLE SEEK JEREMIAH'S COUNSEL

42 Then all the commanders of the armies, along with Johanan son of Kareah, Jezaniah son of Hoshaiah, and all the people from the least to the greatest, approached ² the prophet Jeremiah and said, "May our petition come before you; pray to the LORD your God on our behalf, on behalf of this entire remnant (for few of us remain out of the many, as you can see with your own eyes), ³ that the LORD your God may tell us the way we should go and the thing we should do."

ᴬ41:7 Syr; MT reads *slaughtered them in*   ᴮ41:9 LXX; MT reads *down by the hand of Gedaliah*

⁴ So the prophet Jeremiah said to them, "I have heard. I will now pray to the LORD your God according to your words, and I will tell you every word that the LORD answers you; I won't withhold a word from you."

⁵ And they said to Jeremiah, "May the LORD be a true and faithful witness against us if we don't act according to every word the LORD your God sends you to tell us. ⁶ Whether it is pleasant or unpleasant, we will obey the LORD our God to whom we are sending you so that it may go well with us. We will certainly obey the LORD our God!"

JEREMIAH'S ADVICE TO STAY

⁷ At the end of ten days, the word of the LORD came to Jeremiah, ⁸ and he summoned Johanan son of Kareah, all the commanders of the armies who were with him, and all the people from the least to the greatest.

⁹ He said to them, "This is what the LORD says, the God of Israel to whom you sent me to bring your petition before him: ¹⁰ 'If you will indeed stay in this land, then I will rebuild and not demolish you, and I will plant and not uproot you, because I relent concerning the disaster that I have brought on you. ¹¹ Don't be afraid of the king of Babylon whom you now fear; don't be afraid of him' — this is the LORD's declaration — 'because I am with you to save you and rescue you from him. ¹² I will grant you compassion, and heᴬ will have compassion on you and allow you to return to your own soil.'

¹³ "But if you say, 'We will not stay in this land,' in order to disobey the LORD your God, ¹⁴ and if you say, 'No, instead we'll go to the land of Egypt where we will not see war or hear the sound of the ram's horn or hunger for food, and we'll live there,' ¹⁵ then hear the word of the LORD, remnant of Judah! This is what the LORD of Armies, the God of Israel, says: 'If you are firmly resolved to go to Egypt and stay there for a while, ¹⁶ then the sword you fear will overtake you there in the land of Egypt, and the famine you are worried about will follow on your heelsᴮ there to Egypt, and you will die there. ¹⁷ All who resolve to go to Egypt to stay there for a while will die by the sword, famine, and plague. They will have no survivor or fugitive from the disaster I will bring on them.'

¹⁸ "For this is what the LORD of Armies, the God of Israel, says: 'Just as my anger and fury were poured out on Jerusalem's residents, so will my fury pour out on you if you go to Egypt. You will become an example for cursing, scorn, execration, and disgrace, and you will never see this place again.' ¹⁹ The LORD has spoken concerning you, remnant of Judah: 'Don't go to Egypt.' Know for certain that I have warned you today! ²⁰ You have gone astray at the cost of your livesᶜ because you are the ones who sent me to the LORD your God, saying, 'Pray to the LORD our God on our behalf, and as for all that the LORD our God says, tell it to us, and we'll act accordingly.' ²¹ For I have told you today, but you have not obeyed the LORD your God in everything he has sent me to tell you. ²² Now therefore, know for certain that by the sword, famine, and plague you will die in the place where you desired to go to stay for a while."

ᴬ42:12 LXX reads I   ᴮ42:16 Lit will cling after you   ᶜ42:20 Or You have led your own selves astray

JEREMIAH'S COUNSEL REJECTED

43 When Jeremiah had finished speaking to all the people all the words of the LORD their God — all these words the LORD their God had sent him to give them — ² then Azariah^A son of Hoshaiah, Johanan son of Kareah, and all the other arrogant men responded to Jeremiah, "You are speaking a lie! The LORD our God has not sent you to say, 'You must not go to Egypt to stay there for a while!' ³ Rather, Baruch son of Neriah is inciting you against us to hand us over to the Chaldeans to put us to death or to deport us to Babylon!"

⁴ So Johanan son of Kareah, all the commanders of the armies, and all the people failed to obey the LORD's command to stay in the land of Judah. ⁵ Instead, Johanan son of Kareah and all the commanders of the armies led away the whole remnant of Judah, those who had returned to stay in the land of Judah from all the nations where they had been banished. ⁶ They led away the men, women, children, king's daughters, and everyone whom Nebuzaradan, captain of the guards, had allowed to remain with Gedaliah son of Ahikam son of Shaphan. They also led the prophet Jeremiah and Baruch son of Neriah away. ⁷ They went to the land of Egypt because they did not obey the LORD. They went as far as Tahpanhes.

GOD'S SIGN TO THE PEOPLE IN EGYPT

⁸ Then the word of the LORD came to Jeremiah at Tahpanhes: ⁹ "Pick up some large stones and set them in the mortar of the brick pavement that is at the opening of Pharaoh's palace at Tahpanhes. Do this in the sight of the Judean men ¹⁰ and tell them, 'This is what the LORD of Armies, the God of Israel, says: I will send for my servant Nebuchadnezzar king of Babylon, and I will place his throne on these stones that I have embedded, and he will pitch his pavilion over them. ¹¹ He will come and strike down the land of Egypt — those destined for death, to death; those destined for captivity, to captivity; and those destined for the sword, to the sword. ¹² I^B will kindle a fire in the temples of Egypt's gods, and he will burn them and take them captive. He will clean the land of Egypt as a shepherd picks lice off^C his clothes, and he will leave there unscathed. ¹³ He will smash the sacred pillars of the sun temple^D,E in the land of Egypt and burn the temples of the Egyptian gods.'"

GOD'S JUDGMENT AGAINST HIS PEOPLE IN EGYPT

44 This is the word that came to Jeremiah for all the Jews living in the land of Egypt — at Migdol, Tahpanhes, Memphis, and in the land of Pathros: ² "This is what the LORD of Armies, the God of Israel, says: You have seen all the disaster I brought against Jerusalem and all Judah's cities. Look, they are a ruin today without an inhabitant in them ³ because of the evil they committed to anger me, by going and burning incense to serve other gods that they, you, and your fathers did not know. ⁴ So I sent you all my servants the prophets time and time again,^F saying, 'Don't commit this detestable action that I hate.' ⁵ But they did not

---

^A 43:2 = Jezaniah ^B 43:12 LXX, Syr, Vg read *He* ^C 43:12 Or *will wrap himself in the land of Egypt as a shepherd wraps himself in* ^D 43:13 Or *Beth-shemesh*
^E 43:13 = of Heliopolis ^F 44:4 Lit *prophets, rising up early and sending*

listen or pay attention; they did not turn from their evil or stop burning incense to other gods. ⁶ So my fierce wrath poured out and burned in Judah's cities and Jerusalem's streets so that they became the desolate ruin they are today.

⁷ "So now, this is what the LORD, the God of Armies, the God of Israel, says: Why are you doing such terrible harm to yourselves? You are cutting off man and woman, infant and nursing baby from Judah, leaving yourselves without a remnant. ⁸ You are angering me by the work of your hands. You are burning incense to other gods in the land of Egypt where you have gone to stay for a while. As a result, you will be cut off and become an example for cursing and insult among all the nations of earth. ⁹ Have you forgotten the evils of your fathers, the evils of Judah's kings, the evils of their wives, your own evils, and the evils of your wives that were committed in the land of Judah and in the streets of Jerusalem? ¹⁰ They have not become humble to this day, and they have not feared or followed my instruction or my statutes that I set before you and your ancestors.

¹¹ "Therefore, this is what the LORD of Armies, the God of Israel, says: I am about to set my face against you to bring disaster, to cut off all Judah. ¹² And I will take away the remnant of Judah, those who have set their face to go to the land of Egypt to stay there. All of them will meet their end in the land of Egypt. They will fall by the sword; they will meet their end by famine. From the least to the greatest, they will die by the sword and by famine. Then they will become an example for cursing, scorn, execration, and disgrace. ¹³ I will punish those living in the land of Egypt just as I punished Jerusalem by sword, famine, and plague. ¹⁴ Then the remnant of Judah — those going to live for a while there in the land of Egypt — will have no fugitive or survivor to return to the land of Judah where they are longing^A to return to stay, for they will not return except for a few fugitives."

THE PEOPLE'S STUBBORN RESPONSE

¹⁵ However, all the men who knew that their wives were burning incense to other gods, all the women standing by — a great assembly — and all the people who were living in the land of Egypt at Pathros answered Jeremiah, ¹⁶ "As for the word you spoke to us in the name of the LORD, we are not going to listen to you! ¹⁷ Instead, we will do everything we promised:^B we will burn incense to the queen of heaven^C and offer drink offerings to her just as we, our fathers, our kings, and our officials did in Judah's cities and in Jerusalem's streets. Then we had enough food, we were well off, and we saw no disaster, ¹⁸ but from the time we ceased to burn incense to the queen of heaven and to offer her drink offerings, we have lacked everything, and through sword and famine we have met our end."

¹⁹ And the women said,^D "When we burned incense to the queen of heaven and poured out drink offerings to her, was it apart from our husbands' knowledge that we made sacrificial cakes in her image and poured out drink offerings to her?"

---

^A44:14 Lit lifting up their soul   ^B44:17 Lit do every word that came from our mouth
^C44:17 = Ashtoreth, or Astarte   ^D44:19 LXX, Syr; MT omits And the women said

²⁰ But Jeremiah responded to all the people — the men, women, and all the people who were answering him: ²¹ "As for the incense you burned in Judah's cities and in Jerusalem's streets — you, your fathers, your kings, your officials, and the people of the land — did the LORD not remember them? He brought this to mind. ²² The LORD can no longer bear your evil deeds and the detestable acts you have committed, so your land has become a waste, a desolation, and an example for cursing, without inhabitant, as you see today. ²³ Because you burned incense and sinned against the LORD and didn't obey the LORD and didn't follow his instruction, his statutes, and his testimonies, this disaster has come to you, as you see today."

²⁴ Then Jeremiah said to all the people, including all the women, "Hear the word of the LORD, all you people of Judah who are in the land of Egypt. ²⁵ This is what the LORD of Armies, the God of Israel, says: 'As for you and your wives, you women have spoken with your mouths, and you men fulfilled it by your deeds, saying, "We will keep our vows that we have made to burn incense to the queen of heaven and to pour out drink offerings for her." Go ahead, confirm your vows! Keep your vows!'

²⁶ "Therefore, hear the word of the LORD, all you Judeans who live in the land of Egypt: 'I have sworn by my great name, says the LORD, that my name will never again be invoked by anyone of Judah in all the land of Egypt, saying, "As the Lord GOD lives." ²⁷ I am watching over them for disaster and not for good, and everyone from Judah who is in the land of Egypt will meet his end by sword or famine until they are finished off. ²⁸ Those who escape the sword will return from the land of Egypt to the land of Judah only few in number, and the whole remnant of Judah, the ones going to the land of Egypt to stay there for a while, will know whose word stands, mine or theirs! ²⁹ This will be a sign to you' — this is the LORD's declaration — 'that I will punish you in this place, so you may know that my words of disaster concerning you will certainly come to pass. ³⁰ This is what the LORD says: I am about to hand over Pharaoh Hophra, Egypt's king, to his enemies, to those who intend to take his life, just as I handed over Judah's King Zedekiah to Babylon's King Nebuchadnezzar, who was his enemy, the one who intended to take his life.'"

THE LORD'S MESSAGE TO BARUCH

45 This is the word that the prophet Jeremiah spoke to Baruch son of Neriah when he wrote these words on a scroll at Jeremiah's dictationᴬ in the fourth year of Jehoiakim son of Josiah, king of Judah: ² "This is what the LORD, the God of Israel, says to you, Baruch: ³ 'You have said, "Woe is me, because the LORD has added misery to my pain! I am worn out withᴮ groaning and have found no rest."'

⁴ "This is what you are to say to him: 'This is what the LORD says: "What I have built I am about to demolish, and what I have planted I am about to uproot — the whole land! ⁵ But as for you, do you pursue great things for yourself? Stop pursuing! For I am about to bring disaster on everyone" — this is the LORD's declaration — "but I will grant you your life like the spoils of war wherever you go."'"

ᴬ 45:1 Lit *scroll from Jeremiah's mouth*   ᴮ 45:3 Lit *I labored in my*

PROPHECIES AGAINST THE NATIONS

46 This is the word of the LORD that came to the prophet Jeremiah about the nations:

PROPHECIES AGAINST EGYPT

² About Egypt and the army of Pharaoh Neco, Egypt's king, which was defeated at Carchemish on the Euphrates River by King Nebuchadnezzar of Babylon in the fourth year of Judah's King Jehoiakim son of Josiah:

3   Deploy small shields and large;
    approach for battle!
4   Harness the horses;
    mount the steeds;ᴬ
    take your positions with helmets on!
    Polish the lances;
    put on armor!
5   Why have I seen this?
    They are terrified,
    they are retreating,
    their warriors are crushed,
    they flee headlong,
    they never look back,
    terror is on every side!
        This is the LORD's declaration.
6   The swift cannot flee,
    and the warrior cannot escape!
    In the north by the bank of the Euphrates River,
    they stumble and fall.

7   Who is this, rising like the Nile,
    with waters that churn like rivers?
8   Egypt rises like the Nile,
    and its waters churn like rivers.
    He boasts, "I will go up, I will cover the earth;
    I will destroy cities with their residents."
9   Rise up, you cavalry!
    Race furiously, you chariots!
    Let the warriors march out—
    Cush and Put,
    who are able to handle shields,
    and the men of Lud,
    who are able to handle and string the bow.
10 That day belongs to the Lord, the GOD of Armies,
    a day of vengeance to avenge himself
    against his adversaries.
    The sword will devour and be satisfied;
    it will drink its fill of their blood,
    because it will be a sacrifice to the Lord, the GOD of Armies,
    in the northern land by the Euphrates River.

ᴬ46:4 Or *mount up, riders*

11 Go up to Gilead and get balm,
     Virgin Daughter Egypt!
     You have multiplied remedies in vain;
     there is no healing for you.
12 The nations have heard of your dishonor,
     and your cries fill the earth,
     because warrior stumbles against warrior
     and together both of them have fallen.

13 This is the word the LORD spoke to the prophet Jeremiah about the coming of King Nebuchadnezzar of Babylon to defeat the land of Egypt:

14 Announce it in Egypt, and proclaim it in Migdol!
     Proclaim it in Memphis and in Tahpanhes!
     Say, "Take positions! Prepare yourself,
     for the sword devours all around you."
15 Why have your strong ones been swept away?
     Each has not stood,
     for the LORD has thrust him down.
16 He continues to stumble.
     Indeed, each falls over the other.
     They say, "Get up! Let's return to our people
     and to our native land,
     away from the oppressor's sword."
17 There they will cry out,
     "Pharaoh king of Egypt was all noise;
     he let the opportune moment pass."

18 As I live —
         this is the King's declaration;
         the LORD of Armies is his name —
     the king of Babylon^A will come like Tabor
         among the mountains
     and like Carmel by the sea.
19 Get your bags ready for exile,
     inhabitant of Daughter Egypt!
     For Memphis will become a desolation,
     uninhabited ruins.

20 Egypt is a beautiful young cow,
     but a horsefly from the north is coming against her.^B
21 Even her mercenaries among her
     are like stall-fed calves.
     They too will turn back;
     together they will flee;
     they will not take their stand,
     for the day of their calamity is coming on them,
     the time of their punishment.

---

^A 46:18 Lit He   ^B 46:20 Some Hb mss, LXX, Syr; other Hb mss read *is coming, coming*

22 Egypt will hiss like a slithering snake,^A
  for the enemy will come with an army;
  with axes they will come against her
  like those who cut trees.
23 They will cut down her forest —
    this is the LORD's declaration —
  though it is dense,
  for they are more numerous than locusts;
  they cannot be counted.
24 Daughter Egypt will be put to shame,
  handed over to a northern people.

25 The LORD of Armies, the God of Israel, says, "I am about to punish Amon, god of Thebes, along with Pharaoh, Egypt, her gods, and her kings — Pharaoh and those trusting in him. 26 I will hand them over to those who intend to take their lives — to King Nebuchadnezzar of Babylon and his officers. But after this, Egypt^B will be inhabited again as in ancient times."
  This is the LORD's declaration.

REASSURANCE FOR ISRAEL

27 But you, my servant Jacob, do not be afraid,
  and do not be discouraged, Israel,
  for without fail I will save you from far away,
  and your descendants from the land of their captivity!
  Jacob will return and have calm and quiet
  with no one to frighten him.
28 And you, my servant Jacob, do not be afraid —
    this is the LORD's declaration —
  for I will be with you.
  I will bring destruction on all the nations
  where I have banished you,
  but I will not bring destruction on you.
  I will discipline you with justice,
  and I will by no means leave you unpunished.

PROPHECIES AGAINST THE PHILISTINES

47 This is the word of the LORD that came to the prophet Jeremiah about the Philistines before Pharaoh defeated Gaza. 2 This is what the LORD says:

  Look, water is rising from the north
  and becoming an overflowing wadi.
  It will overflow the land and everything in it,
  the cities and their inhabitants.
  The people will cry out,
  and every inhabitant of the land will wail.
3 At the sound of the stomping hooves of his stallions,
  the rumbling of his chariots,
  and the clatter of their wheels,

^A46:22 Lit Her sound is like a snake as it goes   ^B46:26 Lit it

fathers will not turn back for their sons.
They will be utterly helpless[A]
4   on account of the day that is coming
to destroy all the Philistines,
to cut off from Tyre and Sidon
every remaining ally.
Indeed, the Lord is about to destroy the Philistines,
the remnant of the coastland of Caphtor.[B]
5   Baldness is coming to Gaza;
Ashkelon will become silent.
Remnant of their valley,
how long will you gash yourself?

6   Oh, sword of the Lord!
How long will you be restless?
Go back to your sheath;
be still; be silent!
7   How can it[C] rest
when the Lord has given it a command?
He has assigned it
against Ashkelon and the shore of the sea.

PROPHECIES AGAINST MOAB

48 About Moab, this is what the Lord of Armies, the God of Israel, says:
Woe to Nebo, because it is about to be destroyed;
Kiriathaim will be put to shame; it will be taken captive.
The fortress will be put to shame and dismayed!
2   There is no longer praise for Moab;
they plan harm against her in Heshbon:
Come, let's cut her off from nationhood.
Also, Madmen, you will be silenced;
the sword will follow you.
3   A voice cries out from Horonaim,
"devastation and a crushing blow!"
4   Moab will be shattered;
her little ones will cry out.
5   For on the Ascent to Luhith
they will be weeping continually,[D]
and on the descent to Horonaim
will be heard cries of distress over the destruction:
6   Flee! Save your lives!
Be like a juniper bush[E] in the wilderness.
7   Because you trust in your works and treasures,
you will be captured also.
Chemosh will go into exile
with his priests and officials.

[A]47:3 Lit *Because of weakened hands*   [B]47:4 Probably Crete   [C]47:7 LXX, Vg;
MT reads *you*   [D]48:5 Lit *Luhith, weeping goes up with weeping*   [E]48:6 Or *like*
Aroer; Is 17:2; Jr 48:19

8   The destroyer will move against every town;
    not one town will escape.
    The valley will perish,
    and the plain will be annihilated,
    as the LORD has said.
9   Make Moab a salt marsh,^A
    for she will run away;^B
    her towns will become a desolation,
    without inhabitant.

10 The one who does
    the LORD's business deceitfully^C is cursed,
    and the one who withholds
    his sword from bloodshed is cursed.

11 Moab has been left quiet since his youth,
    settled like wine on its dregs.
    He hasn't been poured from one container
        to another
    or gone into exile.
    So his taste has remained the same,
    and his aroma hasn't changed.
12 Therefore look, the days are coming —
        this is the LORD's declaration —
    when I will send pourers to him,
        who will pour him out.
    They will empty his containers
    and smash his jars.
13 Moab will be put to shame because of Chemosh,
    just as the house of Israel was put to shame
    because of Bethel that they trusted in.

14 How can you say, "We are warriors —
    valiant men for battle"?
15 The destroyer of Moab and its towns
    has come up,^D
    and the best of its young men
    have gone down to slaughter.
        This is the King's declaration;
        the LORD of Armies is his name.
16 Moab's calamity is near at hand;
    his disaster is rushing swiftly.
17 Mourn for him, all you surrounding nations,
    everyone who knows his name.
    Say, "How the mighty scepter is shattered,
    the glorious staff!"

---

^A 48:9 LXX reads *a sign*; Vg reads *a flower*; Syr, Tg read *a crown*   ^B 48:9 Hb
obscure   ^C 48:10 Or *negligently*   ^D 48:15 Or *Moab is destroyed; he has come up
against its cities*

18   Come down from glory; sit on parched ground,
        resident of the daughter of Dibon,
     for the destroyer of Moab has come against you;
        he has destroyed your fortresses.
19   Stand by the highway and watch,
        resident of Aroer!
     Ask him who is fleeing or her who is escaping,
        "What happened?"
20   Moab is put to shame, indeed dismayed.
     Wail and cry out!
     Declare by the Arnon
        that Moab is destroyed.

21 "Judgment has come to the land of the plateau — to Holon, Jahzah, Mephaath, 22 Dibon, Nebo, Beth-diblathaim, 23 Kiriathaim, Beth-gamul, Beth-meon,
24 Kerioth, Bozrah, and all the towns of the land of Moab, those far and near.
25 Moab's horn is chopped off; his arm is shattered."

            This is the LORD's declaration.

26 "Make him drunk, because he has exalted himself against the LORD.
Moab will wallow in his own vomit, and he will also become a laughingstock.
27 Wasn't Israel a laughingstock to you? Was he ever found among thieves?
For whenever you speak of him you shake your head."

28   Abandon the towns! Live in the cliffs,
        residents of Moab!
     Be like a dove
        that nests inside the mouth of a cave.

29   We have heard of Moab's pride,
        great pride, indeed —
     his insolence, arrogance, pride,
        and haughty heart.
30   I know his outburst.
            This is the LORD's declaration.
     It is empty.
     His boast is empty.
31   Therefore, I will wail over Moab.
     I will cry out for Moab, all of it;
        he will moan for the men of Kir-heres.
32   I will weep for you, vine of Sibmah,
        with more than the weeping for Jazer.
     Your tendrils have extended to the sea;
        they have reached to the sea and to Jazer.^A
     The destroyer has fallen on your summer fruit and grape harvest.
33   Gladness and celebration are taken from the fertile field
        and from the land of Moab.
     I have stopped the flow of wine from the winepresses;
        no one will tread with shouts of joy.
     The shouting is not a shout of joy.

---

^A 48:32 Some Hb mss read reached as far as Jazer

³⁴ "There is a cry from Heshbon to Elealeh; they make their voices heard as far as Jahaz — from Zoar to Horonaim and Eglath-shelishiyah — because even the Waters of Nimrim have become desolate. ³⁵ In Moab, I will stop" — this is the LORD's declaration — "the one who offers sacrifices on the high place and burns incense to his gods. ³⁶ Therefore, my heart moans like flutes for Moab, and my heart moans like flutes for the people of Kir-heres. And therefore, the wealth he has gained has perished. ³⁷ Indeed, every head is bald and every beard is chopped short. On every hand is a gash and sackcloth around the waist. ³⁸ On all the rooftops of Moab and in her public squares, everyone is mourning because I have shattered Moab like a jar no one wants." This is the LORD's declaration. ³⁹ "How broken it is! They wail! How Moab has turned his back! He is ashamed. Moab will become a laughingstock and a shock to all those around him."

⁴⁰ For this is what the LORD says:

Look! He will swoop down like an eagle
and spread his wings against Moab.
⁴¹ The towns have^A been captured,
and the strongholds seized.
In that day the heart of Moab's warriors
will be like the heart of a woman with contractions.
⁴² Moab will be destroyed as a people
because he has exalted himself against the LORD.
⁴³ Panic, pit, and trap
await you, resident of Moab.
This is the LORD's declaration.
⁴⁴ He who flees from the panic will fall in the pit,
and he who climbs from the pit
will be captured in the trap,
for I will bring against Moab
the year of their punishment.
This is the LORD's declaration.

⁴⁵ Those who flee will stand exhausted in Heshbon's shadow
because fire has come out from Heshbon
and a flame from within Sihon.
It will devour Moab's forehead
and the skull of the noisemakers.
⁴⁶ Woe to you, Moab!
The people of Chemosh have perished
because your sons have been taken captive
and your daughters have gone into captivity.
⁴⁷ Yet, I will restore the fortunes^B of Moab in the last days.
This is the LORD's declaration.
The judgment on Moab ends here.

PROPHECIES AGAINST AMMON

49 About the Ammonites, this is what the LORD says:
Does Israel have no sons?
Is he without an heir?

^A48:41 Or Kerioth has   ^B48:47 Or will end the captivity

Why then has Milcom^(A,B) dispossessed Gad
and his people settled in their cities?

2 Therefore look, the days are coming —
　　this is the LORD's declaration —
when I will make the shout of battle heard
against Rabbah of the Ammonites.
It will become a desolate mound,
and its surrounding villages will be set on fire.
Israel will dispossess their dispossessors,
says the LORD.

3 Wail, Heshbon, for Ai is devastated;
cry out, daughters of Rabbah!
Clothe yourselves with sackcloth, and lament;
run back and forth within your walls,^(C)
because Milcom will go into exile
together with his priests and officials.

4 Why do you boast about your valleys,
your flowing valley,^(D)
you faithless daughter —
you who trust in your treasures
and say, "Who can attack me?"

5 Look, I am about to bring terror on you —
　　this is the declaration of the Lord GOD of Armies —
from all those around you.
You will be banished, each person headlong,
with no one to gather up the fugitives.

6 But after that, I will restore the fortunes^(E)
of the Ammonites.
This is the LORD's declaration.

PROPHECIES AGAINST EDOM

7 About Edom, this is what the LORD of Armies says:
Is there no longer wisdom in Teman?
Has counsel perished from the prudent?
Has their wisdom rotted away?

8 Run! Turn back! Lie low,
residents of Dedan,
for I will bring Esau's calamity on him
at the time I punish him.

9 If grape harvesters came to you,
wouldn't they leave some gleanings?
Were thieves to come in the night,
they would destroy only what they wanted.

10 But I will strip Esau bare;
I will uncover his secret places.
He will try to hide, but he will be unable.

---

^(A) 49:1 LXX, Syr, Vg; MT reads *Malkam*　^(B) 49:1 = Molech　^(C) 49:3 Or *sheep pens*
^(D) 49:4 Or *about your strength, your ebbing strength*　^(E) 49:6 Or *will end the
captivity, also in v. 39*

His descendants will be destroyed
along with his relatives and neighbors.
He will exist no longer.
¹¹ Abandon your fatherless; I will preserve them;
let your widows trust in me.

¹² For this is what the LORD says: "If those who do not deserve to drink the cup must drink it, can you possibly remain unpunished? You will not remain unpunished, for you must drink it too. ¹³ For by myself I have sworn" — this is the LORD's declaration — "Bozrah ^A will become a desolation, a disgrace, a ruin, and an example for cursing, and all its surrounding cities will become ruins forever."

¹⁴   I have heard an envoy from the LORD;
a messenger has been sent among the nations:
Assemble yourselves to come against her.
Rise up for war!

¹⁵   I will certainly make you insignificant among the nations,
despised among humanity.
¹⁶   As to the terror you cause, ^B
your arrogant heart has deceived you.
You who live in the clefts of the rock, ^C
you who occupy the mountain summit,
though you elevate your nest like the eagles,
even from there I will bring you down.
This is the LORD's declaration.

¹⁷ "Edom will become a desolation. Everyone who passes by her will be appalled and scoff because of all her wounds. ¹⁸ As when Sodom and Gomorrah were overthrown along with their neighbors," says the LORD, "no one will live there; no human being will stay in it even temporarily.

¹⁹ "Look, it will be like a lion coming from the thickets ^D of the Jordan to the watered grazing land. I will chase Edom away from her land in a flash. I will appoint whoever is chosen for her. For who is like me? Who will issue me a summons? Who is the shepherd who can stand against me? "

²⁰ Therefore, hear the plans that the LORD has drawn up against Edom and the strategies he has devised against the people of Teman: The flock's little lambs will certainly be dragged away, and their grazing land will be made desolate because of them. ²¹ At the sound of their fall the earth will quake; the sound of her cry will be heard at the Red Sea. ²² Look! It will be like an eagle soaring upward, then swooping down and spreading its wings over Bozrah. In that day the hearts of Edom's warriors will be like the heart of a woman with contractions.

PROPHECIES AGAINST DAMASCUS

²³ About Damascus:
Hamath and Arpad are put to shame,
for they have heard a bad report and are agitated,

---

^A 49:13 = Edom's capital   ^B 49:16 Lit Your horror   ^C 49:16 = Petra   ^D 49:19 Lit pride like^A the anxious sea that cannot be calmed.

24 Damascus has become weak;
     she has turned to run;
     panic has gripped her.
     Distress and labor pains have seized her
     like a woman in labor.
25 How can the city of praise not be abandoned,
     the town that brings me joy?
26 Therefore, her young men will fall
          in her public squares;
     all the warriors will perish in that day.
          This is the declaration of the Lord of Armies.
27 I will set fire to the wall of Damascus;
     it will consume Ben-hadad's citadels.

PROPHECIES AGAINST KEDAR AND HAZOR

28 About Kedar and the kingdoms of Hazor, which King Nebuchadnezzar of
Babylon defeated, this is what the Lord says:
     Rise up, attack Kedar,
     and destroy the people of the east!
29 They will take their tents and their flocks
     along with their tent curtains
          and all their equipment.
     They will take their camels for themselves.
     They will call out to them,
     "Terror is on every side!"
30 Run! Escape quickly! Lie low,
     residents of Hazor —
          this is the Lord's declaration —
     for King Nebuchadnezzar of Babylon
     has drawn up a plan against you;
     he has devised a strategy against you.

31 Rise up, attack a nation at ease,
     one living in security.
          This is the Lord's declaration.
     They have no doors, not even a gate bar;
     they live alone.
32 Their camels will become plunder,
     and their massive herds of cattle will become spoil.
     I will scatter them to the wind in every direction,
     those who clip the hair on their temples;
     I will bring calamity on them across all their borders.
          This is the Lord's declaration.
33 Hazor will become a jackals' den,
     a desolation forever.
     No one will live there;
     no human being will stay in it even temporarily.

---

^A 49:23 Lit *in*

PROPHECIES AGAINST ELAM

[34] This is the word of the LORD that came to the prophet Jeremiah about Elam[A] at the beginning of the reign of King Zedekiah of Judah. [35] This is what the LORD of Armies says:

> I am about to shatter Elam's bow,
> the source[B] of their might.

[36] I will bring the four winds against Elam
> from the four corners of the heavens,
> and I will scatter them to all these winds.
> There will not be a nation
> to which Elam's banished ones will not go.

[37] I will devastate Elam before their enemies,
> before those who intend to take their lives.
> I will bring disaster on them,
> my burning anger.
>> This is the LORD's declaration.
> I will send the sword after them
> until I finish them off.

[38] I will set my throne in Elam,
> and I will destroy the king and officials from there.
>> This is the LORD's declaration.

[39] Yet, in the last days,
> I will restore the fortunes of Elam.
>> This is the LORD's declaration.

PROPHECIES AGAINST BABYLON

50 This is the word the LORD spoke about Babylon, the land of the Chaldeans, through the prophet Jeremiah:

[2] Announce to the nations;
> proclaim and raise up a signal flag;
> proclaim, and hide nothing.
> Say, "Babylon is captured;
> Bel is put to shame;
> Marduk is terrified."
> Her idols are put to shame;
> her false gods, devastated.

[3] For a nation from the north will attack her;
> it will make her land desolate.
> No one will be living in it —
> both people and animals will escape.[C]

[4] In those days and at that time —
>> this is the LORD's declaration —
> the Israelites and Judeans will come together,
> weeping as they come,
> and will seek the LORD their God.

[5] They will ask about Zion,
> turning their faces to this road.

1318

[A] 49:34 = modern Iran   [B] 49:35 Lit *first*   [C] 50:3 Lit *escape; they will walk*

They will come and join themselves^A to the LORD
in a permanent covenant that will never be forgotten.

6 My people were lost sheep;
their shepherds led them astray,
guiding them the wrong way in the mountains.
They wandered from mountain to hill;
they forgot their resting place.

7 Whoever found them devoured them.
Their adversaries said, "We're not guilty;
instead, they have sinned against the LORD,
their righteous grazing land,
the hope of their ancestors, the LORD."

8 Escape from Babylon;
depart from the Chaldeans' land.
Be like the rams that lead the flock.

9 For I will soon stir up and bring against Babylon
an assembly of great nations from the north country.
They will line up in battle formation against her;
from there she will be captured.
Their arrows will be like a skilled^B warrior
who does not return empty-handed.

10 The Chaldeans will become plunder;
all Babylon's plunderers will be fully satisfied.
This is the LORD's declaration.

11 Because you rejoice,
because you celebrate —
you who plundered my inheritance —
because you frolic like a young cow treading grain
and neigh like stallions,

12 your mother will be utterly humiliated;
she who bore you will be put to shame.
Look! She will lag behind all^C the nations —
an arid wilderness, a desert.

13 Because of the LORD's wrath,
she will not be inhabited;
she will become a desolation, every bit of her.
Everyone who passes through Babylon
will be appalled
and scoff because of all her wounds.

14 Line up in battle formation around Babylon,
all you archers!
Shoot at her! Do not spare an arrow,
for she has sinned against the LORD.

15 Raise a war cry against her on every side!
She has thrown up her hands in surrender;

^A 50:5 LXX; MT reads *Come and join yourselves* ^B 50:9 Some Hb mss, LXX, Syr; other Hb mss read *bereaving* ^C 50:12 Lit *Look! The last of*

1319

her defense towers have fallen;
her walls are demolished.
Since this is the LORD's vengeance,
take your vengeance on her;
as she has done, do the same to her.
¹⁶ Cut off the sower from Babylon
as well as him who wields the sickle at harvest time.
Because of the oppressor's sword,
each will turn to his own people,
each will flee to his own land.

THE RETURN OF GOD'S PEOPLE

¹⁷ Israel is a stray lamb, chased by lions.
The first who devoured him was the king of Assyria;
the last who crushed his bones
was King Nebuchadnezzar of Babylon.

¹⁸ Therefore, this is what the LORD of Armies, the God of Israel, says: I am about to punish the king of Babylon and his land just as I punished the king of Assyria.
¹⁹ I will return Israel to his grazing land,
and he will feed on Carmel and Bashan;
he will be satisfied
in the hill country of Ephraim and of Gilead.
²⁰ In those days and at that time —
this is the LORD's declaration —
one will search for Israel's iniquity,
but there will be none,
and for Judah's sins,
but they will not be found,
for I will forgive those I leave as a remnant.

THE INVASION OF BABYLON

²¹ Attack the land of Merathaim,
and those living in Pekod.
Put them to the sword;
completely destroy them —
this is the LORD's declaration —
do everything I have commanded you.
²² The sound of war is in the land —
a crushing blow!
²³ How the hammer of the whole earth
is cut down and smashed!
What a horror Babylon has become
among the nations!
²⁴ Babylon, I laid a trap for you, and you were caught,
but you did not even know it.
You were found and captured
because you pitted yourself against the LORD.
²⁵ The LORD opened his armory

and brought out his weapons of wrath,
because it is a task of the Lord God of Armies
in the land of the Chaldeans.
26 Come against her from the most distant places.^A
Open her granaries;
pile her up like mounds of grain
and completely destroy her.
Leave her no survivors.
27 Put all her young bulls to the sword;
let them go down to the slaughter.
Woe to them because their day has come,
the time of their punishment.

THE HUMILIATION OF BABYLON

28 There is a voice of fugitives and refugees
from the land of Babylon.
The voice announces in Zion the vengeance of the Lord our God,
the vengeance for his temple.
29 Summon the archers to Babylon,
all who string the bow;
camp all around her; let none escape.
Repay her according to her deeds;
just as she has done, do the same to her,
for she has acted arrogantly against the Lord,
against the Holy One of Israel.
30 Therefore, her young men will fall
in her public squares;
all the warriors will perish in that day.
This is the Lord's declaration.
31 Look, I am against you, you arrogant one —
this is the declaration of
the Lord God of Armies —
for your day has come,
the time when I will punish you.
32 The arrogant will stumble and fall
with no one to pick him up.
I will set fire to his cities,
and it will consume everything around him.

THE DESOLATION OF BABYLON

33 This is what the Lord of Armies says:
Israelites and Judeans alike have been oppressed.
All their captors hold them fast;
they refuse to release them.
34 Their Redeemer is strong;
the Lord of Armies is his name.
He will fervently champion their cause
so that he might bring rest to the earth

^A 50:26 Lit from the end

but turmoil to those who live in Babylon.

³⁵ A sword is over the Chaldeans —
 this is the Lord's declaration —
against those who live in Babylon,
against her officials, and against her sages.

³⁶ A sword is against the diviners,
and they will act foolishly.
A sword is against her heroic warriors,
and they will be terrified.

³⁷ A sword is against his horses and chariots
and against all the foreigners among them,
and they will be like women.
A sword is against her treasuries,
and they will be plundered.

³⁸ A drought will come on her waters,
and they will be dried up.
For it is a land of carved images,
and they go mad because of terrifying things.ᴬ

³⁹ Therefore, desert creaturesᴮ will live with hyenas,
and ostriches will also live in her.
It will never again be inhabited
or lived in through all generations.

⁴⁰ Just as God demolished Sodom and Gomorrah
and their neighboring towns —
 this is the Lord's declaration —
so no one will live there;
no human being will stay in it even temporarily
as a temporary resident.

THE CONQUEST OF BABYLON

⁴¹ Look! A people comes from the north.
A great nation and many kings will be stirred up
from the remote regions of the earth.

⁴² They grasp bow and javelin.
They are cruel and show no mercy.
Their voice roars like the sea,
and they ride on horses,
lined up like men in battle formation
against you, Daughter Babylon.

⁴³ The king of Babylon has heard about them;
his hands have become weak.
Distress has seized him —
pain, like a woman in labor.

⁴⁴ "Look, it will be like a lion coming from the thicketsᶜ of the Jordan to the watered grazing land. I will chase Babylonᴰ away from her land in a flash.

ᴬ50:38 Or *of dreaded gods* ᴮ50:39 Or *desert demons* ᶜ50:44 Lit *pride*
ᴰ50:44 Lit *them*

I will appoint whoever is chosen for her. For who is like me? Who will issue me a summons? Who is the shepherd who can stand against me?"

⁴⁵ Therefore, hear the plans that the LORD has drawn up against Babylon and the strategies he has devised against the land of the Chaldeans: Certainly the flock's little lambs will be dragged away; certainly the grazing land will be made desolate because of them. ⁴⁶ At the sound of Babylon's conquest the earth will quake; a cry will be heard among the nations.

GOD'S JUDGMENT ON BABYLON

51 This is what the LORD says:
I am about to rouse the spirit of a destroyerᴬ against Babylon
and against the population of Leb-qamai.ᴮ,ᶜ

² I will send strangers to Babylon
who will scatter her and strip her land bare,
for they will come against her
from every side in the day of disaster.

³ Don't let the archer string his bow;
don't let him put onᴰ his armor.
Don't spare her young men;
completely destroy her entire army!

⁴ Those who were slain will fall in the land of the Chaldeans,
those who were pierced through, in her streets.

⁵ For Israel and Judah are not left widowed
by their God, the LORD of Armies,
though their land is full of guilt
against the Holy One of Israel.

⁶ Leave Babylon;
save your lives, each of you!
Don't perish because of her guilt.
For this is the time of the LORD's vengeance —
he will pay her what she deserves.

⁷ Babylon was a gold cup in the LORD's hand,
making the whole earth drunk.
The nations drank her wine;
therefore, the nations go mad.

⁸ Suddenly Babylon fell and was shattered.
Wail for her;
get balm for her wound —
perhaps she can be healed.

⁹ We tried to heal Babylon,
but she could not be healed.
Abandon her!
Let each of us go to his own land,
for her judgment extends to the sky
and reaches as far as the clouds.

ᴬ51:1 Or *to stir up a destructive wind*   ᴮ51:1 Lit *heart of my adversaries*
ᶜ51:1 = Chaldeans   ᴰ51:3 Hb obscure

10 The LORD has brought about our vindication;
  come, let's tell in Zion
  what the LORD our God has accomplished.

11 Sharpen the arrows!
  Fill the quivers!^A
  The LORD has roused the spirit
  of the kings of the Medes
  because his plan is aimed at Babylon
  to destroy her,
  for it is the LORD's vengeance,
  vengeance for his temple.

12 Raise up a signal flag
  against the walls of Babylon;
  fortify the watch post;
  set the watchmen in place;
  prepare the ambush.
  For the LORD has both planned and accomplished
  what he has threatened
  against those who live in Babylon.

13 You who reside by abundant water,
  rich in treasures,
  your end has come,
  your life thread is cut.

14 The LORD of Armies has sworn by himself:
  I will fill you up with men as with locusts,
  and they will sing the victory song over you.

15 He made the earth by his power,
  established the world by his wisdom,
  and spread out the heavens by his understanding.

16 When he thunders,^B
  the waters in the heavens are tumultuous,
  and he causes the clouds
  to rise from the ends of the earth.
  He makes lightning for the rain
  and brings the wind from his storehouses.

17 Everyone is stupid and ignorant.
  Every goldsmith is put to shame by his carved image,
  for his cast images are a lie;
  there is no breath in them.

18 They are worthless, a work to be mocked.
  At the time of their punishment they will be destroyed.

19 Jacob's Portion^C is not like these
  because he is the one who formed all things.

---

^A51:11 Or *Grasp the shields!* ^B51:16 Lit *At his giving of the voice*
^C51:19 = The LORD

Israel is the tribe of his inheritance;
the LORD of Armies is his name.

20 You are my war club,
my weapons of war.
With you I will smash nations;
with you I will bring kingdoms to ruin.
21 With you I will smash the horse and its rider;
with you I will smash the chariot and its rider.
22 With you I will smash man and woman;
with you I will smash the old man and the youth;
with you I will smash the young man
and the young woman.
23 With you I will smash the shepherd and his flock;
with you I will smash the farmer and his ox-team.^A
With you I will smash governors and officials.

24 "Before your very eyes, I will repay Babylon and all the residents of
Chaldea for all their evil they have done in Zion."
This is the LORD's declaration.
25 Look, I am against you, devastating mountain.
This is the LORD's declaration.
You devastate the whole earth.
I will stretch out my hand against you,
roll you down from the cliffs,
and turn you into a charred mountain.
26 No one will be able to retrieve a cornerstone
or a foundation stone from you,
because you will become desolate forever.
This is the LORD's declaration.

27 Raise a signal flag in the land;
blow a ram's horn among the nations;
set apart the nations against her.
Summon kingdoms against her —
Ararat, Minni, and Ashkenaz.
Appoint a marshal against her;
bring up horses like a swarm^B of locusts.
28 Set apart the nations for battle against her —
the kings of Media,
her governors and all her officials,
and all the lands they rule.
29 The earth quakes and trembles
because the LORD's intentions against Babylon stand:
to make the land of Babylon a desolation,
without inhabitant.
30 Babylon's warriors have stopped fighting;
they sit in their strongholds.

---

^A 51:23 Lit yoke   ^B 51:27 Hb obscure

Their might is exhausted;
they have become like women.
Babylon's homes have been set ablaze,
her gate bars are shattered.

31 Messenger races to meet messenger,
and herald to meet herald,
to announce to the king of Babylon
that his city has been captured
from end to end.

32 The fords have been seized,
the marshes set on fire,
and the fighting men are terrified.

33 For this is what the LORD of Armies, the God of Israel, says:
Daughter Babylon is like a threshing floor
at the time it is trampled.
In just a little while her harvest time will come.

34 "King Nebuchadnezzar of Babylon has devoured me;
he has crushed me.
He has set me aside like an empty dish;
he has swallowed me like a sea monster;
he filled his belly with my delicacies;
he has vomited me out.[A]

35 Let the violence done to me and my family
be done to Babylon,"
says the inhabitant of Zion.
"Let my blood be on the inhabitants of Chaldea,"
says Jerusalem.

36 Therefore, this is what the LORD says:
I am about to champion your cause
and take vengeance on your behalf;
I will dry up her sea
and make her fountain run dry.

37 Babylon will become a heap of rubble,
a jackals' den,
a desolation and an object of scorn,
without inhabitant.

38 They will roar together like young lions;
they will growl like lion cubs.

39 While they are flushed with heat, I will serve them a feast,
and I will make them drunk so that they celebrate.[B]
Then they will fall asleep forever
and never wake up.
This is the LORD's declaration.

40 I will bring them down like lambs to the slaughter,
like rams together with male goats.

[A]51:34 Lit *has rinsed me off*   [B]51:39 LXX reads *pass out*

41 How Sheshach[A] has been captured,
the praise of the whole earth seized.
What a horror Babylon has become
among the nations!

42 The sea has risen over Babylon;
she is covered with its tumultuous waves.

43 Her cities have become a desolation,
an arid desert,
a land where no one lives,
where no human being even passes through.

44 I will punish Bel in Babylon.
I will make him vomit what he swallowed.
The nations will no longer stream to him;
even Babylon's wall will fall.

45 Come out from among her, my people!
Save your lives, each of you,
from the LORD's burning anger.

46 May you not become cowardly and fearful
when the report is proclaimed in the land,
for the report will come one year,
and then another the next year.
There will be violence in the land
with ruler against ruler.

47 Therefore, look, the days are coming
when I will punish Babylon's carved images.
Her entire land will suffer shame,
and all her slain will lie fallen within her.

48 Heaven and earth and everything in them
will shout for joy over Babylon
because the destroyers from the north
will come against her.
This is the LORD's declaration.

49 Babylon must fall because of the slain of Israel,
even as the slain of the whole earth fell
because of Babylon.

50 You who have escaped the sword,
go and do not stand still!
Remember the LORD from far away,
and let Jerusalem come to your mind.

51 We are ashamed
because we have heard insults.
Humiliation covers our faces
because foreigners have entered
the holy places of the LORD's temple.

[A]51:41 = Babylon

⁵² Therefore, look, the days are coming —
  this is the LORD's declaration —
when I will punish her carved images,
and the wounded will groan
throughout her land.

⁵³ Even if Babylon should ascend
  to the heavens
and fortify her tall fortresses,
destroyers will come against her from me.
  This is the LORD's declaration.

⁵⁴ The sound of a cry from Babylon!
The sound of terrible destruction
from the land of the Chaldeans!

⁵⁵ For the LORD is going to devastate Babylon;
he will silence her mighty voice.
Their waves roar like a huge torrent;
the tumult of their voice resounds,

⁵⁶ for a destroyer is coming against her,
against Babylon.
Her warriors will be captured,
their bows shattered,
for the LORD is a God of retribution;
he will certainly repay.

⁵⁷ I will make her princes and sages drunk,
along with her governors, officials, and warriors.
Then they will fall asleep forever
and never wake up.
  This is the King's declaration;
  the LORD of Armies is his name.

⁵⁸ This is what the LORD of Armies says:
Babylon's thick walls will be totally demolished,
and her high gates set ablaze.
The peoples will have labored for nothing;
the nations will weary themselves only to feed the fire.

⁵⁹ This is what the prophet Jeremiah commanded Seraiah son of Neriah son of Mahseiah, the quartermaster, when he went to Babylon with King Zedekiah of Judah in the fourth year of Zedekiah's reign. ⁶⁰ Jeremiah wrote on one scroll about all the disaster that would come to Babylon; all these words were written against Babylon.

⁶¹ Jeremiah told Seraiah, "When you get to Babylon, see that you read all these words aloud. ⁶² Say, 'LORD, you have threatened to cut off this place so that no one will live in it — people or animals. Indeed, it will remain desolate forever.' ⁶³ When you have finished reading this scroll, tie a stone to it and throw it into the middle of the Euphrates River. ⁶⁴ Then say, 'In the same way, Babylon will sink and never rise again because of the disaster I am bringing on her. They will grow weary.'"

The words of Jeremiah end here.

THE FALL OF JERUSALEM

52 Zedekiah was twenty-one years old when he became king, and he reigned eleven years in Jerusalem. His mother's name was Hamutal daughter of Jeremiah; she was from Libnah. ² Zedekiah did what was evil in the Lord's sight just as Jehoiakim had done. ³ Because of the Lord's anger, it came to the point in Jerusalem and Judah that he finally banished them from his presence. Then Zedekiah rebelled against the king of Babylon.

⁴ In the ninth year of Zedekiah's reign, on the tenth day of the tenth month, King Nebuchadnezzar of Babylon advanced against Jerusalem with his entire army. They laid siege to the city and built a siege wall against it all around. ⁵ The city was under siege until King Zedekiah's eleventh year.

⁶ By the ninth day of the fourth month the famine was so severe in the city that the common people had no food. ⁷ Then the city was broken into, and all the warriors fled. They left the city at night by way of the city gate between the two walls near the king's garden, though the Chaldeans surrounded the city. They made their way along the route to the Arabah. ⁸ The Chaldean army pursued the king and overtook Zedekiah in the plains of Jericho. Zedekiah's entire army left him and scattered. ⁹ The Chaldeans seized the king and brought him to the king of Babylon at Riblah in the land of Hamath, and he passed sentence on him.

¹⁰ At Riblah the king of Babylon slaughtered Zedekiah's sons before his eyes, and he also slaughtered the Judean commanders. ¹¹ Then he blinded Zedekiah and bound him with bronze chains. The king of Babylon brought Zedekiah to Babylon, where he kept him in custody[A] until his dying day.

¹² On the tenth day of the fifth month — which was the nineteenth year of King Nebuchadnezzar, king of Babylon — Nebuzaradan, the captain of the guards, entered Jerusalem as the representative of[B] the king of Babylon. ¹³ He burned the Lord's temple, the king's palace, all the houses of Jerusalem; he burned down all the great houses. ¹⁴ The whole Chaldean army with the captain of the guards tore down all the walls surrounding Jerusalem. ¹⁵ Nebuzaradan, the captain of the guards, deported some of the poorest of the people, as well as the rest of the people who remained in the city, the deserters who had defected to the king of Babylon, and the rest of the craftsmen. ¹⁶ But Nebuzaradan, the captain of the guards, left some of the poorest of the land to be vinedressers and farmers.

¹⁷ Now the Chaldeans broke into pieces the bronze pillars for the Lord's temple and the water carts and the bronze basin[C] that were in the Lord's temple, and they carried all the bronze to Babylon. ¹⁸ They also took the pots, shovels, wick trimmers, sprinkling basins, dishes, and all the bronze articles used in the temple service. ¹⁹ The captain of the guards took away the bowls, firepans, sprinkling basins, pots, lampstands, pans, and drink offering bowls — whatever was gold or silver.

²⁰ As for the two pillars, the one basin, with the twelve bronze oxen under it, and the water carts[D] that King Solomon had made for the Lord's temple, the weight of the bronze of all these articles was beyond measure. ²¹ One pillar was 27 feet[E] tall, had a circumference of 18 feet,[F] was hollow — four

---

[A] 52:11 Lit in a house of guards   [B] 52:12 Lit Jerusalem; he stood before
[C] 52:17 Lit sea   [D] 52:20 LXX, Syr, MT reads oxen under the water carts
[E] 52:21 Lit 18 cubits   [F] 52:21 Lit 12 cubits

fingers thick — 22 and had a bronze capital on top of it. One capital, encircled by bronze grating and pomegranates, stood 7 ½ feet^A high. The second pillar was the same, with pomegranates. 23 Each capital had ninety-six pomegranates all around it. All the pomegranates around the grating numbered one hundred.

24 The captain of the guards also took away Seraiah the chief priest, Zephaniah the priest of the second rank, and the three doorkeepers. 25 From the city he took a court official^B who had been appointed over the warriors; seven trusted royal aides^C found in the city; the secretary of the commander of the army, who enlisted the people of the land for military duty; and sixty men from the common people^D who were found within the city. 26 Nebuzaradan, the captain of the guards, took them and brought them to the king of Babylon at Riblah. 27 The king of Babylon put them to death at Riblah in the land of Hamath. So Judah went into exile from its land.

28 These are the people Nebuchadnezzar deported: in the seventh year, 3,023 Jews; 29 in his eighteenth year,^E 832 people from Jerusalem; 30 in Nebuchadnezzar's twenty-third year, Nebuzaradan, the captain of the guards, deported 745 Jews. Altogether, 4,600 people were deported.

JEHOIACHIN PARDONED

31 On the twenty-fifth day of the twelfth month of the thirty-seventh year of the exile of Judah's King Jehoiachin, King Evil-merodach of Babylon, in the first year of his reign, pardoned King Jehoiachin of Judah and released him from prison. 32 He spoke kindly to him and set his throne above the thrones of the kings who were with him in Babylon. 33 So Jehoiachin changed his prison clothes, and he dined regularly in the presence of the king of Babylon for the rest of his life. 34 As for his allowance, a regular allowance was given to him by the king of Babylon, a portion for each day until the day of his death, for the rest of his life.

---

^A52:22 Lit five cubits   ^B52:25 Or a eunuch   ^C52:25 Lit seven men who look on the king's face   ^D52:25 Lit the people of the land   ^E52:29 Some Hb mss, Syr add he deported

His mercies never end. They are new every morning; great is your faithfulness!

lamentations

 Because of the Lord's faithful love we do not perish, for his mercies never end. They are new every morning; great is your faithfulness! **3:22-23**

ON THE TIMELINE Lamentations was written about 586 BC, after the third deportation of the people of Judah to Babylon, when Nebuchadnezzar completely destroyed the city and the temple.

A LITTLE BACKGROUND The prophet Jeremiah's name has long been associated with this book, and many early texts confirm his authorship. Even though the book lists only one proper name ("Edom," Lm 4:21-22), the book of Lamentations contains unmistakable allusions and historical connections to the events listed so dramatically in 2 Kings 25, 2 Chronicles 36:11-21, and the book of Jeremiah.

MESSAGE & PURPOSE When naming the books of the Hebrew Bible, the first word was often adopted as the name of the whole book. In this case, Lamentations 1:1; 2:1; and 4:1 begin with the typical Hebrew cry of woe, 'ekah, which means "Alas!" Later, rabbis referred to the book more by its contents—qinot, or "lamentations." The suffering described in Lamentations, brought on by the brutal overthrow of Jerusalem by the Babylonian army in 586 BC, was one of the darkest times in Jewish history. The author vividly addresses the extremes of human pain and suffering as few other authors have done in history, making it an important biblical text raising the hard questions that arise during times of pain.

While Lamentations is about pain, it is not a book without hope. The people of Judah had more than enough to weep over, but their united lament was related to their covenant history with God. This anchored their sorrow but also gave their grief specific barriers, lest they become overwhelmed and lose all hope.

GIVE THANKS FOR THE BOOK OF LAMENTATIONS

Lamentations invites us to meet God in the midst of our suffering and teaches us the language of prayer. Instead of offering a set of techniques, easy answers, or inspiring slogans for facing pain and grief, Lamentations gives voice to our pain, reorients our focus to the faithfulness of God, and affirms that He alone is our portion.

THE BOOK OF LAMENTATIONS IN HISTORY

967	550 BC	538	500 BC	457
	586		520	AD 70
			515	

967 — King Solomon builds the temple in Jerusalem

586 — Temple destroyed by Babylonians

538 — Decree of Cyrus allows exiles from Judah to return and rebuild the temple

520 — Temple reconstruction resumes under Darius's decree

515 — Temple reconstruction complete

457 — Ezra's ministry re-establishes worship in Jerusalem

AD 70 — Temple destroyed by the Romans

READ AND UNDERSTAND LAMENTATIONS

The Bible is a complete work in which many stories combine to tell one story. As you read the book of Lamentations, consider reading the additional passages to discover how the whole of Scripture works together.

LAMENT OVER JERUSALEM

א Aleph

1 How[A] she sits alone,
the city once crowded with people!
She who was great among the nations
has become like a widow.
The princess among the provinces
has been put to forced labor.

ב Beth

2 She weeps bitterly during the night,
with tears on her cheeks.
There is no one to offer her comfort,
not one from all her lovers.[B]
All her friends have betrayed her;
they have become her enemies.

ג Gimel

3 Judah has gone into exile
following[C] affliction and harsh slavery;
she lives among the nations
but finds no place to rest.
All her pursuers have overtaken her
in narrow places.

ד Daleth

4 The roads to Zion mourn,
for no one comes to the appointed festivals.
All her gates are deserted;
her priests groan,
her young women grieve,
and she herself is bitter.

ה He

5 Her adversaries have become
her masters;
her enemies are at ease,
for the LORD has made her suffer
because of her many transgressions.
Her children have gone away
as captives before the adversary.

ו Waw

6 All the splendor has vanished
from Daughter Zion.
Her leaders are like stags
that find no pasture;

[A]1:1 The stanzas in Lm 1–4 form an acrostic.   [B]1:2 = Jerusalem's political allies
[C]1:3 Or *because of*

they stumble away exhausted
before the hunter.

ז Zayin

7 During the days of her affliction and homelessness
Jerusalem remembers all her precious belongings
that were hers in days of old.
When her people fell into the adversary's hand,
she had no one to help.
The adversaries looked at her,
laughing over her downfall.

ח Cheth

8 Jerusalem has sinned grievously;
therefore, she has become an object of scorn. ᴬ
All who honored her now despise her,
for they have seen her nakedness.
She herself groans and turns away.

ט Teth

9 Her uncleanness stains her skirts.
She never considered her end.
Her downfall was astonishing;
there was no one to comfort her.
LORD, look on my affliction,
for the enemy boasts.

י Yod

10 The adversary has seized
all her precious belongings.
She has even seen the nations
enter her sanctuary —
those you had forbidden
to enter your assembly.

כ Kaph

11 All her people groan
while they search for bread.
They have traded their precious belongings for food
in order to stay alive.
LORD, look and see
how I have become despised.

ל Lamed

12 Is this nothing to you, all you who pass by?
Look and see!
Is there any pain like mine,
which was dealt out to me,

ᴬ1:8 Or *become impure*

WASH ME

LAMENTATIONS 1; PSALM 32:1-11; PSALM 51:1-6

At first glance, Lamentations does not read like a book of hope. Sin has brought wreckage upon Jerusalem, though she was once great. Her people are hungry, and in their famine and their sorrow they call out to the Lord. Matthew Henry writes, "In this sad condition Jerusalem acknowledged her sin, and entreated the Lord to look upon her case. This is the only way to make ourselves easy under our burdens" (Matthew Henry, *Commentary on Lamentations*).

When I need to ease my burdens, I find myself seeking out warm coffee or "me time," a pedicure or a hot bath. Our modern response to hard times is to look for physical comfort. If my soul is restless, I'm looking for a quick fix and a way to melt away the pain and frustration of the moment.

I know a bubble bath isn't going to wash my soul, but aren't you tempted to believe it might? I want to dip my chin in lavender bubbles and forget that the only way to be truly clean is through repentance.

But Psalm 32 tells us there is true blessing and forgiveness to be found in repentance:

"Then I acknowledged my sin to you and did not conceal my iniquity" (Ps 32:5).

"How joyful is the one whose transgression is forgiven, whose sin is covered!" (Ps 32:1).

When I'm not looking for comfort, I scurry around trying to create life through super-fabulous accomplishments. I feel so much better

when I'm a genius at work, a lovely wife, or the coolest mom. But does my life in the kingdom have anything to do with my talents? Again, my participation in the kingdom of God is rooted in repentance. All my sacrifices and busy actions are just that—"busyness"—unless my heart is willing to repent.

I need to repent, even of my righteousness. My best efforts cannot atone for my sin, nor can my actions earn my salvation (Ps 51:16).

Like the author of Lamentations, I am ultimately incapable of defending my own sin. No amount of comfort or accomplishment can soften my hard heart and free me from judgment. True freedom is only found in forgiveness. Repentance gives life even in the midst of judgment. The author of Lamentations chooses to run to repentance.

We need to be washed of our sin, and only God can do that. It is in our calling out to Him, in acknowledging our sin, that we can enjoy the freedom of being washed clean from our transgressions. It is in repentance that we find life. When I long for peace and spiritual cleansing, rather than reaching for my comfort in earthly pleasures, I have to cry out, "wash away my guilt and cleanse me from my sin" (Ps 51:2).

Run to Him in repentance. Run to Him for peace. Repentance gives life, and it's a blessed sign of God's grace and goodness.

which the LORD made me suffer
on the day of his burning anger?

מ Mem

13 He sent fire from on high into my bones;
he made it descend.[A]
He spread a net for my feet
and turned me back.
He made me desolate,
sick all day long.

נ Nun

14 My transgressions have been formed
into a yoke,[B,C]
fastened together by his hand;
they have been placed on my neck,
and the Lord has broken my strength.
He has handed me over
to those I cannot withstand.

ס Samek

15 The Lord has rejected
all the mighty men within me.
He has summoned an army[D] against me
to crush my young warriors.
The Lord has trampled
Virgin Daughter Judah
like grapes in a winepress.

ע Ayin

16 I weep because of these things;
my eyes flow[E] with tears.
For there is no one nearby to comfort me,
no one to keep me alive.
My children are desolate
because the enemy has prevailed.

פ Pe

17 Zion stretches out her hands;
there is no one to comfort her.
The LORD has issued a decree against Jacob
that his neighbors should be
his adversaries.
Jerusalem has become
something impure among them.

[A]1:13 DSS, LXX; MT reads bones, and it prevailed against them [B]1:14 Some Hb
mss, LXX read He kept watch over my transgressions [C]1:14 Or The yoke of my
transgressions is bound; Hb obscure [D]1:15 Or has announced an appointed
time [E]1:16 Lit my eye, my eye flows

צ *Tsade*

¹⁸ The LORD is just,
for I have rebelled against his command.
Listen, all you people;
look at my pain.
My young women and young men
have gone into captivity.

ק *Qoph*

¹⁹ I called to my lovers,
but they betrayed me.
My priests and elders
perished in the city
while searching for food
to keep themselves alive.

ר *Resh*

²⁰ LORD, see how I am in distress.
I am churning within;
my heart is broken,^A
for I have been very rebellious.
Outside, the sword takes the children;
inside, there is death.

שׁ *Shin*

²¹ People have heard me groaning,
but there is no one to comfort me.
All my enemies have heard of my misfortune;
they are glad that you have caused it.
Bring on the day you have announced,
so that they may become like me.

ת *Taw*

²² Let all their wickedness come before you,
and deal with them
as you have dealt with me
because of all my transgressions.
For my groans are many,
and I am sick at heart.

JUDGMENT ON JERUSALEM

א *Aleph*

2 How the Lord has overshadowed
Daughter Zion with his anger!
He has thrown down Israel's glory
from heaven to earth.
He did not acknowledge his footstool
in the day of his anger.

^A1:20 Lit *is turned within me*

ב *Beth*

2 Without compassion the Lord has swallowed up
all the dwellings of Jacob.
In his wrath he has demolished
the fortified cities of Daughter Judah.
He brought them to the ground
and defiled the kingdom and its leaders.

ג *Gimel*

3 He has cut off every horn of Israel
in his burning anger
and withdrawn his right hand
in the presence of the enemy.
He has blazed against Jacob like a flaming fire
that consumes everything.

ד *Daleth*

4 He has strung his bow like an enemy;
his right hand is positioned like an adversary.
He has killed everyone who was the delight to the eye,
pouring out his wrath like fire
on the tent of Daughter Zion.

ה *He*

5 The Lord is like an enemy;
he has swallowed up Israel.
He swallowed up all its palaces
and destroyed its fortified cities.
He has multiplied mourning and lamentation
within Daughter Judah.

ו *Waw*

6 He has wrecked his temple^A
as if it were merely a shack in a field,^B
destroying his place of meeting.
The Lord has abolished
appointed festivals and Sabbaths in Zion.
He has despised king and priest
in his fierce anger.

ז *Zayin*

7 The Lord has rejected his altar,
repudiated his sanctuary;
he has handed the walls of her palaces
over to the enemy.
They have raised a shout in the house
of the Lord
as on the day of an appointed festival.

---

^A2:6 Lit *booth* ^B2:6 Lit *it were a garden*

ח Cheth

8 The LORD determined to destroy
the wall of Daughter Zion.
He stretched out a measuring line
and did not restrain himself from destroying.
He made the ramparts and walls grieve;
together they waste away.

ט Teth

9 Zion's gates have fallen to the ground;
he has destroyed and shattered the bars
on her gates.
Her king and her leaders live among the nations,
instruction[A] is no more,
and even her prophets receive
no vision from the LORD.

י Yod

10 The elders of Daughter Zion
sit on the ground in silence.
They have thrown dust on their heads
and put on sackcloth.
The young women of Jerusalem
have bowed their heads to the ground.

כ Kaph

11 My eyes are worn out from weeping;
I am churning within.
My heart is poured out in grief[B]
because of the destruction of my dear people,
because infants and nursing babies faint
in the streets of the city.

ל Lamed

12 They cry out to their mothers,
"Where is the grain and wine?"
as they faint like the wounded
in the streets of the city,
as their life pours out
in the arms of their mothers.

מ Mem

13 What can I say on your behalf?
What can I compare you to, Daughter Jerusalem?
What can I liken you to,
so that I may console you, Virgin Daughter Zion?
For your ruin is as vast as the sea.
Who can heal you?

A2:9 Or *the law*   B2:11 Lit *My liver is poured out on the ground*

נ Nun

14 Your prophets saw visions for you
    that were empty and deceptive;[A]
    they did not reveal your iniquity
    and so restore your fortunes.
    They saw pronouncements for you
    that were empty and misleading.

ס Samek

15 All who pass by
    scornfully clap their hands at you.
    They hiss and shake their heads
    at Daughter Jerusalem:
    Is this the city that was called
    the perfection of beauty,
    the joy of the whole earth?

פ Pe

16 All your enemies
    open their mouths against you.
    They hiss and gnash their teeth,
    saying, "We have swallowed her up.
    This is the day we have waited for!
    We have lived to see it."

ע Ayin

17 The Lord has done what he planned;
    he has accomplished his decree,
    which he ordained in days of old.
    He has demolished without compassion,
    letting the enemy gloat over you
    and exalting the horn of your adversaries.

צ Tsade

18 The hearts of the people cry out to the Lord.
    Wall of Daughter Zion,
    let your tears run down like a river
    day and night.
    Give yourself no relief
    and your[B] eyes no rest.

ק Qoph

19 Arise, cry out in the night
    from the first watch of the night.
    Pour out your heart like water
    before the Lord's presence.
    Lift up your hands to him
    for the lives of your children

[A] 2:14 Or insipid [B] 2:18 Lit and the daughter of your

who are fainting from hunger
at the head of every street.

ר Resh

20 LORD, look and consider
to whom you have done this.
Should women eat their own children,
the infants they have nurtured?[A]
Should priests and prophets
be killed in the Lord's sanctuary?

שׁ Shin

21 Both young and old
are lying on the ground in the streets.
My young women and young men
have fallen by the sword.
You have killed them in the day of your anger,
slaughtering without compassion.

ת Taw

22 You summon those who terrorize me[B] on every side,
as if for an appointed festival day;
on the day of the LORD's anger
no one escaped or survived.
My enemy has destroyed
those I nurtured[C] and reared.

HOPE THROUGH GOD'S MERCY

א Aleph

3 I am the man who has seen affliction
under the rod of God's wrath.
2 He has driven me away and forced me to walk
in darkness instead of light.
3 Yes, he repeatedly turns his hand
against me all day long.

ב Beth

4 He has worn away my flesh and skin;
he has broken my bones.
5 He has laid siege against me,
encircling me with bitterness and hardship.
6 He has made me dwell in darkness
like those who have been dead for ages.

ג Gimel

7 He has walled me in so I cannot get out;
he has weighed me down with chains.

[A]2:20 Or *infants in a healthy condition*; Hb obscure   [B]2:22 Or *terrors*
[C]2:22 Or *I bore healthy*; Hb obscure

BUT THIS I CALL TO MIND

LAMENTATIONS 3; REVELATION 1:8

"I have forgotten what prosperity is ..." (Lm 3:17).

It sounds dramatic, but I've had those moments and I bet you have, too. Situations get seriously low. Times get impossibly tough. Not one of us is exempt from the reality of grief, and I don't doubt that every one of us can call to mind a moment when our endurance has threatened to perish.

As we read the words in Lamentations 3, different moments of my life flash into memory. I've never been attacked by a bear or shot with an arrow, but I can certainly recall seasons of "grinding my teeth on gravel," as the lamenter so vividly puts it.

But look at Lamentations 3:21. It's the climax of the entire book of Lamentations, the moment the author's sense of rejection by God shifts to confidence in Him. Pay close attention to these words:

"Yet I call this to mind."

The turning point of Lamentations is not a moment of speculation. No, he's remembering something! The writer is calling to mind a truth he already knows, something that—in spite of the bears and arrows and rocks in his teeth—gives him a sure hope at the very moment his endurance is perishing.

"Because of the LORD's faithful love we do not perish, for his mercies never end. They are new every morning; great is your faithfulness!"

LAMENTATIONS 3:22-23

How does he know? What is this memory he is calling to mind? Is it from his personal life experience, or is he drawing from beyond his own life to his forefathers' history with the Lord of mercy?

Consider how David drew from the testimony of his people in Psalm 22: "Our fathers trusted in you; they trusted, and you rescued them" (v. 4).

I think sometimes we forget God is bigger than what we know of Him from our own personal experience. Because our God is the Alpha and the Omega (Rv 1:8), when we need to call to mind His steadfast love, we get to reach way further back than our own lives.

The God and Creator of the universe has scripted an enormous and lovingly elaborate story of love, provision, and salvation for His people. So we, like the writer of Lamentations, get to call to mind the great deeds and marvelous rescues of our God across generations. He's the God who slayed Goliath, rebuilt Jerusalem's wall, delivered an entire nation from slavery, and rescued sinners by way of the cross. Same God, then and now.

So we call this to mind: our God is faithful. His track record of goodness and mercy reaches back far before and beyond us, pointing to His promises fulfilled, time and time again. It is a record that turns the book of Lamentations on its head, allowing us to return from the darkest night to a light of hope.

⁸ Even when I cry out and plead for help,
he blocks out my prayer.
⁹ He has walled in my ways with blocks of stone;
he has made my paths crooked.

ד Daleth

¹⁰ He is^A a bear waiting in ambush,
a lion in hiding.
¹¹ He forced me off my way and tore me to pieces;
he left me desolate.
¹² He strung his bow
and set me as the target for his arrow.

ה He

¹³ He pierced my kidneys
with shafts from his quiver.
¹⁴ I am a laughingstock to all my people,^B
mocked by their songs all day long.
¹⁵ He filled me with bitterness,
satiated me with wormwood.

ו Waw

¹⁶ He ground my teeth with gravel
and made me cower^C in the dust.
¹⁷ I have been deprived^D of peace;
I have forgotten what prosperity is.
¹⁸ Then I thought, "My future^E is lost,
as well as my hope from the LORD."

ז Zayin

¹⁹ Remember^F my affliction
and my homelessness,
the wormwood and the poison.
²⁰ I continually remember them
and have become depressed.^G
²¹ Yet I call this to mind,
and therefore I have hope:

ח Cheth

²² Because of the LORD's faithful love
we do not perish,^H
for his mercies never end.
²³ They are new every morning;
great is your faithfulness!

---

^A3:10 Lit *is to me* ^B3:14 Some Hb mss, LXX, Vg; other Hb mss, Syr read *all peoples* ^C3:16 Or *and trampled me* ^D3:17 Syr, Vg; MT reads *You deprived my soul* ^E3:18 Or *splendor* ^F3:19 Or *I remember* ^G3:20 Alt Hb tradition reads *and you cause me to collapse* ^H3:22 One Hb mss, Syr, Tg read *The LORD's faithful love, indeed, does not perish*

24 I say, "The LORD is my portion,
    therefore I will put my hope in him."

ט Teth

25 The LORD is good to those who wait for him,
    to the person who seeks him.
26 It is good to wait quietly
    for salvation from the LORD.
27 It is good for a man to bear the yoke
    while he is still young.

י Yod

28 Let him sit alone and be silent,
    for God has disciplined[A] him.
29 Let him put his mouth in the dust —
    perhaps there is still hope.
30 Let him offer his cheek
    to the one who would strike him;
    let him be filled with disgrace.

כ Kaph

31 For the Lord
    will not reject us forever.
32 Even if he causes suffering,
    he will show compassion
    according to the abundance of his faithful love.
33 For he does not enjoy bringing affliction
    or suffering on mankind.

ל Lamed

34 Crushing all the prisoners of the land[B]
    beneath one's feet,
35 denying justice to a man
    in the presence of the Most High,
36 or subverting a person in his lawsuit —
    the Lord does not approve of these things.

מ Mem

37 Who is there who speaks and it happens,
    unless the Lord has ordained it?
38 Do not both adversity and good
    come from the mouth of the Most High?
39 Why should any living person complain,
    any man, because of the punishment for his sins?

נ Nun

40 Let us examine and probe our ways,
    and turn back to the LORD.

A3:28 Lit has laid a burden on   B3:34 Or earth

⁴¹ Let us lift up our hearts and our hands
to God in heaven:
⁴² "We have sinned and rebelled;
you have not forgiven.

ס Samek

⁴³ "You have covered yourself in anger
and pursued us;
you have killed without compassion.
⁴⁴ You have covered yourself with a cloud
so that no prayer can get through.
⁴⁵ You have made us disgusting filth
among the peoples.

פ Pe

⁴⁶ "All our enemies
open their mouths against us.
⁴⁷ We have experienced panic and pitfall,
devastation and destruction."
⁴⁸ My eyes flow with streams of tears
because of the destruction
of my dear people.

ע Ayin

⁴⁹ My eyes overflow unceasingly,
without end,
⁵⁰ until the LORD looks down
from heaven and sees.
⁵¹ My eyes bring me grief
because of the fate of all the women
in my city.

צ Tsade

⁵² For no reason, my enemies^A
hunted me like a bird.
⁵³ They smothered my life in^B a pit
and threw stones on me.
⁵⁴ Water flooded over my head,
and I thought, "I'm going to die!"

ק Qoph

⁵⁵ I called on your name, LORD,
from the depths of the pit.
⁵⁶ You heard my plea:
Do not ignore my cry for relief.
⁵⁷ You came near whenever I called you;
you said, "Do not be afraid."

---

^A3:52 Or Those who were my enemies for no reason   ^B3:53 Or They ended my
life in; Hb obscure

ר Resh

58   You championed my cause, Lord;
    you redeemed my life.
59   LORD, you saw the wrong done to me;
    judge my case.
60   You saw all their vengefulness,
    all their plots against me.

ש Sin / שׁ Shin

61   LORD, you heard their insults,
    all their plots against me.
62   The slander^A and murmuring of my opponents
    attack me all day long.
63   When they sit and when they rise, look,
    I am mocked by their songs.

ת Taw

64   You will pay them back what they deserve, LORD,
    according to the work of their hands.
65   You will give them a heart filled with anguish.^B
    May your curse be on them!
66   You will pursue them in anger
      and destroy them
    under your heavens.^C

TERRORS OF THE BESIEGED CITY

א Aleph

4 How the gold has become tarnished,
  the fine gold become dull!
  The stones of the temple^D lie scattered
  at the head of every street.

ב Beth

2   Zion's precious children —
    once worth their weight in pure gold —
  how they are regarded as clay jars,
    the work of a potter's hands!

ג Gimel

3   Even jackals offer their breasts
    to nurse their young,
  but my dear people have become cruel
    like ostriches in the wilderness.

ד Daleth

4   The nursing baby's tongue
    clings to the roof of his mouth from thirst.

---

^A3:62 Lit lips   ^B3:65 Or them an obstinate heart; Hb obscure   ^C3:66 Lit under
the LORD's heavens   ^D4:1 Or The sacred gems

Infants beg for food,
but no one gives them any.

ה *He*

5 Those who used to eat delicacies
are destitute in the streets;
those who were reared in purple garments
huddle in trash heaps.

ו *Waw*

6 The punishment of my dear people
is greater than that of Sodom,
which was overthrown in an instant
without a hand laid on it.

ז *Zayin*

7 Her dignitaries were brighter than snow,
whiter than milk;
their bodies^A were more ruddy than coral,
their appearance like lapis lazuli.

ח *Cheth*

8 Now they appear darker than soot;
they are not recognized in the streets.
Their skin has shriveled on their bones;
it has become dry like wood.

ט *Teth*

9 Those slain by the sword are better off
than those slain by hunger,
who waste away, pierced with pain
because the fields lack produce.

י *Yod*

10 The hands of compassionate women
have cooked their own children;
they became their food
during the destruction of my dear people.

כ *Kaph*

11 The LORD has exhausted his wrath,
poured out his burning anger;
he has ignited a fire in Zion,
and it has consumed her foundations.

ל *Lamed*

12 The kings of the earth
and all the world's inhabitants did not believe

^A 4:7 Lit *bones*

that an enemy or adversary
could enter Jerusalem's gates.

מ Mem

13 Yet it happened because of the sins of her prophets
and the iniquities of her priests,
who shed the blood of the righteous within her.

נ Nun

14 Blind, they stumbled in the streets,
defiled by this blood,
so that no one dared
to touch their garments.

ס Samek

15 "Stay away! Unclean!" people shouted at them.
"Away, away! Don't touch us!"
So they wandered aimlessly.
It was said among the nations,
"They can stay here no longer."

פ Pe

16 The LORD himself has scattered them;
he no longer watches over them.
The priests are not respected;
the elders find no favor.

ע Ayin

17 All the while our eyes were failing
as we looked in vain for help;
we watched from our towers
for a nation that would not save us.

צ Tsade

18 Our steps were closely followed
so that we could not walk in our streets.
Our end approached; our time ran out.
Our end had come!

ק Qoph

19 Those who chased us were swifter
than eagles in the sky;
they relentlessly pursued us over the mountains
and ambushed us in the wilderness.

ר Resh

20 The LORD's anointed, the breath of our life,^A
was captured in their traps.

---

^A 4:20 Lit nostrils

We had said about him,
"We will live under his protection among the nations."

ש Sin

²¹ So rejoice and be glad, Daughter Edom,
  you resident of the land of Uz!
  Yet the cup will pass to you as well;
  you will get drunk and expose yourself.

ת Taw

²² Daughter Zion, your punishment is complete;
  he will not lengthen your exile.^A
  But he will punish your iniquity, Daughter Edom,
  and will expose your sins.

PRAYER FOR RESTORATION

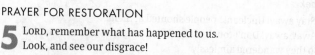

5 Lord, remember what has happened to us.
  Look, and see our disgrace!
² Our inheritance has been turned over to strangers,
  our houses to foreigners.
³ We have become orphans, fatherless;
  our mothers are widows.
⁴ We must pay for the water we drink;
  our wood comes at a price.
⁵ We are closely pursued;
  we are tired, and no one offers us rest.
⁶ We made a treaty with^B Egypt
  and with Assyria, to get enough food.
⁷ Our fathers sinned; they no longer exist,
  but we bear their punishment.
⁸ Slaves rule over us;
  no one rescues us from them.
⁹ We secure our food at the risk of our lives
  because of the sword in the wilderness.
¹⁰ Our skin is as hot^C as an oven
  from the ravages of hunger.
¹¹ Women have been raped in Zion,
  virgins in the cities of Judah.
¹² Princes have been hung up by their hands;
  elders are shown no respect.
¹³ Young men labor at millstones;
  boys stumble under loads of wood.
¹⁴ The elders have left the city gate,
  the young men, their music.
¹⁵ Joy has left our hearts;
  our dancing has turned to mourning.
¹⁶ The crown has fallen from our head.

---

^A 4:22 Or *not deport you again* ^B 5:6 Lit *We gave the hand to* ^C 5:10 Or *black;* Hb obscure

Woe to us, for we have sinned.

17 Because of this, our heart is sick;
because of these, our eyes grow dim:

18 because of Mount Zion, which lies desolate
and has jackals prowling in it.

19 You, LORD, are enthroned forever;
your throne endures from generation to generation.

20 Why do you continually forget us,
abandon us for our entire lives?

21 LORD, bring us back to yourself, so we may return;
renew our days as in former times,

22 unless you have completely rejected us
and are intensely angry with us.

I WILL REMOVE YOUR HEART of STONE AND GIVE YOU A HEART of FLESH

ezekiel

I will give you a new heart and put a new spirit within you; I will remove your heart of stone and give you a heart of flesh. **36:26**

ON THE TIMELINE Ezekiel was written during Judah's time of exile in Babylon, about 593 BC to 571 BC. The last dated oracle in the book occurs in the twenty-seventh year of King Jehoiachin (Ezk 29:17), indicating that Ezekiel's ministry lasted 22 or 23 years. The literary coherence of the book suggests that all editorial work was carried out by a single person, the prophet himself.

A LITTLE BACKGROUND Ezekiel, son of Buzi, was among the approximately ten thousand citizens of Judah deported to Babylon when King Nebuchadnezzar invaded Jerusalem in 597 BC (2Kg 24:10-17). His prophetic call came five years later, in the fifth year of King Jehoiachin's exile (593 BC). Ezekiel was thirty years old when he received his call (Ezk 1:1), the year he should have begun his duties as a priest (Nm 4:3). The prophet lived during the greatest crisis in Israel's history—the destruction of Jerusalem and its temple, and the exile of Judah's leading citizens to Babylon.

MESSAGE & PURPOSE The message of Ezekiel revolves around the fall of Jerusalem in 586 BC. Prior to the announcement of Jerusalem's fall, Ezekiel's message was one of judgment. In this rather scathing review of Israel's history, Ezekiel exposed the nation's moral depravity and absence of spiritual concern (Ezk 2:1-8; 8:7-18; 17:1-21; 20:1-32).

After Jerusalem was destroyed and the nation was in exile, Ezekiel's message became one of hope. God would provide a new heart and a new spirit to enable the people to be faithful and avoid future judgment (Ezk 11:17-20; 36:26-28). The Lord would establish a new temple (Ezk 40–48) and a new way of worship for the people once they were restored.

GIVE THANKS FOR THE BOOK OF EZEKIEL

Though Ezekiel is not often quoted in the New Testament, there are a few notable correlations. The end of Revelation reflects the end of Ezekiel, where the river flows from the presence of God (Ezk 47:1-12; Rv 21:1–22:6), and Ezekiel's depiction of the return of the exiles as resurrected from the dead is comparable to Paul's concept of regeneration (Eph 2:5). The arrangement of the book—announcing judgment in the beginning and declaring restoration at the end—demonstrates that Ezekiel's message was ultimately one of hope in God's sovereign mercy.

THE BOOK OF EZEKIEL IN HISTORY

625 BC   600 BC   575 BC

623

605

597

593 | **586**

573

571

Birth of
Ezekiel

First
Babylonian
invasion of
Judah —
nobility
and princes
taken to
Babylon

Temple and walls of
Jerusalem destroyed
by Nebuchadnezzar

Start of Ezekiel's ministry

Second Babylonian invasion
of Judah — Ezekiel and other
citizens exiled to Babylon

End of
Ezekiel's
ministry

Ezekiel's
vision of the
new temple

READ AND UNDERSTAND EZEKIEL

The Bible is a complete work in which many stories combine to tell one story. As you read the book of Ezekiel, consider reading the additional passages to discover how the whole of Scripture works together.

1

In the thirtieth year, in the fourth month, on the fifth day of the month, while I was among the exiles by the Chebar Canal, the heavens were opened and I saw visions of God. ² On the fifth day of the month — it was the fifth year of King Jehoiachin's exile — ³ the word of the LORD came directly to the priest Ezekiel son of Buzi, in the land of the Chaldeans by the Chebar Canal. The LORD's hand was on him there.

VISION OF THE LORD'S GLORY

⁴ I looked, and there was a whirlwind coming from the north, a huge cloud with fire flashing back and forth and brilliant light all around it. In the center of the fire, there was a gleam like amber. ⁵ The likeness of four living creatures came from it, and this was their appearance: They looked something like a human, ⁶ but each of them had four faces and four wings. ⁷ Their legs were straight, and the soles of their feet were like the hooves of a calf, sparkling like the gleam of polished bronze. ⁸ They had human hands under their wings on their four sides. All four of them had faces and wings. ⁹ Their wings were touching. The creatures did not turn as they moved; each one went straight ahead. ¹⁰ Their faces looked something like the face of a human, and each of the four had the face of a lion on the right, the face of an ox on the left, and the face of an eagle. ¹¹ That is what their faces were like. Their wings were spread upward; each had two wings touching that of another and two wings covering its body. ¹² Each creature went straight ahead. Wherever the Spirit^A wanted to go, they went without turning as they moved.

¹³ The likeness of the living creatures was like the appearance of blazing coals of fire or like torches. Fire was moving back and forth between the living creatures; it was bright, with lightning coming out of it. ¹⁴ The creatures were darting back and forth like flashes of lightning.

¹⁵ When I looked at the living creatures, there was one wheel on the ground beside each of the four-faced creatures. ¹⁶ The appearance of the wheels and their craftsmanship was like the gleam of beryl, and all four had the same likeness. Their appearance and craftsmanship was like a wheel within a wheel. ¹⁷ When they moved, they went in any of the four directions, without turning as they moved. ¹⁸ Their rims were tall and awe-inspiring. Each of their four rims were full of eyes all around. ¹⁹ When the living creatures moved, the wheels moved beside them, and when the creatures rose from the earth, the wheels also rose. ²⁰ Wherever the Spirit wanted to go, the creatures went in the direction the Spirit was moving. The wheels rose alongside them, for the spirit of the living creatures was in the wheels. ²¹ When the creatures moved, the wheels moved; when the creatures stopped, the wheels stopped; and when the creatures rose from the earth, the wheels rose alongside them, for the spirit of the living creatures was in the wheels.

²² Over the heads of the living creatures the likeness of an expanse was spread out. It gleamed like awe-inspiring crystal, ²³ and under the expanse their wings extended one toward another. They each also had two wings covering their bodies. ²⁴ When they moved, I heard the sound of their wings like the roar of a huge torrent, like the voice of the Almighty, and a sound of tumult like the noise of an army. When they stopped, they lowered their wings.

^A 1:12 Or *spirit*, also in v. 20

IN THE WAKE OF HIS GLORY

EZEKIEL 1–3

I felt lost and disoriented, staring out the waiting room window as phone calls and plans were made in the wake of my father's death. I could barely breathe from the weight of my sorrow. I was a senior in college with my whole life ahead of me, but there were so many unchecked boxes on our list of things to do together.

I was a daddy's girl who shared the same naïve optimism and goofy grin as the man who had slipped from this life into eternity. I couldn't reconcile the faithfulness of God with the emptiness I felt. I wrestled with how to move forward, how to serve God with my life when all I had to offer were shattered pieces of a heart no longer bursting with hope and passion.

I needed to see God's hand. I was desperate to hear His answers to my questions of "why?" and "what next?"

God didn't give me answers in that waiting room, but what He did give me was much more intimate, much more needed—the tenderness of His presence and the comfort of His sovereignty.

Can you think of a moment when you desperately needed to see God's hand in your circumstances? A time when you needed to hear His voice before your heart could move forward?

I can't help but think Ezekiel wrestled with similar emotions as he stared out over the Chebar Canal in Babylon. Based on his lineage, Ezekiel had been called to the position of priest from birth, but the temple was gone and God's people had been uprooted from the land of promise. In the midst of shattered hopes and dreams, he must

have wondered if God's great plans for his life were over.

Ezekiel 1:3 tells us, "the word of the LORD came directly to the priest Ezekiel son of Buzi, in the land of the Chaldeans by the Chebar Canal. The LORD's hand was on him there." The rest of the chapter describes a vision God prepared for him as majestic images filled the space as far as his eyes could see. But every image paled in comparison to the most beautiful sight of all. Seated on a lofty throne, wrapped in brilliant light, was the One his soul longed most to behold. **Ezekiel was forever changed by a glimpse of God's glory.**

"The appearance of the brilliant light all around was like that of a rainbow in a cloud on a rainy day. This was the appearance of the likeness of the LORD's glory."

EZEKIEL 1:28

Ezekiel's calling came in the wake of great sorrow and unrest. His ministry began with desperate dependence on divine grace. Nothing less than God's sovereign presence could have prepared Ezekiel for the challenges he would face; and nothing short of God's presence could have sustained him in the midst of it.

In every waiting room, at every crossroads, and through every desperate season, the same is true for us.

²⁵ A voice came from above the expanse over their heads; when they stopped, they lowered their wings. ²⁶ Something like a throne with the appearance of lapis lazuli was above the expanse over their heads. On the throne, high above, was someone who looked like a human. ²⁷ From what seemed to be his waist up, I saw a gleam like amber, with what looked like fire enclosing it all around. From what seemed to be his waist down, I also saw what looked like fire. There was a brilliant light all around him. ²⁸ The appearance of the brilliant light all around was like that of a rainbow in a cloud on a rainy day. This was the appearance of the likeness of the LORD's glory. When I saw it, I fell facedown and heard a voice speaking.

MISSION TO REBELLIOUS ISRAEL

2 He said to me, "Son of man, stand up on your feet and I will speak with you." ² As he spoke to me, the Spirit entered me and set me on my feet, and I listened to the one who was speaking to me. ³ He said to me, "Son of man, I am sending you to the Israelites, to ᴬ the rebellious pagans who have rebelled against me. The Israelites and their ancestors have transgressed against me to this day. ⁴ The descendants are obstinate ᴮ and hardhearted. I am sending you to them, and you must say to them, 'This is what the Lord GOD says.' ⁵ Whether they listen or refuse to listen — for they are a rebellious house — they will know that a prophet has been among them.

⁶ "But you, son of man, do not be afraid of them and do not be afraid of their words, even though briers and thorns are beside you and you live among scorpions. Don't be afraid of their words or discouraged by the look on their faces, for they are a rebellious house. ⁷ Speak my words to them whether they listen or refuse to listen, for they are rebellious.

⁸ "And you, son of man, listen to what I tell you: Do not be rebellious like that rebellious house. Open your mouth and eat what I am giving you." ⁹ So I looked and saw a hand reaching out to me, and there was a written scroll in it. ¹⁰ When he unrolled it before me, it was written on the front and back; words of lamentation, mourning, and woe were written on it.

3 He said to me: "Son of man, eat what you find here. Eat this scroll, then go and speak to the house of Israel." ² So I opened my mouth, and he fed me the scroll. ³ "Son of man," he said to me, "feed your stomach and fill your belly with this scroll I am giving you." So I ate it, and it was as sweet as honey in my mouth.

⁴ Then he said to me: "Son of man, go to the house of Israel and speak my words to them. ⁵ For you are not being sent to a people of unintelligible speech or a difficult language but to the house of Israel — ⁶ not to the many peoples of unintelligible speech or a difficult language, whose words you cannot understand. No doubt, if I sent you to them, they would listen to you. ⁷ But the house of Israel will not want to listen to you because they do not want to listen to me. For the whole house of Israel is hardheaded and hardhearted. ⁸ Look, I have made your face as hard as their faces and your forehead as hard as their foreheads. ⁹ I have made your forehead like a diamond, harder than flint. Don't be afraid of them or discouraged by the look on their faces, though they are a rebellious house."

ᴬ2:3 Or *Israelites and to* ᴮ2:4 Lit *hard of face*

¹⁰ Next he said to me: "Son of man, listen carefully to all my words that I speak to you and take them to heart. ¹¹ Go to your people, the exiles, and speak to them. Tell them, 'This is what the Lord God says,' whether they listen or refuse to listen."

¹² The Spirit then lifted me up, and I heard a loud rumbling sound behind me — bless the glory of the Lord in his place! — ¹³ with the^A sound of the living creatures' wings brushing against each other and the sound of the wheels beside them, a loud rumbling sound. ¹⁴ The Spirit lifted me up and took me away. I left in bitterness and in an angry spirit, and the Lord's hand was on me powerfully. ¹⁵ I came to the exiles at Tel-abib, who were living by the Chebar Canal, and I sat there among them stunned for seven days.

EZEKIEL AS A WATCHMAN

¹⁶ Now at the end of seven days the word of the Lord came to me: ¹⁷ "Son of man, I have made you a watchman over the house of Israel. When you hear a word from my mouth, give them a warning from me. ¹⁸ If I say to the wicked person, 'You will surely die,' but you do not warn him — you don't speak out to warn him about his wicked way in order to save his life — that wicked person will die for his iniquity. Yet I will hold you responsible for his blood. ¹⁹ But if you warn a wicked person and he does not turn from his wickedness or his wicked way, he will die for his iniquity, but you will have rescued yourself. ²⁰ Now if a righteous person turns from his righteousness and acts unjustly, and I put a stumbling block in front of him, he will die. If you did not warn him, he will die because of his sin, and the righteous acts he did will not be remembered. Yet I will hold you responsible for his blood. ²¹ But if you warn the righteous person that he should not sin, and he does not sin, he will indeed live because he listened to your warning, and you will have rescued yourself."

²² The hand of the Lord was on me there, and he said to me, "Get up, go out to the plain, and I will speak with you there." ²³ So I got up and went out to the plain. The Lord's glory was present there, like the glory I had seen by the Chebar Canal, and I fell facedown. ²⁴ The Spirit entered me and set me on my feet. He spoke with me and said: "Go, shut yourself inside your house. ²⁵ As for you, son of man, they will put ropes on you and bind you with them so you cannot go out among them. ²⁶ I will make your tongue stick to the roof of your mouth, and you will be mute and unable to be a mediator for^B them, for they are a rebellious house. ²⁷ But when I speak with you, I will open your mouth, and you will say to them, 'This is what the Lord God says.' Let the one who listens, listen, and let the one who refuses, refuse — for they are a rebellious house.

JERUSALEM'S SIEGE DRAMATIZED

4 "Now you, son of man, take a brick, set it in front of you, and draw the city of Jerusalem on it. ² Then lay siege against it: Construct a siege wall, build a ramp, pitch military camps, and place battering rams against it on all sides. ³ Take an iron plate and set it up as an iron wall between yourself and the city. Face it so that it is under siege, and besiege it. This will be a sign for the house of Israel.

---

^A 3:12-13 Some emend to *behind me as the glory of the Lord rose from his place:* ¹³*the*   ^B 3:26 Or *to rebuke*

⁴ "Then lie down on your left side and place the iniquity ᴬ of the house of Israel on it. You will bear their iniquity for the number of days you lie on your side. ⁵ For I have assigned you the years of their iniquity according to the number of days you lie down, 390 days; so you will bear the iniquity of the house of Israel. ⁶ When you have completed these days, lie down again, but on your right side, and bear the iniquity of the house of Judah. I have assigned you forty days, a day for each year. ⁷ Face the siege of Jerusalem with your arm bared, and prophesy against it. ⁸ Be aware that I will put cords on you so you cannot turn from side to side until you have finished the days of your siege.

⁹ "Also take wheat, barley, beans, lentils, millet, and spelt. Put them in a single container and make them into bread for yourself. You are to eat it during the number of days you lie on your side, 390 days. ¹⁰ The food you eat each day will weigh eight ounces; ᴮ you will eat it at set times. ᶜ ¹¹ You will also drink a ration of water, a sixth of a gallon, ᴰ which you will drink at set times. ¹² You will eat it as you would a barley cake and bake it over dried human excrement in their sight." ¹³ The LORD said, "This is how the Israelites will eat their bread — ceremonially unclean — among the nations where I will banish them."

¹⁴ But I said, "Oh, Lord GOD, I have never been defiled. From my youth until now I have not eaten anything that died naturally or was mauled by wild beasts. And impure meat has never entered my mouth."

¹⁵ He replied to me, "Look, I will let you use cow dung instead of human excrement, and you can make your bread over that." ¹⁶ He said to me, "Son of man, I am going to cut off the supply of bread in Jerusalem. They will anxiously eat food they have weighed out and in dread drink rationed water ¹⁷ for lack of bread and water. Everyone will be devastated and waste away because of their iniquity.

EZEKIEL DRAMATIZES JERUSALEM'S FALL

5 "Now you, son of man, take a sharp sword, use it as you would a barber's razor, and shave your head and beard. Then take a set of scales and divide the hair. ² You are to burn a third of it in the city when the days of the siege have ended; you are to take a third and slash it with the sword all around the city; and you are to scatter a third to the wind, for I will draw a sword to chase after them. ³ But you are to take a few strands from the hair and secure them in the folds of your robe. ⁴ Take some more of them, throw them into the fire, and burn them in it. A fire will spread from it to the whole house of Israel.

⁵ "This is what the Lord GOD says: I have set this Jerusalem in the center of the nations, with countries all around her. ⁶ She has rebelled against my ordinances with more wickedness than the nations, and against my statutes more than the countries that surround her. For her people have rejected my ordinances and have not walked in my statutes.

⁷ "Therefore, this is what the Lord GOD says: Because you have been more insubordinate than the nations around you — you have not walked in my statutes or kept my ordinances; you have not even kept the ordinances of the nations around you — ⁸ therefore, this is what the Lord GOD says: See,

---

ᴬ4:4 Or *punishment*   ᴮ4:10 Lit *20 shekels*   ᶜ4:10 Lit *from time to time,* also in v. 11
ᴰ4:11 Lit *hin*

I myself am against you, Jerusalem, and I will execute judgments within you in the sight of the nations. ⁹ Because of all your detestable practices, I will do to you what I have never done before and what I will never do again. ¹⁰ As a result, fathers will eat their sons within Jerusalem,ᴬ and sons will eat their fathers. I will execute judgments against you and scatter all your survivors to every direction of the wind.

¹¹ "Therefore, as I live" — this is the declaration of the Lord Goᴅ — "I will withdraw and show you no pity, because you have defiled my sanctuary with all your abhorrent acts and detestable practices. Yes, I will not spare you. ¹² A third of your people will die by plague and be consumed by famine within you; a third will fall by the sword all around you; and I will scatter a third to every direction of the wind, and I will draw a sword to chase after them. ¹³ When my anger is spent and I have vented my wrath on them, I will be appeased. Then after I have spent my wrath on them, they will know that I, the Loʀᴅ, have spoken in my jealousy.

¹⁴ "I will make you a ruin and a disgrace among the nations around you, in the sight of everyone who passes by. ¹⁵ So youᴮ will be a disgrace and a taunt, a warning and a horror, to the nations around you when I execute judgments against you in anger, wrath, and furious rebukes. I, the Loʀᴅ, have spoken. ¹⁶ When I shoot deadly arrows of famine at them, arrows for destruction that I will send to destroy you, inhabitants of Jerusalem, I will intensify the famine against you and cut off your supply of bread. ¹⁷ I will send famine and dangerous animals against you. They will leave you childless. Plague and bloodshed will sweep through you, and I will bring a sword against you. I, the Loʀᴅ, have spoken."

PROPHECY AGAINST ISRAEL'S IDOLATRY

6 The word of the Loʀᴅ came to me: ² "Son of man, face the mountains of Israel and prophesy against them. ³ You are to say: Mountains of Israel, hear the word of the Lord Goᴅ! This is what the Lord Goᴅ says to the mountains and the hills, to the ravines and the valleys: I am about to bring a sword against you, and I will destroy your high places. ⁴ Your altars will be desolated and your shrinesᶜ smashed. I will throw down your slain in front of your idols. ⁵ I will lay the corpses of the Israelites in front of their idols and scatter your bones around your altars. ⁶ Wherever you live the cities will be in ruins and the high places will be desolate, so that your altars will lie in ruins and be desecrated,ᴰ your idols smashed and obliterated, your shrines cut down, and what you have made wiped out. ⁷ The slain will fall among you, and you will know that I am the Loʀᴅ.

⁸ "Yet I will leave a remnant when you are scattered among the nations, for throughout the countries there will be some of you who will escape the sword. ⁹ Then your survivors will remember me among the nations where they are taken captive, how I was crushed by their promiscuous hearts that turned away from me and by their eyes that lusted after their idols. They will loathe themselves because of the evil things they did, their detestable actions of every kind. ¹⁰ And they will know that I am the Loʀᴅ; I did not threaten to bring this disaster on them without a reason.

ᴬ5:10 Lit *you* ᴮ5:15 DSS, LXX, Syr, Tg, Vg; MT reads *she* ᶜ6:4 Or *incense altars*, also in v. 6 ᴰ6:6 Hb obscure

LAMENT OVER THE FALL OF JERUSALEM

11 "This is what the Lord God says: Clap your hands, stamp your feet, and cry out over all the evil and detestable practices of the house of Israel, who will fall by the sword, famine, and plague. 12 The one who is far off will die by plague; the one who is near will fall by the sword; and the one who remains and is spared[A] will die of famine. In this way I will exhaust my wrath on them. 13 You will all know that I am the LORD when their slain lie among their idols around their altars, on every high hill, on all the mountaintops, and under every green tree and every leafy oak — the places where they offered pleasing aromas to all their idols. 14 I will stretch out my hand against them, and wherever they live I will make the land a desolate waste, from the wilderness to Diblah.[B] Then they will know that I am the LORD."

ANNOUNCEMENT OF THE END

7 The word of the LORD came to me: 2 "Son of man, this is what the Lord God says to the land of Israel:

An end! The end has come
on the four corners of the earth.
3 The end is now upon you;
I will send my anger against you
and judge you according to your ways.
I will punish you for all your detestable practices.
4 I will not look on you with pity or spare you,
but I will punish you for your ways
and for your detestable practices within you.
Then you will know that I am the LORD."

5 This is what the Lord God says:
Look, one disaster after another is coming!
6 An end has come; the end has come!
It has awakened against you.
Look, it is coming!
7 Doom[C] has come on you,
inhabitants of the land.
The time has come; the day is near.
There will be panic on the mountains
and not celebration.

8 I will pour out my wrath on you very soon;
I will exhaust my anger against you
and judge you according to your ways.
I will punish you for all your detestable practices.
9 I will not look on you with pity or spare you.
I will punish you for your ways
and for your detestable practices within you.
Then you will know
that it is I, the LORD, who strikes.

[A] 6:12 Or besieged [B] 6:14 Some Hb mss, some LXX mss read Riblah; 2Kg 23:33;
Jr 39:5 [C] 7:7 Or A leash; Hb obscure, also in v. 10

10   Here is the day! Here it comes!
     Doom is on its way.
     The rod has blossomed;
     arrogance has bloomed.
11   Violence has grown into a rod of wickedness.
     None of them will remain:
     none of that crowd,
     none of their wealth,
     and none of the eminent[A] among them.

12   The time has come; the day has arrived.
     Let the buyer not rejoice
     and the seller not mourn,
     for wrath is on her whole crowd.
13   The seller will certainly not return
     to what was sold
     as long as he and the buyer remain alive.[B]
     For the vision concerning her whole crowd
     will not be revoked,
     and because of the iniquity of each one,
     none will preserve his life.

14   They have blown the trumpet
     and prepared everything,
     but no one goes to war,
     for my wrath is on her whole crowd.
15   The sword is on the outside;
     plague and famine are on the inside.
     Whoever is in the field will die by the sword,
     and famine and plague will devour
     whoever is in the city.

16   The survivors among them will escape
     and live on the mountains.
     Like doves of the valley,
     all of them will moan,
     each over his own iniquity.
17   All their hands will become weak,
     and all their knees will run with urine.[C]
18   They will put on sackcloth,
     and horror will overwhelm them.
     Shame will cover all their faces,
     and all their heads will be bald.

19   They will throw their silver into the streets,
     and their gold will seem like something filthy.
     Their silver and gold will be unable to save them

[A]7:11 Some Hb mss, Syr, Vg read *and no rest*   [B]7:13 Lit *sold, while still in life is their life*   [C]7:17 Lit *knees will go water*

in the day of the LORD's wrath.
They will not satisfy their appetites
or fill their stomachs,
for these were the stumbling blocks
that brought about their iniquity.

20 He appointed his beautiful ornaments for majesty,
but^A they made their detestable images from them,
their abhorrent things.
Therefore, I have made these
into something filthy to them.

21 I will hand these things over
to foreigners as plunder
and to the wicked of the earth as spoil,
and they will profane them.

22 I will turn my face from them
as they profane my treasured place.
Violent men will enter it and profane it.

23 Forge the chain,
for the land is filled with crimes of bloodshed,
and the city is filled with violence.

24 So I will bring the most evil of nations
to take possession of their houses.
I will put an end to the pride of the strong,
and their sacred places will be profaned.

25 Anguish is coming!
They will look for peace, but there will be none.

26 Disaster after disaster will come,
and there will be rumor after rumor.
Then they will look for a vision from a prophet,
but instruction will perish from the priests
and counsel from the elders.

27 The king will mourn;
the prince will be clothed in grief;
and the hands of the people of the land will tremble.
I will deal with them according to their own conduct,
and I will judge them by their own standards.
Then they will know that I am the LORD.

VISIONARY JOURNEY TO JERUSALEM

8 In the sixth year, in the sixth month, on the fifth day of the month, I was sitting in my house and the elders of Judah were sitting in front of me, and there the hand of the Lord GOD came down on me. ² I looked, and there was someone who looked like a man.^B From what seemed to be his waist down was fire, and from his waist up was something that looked bright, like the gleam of amber. ³ He stretched out what appeared to be a hand and

---

^A 7:20 Or *They turned their beautiful ornaments into objects of pride, and*
^B 8:2 LXX; MT, Vg read *like fire*

took me by the hair of my head. Then the Spirit lifted me up between earth and heaven and carried me in visions of God to Jerusalem, to the entrance of the inner gate that faces north, where the offensive statue that provokes jealousy was located. ⁴I saw the glory of the God of Israel there, like the vision I had seen in the plain.

PAGAN PRACTICES IN THE TEMPLE

⁵The Lord said to me, "Son of man, look toward the north." I looked to the north, and there was this offensive statue north of the Altar Gate, at the entrance. ⁶He said to me, "Son of man, do you see what they are doing here — more detestable acts that the house of Israel is committing — so that I must depart from my sanctuary? You will see even more detestable acts."

⁷Then he brought me to the entrance of the court, and when I looked there was a hole in the wall. ⁸He said to me, "Son of man, dig through the wall." So I dug through the wall and discovered a doorway. ⁹He said to me, "Go in and see the detestable, wicked acts they are committing here."

¹⁰I went in and looked, and there engraved all around the wall was every kind of abhorrent thing — crawling creatures and beasts — as well as all the idols of the house of Israel. ¹¹Seventy elders from the house of Israel were standing before them, with Jaazaniah son of Shaphan standing among them. Each had a firepan in his hand, and a fragrant cloud of incense was rising up. ¹²He said to me, "Son of man, do you see what the elders of the house of Israel are doing in the darkness, each at the shrine of his idol? For they are saying, 'The Lord does not see us. The Lord has abandoned the land.'" ¹³Again he said to me, "You will see even more detestable acts that they are committing."

¹⁴Then he brought me to the entrance of the north gate of the Lord's house, and I saw women sitting there weeping for Tammuz. ¹⁵And he said to me, "Do you see this, son of man? You will see even more detestable acts than these."

¹⁶So he brought me to the inner court of the Lord's house, and there were about twenty-five men at the entrance of the Lord's temple, between the portico and the altar, with their backs to the Lord's temple and their faces turned to the east. They were bowing to the east in worship of the sun. ¹⁷And he said to me, "Do you see this, son of man? Is it not enough for the house of Judah to commit the detestable acts they are doing here, that they must also fill the land with violence and repeatedly anger me, even putting the branch to their nose?ᴬ ¹⁸Therefore I will respond with wrath. I will not show pity or spare them. Though they call loudly in my hearing, I will not listen to them."

VISION OF SLAUGHTER IN JERUSALEM

9 Then he called loudly in my hearing, "Come near, executioners of the city, each of you with a destructive weapon in his hand." ²And I saw six men coming from the direction of the Upper Gate, which faces north, each with a war club in his hand. There was another man among them, clothed in linen, carrying writing equipment. They came and stood beside the bronze altar.

³Then the glory of the God of Israel rose from above the cherub where it had been, to the threshold of the temple. He called to the man clothed in linen and carrying writing equipment. ⁴"Pass throughout the city of Jerusalem,"

ᴬ8:17 Alt Hb tradition reads *my nose*

the Lord said to him, "and put a mark on the foreheads of the men who sigh and groan over all the detestable practices committed in it."

⁵ He spoke to the others in my hearing: "Pass through the city after him and start killing; do not show pity or spare them! ⁶ Slaughter the old men, the young men and women, as well as the children and older women, but do not come near anyone who has the mark. Begin at my sanctuary." So they began with the elders who were in front of the temple. ⁷ Then he said to them, "Defile the temple and fill the courts with the slain. Go!" So they went out killing people in the city.

⁸ While they were killing, I was left alone. And I fell facedown and cried out, "Oh, Lord God! Are you going to destroy the entire remnant of Israel when you pour out your wrath on Jerusalem?"

⁹ He answered me, "The iniquity of the house of Israel and Judah is extremely great; the land is full of bloodshed, and the city full of perversity. For they say, 'The Lord has abandoned the land; he does not see.' ¹⁰ But as for me, I will not show pity or spare them. I will bring their conduct down on their own heads."

¹¹ Then the man clothed in linen and carrying writing equipment reported back, "I have done all that you commanded me."

GOD'S GLORY LEAVES THE TEMPLE

10 Then I looked, and there above the expanse over the heads of the cherubim was something like a throne with the appearance of lapis lazuli. ² The Lord spoke to the man clothed in linen and said, "Go inside the wheelwork beneath the cherubim. Fill your hands with blazing coals from among the cherubim and scatter them over the city." So he went in as I watched.

³ Now the cherubim were standing to the south of the temple when the man went in, and the cloud filled the inner court. ⁴ Then the glory of the Lord rose from above the cherub to the threshold of the temple. The temple was filled with the cloud, and the court was filled with the brightness of the Lord's glory. ⁵ The sound of the cherubim's wings could be heard as far as the outer court; it was like the voice of God Almighty when he speaks.

⁶ After the Lord commanded the man clothed in linen, saying, "Take fire from inside the wheelwork, from among the cherubim," the man went in and stood beside a wheel. ⁷ Then the cherub reached out his hand to the fire that was among them. He took some and put it into the hands of the man clothed in linen, who took it and went out. ⁸ The cherubim appeared to have the form of human hands under their wings.

⁹ I looked, and there were four wheels beside the cherubim, one wheel beside each cherub. The luster of the wheels was like the gleam of beryl. ¹⁰ In appearance, all four looked alike, like a wheel within a wheel. ¹¹ When they moved, they would go in any of the four directions, without pivoting as they moved. But wherever the head faced, they would go in that direction, without pivoting as they went. ¹² Their entire bodies, including their backs, hands, wings, and the wheels that the four of them had, were full of eyes all around. ¹³ As I listened the wheels were called "the wheelwork." ¹⁴ Each one had four faces: one was the face of a cherub, the second the face of a man, the third the face of a lion, and the fourth the face of an eagle.

¹⁵ The cherubim ascended; these were the living creatures I had seen by the Chebar Canal. ¹⁶ When the cherubim moved, the wheels moved beside

them, and when they lifted their wings to rise from the earth, even then the wheels did not veer away from them. ¹⁷ When the cherubim stopped, the wheels stood still, and when they ascended, the wheels ascended with them, for the spirit of the living creatures was in them.

¹⁸ Then the glory of the LORD moved away from the threshold of the temple and stopped above the cherubim. ¹⁹ The cherubim lifted their wings and ascended from the earth right before my eyes; the wheels were beside them as they went. The glory of the God of Israel was above them, and it stopped at the entrance to the eastern gate of the LORD's house.

²⁰ These were the living creatures I had seen beneath the God of Israel by the Chebar Canal, and I recognized that they were cherubim. ²¹ Each had four faces and each had four wings, with what looked something like human hands under their wings. ²² Their faces looked like the same faces I had seen by the Chebar Canal. Each creature went straight ahead.

VISION OF ISRAEL'S CORRUPT LEADERS

11 The Spirit then lifted me up and brought me to the eastern gate of the LORD's house, which faces east, and at the gate's entrance were twenty-five men. Among them I saw Jaazaniah son of Azzur, and Pelatiah son of Benaiah, leaders of the people. ² The LORD ᴬ said to me, "Son of man, these are the men who plot evil and give wicked advice in this city. ³ They are saying, 'Isn't the time near to build houses?ᴮ The city is the pot, and we are the meat.' ⁴ Therefore, prophesy against them. Prophesy, son of man!"

⁵ Then the Spirit of the LORD came on me, and he told me, "You are to say, 'This is what the LORD says: That is what you are thinking, house of Israel; and I know the thoughts that arise in your mind. ⁶ You have multiplied your slain in this city, filling its streets with them.

⁷ "'Therefore, this is what the Lord GOD says: The slain you have put within it are the meat, and the city is the pot, but Iᶜ will take you out of it. ⁸ You fear the sword, so I will bring the sword against you. This is the declaration of the Lord GOD. ⁹ I will take you out of the city and hand you over to foreigners; I will execute judgments against you. ¹⁰ You will fall by the sword, and I will judge you at the border of Israel. Then you will know that I am the LORD. ¹¹ The city will not be a pot for you, and you will not be the meat within it. I will judge you at the border of Israel, ¹² so you will know that I am the LORD, whose statutes you have not followed and whose ordinances you have not practiced. Instead, you have acted according to the ordinances of the nations around you.'"

¹³ Now while I was prophesying, Pelatiah son of Benaiah died. Then I fell facedown and cried out loudly, "Oh, Lord GOD! You are bringing the remnant of Israel to an end!"

PROMISE OF ISRAEL'S RESTORATION

¹⁴ The word of the LORD came to me again: ¹⁵ "Son of man, your own relatives, those who have the right to redeem your property,ᴰ·ᴱ along with the entire house of Israel — all of them — are those to whom the residents of

---

ᴬ11:2 Lit *He*   ᴮ11:3 Or *"The time is not near to build houses.*   ᶜ11:7 Some Hb mss, LXX, Syr, Tg, Vg; other Hb mss read *he*   ᴰ11:15 LXX, Syr read *your relatives, your fellow exiles*   ᴱ11:15 Or *own brothers, your relatives*

Jerusalem have said, 'You are far from the LORD; this land has been given to us as a possession.'

¹⁶"Therefore say, 'This is what the Lord GOD says: Though I sent them far away among the nations and scattered them among the countries, yet for a little while I have been a sanctuary for them in the countries where they have gone.'

¹⁷"Therefore say, 'This is what the Lord GOD says: I will gather you from the peoples and assemble you from the countries where you have been scattered, and I will give you the land of Israel.'

¹⁸"When they arrive there, they will remove all its abhorrent acts and detestable practices from it. ¹⁹I will give them integrity of^A heart and put a new spirit within them; I will remove their heart of stone from their bodies^B and give them a heart of flesh, ²⁰so that they will follow my statutes, keep my ordinances, and practice them. They will be my people, and I will be their God. ²¹But as for those whose hearts pursue their desire for abhorrent acts and detestable practices, I will bring their conduct down on their own heads." This is the declaration of the Lord GOD.

GOD'S GLORY LEAVES JERUSALEM

²²Then the cherubim, with the wheels beside them, lifted their wings, and the glory of the God of Israel was above them. ²³The glory of the LORD rose up from within the city and stopped on the mountain east of the city.^C ²⁴The Spirit lifted me up and brought me to Chaldea and to the exiles in a vision from the Spirit of God. After the vision I had seen left me, ²⁵I spoke to the exiles about all the things the LORD had shown me.

EZEKIEL DRAMATIZES THE EXILE

12 The word of the LORD came to me: ²"Son of man, you are living among a rebellious house. They have eyes to see but do not see, and ears to hear but do not hear, for they are a rebellious house.

³"Now you, son of man, get your bags ready for exile and go into exile in their sight during the day. You will go into exile from your place to another place while they watch; perhaps they will understand, though they are a rebellious house. ⁴During the day, bring out your bags like an exile's bags while they look on. Then in the evening go out in their sight like those going into exile. ⁵As they watch, dig through the wall and take the bags out through it. ⁶And while they look on, lift the bags to your shoulder and take them out in the dark; cover your face so that you cannot see the land. For I have made you a sign to the house of Israel."

⁷So I did just as I was commanded. In the daytime I brought out my bags like an exile's bags. In the evening I dug through the wall by hand; I took them out in the dark, carrying them on my shoulder in their sight.

⁸In the morning the word of the LORD came to me: ⁹"Son of man, hasn't the house of Israel, that rebellious house, asked you, 'What are you doing?' ¹⁰Say to them, 'This is what the Lord GOD says: This pronouncement concerns the prince^D in Jerusalem and the whole house of Israel living there.'^E ¹¹You are to say, 'I am a sign for you. Just as I have done, it will be done to

---

^A11:19 Lit *give them one*   ^B11:19 Lit *flesh*   ^C11:23 = the Mount of Olives   ^D12:10 = King Zedekiah   ^E12:10 Lit *Israel among them*

them; they will go into exile, into captivity.' [12] The prince who is among them will lift his bags to his shoulder in the dark and go out. They[A] will dig through the wall to bring him out through it. He will cover his face so he cannot see the land with his eyes. [13] But I will spread my net over him, and he will be caught in my snare. I will bring him to Babylon, the land of the Chaldeans, yet he will not see it, and he will die there. [14] I will also scatter all the attendants who surround him and all his troops to every direction of the wind, and I will draw a sword to chase after them. [15] They will know that I am the LORD when I disperse them among the nations and scatter them among the countries. [16] But I will spare a few of them from the sword, famine, and plague, so that among the nations where they go they can tell about all their detestable practices. Then they will know that I am the LORD."

EZEKIEL DRAMATIZES ISRAEL'S ANXIETY

[17] The word of the LORD came to me: [18] "Son of man, eat your bread with trembling and drink your water with anxious shaking. [19] Then say to the people of the land, 'This is what the Lord GOD says about the residents of Jerusalem in the land of Israel: They will eat their bread with anxiety and drink their water in dread, for their[B,C] land will be stripped of everything in it because of the violence of all who live there. [20] The inhabited cities will be destroyed, and the land will become dreadful. Then you will know that I am the LORD.'"

A DECEPTIVE PROVERB STOPPED

[21] Again the word of the LORD came to me: [22] "Son of man, what is this proverb you people have about the land of Israel, which goes, 'The days keep passing by, and every vision fails'? [23] Therefore say to them, 'This is what the Lord GOD says: I will put a stop to this proverb, and they will not use it again in Israel.' But say to them, 'The days have arrived, as well as the fulfillment of every vision. [24] For there will no longer be any false vision or flattering divination within the house of Israel. [25] But I, the LORD, will speak whatever message I will speak, and it will be done. It will no longer be delayed. For in your days, rebellious house, I will speak a message and bring it to pass. This is the declaration of the Lord GOD.'"

[26] The word of the LORD came to me: [27] "Son of man, notice that the house of Israel is saying, 'The vision that he sees concerns many years from now; he prophesies about distant times.' [28] Therefore say to them, 'This is what the Lord GOD says: None of my words will be delayed any longer. The message I speak will be fulfilled. This is the declaration of the Lord GOD.'"

ISRAEL'S FALSE PROPHETS CONDEMNED

13 The word of the LORD came to me: [2] "Son of man, prophesy against the prophets of Israel who are prophesying. Say to those who prophesy out of their own imagination, 'Hear the word of the LORD! [3] This is what the Lord GOD says: Woe to the foolish prophets who follow their own spirit and have seen nothing. [4] Your prophets, Israel, are like jackals among ruins. [5] You did not go up to the gaps or restore the wall around the house of

---

Israel so that it might stand in battle on the day of the LORD. [6] They saw false visions and their divinations were a lie. They claimed, "This is the LORD's declaration," when the LORD did not send them, yet they wait for the fulfillment of their message. [7] Didn't you see a false vision and speak a lying divination when you proclaimed, "This is the LORD's declaration," even though I had not spoken?

[8] " 'Therefore, this is what the Lord GOD says: You have spoken falsely and had lying visions; that's why you discover that I am against you. This is the declaration of the Lord GOD. [9] My hand will be against the prophets who see false visions and speak lying divinations. They will not be present in the council of my people or be recorded in the register of the house of Israel, and they will not enter the land of Israel. Then you will know that I am the Lord GOD.

[10] " 'Since they have led my people astray by saying, "Peace," when there is no peace, and since when a flimsy wall is being built, they plaster it with whitewash, [11] therefore, tell those plastering it with whitewash that it will fall. Torrential rain will come, and I will send hailstones plunging[A] down, and a whirlwind will be released. [12] When the wall has fallen, will you not be asked, "Where's the whitewash you plastered on it?"

[13] " 'So this is what the Lord GOD says: I will release a whirlwind in my wrath. Torrential rain will come in my anger, and hailstones will fall in destructive fury. [14] I will demolish the wall you plastered with whitewash and knock it to the ground so that its foundation is exposed. The city will fall, and you will be destroyed within it. Then you will know that I am the LORD. [15] After I exhaust my wrath against the wall and against those who plaster it with whitewash, I will say to you, "The wall is no more and neither are those who plastered it — [16] those prophets of Israel who prophesied to Jerusalem and saw a vision of peace for her when there was no peace." This is the declaration of the Lord GOD.'

[17] "Now you, son of man, face[B] the women among your people who prophesy out of their own imagination, and prophesy against them. [18] Say, 'This is what the Lord GOD says: Woe to the women who sew magic bands on the wrist of every hand and who make veils for the heads of people of every size in order to ensnare lives. Will you ensnare the lives of my people but preserve your own? [19] You profane me among my people for handfuls of barley and scraps of bread; you put those to death who should not die and spare those who should not live, when you lie to my people, who listen to lies.

[20] " 'Therefore, this is what the Lord GOD says: I am against your magic bands with which you ensnare people like birds, and I will tear them from your arms. I will free the people you have ensnared like birds. [21] I will also tear off your veils and rescue my people from your hands, so that they will no longer be prey in your hands. Then you will know that I am the LORD. [22] Because you have disheartened the righteous person with lies (when I intended no distress), and because you have supported[C] the wicked person so that he does not turn from his evil way to save his life, [23] therefore you will no longer see false visions or practice divination. I will rescue my people from your hands. Then you will know that I am the LORD.'"

[A]13:11 One Hb ms, LXX, Vg; other Hb mss read *and you, hailstones, will plunge*
[B]13:17 Lit *set your face*   [C]13:22 Lit *strengthened the hand of*

IDOLATROUS ELDERS PUNISHED

14 Some of the elders of Israel came to me and sat down in front of me. ²Then the word of the LORD came to me: ³"Son of man, these men have set up idols in their hearts and have put their sinful stumbling blocks in front of themselves. Should I actually let them inquire of me?

⁴"Therefore, speak to them and tell them, 'This is what the Lord GOD says: When anyone from the house of Israel sets up idols in his heart and puts his sinful stumbling block in front of himself, and then comes to the prophet, I, the LORD, will answer him appropriately.^A I will answer him according to his many idols, ⁵so that I may take hold of the house of Israel by their hearts. They are all estranged from me because of their idols.'

⁶"Therefore, say to the house of Israel, 'This is what the Lord GOD says: Repent and turn away from your idols; turn your faces away from all your detestable things. ⁷For when anyone from the house of Israel or from the aliens who reside in Israel separates himself from me, setting up idols in his heart and putting his sinful stumbling block in front of himself, and then comes to the prophet to inquire of me, I, the LORD, will answer him myself. ⁸I will turn against that one and make him a sign and a proverb; I will cut him off from among my people. Then you will know that I am the LORD.

⁹"'But if the prophet is deceived and speaks a message, it was I, the LORD, who deceived that prophet. I will stretch out my hand against him and destroy him from among my people Israel. ¹⁰They will bear their punishment — the punishment of the one who inquires will be the same as that of the prophet — ¹¹in order that the house of Israel may no longer stray from following me and no longer defile themselves with all their transgressions. Then they will be my people and I will be their God. This is the declaration of the Lord GOD.'"

FOUR DEVASTATING JUDGMENTS

¹²The word of the LORD came to me: ¹³"Son of man, suppose a land sins against me by acting faithlessly, and I stretch out my hand against it to cut off its supply of bread, to send famine through it, and to wipe out both man and animal from it. ¹⁴Even if these three men — Noah, Daniel, and Job — were in it, they would rescue only themselves by their righteousness." This is the declaration of the Lord GOD.

¹⁵"Suppose I allow dangerous animals to pass through the land and depopulate it so that it becomes desolate, with no one passing through it for fear of the animals. ¹⁶Even if these three men were in it, as I live" — the declaration of the Lord GOD — "they could not rescue their sons or daughters. They alone would be rescued, but the land would be desolate.

¹⁷"Or suppose I bring a sword against that land and say, 'Let a sword pass through it,' so that I wipe out both man and animal from it. ¹⁸Even if these three men were in it, as I live" — the declaration of the Lord GOD — "they could not rescue their sons or daughters, but they alone would be rescued.

¹⁹"Or suppose I send a plague into that land and pour out my wrath on it with bloodshed to wipe out both man and animal from it. ²⁰Even if Noah, Daniel, and Job were in it, as I live" — the declaration of the Lord GOD — "they could not rescue their son or daughter. They would rescue only themselves by their righteousness.

---

^A 14:4 Alt Hb tradition reads *him who comes*

21 "For this is what the Lord God says: How much worse will it be when I send my four devastating judgments against Jerusalem — sword, famine, dangerous animals, and plague — in order to wipe out both man and animal from it! 22 Even so, there will be survivors left in it, sons and daughters who will be brought out. Indeed, they will come out to you, and you will observe their conduct and actions. Then you will be consoled about the devastation I have brought on Jerusalem, about all I have brought on it. 23 They will bring you consolation when you see their conduct and actions, and you will know that it was not without cause that I have done what I did to it." This is the declaration of the Lord God.

PARABLE OF THE USELESS VINE

15 Then the word of the Lord came to me: 2 "Son of man, how does the wood of the vine, that branch among the trees of the forest, compare to any other wood? 3 Can wood be taken from it to make something useful? Or can anyone make a peg from it to hang things on? 4 In fact, it is put into the fire as fuel. The fire devours both of its ends, and the middle is charred. Can it be useful for anything? 5 Even when it was whole it could not be made into a useful object. How much less can it ever be made into anything useful when the fire has devoured it and it is charred!"

6 Therefore, this is what the Lord God says, "Like the wood of the vine among the trees of the forest, which I have given to the fire as fuel, so I will give up the residents of Jerusalem. 7 I will turn against them. They may have escaped from the fire, but it will still consume them. And you will know that I am the Lord when I turn against them. 8 I will make the land desolate because they have acted unfaithfully." This is the declaration of the Lord God.

PARABLE OF GOD'S ADULTEROUS WIFE

16 The word of the Lord came to me again: 2 "Son of man, confront Jerusalem with her detestable practices. 3 You are to say, 'This is what the Lord God says to Jerusalem: Your origin and your birth were in the land of the Canaanites. Your father was an Amorite and your mother a Hethite. 4 As for your birth, your umbilical cord wasn't cut on the day you were born, and you weren't washed clean^A with water. You were not rubbed with salt or wrapped in cloths. 5 No one cared enough about you to do even one of these things out of compassion for you. But you were thrown out into the open field because you were despised on the day you were born.

6 " 'I passed by you and saw you thrashing around in your blood, and I said to you as you lay in your blood, "Live!" Yes, I said to you as you lay in your blood, "Live!"^B 7 I made you thrive^C like plants of the field. You grew up and matured and became very beautiful.^D Your breasts were formed and your hair grew, but you were stark naked.

8 " 'Then I passed by you and saw you, and you were indeed at the age for love. So I spread the edge of my garment over you and covered your nakedness. I pledged myself to you, entered into a covenant with you — this is the declaration of the Lord God — and you became mine. 9 I washed you

---

^A 16:4 Hb obscure   ^B 16:6 Some Hb mss, LXX, Syr omit *Yes, I said to you as you lay in your blood, "Live!"*   ^C 16:7 LXX reads *Thrive; I made you*   ^D 16:7 Or *matured and developed the loveliest of ornaments* with water, rinsed off your blood, and anointed you with oil. ¹⁰ I clothed you in embroidered cloth and provided you with fine leather^ sandals. I also wrapped you in fine linen and covered you with silk. ¹¹ I adorned you with jewelry, putting bracelets on your wrists and a necklace around your neck. ¹² I put a ring in your nose, earrings on your ears, and a beautiful crown on your head. ¹³ So you were adorned with gold and silver, and your clothing was made of fine linen, silk, and embroidered cloth. You ate fine flour, honey, and oil. You became extremely beautiful and attained royalty. ¹⁴ Your fame spread among the nations because of your beauty, for it was perfect through my splendor, which I had bestowed on you. This is the declaration of the Lord God.

¹⁵ "'But you trusted in your beauty and acted like a prostitute because of your fame. You lavished your sexual favors on everyone who passed by. Your beauty became his.^ ¹⁶ You took some of your clothing and made colorful high places for yourself, and you engaged in prostitution on them. These places should not have been built, and this should never have happened!^ ¹⁷ You also took your beautiful jewelry made from the gold and silver I had given you, and you made male images so that you could engage in prostitution with them. ¹⁸ Then you took your embroidered clothing to cover them and set my oil and incense before them. ¹⁹ The food that I gave you — the fine flour, oil, and honey that I fed you — you set it before them as a pleasing aroma. That is what happened. This is the declaration of the Lord God.

²⁰ "'You even took your sons and daughters you bore to me and sacrificed them to these images as food. Wasn't your prostitution enough? ²¹ You slaughtered my children and gave them up when you passed them through the fire to the images. ²² In all your detestable practices and acts of prostitution, you did not remember the days of your youth when you were stark naked and thrashing around in your blood.

²³ "'Then after all your evil — Woe, woe to you! — the declaration of the Lord God — ²⁴ you built yourself a mound and made yourself an elevated place in every square. ²⁵ You built your elevated place at the head of every street and turned your beauty into a detestable thing. You spread your legs to everyone who passed by and increased your prostitution. ²⁶ You engaged in promiscuous acts with Egyptian men, your well-endowed neighbors, and increased your prostitution to anger me.

²⁷ "'Therefore, I stretched out my hand against you and reduced your provisions. I gave you over to the desire of those who hate you, the Philistine women, who were embarrassed by your indecent conduct. ²⁸ Then you engaged in prostitution with the Assyrian men because you were not satisfied. Even though you did this with them, you were still not satisfied. ²⁹ So you extended your prostitution to Chaldea, the land of merchants, but you were not even satisfied with this!

³⁰ "'How your heart was inflamed with lust^B — the declaration of the Lord God — when you did all these things, the acts of a brazen prostitute, ³¹ building your mound at the head of every street and making your elevated place in every square. But you were unlike a prostitute because you scorned payment. ³² You adulterous wife, who receives strangers instead of her husband!

---

^A 16:10,15,16 Hb obscure   ^B 16:30 Or *was sick*

[33] Men give gifts to all prostitutes, but you gave gifts to all your lovers. You bribed them to come to you from all around for your sexual favors. [34] So you were the opposite of other women in your acts of prostitution; no one solicited you. When you paid a fee instead of one being paid to you, you were the opposite.

[35] " 'Therefore, you prostitute, hear the word of the LORD! [36] This is what the Lord GOD says: Because your lust was poured out and your nakedness exposed by your acts of prostitution with your lovers, and because of all your detestable idols and the blood of your children that you gave to them, [37] I am therefore going to gather all the lovers you pleased — all those you loved as well as all those you hated. I will gather them against you from all around and expose your nakedness to them so they see you completely naked. [38] I will judge you the way adulteresses and those who shed blood are judged. Then I will bring about the shedding of your blood in jealous wrath. [39] I will hand you over to them, and they will demolish your mounds and tear down your elevated places. They will strip off your clothes, take your beautiful jewelry, and leave you stark naked. [40] They will bring a mob against you to stone you and to cut you to pieces with their swords. [41] They will burn your houses and execute judgments against you in the sight of many women. I will stop you from being a prostitute, and you will never again pay fees for lovers. [42] So I will satisfy my wrath against you, and my jealousy will turn away from you. Then I will be calm and no longer angry. [43] Because you did not remember the days of your youth but enraged me with all these things, I will also bring your conduct down on your own head. This is the declaration of the Lord GOD. Haven't you committed depravity in addition to all your detestable practices?

[44] " 'Look, everyone who uses proverbs will quote this proverb about you: "Like mother, like daughter." [45] You are the daughter of your mother, who despised her husband and children. You are the sister of your sisters, who despised their husbands and children. Your mother was a Hethite and your father an Amorite. [46] Your older sister was Samaria, who lived with her daughters to the north of you, and your younger sister was Sodom, who lived with her daughters to the south of you. [47] Didn't you walk in their ways and do their detestable practices? It was only a short time before all your ways were more corrupt than theirs.

[48] " 'As I live — the declaration of the Lord GOD — your sister Sodom and her daughters have not behaved as you and your daughters have. [49] Now this was the iniquity of your sister Sodom: She and her daughters had pride, plenty of food, and comfortable security, but didn't support[A] the poor and needy. [50] They were haughty and did detestable acts before me, so I removed them when I saw this.[B] [51] But Samaria did not commit even half your sins. You have multiplied your detestable practices beyond theirs and made your sisters appear righteous by all the detestable acts you have committed. [52] You must also bear your disgrace, since you have helped your sisters out.[C] For they appear more righteous than you because of your sins, which you committed more detestably than they did. So you also, be ashamed and bear your disgrace, since you have made your sisters appear righteous.

[A]16:49 Lit strengthen the hand of   [B]16:50 Or them as you have seen   [C]16:52 Lit you have been the advocate for your sisters

⁵³ " 'I will restore their fortunes, the fortunes of Sodom and her daughters and those of Samaria and her daughters. I will also restoreᴬ your fortunes among them, ⁵⁴ so you will bear your disgrace and be ashamed of all you did when you comforted them. ⁵⁵ As for your sisters, Sodom and her daughters and Samaria and her daughters will return to their former state. You and your daughters will also return to your former state. ⁵⁶ Didn't you treat your sister Sodom as an object of scorn when you were proud, ⁵⁷ before your wickedness was exposed? It was like the time you were scorned by the daughters of Aramᴮ and all those around her, and by the daughters of the Philistines — those who treated you with contempt from every side. ⁵⁸ You yourself must bear the consequences of your depravity and detestable practices — this is the Lord's declaration.

⁵⁹ " 'For this is what the Lord God says: I will deal with you according to what you have done, since you have despised the oath by breaking the covenant. ⁶⁰ But I will remember the covenant I made with you in the days of your youth, and I will establish a permanent covenant with you. ⁶¹ Then you will remember your ways and be ashamed when youᶜ receive your older and younger sisters. I will give them to you as daughters, but not because of your covenant. ⁶² I will establish my covenant with you, and you will know that I am the Lord, ⁶³ so that when I make atonement for all you have done, you will remember and be ashamed, and never open your mouth again because of your disgrace. This is the declaration of the Lord God.' "

PARABLE OF THE EAGLES

17 The word of the Lord came to me: ² "Son of man, pose a riddle and speak a parable to the house of Israel. ³ You are to say, 'This is what the Lord God says: A huge eagle with powerful wings, long feathers, and full plumage of many colors came to Lebanon and took the top of the cedar. ⁴ He plucked off its topmost shoot, brought it to the land of merchants, and set it in a city of traders. ⁵ Then he took some of the land's seed and put it in a fertile field; he set it like a willow, a plantᴰ by abundant water. ⁶ It sprouted and became a spreading vine, low in height with its branches turned toward him, yet its roots stayed under it. So it became a vine, produced branches, and sent out shoots.

⁷ " 'But there was another huge eagle with powerful wings and thick plumage. And this vine bent its roots toward him! It stretched out its branches to him from the plot where it was planted, so that he might water it. ⁸ It had been planted in a good field by abundant water in order to produce branches, bear fruit, and become a splendid vine.'

⁹ "You are to say, 'This is what the Lord God says: Will it flourish? Will he not tear out its roots and strip off its fruit so that it shrivels? All its fresh leaves will wither! Great strength and many people will not be needed to pull it from its roots. ¹⁰ Even though it is planted, will it flourish? Won't it wither completely when the east wind strikes it? It will wither on the plot where it sprouted.' "

¹¹ The word of the Lord came to me: ¹² "Now say to that rebellious house, 'Don't you know what these things mean?' Tell them, 'The king of Babylon

---

ᴬ16:53 LXX, Vg; MT reads *Samaria and her daughters and the fortunes of*
ᴮ16:57 Some Hb mss, Syr read *Edom*   ᶜ16:61 Some LXX mss, Syr read *I*
ᴰ17:5 Hb obscure

came to Jerusalem, took its king and officials, and brought them back with him to Babylon. [13] He took one of the royal family and made a covenant with him, putting him under oath. Then he took away the leading men of the land, [14] so that the kingdom would be humble and not exalt itself but would keep his covenant in order to endure. [15] However, this king revolted against him by sending his ambassadors to Egypt so they might give him horses and a large army. Will he flourish? Will the one who does such things escape? Can he break a covenant and still escape?

[16] "'As I live — this is the declaration of the Lord God — he will die in Babylon, in the land of the king who put him on the throne, whose oath he despised and whose covenant he broke. [17] Pharaoh with his mighty army and vast company will not help him in battle, when ramps are built and siege walls constructed to destroy many lives. [18] He despised the oath by breaking the covenant. He did all these things even though he gave his hand in pledge. He will not escape!

[19] "'Therefore, this is what the Lord God says: As I live, I will bring down on his head my oath that he despised and my covenant that he broke. [20] I will spread my net over him, and he will be caught in my snare. I will bring him to Babylon and execute judgment on him there for the treachery he committed against me. [21] All the fugitives[A] among his troops will fall by the sword, and those who survive will be scattered to every direction of the wind. Then you will know that I, the Lord, have spoken.

[22] "'This is what the Lord God says:

I will take a sprig
from the lofty top of the cedar and plant it.
I will pluck a tender sprig
from its topmost shoots,
and I will plant it
on a high towering mountain.
[23] I will plant it on Israel's high mountain
so that it may bear branches, produce fruit,
and become a majestic cedar.
Birds of every kind will nest under it,
taking shelter in the shade of its branches.
[24] Then all the trees of the field will know
that I am the Lord.
I bring down the tall tree,
and make the low tree tall.
I cause the green tree to wither
and make the withered tree thrive.
I, the Lord, have spoken
and I will do it.'"

PERSONAL RESPONSIBILITY FOR SIN

18 The word of the Lord came to me: [2] "What do you mean by using this proverb concerning the land of Israel:

'The fathers eat sour grapes,
and the children's teeth are set on edge'?

A17:21 Some Hb mss, LXX, Syr, Tg read *choice men*

³ As I live" — this is the declaration of the Lord God — "you will no longer use this proverb in Israel. ⁴ Look, every life belongs to me. The life of the father is like the life of the son — both belong to me. The person who sins is the one who will die.

⁵ "Suppose a man is righteous and does what is just and right: ⁶ He does not eat at the mountain shrinesᴬ or look to the idols of the house of Israel. He does not defile his neighbor's wife or approach a woman during her menstrual impurity. ⁷ He doesn't oppress anyone but returns his collateral to the debtor. He does not commit robbery, but gives his bread to the hungry and covers the naked with clothing. ⁸ He doesn't lend at interest or for profit but keeps his hand from injustice and carries out true justice between men. ⁹ He follows my statutes and keeps my ordinances, acting faithfully. Such a person is righteous; he will certainly live." This is the declaration of the Lord God.

¹⁰ "But suppose the man has a violent son, who sheds blood and does any of these things, ¹¹ though the father has done none of them. Indeed, when the son eats at the mountain shrines and defiles his neighbor's wife, ¹² and when he oppresses the poor and needy, commits robbery, and does not return collateral, and when he looks to the idols, commits detestable acts, ¹³ and lends at interest or for profit, will he live? He will not live! Since he has committed all these detestable acts, he will certainly die. His death will be his own fault.ᴮ

¹⁴ "Now suppose he has a son who sees all the sins his father has committed, and though he sees them, he does not do likewise. ¹⁵ He does not eat at the mountain shrines or look to the idols of the house of Israel. He does not defile his neighbor's wife. ¹⁶ He doesn't oppress anyone, hold collateral, or commit robbery. He gives his bread to the hungry and covers the naked with clothing. ¹⁷ He keeps his hand from harming the poor, not taking interest or profit on a loan. He practices my ordinances and follows my statutes. Such a person will not die for his father's iniquity. He will certainly live.

¹⁸ "As for his father, he will die for his own iniquity because he practiced fraud, robbed his brother, and did among his people what was not good. ¹⁹ But you may ask, 'Why doesn't the son suffer punishment for the father's iniquity?' Since the son has done what is just and right, carefully observing all my statutes, he will certainly live. ²⁰ The person who sins is the one who will die. A son won't suffer punishment for the father's iniquity, and a father won't suffer punishment for the son's iniquity. The righteousness of the righteous person will be on him, and the wickedness of the wicked person will be on him.

²¹ "But if the wicked person turns from all the sins he has committed, keeps all my statutes, and does what is just and right, he will certainly live; he will not die. ²² None of the transgressions he has committed will be held against him. He will live because of the righteousness he has practiced. ²³ Do I take any pleasure in the death of the wicked?" This is the declaration of the Lord God. "Instead, don't I take pleasure when he turns from his ways and lives? ²⁴ But when a righteous person turns from his righteousness and acts unjustly, committing the same detestable acts that the wicked do, will he live? None of the righteous acts he did will be remembered. He will die because of the treachery he has engaged in and the sin he has committed.

ᴬ18:6 Lit the mountains, also in vv. 11, 15   ᴮ18:13 Lit His blood will be on him

²⁵ "But you say, 'The Lord's way isn't fair.' Now listen, house of Israel: Is it my way that is unfair? Instead, isn't it your ways that are unfair? ²⁶ When a righteous person turns from his righteousness and acts unjustly, he will die for this. He will die because of the injustice he has committed. ²⁷ But if a wicked person turns from the wickedness he has committed and does what is just and right, he will preserve his life. ²⁸ He will certainly live because he thought it over and turned from all the transgressions he had committed; he will not die. ²⁹ But the house of Israel says, 'The Lord's way isn't fair.' Is it my ways that are unfair, house of Israel? Instead, isn't it your ways that are unfair?

³⁰ "Therefore, house of Israel, I will judge each one of you according to his ways." This is the declaration of the Lord God. "Repent and turn from all your rebellious acts, so they will not become a sinful stumbling block to you. ³¹ Throw off all the transgressions you have committed, and get yourselves a new heart and a new spirit. Why should you die, house of Israel? ³² For I take no pleasure in anyone's death." This is the declaration of the Lord God. "So repent and live!

A LAMENT FOR ISRAEL'S PRINCES

19 "As for you, take up a lament for the princes of Israel, ² and say:
What was your mother? A lioness!
She lay down among the lions;
she reared her cubs among the young lions.

³   She brought up one of her cubs,
and he became a young lion.
After he learned to tear prey,
he devoured people.

⁴   When the nations heard about him,
he was caught in their pit.
Then they led him away with hooks
to the land of Egypt.

⁵   When she saw that she waited in vain,
that her hope was lost,
she took another of her cubs
and made him a young lion.

⁶   He prowled among the lions,
and he became a young lion.
After he learned to tear prey,
he devoured people.

⁷   He devastated their strongholds^A
and destroyed their cities.
The land and everything in it shuddered
at the sound of his roaring.

⁸   Then the nations from the surrounding provinces
set out against him.
They spread their net over him;
he was caught in their pit.

---

^A19:7 Tg, Aq; MT reads *knew their widows*

9   They put a wooden yoke on him^A with hooks
     and led him away to the king of Babylon.
     They brought him into the fortresses
     so his roar could no longer be heard
     on the mountains of Israel.

10   Your mother was like a vine in your vineyard,^B
     planted by the water;
     it was fruitful and full of branches
     because of abundant water.

11   It had strong branches, fit for
         the scepters of rulers;
     its height towered among the clouds.^C
     So it was conspicuous for its height
     as well as its many branches.

12   But it was uprooted in fury,
     thrown to the ground,
     and the east wind dried up its fruit.
     Its strong branches were torn off and dried up;
     fire consumed them.

13   Now it is planted in the wilderness,
     in a dry and thirsty land.

14   Fire has gone out from its main branch^D
     and has devoured its fruit,
     so that it no longer has a strong branch,
     a scepter for ruling.
This is a lament and should be used as a lament."

ISRAEL'S REBELLION

20 In the seventh year, in the fifth month, on the tenth day of the month, some of Israel's elders came to inquire of the LORD, and they sat down in front of me. ² Then the word of the LORD came to me: ³ "Son of man, speak with the elders of Israel and tell them, 'This is what the Lord GOD says: Are you coming to inquire of me? As I live, I will not let you inquire of me. This is the declaration of the Lord GOD.'

⁴ "Will you pass judgment against them, will you pass judgment, son of man? Explain the detestable practices of their fathers to them. ⁵ Say to them, 'This is what the Lord GOD says: On the day I chose Israel, I swore an oath^E to the descendants of Jacob's house and made myself known to them in the land of Egypt. I swore to them, saying, "I am the LORD your God." ⁶ On that day I swore^F to them that I would bring them out of the land of Egypt into a land I had searched out for them, a land flowing with milk and honey, the most beautiful of all lands. ⁷ I also said to them, "Throw away, each of you, the abhorrent things that you prize,^G and do not defile yourselves with the idols of Egypt. I am the LORD your God."

---

^A 19:9 Or *put him in a cage*   ^B 19:10 Some Hb mss; other Hb mss read *blood*
^C 19:11 Or *thick foliage*   ^D 19:14 Lit *from the branch of its parts*   ^E 20:5 Lit *I lifted my hand*   ^F 20:6 Lit *lifted my hand, also in vv. 15,23,28,42*   ^G 20:7 Lit *things of your eyes*

8 " 'But they rebelled against me and were unwilling to listen to me. None of them threw away the abhorrent things that they prized,^A and they did not abandon the idols of Egypt. So I considered pouring out my wrath on them, exhausting my anger against them within the land of Egypt. 9 But I acted for the sake of my name, so that it would not be profaned in the eyes of the nations they were living among, in whose sight I had made myself known to Israel by bringing them out of Egypt.

10 " 'So I brought them out of the land of Egypt and led them into the wilderness. 11 Then I gave them my statutes and explained my ordinances to them — the person who does them will live by them. 12 I also gave them my Sabbaths to serve as a sign between me and them, so that they would know that I am the LORD who consecrates them.

13 " 'But the house of Israel rebelled against me in the wilderness. They did not follow my statutes and they rejected my ordinances — the person who does them will live by them. They also completely profaned my Sabbaths. So I considered pouring out my wrath on them in the wilderness to put an end to them. 14 But I acted for the sake of my name, so that it would not be profaned in the eyes of the nations in whose sight I had brought them out. 15 However, I swore to them in the wilderness that I would not bring them into the land I had given them — the most beautiful of all lands, flowing with milk and honey — 16 because they rejected my ordinances, profaned my Sabbaths, and did not follow my statutes. For their hearts went after their idols. 17 Yet I spared them from destruction and did not bring them to an end in the wilderness.

18 " 'Then I said to their children in the wilderness, "Don't follow the statutes of your fathers, defile yourselves with their idols, or keep their ordinances. 19 I am the LORD your God. Follow my statutes, keep my ordinances, and practice them. 20 Keep my Sabbaths holy, and they will be a sign between me and you, so you may know that I am the LORD your God."

21 " 'But the children rebelled against me. They did not follow my statutes or carefully keep my ordinances — the person who does them will live by them. They also profaned my Sabbaths. So I considered pouring out my wrath on them and exhausting my anger against them in the wilderness. 22 But I withheld my hand and acted for the sake of my name, so that it would not be profaned in the eyes of the nations in whose sight I brought them out. 23 However, I swore to them in the wilderness that I would disperse them among the nations and scatter them among the countries. 24 For they did not practice my ordinances but rejected my statutes and profaned my Sabbaths, and their eyes were fixed on their fathers' idols. 25 I also gave them statutes that were not good and ordinances they could not live by. 26 When they sacrificed every firstborn in the fire,^B I defiled them through their gifts in order to devastate them so they would know that I am the LORD.'

27 "Therefore, son of man, speak to the house of Israel, and tell them, 'This is what the Lord GOD says: In this way also your fathers blasphemed me by committing treachery against me: 28 When I brought them into the land that I swore to give them and they saw any high hill or leafy tree, they offered their sacrifices and presented their offensive offerings there. They also

---

^A 20:8 Lit *things of their eyes* ^B 20:26 Lit *they made every firstborn pass through the fire* sent up their pleasing aromas and poured out their drink offerings there. ²⁹ So I asked them, "What is this high place you are going to?" And it is still called Bamah^A today.'

³⁰ "Therefore say to the house of Israel, 'This is what the Lord GOD says: Are you defiling yourselves the way your fathers did, and prostituting yourselves with their abhorrent things? ³¹ When you offer your gifts, sacrificing your children in the fire,^B you still continue to defile yourselves with all your idols today. So should I let you inquire of me, house of Israel? As I live — this is the declaration of the Lord GOD — I will not let you inquire of me!

ISRAEL'S RESTORATION

³² "'When you say, "Let us be like the nations, like the clans of other countries, serving wood and stone," what you have in mind will never happen. ³³ As I live — the declaration of the Lord GOD — I will reign over you with a strong hand, an outstretched arm, and outpoured wrath. ³⁴ I will bring you from the peoples and gather you from the countries where you were scattered, with a strong hand, an outstretched arm, and outpoured wrath. ³⁵ I will lead you into the wilderness of the peoples and enter into judgment with you there face to face. ³⁶ Just as I entered into judgment with your fathers in the wilderness of the land of Egypt, so I will enter into judgment with you. This is the declaration of the Lord GOD. ³⁷ I will make you pass under the rod and will bring you into the bond of the covenant. ³⁸ I will purge you of those who rebel and transgress against me. I will bring them out of the land where they live as foreign residents, but they will not enter the land of Israel. Then you will know that I am the LORD.

³⁹ "'As for you, house of Israel, this is what the Lord GOD says: Go and serve your idols, each of you. But afterward you will surely listen to me, and you will no longer defile my holy name with your gifts and idols. ⁴⁰ For on my holy mountain, Israel's high mountain — the declaration of the Lord GOD — there the entire house of Israel, all of them, will serve me in the land. There I will accept them and will require your contributions and choicest gifts, all your holy offerings. ⁴¹ When I bring you from the peoples and gather you from the countries where you have been scattered, I will accept you as a pleasing aroma. And I will demonstrate my holiness through you in the sight of the nations. ⁴² When I lead you into the land of Israel, the land I swore to give your fathers, you will know that I am the LORD. ⁴³ There you will remember your ways and all your deeds by which you have defiled yourself, and you will loathe yourselves for all the evil things you have done. ⁴⁴ You will know that I am the LORD, house of Israel, when I have dealt with you for the sake of my name rather than according to your evil ways and corrupt acts. This is the declaration of the Lord GOD.'"

FIRE IN THE SOUTH

⁴⁵ The word of the LORD came to me: ⁴⁶ "Son of man, face the south and preach against it. Prophesy against the forest land in the Negev, ⁴⁷ and say to the forest there, 'Hear the word of the LORD! This is what the Lord GOD says: I am about to ignite a fire in you, and it will devour every green tree and every dry tree in you. The blazing flame will not be extinguished, and every face

---

^A 20:29 = High Place ^B 20:31 Lit *gifts, making your children pass through the fire* from the south to the north will be scorched by it. ⁴⁸ Then all people will see that I, the Lord, have kindled it. It will not be extinguished.'"

⁴⁹ Then I said, "Oh, Lord God, they are saying of me, 'Isn't he just composing parables?'"

GOD'S SWORD OF JUDGMENT

21 The word of the Lord came to me again: ² "Son of man, face Jerusalem and preach against the sanctuaries. Prophesy against the land of Israel, ³ and say to it, 'This is what the Lord says: I am against you. I will draw my sword from its sheath and cut off from you both the righteous and the wicked. ⁴ Since I will cut off ᴬ both the righteous and the wicked, my sword will therefore come out of its sheath against all people from the south to the north. ⁵ So all people will know that I, the Lord, have taken my sword from its sheath — it will not be sheathed again.'

⁶ "But you, son of man, groan! Groan bitterly with a broken heart ᴮ right before their eyes. ⁷ And when they ask you, 'Why are you groaning?' then say, 'Because of the news that is coming. Every heart will melt, and every hand will become weak. Every spirit will be discouraged, and all knees will run with urine. ᶜ Yes, it is coming and it will happen. This is the declaration of the Lord God.'"

⁸ The word of the Lord came to me: ⁹ "Son of man, prophesy, 'This is what the Lord says!' You are to proclaim,

'A sword! A sword is sharpened
and also polished.
10 It is sharpened for slaughter,
polished to flash like lightning!
Should we rejoice?
The scepter of my son,
the sword despises every tree. ᴰ
11 The sword is given to be polished,
to be grasped in the hand.
It is sharpened, and it is polished,
to be put in the hand of the slayer.'

¹² "Cry out and wail, son of man, for it is against my people. It is against all the princes of Israel! They are given over to the sword with my people. Therefore strike your thigh in grief. ¹³ Surely it will be a trial! And what if the sword despises even the scepter? The scepter will not continue." ᴰ This is the declaration of the Lord God.

¹⁴ "So you, son of man, prophesy and clap your hands together:

Let the sword strike two times, even three.
It is a sword for massacre,
a sword for great massacre —
it surrounds ᴱ them!
15 I have appointed a sword for slaughter ᴰ
at all their gates,
so that their hearts may melt

ᴬ21:4 Lit off from you   ᴮ21:6 Lit insides, or waist   ᶜ21:7 Lit knees will go water
ᴰ21:10,13,15 Hb obscure   ᴱ21:14 Or penetrates

and many may stumble.
Yes! It is ready to flash like lightning;
it is drawn[A] for slaughter.

16 Slash to the right;
turn to the left —
wherever your blade is directed.

17 I also will clap my hands together, and I will satisfy my wrath. I, the LORD, have spoken."

18 The word of the LORD came to me: 19 "Now you, son of man, mark out two roads that the sword of Babylon's king can take. Both of them should originate from the same land. And make a signpost at the fork in the road to each city. 20 Mark out a road that the sword can take to Rabbah of the Ammonites and to Judah into fortified Jerusalem. 21 For the king of Babylon stands at the split in the road, at the fork of the two roads, to practice divination: he shakes the arrows, consults the idols, and observes the liver. 22 The answer marked[B] Jerusalem appears in his right hand, indicating that he should set up battering rams, give the order to[C] slaughter, raise a battle cry, set battering rams against the gates, build a ramp, and construct a siege wall. 23 It will seem like false divination to those who have sworn an oath to the Babylonians,[D] but it will draw attention to their guilt so that they will be captured.

24 "Therefore, this is what the Lord GOD says: Because you have drawn attention to your guilt, exposing your transgressions, so that your sins are revealed in all your actions — since you have done this, you will be captured by them. 25 And you, profane and wicked prince of Israel,[E] the day has come for your punishment.[F]

26 "This is what the Lord GOD says:
Remove the turban, and take off the crown.
Things will not remain as they are;[G]
exalt the lowly and bring down the exalted.

27 A ruin, a ruin,
I will make it a ruin!
Yet this will not happen
until he comes;
I have given the judgment to him.[H]

28 "Now you, son of man, prophesy, and say, 'This is what the Lord GOD says concerning the Ammonites and their contempt.' You are to proclaim,
'A sword! A sword
is drawn for slaughter,
polished to consume, to flash like lightning.

29 While they offer false visions
and lying divinations about you,
the time has come to put you
to the necks of the profane wicked ones;

[A]21:15 Hb obscure   [B]21:22 Lit The divination for   [C]21:22 Lit rams, open the mouth in   [D]21:23 Lit them   [E]21:25 = King Zedekiah   [F]21:25 Lit come in the time of the punishment of the end, also in v. 29   [G]21:26 Lit This not this   [H]21:27 Or comes to whom it rightfully belongs, and I will give it to him

the day has come
for final punishment.

³⁰ " 'Return it to its sheath!

" 'I will judge you^A
in the place where you were created,
in the land of your origin.
³¹ I will pour out my indignation on you;
I will blow the fire of my fury on you.
I will hand you over to brutal men,
skilled at destruction.
³² You will be fuel for the fire.
Your blood will be spilled within the land.
You will not be remembered,
for I, the Lord, have spoken.' "

INDICTMENT OF SINFUL JERUSALEM

22 The word of the Lord came to me: ² "As for you, son of man, will you pass judgment? Will you pass judgment against the city of blood? Then explain all her detestable practices to her. ³ You are to say, 'This is what the Lord God says: A city that sheds blood within her walls so that her time of judgment has come and who makes idols for herself so that she is defiled! ⁴ You are guilty of the blood you have shed, and you are defiled from the idols you have made. You have brought your judgment^B days near and have come to your years of punishment.^C Therefore, I have made you a disgrace to the nations and a mockery to all the lands. ⁵ Those who are near and those far away from you will mock you, you infamous one full of turmoil.

⁶ " 'Look, every prince of Israel within you has used his strength to shed blood. ⁷ Father and mother are treated with contempt, and the resident alien is exploited within you. The fatherless and widow are oppressed in you. ⁸ You despise my holy things and profane my Sabbaths. ⁹ There are men within you who slander in order to shed blood. People who live in you eat at the mountain shrines;^D they commit depraved acts within you. ¹⁰ Men within you have sexual intercourse with their father's wife and violate women during their menstrual impurity. ¹¹ One man within you commits a detestable act with his neighbor's wife; another defiles his daughter-in-law with depravity; and yet another violates his sister, his father's daughter. ¹² People who live in you accept bribes in order to shed blood. You take interest and profit on a loan and brutally extort your neighbors. You have forgotten me. This is the declaration of the Lord God.

¹³ " 'Now look, I clap my hands together against the dishonest profit you have made and against the blood shed among you. ¹⁴ Will your courage endure or your hands be strong in the days when I deal with you? I, the Lord, have spoken, and I will act. ¹⁵ I will disperse you among the nations and scatter you among the countries; I will purge your uncleanness.

---

^A21:30 = the Ammonites ^B22:4 *judgment* supplied for clarity ^C22:4 *punishment* supplied for clarity ^D22:9 Lit *the mountains*

[16] You[A] will be profaned in the sight of the nations. Then you will know that I am the LORD.'"

JERUSALEM AS GOD'S FURNACE

[17] The word of the LORD came to me: [18] "Son of man, the house of Israel has become merely dross to me. All of them are copper, tin, iron, and lead inside the furnace; they are just dross from silver. [19] Therefore, this is what the Lord GOD says: Because all of you have become dross, I am about to gather you into Jerusalem. [20] Just as one gathers silver, copper, iron, lead, and tin into the furnace to blow fire on them and melt them, so I will gather you in my anger and wrath, put you inside, and melt you. [21] Yes, I will gather you together and blow on you with the fire of my fury, and you will be melted within the city. [22] As silver is melted inside a furnace, so you will be melted inside the city. Then you will know that I, the LORD, have poured out my wrath on you."

INDICTMENT OF A SINFUL LAND

[23] The word of the LORD came to me: [24] "Son of man, say to her, 'You are a land that has not been cleansed, that has not received rain in the day of indignation.' [25] The conspiracy of her prophets within her is[B] like a roaring lion tearing its prey: they devour people, seize wealth and valuables, and multiply the widows within her. [26] Her priests do violence to my instruction and profane my holy things. They make no distinction between the holy and the common, and they do not explain the difference between the clean and the unclean. They close their eyes to my Sabbaths, and I am profaned among them.

[27] "Her officials within her are like wolves tearing their prey, shedding blood, and destroying lives in order to make profit dishonestly. [28] Her prophets plaster for them with whitewash by seeing false visions and lying divinations, saying, 'This is what the Lord GOD says,' when the LORD has not spoken. [29] The people of the land have practiced extortion and committed robbery. They have oppressed the poor and needy and unlawfully exploited the resident alien. [30] I searched for a man among them who would repair the wall and stand in the gap before me on behalf of the land so that I might not destroy it, but I found no one. [31] So I have poured out my indignation on them and consumed them with the fire of my fury. I have brought their conduct down on their own heads." This is the declaration of the Lord GOD.

THE TWO IMMORAL SISTERS

23 The word of the LORD came to me again: [2] "Son of man, there were two women, daughters of the same mother, [3] who acted like prostitutes in Egypt, behaving promiscuously in their youth. Their breasts were fondled there, and their virgin nipples caressed. [4] The older one was named Oholah,[C] and her sister was Oholibah.[D] They became mine and gave birth to sons and daughters. As for their names, Oholah represents Samaria and Oholibah represents Jerusalem.

[A]22:16 One Hb ms, LXX, Syr, Vg read I   [B]22:24-25 LXX reads indignation,
[25]whose princes within her are   [C]23:4 = Her Tent   [D]23:4 = My Tent Is in Her

⁵ "Oholah acted like a prostitute even though she was mine. She lusted after her lovers, the Assyrians: warriors ⁶ dressed in blue, governors and prefects, all of them desirable young men, horsemen riding on steeds. ⁷ She offered her sexual favors to them; all of them were the elite of Assyria. She defiled herself with all those she lusted after and with all their idols. ⁸ She didn't give up her promiscuity that began in Egypt, when men slept with her in her youth, caressed her virgin nipples, and poured out their lust on her. ⁹ Therefore, I handed her over to her lovers, the Assyrians she lusted for. ¹⁰ They exposed her nakedness, seized her sons and daughters, and killed her with the sword. Since they executed judgment against her, she became notorious among women.

¹¹ "Now her sister Oholibah saw this, but she was even more depraved in her lust than Oholah, and made her promiscuous acts worse than those of her sister. ¹² She lusted after the Assyrians: governors and prefects, warriors splendidly dressed, horsemen riding on steeds, all of them desirable young men. ¹³ And I saw that she had defiled herself; both of them had taken the same path. ¹⁴ But she increased her promiscuity when she saw male figures carved on the wall, images of the Chaldeans, engraved in bright red, ¹⁵ wearing belts on their waists and flowing turbans on their heads; all of them looked like officers, a depiction of the Babylonians in Chaldea, their native land. ¹⁶ At the sight of them ᴬ she lusted after them and sent messengers to them in Chaldea. ¹⁷ Then the Babylonians came to her, to the bed of love, and defiled her with their lust. But after she was defiled by them, she turned away from them in disgust. ¹⁸ When she flaunted her promiscuity and exposed her nakedness, I turned away from her in disgust just as I turned away from her sister. ¹⁹ Yet she multiplied her acts of promiscuity, remembering the days of her youth when she acted like a prostitute in the land of Egypt ²⁰ and lusted after their lovers, whose sexual members ᴮ were like those of donkeys and whose emission was like that of stallions. ²¹ So you revisited the depravity of your youth, when the Egyptians caressed your nipples to enjoy your youthful breasts.

²² "Therefore, Oholibah, this is what the Lord God says: I am going to incite your lovers against you, those you turned away from in disgust. I will bring them against you from every side: ²³ the Babylonians and all the Chaldeans; Pekod, Shoa, and Koa; and all the Assyrians with them — desirable young men, all of them governors and prefects, officers and administrators, all of them riding on steeds. ²⁴ They will come against you with an assembly of peoples and with weapons, chariots, and ᶜ wagons. They will set themselves against you on every side with large and small shields and helmets. I will delegate judgment to them, and they will judge you by their own standards. ²⁵ When I vent my jealous rage on you, they will deal with you in wrath. They will cut off your nose and ears, and the rest of you ᴰ will fall by the sword. They will seize your sons and daughters, and the rest of you will be consumed by fire. ²⁶ They will strip off your clothes and take your beautiful jewelry. ²⁷ So I will put an end to your depravity and sexual immorality, which began in the land of Egypt, and you will not look longingly at them or remember Egypt anymore.

ᴬ23:16 Lit of her eyes ᴮ23:20 Lit whose flesh ᶜ23:24 LXX reads peoples, from the north, chariots and; Hb obscure ᴰ23:25 Or and your descendants

28 "For this is what the Lord God says: I am going to hand you over to those you hate, to those you turned away from in disgust. 29 They will treat you with hatred, take all you have worked for, and leave you stark naked, so that the shame of your debauchery will be exposed, both your depravity and promiscuity. 30 These things will be done to you because you acted like a prostitute with the nations, defiling yourself with their idols. 31 You have followed the path of your sister, so I will put her cup in your hand."

32 This is what the Lord God says:

"You will drink your sister's cup,
which is deep and wide.
You will be an object of[A] ridicule and scorn,
for it holds so much.
33 You will be filled with drunkenness and grief,
with a cup of devastation and desolation,
the cup of your sister Samaria.
34 You will drink it and drain it;
then you will gnaw its broken pieces,
and tear your breasts.
For I have spoken."
This is the declaration of the Lord God.

35 Therefore, this is what the Lord God says: "Because you have forgotten me and cast me behind your back, you must bear the consequences of your indecency and promiscuity."

36 Then the Lord said to me: "Son of man, will you pass judgment against Oholah and Oholibah? Then declare their detestable practices to them. 37 For they have committed adultery, and blood is on their hands; they have committed adultery with their idols. And the children they bore to me they have sacrificed in the fire[B] as food for the idols. 38 They also did this to me: they defiled my sanctuary on that same day and profaned my Sabbaths. 39 On the same day they slaughtered their children for their idols, they entered my sanctuary to profane it. Yes, that is what they did inside my house.

40 "In addition, they sent for men who came from far away when a messenger was dispatched to them. And look how they came! You bathed, painted your eyes, and adorned yourself with jewelry for them. 41 You sat on a luxurious couch with a table spread before it, on which you had set my incense and oil. 42 The sound of a carefree crowd was there. Drunkards[C] from the desert were brought in, along with common men. They put bracelets on the women's hands and beautiful tiaras on their heads. 43 Then I said concerning this woman worn out by adultery: Will they[D] now have illicit sex with her, even her? 44 Yet they had sex with her as one does with a prostitute. This is how they had sex with Oholah and Oholibah, those depraved women. 45 But righteous men will judge them the way adulteresses and those who shed blood are judged, for they are adulteresses and blood is on their hands.

46 "This is what the Lord God says: Summon[E] an assembly against them and consign them to terror and plunder. 47 The assembly will stone them

---

A23:32 Or It will bring   B23:37 Lit have made pass through the fire   C23:42 Or Sabeans   D23:43 Or They will   E23:46 Or I will summon and cut them down with their swords. They will kill their sons and daughters and burn their houses. ⁴⁸ So I will put an end to depravity in the land, and all the women will be admonished not to imitate your depraved behavior. ⁴⁹ They will punish you for your depravity, and you will bear the consequences for your sins of idolatry. Then you will know that I am the Lord God."

PARABLE OF THE BOILING POT

24 The word of the Lord came to me in the ninth year, in the tenth month, on the tenth day of the month: ² "Son of man, write down today's date, this very day. The king of Babylon has laid siege to Jerusalem this very day. ³ Now speak a parable to the rebellious house. Tell them, 'This is what the Lord God says:

> Put the pot on the fire —
> put it on,
> and then pour water into it!
⁴   Place the pieces of meat in it,
> every good piece —
> thigh and shoulder.
> Fill it with choice bones.
⁵   Take the choicest of the flock
> and also pile up the fuel^A under it.
> Bring it to a boil
> and cook the bones in it.

⁶ " 'Therefore, this is what the Lord God says:
> Woe to the city of bloodshed,
> the pot that has corrosion inside it,
> and its corrosion has not come out of it!
> Empty it piece by piece;
> lots should not be cast for its contents.
⁷   For the blood she shed^B is still within her.
> She put it out on the bare rock;
> she didn't pour it on the ground
> to cover it with dust.
⁸   In order to stir up wrath and take vengeance,
> I have put her blood on the bare rock,
> so that it would not be covered.

⁹ " 'Therefore, this is what the Lord God says:
> Woe to the city of bloodshed!
> I myself will make the pile of kindling large.
¹⁰   Pile on the logs and kindle the fire!
> Cook the meat well
> and mix in the spices!^C,^D
> Let the bones be burned!

---

^A24:5 Lit bones   ^B24:7 Lit For her blood   ^C24:10 Some Hb mss read well; remove the broth; LXX reads fire so that the meat may be cooked and the broth may be reduced   ^D24:10 Or and stir the broth

¹¹ Set the empty pot on its coals
so that it becomes hot and its copper glows.
Then its impurity will melt inside it;
its corrosion will be consumed.

¹² It has frustrated every effort;ᴬ
its thick corrosion will not come off.
Into the fire with its corrosion!

¹³ Because of the depravity
of your uncleanness —
since I tried to purify you,
but you would not be purified
from your uncleanness —
you will not be pure again
until I have satisfied my wrath on you.

¹⁴ I, the LORD, have spoken.
It is coming, and I will do it!
I will not refrain, I will not show pity,
and I will not relent.
Iᴮ will judge you
according to your ways and deeds.
This is the declaration of the Lord GOD.' "

THE DEATH OF EZEKIEL'S WIFE: A SIGN

¹⁵ Then the word of the LORD came to me: ¹⁶ "Son of man, I am about to take the delight of your eyes away from you with a fatal blow. But you must not lament or weep or let your tears flow. ¹⁷ Groan quietly; do not observe mourning rites for the dead. Put on your turban and strap your sandals on your feet; do not cover your mustache or eat the bread of mourners."ᶜ

¹⁸ I spoke to the people in the morning, and my wife died in the evening. The next morning I did just as I was commanded. ¹⁹ Then the people asked me, "Won't you tell us what these things you are doing mean for us?"

²⁰ So I answered them: "The word of the LORD came to me: ²¹ Say to the house of Israel, 'This is what the Lord GOD says: I am about to desecrate my sanctuary, the pride of your power, the delight of your eyes, and the desire of your heart. Also, the sons and daughters you left behind will fall by the sword. ²² Then you will do just as I have done: You will not cover your mustache or eat the bread of mourners. ²³ Your turbans will remain on your heads and your sandals on your feet. You will not lament or weep but will waste away because of your iniquities and will groan to one another. ²⁴ Now Ezekiel will be a sign for you. You will do everything that he has done. When this happens, you will know that I am the Lord GOD.'

²⁵ "As for you, son of man, know that on that day I will take from them their stronghold — their pride and joy, the delight of their eyes, and the longing of their hearts — as well as their sons and daughters. ²⁶ On that day a fugitive will come to you and report the news. ²⁷ On that day your mouth will be opened to talk with him; you will speak and no longer be mute. So you will be a sign for them, and they will know that I am the LORD."

ᴬ24:12 Hb obscure ᴮ24:14 Some Hb mss, LXX, Syr, Tg, Vg; other Hb mss read *They* ᶜ24:17 Lit *men*, also in v. 22

PROPHECIES AGAINST THE NATIONS

JUDGMENT AGAINST AMMON

25 Then the word of the LORD came to me: [2] "Son of man, face the Ammonites and prophesy against them. [3] Say to the Ammonites, 'Hear the word of the Lord GOD: This is what the Lord GOD says: Because you said, "Aha!" about my sanctuary when it was desecrated, about the land of Israel when it was laid waste, and about the house of Judah when they went into exile, [4] therefore I am about to give you to the people of the east as a possession. They will set up their encampments and pitch their tents among you. They will eat your fruit and drink your milk. [5] I will make Rabbah a pasture for camels and Ammon a resting place for sheep. Then you will know that I am the LORD.

[6] "'For this is what the Lord GOD says: Because you clapped your hands, stamped your feet, and rejoiced over the land of Israel with wholehearted contempt, [7] therefore I am about to stretch out my hand against you and give you as plunder to the nations. I will cut you off from the peoples and eliminate you from the countries. I will destroy you, and you will know that I am the LORD.

JUDGMENT AGAINST MOAB

[8] "This is what the Lord GOD says: Because Moab and Seir said, "Look, the house of Judah is like all the other nations." [9] Therefore I am about to expose Moab's flank beginning with its[A] frontier cities, the splendor of the land: Beth-jeshimoth, Baal-meon, and Kiriathaim. [10] I will give it along with Ammon to the people of the east as a possession, so that Ammon will not be remembered among the nations. [11] So I will execute judgments against Moab, and they will know that I am the LORD.

JUDGMENT AGAINST EDOM

[12] "This is what the Lord GOD says: Because Edom acted vengefully against the house of Judah and incurred grievous guilt by taking revenge on them, [13] therefore this is what the Lord GOD says: I will stretch out my hand against Edom and cut off both man and animal from it. I will make it a wasteland; they will fall by the sword from Teman to Dedan. [14] I will take my vengeance on Edom through my people Israel, and they will deal with Edom according to my anger and wrath. So they will know my vengeance. This is the declaration of the Lord GOD.

JUDGMENT AGAINST PHILISTIA

[15] "This is what the Lord GOD says: Because the Philistines acted in vengeance and took revenge with deep contempt, destroying because of their perpetual hatred, [16] therefore this is what the Lord GOD says: I am about to stretch out my hand against the Philistines, cutting off the Cherethites and wiping out what remains of the coastal peoples.[B] [17] I will execute severe vengeance against them with furious rebukes. They will know that I am the LORD when I take my vengeance on them.'"

[A]25:9 Lit with the cities, with its   [B]25:16 Lit the seacoast

THE DOWNFALL OF TYRE

26 In the eleventh year, on the first day of the month, the word of the LORD came to me: ² "Son of man, because Tyre said about Jerusalem, 'Aha! The gateway to the peoples is shattered. She has been turned over to me.ᴬ I will be filled now that she lies in ruins,' ³ therefore this is what the Lord GOD says: See, I am against you, Tyre! I will raise up many nations against you, just as the sea raises its waves. ⁴ They will destroy the walls of Tyre and demolish her towers. I will scrape the soil from her and turn her into a bare rock. ⁵ She will become a place in the sea to spread nets, for I have spoken." This is the declaration of the Lord GOD. "She will become plunder for the nations, ⁶ and her villages on the mainland will be slaughtered by the sword. Then they will know that I am the LORD."

⁷ For this is what the Lord GOD says: "See, I am about to bring King Nebuchadnezzarᴮ of Babylon, king of kings, against Tyre from the north with horses, chariots, cavalry, and a huge assembly of troops. ⁸ He will slaughter your villages on the mainland with the sword. He will set up siege works, build a ramp, and raise a wall of shields against you. ⁹ He will direct the blows of his battering rams against your walls and tear down your towers with his iron tools. ¹⁰ His horses will be so numerous that their dust will cover you. When he enters your gates as an army entering a breached city, your walls will shake from the noise of cavalry, wagons, and chariots. ¹¹ He will trample all your streets with the hooves of his horses. He will slaughter your people with the sword, and your mighty pillars will fall to the ground. ¹² They will take your wealth as spoil and plunder your merchandise. They will also demolish your walls and tear down your beautiful homes. Then they will throw your stones, timber, and soil into the water. ¹³ I will put an end to the noise of your songs, and the sound of your lyres will no longer be heard. ¹⁴ I will turn you into a bare rock, and you will be a place to spread nets. You will never be rebuilt, for I, the LORD, have spoken." This is the declaration of the Lord GOD.

¹⁵ This is what the Lord GOD says to Tyre: "Won't the coasts and islands quake at the sound of your downfall, when the wounded groan and slaughter occurs within you? ¹⁶ All the princes of the sea will descend from their thrones, remove their robes, and strip off their embroidered garments. They will clothe themselves with trembling; they will sit on the ground, tremble continually, and be appalled at you. ¹⁷ Then they will lament for you and say of you,

'How you have perished, city of renown,
you who were populated from the seas!ᶜ
She who was powerful on the sea,
she and all of her inhabitants
inflicted their terror.ᴰ
¹⁸ Now the coastlands tremble
on the day of your downfall;
the islands in the sea
are alarmed by your demise.' "

ᴬ26:2 Or *It has swung open for me* ᴮ26:7 Lit *Nebuchadrezzar* ᶜ26:17 Some LXX mss read *'How you were destroyed from the seas, city of renown!* ᴰ26:17 Lit *and all her inhabitants who put their terror on all her inhabitants;* Hb obscure

[19] For this is what the Lord God says: "When I make you a ruined city like other deserted cities, when I raise up the deep against you so that the mighty waters cover you, [20] then I will bring you down to be with those who descend to the Pit, to the people of antiquity. I will make you dwell in the underworld[A] like[B] the ancient ruins, with those who descend to the Pit, so that you will no longer be inhabited or display your splendor[C] in the land of the living. [21] I will make you an object of horror, and you will no longer exist. You will be sought but will never be found again." This is the declaration of the Lord God.

THE SINKING OF TYRE

27

The word of the Lord came to me: [2] "Now, son of man, lament for Tyre. [3] Say to Tyre, who is located at the entrance of the sea, merchant of the peoples to many coasts and islands, 'This is what the Lord God says:

Tyre, you declared,
"I am perfect in beauty."
[4] Your realm was in the heart of the sea;
your builders perfected your beauty.
[5] They constructed all your planking
with pine trees from Senir.
They took a cedar from Lebanon
to make a mast for you.
[6] They made your oars of oaks from Bashan.
They made your deck of cypress wood
from the coasts of Cyprus,
inlaid with ivory.
[7] Your sail was made of
fine embroidered linen from Egypt,
and served as your banner.
Your awning was of blue and purple fabric
from the coasts of Elishah.
[8] The inhabitants of Sidon and Arvad
were your rowers.
Your wise men were within you, Tyre;
they were your captains.
[9] The elders of Gebal and its wise men
were within you, repairing your leaks.

"'All the ships of the sea and their sailors
came to you to barter for your goods.
[10] Men of Persia, Lud, and Put
were in your army, serving as your warriors.
They hung shields and helmets in you;
they gave you splendor.
[11] Men of Arvad and Helech
were stationed on your walls all around,
and Gammadites were in your towers.

[A]26:20 Lit *the lower parts of the earth*   [B]26:20 Some Hb mss, LXX; other Hb mss, Syr read *in*   [C]26:20 LXX reads *or appear*

They hung their shields^A all around your walls;
they perfected your beauty.

12 " 'Tarshish was your trading partner because of your abundant wealth of every kind. They exchanged silver, iron, tin, and lead for your merchandise. 13 Javan, Tubal, and Meshech were your merchants. They exchanged slaves^B and bronze utensils for your goods. 14 Those from Beth-togarmah exchanged horses, war horses, and mules for your merchandise. 15 Men of Dedan^C were also your merchants; many coasts and islands were your regular markets. They brought back ivory tusks and ebony as your payment. 16 Aram^D was your trading partner because of your numerous products. They exchanged turquoise,^E purple and embroidered cloth, fine linen, coral,^E and rubies^E for your merchandise. 17 Judah and the land of Israel were your merchants. They exchanged wheat from Minnith, meal,^F honey, oil, and balm, for your goods. 18 Damascus was also your trading partner because of your numerous products and your abundant wealth of every kind, trading in wine from Helbon and white wool.^G 19 Vedan^H and Javan from Uzal^E dealt in your merchandise; wrought iron, cassia, and aromatic cane were exchanged for your goods. 20 Dedan was your merchant in saddlecloths for riding. 21 Arabia and all the princes of Kedar were your business partners, trading with you in lambs, rams, and goats. 22 The merchants of Sheba and Raamah traded with you. For your merchandise they exchanged the best of all spices and all kinds of precious stones as well as gold. 23 Haran, Canneh, Eden, the merchants of Sheba, Asshur, and Chilmad traded with you. 24 They were your merchants in choice garments, cloaks of blue and embroidered materials, and multicolored carpets,^E which were bound and secured with cords in your marketplace. 25 Ships of Tarshish were the carriers for your goods.

" 'So you became full and heavily loaded^I
in the heart of the sea.
26 Your rowers have brought you
      onto the high seas,
      but the east wind has wrecked you
      in the heart of the sea.
27 Your wealth, merchandise, and goods,
      your sailors and captains,
      those who repair your leaks,
      those who barter for your goods,
      and all the warriors on board,
      with all the other people within you,
      sink into the heart of the sea
      on the day of your downfall.

28 " 'The countryside shakes
      at the sound of your sailors' cries.

---

^A27:11 Or quivers; Hb obscure   ^B27:13 Lit souls of men   ^C27:15 LXX reads Rhodes   ^D27:16 Some Hb mss, Aq, Syr read Edom   ^E27:16,19,24 Hb obscure ^F27:17 Or resin; Hb obscure   ^G27:18 Or and wool from Zahar   ^H27:19 Or Dan ^I27:25 Or and very glorious

²⁹ All the oarsmen
disembark from their ships.
The sailors and all the captains of the sea
stand on the shore.
³⁰ Because of you, they raise their voices
and cry out bitterly.
They throw dust on their heads;
they roll in ashes.
³¹ They shave their heads because of you
and wrap themselves in sackcloth.
They weep over you
with deep anguish and bitter mourning.

³² " 'In their wailing they lament for you,
mourning over you:
"Who was like Tyre,
silenced^A in the middle of the sea?
³³ When your merchandise was unloaded from the seas,
you satisfied many peoples.
You enriched the kings of the earth
with your abundant wealth and goods.
³⁴ Now you are wrecked by the sea
in the depths of the waters;
your goods and the people within you
have gone down.
³⁵ All the inhabitants of the coasts and islands
are appalled at you.
Their kings shudder with fear;
their faces are contorted.
³⁶ Those who trade among the peoples
scoff^B at you;
you have become an object of horror
and will never exist again." ' "

THE FALL OF TYRE'S RULER

28 The word of the Lord came to me: ² "Son of man, say to the ruler of Tyre, 'This is what the Lord God says: Your^C heart is proud, and you have said, "I am a god; I sit in the seat of gods in the heart of the sea." Yet you are a man and not a god, though you have regarded your heart as that of a god. ³ Yes, you are wiser than Daniel; no secret is hidden from you! ⁴ By your wisdom and understanding you have acquired wealth for yourself. You have acquired gold and silver for your treasuries. ⁵ By your great skill in trading you have increased your wealth, but your heart has become proud because of your wealth.

⁶ " 'Therefore, this is what the Lord God says:
Because you regard your heart as that of a god,
⁷ I am about to bring strangers against you,
ruthless men from the nations.

^A27:32 Hb obscure   ^B27:36 Lit *hiss*   ^C28:2 Lit *Because your*

They will draw their swords
against your magnificent wisdom
and will pierce your splendor.
8 They will bring you down to the Pit,
and you will die a violent death
in the heart of the sea.
9 Will you still say, "I am a god,"
in the presence of those who slay[A] you?
Yet you will be only a man, not a god,
in the hands of those who kill you.
10 You will die the death of the uncircumcised
at the hands of strangers.
For I have spoken.
This is the declaration of the Lord God.'"

A LAMENT FOR TYRE'S KING

11 The word of the Lord came to me: 12 "Son of man, lament for the king of Tyre and say to him, 'This is what the Lord God says:
You were the seal[B] of perfection,[C]
full of wisdom and perfect in beauty.
13 You were in Eden, the garden of God.
Every kind of precious stone covered you:
carnelian, topaz, and diamond,[C]
beryl, onyx, and jasper,
lapis lazuli, turquoise[D] and emerald.[E]
Your mountings and settings were crafted in gold;
they were prepared on the day you were created.
14 You were an anointed guardian cherub,
for[F] I had appointed you.
You were on the holy mountain of God;
you walked among the fiery stones.
15 From the day you were created
you were blameless in your ways
until wickedness was found in you.
16 Through the abundance of your trade,
you were filled with violence, and you sinned.
So I expelled you in disgrace
from the mountain of God,
and banished you, guardian cherub,[G]
from among the fiery stones.
17 Your heart became proud because of your beauty;
For the sake of your splendor
you corrupted your wisdom.
So I threw you down to the ground;[H]
I made you a spectacle before kings.

18 You profaned your sanctuaries
  by the magnitude of your iniquities
  in your dishonest trade.
  So I made fire come from within you,
  and it consumed you.
  I reduced you to ashes on the ground
  in the sight of everyone watching you.
19 All those who know you among the peoples
  are appalled at you.
  You have become an object of horror
  and will never exist again.'"

A PROPHECY AGAINST SIDON

20 The word of the LORD came to me: 21 "Son of man, face Sidon and prophesy against it. 22 You are to say, 'This is what the Lord GOD says:

  Look! I am against you, Sidon,
  and I will display my glory within you.
  They will know that I am the LORD
  when I execute judgments against her
  and demonstrate my holiness through her.
23 I will send a plague against her
  and bloodshed in her streets;
  the slain will fall within her,
  while the sword is against her^A on every side.
  Then they will know that I am the LORD.

24 "'The house of Israel will no longer be hurt by^B prickly briers or painful thorns from all their neighbors who treat them with contempt. Then they will know that I am the Lord GOD.

25 "'This is what the Lord GOD says: When I gather the house of Israel from the peoples where they are scattered, I will demonstrate my holiness through them in the sight of the nations, and they will live in their own land, which I gave to my servant Jacob. 26 They will live there securely, build houses, and plant vineyards. They will live securely when I execute judgments against all their neighbors who treat them with contempt. Then they will know that I am the LORD their God.'"

A PROPHECY OF EGYPT'S RUIN

29 In the tenth year, in the tenth month on the twelfth day of the month, the word of the LORD came to me: 2 "Son of man, face Pharaoh king of Egypt and prophesy against him and against all of Egypt. 3 Speak to him and say, 'This is what the Lord GOD says:

  Look, I am against you, Pharaoh king of Egypt,
  the great monster^C lying in the middle of his Nile,
  who says, "My Nile is my own;
  I made it for myself."
4 I will put hooks in your jaws
  and make the fish of your streams

---

^A28:23 Or *within her by the sword* ^B28:24 Lit *longer have* ^C29:3 Or *crocodile*

cling to your scales.
I will haul you up
from the middle of your Nile,
and all the fish of your streams
will cling to your scales.
5 I will leave you in the desert,
you and all the fish of your streams.
You will fall on the open ground
and will not be taken away
or gathered for burial.
I have given you
to the wild creatures of the earth
and the birds of the sky as food.

6 " 'Then all the inhabitants of Egypt
will know that I am the LORD,
for they[A] have been a staff made of reed
to the house of Israel.
7 When Israel grasped you by the hand,
you splintered, tearing all their shoulders;
when they leaned on you,
you shattered and made all their hips unsteady.[B]

8 " 'Therefore, this is what the Lord GOD says: I am going to bring a sword against you and cut off both man and animal from you. 9 The land of Egypt will be a desolate ruin. Then they will know that I am the LORD. Because you[C] said, "The Nile is my own; I made it," 10 therefore, I am against you and your Nile. I will turn the land of Egypt into ruins, a desolate waste from Migdol to Syene, as far as the border of Cush. 11 No human foot will pass through it, and no animal foot will pass through it. It will be uninhabited for forty years. 12 I will make the land of Egypt a desolation among[D] desolate lands, and its cities will be a desolation among[E] ruined cities for forty years. I will disperse the Egyptians among the nations and scatter them throughout the lands.

13 " 'For this is what the Lord GOD says: At the end of forty years I will gather the Egyptians from the peoples where they were dispersed. 14 I will restore the fortunes of Egypt and bring them back to the land of Pathros, the land of their origin. There they will be a lowly kingdom. 15 Egypt will be the lowliest of kingdoms and will never again exalt itself over the nations. I will make them so small they cannot rule over the nations. 16 It will never again be an object of trust for the house of Israel, drawing attention to their iniquity of turning to the Egyptians. Then they will know that I am the Lord GOD.' "

BABYLON RECEIVES EGYPT AS COMPENSATION

17 In the twenty-seventh year, in the first month, on the first day of the month, the word of the LORD came to me: 18 "Son of man, King Nebuchadnezzar of Babylon made his army labor strenuously against Tyre. Every head was made

---

bald and every shoulder chafed, but he and his army received no compensation from Tyre for the labor he expended against it. [19] Therefore, this is what the Lord GOD says: I am going to give the land of Egypt to King Nebuchadnezzar of Babylon, and he will carry off its wealth, seizing its spoil and taking its plunder. This will be his army's compensation. [20] I have given him the land of Egypt as the pay he labored for, since they worked for me." This is the declaration of the Lord GOD. [21] "In that day I will cause a horn to sprout for the house of Israel, and I will enable you to speak out among them. Then they will know that I am the LORD."

EGYPT'S DOOM

30

The word of the LORD came to me: [2] "Son of man, prophesy and say, 'This is what the Lord GOD says:

Wail, "Woe because of that day!"

[3] For a day is near;
a day belonging to the LORD is near.
It will be a day of clouds,
a time of doom[A] for the nations.

[4] A sword will come against Egypt,
and there will be anguish in Cush
when the slain fall in Egypt,
and its wealth is taken away,
and its foundations are demolished.

[5] Cush, Put, and Lud,
and all the various foreign troops,[B]
plus Libya[C] and the men of the covenant land
will fall by the sword along with them.

[6] This is what the LORD says:
Those who support Egypt will fall,
and its proud strength will collapse.
From Migdol to Syene
they will fall within it by the sword.

This is the declaration of the Lord GOD.

[7] They will be desolate
among[D] desolate lands,
and their cities will lie
among ruined[E] cities.

[8] They will know that I am the LORD
when I set fire to Egypt
and all its allies are shattered.

[9] On that day, messengers will go out from me in ships to terrify confident Cush. Anguish will come over them on the day of Egypt's doom.[F] For indeed it is coming.

[10] "This is what the Lord GOD says:

I will put an end to the hordes[G] of Egypt
by the hand of King Nebuchadnezzar of Babylon.

[A]30:3 of doom supplied for clarity [B]30:5 Or all Arabia [C]30:5 Lit Cub; Hb obscure [D]30:7 Or be the most desolate of [E]30:7 Or will be the most ruined of [F]30:9 Lit of Egypt [G]30:10 Or pomp, or wealth, also in v. 15

11 He along with his people,
   ruthless men from the nations,
   will be brought in to destroy the land.
   They will draw their swords against Egypt
   and fill the land with the slain.
12 I will make the streams dry
   and sell the land to evil men.
   I will bring desolation
   on the land and everything in it
   by the hands of foreigners.
   I, the Lord, have spoken.

13 " 'This is what the Lord God says:
   I will destroy the idols and put an end
   to the false gods in Memphis.
   There will no longer be
   a prince from the land of Egypt.
   And I will instill fear in that land.
14 I will make Pathros desolate,
   set fire to Zoan,
   and execute judgments on Thebes.
15 I will pour out my wrath on Pelusium,
   the stronghold of Egypt,
   and will wipe out the hordes of Thebes.
16 I will set fire to Egypt;
   Pelusium will writhe in anguish,
   Thebes will be breached,
   and Memphis will face foes in broad daylight.ᴬ
17 The young men of Onᴮ and Pi-beseth
   will fall by the sword,
   and those citiesᶜ will go into captivity.
18 The day will be darkᴰ in Tehaphnehes,
   when I break the yoke of Egypt there
   and its proud strength
   comes to an end in the city.
   A cloud will cover Tehaphnehes,ᴱ
   and its surrounding villages will go into captivity.
19 So I will execute judgments against Egypt,
   and they will know that I am the Lord.' "

PHARAOH'S POWER BROKEN

20 In the eleventh year, in the first month, on the seventh day of the month, the word of the Lord came to me: 21 "Son of man, I have broken the arm of Pharaoh king of Egypt. Look, it has not been bandaged — no medicine has been applied and no splint put on to bandage it so that it can grow strong enough to handle a sword. 22 Therefore, this is what the Lord God says: Look!

ᴬ30:16 Or foes daily   ᴮ30:17 LXX, Vg; MT reads iniquity   ᶜ30:17 Or and the women; lit and they   ᴰ30:18 Some Hb mss, LXX, Syr, Tg, Vg; other Hb mss read will withhold   ᴱ30:18 Or Egypt

I am against Pharaoh king of Egypt. I will break his arms, both the strong one and the one already broken, and will make the sword fall from his hand. ²³ I will disperse the Egyptians among the nations and scatter them among the countries. ²⁴ I will strengthen the arms of Babylon's king and place my sword in his hand. But I will break the arms of Pharaoh, and he will groan before him as a mortally wounded man. ²⁵ I will strengthen the arms of Babylon's king, but Pharaoh's arms will fall. They will know that I am the LORD when I place my sword in the hand of Babylon's king and he wields it against the land of Egypt. ²⁶ When I disperse the Egyptians among the nations and scatter them among the countries, they will know that I am the LORD."

DOWNFALL OF EGYPT AND ASSYRIA

31 In the eleventh year, in the third month, on the first day of the month, the word of the LORD came to me: ² "Son of man, say to Pharaoh king of Egypt and to his hordes,

'Who are you like in your greatness?
³ Think of Assyria, a cedar in Lebanon,
  with beautiful branches and shady foliage
  and of lofty height.
  Its top was among the clouds.^A
⁴ The waters caused it to grow;
  the underground springs made it tall,
  directing their rivers all around
  the place where the tree was planted
  and sending their channels
  to all the trees of the field.
⁵ Therefore the cedar became greater in height
  than all the trees of the field.
  Its branches multiplied,
  and its boughs grew long
  as it spread them out
  because of the abundant water.
⁶ All the birds of the sky
  nested in its branches,
  and all the animals of the field
  gave birth beneath its boughs;
  all the great nations lived in its shade.
⁷ It was beautiful in its size,
  in the length of its limbs,
  for its roots extended to abundant water.
⁸ The cedars in God's garden could not eclipse it;
  the pine trees couldn't compare with its branches,
  nor could the plane trees match its boughs.
  No tree in the garden of God
  could compare with it in beauty.
⁹ I made it beautiful with its many limbs,
  and all the trees of Eden,
  which were in God's garden, envied it.

^A31:3 Or *thick foliage,* also in vv. 10,14

10 " 'Therefore, this is what the Lord God says: Since it[A] towered high in stature and set its top among the clouds, and it[B] grew proud on account of its height, 11 I determined to hand it over to a ruler of nations; he would surely deal with it. I banished it because of its wickedness. 12 Foreigners, ruthless men from the nations, cut it down and left it lying. Its limbs fell on the mountains and in every valley; its boughs lay broken in all the earth's ravines. All the peoples of the earth left its shade and abandoned it. 13 All the birds of the sky nested on its fallen trunk, and all the animals of the field were among its boughs. 14 This happened so that no trees planted beside water would become great in height and set their tops among the clouds, and so that no other well-watered trees would reach them in height. For they have all been consigned to death, to the underworld, among the people[C] who descend to the Pit.

15 " 'This is what the Lord God says: I caused grieving on the day the cedar went down to Sheol. I closed off the underground deep because of it:[D] I held back the rivers of the deep, and its abundant water was restrained. I made Lebanon mourn on account of it, and all the trees of the field fainted because of it. 16 I made the nations quake at the sound of its downfall, when I threw it down to Sheol to be with those who descend to the Pit. Then all the trees of Eden, the choice and best of Lebanon, all the well-watered trees, were comforted in the underworld. 17 They too descended with it to Sheol, to those slain by the sword. As its allies[E,F] they had lived in its shade among the nations.

18 " 'Who then are you like in glory and greatness among Eden's trees? You also will be brought down to the underworld to be with the trees of Eden. You will lie among the uncircumcised with those slain by the sword. This is Pharaoh and all his hordes. This is the declaration of the Lord God.' "

A LAMENT FOR PHARAOH

32 In the twelfth year, in the twelfth month, on the first day of the month, the word of the Lord came to me: 2 "Son of man, lament for Pharaoh king of Egypt and say to him,

'You compare yourself to a lion of the nations,
but[G] you are like a monster[H] in the seas.
You thrash about in your rivers,
churn up the waters with your feet,
and muddy the[I] rivers.

3 " 'This is what the Lord God says:
I will spread my net over you
with an assembly of many peoples,
and they[J] will haul you up in my net.
4 I will abandon you on the land
and throw you onto the open field.
I will cause all the birds of the sky

[A]31:10 Syr, Vg; MT, LXX read you   [B]31:10 Lit its heart   [C]31:14 Or the descendants of Adam   [D]31:15 Or I covered it with the underground deep   [E]31:17 LXX, Syr read offspring   [F]31:17 Lit arm   [G]32:2 Or 'Lion of the nations, you are destroyed;   [H]32:2 Or crocodile   [I]32:2 Lit their   [J]32:3 LXX, Vg read I

to settle on you
and let the wild creatures of the entire earth
eat their fill of you.

⁵ I will put your flesh on the mountains
and fill the valleys with your carcass.

⁶ I will drench the land
with the flow of your blood,
even to the mountains;
the ravines will be filled with your gore.

⁷ " 'When I snuff you out,
I will cover the heavens
and darken their stars.
I will cover the sun with a cloud,
and the moon will not give its light.

⁸ I will darken all the shining lights
in the heavens over you,
and will bring darkness on your land.
This is the declaration of the Lord God.

⁹ " 'I will trouble the hearts of many peoples,
when I bring about your destruction
among the nations,
in countries you have not known.

¹⁰ I will cause many peoples to be appalled at you,
and their kings will shudder with fear because of you
when I brandish my sword in front of them.
On the day of your downfall
each of them will tremble
every moment for his life.

¹¹ " 'For this is what the Lord God says:
The sword of Babylon's king
will come against you!

¹² I will make your hordes fall
by the swords of warriors,
all of them ruthless men from the nations.
They will ravage Egypt's pride,
and all its hordes will be destroyed.

¹³ I will slaughter all its cattle
that are beside many waters.
No human foot will churn them again,
and no cattle hooves will disturb them.

¹⁴ Then I will let their waters settle
and will make their rivers flow like oil.
This is the declaration of the Lord God.

¹⁵ When I make the land of Egypt a desolation,
so that it is emptied of everything in it,
when I strike down all who live there,
then they will know that I am the Lord.

16 "The daughters of the nations will chant that lament. They will chant it over Egypt and all its hordes. This is the declaration of the Lord GOD.'"

EGYPT IN SHEOL

17 In the twelfth year,^A on the fifteenth day of the month, the word of the LORD came to me: 18 "Son of man, wail over the hordes of Egypt and bring Egypt and the daughters of mighty nations down to the underworld,^B to be with those who descend to the Pit:

19   Who do you surpass in loveliness?
     Go down and be laid to rest
       with the uncircumcised!

20   They will fall among those slain by the sword.
     A sword is appointed!
     They drag her and all her hordes away.

21   Warrior leaders will speak
     from the middle of Sheol
     about him^C and his allies:
     'They have come down;
     the uncircumcised lie
     slain by the sword.'

22   "Assyria is there with her whole assembly;
     her graves are all around her.
     All of them are slain, fallen by the sword.

23   Her graves are set in the deepest regions
      of the Pit,
     and her assembly is all around her burial place.
     All of them are slain, fallen by the sword —
     those who once spread terror
     in the land of the living.

24   "Elam is there
     with all her hordes around her grave.
     All of them are slain, fallen by the sword —
     those who went down
      to the underworld uncircumcised,
     who once spread their terror
     in the land of the living.
     They bear their disgrace
     with those who descend to the Pit.

25   Among the slain
     they prepare a bed for Elam
     with all her hordes.
     Her graves are all around her.
     All of them are uncircumcised,
     slain by the sword,
     although their terror was once spread

---

^A32:17 LXX reads year, in the first month,   ^B32:18 Lit the lower parts of the earth, also in v. 24   ^C32:21 Either Pharaoh or Egypt

in the land of the living.
They bear their disgrace
with those who descend to the Pit.
They are placed among the slain.

26 "Meshech and Tubal[A] are there,
with all their hordes.
Their graves are all around them.
All of them are uncircumcised, slain by the sword,
although their terror was once spread
in the land of the living.

27 They do not lie down
with the fallen warriors of the uncircumcised,[B]
who went down to Sheol
with their weapons of war,
whose swords were placed under their heads[C]
and their shields[D]
rested on their bones,
although the terror of these warriors
was once in the land of the living.

28 But you will be shattered
and will lie down among the uncircumcised,
with those slain by the sword.

29 "Edom is there, her kings and all her princes,
who, despite their strength, have been placed
among those slain by the sword.
They lie down with the uncircumcised,
with those who descend to the Pit.

30 All the leaders of the north
and all the Sidonians are there.
They went down in shame with the slain,
despite the terror their strength inspired.
They lie down uncircumcised
with those slain by the sword.
They bear their disgrace
with those who descend to the Pit.

31 "Pharaoh will see them
and be comforted over all his hordes —
Pharaoh and his whole army,
slain by the sword."
This is the declaration of the Lord God.

32 "For I will spread my[E] terror
in the land of the living,
so Pharaoh and all his hordes

[A]32:26 Lit Meshech-tubal [B]32:27 LXX reads of antiquity [C]32:27 Or Do they not . . . heads? [D]32:27 Emended; MT reads iniquities [E]32:32 Alt Hb tradition, LXX, Syr read his

will be laid to rest among the uncircumcised,
with those slain by the sword."
This is the declaration of the Lord God.

EZEKIEL AS ISRAEL'S WATCHMAN

33 The word of the Lord came to me: ² "Son of man, speak to your people and tell them, 'Suppose I bring the sword against a land, and the people of that land select a man from among them, appointing him as their watchman. ³ And suppose he sees the sword coming against the land and blows his trumpet to warn the people. ⁴ Then, if anyone hears the sound of the trumpet but ignores the warning, and the sword comes and takes him away, his death will be his own fault.ᴬ ⁵ Since he heard the sound of the trumpet but ignored the warning, his death is his own fault.ᴮ If he had taken warning, he would have saved his life. ⁶ However, suppose the watchman sees the sword coming but doesn't blow the trumpet, so that the people aren't warned, and the sword comes and takes away their lives. Then they have been taken away because of their iniquity, but I will hold the watchman accountable for their blood.'

⁷ "As for you, son of man, I have made you a watchman for the house of Israel. When you hear a word from my mouth, give them a warning from me. ⁸ If I say to the wicked, 'Wicked one, you will surely die,' but you do not speak out to warn him about his way, that wicked person will die for his iniquity, yet I will hold you responsible for his blood. ⁹ But if you warn a wicked person to turn from his way and he doesn't turn from it, he will die for his iniquity, but you will have rescued yourself.

¹⁰ "Now as for you, son of man, say to the house of Israel, 'You have said this: "Our transgressions and our sins are heavy on us, and we are wasting away because of them! How then can we survive?"' ¹¹ Tell them, 'As I live — this is the declaration of the Lord God — I take no pleasure in the death of the wicked, but rather that the wicked person should turn from his way and live. Repent, repent of your evil ways! Why will you die, house of Israel?'

¹² "Now, son of man, say to your people, 'The righteousness of the righteous person will not save him on the day of his transgression; neither will the wickedness of the wicked person cause him to stumble on the day he turns from his wickedness. The righteous person won't be able to survive by his righteousness on the day he sins. ¹³ When I tell the righteous person that he will surely live, but he trusts in his righteousness and acts unjustly, then none of his righteousness will be remembered, and he will die because of the injustice he has committed.

¹⁴ "'So when I tell the wicked person, "You will surely die," but he repents of his sin and does what is just and right — ¹⁵ he returns collateral, makes restitution for what he has stolen, and walks in the statutes of life without committing injustice — he will certainly live; he will not die. ¹⁶ None of the sins he committed will be heldᶜ against him. He has done what is just and right; he will certainly live.

¹⁷ "'But your people say, "The Lord's way isn't fair," even though it is their own way that isn't fair. ¹⁸ When a righteous person turns from his righteousness

---

ᴬ33:4 Lit *his blood will be on his head*   ᴮ33:5 Lit *his blood will be on him*
ᶜ33:16 Lit *remembered*

and commits injustice, he will die for it. [19] But if a wicked person turns from his wickedness and does what is just and right, he will live because of it. [20] Yet you say, "The Lord's way isn't fair." I will judge each of you according to his ways, house of Israel.'"

THE NEWS OF JERUSALEM'S FALL

[21] In the twelfth year of our exile, in the tenth month, on the fifth day of the month, a fugitive from Jerusalem came to me and reported, "The city has been taken!" [22] Now the hand of the LORD had been on me the evening before the fugitive arrived, and he opened my mouth before the man came to me in the morning. So my mouth was opened and I was no longer mute.

ISRAEL'S CONTINUED REBELLION

[23] Then the word of the LORD came to me: [24] "Son of man, those who live in the^A ruins in the land of Israel are saying, 'Abraham was only one person, yet he received possession of the land. But we are many; surely the land has been given to us as a possession.' [25] Therefore say to them, 'This is what the Lord GOD says: You eat meat with blood in it, look to your idols, and shed blood. Should you then receive possession of the land? [26] You have relied on your swords, you have committed detestable acts, and each of you has defiled his neighbor's wife. Should you then receive possession of the land?'

[27] "Tell them this: 'This is what the Lord GOD says: As surely as I live, those who are in the ruins will fall by the sword, those in the open field I have given to wild animals to be devoured, and those in the strongholds and caves will die by plague. [28] I will make the land a desolate waste, and its proud strength will come to an end. The mountains of Israel will become desolate, with no one passing through. [29] They will know that I am the LORD when I make the land a desolate waste because of all the detestable acts they have committed.'

[30] "As for you, son of man, your people are talking about you near the city walls and in the doorways of their houses. One person speaks to another, each saying to his brother, 'Come and hear what the message is that comes from the LORD!' [31] So my people come to you in crowds,^B sit in front of you, and hear your words, but they don't obey them. Their mouths go on passionately, but their hearts pursue dishonest profit. [32] Yes, to them you are like a singer of passionate songs who has a beautiful voice and plays skillfully on an instrument. They hear your words, but they don't obey them. [33] Yet when all this comes true — and it definitely will — then they will know that a prophet has been among them."

THE SHEPHERDS AND GOD'S FLOCK

34 The word of the LORD came to me: [2] "Son of man, prophesy against the shepherds of Israel. Prophesy, and say to them, 'This is what the Lord GOD says to the shepherds: Woe to the shepherds of Israel, who have been feeding themselves! Shouldn't the shepherds feed their flock? [3] You eat the fat, wear the wool, and butcher the fattened animals, but you do not tend the flock. [4] You have not strengthened the weak, healed the sick, bandaged the injured, brought back the strays, or sought the lost. Instead, you have ruled them with violence and cruelty. [5] They were scattered for lack of

^A33:24 Lit these ^B33:31 Lit you like the coming of a people a shepherd; they became food for all the wild animals when they were scattered. ⁶ My flock went astray on all the mountains and every high hill. My flock was scattered over the whole face of the earth, and there was no one searching or seeking for them.

⁷ " 'Therefore, you shepherds, hear the word of the LORD. ⁸ As I live — this is the declaration of the Lord GOD — because my flock, lacking a shepherd, has become prey and food for every wild animal, and because my shepherds do not search for my flock, and because the shepherds feed themselves rather than my flock, ⁹ therefore, you shepherds, hear the word of the LORD!

¹⁰ " 'This is what the Lord GOD says: Look, I am against the shepherds. I will demand my flock from themᴬ and prevent them from shepherding the flock. The shepherds will no longer feed themselves, for I will rescue my flock from their mouths so that they will not be food for them.

¹¹ " 'For this is what the Lord GOD says: See, I myself will search for my flock and look for them. ¹² As a shepherd looks for his sheep on the day he is among his scattered flock, so I will look for my flock. I will rescue them from all the places where they have been scattered on a day of clouds and total darkness. ¹³ I will bring them out from the peoples, gather them from the countries, and bring them to their own soil. I will shepherd them on the mountains of Israel, in the ravines, and in all the inhabited places of the land. ¹⁴ I will tend them in good pasture, and their grazing place will be on Israel's lofty mountains. There they will lie down in a good grazing place; they will feed in rich pasture on the mountains of Israel. ¹⁵ I will tend my flock and let them lie down. This is the declaration of the Lord GOD. ¹⁶ I will seek the lost, bring back the strays, bandage the injured, and strengthen the weak, but I will destroyᴮ the fat and the strong. I will shepherd them with justice.

¹⁷ " 'As for you, my flock, the Lord GOD says this: Look, I am going to judge between one sheep and another, between the rams and goats. ¹⁸ Isn't it enough for you to feed on the good pasture? Must you also trample the rest of the pasture with your feet? Or isn't it enough that you drink the clear water? Must you also muddy the rest with your feet? ¹⁹ Yet my flock has to feed on what your feet have trampled, and drink what your feet have muddied.

²⁰ " 'Therefore, this is what the Lord GOD says to them: See, I myself will judge between the fat sheep and the lean sheep. ²¹ Since you have pushed with flank and shoulder and butted all the weak ones with your horns until you scattered them all over, ²² I will save my flock. They will no longer be prey, and I will judge between one sheep and another. ²³ I will establish over them one shepherd, my servant David, and he will shepherd them. He will tend them himself and will be their shepherd. ²⁴ I, the LORD, will be their God, and my servant David will be a prince among them. I, the LORD, have spoken.

²⁵ " 'I will make a covenant of peace with them and eliminate dangerous creatures from the land, so that they may live securely in the wilderness and sleep in the forest. ²⁶ I will make them and the area around my hill a blessing: I will send down showers in their season; they will be showers of blessing. ²⁷ The trees of the field will yield their fruit, and the land will yield its produce; my flock will be secure in their land. They will know that I am the LORD when I break the bars of their yoke and rescue them from the power of those who enslave them. ²⁸ They will no longer be prey for the nations,

---

and the wild creatures of the earth will not consume them. They will live securely, and no one will frighten them. ²⁹ I will establish for them a place renowned for its agriculture,^ and they will no longer be victims of famine in the land. They will no longer endure the insults of the nations. ³⁰ Then they will know that I, the Lᴏʀᴅ their God, am with them, and that they, the house of Israel, are my people. This is the declaration of the Lord Gᴏᴅ. ³¹ You are my flock, the human flock of my pasture, and I am your God. This is the declaration of the Lord Gᴏᴅ.'"

A PROPHECY AGAINST EDOM

35 The word of the Lᴏʀᴅ came to me: ² "Son of man, face Mount Seir and prophesy against it. ³ Say to it, 'This is what the Lord Gᴏᴅ says:

Look! I am against you, Mount Seir.
I will stretch out my hand against you
and make you a desolate waste.
⁴ I will turn your cities into ruins,
and you will become a desolation.
Then you will know that I am the Lᴏʀᴅ.

⁵ " 'Because you maintained a perpetual hatred and gave the Israelites over to the power of the sword in the time of their disaster, the time of final punishment, ⁶ therefore, as I live — this is the declaration of the Lord Gᴏᴅ — I will destine you for bloodshed, and it will pursue you. Since you did not hate bloodshed, it will pursue you. ⁷ I will make Mount Seir a desolate waste and will cut off from it those who come and go. ⁸ I will fill its mountains with the slain; those slain by the sword will fall on your hills, in your valleys, and in all your ravines. ⁹ I will make you a perpetual desolation; your cities will not be inhabited. Then you will know that I am the Lᴏʀᴅ.

¹⁰ " 'Because you said, "These two nations and two lands will be mine, and we will possess them" — though the Lᴏʀᴅ was there — ¹¹ therefore, as I live — this is the declaration of the Lord Gᴏᴅ — I will treat you according to the anger and jealousy you showed in your hatred of them. I will make myself known among them^B when I judge you. ¹² Then you will know that I, the Lᴏʀᴅ, have heard all the blasphemies you uttered against the mountains of Israel, saying, "They are desolate. They have been given to us to devour!" ¹³ You boasted against me with your mouth, and spoke many words against me. I heard it myself!

¹⁴ " 'This is what the Lord Gᴏᴅ says: While the whole world rejoices, I will make you a desolation. ¹⁵ Just as you rejoiced over the inheritance of the house of Israel because it became a desolation, I will deal the same way with you: you will become a desolation, Mount Seir, and so will all Edom in its entirety. Then they will know that I am the Lᴏʀᴅ.'

RESTORATION OF ISRAEL'S MOUNTAINS

36 "Son of man, prophesy to the mountains of Israel and say, 'Mountains of Israel, hear the word of the Lᴏʀᴅ. ² This is what the Lord Gᴏᴅ says: Because the enemy has said about you, "Aha! The ancient heights have become our possession,"' ³ therefore, prophesy and say: 'This is what

^34:29 LXX, Syr read *a plant of peace*   ^B35:11 LXX reads *you* the Lord God says: Because they have made you desolate and have trampled you from every side, so that you became a possession for the rest of the nations and an object of people's gossip and slander, ⁴ therefore, mountains of Israel, hear the word of the Lord God. This is what the Lord God says to the mountains and hills, to the ravines and valleys, to the desolate ruins and abandoned cities, which have become plunder and a mockery to the rest of the nations all around.

⁵ " 'This is what the Lord God says: Certainly in my burning zeal I speak against the rest of the nations and all of Edom, who took ᴬ my land as their own possession with wholehearted rejoicing and utter contempt so that its pastureland became ᴮ plunder. ⁶ Therefore, prophesy concerning the land of Israel and say to the mountains and hills, to the ravines and valleys: This is what the Lord God says: Look, I speak in my burning zeal because you have endured the insults of the nations. ⁷ Therefore, this is what the Lord God says: I swear ᶜ that the nations all around you will endure their own insults.

⁸ " 'You, mountains of Israel, will produce your branches and bear your fruit for my people Israel, since their arrival is near. ⁹ Look! I am on your side; I will turn toward you, and you will be tilled and sown. ¹⁰ I will fill you with people, with the whole house of Israel in its entirety. The cities will be inhabited and the ruins rebuilt. ¹¹ I will fill you with people and animals, and they will increase and be fruitful. I will make you inhabited as you once were and make you better off than you were before. Then you will know that I am the Lord. ¹² I will cause people, my people Israel, to walk on you; they will possess you, and you will be their inheritance. You will no longer deprive them of their children.

¹³ " 'This is what the Lord God says: Because some are saying to you, "You devour people and deprive your nation of children," ¹⁴ therefore, you will no longer devour people and deprive your nation of children. ᴰ This is the declaration of the Lord God. ¹⁵ I will no longer allow the insults of the nations to be heard against you, and you will not have to endure the reproach of the peoples anymore; you will no longer cause your nation to stumble. ᴱ This is the declaration of the Lord God.' "

RESTORATION OF ISRAEL'S PEOPLE

¹⁶ The word of the Lord came to me: ¹⁷ "Son of man, while the house of Israel lived in their land, they defiled it with their conduct and actions. Their behavior before me was like menstrual impurity. ¹⁸ So I poured out my wrath on them because of the blood they had shed on the land, and because they had defiled it with their idols. ¹⁹ I dispersed them among the nations, and they were scattered among the countries. I judged them according to their conduct and actions. ²⁰ When they came to the nations where they went, they profaned my holy name, because it was said about them, 'These are the people of the Lord, yet they had to leave his land in exile.' ²¹ Then I had concern for my holy name, which the house of Israel profaned among the nations where they went.

ᴬ36:5 Lit gave   ᴮ36:5 Or contempt, to empty it of; Hb obscure   ᶜ36:7 Lit lift up my hand   ᴰ36:14 Alt Hb tradition reads and cause your nation to stumble   ᴱ36:15 Some Hb mss, Tg read no longer bereave your nation of children

REMEMBERING OUR NEWNESS

EZEKIEL 35–36; 2 CORINTHIANS 5:17

Sometimes I'm jealous of those who became believers later in life. I see their passion for the gospel and their understanding of grace that I am only beginning to grasp after twenty years of being a Christ follower. Unlike me, they didn't grow up in Christian circles. They knew the darkness of life without Jesus, and now they walk in the light, deeply grateful and with a firmly rooted belief that they are truly a new creation.

This type of faith reminds me how often I settle for my old way of trying to be good and appear strong, though in truth I am neither. It's easy to forget how the gospel is alive in me, and I am made new.

The prophet Ezekiel speaks often of this newness—a regeneration that only comes from God. He tells the exiled Israelites what God has promised them:

"I will give you a new heart and put a new spirit within you; I will remove your heart of stone and give you a heart of flesh. I will place my Spirit within you and cause you to follow my statutes and carefully observe my ordinances."

EZEKIEL 36:26-27

I love that God doesn't say He'll patch things up with His people. He doesn't offer to put a

Band-Aid over it, wipe the dust off, or ignore the wound. The imagery used here is that of complete renewal. Not a repaired heart, but a new heart.

This theme of transformation continues into the New Testament. It's what Paul is talking about in his letter to the Corinthians when he says, "Therefore, if anyone is in Christ, he is a new creation; the old has passed away, and see, the new has come!" (2Co 5:17).

When we are adopted into God's family, we receive the Holy Spirit, who then transforms our hearts in a way that causes us to want to obey His Word. He changes our desires. **He changes us to our core.**

We may have heard this new creation business many times before, but I think Scripture reminds us of it often—in verses like Galatians 2:20; Philippians 2:13; Hebrews 10:16, to name a few—because our human nature tends to revert to operating as we did before we met Christ. All of us, whether we're lifelong or brand-new believers, need the constant reminder of our newness and the freedom it brings.

How amazing would it be to wake up every day, new to the faith? To rise each morning with fresh eyes to appreciate and be fully aware of our newness in Christ Jesus? I think this is what the Christian life is meant to look like—a daily shedding of the old and breathing in of the new.

May we live a daily response of "yes" to God's invitation of restoration.

²² "Therefore, say to the house of Israel, 'This is what the Lord God says: It is not for your sake that I will act, house of Israel, but for my holy name, which you profaned among the nations where you went. ²³ I will honor the holiness of my great name, which has been profaned among the nations — the name you have profaned among them. The nations will know that I am the Lord — this is the declaration of the Lord God — when I demonstrate my holiness through you in their sight.

²⁴ " 'For I will take you from the nations and gather you from all the countries, and will bring you into your own land. ²⁵ I will also sprinkle clean water on you, and you will be clean. I will cleanse you from all your impurities and all your idols. ²⁶ I will give you a new heart and put a new spirit within you; I will remove your heart of stone^A and give you a heart of flesh. ²⁷ I will place my Spirit within you and cause you to follow my statutes and carefully observe my ordinances. ²⁸ You will live in the land that I gave your fathers; you will be my people, and I will be your God. ²⁹ I will save you from all your uncleanness. I will summon the grain and make it plentiful, and I will not bring famine on you. ³⁰ I will also make the fruit of the trees and the produce of the field plentiful, so that you will no longer experience reproach among the nations on account of famine.

³¹ " 'You will remember your evil ways and your deeds that were not good, and you will loathe yourselves for your iniquities and detestable practices. ³² It is not for your sake that I will act — this is the declaration of the Lord God — let this be known to you. Be ashamed and humiliated because of your ways, house of Israel!

³³ " 'This is what the Lord God says: On the day I cleanse you from all your iniquities, I will cause the cities to be inhabited, and the ruins will be rebuilt. ³⁴ The desolate land will be cultivated instead of lying desolate in the sight of everyone who passes by. ³⁵ They will say, "This land that was desolate has become like the garden of Eden. The cities that were once ruined, desolate, and demolished are now fortified and inhabited." ³⁶ Then the nations that remain around you will know that I, the Lord, have rebuilt what was demolished and have replanted what was desolate. I, the Lord, have spoken and I will do it.

³⁷ " 'This is what the Lord God says: I will respond to the house of Israel and do this for them: I will multiply them in number like a flock.^B ³⁸ So the ruined cities will be filled with a flock of people, just as Jerusalem is filled with a flock of sheep for sacrifice^C during its appointed festivals. Then they will know that I am the Lord.' "

THE VALLEY OF DRY BONES

37 The hand of the Lord was on me, and he brought me out by his Spirit and set me down in the middle of the valley; it was full of bones. ² He led me all around them. There were a great many of them on the surface of the valley, and they were very dry. ³ Then he said to me, "Son of man, can these bones live?"

I replied, "Lord God, only you know."

⁴ He said to me, "Prophesy concerning these bones and say to them: Dry bones, hear the word of the Lord! ⁵ This is what the Lord God says to these

---

^A36:26 Lit stone from your flesh   ^B36:37 Lit flock of people   ^C36:38 Lit as the consecrated flock, as the flock of Jerusalem

bones: I will cause breath to enter you, and you will live. ⁶ I will put tendons on you, make flesh grow on you, and cover you with skin. I will put breath in you so that you come to life. Then you will know that I am the LORD."

⁷ So I prophesied as I had been commanded. While I was prophesying, there was a noise, a rattling sound, and the bones came together, bone to bone. ⁸ As I looked, tendons appeared on them, flesh grew, and skin covered them, but there was no breath in them. ⁹ He said to me, "Prophesy to the breath,ᴬ prophesy, son of man. Say to it: This is what the Lord GOD says: Breath, come from the four winds and breathe into these slain so that they may live!" ¹⁰ So I prophesied as he commanded me; the breath entered them, and they came to life and stood on their feet, a vast army.

¹¹ Then he said to me, "Son of man, these bones are the whole house of Israel. Look how they say, 'Our bones are dried up, and our hope has perished; we are cut off.' ¹² Therefore, prophesy and say to them: 'This is what the Lord GOD says: I am going to open your graves and bring you up from them, my people, and lead you into the land of Israel. ¹³ You will know that I am the LORD, my people, when I open your graves and bring you up from them. ¹⁴ I will put my Spirit in you, and you will live, and I will settle you in your own land. Then you will know that I am the LORD. I have spoken, and I will do it. This is the declaration of the LORD.'"

THE REUNIFICATION OF ISRAEL

¹⁵ The word of the LORD came to me: ¹⁶ "Son of man, take a single stick and write on it: Belonging to Judah and the Israelites associated with him. Then take another stick and write on it: Belonging to Joseph — the stick of Ephraim — and all the house of Israel associated with him. ¹⁷ Then join them together into a single stick so that they become one in your hand. ¹⁸ When your people ask you, 'Won't you explain to us what you mean by these things?' — ¹⁹ tell them, 'This is what the Lord GOD says: I am going to take the stick of Joseph, which is in the hand of Ephraim, and the tribes of Israel associated with him, and put them together with the stick of Judah. I will make them into a single stick so that they become one in my hand.'

²⁰ "When the sticks you have written on are in your hand and in full view of the people, ²¹ tell them, 'This is what the Lord GOD says: I am going to take the Israelites out of the nations where they have gone. I will gather them from all around and bring them into their own land. ²² I will make them one nation in the land, on the mountains of Israel, and one king will rule over all of them. They will no longer be two nations and will no longer be divided into two kingdoms. ²³ They will not defile themselves anymore with their idols, their abhorrent things, and all their transgressions. I will save them from all their apostasies by whichᴮ they sinned, and I will cleanse them. Then they will be my people, and I will be their God. ²⁴ My servant David will be king over them, and there will be one shepherd for all of them. They will follow my ordinances, and keep my statutes and obey them.

²⁵ "They will live in the land that I gave to my servant Jacob, where your fathers lived. They will live in it forever with their children and grandchildren, and my servant David will be their prince forever. ²⁶ I will make a covenant

---

ᴬ37:9 Or wind, or spirit, also in v. 10   ᴮ37:23 Some Hb mss, LXX, Sym; other Hb mss read their settlements where of peace with them; it will be a permanent covenant with them. I will establish and multiply them and will set my sanctuary among them forever. [27] My dwelling place will be with them; I will be their God, and they will be my people. [28] When my sanctuary is among them forever, the nations will know that I, the LORD, sanctify Israel.' "

THE DEFEAT OF GOG

38 The word of the LORD came to me: [2] "Son of man, face Gog, of the land of Magog, the chief prince of[A] Meshech and Tubal. Prophesy against him [3] and say, 'This is what the Lord GOD says: Look, I am against you, Gog, chief prince of Meshech and Tubal. [4] I will turn you around, put hooks in your jaws, and bring you out with all your army, including horses and riders, who are all splendidly dressed, a huge assembly armed with large and small shields, all of them brandishing swords. [5] Persia, Cush, and Put are with them, all of them with shields and helmets; [6] Gomer with all its troops; and Beth-togarmah from the remotest parts of the north along with all its troops — many peoples are with you.

[7] " 'Be prepared and get yourself ready, you and your whole assembly that has been mobilized around you; you will be their guard. [8] After a long time you will be summoned. In the last years you will enter a land that has been restored from war[B] and regathered from many peoples to the mountains of Israel, which had long been a ruin. They were brought out from the peoples, and all of them now live securely. [9] You, all of your troops, and many peoples with you will advance, coming like a thunderstorm; you will be like a cloud covering the land.

[10] " 'This is what the Lord GOD says: On that day, thoughts will arise in your mind, and you will devise an evil plan. [11] You will say, "I will advance against a land of open villages; I will come against a tranquil people who are living securely, all of them living without walls and without bars or gates" — [12] in order to seize spoil and carry off plunder, to turn your hand against ruins now inhabited and against a people gathered from the nations, who have been acquiring cattle and possessions and who live at the center of the world. [13] Sheba and Dedan and the merchants of Tarshish with all its rulers[C] will ask you, "Have you come to seize spoil? Have you mobilized your assembly to carry off plunder, to make off with silver and gold, to take cattle and possessions, to seize plenty of spoil?" '

[14] "Therefore prophesy, son of man, and say to Gog, 'This is what the Lord GOD says: On that day when my people Israel are dwelling securely, will you not know this [15] and come from your place in the remotest parts of the north — you and many peoples with you, who are all riding horses — a huge assembly, a powerful army? [16] You will advance against my people Israel like a cloud covering the land. It will happen in the last days, Gog, that I will bring you against my land so that the nations may know me, when I show myself holy through you in their sight.

[17] " 'This is what the Lord GOD says: Are you the one I spoke about in former times through my servants, the prophets of Israel, who for years prophesied in those times that I would bring you against them? [18] Now on that day, the

---

[A]38:2 Or *the prince of Rosh,*   [B]38:8 Lit *from the sword*   [C]38:13 Lit *young lions,* or *villages* day when Gog comes against the land of Israel — this is the declaration of the Lord GOD — my wrath will flare up.^A 19 I swear in my zeal and fiery rage: On that day there will be a great earthquake in the land of Israel. 20 The fish of the sea, the birds of the sky, the animals of the field, every creature that crawls on the ground, and every human being on the face of the earth will tremble before me. The mountains will be demolished, the cliffs will collapse, and every wall will fall to the ground. 21 I will call for a sword against him on all my mountains — this is the declaration of the Lord GOD — and every man's sword will be against his brother. 22 I will execute judgment on him with plague and bloodshed. I will pour out torrential rain, hailstones, fire, and burning sulfur on him, as well as his troops and the many peoples who are with him. 23 I will display my greatness and holiness, and will reveal myself in the sight of many nations. Then they will know that I am the LORD.'

THE DISPOSAL OF GOG

39 "As for you, son of man, prophesy against Gog and say, 'This is what the Lord GOD says: Look, I am against you, Gog, chief prince of^B Meshech and Tubal. 2 I will turn you around, drive you on, and lead you up from the remotest parts of the north. I will bring you against the mountains of Israel. 3 Then I will knock your bow from your left hand and make your arrows drop from your right hand. 4 You, all your troops, and the peoples who are with you will fall on the mountains of Israel. I will give you as food to every kind of predatory bird and to the wild animals. 5 You will fall on the open field, for I have spoken. This is the declaration of the Lord GOD.

6 " 'I will send fire against Magog and those who live securely on the coasts and islands. Then they will know that I am the LORD. 7 So I will make my holy name known among my people Israel and will no longer allow it to be profaned. Then the nations will know that I am the LORD, the Holy One in Israel. 8 Yes, it is coming, and it will happen. This is the declaration of the Lord GOD. This is the day I have spoken about.

9 " 'Then the inhabitants of Israel's cities will go out, kindle fires, and burn the weapons — the small and large shields, the bows and arrows, the clubs and spears. For seven years they will use them to make fires. 10 They will not gather wood from the countryside or cut it down from the forests, for they will use the weapons to make fires. They will take the loot from those who looted them and plunder those who plundered them. This is the declaration of the Lord GOD.

11 " 'Now on that day I will give Gog a burial place there in Israel — the Travelers' Valley^C east of the Sea. It will block those who travel through, for Gog and all his hordes will be buried there. So it will be called Hordes of Gog^D Valley. 12 The house of Israel will spend seven months burying them in order to cleanse the land. 13 All the people of the land will bury them and their fame will spread on the day I display my glory. This is the declaration of the Lord GOD.

14 " 'They will appoint men on a full-time basis to pass through the land and bury the invaders^E who remain on the surface of the ground, in order to cleanse it. They will make their search at the end of the seven months.

---

^A 38:18 Lit *up in my anger*   ^B 39:1 Or *Gog, prince of Rosh,*   ^C 39:11 Hb obscure
^D 39:11 = Hamon-gog, also in v. 15   ^E 39:14 Or *basis, some to pass through the land, and with them some to bury those*

¹⁵ When they pass through the land and one of them sees a human bone, he will set up a marker next to it until the buriers have buried it in Hordes of Gog Valley. ¹⁶ There will even be a city named Hamonah^A there. So they will cleanse the land.'

¹⁷ "Son of man, this is what the Lord God says: Tell every kind of bird and all the wild animals, 'Assemble and come! Gather from all around to my sacrificial feast that I am slaughtering for you, a great feast on the mountains of Israel; you will eat flesh and drink blood. ¹⁸ You will eat the flesh of mighty men and drink the blood of the earth's princes: rams, lambs, male goats, and all the fattened bulls of Bashan. ¹⁹ You will eat fat until you are satisfied and drink blood until you are drunk, at my sacrificial feast that I have prepared for you. ²⁰ At my table you will eat your fill of horses and riders, of mighty men and all the warriors. This is the declaration of the Lord God.'

ISRAEL'S RESTORATION TO GOD

²¹ "I will display my glory among the nations, and all the nations will see the judgment I have executed and the hand I have laid on them. ²² From that day forward the house of Israel will know that I am the Lord their God. ²³ And the nations will know that the house of Israel went into exile on account of their iniquity, because they dealt unfaithfully with me. Therefore, I hid my face from them and handed them over to their enemies, so that they all fell by the sword. ²⁴ I dealt with them according to their uncleanness and transgressions, and I hid my face from them.

²⁵ "So this is what the Lord God says: Now I will restore the fortunes of Jacob and have compassion on the whole house of Israel, and I will be jealous for my holy name. ²⁶ They will feel remorse for^B,C their disgrace and all the unfaithfulness they committed against me, when they live securely in their land with no one to frighten them. ²⁷ When I bring them back from the peoples and gather them from the countries of their enemies, I will demonstrate my holiness through them in the sight of many nations. ²⁸ They will know that I am the Lord their God when I regather them to their own land after having exiled them among the nations. I will leave none of them behind.^D ²⁹ I will no longer hide my face from them, for I will pour out my Spirit on the house of Israel." This is the declaration of the Lord God.

THE NEW TEMPLE

40 In the twenty-fifth year of our exile, at the beginning of the year, on the tenth day of the month in the fourteenth year after Jerusalem had been captured, on that very day the Lord's hand was on me, and he brought me there. ² In visions of God he took me to the land of Israel and set me down on a very high mountain. On its southern slope was a structure resembling a city. ³ He brought me there, and I saw a man whose appearance was like bronze, with a linen cord and a measuring rod in his hand. He was standing by the city gate. ⁴ He spoke to me: "Son of man, look with your eyes, listen with your ears, and pay attention to everything I am going to show you, for you have been brought here so that I might show it to you. Report everything you see to the house of Israel."

---

^A39:16 In Hb, *Hamonah* is related to the word "horde."   ^B39:26 Some emend to *will forget*   ^C39:26 Lit *will bear*   ^D39:28 Lit *behind there any longer*

THE WALL AND OUTER GATES

[5] Now there was a wall surrounding the outside of the temple. The measuring rod in the man's hand was six units of twenty-one inches;[A] each unit was the standard length plus three inches.[B] He measured the thickness of the wall structure; it was 10 1/2 feet,[C] and its height was the same. [6] Then he came to the gate that faced east and climbed its steps. He measured the threshold of the gate; it was 10 1/2 feet deep — one threshold was 10 1/2 feet deep. [7] Each recess was 10 1/2 feet long and 10 1/2 feet deep, and there was a space of 8 3/4 feet[D] between the recesses. The inner threshold of the gate on the temple side next to the gate's portico was 10 1/2 feet. [8] Next he measured the gate's portico; [9] it[E] was 14 feet,[F] and its jambs were 3 1/2 feet.[G] The gate's portico was on the temple side.

[10] There were three recesses on each side of the east gate, each with the same measurements, and the jambs on either side also had the same measurements. [11] Then he measured the width of the gate's entrance; it was 17 1/2 feet,[H] while the width[I] of the gate was 22 3/4 feet.[J] [12] There was a barrier of 21 inches[K] in front of the recesses on both sides, and the recesses on each side were 10 1/2 feet[L] square. [13] Then he measured the gate from the roof of one recess to the roof of the opposite one; the distance was 43 3/4 feet.[M] The openings of the recesses faced each other. [14] Next, he measured the porch — 105 feet.[N,O] [15] The distance from the front of the gate at the entrance to the front of the gate's portico on the inside was 87 1/2 feet.[P] [16] The recesses and their jambs had beveled windows all around the inside of the gate. The porticoes also had windows all around on the inside. Each jamb was decorated with palm trees.

[17] Then he brought me into the outer court, and there were chambers and a paved surface laid out all around the court. Thirty chambers faced the pavement, [18] which flanked the courtyard's gates and corresponded to the length of the gates; this was the lower pavement. [19] Then he measured the distance from the front of the lower gate to the exterior front of the inner court; it was 175 feet.[Q] This was the east; next the north is described.

[20] He measured the gate of the outer court facing north, both its length and width. [21] Its three recesses on each side, its jambs, and its portico had the same measurements as the first gate: 87 1/2 feet long and 43 3/4 feet wide. [22] Its windows, portico, and palm trees had the same measurements as those of the gate that faced east. Seven steps led up to the gate, and its portico was ahead of them. [23] The inner court had a gate facing the north gate, like the one on the east. He measured the distance from gate to gate; it was 175 feet.

[24] He brought me to the south side, and there was also a gate on the south. He measured its jambs and portico; they had the same measurements as the

others. ²⁵ Both the gate and its portico had windows all around, like the other windows. It was 87 ½ feet long and 43 ¾ feet wide. ²⁶ Its stairway had seven steps, and its portico was ahead of them. It had palm trees on its jambs, one on each side. ²⁷ The inner court had a gate on the south. He measured from gate to gate on the south; it was 175 feet.

THE INNER GATES

²⁸ Then he brought me to the inner court through the south gate. When he measured the south gate, it had the same measurements as the others. ²⁹ Its recesses, jambs, and portico had the same measurements as the others. Both it and its portico had windows all around. It was 87 ½ feet long and 43 ¾ feet wide. ³⁰ (There were porticoes all around, 43 ¾ feet long and 8 ¾ feet wide.^A) ³¹ Its portico faced the outer court, and its jambs were decorated with palm trees. Its stairway had eight steps.

³² Then he brought me to the inner court on the east side. When he measured the gate, it had the same measurements as the others. ³³ Its recesses, jambs, and portico had the same measurements as the others. Both it and its portico had windows all around. It was 87 ½ feet long and 43 ¾ feet wide. ³⁴ Its portico faced the outer court, and its jambs were decorated with palm trees on each side. Its stairway had eight steps.

³⁵ Then he brought me to the north gate. When he measured it, it had the same measurements as the others, ³⁶ as did its recesses, jambs, and portico. It also had windows all around. It was 87 ½ feet long and 43 ¾ feet wide. ³⁷ Its portico^B faced the outer court, and its jambs were decorated with palm trees on each side. Its stairway had eight steps.

ROOMS FOR PREPARING SACRIFICES

³⁸ There was a chamber whose door opened into the gate's portico.^C The burnt offering was to be washed there. ³⁹ Inside the gate's portico there were two tables on each side, on which to slaughter the burnt offering, sin offering, and guilt offering. ⁴⁰ Outside, as one approaches the entrance of the north gate, there were two tables on one side and two more tables on the other side of the gate's portico. ⁴¹ So there were four tables inside the gate and four outside, eight tables in all on which the slaughtering was to be done. ⁴² There were also four tables of cut stone for the burnt offering, each 31 ½ inches^D long, 31 ½ inches wide, and 21 inches high. The utensils used to slaughter the burnt offerings and other sacrifices were placed on them. ⁴³ There were three-inch^E hooks^F fastened all around the inside of the room, and the flesh of the offering was to be laid on the tables.

ROOMS FOR SINGERS AND PRIESTS

⁴⁴ Outside the inner gate, within the inner court, there were chambers for the singers:^G one^H beside the north gate, facing south, and another beside the south^I gate, facing north. ⁴⁵ Then the man said to me: "This chamber that

---

^A 40:30 Some Hb mss, LXX omit v. 30   ^B 40:37 LXX; MT reads *jambs*
^C 40:38 Text emended; MT reads *door was by the jambs, at the gates*
^D 40:42 Lit *one and a half cubits*   ^E 40:43 Lit *one handbreadth*   ^F 40:43 Or
ledges   ^G 40:44 LXX reads *were two chambers*   ^H 40:44 LXX; MT reads *singers,*
which was   ^I 40:44 LXX; MT reads *east*

faces south is for the priests who keep charge of the temple. ⁴⁶ The chamber that faces north is for the priests who keep charge of the altar. These are the sons of Zadok, the ones from the sons of Levi who may approach the LORD to serve him." ⁴⁷ Next he measured the court. It was square, 175 feet long and 175 feet wide. The altar was in front of the temple.

⁴⁸ Then he brought me to the portico of the temple and measured the jambs of the portico; they were 8¾ feet thick on each side. The width of the gate was 24½ feet,ᴬ and the side walls of the gate wereᴮ 5¼ feetᶜ wide on each side. ⁴⁹ The portico was 35 feetᴰ across and 21ᴱ feetᶠ deep, and 10 steps ledᴳ up to it. There were pillars by the jambs, one on each side.

INSIDE THE TEMPLE

41 Next he brought me into the great hall and measured the jambs; on each side the width of the jamb was 10½ feet.ᴴ˒ᴵ ² The width of the entrance was 17½ feet,ᴶ and the side walls of the entrance were 8¾ feetᴷ wide on each side. He also measured the length of the great hall, 70 feet,ᴸ and the width, 35 feet.ᴹ ³ He went inside the next room and measured the jambs at the entrance; they were 3½ feetᴺ wide. The entrance was 10½ feet wide, and the width of the entrance's side walls on each sideᵒ was 12¼ feet.ᴾ ⁴ He then measured the length of the room adjacent to the great hall, 35 feet, and the width, 35 feet. And he said to me, "This is the most holy place."

OUTSIDE THE TEMPLE

⁵ Then he measured the wall of the temple; it was 10½ feet thick. The width of the side rooms all around the temple was 7 feet.ᵠ ⁶ The side rooms were arranged one above another in three stories of thirty rooms each.ᴿ There were ledges on the wall of the temple all around to serve as supports for the side rooms, so that the supports would not be in the temple wall itself. ⁷ The side rooms surrounding the temple widened at each successive story, for the structure surrounding the temple went up by stages. This was the reason for the temple's broadness as it rose. And so, one would go up from the lowest story to the highest by means of the middle one.ˢ

⁸ I saw that the temple had a raised platform surrounding it; this foundation for the side rooms was 10½ feet high.ᵀ ⁹ The thickness of the outer wall of the side rooms was 8¾ feet. The free space between the side rooms of the temple ¹⁰ and the outer chambers was 35 feet wide all around the temple. ¹¹ The side rooms opened into the free space, one entrance toward the north and another to the south. The area of free space was 8¾ feet wide all around.

ᴬ40:48 Lit *14 cubits* ᴮ40:48 LXX; MT omits *24½ feet, and the side walls of the gate were* ᶜ40:48 Lit *three cubits* ᴰ40:49 Lit *20 cubits* ᴱ40:49 LXX; MT reads *19¼* ᶠ40:49 Lit *12 cubits* ᴳ40:49 MT reads *and it was on steps that they would go* ᴴ41:1 LXX; MT reads *jambs; they were 10½ feet wide on each side — the width of the tabernacle* ᴵ41:1 Lit *six cubits*, also in vv. 3,5 ᴶ41:2 Lit *10 cubits* ᴷ41:2 Lit *five cubits*, also in vv. 9,11,12 ᴸ41:2 Lit *40 cubits* ᴹ41:2 Lit *20 cubits*, also in vv. 4,10 ᴺ41:3 Lit *two cubits*, also in v. 22 ᵒ41:3 LXX; MT reads *width of the entrance* ᴾ41:3 Lit *seven cubits* ᵠ41:5 Lit *four cubits* ᴿ41:6 Lit *another three and thirty times* ˢ41:7 Hb obscure ᵀ41:8 Lit *a full rod of six cubits of a joint*; Hb obscure

[12] Now the building that faced the temple yard toward the west was 122 ½ feet[A] wide. The wall of the building was 8 ¾ feet thick on all sides, and the building's length was 157 ½ feet.[B]

[13] Then the man measured the temple; it was 175 feet[C] long. In addition, the temple yard and the building, including its walls, were 175 feet long. [14] The width of the front of the temple along with the temple yard to the east was 175 feet. [15] Next he measured the length of the building facing the temple yard to the west, with its galleries[D] on each side; it was 175 feet.

INTERIOR WOODEN STRUCTURES

The interior of the great hall and the porticoes of the court — [16] the thresholds, the beveled windows, and the balconies all around with their three levels opposite the threshold — were overlaid with wood on all sides. They were paneled from the ground to the windows (but the windows were covered), [17] reaching to the top of the entrance, and as far as the inner temple and on the outside. On every wall all around, on the inside and outside, was a pattern [18] carved with cherubim and palm trees. There was a palm tree between each pair of cherubim. Each cherub had two faces: [19] a human face turned toward the palm tree on one side, and a lion's face turned toward it on the other. They were carved throughout the temple on all sides. [20] Cherubim and palm trees were carved from the ground to the top of the entrance and on the wall of the great hall.

[21] The doorposts of the great hall were square, and the front of the sanctuary had the same appearance. [22] The altar was[E] made of wood, 5 ¼ feet[F] high and 3 ½ feet long.[G] It had corners, and its length[H] and sides were of wood. The man told me, "This is the table that stands before the LORD."

[23] The great hall and the sanctuary each had a double door, [24] and each of the doors had two swinging panels. There were two panels for one door and two for the other. [25] Cherubim and palm trees were carved on the doors of the great hall like those carved on the walls. There was a wooden canopy[I] outside, in front of the portico. [26] There were beveled windows and palm trees on both sides, on the side walls of the portico, the side rooms of the temple, and the canopies.[I]

THE PRIESTS' CHAMBERS

42 Then the man led me out by way of the north gate into the outer court. He brought me to the group of chambers opposite the temple yard and opposite the building to the north. [2] Along the length of the chambers, which was 175 feet,[J] there was an entrance on the north; the width was 87 ½ feet.[K] [3] Opposite the 35 foot space[L] belonging to the inner court and opposite the paved surface belonging to the outer court, the structure rose gallery by gallery in three tiers. [4] In front of the chambers was a walkway toward the inside, 17 ½ feet[M] wide and 175 feet long,[N] and their entrances were on the north. [5] The upper chambers were narrower because the

---

[A]41:12 Lit 70 cubits [B]41:12 Lit 90 cubits [C]41:13 Lit 100 cubits [D]41:15 Or ledges [E]41:21-22 Or and in front of the sanctuary was something that looked like [22]an altar [F]41:22 Lit three cubits [G]41:22 LXX reads long and 3 ½ feet wide [H]41:22 LXX reads base [I]41:25,26 Hb obscure [J]42:2 Lit 100 cubits, also in vv. 4,8 [K]42:2 Lit 50 cubits, also in v. 7 [L]42:3 Lit 20 cubits [M]42:4 Lit 10 cubits [N]42:4 LXX, Syr; MT reads wide, a way of one cubit galleries took away more space from them than from the lower and middle stories of the building. ⁶ For they were arranged in three stories and had no pillars like the pillars of the courts; therefore the upper chambers were set back from the ground more than the lower and middle stories. ⁷ A wall on the outside ran in front of the chambers, parallel to them, toward the outer court; it was 87½ feet long. ⁸ For the chambers on the outer court were 87½ feet long, while those facing the great hall were 175 feet long. ⁹ At the base of these chambers there was an entryway on the east side as one enters them from the outer court.

¹⁰ In the thickness of the wall of the court toward the south,ᴬ there were chambers facing the temple yard and the western building, ¹¹ with a passageway in front of them, just like the chambers that faced north. Their length and width, as well as all their exits, measurements, and entrances, were identical. ¹² The entrance at the beginning of the passageway, the way in front of the correspondingᴮ wall as one enters on the east side, was similar to the entrances of the chambers that were on the south side.

¹³ Then the man said to me, "The northern and southern chambers that face the courtyard are the holy chambers where the priests who approach the Lᴏʀᴅ will eat the most holy offerings. There they will deposit the most holy offerings — the grain offerings, sin offerings, and guilt offerings — for the place is holy. ¹⁴ Once the priests have entered, they are not to go out from the holy area to the outer court until they have removed the clothes they minister in, for these are holy. They are to put on other clothes before they approach the public area."

OUTSIDE DIMENSIONS OF THE TEMPLE COMPLEX

¹⁵ When he finished measuring inside the temple complex, he led me out by way of the gate that faced east and measured all around the complex.

¹⁶ He measured the east side with a measuring rod;
it was 875 feetᶜ by the measuring rod.ᴰ

¹⁷ Heᴱ measured the north side;
it was 875 feet by the measuring rod.

¹⁸ Heᶠ measured the south side;
it was 875 feet by the measuring rod.

¹⁹ Then he turned to the west side
and measured 875 feet by the measuring rod.

²⁰ He measured the temple complex on all four sides. It had a wall all around it, 875 feet long and 875 feet wide, to separate the holy from the common.

RETURN OF THE LORD'S GLORY

43 He led me to the gate, the one that faces east, ² and I saw the glory of the God of Israel coming from the east. His voice sounded like the roar of a huge torrent, and the earth shone with his glory. ³ The vision I saw was like the one I had seen when heᴳ came to destroy the city, and like

---

ᴬ 42:10 LXX; MT reads *east* ᴮ 42:12 Or *protective*; Hb obscure ᶜ 42:16 Lit *500 in rods*, also in vv. 17,18,19 ᴰ 42:16 Lit *rod all around*, also in vv. 17,18,19 ᴱ 42:17 LXX reads *Then he turned to the north and* ᶠ 42:18 LXX reads *Then he turned to the south and* ᴳ 43:3 Some Hb mss, Theod, Vg; other Hb mss, LXX, Syr read *I* the ones I had seen by the Chebar Canal. I fell facedown. ⁴ The glory of the LORD entered the temple by way of the gate that faced east. ⁵ Then the Spirit lifted me up and brought me to the inner court, and the glory of the LORD filled the temple.

⁶ While the man was standing beside me, I heard someone speaking to me from the temple. ⁷ He said to me: "Son of man, this is the place of my throne and the place for the soles of my feet, where I will dwell among the Israelites forever. The house of Israel and their kings will no longer defile my holy name by their religious prostitution and by the corpses ᴬ of their kings at their high places.ᴮ ⁸ Whenever they placed their threshold next to my threshold and their doorposts beside my doorposts, with only a wall between me and them, they were defiling my holy name by the detestable acts they committed. So I destroyed them in my anger. ⁹ Now let them remove their prostitution and the corpses of their kings far from me, and I will dwell among them forever.

¹⁰ "As for you, son of man, describe the temple to the house of Israel, so that they may be ashamed of their iniquities. Let them measure its pattern, ¹¹ and they will be ashamed of all that they have done. Reveal ᶜ the design of the temple to them — its layout with its exits and entrances — its complete design along with all its statutes, design specifications, and laws. Write it down in their sight so that they may observe its complete design and all its statutes and may carry them out. ¹² This is the law of the temple: All its surrounding territory on top of the mountain will be especially holy. Yes, this is the law of the temple.

THE ALTAR

¹³ "These are the measurements of the altar in units of length (each unit being the standard length plus three inches): ᴰ The gutter is 21 inches ᴱ deep and 21 inches wide, with a rim of nine inches ᶠ around its edge. This is the base ᴳ of the altar. ¹⁴ The distance from the gutter on the ground to the lower ledge is 3 ½ feet, ᴴ and the width of the ledge is 21 inches. There are 7 feet ¹ from the small ledge to the large ledge, whose width is also 21 inches. ¹⁵ The altar hearth ᴶ is 7 feet high, and four horns project upward from the hearth. ¹⁶ The hearth is square, 21 feet ᴷ long by 21 feet wide. ¹⁷ The ledge is 24 ½ feet ᴸ long by 24 ½ feet wide, with four equal sides. The rim all around it is 10 ½ inches, ᴹ and its gutter is 21 inches all around it. The altar's steps face east."

¹⁸ Then he said to me: "Son of man, this is what the Lord GOD says: These are the statutes for the altar on the day it is constructed, so that burnt offerings may be sacrificed on it and blood may be splattered on it: ¹⁹ You are to give a bull from the herd as a sin offering to the Levitical priests who are from the offspring of Zadok, who approach me in order to serve me." This is the declaration of the Lord GOD. ²⁰ "You are to take some of its blood and apply it to

---

ᴬ 43:7 Or monuments, also in v. 9   ᴮ 43:7 Some Hb mss, Theod, Tg read their death   ᶜ 43:10-11 LXX, Vg; MT reads pattern. ¹¹And if they are ashamed . . . done, reveal   ᴰ 43:13 Lit in cubits (a cubit being a cubit plus a handbreadth) ᴱ 43:13 Lit one cubit, also in vv. 14,17   ᶠ 43:13 Lit one span   ᴳ 43:13 LXX reads height   ᴴ 43:14 Lit two cubits   ¹ 43:14 Lit four cubits, also in v. 15   ᴶ 43:15 Hb obscure   ᴷ 43:16 Lit 12 cubits   ᴸ 43:17 Lit 14 cubits   ᴹ 43:17 Lit one-half cubit the four horns of the altar, the four corners of the ledge, and all around the rim. In this way you will purify the altar and make atonement for it. ²¹ Then you are to take away the bull for the sin offering, and it must be burned outside the sanctuary in the place appointed for the temple.

²² "On the second day you are to present an unblemished male goat as a sin offering. They will purify the altar just as they did with the bull. ²³ When you have finished the purification, you are to present a young, unblemished bull and an unblemished ram from the flock. ²⁴ You are to present them before the Lord; the priests will throw salt on them and sacrifice them as a burnt offering to the Lord. ²⁵ You will offer a goat for a sin offering each day for seven days. A young bull and a ram from the flock, both unblemished, are also to be offered. ²⁶ For seven days the priests are to make atonement for the altar and cleanse it. In this way they will consecrate it^A ²⁷ and complete the days of purification. Then on the eighth day and afterward, the priests will offer your burnt offerings and fellowship offerings on the altar, and I will accept you." This is the declaration of the Lord God.

THE PRINCE'S PRIVILEGE

44 The man then brought me back toward the sanctuary's outer gate that faced east, and it was closed. ² The Lord said to me: "This gate will remain closed. It will not be opened, and no one will enter through it, because the Lord, the God of Israel, has entered through it. Therefore it will remain closed. ³ The prince himself will sit in the gate to eat a meal before the Lord. He is to enter by way of the portico of the gate and go out the same way."

⁴ Then the man brought me by way of the north gate to the front of the temple. I looked, and the glory of the Lord filled his temple. And I fell facedown. ⁵ The Lord said to me: "Son of man, pay attention; look with your eyes and listen with your ears to everything I tell you about all the statutes and laws of the Lord's temple. Take careful note of the entrance of the temple along with all the exits of the sanctuary.

THE LEVITES' DUTIES AND PRIVILEGES

⁶ "Say to the rebellious people, the house of Israel, 'This is what the Lord God says: I have had enough of all your detestable practices, house of Israel. ⁷ When you brought in foreigners, uncircumcised in both heart and flesh, to occupy my sanctuary, you defiled my temple while you offered my food — the fat and the blood. You^B broke my covenant by all your detestable practices. ⁸ You have not kept charge of my holy things but have appointed others to keep charge of my sanctuary for you.'

⁹ "This is what the Lord God says: No foreigner, uncircumcised in heart and flesh, may enter my sanctuary, not even a foreigner who is among the Israelites. ¹⁰ Surely the Levites who wandered away from me when Israel went astray, and who strayed from me after their idols, will bear the consequences of their iniquity. ¹¹ Yet they will occupy my sanctuary, serving as guards at the temple gates and ministering at the temple. They will slaughter the burnt offerings and other sacrifices for the people and will stand before them to serve them. ¹² Because they ministered to the house

^A 43:26 Lit *will fill its hands*   ^B 44:7 LXX, Syr, Vg; MT reads *They* of Israel before their idols and became a sinful stumbling block to them, therefore I swore an oath[A] against them" — this is the declaration of the Lord God — "that they would bear the consequences of their iniquity. ¹³ They must not approach me to serve me as priests or come near any of my holy things or the most holy things. They will bear their disgrace and the consequences of the detestable acts they committed. ¹⁴ Yet I will make them responsible for the duties of the temple — for all its work and everything done in it.

THE PRIESTS' DUTIES AND PRIVILEGES

¹⁵ "But the Levitical priests descended from Zadok, who kept charge of my sanctuary when the Israelites went astray from me, will approach me to serve me. They will stand before me to offer me fat and blood." This is the declaration of the Lord God. ¹⁶ "They are the ones who may enter my sanctuary and approach my table to serve me. They will keep my mandate. ¹⁷ When they enter the gates of the inner court they are to wear linen garments; they must not have on them anything made of wool when they minister at the gates of the inner court and within it. ¹⁸ They are to wear linen turbans on their heads and linen undergarments around their waists. They are not to put on anything that makes them sweat. ¹⁹ Before they go out to the outer court,[B] to the people, they must take off the clothes they have been ministering in, leave them in the holy chambers, and dress in other clothes so that they do not transmit holiness to the people through their clothes.

²⁰ "They may not shave their heads or let their hair grow long, but are to carefully trim their hair. ²¹ No priest may drink wine before he enters the inner court. ²² He is not to marry a widow or a divorced woman, but may marry only a virgin from the offspring of the house of Israel, or a widow who is the widow of a priest. ²³ They are to teach my people the difference between the holy and the common, and explain to them the difference between the clean and the unclean.

²⁴ "In a dispute, they will officiate as judges and decide the case according to my ordinances. They are to observe my laws and statutes regarding all my appointed festivals, and keep my Sabbaths holy. ²⁵ A priest may not come near a dead person so that he becomes defiled. However, he may defile himself for a father, a mother, a son, a daughter, a brother, or an unmarried sister. ²⁶ After he is cleansed, he is to count off seven days for himself. ²⁷ On the day he goes into the sanctuary, into the inner court to minister in the sanctuary, he is to present his sin offering." This is the declaration of the Lord God.

²⁸ "This will be their inheritance: I am their inheritance. You are to give them no possession in Israel: I am their possession. ²⁹ They will eat the grain offering, the sin offering, and the guilt offering. Everything in Israel that is permanently dedicated to the Lord will belong to them. ³⁰ The best of all the firstfruits of every kind and contribution of every kind from all your gifts will belong to the priests. You are to give your first batch of dough to the priest so that a blessing may rest on your homes. ³¹ The priests may not eat any bird or animal that died naturally or was mauled by wild beasts.

THE SACRED PORTION OF THE LAND

45 "When you divide the land by lot as an inheritance, set aside a donation to the LORD, a holy portion of the land, 8 1/3 miles[A] long and 6 2/3 miles[B] wide. This entire region will be holy. [2] In this area there will be a square section[C] for the sanctuary, 875 by 875 feet,[D] with 87 1/2 feet[E] of open space all around it. [3] From this holy portion,[F] you will measure off an area 8 1/3 miles long and 3 1/3 miles[G] wide, in which the sanctuary, the most holy place, will stand.[H] [4] It will be a holy area of the land to be used by the priests who minister in the sanctuary, who approach to serve the LORD. It will be a place for their houses, as well as a holy area for the sanctuary. [5] There will be another area 8 1/3 miles long and 3 1/3 miles wide for the Levites who minister in the temple; it will be their possession for towns to live in.[I]

[6] "As the property of the city, set aside an area 1 2/3 miles[J] wide and 8 1/3 miles long, adjacent to the holy donation of land. It will be for the whole house of Israel. [7] And the prince will have the area on each side of the holy donation of land and the city's property, adjacent to the holy donation and the city's property, stretching to the west on the west side and to the east on the east side. Its length will correspond to one of the tribal portions from the western boundary to the eastern boundary. [8] This will be his land as a possession in Israel. My princes will no longer oppress my people but give the rest of the land to the house of Israel according to their tribes.

[9] "This is what the Lord GOD says: You have gone too far,[K] princes of Israel! Put away violence and oppression and do what is just and right. Put an end to your evictions of my people." This is the declaration of the Lord GOD. [10] "You are to have honest scales, an honest dry measure,[L] and an honest liquid measure.[M] [11] The dry measure[N] and the liquid measure[O] will be uniform, with the liquid measure containing 5 1/2 gallons[P] and the dry measure holding half a bushel.[P] Their measurement will be a tenth of the standard larger capacity measure.[Q] [12] The shekel[R] will weigh twenty gerahs. Your mina will equal sixty shekels.

THE PEOPLE'S CONTRIBUTION TO THE SACRIFICES

[13] "This is the contribution you are to offer: Three quarts[S] from five bushels[T] of wheat and[U] three quarts from five bushels of barley. [14] The quota of oil in liquid measures[V] will be one percent of every[W] cor. The cor equals ten liquid measures or one standard larger capacity measure,[X] since ten liquid measures equal one standard larger capacity measure. [15] And the quota from the flock is one animal out of every two hundred from the well-watered pastures

---

[A]45:1 Lit 25,000 cubits, also in vv. 3,5,6   [B]45:1 LXX reads 20,000 cubits; MT reads 10,000 cubits   [C]45:2 Lit square all around   [D]45:2 Lit 500 by 500 cubits   [E]45:2 Lit 50 cubits   [F]45:3 Lit this measured portion   [G]45:3 Lit 10,000 cubits, also in v. 5   [H]45:3 Lit be   [I]45:5 LXX; MT, Syr, Tg, Vg read possession — 20 chambers   [J]45:6 Lit 5,000 cubits   [K]45:9 Lit Enough of you   [L]45:10 Lit an honest ephah   [M]45:10 Lit and an honest bath   [N]45:11 Lit The ephah   [O]45:11 Lit the bath   [P]45:11 Lit one-tenth of a homer   [Q]45:11 Lit be based on the homer   [R]45:12 A shekel is about two-fifths of an ounce of silver   [S]45:13 Lit One-sixth of an ephah   [T]45:13 Lit a homer   [U]45:13 LXX, Vg; MT reads and you are to give   [V]45:14 Lit oil, the bath, the oil   [W]45:14 Lit be a tenth of the bath from the   [X]45:14 Lit 10 baths, a homer of Israel. These are for the grain offerings, burnt offerings, and fellowship offerings, to make atonement for the people." This is the declaration of the Lord God. ¹⁶ "All the people of the land must take part in this contribution for the prince in Israel. ¹⁷ Then the burnt offerings, grain offerings, and drink offerings for the festivals, New Moons, and Sabbaths — for all the appointed times of the house of Israel — will be the prince's responsibility. He will provide the sin offerings, grain offerings, burnt offerings, and fellowship offerings to make atonement on behalf of the house of Israel.

¹⁸ "This is what the Lord God says: In the first month, on the first day of the month, you are to take a young, unblemished bull and purify the sanctuary. ¹⁹ The priest is to take some of the blood from the sin offering and apply it to the temple doorposts, the four corners of the altar's ledge, and the doorposts of the gate of the inner court. ²⁰ You are to do the same thing on the seventh day of the month for everyone who sins unintentionally or through ignorance. In this way you will make atonement for the temple.

²¹ "In the first month, on the fourteenth day of the month, you are to celebrate the Passover, a festival of seven days during which unleavened bread will be eaten. ²² On that day the prince will provide a bull as a sin offering on behalf of himself and all the people of the land. ²³ During the seven days of the festival, he will provide seven bulls and seven rams without blemish as a burnt offering to the Lord on each of the seven days, along with a male goat each day for a sin offering. ²⁴ He will also provide a grain offering of half a bushel[A] per bull and half a bushel per ram, along with a gallon[B] of oil for every half bushel. ²⁵ At the festival that begins on the fifteenth day of the seventh month,[C] he will provide the same things for seven days — the same sin offerings, burnt offerings, grain offerings, and oil.

SACRIFICES AT APPOINTED TIMES

46 "This is what the Lord God says: The gate of the inner court that faces east is to be closed during the six days of work, but it will be opened on the Sabbath day and opened on the day of the New Moon. ² The prince should enter from the outside by way of the gate's portico and stand at the gate's doorpost while the priests sacrifice his burnt offerings and fellowship offerings. He will bow in worship at the gate's threshold and then depart, but the gate is not to be closed until evening. ³ The people of the land will also bow in worship before the Lord at the entrance of that gate on the Sabbaths and New Moons.

⁴ "The burnt offering that the prince presents to the Lord on the Sabbath day is to be six unblemished lambs and an unblemished ram. ⁵ The grain offering will be half a bushel[D] with the ram, and the grain offering with the lambs will be whatever he wants to give, as well as a gallon[E] of oil for every half bushel. ⁶ On the day of the New Moon, the burnt offering is to be a young, unblemished bull, as well as six lambs and a ram without blemish. ⁷ He will provide a grain offering of half a bushel with the bull, half a bushel with the ram, and whatever he can afford with the lambs, together with a gallon of oil for every half bushel. ⁸ When the prince enters, he is to go in by way of the gate's portico and go out the same way.

[A] 45:24 Lit an ephah [B] 45:24 Lit a hin [C] 45:25 = the Festival of Shelters
[D] 46:5 Lit an ephah, also in vv. 7,11 [E] 46:5 Lit a hin, also in vv. 7,11

⁹ "When the people of the land come before the LORD at the appointed times, ᴬ whoever enters by way of the north gate to worship is to go out by way of the south gate, and whoever enters by way of the south gate is to go out by way of the north gate. No one may return through the gate by which he entered, but is to go out by the opposite gate. ¹⁰ When the people enter, the prince will enter with them, and when they leave, he will leave. ¹¹ At the festivals and appointed times, the grain offering will be half a bushel with the bull, half a bushel with the ram, and whatever he wants to give with the lambs, along with a gallon of oil for every half bushel.

¹² "When the prince makes a freewill offering, whether a burnt offering or a fellowship offering as a freewill offering to the LORD, the gate that faces east is to be opened for him. He is to offer his burnt offering or fellowship offering just as he does on the Sabbath day. Then he will go out, and the gate is to be closed after he leaves.

¹³ "You are to offer an unblemished year-old male lamb as a daily burnt offering to the LORD; you will offer it every morning. ¹⁴ You are also to prepare a grain offering every morning along with it: three quarts, ᴮ with one-third of a gallon ᶜ of oil to moisten the fine flour — a grain offering to the LORD. This is a permanent statute to be observed regularly. ¹⁵ They will offer the lamb, the grain offering, and the oil every morning as a regular burnt offering.

TRANSFER OF ROYAL LANDS

¹⁶ "This is what the Lord GOD says: If the prince gives a gift to each of his sons as their inheritance, it will belong to his sons. It will become their property by inheritance. ¹⁷ But if he gives a gift from his inheritance to one of his servants, it will belong to that servant until the year of freedom, when it will revert to the prince. His inheritance belongs only to his sons; it is theirs. ¹⁸ The prince must not take any of the people's inheritance, evicting them from their property. He is to provide an inheritance for his sons from his own property, so that none of my people will be displaced from his own property."

THE TEMPLE KITCHENS

¹⁹ Then he brought me through the entrance that was at the side of the gate, into the priests' holy chambers, which faced north. I saw a place there at the far western end. ²⁰ He said to me, "This is the place where the priests will boil the guilt offering and the sin offering, and where they will bake the grain offering, so that they do not bring them into the outer court and transmit holiness to the people." ²¹ Next he brought me into the outer court and led me past its four corners. There was a separate court in each of its corners. ²² In the four corners of the outer court there were enclosed ᴰ courts, 70 feet ᴱ long by 52 ½ feet ᶠ wide. All four corner areas had the same dimensions. ²³ There was a stone wall ᴳ around the inside of them, around the four of them, with ovens built at the base of the walls on all sides. ²⁴ He said to me: "These are the kitchens where those who minister at the temple will cook the people's sacrifices."

ᴬ 46:9 Or the festivals   ᴮ 46:14 Lit one-sixth of an ephah   ᶜ 46:14 Lit one-third of a hin   ᴰ 46:22 Hb obscure   ᴱ 46:22 Lit 40 cubits   ᶠ 46:22 Lit 30 cubits   ᴳ 46:23 Or a row

THE LIFE-GIVING RIVER

47 Then he brought me back to the entrance of the temple and there was water flowing from under the threshold of the temple toward the east, for the temple faced east. The water was coming down from under the south side of the threshold of the temple, south of the altar. ² Next he brought me out by way of the north gate and led me around the outside to the outer gate that faced east; there the water was trickling from the south side. ³ As the man went out east with a measuring line in his hand, he measured off a third of a mile[A] and led me through the water. It came up to my ankles. ⁴ Then he measured off a third of a mile and led me through the water. It came up to my knees. He measured off another third of a mile and led me through the water. It came up to my waist. ⁵ Again he measured off a third of a mile, and it was a river that I could not cross on foot. For the water had risen; it was deep enough to swim in, a river that could not be crossed on foot.

⁶ He asked me, "Do you see this, son of man?" Then he led me back to the bank of the river. ⁷ When I had returned, I saw a very large number of trees along both sides of the riverbank. ⁸ He said to me, "This water flows out to the eastern region and goes down to the Arabah. When it enters the sea, the sea of foul water,[B,C] the water of the sea becomes fresh. ⁹ Every kind of living creature that swarms will live wherever the river flows,[D] and there will be a huge number of fish because this water goes there. Since the water will become fresh, there will be life everywhere the river goes. ¹⁰ Fishermen will stand beside it from En-gedi to En-eglaim.[E] These will become places where nets are spread out to dry. Their fish will consist of many different kinds, like the fish of the Mediterranean Sea. ¹¹ Yet its swamps and marshes will not be healed; they will be left for salt. ¹² All kinds of trees providing food will grow along both banks of the river. Their leaves will not wither, and their fruit will not fail. Each month they will bear fresh fruit because the water comes from the sanctuary. Their fruit will be used for food and their leaves for medicine."

THE BORDERS OF THE LAND

¹³ This is what the Lord God says: "This is[F] the border you will use to divide the land as an inheritance for the twelve tribes of Israel. Joseph will receive two shares. ¹⁴ You will inherit it in equal portions, since I swore[G] to give it to your ancestors. So this land will fall to you as an inheritance.

¹⁵ This is to be the border of the land:

On the north side it will extend from the Mediterranean Sea by way of Hethlon and Lebo-hamath to Zedad, [H] ¹⁶ Berothah, and Sibraim (which is between the border of Damascus and the border of Hamath), as far as Hazer-hatticon, which is on the border of Hauran. ¹⁷ So the border will run from the sea to Hazar-enon at the border of Damascus, with the territory of Hamath to the north. This will be the northern side.

[A]47:3 Lit *1,000 cubits*, also in vv. 4,5   [B]47:8 Or *enters the sea, being brought out to the sea*; Hb obscure   [C]47:8 = the Dead Sea   [D]47:9 LXX, Vg; MT reads *the two rivers flow*   [E]47:10 Two springs near the Dead Sea   [F]47:13 Tg, Vg; Syr reads *The valley of*   [G]47:14 Lit *lifted my hand*   [H]47:15 LXX; MT reads *and Lebo to Zedad, Hamath*; Ezk 48:1

¹⁸ On the east side it will run between Hauran and Damascus, along the Jordan between Gilead and the land of Israel; you will measure from the northern border to the eastern sea.[A] This will be the eastern side.

¹⁹ On the south side it will run from Tamar to the Waters of Meribath-kadesh,[B] and on to the Brook of Egypt as far as the Mediterranean Sea. This will be the southern side.

²⁰ On the west side the Mediterranean Sea will be the border, from the southern border up to a point opposite Lebo-hamath. This will be the western side.

²¹ "You are to divide this land among yourselves according to the tribes of Israel. ²² You will allot it as an inheritance for yourselves and for the aliens residing among you, who have fathered children among you. You will treat them[C] like native-born Israelites; along with you, they will be allotted an inheritance among the tribes of Israel. ²³ In whatever tribe the alien resides, you will assign his inheritance there." This is the declaration of the Lord God.

THE TRIBAL ALLOTMENTS

48 "Now these are the names of the tribes: From the northern end, along the road of Hethlon, to Lebo-hamath as far as Hazar-enon, at the northern border of Damascus, alongside Hamath and extending from the eastern side to the sea, will be Dan — one portion.

² Next to the territory of Dan, from the east side to the west, will be Asher — one portion.

³ Next to the territory of Asher, from the east side to the west, will be Naphtali — one portion.

⁴ Next to the territory of Naphtali, from the east side to the west, will be Manasseh — one portion.

⁵ Next to the territory of Manasseh, from the east side to the west, will be Ephraim — one portion.

⁶ Next to the territory of Ephraim, from the east side to the west, will be Reuben — one portion.

⁷ Next to the territory of Reuben, from the east side to the west, will be Judah — one portion.

⁸ "Next to the territory of Judah, from the east side to the west, will be the portion you donate to the Lord, 8 ⅓ miles[D] wide, and as long as one of the tribal portions from the east side to the west. The sanctuary will be in the middle of it.

⁹ "The special portion you donate to the Lord will be 8 ⅓ miles long and 3 ⅓ miles[E] wide. ¹⁰ This holy donation will be set apart for the priests alone. It will be 8 ⅓ miles long on the northern side, 3 ⅓ miles wide on the western

---

A47:18 = the Dead Sea   B47:19 = Kadesh-barnea   C47:22 Lit *They will be to you*
D48:8 Lit *25,000 cubits*, also in vv. 9,10,13,15,20,21   E48:9 Lit *10,000 cubits*, also in vv. 10,13,18

side, 3 ⅓ miles wide on the eastern side, and 8 ⅓ miles long on the southern side. The LORD's sanctuary will be in the middle of it. ¹¹ It is for the consecrated priests, the sons of Zadok, who kept my charge and did not go astray as the Levites did when the Israelites went astray. ¹² It will be a special donation for them out of the holy donation of the land, a most holy place adjacent to the territory of the Levites.

¹³ "Next to the territory of the priests, the Levites will have an area 8 ⅓ miles long and 3 ⅓ miles wide. The total length will be 8 ⅓ miles and the width 3 ⅓ miles. ¹⁴ They must not sell or exchange any of it, and they must not transfer this choice part of the land, for it is holy to the LORD.

¹⁵ "The remaining area, 1 ⅔ miles ᴬ wide and 8 ⅓ miles long, will be for common use by the city, for both residential and open space. The city will be in the middle of it. ¹⁶ These are the city's measurements:

1 ½ miles ᴮ on the north side;
1 ½ miles on the south side;
1 ½ miles on the east side;
and 1 ½ miles on the west side.
¹⁷ The city's open space will extend:
425 feet ᶜ to the north,
425 feet to the south,
425 feet to the east,
and 425 feet to the west.

¹⁸ "The remainder of the length alongside the holy donation will be 3 ⅓ miles to the east and 3 ⅓ miles to the west. It will run alongside the holy donation. Its produce will be food for the workers of the city. ¹⁹ The city's workers from all the tribes of Israel will cultivate it. ²⁰ The entire donation will be 8 ⅓ miles by 8 ⅓ miles; you are to set apart the holy donation along with the city property as a square area.

²¹ "The remaining area on both sides of the holy donation and the city property will belong to the prince. He will own the land adjacent to the tribal portions, next to the 8 ⅓ miles of the donation as far as the eastern border and ᴰ next to the 8 ⅓ miles of the donation as far as the western border. The holy donation and the sanctuary of the temple will be in the middle of it. ²² Except for the Levitical property and the city property in the middle of the area belonging to the prince, the area between the territory of Judah and that of Benjamin will belong to the prince.

²³ "As for the rest of the tribes:
From the east side to the west, will be Benjamin — one portion.
²⁴ Next to the territory of Benjamin, from the east side to the west, will be Simeon — one portion.
²⁵ Next to the territory of Simeon, from the east side to the west, will be Issachar — one portion.
²⁶ Next to the territory of Issachar, from the east side to the west, will be Zebulun — one portion.
²⁷ Next to the territory of Zebulun, from the east side to the west, will be Gad — one portion.

ᴬ48:15 Lit 5,000 cubits   ᴮ48:16 Lit 4,500 cubits, also in vv. 30,32,33,34
ᶜ48:17 Lit 250 cubits   ᴰ48:21 Lit border, and to the west,

1431

²⁸ Next to the territory of Gad toward the south side, the border will run from Tamar to the Waters of Meribath-kadesh, to the Brook of Egypt, and out to the Mediterranean Sea. ²⁹ This is the land you are to allot as an inheritance to Israel's tribes, and these will be their portions." This is the declaration of the Lord God.

THE NEW CITY

³⁰ "These are the exits of the city:

On the north side, which measures 1 ½ miles, ³¹ there will be three gates facing north, the gates of the city being named for the tribes of Israel: one, the gate of Reuben; one, the gate of Judah; and one, the gate of Levi. ³² On the east side, which is 1 ½ miles, there will be three gates: one, the gate of Joseph; one, the gate of Benjamin; and one, the gate of Dan. ³³ On the south side, which measures 1 ½ miles, there will be three gates: one, the gate of Simeon; one, the gate of Issachar; and one, the gate of Zebulun.

³⁴ On the west side, which is 1 ½ miles, there will be three gates: one, the gate of Gad; one, the gate of Asher; and one, the gate of Naphtali.

³⁵ The perimeter of the city will be six miles,ᴬ and the name of the city from that day on will be, The Lord Is There."

ᴬ48:35 Lit *18,000 cubits*

daniel

 For his dominion is an everlasting dominion, and his kingdom is from generation to generation. **4:34**

ON THE TIMELINE The events in the book of Daniel take place between 605 BC and 535 BC, during the time of the nation of Judah's Babylonian captivity. The book opens after King Nebuchadnezzar's first siege of Judah in 605 BC, when he brought Daniel—along with other captives from the Judean nobility—to Babylon. Nebuchadnezzar's assault of Judah continued in 597 BC and 586 BC, and each time the number of his prisoners grew. Daniel's ministry began when he arrived in Babylon with those first captives, it extended throughout the Babylonian captivity, and concluded after the third year of Cyrus the Great, the Medo-Persian king who overthrew Babylon in 538 BC (Dn 1:21; 10:1).

A LITTLE BACKGROUND Tradition maintains that the prophet Daniel wrote this book sometime shortly after the end of the Babylonian captivity. The book contains retellings of events in his life as well as supernatural predictions of events that took place during the intertestamental period. Daniel is written to the Jewish exiles in Babylon to remind them of God's sovereignty and to encourage them to remain faithful to God even amid their difficult circumstances.

MESSAGE & PURPOSE The theme of the book of Daniel is the hope of the people of God during "the times of the Gentiles," a phrase used by Jesus to refer to the time between the Babylonian captivity and Jesus' return (Lk 21:24). Though it was a lengthy time when God's people lived under ungodly rule, the book of Daniel offers hope in its teaching that, at all times, "the Most High God is ruler over human kingdoms" (Dn 5:21). To encourage Israel's faithfulness to its sovereign God, Daniel recounted examples of godly trust and delivered prophecies of God's ultimate victory.

GIVE THANKS FOR THE BOOK OF DANIEL

Above all, Daniel teaches that the God of Israel is the Sovereign God of the universe, "for his dominion is an everlasting dominion, and his kingdom is from generation to generation" (Dn 4:34). Even when wicked empires have extensive reign, the prophet's words remind us that only the Lord has dominion over all the kingdoms of the earth.

THE BOOK OF DANIEL IN HISTORY

daniel

600 BC

575 BC

605

602

597

586

573

566

Temple
and walls
of Jerusalem
destroyed

Second Babylonian
invasion of Judah

573-566 BC
Nebuchadnezzar's
7 years of insanity

Nebuchadnezzar's
dream of a statue

605-562 BC
Nebuchadnezzar is
king of Babylon

First Babylonian invasion
of Judah — Daniel and
other princes taken into
captivity in Babylon

Daniel's ministry begins

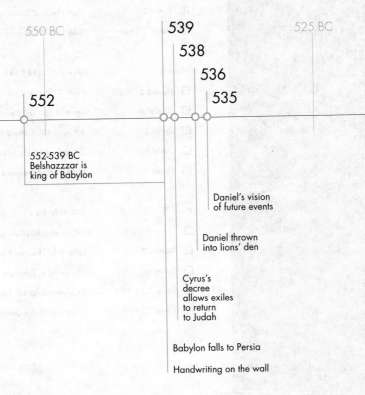

550 BC   539

538

536

525 BC

552

535

552-539 BC
Belshazzzar is
king of Babylon

Daniel's vision
of future events

Daniel thrown
into lions' den

Cyrus's
decree
allows exiles
to return
to Judah

Babylon falls to Persia

Handwriting on the wall

READ AND UNDERSTAND DANIEL

The Bible is a complete work in which many stories combine to tell one story. As you read the book of Daniel, consider reading the additional passages to discover how the whole of Scripture works together.

Week 1	GOING DEEPER
☐ **Daniel 1:1-7**	Psalm 137:1-6; 1 Peter 2:11-12
☐ Daniel 1:8-16	Proverbs 21:2-3; 1 Peter 2:15-16
☐ Daniel 1:17-21	1 Samuel 12:24; James 1:5
☐ Daniel 2:1-24	Psalm 145:1-2; Isaiah 44:6-8
☐ Daniel 2:25-49	Luke 12:11-12; Colossians 3:23

Week 2	GOING DEEPER
☐ **Daniel 3**	Psalm 27; Isaiah 43:2
☐ **Daniel 4**	Proverbs 16:18; 1 Corinthians 1:28
☐ Daniel 5	1 Peter 5:4-7; 1 John 2:15-17
☐ Daniel 6	2 Timothy 3:12-15; 1 Peter 5:8-9
☐ Daniel 7:1-14	Psalm 104:1-5; Hebrews 12:28-29

Week 3	GOING DEEPER
☐ Daniel 7:15-28	Philippians 4:6-7; Colossians 1:15-20
☐ **Daniel 8**	Isaiah 6:1-7; Romans 8:31-39
☐ Daniel 9	1 Kings 9:6-9; Ephesians 2:1-5
☐ Daniel 10:1–12:4	2 Corinthians 10:3-5; Ephesians 6:12
☐ Daniel 12:4-13	2 Peter 3:8-13; Revelation 1:4-8

DANIEL'S CAPTIVITY IN BABYLON

1 In the third year of the reign of King Jehoiakim of Judah, King Nebuchadnezzar^A of Babylon came to Jerusalem and laid siege to it. ² The Lord handed King Jehoiakim of Judah over to him, along with some of the vessels from the house of God. Nebuchadnezzar carried them to the land of Babylon, ᴮ to the house of his god, ᶜ and put the vessels in the treasury of his god.

³ The king ordered Ashpenaz, his chief eunuch, ᴰ to bring some of the Israelites from the royal family and from the nobility — ⁴ young men without any physical defect, good-looking, suitable for instruction in all wisdom, knowledgeable, perceptive, and capable of serving in the king's palace. He was to teach them the Chaldean language and literature. ⁵ The king assigned them daily provisions from the royal food and from the wine that he drank. They were to be trained for three years, and at the end of that time they were to attend the king. ᴱ ⁶ Among them, from the Judahites, were Daniel, Hananiah, Mishael, and Azariah. ⁷ The chief eunuch gave them names; he gave the name Belteshazzar to Daniel, Shadrach to Hananiah, Meshach to Mishael, and Abednego to Azariah.

FAITHFULNESS IN BABYLON

⁸ Daniel determined that he would not defile himself with the king's food or with the wine he drank. So he asked permission from the chief eunuch not to defile himself. ⁹ God had granted Daniel kindness and compassion from the chief eunuch, ¹⁰ yet he said to Daniel, "I fear my lord the king, who assigned your food and drink. What if he sees your faces looking thinner than the other young men your age? You would endanger my life ᶠ with the king."

¹¹ So Daniel said to the guard whom the chief eunuch had assigned to Daniel, Hananiah, Mishael, and Azariah, ¹² "Please test your servants for ten days. Let us be given vegetables to eat and water to drink. ¹³ Then examine our appearance and the appearance of the young men who are eating the king's food, and deal with your servants based on what you see." ¹⁴ He agreed with them about this and tested them for ten days. ¹⁵ At the end of ten days they looked better and healthier ᴳ than all the young men who were eating the king's food. ¹⁶ So the guard continued to remove their food and the wine they were to drink and gave them vegetables.

FAITHFULNESS REWARDED

¹⁷ God gave these four young men knowledge and understanding in every kind of literature and wisdom. Daniel also understood visions and dreams of every kind. ¹⁸ At the end of the time that the king had said to present them, the chief eunuch presented them to Nebuchadnezzar. ¹⁹ The king interviewed them, and among all of them, no one was found equal to Daniel, Hananiah, Mishael, and Azariah. So they began to attend the king. ²⁰ In every matter of wisdom and understanding that the king consulted them about, he found them ten times ᴴ better than all the magicians and mediums in his entire kingdom. ²¹ Daniel remained there until the first year of King Cyrus.

---

^A 1:1 Or Nebuchadrezzar   ᴮ 1:2 Lit *Shinar*   ᶜ 1:2 Or *gods*   ᴰ 1:3 Or *his eunuchs*
ᴱ 1:5 Lit *to stand before the king*   ᶠ 1:10 Lit *would make my head guilty*   ᴳ 1:15 Lit
fatter of flesh   ᴴ 1:20 Lit *hands*

IDENTITY CRISIS

DANIEL 1:1-7; PSALM 137:1-6; PHILIPPIANS 3:20; 1 PETER 2:11-12

I've been known by many names in my life.

My sister still calls me "little one," and I'll always be "baby girl" to my mom. When we get together with extended family, a collective cheer of "Cha-chers!" always greets me. Names matter. Even the silly ones are heavy with meaning and memories.

In the culture of the ancient Near East, a name was actually an indicator of a person's character. Abram and Sarai became Abraham and Sarah after the Lord promised they would be the patriarch and matriarch of many nations (Gn 17:5,15). Jacob's name was changed to Israel (Gn 32:28). Angels appeared in dreams to name Isaac (Gn 17:19), John the Baptist (Lk 1:13), and Jesus (Lk 1:31).

Names are a big deal. And changing names is an even bigger deal—particularly for four "good-looking" Jews plucked out of Jerusalem to serve in the king's court.

Each of the four Jewish exiles were given names by their fathers. The meaning of each name acknowledged the one, true God. But, as a part of their acculturation—in order to make them forget the God of their fathers—the chief official gave them new names with meanings in direct opposition to their upbringing, favoring instead the idolatry of false gods (Dn 1:7).

Daniel (*God Is My Judge*) became
Belteshazzar (*Bel Protect Him*).
Hananiah (*God Has Been Gracious*) became
Shadrach (*The Command of Akku*).

Mishael (*Who Is What God Is?*) became
Meshach (*Who Is What Aku Is?*).
Azariah (*The Lord Has Helped*) became
Abednego (*Servant of Nebo*).

As temporary residents of a foreign land, Daniel, Hananiah, Mishael, and Azariah involuntarily found themselves in a true identity crisis—how can we serve God and Babylon? Is that even possible?

King Nebuchadnezzar did everything he could to "take the Jerusalem out of the Jews," but as we'll see in upcoming chapters, it would go nothing like he'd hoped. These faithful men would remain steadfast in the midst of a cultural cesspool of idolatry.

Like the four Jewish exiles with new names but an unshakable loyalty to their God, Peter encourages us also as "strangers and exiles to abstain from sinful desires" that war against us (1Pt 2:11).

Friends, the world will try to rename you your entire life. You'll call yourself "Christian," and the world will call you a square. God calls you "brand new," and the world will try to tell you you're stuck where you are. God writes "redeemed" across your forehead, and the broken world will try six days from Sunday to make you forget it. But you know, because God's Word tells you, that your "citizenship is in heaven" (Php 3:20).

Let the One who made you also name you, and let that be the only name you'll ever need.

1440

NEBUCHADNEZZAR'S DREAM

2 In the second year of his reign, Nebuchadnezzar had dreams that troubled him, and sleep deserted him. [2] So the king gave orders to summon the magicians, mediums, sorcerers, and Chaldeans[A] to tell the king his dreams. When they came and stood before the king, [3] he said to them, "I have had a dream and am anxious to understand it."

[4] The Chaldeans spoke to the king (Aramaic[B] begins here): "May the king live forever. Tell your servants the dream, and we will give the interpretation."

[5] The king replied to the Chaldeans, "My word is final: If you don't tell me the dream and its interpretation, you will be torn limb from limb,[C] and your houses will be made a garbage dump. [6] But if you make the dream and its interpretation known to me, you'll receive gifts, a reward, and great honor from me. So make the dream and its interpretation known to me."

[7] They answered a second time, "May the king tell the dream to his servants, and we will make known the interpretation."

[8] The king replied, "I know for certain you are trying to gain some time, because you see that my word is final. [9] If you don't tell me the dream, there is one decree for you. You have conspired to tell me something false or fraudulent until the situation changes. So tell me the dream and I will know you can give me its interpretation."

[10] The Chaldeans answered the king, "No one on earth can make known what the king requests. Consequently, no king, however great and powerful, has ever asked anything like this of any magician, medium, or Chaldean. [11] What the king is asking is so difficult that no one can make it known to him except the gods, whose dwelling is not with mortals." [12] Because of this, the king became violently angry and gave orders to destroy all the wise men of Babylon. [13] The decree was issued that the wise men were to be executed, and they searched for Daniel and his friends, to execute them.

[14] Then Daniel responded with tact and discretion to Arioch, the captain of the king's guard,[D] who had gone out to execute the wise men of Babylon. [15] He asked Arioch, the king's officer, "Why is the decree from the king so harsh?"[E] Then Arioch explained the situation to Daniel. [16] So Daniel went and asked the king to give him some time, so that he could give the king the interpretation.

[17] Then Daniel went to his house and told his friends Hananiah, Mishael, and Azariah about the matter, [18] urging them to ask the God of the heavens for mercy concerning this mystery, so Daniel and his friends would not be destroyed with the rest of Babylon's wise men. [19] The mystery was then revealed to Daniel in a vision at night, and Daniel praised the God of the heavens [20] and declared:

> May the name of God
> be praised forever and ever,
> for wisdom and power belong to him.
> [21] He changes the times and seasons;
> he removes kings and establishes kings.
> He gives wisdom to the wise

[A] 2:2 In this chap. Chaldeans are influential Babylonian wise men.
[B] 2:4 Dn 2:4–7:28 is written in Aramaic. [C] 2:5 Lit *be made into limbs*
[D] 2:14 Or *executioners* [E] 2:15 Or *urgent*

and knowledge to those
who have understanding.
²² He reveals the deep and hidden things;
he knows what is in the darkness,
and light dwells with him.
²³ I offer thanks and praise to you,
God of my fathers,
because you have given me
wisdom and power.
And now you have let me know
what we asked of you,
for you have let us know
the king's mystery.^A

²⁴ Therefore Daniel went to Arioch, whom the king had assigned to destroy the wise men of Babylon. He came and said to him, "Don't destroy the wise men of Babylon! Bring me before the king, and I will give him the interpretation."

²⁵ Then Arioch quickly brought Daniel before the king and said to him, "I have found a man among the Judean exiles who can let the king know the interpretation."

²⁶ The king said in reply to Daniel, whose name was Belteshazzar, "Are you able to tell me the dream I had and its interpretation?"

²⁷ Daniel answered the king: "No wise man, medium, magician, or diviner is able to make known to the king the mystery he asked about. ²⁸ But there is a God in heaven who reveals mysteries, and he has let King Nebuchadnezzar know what will happen in the last days. Your dream and the visions that came into your mind as you lay in bed were these: ²⁹ Your Majesty, while you were in your bed, thoughts came to your mind about what will happen in the future.^B The revealer of mysteries has let you know what will happen. ³⁰ As for me, this mystery has been revealed to me, not because I have more wisdom than anyone living, but in order that the interpretation might be made known to the king, and that you may understand the thoughts of your mind.

THE DREAM'S INTERPRETATION

³¹ "Your Majesty, as you were watching, suddenly a colossal statue appeared. That statue, tall and dazzling, was standing in front of you, and its appearance was terrifying. ³² The head of the statue was pure gold, its chest and arms were silver, its stomach and thighs were bronze, ³³ its legs were iron, and its feet were partly iron and partly fired clay. ³⁴ As you were watching, a stone broke off without a hand touching it,^C struck the statue on its feet of iron and fired clay, and crushed them. ³⁵ Then the iron, the fired clay, the bronze, the silver, and the gold were shattered and became like chaff from the summer threshing floors. The wind carried them away, and not a trace of them could be found. But the stone that struck the statue became a great mountain and filled the whole earth.

---

^A 2:23 Lit matter   ^B 2:29 Lit happen after this, also in v. 45   ^C 2:34 Lit off not by hands

³⁶ "This was the dream; now we will tell the king its interpretation. ³⁷ Your Majesty, you are king of kings. The God of the heavens has given you sovereignty, power, strength, and glory. ³⁸ Wherever people live — or wild animals, or birds of the sky — he has handed them over to you and made you ruler over them all. You are the head of gold.

³⁹ "After you, there will arise another kingdom, inferior to yours, and then another, a third kingdom, of bronze, which will rule the whole earth. ⁴⁰ A fourth kingdom will be as strong as iron; for iron crushes and shatters everything, and like iron that smashes, it will crush and smash all the others.^A ⁴¹ You saw the feet and toes, partly of a potter's fired clay and partly of iron — it will be a divided kingdom, though some of the strength of iron will be in it. You saw the iron mixed with clay, ⁴² and that the toes of the feet were partly iron and partly fired clay — part of the kingdom will be strong, and part will be brittle. ⁴³ You saw the iron mixed with clay — the peoples will mix with one another^B but will not hold together, just as iron does not mix with fired clay.

⁴⁴ "In the days of those kings, the God of the heavens will set up a kingdom that will never be destroyed, and this kingdom will not be left to another people. It will crush all these kingdoms and bring them to an end, but will itself endure forever. ⁴⁵ You saw a stone break off from the mountain without a hand touching it,^C and it crushed the iron, bronze, fired clay, silver, and gold. The great God has told the king what will happen in the future. The dream is certain, and its interpretation reliable."

NEBUCHADNEZZAR'S RESPONSE

⁴⁶ Then King Nebuchadnezzar fell facedown, worshiped Daniel, and gave orders to present an offering and incense to him. ⁴⁷ The king said to Daniel, "Your God is indeed God of gods, Lord of kings, and a revealer of mysteries, since you were able to reveal this mystery." ⁴⁸ Then the king promoted Daniel and gave him many generous gifts. He made him ruler over the entire province of Babylon and chief governor over all the wise men of Babylon. ⁴⁹ At Daniel's request, the king appointed Shadrach, Meshach, and Abednego to manage the province of Babylon. But Daniel remained at the king's court.

NEBUCHADNEZZAR'S GOLD STATUE

3 King Nebuchadnezzar made a gold statue, ninety feet high and nine feet wide.^D He set it up on the plain of Dura in the province of Babylon. ² King Nebuchadnezzar sent word to assemble the satraps, prefects, governors, advisers, treasurers, judges, magistrates, and all the rulers of the provinces to attend the dedication of the statue King Nebuchadnezzar had set up. ³ So the satraps, prefects, governors, advisers, treasurers, judges, magistrates, and all the rulers of the provinces assembled for the dedication of the statue the king had set up. Then they stood before the statue Nebuchadnezzar had set up.

⁴ A herald loudly proclaimed, "People of every nation and language, you are commanded: ⁵ When you hear the sound of the horn, flute, zither,^E lyre,^F harp, drum,^G and every kind of music, you are to fall facedown and worship the

---

^A 2:40 Lit all these   ^B 2:43 Lit another in the seed of men   ^C 2:45 Lit mountain, not by hands   ^D 3:1 Lit statue, its height sixty cubits, its width six cubits   ^E 3:5 Or lyre   ^F 3:5 Or sambuke   ^G 3:5 Or pipe

BUT IF NOT, HE IS STILL GOOD

DANIEL 3; PSALM 27; ISAIAH 43:2

It was 1940, and the German Wehrmacht had the British Expeditionary and French forces surrounded at Dunkirk, on the northern coast of France. The British Navy couldn't rescue them, and they couldn't fight their way out. It looked like no one was going to survive.

The British and French would be safe if they could get across the English Channel and out of France. But an evacuation was impossible. A British officer sent a three-word telegram to the war offices in London:

"But if not . . ."

This powerful phrase communicated to the people at home the true straits of the men stranded at Dunkirk (Winston Churchill, *Their Finest Hour*).

Shadrach, Meshach, and Abednego expressed the same sentiment in response to their sentence to be thrown into the fiery furnace.

"If the God we serve exists, then he can rescue us from the furnace of blazing fire, and he can rescue us from the power of you, the king. But even if he does not rescue us, we want you as king to know that we will not serve your gods or worship the gold statue you set up" (Dn 3:17-18).

Translation: the situation looks hopeless, and we pray God will save us. But even if He doesn't, we will still be faithful.

In case you're still holding your breath about those stranded soldiers, exhale. Under the cover of fog and night, in small fishing boats, pleasure cruisers, and all manner of small watercraft,

piloted by the good people who lived on that coast, 338,000 men were saved.

The story of Shadrach, Meshach, and Abednego has a happy ending too. And their words still have the power to teach us. They knew they served a God greater than kings and armies.

Though the powers of this world threaten us, taunting, "who is the god who can rescue you from my power?" (Dn 3:15), we serve the God who can save.

God doesn't promise to save us from the flames. But He has promised to be with us as we walk through the fire—and to either rescue us in this life, or through death for our eternal salvation (Is 43).

That's comforting and scary, right? Those brave words spoken by brave men sound amazing, but I'm a little nervous when it comes to getting my own hair singed.

Lord, give us confidence in your words. Forge courage for us in the midst of a hostile world. Steel our nerves for long, hard days of quiet faithfulness. Resolve our hearts to follow you in momentous decisions and small choices. Build in us a brave resistance to evil.

Then, when the day of testing comes, we can bravely go into the fire and know that whether we live or die, we serve a God like no other—a God who is able to save.

But even if He does not, we will serve Him still.

gold statue that King Nebuchadnezzar has set up. ⁶ But whoever does not fall down and worship will immediately be thrown into a furnace of blazing fire."

⁷ Therefore, when all the people heard the sound of the horn, flute, zither, lyre, harp, and every kind of music, people of every nation and language fell down and worshiped the gold statue that King Nebuchadnezzar had set up.

THE FURNACE OF BLAZING FIRE

⁸ Some Chaldeans took this occasion to come forward and maliciously accuse^A the Jews. ⁹ They said to King Nebuchadnezzar, "May the king live forever. ¹⁰ You as king have issued a decree that everyone who hears the sound of the horn, flute, zither, lyre, harp, drum, and every kind of music must fall down and worship the gold statue. ¹¹ Whoever does not fall down and worship will be thrown into a furnace of blazing fire. ¹² There are some Jews you have appointed to manage the province of Babylon: Shadrach, Meshach, and Abednego. These men have ignored you, the king; they do not serve your gods or worship the gold statue you have set up."

¹³ Then in a furious rage Nebuchadnezzar gave orders to bring in Shadrach, Meshach, and Abednego. So these men were brought before the king. ¹⁴ Nebuchadnezzar asked them, "Shadrach, Meshach, and Abednego, is it true that you don't serve my gods or worship the gold statue I have set up? ¹⁵ Now if you're ready, when you hear the sound of the horn, flute, zither, lyre, harp, drum, and every kind of music, fall down and worship the statue I made. But if you don't worship it, you will immediately be thrown into a furnace of blazing fire — and who is the god who can rescue you from my power? "

¹⁶ Shadrach, Meshach, and Abednego replied to the king, "Nebuchadnezzar, we don't need to give you an answer to this question. ¹⁷ If the God we serve exists, then he can rescue us from the furnace of blazing fire, and he can^B rescue us from the power of you, the king. ¹⁸ But even if he does not rescue us,^C we want you as king to know that we will not serve your gods or worship the gold statue you set up."

¹⁹ Then Nebuchadnezzar was filled with rage, and the expression on his face changed toward Shadrach, Meshach, and Abednego. He gave orders to heat the furnace seven times more than was customary, ²⁰ and he commanded some of the best soldiers in his army to tie up Shadrach, Meshach, and Abednego and throw them into the furnace of blazing fire. ²¹ So these men, in their trousers, robes, head coverings,^D and other clothes, were tied up and thrown into the furnace of blazing fire. ²² Since the king's command was so urgent^E and the furnace extremely hot, the raging flames^F killed those men who carried Shadrach, Meshach, and Abednego up. ²³ And these three men, Shadrach, Meshach, and Abednego fell, bound, into the furnace of blazing fire.

DELIVERED FROM THE FIRE

²⁴ Then King Nebuchadnezzar jumped up in alarm. He said to his advisers, "Didn't we throw three men, bound, into the fire? "

"Yes, of course, Your Majesty," they replied to the king.

---

^A 3:8 Lit and eat the pieces of   ^B 3:17 Or If the God whom we serve is willing to save us from the furnace of blazing fire, then he will   ^C 3:18 Lit But if not
^D 3:21 The identity of these articles of clothing is uncertain.   ^E 3:22 Or harsh
^F 3:22 Lit the flame of the fire

²⁵ He exclaimed, "Look! I see four men, not tied, walking around in the fire unharmed; and the fourth looks like a son of the gods."ᴬ

²⁶ Nebuchadnezzar then approached the door of the furnace of blazing fire and called: "Shadrach, Meshach, and Abednego, you servants of the Most High God — come out!" So Shadrach, Meshach, and Abednego came out of the fire. ²⁷ When the satraps, prefects, governors, and the king's advisers gathered around, they saw that the fire had no effect onᴮ the bodies of these men: not a hair of their heads was singed, their robes were unaffected, and there was no smell of fire on them. ²⁸ Nebuchadnezzar exclaimed, "Praise to the God of Shadrach, Meshach, and Abednego! He sent his angelᶜ and rescued his servants who trusted in him. They violated the king's command and risked their lives rather than serve or worship any god except their own God. ²⁹ Therefore I issue a decree that anyone of any people, nation, or language who says anything offensive against the God of Shadrach, Meshach, and Abednego will be torn limb from limb and his house made a garbage dump. For there is no other god who is able to deliver like this." ³⁰ Then the king rewarded Shadrach, Meshach, and Abednego in the province of Babylon.

NEBUCHADNEZZAR'S PROCLAMATION

4 King Nebuchadnezzar,

To those of every people, nation, and language, who live on the whole earth:

May your prosperity increase. ² I am pleased to tell you about the miracles and wonders the Most High God has done for me.

³ How great are his miracles,
and how mighty his wonders!
His kingdom is an eternal kingdom,
and his dominion is from generation to generation.

THE DREAM

⁴ I, Nebuchadnezzar, was at ease in my house and flourishing in my palace. ⁵ I had a dream, and it frightened me; while in my bed, the images and visions in my mind alarmed me. ⁶ So I issued a decree to bring all the wise men of Babylon to me in order that they might make the dream's interpretation known to me. ⁷ When the magicians, mediums, Chaldeans, and diviners came in, I told them the dream, but they could not make its interpretation known to me.

⁸ Finally Daniel, named Belteshazzar after the name of my god — and a spirit of the holy gods is in him — came before me. I told him the dream: ⁹ "Belteshazzar, head of the magicians, because I know that you have the spirit of the holy gods and that no mystery puzzles you, explain to me the visions of my dream that I saw, and its interpretation. ¹⁰ In the visions of my mind as I was lying in bed, I saw this:

There was a tree in the middle of the earth,
and it was very tall.

ᴬ3:25 Or of a divine being ᴮ3:27 Lit fire had not overcome ᶜ3:28 Or messenger

NO LOST CAUSES

DANIEL 4; PROVERBS 16:18; 1 CORINTHIANS 1:28

What am I really saying when I write off another person in my heart? Am I saying they're beyond repair, that they're not worth waiting for, praying for, hoping for?

Am I saying the gospel isn't big enough for them, that God's arms of compassion and grace aren't long enough to reach them?

Were I Daniel, I would have thought all those things about Nebuchadnezzar.

When Nebuchadnezzar wasn't spending his time expanding his kingdom, he was admiring it, worshiping it, and ordering others to do the same. For crying out loud, he nearly had people killed for not being able to describe his own dreams back to him! Had a licensed psychologist been handy, I'm pretty sure the king would have been diagnosed with grade-A narcissism.

All of this took place under the watchful eye of a God who sees, pursues, loves, and forgives. **With the one true God on the scene, no one is a lost cause.**

God's grace to the proud king came in the form of a man who could interpret dreams. When Nebuchadnezzar had an inexplicable dream about a great tree, he called Daniel in to interpret it. Daniel explained that Nebuchadnezzar himself was the magnificent tree and that God was going to humble him in a dramatic way.

Can you believe what happened next? The king literally went mad and started grazing in the field like a wild animal. Nebuchadnezzar was brought low to the point of losing himself

completely. But when God restored the king's sanity, He also restored his spirit, and Nebuchadnezzar praised God:

"But at the end of those days, I, Nebuchadnezzar, looked up to heaven, and my sanity returned to me. Then I praised the Most High and honored and glorified him who lives forever:

"For his dominion is an everlasting dominion, and his kingdom is from generation to generation."

DANIEL 4:34

This is an exclamation point moment! The king who had the whole world at his fingertips bows low before the God of heaven and proclaims, "All the inhabitants of the earth are counted as nothing" before the Most High King (Dn 4:35). This, coming from a man who most definitely prized being counted as something.

In a remarkable example of God's boundless grace, Nebuchadnezzar is transformed from destructive pride and self-exaltation to restorative humility.

You and I need God's grace and Christ's sacrifice as much as anyone else on this vast, sinner-filled earth. When we are confused, distracted, or proud, may we remember the beautifully disarming image of this pompous king returning from the field to praise the God of heaven.

11 The tree grew large and strong;
   its top reached to the sky,
   and it was visible to the ends of the^A earth.
12 Its leaves were beautiful, its fruit was abundant,
   and on it was food for all.
   Wild animals found shelter under it,
   the birds of the sky lived in its branches,
   and every creature was fed from it.

13 "As I was lying in my bed, I also saw in the visions of my mind a watcher, a holy one,^B coming down from heaven. 14 He called out loudly:
   Cut down the tree and chop off its branches;
   strip off its leaves and scatter its fruit.
   Let the animals flee from under it,
   and the birds from its branches.
15 But leave the stump with its roots in the ground
   and with a band of iron and bronze around it
   in the tender grass of the field.
   Let him be drenched with dew from the sky
   and share the plants of the earth
   with the animals.
16 Let his mind be changed from that of a human,
   and let him be given the mind of an animal
   for seven periods of time.^C,D
17 This word is by decree of the watchers,
   and the decision is by command
      from the holy ones.
   This is so that the living will know
   that the Most High is ruler
   over human kingdoms.
   He gives them to anyone he wants
   and sets the lowliest of people over them.
18 This is the dream that I, King Nebuchadnezzar, had. Now, Belteshazzar, tell me the interpretation, because none of the wise men of my kingdom can make the interpretation known to me. But you can, because you have a spirit of the holy gods."

THE DREAM INTERPRETED

19 Then Daniel, whose name is Belteshazzar, was stunned for a moment, and his thoughts alarmed him. The king said, "Belteshazzar, don't let the dream or its interpretation alarm you."

Belteshazzar answered, "My lord, may the dream apply to those who hate you, and its interpretation to your enemies! 20 The tree you saw, which grew large and strong, whose top reached to the sky and was visible to the whole earth, 21 and whose leaves were beautiful and its fruit abundant — and on it was food for all, under it the wild animals lived, and in its branches the birds of the sky lived — 22 that tree is you, Your Majesty. For you have become

---

^A 4:11 Lit *of all the*   ^B 4:13 = an angel   ^C 4:16 Lit *animal as seven times pass over him*   ^D 4:16 Perhaps seven years great and strong: your greatness has grown and even reaches the sky, and your dominion extends to the ends of the earth.

²³ "The king saw a watcher, a holy one, coming down from heaven and saying, 'Cut down the tree and destroy it, but leave the stump with its roots in the ground and with a band of iron and bronze around it in the tender grass of the field. Let him be drenched with dew from the sky and share food with the wild animals for seven periods of time.' ²⁴ This is the interpretation, Your Majesty, and this is the decree of the Most High that has been issued against my lord the king: ²⁵ You will be driven away from people to live with the wild animals. You will feed on grass like cattle and be drenched with dew from the sky for seven periods of time, until you acknowledge that the Most High is ruler over human kingdoms, and he gives them to anyone he wants. ²⁶ As for the command to leave the tree's stump with its roots, your kingdom will be restored ᴬ to you as soon as you acknowledge that Heaven ᴮ rules. ²⁷ Therefore, may my advice seem good to you my king. Separate yourself from your sins by doing what is right, and from your injustices by showing mercy to the needy. Perhaps there will be an extension of your prosperity."

THE SENTENCE EXECUTED

²⁸ All this happened to King Nebuchadnezzar. ²⁹ At the end of twelve months, as he was walking on the roof of the royal palace in Babylon, ³⁰ the king exclaimed, "Is this not Babylon the Great that I have built to be a royal residence by my vast power and for my majestic glory?"

³¹ While the words were still in the king's mouth, a voice came from heaven: "King Nebuchadnezzar, to you it is declared that the kingdom has departed from you. ³² You will be driven away from people to live with the wild animals, and you will feed on grass like cattle for seven periods of time, until you acknowledge that the Most High is ruler over human kingdoms, and he gives them to anyone he wants."

³³ At that moment the message against Nebuchadnezzar was fulfilled. He was driven away from people. He ate grass like cattle, and his body was drenched with dew from the sky, until his hair grew like eagles' feathers and his nails like birds' claws.

NEBUCHADNEZZAR'S PRAISE

³⁴ But at the end of those days, I, Nebuchadnezzar, looked up to heaven, and my sanity returned to me. Then I praised the Most High and honored and glorified him who lives forever:

> For his dominion is an everlasting dominion,
> and his kingdom is from generation to generation.
³⁵   All the inhabitants of the earth are counted as nothing,
> and he does what he wants with the army of heaven
> and the inhabitants of the earth.
> There is no one who can block his hand
> or say to him, "What have you done?"

³⁶ At that time my sanity returned to me, and my majesty and splendor returned to me for the glory of my kingdom. My advisers and my nobles sought me out, I was reestablished over my kingdom, and even more greatness

came to me. ³⁷ Now I, Nebuchadnezzar, praise, exalt, and glorify the King of the heavens, because all his works are true and his ways are just. He is able to humble those who walk in pride.

BELSHAZZAR'S FEAST

5 King Belshazzar held a great feast for a thousand of his nobles and drank wine in their presence. ² Under the influence of ᴬ the wine, Belshazzar gave orders to bring in the gold and silver vessels that his predecessor ᴮ Nebuchadnezzar had taken from the temple in Jerusalem, so that the king and his nobles, wives, and concubines could drink from them. ³ So they brought in the gold ᶜ vessels that had been taken from the temple, the house of God in Jerusalem, and the king and his nobles, wives, and concubines drank from them. ⁴ They drank the wine and praised their gods made of gold and silver, bronze, iron, wood, and stone.

THE HANDWRITING ON THE WALL

⁵ At that moment the fingers of a man's hand appeared and began writing on the plaster of the king's palace wall next to the lampstand. As the king watched the hand ᴰ that was writing, ⁶ his face turned pale, ᴱ and his thoughts so terrified him that he soiled himself ᶠ and his knees knocked together. ⁷ The king shouted to bring in the mediums, Chaldeans, and diviners. He said to these wise men of Babylon, "Whoever reads this inscription and gives me its interpretation will be clothed in purple, have a gold chain around his neck, and have the third highest position in the kingdom." ⁸ So all the king's wise men came in, but none could read the inscription or make its interpretation known to him. ⁹ Then King Belshazzar became even more terrified, his face turned pale, ᴳ and his nobles were bewildered.

¹⁰ Because of the outcry of the king and his nobles, the queen ᴴ came to the banquet hall. "May the king live forever," she said. "Don't let your thoughts terrify you or your face be pale.ᴵ ¹¹ There is a man in your kingdom who has a spirit of the holy gods in him. In the days of your predecessor he was found to have insight, intelligence, and wisdom like the wisdom of the gods. Your predecessor, King Nebuchadnezzar, appointed him chief of the magicians, mediums, Chaldeans, and diviners. Your own predecessor, the king, ¹² did this because Daniel, the one the king named Belteshazzar, was found to have an extraordinary spirit, knowledge and intelligence, and the ability to interpret dreams, explain riddles, and solve problems. Therefore, summon Daniel, and he will give the interpretation."

DANIEL BEFORE THE KING

¹³ Then Daniel was brought before the king. The king said to him, "Are you Daniel, one of the Judean exiles that my predecessor the king brought from Judah? ¹⁴ I've heard that you have a spirit of the gods in you, and that insight, intelligence, and extraordinary wisdom are found in you. ¹⁵ Now the wise

---

ᴬ5:2 Or *When he tasted*   ᴮ5:2 Or *father,* or *grandfather*   ᶜ5:3 Theod, Vg add *and silver*   ᴰ5:5 Lit *part of the hand*   ᴱ5:5-6 Lit *writing, ⁶the king's brightness changed*   ᶠ5:6 Lit *that the knots of his loins were loosed*   ᴳ5:9 Lit *his brightness changed on him*   ᴴ5:10 Perhaps *the queen mother*   ᴵ5:10 Lit *your brightness change* men and mediums were brought before me to read this inscription and make its interpretation known to me, but they could not give its interpretation. 16 However, I have heard about you that you can give interpretations and solve problems. Therefore, if you can read this inscription and give me its interpretation, you will be clothed in purple, have a gold chain around your neck, and have the third highest position in the kingdom."

17 Then Daniel answered the king, "You may keep your gifts and give your rewards to someone else; however, I will read the inscription for the king and make the interpretation known to him. 18 Your Majesty, the Most High God gave sovereignty, greatness, glory, and majesty to your predecessor Nebuchadnezzar. 19 Because of the greatness he gave him, all peoples, nations, and languages were terrified and fearful of him. He killed anyone he wanted and kept alive anyone he wanted; he exalted anyone he wanted and humbled anyone he wanted. 20 But when his heart was exalted and his spirit became arrogant, he was deposed from his royal throne and his glory was taken from him. 21 He was driven away from people, his mind was like an animal's, he lived with the wild donkeys, he was fed grass like cattle, and his body was drenched with dew from the sky until he acknowledged that the Most High God is ruler over human kingdoms and sets anyone he wants over them.

22 "But you his successor, Belshazzar, have not humbled your heart, even though you knew all this. 23 Instead, you have exalted yourself against the Lord of the heavens. The vessels from his house were brought to you, and as you and your nobles, wives, and concubines drank wine from them, you praised the gods made of silver and gold, bronze, iron, wood, and stone, which do not see or hear or understand. But you have not glorified the God who holds your life-breath in his hand and who controls the whole course of your life.^A 24 Therefore, he sent the hand, and this writing was inscribed.

THE INSCRIPTION'S INTERPRETATION

25 "This is the writing that was inscribed: MENE, MENE, TEKEL, and PARSIN. 26 This is the interpretation of the message:

'Mene'^B means that God has numbered^C the days of your kingdom and brought it to an end.

27 'Tekel'^D means that you have been weighed^E on the balance and found deficient.

28 'Peres'^F,G means that your kingdom has been divided and given to the Medes and Persians."^H

29 Then Belshazzar gave an order, and they clothed Daniel in purple, placed a gold chain around his neck, and issued a proclamation concerning him that he should be the third ruler in the kingdom.

30 That very night Belshazzar the king of the Chaldeans was killed, 31 and Darius the Mede received the kingdom at the age of sixty-two.

---

^A 5:23 Lit and all your ways belong to him ^B 5:26 Or a mina ^C 5:26 The Aramaic word for numbered sounds like mene. ^D 5:27 Or a shekel ^E 5:27 The Aramaic word for weighed sounds like tekel. ^F 5:28 Or half a shekel ^G 5:28 In Aramaic, the word peres is the sg form of "parsin" in v. 25. ^H 5:28 The Aramaic word for divided and Persians sounds like peres.

THE PLOT AGAINST DANIEL

6 Darius decided[A] to appoint 120 satraps over the kingdom, stationed throughout the realm, [2] and over them three administrators, including Daniel. These satraps would be accountable to them so that the king would not be defrauded. [3] Daniel[B] distinguished himself above the administrators and satraps because he had an extraordinary spirit, so the king planned to set him over the whole realm. [4] The administrators and satraps, therefore, kept trying to find a charge against Daniel regarding the kingdom. But they could find no charge or corruption, for he was trustworthy, and no negligence or corruption was found in him. [5] Then these men said, "We will never find any charge against this Daniel unless we find something against him concerning the law of his God."

[6] So the administrators and satraps went together to the king and said to him, "May King Darius live forever. [7] All the administrators of the kingdom, the prefects, satraps, advisers, and governors have agreed that the king should establish an ordinance and enforce an edict that for thirty days, anyone who petitions any god or man except you, the king, will be thrown into the lions' den. [8] Therefore, Your Majesty, establish the edict and sign the document so that, as a law of the Medes and Persians, it is irrevocable and cannot be changed." [9] So King Darius signed the written edict.

DANIEL IN THE LIONS' DEN

[10] When Daniel learned that the document had been signed, he went into his house. The windows in its upstairs room opened toward Jerusalem, and three times a day he got down on his knees, prayed, and gave thanks to his God, just as he had done before. [11] Then these men went as a group and found Daniel petitioning and imploring his God. [12] So they approached the king and asked about his edict: "Didn't you sign an edict that for thirty days any person who petitions any god or man except you, the king, will be thrown into the lions' den?"

The king answered, "As a law of the Medes and Persians, the order stands[C] and is irrevocable."

[13] Then they replied to the king, "Daniel, one of the Judean exiles, has ignored you, the king, and the edict you signed, for he prays three times a day." [14] As soon as the king heard this, he was very displeased; he set his mind on rescuing Daniel and made every effort until sundown to deliver him.

[15] Then these men went together to the king and said to him, "You know, Your Majesty, that it is a law of the Medes and Persians that no edict or ordinance the king establishes can be changed."

[16] So the king gave the order, and they brought Daniel and threw him into the lions' den. The king said to Daniel, "May your God, whom you continually serve, rescue you!" [17] A stone was brought and placed over the mouth of the den. The king sealed it with his own signet ring and with the signet rings of his nobles, so that nothing in regard to Daniel could be changed. [18] Then the king went to his palace and spent the night fasting. No diversions[D] were brought to him, and he could not sleep.

A6:1 Lit *It was pleasing before Darius*   B6:3 Lit *Now this Daniel*   C6:12 Lit *the word is certain*   D6:18 Aramaic obscure

DANIEL RELEASED

¹⁹ At the first light of dawn the king got up and hurried to the lions' den. ²⁰ When he reached the den, he cried out in anguish to Daniel. "Daniel, servant of the living God," the king said, ᴬ "has your God, whom you continually serve, been able to rescue you from the lions?"

²¹ Then Daniel spoke with the king: "May the king live forever. ²² My God sent his angel and shut the lions' mouths; and they haven't harmed me, for I was found innocent before him. And also before you, Your Majesty, I have not done harm."

²³ The king was overjoyed and gave orders to take Daniel out of the den. When Daniel was brought up from the den, he was found to be unharmed, for he trusted in his God. ²⁴ The king then gave the command, and those men who had maliciously accused Daniel ᴮ were brought and thrown into the lions' den — they, their children, and their wives. They had not reached the bottom of the den before the lions overpowered them and crushed all their bones.

DARIUS HONORS GOD

²⁵ Then King Darius wrote to those of every people, nation, and language who live on the whole earth: "May your prosperity abound. ²⁶ I issue a decree that in all my royal dominion, people must tremble in fear before the God of Daniel:

> For he is the living God,
> and he endures forever;
> his kingdom will never be destroyed,
> and his dominion has no end.
> ²⁷ He rescues and delivers;
> he performs signs and wonders
> in the heavens and on the earth,
> for he has rescued Daniel
> from the power of the lions."

²⁸ So Daniel prospered during the reign of Darius and ᶜ the reign of Cyrus the Persian.

DANIEL'S VISION OF THE FOUR BEASTS

7 In the first year of King Belshazzar of Babylon, Daniel had a dream with visions in his mind as he was lying in his bed. He wrote down the dream, and here is the summary ᴰ of his account. ² Daniel said, "In my vision at night I was watching, and suddenly the four winds of heaven stirred up the great sea. ³ Four huge beasts came up from the sea, each different from the other.

⁴ "The first was like a lion but had eagle's wings. I continued watching until its wings were torn off. It was lifted up from the ground, set on its feet like a man, and given a human mind.

⁵ "Suddenly, another beast appeared, a second one, that looked like a bear. It was raised up on one side, with three ribs in its mouth between its teeth. It was told, 'Get up! Gorge yourself on flesh.'

⁶ "After this, while I was watching, suddenly another beast appeared. It was like a leopard with four wings of a bird on its back. It had four heads, and it was given dominion.

ᴬ 6:20 Lit said to Daniel   ᴮ 6:24 Lit had eaten his pieces   ᶜ 6:28 Or Darius, even
ᴰ 7:1 Lit beginning

⁷ "After this, while I was watching in the night visions, suddenly a fourth beast appeared, frightening and dreadful, and incredibly strong, with large iron teeth. It devoured and crushed, and it trampled with its feet whatever was left. It was different from all the beasts before it, and it had ten horns.

⁸ "While I was considering the horns, suddenly another horn, a little one, came up among them, and three of the first horns were uprooted before it. And suddenly in this horn there were eyes like the eyes of a human and a mouth that was speaking arrogantly.

THE ANCIENT OF DAYS AND THE SON OF MAN

⁹ "As I kept watching,

thrones were set in place,
and the Ancient of Days took his seat.
His clothing was white like snow,
and the hair of his head like whitest wool.
His throne was flaming fire;
its wheels were blazing fire.
¹⁰   A river of fire was flowing,
coming out from his presence.
Thousands upon thousands served him;
ten thousand times ten thousand stood before him.
The court was convened,
and the books were opened.

¹¹ "I watched, then, because of the sound of the arrogant words the horn was speaking. As I continued watching, the beast was killed and its body destroyed and given over to the burning fire. ¹² As for the rest of the beasts, their dominion was removed, but an extension of life was granted to them for a certain period of time. ¹³ I continued watching in the night visions,

and suddenly one like a son of man
was coming with the clouds of heaven.
He approached the Ancient of Days
and was escorted before him.
¹⁴   He was given dominion,
and glory, and a kingdom;
so that those of every people,
nation, and language
should serve him.
His dominion is an everlasting dominion
that will not pass away,
and his kingdom is one
that will not be destroyed.

INTERPRETATION OF THE VISION

¹⁵ "As for me, Daniel, my spirit was deeply distressed within me,^A and the visions in my mind terrified me. ¹⁶ I approached one of those who were standing by and asked him to clarify all this. So he let me know the interpretation of these things: ¹⁷ "These huge beasts, four in number, are four kings who

---

^A7:15 Lit *was distressed in the middle of its sheath*

will rise from the earth. [18] But the holy ones of the Most High will receive the kingdom and possess it forever, yes, forever and ever.'

[19] "Then I wanted to be clear about the fourth beast, the one different from all the others, extremely terrifying, with iron teeth and bronze claws, devouring, crushing, and trampling with its feet whatever was left. [20] I also wanted to know about the ten horns on its head and about the other horn that came up, before which three fell — the horn that had eyes, and a mouth that spoke arrogantly, and that looked bigger than the others. [21] As I was watching, this horn waged war against the holy ones and was prevailing over them [22] until the Ancient of Days arrived and a judgment was given in favor of the holy ones of the Most High, for the time had come, and the holy ones took possession of the kingdom.

[23] "This is what he said: 'The fourth beast will be a fourth kingdom on the earth, different from all the other kingdoms. It will devour the whole earth, trample it down, and crush it. [24] The ten horns are ten kings who will rise from this kingdom. Another king, different from the previous ones, will rise after them and subdue three kings. [25] He will speak words against the Most High and oppress[A] the holy ones of the Most High. He will intend to change religious festivals[B] and laws, and the holy ones will be handed over to him for a time, times, and half a time.[C] [26] But the court will convene, and his dominion will be taken away, to be completely destroyed forever. [27] The kingdom, dominion, and greatness of the kingdoms under all of heaven will be given to the people, the holy ones of the Most High. His kingdom will be an everlasting kingdom, and all rulers will serve and obey him.'

[28] "This is the end of the account. As for me, Daniel, my thoughts terrified me greatly, and my face turned pale,[D] but I kept the matter to myself."

THE VISION OF A RAM AND A GOAT

8 In the third year of King Belshazzar's reign, a vision appeared to me, Daniel, after the one that had appeared to me earlier. [2] I saw the vision, and as I watched, I was in the fortress city of Susa, in the province of Elam. I saw in the vision that I was beside the Ulai Canal. [3] I looked up,[E] and there was a ram standing beside the canal. He had two horns. The two horns were long, but one was longer than the other, and the longer one came up last. [4] I saw the ram charging to the west, the north, and the south. No animal could stand against him, and there was no rescue from his power. He did whatever he wanted and became great.

[5] As I was observing, a male goat appeared, coming from the west across the surface of the entire earth without touching the ground. The goat had a conspicuous horn[F] between his eyes. [6] He came toward the two-horned ram I had seen standing beside the canal and rushed at him with savage fury. [7] I saw him approaching the ram, and infuriated with him, he struck the ram, breaking his two horns, and the ram was not strong enough to stand against him. The goat threw him to the ground and trampled him, and there was no one to rescue the ram from his power. [8] Then the male goat acted even more arrogantly, but when he became powerful, the large horn

---

[A]7:25 Lit *wear out* [B]7:25 Lit *change times* [C]7:25 Or *for three and a half years*
[D]7:28 Lit *my brightness changed on me* [E]8:3 Lit *I lifted my eyes and looked*
[F]8:5 Lit *a horn of a vision*

GOOD NEWS IN UNLIKELY PLACES

DANIEL 8; ISAIAH 6:1-7; ROMANS 8:31-39; 2 PETER 1:3

What can a ram, a goat, and more horns than a marching band teach us about God? That's the riddle we discover in Daniel 8.

In the Bible, horns almost always represent power, dominion, and authority. The horns in Daniel's vision are no exception, but they're tricky to make sense of. Stick with me. Because the Bible is true, even the parts that are confusing or hard to understand are good news.

Gabriel appears to Daniel in Daniel 8:15 to explain his vision. Here is the gist of the angel's explanation:

- The two-horned ram represents the kings of Media and Persia (Dn 8:3-4,20).

- The shaggy goat represents the Greek Empire (Dn 8:5-7,21).

- Specifically, the large horn between his eyes is understood to be Alexander the Great (Dn 8:8,21).

- Historically, after Alexander the Great's death in 323 BC, four smaller rulers (horns) rose in his place, but none were as powerful as him (Dn 8:8,22).

Gabriel goes on to talk about the little horn, "a ruthless king, skilled in intrigue," who causes "deceit to prosper" (Dn 8:23,25). This horn is widely believed to be Antiochus Epiphanes (who reigned much later, from 175–164 BC), a wicked ruler who desecrated the temple by sacrificing pigs on the altar and setting it up as a shrine to Zeus.

The dream forecasted many more years of persecution for the Jews, and this was incredibly sad for Daniel to learn. Daniel had been praying for deliverance for God's people, but this dream meant he wouldn't live to see it. Terrible leaders and violent conquerors lay ahead and things were going to get worse for God's people before they got better. No wonder verse 27 tells us Daniel "was overcome and lay sick for days."

Maybe you feel like Daniel today. Maybe you're learning firsthand that God's deliverance is rarely quick or tidy. Perhaps you're beginning to understand, as the Israelites discovered, that God doesn't always take us out of pain or heartache. Instead, He gives us everything we need to persevere (2Co 12:9; 2Pt 1:3).

Because the Bible is true, we can look all manner of persecution in the face and have confidence that nothing in the present or future can separate us from the love of God in Christ Jesus (Rm 8:38-39).

We can rise up and go about the King's business as Daniel did (Dn 8:27). Even when we don't understand. Even when we're overwhelmed. Because the greatest evils in the world will come face to face with the Prince of princes and "will be broken—not by human hands" (Dn 8:25).

Thanks be to God.

was broken. Four conspicuous horns came up in its place, pointing toward the four winds of heaven.

THE LITTLE HORN

[9] From one of them a little horn emerged and grew extensively toward the south and the east and toward the beautiful land.[A] [10] It grew as high as the heavenly army, made some of the army and some of the stars[B] fall to the earth, and trampled them. [11] It acted arrogantly even against the Prince of the heavenly army; it revoked his regular sacrifice and overthrew the place of his sanctuary. [12] In the rebellion, the army was given up, together with the regular sacrifice. The horn threw truth to the ground and was successful in what it did.

[13] Then I heard a holy one speaking, and another holy one said to the speaker, "How long will the events of this vision last — the regular sacrifice, the rebellion that makes desolate, and the giving over of the sanctuary and of the army to be trampled?"

[14] He said to me,[C] "For 2,300 evenings and mornings; then the sanctuary will be restored."

INTERPRETATION OF THE VISION

[15] While I, Daniel, was watching the vision and trying to understand it, there stood before me someone who appeared to be a man. [16] I heard a human voice calling from the middle of the Ulai: "Gabriel, explain the vision to this man."

[17] So he approached where I was standing; when he came near, I was terrified and fell facedown. "Son of man," he said to me, "understand that the vision refers to the time of the end." [18] While he was speaking to me, I fell into a deep sleep, with my face to the ground. Then he touched me, made me stand up, [19] and said, "I am here to tell you what will happen at the conclusion of the time of wrath, because it refers to the appointed time of the end. [20] The two-horned ram that you saw represents the kings of Media and Persia. [21] The shaggy goat represents the king of Greece, and the large horn between his eyes represents the first king.[D] [22] The four horns that took the place of the broken horn represent four kingdoms. They will rise from that nation, but without its power.

[23] Near the end of their kingdoms,
 when the rebels have reached
 the full measure of their sin,[E]
 a ruthless[F] king, skilled in intrigue,[G]
 will come to the throne.
[24] His power will be great,
 but it will not be his own.
 He will cause outrageous destruction
 and succeed in whatever he does.
 He will destroy the powerful
 along with the holy people.
[25] He will cause deceit to prosper

[A]8:9 = Israel [B]8:10 Or some of the army, that is, some of the stars [C]8:14 LXX, Theod, Syr, Vg read him [D]8:21 = Alexander the Great [E]8:23 Lit have become complete [F]8:23 Lit strong of face [G]8:23 Lit king, and understanding riddles

through his cunning and by his influence,
and in his own mind he will exalt himself.
He will destroy many in a time of peace;
he will even stand against the Prince of princes.
Yet he will be broken — not by human hands.
26 The vision of the evenings and the mornings
that has been told is true.
Now you are to seal up the vision
because it refers to many days in the future."

27 I, Daniel, was overcome and lay sick for days. Then I got up and went about the king's business. I was greatly disturbed by the vision and could not understand it.

DANIEL'S PRAYER

9 In the first year of Darius, the son of Ahasuerus, a Mede by birth, who was made king over the Chaldean kingdom — 2 in the first year of his reign, I, Daniel, understood from the books according to the word of the LORD to the prophet Jeremiah that the number of years for the desolation of Jerusalem would be seventy. 3 So I turned my attention to the Lord God to seek him by prayer and petitions, with fasting, sackcloth, and ashes.

4 I prayed to the LORD my God and confessed:

Ah, Lord — the great and awe-inspiring God who keeps his gracious covenant with those who love him and keep his commands — 5 we have sinned, done wrong, acted wickedly, rebelled, and turned away from your commands and ordinances. 6 We have not listened to your servants the prophets, who spoke in your name to our kings, leaders, fathers, and all the people of the land.

7 Lord, righteousness belongs to you, but this day public shame belongs to us: the men of Judah, the residents of Jerusalem, and all Israel — those who are near and those who are far, in all the countries where you have banished them because of the disloyalty they have shown toward you. 8 LORD, public shame belongs to us, our kings, our leaders, and our fathers, because we have sinned against you. 9 Compassion and forgiveness belong to the Lord our God, though we have rebelled against him 10 and have not obeyed the LORD our God by following his instructions that he set before us through his servants the prophets.

11 All Israel has broken your law and turned away, refusing to obey you. The promised curse^A written in the law of Moses, the servant of God, has been poured out on us because we have sinned against him. 12 He has carried out his words that he spoke against us and against our rulers^B by bringing on us a disaster that is so great that nothing like what has been done to Jerusalem has ever been done under all of heaven. 13 Just as it is written in the law of Moses, all this disaster has come on us, yet we have not sought the favor of the LORD our God by turning from our iniquities and paying attention to your truth. 14 So the LORD

^A9:11 Lit *The curse and the oath*   ^B9:12 Lit *against rulers who ruled us* kept the disaster in mind and brought it on us, for the Lord our God is righteous in all he has done. But we have not obeyed him.

¹⁵ Now, Lord our God, who brought your people out of the land of Egypt with a strong hand and made your name renowned as it is this day, we have sinned, we have acted wickedly. ¹⁶ Lord, in keeping with all your righteous acts, may your anger and wrath turn away from your city Jerusalem, your holy mountain; for because of our sins and the iniquities of our fathers, Jerusalem and your people have become an object of ridicule to all those around us.

¹⁷ Therefore, our God, hear the prayer and the petitions of your servant. Make your face shine on your desolate sanctuary for the Lord's sake. ¹⁸ Listen closely,^A my God, and hear. Open your eyes and see our desolations and the city that bears your name. For we are not presenting our petitions before you based on our righteous acts, but based on your abundant compassion. ¹⁹ Lord, hear! Lord, forgive! Lord, listen and act! My God, for your own sake, do not delay, because your city and your people bear your name.

THE SEVENTY WEEKS OF YEARS

²⁰ While I was speaking, praying, confessing my sin and the sin of my people Israel, and presenting my petition before the Lord my God concerning the holy mountain of my God — ²¹ while I was praying, Gabriel, the man I had seen in the first vision, reached me in my extreme weariness, about the time of the evening offering. ²² He gave me this explanation: "Daniel, I've come now to give you understanding. ²³ At the beginning of your petitions an answer went out, and I have come to give it, for you are treasured by God.^B So consider the message and understand the vision:

24 Seventy weeks are decreed
   about your people and your holy city —
   to bring the rebellion to an end,
   to put a stop to sin,
   to atone for iniquity,
   to bring in everlasting righteousness,
   to seal up vision and prophecy,
   and to anoint the most holy place.
25 Know and understand this:
   From the issuing of the decree
   to restore and rebuild Jerusalem
   until an Anointed One, the ruler,^C
   will be seven weeks and sixty-two weeks.
   It will be rebuilt with a plaza and a moat,
   but in difficult times.
26 After those sixty-two weeks
   the Anointed One will be cut off
   and will have nothing.

> The people of the coming ruler
> will destroy the city and the sanctuary.[A]
> The[B] end will come with a flood,
> and until the end there will be[c] war;
> desolations are decreed.

27 > He will make a firm covenant[D]
> with many for one week,
> but in the middle of the week
> he will put a stop to sacrifice and offering.
> And the abomination of desolation
> will be on a wing of the temple[E,F]
> until the decreed destruction
> is poured out on the desolator."

VISION OF A GLORIOUS ONE

10 In the third year of King Cyrus of Persia, a message was revealed to Daniel, who was named Belteshazzar. The message was true and was about a great conflict. He understood the message and had understanding of the vision.

[2] In those days I, Daniel, was mourning for three full weeks. [3] I didn't eat any rich food, no meat or wine entered my mouth, and I didn't put any oil on my body until the three weeks were over. [4] On the twenty-fourth day of the first month,[G] as I was standing on the bank of the great river, the Tigris, [5] I looked up, and there was a man dressed in linen, with a belt of gold from Uphaz[H] around his waist. [6] His body was like beryl,[I] his face like the brilliance of lightning, his eyes like flaming torches, his arms and feet like the gleam of polished bronze, and the sound of his words like the sound of a multitude.

[7] Only I, Daniel, saw the vision. The men who were with me did not see it, but a great terror fell on them, and they ran and hid. [8] I was left alone, looking at this great vision. No strength was left in me; my face grew deathly pale,[J] and I was powerless. [9] I heard the words he said, and when I heard them I fell into a deep sleep,[K] with my face to the ground.

ANGELIC CONFLICT

[10] Suddenly, a hand touched me and set me shaking on my hands and knees. [11] He said to me, "Daniel, you are a man treasured by God.[L] Understand the words that I'm saying to you. Stand on your feet, for I have now been sent to you." After he said this to me, I stood trembling.

[12] "Don't be afraid, Daniel," he said to me, "for from the first day that you purposed to understand and to humble yourself before your God, your prayers

---

[A]9:26 MT; Theod, some mss read *The city and the sanctuary will be destroyed when the ruler comes.*   [B]9:26 Lit *Its,* or *His*   [c]9:26 Or *end of a*   [D]9:27 Or *will enforce a covenant*   [E]9:27 LXX; MT reads *of abominations*   [F]9:27 Or *And the desolator will be on the wing of abominations,* or *And the desolator will come on the wings of monsters* (or *of horror*); Hb obscure   [G]10:4 = Nisan (March–April)   [H]10:5 Some Hb mss read *Ophir*   [I]10:6 The identity of this stone is uncertain.   [J]10:8 Lit *my splendor was turned on me to ruin*   [K]10:9 Lit *a sleep on my face*   [L]10:11 *by God* added for clarity, also in v. 19

were heard. I have come because of your prayers. ¹³But the prince of the kingdom of Persia opposed me for twenty-one days. Then Michael, one of the chief princes, came to help me after I had been left there with the kings of Persia. ¹⁴Now I have come to help you understand what will happen to your people in the last days, for the vision refers to those days."

¹⁵While he was saying these words to me, I turned my face toward the ground and was speechless. ¹⁶Suddenly one with human likeness touched my lips. I opened my mouth and said to the one standing in front of me, "My lord, because of the vision, anguish overwhelms me and I am powerless. ¹⁷How can someone like me, your servant,ᴬ speak with someone like you, my lord? Now I have no strength, and there is no breath in me."

¹⁸Then the one with a human appearance touched me again and strengthened me. ¹⁹He said, "Don't be afraid, you who areᴮ treasured by God. Peace to you; be very strong!"

As he spoke to me, I was strengthened and said, "Let my lord speak, for you have strengthened me."

²⁰He said, "Do you know why I've come to you? I must return at once to fight against the prince of Persia, and when I leave, the prince of Greece will come. ²¹However, I will tell you what is recorded in the book of truth. (No one has the courage to support me against those princes except Michael, your prince.

11 ¹In the first year of Darius the Mede, I stood up to strengthen and protect him.) ²Now I will tell you the truth.

PROPHECIES ABOUT PERSIA AND GREECE

"Three more kings will arise in Persia, and the fourth will be far richer than the others. By the power he gains through his riches, he will stir up everyone against the kingdom of Greece. ³Then a warrior king will arise; he will rule a vast realm and do whatever he wants. ⁴But as soon as he is established, his kingdom will be broken up and divided to the four winds of heaven, but not to his descendants; it will not be the same kingdom that he ruled, because his kingdom will be uprooted and will go to others besides them.

KINGS OF THE SOUTH AND THE NORTH

⁵"The king of the South will grow powerful, but one of his commanders will grow more powerful and will rule a kingdom greater than his. ⁶After some years they will form an alliance, and the daughter of the king of the South will go to the king of the North to seal the agreement. She will not retain power, and his strength will not endure. She will be given up, together with her entourage, her father,ᶜ and the one who supported her during those times. ⁷In the place of the king of the South, one from her familyᴰ will rise up, come against the army, and enter the fortress of the king of the North. He will take action against them and triumph. ⁸He will take even their gods captive to Egypt, with their metal images and their precious articles of silver and gold. For some years he will stay away from the king of the North, ⁹who will enter the kingdom of the king of the South and then return to his own land.

ᴬ10:17 Lit Can I, a servant of my lord   ᴮ10:19 Lit afraid, man   ᶜ11:6 Some Hb mss, Theod read the child; Syr, Vg read her children   ᴰ11:7 Lit from the shoot of her roots

¹⁰ "His sons will mobilize for war and assemble a large number of armed forces. They will advance, sweeping through like a flood,ᴬ and will again wage war as far as his fortress. ¹¹ Infuriated, the king of the South will march out to fight with the king of the North, who will raise a large army, but they will be handed over to his enemy. ¹² When the army is carried off, he will become arrogant and cause tens of thousands to fall, but he will not triumph. ¹³ The king of the North will again raise a multitude larger than the first. After some yearsᴮ he will advance with a great army and many supplies.

¹⁴ "In those times many will rise up against the king of the South. Violent ones among your own people will assert themselves to fulfill a vision, but they will fail. ¹⁵ Then the king of the North will come, build up a siege ramp, and capture a well-fortified city. The forces of the South will not stand; even their select troops will not be able to resist. ¹⁶ The king of the North who comes against him will do whatever he wants, and no one can oppose him. He will establish himself in the beautiful landᶜ with total destruction in his hand. ¹⁷ He will resolve to come with the force of his whole kingdom and will reach an agreement with him.ᴰ He will give him a daughter in marriageᴱ to destroy it,ᶠ but she will not stand with him or support him. ¹⁸ Then he will turn his attention to the coasts and islandsᴳ and capture many. But a commander will put an end to his taunting; instead, he will turn his taunts against him. ¹⁹ He will turn his attention back to the fortresses of his own land, but he will stumble, fall, and be no more.

²⁰ "In his place one will arise who will send out a tax collector for the glory of the kingdom; but within a few days he will be broken, though not in angerᴴ or in battle.

²¹ "In his place a despised person will arise; royal honors will not be given to him, but he will come during a time of peaceᴵ and seize the kingdom by intrigue. ²² A flood of forces will be swept away before him; they will be broken, as well as the covenant prince. ²³ After an alliance is made with him, he will act deceitfully. He will rise to power with a small nation.ᴶ ²⁴ During a time of peace,ᴷ he will come into the richest parts of the province and do what his fathers and predecessors never did. He will lavish plunder, loot, and wealth on his followers, and he will make plans against fortified cities, but only for a time.

²⁵ "With a large army he will stir up his power and his courage against the king of the South. The king of the South will prepare for battle with an extremely large and powerful army, but he will not succeed, because plots will be made against him. ²⁶ Those who eat his provisions will destroy him; his army will be swept away, and many will fall slain. ²⁷ The two kings, whose hearts are bent on evil, will speak lies at the same table but to no avail, for still the end will come at the appointed time. ²⁸ The king of the North will return to his land with great wealth, but his heart will be set against the holy covenant;ᴸ he will take action, then return to his own land.

ᴬ11:10 Lit *advance and overflow and pass through*   ᴮ11:13 Lit *At the end of the times*   ᶜ11:16 = Israel   ᴰ11:17 = the king of the South   ᴱ11:17 Lit *him the daughter of women*   ᶠ11:17 Perhaps the kingdom   ᴳ11:18 of the Mediterranean   ᴴ11:20 Or *not openly*   ᴵ11:21 Or *come without warning*   ᴶ11:23 Or *a few people*   ᴷ11:24 Or *Without warning*   ᴸ11:28 Or *the Jewish people and religion*

²⁹ "At the appointed time he will come again to the South, but this time^A will not be like the first. ³⁰ Ships of Kittim^B will come against him, and being intimidated, he will withdraw. Then he will rage against the holy covenant and take action. On his return, he will favor those who abandon the holy covenant. ³¹ His forces will rise up and desecrate the temple fortress. They will abolish the regular sacrifice and set up the abomination of desolation. ³² With flattery he will corrupt those who act wickedly toward the covenant, but the people who know their God will be strong and take action. ³³ Those who have insight among the people will give understanding to many, yet they will fall by the sword and flame, and be captured and plundered for a time. ³⁴ When they fall, they will be helped by some, but many others will join them insincerely. ³⁵ Some of those who have insight will fall so that they may be refined, purified, and cleansed until the time of the end, for it will still come at the appointed time.

³⁶ "Then the king will do whatever he wants. He will exalt and magnify himself above every god, and he will say outrageous things against the God of gods. He will be successful until the time of wrath is completed, because what has been decreed will be accomplished. ³⁷ He will not show regard for the gods^C of his fathers, the god desired by women, or for any other god, because he will magnify himself above all. ³⁸ Instead, he will honor a god of fortresses — a god his fathers did not know — with gold, silver, precious stones, and riches. ³⁹ He will deal with the strongest fortresses with the help of a foreign god. He will greatly honor those who acknowledge him,^D making them rulers over many and distributing land as a reward.

⁴⁰ "At the time of the end, the king of the South will engage him in battle, but the king of the North will storm against him with chariots, horsemen, and many ships. He will invade countries and sweep through them like a flood. ⁴¹ He will also invade the beautiful land, and many will fall. But these will escape from his power: Edom, Moab, and the prominent people^E of the Ammonites. ⁴² He will extend his power against the countries, and not even the land of Egypt will escape. ⁴³ He will get control over the hidden treasures of gold and silver and over all the riches of Egypt. The Libyans and Cushites will also be in submission.^F ⁴⁴ But reports from the east and the north will terrify him, and he will go out with great fury to annihilate and completely destroy many. ⁴⁵ He will pitch his royal tents between the sea and^G the beautiful holy mountain, but he will meet his end with no one to help him.

12

At that time
Michael, the great prince
who stands watch over your people, will rise up.
There will be a time of distress
such as never has occurred
since nations came into being until that time.
But at that time all your people
who are found written in the book will escape.
² Many who sleep in the dust
of the earth will awake,

---

^A 11:29 Lit *but the last*   ^B 11:30 = the Romans   ^C 11:37 Or *God*   ^D 11:39 Or *those he acknowledges*   ^E 11:41 Lit *the first*   ^F 11:43 Lit *Cushites at his steps*
^G 11:45 Or *the seas at*

some to eternal life,
and some to disgrace and eternal contempt.
³ Those who have insight will shine
like the bright expanse of the heavens,
and those who lead many to righteousness,
like the stars forever and ever.

⁴ "But you, Daniel, keep these words secret and seal the book until the time of the end. Many will roam about, and knowledge will increase."ᴬ

⁵ Then I, Daniel, looked, and two others were standing there, one on this bank of the river and one on the other. ⁶ One of them said to the man dressed in linen, who was above the water of the river, "How long until the end of these wondrous things?" ⁷ Then I heard the man dressed in linen, who was above the water of the river. He raised both his hands ᴮ toward heaven and swore by him who lives eternally that it would be for a time, times, and half a time. When the power of the holy people is shattered, all these things will be completed.

⁸ I heard but did not understand. So I asked, "My lord, what will be the outcome of these things?"

⁹ He said, "Go on your way, Daniel, for the words are secret and sealed until the time of the end. ¹⁰ Many will be purified, cleansed, and refined, but the wicked will act wickedly; none of the wicked will understand, but those who have insight will understand. ¹¹ From the time the daily sacrifice is abolished and the abomination of desolation is set up, there will be 1,290 days. ¹² Happy is the one who waits for and reaches 1,335 days. ¹³ But as for you, go on your way to the end;ᶜ you will rest, and then you will stand to receive your allotted inheritance at the end of the days."

ᴬ12:4 LXX reads *and the earth will be filled with unrighteousness* ᴮ12:7 Lit *raised his right and his left* ᶜ12:13 LXX omits *to the end*

For I Desire Faithful Love & Love NOT SACRIFICE

hosea

 For I desire faithful love and not sacrifice, the knowledge of God rather than burnt offerings. **6:6**

ON THE TIMELINE Hosea's ministry to the nation of Israel occurred over a thirty-year period, approximately 753 BC to 725 BC. Shortly after Hosea's final message, Israel was overthrown by Assyria and the people were taken into captivity, in 722 BC.

A LITTLE BACKGROUND One of the most autobiographical of the Prophetic Books, Hosea opens with the account of Hosea's divinely commissioned marriage to the promiscuous Gomer and the odd names of their three children. Apart from this information about his immediate family, hardly anything is known about Hosea.

MESSAGE & PURPOSE The nation of Israel was crumbling. After the death of Jeroboam II in 753 BC, Israel sank into near anarchy, going through six kings in about thirty years. Assyria regained power and eventually destroyed Israel. Hosea made clear that this devastation was God's judgment for Israel's sins, as well as a means of calling His people back to Himself.

The Lord's message through Hosea to the people of Israel was simple: stop their promiscuity and idolatry and return to God in humility and faithfulness. Hosea reminded Israel that their present distress was the Lord's discipline, which would continue until they returned to Him.

GIVE THANKS FOR THE BOOK OF HOSEA

The book of Hosea compares the relationship between God and His people to a real-life marriage of Hosea and his wife, drawing a parallel between spiritual and marital unfaithfulness. Like a marriage partner, God is deeply involved in our lives and is pained when we go our own way. Often God's people have failed to demonstrate wholehearted love and faithfulness to Him, but nothing can quench God's love for them. He stands ready to forgive and restore those who turn to Him in repentance. In buying Gomer's freedom, Hosea pointed ahead to God's love perfectly expressed in Christ, who bought the freedom of His bride, the Church, with His own life.

THE BOOK OF HOSEA IN HISTORY

775 BC   750 BC   725 BC

753

735

793

732   722

Jeroboam II
becomes
king of Israel

Zechariah
becomes king
of Israel

Hosea's
prophetic
ministry begins

Israel invaded
and taken captive
by Assyria

End of Hosea's
ministry

Hoshea's reign begins—
the last king of Israel

Damascus and Israel attack
Jerusalem and Judah

READ AND UNDERSTAND HOSEA

The Bible is a complete work in which many stories combine to tell one story. As you read the book of Hosea, consider reading the additional passages to discover how the whole of Scripture works together.

1 The word of the LORD that came to Hosea son of Beeri during the reigns of Uzziah, Jotham, Ahaz, and Hezekiah, kings of Judah, and of Jeroboam son of Jehoash, king of Israel.

HOSEA'S MARRIAGE AND CHILDREN

² When the LORD first spoke to Hosea, he said this to him:

Go and marry a woman of promiscuity,
and have children of promiscuity,
for the land is committing blatant acts of promiscuity
by abandoning the LORD.

³ So he went and married Gomer daughter of Diblaim, and she conceived and bore him a son. ⁴ Then the LORD said to him:

Name him Jezreel,ᴬ for in a little while
I will bring the bloodshed of Jezreel
on the house of Jehu
and put an end to the kingdom
of the house of Israel.
⁵ On that day I will break the bow of Israel
in the Valley of Jezreel.

⁶ She conceived again and gave birth to a daughter, and the LORD said to him:

Name her Lo-ruhamah,ᴮ
for I will no longer have compassion
on the house of Israel.
I will certainly take them away.
⁷ But I will have compassion on the house of Judah,
and I will deliver them by the LORD their God.
I will not deliver them by bow, sword, or war,
or by horses and cavalry.

⁸ After Gomer had weaned Lo-ruhamah, she conceived and gave birth to a son. ⁹ Then the LORD said:

Name him Lo-ammi,ᶜ
for you are not my people,
and I will not be your God.ᴰ
¹⁰ Yet the number of the Israelites
will be like the sand of the sea,
which cannot be measured or counted.
And in the place where they were told:
You are not my people,
they will be called: Sons of the living God.
¹¹ And the Judeans and the Israelites
will be gathered together.
They will appoint for themselves a single ruler
and go up fromᴱ the land.
For the day of Jezreel will be great.

ᴬ1:4 = God Sows   ᴮ1:6 = No Compassion   ᶜ1:9 = Not My People   ᴰ1:9 Lit *not be yours*   ᴱ1:11 Or *and flourish in*; Hb obscure

2 Call^A your brothers: My People
and your sisters: Compassion.

ISRAEL'S ADULTERY REBUKED

2 Rebuke your mother; rebuke her.
For she is not my wife and I am not her husband.
Let her remove the promiscuous look from her face
and her adultery from between her breasts.

3 Otherwise, I will strip her naked
and expose her as she was on the day of her birth.
I will make her like a desert
and like a parched land,
and I will let her die of thirst.

4 I will have no compassion on her children
because they are the children of promiscuity.

5 Yes, their mother is promiscuous;
she conceived them and acted shamefully.
For she thought, "I will follow my lovers,
the men who give me my food and water,
my wool and flax, my oil and drink."

6 Therefore, this is what I will do:
I will block her^B way with thorns;
I will enclose her with a wall,
so that she cannot find her paths.

7 She will pursue her lovers but not catch them;
she will look for them but not find them.
Then she will think,
"I will go back to my former husband,
for then it was better for me than now."

8 She does not recognize
that it is I who gave her the grain,
the new wine, and the fresh oil.
I lavished silver and gold on her,
which they used for Baal.

9 Therefore, I will take back my grain in its time
and my new wine in its season;
I will take away my wool and linen,
which were to cover her nakedness.

10 Now I will expose her shame
in the sight of her lovers,
and no one will rescue her from my power.

11 I will put an end to all her celebrations:
her feasts, New Moons, and Sabbaths —
all her festivals.

12 I will devastate her vines and fig trees.
She thinks that these are her wages
that her lovers have given her.
I will turn them into a thicket,

---

^A 2:1 Lit *Say to*   ^B 2:6 LXX, Syr; MT reads *your*

and the wild animals will eat them.

13 And I will punish her for the days of the Baals,
to which she burned incense.
She put on her rings and her jewelry
and followed her lovers,
but she forgot me.
This is the LORD's declaration.

ISRAEL'S ADULTERY FORGIVEN

14 Therefore, I am going to persuade her,
lead her to the wilderness,
and speak tenderly to her.ᴬ

15 There I will give her vineyards back to her
and make the Valley of Achorᴮ
into a gateway of hope.
There she will respond as she did
in the days of her youth,
as in the day she came out of the land of Egypt.

16 In that day —
this is the LORD's declaration —
you will call me, "My husband,"
and no longer call me, "My Baal."ᶜ

17 For I will remove the names of the Baals
from her mouth;
they will no longer be remembered by their names.

18 On that day I will make a covenant for them
with the wild animals, the birds of the sky,
and the creatures that crawl on the ground.
I will shatter bow, sword,
and weapons of war in the landᴰ
and will enable the people to rest securely.

19 I will take you to be my wife forever.
I will take you to be my wife in righteousness,
justice, love, and compassion.

20 I will take you to be my wife in faithfulness,
and you will know the LORD.

21 On that day I will respond —
this is the LORD's declaration.
I will respond to the sky,
and it will respond to the earth.

22 The earth will respond to the grain,
the new wine, and the fresh oil,
and they will respond to Jezreel.

23 I will sow herᴱ in the land for myself,
and I will have compassion
on Lo-ruhamah;
I will say to Lo-ammi:

ᴬ2:14 Lit *speak to her heart*   ᴮ2:15 = Trouble   ᶜ2:16 Or *My Master*   ᴰ2:18 Or
war on the earth   ᴱ2:23 = Israel

You are my people,
and he will say, "You are my God."

WAITING FOR RESTORATION

3 Then the LORD said to me, "Go again; show love to a woman who is loved by another man and is an adulteress, just as the LORD loves the Israelites though they turn to other gods and love raisin cakes."

² So I bought her for fifteen shekels of silver and five bushels of barley.[A,B] ³ I said to her, "You are to live with me many days. You must not be promiscuous or belong to any man, and I will act the same way toward you."

⁴ For the Israelites must live many days without king or prince, without sacrifice or sacred pillar, and without ephod or household idols. ⁵ Afterward, the people of Israel will return and seek the LORD their God and David their king. They will come with awe to the LORD and to his goodness in the last days.

GOD'S CASE AGAINST ISRAEL

4 Hear the word of the LORD, people of Israel,
for the LORD has a case
against the inhabitants of the land:
There is no truth, no faithful love,
and no knowledge of God in the land!
² Cursing, lying, murder, stealing,
and adultery are rampant;
one act of bloodshed follows another.
³ For this reason the land mourns,
and everyone who lives in it languishes,
along with the wild animals
and the birds of the sky;
even the fish of the sea disappear.
⁴ But let no one dispute; let no one argue,
for my case is against you priests.[C,D]
⁵ You will stumble by day;
the prophet will also stumble with you by night.
And I will destroy your mother.
⁶ My people are destroyed for lack of knowledge.
Because you have rejected knowledge,
I will reject you from serving as my priest.
Since you have forgotten the law of your God,
I will also forget your sons.

⁷ The more they multiplied,
the more they sinned against me.
I[E] will change their[F] honor into disgrace.
⁸ They feed on the sin[G] of my people;
they have an appetite for their iniquity.

[A] 3:2 LXX reads *barley and a measure of wine* [B] 3:2 Lit *silver, a homer of barley, and a lethek of barley* [C] 4:4 Text emended; MT reads *argue, and your people are like those contending with a priest* [D] 4:4 Hb obscure [E] 4:7 Alt Hb tradition, Syr, Tg read *They* [F] 4:7 Alt Hb tradition reads *my* [G] 4:8 Or *sin offerings*

⁹ The same judgment will happen
to both people and priests.
I will punish them for their ways
and repay them for their deeds.
¹⁰ They will eat but not be satisfied;
they will be promiscuous but not multiply.
For they have abandoned
their devotion to the LORD.
¹¹ Promiscuity, wine, and new wine
take away one's understanding.

¹² My people consult their wooden idols,
and their divining rods inform them.
For a spirit of promiscuity leads them astray;
they act promiscuously
in disobedience to ᴬ their God.
¹³ They sacrifice on the mountaintops,
and they burn offerings on the hills,
and under oaks, poplars, and terebinths,
because their shade is pleasant.
And so your daughters act promiscuously
and your daughters-in-law commit adultery.
¹⁴ I will not punish your daughters
when they act promiscuously
or your daughters-in-law
when they commit adultery,
for the men themselves go off with prostitutes
and make sacrifices with cult prostitutes.
People without discernment are doomed.

WARNINGS FOR ISRAEL AND JUDAH

¹⁵ Israel, if you act promiscuously,
don't let Judah become guilty!
Do not go to Gilgal
or make a pilgrimage to Beth-aven, ᴮ
and do not swear an oath: As the LORD lives!
¹⁶ For Israel is as obstinate as a stubborn cow.
Can the LORD now shepherd them
like a lamb in an open meadow?
¹⁷ Ephraim is attached to idols;
leave him alone!
¹⁸ When their drinking is over,
they turn to promiscuity.
Israel's leaders ᶜ fervently love disgrace. ᴰ
¹⁹ A wind with its wings will carry them off, ᴱ
and they will be ashamed of their sacrifices.

ᴬ4:12 Lit *promiscuously from under*   ᴮ4:15 = House of Wickedness   ᶜ4:18 Lit
Her shields; Ps 47:9; 89:18   ᴰ4:18 Hb obscure   ᴱ4:19 Lit *wind will bind it in
its wings*

5

Hear this, priests!
Pay attention, house of Israel!
Listen, royal house!
For the judgment applies to you
because you have been a snare at Mizpah
and a net spread out on Tabor.

2 Rebels are deeply involved in slaughter;
I will be a punishment for all of them.^A

3 I know Ephraim,
and Israel is not hidden from me.
For now, Ephraim,
you have acted promiscuously;
Israel is defiled.

4 Their actions do not allow them
to return to their God,
for a spirit of promiscuity is among them,
and they do not know the LORD.

5 Israel's arrogance testifies against them.^B
Both Israel and Ephraim stumble
because of their iniquity;
even Judah will stumble with them.

6 They go with their flocks and herds
to seek the LORD
but do not find him;
he has withdrawn from them.

7 They betrayed the LORD;
indeed, they gave birth to illegitimate children.
Now the New Moon will devour them
along with their fields.

8 Blow the horn in Gibeah,
the trumpet in Ramah;
raise the war cry in Beth-aven:
Look behind you,^C Benjamin!

9 Ephraim will become a desolation
on the day of punishment;
I announce what is certain
among the tribes of Israel.

10 The princes of Judah are like those
who move boundary markers;
I will pour out my fury on them like water.

11 Ephraim is oppressed, crushed in judgment,
for he is determined to follow what is worthless.^D

12 So I am like rot to Ephraim
and like decay to the house of Judah.

13 When Ephraim saw his sickness
and Judah his wound,

---

^A 5:2 Hb obscure ^B 5:5 Lit *against his face* ^C 5:8 Or *We will follow you*
^D 5:11 Or *follow a command*; Hb obscure

Ephraim went to Assyria
and sent a delegation to the great king.[A]
But he cannot cure you or heal your wound.
14   For I am like a lion to Ephraim
and like a young lion to the house of Judah.
Yes, I will tear them to pieces and depart.
I will carry them off,
and no one can rescue them.
15   I will depart and return to my place
until they recognize their guilt and seek my face;
they will search for me in their distress.

A CALL TO REPENTANCE

6 Come, let us return to the LORD.
For he has torn us,
and he will heal us;
he has wounded us,
and he will bind up our wounds.
2   He will revive us after two days,
and on the third day he will raise us up
so we can live in his presence.
3   Let us strive to know the LORD.
His appearance is as sure as the dawn.
He will come to us like the rain,
like the spring showers that water the land.

THE LORD'S FIRST LAMENT

4   What am I going to do with you, Ephraim?
What am I going to do with you, Judah?
Your love is like the morning mist
and like the early dew that vanishes.
5   This is why I have used the prophets
to cut them down;[B]
I have killed them with the words from my mouth.
My judgment strikes like lightning.[C]
6   For I desire faithful love and not sacrifice,
the knowledge of God rather than burnt offerings.

7   But they, like Adam,[D] have violated the covenant;
there they have betrayed me.
8   Gilead is a city of evildoers,
tracked with bloody footprints.
9   Like raiders who wait in ambush for someone,
a band of priests murders on the road to Shechem.
They commit atrocities.
10   I have seen something horrible in the house of Israel:

[A]5:13 Or to King Yareb   [B]6:5 Or have cut down the prophets   [C]6:5 LXX, Syr,
Tg; MT reads Your judgments go out as light   [D]6:7 Or they, as at Adam, or they,
like men,

FAITHFUL LOVE, NOT SACRIFICE

HOSEA 6:1–7:2; MATTHEW 12:1-8

As a church culture kid, brought up on the lap of youth group events, Christian concerts, Bible camp, and the Awana Olympics, I somehow got the impression that overseas mission work was the highest calling a Christian could have. I truly and passionately loved God, so if that's where the faith-action was, then that's where I wanted to be.

To a wide-eyed high schooler, anxious for adventure and an uncommon life, the abnormality of mission work appealed to me. I was ready to sacrifice big for God. But if I'm honest, that was mostly because I thought a missionary life sounded kind of flashy—daring, and even religiously "successful."

I took a handful of short-term trips (which, in all reality, probably benefitted me more than the people I went to serve), but I never became a career missionary, not in the way I had pictured, anyway. I was willing, but God had a different plan for my life. Today, my "mission field" looks strangely more like my childhood home than the jungles of the Amazon.

Maybe you've wrestled through that tension too. Can we be faithful to God in the ordinary, or do we have to do "big things" for God for our faith to be legitimate?

In Ephesians 4:1, Paul urges believers to "live worthy of the calling [we] have received." But what does that actually look like? Hosea 6:6 helps us:

"For I desire faithful love and not sacrifice, the knowledge of God rather than burnt offerings."

This verse shows us what God considers the highest devotion to Him, what He wants most: faithful love over sacrifice, a relationship with Him over our offerings.

Have you ever had a nagging suspicion that giant sacrifices come more easily than quiet faithfulness? I have. It was easier to dream of living in a foreign land, leading whole villages to Christ, than it is to actually live a quiet, largely unknown, completely unflashy, but faithful life. To be loyal to God even when His plan for me doesn't make for a great Christmas card.

God still expected the Israelites to bring the prescribed offerings and sacrifices to the altar. But those things weren't what He wanted most of all.

So why would God prefer loyalty and faithfulness over big sacrifices? The answer is the echo of the love story woven throughout the Bible's pages: **God wants our hearts. He is jealous for our affection.** He wants loyalty and faithfulness because that's what you bring to the table when you are hopelessly in love with someone. He wants us to be head-over-heels for Him, and when we are, sacrifices will come easily.

Whether our faithfulness takes us to the ends of the earth or leaves us right where we are, remember what He's really after: us.

Ephraim's promiscuity is there; Israel is defiled.

11 A harvest is also appointed for you, Judah.

When I[A] return my people from captivity,
7 ¹ when I heal Israel,
the iniquity of Ephraim and the crimes of Samaria
will be exposed.
For they practice fraud;
a thief breaks in;
a raiding party pillages outside.

2 But they never consider that I remember all their evil.
Now their actions are all around them;
they are right in front of my face.

ISRAEL'S CORRUPTION

3 They please the king with their evil,
the princes with their lies.

4 All of them commit adultery;
they are like an oven heated by a baker
who stops stirring the fire
from the kneading of the dough until it is leavened.

5 On the day of our king,
the princes are sick with the heat of wine —
there is a conspiracy with traitors.[B]

6 For they — their hearts like an oven —
draw him into their oven.
Their anger smolders all night;
in the morning it blazes like a flaming fire.

7 All of them are as hot as an oven,
and they consume their rulers.
All their kings fall;
not one of them calls on me.[C]

8 Ephraim has allowed himself to get mixed up with the nations.
Ephraim is unturned bread baked on a griddle.

9 Foreigners consume his strength,
but he does not notice.
Even his hair is streaked with gray,
but he does not notice.

10 Israel's arrogance testifies against them,[D]
yet they do not return to the LORD their God,
and for all this, they do not seek him.

11 So Ephraim has become like a silly, senseless dove;
they call to Egypt, and they go to Assyria.

12 As they are going, I will spread my net over them;

[A]6:11 Or you. Judah, when I   [B]7:5 Lit wine — he stretches out his hand to scorners; Hb obscure   [C]7:3-7 These vv. may refer to a king's assassination; Hb obscure.   [D]7:10 Lit against his face

GOD HAS NOT CHANGED

HOSEA 7:3–8:14; ROMANS 9:22-26

"Ephraim has allowed himself to get mixed up with the nations. Ephraim is unturned bread baked on a griddle. Foreigners consume his strength, but he does not notice. Even his hair is streaked with gray, but he does not notice. Israel's arrogance testifies against them, yet they do not return to the LORD their God, and for all this, they do not seek him."

HOSEA 7:8-10

Have you noticed something here?

Ephraim (the largest of the ten northern tribes, whose name is sometimes used to refer to Israel as a whole) has become an out-of-control mess. Meanwhile, the people of Israel are so crazed with self-indulgence they can hardly tell what day it is. But I can't help standing back a bit and noticing, in all of Israel's wayward mindlessness as they run to Egypt and Assyria and every which way, God hasn't changed.

Oh, He's definitely watching. He sees them spiraling out of control, tossing their reputation out the window. He hears the other nations all whispering to each other about "God's chosen people" killing off their leaders, one by one, and getting fresh starts from their God, only to get all muddy again (Hs 7:16).

Israel is two-faced and double-tongued.

But if we turn our attention from the squeaky wheel for a moment—if we tune out all the noise—we'll notice this: God has not changed.

He has but one face and one tongue. One unrelenting love for His bride.

We want this passage to be about the rogue bride, or the prodigal son, and how Israel can't seem to get it right. But it isn't. It's about God.

God's character never changes. His one face is righteousness. His one Word is holiness. His one undying call to His people is love.

As the ever-faithful Groom, God remains. Even as His anger burns over the unfaithfulness of His bride, He forgives her. He provides for her. He gives her a fresh start. And in His severe mercy, He even withholds good things from her so that she might return to Him. While Israel hedges its bets on other gods, the Groom has all His focus on His one, true love.

Maybe you don't need me to spell it out for you today, but in case you do, hear this: you are His one, true love. Wherever you are, whatever you've done, whatever anyone else thinks of you, and however long it's been since the last time you called Him your Groom—He hasn't changed, and neither has His love for you.

"But God proves his own love for us in that while we were still sinners, Christ died for us."

ROMANS 5:8

I will bring them down like birds of the sky.
I will discipline them in accordance
with the news that reaches[A] their assembly.

THE LORD'S SECOND LAMENT

13 Woe to them, for they fled from me;
destruction to them, for they rebelled
against me!
Though I want to redeem them,
they speak lies against me.
14 They do not cry to me from their hearts;
rather, they wail on their beds.
They slash themselves[B] for grain and new wine;
they turn away from me.
15 I trained and strengthened their arms,
but they plot evil against me.
16 They turn, but not to what is above;[C]
they are like a faulty bow.
Their leaders will fall by the sword
because of their insolent tongue.
They will be ridiculed for this in the land of Egypt.

ISRAEL'S FALSE HOPES

8 Put the horn to your mouth!
One like an eagle comes
against the house of the LORD,
because they transgress my covenant
and rebel against my law.
2 Israel cries out to me,
"My God, we know you!"
3 Israel has rejected what is good;
an enemy will pursue him.

4 They have installed kings,
but not through me.
They have appointed leaders,
but without my approval.
They make their silver and gold
into idols for themselves
for their own destruction.[D]
5 Your calf-idol[E] is rejected, Samaria.
My anger burns against them.
How long will they be incapable of innocence?
6 For this thing is from Israel —
a craftsman made it, and it is not God.
The calf of Samaria will be smashed to bits!

[A]7:12 Lit news to   [B]7:14 Some Hb mss, LXX; other Hb mss read They stay
[C]7:16 Some emend to turn to what is useless   [D]8:4 Lit themselves that it might be
cut off   [E]8:5 Lit calf

7 Indeed, they sow the wind
  and reap the whirlwind.
  There is no standing grain;
  what sprouts fails to yield flour.
  Even if they did,
  foreigners would swallow it up.

8 Israel is swallowed up!
  Now they are among the nations
  like discarded pottery.

9 For they have gone up to Assyria
  like a wild donkey going off on its own.
  Ephraim has paid for love.

10 Even though they hire lovers among the nations,
   I will now round them up,
   and they will begin to decrease in number
   under the burden of the king and leaders.

11 When Ephraim multiplied his altars for sin,
   they became his altars for sinning.

12 Though I were to write out for him
   ten thousand points of my instruction,
   they would be^A regarded as something strange.

13 Though they offer sacrificial gifts^B
   and eat the flesh,
   the Lord does not accept them.
   Now he will remember their guilt
   and punish their sins;
   they will return to Egypt.

14 Israel has forgotten his Maker and built palaces;
   Judah has also multiplied fortified cities.
   I will send fire on their cities,
   and it will consume their citadels.

THE COMING EXILE

9 Israel, do not rejoice jubilantly as the nations do,
  for you have acted promiscuously, leaving your God.
  You love the wages of a prostitute
  on every grain-threshing floor.

2 Threshing floor and wine vat will not sustain them,
  and the new wine will fail them.

3 They will not stay in the land of the Lord.
  Instead, Ephraim will return to Egypt,
  and they will eat unclean food in Assyria.

4 They will not pour out
  their wine offerings to the Lord,
  and their sacrifices will not please him.
  Their food will be like the bread of mourners;

---

^A 8:12 Or *Though I wrote out . . . instruction, they are*   ^B 8:13 Hb obscure

all who eat it become defiled.
For their bread will be for their appetites alone;
it will not enter the house of the LORD.

5 What will you do on a festival day,
on the day of the LORD's feast?

6 For even if they flee from devastation,
Egypt will gather them, and Memphis will bury them.
Thistles will take possession of their precious silver;
thorns will invade their tents.

7 The days of punishment have come;
the days of retribution have come.
Let Israel recognize it!
The prophet is a fool,
and the inspired man is insane,
because of the magnitude
of your iniquity and hostility.

8 Ephraim's watchman is with my God.
Yet the prophet encounters a bird trap
on all his pathways.
Hostility is in the house of his God!

9 They have deeply corrupted themselves
as in the days of Gibeah.
He will remember their iniquity;
he will punish their sins.

EPHRAIM BEREAVED OF OFFSPRING

10 I discovered Israel
like grapes in the wilderness.
I saw your fathers
like the first fruit of the fig tree in its first season.
But they went to Baal-peor,
consecrated themselves to Shame, [A]
and became abhorrent,
like the thing they loved.

11 Ephraim's glory will fly away like a bird:
no birth, no pregnancy, no conception.

12 Even if they raise children,
I will bereave them of each one.
Yes, woe to them when I depart from them!

13 I have seen Ephraim like Tyre,
planted in a meadow,
so Ephraim will bring out his children
to the executioner.

14 Give them, LORD —
What should you give?
Give them a womb that miscarries
and breasts that are dry!

A 9:10 = Baal

15 All their evil appears at Gilgal,
    for there I began to hate them.
    I will drive them from my house
    because of their evil, wicked actions.
    I will no longer love them;
    all their leaders are rebellious.
16 Ephraim is struck down;
    their roots are withered;
    they cannot bear fruit.
    Even if they bear children,
    I will kill the precious offspring of their wombs.
17 My God will reject them
    because they have not listened to him;
    they will become wanderers among the nations.

THE VINE AND THE CALF

10 Israel is a lush[A] vine;
    it yields fruit for itself.
    The more his fruit increased,
    the more he increased the altars.
    The better his land produced,
    the better they made the sacred pillars.
2 Their hearts are devious;[B]
    now they must bear their guilt.
    The LORD will break down their altars
    and demolish their sacred pillars.
3 In fact, they are now saying,
    "We have no king!
    For we do not fear the LORD.
    What can a king do for us?"
4 They speak mere words,
    taking false oaths while making covenants.
    So lawsuits break out
    like poisonous weeds in the furrows of a field.

5 The residents of Samaria will have anxiety
    over the calf of Beth-aven.
    Indeed, its idolatrous priests rejoiced over it;
    the people will mourn over it,
    over its glory.
    It will certainly go into exile.
6 The calf itself will be taken to Assyria
    as an offering to the great king.[C]
    Ephraim will experience shame;
    Israel will be ashamed of its counsel.
7 Samaria's king will disappear[D]
    like foam[E] on the surface of the water.

A10:1 Or ravaged   B10:2 Or divided   C10:6 Or to King Yareb   D10:7 Or will
be cut off   E10:7 Or a stick

HIS DISCIPLINE IS LOVING

HOSEA 9–10; MATTHEW 11:28

There are some passages of Scripture that are really hard to read because they don't tell us pleasant things. This passage in Hosea is one of them; it talks to us about sin and its undeniable consequences.

I like it best when I can imagine Jesus patting me on the shoulder, saying, "Well done, good and faithful servant" (Mt 25:23). But instead of patting me on the back, Hosea 10 kicks me in the pants.

Why would God say all this to us? Why can't we skip over the nasty parts and hear about something nice instead?

The truth is, we cannot fully understand the gospel without this very real and difficult realization of sin. The gospel isn't a "skip over the difficult stuff" message. It's the answer to an ugly, deeply rooted problem in our hearts. On their own, our hearts aren't naturally inclined to seek the Lord and do what's right.

We may like to claim a kind of made-up righteousness of our own, but those are "mere words" and "false oaths" (Hs 10:4). In truth, apart from God's bountiful grace, we are like Israel. Our actions reveal what we really believe, that "we do not fear the LORD" (Hs 10:3). That's frightening because Hosea tells us where all this leads: shame, judgment, and war.

But even in this passage about the darkness of sin, God shines a light for us. When God calls us to "sow righteousness" (Hs 10:12), He's not simply commanding us—He's also beckoning to us. **God is throwing a rope down into the well to pull us up out of the darkness and muck of our sin.**

From the deep pit of our own destruction and despair, we hear a steady, loving voice calling even now:

"Sow righteousness for yourselves and reap faithful love; break up your unplowed ground. It is time to seek the LORD until he comes and sends righteousness on you like the rain" (Hs 10:12). "Come to me, all of you who are weary and burdened, and I will give you rest" (Mt 11:28).

Hosea is a book about God's wooing of an undeserving people. While the reality of our sin may make us want to run from God, the reminder that He desires good for us, not destruction, draws us close. Difficult passages like this remind us that God longs for our wandering hearts to return to Him and receive His cleansing grace.

Let's not wallow in our shame, but instead run with abandon back to our loving Father. As we do, He will continue to pursue us as He always has, to rescue us from even the deepest darkness of our hearts.

8 The high places of Aven, the sin of Israel,
  will be destroyed;
  thorns and thistles will grow
      over their altars.
  They will say to the mountains, "Cover us!"
  and to the hills, "Fall on us!"

ISRAEL'S DEFEAT BECAUSE OF SIN

9 Israel, you have sinned
  since the days of Gibeah;
  they have taken their stand there.
  Will not war against the unjust
  overtake them in Gibeah?

10 I will discipline them at my discretion;
  nations will be gathered against them
  to put them in bondage^A
  for their double iniquity.

11 Ephraim is a well-trained calf
  that loves to thresh,
  but I will place a yoke on^B her fine neck.
  I will harness Ephraim;
  Judah will plow;
  Jacob will do the final plowing.

12 Sow righteousness for yourselves
  and reap faithful love;
  break up your unplowed ground.
  It is time to seek the LORD
  until he comes and sends righteousness
  on you like the rain.

13 You have plowed wickedness
      and reaped injustice;
  you have eaten the fruit of lies.
  Because you have trusted in your own way^C
  and in your large number of soldiers,

14 the roar of battle will rise
      against your people,
  and all your fortifications will be demolished
  in a day of war,
  like Shalman's destruction of Beth-arbel.
  Mothers will be dashed to pieces
  along with their children.

15 So it will be done to you, Bethel,
  because of your extreme evil.
  At dawn the king of Israel
      will be totally destroyed.

---

^A10:10 LXX, Syr, Vg read *against them when they are disciplined* ^B10:11 Lit *will pass over* ^C10:13 LXX reads *your chariots*

THE LORD'S LOVE FOR ISRAEL

11 When Israel was a child, I loved him,
and out of Egypt I called my son.
2 Israel called to the Egyptians
even as Israel was leaving them. [A]
They kept sacrificing to the Baals
and burning offerings to idols.
3 It was I who taught Ephraim to walk,
taking them [B] by the hand, [C]
but they never knew that I healed them.
4 I led them with human cords,
with ropes of love.
To them I was like one
who eases the yoke from their jaws;
I bent down to give them food.
5 Israel will not return to the land of Egypt
and Assyria will be his king,
because they refused to repent.
6 A sword will whirl through his cities;
it will destroy and devour the bars of his gates, [D]
because of their schemes.
7 My people are bent on turning from me.
Though they call to him on high,
he will not exalt them at all.

8 How can I give you up, Ephraim?
How can I surrender you, Israel?
How can I make you like Admah?
How can I treat you like Zeboiim?
I have had a change of heart;
my compassion is stirred!
9 I will not vent the full fury of my anger;
I will not turn back to destroy Ephraim.
For I am God and not man,
the Holy One among you;
I will not come in rage. [E]
10 They will follow the LORD;
he will roar like a lion.
When he roars,
his children will come trembling from the west.
11 They will be roused like birds from Egypt
and like doves from the land of Assyria.
Then I will settle them in their homes.
This is the LORD's declaration.
12 Ephraim surrounds me with lies,
the house of Israel, with deceit.

[A]11:2 Lit *They called to them; thus they went from before them* [B]11:3 LXX, Syr, Vg; MT reads *him* [C]11:3 Lit *them on his arms* [D]11:6 Or *devour his empty talkers, or devour his limbs*; Hb obscure [E]11:9 Or *come into any city*; Hb obscure

Judah still wanders with God
and is faithful to the holy ones.[A]

GOD'S CASE AGAINST JACOB'S HEIRS

12 Ephraim chases[B] the wind
and pursues the east wind.
He continually multiplies lies and violence.
He makes a covenant with Assyria,
and olive oil is carried to Egypt.

2 The LORD also has a dispute with Judah.
He is about to punish Jacob according to his conduct;
he will repay him based on his actions.

3 In the womb he grasped his brother's heel,
and as an adult he wrestled with God.

4 Jacob struggled with the angel and prevailed;
he wept and sought his favor.
He found him at Bethel,
and there he spoke with him.[C]

5 The LORD is the God of Armies;
the LORD is his name.

6 But you must return to your God.
Maintain love and justice,
and always put your hope in God.

7 A merchant loves to extort
with dishonest scales in his hands.

8 But Ephraim thinks,
"How rich I have become;
I made it all myself.
In all my earnings,
no one can find any iniquity in me
that I can be punished for!"[D]

JUDGMENT ON APOSTATE ISRAEL

9 I have been the LORD your God
ever since[E] the land of Egypt.
I will make you live in tents again,
as in the festival days.

10 I will speak through the prophets
and grant many visions;
I will give parables through the prophets.

11 Since Gilead is full of evil,
they will certainly come to nothing.
They sacrifice bulls in Gilgal;
even their altars will be like piles of rocks
on the furrows of a field.

[A]11:12 Hb obscure [B]12:1 Or grazes on, or tends [C]12:4 LXX, Syr; MT reads us
[D]12:8 Lit iniquity which is sin [E]12:9 LXX reads God who brought you out of

FURTHER INDICTMENT OF JACOB'S HEIRS

12 Jacob fled to the territory of Aram.
Israel worked to earn a wife;
he tended flocks for a wife.
13 The LORD brought Israel from Egypt
by a prophet,
and Israel was tended by a prophet.

14 Ephraim has provoked bitter anger,
so his Lord will leave his bloodguilt on him
and repay him for his contempt.

13 When Ephraim spoke, there was trembling;
he was exalted in Israel.
But he incurred guilt through Baal and died.

2 Now they continue to sin
and make themselves a cast image,
idols skillfully made from their silver,
all of them the work of craftsmen.
People say about them,
"Let the men who sacrifice^A kiss the calves."
3 Therefore, they will be like the morning mist,
like the early dew that vanishes,
like chaff blown from a threshing floor,
or like smoke from a window.

DEATH AND RESURRECTION

4 I have been the LORD your God
ever since^B the land of Egypt;
you know no God but me,
and no Savior exists besides me.
5 I knew^C you in the wilderness,
in the land of drought.
6 When they had pasture,
they became satisfied;
they were satisfied,
and their hearts became proud.
Therefore they forgot me.
7 So I will be like a lion to them;
I will lurk like a leopard on the path.
8 I will attack them
like a bear robbed of her cubs
and tear open the rib cage
over their hearts.
I will devour them there like a lioness,
like a wild beast that would rip them open.

---

^A 13:2 Or "Those who make human sacrifices ^B 13:4 DSS, LXX read God who
brought you out of ^C 13:5 LXX, Syr read fed

9   I will destroy you, Israel;
    you have no help but me.[A]

10 Where now is your king,[B]
    that he may save you in all your cities,
    and the[C] rulers[D] you demanded, saying,
    "Give me a king and leaders"?
11 I give you a king in my anger
    and take away a king in my wrath.
12 Ephraim's guilt is preserved;
    his sin is stored up.
13 Labor pains come on him.
    He is not a wise son;
    when the time comes,
    he will not be born.[E]

14 I will ransom them from the power of Sheol.
    I will redeem[F] them from death.
    Death, where are your barbs?
    Sheol, where is your sting?
    Compassion is hidden from my eyes.

THE COMING JUDGMENT

15 Although he flourishes among his brothers,[G]
    an east wind will come,
    a wind from the LORD rising up from the desert.
    His water source will fail,
    and his spring will run dry.
    The wind[H] will plunder the treasury
    of every precious item.

16 Samaria will bear her guilt
    because she has rebelled against her God.
    They will fall by the sword;
    their children will be dashed to pieces,
    and their pregnant women ripped open.

A PLEA TO REPENT

14 Israel, return to the LORD your God,
    for you have stumbled in your iniquity.
2   Take words of repentance with you
    and return to the LORD.
    Say to him: "Forgive all our iniquity
    and accept what is good,

[A] 13:9 LXX reads *At your destruction, Israel, who will help you?*   [B] 13:10 LXX, Syr,
Vg; MT reads *I will be your king*   [C] 13:10 Lit *your*   [D] 13:10 Or *judges*
[E] 13:13 Lit *he will not present himself at the opening of the womb for sons*
[F] 13:14 Or *Should I ransom . . . ? Should I redeem . . . ?*   [G] 13:15 Or *among reeds*
[H] 13:15 Probably the Assyrian king

so that we may repay you
with praise[A] from our[B] lips.
3 Assyria will not save us,
we will not ride on horses,
and we will no longer proclaim, 'Our gods!'
to the work of our hands.
For the fatherless receives compassion in you."

A PROMISE OF RESTORATION

4 I will heal their apostasy;
I will freely love them,
for my anger will have turned from him.
5 I will be like the dew to Israel;
he will blossom like the lily
and take root like the cedars of Lebanon.
6 His new branches will spread,
and his splendor will be like the olive tree,
his fragrance, like the forest of Lebanon.
7 The people will return and live beneath his shade.
They will grow grain
and blossom like the vine.
His renown will be like the wine of Lebanon.

8 Ephraim, why should I[C] have anything more
to do with idols?
It is I who answer and watch over him.
I am like a flourishing pine tree;
your fruit comes from me.

9 Let whoever is wise understand these things,
and whoever is insightful recognize them.
For the ways of the LORD are right,
and the righteous walk in them,
but the rebellious stumble in them.

[A]14:2 LXX reads with the fruit [B]14:2 Lit repay the bulls of our
[C]14:8 LXX reads he

RETURN TO THE LORD YOUR GOD

joel

Tear your hearts, not just your clothes, and return to the LORD your God. For he is gracious and compassionate, slow to anger, abounding in faithful love, and he relents from sending disaster. **2:13**

ON THE TIMELINE While the book of Joel is difficult to date, many scholars believe it was written around 830 BC. Joel's message was given to the nation of Judah, the southern kingdom in Israel, during the height of the monarchy. According to this date, Joel's message would have been given to Judah roughly 250 years before the Babylonian exile (586 BC).

A LITTLE BACKGROUND The book of Joel is one of the shortest in the Old Testament. Its author, Joel (Hebrew for "The LORD is God"), is the son of Pethuel. He is not easily identified with the other Joels of Scripture (1Sm 8:2; 1Ch 4:35; Ezr 10:43; Neh 11:9), leaving us only this book to know him, his calling from God, and his message. The book itself gives no biographical information other than his father's name.

MESSAGE & PURPOSE Joel's message was concerned primarily with motivating repentance by proclaiming the "day of the LORD." The locust plague is understood as judgment from God and a harbinger of the "day of the LORD" (Jl 1:2-20, especially v. 15). Joel also announced an even worse judgment—one that would come through a human army (Jl 2:1-11).

The phrase "day of the LORD" is prominent in the book of Joel and describes the judgment day of God. Joel showed that judgment could be directed both against the nation of Judah and against the "nations" as a whole. In addition to the more general theme of judgment, Joel also pointed to a day when God will make Himself known through His judgments.

GIVE THANKS FOR THE BOOK OF JOEL

The book of Joel shows us the Creator and Redeemer God of all the universe in complete control of nature. Joel preached that the God of judgment also is a God of mercy who stands ready to redeem and restore when His people come before Him in repentance. This book points to a time when the Spirit of God would be present upon all people. On the day of Pentecost, Peter proclaimed that the new day of Spirit-filled discipleship, foretold by Joel, had arrived (Ac 2:17-21).

THE BOOK OF JOEL IN HISTORY

900 BC   800 BC   700 BC   600 BC

835

830

931   **722**   **605**

Joel's prophetic
ministry

Kingdom of Israel
divided into Israel
and Judah

First Babylonian
siege of Judah

Joash becomes
king of Judah

Israel invaded
and taken captive
by Assyria

READ AND UNDERSTAND JOEL

The Bible is a complete work in which many stories combine to tell one story. As you read the book of Joel, consider reading the additional passages to discover how the whole of Scripture works together.

1 The word of the LORD that came to Joel son of Pethuel:

A PLAGUE OF LOCUSTS

2 Hear this, you elders;
   listen, all you inhabitants of the land.
   Has anything like this
      ever happened in your days
   or in the days of your ancestors?
3 Tell your children about it,
   and let your children tell their children,
   and their children the next generation.
4 What the devouring locust has left,
   the swarming locust has eaten;
   what the swarming locust has left,
   the young locust has eaten;
   and what the young locust has left,
   the destroying locust has eaten.

5 Wake up, you drunkards, and weep;
   wail, all you wine drinkers,
   because of the sweet wine,
   for it has been taken from your mouth.
6 For a nation has invaded my land,
   powerful and without number;
   its teeth are the teeth of a lion,
   and it has the fangs of a lioness.
7 It has devastated my grapevine
   and splintered my fig tree.
   It has stripped off its bark and thrown it away;
   its branches have turned white.
8 Grieve like a young woman dressed in sackcloth,
   mourning for the husband of her youth.
9 Grain and drink offerings have been cut off
   from the house of the LORD;
   the priests, who are ministers of the LORD, mourn.
10 The fields are destroyed;
   the land grieves;
   indeed, the grain is destroyed;
   the new wine is dried up;
   and the fresh oil fails.
11 Be ashamed, you farmers,
   wail, you vinedressers,^A
   over the wheat and the barley,
   because the harvest of the field has perished.
12 The grapevine is dried up,
   and the fig tree is withered;
   the pomegranate, the date palm, and the apple —

---

^A1:11 Or *The farmers are dismayed, the vinedressers wail*

all the trees of the orchard — have withered.
Indeed, human joy has dried up.

13 Dress in sackcloth and lament, you priests;
wail, you ministers of the altar.
Come and spend the night in sackcloth,
you ministers of my God,
because grain and drink offerings
are withheld from the house of your God.
14 Announce a sacred fast;
proclaim an assembly!
Gather the elders
and all the residents of the land
at the house of the LORD your God,
and cry out to the LORD.

THE DAY OF THE LORD

15 Woe because of that day!
For the day of the LORD is near
and will come as devastation from the Almighty.
16 Hasn't the food been cut off
before our eyes,
joy and gladness
from the house of our God?
17 The seeds lie shriveled in their casings.^A
The storehouses are in ruin,
and the granaries are broken down,
because the grain has withered away.
18 How the animals groan!
The herds of cattle wander in confusion
since they have no pasture.
Even the flocks of sheep and goats suffer punishment.
19 I call to you, LORD,
for fire has consumed
the pastures of the wilderness,
and flames have devoured
all the trees of the orchard.
20 Even the wild animals cry out to^B you,
for the river beds are dried up,
and fire has consumed
the pastures of the wilderness.

2 Blow the horn in Zion;
sound the alarm on my holy mountain!
Let all the residents of the land tremble,
for the day of the LORD is coming;
in fact, it is near —
2 a day of darkness and gloom,

---

^A1:17 Or clods; Hb obscure   ^B1:20 Or animals pant for; Hb obscure

a day of clouds and total darkness,
like the dawn spreading over the mountains;
a great and strong people appears,
such as never existed in ages past
and never will again
in all the generations to come.

³ A fire devours in front of them,
and behind them a flame blazes.
The land in front of them
is like the garden of Eden,
but behind them,
it is like a desert wasteland;
there is no escape from them.
⁴ Their appearance is like that of horses,
and they gallop like war horses.
⁵ They bound on the tops of the mountains.
Their sound is like the sound of chariots,
like the sound of fiery flames consuming stubble,
like a mighty army deployed for war.

⁶ Nations writhe in horror before them;
all faces turn pale.
⁷ They attack as warriors attack;
they scale walls as men of war do.
Each goes on his own path,
and they do not change their course.
⁸ They do not push each other;
each proceeds on his own path.
They dodge the arrows, never stopping.
⁹ They storm the city;
they run on the wall;
they climb into the houses;
they enter through the windows like thieves.

¹⁰ The earth quakes before them;
the sky shakes.
The sun and moon grow dark,
and the stars cease their shining.
¹¹ The Lord makes his voice heard
in the presence of his army.
His camp is very large;
those who carry out his command are powerful.
Indeed, the day of the Lord is terrible and dreadful —
who can endure it?

GOD'S CALL FOR REPENTANCE

¹² Even now —
  this is the Lord's declaration —
turn to me with all your heart,

FIRST THINGS FIRST

JOEL 2:12-17; MARK 1:14-15; LUKE 15:11-32

"Repent and believe."

They're the words Christ uses in the Gospel of Mark to begin His earthly ministry (Mk 1:15). But isn't it funny how quickly we skate past that first part? Believing is beautiful, but repentance is less glamorous. Yet, right out of the gate, Jesus' ministry began with a call for us to repent of our sin and believe He came to save us.

If we skip repentance, what do we believe He saves us from?

I spent thirty years hearing the story of the Prodigal Son one way: a young foolish son squanders his inheritance, only to crawl back home when he had nowhere else to turn. To me, the story was always more about the father. I assumed the lesson here was that I should be as forgiving of foolish people as he was.

Years passed, and as I read the story anew, I realized I'm not the father in this scenario. I'm the young fool. The story is as much about repentance as it is about forgiveness.

Scripture tells us the son came to his senses. He found clear eyes to look around and see the mess he'd made, then delivered a simple yet profound confession and repentance to his father: "Father, I have sinned against heaven and in your sight. I'm no longer worthy to be called your son" (Lk 15:21).

Repentance wasn't easy. The son wasn't even sure if his father would take him back. But the father received him with open arms as a beloved son.

If Christ calls us to repent and believe, let's not skip the first step. In doing so, we miss the fullness of the gospel. Let's listen closely and hear the call to repentance spoken by the prophet Joel on behalf of God Himself:

"Even now—this is the LORD's declaration—turn to me with all your heart, with fasting, weeping, and mourning. Tear your hearts, not just your clothes, and return to the LORD your God. For he is gracious and compassionate, slow to anger, abounding in faithful love, and he relents from sending disaster."

JOEL 2:12-13

Let's rend our hearts, like the prophet Joel said. But let's do so with the confidence that we are returning to a Father who will receive us with open arms and forgive us. He will delight in us with singing (Zph 3:17)! When our repentance is at its deepest, the joy of our salvation is at its highest.

with fasting, weeping, and mourning.

13 Tear your hearts,
not just your clothes,
and return to the LORD your God.
For he is gracious and compassionate,
slow to anger, abounding in faithful love,
and he relents from sending disaster.

14 Who knows? He may turn and relent
and leave a blessing behind him,
so you can offer grain and wine
to the LORD your God.

15 Blow the horn in Zion!
Announce a sacred fast;
proclaim an assembly.

16 Gather the people;
sanctify the congregation;
assemble the aged;^A
gather the infants,
even babies nursing at the breast.
Let the groom leave his bedroom,
and the bride her honeymoon chamber.

17 Let the priests, the LORD's ministers,
weep between the portico and the altar.
Let them say:
"Have pity on your people, LORD,
and do not make your inheritance
a disgrace,
an object of scorn among the nations.
Why should it be said among the peoples,
'Where is their God?'"

GOD'S RESPONSE TO HIS PEOPLE

18 Then the LORD became jealous for his land and spared his people. 19 The
LORD answered his people:

Look, I am about to send you
grain, new wine, and fresh oil.
You will be satiated with them,
and I will no longer make you
a disgrace among the nations.

20 I will drive the northerner far from you
and banish him to a dry and desolate land,
his front ranks into the Dead Sea,
and his rear guard into the Mediterranean Sea.
His stench will rise;
yes, his rotten smell will rise,
for he has done astonishing things.

^A2:16 Or *elders*

21 Don't be afraid, land;
   rejoice and be glad,
   for the LORD has done astonishing things.
22 Don't be afraid, wild animals,
   for the wilderness pastures have turned green,
   the trees bear their fruit,
   and the fig tree and grapevine yield their riches.
23 Children of Zion, rejoice and be glad
   in the LORD your God,
   because he gives you the autumn rain
   for your vindication.^A
   He sends showers for you,
   both autumn and spring rain as before.
24 The threshing floors will be full of grain,
   and the vats will overflow
   with new wine and fresh oil.

25 I will repay you for the years
   that the swarming locust ate,
   the young locust, the destroying locust,
   and the devouring locust —
   my great army that I sent against you.
26 You will have plenty to eat and be satisfied.
   You will praise the name of the LORD your God,
   who has dealt wondrously with you.
   My people will never again be put to shame.
27 You will know that I am present in Israel
   and that I am the LORD your God,
   and there is no other.
   My people will never again be put to shame.

GOD'S PROMISE OF HIS SPIRIT

28 After this
   I will pour out my Spirit on all humanity;
   then your sons and your daughters will prophesy,
   your old men will have dreams,
   and your young men will see visions.
29 I will even pour out my Spirit
   on the male and female slaves in those days.
30 I will display wonders
   in the heavens and on the earth:
   blood, fire, and columns of smoke.
31 The sun will be turned to darkness
   and the moon to blood
   before the great and terrible day of the LORD comes.
32 Then everyone who calls
   on the name of the LORD will be saved,
   for there will be an escape

---

^A 2:23 Or righteousness

for those on Mount Zion and in Jerusalem,
as the LORD promised,
among the survivors the LORD calls.

JUDGMENT OF THE NATIONS

3 Yes, in those days and at that time,
when I restore the fortunes of Judah and Jerusalem,

2 I will gather all the nations
and take them to the Valley of Jehoshaphat.ᴬ
I will enter into judgment with them there
because of my people, my inheritance Israel.
The nations have scattered the Israelites
in foreign countries
and divided up my land.

3 They cast lots for my people;
they bartered a boy for a prostitute
and sold a girl for wine to drink.

⁴ And also: Tyre, Sidon, and all the territories of Philistia — what are you to me? Are you paying me back or trying to get even with me? I will quickly bring retribution on your heads. ⁵ For you took my silver and gold and carried my finest treasures to your temples. ⁶ You sold the people of Judah and Jerusalem to the Greeks to remove them far from their own territory. ⁷ Look, I am about to rouse them up from the place where you sold them; I will bring retribution on your heads. ⁸ I will sell your sons and daughters to the people of Judah, and they will sell them to the Sabeans,ᴮ to a distant nation, for the LORD has spoken.

9 Proclaim this among the nations:
Prepare for holy war;
rouse the warriors;
let all the men of war advance and attack!

10 Beat your plows into swords
and your pruning knives into spears.
Let even the weakling say, "I am a warrior."

11 Come quickly,ᶜ all you surrounding nations;
gather yourselves.
Bring down your warriors there, LORD.

12 Let the nations be roused
and come to the Valley of Jehoshaphat,
for there I will sit down
to judge all the surrounding nations.

13 Swing the sickle
because the harvest is ripe.
Come and trample the grapes
because the winepress is full;

ᴬ3:2 = The LORD Will Judge   ᴮ3:8 Probably the south Arabian kingdom of Sheba (modern Yemen)   ᶜ3:11 LXX, Syr, Tg read *Gather yourselves and come*; Hb obscure

the wine vats overflow
because the wickedness of the nations is extreme.

14 Multitudes, multitudes
in the valley of decision!
For the day of the Lord is near
in the valley of decision.
15 The sun and moon will grow dark,
and the stars will cease their shining.
16 The Lord will roar from Zion
and make his voice heard from Jerusalem;
heaven and earth will shake.
But the Lord will be a refuge for his people,
a stronghold for the Israelites.

ISRAEL BLESSED

17 Then you will know
that I am the Lord your God,
who dwells in Zion, my holy mountain.
Jerusalem will be holy,
and foreigners will never overrun it again.
18 In that day
the mountains will drip with sweet wine,
and the hills will flow with milk.
All the streams of Judah will flow with water,
and a spring will issue from the Lord's house,
watering the Valley of Acacias.^A
19 Egypt will become desolate,
and Edom a desert wasteland,
because of the violence done to the people of Judah
in whose land they shed innocent blood.
20 But Judah will be inhabited forever,
and Jerusalem from generation to generation.
21 I will pardon their bloodguilt,^B
which I have not pardoned,
for the Lord dwells in Zion.

A 3:18 Or *Shittim*   B 3:21 LXX, Syr read *I will avenge their blood*

But let
JUSTICE
flow like water
& RIGHTEOUSNESS
like an unfailing
Stream

amos

 But let justice flow like water, and righteousness, like an unfailing stream. **5:24**

ON THE TIMELINE Amos prophesied during the reigns of Uzziah of Judah (792–740 BC) and Jeroboam II of Israel (793–753 BC). This was a time of great prosperity for both nations, and the weakened condition of their enemies meant great military success. Amos's prophecy to Israel occurred around 760 BC, about forty years before Israel was destroyed by Assyria and 175 years before Judah's destruction and exile.

A LITTLE BACKGROUND Amos was a shepherd from Tekoa, a village about ten miles south of Jerusalem. God called Amos to go north and prophesy against Samaria and the kingdom of Israel. Though we do not know how long he was in the north, it appears to have been a fairly short time. Amos provoked a great deal of opposition and anger, as illustrated by his encounter with Amaziah, the priest of Bethel (Am 7:10-17). He wrote his book, a summary of his prophecies, after his return to Judah.

MESSAGE & PURPOSE God's right to judge the earth was the centerpiece of Amos's message. He proclaimed that God is impartial and fair, judging each nation appropriately, and neither Jew nor Gentile is exempt from divine judgment. In Amos's prophecies, the Gentiles are punished for their crimes against humanity, while the Jews are judged by the demands of the Mosaic law (Am 1:3–2:5). Even after judgment, when it seems all hope is lost (Am 9:1-4), God is able to bring about redemption and salvation (Am 9:13-15). Israel's hope—and humanity's hope—is in the line of David, which God will raise up to establish His kingdom (Am 9:11-12). We now know this prophesy is fulfilled in Jesus Christ.

GIVE THANKS FOR THE BOOK OF AMOS

Amos reminds us of the sovereignty of God in His involvement with His people. His message emphasized the coming "day of the LORD," which had current implications for Amos's contemporaries, and future implications for the modern reader as we await the coming day of Christ's return.

THE BOOK OF AMOS IN HISTORY

775 BC   750 BC   725 BC

760

793   **755**

792   **753**   **740**   **722**

Uzziah becomes
king of Judah

Jeroboam II becomes
king of Israel

760-
755 BC
Amos's
prophetic
ministry
in Israel

End of
Jeroboam II's
reign in Israel

End of
Uzziah's reign
in Judah

Israel
invaded
and taken
captive by
Assyria

READ AND UNDERSTAND AMOS

The Bible is a complete work in which many stories combine to tell one story. As you read the book of Amos, consider reading the additional passages to discover how the whole of Scripture works together.

1

The words of Amos, who was one of the sheep breeders[A] from Tekoa — what he saw regarding Israel in the days of King Uzziah of Judah and Jeroboam son of Jehoash, king of Israel, two years before the earthquake. [2] He said:

The LORD roars from Zion
and makes his voice heard from Jerusalem;
the pastures of the shepherds mourn,[B]
and the summit of Carmel withers.

JUDGMENT ON ISRAEL'S NEIGHBORS

[3] The LORD says:

I will not relent from punishing Damascus
for three crimes, even four,
because they threshed Gilead with iron sledges.
[4] Therefore, I will send fire against Hazael's palace,
and it will consume Ben-hadad's citadels.
[5] I will break down the gates[C] of Damascus.
I will cut off the ruler from the Valley of Aven,
and the one who wields the scepter from Beth-eden.
The people of Aram will be exiled to Kir.
The LORD has spoken.

[6] The LORD says:

I will not relent from punishing Gaza
for three crimes, even four,
because they exiled a whole community,
handing them over to Edom.
[7] Therefore, I will send fire against the walls of Gaza,
and it will consume its citadels.
[8] I will cut off the ruler from Ashdod,
and the one who wields the scepter from Ashkelon.
I will also turn my hand against Ekron,
and the remainder of the Philistines will perish.
The Lord GOD has spoken.

[9] The LORD says:

I will not relent from punishing Tyre
for three crimes, even four,
because they handed over
a whole community of exiles to Edom
and broke[D] a treaty of brotherhood.
[10] Therefore, I will send fire against the walls of Tyre,
and it will consume its citadels.

[11] The LORD says:

I will not relent from punishing Edom
for three crimes, even four,

[A]1:1 Or the shepherds [B]1:2 Or dry up [C]1:5 Lit gate bars [D]1:9 Lit and did not remember

because he pursued his brother with the sword.
He stifled his compassion,
   his anger tore at him continually,
   and he harbored his rage incessantly.
¹² Therefore, I will send fire against Teman,
   and it will consume the citadels of Bozrah.

¹³ The Lord says:
I will not relent from punishing the Ammonites
   for three crimes, even four,
because they ripped open
   the pregnant women of Gilead
   in order to enlarge their territory.
¹⁴ Therefore, I will set fire to the walls of Rabbah,
   and it will consume its citadels.
There will be shouting on the day of battle
   and a violent wind on the day of the storm.
¹⁵ Their king and his princes
   will go into exile together.
   The Lord has spoken.

2 The Lord says:
I will not relent from punishing Moab
   for three crimes, even four,
because he burned the bones
   of the king of Edom to lime.
² Therefore, I will send fire against Moab,
   and it will consume the citadels of Kerioth.
Moab will die with a tumult,
   with shouting and the sound of the ram's horn.
³ I will cut off the judge from the land
   and kill all its officials with him.
   The Lord has spoken.

JUDGMENT ON JUDAH

⁴ The Lord says:
I will not relent from punishing Judah
   for three crimes, even four,
because they have rejected the instruction of the Lord
   and have not kept his statutes.
The lies that their ancestors followed
   have led them astray.
⁵ Therefore, I will send fire against Judah,
   and it will consume the citadels of Jerusalem.

JUDGMENT ON ISRAEL

⁶ The Lord says:
I will not relent from punishing Israel
   for three crimes, even four,
because they sell a righteous person for silver

and a needy person for a pair of sandals.
7 They trample the heads of the poor
on the dust of the ground
and obstruct the path of the needy.
A man and his father have sexual relations
with the same girl,
profaning my holy name.
8 They stretch out beside every altar
on garments taken as collateral,
and in the house of their God
they drink wine obtained through fines.

9 Yet I destroyed the Amorite as Israel advanced;
his height was like the cedars,
and he was as sturdy as the oaks;
I destroyed his fruit above and his roots beneath.
10 And I brought you from the land of Egypt
and led you forty years in the wilderness
in order to possess the land of the Amorite.
11 I raised up some of your sons as prophets
and some of your young men as Nazirites.
Is this not the case, Israelites?
This is the LORD's declaration.
12 But you made the Nazirites drink wine
and commanded the prophets,
"Do not prophesy."
13 Look, I am about to crush^A you in your place
as a wagon crushes when full of grain.
14 Escape will fail the swift,
the strong one will not maintain his strength,
and the warrior will not save his life.
15 The archer will not stand his ground,
the one who is swift of foot
will not save himself,
and the one riding a horse will not save his life.
16 Even the most courageous of the warriors
will flee naked on that day —
this is the LORD's declaration.

GOD'S REASONS FOR PUNISHING ISRAEL

3 Listen to this message that the LORD has spoken against you, Israelites,
against the entire clan that I brought from the land of Egypt:
2 I have known only you
out of all the clans of the earth;
therefore, I will punish you for all your iniquities.
3 Can two walk together
without agreeing to meet?
4 Does a lion roar in the forest

^A2:13 Or *hinder*; Hb obscure

when it has no prey?
Does a young lion growl from its lair
unless it has captured something?
5 Does a bird land in a trap on the ground
if there is no bait for it?
Does a trap spring from the ground
when it has caught nothing?
6 If a ram's horn is blown in a city,
aren't people afraid?
If a disaster occurs in a city,
hasn't the LORD done it?
7 Indeed, the Lord GOD does nothing
without revealing his counsel
to his servants the prophets.
8 A lion has roared;
who will not fear?
The Lord GOD has spoken;
who will not prophesy?

9 Proclaim on the citadels in Ashdod
and on the citadels in the land of Egypt:
Assemble on the mountains of Samaria,
and see the great turmoil in the city
and the acts of oppression within it.
10 The people are incapable of doing right —
this is the LORD's declaration —
those who store up violence and destruction
in their citadels.
11 Therefore, the Lord GOD says:
An enemy will surround the land;
he will destroy your strongholds
and plunder your citadels.

12 The LORD says:
As the shepherd snatches two legs
or a piece of an ear
from the lion's mouth,
so the Israelites who live in Samaria
will be rescued
with only the corner of a bed
or the^A cushion^B of a couch.^C

13 Listen and testify against the house of Jacob —
this is the declaration of the Lord GOD,
the God of Armies.
14 I will punish the altars of Bethel

---

^A3:12 Or *Israelites will be rescued, those who sit in Samaria on a corner of a
bed or a* ^B3:12 Hb obscure ^C3:12 LXX, Aq, Sym, Theod, Syr, Tg, Vg read *or in
Damascus*

on the day I punish Israel for its crimes;
the horns of the altar will be cut off
and fall to the ground.
¹⁵ I will demolish the winter house
and the summer house;
the houses inlaid with ivory will be destroyed,
and the great houses will come to an end.
This is the LORD's declaration.

SOCIAL AND SPIRITUAL CORRUPTION

4 Listen to this message, you cows of Bashan
who are on the hill of Samaria,
women who oppress the poor
and crush the needy,
who say to their husbands,
"Bring us something to drink."

² The Lord GOD has sworn by his holiness:
Look, the days are coming^A
when you will be taken away with hooks,
every last one of you with fishhooks.
³ You will go through breaches in the wall,
each woman straight ahead,
and you will be driven along toward Harmon.
This is the LORD's declaration.

⁴ Come to Bethel and rebel;
rebel even more at Gilgal!
Bring your sacrifices every morning,
your tenths every three days.
⁵ Offer leavened bread as a thank offering,
and loudly proclaim your freewill offerings,
for that is what you Israelites love to do!
This is the declaration of the Lord GOD.

GOD'S DISCIPLINE AND ISRAEL'S APOSTASY

⁶ I gave you absolutely nothing to eat^B
in all your cities,
a shortage of food in all your communities,
yet you did not return to me.
This is the LORD's declaration.

⁷ I also withheld the rain from you
while there were still three months until harvest.
I sent rain on one city
but no rain on another.
One field received rain
while a field with no rain withered.

^A4:2 Lit *coming on you*   ^B4:6 Lit *you cleanness of teeth*

8 Two or three cities staggered
to another city to drink water
but were not satisfied,
yet you did not return to me.
    This is the LORD's declaration.

9 I struck you with blight and mildew;
the locust devoured
your many gardens and vineyards,
your fig trees and olive trees,
yet you did not return to me.
    This is the LORD's declaration.

10 I sent plagues like those of Egypt;
I killed your young men with the sword,
along with your captured horses.
I caused the stench of your camp
to fill your nostrils,
yet you did not return to me.
    This is the LORD's declaration.

11 I overthrew some of you
as I^A overthrew Sodom and Gomorrah,
and you were like a burning stick
snatched from a fire,
yet you did not return to me —
    This is the LORD's declaration.

12 Therefore, Israel, that is what I will do to you,
and since I will do that to you,
Israel, prepare to meet your God!
13 He is here:
the one who forms the mountains,
creates the wind,
and reveals his thoughts to man,
the one who makes the dawn out of darkness
and strides on the heights of the earth.
The LORD, the God of Armies, is his name.

LAMENTATION FOR ISRAEL

5 Listen to this message that I am singing for you, a lament, house of Israel:
2 She has fallen;
Virgin Israel will never rise again.
She lies abandoned on her land
with no one to raise her up.
3 For the Lord GOD says:
The city that marches out a thousand strong
will have only a hundred left,

LET JUSTICE FLOW

AMOS 5; MICAH 6:8; PHILIPPIANS 4:8-9

The bright eastern sunrise casts a rolling shadow of our car as we hurry through the green hills and over the back roads. The flowers on my new dress echo the fresh fields of purple violets and cheery goldenrods growing alongside the road. But I stare down at the idyllic shadow riding in the wildflowers beside us and scowl. My husband is driving too fast. In fact, we have all been driving a little too fast this morning. The children are using their shrill voices to holler ridiculous, annoying, and irrelevant commentaries. And I've started stress-biting my nails and fantasizing about running away to Italy where everything would be better.

It's Sunday morning. You might think our family would be at our best on the way to church, but we are at our bottom-of-the-barrel worst. We are habitually self-focused, and the pressure of Sunday morning always brings out the truth. But if we can't exercise goodness, patience, and justice on Sunday morning, how can we dream of walking rightly with God any other day of the week?

In the days of Amos, Israel shared my Sunday morning conundrum. They were self-focused and arrogant in the midst of all their sacrifices and rituals. Amos's words exhort us, as much as the Israelites, to look to God first. Even in their songs of praise to Him, they were thinking of themselves. This is why God admonishes them:

> "Do not seek Bethel or go to Gilgal or journey to Beer-sheba, for Gilgal will certainly go into exile, and Bethel will come to nothing."
>
> AMOS 5:5

They were looking to their own worship practices, and looking around at what other people were doing, rather than to the God they were supposed to be worshiping.

Any time we turn our eyes from Christ and seek to please God in our own strength, in our own way, this inevitably leads to injustice. We deny the preeminence of Christ when we try to do things our own way. If we begin with faulty foundations, it is inevitable that anything we build will fall short. We will turn justice to wormwood and throw righteousness to the ground (Am 5:7).

How then can we ever practice righteousness? How can we correct injustice? God declares: "Seek me and live" (Am 5:4). For His justice will "flow like water," and righteousness comes from Christ in "an unfailing stream" (Am 5:24).

Justice and righteousness do not come from us. Even in the best of circumstances, on the very sunniest of Sunday mornings, we still fall short. But God has proven that He is faithful.

To Israel in the wilderness, He was the stream in a dry and thirsty land. He rescues the captives, feeds the hungry, and it is He who gives justice to the poor.

and the one that marches out a hundred strong
will have only ten left in the house of Israel.

SEEK GOD AND LIVE

⁴ For the LORD says to the house of Israel:
Seek me and live!
⁵ Do not seek Bethel
or go to Gilgal
or journey to Beer-sheba,
for Gilgal will certainly go into exile,
and Bethel will come to nothing.
⁶ Seek the LORD and live,
or he will spread like fire
throughout the house of Joseph;
it will consume everything
with no one at Bethel to extinguish it.
⁷ Those who turn justice into wormwood
also throw righteousness to the ground.

⁸ The one who made the Pleiades and Orion,
who turns darkness ᴬ into dawn
and darkens day into night,
who summons the water of the sea
and pours it out over the surface of the earth —
the LORD is his name.
⁹ He brings destruction ᴮ on the strong, ᶜ
and it falls on the fortress.

¹⁰ They hate the one who convicts the guilty
at the city gate,
and they despise the one who speaks
with integrity.
¹¹ Therefore, because you trample on the poor
and exact a grain tax from him,
you will never live in the houses of cut stone
you have built;
you will never drink the wine
from the lush vineyards
you have planted.
¹² For I know your crimes are many
and your sins innumerable.
They oppress the righteous, take a bribe,
and deprive the poor of justice at the city gates.
¹³ Therefore, those who have insight
will keep silent ᴰ
at such a time,
for the days are evil.

ᴬ 5:8 Or *turns the shadow of death*   ᴮ 5:9 Hb obscure   ᶜ 5:9 Or *stronghold*
ᴰ 5:13 Or *who are prudent will perish*

¹⁴ Pursue good and not evil
so that you may live,
and the LORD, the God of Armies,
will be with you
as you have claimed.
¹⁵ Hate evil and love good;
establish justice in the city gate.
Perhaps the LORD, the God of Armies,
    will be gracious
to the remnant of Joseph.

¹⁶ Therefore the LORD, the God of Armies, the Lord, says:
There will be wailing in all the public squares;
they will cry out in anguish^A in all the streets.
The farmer will be called on to mourn,
and professional mourners^B to wail.
¹⁷ There will be wailing in all the vineyards,
for I will pass among you.
The LORD has spoken.

THE DAY OF THE LORD

¹⁸ Woe to you who long for the day of the LORD!
What will the day of the LORD be for you?
It will be darkness and not light.
¹⁹ It will be like a man who flees from a lion
only to have a bear confront him.
He goes home and rests his hand against the wall
only to have a snake bite him.
²⁰ Won't the day of the LORD
be darkness rather than light,
even gloom without any brightness in it?
²¹ I hate, I despise, your feasts!
I can't stand the stench
of your solemn assemblies.
²² Even if you offer me
your burnt offerings and grain offerings,
I will not accept them;
I will have no regard
for your fellowship offerings
    of fattened cattle.
²³ Take away from me the noise of your songs!
I will not listen to the music of your harps.
²⁴ But let justice flow like water,
and righteousness, like an unfailing stream.

²⁵ "House of Israel, was it sacrifices and grain offerings that you present-
ed to me during the forty years in the wilderness? ²⁶ But you have taken up^C

---

^A5:16 Lit *will say, "Alas! Alas!"* ^B5:16 Lit *and those skilled in lamentation*
^C5:26 Or *you will lift up*

Sakkuth your king and Kaiwan your star god,^A images you have made for yourselves. ²⁷ So I will send you into exile beyond Damascus." The LORD, the God of Armies, is his name. He has spoken.

WOE TO THE COMPLACENT

6 Woe to those who are at ease in Zion
and to those who feel secure on the hill of Samaria —
the notable people in this first of the nations,
those the house of Israel comes to.

² Cross over to Calneh and see;
go from there to great Hamath;
then go down to Gath of the Philistines.
Are you better than these kingdoms?
Is their territory larger than yours?

³ You dismiss any thought of the evil day
and bring in a reign of violence.

⁴ They lie on beds inlaid with ivory,
sprawled out on their couches,
and dine on lambs from the flock
and calves from the stall.

⁵ They improvise songs^B to the sound of the harp
and invent^C their own musical instruments
like David.

⁶ They drink wine by the bowlful
and anoint themselves with the finest oils
but do not grieve over the ruin of Joseph.

⁷ Therefore, they will now go into exile
as the first of the captives,
and the feasting of those who sprawl out
will come to an end.

ISRAEL'S PRIDE JUDGED

⁸ The Lord GOD has sworn by himself — this is the declaration of the LORD, the God of Armies:

I loathe Jacob's pride
and hate his citadels,
so I will hand over the city and everything in it.

⁹ And if there are ten men left in one house, they will die. ¹⁰ A close relative^D and burner^E will remove his corpse^F from the house. He will call to someone in the inner recesses of the house, "Any more with you?"

That person will reply, "None."

Then he will say, "Silence, because the LORD's name must not be invoked."

¹¹ For the LORD commands:

---

^A 5:26 LXX reads *taken up the tent of Molech and the star of your god Rephan;*
Ac 7:43 ^B 6:5 Hb obscure ^C 6:5 Or *compose on* ^D 6:10 Lit *His uncle*
^E 6:10 A burner of incense, a memorial fire, or a body; Hb obscure ^F 6:10 Lit
remove bones

The large house will be smashed to pieces,
and the small house to rubble.

12 Do horses gallop on the cliffs?
Does anyone plow there with oxen?[A]
Yet you have turned justice into poison
and the fruit of righteousness into wormwood —
13 you who rejoice over Lo-debar
and say, "Didn't we capture Karnaim
for ourselves by our own strength?"
14 But look, I am raising up a nation
against you, house of Israel —
this is the declaration of the Lord,
the GOD of Armies —
and they will oppress you
from the entrance of Hamath[B]
to the Brook of the Arabah.[C]

FIRST VISION: LOCUSTS

7 The Lord GOD showed me this: He was forming a swarm of locusts at the time the spring crop first began to sprout — after the cutting of the king's hay. 2 When the locusts finished eating the vegetation of the land, I said, "Lord GOD, please forgive! How will Jacob survive since he is so small?"

3 The LORD relented concerning this. "It will not happen," he said.

SECOND VISION: FIRE

4 The Lord GOD showed me this: The Lord GOD was calling for a judgment by fire. It consumed the great deep and devoured the land. 5 Then I said, "Lord GOD, please stop! How will Jacob survive since he is so small?"

6 The LORD relented concerning this. "This will not happen either," said the Lord GOD.

THIRD VISION: A PLUMB LINE

7 He showed me this: The Lord was standing there by a vertical wall with a plumb line in his hand. 8 The LORD asked me, "What do you see, Amos?"

I replied, "A plumb line."

Then the Lord said, "I am setting a plumb line among my people Israel; I will no longer spare them:

9 Isaac's high places will be deserted,
and Israel's sanctuaries will be in ruins;
I will rise up against the house of Jeroboam
with a sword."

AMAZIAH'S OPPOSITION

10 Amaziah the priest of Bethel sent word to King Jeroboam of Israel, saying, "Amos has conspired against you right here in the house of Israel. The

[A]6:12 Some emend to *plow the sea*   [B]6:14 Or *from Lebo-hamath*   [C]6:14 Probably the Valley of Zared at the southeast end of the Dead Sea

1518

land cannot endure all his words, ¹¹ for Amos has said this: 'Jeroboam will die by the sword, and Israel will certainly go into exile from its homeland.' "

¹² Then Amaziah said to Amos, "Go away, you seer! Flee to the land of Judah. Earn your living ^A and give your prophecies there, ¹³ but don't ever prophesy at Bethel again, for it is the king's sanctuary and a royal temple."

¹⁴ So Amos answered Amaziah, "I was ^B not a prophet or the son of a prophet; ^C rather, I was ^B a herdsman, and I took care of sycamore figs. ¹⁵ But the LORD took me from following the flock and said to me, 'Go, prophesy to my people Israel.' "

¹⁶ Now hear the word of the LORD. You say:

Do not prophesy against Israel;
do not preach against the house of Isaac.

¹⁷ Therefore, this is what the LORD says:

Your wife will be a prostitute in the city,
your sons and daughters will fall
    by the sword,
and your land will be divided up
with a measuring line.
You yourself will die on pagan ^D soil,
and Israel will certainly go into exile
from its homeland.

FOURTH VISION: A BASKET OF SUMMER FRUIT

8 The Lord GOD showed me this: a basket of summer fruit. ² He asked me, "What do you see, Amos?"

I replied, "A basket of summer fruit." ^E

The LORD said to me, "The end has come for my people Israel; I will no longer spare them. ³ In that day the temple ^F songs will become wailing" — this is the Lord GOD's declaration. "Many dead bodies, thrown everywhere! Silence!"

⁴   Hear this, you who trample on the needy
    and do away with the poor of the land,
⁵   asking, "When will the New Moon be over
    so we may sell grain,
    and the Sabbath,
    so we may market wheat?
    We can reduce the measure
    while increasing the price ^G
    and cheat with dishonest scales.
⁶   We can buy the poor with silver
    and the needy for a pair of sandals
    and even sell the chaff!"

⁷ The LORD has sworn by the Pride of Jacob: ^H
    I will never forget all their deeds.

---

⁸ Because of this, won't the land quake
and all who dwell in it mourn?
All of it will rise like the Nile;
it will surge and then subside
like the Nile in Egypt.

⁹ And in that day —
this is the declaration of the Lord GOD —
I will make the sun go down at noon;
I will darken the land in the daytime.

¹⁰ I will turn your feasts into mourning
and all your songs into lamentation;
I will cause everyoneᴬ to wear sackcloth
and every head to be shaved.
I will make that grief
like mourning for an only son
and its outcome like a bitter day.

¹¹ Look, the days are coming —
this is the declaration of the Lord GOD —
when I will send a famine through the land:
not a famine of bread or a thirst for water,
but of hearing the words of the LORD.

¹² People will stagger from sea to sea
and roam from north to east
seeking the word of the LORD,
but they will not find it.

¹³ In that day the beautiful young women,
the young men also, will faint from thirst.

¹⁴ Those who swear by the guilt of Samaria
and say, "As your god lives, Dan,"
or, "As the wayᴮ·ᶜ of Beer-sheba lives" —
they will fall, never to rise again.

FIFTH VISION: THE LORD BESIDE THE ALTAR

9 I saw the Lord standing beside the altar, and he said:
Strike the capitals of the pillars
so that the thresholds shake;
knock them down on the heads of all the people.
Then I will kill the rest of them with the sword.
None of those who flee will get away;
none of the fugitives will escape.

² If they dig down to Sheol,
from there my hand will take them;
if they climb up to heaven,
from there I will bring them down.

³ If they hide
on the top of Carmel,

ᴬ8:10 Lit every waist ᴮ8:14 LXX reads god ᶜ8:14 Or power

from there I will track them down
and seize them;
if they conceal themselves
from my sight on the sea floor,
from there I will command
the sea serpent to bite them.
4 And if they are driven
by their enemies into captivity,
from there I will command
the sword to kill them.
I will keep my eye on them
for harm and not for good.

5 The Lord, the GOD of Armies —
he touches the earth;
it melts, and all who dwell in it mourn;
all of it rises like the Nile
and subsides like the Nile of Egypt.
6 He builds his upper chambers
in the heavens
and lays the foundation of his vault
on the earth.
He summons the water of the sea
and pours it out over the surface of the earth.
The LORD is his name.

ANNOUNCEMENT OF JUDGMENT

7 Israelites, are you not like the Cushites to me?
This is the LORD's declaration.
Didn't I bring Israel from the land of Egypt,
the Philistines from Caphtor,^A
and the Arameans from Kir?
8 Look, the eyes of the Lord GOD
are on the sinful kingdom,
and I will obliterate it
from the face of the earth.
However, I will not totally destroy
the house of Jacob —
this is the LORD's declaration —
9 for I am about to give the command,
and I will shake the house of Israel
among all the nations,
as one shakes a sieve,
but not a pebble will fall to the ground.
10 All the sinners among my people
who say: "Disaster will never overtake^B
or confront us,"
will die by the sword.

---

^A 9:7 Probably Crete   ^B 9:10 Or *You will not let disaster come near*

ANNOUNCEMENT OF RESTORATION

11 In that day
I will restore the fallen shelter of David:
I will repair its gaps,
restore its ruins,
and rebuild it as in the days of old,
12 so that they may possess
the remnant of Edom
and all the nations
that bear my name^ —
this is the declaration of the LORD; he will do this.

13 Look, the days are coming —
this is the LORD's declaration —
when the plowman will overtake the reaper
and the one who treads grapes,
the sower of seed.
The mountains will drip with sweet wine,
and all the hills will flow with it.
14 I will restore the fortunes of my people Israel.^B
They will rebuild and occupy ruined cities,
plant vineyards and drink their wine,
make gardens and eat their produce.
15 I will plant them on their land,
and they will never again be uprooted
from the land I have given them.
The LORD your God has spoken.

^9:12 LXX reads so that the remnant of man and all the nations . . . may seek me;
Ac 15:17 ^B9:14 Or restore my people Israel from captivity

obadiah

 Saviors will ascend Mount Zion to rule over the hill country of Esau, but the kingdom will be the LORD's. **VERSE 21**

ON THE TIMELINE The time of the writing of Obadiah is disputed, with a wide variety of proposed dates from the tenth to the fifth centuries BC, depending on when the invasion and plunder of Jerusalem occurred (Ob 11-14). The two most popular views claim that Obadiah was written during the reign of King Jehoram of Judah (around 848–841 BC) or shortly after the final destruction of Jerusalem by the Babylonians (586 BC).

A LITTLE BACKGROUND Obadiah was presumably the author of this book, but nothing else is known about him. His common Hebrew name, meaning "servant of the LORD," is shared by at least a dozen other people in the Old Testament.

Many Prophetic Books contain prophecies against multiple nations, but the book of Obadiah focuses exclusively on the nation of Edom. Edom was the nation that descended from Esau, Jacob's twin brother and firstborn son of Isaac. Like Amos, Obadiah's short message centers on the approaching "day of the LORD," but it comes with a promise that Israel will possess the land of Edom.

MESSAGE & PURPOSE The Lord's judgment was predicted for Edom because of its arrogance in trusting geographical security (Ob 3-5), diplomatic treaties (Ob 7), and the counsel of its famed wise men (Ob 8; Jr 49:7) instead of the true God of Israel.

Obadiah spoke of the nearness of the "day of the LORD" (Is 13:6; Jl 1:15; Zph 1:7,14), focusing on the darkness and gloom of the Lord's wrath (Is 13:6-13; Jl 2:1-3; Zph 1:7-18; 2:2). Obadiah also emphasized the dual nature of the "day of the LORD." It would bring judgment on the historical nation Edom and "Edom" as symbolic of Israel's enemies (Ob 15) while, at the same time, bringing salvation for the nation of Israel (Jl 2:30-32; Zph 2:1-10; 3:8-16).

GIVE THANKS FOR THE BOOK OF OBADIAH

Like the book of Revelation—which proclaims the downfall of the persecuting Roman Empire—the book of Obadiah upholds faith in God's just government and hope in the triumph of His will. Its message reorients aching hearts to the truth that God is on His throne and He faithfully cares for His own.

THE BOOK OF OBADIAH IN HISTORY

900 BC   700 BC

1966

   1406   982   850   594

                                                     586

David resists
Edom's invasion
of Israel and
subjects Edom
to Israelite rule

Edom rebels
against Judah's rule
and becomes an
independent state

Edom
commits
hostilities
against Jud[e]

Obadiah's
prophecy
of the
destruction
of Edom

The Israelites
extend their
journey to
Canaan
in order to
bypass the
land of Edom

Approximate
year of Esau's
marriage —
Edomites descend
from Esau

Edom
becomes
Judah's
ally in
resisting the
Babylonians

READ AND UNDERSTAND OBADIAH

The Bible is a complete work in which many stories combine to tell one story. As you read the book of Obadiah, consider reading the additional passages to discover how the whole of Scripture works together.

The vision of Obadiah.

EDOM'S CERTAIN JUDGMENT

This is what the Lord God has said about Edom:
> We have heard a message from the LORD;
> an envoy has been sent among the nations:
> "Rise up, and let us go to war against her."[A]

2 Look, I will make you insignificant
among the nations;
you will be deeply despised.
3 Your arrogant heart has deceived you,
you who live in clefts of the rock[B,C]
in your home on the heights,
who say to yourself,
"Who can bring me down to the ground?"
4 Though you seem to soar[D] like an eagle
and make your nest among the stars,
even from there I will bring you down.
> This is the LORD's declaration.

5 If thieves came to you,
if marauders by night —
how ravaged you would be! —
wouldn't they steal only what they wanted?
If grape pickers came to you,
wouldn't they leave some grapes?
6 How Esau will be pillaged,
his hidden treasures searched out!
7 Everyone who has a treaty with you
will drive you to the border;
everyone at peace with you
will deceive and conquer you.
Those who eat your bread
will set[E] a trap for you.
He will be unaware of it.
8 In that day —
> this is the LORD's declaration —
will I not eliminate the wise ones of Edom
and those who understand
from the hill country of Esau?
9 Teman,[F] your warriors will be terrified
so that everyone from the hill country of Esau
will be destroyed by slaughter.

[A]1 = Edom   [B]3 Or in Sela; probably = Petra   [C]3 Probably Petra   [D]4 Or to build high   [E]7 Some LXX mss, Sym, Tg, Vg; MT reads They will set your bread as   [F]9 = a region or city in Edom

THE KINGDOM IS THE LORD'S

OBADIAH 19-21; EZEKIEL 25:12-14

My dad started prepping me for a career in politics at age 5.

It was the Reagan/Carter election year, and he quizzed me on the merits of each candidate while I snacked on graham crackers in the front seat of his blue sedan. He reminded me of the policies of our forefathers and refused to give me a pass on listening to talk radio. I took the bait—hook, line, and sinker—becoming a political analyst with aspirations to run for office at a young age.

My first job after graduation was as a newspaper reporter. One day, the paper received an "anonymous" email from a reader:

"I love the style of your new reporter," it said. "Please consider putting her on the political beat."

Turns out that email was from my dad. His political dreams for me lived on (embarrassing as they were!).

With that kind of background, you can imagine how things ratchet up to a fever pitch for me during an election year. Every four years I get swept up in the idea that some candidate or political party will fix what's wrong in our country. But the truth is, the world has yet to produce one political savior.

This pattern is true for every nation in every era of history. Take a look at some biblical politics for proof:

- King Saul was initially a good king, who eventually turned his back on God and cost himself the throne and God's favor (1Sm 13).
- The people loved King David, but he had a massive moral failure and was forced to flee a rebellion led by his own son (2Sm 11).
- King Herod was so egotistical he ordered his own people massacred (Mt 2:16).

Every human leader in the history of the world has fallen short of their promises. It's not that politics don't matter, it's that, well . . . maybe they don't matter as much as we think they do.

Obadiah is a short little book that prophesies the end of the nation of Edom. But the prophecy ends with the bottom line for all nations:

"Saviors will ascend Mount Zion to rule over the hill country of Esau, but the kingdom will be the LORD's."

OBADIAH 21

Here's a paraphrase for a politics-lovin', all American girl like myself: Candidates will come and go, but **God and His kingdom will stand forever.**

In every era and election cycle, God is on His throne. Kings and congressman will rise and fall, but God's power and influence will stand through eternity. The kingdom will be the Lord's.

EDOM'S SINS AGAINST JUDAH

¹⁰ You will be covered with shame
and destroyed forever
because of violence done to your brother Jacob.
¹¹ On the day you stood aloof,
on the day strangers captured his wealth,ᴬ
while foreigners entered his city gate
and cast lots for Jerusalem,
you were just like one of them.
¹² Do notᴮ gloat over your brother
in the day of his calamity;
do not rejoice over the people of Judah
in the day of their destruction;
do not boastfully mockᶜ
in the day of distress.
¹³ Do not enter my people's city gate
in the day of their disaster.
Yes, you — do not gloat over their misery
in the day of their disaster,
and do not appropriate their possessions
in the day of their disaster.
¹⁴ Do not stand at the crossroadsᴰ
to cut off their fugitives,
and do not hand over their survivors
in the day of distress.

JUDGMENT OF THE NATIONS

¹⁵ For the day of the Lᴏʀᴅ is near,
against all the nations.
As you have done, it will be done to you;
what you deserve will return on your own head.
¹⁶ As you have drunk on my holy mountain,
so all the nations will drink continually.
They will drink and gulp down
and be as though they had never been.
¹⁷ But there will be a deliverance on Mount Zion,
and it will be holy;
the house of Jacob will dispossess
those who dispossessed them.ᴱ
¹⁸ Then the house of Jacob will be a blazing fire,
and the house of Joseph, a burning flame,
but the house of Esau will be stubble;
Jacobᶠ will set them on fire and consume Edom.ᴳ
Therefore no survivor will remain
of the house of Esau,
for the Lᴏʀᴅ has spoken.

ᴬ11 Or forces   ᴮ12-14 Or You should not throughout vv. 12-14   ᶜ12 Lit not make
your mouth big   ᴰ14 Hb obscure   ᴱ17 DSS, LXX, Syr, Vg, Tg; MT reads Jacob
will possess its inheritance   ᶠ18 Lit they   ᴳ18 Lit them

FUTURE BLESSING FOR ISRAEL

¹⁹ People from the Negev will possess
the hill country of Esau;
those from the Judean foothills will possess
the land of the Philistines.
They^A will possess
the territories of Ephraim and Samaria,
while Benjamin will possess Gilead.

²⁰ The exiles of the Israelites who are in Halah^B
and who are among the Canaanites as far as Zarephath
as well as the exiles of Jerusalem who are in Sepharad
will possess the cities of the Negev.

²¹ Saviors^C will ascend Mount Zion
to rule over the hill country of Esau,
but the kingdom will be the LORD's.

---

^A19 = The house of Jacob   ^B20 Or *of this host of the Israelites*; Hb obscure
^C21 Or *Those who have been delivered*

YOU ARE A

Gracious & Compassionate God

jonah

I knew that you are a gracious and compassionate God, slow to anger, abounding in faithful love, and one who relents from sending disaster. **4:2**

ON THE TIMELINE Jonah proclaimed his message to the city of Nineveh sometime in the first half of the eighth century BC, approximately 760 BC. His message predates the fall of the northern kingdom of Israel to Assyria in 722 BC. Jonah also appears in 2 Kings 14:25, as a prophet from Gath-hepher in the territory of Zebulun in northern Israel who predicted the restoration of the northern kingdom's boundaries during the reign of Jeroboam II (ca 793–753 BC). This book about Jonah could have been composed at any time from the eighth century to the end of the Old Testament period. The authorship of the narrative is anonymous.

A LITTLE BACKGROUND Jonah was called to preach to the city of Nineveh, a major Assyrian city filled with cruel people who were longtime enemies of Israel. Assyrian artwork emphasizes war, including scenes of execution, beheadings, and torture. This explains Jonah's reluctance to preach to this infamous city of warlike people.

MESSAGE & PURPOSE Jonah's message emphasizes God's compassion for and pursuit of the Gentiles. In Jonah 1, Gentile sailors learn to revere and worship Israel's God. And in Jonah 3, Nineveh's repentance shows that Gentiles, too, can be saved. God's "gracious and compassionate" (Jnh 4:2) actions toward Nineveh show that the God of the OT is a God of grace.

The book of Jonah also portrays the sovereign power of God over the natural world. God can create a storm (Jnh 1:4), miraculously raise up a plant, as well as a worm to kill it (Jnh 4:6-7), and use a great fish to swallow and save a wayward prophet like Jonah (Jnh 1:17).

Centrally, the book of Jonah expresses the futility of running from God. The trouble Jonah got into when he tried to escape God's calling is a warning to readers that running from God is futile and only invites unnecessary hardship.

GIVE THANKS FOR THE BOOK OF JONAH

The book of Jonah shows God's gift of salvation offered to the whole world (not just Israel), His power over nature, and the futility of ignoring His instruction. Jonah's time in the fish foreshadows Jesus' burial and resurrection, and Jonah's flawed ministry points to Jesus' better, perfect ministry (Mt 12:38-45; Lk 11:24-32).

THE BOOK OF JONAH IN HISTORY

750 BC   650 BC   550

1900

760   **722**

701

Assyria
invades
Judah

Jonah
travels to
Nineveh

Israel falls
to Assyria

Nineveh
established
as prominent
Assyrian city

630

612

609

Fall of
Assyria

Fall of Nineveh

Nahum's
prophecy
against
Nineveh

READ AND UNDERSTAND JONAH

The Bible is a complete work in which many stories combine to tell one story. As you read the book of Jonah, consider reading the additional passages to discover how the whole of Scripture works together.

JONAH'S FLIGHT

1 The word of the LORD came to Jonah son of Amittai: ² "Get up! Go to the great city of Nineveh and preach against it because their evil has come up before me." ³ Jonah got up to flee to Tarshish from the LORD's presence. He went down to Joppa and found a ship going to Tarshish. He paid the fare and went down into it to go with them to Tarshish from the LORD's presence.

⁴ But the LORD threw a great wind onto the sea, and such a great storm arose on the sea that the ship threatened to break apart. ⁵ The sailors were afraid, and each cried out to his god. They threw the ship's cargo into the sea to lighten the load. Meanwhile, Jonah had gone down to the lowest part of the vessel and had stretched out and fallen into a deep sleep.

⁶ The captain approached him and said, "What are you doing sound asleep? Get up! Call to your god.ᴬ Maybe this god will consider us, and we won't perish."

⁷ "Come on!" the sailors said to each other. "Let's cast lots. Then we'll know who is to blame for this trouble we're in." So they cast lots, and the lot singled out Jonah. ⁸ Then they said to him, "Tell us who is to blame for this trouble we're in. What is your business, and where are you from? What is your country, and what people are you from?"

⁹ He answered them, "I'm a Hebrew. I worshipᴮ the LORD, the God of the heavens, who made the sea and the dry land."

¹⁰ Then the men were seized by a great fear and said to him, "What is this you've done?" The men knew he was fleeing from the LORD's presence because he had told them. ¹¹ So they said to him, "What should we do to you so that the sea will calm down for us?" For the sea was getting worse and worse.

¹² He answered them, "Pick me up and throw me into the sea so that it will calm down for you, for I know that I'm to blame for this great storm that is against you." ¹³ Nevertheless, the men rowed hard to get back to dry land, but they couldn't because the sea was raging against them more and more.

¹⁴ So they called out to the LORD: "Please, LORD, don't let us perish because of this man's life, and don't charge us with innocent blood! For you, LORD, have done just as you pleased." ¹⁵ Then they picked up Jonah and threw him into the sea, and the sea stopped its raging. ¹⁶ The men were seized by great fear of the LORD, and they offered a sacrifice to the LORD and made vows.

¹⁷ The LORD appointed a great fish to swallow Jonah, and Jonah was in the belly of the fish three days and three nights.

JONAH'S PRAYER

2 Jonah prayed to the LORD his God from the belly of the fish:
² I called to the LORD in my distress,
and he answered me.
I cried out for help from deep insideᶜ Sheol;
you heard my voice.
³ You threw me into the depths,
into the heart of the seas,
and the currentᴰ overcame me.
All your breakers and your billows swept over me.

ᴬ1:6 Or *God* ᴮ1:9 Or *fear* ᶜ2:2 Lit *from the stomach of* ᴰ2:3 Lit *river*

GOD'S PURSUIT

JONAH 1; PSALM 139:7-8; NAHUM 3:1-7

Pulling the coarse blanket tighter and rolling over, Jonah sighed as he sank deeper into sleep. The warm dark cabin around him creaked and groaned as the waves outside surged with increasing intensity. The sailors above deck scanned the horizon and glanced anxiously up at a grey sky heavy with the strength of the Lord Almighty. God was coming for Jonah.

The prophet was running away, but God pursued him like only the Creator and Lord of the sea could: with a furious ocean tempest. Jonah tried to flee from the very presence of the Lord and he thought he could hide if he found an old boat heading in a new direction.

But God is fierce and awesome in His pursuit. Jonah never had a chance of hiding. Even the inanimate dice the sailors used to cast lots pointed him out as the one running from God (Jnh 1:7). All creation seemed to be shouting, "Return!" God uses wind and waves, pennies and dice—everything in creation stands by to obey its Creator. In the face of the deafening storm and sure signs, the sailors feared for their lives, and looked to Jonah with eyes of blame and hands ready to heave-ho.

God's pursuit is relentless exactly because He is so loving. He could've crushed Jonah under a tremendous sea surge and found another man. Jonah had his chance, and he clearly took the coward's way

out, right? God gave him a clear instruction (something we all long for), and Jonah ran like a frightened child in the other direction. Why didn't God give up on Jonah?

God wanted Jonah. Goodness, isn't that amazing? I sometimes feel like I'm a sub-standard version of the person who should actually be living my life. And the truth is, I do fall short. I do worry that there is someone who would be a better mother to my kids, wife to my husband, friend to my friends. But despite my imperfections and failings, I am the best mother for my children, wife to my husband, and friend to my friends! God gives specific callings to specific people (Eph 2:10). That means God wants me for my particular calling and life.

We can't escape God and His storm gale of purpose. He pursues us with love that is filled with a beautiful intensity unlike anything else we have ever known.

"Where can I go to escape your Spirit? Where can I flee from your presence? If I go up to heaven, you are there; if I make my bed in Sheol, you are there."

PSALM 139:7-8

---

⁴ But I said, "I have been banished
from your sight,
yet I will look once more ᴬ
toward your holy temple.
⁵ The water engulfed me up to the neck; ᴮ
the watery depths overcame me;
seaweed was wrapped around my head.
⁶ I sank to the foundations of the mountains,
the earth's gates shut behind me forever!
Then you raised my life from the Pit,
Lᴏʀᴅ my God!
⁷ As my life was fading away,
I remembered the Lᴏʀᴅ,
and my prayer came to you,
to your holy temple.
⁸ Those who cherish worthless idols
abandon their faithful love,
⁹ but as for me, I will sacrifice to you
with a voice of thanksgiving.
I will fulfill what I have vowed.
Salvation ᶜ belongs to the Lᴏʀᴅ."

¹⁰ Then the Lᴏʀᴅ commanded the fish, and it vomited Jonah onto dry land.

JONAH'S PREACHING

3 The word of the Lᴏʀᴅ came to Jonah a second time: ² "Get up! Go to the great city of Nineveh and preach the message that I tell you." ³ Jonah got up and went to Nineveh according to the Lᴏʀᴅ's command.

Now Nineveh was an extremely great city, ᴰ a three-day walk. ⁴ Jonah set out on the first day of his walk in the city and proclaimed, "In forty days Nineveh will be demolished!" ⁵ Then the people of Nineveh believed God. They proclaimed a fast and dressed in sackcloth — from the greatest of them to the least.

⁶ When word reached the king of Nineveh, he got up from his throne, took off his royal robe, put on sackcloth, and sat in ashes. ⁷ Then he issued a decree in Nineveh:

By order of the king and his nobles: No person or animal, herd or flock, is to taste anything at all. They must not eat or drink water. ⁸ Furthermore, both people and animals must be covered with sackcloth, and everyone must call out earnestly to God. Each must turn from his evil ways and from his wrongdoing. ᴱ ⁹ Who knows? God may turn and relent; he may turn from his burning anger so that we will not perish.

¹⁰ God saw their actions — that they had turned from their evil ways — so God relented from the disaster he had threatened them with. And he did not do it.

ᴬ2:4 LXX reads *said, "Indeed, will I look . . . ?*   ᴮ2:5 Or *me, threatening my life*   ᶜ2:9 Or *Deliverance*   ᴰ3:3 Or *was a great city to God*   ᴱ3:8 Or *injustice, or violence*

GENUINE REPENTANCE

Nineveh was the worst.

A chief city in the already brutal and wicked Assyrian empire, Nineveh removed the noses and ears of their prisoners to mark and maim them for life. And like most Mesopotamian civilizations, their culture was immoral and generally terrifying—temple prostitution, child sacrifice, and infanticide.

I love my ears and nose, so I understand why Jonah didn't want to go.

These are the people who heard God's call to repentance. They listened to Jonah and to God. And they repented. They stopped, tore their clothes, rubbed their faces in the fireplace, and gave up eating. They were desperate to get God's attention.

God had mercy on even these most wicked people. They didn't know they were that wicked until God arrested them in their sin. But this story is only marginally about the repentant Ninevite hearts. Primarily, this is a story about God's mercy and forgiveness.

God calls them to repent, and they respond by fasting.

Fasting hurts. It is tangible and practical repentance, and repentance must change how we live our lives. We turn from the things that give us false comfort, and only have God.

For the Ninevites, fasting meant giving up their means of power and energy, and depending only on God for power in a very real way. They humbled themselves publicly and didn't hold back for pride or fear of what others would

think. Even the king—who held an almost god-like status in the culture and had everything to lose—humbled himself, bowing before the one true God. It was a culture-wide repentance, extending from the greatest to the least.

Their repentance was not chiefly about how sorry they felt, but about casting themselves wholly upon God's mercy. It wasn't about what they could bring to the table. Rather, they said, "Who knows? God may turn and relent" (Jnh 3:9). They recognized that repentance is about what God is doing, not what we can do to gain any kind of merit.

Mercy is not a matter of merit; it is God's gift.

Even though Nineveh was awful by any standard, God had mercy on them. This is good news, because the truth is we are all more like the Ninevites than we are like God. I know I am. I don't gouge eyes out, yet pride, envy, and wrath are always within arm's reach for me.

"But I received mercy for this reason, so that in me, the worst of them, Christ Jesus might demonstrate his extraordinary patience as an example to those who would believe in him for eternal life."

1 TIMOTHY 1:16

The story of Nineveh's repentance is about God's perfect patience, His deep mercy, and His profound forgiveness. Thanks be to God.

JONAH'S ANGER

4 Jonah was greatly displeased and became furious. ² He prayed to the LORD: "Please, LORD, isn't this what I thought while I was still in my own country? That's why I fled toward Tarshish in the first place. I knew that you are a gracious and compassionate God, slow to anger, abounding in faithful love, and one who relents from sending disaster. ³ And now, LORD, take my life from me, for it is better for me to die than to live."

⁴ The LORD asked, "Is it right for you to be angry?"

⁵ Jonah left the city and found a place east of it. He made himself a shelter there and sat in its shade to see what would happen to the city. ⁶ Then the LORD God appointed a plant, and it grew over Jonah to provide shade for his head to rescue him from his trouble.ᴬ Jonah was greatly pleased with the plant. ⁷ When dawn came the next day, God appointed a worm that attacked the plant, and it withered.

⁸ As the sun was rising, God appointed a scorching east wind. The sun beat down on Jonah's head so much that he almost fainted, and he wanted to die. He said, "It's better for me to die than to live."

⁹ Then God asked Jonah, "Is it right for you to be angry about the plant?"

"Yes, it's right!" he replied. "I'm angry enough to die!"

¹⁰ So the LORD said, "You cared about the plant, which you did not labor over and did not grow. It appeared in a night and perished in a night. ¹¹ But may I not care about the great city of Nineveh, which has more than a hundred and twenty thousand people who cannot distinguish between their right and their left, as well as many animals?"

ᴬ4:6 Or disaster, or evil

Act Justly,
Love Faithfulness,
Walk Humbly
with
Your God

micah

Mankind, he has told each of you what is good and what it is the LORD requires of you: to act justly, to love faithfulness, and to walk humbly with your God. **6:8**

ON THE TIMELINE Micah's ministry likely began late in Jotham's reign and ended early in Hezekiah's, dating between 750 and 690 BC. His reference to the future judgment of Samaria (Mc 1:6) shows that his ministry began some time before Israel's destruction in 722 BC, indicating that Micah's ministry overlapped Isaiah's.

A LITTLE BACKGROUND Micah's hometown of Moresheth-gath (Mc 1:1,14) in the lowlands of Judah was about twenty-five miles southwest of Jerusalem. The mentioning of his hometown suggests that Micah probably ministered elsewhere, including Jerusalem. Since no genealogy is given, we can presume he did not come from a prominent family. Micah was a skilled orator, a master of metaphors with a genius for wordplay and blunt, vivid imagery. Few prophets saw the future more clearly. Micah prophesied the fall of Samaria (Mc 1:5-9), Jerusalem's destruction (Mc 1:1-16; 3:12), the Babylonian captivity and return from exile (Mc 4:6-10), as well as the birth of Christ in Bethlehem (Mc 5:2).

MESSAGE & PURPOSE Micah sought "to proclaim to Jacob his rebellion and to Israel his sin" (Mc 3:8), pronouncing God's judgment in an effort to call His people to repentance. Injustice was rampant in Israel at the time (Mc 2:1-2; 3:1-3; 6:10-11), and the people would suffer destruction and exile (Mc 1:10-16), silence from God (Mc 3:6-7), and frustration (Mc 6:13-16). But Micah balanced his prophecy with hope of a remnant spared through God's judgment and a glorious future restoration (Mc 2:12-13; 4:1-5; 5:5-9; 7:8-20).

GIVE THANKS FOR THE BOOK OF MICAH

Micah's holy and just God demands holiness and justice from all people. This is the "good" He requires (Mc 6:8). The people had grown content to go through religious motions while carrying out very little genuine devotion. Even the religious leaders chose to speak popular messages in order to support their standard of living. Micah preached that true religion comes from a heart tuned to God, resulting in godly living. As such, religion and ethics are inseparable. People who refuse to repent will face God's judgment, but the faithful will find His salvation and be led by God's king, who would usher in His peace and prosperity.

THE BOOK OF MICAH IN HISTORY

740 BC   725 BC   710 BC   695 BC

750

735

Ahaz
becomes
king of
Judah

Start of Micah's
prophetic ministry

722

716

Hezekiah
becomes
king of
Judah

Israel taken
captive by
Assyria

701

696

Manasseh
becomes
king of
Judah

Assyria
invades
Judah

690

End of
Micah's
ministry

READ AND UNDERSTAND MICAH

The Bible is a complete work in which many stories combine to tell one story. As you read the book of Micah, consider reading the additional passages to discover how the whole of Scripture works together.

1 The word of the Lord that came to Micah the Moreshite — what he saw regarding Samaria and Jerusalem in the days of Jotham, Ahaz, and Hezekiah, kings of Judah.

COMING JUDGMENT ON ISRAEL

2 Listen, all you peoples;
pay attention, earth^A and everyone in it!
The Lord God will be a witness against you,
the Lord, from his holy temple.

3 Look, the Lord is leaving his place
and coming down to trample
the heights^B of the earth.

4 The mountains will melt beneath him,
and the valleys will split apart,
like wax near a fire,
like water cascading down a mountainside.

5 All this will happen because of Jacob's rebellion
and the sins of the house of Israel.
What is the rebellion of Jacob?
Isn't it Samaria?
And what is the high place of Judah?
Isn't it Jerusalem?

6 Therefore, I will make Samaria
a heap of ruins in the countryside,
a planting area for a vineyard.
I will roll her stones into the valley
and expose her foundations.

7 All her carved images will be smashed to pieces;
all her wages will be burned in the fire,
and I will destroy all her idols.
Since she collected the wages of a prostitute,
they will be used again for a prostitute.

MICAH'S LAMENT

8 Because of this I will lament and wail;
I will walk barefoot and naked.
I will howl like the jackals
and mourn like ostriches.^C

9 For her wound is incurable
and has reached even Judah;
it has approached my people's city gate,
as far as Jerusalem.

10 Don't announce it in Gath,
don't weep at all.
Roll in the dust in Beth-leaphrah.

11 Depart in shameful nakedness,

---

^A1:2 Or *land*   ^B1:3 Or *high places*   ^C1:8 Or *eagle owls*; lit *daughters of the desert*

you residents of Shaphir;
the residents of Zaanan will not come out.
Beth-ezel is lamenting;
its support^A is taken from you.

¹² Though the residents of Maroth
anxiously wait for something good,
disaster has come from the LORD
to the gate of Jerusalem.

¹³ Harness the horses to the chariot,
you residents of Lachish.
This was the beginning of sin for Daughter Zion
because Israel's acts of rebellion
can be traced to you.

¹⁴ Therefore, send farewell gifts to Moresheth-gath;
the houses of Achzib are a deception
to the kings of Israel.

¹⁵ I will again bring a conqueror
against you who live in Mareshah.
The nobility^B of Israel will come to Adullam.

¹⁶ Shave yourselves bald and cut off your hair
in sorrow for your precious children;
make yourselves as bald as an eagle,
for they have been taken from you into exile.

OPPRESSORS JUDGED

2 Woe to those who dream up wickedness
and prepare evil plans on their beds!
At morning light they accomplish it
because the power is in their hands.

² They covet fields and seize them;
they also take houses.
They deprive a man of his home,
a person of his inheritance.

³ Therefore, the LORD says:
I am now planning a disaster
against this nation;
you cannot free your necks from it.
Then you will not walk so proudly
because it will be an evil time.

⁴ In that day one will take up a taunt against you
and lament mournfully, saying,
"We are totally ruined!
He measures out the allotted land
of my people.
How he removes it from me!
He allots our fields to traitors."

⁵ Therefore, there will be no one

---

^A1:11 Lit *its standing place*; Hb obscure   ^B1:15 Lit *glory*

in the assembly of the Lord
to divide the land by casting lots.^A

GOD'S WORD REJECTED

⁶ "Quit your preaching," they^B preach.
"They should not preach these things;
shame will not overtake us."^C

⁷ House of Jacob, should it be asked,
"Is the Spirit of the Lord impatient?
Are these the things he does?"
Don't my words bring good
to the one who walks uprightly?

⁸ But recently my people have risen up
like an enemy:
You strip off the splendid robe
from those who are passing through confidently,
like those returning from war.

⁹ You force the women of my people
out of their comfortable homes,
and you take my blessing^D
from their children forever.

¹⁰ Get up and leave,
for this is not your place of rest
because defilement brings destruction —
a grievous destruction!

¹¹ If a man comes
and utters empty lies —
"I will preach to you about wine and beer" —
he would be just the preacher for this people!

THE REMNANT REGATHERED

¹² I will indeed gather all of you, Jacob;
I will collect the remnant of Israel.
I will bring them together like sheep in a pen,
like a flock in the middle of its pasture.
It will be noisy with people.

¹³ One who breaks open the way
will advance before them;
they will break out, pass through the city gate,
and leave by it.
Their King will pass through before them,
the Lord as their leader.

UNJUST LEADERS JUDGED

3 Then I said, "Now listen, leaders of Jacob,
you rulers of the house of Israel.
Aren't you supposed to know what is just?

---

^A2:5 Lit Lord stretching the measuring line by lot ^B2:6 = the prophets ^C2:6 Text emended; MT reads things. Shame will not depart ^D2:9 Perhaps the land

² You hate good and love evil.
You tear off people's skin
and strip their flesh from their bones.
³ You eat the flesh of my people
after you strip their skin from them
and break their bones.
You chop them up
like flesh for the cooking pot,
like meat in a cauldron."
⁴ Then they will cry out to the LORD,
but he will not answer them.
He will hide his face from them at that time
because of the crimes they have committed.

FALSE PROPHETS JUDGED

⁵ This is what the LORD says
concerning the prophets
who lead my people astray,
who proclaim peace
when they have food to sink their teeth into
but declare war against the one
who puts nothing in their mouths.
⁶ Therefore, it will be night for you —
without visions;
it will grow dark for you —
without divination.
The sun will set on these prophets,
and the daylight will turn black over them.
⁷ Then the seers will be ashamed
and the diviners disappointed.
They will all cover their mouths^A
because there will be no answer from God.

⁸ As for me, however, I am filled with power
by the Spirit of the LORD,
with justice and courage,
to proclaim to Jacob his rebellion
and to Israel his sin.

ZION'S DESTRUCTION

⁹ Listen to this, leaders of the house of Jacob,
you rulers of the house of Israel,
who abhor justice
and pervert everything that is right,
¹⁰ who build Zion with bloodshed
and Jerusalem with injustice.
¹¹ Her leaders issue rulings for a bribe,
her priests teach for payment,

---

^A3:7 Lit mustache

and her prophets practice divination for silver.
Yet they lean on the LORD, saying,
"Isn't the LORD among us?
No disaster will overtake us."

¹² Therefore, because of you,
Zion will be plowed like a field,
Jerusalem will become ruins,
and the temple's mountain
will be a high thicket.

THE LORD'S RULE FROM RESTORED ZION

4 In the last days
the mountain of the LORD's house
will be established
at the top of the mountains
and will be raised above the hills.
Peoples will stream to it,

² and many nations will come and say,
"Come, let us go up to the mountain of the LORD,
to the house of the God of Jacob.
He will teach us about his ways
so we may walk in his paths."
For instruction will go out of Zion
and the word of the LORD from Jerusalem.

³ He will settle disputes among many peoples
and provide arbitration for strong nations
that are far away.
They will beat their swords into plows
and their spears into pruning knives.
Nation will not take up the sword against nation,
and they will never again train for war.

⁴ But each person will sit under his grapevine
and under his fig tree
with no one to frighten him.
For the mouth of the LORD of Armies
has spoken.

⁵ Though all the peoples each walk
in the name of their gods,
we will walk in the name of the LORD our God
forever and ever.

⁶ On that day —
this is the LORD's declaration —
I will assemble the lame
and gather the scattered,
those I have injured.

⁷ I will make the lame into a remnant,
those far removed into a strong nation.
Then the LORD will reign over them in Mount Zion
from this time on and forever.

8 And you, watchtower for the flock,
fortified hill[A] of Daughter Zion,
the former rule will come to you;
sovereignty will come to Daughter Jerusalem.

FROM EXILE TO VICTORY

9 Now, why are you shouting loudly?
Is there no king with you?
Has your counselor perished
so that anguish grips you like a woman in labor?

10 Writhe and cry out,[B] Daughter Zion,
like a woman in labor,
for now you will leave the city
and camp in the open fields.
You will go to Babylon;
there you will be rescued;
there the LORD will redeem you
from the grasp of your enemies!

11 Many nations have now assembled against you;
they say, "Let her be defiled,
and let us feast our eyes on Zion."

12 But they do not know the LORD's intentions
or understand his plan,
that he has gathered them
like sheaves to the threshing floor.

13 Rise and thresh, Daughter Zion,
for I will make your horns iron
and your hooves bronze
so you can crush many peoples.
Then you[C] will set apart their plunder
for the LORD,
their wealth for the Lord of the whole earth.

FROM DEFEATED RULER TO CONQUERING KING

5 Now, daughter who is under attack,
you slash yourself in grief;
a siege is set against us!
They are striking the judge of Israel
on the cheek with a rod.

2 Bethlehem Ephrathah,
you are small among the clans of Judah;
one will come from you
to be ruler over Israel for me.
His origin[D] is from antiquity,
from ancient times.

3 Therefore, Israel will be abandoned until the time
when she who is in labor has given birth;

A 4:8 Or *flock, Ophel*   B 4:10 Hb obscure   C 4:13 LXX, Syr, Tg; MT reads *I*
D 5:2 Lit *His going out*

then the rest of the ruler's brothers will return
to the people of Israel.
⁴ He will stand and shepherd them
in the strength of the LORD,
in the majestic name of the LORD his God.
They will live securely,
for then his greatness will extend
to the ends of the earth.
⁵ He will be their peace.
When Assyria invades our land,
when it marches against our fortresses,
we will raise against it seven shepherds,
even eight leaders of men.
⁶ They will shepherd the land of Assyria with the sword,
the land of Nimrod with a drawn blade.ᴬ
So he will rescue us from Assyria
when it invades our land,
when it marches against our territory.

THE GLORIOUS AND PURIFIED REMNANT

⁷ Then the remnant of Jacob
will be among many peoples
like dew from the LORD,
like showers on the grass,
which do not wait for anyone
or linger for mankind.
⁸ Then the remnant of Jacob
will be among the nations, among many peoples,
like a lion among animals of the forest,
like a young lion among flocks of sheep,
which tramples and tears as it passes through,
and there is no one to rescue them.
⁹ Your hand will be lifted up against your adversaries,
and all your enemies will be destroyed.

¹⁰ In that day —
    this is the LORD's declaration —
I will remove your horses from you
and wreck your chariots.
¹¹ I will remove the cities of your land
and tear down all your fortresses.
¹² I will remove sorceries from your hands,
and you will not have any more fortune-tellers.
¹³ I will remove your carved images
and sacred pillars from you
so that you will no longer worship
the work of your hands.
¹⁴ I will pull up the Asherah poles from among you

ᴬ5:6 Aq, Vg; MT, Sym read *Nimrod at its gateways*

and demolish your cities.^A

15 I will take vengeance in anger and wrath
   against the nations that have not obeyed me.

GOD'S LAWSUIT AGAINST JUDAH

6 Now listen to what the LORD is saying:
   Rise, plead your case before the mountains,
   and let the hills hear your complaint.^B

2 Listen to the LORD's lawsuit,
   you mountains and enduring foundations
      of the earth,
   because the LORD has a case against his people,
   and he will argue it against Israel.

3 My people, what have I done to you,
   or how have I wearied you?
   Testify against me!

4 Indeed, I brought you up from the land of Egypt
   and redeemed you from that place of slavery.
   I sent Moses, Aaron, and Miriam ahead of you.

5 My people,
   remember what King Balak of Moab proposed,
   what Balaam son of Beor answered him,
   and what happened from the Acacia Grove^C
      to Gilgal
   so that you may acknowledge
   the LORD's righteous acts.

6 What should I bring before the LORD
   when I come to bow before God on high?
   Should I come before him with burnt offerings,
   with year-old calves?

7 Would the LORD be pleased with thousands of rams
   or with ten thousand streams of oil?
   Should I give my firstborn for my transgression,
   the offspring of my body for my own sin?

8 Mankind, he has told each of you what is good
   and what it is the LORD requires of you:
   to act justly,
   to love faithfulness,
   and to walk humbly with your God.

VERDICT OF JUDGMENT

9 The voice of the LORD calls out to the city^D
   (and it is wise to fear your name):
   "Pay attention to the rod
   and the one who ordained it.^E

---

^A5:14 Or *shrines* ^B6:1 Lit *voice* ^C6:5 Or *from Shittim* ^D6:9 = Jerusalem
^E6:9 Or *attention, you tribe. Who has ordained it?*; Hb obscure

BORROWED MERIT BADGES

MICAH 6

They say women love a man in uniform, but they may not have been talking about the Boy Scouts. Unfortunately, no one relayed this message to my kerchief-wearing, popcorn-selling, Eagle Scout of a little brother.

With socks to his knees and badges across his chest, he'd proudly hold up his fingers, reciting the Boy Scout Motto every night before brushing his teeth. His newfound pack became his identity, and while it didn't earn him a swarm of girlfriends, it certainly brought the shy boy out of his shell. He threw himself into first aid, emergency preparedness, environmental science, and camping, checking off as many merit badge requirements as possible.

In Micah 6, that's exactly what the Israelites were hoping for: a checklist for how to please God. They had failed at manufacturing goodness for themselves, and their idols hadn't produced any fruit. Assuming the answer was to work harder, they wondered when God would ever be satisfied with what they had to offer.

Israel wanted to earn their ranking in faith through burnt offerings, year-old calves, rams, and streams of oil, but even these expensive gifts were not an equal trade for righteousness. But the instructions God provided were not what they expected.

"Mankind, he has told each of you what is good and what it is the LORD requires of you: to act justly, to love faithfulness, and to walk humbly with your God."

MICAH 6:8

Upon hearing these words from the prophet, I bet the Israelites were ready to tie their kerchiefs around their necks and get to work achieving their merit badges with God. But looking at the specific commands, we can guess they became a little confused when they realized everything had already been accomplished. Their assigned tasks did not require sacrifice, strength, or anything else the Israelites could offer. They were simply called to mirror the character of God.

Instead of giving them rules to follow, He provided built-in sufficiency, pointing forward to the boxes He'd checkmark later on the cross.

We, like Israel, forget that the only merit we have is the blood of the Messiah.

We can only act justly because we have been justified through Christ.

We can only love faithfulness because He defined it for us on the cross.

We can only walk humbly because His footsteps went before us.

We can only be with our God because Christ joined us to Him.

The only thing left on our to-do list is to treasure how good He is to us. May we never grow tired of checking that box.

¹⁰ Are there still^A the treasures of wickedness
and the accursed short measure
in the house of the wicked?

¹¹ Can I excuse wicked scales
or bags of deceptive weights?

¹² For the wealthy of the city are full of violence,
and its residents speak lies;
the tongues in their mouths are deceitful.

¹³ "As a result, I have begun to strike you severely,^B
bringing desolation because of your sins.

¹⁴ You will eat but not be satisfied,
for there will be hunger within you.
What you acquire, you cannot save,
and what you do save,
I will give to the sword.^A

¹⁵ You will sow but not reap;
you will press olives
but not anoint yourself with oil;
and you will tread grapes
but not drink the wine.

¹⁶ The statutes of Omri
and all the practices of Ahab's house
have been observed;
you have followed their policies.
Therefore, I will make you a desolate place
and the city's^C residents an object of contempt;^D
you will bear the scorn of my people."^E

ISRAEL'S MORAL DECLINE

7 How sad for me!
For I am like one who —
when the summer fruit has been gathered
after the gleaning of the grape harvest —
finds no grape cluster to eat,
no early fig, which I crave.

² Faithful people have vanished from the land;
there is no one upright among the people.
All of them wait in ambush to shed blood;
they hunt each other with a net.

³ Both hands are good at accomplishing evil:
the official and the judge demand a bribe;
when the powerful man communicates his evil desire,
they plot it together.

⁴ The best of them is like a brier;
the most upright is worse than a hedge of thorns.

---

^A6:10,14 Hb obscure   ^B6:13 LXX, Aq, Theod, Syr, Vg; MT reads *I have made you sick by striking you down*   ^C6:16 Lit *and its*   ^D6:16 Lit *residents a hissing*
^E6:16 LXX reads *of the peoples*

The day of your watchmen,
the day of your punishment, is coming;
at this time their panic is here.
⁵ Do not rely on a friend;
don't trust in a close companion.
Seal your mouth
from the woman who lies in your arms.
⁶ Surely a son considers his father a fool,
a daughter opposes her mother,
and a daughter-in-law is against her mother-in-law;
a man's enemies are the men of his own household.
⁷ But I will look to the LORD;
I will wait for the God of my salvation.
My God will hear me.

ZION'S VINDICATION

⁸ Do not rejoice over me, my enemy!
Though I have fallen, I will stand up;
though I sit in darkness,
the LORD will be my light.
⁹ Because I have sinned against him,
I must endure the LORD's rage
until he champions my cause
and establishes justice for me.
He will bring me into the light;
I will see his salvation.ᴬ
¹⁰ Then my enemy will see,
and she will be covered with shame,
the one who said to me,
"Where is the LORD your God?"
My eyes will look at her in triumph;
at that time she will be trampled
like mud in the streets.

¹¹ A day will come for rebuilding your walls;
on that day your boundary will be extended.
¹² On that day people will come to you
from Assyria and the cities of Egypt,
even from Egypt to the Euphrates River
and from sea to sea
and mountain to mountain.
¹³ Then the earth will become a wasteland
because of its inhabitants
and as a result of their actions.

MICAH'S PRAYER ANSWERED

¹⁴ Shepherd your people with your staff,
the flock that is your possession.

ᴬ7:9 Or *righteousness*

They live alone in a woodland
surrounded by pastures.
Let them graze in Bashan and Gilead
as in ancient times.

¹⁵ I will perform miracles for them^A
as in the days of your exodus
from the land of Egypt.
¹⁶ Nations will see and be ashamed
of^B all their power.
They will put their hands over their mouths,
and their ears will become deaf.
¹⁷ They will lick the dust like a snake;
they will come trembling out of their hiding places
like reptiles slithering on the ground.
They will tremble in the presence of the LORD our God;
they will stand in awe of you.

¹⁸ Who is a God like you,
forgiving iniquity and passing over rebellion
for the remnant of his inheritance?
He does not hold on to his anger forever
because he delights in faithful love.
¹⁹ He will again have compassion on us;
he will vanquish our iniquities.
You will cast all our^C sins
into the depths of the sea.
²⁰ You will show loyalty to Jacob
and faithful love to Abraham,
as you swore to our fathers
from days long ago.

---

^A7:15 = Israel ^B7:16 Or *ashamed in spite of* ^C7:19 Some Hb mss, LXX, Syr, Vg; other Hb mss read *their*

He cares for those who take refuge in Him

nahum

The Lord is good, a stronghold in a day of distress; he cares for those who take refuge in him. **1:7**

ON THE TIMELINE Nahum was written sometime between the capture and downfall of Thebes (the capital of Egypt) in 663 BC, and the destruction of Nineveh in 612 BC. The northern kingdom of Israel had been overthrown by Assyria about a century earlier, and Nahum's message was meant to bring comfort to the remaining kingdom of Judah as it pronounced God's judgment on the enemies of God's people. Jonah's message to Nineveh occurred about one-hundred years prior to Nahum's. While God relented from sending judgment on Nineveh in Jonah's day, Nahum announced that God's judgment against this wicked nation was now certain.

A LITTLE BACKGROUND Nahum the Elkoshite (Nah 1:1) is the only person identified by that name in the Old Testament. Like Jonah in the previous century, Nahum prophesied judgment upon Nineveh. The Ninevites in Jonah's time had repented (Jnh 3), but now that Nineveh's leaders had resumed their wicked actions, God called Nahum to reaffirm God's coming judgment. Ironically, Nahum's Hebrew name means "comfort"—comfort for Judah (Nah 1:12-15) because it's cruel overlord Assyria would be punished without any "comforters" (Nah 3:7).

MESSAGE & PURPOSE The main theme of the book of Nahum is the impending judgment of Nineveh by the Lord (Nah 1:1,8; 2:8-13; 3:7-19) by which He would deliver His people (Nah 1:12-15). The Lord would punish Nineveh in the same way they had mistreated their enemies. The character of God, portrayed as a powerful but caring warrior (Nah 1:2-7), was the propelling force behind Nineveh's judgment. The portrait of a God of wrath is consistent with His promise to avenge the blood of His servants (Dt 32:35-36, 42-43). He was "good" (or kind) to those who took refuge in Him (Nah 1:7), while bringing destruction on His unrepentant enemies, including Nineveh (Nah 1:8).

GIVE THANKS FOR THE BOOK OF NAHUM

The book of Nahum provides a great view of a powerful and just God who maintains His absolute moral standards and offers hope to those who are despised and downtrodden. Nahum teaches us to trust in God. Even when our situation seems hopeless, Nahum's message reminds us that God will stand with those who belong to Him.

THE BOOK OF NAHUM IN HISTORY

750

650

55

1900

760

722

630

612

701

609

Jonah
travels to
Nineveh

Assyria
invades
Judah

Fall of Assyria

Nineveh
established
as prominent
Assyrian city

Israel falls
to Assyria

Fall of Nineveh

Nahum's
prophecy
against
Nineveh

READ AND UNDERSTAND NAHUM

The Bible is a complete work in which many stories combine to tell one story. As you read the book of Nahum, consider reading the additional passages to discover how the whole of Scripture works together.

1 The pronouncement concerning Nineveh. The book of the vision of Nahum the Elkoshite.

GOD'S VENGEANCE

² The Lord is a jealous and avenging God;
the Lord takes vengeance
and is fierce in ᴬ wrath.
The Lord takes vengeance against his foes;
he is furious with his enemies.
³ The Lord is slow to anger but great
in power;
the Lord will never leave
the guilty unpunished.
His path is in the whirlwind and storm,
and clouds are the dust beneath his feet.
⁴ He rebukes the sea and dries it up,
and he makes all the rivers run dry.
Bashan and Carmel wither;
even the flower of Lebanon withers.
⁵ The mountains quake before him,
and the hills melt;
the earth trembles ᴮ,ᶜ at his presence —
the world and all who live in it.
⁶ Who can withstand his indignation?
Who can endure his burning anger?
His wrath is poured out like fire;
even rocks are shattered before him.

DESTRUCTION OF NINEVEH

⁷ The Lord is good,
a stronghold in a day of distress;
he cares for those who take refuge in him.
⁸ But he will completely destroy Nineveh ᴰ
with an overwhelming flood,
and he will chase his enemies
into darkness.

⁹ Whatever you ᴱ plot against the Lord,
he will bring it to complete destruction;
oppression will not rise up a second time.
¹⁰ For they will be consumed
like entangled thorns,
like the drink of a drunkard
and like straw that is fully dry. ᶠ
¹¹ One has gone out from you, ᴳ
who plots evil against the Lord,
and is a wicked counselor.

ᴬ1:2 Lit *is a master of*   ᴮ1:5 Some emend to *earth is laid waste*   ᶜ1:5 Lit *lifts*
ᴰ1:8 Lit *her place*   ᴱ1:9 = Nineveh   ᶠ1:10 Hb obscure   ᴳ1:11 Possibly Nineveh

OUR ONLY STRONGHOLD

NAHUM 1:7-15; 2 KINGS 17-19; PSALM 62

The Assyrians had certainly been warned. First, God sent Jonah, and the Ninevites scrambled into sackcloth and ashes to repent and save their city from destruction. But halfway repentance doesn't last. Before long, they rejoined the Assyrian empire to decimate Jerusalem, shame their king, and scoff at the God of Israel.

But God is not mocked (Gl 6:7), and even while the Assyrians celebrated their fresh conquest, God's thunderous judgment was already rumbling in the distance. When they were established in battle formation against Israel, an angel of the Lord went out and struck down 185,000 in the camp of the Assyrians (2Kg 19:35).

Almost a century later, the Assyrians again rose in their bloodthirsty power. God's prophet, Nahum, prophesied the final destruction of Nineveh, their capital city. God's patience for their sin lasted hundreds of years, but His forbearance for sin does not last forever. Nahum declared God's judgment on Assyria, "Though they are strong and numerous, they will be mowed down, and he will pass away" (Nah 1:12).

I'll be honest. These words of judgment feel final and heavy. I can't help but feel a shameful kinship with the Ninevites, and this valuation of sin makes me fidget. I think I find a common ground with the Ninevites because they did repent, and that's the thing we're supposed to do, right? I find myself repenting all the time, but am I truly repenting and turning in the other direction? Or am I repenting, then returning to my sin? Should I expect God to extend favor to me for a job half done?

Indeed, as Matthew Henry says, "Humble suppliants will find him gracious, but scornful beggars will not find him easy" (*Matthew Henry's Commentary on the Whole Bible*, Volume 4). *Lord, teach me to be a humble suppliant, and not a scornful beggar!* When I repent but return again to my sin, I make a mockery of repentance and scorn God's mercy.

We often identify with the hero or the victim in a story, but rarely are we willing to consider that we might be the villain. The judgment for the unrepentant Assyrians could also be for unrepentant stay-at-home moms, or unrepentant Sunday school teachers, or even unrepentant devotional writers.

God is serious about repentance, but even our repentance is dependent on the grace given to us in Christ Jesus. God's Word promises that if we confess our sins, "he is faithful and righteous to forgive us our sins and to cleanse us from all unrighteousness" (1Jn 1:9).

Those who humble themselves before our just and compassionate God receive eternal refuge, even from the storm of their own sin.

"The Lord is good, a stronghold in a day of distress; he cares for those who take refuge in him."

NAHUM 1:7

PROMISE OF JUDAH'S DELIVERANCE

¹²This is what the LORD says:

Though they are strong[A] and numerous,
they will still be mowed down,
and he[B] will pass away.
Though I have punished you,[C]
I will punish you no longer.

¹³ For I will now break off his yoke from you
and tear off your shackles.

THE ASSYRIAN KING'S DEMISE

¹⁴The LORD has issued an order concerning you:

There will be no offspring
to carry on your name.[D]
I will eliminate the carved idol and cast image
from the house of your gods;
I will prepare your grave,
for you are contemptible.

¹⁵ Look to the mountains —
the feet of the herald,
who proclaims peace.
Celebrate your festivals, Judah;
fulfill your vows.
For the wicked one will never again
march through you;
he will be entirely wiped out.

ATTACK AGAINST NINEVEH

2 One who scatters is coming up against you.
Man the fortifications!
Watch the road!
Brace[E] yourself!
Summon all your strength!

² For the LORD will restore the majesty
of Jacob,
yes,[F] the majesty of Israel,
though ravagers have ravaged them
and ruined their vine branches.

³ The shields of his[G] warriors are dyed red;
the valiant men are dressed in scarlet.
The fittings of the chariot flash like fire
on the day of its battle preparations,
and the spears are brandished.

[A]1:12 Lit intact   [B]1:12 Either the king of Assyria or his army   [C]1:12 = Judah
[D]1:14 Lit It will not be sown from your name any longer   [E]2:1 Lit Strengthen
[F]2:2 Or like   [G]2:3 = the army commander attacking Nineveh

4 The chariots dash madly through the streets;
  they rush around in the plazas.
  They look like torches;
  they dart back and forth like lightning.
5 He gives orders to his officers;
  they stumble as they advance.
  They race to its wall;
  the protective shield is set in place.
6 The river gates are opened,
  and the palace erodes away.

7 Beauty [A] is stripped; [B]
  she is carried away;
  her ladies-in-waiting moan
  like the sound of doves
  and beat their breasts.
8 Nineveh has been like a pool of water
  from her first days, [B]
  but they are fleeing.
  "Stop! Stop!" they cry,
  but no one turns back.
9 "Plunder the silver! Plunder the gold!"
  There is no end to the treasure,
  an abundance of every precious thing.
10 Desolation, decimation, devastation!
  Hearts melt,
  knees tremble,
  insides churn,
  every face grows pale!

11 Where is the lions' lair,
  or the feeding ground of the young lions,
  where the lion and lioness prowled,
  and the lion's cub,
  with nothing to frighten them away?
12 The lion mauled whatever its cubs needed
  and strangled prey for its lionesses.
  It filled up its dens with the kill,
  and its lairs with mauled prey.
13 Beware, I am against you.
    This is the declaration of the LORD
    of Armies.
  I will make your chariots go up in smoke, [C]
  and the sword will devour your young lions.
  I will cut off your prey from the earth,
  and the sound of your messengers
  will never be heard again.

NINEVEH'S DOWNFALL

3 Woe to the city of blood,
totally deceitful,
full of plunder,
never without prey.
² The crack of the whip
and rumble of the wheel,
galloping horse
and jolting chariot!
³ Charging horseman,
flashing sword,
shining spear;
heaps of slain,
mounds of corpses,
dead bodies without end —
they stumble over their dead.
⁴ Because of the continual prostitution of the prostitute,
the attractive mistress of sorcery,
who treats nations and clans like merchandise
by her prostitution and sorcery,
⁵ I am against you.
This is the declaration of the LORD of Armies.
I will lift your skirts over your face
and display your nakedness to nations,
your shame to kingdoms.
⁶ I will throw filth on you
and treat you with contempt;
I will make a spectacle of you.
⁷ Then all who see you will recoil from you, saying,
"Nineveh is devastated;
who will show sympathy to her?"
Where can I find anyone to comfort you?

⁸ Are you better than Thebes ᴬ
that sat along the Nile
with water surrounding her,
whose rampart was the sea,
the river ᴮ,ᶜ her wall?
⁹ Cush and Egypt were her endless source of strength;
Put and Libya were among her ᴰ allies.
¹⁰ Yet she became an exile;
she went into captivity.
Her children were also dashed to pieces
at the head of every street.
They cast lots for her dignitaries,
and all her nobles were bound in chains.
¹¹ You ᴱ also will become drunk;

ᴬ3:8 Hb *No-amon* ᴮ3:8 LXX, Syr, Vg read *water* ᶜ3:8 Lit *sea from sea*
ᴰ3:9 Lit *your* ᴱ3:11 = Nineveh

you will hide.^A
You also will seek refuge from the enemy.

12 All your fortresses are fig trees
with figs that ripened first;
when shaken, they fall —
right into the mouth of the eater!

13 Look, your troops are like women among you;
your land's city gates
are wide open to your enemies.
Fire will devour the bars of your gates.

14 Draw water for the siege;
strengthen your fortresses.
Step into the clay and tread the mortar;
take hold of the brick-mold!
15 The fire will devour you there;
the sword will cut you down.
It will devour you like the young locust.
Multiply yourselves like the young locust;
multiply like the swarming locust!
16 You have made your merchants
more numerous than the stars of the sky.
The young locust strips^B the land
and flies away.
17 Your court officials are like the swarming locust,
and your scribes like clouds of locusts,
which settle on the walls on a cold day;
when the sun rises, they take off,
and no one knows where they are.

18 King of Assyria, your shepherds slumber;
your officers sleep.
Your people are scattered across the mountains
with no one to gather them together.
19 There is no remedy for your injury;
your wound is severe.
All who hear the news about you
will clap their hands because of you,
for who has not experienced
your constant cruelty?

yet I will celebrate in the Lord; I will rejoice in the God of my salvation! The Lord my Lord is my strength; He makes my feet like those of a deer and enables me to walk on mountain heights!

habakkuk

Yet I will celebrate in the LORD; I will rejoice in the God of my salvation! The LORD my Lord is my strength; he makes my feet like those of a deer and enables me to walk on mountain heights! **3:18-19**

ON THE TIMELINE Habakkuk likely wrote his prophecy after the death of King Josiah of Judah in 609 BC, but before the devastations of Judah in 597 BC and 586 BC. This dates the prophecy to the reign of Jehoiakim (around 609–599 BC), probably in the period of Egyptian domination before Babylon invaded Judah (609–605 BC).

A LITTLE BACKGROUND Rather than speaking to the people on God's behalf, Habakkuk spoke to God on behalf of the people. The entire small book of Habakkuk is a conversation between Habakkuk and the Lord. This conversation predicts the Babylonian devastation of Judah (Hab 1:5-11), a prophecy fulfilled when Nebuchadnezzar invaded Jerusalem and destroyed the temple (586 BC). Habakkuk also predicts Babylon's own day of reckoning (Hab 2:6-20), which occurred when Cyrus of Persia conquered Babylon in 539 BC.

MESSAGE & PURPOSE Habakkuk deals with the human problem of understanding God's ways: How can God allow injustice to prevail (Hab 1:3)? Why does God use the more wicked Babylonians to punish the less wicked Judeans (Hab 1:13)? How long will God allow evildoers to dominate the world (Hab 1:17)? Rather than giving clear answers to these questions Habakkuk raised, God instructed the godly to have faith (Hab 2:4).

Habakkuk also demonstrates the greatness of God: He is eternally alive (Hab 1:12), He can raise up nations to accomplish His purposes (Hab 1:6), and He shakes the world through pestilence and war (Hab 3:2-15). Though God may use the wicked acts of men for His good purposes and allow evil to prevail for a time, ultimately the wicked will pay for their crimes (Hab 2:6-14) and God will come to save His people and crush the wicked (Hab 3:13-15).

GIVE THANKS FOR THE BOOK OF HABAKKUK

The book of Habakkuk addresses the common struggle to understand God's actions in the world while calling us to faith in God's good purposes. Habakkuk's message that the righteous will live by faith prepared the way for the greater understanding of this truth in the New Testament, which emphasizes salvation through faith in Christ (Rm 1:17; Gl 3:11; Heb 10:38-39).

THE BOOK OF HABAKKUK IN HISTORY

610 BC   600 BC   590

609

King Josiah
of Judah dies

Pharaoh Necho
invades Judah

Start of Habakkuk's ministry

605

First Babylonian
siege of Judah

598

End of Habakkuk's
prophetic ministry

Second Babylonian invasion

People of Judah taken into exile

597

Jehoiachin becomes
king of Judah

READ AND UNDERSTAND HABAKKUK

The Bible is a complete work in which many stories combine to tell one story. As you read the book of Habakkuk, consider reading the additional passages to discover how the whole of Scripture works together.

1

The pronouncement that the prophet Habakkuk saw.

HABAKKUK'S FIRST PRAYER

2 How long, LORD, must I call for help
and you do not listen
or cry out to you about violence
and you do not save?
3 Why do you force me to look at injustice?
Why do you tolerate[A] wrongdoing?
Oppression and violence are right
in front of me.
Strife is ongoing, and conflict escalates.
4 This is why the law is ineffective
and justice never emerges.
For the wicked restrict the righteous;
therefore, justice comes out perverted.

GOD'S FIRST ANSWER

5 Look at the nations[B] and observe —
be utterly astounded!
For I am doing something in your days
that you will not believe
when you hear about it.
6 Look! I am raising up the Chaldeans,[C]
that bitter, impetuous nation
that marches across the earth's open spaces
to seize territories not its own.
7 They are fierce and terrifying;
their views of justice and sovereignty
stem from themselves.
8 Their horses are swifter than leopards
and more fierce[D] than wolves of the night.
Their horsemen charge ahead;
their horsemen come from distant lands.
They fly like eagles, swooping to devour.
9 All of them come to do violence;
their faces are set in determination.[E]
They gather prisoners like sand.
10 They mock kings,
and rulers are a joke to them.
They laugh at every fortress
and build siege ramps to capture it.
11 Then they sweep by like the wind
and pass through.
They are guilty;[F] their strength is their god.

A 1:3 Lit observe, also in v. 13   B 1:5 DSS, LXX, Syr read Look, you treacherous
people   C 1:6 = the Babylonians   D 1:8 Or and quicker   E 1:9 Hb obscure
F 1:11 Or wind, and transgress and incur guilt

HABAKKUK'S SECOND PRAYER

12 Are you not from eternity, LORD my God?
My Holy One, you^A will not die.
LORD, you appointed them to execute judgment;
my Rock, you destined them to punish us.

13 Your eyes are too pure to look on evil,
and you cannot tolerate wrongdoing.
So why do you tolerate those
who are treacherous?
Why are you silent
while one^B who is wicked swallows up
one^C who is more righteous than himself?

14 You have made mankind
like the fish of the sea,
like marine creatures that have no ruler.

15 The Chaldeans pull them all up with a hook,
catch them in their dragnet,
and gather them in their fishing net;
that is why they are glad and rejoice.

16 That is why they sacrifice to their dragnet
and burn incense to their fishing net,
for by these things their portion is rich
and their food plentiful.

17 Will they therefore empty their net
and continually slaughter nations
without mercy?

HABAKKUK WAITS FOR GOD'S RESPONSE

2 I will stand at my guard post
and station myself on the lookout tower.
I will watch to see what he will say to me
and what I should^D reply about my complaint.

GOD'S SECOND ANSWER

2 The LORD answered me:
Write down this vision;
clearly inscribe it on tablets
so one may easily read it.^E

3 For the vision is yet for the appointed time;
it testifies about the end and will not lie.
Though it delays, wait for it,
since it will certainly come and not be late.

4 Look, his ego is inflated;^F
he is without integrity.
But the righteous one will live by his faith.^G

5 Moreover, wine^H betrays;

---

^A1:12 Alt Hb tradition reads *we* ^B1:13 = Babylon ^C1:13 = Judah ^D2:1 Syr
reads *what he will* ^E2:2 Lit *one who reads in it may run* ^F2:4 Hb obscure
^G2:4 Or *faithfulness* ^H2:5 DSS read *wealth*

an arrogant man is never at rest.^A
He enlarges his appetite like Sheol,
and like Death he is never satisfied.
He gathers all the nations to himself;
he collects all the peoples for himself.

THE FIVE WOE ORACLES

⁶ Won't all of these take up a taunt against him,
with mockery and riddles about him?
They will say:

Woe to him who amasses what is not his —
how much longer? —
and loads himself with goods taken in pledge.
⁷ Won't your creditors suddenly arise,
and those who disturb you wake up?
Then you will become spoil for them.
⁸ Since you have plundered many nations,
all the peoples who remain will plunder you —
because of human bloodshed
and violence against lands, cities,
and all who live in them.

⁹ Woe to him who dishonestly makes
wealth for his house^B
to place his nest on high,
to escape the grasp of disaster!
¹⁰ You have planned shame for your house
by wiping out many peoples
and sinning against your own self.
¹¹ For the stones will cry out from the wall,
and the rafters will answer them
from the woodwork.

¹² Woe to him who builds a city with bloodshed
and founds a town with injustice!
¹³ Is it not from the LORD of Armies
that the peoples labor only to fuel the fire
and countries exhaust themselves for nothing?
¹⁴ For the earth will be filled
with the knowledge of the LORD's glory,
as the water covers the sea.

¹⁵ Woe to him who gives his neighbors drink,
pouring out your wrath^C
and even making them drunk,
in order to look at their nakedness!
¹⁶ You will be filled with disgrace instead of glory.

---

^A2:5 Or *man does not endure*; Hb obscure   ^B2:9 Or *dynasty*   ^C2:15 Or *venom*

You also — drink,
and expose your uncircumcision!^A
The cup in the LORD's right hand
will come around to you,
and utter disgrace will cover your glory.
¹⁷ For your violence against Lebanon
will overwhelm you;
the destruction of animals will terrify you^B
because of your human bloodshed and violence
against lands, cities, and all who live in them.

¹⁸ What use is a carved idol
after its craftsman carves it?
It is only a cast image, a teacher of lies.
For the one who crafts its shape trusts in it
and makes idols that cannot speak.
¹⁹ Woe to him who says to wood: Wake up!
or to mute stone: Come alive!
Can it teach?
Look! It may be plated with gold and silver,
yet there is no breath in it at all.

²⁰ But the LORD is in his holy temple;
let the whole earth
be silent in his presence.

HABAKKUK'S THIRD PRAYER

3 A prayer of the prophet Habakkuk. According to *Shigionoth.*^C
² LORD, I have heard the report about you;
LORD, I stand in awe of your deeds.
Revive your work in these years;
make it known in these years.
In your wrath remember mercy!

³ God comes from Teman,
the Holy One from Mount Paran.
His splendor covers the heavens,
and the earth is full of his praise.   *Selah*
⁴ His brilliance is like light;
rays are flashing from his hand.
This is where his power is hidden.
⁵ Plague goes before him,
and pestilence follows in his steps.
⁶ He stands and shakes^D the earth;
he looks and startles the nations.
The age-old mountains break apart;

---

^A2:16 DSS, LXX, Aq, Syr, Vg read *and stagger* ^B2:17 DSS, LXX, Aq, Syr, Tg, Vg;
MT reads *them* ^C3:1 Perhaps a passionate song with rapid changes of rhythm,
or a dirge ^D3:6 Or *surveys*

YET I WILL CELEBRATE

HABAKKUK 3:16-19; PSALM 17; JOHN 1:14-18

When was the last time you really, really wanted something? Dig deeper than a juicy steak and a great new pair of shoes. Picture something you not only desire with your mind, but something your entire body and soul groan and ache for.

Whatever it is, however long you've wanted it, I bet you're thinking about it now. You've probably forced a swallow and gotten a little bit stiller. I get that feeling too.

I know they say it's hard sometimes to differentiate between wants and needs. I'm honestly not sure where mine lands, but I'll tell you anyway: I've always really, really wanted a dad.

Oh, I prayed. I asked, and I waited, and I hoped. But like Habakkuk's prayer in chapter 3, the fig tree did not blossom. There was no fruit on the vines, and the flock was cut off from the fold. My prayer for the earthly father I'd envisioned was met with a "no" from the Lord.

We all have heart longings like this—big ones and small ones. We have wants that last a day and some that last a lifetime. We long to be needed and known. We long to feel accepted and free.

Not only that, but we also have pressing, immediate needs. We are unemployed. We are out of groceries. We are supposed to leave on family vacation in a few hours, and the engine light just came on. We have human body aches. We are in want of health and healing. We need justice and mercy and for our checkbooks to balance. Sometimes we get the things. Sometimes we don't.

But look what Habakkuk says at the end of his prayer, after he's listed out all of his legitimate needs that seem to have gone unnoticed by the God he unwaveringly serves:

"Yet I will celebrate in the LORD; I will rejoice in the God of my salvation!"

HABAKKUK 3:18

Let's sit for a moment, having acknowledged those fields and flocks and fig trees we have asked the Lord to provide for us—our deepest heart-longings and our most immediate stressors.

Ask the Holy Spirit to use the truth of Habakkuk's prayer to encourage you.

"The LORD my Lord is my strength; he makes my feet like those of a deer and enables me to walk on mountain heights!"

HABAKKUK 3:19

Even if God doesn't answer our prayers how we'd like Him to, even if we don't get what we're yearning for, **He promises to be our strength.** He grants us exactly what we need and gives us grace to follow Him. May we celebrate in Him.

the ancient hills sink down.
His pathways are ancient.
7 I see the tents of Cushan[A] in distress;
the tent curtains of the land of Midian tremble.

8 Are you angry at the rivers, LORD?
Is your wrath against the rivers?
Or is your rage against the sea
when you ride on your horses,
your victorious chariot?
9 You took the sheath from your bow;
the arrows are ready[B] to be used with an oath.[C]   *Selah*
You split the earth with rivers.
10 The mountains see you and shudder;
a downpour of water sweeps by.
The deep roars with its voice
and lifts its waves[D] high.
11 Sun and moon stand still in their lofty residence,
at the flash of your flying arrows,
at the brightness of your shining spear.
12 You march across the earth with indignation;
you trample down the nations in wrath.
13 You come out to save your people,
to save your anointed.[E]
You crush the leader of the house of the wicked
and strip him from foot[F] to neck.   *Selah*
14 You pierce his head
with his own spears;
his warriors storm out to scatter us,
gloating as if ready to secretly devour the weak.
15 You tread the sea with your horses,
stirring up the vast water.

HABAKKUK'S CONFIDENCE IN GOD EXPRESSED

16 I heard, and I trembled within;
my lips quivered at the sound.
Rottenness entered my bones;
I trembled where I stood.
Now I must quietly wait for the day of distress
to come against the people invading us.
17 Though the fig tree does not bud
and there is no fruit on the vines,
though the olive crop fails
and the fields produce no food,
though the flocks disappear from the pen
and there are no herds in the stalls,
18 yet I will celebrate in the LORD;
I will rejoice in the God of my salvation!

[A]3:7 = Midian   [B]3:9 Or set   [C]3:9 Hb obscure   [D]3:10 Lit *hands*   [E]3:13 The
Davidic king or the nation of Israel   [F]3:13 Lit *foundation*

¹⁹ The Lord my Lord is my strength;
he makes my feet like those of a deer
and enables me to walk on mountain heights!
For the choir director: on^A stringed instruments.

---

^A 3:19 Lit *on my*

zephaniah

 The Lord your God is among you, a warrior who saves. He will rejoice over you with gladness. He will be quiet in his love. He will delight in you with singing. **3:17**

ON THE TIMELINE Evidence in the text indicates the book of Zephaniah was written sometime between 640 and 612 BC. Zephaniah 1:1 refers to King Josiah's reign (around 640–609 BC), and Zephaniah 2:13-15 prophesies Nineveh's fall, which occurred in 612 BC. This message was given to Judah about a decade before the first deportation to Babylon in 605 BC.

A LITTLE BACKGROUND King Josiah's father, King Amon (Zph 1:1), was a wicked man, as was his father before him, King Manasseh (2Kg 21:1-7,11,16, 20-22). This heritage of wickedness helps explain the rampant idolatry in the land when Josiah inherited the throne in 640 BC. While the new king struggled to squelch idolatry in Judah (Zph 1:4-9), orthodox and "pagan priests" led worship of the Lord while also bowing before Baal, Molech, and other pagan gods (Zph 1:4-6). The public reading of the book of the law (ca 621 BC) helped bring the people to repentance, prompting them to tear down the altars to their false gods (Zph 1:3-4; 2Kg 23:1-14).

MESSAGE & PURPOSE In view of the impending destruction of the "day of the Lord" (Zph 1:7-18; 2:2-3), Zephaniah's primary purpose was to extend an urgent invitation. He urged the people of Judah to seek the Lord alone in righteousness and humility (Zph 2:1-3). The immediate purpose was to warn idolatrous Judah of the Lord's imminent judgment (Zph 1:4-13), but the ultimate purpose was to call out a "remnant" from all nations (Zph 2:7-9; 3:9-10,12-13) to trust in the Lord.

GIVE THANKS FOR THE BOOK OF ZEPHANIAH

The promise of a remnant illustrates God's amazing grace alongside His just wrath toward the wicked (Nah 1:2-8). God would judge the proud (2:8-11,13-15; 3:11) and preserve the humble, and Zephaniah invited everyone who humbly obeyed the Lord to seek Him for deliverance (2:2-3). The New Testament highlights the beautiful truth that all people are invited to be part of what Paul calls "remnant chosen by grace" (Rm 11:5)—those who receive eternal salvation through faith in Christ.

THE BOOK OF ZEPHANIAH IN HISTORY

635 BC   625 BC   615 BC

| | 626 | | 612 |

640   631   621   612

Josiah becomes   Josiah's   Book of the Law is found   Fall of Nineveh
king of Judah   initial   and read publicly,
                         reforms   continuing Josiah's reforms   End of
                                  Zephaniah's   Zephaniah's
                                  prophetic call   ministry

READ AND UNDERSTAND ZEPHANIAH

The Bible is a complete work in which many stories combine to tell one story. As you read the book of Zephaniah, consider reading the additional passages to discover how the whole of Scripture works together.

1 The word of the LORD that came to Zephaniah son of Cushi, son of Gedaliah, son of Amariah, son of Hezekiah, in the days of Josiah son of Amon, king of Judah.

THE GREAT DAY OF THE LORD

2 I will completely sweep away everything
from the face of the earth —
    this is the LORD's declaration.
3 I will sweep away people and animals;
I will sweep away the birds of the sky
and the fish of the sea,
and the ruins^A along with the wicked.
I will cut off mankind
from the face of the earth.
    This is the LORD's declaration.

4 I will stretch out my hand against Judah
and against all the residents of Jerusalem.
I will cut off every vestige of Baal
from this place,
the names of the pagan priests
along with the priests;
5 those who bow in worship on the rooftops
to the stars in the sky;
those who bow and pledge loyalty to the LORD
but also pledge loyalty to Milcom;^B
6 and those who turn back from following
    the LORD,
who do not seek the LORD or inquire of him.
7 Be silent in the presence of the Lord GOD,
for the day of the LORD is near.
Indeed, the LORD has prepared a sacrifice;
he has consecrated his guests.

8 On the day of the LORD's sacrifice
I will punish the officials, the king's sons,
and all who are dressed in foreign clothing.
9 On that day I will punish
all who skip over the threshold,^C
who fill their master's house
with violence and deceit.

10 On that day —
    this is the LORD's declaration —
there will be an outcry from the Fish Gate,
a wailing from the Second District,
and a loud crashing from the hills.

---

^A 1:3 Perhaps objects connected with idolatry   ^B 1:5 Some LXX mss, Syr, Vg; MT, other LXX mss read *their king*   ^C 1:9 Hb obscure

11   Wail, you residents of the Hollow,[A]
       for all the merchants[B] will be silenced;
       all those loaded with silver will be cut off.

12   And at that time I will search Jerusalem with lamps
       and punish those who settle down comfortably,[C]
       who say to themselves:
       The Lord will not do good or evil.

13   Their wealth will become plunder
       and their houses a ruin.
       They will build houses but never live in them,
       plant vineyards but never drink their wine.

14   The great day of the Lord is near,
       near and rapidly approaching.
       Listen, the day of the Lord —
       then the warrior's cry is bitter.

15   That day is a day of wrath,
       a day of trouble and distress,
       a day of destruction and desolation,
       a day of darkness and gloom,
       a day of clouds and total darkness,

16   a day of trumpet blast and battle cry
       against the fortified cities,
       and against the high corner towers.

17   I will bring distress on mankind,
       and they will walk like the blind
       because they have sinned against the Lord.
       Their blood will be poured out like dust
       and their flesh like dung.

18   Their silver and their gold
       will be unable to rescue them
       on the day of the Lord's wrath.
       The whole earth will be consumed
       by the fire of his jealousy,
       for he will make a complete,
       yes, a horrifying end
       of all the inhabitants of the earth.

A CALL TO REPENTANCE

2   Gather yourselves together;
     gather together, undesirable[D] nation,

2   before the decree takes effect
       and the day passes like chaff,
       before the burning of the Lord's anger overtakes you,
       before the day of the Lord's anger overtakes you.

3   Seek the Lord, all you humble of the earth,

[A]1:11 Or the market district   [B]1:11 Or Canaanites   [C]1:12 Lit who thicken on their dregs   [D]2:1 Or shameless

who carry out what he commands.
Seek righteousness, seek humility;
perhaps you will be concealed
on the day of the LORD's anger.

JUDGMENT AGAINST THE NATIONS

⁴ For Gaza will be abandoned,
and Ashkelon will become a ruin.
Ashdod will be driven out at noon,
and Ekron will be uprooted.
⁵ Woe, inhabitants of the seacoast,
nation of the Cherethites!^A
The word of the LORD is against you,
Canaan, land of the Philistines:
I will destroy you until there is no one left.
⁶ The seacoast will become pasturelands
with caves for shepherds and pens for sheep.
⁷ The coastland will belong
to the remnant of the house of Judah;
they will find pasture there.
They will lie down in the evening
among the houses of Ashkelon,
for the LORD their God will return to them
and restore their fortunes.

⁸ I have heard the taunting of Moab
and the insults of the Ammonites,
who have taunted my people
and threatened their territory.
⁹ Therefore, as I live —
this is the declaration of the LORD of Armies,
the God of Israel —
Moab will be like Sodom
and the Ammonites like Gomorrah:
a place overgrown with weeds,
a salt pit, and a perpetual wasteland.
The remnant of my people will plunder them;
the remainder of my nation will dispossess them.
¹⁰ This is what they get for their pride,
because they have taunted and acted arrogantly
against the people of the LORD of Armies.
¹¹ The LORD will be terrifying to them
when he starves all the gods of the earth.
Then all the distant coasts and islands of the nations
will bow in worship to him,
each in its own place.

¹² You Cushites will also be slain by my sword.

^A2:5 = Sea Peoples

13 He will also stretch out his hand against the north
   and destroy Assyria;
   he will make Nineveh a desolate ruin,
   dry as the desert.
14 Herds will lie down in the middle of it,
   every kind of wild animal.ᴬ
   Both eagle owlsᴮ and heronsᶜ
   will roost in the capitals of its pillars.
   Their calls will soundᴰ from the window,
   but devastationᴱ will be on the threshold,
   for he will expose the cedar work.ᶠ
15 This is the jubilant city
   that lives in security,
   that thinks to herself:
   I exist, and there is no one else.
   What a desolation she has become,
   a place for wild animals to lie down!
   Everyone who passes by her
   scoffsᴳ and shakes his fist.

WOE TO OPPRESSIVE JERUSALEM

3 Woe to the city that is rebelliousᴴ and defiled,
   the oppressive city!
2 She has not obeyed;
   she has not accepted discipline.
   She has not trusted in the LORD;
   she has not drawn near to her God.
3 Theᴵ princes within her are roaring lions;
   her judges are wolves of the night,
   which leave nothing forᴶ the morning.
4 Her prophets are reckless —
   treacherous men.
   Her priests profane the sanctuary;
   they do violence to instruction.
5 The righteous LORD is in her;
   he does no wrong.
   He applies his justice morning by morning;
   he does not fail at dawn,
   yet the one who does wrong knows no shame.

6 I have cut off nations;
   their corner towers are destroyed.
   I have laid waste their streets,
   with no one to pass through.
   Their cities lie devastated,
   without a person, without an inhabitant.

ᴬ2:14 Lit every wild animal of a nation   ᴮ2:14 Or the pelicans   ᶜ2:14 Or the
hedgehogs   ᴰ2:14 Lit sing   ᴱ2:14 LXX, Vg read ravens   ᶠ2:14 Hb obscure
ᴳ2:15 Or hisses   ᴴ3:1 Or filthy   ᴵ3:3 Lit Her   ᴶ3:3 Or that had nothing to gnaw in

GOD WITH YOU

ZEPHANIAH 3:9-20; ISAIAH 30:18

When Kaitlin joined me to work in my 10'x10' office, I was skeptical. She was young and vibrant, with a big loud laugh, and I was tired, pregnant, and very task-oriented. The weather had already turned the tiny space humid, and I did not need to keep track of another person.

But then I did. I did need one more person. I needed Kaitlin. By the end of that summer we were working together as happily as little girls who had just learned to make friendship bracelets at summer camp. Then one morning, before the sun had even started to warm the day, a heartbreaking tragedy visited her family, and her younger brother was dead. And summer was over.

Suddenly I had no idea how to love my new person. How do you comfort someone when their world stops? You sit. I sat next to my now beloved girl, and tried not to say anything stupid. My words weren't going to work some kind of magic. Her gorgeous, genius brother was gone. Her suffering was real.

We know there is no greater comfort, no greater surety, than God's own character. My stuttering, stumbling attempts to love and give comfort only have life because God is who He is.

But summer did come again, and on the first anniversary of her brother's death I searched for something loving to do or say. Realizing the inadequacy of whatever clumsy thing I might share, I opened my Bible, and hurriedly wrote out Zephaniah 3:17 on a card for Kaitlin:

"The LORD your God is among you, a warrior who saves. He will rejoice over you with gladness. He will be quiet in his love. He will delight in you with singing."

I left it on her desk and walked away like an awkward twelve-year-old, because I'm still not great with emotions. But I wanted to give love and comfort.

"This is the first verse I ever memorized!" Kaitlin smiled. "Thank you."

Our God is a living and active God. In spite of our paltry efforts, He still makes something beautiful out of our nothing, and more than that, He takes joy in us—He delights in us! **He delights to be among us, and even to save us.**

God connected the dots in spite of my shortcomings. He used His own words to comfort my friend, because His words and character are timeless and true. We can find rest in His steadfast love.

Summer will change into fall every year for the rest of our lives. The sad things often don't go away, but as we face these seasons, God remains unchanged. He promises to rejoice over us with gladness, bring us quietness with His love, and delight in us with shouts of joy.

This is our hope: our God, who delights in mercy, is with us.

7   I thought: You will certainly fear me
    and accept correction.
    Then her dwelling place^A
    would not be cut off
    based on all that I had allocated to her.
    However, they became more corrupt
    in all their actions.
8   Therefore, wait for me —
        this is the LORD's declaration —
    until the day I rise up for plunder.^B
    For my decision is to gather nations,
    to assemble kingdoms,
    in order to pour out my indignation on them,
    all my burning anger;
    for the whole earth will be consumed
    by the fire of my jealousy.

FINAL RESTORATION PROMISED

9   For I will then restore
    pure speech to the peoples
    so that all of them may call
    on the name of the LORD
    and serve him with a single purpose.^C
10 From beyond the rivers of Cush
    my supplicants, my dispersed people,
    will bring an offering to me.
11 On that day you^D will not be put to shame
    because of everything you have done
    in rebelling against me.
    For then I will remove
    from among you your jubilant, arrogant people,
    and you will never again be haughty
    on my holy mountain.
12 I will leave
    a meek and humble people among you,
    and they will take refuge in the name of the LORD.
13 The remnant of Israel will no longer
    do wrong or tell lies;
    a deceitful tongue will not be found
    in their mouths.
    They will pasture and lie down,
    with nothing to make them afraid.

14 Sing for joy, Daughter Zion;
    shout loudly, Israel!
    Be glad and celebrate with all your heart,
    Daughter Jerusalem!

---

^A3:7 LXX, Syr read *her eyes*   ^B3:8 LXX, Syr read *for a witness*; Vg reads *up forever*
^C3:9 Lit *with one shoulder*   ^D3:11 = Israel

¹⁵ The LORD has removed your punishment;
he has turned back your enemy.
The King of Israel, the LORD, is among you;
you need no longer fear harm.

¹⁶ On that day it will be said to Jerusalem:
"Do not fear;
Zion, do not let your hands grow weak.

¹⁷ The LORD your God is among you,
a warrior who saves.
He will rejoice over you with gladness.
He will be quiet^A in his love.
He will delight in you with singing."

¹⁸ I will gather those who have been driven
from the appointed festivals;
they will be a tribute from you^B
and a reproach on her.^C

¹⁹ Yes, at that time
I will deal with all who oppress you.
I will save the lame and gather the outcasts;
I will make those who were disgraced
throughout the earth
receive praise and fame.

²⁰ At that time I will bring you^D back,
yes, at the time I will gather you.
I will give you fame and praise
among all the peoples of the earth,
when I restore your fortunes before your eyes.
The LORD has spoken.

---

^A3:17 LXX, Syr read *He will renew you*   ^B3:18 = Jerusalem   ^C3:18 Hb obscure
^D3:20 = people of Israel

I will provide peace in this place

haggai

 "The final glory of this house will be greater than the first," says the LORD of Armies. "I will provide peace in this place" — this is the declaration of the LORD of Armies. **2:9**

ON THE TIMELINE Haggai is written to the people in post-exilic Jerusalem, about 520 BC. The temple had been destroyed in 586 BC, during Nebuchadnezzar's final siege of Jerusalem, and Haggai's message encouraged the returned people to continue the rebuilding of the temple. There is no statement specifically identifying who wrote this book, but the words recorded are repeatedly connected to what God spoke to the prophet Haggai (Hg 1:1,3,13; 2:1,10,14,20).

A LITTLE BACKGROUND After the Persian king Cyrus defeated Babylon, he issued a decree in 538 BC which allowed the exiled nations in Babylon to return to their homelands (Ezr 1:1-4). Because of this, Sheshbazzar (Ezr 1:8-11) led about 43,000 Jewish pilgrims back to Judah to rebuild the temple in Jerusalem (Ezr 2:64-65). After the Samaritan people frustrated the rebuilding efforts and a new governor of the region refused to approve the construction, the Jews began to lose hope. However, in 520 BC, Darius (now king of Persia) issued a decree, which allowed the Jews to continue rebuilding the temple.

MESSAGE & PURPOSE Haggai challenged the discouraged people in Jerusalem to examine the way they were living. He called them to set new priorities that would please God, glorifying God in their rebuilding the temple. Haggai argues that the people should not focus on their own needs (Hg 1:4), become discouraged because the temple was not as glorious as Solomon's (Hg 2:3), be unclean and unholy (Hg 2:10-14), or feel useless and powerless (Hg 2:20-23). The restoration of the temple was a sign that God had not revoked His covenant. It showed He was with the remnant and His promises were indeed being fulfilled.

GIVE THANKS FOR THE BOOK OF HAGGAI

Haggai admonished the post-exilic Jews living in Jerusalem to choose God over what made them comfortable or happy. Their response to this challenge would be reflected in their work on the temple. In the New Testament, Jesus echoed Haggai's message: "But seek first the kingdom of God and his righteousness, and all these things will be provided for you" (Mt 6:33).

THE BOOK OF HAGGAI IN HISTORY

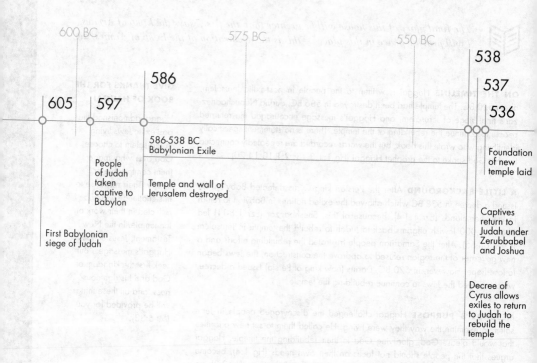

600 BC — 575 BC — 550 BC

538

586

537

536

605

597

586-538 BC
Babylonian Exile

Foundation
of new
temple laid

People
of Judah
taken
captive to
Babylon

Temple and wall of
Jerusalem destroyed

First Babylonian
siege of Judah

Captives
return to
Judah under
Zerubbabel
and Joshua

Decree of
Cyrus allows
exiles to return
to Judah to
rebuild the
temple

500 BC

475 BC

515

520

457

520-515 BC
Zechariah's
ministry

Temple construction
complete

Ezra's ministry
reestablishes
worship in
Jerusalem

Decree of Darius to continue
rebuilding the temple in Jerusalem

Haggai's ministry

READ AND UNDERSTAND HAGGAI

The Bible is a complete work in which many stories combine to tell one story. As you read the book of Haggai, consider reading the additional passages to discover how the whole of Scripture works together.

Week 1		GOING DEEPER
☐	Haggai 1:1-11	Ezra 4:24–5:5
☐	Haggai 1:12-15	Ephesians 2:19–22
☐	**Haggai 2:1-9**	Romans 8:9–10
☐	Haggai 2:10-19	Ezra 6:6–22
☐	Haggai 2:20-23	Hebrews 12:26

COMMAND TO REBUILD THE TEMPLE

1 In the second year of King Darius,[A] on the first day of the sixth month, the word of the LORD came through the prophet Haggai to Zerubbabel son of Shealtiel, the governor of Judah, and to Joshua son of Jehozadak, the high priest:

2 "The LORD of Armies says this: These people say: The time has not come for the house of the LORD to be rebuilt."

3 The word of the LORD came through the prophet Haggai: 4 "Is it a time for you yourselves to live in your paneled houses, while this house[B] lies in ruins?" 5 Now, the LORD of Armies says this: "Think carefully about[C] your ways:

6 You have planted much
but harvested little.
You eat
but never have enough to be satisfied.
You drink
but never have enough to be happy.
You put on clothes
but never have enough to get warm.
The wage earner puts his wages
into a bag with a hole in it."

7 The LORD of Armies says this: "Think carefully about your ways. 8 Go up into the hills, bring down lumber, and build the house; and I will be pleased with it and be glorified," says the LORD. 9 "You expected much, but then it amounted to little. When you brought the harvest to your house, I ruined[D] it. Why?" This is the declaration of the LORD of Armies. "Because my house still lies in ruins, while each of you is busy with his own house.

10 So on your account,[E]
the skies have withheld the dew
and the land its crops.
11 I have summoned a drought
on the fields and the hills,
on the grain, new wine, fresh oil,
and whatever the ground yields,
on man and animal,
and on all that your hands produce."

THE PEOPLE'S RESPONSE

12 Then Zerubbabel son of Shealtiel, the high priest Joshua son of Jehozadak, and the entire remnant of the people obeyed the LORD their God and the words of the prophet Haggai, because the LORD their God had sent him. So the people feared the LORD.

13 Then Haggai, the LORD's messenger, delivered the LORD's message to the people: "I am with you — this is the LORD's declaration."

14 The LORD roused the spirit of Zerubbabel son of Shealtiel, governor of Judah, the spirit of the high priest Joshua son of Jehozadak, and the spirit of all the remnant of the people. They began work on the house of the LORD

A1:1 King of Persia reigned 522–486 BC   B1:4 = the temple   C1:5 Lit *Place your heart on*, also in v. 7   D1:9 Lit *blew on*   E1:10 Or *So above you*

CHRIST, THE LIVING TEMPLE

HAGGAI 2:1-9; JOHN 2:19-22

When my twins were young I used to think about how I had to touch every morsel of food that went into their bodies. It felt like the cycle would never end, and they would never be satisfied. I remember sitting hunched over in front of their high chairs and crying as I spooned food into one mouth and then the other, back and forth, feeling hopeless. Depression can cast a dark haze over anything, but I felt like I would never see sunlight again and escape from baby-feeding prison.

Have you ever felt discouraged because your appointed task feels insignificant in God's kingdom? You work and work, but everything you do seems to stay in the shadows.

That's what was happening with the people of God after seventy years in exile. After so much suffering, they finally returned home. The city was ransacked and the temple destroyed. Instead of a shining city surrounded by family and protected by walls, they had tarnished dreams, crumpled expectations, and aching loneliness. How could they ever recover the splendor of the former Jerusalem? How could they ever rebuild the temple, the very "house of God"?

The place where they had once experienced God's glory had turned to dust and ashes. Their hearts were weighed down and devoid of hope. Why should they get down to business and rebuild the temple if they'd never be able to recover the glory of the former building?

Many years have passed since the days of Haggai, but the same struggle that existed in the hearts of God's people then often burdens your heart and mine. We don't have to go into exile to run the risk of forgetting who we are. Discouragement happens to all of us. When we look around and see only rubble, sin, and insufficiency, we feel overwhelmed and wonder whether our small labors will bear fruit some day.

It's exactly in those conditions that God spoke through the prophet Haggai.

"'The final glory of this house will be greater than the first,' says the LORD of Armies. 'I will provide peace in this place'—this is the declaration of the LORD of Armies."

HAGGAI 2:9

These words were a foreshadowing of the words of our Savior: "Jesus answered, 'Destroy this temple, and I will raise it up in three days'" (Jn 2:19).

The day Christ rose from the dead, our temple was rebuilt forever. As the Hebrews placed their hope in a future building, today we find hope in our living Temple. Our salvation rests on the Cornerstone (Ps 118:22). Christ's work accomplished it all. He alone gives our kingdom work eternal value. All glory and thanks be to Him.

of Armies, their God, [15] on the twenty-fourth day of the sixth month, in the second year of King Darius.

ENCOURAGEMENT AND PROMISE

2 On the twenty-first day of the seventh month, the word of the LORD came through the prophet Haggai: [2] "Speak to Zerubbabel son of Shealtiel, governor of Judah, to the high priest Joshua son of Jehozadak, and to the remnant of the people: [3] 'Who is left among you who saw this house in its former glory? How does it look to you now? Doesn't it seem to you like nothing by comparison? [4] Even so, be strong, Zerubbabel — this is the LORD's declaration. Be strong, Joshua son of Jehozadak, high priest. Be strong, all you people of the land — this is the LORD's declaration. Work! For I am with you — the declaration of the LORD of Armies. [5] This is the promise I made to you when you came out of Egypt, and my Spirit is present among you; don't be afraid.' "

[6] For the LORD of Armies says this: "Once more, in a little while, I am going to shake the heavens and the earth, the sea and the dry land. [7] I will shake all the nations so that the treasures of all the nations will come, and I will fill this house with glory," says the LORD of Armies. [8] "The silver and gold belong to me" — this is the declaration of the LORD of Armies. [9] "The final glory of this house[A] will be greater than the first," says the LORD of Armies. "I will provide peace in this place" — this is the declaration of the LORD of Armies.

FROM DEPRIVATION TO BLESSING

[10] On the twenty-fourth day of the ninth month, in the second year of Darius, the word of the LORD came to the prophet Haggai: [11] "This is what the LORD of Armies says: Ask the priests for a ruling. [12] If a man is carrying consecrated meat in the fold of his garment, and it touches bread, stew, wine, oil, or any other food, does it become holy?"

The priests answered, "No."

[13] Then Haggai asked, "If someone defiled by contact with a corpse touches any of these, does it become defiled?"

The priests answered, "It becomes defiled."

[14] Then Haggai replied, "So is this people, and so is this nation before me — this is the LORD's declaration. And so is every work of their hands; even what they offer there is defiled.

[15] "Now from this day on, think carefully: Before one stone was placed on another in the LORD's temple, [16] what state were you in?[B] When someone came to a grain heap of twenty measures, it only amounted to ten; when one came to the winepress to dip fifty measures from the vat, it only amounted to twenty. [17] I struck you — all the work of your hands — with blight, mildew, and hail, but you didn't turn to me — this is the LORD's declaration. [18] "From this day on, think carefully; from the twenty-fourth day of the ninth month, from the day the foundation of the LORD's temple was laid; think carefully. [19] Is there still seed left in the granary? The vine, the fig, the pomegranate, and the olive tree have not yet produced. But from this day on I will bless you."

[A]2:9 Or *The glory of this latter house*   [B]2:16 Hb obscure

PROMISE TO ZERUBBABEL

[20] The word of the LORD came to Haggai a second time on the twenty-fourth day of the month: [21] "Speak to Zerubbabel, governor of Judah: I am going to shake the heavens and the earth. [22] I will overturn royal thrones and destroy the power of the Gentile kingdoms. I will overturn chariots and their riders. Horses and their riders will fall, each by his brother's sword. [23] On that day" — this is the declaration of the LORD of Armies — "I will take you, Zerubbabel son of Shealtiel, my servant" — this is the LORD's declaration — "and make you like my signet ring, for I have chosen you." This is the declaration of the LORD of Armies.

I WILL REFINE THEM AS SILVER IS REFINED AND TEST THEM AS GOLD IS TESTED.

zechariah

I will put this third through the fire; I will refine them as silver is refined and test them as gold is tested. They will call on my name, and I will answer them. I will say: They are my people, and they will say: The LORD is our God. **13:9**

ON THE TIMELINE The book of Zechariah was written to the people in post-exilic Jerusalem, between 520 BC and 516 BC. The temple had been destroyed in 586 BC during Nebuchadnezzar's final siege of Jerusalem, and Zechariah's message encourages the returned people to continue the rebuilding of the temple.

A LITTLE BACKGROUND A key moment in the history of Israel came after King Cyrus of Persia granted the captives permission to return to Judah (538 BC). The chosen people had come through one of the worst experiences possible in the ancient world, and now the exiles who made the long trek back to Judah were faced with the challenge of reestablishing Jerusalem and the temple.

Zechariah, a priest and the author of this book, returned to Judah with the former exiles (Neh 12:16). He was a contemporary of Haggai. Though the two prophets are not known to have worked together, they had similar missions and are both credited with the successful reconstruction of the temple (Ezr 5:1-2; 6:14).

MESSAGE & PURPOSE The message of Zechariah was both encouraging and challenging for God's people. With God's help and provision, nothing would be impossible, not even rebuilding the temple. But Zechariah was concerned with more than bricks and mortar. The fundamental point of his message was the covenant between the Lord and the Israelites. God desired more than a rebuilt temple and city; He desired a restored relationship with His people. Because their ancestors failed to obey the law, God caused surrounding nations to punish His people. The nation had been allowed to return to their homeland, but the question still remained as to whether they had learned the hard lesson and would honor the terms of the covenant.

GIVE THANKS FOR THE BOOK OF ZECHARIAH

The book of Zechariah is full of the language of judgment, but it is also full of God's promises. From beginning to end, the Bible tells the story of God's redemptive plan, culminating in God's triumph over evil and salvation for sinners through the cross of Jesus Christ. Zechariah's prophecies anticipate this grand culmination of history, describing a coming glorious king, a God who triumphs over all, and a world with all wrongs corrected. These promises set the stage for God's future kingdom, as evidenced by the quotes and allusions to Zechariah in the New Testament.

THE BOOK OF ZECHARIAH IN HISTORY

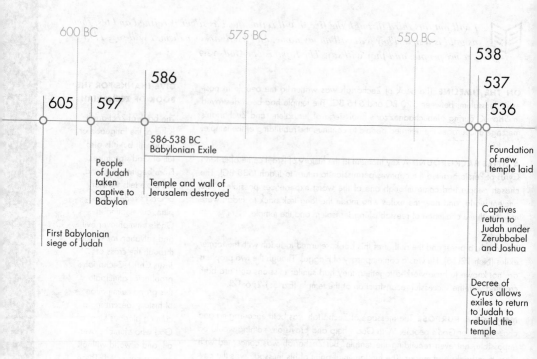

600 BC	575 BC	550 BC	538
	586		537
			536
605	597		

586-538 BC
Babylonian Exile

People of Judah taken captive to Babylon

Temple and wall of Jerusalem destroyed

First Babylonian siege of Judah

Foundation of new temple laid

Captives return to Judah under Zerubbabel and Joshua

Decree of Cyrus allows exiles to return to Judah to rebuild the temple

500 BC   475 BC

515

520

520-515 BC
Zechariah's
ministry

Temple construction
complete

457

Ezra's ministry
reestablishes
worship in
Jerusalem

Decree of Darius to continue
rebuilding the temple in Jerusalem

Haggai's ministry

READ AND UNDERSTAND ZECHARIAH

The Bible is a complete work in which many stories combine to tell one story. As you read the book of Zechariah, consider reading the additional passages to discover how the whole of Scripture works together.

A PLEA FOR REPENTANCE

1 In the eighth month, in the second year of Darius, the word of the Lord came to the prophet Zechariah son of Berechiah, son of Iddo: ² "The Lord was extremely angry with your ancestors. ³ So tell the people, 'This is what the Lord of Armies says: Return to me — this is the declaration of the Lord of Armies — and I will return to you, says the Lord of Armies. ⁴ Do not be like your ancestors; the earlier prophets proclaimed to them: This is what the Lord of Armies says: Turn from your evil ways and your evil deeds. But they did not listen or pay attention to me — this is the Lord's declaration. ⁵ Where are your ancestors now? And do the prophets live forever? ⁶ But didn't my words and my statutes that I commanded my servants the prophets overtake your ancestors?'"

So the people repented and said, "As the Lord of Armies decided to deal with us for our ways and our deeds, so he has dealt with us."

THE NIGHT VISIONS

⁷ On the twenty-fourth day of the eleventh month, which is the month of Shebat, in the second year of Darius, the word of the Lord came to the prophet Zechariah son of Berechiah, son of Iddo:

FIRST VISION: HORSEMEN

⁸ I looked out in the night and saw a man riding on a chestnut ᴬ horse. He was standing among the myrtle trees in the valley. ᴮ Behind him were chestnut, brown, and white horses. ⁹ I asked, "What are these, my lord?"

The angel who was talking to me replied, "I will show you what they are."

¹⁰ Then the man standing among the myrtle trees explained, "They are the ones the Lord has sent to patrol the earth."

¹¹ They reported to the angel of the Lord standing among the myrtle trees, "We have patrolled the earth, and right now the whole earth is calm and quiet."

¹² Then the angel of the Lord responded, "How long, Lord of Armies, will you withhold mercy from Jerusalem and the cities of Judah that you have been angry with these seventy years?" ¹³ The Lord replied with kind and comforting words to the angel who was speaking with me.

¹⁴ So the angel who was speaking with me said, "Proclaim: The Lord of Armies says: I am extremely jealous for Jerusalem and Zion. ¹⁵ I am fiercely angry with the nations that are at ease, for I was a little angry, but they made the destruction worse. ᶜ ¹⁶ Therefore, this is what the Lord says: In mercy, I have returned to Jerusalem; my house will be rebuilt within it — this is the declaration of the Lord of Armies — and a measuring line will be stretched out over Jerusalem.

¹⁷ "Proclaim further: This is what the Lord of Armies says: My cities will again overflow with prosperity; the Lord will once more comfort Zion and again choose Jerusalem."

SECOND VISION: FOUR HORNS AND CRAFTSMEN

¹⁸ Then I looked up and saw four horns. ¹⁹ So I asked the angel who was speaking with me, "What are these?"

[handwritten margin note: even when you think you've done everything for God to stop loving you, you haven't!!!]

ᴬ 1:8 Lit *red*   ᴮ 1:8 Lit *depths*   ᶜ 1:15 Lit *they helped for evil*

And he said to me, "These are the horns that scattered Judah, Israel, and Jerusalem."

²⁰ Then the LORD showed me four craftsmen. ²¹ I asked, "What are they coming to do?"

He replied, "These are the horns that scattered Judah so no one could raise his head. These craftsmen have come to terrify them, to cut off^A the horns of the nations that raised a horn against the land of Judah to scatter it."

THIRD VISION: SURVEYOR

2 I looked up and saw a man with a measuring line in his hand. ² I asked, "Where are you going?"

He answered me, "To measure Jerusalem to determine its width and length."

³ Then the angel who was speaking with me went out, and another angel went out to meet him. ⁴ He said to him, "Run and tell this young man: Jerusalem will be inhabited without walls because of the number of people and livestock in it." ⁵ The declaration of the LORD: "I myself will be a wall of fire around it, and I will be the glory within it."

⁶ "Listen! Listen! Flee from the land of the north" — this is the LORD's declaration — "for I have scattered you like the four winds of heaven" — this is the LORD's declaration. ⁷ "Listen, Zion! Escape, you who are living with Daughter Babylon." ⁸ For the LORD of Armies says this: "In pursuit of his glory, he sent me against the nations plundering you, for whoever touches you touches the pupil^B of my^C eye. ⁹ For look, I am raising my hand against them, and they will become plunder for their own servants. Then you will know that the LORD of Armies has sent me.

¹⁰ "Daughter Zion, shout for joy and be glad, for I am coming to dwell among you" — this is the LORD's declaration. ¹¹ "Many nations will join themselves to the LORD on that day and become my^D people. I will dwell among you, and you will know that the LORD of Armies has sent me to you. ¹² The LORD will take possession of Judah as his portion in the Holy Land, and he will once again choose Jerusalem. ¹³ Let all people be silent before the LORD, for from his holy dwelling he has roused himself."

FOURTH VISION: HIGH PRIEST AND BRANCH

3 Then he showed me the high priest Joshua standing before the angel of the LORD, with Satan^E standing at his right side to accuse him. ² The LORD^F said to Satan: "The LORD rebuke you, Satan! May the LORD who has chosen Jerusalem rebuke you! Isn't this man a burning stick snatched from the fire?"

³ Now Joshua was dressed with filthy^G clothes as he stood before the angel. ⁴ So the angel of the LORD^H spoke to those^I standing before him, "Take off his filthy clothes!" Then he said to him, "See, I have removed your iniquity from you, and I will clothe you with festive robes."

⁵ Then I said, "Let them put a clean turban on his head." So a clean turban was placed on his head, and they clothed him in garments while the angel of the LORD was standing nearby.

^A 1:21 Lit *throw down*   ^B 2:8 Or *apple*   ^C 2:8 Alt Hb tradition; MT reads *his*
^D 2:11 LXX, Syr read *his*   ^E 3:1 Or *the accuser*   ^F 3:2 Syr reads *The Angel of the LORD*
^G 3:3 Probably stained with human excrement   ^H 3:4 Lit *he*   ^I 3:4 = the angels

⁶ Then the angel of the LORD charged Joshua: ⁷ "This is what the LORD of Armies says: If you walk in my ways and keep my mandates, you will both rule my house and take care of my courts; I will also grant you access among these who are standing here.

⁸ "Listen, High Priest Joshua, you and your colleagues sitting before you; indeed, these men are a sign that I am about to bring my servant, the Branch. ⁹ Notice the stone I have set before Joshua; on that one stone are seven eyes. I will engrave an inscription on it" — this is the declaration of the LORD of Armies — "and I will take away the iniquity of this land in a single day. ¹⁰ On that day, each of you will invite his neighbor to sit under his vine and fig tree." This is the declaration of the LORD of Armies.

FIFTH VISION: GOLD LAMPSTAND

4 The angel who was speaking with me then returned and roused me as one awakened out of sleep. ² He asked me, "What do you see?"

I replied, "I see a solid gold lampstand with a bowl at the top. The lampstand also has seven lamps at the top with seven spouts for each ofᴬ the lamps. ³ There are also two olive trees beside it, one on the right of the bowl and the other on its left."

⁴ Then I asked the angel who was speaking with me, "What are these, my lord?"

⁵ "Don't you know what they are?" replied the angel who was speaking with me.

I said, "No, my lord."

⁶ So he answered me, "This is the word of the LORD to Zerubbabel: 'Not by strength or by might, but by my Spirit,' says the LORD of Armies. ⁷ 'What are you, great mountain? Before Zerubbabel you will become a plain. And he will bring out the capstone accompanied by shouts of: Grace, grace to it!'"

⁸ Then the word of the LORD came to me: ⁹ "Zerubbabel's hands have laid the foundation of this house, and his hands will complete it. Then you will know that the LORD of Armies has sent me to you. ¹⁰ For who despises the day of small things? These seven eyes of the LORD, which scan throughout the whole earth, will rejoice when they see the ceremonial stoneᴮ in Zerubbabel's hand."

¹¹ I asked him, "What are the two olive trees on the right and left of the lampstand?" ¹² And I questioned him further, "What are the two streamsᶜ of the olive trees, from which the golden oil is pouring through the two golden conduits?"

¹³ Then he inquired of me, "Don't you know what these are?"

"No, my lord," I replied.

¹⁴ "These are the two anointed ones,"ᴰ he said, "who stand by the Lord of the whole earth."

SIXTH VISION: FLYING SCROLL

5 I looked up again and saw a flying scroll. ² "What do you see?" he asked me. "I see a flying scroll," I replied, "thirty feetᴱ long and fifteen feetᶠ wide."

³ Then he said to me, "This is the curse that is going out over the whole land, for everyone who is a thief, contrary to what is written on one side,

---

ᴬ 4:2 Or seven lips to ᴮ 4:10 Lit the tin stone ᶜ 4:12 Or branches ᴰ 4:14 = Joshua and Zerubbabel ᴱ 5:2 Lit 20 cubits ᶠ 5:2 Lit 10 cubits has gone unpunished,[A] and everyone who swears falsely, contrary to what is written on the other side, has gone unpunished. [4] I will send it out," — this is the declaration of the LORD of Armies — "and it will enter the house of the thief and the house of the one who swears falsely by my name. It will stay inside his house and destroy it along with its timbers and stones."

SEVENTH VISION: WOMAN IN THE BASKET

[5] Then the angel who was speaking with me came forward and told me, "Look up and see what this is that is approaching."

[6] So I asked, "What is it?"

He responded, "It's a measuring basket[B] that is approaching." And he continued, "This is their iniquity[C] in all the land." [7] Then a lead cover was lifted, and there was a woman sitting inside the basket. [8] "This is Wickedness," he said. He shoved her down into the basket and pushed the lead weight over its opening. [9] Then I looked up and saw two women approaching with the wind in their wings. Their wings were like those of a stork, and they lifted up the basket between earth and sky.

[10] So I asked the angel who was speaking with me, "Where are they taking the basket?"

[11] "To build a shrine for it in the land of Shinar," he told me. "When that is ready, the basket will be placed there on its pedestal."

EIGHTH VISION: FOUR CHARIOTS

6 Then I looked up again and saw four chariots coming from between two mountains. The mountains were made of bronze. [2] The first chariot had chestnut[D] horses, the second chariot black horses, [3] the third chariot white horses, and the fourth chariot dappled horses — all strong horses. [4] So I inquired of the angel who was speaking with me, "What are these, my lord?"

[5] The angel told me, "These are the four spirits[E] of heaven going out after presenting themselves to the Lord of the whole earth. [6] The one with the black horses is going to the land of the north, the white horses are going after them, but the dappled horses are going to the land of the south." [7] As the strong horses went out, they wanted to go patrol the earth, and the LORD said, "Go, patrol the earth." So they patrolled the earth. [8] Then he summoned me saying, "See, those going to the land of the north have pacified my Spirit in the northern land."

CROWNING OF THE BRANCH

[9] The word of the LORD came to me: [10] "Take an offering from the exiles, from Heldai, Tobijah, and Jedaiah, who have arrived from Babylon, and go that same day to the house of Josiah son of Zephaniah. [11] Take silver and gold, make a crown,[F] and place it on the head of Joshua son of Jehozadak, the high priest. [12] You are to tell him: This is what the LORD of Armies says: Here is a man whose name is Branch; he will branch out from his place and build the LORD's temple. [13] Yes, he will build the LORD's temple; he will be clothed in splendor and will sit on his throne and rule. There will also be a priest on his throne, and there will be peaceful counsel between the two of them.

[A]5:3 Or *side, will be removed*   [B]5:6 Lit *It's an ephah*   [C]5:6 One Hb ms, LXX, Syr; other Hb mss read *eye*   [D]6:2 Lit *red*   [E]6:5 Or *winds*   [F]6:11 Lit *crowns*

¹⁴ The crown will reside in the LORD's temple as a memorial to Heldai, Tobijah, Jedaiah, and Hen ^A son of Zephaniah. ¹⁵ People who are far off will come and build the LORD's temple, and you will know that the LORD of Armies has sent me to you. This will happen when you fully obey the LORD your God."

DISOBEDIENCE AND FASTING

7 In the fourth year of King Darius, the word of the LORD came to Zechariah on the fourth day of the ninth month, which is Chislev. ² Now the people of Bethel had sent Sharezer, Regem-melech, and their men to plead for the LORD's favor ³ by asking the priests who were at the house of the LORD of Armies as well as the prophets, "Should we mourn and fast in the fifth month as we have done these many years?"

⁴ Then the word of the LORD of Armies came to me: ⁵ "Ask all the people of the land and the priests: When you fasted and lamented in the fifth and in the seventh months for these seventy years, did you really fast for me? ⁶ When you eat and drink, don't you eat and drink simply for yourselves? ⁷ Aren't these the words that the LORD proclaimed through the earlier prophets when Jerusalem was inhabited and secure, ⁸ along with its surrounding cities, and when the southern region and the Judean foothills were inhabited?"

⁸ The word of the LORD came to Zechariah: ⁹ "The LORD of Armies says this: 'Make fair decisions. Show faithful love and compassion to one another. ¹⁰ Do not oppress the widow or the fatherless, the resident alien or the poor, and do not plot evil in your hearts against one another.' ¹¹ But they refused to pay attention and turned a stubborn shoulder; they closed their ears so they could not hear. ¹² They made their hearts like a rock so as not to obey the law or the words that the LORD of Armies had sent by his Spirit through the earlier prophets. Therefore intense anger came from the LORD of Armies. ¹³ Just as he had called, and they would not listen, so when they called, I would not listen, says the LORD of Armies. ¹⁴ I scattered them with a windstorm over all the nations that had not known them, and the land was left desolate behind them, with no one coming or going. They turned a pleasant land into a desolation."

OBEDIENCE AND FEASTING

8 The word of the LORD of Armies came: ² The LORD of Armies says this: "I am extremely jealous for Zion; I am jealous for her with great wrath." ³ The LORD says this: "I will return to Zion and live in Jerusalem. Then Jerusalem will be called the Faithful City; the mountain of the LORD of Armies will be called the Holy Mountain." ⁴ The LORD of Armies says this: "Old men and women will again sit along the streets of Jerusalem, each with a staff in hand because of advanced age. ⁵ The streets of the city will be filled with boys and girls playing in them." ⁶ The LORD of Armies says this: "Though it may seem impossible to the remnant of this people in those days, should it also seem impossible to me?" — this is the declaration of the LORD of Armies. ⁷ The LORD of Armies says this: "I will save my people from the land of the east and the land of the west. ^C ⁸ I will bring them back to live in Jerusalem. They will be my people, and I will be their faithful and righteous God."

---

^A 6:14 Probably Josiah   ^B 7:7 Or prosperous   ^C 8:7 Lit sunset

GENUINE FAITHFULNESS

ZECHARIAH 7–8

When I'm about to make a big decision, I pray and ask for God's direction.

Seated on the braided rug in my bedroom, clutching a faintly scented teenage boy's sweatshirt, all fourteen years of me hoped for a boyfriend to take to the hay maze: "God, please help me choose between Chris and Brandon!" After praying, I would feel my Christian duty complete, choose the boy with cuter hair, and sigh with confident assurance that my prayer for discernment had pointed me in the direction I was already headed.

I'm afraid I still do this as an adult. Maybe I add a twenty-four-hour fast to my prayer for discernment, but what I'm looking for is some kind of magical arrow from heaven to justify what I want to do in my heart.

This is kind of what was happening in Zechariah's time with the captive Jews in Babylon. For over seventy years they had been displaced, and during those long years they had regular periods of fasting to commemorate the devastating indignities suffered during their removal from Jerusalem.

This particular fast commemorated the destruction of the temple. But they were starting to wonder, *Should we keep weeping about this, teaching it to our children, and do we have to keep fasting, or have we grieved enough?* At this time, temple reconstruction was already on the horizon, so the uprooted Israelites had a fair reason to wonder if they could skip the fast.

Instead of striking this fast from their calendars, they asked God. They had been religiously observing the fast, and when they considered changing their pattern, they consulted God. They had checked all the boxes and fulfilled God's requirements. What else were they supposed to do?

Does our enthusiasm for the appearance of doing right overshadow learning how to actually do what is right? **Do we have more regard for looking like we are faithful, rather than examining our hearts and genuinely being faithful?**

Our righteous actions, if they are not done to please God, follow His Word, and give Him glory, are empty. When our prayers for direction are directed more towards our own will than God's, we mock Him, and God will not be mocked. Truly, "just as he had called, and they would not listen, so when they called, I would not listen" (Zch 7:13).

My immediate response is: *Ok, I'll try harder! I'll pray with more sincerity, fast with more intention, and stop trying to eclipse God's will with my own. Yes!*

But, like the captive Israelites, it's not about getting my fasting schedule exactly right, or earning a perfect score in "Christian-ing." God calls us to stop scrambling. He calls us to do the thing we don't want to do: repent of our sins and trust in the finished work of Christ on our behalf.

⁹ The Lᴏʀᴅ of Armies says this: "Let your hands be strong, you who now hear these words that the prophets spoke when the foundations were laid for the rebuilding of the temple, the house of the Lᴏʀᴅ of Armies. ¹⁰ For prior to those days neither man nor animal had wages. There was no safety from the enemy for anyone who came or went, for I turned everyone against his neighbor. ¹¹ But now, I will not treat the remnant of this people as in the former days" — this is the declaration of the Lᴏʀᴅ of Armies. ¹² "For they will sow in peace: the vine will yield its fruit, the land will yield its produce, and the skies will yield their dew. I will give the remnant of this people all these things as an inheritance. ¹³ As you have been a curse among the nations, house of Judah and house of Israel, so I will save you, and you will be a blessing. Don't be afraid; let your hands be strong." ¹⁴ For the Lᴏʀᴅ of Armies says this: "As I resolved to treat you badly when your fathers provoked me to anger, and I did not relent," says the Lᴏʀᴅ of Armies, ¹⁵ "so I have resolved again in these days to do what is good to Jerusalem and the house of Judah. Don't be afraid. ¹⁶ These are the things you must do: Speak truth to one another; make true and sound decisions within your city gates. ¹⁷ Do not plot evil in your hearts against your neighbor, and do not love perjury, for I hate all this" — this is the Lᴏʀᴅ's declaration.

¹⁸ Then the word of the Lᴏʀᴅ of Armies came to me: ¹⁹ The Lᴏʀᴅ of Armies says this: "The fast of the fourth month, the fast of the fifth, the fast of the seventh, and the fast of the tenth will become times of joy, gladness, and cheerful festivals for the house of Judah. Therefore, love truth and peace." ²⁰ The Lᴏʀᴅ of Armies says this: "Peoples will yet come, the residents of many cities; ²¹ the residents of one city will go to another, saying: Let's go at once to plead for the Lᴏʀᴅ's favor and to seek the Lᴏʀᴅ of Armies. I am also going. ²² Many peoples and strong nations will come to seek the Lᴏʀᴅ of Armies in Jerusalem and to plead for the Lᴏʀᴅ's favor." ²³ The Lᴏʀᴅ of Armies says this: "In those days, ten men from nations of every language will grab the robe of a Jewish man tightly, urging: Let us go with you, for we have heard that God is with you."

JUDGMENT OF ZION'S ENEMIES

 A pronouncement:
The word of the Lᴏʀᴅ
is against the land of Hadrach,
and Damascus is its resting place —
for the eyes of humanity
and all the tribes of Israel
are on the Lᴏʀᴅᴬ —

² and also against Hamath, which borders it,
as well as Tyre and Sidon,
though they are very shrewd.

³ Tyre has built herself a fortress;
she has heaped up silver like dust
and gold like the dirt of the streets.

⁴ Listen! The Lord will impoverish her
and cast her wealth into the sea;

---

she herself will be consumed by fire.

5 Ashkelon will see it and be afraid;
Gaza too, and will writhe in great pain,
as will Ekron, for her hope will fail.
There will cease to be a king in Gaza,
and Ashkelon will become uninhabited.
6 A mongrel people will live in Ashdod,
and I will destroy the pride of the Philistines.
7 I will remove the blood from their mouths
and the abhorrent things
from between their teeth.
Then they too will become a remnant for our God;
they will become like a clan in Judah
and Ekron like the Jebusites.
8 I will encamp at my house as a guard,
against those who march back and forth,
and no oppressor will march against them again,
for now I have seen with my own eyes.

THE COMING OF ZION'S KING

9 Rejoice greatly, Daughter Zion!
Shout in triumph, Daughter Jerusalem!
Look, your King is coming to you;
he is righteous and victorious,[A]
humble and riding on a donkey,
on a colt, the foal of a donkey.
10 I will cut off the chariot from Ephraim
and the horse from Jerusalem.
The bow of war will be removed,
and he will proclaim peace to the nations.
His dominion will extend from sea to sea,
from the Euphrates River
to the ends of the earth.
11 As for you,
because of the blood of your covenant,
I will release your prisoners
from the waterless cistern.
12 Return to a stronghold,
you prisoners who have hope;
today I declare that I will restore double to you.
13 For I will bend Judah as my bow;
I will fill that bow with Ephraim.
I will rouse your sons, Zion,
against your sons, Greece.[B]
I will make you like a warrior's sword.
14 Then the LORD will appear over them,
and his arrow will fly like lightning.
The Lord GOD will sound the trumpet

[A]9:9 Or and has salvation   [B]9:13 Lit Javan

and advance with the southern storms.
¹⁵ The LORD of Armies will defend them.
They will consume and conquer with slingstones;
they will drink and be rowdy as if with wine.
They will be as full as the sprinkling basin,
like those at the corners of the altar.
¹⁶ The LORD their God will save them on that day
as the flock of his people;
for they are like jewels in a crown,
sparkling over his land.
¹⁷ How lovely and beautiful!
Grain will make the young men flourish,
and new wine, the young women.

THE LORD RESTORES HIS PEOPLE

10 Ask the LORD for rain
in the season of spring rain.
The LORD makes the rain clouds,
and he will give them showers of rain
and crops in the field for everyone.
² For the idols speak falsehood,
and the diviners see illusions;
they relate empty dreams
and offer empty comfort.
Therefore the people wander like sheep;
they suffer affliction because there is no shepherd.
³ My anger burns against the shepherds,
so I will punish the leaders.ᴬ
For the LORD of Armies has tended his flock,
the house of Judah;
he will make them like his majestic steed in battle.
⁴ The cornerstone will come from Judah.ᴮ
The tent peg will come from them
and also the battle bow and everyᶜ ruler.
Together ⁵ they will be like warriors in battle
trampling down the mud of the streets.
They will fight because the LORD is with them,
and they will put horsemen to shame.
⁶ I will strengthen the house of Judah
and deliver the house of Joseph.ᴰ
I will restoreᴱ them
because I have compassion on them,
and they will be
as though I had never rejected them.
For I am the LORD their God,
and I will answer them.
⁷ Ephraim will be like a warrior,

ᴬ10:3 Lit *male goats*   ᴮ10:4 Lit *him*   ᶜ10:4 Lit *also from him the . . . , from him every*   ᴰ10:6 = the northern kingdom   ᴱ10:6 Other Hb mss, LXX read *settle*

and their hearts will be glad as if with wine.
Their children will see it and be glad;
their hearts will rejoice in the LORD.

8   I will whistle and gather them
    because I have redeemed them;
    they will be as numerous as they once were.
9   Though I sow them among the nations,
    they will remember me in the distant lands;
    they and their children will live and return.
10 I will bring them back from the land of Egypt
    and gather them from Assyria.
    I will bring them to the land of Gilead
    and to Lebanon,
    but it will not be enough for them.
11 The LORD^A will pass through the sea of distress
    and strike the waves of the sea;
    all the depths of the Nile will dry up.
    The pride of Assyria will be brought down,
    and the scepter of Egypt will come to an end.
12 I will strengthen them in the LORD,
    and they will march in his name —
        this is the LORD's declaration.

ISRAEL'S SHEPHERDS: GOOD AND BAD

11 Open your gates, Lebanon,
    and fire will consume your cedars.
2   Wail, cypress, for the cedar has fallen;
    the glorious trees are destroyed!
    Wail, oaks of Bashan,
    for the stately forest has fallen!
3   Listen to the wail of the shepherds,
    for their glory is destroyed.
    Listen to the roar of young lions,
    for the thickets of the Jordan are^B destroyed.

⁴ The LORD my God says this: "Shepherd the flock intended for slaughter. ⁵ Those who buy them slaughter them but are not punished. Those who sell them say: Blessed be the LORD because I have become rich! Even their own shepherds have no compassion for them. ⁶ Indeed, I will no longer have compassion on the inhabitants of the land" — this is the LORD's declaration. "Instead, I will turn everyone over to his neighbor and his king. They will devastate the land, and I will not rescue it from their hand."

⁷ So I shepherded the flock intended for slaughter, the oppressed of the flock.^C I took two staffs, calling one Favor and the other Union, and I shepherded the flock. ⁸ In one month I got rid of three shepherds. I became impatient with them, and they also detested me. ⁹ Then I said, "I will no longer

---

^A 10:11 Lit *He*   ^B 11:3 Lit *for the majesty of the Jordan is*   ^C 11:7 LXX reads *slaughter that belonged to the sheep merchants* shepherd you. Let what is dying die, and let what is perishing perish; let the rest devour each other's flesh." [10] Next I took my staff called Favor and cut it in two, annulling the covenant I had made with all the peoples. [11] It was annulled on that day, and so the oppressed of the flock[A] who were watching me knew that it was the word of the LORD. [12] Then I said to them, "If it seems right to you, give me my wages; but if not, keep them." So they weighed my wages, thirty pieces of silver.

[13] "Throw it to the potter,"[B] the LORD said to me — this magnificent price I was valued by them. So I took the thirty pieces of silver and threw it into the house of the LORD, to the potter.[C] [14] Then I cut in two my second staff, Union, annulling the brotherhood between Judah and Israel.

[15] The LORD also said to me: "Take the equipment of a foolish shepherd. [16] I am about to raise up a shepherd in the land who will not care for those who are perishing, and he will not seek the lost[D] or heal the broken. He will not sustain the healthy,[E] but he will devour the flesh of the fat sheep and tear off their hooves.

[17]   Woe to the worthless shepherd
      who deserts the flock!
      May a sword strike[F] his arm
      and his right eye!
      May his arm wither away
      and his right eye go completely blind!"

JUDAH'S SECURITY

12 A pronouncement:
      The word of the LORD concerning Israel.
      A declaration of the LORD,
      who stretched out the heavens,
      laid the foundation of the earth,
      and formed the spirit of man within him.

[2] "Look, I will make Jerusalem a cup that causes staggering for the peoples who surround the city. The siege against Jerusalem will also involve Judah. [3] On that day I will make Jerusalem a heavy stone for all the peoples; all who try to lift it will injure themselves severely when all the nations of the earth gather against her. [4] On that day" — this is the LORD's declaration — "I will strike every horse with panic and its rider with madness. I will keep a watchful eye on the house of Judah but strike all the horses of the nations with blindness. [5] Then each of the leaders of Judah will think to himself: The residents of Jerusalem are my strength through the LORD of Armies, their God. [6] On that day I will make the leaders of Judah like a firepot in a woodpile, like a flaming torch among sheaves; they will consume all the peoples around them on the right and the left, while Jerusalem continues to be inhabited on its site, in Jerusalem. [7] The LORD will save the tents of Judah first, so that the glory of David's house and the glory of Jerusalem's residents may not be greater than that of Judah. [8] On that day the LORD will defend the

---

[A] 11:11 LXX reads *and the sheep merchants*   [B] 11:13 Syr reads *treasury*
[C] 11:13 One Hb ms, Syr read *treasury*   [D] 11:16 Or *young*   [E] 11:16 Or *exhausted*
[F] 11:17 Lit *be against*

A NEW AND BETTER TEMPLE

ZECHARIAH 12; LUKE 7:11-17

It's one of my favorite sentences in the entire Bible.

"And Jesus gave him to his mother" (Lk 7:15).

The story of the widow of Nain, found in Luke 7:11-17, tells us tons about the tenderness of God. Jesus and the disciples were traveling when they ran into a funeral procession. They stepped aside as a dead man was being carried out for burial. The Bible tells us there was a large crowd around the body, but one mourner in particular pulled at Jesus' heartstrings.

The boy's mother. (The text doesn't tell us exactly how old he was, but it doesn't matter. He was still his mother's boy.)

No mother should have to be graveside as her child is buried, but this woman's situation was particularly desperate. She was a widow and this was her only son. This funeral meant she was socially, economically, and emotionally bankrupt. She would be forced to bury her future alongside her only son. Her grief is almost palpable.

But the grieving mother at the gates of Nain was among the first to see the Savior in action. Moved with compassion, He resurrected her dead son and tenderly handed the boy back to her. The profound grief of a mother who had lost everything was matched by the profound power of the long-awaited Savior.

Rewind half a century and we find a similar story tucked in the prophetic book of Zechariah.

Zechariah prophesied to a ragtag bunch of Israelites returning from Babylonian captivity.

Inspired by the Word of the Lord, Zechariah looked at the pile of rubble that remained in Jerusalem and saw the walls rebuilt. But he also looked past the temple of stone and saw the new and better Temple—Jesus Christ.

"Then I will pour out a spirit of grace and prayer on the house of David and the residents of Jerusalem, and they will look at me whom they pierced. They will mourn for him as one mourns for an only child and weep bitterly for him as one weeps for a firstborn."

ZECHARIAH 12:10

Zechariah didn't get to know the rest of the story. No wonder he imagined grief like that of parents who've lost their only child. If Jesus' funeral had been the last chapter, there would not be a veil black enough to demonstrate our mourning.

But the grave did not have the final say. Like Jesus showed compassion and power to the widow of Nain in her distress, He would demonstrate compassion through the cross and power over death through the resurrection. **He made a way to take the rubble of our sin-shattered lives and turn it into redemption.**

Jesus Christ offers us the same beautiful trade He extended to a grieving mother and a visionary prophet: life instead of death, freedom instead of shackles, joy instead of grief.

inhabitants of Jerusalem, so that on that day the one who is weakest among them will be like David on that day, and the house of David will be like God, like the angel of the LORD, before them. ⁹ On that day I will set out to destroy all the nations that come against Jerusalem.

MOURNING FOR THE PIERCED ONE

¹⁰ "Then I will pour out a spirit ᴬ of grace and prayer on the house of David and the residents of Jerusalem, and they will look at ᴮ me whom they pierced. They will mourn for him as one mourns for an only child and weep bitterly for him as one weeps for a firstborn. ¹¹ On that day the mourning in Jerusalem will be as great as the mourning of Hadad-rimmon in the plain of Megiddo. ¹² The land will mourn, every family by itself: the family of David's house by itself and their women by themselves; the family of Nathan's ᶜ house by itself and their women by themselves; ¹³ the family of Levi's house by itself and their women by themselves; the family of Shimei ᴰ by itself and their women by themselves; ¹⁴ all the remaining families, every family by itself, and their women by themselves.

GOD'S PEOPLE CLEANSED

13 "On that day a fountain will be opened for the house of David and for the residents of Jerusalem, to wash away sin and impurity. ² On that day" — this is the declaration of the LORD of Armies — "I will remove the names of the idols from the land, and they will no longer be remembered. I will banish the prophets ᴱ and the unclean spirit from the land. ³ If a man still prophesies, his father and his mother who bore him will say to him: You cannot remain alive because you have spoken a lie in the name of the LORD. When he prophesies, his father and his mother who bore him will pierce him through. ⁴ On that day every prophet will be ashamed of his vision when he prophesies; they will not put on a hairy cloak in order to deceive. ⁵ He will say: I am not a prophet; I work the land, for a man purchased ᶠ me as a servant since my youth. ⁶ If someone asks him: What are these wounds on your chest? ᴳ — then he will answer: I received the wounds in the house of my friends.

⁷ Sword, awake against my shepherd,
   against the man who is my associate —
      this is the declaration of the LORD of Armies.
   Strike the shepherd, and the sheep will be scattered;
   I will turn my hand against the little ones.

⁸ In the whole land —
      this is the LORD's declaration —
   two-thirds ᴴ will be cut off and die,
   but a third will be left in it.

⁹ I will put this third through the fire;
   I will refine them as silver is refined
   and test them as gold is tested.
   They will call on my name,

ᴬ 12:10 Or *out the Spirit*   ᴮ 12:10 Or *to*   ᶜ 12:12 = a son of David   ᴰ 12:13 = a descendant of Levi   ᴱ 13:2 = false prophets   ᶠ 13:5 Or *sold*   ᴳ 13:6 Lit *wounds between your hands*   ᴴ 13:8 Lit *two-thirds in it*

THE REFINER'S FIRE

ZECHARIAH 13; PSALM 66:10-12; 1 PETER 1:3-12

From a distance, fire is inviting. A single torch can light a pathway; a few logs can warm a room. But come too close to the flame and you'll get burned. It doesn't take long to discover a certain amount of caution is necessary when it comes to life's fires, both the literal and metaphorical kind.

Scripture uses fire to describe the process of purification. Psalm 66:10 says, "For you, God, tested us; you refined us as silver is refined." Fire symbolizes the character of God because He is flawless—pure in every sense of the word. He is a "consuming fire" (Heb 12:29); His glory radiates like an infinite flame. To draw near to God is to experience the heat of His holiness in a way that purifies us from the inside out. His is no ordinary flame; He is wholly loving and good. "We went through fire and water," the psalmist writes, "but you brought us out to abundance" (Ps 66:12).

In Zechariah 13, the prophet pointed to a time in the future when the Lord would set all things right. His words were first delivered to a remnant of Israel who had survived the exile and come home to Jerusalem; a people who would quickly forget God's faithfulness and once again rebel. Even then God would pour out His mercy on His people and draw them back to Himself. His anger would burn against their idolatry, but His grace would temper the flames. True to His character and faithful to His covenant, a remnant would always be spared.

As the fire of His holiness refined them, the comfort of His grace defined them.

> "I will put this third through the fire; I will refine them as silver is refined and test them as gold is tested. They will call on my name, and I will answer them. I will say: They are my people, and they will say: The LORD is our God."
>
> ZECHARIAH 13:9

This is the promise to all who belong to God in Christ: He will claim us, keep us, and refine us until we reach eternity. In His goodness and sovereignty, God uses the fire of His holiness and even the circumstances of our lives to shape us and make us more like Jesus. He is pleased to display His glory in us, purifying and strengthening us from the inside out.

The God who is a consuming fire is also our merciful Savior, graciously drawing sinners to Himself and calling them by name. We can trust Him.

> "You rejoice in this, even though now for a short time, if necessary, you suffer grief in various trials so that the proven character of your faith—more valuable than gold which, though perishable, is refined by fire—may result in praise, glory, and honor at the revelation of Jesus Christ."
>
> 1 PETER 1:6-7

and I will answer them.
I will say: They are my people,
and they will say: The Lord is our God."

THE LORD'S TRIUMPH AND REIGN

14 Look, a day belonging to the Lord is coming when the plunder taken from you will be divided in your presence. ²I will gather all the nations against Jerusalem for battle. The city will be captured, the houses looted, and the women raped. Half the city will go into exile, but the rest of the people will not be removed from the city.

³Then the Lord will go out to fight against those nations as he fights on a day of battle. ⁴On that day his feet will stand on the Mount of Olives, which faces Jerusalem on the east. The Mount of Olives will be split in half from east to west, forming a huge valley, so that half the mountain will move to the north and half to the south. ⁵You will flee by my mountain valley,^A for the valley of the mountains will extend to Azal. You will flee as you fled^B from the earthquake in the days of King Uzziah of Judah. Then the Lord my God will come and all the holy ones with him.^C

⁶On that day there will be no light; the sunlight and moonlight will diminish.^D,E 7 It will be a unique day known only to the Lord, without day or night, but there will be light at evening.

⁸On that day living water will flow out from Jerusalem, half of it toward the eastern sea^F and the other half toward the western sea,^G in summer and winter alike. ⁹On that day the Lord will become King over the whole earth — the Lord alone, and his name alone. ¹⁰All the land from Geba to Rimmon south of Jerusalem will be changed into a plain. But Jerusalem will be raised up and will remain^H on its site from the Benjamin Gate to the place of the First Gate,^I to the Corner Gate, and from the Tower of Hananel to the royal winepresses. ¹¹People will live there, and never again will there be a curse of complete destruction. So Jerusalem will dwell in security.

¹²This will be the plague with which the Lord strikes all the people who have warred against Jerusalem: their flesh will rot while they stand on their feet, their eyes will rot in their sockets, and their tongues will rot in their mouths. ¹³On that day a great panic from the Lord will be among them, so that each will seize the hand of another, and the hand of one will rise against the other. ¹⁴Judah will also fight at Jerusalem, and the wealth of all the surrounding nations will be collected: gold, silver, and clothing in great abundance. ¹⁵The same plague as the previous one will strike^J the horses, mules, camels, donkeys, and all the animals that are in those camps.

¹⁶Then all the survivors from the nations that came against Jerusalem will go up year after year to worship the King, the Lord of Armies, and to celebrate the Festival of Shelters. ¹⁷Should any of the families of the earth not go up to Jerusalem to worship the King, the Lord of Armies, rain will

---

^A14:5 Some Hb mss, LXX, Sym, Tg read *The valley of my mountains will be blocked* ^B14:5 LXX reads *It will be blocked as it was blocked* ^C14:5 Some Hb mss, LXX, Vg, Tg, Syr; other Hb mss read *you* ^D14:6 LXX, Sym, Syr, Tg, Vg read *no light or cold or ice* ^E14:6 Lit *no light; the precious ones will congeal* ^F14:8 = the Dead Sea ^G14:8 = the Mediterranean Sea ^H14:10 Or *will be inhabited* ^I14:10 Or *the former gate* ^J14:15 Lit *be on* not fall on them. [18] And if the people[A] of Egypt will not go up and enter, then rain will not fall on them; this will be the plague the LORD inflicts on the nations who do not go up to celebrate the Festival of Shelters. [19] This will be the punishment of Egypt and all the nations that do not go up to celebrate the Festival of Shelters.

[20] On that day, the words HOLY TO THE LORD will be on the bells of the horses. The pots in the house of the LORD will be like the sprinkling basins before the altar. [21] Every pot in Jerusalem and in Judah will be holy to the LORD of Armies. All who sacrifice will come and use the pots to cook in. And on that day there will no longer be a Canaanite[B] in the house of the LORD of Armies.

THE SUN OF RIGHTEOUSNESS WILL RISE WITH HEALING IN ITS WINGS

malachi

But for you who fear my name, the sun of righteousness will rise with healing in its wings, and you will go out and playfully jump like calves from the stall. **4:2**

ON THE TIMELINE Although the book of Malachi is not dated by a reference to a specific ruler or specific event, evidence within the text—and its position in the canon—favors a postexilic date. The temple had been rebuilt (515 BC) and worship had been reestablished there (Mal 1:6-11; 2:1-3; 3:1,10). The social and religious problems that Malachi addressed reflect the situation portrayed in Ezra 9 and 10 and Nehemiah 5 and 13, suggesting dates not long before Ezra's return to Judah (about 460 BC). Based on this, we can date Malachi close to the time of Esther.

A LITTLE BACKGROUND Nothing is known about the author except his name, Malachi. The book emphasizes the message rather than the messenger; God is the speaker in about 47 of the 55 verses. The one prophesied in Malachi 3:1 to "clear the way" for God to come to His temple is identified as *malakiy* in the Hebrew, which means, "My messenger," a word identical to the name of the book's author.

MESSAGE & PURPOSE Malachi called out Judah's sins by quoting their own words, repeating their own thoughts, and describing their own attitudes (Mal 1:2; 2:14; 3:7-8). God commanded sincere worship with genuine faith and humility. Instead, the priests failed to fear God and to serve the people conscientiously during difficult times. This certainly contributed to Judah's indifference toward God.

As other incentives to obedience, Malachi pointed to God's demonstrations of love for Israel (Mal 1:2), their spiritual and covenant unity with God and with one another (Mal 2:10), and a coming day of salvation and blessing for those who fear Him (Mal 3:1-6,16–4:3).

GIVE THANKS FOR THE BOOK OF MALACHI

Malachi is the last prophetic message from God before the close of the Old Testament period. The book is a fitting conclusion to the OT and a transition for understanding the kingdom proclamation in the New Testament. Malachi reminds us that we have a great, loving, and holy God, who has unchanging and glorious purposes for His people. This God calls us to genuine worship, to fidelity to Himself and to one another, and to expectant faith in what He is doing and says He will do in this world and for His people.

THE BOOK OF MALACHI IN HISTORY

500 BC   475 BC   450 BC

479

515   **486**   **474**   **465**   **457**   **444**

Temple
reconstruction
completed in
Jerusalem

479-
474 BC
Malachi's
ministry in
Jerusalem

Haman's
plot to
destroy
the Jews

Victory of
the Jews

Ezra's ministry
reestablishes
worship in
Jerusalem

Nehemiah
rebuilds
walls of
Jerusalem

Esther
made
queen
of Persia

End of Ahasuerus's
reign in Persia

Ahasuerus
becomes king
of Persia

READ AND UNDERSTAND MALACHI

The Bible is a complete work in which many stories combine to tell one story. As you read the book of Malachi, consider reading the additional passages to discover how the whole of Scripture works together.

THE LORD'S LOVE FOR ISRAEL

1 A pronouncement:
The word of the LORD to Israel through Malachi.[A]

² "I have loved you," says the LORD.

Yet you ask, "How have you loved us?"

"Wasn't Esau Jacob's brother?" This is the LORD's declaration. "Even so, I loved Jacob, ³ but I hated Esau. I turned his mountains into a wasteland, and gave his inheritance to the desert jackals."

⁴ Though Edom says: "We have been devastated, but we will rebuild[B] the ruins," the LORD of Armies says this: "They may build, but I will demolish. They will be called a wicked country and the people the LORD has cursed[C] forever. ⁵ Your own eyes will see this, and you yourselves will say, 'The LORD is great, even beyond[D] the borders of Israel.'

DISOBEDIENCE OF THE PRIESTS

⁶ "A son honors his father, and a servant his master. But if I am a father, where is my honor? And if I am a master, where is your fear of me? says the LORD of Armies to you priests, who despise my name."

Yet you ask: "How have we despised your name?"

⁷ "By presenting defiled food on my altar."

"How have we defiled you?" you ask.

When you say: "The LORD's table is contemptible."

⁸ "When you present a blind animal for sacrifice, is it not wrong? And when you present a lame or sick animal, is it not wrong? Bring it to your governor! Would he be pleased with you or show you favor?" asks the LORD of Armies. ⁹ "And now plead for God's favor. Will he be gracious to us? Since this has come from your hands, will he show any of you favor?" asks the LORD of Armies. ¹⁰ "I wish one of you would shut the temple doors, so that you would no longer kindle a useless fire on my altar! I am not pleased with you," says the LORD of Armies, "and I will accept no offering from your hands.

¹¹ "My name will be great among the nations, from the rising of the sun to its setting. Incense[E] and pure offerings will be presented in my name in every place because my name will be great among the nations,"[F] says the LORD of Armies.

¹² "But you are profaning it when you say: 'The Lord's table is defiled, and its product, its food, is contemptible.' ¹³ You also say: 'Look, what a nuisance!' And you scorn[G] it,"[H] says the LORD of Armies. "You bring stolen,[I] lame, or sick animals. You bring this as an offering! Am I to accept that from your hands?" asks the LORD.

¹⁴ "The deceiver is cursed who has an acceptable male in his flock and makes a vow but sacrifices a defective animal to the Lord. For I am a great King," says the LORD of Armies, "and my name will be feared among the nations.

A1:1 = My Messenger   B1:4 Or *will return and build*   C1:4 Or LORD *is angry with*
D1:5 Or *great over*   E1:11 Or *Burnt offerings*   F1:11 Or *is great . . . are presented
. . . is great*   G1:13 Lit *blow at*   H1:13 Alt Hb tradition reads *me*
I1:13 Or *injured*

WARNING TO THE PRIESTS

2 "Therefore, this decree is for you priests: [2] If you don't listen, and if you don't take it to heart to honor my name," says the LORD of Armies, "I will send a curse among you, and I will curse your blessings. In fact, I have already begun to curse them because you are not taking it to heart.

[3] "Look, I am going to rebuke your descendants, and I will spread animal waste[A] over your faces, the waste from your festival sacrifices, and you will be taken away with it. [4] Then you will know that I sent you this decree, so that my covenant with Levi may continue," says the LORD of Armies. [5] "My covenant with him was one of life and peace, and I gave these to him; it called for reverence, and he revered me and stood in awe of my name. [6] True instruction was in his mouth, and nothing wrong was found on his lips. He walked with me in peace and integrity and turned many from iniquity. [7] For the lips of a priest should guard knowledge, and people should desire instruction from his mouth, because he is the messenger of the LORD of Armies.

[8] "You, on the other hand, have turned from the way. You have caused many to stumble by your instruction. You have violated[B] the covenant of Levi," says the LORD of Armies. [9] "So I in turn have made you despised and humiliated before all the people because you are not keeping my ways but are showing partiality in your instruction."

JUDAH'S MARITAL UNFAITHFULNESS

[10] Don't all of us have one Father? Didn't one God create us? Why then do we act treacherously against one another, profaning the covenant of our fathers? [11] Judah has acted treacherously, and a detestable act has been done in Israel and in Jerusalem. For Judah has profaned the LORD's sanctuary,[C] which he loves, and has married the daughter of a foreign god.[D] [12] May the LORD cut off from the tents of Jacob the man who does this, whoever he may be,[E] even if he presents an offering to the LORD of Armies.

[13] This is another thing you do. You are covering the LORD's altar with tears, with weeping and groaning, because he no longer respects your offerings or receives them gladly from your hands.

[14] And you ask, "Why?" Because even though the LORD has been a witness between you and the wife of your youth, you have acted treacherously against her. She was your marriage partner and your wife by covenant. [15] Didn't God make them one and give them a portion of spirit? What is the one seeking?[E] Godly offspring. So watch yourselves carefully,[F] so that no one acts treacherously against the wife of his[G] youth. [16] "If he hates and divorces his wife," says the LORD God of Israel, "he[H] covers his garment with injustice," says the LORD of Armies. Therefore, watch yourselves carefully,[I] and do not act treacherously.

JUDGMENT AT THE LORD'S COMING

[17] You have wearied the LORD with your words.

A2:3 Dung or entrails   B2:8 Lit *corrupted*   C2:11 Or *profaned what is holy to the LORD*   D2:11 = a woman who worshiped a foreign god   E2:12,15 Hb obscure   F2:15 Lit *So guard yourselves in your spirit*   G2:15 Lit *your*   H2:16 Or *The LORD God of Israel says that he hates divorce and the one who*   I2:16 Lit *Therefore, guard yourselves in your spirit*

Yet you ask, "How have we wearied him?"

When you say, "Everyone who does what is evil is good in the LORD's sight, and he is delighted with them, or else where is the God of justice?"

3 "See, I am going to send my messenger, and he will clear the way before me. Then the Lord you seek will suddenly come to his temple, the Messenger of the covenant you delight in — see, he is coming," says the LORD of Armies. ² But who can endure the day of his coming? And who will be able to stand when he appears? For he will be like a refiner's fire and like launderer's bleach.^A ³ He will be like a refiner and purifier of silver; he will purify the sons of Levi and refine them like gold and silver. Then they will present offerings to the LORD in righteousness. ⁴ And the offerings of Judah and Jerusalem will please the LORD as in days of old and years gone by.

⁵ "I will come to you in judgment, and I will be ready to witness against sorcerers and adulterers; against those who swear falsely; against those who oppress the hired worker, the widow, and the fatherless; and against those who deny justice to the resident alien. They do not fear me," says the LORD of Armies. ⁶ "Because I, the LORD, have not changed, you descendants of Jacob have not been destroyed.^B

ROBBING GOD

⁷ "Since the days of your fathers, you have turned from my statutes; you have not kept them. Return to me, and I will return to you," says the LORD of Armies.

Yet you ask, "How can we return?"

⁸ "Will a man rob God? Yet you are robbing me!"

"How do we rob you?" you ask.

"By not making the payments of the tenth and the contributions. ⁹ You are suffering under a curse, yet^C you — the whole nation — are still robbing me. ¹⁰ Bring the full tenth into the storehouse so that there may be food in my house. Test me in this way," says the LORD of Armies. "See if I will not open the floodgates of heaven and pour out a blessing for you without measure. ¹¹ I will rebuke the devourer^D for you, so that it will not ruin the produce of your land and your vine in your field will not fail to produce fruit," says the LORD of Armies. ¹² "Then all the nations will consider you fortunate, for you will be a delightful land," says the LORD of Armies.

THE RIGHTEOUS AND THE WICKED

¹³ "Your words against me are harsh," says the LORD.

Yet you ask, "What have we spoken against you?"

¹⁴ You have said: "It is useless to serve God. What have we gained by keeping his requirements and walking mournfully before the LORD of Armies? ¹⁵ So now we consider the arrogant to be fortunate. Not only do those who commit wickedness prosper, they even test God and escape."

¹⁶ At that time those who feared the LORD spoke to one another. The LORD took notice and listened. So a book of remembrance was written before him for those who feared the LORD and had high regard for his name. ¹⁷ "They will be mine," says the LORD of Armies, "my own possession on the day I am preparing. I will have compassion on them as a man has compassion

---

^A3:2 Lit *cleansing agent*   ^B3:6 Or *Because I, the LORD, do not change, you descendants of Jacob are not destroyed*   ^C3:9 Or *because*   ^D3:11 Perhaps locusts

THE SON OF RIGHTEOUSNESS

MALACHI 4; REVELATION 22:16-21

As uncomfortable as it is to read words of judgment in the Bible, it does not make them any less important or true. We need to hear them. The prophet Malachi told it in no uncertain terms: the day was coming, "burning like a furnace." The wicked would meet their match; the arrogant would become like ash in the fire (Mal 4:1).

The images make me squirm. I so desperately want justice and, at the very same time, I don't want it. I want to have my justice cake and be perfectly comfortable too. But if all is to be made right—if the perfect justice of the Lord is to come and cover the earth—then that justice must also come for me. It is for my arrogance. It is for the darkest corners of my heart that can only be described as wicked. The day is coming when all the darkness will be consumed by the holy fire of God's presence. That is a promise from God's Word.

But thanks be to God that the promise does not end there.

"But for you who fear my name, the sun of righteousness will rise with healing in its wings, and you will go out and playfully jump like calves from the stall."

MALACHI 4:2

Is there anything more opposite the gloom of impending destruction than a young, gleeful cow leaping out of her stall, strong legs trampling fear and darkness? Is there anything more freeing than being pulled from a darkness of our own making into never-ending light?

That promise is for you and me. We are due justice, but we are given healing. We are owed destruction, but we are made to leap with joy.

The prophet was speaking of the glorious day when Immanuel would come—the day our rescue would begin and the day it would be fulfilled. God would dwell in flesh, the holy fire of the Almighty bottled up in human skin. Our God would descend to us and then extend to us the ultimate invitation:

"Let the one who is thirsty come. Let the one who desires take the water of life as a gift."

REVELATION 22:17

The Son of Righteousness shall rise and, yes, the wicked will not withstand the light of His holy justice. But for the thirsty ones who will admit their thirst and ask for that life-giving drink of grace, with Him comes salvation.

Jesus brings healing and freedom. He brings mercy and wholeness. He brings a hope that has us leaping from the stalls! Thanks be to Him.

"For you were once darkness, but now you are light in the Lord. Live as children of light."

EPHESIANS 5:8

---

on his son who serves him. [18] So you will again see the difference between the righteous and the wicked, between one who serves God and one who does not serve him.

THE DAY OF THE LORD

4 "For look, the day is coming, burning like a furnace, when all the arrogant and everyone who commits wickedness will become stubble. The coming day will consume them," says the LORD of Armies, "not leaving them root or branches. [2] But for you who fear my name, the sun of righteousness will rise with healing in its wings, and you will go out and playfully jump like calves from the stall.[A] [3] You will trample the wicked, for they will be ashes under the soles of your feet on the day I am preparing," says the LORD of Armies.

A FINAL WARNING

[4] "Remember the instruction of Moses my servant, the statutes and ordinances I commanded him at Horeb for all Israel. [5] Look, I am going to send you the prophet Elijah before the great and terrible day of the LORD comes. [6] And he will turn the hearts of fathers to their children and the hearts of children to their fathers. Otherwise, I will come and strike the land[B] with a curse."

[A]4:2 Or like stall-fed calves [B]4:6 Or earth

the NEW TESTAMENT

Repent
BECAUSE THE
KINGDOM
of
HEAVEN
HAS COME NEAR

matthew

 From then on Jesus began to preach, "Repent, because the kingdom of heaven has come near." **4:17**

ON THE TIMELINE Matthew was written in the first century, around AD 60, before the fall of the temple in Jerusalem (AD 70). The events of Matthew took place during the life of Christ, between roughly 5 BC and AD 33.

A LITTLE BACKGROUND Though he did not identify himself in the text, the early church unanimously affirmed that the apostle Matthew authored the Gospel of Matthew. Most scholars believe that Matthew used Mark's Gospel in writing his own. If this is correct, Matthew's Gospel was written after Mark's, though the date of Mark's Gospel is also a bit of a mystery. Irenaeus (ca AD 180) claimed that Mark wrote his Gospel after Peter's death in the mid-60s. However, Clement of Alexandria, who wrote only twenty years after Irenaeus, claimed that Mark wrote his Gospel while Peter was still alive.

MESSAGE & PURPOSE It seems fitting that the first book of the New Testament begins with the words: "An account of the genealogy of Jesus Christ." This Gospel was written from a strong Jewish perspective to show that Jesus truly is the Messiah and coming King promised in the Old Testament.

Matthew presents an eyewitness testimony of the ministry of Jesus and emphasizes certain theological truths:

1. Jesus is the Messiah, the long-awaited King of God's people.
2. Jesus is the new Abraham, the founder of a new spiritual Israel consisting of all people (both Jews and Gentiles) who choose to follow Him.
3. Jesus is the new Moses, the deliverer, instructor, and mediator of God's people.
4. Jesus is the Immanuel, the virgin-born Son of God who fulfills the promises of the OT.

GIVE THANKS FOR THE GOSPEL OF MATTHEW

As the first book in the NT, the Gospel of Matthew serves as a gateway between the two testaments. Of the NT books, and certainly of the four Gospels, Matthew makes the most direct connections to the OT. Matthew gave us God's entire plan from Genesis to Revelation, and he referred to Hebrew prophecies about sixty times. He also looked forward by discussing not only the Messiah's coming and His ministry, but also His future plan for His Church and kingdom.

SUNDAY
Jesus descends from
Bethany and enters
the temple precincts

SUNDAY NI
Jesus returns
Bethany to lo
with His frien

MT. OF OLI

TUESDAY
Jesus teaches H
disciples about
end times on the
Mount of Olives

9 FRIDAY MORNING
Jesus is crucified

ANTONIA FORTRESS

MONDAY
Jesus cleanses the temple

TEMPLE MOUNT

GETHSEMANE

3 THURSDAY NI
Jesus is arreste

8 FRIDAY MORNING
Jesus again
before Pilate

**5 FRIDAY
DAYBREAK**
Jesus before
the Sanhedrin

6 FRIDAY DAYBREAK
Jesus before Pilate

4 THURSDAY/FRIDAY
Jesus is taken to
the house of Caiaphas
for a preliminary hearing

UPPER CITY

7 FRIDAY MORNING
Jesus before
Herod Antipas

2 THURSDAY EVENING
Jesus retires to
Gethsemane with
His disciples

1 THURSDAY
Jesus shares
the Passover
meal with His
disciples

LOWER CITY

Hinnom Valley

JOSEPHUS' THIRD NORTH WALL

JOSEPHUS' SECOND NORTH WALL

Kidron Valley

THE PASSION WEEK IN JERUSALEM

READ AND UNDERSTAND MATTHEW

The Bible is a complete work in which many stories combine to tell one story. As you read the Gospel of Matthew, consider reading the additional passages to discover how the whole of Scripture works together.

THE GENEALOGY OF JESUS CHRIST

1 An account of the genealogy of Jesus Christ, the Son of David, the Son of Abraham:

FROM ABRAHAM TO DAVID

2   Abraham fathered[A] Isaac,
Isaac fathered Jacob,
Jacob fathered Judah and his brothers,
3   Judah fathered Perez and Zerah by Tamar,
Perez fathered Hezron,
Hezron fathered Aram,
4   Aram fathered Amminadab,
Amminadab fathered Nahshon,
Nahshon fathered Salmon,
5   Salmon fathered Boaz by Rahab,
Boaz fathered Obed by Ruth,
Obed fathered Jesse,
6   and Jesse fathered King David.

FROM DAVID TO THE BABYLONIAN EXILE

David fathered Solomon[B] by Uriah's wife,
7   Solomon fathered Rehoboam,
Rehoboam fathered Abijah,
Abijah fathered Asa,[C]
8   Asa[C] fathered Jehoshaphat,
Jehoshaphat fathered Joram,[D]
Joram fathered Uzziah,
9   Uzziah fathered Jotham,
Jotham fathered Ahaz,
Ahaz fathered Hezekiah,
10   Hezekiah fathered Manasseh,
Manasseh fathered Amon,[E]
Amon fathered Josiah,
11   and Josiah fathered Jeconiah and his brothers
at the time of the exile to Babylon.

FROM THE EXILE TO THE CHRIST

12   After the exile to Babylon
Jeconiah fathered Shealtiel,
Shealtiel fathered Zerubbabel,
13   Zerubbabel fathered Abiud,
Abiud fathered Eliakim,
Eliakim fathered Azor,
14   Azor fathered Zadok,
Zadok fathered Achim,
Achim fathered Eliud,

[A]1:2 In vv. 2-16 either a son, as here, or a later descendant, as in v. 8
[B]1:6 Other mss add *King*   [C]1:7,8 Other mss read *Asaph*   [D]1:8 = Jehoram
[E]1:10 Other mss read *Amos*

15 Eliud fathered Eleazar,
Eleazar fathered Matthan,
Matthan fathered Jacob,
16 and Jacob fathered Joseph the husband of Mary,
who gave birth to Jesus who is called the Christ.

17 So all the generations from Abraham to David were fourteen generations; and from David until the exile to Babylon, fourteen generations; and from the exile to Babylon until the Christ, fourteen generations.

THE NATIVITY OF THE CHRIST

18 The birth of Jesus Christ came about this way: After his mother Mary had been engaged^A to Joseph, it was discovered before they came together that she was pregnant from the Holy Spirit. 19 So her husband Joseph, being a righteous man, and not wanting to disgrace her publicly, decided to divorce her secretly.

20 But after he had considered these things, an angel of the Lord appeared to him in a dream, saying, "Joseph, son of David, don't be afraid to take Mary as your wife, because what has been conceived in her is from the Holy Spirit. 21 She will give birth to a son, and you are to name him Jesus, because he will save his people from their sins."

22 Now all this took place to fulfill what was spoken by the Lord through the prophet:

23 **See, the virgin will become pregnant
and give birth to a son,
and they will name him Immanuel**,^B

which is translated "God is with us."

24 When Joseph woke up, he did as the Lord's angel had commanded him. He married her 25 but did not have sexual relations with her until she gave birth to a son.^C And he named him Jesus.

WISE MEN VISIT THE KING

2 After Jesus was born in Bethlehem of Judea in the days of King Herod, wise men from the east arrived in Jerusalem, 2 saying, "Where is he who has been born king of the Jews? For we saw his star at its rising and have come to worship him."^D

3 When King Herod heard this, he was deeply disturbed, and all Jerusalem with him. 4 So he assembled all the chief priests and scribes of the people and asked them where the Christ would be born.

5 "In Bethlehem of Judea," they told him, "because this is what was written by the prophet:

6 **And you, Bethlehem**, in the land of Judah,
are by no means **least among the rulers of Judah:
Because out of you will come a ruler
who will shepherd my people Israel**."^E

7 Then Herod secretly summoned the wise men and asked them the exact time the star appeared. 8 He sent them to Bethlehem and said, "Go and

---

^A1:18 Or betrothed   ^B1:23 Is 7:14   ^C1:25 Other mss read to her firstborn son
^D2:2 Or to pay him homage   ^E2:6 Mc 5:2

AN EDICT OF DEATH

MATTHEW 1–2; ISAIAH 7:14; ISAIAH 9:2-7; ISAIAH 11:1-9; MICAH 5:2

I like it when things go according to plan. More specifically, my plan. But the world doesn't revolve around me, and sometimes plans have to change. When they do, I usually remain pretty open to those changes (meaning, I hyperventilate and break out in a cold sweat).

I wonder if that's what happened to Mary after the wise men left. In the middle of the night Joseph suddenly woke her, packed up their toddler, and took their family to Egypt. I'm sure this wasn't what she'd planned for them, especially when an angel of God told them both that said toddler was the Son of the Most High (Lk 1:32).

Mary's best-laid plans couldn't hold up under this somber truth: the Messiah sent to bring life was targeted by an edict of death. It may not have been Mary's plan to flee, but she could rest assured that what was happening to their family wasn't outside of God's plan—nothing ever is.

Matthew's Gospel tells us of God's unwavering plan to save His people. Despite the wickedness and darkness surrounding the birth of Christ, nothing could thwart the redemption God had been orchestrating since the beginning of time. It was finally time for the Messiah to come.

Referencing one Old Testament prophecy after another, Matthew proves how this child from

Bethlehem is the Messiah the Jews had been waiting for—the heir to David's throne, the rightful King of Israel, the One to save His people and to bring redemption to the world. He was the fulfillment of God's ultimate plan.

Like Jesus, we come into this world under an edict of death. His was physical. Ours is spiritual. Through Adam we all inherit sin, and the punishment we all deserve for that sin is death (Rm 6:23). Jesus, however, being conceived of the Holy Spirit, didn't inherit this same sin nature.

Yet, Christ accepted death for us. Jesus took on the punishment we deserve as sinners, surrendering Himself to death on the cross—a death He willingly received for the joy set before Him: the salvation of His people (Heb 12:2).

I've always wondered whether Mary and Joseph panicked or remained steadfast in their faith in the twists and turns surrounding Jesus' early years. After all, they were real people, with real hopes, dreams, and plans for their family. But they believed their God and followed where He led, even though it may have been outside of their plan.

I pray our faith, too, would hold fast under pressure, resting on God's plans and not our own. Amen.

search carefully for the child. When you find him, report back to me so that I too can go and worship him."ᴬ

⁹ After hearing the king, they went on their way. And there it was — the star they had seen at its rising. It led them until it came and stopped above the place where the child was. ¹⁰ When they saw the star, they were overwhelmed with joy. ¹¹ Entering the house, they saw the child with Mary his mother, and falling to their knees, they worshiped him. ᴮ Then they opened their treasures and presented him with gifts: gold, frankincense, and myrrh. ¹² And being warned in a dream not to go back to Herod, they returned to their own country by another route.

THE FLIGHT INTO EGYPT

¹³ After they were gone, an angel of the Lord appeared to Joseph in a dream, saying, "Get up! Take the child and his mother, flee to Egypt, and stay there until I tell you. For Herod is about to search for the child to kill him." ¹⁴ So he got up, took the child and his mother during the night, and escaped to Egypt. ¹⁵ He stayed there until Herod's death, so that what was spoken by the Lord through the prophet might be fulfilled: **Out of Egypt I called my Son.**ᶜ

THE MASSACRE OF THE INNOCENTS

¹⁶ Then Herod, when he realized that he had been outwitted by the wise men, flew into a rage. He gave orders to massacre all the boys in and around Bethlehem who were two years old and under, in keeping with the time he had learned from the wise men. ¹⁷ Then what was spoken through Jeremiah the prophet was fulfilled:

¹⁸ **A voice was heard in Ramah,**
weeping,ᴰ **and great mourning,**
Rachel weeping for her children;
and she refused to be consoled,
because they are no more.ᴱ

THE RETURN TO NAZARETH

¹⁹ After Herod died, an angel of the Lord appeared in a dream to Joseph in Egypt, ²⁰ saying, "Get up, take the child and his mother, and go to the land of Israel, because those who intended to kill the child are dead." ²¹ So he got up, took the child and his mother, and entered the land of Israel. ²² But when he heard that Archelaus was ruling over Judea in place of his father Herod, he was afraid to go there. And being warned in a dream, he withdrew to the region of Galilee. ²³ Then he went and settled in a town called Nazareth to fulfill what was spoken through the prophets, that he would be called a Nazarene.

THE HERALD OF THE CHRIST

3 In those days John the Baptist came, preaching in the wilderness of Judea ² and saying, "Repent, because the kingdom of heaven has come near!" ³ For he is the one spoken of through the prophet Isaiah, who said:

ᴬ2:8 Or *and pay him homage*   ᴮ2:11 Or *they paid him homage*   ᶜ2:15 Hs 11:1
ᴰ2:18 Other mss read *Ramah, lamentation, and weeping,*   ᴱ2:18 Jr 31:15

> A voice of one crying out in the wilderness:
> Prepare the way for the Lord;
> make his paths straight!ᴬ

⁴ Now John had a camel-hair garment with a leather belt around his waist, and his food was locusts and wild honey. ⁵ Then people from Jerusalem, all Judea, and all the vicinity of the Jordan were going out to him, ⁶ and they were baptized by him in the Jordan River, confessing their sins.

⁷ When he saw many of the Pharisees and Sadducees coming to his baptism, he said to them, "Brood of vipers! Who warned you to flee from the coming wrath? ⁸ Therefore produce fruit consistent withᴮ repentance. ⁹ And don't presume to say to yourselves, 'We have Abraham as our father.' For I tell you that God is able to raise up children for Abraham from these stones. ¹⁰ The ax is already at the root of the trees. Therefore, every tree that doesn't produce good fruit will be cut down and thrown into the fire.

¹¹ "I baptize you withᶜ water for repentance, but the one who is coming after me is more powerful than I. I am not worthy to removeᴰ his sandals. He himself will baptize you with the Holy Spirit and fire. ¹² His winnowing shovel is in his hand, and he will clear his threshing floor and gather his wheat into the barn. But the chaff he will burn with fire that never goes out."

THE BAPTISM OF JESUS

¹³ Then Jesus came from Galilee to John at the Jordan, to be baptized by him. ¹⁴ But John tried to stop him, saying, "I need to be baptized by you, and yet you come to me?"

¹⁵ Jesus answered him, "Allow it for now, because this is the way for us to fulfill all righteousness." Then John allowed him to be baptized.

¹⁶ When Jesus was baptized, he went up immediately from the water. The heavens suddenly opened for him,ᴱ and he saw the Spirit of God descending like a dove and coming down on him. ¹⁷ And a voice from heaven said: "This is my beloved Son, with whom I am well-pleased."

THE TEMPTATION OF JESUS

4 Then Jesus was led up by the Spirit into the wilderness to be tempted by the devil. ² After he had fasted forty days and forty nights, he was hungry. ³ Then the tempter approached him and said, "If you are the Son of God, tell these stones to become bread."

⁴ He answered, "It is written: **Man must not live on bread alone but on every word that comes from the mouth of God.**"ᶠ

⁵ Then the devil took him to the holy city, had him stand on the pinnacle of the temple, ⁶ and said to him, "If you are the Son of God, throw yourself down. For it is written:

> He will give his angels orders concerning you,
> and they will support you with their hands
> so that you will not strike
> your foot against a stone."ᴳ

ᴬ3:3 Is 40:3 ᴮ3:8 Lit *fruit worthy of* ᶜ3:11 Or *in* ᴰ3:11 Or *to carry*
ᴱ3:16 Other mss omit *for him* ᶠ4:4 Dt 8:3 ᴳ4:6 Ps 91:11-12

⁷ Jesus told him, "It is also written: **Do not test the Lord your God."**ᴬ

⁸ Again, the devil took him to a very high mountain and showed him all the kingdoms of the world and their splendor. ⁹ And he said to him, "I will give you all these things if you will fall down and worship me."ᴮ

¹⁰ Then Jesus told him, "Go away,ᶜ Satan! For it is written: **Worship the Lord your God, and serve only him."**ᴰ

¹¹ Then the devil left him, and angels came and began to serve him.

MINISTRY IN GALILEE

¹² When he heard that John had been arrested, he withdrew into Galilee. ¹³ He left Nazareth and went to live in Capernaum by the sea, in the region of Zebulun and Naphtali. ¹⁴ This was to fulfill what was spoken through the prophet Isaiah:

¹⁵　Land of Zebulun and land of Naphtali,
　　along the road by the sea, beyond the Jordan,
　　Galilee of the Gentiles.
¹⁶　The people who live in darkness
　　have seen a great light,
　　and for those living in the land of the shadow of death,
　　a light has dawned.ᴱ'ᶠ

¹⁷ From then on Jesus began to preach, "Repent, because the kingdom of heaven has come near."

THE FIRST DISCIPLES

¹⁸ As he was walking along the Sea of Galilee, he saw two brothers, Simon (who is called Peter), and his brother Andrew. They were casting a net into the sea — for they were fishermen. ¹⁹ "Follow me," he told them, "and I will make you fish forᴳ people." ²⁰ Immediately they left their nets and followed him.

²¹ Going on from there, he saw two other brothers, James the son of Zebedee, and his brother John. They were in a boat with Zebedee their father, preparing their nets, and he called them. ²² Immediately they left the boat and their father and followed him.

TEACHING, PREACHING, AND HEALING

²³ Now Jesus began to go all over Galilee, teaching in their synagogues, preaching the good news of the kingdom, and healing everyᴴ disease and sicknessᴵ among the people. ²⁴ Then the news about him spread throughout Syria. So they brought to him all those who were afflicted, those suffering from various diseases and intense pains, the demon-possessed, the epileptics, and the paralytics. And he healed them. ²⁵ Large crowds followed him from Galilee, the Decapolis, Jerusalem, Judea, and beyond the Jordan.

ᴬ4:7 Dt 6:16　ᴮ4:9 Or and pay me homage　ᶜ4:10 Other mss read "Get behind me　ᴰ4:10 Dt 6:13　ᴱ4:16 Lit dawned on them　ᶠ4:15-16 Is 9:1-2　ᴳ4:19 Or you fishers of　ᴴ4:23 Or every kind of　ᴵ4:23 Or physical ailment

THE SERMON ON THE MOUNT

5 When he saw the crowds, he went up on the mountain, and after he sat down, his disciples came to him. ² Then^A he began to teach them, saying:

THE BEATITUDES

³ "Blessed are the poor in spirit,
for the kingdom of heaven is theirs.

⁴ Blessed are those who mourn,
for they will be comforted.

⁵ Blessed are the humble,
for they will inherit the earth.

⁶ Blessed are those who hunger and thirst for righteousness,
for they will be filled.

⁷ Blessed are the merciful,
for they will be shown mercy.

⁸ Blessed are the pure in heart,
for they will see God.

⁹ Blessed are the peacemakers,
for they will be called sons of God.

¹⁰ Blessed are those who are persecuted because of righteousness,
for the kingdom of heaven is theirs.

¹¹ "You are blessed when they insult you and persecute you and falsely say every kind of evil against you because of me. ¹² Be glad and rejoice, because your reward is great in heaven. For that is how they persecuted the prophets who were before you.

BELIEVERS ARE SALT AND LIGHT

¹³ "You are the salt of the earth. But if the salt should lose its taste, how can it be made salty?^B It's no longer good for anything but to be thrown out and trampled under people's feet.

¹⁴ "You are the light of the world. A city situated on a hill cannot be hidden. ¹⁵ No one lights a lamp and puts it under a basket, but rather on a lampstand, and it gives light for all who are in the house. ¹⁶ In the same way, let your light shine before others, so that they may see your good works and give glory to your Father in heaven.

CHRIST FULFILLS THE LAW

¹⁷ "Don't think that I came to abolish the Law or the Prophets. I did not come to abolish but to fulfill. ¹⁸ For truly I tell you, until heaven and earth pass away, not the smallest letter^C or one stroke of a letter will pass away from the law until all things are accomplished. ¹⁹ Therefore, whoever breaks one of the least of these commands and teaches others to do the same will be called least in the kingdom of heaven. But whoever does and teaches these commands will be called great in the kingdom of heaven. ²⁰ For I tell you, unless your righteousness surpasses that of the scribes and Pharisees, you will never get into the kingdom of heaven.

---

^A 5:2 Lit *Then opening his mouth* ^B 5:13 Or *how can the earth be salted?*
^C 5:18 Or *not one iota; iota is the smallest letter of the Gk alphabet.*

MURDER BEGINS IN THE HEART

[21] "You have heard that it was said to our ancestors, **Do not murder,**[A] and whoever murders will be subject to judgment. [22] But I tell you, everyone who is angry with his brother or sister[B] will be subject to judgment. Whoever insults[C] his brother or sister, will be subject to the court.[D] Whoever says, 'You fool!' will be subject to hellfire.[E] [23] So if you are offering your gift on the altar, and there you remember that your brother or sister has something against you, [24] leave your gift there in front of the altar. First go and be reconciled with your brother or sister, and then come and offer your gift. [25] Reach a settlement quickly with your adversary while you're on the way with him to the court, or your adversary will hand you over to the judge, and the judge to[F] the officer, and you will be thrown into prison. [26] Truly I tell you, you will never get out of there until you have paid the last penny.[G]

ADULTERY BEGINS IN THE HEART

[27] "You have heard that it was said, **Do not commit adultery.**[H] [28] But I tell you, everyone who looks at a woman lustfully has already committed adultery with her in his heart. [29] If your right eye causes you to sin, gouge it out and throw it away. For it is better that you lose one of the parts of your body than for your whole body to be thrown into hell. [30] And if your right hand causes you to sin, cut it off and throw it away. For it is better that you lose one of the parts of your body than for your whole body to go into hell.

DIVORCE PRACTICES CENSURED

[31] "It was also said, **Whoever divorces his wife must give her a written notice of divorce.**[I] [32] But I tell you, everyone who divorces his wife, except in a case of sexual immorality, causes her to commit adultery. And whoever marries a divorced woman commits adultery.

TELL THE TRUTH

[33] "Again, you have heard that it was said to our ancestors, **You must not break your oath, but you must keep your oaths to the Lord.**[J] [34] But I tell you, don't take an oath at all: either by heaven, because it is God's throne; [35] or by the earth, because it is his footstool; or by Jerusalem, because it is the city of the great King. [36] Do not swear by your head, because you cannot make a single hair white or black. [37] But let your 'yes' mean 'yes,' and your 'no' mean 'no.' Anything more than this is from the evil one.

GO THE SECOND MILE

[38] "You have heard that it was said, **An eye for an eye and a tooth for a tooth.**[K] [39] But I tell you, don't resist[L] an evildoer. On the contrary, if anyone slaps you

---

[A]5:21 Ex 20:13; Dt 5:17   [B]5:22 Other mss add *without a cause*   [C]5:22 Lit *Whoever says 'Raca'*; an Aramaic term of abuse that puts someone down, insulting one's intelligence   [D]5:22 Lit *Sanhedrin*   [E]5:22 Lit *the gehenna of fire*   [F]5:25 Other mss read *judge will hand you over to*   [G]5:26 Lit *quadrans,* the smallest and least valuable Roman coin, worth 1/64 of a daily wage   [H]5:27 Ex 20:14; Dt 5:18   [I]5:31 Dt 24:1   [J]5:33 Lv 19:12; Nm 30:2; Dt 23:21   [K]5:38 Ex 21:24; Lv 24:20; Dt 19:21   [L]5:39 Or *don't set yourself against,* or *don't retaliate against* on your right cheek, turn the other to him also. ⁴⁰ As for the one who wants to sue you and take away your shirt, let him have your coat as well. ⁴¹ And if anyone forces you to go one mile, go with him two. ⁴² Give to the one who asks you, and don't turn away from the one who wants to borrow from you.

LOVE YOUR ENEMIES

⁴³ "You have heard that it was said, **Love your neighbor**ᴬ and hate your enemy. ⁴⁴ But I tell you, love your enemiesᴮ and pray for those whoᶜ persecute you, ⁴⁵ so that you may beᴰ children of your Father in heaven. For he causes his sun to rise on the evil and the good, and sends rain on the righteous and the unrighteous. ⁴⁶ For if you love those who love you, what reward will you have? Don't even the tax collectors do the same? ⁴⁷ And if you greet only your brothers and sisters, what are you doing out of the ordinary?ᴱ Don't even the Gentilesᶠ do the same? ⁴⁸ Be perfect, therefore, as your heavenly Father is perfect.

HOW TO GIVE

6 "Be careful not to practice your righteousnessᴳ in front of others to be seen by them. Otherwise, you have no reward with your Father in heaven. ² So whenever you give to the poor, don't sound a trumpet before you, as the hypocrites do in the synagogues and on the streets, to be applauded by people. Truly I tell you, they have their reward. ³ But when you give to the poor, don't let your left hand know what your right hand is doing, ⁴ so that your giving may be in secret. And your Father who sees in secret will reward you.ᴴ

HOW TO PRAY

⁵ "Whenever you pray, you must not be like the hypocrites, because they love to pray standing in the synagogues and on the street corners to be seen by people. Truly I tell you, they have their reward. ⁶ But when you pray, go into your private room, shut your door, and pray to your Father who is in secret. And your Father who sees in secret will reward you.ᴵ ⁷ When you pray, don't babble like the Gentiles, since they imagine they'll be heard for their many words. ⁸ Don't be like them, because your Father knows the things you need before you ask him.

THE LORD'S PRAYER

⁹ "Therefore, you should pray like this:

Our Father in heaven,
your name be honored as holy.
¹⁰   Your kingdom come.
Your will be done
on earth as it is in heaven.
¹¹   Give us today our daily bread.ᴶ

ᴬ5:43 Lv 19:18 ᴮ5:44 Other mss add *bless those who curse you, do good to those who hate you,* ᶜ5:44 Other mss add *mistreat you and* ᴰ5:45 Or *may become,* or *may show yourselves to be* ᴱ5:47 Or *doing that is superior;* lit *doing more* ᶠ5:47 Other mss read *tax collectors* ᴳ6:1 Other mss read *charitable giving* ᴴ6:4 Other mss read *will himself reward you openly* ᴵ6:6 Other mss add *openly* ᴶ6:11 Or *our necessary bread,* or *our bread for tomorrow*

12 And forgive us our debts,
   as we also have forgiven our debtors.
13 And do not bring us into[A] temptation,
   but deliver us from the evil one.[B]

14 "For if you forgive others their offenses, your heavenly Father will forgive you as well. 15 But if you don't forgive others,[C] your Father will not forgive your offenses.

HOW TO FAST

16 "Whenever you fast, don't be gloomy like the hypocrites. For they make their faces unattractive[D] so that their fasting is obvious to people. Truly I tell you, they have their reward. 17 But when you fast, put oil on your head and wash your face, 18 so that your fasting isn't obvious to others but to your Father who is in secret. And your Father who sees in secret will reward you.[E]

GOD AND POSSESSIONS

19 "Don't store up for yourselves treasures[F] on earth, where moth and rust destroy and where thieves break in and steal. 20 But store up for yourselves treasures in heaven, where neither moth nor rust destroys, and where thieves don't break in and steal. 21 For where your treasure is, there your heart will be also.

22 "The eye is the lamp of the body. If your eye is healthy, your whole body will be full of light. 23 But if your eye is bad, your whole body will be full of darkness. So if the light within you is darkness, how deep is that darkness!

24 "No one can serve two masters, since either he will hate one and love the other, or he will be devoted to one and despise the other. You cannot serve both God and money.

THE CURE FOR ANXIETY

25 "Therefore I tell you: Don't worry about your life, what you will eat or what you will drink; or about your body, what you will wear. Isn't life more than food and the body more than clothing? 26 Consider the birds of the sky: They don't sow or reap or gather into barns, yet your heavenly Father feeds them. Aren't you worth more than they? 27 Can any of you add one moment to his life span[G] by worrying? 28 And why do you worry about clothes? Observe how the wildflowers of the field grow: They don't labor or spin thread. 29 Yet I tell you that not even Solomon in all his splendor was adorned like one of these. 30 If that's how God clothes the grass of the field, which is here today and thrown into the furnace tomorrow, won't he do much more for you — you of little faith? 31 So don't worry, saying, 'What will we eat?' or 'What will we drink?' or 'What will we wear?' 32 For the Gentiles eagerly seek all these things, and your heavenly Father knows that you need them. 33 But seek first the kingdom of God[H] and his righteousness, and all these things

---

[A]6:13 Or do not cause us to come into [B]6:13 Or from evil; some later mss add
For yours is the kingdom and the power and the glory forever. Amen.
[C]6:15 Other mss add their wrongdoing [D]6:16 Or unrecognizable, or disfigured
[E]6:18 Other mss add openly [F]6:19 Or valuables [G]6:27 Or add a single cubit
to his height [H]6:33 Other mss omit of God

SPECTACLE OR SACRED?

MATTHEW 6–7; 2 CORINTHIANS 11:2; EPHESIANS 5:22-33; REVELATION 19:6-9

Pull up a chair, girls. We're about to have a conversation about intimacy. Yep—"husband and wife" intimacy. It may very well make you blush, but I promise to keep it PG, and I promise it's all part of a very important point.

The Bible often refers to the Church as the bride of Christ (2Co 11:2; Eph 5:22-33). Our relationship with Jesus is like a marriage—but in a perfect way. He makes us beautiful, then admires us as we walk down the aisle toward Him on our wedding day (Rv 19:6-9). Perfectly pure. Impeccably white. Kind of awesome.

So now comes that part about intimacy.

Let's say, physically speaking, there are varying levels of intimacy. Those levels might begin with any sort of public display of affection and graduate all the way to the most intimate, behind closed doors, one-flesh moments only shared between a husband and wife. It's really nobody's business and it's deeply personal. A husband and wife are, indeed, one flesh. The intimate covenant they share, like Christ's covenant with us, is sacred.

When it comes to our relationship with God, it can be the same way. There's PDA and then there's sacred intimacy. There are grand public gestures of skywriting and singing telegrams (praying on the street corner "to be seen by people," as Matthew put it in 6:5). And then there is the love language of God: taking time in secret to show Him the only affections you're chasing after are His—pursuing Him privately, closing the doors, enjoying sacred intimacy.

Any relationship that only goes as deep as public displays, or mere physical intimacy without an emotional bond, is not true intimacy. This is what Jesus warns the crowds about in Matthew 6: "Be careful not to practice your righteousness in front of others to be seen by them. Otherwise, you will have no reward with your Father in heaven" (v. 1).

Jesus doesn't want your love to be a spectacle. He wants it to be sacred.

In a marriage, intimacy takes intentionality. Sometimes it takes scheduling regular dates on the calendar, even committing to block out distractions and making space for *ahem* intimacy on a regular basis. Intimacy can be enjoyed organically, only when it is supported intentionally.

"But when you pray, go into your private room, shut your door, and pray to your Father who is in secret."

MATTHEW 6:6

How are you pursuing intimacy as the bride of Christ? Are you intentionally closing the doors, scheduling dates, and setting aside time in order for your relationship to deepen, or are you publicly kissing Him, then living as strangers at home?

Is your prayer life simply a spectacle, or is it spectacularly sacred?

will be provided for you. [34] Therefore don't worry about tomorrow, because tomorrow will worry about itself. Each day has enough trouble of its own.

DO NOT JUDGE

7 "Do not judge, so that you won't be judged. [2] For you will be judged by the same standard with which you judge others, and you will be measured by the same measure you use. [3] Why do you look at the splinter in your brother's eye but don't notice the beam of wood in your own eye? [4] Or how can you say to your brother, 'Let me take the splinter out of your eye,' and look, there's a beam of wood in your own eye? [5] Hypocrite! First take the beam of wood out of your eye, and then you will see clearly to take the splinter out of your brother's eye. [6] Don't give what is holy to dogs or toss your pearls before pigs, or they will trample them under their feet, turn, and tear you to pieces.

ASK, SEARCH, KNOCK

[7] "Ask, and it will be given to you. Seek, and you will find. Knock, and the door[A] will be opened to you. [8] For everyone who asks receives, and the one who seeks finds, and to the one who knocks, the door will be opened. [9] Who among you, if his son asks him for bread, will give him a stone? [10] Or if he asks for a fish, will give him a snake? [11] If you then, who are evil, know how to give good gifts to your children, how much more will your Father in heaven give good things to those who ask him. [12] Therefore, whatever you want others to do for you, do also the same for them, for this is the Law and the Prophets.

ENTERING THE KINGDOM

[13] "Enter through the narrow gate. For the gate is wide and the road broad that leads to destruction, and there are many who go through it. [14] How narrow is the gate and difficult the road that leads to life, and few find it.

[15] "Be on your guard against false prophets who come to you in sheep's clothing but inwardly are ravaging wolves. [16] You'll recognize them by their fruit. Are grapes gathered from thornbushes or figs from thistles? [17] In the same way, every good tree produces good fruit, but a bad tree produces bad fruit. [18] A good tree can't produce bad fruit; neither can a bad tree produce good fruit. [19] Every tree that doesn't produce good fruit is cut down and thrown into the fire. [20] So you'll recognize them by their fruit.

[21] "Not everyone who says to me, 'Lord, Lord,' will enter the kingdom of heaven, but only the one who does the will of my Father in heaven. [22] On that day many will say to me, 'Lord, Lord, didn't we prophesy in your name, drive out demons in your name, and do many miracles in your name?' [23] Then I will announce to them, 'I never knew you. **Depart from me, you lawbreakers!**'[B,C]

THE TWO FOUNDATIONS

[24] "Therefore, everyone who hears these words of mine and acts on them will be like a wise man who built his house on the rock. [25] The rain fell, the rivers rose, and the winds blew and pounded that house. Yet it didn't collapse, because its foundation was on the rock. [26] But everyone who hears these words of mine and doesn't act on them will be like a foolish man who

---

A7:7 Lit and it   B7:23 Lit you who work lawlessness   C7:23 Ps 6:8

built his house on the sand. ²⁷ The rain fell, the rivers rose, the winds blew and pounded that house, and it collapsed. It collapsed with a great crash."

²⁸ When Jesus had finished saying these things, the crowds were astonished at his teaching, ²⁹ because he was teaching them like one who had authority, and not like their scribes.

A MAN CLEANSED

8 When he came down from the mountain, large crowds followed him. ² Right away a man with leprosy⁴ came up and knelt before him, saying, "Lord, if you are willing, you can make me clean."

³ Reaching out his hand, Jesus touched him, saying, "I am willing; be made clean." Immediately his leprosy was cleansed. ⁴ Then Jesus told him, "See that you don't tell anyone; but go, show yourself to the priest, and offer the gift that Moses commanded, as a testimony to them."

A CENTURION'S FAITH

⁵ When he entered Capernaum, a centurion came to him, pleading with him, ⁶ "Lord, my servant is lying at home paralyzed, in terrible agony."

⁷ He said to him, "Am I to come and heal him?"ᴮ

⁸ "Lord," the centurion replied, "I am not worthy to have you come under my roof. But just say the word, and my servant will be healed. ⁹ For I too am a man under authority, having soldiers under my command.ᶜ I say to this one, 'Go,' and he goes; and to another, 'Come,' and he comes; and to my servant, 'Do this!' and he does it."

¹⁰ Hearing this, Jesus was amazed and said to those following him, "Truly I tell you, I have not found anyone in Israel with so great a faith. ¹¹ I tell you that many will come from east and west to share the banquetᴰ with Abraham, Isaac, and Jacob in the kingdom of heaven. ¹² But the sons of the kingdom will be thrown into the outer darkness where there will be weeping and gnashing of teeth." ¹³ Then Jesus told the centurion, "Go. As you have believed, let it be done for you." And his servant was healed that very moment.ᴱ

HEALINGS AT CAPERNAUM

¹⁴ Jesus went into Peter's house and saw his mother-in-law lying in bed with a fever. ¹⁵ So he touched her hand, and the fever left her. Then she got up and began to serve him. ¹⁶ When evening came, they brought to him many who were demon-possessed. He drove out the spirits with a word and healed all who were sick, ¹⁷ so that what was spoken through the prophet Isaiah might be fulfilled:

**He himself took our weaknesses
and carried our diseases.**ᶠ

THE COST OF FOLLOWING JESUS

¹⁸ When Jesus saw a large crowdᴳ around him, he gave the order to go to the other side of the sea. ¹⁹ A scribe approached him and said, "Teacher, I will follow you wherever you go."

ᴬ8:2 Gk *lepros*; a term for various skin diseases, also in v. 3; see Lv 13–14
ᴮ8:7 Or "*I will come and heal him.*"   ᶜ8:9 Lit *under me*   ᴰ8:11 Lit *recline at the table*   ᴱ8:13 Or *that hour*; lit *very hour*   ᶠ8:17 Is 53:4   ᴳ8:18 Other mss read *saw large crowds*

²⁰ Jesus told him, "Foxes have dens, and birds of the sky have nests, but the Son of Man has no place to lay his head."

²¹ "Lord," another of his disciples said, "first let me go bury my father."

²² But Jesus told him, "Follow me, and let the dead bury their own dead."

WIND AND WAVES OBEY JESUS

²³ As he got into the boat, his disciples followed him. ²⁴ Suddenly, a violent storm arose on the sea, so that the boat was being swamped by the waves — but Jesus kept sleeping. ²⁵ So the disciples came and woke him up, saying, "Lord, save us! We're going to die!"

²⁶ He said to them, "Why are you afraid, you of little faith?" Then he got up and rebuked the winds and the sea, and there was a great calm.

²⁷ The men were amazed and asked, "What kind of man is this? Even the winds and the sea obey him!"

DEMONS DRIVEN OUT BY JESUS

²⁸ When he had come to the other side, to the region of the Gadarenes,^A two demon-possessed men met him as they came out of the tombs. They were so violent that no one could pass that way. ²⁹ Suddenly they shouted, "What do you have to do with us,^B Son of God? Have you come here to torment us before the time?"

³⁰ A long way off from them, a large herd of pigs was feeding. ³¹ "If you drive us out," the demons begged him, "send us into the herd of pigs."

³² "Go!" he told them. So when they had come out, they entered the pigs, and the whole herd rushed down the steep bank into the sea and perished in the water. ³³ Then the men who tended them fled. They went into the city and reported everything, especially what had happened to those who were demon-possessed. ³⁴ At that, the whole town went out to meet Jesus. When they saw him, they begged him to leave their region.

THE SON OF MAN FORGIVES AND HEALS

9 So he got into a boat, crossed over, and came to his own town. ² Just then some men^C brought to him a paralytic lying on a stretcher. Seeing their faith, Jesus told the paralytic, "Have courage, son, your sins are forgiven."

³ At this, some of the scribes said to themselves, "He's blaspheming!"

⁴ Perceiving their thoughts, Jesus said, "Why are you thinking evil things in your hearts?^D ⁵ For which is easier: to say, 'Your sins are forgiven,' or to say, 'Get up and walk'? ⁶ But so that you may know that the Son of Man has authority on earth to forgive sins" — then he told the paralytic, "Get up, take your stretcher, and go home." ⁷ So he got up and went home. ⁸ When the crowds saw this, they were awestruck^E,^F and gave glory to God, who had given such authority to men.

THE CALL OF MATTHEW

⁹ As Jesus went on from there, he saw a man named Matthew sitting at the toll booth, and he said to him, "Follow me," and he got up and followed him.

---

^A8:28 Other mss read *Gergesenes* ^B8:29 Other mss add *Jesus* ^C9:2 Lit *then they* ^D9:4 Or *minds* ^E9:8 Other mss read *amazed* ^F9:8 Lit *afraid*

¹⁰ While he was reclining at the table in the house, many tax collectors and sinners came to eat with Jesus and his disciples. ¹¹ When the Pharisees saw this, they asked his disciples, "Why does your teacher eat with tax collectors and sinners?"

¹² Now when he heard this, he said, "It is not those who are well who need a doctor, but those who are sick. ¹³ Go and learn what this means: **I desire mercy and not sacrifice.** ᴬ For I didn't come to call the righteous, but sinners." ᴮ

A QUESTION ABOUT FASTING

¹⁴ Then John's disciples came to him, saying, "Why do we and the Pharisees fast often, but your disciples do not fast?"

¹⁵ Jesus said to them, "Can the wedding guests ᶜ be sad while the groom is with them? The time ᴰ will come when the groom will be taken away from them, and then they will fast. ¹⁶ No one patches an old garment with unshrunk cloth, because the patch pulls away from the garment and makes the tear worse. ¹⁷ And no one puts ᴱ new wine into old wineskins. Otherwise, the skins burst, the wine spills out, and the skins are ruined. No, they put new wine into fresh wineskins, and both are preserved."

A GIRL RESTORED AND A WOMAN HEALED

¹⁸ As he was telling them these things, suddenly one of the leaders came and knelt down before him, saying, "My daughter just died, ᶠ but come and lay your hand on her, and she will live." ¹⁹ So Jesus and his disciples got up and followed him.

²⁰ Just then, a woman who had suffered from bleeding for twelve years approached from behind and touched the end of his robe, ²¹ for she said to herself, "If I can just touch his robe, I'll be made well." ᴳ

²² Jesus turned and saw her. "Have courage, daughter," he said. "Your faith has saved you." ᴴ And the woman was made well from that moment. ᴵ

²³ When Jesus came to the leader's house, he saw the flute players and a crowd lamenting loudly. ²⁴ "Leave," he said, "because the girl is not dead but asleep." And they laughed at him. ²⁵ After the crowd had been put outside, he went in and took her by the hand, and the girl got up. ²⁶ Then news of this spread throughout that whole area.

HEALING THE BLIND

²⁷ As Jesus went on from there, two blind men followed him, calling out, "Have mercy on us, Son of David!"

²⁸ When he entered the house, the blind men approached him, and Jesus said to them, "Do you believe that I can do this?"

They said to him, "Yes, Lord."

²⁹ Then he touched their eyes, saying, "Let it be done for you according to your faith." ³⁰ And their eyes were opened. Then Jesus warned them sternly, "Be sure that no one finds out." ³¹ But they went out and spread the news about him throughout that whole area.

ᴬ9:13 Hs 6:6   ᴮ9:13 Other mss add *to repentance*   ᶜ9:15 Lit *the sons of the bridal chamber*   ᴰ9:15 Lit *days*   ᴱ9:17 Lit *And they do not put*   ᶠ9:18 Lit *daughter has now come to the end*   ᴳ9:21 Or *be saved*   ᴴ9:22 Or *has made you well* ᴵ9:22 Lit *hour*

DRIVING OUT A DEMON

³² Just as they were going out, a demon-possessed man who was unable to speak was brought to him. ³³ When the demon had been driven out, the man who had been mute spoke, and the crowds were amazed, saying, "Nothing like this has ever been seen in Israel!"

³⁴ But the Pharisees said, "He drives out demons by the ruler of the demons."

THE LORD OF THE HARVEST

³⁵ Jesus continued going around to all the towns and villages, teaching in their synagogues, preaching the good news of the kingdom, and healing every ^A disease and every sickness. ^B,C ³⁶ When he saw the crowds, he felt compassion for them, because they were distressed and dejected, like sheep without a shepherd. ³⁷ Then he said to his disciples, "The harvest is abundant, but the workers are few. ³⁸ Therefore, pray to the Lord of the harvest to send out workers into his harvest."

COMMISSIONING THE TWELVE

10 Summoning his twelve disciples, he gave them authority over unclean spirits, to drive them out and to heal every ^A disease and sickness. ^C ² These are the names of the twelve apostles: First, Simon, who is called Peter, and Andrew his brother; James the son of Zebedee, and John his brother; ³ Philip and Bartholomew; Thomas and Matthew the tax collector; James the son of Alphaeus, and Thaddaeus; ^D ⁴ Simon the Zealot, ^E and Judas Iscariot, who also betrayed him.

⁵ Jesus sent out these twelve after giving them instructions: "Don't take the road that leads to the Gentiles, and don't enter any Samaritan town. ⁶ Instead, go to the lost sheep of the house of Israel. ⁷ As you go, proclaim: 'The kingdom of heaven has come near.' ⁸ Heal the sick, raise the dead, cleanse those with leprosy, ^F drive out demons. Freely you received, freely give. ⁹ Don't acquire gold, silver, or copper for your money-belts. ¹⁰ Don't take a traveling bag for the road, or an extra shirt, sandals, or a staff, for the worker is worthy of his food. ¹¹ When you enter any town or village, find out who is worthy, and stay there until you leave. ¹² Greet a household when you enter it, ¹³ and if the household is worthy, let your peace be on it; but if it is unworthy, let your peace return to you. ¹⁴ If anyone does not welcome you or listen to your words, shake the dust off your feet when you leave that house or town. ¹⁵ Truly I tell you, it will be more tolerable on the day of judgment for the land of Sodom and Gomorrah than for that town.

PERSECUTIONS PREDICTED

¹⁶ "Look, I'm sending you out like sheep among wolves. Therefore be as shrewd as serpents and as innocent as doves. ¹⁷ Beware of them, because they will hand you over to local courts ^G and flog you in their synagogues. ¹⁸ You will even be brought before governors and kings because of me, to bear

---

^A 9:35; 10:1 Or *every kind of* ^B 9:35 Other mss add *among the people*
^C 9:35; 10:1 Or *physical ailment* ^D 10:3 Other mss read *and Lebbaeus, whose surname was Thaddaeus* ^E 10:4 Lit *the Cananaean* ^F 10:8 Gk *lepros*; a term for various skin diseases; see Lv 13–14 ^G 10:17 Or *sanhedrins*

witness to them and to the Gentiles. ¹⁹ But when they hand you over, don't worry about how or what you are to speak. For you will be given what to say at that hour, ²⁰ because it isn't you speaking, but the Spirit of your Father is speaking through you.

²¹ "Brother will betray brother to death, and a father his child. Children will rise up against parents and have them put to death. ²² You will be hated by everyone because of my name. But the one who endures to the end will be saved. ²³ When they persecute you in one town, flee to another. For truly I tell you, you will not have gone through the towns of Israel before the Son of Man comes. ²⁴ A disciple^A is not above his teacher, or a slave above his master. ²⁵ It is enough for a disciple to become like his teacher and a slave like his master. If they called the head of the house 'Beelzebul,' how much more the members of his household!

FEAR GOD

²⁶ "Therefore, don't be afraid of them, since there is nothing covered that won't be uncovered and nothing hidden that won't be made known. ²⁷ What I tell you in the dark, speak in the light. What you hear in a whisper,^B proclaim on the housetops. ²⁸ Don't fear those who kill the body but are not able to kill the soul; rather, fear him who is able to destroy both soul and body in hell. ²⁹ Aren't two sparrows sold for a penny?^C Yet not one of them falls to the ground without your Father's consent.^D ³⁰ But even the hairs of your head have all been counted. ³¹ So don't be afraid; you are worth more than many sparrows.

ACKNOWLEDGING CHRIST

³² "Therefore, everyone who will acknowledge me before others, I will also acknowledge him before my Father in heaven. ³³ But whoever denies me before others, I will also deny him before my Father in heaven. ³⁴ Don't assume that I came to bring peace on the earth. I did not come to bring peace, but a sword. ³⁵ For I came to turn

> a man against his father,
> a daughter against her mother,
> a daughter-in-law against her mother-in-law;
> ³⁶ and a man's enemies will be
> the members of his household.^E

³⁷ The one who loves a father or mother more than me is not worthy of me; the one who loves a son or daughter more than me is not worthy of me. ³⁸ And whoever doesn't take up his cross and follow me is not worthy of me. ³⁹ Anyone who finds his life will lose it, and anyone who loses his life because of me will find it.

A CUP OF COLD WATER

⁴⁰ "The one who welcomes you welcomes me, and the one who welcomes me welcomes him who sent me. ⁴¹ Anyone who welcomes a prophet because he is a prophet^F will receive a prophet's reward. And anyone who welcomes a

---

^A 10:24 Or student   ^B 10:27 Lit in the ear   ^C 10:29 Gk assarion, a small copper coin   ^D 10:29 Lit ground apart from your Father   ^E 10:35-36 Mc 7:6   ^F 10:41 Lit prophet in the name of a prophet righteous person because he's righteous[A] will receive a righteous person's reward. [42] And whoever gives even a cup of cold water to one of these little ones because he is a disciple,[B] truly I tell you, he will never lose his reward."

JOHN THE BAPTIST DOUBTS

11 When Jesus had finished giving instructions to his twelve disciples, he moved on from there to teach and preach in their towns. [2] Now when John heard in prison what the Christ was doing, he sent a message through his disciples [3] and asked him, "Are you the one who is to come, or should we expect someone else?"

[4] Jesus replied to them, "Go and report to John what you hear and see: [5] The blind receive their sight, the lame walk, those with leprosy[C] are cleansed, the deaf hear, the dead are raised, and the poor are told the good news, [6] and blessed is the one who isn't offended by me."

[7] As these men were leaving, Jesus began to speak to the crowds about John: "What did you go out into the wilderness to see? A reed swaying in the wind? [8] What then did you go out to see? A man dressed in soft clothes? See, those who wear soft clothes are in royal palaces. [9] What then did you go out to see? A prophet? Yes, I tell you, and more than a prophet. [10] This is the one about whom it is written:

> See, I am sending my messenger ahead of you;
> he will prepare your way before you.[D]

[11] "Truly I tell you, among those born of women no one greater than John the Baptist has appeared,[E] but the least in the kingdom of heaven is greater than he. [12] From the days of John the Baptist until now, the kingdom of heaven has been suffering violence,[F] and the violent have been seizing it by force. [13] For all the prophets and the law prophesied until John. [14] And if you're willing to accept it, he is the Elijah who is to come. [15] Let anyone who has ears[G] listen.

AN UNRESPONSIVE GENERATION

[16] "To what should I compare this generation? It's like children sitting in the marketplaces who call out to other children:

[17] We played the flute for you,
> but you didn't dance;
> we sang a lament,
> but you didn't mourn![H]

[18] For John came neither eating nor drinking, and they say, 'He has a demon!' [19] The Son of Man came eating and drinking, and they say, 'Look, a glutton and a drunkard, a friend of tax collectors and sinners!' Yet wisdom is vindicated[I] by her deeds."[J]

[20] Then he proceeded to denounce the towns where most of his miracles were done, because they did not repent: [21] "Woe to you, Chorazin! Woe to you, Bethsaida! For if the miracles that were done in you had been done in Tyre and Sidon, they would have repented in sackcloth and ashes long ago. [22] But

---

[A]10:41 Lit *person in the name of a righteous person*   [B]10:42 Lit *little ones in the name of a disciple*   [C]11:5 Gk *lepros*; a term for various skin diseases; see Lv 13–14   [D]11:10 Mal 3:1   [E]11:11 Lit *arisen*   [F]11:12 Or *has been forcefully advancing*   [G]11:15 Other mss add *to hear*   [H]11:17 Or *beat your chests in grief*   [I]11:19 Or *declared right*   [J]11:19 Other mss read *children*

I tell you, it will be more tolerable for Tyre and Sidon on the day of judgment than for you. ²³ And you, Capernaum, will you be exalted to heaven? No, you will go down to Hades. For if the miracles that were done in you had been done in Sodom, it would have remained until today. ²⁴ But I tell you, it will be more tolerable for the land of Sodom on the day of judgment than for you."

THE SON GIVES KNOWLEDGE AND REST

²⁵ At that time Jesus said, "I praise you, Father, Lord of heaven and earth, because you have hidden these things from the wise and intelligent and revealed them to infants. ²⁶ Yes, Father, because this was your good pleasure.ᴬ ²⁷ All things have been entrusted to me by my Father. No one knows the Son except the Father, and no one knows the Father except the Son and anyone to whom the Son desiresᴮ to reveal him.

²⁸ "Come to me, all of you who are weary and burdened, and I will give you rest. ²⁹ Take up my yoke and learn from me, because I am lowly and humble in heart, and you will find rest for your souls. ³⁰ For my yoke is easy and my burden is light."

LORD OF THE SABBATH

12 At that time Jesus passed through the grainfields on the Sabbath. His disciples were hungry and began to pick and eat some heads of grain. ² When the Pharisees saw this, they said to him, "See, your disciples are doing what is not lawful to do on the Sabbath."

³ He said to them, "Haven't you read what David did when he and those who were with him were hungry: ⁴ how he entered the house of God, and they ateᶜ the bread of the Presence — which is not lawful for him or for those with him to eat, but only for the priests? ⁵ Or haven't you read in the law that on Sabbath days the priests in the temple violate the Sabbath and are innocent? ⁶ I tell you that something greater than the temple is here. ⁷ If you had known what this means, **I desire mercy and not sacrifice,** ᴰ you would not have condemned the innocent. ⁸ For the Son of Man is Lord of the Sabbath."

THE MAN WITH THE SHRIVELED HAND

⁹ Moving on from there, he entered their synagogue. ¹⁰ There he saw a man who had a shriveled hand, and in order to accuse him they asked him, "Is it lawful to heal on the Sabbath?"

¹¹ He replied to them, "Who among you, if he had a sheep that fell into a pit on the Sabbath, wouldn't take hold of it and lift it out? ¹² A person is worth far more than a sheep; so it is lawful to do what is good on the Sabbath."

¹³ Then he told the man, "Stretch out your hand." So he stretched it out, and it was restored, as good as the other. ¹⁴ But the Pharisees went out and plotted against him, how they might kill him.

THE SERVANT OF THE LORD

¹⁵ Jesus was aware of this and withdrew. Large crowdsᴱ followed him, and he healed them all. ¹⁶ He warned them not to make him known, ¹⁷ so that what was spoken through the prophet Isaiah might be fulfilled:

ᴬ11:26 Lit was well-pleasing in your sight   ᴮ11:27 Or wills, or chooses
ᶜ12:4 Other mss read he ate   ᴰ12:7 Hs 6:6   ᴱ12:15 Other mss read Many

18 Here is my servant whom I have chosen,
    my beloved in whom I delight;
    I will put my Spirit on him,
    and he will proclaim justice to the nations.
19 He will not argue or shout,
    and no one will hear his voice in the streets.
20 He will not break a bruised reed,
    and he will not put out a smoldering wick,
    until he has led justice to victory.[A]
21 The nations will put their hope in his name.[B]

A HOUSE DIVIDED

22 Then a demon-possessed man who was blind and unable to speak was brought to him. He healed him, so that the man[C] could both speak and see. 23 All the crowds were astounded and said, "Could this be the Son of David?"

24 When the Pharisees heard this, they said, "This man drives out demons only by Beelzebul, the ruler of the demons."

25 Knowing their thoughts, he told them: "Every kingdom divided against itself is headed for destruction, and no city or house divided against itself will stand. 26 If Satan drives out Satan, he is divided against himself. How then will his kingdom stand? 27 And if I drive out demons by Beelzebul, by whom do your sons drive them out? For this reason they will be your judges. 28 If I drive out demons by the Spirit of God, then the kingdom of God has come upon you. 29 How can someone enter a strong man's house and steal his possessions unless he first ties up the strong man? Then he can plunder his house. 30 Anyone who is not with me is against me, and anyone who does not gather with me scatters. 31 Therefore, I tell you, people will be forgiven every sin and blasphemy, but the blasphemy against[D] the Spirit will not be forgiven.[E] 32 Whoever speaks a word against the Son of Man, it will be forgiven him; but whoever speaks against the Holy Spirit, it will not be forgiven him, either in this age or in the one to come.

A TREE AND ITS FRUIT

33 "Either make the tree good and its fruit will be good, or make the tree bad[F] and its fruit will be bad; for a tree is known by its fruit. 34 Brood of vipers! How can you speak good things when you are evil? For the mouth speaks from the overflow of the heart. 35 A good person produces good things from his storeroom of good, and an evil person produces evil things from his storeroom of evil. 36 I tell you that on the day of judgment people will have to account for every careless[G] word they speak.[H] 37 For by your words you will be acquitted, and by your words you will be condemned."

THE SIGN OF JONAH

38 Then some of the scribes and Pharisees said to him, "Teacher, we want to see a sign from you."

[A]12:20 Or until he has successfully put forth justice   [B]12:18-21 Is 42:1-4
[C]12:22 Lit mute   [D]12:31 Or of   [E]12:31 Other mss add people   [F]12:33 Or decayed; lit rotten   [G]12:36 Lit worthless   [H]12:36 Lit will speak

³⁹ He answered them, "An evil and adulterous generation demands a sign, but no sign will be given to it except the sign of the prophet Jonah. ⁴⁰ For as Jonah was in the belly of the huge fish⁴ three days and three nights, so the Son of Man will be in the heart of the earth three days and three nights. ⁴¹ The men of Nineveh will stand up at the judgment with this generation and condemn it, because they repented at Jonah's preaching; and look — something greater than Jonah is here. ⁴² The queen of the south will rise up at the judgment with this generation and condemn it, because she came from the ends of the earth to hear the wisdom of Solomon; and look — something greater than Solomon is here.

AN UNCLEAN SPIRIT'S RETURN

⁴³ "When an unclean spirit comes out of a person, it roams through waterless places looking for rest but doesn't find any. ⁴⁴ Then it says, 'I'll go back to my house that I came from.' Returning, it finds the house vacant, swept, and put in order. ⁴⁵ Then it goes and brings with it seven other spirits more evil than itself, and they enter and settle down there. As a result, that person's last condition is worse than the first. That's how it will also be with this evil generation."

TRUE RELATIONSHIPS

⁴⁶ While he was still speaking with the crowds, his mother and brothers were standing outside wanting to speak to him. ⁴⁷ Someone told him, "Look, your mother and your brothers are standing outside, wanting to speak to you."ᴮ

⁴⁸ He replied to the one who was speaking to him, "Who is my mother and who are my brothers?" ⁴⁹ Stretching out his hand toward his disciples, he said, "Here are my mother and my brothers! ⁵⁰ For whoever does the will of my Father in heaven is my brother and sister and mother."

THE PARABLE OF THE SOWER

13 On that day Jesus went out of the house and was sitting by the sea. ² Such large crowds gathered around him that he got into a boat and sat down, while the whole crowd stood on the shore.

³ Then he told them many things in parables, saying: "Consider the sower who went out to sow. ⁴ As he sowed, some seed fell along the path, and the birds came and devoured them. ⁵ Other seed fell on rocky ground where it didn't have much soil, and it grew up quickly since the soil wasn't deep. ⁶ But when the sun came up, it was scorched, and since it had no root, it withered away. ⁷ Other seed fell among thorns, and the thorns came up and choked it. ⁸ Still other seed fell on good ground and produced fruit: some a hundred, some sixty, and some thirty times what was sown. ⁹ Let anyone who has earsᶜ listen."

WHY JESUS USED PARABLES

¹⁰ Then the disciples came up and asked him, "Why are you speaking to them in parables?"

ᴬ12:40 Or sea creature; Jnh 1:17   ᴮ12:47 Other mss omit this v.   ᶜ13:9 Other mss add to hear

[11] He answered, "Because the secrets of the kingdom of heaven have been given for you to know, but it has not been given to them. [12] For whoever has, more will be given to him, and he will have more than enough; but whoever does not have, even what he has will be taken away from him. [13] That is why I speak to them in parables, because looking they do not see, and hearing they do not listen or understand. [14] Isaiah's prophecy is fulfilled in them, which says:

> You will listen and listen,
> but never understand;
> you will look and look,
> but never perceive.
> [15] For this people's heart has grown callous;
> their ears are hard of hearing,
> and they have shut their eyes;
> otherwise they might see with their eyes,
> and hear with their ears, and
> understand with their hearts,
> and turn back —
> and I would heal them.[A]

[16] "Blessed are your eyes because they do see, and your ears because they do hear. [17] For truly I tell you, many prophets and righteous people longed to see the things you see but didn't see them, to hear the things you hear but didn't hear them.

THE PARABLE OF THE SOWER EXPLAINED

[18] "So listen to the parable of the sower: [19] When anyone hears the word about the kingdom and doesn't understand it, the evil one comes and snatches away what was sown in his heart. This is the one sown along the path. [20] And the one sown on rocky ground — this is one who hears the word and immediately receives it with joy. [21] But he has no root and is short-lived. When distress or persecution comes because of the word, immediately he falls away. [22] Now the one sown among the thorns — this is one who hears the word, but the worries of this age and the deceitfulness[B] of wealth choke the word, and it becomes unfruitful. [23] But the one sown on the good ground — this is one who hears and understands the word, who does produce fruit and yields: some a hundred, some sixty, some thirty times what was sown."

THE PARABLE OF THE WHEAT AND THE WEEDS

[24] He presented another parable to them: "The kingdom of heaven may be compared to a man who sowed good seed in his field. [25] But while people were sleeping, his enemy came, sowed weeds among the wheat, and left. [26] When the plants sprouted and produced grain, then the weeds also appeared. [27] The landowner's servants came to him and said, 'Master, didn't you sow good seed in your field? Then where did the weeds come from?'

[28] "'An enemy did this,' he told them.

"'So, do you want us to go and pull them up?' the servants asked him.

[29] "'No,' he said. 'When you pull up the weeds, you might also uproot the wheat with them. [30] Let both grow together until the harvest. At harvest time

---

[A] 13:14-15 Is 6:9-10 [B] 13:22 Or pleasure

I'll tell the reapers: Gather the weeds first and tie them in bundles to burn them, but collect the wheat in my barn.'"

THE PARABLES OF THE MUSTARD SEED AND OF THE LEAVEN

[31] He presented another parable to them: "The kingdom of heaven is like a mustard seed that a man took and sowed in his field. [32] It's the smallest of all the seeds, but when grown, it's taller than the garden plants and becomes a tree, so that the birds of the sky come and nest in its branches."

[33] He told them another parable: "The kingdom of heaven is like leaven[A] that a woman took and mixed into fifty pounds[B] of flour until all of it was leavened."

USING PARABLES FULFILLS PROPHECY

[34] Jesus told the crowds all these things in parables, and he did not tell them anything without a parable, [35] so that what was spoken through the prophet might be fulfilled:

I will open my mouth in parables;
I will declare things kept secret
from the foundation of the world.[C,D]

JESUS INTERPRETS THE PARABLE OF THE WHEAT AND THE WEEDS

[36] Then he left the crowds and went into the house. His disciples approached him and said, "Explain to us the parable of the weeds in the field."

[37] He replied: "The one who sows the good seed is the Son of Man; [38] the field is the world; and the good seed — these are the children of the kingdom. The weeds are the children of the evil one, [39] and the enemy who sowed them is the devil. The harvest is the end of the age, and the harvesters are angels. [40] Therefore, just as the weeds are gathered and burned in the fire, so it will be at the end of the age. [41] The Son of Man will send out his angels, and they will gather from his kingdom all who cause sin[E] and those guilty of lawlessness.[F] [42] They will throw them into the blazing furnace where there will be weeping and gnashing of teeth. [43] Then the righteous will shine like the sun in their Father's kingdom. Let anyone who has ears[G] listen.

THE PARABLES OF THE HIDDEN TREASURE AND OF THE PRICELESS PEARL

[44] "The kingdom of heaven is like treasure, buried in a field, that a man found and reburied. Then in his joy he goes and sells everything he has and buys that field.

[45] "Again, the kingdom of heaven is like a merchant in search of fine pearls. [46] When he found one priceless[H] pearl, he went and sold everything he had and bought it.

THE PARABLE OF THE NET

[47] "Again, the kingdom of heaven is like a large net thrown into the sea. It collected every kind of fish, [48] and when it was full, they dragged it ashore, sat

---

[A]13:33 Or yeast   [B]13:33 Lit three sata ; about 40 liters   [C]13:35 Some mss omit of the world   [D]13:35 Ps 78:2   [E]13:41 Or stumbling   [F]13:41 Or those who do lawlessness   [G]13:43 Other mss add to hear   [H]13:46 Or very precious down, and gathered the good fish into containers, but threw out the worthless ones. ⁴⁹ So it will be at the end of the age. The angels will go out, separate the evil people from the righteous, ⁵⁰ and throw them into the blazing furnace, where there will be weeping and gnashing of teeth.

THE STOREHOUSE OF TRUTH

⁵¹ "Have you understood all these things?" ᴬ

They answered him, "Yes."

⁵² "Therefore," he said to them, "every teacher of the law ᴮ who has become a disciple in the kingdom of heaven is like the owner of a house who brings out of his storeroom treasures new and old."

REJECTION AT NAZARETH

⁵³ When Jesus had finished these parables, he left there. ⁵⁴ He went to his hometown and began to teach them in their synagogue, so that they were astonished and said, "Where did this man get this wisdom and these miraculous powers? ⁵⁵ Isn't this the carpenter's son? Isn't his mother called Mary, and his brothers James, Joseph, ᶜ Simon, and Judas? ⁵⁶ And his sisters, aren't they all with us? So where does he get all these things?" ⁵⁷ And they were offended by him.

Jesus said to them, "A prophet is not without honor except in his hometown and in his household." ⁵⁸ And he did not do many miracles there because of their unbelief.

JOHN THE BAPTIST BEHEADED

14 At that time Herod the tetrarch heard the report about Jesus. ² "This is John the Baptist," he told his servants. "He has been raised from the dead, and that's why miraculous powers are at work in him."

³ For Herod had arrested John, chained ᴰ him, and put him in prison on account of Herodias, his brother Philip's wife, ⁴ since John had been telling him, "It's not lawful for you to have her." ⁵ Though Herod wanted to kill John, he feared the crowd since they regarded John as a prophet.

⁶ When Herod's birthday celebration came, Herodias's daughter danced before them ᴱ and pleased Herod. ⁷ So he promised with an oath to give her whatever she asked. ⁸ Prompted by her mother, she answered, "Give me John the Baptist's head here on a platter." ⁹ Although the king regretted it, he commanded that it be granted because of his oaths and his guests. ¹⁰ So he sent orders and had John beheaded in the prison. ¹¹ His head was brought on a platter and given to the girl, who carried it to her mother. ¹² Then his disciples came, removed the corpse, ꜰ buried it, and went and reported to Jesus.

FEEDING OF THE FIVE THOUSAND

¹³ When Jesus heard about it, he withdrew from there by boat to a remote place to be alone. When the crowds heard this, they followed him on foot from the towns. ¹⁴ When he went ashore, ᴳ he saw a large crowd, had compassion on them, and healed their sick.

ᴬ13:51 Other mss add *Jesus asked them* ᴮ13:52 Or *every scribe* ᶜ13:55 Other mss read *Joses*; Mk 6:3 ᴰ14:3 Or *bound* ᴱ14:6 Lit *danced in the middle* ꜰ14:12 Other mss read *body* ᴳ14:14 Lit *Coming out* (of the boat)

¹⁵ When evening came, the disciples approached him and said, "This place is deserted, and it is already late.[A] Send the crowds away so that they can go into the villages and buy food for themselves."

¹⁶ "They don't need to go away," Jesus told them. "You give them something to eat."

¹⁷ "But we only have five loaves and two fish here," they said to him.

¹⁸ "Bring them here to me," he said. ¹⁹ Then he commanded the crowds to sit down on the grass. He took the five loaves and the two fish, and looking up to heaven, he blessed them. He broke the loaves and gave them to the disciples, and the disciples gave them to the crowds. ²⁰ Everyone ate and was satisfied. They picked up twelve baskets full of leftover pieces. ²¹ Now those who ate were about five thousand men, besides women and children.

WALKING ON THE WATER

²² Immediately he[B] made the disciples get into the boat and go ahead of him to the other side, while he dismissed the crowds. ²³ After dismissing the crowds, he went up on the mountain by himself to pray. Well into the night, he was there alone. ²⁴ Meanwhile, the boat was already some distance[C] from land,[D] battered by the waves, because the wind was against them. ²⁵ Jesus came toward them walking on the sea very early in the morning.[E] ²⁶ When the disciples saw him walking on the sea, they were terrified. "It's a ghost!" they said, and they cried out in fear.

²⁷ Immediately Jesus spoke to them. "Have courage! It is I. Don't be afraid."

²⁸ "Lord, if it's you," Peter answered him, "command me to come to you on the water."

²⁹ He said, "Come."

And climbing out of the boat, Peter started walking on the water and came toward Jesus. ³⁰ But when he saw the strength of the wind,[F] he was afraid, and beginning to sink he cried out, "Lord, save me!"

³¹ Immediately Jesus reached out his hand, caught hold of him, and said to him, "You of little faith, why did you doubt?"

³² When they got into the boat, the wind ceased. ³³ Then those in the boat worshiped him and said, "Truly you are the Son of God."

MIRACULOUS HEALINGS

³⁴ When they had crossed over, they came to shore at Gennesaret. ³⁵ When the men of that place recognized him, they alerted the whole vicinity and brought to him all who were sick. ³⁶ They begged him that they might only touch the end of his robe, and as many as touched it were healed.

THE TRADITION OF THE ELDERS

15 Then Jesus was approached by Pharisees and scribes from Jerusalem, who asked, ² "Why do your disciples break the tradition of the elders? For they don't wash their hands when they eat."[G]

[A]14:15 Lit and the time (for the evening meal) has already passed
[B]14:22 Other mss read Jesus   [C]14:24 Lit already many stadia; one stadion
= 600 feet   [D]14:24 Other mss read already in the middle of the sea
[E]14:25 Lit fourth watch of the night = 3 to 6 a.m.   [F]14:30 Other mss read saw
the wind   [G]15:2 Lit eat bread = eat a meal

³ He answered them, "Why do you break God's commandment because of your tradition? ⁴ For God said:^A **Honor your father and your mother;**^B and, **Whoever speaks evil of father or mother must be put to death.**^C ⁵ But you say, 'Whoever tells his father or mother, "Whatever benefit you might have received from me is a gift committed to the temple," ⁶ he does not have to honor his father.'^D In this way, you have nullified the word of God^E because of your tradition. ⁷ Hypocrites! Isaiah prophesied correctly about you when he said:

⁸ This people^F honors me with their lips,
   but their heart is far from me.
⁹ They worship me in vain,
   teaching as doctrines human commands."^G

DEFILEMENT IS FROM WITHIN

¹⁰ Summoning the crowd, he told them, "Listen and understand: ¹¹ It's not what goes into the mouth that defiles a person, but what comes out of the mouth — this defiles a person."

¹² Then the disciples came up and told him, "Do you know that the Pharisees took offense when they heard what you said?"

¹³ He replied, "Every plant that my heavenly Father didn't plant will be uprooted. ¹⁴ Leave them alone! They are blind guides.^H And if the blind guide the blind, both will fall into a pit."

¹⁵ Then Peter said, "Explain this parable to us."

¹⁶ "Do you still lack understanding?" he^I asked. ¹⁷ "Don't you realize^J that whatever goes into the mouth passes into the stomach and is eliminated?^K ¹⁸ But what comes out of the mouth comes from the heart, and this defiles a person. ¹⁹ For from the heart come evil thoughts, murders, adulteries, sexual immoralities, thefts, false testimonies, slander. ²⁰ These are the things that defile a person; but eating with unwashed hands does not defile a person."

A GENTILE MOTHER'S FAITH

²¹ When Jesus left there, he withdrew to the area of Tyre and Sidon. ²² Just then a Canaanite woman from that region came and kept crying out,^L "Have mercy on me, Lord, Son of David! My daughter is severely tormented by a demon."

²³ Jesus did not say a word to her. His disciples approached him and urged him, "Send her away because she's crying out after us."

²⁴ He replied, "I was sent only to the lost sheep of the house of Israel."

²⁵ But she came, knelt before him, and said, "Lord, help me!"

²⁶ He answered, "It isn't right to take the children's bread and throw it to the dogs."

²⁷ "Yes, Lord," she said, "yet even the dogs eat the crumbs that fall from their masters' table."

---

^A 15:4 Other mss read *commanded, saying*   ^B 15:4 Ex 20:12; Dt 5:16
^C 15:4 Ex 21:17; Lv 20:9   ^D 15:6 Other mss read *then he does not have to honor his father or mother*   ^E 15:6 Other mss read *commandment*   ^F 15:8 Other mss add *draw near to me with their mouths, and*   ^G 15:8-9 Is 29:13 LXX
^H 15:14 Other mss add *for the blind*   ^I 15:16 Other mss read *Jesus*
^J 15:17 Other mss add *yet*   ^K 15:17 Lit *and goes out into the toilet*   ^L 15:22 Other mss read *and cried out to him*

²⁸ Then Jesus replied to her, "Woman, your faith is great. Let it be done for you as you want." And from that moment^A her daughter was healed.

HEALING MANY PEOPLE

²⁹ Moving on from there, Jesus passed along the Sea of Galilee. He went up on a mountain and sat there, ³⁰ and large crowds came to him, including the lame, the blind, the crippled, those unable to speak, and many others. They put them at his feet, and he healed them. ³¹ So the crowd was amazed when they saw those unable to speak talking, the crippled restored, the lame walking, and the blind seeing, and they gave glory to the God of Israel.

FEEDING OF THE FOUR THOUSAND

³² Jesus called his disciples and said, "I have compassion on the crowd, because they've already stayed with me three days and have nothing to eat. I don't want to send them away hungry, otherwise they might collapse on the way."

³³ The disciples said to him, "Where could we get enough bread in this desolate place to feed such a crowd?"

³⁴ "How many loaves do you have?" Jesus asked them.

"Seven," they said, "and a few small fish."

³⁵ After commanding the crowd to sit down on the ground, ³⁶ he took the seven loaves and the fish, gave thanks, broke them, and gave them to the disciples, and the disciples gave them to the crowds. ³⁷ They all ate and were satisfied. They collected the leftover pieces — seven large baskets full. ³⁸ Now there were four thousand men who had eaten, besides women and children. ³⁹ After dismissing the crowds, he got into the boat and went to the region of Magadan.^B

THE LEAVEN OF THE PHARISEES AND THE SADDUCEES

16 The Pharisees and Sadducees approached, and tested him, asking him to show them a sign from heaven. ² He replied, "When evening comes you say, 'It will be good weather because the sky is red.' ³ And in the morning, 'Today will be stormy because the sky is red and threatening.' You^C know how to read the appearance of the sky, but you can't read the signs of the times.^D ⁴ An evil and adulterous generation demands a sign, but no sign will be given to it except the sign of^E Jonah." Then he left them and went away.

⁵ The disciples reached the other shore,^F and they had forgotten to take bread. ⁶ Then Jesus told them, "Watch out and beware of the leaven^G of the Pharisees and Sadducees."

⁷ They were discussing among themselves, "We didn't bring any bread."

⁸ Aware of this, Jesus said, "You of little faith, why are you discussing among yourselves that you do not have bread? ⁹ Don't you understand yet? Don't you remember the five loaves for the five thousand and how many baskets you collected? ¹⁰ Or the seven loaves for the four thousand and how many large baskets you collected? ¹¹ Why is it you don't understand that when I told you, 'Beware of the leaven of the Pharisees and Sadducees,' it wasn't

---

^A 15:28 Lit hour   ^B 15:39 Other mss read Magdala   ^C 16:3 Other mss read Hypocrites! You   ^D 16:2-3 Other mss omit When (v. 2) through end of v. 3   ^E 16:4 Other mss add the prophet   ^F 16:5 Lit disciples went to the other side   ^G 16:6 Or yeast, also in vv. 11,12 about bread?" ¹² Then they understood that he had not told them to beware of the leaven in bread, but of the teaching of the Pharisees and Sadducees.

PETER'S CONFESSION OF THE MESSIAH

¹³ When Jesus came to the region of Caesarea Philippi,ᴬ he asked his disciples, "Who do people say that the Son of Man is?"ᴮ

¹⁴ They replied, "Some say John the Baptist; others, Elijah; still others, Jeremiah or one of the prophets."

¹⁵ "But you," he asked them, "who do you say that I am?"

¹⁶ Simon Peter answered, "You are the Messiah, the Son of the living God."

¹⁷ Jesus responded, "Blessed are you, Simon son of Jonah,ᶜ because flesh and blood did not reveal this to you, but my Father in heaven. ¹⁸ And I also say to you that you are Peter, and on this rock I will build my church, and the gates of Hades will not overpower it. ¹⁹ I will give you the keys of the kingdom of heaven, and whatever you bind on earth will have been boundᴰ in heaven, and whatever you loose on earth will have been loosedᴱ in heaven." ²⁰ Then he gave the disciples orders to tell no one that he wasᶠ the Messiah.

HIS DEATH AND RESURRECTION PREDICTED

²¹ From then on Jesus began to point out to his disciples that it was necessary for him to go to Jerusalem and suffer many things from the elders, chief priests, and scribes, be killed, and be raised the third day. ²² Peter took him aside and began to rebuke him, "Oh no,ᴳ Lord! This will never happen to you!"

²³ Jesus turned and told Peter, "Get behind me, Satan! You are a hindrance to me because you're not thinking about God's concernsᴴ but human concerns."

TAKE UP YOUR CROSS

²⁴ Then Jesus said to his disciples, "If anyone wants to follow after me, let him deny himself, take up his cross, and follow me. ²⁵ For whoever wants to save his life will lose it, but whoever loses his life because of me will find it. ²⁶ For what will it benefit someone if he gains the whole world yet loses his life? Or what will anyone give in exchange for his life? ²⁷ For the Son of Man is going to come with his angels in the glory of his Father, and then he will reward each according to what he has done. ²⁸ Truly I tell you, there are some standing here who will not taste death until they see the Son of Man coming in his kingdom."

THE TRANSFIGURATION

17 After six days Jesus took Peter, James, and his brother John and led them up on a high mountain by themselves. ² He was transfigured in front of them, and his face shone like the sun; his clothes became as white as the light. ³ Suddenly, Moses and Elijah appeared to them, talking with him.

ᴬ16:13 A town north of Galilee at the base of Mount Hermon ᴮ16:13 Other mss read that I, the Son of Man, am ᶜ16:17 Or son of John ᴰ16:19 Or earth will be bound ᴱ16:19 Or earth will be loosed ᶠ16:20 Other mss add Jesus ᴳ16:22 Lit "Mercy to you = "May God have mercy on you ᴴ16:23 Lit about the things of God

4 Then Peter said to Jesus, "Lord, it's good for us to be here. If you want, I will set up[A] three shelters here: one for you, one for Moses, and one for Elijah."

5 While he was still speaking, suddenly a bright cloud covered[B] them, and a voice from the cloud said: "This is my beloved Son, with whom I am well-pleased. Listen to him!" 6 When the disciples heard this, they fell facedown and were terrified.

7 Jesus came up, touched them, and said, "Get up; don't be afraid." 8 When they looked up they saw no one except Jesus alone.

9 As they were coming down the mountain, Jesus commanded them, "Don't tell anyone about the vision until the Son of Man is raised[C] from the dead."

10 So the disciples asked him, "Why then do the scribes say that Elijah must come first?"

11 "Elijah is coming[D] and will restore everything," he replied.[E] 12 "But I tell you: Elijah has already come, and they didn't recognize him. On the contrary, they did whatever they pleased to him. In the same way the Son of Man is going to suffer at their hands." 13 Then the disciples understood that he had spoken to them about John the Baptist.

THE POWER OF JESUS OVER A DEMON

14 When they reached the crowd, a man approached and knelt down before him. 15 "Lord," he said, "have mercy on my son, because he has seizures[F] and suffers terribly. He often falls into the fire and often into the water. 16 I brought him to your disciples, but they couldn't heal him."

17 Jesus replied, "You unbelieving and perverse generation, how long will I be with you? How long must I put up with you? Bring him here to me." 18 Then Jesus rebuked the demon,[G] and it[H] came out of him, and from that moment[I] the boy was healed.

19 Then the disciples approached Jesus privately and said, "Why couldn't we drive it out?"

20 "Because of your little faith," he[J] told them. "For truly I tell you, if you have faith the size of[K] a mustard seed, you will tell this mountain, 'Move from here to there,' and it will move. Nothing will be impossible for you."[L]

THE SECOND PREDICTION OF HIS DEATH

22 As they were gathering together[M] in Galilee, Jesus told them, "The Son of Man is about to be betrayed into the hands of men. 23 They will kill him, and on the third day he will be raised up." And they were deeply distressed.

PAYING THE TEMPLE TAX

24 When they came to Capernaum, those who collected the temple tax approached Peter and said, "Doesn't your teacher pay the temple tax?"

25 "Yes," he said.

A17:4 Other mss read *Let's make*   B17:5 Or *enveloped*; Ex 40:34-35
C17:9 Other mss read *Man has risen*   D17:11 Other mss add *first*   E17:11 Other mss read *Jesus said to them*   F17:15 Lit *he is moonstruck*; thought to be a form of epilepsy   G17:18 Lit *rebuked him, or it*   H17:18 Lit *the demon*   I17:18 Lit *hour*   J17:20 Other mss read *your unbelief, Jesus*   K17:20 Lit *faith like*   L17:20 Some mss include v. 21: *"However, this kind does not come out except by prayer and fasting."*   M17:22 Other mss read *were staying*

When he went into the house, Jesus spoke to him first,ᴬ "What do you think, Simon? From whom do earthly kings collect tariffs or taxes? From their sons or from strangers?"ᴮ

²⁶ "From strangers," he said.ᶜ

"Then the sons are free," Jesus told him. ²⁷ "But, so we won't offend them, go to the sea, cast in a fishhook, and take the first fish that you catch. When you open its mouth you'll find a coin.ᴰ Take it and give it to them for me and you."

WHO IS THE GREATEST?

18 At that timeᴱ the disciples came to Jesus and asked, "So who is greatest in the kingdom of heaven?" ² He called a child and had him stand among them. ³ "Truly I tell you," he said, "unless you turn and become like children, you will never enter the kingdom of heaven. ⁴ Therefore, whoever humbles himself like this child — this one is the greatest in the kingdom of heaven. ⁵ And whoever welcomesᶠ one child like this in my name welcomes me.

⁶ "But whoever causes one of these little ones who believe in me to fall away — it would be better for him if a heavy millstone were hung around his neck and he were drowned in the depths of the sea. ⁷ Woe to the world because of offenses. For offenses will inevitably come, but woe to that person by whom the offense comes. ⁸ If your hand or your foot causes you to fall away, cut it off and throw it away. It is better for you to enter life maimed or lame than to have two hands or two feet and be thrown into the eternal fire. ⁹ And if your eye causes you to fall away, gouge it out and throw it away. It is better for you to enter life with one eye than to have two eyes and be thrown into hellfire.ᴳ

THE PARABLE OF THE LOST SHEEP

¹⁰ "See to it that you don't despise one of these little ones, because I tell you that in heaven their angels continually view the face of my Father in heaven.ᴴ ¹² What do you think? If someone has a hundred sheep, and one of them goes astray, won't he leave the ninety-nine on the hillside and go and search for the stray? ¹³ And if he finds it, truly I tell you, he rejoices over that sheepᴵ more than over the ninety-nine that did not go astray. ¹⁴ In the same way, it is not the will of your Father in heaven that one of these little ones perish.

RESTORING A BROTHER

¹⁵ "If your brother sins against you,ᴶ go and rebuke him in private.ᴷ If he listens to you, you have won your brother. ¹⁶ But if he won't listen, take one or two others with you, so that **by the testimony**ᴸ **of two or three witnesses every fact may be established.**ᴹ ¹⁷ If he doesn't pay attention to them, tell the church.ᴺ If he doesn't pay attention even to the church, let him be like a Gentile and a tax collector to you. ¹⁸ Truly I tell you, whatever you bind on

---

ᴬ17:25 Lit Jesus anticipated him by saying   ᴮ17:25 Or foreigners   ᶜ17:26 Other mss read Peter said to him   ᴰ17:27 Gk stater, worth 2 double-drachmas   ᴱ18:1 Lit hour   ᶠ18:5 Or receives   ᴳ18:9 Lit gehenna of fire   ᴴ18:10 Some mss include v. 11: For the Son of Man has come to save the lost.   ᴵ18:13 Lit over it   ᴶ18:15 Other mss omit against you   ᴷ18:15 Lit him between you and him alone   ᴸ18:16 Lit mouth   ᴹ18:16 Dt 19:15   ᴺ18:17 Or congregation

THE GREAT MERCY OF GOD

MATTHEW 17–18

In Matthew 18, Jesus tells the parable of a servant who owes his master a huge sum. As in, more than he could pay back over several lifetimes—that kind of huge. The servant begs for mercy, and the master pardons the entire debt. But then, that servant turns around and finds somebody who owes him not much—a tiny fraction of his own pardoned debt—and starts choking him to give back his money.

Although I don't actually put my hands on the throat of those who owe me, I do choke other people with my lack of mercy and forgiveness. The huge disparity in this passage is an opportunity for me to see how God is God and I am not.

Jesus' story forces me to look at the truth. I don't love this, because I really want to think of myself as merciful and forgiving. In fact, I actually want to be merciful and forgiving. This parable shows me that even my best efforts are little more than drops in the bucket. My forgiveness is in a chronic state of "too little too late."

My mercy is a pantomime show using shadow puppets and a flashlight, while God's mercy is opening night on Broadway. Spurgeon explained it this way: "God's mercy is so great that you may sooner drain the sea of its water, or deprive the sun of its light, or make space too narrow, than diminish the great mercy of God" (C.H. Spurgeon, *From Death to Life*).

The vastness of God's never-ending mercy *should* give us an overwhelmed and inadequate feeling. Our need for forgiveness is enormous! Grasping that need is actually the first step to understanding the gospel.

Our trespasses against God are greater by far than anyone's trespasses against us.

It's difficult to remember mercy when someone hurts you. Some of us have been hurt so badly it feels like everything is ruined—that nothing can restore what's been taken from us. The very thought of the offense can fill you with fear and loathing.

Now, remember this: in order to forgive us, Christ had to die for us. He took the curse that we brought to Him and gave up everything so He could give us mercy (Gl 3:13). This is staggering.

True forgiveness costs everything. But God loves us so much, He freely gave everything. While this passage does remind us that we are like the unforgiving slave, the bigger truth here is that God is our compassionate master and He piles love and forgiveness on us all.

The gospel is true! God's great love and mercy for us are greater than all our sins.

Wonderful the matchless grace of Jesus,
Deeper than the mighty rolling sea;
Wonderful grace, all sufficient for me, for even me.
Broader than the scope of my transgressions,
Greater far than all my sin and shame,
O magnify the precious Name of Jesus.
Praise His Name!

HALDOR LILLENAS, "WONDERFUL GRACE OF JESUS"

earth will have been bound[A] in heaven, and whatever you loose on earth will have been loosed[B] in heaven. ¹⁹ Again, truly I tell you, if two of you on earth agree about any matter that you[C] pray for, it will be done for you[D] by my Father in heaven. ²⁰ For where two or three are gathered together in my name, I am there among them."

THE PARABLE OF THE UNFORGIVING SERVANT

²¹ Then Peter approached him and asked, "Lord, how many times shall I forgive my brother or sister who sins against me? As many as seven times?"

²² "I tell you, not as many as seven," Jesus replied, "but seventy times seven.[E]

²³ "For this reason, the kingdom of heaven can be compared to a king who wanted to settle accounts with his servants. ²⁴ When he began to settle accounts, one who owed ten thousand talents[F] was brought before him. ²⁵ Since he did not have the money to pay it back, his master commanded that he, his wife, his children, and everything he had be sold to pay the debt.

²⁶ "At this, the servant fell facedown before him and said, 'Be patient with me, and I will pay you everything.' ²⁷ Then the master of that servant had compassion, released him, and forgave him the loan.

²⁸ "That servant went out and found one of his fellow servants who owed him a hundred denarii.[G] He grabbed him, started choking him, and said, 'Pay what you owe!'

²⁹ "At this, his fellow servant fell down[H] and began begging him, 'Be patient with me, and I will pay you back.' ³⁰ But he wasn't willing. Instead, he went and threw him into prison until he could pay what was owed. ³¹ When the other servants saw what had taken place, they were deeply distressed and went and reported to their master everything that had happened. ³² Then, after he had summoned him, his master said to him, 'You wicked servant! I forgave you all that debt because you begged me. ³³ Shouldn't you also have had mercy on your fellow servant, as I had mercy on you?' ³⁴ And because he was angry, his master handed him over to the jailers to be tortured until he could pay everything that was owed. ³⁵ So also my heavenly Father will do to you unless every one of you forgives his brother or sister[I] from your[J] heart."

THE QUESTION OF DIVORCE

19 When Jesus had finished saying these things, he departed from Galilee and went to the region of Judea across the Jordan. ² Large crowds followed him, and he healed them there. ³ Some Pharisees approached him to test him. They asked, "Is it lawful for a man to divorce his wife on any grounds?"

⁴ "Haven't you read," he replied, "that he who created[K] them in the beginning **made them male and female,[L]** ⁵ and he also said, '**For this reason a man will leave his father and mother and be joined to his wife, and the**

[A]18:18 Or *earth will be bound* [B]18:18 Or *earth will be loosed* [C]18:19 Lit *they*
[D]18:19 Lit *for them* [E]18:22 Or *but seventy-seven times* [F]18:24 A talent is worth about 6,000 denarii, or twenty years' wages for a laborer [G]18:28 A denarius = one day's wage [H]18:29 Other mss add *at his feet* [I]18:35 Other mss add *their trespasses* [J]18:35 Lit *his* [K]19:4 Other mss read *made* [L]19:4 Gn 1:27; 5:2

two will become one flesh'?[A] 6 So they are no longer two, but one flesh. Therefore, what God has joined together, let no one separate."

7 "Why then," they asked him, "did Moses command us to give divorce papers and to send her away?"

8 He told them, "Moses permitted you to divorce your wives because of the hardness of your hearts, but it was not like that from the beginning. 9 I tell you, whoever divorces his wife, except for sexual immorality, and marries another commits adultery."[B]

10 His disciples said to him, "If the relationship of a man with his wife is like this, it's better not to marry."

11 He responded, "Not everyone can accept this saying, but only those to whom it has been given. 12 For there are eunuchs who were born that way from their mother's womb, there are eunuchs who were made by men, and there are eunuchs who have made themselves that way because of the kingdom of heaven. The one who is able to accept it should accept it."

BLESSING THE CHILDREN

13 Then children were brought to Jesus for him to place his hands on them and pray, but the disciples rebuked them. 14 Jesus said, "Leave the children alone, and don't try to keep them from coming to me, because the kingdom of heaven belongs to such as these."[C] 15 After placing his hands on them, he went on from there.

THE RICH YOUNG RULER

16 Just then someone came up and asked him, "Teacher, what good must I do to have eternal life?"

17 "Why do you ask me about what is good?"[D] he said to him. "There is only one who is good.[E] If you want to enter into life, keep the commandments."

18 "Which ones?" he asked him.

Jesus answered: **Do not murder; do not commit adultery; do not steal; do not bear false witness;** 19 **honor your father and your mother; and love your neighbor as yourself.**[F]

20 "I have kept all these,"[G] the young man told him. "What do I still lack?"

21 "If you want to be perfect,"[H] Jesus said to him, "go, sell your belongings and give to the poor, and you will have treasure in heaven. Then come, follow me."

22 When the young man heard that, he went away grieving, because he had many possessions.

POSSESSIONS AND THE KINGDOM

23 Jesus said to his disciples, "Truly I tell you, it will be hard for a rich person to enter the kingdom of heaven. 24 Again I tell you, it is easier for a camel to go through the eye of a needle than for a rich person to enter the kingdom of God."

[A]19:5 Gn 2:24 [B]19:9 Other mss add *Also whoever marries a divorced woman commits adultery*; Mt 5:32 [C]19:14 Lit *heaven is of such ones* [D]19:17 Other mss read *"Why do you call me good?"* [E]19:17 Other mss read *"No one is good but one — God* [F]19:18-19 Ex 20:12-16; Lv 19:18; Dt 5:16-20 [G]19:20 Other mss add *from my youth* [H]19:21 Or *complete*

²⁵ When the disciples heard this, they were utterly astonished and asked, "Then who can be saved?"

²⁶ Jesus looked at them and said, "With man this is impossible, but with God all things are possible."

²⁷ Then Peter responded to him, "See, we have left everything and followed you. So what will there be for us?"

²⁸ Jesus said to them, "Truly I tell you, in the renewal of all things, when the Son of Man sits on his glorious throne, you who have followed me will also sit on twelve thrones, judging the twelve tribes of Israel. ²⁹ And everyone who has left houses or brothers or sisters or father or motherᴬ or children or fields because of my name will receive a hundred times more and will inherit eternal life. ³⁰ But many who are first will be last, and the last first.

THE PARABLE OF THE VINEYARD WORKERS

20 "For the kingdom of heaven is like a landowner who went out early in the morning to hire workers for his vineyard. ² After agreeing with the workers on one denarius,ᴮ he sent them into his vineyard for the day. ³ When he went out about nine in the morning,ᶜ he saw others standing in the marketplace doing nothing. ⁴ He said to them, 'You also go into my vineyard, and I'll give you whatever is right.' So off they went. ⁵ About noon and about three,ᴰ he went out again and did the same thing. ⁶ Then about fiveᴱ he went and found others standing aroundᶠ and said to them, 'Why have you been standing here all day doing nothing?'

⁷ " 'Because no one hired us,' they said to him.

" 'You also go into my vineyard,' he told them.ᴳ ⁸ When evening came, the owner of the vineyard told his foreman, 'Call the workers and give them their pay, starting with the last and ending with the first.'

⁹ "When those who were hired about five came, they each received one denarius. ¹⁰ So when the first ones came, they assumed they would get more, but they also received a denarius each. ¹¹ When they received it, they began to complain to the landowner: ¹² 'These last men put in one hour, and you made them equal to us who bore the burden of the day's work and the burning heat.'

¹³ "He replied to one of them, 'Friend, I'm doing you no wrong. Didn't you agree with me on a denarius? ¹⁴ Take what's yours and go. I want to give this last man the same as I gave you. ¹⁵ Don't I have the right to do what I want with what is mine? Are you jealousᴴ because I'm generous?'ᴵ

¹⁶ "So the last will be first, and the first last."ᴶ

THE THIRD PREDICTION OF HIS DEATH

¹⁷ While going up to Jerusalem, Jesus took the twelve disciples aside privately and said to them on the way, ¹⁸ "See, we are going up to Jerusalem. The Son of Man will be handed over to the chief priests and scribes, and they

---

ᴬ19:29 Other mss add *or wife* ᴮ20:2 A denarius = one day's wage, also in vv. 9,10,13 ᶜ20:3 Lit *about the third hour* ᴰ20:5 Lit *about the sixth hour and the ninth hour* ᴱ20:6 Lit *about the eleventh hour*, also in v. 9 ᶠ20:6 Other mss add *doing nothing* ᴳ20:7 Other mss add *'and you'll get whatever is right.'*
ᴴ20:15 Lit *Is your eye evil*; an idiom for jealousy or stinginess ᴵ20:15 Lit *good*
ᴶ20:16 Other mss add *"For many are called, but few are chosen."*

will condemn him to death. ¹⁹ They will hand him over to the Gentiles to be mocked, flogged, ᴬ and crucified, and on the third day he will be raised. "ᴮ

SUFFERING AND SERVICE

²⁰ Then the mother of Zebedee's sons approached him with her sons. She knelt down to ask him for something. ²¹ "What do you want?" he asked her.

"Promise," ᶜ she said to him, "that these two sons of mine may sit, one on your right and the other on your left, in your kingdom."

²² Jesus answered, "You don't know what you're asking. Are you able to drink the cup that I am about to drink?" ᴰ

"We are able," they said to him.

²³ He told them, "You will indeed drink my cup, ᴱ but to sit at my right and left is not mine to give; instead, it is for those for whom it has been prepared by my Father."

²⁴ When the ten disciples heard this, they became indignant with the two brothers. ²⁵ Jesus called them over and said, "You know that the rulers of the Gentiles lord it over them, and those in high positions act as tyrants over them. ²⁶ It must not be like that among you. On the contrary, whoever wants to become great among you must be your servant, ²⁷ and whoever wants to be first among you must be your slave; ²⁸ just as the Son of Man did not come to be served, but to serve, and to give his life as a ransom for many."

TWO BLIND MEN HEALED

²⁹ As they were leaving Jericho, a large crowd followed him. ³⁰ There were two blind men sitting by the road. When they heard that Jesus was passing by, they cried out, "Lord, have mercy on us, Son of David!" ³¹ The crowd demanded that they keep quiet, but they cried out all the more, "Lord, have mercy on us, Son of David!"

³² Jesus stopped, called them, and said, "What do you want me to do for you?"

³³ "Lord," they said to him, "open our eyes." ³⁴ Moved with compassion, Jesus touched their eyes. Immediately they could see, and they followed him.

THE TRIUMPHAL ENTRY

21 When they approached Jerusalem and came to Bethphage at the Mount of Olives, Jesus then sent two disciples, ² telling them, "Go into the village ahead of you. At once you will find a donkey tied there with her colt. Untie them and bring them to me. ³ If anyone says anything to you, say that the Lord needs them, and he will send them at once."

⁴ This took place so that what was spoken through the prophet might be fulfilled:

⁵   Tell Daughter Zion,
    "See, your King is coming to you,
    gentle, and mounted on a donkey,
    and on a colt,
    the foal of a donkey."ᶠ

ᴬ20:19 Or *scourged*   ᴮ20:19 Other mss read *will rise again*   ᶜ20:21 Lit *Say*
ᴰ20:22 Other mss add *and (or) to be baptized with the baptism which I am baptized?"*   ᴱ20:23 Other mss add *and be baptized with the baptism with which I am baptized.*   ᶠ21:5 Is 62:11; Zch 9:9

HOSANNA

MATTHEW 21–22; REVELATION 7:9-12

Only Jesus knew the gravity of what the crowd was asking when they shouted "Hosanna!" that day.

It was a shout of adoration but it was also a plea, because the word "Hosanna" literally means, "Come save us now!" And this is exactly what He would do.

The next day, Jesus walked into the temple, flipping over tables and tossing money to the floor. The hosanna-shouters must have been shocked to see the man on the donkey driving the sellers out of the temple with such authority. "My house will be called a house of prayer," Jesus said to them. "But you are making it a den of thieves!" (Mt 21:13).

But it's what He did next that was truly radical: He invited the least inside.

The blind, the lame, the children all came in and Jesus welcomed them, healed them, and confirmed their place with Him (Mt 21:14-15). He cleared out those who had profaned the temple and ushered in those who humbly sought after God.

When I picture the scene I can see myself in the wings, on the outside looking in. I am nervous, I am afraid, but I am drawn to this house of God, and so I watch and wait. Those inside seem to have it together, bringing riches rather than sacrifice, doing religion like a business.

All I have is this humble offering in my hands carried the long journey from my home, over rocky roads and mistake-laden miles.

Then I see Him. And right before my eyes I watch Him turn it on its side, all the pretension and injustice and darkness that kept me at bay. He sends out those who've come not for God but for gods.

And then? He looks me in the eye. Me. Lame, frightened, filthy from days of travel. He looks at me and sees me. He motions for me to come in and then He tells me I belong.

I had cried out "Hosanna! Save me!" not knowing what I was really asking. And He rode on through the streets and into the city, knowing exactly what was coming. He would soon die, but not before He cleansed His house of prayer and invited me in.

This is our Christ! He welcomes in the defenseless and He becomes their defense. He brings the weak to Himself and makes them strong. He desires not the shiny sacrifices our pride wishes to bring, but only a heart that is stayed on Him. He saves us when we call out to Him.

Only He knows what our hearts truly need as we cry out, "Hosanna!" He knew it even then.

⁶ The disciples went and did just as Jesus directed them. ⁷ They brought the donkey and the colt; then they laid their clothes on them, and he sat on them. ⁸ A very large crowd spread their clothes on the road; others were cutting branches from the trees and spreading them on the road. ⁹ Then the crowds who went ahead of him and those who followed shouted:

Hosanna to the Son of David!

Blessed is he who comes in the name of the Lord![A]

Hosanna in the highest heaven!

¹⁰ When he entered Jerusalem, the whole city was in an uproar, saying, "Who is this?" ¹¹ The crowds were saying, "This is the prophet Jesus from Nazareth in Galilee."

CLEANSING THE TEMPLE

¹² Jesus went into the temple[B] and threw out all those buying and selling. He overturned the tables of the money changers and the chairs of those selling doves. ¹³ He said to them, "It is written, **my house will be called a house of prayer,**[C] but you are making it **a den of thieves!**"[D]

CHILDREN PRAISE JESUS

¹⁴ The blind and the lame came to him in the temple, and he healed them. ¹⁵ When the chief priests and the scribes saw the wonders that he did and the children shouting in the temple, "*Hosanna* to the Son of David!" they were indignant ¹⁶ and said to him, "Do you hear what these children are saying?"

Jesus replied, "Yes, have you never read:

You have prepared[E] **praise**

from the mouths of infants and nursing babies?"[F]

¹⁷ Then he left them, went out of the city to Bethany, and spent the night there.

THE BARREN FIG TREE

¹⁸ Early in the morning, as he was returning to the city, he was hungry. ¹⁹ Seeing a lone fig tree by the road, he went up to it and found nothing on it except leaves. And he said to it, "May no fruit ever come from you again!" At once the fig tree withered.

²⁰ When the disciples saw it, they were amazed and said, "How did the fig tree wither so quickly?"

²¹ Jesus answered them, "Truly I tell you, if you have faith and do not doubt, you will not only do what was done to the fig tree, but even if you tell this mountain, 'Be lifted up and thrown into the sea,' it will be done. ²² And if you believe, you will receive whatever you ask for in prayer."

THE AUTHORITY OF JESUS CHALLENGED

²³ When he entered the temple, the chief priests and the elders of the people came to him as he was teaching and said, "By what authority are you doing these things? Who gave you this authority?"

[A]21:9 Ps 118:25-26 [B]21:12 Other mss add *of God* [C]21:13 Is 56:7
[D]21:13 Jr 7:11 [E]21:16 Or *restored* [F]21:16 Ps 8:2

24 Jesus answered them, "I will also ask you one question, and if you answer it for me, then I will tell you by what authority I do these things. 25 Did John's baptism come from heaven, or was it of human origin?"

They discussed it among themselves, "If we say, 'From heaven,' he will say to us, 'Then why didn't you believe him?' 26 But if we say, 'Of human origin,' we're afraid of the crowd, because everyone considers John to be a prophet." 27 So they answered Jesus, "We don't know."

And he said to them, "Neither will I tell you by what authority I do these things.

THE PARABLE OF THE TWO SONS

28 "What do you think? A man had two sons. He went to the first and said, 'My son, go work in the vineyard today.'

29 "He answered, 'I don't want to,' but later he changed his mind and went. 30 Then the man went to the other and said the same thing. 'I will, sir,' he answered, but he didn't go. 31 Which of the two did his father's will?"

They said, "The first."

Jesus said to them, "Truly I tell you, tax collectors and prostitutes are entering the kingdom of God before you. 32 For John came to you in the way of righteousness, and you didn't believe him. Tax collectors and prostitutes did believe him; but you, when you saw it, didn't even change your minds then and believe him.

THE PARABLE OF THE VINEYARD OWNER

33 "Listen to another parable: There was a landowner, who planted a vineyard, put a fence around it, dug a winepress in it, and built a watchtower. He leased it to tenant farmers and went away. 34 When the time came to harvest fruit, he sent his servants to the farmers to collect his fruit. 35 The farmers took his servants, beat one, killed another, and stoned a third. 36 Again, he sent other servants, more than the first group, and they did the same to them. 37 Finally, he sent his son to them. 'They will respect my son,' he said.

38 "But when the tenant farmers saw the son, they said to each other, 'This is the heir. Come, let's kill him and take his inheritance.' 39 So they seized him, threw him out of the vineyard, and killed him. 40 Therefore, when the owner of the vineyard comes, what will he do to those farmers?"

41 "He will completely destroy those terrible men," they told him, "and lease his vineyard to other farmers who will give him his fruit at the harvest."

42 Jesus said to them, "Have you never read in the Scriptures:

**The stone that the builders rejected
has become the cornerstone.** A
**This is what the Lord has done
and it is wonderful in our eyes?** B

43 Therefore I tell you, the kingdom of God will be taken away from you and given to a people producing its fruit. 44 Whoever falls on this stone will be broken to pieces; but on whomever it falls, it will shatter him." C

A 21:42 Lit *the head of the corner*   B 21:42 Ps 118:22-23   C 21:44 Some mss omit this verse

⁴⁵ When the chief priests and the Pharisees heard his parables, they knew he was speaking about them. ⁴⁶ Although they were looking for a way to arrest him, they feared the crowds, because the people regarded him as a prophet.

THE PARABLE OF THE WEDDING BANQUET

22 Once more Jesus spoke to them in parables: ² "The kingdom of heaven is like a king who gave a wedding banquet for his son. ³ He sent his servants to summon those invited to the banquet, but they didn't want to come. ⁴ Again, he sent out other servants and said, 'Tell those who are invited: See, I've prepared my dinner; my oxen and fattened cattle have been slaughtered, and everything is ready. Come to the wedding banquet.'

⁵ "But they paid no attention and went away, one to his own farm, another to his business, ⁶ while the rest seized his servants, mistreated them, and killed them. ⁷ The king ᴬ was enraged, and he sent out his troops, killed those murderers, and burned down their city.

⁸ "Then he told his servants, 'The banquet is ready, but those who were invited were not worthy. ⁹ Go then to where the roads exit the city and invite everyone you find to the banquet.' ¹⁰ So those servants went out on the roads and gathered everyone they found, both evil and good. The wedding banquet ᴮ was filled with guests. ᶜ ¹¹ When the king came in to see the guests, he saw a man there who was not dressed for a wedding. ¹² So he said to him, 'Friend, how did you get in here without wedding clothes?' The man was speechless.

¹³ "Then the king told the attendants, 'Tie him up hand and foot, ᴰ and throw him into the outer darkness, where there will be weeping and gnashing of teeth.'

¹⁴ "For many are invited, but few are chosen."

GOD AND CAESAR

¹⁵ Then the Pharisees went and plotted how to trap him by what he said. ᴱ ¹⁶ So they sent their disciples to him, along with the Herodians. "Teacher," they said, "we know that you are truthful and teach truthfully the way of God. You don't care what anyone thinks nor do you show partiality. ᶠ ¹⁷ Tell us, then, what you think. Is it lawful to pay taxes to Caesar or not?"

¹⁸ Perceiving their malicious intent, Jesus said, "Why are you testing me, hypocrites? ¹⁹ Show me the coin used for the tax." They brought him a denarius. ᴳ ²⁰ "Whose image and inscription is this?" he asked them.

²¹ "Caesar's," they said to him.

Then he said to them, "Give, then, to Caesar the things that are Caesar's, and to God the things that are God's." ²² When they heard this, they were amazed. So they left him and went away.

THE SADDUCEES AND THE RESURRECTION

²³ That same day some Sadducees, who say there is no resurrection, came up to him and questioned him: ²⁴ "Teacher, Moses said, **if a man dies, having no children, his brother is to marry his wife and raise up offspring for his brother.** ᴴ ²⁵ Now there were seven brothers among us. The first got

---

ᴬ22:7 Other mss read *But when the (that) king heard about it he*   ᴮ22:10 Other mss read *wedding hall*   ᶜ22:10 Lit *those reclining* (to eat)   ᴰ22:13 Other mss add *take him away*   ᴱ22:15 Lit *trap him in a word*   ᶠ22:16 Lit *don't look on the face of men*   ᴳ22:19 A denarius = one day's wage   ᴴ22:24 Dt 25:5

married and died. Having no offspring, he left his wife to his brother. [26] The same thing happened to the second also, and the third, and so on to all seven. [27] Last of all, the woman died. [28] In the resurrection, then, whose wife will she be of the seven? For they all had married her."[A]

[29] Jesus answered them, "You are mistaken, because you don't know the Scriptures or the power of God. [30] For in the resurrection they neither marry nor are given in marriage but are like[B] angels in heaven. [31] Now concerning the resurrection of the dead, haven't you read what was spoken to you by God: [32] **I am the God of Abraham and the God of Isaac and the God of Jacob?**[C] He[D] is not the God of the dead, but of the living."

[33] And when the crowds heard this, they were astonished at his teaching.

THE PRIMARY COMMANDS

[34] When the Pharisees heard that he had silenced the Sadducees, they came together. [35] And one of them, an expert in the law, asked a question to test him: [36] "Teacher, which command in the law is the greatest?"

[37] He said to him, "**Love the Lord your God with all your heart, with all your soul, and with all your mind.**[E] [38] This is the greatest and most important[F] command. [39] The second is like it: **Love your neighbor as yourself.**[G] [40] All the Law and the Prophets depend[H] on these two commands."

THE QUESTION ABOUT THE CHRIST

[41] While the Pharisees were together, Jesus questioned them, [42] "What do you think about the Messiah? Whose son is he?"

They replied, "David's."

[43] He asked them, "How is it then that David, inspired by the Spirit,[I] calls him 'Lord':

[44]   **The Lord declared to my Lord,**
      'Sit at my right hand
      until I put your enemies under your feet'?[J,K]

[45] "If David calls him 'Lord,' how then can he be his son?" [46] No one was able to answer him at all,[L] and from that day no one dared to question him anymore.

RELIGIOUS HYPOCRITES DENOUNCED

23 Then Jesus spoke to the crowds and to his disciples: [2] "The scribes and the Pharisees are seated in the chair of Moses. [3] Therefore do whatever they tell you, and observe it. But don't do what they do, because they don't practice what they teach. [4] They tie up heavy loads that are hard to carry[M] and put them on people's shoulders, but they themselves aren't willing to lift a finger to move them. [5] They do everything[N] to be seen by others: They enlarge their phylacteries and lengthen their tassels.[O] [6] They love the place of honor at banquets, the front seats in the synagogues, [7] greetings in the marketplaces, and to be called 'Rabbi' by people.

[A]22:28 Lit all had her   [B]22:30 Other mss add God's   [C]22:32 Ex 3:6,15-16
[D]22:32 Other mss read God   [E]22:37 Dt 6:5   [F]22:38 Lit and first
[G]22:39 Lv 19:18   [H]22:40 Or hang   [I]22:43 Lit David in Spirit   [J]22:44 Other
mss read until I make your enemies your footstool'   [K]22:44 Ps 110:1   [L]22:46 Lit
answer him a word   [M]23:4 Other mss omit that are hard to carry   [N]23:5 Lit do
all their works   [O]23:5 Other mss add on their robes

⁸ "But you are not to be called 'Rabbi,' because you have one Teacher,ᴬ and you are all brothers and sisters. ⁹ Do not call anyone on earth your father, because you have one Father, who is in heaven. ¹⁰ You are not to be called instructors either, because you have one Instructor, the Messiah. ¹¹ The greatest among you will be your servant. ¹² Whoever exalts himself will be humbled, and whoever humbles himself will be exalted.

¹³ "Woe to you, scribes and Pharisees, hypocrites! You shut the door of the kingdom of heaven in people's faces. For you don't go in, and you don't allow those entering to go in.ᴮ

¹⁵ "Woe to you, scribes and Pharisees, hypocrites! You travel over land and sea to make one convert, and when he becomes one, you make him twice as fit for hellᶜ as you are!

¹⁶ "Woe to you, blind guides, who say, 'Whoever takes an oath by the temple, it means nothing. But whoever takes an oath by the gold of the temple is bound by his oath.'ᴰ ¹⁷ Blind fools! For which is greater, the gold or the temple that sanctified the gold? ¹⁸ Also, 'Whoever takes an oath by the altar, it means nothing; but whoever takes an oath by the gift that is on it is bound by his oath.' ¹⁹ Blind people!ᴱ For which is greater, the gift or the altar that sanctifies the gift? ²⁰ Therefore, the one who takes an oath by the altar takes an oath by it and by everything on it. ²¹ The one who takes an oath by the temple takes an oath by it and by him who dwells in it. ²² And the one who takes an oath by heaven takes an oath by God's throne and by him who sits on it.

²³ "Woe to you, scribes and Pharisees, hypocrites! You pay a tenth ofᶠ mint, dill, and cumin, and yet you have neglected the more important matters of the law — justice, mercy, and faithfulness.ᴳ These things should have been done without neglecting the others. ²⁴ Blind guides! You strain out a gnat, but gulp down a camel!

²⁵ "Woe to you, scribes and Pharisees, hypocrites! You clean the outside of the cup and dish, but inside they are full of greedᴴ and self-indulgence. ²⁶ Blind Pharisee! First clean the inside of the cup,ᴵ so that the outside of itᴶ may also become clean.

²⁷ "Woe to you, scribes and Pharisees, hypocrites! You are like whitewashed tombs, which appear beautiful on the outside, but inside are full of the bones of the dead and every kind of impurity. ²⁸ In the same way, on the outside you seem righteous to people, but inside you are full of hypocrisy and lawlessness.

²⁹ "Woe to you, scribes and Pharisees, hypocrites! You build the tombs of the prophets and decorate the graves of the righteous, ³⁰ and you say, 'If we had lived in the days of our ancestors, we wouldn't have taken part with them in shedding the prophets' blood.' ³¹ So you testify against yourselves that you are descendants of those who murdered the prophets. ³² Fill up, then, the measure of your ancestors' sins!

ᴬ23:8 Other mss add *the Christ* ᴮ23:13 Some mss include v. 14: *"Woe to you, scribes and Pharisees, hypocrites! You devour widows' houses and make long prayers just for show. This is why you will receive a harsher punishment.*
ᶜ23:15 Lit *twice the son of gehenna* ᴰ23:16 Lit *is obligated*, also in v. 18
ᴱ23:19 Other mss read *Fools and blind* ᶠ23:23 Or *You tithe* ᴳ23:23 Or *faith*
ᴴ23:25 Or *full of violence* ᴵ23:26 Other mss add *and dish* ᴶ23:26 Other mss read *of them*

[33] "Snakes! Brood of vipers! How can you escape being condemned to hell?[A] [34] This is why I am sending you prophets, sages, and scribes. Some of them you will kill and crucify, and some of them you will flog in your synagogues and pursue from town to town. [35] So all the righteous blood shed on the earth will be charged to you,[B] from the blood of righteous Abel to the blood of Zechariah, son of Berechiah, whom you murdered between the sanctuary and the altar. [36] Truly I tell you, all these things will come on this generation.

JESUS'S LAMENTING OVER JERUSALEM

[37] "Jerusalem, Jerusalem, who kills the prophets and stones those who are sent to her. How often I wanted to gather your children together, as a hen gathers her chicks[C] under her wings, but you were not willing! [38] See, your house is left to you desolate. [39] For I tell you, you will not see me again until you say, '**Blessed is he who comes in the name of the Lord**'!"[D]

DESTRUCTION OF THE TEMPLE PREDICTED

24 As Jesus left and was going out of the temple, his disciples came up and called his attention to its buildings. [2] He replied to them, "Do you see all these things? Truly I tell you, not one stone will be left here on another that will not be thrown down."

SIGNS OF THE END OF THE AGE

[3] While he was sitting on the Mount of Olives, the disciples approached him privately and said, "Tell us, when will these things happen? And what is the sign of your coming and of the end of the age?"

[4] Jesus replied to them: "Watch out that no one deceives you. [5] For many will come in my name, saying, 'I am the Messiah,' and they will deceive many. [6] You are going to hear of wars and rumors of wars. See that you are not alarmed, because these things must take place, but the end is not yet. [7] For nation will rise up against nation, and kingdom against kingdom. There will be famines[E] and earthquakes in various places. [8] All these events are the beginning of labor pains.

PERSECUTIONS PREDICTED

[9] "Then they will hand you over to be persecuted, and they will kill you. You will be hated by all nations because of my name. [10] Then many will fall away, betray one another, and hate one another. [11] Many false prophets will rise up and deceive many. [12] Because lawlessness will multiply, the love of many will grow cold. [13] But the one who endures to the end will be saved. [14] This good news of the kingdom will be proclaimed in all the world[F] as a testimony to all nations, and then the end will come.

THE GREAT TRIBULATION

[15] "So when you see **the abomination of desolation**,[G] spoken of by the prophet Daniel, standing in the holy place" (let the reader understand), [16] "then

---

[A]23:33 Lit escape from the judgment of gehenna   [B]23:35 Lit will come on you
[C]23:37 Or as a mother bird gathers her young   [D]23:39 Ps 118:26   [E]24:7 Other mss add epidemics   [F]24:14 Or in all the inhabited earth   [G]24:15 Dn 9:27

those in Judea must flee to the mountains. [17] A man on the housetop[A] must not come down to get things out of his house, [18] and a man in the field must not go back to get his coat. [19] Woe to pregnant women and nursing mothers in those days! [20] Pray that your escape may not be in winter or on a Sabbath. [21] For at that time there will be great distress, [B] the kind that hasn't taken place from the beginning of the world until now and never will again. [22] Unless those days were cut short, no one would[C] be saved. But those days will be cut short because of the elect.

[23] "If anyone tells you then, 'See, here is the Messiah!' or, 'Over here!' do not believe it. [24] For false messiahs and false prophets will arise and perform great signs and wonders to lead astray, if possible, even the elect. [25] Take note: I have told you in advance. [26] So if they tell you, 'See, he's in the wilderness!' don't go out; or, 'See, he's in the storerooms!' do not believe it. [27] For as the lightning comes from the east and flashes as far as the west, so will be the coming of the Son of Man. [28] Wherever the carcass is, there the vultures[D] will gather.

THE COMING OF THE SON OF MAN

[29] "Immediately after the distress of those days, the sun will be darkened, and the moon will not shed its light; the stars will fall from the sky, and the powers of the heavens will be shaken. [30] Then the sign of the Son of Man will appear in the sky, and then all the peoples of the earth[E] will mourn;[F] and they will see the Son of Man coming on the clouds of heaven with power and great glory. [31] He will send out his angels with a loud trumpet, and they will gather his elect from the four winds, from one end of the sky to the other.

THE PARABLE OF THE FIG TREE

[32] "Learn this lesson from the fig tree: As soon as its branch becomes tender and sprouts leaves, you know that summer is near. [33] In the same way, when you see all these things, recognize[G] that he[H] is near — at the door. [34] Truly I tell you, this generation will certainly not pass away until all these things take place. [35] Heaven and earth will pass away, but my words will never pass away.

NO ONE KNOWS THE DAY OR HOUR

[36] "Now concerning that day and hour no one knows — neither the angels of heaven nor the Son[I] — except the Father alone. [37] As the days of Noah were, so the coming of the Son of Man will be. [38] For in those days before the flood they were eating and drinking, marrying and giving in marriage, until the day Noah boarded the ark. [39] They didn't know until the flood came and swept them all away. This is the way the coming of the Son of Man will be. [40] Then two men will be in the field; one will be taken and one left. [41] Two women will be grinding grain with a hand mill; one will be taken and one left. [42] Therefore be alert, since you don't know what day[J] your Lord is coming. [43] But know this: If the homeowner had known what time[K] the thief was

---

[A]24:17 Or roof   [B]24:21 Or tribulation, also in v. 29   [C]24:22 Lit short, all flesh would not   [D]24:28 Or eagles   [E]24:30 Or all the tribes of the land   [F]24:30 Lit will beat; that is, beat their chests   [G]24:33 Or things, you know   [H]24:33 Or it; that is, summer   [I]24:36 Other mss omit nor the Son   [J]24:42 Other mss read hour; = time   [K]24:43 Lit watch; a division of the night in ancient times coming, he would have stayed alert and not let his house be broken into. [44] This is why you are also to be ready, because the Son of Man is coming at an hour you do not expect.

FAITHFUL SERVICE TO CHRIST

[45] "Who then is a faithful and wise servant, whom his master has put in charge of his household, to give them food at the proper time? [46] Blessed is that servant whom the master finds doing his job when he comes. [47] Truly I tell you, he will put him in charge of all his possessions. [48] But if that wicked servant says in his heart, 'My master is delayed,' [49] and starts to beat his fellow servants, and eats and drinks with drunkards, [50] that servant's master will come on a day he does not expect him and at an hour he does not know. [51] He will cut him to pieces and assign him a place with the hypocrites, where there will be weeping and gnashing of teeth.

THE PARABLE OF THE TEN VIRGINS

25 "At that time the kingdom of heaven will be like ten virgins[A] who took their lamps[B] and went out to meet the groom. [2] Five of them were foolish and five were wise. [3] When the foolish took their lamps, they didn't take oil with them; [4] but the wise ones took oil in their flasks with their lamps. [5] When the groom was delayed, they all became drowsy and fell asleep.

[6] "In the middle of the night there was a shout: 'Here's the groom! Come out to meet him.'

[7] "Then all the virgins got up and trimmed their lamps. [8] The foolish ones said to the wise ones, 'Give us some of your oil, because our lamps are going out.'

[9] "The wise ones answered, 'No, there won't be enough for us and for you. Go instead to those who sell oil, and buy some for yourselves.'

[10] "When they had gone to buy some, the groom arrived, and those who were ready went in with him to the wedding banquet, and the door was shut. [11] Later the rest of the virgins also came and said, 'Master, master, open up for us!'

[12] "He replied, 'Truly I tell you, I don't know you!'

[13] "Therefore be alert, because you don't know either the day or the hour.[C]

THE PARABLE OF THE TALENTS

[14] "For it is just like a man about to go on a journey. He called his own servants and entrusted his possessions to them. [15] To one he gave five talents,[D] to another two talents, and to another one talent, depending on each one's ability. Then he went on a journey. Immediately [16] the man who had received five talents went, put them to work, and earned five more. [17] In the same way the man with two earned two more. [18] But the man who had received one talent went off, dug a hole in the ground, and hid his master's money.

[19] "After a long time the master of those servants came and settled accounts with them. [20] The man who had received five talents approached, presented five more talents, and said, 'Master, you gave me five talents. See, I've earned five more talents.'

[A]25:1 Or *bridesmaids* [B]25:1 Or *torches*, also in vv. 3,4,7,8 [C]25:13 Other mss add *in which the Son of Man is coming.* [D]25:15 A talent is worth about 6,000 denarii, or twenty years' wages for a laborer

²¹ "His master said to him, 'Well done, good and faithful servant! You were faithful over a few things; I will put you in charge of many things. Share your master's joy.'

²² "The man with two talents also approached. He said, 'Master, you gave me two talents. See, I've earned two more talents.'

²³ "His master said to him, 'Well done, good and faithful servant! You were faithful over a few things; I will put you in charge of many things. Share your master's joy.'

²⁴ "The man who had received one talent also approached and said, 'Master, I know you. You're a harsh man, reaping where you haven't sown and gathering where you haven't scattered seed. ²⁵ So I was afraid and went off and hid your talent in the ground. See, you have what is yours.'

²⁶ "His master replied to him, 'You evil, lazy servant! If you knew that I reap where I haven't sown and gather where I haven't scattered, ²⁷ then^A you should have deposited my money with the bankers, and I would have received my money^B back with interest when I returned.

²⁸ " 'So take the talent from him and give it to the one who has ten talents. ²⁹ For to everyone who has, more will be given, and he will have more than enough. But from the one who does not have, even what he has will be taken away from him. ³⁰ And throw this good-for-nothing servant into the outer darkness, where there will be weeping and gnashing of teeth.'

THE SHEEP AND THE GOATS

³¹ "When the Son of Man comes in his glory, and all the angels^C with him, then he will sit on his glorious throne. ³² All the nations^D will be gathered before him, and he will separate them one from another, just as a shepherd separates the sheep from the goats. ³³ He will put the sheep on his right and the goats on the left. ³⁴ Then the King will say to those on his right, 'Come, you who are blessed by my Father; inherit the kingdom prepared for you from the foundation of the world.

³⁵ " 'For I was hungry and you gave me something to eat; I was thirsty and you gave me something to drink; I was a stranger and you took me in; ³⁶ I was naked and you clothed me; I was sick and you took care of me; I was in prison and you visited me.'

³⁷ "Then the righteous will answer him, 'Lord, when did we see you hungry and feed you, or thirsty and give you something to drink? ³⁸ When did we see you a stranger and take you in, or without clothes and clothe you? ³⁹ When did we see you sick, or in prison, and visit you?'

⁴⁰ "And the King will answer them, 'Truly I tell you, whatever you did for one of the least of these brothers and sisters of mine, you did for me.'

⁴¹ "Then he will also say to those on the left, 'Depart from me, you who are cursed, into the eternal fire prepared for the devil and his angels! ⁴² For I was hungry and you gave me nothing to eat; I was thirsty and you gave me nothing to drink; ⁴³ I was a stranger and you didn't take me in; I was naked and you didn't clothe me, sick and in prison and you didn't take care of me.'

---

^A 25:26-27 Or So you knew . . . scattered? Then (as a question) ^B 25:27 Lit received what is mine ^C 25:31 Other mss read holy angels ^D 25:32 Or the Gentiles

[44] "Then they too will answer, 'Lord, when did we see you hungry, or thirsty, or a stranger, or without clothes, or sick, or in prison, and not help you?'

[45] "Then he will answer them, 'Truly I tell you, whatever you did not do for one of the least of these, you did not do for me.'

[46] "And they will go away into eternal punishment, but the righteous into eternal life."

THE PLOT TO KILL JESUS

26 When Jesus had finished saying all these things, he told his disciples, [2] "You know[A] that the Passover takes place after two days, and the Son of Man will be handed over to be crucified."

[3] Then the chief priests[B] and the elders of the people assembled in the courtyard of the high priest, who was named Caiaphas, [4] and they conspired to arrest Jesus in a treacherous way and kill him. [5] "Not during the festival," they said, "so there won't be rioting among the people."

THE ANOINTING AT BETHANY

[6] While Jesus was in Bethany at the house of Simon the leper,[C] [7] a woman approached him with an alabaster jar of very expensive perfume. She poured it on his head as he was reclining at the table. [8] When the disciples saw it, they were indignant. "Why this waste?" they asked. [9] "This might have been sold for a great deal and given to the poor."

[10] Aware of this, Jesus said to them, "Why are you bothering this woman? She has done a noble thing for me. [11] You always have the poor with you, but you do not always have me. [12] By pouring this perfume on my body, she has prepared me for burial. [13] Truly I tell you, wherever this gospel is proclaimed in the whole world, what she has done will also be told in memory of her."

[14] Then one of the Twelve, the man called Judas Iscariot, went to the chief priests [15] and said, "What are you willing to give me if I hand him over to you?" So they weighed out thirty pieces of silver for him. [16] And from that time he started looking for a good opportunity to betray him.

BETRAYAL AT THE PASSOVER

[17] On the first day of Unleavened Bread the disciples came to Jesus and asked, "Where do you want us to make preparations for you to eat the Passover?"

[18] "Go into the city to a certain man," he said, "and tell him, 'The Teacher says: My time is near; I am celebrating the Passover at your place[D] with my disciples.'" [19] So the disciples did as Jesus had directed them and prepared the Passover. [20] When evening came, he was reclining at the table with the Twelve. [21] While they were eating, he said, "Truly I tell you, one of you will betray me."

[22] Deeply distressed, each one began to say to him, "Surely not I, Lord?"

[23] He replied, "The one who dipped his hand with me in the bowl — he will betray me. [24] The Son of Man will go just as it is written about him, but woe to that man by whom the Son of Man is betrayed! It would have been better for him if he had not been born."

[A] 26:2 Or "Know (as a command) [B] 26:3 Other mss add and the scribes
[C] 26:6 Gk lepros; a term for various skin diseases; see Lv 13–14 [D] 26:18 Lit
Passover with you

²⁵ Judas, his betrayer, replied, "Surely not I, Rabbi?"

"You have said it," he told him.

THE FIRST LORD'S SUPPER

²⁶ As they were eating, Jesus took bread, blessed and broke it, gave it to the disciples, and said, "Take and eat it; this is my body." ²⁷ Then he took a cup, and after giving thanks, he gave it to them and said, "Drink from it, all of you. ²⁸ For this is my blood of the covenant,ᴬ which is poured out for many for the forgiveness of sins. ²⁹ But I tell you, I will not drink from this fruit of the vine from now on until that day when I drink it new with you in my Father's kingdom." ³⁰ After singing a hymn, they went out to the Mount of Olives.

PETER'S DENIAL PREDICTED

³¹ Then Jesus said to them, "Tonight all of you will fall away because of me, for it is written:

I will strike the shepherd,

and the sheep of the flock will be scattered.ᴮ

³² But after I have risen, I will go ahead of you to Galilee."

³³ Peter told him, "Even if everyone falls away because of you, I will never fall away."

³⁴ "Truly I tell you," Jesus said to him, "tonight, before the rooster crows, you will deny me three times."

³⁵ "Even if I have to die with you," Peter told him, "I will never deny you," and all the disciples said the same thing.

THE PRAYER IN THE GARDEN

³⁶ Then Jesus came with them to a place called Gethsemane, and he told the disciples, "Sit here while I go over there and pray." ³⁷ Taking along Peter and the two sons of Zebedee, he began to be sorrowful and troubled. ³⁸ He said to them, "I am deeply grievedᶜ to the point of death. Remain here and stay awake with me." ³⁹ Going a little farther,ᴰ he fell facedown and prayed, "My Father, if it is possible, let this cup pass from me. Yet not as I will, but as you will."

⁴⁰ Then he came to the disciples and found them sleeping. He asked Peter, "So, couldn't you stay awake with me one hour? ⁴¹ Stay awake and pray, so that you won't enter into temptation. The spirit is willing, but the flesh is weak."

⁴² Again, a second time, he went away and prayed, "My Father, if thisᴱ cannot passᶠ unless I drink it, your will be done." ⁴³ And he came again and found them sleeping, because they could not keep their eyes open.

⁴⁴ After leaving them, he went away again and prayed a third time, saying the same thing once more. ⁴⁵ Then he came to the disciples and said to them, "Are you still sleeping and resting? See, the time is near. The Son of Man is betrayed into the hands of sinners. ⁴⁶ Get up; let's go. See, my betrayer is near."

JUDAS'S BETRAYAL OF JESUS

⁴⁷ While he was still speaking, Judas, one of the Twelve, suddenly arrived. A large mob with swords and clubs was with him from the chief priests and

---

ᴬ26:28 Other mss read *new covenant* ᴮ26:31 Zch 13:7 ᶜ26:38 Lit *"My soul is swallowed up in sorrow* ᴰ26:39 Other mss read *Drawing nearer* ᴱ26:42 Other mss add *cup* ᶠ26:42 Other mss add *from me* elders of the people. [48] His betrayer had given them a sign: "The one I kiss, he's the one; arrest him." [49] So immediately he went up to Jesus and said, "Greetings, Rabbi!" and kissed him.

[50] "Friend," Jesus asked him, "why have you come?" [A]

Then they came up, took hold of Jesus, and arrested him. [51] At that moment one of those with Jesus reached out his hand and drew his sword. He struck the high priest's servant and cut off his ear.

[52] Then Jesus told him, "Put your sword back in its place because all who take up the sword will perish by the sword. [53] Or do you think that I cannot call on my Father, and he will provide me here and now with more than twelve legions of angels? [54] How, then, would the Scriptures be fulfilled that say it must happen this way?"

[55] At that time Jesus said to the crowds, "Have you come out with swords and clubs, as if I were a criminal, [B] to capture me? Every day I used to sit, teaching in the temple, and you didn't arrest me. [56] But all this has happened so that the writings of the prophets would be fulfilled." Then all the disciples deserted him and ran away.

JESUS FACES THE SANHEDRIN

[57] Those who had arrested Jesus led him away to Caiaphas the high priest, where the scribes and the elders had convened. [58] Peter was following him at a distance right to the high priest's courtyard. He went in and was sitting with the servants to see the outcome.

[59] The chief priests and the whole Sanhedrin were looking for false testimony against Jesus so that they could put him to death, [60] but they could not find any, even though many false witnesses came forward. [C] Finally, two [D] who came forward [61] stated, "This man said, 'I can destroy the temple of God and rebuild it in three days.'"

[62] The high priest stood up and said to him, "Don't you have an answer to what these men are testifying against you?" [63] But Jesus kept silent. The high priest said to him, "I charge you under oath by the living God: Tell us if you are the Messiah, the Son of God."

[64] "You have said it," Jesus told him. "But I tell you, in the future [E] you will see **the Son of Man seated at the right hand** of Power and **coming on the clouds of heaven.**" [F]

[65] Then the high priest tore his robes and said, "He has blasphemed! Why do we still need witnesses? See, now you've heard the blasphemy. [66] What is your decision?"

They answered, "He deserves death!" [67] Then they spat in his face and beat him; others slapped him [68] and said, "Prophesy to us, Messiah! Who was it that hit you?"

PETER DENIES HIS LORD

[69] Now Peter was sitting outside in the courtyard. A servant girl approached him and said, "You were with Jesus the Galilean too."

[A]26:50 Or *Jesus told him, "do what you have come for."* [B]26:55 Lit *as against a criminal* [C]26:60 Other mss add *they found none* [D]26:60 Other mss add *false witnesses* [E]26:64 Lit *you, from now* [F]26:64 Ps 110:1; Dn 7:13

[70] But he denied it in front of everyone: "I don't know what you're talking about."

[71] When he had gone out to the gateway, another woman saw him and told those who were there, "This man was with Jesus the Nazarene!"

[72] And again he denied it with an oath: "I don't know the man!"

[73] After a little while those standing there approached and said to Peter, "You really are one of them, since even your accent[A] gives you away."

[74] Then he started to curse and to swear with an oath, "I don't know the man!" Immediately a rooster crowed, [75] and Peter remembered the words Jesus had spoken, "Before the rooster crows, you will deny me three times." And he went outside and wept bitterly.

JESUS HANDED OVER TO PILATE

27 When daybreak came, all the chief priests and the elders of the people plotted against Jesus to put him to death. [2] After tying him up, they led him away and handed him over to Pilate,[B] the governor.

JUDAS HANGS HIMSELF

[3] Then Judas, his betrayer, seeing that Jesus had been condemned, was full of remorse and returned the thirty pieces of silver to the chief priests and elders. [4] "I have sinned by betraying innocent blood," he said.

"What's that to us?" they said. "See to it yourself!" [5] So he threw the silver into the temple and departed. Then he went and hanged himself.

[6] The chief priests took the silver and said, "It's not permitted to put it into the temple treasury, since it is blood money." [7] They conferred together and bought the potter's field with it as a burial place for foreigners. [8] Therefore that field has been called "Blood Field" to this day. [9] Then what was spoken through the prophet Jeremiah was fulfilled: **They took[C] the thirty pieces of silver, the price of him whose price was set by the Israelites, [10] and they gave[D] them for the potter's field, as the Lord directed me.[E]**

JESUS FACES THE GOVERNOR

[11] Now Jesus stood before the governor. "Are you the King of the Jews?" the governor asked him.

Jesus answered, "You say so." [12] While he was being accused by the chief priests and elders, he didn't answer.

[13] Then Pilate said to him, "Don't you hear how much they are testifying against you?" [14] But he didn't answer him on even one charge, so that the governor was quite amazed.

JESUS OR BARABBAS

[15] At the festival the governor's custom was to release to the crowd a prisoner they wanted. [16] At that time they had a notorious prisoner called Barabbas.[F] [17] So when they had gathered together, Pilate said to them, "Who is it you want me to release for you — Barabbas, or Jesus who is called Christ?" [18] For he knew it was because of envy that they had handed him over.

[A]26:73 Or *speech*   [B]27:2 Other mss read *Pontius Pilate*   [C]27:9 Or *I took*
[D]27:10 Some mss read *I gave*   [E]27:9-10 Jr 32:6-9; Zch 11:12-13   [F]27:16 Other
mss read *Jesus Barabbas*, also in v. 17

JESUS IS KING

MATTHEW 27–28; REVELATION 19:11-16

My parents like to tell this story about me as a three-year-old.

My sisters and I had a babysitter for the night, and my mom had made us brownies to have as a snack, with the instruction that we were each allowed one brownie. After the first brownie, I toddled my way back to the kitchen and reached for a second.

"No, Andrea," said the babysitter. "You can only have one." I looked at her, and with a scrunched up face and my hands on my hips, I declared, "You're not the boss!" At the time I had a speech impediment that softened my "r"s, so you can imagine how intimidating this sounded to my babysitter.

I still have authority issues. Authority threatens my freedom. It says I am not in charge, not the boss of my own life. Yet, as Christians, we aren't meant to live under the authority of our own rule. We have a King!

The Kingship of Jesus is highlighted in Matthew's account of the crucifixion. It was a Roman custom to name the crime of the offender on a plaque and place it above the criminal's head as he hung on the cross. Because Pilate said Jesus had committed no real crime, he ordered this inscription instead:

*"THIS IS JESUS,
THE KING OF THE JEWS."*

MATTHEW 27:37

It was a label given in contempt that could not have been more correct.

Scripture tells us Jesus is not only King of the Jews, but He is the King. As Revelation 19:16 says, "he has a name written on his robe and on his thigh:

"KING OF KINGS AND LORD OF LORDS."

Still, I more often refer to Jesus as my Savior rather than my King. Charles Spurgeon says this is our tendency: "Men might be willing for Christ to save them, but not for Him to reign over them" (C.H. Spurgeon, *The King of the Jews*).

Acknowledging that Jesus reigns over me means acknowledging that I am not in control. But His kingship also means He is involved in the everyday—that His sovereignty covers even the nitty gritty of life. There is accountability that says we are called to a new, gospel way of living, and there is grace that says we aren't doing this on our own. Both threaten our autonomy.

So we have to ask ourselves, who's the boss here? Me, or Jesus?

When we bow to Jesus as our King, we receive what we are most afraid of losing in the face of authority: freedom. Real freedom.

"So if the Son sets you free, you really will be free" (Jn 8:36).

That's the type of freedom I want. Not the kind that creates the illusion of my own control, but the kind that comes with the cross. The kind that says Jesus is the King of the Jews, and He is the King of me.

¹⁹ While he was sitting on the judge's bench, his wife sent word to him, "Have nothing to do with that righteous man, for today I've suffered terribly in a dream because of him."

²⁰ The chief priests and the elders, however, persuaded the crowds to ask for Barabbas and to execute Jesus. ²¹ The governor asked them, "Which of the two do you want me to release for you?"

"Barabbas!" they answered.

²² Pilate asked them, "What should I do then with Jesus, who is called Christ?" They all answered, "Crucify him!"

²³ Then he said, "Why? What has he done wrong?"

But they kept shouting all the more, "Crucify him!"

²⁴ When Pilate saw that he was getting nowhere, but that a riot was starting instead, he took some water, washed his hands in front of the crowd, and said, "I am innocent of this man's blood.ᴬ See to it yourselves!"

²⁵ All the people answered, "His blood be on us and on our children!" ²⁶ Then he released Barabbas to them and, after having Jesus flogged, handed him over to be crucified.

MOCKED BY THE MILITARY

²⁷ Then the governor's soldiers took Jesus into the governor's residence and gathered the whole companyᴮ around him. ²⁸ They stripped him and dressed him in a scarlet robe. ²⁹ They twisted together a crown of thorns, put it on his head, and placed a staff in his right hand. And they knelt down before him and mocked him: "Hail, King of the Jews!" ³⁰ Then they spat on him, took the staff, and kept hitting him on the head. ³¹ After they had mocked him, they stripped him of the robe, put his own clothes on him, and led him away to crucify him.

CRUCIFIED BETWEEN TWO CRIMINALS

³² As they were going out, they found a Cyrenian man named Simon. They forced him to carry his cross. ³³ When they came to a place called *Golgotha* (which means Place of the Skull), ³⁴ they gave him wineᶜ mixed with gall to drink. But when he tasted it, he refused to drink it. ³⁵ After crucifying him, they divided his clothes by casting lots.ᴰ ³⁶ Then they sat down and were guarding him there. ³⁷ Above his head they put up the charge against him in writing: This Is Jesus, the King of the Jews.

³⁸ Then two criminalsᴱ were crucified with him, one on the right and one on the left. ³⁹ Those who passed by were yelling insults atᶠ him, shaking their heads ⁴⁰ and saying, "You who would destroy the temple and rebuild it in three days, save yourself! If you are the Son of God, come down from the cross!" ⁴¹ In the same way the chief priests, with the scribes and elders,ᴳ mocked him and said, ⁴² "He saved others, but he cannot save himself! He is the King of Israel! Let himᴴ come down now from the cross, and we will believe in

---

ᴬ27:24 Other mss read *this righteous man's blood* ᴮ27:27 Lit *cohort*
ᶜ27:34 Other mss read *sour wine* ᴰ27:35 Other mss add *that what was spoken by the prophet might be fulfilled: "They divided my clothes among them, and for my clothing they cast lots."* ᴱ27:38 Or *revolutionaries* ᶠ27:39 Lit *passed by blasphemed,* or *were blaspheming* ᴳ27:41 Other mss add *and Pharisees*
ᴴ27:42 Other mss read *If he . . . Israel, let him*

him. [43] He trusts in God; let God rescue him now — if he takes pleasure in him![A] For he said, 'I am the Son of God.'" [44] In the same way even the criminals who were crucified with him taunted him.

THE DEATH OF JESUS

[45] From noon until three in the afternoon[B] darkness came over the whole land.[C] [46] About three in the afternoon Jesus cried out with a loud voice, "*Elí, Elí, lemá[D] sabachtháni?*" that is, "**My God, my God, why have you abandoned me?**"[E]

[47] When some of those standing there heard this, they said, "He's calling for Elijah."

[48] Immediately one of them ran and got a sponge, filled it with sour wine, put it on a stick, and offered him a drink. [49] But the rest said, "Let's see if Elijah comes to save him."

[50] But Jesus cried out again with a loud voice and gave up his spirit. [51] Suddenly, the curtain of the sanctuary was torn in two from top to bottom, the earth quaked, and the rocks were split. [52] The tombs were also opened and many bodies of the saints who had fallen asleep were raised. [53] And they came out of the tombs after his resurrection, entered the holy city, and appeared to many.

[54] When the centurion and those with him, who were keeping watch over Jesus, saw the earthquake and the things that had happened, they were terrified and said, "Truly this man was the Son of God!"

[55] Many women who had followed Jesus from Galilee and looked after him were there, watching from a distance. [56] Among them were Mary Magdalene, Mary the mother of James and Joseph, and the mother of Zebedee's sons.

THE BURIAL OF JESUS

[57] When it was evening, a rich man from Arimathea named Joseph came, who himself had also become a disciple of Jesus. [58] He approached Pilate and asked for Jesus's body. Then Pilate ordered that it[F] be released. [59] So Joseph took the body, wrapped it in clean, fine linen, [60] and placed it in his new tomb, which he had cut into the rock. He left after rolling a great stone against the entrance of the tomb. [61] Mary Magdalene and the other Mary were seated there, facing the tomb.

THE CLOSELY GUARDED TOMB

[62] The next day, which followed the preparation day, the chief priests and the Pharisees gathered before Pilate [63] and said, "Sir, we remember that while this deceiver was still alive he said, 'After three days I will rise again.' [64] So give orders that the tomb be made secure until the third day. Otherwise, his disciples may come, steal him, and tell the people, 'He has been raised from the dead,' and the last deception will be worse than the first."

[65] "You have[G] a guard of soldiers," Pilate told them. "Go and make it as secure as you know how." [66] They went and secured the tomb by setting a seal on the stone and placing the guard.

[A]27:43 Or *if he wants him* [B]27:45 Lit *From the sixth hour to the ninth hour*
[C]27:45 Or *whole earth* [D]27:46 Some mss read *lama*; other mss read *lima*
[E]27:46 Ps 22:1 [F]27:58 Other mss read *that the body* [G]27:65 Or *"Take*

RESURRECTION MORNING

28

After the Sabbath, as the first day of the week was dawning, Mary Magdalene and the other Mary went to view the tomb. [2] There was a violent earthquake, because an angel of the Lord descended from heaven and approached the tomb. He rolled back the stone and was sitting on it. [3] His appearance was like lightning, and his clothing was as white as snow. [4] The guards were so shaken by fear of him that they became like dead men.

[5] The angel told the women, "Don't be afraid, because I know you are looking for Jesus who was crucified. [6] He is not here. For he has risen, just as he said. Come and see the place where he lay. [7] Then go quickly and tell his disciples, 'He has risen from the dead and indeed he is going ahead of you to Galilee; you will see him there.' Listen, I have told you."

[8] So, departing quickly from the tomb with fear and great joy, they ran to tell his disciples the news. [9] Just then[A] Jesus met them and said, "Greetings!" They came up, took hold of his feet, and worshiped him. [10] Then Jesus told them, "Do not be afraid. Go and tell my brothers to leave for Galilee, and they will see me there."

THE SOLDIERS BRIBED TO LIE

[11] As they were on their way, some of the guards came into the city and reported to the chief priests everything that had happened. [12] After the priests[B] had assembled with the elders and agreed on a plan, they gave the soldiers a large sum of money [13] and told them, "Say this, 'His disciples came during the night and stole him while we were sleeping.' [14] If this reaches the governor's ears, we will deal with[C] him and keep you out of trouble." [15] They took the money and did as they were instructed, and this story has been spread among Jewish people to this day.

THE GREAT COMMISSION

[16] The eleven disciples traveled to Galilee, to the mountain where Jesus had directed them. [17] When they saw him, they worshiped,[D] but some doubted. [18] Jesus came near and said to them, "All authority has been given to me in heaven and on earth. [19] Go, therefore, and make disciples of[E] all nations, baptizing them in the name of the Father and of the Son and of the Holy Spirit, [20] teaching them to observe everything I have commanded you. And remember,[F] I am with you always,[G] to the end of the age."

[A]28:9 Other mss add *as they were on their way to tell the news to his disciples*
[B]28:12 Lit *After they*   [C]28:14 Lit *will persuade*   [D]28:17 Other mss add *him*
[E]28:19 Or *and disciple*   [F]28:20 Lit *see*   [G]28:20 Lit *all the days*

mark

For even the Son of Man did not come to be served, but to serve, and to give his life as a ransom for many. **10:45**

ON THE TIMELINE Most Bible scholars are convinced Mark was the earliest Gospel written and that it served as one of the sources for the writing of Matthew and Luke. It is believed Mark wrote his Gospel between AD 64 and 68. The events in the Gospel of Mark take place during Jesus' ministry, around AD 30–33.

A LITTLE BACKGROUND The Gospel of Mark is anonymous, though the author is believed to be John Mark. John Mark was the son of a widow named Mary, in whose house the church in Jerusalem sometimes gathered (Ac 12:12-17) and where Jesus possibly ate the Last Supper with His disciples.

According to the early church fathers, Mark wrote his Gospel in Rome either just before or soon after Peter's martyrdom. Because Mark wrote primarily for Roman Gentiles, he explained Jewish customs, translated Aramaic words and phrases into Greek, used Latin terms rather than their Greek equivalents, and rarely quoted from the Old Testament.

MESSAGE & PURPOSE Mark's Gospel is a narrative about Jesus, and Mark identified this theme in the first verse: "the gospel of Jesus Christ, the Son of God." The major emphasis of Mark's Gospel is that Jesus is the divine Son of God, as announced by God at Jesus' baptism (Mk 1:11). Demons and unclean spirits recognized and acknowledged Jesus' divinity in Mark 3:11 and 5:7, and God reaffirmed it at the transfiguration in Mark 9:7. Jesus taught it parabolically in Mark 12:1-12, hinted at it in 13:32, and confessed it directly in 14:61-62. Finally, the Roman centurion confessed it openly and without qualification in Mark 15:39. Thus, Mark's purpose was to summon people to repent and believe the good news of Jesus Christ, the Messiah, the Son of God (Mk 1:1,15).

GIVE THANKS FOR THE GOSPEL OF MARK

Many concepts of the Messiah existed in Jesus' day, and several individuals laid claim to the title. What Mark contributes to the canon is a clarification of the concept of Messiah and a redefining of the term. Mark gives us a strong picture of both the divine and human sides of Jesus, with special emphasis given to Jesus' humanity and emotions.

THE ROMAN EMPIRE
IN JESUS' TIME

READ AND UNDERSTAND MARK

The Bible is a complete work in which many stories combine to tell one story. As you read the Gospel of Mark, consider reading the additional passages to discover how the whole of Scripture works together.

THE MESSIAH'S HERALD

1 The beginning of the gospel of Jesus Christ, the Son of God.[A] [2] As it is written in Isaiah the prophet:[B]

See, I am sending my messenger ahead of you;
he will prepare your way.[C,D]

[3] A voice of one crying out in the wilderness:
Prepare the way for the Lord;
make his paths straight![E]

[4] John came baptizing[F] in the wilderness and proclaiming a baptism of repentance for the forgiveness of sins. [5] The whole Judean countryside and all the people of Jerusalem were going out to him, and they were baptized by him in the Jordan River, confessing their sins. [6] John wore a camel-hair garment with a leather belt around his waist and ate locusts and wild honey.

[7] He proclaimed, "One who is more powerful than I am is coming after me. I am not worthy to stoop down and untie the strap of his sandals. [8] I baptize you with[G] water, but he will baptize you with the Holy Spirit."

THE BAPTISM OF JESUS

[9] In those days Jesus came from Nazareth in Galilee and was baptized in the Jordan by John. [10] As soon as he came up out of the water, he saw the heavens being torn open and the Spirit descending on him like a dove. [11] And a voice came from heaven: "You are my beloved Son; with you I am well-pleased."

THE TEMPTATION OF JESUS

[12] Immediately the Spirit drove him into the wilderness. [13] He was in the wilderness forty days, being tempted by Satan. He was with the wild animals, and the angels were serving him.

MINISTRY IN GALILEE

[14] After John was arrested, Jesus went to Galilee, proclaiming the good news[H,I] of God: [15] "The time is fulfilled, and the kingdom of God has come near. Repent and believe the good news!"

THE FIRST DISCIPLES

[16] As he passed alongside the Sea of Galilee, he saw Simon and Andrew, Simon's brother, casting a net into the sea — for they were fishermen. [17] "Follow me," Jesus told them, "and I will make you fish for[J] people." [18] Immediately they left their nets and followed him. [19] Going on a little farther, he saw James the son of Zebedee and his brother John in a boat putting their nets in order. [20] Immediately he called them, and they left their father Zebedee in the boat with the hired men and followed him.

DRIVING OUT AN UNCLEAN SPIRIT

[21] They went into Capernaum, and right away he entered the synagogue on the Sabbath and began to teach. [22] They were astonished at his teaching

---

REPENT AND BELIEVE

MARK 1; EPHESIANS 2:1-5

Repentance is the life-giving rhythm of the Christian life. It restores hope, fuels joy, tells our fears, "lie in quiet confidence" (Is 30:15). This is the way it should be.

But there was a time when it wasn't that way for me.

After following Jesus for more than thirty years, the need for repentance hardened like a layer of frost over my soul. I wanted to repent, but I couldn't. I felt frozen. Fear and accusations assaulted my mind almost daily.

What if I don't repent the right way?
What if I'm not repenting enough?
How could I have failed again?
How can I come into His presence after this?

Clear as hindsight, I can now see that repentance had become my way of proving I was worthy of God's forgiveness. I would repent for messing up again, and my heavenly Father would extend mercy. But, in my mind, my standing with God was dependent on my ability to get things right—and if I got things right, eventually repentance should become unnecessary. Oh, the confusion and distortion that comes when we forget the gospel of Jesus Christ!

Though gloriously redeemed by Jesus, my heart had become shackled by chains of unbelief, dramatically impacting the way I repented (or didn't repent). I simply could not believe that Jesus accepted me, mess and all, and that He

didn't throw up His hands at my incessant need for forgiveness.

Who even wants to hang out with—let alone love and die for—hopelessly broken, messed up failures who can't ever get it right?

Only Jesus. Only the Messiah who tenderly said, "I have not come to call the righteous, but sinners to repentance" (Lk 5:32).

You see, "Jesus Loves Me" isn't only a song we learn as children; it's the anchor of truth upon which our faith rests. We're free to admit the depth of our need and the messiness of our realities when we believe that nothing—not even our sin—can separate us from the love of Jesus.

Repentance and belief are two sides of the same beautiful coin. Repentance flows freely when we believe our sins have already been forgiven—past, present, and future.

Jesus, because of His great love for us, came to seek and save us while we were still dead in our trespasses (Eph 2:5). Knowing this kind of unmerited love and kindness changes us. It makes our repentance, our returning to God, as natural as breathing. It restores our relationship with Him.

Friend, don't repent to earn God's love. Repent because you are deeply loved by the God who already secured your forgiveness. Thanks be to Him.

because he was teaching them as one who had authority, and not like the scribes.

²³ Just then a man with an unclean spirit was in their synagogue. He cried out, ²⁴ "What do you have to do with us, Jesus of Nazareth? Have you come to destroy us? I know who you are — the Holy One of God!"

²⁵ Jesus rebuked him saying, "Be silent, and come out of him!" ²⁶ And the unclean spirit threw him into convulsions, shouted with a loud voice, and came out of him.

²⁷ They were all amazed, and so they began to ask each other: "What is this? A new teaching with authority!ᴬ He commands even the unclean spirits, and they obey him." ²⁸ At once the news about him spread throughout the entire vicinity of Galilee.

HEALINGS AT CAPERNAUM

²⁹ As soon as they left the synagogue, they went into Simon and Andrew's house with James and John. ³⁰ Simon's mother-in-law was lying in bed with a fever, and they told him about her at once. ³¹ So he went to her, took her by the hand, and raised her up. The fever left her,ᴮ and she began to serve them.

³² When evening came, after the sun had set, they brought to him all those who were sick and demon-possessed. ³³ The whole town was assembled at the door, ³⁴ and he healed many who were sick with various diseases and drove out many demons. And he would not permit the demons to speak, because they knew him.

PREACHING IN GALILEE

³⁵ Very early in the morning, while it was still dark, he got up, went out, and made his way to a deserted place; and there he was praying. ³⁶ Simon and his companions searched for him, ³⁷ and when they found him they said, "Everyone is looking for you."

³⁸ And he said to them, "Let's go on to the neighboring villages so that I may preach there too. This is why I have come."

A MAN CLEANSED

³⁹ He went into all of Galilee, preaching in their synagogues and driving out demons. ⁴⁰ Then a man with leprosyᶜ came to him and, on his knees,ᴰ begged him: "If you are willing, you can make me clean." ⁴¹ Moved with compassion,ᴱ Jesus reached out his hand and touched him. "I am willing," he told him. "Be made clean." ⁴² Immediately the leprosy left him, and he was made clean. ⁴³ Then he sternly warned him and sent him away at once, ⁴⁴ telling him, "See that you say nothing to anyone; but go and show yourself to the priest, and offer what Moses commanded for your cleansing, as a testimony to them."ᶠ ⁴⁵ Yet he went out and began to proclaim it widely and to spread the news, with the result that Jesus could no longer enter a town openly. But he was out in deserted places, and they came to him from everywhere.

ᴬ1:27 Other mss read "What is this? What is this new teaching? For with authority ᴮ1:31 Other mss add at once ᶜ1:40 Gk lepros; a term for various skin diseases, also in v. 42; see Lv 13–14 ᴰ1:40 Other mss omit on his knees ᴱ1:41 Other mss Moved with indignation ᶠ1:44 Or against them

THE SON OF MAN FORGIVES AND HEALS

2 When he entered Capernaum again after some days, it was reported that he was at home. ² So many people gathered together that there was no more room, not even in the doorway, and he was speaking the word to them. ³ They came to him bringing a paralytic, carried by four of them. ⁴ Since they were not able to bring him to ᴬ Jesus because of the crowd, they removed the roof above him, and after digging through it, they lowered the mat on which the paralytic was lying. ⁵ Seeing their faith, Jesus told the paralytic, "Son, your sins are forgiven."

⁶ But some of the scribes were sitting there, questioning in their hearts: ⁷ "Why does he speak like this? He's blaspheming! Who can forgive sins but God alone?"

⁸ Right away Jesus perceived in his spirit that they were thinking like this within themselves and said to them, "Why are you thinking these things in your hearts? ⁹ Which is easier: to say to the paralytic, 'Your sins are forgiven,' or to say, 'Get up, take your mat, and walk'? ¹⁰ But so that you may know that the Son of Man has authority on earth to forgive sins" — he told the paralytic — ¹¹ "I tell you: get up, take your mat, and go home."

¹² Immediately he got up, took the mat, and went out in front of everyone. As a result, they were all astounded and gave glory to God, saying, "We have never seen anything like this!"

THE CALL OF LEVI

¹³ Jesus went out again beside the sea. The whole crowd was coming to him, and he was teaching them. ¹⁴ Then, passing by, he saw Levi the son of Alphaeus sitting at the toll booth, and he said to him, "Follow me," and he got up and followed him.

¹⁵ While he was reclining at the table in Levi's house, many tax collectors and sinners were eating ᴮ with Jesus and his disciples, for there were many who were following him. ¹⁶ When the scribes who were Pharisees ᶜ saw that he was eating with sinners and tax collectors, they asked his disciples, "Why does he eat ᴰ with tax collectors and sinners?"

¹⁷ When Jesus heard this, he told them, "It is not those who are well who need a doctor, but those who are sick. I didn't come to call the righteous, but sinners."

A QUESTION ABOUT FASTING

¹⁸ Now John's disciples and the Pharisees ᴱ were fasting. People came and asked him, "Why do John's disciples and the Pharisees' disciples fast, but your disciples do not fast?"

¹⁹ Jesus said to them, "The wedding guests cannot fast while the groom is with them, can they? As long as they have the groom with them, they cannot fast. ²⁰ But the time ᶠ will come when the groom will be taken away from them, and then they will fast on that day. ²¹ No one sews a patch of unshrunk cloth on an old garment. Otherwise, the new patch pulls away from the old cloth, and a worse tear is made. ²² And no one puts new wine into old wineskins.

ᴬ2:4 Other mss read *able to get near* ᴮ2:15 Lit *reclining together* ᶜ2:16 Other mss read *scribes and Pharisees* ᴰ2:16 Other mss add *and drink* ᴱ2:18 Other mss read *The disciples of John and of the Pharisees* ᶠ2:20 Or *the days*

Otherwise, the wine will burst the skins, and the wine is lost as well as the skins. No, new wine is put into fresh wineskins."

LORD OF THE SABBATH

²³ On the Sabbath he was going through the grainfields, and his disciples began to make their way, picking some heads of grain. ²⁴ The Pharisees said to him, "Look, why are they doing what is not lawful on the Sabbath?"

²⁵ He said to them, "Have you never read what David and those who were with him did when he was in need and hungry — ²⁶ how he entered the house of God in the time of Abiathar the high priest and ate the bread of the Presence — which is not lawful for anyone to eat except the priests — and also gave some to his companions?" ²⁷ Then he told them, "The Sabbath was made for^A man and not man for the Sabbath. ²⁸ So then, the Son of Man is Lord even of the Sabbath."

3 Jesus entered the synagogue again, and a man was there who had a shriveled hand. ² In order to accuse him, they were watching him closely to see whether he would heal him on the Sabbath. ³ He told the man with the shriveled hand, "Stand before us." ⁴ Then he said to them, "Is it lawful to do good on the Sabbath or to do evil, to save life or to kill?" But they were silent. ⁵ After looking around at them with anger, he was grieved at the hardness of their hearts and told the man, "Stretch out your hand." So he stretched it out, and his hand was restored. ⁶ Immediately the Pharisees went out and started plotting with the Herodians against him, how they might kill him.

MINISTERING TO THE MULTITUDE

⁷ Jesus departed with his disciples to the sea, and a large crowd followed from Galilee, and a large crowd followed from Judea, ⁸ Jerusalem, Idumea, beyond the Jordan, and around Tyre and Sidon. The large crowd came to him because they heard about everything he was doing. ⁹ Then he told his disciples to have a small boat ready for him, so that the crowd wouldn't crush him. ¹⁰ Since he had healed many, all who had diseases were pressing toward him to touch him. ¹¹ Whenever the unclean spirits saw him, they fell down before him and cried out, "You are the Son of God!" ¹² And he would strongly warn them not to make him known.

THE TWELVE APOSTLES

¹³ Jesus went up the mountain and summoned those he wanted, and they came to him. ¹⁴ He appointed twelve, whom he also named apostles,^B to be with him, to send them out to preach, ¹⁵ and to have authority to^C drive out demons. ¹⁶ He appointed the Twelve:^D To Simon, he gave the name Peter; ¹⁷ and to James the son of Zebedee, and to his brother John, he gave the name "Boanerges" (that is, "Sons of Thunder"); ¹⁸ Andrew; Philip and Bartholomew; Matthew and Thomas; James the son of Alphaeus, and Thaddaeus; Simon the Zealot, ¹⁹ and Judas Iscariot, who also betrayed him.

---

^A2:27 Or *because of*   ^B3:14 Other mss omit *he also named them apostles*
^C3:15 Other mss add *heal diseases, and to*   ^D3:16 Other mss omit *He appointed the Twelve*

A HOUSE DIVIDED

²⁰ Jesus entered a house, and the crowd gathered again so that they were not even able to eat.ᴬ ²¹ When his family heard this, they set out to restrain him, because they said, "He's out of his mind."

²² The scribes who had come down from Jerusalem said, "He is possessed by Beelzebul," and, "He drives out demons by the ruler of the demons."

²³ So he summoned them and spoke to them in parables: "How can Satan drive out Satan? ²⁴ If a kingdom is divided against itself, that kingdom cannot stand. ²⁵ If a house is divided against itself, that house cannot stand. ²⁶ And if Satan opposes himself and is divided, he cannot stand but is finished. ²⁷ But no one can enter a strong man's house and plunder his possessions unless he first ties up the strong man. Then he can plunder his house.

²⁸ "Truly I tell you, people will be forgiven for all sins and whatever blasphemies they utter. ²⁹ But whoever blasphemes against the Holy Spirit never has forgiveness, but is guilty of an eternal sin"ᴮ — ³⁰ because they were saying, "He has an unclean spirit."

TRUE RELATIONSHIPS

³¹ His mother and his brothers came, and standing outside, they sent word to him and called him. ³² A crowd was sitting around him and told him, "Look, your mother, your brothers, and your sistersᶜ are outside asking for you."

³³ He replied to them, "Who are my mother and my brothers?" ³⁴ Looking at those sitting in a circle around him, he said, "Here are my mother and my brothers! ³⁵ Whoever does the will of God is my brother and sister and mother."

THE PARABLE OF THE SOWER

4 Again he began to teach by the sea, and a very large crowd gathered around him. So he got into a boat on the sea and sat down, while the whole crowd was by the sea on the shore. ² He taught them many things in parables, and in his teaching he said to them: ³ "Listen! Consider the sower who went out to sow. ⁴ As he sowed, some seed fell along the path, and the birds came and devoured it. ⁵ Other seed fell on rocky ground where it didn't have much soil, and it grew up quickly, since the soil wasn't deep. ⁶ When the sun came up, it was scorched, and since it had no root, it withered away. ⁷ Other seed fell among thorns, and the thorns came up and choked it, and it didn't produce fruit. ⁸ Still other seed fell on good ground and it grew up, producing fruit that increased thirty, sixty, and a hundred times." ⁹ Then he said, "Let anyone who has ears to hear listen."

WHY JESUS USED PARABLES

¹⁰ When he was alone, those around him with the Twelve asked him about the parables. ¹¹ He answered them, "The secret of the kingdom of God has been given to you, but to those outside, everything comes in parables ¹² so that

> they may indeed look,
> and yet not perceive;

ᴬ3:20 Or eat a meal; lit eat bread ᴮ3:29 Other mss read is subject to eternal judgment ᶜ3:32 Other mss omit and your sisters

they may indeed listen,
and yet not understand;
otherwise, they might turn back
and be forgiven."[A,B]

THE PARABLE OF THE SOWER EXPLAINED

[13] Then he said to them: "Don't you understand this parable? How then will you understand all of the parables? [14] The sower sows the word. [15] Some are like the word sown on the path. When they hear, immediately Satan comes and takes away the word sown in them.[C] [16] And others are like seed sown on rocky ground. When they hear the word, immediately they receive it with joy. [17] But they have no root; they are short-lived. When distress or persecution comes because of the word, they immediately fall away. [18] Others are like seed sown among thorns; these are the ones who hear the word, [19] but the worries of this age, the deceitfulness[D] of wealth, and the desires for other things enter in and choke the word, and it becomes unfruitful. [20] And those like seed sown on good ground hear the word, welcome it, and produce fruit thirty, sixty, and a hundred times what was sown."

USING YOUR LIGHT

[21] He also said to them, "Is a lamp brought in to be put under a basket or under a bed? Isn't it to be put on a lampstand? [22] For there is nothing hidden that will not be revealed, and nothing concealed that will not be brought to light. [23] If anyone has ears to hear, let him listen." [24] And he said to them, "Pay attention to what you hear. By the measure you use, it will be measured to you — and more will be added to you. [25] For whoever has, more will be given to him, and whoever does not have, even what he has will be taken away from him."

THE PARABLE OF THE GROWING SEED

[26] "The kingdom of God is like this," he said. "A man scatters seed on the ground. [27] He sleeps and rises night and day; the seed sprouts and grows, although he doesn't know how. [28] The soil produces a crop by itself — first the blade, then the head, and then the full grain on the head. [29] As soon as the crop is ready, he sends for the sickle, because the harvest has come."

THE PARABLE OF THE MUSTARD SEED

[30] And he said, "With what can we compare the kingdom of God, or what parable can we use to describe it? [31] It's like a mustard seed that, when sown upon the soil, is the smallest of all the seeds on the ground. [32] And when sown, it comes up and grows taller than all the garden plants, and produces large branches, so that the birds of the sky can nest in its shade."

USING PARABLES

[33] He was speaking the word to them with many parables like these, as they were able to understand. [34] He did not speak to them without a parable. Privately, however, he explained everything to his own disciples.

[A]4:12 Other mss read and their sins be forgiven them   [B]4:12 Is 6:9-10
[C]4:15 Other mss read in their hearts   [D]4:19 Or seduction

ARISE

MARK 5; ACTS 9:39-41

We don't know a lot about Jairus's daughter.

We know she was young, about twelve years old. We know her father was a ruler in the synagogue, and he grieved at the thought of losing his daughter. Was she his only child or the baby of a big family? Had they long prayed for her healing, or had she fallen ill quickly, without warning? Many details of her story are a mystery.

Here's what else we know: her father's faith led him to Jesus, the only One with the ability to save his daughter.

Jesus went, stopping along the way to minister to a woman who had been bleeding for twelve long years. While Jesus was tending to this woman, a man from Jairus's household came to tell Jesus not to bother—the child was already dead. But Jesus went anyway. He quieted the ones who did not believe, the people in the house weeping and wailing. And though she was already dead, Jesus went to the little girl and said one thing: "get up" (Mk 5:41).

And she did.

Is He calling you to do the same today?

Hear this: it doesn't matter who you were before He told you to get up. In fact, I love how little we know about the characters in this story because it speaks volumes about who our Savior is. There

was only faith by the grace He supplied— everything else was Him bringing death to life.

We don't know what happened next. Did her whole family place their trust in Jesus? Did she go on to become a passionate follower of Christ because He saved her in such an extravagant way? We don't know, and that's okay. Because nothing could change what happened that day.

The new basis of her identity was this: she was dead, and Jesus brought her back to life. If you believe in Him, that's your story too.

Last year, last week, even what you did last night does not define you. Your sin, your shame, your accolades, your family name—none of these details matter compared to the truth of who He is and who you are in Him. The fruit God produces after He raises you from the dead can be beautiful and glorifying to God, but you are everything you are because of the moment when He said, "Little girl, I say to you, get up."

You are everything you are because He brought you back.

You are everything you are because you are loved.

You are everything you are because you've been made alive.

No sin in your life is beyond the power of Christ's forgiveness, and no brokenness is beyond the reach of His healing, restoring touch. It's time to get up. *Arise.*

WIND AND WAVES OBEY JESUS

³⁵ On that day, when evening had come, he told them, "Let's cross over to the other side of the sea." ³⁶ So they left the crowd and took him along since he was in the boat. And other boats were with him. ³⁷ A great windstorm arose, and the waves were breaking over the boat, so that the boat was already being swamped. ³⁸ He was in the stern, sleeping on the cushion. So they woke him up and said to him, "Teacher! Don't you care that we're going to die?"

³⁹ He got up, rebuked the wind, and said to the sea, "Silence! Be still!" The wind ceased, and there was a great calm. ⁴⁰ Then he said to them, "Why are you afraid? Do you still have no faith?"

⁴¹ And they were terrified[A] and asked one another, "Who then is this? Even the wind and the sea obey him!"

DEMONS DRIVEN OUT BY JESUS

5 They came to the other side of the sea, to the region of the Gerasenes.[B] ² As soon as he got out of the boat, a man with an unclean spirit came out of the tombs and met him. ³ He lived in the tombs, and no one was able to restrain him anymore — not even with a chain — ⁴ because he often had been bound with shackles and chains, but had torn the chains apart and smashed the shackles. No one was strong enough to subdue him. ⁵ Night and day among the tombs and on the mountains, he was always crying out and cutting himself with stones.

⁶ When he saw Jesus from a distance, he ran and knelt down before him. ⁷ And he cried out with a loud voice, "What do you have to do with me, Jesus, Son of the Most High God? I beg you before God, don't torment me!" ⁸ For he had told him, "Come out of the man, you unclean spirit!"

⁹ "What is your name?" he asked him.

"My name is Legion," he answered him, "because we are many." ¹⁰ And he begged him earnestly not to send them out of the region.

¹¹ A large herd of pigs was there, feeding on the hillside. ¹² The demons[C] begged him, "Send us to the pigs, so that we may enter them." ¹³ So he gave them permission, and the unclean spirits came out and entered the pigs. The herd of about two thousand rushed down the steep bank into the sea and drowned there.

¹⁴ The men who tended them[D] ran off and reported it in the town and the countryside, and people went to see what had happened. ¹⁵ They came to Jesus and saw the man who had been demon-possessed, sitting there, dressed and in his right mind; and they were afraid. ¹⁶ Those who had seen it described to them what had happened to the demon-possessed man and told about the pigs. ¹⁷ Then they began to beg him to leave their region.

¹⁸ As he was getting into the boat, the man who had been demon-possessed begged him earnestly that he might remain with him. ¹⁹ Jesus did not let him but told him, "Go home to your own people, and report to them how much the Lord has done for you and how he has had mercy on you." ²⁰ So he went out and began to proclaim in the Decapolis how much Jesus had done for him, and they were all amazed.

[A] 4:41 Or *were filled with awe*   [B] 5:1 Some mss read *Gadarenes*; other mss read *Gergesenes*   [C] 5:12 Other mss read *All the demons*   [D] 5:14 Other mss read *tended the pigs*

A GIRL RESTORED AND A WOMAN HEALED

²¹ When Jesus had crossed over again by boat^A to the other side, a large crowd gathered around him while he was by the sea. ²² One of the synagogue leaders, named Jairus, came, and when he saw Jesus, he fell at his feet ²³ and begged him earnestly, "My little daughter is dying. Come and lay your hands on her so that she can get well^B and live." ²⁴ So Jesus went with him, and a large crowd was following and pressing against him.

²⁵ Now a woman suffering from bleeding for twelve years ²⁶ had endured much under many doctors. She had spent everything she had and was not helped at all. On the contrary, she became worse. ²⁷ Having heard about Jesus, she came up behind him in the crowd and touched his clothing. ²⁸ For she said, "If I just touch his clothes, I'll be made well." ²⁹ Instantly her flow of blood ceased, and she sensed in her body that she was healed of her affliction.

³⁰ At once Jesus realized in himself that power had gone out from him. He turned around in the crowd and said, "Who touched my clothes?"

³¹ His disciples said to him, "You see the crowd pressing against you, and yet you say, 'Who touched me?'"

³² But he was looking around to see who had done this. ³³ The woman, with fear and trembling, knowing what had happened to her, came and fell down before him, and told him the whole truth. ³⁴ "Daughter," he said to her, "your faith has saved you. Go in peace and be healed from your affliction."

³⁵ While he was still speaking, people came from the synagogue leader's house and said, "Your daughter is dead. Why bother the teacher anymore?"

³⁶ When Jesus overheard^C what was said, he told the synagogue leader, "Don't be afraid. Only believe." ³⁷ He did not let anyone accompany him except Peter, James, and John, James's brother. ³⁸ They came to the leader's house, and he saw a commotion — people weeping and wailing loudly. ³⁹ He went in and said to them, "Why are you making a commotion and weeping? The child is not dead but asleep." ⁴⁰ They laughed at him, but he put them all outside. He took the child's father, mother, and those who were with him, and entered the place where the child was. ⁴¹ Then he took the child by the hand and said to her, "*Talitha koum*"^D (which is translated, "Little girl, I say to you, get up"). ⁴² Immediately the girl got up and began to walk. (She was twelve years old.) At this they were utterly astounded. ⁴³ Then he gave them strict orders that no one should know about this and told them to give her something to eat.

REJECTION AT NAZARETH

6 He left there and came to his hometown, and his disciples followed him. ² When the Sabbath came, he began to teach in the synagogue, and many who heard him were astonished. "Where did this man get these things?" they said. "What is this wisdom that has been given to him, and how are these miracles performed by his hands? ³ Isn't this the carpenter, the son of Mary, and the brother of James, Joses, Judas, and Simon? And aren't his sisters here with us?" So they were offended by him.

⁴ Jesus said to them, "A prophet is not without honor except in his hometown, among his relatives, and in his household." ⁵ He was not able to do a

---

^A 5:21 Other mss omit *by boat* ^B 5:23 Or *she might be saved* ^C 5:36 Or *ignored*
^D 5:41 An Aramaic expression

miracle there, except that he laid his hands on a few sick people and healed them. [6] And he was amazed at their unbelief. He was going around the villages teaching.

COMMISSIONING THE TWELVE

[7] He summoned the Twelve and began to send them out in pairs and gave them authority over unclean spirits. [8] He instructed them to take nothing for the road except a staff — no bread, no traveling bag, no money in their belts, [9] but to wear sandals and not put on an extra shirt. [10] He said to them, "Whenever you enter a house, stay there until you leave that place. [11] If any place does not welcome you or listen to you, when you leave there, shake the dust off your feet as a testimony against them."[A] [12] So they went out and preached that people should repent. [13] They drove out many demons, anointed many sick people with oil and healed them.

JOHN THE BAPTIST BEHEADED

[14] King Herod heard about it, because Jesus's name had become well known. Some[B] said, "John the Baptist has been raised from the dead, and that's why miraculous powers are at work in him." [15] But others said, "He's Elijah." Still others said, "He's a prophet, like one of the prophets from long ago."

[16] When Herod heard of it, he said, "John, the one I beheaded, has been raised!"

[17] For Herod himself had given orders to arrest John and to chain him in prison on account of Herodias, his brother Philip's wife, because he had married her. [18] John had been telling Herod, "It is not lawful for you to have your brother's wife." [19] So Herodias held a grudge against him and wanted to kill him. But she could not, [20] because Herod feared John and protected him, knowing he was a righteous and holy man. When Herod heard him he would be very perplexed,[C] and yet he liked to listen to him.

[21] An opportune time came on his birthday, when Herod gave a banquet for his nobles, military commanders, and the leading men of Galilee. [22] When Herodias's own daughter[D] came in and danced, she pleased Herod and his guests. The king said to the girl, "Ask me whatever you want, and I'll give it to you." [23] He promised her with an oath: "Whatever you ask me I will give you, up to half my kingdom."

[24] She went out and said to her mother, "What should I ask for?"

"John the Baptist's head," she said.

[25] At once she hurried to the king and said, "I want you to give me John the Baptist's head on a platter immediately." [26] Although the king was deeply distressed, because of his oaths and the guests[E] he did not want to refuse her. [27] The king immediately sent for an executioner and commanded him to bring John's head. So he went and beheaded him in prison, [28] brought his head on a platter, and gave it to the girl. Then the girl gave it to her mother. [29] When John's disciples heard about it, they came and removed his corpse and placed it in a tomb.

[A]6:11 Other mss add *Truly I tell you, it will be more tolerable for Sodom or Gomorrah on judgment day than for that town.*   [B]6:14 Other mss read *He*   [C]6:20 Other mss read *When he heard him, he did many things*   [D]6:22 Other mss read *When his daughter Herodias*   [E]6:26 Lit *and those reclining at the table*

FEEDING OF THE FIVE THOUSAND

[30] The apostles gathered around Jesus and reported to him all that they had done and taught. [31] He said to them, "Come away by yourselves to a remote place and rest for a while." For many people were coming and going, and they did not even have time to eat.

[32] So they went away in the boat by themselves to a remote place, [33] but many saw them leaving and recognized them, and they ran on foot from all the towns and arrived ahead of them.[A]

[34] When he went ashore, he saw a large crowd and had compassion on them, because they were like sheep without a shepherd. Then he began to teach them many things.

[35] When it grew late, his disciples approached him and said, "This place is deserted, and it is already late. [36] Send them away so that they can go into the surrounding countryside and villages to buy themselves something to eat."

[37] "You give them something to eat," he responded.

They said to him, "Should we go and buy two hundred denarii[B] worth of bread and give them something to eat?"

[38] He asked them, "How many loaves do you have? Go and see."

When they found out they said, "Five, and two fish." [39] Then he instructed them to have all the people sit down in groups on the green grass. [40] So they sat down in groups of hundreds and fifties. [41] He took the five loaves and the two fish, and looking up to heaven, he blessed and broke the loaves. He kept giving them to his disciples to set before the people. He also divided the two fish among them all. [42] Everyone ate and was satisfied. [43] They picked up twelve baskets full of pieces of bread and fish. [44] Now those who had eaten the loaves were five thousand men.

WALKING ON THE WATER

[45] Immediately he made his disciples get into the boat and go ahead of him to the other side, to Bethsaida, while he dismissed the crowd. [46] After he said good-bye to them, he went away to the mountain to pray. [47] Well into the night, the boat was in the middle of the sea, and he was alone on the land. [48] He saw them straining at the oars,[C] because the wind was against them. Very early in the morning[D] he came toward them walking on the sea and wanted to pass by them. [49] When they saw him walking on the sea, they thought it was a ghost and cried out, [50] because they all saw him and were terrified. Immediately he spoke with them and said, "Have courage! It is I. Don't be afraid." [51] Then he got into the boat with them, and the wind ceased. They were completely astounded, [52] because they had not understood about the loaves. Instead, their hearts were hardened.

MIRACULOUS HEALINGS

[53] When they had crossed over, they came to shore at Gennesaret and anchored there.

[A]6:33 Other mss add *and gathered around him*   [B]6:37 A denarius = one day's wage   [C]6:48 Or *them being battered as they rowed*   [D]6:48 Lit *Around the fourth watch of the night* = 3 to 6 a.m.

⁵⁴ As they got out of the boat, people immediately recognized him. ⁵⁵ They hurried throughout that region and began to carry the sick on mats to wherever they heard he was. ⁵⁶ Wherever he went, into villages, towns, or the country, they laid the sick in the marketplaces and begged him that they might touch just the end of his robe. And everyone who touched it was healed.

THE TRADITIONS OF THE ELDERS

7 The Pharisees and some of the scribes who had come from Jerusalem gathered around him. ² They observed that some of his disciples were eating bread with unclean — that is, unwashed — hands. ³ (For the Pharisees and all the Jews do not eat unless they give their hands a ceremonial washing, keeping the tradition of the elders. ⁴ When they come from the marketplace, they do not eat unless they have washed. And there are many other customs they have received and keep, like the washing of cups, pitchers, kettles, and dining couches.ᴬ) ⁵ So the Pharisees and the scribes asked him, "Why don't your disciples live according to the tradition of the elders, instead of eating bread with ceremonially unclean ᴮ hands?"

⁶ He answered them, "Isaiah prophesied correctly about you hypocrites, as it is written:

This people honors me with their lips,
but their heart is far from me.
⁷ **They worship me in vain,**
teaching as doctrines human commands.ᶜ

⁸ Abandoning the command of God, you hold on to human tradition."ᴰ ⁹ He also said to them, "You have a fine way of invalidating God's command in order to set upᴱ your tradition! ¹⁰ For Moses said: **Honor your father and your mother;**ᶠ and **Whoever speaks evil of father or mother must be put to death.** ᴳ ¹¹ But you say, 'If anyone tells his father or mother: Whatever benefit you might have received from me is *corban*'" (that is, an offering devoted to God), ¹² "you no longer let him do anything for his father or mother. ¹³ You nullify the word of God by your tradition that you have handed down. And you do many other similar things."

¹⁴ Summoning the crowd again, he told them, "Listen to me, all of you, and understand: ¹⁵ Nothing that goes into a person from outside can defile him but the things that come out of a person are what defile him."ᴴ

¹⁷ When he went into the house away from the crowd, his disciples asked him about the parable. ¹⁸ He said to them, "Are you also as lacking in understanding? Don't you realize that nothing going into a person from the outside can defile him? ¹⁹ For it doesn't go into his heart but into the stomach and is eliminated" (thus he declared all foods cleanᴵ). ²⁰ And he said, "What comes out of a person is what defiles him. ²¹ For from within, out of people's hearts, come evil thoughts, sexual immoralities, thefts, murders, ²² adulteries, greed,

---

ᴬ7:4 Other mss omit *and dining couches* ᴮ7:5 Other mss read *with unwashed*
ᶜ7:6-7 Is 29:13 ᴰ7:8 Other mss add *The washing of jugs, and cups, and many other similar things you practice.* ᴱ7:9 Or *to maintain* ᶠ7:10 Ex 20:12; Dt 5:16
ᴳ7:10 Ex 21:17; Lv 20:9 ᴴ7:15 Some mss include v. 16: *"If anyone has ears to hear, let him listen."* ᴵ7:19 Other mss read *is eliminated, making all foods clean"*

evil actions, deceit, self-indulgence, envy,^ slander, pride, and foolishness. 23 All these evil things come from within and defile a person."

A GENTILE MOTHER'S FAITH

24 He got up and departed from there to the region of Tyre.^B He entered a house and did not want anyone to know it, but he could not escape notice. 25 Instead, immediately after hearing about him, a woman whose little daughter had an unclean spirit came and fell at his feet. 26 The woman was a Gentile,^C a Syrophoenician by birth, and she was asking him to cast the demon out of her daughter. 27 He said to her, "Let the children be fed first, because it isn't right to take the children's bread and throw it to the dogs."

28 But she replied to him, "Lord, even the dogs under the table eat the children's crumbs."

29 Then he told her, "Because of this reply, you may go. The demon has left your daughter." 30 When she went back to her home, she found her child lying on the bed, and the demon was gone.

JESUS DOES EVERYTHING WELL

31 Again, leaving the region of Tyre, he went by way of Sidon to the Sea of Galilee, through^D the region of the Decapolis. 32 They brought to him a deaf man who had difficulty speaking and begged Jesus to lay his hand on him. 33 So he took him away from the crowd in private. After putting his fingers in the man's ears and spitting, he touched his tongue. 34 Looking up to heaven, he sighed deeply and said to him, *"Ephphatha!"*^E (that is, "Be opened!"). 35 Immediately his ears were opened, his tongue was loosened, and he began to speak clearly. 36 He ordered them to tell no one, but the more he ordered them, the more they proclaimed it.

37 They were extremely astonished and said, "He has done everything well. He even makes the deaf hear and the mute speak."

FEEDING FOUR THOUSAND

8 In those days there was again a large crowd, and they had nothing to eat. He called the disciples and said to them, 2 "I have compassion on the crowd, because they've already stayed with me three days and have nothing to eat. 3 If I send them home hungry, they will collapse on the way, and some of them have come a long distance."

4 His disciples answered him, "Where can anyone get enough bread here in this desolate place to feed these people?"

5 "How many loaves do you have?" he asked them.

"Seven," they said. 6 He commanded the crowd to sit down on the ground. Taking the seven loaves, he gave thanks, broke them, and gave them to his disciples to set before the people. So they served them to the crowd. 7 They also had a few small fish, and after he had blessed them, he said these were to be served as well. 8 They ate and were satisfied. Then they collected seven large baskets of leftover pieces. 9 About four thousand were there. He dismissed them. 10 And he immediately got into the boat with his disciples and went to the district of Dalmanutha.

---

^7:22 Or evil eye ^B7:24 Many early mss add *and Sidon* ^C7:26 Or *a Greek (speaker)* ^D7:31 Or *into* ^E7:34 An Aramaic expression

THE LEAVEN OF THE PHARISEES AND HEROD

[11] The Pharisees came and began to argue with him, demanding of him a sign from heaven to test him. [12] Sighing deeply in his spirit, he said, "Why does this generation demand a sign? Truly I tell you, no sign will be given to this generation." [13] Then he left them, got back into the boat, and went to the other side.

[14] The disciples had forgotten to take bread and had only one loaf with them in the boat. [15] Then he gave them strict orders: "Watch out! Beware of the leaven[A] of the Pharisees and the leaven of Herod." [16] They were discussing among themselves that they did not have any bread. [17] Aware of this, he said to them, "Why are you discussing the fact you have no bread? Don't you understand or comprehend? Do you have hardened hearts? [18] **Do you have eyes and not see; do you have ears and not hear?**[B] And do you not remember? [19] When I broke the five loaves for the five thousand, how many baskets full of leftovers did you collect?"

"Twelve," they told him.

[20] "When I broke the seven loaves for the four thousand, how many baskets full of pieces did you collect?"

"Seven," they said.

[21] And he said to them, "Don't you understand yet?"

HEALING A BLIND MAN

[22] They came to Bethsaida. They brought a blind man to him and begged him to touch him. [23] He took the blind man by the hand and brought him out of the village. Spitting on his eyes and laying his hands on him, he asked him, "Do you see anything?"

[24] He looked up and said, "I see people — they look like trees walking."

[25] Again Jesus placed his hands on the man's eyes. The man looked intently and his sight was restored and he saw everything clearly. [26] Then he sent him home, saying, "Don't even go into the village."[C]

PETER'S CONFESSION OF THE MESSIAH

[27] Jesus went out with his disciples to the villages of Caesarea Philippi. And on the road he asked his disciples, "Who do people say that I am?"

[28] They answered him, "John the Baptist; others, Elijah; still others, one of the prophets."

[29] "But you," he asked them, "who do you say that I am?"

Peter answered him, "You are the Messiah." [30] And he strictly warned them to tell no one about him.

HIS DEATH AND RESURRECTION PREDICTED

[31] Then he began to teach them that it was necessary for the Son of Man to suffer many things and be rejected by the elders, chief priests, and scribes, be killed, and rise after three days. [32] He spoke openly about this. Peter took him aside and began to rebuke him. [33] But turning around and looking at his disciples, he rebuked Peter and said, "Get behind me, Satan! You are not thinking about God's concerns[D] but human concerns."

[A]8:15 Or yeast [B]8:18 Jr 5:21; Ezk 12:2 [C]8:26 Other mss add *or tell anyone in the village* [D]8:33 Or *about the things of God*

TAKE UP YOUR CROSS

[34] Calling the crowd along with his disciples, he said to them, "If anyone wants to follow after me, let him deny himself, take up his cross, and follow me. [35] For whoever wants to save his life will lose it, but whoever loses his life because of me and the gospel will save it. [36] For what does it benefit someone to gain the whole world and yet lose his life? [37] What can anyone give in exchange for his life? [38] For whoever is ashamed of me and my words in this adulterous and sinful generation, the Son of Man will also be ashamed of him when he comes in the glory of his Father with the holy angels."

9 Then he said to them, "Truly I tell you, there are some standing here who will not taste death until they see the kingdom of God come in power."

THE TRANSFIGURATION

[2] After six days Jesus took Peter, James, and John and led them up a high mountain by themselves to be alone. He was transfigured in front of them, [3] and his clothes became dazzling — extremely white as no launderer on earth could whiten them. [4] Elijah appeared to them with Moses, and they were talking with Jesus. [5] Peter said to Jesus, "Rabbi, it's good for us to be here. Let us set up three shelters: one for you, one for Moses, and one for Elijah" — [6] because he did not know what to say, since they were terrified.

[7] A cloud appeared, overshadowing them, and a voice came from the cloud: "This is my beloved Son; listen to him!"

[8] Suddenly, looking around, they no longer saw anyone with them except Jesus.

[9] As they were coming down the mountain, he ordered them to tell no one what they had seen until the Son of Man had risen from the dead. [10] They kept this word to themselves, questioning what "rising from the dead" meant.

[11] Then they asked him, "Why do the scribes say that Elijah must come first?"

[12] "Elijah does come first and restores all things," he replied. "Why then is it written that the Son of Man must suffer many things and be treated with contempt? [13] But I tell you that Elijah has come, and they did whatever they pleased to him, just as it is written about him."

THE POWER OF FAITH OVER A DEMON

[14] When they came to the disciples, they saw a large crowd around them and scribes disputing with them. [15] When the whole crowd saw him, they were amazed and ran to greet him. [16] He asked them, "What are you arguing with them about?"

[17] Someone from the crowd answered him, "Teacher, I brought my son to you. He has a spirit that makes him unable to speak. [18] Whenever it seizes him, it throws him down, and he foams at the mouth, grinds his teeth, and becomes rigid. I asked your disciples to drive it out, but they couldn't."

[19] He replied to them, "You unbelieving generation, how long will I be with you? How long must I put up with you? Bring him to me." [20] So they brought the boy to him. When the spirit saw him, it immediately threw the boy into convulsions. He fell to the ground and rolled around, foaming at the mouth. [21] "How long has this been happening to him?" Jesus asked his father.

"From childhood," he said. [22] "And many times it has thrown him into fire or water to destroy him. But if you can do anything, have compassion on us and help us."

²³ Jesus said to him, " 'If you can'?ᴬ Everything is possible for the one who believes."

²⁴ Immediately the father of the boy cried out, "I do believe; help my unbelief!"

²⁵ When Jesus saw that a crowd was quickly gathering, he rebuked the unclean spirit, saying to it, "You mute and deaf spirit, I command you: Come out of him and never enter him again."

²⁶ Then it came out, shrieking and throwing himᴮ into terrible convulsions. The boy became like a corpse, so that many said, "He's dead." ²⁷ But Jesus, taking him by the hand, raised him, and he stood up.

²⁸ After he had gone into the house, his disciples asked him privately, "Why couldn't we drive it out?"

²⁹ And he told them, "This kind can come out by nothing but prayer."ᶜ

THE SECOND PREDICTION OF HIS DEATH

³⁰ Then they left that place and made their way through Galilee, but he did not want anyone to know it. ³¹ For he was teaching his disciples and telling them, "The Son of Man is going to be betrayedᴰ into the hands of men. They will kill him, and after he is killed, he will rise three days later." ³² But they did not understand this statement, and they were afraid to ask him.

WHO IS THE GREATEST?

³³ They came to Capernaum. When he was in the house, he asked them, "What were you arguing about on the way?" ³⁴ But they were silent, because on the way they had been arguing with one another about who was the greatest. ³⁵ Sitting down, he called the Twelve and said to them, "If anyone wants to be first, he must be last and servant of all." ³⁶ He took a child, had him stand among them, and taking him in his arms, he said to them, ³⁷ "Whoever welcomesᴱ one little child such as this in my name welcomes me. And whoever welcomes me does not welcome me, but him who sent me."

IN HIS NAME

³⁸ John said to him, "Teacher, we saw someoneᶠ driving out demons in your name, and we tried to stop him because he wasn't following us."

³⁹ "Don't stop him," said Jesus, "because there is no one who will perform a miracle in my name who can soon afterward speak evil of me. ⁴⁰ For whoever is not against us is for us. ⁴¹ And whoever gives you a cup of water to drink in my name, because you belong to Christ — truly I tell you, he will never lose his reward.

WARNINGS FROM JESUS

⁴² "But whoever causes one of these little ones who believe in me to fall away — it would be better for him if a heavy millstone were hung around his neck and he were thrown into the sea.

⁴³ "And if your hand causes you to fall away, cut it off. It is better for you to enter life maimed than to have two hands and go to hell, the unquenchable

---

ᴬ9:23 Other mss add *believe*   ᴮ9:26 Other mss omit *him*   ᶜ9:29 Other mss add *and fasting*   ᴰ9:31 Or *handed over*   ᴱ9:37 Or *"Whoever receives*
ᶠ9:38 Other mss add *who didn't go along with us*

THE TRUE SIZE OF OUR RANSOM

MARK 10; MATTHEW 20:20-28

I'm a considerably tall girl still looking for her exceptionally tall guy.

You see, I have dated really nice, yet average-height, guys before, and it's gone great. That is, up until . . . *the group bowling date.* I'll never know why that's a relationship milestone, but for me, it apparently is.

Prior to this point in the relationship, I can manage to pull off a dainty persona. Then comes the moment my gentleman-of-a-date asks for my shoe size. In an attempt to guess a size smaller than his feet, I casually offer a number that will make him think about how adorable I am as he carries our shoes side by side all the way back to our lane. I'll bend my feet in half like one of Cinderella's stepsisters to make them fit, thus maintaining my dainty charade.

But then it happens: a few spares, splits, and gutter balls in, he will inevitably notice me wince my way to the ball return. He'll comment on my "cute" blisters, made evident by my now-red socks. The truth that I need a bigger size won't stay hidden.

In Mark 10, the disciples have a similarly embarrassing conversation with Jesus. They are pumped up by their new connection to the King of kings, hoping to squeeze into a position at His right hand. But they are so puffed up with pride, they're oblivious to their true needs.

Jesus points to their red, blistered hearts, saying, "whoever wants to become great among you will be your servant" (Mk 10:43). It's as if He's

saying, *Don't you know you need something bigger than position and power?*

The disciples are blind to the amount of debt their sin has accrued. Their pride wants to minimize the weight of the debt and the price demanded to relieve it, but the truth is this:

"For even the Son of Man did not come to be served, but to serve, and to give his life as a ransom for many."

MARK 10:45

The word "ransom" here is *lutron* in Greek—a word historically used when referring to ransom in the realm of warfare. In Mark's day, when someone was a prisoner of war, there were typically two options left for him or her: slavery or death. Unless, on the very rare occasion, someone rescued them by paying the ransom for their release.

The same is true for us: without Christ, our only option is slavery to sin and death. By blinding ourselves to the debt we owe, our eyes remain closed to the One who already paid it. Christ isn't just giving us an example of humility here; He's showing us the only way out.

May we be ever reminded of the true size of our ransom so that we never forget the size of our rescue.

fire. [A] 45 And if your foot causes you to fall away, cut it off. It is better for you to enter life lame than to have two feet and be thrown into hell. [B] 47 And if your eye causes you to fall away, gouge it out. It is better for you to enter the kingdom of God with one eye than to have two eyes and be thrown into hell, 48 where **their worm does not die, and the fire is not quenched.** [C] 49 For everyone will be salted with fire. [D,E] 50 Salt is good, but if the salt should lose its flavor, how can you season it? Have salt among yourselves, and be at peace with one another."

THE QUESTION OF DIVORCE

10 He set out from there and went to the region of Judea and across the Jordan. Then crowds converged on him again, and as was his custom he taught them again.

2 Some Pharisees came to test him, asking, "Is it lawful for a man to divorce his wife?"

3 He replied to them, "What did Moses command you?"

4 They said, "Moses permitted us to write divorce papers and send her away."

5 But Jesus told them, "He wrote this command for you because of the hardness of your hearts. 6 But from the beginning of creation God [F] **made them male and female.** [G] 7 **For this reason a man will leave his father and mother** [H] 8 **and the two will become one flesh.** [I] So they are no longer two, but one flesh. 9 Therefore what God has joined together, let no one separate."

10 When they were in the house again, the disciples questioned him about this matter. 11 He said to them, "Whoever divorces his wife and marries another commits adultery against her. 12 Also, if she divorces her husband and marries another, she commits adultery."

BLESSING THE CHILDREN

13 People were bringing little children to him in order that he might touch them, but the disciples rebuked them. 14 When Jesus saw it, he was indignant and said to them, "Let the little children come to me. Don't stop them, because the kingdom of God belongs to such as these. 15 Truly I tell you, whoever does not receive [J] the kingdom of God like a little child will never enter it." 16 After taking them in his arms, he laid his hands on them and blessed them.

THE RICH YOUNG RULER

17 As he was setting out on a journey, a man ran up, knelt down before him, and asked him, "Good teacher, what must I do to inherit eternal life?"

18 "Why do you call me good?" Jesus asked him. "No one is good except God alone. 19 You know the commandments: **Do not murder; do not commit adultery; do not steal; do not bear false witness; do not defraud; honor your father and mother.**" [K]

[A]9:43 Some mss include v. 44: *Where their worm does not die, and the fire is not quenched.* [B]9:45 Some mss include v. 46: *Where their worm does not die, and the fire is not quenched.* [C]9:48 Is 66:24 [D]9:49 Other mss add *and every sacrifice will be salted with salt* [E]9:49 Lv 2:13; Ezk 43:24 [F]10:6 Other mss omit *God* [G]10:6 Gn 1:27; 5:2 [H]10:7 Some mss add *and be joined to his wife* [I]10:7-8 Gn 2:24 [J]10:15 Or *not welcome* [K]10:19 Ex 20:12-16; Dt 5:16-20

²⁰ He said to him, "Teacher, I have kept all these from my youth."

²¹ Looking at him, Jesus loved him and said to him, "You lack one thing: Go, sell all you have and give to the poor, and you will have treasure in heaven. Then come, ᴬ follow me." ²² But he was dismayed by this demand, and he went away grieving, because he had many possessions.

POSSESSIONS AND THE KINGDOM

²³ Jesus looked around and said to his disciples, "How hard it is for those who have wealth to enter the kingdom of God!"

²⁴ The disciples were astonished at his words. Again Jesus said to them, "Children, how hard it is ᴮ to enter the kingdom of God! ²⁵ It is easier for a camel to go through the eye of a needle than for a rich person to enter the kingdom of God."

²⁶ They were even more astonished, saying to one another, "Then who can be saved?"

²⁷ Looking at them, Jesus said, "With man it is impossible, but not with God, because all things are possible with God."

²⁸ Peter began to tell him, "Look, we have left everything and followed you."

²⁹ "Truly I tell you," Jesus said, "there is no one who has left house or brothers or sisters or mother or father ᶜ or children or fields for my sake and for the sake of the gospel, ³⁰ who will not receive a hundred times more, now at this time — houses, brothers and sisters, mothers and children, and fields, with persecutions — and eternal life in the age to come. ³¹ But many who are first will be last, and the last first."

THE THIRD PREDICTION OF HIS DEATH

³² They were on the road, going up to Jerusalem, and Jesus was walking ahead of them. The disciples were astonished, but those who followed him were afraid. Taking the Twelve aside again, he began to tell them the things that would happen to him. ³³ "See, we are going up to Jerusalem. The Son of Man will be handed over to the chief priests and the scribes, and they will condemn him to death. Then they will hand him over to the Gentiles, ³⁴ and they will mock him, spit on him, flog ᴰ him, and kill him, and he will rise after three days."

SUFFERING AND SERVICE

³⁵ James and John, the sons of Zebedee, approached him and said, "Teacher, we want you to do whatever we ask you."

³⁶ "What do you want me to do for you?" he asked them.

³⁷ They answered him, "Allow us to sit at your right and at your left in your glory."

³⁸ Jesus said to them, "You don't know what you're asking. Are you able to drink the cup I drink or to be baptized with the baptism I am baptized with?"

³⁹ "We are able," they told him.

Jesus said to them, "You will drink the cup I drink, and you will be baptized with the baptism I am baptized with. ⁴⁰ But to sit at my right or left is not mine to give; instead, it is for those for whom it has been prepared."

ᴬ 10:21 Other mss add *taking up the cross, and*   ᴮ 10:24 Other mss add *for those trusting in wealth*   ᶜ 10:29 Other mss add *or wife*   ᴰ 10:34 Or *scourge*

[41] When the ten disciples heard this, they began to be indignant with James and John. [42] Jesus called them over and said to them, "You know that those who are regarded as rulers of the Gentiles lord it over them, and those in high positions act as tyrants over them. [43] But it is not so among you. On the contrary, whoever wants to become great among you will be your servant, [44] and whoever wants to be first among you will be a slave to all. [45] For even the Son of Man did not come to be served, but to serve, and to give his life as a ransom for many."[A]

A BLIND MAN HEALED

[46] They came to Jericho. And as he was leaving Jericho with his disciples and a large crowd, Bartimaeus (the son of Timaeus), a blind beggar, was sitting by the road. [47] When he heard that it was Jesus of Nazareth, he began to cry out, "Jesus, Son of David, have mercy on me!" [48] Many warned him to keep quiet, but he was crying out all the more, "Have mercy on me, Son of David!"

[49] Jesus stopped and said, "Call him."

So they called the blind man and said to him, "Have courage! Get up; he's calling for you." [50] He threw off his coat, jumped up, and came to Jesus.

[51] Then Jesus answered him, "What do you want me to do for you?"

"Rabboni,"[B] the blind man said to him, "I want to see."

[52] Jesus said to him, "Go, your faith has saved you." Immediately he could see and began to follow Jesus on the road.

THE TRIUMPHAL ENTRY

11 When they approached Jerusalem, at Bethphage and Bethany near the Mount of Olives, he sent two of his disciples [2] and told them, "Go into the village ahead of you. As soon as you enter it, you will find a colt tied there, on which no one has ever sat. Untie it and bring it. [3] If anyone says to you, 'Why are you doing this?' say, 'The Lord needs it and will send it back here right away.'"

[4] So they went and found a colt outside in the street, tied by a door. They untied it, [5] and some of those standing there said to them, "What are you doing, untying the colt?" [6] They answered them just as Jesus had said; so they let them go.

[7] They brought the colt to Jesus and threw their clothes on it, and he sat on it. [8] Many people spread their clothes on the road, and others spread leafy branches cut from the fields.[C] [9] Those who went ahead and those who followed shouted:

Hosanna!
**Blessed is he who comes
in the name of the Lord!**[D]
[10] Blessed is the coming kingdom
of our father David!
Hosanna in the highest heaven!

[11] He went into Jerusalem and into the temple. After looking around at everything, since it was already late, he went out to Bethany with the Twelve.

[A]10:45 Or *in the place of many*; Is 53:10-12   [B]10:51 Hb word for *my lord*
[C]11:8 Other mss read *others were cutting leafy branches from the trees and spreading them on the road*   [D]11:9 Ps 118:26

THE BARREN FIG TREE IS CURSED

[12] The next day when they went out from Bethany, he was hungry. [13] Seeing in the distance a fig tree with leaves, he went to find out if there was anything on it. When he came to it, he found nothing but leaves; for it was not the season for figs. [14] He said to it, "May no one ever eat fruit from you again!" And his disciples heard it.

CLEANSING THE TEMPLE

[15] They came to Jerusalem, and he went into the temple and began to throw out those buying and selling. He overturned the tables of the money changers and the chairs of those selling doves, [16] and would not permit anyone to carry goods through the temple. [17] He was teaching them: "Is it not written, **My house will be called a house of prayer for all nations?**[A] But you have made it **a den of thieves!**"[B]

[18] The chief priests and the scribes heard it and started looking for a way to kill him. For they were afraid of him, because the whole crowd was astonished by his teaching.

[19] Whenever evening came, they would go out of the city.

THE BARREN FIG TREE IS WITHERED

[20] Early in the morning, as they were passing by, they saw the fig tree withered from the roots up. [21] Then Peter remembered and said to him, "Rabbi, look! The fig tree that you cursed has withered."

[22] Jesus replied to them, "Have faith in God. [23] Truly I tell you, if anyone says to this mountain, 'Be lifted up and thrown into the sea,' and does not doubt in his heart, but believes that what he says will happen, it will be done for him. [24] Therefore I tell you, everything you pray and ask for — believe that you have received[C] it and it will be yours. [25] And whenever you stand praying, if you have anything against anyone, forgive him, so that your Father in heaven will also forgive you your wrongdoing."[D]

THE AUTHORITY OF JESUS CHALLENGED

[27] They came again to Jerusalem. As he was walking in the temple, the chief priests, the scribes, and the elders came [28] and asked him, "By what authority are you doing these things? Who gave you this authority to do these things?"

[29] Jesus said to them, "I will ask you one question; then answer me, and I will tell you by what authority I do these things. [30] Was John's baptism from heaven or of human origin? Answer me."

[31] They discussed it among themselves: "If we say, 'From heaven,' he will say, 'Then why didn't you believe him?' [32] But if we say, 'Of human origin'" — they were afraid of the crowd, because everyone thought that John was truly a prophet. [33] So they answered Jesus, "We don't know."

And Jesus said to them, "Neither will I tell you by what authority I do these things."

[A]11:17 Is 56:7 [B]11:17 Jr 7:11 [C]11:24 Some mss read *you receive*; other mss read *you will receive* [D]11:25 Some mss include v. 26: *"But if you don't forgive, neither will your Father in heaven forgive your wrongdoing."*

THE PARABLE OF THE VINEYARD OWNER

12 He began to speak to them in parables: "A man planted a vineyard, put a fence around it, dug out a pit for a winepress, and built a watchtower. Then he leased it to tenant farmers and went away. ² At harvest time he sent a servant to the farmers to collect some of the fruit of the vineyard from them. ³ But they took him, beat him, and sent him away empty-handed. ⁴ Again he sent another servant to them, and they ᴬ hit him on the head and treated him shamefully. ᴮ ⁵ Then he sent another, and they killed that one. He also sent many others; some they beat, and others they killed. ⁶ He still had one to send, a beloved son. Finally he sent him to them, saying, 'They will respect my son.' ⁷ But those tenant farmers said to one another, 'This is the heir. Come, let's kill him, and the inheritance will be ours.' ⁸ So they seized him, killed him, and threw him out of the vineyard. ⁹ What then will the owner ᶜ of the vineyard do? He will come and kill the farmers and give the vineyard to others. ¹⁰ Haven't you read this Scripture:

**The stone that the builders rejected
has become the cornerstone.**
¹¹ **This came about from the Lord
and is wonderful in our eyes?** " ᴰ

¹² They were looking for a way to arrest him but feared the crowd because they knew he had spoken this parable against them. So they left him and went away.

GOD AND CAESAR

¹³ Then they sent some of the Pharisees and the Herodians to Jesus to trap him in his words. ¹⁴ When they came, they said to him, "Teacher, we know you are truthful and don't care what anyone thinks, nor do you show partiality but teach the way of God truthfully. Is it lawful to pay taxes to Caesar or not? Should we pay or shouldn't we?"

¹⁵ But knowing their hypocrisy, he said to them, "Why are you testing me? Bring me a denarius ᴱ to look at." ¹⁶ They brought a coin. "Whose image and inscription is this?" he asked them.

"Caesar's," they replied.

¹⁷ Jesus told them, "Give to Caesar the things that are Caesar's, and to God the things that are God's." And they were utterly amazed at him.

THE SADDUCEES AND THE RESURRECTION

¹⁸ Sadducees, who say there is no resurrection, came to him and questioned him: ¹⁹ "Teacher, Moses wrote for us that **if a man's brother dies**, leaving a wife behind but **no child, that man should take the wife and raise up offspring for his brother.** ᶠ ²⁰ There were seven brothers. The first married a woman, and dying, left no offspring. ²¹ The second also took her, and he died, leaving no offspring. And the third likewise. ²² None of the seven ᴳ left offspring. Last of all, the woman died too. ²³ In the resurrection, when they rise, ᴴ whose wife will she be, since the seven had married her?"

ᴬ 12:4 Other mss add *threw stones and* ᴮ 12:4 Other mss add *and sent him off*
ᶜ 12:9 Or *lord* ᴰ 12:10-11 Ps 118:22-23 ᴱ 12:15 A denarius = one day's wage
ᶠ 12:19 Gn 38:8; Dt 25:5 ᴳ 12:22 Other mss add *had taken her and*
ᴴ 12:23 Other mss omit *when they rise*

²⁴ Jesus spoke to them, "Isn't this the reason why you're mistaken: you don't know the Scriptures or the power of God? ²⁵ For when they rise from the dead, they neither marry nor are given in marriage but are like angels in heaven. ²⁶ And as for the dead being raised — haven't you read in the book of Moses, in the passage about the burning bush, how God said to him: **I am the God of Abraham and the God of Isaac and the God of Jacob?**ᴬ ²⁷ He is not the God of the dead but of the living. You are badly mistaken."

THE PRIMARY COMMANDS

²⁸ One of the scribes approached. When he heard them debating and saw that Jesus answered them well, he asked him, "Which command is the most important of all?"

²⁹ Jesus answered, "The most importantᴮ is **Listen, O Israel! The Lord our God, the Lord is one.**ᶜ ³⁰ **Love the Lord your God with all your heart, with all your soul, with all your mind, and with all your strength.**ᴰ,ᴱ ³¹ The second is, **Love your neighbor as yourself.**ᶠ There is no other command greater than these."

³² Then the scribe said to him, "You are right, teacher. You have correctly said that he is one, and there is no one else except him. ³³ And to love him with all your heart, with all your understanding,ᴳ and with all your strength, and to love your neighbor as yourself, is far more important than all the burnt offerings and sacrifices."

³⁴ When Jesus saw that he answered wisely, he said to him, "You are not far from the kingdom of God." And no one dared to question him any longer.

THE QUESTION ABOUT THE CHRIST

³⁵ While Jesus was teaching in the temple, he asked, "How can the scribes say that the Messiah is the son of David? ³⁶ David himself says by the Holy Spirit:

> The Lord declared to my Lord,
> 'Sit at my right hand
> until I put your enemies under your feet.'ᴴ

³⁷ David himself calls him 'Lord'; how then can he be his son?" And the large crowd was listening to him with delight.

WARNING AGAINST THE SCRIBES

³⁸ He also said in his teaching, "Beware of the scribes, who want to go around in long robes and who want greetings in the marketplaces, ³⁹ the best seats in the synagogues, and the places of honor at banquets. ⁴⁰ They devour widows' houses and say long prayers just for show. These will receive harsher judgment."

THE WIDOW'S GIFT

⁴¹ Sitting across from the temple treasury, he watched how the crowd dropped money into the treasury. Many rich people were putting in large sums. ⁴² Then a poor widow came and dropped in two tiny coins worth very little.

ᴬ12:26 Ex 3:6,15-16 ᴮ12:29 Other mss add *of all the commands* ᶜ12:29 Or *the Lord our God is Lord alone.* ᴰ12:30 Other mss add *This is the first commandment.* ᴱ12:30 Dt 6:4-5; Jos 22:5 ᶠ12:31 Lv 19:18 ᴳ12:33 Other mss add *with all your soul* ᴴ12:36 Ps 110:1

[43] Summoning his disciples, he said to them, "Truly I tell you, this poor widow has put more into the treasury than all the others. [44] For they all gave out of their surplus, but she out of her poverty has put in everything she had — all she had to live on."

DESTRUCTION OF THE TEMPLE PREDICTED

13 As he was going out of the temple, one of his disciples said to him, "Teacher, look! What massive stones! What impressive buildings!"
[2] Jesus said to him, "Do you see these great buildings? Not one stone will be left upon another — all will be thrown down."

SIGNS OF THE END OF THE AGE

[3] While he was sitting on the Mount of Olives across from the temple, Peter, James, John, and Andrew asked him privately, [4] "Tell us, when will these things happen? And what will be the sign when all these things are about to be accomplished?"

[5] Jesus told them, "Watch out that no one deceives you. [6] Many will come in my name, saying, 'I am he,' and they will deceive many. [7] When you hear of wars and rumors of wars, don't be alarmed; these things must take place, but it is not yet the end. [8] For nation will rise up against nation, and kingdom against kingdom. There will be earthquakes in various places, and famines.[A] These are the beginning of birth pains.

PERSECUTIONS PREDICTED

[9] "But you, be on your guard! They will hand you over to local courts,[B] and you will be flogged in the synagogues. You will stand before governors and kings because of me, as a witness to them. [10] And it is necessary that the gospel be preached to all nations. [11] So when they arrest you and hand you over, don't worry beforehand what you will say, but say whatever is given to you at that time, for it isn't you speaking, but the Holy Spirit.

[12] "Brother will betray brother to death, and a father his child. Children will rise up against parents and have them put to death. [13] You will be hated by everyone because of my name, but the one who endures to the end will be saved.

THE GREAT TRIBULATION

[14] "When you see **the abomination of desolation**[C] standing where it should not be" (let the reader understand), "then those in Judea must flee to the mountains. [15] A man on the housetop must not come down or go in to get anything out of his house, [16] and a man in the field must not go back to get his coat. [17] Woe to pregnant women and nursing mothers in those days!

[18] "Pray it[D] won't happen in winter. [19] For those will be days of tribulation, the kind that hasn't been from the beginning of creation until now and never will be again. [20] If the Lord had not cut those days short, no one would be saved. But he cut those days short for the sake of the elect, whom he chose.

[21] "Then if anyone tells you, 'See, here is the Messiah! See, there!' do not believe it. [22] For false messiahs and false prophets will arise and will perform

---

[A] 13:8 Other mss add *and disturbances*   [B] 13:9 Or *sanhedrins*   [C] 13:14 Dn 9:27
[D] 13:18 Other mss read *"Pray that your escape*

signs and wonders to lead astray, if possible, the elect. ²³ And you must watch! I have told you everything in advance.

THE COMING OF THE SON OF MAN

²⁴ "But in those days, after that tribulation: The sun will be darkened, and the moon will not shed its light; ²⁵ the stars will be falling from the sky, and the powers in the heavens will be shaken. ²⁶ Then they will see the Son of Man coming in clouds with great power and glory. ²⁷ He will send out the angels and gather his elect from the four winds, from the ends of the earth to the ends of heaven.

THE PARABLE OF THE FIG TREE

²⁸ "Learn this lesson from the fig tree: As soon as its branch becomes tender and sprouts leaves, you know that summer is near. ²⁹ In the same way, when you see these things happening, recognize^A that he^B is near — at the door.

³⁰ "Truly I tell you, this generation will certainly not pass away until all these things take place. ³¹ Heaven and earth will pass away, but my words will never pass away.

NO ONE KNOWS THE DAY OR HOUR

³² "Now concerning that day or hour no one knows — neither the angels in heaven nor the Son — but only the Father.

³³ "Watch! Be alert!^C For you don't know when the time is coming.

³⁴ "It is like a man on a journey, who left his house, gave authority to his servants, gave each one his work, and commanded the doorkeeper to be alert. ³⁵ Therefore be alert, since you don't know when the master of the house is coming — whether in the evening or at midnight or at the crowing of the rooster or early in the morning. ³⁶ Otherwise, when he comes suddenly he might find you sleeping. ³⁷ And what I say to you, I say to everyone: Be alert!"

THE PLOT TO KILL JESUS

14 It was two days before the Passover and the Festival of Unleavened Bread. The chief priests and the scribes were looking for a cunning way to arrest Jesus and kill him. ² "Not during the festival," they said, "so that there won't be a riot among the people."

THE ANOINTING AT BETHANY

³ While he was in Bethany at the house of Simon the leper,^D as he was reclining at the table, a woman came with an alabaster jar of very expensive perfume of pure nard. She broke the jar and poured it on his head. ⁴ But some were expressing indignation to one another: "Why has this perfume been wasted? ⁵ For this perfume might have been sold for more than three hundred denarii^E and given to the poor." And they began to scold her.

⁶ Jesus replied, "Leave her alone. Why are you bothering her? She has done a noble thing for me. ⁷ You always have the poor with you, and you can do what is good for them whenever you want, but you do not always have me.

---

^A13:29 Or you know   ^B13:29 Or it   ^C13:33 Other mss add and pray   ^D14:3 Gk lepros; a term for various skin diseases; see Lv 13–14   ^E14:5 A denarius = one day's wage

WE CANNOT WASH OUR HANDS OF THIS

MARK 14; MARK 15:1-20; MATTHEW 27:24; ROMANS 3:23-25

We all want justice. We want the guilty punished and the innocent set free, preferably in a tidy, sixty-minute time slot. But reality rarely plays out like our favorite detective show. The world's lack of perfect and timely justice is one bitter pill we have to swallow when reading about Jesus' many trials. Have you ever tallied them up?

He appeared before Annas (former high priest and father-in-law to Caiaphas), who handed down no verdict, passing Jesus up the political ladder (Jn 18:12-24).

He appeared before the Sanhedrin (basically the ancient Supreme Court of religious leaders), and the trial was a circus marked by conflicting testimonies. The web of lies woven by those hungry to see Jesus punished couldn't hold up (Mk 14:55-59).

He appeared before Caiaphas (the reigning high priest), where He remained silent throughout questioning until asked, "Are you the Messiah?" Jesus replied, "I am," and Caiaphas claimed blasphemy (Mk 14:60-64).

He appeared before Pilate (a Roman government official), who knew the religious leaders had targeted Jesus out of jealousy. But they stirred up the crowd against Him, and Pilate released Barabbas instead (Mk 15:10-11).

He appeared before Herod Antipas (the ruler of the Galileans), who wanted a dog and pony show, not a trial. When Jesus refused to perform miracles, He was sent back to Pilate (Lk 23:6-12).

He appeared before Pilate again, who recognized Jesus' innocence but feared His release meant political suicide. Distancing himself from the impending guilty verdict, Pilate declared, "I am innocent of this man's blood. See to it yourselves!" (Mt 27:24).

That's six trials. Six times Jesus was brought before judges who were not interested in the truth. Six times He appeared before officials on trumped-up charges and listened to people shout lies and false accusations. Not only that, but even after Pilate became convinced of Jesus' innocence, he still passed a sentence on Jesus as if Jesus was guilty.

Lady justice would be mortified. I am mortified.

I'm tempted to assume Pilate's position, to simply wash my hands of these shenanigans and shake my head at a justice system that was clearly broken. But it was not the justice system that failed Jesus. It was me.

Any judge or jury looking for guilt could find the evidence stacked overwhelmingly against me. I am a sinner, guilty of falling short of the glory of God (Rm 3:23).

But Jesus took my place. He took yours.

We cannot simply wash our hands of the truth that Jesus, who never sinned, took the punishment for our sin. He absorbed all the accusations so the enemy could no longer accuse us. Jesus endured the "guilty" verdict six times so we could be declared "not guilty" for all eternity.

What Jesus offers us is something far beyond what His kangaroo court could have ever imagined. He offers us radical, unmerited, irreversible redemption.

[8] She has done what she could; she has anointed my body in advance for burial. [9] Truly I tell you, wherever the gospel is proclaimed in the whole world, what she has done will also be told in memory of her."

[10] Then Judas Iscariot, one of the Twelve, went to the chief priests to betray Jesus to them. [11] And when they heard this, they were glad and promised to give him money. So he started looking for a good opportunity to betray him.

PREPARATION FOR PASSOVER

[12] On the first day of Unleavened Bread, when they sacrifice the Passover lamb, his disciples asked him, "Where do you want us to go and prepare the Passover so that you may eat it?"

[13] So he sent two of his disciples and told them, "Go into the city, and a man carrying a jar of water will meet you. Follow him. [14] Wherever he enters, tell the owner of the house, 'The Teacher says, "Where is my guest room where I may eat the Passover with my disciples?" ' [15] He will show you a large room upstairs, furnished and ready. Make the preparations for us there." [16] So the disciples went out, entered the city, and found it just as he had told them, and they prepared the Passover.

BETRAYAL AT THE PASSOVER

[17] When evening came, he arrived with the Twelve. [18] While they were reclining and eating, Jesus said, "Truly I tell you, one of you will betray me — one who is eating with me."

[19] They began to be distressed and to say to him one by one, "Surely not I?"

[20] He said to them, "It is one of the Twelve — the one who is dipping bread in the bowl with me. [21] For the Son of Man will go just as it is written about him, but woe to that man by whom the Son of Man is betrayed! It would have been better for him if he had not been born."

THE FIRST LORD'S SUPPER

[22] As they were eating, he took bread, blessed and broke it, gave it to them, and said, "Take it; this is my body." [23] Then he took a cup, and after giving thanks, he gave it to them, and they all drank from it. [24] He said to them, "This is my blood of the covenant,[A] which is poured out for many. [25] Truly I tell you, I will no longer drink of the fruit of the vine until that day when I drink it new[B] in the kingdom of God."

[26] After singing a hymn, they went out to the Mount of Olives.

PETER'S DENIAL PREDICTED

[27] Then Jesus said to them, "All of you will fall away,[C] because it is written:

I will strike the shepherd,
and the sheep will be scattered.[D]

[28] But after I have risen, I will go ahead of you to Galilee."

[29] Peter told him, "Even if everyone falls away, I will not."

[30] "Truly I tell you," Jesus said to him, "today, this very night, before the rooster crows twice, you will deny me three times."

[A]14:24 Other mss read the new covenant   [B]14:25 Or drink new wine; lit drink it new   [C]14:27 Other mss add because of me this night   [D]14:27 Zch 13:7

[31] But he kept insisting, "If I have to die with you, I will never deny you." And they all said the same thing.

THE PRAYER IN THE GARDEN

[32] Then they came to a place named Gethsemane, and he told his disciples, "Sit here while I pray." [33] He took Peter, James, and John with him, and he began to be deeply distressed and troubled. [34] He said to them, "I am deeply grieved[A] to the point of death. Remain here and stay awake." [35] He went a little farther, fell to the ground, and prayed that if it were possible, the hour might pass from him. [36] And he said, "*Abba*,[B] Father! All things are possible for you. Take this cup away from me. Nevertheless, not what I will, but what you will." [37] Then he came and found them sleeping. He said to Peter, "Simon, are you sleeping? Couldn't you stay awake one hour? [38] Stay awake and pray so that you won't enter into temptation.[C] The spirit is willing, but the flesh is weak." [39] Once again he went away and prayed, saying the same thing. [40] And again he came and found them sleeping, because they could not keep their eyes open. They did not know what to say to him. [41] Then he came a third time and said to them, "Are you still sleeping and resting? Enough! The time has come. See, the Son of Man is betrayed into the hands of sinners. [42] Get up; let's go. See, my betrayer is near."

JUDAS'S BETRAYAL OF JESUS

[43] While he was still speaking, Judas, one of the Twelve, suddenly arrived. With him was a mob, with swords and clubs, from the chief priests, the scribes, and the elders. [44] His betrayer had given them a signal. "The one I kiss," he said, "he's the one; arrest him and take him away under guard." [45] So when he came, immediately he went up to Jesus and said, "Rabbi!" and kissed him. [46] They took hold of him and arrested him. [47] One of those who stood by drew his sword, struck the high priest's servant, and cut off his ear.

[48] Jesus said to them, "Have you come out with swords and clubs, as if I were a criminal,[D] to capture me? [49] Every day I was among you, teaching in the temple, and you didn't arrest me. But the Scriptures must be fulfilled."

[50] Then they all deserted him and ran away. [51] Now a certain young man, wearing nothing but a linen cloth, was following him. They caught hold of him, [52] but he left the linen cloth behind and ran away naked.

JESUS FACES THE SANHEDRIN

[53] They led Jesus away to the high priest, and all the chief priests, the elders, and the scribes assembled. [54] Peter followed him at a distance, right into the high priest's courtyard. He was sitting with the servants,[E] warming himself by the fire.

[55] The chief priests and the whole Sanhedrin were looking for testimony against Jesus to put him to death, but they could not find any. [56] For many were giving false testimony against him, and the testimonies did not agree. [57] Some stood up and gave false testimony against him, stating, [58] "We heard him say, 'I will destroy this temple made with human hands, and in three

---

[A] 14:34 Or "My soul is swallowed up in sorrow   [B] 14:36 Aramaic for father
[C] 14:38 Or won't be put to the test   [D] 14:48 Or insurrectionist   [E] 14:54 Or temple police, or officers, also in v. 65

days I will build another not made by hands.'" 59 Yet their testimony did not agree even on this.

60 Then the high priest stood up before them all and questioned Jesus, "Don't you have an answer to what these men are testifying against you?" 61 But he kept silent and did not answer. Again the high priest questioned him, "Are you the Messiah, the Son of the Blessed One?"

62 "I am," said Jesus, "and you will see **the Son of Man seated at the right hand** of Power and **coming with the clouds of heaven.**"ᴬ

63 Then the high priest tore his robes and said, "Why do we still need witnesses? 64 You have heard the blasphemy. What is your decision?" They all condemned him as deserving death.

65 Then some began to spit on him, to blindfold him, and to beat him, saying, "Prophesy!" The temple servants also took him and slapped him.

PETER DENIES HIS LORD

66 While Peter was in the courtyard below, one of the high priest's maidservants came. 67 When she saw Peter warming himself, she looked at him and said, "You also were with Jesus, the man from Nazareth."

68 But he denied it: "I don't know or understand what you're talking about." Then he went out to the entryway,ᴮ and a rooster crowed.ᶜ

69 When the maidservant saw him again, she began to tell those standing nearby, "This man is one of them."

70 But again he denied it. After a little while those standing there said to Peter again, "You certainly are one of them, since you're also a Galilean."ᴰ

71 Then he started to curse and swear, "I don't know this man you're talking about!"

72 Immediately a rooster crowed a second time, and Peter remembered when Jesus had spoken the word to him, "Before the rooster crows twice, you will deny me three times." And he broke down and wept.

JESUS FACES PILATE

15 As soon as it was morning, having held a meeting with the elders, scribes, and the whole Sanhedrin, the chief priests tied Jesus up, led him away, and handed him over to Pilate.

2 So Pilate asked him, "Are you the King of the Jews?"

He answered him, "You say so."

3 And the chief priests accused him of many things. 4 Pilate questioned him again, "Aren't you going to answer? Look how many things they are accusing you of!" 5 But Jesus still did not answer, and so Pilate was amazed.

JESUS OR BARABBAS

6 At the festival Pilate used to release for the people a prisoner whom they requested. 7 There was one named Barabbas, who was in prison with rebels who had committed murder during the rebellion. 8 The crowd came up and began to ask Pilate to do for them as was his custom. 9 Pilate answered them, "Do you want me to release the King of the Jews for you?" 10 For he knew it was because of envy that the chief priests had handed him over. 11 But the

---

ᴬ14:62 Ps 110:1; Dn 7:13   ᴮ14:68 Or forecourt   ᶜ14:68 Other mss omit and a rooster crowed   ᴰ14:70 Other mss add and your speech shows it chief priests stirred up the crowd so that he would release Barabbas to them instead. [12] Pilate asked them again, "Then what do you want me to do with the one you call the King of the Jews?"

[13] Again they shouted, "Crucify him!"

[14] Pilate said to them, "Why? What has he done wrong?"

But they shouted all the more, "Crucify him!"

[15] Wanting to satisfy the crowd, Pilate released Barabbas to them; and after having Jesus flogged, he handed him over to be crucified.

MOCKED BY THE MILITARY

[16] The soldiers led him away into the palace (that is, the governor's residence) and called the whole company together. [17] They dressed him in a purple robe, twisted together a crown of thorns, and put it on him. [18] And they began to salute him, "Hail, King of the Jews!" [19] They were hitting him on the head with a stick and spitting on him. Getting down on their knees, they were paying him homage. [20] After they had mocked him, they stripped him of the purple robe and put his clothes on him.

CRUCIFIED BETWEEN TWO CRIMINALS

They led him out to crucify him. [21] They forced a man coming in from the country, who was passing by, to carry Jesus's cross. He was Simon of Cyrene, the father of Alexander and Rufus.

[22] They brought Jesus to the place called *Golgotha* (which means Place of the Skull). [23] They tried to give him wine mixed with myrrh, but he did not take it.

[24] Then they crucified him and divided his clothes, casting lots for them to decide what each would get. [25] Now it was nine in the morning[A] when they crucified him. [26] The inscription of the charge written against him was: THE KING OF THE JEWS. [27] They crucified two criminals[B] with him, one on his right and one on his left.[C]

[29] Those who passed by were yelling insults at[D] him, shaking their heads, and saying, "Ha! The one who would destroy the temple and rebuild it in three days, [30] save yourself by coming down from the cross!" [31] In the same way, the chief priests with the scribes were mocking him among themselves and saying, "He saved others, but he cannot save himself! [32] Let the Messiah, the King of Israel, come down now from the cross, so that we may see and believe." Even those who were crucified with him taunted him.

THE DEATH OF JESUS

[33] When it was noon,[E] darkness came over the whole land until three in the afternoon.[F] [34] And at three Jesus cried out with a loud voice, "*Eloi, Eloi, lemá sabachtháni?*" which is translated, "**My God, my God, why have you abandoned me?**"[G]

[35] When some of those standing there heard this, they said, "See, he's calling for Elijah."

[A]15:25 Lit *was the third hour*   [B]15:27 Or *revolutionaries*   [C]15:27 Some mss include v. 28: *So the Scripture was fulfilled that says: And he was counted among criminals.*   [D]15:29 Or *passed by blasphemed*   [E]15:33 Lit *the sixth hour*   [F]15:33 Lit *the ninth hour*, also in v. 34   [G]15:34 Ps 22:1

IT IS FINISHED

MARK 15; JOHN 19:30; COLOSSIANS 1:22

Take one glance at the headlines and you'll see evidence of the darkness that permeates our world. Hatred, violence, and every form of brokenness flash across our screens in high-definition. Since sin entered the garden of Eden, evil has worked its way into every corner of existence. Through one act of rebellion, death came on the scene and dominated the storyline, separating us from the glory of life in God's presence (Gn 3:1-24).

We hate death, and rightly so. It's the opposite of what we were created for (Rm 5:12). It feels empty and leaves an ache in our souls. But it was never the end of the story. Through one act of redemption, death was defeated and grace permeated the void that had been left in its wake (2Tm 1:10).

On the darkest day in history, the Light of the world brought hope in the most unlikely of ways. The Son of God willingly embraced the curse of death so we might taste eternal life.

We may know the story well. Maybe we've read it countless times—a story about death, yet profoundly full of life. Mark 15 describes the events in detail. Even so, it's impossible to fully comprehend the significance of what took place on that day when the storyline of all humanity took a dramatic turn. It was a glorious plot twist the Author had been orchestrating since the beginning.

Hanging high on a cross between two thieves, the Son of God cried out in anguish as the weight of our sins met the wrath of God's judgment. Jesus gave up His Spirit in a willful act of obedience that altered eternity. In that moment, the temple curtain was torn from top to bottom, signifying that what once separated us from God's holy presence had been torn away by God Himself. The miracle of redemption was completed as the spotless Lamb of God died in our place.

Our past, present, and future are inextricably tied to these three words that still echo into eternity:

"It is finished."

JOHN 19:30

Christ's grace has healed our brokenness. His sacrifice has given us hope for today, tomorrow, and forever. **What sin unraveled in the garden, our Savior restored on the cross.**

The fear of death has been replaced by the glory of redemption. "But now," as the apostle Paul said, "he has reconciled you by his physical body through his death, to present you holy, faultless, and blameless before him" (Col 1:22). This is good news! (Really, really, really good news!)

We know the end of the story (see Mark 16; Matthew 28). Jesus' resurrection defeated death once and for all. Though darkness is still visible in our world today, it has no power over those who belong to the Light (1Th 5:5).

³⁶ Someone ran and filled a sponge with sour wine, fixed it on a stick, offered him a drink, and said, "Let's see if Elijah comes to take him down."

³⁷ Jesus let out a loud cry and breathed his last. ³⁸ Then the curtain of the temple was torn in two from top to bottom. ³⁹ When the centurion, who was standing opposite him, saw the way heᴬ breathed his last, he said, "Truly this man was the Son of God! "ᴮ

⁴⁰ There were also women watching from a distance. Among them were Mary Magdalene, Mary the mother of James the younger and of Joses, and Salome. ⁴¹ In Galilee these women followed him and took care of him. Many other women had come up with him to Jerusalem.

THE BURIAL OF JESUS

⁴² When it was already evening, because it was the day of preparation (that is, the day before the Sabbath), ⁴³ Joseph of Arimathea, a prominent member of the Sanhedrin who was himself looking forward to the kingdom of God, came and boldly went to Pilate and asked for Jesus's body. ⁴⁴ Pilate was surprised that he was already dead. Summoning the centurion, he asked him whether he had already died. ⁴⁵ When he found out from the centurion, he gave the corpse to Joseph. ⁴⁶ After he bought some linen cloth, Joseph took him down and wrapped him in the linen. Then he laid him in a tomb cut out of the rock and rolled a stone against the entrance to the tomb. ⁴⁷ Mary Magdalene and Mary the mother of Joses were watching where he was laid.

RESURRECTION MORNING

16 When the Sabbath was over, Mary Magdalene, Mary the mother of James, and Salome bought spices, so that they could go and anoint him. ² Very early in the morning, on the first day of the week, they went to the tomb at sunrise. ³ They were saying to one another, "Who will roll away the stone from the entrance to the tomb for us?" ⁴ Looking up, they noticed that the stone — which was very large — had been rolled away.

⁵ When they entered the tomb, they saw a young man dressed in a white robe sitting on the right side; they were alarmed. ⁶ "Don't be alarmed," he told them. "You are looking for Jesus of Nazareth, who was crucified. He has risen! He is not here. See the place where they put him. ⁷ But go, tell his disciples and Peter, 'He is going ahead of you to Galilee; you will see him there just as he told you.'"

⁸ They went out and ran from the tomb, because trembling and astonishment overwhelmed them. And they said nothing to anyone, since they were afraid.

[Some of the earliest mss conclude with 16:8.]ᶜ

THE LONGER ENDING OF MARK: APPEARANCES OF THE RISEN LORD

[⁹ Early on the first day of the week, after he had risen, he appeared first to Mary Magdalene, out of whom he had driven seven demons. ¹⁰ She went and reported to those who had been with him, as they were mourning and weeping. ¹¹ Yet, when they heard that he was alive and had been seen by her, they did not believe it.

¹² After this, he appeared in a different form to two of them walking on their way into the country. ¹³ And they went and reported it to the rest, who did not believe them either.

THE GREAT COMMISSION

¹⁴ Later he appeared to the Eleven themselves as they were reclining at the table. He rebuked their unbelief and hardness of heart, because they did not believe those who saw him after he had risen. ¹⁵ Then he said to them, "Go into all the world and preach the gospel to all creation. ¹⁶ Whoever believes and is baptized will be saved, but whoever does not believe will be condemned. ¹⁷ And these signs will accompany those who believe: In my name they will drive out demons; they will speak in new tongues;ᴬ ¹⁸ they will pick up snakes;ᴮ if they should drink anything deadly, it will not harm them; they will lay hands on the sick, and they will get well."

THE ASCENSION

¹⁹ So the Lord Jesus, after speaking to them, was taken up into heaven and sat down at the right hand of God. ²⁰ And they went out and preached everywhere, while the Lord worked with them and confirmed the word by the accompanying signs.]

ᴬ16:17 = languages   ᴮ16:18 Other mss add *with their hands*

FOR THE SON OF MAN HAS COME TO SEEK & TO SAVE THE LOST

luke

 For the Son of Man has come to seek and to save the lost. **19:10**

ON THE TIMELINE The third Gospel is commonly believed to have been written by the same author, and around the same time, as the book of Acts. Considerable evidence points to Luke as the writer of both books, including Acts 1:1-3, which identifies Acts as a sequel to Luke. The events at the end of Acts occurred around AD 62–63, indicating that both Luke and Acts were most likely written in the early to mid-60s. The events of the Gospel of Luke occur around the life of Christ, from about 5 BC to AD 33.

A LITTLE BACKGROUND Like Acts, Luke's Gospel is addressed to "most honorable Theophilus" (Lk 1:3), about whom nothing else is known. The Greek name Theophilus means "lover of God" and implies he was a Gentile, probably Greek. He seems to have been a relatively new believer, recently instructed about Jesus and the Christian faith. Luke's profession as a medical doctor gives his Gospel a unique focus on Jesus' humanity and the role of Christ as the Suffering Servant (Is 53).

MESSAGE & PURPOSE The Gospel of Luke is a carefully researched (Lk 1:3) and selective presentation of the person and life of Jesus Christ. The book is designed to strengthen the faith of believers (Lk 1:3-4) and challenge the misconceptions of unbelievers, especially those from a Greek background. Luke's Gospel is a well-balanced portrait of Jesus, skillfully emphasizing His divinity and perfect humanity.

GIVE THANKS FOR THE GOSPEL OF LUKE

Some 35 percent of the material in the Gospel of Luke is unique, so there is a great deal we would not know if this book had not been included in the Bible. These distinct passages include the births of John the Baptist and Jesus (Lk 2–3), the retellings of Jesus' childhood and pre-ministry adult life (Lk 2:40-52), a genealogy that emphasizes different aspects of Jesus' ancestry than the genealogy in Matthew (Lk 3:23-38), additional information about Jesus' journey to Jerusalem (Lk 9:51–19:44), and a different take on the destruction of the temple (Lk 21:5-38). Also specific to Luke are the account of the Emmaus Road and the only description in the Gospels of Jesus' ascension into heaven (Lk 24:13-53).

KEY CHARACTERISTICS OF CHRIST IN THE GOSPELS

CHARACTERISTIC	EXPLANATION	MATTHEW	MARK	LUKE	JOHN
Jesus is the Son of God.	Through the authors, the disciples, the Gentiles, and Jesus Himself, all four gospels testify that Christ is the Son of God.	16:15-16; 27:54	1:1	22:70-71	8:24
Jesus is God who became human.	Jesus is both fully God and fully man. The deity and humanity of Jesus are displayed through the testimony of the gospel writers and the disciples.	2:11	8:27-30	9:28-36	1:1-2,14; 20:28
Jesus is the Christ, the Messiah.	Jesus is the Messiah, the promised deliverer of the nation of Israel and of all humanity.	26:63-64	14:61-62	9:20	4:25-26
Jesus came to save sinners.	Jesus' purpose on earth was to save sinners by taking their punishment on Himself.	9:13	2:17	5:32	12:47
Jesus has power to forgive sins.	Because He is God, Jesus has the authority to forgive sins.	9:1-8	2:9-12	24:47	8:2-11
Jesus has authority over death.	Jesus has power to raise the dead. He conquered death through His perfect life, sacrificial death, and glorious resurrection.	28:5-6	5:22-24, 35-42	24:5-6	11:1-44
Jesus has power to give eternal life.	God has given Jesus authority to grant eternal life to all those who believe in Him.	8:5-13	9:1	23:43	10:28; 17:2
Jesus healed the sick.	Jesus has power over all physical sickness. While on earth, He healed many people, from those with skin diseases and fevers to those blind and lame from birth.	8:5-13	1:32-34	5:12-15	9:1-17
Jesus taught with authority.	As the Son of God, Jesus has authority over heaven and earth.	7:29	1:21-22	8:22-25	6:16-21
Jesus is compassionate.	Jesus showed compassion for all people—those who were lost and those who followed Him.	9:36	1:41; 8:2	23:34	5:5-9
Jesus experienced sorrow.	Jesus experienced sorrow and many other emotions.	26:38	10:14	22:44	11:35
Jesus never disobeyed God.	Jesus lived a perfect life without sin. Even though He was tempted, He modeled how to use Scripture to resist temptation.	4:1-11	1:12-13	22:42	8:46

READ AND UNDERSTAND LUKE

The Bible is a complete work in which many stories combine to tell one story. As you read the Gospel of Luke, consider reading the additional passages to discover how the whole of Scripture works together.

LUKE 1

Handwritten annotations (left margin and around text):

Fun fact: Luke was a Gentile

Q: Who is Theophilus? Is his name symbolic?

A: Roman govt. official. Theophilus → friend of God, beloved by God, lover of God

* what it means to me:
— Paul also wrote to all Christians. Theophilus is symbolic of God's children, those beloved by God.

* what others say:
— Theophilus was likely a new believer, making this a great book for 1st time Bible readers

:13 & 20 — Lesson: don't pray for something & then be scared or doubtful when God answers it

Q: significance? →

A: The angel would have been standing next to the altar of showbread just like Jesus is the "bread of life"/"living bread"

:13 — Zechariah had probably given up on praying for a son cause he was old and Elizabeth was barren but GOD'S LOVE NEVER FAILS

God's plan for John's life

these are REAL people

Even Zechariah doubted God. He wasn't perfectly blameless

"I am an old man" vs. "I am Gabriel...sent [by God]"

20 — "When we don't believe God's promise for our lives, we destroy our ability to enjoy it" (Enduring Word)

24 — John is not by miraculous conception like Jesus

Elizabeth: GLORY BE TO GOD!!

THE DEDICATION TO THEOPHILUS

1 Many have undertaken to compile a narrative about the events that have been fulfilled[A] among us, [2] just as the original eyewitnesses and servants of the word handed them down to us. [3] It also seemed good to me, since I have carefully investigated everything from the very first, to write to you in an orderly sequence, most honorable Theophilus, [4] so that you may know the certainty of the things about which you have been instructed.[B]

(handwritten): 1:1 — references other Gospel writers
1:2 — references the Apostles

GABRIEL PREDICTS JOHN'S BIRTH

[5] In the days of King Herod of Judea, there was a priest of Abijah's division named Zechariah. His wife was from the daughters of Aaron, and her name was Elizabeth. [6] Both were righteous in God's sight, living without blame according to all the commands and requirements of the Lord. [7] But they had no children because Elizabeth could not conceive, and both of them were well along in years. *(handwritten): Parallel to Abraham & Sarah suggests something big is happening* [8] When his division was on duty and he was serving as priest before God, [9] it happened that he was chosen by lot, according to the custom of the priesthood, to enter the sanctuary of the Lord and burn incense. [10] At the hour of incense the whole assembly of the people was praying outside. [11] An angel of the Lord appeared to him, standing to the right of the altar of incense. [12] When Zechariah saw him, he was terrified and overcome with fear. [13] But the angel said to him: "Do not be afraid, Zechariah, because your prayer has been heard. Your wife Elizabeth will bear you a son, and you will name him John. [14] There will be joy and delight for you, and many will rejoice at his birth. [15] For he will be great in the sight of the Lord and will never drink wine or beer. He will be filled with the Holy Spirit while still in his mother's womb. [16] He will turn many of the children of Israel to the Lord their God. [17] And he will go before him in the spirit and power of Elijah, to turn the hearts of fathers to their children, and the disobedient to the understanding of the righteous, to make ready for the Lord a prepared people." *(handwritten): STRIVE TO BE LIKE JOHN*

[18] "How can I know this?" Zechariah asked the angel. "For I am an old man, and my wife is well along in years." [19] The angel answered him, "I am Gabriel, who stands in the presence of God, and I was sent to speak to you and tell you this good news. [20] Now listen. You will become silent and unable to speak until the day these things take place, because you did not believe my words, which will be fulfilled in their proper time."

[21] Meanwhile, the people were waiting for Zechariah, amazed that he stayed so long in the sanctuary. [22] When he did come out, he could not speak to them. Then they realized that he had seen a vision in the sanctuary. He was making signs to them and remained speechless. [23] When the days of his ministry were completed, he went back home.

(handwritten): 1:25

[24] After these days his wife Elizabeth conceived and kept herself in seclusion for five months. She said, [25] "The Lord has done this for me. He has looked with favor in these days to take away my disgrace among the people."

[A] 1:1 Or events that have been accomplished, or events most surely believed
[B] 1:4 Or informed

(handwritten): He has looked on me with favor

1734

to serve him without fear
75 in holiness and righteousness
   in his presence all our days.
76 And you, child, will be called
   a prophet of the Most High,
   for you will go before the Lord
   to prepare his ways,
77 to give his people knowledge of salvation
   through the forgiveness of their sins.
78 Because of our God's merciful compassion,
   the dawn from on high will visit us
79 to shine on those who live in darkness
   and the shadow of death,
   to guide our feet into the way of peace.

80 The child grew up and became spiritually strong, and he was in the wilderness until the day of his public appearance to Israel.

THE BIRTH OF JESUS

2 In those days a decree went out from Caesar Augustus that the whole empire[A] should be registered. [2] This first registration took place while[B] Quirinius was governing Syria. [3] So everyone went to be registered, each to his own town.

[4] Joseph also went up from the town of Nazareth in Galilee, to Judea, to the city of David, which is called Bethlehem, because he was of the house and family line of David, [5] to be registered along with Mary, who was engaged to him[C] and was pregnant. [6] While they were there, the time came for her to give birth. [7] Then she gave birth to her firstborn son, and she wrapped him tightly in cloth and laid him in a manger,[D] because there was no guest room available for them.

THE SHEPHERDS AND THE ANGELS

[8] In the same region, shepherds were staying out in the fields and keeping watch at night over their flock. [9] Then an angel of the Lord stood before them, and the glory of the Lord shone around them, and they were terrified.[E] [10] But the angel said to them, "Don't be afraid, for look, I proclaim to you good news of great joy that will be for all the people:[F] [11] Today in the city of David a Savior was born for you, who is the Messiah, the Lord. [12] This will be the sign for you: You will find a baby wrapped tightly in cloth and lying in a manger."

[13] Suddenly there was a multitude of the heavenly host[G] with the angel, praising God and saying:

14 Glory to God in the highest heaven,
    and peace on earth to people he favors![H,I]

A2:1 Or the whole inhabited world B2:2 Or This registration was the first while, or This registration was before C2:5 Lit betrothed D2:7 Or feeding trough, also in vv. 12,16 E2:9 Lit they feared a great fear F2:10 Or the whole nation G2:13 Lit heavenly army H2:14 Other mss read earth good will to people I2:14 Or earth to men of good will

SAVORING HIS PROMISES

LUKE 2; JOHN 19:25-30

I don't know about birthing babies, but I can tell you about making noodles.

It began as a fun skill to impress party guests and my one-day husband, but as I ducked into the stone kitchen in the center of Florence, Italy, I soon realized pasta making is not an idle pastime, but a sacred trust. I tied back my hair and took a deep breath.

While the instructor demonstrated at the front of the kitchen, I did my best to follow along. Finally, I sliced off one string of dough from my kneaded flour-water mixture, holding it up, proud and tired.

"Again," I was instructed. I resumed kneading and rolling and slicing, holding up my second piece with a little less pride.

"Hold it up to the first," I was told. Placing the pieces in line for comparison revealed two straggly opposites. My brow furrowed. Fine tuning the individual pasta pieces was a disciplined craft, and considering each new piece in light of the original became a satisfying and enlightening exercise.

As I worked the dough with my hands that day, it became clear that this was the Italian way: savoring over striving.

I think Mary of Nazareth would have understood. Though she had plenty of chances to act from her flesh, Mary opted to serve the Lord by savoring her collection of things she knew to be true.

When Jesus was born, others jumped up to share the good news. "But Mary was treasuring up all these things in her heart and meditating on them" (Lk 2:19).

Later, instead of flying off the handle when she finds her son in the temple after three days of searching, Mary "kept all these things in her heart" (Lk 2:51).

If I were Mary, I'd have asked for a hall pass on suffering, but Scripture tells us that being the favored mother of Jesus came instead with an extra heap of heartache. In fact, the old cleric Simeon prophesied that a sword would pierce her soul because of Him (Lk 2:35). Mary would suffer greatly as the mother of Jesus.

Mary was the only person Scripture recorded as present at both Jesus' birth and crucifixion. Did "treasuring it all" mean passively standing by? No! I believe Mary was busy fiercely clinging to the treasured promises of God, holding up each unfolding circumstance to what she knew to be true. As if carefully crafting an elegant Italian dish, Mary was actively fighting for the truth with the Truth. **She held up the events of her life against the truth of God, savoring His promises over her striving.**

LESSON

As servants of the Lord, let's remember to savor the truth of Jesus, always holding up our unfolding circumstances to what God's Word tells us is true.

[15] When the angels had left them and returned to heaven, the shepherds said to one another, "Let's go straight to Bethlehem and see what has happened, which the Lord has made known to us."

[16] They hurried off and found both Mary and Joseph, and the baby who was lying in the manger. [17] After seeing them, they reported the message they were told about this child, [18] and all who heard it were amazed at what the shepherds said to them. [19] But Mary was treasuring up all these things in her heart and meditating on them. [20] The shepherds returned, glorifying and praising God for all the things they had seen and heard, which were just as they had been told.

THE CIRCUMCISION AND PRESENTATION OF JESUS

[21] When the eight days were completed for his circumcision, he was named Jesus — the name given by the angel before he was conceived. [22] And when the days of their purification according to the law of Moses were finished, they brought him up to Jerusalem to present him to the Lord [23] (just as it is written in the law of the Lord, **Every firstborn male will be dedicated[A] to the Lord**[B]) [24] and to offer a sacrifice (according to what is stated in the law of the Lord, **a pair of turtledoves or two young pigeons**[C]).

SIMEON'S PROPHETIC PRAISE

[25] There was a man in Jerusalem whose name was Simeon. This man was righteous and devout, looking forward to Israel's consolation, and the Holy Spirit was on him. [26] It had been revealed to him by the Holy Spirit that he would not see death before he saw the Lord's Messiah. [27] Guided by the Spirit, he entered the temple. When the parents brought in the child Jesus to perform for him what was customary under the law, [28] Simeon took him up in his arms, praised God, and said,

[29] Now, Master,
you can dismiss your servant in peace,
as you promised.
[30] For my eyes have seen your salvation.
[31] You have prepared it
in the presence of all peoples —
[32] a light for revelation to the Gentiles[D]
and glory to your people Israel.

[33] His father and mother[E] were amazed at what was being said about him. [34] Then Simeon blessed them and told his mother Mary: "Indeed, this child is destined to cause the fall and rise of many in Israel and to be a sign that will be opposed[F] — [35] and a sword will pierce your own soul — that the thoughts[G] of many hearts may be revealed."

ANNA'S TESTIMONY

[36] There was also a prophetess, Anna, a daughter of Phanuel, of the tribe of Asher. She was well along in years, having lived with her husband seven

---

[A]2:23 Lit be called holy [B]2:23 Ex 13:2,12 [C]2:24 Lv 5:11; 12:8 [D]2:32 Or the nations [E]2:33 Other mss read But Joseph and his mother [F]2:34 Or spoken against [G]2:35 Or schemes

Lesson:
Simeon and Anna
were both devout
servants of God
who held onto
hope and faith
and God provided
for their wants &
needs

years after her marriage,[A] [37] and was a widow for eighty-four years.[B] She did not leave the temple, serving God night and day with fasting and prayers. [38] At that very moment,[C] she came up and began to thank God and to speak about him to all who were looking forward to the redemption of Jerusalem.[D]

THE FAMILY'S RETURN TO NAZARETH

[39] When they had completed everything according to the law of the Lord, they returned to Galilee, to their own town of Nazareth. [40] The boy grew up and became strong, filled with wisdom, and God's grace was on him.

IN HIS FATHER'S HOUSE

[41] Every year his parents traveled to Jerusalem for the Passover Festival. [42] When he was twelve years old, they went up according to the custom of the festival. [43] After those days were over, as they were returning, the boy Jesus stayed behind in Jerusalem, but his parents[E] did not know it. [44] Assuming he was in the traveling party, they went a day's journey. Then they began looking for him among their relatives and friends. [45] When they did not find him, they returned to Jerusalem to search for him. [46] After three days, they found him in the temple sitting among the teachers, listening to them and asking them questions. [47] And all those who heard him were astounded at his understanding and his answers. [48] When his parents saw him, they were astonished, and his mother said to him, "Son, why have you treated us like this? Your father and I have been anxiously searching for you."

[49] "Why were you searching for me?" he asked them. "Didn't you know that it was necessary for me to be in my Father's house?"[F] [50] But they did not understand what he said to them.

IN FAVOR WITH GOD AND WITH PEOPLE

[51] Then he went down with them and came to Nazareth and was obedient to them. His mother kept all these things in her heart. [52] And Jesus increased in wisdom and stature, and in favor with God and with people.

THE MESSIAH'S HERALD

3 In the fifteenth year of the reign of Tiberius Caesar, while Pontius Pilate was governor of Judea, Herod was tetrarch[G] of Galilee, his brother Philip tetrarch of the region of Iturea and Trachonitis, and Lysanias tetrarch of Abilene, [2] during the high priesthood of Annas and Caiaphas, God's word came to John the son of Zechariah in the wilderness. [3] He went into all the vicinity of the Jordan, proclaiming a baptism of repentance for the forgiveness of sins, [4] as it is written in the book of the words of the prophet Isaiah:

A voice of one crying out in the wilderness:
Prepare the way for the Lord;
make his paths straight!
[5] Every valley will be filled,

[A]2:36 Lit years from her virginity   [B]2:37 Or she was a widow until the age of eighty-four   [C]2:38 Lit very hour   [D]2:38 Other mss read in Jerusalem
[E]2:43 Other mss read but Joseph and his mother   [F]2:49 Or be involved in my Father's interests (or things), or be among my Father's people   [G]3:1 Or ruler

and every mountain and hill will be made low;[A]
the crooked will become straight,
the rough ways smooth,
⁶ and everyone will see the salvation of God.[B]

⁷ He then said to the crowds who came out to be baptized by him, "Brood of vipers! Who warned you to flee from the coming wrath? ⁸ Therefore produce fruit consistent with repentance. And don't start saying to yourselves, 'We have Abraham as our father,' for I tell you that God is able to raise up children for Abraham from these stones. ⁹ The ax is already at the root of the trees. Therefore, every tree that doesn't produce good fruit will be cut down and thrown into the fire."

¹⁰ "What then should we do?" the crowds were asking him.

¹¹ He replied to them, "The one who has two shirts must share with someone who has none, and the one who has food must do the same."

¹² Tax collectors also came to be baptized, and they asked him, "Teacher, what should we do?"

¹³ He told them, "Don't collect any more than what you have been authorized."

¹⁴ Some soldiers also questioned him, "What should we do?"

He said to them, "Don't take money from anyone by force or false accusation, and be satisfied with your wages."

¹⁵ Now the people were waiting expectantly, and all of them were questioning in their hearts whether John might be the Messiah. ¹⁶ John answered them all, "I baptize you with water, but one who is more powerful than I am is coming. I am not worthy to untie the strap of his sandals. He will baptize you with[C] the Holy Spirit and fire. ¹⁷ His winnowing shovel is in his hand to clear his threshing floor and gather the wheat into his barn, but the chaff he will burn with fire that never goes out." ¹⁸ Then, along with many other exhortations, he proclaimed good news to the people. ¹⁹ But when John rebuked Herod the tetrarch because of Herodias, his brother's wife, and all the evil things he had done, ²⁰ Herod added this to everything else — he locked up John in prison.

THE BAPTISM OF JESUS

²¹ When all the people were baptized, Jesus also was baptized. As he was praying, heaven opened, ²² and the Holy Spirit descended on him in a physical appearance like a dove. And a voice came from heaven: "You are my beloved Son; with you I am well-pleased."

THE GENEALOGY OF JESUS CHRIST

²³ As he began his ministry, Jesus was about thirty years old and was thought to be the
son of Joseph, son of Heli,
²⁴ son of Matthat, son of Levi,
son of Melchi, son of Jannai,
son of Joseph, ²⁵ son of Mattathias,
son of Amos, son of Nahum,

A 3:5 Lit *be humbled*   B 3:4-6 Is 40:3-5   C 3:16 Or *in*

son of Esli, son of Naggai,
26 son of Maath, son of Mattathias,
son of Semein, son of Josech,
son of Joda, 27 son of Joanan,
son of Rhesa, son of Zerubbabel,
son of Shealtiel, son of Neri,
28 son of Melchi, son of Addi,
son of Cosam, son of Elmadam,
son of Er, 29 son of Joshua,
son of Eliezer, son of Jorim,
son of Matthat, son of Levi,
30 son of Simeon, son of Judah,
son of Joseph, son of Jonam,
son of Eliakim, 31 son of Melea,
son of Menna, son of Mattatha,
son of Nathan, son of David,
32 son of Jesse, son of Obed,
son of Boaz, son of Salmon, A
son of Nahshon, 33 son of Amminadab,
son of Ram, B son of Hezron,
son of Perez, son of Judah,
34 son of Jacob, son of Isaac,
son of Abraham, son of Terah,
son of Nahor, 35 son of Serug,
son of Reu, son of Peleg,
son of Eber, son of Shelah,
36 son of Cainan, son of Arphaxad,
son of Shem, son of Noah,
son of Lamech, 37 son of Methuselah,
son of Enoch, son of Jared,
son of Mahalalel, son of Cainan,
38 son of Enos, son of Seth,
son of Adam, son of God.

THE TEMPTATION OF JESUS

4 Then Jesus left the Jordan, full of the Holy Spirit, and was led by the Spirit in the wilderness 2 for forty days to be tempted by the devil. He ate nothing during those days, and when they were over, he was hungry. 3 The devil said to him, "If you are the Son of God, tell this stone to become bread."

4 But Jesus answered him, "It is written: **Man must not live on bread alone.**" C,D

5 So he took him up E and showed him all the kingdoms of the world in a moment of time. 6 The devil said to him, "I will give you their splendor and all this authority, because it has been given over to me, and I can give it to anyone I want. 7 If you, then, will worship me, F all will be yours."

A 3:32 Other mss read *Sala* B 3:33 Other mss read *Amminadab, son of Aram, son of Joram*; other mss read *Amminadab, son of Admin, son of Arni* C 4:4 Other mss add *but on every word of God* D 4:4 Dt 8:3 E 4:5 Other mss read *So the devil took him up on a high mountain* F 4:7 Lit *will fall down before me*

⁸ And Jesus answered him,ᴬ "It is written: **Worship the Lord your God, and serve him only.**"ᴮ

⁹ So he took him to Jerusalem, had him stand on the pinnacle of the temple, and said to him, "If you are the Son of God, throw yourself down from here. ¹⁰ For it is written:

He will give his angels orders concerning you,
  to protect you,ᶜ ¹¹ **and**
they will support you with their hands,
  so that you will not strike
your foot against a stone."ᴰ

¹² And Jesus answered him, "It is said: **Do not test the Lord your God.**"ᴱ

¹³ After the devil had finished every temptation, he departed from him for a time.

MINISTRY IN GALILEE

¹⁴ Then Jesus returned to Galilee in the power of the Spirit, and news about him spread throughout the entire vicinity. ¹⁵ He was teaching in their synagogues, being praisedᶠ by everyone.

REJECTION AT NAZARETH

¹⁶ He came to Nazareth, where he had been brought up. As usual, he entered the synagogue on the Sabbath day and stood up to read. ¹⁷ The scroll of the prophet Isaiah was given to him, and unrolling the scroll, he found the place where it was written:

¹⁸ **The Spirit of the Lord is on me,**
  because he has anointed me
  to preach good news to the poor.
  He has sent meᴳ
  to proclaim releaseᴴ **to the captives**
  and recovery of sight to the blind,
  to set free the oppressed,
¹⁹   **to proclaim the year of the Lord's favor.**ᴵ

²⁰ He then rolled up the scroll, gave it back to the attendant, and sat down. And the eyes of everyone in the synagogue were fixed on him. ²¹ He began by saying to them, "Today as you listen, this Scripture has been fulfilled."

²² They were all speaking well of himᴶ and were amazed by the gracious words that came from his mouth; yet they said, "Isn't this Joseph's son?"

²³ Then he said to them, "No doubt you will quote this proverbᴷ to me: 'Doctor, heal yourself. What we've heard that took place in Capernaum, do here in your hometown also.'"

²⁴ He also said, "Truly I tell you, no prophet is accepted in his hometown. ²⁵ But I say to you, there were certainly many widows in Israel in Elijah's days, when the sky was shut up for three years and six months while a great famine came over all the land. ²⁶ Yet Elijah was not sent to any of them except a

---

ᴬ4:8 Other mss add *"Get behind me, Satan!* ᴮ4:8 Dt 6:13 ᶜ4:10 Ps 91:11
ᴰ4:11 Ps 91:12 ᴱ4:12 Dt 6:16 ᶠ4:15 Or *glorified* ᴳ4:18 Other mss add *to heal the brokenhearted,* ᴴ4:18 Or *freedom,* or *forgiveness* ᴵ4:18-19 Is 61:1-2 ᴶ4:22 Or *They were testifying against him* ᴷ4:23 Or *parable*

widow at Zarephath in Sidon. ²⁷ And in the prophet Elisha's time, there were many in Israel who had leprosy,ᴬ and yet not one of them was cleansed except Naaman the Syrian."

²⁸ When they heard this, everyone in the synagogue was enraged. ²⁹ They got up, drove him out of town, and brought him to the edge of the hill that their town was built on, intending to hurl him over the cliff. ³⁰ But he passed right through the crowd and went on his way.

DRIVING OUT AN UNCLEAN SPIRIT

³¹ Then he went down to Capernaum, a town in Galilee, and was teaching them on the Sabbath. ³² They were astonished at his teaching because his message had authority. ³³ In the synagogue there was a man with an unclean demonic spirit who cried out with a loud voice, ³⁴ "Leave us alone! What do you have to do with us, Jesus of Nazareth? Have you come to destroy us? I know who you are — the Holy One of God!"

³⁵ But Jesus rebuked him and said, "Be silent and come out of him!" And throwing him down before them, the demon came out of him without hurting him at all.

³⁶ Amazement came over them all, and they were saying to one another, "What is this message? For he commands the unclean spirits with authority and power, and they come out!" ³⁷ And news about him began to go out to every place in the vicinity.

HEALINGS AT CAPERNAUM

³⁸ After he left the synagogue, he entered Simon's house. Simon's mother-in-law was suffering from a high fever, and they asked him about her. ³⁹ So he stood over her and rebuked the fever, and it left her. She got up immediately and began to serve them.

⁴⁰ When the sun was setting, all those who had anyone sick with various diseases brought them to him. As he laid his hands on each one of them, he healed them. ⁴¹ Also, demons were coming out of many, shouting and saying, "You are the Son of God!" But he rebuked them and would not allow them to speak, because they knew he was the Christ.

⁴² When it was day, he went out and made his way to a deserted place. But the crowds were searching for him. They came to him and tried to keep him from leaving them. ⁴³ But he said to them, "It is necessary for me to proclaim the good news about the kingdom of God to the other towns also, because I was sent for this purpose." ⁴⁴ And he was preaching in the synagogues of Judea.ᴮ

THE FIRST DISCIPLES

5 As the crowd was pressing in on Jesus to hear God's word, he was standing by Lake Gennesaret. ² He saw two boats at the edge of the lake; the fishermen had left them and were washing their nets. ³ He got into one of the boats, which belonged to Simon, and asked him to put out a little from the land. Then he sat down and was teaching the crowds from the boat.

⁴ When he had finished speaking, he said to Simon, "Put out into deep water and let down your nets for a catch."

ᴬ4:27 Gk *lepros*; a term for various skin diseases; see Lv 13–14   ᴮ4:44 Other mss read *Galilee*

5 "Master," Simon replied, "we've worked hard all night long and caught nothing. But if you say so, I'll let down the nets."^A

6 When they did this, they caught a great number of fish, and their nets^A began to tear. 7 So they signaled to their partners in the other boat to come and help them; they came and filled both boats so full that they began to sink.

8 When Simon Peter saw this, he fell at Jesus's knees and said, "Go away from me, because I'm a sinful man, Lord!" 9 For he and all those with him were amazed at the catch of fish they had taken, 10 and so were James and John, Zebedee's sons, who were Simon's partners.

"Don't be afraid," Jesus told Simon. "From now on you will be catching people." 11 Then they brought the boats to land, left everything, and followed him.

A MAN CLEANSED

12 While he was in one of the towns, a man was there who had leprosy^B all over him. He saw Jesus, fell facedown, and begged him: "Lord, if you are willing, you can make me clean."

13 Reaching out his hand, Jesus touched him, saying, "I am willing; be made clean," and immediately the leprosy left him. 14 Then he ordered him to tell no one: "But go and show yourself to the priest, and offer what Moses commanded for your cleansing as a testimony to them."

15 But the news^C about him spread even more, and large crowds would come together to hear him and to be healed of their sicknesses. 16 Yet he often withdrew to deserted places and prayed.

THE SON OF MAN FORGIVES AND HEALS

17 On one of those days while he was teaching, Pharisees and teachers of the law were sitting there who had come from every village of Galilee and Judea, and also from Jerusalem. And the Lord's power to heal was in him. 18 Just then some men came, carrying on a stretcher a man who was paralyzed. They tried to bring him in and set him down before him. 19 Since they could not find a way to bring him in because of the crowd, they went up on the roof and lowered him on the stretcher through the roof tiles into the middle of the crowd before Jesus.

20 Seeing their faith he said, "Friend,^D your sins are forgiven."

21 Then the scribes and the Pharisees began to think to themselves: "Who is this man who speaks blasphemies? Who can forgive sins but God alone?"

22 But perceiving their thoughts, Jesus replied to them, "Why are you thinking this in your hearts?^E 23 Which is easier: to say, 'Your sins are forgiven,' or to say, 'Get up and walk'? 24 But so that you may know that the Son of Man has authority on earth to forgive sins" — he told the paralyzed man, "I tell you: Get up, take your stretcher, and go home."

25 Immediately he got up before them, picked up what he had been lying on, and went home glorifying God. 26 Then everyone was astounded, and they were giving glory to God. And they were filled with awe and said, "We have seen incredible things today."

---

^A5:5,6 Other mss read *net* (Gk sg)   ^B5:12 Gk *lepros*; a term for various skin diseases, also in v. 13; see Lv 13–14   ^C5:15 Lit *the word*   ^D5:20 Lit "*Man*"
^E5:22 Or *minds*

THE CALL OF LEVI

27 After this, Jesus went out and saw a tax collector named Levi sitting at the tax office, and he said to him, "Follow me." 28 So, leaving everything behind, he got up and began to follow him.

29 Then Levi hosted a grand banquet for him at his house. Now there was a large crowd of tax collectors and others who were guests^A with them. 30 But the Pharisees and their scribes were complaining to his disciples, "Why do you eat and drink with tax collectors and sinners?"

31 Jesus replied to them, "It is not those who are healthy who need a doctor, but those who are sick. 32 I have not come to call the righteous, but sinners to repentance."

A QUESTION ABOUT FASTING

33 Then they said to him, "John's disciples fast often and say prayers, and those of the Pharisees do the same, but yours eat and drink."^B

34 Jesus said to them, "You can't make the wedding guests fast while the groom is with them, can you? 35 But the time^C will come when the groom will be taken away from them — then they will fast in those days."

36 He also told them a parable: "No one tears a patch from a new garment and puts it on an old garment. Otherwise, not only will he tear the new, but also the piece from the new garment will not match the old. 37 And no one puts new wine into old wineskins. Otherwise, the new wine will burst the skins, it will spill, and the skins will be ruined. 38 No, new wine is put into fresh wineskins.^D 39 And no one, after drinking old wine, wants new, because he says, 'The old is better.'"^E

LORD OF THE SABBATH

6 On a Sabbath, he passed through the grainfields. His disciples were picking heads of grain, rubbing them in their hands, and eating them. 2 But some of the Pharisees said, "Why are you doing what is not lawful on the Sabbath?"

3 Jesus answered them, "Haven't you read what David and those who were with him did when he was hungry — 4 how he entered the house of God and took and ate the bread of the Presence, which is not lawful for any but the priests to eat? He even gave some to those who were with him." 5 Then he told them, "The Son of Man is Lord of the Sabbath."

6 On another Sabbath he entered the synagogue and was teaching. A man was there whose right hand was shriveled. 7 The scribes and Pharisees were watching him closely, to see if he would heal on the Sabbath, so that they could find a charge against him. 8 But he knew their thoughts and told the man with the shriveled hand, "Get up and stand here."^F So he got up and stood there. 9 Then Jesus said to them, "I ask you: Is it lawful to do good on the Sabbath or to do evil, to save life or to destroy it?" 10 After looking around at them all, he told him, "Stretch out your hand." He did, and his hand was restored.^G 11 They, however, were filled with rage and started discussing with one another what they might do to Jesus.

---

^A 5:29 Lit were reclining   ^B 5:33 Other mss read "Why do John's . . . drink?" (as a question)   ^C 5:35 Lit days   ^D 5:38 Other mss add And so both are preserved.
^E 5:39 Other mss read is good   ^F 6:8 Lit stand in the middle   ^G 6:10 Other mss add as sound as the other

THE TWELVE APOSTLES

[12] During those days he went out to the mountain to pray and spent all night in prayer to God. [13] When daylight came, he summoned his disciples, and he chose twelve of them, whom he also named apostles: [14] Simon, whom he also named Peter, and Andrew his brother; James and John; Philip and Bartholomew; [15] Matthew and Thomas; James the son of Alphaeus, and Simon called the Zealot; [16] Judas the son of James, and Judas Iscariot, who became a traitor.

TEACHING AND HEALING

[17] After coming down with them, he stood on a level place with a large crowd of his disciples and a great number of people from all Judea and Jerusalem and from the seacoast of Tyre and Sidon. [18] They came to hear him and to be healed of their diseases; and those tormented by unclean spirits were made well. [19] The whole crowd was trying to touch him, because power was coming out from him and healing them all.

THE BEATITUDES

[20] Then looking up at his disciples, he said:

Blessed are you who are poor,
because the kingdom of God is yours.
[21] Blessed are you who are now hungry,
because you will be filled.
Blessed are you who weep now,
because you will laugh.
[22] Blessed are you when people hate you,
when they exclude you, insult you,
and slander your name as evil
because of the Son of Man.

[23] "Rejoice in that day and leap for joy. Take note — your reward is great in heaven, for this is the way their ancestors used to treat the prophets.

WOE TO THE SELF-SATISFIED

[24] But woe to you who are rich,
for you have received your comfort.
[25] Woe to you who are now full,
for you will be hungry.
Woe to you^A who are now laughing,
for you will mourn and weep.
[26] Woe to you^A
when all people speak well of you,
for this is the way their ancestors
used to treat the false prophets.

LOVE YOUR ENEMIES

[27] "But I say to you who listen: Love your enemies, do what is good to those who hate you, [28] bless those who curse you, pray for those who mistreat you. [29] If anyone hits you on the cheek, offer the other also. And if anyone takes away your coat, don't hold back your shirt either. [30] Give to everyone

Turn the other cheek

---

^A6:25,26 Other mss omit *to you*

who asks you, and from someone who takes your things, don't ask for them back. [31] Just as you want others to do for you, do the same for them. [32] If you love those who love you, what credit is that to you? Even sinners love those who love them. [33] If you do what is good to those who are good to you, what credit is that to you? Even sinners do that. [34] And if you lend to those from whom you expect to receive, what credit is that to you? Even sinners lend to sinners to be repaid in full. [35] But love your enemies, do what is good, and lend, expecting nothing in return. Then your reward will be great, and you will be children of the Most High. For he is gracious to the ungrateful and evil. [36] Be merciful, just as your Father also is merciful.

DO NOT JUDGE

[37] "Do not judge, and you will not be judged. Do not condemn, and you will not be condemned. Forgive, and you will be forgiven. [38] Give, and it will be given to you; a good measure — pressed down, shaken together, and running over — will be poured into your lap. For with the measure you use, it will be measured back to you."

[39] He also told them a parable: "Can the blind guide the blind? Won't they both fall into a pit? [40] A disciple is not above his teacher, but everyone who is fully trained will be like his teacher.

[41] "Why do you look at the splinter in your brother's eye, but don't notice the beam of wood in your own eye? [42] Or how can you say to your brother, 'Brother, let me take out the splinter that is in your eye,' when you yourself don't see the beam of wood in your eye? Hypocrite! First take the beam of wood out of your eye, and then you will see clearly to take out the splinter in your brother's eye.

A TREE AND ITS FRUIT

[43] "A good tree doesn't produce bad fruit; on the other hand, a bad tree doesn't produce good fruit.^A [44] For each tree is known by its own fruit. Figs aren't gathered from thornbushes, or grapes picked from a bramble bush. [45] A good person produces good out of the good stored up in his heart. An evil person produces evil out of the evil stored up in his heart, for his mouth speaks from the overflow of the heart.

THE TWO FOUNDATIONS

[46] "Why do you call me 'Lord, Lord,' and don't do the things I say? [47] I will show you what someone is like who comes to me, hears my words, and acts on them: [48] He is like a man building a house, who dug deep and laid the foundation on the rock. When the flood came, the river crashed against that house and couldn't shake it, because it was well built. [49] But the one who hears and does not act is like a man who built a house on the ground without a foundation. The river crashed against it, and immediately it collapsed. And the destruction of that house was great."

A CENTURION'S FAITH

7 When he had concluded saying all this to the people who were listening, he entered Capernaum. [2] A centurion's servant, who was highly valued by him, was sick and about to die. [3] When the centurion heard about

^6:43 Lit on the other hand, again, a bad tree doesn't produce good fruit

Jesus, he sent some Jewish elders to him, requesting him to come and save the life of his servant. ⁴ When they reached Jesus, they pleaded with him earnestly, saying, "He is worthy for you to grant this, ⁵ because he loves our nation and has built us a synagogue."

⁶ Jesus went with them, and when he was not far from the house, the centurion sent friends to tell him, "Lord, don't trouble yourself, since I am not worthy to have you come under my roof. ⁷ That is why I didn't even consider myself worthy to come to you. But say the word, and my servant will be healed.^A ⁸ For I too am a man placed under authority, having soldiers under my command. I say to this one, 'Go,' and he goes; and to another, 'Come,' and he comes; and to my servant, 'Do this,' and he does it."

⁹ Jesus heard this and was amazed at him, and turning to the crowd following him, he said, "I tell you, I have not found so great a faith even in Israel." ¹⁰ When those who had been sent returned to the house, they found the servant in good health.

A WIDOW'S SON RAISED TO LIFE

¹¹ Afterward he was on his way to a town called Nain. His disciples and a large crowd were traveling with him. ¹² Just as he neared the gate of the town, a dead man was being carried out. He was his mother's only son, and she was a widow. A large crowd from the city was also with her. ¹³ When the Lord saw her, he had compassion on her and said, "Don't weep." ¹⁴ Then he came up and touched the open coffin, and the pallbearers stopped. And he said, "Young man, I tell you, get up!"

¹⁵ The dead man sat up and began to speak, and Jesus gave him to his mother. ¹⁶ Then fear^B came over everyone, and they glorified God, saying, "A great prophet has risen among us," and "God has visited^C his people." ¹⁷ This report about him went throughout Judea and all the vicinity.

IN PRAISE OF JOHN THE BAPTIST

¹⁸ Then John's disciples told him about all these things. So John summoned two of his disciples ¹⁹ and sent them to the Lord, asking, "Are you the one who is to come, or should we expect someone else?"

²⁰ When the men reached him, they said, "John the Baptist sent us to ask you, 'Are you the one who is to come, or should we expect someone else?'"

²¹ At that time Jesus healed many people of diseases, afflictions, and evil spirits, and he granted sight to many blind people. ²² He replied to them, "Go and report to John what you have seen and heard: The blind receive their sight, the lame walk, those with leprosy^D are cleansed, the deaf hear, the dead are raised, and the poor are told the good news, ²³ and blessed is the one who isn't offended by me."

²⁴ After John's messengers left, he began to speak to the crowds about John: "What did you go out into the wilderness to see? A reed swaying in the wind? ²⁵ What then did you go out to see? A man dressed in soft clothes? See, those who are splendidly dressed and live in luxury are in royal palaces. ²⁶ What then did you go out to see? A prophet? Yes, I tell you, and more than a prophet. ²⁷ This is the one about whom it is written:

---

^A 7:7 Other mss read and let my servant be healed   ^B 7:16 Or awe   ^C 7:16 Or come to help   ^D 7:22 Gk lepros; a term for various skin diseases; see Lv 13–14

> See, I am sending my messenger
> ahead of you;
> he will prepare your way before you. ^

²⁸ I tell you, among those born of women no one is greater than John, ᴮ but the least in the kingdom of God is greater than he."

²⁹ (And when all the people, including the tax collectors, heard this, they acknowledged God's way of righteousness, because they had been baptized with John's baptism. ³⁰ But since the Pharisees and experts in the law had not been baptized by him, they rejected the plan of God for themselves.)

AN UNRESPONSIVE GENERATION

³¹ "To what then should I compare the people of this generation, and what are they like? ³² They are like children sitting in the marketplace and calling to each other:

> We played the flute for you,
> but you didn't dance;
> we sang a lament,
> but you didn't weep!

³³ For John the Baptist did not come eating bread or drinking wine, and you say, 'He has a demon!' ³⁴ The Son of Man has come eating and drinking, and you say, 'Look, a glutton and a drunkard, a friend of tax collectors and sinners!' ³⁵ Yet wisdom is vindicated by all her children."

MUCH FORGIVENESS, MUCH LOVE

³⁶ Then one of the Pharisees invited him to eat with him. He entered the Pharisee's house and reclined at the table. ³⁷ And a woman in the town who was a sinner found out that Jesus was reclining at the table in the Pharisee's house. She brought an alabaster jar of perfume ³⁸ and stood behind him at his feet, weeping, and began to wash his feet with her tears. She wiped his feet with her hair, kissing them and anointing them with the perfume.

³⁹ When the Pharisee who had invited him saw this, he said to himself, "This man, if he were a prophet, would know who and what kind of woman this is who is touching him — she's a sinner!"

⁴⁰ Jesus replied to him, "Simon, I have something to say to you."

He said, "Say it, teacher."

⁴¹ "A creditor had two debtors. One owed five hundred denarii, ᶜ and the other fifty. ⁴² Since they could not pay it back, he graciously forgave them both. So, which of them will love him more?"

⁴³ Simon answered, "I suppose the one he forgave more."

"You have judged correctly," he told him. ⁴⁴ Turning to the woman, he said to Simon, "Do you see this woman? I entered your house; you gave me no water for my feet, but she, with her tears, has washed my feet and wiped them with her hair. ⁴⁵ You gave me no kiss, but she hasn't stopped kissing my feet since I came in. ⁴⁶ You didn't anoint my head with olive oil, but she has anointed my feet with perfume. ⁴⁷ Therefore I tell you, her many sins have been forgiven; that's why she loved much. But the one who is forgiven little, loves little." ⁴⁸ Then he said to her, "Your sins are forgiven."

---

^7:27 Mal 3:1   ᴮ7:28 Other mss read *women is not a greater prophet than John the Baptist*   ᶜ7:41 A denarius = one day's wage

[49] Those who were at the table with him began to say among themselves, "Who is this man who even forgives sins?"

[50] And he said to the woman, "Your faith has saved you. Go in peace."

MANY WOMEN SUPPORT CHRIST'S WORK

8 Afterward he was traveling from one town and village to another, preaching and telling the good news of the kingdom of God. The Twelve were with him, [2] and also some women who had been healed of evil spirits and sicknesses: Mary, called Magdalene (seven demons had come out of her); [3] Joanna the wife of Chuza, Herod's steward; Susanna; and many others who were supporting them from their possessions.

THE PARABLE OF THE SOWER

[4] As a large crowd was gathering, and people were coming to Jesus from every town, he said in a parable: [5] "A sower went out to sow his seed. As he sowed, some seed fell along the path; it was trampled on, and the birds of the sky devoured it. [6] Other seed fell on the rock; when it grew up, it withered away, since it lacked moisture. [7] Other seed fell among thorns; the thorns grew up with it and choked it. [8] Still other seed fell on good ground; when it grew up, it produced fruit: a hundred times what was sown." As he said this, he called out, "Let anyone who has ears to hear listen."

WHY JESUS USED PARABLES

[9] Then his disciples asked him, "What does this parable mean?" [10] So he said, "The secrets of the kingdom of God have been given for you to know, but to the rest it is in parables, so that

**Looking they may not see,
and hearing they may not understand.**[A]

THE PARABLE OF THE SOWER EXPLAINED

[11] "This is the meaning of the parable: The seed is the word of God. [12] The seed along the path are those who have heard and then the devil comes and takes away the word from their hearts, so that they may not believe and be saved. [13] And the seed on the rock are those who, when they hear, receive the word with joy. Having no root, these believe for a while and fall away in a time of testing. [14] As for the seed that fell among thorns, these are the ones who, when they have heard, go on their way and are choked with worries, riches, and pleasures of life, and produce no mature fruit. [15] But the seed in the good ground — these are the ones who, having heard the word with an honest and good heart, hold on to it and by enduring, produce fruit.

USING YOUR LIGHT

[16] "No one, after lighting a lamp, covers it with a basket or puts it under a bed, but puts it on a lampstand so that those who come in may see its light. [17] For nothing is concealed that won't be revealed, and nothing hidden that won't be made known and brought to light. [18] Therefore take care how you listen. For whoever has, more will be given to him; and whoever does not have, even what he thinks he has will be taken away from him."

A 8:10 Is 6:9

TRUE RELATIONSHIPS

[19] Then his mother and brothers came to him, but they could not meet with him because of the crowd. [20] He was told, "Your mother and your brothers are standing outside, wanting to see you."

[21] But he replied to them, "My mother and my brothers are those who hear and do the word of God."

WIND AND WAVES OBEY JESUS

[22] One day he and his disciples got into a boat, and he told them, "Let's cross over to the other side of the lake." So they set out, [23] and as they were sailing he fell asleep. Then a fierce windstorm came down on the lake; they were being swamped and were in danger. [24] They came and woke him up, saying, "Master, Master, we're going to die!"

Then he got up and rebuked the wind and the raging waves. So they ceased, and there was a calm. [25] He said to them, "Where is your faith?"

They were fearful and amazed, asking one another, "Who then is this? He commands even the winds and the waves, and they obey him!"

DEMONS DRIVEN OUT BY JESUS

[26] Then they sailed to the region of the Gerasenes,^A which is opposite Galilee. [27] When he got out on land, a demon-possessed man from the town met him. For a long time he had worn no clothes and did not stay in a house but in the tombs. [28] When he saw Jesus, he cried out, fell down before him, and said in a loud voice, "What do you have to do with me, Jesus, Son of the Most High God? I beg you, don't torment me!" [29] For he had commanded the unclean spirit to come out of the man. Many times it had seized him, and though he was guarded, bound by chains and shackles, he would snap the restraints and be driven by the demon into deserted places.

[30] "What is your name?" Jesus asked him.

"Legion," he said, because many demons had entered him. [31] And they begged him not to banish them to the abyss.

[32] A large herd of pigs was there, feeding on the hillside. The demons begged him to permit them to enter the pigs, and he gave them permission. [33] The demons came out of the man and entered the pigs, and the herd rushed down the steep bank into the lake and drowned.

[34] When the men who tended them saw what had happened, they ran off and reported it in the town and in the countryside. [35] Then people went out to see what had happened. They came to Jesus and found the man the demons had departed from, sitting at Jesus's feet, dressed and in his right mind. And they were afraid. [36] Meanwhile, the eyewitnesses reported to them how the demon-possessed man was delivered. [37] Then all the people of the Gerasene region^A asked him to leave them, because they were gripped by great fear. So getting into the boat, he returned.

[38] The man from whom the demons had departed begged him earnestly to be with him. But he sent him away and said, [39] "Go back to your home, and tell all that God has done for you." And off he went, proclaiming throughout the town how much Jesus had done for him.

^A 8:26,37 Other mss read *the Gadarenes*

A GIRL RESTORED AND A WOMAN HEALED

⁴⁰ When Jesus returned, the crowd welcomed him, for they were all expecting him. ⁴¹ Just then, a man named Jairus came. He was a leader of the synagogue. He fell down at Jesus's feet and pleaded with him to come to his house, ⁴² because he had an only daughter about twelve years old, and she was dying.

While he was going, the crowds were nearly crushing him. ⁴³ A woman suffering from bleeding for twelve years, who had spent all she had on doctors[A] and yet could not be healed by any, ⁴⁴ approached from behind and touched the end of his robe. Instantly her bleeding stopped.

⁴⁵ "Who touched me?" Jesus asked.

When they all denied it, Peter[B] said, "Master, the crowds are hemming you in and pressing against you."[C]

⁴⁶ "Someone did touch me," said Jesus. "I know that power has gone out from me." ⁴⁷ When the woman saw that she was discovered, she came trembling and fell down before him. In the presence of all the people, she declared the reason she had touched him and how she was instantly healed. ⁴⁸ "Daughter," he said to her, "your faith has saved you.[D] Go in peace."

⁴⁹ While he was still speaking, someone came from the synagogue leader's house and said, "Your daughter is dead. Don't bother the teacher anymore."

⁵⁰ When Jesus heard it, he answered him, "Don't be afraid. Only believe, and she will be saved."[E] ⁵¹ After he came to the house, he let no one enter with him except Peter, John, James, and the child's father and mother. ⁵² Everyone was crying and mourning for her. But he said, "Stop crying, because she is not dead but asleep."

⁵³ They laughed at him, because they knew she was dead. ⁵⁴ So he[F] took her by the hand and called out, "Child, get up!" ⁵⁵ Her spirit returned, and she got up at once. Then he gave orders that she be given something to eat. ⁵⁶ Her parents were astounded, but he instructed them to tell no one what had happened.

COMMISSIONING THE TWELVE

9 Summoning the Twelve, he gave them power and authority over all the demons and to heal diseases. ² Then he sent them to proclaim the kingdom of God and to heal the sick.

³ "Take nothing for the road," he told them, "no staff, no traveling bag, no bread, no money; and don't take an extra shirt. ⁴ Whatever house you enter, stay there and leave from there. ⁵ If they do not welcome you, when you leave that town, shake off the dust from your feet as a testimony against them."

⁶ So they went out and traveled from village to village, proclaiming the good news and healing everywhere.

HEROD'S DESIRE TO SEE JESUS

⁷ Herod the tetrarch heard about everything that was going on. He was perplexed, because some said that John had been raised from the dead, ⁸ some that Elijah had appeared, and others that one of the ancient prophets had

---

[A]8:43 Other mss omit *who had spent all she had on doctors*   [B]8:45 Other mss add *and those with him*   [C]8:45 Other mss add *and you say, 'Who touched me?'*   [D]8:48 Or *has made you well*   [E]8:50 Or *she will be made well*   [F]8:54 Other mss add *having put them all outside* risen. ⁹ "I beheaded John," Herod said, "but who is this I hear such things about?" And he wanted to see him.

FEEDING OF THE FIVE THOUSAND

¹⁰ When the apostles returned, they reported to Jesus all that they had done. He took them along and withdrew privately to a ᴬ town called Bethsaida. ¹¹ When the crowds found out, they followed him. He welcomed them, spoke to them about the kingdom of God, and healed those who needed healing.

¹² Late in the day, the Twelve approached and said to him, "Send the crowd away, so that they can go into the surrounding villages and countryside to find food and lodging, because we are in a deserted place here."

¹³ "You give them something to eat," he told them.

"We have no more than five loaves and two fish," they said, "unless we go and buy food for all these people." ¹⁴ (For about five thousand men were there.)

Then he told his disciples, "Have them sit down ᴮ in groups of about fifty each." ¹⁵ They did what he said, and had them all sit down. ¹⁶ Then he took the five loaves and the two fish, and looking up to heaven, he blessed and broke them. He kept giving them to the disciples to set before the crowd. ¹⁷ Everyone ate and was filled. They picked up twelve baskets of leftover pieces.

PETER'S CONFESSION OF THE MESSIAH

¹⁸ While he was praying in private and his disciples were with him, he asked them, "Who do the crowds say that I am?"

¹⁹ They answered, "John the Baptist; others, Elijah; still others, that one of the ancient prophets has come back." ᶜ

²⁰ "But you," he asked them, "who do you say that I am?"

Peter answered, "God's Messiah."

HIS DEATH AND RESURRECTION PREDICTED

²¹ But he strictly warned and instructed them to tell this to no one, ²² saying, "It is necessary that the Son of Man suffer many things and be rejected by the elders, chief priests, and scribes, be killed, and be raised the third day."

TAKE UP YOUR CROSS

²³ Then he said to them all, "If anyone wants to follow after ᴰ me, let him deny himself, take up his cross daily, ᴱ and follow me. ²⁴ For whoever wants to save his life will lose it, but whoever loses his life because of me will save it. ²⁵ For what does it benefit someone if he gains the whole world, and yet loses or forfeits himself? ²⁶ For whoever is ashamed of me and my words, the Son of Man will be ashamed of him when he comes in his glory and that of the Father and the holy angels. ²⁷ Truly I tell you, there are some standing here who will not taste death until they see the kingdom of God."

THE TRANSFIGURATION

²⁸ About eight days after this conversation, he took along Peter, John, and James and went up on the mountain to pray. ²⁹ As he was praying, the appearance of his face changed, and his clothes became dazzling white. ³⁰ Suddenly,

---

ᴬ 9:10 Other mss add *deserted place near a* ᴮ 9:14 Lit *them recline* ᶜ 9:19 Lit *has risen* ᴰ 9:23 Lit *come after* ᴱ 9:23 Other mss omit *daily* two men were talking with him — Moses and Elijah. [31] They appeared in glory and were speaking of his departure, which he was about to accomplish in Jerusalem.

[32] Peter and those with him were in a deep sleep,[A] and when they became fully awake, they saw his glory and the two men who were standing with him. [33] As the two men were departing from him, Peter said to Jesus, "Master, it's good for us to be here. Let us set up three shelters: one for you, one for Moses, and one for Elijah" — not knowing what he was saying.

[34] While he was saying this, a cloud appeared and overshadowed them. They became afraid as they entered the cloud. [35] Then a voice came from the cloud, saying: "This is my Son, the Chosen One;[B] listen to him!"

[36] After the voice had spoken, Jesus was found alone. They kept silent, and at that time told no one what they had seen.

THE POWER OF JESUS OVER A DEMON

[37] The next day, when they came down from the mountain, a large crowd met him. [38] Just then a man from the crowd cried out, "Teacher, I beg you to look at my son, because he's my only child. [39] A spirit seizes him; suddenly he shrieks, and it throws him into convulsions until he foams at the mouth; severely bruising him, it scarcely ever leaves him. [40] I begged your disciples to drive it out, but they couldn't."

[41] Jesus replied, "You unbelieving and perverse[C] generation, how long will I be with you and put up with you? Bring your son here."

[42] As the boy was still approaching, the demon knocked him down and threw him into severe convulsions. But Jesus rebuked the unclean spirit, healed the boy, and gave him back to his father. [43] And they were all astonished at the greatness of God.

THE SECOND PREDICTION OF HIS DEATH

While everyone was amazed at all the things he was doing, he told his disciples, [44] "Let these words sink in:[D] The Son of Man is about to be betrayed into the hands of men."

[45] But they did not understand this statement; it was concealed from them so that they could not grasp it, and they were afraid to ask him about it.

WHO IS THE GREATEST?

[46] An argument started among them about who was the greatest of them. [47] But Jesus, knowing their inner thoughts,[E] took a little child and had him stand next to him. [48] He told them, "Whoever welcomes[F] this little child in my name welcomes me. And whoever welcomes me welcomes him who sent me. For whoever is least among you — this one is great."

IN HIS NAME

[49] John responded, "Master, we saw someone driving out demons in your name, and we tried to stop him because he does not follow us."

[A]9:32 Lit *were weighed down with sleep*   [B]9:35 Other mss read *the Beloved*
[C]9:41 Or *corrupt*, or *perverted*, or *twisted*; Dt 32:5   [D]9:44 Lit *"Put these words in your ears*   [E]9:47 Lit *the thoughts of their hearts*   [F]9:48 Or *receives*, throughout the verse

⁵⁰ "Don't stop him," Jesus told him, "because whoever is not against you is for you."ᴬ

THE JOURNEY TO JERUSALEM

⁵¹ When the days were coming to a close for him to be taken up, he determinedᴮ to journey to Jerusalem. ⁵² He sent messengers ahead of himself, and on the way they entered a village of the Samaritans to make preparations for him. ⁵³ But they did not welcome him, because he determined to journey to Jerusalem. ⁵⁴ When the disciples James and John saw this, they said, "Lord, do you want us to call down fire from heaven to consume them?"ᶜ

⁵⁵ But he turned and rebuked them,ᴰ ⁵⁶ and they went to another village.

FOLLOWING JESUS

⁵⁷ As they were traveling on the road someone said to him, "I will follow you wherever you go."

⁵⁸ Jesus told him, "Foxes have dens, and birds of the sky have nests, but the Son of Man has no place to lay his head." ⁵⁹ Then he said to another, "Follow me."

"Lord," he said, "first let me go bury my father."

⁶⁰ But he told him, "Let the dead bury their own dead, but you go and spread the news of the kingdom of God."

⁶¹ Another said, "I will follow you, Lord, but first let me go and say goodbye to those at my house."

⁶² But Jesus said to him, "No one who puts his hand to the plow and looks back is fit for the kingdom of God."

SENDING OUT THE SEVENTY-TWO

10 After this, the Lord appointed seventy-twoᴱ others, and he sent them ahead of him in pairs to every town and place where he himself was about to go. ² He told them, "The harvest is abundant, but the workers are few. Therefore, pray to the Lord of the harvest to send out workers into his harvest. ³ Now go; I'm sending you out like lambs among wolves. ⁴ Don't carry a money-bag, traveling bag, or sandals; don't greet anyone along the road. ⁵ Whatever house you enter, first say, 'Peace to this household.' ⁶ If a person of peace is there, your peace will rest on him; but if not, it will return to you. ⁷ Remain in the same house, eating and drinking what they offer, for the worker is worthy of his wages. Don't move from house to house. ⁸ When you enter any town, and they welcome you, eat the things set before you. ⁹ Heal the sick who are there, and tell them, 'The kingdom of God has come near you.' ¹⁰ When you enter any town, and they don't welcome you, go out into its streets and say, ¹¹ 'We are wiping off even the dust of your town that clings to our feet as a witness against you. Know this for certain: The kingdom of God has come near.' ¹² I tell you, on that day it will be more tolerable for Sodom than for that town.

ᴬ9:50 Other mss read against us is for us   ᴮ9:51 Lit he stiffened his face to go; Is 50:7   ᶜ9:54 Other mss add as Elijah also did   ᴰ9:55-56 Other mss add and said, "You don't know what kind of spirit you belong to. ⁵⁶For the Son of Man did not come to destroy people's lives but to save them,"   ᴱ10:1 Other mss read seventy

UNREPENTANT TOWNS

¹³ "Woe to you, Chorazin! Woe to you, Bethsaida! For if the miracles that were done in you had been done in Tyre and Sidon, they would have repented long ago, sitting in sackcloth and ashes. ¹⁴ But it will be more tolerable for Tyre and Sidon at the judgment than for you. ¹⁵ And you, Capernaum, will you be exalted to heaven? No, you will go down to Hades. ¹⁶ Whoever listens to you listens to me. Whoever rejects you rejects me. And whoever rejects me rejects the one who sent me."

THE RETURN OF THE SEVENTY-TWO

¹⁷ The seventy-two ᴬ returned with joy, saying, "Lord, even the demons submit to us in your name."

¹⁸ He said to them, "I watched Satan fall from heaven like lightning. ¹⁹ Look, I have given you the authority to trample on snakes and scorpions and over all the power of the enemy; nothing at all will harm you. ²⁰ However, don't rejoice that ᴮ the spirits submit to you, but rejoice that your names are written in heaven."

THE SON REVEALS THE FATHER

²¹ At that time he ᶜ rejoiced in the Holy ᴰ Spirit and said, "I praise ᴱ you, Father, Lord of heaven and earth, because you have hidden these things from the wise and intelligent and revealed them to infants. Yes, Father, because this was your good pleasure. ᶠ ²² All things have ᴳ been entrusted to me by my Father. No one knows who the Son is except the Father, and who the Father is except the Son, and anyone to whom the Son desires ᴴ to reveal him."

²³ Then turning to his disciples he said privately, "Blessed are the eyes that see the things you see! ²⁴ For I tell you that many prophets and kings wanted to see the things you see but didn't see them; to hear the things you hear but didn't hear them."

THE PARABLE OF THE GOOD SAMARITAN

²⁵ Then an expert in the law stood up to test him, saying, "Teacher, what must I do to inherit eternal life?"

²⁶ "What is written in the law?" he asked him. "How do you read it?"

²⁷ He answered, **"Love the Lord your God with all your heart, with all your soul, with all your strength, and with all your mind,"** and **"your neighbor as yourself."** ᴵ

²⁸ "You've answered correctly," he told him. "Do this and you will live."

²⁹ But wanting to justify himself, he asked Jesus, "And who is my neighbor?"

³⁰ Jesus took up the question and said: "A man was going down from Jerusalem to Jericho and fell into the hands of robbers. They stripped him, beat him up, and fled, leaving him half dead. ³¹ A priest happened to be going down that road. When he saw him, he passed by on the other side. ³² In the same way, a Levite, when he arrived at the place and saw him, passed

---

ᴬ10:17 Other mss read *The seventy*   ᴮ10:20 Lit *don't rejoice in this, that*
ᶜ10:21 Other mss read *Jesus*   ᴰ10:21 Other mss omit *Holy*   ᴱ10:21 Or *thank*, or
confess   ᶠ10:21 Lit *was well-pleasing in your sight*   ᴳ10:22 Other mss read *And
turning to the disciples, he said, "Everything has*   ᴴ10:22 Or *wills*, or *chooses*
ᴵ10:27 Lv 19:18; Dt 6:5

THE POWER OF HIS PRESENCE

LUKE 10; PSALM 16; ROMANS 10:14-17

I have a dear friend who appears to effortlessly exhibit the gift of hospitality. Her historic home is beautifully decorated, warm, and inviting. Her guests feel at ease the moment they pull in the driveway, and the front porch beckons you to stay a while. I can't help but feel comfortable when I'm with her.

But over the years, I've realized something: that feeling I get when I spend time with my friend has little to do with her home or her skills as a hostess. It has everything to do with her character. On a daily basis, she lingers in the presence of Jesus. His kindness, faithfulness, and grace fill her up and spill out in the ways she serves others. This is what makes her home truly special.

I'll be the first to admit that my task-oriented, detail-obsessed personality is often consumed with lesser things. There are times I'm more concerned with the quality of my service than the motivation of my heart. That's why this passage of Scripture makes me shift uncomfortably in my seat.

The story of Mary and Martha appears, at first glance, to be about two sisters and their vastly different approaches to life. But in truth, it is centered on the Savior who loved them both deeply.

Martha was wired for action, highly motivated, and created with a deep desire to serve. But at times, those strengths led to struggles. She strained to balance the beauty of how she was made with her ultimate purpose—enjoying and glorifying her Savior. She busied herself with details, presentation, and chores, losing sight of her priorities in the process. The cycle left her feeling weary and frustrated.

Jesus responded to Martha's meltdown with astounding grace and affection, saying,

---

"Martha, Martha, you are worried and upset about many things, but one thing is necessary. Mary has made the right choice, and it will not be taken away from her."

LUKE 10:41-42

This was not a lecture. It was much more than that. **The God of mercy met Martha in her weakness and offered her the cure for her weary heart.**

Martha had allowed the urgency of temporary tasks to distract her from the glory of eternal truths. She missed the significance of the invitation to sit at the feet of Jesus and experience His nearness. Martha's acts of service had become more about her efforts than loving the One she served.

We are all Marthas at times. Driven by expectations and prone to empty pursuits, we struggle to sit still long enough to let truth take root in our hearts. When we are distracted by our to-do lists and striving, may we remember there is only one cure for our weary hearts: the power of Jesus' presence. Let's rest at His feet today.

by on the other side. ³³ But a Samaritan on his journey came up to him, and when he saw the man, he had compassion. ³⁴ He went over to him and bandaged his wounds, pouring on olive oil and wine. Then he put him on his own animal, brought him to an inn, and took care of him. ³⁵ The next day ᴬ he took out two denarii, ᴮ gave them to the innkeeper, and said, 'Take care of him. When I come back I'll reimburse you for whatever extra you spend.'

³⁶ "Which of these three do you think proved to be a neighbor to the man who fell into the hands of the robbers?"

³⁷ "The one who showed mercy to him," he said.

Then Jesus told him, "Go and do the same."

MARTHA AND MARY

³⁸ While they were traveling, he entered a village, and a woman named Martha welcomed him into her home. ᶜ ³⁹ She had a sister named Mary, who also sat at the Lord's ᴰ feet and was listening to what he said. ᴱ ⁴⁰ But Martha was distracted by her many tasks, and she came up and asked, "Lord, don't you care that my sister has left me to serve alone? So tell her to give me a hand." ᶠ

⁴¹ The Lord ᴳ answered her, "Martha, Martha, you are worried and upset about many things, ⁴² but one thing is necessary. ᴴ Mary has made the right choice, ¹ and it will not be taken away from her."

THE LORD'S PRAYER

11 He was praying in a certain place, and when he finished, one of his disciples said to him, "Lord, teach us to pray, just as John also taught his disciples."

² He said to them, "Whenever you pray, say,

Father, ᴶ
your name be honored as holy.
Your kingdom come. ᴷ
³   Give us each day our daily bread. ᴸ
⁴   And forgive us our sins,
    for we ourselves also forgive everyone
    in debt to us. ᴹ
    And do not bring us into temptation." ᴺ

ASK, SEARCH, KNOCK

⁵ He also said to them: "Suppose one of you ᴼ has a friend and goes to him at midnight and says to him, 'Friend, lend me three loaves of bread, ⁶ because a friend of mine on a journey has come to me, and I don't have anything to offer him.' ⁷ Then he will answer from inside and say, 'Don't bother me! The

---

ᴬ 10:35 Other mss add *as he was leaving*   ᴮ 10:35 A denarius = one day's wage.   ᶜ 10:38 Other mss omit *into her home*   ᴰ 10:39 Other mss read *at Jesus's* ᴱ 10:39 Lit *to his word*, or *message*   ᶠ 10:40 Or *tell her to help me*   ᴳ 10:41 Other mss read *Jesus*   ᴴ 10:42 Some mss read *few things are necessary*, or *only one* ¹ 10:42 Lit *has chosen the good part*, or *has chosen the better portion* ; = the right meal   ᴶ 11:2 Other mss read *Our Father in heaven*   ᴷ 11:2 Other mss add *Your will be done on earth as it is in heaven*   ᴸ 11:3 Or *our bread for tomorrow* ᴹ 11:4 Or *everyone who wrongs us*   ᴺ 11:4 Other mss add *But deliver us from the evil one*   ᴼ 11:5 Lit *Who of you* door is already locked, and my children and I have gone to bed. I can't get up to give you anything.' [8] I tell you, even though he won't get up and give him anything because he is his friend, yet because of his friend's shameless boldness,[A] he will get up and give him as much as he needs.

[9] "So I say to you, ask, and it will be given to you. Seek, and you will find. Knock, and the door will be opened to you. [10] For everyone who asks receives, and the one who seeks finds, and to the one who knocks, the door will be opened. [11] What father among you, if his son[B] asks for a fish, will give him a snake instead of a fish? [12] Or if he asks for an egg, will give him a scorpion? [13] If you then, who are evil, know how to give good gifts to your children, how much more will the heavenly Father give the Holy Spirit to those who ask him?"

A HOUSE DIVIDED

[14] Now he was driving out a demon that was mute. When the demon came out, the man who had been mute spoke, and the crowds were amazed. [15] But some of them said, "He drives out demons by Beelzebul, the ruler of the demons." [16] And others, as a test, were demanding of him a sign from heaven.

[17] Knowing their thoughts, he told them, "Every kingdom divided against itself is headed for destruction, and a house divided against itself falls. [18] If Satan also is divided against himself, how will his kingdom stand? For you say I drive out demons by Beelzebul. [19] And if I drive out demons by Beelzebul, by whom do your sons drive them out? For this reason they will be your judges. [20] If I drive out demons by the finger of God, then the kingdom of God has come upon you. [21] When a strong man, fully armed, guards his estate, his possessions are secure. [22] But when one stronger than he attacks and overpowers him, he takes from him all his weapons[C] he trusted in, and divides up his plunder. [23] Anyone who is not with me is against me, and anyone who does not gather with me scatters.

AN UNCLEAN SPIRIT'S RETURN

[24] "When an unclean spirit comes out of a person, it roams through waterless places looking for rest, and not finding rest, it then[D] says, 'I'll go back to my house that I came from.' [25] Returning, it finds the house swept and put in order. [26] Then it goes and brings seven other spirits more evil than itself, and they enter and settle down there. As a result, that person's last condition is worse than the first."

TRUE BLESSEDNESS

[27] As he was saying these things, a woman from the crowd raised her voice and said to him, "Blessed is the womb that bore you and the one who nursed you!"

[28] He said, "Rather, blessed are those who hear the word of God and keep it."

THE SIGN OF JONAH

[29] As the crowds were increasing, he began saying: "This generation is an evil generation. It demands a sign, but no sign will be given to it except the

---

[A] 11:8 Or *persistence* [B] 11:11 Other mss read *son asks for bread, would give him a stone? Or if he* [C] 11:22 Gk *panoplia*, the armor and weapons of a foot soldier; Eph 6:11,13 [D] 11:24 Other mss omit *then* sign of Jonah.^A ³⁰ For just as Jonah became a sign to the people of Nineveh, so also the Son of Man will be to this generation. ³¹ The queen of the south will rise up at the judgment with the men of this generation and condemn them, because she came from the ends of the earth to hear the wisdom of Solomon, and look — something greater than Solomon is here. ³² The men of Nineveh will stand up at the judgment with this generation and condemn it, because they repented at Jonah's preaching, and look — something greater than Jonah is here.

THE LAMP OF THE BODY

³³ "No one lights a lamp and puts it in the cellar or under a basket,^B but on a lampstand, so that those who come in may see its light. ³⁴ Your eye is the lamp of the body. When your eye is healthy, your whole body is also full of light. But when it is bad, your body is also full of darkness. ³⁵ Take care, then, that the light in you is not darkness. ³⁶ If, therefore, your whole body is full of light, with no part of it in darkness, it will be entirely illuminated, as when a lamp shines its light on you."

RELIGIOUS HYPOCRISY DENOUNCED

³⁷ As he was speaking, a Pharisee asked him to dine with him. So he went in and reclined at the table. ³⁸ When the Pharisee saw this, he was amazed that he did not first perform the ritual washing^C before dinner. ³⁹ But the Lord said to him, "Now you Pharisees clean the outside of the cup and dish, but inside you are full of greed and evil. ⁴⁰ Fools! Didn't he who made the outside make the inside too? ⁴¹ But give from what is within to the poor,^D and then everything is clean for you.

⁴² "But woe to you Pharisees! You give a tenth^E of mint, rue, and every kind of herb, and you bypass^F justice and love for God.^G These things you should have done without neglecting the others.

⁴³ "Woe to you Pharisees! You love the front seat in the synagogues and greetings in the marketplaces.

⁴⁴ "Woe to you!^H You are like unmarked graves; the people who walk over them don't know it."

⁴⁵ One of the experts in the law answered him, "Teacher, when you say these things you insult us too."

⁴⁶ Then he said: "Woe also to you experts in the law! You load people with burdens that are hard to carry, and yet you yourselves don't touch these burdens with one of your fingers.

⁴⁷ "Woe to you! You build tombs^I for the prophets, and your fathers killed them. ⁴⁸ Therefore, you are witnesses that you approve^J the deeds of your fathers, for they killed them, and you build their monuments.^K ⁴⁹ Because of this, the wisdom of God said, 'I will send them prophets and apostles, and some of them they will kill and persecute,' ⁵⁰ so that this generation may be held responsible for the blood of all the prophets shed since the foundation

---

^A11:29 Other mss add *the prophet* ^B11:33 Other mss omit *or under a basket*
^C11:38 Lit *he did not first wash* ^D11:41 Or *But donate from the heart as charity*
^E11:42 Or *a tithe* ^F11:42 Or *neglect* ^G11:42 Lit *the justice and the love of God*
^H11:44 Other mss add *scribes and Pharisees, hypocrites!* ^I11:47 Or *graves*
^J11:48 Lit *witnesses and approve* ^K11:48 Other mss omit *their monuments*

of the world^A — ^51 from the blood of Abel to the blood of Zechariah, who perished between the altar and the sanctuary.

"Yes, I tell you, this generation will be held responsible.^B

^52 "Woe to you experts in the law! You have taken away the key to knowledge. You didn't go in yourselves, and you hindered those who were trying to go in."

^53 When he left there,^C the scribes and the Pharisees began to oppose him fiercely and to cross-examine him about many things; ^54 they were lying in wait for him to trap him in something he said.^D

BEWARE OF RELIGIOUS HYPOCRISY

12 Meanwhile, a crowd of many thousands came together, so that they were trampling on one another. He began to say to his disciples first, "Be on your guard against the leaven^E of the Pharisees, which is hypocrisy. ^2 There is nothing covered that won't be uncovered, nothing hidden that won't be made known. ^3 Therefore, whatever you have said in the dark will be heard in the light, and what you have whispered in an ear in private rooms will be proclaimed on the housetops.

FEAR GOD

^4 "I say to you, my friends, don't fear those who kill the body, and after that can do nothing more. ^5 But I will show you the one to fear: Fear him who has authority to throw people into hell after death. Yes, I say to you, this is the one to fear! ^6 Aren't five sparrows sold for two pennies?^F Yet not one of them is forgotten in God's sight. ^7 Indeed, the hairs of your head are all counted. Don't be afraid; you are worth more than many sparrows.

ACKNOWLEDGING CHRIST

^8 "And I say to you, anyone who acknowledges me before others, the Son of Man will also acknowledge him before the angels of God, ^9 but whoever denies me before others will be denied before the angels of God. ^10 Anyone who speaks a word against the Son of Man will be forgiven, but the one who blasphemes against the Holy Spirit will not be forgiven. ^11 Whenever they bring you before synagogues and rulers and authorities, don't worry about how you should defend yourselves or what you should say. ^12 For the Holy Spirit will teach you at that very hour what must be said."

THE PARABLE OF THE RICH FOOL

^13 Someone from the crowd said to him, "Teacher, tell my brother to divide the inheritance with me."

^14 "Friend,"^G he said to him, "who appointed me a judge or arbitrator over you?" ^15 He then told them, "Watch out and be on guard against all greed, because one's life is not in the abundance of his possessions."

^16 Then he told them a parable: "A rich man's land was very productive. ^17 He thought to himself, 'What should I do, since I don't have anywhere to

---

^A11:50 Lit so that the blood of all . . . world may be required of this generation,
^B11:51 Lit you, it will be required of this generation   ^C11:53 Other mss read
And as he was saying these things to them   ^D11:54 Other mss add so that they
might bring charges against him   ^E12:1 Or yeast   ^F12:6 Lit two assaria; a small
copper coin   ^G12:14 Lit Man

CONSIDER THE RAVENS

LUKE 12; PSALM 91:1-4

Leaning against the window, I argued, "That's a Pileated Woodpecker!" My husband and son, surrounded by bird identification books countered, "Red-Headed Woodpecker, for sure." I strained my eyes and looked up to the dying walnut tree for the pair of big birds nesting in the topmost branch, trying to see if the gorgeous redheads were crested or round.

The world of computers, catalogs, and vacuuming often sucks my focus and I can go hours without even looking outside. Maybe that's why I love bird watching. It gives me a sense of the place I'm in, allowing me to stop and notice God's world.

In Luke 12, Jesus invites His disciples to look at creation so they can learn about God's providence. "Consider the ravens", He enjoins. "They don't sow or reap; they don't have a storeroom or a barn; yet God feeds them" (Lk 12:24).

When I remember this story, I always get the birds mixed up. I remember it as, "Consider the sparrows." Sparrows are adorable, tiny, flighty things. Obviously, God would take care of the darling sparrows. Bless them.

But Jesus said ravens—big, black, ominous, croaking ravens. Ravens appear frequently in our myths, stories, and symbols. Remember Edgar Allen Poe's raven speaking, "Nevermore," or the portentous Tower of London ravens? The raven also appears in Tolkien's *The Hobbit*, and Shakespeare's *Othello*. In all its manifestations, the raven is not an omen of sunshine and happiness. But God cares for these birds.

If I were to associate myself with a bird, on my bad days I might choose a raven, or a turkey, or probably a crow. Regardless, Jesus nudges me, "Aren't you worth much more than the birds?" (Lk 12:24). He's not asking me to imagine. He's asking me to look. God is taking care of the ravens. It's a fact. They are a little creepy, but God's got them.

When life gets weird and scary, I panic and think I have to take care of myself. We all scramble and forget to look outside our windows and outside of ourselves. We get tied down by the things man has created instead of considering what God has created. Instead of looking at more spreadsheets and emails when things are scary, we can open our eyes and consider God's creation.

God's continual provision is always before our eyes. It's His common grace that keeps the sun rising and the earth turning. It's God's good providence that keeps His creatures fed and clothed. Indeed, it is His grace that runs before us and behind us, keeping us secure in a way our own worrying, striving, and scheming could never achieve.

When fear creeps in and crowds your mind and your heart, look outward and consider the ravens.

store my crops? ¹⁸ I will do this,' he said. 'I'll tear down my barns and build bigger ones and store all my grain and my goods there. ¹⁹ Then I'll say to myself, "You have many goods stored up for many years. Take it easy; eat, drink, and enjoy yourself." '

²⁰ "But God said to him, 'You fool! This very night your life is demanded of you. And the things you have prepared — whose will they be?'

²¹ "That's how it is with the one who stores up treasure for himself and is not rich toward God."

THE CURE FOR ANXIETY

²² Then he said to his disciples: "Therefore I tell you, don't worry about your life, what you will eat; or about the body, what you will wear. ²³ For life is more than food and the body more than clothing. ²⁴ Consider the ravens: They don't sow or reap; they don't have a storeroom or a barn; yet God feeds them. Aren't you worth much more than the birds? ²⁵ Can any of you add one moment to his life span^A by worrying? ²⁶ If then you're not able to do even a little thing, why worry about the rest?

²⁷ "Consider how the wildflowers grow: They don't labor or spin thread. Yet I tell you, not even Solomon in all his splendor was adorned like one of these. ²⁸ If that's how God clothes the grass, which is in the field today and is thrown into the furnace tomorrow, how much more will he do for you — you of little faith? ²⁹ Don't strive for what you should eat and what you should drink, and don't be anxious. ³⁰ For the Gentile world eagerly seeks all these things, and your Father knows that you need them.

³¹ "But seek his kingdom, and these things will be provided for you. ³² Don't be afraid, little flock, because your Father delights to give you the kingdom. ³³ Sell your possessions and give to the poor. Make money-bags for yourselves that won't grow old, an inexhaustible treasure in heaven, where no thief comes near and no moth destroys. ³⁴ For where your treasure is, there your heart will be also.

READY FOR THE MASTER'S RETURN

³⁵ "Be ready for service^B and have your lamps lit. ³⁶ You are to be like people waiting for their master to return from the wedding banquet so that when he comes and knocks, they can open the door for him at once. ³⁷ Blessed will be those servants the master finds alert when he comes. Truly I tell you, he will get ready,^C have them recline at the table, then come and serve them. ³⁸ If he comes in the middle of the night, or even near dawn,^D and finds them alert, blessed are those servants. ³⁹ But know this: If the homeowner had known at what hour the thief was coming, he would not have let his house be broken into. ⁴⁰ You also be ready, because the Son of Man is coming at an hour you do not expect."

REWARDS AND PUNISHMENT

⁴¹ "Lord," Peter asked, "are you telling this parable to us or to everyone?"

⁴² The Lord said: "Who then is the faithful and sensible manager his master will put in charge of his household servants to give them their allotted

---

^A 12:25 Or *add a cubit to his height* ^B 12:35 Lit *"Let your loins be girded;*
an idiom for tying up loose outer clothing in preparation for action; Ex 12:11
^C 12:37 Lit *will gird himself* ^D 12:38 Lit *even in the second or third watch*

food at the proper time? ⁴³ Blessed is that servant whom the master finds doing his job when he comes. ⁴⁴ Truly I tell you, he will put him in charge of all his possessions. ⁴⁵ But if that servant says in his heart, 'My master is delaying his coming,' and starts to beat the male and female servants, and to eat and drink and get drunk, ⁴⁶ that servant's master will come on a day he does not expect him and at an hour he does not know. He will cut him to pieces ᴬ and assign him a place with the unfaithful. ᴮ ⁴⁷ And that servant who knew his master's will and didn't prepare himself or do it ᶜ will be severely beaten. ⁴⁸ But the one who did not know and did what deserved punishment will receive a light beating. From everyone who has been given much, much will be required; and from the one who has been entrusted with much, even more will be expected. ᴰ

NOT PEACE BUT DIVISION

⁴⁹ "I came to bring fire on the earth, and how I wish it were already set ablaze! ⁵⁰ But I have a baptism to undergo, and how it consumes me until it is finished! ⁵¹ Do you think that I came here to bring peace on the earth? No, I tell you, but rather division. ⁵² From now on, five in one household will be divided: three against two, and two against three.

⁵³ **They will be divided, father against son,**
    son against father,
    mother against daughter,
    daughter against mother,
    mother-in-law against her daughter-in-law,
    and daughter-in-law against mother-in-law." ᴱ

INTERPRETING THE TIME

⁵⁴ He also said to the crowds: "When you see a cloud rising in the west, right away you say, 'A storm is coming,' and so it does. ⁵⁵ And when the south wind is blowing, you say, 'It's going to be hot,' and it is. ⁵⁶ Hypocrites! You know how to interpret the appearance of the earth and the sky, but why don't you know how to interpret this present time?

SETTLING ACCOUNTS

⁵⁷ "Why don't you judge for yourselves what is right? ⁵⁸ As you are going with your adversary to the ruler, make an effort to settle with him on the way. Then he won't drag you before the judge, the judge hand you over to the bailiff, and the bailiff throw you into prison. ⁵⁹ I tell you, you will never get out of there until you have paid the last cent." ᶠ

REPENT OR PERISH

13 At that time, some people came and reported to him about the Galileans whose blood Pilate had mixed with their sacrifices. ² And he ᴳ responded to them, "Do you think that these Galileans were more sinful than all the other Galileans because they suffered these things? ³ No, I tell you; but unless you repent, you will all perish as well. ⁴ Or those eighteen

---

ᴬ 12:46 Lit *him in two* ᴮ 12:46 Or *unbelievers* ᶜ 12:47 Lit *or do toward his will,*
ᴰ 12:48 Or *much* ᴱ 12:53 Mc 7:6 ᶠ 12:59 Gk *lepton,* the smallest and least
valuable copper coin in use ᴳ 13:2 Other mss read *Jesus*

that the tower in Siloam fell on and killed — do you think they were more sinful than all the other people who live in Jerusalem? [5] No, I tell you; but unless you repent, you will all perish as well."

THE PARABLE OF THE BARREN FIG TREE

[6] And he told this parable: "A man had a fig tree that was planted in his vineyard. He came looking for fruit on it and found none. [7] He told the vineyard worker, 'Listen, for three years I have come looking for fruit on this fig tree and haven't found any. Cut it down! Why should it even waste the soil?'

[8] "But he replied to him, 'Sir,[A] leave it this year also, until I dig around it and fertilize it. [9] Perhaps it will produce fruit next year, but if not, you can cut it down.'"

HEALING A DAUGHTER OF ABRAHAM

[10] As he was teaching in one of the synagogues on the Sabbath, [11] a woman was there who had been disabled by a spirit[B] for over eighteen years. She was bent over and could not straighten up at all.[C] [12] When Jesus saw her, he called out to her,[D] "Woman, you are free of your disability." [13] Then he laid his hands on her, and instantly she was restored and began to glorify God.

[14] But the leader of the synagogue, indignant because Jesus had healed on the Sabbath, responded by telling the crowd, "There are six days when work should be done; therefore come on those days and be healed and not on the Sabbath day."

[15] But the Lord answered him and said, "Hypocrites! Doesn't each one of you untie his ox or donkey from the feeding trough on the Sabbath and lead it to water? [16] Satan has bound this woman, a daughter of Abraham, for eighteen years — shouldn't she be untied from this bondage[E] on the Sabbath day?"

[17] When he had said these things, all his adversaries were humiliated, but the whole crowd was rejoicing over all the glorious things he was doing.

THE PARABLES OF THE MUSTARD SEED AND OF THE LEAVEN

[18] He said, therefore, "What is the kingdom of God like, and what can I compare it to? [19] It's like a mustard seed that a man took and sowed in his garden. It grew and became a tree, and the birds of the sky nested in its branches."

[20] Again he said, "What can I compare the kingdom of God to? [21] It's like leaven[F] that a woman took and mixed into fifty pounds[G] of flour until all of it was leavened."

THE NARROW WAY

[22] He went through one town and village after another, teaching and making his way to Jerusalem. [23] "Lord," someone asked him, "are only a few people going to be saved?"

He said to them, [24] "Make every effort to enter through the narrow door, because I tell you, many will try to enter and won't be able [25] once the homeowner gets up and shuts the door. Then you will stand outside and knock on

---

the door, saying, 'Lord, open up for us!' He will answer you, 'I don't know you or where you're from.' ²⁶ Then you will say, 'We ate and drank in your presence, and you taught in our streets.' ²⁷ But he will say, 'I tell you, I don't know you or where you're from. Get away from me, all you evildoers!' ²⁸ There will be weeping and gnashing of teeth in that place, when you see Abraham, Isaac, Jacob, and all the prophets in the kingdom of God, but yourselves thrown out. ²⁹ They will come from east and west, from north and south, to share the banquet^A in the kingdom of God. ³⁰ Note this: Some who are last will be first, and some who are first will be last."

JESUS AND HEROD ANTIPAS

³¹ At that time some Pharisees came and told him, "Go, get out of here. Herod wants to kill you."

³² He said to them, "Go tell that fox, 'Look, I'm driving out demons and performing healings today and tomorrow, and on the third day I will complete my work.'^B ³³ Yet it is necessary that I travel today, tomorrow, and the next day, because it is not possible for a prophet to perish outside of Jerusalem.

JESUS'S LAMENTATION OVER JERUSALEM

³⁴ "Jerusalem, Jerusalem, who kills the prophets and stones those who are sent to her. How often I wanted to gather your children together, as a hen gathers her chicks under her wings, but you were not willing! ³⁵ See, your house is abandoned to you. I tell you, you will not see me until the time comes when^C you say, **'Blessed is he who comes in the name of the Lord'!**"^D

A SABBATH CONTROVERSY

14 One Sabbath, when he went in to eat^E at the house of one of the leading Pharisees, they were watching him closely. ² There in front of him was a man whose body was swollen with fluid. ³ In response, Jesus asked the law experts and the Pharisees, "Is it lawful to heal on the Sabbath or not?" ⁴ But they kept silent. He took the man, healed him, and sent him away. ⁵ And to them, he said, "Which of you whose son or ox falls into a well, will not immediately pull him out on the Sabbath day?" ⁶ They could find no answer to these things.

TEACHINGS ON HUMILITY

⁷ He told a parable to those who were invited, when he noticed how they would choose the best places for themselves: ⁸ "When you are invited by someone to a wedding banquet, don't recline at the best place, because a more distinguished person than you may have been invited by your host. ⁹ The one who invited both of you may come and say to you, 'Give your place to this man,' and then in humiliation, you will proceed to take the lowest place.

¹⁰ "But when you are invited, go and recline in the lowest place, so that when the one who invited you comes, he will say to you, 'Friend, move up higher.' You will then be honored in the presence of all the other guests. ¹¹ For everyone who exalts himself will be humbled, and the one who humbles himself will be exalted."

---

^A 13:29 Lit recline at the table   ^B 13:32 Lit I will be finished   ^C 13:35 Other mss omit the time comes when   ^D 13:35 Ps 118:26   ^E 14:1 Lit eat bread

[12] He also said to the one who had invited him, "When you give a lunch or a dinner, don't invite your friends, your brothers or sisters, your relatives, or your rich neighbors, because they might invite you back, and you would be repaid. [13] On the contrary, when you host a banquet, invite those who are poor, maimed, lame, or blind. [14] And you will be blessed, because they cannot repay you; for you will be repaid at the resurrection of the righteous."

THE PARABLE OF THE LARGE BANQUET

[15] When one of those who reclined at the table with him heard these things, he said to him, "Blessed is the one who will eat bread in the kingdom of God!"

[16] Then he told him: "A man was giving a large banquet and invited many. [17] At the time of the banquet, he sent his servant to tell those who were invited, 'Come, because everything is now ready.'

[18] "But without exception[A] they all began to make excuses. The first one said to him, 'I have bought a field, and I must go out and see it. I ask you to excuse me.'

[19] "Another said, 'I have bought five yoke of oxen, and I'm going to try them out. I ask you to excuse me.'

[20] "And another said, 'I just got married, and therefore I'm unable to come.'

[21] "So the servant came back and reported these things to his master. Then in anger, the master of the house told his servant, 'Go out quickly into the streets and alleys of the city, and bring in here the poor, maimed, blind, and lame.'

[22] " 'Master,' the servant said, 'what you ordered has been done, and there's still room.'

[23] "Then the master told the servant, 'Go out into the highways and hedges and make them come in, so that my house may be filled. [24] For I tell you, not one of those people who were invited will enjoy my banquet.' "

THE COST OF FOLLOWING JESUS

[25] Now great crowds were traveling with him. So he turned and said to them: [26] "If anyone comes to me and does not hate his own father and mother, wife and children, brothers and sisters — yes, and even his own life — he cannot be my disciple. [27] Whoever does not bear his own cross and come after me cannot be my disciple.

[28] "For which of you, wanting to build a tower, doesn't first sit down and calculate the cost to see if he has enough to complete it? [29] Otherwise, after he has laid the foundation and cannot finish it, all the onlookers will begin to ridicule him, [30] saying, 'This man started to build and wasn't able to finish.'

[31] "Or what king, going to war against another king, will not first sit down and decide if he is able with ten thousand to oppose the one who comes against him with twenty thousand? [32] If not, while the other is still far off, he sends a delegation and asks for terms of peace. [33] In the same way, therefore, every one of you who does not renounce[B] all his possessions cannot be my disciple.

[34] "Now, salt is good, but if salt should lose its taste, how will it be made salty? [35] It isn't fit for the soil or for the manure pile; they throw it out. Let anyone who has ears to hear listen."

[A]14:18 Lit "And from one (voice)   [B]14:33 Or leave

THE PARABLE OF THE LOST SHEEP

15 All the tax collectors and sinners were approaching to listen to him. ² And the Pharisees and scribes were complaining, "This man welcomes sinners and eats with them."

³ So he told them this parable: ⁴ "What man among you, who has a hundred sheep and loses one of them, does not leave the ninety-nine in the open field ᴬ and go after the lost one until he finds it? ⁵ When he has found it, he joyfully puts it on his shoulders, ⁶ and coming home, he calls his friends and neighbors together, saying to them, 'Rejoice with me, because I have found my lost sheep!' ⁷ I tell you, in the same way, there will be more joy in heaven over one sinner who repents than over ninety-nine righteous people who don't need repentance.

THE PARABLE OF THE LOST COIN

⁸ "Or what woman who has ten silver coins, ᴮ,ᶜ if she loses one coin, does not light a lamp, sweep the house, and search carefully until she finds it? ⁹ When she finds it, she calls her friends and neighbors together, saying, 'Rejoice with me, because I have found the silver coin I lost!' ¹⁰ I tell you, in the same way, there is joy in the presence of God's angels over one sinner who repents."

THE PARABLE OF THE LOST SON

¹¹ He also said: "A man had two sons. ¹² The younger of them said to his father, 'Father, give me the share of the estate I have coming to me.' So he distributed the assets ᴰ to them. ¹³ Not many days later, the younger son gathered together all he had and traveled to a distant country, where he squandered his estate in foolish living. ¹⁴ After he had spent everything, a severe famine struck that country, and he had nothing. ᴱ ¹⁵ Then he went to work for one of the citizens of that country, who sent him into his fields to feed pigs. ¹⁶ He longed to eat his fill from ᶠ the pods that the pigs were eating, but no one would give him anything. ¹⁷ When he came to his senses, ᴳ he said, 'How many of my father's hired workers have more than enough food, and here I am dying of hunger! ᴴ ¹⁸ I'll get up, go to my father, and say to him, "Father, I have sinned against heaven and in your sight. ¹⁹ I'm no longer worthy to be called your son. Make me like one of your hired workers."' ²⁰ So he got up and went to his father. But while the son was still a long way off, his father saw him and was filled with compassion. He ran, threw his arms around his neck, and kissed him. ²¹ The son said to him, 'Father, I have sinned against heaven and in your sight. I'm no longer worthy to be called your son.'

²² "But the father told his servants, 'Quick! Bring out the best robe and put it on him; put a ring on his finger and sandals on his feet. ²³ Then bring the fattened calf and slaughter it, and let's celebrate with a feast, ²⁴ because this son of mine was dead and is alive again; he was lost and is found!' So they began to celebrate.

ᴬ15:4 Or *the wilderness* ᴮ15:8 Gk *ten drachmas* ᶜ15:8 A Gk drachma was equivalent to a Roman denarius = one day's wage ᴰ15:12 Or *life,* or *livelihood,* also in v. 30 ᴱ15:14 Lit *and he began to be in need* ᶠ15:16 Other mss read *to fill his stomach with* ᴳ15:17 Lit *to himself* ᴴ15:17 Or *dying in the famine*; v. 14

²⁵ "Now his older son was in the field; as he came near the house, he heard music and dancing. ²⁶ So he summoned one of the servants, questioning what these things meant. ²⁷ 'Your brother is here,' he told him, 'and your father has slaughtered the fattened calf because he has him back safe and sound.'^A

²⁸ "Then he became angry and didn't want to go in. So his father came out and pleaded with him. ²⁹ But he replied to his father, 'Look, I have been slaving many years for you, and I have never disobeyed your orders, yet you never gave me a goat so that I could celebrate with my friends. ³⁰ But when this son of yours came, who has devoured your assets^B with prostitutes, you slaughtered the fattened calf for him.'

³¹ "'Son,'^C he said to him, 'you are always with me, and everything I have is yours. ³² But we had to celebrate and rejoice, because this brother of yours was dead and is alive again; he was lost and is found.'"

THE PARABLE OF THE DISHONEST MANAGER

16 Now he said to the disciples: "There was a rich man who received an accusation that his manager was squandering his possessions. ² So he called the manager in and asked, 'What is this I hear about you? Give an account of your management, because you can no longer be my manager.'

³ "Then the manager said to himself, 'What will I do since my master is taking the management away from me? I'm not strong enough to dig; I'm ashamed to beg. ⁴ I know what I'll do so that when I'm removed from management, people will welcome me into their homes.'

⁵ "So he summoned each one of his master's debtors. 'How much do you owe my master?' he asked the first one.

⁶ "'A hundred measures of olive oil,' he said.

"'Take your invoice,' he told him, 'sit down quickly, and write fifty.'

⁷ "Next he asked another, 'How much do you owe?'

"'A hundred measures of wheat,' he said.

"'Take your invoice,' he told him, 'and write eighty.'

⁸ "The master praised the unrighteous manager because he had acted shrewdly. For the children of this age are more shrewd than the children of light in dealing with their own people.^D ⁹ And I tell you, make friends for yourselves by means of worldly wealth^E so that when it fails,^F they may welcome you into eternal dwellings. ¹⁰ Whoever is faithful in very little is also faithful in much, and whoever is unrighteous in very little is also unrighteous in much. ¹¹ So if you have not been faithful with worldly wealth, who will trust you with what is genuine? ¹² And if you have not been faithful with what belongs to someone else, who will give you what is your own? ¹³ No servant can serve two masters, since either he will hate one and love the other, or he will be devoted to one and despise the other. You cannot serve both God and money."

---

^A15:27 Lit *him back healthy*   ^B15:30 Or *life,* or *livelihood*   ^C15:31 Lit *Child*
^D16:8 Lit *own generation*   ^E16:9 Lit *unrighteous money,* also in v. 11
^F16:9 Other mss read *when you fail,* or *pass away*

KINGDOM VALUES

¹⁴ The Pharisees, who were lovers of money, were listening to all these things and scoffing at him. ¹⁵ And he told them, "You are the ones who justify yourselves in the sight of others, but God knows your hearts. For what is highly admired by people is revolting in God's sight.

¹⁶ "The Law and the Prophets were until John; since then, the good news of the kingdom of God has been proclaimed, and everyone is urgently invited to enter it.ᴬ ¹⁷ But it is easier for heaven and earth to pass away than for one stroke of a letter in the law to drop out.

¹⁸ "Everyone who divorces his wife and marries another woman commits adultery, and everyone who marries a woman divorced from her husband commits adultery.

THE RICH MAN AND LAZARUS

¹⁹ "There was a rich man who would dress in purple and fine linen, feasting lavishly every day. ²⁰ But a poor man named Lazarus, covered with sores, was lying at his gate. ²¹ He longed to be filled with what fell from the rich man's table, but instead the dogs would come and lick his sores. ²² One day the poor man died and was carried away by the angels to Abraham's side.ᴮ The rich man also died and was buried. ²³ And being in torment in Hades, he looked up and saw Abraham a long way off, with Lazarus at his side. ²⁴ 'Father Abraham!' he called out, 'Have mercy on me and send Lazarus to dip the tip of his finger in water and cool my tongue, because I am in agony in this flame!'

²⁵ "'Son,'ᶜ Abraham said, 'remember that during your life you received your good things, just as Lazarus received bad things, but now he is comforted here, while you are in agony. ²⁶ Besides all this, a great chasm has been fixed between us and you, so that those who want to pass over from here to you cannot; neither can those from there cross over to us.'

²⁷ "'Father,' he said, 'then I beg you to send him to my father's house — ²⁸ because I have five brothers — to warn them, so they won't also come to this place of torment.'

²⁹ "But Abraham said, 'They have Moses and the prophets; they should listen to them.'

³⁰ "'No, father Abraham,' he said. 'But if someone from the dead goes to them, they will repent.'

³¹ "But he told him, 'If they don't listen to Moses and the prophets, they will not be persuaded if someone rises from the dead.'"

WARNINGS FROM JESUS

17 He said to his disciples, "Offenses will certainly come,ᴰ but woe to the one through whom they come! ² It would be better for him if a millstone were hung around his neck and he were thrown into the sea than for him to cause one of these little ones to stumble. ³ Be on your guard. If your brother sins,ᴱ rebuke him, and if he repents, forgive him. ⁴ And if he sins against you seven times in a day, and comes back to you seven times, saying, 'I repent,' you must forgive him."

ᴬ 16:16 Or everyone is forcing his way into it   ᴮ 16:22 Or to Abraham's bosom; lit to the fold of Abraham's robe; Jn 13:23   ᶜ 16:25 Lit Child   ᴰ 17:1 Lit "It is impossible for offenses not to come   ᴱ 17:3 Other mss add against you

FAITH AND DUTY

⁵ The apostles said to the Lord, "Increase our faith."

⁶ "If you have faith the size of ᴬ a mustard seed," the Lord said, "you can say to this mulberry tree, 'Be uprooted and planted in the sea,' and it will obey you.

⁷ "Which one of you having a servant tending sheep or plowing will say to him when he comes in from the field, 'Come at once and sit down to eat'? ⁸ Instead, will he not tell him, 'Prepare something for me to eat, get ready, and serve me while I eat and drink; later you can eat and drink'? ⁹ Does he thank that servant because he did what was commanded? ᴮ ¹⁰ In the same way, when you have done all that you were commanded, you should say, 'We are worthless servants; we've only done our duty.'"

TEN MEN HEALED

¹¹ While traveling to Jerusalem, he passed between ᶜ Samaria and Galilee. ¹² As he entered a village, ten men with leprosy ᴰ met him. They stood at a distance ¹³ and raised their voices, saying, "Jesus, Master, have mercy on us!" ¹⁴ When he saw them, he told them, "Go and show yourselves to the priests." And while they were going, they were cleansed.

¹⁵ But one of them, seeing that he was healed, returned and, with a loud voice, gave glory to God. ¹⁶ He fell facedown at his feet, thanking him. And he was a Samaritan.

¹⁷ Then Jesus said, "Were not ten cleansed? Where are the nine? ¹⁸ Didn't any return to give glory to God except this foreigner?" ¹⁹ And he told him, "Get up and go on your way. Your faith has saved you." ᴱ

THE COMING OF THE KINGDOM

²⁰ Being asked by the Pharisees when the kingdom of God would come, he answered them, "The kingdom of God is not coming with something observable; ²¹ no one will say, ᶠ 'See here!' or 'There!' For you see, the kingdom of God is in your midst." ᴳ

²² Then he told the disciples: "The days are coming when you will long to see one of the days of the Son of Man, but you won't see it. ²³ They will say to you, 'See there!' or 'See here!' Don't follow or run after them. ²⁴ For as the lightning flashes from horizon to horizon and lights up the sky, so the Son of Man will be in his day. ²⁵ But first it is necessary that he suffer many things and be rejected by this generation.

²⁶ "Just as it was in the days of Noah, so it will be in the days of the Son of Man: ²⁷ People went on eating, drinking, marrying and giving in marriage until the day Noah boarded the ark, and the flood came and destroyed them all. ²⁸ It will be the same as it was in the days of Lot: People went on eating, drinking, buying, selling, planting, building. ²⁹ But on the day Lot left Sodom, fire and sulfur rained from heaven and destroyed them all. ³⁰ It will be like that on the day the Son of Man is revealed. ³¹ On that day, a man on the housetop, whose belongings are in the house, must not

---

ᴬ17:6 Lit faith like   ᴮ17:9 Other mss add I don't think so   ᶜ17:11 Other mss read through the middle of   ᴰ17:12 Gk lepros; a term for various skin diseases; see Lv 13–14   ᴱ17:19 Or faith has made you well   ᶠ17:21 Lit they will not say   ᴳ17:21 Or within you come down to get them. Likewise the man who is in the field must not turn back. ³² Remember Lot's wife! ³³ Whoever tries to make his life secure[A,B] will lose it, and whoever loses his life will preserve it. ³⁴ I tell you, on that night two will be in one bed; one will be taken and the other will be left. ³⁵ Two women will be grinding grain together; one will be taken and the other left."[C]

³⁷ "Where, Lord?" they asked him.

He said to them, "Where the corpse is, there also the vultures will be gathered."

THE PARABLE OF THE PERSISTENT WIDOW

18 Now he told them a parable on the need for them to pray always and not give up. ² "There was a judge in a certain town who didn't fear God or respect people. ³ And a widow in that town kept coming to him, saying, 'Give me justice against my adversary.'

⁴ "For a while he was unwilling, but later he said to himself, 'Even though I don't fear God or respect people, ⁵ yet because this widow keeps pestering me,[D] I will give her justice, so that she doesn't wear me out[E] by her persistent coming.'"

⁶ Then the Lord said, "Listen to what the unjust judge says. ⁷ Will not God grant justice to his elect who cry out to him day and night? Will he delay helping them?[F] ⁸ I tell you that he will swiftly grant them justice. Nevertheless, when the Son of Man comes, will he find faith on earth?"

THE PARABLE OF THE PHARISEE AND THE TAX COLLECTOR

⁹ He also told this parable to some who trusted in themselves that they were righteous and looked down on everyone else: ¹⁰ "Two men went up to the temple to pray, one a Pharisee and the other a tax collector. ¹¹ The Pharisee was standing and praying like this about himself:[G] 'God, I thank you that I'm not like other people — greedy, unrighteous, adulterers, or even like this tax collector. ¹² I fast twice a week; I give a tenth[H] of everything I get.'

¹³ "But the tax collector, standing far off, would not even raise his eyes to heaven but kept striking his chest and saying, 'God, have mercy on me,[I] a sinner!' ¹⁴ I tell you, this one went down to his house justified rather than the other; because everyone who exalts himself will be humbled, but the one who humbles himself will be exalted."

BLESSING THE CHILDREN

¹⁵ People were bringing infants to him so he might touch them, but when the disciples saw it, they rebuked them. ¹⁶ Jesus, however, invited them: "Let the little children come to me, and don't stop them, because the kingdom of God belongs to such as these. ¹⁷ Truly I tell you, whoever does not receive the kingdom of God like a little child will never enter it."

[A] 17:33 Other mss read *to save his life* [B] 17:33 Or *tries to retain his life*
[C] 17:35 Some mss include v. 36: *"Two will be in a field: One will be taken, and the other will be left. "* [D] 18:5 Lit *widow causes me trouble* [E] 18:5 Or *doesn't ruin my reputation* [F] 18:7 Or *Will he put up with them?* [G] 18:11 Or *by himself* [H] 18:12 Or *give tithes* [I] 18:13 Or *God, turn your wrath from me*

THE RICH YOUNG RULER

[18] A ruler asked him, "Good teacher, what must I do to inherit eternal life?"

[19] "Why do you call me good?" Jesus asked him. "No one is good except God alone. [20] You know the commandments: **Do not commit adultery; do not murder; do not steal; do not bear false witness; honor your father and mother.**"[A]

[21] "I have kept all these from my youth," he said.

[22] When Jesus heard this, he told him, "You still lack one thing: Sell all you have and distribute it to the poor, and you will have treasure in heaven. Then come, follow me."

[23] After he heard this, he became extremely sad, because he was very rich.

POSSESSIONS AND THE KINGDOM

[24] Seeing that he became sad,[B] Jesus said, "How hard it is for those who have wealth to enter the kingdom of God! [25] For it is easier for a camel to go through the eye of a needle than for a rich person to enter the kingdom of God."

[26] Those who heard this asked, "Then who can be saved?"

[27] He replied, "What is impossible with man is possible with God."

[28] Then Peter said, "Look, we have left what we had and followed you."

[29] So he said to them, "Truly I tell you, there is no one who has left a house, wife or brothers or sisters, parents or children because of the kingdom of God, [30] who will not receive many times more at this time, and eternal life in the age to come."

THE THIRD PREDICTION OF HIS DEATH

[31] Then he took the Twelve aside and told them, "See, we are going up to Jerusalem. Everything that is written through the prophets about the Son of Man will be accomplished. [32] For he will be handed over to the Gentiles, and he will be mocked, insulted, spit on; [33] and after they flog him, they will kill him, and he will rise on the third day."

[34] They understood none of these things. The meaning of the saying[C] was hidden from them, and they did not grasp what was said.

A BLIND MAN RECEIVES HIS SIGHT

[35] As he approached Jericho, a blind man was sitting by the road begging. [36] Hearing a crowd passing by, he inquired what was happening. [37] "Jesus of Nazareth is passing by," they told him.

[38] So he called out, "Jesus, Son of David, have mercy on me!" [39] Then those in front told him to keep quiet,[D] but he kept crying out all the more, "Son of David, have mercy on me!"

[40] Jesus stopped and commanded that he be brought to him. When he came closer, he asked him, [41] "What do you want me to do for you?"

"Lord," he said, "I want to see."

[42] "Receive your sight." Jesus told him. "Your faith has saved you." [43] Instantly he could see, and he began to follow him, glorifying God. All the people, when they saw it, gave praise to God.

[A]18:20 Ex 20:12-16; Dt 5:16-20 [B]18:24 Other mss omit *he became sad*
[C]18:34 Lit *This saying* [D]18:39 Or *those in front rebuked him*

JESUS VISITS ZACCHAEUS

19 He entered Jericho and was passing through. ² There was a man named Zacchaeus who was a chief tax collector, and he was rich. ³ He was trying to see who Jesus was, but he was not able because of the crowd, since he was a short man. ⁴ So running ahead, he climbed up a sycamore tree to see Jesus, since he was about to pass that way. ⁵ When Jesus came to the place, he looked up and said to him, "Zacchaeus, hurry and come down because today it is necessary for me to stay at your house."

⁶ So he quickly came down and welcomed him joyfully. ⁷ All who saw it began to complain, "He's gone to stay with a sinful man."

⁸ But Zacchaeus stood there and said to the Lord, "Look, I'll give half of my possessions to the poor, Lord. And if I have extorted anything from anyone, I'll pay back four times as much."

⁹ "Today salvation has come to this house," Jesus told him, "because he too is a son of Abraham. ¹⁰ For the Son of Man has come to seek and to save the lost."

THE PARABLE OF THE TEN MINAS

¹¹ As they were listening to this, he went on to tell a parable because he was near Jerusalem, and they thought the kingdom of God was going to appear right away.

¹² Therefore he said: "A nobleman traveled to a far country to receive for himself authority to be king ᴬ and then to return. ¹³ He called ten of his servants, gave them ten minas, ᴮ and told them, 'Engage in business until I come back.'

¹⁴ "But his subjects hated him and sent a delegation after him, saying, 'We don't want this man to rule over us.'

¹⁵ "At his return, having received the authority to be king, he summoned those servants he had given the money to, so that he could find out how much they had made in business. ¹⁶ The first came forward and said, 'Master, your mina has earned ten more minas.'

¹⁷ " 'Well done, good ᶜ servant!' he told him. 'Because you have been faithful in a very small matter, have authority over ten towns.'

¹⁸ "The second came and said, 'Master, your mina has made five minas.'

¹⁹ "So he said to him, 'You will be over five towns.'

²⁰ "And another came and said, 'Master, here is your mina. I have kept it safe in a cloth ²¹ because I was afraid of you since you're a harsh man: you collect what you didn't deposit and reap what you didn't sow.'

²² "He told him, 'I will condemn you by what you have said, you evil servant! If you knew I was a harsh man, collecting what I didn't deposit and reaping what I didn't sow, ²³ why, then, didn't you put my money in the bank? And when I returned, I would have collected it with interest.' ²⁴ So he said to those standing there, 'Take the mina away from him and give it to the one who has ten minas.'

²⁵ "But they said to him, 'Master, he has ten minas.'

²⁶ " 'I tell you, that to everyone who has, more will be given; and from the one who does not have, even what he does have will be taken away. ²⁷ But bring here these enemies of mine, who did not want me to rule over them, and slaughter ᴰ them in my presence.' "

ᴬ 19:12 Lit *to receive for himself a kingdom*, or *sovereignty*, also in v. 15
ᴮ 19:13 = Gk coin worth a hundred drachmas or about a hundred days' wages
ᶜ 19:17 Or *capable*   ᴰ 19:27 Or *execute*

HE SEEKS US OUT

LUKE 18–19; JOHN 6:44

Where do you land on the chicken vs. egg debate? Did the egg come first, or was it the chicken? (Psst . . . the answers are totally in the textbook. Check out Genesis 1:21.)

Zacchaeus's story answers another chicken-or-egg-like scenario. When it comes to salvation, who initiates? Does God call us to Him or do we call out to God? If you grew up going to church, you probably learned to sing Zacchaeus's story, found in Luke 19:1-10, like this:

"Zacchaeus was a wee little man,
A wee little man was he."

Having children sing this song about me for centuries is not exactly a legacy I'd choose, but the facts are that Zacchaeus was, well . . . short (Lk 19:3). Poor Zacchaeus gets plenty of flak for his small frame, but it was his tiny heart that was the real problem. He tried to see Jesus, but couldn't because of his height. Even more troubling, he tried to see Jesus, but couldn't because of his heart.

You see, Zacchaeus had a sin problem. We know this because the crowds blared it at full volume (Lk 19:7). We have a sin problem, too, regardless of whether or not other people see it and shout it from a bullhorn. But while we wallowed in our sinful state, unable to throw ourselves a life raft, Jesus initiated the reconciliation we didn't even know we needed (Rm 5:8).

We see this clearly in Zacchaeus's story. He was content to watch Jesus as He passed, to hide in the bushes, like the paparazzi watching

a celebrity from a distance. But Jesus looked up at His image-bearer perched in a tree and desired a right relationship with him. Not willing to walk on by, Jesus sought Zacchaeus out.

The next part of Zacchaeus's story carries great weight for all people, big and small:

"Today salvation has come to this house," Jesus told him, "because he too is a son of Abraham. For the Son of Man has come to seek and to save the lost" (Lk 19:9-10).

Jesus didn't only come to save. He came to seek and save. Through His death on the cross, He accomplished the work those who believe require to be made right with God. He says it this way in John 6:44:

"No one can come to me unless the Father who sent me draws him, and I will raise him up on the last day."

The life-changing, earth-shaking, curtain-ripping message of the gospel is that we are helpless to save ourselves from sin, or to clean ourselves up enough to stand before a holy God. Unless the Lord gives us eyes to see it, we cannot even fathom our need for Him. And yet, in love, He turns toward us, not away from us, and makes a way for us to be spared the punishment for our sin.

What grace!

THE TRIUMPHAL ENTRY

²⁸ When he had said these things, he went on ahead, going up to Jerusalem. ²⁹ As he approached Bethphage and Bethany, at the place called the Mount of Olives, he sent two of the disciples ³⁰ and said, "Go into the village ahead of you. As you enter it, you will find a colt tied there, on which no one has ever sat. Untie it and bring it. ³¹ If anyone asks you, 'Why are you untying it?' say this: 'The Lord needs it.'"

³² So those who were sent left and found it just as he had told them. ³³ As they were untying the colt, its owners said to them, "Why are you untying the colt?"

³⁴ "The Lord needs it," they said. ³⁵ Then they brought it to Jesus, and after throwing their clothes on the colt, they helped Jesus get on it. ³⁶ As he was going along, they were spreading their clothes on the road. ³⁷ Now he came near the path down the Mount of Olives, and the whole crowd of the disciples began to praise God joyfully with a loud voice for all the miracles they had seen:

³⁸ **Blessed is the King who comes**
in the name of the Lord.ᴬ
Peace in heaven
and glory in the highest heaven!

³⁹ Some of the Pharisees from the crowd told him, "Teacher, rebuke your disciples."

⁴⁰ He answered, "I tell you, if they were to keep silent, the stones would cry out."

JESUS'S LOVE FOR JERUSALEM

⁴¹ As he approached and saw the city, he wept for it, ⁴² saying, "If you knew this day what would bring peace — but now it is hidden from your eyes. ⁴³ For the days will come on you when your enemies will build a barricade around you, surround you, and hem you in on every side. ⁴⁴ They will crush you and your children among you to the ground, and they will not leave one stone on another in your midst, because you did not recognize the time when God visited you."

CLEANSING THE TEMPLE

⁴⁵ He went into the temple and began to throw out those who were selling, ᴮ ⁴⁶ and he said, "It is written, **my house will be a house of prayer**, but you have made it **a den of thieves!**"ᶜ

⁴⁷ Every day he was teaching in the temple. The chief priests, the scribes, and the leaders of the people were looking for a way to kill him, ⁴⁸ but they could not find a way to do it, because all the people were captivated by what they heard.

THE AUTHORITY OF JESUS CHALLENGED

20 One day as he was teaching the people in the temple and proclaiming the good news, the chief priests and the scribes, with the elders, came ² and said to him: "Tell us, by what authority are you doing these things? Who is it who gave you this authority?"

ᴬ19:38 Ps 118:26 ᴮ19:45 Other mss add *and buying in it* ᶜ19:46 Is 56:7; Jr 7:11

³ He answered them, "I will also ask you a question. Tell me, ⁴ was the baptism of John from heaven or of human origin?"

⁵ They discussed it among themselves: "If we say, 'From heaven,' he will say, 'Why didn't you believe him?' ⁶ But if we say, 'Of human origin,' all the people will stone us, because they are convinced that John was a prophet." ⁷ So they answered that they did not know its origin.

⁸ And Jesus said to them, "Neither will I tell you by what authority I do these things."

THE PARABLE OF THE VINEYARD OWNER

⁹ Now he began to tell the people this parable: "A man planted a vineyard, leased it to tenant farmers, and went away for a long time. ¹⁰ At harvest time he sent a servant to the farmers so that they might give him some fruit from the vineyard. But the farmers beat him and sent him away empty-handed. ¹¹ He sent yet another servant, but they beat that one too, treated him shamefully, and sent him away empty-handed. ¹² And he sent yet a third, but they wounded this one too and threw him out.

¹³ "Then the owner of the vineyard said, 'What should I do? I will send my beloved son. Perhaps ᴬ they will respect him.'

¹⁴ "But when the tenant farmers saw him, they discussed it among themselves and said, 'This is the heir. Let's kill him, so that the inheritance will be ours.' ¹⁵ So they threw him out of the vineyard and killed him.

"What then will the owner of the vineyard do to them? ¹⁶ He will come and kill those farmers and give the vineyard to others."

But when they heard this they said, "That must never happen!"

¹⁷ But he looked at them and said, "Then what is the meaning of this Scripture: ᴮ

The stone that the builders rejected
has become the cornerstone? ᶜ

¹⁸ Everyone who falls on that stone will be broken to pieces, but on whomever it falls, it will shatter him."

¹⁹ Then the scribes and the chief priests looked for a way to get their hands on him that very hour, because they knew he had told this parable against them, but they feared the people.

GOD AND CAESAR

²⁰ They watched closely and sent spies who pretended to be righteous, ᴰ so that they could catch him in what he said, to hand him over to the governor's rule and authority. ²¹ They questioned him, "Teacher, we know that you speak and teach correctly, and you don't show partiality ᴱ but teach truthfully the way of God. ²² Is it lawful for us to pay taxes to Caesar or not?"

²³ But detecting their craftiness, he said to them, ᶠ ²⁴ "Show me a denarius. ᴳ Whose image and inscription does it have?"

"Caesar's," they said.

²⁵ "Well then," he told them, "give to Caesar the things that are Caesar's, and to God the things that are God's."

ᴬ20:13 Other mss add *when they see him*   ᴮ20:17 Lit *"What then is this that is written*   ᶜ20:17 Ps 118:22   ᴰ20:20 Or *upright*   ᴱ20:21 Lit *you don't receive a face*   ᶠ20:23 Other mss add *"Why are you testing me?*   ᴳ20:24 A denarius = one day's wage

26 They were not able to catch him in what he said in public, and being amazed at his answer, they became silent.

THE SADDUCEES AND THE RESURRECTION

27 Some of the Sadducees, who say there is no resurrection, came up and questioned him: 28 "Teacher, Moses wrote for us that **if a man's brother** has a wife, and **dies childless, his brother should take the wife and produce offspring for his brother.**[A] 29 Now there were seven brothers. The first took a wife and died without children. 30 Also the second[B] 31 and the third took her. In the same way, all seven died and left no children. 32 Finally, the woman died too. 33 In the resurrection, therefore, whose wife will the woman be? For all seven had married her."

34 Jesus told them, "The children of this age marry and are given in marriage. 35 But those who are counted worthy to take part in that age and in the resurrection from the dead neither marry nor are given in marriage. 36 For they can no longer die, because they are like angels and are children of God, since they are children of the resurrection. 37 Moses even indicated in the passage about the burning bush that the dead are raised, where he calls the Lord **the God of Abraham and the God of Isaac and the God of Jacob.**[C] 38 He is not the God of the dead but of the living, because all are living to[D] him."

39 Some of the scribes answered, "Teacher, you have spoken well." 40 And they no longer dared to ask him anything.

THE QUESTION ABOUT THE CHRIST

41 Then he said to them, "How can they say that the Christ is the son of David? 42 For David himself says in the Book of Psalms:

> **The Lord declared to my Lord,**
>   **'Sit at my right hand**
> 43   **until I make your enemies your footstool.'**[E]

44 David calls him 'Lord'; how then can the Christ be his son?"

WARNING AGAINST THE SCRIBES

45 While all the people were listening, he said to his disciples, 46 "Beware of the scribes, who want to go around in long robes and who love greetings in the marketplaces, the best seats in the synagogues, and the places of honor at banquets. 47 They devour widows' houses and say long prayers just for show. These will receive harsher judgment."[F]

THE WIDOW'S GIFT

21 He looked up and saw the rich dropping their offerings into the temple treasury. 2 He also saw a poor widow dropping in two tiny coins.[G] 3 "Truly I tell you," he said, "this poor widow has put in more than all of them. 4 For all these people have put in gifts out of their surplus, but she out of her poverty has put in all she had to live on."

[A]20:28 Dt 25:5 [B]20:30 Other mss add *took her as wife, and he died without children* [C]20:37 Ex 3:6,15 [D]20:38 Or *with* [E]20:42-43 Ps 110:1
[F]20:47 Or *judgment* [G]21:2 Lit *two lepta; the lepton was the smallest and least valuable Gk coin in use.*

DESTRUCTION OF THE TEMPLE PREDICTED

⁵ As some were talking about the temple, how it was adorned with beautiful stones and gifts dedicated to God, he said, ⁶ "These things that you see — the days will come when not one stone will be left on another that will not be thrown down."

SIGNS OF THE END OF THE AGE

⁷ "Teacher," they asked him, "so when will these things happen? And what will be the sign when these things are about to take place?"

⁸ Then he said, "Watch out that you are not deceived. For many will come in my name, saying, 'I am he,' and, 'The time is near.' Don't follow them. ⁹ When you hear of wars and rebellions,ᴬ don't be alarmed. Indeed, it is necessary that these things take place first, but the end won't come right away."

¹⁰ Then he told them: "Nation will be raised up against nation, and kingdom against kingdom. ¹¹ There will be violent earthquakes, and famines and plagues in various places, and there will be terrifying sights and great signs from heaven. ¹² But before all these things, they will lay their hands on you and persecute you. They will hand you over to the synagogues and prisons, and you will be brought before kings and governors because of my name. ¹³ This will give you an opportunity to bear witness. ¹⁴ Therefore make up your mindsᴮ not to prepare your defense ahead of time, ¹⁵ for I will give you such words and a wisdom that none of your adversaries will be able to resist or contradict. ¹⁶ You will even be betrayed by parents, brothers, relatives, and friends. They will kill some of you. ¹⁷ You will be hated by everyone because of my name, ¹⁸ but not a hair of your head will be lost. ¹⁹ By your endurance, gainᶜ your lives.

THE DESTRUCTION OF JERUSALEM

²⁰ "When you see Jerusalem surrounded by armies, then recognize that its desolation has come near. ²¹ Then those in Judea must flee to the mountains. Those inside the city must leave it, and those who are in the country must not enter it, ²² because these are days of vengeance to fulfill all the things that are written. ²³ Woe to pregnant women and nursing mothers in those days, for there will be great distress in the landᴰ and wrath against this people. ²⁴ They will be killed by the swordᴱ and be led captive into all the nations, and Jerusalem will be trampled by the Gentilesᶠ until the times of the Gentiles are fulfilled.

THE COMING OF THE SON OF MAN

²⁵ "Then there will be signs in the sun, moon, and stars; and there will be anguish on the earth among nations bewildered by the roaring of the sea and the waves. ²⁶ People will faint from fear and expectation of the things that are coming on the world, because the powers of the heavens will be shaken. ²⁷ Then they will see the Son of Man coming in a cloud with power and great glory. ²⁸ But when these things begin to take place, stand up and lift up your heads, because your redemption is near."

ᴬ21:9 Or insurrections, or revolutions, or chaos   ᴮ21:14 Lit Therefore place (determine) in your hearts   ᶜ21:19 Other mss read endurance, you will gain   ᴰ21:23 Or the earth   ᴱ21:24 Lit will fall by the edge of the sword   ᶠ21:24 Or nations

THE PARABLE OF THE FIG TREE

²⁹ Then he told them a parable: "Look at the fig tree, and all the trees. ³⁰ As soon as they put out leaves you can see for yourselves and recognize that summer is already near. ³¹ In the same way, when you see these things happening, recognize^A that the kingdom of God is near. ³² Truly I tell you, this generation will certainly not pass away until all things take place. ³³ Heaven and earth will pass away, but my words will never pass away.

THE NEED FOR WATCHFULNESS

³⁴ "Be on your guard, so that your minds are not dulled^B from carousing,^C drunkenness, and worries of life, or that day will come on you unexpectedly ³⁵ like a trap. For it will come on all who live on the face of the whole earth. ³⁶ But be alert at all times, praying that you may have strength^D to escape all these things that are going to take place and to stand before the Son of Man."

³⁷ During the day, he was teaching in the temple, but in the evening he would go out and spend the night on what is called the Mount of Olives. ³⁸ Then all the people would come early in the morning to hear him in the temple.

THE PLOT TO KILL JESUS

22 The Festival of Unleavened Bread, which is called Passover, was approaching. ² The chief priests and the scribes were looking for a way to put him to death, because they were afraid of the people.

³ Then Satan entered Judas, called Iscariot, who was numbered among the Twelve. ⁴ He went away and discussed with the chief priests and temple police how he could hand him over to them. ⁵ They were glad and agreed to give him silver.^E ⁶ So he accepted the offer and started looking for a good opportunity to betray him to them when the crowd was not present.

PREPARATION FOR PASSOVER

⁷ Then the Day of Unleavened Bread came when the Passover lamb had to be sacrificed. ⁸ Jesus sent Peter and John, saying, "Go and make preparations for us to eat the Passover."

⁹ "Where do you want us to prepare it?" they asked him.

¹⁰ "Listen," he said to them, "when you've entered the city, a man carrying a water jug will meet you. Follow him into the house he enters. ¹¹ Tell the owner of the house, 'The Teacher asks you, "Where is the guest room where I can eat the Passover with my disciples?"' ¹² Then he will show you a large, furnished room upstairs. Make the preparations there."

¹³ So they went and found it just as he had told them, and they prepared the Passover.

THE FIRST LORD'S SUPPER

¹⁴ When the hour came, he reclined at the table, and the apostles with him. ¹⁵ Then he said to them, "I have fervently desired to eat this Passover with you before I suffer. ¹⁶ For I tell you, I will not eat it again^F until it is fulfilled in the kingdom of God." ¹⁷ Then he took a cup, and after

---

^A21:31 Or you know ^B21:34 Lit your hearts are not weighed down ^C21:34 Or hangovers ^D21:36 Other mss read you may be counted worthy ^E22:5 Or money ^F22:16 Other mss omit again giving thanks, he said, "Take this and share it among yourselves. [18] For I tell you, from now on I will not drink of the fruit of the vine until the kingdom of God comes."

[19] And he took bread, gave thanks, broke it, gave it to them, and said, "This is my body, which is given for you. Do this in remembrance of me."

[20] In the same way he also took the cup after supper and said, "This cup is the new covenant in my blood, which is poured out for you.[A] [21] But look, the hand of the one betraying me is at the table with me. [22] For the Son of Man will go away as it has been determined, but woe to that man by whom he is betrayed!"

[23] So they began to argue among themselves which of them it could be who was going to do it.

THE DISPUTE OVER GREATNESS

[24] Then a dispute also arose among them about who should be considered the greatest. [25] But he said to them, "The kings of the Gentiles lord it over them, and those who have authority over them have themselves called[B] 'Benefactors.' [26] It is not to be like that among you. On the contrary, whoever is greatest among you should become like the youngest, and whoever leads, like the one serving. [27] For who is greater, the one at the table or the one serving? Isn't it the one at the table? But I am among you as the one who serves. [28] You are those who stood by me in my trials. [29] I bestow on you a kingdom, just as my Father bestowed one on me, [30] so that you may eat and drink at my table in my kingdom. And you will sit on thrones judging the twelve tribes of Israel.

PETER'S DENIAL PREDICTED

[31] "Simon, Simon,[C] look out. Satan has asked to sift you like wheat. [32] But I have prayed for you that your faith may not fail. And you, when you have turned back, strengthen your brothers."

[33] "Lord," he told him, "I'm ready to go with you both to prison and to death."

[34] "I tell you, Peter," he said, "the rooster will not crow today until[D] you deny three times that you know me."

BE READY FOR TROUBLE

[35] He also said to them, "When I sent you out without money-bag, traveling bag, or sandals, did you lack anything?"

"Not a thing," they said.

[36] Then he said to them, "But now, whoever has a money-bag should take it, and also a traveling bag. And whoever doesn't have a sword should sell his robe and buy one. [37] For I tell you, what is written must be fulfilled in me:[E] **And he was counted among the lawless.**[F] Yes, what is written about me is coming to its fulfillment."

[38] "Lord," they said, "look, here are two swords."

"That is enough!" he told them.

[A]22:19-20 Other mss omit *which is given for you* (v. 19) through the end of v. 20
[B]22:25 Or *them call themselves*   [C]22:31 Other mss read *Then the Lord said, "Simon, Simon*   [D]22:34 Other mss read *before*   [E]22:37 Or *it is necessary that what is written be fulfilled in me*   [F]22:37 Is 53:12

THE PRAYER IN THE GARDEN

[39] He went out and made his way as usual to the Mount of Olives, and the disciples followed him. [40] When he reached the place, he told them, "Pray that you may not fall into temptation." [41] Then he withdrew from them about a stone's throw, knelt down, and began to pray, [42] "Father, if you are willing, take this cup away from me — nevertheless, not my will, but yours, be done."

[43] Then an angel from heaven appeared to him, strengthening him. [44] Being in anguish, he prayed more fervently, and his sweat became like drops of blood falling to the ground.[A] [45] When he got up from prayer and came to the disciples, he found them sleeping, exhausted from their grief. [46] "Why are you sleeping?" he asked them. "Get up and pray, so that you won't fall into temptation."

JUDAS'S BETRAYAL OF JESUS

[47] While he was still speaking, suddenly a mob came, and one of the Twelve named Judas was leading them. He came near Jesus to kiss him, [48] but Jesus said to him, "Judas, are you betraying the Son of Man with a kiss?"

[49] When those around him saw what was going to happen, they asked, "Lord, should we strike with the sword?" [50] Then one of them struck the high priest's servant and cut off his right ear.

[51] But Jesus responded, "No more of this!" And touching his ear, he healed him. [52] Then Jesus said to the chief priests, temple police, and the elders who had come for him, "Have you come out with swords and clubs as if I were a criminal?[B] [53] Every day while I was with you in the temple, you never laid a hand on me. But this is your hour — and the dominion of darkness."

PETER DENIES HIS LORD

[54] They seized him, led him away, and brought him into the high priest's house. Meanwhile Peter was following at a distance. [55] They lit a fire in the middle of the courtyard and sat down together, and Peter sat among them. [56] When a servant saw him sitting in the light, and looked closely at him, she said, "This man was with him too."

[57] But he denied it: "Woman, I don't know him."

[58] After a little while, someone else saw him and said, "You're one of them too."

"Man, I am not!" Peter said.

[59] About an hour later, another kept insisting, "This man was certainly with him, since he's also a Galilean."

[60] But Peter said, "Man, I don't know what you're talking about!" Immediately, while he was still speaking, a rooster crowed. [61] Then the Lord turned and looked at Peter. So Peter remembered the word of the Lord, how he had said to him, "Before the rooster crows today, you will deny me three times." [62] And he went outside and wept bitterly.

JESUS MOCKED AND BEATEN

[63] The men who were holding Jesus started mocking and beating him. [64] After blindfolding him, they kept[C] asking, "Prophesy! Who was it that hit you?" [65] And they were saying many other blasphemous things to him.

[A]22:43-44 Other mss omit vv. 43-44   [B]22:52 Lit as against a thief, or a bandit
[C]22:64 Other mss add striking him on the face and

JESUS FACES THE SANHEDRIN

⁶⁶ When daylight came, the elders ᴬ of the people, both the chief priests and the scribes, convened and brought him before their Sanhedrin. ⁶⁷ They said, "If you are the Messiah, tell us."

But he said to them, "If I do tell you, you will not believe. ⁶⁸ And if I ask you, you will not answer. ⁶⁹ But from now on, the Son of Man will be seated at the right hand of the power of God."

⁷⁰ They all asked, "Are you, then, the Son of God?"

And he said to them, "You say that I am."

⁷¹ "Why do we need any more testimony," they said, "since we've heard it ourselves from his mouth?"

JESUS FACES PILATE

23 Then their whole assembly rose up and brought him before Pilate. ² They began to accuse him, saying, "We found this man misleading our nation, opposing payment of taxes to Caesar, and saying that he himself is the Messiah, a king."

³ So Pilate asked him, "Are you the king of the Jews?"

He answered him, "You say so." ᴮ

⁴ Pilate then told the chief priests and the crowds, "I find no grounds for charging this man."

⁵ But they kept insisting, "He stirs up the people, teaching throughout all Judea, from Galilee where he started even to here."

JESUS FACES HEROD ANTIPAS

⁶ When Pilate heard this, ᶜ he asked if the man was a Galilean. ⁷ Finding that he was under Herod's jurisdiction, he sent him to Herod, who was also in Jerusalem during those days. ⁸ Herod was very glad to see Jesus; for a long time he had wanted to see him because he had heard about him and was hoping to see some miracle ᴰ performed by him. ⁹ So he kept asking him questions, but Jesus did not answer him. ¹⁰ The chief priests and the scribes stood by, vehemently accusing him. ¹¹ Then Herod, with his soldiers, treated him with contempt, mocked him, dressed him in bright clothing, and sent him back to Pilate. ¹² That very day Herod and Pilate became friends. ᴱ Previously, they had been enemies.

JESUS OR BARABBAS

¹³ Pilate called together the chief priests, the leaders, and the people, ¹⁴ and said to them, "You have brought me this man as one who misleads the people. But in fact, after examining him in your presence, I have found no grounds to charge this man with those things you accuse him of. ¹⁵ Neither has Herod, because he sent him back to us. Clearly, he has done nothing to deserve death. ¹⁶ Therefore, I will have him whipped ᶠ and then release him." ᴳ

ᴬ22:66 Or *council of elders*   ᴮ23:3 Or *"That is true."*   ᶜ23:6 Other mss read *heard "Galilee"*   ᴰ23:8 Or *sign*   ᴱ23:12 Lit *friends with one another*   ᶠ23:16 Gk *paideuo*; to discipline or *"teach a lesson"*   ᴳ23:16 Some mss include v. 17: *For according to the festival he had to release someone to them.*

DON'T LOOK AWAY

LUKE 23; 1 PETER 2:21-25

I don't walk by caskets and I don't go to gravesites. Whenever possible, I prefer to avoid staring death in the face.

It's not surprising then, that I often steer clear of the passages detailing Jesus' death. I might give them a quick skim a couple times a year, but I never sit still with them for long, or meditate on them like I do other parts of the Bible. I can't bear to look too closely.

But I need to. We all do.

Let's put the rubber gloves aside and refuse to sanitize this part of the story. Would you take a minute and read the account right now? It's here, in Luke 23:26-56.

When I force my eyeballs to take in the full account, I see the gory details I'd rather gloss over.

The prophecy about the dreadful day to come (Lk 23:28-30).
The crucifixion at a place called "The Skull" (Lk 23:33).
The humiliating game for His clothes (Lk 23:34).
The mocking (Lk 23:35-38).
The insults (Lk 23:39).
The oppressive darkness (Lk 23:44).

This is as gut wrenching as death gets. I want to look away, don't you? But when we look closely at the narrative, we see a group of people who dared to stay. "But all who knew him, including the women who had followed him from Galilee, stood at a distance, watching these things" (Lk 23:49).

John 19:25 tells us this circle of onlookers included Jesus' mother Mary, His aunt, a family friend, and Mary Magdalene. Some had seen Him wrapped in swaddling clothes and lying in a manger. Some had seen Him drive out demons and heal the sick. All four women had been forever changed.

Like mamas who stick close to their babies in the ER, these women dug in their heels and stayed for the darkest moment in history. Jesus was doing a monumental saving work for them on the cross. They did what they could in return. **They refused to look away.**

As Christ followers, we need to circle up at the base of the cross often. When we do, we see the gravity of our sin. Though we're experts at rug sweeping, justifying, and deflecting blame when it comes to our sin, a hard look at the cross reminds us what serious business it really is.

It's horrific and hard and heart wrenching to watch, but it's a fitting punishment for our rebellion against the loving God who created us. When we gloss over what Jesus endured for us, we miss something huge: there was no cost He was unwilling to pay to rescue us.

"He himself bore our sins in his body on the tree . . ."

1 PETER 2:24

Jesus, teach us not to look away.

¹⁸ Then they all cried out together, "Take this man away! Release Barabbas to us!" ¹⁹ (He had been thrown into prison for a rebellion that had taken place in the city, and for murder.)

²⁰ Wanting to release Jesus, Pilate addressed them again, ²¹ but they kept shouting, "Crucify! Crucify him!"

²² A third time he said to them, "Why? What has this man done wrong? I have found in him no grounds for the death penalty. Therefore, I will have him whipped and then release him."

²³ But they kept up the pressure, demanding with loud voices that he be crucified, and their voices ᴬ won out. ²⁴ So Pilate decided to grant their demand ²⁵ and released the one they were asking for, who had been thrown into prison for rebellion and murder. But he handed Jesus over to their will.

THE WAY TO THE CROSS

²⁶ As they led him away, they seized Simon, a Cyrenian, who was coming in from the country, and laid the cross on him to carry behind Jesus. ²⁷ A large crowd of people followed him, including women who were mourning and lamenting him. ²⁸ But turning to them, Jesus said, "Daughters of Jerusalem, do not weep for me, but weep for yourselves and your children. ²⁹ Look, the days are coming when they will say, 'Blessed are the women without children, the wombs that never bore, and the breasts that never nursed!' ³⁰ Then they will begin to say to the mountains, 'Fall on us!' and to the hills, 'Cover us!' ᴮ ³¹ For if they do these things when the wood is green, what will happen when it is dry?"

CRUCIFIED BETWEEN TWO CRIMINALS

³² Two others — criminals — were also led away to be executed with him. ³³ When they arrived at the place called The Skull, they crucified him there, along with the criminals, one on the right and one on the left. ³⁴ Then Jesus said, "Father, forgive them, because they do not know what they are doing." ᶜ And they divided his clothes and cast lots.

³⁵ The people stood watching, and even the leaders were scoffing: "He saved others; let him save himself if this is God's Messiah, the Chosen One!" ³⁶ The soldiers also mocked him. They came offering him sour wine ³⁷ and said, "If you are the King of the Jews, save yourself!"

³⁸ An inscription was above him: ᴰ THIS IS THE KING OF THE JEWS.

³⁹ Then one of the criminals hanging there began to yell insults at ᴱ him: "Aren't you the Messiah? Save yourself and us!"

⁴⁰ But the other answered, rebuking him: "Don't you even fear God, since you are undergoing the same punishment? ⁴¹ We are punished justly, because we're getting back what we deserve for the things we did, but this man has done nothing wrong." ⁴² Then he said, "Jesus, remember me ᶠ when you come into your kingdom."

⁴³ And he said to him, "Truly I tell you, today you will be with me in paradise."

ᴬ 23:23 Other mss add *and those of the chief priests* ᴮ 23:30 Hs 10:8
ᶜ 23:34 Other mss omit *Then Jesus said, "Father, forgive them, because they do not know what they are doing."* ᴰ 23:38 Other mss add *written in Greek, Latin, and Hebrew letters* ᴱ 23:39 Or *began to blaspheme* ᶠ 23:42 Other mss add *Lord*

THE DEATH OF JESUS

⁴⁴ It was now about noon,^A and darkness came over the whole land^B until three,^C ⁴⁵ because the sun's light failed.^D The curtain of the sanctuary was split down the middle. ⁴⁶ And Jesus called out with a loud voice, "Father, **into your hands I entrust my spirit**."^E Saying this, he breathed his last.

⁴⁷ When the centurion saw what happened, he began to glorify God, saying, "This man really was righteous!"^F ⁴⁸ All the crowds that had gathered for this spectacle, when they saw what had taken place, went home, striking their chests. ⁴⁹ But all who knew him, including the women who had followed him from Galilee, stood at a distance, watching these things.

THE BURIAL OF JESUS

⁵⁰ There was a good and righteous man named Joseph, a member of the Sanhedrin, ⁵¹ who had not agreed with their plan and action. He was from Arimathea, a Judean town, and was looking forward to the kingdom of God. ⁵² He approached Pilate and asked for Jesus's body. ⁵³ Taking it down, he wrapped it in fine linen and placed it in a tomb cut into the rock, where no one had ever been placed.^G ⁵⁴ It was the preparation day, and the Sabbath was about to begin.^H ⁵⁵ The women who had come with him from Galilee followed along and observed the tomb and how his body was placed. ⁵⁶ Then they returned and prepared spices and perfumes. And they rested on the Sabbath according to the commandment.

RESURRECTION MORNING

24 On the first day of the week, very early in the morning, they^I came to the tomb, bringing the spices they had prepared. ² They found the stone rolled away from the tomb. ³ They went in but did not find the body of the Lord Jesus. ⁴ While they were perplexed about this, suddenly two men stood by them in dazzling clothes. ⁵ So the women were terrified and bowed down to the ground.

"Why are you looking for the living among the dead?" asked the men. ⁶ "He is not here, but he has risen! Remember how he spoke to you when he was still in Galilee, ⁷ saying, 'It is necessary that the Son of Man be betrayed into the hands of sinful men, be crucified, and rise on the third day'?" ⁸ And they remembered his words.

⁹ Returning from the tomb, they reported all these things to the Eleven and to all the rest. ¹⁰ Mary Magdalene, Joanna, Mary the mother of James, and the other women with them were telling the apostles these things. ¹¹ But these words seemed like nonsense to them, and they did not believe the women. ¹² Peter, however, got up and ran to the tomb. When he stooped to look in, he saw only the linen cloths.^J So he went away, amazed at what had happened.

---

^A23:44 Lit about the sixth hour   ^B23:44 Or whole earth   ^C23:44 Lit the ninth hour   ^D23:45 Other mss read three, and the sun was darkened   ^E23:46 Ps 31:5   ^F23:47 Or innocent   ^G23:53 Or interred, or laid   ^H23:54 Lit was dawning   ^I24:1 Other mss add and other women with them   ^J24:12 Other mss add lying there

GOD'S WORK IN THE MUNDANE

LUKE 24; PHILIPPIANS 2:8-11; 1 JOHN 1:1-3

God must care about the mundane because there seems to be an awful lot of it.

Sure, the Christian life has some bells and whistles—moments of great kingdom victory, ministry milestones, and emotional connections with the God of the universe. But there are also a lot of noses to wipe and toilets to clean. There are oodles of motions to simply go through and as many plain ol' Tuesdays as Spirit-filled Sundays.

I have to fight the temptation to believe God is only at work in the big stuff. In fact, Scripture illustrates an inverse reality. **Often, God is doing something big in moments that seem small.**

Here, in Luke 24, we see God do the biggest thing He's done since He spoke all of creation into existence. Jesus had been crucified to take the punishment for our sin (Lk 23:26-49), then laid in a borrowed tomb (Lk 23:50-56). None of that would've amounted to a hill of beans without this:

"He is not here, but he has risen!"

LUKE 24:6

As a fan of pomp and circumstance, I can think of at least a hundred ways I would've announced this news. A parade? A skywriter? A big musical number put on by the trumpets of heaven?

But Jesus took a different approach. He chose obscure people in the middle of mundane

moments to be the mouthpieces for this radical news: death had been defeated once and for all (1Pt 3:18).

Jesus could've appeared to Pilate, or Herod, or the Pharisees, and forced them to eat crow. Instead, the news of the resurrection was given first to a group of women whose testimony would be inadmissible or ignored in a court of law.

In Luke 24:13, we find two obscure disciples, Cleopas and one who goes unnamed, walking to a little village called Emmaus. Jesus joins them on their walk, but again, refuses to make a flashy entrance. He simply joins the conversation.

Think about every mundane moment in your life. Every season where it feels like God isn't doing a thing. Every time you've thought, *I'm a nobody. God can't use me.* Then read these passages again.

Jesus announced His resurrection from the dead to an unknown disciple, walking down an unnamed road, to an unimportant town. *Ta-da!*

From there He moved on to a little room filled with eleven disciples. Instead of saying "I'm alive!" He said, "Do you have anything here to eat?" (Lk 24:41). See it? Big stuff in the little stuff.

Every marketing team in the world would call this a mistake. But Jesus knows how to multiply loaves and fishes (Mt 14:13-21). The message He entrusted to nobodies somehow made it to our ears and hearts two thousand years later.

May we learn to see God's hand in the mundane and as we walk our own Emmaus roads.

THE EMMAUS DISCIPLES

¹³ Now that same day two of them were on their way to a village called Emmaus, which was about seven miles^A from Jerusalem. ¹⁴ Together they were discussing everything that had taken place. ¹⁵ And while they were discussing and arguing, Jesus himself came near and began to walk along with them. ¹⁶ But they^B were prevented from recognizing him. ¹⁷ Then he asked them, "What is this dispute that you're having^C with each other as you are walking?" And they stopped walking and looked discouraged.

¹⁸ The one named Cleopas answered him, "Are you the only visitor in Jerusalem who doesn't know the things that happened there in these days?"

¹⁹ "What things?" he asked them.

So they said to him, "The things concerning Jesus of Nazareth, who was a prophet powerful in action and speech before God and all the people, ²⁰ and how our chief priests and leaders handed him over to be sentenced to death, and they crucified him. ²¹ But we were hoping that he was the one who was about to redeem Israel. Besides all this, it's the third day since these things happened. ²² Moreover, some women from our group astounded us. They arrived early at the tomb, ²³ and when they didn't find his body, they came and reported that they had seen a vision of angels who said he was alive. ²⁴ Some of those who were with us went to the tomb and found it just as the women had said, but they didn't see him."

²⁵ He said to them, "How foolish you are, and how slow^D to believe all that the prophets have spoken! ²⁶ Wasn't it necessary for the Messiah to suffer these things and enter into his glory?" ²⁷ Then beginning with Moses and all the Prophets, he interpreted for them the things concerning himself in all the Scriptures.

²⁸ They came near the village where they were going, and he gave the impression that he was going farther. ²⁹ But they urged him, "Stay with us, because it's almost evening, and now the day is almost over." So he went in to stay with them.

³⁰ It was as he reclined at the table with them that he took the bread, blessed and broke it, and gave it to them. ³¹ Then their eyes were opened, and they recognized him, but he disappeared from their sight. ³² They said to each other, "Weren't our hearts burning within us while he was talking with us on the road and explaining the Scriptures to us?" ³³ That very hour they got up and returned to Jerusalem. They found the Eleven and those with them gathered together, ³⁴ who said, "The Lord has truly been raised and has appeared to Simon!" ³⁵ Then they began to describe what had happened on the road and how he was made known to them in the breaking of the bread.

THE REALITY OF THE RISEN JESUS

³⁶ As they were saying these things, he himself stood in their midst. He said to them, "Peace to you!" ³⁷ But they were startled and terrified and thought they were seeing a ghost. ³⁸ "Why are you troubled?" he asked them. "And why do doubts arise in your hearts? ³⁹ Look at my hands and my feet, that it is I myself! Touch me and see, because a ghost does not have flesh and bones

---

^A 24:13 Lit *about sixty stadia*; one stadion = 600 feet   ^B 24:16 Lit *their eyes*
^C 24:17 Lit *"What are these words that you are exchanging*   ^D 24:25 Lit *slow of heart*

as you can see I have." ⁴⁰ Having said this, he showed them his hands and feet. ⁴¹ But while they still were amazed and in disbelief because of their joy, he asked them, "Do you have anything here to eat?" ⁴² So they gave him a piece of a broiled fish,ᴬ ⁴³ and he took it and ate in their presence.

⁴⁴ He told them, "These are my words that I spoke to you while I was still with you — that everything written about me in the Law of Moses, the Prophets, and the Psalms must be fulfilled." ⁴⁵ Then he opened their minds to understand the Scriptures. ⁴⁶ He also said to them, "This is what is written:ᴮ The Messiah would suffer and rise from the dead the third day, ⁴⁷ and repentance forᶜ forgiveness of sins would be proclaimed in his name to all the nations, beginning at Jerusalem. ⁴⁸ You are witnesses of these things. ⁴⁹ And look, I am sending youᴰ what my Father promised. As for you, stay in the cityᴱ until you are empoweredᶠ from on high."

THE ASCENSION OF JESUS

⁵⁰ Then he led them out to the vicinity of Bethany, and lifting up his hands he blessed them. ⁵¹ And while he was blessing them, he left them and was carried up into heaven. ⁵² After worshiping him, they returned to Jerusalem with great joy. ⁵³ And they were continually in the temple praising God.ᴳ

ᴬ 24:42 Other mss add *and some honeycomb*   ᴮ 24:46 Other mss add *and thus it was necessary that*   ᶜ 24:47 Many mss read *repentance and*   ᴰ 24:49 Lit *upon you*   ᴱ 24:49 Other mss add *of Jerusalem*   ᶠ 24:49 Lit *clothed with power*   ᴳ 24:53 Other mss read *praising and blessing God. Amen.*

IN THE BEGINNING WAS THE WORD

john

In the beginning was the Word, and the Word was with God, and the Word was God. **1:1**

ON THE TIMELINE The Gospel of John was most likely written between AD 70 (the date of the destruction of the temple) and AD 100 (the end of John's life). The events in John's Gospel occur during Jesus' ministry, about AD 30–33.

A LITTLE BACKGROUND John's original audience was probably composed of people in the larger Greco-Roman world in Ephesus and beyond, toward the close of the first century AD. John frequently explained Jewish customs and Palestinian geography and translated Aramaic terms into Greek.

Of all the New Testament books, the Gospel of John most clearly teaches the deity and preexistence of Christ (Jn 1:1-2,18; 8:58; 17:5, 24; 20:28). John provides proof of Jesus' messiahship by:

1. Narrating seven messianic signs
2. Providing Jesus' seven "I am" statements
3. Including specific fulfillment quotations, especially at Jesus' death
4. Showing how Jesus fulfilled the symbolism inherent in a variety of Jewish festivals and institutions.

MESSAGE & PURPOSE The purpose statement in John 20:30-31 indicates that John wrote his Gospel with the purpose of reaching unbelievers. If the Gospel of John was written after the destruction of the Jewish temple in Jerusalem, it is likely that John sought to present Jesus as the new temple and center of worship for God's people, a replacement of the old sanctuary.

John emphasized the deity of Jesus in the prologue to his Gospel. The prologue affirms that He is the eternal Word (*logos* in the Greek) who was with God and was God. Jesus used the significant phrase "I am" seven times in John, claiming the personal name of God as His own.

GIVE THANKS FOR THE GOSPEL OF JOHN

The Gospel of John is different from the Synoptic Gospels—Matthew, Mark, and Luke—in that over ninety percent of its material is unique. John's Gospel does not focus on the miracles, parables, and public speeches that are so prominent in the other accounts. Instead, John emphasizes the identity of Jesus as the Son of God and how we, as believers, should respond to His teachings.

JESUS' FINAL HOURS*

THURSDAY

6p.m. 7p.m. 9p.m.

Jesus prays for
His disciples,
for all believers,
and for Himself

Jesus washes His
disciples' feet

Jesus celebrates Passover
with His disciples

FRIDAY

12a.m.

Jesus and His disciples in
the garden of Gethsemane

3a.m.

4a.m.

Jesus before Annas

Peter denies Jesus

Jesus arrested

* Times are approximate.

6a.m.

7a.m.

8a.m

9a.m.

10a.m.

12p.m.

3p.m.

4p.m.

5p.m.

6p.m.

Jesus crucified

Darkness covers the land

Jesus taken down from the cross

Sabbath begins

Jesus buried

Jesus led away to Calvary

Jesus mocked while on the cross

Jesus sentenced to death

Jesus gives up His spirit

The earthquake, the curtain torn, and many dead are raised

Jesus stands trial before Pilate and Herod

READ AND UNDERSTAND JOHN

The Bible is a complete work in which many stories combine to tell one story. As you read the Gospel of John, consider reading the additional passages to discover how the whole of Scripture works together.

Week 1	GOING DEEPER
☐ **John 1**	Isaiah 55:10-11; Hebrews 1:1-4
☐ John 2	Psalm 69:9; 104:14-15
☐ **John 3**	Ezekiel 36:25-27; 1 Timothy 2:5-6
☐ **John 4**	2 Kings 17:24-31; Isaiah 55:1-3
☐ John 5	Exodus 20:8-11; 1 Thessalonians 4:13-18

Week 2	GOING DEEPER
☐ John 6	Psalm 29:10-11; Acts 3:22-23
☐ John 7:1-52	Leviticus 23:39-41; Joel 2:28-29
☐ **John 7:53-8:59**	Romans 2:25-29; 1 John 1:5-7
☐ John 9	Genesis 2:7; Romans 1:18-20
☐ John 10	Numbers 27:16-17; Micah 2:12-13

Week 3	GOING DEEPER
☐ John 11	Daniel 12:2-3; 1 Thessalonians 4:13-14
☐ John 12	Psalm 118:25-26; Isaiah 6:10; 53:1
☐ **John 13**	Psalm 31:9-10; Romans 3:21-26
☐ John 14	Ezekiel 1:26-28; Isaiah 28:16
☐ **John 15**	Hosea 14:4-8; Zephaniah 3:14-17

Week 4	GOING DEEPER
☐ John 16	Isaiah 32:14-18; Romans 8:12-17
☐ John 17	Isaiah 42:8; 1 John 5:20
☐ John 18	Jeremiah 25:15-17; Daniel 7:14
☐ **John 19-20**	Psalm 22:1-8; 1 Peter 2:22-25
☐ **John 21**	Hebrews 2:17-18; 1 Peter 5:1-4

PROLOGUE

1 In the beginning was the Word, and the Word was with God, and the Word was God. ² He was with God in the beginning. ³ All things were created through him, and apart from him not one thing was created that has been created. ⁴ In him was life,ᴬ and that life was the light of men. ⁵ That light shines in the darkness, and yet the darkness did not overcomeᴮ it.

⁶ There was a man sent from God whose name was John. ⁷ He came as a witness to testify about the light, so that all might believe through him.ᶜ ⁸ He was not the light, but he came to testify about the light. ⁹ The true light that gives light to everyone, was coming into the world.ᴰ

¹⁰ He was in the world, and the world was created through him, and yet the world did not recognize him. ¹¹ He came to his own, and his own people did not receive him. ¹² But to all who did receive him, he gave them the right to beᴱ children of God, to those who believe in his name, ¹³ who were born, not of natural descent,ᶠ or of the will of the flesh, or of the will of man,ᴳ but of God.

¹⁴ The Word became flesh and dweltᴴ among us. We observed his glory, the glory as the one and only Sonᴵ from the Father, full of grace and truth. ¹⁵ (John testified concerning him and exclaimed, "This was the one of whom I said, 'The one coming after me ranks ahead of me, because he existed before me.' ") ¹⁶ Indeed, we have all received grace uponᴶ grace from his fullness, ¹⁷ for the law was given through Moses; grace and truth came through Jesus Christ. ¹⁸ No one has ever seen God. The one and only Son, who is himself God and is at the Father's side ᴷ —he has revealed him.

JOHN THE BAPTIST'S TESTIMONY

¹⁹ This was John's testimony when the Jews from Jerusalem sent priests and Levites to ask him, "Who are you?"

²⁰ He didn't deny it but confessed: "I am not the Messiah."

²¹ "What then?" they asked him. "Are you Elijah?"

"I am not," he said.

"Are you the Prophet?"

"No," he answered.

²² "Who are you, then?" they asked. "We need to give an answer to those who sent us. What can you tell us about yourself?"

²³ He said, "I am a **voice of one crying out in the wilderness: Make straight the way of the Lord** ᴸ — just as Isaiah the prophet said."

²⁴ Now they had been sent from the Pharisees. ²⁵ So they asked him, "Why then do you baptize if you aren't the Messiah, or Elijah, or the Prophet?"

ᴬ1:3-4 Other punctuation is possible: . . . *not one thing was created. What was created in him was life* ᴮ1:5 Or *grasp,* or *comprehend,* or *overtake;* Jn 12:35 ᶜ1:7 Or *it (the light)* ᴰ1:9 Or *The true light who comes into the world gives light to everyone,* or *The true light enlightens everyone coming into the world.* ᴱ1:12 Or *become* ᶠ1:13 Lit *blood* ᴳ1:13 Or *not of human lineage, or of human capacity, or of human volition* ᴴ1:14 Or *and dwelt in a tent;* lit *and tabernacled* ᴵ1:14 *Son* is implied from the reference to the Father and from Gk usage. ᴶ1:16 Or *in place of* ᴷ1:18 Other mss read *The one and only Son, who is at the Father's side* ᴸ1:23 Is 40:3

JESUS IS THE WORD

JOHN 1; ISAIAH 55:10-11; HEBREWS 1:1-4

Gathered around the living room, we remained seated as the doorbell continued to ring. We didn't need another casserole or vase of sympathy flowers; we needed words.

Void of compassion, the blank document—an unforeseen obituary—stared back at us, wringing all adjectives of their meaning, one after another. Each suggested description seemed to shrink our beloved boy, the one who held the titles of both my best friend and younger brother, into someone foreign and unrecognizable. The task of fitting all of his life and all of our love into one small newspaper column was exhausting, so we traded our pencils for pillows and gave up for the night.

A few hours later, unable to sleep, I rolled over to see a small beam of light coming from downstairs, and decided to follow it. I found my sleepy-eyed father furiously scribbling notes on a stack of white index cards. Between the light blue lines were favorite stories, memorable quotes, and beloved quirks. My dad handed me a stack, and as the dark sky faded into morning, our collection of cards finally created the outline of something familiar—someone familiar.

I imagine the Apostle John sitting down to translate the encounters he'd had with Jesus into suitable words. To him, Jesus was not a faraway character, but a trusted friend and beloved Savior. Writing these words, this Gospel account, John probably recalled intimate details about Jesus—the way He smelled, what His favorite foods were, the sound of His laugh. He could clearly call to mind the expressions his friend made when feeling tired or excited or somber. Yet, John undertook the task of assembling words to describe the heaven-sent

Son of God to those of us who didn't know Jesus in the flesh.

John must have had a wealth of stories to choose from when deciding how to open his eyewitness account. But, through the Holy Spirit's inspiration, this dear friend of Jesus begins his narrative with the thing that identified Jesus most:

"In the beginning was the Word, and the Word was with God, and the Word was God."

JOHN 1:1

After years of witnessing Jesus' parables, miracles, and interactions firsthand, John presents Jesus as the Word—a tangible love letter from God. **Jesus did not come to merely deliver a message from God— He Himself is the message.**

"The Word became flesh and dwelt among us. We observed his glory, the glory as the one and only Son from the Father, full of grace and truth."

JOHN 1:14

The Apostle John's words are not only the beginning to another chapter in the Bible, they are the beginning to understanding who Jesus is. He is our promised Savior. He is the One who has been with God from the beginning. He is the Word.

²⁶"I baptize with^A water," John answered them. "Someone stands among you, but you don't know him. ²⁷ He is the one coming after me,^B whose sandal strap I'm not worthy to untie." ²⁸ All this happened in Bethany^C across the Jordan, where John was baptizing.

THE LAMB OF GOD

²⁹ The next day John saw Jesus coming toward him and said, "Here is the Lamb of God, who takes away the sin of the world! ³⁰ This is the one I told you about: 'After me comes a man who ranks ahead of me, because he existed before me.' ³¹ I didn't know him, but I came baptizing with water so he might be revealed to Israel." ³² And John testified, "I saw the Spirit descending from heaven like a dove, and he rested on him. ³³ I didn't know him, but he who sent me to baptize with water told me, 'The one you see the Spirit descending and resting on — he is the one who baptizes with the Holy Spirit.' ³⁴ I have seen and testified that this is the Son of God."^D

³⁵ The next day, John was standing with two of his disciples. ³⁶ When he saw Jesus passing by, he said, "Look, the Lamb of God!"

³⁷ The two disciples heard him say this and followed Jesus. ³⁸ When Jesus turned and noticed them following him, he asked them, "What are you looking for?"

They said to him, "Rabbi" (which means "Teacher"), "where are you staying?"

³⁹ "Come and you'll see," he replied. So they went and saw where he was staying, and they stayed with him that day. It was about four in the afternoon.^E

⁴⁰ Andrew, Simon Peter's brother, was one of the two who heard John and followed him. ⁴¹ He first found his own brother Simon and told him, "We have found the Messiah"^F (which is translated "the Christ"), ⁴² and he brought Simon to Jesus.

When Jesus saw him, he said, "You are Simon, son of John.^G You will be called Cephas" (which is translated "Peter"^H).

PHILIP AND NATHANAEL

⁴³ The next day Jesus^I decided to leave for Galilee. He found Philip and told him, "Follow me."

⁴⁴ Now Philip was from Bethsaida, the hometown of Andrew and Peter. ⁴⁵ Philip found Nathanael and told him, "We have found the one Moses wrote about in the law (and so did the prophets): Jesus the son of Joseph, from Nazareth."

⁴⁶ "Can anything good come out of Nazareth?" Nathanael asked him.

"Come and see," Philip answered.

⁴⁷ Then Jesus saw Nathanael coming toward him and said about him, "Here truly is an Israelite in whom there is no deceit."

⁴⁸ "How do you know me?" Nathanael asked.

"Before Philip called you, when you were under the fig tree, I saw you," Jesus answered.

---

^A1:26 Or *in*, also in vv. 31,33   ^B1:27 Other mss add *who came before me*
^C1:28 Other mss read *in Bethabara*   ^D1:34 Other mss read *is the Chosen One of God*   ^E1:39 Lit *about the tenth hour*   ^F1:41 Both Hb *Messiah* and Gk *Christos* mean "anointed one"   ^G1:42 Other mss read *"Simon, son of Jonah*   ^H1:42 Both Aramaic *Cephas* and Gk *Petros* mean "rock"   ^I1:43 Lit *he*

⁴⁹ "Rabbi," Nathanael replied, "You are the Son of God; you are the King of Israel!"

⁵⁰ Jesus responded to him, "Do you believe because I told you I saw you under the fig tree? You will see greater things than this." ⁵¹ Then he said, "Truly I tell you, you will see heaven opened and the angels of God ascending and descending on the Son of Man."

THE FIRST SIGN: TURNING WATER INTO WINE

2 On the third day a wedding took place in Cana of Galilee. Jesus's mother was there, and ² Jesus and his disciples were invited to the wedding as well. ³ When the wine ran out, Jesus's mother told him, "They don't have any wine."

⁴ "What does that have to do with you and me,ᴬ woman?" Jesus asked. "My hour has not yet come."

⁵ "Do whatever he tells you," his mother told the servants.

⁶ Now six stone water jars had been set there for Jewish purification. Each contained twenty or thirty gallons.ᴮ

⁷ "Fill the jars with water," Jesus told them. So they filled them to the brim. ⁸ Then he said to them, "Now draw some out and take it to the headwaiter."ᶜ And they did.

⁹ When the headwaiter tasted the water (after it had become wine), he did not know where it came from — though the servants who had drawn the water knew. He called the groom ¹⁰ and told him, "Everyone sets out the fine wine first, then, after people are drunk, the inferior. But you have kept the fine wine until now."

¹¹ Jesus did this, the first of his signs, in Cana of Galilee. He revealed his glory, and his disciples believed in him.

¹² After this, he went down to Capernaum, together with his mother, his brothers, and his disciples, and they stayed there only a few days.

CLEANSING THE TEMPLE

¹³ The Jewish Passover was near, and so Jesus went up to Jerusalem. ¹⁴ In the temple he found people selling oxen, sheep, and doves, and he also found the money changers sitting there. ¹⁵ After making a whip out of cords, he drove everyone out of the temple with their sheep and oxen. He also poured out the money changers' coins and overturned the tables. ¹⁶ He told those who were selling doves, "Get these things out of here! Stop turning my Father's house into a marketplace!"ᴰ

¹⁷ And his disciples remembered that it is written: **Zeal for your house will consume me.**ᴱ

¹⁸ So the Jews replied to him, "What sign will you show us for doing these things?"

¹⁹ Jesus answered, "Destroy this temple,ᶠ and I will raise it up in three days."

²⁰ Therefore the Jews said, "This temple took forty-six years to build,ᴳ and will you raise it up in three days?"

ᴬ2:4 Or "You and I see things differently; lit "What to me and to you; Mt 8:29; Mk 1:24; 5:7; Lk 8:28   ᴮ2:6 Lit two or three measures   ᶜ2:8 Lit ruler of the table   ᴰ2:16 Lit a house of business   ᴱ2:17 Ps 69:9   ᶠ2:19 Or sanctuary, also in vv. 20,21   ᴳ2:20 Or was built forty-six years ago

²¹ But he was speaking about the temple of his body. ²² So when he was raised from the dead, his disciples remembered that he had said this, and they believed the Scripture and the statement Jesus had made.

²³ While he was in Jerusalem during the Passover Festival, many believed in his name when they saw the signs he was doing. ²⁴ Jesus, however, would not entrust himself to them, since he knew them all ²⁵ and because he did not need anyone to testify about man; for he himself knew what was in man.

JESUS AND NICODEMUS

3 There was a man from the Pharisees named Nicodemus, a ruler of the Jews. ² This man came to him at night and said, "Rabbi, we know that you are a teacher who has come from God, for no one could perform these signs you do unless God were with him."

³ Jesus replied, "Truly I tell you, unless someone is born again,ᴬ he cannot see the kingdom of God."

⁴ "How can anyone be born when he is old?" Nicodemus asked him. "Can he enter his mother's womb a second time and be born?"

⁵ Jesus answered, "Truly I tell you, unless someone is born of water and the Spirit, he cannot enter the kingdom of God. ⁶ Whatever is born of the flesh is flesh, and whatever is born of the Spirit is spirit. ⁷ Do not be amazed that I told you that you must be born again. ⁸ The wind blows where it pleases, and you hear its sound, but you don't know where it comes from or where it is going. So it is with everyone born of the Spirit."

⁹ "How can these things be?" asked Nicodemus.

¹⁰ "Are you a teacherᴮ of Israel and don't know these things?" Jesus replied. ¹¹ "Truly I tell you, we speak what we know and we testify to what we have seen, but you do not accept our testimony. ¹² If I have told you about earthly things and you don't believe, how will you believe if I tell you about heavenly things? ¹³ No one has ascended into heaven except the one who descended from heaven — the Son of Man.ᶜ

¹⁴ "Just as Moses lifted up the snake in the wilderness, so the Son of Man must be lifted up, ¹⁵ so that everyone who believes in him mayᴰ have eternal life. ¹⁶ For God loved the world in this way:ᴱ He gaveᶠ his one and only Son, so that everyone who believes in him will not perish but have eternal life. ¹⁷ For God did not send his Son into the world to condemn the world, but to save the world through him. ¹⁸ Anyone who believes in him is not condemned, but anyone who does not believe is already condemned, because he has not believed in the name of the one and only Son of God. ¹⁹ This is the judgment: The light has come into the world, and people loved darkness rather than the light because their deeds were evil. ²⁰ For everyone who does evil hates the light and avoids it,ᴳ so that his deeds may not be exposed. ²¹ But anyone who lives byᴴ the truth comes to the light, so that his works may be shown to be accomplished by God."

ᴬ3:3 Or *from above, also in v. 7*   ᴮ3:10 Or *the teacher*   ᶜ3:13 Other mss add *who is in heaven*   ᴰ3:15 Other mss add *not perish, but*   ᴱ3:16 Or *this much*   ᶠ3:16 Or *For in this way God loved the world, and so he gave*, or *For God so loved the world that he gave*   ᴳ3:20 Lit *and does not come to the light*   ᴴ3:21 Lit *who does*

WHY WE STILL NEED JOHN 3:16

JOHN 3; EZEKIEL 36:25-27; 1 TIMOTHY 2:5-6

John 3:16 wins the prize for the most well-worn verse in the Bible. Scribbled on bathroom stalls, held high on signs at basketball games, or added to the gear of NFL quarterbacks, John 3:16 is seemingly everywhere. When things become familiar, they sometimes lose their ability to "wow" us. But we still need John 3:16.

In John 3, we find Jesus in a clandestine conversation with Nicodemus, a Pharisee and influential Jew (Jn 3:1). Nicodemus was trying to wrap his well-educated, powerful brain around the fact that the Savior of His people didn't look like, act like, or teach like Nicodemus thought he should. What Nicodemus was really wrestling with was the gospel.

I've always had a soft spot for Nicodemus, probably because I've stepped into the ring and gone a few rounds with the gospel myself. There is a tiny corner of my mind and heart that gets it: I am a sinner, deserving of eternal separation from a holy God. Through His death on the cross, Jesus paid the penalty for my sin and made a way for me to be reconciled to the Father (Rm 6:23). But I struggle to convince my whole self that the gospel can be this simple.

Surely, I need a lot of good works to save me.
I mess up so often, God must have changed His mind about me.
Maybe if I run myself ragged, involving myself in every possible ministry, I will please God.

These are the things I tell myself nearly as often as John 3:16 shows up on the side of a semi-truck. It's what we see when we read between the lines when Nicodemus said to Jesus, "How

can anyone be born when he is old? . . . Can he enter his mother's womb a second time and be born?" (Jn 3:4).

A few short verses later, we see Nicodemus finally collide with gospel truth:

"For God loved the world in this way: He gave his one and only Son, so that everyone who believes in him will not perish but have eternal life."

JOHN 3:16

This is so good! Let's keep reading:

"For God did not send his Son into the world to condemn the world, but to save the world through him."

JOHN 3:17

When I try to create a list of requirements for my salvation, I do so out of fear and forgetfulness—like Nicodemus. I'm fearful of being punished and forgetful of God's character. But God loves us so much! That's why He sent Jesus here—not to condemn us but to save us. His perfect plan for salvation is laid out for us in John 3:16-17.

May these words from our Savior never grow stale in our hearts and minds, and may we never grow tired of hearing them.

JESUS AND JOHN THE BAPTIST

²² After this, Jesus and his disciples went to the Judean countryside, where he spent time with them and baptized.

²³ John also was baptizing in Aenon near Salim, because there was plenty of water there. People were coming and being baptized, ²⁴ since John had not yet been thrown into prison.

²⁵ Then a dispute arose between John's disciples and a Jew[A] about purification. ²⁶ So they came to John and told him, "Rabbi, the one you testified about, and who was with you across the Jordan, is baptizing — and everyone is going to him."

²⁷ John responded, "No one can receive anything unless it has been given to him from heaven. ²⁸ You yourselves can testify that I said, 'I am not the Messiah, but I've been sent ahead of him.' ²⁹ He who has the bride is the groom. But the groom's friend, who stands by and listens for him, rejoices greatly[B] at the groom's voice. So this joy of mine is complete. ³⁰ He must increase, but I must decrease."

THE ONE FROM HEAVEN

³¹ The one who comes from above is above all. The one who is from the earth is earthly and speaks in earthly terms.[C] The one who comes from heaven is above all. ³² He testifies to what he has seen and heard, and yet no one accepts his testimony. ³³ The one who has accepted his testimony has affirmed that God is true. ³⁴ For the one whom God sent speaks God's words, since he[D] gives the Spirit without measure. ³⁵ The Father loves the Son and has given all things into his hands. ³⁶ The one who believes in the Son has eternal life, but the one who rejects the Son[E] will not see life; instead, the wrath of God remains on him.

JESUS AND THE SAMARITAN WOMAN

4 When Jesus[F] learned that the Pharisees had heard he was making and baptizing more disciples than John ² (though Jesus himself was not baptizing, but his disciples were), ³ he left Judea and went again to Galilee. ⁴ He had to travel through Samaria; ⁵ so he came to a town of Samaria called Sychar near the property[G] that Jacob had given his son Joseph. ⁶ Jacob's well was there, and Jesus, worn out from his journey, sat down at the well. It was about noon.[H]

⁷ A woman of Samaria came to draw water.

"Give me a drink," Jesus said to her, ⁸ because his disciples had gone into town to buy food.

⁹ "How is it that you, a Jew, ask for a drink from me, a Samaritan woman?" she asked him. For Jews do not associate with[I] Samaritans.[J]

¹⁰ Jesus answered, "If you knew the gift of God, and who is saying to you, 'Give me a drink,' you would ask him, and he would give you living water."

¹¹ "Sir," said the woman, "you don't even have a bucket, and the well is deep. So where do you get this 'living water'? ¹² You aren't greater than our

---

[A]3:25 Other mss read and the Jews   [B]3:29 Lit with joy rejoices   [C]3:31 Or of earthly things   [D]3:34 Other mss read since God   [E]3:36 Or refuses to believe in the Son, or disobeys the Son   [F]4:1 Other mss read the Lord   [G]4:5 Lit piece of land   [H]4:6 Lit about the sixth hour   [I]4:9 Or do not share vessels with   [J]4:9 Other mss omit For Jews do not associate with Samaritans.

father Jacob, are you? He gave us the well and drank from it himself, as did his sons and livestock."

¹³ Jesus said, "Everyone who drinks from this water will get thirsty again. ¹⁴ But whoever drinks from the water that I will give him will never get thirsty again. In fact, the water I will give him will become a well^A of water spring-ing up in him for eternal life."

¹⁵ "Sir," the woman said to him, "give me this water so that I won't get thirsty and come here to draw water."

¹⁶ "Go call your husband," he told her, "and come back here."

¹⁷ "I don't have a husband," she answered.

"You have correctly said, 'I don't have a husband,'" Jesus said. ¹⁸ "For you've had five husbands, and the man you now have is not your husband. What you have said is true."

¹⁹ "Sir," the woman replied, "I see that you are a prophet. ²⁰ Our fathers worshiped on this mountain, but you Jews say that the place to worship is in Jerusalem."

²¹ Jesus told her, "Believe me, woman, an hour is coming when you will worship the Father neither on this mountain nor in Jerusalem. ²² You Samar-itans worship what you do not know. We worship what we do know, because salvation is from the Jews. ²³ But an hour is coming, and is now here, when the true worshipers will worship the Father in Spirit and in truth.^B Yes, the Father wants such people to worship him. ²⁴ God is spirit, and those who worship him must worship in Spirit and in truth."

²⁵ The woman said to him, "I know that the Messiah is coming" (who is called Christ). "When he comes, he will explain everything to us."

²⁶ Jesus told her, "I, the one speaking to you, am he."

THE RIPENED HARVEST

²⁷ Just then his disciples arrived, and they were amazed that he was talking with a woman. Yet no one said, "What do you want?" or "Why are you talk-ing with her?"

²⁸ Then the woman left her water jar, went into town, and told the peo-ple, ²⁹ "Come, see a man who told me everything I ever did. Could this be the Messiah?" ³⁰ They left the town and made their way to him.

³¹ In the meantime the disciples kept urging him, "Rabbi, eat something."

³² But he said, "I have food to eat that you don't know about."

³³ The disciples said to one another, "Could someone have brought him something to eat?"

³⁴ "My food is to do the will of him who sent me and to finish his work," Jesus told them. ³⁵ "Don't you say, 'There are still four more months, and then comes the harvest'? Listen to what I'm telling you: Open^C your eyes and look at the fields, because they are ready^D for harvest. ³⁶ The reaper is already receiving pay and gathering fruit for eternal life, so that the sower and reaper can rejoice together. ³⁷ For in this case the saying is true: 'One sows and another reaps.' ³⁸ I sent you to reap what you didn't labor for; others have labored, and you have benefited from^E their labor."

---

^A4:14 Or spring   ^B4:23 Or in spirit and truth, also in v. 24   ^C4:35 Lit Raise
^D4:35 Lit white   ^E4:38 Lit you have entered into

GIVE ME WATER

JOHN 4; 2 KINGS 17:24-31; ISAIAH 55:1-3

I wonder if she spotted Him from a distance, a man sitting at the well alone—her well, the one she visited daily. I wonder if, as she drew closer, she could make out Jesus' face and recognize His nationality. A man—a Jewish man—sitting at her well?

She approached, probably confused. Maybe even a bit afraid. Then, Jesus spoke to her.

In this story from John 4, Jesus broke through at least three cultural and social barriers of His time:

- He spoke to a woman, and traditionally, Jewish men were not to be seen conversing with women.
- He spoke to a Samaritan, and as the Scripture says, Jews had no dealings with Samaritans at the time (Jn 4:9).
- He spoke to a woman He knew was an "adulteress"—a woman who had more than one husband and was with a man she wasn't married to.

Yet, Jesus spoke to her. A woman. A Samaritan. A sinner.

And He didn't just say hello. Over the course of their brief and profound conversation, He offered her the gift of a lifetime: living water, eternal life. "But whoever drinks from the water that I will give him will never get thirsty again," Jesus said to her (Jn 4:14).

"Sir," she said, "give me this water, so that I won't get thirsty and come here to draw water" (Jn 4:15).

There she was, standing beside the Messiah in the flesh, and she didn't fully understand what He was telling her. She took His offer of living water literally. She didn't get it—not yet.

I love this part so much because it paints such a real and beautiful picture of grace. You don't have to fully "get it" to receive it.

That part is hard for me, a lifelong Christ follower, to accept. Unlike the Samaritan woman, I have the knowledge. I like to think that I know Jesus and His story, that I know the right answers and theology. But this story says the gift of Christ is for anyone who wants to receive it—no matter how little you know, how little you have been taught, or how wayward you have lived. Grace reminds us how level the playing field is.

The Samaritan woman wanted what Jesus offered. She knew this if she knew nothing else. "Give me this water," she said. And that's all she had to say.

That's all we have to say, too. From the woman frantically checking all her Bible-study boxes to the woman buried under the weight of past sin and shame, this promise is for all of us. Because we're all thirsty. We're all weary. **We are all desperate for the Jesus who stands at the well offering the exact and only thing we need.**

"Give me this water," we say, breathless and tired. And He does.

THE SAVIOR OF THE WORLD

[39] Now many Samaritans from that town believed in him because of what the woman said[A] when she testified, "He told me everything I ever did." [40] So when the Samaritans came to him, they asked him to stay with them, and he stayed there two days. [41] Many more believed because of what he said. [B] [42] And they told the woman, "We no longer believe because of what you said, since we have heard for ourselves and know that this really is the Savior of the world."[C]

A GALILEAN WELCOME

[43] After two days he left there for Galilee. [44] (Jesus himself had testified that a prophet has no honor in his own country.) [45] When they entered Galilee, the Galileans welcomed him because they had seen everything he did in Jerusalem during the festival. For they also had gone to the festival.

THE SECOND SIGN: HEALING AN OFFICIAL'S SON

[46] He went again to Cana of Galilee, where he had turned the water into wine. There was a certain royal official whose son was ill at Capernaum. [47] When this man heard that Jesus had come from Judea into Galilee, he went to him and pleaded with him to come down and heal his son, since he was about to die.

[48] Jesus told him, "Unless you people see signs and wonders, you will not believe."

[49] "Sir," the official said to him, "come down before my boy dies."

[50] "Go," Jesus told him, "your son will live." The man believed what[D] Jesus said to him and departed.

[51] While he was still going down, his servants met him saying that his boy was alive. [52] He asked them at what time he got better. "Yesterday at one in the afternoon[E] the fever left him," they answered. [53] The father realized this was the very hour at which Jesus had told him, "Your son will live." So he himself believed, along with his whole household.

[54] Now this was also the second sign Jesus performed after he came from Judea to Galilee.

THE THIRD SIGN: HEALING THE SICK

5 After this, a Jewish festival took place, and Jesus went up to Jerusalem. [2] By the Sheep Gate in Jerusalem there is a pool, called Bethesda[F] in Aramaic, which has five colonnades. [3] Within these lay a large number of the disabled — blind, lame, and paralyzed. [G]

[5] One man was there who had been disabled for thirty-eight years. [6] When Jesus saw him lying there and realized he had already been there a long time, he said to him, "Do you want to get well?"

[7] "Sir," the disabled man answered, "I have no one to put me into the pool when the water is stirred up, but while I'm coming, someone goes down ahead of me."

[A]4:39 Lit because of the woman's word   [B]4:41 Lit because of his word
[C]4:42 Other mss add , the Messiah   [D]4:50 Lit the word   [E]4:52 Lit at the seventh hour   [F]5:2 Some mss read Bethzatha; other mss read Bethsaida   [G]5:3 Some mss include vv. 3b-4: — waiting for the moving of the water, [4]because an angel would go down into the pool from time to time and stir up the water. Then the first one who got in after the water was stirred up recovered from whatever ailment he had.

[8] "Get up," Jesus told him, "pick up your mat and walk." [9] Instantly the man got well, picked up his mat, and started to walk.

Now that day was the Sabbath, [10] and so the Jews said to the man who had been healed, "This is the Sabbath. The law prohibits you from picking up your mat."

[11] He replied, "The man who made me well told me, 'Pick up your mat and walk.'"

[12] "Who is this man who told you, 'Pick up your mat and walk'?" they asked. [13] But the man who was healed did not know who it was, because Jesus had slipped away into the crowd that was there.[A]

[14] After this, Jesus found him in the temple and said to him, "See, you are well. Do not sin anymore, so that something worse doesn't happen to you." [15] The man went and reported to the Jews that it was Jesus who had made him well. [16] Therefore, the Jews began persecuting Jesus[B] because he was doing these things on the Sabbath.

HONORING THE FATHER AND THE SON

[17] Jesus responded to them, "My Father is still working, and I am working also." [18] This is why the Jews began trying all the more to kill him: Not only was he breaking the Sabbath, but he was even calling God his own Father, making himself equal to God.

[19] Jesus replied, "Truly I tell you, the Son is not able to do anything on his own, but only what he sees the Father doing. For whatever the Father[C] does, the Son likewise does these things. [20] For the Father loves the Son and shows him everything he is doing, and he will show him greater works than these so that you will be amazed. [21] And just as the Father raises the dead and gives them life, so the Son also gives life to whom he wants. [22] The Father, in fact, judges no one but has given all judgment to the Son, [23] so that all people may honor the Son just as they honor the Father. Anyone who does not honor the Son does not honor the Father who sent him.

LIFE AND JUDGMENT

[24] "Truly I tell you, anyone who hears my word and believes him who sent me has eternal life and will not come under judgment but has passed from death to life.

[25] "Truly I tell you, an hour is coming, and is now here, when the dead will hear the voice of the Son of God, and those who hear will live. [26] For just as the Father has life in himself, so also he has granted to the Son to have life in himself. [27] And he has granted him the right to pass judgment, because he is the Son of Man. [28] Do not be amazed at this, because a time is coming when all who are in the graves will hear his voice [29] and come out — those who have done good things, to the resurrection of life, but those who have done wicked things, to the resurrection of condemnation.

[30] "I can do nothing on my own. I judge only as I hear, and my judgment is just, because I do not seek my own will, but the will of him who sent me.

WITNESSES TO JESUS

[31] "If I testify about myself, my testimony is not true. [32] There is another who testifies about me, and I know that the testimony he gives about me is true.

[A] 5:13 Lit slipped away, there being a crowd in that place   [B] 5:16 Other mss add and trying to kill him   [C] 5:19 Lit whatever that one

³³ You sent messengers to John, and he testified to the truth. ³⁴ I don't receive human testimony, but I say these things so that you may be saved. ³⁵ John^ was a burning and shining lamp, and you were willing to rejoice for a while in his light.

³⁶ "But I have a greater testimony than John's because of the works that the Father has given me to accomplish. These very works I am doing testify about me that the Father has sent me. ³⁷ The Father who sent me has himself testified about me. You have not heard his voice at any time, and you haven't seen his form. ³⁸ You don't have his word residing in you, because you don't believe the one he sent. ³⁹ You pore over the Scriptures because you think you have eternal life in them, and yet they testify about me. ⁴⁰ But you are not willing to come to me so that you may have life.

⁴¹ "I do not accept glory from people, ⁴² but I know you — that you have no love for God within you. ⁴³ I have come in my Father's name, and yet you don't accept me. If someone else comes in his own name, you will accept him. ⁴⁴ How can you believe, since you accept glory from one another but don't seek the glory that comes from the only God? ⁴⁵ Do not think that I will accuse you to the Father. Your accuser is Moses, on whom you have set your hope. ⁴⁶ For if you believed Moses, you would believe me, because he wrote about me. ⁴⁷ But if you don't believe what he wrote, how will you believe my words?"

THE FOURTH SIGN: FEEDING OF THE FIVE THOUSAND

6 After this, Jesus crossed the Sea of Galilee (or Tiberias). ² A huge crowd was following him because they saw the signs that he was performing by healing the sick. ³ Jesus went up a mountain and sat down there with his disciples.

⁴ Now the Passover, a Jewish festival, was near. ⁵ So when Jesus looked up and noticed a huge crowd coming toward him, he asked Philip, "Where will we buy bread so that these people can eat?" ⁶ He asked this to test him, for he himself knew what he was going to do.

⁷ Philip answered him, "Two hundred denarii^B worth of bread wouldn't be enough for each of them to have a little."

⁸ One of his disciples, Andrew, Simon Peter's brother, said to him, ⁹ "There's a boy here who has five barley loaves and two fish — but what are they for so many?"

¹⁰ Jesus said, "Have the people sit down."

There was plenty of grass in that place; so they sat down. The men numbered about five thousand. ¹¹ Then Jesus took the loaves, and after giving thanks he distributed them to those who were seated — so also with the fish, as much as they wanted.

¹² When they were full, he told his disciples, "Collect the leftovers so that nothing is wasted." ¹³ So they collected them and filled twelve baskets with the pieces from the five barley loaves that were left over by those who had eaten.

¹⁴ When the people saw the sign^C he had done, they said, "This truly is the Prophet who is to come into the world."

¹⁵ Therefore, when Jesus realized that they were about to come and take him by force to make him king, he withdrew again to the mountain by himself.

---

^5:35 Lit *That man*   ^6:7 A denarius = one day's wage   ^6:14 Other mss read *signs*

THE FIFTH SIGN: WALKING ON WATER

¹⁶ When evening came, his disciples went down to the sea, ¹⁷ got into a boat, and started across the sea to Capernaum. Darkness had already set in, but Jesus had not yet come to them. ¹⁸ A high wind arose, and the sea began to churn. ¹⁹ After they had rowed about three or four miles,[A] they saw Jesus walking on the sea. He was coming near the boat, and they were afraid. ²⁰ But he said to them, "It is I.[B] Don't be afraid." ²¹ Then they were willing to take him on board, and at once the boat was at the shore where they were heading.

THE BREAD OF LIFE

²² The next day, the crowd that had stayed on the other side of the sea saw there had been only one boat.[C] They also saw that Jesus had not boarded the boat with his disciples, but that his disciples had gone off alone. ²³ Some boats from Tiberias came near the place where they had eaten the bread after the Lord had given thanks. ²⁴ When the crowd saw that neither Jesus nor his disciples were there, they got into the boats and went to Capernaum looking for Jesus. ²⁵ When they found him on the other side of the sea, they said to him, "Rabbi, when did you get here?"

²⁶ Jesus answered, "Truly I tell you, you are looking for me, not because you saw[D] the signs, but because you ate the loaves and were filled. ²⁷ Don't work for the food that perishes but for the food that lasts for eternal life, which the Son of Man will give you, because God the Father has set his seal of approval on him."

²⁸ "What can we do to perform the works of God?" they asked.

²⁹ Jesus replied, "This is the work of God — that you believe in the one he has sent."

³⁰ "What sign, then, are you going to do so we may see and believe you?" they asked. "What are you going to perform? ³¹ Our ancestors ate the manna in the wilderness, just as it is written: **He gave them bread from heaven to eat.**"[E]

³² Jesus said to them, "Truly I tell you, Moses didn't give you the bread from heaven, but my Father gives you the true bread from heaven. ³³ For the bread of God is the one who comes down from heaven and gives life to the world."

³⁴ Then they said, "Sir, give us this bread always."

³⁵ "I am the bread of life," Jesus told them. "No one who comes to me will ever be hungry, and no one who believes in me will ever be thirsty again. ³⁶ But as I told you, you've seen me,[F] and yet you do not believe. ³⁷ Everyone the Father gives me will come to me, and the one who comes to me I will never cast out. ³⁸ For I have come down from heaven, not to do my own will, but the will of him who sent me. ³⁹ This is the will of him who sent me: that I should lose none of those he has given me but should raise them up on the last day. ⁴⁰ For this is the will of my Father: that everyone who sees the Son and believes in him will have eternal life, and I will raise him up on the last day."

⁴¹ Therefore the Jews started complaining about him because he said, "I am the bread that came down from heaven." ⁴² They were saying, "Isn't this Jesus the son of Joseph, whose father and mother we know? How can he now say, 'I have come down from heaven'?"

[A] 6:19 Lit *twenty-five or thirty stadia*; one *stadion* = 600 feet [B] 6:20 Lit *"I am*
[C] 6:22 Other mss add *into which his disciples had entered* [D] 6:26 Or *perceived*
[E] 6:31 Ex 16:4; Ps 78:24 [F] 6:36 Other mss omit *me*

43 Jesus answered them, "Stop complaining among yourselves. 44 No one can come to me unless the Father who sent me draws[A] him, and I will raise him up on the last day. 45 It is written in the Prophets: **And they will all be taught by God.**[B] Everyone who has listened to and learned from the Father comes to me — 46 not that anyone has seen the Father except the one who is from God. He has seen the Father.

47 "Truly I tell you, anyone who believes[C] has eternal life. 48 I am the bread of life. 49 Your ancestors ate the manna in the wilderness, and they died. 50 This is the bread that comes down from heaven so that anyone may eat of it and not die. 51 I am the living bread that came down from heaven. If anyone eats of this bread he will live forever. The bread that I will give for the life of the world is my flesh."

52 At that, the Jews argued among themselves, "How can this man give us his flesh to eat?"

53 So Jesus said to them, "Truly I tell you, unless you eat the flesh of the Son of Man and drink his blood, you do not have life in yourselves. 54 The one who eats my flesh and drinks my blood has eternal life, and I will raise him up on the last day, 55 because my flesh is true food and my blood is true drink. 56 The one who eats my flesh and drinks my blood remains in me, and I in him. 57 Just as the living Father sent me and I live because of the Father, so the one who feeds on me will live because of me. 58 This is the bread that came down from heaven; it is not like the manna[D] your ancestors ate — and they died. The one who eats this bread will live forever."

59 He said these things while teaching in the synagogue in Capernaum.

MANY DISCIPLES DESERT JESUS

60 Therefore, when many of his disciples heard this, they said, "This teaching is hard. Who can accept[E] it?"

61 Jesus, knowing in himself that his disciples were complaining about this, asked them, "Does this offend you? 62 Then what if you were to observe the Son of Man ascending to where he was before? 63 The Spirit is the one who gives life. The flesh doesn't help at all. The words that I have spoken to you are spirit and are life. 64 But there are some among you who don't believe." (For Jesus knew from the beginning those who did not[F] believe and the one who would betray him.) 65 He said, "This is why I told you that no one can come to me unless it is granted to him by the Father."

66 From that moment[G] many of his disciples turned back and no longer accompanied him. 67 So Jesus said to the Twelve, "You don't want to go away too, do you?"

68 Simon Peter answered, "Lord, to whom will we go? You have the words of eternal life. 69 We have come to believe and know that you are the Holy One of God."[H]

70 Jesus replied to them, "Didn't I choose you, the Twelve? Yet one of you is a devil."[71] He was referring to Judas, Simon Iscariot's son,[I] one of the Twelve, because he was going to betray him.

[A]6:44 Or *brings,* or *leads*   [B]6:45 Is 54:13   [C]6:47 Other mss add *in me*
[D]6:58 Other mss omit *the manna*   [E]6:60 Lit *hear*   [F]6:64 Other mss omit *not*
[G]6:66 Or *Because of this*   [H]6:69 Other mss read *you are the Messiah, the Son of the Living God*   [I]6:71 Or *Judas Iscariot, Simon's son*

THE UNBELIEF OF JESUS'S BROTHERS

7 After this, Jesus traveled in Galilee, since he did not want to travel in Judea because the Jews were trying to kill him. ² The Jewish Festival of Shelters^A was near. ³ So his brothers said to him, "Leave here and go to Judea so your disciples can see your works that you are doing. ⁴ For no one does anything in secret while he's seeking public recognition. If you do these things, show yourself to the world." ⁵ (For not even his brothers believed in him.)

⁶ Jesus told them, "My time has not yet arrived, but your time is always at hand. ⁷ The world cannot hate you, but it does hate me because I testify about it — that its works are evil. ⁸ Go up to the festival yourselves. I'm not going up to this festival,^B because my time has not yet fully come." ⁹ After he had said these things, he stayed in Galilee.

JESUS AT THE FESTIVAL OF SHELTERS

¹⁰ After his brothers had gone up to the festival, then he also went up, not openly but secretly. ¹¹ The Jews were looking for him at the festival and saying, "Where is he?" ¹² And there was a lot of murmuring about him among the crowds. Some were saying, "He's a good man." Others were saying, "No, on the contrary, he's deceiving the people." ¹³ Still, nobody was talking publicly about him for fear of the Jews.

¹⁴ When the festival was already half over, Jesus went up into the temple and began to teach. ¹⁵ Then the Jews were amazed and said, "How is this man so learned, since he hasn't been trained?"

¹⁶ Jesus answered them, "My teaching isn't mine but is from the one who sent me. ¹⁷ If anyone wants to do his will, he will know whether the teaching is from God or whether I am speaking on my own. ¹⁸ The one who speaks on his own seeks his own glory; but he who seeks the glory of the one who sent him is true, and there is no unrighteousness in him. ¹⁹ Didn't Moses give you the law? Yet none of you keeps the law. Why are you trying to kill me?"

²⁰ "You have a demon!" the crowd responded. "Who is trying to kill you?"

²¹ "I performed one work, and you are all amazed," Jesus answered. ²² "This is why Moses has given you circumcision — not that it comes from Moses but from the fathers — and you circumcise a man on the Sabbath. ²³ If a man receives circumcision on the Sabbath so that the law of Moses won't be broken, are you angry at me because I made a man entirely well on the Sabbath? ²⁴ Stop judging according to outward appearances; rather judge according to righteous judgment."

THE IDENTITY OF THE MESSIAH

²⁵ Some of the people of Jerusalem were saying, "Isn't this the man they are trying to kill? ²⁶ Yet, look, he's speaking publicly and they're saying nothing to him. Can it be true that the authorities know he is the Messiah? ²⁷ But we know where this man is from. When the Messiah comes, nobody will know where he is from."

²⁸ As he was teaching in the temple, Jesus cried out, "You know me and you know where I am from. Yet I have not come on my own, but the one who sent me is true. You don't know him; ²⁹ I know him because I am from him, and he sent me."

---

^A 7:2 Or *Tabernacles*, or *Booths*   ^B 7:8 Other mss add *yet*

³⁰ Then they tried to seize him. Yet no one laid a hand on him because his hour had not yet come. ³¹ However, many from the crowd believed in him and said, "When the Messiah comes, he won't perform more signs than this man has done, will he?" ³² The Pharisees heard the crowd murmuring these things about him, and so the chief priests and the Pharisees sent servants^A to arrest him.

³³ Then Jesus said, "I am only with you for a short time. Then I'm going to the one who sent me. ³⁴ You will look for me, but you will not find me; and where I am, you cannot come."

³⁵ Then the Jews said to one another, "Where does he intend to go so we won't find him? He doesn't intend to go to the Jewish people dispersed^B among the Greeks and teach the Greeks, does he? ³⁶ What is this remark he made: 'You will look for me, and you will not find me; and where I am, you cannot come'?"

THE PROMISE OF THE SPIRIT

³⁷ On the last and most important day of the festival, Jesus stood up and cried out, "If anyone is thirsty, let him come to me^C and drink. ³⁸ The one who believes in me, as the Scripture has said, will have streams of living water flow from deep within him." ³⁹ He said this about the Spirit. Those who believed in Jesus were going to receive the Spirit, for the Spirit^D had not yet been given^E because Jesus had not yet been glorified.

THE PEOPLE ARE DIVIDED OVER JESUS

⁴⁰ When some from the crowd heard these words, they said, "This truly is the Prophet." ⁴¹ Others said, "This is the Messiah." But some said, "Surely the Messiah doesn't come from Galilee, does he? ⁴² Doesn't the Scripture say that the Messiah comes from David's offspring^F and from the town of Bethlehem, where David lived?" ⁴³ So the crowd was divided because of him. ⁴⁴ Some of them wanted to seize him, but no one laid hands on him.

DEBATE OVER JESUS'S CLAIMS

⁴⁵ Then the servants came to the chief priests and Pharisees, who asked them, "Why didn't you bring him?"

⁴⁶ The servants answered, "No man ever spoke like this!"^G

⁴⁷ Then the Pharisees responded to them: "Are you fooled too? ⁴⁸ Have any of the rulers or Pharisees believed in him? ⁴⁹ But this crowd, which doesn't know the law, is accursed."

⁵⁰ Nicodemus — the one who came to him previously and who was one of them — said to them, ⁵¹ "Our law doesn't judge a man before it hears from him and knows what he's doing, does it?"

⁵² "You aren't from Galilee too, are you?" they replied. "Investigate and you will see that no prophet arises from Galilee."

[The earliest mss do not include 7:53–8:11.]^H

---

^A7:32 Or temple police, or officers, also in vv. 45,46   ^B7:35 Gk diaspora; Jewish people scattered throughout Gentile lands   ^C7:37 Other mss omit to me   ^D7:39 Other mss read Holy Spirit   ^E7:39 Lit the Spirit was not yet   ^F7:42 Lit seed   ^G7:46 Other mss read like this man   ^H7:53–8:11 Other mss include all or some of the passage after Jn 7:36,44,52; 21:25; or Lk 21:38.

8 [53 Then each one went to his house. 1 But Jesus went to the Mount of Olives.

AN ADULTERESS FORGIVEN

2 At dawn he went to the temple again, and all the people were coming to him. He sat down and began to teach them.

3 Then the scribes and the Pharisees brought a woman caught in adultery, making her stand in the center. 4 "Teacher," they said to him, "this woman was caught in the act of committing adultery. 5 In the law Moses commanded us to stone such women. So what do you say?" 6 They asked this to trap him, in order that they might have evidence to accuse him.

Jesus stooped down and started writing on the ground with his finger. 7 When they persisted in questioning him, he stood up and said to them, "The one without sin among you should be the first to throw a stone at her." 8 Then he stooped down again and continued writing on the ground. 9 When they heard this, they left one by one, starting with the older men. Only he was left, with the woman in the center. 10 When Jesus stood up, he said to her, "Woman, where are they? Has no one condemned you?"

11 "No one, Lord,"^A she answered.

"Neither do I condemn you," said Jesus. "Go, and from now on do not sin anymore."]

THE LIGHT OF THE WORLD

12 Jesus spoke to them again: "I am the light of the world. Anyone who follows me will never walk in the darkness but will have the light of life."

13 So the Pharisees said to him, "You are testifying about yourself. Your testimony is not valid."

14 "Even if I testify about myself," Jesus replied, "My testimony is true, because I know where I came from and where I'm going. But you don't know where I come from or where I'm going. 15 You judge by human standards.^B I judge no one. 16 And if I do judge, my judgment is true, because it is not I alone who judge, but I and the Father who sent me. 17 Even in your law it is written that the testimony of two witnesses is true. 18 I am the one who testifies about myself, and the Father who sent me testifies about me."

19 Then they asked him, "Where is your Father?"

"You know neither me nor my Father," Jesus answered. "If you knew me, you would also know my Father." 20 He spoke these words by the treasury, while teaching in the temple. But no one seized him, because his hour had not yet come.

JESUS PREDICTS HIS DEPARTURE

21 Then he said to them again, "I'm going away; you will look for me, and you will die in your sin. Where I'm going, you cannot come."

22 So the Jews said again, "He won't kill himself, will he, since he says, 'Where I'm going, you cannot come'?"

---

^A8:11 Or Sir; Jn 4:15,49; 5:7; 6:34; 9:36 ^B8:15 Lit You judge according to the flesh

THERE IS GRACE

JOHN 7:53–8:59; MARK 2:15-17; ROMANS 8:1-6

"Go, and from now on do not sin anymore" (Jn 8:11).

We're familiar with the charge. But do you remember the beginning of the story? The way the Pharisees brought the adulterous woman before Jesus, a human pawn in their attempted power play?

She was guilty. There was no question. She had been caught in the act.

Oh, the emotions she must have felt. She was already considered "less than" in her world simply by virtue of being a woman. But now she had been found committing a despicable sin and dragged by the religious leaders themselves to stand before the man who called Himself the Son of God.

Guilt.
Humiliation.
Shame.
Staggering fear.

When I close my eyes, I can see her there. Her eyes focused on the ground in front of her feet, unable to look this so-called Messiah in the face. Could what they've said about Him be true? She listened as her accusers made public her secret sin, cringing at the judgment in their tone, flinching at every move for fear a stone might fly.

She waited for the inevitable. And then she saw His hand.

He started writing, right there in the sand, and suddenly everything changed.

"Are you without sin?" He asked those gathered around. "Then go ahead; throw your stones" (Jn 8:7).

Nothing. No one dared move. And so He did it again. He wrote more words there on the ground as His unanswered question hung in the air. But this time, they fled. One at a time, they walked away. Her accusers vanished, and she was left standing face to face with Jesus.

"Neither do I condemn you" (Jn 8:11).

Oh, that phrase, it makes my heart skip a beat! She was absolutely guilty, a sinner with no defense. And yet the sinless Savior looked at her—like He looks at me and you—and said there is grace even for this.

There is grace because our God is both perfectly just and perfectly merciful.
He doesn't merely forgo the punishment due our sin—that wouldn't be true justice. He takes our punishment on Himself. He doesn't simply pity our situation—that would not be true mercy. He receives us as we are and heals us with His love.

Do you come to Jesus in guilt today? In sin and humiliation? Does your chest tighten at the sound of the Accuser in your ear, whispering quietly your secret sin or shouting loudly your deepest shame? Call on the name of Jesus. Let His grace be your defense.

Galatians 5:1 says, "For freedom, Christ set us free. Stand firm then and don't submit again to a yoke of slavery." Or, in the words of our dear Savior, "Go, and from now on do not sin anymore."

It's just you and Him now. The pious have all fled. Receive and walk in His forgiveness today.

23 "You are from below," he told them, "I am from above. You are of this world; I am not of this world. 24 Therefore I told you that you will die in your sins. For if you do not believe that I am he, you will die in your sins."

25 "Who are you?" they questioned.

"Exactly what I've been telling you from the very beginning," Jesus told them. 26 "I have many things to say and to judge about you, but the one who sent me is true, and what I have heard from him — these things I tell the world."

27 They did not know he was speaking to them about the Father. 28 So Jesus said to them, "When you lift up the Son of Man, then you will know that I am he, and that I do nothing on my own. But just as the Father taught me, I say these things. 29 The one who sent me is with me. He has not left me alone, because I always do what pleases him."

TRUTH AND FREEDOM

30 As he was saying these things, many believed in him.

31 Then Jesus said to the Jews who had believed him, "If you continue in my word,^A you really are my disciples. 32 You will know the truth, and the truth will set you free."

33 "We are descendants^B of Abraham," they answered him, "and we have never been enslaved to anyone. How can you say, 'You will become free'?"

34 Jesus responded, "Truly I tell you, everyone who commits sin is a slave of sin. 35 A slave does not remain in the household forever, but a son does remain forever. 36 So if the Son sets you free, you really will be free. 37 I know you are descendants of Abraham, but you are trying to kill me because my word has no place among you. 38 I speak what I have seen in the presence of the Father;^C so then, you do what you have heard from your father."

39 "Our father is Abraham," they replied.

"If you were Abraham's children," Jesus told them, "you would do what Abraham did. 40 But now you are trying to kill me, a man who has told you the truth that I heard from God. Abraham did not do this. 41 You're doing what your father does."

"We weren't born of sexual immorality," they said. "We have one Father — God."

42 Jesus said to them, "If God were your Father, you would love me, because I came from God and I am here. For I didn't come on my own, but he sent me. 43 Why don't you understand what I say? Because you cannot listen to^D my word. 44 You are of your father the devil, and you want to carry out your father's desires. He was a murderer from the beginning and does not stand in the truth, because there is no truth in him. When he tells a lie, he speaks from his own nature,^E because he is a liar and the father of lies. 45 Yet because I tell the truth, you do not believe me. 46 Who among you can convict me of sin? If I am telling the truth, why don't you believe me? 47 The one who is from God listens to God's words. This is why you don't listen, because you are not from God."

^A8:31 Or my teaching, or my message, also in v. 37 ^B8:33 Or offspring; lit seed, also in v. 37; Jn 7:42 ^C8:38 Other mss read of my Father ^D8:43 Or cannot hear ^E8:44 Lit from his own things

JESUS AND ABRAHAM

⁴⁸ The Jews responded to him, "Aren't we right in saying that you're a Samaritan and have a demon?"

⁴⁹ "I do not have a demon," Jesus answered. "On the contrary, I honor my Father and you dishonor me. ⁵⁰ I do not seek my own glory; there is one who seeks it and judges. ⁵¹ Truly I tell you, if anyone keeps my word, he will never see death."

⁵² Then the Jews said, "Now we know you have a demon. Abraham died and so did the prophets. You say, 'If anyone keeps my word, he will never taste death.' ⁵³ Are you greater than our father Abraham who died? And the prophets died. Who do you claim to be?"

⁵⁴ "If I glorify myself," Jesus answered, "my glory is nothing. My Father — about whom you say, 'He is our God' — he is the one who glorifies me. ⁵⁵ You do not know him, but I know him. If I were to say I don't know him, I would be a liar like you. But I do know him, and I keep his word. ⁵⁶ Your father Abraham rejoiced to see my day; he saw it and was glad."

⁵⁷ The Jews replied, "You aren't fifty years old yet, and you've seen Abraham?"^A

⁵⁸ Jesus said to them, "Truly I tell you, before Abraham was, I am."

⁵⁹ So they picked up stones to throw at him. But Jesus was hidden^B and went out of the temple.^C

THE SIXTH SIGN: HEALING A MAN BORN BLIND

9 As he was passing by, he saw a man blind from birth. ² His disciples asked him: "Rabbi, who sinned, this man or his parents, that he was born blind?"

³ "Neither this man nor his parents sinned," Jesus answered. "This came about so that God's works might be displayed in him. ⁴ We^D must do the works of him who sent me^E while it is day. Night is coming when no one can work. ⁵ As long as I am in the world, I am the light of the world."

⁶ After he said these things he spit on the ground, made some mud from the saliva, and spread the mud on his eyes. ⁷ "Go," he told him, "wash in the pool of Siloam" (which means "Sent"). So he left, washed, and came back seeing.

⁸ His neighbors and those who had seen him before as a beggar said, "Isn't this the one who used to sit begging?" ⁹ Some said, "He's the one." Others were saying, "No, but he looks like him."

He kept saying, "I'm the one."

¹⁰ So they asked him, "Then how were your eyes opened?"

¹¹ He answered, "The man called Jesus made mud, spread it on my eyes, and told me, 'Go to Siloam and wash.' So when I went and washed I received my sight."

¹² "Where is he?" they asked.

"I don't know," he said.

---

^A 8:57 Other mss read *and Abraham has seen you?* ^B 8:59 Or *Jesus hid himself*
^C 8:59 Other mss add *and having gone through their midst, he passed by*
^D 9:4 Other mss read *I* ^E 9:4 Other mss read *us*

THE HEALED MAN'S TESTIMONY

¹³ They brought the man who used to be blind to the Pharisees. ¹⁴ The day that Jesus made the mud and opened his eyes was a Sabbath. ¹⁵ Then the Pharisees asked him again how he received his sight.

"He put mud on my eyes," he told them. "I washed and I can see."

¹⁶ Some of the Pharisees said, "This man is not from God, because he doesn't keep the Sabbath." But others were saying, "How can a sinful man perform such signs?" And there was a division among them.

¹⁷ Again they asked the blind man, "What do you say about him, since he opened your eyes?"

"He's a prophet," he said.

¹⁸ The Jews did not believe this about him — that he was blind and received sight — until they summoned the parents of the one who had received his sight.

¹⁹ They asked them, "Is this your son, the one you say was born blind? How then does he now see?"

²⁰ "We know this is our son and that he was born blind," his parents answered. ²¹ "But we don't know how he now sees, and we don't know who opened his eyes. Ask him; he's of age. He will speak for himself." ²² His parents said these things because they were afraid of the Jews, since the Jews had already agreed that if anyone confessed him as the Messiah, he would be banned from the synagogue. ²³ This is why his parents said, "He's of age; ask him."

²⁴ So a second time they summoned the man who had been blind and told him, "Give glory to God. We know that this man is a sinner."

²⁵ He answered, "Whether or not he's a sinner, I don't know. One thing I do know: I was blind, and now I can see!"

²⁶ Then they asked him, "What did he do to you? How did he open your eyes?"

²⁷ "I already told you," he said, "and you didn't listen. Why do you want to hear it again? You don't want to become his disciples too, do you?"

²⁸ They ridiculed him: "You're that man's disciple, but we're Moses's disciples. ²⁹ We know that God has spoken to Moses. But this man — we don't know where he's from."

³⁰ "This is an amazing thing!" the man told them. "You don't know where he is from, and yet he opened my eyes. ³¹ We know that God doesn't listen to sinners, but if anyone is God-fearing and does his will, he listens to him. ³² Throughout history^A no one has ever heard of someone opening the eyes of a person born blind. ³³ If this man were not from God, he wouldn't be able to do anything."

³⁴ "You were born entirely in sin," they replied, "and are you trying to teach us?" Then they threw him out.

SPIRITUAL BLINDNESS

³⁵ Jesus heard that they had thrown the man out, and when he found him, he asked, "Do you believe in the Son of Man?"^B

³⁶ "Who is he, Sir, that I may believe in him?" he asked.

³⁷ Jesus answered, "You have seen him; in fact, he is the one speaking with you."

---

^A 9:32 Lit *From the age* ^B 9:35 Other mss read *the Son of God*

³⁸ "I believe, Lord!" he said, and he worshiped him.

³⁹ Jesus said, "I came into this world for judgment, in order that those who do not see will see and those who do see will become blind."

⁴⁰ Some of the Pharisees who were with him heard these things and asked him, "We aren't blind too, are we?"

⁴¹ "If you were blind," Jesus told them, "you wouldn't have sin. But now that you say, 'We see,' your sin remains.

THE GOOD SHEPHERD

10 "Truly I tell you, anyone who doesn't enter the sheep pen by the gate but climbs in some other way is a thief and a robber. ² The one who enters by the gate is the shepherd of the sheep. ³ The gatekeeper opens it for him, and the sheep hear his voice. He calls his own sheep by name and leads them out. ⁴ When he has brought all his own outside, he goes ahead of them. The sheep follow him because they know his voice. ⁵ They will never follow a stranger; instead they will run away from him, because they don't know the voice of strangers." ⁶ Jesus gave them this figure of speech, but they did not understand what he was telling them.

⁷ Jesus said again, "Truly I tell you, I am the gate for the sheep. ⁸ All who came before meᴬ are thieves and robbers, but the sheep didn't listen to them. ⁹ I am the gate. If anyone enters by me, he will be saved and will come in and go out and find pasture. ¹⁰ A thief comes only to steal and kill and destroy. I have come so that they may have life and have it in abundance.

¹¹ "I am the good shepherd. The good shepherd lays down his life for the sheep. ¹² The hired hand, since he is not the shepherd and doesn't own the sheep, leaves themᴮ and runs away when he sees a wolf coming. The wolf then snatches and scatters them. ¹³ This happens because he is a hired hand and doesn't care about the sheep.

¹⁴ "I am the good shepherd. I know my own, and my own know me, ¹⁵ just as the Father knows me, and I know the Father. I lay down my life for the sheep. ¹⁶ But I have other sheep that are not from this sheep pen; I must bring them also, and they will listen to my voice. Then there will be one flock, one shepherd. ¹⁷ This is why the Father loves me, because I lay down my life so that I may take it up again. ¹⁸ No one takes it from me, but I lay it down on my own. I have the right to lay it down, and I have the right to take it up again. I have received this command from my Father."

¹⁹ Again the Jews were divided because of these words. ²⁰ Many of them were saying, "He has a demon and he's crazy. Why do you listen to him?" ²¹ Others were saying, "These aren't the words of someone who is demon-possessed. Can a demon open the eyes of the blind?"

JESUS AT THE FESTIVAL OF DEDICATION

²² Then the Festival of Dedication took place in Jerusalem, and it was winter. ²³ Jesus was walking in the temple in Solomon's Colonnade. ²⁴ The Jews surrounded him and asked, "How long are you going to keep us in suspense?ᶜ If you are the Messiah, tell us plainly."ᴰ

ᴬ10:8 Other mss omit *before me*   ᴮ10:12 Lit *leaves the sheep*   ᶜ10:24 Lit *"How long are you taking away our life?*   ᴰ10:24 Or *openly,* or *publicly*

[25] "I did tell you and you don't believe," Jesus answered them. "The works that I do in my Father's name testify about me. [26] But you don't believe because you are not of my sheep.[A] [27] My sheep hear my voice, I know them, and they follow me. [28] I give them eternal life, and they will never perish. No one will snatch them out of my hand. [29] My Father, who has given them to me, is greater than all. No one is able to snatch them out of the Father's hand. [30] I and the Father are one."

RENEWED EFFORTS TO STONE JESUS

[31] Again the Jews picked up rocks to stone him.

[32] Jesus replied, "I have shown you many good works from the Father. For which of these works are you stoning me?"

[33] "We aren't stoning you for a good work," the Jews answered, "but for blasphemy, because you — being a man — make yourself God."

[34] Jesus answered them, "Isn't it written in your law,[B] **I said, you are gods?**[C] [35] If he called those whom the word of God came to 'gods' — and the Scripture cannot be broken — [36] do you say, 'You are blaspheming' to the one the Father set apart and sent into the world, because I said: I am the Son of God? [37] If I am not doing my Father's works, don't believe me. [38] But if I am doing them and you don't believe me, believe the works. This way you will know and understand[D] that the Father is in me and I in the Father." [39] Then they were trying again to seize him, but he eluded their grasp.

MANY BEYOND THE JORDAN BELIEVE IN JESUS

[40] So he departed again across the Jordan to the place where John had been baptizing earlier, and he remained there. [41] Many came to him and said, "John never did a sign, but everything John said about this man was true." [42] And many believed in him there.

LAZARUS DIES AT BETHANY

11 Now a man was sick, Lazarus from Bethany, the village of Mary and her sister Martha. [2] Mary was the one who anointed the Lord with perfume and wiped his feet with her hair, and it was her brother Lazarus who was sick. [3] So the sisters sent a message to him: "Lord, the one you love is sick."

[4] When Jesus heard it, he said, "This sickness will not end in death but is for the glory of God, so that the Son of God may be glorified through it." [5] Now Jesus loved Martha, her sister, and Lazarus. [6] So when he heard that he was sick, he stayed two more days in the place where he was. [7] Then after that, he said to the disciples, "Let's go to Judea again."

[8] "Rabbi," the disciples told him, "just now the Jews tried to stone you, and you're going there again?"

[9] "Aren't there twelve hours in a day?" Jesus answered. "If anyone walks during the day, he doesn't stumble, because he sees the light of this world. [10] But if anyone walks during the night, he does stumble, because the light is not in him."

[11] He said this, and then he told them, "Our friend Lazarus has fallen asleep, but I'm on my way to wake him up."

[A]10:26 Other mss add *just as I told you*   [B]10:34 Other mss read *in the scripture*
[C]10:34 Ps 82:6   [D]10:38 Other mss read *know and believe*

¹²Then the disciples said to him, "Lord, if he has fallen asleep, he will get well." ¹³Jesus, however, was speaking about his death, but they thought he was speaking about natural sleep. ¹⁴So Jesus then told them plainly, "Lazarus has died. ¹⁵I'm glad for you that I wasn't there so that you may believe. But let's go to him."

¹⁶Then Thomas (called "Twin"ᴬ) said to his fellow disciples, "Let's go too so that we may die with him."

THE RESURRECTION AND THE LIFE

¹⁷When Jesus arrived, he found that Lazarus had already been in the tomb four days. ¹⁸Bethany was near Jerusalem (less than two milesᴮ away). ¹⁹Many of the Jews had come to Martha and Mary to comfort them about their brother.

²⁰As soon as Martha heard that Jesus was coming, she went to meet him, but Mary remained seated in the house. ²¹Then Martha said to Jesus, "Lord, if you had been here, my brother wouldn't have died. ²²Yet even now I know that whatever you ask from God, God will give you."

²³"Your brother will rise again," Jesus told her.

²⁴Martha said to him, "I know that he will rise again in the resurrection at the last day."

²⁵Jesus said to her, "I am the resurrection and the life. The one who believes in me, even if he dies, will live. ²⁶Everyone who lives and believes in me will never die. Do you believe this?"

²⁷"Yes, Lord," she told him, "I believe you are the Messiah, the Son of God, who comes into the world."

JESUS SHARES THE SORROW OF DEATH

²⁸Having said this, she went back and called her sister Mary, saying in private, "The Teacher is here and is calling for you."

²⁹As soon as Mary heard this, she got up quickly and went to him. ³⁰Jesus had not yet come into the village but was still in the place where Martha had met him. ³¹The Jews who were with her in the house consoling her saw that Mary got up quickly and went out. They followed her, supposing that she was going to the tomb to cry there.

³²As soon as Mary came to where Jesus was and saw him, she fell at his feet and told him, "Lord, if you had been here, my brother would not have died!"

³³When Jesus saw her crying, and the Jews who had come with her crying, he was deeply movedᶜ in his spirit and troubled. ³⁴"Where have you put him?" he asked.

"Lord," they told him, "come and see."

³⁵Jesus wept.

³⁶So the Jews said, "See how he loved him!" ³⁷But some of them said, "Couldn't he who opened the blind man's eyes also have kept this man from dying?"

THE SEVENTH SIGN: RAISING LAZARUS FROM THE DEAD

³⁸Then Jesus, deeply moved again, came to the tomb. It was a cave, and a stone was lying against it. ³⁹"Remove the stone," Jesus said.

ᴬ11:16 Gk Didymus ᴮ11:18 Lit fifteen stadia; one stadion = 600 feet ᶜ11:33 Or angry, also in v. 38

Martha, the dead man's sister, told him, "Lord, there is already a stench because he has been dead four days."

⁴⁰ Jesus said to her, "Didn't I tell you that if you believed you would see the glory of God?"

⁴¹ So they removed the stone. Then Jesus raised his eyes and said, "Father, I thank you that you heard me. ⁴² I know that you always hear me, but because of the crowd standing here I said this, so that they may believe you sent me." ⁴³ After he said this, he shouted with a loud voice, "Lazarus, come out!" ⁴⁴ The dead man came out bound hand and foot with linen strips and with his face wrapped in a cloth. Jesus said to them, "Unwrap him and let him go."

THE PLOT TO KILL JESUS

⁴⁵ Therefore, many of the Jews who came to Mary and saw what he did believed in him. ⁴⁶ But some of them went to the Pharisees and told them what Jesus had done.

⁴⁷ So the chief priests and the Pharisees convened the Sanhedrin and were saying, "What are we going to do since this man is doing many signs? ⁴⁸ If we let him go on like this, everyone will believe in him, and the Romans will come and take away both our place and our nation."

⁴⁹ One of them, Caiaphas, who was high priest that year, said to them, "You know nothing at all! ⁵⁰ You're not considering that it is to your^A advantage that one man should die for the people rather than the whole nation perish." ⁵¹ He did not say this on his own, but being high priest that year he prophesied that Jesus was going to die for the nation, ⁵² and not for the nation only, but also to unite the scattered children of God. ⁵³ So from that day on they plotted to kill him.

⁵⁴ Jesus therefore no longer walked openly among the Jews but departed from there to the countryside near the wilderness, to a town called Ephraim, and he stayed there with the disciples.

⁵⁵ Now the Jewish Passover was near, and many went up to Jerusalem from the country to purify themselves before the Passover. ⁵⁶ They were looking for Jesus and asking one another as they stood in the temple: "What do you think? He won't come to the festival, will he?" ⁵⁷ The chief priests and the Pharisees had given orders that if anyone knew where he was, he should report it so that they could arrest him.

THE ANOINTING AT BETHANY

12 Six days before the Passover, Jesus came to Bethany where Lazarus^B was, the one Jesus had raised from the dead. ² So they gave a dinner for him there; Martha was serving them, and Lazarus was one of those reclining at the table with him. ³ Then Mary took a pound of perfume, pure and expensive nard, anointed Jesus's feet, and wiped his feet with her hair. So the house was filled with the fragrance of the perfume.

⁴ Then one of his disciples, Judas Iscariot (who was about to betray him), said, ⁵ "Why wasn't this perfume sold for three hundred denarii^C and given to the poor?" ⁶ He didn't say this because he cared about the poor but

---

^A 11:50 Other mss read *to our* ^B 12:1 Other mss read *Lazarus who died*
^C 12:5 A denarius = one day's wage

because he was a thief. He was in charge of the money-bag and would steal part of what was put in it.

⁷ Jesus answered, "Leave her alone; she has kept it for the day of my burial. ⁸ For you always have the poor with you, but you do not always have me."

THE DECISION TO KILL LAZARUS

⁹ Then a large crowd of the Jews learned he was there. They came not only because of Jesus but also to see Lazarus, the one he had raised from the dead. ¹⁰ But the chief priests had decided to kill Lazarus also, ¹¹ because he was the reason many of the Jews were deserting them ᴬ and believing in Jesus.

THE TRIUMPHAL ENTRY

¹² The next day, when the large crowd that had come to the festival heard that Jesus was coming to Jerusalem, ¹³ they took palm branches and went out to meet him. They kept shouting:

> "*Hosanna!*
>
> **Blessed is he who comes in the name of the Lord** ᴮ — the King of Israel!"

¹⁴ Jesus found a young donkey and sat on it, just as it is written:

> ¹⁵   **Do not be afraid,**
>
> **Daughter Zion. Look, your King is coming,**
>
> **sitting on a donkey's colt.** ᶜ

¹⁶ His disciples did not understand these things at first. However, when Jesus was glorified, then they remembered that these things had been written about him and that they had done these things to him.

¹⁷ Meanwhile, the crowd, which had been with him when he called Lazarus out of the tomb and raised him from the dead, continued to testify. ᴰ ¹⁸ This is also why the crowd met him, because they heard he had done this sign. ¹⁹ Then the Pharisees said to one another, "You see? You've accomplished nothing. Look, the world has gone after him!"

JESUS PREDICTS HIS CRUCIFIXION

²⁰ Now some Greeks were among those who went up to worship at the festival. ²¹ So they came to Philip, who was from Bethsaida in Galilee, and requested of him, "Sir, we want to see Jesus." ²² Philip went and told Andrew; then Andrew and Philip went and told Jesus.

²³ Jesus replied to them, "The hour has come for the Son of Man to be glorified. ²⁴ Truly I tell you, unless a grain of wheat falls to the ground and dies, it remains by itself. But if it dies, it produces much fruit. ²⁵ The one who loves his life will lose it, and the one who hates his life in this world will keep it for eternal life. ²⁶ If anyone serves me, he must follow me. Where I am, there my servant also will be. If anyone serves me, the Father will honor him.

²⁷ "Now my soul is troubled. What should I say — Father, save me from this hour? But that is why I came to this hour. ²⁸ Father, glorify your name." ᴱ

Then a voice came from heaven: "I have glorified it, and I will glorify it again."

ᴬ 12:11 Lit *going away*   ᴮ 12:13 Ps 118:25-26   ᶜ 12:15 Zch 9:9   ᴰ 12:17 Other mss read *Meanwhile the crowd, which had been with him, continued to testify that he had called Lazarus out of the tomb and raised him from the dead.*
ᴱ 12:28 Other mss read *your Son*

29 The crowd standing there heard it and said it was thunder. Others said, "An angel has spoken to him."

30 Jesus responded, "This voice came, not for me, but for you. 31 Now is the judgment of this world. Now the ruler of this world will be cast out. 32 As for me, if I am lifted up^A from the earth I will draw all people to myself." 33 He said this to indicate what kind of death he was about to die.

34 Then the crowd replied to him, "We have heard from the law that the Messiah will remain forever. So how can you say, 'The Son of Man must be lifted up'? Who is this Son of Man?"

35 Jesus answered, "The light will be with you only a little longer. Walk while you have the light so that darkness doesn't overtake you. The one who walks in darkness doesn't know where he's going. 36 While you have the light, believe in the light so that you may become children of light." Jesus said this, then went away and hid from them.

ISAIAH'S PROPHECIES FULFILLED

37 Even though he had performed so many signs in their presence, they did not believe in him. 38 This was to fulfill the word of Isaiah the prophet, who said:^B

> **Lord, who has believed our message?**
> **And to whom has the arm of the Lord been revealed?**^C

39 This is why they were unable to believe, because Isaiah also said:

40   **He has blinded their eyes**
   and hardened their hearts,
   so that they would not see with their eyes
   or understand with their hearts,
   and turn,
   and I would heal them.^D

41 Isaiah said these things because^E he saw his glory and spoke about him.

42 Nevertheless, many did believe in him even among the rulers, but because of the Pharisees they did not confess him, so that they would not be banned from the synagogue. 43 For they loved human praise more than praise from God.

A SUMMARY OF JESUS'S MISSION

44 Jesus cried out, "The one who believes in me believes not in me, but in him who sent me. 45 And the one who sees me sees him who sent me. 46 I have come as light into the world, so that everyone who believes in me would not remain in darkness. 47 If anyone hears my words and doesn't keep them, I do not judge him; for I did not come to judge the world but to save the world. 48 The one who rejects me and doesn't receive my sayings has this as his judge:^F The word I have spoken will judge him on the last day. 49 For I have not spoken on my own, but the Father himself who sent me has given me a command to say everything I have said. 50 I know that his command is eternal life. So the things that I speak, I speak just as the Father has told me."

---

^A12:32 Or *exalted*, also in v. 34   ^B12:38 Lit *which he said*   ^C12:38 Is 53:1
^D12:40 Is 6:10   ^E12:41 Other mss read *when*   ^F12:48 Lit *has the one judging him*

JESUS WASHES HIS DISCIPLES' FEET

13 Before the Passover Festival, Jesus knew that his hour had come to depart from this world to the Father. Having loved his own who were in the world, he loved them to the end.

2 Now when it was time for supper, the devil had already put it into the heart of Judas, Simon Iscariot's son,^A to betray him. 3 Jesus knew that the Father had given everything into his hands, that he had come from God, and that he was going back to God. 4 So he got up from supper, laid aside his outer clothing, took a towel, and tied it around himself. 5 Next, he poured water into a basin and began to wash his disciples' feet and to dry them with the towel tied around him.

6 He came to Simon Peter, who asked him, "Lord, are you going to wash my feet?"

7 Jesus answered him, "What I'm doing you don't realize now, but afterward you will understand."

8 "You will never wash my feet," Peter said.

Jesus replied, "If I don't wash you, you have no part with me."

9 Simon Peter said to him, "Lord, not only my feet, but also my hands and my head."

10 "One who has bathed," Jesus told him, "doesn't need to wash anything except his feet, but he is completely clean. You are clean, but not all of you." 11 For he knew who would betray him. This is why he said, "Not all of you are clean."

THE MEANING OF FOOT WASHING

12 When Jesus had washed their feet and put on his outer clothing, he reclined again and said to them, "Do you know what I have done for you? 13 You call me Teacher and Lord — and you are speaking rightly, since that is what I am. 14 So if I, your Lord and Teacher, have washed your feet, you also ought to wash one another's feet. 15 For I have given you an example, that you also should do just as I have done for you.

16 "Truly I tell you, a servant is not greater than his master,^B and a messenger is not greater than the one who sent him. 17 If you know these things, you are blessed if you do them.

18 "I'm not speaking about all of you; I know those I have chosen. But the Scripture must be fulfilled: **The one who eats my bread**^C **has raised his heel against me.**^D 19 I am telling you now before it happens, so that when it does happen you will believe that I am he. 20 Truly I tell you, whoever receives anyone I send receives me, and the one who receives me receives him who sent me."

JUDAS'S BETRAYAL PREDICTED

21 When Jesus had said this, he was troubled in his spirit and testified, "Truly I tell you, one of you will betray me."

22 The disciples started looking at one another — uncertain which one he was speaking about. 23 One of his disciples, the one Jesus loved, was

---

^A 13:2 Or *Judas Iscariot, Simon's son*   ^B 13:16 Or *lord*   ^C 13:18 Other mss read *eats bread with me*   ^D 13:18 Ps 41:9

THE TRUE JESUS

JOHN 13; ISAIAH 53

I've heard it said that suffering reveals the real you. What comes out of our mouths when life squeezes us in its vise grip is the stuff we're really made of.

At the Last Supper, we find Jesus in the tightest situation imaginable. He knows unthinkable suffering is right around the corner. Since His disciples are still presuming He is going to lead a government takeover, it's a burden He must carry alone. Jesus knows there will be no military coup. He will secure the kingdom victory, but through suffering—not conquest.

In that crucible of suffering, the real Jesus shines through. We don't catch one hint of self-pity or bitterness in His words or actions. He would soon be poured out on our behalf, yet Jesus remained faithful to who He is and what He came to do.

He never stopped teaching. Using bread and wine for an object lesson of cosmic consequences, Jesus taught truths in advance that His disciples would not grasp until He was gone (Jn 12:16). As modern Christ followers, we have access to this Upper Room as a classroom. We're able to wrestle with the lessons of His atoning sacrifice every time we come to take communion.

He never stopped serving. Knowing that within hours His own body would be nailed to a tree, Jesus took the time to wash His disciples' feet. "So if I, your Lord and Teacher, have washed your feet, you also ought to wash one another's feet. For I have given you an example, that you also should do just as I have done for you" (Jn 13:14-15). This moment wasn't mere ritual. Jesus was showing them how to care for one another after He departed.

He never stopped loving. When I study the Last Supper, I am most grateful for this truth: "Having loved his own who were in the world, he loved them to the end" (Jn 13:1). To the end. Our Savior never stopped loving the undeserving, helpless sinners He came to die for. He never chose hatred or contempt. He didn't shame or ostracize Judas, the one who would sell Him out for a few silver coins. Instead of pointing His finger at him, Jesus offered him bread.

When hard-pressed on every side, Jesus never resented the sacrifice He chose to make on our behalf. It was in His suffering that our Savior displayed His true strength.

"But he was pierced because of our rebellion, crushed because of our iniquities; punishment for our peace was on him, and we are healed by his wounds."

ISAIAH 53:5

---

reclining close beside Jesus.[A] 24 Simon Peter motioned to him to find out who it was he was talking about. 25 So he leaned back against Jesus and asked him, "Lord, who is it?"

26 Jesus replied, "He's the one I give the piece of bread to after I have dipped it." When he had dipped the bread, he gave it to Judas, Simon Iscariot's son.[B] 27 After Judas ate the piece of bread, Satan entered him. So Jesus told him, "What you're doing, do quickly."

28 None of those reclining at the table knew why he said this to him. 29 Since Judas kept the money-bag, some thought that Jesus was telling him, "Buy what we need for the festival," or that he should give something to the poor. 30 After receiving the piece of bread, he immediately left. And it was night.

THE NEW COMMAND

31 When he had left, Jesus said, "Now the Son of Man is glorified, and God is glorified in him. 32 If God is glorified in him,[C] God will also glorify him in himself and will glorify him at once. 33 Children, I am with you a little while longer. You will look for me, and just as I told the Jews, so now I tell you: 'Where I am going, you cannot come.'

34 "I give you a new command: Love one another. Just as I have loved you, you are also to love one another. 35 By this everyone will know that you are my disciples, if you love one another."

PETER'S DENIALS PREDICTED

36 "Lord," Simon Peter said to him, "where are you going?"

Jesus answered, "Where I am going you cannot follow me now, but you will follow later."

37 "Lord," Peter asked, "why can't I follow you now? I will lay down my life for you."

38 Jesus replied, "Will you lay down your life for me? Truly I tell you, a rooster will not crow until you have denied me three times.

THE WAY TO THE FATHER

14 "Don't let your heart be troubled. Believe[D] in God; believe also in me. 2 In my Father's house are many rooms; if not, I would have told you. I am going away to prepare a place for you. 3 If I go away and prepare a place for you, I will come again and take you to myself, so that where I am you may be also. 4 You know the way to where I am going."[E]

5 "Lord," Thomas said, "we don't know where you're going. How can we know the way?"

6 Jesus told him, "I am the way, the truth, and the life. No one comes to the Father except through me. 7 If you know me, you will also know[F] my Father. From now on you do know him and have seen him."

[A]13:23 Lit reclining at Jesus's breast; that is, on his right; Jn 1:18
[B]13:26 Or Judas Iscariot, Simon's son   [C]13:32 Other mss omit If God is glorified in him   [D]14:1 Or You believe   [E]14:4 Other mss read this verse: And you know where I am going, and you know the way   [F]14:7 Other mss read If you had known me, you would have known

JESUS REVEALS THE FATHER

[8] "Lord," said Philip, "show us the Father, and that's enough for us."

[9] Jesus said to him, "Have I been among you all this time and you do not know me, Philip? The one who has seen me has seen the Father. How can you say, 'Show us the Father'? [10] Don't you believe that I am in the Father and the Father is in me? The words I speak to you I do not speak on my own. The Father who lives in me does his works. [11] Believe me that I am in the Father and the Father is in me. Otherwise, believe[A] because of the works themselves.

PRAYING IN JESUS'S NAME

[12] "Truly I tell you, the one who believes in me will also do the works that I do. And he will do even greater works than these, because I am going to the Father. [13] Whatever you ask in my name, I will do it so that the Father may be glorified in the Son. [14] If you ask me[B] anything in my name, I will do it.[C]

ANOTHER COUNSELOR PROMISED

[15] "If you love me, you will keep[D] my commands. [16] And I will ask the Father, and he will give you another Counselor[E] to be with you forever. [17] He is the Spirit of truth. The world is unable to receive him because it doesn't see him or know him. But you do know him, because he remains with you and will be[F] in you.

THE FATHER, THE SON, AND THE HOLY SPIRIT

[18] "I will not leave you as orphans; I am coming to you. [19] In a little while the world will no longer see me, but you will see me. Because I live, you will live too. [20] On that day you will know that I am in my Father, you are in me, and I am in you. [21] The one who has my commands and keeps them is the one who loves me. And the one who loves me will be loved by my Father. I also will love him and will reveal myself to him."

[22] Judas (not Iscariot) said to him, "Lord, how is it you're going to reveal yourself to us and not to the world?"

[23] Jesus answered, "If anyone loves me, he will keep my word. My Father will love him, and we will come to him and make our home with him. [24] The one who doesn't love me will not keep my words. The word that you hear is not mine but is from the Father who sent me.

[25] "I have spoken these things to you while I remain with you. [26] But the Counselor, the Holy Spirit, whom the Father will send in my name, will teach you all things and remind you of everything I have told you.

JESUS'S GIFT OF PEACE

[27] "Peace I leave with you. My peace I give to you. I do not give to you as the world gives. Don't let your heart be troubled or fearful. [28] You have heard me tell you, 'I am going away and I am coming to you.' If you loved me, you would rejoice that I am going to the Father, because the Father

---

[A] 14:11 Other mss read *believe me* [B] 14:14 Other mss omit *me* [C] 14:14 Other mss omit all of v. 14 [D] 14:15 Other mss read *"If you love me, keep* (as a command) [E] 14:16 Or *advocate,* or *comforter,* also in v. 26 [F] 14:17 Other mss read *and is* is greater than I. ²⁹ I have told you now before it happens so that when it does happen you may believe. ³⁰ I will not talk with you much longer, because the ruler of the world is coming. He has no power over me.^A ³¹ On the contrary, so that the world may know that I love the Father, I do as the Father commanded me.

"Get up; let's leave this place.

THE VINE AND THE BRANCHES

15 "I am the true vine, and my Father is the gardener. ² Every branch in me that does not produce fruit he removes, and he prunes every branch that produces fruit so that it will produce more fruit. ³ You are already clean because of the word I have spoken to you. ⁴ Remain in me, and I in you. Just as a branch is unable to produce fruit by itself unless it remains on the vine, neither can you unless you remain in me. ⁵ I am the vine; you are the branches. The one who remains in me and I in him produces much fruit, because you can do nothing without me. ⁶ If anyone does not remain in me, he is thrown aside like a branch and he withers. They gather them, throw them into the fire, and they are burned. ⁷ If you remain in me and my words remain in you, ask whatever you want and it will be done for you. ⁸ My Father is glorified by this: that you produce much fruit and prove to be^B my disciples.

CHRISTLIKE LOVE

⁹ "As the Father has loved me, I have also loved you. Remain in my love. ¹⁰ If you keep my commands you will remain in my love, just as I have kept my Father's commands and remain in his love.

¹¹ "I have told you these things so that my joy may be in you and your joy may be complete.

¹² "This is my command: Love one another as I have loved you. ¹³ No one has greater love than this: to lay down his life for his friends. ¹⁴ You are my friends if you do what I command you. ¹⁵ I do not call you servants anymore, because a servant doesn't know what his master^C is doing. I have called you friends, because I have made known to you everything I have heard from my Father. ¹⁶ You did not choose me, but I chose you. I appointed you to go and produce fruit and that your fruit should remain, so that whatever you ask the Father in my name, he will give you.

¹⁷ "This is what I command you: Love one another.

PERSECUTIONS PREDICTED

¹⁸ "If the world hates you, understand that it hated me before it hated you. ¹⁹ If you were of the world, the world would love you as its own. However, because you are not of the world, but I have chosen you out of it, the world hates you. ²⁰ Remember the word I spoke to you: 'A servant is not greater than his master.' If they persecuted me, they will also persecute you. If they kept my word, they will also keep yours. ²¹ But they will do all these things to you on account of my name, because they don't know the one who sent me. ²² If I had not come and spoken to them, they would not be guilty of sin. Now they have no excuse for their sin. ²³ The one who hates me also hates

---

^A14:30 Lit *He has nothing in me*   ^B15:8 Or *and become*   ^C15:15 Or *lord*

REMAIN

JOHN 15

I'm the Queen of Focusing on the Wrong Things.

My daughter makes an amazing piece of eight-year-old art and declares it dedicated to her mom (that's me!)—and I silently lament the sea of paper covering the floor and the glue stick smashed into all the creases of the dining room table.

A long-lost friend says she and her family are coming to visit for a weekend—and I spend more time worrying about the condition of the guest room than rejoicing in the long conversations and late-night laughter to come.

My husband spends hours creating new storage solutions for our mudroom (slash laundry room, slash pantry, slash coat closet, slash place the dog stays during dinner so she won't eat food off our plates)—and I involuntarily scowl that my tired, dirty, three-compartment clothes hamper will no longer fit. (Three compartments! You can understand my sadness.)

And here, in John 15, Jesus says this:

"Remain in me, and I in you. Just as a branch is unable to produce fruit by itself unless it remains on the vine, neither can you unless you remain in me. I am the vine; you are the branches. The one who remains in me and I in him produces much fruit, because you can do nothing without me."

JOHN 15:4-5

But do you know what I hear? I hear, "Bear fruit." Or, to be more specific, "Hey, you, why aren't you bearing fruit?"

I, the Queen of Focusing on the Wrong Things, read Jesus' words and hear all of the goal and none of the grace. I want the end but forget the means.

Yes, bear fruit. Yes, love others. Yes, give grace to a world that will misunderstand and even hate us. But look back through John 15. Jesus is not commanding His disciples to bear fruit. The command is to remain! When we remain—when we abide in the never-ending, unconditional, forever love of Christ—then the fruit will come. But only then.

We bear fruit when, and only when, we are grafted into the True Vine. His Holy Spirit in us is the fruit producer; we are simply the branches who have the privilege of displaying His fruit.

Jesus Christ comes to make us new. He comes to redeem the dead branches that we are and give us abundant life! Remaining in Him—resting, dwelling, abiding in Him—is the only source of our strength, our goodness, our fruit. Let's focus our eyes on the True Vine today. Let's be about the business of remaining in Jesus, and trust His Spirit to be about the business of bearing fruit in our lives.

my Father. ²⁴ If I had not done the works among them that no one else has done, they would not be guilty of sin. Now they have seen and hated both me and my Father. ²⁵ But this happened so that the statement written in their law might be fulfilled: **They hated me for no reason.** ^A

THE COUNSELOR'S MINISTRY

²⁶ "When the Counselor comes, the one I will send to you from the Father — the Spirit of truth who proceeds from the Father — he will testify about me. ²⁷ You also will testify, because you have been with me from the beginning.

16 "I have told you these things to keep you from stumbling. ² They will ban you from the synagogues. In fact, a time is coming when anyone who kills you will think he is offering service to God. ³ They will do these things because they haven't known the Father or me. ⁴ But I have told you these things so that when their time ^B comes you will remember I told them to you. I didn't tell you these things from the beginning, because I was with you. ⁵ But now I am going away to him who sent me, and not one of you asks me, 'Where are you going?' ⁶ Yet, because I have spoken these things to you, sorrow has filled your heart. ⁷ Nevertheless, I am telling you the truth. It is for your benefit that I go away, because if I don't go away the Counselor will not come to you. If I go, I will send him to you. ⁸ When he comes, he will convict the world about sin, righteousness, and judgment: ⁹ About sin, because they do not believe in me; ¹⁰ about righteousness, because I am going to the Father and you will no longer see me; ¹¹ and about judgment, because the ruler of this world has been judged.

¹² "I still have many things to tell you, but you can't bear them now. ¹³ When the Spirit of truth comes, he will guide you into all the truth. For he will not speak on his own, but he will speak whatever he hears. He will also declare to you what is to come. ¹⁴ He will glorify me, because he will take from what is mine and declare it to you. ¹⁵ Everything the Father has is mine. This is why I told you that he takes from what is mine and will declare it to you.

SORROW TURNED TO JOY

¹⁶ "A little while and you will no longer see me; again a little while and you will see me." ^C

¹⁷ Then some of his disciples said to one another, "What is this he's telling us: 'A little while and you will not see me; again a little while and you will see me' and, 'Because I am going to the Father'?" ¹⁸ They said, "What is this he is saying, ^D 'A little while'? We don't know what he's talking about."

¹⁹ Jesus knew they wanted to ask him, and so he said to them, "Are you asking one another about what I said, 'A little while and you will not see me; again a little while and you will see me'? ²⁰ Truly I tell you, you will weep and mourn, but the world will rejoice. You will become sorrowful, but your sorrow will turn to joy. ²¹ When a woman is in labor, she has pain because her time has come. But when she has given birth to a child, she no longer remembers the suffering because of the joy that a person has been born into the

---

^A 15:25 Ps 69:4   ^B 16:4 Other mss read *when the time*   ^C 16:16 Other mss add *because I am going to the Father*   ^D 16:18 Other mss omit *he is saying* world. ²² So you also have sorrow^A now. But I will see you again. Your hearts will rejoice, and no one will take away your joy from you.

²³ "In that day you will not ask me anything. Truly I tell you, anything you ask the Father in my name, he will give you. ²⁴ Until now you have asked for nothing in my name. Ask and you will receive, so that your joy may be complete.

JESUS THE VICTOR

²⁵ "I have spoken these things to you in figures of speech. A time is coming when I will no longer speak to you in figures, but I will tell you plainly about the Father. ²⁶ On that day you will ask in my name, and I am not telling you that I will ask the Father on your behalf. ²⁷ For the Father himself loves you, because you have loved me and have believed that I came from God.^B ²⁸ I came from the Father and have come into the world. Again, I am leaving the world and going to the Father."

²⁹ His disciples said, "Look, now you're speaking plainly and not using any figurative language. ³⁰ Now we know that you know everything and don't need anyone to question you. By this we believe that you came from God."

³¹ Jesus responded to them, "Do you now believe? ³² Indeed, an hour is coming, and has come, when each of you will be scattered to his own home, and you will leave me alone. Yet I am not alone, because the Father is with me. ³³ I have told you these things so that in me you may have peace. You will have suffering in this world. Be courageous! I have conquered the world."

JESUS PRAYS FOR HIMSELF

17 Jesus spoke these things, looked up to heaven, and said: "Father, the hour has come. Glorify your Son so that the Son may glorify you, ² since you gave him authority over all flesh,^C so that he may give eternal life to everyone you have given him. ³ This is eternal life: that they may know you, the only true God, and the one you have sent — Jesus Christ. ⁴ I have glorified you on the earth by completing the work you gave me to do. ⁵ Now, Father, glorify me in your presence with that glory I had with you before the world existed.

JESUS PRAYS FOR HIS DISCIPLES

⁶ "I have revealed your name to the people you gave me from the world. They were yours, you gave them to me, and they have kept your word. ⁷ Now they know that everything you have given me is from you, ⁸ because I have given them the words you gave me. They have received them and have known for certain that I came from you. They have believed that you sent me.

⁹ "I pray^D for them. I am not praying for the world but for those you have given me, because they are yours. ¹⁰ Everything I have is yours, and everything you have is mine, and I am glorified in them. ¹¹ I am no longer in the world, but they are in the world, and I am coming to you. Holy Father, protect^E them by your name that you have given me, so that they may be one as we are one. ¹² While I was with them, I was protecting them by your name

---

^A16:22 Other mss read *will have sorrow* ^B16:27 Other mss read *from the Father*
^C17:2 Or *people* ^D17:9 Lit *ask* (throughout this passage) ^E17:11 Lit *keep*
(throughout this passage)

that you have given me. I guarded them and not one of them is lost, except the son of destruction,^A so that the Scripture may be fulfilled. ¹³ Now I am coming to you, and I speak these things in the world so that they may have my joy completed in them. ¹⁴ I have given them your word. The world hated them because they are not of the world, just as I am not of the world. ¹⁵ I am not praying that you take them out of the world but that you protect them from the evil one. ¹⁶ They are not of the world, just as I am not of the world. ¹⁷ Sanctify them by the truth; your word is truth. ¹⁸ As you sent me into the world, I also have sent them into the world. ¹⁹ I sanctify myself for them, so that they also may be sanctified by the truth.

JESUS PRAYS FOR ALL BELIEVERS

²⁰ "I pray not only for these, but also for those who believe in me through their word. ²¹ May they all be one, as you, Father, are in me and I am in you. May they also be^B in us, so that the world may believe you sent me. ²² I have given them the glory you have given me, so that they may be one as we are one. ²³ I am in them and you are in me, so that they may be made completely one, that the world may know you have sent me and have loved them as you have loved me.

²⁴ "Father, I want those you have given me to be with me where I am, so that they will see my glory, which you have given me because you loved me before the world's foundation. ²⁵ Righteous Father, the world has not known you. However, I have known you, and they have known that you sent me. ²⁶ I made your name known to them and will continue to make it known, so that the love you have loved me with may be in them and I may be in them."

JESUS BETRAYED

18 After Jesus had said these things, he went out with his disciples across the Kidron Valley, where there was a garden, and he and his disciples went into it. ² Judas, who betrayed him, also knew the place, because Jesus often met there with his disciples. ³ So Judas took a company of soldiers and some officials^C from the chief priests and the Pharisees and came there with lanterns, torches, and weapons.

⁴ Then Jesus, knowing everything that was about to happen to him, went out and said to them, "Who is it that you're seeking?"

⁵ "Jesus of Nazareth," they answered.

"I am he," Jesus told them.

Judas, who betrayed him, was also standing with them. ⁶ When Jesus told them, "I am he," they stepped back and fell to the ground.

⁷ Then he asked them again, "Who is it that you're seeking?"

"Jesus of Nazareth," they said.

⁸ "I told you I am he," Jesus replied. "So if you're looking for me, let these men go." ⁹ This was to fulfill the words he had said: "I have not lost one of those you have given me."

¹⁰ Then Simon Peter, who had a sword, drew it, struck the high priest's servant, and cut off his right ear. (The servant's name was Malchus.)

---

^A 17:12 The one destined for destruction, loss, or perdition ^B 17:21 Other mss add *one* ^C 18:3 Or *temple police*, or *officers*, also in vv. 12,18,22

¹¹ At that, Jesus said to Peter, "Put your sword away! Am I not to drink the cup the Father has given me?"

JESUS ARRESTED AND TAKEN TO ANNAS

¹² Then the company of soldiers, the commander, and the Jewish officials arrested Jesus and tied him up. ¹³ First they led him to Annas, since he was the father-in-law of Caiaphas, who was high priest that year. ¹⁴ Caiaphas was the one who had advised the Jews that it would be better for one man to die for the people.

PETER DENIES JESUS

¹⁵ Simon Peter was following Jesus, as was another disciple. That disciple was an acquaintance of the high priest; so he went with Jesus into the high priest's courtyard. ¹⁶ But Peter remained standing outside by the door. So the other disciple, the one known to the high priest, went out and spoke to the girl who was the doorkeeper and brought Peter in.

¹⁷ Then the servant girl who was the doorkeeper said to Peter, "You aren't one of this man's disciples too, are you?"

"I am not," he said. ¹⁸ Now the servants and the officials had made a charcoal fire, because it was cold. They were standing there warming themselves, and Peter was standing with them, warming himself.

JESUS BEFORE ANNAS

¹⁹ The high priest questioned Jesus about his disciples and about his teaching.

²⁰ "I have spoken openly to the world," Jesus answered him. "I have always taught in the synagogue and in the temple, where all the Jews congregate, and I haven't spoken anything in secret. ²¹ Why do you question me? Question those who heard what I told them. Look, they know what I said."

²² When he had said these things, one of the officials standing by slapped Jesus, saying, "Is this the way you answer the high priest?"

²³ "If I have spoken wrongly," Jesus answered him, "give evidence^A about the wrong; but if rightly, why do you hit me?" ²⁴ Then Annas sent him bound to Caiaphas the high priest.

PETER DENIES JESUS TWICE MORE

²⁵ Now Simon Peter was standing and warming himself. They said to him, "You aren't one of his disciples too, are you?"

He denied it and said, "I am not."

²⁶ One of the high priest's servants, a relative of the man whose ear Peter had cut off, said, "Didn't I see you with him in the garden?" ²⁷ Peter denied it again. Immediately a rooster crowed.

JESUS BEFORE PILATE

²⁸ Then they led Jesus from Caiaphas to the governor's headquarters. It was early morning. They did not enter the headquarters themselves; otherwise they would be defiled and unable to eat the Passover.

²⁹ So Pilate came out to them and said, "What charge do you bring against this man?"

---

^A18:23 Or him, "testify

³⁰ They answered him, "If this man weren't a criminal,^A we wouldn't have handed him over to you."

³¹ Pilate told them, "You take him and judge him according to your law."

"It's not legal for us to put anyone to death," the Jews declared. ³² They said this so that Jesus's words might be fulfilled indicating what kind of death he was going to die.

³³ Then Pilate went back into the headquarters, summoned Jesus, and said to him, "Are you the King of the Jews?"

³⁴ Jesus answered, "Are you asking this on your own, or have others told you about me?"

³⁵ "I'm not a Jew, am I?" Pilate replied. "Your own nation and the chief priests handed you over to me. What have you done?"

³⁶ "My kingdom is not of this world," said Jesus. "If my kingdom were of this world, my servants would fight, so that I wouldn't be handed over to the Jews. But as it is,^B my kingdom is not from here."

³⁷ "You are a king then?" Pilate asked.

"You say that I'm a king," Jesus replied. "I was born for this, and I have come into the world for this: to testify to the truth. Everyone who is of the truth listens to my voice."

³⁸ "What is truth?" said Pilate.

JESUS OR BARABBAS

After he had said this, he went out to the Jews again and told them, "I find no grounds for charging him. ³⁹ You have a custom that I release one prisoner to you at the Passover. So, do you want me to release to you the King of the Jews?"

⁴⁰ They shouted back, "Not this man, but Barabbas!" Now Barabbas was a revolutionary.^C

JESUS FLOGGED AND MOCKED

19 Then Pilate took Jesus and had him flogged. ² The soldiers also twisted together a crown of thorns, put it on his head, and clothed him in a purple robe. ³ And they kept coming up to him and saying, "Hail, King of the Jews!" and were slapping his face.

⁴ Pilate went outside again and said to them, "Look, I'm bringing him out to you to let you know I find no grounds for charging him." ⁵ Then Jesus came out wearing the crown of thorns and the purple robe. Pilate said to them, "Here is the man!"

PILATE SENTENCES JESUS TO DEATH

⁶ When the chief priests and the temple servants^D saw him, they shouted, "Crucify! Crucify!"

Pilate responded, "Take him and crucify him yourselves, since I find no grounds for charging him."

⁷ "We have a law," the Jews replied to him, "and according to that law he ought to die, because he made himself the Son of God."

⁸ When Pilate heard this statement, he was more afraid than ever. ⁹ He went back into the headquarters and asked Jesus, "Where are you from?"

---

^A 18:30 Lit *an evil doer*   ^B 18:36 Or *But now*   ^C 18:40 Or *robber*; see Jn 10:1,8 for the same Gk word used here   ^D 19:6 Or *temple police*, or *officers*

But Jesus did not give him an answer. [10] So Pilate said to him, "Do you refuse to speak to me? Don't you know that I have the authority to release you and the authority to crucify you?"

[11] "You would have no authority over me at all," Jesus answered him, "if it hadn't been given you from above. This is why the one who handed me over to you has the greater sin."

[12] From that moment Pilate kept trying[A] to release him. But the Jews shouted, "If you release this man, you are not Caesar's friend. Anyone who makes himself a king opposes Caesar!"

[13] When Pilate heard these words, he brought Jesus outside. He sat down on the judge's seat in a place called the Stone Pavement (but in Aramaic,[B] Gabbatha). [14] It was the preparation day for the Passover, and it was about noon.[C] Then he told the Jews, "Here is your king!"

[15] They shouted, "Take him away! Take him away! Crucify him!"

Pilate said to them, "Should I crucify your king?"

"We have no king but Caesar!" the chief priests answered.

[16] Then he handed him over to be crucified.

THE CRUCIFIXION

Then they took Jesus away.[D] [17] Carrying the cross by himself, he went out to what is called Place of the Skull, which in Aramaic is called *Golgotha*. [18] There they crucified him and two others with him, one on either side, with Jesus in the middle. [19] Pilate also had a sign made and put on the cross. It said: JESUS OF NAZARETH, THE KING OF THE JEWS. [20] Many of the Jews read this sign, because the place where Jesus was crucified was near the city, and it was written in Aramaic, Latin, and Greek. [21] So the chief priests of the Jews said to Pilate, "Don't write, 'The King of the Jews,' but that he said, 'I am the King of the Jews.'"

[22] Pilate replied, "What I have written, I have written."

[23] When the soldiers crucified Jesus, they took his clothes and divided them into four parts, a part for each soldier. They also took the tunic, which was seamless, woven in one piece from the top. [24] So they said to one another, "Let's not tear it, but cast lots for it, to see who gets it." This happened that the Scripture might be fulfilled that says: **They divided my clothes among themselves, and they cast lots for my clothing.**[E] This is what the soldiers did.

JESUS'S PROVISION FOR HIS MOTHER

[25] Standing by the cross of Jesus were his mother, his mother's sister, Mary the wife of Clopas, and Mary Magdalene. [26] When Jesus saw his mother and the disciple he loved standing there, he said to his mother, "Woman, here is your son." [27] Then he said to the disciple, "Here is your mother." And from that hour the disciple took her into his home.

THE FINISHED WORK OF JESUS

[28] After this, when Jesus knew that everything was now finished that the Scripture might be fulfilled, he said, "I'm thirsty." [29] A jar full of sour wine

---

[A] 19:12 Lit *Pilate was trying*   [B] 19:13 Or *Hebrew*, also in vv. 17,20   [C] 19:14 Lit *about the sixth hour*   [D] 19:16 Other mss add *and led him out*   [E] 19:24 Ps 22:18

1835

was sitting there; so they fixed a sponge full of sour wine on a hyssop branch and held it up to his mouth. ³⁰ When Jesus had received the sour wine, he said, "It is finished." Then bowing his head, he gave up his spirit.

JESUS'S SIDE PIERCED

³¹ Since it was the preparation day, the Jews did not want the bodies to remain on the cross on the Sabbath (for that Sabbath was a special ᴬ day). They requested that Pilate have the men's legs broken and that their bodies be taken away. ³² So the soldiers came and broke the legs of the first man and of the other one who had been crucified with him. ³³ When they came to Jesus, they did not break his legs since they saw that he was already dead. ³⁴ But one of the soldiers pierced his side with a spear, and at once blood and water came out. ³⁵ He who saw this has testified so that you also may believe. His testimony is true, and he knows he is telling the truth. ³⁶ For these things happened so that the Scripture would be fulfilled: **Not one of his bones will be broken.** ᴮ ³⁷ Also, another Scripture says: **They will look at the one they pierced.** ᶜ

JESUS'S BURIAL

³⁸ After this, Joseph of Arimathea, who was a disciple of Jesus — but secretly because of his fear of the Jews — asked Pilate that he might remove Jesus's body. Pilate gave him permission; so he came and took his body away. ³⁹ Nicodemus (who had previously come to him at night) also came, bringing a mixture of about seventy-five pounds ᴰ of myrrh and aloes. ⁴⁰ They took Jesus's body and wrapped it in linen cloths with the fragrant spices, according to the burial custom of the Jews. ⁴¹ There was a garden in the place where he was crucified. A new tomb was in the garden; no one had yet been placed in it. ⁴² They placed Jesus there because of the Jewish day of preparation and since the tomb was nearby.

THE EMPTY TOMB

20 On the first day of the week Mary Magdalene came to the tomb early, while it was still dark. She saw that the stone had been removed from the tomb. ² So she went running to Simon Peter and to the other disciple, the one Jesus loved, and said to them, "They've taken the Lord out of the tomb, and we don't know where they've put him!"

³ At that, Peter and the other disciple went out, heading for the tomb. ⁴ The two were running together, but the other disciple outran Peter and got to the tomb first. ⁵ Stooping down, he saw the linen cloths lying there, but he did not go in. ⁶ Then, following him, Simon Peter also came. He entered the tomb and saw the linen cloths lying there. ⁷ The wrapping that had been on his head was not lying with the linen cloths but was folded up in a separate place by itself. ⁸ The other disciple, who had reached the tomb first, then also went in, saw, and believed. ⁹ For they did not yet understand the Scripture that he must rise from the dead. ¹⁰ Then the disciples returned to the place where they were staying.

ᴬ19:31 Lit *great* ᴮ19:36 Ex 12:46; Nm 9:12; Ps 34:20 ᶜ19:37 Zch 12:10
ᴰ19:39 Lit *a hundred litrai*; a Roman *litrai* = 12 ounces

BACK TO THE GARDEN

JOHN 19–20; LUKE 23–24

When Christ was crucified, Mary Magdalene did not leave His side.

She was there when He breathed His last. She was there when He was buried. There is no mention of the disciples as they lay Him in the tomb that day, only "the women who had come with Him from Galilee" (Lk 23:55).

While others were no doubt lost in their sorrow, it was Mary Magdalene who went home to prepare the burial spices. It was Mary who showed up the morning of the third day to apply the ointments. It was Mary who was the first to see Jesus no longer in the grave. As you read of their encounter in John 20, try to imagine what it was like to be in the garden that day, seeking your Lord through your tears.

Mary needed to see Jesus. She needed to find her friend and healer.

How emotional these days of mourning, waiting, and searching must have been for Mary. But you know what? I want this kind of relationship with Christ, this sort of intimacy with the one who saved my soul. Don't you?

The angel at the empty tomb said to her, "Remember how he spoke to you when he was still in Galilee, saying, 'It is necessary that the Son of Man be betrayed into the hands of sinful men, be crucified, and rise on the third day'?" (Lk 24:6-7). And Mary remembered. Because she'd been there, following Jesus, listening to His every word.

Then He appeared, right there where she knelt weeping.

"Mary," Jesus said.

"Rabboni!" she cried (Jn 20:16). It means "teacher" in Aramaic. Her beloved Lord had appeared before her eyes. He was alive!

Sister in Christ, you are no less a daughter, a follower, or a friend of Jesus than Mary Magdalene. **The hope that surged in Mary's heart upon seeing her risen Lord is the same hope offered you by His finished work on the cross and His victory over the grave.**

Jesus gave Mary life when He healed her, and He made that life eternal when He emerged from the tomb. In the garden that day, He secured her rescue—and ours.

C. Austin Miles wrote a hymn about that meeting in the garden, one of my grandmother's favorites:

I come to the garden alone
While the dew is still on the roses
And the voice I hear falling on my ear
The Son of God discloses.
And He walks with me, and He talks with me,
And He tells me I am His own;
And the joy we share as we tarry there,
None other has ever known.

C. AUSTIN MILES, "IN THE GARDEN"

Go to the garden today. Listen for the voice of the risen Christ. Hear Him tell you that you are His own. Because the resurrection is true, you always will be.

MARY MAGDALENE SEES THE RISEN LORD

[11] But Mary stood outside the tomb, crying. As she was crying, she stooped to look into the tomb. [12] She saw two angels in white sitting where Jesus's body had been lying, one at the head and the other at the feet. [13] They said to her, "Woman, why are you crying?"

"Because they've taken away my Lord," she told them, "and I don't know where they've put him."

[14] Having said this, she turned around and saw Jesus standing there, but she did not know it was Jesus. [15] "Woman," Jesus said to her, "why are you crying? Who is it that you're seeking?"

Supposing he was the gardener, she replied, "Sir, if you've carried him away, tell me where you've put him, and I will take him away."

[16] Jesus said to her, "Mary."

Turning around, she said to him in Aramaic,[A] "*Rabboni!*" — which means "Teacher."

[17] "Don't cling to me," Jesus told her, "since I have not yet ascended to the Father. But go to my brothers and tell them that I am ascending to my Father and your Father, to my God and your God."

[18] Mary Magdalene went and announced to the disciples, "I have seen the Lord!" And she told them what[B] he had said to her.

THE DISCIPLES COMMISSIONED

[19] When it was evening of that first day of the week, the disciples were gathered together with the doors locked because they feared the Jews. Jesus came, stood among them, and said to them, "Peace be with you." [20] Having said this, he showed them his hands and his side. So the disciples rejoiced when they saw the Lord. [21] Jesus said to them again, "Peace be with you. As the Father has sent me, I also send you." [22] After saying this, he breathed on them and said,[C] "Receive the Holy Spirit. [23] If you forgive the sins of any, they are forgiven them; if you retain the sins of any, they are retained."

THOMAS SEES AND BELIEVES

[24] But Thomas (called "Twin"[D]), one of the Twelve, was not with them when Jesus came. [25] So the other disciples were telling him, "We've seen the Lord!"

But he said to them, "If I don't see the mark of the nails in his hands, put my finger into the mark of the nails, and put my hand into his side, I will never believe."

[26] A week later his disciples were indoors again, and Thomas was with them. Even though the doors were locked, Jesus came and stood among them and said, "Peace be with you." [27] Then he said to Thomas, "Put your finger here and look at my hands. Reach out your hand and put it into my side. Don't be faithless, but believe." [28] Thomas responded to him, "My Lord and my God!" [29] Jesus said, "Because you have seen me, you have believed.[E] Blessed are those who have not seen and yet believe."

[A] 20:16 Or Hebrew [B] 20:18 Lit these things [C] 20:22 Lit he breathed and said to them [D] 20:24 Gk Didymus [E] 20:29 Or have you believed?

THE PURPOSE OF THIS GOSPEL

30 Jesus performed many other signs in the presence of his disciples that are not written in this book. 31 But these are written so that you may believe that Jesus is the Messiah, the Son of God,^A and that by believing you may have life in his name.

JESUS'S THIRD APPEARANCE TO THE DISCIPLES

21 After this, Jesus revealed himself again to his disciples by the Sea of Tiberias. He revealed himself in this way:

2 Simon Peter, Thomas (called "Twin"^B), Nathanael from Cana of Galilee, Zebedee's sons, and two others of his disciples were together.

3 "I'm going fishing," Simon Peter said to them.

"We're coming with you," they told him. They went out and got into the boat, but that night they caught nothing.

4 When daybreak came, Jesus stood on the shore, but the disciples did not know it was Jesus. 5 "Friends,"^C Jesus called to them, "you don't have any fish, do you?"

"No," they answered.

6 "Cast the net on the right side of the boat," he told them, "and you'll find some." So they did,^D and they were unable to haul it in because of the large number of fish. 7 The disciple, the one Jesus loved, said to Peter, "It is the Lord!"

When Simon Peter heard that it was the Lord, he tied his outer clothing around him (for he had taken it off) and plunged into the sea. 8 Since they were not far from land (about a hundred yards^E away), the other disciples came in the boat, dragging the net full of fish.

9 When they got out on land, they saw a charcoal fire there, with fish lying on it, and bread. 10 "Bring some of the fish you've just caught," Jesus told them. 11 So Simon Peter climbed up and hauled the net ashore, full of large fish — 153 of them. Even though there were so many, the net was not torn.

12 "Come and have breakfast," Jesus told them. None of the disciples dared ask him, "Who are you?" because they knew it was the Lord. 13 Jesus came, took the bread, and gave it to them. He did the same with the fish. 14 This was now the third time Jesus appeared^F to the disciples after he was raised from the dead.

JESUS'S THREEFOLD RESTORATION OF PETER

15 When they had eaten breakfast, Jesus asked Simon Peter, "Simon, son of John,^G do you love me more than these?"

"Yes, Lord," he said to him, "you know that I love you."

"Feed my lambs," he told him. 16 A second time he asked him, "Simon, son of John, do you love me?"

"Yes, Lord," he said to him, "you know that I love you."

"Shepherd my sheep," he told him.

17 He asked him the third time, "Simon, son of John, do you love me?"

---

^A20:31 Or that the Messiah, the Son of God, is Jesus ^B21:2 Gk Didymus
^C21:5 Lit "Children" ^D21:6 Lit they cast ^E21:8 Lit about two hundred cubits
^F21:14 Lit was revealed (v. 1) ^G21:15-17 Other mss read "Simon, son of Jonah; Mt 16:17; Jn 1:42

THE MINISTRY OF PANCAKES

JOHN 21

I was the very pregnant, sick, and tired mama of a demanding toddler. My brain was so clouded by pregnancy hormones and sleep deprivation that I didn't know what I needed or how to ask for help.

So Mandy made me pancakes.

Mandy and I weren't friends, exactly. We mostly smiled at each other in the halls of our church, but she called me one evening with this invitation: "Come over tomorrow morning, first thing. Bring your little guy and stay in your jammies. I'm going to make you pancakes."

Not typically the kind of gal to show up at a stranger's house in my pajamas, I'm surprised I accepted her offer. I'm usually more of a "spiff everything up and look like you have it together" kind of girl. Even so, the next morning we headed over to Mandy's in our comfies.

Those were the best pancakes of my life. Food eaten on dishes I didn't have to wash was a lifeline of sorts. That moment of simple compassion stuck with me long after I cleaned (okay fine, licked) my plate and headed home.

Years later I was surprised to find a similar story in John 21.

After a night of fruitless fishing to punctuate the best and worst months of their lives, Peter, James, John, and a handful of other disciples found themselves staring out at the same waves Jesus had walked upon (Jn 6:1, 9).

Everything had changed since then. Jesus had been arrested, crucified, and buried. Their hopes were dashed and they scattered, fearing for their lives. Peter's grief was compounded by the agonizing memory that he denied the Savior not once, not twice, but three times (Jn 18:15-18, 25-27).

Almost immediately after everything went so terribly wrong, Jesus started setting it right again. His death was trumped by His resurrection. His scared disciples were refocused by His return. Even Peter's denials got reversed.

Jesus called His fishing friends to the shore. Peter was so anxious to be with his Savior that he jumped right out of the boat fully clothed (Jn 21:7). When they got to shore, they found that Jesus had made them breakfast.

It was a simple gesture that demonstrated profound care and compassion. **Jesus tenderly met His friends' physical needs before offering an even better portion.**

During a post-breakfast stroll, Jesus gave Peter not one, not two, but three chances to declare his love. For every denial, Peter got to make a proclamation (Jn 21:15-17). Though sinned against, Jesus initiated reconciliation and offered tender mercies.

Perhaps emulating Jesus is simpler than we think. Offer grace. Pursue reconciliation. Forgive freely. Whenever possible, love others well by serving them. Pancakes optional.

Peter was grieved that he asked him the third time, "Do you love me?" He said, "Lord, you know everything; you know that I love you."

"Feed my sheep," Jesus said. [18] "Truly I tell you, when you were younger, you would tie your belt and walk wherever you wanted. But when you grow old, you will stretch out your hands and someone else will tie you and carry you where you don't want to go." [19] He said this to indicate by what kind of death Peter would glorify God. After saying this, he told him, "Follow me."

CORRECTING A FALSE REPORT

[20] So Peter turned around and saw the disciple Jesus loved following them, the one who had leaned back against Jesus at the supper and asked, "Lord, who is the one that's going to betray you?" [21] When Peter saw him, he said to Jesus, "Lord, what about him?"

[22] "If I want him to remain until I come," Jesus answered, "what is that to you? As for you, follow me."

[23] So this rumor[A] spread to the brothers and sisters that this disciple would not die. Yet Jesus did not tell him that he would not die, but, "If I want him to remain until I come, what is that to you?"

EPILOGUE

[24] This is the disciple who testifies to these things and who wrote them down. We know that his testimony is true.

[25] And there are also many other things that Jesus did, which, if every one of them were written down, I suppose not even the world itself could contain the books[B] that would be written.

[A]21:23 Lit *this word*   [B]21:25 Lit *scroll*

And You
Will Be My
Witnesses

acts

 But you will receive power when the Holy Spirit has come on you, and you will be my witnesses in Jerusalem, in all Judea and Samaria, and to the end of the earth. **1:8**

ON THE TIMELINE The book of Acts is traditionally credited to a physician named Luke, a traveling companion of Paul and author of the Gospel of Luke. Both Luke and Acts are believed to have been written at the same time, during the early to mid AD 60s, likely during Paul's imprisonment in Rome. The events in Acts took place after the death of Christ in AD 33 and conclude in AD 62.

A LITTLE BACKGROUND Acts provides biographical glimpses of some of the early apostles as they spread the news of the gospel first in Jerusalem and then to the world around the Mediterranean. Peter, Philip, and a few others were responsible for the Church's growth into Jerusalem, Judea, and Samaria, while Paul primarily focused on ministry to the Gentiles.

Paul's typical missionary strategy was to go to a familiar place in each city he visited, usually a synagogue, and proclaim the gospel first to local Jews. The speed with which he shifted his focus to Gentiles outside the synagogue depended on how Jews received him within the synagogue. Before leaving a town, Paul united Jewish and Gentile converts to form a local church.

MESSAGE & PURPOSE The book of Acts emphasizes the work of God through the Holy Spirit in the lives of people who devoted themselves to Jesus Christ, especially Paul as he led the Gentile missionary endeavor. The Christian church was built, city-by-city, through the dynamic power of the Spirit working through chosen vessels.

GIVE THANKS FOR THE BOOK OF ACTS

The book of Acts ties together the other books of the New Testament by providing the rest of the story told in the Gospels. The gospel of Jesus Christ and the message of the kingdom of God did not end with Jesus' ascension to heaven forty days after His resurrection, but it continued in the lives of His followers. Acts shows us how Jesus' call to take the gospel into the world was carried out by the apostles and other believers through the power of the Holy Spirit. It also gives us the context for much of the NT, especially the letters Paul wrote to the churches he helped establish during his missionary journeys.

ROME

THREE
TAVERNS

PUTEOLI

POMPEII

ITALIA

MACEDONIA

PHILIPPI   NEAPOL

AMPHIPOLIS

THESSALONICA

BEREA

APOLLONIA

RHEGIUM

SICILY

SYRACUSE

CORINTH

ATHENS

CENCHREAE

Ship wrecks into reef
and all swim ashore

Ship lost at sea

MALTA

MEDITERRANE

PAUL'S MISSIONARY JOURNEYS

1ST MISSIONARY JOURNEY ·············▸
2ND MISSIONARY JOURNEY ‐ ‐ ‐ ‐ ▸
3RD MISSIONARY JOURNEY ‐·‐·‐·▸
JOURNEY TO ROME ————▸

THRACE

ASIA

GALATIA

CAPPADOCIA

TROAS
ADRAMYTTIUM
OS
MITYLENE
PERGAMUM
SMYRNA
EPHESUS
MILETUS
LAODICEA

ANTIOCH
IN PISIDIA
ICONIUM
LYSTRA
DERBE
TARSUS
PAMPHYLIA
CILICIA
ATTALIA
PERGA
LYCIA
CNIDUS
PATARA
MYRA
RHODES

ANTIOCH
SELEUCIA
PIERIA
SYRIA

SALAMIS
CYPRUS
PAPHOS

DAMASCUS

FAIR HAVENS
LASEA
SALMONE
CRETE

SEA

TYRE
PTOLEMAIS
CAESAREA
MARITIMA
JERUSALEM
JUDEA

READ AND UNDERSTAND ACTS

The Bible is a complete work in which many stories combine to tell one story. As you read the book of Acts, consider reading the additional passages to discover how the whole of Scripture works together.

READ AND
UNDERSTAND
ACTS

PROLOGUE

1 I wrote the first narrative, Theophilus, about all that Jesus began to do and teach [2] until the day he was taken up, after he had given instructions through the Holy Spirit to the apostles he had chosen. [3] After he had suffered, he also presented himself alive to them by many convincing proofs, appearing to them over a period of forty days and speaking about the kingdom of God.

THE HOLY SPIRIT PROMISED

[4] While he was[A] with them, he commanded them not to leave Jerusalem, but to wait for the Father's promise. "Which," he said, "you have heard me speak about; [5] for John baptized with water, but you will be baptized with the Holy Spirit in a few days."

[6] So when they had come together, they asked him, "Lord, are you restoring the kingdom to Israel at this time?"

[7] He said to them, "It is not for you to know times or periods that the Father has set by his own authority. [8] But you will receive power when the Holy Spirit has come on you, and you will be my witnesses in Jerusalem, in all Judea and Samaria, and to the end of the earth."

THE ASCENSION

[9] After he had said this, he was taken up as they were watching, and a cloud took him out of their sight. [10] While he was going, they were gazing into heaven, and suddenly two men in white clothes stood by them. [11] They said, "Men of Galilee, why do you stand looking up into heaven? This same Jesus, who has been taken from you into heaven, will come in the same way that you have seen him going into heaven."

UNITED IN PRAYER

[12] Then they returned to Jerusalem from the Mount of Olives, which is near Jerusalem — a Sabbath day's journey away. [13] When they arrived, they went to the room upstairs where they were staying: Peter, John, James, Andrew, Philip, Thomas, Bartholomew, Matthew, James the son of Alphaeus, Simon the Zealot, and Judas the son of James. [14] They all were continually united in prayer,[B] along with the women, including Mary the mother of Jesus, and his brothers.

MATTHIAS CHOSEN

[15] In those days Peter stood up among the brothers and sisters[C] — the number of people who were together was about a hundred and twenty — and said: [16] "Brothers and sisters, it was necessary that the Scripture be fulfilled that the Holy Spirit through the mouth of David foretold about Judas, who became a guide to those who arrested Jesus. [17] For he was one of our number and shared in this ministry." [18] Now this man acquired a field with his unrighteous wages. He fell headfirst, his body burst open and his intestines spilled out. [19] This became known to all the residents of Jerusalem, so that in their own language that field is called *Hakeldama* (that is, Field of Blood). [20] "For it is written in the Book of Psalms:

[A] 1:4 Or *he was eating*, or *he was lodging* [B] 1:14 Other mss add *and petition*
[C] 1:15 Other mss read *disciples*

WELCOME TO THE FIRST STRING

ACTS 1; MATTHEW 28:16-20

I've always been on the B Team.

My athletic dreams died in fourth grade when I was cut from a basketball team in a league where cuts weren't officially allowed. Evidently, I'm a glutton for punishment because I kept trying out for sports teams into my high school years. I even donned a couple uniforms, but I was always second string.

I may be best suited for warming the bench in sports, but in the kingdom of God, I'm a starter. So are you. He puts us all in the game in this final charge:

"But you will receive power when the Holy Spirit has come on you, and you will be my witnesses in Jerusalem, in all Judea and Samaria, and to the end of the earth."

ACTS 1:8

Please excuse the continued sports analogy, but this moment between Jesus and His disciples is the huddle before the game goes into overtime. Jesus arrived on earth as a baby, shook up the political and spiritual climate during His brief ministry, died and rose again for the sins of humanity, and spent forty days on earth in His resurrected body. All that remained was to run the ball into the end zone. Instead, Jesus looked at His disciples and passed. He didn't need them for that final play, but He invited them onto the field nonetheless.

This is how God, in His sovereign goodness, has chosen to spread His good news. We have the privilege of being Christ's witnesses, telling what He's done in every corner of our world.

Jesus gave the charge to a small band of followers in Jerusalem—a moment 2,000 years and 6,500 miles removed from where I sit. Yet, His words were as descriptive as they were prescriptive. What started in Jerusalem went on to send shock waves to surrounding territories in the Middle East (Judea and Samaria). And it keeps on spreading.

The unifying and liberating message of the gospel of Jesus permeates geographical, political, and socioeconomic barriers. No longer bound to a handful of Jewish men, it is now the treasure and mission of millions of Christians around the world.

Jesus did all the work. He accomplished our redemption on the cross. **But by His grace and through His power, we are the conduit that carries that good news to the hurting and the broken, the wayward and the enslaved.**

You and I are called to more than bench warming in the kingdom of God. Amazingly, He has chosen us, best suited for the second or third string, to tell the world about our Savior. He's given us the Holy Spirit, the very thing we need to carry out the mission, and the victory has already been won (Jn 16:33; 2Pt 1:3). Thanks be to God!

Let his dwelling become desolate;
let no one live in it;[A] and
Let someone else take his position.[B]

[21] "Therefore, from among the men who have accompanied us during the whole time the Lord Jesus went in and out among us — [22] beginning from the baptism of John until the day he was taken up from us — from among these, it is necessary that one become a witness with us of his resurrection."

[23] So they proposed two: Joseph, called Barsabbas, who was also known as Justus, and Matthias. [24] Then they prayed, "You, Lord, know everyone's hearts; show which of these two you have chosen [25] to take the place[C] in this apostolic ministry that Judas left to go where he belongs." [26] Then they cast lots for them, and the lot fell to Matthias and he was added to the eleven apostles.

PENTECOST

2 When the day of Pentecost had arrived, they were all together in one place. [2] Suddenly a sound like that of a violent rushing wind came from heaven, and it filled the whole house where they were staying. [3] They saw tongues like flames of fire that separated and rested on each one of them. [4] Then they were all filled with the Holy Spirit and began to speak in different tongues,[D] as the Spirit enabled them.

[5] Now there were Jews staying in Jerusalem, devout people from every nation under heaven. [6] When this sound occurred, a crowd came together and was confused because each one heard them speaking in his own language. [7] They were astounded and amazed, saying,[E] "Look, aren't all these who are speaking Galileans? [8] How is it that each of us can hear them in our own native language? [9] Parthians, Medes, Elamites; those who live in Mesopotamia, in Judea and Cappadocia, Pontus and Asia, [10] Phrygia and Pamphylia, Egypt and the parts of Libya near Cyrene; visitors from Rome (both Jews and converts), [11] Cretans and Arabs — we hear them declaring the magnificent acts of God in our own tongues." [12] They were all astounded and perplexed, saying to one another, "What does this mean?" [13] But some sneered and said, "They're drunk on new wine."

PETER'S SERMON

[14] Peter stood up with the Eleven, raised his voice, and proclaimed to them: "Fellow Jews and all you residents of Jerusalem, let me explain this to you and pay attention to my words. [15] For these people are not drunk, as you suppose, since it's only nine in the morning.[F] [16] On the contrary, this is what was spoken through the prophet Joel:

[17]   And it will be in the last days, says God,
        that I will pour out my Spirit on all people;
        then your sons and your daughters will prophesy,
        your young men will see visions,
        and your old men will dream dreams.
[18]   I will even pour out my Spirit

[A]1:20 Ps 69:25   [B]1:20 Ps 109:8   [C]1:25 Other mss read *to share*
[D]2:4 languages, also in v. 11   [E]2:7 Other mss add *to one another*   [F]2:15 Lit *it's the third hour of the day*

on my servants in those days, both men and women
and they will prophesy.
19 I will display wonders in the heaven above
and signs on the earth below:
blood and fire and a cloud of smoke.
20 The sun will be turned to darkness
and the moon to blood
before the great and glorious day of the Lord comes.
21 Then everyone who calls
on the name of the Lord will be saved.[A]

22 "Fellow Israelites, listen to these words: This Jesus of Nazareth was a man attested to you by God with miracles, wonders, and signs that God did among you through him, just as you yourselves know. 23 Though he was delivered up according to God's determined plan and foreknowledge, you used[B] lawless people to nail him to a cross and kill him. 24 God raised him up, ending the pains of death, because it was not possible for him to be held by death. 25 For David says of him:

I saw the Lord ever before me;
because he is at my right hand,
I will not be shaken.
26 Therefore my heart is glad
and my tongue rejoices.
Moreover, my flesh will rest in hope,
27 because you will not abandon me in Hades
or allow your holy one to see decay.
28 You have revealed the paths of life to me;
you will fill me with gladness
in your presence.[C]

29 "Brothers and sisters, I can confidently speak to you about the patriarch David: He is both dead and buried, and his tomb is with us to this day. 30 Since he was a prophet, he knew that God had sworn an oath to him to seat one of his descendants[D] on his throne. 31 Seeing what was to come, he spoke concerning the resurrection of the Messiah: He[E] was not abandoned in Hades, and his flesh did not experience decay.[F]

32 "God has raised this Jesus; we are all witnesses of this. 33 Therefore, since he has been exalted to the right hand of God and has received from the Father the promised Holy Spirit, he has poured out what you both see and hear. 34 For it was not David who ascended into the heavens, but he himself says:

The Lord declared to my Lord,
'Sit at my right hand
35 until I make your enemies your footstool.'[G]

36 "Therefore let all the house of Israel know with certainty that God has made this Jesus, whom you crucified, both Lord and Messiah."

[A]2:17-21 Jl 2:28-32 [B]2:23 Other mss read *you have taken* [C]2:25-28 Ps 16:8-11
[D]2:30 Other mss add *according to the flesh to raise up the Messiah*
[E]2:31 Other mss read *His soul* [F]2:31 Ps 16:10 [G]2:34-35 Ps 110:1

BREAKING BREAD

ACTS 2; LUKE 22:14-20; 1 CORINTHIANS 11:23-26

My grandma was born two years before the Stock Market crashed in 1929. She spent her childhood on a farm in Iowa in the middle of the Great Depression, raised in a family who knew what it was to have very little. They worked hard, yet still had just enough to get by. Hers was an entire generation eager to avoid going without ever again. Those experiences taught her to save everything.

Now, eighty years later, she still pinches pennies, but her reasons for saving are different than they were in the 1930s. No longer fearful of going hungry, she gives freely and selflessly because she has an abundance of resources. I've never known her to think twice before offering to help someone in need.

In the New Testament we find a group of believers as generous as my grandma. Acts describes how the early Church lived from a place of confidence and security, sure that God would meet all their needs. Instead of holding their possessions tightly out of fear, they shared freely with one another. I have a hard time looking at the way they lived without feeling convicted for freaking out when my roommate asks to borrow my favorite sweater.

What was their secret?

Every day, the early Church devoted themselves to meeting together.
Every day, they gathered together at the temple and in each other's homes.
Every day, they broke bread.

Every day.

At first glance, this may give us warm, happy feelings and images of the early Church gathered together for breakfast. But they weren't sharing *any* meal. They shared *the* meal. Not simply sitting around a kitchen table for pancakes, they were gathered at the Lord's table for communion.

When Jesus broke bread at the Last Supper, He commanded His disciples to continue the practice (Lk 22:14-20). He wants us to continue to break bread together, too, for two reasons: to remember Him and to proclaim His death and resurrection until He returns (1Co 11:25-26).

In Acts, we see a group of believers who remembered Jesus' sacrifice every day. Every day, they broke bread, remembering how His body was broken on the cross for their sins. Every day, they remembered the redemption they'd been offered and the gift they'd received through faith.

Each and every day, they remembered Jesus, and it changed the way they lived.

Taking communion reminds us of the new covenant God established through Jesus. We remember that our God keeps His promises, that He's granted us life and redemption through Jesus. We remember that through faith alone we are saved, all because of what Christ has done (Eph 2:8). Let us be faithful to always remember His sacrifice, to model the generosity of the early Church, and to praise God together with joyful and humble hearts.

CALL TO REPENTANCE

³⁷ When they heard this, they were pierced to the heart and said to Peter and the rest of the apostles: "Brothers, what should we do?"

³⁸ Peter replied, "Repent and be baptized, each of you, in the name of Jesus Christ for the forgiveness of your sins, and you will receive the gift of the Holy Spirit. ³⁹ For the promise is for you and for your children, and for all who are far off, as many as the Lord our God will call." ⁴⁰ With many other words he testified and strongly urged them, saying, "Be saved from this corrupt^A generation!" ⁴¹ So those who accepted his message were baptized, and that day about three thousand people were added to them.

A GENEROUS AND GROWING CHURCH

⁴² They devoted themselves to the apostles' teaching, to the fellowship, to the breaking of bread, and to prayer.

⁴³ Everyone was filled with awe, and many wonders and signs were being performed through the apostles. ⁴⁴ Now all the believers were together and held all things in common. ⁴⁵ They sold their possessions and property and distributed the proceeds to all, as any had need. ⁴⁶ Every day they devoted themselves to meeting together in the temple, and broke bread from house to house. They ate their food with joyful and sincere hearts, ⁴⁷ praising God and enjoying the favor of all the people. Every day the Lord added to their number^B those who were being saved.

HEALING OF A LAME MAN

3 Now Peter and John were going up to the temple for the time of prayer at three in the afternoon.^C ² A man who was lame from birth was being carried there. He was placed each day at the temple gate called Beautiful, so that he could beg from those entering the temple. ³ When he saw Peter and John about to enter the temple, he asked for money. ⁴ Peter, along with John, looked straight at him and said, "Look at us." ⁵ So he turned to them, expecting to get something from them. ⁶ But Peter said, "I don't have silver or gold, but what I do have, I give you: In the name of Jesus Christ of Nazareth, get up and walk!" ⁷ Then, taking him by the right hand he raised him up, and at once his feet and ankles became strong. ⁸ So he jumped up and started to walk, and he entered the temple with them — walking, leaping, and praising God. ⁹ All the people saw him walking and praising God, ¹⁰ and they recognized that he was the one who used to sit and beg at the Beautiful Gate of the temple. So they were filled with awe and astonishment at what had happened to him.

PREACHING IN SOLOMON'S COLONNADE

¹¹ While he^D was holding on to Peter and John, all the people, utterly astonished, ran toward them in what is called Solomon's Colonnade. ¹² When Peter saw this, he addressed the people: "Fellow Israelites, why are you amazed at this? Why do you stare at us, as though we had made him walk by our own power or godliness? ¹³ The God of Abraham, Isaac, and Jacob, the God of our ancestors, has glorified his servant Jesus, whom you handed over and

---

^A 2:40 Or *crooked, or twisted*   ^B 2:47 Other mss read *to the church*   ^C 3:1 Lit *at the ninth hour*   ^D 3:11 Other mss read *the lame man who was healed* denied before Pilate, though he had decided to release him. [14] You denied the Holy and Righteous One and asked to have a murderer released to you. [15] You killed the source[A] of life, whom God raised from the dead; we are witnesses of this. [16] By faith in his name, his name has made this man strong, whom you see and know. So the faith that comes through Jesus has given him this perfect health in front of all of you.

[17] "And now, brothers and sisters, I know that you acted in ignorance, just as your leaders also did. [18] In this way God fulfilled what he had predicted through all the prophets — that his Messiah would suffer. [19] Therefore repent and turn back, so that your sins may be wiped out, [20] that seasons of refreshing may come from the presence of the Lord, and that he may send Jesus, who has been appointed for you as the Messiah. [21] Heaven must receive him until the time of the restoration of all things, which God spoke about through his holy prophets from the beginning. [22] Moses said:[B] **The Lord your God will raise up for you a prophet like me from among your brothers and sisters. You must listen to everything he tells you.** [23] **And everyone who does not listen to that prophet will be completely cut off from the people.**[C]

[24] "In addition, all the prophets who have spoken, from Samuel and those after him, have also foretold these days. [25] You are the sons[D] of the prophets and of the covenant that God made with your ancestors, saying to Abraham, **And all the families of the earth will be blessed through your offspring.**[E] [26] God raised up his servant[F] and sent him first to you to bless you by turning each of you from your evil ways."

PETER AND JOHN ARRESTED

4 While they were speaking to the people, the priests, the captain of the temple police, and the Sadducees confronted them, [2] because they were annoyed that they were teaching the people and proclaiming in Jesus the resurrection of the dead. [3] So they seized them and took them into custody until the next day since it was already evening. [4] But many of those who heard the message believed, and the number of the men[G] came to about five thousand.

PETER AND JOHN FACE THE JEWISH LEADERSHIP

[5] The next day, their rulers, elders, and scribes assembled in Jerusalem [6] with Annas the high priest, Caiaphas, John, Alexander, and all the members of the high-priestly family. [7] After they had Peter and John stand before them, they began to question them: "By what power or in what name have you done this?"

[8] Then Peter was filled with the Holy Spirit and said to them, "Rulers of the people and elders:[H] [9] If we are being examined today about a good deed done to a disabled man, by what means he was healed, [10] let it be known to all of you and to all the people of Israel, that by the name of Jesus Christ of Nazareth, whom you crucified and whom God raised from the dead — by him this man is standing here before you healthy. [11] This Jesus is

the stone rejected by you builders,
which has become the cornerstone.[I]

[A]3:15 Or the Prince, or the Ruler   [B]3:22 Other mss add to the fathers
[C]3:22-23 Dt 18:15-19   [D]3:25 = heirs   [E]3:25 Gn 12:3; 18:18; 22:18; 26:4
[F]3:26 Other mss add Jesus   [G]4:4 Or people   [H]4:8 Other mss add of Israel
[I]4:11 Ps 118:22

[12] There is salvation in no one else, for there is no other name under heaven given to people by which we must be saved."

THE BOLDNESS OF THE DISCIPLES

[13] When they observed the boldness of Peter and John and realized that they were uneducated and untrained men, they were amazed and recognized that they had been with Jesus. [14] And since they saw the man who had been healed standing with them, they had nothing to say in opposition. [15] After they ordered them to leave the Sanhedrin, they conferred among themselves, [16] saying, "What should we do with these men? For an obvious sign has been done through them, clear to everyone living in Jerusalem, and we cannot deny it. [17] But so that this does not spread any further among the people, let's threaten them against speaking to anyone in this name again." [18] So they called for them and ordered them not to speak or teach at all in the name of Jesus.

[19] Peter and John answered them, "Whether it's right in the sight of God for us to listen to you rather than to God, you decide; [20] for we are unable to stop speaking about what we have seen and heard."

[21] After threatening them further, they released them. They found no way to punish them because the people were all giving glory to God over what had been done. [22] For this sign of healing had been performed on a man over forty years old.

PRAYER FOR BOLDNESS

[23] After they were released, they went to their own people and reported everything the chief priests and the elders had said to them. [24] When they heard this, they raised their voices together to God and said, "Master, you are the one who made the heaven, the earth, and the sea, and everything in them. [25] You said through the Holy Spirit, by the mouth of our father David your servant:[A]

> Why do the Gentiles rage
> and the peoples plot futile things?
> [26] The kings of the earth take their stand
> and the rulers assemble together
> against the Lord and against his Messiah.[B]

[27] "For, in fact, in this city both Herod and Pontius Pilate, with the Gentiles and the people of Israel, assembled together against your holy servant Jesus, whom you anointed, [28] to do whatever your hand and your will had predestined to take place. [29] And now, Lord, consider their threats, and grant that your servants may speak your word with all boldness, [30] while you stretch out your hand for healing, and signs and wonders are performed through the name of your holy servant Jesus." [31] When they had prayed, the place where they were assembled was shaken, and they were all filled with the Holy Spirit and began to speak the word of God boldly.

ALL THINGS IN COMMON

[32] Now the entire group of those who believed were of one heart and mind, and no one claimed that any of his possessions was his own, but instead they

---

[A]4:25 Other mss read *through the mouth of David your servant* [B]4:25-26 Ps 2:1-2 held everything in common. ³³ With great power the apostles were giving testimony to the resurrection of the Lord Jesus, and great grace was on all of them. ³⁴ For there was not a needy person among them because all those who owned lands or houses sold them, brought the proceeds of what was sold, ³⁵ and laid them at the apostles' feet. This was then distributed to each person as any had need.

³⁶ Joseph, a Levite from Cyprus by birth, the one the apostles called Barnabas (which is translated Son of Encouragement), ³⁷ sold a field he owned, brought the money, and laid it at the apostles' feet.

LYING TO THE HOLY SPIRIT

5 But a man named Ananias, with his wife Sapphira, sold a piece of property. ² However, he kept back part of the proceeds with his wife's knowledge, and brought a portion of it and laid it at the apostles' feet.

³ "Ananias," Peter asked, "why has Satan filled your heart to lie to the Holy Spirit and keep back part of the proceeds of the land? ⁴ Wasn't it yours while you possessed it? And after it was sold, wasn't it at your disposal? Why is it that you planned this thing in your heart? You have not lied to people but to God." ⁵ When he heard these words, Ananias dropped dead, and a great fear came on all who heard. ⁶ The young men got up, wrapped his body, carried him out, and buried him.

⁷ About three hours later, his wife came in, not knowing what had happened. ⁸ "Tell me," Peter asked her, "did you sell the land for this price?"

"Yes," she said, "for that price."

⁹ Then Peter said to her, "Why did you agree to test the Spirit of the Lord? Look, the feet of those who have buried your husband are at the door, and they will carry you out."

¹⁰ Instantly she dropped dead at his feet. When the young men came in, they found her dead, carried her out, and buried her beside her husband. ¹¹ Then great fear came on the whole church and on all who heard these things.

APOSTOLIC SIGNS AND WONDERS

¹² Many signs and wonders were being done among the people through the hands of the apostles. They were all together in Solomon's Colonnade. ¹³ No one else dared to join them, but the people spoke well of them. ¹⁴ Believers were added to the Lord in increasing numbers — multitudes of both men and women. ¹⁵ As a result, they would carry the sick out into the streets and lay them on cots and mats so that when Peter came by, at least his shadow might fall on some of them. ¹⁶ In addition, a multitude came together from the towns surrounding Jerusalem, bringing the sick and those who were tormented by unclean spirits, and they were all healed.

IN AND OUT OF PRISON

¹⁷ Then the high priest rose up. He and all who were with him, who belonged to the party of the Sadducees, were filled with jealousy. ¹⁸ So they arrested the apostles and put them in the public jail. ¹⁹ But an angel of the Lord opened the doors of the jail during the night, brought them out, and said, ²⁰ "Go and stand in the temple, and tell the people all about this life." ²¹ Hearing this, they entered the temple at daybreak and began to teach.

THE APOSTLES ON TRIAL AGAIN

When the high priest and those who were with him arrived, they convened the Sanhedrin — the full council of the Israelites — and sent orders to the jail to have them brought. ²² But when the servants ^A^ got there, they did not find them in the jail, so they returned and reported, ²³ "We found the jail securely locked, with the guards standing in front of the doors, but when we opened them, we found no one inside." ²⁴ As ^B^ the captain of the temple police and the chief priests heard these things, they were baffled about them, wondering what would come of this.

²⁵ Someone came and reported to them, "Look! The men you put in jail are standing in the temple and teaching the people." ²⁶ Then the commander went with the servants and brought them in without force, because they were afraid the people might stone them. ²⁷ After they brought them in, they had them stand before the Sanhedrin, and the high priest asked, ²⁸ "Didn't we strictly order you not to teach in this name? Look, you have filled Jerusalem with your teaching and are determined to make us guilty of this man's blood."

²⁹ Peter and the apostles replied, "We must obey God rather than people. ³⁰ The God of our ancestors raised up Jesus, whom you had murdered by hanging him on a tree. ³¹ God exalted this man to his right hand as ruler and Savior, to give repentance to Israel and forgiveness of sins. ³² We are witnesses of these things, and so is the Holy Spirit whom God has given to those who obey him."

GAMALIEL'S ADVICE

³³ When they heard this, they were enraged and wanted to kill them. ³⁴ But a Pharisee named Gamaliel, a teacher of the law who was respected by all the people, stood up in the Sanhedrin and ordered the men ^C^ to be taken outside for a little while. ³⁵ He said to them, "Men of Israel, be careful about what you're about to do to these men. ³⁶ Some time ago Theudas rose up, claiming to be somebody, and a group of about four hundred men rallied to him. He was killed, and all his followers were dispersed and came to nothing. ³⁷ After this man, Judas the Galilean rose up in the days of the census and attracted a following. He also perished, and all his followers were scattered. ³⁸ So in the present case, I tell you, stay away from these men and leave them alone. For if this plan or this work is of human origin, it will fail; ³⁹ but if it is of God, you will not be able to overthrow them. You may even be found fighting against God." They were persuaded by him. ⁴⁰ After they called in the apostles and had them flogged, they ordered them not to speak in the name of Jesus and released them. ⁴¹ Then they went out from the presence of the Sanhedrin, rejoicing that they were counted worthy to be treated shamefully on behalf of the Name. ^D^ ⁴² Every day in the temple, and in various homes, they continued teaching and proclaiming the good news that Jesus is the Messiah.

---

^A^5:22 Or *temple police*, or *officers*, also in v. 26　^B^5:24 Other mss add *the high priest and*　^C^5:34 Other mss read *apostles*　^D^5:41 Other mss add *of Jesus*, or *of Christ*

SEVEN CHOSEN TO SERVE

6 In those days, as the disciples were increasing in number, there arose a complaint by the Hellenistic Jews against the Hebraic Jews that their widows were being overlooked in the daily distribution. ² The Twelve summoned the whole company of the disciples and said, "It would not be right for us to give up preaching the word of God to wait on tables. ³ Brothers and sisters, select from among you seven men of good reputation, full of the Spirit and wisdom, whom we can appoint to this duty. ⁴ But we will devote ourselves to prayer and to the ministry of the word." ⁵ This proposal pleased the whole company. So they chose Stephen, a man full of faith and the Holy Spirit, and Philip, Prochorus, Nicanor, Timon, Parmenas, and Nicolaus, a convert from Antioch. ⁶ They had them stand before the apostles, who prayed and laid their hands on them.

⁷ So the word of God spread, the disciples in Jerusalem increased greatly in number, and a large group of priests became obedient to the faith.

STEPHEN ACCUSED OF BLASPHEMY

⁸ Now Stephen, full of grace and power, was performing great wonders and signs among the people. ⁹ Opposition arose, however, from some members of the Freedmen's Synagogue, composed of both Cyrenians and Alexandrians, and some from Cilicia and Asia, and they began to argue with Stephen. ¹⁰ But they were unable to stand up against his wisdom and the Spirit by whom he was speaking.

¹¹ Then they secretly persuaded some men to say, "We heard him speaking blasphemous words against Moses and God." ¹² They stirred up the people, the elders, and the scribes; so they came, seized him, and took him to the Sanhedrin. ¹³ They also presented false witnesses who said, "This man never stops speaking against this holy place and the law. ¹⁴ For we heard him say that this Jesus of Nazareth will destroy this place and change the customs that Moses handed down to us." ¹⁵ And all who were sitting in the Sanhedrin looked intently at him and saw that his face was like the face of an angel.

STEPHEN'S SERMON

7 "Are these things true?" the high priest asked.

² "Brothers and fathers," he replied, "listen: The God of glory appeared to our father Abraham when he was in Mesopotamia, before he settled in Haran, ³ and said to him: **Leave your country and relatives, and come to the land that I will show you.**ᴬ

⁴ "Then he left the land of the Chaldeans and settled in Haran. From there, after his father died, God had him move to this land in which you are now living. ⁵ He didn't give him an inheritance in it — not even a foot of ground — but he promised to give it to him as a possession, and to his descendants after him, even though he was childless. ⁶ God spoke in this way: **His descendants would be strangers in a foreign country, and they would enslave and oppress them for four hundred years.** ⁷ **I will judge the nation that they will serve as slaves,** God said. **After this, they will come out and worship me in this place.**ᴮ ⁸ And so he gave Abraham the covenant of circumcision. After this, he fathered Isaac and circumcised him on the eighth day. Isaac became the father of Jacob, and Jacob became the father of the twelve patriarchs.

ᴬ7:3 Gn 12:1   ᴮ7:6-7 Gn 15:13-14

THE ZEAL OF THE SPIRIT

ACTS 7:1-53

I know all Scripture is ultimately about God. Still, I find myself putting undue emphasis on the other, oh-so-human characters in the story. I'd always walked away from Acts 7 in awe of Stephen. What faith! What courage! What knowledge of Scripture! But one day, I saw it.

Stephen isn't the hero of this story. The Holy Spirit is.

Now when I read this passage, the role of the Holy Spirit jumps out like it's written in neon lights. Here's what I see:

The Holy Spirit gave Stephen his edge. Stephen was in this situation in Acts 7 because of what happened the chapter before. The Holy Spirit filled Stephen with "grace and power," enabling him to perform amazing signs and wonders (Ac 6:8-10). The religious leaders didn't understand this, so they dragged him to the Sanhedrin under charges of blasphemy.

The Holy Spirit gave Stephen the words to say. During Jesus' ministry, He said this to His disciples: "So when they arrest you and hand you over, don't worry beforehand what you will say, but say whatever is given to you at that time, for it isn't you speaking, but the Holy Spirit" (Mk 13:11). Stephen's situation was exactly that. Face shining like an angel (Ac 6:15), he stood before the Sanhedrin and gave a comprehensive history of God's people, while the faces of the religious leaders flamed with anger.

Stephen's message was all about the Spirit. The chapter might sound like a history lesson to us, but the Holy Spirit was hurling a verbal spear right at the Sanhedrin's unbelieving hearts. Every time God had changed the system or sent the Israelites a message, they had resisted, turning to idols or killing the messengers—like they were doing now. Verse 51 was the clincher: "You stiff-necked people with uncircumcised hearts and ears! You are always resisting the Holy Spirit; as your ancestors did, you do also."

The Spirit enabled Stephen to forgive his enemies. As Stephen was stoned, Scripture tells us again that he was "full of the Holy Spirit" (Ac 7:55). As he died at the hands of those who claimed to have the corner on religion, he did something unfathomable: he forgave them (Ac 7:60). Nothing but the Holy Spirit's power could produce that kind of radical grace.

It is appropriate to acknowledge the steadfastness and courage of our beloved martyr, Stephen. But let us never forget the God who indwelled and empowered him.

The Holy Spirit stood before the Sanhedrin that day. The Holy Spirit spoke words of truth. And, as the accusations and stones flew, the Holy Spirit ministered peace to our brother, Stephen. May we never try to explain that Spirit away.

THE PATRIARCHS IN EGYPT

⁹ "The patriarchs became jealous of Joseph and sold him into Egypt, but God was with him ¹⁰ and rescued him out of all his troubles. He gave him favor and wisdom in the sight of Pharaoh, king of Egypt, who appointed him ruler over Egypt and over his whole household. ¹¹ Now a famine and great suffering came over all of Egypt and Canaan, and our ancestors could find no food. ¹² When Jacob heard there was grain in Egypt, he sent our ancestors there the first time. ¹³ The second time, Joseph revealed himself to his brothers, and Joseph's family became known to Pharaoh. ¹⁴ Joseph invited his father Jacob and all his relatives, seventy-five people in all, ¹⁵ and Jacob went down to Egypt. He and our ancestors died there, ¹⁶ were carried back to Shechem, and were placed in the tomb that Abraham had bought for a sum of silver from the sons of Hamor in Shechem.

MOSES, A REJECTED SAVIOR

¹⁷ "As the time was approaching to fulfill the promise that God had made to Abraham, the people flourished and multiplied in Egypt ¹⁸ until a different king who did not know Joseph ruled over Egypt.ᴬ ¹⁹ He dealt deceitfully with our race and oppressed our ancestors by making them abandon their infants outside so that they wouldn't survive. ²⁰ At this time Moses was born, and he was beautiful in God's sight. He was cared for in his father's home for three months. ²¹ When he was put outside, Pharaoh's daughter adopted and raised him as her own son. ²² So Moses was educated in all the wisdom of the Egyptians and was powerful in his speech and actions.

²³ "When he was forty years old, he decided to visit his own people, the Israelites. ²⁴ When he saw one of them being mistreated, he came to his rescue and avenged the oppressed man by striking down the Egyptian. ²⁵ He assumed his people would understand that God would give them deliverance through him, but they did not understand. ²⁶ The next day he showed up while they were fighting and tried to reconcile them peacefully, saying, 'Men, you are brothers. Why are you mistreating each other?'

²⁷ "But the one who was mistreating his neighbor pushed Moses aside, saying: **Who appointed you a ruler and a judge over us? ²⁸ Do you want to kill me, the same way you killed the Egyptian yesterday?**ᴮ

²⁹ "When he heard this, Moses fled and became an exile in the land of Midian, where he became the father of two sons. ³⁰ After forty years had passed, an angelᶜ appeared to him in the wilderness of Mount Sinai, in the flame of a burning bush. ³¹ When Moses saw it, he was amazed at the sight. As he was approaching to look at it, the voice of the Lord came: ³² **I am the God of your ancestors — the God of Abraham, of Isaac, and of Jacob.**ᴰ Moses began to tremble and did not dare to look.

³³ "The Lord said to him: **Take off the sandals from your feet, because the place where you are standing is holy ground. ³⁴ I have certainly seen the oppression of my people in Egypt; I have heard their groaning and have come down to set them free. And now, come, I will send you to Egypt.**ᴱ

³⁵ "This Moses, whom they rejected when they said, **Who appointed you a ruler and a judge?**ᴮ — this one God sent as a ruler and a deliverer through

---

ᴬ7:18 Other mss omit *over Egypt*   ᴮ7:27-28,35 Ex 2:14   ᶜ7:30 Other mss add *of the Lord*   ᴰ7:32 Ex 3:6,15   ᴱ7:33-34 Ex 3:5,7-8,10 the angel who appeared to him in the bush. ³⁶ This man led them out and performed wonders and signs in the land of Egypt, at the Red Sea, and in the wilderness for forty years.

ISRAEL'S REBELLION AGAINST GOD

³⁷ "This is the Moses who said to the Israelites: **God**ᴬ **will raise up for you a prophet like me from among your brothers and sisters.**ᴮ ³⁸ He is the one who was in the assembly in the wilderness, with the angel who spoke to him on Mount Sinai, and with our ancestors. He received living oracles to give to us. ³⁹ Our ancestors were unwilling to obey him. Instead, they pushed him aside, and in their hearts turned back to Egypt. ⁴⁰ They told Aaron: **Make us gods who will go before us. As for this Moses who brought us out of the land of Egypt, we don't know what's happened to him.**ᶜ ⁴¹ They even made a calf in those days, offered sacrifice to the idol, and were celebrating what their hands had made. ⁴² God turned away and gave them up to worship the stars of heaven, as it is written in the book of the prophets:

> House of Israel, did you bring me offerings and sacrifices
> for forty years in the wilderness?
> ⁴³ You took up the tent of Moloch
> and the star of your god Rephan,
> the images that you made to worship.
> So I will send you into exile beyond Babylon.ᴰ

GOD'S REAL TABERNACLE

⁴⁴ "Our ancestors had the tabernacle of the testimony in the wilderness, just as he who spoke to Moses commanded him to make it according to the pattern he had seen. ⁴⁵ Our ancestors in turn received it and with Joshua brought it in when they dispossessed the nations that God drove out before them, until the days of David. ⁴⁶ He found favor in God's sight and asked that he might provide a dwelling place for the Godᴱ of Jacob. ⁴⁷ It was Solomon, rather, who built him a house, ⁴⁸ but the Most High does not dwell in sanctuaries made with hands, as the prophet says:

> ⁴⁹ Heaven is my throne,
> and the earth my footstool.
> What sort of house will you build for me?
> says the Lord,
> or what will be my resting place?
> ⁵⁰ Did not my hand make all these things?ᶠ

RESISTING THE HOLY SPIRIT

⁵¹ "You stiff-necked people with uncircumcised hearts and ears! You are always resisting the Holy Spirit. As your ancestors did, you do also. ⁵² Which of the prophets did your ancestors not persecute? They even killed those who foretold the coming of the Righteous One, whose betrayers and murderers you have now become. ⁵³ You received the law under the direction of angels and yet have not kept it."

ᴬ7:37 Other mss read *The Lord your God* ᴮ7:37 Dt 18:15 ᶜ7:40 Ex 32:1,23
ᴰ7:42-43 Am 5:25-27 ᴱ7:46 Other mss read *house* ᶠ7:49-50 Is 66:1-2

THE FIRST CHRISTIAN MARTYR

[54] When they heard these things, they were enraged[A] and gnashed their teeth at him. [55] Stephen, full of the Holy Spirit, gazed into heaven. He saw the glory of God, and Jesus standing at the right hand of God. [56] He said, "Look, I see the heavens opened and the Son of Man standing at the right hand of God!"

[57] They yelled at the top of their voices, covered their ears, and together rushed against him. [58] They dragged him out of the city and began to stone him. And the witnesses laid their garments at the feet of a young man named Saul. [59] While they were stoning Stephen, he called out: "Lord Jesus, receive my spirit!" [60] He knelt down and cried out with a loud voice, "Lord, do not hold this sin against them!" And after saying this, he died.[B]

SAUL THE PERSECUTOR

8 Saul agreed with putting him to death.

On that day a severe persecution broke out against the church in Jerusalem, and all except the apostles were scattered throughout the land of Judea and Samaria. [2] Devout men buried Stephen and mourned deeply over him. [3] Saul, however, was ravaging the church. He would enter house after house, drag off men and women, and put them in prison.

PHILIP IN SAMARIA

[4] So those who were scattered went on their way preaching the word. [5] Philip went down to a[C] city in Samaria and proclaimed the Messiah to them. [6] The crowds were all paying attention to what Philip said, as they listened and saw the signs he was performing. [7] For unclean spirits, crying out with a loud voice, came out of many who were possessed, and many who were paralyzed and lame were healed. [8] So there was great joy in that city.

THE RESPONSE OF SIMON

[9] A man named Simon had previously practiced sorcery in that city and amazed the Samaritan people, while claiming to be somebody great. [10] They all paid attention to him, from the least of them to the greatest, and they said, "This man is called the Great Power of God."[D] [11] They were attentive to him because he had amazed them with his sorceries for a long time. [12] But when they believed Philip, as he proclaimed the good news about the kingdom of God and the name of Jesus Christ, both men and women were baptized. [13] Even Simon himself believed. And after he was baptized, he followed Philip everywhere and was amazed as he observed the signs and great miracles that were being performed.

SIMON'S SIN

[14] When the apostles who were at Jerusalem heard that Samaria had received the word of God, they sent Peter and John to them. [15] After they went down there, they prayed for them so the Samaritans might receive the Holy Spirit because he had not yet come down on any of them. [16] (They had only been baptized in the name of the Lord Jesus.) [17] Then Peter and John laid their hands on them, and they received the Holy Spirit.

[A]7:54 Or were cut to the quick [B]7:60 Lit he fell asleep [C]8:5 Other mss read the
[D]8:10 Or "This is the power of God called Great

18 When Simon saw that the Spirit^A was given through the laying on of the apostles' hands, he offered them money, 19 saying, "Give me this power also so that anyone I lay hands on may receive the Holy Spirit."

20 But Peter told him, "May your silver be destroyed with you, because you thought you could obtain the gift of God with money! 21 You have no part or share in this matter, because your heart is not right before God. 22 Therefore repent of this wickedness of yours, and pray to the Lord that, if possible, your heart's intent may be forgiven. 23 For I see you are poisoned by bitterness and bound by wickedness."

24 "Pray to the Lord for me," Simon replied, "so that nothing you have said may happen to me."

25 So, after they had testified and spoken the word of the Lord, they traveled back to Jerusalem, preaching the gospel in many villages of the Samaritans.

THE CONVERSION OF THE ETHIOPIAN OFFICIAL

26 An angel of the Lord spoke to Philip: "Get up and go south to the road that goes down from Jerusalem to Gaza." (This is the desert road.^B) 27 So he got up and went. There was an Ethiopian man, a eunuch and high official of Candace, queen of the Ethiopians, who was in charge of her entire treasury. He had come to worship in Jerusalem 28 and was sitting in his chariot on his way home, reading the prophet Isaiah aloud.

29 The Spirit told Philip, "Go and join that chariot."

30 When Philip ran up to it, he heard him reading the prophet Isaiah, and said, "Do you understand what you're reading?"

31 "How can I," he said, "unless someone guides me?" So he invited Philip to come up and sit with him. 32 Now the Scripture passage he was reading was this:

He was led like a sheep to the slaughter,
and as a lamb is silent before its shearer,
so he does not open his mouth.
33 In his humiliation justice was denied him.
Who will describe his generation?
For his life is taken from the earth.^C

34 The eunuch said to Philip, "I ask you, who is the prophet saying this about — himself or someone else?" 35 Philip proceeded to tell him the good news about Jesus, beginning with that Scripture.

36 As they were traveling down the road, they came to some water. The eunuch said, "Look, there's water. What would keep me from being baptized?"^D 38 So he ordered the chariot to stop, and both Philip and the eunuch went down into the water, and he baptized him. 39 When they came up out of the water, the Spirit of the Lord carried Philip away, and the eunuch did not see him any longer but went on his way rejoicing. 40 Philip appeared in^E Azotus,^F and he was traveling and preaching the gospel in all the towns until he came to Caesarea.

---

^A 8:18 Other mss add Holy   ^B 8:26 Or is a desert place   ^C 8:32-33 Is 53:7-8
^D 8:36 Some mss include v. 37: Philip said, "If you believe with all your heart you may." And he replied, "I believe that Jesus Christ is the Son of God."   ^E 8:40 Or Philip was found at, or Philip found himself in   ^F 8:40 Or Ashdod

THE DAMASCUS ROAD

9 Now Saul was still breathing threats and murder against the disciples of the Lord. He went to the high priest ² and requested letters from him to the synagogues in Damascus, so that if he found any men or women who belonged to the Way, he might bring them as prisoners to Jerusalem. ³ As he traveled and was nearing Damascus, a light from heaven suddenly flashed around him. ⁴ Falling to the ground, he heard a voice saying to him, "Saul, Saul, why are you persecuting me?"

⁵ "Who are you, Lord?" Saul said.

"I am Jesus, the one you are persecuting," he replied. ⁶ "But get up and go into the city, and you will be told what you must do."

⁷ The men who were traveling with him stood speechless, hearing the sound but seeing no one. ⁸ Saul got up from the ground, and though his eyes were open, he could see nothing. So they took him by the hand and led him into Damascus. ⁹ He was unable to see for three days and did not eat or drink.

SAUL'S BAPTISM

¹⁰ There was a disciple in Damascus named Ananias, and the Lord said to him in a vision, "Ananias."

"Here I am, Lord," he replied.

¹¹ "Get up and go to the street called Straight," the Lord said to him, "to the house of Judas, and ask for a man from Tarsus named Saul, since he is praying there. ¹² In a vision^A he has seen a man named Ananias coming in and placing his hands on him so that he may regain his sight."

¹³ "Lord," Ananias answered, "I have heard from many people about this man, how much harm he has done to your saints in Jerusalem. ¹⁴ And he has authority here from the chief priests to arrest all who call on your name."

¹⁵ But the Lord said to him, "Go, for this man is my chosen instrument to take my name to Gentiles, kings, and Israelites. ¹⁶ I will show him how much he must suffer for my name."

¹⁷ Ananias went and entered the house. He placed his hands on him and said, "Brother Saul, the Lord Jesus, who appeared to you on the road you were traveling, has sent me so that you may regain your sight and be filled with the Holy Spirit."

¹⁸ At once something like scales fell from his eyes, and he regained his sight. Then he got up and was baptized. ¹⁹ And after taking some food, he regained his strength.

SAUL PROCLAIMING THE MESSIAH

Saul was with the disciples in Damascus for some time. ²⁰ Immediately he began proclaiming Jesus in the synagogues: "He is the Son of God."

²¹ All who heard him were astounded and said, "Isn't this the man in Jerusalem who was causing havoc for those who called on this name and came here for the purpose of taking them as prisoners to the chief priests?"

²² But Saul grew stronger and kept confounding the Jews who lived in Damascus by proving that Jesus is the Messiah.

²³ After many days had passed, the Jews conspired to kill him, ²⁴ but Saul learned of their plot. So they were watching the gates day and night intending

^A 9:12 Other mss omit *In a vision*

to kill him, ²⁵ but his disciples took him by night and lowered him in a large basket through an opening in the wall.

SAUL IN JERUSALEM

²⁶ When he arrived in Jerusalem, he tried to join the disciples, but they were all afraid of him, since they did not believe he was a disciple. ²⁷ Barnabas, however, took him and brought him to the apostles and explained to them how Saul had seen the Lord on the road and that the Lord had talked to him, and how in Damascus he had spoken boldly in the name of Jesus. ²⁸ Saul was coming and going with them in Jerusalem, speaking boldly in the name of the Lord. ²⁹ He conversed and debated with the Hellenistic Jews, but they tried to kill him. ³⁰ When the brothers found out, they took him down to Caesarea and sent him off to Tarsus.

THE CHURCH'S GROWTH

³¹ So the church throughout all Judea, Galilee, and Samaria had peace and was strengthened. Living in the fear of the Lord and encouraged by the Holy Spirit, it increased in numbers.

THE HEALING OF AENEAS

³² As Peter was traveling from place to place, he also came down to the saints who lived in Lydda. ³³ There he found a man named Aeneas, who was paralyzed and had been bedridden for eight years. ³⁴ Peter said to him, "Aeneas, Jesus Christ heals you. Get up and make your bed,"ᴬ and immediately he got up. ³⁵ So all who lived in Lydda and Sharon saw him and turned to the Lord.

DORCAS RESTORED TO LIFE

³⁶ In Joppa there was a disciple named Tabitha (which is translated Dorcas). She was always doing good works and acts of charity. ³⁷ About that time she became sick and died. After washing her, they placed her in a room upstairs. ³⁸ Since Lydda was near Joppa, the disciples heard that Peter was there and sent two men to him who urged him, "Don't delay in coming with us." ³⁹ Peter got up and went with them. When he arrived, they led him to the room upstairs. And all the widows approached him, weeping and showing him the robes and clothes that Dorcas had made while she was with them. ⁴⁰ Peter sent them all out of the room. He knelt down, prayed, and turning toward the body said, "Tabitha, get up." She opened her eyes, saw Peter, and sat up. ⁴¹ He gave her his hand and helped her stand up. He called the saints and widows and presented her alive. ⁴² This became known throughout Joppa, and many believed in the Lord. ⁴³ Peter stayed for some time in Joppa with Simon, a leather tanner.

CORNELIUS'S VISION

10 There was a man in Caesarea named Cornelius, a centurion of what was called the Italian Regiment. ² He was a devout man and feared God along with his whole household. He did many charitable deeds for the Jewish people and always prayed to God. ³ About three in the afternoonᴮ he distinctly saw in a vision an angel of God who came in and said to him, "Cornelius."

ᴬ9:34 Or and get ready to eat   ᴮ10:3 Lit About the ninth hour

⁴ Staring at him in awe, he said, "What is it, Lord?"

The angel told him, "Your prayers and your acts of charity have ascended as a memorial offering before God. ⁵ Now send men to Joppa and call for Simon, who is also named Peter. ⁶ He is lodging with Simon, a tanner, whose house is by the sea."

⁷ When the angel who spoke to him had gone, he called two of his household servants and a devout soldier, who was one of those who attended him. ⁸ After explaining everything to them, he sent them to Joppa.

PETER'S VISION

⁹ The next day, as they were traveling and nearing the city, Peter went up to pray on the roof about noon. ^ ¹⁰ He became hungry and wanted to eat, but while they were preparing something, he fell into a trance. ¹¹ He saw heaven opened and an object that resembled a large sheet coming down, being lowered by its four corners to the earth. ¹² In it were all the four-footed animals and reptiles of the earth, and the birds of the sky. ¹³ A voice said to him, "Get up, Peter; kill and eat."

¹⁴ "No, Lord!" Peter said. "For I have never eaten anything impure and ritually unclean."

¹⁵ Again, a second time, the voice said to him, "What God has made clean, do not call impure." ¹⁶ This happened three times, and suddenly the object was taken up into heaven.

PETER VISITS CORNELIUS

¹⁷ While Peter was deeply perplexed about what the vision he had seen might mean, right away the men who had been sent by Cornelius, having asked directions to Simon's house, stood at the gate. ¹⁸ They called out, asking if Simon, who was also named Peter, was lodging there.

¹⁹ While Peter was thinking about the vision, the Spirit told him, "Three men are here looking for you. ²⁰ Get up, go downstairs, and go with them with no doubts at all, because I have sent them."

²¹ Then Peter went down to the men and said, "Here I am, the one you're looking for. What is the reason you're here?"

²² They said, "Cornelius, a centurion, an upright and God-fearing man, who has a good reputation with the whole Jewish nation, was divinely directed by a holy angel to call you to his house and to hear a message from you." ²³ Peter then invited them in and gave them lodging.

The next day he got up and set out with them, and some of the brothers from Joppa went with him. ²⁴ The following day he entered Caesarea. Now Cornelius was expecting them and had called together his relatives and close friends. ²⁵ When Peter entered, Cornelius met him, fell at his feet, and worshiped him.

²⁶ But Peter lifted him up and said, "Stand up. I myself am also a man." ²⁷ While talking with him, he went in and found a large gathering of people. ²⁸ Peter said to them, "You know it's forbidden for a Jewish man to associate with or visit a foreigner, but God has shown me that I must not call any person impure or unclean. ²⁹ That's why I came without any objection when I was sent for. So may I ask why you sent for me?"

^10:9 Lit about the sixth hour

30 Cornelius replied, "Four days ago at this hour, at three in the afternoon,^A I was^B praying in my house. Just then a man in dazzling clothing stood before me 31 and said, 'Cornelius, your prayer has been heard, and your acts of charity have been remembered in God's sight. 32 Therefore send someone to Joppa and invite Simon here, who is also named Peter. He is lodging in Simon the tanner's house by the sea.'^C 33 So I immediately sent for you, and it was good of you to come. So now we are all in the presence of God to hear everything you have been commanded by the Lord."

GOOD NEWS FOR GENTILES

34 Peter began to speak: "Now I truly understand that God doesn't show favoritism, 35 but in every nation the person who fears him and does what is right is acceptable to him. 36 He sent the message to the Israelites, proclaiming the good news of peace through Jesus Christ — he is Lord of all. 37 You know the events that took place throughout all Judea, beginning from Galilee after the baptism that John preached: 38 how God anointed Jesus of Nazareth with the Holy Spirit and with power, and how he went about doing good and healing all who were under the tyranny of the devil, because God was with him. 39 We ourselves are witnesses of everything he did in both the Judean country and in Jerusalem, and yet they killed him by hanging him on a tree. 40 God raised up this man on the third day and caused him to be seen, 41 not by all the people, but by us whom God appointed as witnesses, who ate and drank with him after he rose from the dead. 42 He commanded us to preach to the people and to testify that he is the one appointed by God to be the judge of the living and the dead. 43 All the prophets testify about him that through his name everyone who believes in him receives forgiveness of sins."

GENTILE CONVERSION AND BAPTISM

44 While Peter was still speaking these words, the Holy Spirit came down on all those who heard the message. 45 The circumcised believers who had come with Peter were amazed because the gift of the Holy Spirit had been poured out even on the Gentiles. 46 For they heard them speaking in other tongues^D and declaring the greatness of God.

Then Peter responded, 47 "Can anyone withhold water and prevent these people from being baptized, who have received the Holy Spirit just as we have?" 48 He commanded them to be baptized in the name of Jesus Christ. Then they asked him to stay for a few days.

GENTILE SALVATION DEFENDED

11 The apostles and the brothers and sisters who were throughout Judea heard that the Gentiles had also received the word of God. 2 When Peter went up to Jerusalem, the circumcision party criticized him, 3 saying, "You went to uncircumcised men and ate with them."

4 Peter began to explain to them step by step: 5 "I was in the town of Joppa praying, and I saw, in a trance, an object that resembled a large sheet coming down, being lowered by its four corners from heaven, and it came to me.

---

^A 10:30 Lit at the ninth hour   ^B 10:30 Other mss add fasting and   ^C 10:32 Other mss add When he arrives, he will speak to you.   ^D 10:46 languages

⁶ When I looked closely and considered it, I saw the four-footed animals of the earth, the wild beasts, the reptiles, and the birds of the sky. ⁷ I also heard a voice telling me, 'Get up, Peter; kill and eat.'

⁸ " 'No, Lord!' I said. 'For nothing impure or ritually unclean has ever entered my mouth.' ⁹ But a voice answered from heaven a second time, 'What God has made clean, you must not call impure.'

¹⁰ "Now this happened three times, and everything was drawn up again into heaven. ¹¹ At that very moment, three men who had been sent to me from Caesarea arrived at the house where we were. ¹² The Spirit told me to accompany them with no doubts at all. These six brothers also accompanied me, and we went into the man's house. ¹³ He reported to us how he had seen the angel standing in his house and saying, 'Send ᴬ to Joppa, and call for Simon, who is also named Peter. ¹⁴ He will speak a message to you by which you and all your household will be saved.'

¹⁵ "As I began to speak, the Holy Spirit came down on them, just as on us at the beginning. ¹⁶ I remembered the word of the Lord, how he said, 'John baptized with water, but you will be baptized with the Holy Spirit.' ¹⁷ If, then, God gave them the same gift that he also gave to us when we believed in the Lord Jesus Christ, how could I possibly hinder God?"

¹⁸ When they heard this they became silent. And they glorified God, saying, "So then, God has given repentance resulting in life even to the Gentiles."

THE CHURCH IN ANTIOCH

¹⁹ Now those who had been scattered as a result of the persecution that started because of Stephen made their way as far as Phoenicia, Cyprus, and Antioch, speaking the word to no one except Jews. ²⁰ But there were some of them, men from Cyprus and Cyrene, who came to Antioch and began speaking to the Greeks ᴮ also, proclaiming the good news about the Lord Jesus. ²¹ The Lord's hand was with them, and a large number who believed turned to the Lord. ²² News about them reached ᶜ the church in Jerusalem, and they sent out Barnabas to travel ᴰ as far as Antioch. ²³ When he arrived and saw the grace of God, he was glad and encouraged all of them to remain true to the Lord with devoted hearts, ²⁴ for he was a good man, full of the Holy Spirit and of faith. And large numbers of people were added to the Lord.

²⁵ Then he ᴱ went to Tarsus to search for Saul, ²⁶ and when he found him he brought him to Antioch. For a whole year they met with the church and taught large numbers. The disciples were first called Christians at Antioch.

FAMINE RELIEF

²⁷ In those days some prophets came down from Jerusalem to Antioch. ²⁸ One of them, named Agabus, stood up and predicted by the Spirit that there would be a severe famine throughout the Roman world. ᶠ This took place during the reign of Claudius. ²⁹ Each of the disciples, according to his ability, determined to send relief to the brothers and sisters who lived in Judea. ³⁰ They did this, sending it to the elders by means of Barnabas and Saul.

ᴬ 11:13 Other mss add men   ᴮ 11:20 Lit Hellenists   ᶜ 11:22 Lit reached the ears of
ᴰ 11:22 Other mss omit to travel   ᴱ 11:25 Other mss read Barnabas   ᶠ 11:28 Or
the whole world

JAMES MARTYRED AND PETER JAILED

12 About that time King Herod violently attacked some who belonged to the church, [2] and he executed James, John's brother, with the sword. [3] When he saw that it pleased the Jews, he proceeded to arrest Peter too, during the Festival of Unleavened Bread. [4] After the arrest, he put him in prison and assigned four squads of four soldiers each to guard him, intending to bring him out to the people after the Passover. [5] So Peter was kept in prison, but the church was praying fervently to God for him.

PETER RESCUED

[6] When Herod was about to bring him out for trial, that very night Peter, bound with two chains, was sleeping between two soldiers, while the sentries in front of the door guarded the prison. [7] Suddenly an angel of the Lord appeared, and a light shone in the cell. Striking Peter on the side, he woke him up and said, "Quick, get up!" And the chains fell off his wrists. [8] "Get dressed," the angel told him, "and put on your sandals." And he did. "Wrap your cloak around you," he told him, "and follow me." [9] So he went out and followed, and he did not know that what the angel did was really happening, but he thought he was seeing a vision. [10] After they passed the first and second guards, they came to the iron gate that leads into the city, which opened to them by itself. They went outside and passed one street, and suddenly the angel left him.

[11] When Peter came to himself, he said, "Now I know for certain that the Lord has sent his angel and rescued me from Herod's grasp and from all that the Jewish people expected." [12] As soon as he realized this, he went to the house of Mary, the mother of John Mark, ^A where many had assembled and were praying. [13] He knocked at the door of the outer gate, and a servant named Rhoda came to answer. [14] She recognized Peter's voice, and because of her joy, she did not open the gate but ran in and announced that Peter was standing at the outer gate.

[15] "You're out of your mind!" they told her. But she kept insisting that it was true, and they said, "It's his angel." [16] Peter, however, kept on knocking, and when they opened the door and saw him, they were amazed.

[17] Motioning to them with his hand to be silent, he described to them how the Lord had brought him out of the prison. "Tell these things to James and the brothers," he said, and he left and went to another place.

[18] At daylight, there was a great commotion among the soldiers as to what had become of Peter. [19] After Herod had searched and did not find him, he interrogated the guards and ordered their execution. Then Herod went down from Judea to Caesarea and stayed there.

HEROD'S DEATH

[20] Herod had been very angry with the people of Tyre and Sidon. Together they presented themselves before him. After winning over Blastus, who was in charge of the king's bedroom, they asked for peace, because their country was supplied with food from the king's country. [21] On an appointed day, dressed in royal robes and seated on the throne, Herod delivered a speech to them. [22] The assembled people began to shout, "It's the voice of a god and

---

^A 12:12 Lit *John who was called Mark*

not of a man!" ²³ At once an angel of the Lord struck him because he did not give the glory to God, and he was eaten by worms and died.

²⁴ But the word of God flourished and multiplied. ²⁵ After they had completed their relief mission, Barnabas and Saul returned to[A] Jerusalem, taking along John who was called Mark.

PREPARING FOR THE MISSION FIELD

13 Now in the church at Antioch there were prophets and teachers: Barnabas, Simeon who was called Niger, Lucius of Cyrene, Manaen, a close friend of Herod the tetrarch, and Saul.

² As they were worshiping[B] the Lord and fasting, the Holy Spirit said, "Set apart for me Barnabas and Saul for the work to which I have called them." ³ Then after they had fasted, prayed, and laid hands on them, they sent them off.

THE MISSION TO CYPRUS

⁴ So being sent out by the Holy Spirit, they went down to Seleucia, and from there they sailed to Cyprus. ⁵ Arriving in Salamis, they proclaimed the word of God in the Jewish synagogues. They also had John as their assistant. ⁶ When they had traveled the whole island as far as Paphos, they came across a sorcerer, a Jewish false prophet named Bar-Jesus. ⁷ He was with the proconsul, Sergius Paulus, an intelligent man. This man summoned Barnabas and Saul and wanted to hear the word of God. ⁸ But Elymas the sorcerer (that is the meaning of his name) opposed them and tried to turn the proconsul away from the faith.

⁹ But Saul — also called Paul — filled with the Holy Spirit, stared straight at Elymas ¹⁰ and said, "You are full of all kinds of deceit and trickery, you son of the devil and enemy of all that is right. Won't you ever stop perverting the straight paths of the Lord? ¹¹ Now, look, the Lord's hand is against you. You are going to be blind, and will not see the sun for a time." Immediately a mist and darkness fell on him, and he went around seeking someone to lead him by the hand.

¹² Then, when he saw what happened, the proconsul believed, because he was astonished at the teaching of the Lord.

PAUL'S SERMON IN ANTIOCH OF PISIDIA

¹³ Paul and his companions set sail from Paphos and came to Perga in Pamphylia, but John left them and went back to Jerusalem. ¹⁴ They continued their journey from Perga and reached Pisidian Antioch. On the Sabbath day they went into the synagogue and sat down. ¹⁵ After the reading of the Law and the Prophets, the leaders of the synagogue sent word to them, saying, "Brothers, if you have any word of encouragement for the people, you can speak."

¹⁶ Paul stood up and motioned with his hand and said: "Fellow Israelites, and you who fear God, listen! ¹⁷ The God of this people Israel chose our ancestors, made the people prosper during their stay in the land of Egypt, and led them out of it with a mighty[C] arm. ¹⁸ And for about forty years he put up with them[D] in the wilderness; ¹⁹ and after destroying seven nations in the land of Canaan, he gave them their land as an inheritance. ²⁰ This all took

---

[A]12:25 Other mss read *from*   [B]13:2 Or *were ministering to*   [C]13:17 Lit *with an uplifted*   [D]13:18 Other mss read *he cared for them* about 450 years. After this, he gave them judges until Samuel the prophet. [21] Then they asked for a king, and God gave them Saul the son of Kish, a man of the tribe of Benjamin, for forty years. [22] After removing him, he raised up David as their king and testified about him: '**I have found David** the son of Jesse to be **a man after my own heart,**[A] who will carry out all my will.'

[23] "From this man's descendants, as he promised, God brought to Israel the Savior, Jesus.[B] [24] Before his coming to public attention, John had previously proclaimed a baptism of repentance to all the people of Israel. [25] Now as John was completing his mission, he said, 'Who do you think I am? I am not the one. But one is coming after me, and I am not worthy to untie the sandals on his feet.'

[26] "Brothers and sisters, children of Abraham's race, and those among you who fear God, it is to us that the word of this salvation has been sent. [27] Since the residents of Jerusalem and their rulers did not recognize him or the sayings of the prophets that are read every Sabbath, they have fulfilled their words by condemning him. [28] Though they found no grounds for the death sentence, they asked Pilate to have him killed. [29] When they had carried out all that had been written about him, they took him down from the tree and put him in a tomb. [30] But God raised him from the dead, [31] and he appeared for many days to those who came up with him from Galilee to Jerusalem, who are now his witnesses to the people. [32] And we ourselves proclaim to you the good news of the promise that was made to our ancestors. [33] God has fulfilled this for us, their children, by raising up Jesus, as it is written in the second Psalm:

You are my Son;
today I have become your Father.[C,D]

[34] As to his raising him from the dead, never to return to decay, he has spoken in this way, **I will give you the holy and sure promises of David.**[E] [35] Therefore he also says in another passage, **You will not let your Holy One see decay.**[F] [36] For David, after serving God's purpose in his own generation, fell asleep, was buried with his fathers, and decayed, [37] but the one God raised up did not decay. [38] Therefore, let it be known to you, brothers and sisters, that through this man forgiveness of sins is being proclaimed to you. [39] Everyone who believes is justified[G] through him from everything that you could not be justified from through the law of Moses. [40] So beware that what is said in the prophets does not happen to you:

[41] **Look, you scoffers,**
marvel and vanish away,
because I am doing a work in your days,
a work that you will never believe,
even if someone were to explain it to you."[H]

PAUL AND BARNABAS IN ANTIOCH

[42] As they were leaving, the people[I] urged them to speak about these matters the following Sabbath. [43] After the synagogue had been dismissed, many of

---

[A]13:22 1Sm 13:14; Ps 89:20 [B]13:23 Other mss read *brought salvation*
[C]13:33 Or *I have begotten you* [D]13:33 Ps 2:7 [E]13:34 Is 55:3 [F]13:35 Ps
16:10 [G]13:39 Or *freed,* also later in this verse [H]13:41 Hab 1:5 [I]13:42 Other
mss read *they were leaving the synagogue of the Jews, the Gentiles*

the Jews and devout converts to Judaism followed Paul and Barnabas, who were speaking with them and urging them to continue in the grace of God.

⁴⁴ The following Sabbath almost the whole town assembled to hear the word of the Lord.^ ⁴⁵ But when the Jews saw the crowds, they were filled with jealousy and began to contradict what Paul was saying, insulting him. ⁴⁶ Paul and Barnabas boldly replied, "It was necessary that the word of God be spoken to you first. Since you reject it and judge yourselves unworthy of eternal life, we are turning to the Gentiles. ⁴⁷ For this is what the Lord has commanded us:

**I have made you
a light for the Gentiles
to bring salvation
to the end of the earth."**ᴮ

⁴⁸ When the Gentiles heard this, they rejoiced and honored the word of the Lord, and all who had been appointed to eternal life believed. ⁴⁹ The word of the Lord spread through the whole region. ⁵⁰ But the Jews incited the prominent God-fearing women and the leading men of the city. They stirred up persecution against Paul and Barnabas and expelled them from their district. ⁵¹ But Paul and Barnabas shook the dust off their feet against them and went to Iconium. ⁵² And the disciples were filled with joy and the Holy Spirit.

GROWTH AND PERSECUTION IN ICONIUM

14 In Iconium they entered the Jewish synagogue, as usual, and spoke in such a way that a great number of both Jews and Greeks believed. ² But the unbelieving Jews stirred up the Gentiles and poisoned their minds against the brothers. ³ So they stayed there a long time and spoke boldly for the Lord, who testified to the message of his grace by enabling them to do signs and wonders. ⁴ But the people of the city were divided, some siding with the Jews and others with the apostles. ⁵ When an attempt was made by both the Gentiles and Jews, with their rulers, to mistreat and stone them, ⁶ they found out about it and fled to the Lycaonian towns of Lystra and Derbe and to the surrounding countryside. ⁷ There they continued preaching the gospel.

MISTAKEN FOR GODS IN LYSTRA

⁸ In Lystra a man was sitting who was without strength in his feet, had never walked, and had been lame from birth. ⁹ He listened as Paul spoke. After looking directly at him and seeing that he had faith to be healed, ¹⁰ Paul said in a loud voice, "Stand up on your feet!" And he jumped up and began to walk around.

¹¹ When the crowds saw what Paul had done, they shouted, saying in the Lycaonian language, "The gods have come down to us in human form!" ¹² Barnabas they called Zeus, and Paul, Hermes, because he was the chief speaker. ¹³ The priest of Zeus, whose temple was just outside the town, brought bulls and wreaths to the gates because he intended, with the crowds, to offer sacrifice.

¹⁴ The apostles Barnabas and Paul tore their robes when they heard this and rushed into the crowd, shouting: ¹⁵ "People! Why are you doing these things? We are people also, just like you, and we are proclaiming good news

^13:44 Other mss read *of God* ᴮ13:47 Is 49:6

to you, that you turn from these worthless things to the living God, **who made the heaven, the earth, the sea, and everything in them.**[A] [16] In past generations he allowed all the nations to go their own way, [17] although he did not leave himself without a witness, since he did what is good by giving you rain from heaven and fruitful seasons and filling you with food and your[B] hearts with joy." [18] Even though they said these things, they barely stopped the crowds from sacrificing to them.

[19] Some Jews came from Antioch and Iconium, and when they won over the crowds, they stoned Paul and dragged him out of the city, thinking he was dead. [20] After the disciples gathered around him, he got up and went into the town. The next day he left with Barnabas for Derbe.

CHURCH PLANTING

[21] After they had preached the gospel in that town and made many disciples, they returned to Lystra, to Iconium, and to Antioch, [22] strengthening the[C] disciples by encouraging them to continue in the faith and by telling them, "It is necessary to go through many hardships to enter the kingdom of God." [23] When they had appointed elders for them in every church and prayed with fasting, they committed them to the Lord in whom they had believed.

[24] They passed through Pisidia and came to Pamphylia. [25] After they had spoken the word in Perga, they went down to Attalia. [26] From there they sailed back to Antioch where they had been commended to the grace of God for the work they had now completed. [27] After they arrived and gathered the church together, they reported everything God had done with them and that he had opened the door of faith to the Gentiles. [28] And they spent a considerable time with the disciples.

DISPUTE IN ANTIOCH

15 Some men came down from Judea and began to teach the brothers: "Unless you are circumcised according to the custom prescribed by Moses, you cannot be saved." [2] After Paul and Barnabas had engaged them in serious argument and debate, Paul and Barnabas and some others were appointed to go up to the apostles and elders in Jerusalem about this issue. [3] When they had been sent on their way by the church, they passed through both Phoenicia and Samaria, describing in detail the conversion of the Gentiles, and they brought great joy to all the brothers and sisters.

[4] When they arrived at Jerusalem, they were welcomed by the church, the apostles, and the elders, and they reported all that God had done with them. [5] But some of the believers who belonged to the party of the Pharisees stood up and said, "It is necessary to circumcise them and to command them to keep the law of Moses."

THE JERUSALEM COUNCIL

[6] The apostles and the elders gathered to consider this matter. [7] After there had been much debate, Peter stood up and said to them: "Brothers and sisters, you are aware that in the early days God made a choice among you,[D] that by my mouth the Gentiles would hear the gospel message and believe.

[A]14:15 Ex 20:11; Ps 146:6   [B]14:17 Other mss read *our*   [C]14:22 Lit *the souls of the*   [D]15:7 Other mss read *us*

SAVED BY GRACE ALONE

ACTS 15:1-35; ROMANS 2:17-24; GALATIANS 2:21

I imagine them gathered in a dark, dimly lit room. The group of Jewish men, newly converted to Christianity, huddled together in deep discussion. Their topic was this: Do Gentile Christians need to be circumcised in order to be saved?

It was a serious question at the time. So serious that this meeting is recorded in history as the Jerusalem Council.

Things got heated at the Council. Paul disagreed with the Pharisees. Barnabas backed Paul. The Pharisees pulled out their scrolls and began reciting Moses' words from long ago. What would they decide? Who would have the final say?

Finally, Peter stood up, quieted the group, and settled the matter. "We believe that we are saved through the grace of the Lord Jesus in the same way they are" (Ac 15:11).

Before Jesus, the chosen people of Israel had been instructed to do things a certain way. Abiding by the law set them apart, and circumcision was part of the law. After the cross of Christ, however, it was possible for all Gentiles—those with no knowledge of the law—to be adopted into God's family and be saved. The Jews had faithfully done their thing for hundreds of years, and then suddenly, anyone was allowed into their club.

If I were a Jewish Christian, I'd be upset too. *What do you mean the Gentiles are included?*

I've been following the law my entire life. Ever heard of seniority?

We had a rule in our house growing up. The oldest daughter in the car rode shotgun. I was committed to this rule. If my little sister tried to slide up front, I'd remind her I was older and, therefore, deserved the front seat.

I had seniority in the car, and I've carried this sense of entitlement with me elsewhere in life. Maybe you have, too. In our sinful human nature we size each other up, deciphering who is worthy and who isn't. Who has earned the shotgun seat and who needs to wait a few years.

The debate of the Jerusalem Council might be a debate we need to have with our own hearts. The truth the Holy Spirit revealed that day is still true. **When it comes to salvation through Christ, God doesn't take seniority into account. He looks only at the heart** (1Sm 16:7). He doesn't look at our previous religious affiliations, or knowledge of the law. He doesn't look at our age or talent or holiness or lack thereof. In His eyes, we are made worthy by the blood of Jesus alone.

Let's not revert to the old way of the law. As Paul warns, let us not "set aside the grace of God" (Gl 2:21). Instead, let's set grace at our core. Let's view others and ourselves through its lens, so the people of today can know us by our love rather than our rules.

⁸ And God, who knows the heart, bore witness to them by giving them the Holy Spirit, just as he also did to us. ⁹ He made no distinction between us and them, cleansing their hearts by faith. ¹⁰ Now then, why are you testing God by putting a yoke on the disciples' necks that neither our ancestors nor we have been able to bear? ¹¹ On the contrary, we believe that we are saved through the grace of the Lord Jesus in the same way they are."

¹² The whole assembly became silent and listened to Barnabas and Paul describe all the signs and wonders God had done through them among the Gentiles. ¹³ After they stopped speaking, James responded: "Brothers and sisters, listen to me. ¹⁴ Simeon^A has reported how God first intervened to take from the Gentiles a people for his name. ¹⁵ And the words of the prophets agree with this, as it is written:

¹⁶ **After these things I will return**
   and rebuild David's fallen tent.
   I will rebuild its ruins
   and set it up again,
¹⁷ **so the rest of humanity**
   may seek the Lord —
   even all the Gentiles
   who are called by my name —
   declares the Lord
   who makes these things ¹⁸ **known from long ago.** ^{B,C}

¹⁹ Therefore, in my judgment, we should not cause difficulties for those among the Gentiles who turn to God, ²⁰ but instead we should write to them to abstain from things polluted by idols, from sexual immorality, from eating anything that has been strangled, and from blood. ²¹ For since ancient times, Moses has had those who proclaim him in every city, and every Sabbath day he is read aloud in the synagogues."

THE LETTER TO THE GENTILE BELIEVERS

²² Then the apostles and the elders, with the whole church, decided to select men who were among them and to send them to Antioch with Paul and Barnabas: Judas, called Barsabbas, and Silas, both leading men among the brothers. ²³ They wrote:

"From the apostles and the elders, your brothers,
To the brothers and sisters among the Gentiles in Antioch, Syria, and Cilicia:
Greetings.
²⁴ Since we have heard that some without our authorization went out from us and troubled you with their words and unsettled your hearts, ^D ²⁵ we have unanimously decided to select men and send them to you along with our dearly loved Barnabas and Paul, ²⁶ who have risked their lives for the name of our Lord Jesus Christ. ²⁷ Therefore we have sent Judas and Silas, who will personally report the same things by word of mouth. ²⁸ For it was the Holy Spirit's decision — and ours — not to

^A15:14 Simon (Peter)   ^B15:17-18 Other mss read *says the Lord who does all these things. Known to God from long ago are all his works.*   ^C15:16-18 Am 9:11-12; Is 45:21   ^D15:24 Other mss add *by saying, 'Be circumcised and keep the law,'*

place further burdens on you beyond these requirements: [29] that you abstain from food offered to idols, from blood, from eating anything that has been strangled, and from sexual immorality. You will do well if you keep yourselves from these things. Farewell."

THE OUTCOME OF THE JERUSALEM LETTER

[30] So they were sent off and went down to Antioch, and after gathering the assembly, they delivered the letter. [31] When they read it, they rejoiced because of its encouragement. [32] Both Judas and Silas, who were also prophets themselves, encouraged the brothers and sisters and strengthened them with a long message. [33] After spending some time there, they were sent back in peace by the brothers and sisters to those who had sent them. [A,B] [35] But Paul and Barnabas, along with many others, remained in Antioch, teaching and proclaiming the word of the Lord.

PAUL AND BARNABAS PART COMPANY

[36] After some time had passed, Paul said to Barnabas, "Let's go back and visit the brothers and sisters in every town where we have preached the word of the Lord and see how they're doing." [37] Barnabas wanted to take along John Mark. [C] [38] But Paul insisted that they should not take along this man who had deserted them in Pamphylia and had not gone on with them to the work. [39] They had such a sharp disagreement that they parted company, and Barnabas took Mark with him and sailed off to Cyprus. [40] But Paul chose Silas and departed, after being commended by the brothers and sisters to the grace of the Lord. [41] He traveled through Syria and Cilicia, strengthening the churches.

PAUL SELECTS TIMOTHY

16 Paul went on to Derbe and Lystra, where there was a disciple named Timothy, the son of a believing Jewish woman, but his father was a Greek. [2] The brothers and sisters at Lystra and Iconium spoke highly of him. [3] Paul wanted Timothy to go with him; so he took him and circumcised him because of the Jews who were in those places, since they all knew that his father was a Greek. [4] As they traveled through the towns, they delivered the decisions reached by the apostles and elders at Jerusalem for the people to observe. [5] So the churches were strengthened in the faith and grew daily in numbers.

EVANGELIZATION OF EUROPE

[6] They went through the region of Phrygia and Galatia; they had been forbidden by the Holy Spirit to speak the word in Asia. [7] When they came to Mysia, they tried to go into Bithynia, but the Spirit of Jesus did not allow them. [8] Passing by Mysia they went down to Troas. [9] During the night Paul had a vision in which a Macedonian man was standing and pleading with him, "Cross over to Macedonia and help us!" [10] After he had seen the vision, we immediately made efforts to set out for Macedonia, concluding that God had called us to preach the gospel to them.

[A] 15:33 Other mss read *the brothers to the apostles*   [B] 15:33 Other mss add v. 34: *But Silas decided to stay there.*   [C] 15:37 Lit *John who was called Mark*

LYDIA'S CONVERSION

[11] From Troas we put out to sea and sailed straight for Samothrace, the next day to Neapolis, [12] and from there to Philippi, a Roman colony and a leading city of the district of Macedonia. We stayed in that city for several days. [13] On the Sabbath day we went outside the city gate by the river, where we expected to find a place of prayer. We sat down and spoke to the women gathered there. [14] A God-fearing woman named Lydia, a dealer in purple cloth from the city of Thyatira, was listening. The Lord opened her heart to respond to what Paul was saying. [15] After she and her household were baptized, she urged us, "If you consider me a believer in the Lord, come and stay at my house." And she persuaded us.

PAUL AND SILAS IN PRISON

[16] Once, as we were on our way to prayer, a slave girl met us who had a spirit by which she predicted the future. She made a large profit for her owners by fortune-telling. [17] As she followed Paul and us she cried out, "These men, who are proclaiming to you[A] the way of salvation, are the servants of the Most High God." [18] She did this for many days.

Paul was greatly annoyed. Turning to the spirit, he said, "I command you in the name of Jesus Christ to come out of her!" And it came out right away.

[19] When her owners realized that their hope of profit was gone, they seized Paul and Silas and dragged them into the marketplace to the authorities. [20] Bringing them before the chief magistrates, they said, "These men are seriously disturbing our city. They are Jews [21] and are promoting customs that are not legal for us as Romans to adopt or practice." [22] The crowd joined in the attack against them, and the chief magistrates stripped off their clothes and ordered them to be beaten with rods. [23] After they had severely flogged them, they threw them in jail, ordering the jailer to guard them carefully. [24] Receiving such an order, he put them into the inner prison and secured their feet in the stocks.

A MIDNIGHT DELIVERANCE

[25] About midnight Paul and Silas were praying and singing hymns to God, and the prisoners were listening to them. [26] Suddenly there was such a violent earthquake that the foundations of the jail were shaken, and immediately all the doors were opened, and everyone's chains came loose. [27] When the jailer woke up and saw the doors of the prison standing open, he drew his sword and was going to kill himself, since he thought the prisoners had escaped. [28] But Paul called out in a loud voice, "Don't harm yourself, because we're all here!"

[29] The jailer called for lights, rushed in, and fell down trembling before Paul and Silas. [30] He escorted them out and said, "Sirs, what must I do to be saved?" [31] They said, "Believe in the Lord Jesus, and you will be saved — you and your household." [32] And they spoke the word of the Lord to him along with everyone in his house. [33] He took them the same hour of the night and washed their wounds. Right away he and all his family were baptized. [34] He brought them into his house, set a meal before them, and rejoiced because he had come to believe in God with his entire household.

[A] 16:17 Other mss read us

AN OFFICIAL APOLOGY

[35] When daylight came, the chief magistrates sent the police to say, "Release those men."

[36] The jailer reported these words to Paul: "The magistrates have sent orders for you to be released. So come out now and go in peace."

[37] But Paul said to them, "They beat us in public without a trial, although we are Roman citizens, and threw us in jail. And now are they going to send us away secretly? Certainly not! On the contrary, let them come themselves and escort us out."

[38] The police reported these words to the magistrates. They were afraid when they heard that Paul and Silas were Roman citizens. [39] So they came to appease them, and escorting them from prison, they urged them to leave town. [40] After leaving the jail, they came to Lydia's house, where they saw and encouraged the brothers and sisters, and departed.

A SHORT MINISTRY IN THESSALONICA

17 After they passed through Amphipolis and Apollonia, they came to Thessalonica, where there was a Jewish synagogue. [2] As usual, Paul went into the synagogue, and on three Sabbath days reasoned with them from the Scriptures, [3] explaining and proving that it was necessary for the Messiah to suffer and rise from the dead: "This Jesus I am proclaiming to you is the Messiah." [4] Some of them were persuaded and joined Paul and Silas, including a large number of God-fearing Greeks, as well as a number of the leading women.

RIOT IN THE CITY

[5] But the Jews became jealous, and they brought together some wicked men from the marketplace, formed a mob, and started a riot in the city. Attacking Jason's house, they searched for them to bring them out to the public assembly. [6] When they did not find them, they dragged Jason and some of the brothers before the city officials, shouting, "These men who have turned the world upside down have come here too, [7] and Jason has welcomed them. They are all acting contrary to Caesar's decrees, saying that there is another king — Jesus." [8] The crowd and city officials who heard these things were upset. [9] After taking a security bond from Jason and the others, they released them.

THE BEREANS SEARCH THE SCRIPTURES

[10] As soon as it was night, the brothers and sisters sent Paul and Silas away to Berea. Upon arrival, they went into the synagogue of the Jews. [11] The people here were of more noble character than those in Thessalonica, since they received the word with eagerness and examined the Scriptures daily to see if these things were so. [12] Consequently, many of them believed, including a number of the prominent Greek women as well as men. [13] But when the Jews from Thessalonica found out that the word of God had been proclaimed by Paul at Berea, they came there too, agitating and upsetting[A] the crowds. [14] Then the brothers and sisters immediately sent Paul away to go to the coast, but Silas and Timothy stayed on there. [15] Those who escorted Paul brought him as far as Athens, and after receiving instructions for Silas and Timothy to come to him as quickly as possible, they departed.

[A] 17:13 Other mss omit *and upsetting*

PAUL IN ATHENS

[16] While Paul was waiting for them in Athens, he was deeply distressed when he saw that the city was full of idols. [17] So he reasoned in the synagogue with the Jews and with those who worshiped God, as well as in the marketplace every day with those who happened to be there. [18] Some of the Epicurean and Stoic philosophers also debated with him. Some said, "What is this ignorant show-off[A] trying to say?"

Others replied, "He seems to be a preacher of foreign deities" — because he was telling the good news about Jesus and the resurrection.

[19] They took him and brought him to the Areopagus,[B] and said, "May we learn about this new teaching you are presenting? [20] Because what you say sounds strange to us, and we want to know what these things mean." [21] Now all the Athenians and the foreigners residing there spent their time on nothing else but telling or hearing something new.

THE AREOPAGUS ADDRESS

[22] Paul stood in the middle of the Areopagus and said: "People of Athens! I see that you are extremely religious in every respect. [23] For as I was passing through and observing the objects of your worship, I even found an altar on which was inscribed: 'To an Unknown God.' Therefore, what you worship in ignorance, this I proclaim to you. [24] The God who made the world and everything in it — he is Lord of heaven and earth — does not live in shrines made by hands. [25] Neither is he served by human hands, as though he needed anything, since he himself gives everyone life and breath and all things. [26] From one man[C] he has made every nationality to live over the whole earth and has determined their appointed times and the boundaries of where they live. [27] He did this so that they might seek God, and perhaps they might reach out and find him, though he is not far from each one of us. [28] For in him we live and move and have our being, as even some of your own poets have said, 'For we are also his offspring.' [29] Since we are God's offspring then, we shouldn't think that the divine nature is like gold or silver or stone, an image fashioned by human art and imagination.

[30] "Therefore, having overlooked the times of ignorance, God now commands all people everywhere to repent, [31] because he has set a day when he is going to judge the world in righteousness by the man he has appointed. He has provided proof of this to everyone by raising him from the dead."

[32] When they heard about the resurrection of the dead, some began to ridicule him, but others said, "We'd like to hear from you again about this." [33] So Paul left their presence. [34] However, some people joined him and believed, including Dionysius the Areopagite, a woman named Damaris, and others with them.

FOUNDING THE CORINTHIAN CHURCH

18 After this, he[D] left Athens and went to Corinth, [2] where he found a Jew named Aquila, a native of Pontus, who had recently come from Italy with his wife Priscilla because Claudius had ordered all the Jews to leave Rome. Paul came to them, [3] and since they were of the same occupation,

---

[A]17:18 Lit *this seed picker* [B]17:19 Or *Mars Hill* [C]17:26 Other mss read *blood*
[D]18:1 Other mss read *Paul*

tentmakers by trade, he stayed with them and worked. [4] He reasoned in the synagogue every Sabbath and tried to persuade both Jews and Greeks.

[5] When Silas and Timothy arrived from Macedonia, Paul devoted himself to preaching the word[A] and testified to the Jews that Jesus is the Messiah. [6] When they resisted and blasphemed, he shook out his clothes and told them, "Your blood is on your own heads! I am innocent. [B] From now on I will go to the Gentiles." [7] So he left there and went to the house of a man named Titius Justus, a worshiper of God, whose house was next door to the synagogue. [8] Crispus, the leader of the synagogue, believed in the Lord, along with his whole household. Many of the Corinthians, when they heard, believed and were baptized.

[9] The Lord said to Paul in a night vision, "Don't be afraid, but keep on speaking and don't be silent. [10] For I am with you, and no one will lay a hand on you to hurt you, because I have many people in this city." [11] He stayed there a year and a half, teaching the word of God among them.

[12] While Gallio was proconsul of Achaia, the Jews made a united attack against Paul and brought him to the tribunal. [13] "This man," they said, " is persuading people to worship God in ways contrary to the law."

[14] As Paul was about to open his mouth, Gallio said to the Jews, "If it were a matter of wrongdoing or of a serious crime, it would be reasonable for me to put up with you Jews. [15] But if these are questions about words, names, and your own law, see to it yourselves. I refuse to be a judge of such things." [16] So he drove them from the tribunal. [17] And they all[C] seized Sosthenes, the leader of the synagogue, and beat him in front of the tribunal, but none of these things mattered to Gallio.

THE RETURN TRIP TO ANTIOCH

[18] After staying for some time, Paul said farewell to the brothers and sisters and sailed away to Syria, accompanied by Priscilla and Aquila. He shaved his head at Cenchreae because of a vow he had taken. [19] When they reached Ephesus he left them there, but he himself entered the synagogue and debated with the Jews. [20] When they asked him to stay for a longer time, he declined, [21] but he said farewell and added,[D] "I'll come back to you again, if God wills." Then he set sail from Ephesus.

[22] On landing at Caesarea, he went up to Jerusalem and greeted the church, then went down to Antioch.

[23] After spending some time there, he set out, traveling through one place after another in the region of Galatia and Phrygia, strengthening all the disciples.

THE ELOQUENT APOLLOS

[24] Now a Jew named Apollos, a native Alexandrian, an eloquent man who was competent in the use of the Scriptures, arrived in Ephesus. [25] He had been instructed in the way of the Lord; and being fervent in spirit,[E] he was speaking and teaching accurately about Jesus, although he knew only John's baptism. [26] He began to speak boldly in the synagogue. After Priscilla and

---

[A] 18:5 Other mss read *was urged by the Spirit* [B] 18:6 Lit *clean* [C] 18:17 Other mss read *Then all the Greeks* [D] 18:21 Other mss add *"By all means it is necessary to keep the coming festival in Jerusalem. But* [E] 18:25 Or *in the Spirit*

Aquila heard him, they took him aside^A and explained the way of God to him more accurately. ²⁷ When he wanted to cross over to Achaia, the brothers and sisters wrote to the disciples to welcome him. After he arrived, he was a great help to those who by grace had believed. ²⁸ For he vigorously refuted the Jews in public, demonstrating through the Scriptures that Jesus is the Messiah.

TWELVE DISCIPLES OF JOHN THE BAPTIST

19 While Apollos was in Corinth, Paul traveled through the interior regions and came to Ephesus. He found some disciples ² and asked them, "Did you receive the Holy Spirit when you believed?"

"No," they told him, "we haven't even heard that there is a Holy Spirit."

³ "Into what then were you baptized?" he asked them.

"Into John's baptism," they replied.

⁴ Paul said, "John baptized with a baptism of repentance, telling the people that they should believe in the one who would come after him, that is, in Jesus."

⁵ When they heard this, they were baptized into the name of the Lord Jesus. ⁶ And when Paul had laid his hands on them, the Holy Spirit came on them, and they began to speak in other tongues^B and to prophesy. ⁷ Now there were about twelve men in all.

IN THE LECTURE HALL OF TYRANNUS

⁸ Paul entered the synagogue and spoke boldly over a period of three months, arguing and persuading them about the kingdom of God. ⁹ But when some became hardened and would not believe, slandering the Way in front of the crowd, he withdrew from them, taking the disciples, and conducted discussions every day in the lecture hall of Tyrannus. ¹⁰ This went on for two years, so that all the residents of Asia, both Jews and Greeks, heard the word of the Lord.

DEMONISM DEFEATED AT EPHESUS

¹¹ God was performing extraordinary miracles by Paul's hands, ¹² so that even facecloths or aprons^C that had touched his skin were brought to the sick, and the diseases left them, and the evil spirits came out of them.

¹³ Now some of the itinerant Jewish exorcists also attempted to pronounce the name of the Lord Jesus over those who had evil spirits, saying, "I command you by the Jesus that Paul preaches!" ¹⁴ Seven sons of Sceva, a Jewish high priest, were doing this. ¹⁵ The evil spirit answered them, "I know Jesus, and I recognize Paul — but who are you?" ¹⁶ Then the man who had the evil spirit jumped on them, overpowered them all, and prevailed against them, so that they ran out of that house naked and wounded. ¹⁷ When this became known to everyone who lived in Ephesus, both Jews and Greeks, they became afraid, and the name of the Lord Jesus was held in high esteem.

¹⁸ And many who had become believers came confessing and disclosing their practices, ¹⁹ while many of those who had practiced magic collected their books and burned them in front of everyone. So they calculated their value and found it to be fifty thousand pieces of silver. ²⁰ In this way the word of the Lord flourished and prevailed.

---

^A 18:26 Lit *they received him*   ^B 19:6 languages   ^C 19:12 Or *sweat cloths*

THE RIOT IN EPHESUS

[21] After these events, Paul resolved by the Spirit[A] to pass through Macedonia and Achaia and go to Jerusalem. "After I've been there," he said, "It is necessary for me to see Rome as well." [22] After sending to Macedonia two of those who assisted him, Timothy and Erastus, he himself stayed in Asia for a while.

[23] About that time there was a major disturbance about the Way. [24] For a person named Demetrius, a silversmith who made silver shrines of Artemis, provided a great deal of business for the craftsmen. [25] When he had assembled them, as well as the workers engaged in this type of business, he said: "Men, you know that our prosperity is derived from this business. [26] You see and hear that not only in Ephesus, but in almost all of Asia, this man Paul has persuaded and misled a considerable number of people by saying that gods made by hand are not gods. [27] Not only do we run a risk that our business may be discredited, but also that the temple of the great goddess Artemis may be despised and her magnificence come to the verge of ruin — the very one all of Asia and the world worship."

[28] When they had heard this, they were filled with rage and began to cry out, "Great is Artemis of the Ephesians!" [29] So the city was filled with confusion, and they rushed all together into the amphitheater, dragging along Gaius and Aristarchus, Macedonians who were Paul's traveling companions. [30] Although Paul wanted to go in before the people, the disciples did not let him. [31] Even some of the provincial officials of Asia, who were his friends, sent word to him, pleading with him not to venture[B] into the amphitheater. [32] Some were shouting one thing and some another, because the assembly was in confusion, and most of them did not know why they had come together. [33] Some Jews in the crowd gave instructions to Alexander[C] after they pushed him to the front. Motioning with his hand, Alexander wanted to make his defense to the people. [34] But when they recognized that he was a Jew, they all shouted in unison for about two hours: "Great is Artemis of the Ephesians!"

[35] When the city clerk had calmed the crowd down, he said, "People of Ephesus! What person is there who doesn't know that the city of the Ephesians is the temple guardian of the great[D] Artemis, and of the image that fell from heaven? [36] Therefore, since these things are undeniable, you must keep calm and not do anything rash. [37] For you have brought these men here who are not temple robbers or blasphemers of our[E] goddess. [38] So if Demetrius and the craftsmen who are with him have a case against anyone, the courts are in session, and there are proconsuls. Let them bring charges against one another. [39] But if you seek anything further, it must be decided in a legal assembly. [40] In fact, we run a risk of being charged with rioting for what happened today, since there is no justification that we can give as a reason for this disturbance." [41] After saying this, he dismissed the assembly.

PAUL IN MACEDONIA

20 After the uproar was over, Paul sent for the disciples, encouraged them, and after saying farewell, departed to go to Macedonia. [2] And when he had passed through those areas and offered them many words of encouragement, he came to Greece [3] and stayed three months. The

---

[A]19:21 Or *in his spirit*   [B]19:31 Lit *not to give himself*   [C]19:33 Or *thought it was about Alexander*   [D]19:35 Other mss add *goddess*   [E]19:37 Other mss read *your*

Jews plotted against him when he was about to set sail for Syria, and so he decided to go back through Macedonia. [4] He was accompanied[A] by Sopater son of Pyrrhus[B] from Berea, Aristarchus and Secundus from Thessalonica, Gaius from Derbe, Timothy, and Tychicus and Trophimus from the province of Asia. [5] These men went on ahead and waited for us in Troas, [6] but we sailed away from Philippi after the Festival of Unleavened Bread. In five days we reached them at Troas, where we spent seven days.

EUTYCHUS REVIVED AT TROAS

[7] On the first day of the week, we[C] assembled to break bread. Paul spoke to them, and since he was about to depart the next day, he kept on talking until midnight. [8] There were many lamps in the room upstairs where we were assembled, [9] and a young man named Eutychus was sitting on a window sill and sank into a deep sleep as Paul kept on talking. When he was overcome by sleep, he fell down from the third story and was picked up dead. [10] But Paul went down, bent over him, embraced him, and said, "Don't be alarmed, because he's alive." [11] After going upstairs, breaking the bread, and eating, Paul talked a long time until dawn. Then he left. [12] They brought the boy home alive and were greatly comforted.

FROM TROAS TO MILETUS

[13] We went on ahead to the ship and sailed for Assos, where we were going to take Paul on board, because these were his instructions, since he himself was going by land. [14] When he met us at Assos, we took him on board and went on to Mitylene. [15] Sailing from there, the next day we arrived off Chios. The following day we crossed over to Samos, and[D] the day after, we came to Miletus. [16] For Paul had decided to sail past Ephesus to avoid spending time in the province of Asia, because he was hurrying to be in Jerusalem, if possible, for the day of Pentecost.

FAREWELL ADDRESS TO THE EPHESIAN ELDERS

[17] Now from Miletus, he sent to Ephesus and summoned the elders of the church. [18] When they came to him, he said to them: "You know, from the first day I set foot in Asia, how I was with you the whole time, [19] serving the Lord with all humility, with tears, and during the trials that came to me through the plots of the Jews. [20] You know that I did not avoid proclaiming to you anything that was profitable or from teaching you publicly and from house to house. [21] I testified to both Jews and Greeks about repentance toward God and faith in our Lord Jesus.

[22] "And now I am on my way to Jerusalem, compelled by the Spirit,[E] not knowing what I will encounter there, [23] except that in every town the Holy Spirit warns me that chains and afflictions are waiting for me. [24] But I consider my life of no value to myself; my purpose is to finish my course[F] and the ministry I received from the Lord Jesus, to testify to the gospel of God's grace.

[25] "And now I know that none of you, among whom I went about preaching the kingdom, will ever see me again. [26] Therefore I declare to you this

---

[A]20:4 Other mss add *to Asia* [B]20:4 Other mss omit *son of Pyrrhus*
[C]20:7 Other mss read *the disciples* [D]20:15 Other mss add *after staying at Trogyllium* [E]20:22 Or *in my spirit* [F]20:24 Other mss add *with joy*

AN UNUSUAL EULOGY

ACTS 20; PHILIPPIANS 1:20-21

I imagine the best compliments I'll never hear will be given at my funeral. Wouldn't we all like to be a fly on the wall when our people gather to tell us goodbye?

In Acts 20, Paul attended a pre-funeral of sorts in his own honor. He knew he'd never again see the elders of the Ephesian church, men he had worked beside for more than three years (vv. 25, 31). It was a tough goodbye (vv. 37-38).

In this heartsick moment, the apostle delivered his own eulogy and his final sermon in one passionate farewell address. He didn't sugarcoat his leaving or offer his mourning friends empty platitudes. Instead, in true Paul fashion, he went for the spiritual jugular with three unconventional funeral themes.

Trouble awaits. In the thick of our grief, the last thing we want to see is more pain on the horizon. Funeral messages tend to focus on the day when our troubles will be no more, but Paul knew "chains and afflictions" were waiting for him, no matter where he went (Ac 20:23).

We don't have to be able to see around corners to count on future suffering (Jn 16:33). This side of heaven, trouble awaits us all. Yet, Paul was undaunted by the knowledge that trouble was coming. The promises of Christ made every chain feel light as a feather (2Co 4:17).

My life is nothing. I'll be honest; the reason I'd want to attend my own funeral is to hear how important I was to people. But Paul flips that idea on its head. Though the end was near, he refused to elevate himself. Instead, he championed the gospel: "But I consider my life of no value to myself" (Ac 20:24).

Paul exchanged the universal human obsession with self for an obsession with Christ. What would change if we saw our lives as nothing and the gospel as absolutely everything?

Grace is your inheritance. After a funeral, there's often a will to be read or an estate to be divvied up. But the inheritance Paul offered the Ephesian elders had nothing to do with bank accounts or property lines. "And now I commit you to God and to the word of his grace, which is able to build you up and to give you an inheritance among all who are sanctified" (Ac 20:32).

When mourners are gathered around our graves, will God's grace be the gift we left behind?

Ecclesiastes 7:2 encourages us to spend more time at funerals than festivals. This isn't macabre advice, but a reminder that there will be a funeral for each of us some day. When mourners gather to cry for me, I hope they look at my life and hear echoes of Paul's final sermon:

She faced trouble. It was nothing compared to the cause of Christ. Grace is her inheritance.

day that I am innocent[A] of the blood of all of you, [27] because I did not avoid declaring to you the whole plan of God. [28] Be on guard for yourselves and for all the flock of which the Holy Spirit has appointed you as overseers, to shepherd the church of God,[B] which he purchased with his own blood. [29] I know that after my departure savage wolves will come in among you, not sparing the flock. [30] Men will rise up even from your own number and distort the truth to lure the disciples into following them. [31] Therefore be on the alert, remembering that night and day for three years I never stopped warning each one of you with tears.

[32] "And now[C] I commit you to God and to the word of his grace, which is able to build you up and to give you an inheritance among all who are sanctified. [33] I have not coveted anyone's silver or gold or clothing. [34] You yourselves know that I worked with my own hands to support myself and those who are with me. [35] In every way I've shown you that it is necessary to help the weak by laboring like this and to remember the words of the Lord Jesus, because he said, 'It is more blessed to give than to receive.' "

[36] After he said this, he knelt down and prayed with all of them. [37] There were many tears shed by everyone. They embraced Paul and kissed him, [38] grieving most of all over his statement that they would never see his face again. And they accompanied him to the ship.

WARNINGS ON THE JOURNEY TO JERUSALEM

21 After we tore ourselves away from them, we set sail straight for Cos, the next day to Rhodes, and from there to Patara. [2] Finding a ship crossing over to Phoenicia, we boarded and set sail. [3] After we sighted Cyprus, passing to the south of it,[D] we sailed on to Syria and arrived at Tyre, since the ship was to unload its cargo there. [4] We sought out the disciples and stayed there seven days. Through the Spirit they told Paul not to go to Jerusalem. [5] When our time had come to an end, we left to continue our journey, while all of them, with their wives and children, accompanied us out of the city. After kneeling down on the beach to pray, [6] we said farewell to one another and boarded the ship, and they returned home.

[7] When we completed our voyage[E] from Tyre, we reached Ptolemais, where we greeted the brothers and sisters and stayed with them for a day. [8] The next day we left and came to Caesarea, where we entered the house of Philip the evangelist, who was one of the Seven, and stayed with him. [9] This man had four virgin daughters who prophesied.

[10] After we had been there for several days, a prophet named Agabus came down from Judea. [11] He came to us, took Paul's belt, tied his own feet and hands, and said, "This is what the Holy Spirit says: 'In this way the Jews in Jerusalem will bind the man who owns this belt and deliver him over to the Gentiles.' " [12] When we heard this, both we and the local people pleaded with him not to go up to Jerusalem.

[13] Then Paul replied, "What are you doing, weeping and breaking my heart? For I am ready not only to be bound but also to die in Jerusalem for the name of the Lord Jesus."

[A]20:26 Lit *clean*   [B]20:28 Some mss read *church of the Lord*; other mss read *church of the Lord and God*   [C]20:32 Other mss add *brothers and sisters*
[D]21:3 Lit *leaving it on the left*   [E]21:7 Or *As we continued our voyage*

[14] Since he would not be persuaded, we said no more except, "The Lord's will be done."

CONFLICT OVER THE GENTILE MISSION

[15] After this we got ready and went up to Jerusalem. [16] Some of the disciples from Caesarea also went with us and brought us to Mnason of Cyprus, an early disciple, with whom we were to stay.

[17] When we reached Jerusalem, the brothers and sisters welcomed us warmly. [18] The following day Paul went in with us to James, and all the elders were present. [19] After greeting them, he reported in detail what God had done among the Gentiles through his ministry.

[20] When they heard it, they glorified God and said, "You see, brother, how many thousands of Jews there are who have believed, and they are all zealous for the law. [21] But they have been informed about you — that you are teaching all the Jews who are among the Gentiles to abandon Moses, telling them not to circumcise their children or to live according to our customs. [22] So what is to be done?[A] They will certainly hear that you've come. [23] Therefore do what we tell you: We have four men who have made a vow. [24] Take these men, purify yourself along with them, and pay for them to get their heads shaved. Then everyone will know that what they were told about you amounts to nothing, but that you yourself are also careful about observing the law. [25] With regard to the Gentiles who have believed, we have written a letter containing our decision that[B] they should keep themselves from food sacrificed to idols, from blood, from what is strangled, and from sexual immorality."

THE RIOT IN THE TEMPLE

[26] So the next day, Paul took the men, having purified himself along with them, and entered the temple, announcing the completion of the purification days when the offering would be made for each of them. [27] When the seven days were nearly over, some Jews from the province of Asia saw him in the temple, stirred up the whole crowd, and seized him, [28] shouting, "Fellow Israelites, help! This is the man who teaches everyone everywhere against our people, our law, and this place. What's more, he also brought Greeks into the temple and has defiled this holy place." [29] For they had previously seen Trophimus the Ephesian in the city with him, and they supposed that Paul had brought him into the temple.

[30] The whole city was stirred up, and the people rushed together. They seized Paul, dragged him out of the temple, and at once the gates were shut. [31] As they were trying to kill him, word went up to the commander of the regiment that all Jerusalem was in chaos. [32] Taking along soldiers and centurions, he immediately ran down to them. Seeing the commander and the soldiers, they stopped beating Paul. [33] Then the commander approached, took him into custody, and ordered him to be bound with two chains. He asked who he was and what he had done. [34] Some in the crowd were shouting one thing and some another. Since he was not able to get reliable information because of the uproar, he ordered him to be taken into the barracks. [35] When

---

[A]21:22 Other mss add *A multitude has to come together, since* [B]21:25 Other mss add *they should observe no such thing, except that*

Paul got to the steps, he had to be carried by the soldiers because of the violence of the crowd, ³⁶ for the mass of people followed, yelling, "Get rid of him!"

PAUL'S DEFENSE BEFORE THE JERUSALEM MOB

³⁷ As he was about to be brought into the barracks, Paul said to the commander, "Am I allowed to say something to you?"

He replied, "You know how to speak Greek? ³⁸ Aren't you the Egyptian who started a revolt some time ago and led four thousand men of the Assassins into the wilderness?"

³⁹ Paul said, "I am a Jewish man from Tarsus of Cilicia, a citizen of an important city. Now I ask you, let me speak to the people."

⁴⁰ After he had given permission, Paul stood on the steps and motioned with his hand to the people. When there was a great hush, he addressed them

22 in Aramaic:ᴬ ¹ "Brothers and fathers, listen now to my defense before you." ² When they heard that he was addressing them in Aramaic,ᴬ they became even quieter. ³ He continued, "I am a Jew, born in Tarsus of Cilicia but brought up in this city, educated at the feet of Gamaliel according to the law of our ancestors. I was zealous for God, just as all of you are today. ⁴ I persecuted this Way to the death, arresting and putting both men and women in jail, ⁵ as both the high priest and the whole council of elders can testify about me. After I received letters from them to the brothers, I traveled to Damascus to arrest those who were there and bring them to Jerusalem to be punished.

PAUL'S TESTIMONY

⁶ "As I was traveling and approaching Damascus, about noon an intense light from heaven suddenly flashed around me. ⁷ I fell to the ground and heard a voice saying to me, 'Saul, Saul, why are you persecuting me?'

⁸ "I answered, 'Who are you, Lord?'

"He said to me, 'I am Jesus of Nazareth, the one you are persecuting.' ⁹ Now those who were with me saw the light,ᴮ but they did not hear the voice of the one who was speaking to me.

¹⁰ "I said, 'What should I do, Lord?'

"The Lord told me, 'Get up and go into Damascus, and there you will be told everything that you have been assigned to do.'

¹¹ "Since I couldn't see because of the brightness of the light,ᶜ I was led by the hand by those who were with me, and went into Damascus. ¹² Someone named Ananias, a devout man according to the law, who had a good reputation with all the Jews living there, ¹³ came and stood by me and said, 'Brother Saul, regain your sight.' And in that very hour I looked up and saw him. ¹⁴ And he said, 'The God of our ancestors has appointed you to know his will, to see the Righteous One, and to hear the words from his mouth, ¹⁵ since you will be a witness for him to all people of what you have seen and heard. ¹⁶ And now, why are you delaying? Get up and be baptized, and wash away your sins, calling on his name.'

¹⁷ "After I returned to Jerusalem and was praying in the temple, I fell into a trance ¹⁸ and saw him telling me, 'Hurry and get out of Jerusalem quickly, because they will not accept your testimony about me.'

ᴬ 21:40; 22:2 Or Hebrew ᴮ 22:9 Other mss add and were afraid ᶜ 22:11 Lit the glory of that light

[19] "But I said, 'Lord, they know that in synagogue after synagogue I had those who believed in you imprisoned and beaten. [20] And when the blood of your witness Stephen was being shed, I stood there giving approval[A] and guarding the clothes of those who killed him.'

[21] "He said to me, 'Go, because I will send you far away to the Gentiles.' "

PAUL'S ROMAN PROTECTION

[22] They listened to him up to this point. Then they raised their voices, shouting, "Wipe this man off the face of the earth! He should not be allowed to live! "

[23] As they were yelling and flinging aside their garments and throwing dust into the air, [24] the commander ordered him to be brought into the barracks, directing that he be interrogated with the scourge to discover the reason they were shouting against him like this. [25] As they stretched him out for the lash, Paul said to the centurion standing by, "Is it legal for you to scourge a man who is a Roman citizen and is uncondemned? "

[26] When the centurion heard this, he went and reported to the commander, saying, "What are you going to do? For this man is a Roman citizen."

[27] The commander came and said to him, "Tell me, are you a Roman citizen? "

"Yes," he said.

[28] The commander replied, "I bought this citizenship for a large amount of money."

"But I was born a citizen," Paul said.

[29] So those who were about to examine him withdrew from him immediately. The commander too was alarmed when he realized Paul was a Roman citizen and he had bound him.

PAUL BEFORE THE SANHEDRIN

[30] The next day, since he wanted to find out exactly why Paul was being accused by the Jews, he released him[B] and instructed the chief priests and all the Sanhedrin to convene. He brought Paul down and placed him before

23 them. [1] Paul looked straight at the Sanhedrin and said, "Brothers, I have lived my life before God in all good conscience to this day." [2] The high priest Ananias ordered those who were standing next to him to strike him on the mouth. [3] Then Paul said to him, "God is going to strike you, you whitewashed wall! You are sitting there judging me according to the law, and yet in violation of the law are you ordering me to be struck? "

[4] Those standing nearby said, "Do you dare revile God's high priest? "

[5] "I did not know, brothers, that he was the high priest," replied Paul. "For it is written, **You must not speak evil of a ruler of your people.**"[C] [6] When Paul realized that one part of them were Sadducees and the other part were Pharisees, he cried out in the Sanhedrin, "Brothers, I am a Pharisee, a son of Pharisees. I am being judged because of the hope of the resurrection of the dead! " [7] When he said this, a dispute broke out between the Pharisees and the Sadducees, and the assembly was divided. [8] For the Sadducees say there is no resurrection, and neither angel nor spirit, but the Pharisees affirm them all.

[A]22:20 Other mss add *of his murder* [B]22:30 Other mss add *from his chains*
[C]23:5 Ex 22:28

⁹ The shouting grew loud, and some of the scribes of the Pharisees' party got up and argued vehemently: "We find nothing evil in this man. What if a spirit or an angel has spoken to him?" ᴬ

¹⁰ When the dispute became violent, the commander feared that Paul might be torn apart by them and ordered the troops to go down, take him away from them, and bring him into the barracks. ¹¹ The following night, the Lord stood by him and said, "Have courage! For as you have testified about me in Jerusalem, so it is necessary for you to testify in Rome."

THE PLOT AGAINST PAUL

¹² When it was morning, the Jews formed a conspiracy and bound themselves under a curse not to eat or drink until they had killed Paul. ¹³ There were more than forty who had formed this plot. ¹⁴ These men went to the chief priests and elders and said, "We have bound ourselves under a solemn curse that we won't eat anything until we have killed Paul. ¹⁵ So now you, along with the Sanhedrin, make a request to the commander that he bring him down to you ᴮ as if you were going to investigate his case more thoroughly. But, before he gets near, we are ready to kill him."

¹⁶ But the son of Paul's sister, hearing about their ambush, came and entered the barracks and reported it to Paul. ¹⁷ Paul called one of the centurions and said, "Take this young man to the commander, because he has something to report to him."

¹⁸ So he took him, brought him to the commander, and said, "The prisoner Paul called me and asked me to bring this young man to you, because he has something to tell you."

¹⁹ The commander took him by the hand, led him aside, and inquired privately, "What is it you have to report to me?"

²⁰ "The Jews," he said, "have agreed to ask you to bring Paul down to the Sanhedrin tomorrow, as though they are going to hold a somewhat more careful inquiry about him. ²¹ Don't let them persuade you, because there are more than forty of them lying in ambush — men who have bound themselves under a curse not to eat or drink until they have killed him. Now they are ready, waiting for your consent."

²² So the commander dismissed the young man and instructed him, "Don't tell anyone that you have informed me about this."

TO CAESAREA BY NIGHT

²³ He summoned two of his centurions and said, "Get two hundred soldiers ready with seventy cavalry and two hundred spearmen to go to Caesarea at nine tonight. ᶜ ²⁴ Also provide mounts for Paul to ride and bring him safely to Felix the governor."

²⁵ He wrote the following letter: ᴰ

²⁶ Claudius Lysias,

To the most excellent governor Felix:

Greetings.

²⁷ When this man had been seized by the Jews and was about to be killed by them, I arrived with my troops and rescued him because I learned

---

ᴬ 23:9 Other mss add *Let us not fight God.*   ᴮ 23:15 Other mss add *tomorrow*
ᶜ 23:23 Lit *at the third hour tonight*   ᴰ 23:25 Or *He wrote a letter to this effect:*

that he is a Roman citizen. [28] Wanting to know the charge they were accusing him of, I brought him down before their Sanhedrin. [29] I found out that the accusations were concerning questions of their law, and that there was no charge that merited death or imprisonment. [30] When I was informed that there was a plot against the man,[A] I sent him to you right away. I also ordered his accusers to state their case against him in your presence.[B]

[31] So the soldiers took Paul during the night and brought him to Antipatris as they were ordered. [32] The next day, they returned to the barracks, allowing the cavalry to go on with him. [33] When these men entered Caesarea and delivered the letter to the governor, they also presented Paul to him. [34] After he[C] read it, he asked what province he was from. When he learned he was from Cilicia, [35] he said, "I will give you a hearing whenever your accusers also get here." He ordered that he be kept under guard in Herod's palace.[D]

THE ACCUSATION AGAINST PAUL

24 Five days later Ananias the high priest came down with some elders and a lawyer named Tertullus. These men presented their case against Paul to the governor. [2] When Paul was called in, Tertullus began to accuse him and said: "We enjoy great peace because of you, and reforms are taking place for the benefit of this nation because of your foresight. [3] We acknowledge this in every way and everywhere, most excellent Felix, with utmost gratitude. [4] But, so that I will not burden you any further, I request that you would be kind enough to give us a brief hearing. [5] For we have found this man to be a plague, an agitator among all the Jews throughout the Roman world, and a ringleader of the sect of the Nazarenes. [6] He even tried to desecrate the temple, and so we apprehended him.[E] By examining him yourself you will be able to discern the truth about these charges we are bringing against him." [9] The Jews also joined in the attack, alleging that these things were true.

PAUL'S DEFENSE BEFORE FELIX

[10] When the governor motioned for him to speak, Paul replied: "Because I know you have been a judge of this nation for many years, I am glad to offer my defense in what concerns me. [11] You can verify for yourself that it is no more than twelve days since I went up to worship in Jerusalem. [12] They didn't find me arguing with anyone or causing a disturbance among the crowd, either in the temple or in the synagogues or anywhere in the city. [13] Neither can they prove the charges they are now making against me. [14] But I admit this to you: I worship the God of my ancestors according to the Way, which they call a sect, believing everything that is in accordance with the law and written in the prophets. [15] I have a hope in God, which these men

---

[A]23:30 Other mss add *by the Jews*   [B]23:30 Other mss add *Farewell*
[C]23:34 Other mss read *the governor*   [D]23:35 Or *headquarters*   [E]24:6 Some mss include vv. 6b-8a: *and wanted to judge him according to our law.* [7]*But Lysias the commander came and took him from our hands with great force,* [8]*commanding his accusers to come to you.*

themselves also accept, that there will be a resurrection,^A both of the righteous and the unrighteous. ¹⁶ I always strive to have a clear conscience toward God and men. ¹⁷ After many years, I came to bring charitable gifts and offerings to my people. ¹⁸ While I was doing this, some Jews from Asia found me ritually purified in the temple, without a crowd and without any uproar. ¹⁹ It is they who ought to be here before you to bring charges, if they have anything against me. ²⁰ Or let these men here state what wrongdoing they found in me when I stood before the Sanhedrin, ²¹ other than this one statement I shouted while standing among them, 'Today I am on trial before you concerning the resurrection of the dead.'"

THE VERDICT POSTPONED

²² Since Felix was well informed about the Way, he adjourned the hearing, saying, "When Lysias the commander comes down, I will decide your case." ²³ He ordered that the centurion keep Paul under guard, though he could have some freedom, and that he should not prevent any of his friends from meeting^B his needs.

²⁴ Several days later, when Felix came with his wife Drusilla, who was Jewish, he sent for Paul and listened to him on the subject of faith in Christ Jesus. ²⁵ Now as he spoke about righteousness, self-control, and the judgment to come, Felix became afraid and replied, "Leave for now, but when I have an opportunity I'll call for you." ²⁶ At the same time he was also hoping that Paul would offer him money.^C So he sent for him quite often and conversed with him.

²⁷ After two years had passed, Porcius Festus succeeded Felix, and because Felix wanted to do the Jews a favor, he left Paul in prison.

APPEAL TO CAESAR

25 Three days after Festus arrived in the province, he went up to Jerusalem from Caesarea. ² The chief priests and the leaders of the Jews presented their case against Paul to him; and they appealed, ³ asking for a favor against Paul, that Festus summon him to Jerusalem. They were, in fact, preparing an ambush along the road to kill him. ⁴ Festus, however, answered that Paul should be kept at Caesarea, and that he himself was about to go there shortly. ⁵ "Therefore," he said, "let those of you who have authority go down with me and accuse him, if he has done anything wrong."

⁶ When he had spent not more than eight or ten days among them, he went down to Caesarea. The next day, seated at the tribunal, he commanded Paul to be brought in. ⁷ When he arrived, the Jews who had come down from Jerusalem stood around him and brought many serious charges that they were not able to prove. ⁸ Then Paul made his defense: "Neither against the Jewish law, nor against the temple, nor against Caesar have I sinned in any way."

⁹ But Festus, wanting to do the Jews a favor, replied to Paul, "Are you willing to go up to Jerusalem to be tried before me there on these charges?"

¹⁰ Paul replied: "I am standing at Caesar's tribunal, where I ought to be tried. I have done no wrong to the Jews, as even you yourself know very well. ¹¹ If then I did anything wrong and am deserving of death, I am not trying

---

^A 24:15 Other mss add *of the dead*   ^B 24:23 Other mss add *or visiting*
^C 24:26 Other mss add *so that he might release him*

to escape death; but if there is nothing to what these men accuse me of, no one can give me up to them. I appeal to Caesar!"

[12] Then after Festus conferred with his council, he replied, "You have appealed to Caesar; to Caesar you will go."

KING AGRIPPA AND BERNICE VISIT FESTUS

[13] Several days later, King Agrippa and Bernice arrived in Caesarea and paid a courtesy call on Festus. [14] Since they were staying there several days, Festus presented Paul's case to the king, saying, "There's a man who was left as a prisoner by Felix. [15] When I was in Jerusalem, the chief priests and the elders of the Jews presented their case and asked that he be condemned. [16] I answered them that it is not the Roman custom to give someone up[A] before the accused faces the accusers and has an opportunity for a defense against the charges. [17] So when they had assembled here, I did not delay. The next day I took my seat at the tribunal and ordered the man to be brought in. [18] The accusers stood up but brought no charge against him of the evils I was expecting. [19] Instead they had some disagreements with him about their own religion and about a certain Jesus, a dead man Paul claimed to be alive. [20] Since I was at a loss in a dispute over such things, I asked him if he wanted to go to Jerusalem and be tried there regarding these matters. [21] But when Paul appealed to be held for trial by the Emperor,[B] I ordered him to be kept in custody until I could send him to Caesar."

[22] Agrippa said to Festus, "I would like to hear the man myself."

"Tomorrow you will hear him," he replied.

PAUL BEFORE AGRIPPA

[23] So the next day, Agrippa and Bernice came with great pomp and entered the auditorium with the military commanders and prominent men of the city. When Festus gave the command, Paul was brought in. [24] Then Festus said: "King Agrippa and all men present with us, you see this man. The whole Jewish community has appealed to me concerning him, both in Jerusalem and here, shouting that he should not live any longer. [25] I found that he had not done anything deserving of death, but when he himself appealed to the Emperor, I decided to send him. [26] I have nothing definite to write to my lord about him. Therefore, I have brought him before all of you, and especially before you, King Agrippa, so that after this examination is over, I may have something to write. [27] For it seems unreasonable to me to send a prisoner without indicating the charges against him."

PAUL'S DEFENSE BEFORE AGRIPPA

26 Agrippa said to Paul, "You have permission to speak for yourself." Then Paul stretched out his hand and began his defense: [2] "I consider myself fortunate, that it is before you, King Agrippa, I am to make my defense today against all the accusations of the Jews, [3] especially since you are very knowledgeable about all the Jewish customs and controversies. Therefore I beg you to listen to me patiently.

[4] "All the Jews know my way of life from my youth, which was spent from the beginning among my own people and in Jerusalem. [5] They have known

[A]25:16 Other mss add *to destruction*   [B]25:21 Lit *his majesty,* also in v. 25

me for a long time, if they are willing to testify, that according to the strict-est sect of our religion I lived as a Pharisee. [6] And now I stand on trial because of the hope in what God promised to our ancestors, [7] the promise our twelve tribes hope to reach as they earnestly serve him night and day. King Agrippa, I am being accused by the Jews because of this hope. [8] Why do any of you consider it incredible that God raises the dead? [9] In fact, I myself was convinced that it was necessary to do many things in opposition to the name of Jesus of Nazareth. [10] I actually did this in Jerusalem, and I locked up many of the saints in prison, since I had received authority for that from the chief priests. When they were put to death, I was in agreement against them. [11] In all the synagogues I often punished them and tried to make them blaspheme. Since I was terribly enraged at them, I pursued them even to foreign cities.

PAUL'S ACCOUNT OF HIS CONVERSION AND COMMISSION

[12] "I was traveling to Damascus under these circumstances with authority and a commission from the chief priests. [13] King Agrippa, while on the road at midday, I saw a light from heaven brighter than the sun, shining around me and those traveling with me. [14] We all fell to the ground, and I heard a voice speaking to me in Aramaic,[A] 'Saul, Saul, why are you persecuting me? It is hard for you to kick against the goads.'

[15] "I asked, 'Who are you, Lord?'

"And the Lord replied: 'I am Jesus, the one you are persecuting. [16] But get up and stand on your feet. For I have appeared to you for this purpose, to appoint you as a servant and a witness of what you have seen and will see of me. [17] I will rescue you from your people and from the Gentiles. I am sending you to them [18] to open their eyes so that they may turn[B] from darkness to light and from the power of Satan to God, that they may receive forgiveness of sins and a share among those who are sanctified by faith in me.'

[19] "So then, King Agrippa, I was not disobedient to the heavenly vision. [20] Instead, I preached to those in Damascus first, and to those in Jerusalem and in all the region of Judea, and to the Gentiles, that they should repent and turn to God, and do works worthy of repentance. [21] For this reason the Jews seized me in the temple and were trying to kill me. [22] To this very day, I have had help from God, and I stand and testify to both small and great, saying nothing other than what the prophets and Moses said would take place — [23] that the Messiah must suffer, and that, as the first to rise from the dead, he would proclaim light to our people and to the Gentiles."

AGRIPPA NOT QUITE PERSUADED

[24] As he was saying these things in his defense, Festus exclaimed in a loud voice, "You're out of your mind, Paul! Too much study is driving you mad."

[25] But Paul replied, "I'm not out of my mind, most excellent Festus. On the contrary, I'm speaking words of truth and good judgment. [26] For the king knows about these matters, and I can speak boldly to him. For I am convinced that none of these things has escaped his notice, since this was not done in a corner. [27] King Agrippa, do you believe the prophets? I know you believe."

A26:14 Or *Hebrew*   B26:18 Or *to turn them*

²⁸ Agrippa said to Paul, "Are you going to persuade me to become a Christian so easily?"ᴬ

²⁹ "I wish before God," replied Paul, "that whether easily or with difficulty,ᴮ not only you but all who listen to me today might become as I am — except for these chains."

³⁰ The king, the governor, Bernice, and those sitting with them got up, ³¹ and when they had left they talked with each other and said, "This man is not doing anything to deserve death or imprisonment."

³² Agrippa said to Festus, "This man could have been released if he had not appealed to Caesar."

SAILING FOR ROME

27 When it was decided that we were to sail to Italy, they handed over Paul and some other prisoners to a centurion named Julius, of the Imperial Regiment.ᶜ ² When we had boarded a ship of Adramyttium, we put to sea, intending to sail to ports along the coast of Asia. Aristarchus, a Macedonian of Thessalonica, was with us. ³ The next day we put in at Sidon, and Julius treated Paul kindly and allowed him to go to his friends to receive their care. ⁴ When we had put out to sea from there, we sailed along the northern coastᴰ of Cyprus because the winds were against us. ⁵ After sailing through the open sea off Cilicia and Pamphylia, we reached Myra in Lycia. ⁶ There the centurion found an Alexandrian ship sailing for Italy and put us on board. ⁷ Sailing slowly for many days, with difficulty we arrived off Cnidus. Since the wind did not allow us to approach it, we sailed along the south side of Crete off Salmone. ⁸ With still more difficulty we sailed along the coast and came to a place called Fair Havens near the city of Lasea.

PAUL'S ADVICE IGNORED

⁹ By now much time had passed, and the voyage was already dangerous. Since the Day of Atonementᴱ was already over, Paul gave his advice ¹⁰ and told them, "Men, I can see that this voyage is headed toward disaster and heavy loss, not only of the cargo and the ship but also of our lives." ¹¹ But the centurion paid attention to the captain and the owner of the ship rather than to what Paul said. ¹² Since the harbor was unsuitable to winter in, the majority decided to set sail from there, hoping somehow to reach Phoenix, a harbor on Crete facing the southwest and northwest, and to winter there.

STORM-TOSSED SHIP

¹³ When a gentle south wind sprang up, they thought they had achieved their purpose. They weighed anchor and sailed along the shore of Crete. ¹⁴ But before long, a fierce wind called the "northeaster" rushed down from the island. ¹⁵ Since the ship was caught and unable to head into the wind, we gave way to it and were driven along. ¹⁶ After running under the shelter of a little island called Cauda,ᶠ we were barely able to get control of the skiff. ¹⁷ After hoisting it up, they used ropes and tackle and girded the ship. Fearing they would run aground on the Syrtis, they lowered the drift-anchor, and in this

---

ᴬ26:28 Or so quickly ᴮ26:29 Or whether a short time or long ᶜ27:1 Or Augustan Cohort ᴰ27:4 Lit sailed under the lee, also in v. 7 ᴱ27:9 Lit the Fast ᶠ27:16 Or Clauda way they were driven along. ¹⁸ Because we were being severely battered by the storm, they began to jettison the cargo the next day. ¹⁹ On the third day, they threw the ship's tackle overboard with their own hands. ²⁰ For many days neither sun nor stars appeared, and the severe storm kept raging. Finally all hope was fading that we would be saved.

²¹ Since they had been without food for a long time, Paul then stood up among them and said, "You men should have followed my advice not to sail from Crete and sustain this damage and loss. ²² Now I urge you to take courage, because there will be no loss of any of your lives, but only of the ship. ²³ For last night an angel of the God I belong to and serve stood by me ²⁴ and said, 'Don't be afraid, Paul. It is necessary for you to appear before Caesar. And indeed, God has graciously given you all those who are sailing with you.' ²⁵ So take courage, men, because I believe God that it will be just the way it was told to me. ²⁶ But we have to run aground on some island."

²⁷ When the fourteenth night came, we were drifting in the Adriatic Sea, and about midnight the sailors thought they were approaching land. ²⁸ They took soundings and found it to be a hundred and twenty feet^A deep; when they had sailed a little farther and sounded again, they found it to be ninety feet^B deep. ²⁹ Then, fearing we might run aground on the rocks, they dropped four anchors from the stern and prayed for daylight to come. ³⁰ Some sailors tried to escape from the ship; they had let down the skiff into the sea, pretending that they were going to put out anchors from the bow. ³¹ Paul said to the centurion and the soldiers, "Unless these men stay in the ship, you cannot be saved." ³² Then the soldiers cut the ropes holding the skiff and let it drop away.

³³ When it was about daylight, Paul urged them all to take food, saying, "Today is the fourteenth day that you have been waiting and going without food, having eaten nothing. ³⁴ So I urge you to take some food. For this is for your survival, since none of you will lose a hair from your head." ³⁵ After he said these things and had taken some bread, he gave thanks to God in the presence of all of them, and after he broke it, he began to eat. ³⁶ They all were encouraged and took food themselves. ³⁷ In all there were 276 of us on the ship. ³⁸ When they had eaten enough, they began to lighten the ship by throwing the grain overboard into the sea.

SHIPWRECK

³⁹ When daylight came, they did not recognize the land but sighted a bay with a beach. They planned to run the ship ashore if they could. ⁴⁰ After cutting loose the anchors, they left them in the sea, at the same time loosening the ropes that held the rudders. Then they hoisted the foresail to the wind and headed for the beach. ⁴¹ But they struck a sandbar and ran the ship aground. The bow jammed fast and remained immovable, while the stern began to break up by the pounding of the waves. ⁴² The soldiers' plan was to kill the prisoners so that no one could swim away and escape. ⁴³ But the centurion kept them from carrying out their plan because he wanted to save Paul, and so he ordered those who could swim to jump overboard first and get to land. ⁴⁴ The rest were to follow, some on planks and some on debris from the ship. In this way, everyone safely reached the shore.

---

^A 27:28 Lit twenty fathoms   ^B 27:28 Lit fifteen fathoms

MALTA'S HOSPITALITY

28 Once safely ashore, we then learned that the island was called Malta. ² The local people showed us extraordinary kindness. They lit a fire and took us all in, since it was raining and cold. ³ As Paul gathered a bundle of brushwood and put it on the fire, a viper came out because of the heat and fastened itself on his hand. ⁴ When the local people saw the snake hanging from his hand, they said to one another, "This man, no doubt, is a murderer. Even though he has escaped the sea, Justice has not allowed him to live." ⁵ But he shook the snake off into the fire and suffered no harm. ⁶ They expected that he would begin to swell up or suddenly drop dead. After they waited a long time and saw nothing unusual happen to him, they changed their minds and said he was a god.

MINISTRY IN MALTA

⁷ Now in the area around that place was an estate belonging to the leading man of the island, named Publius, who welcomed us and entertained us hospitably for three days. ⁸ Publius's father was in bed suffering from fever and dysentery. Paul went to him, and praying and laying his hands on him, he healed him. ⁹ After this, the rest of those on the island who had diseases also came and were healed. ¹⁰ So they heaped many honors on us, and when we sailed, they gave us what we needed.

ROME AT LAST

¹¹ After three months we set sail in an Alexandrian ship that had wintered at the island, with the Twin Gods^A as its figurehead. ¹² Putting in at Syracuse, we stayed three days. ¹³ From there, after making a circuit along the coast,^B we reached Rhegium. After one day a south wind sprang up, and the second day we came to Puteoli. ¹⁴ There we found brothers and sisters and were invited to stay a week with them. And so we came to Rome. ¹⁵ Now the brothers and sisters from there had heard the news about us and had come to meet us as far as the Forum of Appius and the Three Taverns. When Paul saw them, he thanked God and took courage. ¹⁶ When we entered Rome,^C Paul was allowed to live by himself with the soldier who guarded him.

PAUL'S FIRST INTERVIEW WITH ROMAN JEWS

¹⁷ After three days he called together the leaders of the Jews. When they had gathered he said to them: "Brothers, although I have done nothing against our people or the customs of our ancestors, I was delivered as a prisoner from Jerusalem into the hands of the Romans. ¹⁸ After they examined me, they wanted to release me, since there was no reason for the death penalty in my case. ¹⁹ Because the Jews objected, I was compelled to appeal to Caesar; even though I had no charge to bring against my people. ²⁰ For this reason I've asked to see you and speak to you. In fact, it is for the hope of Israel that I'm wearing this chain."

²¹ Then they said to him, "We haven't received any letters about you from Judea. None of the brothers has come and reported or spoken anything evil

---

^A 28:11 Gk *Dioscuri*, twin sons of Zeus, Castor and Pollux   ^B 28:13 Other mss read *From there, casting off,*   ^C 28:16 Other mss add *the centurion turned the prisoners over to the military commander; but* about you. [22] But we want to hear what your views are, since we know that people everywhere are speaking against this sect."

THE RESPONSE TO PAUL'S MESSAGE

[23] After arranging a day with him, many came to him at his lodging. From dawn to dusk he expounded and testified about the kingdom of God. He tried to persuade them about Jesus from both the Law of Moses and the Prophets. [24] Some were persuaded by what he said, but others did not believe.

[25] Disagreeing among themselves, they began to leave after Paul made one statement:[A] "The Holy Spirit was right in saying to your[B] ancestors through the prophet Isaiah [26] when he said,

> Go to these people and say:
> You will always be listening,
> but never understanding;
> and you will always be looking,
> but never perceiving.
> [27] For the hearts of these people
> have grown callous,
> their ears are hard of hearing,
> and they have shut their eyes;
> otherwise they might see with their eyes
> and hear with their ears,
> understand with their heart
> and turn,
> and I would heal them.[C]

[28] Therefore, let it be known to you that this salvation of God has been sent to the Gentiles; they will listen." [D]

PAUL'S MINISTRY UNHINDERED

[30] Paul stayed two whole years in his own rented house. And he welcomed all who visited him, [31] proclaiming the kingdom of God and teaching about the Lord Jesus Christ with all boldness and without hindrance.

[A]28:25 Or after they began to leave, Paul made one statement   [B]28:25 Other mss read our   [C]28:26-27 Is 6:9-10   [D]28:28 Some mss include v. 29: After he said these things, the Jews departed, while engaging in a vigorous debate among themselves.

THEY are JUSTIFIED freely BY HIS grace

romans

 For all have sinned and fall short of the glory of God. They are justified freely by his grace through the redemption that is in Christ Jesus. **3:23-24**

ON THE TIMELINE The indisputable author of the book of Romans is the Apostle Paul. From the book of Acts and statements made in Romans, we learn that Paul wrote this letter while he was in Corinth in the spring of AD 57, while on his way to Jerusalem to deliver an offering from the Gentile churches to poor Jewish Christians (Ac 20:3; Rm 15:25-29). This places the writing of Romans at the end of Paul's third missionary journey.

A LITTLE BACKGROUND The imposing city of Rome was the primary destination for this letter. Some manuscripts, however, lack the phrase "in Rome" (Rm 1:7), giving some support to the conclusion that Paul intended an even wider audience for the letter. The origin of the Roman house churches is unknown, though their foundations can be traced back to the "visitors from Rome, both Jews and converts" who came to Jerusalem at Pentecost (Ac 2:10), many of whom converted to Christianity (Ac 2:41).

MESSAGE & PURPOSE Paul's letter to the Roman house churches has been a favorite among the New Testament writings for its theological and pastoral influence. It focuses on the doctrine of salvation, including the practical implications for believers as they live out the salvation given to them through Jesus Christ. Paul's purpose in writing the letter was to impart spiritual strength to the believers at Rome (Rm 1:11-12; 16:25-26). He asked for prayer for the difficult task he was undertaking (Rm 15:30-31) and that he might be able to visit them (Rm 15:32). Paul also hoped to enlist the Roman churches to support a mission to the west (Rm 15:23-29). In response to Jewish-Gentile tensions, Paul included an exposition of what is essential to Christianity and what are matters of indifference.

GIVE THANKS FOR THE BOOK OF ROMANS

In the book of Romans, Paul emphasized righteousness and justification by grace through faith to a depth and detail not found elsewhere in the Bible. Paul also mapped out the spread of human sin and its results in both believers and nonbelievers. In Romans 6–8, Paul gave the most comprehensive development of our union with Christ and the Spirit's work in us.

ROME IN THE AGE
OF THE EARLY CHURCH

READ AND UNDERSTAND ROMANS

The Bible is a complete work in which many stories combine to tell one story. As you read the book of Romans, consider reading the additional passages to discover how the whole of Scripture works together.

THE GOSPEL OF GOD FOR ROME

1 Paul, a servant of Christ Jesus, called as an apostle[A] and set apart for the gospel of God — [2] which he promised beforehand through his prophets in the Holy Scriptures — [3] concerning his Son, Jesus Christ our Lord, who was a descendant of David[B] according to the flesh [4] and was appointed to be the powerful Son of God according to the Spirit of holiness[C] by the resurrection of the dead. [5] Through him we have received grace and apostleship to bring about[D] the obedience of faith for the sake of his name among all the Gentiles, [E] [6] including you who are also called by Jesus Christ.

[7] To all who are in Rome, loved by God, called as saints.

Grace to you and peace from God our Father and the Lord Jesus Christ.

PAUL'S DESIRE TO VISIT ROME

[8] First, I thank my God through Jesus Christ for all of you because the news of your faith[F] is being reported in all the world. [9] God is my witness, whom I serve with my spirit in telling the good news about his Son — that I constantly mention you, [10] always asking in my prayers that if it is somehow in God's will, I may now at last succeed in coming to you. [11] For I want very much to see you, so that I may impart to you some spiritual gift to strengthen you, [12] that is, to be mutually encouraged by each other's faith, both yours and mine.

[13] Now I don't want you to be unaware, brothers and sisters, that I often planned to come to you (but was prevented until now) in order that I might have a fruitful ministry[G] among you, just as I have had among the rest of the Gentiles. [14] I am obligated both to Greeks and barbarians, [H] both to the wise and the foolish. [15] So I am eager to preach the gospel to you also who are in Rome.

THE RIGHTEOUS WILL LIVE BY FAITH

[16] For I am not ashamed of the gospel, [I] because it is the power of God for salvation to everyone who believes, first to the Jew, and also to the Greek. [17] For in it the righteousness of God is revealed from faith to faith, [J] just as it is written: **The righteous will live by faith.** [K,L]

THE GUILT OF THE GENTILE WORLD

[18] For God's wrath is revealed from heaven against all godlessness and unrighteousness of people who by their unrighteousness suppress the truth, [19] since what can be known[M] about God is evident among them, because God has shown it to them. [20] For his invisible attributes, that is, his eternal power and divine nature, have been clearly seen since the creation of the world, being understood through what he has made. As a result, people are without excuse. [21] For though they knew God, they did not glorify him as God or show gratitude. Instead, their thinking became worthless, and their senseless hearts were darkened. [22] Claiming to be wise, they became fools [23] and

---

[A]1:1 Or *Jesus, a called apostle*   [B]1:3 Lit *was of the seed of David*   [C]1:4 Or *the spirit of holiness, or the Holy Spirit*   [D]1:5 Or *him for*; lit *him into*   [E]1:5 Or *nations, also in v. 13*   [F]1:8 Or *because your faith*   [G]1:13 Lit *have some fruit*   [H]1:14 Or *non-Greeks*   [I]1:16 Other mss add *of Christ*   [J]1:17 Or *revealed out of faith into faith*   [K]1:17 Or *The one who is righteous by faith will live*   [L]1:17 Hab 2:4   [M]1:19 Or *what is known* exchanged the glory of the immortal God for images resembling mortal man, birds, four-footed animals, and reptiles. [24] Therefore God delivered them over in the desires of their hearts to sexual impurity, so that their bodies were degraded among themselves. [25] They exchanged the truth of God for a lie, and worshiped and served what has been created instead of the Creator, who is praised forever. Amen.

FROM IDOLATRY TO DEPRAVITY

[26] For this reason God delivered them over to disgraceful passions. Their women[A] exchanged natural sexual relations[B] for unnatural ones. [27] The men[C] in the same way also left natural relations with women and were inflamed in their lust for one another. Men committed shameless acts with men and received in their own persons[D] the appropriate penalty of their error.

[28] And because they did not think it worthwhile to acknowledge God, God delivered them over to a corrupt mind so that they do what is not right. [29] They are filled with all unrighteousness,[E] evil, greed, and wickedness. They are full of envy, murder, quarrels, deceit, and malice. They are gossips, [30] slanderers, God-haters, arrogant, proud, boastful, inventors of evil, disobedient to parents, [31] senseless, untrustworthy, unloving,[F] and unmerciful. [32] Although they know God's just sentence — that those who practice such things deserve to die[G] — they not only do them, but even applaud[H] others who practice them.

GOD'S RIGHTEOUS JUDGMENT

2 Therefore, every one of you[I] who judges is without excuse. For when you judge another, you condemn yourself, since you, the judge, do the same things. [2] We know that God's judgment on those who do such things is based on the truth. [3] Do you really think — anyone of you who judges those who do such things yet do the same — that you will escape God's judgment? [4] Or do you despise the riches of his kindness, restraint, and patience, not recognizing[J] that God's kindness is intended to lead you to repentance? [5] Because of your hardened and unrepentant heart you are storing up wrath for yourself in the day of wrath, when God's righteous judgment is revealed. [6] **He will repay each one according to his works:**[K] [7] eternal life to those who by persistence in doing good seek glory, honor, and immortality; [8] but wrath and anger to those who are self-seeking and disobey the truth while obeying unrighteousness. [9] There will be affliction and distress for every human being who does evil, first to the Jew, and also to the Greek; [10] but glory, honor, and peace for everyone who does what is good, first to the Jew, and also to the Greek. [11] For there is no favoritism with God.

[12] All who sin without the law will also perish without the law, and all who sin under[L] the law will be judged by the law. [13] For the hearers of the law are not righteous before God, but the doers of the law will be justified.[M]

[A] 1:26 Lit *females*, also in v. 27   [B] 1:26 Lit *natural use*, also in v. 27
[C] 1:27 Lit *males*, also later in v.   [D] 1:27 Or *in themselves* [E] 1:29 Other mss add *sexual immorality*   [F] 1:31 Other mss add *unforgiving* [G] 1:32 Lit *things are worthy of death* [H] 1:32 Lit *even take pleasure in* [I] 2:1 Lit *Therefore, O man, every one* [J] 2:4 Or *patience, because you do not recognize* [K] 2:6 Ps 62:12; Pr 24:12 [L] 2:12 Lit *in* [M] 2:13 Or *acquitted*

[14] So, when Gentiles, who do not by nature have the law, do[A] what the law demands, they are a law to themselves even though they do not have the law. [15] They show that the work of the law[B] is written on their hearts. Their consciences confirm this. Their competing thoughts either accuse or even excuse them[C] [16] on the day when God judges what people have kept secret, according to my gospel through Christ Jesus.

JEWISH VIOLATION OF THE LAW

[17] Now if[D] you call yourself a Jew, and rely on the law, and boast in God, [18] and know his will, and approve the things that are superior, being instructed from the law, [19] and if you are convinced that you are a guide for the blind, a light to those in darkness, [20] an instructor of the ignorant, a teacher of the immature, having the embodiment of knowledge and truth in the law — [21] you then, who teach another, don't you teach yourself? You who preach, "You must not steal" — do you steal? [22] You who say, "You must not commit adultery" — do you commit adultery? You who detest idols, do you rob their temples? [23] You who boast in the law, do you dishonor God by breaking the law? [24] For, as it is written: **The name of God is blasphemed among the Gentiles because of you.**[E]

CIRCUMCISION OF THE HEART

[25] Circumcision benefits you if you observe the law, but if you are a lawbreaker, your circumcision has become uncircumcision. [26] So if an uncircumcised man keeps the law's requirements, will not his uncircumcision be counted as circumcision? [27] A man who is physically uncircumcised, but who keeps the law, will judge you who are a lawbreaker in spite of having the letter of the law and circumcision. [28] For a person is not a Jew who is one outwardly, and true circumcision is not something visible in the flesh. [29] On the contrary, a person is a Jew who is one inwardly, and circumcision is of the heart — by the Spirit, not the letter.[F] That person's praise is not from people but from God.

PAUL ANSWERS AN OBJECTION

3 So what advantage does the Jew have? Or what is the benefit of circumcision? [2] Considerable in every way. First, they were entrusted with the very words of God. [3] What then? If some were unfaithful, will their unfaithfulness nullify God's faithfulness? [4] Absolutely not! Let God be true, even though everyone is a liar, as it is written:

That you may be justified in your words
and triumph when you judge.[G]

[5] But if our unrighteousness highlights[H] God's righteousness, what are we to say? I am using a human argument:[I] Is God unrighteous to inflict wrath? [6] Absolutely not! Otherwise, how will God judge the world? [7] But if by my lie God's truth abounds to his glory, why am I also still being

---

[A]2:14 Or *who do not have the law, instinctively do*   [B]2:15 The code of conduct required by the law   [C]2:15 Internal debate, either in a person or among the pagan moralists   [D]2:17 Other mss read *Look* —   [E]2:24 Is 52:5   [F]2:29 Or *heart — spiritually, not literally*   [G]3:4 Ps 51:4   [H]3:5 Or *shows,* or *demonstrates*
[I]3:5 Lit *I speak as a man*

GOOD NEWS FOR SINNERS

ROMANS 3; PSALM 14; ECCLESIASTES 7:20

"For all have sinned and fall short of the glory of God."

If you read Paul's letters enough, you're bound to catch this recurring theme.

Why did he find it so important for believers in the first century (and us!) to understand they were sinners?

Because God loves sinners.

"But God proves his own love for us in that while we were still sinners, Christ died for us!" (Rm 5:8).

Jesus came to earth for sinners. He lived, died, and rose again for sinners. He forgives sinners. And sinners who place their faith in Him are welcomed into His family.

That's really good news for sinners, right? And Scripture leaves no doubt. You, me, and every person on earth . . . we're all sinners. That's the bottom line Paul lays out in Romans 3:23.

We're all broken, needy, and messed-up in a way that simply being "good" can never fix.

Since the garden of Eden, our identity as humans has been marked by our tendency to rebel against God. That's why we can never behave our way into a right relationship with Him. The most well-behaved, law-abiding, church-attending, choir-singing, modest-dressing, moralistic person alive, apart from Jesus Christ, is still dead in her trespasses and sins (Eph 2:1).

The heartbeat of the gospel is not, "Clean up your act, obey the rules, and God will forgive you." That's moralism, not Christianity. Any one of us who has ever tried to be a perfect person, even for a day, knows that approach simply doesn't work. That false gospel stands in direct contradiction to the true one: Christ died for sinners. Because He loves us, remember?

Do we encourage each other—and ourselves—to obedience? Absolutely! But let's also remember that righteousness does not come through our obedience. Right standing with God comes only through faith in Jesus—His works and not our own. As Paul says in verse 24, "They are justified freely by his grace through the redemption that is in Christ Jesus."

Through Jesus, grace flows freely to sinners of all ages. Through Jesus, those guilty and condemned are declared righteous—justified by His sacrifice, by grace through faith. And through Jesus, polluted sinners exchange filthy rags for robes of righteousness.

"I rejoice greatly in the LORD, I exult in my God; for he has clothed me with the garments of salvation and wrapped me in a robe of righteousness . . ."

ISAIAH 61:10

---

judged as a sinner? [8] And why not say, just as some people slanderously claim we say, "Let us do what is evil so that good may come"? Their condemnation is deserved!

THE WHOLE WORLD GUILTY BEFORE GOD

[9] What then? Are we any better off?[A] Not at all! For we have already charged that both Jews and Gentiles[B] are all under sin,[C] [10] as it is written:

There is no one righteous, not even one.
[11] There is no one who understands;
there is no one who seeks God.
[12] All have turned away;
all alike have become worthless.
There is no one who does what is good,
not even one.[D]
[13] Their throat is an open grave;
they deceive with their tongues.[E]
Vipers' venom is under their lips.[F]
[14] Their mouth is full of cursing and bitterness.[G]
[15] Their feet are swift to shed blood;
[16] ruin and wretchedness are in their paths,
[17] and the path of peace they have not known.[H]
[18] There is no fear of God before their eyes.[I]

[19] Now we know that whatever the law says, it speaks to those who are subject to the law,[J] so that every mouth may be shut and the whole world may become subject to God's judgment.[K] [20] For no one will be justified[L] in his sight by the works of the law, because the knowledge of sin comes through the law.

THE RIGHTEOUSNESS OF GOD THROUGH FAITH

[21] But now, apart from the law, the righteousness of God has been revealed, attested by the Law and the Prophets.[M] [22] The righteousness of God is through faith in Jesus Christ[N] to all who believe, since there is no distinction. [23] For all have sinned and fall short of the[O] glory of God. [24] They are justified freely by his grace through the redemption that is in Christ Jesus. [25] God presented him as an atoning sacrifice[P] in his blood, received through faith, to demonstrate his righteousness, because in his restraint God passed over the sins previously committed. [26] God presented him to demonstrate his righteousness at the present time, so that he would be righteous and declare righteous[Q] the one who has faith in Jesus.

[A]3:9 Are we Jews any better than the Gentiles?   [B]3:9 Lit Greeks   [C]3:9 Under sin's power or dominion   [D]3:10-12 Ps 14:1-3; 53:1-3; Ec 7:20   [E]3:13 Ps 5:9
[F]3:13 Ps 140:3   [G]3:14 Ps 10:7   [H]3:15-17 Is 59:7-8   [I]3:18 Ps 36:1   [J]3:19 Lit those in the law   [K]3:19 Or become guilty before God, or may be accountable to God   [L]3:20 Or will be declared righteous, or will be acquitted   [M]3:21 When capitalized, the Law and the Prophets = OT   [N]3:22 Or through the faithfulness of Jesus Christ   [O]3:23 Or and lack the   [P]3:25 Or a propitiation, or a place of atonement   [Q]3:26 Or and justify, or and acquit

BOASTING EXCLUDED

²⁷ Where, then, is boasting? It is excluded. By what kind of law?ᴬ By one of works? No, on the contrary, by a lawᴮ of faith. ²⁸ For we conclude that a person is justified by faith apart from the works of the law. ²⁹ Or is God the God of Jews only? Is he not the God of Gentiles too? Yes, of Gentiles too, ³⁰ since there is one God who will justify the circumcised by faith and the uncircumcised through faith. ³¹ Do we then nullify the law through faith? Absolutely not! On the contrary, we uphold the law.

ABRAHAM JUSTIFIED BY FAITH

4 What then will we say that Abraham, our forefather according to the flesh, has found?ᶜ ² If Abraham was justifiedᴰ by works, he has something to boast about — but not before God. ³ For what does the Scripture say? **Abraham believed God, and it was credited to him for righteousness.**ᴱ ⁴ Now to the one who works, pay is not credited as a gift, but as something owed. ⁵ But to the one who does not work, but believes on him who declares the ungodly to be righteous, his faith is credited for righteousness.

DAVID CELEBRATING THE SAME TRUTH

⁶ Just as David also speaks of the blessing of the person to whom God credits righteousness apart from works:

> ⁷ **Blessed are those whose lawless acts are forgiven**
> **and whose sins are covered.**
> ⁸ **Blessed is the person**
> **the Lord will never charge with sin.**ᶠ

ABRAHAM JUSTIFIED BEFORE CIRCUMCISION

⁹ Is this blessing only for the circumcised, then? Or is it also for the uncircumcised? For we say, **Faith was credited to Abraham for righteousness.**ᴱ ¹⁰ In what way then was it credited — while he was circumcised, or uncircumcised? It was not while he was circumcised, but uncircumcised. ¹¹ And he received the sign of circumcision as a seal of the righteousness that he had by faithᴳ while still uncircumcised. This was to make him the father of all who believe but are not circumcised, so that righteousness may be credited to them also. ¹² And he became the father of the circumcised, who are not only circumcised but who also follow in the footsteps of the faith our father Abraham had while he was still uncircumcised.

THE PROMISE GRANTED THROUGH FAITH

¹³ For the promise to Abraham or to his descendants that he would inherit the world was not through the law, but through the righteousness that comes by faith. ¹⁴ If those who are of the law are heirs, faith is made empty and the promise nullified, ¹⁵ because the law produces wrath. And where there is no law, there is no transgression.

ᴬ3:27 Or *what principle?* ᴮ3:27 Or *a principle* ᶜ4:1 Or *What then shall we say? Have we found Abraham to be our forefather according to the flesh?* or *What, then, shall we say that Abraham our forefather found according to the flesh?* ᴰ4:2 Or *was declared righteous,* or *was acquitted* ᴱ4:3,9 Gn 15:6 ᶠ4:7-8 Ps 32:1-2 ᴳ4:11 Lit *righteousness of faith,* also in v. 13

[16] This is why the promise is by faith, so that it may be according to grace, to guarantee it to all the descendants — not only to those who are of the law [A] but also to those who are of Abraham's faith. He is the father of us all. [17] As it is written: **I have made you the father of many nations.** [B] He is our father in God's sight, in whom Abraham believed — the God who gives life to the dead and calls things into existence that do not exist. [18] He believed, hoping against hope, so that he became **the father of many nations** [B] according to what had been spoken: **So will your descendants be.** [C] [19] He did not weaken in faith when he considered [D] his own body to be already dead (since he was about a hundred years old) and also the deadness of Sarah's womb. [20] He did not waver in unbelief at God's promise but was strengthened in his faith and gave glory to God, [21] because he was fully convinced that what God had promised, he was also able to do. [22] Therefore, **it was credited to him for righteousness.** [E] [23] Now **it was credited to him** [E] was not written for Abraham alone, [24] but also for us. It will be credited to us who believe in him who raised Jesus our Lord from the dead. [25] He was delivered up for [F] our trespasses and raised for our justification.

FAITH TRIUMPHS

5 Therefore, since we have been declared righteous by faith, we have peace [G] with God through our Lord Jesus Christ. [2] We have also obtained access through him by faith [H] into this grace in which we stand, and we rejoice [I] in the hope of the glory of God. [3] And not only that, but we also rejoice in our afflictions, because we know that affliction produces endurance, [4] endurance produces proven character, and proven character produces hope. [5] This hope will not disappoint us, because God's love has been poured out in our hearts through the Holy Spirit who was given to us.

THOSE DECLARED RIGHTEOUS ARE RECONCILED

[6] For while we were still helpless, at the right time, Christ died for the ungodly. [7] For rarely will someone die for a just person — though for a good person perhaps someone might even dare to die. [8] But God proves his own love for us in that while we were still sinners, Christ died for us. [9] How much more then, since we have now been declared righteous by his blood, will we be saved through him from wrath. [10] For if, while we were enemies, we were reconciled to God through the death of his Son, then how much more, having been reconciled, will we be saved by his life. [11] And not only that, but we also rejoice in God through our Lord Jesus Christ, through whom we have now received this reconciliation.

DEATH THROUGH ADAM AND LIFE THROUGH CHRIST

[12] Therefore, just as sin entered the world through one man, and death through sin, in this way death spread to all people, because all sinned. [J] [13] In fact, sin

---

[A] 4:16 Or *not to those who are of the law only*   [B] 4:17,18 Gn 17:5
[C] 4:18 Gn 15:5   [D] 4:19 Other mss read *He did not consider*   [E] 4:22,23 Gn 15:6
[F] 4:25 Or *because of*   [G] 5:1 Other mss read *faith, let us have peace,* which can also be translated *faith, let us grasp the fact that we have peace*   [H] 5:2 Other mss omit *by faith*   [I] 5:2 Lit *boast,* also in vv. 3, 11   [J] 5:12 Or *have sinned*

was in the world before the law, but sin is not charged to a person's account when there is no law. [14] Nevertheless, death reigned from Adam to Moses, even over those who did not sin in the likeness of Adam's transgression. He is a type of the Coming One.

[15] But the gift is not like the trespass. For if by the one man's trespass the many died, how much more have the grace of God and the gift which comes through the grace of the one man Jesus Christ overflowed to the many. [16] And the gift is not like the one man's sin, because from one sin came the judgment, resulting in condemnation, but from many trespasses came the gift, resulting in justification.[A] [17] Since by the one man's trespass, death reigned through that one man, how much more will those who receive the overflow of grace and the gift of righteousness reign in life through the one man, Jesus Christ.

[18] So then, as through one trespass there is condemnation for everyone, so also through one righteous act there is justification leading to life for everyone. [19] For just as through one man's disobedience the many were made sinners, so also through the one man's obedience the many will be made righteous. [20] The law came along to multiply the trespass. But where sin multiplied, grace multiplied even more [21] so that, just as sin reigned in death, so also grace will reign through righteousness, resulting in eternal life through Jesus Christ our Lord.

THE NEW LIFE IN CHRIST

6 What should we say then? Should we continue in sin so that grace may multiply? [2] Absolutely not! How can we who died to sin still live in it? [3] Or are you unaware that all of us who were baptized into Christ Jesus were baptized into his death? [4] Therefore we were buried with him by baptism into death, in order that, just as Christ was raised from the dead by the glory of the Father, so we too may walk in newness[B] of life. [5] For if we have been united with him in the likeness of his death, we will certainly also be[C] in the likeness of his resurrection. [6] For we know that our old self[D] was crucified with him so that the body ruled by sin[E] might be rendered powerless so that we may no longer be enslaved to sin, [7] since a person who has died is freed[F] from sin. [8] Now if we died with Christ, we believe that we will also live with him, [9] because we know that Christ, having been raised from the dead, will not die again. Death no longer rules over him. [10] For the death he died, he died to sin once for all time; but the life he lives, he lives to God. [11] So, you too consider yourselves dead to sin and alive to God in Christ Jesus.[G]

[12] Therefore do not let sin reign in your mortal body, so that you obey[H] its desires. [13] And do not offer any parts[I] of it to sin as weapons for unrighteousness. But as those who are alive from the dead, offer yourselves to God, and all the parts of yourselves to God as weapons for righteousness. [14] For sin will not rule over you, because you are not under the law but under grace.

[A] 5:16 Or acquittal [B] 6:4 Or a new way [C] 6:5 Be joined with him [D] 6:6 Lit man [E] 6:6 Lit that the body of sin [F] 6:7 Or justified; lit acquitted [G] 6:11 Other mss add our Lord [H] 6:12 Other mss add sin (lit it) in [I] 6:13 Or members, also in v. 19

1909

FROM SLAVES OF SIN TO SLAVES OF GOD

[15] What then? Should we sin because we are not under the law but under grace? Absolutely not! [16] Don't you know that if you offer yourselves to someone[A] as obedient slaves, you are slaves of that one you obey — either of sin leading to death or of obedience leading to righteousness? [17] But thank God that, although you used to be slaves of sin, you obeyed from the heart that pattern of teaching to which you were handed[B] over, [18] and having been set free from sin, you became enslaved to righteousness. [19] I am using a human analogy because of the weakness of your flesh.[C] For just as you offered the parts of yourselves as slaves to impurity, and to greater and greater lawlessness, so now offer them as slaves to righteousness, which results in sanctification. [20] For when you were slaves of sin, you were free with regard to righteousness.[D] [21] So what fruit was produced[E] then from the things you are now ashamed of? The outcome of those things is death. [22] But now, since you have been set free from sin and have become enslaved to God, you have your fruit, which results in sanctification — and the outcome is eternal life! [23] For the wages of sin is death, but the gift of God is eternal life in Christ Jesus our Lord.

AN ILLUSTRATION FROM MARRIAGE

7 Since I am speaking to those who know the law, brothers and sisters, don't you know that the law rules over someone as long as he lives? [2] For example, a married woman is legally bound to her husband while he lives. But if her husband dies, she is released from the law regarding the husband. [3] So then, if she is married to another man while her husband is living, she will be called an adulteress. But if her husband dies, she is free from that law. Then, if she is married to another man, she is not an adulteress.

[4] Therefore, my brothers and sisters, you also were put to death in relation to the law through the body of Christ so that you may belong to another. You belong to him who was raised from the dead in order that we may bear fruit for God. [5] For when we were in the flesh, the sinful passions aroused through the law were working in us[F] to bear fruit for death. [6] But now we have been released from the law, since we have died to what held us, so that we may serve in the newness of the Spirit and not in the old letter of the law.

SIN'S USE OF THE LAW

[7] What should we say then? Is the law sin? Absolutely not! On the contrary, I would not have known sin if it were not for the law. For example, I would not have known what it is to covet if the law had not said, **Do not covet.**[G] [8] And sin, seizing an opportunity through the commandment, produced in me coveting of every kind. For apart from the law sin is dead. [9] Once I was alive apart from the law, but when the commandment came, sin sprang to life again [10] and I died. The commandment that was meant for life resulted in death for me. [11] For sin, seizing an opportunity through the commandment, deceived me, and through it killed me. [12] So then, the

---

[A]6:16 Lit that to whom you offer yourselves   [B]6:17 Or entrusted   [C]6:19 Or your human nature   [D]6:20 Lit free to righteousness   [E]6:21 Lit what fruit do you have   [F]7:5 Lit in our members   [G]7:7 Ex 20:17

law is holy, and the commandment is holy and just and good. ¹³ Therefore, did what is good become death to me? Absolutely not! On the contrary, sin, in order to be recognized as sin, was producing death in me through what is good, so that through the commandment, sin might become sinful beyond measure.

THE PROBLEM OF SIN IN US

¹⁴ For we know that the law is spiritual, but I am of the flesh,ᴬ sold as a slave to sin.ᴮ ¹⁵ For I do not understand what I am doing, because I do not practice what I want to do, but I do what I hate. ¹⁶ Now if I do what I do not want to do, I agree with the law that it is good. ¹⁷ So now I am no longer the one doing it, but it is sin living in me. ¹⁸ For I know that nothing good lives in me, that is, in my flesh. For the desire to do what is good is with me, but there is no ability to do it. ¹⁹ For I do not do the good that I want to do, but I practice the evil that I do not want to do. ²⁰ Now if I do what I do not want, I am no longer the one that does it, but it is the sin that lives in me. ²¹ So I discover this law:ᶜ When I want to do what is good,ᴰ evil is present with me. ²² For in my inner selfᴱ I delight in God's law, ²³ but I see a different law in the parts of my body,ᶠ waging war against the law of my mind and taking me prisoner to the law of sin in the parts of my body. ²⁴ What a wretched man I am! Who will rescue me from this body of death? ²⁵ Thanks be to God through Jesus Christ our Lord! So then, with my mind I myself am serving the law of God, but with my flesh, the law of sin.

THE LIFE-GIVING SPIRIT

8 Therefore, there is now no condemnation for those in Christ Jesus,ᴳ ² because the law of the Spirit of life in Christ Jesus has set youᴴ free from the law of sin and death. ³ What the law could not do since it was weakened by the flesh, God did. He condemned sin in the flesh by sending his own Son in the likeness of sinful flesh as a sin offering,ᴵ ⁴ in order that the law's requirement would be fulfilled in us who do not walk according to the flesh but according to the Spirit. ⁵ For those who live according to the flesh have their minds set on the things of the flesh, but those who live according to the Spirit have their minds set on the things of the Spirit. ⁶ Now the mind-set of the flesh is death, but the mind-set of the Spirit is life and peace. ⁷ The mind-set of the flesh is hostile to God because it does not submit to God's law. Indeed, it is unable to do so. ⁸ Those who are in the flesh cannot please God. ⁹ You, however, are not in the flesh, but in the Spirit, if indeed the Spirit of God lives in you. If anyone does not have the Spirit of Christ, he does not belong to him. ¹⁰ Now if Christ is in you, the body is dead because of sin, but the Spiritᴶ gives lifeᴷ because of righteousness. ¹¹ And if the Spirit of him who raised Jesus from the dead lives in you, then he who raised Christ from the dead will also bring your mortal bodies to life throughᴸ his Spirit who lives in you.

ᴬ7:14 Or unspiritual ᴮ7:14 Lit under sin ᶜ7:21 Or principle ᴰ7:21 Or
I find with respect to the law that when I want to do good ᴱ7:22 Lit inner man
ᶠ7:23 Lit my members ᴳ8:1 Other mss add who do not walk according to the
flesh but according to the Spirit ᴴ8:2 Other mss read me ᴵ8:3 Or for sin
ᴶ8:10 Or spirit ᴷ8:10 Or your spirit is alive ᴸ8:11 Other mss read because of

COME TO JESUS

ROMANS 8; PSALM 51

What can separate me from the love of God in Christ? Romans 8 says, "nothing," but I had my doubts.

I bet I prayed "The Sinner's Prayer" twenty times growing up. I was always so afraid I'd missed something, or paranoid I'd somehow nullified my salvation since the last time I said the magic words. A full thirty years after the first time I prayed, I now know: there is nothing magical about it.

My words don't save me. Jesus saves me. My response is to repent of my sins and believe He saves me (Mk 1:15).

Romans 10:9 says, "If you confess with your mouth, 'Jesus is Lord,' and believe in your heart that God raised him from the dead, you will be saved." This is beautiful and true, yet it's easy to see how we misconstrue these words to make them about us. We focus on the exact words we said, the exact time and place we knelt. We make our coming to Christ about our circumstances rather than our Savior.

The Apostle Paul got it. He wrote in Galatians 2:21:

"I do not set aside the grace of God, for if righteousness comes through the law, then Christ died for nothing."

It was never about where or how or with what words I came to Christ.

It was never about what I was doing. It was always about what He did for me.

The depth of our need for Jesus is so vast that even our act of coming to Him is flawed, but He is not surprised by this. He knows us fully and loves us still (Ps 139; Gl 2:20). He came to make everything right, including our half-heartedness and our ill intentions. Whether we turn to Him for the first time or the hundredth, He never leaves us or forsakes us.

Repentance is not about saving or re-saving myself. Jesus already secured my redemption. Repentance is always and only about His grace. There is no condemnation for those now in Christ Jesus (Rm 8:1).

If you long to confess your sin and believe Jesus today, don't worry about the circumstances. Don't wait for the perfect time, the perfect place—even the perfect words. As the hymn writer Joseph Hart put it, "If you tarry till you're better, you will never come at all" (Joseph Hart, "Come, Ye Sinners, Poor and Needy").

Come as you are and bare your soul. Cry out like David cried out in Psalm 51, confessing honestly and openly before the God who made you and promises to make you new (2Co 5:17), who loves you and stands ready to save. Then come back day after day. Walk daily in the grace you first received, knowing there is nothing you can do or not do to reverse the rescue His cross secured. Thanks be to our God!

THE HOLY SPIRIT'S MINISTRIES

[12] So then, brothers and sisters, we are not obligated to the flesh to live according to the flesh, [13] because if you live according to the flesh, you are going to die. But if by the Spirit you put to death the deeds of the body, you will live. [14] For all those led by God's Spirit are God's sons. [15] For you did not receive a spirit of slavery to fall back into fear. Instead, you received the Spirit of adoption, by whom we cry out, "*Abba*,[A] Father!" [16] The Spirit himself testifies together with our spirit that we are God's children, [17] and if children, also heirs — heirs of God and coheirs with Christ — if indeed we suffer with him so that we may also be glorified with him.

FROM GROANS TO GLORY

[18] For I consider that the sufferings of this present time are not worth comparing with the glory that is going to be revealed to us. [19] For the creation eagerly waits with anticipation for God's sons to be revealed. [20] For the creation was subjected to futility — not willingly, but because of him who subjected it — in the hope [21] that the creation itself will also be set free from the bondage to decay into the glorious freedom of God's children. [22] For we know that the whole creation has been groaning together with labor pains until now. [23] Not only that, but we ourselves who have the Spirit as the firstfruits — we also groan within ourselves, eagerly waiting for adoption, the redemption of our bodies. [24] Now in this hope we were saved, but hope that is seen is not hope, because who hopes for what he sees? [25] Now if we hope for what we do not see, we eagerly wait for it with patience.

[26] In the same way the Spirit also helps us in our weakness, because we do not know what to pray for as we should, but the Spirit himself intercedes for us[B] with unspoken groanings. [27] And he who searches our hearts knows the mind of the Spirit, because he intercedes for the saints according to the will of God.

[28] We know that all things work together[C] for the good[D] of those who love God, who are called according to his purpose. [29] For those he foreknew he also predestined to be conformed to the image of his Son, so that he would be the firstborn among many brothers and sisters. [30] And those he predestined, he also called; and those he called, he also justified; and those he justified, he also glorified.

THE BELIEVER'S TRIUMPH

[31] What then are we to say about these things? If God is for us, who is against us? [32] He did not even spare his own Son but offered him up for us all. How will he not also with him grant us everything? [33] Who can bring an accusation against God's elect? God is the one who justifies. [34] Who is the one who condemns? Christ Jesus is the one who died, but even more, has been raised; he also is at the right hand of God and intercedes for us. [35] Who can separate us from the love of Christ? Can affliction or distress or persecution or famine or nakedness or danger or sword? [36] As it is written:

Because of you
we are being put to death all day long;

[A]8:15 Aramaic for *father*   [B]8:26 Some mss omit *for us*   [C]8:28 Other mss read *that God works together in all things*   [D]8:28 The ultimate good

we are counted as sheep to be slaughtered.[A] [37] No, in all these things we are more than conquerors through him who loved us. [38] For I am persuaded that neither death nor life, nor angels nor rulers, nor things present nor things to come, nor powers, [39] nor height nor depth, nor any other created thing will be able to separate us from the love of God that is in Christ Jesus our Lord.

ISRAEL'S REJECTION OF CHRIST

9 I speak the truth in Christ — I am not lying; my conscience testifies to me through the Holy Spirit[B] — [2] that I have great sorrow and unceasing anguish in my heart. [3] For I could wish that I myself were cursed and cut off[C] from Christ for the benefit of my brothers and sisters, my own flesh and blood. [4] They are Israelites, and to them belong the adoption, the glory, the covenants, the giving of the law, the temple service, and the promises. [5] The ancestors are theirs, and from them, by physical descent,[D] came the Christ, who is God over all, praised forever.[E] Amen.

GOD'S GRACIOUS ELECTION OF ISRAEL

[6] Now it is not as though the word of God has failed, because not all who are descended from Israel are Israel. [7] Neither are all of Abraham's children his descendants.[F] On the contrary, **your offspring will be traced**[G] **through Isaac.**[H] [8] That is, it is not the children by physical descent[I] who are God's children, but the children of the promise are considered to be the offspring. [9] For this is the statement of the promise: **At this time I will come, and Sarah will have a son.**[J] [10] And not only that, but Rebekah conceived children through one man, our father Isaac. [11] For though her sons had not been born yet or done anything good or bad, so that God's purpose according to election might stand — [12] not from works but from the one who calls — she was told, **The older will serve the younger.**[K] [13] As it is written: **I have loved Jacob, but I have hated Esau.**[L]

GOD'S SELECTION IS JUST

[14] What should we say then? Is there injustice with God? Absolutely not! [15] For he tells Moses, **I will show mercy to whom I will show mercy, and I will have compassion on whom I will have compassion.**[M] [16] So then, it does not depend on human will or effort but on God who shows mercy. [17] For the Scripture tells Pharaoh, **I raised you up for this reason so that I may display my power in you and that my name may be proclaimed in the whole earth.**[N] [18] So then, he has mercy on whom he wants to have mercy and he hardens whom he wants to harden.

[19] You will say to me, therefore, "Why then does he still find fault? For who can resist his will?" [20] But who are you, a mere man, to talk back to God? Will what is formed say to the one who formed it, "Why did you make

---

[A] 8:36 Ps 44:22   [B] 9:1 Or testifying with me by the Holy Spirit   [C] 9:3 Lit to be anathema   [D] 9:5 Lit them, according to the flesh   [E] 9:5 Or the Messiah, the one who is over all, the God who is blessed forever, or Messiah. God, who is over all, be blessed forever   [F] 9:7 Lit seed   [G] 9:7 Lit called   [H] 9:7 Gn 21:12   [I] 9:8 Lit children of the flesh   [J] 9:9 Gn 18:10,14   [K] 9:12 Gn 25:23   [L] 9:13 Mal 1:2-3   [M] 9:15 Ex 33:19   [N] 9:17 Ex 9:16

me like this?" [21] Or has the potter no right over the clay, to make from the same lump one piece of pottery for honor and another for dishonor? [22] And what if God, wanting to display his wrath and to make his power known, endured with much patience objects of wrath prepared for destruction? [23] And what if he did this to make known the riches of his glory on objects of mercy that he prepared beforehand for glory — [24] on us, the ones he also called, not only from the Jews but also from the Gentiles? [25] As it [A] also says in Hosea,

> I will call Not My People, My People,
> and she who is Unloved, Beloved. [B]

[26]
> And it will be in the place where they were told,
> you are not my people,
> there they will be called sons of the living God. [C]

[27] But Isaiah cries out concerning Israel,

> Though the number of Israelites
> is like the sand of the sea,
> only the remnant will be saved;

[28]
> since the Lord will execute his sentence
> completely and decisively on the earth. [D,E]

[29] And just as Isaiah predicted:

> If the Lord of Hosts [F] had not left us offspring,
> we would have become like Sodom,
> and we would have been made like Gomorrah. [G]

ISRAEL'S PRESENT STATE

[30] What should we say then? Gentiles, who did not pursue righteousness, have obtained righteousness — namely the righteousness that comes from faith. [31] But Israel, pursuing the law of righteousness, has not achieved the righteousness of the law. [H] [32] Why is that? Because they did not pursue it by faith, but as if it were by works. [I] They stumbled over the stumbling stone. [33] As it is written,

> Look, I am putting a stone in Zion to stumble over
> and a rock to trip over,
> and the one who believes on him
> will not be put to shame. [J]

RIGHTEOUSNESS BY FAITH ALONE

10 Brothers and sisters, my heart's desire and prayer to God concerning them [K] is for their salvation. [2] I can testify about them that they have zeal for God, but not according to knowledge. [3] Since they are ignorant of the righteousness of God and attempted to establish their own righteousness, they have not submitted to God's righteousness. [4] For Christ is the end [L] of the law for righteousness to everyone who believes, [5] since Moses writes about the righteousness that is from the law: **The one who does**

[A] 9:25 Or he   [B] 9:25 Hs 2:23   [C] 9:26 Hs 1:10   [D] 9:28 Or land   [E] 9:27-28 Is 10:22-23; 28:22; Hs 1:10   [F] 9:29 Gk Sabaoth; or the Lord of Armies
[G] 9:29 Is 1:9   [H] 9:31 Other mss read the law for righteousness   [I] 9:32 Other mss add of the law   [J] 9:33 Is 8:14; 28:16   [K] 10:1 Other mss read God for Israel
[L] 10:4 Or goal

FAITH ALONE (FOR REAL)

ROMANS 10; GALATIANS 2:20-22

I sat on the plush, cream-colored sofa, helping my mentor fold laundry while her two-year-old played on the floor. I was a senior in college, involved in campus ministry and leading a Bible study, and I enthusiastically updated her on both endeavors. I'd begun telling yet another story when she calmly interrupted me with a simple, matter-of-fact statement: "You believe in a works-based gospel."

We'd known each other a while, and her statement stunned me. *Was she serious?*

I quickly brushed it off in the moment. But later that week, I found myself kneeling by the side of my bed, soaking my plaid, purple bedspread with tears. She was right.

There I was, wallowing in my sin, wanting desperately to be back in the loving arms of my Savior. I had asked for forgiveness, but the relief wasn't coming. As I poured my guilty conscience onto the pages of my journal, I was struck by one word: time.

That's what I thought I needed: time. I didn't really want forgiveness. I wanted time—enough time to fill my life up with the right things, the good things, to settle the score. It was salvation by works at its worst.

All my striving, all my desire to put time between myself and my mistakes, it was another attempt to earn my salvation through my own effort. Rather than trusting the work of Christ on the cross for my righteousness, I had become dependent on my own actions to save me.

I was living exactly like the Israelites Paul describes in Romans 10:3:

"Since they are ignorant of the righteousness of God and attempted to establish their own righteousness, they have not submitted to God's righteousness."

After Christ's death and resurrection, Israel was still working hard to keep the Law of Moses in order to gain righteousness. They were working to save themselves, forgetting that "Christ is the end of the law for righteousness to everyone who believes" (Rm 10:4).

The law, our works, the right things—they were never supposed to save us. God had planned our salvation and redemption through Jesus Christ all along. Christ is the only perfect fulfillment, the only victory we have over sin and death. His perfect life allows us to be justified through our faith alone. Faith and nothing else—just Jesus.

As I knelt beside my bed that day, I realized Jesus truly was all I needed. His sacrifice covered me then, despite all my striving, and it covers me today. I need His righteousness, not my own. He is enough.

Friends, no matter what our past, present, or future holds, the only work that can save us is the work Christ completed on the cross. May we call on the name of the Lord and be saved.

these things will live by them.^{A 6} But the righteousness that comes from faith speaks like this: **Do not say in your heart, "Who will go up to heaven?"** ^B that is, to bring Christ down ⁷ or, **"Who will go down into the abyss?"** ^C that is, to bring Christ up from the dead. ⁸ On the contrary, what does it say? **The message is near you, in your mouth and in your heart.** ^D This is the message of faith that we proclaim: ⁹ If you confess with your mouth, "Jesus is Lord," and believe in your heart that God raised him from the dead, you will be saved. ¹⁰ One believes with the heart, resulting in righteousness, and one confesses with the mouth, resulting in salvation. ¹¹ For the Scripture says, **Everyone who believes on him will not be put to shame,** ^{E 12} since there is no distinction between Jew and Greek, because the same Lord of all richly blesses all who call on him. ¹³ For **everyone who calls on the name of the Lord will be saved.** ^F

ISRAEL'S REJECTION OF THE MESSAGE

¹⁴ How, then, can they call on him they have not believed in? And how can they believe without hearing about him? And how can they hear without a preacher? ¹⁵ And how can they preach unless they are sent? As it is written: **How beautiful** ^G **are the feet of those who bring good news.** ^{H 16} But not all obeyed the gospel. For Isaiah says, **Lord, who has believed our message?** ^I ¹⁷ So faith comes from what is heard, and what is heard comes through the message about Christ. ^{J 18} But I ask, "Did they not hear?" Yes, they did:

> Their voice has gone out to the whole earth,
> and their words to the ends of the world. ^K

¹⁹ But I ask, "Did Israel not understand?" First, Moses said,

> I will make you jealous
> of those who are not a nation;
> I will make you angry by a nation
> that lacks understanding. ^L

²⁰ And Isaiah says boldly,

> I was found
> by those who were not looking for me;
> I revealed myself
> to those who were not asking for me. ^M

²¹ But to Israel he says, **All day long I have held out my hands to a disobedient and defiant people.** ^N

ISRAEL'S REJECTION NOT TOTAL

11 I ask, then, has God rejected his people? Absolutely not! For I too am an Israelite, a descendant of Abraham, from the tribe of Benjamin. ² God has not rejected his people whom he foreknew. Or don't you know what the Scripture says in the passage about Elijah — how he pleads with God against Israel? ³ **Lord, they have killed your prophets and torn down your altars. I am the only one left, and they are trying to take my life!** ^O

---

^A10:5 Lv 18:5   ^B10:6 Dt 9:4; 30:12   ^C10:7 Dt 30:13   ^D10:8 Dt 30:14
^E10:11 Is 28:16   ^F10:13 Jl 2:32   ^G10:15 Or *welcome,* or *timely*
^H10:15 Is 52:7; Nah 1:15   ^I10:16 Is 53:1   ^J10:17 Other mss read *God*
^K10:18 Ps 19:4   ^L10:19 Dt 32:21   ^M10:20 Is 65:1   ^N10:21 Is 65:2
^O11:3 1Kg 19:10,14

⁴ But what was God's answer to him? **I have left seven thousand for myself who have not bowed down to Baal.**^A ⁵ In the same way, then, there is also at the present time a remnant chosen by grace. ⁶ Now if by grace, then it is not by works; otherwise grace ceases to be grace.^B

⁷ What then? Israel did not find what it was looking for, but the elect did find it. The rest were hardened, ⁸ as it is written,

> God gave them a spirit of stupor,
> eyes that cannot see
> and ears that cannot hear,
> to this day.^C

⁹ And David says,

> Let their table become a snare and a trap,
> a pitfall and a retribution to them.
> ¹⁰ Let their eyes be darkened so that they cannot see,
> and their backs be bent continually.^D

ISRAEL'S REJECTION NOT FINAL

¹¹ I ask, then, have they stumbled so as to fall? Absolutely not! On the contrary, by their transgression, salvation has come to the Gentiles to make Israel jealous. ¹² Now if their transgression brings riches for the world, and their failure riches for the Gentiles, how much more will their fullness bring!

¹³ Now I am speaking to you Gentiles. Insofar as I am an apostle to the Gentiles, I magnify my ministry, ¹⁴ if I might somehow make my own people^E jealous and save some of them. ¹⁵ For if their rejection brings reconciliation to the world, what will their acceptance mean but life from the dead? ¹⁶ Now if the firstfruits are holy, so is the whole batch. And if the root is holy, so are the branches.

¹⁷ Now if some of the branches were broken off, and you, though a wild olive branch, were grafted in among them and have come to share in the rich root^F of the cultivated olive tree, ¹⁸ do not boast that you are better than those branches. But if you do boast — you do not sustain the root, but the root sustains you. ¹⁹ Then you will say, "Branches were broken off so that I might be grafted in." ²⁰ True enough; they were broken off because of unbelief, but you stand by faith. Do not be arrogant, but beware,^G ²¹ because if God did not spare the natural branches, he will not spare you either. ²² Therefore, consider God's kindness and severity: severity toward those who have fallen but God's kindness toward you — if you remain in his kindness. Otherwise you too will be cut off. ²³ And even they, if they do not remain in unbelief, will be grafted in, because God has the power to graft them in again. ²⁴ For if you were cut off from your native wild olive tree and against nature were grafted into a cultivated olive tree, how much more will these — the natural branches — be grafted into their own olive tree?

²⁵ I don't want you to be ignorant of this mystery, brothers and sisters, so that you will not be conceited: A partial hardening has come upon Israel

---

^A 11:4 1Kg 19:18   ^B 11:6 Other mss add *But if of works it is no longer grace; otherwise work is no longer work.*   ^C 11:8 Dt 29:4; Is 29:10
^D 11:9-10 Ps 69:22-23   ^E 11:14 Lit *flesh*   ^F 11:17 Other mss read *the root and the richness*   ^G 11:20 Lit *fear*

until the fullness of the Gentiles has come in. ²⁶ And in this way all^A Israel will be saved, as it is written,

> The Deliverer will come from Zion;
> he will turn godlessness away from Jacob.
> ²⁷ And this will be my covenant with them ^B
> when I take away their sins. ^C

²⁸ Regarding the gospel, they are enemies for your advantage, but regarding election, they are loved because of the patriarchs, ²⁹ since God's gracious gifts and calling are irrevocable. ^D ³⁰ As you once disobeyed God but now have received mercy through their disobedience, ³¹ so they too have now disobeyed, resulting in mercy to you, so that they also may now^E receive mercy. ³² For God has imprisoned all in disobedience so that he may have mercy on all.

A HYMN OF PRAISE

> ³³ Oh, the depth of the riches
> both of the wisdom and of the knowledge of God!
> How unsearchable his judgments
> and untraceable his ways!
> ³⁴ For who has known the mind of the Lord?
> Or who has been his counselor?
> ³⁵ And who has ever given to God,
> that he should be repaid?^F
> ³⁶ For from him and through him
> and to him are all things.
> To him be the glory forever. Amen.

A LIVING SACRIFICE

12 Therefore, brothers and sisters, in view of the mercies of God, I urge you to present your bodies as a living sacrifice, holy and pleasing to God; this is your true worship.^G ² Do not be conformed to this age, but be transformed by the renewing of your mind, so that you may discern what is the good, pleasing, and perfect will of God.

MANY GIFTS BUT ONE BODY

³ For by the grace given to me, I tell everyone among you not to think of himself more highly than he should think. Instead, think sensibly, as God has distributed a measure of faith to each one. ⁴ Now as we have many parts in one body, and all the parts do not have the same function, ⁵ in the same way we who are many are one body in Christ and individually members of one another. ⁶ According to the grace given to us, we have different gifts: If prophecy, use it according to the proportion of one's^H faith; ⁷ if service, use it in service; if teaching, in teaching; ⁸ if exhorting, in exhortation; giving, with generosity; leading, with diligence; showing mercy, with cheerfulness.

---

^A11:26 Or And then all   ^B11:26-27 Is 59:20-21   ^C11:27 Jr 31:31-34   ^D11:29 Or are not taken back   ^E11:31 Other mss omit now   ^F11:34-35 Jb 41:11; Is 40:13; Jr 23:18   ^G12:1 Or your reasonable service   ^H12:6 Or the, also in v. 19

RENEWED MINDS

ROMANS 12–13; HEBREWS 13:15-16

Personal discipline isn't one of my stronger gifts. In other words, I stink at it.

I'm the one in my family who excitedly asks who wants to go get ice cream rather than stick to our sensible meal plan. I'm notorious for drafting a shiny new routine that lasts for three days before I'm ready for spontaneity again. Despite my best efforts to implement structure in my life, I'm all over the place. I've come to accept that flexibility is part of who God made me to be.

But here's the truth. For me, that acceptance spills over into a lack of spiritual discipline. The world tells us fulfilling every desire in every moment is a sign of happiness and freedom, but I can say from experience that ignoring spiritual disciplines leads to chains, not freedom.

"Do not be conformed to this age, but be transformed by the renewing of your mind," Paul says in Romans 12:2, and I find myself staring longingly at the words.

I want that.

I tried renewing my mind by going to church, but I didn't make time to do the same at home. I'd sit half-dazed in front of my computer, reading about fall fashion trends rather than reading my Bible. I'd watch one more episode of my favorite show and skip my prayer time. I wanted to read my Bible and pray and obey Romans 12:2, but my desires for distraction and gluttony grew.

I couldn't control them on my own, no matter how guilty I felt or how firmly I said that tomorrow was the day I would change.

I wanted a renewed mind, but I'd forgotten that our lives are only truly transformed in the presence of the living God.

Have you ever felt a simple desire grow beyond your control? Maybe your struggle is the opposite of mine, and routine and productivity are the desires that take the place of true renewal. Or perhaps your days are bound by a structure that you don't want God to bend, a rigidity where spending time with Him in Scripture and in prayer are items on a checklist rather than intimate interaction with your heavenly Father.

Spiritual disciplines are tools that lift our eyes from our circumstances and desires and focus our hearts on God's presence. Fasting, prayer, Bible study—they're all disciplines that renew our minds and refresh our spirits. But they're different from a resolution, a diet, or an exercise regimen because they aren't sustained in our own willpower. Instead, spiritual disciplines are rooted in the Spirit's work in us. God is the Giver. We are the recipients. He empowers. We surrender.

Whatever our personality, no matter how God created us, we are all His image-bearers (Gn 1:26-27). Spiritual disciplines are gifts from our loving Father to make us more like Him.

CHRISTIAN ETHICS

[9] Let love be without hypocrisy. Detest evil; cling to what is good. [10] Love one another deeply as brothers and sisters. Outdo one another in showing honor. [11] Do not lack diligence in zeal; be fervent in the Spirit;[A] serve the Lord. [12] Rejoice in hope; be patient in affliction; be persistent in prayer. [13] Share with the saints in their needs; pursue hospitality. [14] Bless those who persecute you; bless and do not curse. [15] Rejoice with those who rejoice; weep with those who weep. [16] Live in harmony with one another. Do not be proud; instead, associate with the humble. Do not be wise in your own estimation. [17] Do not repay anyone evil for evil. Give careful thought to do what is honorable in everyone's eyes. [18] If possible, as far as it depends on you, live at peace with everyone. [19] Friends, do not avenge yourselves; instead, leave room for God's wrath, because it is written, **Vengeance belongs to me; I will repay**,[B] says the Lord. [20] But

> **If your enemy is hungry, feed him.**
> **If he is thirsty, give him something to drink.**
> **For in so doing**
> **you will be heaping fiery coals on his head.**[C]

[21] Do not be conquered by evil, but conquer evil with good.

A CHRISTIAN'S DUTIES TO THE STATE

13 Let everyone submit to the governing authorities, since there is no authority except from God, and the authorities that exist are instituted by God. [2] So then, the one who resists the authority is opposing God's command, and those who oppose it will bring judgment on themselves. [3] For rulers are not a terror to good conduct, but to bad. Do you want to be unafraid of the authority? Do what is good, and you will have its approval. [4] For it is God's servant for your good. But if you do wrong, be afraid, because it does not carry the sword for no reason. For it is God's servant, an avenger that brings wrath on the one who does wrong. [5] Therefore, you must submit, not only because of wrath but also because of your conscience. [6] And for this reason you pay taxes, since the authorities are God's servants, continually attending to these tasks.[D] [7] Pay your obligations to everyone: taxes to those you owe taxes, tolls to those you owe tolls, respect to those you owe respect, and honor to those you owe honor.

LOVE, OUR PRIMARY DUTY

[8] Do not owe anyone anything, except to love one another, for the one who loves another has fulfilled the law. [9] The commandments, **Do not commit adultery; do not murder; do not steal;**[E] **do not covet;**[F] and any other commandment, are summed up by this commandment: **Love your neighbor as yourself.**[G] [10] Love does no wrong to a neighbor. Love, therefore, is the fulfillment of the law.

PUT ON CHRIST

[11] Besides this, since you know the time, it is already the hour for you[H] to wake up from sleep, because now our salvation is nearer than when we first

---

[A] 12:11 Or *in spirit*   [B] 12:19 Dt 32:35   [C] 12:20 Pr 25:21-22   [D] 13:6 Lit *to this very thing*   [E] 13:9 Other mss add *do not bear false witness*   [F] 13:9 Ex 20:13-17; Dt 5:17-21   [G] 13:9 Lv 19:18   [H] 13:11 Other mss read *for us* believed. [12] The night is nearly over, and the day is near; so let us discard the deeds of darkness and put on the armor of light. [13] Let us walk with decency, as in the daytime: not in carousing and drunkenness; not in sexual impurity and promiscuity; not in quarreling and jealousy. [14] But put on the Lord Jesus Christ, and don't make plans to gratify the desires of the flesh.

THE LAW OF LIBERTY

14 Accept anyone who is weak in faith, but don't argue about disputed matters. [2] One person believes he may eat anything, while one who is weak eats only vegetables. [3] One who eats must not look down on one who does not eat, and one who does not eat must not judge one who does, because God has accepted him. [4] Who are you to judge another's household servant? Before his own Lord he stands or falls. And he will stand, because the Lord is able[A] to make him stand.

[5] One person judges one day to be more important than another day. Someone else judges every day to be the same. Let each one be fully convinced in his own mind. [6] Whoever observes the day, observes it for the honor of the Lord.[B] Whoever eats, eats for the Lord, since he gives thanks to God; and whoever does not eat, it is for the Lord that he does not eat it, and he gives thanks to God. [7] For none of us lives for himself, and no one dies for himself. [8] If we live, we live for the Lord; and if we die, we die for the Lord. Therefore, whether we live or die, we belong to the Lord. [9] Christ died and returned to life for this: that he might be Lord over both the dead and the living. [10] But you, why do you judge your brother or sister? Or you, why do you despise your brother or sister? For we will all stand before the judgment seat of God.[C] [11] For it is written,

As I live, says the Lord,
    every knee will bow to me,
    and every tongue will give praise to God.[D]

[12] So then, each of us will give an account of himself to God.

THE LAW OF LOVE

[13] Therefore, let us no longer judge one another. Instead decide never to put a stumbling block or pitfall in the way of your brother or sister. [14] I know and am persuaded in the Lord Jesus that nothing is unclean in itself. Still, to someone who considers a thing to be unclean, to that one it is unclean. [15] For if your brother or sister is hurt by what you eat, you are no longer walking according to love. Do not destroy, by what you eat, someone for whom Christ died. [16] Therefore, do not let your good be slandered, [17] for the kingdom of God is not eating and drinking, but righteousness, peace, and joy in the Holy Spirit. [18] Whoever serves Christ in this way is acceptable to God and receives human approval.

[19] So then, let us pursue what promotes peace and what builds up one another. [20] Do not tear down God's work because of food. Everything is clean, but it is wrong to make someone fall by what he eats. [21] It is a good thing not to eat meat, or drink wine, or do anything that makes your brother or sister

---

[A]14:4 Other mss read *For God has the power*   [B]14:6 Other mss add *but whoever does not observe the day, it is to the Lord that he does not observe it*   [C]14:10 Other mss read *of Christ*   [D]14:11 Is 45:23; 49:18

stumble.[A] 22 Whatever you believe about these things, keep between yourself and God. Blessed is the one who does not condemn himself by what he approves. 23 But whoever doubts stands condemned if he eats, because his eating is not from faith,[B] and everything that is not from faith is sin.

PLEASING OTHERS, NOT OURSELVES

15 Now we who are strong have an obligation to bear the weaknesses of those without strength, and not to please ourselves. 2 Each one of us is to please his neighbor for his good, to build him up. 3 For even Christ did not please himself. On the contrary, as it is written, **The insults of those who insult you have fallen on me.**[C] 4 For whatever was written in the past was written for our instruction, so that we may have hope through endurance and through the encouragement from the Scriptures. 5 Now may the God who gives[D] endurance and encouragement grant you to live in harmony with one another, according to Christ Jesus, 6 so that you may glorify the God and Father of our Lord Jesus Christ with one mind and one voice.

GLORIFYING GOD TOGETHER

7 Therefore accept one another, just as Christ also accepted you, to the glory of God. 8 For I say that Christ became a servant of the circumcised[E] on behalf of God's truth, to confirm the promises to the fathers, 9 and so that Gentiles may glorify God for his mercy. As it is written,

> **Therefore I will praise you among the Gentiles,**
> **and I will sing praise to your name.**[F]

10 Again it says, **Rejoice, you Gentiles, with his people!**[G] 11 And again,

> **Praise the Lord, all you Gentiles;**
> **let all the peoples praise him!**[H]

12 And again, Isaiah says,

> **The root of Jesse will appear,**
> **the one who rises to rule the Gentiles;**
> **the Gentiles will hope in him.**[I]

13 Now may the God of hope fill you with all joy and peace as you believe so that you may overflow with hope by the power of the Holy Spirit.

FROM JERUSALEM TO ILLYRICUM

14 My brothers and sisters, I myself am convinced about you that you also are full of goodness, filled with all knowledge, and able to instruct one another. 15 Nevertheless, I have written to remind you more boldly on some points[J] because of the grace given me by God 16 to be a minister of Christ Jesus to the Gentiles, serving as a priest of the gospel of God. My purpose is that the Gentiles may be an acceptable offering, sanctified by the Holy Spirit. 17 Therefore I have reason to boast in Christ Jesus regarding what pertains to God. 18 For I would not dare say anything except what Christ has accomplished through me by word and deed for the obedience of the Gentiles, 19 by the power of miraculous signs and wonders, and by the power of God's Spirit.

As a result, I have fully proclaimed the gospel of Christ from Jerusalem all the way around to Illyricum.^A ^20 My aim is to preach the gospel where Christ has not been named, so that I will not build on someone else's foundation, ^21 but, as it is written,

> Those who were not told about him will see,
> and those who have not heard will understand.^B

PAUL'S TRAVEL PLANS

^22 That is why I have been prevented many times from coming to you. ^23 But now I no longer have any work to do in these regions,^C and I have strongly desired for many years to come to you ^24 whenever I travel to Spain.^D For I hope to see you when I pass through and to be assisted by you for my journey there, once I have first enjoyed your company for a while. ^25 Right now I am traveling to Jerusalem to serve the saints, ^26 because Macedonia and Achaia were pleased to make a contribution for the poor among the saints in Jerusalem. ^27 Yes, they were pleased, and indeed are indebted to them. For if the Gentiles have shared in their spiritual benefits, then they are obligated to minister to them in material needs. ^28 So when I have finished this and safely delivered the funds^E to them,^F I will visit you on the way to Spain. ^29 I know that when I come to you, I will come in the fullness of the blessing^G of Christ.

^30 Now I appeal to you, brothers and sisters, through our Lord Jesus Christ and through the love of the Spirit, to strive together with me in fervent prayers to God on my behalf. ^31 Pray that I may be rescued from the unbelievers in Judea, that my ministry to^H Jerusalem may be acceptable to the saints, ^32 and that, by God's will, I may come to you with joy and be refreshed together with you.

^33 May the God of peace be with all of you. Amen.

PAUL'S COMMENDATION OF PHOEBE

16 I commend to you our sister Phoebe, who is a servant^I of the church in Cenchreae. ^2 So you should welcome her in the Lord in a manner worthy of the saints and assist her in whatever matter she may require your help. For indeed she has been a benefactor of many — and of me also.

GREETING TO ROMAN CHRISTIANS

^3 Give my greetings to Prisca^J and Aquila, my coworkers in Christ Jesus, ^4 who risked their own necks for my life. Not only do I thank them, but so do all the Gentile churches. ^5 Greet also the church that meets in their home. Greet my dear friend Epaenetus, who is the first convert^K to Christ from Asia.^L ^6 Greet Mary,^M who has worked very hard for you.^N ^7 Greet Andronicus and Junia, my fellow Jews^O and fellow prisoners. They are noteworthy in the eyes of

---

^A 15:19 A Roman province northwest of Greece on the eastern shore of the Adriatic Sea   ^B 15:21 Is 52:15   ^C 15:23 Lit now, having no longer a place in these parts   ^D 15:24 Other mss add I will come to you.   ^E 15:28 Lit delivered this fruit   ^F 15:28 Or and placed my seal of approval on this fruit for them   ^G 15:29 Other mss add of the gospel   ^H 15:31 Lit that my service for   ^I 16:1 Others interpret this term in a technical sense: deacon, or deaconess, or minister, or courier   ^J 16:3 Traditionally, Priscilla, as in Ac 18:2,18,26   ^K 16:5 Lit the firstfruits   ^L 16:5 Other mss read Achaia   ^M 16:6 Or Maria   ^N 16:6 Other mss read us   ^O 16:7 Or family members the apostles, [A] and they were also in Christ before me. [8] Greet Ampliatus, my dear friend in the Lord. [9] Greet Urbanus, our coworker in Christ, and my dear friend Stachys. [10] Greet Apelles, who is approved in Christ. Greet those who belong to the household of Aristobulus. [11] Greet Herodion, my fellow Jew. [B] Greet those who belong to the household of Narcissus who are in the Lord. [12] Greet Tryphaena and Tryphosa, who have worked hard in the Lord. Greet my dear friend Persis, who has worked very hard in the Lord. [13] Greet Rufus, chosen in the Lord; also his mother — and mine. [14] Greet Asyncritus, Phlegon, Hermes, Patrobas, Hermas, and the brothers and sisters who are with them. [15] Greet Philologus and Julia, Nereus and his sister, and Olympas, and all the saints who are with them. [16] Greet one another with a holy kiss. All the churches of Christ send you greetings.

WARNING AGAINST DIVISIVE PEOPLE

[17] Now I urge you, brothers and sisters, to watch out for those who create divisions and obstacles contrary to the teaching that you learned. Avoid them, [18] because such people do not serve our Lord Christ but their own appetites. [C] They deceive the hearts of the unsuspecting with smooth talk and flattering words.

PAUL'S GRACIOUS CONCLUSION

[19] The report of your obedience has reached everyone. Therefore I rejoice over you, but I want you to be wise about what is good, and yet innocent about what is evil. [20] The God of peace will soon crush Satan under your feet. The grace of our Lord Jesus be with you.

[21] Timothy, my coworker, and Lucius, Jason, and Sosipater, my fellow countrymen, greet you.

[22] I Tertius, who wrote this letter, greet you in the Lord. [D]

[23] Gaius, who is host to me and to the whole church, greets you. Erastus, the city treasurer, and our brother Quartus greet you. [E]

GLORY TO GOD

[25] Now to him who is able to strengthen you according to my gospel and the proclamation about Jesus Christ, according to the revelation of the mystery kept silent for long ages [26] but now revealed and made known through the prophetic Scriptures, according to the command of the eternal God to advance the obedience of faith among all the Gentiles — [27] to the only wise God, through Jesus Christ — to him be the glory forever! [F] Amen.

[A]16:7 Or They are noteworthy among the apostles   [B]16:11 Or family member
[C]16:18 Lit belly   [D]16:22 Or letter in the Lord, greet you   [E]16:23 Some mss
include v. 24: The grace of our Lord Jesus Christ be with you all.
[F]16:25-27 Other mss have these vv. at the end of chap. 14 or 15.

YOU WERE CALLED by HIM INTO fellowship WITH HIS SON

1 corinthians

God is faithful; you were called by him into fellowship with his Son, Jesus Christ our Lord. **1:9**

ON THE TIMELINE Paul wrote his first letter to the Corinthian church during the last year of his three-year ministry at Ephesus, probably a few weeks before Pentecost in the spring of AD 56 (1Co 15:32; 16:8; Ac 20:31).

A LITTLE BACKGROUND First Corinthians is the second letter Paul wrote to the Corinthian church. His earlier letter to Corinth, which is not included in the canon of Scripture but is referenced in 1 Corinthians 5:9, warned them not to associate with the sexually immoral. The writing of this second letter, 1 Corinthians, was prompted by reports of rivalry within the church (1Co 1:11). Paul addressed this in his letter, along with other troubling issues, including an incestuous relationship among the membership (1Co 5:1), division that arose during observance of the Lord's Supper (1Co 11:18), and confusion over the resurrection of the dead (1Co 15:12). As he was writing this letter to the Corinthian church, he must have received a letter from them asking his opinion on various issues (1Co 7:1,25; 8:1; 16:1) because he included replies to those concerns as well.

MESSAGE & PURPOSE First Corinthians is the most literary of Paul's letters, using stylistic devices like irony, repetition, alliteration, and other wordplays to communicate to his readers the necessity of accepting the Lord's authority over their lives. Jesus is Lord and believers are His possession: this is the main theme of Paul's letter. For Paul, whatever issue was discussed, the answer was always addressed with a reminder of the Lord's authority over them (1Co 1:2,10).

In addition to motivating the Corinthian church to acknowledge the Lord's ownership of them, Paul wrote 1 Corinthians to set forth the implications for their lives. Within this theme of Christ's authority, Paul addressed key topics such as Christian unity, morality, the role of women, spiritual gifts, love, and the resurrection.

GIVE THANKS FOR THE BOOK OF 1 CORINTHIANS

First Corinthians contributes greatly to our understanding of the Christian life, ministry, and relationships by showing us how the members of the Church—Christ's body—are to function together. Paul gave specific solutions to specific problems, but the underlying answer to them all is for the Church and its members to live Christ-centered lives.

THE BOOK OF 1 CORINTHIANS IN HISTORY

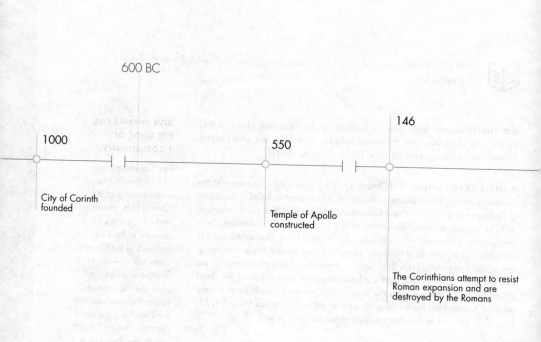

600 BC

146

1000

550

City of Corinth founded

Temple of Apollo constructed

The Corinthians attempt to resist Roman expansion and are destroyed by the Romans

100 BC

AD 1

44

50-51

56

57

Paul spends a few
months in Corinth
writing Romans

Paul writes
1 and 2 Corinthians

Paul spends 18 months in
Corinth planting a church

Paul's hearing before
Corinth's proconsul Gallio

Julius Caesar rebuilds Corinth
as a colony of Rome

READ AND UNDERSTAND 1 CORINTHIANS

The Bible is a complete work in which many stories combine to tell one story. As you read the book of 1 Corinthians, consider reading the additional passages to discover how the whole of Scripture works together.

GREETING

1

Paul, called as an apostle of Christ Jesus by God's will, and Sosthenes our brother:

² To the church of God at Corinth, to those sanctified in Christ Jesus, called as saints, with all those in every place who call on the name of Jesus Christ our Lord — both their Lord and ours.

³ Grace to you and peace from God our Father and the Lord Jesus Christ.

THANKSGIVING

⁴ I always thank my God for you because of the grace of God given to you in Christ Jesus, ⁵ that you were enriched in him in every way, in all speech and all knowledge. ⁶ In this way, the testimony about Christ was confirmed among you, ⁷ so that you do not lack any spiritual gift as you eagerly wait for the revelation of our Lord Jesus Christ. ⁸ He will also strengthen you to the end, so that you will be blameless in the day of our Lord Jesus Christ. ⁹ God is faithful; you were called by him into fellowship with his Son, Jesus Christ our Lord.

DIVISIONS AT CORINTH

¹⁰ Now I urge you, brothers and sisters, in the name of our Lord Jesus Christ, that all of you agree in what you say, that there be no divisions among you, and that you be united with the same understanding and the same conviction. ¹¹ For it has been reported to me about you, my brothers and sisters, by members of Chloe's people, that there is rivalry among you. ¹² What I am saying is this: One of you says, "I belong to Paul," or "I belong to Apollos," or "I belong to Cephas," or "I belong to Christ." ¹³ Is Christ divided? Was Paul crucified for you? Or were you baptized in Paul's name? ¹⁴ I thank God^{A,B} that I baptized none of you except Crispus and Gaius, ¹⁵ so that no one can say you were baptized in my name. ¹⁶ I did, in fact, baptize the household of Stephanas; beyond that, I don't recall if I baptized anyone else. ¹⁷ For Christ did not send me to baptize, but to preach the gospel — not with eloquent wisdom, so that the cross of Christ will not be emptied of its effect.

CHRIST THE POWER AND WISDOM OF GOD

¹⁸ For the word of the cross is foolishness to those who are perishing, but it is the power of God to us who are being saved. ¹⁹ For it is written,

I will destroy the wisdom of the wise,
and I will set aside the intelligence of the intelligent.^{C}

²⁰ Where is the one who is wise? Where is the teacher of the law?^{D} Where is the debater of this age? Hasn't God made the world's wisdom foolish? ²¹ For since, in God's wisdom, the world did not know God through wisdom, God was pleased to save those who believe through the foolishness of what is preached. ²² For the Jews ask for signs and the Greeks seek wisdom, ²³ but we preach Christ crucified, a stumbling block to the Jews and foolishness to the Gentiles.^{E} ²⁴ Yet to those who are called, both Jews and Greeks, Christ is the power of God and the wisdom of God, ²⁵ because God's foolishness is wiser than human wisdom, and God's weakness is stronger than human strength.

---

^{A}1:14 Other mss omit God   ^{B}1:14 Or I am thankful   ^{C}1:19 Is 29:14
^{D}1:20 Or scholar   ^{E}1:23 Other mss read Greeks

DISSOLVING THE SUPER GLUE COMPLEX

1 CORINTHIANS 1; ROMANS 8:38-39

I have a nasty habit of seeing myself as a big ol' bottle of Super Glue. I like to think I'm the one who holds everything together—my marriage, my children, my work, my friendships. I worry that if I don't keep every plate spinning 100% of the time, everything I love and cherish will come apart at the seams.

Super Glue complex has oozed its way into my theology, too, causing me to worry that my standing with God is somehow dependent upon me.

Am I growing in Christ enough?
Am I sinning too much?
Am I doing enough kingdom work?

These anxious thoughts are always nearby, hovering on the fringes of my faith. My time in the Word becomes another way to earn gold stars with both God and man, and hopefully, stave off judgment and rejection. This makes it rather easy to ignore all those passages about the Sabbath—if I stop hustling and take time to rest, my life might fall apart.

Can you relate to the Super Glue complex? Perhaps as a byproduct of being women raised on the idea that we can do it all, we've decided the world will stop spinning if we don't. But God's Word gives us a refreshing reality check.

"God is faithful; you were called by him into fellowship with his Son, Jesus Christ our Lord."

1 CORINTHIANS 1:9

In declaring God's faithfulness, Paul was repeating the theme that all of Scripture declares:

Adam and Eve sinned, but God faithfully cared for them.
The Israelites were idol-worshiping grumblers, but God ushered them into the promised land.
God's people are described as a wayward and cheating wife in the book of Hosea, but God lovingly and faithfully pursues us.
We are sinful and deserve to be removed from God's presence, but Jesus died so we could be accepted.

This is the drum that beats steadily from Genesis to Revelation: God is faithful.
It is God who called us into fellowship with Him. And it is God's faithfulness keeping our fellowship with Him intact.

I know, Super Glue girls, it feels too simple. Shouldn't we have to jump through hoops, flex our muscles, or check some boxes to be right with God?

Nope. Nope. And nope again.

We are free to stop spinning plates to earn God's favor and instead join the chorus echoing throughout all of Scripture: God is faithful!

"For I am persuaded that neither death nor life, nor angels nor rulers, nor things present nor things to come, nor powers, nor height nor depth, nor any other created thing will be able to separate us from the love of God that is in Christ Jesus our Lord" (Rm 8:38-39).

BOASTING ONLY IN THE LORD

²⁶ Brothers and sisters, consider your calling: Not many were wise from a human perspective,^A not many powerful, not many of noble birth. ²⁷ Instead, God has chosen what is foolish in the world to shame the wise, and God has chosen what is weak in the world to shame the strong. ²⁸ God has chosen what is insignificant and despised in the world — what is viewed as nothing — to bring to nothing what is viewed as something, ²⁹ so that no one^B may boast in his presence. ³⁰ It is from him that you are in Christ Jesus, who became wisdom from God for us — our righteousness, sanctification, and redemption — ³¹ in order that, as it is written: **Let the one who boasts, boast in the Lord.**^C

PAUL'S PROCLAMATION

2 When I came to you, brothers and sisters, announcing the mystery^D of God to you, I did not come with brilliance of speech or wisdom. ² I decided to know nothing among you except Jesus Christ and him crucified. ³ I came to you in weakness, in fear, and in much trembling. ⁴ My speech and my preaching were not with persuasive words of wisdom^E but with a demonstration of the Spirit's power, ⁵ so that your faith might not be based on human wisdom but on God's power.

SPIRITUAL WISDOM

⁶ We do, however, speak a wisdom among the mature, but not a wisdom of this age, or of the rulers of this age, who are coming to nothing. ⁷ On the contrary, we speak God's hidden wisdom in a mystery, a wisdom God predestined before the ages for our glory. ⁸ None of the rulers of this age knew this wisdom, because if they had known it, they would not have crucified the Lord of glory. ⁹ But as it is written,

> **What no eye has seen, no ear has heard,**
> **and no human heart has conceived —**
> **God has prepared these things for those who love him.**^F

¹⁰ Now God has revealed these things to us by the Spirit, since the Spirit searches everything, even the depths of God. ¹¹ For who knows a person's thoughts^G except his spirit within him? In the same way, no one knows the thoughts of God except the Spirit of God. ¹² Now we have not received the spirit of the world, but the Spirit who comes from God, so that we may understand what has been freely given to us by God. ¹³ We also speak these things, not in words taught by human wisdom, but in those taught by the Spirit, explaining spiritual things to spiritual people.^H ¹⁴ But the person without the Spirit^I does not receive what comes from God's Spirit, because it is foolishness to him; he is not able to understand it since it is evaluated^J spiritually. ¹⁵ The spiritual person, however, can evaluate^K everything, and yet he himself cannot be evaluated by anyone. ¹⁶ For

> **who has known the Lord's mind,**
> **that he may instruct him?**^L

But we have the mind of Christ.

---

^A1:26 Lit wise according to the flesh   ^B1:29 Lit that not all flesh   ^C1:31 Jr 9:24
^D2:1 Other mss read testimony   ^E2:4 Other mss read human wisdom   ^F2:9 Is
52:15; 64:4   ^G2:11 Or things   ^H2:13 Or things with spiritual words   ^I2:14 Lit
natural person   ^J2:14 Or judged, or discerned, also in v. 15   ^K2:15 Or judge,
or discern   ^L2:16 Is 40:13

THE PROBLEM OF IMMATURITY

3 For my part, brothers and sisters, I was not able to speak to you as spiritual people but as people of the flesh, as babies in Christ. ² I gave you milk to drink, not solid food, since you were not yet ready for it. In fact, you are still not ready, ³ because you are still worldly. For since there is envy and strife[A] among you, are you not worldly and behaving like mere humans? ⁴ For whenever someone says, "I belong to Paul," and another, "I belong to Apollos," are you not acting like mere humans?

THE ROLE OF GOD'S SERVANTS

⁵ What then is Apollos? What is Paul? They are servants through whom you believed, and each has the role the Lord has given. ⁶ I planted, Apollos watered, but God gave the growth. ⁷ So then neither the one who plants nor the one who waters is anything, but only God who gives the growth. ⁸ Now he who plants and he who waters are one,[B] and each will receive his own reward according to his own labor. ⁹ For we are God's coworkers.[C] You are God's field, God's building.

¹⁰ According to God's grace that was given to me, I have laid a foundation as a skilled master builder,[D] and another builds on it. But each one is to be careful how he builds on it. ¹¹ For no one can lay any other foundation than what has been laid down. That foundation is Jesus Christ. ¹² If anyone builds on the foundation with gold, silver, costly stones, wood, hay, or straw, ¹³ each one's work will become obvious. For the day will disclose it, because it will be revealed by fire; the fire will test the quality of each one's work. ¹⁴ If anyone's work that he has built survives, he will receive a reward. ¹⁵ If anyone's work is burned up, he will experience[E] loss, but he himself will be saved — but only as through fire.

¹⁶ Don't you yourselves know that you are God's temple and that the Spirit of God lives in you? ¹⁷ If anyone destroys God's temple, God will destroy him; for God's temple is holy, and that is what you are.

THE FOLLY OF HUMAN WISDOM

¹⁸ Let no one deceive himself. If anyone among you thinks he is wise in this age, let him become a fool so that he can become wise. ¹⁹ For the wisdom of this world is foolishness with God, since it is written, **He catches the wise in their craftiness;**[F] ²⁰ and again, **The Lord knows that the reasonings of the wise are futile.**[G] ²¹ So let no one boast in human leaders, for everything is yours — ²² whether Paul or Apollos or Cephas or the world or life or death or things present or things to come — everything is yours, ²³ and you belong to Christ, and Christ belongs to God.

THE FAITHFUL MANAGER

4 A person should think of us in this way: as servants of Christ and managers of the mysteries of God. ² In this regard, it is required that managers be found faithful. ³ It is of little importance to me that I should be judged by you or by any human court.[H] In fact, I don't even judge myself. ⁴ For I am not

---

[A] 3:3 Other mss add *and divisions*   [B] 3:8 Or *of equal status,* or *united in purpose*
[C] 3:9 Or *are coworkers belonging to God*   [D] 3:10 Or *wise master builder*
[E] 3:15 Or *suffer*   [F] 3:19 Jb 5:13   [G] 3:20 Ps 94:11   [H] 4:3 Lit *a human day*

conscious of anything against myself, but I am not justified by this. It is the Lord who judges me. ⁵ So don't judge anything prematurely, before the Lord comes, who will both bring to light what is hidden in darkness and reveal the intentions of the hearts. And then praise will come to each one from God.

THE APOSTLES' EXAMPLE OF HUMILITY

⁶ Now, brothers and sisters, I have applied these things to myself and Apollos for your benefit, so that you may learn from us the meaning of the saying: "Nothing beyond what is written." The purpose is that none of you will be arrogant, favoring one person over another. ⁷ For who makes you so superior? What do you have that you didn't receive? If, in fact, you did receive it, why do you boast as if you hadn't received it? ⁸ You are already full! You are already rich! You have begun to reign as kings without us — and I wish you did reign, so that we could also reign with you! ⁹ For I think God has displayed us, the apostles, in last place, like men condemned to die: We have become a spectacle to the world, both to angels and to people. ¹⁰ We are fools for Christ, but you are wise in Christ! We are weak, but you are strong! You are distinguished, but we are dishonored! ¹¹ Up to the present hour we are both hungry and thirsty; we are poorly clothed, roughly treated, homeless; ¹² we labor, working with our own hands. When we are reviled, we bless; when we are persecuted, we endure it; ¹³ when we are slandered, we respond graciously. Even now, we are like the scum of the earth, like everyone's garbage.

PAUL'S FATHERLY CARE

¹⁴ I'm not writing this to shame you, but to warn you as my dear children. ¹⁵ For you may have countless instructors in Christ, but you don't have many fathers. For I became your father in Christ Jesus through the gospel. ¹⁶ Therefore I urge you to imitate me. ¹⁷ This is why I have sent Timothy to you. He is my dearly loved and faithful child in the Lord. He will remind you about my ways in Christ Jesus, just as I teach everywhere in every church.

¹⁸ Now some are arrogant, as though I were not coming to you. ¹⁹ But I will come to you soon, if the Lord wills, and I will find out not the talk, but the power of those who are arrogant. ²⁰ For the kingdom of God is not a matter of talk but of power. ²¹ What do you want? Should I come to you with a rod, or in love and a spirit of gentleness?

IMMORAL CHURCH MEMBERS

5 It is actually reported that there is sexual immorality among you, and the kind of sexual immorality that is not even tolerated^A among the Gentiles — a man is sleeping with his father's wife. ² And you are arrogant! Shouldn't you be filled with grief and remove from your congregation the one who did this? ³ Even though I am absent in the body, I am present in spirit. As one who is present with you in this way, I have already pronounced judgment on the one who has been doing such a thing. ⁴ When you are assembled in the name of our Lord Jesus, and I am with you in spirit, with the power of our Lord Jesus, ⁵ hand that one over to Satan for the destruction of the flesh, so that his spirit may be saved in the day of the Lord.

^A5:1 Other mss read *named*

⁶ Your boasting is not good. Don't you know that a little leaven^A^ leavens the whole batch of dough? ⁷ Clean out the old leaven so that you may be a new unleavened batch, as indeed you are. For Christ our Passover lamb has been sacrificed.^B^ ⁸ Therefore, let us observe the feast, not with old leaven or with the leaven of malice and evil, but with the unleavened bread of sincerity and truth.

CHURCH DISCIPLINE

⁹ I wrote to you in a letter not to associate with sexually immoral people. ¹⁰ I did not mean the immoral people of this world or the greedy and swindlers or idolaters; otherwise you would have to leave the world. ¹¹ But actually, I wrote^C^ you not to associate with anyone who claims to be a brother or sister and is sexually immoral or greedy, an idolater or verbally abusive, a drunkard or a swindler. Do not even eat with such a person. ¹² For what business is it of mine to judge outsiders? Don't you judge those who are inside? ¹³ God judges outsiders. **Remove the evil person from among you.**^D^

LAWSUITS AMONG BELIEVERS

6 If any of you has a dispute against another, how dare you take it to court before the unrighteous,^E^ and not before the saints? ² Or don't you know that the saints will judge the world? And if the world is judged by you, are you unworthy to judge the trivial cases? ³ Don't you know that we will judge angels — how much more matters of this life? ⁴ So if you have such matters, do you appoint as your judges those who have no standing in the church? ⁵ I say this to your shame! Can it be that there is not one wise person among you who is able to arbitrate between fellow believers? ⁶ Instead, brother goes to court against brother, and that before unbelievers!

⁷ As it is, to have legal disputes against one another is already a defeat for you. Why not rather be wronged? Why not rather be cheated? ⁸ Instead, you yourselves do wrong and cheat — and you do this to brothers and sisters! ⁹ Don't you know that the unrighteous will not inherit God's kingdom? Do not be deceived: No sexually immoral people, idolaters, adulterers, or males who have sex with males,^F^ ¹⁰ no thieves, greedy people, drunkards, verbally abusive people, or swindlers will inherit God's kingdom. ¹¹ And some of you used to be like this. But you were washed, you were sanctified, you were justified in the name of the Lord Jesus Christ and by the Spirit of our God.

GLORIFYING GOD IN BODY AND SPIRIT

¹² "Everything is permissible for me," but not everything is beneficial. "Everything is permissible for me," but I will not be mastered by anything. ¹³ "Food is for the stomach and the stomach for food," and God will do away with both of them. However, the body is not for sexual immorality but for the Lord, and the Lord for the body. ¹⁴ God raised up the Lord and will also raise us up by his power. ¹⁵ Don't you know that your bodies are a part of Christ's body? So should I take a part of Christ's body and make it part of a prostitute? Absolutely not! ¹⁶ Don't you know that anyone joined to a prostitute is one body

---

^A^5:6 Or *yeast,* also in vv. 7,8   ^B^5:7 Other mss add *for us*   ^C^5:11 Or *But now I am writing*   ^D^5:13 Dt 17:7   ^E^6:1 Unbelievers; v. 6   ^F^6:9 Both passive and active participants in homosexual acts with her? For Scripture says, **The two will become one flesh.**[A] [17] But anyone joined to the Lord is one spirit with him.

[18] Flee sexual immorality! Every other sin[B] a person commits is outside the body, but the person who is sexually immoral sins against his own body. [19] Don't you know that your body is a temple of the Holy Spirit who is in you, whom you have from God? You are not your own, [20] for you were bought at a price. So glorify God with your body.[C]

PRINCIPLES OF MARRIAGE

7 Now in response to the matters you wrote[D] about: "It is good for a man not to use[E] a woman for sex." [2] But because sexual immorality is so common,[F] each man should have sexual relations with his own wife, and each woman should have sexual relations with her own husband. [3] A husband should fulfill his marital duty to his wife, and likewise a wife to her husband. [4] A wife does not have the right over her own body, but her husband does. In the same way, a husband does not have the right over his own body, but his wife does. [5] Do not deprive one another — except when you agree for a time, to devote yourselves to[G] prayer. Then come together again; otherwise, Satan may tempt you because of your lack of self-control. [6] I say this as a concession, not as a command. [7] I wish that all people were as I am. But each has his own gift from God, one person has this gift, another has that.

A WORD TO THE UNMARRIED

[8] I say to the unmarried[H] and to widows: It is good for them if they remain as I am. [9] But if they do not have self-control, they should marry, since it is better to marry than to burn with desire.

ABOUT MARRIED PEOPLE

[10] To the married I give this command — not I, but the Lord — a wife is not to leave[I] her husband. [11] But if she does leave, she must remain unmarried or be reconciled to her husband — and a husband is not to divorce his wife. [12] But I (not the Lord) say to the rest: If any brother has an unbelieving wife and she is willing to live with him, he must not divorce her. [13] Also, if any woman has an unbelieving husband and he is willing to live with her, she must not divorce her husband. [14] For the unbelieving husband is made holy by the wife, and the unbelieving wife is made holy by the husband.[J] Otherwise your children would be unclean, but as it is they are holy. [15] But if the unbeliever leaves, let him leave. A brother or a sister is not bound in such cases. God has called you[K] to live in peace. [16] Wife, for all you know, you might save your husband. Husband, for all you know, you might save your wife.[L]

[A]6:16 Gn 2:24 [B]6:18 Lit *Every sin* [C]6:20 Other mss add *and in your spirit, which belong to God.* [D]7:1 Other mss add *to me* [E]7:1 Lit *"It is good for a man not to touch a woman* [F]7:2 Lit *because of immoralities* [G]7:5 Other mss add *fasting and to* [H]7:8 Or *widowers* [I]7:10 Or *separate from*, or *divorce* [J]7:14 Lit *the brother* [K]7:15 Other mss read *us* [L]7:16 Or *Wife, how do you know that you will save your husband? Husband, how do you know that you will save your wife?*

VARIOUS SITUATIONS OF LIFE

¹⁷ Let each one live his life in the situation the Lord assigned when God called him.ᴬ This is what I command in all the churches. ¹⁸ Was anyone already circumcised when he was called? He should not undo his circumcision. Was anyone called while uncircumcised? He should not get circumcised. ¹⁹ Circumcision does not matter and uncircumcision does not matter. Keeping God's commands is what matters. ²⁰ Let each of you remain in the situationᴮ in which he was called. ²¹ Were you called while a slave? Don't let it concern you. But if you can become free, by all means take the opportunity.ᶜ ²² For he who is called by the Lord as a slave is the Lord's freedman. Likewise he who is called as a free man is Christ's slave. ²³ You were bought at a price; do not become slaves of people. ²⁴ Brothers and sisters, each person is to remain with God in the situation in which he was called.

ABOUT THE UNMARRIED AND WIDOWS

²⁵ Now about virgins:ᴰ I have no command from the Lord, but I do give an opinion as one who by the Lord's mercy is faithful. ²⁶ Because of the present distress, I think that it is good for a man to remain as he is. ²⁷ Are you bound to a wife? Do not seek to be released. Are you released from a wife? Do not seek a wife. ²⁸ However, if you do get married, you have not sinned, and if a virginᴱ marries, she has not sinned. But such people will have trouble in this life,ᶠ and I am trying to spare you.

²⁹ This is what I mean, brothers and sisters: The time is limited, so from now on those who have wives should be as though they had none, ³⁰ those who weep as though they did not weep, those who rejoice as though they did not rejoice, those who buy as though they didn't own anything, ³¹ and those who use the world as though they did not make full use of it. For this world in its current form is passing away.

³² I want you to be without concerns. The unmarried man is concerned about the things of the Lord — how he may please the Lord. ³³ But the married man is concerned about the things of the world — how he may please his wife — ³⁴ and his interests are divided. The unmarried woman or virgin is concerned about the things of the Lord, so that she may be holy both in body and in spirit. But the married woman is concerned about the things of the world — how she may please her husband. ³⁵ I am saying this for your own benefit, not to put a restraint on you, but to promote what is proper and so that you may be devoted to the Lord without distraction.

³⁶ If any man thinks he is acting improperly toward the virgin he is engaged to, if she is getting beyond the usual age for marriage, and he feels he should marry — he can do what he wants. He is not sinning; they can get married. ³⁷ But he who stands firm in his heart (who is under no compulsion, but has control over his own will) and has decided in his heart to keep her as his fiancée, will do well. ³⁸ So then he who marries his fiancée does well, but he who does not marry will do better.ᴳ

ᴬ7:17 Lit called each   ᴮ7:20 Lit in the calling   ᶜ7:21 Or But even though you can become free, make the most of your position as a slave   ᴰ7:25 Or betrothed, or those not yet married   ᴱ7:28 Or betrothed woman   ᶠ7:28 Lit in the flesh   ᴳ7:36-38 Or ³⁶ If any man thinks he is acting improperly toward his virgin daughter, if she is getting beyond the usual age for marriage, and he feels she

³⁹ A wife is bound^A as long as her husband is living. But if her husband dies, she is free to be married to anyone she wants — only in the Lord. ⁴⁰ But she is happier if she remains as she is, in my opinion. And I think that I also have the Spirit of God.

FOOD OFFERED TO IDOLS

8 Now about food sacrificed to idols: We know that "we all have knowledge." Knowledge puffs up, but love builds up. ² If anyone thinks he knows anything, he does not yet know it as he ought to know it. ³ But if anyone loves God, he is known by him.

⁴ About eating food sacrificed to idols, then, we know that "an idol is nothing in the world,"^B and that "there is no God but one." ⁵ For even if there are so-called gods, whether in heaven or on earth — as there are many "gods" and many "lords" — ⁶ yet for us there is one God, the Father. All things are from him, and we exist for him. And there is one Lord, Jesus Christ. All things are through him, and we exist through him.

⁷ However, not everyone has this knowledge. Some have been so used to idolatry up until now that when they eat food sacrificed to an idol, their conscience, being weak, is defiled. ⁸ Food will not bring us close to God.^C We are not worse off if we don't eat, and we are not better if we do eat. ⁹ But be careful that this right of yours in no way becomes a stumbling block to the weak. ¹⁰ For if someone sees you, the one who has knowledge, dining in an idol's temple, won't his weak conscience be encouraged^D to eat food offered to idols? ¹¹ So the weak person, the brother or sister for whom Christ died, is ruined^E by your knowledge. ¹² Now when you sin like this against brothers and sisters and wound their weak conscience, you are sinning against Christ. ¹³ Therefore, if food causes my brother or sister to fall, I will never again eat meat, so that I won't cause my brother or sister to fall.

PAUL'S EXAMPLE AS AN APOSTLE

9 Am I not free? Am I not an apostle? Have I not seen Jesus our Lord? Are you not my work in the Lord? ² If I am not an apostle to others, at least I am to you, because you are the seal of my apostleship in the Lord.

³ My defense to those who examine me is this: ⁴ Don't we have the right to eat and drink? ⁵ Don't we have the right to be accompanied by a believing wife^F like the other apostles, the Lord's brothers, and Cephas? ⁶ Or do only Barnabas and I have no right to refrain from working? ⁷ Who serves as a soldier at his own expense? Who plants a vineyard and does not eat its fruit? Or who shepherds a flock and does not drink the milk from the flock?

⁸ Am I saying this from a human perspective? Doesn't the law also say the same thing? ⁹ For it is written in the law of Moses, **Do not muzzle an ox while it treads out grain.**^G Is God really concerned about oxen? ¹⁰ Isn't he really

---

should marry — he can do what he wants. He is not sinning; she can get married. ³⁷ But he who stands firm in his heart (who is under no compulsion, but has control over his own will) and has decided in his heart to keep his own virgin daughter will do well. ³⁸ So then he who gives his own virgin daughter in marriage does well, but he who does not give his own virgin daughter in marriage will do better.

^A 7:39 Other mss add *by law*   ^B 8:4 Or *an idol has no real existence*   ^C 8:8 Or *bring us before* (the judgment seat of) *God*   ^D 8:10 Or *built up*   ^E 8:11 Or *destroyed*   ^F 9:5 Lit *a sister as a wife*   ^G 9:9 Dt 25:4

saying it for our sake? Yes, this is written for our sake, because he who plows ought to plow in hope, and he who threshes should thresh in hope of sharing the crop. ¹¹ If we have sown spiritual things for you, is it too much if we reap material benefits from you? ¹² If others have this right to receive benefits from you, don't we even more? Nevertheless, we have not made use of this right; instead, we endure everything so that we will not hinder the gospel of Christ.

¹³ Don't you know that those who perform the temple services eat the food from the temple, and those who serve at the altar share in the offerings of the altar? ¹⁴ In the same way, the Lord has commanded that those who preach the gospel should earn their living by the gospel.

¹⁵ For my part I have used none of these rights, nor have I written these things that they may be applied in my case. For it would be better for me to die than for anyone to deprive me of my boast! ¹⁶ For if I preach the gospel, I have no reason to boast, because I am compelled to preach^A — and woe to me if I do not preach the gospel! ¹⁷ For if I do this willingly, I have a reward, but if unwillingly, I am entrusted with a commission. ¹⁸ What then is my reward? To preach the gospel and offer it free of charge and not make full use of my rights in the gospel.

¹⁹ Although I am free from all and not anyone's slave, I have made myself a slave to everyone, in order to win more people. ²⁰ To the Jews I became like a Jew, to win Jews; to those under the law, like one under the law — though I myself am not under the law^B — to win those under the law. ²¹ To those who are without the law, like one without the law — though I am not without God's law but under the law of Christ — to win those without the law. ²² To the weak I became weak, in order to win the weak. I have become all things to all people, so that I may by every possible means save some. ²³ Now I do all this because of the gospel, so that I may share in the blessings.

²⁴ Don't you know that the runners in a stadium all race, but only one receives the prize? Run in such a way to win the prize. ²⁵ Now everyone who competes exercises self-control in everything. They do it to receive a perishable crown, but we an imperishable crown. ²⁶ So I do not run like one who runs aimlessly or box like one beating the air. ²⁷ Instead, I discipline my body and bring it under strict control, so that after preaching to others, I myself will not be disqualified.

WARNINGS FROM ISRAEL'S PAST

10 Now I do not want you to be unaware, brothers and sisters, that our ancestors were all under the cloud, all passed through the sea, ² and all were baptized into Moses in the cloud and in the sea. ³ They all ate the same spiritual food, ⁴ and all drank the same spiritual drink. For they drank from the spiritual rock that followed them, and that rock was Christ. ⁵ Nevertheless God was not pleased with most of them, since they were struck down in the wilderness.

⁶ Now these things took place as examples for us, so that we will not desire evil things as they did.^C ⁷ Don't become idolaters as some of them were; as it is written, **The people sat down to eat and drink, and got up to party.**^D,E ⁸ Let us not commit sexual immorality as some of them did,^F and in

---

^A 9:16 Lit because necessity is laid upon me   ^B 9:20 Other mss omit though I myself am not under the law   ^C 10:6 Lit they desired   ^D 10:7 Or to dance   ^E 10:7 Ex 32:6   ^F 10:8 Lit them committed sexual immorality a single day twenty-three thousand people died. [9] Let us not test Christ as some of them did[A] and were destroyed by snakes. [10] And don't complain as some of them did,[B] and were killed by the destroyer.[C] [11] These things happened to them as examples, and they were written for our instruction, on whom the ends of the ages[D] have come. [12] So, whoever thinks he stands must be careful not to fall. [13] No temptation has come upon you except what is common to humanity. But God is faithful; he will not allow you to be tempted beyond what you are able, but with the temptation he will also provide a way out so that you may be able to bear it.

WARNING AGAINST IDOLATRY

[14] So then, my dear friends, flee from idolatry. [15] I am speaking as to sensible people. Judge for yourselves what I am saying. [16] The cup of blessing that we bless, is it not a sharing in the blood of Christ? The bread that we break, is it not a sharing in the body of Christ? [17] Because there is one bread, we who are many are one body, since all of us share the one bread. [18] Consider the people of Israel.[E] Do not those who eat the sacrifices participate in the altar? [19] What am I saying then? That food sacrificed to idols is anything, or that an idol is anything? [20] No, but I do say that what they[F] sacrifice, they sacrifice to demons and not to God. I do not want you to be participants with demons! [21] You cannot drink the cup of the Lord and the cup of demons. You cannot share in the Lord's table and the table of demons. [22] Or are we provoking the Lord to jealousy? Are we stronger than he?

CHRISTIAN LIBERTY

[23] "Everything is permissible,"[G] but not everything is beneficial. "Everything is permissible,"[G] but not everything builds up. [24] No one is to seek his own good, but the good of the other person.

[25] Eat everything that is sold in the meat market, without raising questions for the sake of conscience, [26] since **the earth is the Lord's, and all that is in it.**[H] [27] If any of the unbelievers invites you over and you want to go, eat everything that is set before you, without raising questions for the sake of conscience. [28] But if someone says to you, "This is food from a sacrifice," do not eat it, out of consideration for the one who told you, and for the sake of conscience.[I] [29] I do not mean your own conscience, but the other person's. For why is my freedom judged by another person's conscience? [30] If I partake with thanksgiving, why am I criticized because of something for which I give thanks?

[31] So, whether you eat or drink, or whatever you do, do everything for the glory of God. [32] Give no offense to Jews or Greeks or the church of God, [33] just as I also try to please everyone in everything, not seeking my own

11 benefit, but the benefit of many, so that they may be saved. [1] Imitate me, as I also imitate Christ.

[A]10:9 Lit them tested [B]10:10 Lit them complained [C]10:10 Or the destroying angel [D]10:11 Or goals of the ages, or culmination of the ages [E]10:18 Lit Look at Israel according to the flesh [F]10:20 Other mss read Gentiles [G]10:23 Other mss add for me [H]10:26 Ps 24:1 [I]10:28 Other mss add "For the earth is the Lord's and all that is in it."

INSTRUCTIONS ABOUT HEAD COVERINGS

[2] Now I praise you[A] because you remember me in everything and hold fast to the traditions just as I delivered them to you. [3] But I want you to know that Christ is the head of every man, and the man is the head of the woman,[B] and God is the head of Christ. [4] Every man who prays or prophesies with something on his head dishonors his head. [5] Every woman who prays or prophesies with her head uncovered dishonors her head, since that is one and the same as having her head shaved. [6] For if a woman doesn't cover her head, she should have her hair cut off. But if it is disgraceful for a woman to have her hair cut off or her head shaved, let her head be covered.

[7] A man should not cover his head, because he is the image and glory of God. So too, woman is the glory of man. [8] For man did not come from woman, but woman came from man. [9] Neither was man created for the sake of woman, but woman for the sake of man. [10] This is why a woman should have a symbol of authority on her head, because of the angels. [11] In the Lord, however, woman is not independent of man, and man is not independent of woman. [12] For just as woman came from man, so man comes through woman, and all things come from God.

[13] Judge for yourselves: Is it proper for a woman to pray to God with her head uncovered? [14] Does not even nature itself teach you that if a man has long hair it is a disgrace to him, [15] but that if a woman has long hair, it is her glory? For her hair is given to her[C] as a covering. [16] If anyone wants to argue about this, we have no other[D] custom, nor do the churches of God.

THE LORD'S SUPPER

[17] Now in giving this instruction I do not praise you, since you come together not for the better but for the worse. [18] For to begin with, I hear that when you come together as a church there are divisions among you, and in part I believe it. [19] Indeed, it is necessary that there be factions among you, so that those who are approved may be recognized among you. [20] When you come together, then, it is not to eat the Lord's Supper. [21] For at the meal, each one eats his own supper.[E] So one person is hungry while another gets drunk! [22] Don't you have homes in which to eat and drink? Or do you despise the church of God and humiliate those who have nothing? What should I say to you? Should I praise you? I do not praise you in this matter!

[23] For I received from the Lord what I also passed on to you: On the night when he was betrayed, the Lord Jesus took bread, [24] and when he had given thanks, broke it, and said,[F] "This is my body, which is[G] for you. Do this in remembrance of me."

[25] In the same way also he took the cup, after supper, and said, "This cup is the new covenant in my blood. Do this, as often as you drink it, in remembrance of me." [26] For as often as you eat this bread and drink the cup, you proclaim the Lord's death until he comes.

[A]11:2 Other mss add brothers,   [B]11:3 Or the husband is the head of the wife
[C]11:15 Other mss omit to her   [D]11:16 Or no such   [E]11:21 Or eats his own supper ahead of others   [F]11:24 Other mss add "Take, eat.   [G]11:24 Other mss add broken

SELF-EXAMINATION

27 So then, whoever eats the bread or drinks the cup of the Lord in an unworthy manner will be guilty of sin against the body^A and blood of the Lord. 28 Let a person examine himself; in this way let him eat the bread and drink from the cup. 29 For whoever eats and drinks without recognizing the body,^B eats and drinks judgment on himself. 30 This is why many are sick and ill among you, and many have fallen asleep. 31 If we were properly judging ourselves, we would not be judged, 32 but when we are judged by the Lord, we are disciplined, so that we may not be condemned with the world.

33 Therefore, my brothers and sisters, when you come together to eat, welcome one another.^C 34 If anyone is hungry, he should eat at home, so that when you gather together you will not come under judgment. I will give instructions about the other matters whenever I come.

DIVERSITY OF SPIRITUAL GIFTS

12 Now concerning spiritual gifts:^D brothers and sisters, I do not want you to be unaware. 2 You know that when you were pagans, you used to be enticed and led astray by mute idols. 3 Therefore I want you to know that no one speaking by the Spirit of God says, "Jesus is cursed," and no one can say, "Jesus is Lord," except by the Holy Spirit.

4 Now there are different gifts, but the same Spirit. 5 There are different ministries, but the same Lord. 6 And there are different activities, but the same God produces each gift in each person. 7 A manifestation of the Spirit is given to each person for the common good: 8 to one is given a message of wisdom through the Spirit, to another, a message of knowledge by the same Spirit, 9 to another, faith by the same Spirit, to another, gifts of healing by the one Spirit, 10 to another, the performing of miracles, to another, prophecy, to another, distinguishing between spirits, to another, different kinds of tongues,^E to another, interpretation of tongues. 11 One and the same Spirit is active in all these, distributing to each person as he wills.

UNITY YET DIVERSITY IN THE BODY

12 For just as the body is one and has many parts, and all the parts of that body, though many, are one body — so also is Christ. 13 For we were all baptized by^F one Spirit into one body — whether Jews or Greeks, whether slaves or free — and we were all given one Spirit to drink. 14 Indeed, the body is not one part but many. 15 If the foot should say, "Because I'm not a hand, I don't belong to the body," it is not for that reason any less a part of the body. 16 And if the ear should say, "Because I'm not an eye, I don't belong to the body," it is not for that reason any less a part of the body. 17 If the whole body were an eye, where would the hearing be? If the whole body were an ear, where would the sense of smell be? 18 But as it is, God has arranged each one of the parts in the body just as he wanted. 19 And if they were all the same part, where would the body be? 20 As it is, there are many parts, but one body. 21 The eye cannot say to the hand, "I don't need you!" Or again, the head can't say to the feet, "I don't need you!" 22 On the contrary, those parts of the body that are

---

^A 11:27 Lit be guilty of the body   ^B 11:29 Other mss read drinks unworthily, not discerning the Lord's body   ^C 11:33 Or wait for one another   ^D 12:1 Or spiritual things, or spiritual people   ^E 12:10 languages   ^F 12:13 Or with, or in weaker are indispensable. [23] And those parts of the body that we consider less honorable, we clothe these with greater honor, and our unrespectable parts are treated with greater respect, [24] which our respectable parts do not need.

Instead, God has put the body together, giving greater honor to the less honorable, [25] so that there would be no division in the body, but that the members would have the same concern for each other. [26] So if one member suffers, all the members suffer with it; if one member is honored, all the members rejoice with it.

[27] Now you are the body of Christ, and individual members of it. [28] And God has appointed these in the church: first apostles, second prophets, third teachers, next miracles, then gifts of healing, helping, administrating, various kinds of tongues.[A] [29] Are all apostles? Are all prophets? Are all teachers? Do all do miracles? [30] Do all have gifts of healing? Do all speak in other tongues? Do all interpret? [31] But desire the greater gifts. And I will show you an even better way.

LOVE: THE SUPERIOR WAY

13 If I speak human or angelic tongues[B] but do not have love, I am a noisy gong or a clanging cymbal. [2] If I have the gift of prophecy and understand all mysteries and all knowledge, and if I have all faith so that I can move mountains but do not have love, I am nothing. [3] And if I give away all my possessions, and if I give over my body in order to boast[C] but do not have love, I gain nothing.

[4] Love is patient, love is kind. Love does not envy, is not boastful, is not arrogant, [5] is not rude, is not self-seeking, is not irritable, and does not keep a record of wrongs. [6] Love finds no joy in unrighteousness but rejoices in the truth. [7] It bears all things, believes all things, hopes all things, endures all things.

[8] Love never ends. But as for prophecies, they will come to an end; as for tongues, they will cease; as for knowledge, it will come to an end. [9] For we know in part, and we prophesy in part, [10] but when the perfect comes, the partial will come to an end. [11] When I was a child, I spoke like a child, I thought like a child, I reasoned like a child. When I became a man, I put aside childish things. [12] For now we see only a reflection[D] as in a mirror, but then face to face. Now I know in part, but then I will know fully, as I am fully known. [13] Now these three remain: faith, hope, and love — but the greatest of these is love.

PROPHECY: A SUPERIOR GIFT

14 Pursue love and desire spiritual gifts, and especially that you may prophesy. [2] For the person who speaks in another tongue[E] is not speaking to people but to God, since no one understands him; he speaks mysteries in the Spirit.[F] [3] On the other hand, the person who prophesies speaks to people for their strengthening,[G] encouragement, and consolation. [4] The person who speaks in another tongue builds himself up, but the one who prophesies builds up the church. [5] I wish all of you spoke in other tongues,[H] but even more that you prophesied. The person who prophesies

---

[A]12:28 languages, also in v. 30   [B]13:1 languages, also in v. 8   [C]13:3 Other mss read *body to be burned*   [D]13:12 Lit *we see indirectly*   [E]14:2 language, also in vv. 4,13,14,19,26,27   [F]14:2 Or *in spirit,* or *in his spirit*   [G]14:3 Lit *building up*   [H]14:5 languages, also in vv. 6,18,21,22,23,39 is greater than the person who speaks in tongues, unless he interprets so that the church may be built up.

⁶ So now, brothers and sisters, if I come to you speaking in other tongues, how will I benefit you unless I speak to you with a revelation or knowledge or prophecy or teaching? ⁷ Even lifeless instruments that produce sounds — whether flute or harp — if they don't make a distinction in the notes, how will what is played on the flute or harp be recognized? ⁸ In fact, if the bugle makes an unclear sound, who will prepare for battle? ⁹ In the same way, unless you use your tongue for intelligible speech, how will what is spoken be known? For you will be speaking into the air. ¹⁰ There are doubtless many different kinds of languages in the world, none is without meaning. ¹¹ Therefore, if I do not know the meaning of the language, I will be a foreigner^A to the speaker, and the speaker will be a foreigner to me. ¹² So also you — since you are zealous for spiritual gifts,^B seek to excel in building up the church.

¹³ Therefore the person who speaks in another tongue should pray that he can interpret. ¹⁴ For if I pray in another tongue, my spirit prays, but my understanding is unfruitful. ¹⁵ What then? I will pray with the spirit, and I will also pray with my understanding. I will sing praise with the spirit, and I will also sing praise with my understanding. ¹⁶ Otherwise, if you praise with the spirit,^C how will the outsider^D say "Amen" at your giving of thanks, since he does not know what you are saying? ¹⁷ For you may very well be giving thanks, but the other person is not being built up. ¹⁸ I thank God that I speak in other tongues more than all of you; ¹⁹ yet in the church I would rather speak five words with my understanding, in order to teach others also, than ten thousand words in another tongue.

²⁰ Brothers and sisters, don't be childish in your thinking, but be infants in regard to evil and adult in your thinking. ²¹ It is written in the law,

> **I will speak to this people**
> **by people of other tongues**
> **and by the lips of foreigners,**
> **and even then, they will not listen to me,**^E

says the Lord. ²² Speaking in other tongues, then, is intended as a sign, not for believers but for unbelievers, while prophecy is not for unbelievers but for believers. ²³ If, therefore, the whole church assembles together and all are speaking in other tongues and people who are outsiders or unbelievers come in, will they not say that you are out of your minds? ²⁴ But if all are prophesying and some unbeliever or outsider comes in, he is convicted by all and is called to account by all. ²⁵ The secrets of his heart will be revealed, and as a result he will fall facedown and worship God, proclaiming, "God is really among you."

ORDER IN CHURCH MEETINGS

²⁶ What then, brothers and sisters? Whenever you come together, each one^F has a hymn, a teaching, a revelation, another tongue, or an interpretation. Everything is to be done for building up. ²⁷ If anyone speaks in another tongue, there are to be only two, or at the most three, each in turn, and let someone

---

^A 14:11 Gk *barbaros*, or *barbarian*   ^B 14:12 Lit *zealous of spirits*   ^C 14:16 Or *praise by the Spirit*   ^D 14:16 Lit *the one filling the place of the uninformed*   ^E 14:21 Is 28:11-12   ^F 14:26 Other mss add *of you* interpret. [28] But if there is no interpreter, that person is to keep silent in the church and speak to himself and God. [29] Two or three prophets should speak, and the others should evaluate. [30] But if something has been revealed to another person sitting there, the first prophet should be silent. [31] For you can all prophesy one by one, so that everyone may learn and everyone may be encouraged. [32] And the prophets' spirits are subject to the prophets, [33] since God is not a God of disorder but of peace.

As in all the churches of the saints, [34] the women[A] should be silent in the churches, for they are not permitted to speak, but are to submit themselves, as the law also says. [35] If they want to learn something, let them ask their own husbands at home, since it is disgraceful for a woman to speak in the church. [36] Or did the word of God originate from you, or did it come to you only?

[37] If anyone thinks he is a prophet or spiritual, he should recognize that what I write to you is the Lord's command. [38] If anyone ignores this, he will be ignored.[B] [39] So then, my brothers and sisters, be eager to prophesy, and do not forbid speaking in other tongues. [40] But everything is to be done decently and in order.

RESURRECTION ESSENTIAL TO THE GOSPEL

15 Now I want to make clear for you, brothers and sisters, the gospel I preached to you, which you received, on which you have taken your stand [2] and by which you are being saved, if you hold to the message I preached to you — unless you believed in vain. [3] For I passed on to you as most important what I also received: that Christ died for our sins according to the Scriptures, [4] that he was buried, that he was raised on the third day according to the Scriptures, [5] and that he appeared to Cephas, then to the Twelve. [6] Then he appeared to over five hundred brothers and sisters at one time; most of them are still alive, but some have fallen asleep. [7] Then he appeared to James, then to all the apostles. [8] Last of all, as to one born at the wrong time,[C] he also appeared to me.

[9] For I am the least of the apostles, not worthy to be called an apostle, because I persecuted the church of God. [10] But by the grace of God I am what I am, and his grace toward me was not in vain. On the contrary, I worked harder than any of them, yet not I, but the grace of God that was with me. [11] Whether, then, it is I or they, so we proclaim and so you have believed.

RESURRECTION ESSENTIAL TO THE FAITH

[12] Now if Christ is proclaimed as raised from the dead, how can some of you say, "There is no resurrection of the dead"? [13] If there is no resurrection of the dead, then not even Christ has been raised; [14] and if Christ has not been raised, then our proclamation is in vain, and so is your faith.[D] [15] Moreover, we are found to be false witnesses about God, because we have testified wrongly about God that he raised up Christ — whom he did not raise up, if in fact the dead are not raised. [16] For if the dead are not raised, not even Christ has been raised. [17] And if Christ has not been raised, your faith is worthless; you

---

A14:34 Other mss read *your women*   B14:38 Other mss read *he should be ignored*   C15:8 Or *one whose birth was unusual*   D15:14 Or *proclamation is useless, and your faith also is useless,* or *proclamation is empty, and your faith also is empty* are still in your sins. ¹⁸ Those, then, who have fallen asleep in Christ have also perished. ¹⁹ If we have put our hope in Christ for this life only, we should be pitied more than anyone.

CHRIST'S RESURRECTION GUARANTEES OURS

²⁰ But as it is, Christ has been raised from the dead, the firstfruits of those who have fallen asleep. ²¹ For since death came through a man, the resurrection of the dead also comes through a man. ²² For just as in Adam all die, so also in Christ all will be made alive.

²³ But each in his own order: Christ, the firstfruits; afterward, at his coming, those who belong to Christ. ²⁴ Then comes the end, when he hands over the kingdom to God the Father, when he abolishes all rule and all authority and power. ²⁵ For he must reign until he puts all his enemies under his feet. ²⁶ The last enemy to be abolished is death. ²⁷ For **God has put everything under his feet.**ᴬ Now when it says "everything" is put under him, it is obvious that he who puts everything under him is the exception. ²⁸ When everything is subject to Christ, then the Son himself will also be subject to the one who subjected everything to him, so that God may be all in all.

RESURRECTION SUPPORTED BY CHRISTIAN EXPERIENCE

²⁹ Otherwise what will they do who are being baptized for the dead?ᴮ If the dead are not raised at all, then why are people baptized for them?ᶜ ³⁰ Why are we in danger every hour? ³¹ I face death every day, as surely as I may boast about you, brothers and sisters, in Christ Jesus our Lord. ³² If I fought wild beasts in Ephesus as a mere man, what good did that do me? If the dead are not raised, **Let us eat and drink, for tomorrow we die.**ᴰ ³³ Do not be deceived: "Bad company corrupts good morals." ³⁴ Come to your sensesᴱ and stop sinning; for some people are ignorant about God. I say this to your shame.

THE NATURE OF THE RESURRECTION BODY

³⁵ But someone will ask, "How are the dead raised? What kind of body will they have when they come?" ³⁶ You fool! What you sow does not come to life unless it dies. ³⁷ And as for what you sow — you are not sowing the body that will be, but only a seed, perhaps of wheat or another grain. ³⁸ But God gives it a body as he wants, and to each of the seeds its own body. ³⁹ Not all flesh is the same flesh; there is one flesh for humans, another for animals, another for birds, and another for fish. ⁴⁰ There are heavenly bodies and earthly bodies, but the splendor of the heavenly bodies is different from that of the earthly ones. ⁴¹ There is a splendor of the sun, another of the moon, and another of the stars; in fact, one star differs from another star in splendor. ⁴² So it is with the resurrection of the dead: Sown in corruption, raised in incorruption; ⁴³ sown in dishonor, raised in glory; sown in weakness, raised in power; ⁴⁴ sown a natural body, raised a spiritual body. If there is a natural body, there is also a spiritual body. ⁴⁵ So it is written, **The first man Adam became a living being;**ᶠ the last Adam became a life-giving spirit. ⁴⁶ However, the spiritual is not first, but the natural, then the spiritual.

ᴬ15:27 Ps 8:6 ᴮ15:29 Or *baptized on account of the dead* ᶜ15:29 Other mss read *for the dead* ᴰ15:32 Is 22:13 ᴱ15:34 Lit *Sober up* ᶠ15:45 Gn 2:7

WHY THE RESURRECTION MATTERS

1 CORINTHIANS 15; ROMANS 6:1-5; HEBREWS 2:5-9

Thirty of us gathered at the river's edge on a warm spring afternoon to witness the baptism of my middle child. His daddy did the honors. I saw it all through a cloudy filter because my eyes were filled with happy tears.

Every single baptism, not just the ones involving my precious family, chokes me up because baptism tells a story I desperately need to hear. It is a parable of the gospel, a retelling of the greatest story ever told. Jesus died and was buried to pay the penalty for our sin. Then He rose again in victory!

Whether you come from a tradition of dunkers or sprinklers, the symbolism remains: baptism declares that we, as Christians, are buried with Christ, and then raised to walk in newness of life (Rm 6:4). But what if the story had stopped at the cross? What then?

In 1 Corinthians 15, Paul delivers the most thorough discussion of the resurrection in the entire Bible. It's a section of Scripture that is equal parts seminary-level theology and emotional appeal. Would you take a minute and read the entire chapter right now? I'll stay right here.

Paul needed to address the resurrection so exhaustively because the church in Corinth was confused about its validity and purpose. This confusion manifested in the practice of baptizing the dead (1Co 15:29). Baptism was intended to paint a picture of new life in Christ, but that picture was blurred by a misunderstanding of why Christ was raised.

We don't baptize the dead anymore, but we are still capable of misunderstanding the

resurrection or, at the very least, glossing it over. Since the work of salvation was accomplished on the cross, why does the resurrection matter, anyway?

Paul cut to the chase, explaining it this way:

"And if Christ has not been raised, your faith is worthless; you are still in your sins."

1 CORINTHIANS 15:17

If the resurrection didn't happen or doesn't matter, you and I are back at square one. You see, we didn't only need Jesus to pay the penalty for sin. We needed Him to conquer the consequence of sin—death (Rm 6:23). Before Christ, we were all dead in our trespasses and sins (Eph 2:11). Christ paid the price to forgive our sins and remove the punishment.

In other words, "The last enemy to be abolished is death" (1Co 15:26).

If Christ's story ended in death, so would ours. Imagine it like the most epic movie in history, ending with the tragic death of the main character and his love. If Christ had not been raised, our faith would be useless and our stories, tragic. But friends, He was raised!

May our lives forever tell this story: "Death has been swallowed up in victory . . . thanks be to God, who gives us the victory through our Lord Jesus Christ!" (1Co 15:54, 57).

47 The first man was from the earth, a man of dust; the second man is[A] from heaven. 48 Like the man of dust, so are those who are of the dust; like the man of heaven, so are those who are of heaven. 49 And just as we have borne the image of the man of dust, we will also bear the image of the man of heaven.

VICTORIOUS RESURRECTION

50 What I am saying, brothers and sisters, is this: Flesh and blood cannot inherit the kingdom of God, nor can corruption inherit incorruption. 51 Listen, I am telling you a mystery: We will not all fall asleep, but we will all be changed, 52 in a moment, in the twinkling of an eye, at the last trumpet. For the trumpet will sound, and the dead will be raised incorruptible, and we will be changed. 53 For this corruptible body must be clothed with incorruptibility, and this mortal body must be clothed with immortality. 54 When this corruptible body is clothed with incorruptibility, and this mortal body is clothed with immortality, then the saying that is written will take place:

Death has been swallowed up in victory.[B]
55   **Where, death, is your victory?**
       Where, death, is your sting?[C]

56 The sting of death is sin, and the power of sin is the law. 57 But thanks be to God, who gives us the victory through our Lord Jesus Christ!

58 Therefore, my dear brothers and sisters, be steadfast, immovable, always excelling in the Lord's work, because you know that your labor in the Lord is not in vain.

COLLECTION FOR THE JERUSALEM CHURCH

16 Now about the collection for the saints: Do the same as I instructed the Galatian churches. 2 On the first day of the week, each of you is to set something aside and save in keeping with how he is prospering, so that no collections will need to be made when I come. 3 When I arrive, I will send with letters those you recommend to carry your gift to Jerusalem. 4 If it is suitable for me to go as well, they will travel with me.

PAUL'S TRAVEL PLANS

5 I will come to you after I pass through Macedonia — for I will be traveling through Macedonia — 6 and perhaps I will remain with you or even spend the winter, so that you may send me on my way wherever I go. 7 I don't want to see you now just in passing, since I hope to spend some time with you, if the Lord allows. 8 But I will stay in Ephesus until Pentecost, 9 because a wide door for effective ministry has opened for me[D] — yet many oppose me. 10 If Timothy comes, see that he has nothing to fear while with you, because he is doing the Lord's work, just as I am. 11 So let no one look down on him. Send him on his way in peace so that he can come to me, because I am expecting him with the brothers.

12 Now about our brother Apollos: I strongly urged him to come to you with the brothers, but he was not at all willing to come now. However, he will come when he has an opportunity.

A 15:47 Other mss add *the Lord*   B 15:54 Is 25:8   C 15:55 Hs 13:14   D 16:9 Lit *door has opened to me, great and effective*

FINAL EXHORTATION

[13] Be alert, stand firm in the faith, be courageous,[A] be strong. [14] Do everything in love.

[15] Brothers and sisters, you know the household of Stephanas: They are the firstfruits of Achaia and have devoted themselves to serving the saints. I urge you [16] also to submit to such people, and to everyone who works and labors with them. [17] I am delighted to have Stephanas, Fortunatus, and Achaicus present, because these men have made up for your absence. [18] For they have refreshed my spirit and yours. Therefore recognize such people.

CONCLUSION

[19] The churches of Asia send you greetings. Aquila and Priscilla send you greetings warmly in the Lord, along with the church that meets in their home. [20] All the brothers and sisters send you greetings. Greet one another with a holy kiss.

[21] This greeting is in my own hand — Paul. [22] If anyone does not love the Lord, a curse be on him. Our Lord, come![B] [23] The grace of the Lord Jesus be with you. [24] My love be with all of you in Christ Jesus.

---

^A16:13 Lit *act like men*   ^B16:22 Aramaic *Marana tha*

MY GRACE IS SUFICIENT FOR YOU

2 corinthians

But he said to me, "My grace is sufficient for you, for my power is perfected in weakness." Therefore, I will most gladly boast all the more about my weaknesses, so that Christ's power may reside in me. **12:9**

ON THE TIMELINE Paul wrote 2 Corinthians around AD 56 during his third missionary journey. He included more personal information about himself here than in any of his other letters.

A LITTLE BACKGROUND First Corinthians was not well received by the church at Corinth. Timothy had returned to Paul in Ephesus (1Co 4:17; 16:10) and reported that the church was still greatly troubled, in part due to the arrival in Corinth of "false apostles" (2Co 11:13-15). These were perhaps Judaizers, asking Corinthian believers of Gentile heritage to live according to Mosaic regulations (Gl 2:14). Paul visited Corinth a second time, describing this visit as sorrowful or "painful" (2Co 2:1; 13:2).

Paul then wrote a (now lost) severe letter of stinging rebuke to Corinth from Ephesus (2Co 2:3-4,9). After delivering the letter to Corinth, Titus came to Paul with the news that most of the Corinthian church had repented. Paul decided to write to them one more time, in the letter now known as 2 Corinthians, expressing his relief but still pleading with an unrepentant minority. He promised to come to Corinth a third time (2Co 12:14; 13:1), which he did while on his way to Jerusalem (Ac 20:2-3).

MESSAGE & PURPOSE A number of important doctrines are taught in the epistle, yet its greatest value may be that it reveals the heart and spirit of one of the most effective ministers of all time. Paul wrote to the Corinthian Christians mainly to express his joy that the majority had been restored to him, to ask for an offering on behalf of the poor saints in Jerusalem, and to defend his ministry as an apostle to the minority of unrepentant Corinthian believers.

GIVE THANKS FOR THE BOOK OF 2 CORINTHIANS

Second Corinthians contributes to our understanding of ministry by teaching us four key truths: (1) God, in Christ, is reconciling the world to Himself and has given to us a ministry of reconciliation; (2) true ministry in Christ's name involves both suffering and victory; (3) serving Christ means ministering in His name to every need of the people; and (4) leaders in ministry need support and trust from those to whom they minister.

CORINTH AND
SURROUNDING CITIES

READ AND UNDERSTAND 2 CORINTHIANS

The Bible is a complete work in which many stories combine to tell one story. As you read the book of 2 Corinthians, consider reading the additional passages to discover how the whole of Scripture works together.

GREETING

1 Paul, an apostle of Christ Jesus by God's will, and Timothy our ^A brother:
To the church of God at Corinth, with all the saints who are throughout Achaia.

² Grace to you and peace from God our Father and the Lord Jesus Christ.

THE GOD OF COMFORT

³ Blessed be the God and Father of our Lord Jesus Christ, the Father of mercies and the God of all comfort. ⁴ He comforts us in all our affliction, ^B so that we may be able to comfort those who are in any kind of affliction, through the comfort we ourselves receive from God. ⁵ For just as the sufferings of Christ overflow to us, so also through Christ our comfort overflows. ⁶ If we are afflicted, it is for your comfort and salvation. If we are comforted, it is for your comfort, which produces in you patient endurance of the same sufferings that we suffer. ⁷ And our hope for you is firm, because we know that as you share in the sufferings, so you will also share in the comfort.

⁸ We don't want you to be unaware, brothers and sisters, of our affliction that took place in Asia. We were completely overwhelmed — beyond our strength — so that we even despaired of life itself. ⁹ Indeed, we felt that we had received the sentence of death, so that we would not trust in ourselves but in God who raises the dead. ¹⁰ He has delivered us from such a terrible death, and he will deliver us. We have put our hope in him that he will deliver us again ¹¹ while you join in helping us by your prayers. Then many will give thanks on our ^C behalf for the gift that came to us through the prayers of many.

A CLEAR CONSCIENCE

¹² Indeed, this is our boast: The testimony of our conscience is that we have conducted ourselves in the world, and especially toward you, with godly sincerity and purity, not by human wisdom but by God's grace. ¹³ For we are writing nothing to you other than what you can read and also understand. I hope you will understand completely — ¹⁴ just as you have partially understood us — that we are your reason for pride, just as you also are ours in the day of our ^D Lord Jesus.

A VISIT POSTPONED

¹⁵ Because of this confidence, I planned to come to you first, so that you could have a second benefit, ^E ¹⁶ and to visit you on my way to Macedonia, and then come to you again from Macedonia and be helped by you on my journey to Judea. ¹⁷ Now when I planned this, was I of two minds? Or what I plan, do I plan in a purely human ^F way so that I say "Yes, yes" and "No, no" at the same time? ¹⁸ As God is faithful, our message to you is not "Yes and no." ¹⁹ For the Son of God, Jesus Christ, whom we proclaimed among you — Silvanus, ^G Timothy, and I — did not become "Yes and no." On the contrary, in him it is always "Yes." ²⁰ For every one of God's promises is "Yes" in him. Therefore, through him we also say "Amen" to the glory of God. ²¹ Now it is

---

^A1:1 Lit *the*   ^B1:4 Or *trouble, or tribulation, or trials, or oppression*   ^C1:11 Other mss read *your*   ^D1:14 Other mss omit *our*   ^E1:15 Other mss read *a second joy*   ^F1:17 Or *a worldly, or a fleshly, or a selfish*   ^G1:19 Or *Silas* ; Ac 15:22-32; 16:19-40; 17:1-16

God who strengthens us together with you in Christ, and who has anointed us. ²² He has also put his seal on us and given us the Spirit in our hearts as a down payment.

²³ I call on God as a witness, on my life, that it was to spare you that I did not come to Corinth. ²⁴ I do not mean that we lord it over your faith, but we are **2** workers with you for your joy, because you stand firm in your faith. ¹ In fact, I made up my mind about this: I would not come to you on another painful visit.ᴬ ² For if I cause you pain, then who will cheer me other than the one being hurt by me?ᴮ ³ I wrote this very thing so that when I came I wouldn't have pain from those who ought to give me joy, because I am confident about all of you that my joy will also be yours. ⁴ For I wrote to you with many tears out of an extremely troubled and anguished heart — not to cause you pain, but that you should know the abundant love I have for you.

A SINNER FORGIVEN

⁵ If anyone has caused pain, he has caused pain not so much to me but to some degree — not to exaggerate — to all of you. ⁶ This punishment by the majority is sufficient for that person. ⁷ As a result, you should instead forgive and comfort him. Otherwise, he may be overwhelmed by excessive grief. ⁸ Therefore I urge you to reaffirm your love to him. ⁹ I wrote for this purpose: to test your character to see if you are obedient in everything. ¹⁰ Anyone you forgive, I do too. For what I have forgiven — if I have forgiven anything — it is for your benefit in the presence of Christ, ¹¹ so that we may not be taken advantage of by Satan. For we are not ignorant of his schemes.

A TRIP TO MACEDONIA

¹² When I came to Troas to preach the gospel of Christ, even though the Lord opened a door for me, ¹³ I had no rest in my spirit because I did not find my brother Titus. Instead, I said good-bye to them and left for Macedonia.

A MINISTRY OF LIFE OR DEATH

¹⁴ But thanks be to God, who always leads us in Christ's triumphal procession and through us spreads the aroma of the knowledge of him in every place. ¹⁵ For to God we are the fragrance of Christ among those who are being saved and among those who are perishing. ¹⁶ To some we are an aroma of death leading to death, but to others, an aroma of life leading to life. Who is adequate for these things? ¹⁷ For we do not market the word of God for profit like so many.ᶜ On the contrary, we speak with sincerity in Christ, as from God and before God.

LIVING LETTERS

3 Are we beginning to commend ourselves again? Or do we need, like some, letters of recommendation to you or from you? ² You yourselves are our letter, written on our hearts, known and read by everyone. ³ You show that you are Christ's letter, deliveredᴰ by us, not written with ink but with the Spirit of the living God — not on tablets of stone but on tablets of human hearts.ᴱ

ᴬ2:1 Lit *not again in sorrow to come to you*   ᴮ2:2 Lit *the one pained*
ᶜ2:17 Other mss read *like the rest*   ᴰ3:3 Lit *ministered to*   ᴱ3:3 Lit *fleshly hearts*

PAUL'S COMPETENCE

⁴ Such is the confidence we have through Christ before God. ⁵ It is not that we are competent in⁴ ourselves to claim anything as coming from ourselves, but our adequacy is from God. ⁶ He has made us competent to be ministers of a new covenant, not of the letter, but of the Spirit. For the letter kills, but the Spirit gives life.

NEW COVENANT MINISTRY

⁷ Now if the ministry that brought death, chiseled in letters on stones, came with glory, so that the Israelites were not able to gaze steadily at Moses's face because of its glory, which was set aside, ⁸ how will the ministry of the Spirit not be more glorious? ⁹ For if the ministry that brought condemnation had glory, the ministry that brings righteousness overflows with even more glory. ¹⁰ In fact, what had been glorious is not glorious now by comparison because of the glory that surpasses it. ¹¹ For if what was set aside was glorious, what endures will be even more glorious.

¹² Since, then, we have such a hope, we act with great boldness. ¹³ We are not like Moses, who used to put a veil over his face to prevent the Israelites from gazing steadily until the end⁸ of the glory of what was being set aside, ¹⁴ but their minds were hardened. For to this day, at the reading of the old covenant, the same veil remains; it is not lifted, because it is set aside only in Christ. ¹⁵ Yet still today, whenever Moses is read, a veil lies over their hearts, ¹⁶ but whenever a person turns to the Lord, the veil is removed. ¹⁷ Now the Lord is the Spirit, and where the Spirit of the Lord is, there is freedom. ¹⁸ We all, with unveiled faces, are looking as in a mirror at⁶ the glory of the Lord and are being transformed into the same image from glory to glory; this is from the Lord who is the Spirit.ᴰ

THE LIGHT OF THE GOSPEL

4 Therefore, since we have this ministry because we were shown mercy, we do not give up. ² Instead, we have renounced secret and shameful things, not acting deceitfully or distorting the word of God, but commending ourselves before God to everyone's conscience by an open display of the truth. ³ But if our gospel is veiled, it is veiled to those who are perishing. ⁴ In their case, the god of this age has blinded the minds of the unbelievers to keep them from seeing the light of the gospel of the glory of Christ,ᴱ who is the image of God. ⁵ For we are not proclaiming ourselves but Jesus Christ as Lord, and ourselves as your servants for Jesus's sake. ⁶ For God who said, "Let light shine out of darkness," has shone in our hearts to give the light of the knowledge of God's glory in the face of Jesus Christ.

TREASURE IN CLAY JARS

⁷ Now we have this treasure in clay jars, so that this extraordinary power may be from God and not from us. ⁸ We are afflicted in every way but not crushed; we are perplexed but not in despair; ⁹ we are persecuted but not abandoned; we are struck down but not destroyed. ¹⁰ We always carry the

---

ᴬ3:5 Lit from   ᴮ3:13 Or at the outcome   ᶜ3:18 Or are reflecting   ᴰ3:18 Or from the Spirit of the Lord, or from the Lord, the Spirit   ᴱ4:4 Or the gospel of the glorious Christ, or the glorious gospel of Christ death of Jesus in our body, so that the life of Jesus may also be displayed in our body. ¹¹ For we who live are always being given over to death for Jesus's sake, so that Jesus's life may also be displayed in our mortal flesh. ¹² So then, death is at work in us, but life in you. ¹³ And since we have the same spirit of faith in keeping with what is written, **I believed, therefore I spoke,** ^A we also believe, and therefore speak. ¹⁴ For we know that the one who raised the Lord Jesus will also raise us with Jesus and present us with you. ¹⁵ Indeed, everything is for your benefit so that, as grace extends through more and more people, it may cause thanksgiving to increase to the glory of God.

¹⁶ Therefore we do not give up. Even though our outer person is being destroyed, our inner person is being renewed day by day. ¹⁷ For our momentary light affliction is producing for us an absolutely incomparable eternal weight of glory. ¹⁸ So we do not focus on what is seen, but on what is unseen. For what is seen is temporary, but what is unseen is eternal.

OUR FUTURE AFTER DEATH

5 For we know that if our earthly tent we live in is destroyed, we have a building from God, an eternal dwelling in the heavens, not made with hands. ² Indeed, we groan in this tent, desiring to put on our heavenly dwelling, ³ since, when we have taken it off, ^B we will not be found naked. ⁴ Indeed, we groan while we are in this tent, burdened as we are, because we do not want to be unclothed but clothed, so that mortality may be swallowed up by life. ⁵ Now the one who prepared us for this very purpose is God, who gave us the Spirit as a down payment.

⁶ So we are always confident and know that while we are at home in the body we are away from the Lord. ⁷ For we walk by faith, not by sight. ⁸ In fact, we are confident, and we would prefer to be away from the body and at home with the Lord. ⁹ Therefore, whether we are at home or away, we make it our aim to be pleasing to him. ¹⁰ For we must all appear before the judgment seat of Christ, so that each may be repaid for what he has done in the body, whether good or evil.

¹¹ Therefore, since we know the fear of the Lord, we try to persuade people. What we are is plain to God, and I hope it is also plain to your consciences. ¹² We are not commending ourselves to you again, but giving you an opportunity to be proud of us, so that you may have a reply for those who take pride in outward appearance rather than in the heart. ¹³ For if we are out of our mind, it is for God; if we are in our right mind, it is for you. ¹⁴ For the love of Christ compels us, since we have reached this conclusion: If one died for all, then all died. ¹⁵ And he died for all so that those who live should no longer live for themselves, but for the one who died for them and was raised.

THE MINISTRY OF RECONCILIATION

¹⁶ From now on, then, we do not know anyone from a worldly perspective. ^C Even if we have known Christ from a worldly perspective, ^D yet now we no longer know him in this way. ¹⁷ Therefore, if anyone is in Christ, he is a new creation; the old has passed away, and see, the new has ^E come! ¹⁸ Everything

---

^A 4:13 Ps 116:10 LXX   ^B 5:3 Other mss read *when we have put on*   ^C 5:16 Lit
anyone according to the flesh   ^D 5:16 Lit *Christ according to the flesh*
^E 5:17 Other mss read *look, all new things have*

is from God, who has reconciled us to himself through Christ and has given us the ministry of reconciliation. [19] That is, in Christ, God was reconciling the world to himself, not counting their trespasses against them, and he has committed the message of reconciliation to us.

[20] Therefore, we are ambassadors for Christ, since God is making his appeal through us. We plead on Christ's behalf: "Be reconciled to God." [21] He made the one who did not know sin to be sin[A] for us, so that in him we might become the righteousness of God.

6 Working together with him, we also appeal to you, "Don't receive the grace of God in vain." [2] For he says:

At an acceptable time I listened to you,
and in the day of salvation I helped you.[B]

See, now is the acceptable time; now is the day of salvation!

THE CHARACTER OF PAUL'S MINISTRY

[3] We are not giving anyone an occasion for offense, so that the ministry will not be blamed. [4] Instead, as God's ministers, we commend ourselves in everything: by great endurance, by afflictions, by hardships, by difficulties, [5] by beatings, by imprisonments, by riots, by labors, by sleepless nights, by times of hunger, [6] by purity, by knowledge, by patience, by kindness, by the Holy Spirit, by sincere love, [7] by the word of truth,[C] by the power of God; through weapons of righteousness for the right hand and the left, [8] through glory and dishonor, through slander and good report; regarded as deceivers, yet true; [9] as unknown, yet recognized; as dying, yet see — we live; as being disciplined, yet not killed; [10] as grieving, yet always rejoicing; as poor, yet enriching many; as having nothing, yet possessing everything. [11] We have spoken openly to you, Corinthians; our heart has been opened wide. [12] We are not withholding our affection from you, but you are withholding yours from us. [13] I speak as to my children; as a proper response, open your heart to us.

SEPARATION TO GOD

[14] Don't become partners with those who do not believe. For what partnership is there between righteousness and lawlessness? Or what fellowship does light have with darkness? [15] What agreement does Christ have with Belial?[D] Or what does a believer have in common with an unbeliever? [16] And what agreement does the temple of God have with idols? For we[E] are the temple of the living God, as God said:

I will dwell
and walk among them,
and I will be their God,
and they will be my people.[F]

[17]   **Therefore, come out from among them**
and be separate, says the Lord;
do not touch any unclean thing,
and I will welcome you.[G]

[A]5:21 Or *be a sin offering*   [B]6:2 Is 49:8   [C]6:7 Or *by truthful speech*
[D]6:15 Or *Beliar*   [E]6:16 Other mss read *you*   [F]6:16 Lv 26:12; Jr 31:33; 32:38;
Ezk 37:26   [G]6:17 Is 52:11

GODLY GRIEF

2 CORINTHIANS 6–7; LAMENTATIONS 3:19-24; ACTS 3:19

I'm an avoider. I avoid uncomfortable topics and decisions. I avoid unfortunate feelings and situations. I avoid watching the news when I can get away with it, and I've been known to avoid eye contact with the homeless vendor selling newspapers on the corner.

I avoid grief and suffering because I don't want to experience grief and suffering. I can't solve them, can't explain them away—I can only enter in, and honestly, I'd rather not. The only way to get to the other side of these mountains is to walk through them. Over, under, and around are not options.

I avoid acknowledging my sin for the same reason. It's uncomfortable, painful, something I can't solve or explain away. I fall deathly short, like we all do (Rm 3:23; 6:23). The darkness I'm capable of is shocking. *Who wants to admit such a thing?*

Acknowledging sin and its consequences is a difficult, achy, and emotionally invasive procedure. But a beautiful thing happens when we take that hard road through the mountain: we do not travel alone. Jesus is with us as God's Word convicts our hearts. Jesus is with us as the Holy Spirit reveals our desperate need. Jesus is with us as our knees buckle at the devastation around us and within us. **He is by our side to administer the salve of grace the moment each sin-wound is revealed.**

Somewhere in the thick of this ongoing heart surgery we begin to understand: Only in seeing the depth of our sin can we see the unmatched grace and glory of the cross.

Lamentations tells of God's people standing among the ruins of Jerusalem, singing painful poems of lament (Lm 1:7). There in the rubble, they worshiped. They repented. They claimed what they knew to be true—God is faithful, even here and now.

"Because of the LORD's faithful love we do not perish, for his mercies never end. They are new every morning; great is your faithfulness!"

LAMENTATIONS 3:22-23

Like God's people standing among the temple ruins, you and I stand in the midst of wreckage today—broken churches, broken families, broken bodies, broken hopes. The consequences of sin are ugly, and it hurts to look full on at the darkness. We grieve our sinful state with honest questions and hot tears and loud lamenting. But this is the kind of godly grief that brings the Apostle Paul to rejoice! Not because grief is painless or petty—it most certainly is not—but because godly grief leads to repentance (2Co 7:9-10).

Let us look on our sin and look longer at the Cross. Look to the One who does not avoid our suffering but enters in, who does not despise our brokenness but redeems it. May our tears of grief lead us to repentance, and may we receive refreshment for our souls (Ac 3:19).

> ¹⁸ And **I will be a Father** to you,
> **and** you will be **sons** and daughters **to me,**
> **says the Lord Almighty.**^A

7 So then, dear friends, since we have these promises, let us cleanse ourselves from every impurity of the flesh and spirit, bringing holiness to completion^B in the fear of God.

JOY AND REPENTANCE

² Make room for us in your hearts. We have wronged no one, corrupted no one, taken advantage of no one. ³ I don't say this to condemn you, since I have already said that you are in our hearts, to die together and to live together. ⁴ I am very frank with you; I have great pride in you. I am filled with encouragement; I am overflowing with joy in all our afflictions.

⁵ In fact, when we came into Macedonia, we^C had no rest. Instead, we were troubled in every way: conflicts on the outside, fears within. ⁶ But God, who comforts the downcast, comforted us by the arrival of Titus, ⁷ and not only by his arrival but also by the comfort he received from you. He told us about your deep longing, your sorrow, and your zeal for me, so that I rejoiced even more. ⁸ For even if I grieved you with my letter, I don't regret it. And if I regretted it — since I saw that the letter grieved you, yet only for a while — ⁹ I now rejoice, not because you were grieved, but because your grief led to repentance. For you were grieved as God willed, so that you didn't experience any loss from us. ¹⁰ For godly grief produces a repentance that leads to salvation without regret, but worldly grief produces death. ¹¹ For consider how much diligence this very thing — this grieving as God wills — has produced in you: what a desire to clear yourselves, what indignation, what fear, what deep longing, what zeal, what justice! In every way you showed yourselves to be pure in this matter. ¹² So even though I wrote to you, it was not because of the one who did wrong, or because of the one who was wronged, but in order that your devotion to us might be made plain to you in the sight of God. ¹³ For this reason we have been comforted.

In addition to our own comfort, we rejoiced even more over the joy Titus had, because his spirit was refreshed by all of you. ¹⁴ For if I have made any boast to him about you, I have not been disappointed; but as I have spoken everything to you in truth, so our boasting to Titus has also turned out to be the truth. ¹⁵ And his affection toward you is even greater as he remembers the obedience of all of you, and how you received him with fear and trembling. ¹⁶ I rejoice that I have complete confidence in you.

APPEAL TO COMPLETE THE COLLECTION

8 We want you to know, brothers and sisters, about the grace of God that was given to the churches of Macedonia: ² During a severe trial brought about by affliction, their abundant joy and their extreme poverty overflowed in a wealth of generosity on their part. ³ I can testify that, according to their ability and even beyond their ability, of their own accord, ⁴ they begged us

---

^A 6:18 2Sm 7:14; Is 43:6; 49:22; 60:4; Hs 1:10   ^B 7:1 Or *spirit, perfecting holiness*   ^C 7:5 Lit *our flesh* earnestly for the privilege of sharing in the ministry to the saints, [5] and not just as we had hoped. Instead, they gave themselves first to the Lord and then to us by God's will. [6] So we urged Titus that just as he had begun, so he should also complete among you this act of grace.

[7] Now as you excel in everything — in faith, speech, knowledge, and in all diligence, and in your love for us [A] — excel also in this act of grace. [8] I am not saying this as a command. Rather, by means of the diligence of others, I am testing the genuineness of your love. [9] For you know the grace of our Lord Jesus Christ: Though he was rich, for your sake he became poor, so that by his poverty you might become rich. [10] And in this matter I am giving advice because it is profitable for you, who began last year not only to do something but also to want to do it. [11] Now also finish the task, so that just as there was an eager desire, there may also be a completion, according to what you have. [12] For if the eagerness is there, the gift is acceptable according to what a person has, not according to what he does not have. [13] It is not that there should be relief for others and hardship for you, but it is a question of equality. [B] [14] At the present time your surplus is available for their need, so that their abundance may in turn meet your need, in order that there may be equality. [15] As it is written: **The person who had much did not have too much, and the person who had little did not have too little.** [C]

ADMINISTRATION OF THE COLLECTION

[16] Thanks be to God, who put the same concern for you into the heart of Titus. [17] For he welcomed our appeal and, being very diligent, went out to you by his own choice. [18] We have sent with him the brother who is praised among all the churches for his gospel ministry. [D] [19] And not only that, but he was also appointed by the churches to accompany us with this gracious gift that we are administering for the glory of the Lord himself and to show our eagerness to help. [20] We are taking this precaution so that no one will criticize us about this large sum that we are administering. [21] Indeed, we are giving careful thought to do what is right, not only before the Lord but also before people. [22] We have also sent with them our brother. We have often tested him in many circumstances and found him to be diligent — and now even more diligent because of his great confidence in you. [23] As for Titus, he is my partner and coworker for you; as for our brothers, they are the messengers of the churches, the glory of Christ. [24] Therefore, show them proof before the churches of your love and of our boasting about you.

MOTIVATIONS FOR GIVING

9 Now concerning the ministry to the saints, it is unnecessary for me to write to you. [2] For I know your eagerness, and I boast about you to the Macedonians: "Achaia has been ready since last year," and your zeal has stirred up most of them. [3] But I am sending the brothers so that our boasting about you in this matter would not prove empty, and so that you would be ready just as I said. [4] Otherwise, if any Macedonians come with me and find you unprepared, we, not to mention you, would be put to shame in that situation. [E] [5] Therefore I considered it necessary to urge the brothers to go

---

[A] 8:7 Other mss read *in our love for you* [B] 8:13 Lit *but from equality* [C] 8:15 Ex 16:18 [D] 8:18 Lit *churches, in the gospel* [E] 9:4 Or *in this confidence* on ahead to you and arrange in advance the generous gift you promised, so that it will be ready as a gift and not as an extortion.

⁶ The point is this:^A The person who sows sparingly will also reap sparingly, and the person who sows generously will also reap generously. ⁷ Each person should do as he has decided in his heart — not reluctantly or out of compulsion, since God loves a cheerful giver. ⁸ And God is able to make every grace overflow to you, so that in every way, always having everything you need, you may excel in every good work. ⁹ As it is written:

> He distributed freely;
> he gave to the poor;
> his righteousness endures forever.^B

¹⁰ Now the one who provides seed for the sower and bread for food will also provide and multiply your seed and increase the harvest of your righteousness. ¹¹ You will be enriched in every way for all generosity, which produces thanksgiving to God through us. ¹² For the ministry of this service is not only supplying the needs of the saints but is also overflowing in many expressions of thanks to God. ¹³ Because of the proof provided by this ministry, they will glorify God for your obedient confession of the gospel of Christ, and for your generosity in sharing with them and with everyone. ¹⁴ And as they pray on your behalf, they will have deep affection for you because of the surpassing grace of God in you. ¹⁵ Thanks be to God for his indescribable gift!

PAUL'S APOSTOLIC AUTHORITY

10 Now I Paul, myself, appeal to you by the meekness and gentleness of Christ — I who am humble among you in person but bold toward you when absent. ² I beg you that when I am present I will not need to be bold with the confidence by which I plan to challenge certain people who think we are behaving according to the flesh. ³ For although we live in the flesh, we do not wage war according to the flesh, ⁴ since the weapons of our warfare are not of the flesh, but are powerful through God for the demolition of strongholds. We demolish arguments ⁵ and every proud thing that is raised up against the knowledge of God, and we take every thought captive to obey Christ. ⁶ And we are ready to punish any disobedience, once your obedience is complete.

⁷ Look at what is obvious.^C If anyone is confident that he belongs to Christ, let him remind himself of this: Just as he belongs to Christ, so do we. ⁸ For if I boast a little too much about our authority, which the Lord gave for building you up and not for tearing you down, I will not be put to shame. ⁹ I don't want to seem as though I am trying to terrify you with my letters. ¹⁰ For it is said, "His letters are weighty and powerful, but his physical presence is weak and his public speaking amounts to nothing." ¹¹ Let such a person consider this: What we are in our letters, when we are absent, we will also be in our actions when we are present.

¹² For we don't dare classify or compare ourselves with some who commend themselves. But in measuring themselves by themselves and comparing themselves to themselves, they lack understanding. ¹³ We, however, will not boast beyond measure but according to the measure of the area of ministry that God has assigned to us, which reaches even to you. ¹⁴ For we are not overextending ourselves, as if we had not reached you, since we have

---

^A 9:6 Lit *And this* ^B 9:9 Ps 112:9 ^C 10:7 Or *You are looking at things outwardly* come to you with the gospel of Christ. ¹⁵ We are not boasting beyond measure about other people's labors. On the contrary, we have the hope that as your faith increases, our area of ministry will be greatly enlarged, ¹⁶ so that we may preach the gospel to the regions beyond you without boasting about what has already been done in someone else's area of ministry. ¹⁷ So **let the one who boasts, boast in the Lord.**[A] ¹⁸ For it is not the one commending himself who is approved, but the one the Lord commends.

PAUL AND THE FALSE APOSTLES

11 I wish you would put up with a little foolishness from me. Yes, do put up with me![B] ² For I am jealous for you with a godly jealousy, because I have promised you in marriage to one husband — to present a pure virgin to Christ. ³ But I fear that, as the serpent deceived Eve by his cunning, your minds may be seduced from a sincere and pure[C] devotion to Christ. ⁴ For if a person comes and preaches another Jesus, whom we did not preach, or you receive a different spirit, which you had not received, or a different gospel, which you had not accepted, you put up with it splendidly!

⁵ Now I consider myself in no way inferior to those "super-apostles." ⁶ Even if I am untrained in public speaking, I am certainly not untrained in knowledge. Indeed, we have in every way made that clear to you in everything. ⁷ Or did I commit a sin by humbling myself so that you might be exalted, because I preached the gospel of God to you free of charge? ⁸ I robbed other churches by taking pay from them to minister to you. ⁹ When I was present with you and in need, I did not burden anyone, since the brothers who came from Macedonia supplied my needs. I have kept myself, and will keep myself, from burdening you in any way. ¹⁰ As the truth of Christ is in me, this boasting of mine will not be stopped[D] in the regions of Achaia. ¹¹ Why? Because I don't love you? God knows I do!

¹² But I will continue to do what I am doing, in order to deny[E] an opportunity to those who want to be regarded as our equals in what they boast about. ¹³ For such people are false apostles, deceitful workers, disguising themselves as apostles of Christ. ¹⁴ And no wonder! For Satan disguises himself as an angel of light. ¹⁵ So it is no great surprise if his servants also disguise themselves as servants of righteousness. Their end will be according to their works.

PAUL'S SUFFERINGS FOR CHRIST

¹⁶ I repeat: Let no one consider me a fool. But if you do, at least accept me as a fool so that I can also boast a little. ¹⁷ What I am saying in this matter[F] of boasting, I don't speak as the Lord would, but as it were, foolishly. ¹⁸ Since many boast according to the flesh, I will also boast. ¹⁹ For you, being so wise, gladly put up with fools! ²⁰ In fact, you put up with it if someone enslaves you, if someone exploits you, if someone takes advantage of you, if someone is arrogant toward you, if someone slaps you in the face. ²¹ I say this to our shame: We have been too weak for that!

But in whatever anyone dares to boast — I am talking foolishly — I also dare: ²² Are they Hebrews? So am I. Are they Israelites? So am I. Are they the

---

[A]10:17 Jr 9:24 [B]11:1 Or *Yes, you are putting up with me* [C]11:3 Other mss omit *and pure* [D]11:10 Or *silenced* [E]11:12 Lit *cut off* [F]11:17 Or *business*, or *confidence* descendants of Abraham? So am I. ²³ Are they servants of Christ? I'm talking like a madman — I'm a better one: with far more labors, many more imprisonments, far worse beatings, many times near death.

²⁴ Five times I received the forty lashes minus one from the Jews. ²⁵ Three times I was beaten with rods. Once I received a stoning. Three times I was shipwrecked. I have spent a night and a day in the open sea. ²⁶ On frequent journeys, I faced dangers from rivers, dangers from robbers, dangers from my own people, dangers from Gentiles, dangers in the city, dangers in the wilderness, dangers at sea, and dangers among false brothers; ²⁷ toil and hardship, many sleepless nights, hunger and thirst, often without food, cold, and without clothing. ²⁸ Not to mention ᴬ other things, there is the daily pressure on me: my concern for all the churches. ²⁹ Who is weak, and I am not weak? Who is made to stumble, and I do not burn with indignation?

³⁰ If boasting is necessary, I will boast about my weaknesses. ³¹ The God and Father of the Lord Jesus, who is blessed forever, knows I am not lying. ³² In Damascus, a ruler ᴮ under King Aretas guarded the city of Damascus in order to arrest me. ³³ So I was let down in a basket through a window in the wall and escaped from his hands.

SUFFICIENT GRACE

12 Boasting is necessary. It is not profitable, but I will move on to visions and revelations of the Lord. ² I know a man in Christ who was caught up to the third heaven fourteen years ago. Whether he was in the body or out of the body, I don't know; God knows. ³ I know that this man — whether in the body or out of the body I don't know; God knows — ⁴ was caught up into paradise and heard inexpressible words, which a human being is not allowed to speak. ⁵ I will boast about this person, but not about myself, except of my weaknesses.

⁶ For if I want to boast, I wouldn't be a fool, because I would be telling the truth. But I will spare you, so that no one can credit me with something beyond what he sees in me or hears from me, ⁷ especially because of the extraordinary revelations. Therefore, so that I would not exalt myself, a thorn in the flesh was given to me, a messenger of Satan to torment me so that I would not exalt myself. ⁸ Concerning this, I pleaded with the Lord three times that it would leave me. ⁹ But he said to me, "My grace is sufficient for you, for my power is perfected in weakness."

Therefore, I will most gladly boast all the more about my weaknesses, so that Christ's power may reside in me. ¹⁰ So I take pleasure in weaknesses, insults, hardships, persecutions, and in difficulties, for the sake of Christ. For when I am weak, then I am strong.

SIGNS OF AN APOSTLE

¹¹ I have been a fool; you forced it on me. You ought to have commended me, since I am not in any way inferior to those "super-apostles," even though I am nothing. ¹² The signs of an apostle were performed with unfailing endurance among you, including signs and wonders and miracles. ¹³ So in what way are you worse off than the other churches, except that I personally did not burden you? Forgive me for this wrong!

ᴬ11:28 Lit Apart from   ᴮ11:32 Gk ethnarches; a leader of an ethnic community

CHRIST'S SUFFICIENCY

2 CORINTHIANS 12–13; MARK 14:32-36

Early in my first pregnancy, doctors discovered there was something wrong. My tiny baby's bladder was blocked and his kidneys would not develop correctly.

As the weeks ticked by and ultrasounds showed the problem worsening, I didn't know how to pray.

One evening at a church service, I listened as the band belted out this chorus: "Your grace is enough for me . . ." And I found myself at a fork in the road.

Was God's grace sufficient for sick babies? Was it sufficient for desperate prayers that seemed to go unanswered? Was it enough for this, right here and now?

My knees hit the floor and I made a choice. Though I desperately wanted God to take away the blockage in my unborn baby's bladder, I would choose to believe His grace was sufficient for the healing and for the alternate outcome of a baby with bad kidneys.

That sweet baby boy is now a rowdy first grader with permanent kidney damage. And I am a mama forever changed by the reality of Christ's sufficiency.

I'm not crazy about the restrictions my child has, or our regular trips to specialists, or the seemingly chronic fear that his condition will worsen. But I've yet to face a worry, a doctor, or a limitation that God's grace isn't big enough to cover. I keep praying for God to heal my boy,

and I keep falling to my knees, declaring Christ as sufficient. And He is.

Paul knew this rhythm. In 2 Corinthians 12, he described a "thorn in the flesh" (v. 7), something he wanted God to take away. But for whatever reason, God did not. I'm grateful Paul spared us more detail; it helps us see ourselves in his place. We all have a thorn or two, don't we? We all have something that pokes and prods at our hearts, something we've asked God over and over again to remove, but so far, He has not.

When Paul asked God to remove the thorn, He answered him, saying,

---

"My grace is sufficient for you, for my power is perfected in weakness. Therefore, I will most gladly boast all the more about my weaknesses, so that Christ's power may reside in me."

2 CORINTHIANS 12:9

Paul didn't see God's answer as a glass-half-empty truth. Instead, He found good reason to brag about his own shortcomings.

Our insufficiency helps us press into Christ's sufficiency. I have a friend who says it this way: "Anything that causes us to depend on Christ is a good thing." When we lean on Him, we will always, always, always find Him strong enough to hold us up.

PAUL'S CONCERN FOR THE CORINTHIANS

¹⁴ Look, I am ready to come to you this third time. I will not burden you, since I am not seeking what is yours, but you. For children ought not save up for their parents, but parents for their children. ¹⁵ I will most gladly spend and be spent for you.ᴬ If I love you more, am I to be loved less? ¹⁶ Now granted, I did not burden you; yet sly as I am, I took you in by deceit! ¹⁷ Did I take advantage of you by any of those I sent you? ¹⁸ I urged Titus to go, and I sent the brother with him. Titus didn't take advantage of you, did he? Didn't we walk in the same spirit and in the same footsteps?

¹⁹ Have you been thinking all along that we were defending ourselves to you? No, in the sight of God we are speaking in Christ, and everything, dear friends, is for building you up. ²⁰ For I fear that perhaps when I come I will not find you to be what I want, and you may not find me to be what you want. Perhaps there will be quarreling, jealousy, angry outbursts, selfish ambitions, slander, gossip, arrogance, and disorder. ²¹ I fear that when I come my God will againᴮ humiliate me in your presence, and I will grieve for many who sinned before and have not repented of the moral impurity, sexual immorality, and sensuality they practiced.

FINAL WARNINGS AND EXHORTATIONS

13 This is the third time I am coming to you. **Every matter must be established by the testimony of two or three witnesses.**ᶜ ² I gave a warning when I was present the second time, and now I give a warning while I am absent to those who sinned before and to all the rest: If I come again, I will not be lenient, ³ since you seek proof of Christ speaking in me. He is not weak in dealing with you, but powerful among you. ⁴ For he was crucified in weakness, but he lives by the power of God. For we also are weak in him, but in dealing with you we will live with him by God's power.

⁵ Test yourselves to see if you are in the faith. Examine yourselves. Or do you yourselves not recognize that Jesus Christ is in you? — unless you fail the test.ᴰ ⁶ And I hope you will recognize that we ourselves do not fail the test. ⁷ But we pray to God that you do nothing wrong — not that we may appear to pass the test, but that you may do what is right, even though we may appear to fail. ⁸ For we can't do anything against the truth, but only for the truth. ⁹ We rejoice when we are weak and you are strong. We also pray that you become fully mature.ᴱ ¹⁰ This is why I am writing these things while absent, so that when I am there I may not have to deal harshly with you, in keeping with the authority the Lord gave me for building up and not for tearing down.

¹¹ Finally, brothers and sisters, rejoice.ᶠ Become mature, be encouraged,ᴳ be of the same mind, be at peace, and the God of love and peace will be with you. ¹² Greet one another with a holy kiss. All the saints send you greetings.

¹³ The grace of the Lord Jesus Christ, and the love of God, and the fellowship of the Holy Spirit be with you all.ᴴ

ᴬ12:15 Lit for your souls, or for your lives   ᴮ12:21 Or come again my God will
ᶜ13:1 Dt 17:6; 19:15   ᴰ13:5 Or you are disqualified, or you are counterfeit
ᴱ13:9 Or become complete, or be restored   ᶠ13:11 Or farewell   ᴳ13:11 Or listen to my appeal   ᴴ13:12-13 Some translations divide these two vv. into three vv. so that v. 13 begins with All the saints . . . and v. 14 begins with The grace of . . .

I do not
set Aside the
grace
of God

galatians

 I do not set aside the grace of God, for if righteousness comes through the law, then Christ died for nothing. **2:21**

ON THE TIMELINE Possible dates range from AD 48, just before the Jerusalem Council, to AD 56, if written around the same time as the book of Romans, during Paul's third missionary journey. Though certainty is not possible, AD 48 seems most likely given all the evidence.

A LITTLE BACKGROUND The term "Galatians" was used both ethnically and politically in the New Testament era, making it unclear where the Galatian churches were actually located. If understood ethnically, the founding of the Galatian churches is only implied in the NT. Paul "went through the region of Phrygia and Galatia" (Ac 16:6), in north central Asia Minor, during his second missionary journey and again later (Ac 18:23; 19:1). A group from Gaul (modern France) invaded that area in the third century BC, and it became known as Galatia.

Understood politically, "Galatians" can refer to those living in the southern part of the Roman province of Galatia, a different area entirely. That region included the cities of Pisidian Antioch, Iconium, Lystra, and Derbe, where Paul worked to plant churches (Ac 13:14–14:23).

MESSAGE & PURPOSE Galatians, which is probably the earliest of Paul's letters, is also his most intense, proclaiming the truth that sinners are justified and live godly lives by trusting in Jesus alone. Paul wrote Galatians to clarify and defend "the truth of the gospel" (Gl 2:5,16) in the face of a false gospel. He did this by defending his authority as an apostle, considering the Old Testament basis of the gospel message, and demonstrating how the gospel message worked practically in daily Christian living.

GIVE THANKS FOR THE BOOK OF GALATIANS

Galatians teaches extensively about the ministry of the Holy Spirit in relation to the Christian life. After the Spirit's role in the ministry of adoption (Gl 4:5-6), believers are commanded to "walk by the Spirit" (Gl 5:16), be "led by the Spirit" (Gl 5:18), and "keep in step with the Spirit" (Gl 5:25), as well as "sows to the Spirit" and "reap" the related eternal harvest (Gl 6:8). The moment-by-moment outcome of that kind of sensitivity to the ministry of the Holy Spirit is what is meant by "the fruit of the Spirit" (Gl 5:22-23).

GALATIA

READ AND UNDERSTAND GALATIANS

The Bible is a complete work in which many stories combine to tell one story. As you read the book of Galatians, consider reading the additional passages to discover how the whole of Scripture works together.

GREETING

1 Paul, an apostle — not from men or by man, but by Jesus Christ and God the Father who raised him from the dead — ² and all the brothers who are with me:

To the churches of Galatia.

³ Grace to you and peace from God the Father and our Lord^A Jesus Christ, ⁴ who gave himself for our sins to rescue us from this present evil age, according to the will of our God and Father. ⁵ To him be the glory forever and ever. Amen.

NO OTHER GOSPEL

⁶ I am amazed that you are so quickly turning away from him who called you by the grace of Christ and are turning to a different gospel — ⁷ not that there is another gospel, but there are some who are troubling you and want to distort the gospel of Christ. ⁸ But even if we or an angel from heaven should preach to you a gospel contrary to what we have preached to you, a curse be on him!^B ⁹ As we have said before, I now say again: If anyone is preaching to you a gospel contrary to what you received, a curse be on him!

¹⁰ For am I now trying to persuade people,^C or God? Or am I striving to please people? If I were still trying to please people, I would not be a servant of Christ.

PAUL DEFENDS HIS APOSTLESHIP

¹¹ For I want you to know, brothers and sisters, that the gospel preached by me is not of human origin. ¹² For I did not receive it from a human source and I was not taught it, but it came by a revelation of Jesus Christ.

¹³ For you have heard about my former way of life in Judaism: I intensely persecuted God's church and tried to destroy it. ¹⁴ I advanced in Judaism beyond many contemporaries among my people, because I was extremely zealous for the traditions of my ancestors. ¹⁵ But when God, who from my mother's womb set me apart and called me by his grace, was pleased ¹⁶ to reveal his Son in me, so that I could preach him among the Gentiles, I did not immediately consult with anyone.^D ¹⁷ I did not go up to Jerusalem to those who had become apostles before me; instead I went to Arabia and came back to Damascus.

¹⁸ Then after three years I did go up to Jerusalem to get to know Cephas,^E and I stayed with him fifteen days. ¹⁹ But I didn't see any of the other apostles except James, the Lord's brother. ²⁰ I declare in the sight of God: I am not lying in what I write to you.

²¹ Afterward, I went to the regions of Syria and Cilicia. ²² I remained personally unknown to the Judean churches that are in Christ. ²³ They simply kept hearing: "He who formerly persecuted us now preaches the faith he once tried to destroy." ²⁴ And they glorified God because of me.^F

---

^A1:3 Other mss read *God our Father and the Lord*   ^B1:8 Or *you, let him be condemned*, or *you, let him be condemned to hell*; Gk *anathema*   ^C1:10 Or *win the approval of people*   ^D1:16 Lit *flesh and blood*   ^E1:18 Other mss read *Peter*   ^F1:24 Or *in me*

PAUL DEFENDS HIS GOSPEL AT JERUSALEM

2 Then after fourteen years I went up again to Jerusalem with Barnabas, taking Titus along also. [2] I went up according to a revelation and presented to them the gospel I preach among the Gentiles, but privately to those recognized as leaders. I wanted to be sure I was not running, and had not been running, in vain. [3] But not even Titus, who was with me, was compelled to be circumcised, even though he was a Greek. [4] This matter arose because some false brothers had infiltrated our ranks to spy on the freedom we have in Christ Jesus in order to enslave us. [5] But we did not give up and submit to these people for even a moment, so that the truth of the gospel would be preserved for you.

[6] Now from those recognized as important (what they[A] once were makes no difference to me; God does not show favoritism[B]) — they added nothing to me. [7] On the contrary, they saw that I had been entrusted with the gospel for the uncircumcised, just as Peter was for the circumcised, [8] since the one at work in Peter for an apostleship to the circumcised was also at work in me for the Gentiles. [9] When James, Cephas,[C] and John — those recognized as pillars — acknowledged the grace that had been given to me, they gave the right hand of fellowship to me and Barnabas, agreeing that we should go to the Gentiles and they to the circumcised. [10] They asked only that we would remember the poor, which I had made every effort to do.

FREEDOM FROM THE LAW

[11] But when Cephas[C] came to Antioch, I opposed him to his face because he stood condemned.[D] [12] For he regularly ate with the Gentiles before certain men came from James. However, when they came, he withdrew and separated himself, because he feared those from the circumcision party. [13] Then the rest of the Jews joined his hypocrisy, so that even Barnabas was led astray by their hypocrisy. [14] But when I saw that they were deviating from the truth of the gospel, I told Cephas[C] in front of everyone, "If you, who are a Jew, live like a Gentile and not like a Jew, how can you compel Gentiles to live like Jews?"[E]

[15] We are Jews by birth and not "Gentile sinners," [16] and yet because we know that a person is not justified by the works of the law but by faith in Jesus Christ,[F] even we ourselves have believed in Christ Jesus. This was so that we might be justified by faith in Christ[G] and not by the works of the law, because by the works of the law no human being will[H] be justified. [17] But if we ourselves are also found to be "sinners" while seeking to be justified by Christ, is Christ then a promoter[I] of sin? Absolutely not! [18] If I rebuild those things that I tore down, I show myself to be a lawbreaker. [19] For through the law I died to the law, so that I might live for God. [20] I have been crucified with Christ, and I no longer live, but Christ lives in me. The life I now live in the body,[J] I live by faith in the Son of God, who loved me and

---

[A]2:6 Lit the recognized ones   [B]2:6 Or God is not a respecter of persons; lit God does not receive the face of man   [C]2:9,11,14 Other mss read Peter   [D]2:11 Or he was in the wrong   [E]2:14 Some translations continue the quotation through v. 16 or v. 21.   [F]2:16 Or by the faithfulness of Jesus Christ   [G]2:16 Or by the faithfulness of Christ   [H]2:16 Lit law all flesh will not   [I]2:17 Or servant   [J]2:20 Lit flesh

FREEDOM FROM THE LAW

GALATIANS 2:11-21; ACTS 15; EPHESIANS 2:8-9

We call it the Goodbye Tour. I can't leave anywhere—a party, a church gathering, even a workday—until I've told everyone goodbye. I can't help it. I need you to know I love you. Okay, and yes, I need to know you love me too.

I could list more of these "just in case" habits in my life. They are those things I do when I think I know something, but the unbelief flickers bright enough to push me to do a little bit more, to be double sure I'm in the clear. It's harmless enough when we're talking about the Goodbye Tour. But "just in case" has sobering implications when it comes to my faith in Christ and His gospel.

Here in Galatians, Paul is really fired up about protecting "the truth of the gospel" (a phrase he uses repeatedly—see Galatians 2:5,14) and really fed up with those preaching a different gospel. In this passage, Paul calls Peter out for promoting a false gospel. Yes, that Peter. Disciple of Christ, one of the Twelve, also known as Cephas.

Peter had distanced himself from the Gentiles in the presence of his ethnically Jewish buddies, insisting the Gentiles act like Jews in order to be brought into the family of God. Peter and others with him began reverting to the belief that circumcision was still required for salvation (a belief the Jerusalem Council would refute in Acts 15). This, Paul pointed out, was ridiculous, since not even the most righteous Jew was saved by works (Gl 2:16).

Grace through faith in Jesus: this is the true gospel.

Peter knew firsthand you can't walk on water when you're sinking in doubt. He knew you can't believe Jesus with all your heart when you're denying Him with your lips. Peter wanted to have an unwavering faith—you can almost hear it in his voice when Jesus so gently restores him in John 21:15-17—but he struggled.

Isn't that exactly what we do? What we all do? We want to believe the gospel is truly unearned grace, but unbelief creeps in and we do a little something in an attempt to earn our salvation . . . just in case.

But the law does not free us. Christ frees us.

When God has declared us righteous in Christ, we need not ask, "But are you sure we're okay?" His promise is sure! Rather than turning to our "doing" to relieve our doubt, we turn back to Him, in confession, repentance, and worship. After all, if Christ's righteousness covers all our sin—and it truly does!—then it also covers our sin of unbelief.

"For if righteousness comes through the law, then Christ died for nothing."

GALATIANS 2:21

---

gave himself for me. [21] I do not set aside the grace of God, for if righteousness comes through the law, then Christ died for nothing.

JUSTIFICATION THROUGH FAITH

3 You foolish Galatians! Who has cast a spell on you,[A] before whose eyes Jesus Christ was publicly portrayed[B] as crucified? [2] I only want to learn this from you: Did you receive the Spirit by the works of the law or by believing what you heard?[C] [3] Are you so foolish? After beginning by the Spirit, are you now finishing by the flesh? [4] Did you experience[D] so much for nothing — if in fact it was for nothing? [5] So then, does God give you the Spirit and work miracles among you by your doing the works of the law? Or is it by believing what you heard — [6] just like Abraham who **believed God, and it was credited to him for righteousness?**[E]

[7] You know, then, that those who have faith, these are Abraham's sons. [8] Now the Scripture saw in advance that God would justify the Gentiles by faith and proclaimed the gospel ahead of time to Abraham, saying, **All the nations**[F] **will be blessed through you.**[G] [9] Consequently those who have faith are blessed with Abraham, who had faith.[H]

LAW AND PROMISE

[10] For all who rely on the works of the law are under a curse, because it is written, **Everyone who does not do everything written in the book of the law is cursed.**[I] [11] Now it is clear that no one is justified before God by the law, because **the righteous will live by faith.**[J] [12] But the law is not based on faith; instead, **the one who does these things will live by them.**[K] [13] Christ redeemed us from the curse of the law by becoming a curse for us, because it is written, **Cursed is everyone who is hung on a tree.**[L] [14] The purpose was that the blessing of Abraham would come to the Gentiles by Christ Jesus, so that we could receive the promised Spirit through faith.

[15] Brothers and sisters, I'm using a human illustration. No one sets aside or makes additions to a validated human will.[M] [16] Now the promises were spoken to Abraham and to his seed. He does not say "and to seeds," as though referring to many, but referring to one, **and to your seed,**[N] who is Christ. [17] My point is this: The law, which came 430 years later, does not invalidate a covenant previously established by God[O] and thus cancel the promise. [18] For if the inheritance is based on the law, it is no longer based on the promise; but God has graciously given it to Abraham through the promise.

THE PURPOSE OF THE LAW

[19] Why then was the law given? It was added for the sake of transgressions[P] until the Seed to whom the promise was made would come. The law was put into effect through angels by means of a mediator. [20] Now a mediator is not just for one person alone, but God is one. [21] Is the law therefore contrary to

---

[A]3:1 Other mss add *not to obey the truth*   [B]3:1 Other mss add *among you*
[C]3:2 Lit *hearing with faith,* also in v. 5   [D]3:4 Or *suffer*   [E]3:6 Gn 15:6
[F]3:8 Or *Gentiles*   [G]3:8 Gn 12:3; 18:18   [H]3:9 Or *with believing Abraham*
[I]3:10 Dt 27:26   [J]3:11 Hab 2:4   [K]3:12 Lv 18:5   [L]3:13 Dt 21:23   [M]3:15 Or
a human covenant that has been ratified   [N]3:16 Gn 12:7; 13:15; 17:8; 24:7
[O]3:17 Other mss add *in Christ*   [P]3:19 Or *because of transgressions*

God's promises? Absolutely not! For if the law had been granted with the ability to give life, then righteousness would certainly be on the basis of the law. ²² But the Scripture imprisoned everything under sin's power,^ so that the promise might be given on the basis of faith in Jesus Christ to those who believe. ²³ Before this faith came, we were confined under the law, imprisoned until the coming faith was revealed. ²⁴ The law, then, was our guardian until Christ, so that we could be justified by faith. ²⁵ But since that faith has come, we are no longer under a guardian, ²⁶ for through faith you are all sons of God in Christ Jesus.

SONS AND HEIRS

²⁷ For those of you who were baptized into Christ have been clothed with Christ. ²⁸ There is no Jew or Greek, slave or free, male and female; since you are all one in Christ Jesus. ²⁹ And if you belong to Christ, then you are Abraham's seed, heirs according to the promise. ¹ Now I say that as long as **4** the heir is a child, he differs in no way from a slave, though he is the owner of everything. ² Instead, he is under guardians and trustees until the time set by his father. ³ In the same way we also, when we were children, were in slavery under the elements ᴮ of the world. ⁴ When the time came to completion, God sent his Son, born of a woman, born under the law, ⁵ to redeem those under the law, so that we might receive adoption as sons. ⁶ And because you are sons, God sent the Spirit of his Son into our ᶜ hearts, crying, "*Abba,*ᴰ Father!"⁷ So you are no longer a slave but a son, and if a son, then God has made you an heir.

PAUL'S CONCERN FOR THE GALATIANS

⁸ But in the past, since you didn't know God, you were enslaved to things ᴱ that by nature are not gods. ⁹ But now, since you know God, or rather have become known by God, how can you turn back again to the weak and worthless elements? Do you want to be enslaved to them all over again? ¹⁰ You are observing special days, months, seasons, and years. ¹¹ I am fearful for you, that perhaps my labor for you has been wasted.

¹² I beg you, brothers and sisters: Become like me, for I also became like you. You have not wronged me; ¹³ you know ᶠ that previously I preached the gospel to you because of a weakness of the flesh. ¹⁴ You did not despise or reject me though my physical condition was a trial for you. ᴳ On the contrary, you received me as an angel of God, as Christ Jesus himself.

¹⁵ Where, then, is your blessing? For I testify to you that, if possible, you would have torn out your eyes and given them to me. ¹⁶ So then, have I become your enemy because I told you the truth? ¹⁷ They court you eagerly, but not for good. They want to exclude you from me, so that you would pursue them. ¹⁸ But it is always good to be pursued ᴴ in a good manner — and not just when I am with you. ¹⁹ My children, I am again suffering labor pains for you until Christ is formed in you. ²⁰ I would like to be with

---

^3:22 Lit *under sin*   ᴮ4:3 Or *spirits,* or *principles*   ᶜ4:6 Other mss read *your*   ᴰ4:6 Aramaic for *father*   ᴱ4:8 Or *beings*   ᶠ4:12-13 Or ¹² *Become like I am, because I — inasmuch as you are brothers and sisters — am not requesting anything of you. You wronged me.* ¹³ *You know*   ᴳ4:14 Other mss read *me*   ᴴ4:18 Lit *zealously courted* you right now and change my tone of voice, because I don't know what to do about you.

SARAH AND HAGAR: TWO COVENANTS

²¹ Tell me, you who want to be under the law, don't you hear the law? ²² For it is written that Abraham had two sons, one by a slave and the other by a free woman. ²³ But the one by the slave was born as a result of the flesh, while the one by the free woman was born through promise. ²⁴ These things are being taken figuratively, for the women represent two covenants. One is from Mount Sinai and bears children into slavery — this is Hagar. ²⁵ Now Hagar represents Mount Sinai in Arabia and corresponds to the present Jerusalem, for she is in slavery with her children. ²⁶ But the Jerusalem above is free, and she is our mother. ²⁷ For it is written,

> Rejoice, childless woman,
> unable to give birth.
> Burst into song and shout,
> you who are not in labor,
> for the children of the desolate woman will be many,
> more numerous than those
> of the woman who has a husband.ᴬ

²⁸ Now you too, brothers and sisters, like Isaac, are children of promise. ²⁹ But just as then the child born as a result of the flesh persecuted the one born as a result of the Spirit, so also now. ³⁰ But what does the Scripture say? **"Drive out the slave and her son, for the son of the slave will never be a coheir with the son of the free woman."**ᴮ ³¹ Therefore, brothers and sisters, we are not children of a slave but of the free woman.

FREEDOM OF THE CHRISTIAN

5 For freedom, Christ set us free. Stand firm then and don't submit again to a yoke of slavery. ² Take note! I, Paul, am telling you that if you get yourselves circumcised, Christ will not benefit you at all. ³ Again I testify to every man who gets himself circumcised that he is obligated to do the entire law. ⁴ You who are trying to be justified by the law are alienated from Christ; you have fallen from grace. ⁵ For we eagerly await through the Spirit, by faith, the hope of righteousness. ⁶ For in Christ Jesus neither circumcision nor uncircumcision accomplishes anything; what matters is faith working through love.

⁷ You were running well. Who prevented you from being persuaded regarding the truth?ᶜ ⁸ This persuasion does not come from the one who calls you. ⁹ A little leavenᴰ leavens the whole batch of dough. ¹⁰ I myself am persuaded in the Lord you will not accept any other view. But whoever it is that is confusing you will pay the penalty. ¹¹ Now brothers and sisters, if I still preach circumcision, why am I still persecuted? In that case the offense of the cross has been abolished. ¹² I wish those who are disturbing you might also let themselves be mutilated!

¹³ For you were called to be free, brothers and sisters; only don't use this freedom as an opportunityᴱ for the flesh, but serve one another through

---

ᴬ4:27 Is 54:1   ᴮ4:30 Gn 21:10   ᶜ5:7 Or *obeying the truth*   ᴰ5:9 Or *yeast*
ᴱ5:13 Lit *a pretext;* a military term for abuse of position

THE SPIRIT'S FRUIT

GALATIANS 5:16-26; ROMANS 7:14-19; ROMANS 8:5-7

Haircut days are some of the best days.

I love sitting in the chair, making small talk with my stylist, knowing that my hair will be better for the time I spent with her. I have no problem showing up with a dirty bun piled high on my head, no issue relinquishing creative control while we chat. I am perfectly willing to come as I am and let her do the work. We have a relationship, she and I, and I trust her to do magical things with my wayward locks.

Since she is the professional and I am not, barging into our appointment and taking over the scissors would be a bad move on my part. Trying to commandeer the process would not only be silly, it would have unsightly consequences. (My one attempt at a self bang-trim was proof of this.)

As I read this passage in Galatians, it's clear that the me who seeks to bear fruit for God's kingdom could stand to take a few tips from the me who sits in the salon chair. **I don't want to insist on creating my own goodness; I want to learn the art of trusting the only One who is truly good.**

The Apostle Paul offers a clear contrast between our rotten, self-made fruit and the good, God-made fruit of the Holy Spirit: "Now the works of the flesh are obvious . . ." (insert long list of rotten fruit here). "But the fruit of the Spirit is love, joy, peace, patience, kindness, goodness, faithfulness, gentleness, and self-control. The law is not against such things" (Gl 5:19,22).

Until we repent of our sin and lean wholly on the perfection of Jesus, we remain stuck in a cycle of rotten fruit, powerless to break free. Even our "good" works cannot gain us entrance to the kingdom of God. But when we call out to Christ for salvation, we receive mercy, forgiveness, and freedom—and we receive the Holy Spirit, a gift promised by Christ Himself.

In John 14:15, Jesus issued His disciples a tall yet serious order: "If you love me, you will keep my commands." Easier said than done, they may have thought. But Jesus didn't stop there; He explained how they are to keep His commands. "I will ask the Father, and he will give you another Counselor to be with you forever" (Jn 14:16). This was more than a to-do—this was His Spirit at work in them!

The fruit of the Spirit is not borne of our best efforts. It is borne only of the Spirit. Only by abiding in Him—resting in His goodness and trusting Him to do the hard work of redemption on our behalf—can we bear fruit.

Let's repent of every drop of goodness we've tried to squeeze out on our own, relying instead on the perfect life and love of Christ.

love. ¹⁴ For the whole law is fulfilled in one statement: **Love your neighbor as yourself.**ᴬ ¹⁵ But if you bite and devour one another, watch out, or you will be consumed by one another.

THE SPIRIT VERSUS THE FLESH

¹⁶ I say then, walk by the Spirit and you will certainly not carry out the desire of the flesh. ¹⁷ For the flesh desires what is against the Spirit, and the Spirit desires what is against the flesh; these are opposed to each other, so that you don't do what you want. ¹⁸ But if you are led by the Spirit, you are not under the law.

¹⁹ Now the works of the flesh are obvious:ᴮ sexual immorality, moral impurity, promiscuity, ²⁰ idolatry, sorcery, hatreds, strife, jealousy, outbursts of anger, selfish ambitions, dissensions, factions, ²¹ envy,ᶜ drunkenness, carousing, and anything similar. I am warning you about these things — as I warned you before — that those who practice such things will not inherit the kingdom of God.

²² But the fruit of the Spirit is love, joy, peace, patience, kindness, goodness, faithfulness, ²³ gentleness, and self-control. The law is not against such things.ᴰ ²⁴ Now those who belong to Christ Jesus have crucified the flesh with its passions and desires. ²⁵ If we live by the Spirit, let us also keep in step with the Spirit. ²⁶ Let us not become conceited, provoking one another, envying one another.

CARRY ONE ANOTHER'S BURDENS

6 Brothers and sisters, if someone is overtaken in any wrongdoing, you who are spiritual, restore such a person with a gentle spirit,ᴱ watching out for yourselves so that you also won't be tempted. ² Carry one another's burdens; in this way you will fulfill the law of Christ. ³ For if anyone considers himself to be something when he is nothing, he deceives himself. ⁴ Let each person examine his own work, and then he can take pride in himself alone, and not compare himself with someone else. ⁵ For each person will have to carry his own load.

⁶ Let the one who is taught the word share all his good things with the teacher. ⁷ Don't be deceived: God is not mocked. For whatever a person sows he will also reap, ⁸ because the one who sows to his flesh will reap destruction from the flesh, but the one who sows to the Spirit will reap eternal life from the Spirit. ⁹ Let us not get tired of doing good, for we will reap at the proper time if we don't give up. ¹⁰ Therefore, as we have opportunity, let us work for the good of all, especially for those who belong to the household of faith.

CONCLUDING EXHORTATION

¹¹ Look at what large letters I use as I write to you in my own handwriting. ¹² Those who want to make a good impression in the flesh are the ones who would compel you to be circumcised — but only to avoid being persecuted for the cross of Christ. ¹³ For even the circumcised don't keep the law themselves, and yet they want you to be circumcised in order to boast about your flesh. ¹⁴ But as for me, I will never boast about anything except the cross of

---

ᴬ5:14 Lv 19:18   ᴮ5:19 Other mss add *adultery,*   ᶜ5:21 Other mss add *murders,*
ᴰ5:23 Or *Against such things there is no law*   ᴱ6:1 Or *with the Spirit of gentleness*

our Lord Jesus Christ. The world has been crucified to me through the cross, and I to the world. [15] For[A] both circumcision and uncircumcision mean nothing; what matters instead is a new creation. [16] May peace come to all those who follow this standard, and mercy even to the Israel of God![B]

[17] From now on, let no one cause me trouble, because I bear on my body the marks of Jesus. [18] Brothers and sisters, the grace of our Lord Jesus Christ be with your spirit. Amen.

[A]6:15 Other mss add *in Christ Jesus*   [B]6:16 Or *And for those who follow this standard, may peace and mercy be upon them, even upon the Israel of God,* or *And as many who will follow this standard, peace be upon them and mercy even upon the Israel of God.*

you are
saved by
grace
through
Faith

ephesians

 For you are saved by grace through faith, and this is not from yourselves; it is God's gift — not from works, so that no one can boast. **2:8-9**

ON THE TIMELINE Paul, the clearly identified author of Ephesians (Eph 1:1), wrote the letter while in prison (Eph 3:1; 4:1; 6:20). There is disagreement concerning whether he was imprisoned in Caesarea (Ac 24:22) or Rome (Ac 28:30) at the time, but tradition suggests Paul wrote the letter from Rome around AD 60–61. This would have been while Paul was under house arrest awaiting his appeal before Caesar (Ac 28:23-31). Paul most likely wrote Philippians, Colossians and Philemon during the same imprisonment.

A LITTLE BACKGROUND Relatively little is known about the recipients of Ephesians. In fact, some important and early manuscripts do not contain the words "at Ephesus" (Eph 1:1). The letter was carried to its destination by Tychicus, who in Ephesians 6:21 and Colossians 4:7 is identified as Paul's messenger. Since Paul notes in both letters that Tychicus would inform the churches of Paul's situation, we can assume the letters to the Ephesians and the Colossians were delivered at the same time.

MESSAGE & PURPOSE The overall theme of Ephesians is the unity of the Church in Christ, through the power of the Spirit. The doctrine of the new creation corrects the misguided view that God accepts the Jew and rejects the Gentile. Paul teaches that this distinction was abolished at Christ's sacrificial death, and no hindrance remains to reuniting all humanity as the people of God, with Christ as the head (Eph 1:22-23). The new body, the Church, has been endowed with the power of the Holy Spirit to enable the members to live out their new lives (Eph 1:3–2:10) and put into practice Christ's standards (Eph 4:1–6:9).

GIVE THANKS FOR THE BOOK OF EPHESIANS

Paul's letter to the Ephesians is an anthem to the sovereign grace of God displayed toward sinners in Christ. It contains some of the worst news ("you were dead in your trespasses and sins," Eph 2:1) and best news ("but God . . . made us alive with Christ," Eph 2:4-5) in all of Scripture. In view of this grace, Paul calls believers to "live worthy of the calling" (Eph 4:1) we have received.

EPHESUS AND
SURROUNDING CITIES

READ AND UNDERSTAND EPHESIANS

The Bible is a complete work in which many stories combine to tell one story. As you read the book of Ephesians, consider reading the additional passages to discover how the whole of Scripture works together.

GREETING

1 Paul, an apostle of Christ Jesus by God's will:
To the faithful saints in Christ Jesus[A] at Ephesus.[B]

[2] Grace to you and peace from God our Father and the Lord Jesus Christ.

GOD'S RICH BLESSINGS

[3] Blessed is the God and Father of our Lord Jesus Christ, who has blessed us with every spiritual blessing in the heavens in Christ. [4] For he chose us in him, before the foundation of the world, to be holy and blameless in love before him.[C] [5] He predestined us to be adopted as sons through Jesus Christ for himself, according to the good pleasure of his will, [6] to the praise of his glorious grace that he lavished on us in the Beloved One.

[7] In him we have redemption through his blood, the forgiveness of our trespasses, according to the riches of his grace [8] that he richly poured out on us with all wisdom and understanding.[D] [9] He made known to us the mystery of his will, according to his good pleasure that he purposed in Christ [10] as a plan for the right time[E] — to bring everything together in Christ, both things in heaven and things on earth in him.

[11] In him we have also received an inheritance,[F] because we were predestined according to the plan of the one who works out everything in agreement with the purpose of his will, [12] so that we who had already put our hope in Christ might bring praise to his glory.

[13] In him you also were sealed with the promised Holy Spirit when you heard the word of truth, the gospel of your salvation, and when you believed. [14] The Holy Spirit is the down payment of our inheritance, until the redemption of the possession, to the praise of his glory.

PRAYER FOR SPIRITUAL INSIGHT

[15] This is why, since I heard about your faith in the Lord Jesus and your love for all the saints, [16] I never stop giving thanks for you as I remember you in my prayers. [17] I pray that the God of our Lord Jesus Christ, the glorious Father,[G] would give you the Spirit[H] of wisdom and revelation in the knowledge of him. [18] I pray that the eyes of your heart may be enlightened so that you may know what is the hope of his calling, what is the wealth of his glorious inheritance in the saints, [19] and what is the immeasurable greatness of his power toward us who believe, according to the mighty working of his strength.

GOD'S POWER IN CHRIST

[20] He exercised this power in Christ by raising him from the dead and seating him at his right hand in the heavens — [21] far above every ruler and authority, power and dominion, and every title given,[I] not only in this age but also in the one to come. [22] And **he subjected everything under his feet**[J] and appointed him[K] as head over everything for the church, [23] which is his body, the fullness of the one who fills all things in every way.

[A] 1:1 Or *to the saints, the believers in Christ Jesus* [B] 1:1 Other mss omit *at Ephesus* [C] 1:4 Or *in his sight. In love* [D] 1:8 Or *on us. With all wisdom and understanding* [E] 1:10 Or *the fulfillment of times* [F] 1:11 Or *In him we are also an inheritance,* [G] 1:17 Or *the Father of glory* [H] 1:17 Or *a spirit* [I] 1:21 Lit *every name named* [J] 1:22 Ps 8:6 [K] 1:22 Lit *gave him*

FROM DEATH TO LIFE

2 And you were dead in your trespasses and sins ² in which you previously lived according to the ways of this world, according to the ruler of the power of the air, the spirit now working in the disobedient.ᴬ ³ We too all previously lived among them in our fleshly desires, carrying out the inclinations of our flesh and thoughts, and we were by nature children under wrath as the others were also. ⁴ But God, who is rich in mercy, because of his great love that he had for us,ᴮ ⁵ made us alive with Christ even though we were dead in trespasses. You are saved by grace! ⁶ He also raised us up with him and seated us with him in the heavens in Christ Jesus, ⁷ so that in the coming ages he might display the immeasurable riches of his grace through his kindness to us in Christ Jesus. ⁸ For you are saved by grace through faith, and this is not from yourselves; it is God's gift — ⁹ not from works, so that no one can boast. ¹⁰ For we are his workmanship, created in Christ Jesus for good works, which God prepared ahead of time for us to do.

UNITY IN CHRIST

¹¹ So then, remember that at one time you were Gentiles in the flesh — called "the uncircumcised" by those called "the circumcised," which is done in the flesh by human hands. ¹² At that time you were without Christ, excluded from the citizenship of Israel, and foreigners to the covenants of promise, without hope and without God in the world. ¹³ But now in Christ Jesus, you who were far away have been brought near by the blood of Christ. ¹⁴ For he is our peace, who made both groups one and tore down the dividing wall of hostility. In his flesh, ¹⁵ he made of no effect the law consisting of commands and expressed in regulations, so that he might create in himself one new man from the two, resulting in peace. ¹⁶ He did this so that he might reconcile both to God in one body through the cross by which he put the hostility to death.ᶜ ¹⁷ He came and proclaimed the good news of peace to you who were far away and peace to those who were near. ¹⁸ For through him we both have access in one Spirit to the Father. ¹⁹ So then you are no longer foreigners and strangers, but fellow citizens with the saints, and members of God's household, ²⁰ built on the foundation of the apostles and prophets, with Christ Jesus himself as the cornerstone. ²¹ In him the whole building, being put together, grows into a holy temple in the Lord. ²² In him you are also being built together for God's dwelling in the Spirit.

PAUL'S MINISTRY TO THE GENTILES

3 For this reason, I, Paul, the prisoner of Christ Jesus on behalf of you Gentiles — ² you have heard, haven't you, about the administration of God's grace that he gave to me for you? ³ The mystery was made known to me by revelation, as I have briefly written above. ⁴ By reading this you are able to understand my insight into the mystery of Christ. ⁵ This was not made known to peopleᴰ in other generations as it is now revealed to his holy apostles and prophets by the Spirit: ⁶ The Gentiles are coheirs, members of the same body, and partners in the promise in Christ Jesus through the gospel.

ᴬ2:2 Lit *sons of disobedience*   ᴮ2:4 Lit *love with which he loved us*   ᶜ2:16 Or *death in himself*   ᴰ3:5 Lit *to the sons of men*

WALK IN THEM

EPHESIANS 2:1-10; MATTHEW 20:27-28; HEBREWS 12:2

Maybe the secret to doing big things for the kingdom is in making peace with this sentence: "I can't do this!"

Since giving my life to Christ, I've said those words a few billion times.

When Scripture compelled me to teach other women God's Word, my first thought was, "I can't do this!" When I left my predictable job for the unpredictability of a writing career, I spent years (yes, years) in tears, thinking, "I can't do this!" When I decided to see my own children as a mission field, the weight of that made me groan, "I can't do this!"

To even put these words on this page, to try to say something worthy of the remarkable Word of God, makes me want to throw my hands up and scream, "I can't do this!"

Jesus calls His followers to a life of selfless, sacrificial service (Mt 20:27-28), but our good works are not built on elbow grease and effort. They are the byproduct of dependence on our Savior. As we go about our kingdom work, we desperately need a grasp on this truth:

"For we are his workmanship, created in Christ Jesus for good works, which God prepared ahead of time for us to do" (Eph 2:10).

When we live fruitful lives, freely serving others, we are in the sweet spot God designed us for—but pay close attention to Who does all the heavy lifting.

". . . which God prepared ahead of time for us to do."

All the prep work has been done. The heart change necessary to pry our eyes off ourselves and direct them to see the needs of others is His specialty. The fruit of our labors is not our responsibility; it's His (Jn 15:1-4). What's our job? To walk on the path God has paved for us, "keeping our eyes on Jesus, the source and perfecter of our faith" (Heb 12:2).

If we rewind a couple of verses back in the passage, we find the beauty of the gospel on full display:

"For you are saved by grace through faith, and this is not from yourselves; it is God's gift—not from works, so that no one can boast."

EPHESIANS 2:8-9

Salvation is a gift given freely to us by God. Our good works are a fruit of that gift, but never the cause of it. **Even our good works are God's gift to us.**

In the face of the work God calls us to, our inadequacy tees us up to remember and cling to the gospel of Jesus. Instead of insisting, "I can't do this," let's declare these truths instead:

God made me.

He has prepared this good work in advance for me.

By His grace I will walk in obedience, one step at a time.

⁷ I was made a servant of this gospel by the gift of God's grace that was given to me by the working of his power.

⁸ This grace was given to me — the least of all the saints — to proclaim to the Gentiles the incalculable riches of Christ, ⁹ and to shed light for all about the administration of the mystery hidden for ages in God who created all things. ¹⁰ This is so that God's multi-faceted wisdom may now be made known through the church to the rulers and authorities in the heavens. ¹¹ This is according to his eternal purpose accomplished in Christ Jesus our Lord. ¹² In him we have boldness and confident access through faith in him.ᴬ ¹³ So then I ask you not to be discouraged over my afflictions on your behalf, for they are your glory.

PRAYER FOR SPIRITUAL POWER

¹⁴ For this reason I kneel before the Fatherᴮ ¹⁵ from whom every family in heaven and on earth is named. ¹⁶ I pray that he may grant you, according to the riches of his glory, to be strengthened with power in your inner being through his Spirit, ¹⁷ and that Christ may dwell in your hearts through faith. I pray that you, being rooted and firmly established in love, ¹⁸ may be able to comprehend with all the saints what is the length and width, height and depth of God's love, ¹⁹ and to know Christ's love that surpasses knowledge, so that you may be filled with all the fullness of God.

²⁰ Now to him who is able to do above and beyond all that we ask or think according to the power that works in us — ²¹ to him be glory in the church and in Christ Jesus to all generations, forever and ever. Amen.

UNITY AND DIVERSITY IN THE BODY OF CHRIST

4 Therefore I, the prisoner in the Lord, urge you to live worthy of the calling you have received, ² with all humility and gentleness, with patience, bearing with one another in love, ³ making every effort to keep the unity of the Spirit through the bond of peace. ⁴ There is one body and one Spirit — just as you were called to one hopeᶜ at your calling — ⁵ one Lord, one faith, one baptism, ⁶ one God and Father of all, who is above all and through all and in all.

⁷ Now grace was given to each one of us according to the measure of Christ's gift. ⁸ For it says:

When he ascended on high,
he took the captives captive;
he gave gifts to people.ᴰ

⁹ But what does "he ascended" mean except that heᴱ also descended to the lower parts of the earth?ᶠ ¹⁰ The one who descended is also the one who ascended far above all the heavens, to fill all things. ¹¹ And he himself gave some to be apostles, some prophets, some evangelists, some pastors and teachers, ¹² equipping the saints for the work of ministry, to build up the body of Christ, ¹³ until we all reach unity in the faith and in the knowledge of God's Son, growing into maturity with a stature measured by Christ's fullness. ¹⁴ Then we will no longer be little children, tossed by the waves and blown around

---

ᴬ3:12 Or through his faithfulness   ᴮ3:14 Other mss add of our Lord Jesus Christ   ᶜ4:4 Lit called in one hope   ᴰ4:8 Ps 68:18   ᴱ4:9 Other mss add first   ᶠ4:9 Or the lower parts, namely, the earth by every wind of teaching, by human cunning with cleverness in the techniques of deceit. [15] But speaking the truth in love, let us grow in every way into him who is the head — Christ. [16] From him the whole body, fitted and knit together by every supporting ligament, promotes the growth of the body for building up itself in love by the proper working of each individual part.

LIVING THE NEW LIFE

[17] Therefore, I say this and testify in the Lord: You should no longer live as the Gentiles live, in the futility of their thoughts. [18] They are darkened in their understanding, excluded from the life of God, because of the ignorance that is in them and because [A] of the hardness of their hearts. [19] They became callous and gave themselves over to promiscuity for the practice of every kind of impurity with a desire for more and more. [B]

[20] But that is not how you came to know Christ, [21] assuming you heard about him and were taught by him, as the truth is in Jesus, [22] to take off [C] your former way of life, the old self that is corrupted by deceitful desires, [23] to be renewed [D] in the spirit of your minds, [24] and to put on [E] the new self, the one created according to God's likeness in righteousness and purity of the truth.

[25] Therefore, putting away lying, **speak the truth, each one to his neighbor,** [F] because we are members of one another. [26] **Be angry and do not sin.** [G] Don't let the sun go down on your anger, [27] and don't give the devil an opportunity. [28] Let the thief no longer steal. Instead, he is to do honest work with his own hands, so that he has something to share with anyone in need. [29] No foul language should come from your mouth, but only what is good for building up someone in need, [H] so that it gives grace to those who hear. [30] And don't grieve God's Holy Spirit. You were sealed by him [I] for the day of redemption. [31] Let all bitterness, anger and wrath, shouting and slander be removed from you, along with all malice. [32] And be kind and compassionate to one another, forgiving one another, just as God also forgave you [J] in Christ.

5 Therefore, be imitators of God, as dearly loved children, [2] and walk in love, as Christ also loved us and gave himself for us, a sacrificial and fragrant offering to God. [3] But sexual immorality and any impurity or greed should not even be heard of [K] among you, as is proper for saints. [4] Obscene and foolish talking or crude joking are not suitable, but rather giving thanks. [5] For know and recognize this: Every sexually immoral or impure or greedy person, who is an idolater, does not have an inheritance in the kingdom of Christ and of God.

LIGHT VERSUS DARKNESS

[6] Let no one deceive you with empty arguments, for God's wrath is coming on the disobedient [L] because of these things. [7] Therefore, do not become their partners. [8] For you were once darkness, but now you are light in the Lord. Live as children of light — [9] for the fruit of the light [M] consists of all

---

[A] 4:18 Or *in them because* [B] 4:19 Lit *with greediness* [C] 4:21-22 Or *Jesus. This means: take off* (as a command) [D] 4:22-23 Or *desires; renew* (as a command) [E] 4:23-24 Or *minds; and put on* (as a command) [F] 4:25 Zch 8:16 [G] 4:26 Ps 4:4 [H] 4:29 Lit *for the building up of the need* [I] 4:30 Or *Spirit, by whom you were sealed* [J] 4:32 Other mss read *us* [K] 5:3 Or *be named* [L] 5:6 Lit *sons of disobedience* [M] 5:9 Other mss read *fruit of the Spirit* goodness, righteousness, and truth — [10] testing what is pleasing to the Lord. [11] Don't participate in the fruitless works of darkness, but instead expose them. [12] For it is shameful even to mention what is done by them in secret. [13] Everything exposed by the light is made visible, [14] for what makes everything visible is light. Therefore it is said:

> Get up, sleeper, and rise up from the dead,
> and Christ will shine on you.

CONSISTENCY IN THE CHRISTIAN LIFE

[15] Pay careful attention, then, to how you live — not as unwise people but as wise — [16] making the most of the time,[A] because the days are evil. [17] So don't be foolish, but understand what the Lord's will is. [18] And don't get drunk with wine, which leads to reckless living, but be filled by the Spirit: [19] speaking to one another in psalms, hymns, and spiritual songs, singing and making music with your heart to the Lord, [20] giving thanks always for everything to God the Father in the name of our Lord Jesus Christ, [21] submitting to one another in the fear of Christ.

WIVES AND HUSBANDS

[22] Wives, submit[B] to your husbands as to the Lord, [23] because the husband is the head of the wife as Christ is the head of the church. He is the Savior of the body. [24] Now as the church submits to Christ, so also wives are to submit to their husbands in everything. [25] Husbands, love your wives, just as Christ loved the church and gave himself for her [26] to make her holy, cleansing[C] her with the washing of water by the word. [27] He did this to present the church to himself in splendor, without spot or wrinkle or anything like that, but holy and blameless. [28] In the same way, husbands are to love their wives as their own bodies. He who loves his wife loves himself. [29] For no one ever hates his own flesh but provides and cares for it, just as Christ does for the church, [30] since we are members of his body.[D] [31] **For this reason a man will leave his father and mother and be joined to his wife, and the two will become one flesh.**[E] [32] This mystery is profound, but I am talking about Christ and the church. [33] To sum up, each one of you is to love his wife as himself, and the wife is to respect her husband.

CHILDREN AND PARENTS

6 Children, obey your parents in the Lord, because this is right. [2] **Honor your father and mother**, which is the first commandment with a promise, [3] **so that it may go well with you and that you may have a long life in the land.**[F,G] [4] Fathers, don't stir up anger in your children, but bring them up in the training and instruction of the Lord.

SLAVES AND MASTERS

[5] Slaves, obey your human[H] masters with fear and trembling, in the sincerity of your heart, as you would Christ. [6] Don't work only while being watched, as people-pleasers, but as slaves of Christ, do God's will from your heart.

[A] 5:16 Lit *buying back the time* [B] 5:22 Other mss omit *submit* [C] 5:26 Or *having cleansed* [D] 5:30 Other mss add *and of his flesh and of his bones* [E] 5:31 Gn 2:24 [F] 6:3 Or *life on the earth* [G] 6:2-3 Ex 20:12 [H] 6:5 Lit *according to the flesh*

READY FOR BATTLE

EPHESIANS 6:10-24; EPHESIANS 4:22-24; REVELATION 12:7-12

You and I could gather around our Bibles today like we were kids in Sunday school, felt board placed front and center. We'd label the felt man with his felt armor, giving each other a pep talk about putting on the full armor of God. The conversation would be worthwhile, but I'm wondering if we could dig a little deeper together?

What is this spiritual battle Paul has us suiting up for in the first place? To find the answer, let's hop over to Revelation 12.

The text describes a dramatic event where "the ancient serpent, who is called the devil and Satan, the one who deceives the whole world" is thrown out of heaven with all his angels (Rv 12:9). We know how the story ends: death and Satan are conquered by the perfect sacrifice of Jesus, the Lamb, on the cross (Amen!). But right now, the enemy is on this earth and he knows his time is limited (Rv 12:12).

Paul entreated the Ephesians to dress for battle because the battle is real and ongoing. The evil one has been defeated, but he's not going down without a fight. He lives to destroy goodness and steal the true life that only Christ can bring (Jn 10:10).

This is no ordinary battle, and it calls for extraordinary armor.

You and I are not average soldiers. We are co-heirs with the Great High Priest, children of the undefeated King—a King who is often described as our shield (Gn 15:1). What's more, Isaiah describes the coming Messiah as wearing a belt of righteousness and faithfulness (Is 11:5), righteousness like a breastplate, and a helmet of salvation (Is 59:17).

Now, back to Paul's letter—he already reminded the believers of their new spiritual clothing two chapters earlier. "Take off your former way of life, the old self," he said, and you "put on the new self" in Christ (Eph 4:22-24). He wrote it in his letter to the Romans, too: "Put on the Lord Jesus Christ" (Rm 13:14).

This armor is all His—His truth, His righteousness, His salvation, His Word. Jesus fought the battle and won, and He laid the armor of victory upon us.

So, yes, suit up today. Pray earnestly at all times and "with every prayer and request," like Paul describes. Pray for boldness—not to proclaim all the answers, but to proclaim the mysterious gospel (Eph 6:18-19).

It is indeed a battle—a battle both won and ongoing. But you and I were made to fight it. Not by armor of our own making, but by the already tried and true armor of the Mighty One, our High Priest, our Messiah and King. To Him be the glory, forever.

[7] Serve with a good attitude, as to the Lord and not to people, [8] knowing that whatever good each one does, slave or free, he will receive this back from the Lord. [9] And masters, treat your slaves the same way, without threatening them, because you know that both their Master and yours is in heaven, and there is no favoritism with him.

CHRISTIAN WARFARE

[10] Finally, be strengthened by the Lord and by his vast strength. [11] Put on the full armor of God so that you can stand against the schemes of the devil. [12] For our struggle is not against flesh and blood, but against the rulers, against the authorities, against the cosmic powers of this darkness, against evil, spiritual forces in the heavens. [13] For this reason take up the full armor of God, so that you may be able to resist in the evil day, and having prepared everything, to take your stand. [14] Stand, therefore, with truth like a belt around your waist, righteousness like armor on your chest, [15] and your feet sandaled with readiness for the gospel of peace. [16] In every situation take up the shield of faith with which you can extinguish all the flaming arrows of the evil one. [17] Take the helmet of salvation and the sword of the Spirit — which is the word of God. [18] Pray at all times in the Spirit with every prayer and request, and stay alert with all perseverance and intercession for all the saints. [19] Pray also for me, that the message may be given to me when I open my mouth to make known with boldness the mystery of the gospel. [20] For this I am an ambassador in chains. Pray that I might be bold enough to speak about it as I should.

PAUL'S FAREWELL

[21] Tychicus, our dearly loved brother and faithful servant[A] in the Lord, will tell you all the news about me so that you may be informed. [22] I am sending him to you for this very reason, to let you know how we are and to encourage your hearts.

[23] Peace to the brothers and sisters, and love with faith, from God the Father and the Lord Jesus Christ. [24] Grace be with all who have undying love for our Lord Jesus Christ.[B,C]

[A]6:21 Or deacon   [B]6:24 Other mss add Amen.   [C]6:24 Lit all who love our Lord Jesus Christ in incorruption to live is christ and to die is gain

philippians

 For me, to live is Christ and to die is gain. **1:21**

ON THE TIMELINE The traditional date for the writing of Philippians is during Paul's first Roman imprisonment in AD 60–62. Paul planted the church at Philippi during his second missionary journey, around AD 51, in response to his "Macedonian vision" (Ac 16:9-10). The church at Philippi was the first church in Europe (Ac 16).

A LITTLE BACKGROUND Philippi, the ancient city of Krenides, had military significance. Renamed after Alexander the Great's father, Philip of Macedon, Philippi became the capital of the Greek Empire in 332 BC. After the Roman conquest of Greece and Julius Caesar's death in 44 BC, Philippi was declared a Roman colony. The people of Philippi were knowledgeable of their rich history and social structure, and Paul uses military and political metaphors to communicate with the Philippians in his letter.

MESSAGE & PURPOSE Philippians is Paul's most warmly personal letter. After initial difficulties in the city of Philippi (Ac 16), a strong bond developed between Paul and the converts there. Paul wrote to thank the church for a gift they had recently sent him in prison and to inform them of his circumstances.

Although Paul was concerned about the divided Christian community at Philippi, his outlook was strengthened by the knowledge that Christ was being magnified. Paul's faith was the foundation of his optimism. Whether he lived or died, whether he continued his service to others or went to be in Christ's presence, whether he was appreciated or not—Paul wanted Christ to be glorified. His letter to the church at Philippi includes messages of unity (Php 1:27–2:18), freedom from legalism (Php 3:2-21), salvation (Php 2:6-8), stewardship (Php 4:10-20), and imitation of Christ's humility (Php 2:5-11).

GIVE THANKS FOR THE BOOK OF PHILIPPIANS

Paul's letter to the Philippians teaches us about genuine Christian living. While nearly every theme introduced can also be found elsewhere in Scripture, it is within Paul's letter to the church at Philippi that we can really see how those themes and messages impact our lives. Philippians contributes to our understanding of Christian commitment and what it means to be Christlike.

PHILIPPI AND
SURROUNDING CITIES

READ AND UNDERSTAND PHILIPPIANS

The Bible is a complete work in which many stories combine to tell one story. As you read the book of Philippians, consider reading the additional passages to discover how the whole of Scripture works together.

GREETING

1 Paul and Timothy, servants of Christ Jesus:
To all the saints in Christ Jesus who are in Philippi, including the overseers and deacons.

[2] Grace to you and peace from God our Father and the Lord Jesus Christ.

THANKSGIVING AND PRAYER

[3] I give thanks to my God for every remembrance of you,[A] [4] always praying with joy for all of you in my every prayer, [5] because of your partnership in the gospel from the first day until now. [6] I am sure of this, that he who started a good work in you[B] will carry it on to completion until the day of Christ Jesus. [7] Indeed, it is right for me to think this way about all of you, because I have you in my heart,[C] and you are all partners with me in grace, both in my imprisonment and in the defense and confirmation of the gospel. [8] For God is my witness, how deeply I miss all of you with the affection of Christ Jesus. [9] And I pray this: that your love will keep on growing in knowledge and every kind of discernment, [10] so that you may approve the things that are superior and may be pure and blameless in the day of Christ, [11] filled with the fruit of righteousness that comes through Jesus Christ to the glory and praise of God.

ADVANCE OF THE GOSPEL

[12] Now I want you to know, brothers and sisters, that what has happened to me has actually advanced the gospel, [13] so that it has become known throughout the whole imperial guard, and to everyone else, that my imprisonment is because I am in Christ. [14] Most of the brothers have gained confidence in the Lord from my imprisonment and dare even more to speak the word[D] fearlessly. [15] To be sure, some preach Christ out of envy and rivalry, but others out of good will. [16] These preach out of love, knowing that I am appointed for the defense of the gospel; [17] the others proclaim Christ out of selfish ambition, not sincerely, thinking that they will cause me trouble in my imprisonment. [18] What does it matter? Only that in every way, whether from false motives or true, Christ is proclaimed, and in this I rejoice. Yes, and I will continue to rejoice [19] because I know this will lead to my salvation[E] through your prayers and help from the Spirit of Jesus Christ. [20] My eager expectation and hope is that I will not be ashamed about anything, but that now as always, with all courage, Christ will be highly honored in my body, whether by life or by death.

LIVING IS CHRIST

[21] For me, to live is Christ and to die is gain. [22] Now if I live on in the flesh, this means fruitful work for me; and I don't know which one I should choose. [23] I am torn between the two. I long to depart and be with Christ — which is far better — [24] but to remain in the flesh is more necessary for your sake. [25] Since I am persuaded of this, I know that I will remain and continue with all of you for your progress and joy in the faith, [26] so that, because of my coming to you again, your boasting in Christ Jesus may abound.

[A] 1:3 Or *for your every remembrance of me*   [B] 1:6 Or *work among you*
[C] 1:7 Or *because you have me in your heart*   [D] 1:14 Other mss add *of God*
[E] 1:19 Or *vindication*

UNCONVENTIONAL JOY

PHILIPPIANS 1:12-26; PHILIPPIANS 4:1

Philippians reads like a greatest hits of the Bible. Like all my favorite pop songs, I can half-finish every line. What's so popular about this epistle? Why have we heard it quoted in so many sermons and seen it posted as inspiration in so many locker rooms?

Because this is the epistle of joy! It's full of loving encouragement—a massively quotable and happy book. But Paul wrote it from prison. Nothing says joy like prison. Wait, what?

How did Paul write this merry letter from behind bars? Our biggest hint is found in the first chapter, Philippians 1:21:

"For me, to live is Christ and to die is gain."

Paul's joy did not come from frolicking in a meadow, free from chains. It did not come from self-satisfaction or his favorite foods. Because he knew the gospel is true, **Paul's joy came only from Christ.**

In this little letter to the Philippians, Paul shares three unexpected places where Christ brings us joy.

Christ gives joy in community. Paul founded the church at Philippi, and they supported him financially so he could keep spreading the good news. These were his people, and he loved them. In fact, he called them "my joy" (Php 4:1) and referred to them as family, underscoring

their unity in Christ (Php 2:19). This loving family imagery matters because the church at Philippi was mostly Gentiles, and there was still a lot of debate about whether these outsiders were all the way welcome. Paul emphasized the value of every person and role, reiterating that we all have a place in the community of the Church, even in hard times.

Christ gives joy in persecution. The city of Philippi became a Roman colony in 31 BC, which came with some privileges. The Philippians were proud of their earthly citizenship (Ac 16:21), but Paul directs them to find joy in heavenly citizenship (Php 3:20). With his eyes fixed on heavenly citizenship, Paul was able to find joy while he was persecuted in prison. Paul actually exults in his tribulations and rejoices in sufferings for the sake of Christ (Rm 5:3; Col 1:24).

Christ gives joy in humility. Paul wrote a beautiful hymn on the humility of Christ in the second chapter of his letter, and he echoes this language when he calls himself a servant (Php 1:1). Paul's language, in light of his present uncomfortable living conditions, forces us to consider the radical idea that joy actually comes not through glory, but humility. We can find joy in Christ when, like Him, we clothe ourselves in humility (1Pt 5:5).

As you read this letter of unconventional joy, look for the joy of Christ in unexpected places—in the corners of your community, in the reality of pain, and in the freedom of humility. Because the gospel is true, life in Christ is true life indeed.

²⁷ Just one thing: As citizens of heaven, live your life worthy of the gospel of Christ. Then, whether I come and see you or am absent, I will hear about you that you are standing firm in one spirit, in one accord,^A contending together for the faith of the gospel, ²⁸ not being frightened in any way by your opponents. This is a sign of destruction for them, but of your salvation — and this is from God. ²⁹ For it has been granted to you on Christ's behalf not only to believe in him, but also to suffer for him, ³⁰ since you are engaged in the same struggle that you saw I had and now hear that I have.

CHRISTIAN HUMILITY

2 If then there is any encouragement in Christ, if any consolation of love, if any fellowship with the Spirit, if any affection and mercy, ² make my joy complete by thinking the same way, having the same love, united in spirit, intent on one purpose. ³ Do nothing out of selfish ambition or conceit, but in humility consider others as more important than yourselves. ⁴ Everyone should look out not only for his own interests, but also for the interests of others.

CHRIST'S HUMILITY AND EXALTATION

⁵ Adopt the same attitude as that of Christ Jesus,
⁶   who, existing in the form of God,
   did not consider equality with God
   as something to be exploited.^B
⁷   Instead he emptied himself
   by assuming the form of a servant,
   taking on the likeness of humanity.
   And when he had come as a man,
⁸   he humbled himself by becoming obedient
   to the point of death —
   even to death on a cross.
⁹   For this reason God highly exalted him
   and gave him the name
   that is above every name,
¹⁰   so that at the name of Jesus
   every knee will bow —
   in heaven and on earth
   and under the earth —
¹¹   and every tongue will confess
   that Jesus Christ is Lord,
   to the glory of God the Father.

LIGHTS IN THE WORLD

¹² Therefore, my dear friends, just as you have always obeyed, so now, not only in my presence but even more in my absence, work out your own salvation with fear and trembling. ¹³ For it is God who is working in you both to will and to work according to his good purpose. ¹⁴ Do everything without grumbling and arguing, ¹⁵ so that you may be blameless and pure, children of God who are faultless in a crooked and perverted generation, among whom

^A1:27 Lit *soul*   ^B2:6 Or *to be grasped,* or *to be held on to*

you shine like stars in the world, [16] by holding firm to the word of life. Then I can boast in the day of Christ that I didn't run or labor for nothing. [17] But even if I am poured out as a drink offering on the sacrificial service of your faith, I am glad and rejoice with all of you. [18] In the same way you should also be glad and rejoice with me.

TIMOTHY AND EPAPHRODITUS

[19] Now I hope in the Lord Jesus to send Timothy to you soon so that I too may be encouraged by news about you. [20] For I have no one else like-minded who will genuinely care about your interests; [21] all seek their own interests, not those of Jesus Christ. [22] But you know his proven character, because he has served with me in the gospel ministry like a son with a father. [23] Therefore, I hope to send him as soon as I see how things go with me. [24] I am confident in the Lord that I myself will also come soon.

[25] But I considered it necessary to send you Epaphroditus — my brother, coworker, and fellow soldier, as well as your messenger and minister to my need — [26] since he has been longing for all of you and was distressed because you heard that he was sick. [27] Indeed, he was so sick that he nearly died. However, God had mercy on him, and not only on him but also on me, so that I would not have sorrow upon sorrow. [28] For this reason, I am very eager to send him so that you may rejoice again when you see him and I may be less anxious. [29] Therefore, welcome him in the Lord with great joy and hold people like him in honor, [30] because he came close to death for the work of Christ, risking his life to make up what was lacking in your ministry to me.

KNOWING CHRIST

3 In addition, my brothers and sisters, rejoice in the Lord. To write to you again about this is no trouble for me and is a safeguard for you. [2] Watch out for the dogs, watch out for the evil workers, watch out for those who mutilate the flesh. [3] For we are the circumcision, the ones who worship by the Spirit of God, boast in Christ Jesus, and do not put confidence in the flesh — [4] although I have reasons for confidence in the flesh. If anyone else thinks he has grounds for confidence in the flesh, I have more: [5] circumcised the eighth day; of the nation of Israel, of the tribe of Benjamin, a Hebrew born of Hebrews; regarding the law, a Pharisee; [6] regarding zeal, persecuting the church; regarding the righteousness that is in the law, blameless.

[7] But everything that was a gain to me, I have considered to be a loss because of Christ. [8] More than that, I also consider everything to be a loss in view of the surpassing value of knowing Christ Jesus my Lord. Because of him I have suffered the loss of all things and consider them as dung, so that I may gain Christ [9] and be found in him, not having a righteousness of my own from the law, but one that is through faith in Christ[A] — the righteousness from God based on faith. [10] My goal is to know him and the power of his resurrection and the fellowship of his sufferings, being conformed to his death, [11] assuming that I will somehow reach the resurrection from among the dead.

[A] 3:9 Or *through the faithfulness of Christ*

REACHING FORWARD TO GOD'S GOAL

[12] Not that I have already reached the goal or am already perfect, but I make every effort to take hold of it because I also have been taken hold of by Christ Jesus. [13] Brothers and sisters, I do not[A] consider myself to have taken hold of it. But one thing I do: Forgetting what is behind and reaching forward to what is ahead, [14] I pursue as my goal the prize promised by God's heavenly[B] call in Christ Jesus. [15] Therefore, let all of us who are mature think this way. And if you think differently about anything, God will reveal this also to you. [16] In any case, we should live up to whatever truth we have attained. [17] Join in imitating me, brothers and sisters, and pay careful attention to those who live according to the example you have in us. [18] For I have often told you, and now say again with tears, that many live as enemies of the cross of Christ. [19] Their end is destruction; their god is their stomach; their glory is in their shame. They are focused on earthly things, [20] but our citizenship is in heaven, and we eagerly wait for a Savior from there, the Lord Jesus Christ. [21] He will transform the body of our humble condition into the likeness of his glorious body, by the power that enables him to subject everything to himself.

4 So then, my dearly loved and longed for brothers and sisters, my joy and crown, in this manner stand firm in the Lord, dear friends.

PRACTICAL COUNSEL

[2] I urge Euodia and I urge Syntyche to agree in the Lord. [3] Yes, I also ask you, true partner,[C] to help these women who have contended for the gospel at my side, along with Clement and the rest of my coworkers whose names are in the book of life. [4] Rejoice in the Lord always. I will say it again: Rejoice! [5] Let your graciousness[D] be known to everyone. The Lord is near. [6] Don't worry about anything, but in everything, through prayer and petition with thanksgiving, present your requests to God. [7] And the peace of God, which surpasses all understanding, will guard your hearts and minds in Christ Jesus.

[8] Finally[E] brothers and sisters, whatever is true, whatever is honorable, whatever is just, whatever is pure, whatever is lovely, whatever is commendable — if there is any moral excellence and if there is anything praiseworthy — dwell on these things. [9] Do what you have learned and received and heard from me, and seen in me, and the God of peace will be with you.

APPRECIATION OF SUPPORT

[10] I rejoiced in the Lord greatly because once again you renewed your care for me. You were, in fact, concerned about me but lacked the opportunity to show it. [11] I don't say this out of need, for I have learned to be content in whatever circumstances I find myself. [12] I know both how to make do with little, and I know how to make do with a lot. In any and all circumstances I have learned the secret of being content — whether well fed or hungry, whether in abundance or in need. [13] I am able to do all things through him[F] who strengthens me. [14] Still, you did well by partnering with me in my hardship.

[15] And you Philippians know that in the early days of the gospel, when I left Macedonia, no church shared with me in the matter of giving and receiving

---

[A] 3:13 Other mss read *not yet*   [B] 3:14 Or *upward*   [C] 4:3 Or *true Syzygus,* possibly a person's name   [D] 4:5 Or *gentleness*   [E] 4:8 Or *In addition*   [F] 4:13 Other mss read *Christ*

ALL WE NEED

PHILIPPIANS 4:10-23; 2 PETER 1:3

Imagine you wrote a book about your life—let's say it's a spiritual memoir. Would the title be something dramatic and decisive, like "Tales of Triumph" or "Leap of Faith"? Maybe it would follow more along the lines of "Carefully Calculated Efforts" or "Risk Averse, Partially Trusting Hop."

I've never been much of a leaper myself. If God calls me to something, my ideal scenario is to send someone ahead to see what I'm in for. I need someone to take a look at what's on the other side and send back a postcard with a full report. Then I can make an educated decision: *Is it worth the leap or not?*

If you, too, are a partially-trusting hopper, I have good news! Philippians is that postcard. Paul has gone to that most faithful, gospel-believing, Christ-trusting place where so many of us long to go, and he's sent back a letter to describe his panoramic view from the other end of the journey.

Philippians 4 is the close of what could, for all Paul knows, be his last letter. He's witnessed firsthand the life-changing power of the gospel and the saving grace of Jesus Christ. He's endured sacrifice, struggle, and suffering. And, as he says in Philippians 4:12, he knows how to have a little and how to have a lot. Sitting in prison at the possible end of it all, Paul delivers his final sentiments with profound joy and certainty:

In Christ I have all I need. And, friends, so do you.

Tucked inside Paul's beautiful litany of faith is the very verse we Christians like to use—and misuse—to talk ourselves out of those faith slumps we'll likely write about in our book: "I am able to do all things through him who strengthens me" (Php 4:13).

Notice: **Christ's strength in Paul produces something far richer than achievement; it produces contentment.** Christ's strength in me fuels something far more significant than my best efforts; it fuels my faith.

Like Paul, we will know what it is to have a little and what it is to have a lot. Like Paul, our story will include sacrifice, struggle, and suffering. And like him, we have been given profound joy and unending riches in the gospel and glory of Jesus Christ. The God who provided for Paul—and for the church at Philippi, as well as for generation after generation of believers who have come before us—also supplies all our needs "according to his riches in glory in Christ Jesus" (Php 4:19).

May His strength be our contentment. May His grace fuel our faith. And may the message of our story be simply this:

In Christ I have all I need. And, friends, so do you.

except you alone. ¹⁶ For even in Thessalonica you sent gifts for my need several times. ¹⁷ Not that I seek the gift, but I seek the profit ^A that is increasing to your account. ¹⁸ But I have received everything in full, and I have an abundance. I am fully supplied, ^B having received from Epaphroditus what you provided — a fragrant offering, an acceptable sacrifice, pleasing to God. ¹⁹ And my God will supply all your needs according to his riches in glory in Christ Jesus. ²⁰ Now to our God and Father be glory forever and ever. Amen.

FINAL GREETINGS

²¹ Greet every saint in Christ Jesus. The brothers who are with me send you greetings. ²² All the saints send you greetings, especially those who belong to Caesar's household. ²³ The grace of the Lord Jesus Christ be with your spirit. ^C

---

^A 4:17 Lit fruit ^B 4:18 Or Here, then, is my receipt for everything, I have an abundance, for I am fully supplied ^C 4:23 Other mss add Amen.

He Is Before
All Things
and By Him
All Things
hold together

colossians

 He is before all things, and by him all things hold together. **1:17**

ON THE TIMELINE Paul wrote Colossians during his first Roman imprisonment (Col 4:3,10,18) in the early AD 60s. Together with Ephesians, Philippians, and Philemon, Paul's letter to the Colossians is commonly classified as a "prison epistle."

A LITTLE BACKGROUND During his ministry in Ephesus (Ac 19:10), Paul sent Epaphras to spread the gospel in the Lycus Valley. Epaphras subsequently established the church at Colossae (Col 1:7; 4:12-13). The city's population consisted mostly of Phrygians and Greeks, but it also included a significant number of Jews. Likewise, the church was composed mostly of Gentiles (Col 1:21, 27; 2:13), but it also had Jewish members (Col 2:11,16,18,21; 3:11). When Epaphras (Phm 23) informed Paul of certain heretical teachings that had spread there, Paul wrote the letter to the Colossians as a theological antidote.

MESSAGE & PURPOSE Paul wrote this letter to counter the "Colossian heresy" that he considered contrary to the gospel of Jesus Christ. The false teaching is identified as a "philosophy" (Col 2:8), presumably drawn from some Hellenistic traditions as indicated by the references to the "fullness" (Col 1:19), the "elements of the world" (Col 2:8,20), "wisdom" (Col 2:3,23), and "self-made religion" (Col 2:23).

This false gospel contained several Jewish elements, from circumcision (Col 2:11; 3:11) and "human tradition" (Col 2:8), to Sabbath observance, food regulations, festival participation (Col 2:16), and more. Paul addressed this combination of philosophies by teaching a proper understanding of the gospel of Jesus Christ and its appropriate implications for Christian salvation (Col 2:10,13,20; 3:1,11-12,17) and conduct (Col 3:5–4:6).

GIVE THANKS FOR THE BOOK OF COLOSSIANS

Colossians provides one of the Bible's fullest expressions of the deity and supremacy of Christ. This is most evident in the magnificent hymn of praise found in Colossians 1:15-20, which sets forth Christ as the image of the invisible God, the Creator and sustainer of the universe. He is the head of His body, the Church, and the One through whom forgiveness is possible.

COLOSSAE AND
SURROUNDING CITIES

READ AND UNDERSTAND COLOSSIANS

The Bible is a complete work in which many stories combine to tell one story. As you read the book of Colossians, consider reading the additional passages to discover how the whole of Scripture works together.

GREETING

1 Paul, an apostle of Christ Jesus by God's will, and Timothy our brother: ² To the saints in Christ at Colossae, who are faithful brothers and sisters. Grace to you and peace from God our Father.^A

THANKSGIVING

³ We always thank God, the Father of our Lord Jesus Christ, when we pray for you, ⁴ for we have heard of your faith in Christ Jesus and of the love you have for all the saints ⁵ because of the hope reserved for you in heaven. You have already heard about this hope in the word of truth, the gospel ⁶ that has come to you. It is bearing fruit and growing all over the world, just as it has among you since the day you heard it and came to truly appreciate God's grace.^B ⁷ You learned this from Epaphras, our dearly loved fellow servant. He is a faithful minister of Christ on your^C behalf, ⁸ and he has told us about your love in the Spirit.

PRAYER FOR SPIRITUAL GROWTH

⁹ For this reason also, since the day we heard this, we haven't stopped praying for you. We are asking that you may be filled with the knowledge of his will in all wisdom and spiritual understanding,^D ¹⁰ so that you may walk worthy of the Lord, fully pleasing to him: bearing fruit in every good work and growing in the knowledge of God, ¹¹ being strengthened with all power, according to his glorious might, so that you may have great endurance and patience, joyfully ¹² giving thanks to the Father, who has enabled you^E to share in the saints' inheritance in the light. ¹³ He has rescued us from the domain of darkness and transferred us into the kingdom of the Son he loves. ¹⁴ In him we have redemption,^F the forgiveness of sins.

THE CENTRALITY OF CHRIST

¹⁵ He is the image of the invisible God,
the firstborn over all creation.
¹⁶ For everything was created by him,
in heaven and on earth,
the visible and the invisible,
whether thrones or dominions
or rulers or authorities —
all things have been created through him and for him.
¹⁷ He is before all things,
and by him all things hold together.
¹⁸ He is also the head of the body, the church;
he is the beginning,
the firstborn from the dead,
so that he might come to have
first place in everything.
¹⁹ For God was pleased to have
all his fullness dwell in him,

---

^A1:2 Other mss add *and the Lord Jesus Christ* ^B1:6 Or *and truly recognized God's grace* ^C1:7 Other mss read *our* ^D1:9 Or *all spiritual wisdom and understanding* ^E1:12 Other mss read *us* ^F1:14 Other mss add *through his blood*

KNOWING WHO JESUS IS

COLOSSIANS 1:15-23; 1 CORINTHIANS 8:5-6; JUDE 24-25

Every Tuesday I meet my mentor for a walk in the woods. We stroll on the dirt path that meanders through pine and California Oak trees, taking note of the wildflowers that change with the seasons. The path takes us to a picnic bench with a stunning backdrop of the Cleveland National Forest. Majestic mountains reach to the sky.

There we sit for an hour or more, in deep conversation about God. Our dialogue usually takes the form of these questions: Who do you believe God is? Who or what has influenced that belief? Is it true?

Our conversations have made me realize how easy it is to be influenced by the world's view of God. Culture can easily distract and misguide us unless we know, really know, who God is by reading His Word and believing its truth (Col 2:7).

Paul understood well the need to know Christ, and he emphasized this vital truth as he ministered the good news of redemption to others. A man named Epaphras, believed to be the founder and leader of the Colossian church, visited Paul in prison and requested his help in dealing with the false teaching confronting the church. Paul wrote this compelling letter to the Colossians, including a statement of faith exalting the supremacy of Christ in both creation and redemption.

According to God's Word—and the hymn of the church as "sung" by Paul in Colossians 1:15-20 —this is who Christ is:

He is the image of the invisible God.
He is the firstborn over all creation.
He is the creator of everything in heaven and on earth.
He is before all things.
He is the One who holds all things together.
He is the head of the church.
He is the beginning.
He is the One in whom all the fullness of God dwells.
He is the reconciler of all things.
He is the ultimate peacemaker.

Take a moment to soak in these truths. Read Colossians 1:15-20 silently, shout them aloud, or even sing them with joy! Ask God for fresh eyes to see the divine nature of Christ, and give thanks for a Savior who is all of these incredible things.

He is the One who created you and called you, who holds all things together today. He is the beginning and the end. He is the loving God who took on flesh and made peace with His children through the blood of His cross.

Paul's hymn of adoration is a reminder for us that Christ is alive—present in our world, in our communities, and in us, that we may be resurrected in new life. Who Christ is has not changed, no matter the view from where we sit today.

²⁰ and through him to reconcile
everything to himself,
whether things on earth or things in heaven,
by making peace
through his blood, shed on the cross.ᴬ

²¹ Once you were alienated and hostile in your minds expressed in your evil actions. ²² But now he has reconciled you by his physical body through his death, to present you holy, faultless, and blameless before him — ²³ if indeed you remain grounded and steadfast in the faith and are not shifted away from the hope of the gospel that you heard. This gospel has been proclaimed in all creation under heaven, and I, Paul, have become a servant of it.

PAUL'S MINISTRY

²⁴ Now I rejoice in my sufferings for you, and I am completing in my flesh what is lacking in Christ's afflictions for his body, that is, the church. ²⁵ I have become its servant, according to God's commission that was given to me for you, to make the word of God fully known, ²⁶ the mystery hidden for ages and generations but now revealed to his saints. ²⁷ God wanted to make known among the Gentiles the glorious wealth of this mystery, which is Christ in you, the hope of glory. ²⁸ We proclaim him, warning and teaching everyone with all wisdom, so that we may present everyone mature in Christ. ²⁹ I labor for this, striving with his strength that works powerfully in me.

2 For I want you to know how greatly I am struggling for you, for those in Laodicea, and for all who have not seen me in person. ² I want their hearts to be encouraged and joined together in love, so that they may have all the riches of complete understanding and have the knowledge of God's mystery — Christ.ᴮ ³ In him are hidden all the treasures of wisdom and knowledge.

CHRIST VERSUS THE COLOSSIAN HERESY

⁴ I am saying this so that no one will deceive you with arguments that sound reasonable. ⁵ For I may be absent in body, but I am with you in spirit, rejoicing to see how well ordered you are and the strength of your faith in Christ.

⁶ So then, just as you have received Christ Jesus as Lord, continue to live in him, ⁷ being rooted and built up in him and established in the faith, just as you were taught, and overflowing with gratitude.

⁸ Be careful that no one takes you captive through philosophy and empty deceit based on human tradition, based on the elements of the world, rather than Christ. ⁹ For the entire fullness of God's nature dwells bodilyᶜ in Christ, ¹⁰ and you have been filled by him, who is the head over every ruler and authority. ¹¹ You were also circumcised in him with a circumcision not done with hands, by putting off the body of flesh, in the circumcision of Christ, ¹² when you were buried with him in baptism, in which you were

---

ᴬ1:20 Other mss add *through him*   ᴮ2:2 Other mss read *mystery of God, both of the Father and of Christ*; other ms variations exist on this v.   ᶜ2:9 Or *nature lives in a human body* also raised with him through faith in the working of God, who raised him from the dead. [13] And when you were dead in trespasses and in the uncircumcision of your flesh, he made you alive with him and forgave us all our trespasses. [14] He erased the certificate of debt, with its obligations, that was against us and opposed to us, and has taken it away by nailing it to the cross. [15] He disarmed the rulers and authorities and disgraced them publicly; he triumphed over them in him. [A]

[16] Therefore, don't let anyone judge you in regard to food and drink or in the matter of a festival or a new moon or a Sabbath day. [B] [17] These are a shadow of what was to come; the substance is [C] Christ. [18] Let no one condemn [D] you by delighting in ascetic practices and the worship of angels, claiming access to a visionary realm. Such people are inflated by empty notions of their unspiritual [E] mind. [19] He doesn't hold on to the head, from whom the whole body, nourished and held together by its ligaments and tendons, grows with growth from God.

[20] If you died with Christ to the elements of this world, why do you live as if you still belonged to the world? Why do you submit to regulations: [21] "Don't handle, don't taste, don't touch"? [22] All these regulations refer to what is destined to perish by being used up; they are human commands and doctrines. [23] Although these have a reputation for wisdom by promoting self-made religion, false humility, and severe treatment of the body, they are not of any value in curbing self-indulgence. [F]

THE LIFE OF THE NEW MAN

3 So if you have been raised with Christ, seek the things above, where Christ is, seated at the right hand of God. [2] Set your minds on things above, not on earthly things. [3] For you died, and your life is hidden with Christ in God. [4] When Christ, who is your [G] life, appears, then you also will appear with him in glory.

[5] Therefore, put to death what belongs to your earthly nature: sexual immorality, impurity, lust, evil desire, and greed, which is idolatry. [6] Because of these, God's wrath is coming upon the disobedient, [H] [7] and you once walked in these things when you were living in them. [8] But now, put away all the following: anger, wrath, malice, slander, and filthy language from your mouth. [9] Do not lie to one another, since you have put off the old self with its practices [10] and have put on the new self. You are being renewed in knowledge according to the image of your [I] Creator. [11] In Christ there is not Greek and Jew, circumcision and uncircumcision, barbarian, Scythian, slave and free; but Christ is all and in all.

THE CHRISTIAN LIFE

[12] Therefore, as God's chosen ones, holy and dearly loved, put on compassion, kindness, humility, gentleness, and patience, [13] bearing with one another and forgiving one another if anyone has a grievance against another. Just as the Lord has forgiven you, so you are also to forgive. [14] Above all, put

---

[A] 2:15 Or *them through it* [B] 2:16 Or *or sabbaths* [C] 2:17 Or *substance belongs to* [D] 2:18 Or *disqualify* [E] 2:18 Lit *fleshly* [F] 2:23 Lit *value against indulgence of the flesh* [G] 3:4 Other mss read *our* [H] 3:6 Other mss omit *upon the disobedient* [I] 3:10 Lit *his*

FIX YOUR EYES

COLOSSIANS 3:1-17; PHILIPPIANS 4:4-7

My bedroom can be a scary sight. From un-packed suitcases and dirty clothes, to unopened mail and several dozen sticky notes decorated by my two-year-old—it can look like a bomb went off in there.

The state of my bedroom often matches the state of my heart. It's a mess in there. I'm looking at the clutter and the to-do list of things left undone, and all the lies start coming.

You're terrible at life.
You're worthless.
You can't get anything right.

I'm stressed and anxious, overwhelmed and sleep-deprived, and the weight of it all makes my shoulders tight. But then I read this:

"Set your minds on things above, not on earthly things."

COLOSSIANS 3:2

This verse always reminds me of a Robert Mur-ray M'Cheyne quote my pastor once shared with us: "For every look at yourself, take ten looks at Christ" (Andrew Bonar, *Memoir and Remains of the Rev. Robert Murray M'Cheyne*).

Years ago, we practiced this with our small group. We'd sit around and share what life was throwing at us, and for each struggle, we'd move our eyes together from the trial to the cross—to the promises God has given and the life He's called us to live. That practice was, and still is, transformative for me.

As I turn my mind from the messes in-side and around me to the face of Jesus, something shifts. I remember His love and how He covers me, even when I'm a wreck (Col 3:3). I remember He's a God who is not afraid of our messes, but instead, enters right into the middle of them.

I remember that I'm no longer a slave to sin (Rm 6:6). I may struggle with the same junk over and over again, but each struggle is an opportunity to put off the old self and take hold of that which Jesus has already taken hold of for me (Col 3:5-11; Php 3:12).

When my house and heart are a mess, I get to choose how I think. I can choose to let the peace of God control my heart and mind (Php 4:7). And I can choose to be thankful, even when life breaks my heart and doesn't turn out like I wish it would.

Sisters, we are God's beloved children, redeemed by Him and called by name (Is 43:1; Eph 5:1). And that changes everything. **Christ Jesus has freed us to fix our eyes on Him** (Heb 12:2). So, instead of focusing on ourselves today—on what we've done or left undone, on how we ache, or on how we wish things were different than they are—let's turn our eyes, over and over again, toward the One who knows and loves us best.

on love, which is the perfect bond of unity. ¹⁵ And let the peace of Christ, to which you were also called in one body, rule your hearts. And be thankful. ¹⁶ Let the word of Christ dwell richly among you, in all wisdom teaching and admonishing one another through psalms, hymns, and spiritual songs,ᴬ singing to God with gratitude in your hearts. ¹⁷ And whatever you do, in word or in deed, do everything in the name of the Lord Jesus, giving thanks to God the Father through him.

CHRIST IN YOUR HOME

¹⁸ Wives, submit yourselves to your husbands, as is fitting in the Lord. ¹⁹ Husbands, love your wives and don't be bitter toward them. ²⁰ Children, obey your parents in everything, for this pleases the Lord. ²¹ Fathers, do not exasperate your children, so that they won't become discouraged. ²² Slaves, obey your human masters in everything. Don't work only while being watched, as people-pleasers, but work wholeheartedly, fearing the Lord. ²³ Whatever you do, do it from the heart, as something done for the Lord and not for people, ²⁴ knowing that you will receive the reward of an inheritance from the Lord. You serve the Lord Christ. ²⁵ For the wrongdoer will be paid back for whatever wrong he has done, and there is no favoritism.

4 Masters, deal with your slaves justly and fairly, since you know that you too have a Master in heaven.

SPEAKING TO GOD AND OTHERS

² Devote yourselves to prayer; stay alert in it with thanksgiving. ³ At the same time, pray also for us that God may open a door to us for the word, to speak the mystery of Christ, for which I am in chains, ⁴ so that I may make it known as I should. ⁵ Act wisely toward outsiders, making the most of the time. ⁶ Let your speech always be gracious, seasoned with salt, so that you may know how you should answer each person.

FINAL GREETINGS

⁷ Tychicus, our dearly loved brother, faithful minister, and fellow servant in the Lord, will tell you all the news about me. ⁸ I have sent him to you for this very purpose, so that you may know how we areᴮ and so that he may encourage your hearts. ⁹ He is coming with Onesimus, a faithful and dearly loved brother, who is one of you. They will tell you about everything here.

¹⁰ Aristarchus, my fellow prisoner, sends you greetings, as does Mark, Barnabas's cousin (concerning whom you have received instructions: if he comes to you, welcome him), ¹¹ and so does Jesus who is called Justus. These alone of the circumcised are my coworkers for the kingdom of God, and they have been a comfort to me. ¹² Epaphras, who is one of you, a servant of Christ Jesus, sends you greetings. He is always wrestling for you in his prayers, so that you can stand mature and fully assuredᶜ in everything God wills. ¹³ For I testify about him that he works hardᴰ for you, for those in Laodicea, and for those in Hierapolis. ¹⁴ Luke, the dearly loved physician, and Demas send you greetings. ¹⁵ Give my greetings to the brothers and sisters

---

ᴬ3:16 Or *and songs prompted by the Spirit*   ᴮ4:8 Other mss read *that he may know how you are*   ᶜ4:12 Other mss read *and complete*   ᴰ4:13 Other mss read *he has a great zeal* in Laodicea, and to Nympha and the church in her home. [16] After this letter has been read at your gathering, have it read also in the church of the Laodiceans; and see that you also read the letter from Laodicea. [17] And tell Archippus, "Pay attention to the ministry you have received in the Lord, so that you can accomplish it."

[18] I, Paul, am writing this greeting with my own hand. Remember my chains. Grace be with you. ^A

^A 4:18 Other mss add *Amen.*

1 thessalonians

 Rejoice always, pray constantly, give thanks in everything; for this is God's will for you in Christ Jesus. **5:16-18**

ON THE TIMELINE First Thessalonians can be reliably dated at AD 50 or 51, between Paul's second and third missionary journeys.

A LITTLE BACKGROUND Thessalonica was the capital and major port of the Roman province of Macedonia, with a population of about 200,000. Loyal to Caesar, the city of Thessalonica was filled with pagan worshipers of idols, the full pantheon of Greek and Roman gods, and was well known for its emperor worship.

MESSAGE & PURPOSE Timothy reported to Paul that although the church at Thessalonica was suffering affliction, they were holding fast to the faith. Though they had some doctrinal misunderstandings, they were laboring for the Lord out of love and patiently hoping for the return of Christ. Paul wrote to encourage the church in their faith; to remind them that sanctification was God's will for them, and to correct misunderstandings about end-time events.

First Thessalonians presents four major themes:
1. *Paul's conduct of his ministry* – Paul's ministry centered on two aspects: the communication of the Word of God and the sharing of his life (1Th 2:8). Paul's motives were to please God (1Th 2:4; 4:1) and to express his concern for the Thessalonians' welfare (1Th 2:8).
2. *Persecution* – The Thessalonian church was founded in the midst of persecution. Paul encouraged the believers there to not be shaken by these afflictions because Christians are "going to experience affliction" (1Th 3:3-4).
3. *Sanctification* – Salvation isn't finished once a person believes in Christ and receives forgiveness of sins. Paul's prayer for the believers at Thessalonica in 1 Thessalonians 3:13 was that God would establish their hearts blameless in holiness before God.
4. *The second coming of Christ* – Jesus' return is mentioned in every chapter of 1 Thessalonians.

GIVE THANKS FOR THE BOOK OF 1 THESSALONIANS

First Thessalonians contributes to our understanding of the second coming of Christ. Paul wrote to correct misunderstandings of this doctrine, and in the process he showed us that Christ's return gives us true hope.

THE BOOK OF 1 THESSALONIANS IN HISTORY

150 BC

100 BC

168

146

First Jewish
community in
Thessalonica

Thessalonica
becomes capital of
the Roman province
of Macedonia

* Herod killed all boys two years old and younger in Bethlehem because the
star had appeared to the wise men approximately two years prior,
presumably at the moment of Jesus' birth. Since Herod died in 4 BC and
since Jesus was born roughly two years before Herod ordered the massacre
of the Bethlehem boys, it seems that Jesus was born in 5 BC or 6 BC.

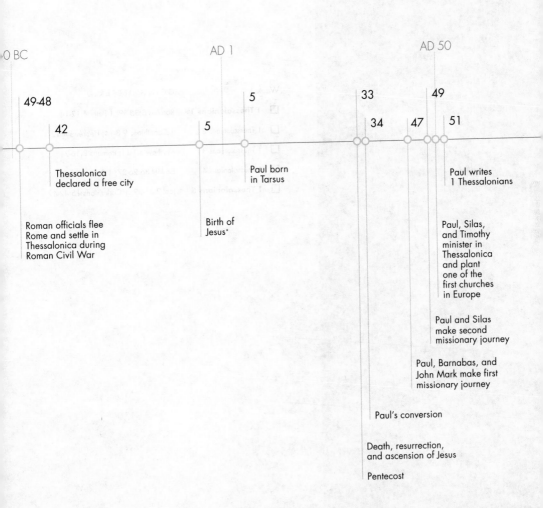

0 BC   AD 1   AD 50

49-48

42

5

5

33

34

47

49

51

Thessalonica
declared a free city

Paul born
in Tarsus

Paul writes
1 Thessalonians

Roman officials flee
Rome and settle in
Thessalonica during
Roman Civil War

Birth of
Jesus*

Paul, Silas,
and Timothy
minister in
Thessalonica
and plant
one of the
first churches
in Europe

Paul and Silas
make second
missionary journey

Paul, Barnabas, and
John Mark make first
missionary journey

Paul's conversion

Death, resurrection,
and ascension of Jesus

Pentecost

READ AND UNDERSTAND
1 THESSALONIANS

The Bible is a complete work in which many stories combine to tell one story. As you read the book of 1 Thessalonians, consider reading the additional passages to discover how the whole of Scripture works together.

GREETING

1 Paul, Silvanus,[A] and Timothy:

To the church of the Thessalonians in God the Father and the Lord Jesus Christ.

Grace to you and peace.[B]

THANKSGIVING

[2] We always thank God for all of you, making mention of you constantly in our prayers. [3] We recall, in the presence of our God and Father, your work produced by faith, your labor motivated by love, and your endurance inspired by hope in our Lord Jesus Christ. [4] For we know, brothers and sisters loved by God, that he has chosen you, [5] because our gospel did not come to you in word only, but also in power, in the Holy Spirit, and with full assurance. You know how we lived among you for your benefit, [6] and you yourselves became imitators of us and of the Lord when, in spite of severe persecution, you welcomed the message with joy from the Holy Spirit. [7] As a result, you became an example to all the believers in Macedonia and Achaia. [8] For the word of the Lord rang out from you, not only in Macedonia and Achaia, but in every place that your faith[C] in God has gone out. Therefore, we don't need to say anything, [9] for they themselves report[D] what kind of reception we had from you: how you turned to God from idols to serve the living and true God [10] and to wait for his Son from heaven, whom he raised from the dead — Jesus, who rescues us from the coming wrath.

PAUL'S CONDUCT

2 For you yourselves know, brothers and sisters, that our visit with you was not without result. [2] On the contrary, after we had previously suffered and were treated outrageously in Philippi, as you know, we were emboldened by our God to speak the gospel of God to you in spite of great opposition. [3] For our exhortation didn't come from error or impurity or an intent to deceive. [4] Instead, just as we have been approved by God to be entrusted with the gospel, so we speak, not to please people, but rather God, who examines our hearts. [5] For we never used flattering speech, as you know, or had greedy motives — God is our witness — [6] and we didn't seek glory from people, either from you or from others. [7] Although we could have been a burden as Christ's apostles, instead we were gentle[E] among you, as a nurse[F] nurtures her own children. [8] We cared so much for you that we were pleased to share with you not only the gospel of God but also our own lives, because you had become dear to us. [9] For you remember our labor and hardship, brothers and sisters. Working night and day so that we would not burden any of you, we preached God's gospel to you. [10] You are witnesses, and so is God, of how devoutly, righteously, and blamelessly we conducted ourselves with you believers. [11] As you know, like a father with his own children, [12] we encouraged, comforted, and implored each one of you to live worthy of God, who calls you into his own kingdom and glory.

[A]1:1 Or *Silas*; Ac 15:22-32; 16:19-40; 17:1-16   [B]1:1 Other mss add *from God our Father and the Lord Jesus Christ*   [C]1:8 Or *in every place news of your faith*   [D]1:9 Lit *report about us*   [E]2:7 Many mss read *infants*   [F]2:7 Or *nursing mother*

GRACE AND PEACE

1 THESSALONIANS 1; ACTS 20:24; 2 CORINTHIANS 11:1-6,12-15

"Grace to you and peace" (1Th 1:1).

Mark it in your Bibles, girls—these words are not here in 1 Thessalonians by coincidence. Grace and peace are the words the Apostle Paul used to greet the Christians in Rome, the churches of Corinth, Galatia, Ephesus, Philippi, Colossae, and Thessalonica, as well as his brothers in the faith—Timothy, Titus, and Philemon.

Clearly, these words were important to Paul and the first-century believers he wrote to. It's worth pausing a moment for a brief word study. Shall we?

The Greek word for "grace" used here is *charis* (khar'-ece), which means "an undeserved act of kindness." This is Paul's way of reminding each church that everything we have in Christ is unearned and cannot be repaid.

The Greek word for "peace" used here is *eiréné* (i-ray'-nay), which means "a sense of health, welfare or wholeness."

Each time "grace and peace" kicks off one of Paul's Epistles, they always come in that order: first grace, then peace. **There can be no wholeness apart from Christ's kindness.**

In almost all thirteen of his letters, "grace to you and peace" is followed by a note of thanksgiving. As Paul expressed his gratefulness for the church in Thessalonica, we learn of the trials they had overcome. The believers had endured severe persecution, yet they still embraced the truth of the gospel. They left their former way of life, turned from idols, and served the one true God.

The kindness of Christ had extended to the people in Thessalonica through the power of the Holy Spirit. Because the believers received the gospel with "full assurance" (1Th 1:5), they were able to experience wholeness in Christ despite great difficulty.

The church in Thessalonica was undeserving. They worshiped idols, not the true God. Yet God sent the message of the gospel to them despite their wickedness. Through the power of the Holy Spirit, they believed the truth and turned from their evil ways. Then, the people remained steadfast in their faith, endured trials and persecutions, and continued to spread the message of Christ. Their assurance in the message granted them peace and wholeness. This was grace and peace in action.

Paul's words extend beyond the first century all the way to you and me. By the power of the Holy Spirit, these words in 1 Thessalonians are still "living and effective" (Heb 4:12). They offer all of us grace and peace and encourage us to follow God and His Son, who was raised from the dead. They urge us to lean wholly on faith in Christ's crucifixion and resurrection.

The Greek roots help us dig a little deeper, but the message remains as simple as five words: "Grace to you and peace."

Salvation is unearned kindness and it brings wholeness. May these words in 1 Thessalonians call us to endure in faith and wait expectantly for Christ's return.

Grace and peace, dear friends.

RECEPTION AND OPPOSITION TO THE MESSAGE

¹³ This is why we constantly thank God, because when you received the word of God that you heard from us, you welcomed it not as a human message, but as it truly is, the word of God, which also works effectively in you who believe. ¹⁴ For you, brothers and sisters, became imitators of God's churches in Christ Jesus that are in Judea, since you have also suffered the same things from people of your own country, just as they did from the Jews ¹⁵ who killed the Lord Jesus and the prophets and persecuted us. They displease God and are hostile to everyone, ¹⁶ by keeping us from speaking to the Gentiles so that they may be saved. As a result, they are constantly filling up their sins to the limit, and wrath has overtaken them at last.ᴬ

PAUL'S DESIRE TO SEE THEM

¹⁷ But as for us, brothers and sisters, after we were forced to leave youᴮ for a short time (in person, not in heart), we greatly desired and made every effort to return and see you face to face. ¹⁸ So we wanted to come to you — even I, Paul, time and again — but Satan hindered us. ¹⁹ For who is our hope or joy or crown of boasting in the presence of our Lord Jesus at his coming? Is it not you? ²⁰ Indeed you are our glory and joy!

ANXIETY IN ATHENS

3 Therefore, when we could no longer stand it, we thought it was better to be left alone in Athens. ² And we sent Timothy, our brother and God's coworkerᶜ in the gospel of Christ, to strengthen and encourage you concerning your faith, ³ so that no one will be shaken by these afflictions. For you yourselves know that we are appointed to this. ⁴ In fact, when we were with you, we told you in advance that we were going to experience affliction, and as you know, it happened. ⁵ For this reason, when I could no longer stand it, I also sent him to find out about your faith, fearing that the tempter had tempted you and that our labor might be for nothing.

ENCOURAGED BY TIMOTHY

⁶ But now Timothy has come to us from you and brought us good news about your faith and love. He reported that you always have good memories of us and that you long to see us, as we also long to see you. ⁷ Therefore, brothers and sisters, in all our distress and affliction, we were encouraged about you through your faith. ⁸ For now we live, if you stand firm in the Lord. ⁹ How can we thank God for you in return for all the joy we experience before our God because of you, ¹⁰ as we pray very earnestly night and day to see you face to face and to complete what is lacking in your faith?

PRAYER FOR THE CHURCH

¹¹ Now may our God and Father himself, and our Lord Jesus, direct our way to you. ¹² And may the Lord cause you to increase and overflow with love for one another and for everyone, just as we do for you. ¹³ May he make your hearts blameless in holiness before our God and Father at the coming of our Lord Jesus with all his saints. Amen.ᴰ

ᴬ2:16 Or to the end　ᴮ2:17 Lit orphaned from you　ᶜ3:2 Other mss read servant
ᴰ3:13 Other mss omit Amen.

THE CALL TO SANCTIFICATION

4 Additionally then, brothers and sisters, we ask and encourage you in the Lord Jesus, that as you have received instruction from us on how you should live and please God — as you are doing[A] — do this even more. [2] For you know what commands we gave you through the Lord Jesus.

[3] For this is God's will, your sanctification: that you keep away from sexual immorality, [4] that each of you knows how to control his own body[B] in holiness and honor, [5] not with lustful passions, like the Gentiles, who don't know God. [6] This means one must not transgress against and take advantage of a brother or sister in this manner, because the Lord is an avenger of all these offenses, as we also previously told and warned you. [7] For God has not called us to impurity but to live in holiness. [8] Consequently, anyone who rejects this does not reject man, but God, who gives you his Holy Spirit.

LOVING AND WORKING

[9] About brotherly love: You don't need me to write you because you yourselves are taught by God to love one another. [10] In fact, you are doing this toward all the brothers and sisters in the entire region of Macedonia. But we encourage you, brothers and sisters, to do this even more, [11] to seek to lead a quiet life, to mind your own business,[C] and to work with your own hands, as we commanded you, [12] so that you may behave properly in the presence of outsiders and not be dependent on anyone.[D]

THE COMFORT OF CHRIST'S COMING

[13] We do not want you to be uninformed, brothers and sisters, concerning those who are asleep, so that you will not grieve like the rest, who have no hope. [14] For if we believe that Jesus died and rose again, in the same way, through Jesus, God will bring with him those who have fallen asleep. [15] For we say this to you by a word from the Lord: We who are still alive at the Lord's coming will certainly not precede those who have fallen asleep. [16] For the Lord himself will descend from heaven with a shout,[E] with the archangel's voice, and with the trumpet of God, and the dead in Christ will rise first. [17] Then we who are still alive, who are left, will be caught up together with them in the clouds to meet the Lord in the air, and so we will always be with the Lord. [18] Therefore encourage[F] one another with these words.

THE DAY OF THE LORD

5 About the times and the seasons: Brothers and sisters, you do not need anything to be written to you. [2] For you yourselves know very well that the day of the Lord will come just like a thief in the night. [3] When they say, "Peace and security," then sudden destruction will come upon them, like labor pains on a pregnant woman, and they will not escape. [4] But you, brothers and sisters, are not in the dark, for this day to surprise you like a thief. [5] For you are all children of light and children of the day. We do not belong to the night or the darkness. [6] So then, let us not sleep, like the rest, but let us stay awake and be self-controlled. [7] For those who sleep, sleep at night, and those

---

[A] 4:1 Lit walking   [B] 4:4 Or to acquire his own wife; lit to possess his own vessel
[C] 4:11 Lit to practice one's own things   [D] 4:12 Or not need anything, or not be in need   [E] 4:16 Or command   [F] 4:18 Or comfort

IN EVERYTHING, GIVE THANKS

1 THESSALONIANS 5; PSALM 105

What is God's will for my life?

Oh, the anxious hours I've spent with this question on repeat, searching for a spiritual formula to solve life's riddles. My college years especially were a mishmash of trusting the Lord with newfound abandon yet agonizing over every decision. *What am I supposed to study? Am I supposed to go on this mission trip or that one? Should I break up with this boy? Should we get back together?*

The weight of my young world balanced precariously on so many question marks. Sometimes it still does.

The uncertainties I've faced in each phase of life have felt big and I've felt small, like life is the sum of a million puzzles, most of them missing a piece (or ten). But as the years pass and draw me closer to the Lord, a surprising truth has become clear: **God's will is not a problem to be solved.**

God's Word tells me His faithfulness does not depend on my wisdom (Lm 3:22-24).

God's Word tells me His grace does not depend on my performance (Eph 2:8-9).

God's Word tells me that no matter what shape my life takes, His steadfastness and goodness trump whatever is going on around me (Ps 136).

Friends, our circumstances are big, but our God is bigger. And as we learn to trust the bigness of our God and the sureness of His sovereignty, we find that His will is not just a path—it is also a way of walking.

In his letter to the church at Thessalonica, Paul reduces all our agonizing life questions to a non-formula so simple it makes the perfectionists among us a little crazy:

"Rejoice always, pray constantly, give thanks in everything; for this is God's will for you in Christ Jesus."

1 THESSALONIANS 5:16-18

No hoops to jump through. No tests to pass. No situational tidiness required. Only actively resting in the goodness of our God.

Why an active resting? Because rejoicing is not a passive pursuit. Thanksgiving is not an emotion. We are to declare God's goodness in every circumstance. We are to let the world know what He has done and what He is doing. We are to pray to Him, seek Him, and give Him thanks with an expectant, joyful heart. This is God's will for us in Jesus.

There are heartaches among us today. So many question marks, so much waiting, so many puzzles missing a piece. But He is good. **In everything, He is good.**

God's love for you is steadfast, no matter the path you're walking. His promises hold even when your world is crumbling. It is not up to you to be the god of your circumstances. It is for you to give thanks to the One who is greater than any circumstance you will ever face.

who get drunk, get drunk at night. [8] But since we belong to the day, let us be self-controlled and put on the armor of faith and love, and a helmet of the hope of salvation. [9] For God did not appoint us to wrath, but to obtain salvation through our Lord Jesus Christ, [10] who died for us, so that whether we are awake or asleep, we may live together with him. [11] Therefore encourage one another and build each other up as you are already doing.

EXHORTATIONS AND BLESSINGS

[12] Now we ask you, brothers and sisters, to give recognition to those who labor among you and lead you[A] in the Lord and admonish you, [13] and to regard them very highly in love because of their work. Be at peace among yourselves. [14] And we exhort you, brothers and sisters: warn those who are idle,[B] comfort the discouraged, help the weak, be patient with everyone. [15] See to it that no one repays evil for evil to anyone, but always pursue what is good for one another and for all. [16] Rejoice always, [17] pray constantly, [18] give thanks in everything; for this is God's will for you in Christ Jesus. [19] Don't stifle the Spirit. [20] Don't despise prophecies, [21] but test all things. Hold on to what is good. [22] Stay away from every kind of evil.

[23] Now may the God of peace himself sanctify you completely. And may your whole spirit, soul, and body be kept sound and blameless at the coming of our Lord Jesus Christ. [24] He who calls you is faithful; he will do it. [25] Brothers and sisters, pray for us also. [26] Greet all the brothers and sisters with a holy kiss. [27] I charge you by the Lord that this letter be read to all the brothers and sisters. [28] The grace of our Lord Jesus Christ be with you.

A 5:12 Or care for you   B 5:14 Or who are disorderly, or who are undisciplined

May the Lord direct your hearts to God's love and Christ's endurance

2 thessalonians

 May the Lord direct your hearts to God's love and Christ's endurance. **3:5**

ON THE TIMELINE While there are few indicators about the date and place of writing of 2 Thessalonians, it was probably written from Corinth around AD 50–51, shortly after 1 Thessalonians.

A LITTLE BACKGROUND Following up on his first letter to the Thessalonians, Paul wrote to give further clarification on how to live the Christian life in light of the return of Christ. The Thessalonian believers were called to stand firm and live useful lives because the return of Christ might be in the distant future.

MESSAGE & PURPOSE Paul wrote in part to encourage the Thessalonian believers to stand firm in truth in the midst of persecution (2Th 2:13-15) and to assure them that God would judge those afflicting them (2Th 1:6-9). The short letter addresses the present need of the congregation by focusing on four main themes:

1. *The greatness of God* – God elects (2Th 2:13), calls (2Th 1:11; 2:14), and saves His Church, and His purpose on earth will continue until Christ's return.

2. *The second coming* – The second coming is seen here in terms of the overthrow of all evil, especially the "man of lawlessness" (2Th 2:3).

3. *The day of the LORD* – The "day of the LORD" was coming, though several things must happen first, including the arrival of "the apostasy" and the revelation of "the man of lawlessness" (2Th 2:1-3).

4. *Life and work* – Paul addressed the issue of people he called "busybodies" and who appeared to be idle (2Th 3:6-12). Christians are to work and not interfere with the work of others.

GIVE THANKS FOR THE BOOK OF 2 THESSALONIANS

Second Thessalonians continues and further amplifies some of the same themes as 1 Thessalonians: persecution, sanctification, and end-time events associated with the second coming of Christ. The letter proclaims salvation in Christ—a salvation that will be consummated when Christ comes again to overthrow all evil and bring rest and glory to His own. Meanwhile, God loves His people and gives them great comfort and hope, even in the midst of persecution (2Th 2:16).

THE BOOK OF 2 THESSALONIANS IN HISTORY

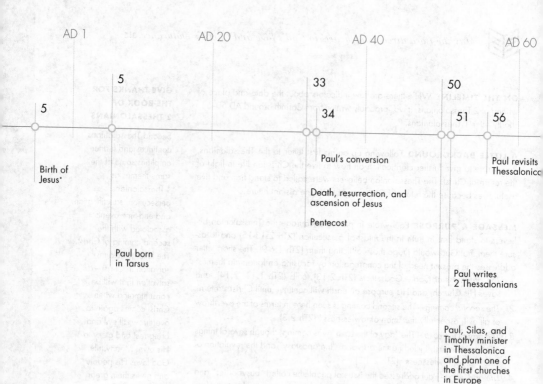

AD 1

AD 20

AD 40

AD 60

5

5

33

34

50

51

56

Birth of Jesus*

Paul born in Tarsus

Paul's conversion

Death, resurrection, and ascension of Jesus

Pentecost

Paul writes 2 Thessalonians

Paul, Silas, and Timothy minister in Thessalonica and plant one of the first churches in Europe

Paul revisits Thessalonica

* Herod killed all boys two years old and younger in Bethlehem because the star had appeared to the wise men approximately two years prior, presumably at the moment of Jesus' birth. Since Herod died in 4 BC and since Jesus was born roughly two years before Herod ordered the massacre of the Bethlehem boys, it seems that Jesus was born in 5 BC or 6 BC.

READ AND UNDERSTAND
2 THESSALONIANS

The Bible is a complete work in which many stories combine to tell one story. As you read the book of 2 Thessalonians, consider reading the additional passages to discover how the whole of Scripture works together.

GREETING

1 Paul, Silvanus, [A] and Timothy:
To the church of the Thessalonians in God our Father and the Lord Jesus Christ.

² Grace to you and peace from God our Father and the Lord Jesus Christ.

GOD'S JUDGMENT AND GLORY

³ We ought to thank God always for you, brothers and sisters, and rightly so, since your faith is flourishing and the love each one of you has for one another is increasing. ⁴ Therefore, we ourselves boast about you among God's churches — about your perseverance and faith in all the persecutions and afflictions that you are enduring. ⁵ It is clear evidence of God's righteous judgment that you will be counted worthy of God's kingdom, for which you also are suffering, ⁶ since it is just for God to repay with affliction those who afflict you ⁷ and to give relief to you who are afflicted, along with us. This will take place at the revelation of the Lord Jesus from heaven with his powerful angels, ⁸ when he takes vengeance with flaming fire on those who don't know God and on those who don't obey the gospel of our Lord Jesus. ⁹ They will pay the penalty of eternal destruction from the Lord's presence and from his glorious strength ¹⁰ on that day when he comes to be glorified by his saints and to be marveled at by all those who have believed, because our testimony among you was believed. ¹¹ In view of this, we always pray for you that our God will make you worthy of his calling, and by his power fulfill your every desire to do good [B] and your work produced by faith, ¹² so that the name of our Lord Jesus will be glorified by you, and you by him, according to the grace of our God and the Lord Jesus Christ.

THE MAN OF LAWLESSNESS

2 Now concerning the coming of our Lord Jesus Christ and our being gathered to him: We ask you, brothers and sisters, ² not to be easily upset or troubled, either by a prophecy [C] or by a message or by a letter supposedly from us, alleging that the day of the Lord [D] has come. ³ Don't let anyone deceive you in any way. For that day will not come unless the apostasy [E] comes first and the man of lawlessness [F] is revealed, the man doomed to destruction. ⁴ He opposes and exalts himself above every so-called god or object of worship, so that he sits [G] in God's temple, proclaiming that he himself is God.

⁵ Don't you remember that when I was still with you I used to tell you about this? ⁶ And you know what currently restrains him, so that he will be revealed in his time. ⁷ For the mystery of lawlessness is already at work, but the one now restraining will do so until he is out of the way, ⁸ and then the lawless one will be revealed. The Lord Jesus will destroy him with the breath of his mouth and will bring him to nothing at the appearance of his coming. ⁹ The coming of the lawless one is based on Satan's working, with all kinds of false miracles, signs, and wonders, ¹⁰ and with every wicked deception among those who are perishing. They perish because they did not accept the love

---

[A] 1:1 Or *Silas*; Ac 15:22-32; 16:19-40; 17:1-16   [B] 1:11 Or *power bring to fruition your desire to do good*   [C] 2:2 Or *spiritual utterance*   [D] 2:2 Other mss read *Christ*   [E] 2:3 Or *rebellion*   [F] 2:3 Other mss read *man of sin*   [G] 2:4 Other mss add *as God* of the truth and so be saved. [11] For this reason God sends them a strong delusion so that they will believe the lie, [12] so that all will be condemned — those who did not believe the truth but delighted in unrighteousness.

STAND FIRM

[13] But we ought to thank God always for you, brothers and sisters loved by the Lord, because from the beginning[A] God has chosen you for salvation through sanctification by the Spirit and through belief in the truth. [14] He called you to this through our gospel, so that you might obtain the glory of our Lord Jesus Christ. [15] So then, brothers and sisters, stand firm and hold to the traditions you were taught, whether by what we said or what we wrote.

[16] May our Lord Jesus Christ himself and God our Father, who has loved us and given us eternal encouragement and good hope by grace, [17] encourage your hearts and strengthen you in every good work and word.

PRAY FOR US

3 In addition, brothers and sisters, pray for us that the word of the Lord may spread rapidly and be honored, just as it was with you, [2] and that we may be delivered from wicked and evil people, for not all have faith.[B] [3] But the Lord is faithful; he will strengthen and guard you from the evil one. [4] We have confidence in the Lord about you, that you are doing and will continue to do what we command. [5] May the Lord direct your hearts to God's love and Christ's endurance.

WARNING AGAINST IRRESPONSIBLE BEHAVIOR

[6] Now we command you, brothers and sisters, in the name of our Lord Jesus Christ, to keep away from every brother or sister who is idle and does not live according to the tradition received from us. [7] For you yourselves know how you should imitate us: We were not idle among you; [8] we did not eat anyone's food free of charge; instead, we labored and toiled, working night and day, so that we would not be a burden to any of you. [9] It is not that we don't have the right to support, but we did it to make ourselves an example to you so that you would imitate us. [10] In fact, when we were with you, this is what we commanded you: "If anyone isn't willing to work, he should not eat." [11] For we hear that there are some among you who are idle. They are not busy but busybodies. [12] Now we command and exhort such people by the Lord Jesus Christ to work quietly and provide for themselves.[C] [13] But as for you, brothers and sisters, do not grow weary in doing good.

[14] If anyone does not obey our instruction in this letter, take note of that person; don't associate with him, so that he may be ashamed. [15] Yet don't consider him as an enemy, but warn him as a brother.

FINAL GREETINGS

[16] May the Lord of peace himself give you peace always in every way. The Lord be with all of you. [17] I, Paul, am writing this greeting with my own hand, which is an authenticating mark in every letter; this is how I write. [18] The grace of our Lord Jesus Christ be with you all.

[A]2:13 Other mss read *because as a firstfruit* [B]3:2 Or *for the faith is not in everyone* [C]3:12 Lit *they may eat their own bread*

GRABBING ON TO CHRIST'S ENDURANCE

2 THESSALONIANS 3:1-5; 1 PETER 5:8-11

I try not to follow ambulances, rubberneck at traffic accidents, or stare when someone drops a whole bag of marbles on the ground. But when something goes terribly wrong, somehow we all want to turn our heads to watch. I think it comes from twin desires to help but also gawk.

Recently, my eight-year-old and I walked into the food court of our local mall. There we found ourselves pushed to the front of a crowd that must have been nearing a hundred people. They were encircling a lifeless boy on the floor who looked to be no more than two years old. Together, we stood helpless, looking on while EMTs performed CPR on his little body.

I don't know a lot about medicine, but I do know you only implement CPR if there is no pulse or breathing. It's our way of manually keeping a body going. Since that was already being done, there was really nothing left for the other one hundred of us to do.

And so we all stood still and watched. His mother didn't cry; she paced, she moaned, she shouted. We felt powerless to help the child or his mother. It was shocking to see so many people standing there, hands at their sides, while the battle between life and death was fought right in front of us.

It's awful to face our own powerlessness. I like to really lean my shoulder into a job and then promptly see a result for my effort. But when it comes down to it, when things are really important, I'm like that crowd of people, rendered helpless, left watching and waiting.

In 2 Thessalonians 3:5, Paul prays, "May the Lord direct your hearts to God's love and Christ's endurance." The whole Christian walk is one of dependence. The air we breathe, the gravity that holds us to the earth, and the ability to wonder at it—it all comes from God's common grace. We have no endurance apart from the endurance of Christ.

Moments of calamity and tragedy unveil our deep neediness and utter helplessness. They direct us to our only strength and recourse, which is Christ.

When we saw the baby and his mother in crisis, I took my little girl by the hand and led her around the corner where we found a quiet spot to pray. But even our prayers are recognition of our enormous need. Prayer is not about what we do, but about running to the God who can do all things. It is an avenue for God to impart His love and endurance to us.

What a tremendous grace this is, to know the God who loves perfectly, to be in relationship with the God who endures endlessly. In the face of our overwhelming sorrows, His is the real strength in our ever-present weakness.

Christ Jesus came into the world to save sinners

1 timothy

 This saying is trustworthy and deserving of full acceptance: "Christ Jesus came into the world to save sinners"—and I am the worst of them. **1:15**

ON THE TIMELINE Paul most likely wrote 1 Timothy after the time covered in the book of Acts (after AD 62). While Acts closes with Paul in prison, it is believed that Paul was then released and continued his work around the Mediterranean, perhaps even reaching Spain (Rm 15:22-29). First Timothy was written during this period of further mission work, likely around AD 63.

A LITTLE BACKGROUND Timothy, a native of Lystra, may have been converted on Paul's first missionary journey (Ac 14:6-23). Paul referred to Timothy as his child in the Lord (1Tm 1:2; 1Co 4:17). When Paul came to Lystra on his second journey, Timothy was a disciple who was well respected by the believers (Ac 16:1-2). Paul asked Timothy to accompany him and Silas as he moved westward. Timothy not only accompanied Paul but also was sent on many crucial missions by Paul (Ac 17:14-15; 18:5; 19:22; 20:4). When Paul was unable to go to Corinth, he sent Timothy to represent him and his teachings (1Co 4:17). Later when Paul was in prison, he sent Timothy to Philippi (Php 2:19) and then to Ephesus, where it's believed Timothy was when Paul wrote 1 Timothy.

MESSAGE & PURPOSE The epistle contains instructions concerning order and structure in the church and political advice for the young pastor. One important theme in this and the other two Pastoral Epistles (2 Timothy and Titus) is sound teaching. Paul urged Timothy and Titus to confront the false teaching with sound teaching and sound doctrine. The Greek word for "sound" occurs ten times in these three letters (1Tm 1:10; 6:3; 2Tm 1:7,13; 4:3; Ti 1:9,13; 2:1-2,8).

GIVE THANKS FOR THE BOOK OF 1 TIMOTHY

First Timothy offers rich theological and ethical wisdom. Paul draws clear connections between doctrine and ethics, belief and behavior. While 1 Timothy and the other Pastoral Epistles were not intended to provide a detailed account of church government, they do provide some significant insights on this topic. The lists of characteristics for overseers (1Tm 3:1-7; Ti 1:5-9) and deacons (1Tm 3:8-13), for example, are the only such lists in the New Testament.

THE BOOK OF 1 TIMOTHY IN HISTORY

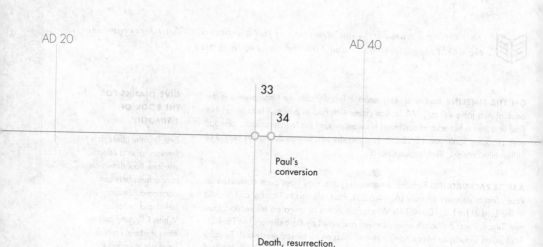

AD 20

AD 40

33

34

Paul's
conversion

Death, resurrection,
and ascension of Jesus

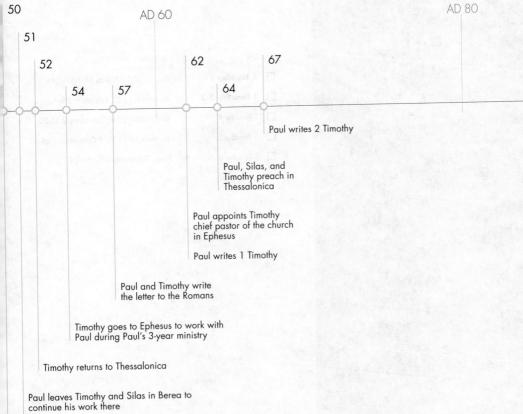

50

51

AD 60

52

62

67

54   57

64

Paul writes 2 Timothy

Paul, Silas, and
Timothy preach in
Thessalonica

Paul appoints Timothy
chief pastor of the church
in Ephesus

Paul writes 1 Timothy

Paul and Timothy write
the letter to the Romans

Timothy goes to Ephesus to work with
Paul during Paul's 3-year ministry

Timothy returns to Thessalonica

Paul leaves Timothy and Silas in Berea to
continue his work there

Timothy and Paul are reunited in Athens

Paul and Silas come to Lystra and take Timothy
with them on their second missionary journey

AD 80

READ AND UNDERSTAND 1 TIMOTHY

The Bible is a complete work in which many stories combine to tell one story. As you read the book of 1 Timothy, consider reading the additional passages to discover how the whole of Scripture works together.

GREETING

1 Paul, an apostle of Christ Jesus by the command of God our Savior and of Christ Jesus our hope:

² To Timothy, my true son in the faith.

Grace, mercy, and peace from God the ᴬ Father and Christ Jesus our Lord.

FALSE DOCTRINE AND MISUSE OF THE LAW

³ As I urged you when I went to Macedonia, remain in Ephesus so that you may instruct certain people not to teach false doctrine ⁴ or to pay attention to myths and endless genealogies. These promote empty speculations rather than God's plan, which operates by faith. ⁵ Now the goal of our instruction is love that comes from a pure heart, a good conscience, and a sincere faith. ⁶ Some have departed from these and turned aside to fruitless discussion. ⁷ They want to be teachers of the law, although they don't understand what they are saying or what they are insisting on. ⁸ But we know that the law is good, provided one uses it legitimately. ⁹ We know that the law is not meant for a righteous person, but for the lawless and rebellious, for the ungodly and sinful, for the unholy and irreverent, for those who kill their fathers and mothers, for murderers, ¹⁰ for the sexually immoral and homosexuals, for slave traders, liars, perjurers, and for whatever else is contrary to the sound teaching ¹¹ that conforms to the gospel concerning the glory of the blessed God, which was entrusted to me.

PAUL'S TESTIMONY

¹² I give thanks to Christ Jesus our Lord who has strengthened me, because he considered me faithful, appointing me to the ministry — ¹³ even though I was formerly a blasphemer, a persecutor, and an arrogant man. But I received mercy because I acted out of ignorance in unbelief, ¹⁴ and the grace of our Lord overflowed, along with the faith and love that are in Christ Jesus. ¹⁵ This saying is trustworthy and deserving of full acceptance: "Christ Jesus came into the world to save sinners" — and I am the worst of them. ¹⁶ But I received mercy for this reason, so that in me, the worst of them, Christ Jesus might demonstrate his extraordinary patience as an example to those who would believe in him for eternal life. ¹⁷ Now to the King eternal, immortal, invisible, the only ᴮ God, be honor and glory forever and ever. Amen.

ENGAGE IN BATTLE

¹⁸ Timothy, my son, I am giving you this instruction in keeping with the prophecies previously made about you, so that by recalling them you may fight the good fight, ¹⁹ having faith and a good conscience. Some have rejected these and have shipwrecked their faith. ²⁰ Among them are Hymenaeus and Alexander, whom I have delivered to Satan, so that they may be taught not to blaspheme.

INSTRUCTIONS ON PRAYER

2 First of all, then, I urge that petitions, prayers, intercessions, and thanksgivings be made for everyone, ² for kings and all those who are in authority, so that we may lead a tranquil and quiet life in all godliness and

---

ᴬ1:2 Other mss read *our* ᴮ1:17 Other mss add *wise*

THE WORST

1 TIMOTHY 1; ROMANS 5:6-8

They may not look like a formidable foe, but the bookshelves at my office nearly did me in. These floor-to-ceiling units store beautiful product, ready to be shipped. Putting them together, however, was not so pretty.

On move-in day, I bravely rolled up my sleeves, thinking, *how bad could it be?* I watched my coworkers breeze through the process, knowing exactly where to place each dowel, cam, and screw. Meanwhile, I was still comparing the parts in my hand to the instructions, hoping that if I looked distressed enough the bookshelves might magically assemble themselves.

Somehow, at the end of the day, all the bookshelves were standing tall, but I couldn't help but overhear someone kid in my direction, "Building bookcases is definitely not one of her spiritual gifts." I wholeheartedly agree. I'm the worst at a few things, including carpentry, water skiing, and eating leftovers. On the other hand, there are some things I take pride in doing well, like public speaking, typing really fast, and knowing all the lyrics to my favorite Broadway hits.

Isn't that how it goes? I want to avoid dwelling on my faults, so I immediately justify them with my strengths. But applying this same earn-my-keep principle to the gospel won't work.

Paul writes, "This saying is trustworthy and deserving of full acceptance: 'Christ Jesus came into the world to save sinners'—and I am the worst of them" (1Tm 1:15).

The worst of them. Period. Paul doesn't follow this with a statement to justify his flaws or qualify himself for a Savior, and neither can I.

We instinctively operate out of our sin. But the crazy-beautiful reality of the gospel is that Jesus takes our weaknesses and uses them to magnify His strength. Paul describes this in 1 Timothy 1:16:

"But I received mercy for this reason, so that in me, the worst of them, Christ Jesus might demonstrate his extraordinary patience as an example to those who would believe in him for eternal life."

Oh, the patience and mercy of our Savior!

When we leap into these grace-granting conditions fashioned by Jesus, we can become disoriented. We want to shake our fists at the law for revealing our powerlessness over our sin (Rm 7:7). But we also need the law—we need outside direction to lead us away from our inward wickedness. God's law itself is good and its goal is love (1Tm 1:5).

May we trust the Lord and His law, allowing our weakness and our strength to fade into His mercy and perfection. He loves us at our very worst, and I'm so very grateful.

dignity. [3] This is good, and it pleases God our Savior, [4] who wants everyone to be saved and to come to the knowledge of the truth.

[5] For there is one God and one mediator between God and humanity, the man Christ Jesus, [6] who gave himself as a ransom for all, a testimony at the proper time.

[7] For this I was appointed a herald, an apostle (I am telling the truth;[A] I am not lying), and a teacher of the Gentiles in faith and truth.

INSTRUCTIONS TO MEN AND WOMEN

[8] Therefore, I want the men in every place to pray, lifting up holy hands without anger or argument. [9] Also, the women are to dress themselves in modest clothing, with decency and good sense, not with elaborate hairstyles, gold, pearls, or expensive apparel, [10] but with good works, as is proper for women who profess to worship God. [11] A woman is to learn quietly with full submission. [12] I do not allow a woman to teach or to have authority over a man; instead, she is to remain quiet. [13] For Adam was formed first, then Eve. [14] And Adam was not deceived, but the woman was deceived and transgressed. [15] But she will be saved through childbearing, if they continue in faith, love, and holiness, with good sense.

QUALIFICATIONS FOR OVERSEERS AND DEACONS

3 This saying is trustworthy: "If anyone aspires to be an overseer,[B] he desires a noble work." [2] An overseer, therefore, must be above reproach, the husband of one wife, self-controlled, sensible, respectable, hospitable, able to teach, [3] not an excessive drinker, not a bully but gentle, not quarrelsome, not greedy. [4] He must manage his own household competently and have his children under control with all dignity. [5] (If anyone does not know how to manage his own household, how will he take care of God's church?) [6] He must not be a new convert, or he might become conceited and incur the same condemnation as the devil. [7] Furthermore, he must have a good reputation among outsiders, so that he does not fall into disgrace and the devil's trap.

[8] Deacons, likewise, should be worthy of respect, not hypocritical, not drinking a lot of wine, not greedy for money, [9] holding the mystery of the faith with a clear conscience. [10] They must also be tested first; if they prove blameless, then they can serve as deacons. [11] Wives,[C] too, must be worthy of respect, not slanderers, self-controlled, faithful in everything. [12] Deacons are to be husbands of one wife, managing their children and their own households competently. [13] For those who have served well as deacons acquire a good standing for themselves and great boldness in the faith that is in Christ Jesus.

THE MYSTERY OF GODLINESS

[14] I write these things to you, hoping to come to you soon. [15] But if I should be delayed, I have written so that you will know how people ought to conduct themselves in God's household, which is the church of the living God, the pillar and foundation of the truth. [16] And most certainly, the mystery of godliness is great:

A 2:7 Other mss add *in Christ* B 3:1 Or *bishop, pastor* C 3:11 Or *The women*

OUR ANTHEM

1 TIMOTHY 2-3; 1 TIMOTHY 5:6-14; EPHESIANS 5:19-20

The hymn "In Christ Alone" has been my church's unofficial anthem for several years now. I say "anthem" because whenever the worship leader begins to play the familiar chords, the energy in the room changes. Everyone's attention seems to become more focused, both forward and upward. People stand without prompting, and by the end of the song, we're all sort of yell-singing our favorite line: "Up from the grave He rose again!" We are declaring in this anthem what we believe. We're reminding each other of what's true, and the power of this is tangible in the room.

Perhaps this is why Paul slipped a hymn into his instructions for Timothy. "The mystery of godliness is great," he says in 1 Timothy 3:16. He then explains what that mystery is by using lines from what some scholars believe was a popular hymn of his time:

"He was manifested in the flesh, vindicated in the Spirit, seen by angels, preached among the nations, believed on in the world, taken up in glory."

1 TIMOTHY 3:16

These are the basic tenets of Christianity—truths Timothy knew well. Paul understood our human tendency to forget the truth and simply begin to follow a religion or set of rules for the sake

of following something. Using the power of an anthem—his "In Christ Alone," shall we say—Paul reminds Timothy of the gospel before diving into further spiritual instruction. We need the same thing.

There's a method to our godliness, and it's crucial to understand the reason behind what we do and who we live for if we're going to stand strong in our faith.

In almost the same breath that he declares the mystery of godliness, Paul also delivers a warning to Timothy, saying that in later times there will be false teachers, deceitful spirits, and many who depart from the faith (1Tm 4:1-2).

Paul was right. Heresy, deceit, and hypocrisy are not only things of the future; they are rampant in our world now. Knowing, understanding, and believing the mystery of godliness—the gospel of Jesus Christ—is more crucial than ever. Without God's truth as our anchor, we will float from here to there with each person who enters our lives touting a new philosophy or theology (Jms 1:6). But with our anthem close to our hearts, we remember who Jesus is and we can distinguish His truth from the lies.

Just as Paul did in his letter to Timothy, we must remember and remind one another of what is true. We declare our anthem to one another again and again, "giving thanks always for everything to God the Father in the name of our Lord Jesus Christ" (Eph 5:19-20). Amen.

He[A] was manifested in the flesh,
vindicated in the Spirit,
seen by angels,
preached among the nations,
believed on in the world,
taken up in glory.

DEMONIC INFLUENCE

4 Now the Spirit explicitly says that in later times some will depart from the faith, paying attention to deceitful spirits and the teachings of demons, ² through the hypocrisy of liars whose consciences are seared. ³ They forbid marriage and demand abstinence from foods that God created to be received with gratitude by those who believe and know the truth. ⁴ For everything created by God is good, and nothing is to be rejected if it is received with thanksgiving, ⁵ since it is sanctified by the word of God and by prayer.

A GOOD SERVANT OF JESUS CHRIST

⁶ If you point these things out to the brothers and sisters, you will be a good servant of Christ Jesus, nourished by the words of the faith and the good teaching that you have followed. ⁷ But have nothing to do with pointless and silly myths. Rather, train yourself in godliness. ⁸ For the training of the body has limited benefit, but godliness is beneficial in every way, since it holds promise for the present life and also for the life to come. ⁹ This saying is trustworthy and deserves full acceptance. ¹⁰ For this reason we labor and strive,[B] because we have put our hope in the living God, who is the Savior of all people, especially of those who believe.

INSTRUCTIONS FOR MINISTRY

¹¹ Command and teach these things. ¹² Don't let anyone despise your youth, but set an example for the believers in speech, in conduct, in love,[C] in faith, and in purity. ¹³ Until I come, give your attention to public reading, exhortation, and teaching. ¹⁴ Don't neglect the gift that is in you; it was given to you through prophecy, with the laying on of hands by the council of elders. ¹⁵ Practice these things; be committed to them, so that your progress may be evident to all. ¹⁶ Pay close attention to your life and your teaching; persevere in these things, for in doing this you will save both yourself and your hearers.

5 Don't rebuke an older man, but exhort him as a father, younger men as brothers, ² older women as mothers, and the younger women as sisters with all purity.

THE SUPPORT OF WIDOWS

³ Support[D] widows who are genuinely in need. ⁴ But if any widow has children or grandchildren, let them learn to practice godliness toward their own family first and to repay their parents, for this pleases God. ⁵ The widow who is truly in need and left all alone has put her hope in God and continues night and day in her petitions and prayers; ⁶ however, she who is self-indulgent is dead even while she lives. ⁷ Command this also, so that they will be above

---

[A]3:16 Other mss read *God*   [B]4:10 Other mss read *and suffer reproach*
[C]4:12 Other mss add *in spirit,*   [D]5:3 Lit *Honor*

reproach. [8] But if anyone does not provide for his own family, especially for his own household, he has denied the faith and is worse than an unbeliever.

[9] No widow is to be enrolled on the list for support unless she is at least sixty years old, has been the wife of one husband, [10] and is well known for good works — that is, if she has brought up children, shown hospitality, washed the saints' feet, helped the afflicted, and devoted herself to every good work. [11] But refuse to enroll younger widows, for when they are drawn away from Christ by desire, they want to marry [12] and will therefore receive condemnation because they have renounced their original pledge. [13] At the same time, they also learn to be idle, going from house to house; they are not only idle, but are also gossips and busybodies, saying things they shouldn't say. [14] Therefore, I want younger women to marry, have children, manage their households, and give the adversary no opportunity to accuse us. [15] For some have already turned away to follow Satan. [16] If any[A] believing woman has widows in her family, let her help them. Let the church not be burdened, so that it can help widows in genuine need.

HONORING THE ELDERS

[17] The elders who are good leaders are to be considered worthy of double honor,[B] especially those who work hard at preaching and teaching. [18] For the Scripture says: **Do not muzzle an ox while it is treading out the grain,**[C] and "The worker is worthy of his wages."

[19] Don't accept an accusation against an elder unless it is supported by two or three witnesses. [20] Publicly rebuke those who sin, so that the rest will be afraid. [21] I solemnly charge you before God and Christ Jesus and the elect angels to observe these things without prejudice, doing nothing out of favoritism. [22] Don't be too quick to appoint[D] anyone as an elder, and don't share in the sins of others. Keep yourself pure. [23] Don't continue drinking only water, but use a little wine because of your stomach and your frequent illnesses. [24] Some people's sins are obvious, preceding them to judgment, but the sins of others surface[E] later. [25] Likewise, good works are obvious, and those that are not obvious cannot remain hidden.

HONORING MASTERS

6 All who are under the yoke as slaves should regard their own masters[F] as worthy of all respect, so that God's name and his teaching will not be blasphemed. [2] Let those who have believing masters not be disrespectful to them because they are brothers, but serve them even better, since those who benefit from their service are believers and dearly loved.[G]

FALSE DOCTRINE AND HUMAN GREED

Teach and encourage these things. [3] If anyone teaches false doctrine and does not agree with the sound teaching of our Lord Jesus Christ and with the teaching that promotes godliness, [4] he is conceited and understands nothing, but has an unhealthy interest in disputes and arguments over words.

[A] 5:16 Other mss add *believing man or*   [B] 5:17 Or *of respect and remuneration*
[C] 5:18 Dt 25:4   [D] 5:22 Lit *to lay hands on*   [E] 5:24 Lit *follow*   [F] 6:1 Or *owners*
[G] 6:2 Or *because, as believers who are dearly loved, they are devoted to others' welfare*

From these come envy, quarreling, slander, evil suspicions, [5] and constant disagreement among people whose minds are depraved and deprived of the truth, who imagine that godliness is a way to material gain. [A] [6] But godliness with contentment is great gain. [7] For we brought nothing into the world, and [B] we can take nothing out. [8] If we have food and clothing, [C] we will be content with these. [9] But those who want to be rich fall into temptation, a trap, and many foolish and harmful desires, which plunge people into ruin and destruction. [10] For the love of money is a root [D] of all kinds of evil, and by craving it, some have wandered away from the faith and pierced themselves with many griefs.

FIGHT THE GOOD FIGHT

[11] But you, man of God, flee from these things, and pursue righteousness, godliness, faith, love, endurance, and gentleness. [12] Fight the good fight of the faith. Take hold of eternal life to which you were called and about which you have made a good confession in the presence of many witnesses. [13] In the presence of God, who gives life to all, and of Christ Jesus, who gave a good confession before Pontius Pilate, I charge you [14] to keep this command without fault or failure until the appearing of our Lord Jesus Christ. [15] God will bring this about in his own time. He is the blessed and only Sovereign, the King of kings, and the Lord of lords, [16] who alone is immortal and who lives in unapproachable light, whom no one has seen or can see, to him be honor and eternal power. Amen.

INSTRUCTIONS TO THE RICH

[17] Instruct those who are rich in the present age not to be arrogant or to set their hope on the uncertainty of wealth, but on God, [E] who richly provides us with all things to enjoy. [18] Instruct them to do what is good, to be rich in good works, to be generous and willing to share, [19] storing up treasure for themselves as a good foundation for the coming age, so that they may take hold of what is truly life.

GUARD THE HERITAGE

[20] Timothy, guard what has been entrusted to you, avoiding irreverent and empty speech and contradictions from what is falsely called knowledge. [21] By professing it, some people have departed from the faith.

Grace be with you all.

[A] 6:5 Other mss add *From such people withdraw yourself.* [B] 6:7 Other mss add *it is clear that* [C] 6:8 Or *food and shelter* [D] 6:10 Or *is the root* [E] 6:17 Other mss read *on the living God*

all scripture
is inspired
by God

2 timothy

 All Scripture is inspired by God and is profitable for teaching, for rebuking, for correcting, for training in righteousness, so that the man of God may be complete, equipped for every good work. **3:16-17**

ON THE TIMELINE During Paul's final imprisonment, he wrote this letter to request another visit from Timothy and to give final exhortations as he anticipated his martyrdom. Second Timothy was written during the final days before Paul's death in AD 67 or 68.

A LITTLE BACKGROUND Timothy was a friend and trusted coworker of Paul. When Timothy was a child, his mother Eunice and his grandmother Lois taught him the Scriptures (2Tm 1:5; 3:15). In this highly personal letter, Paul reminds Timothy of his godly heritage and urged him to keep ablaze the gift God imparted to him when Paul set him apart for ministry. Knowing that his time was short and that winter was approaching, Paul urged him to come soon. Although written in extremely difficult circumstances, this letter exudes thanksgiving and hope in a future secure in Christ.

MESSAGE & PURPOSE After reminding Timothy of his rich heritage and the gift God had planted within him, Paul urged Timothy to be strong in Jesus Christ. He used the metaphors of a good soldier, an athlete, and a hardworking farmer when describing the Christian's calling. The purpose of that calling is so all those called "may obtain salvation, which is in Christ Jesus" (2Tm 2:10). Timothy was to be one who would be "correctly teaching the word of truth" (2Tm 2:15) in the face of those who mishandled skills as he led God's people (2Tm 2:23-26). Scripture, God's inspired Word, is to be the foundation for his teaching, designed to make believers complete and equipped for every good work.

GIVE THANKS FOR THE BOOK OF 2 TIMOTHY

As Paul built up church leaders, he expressed concern for the spread of the truth of the gospel. He referred to the gospel as "the faith" (1Tm 3:9; 2Tm 4:7; Ti 1:13); "the truth" (1Tm 4:3; 2Tm 2:25; Ti 1:1); sound or healthy teaching (1Tm 1:10; 2Tm 1:13; 4:3; Ti 1:9; 2:1); and godliness or sound religion (1Tm 3:16; 6:3; Ti 1:1). Paul may have used these terms because they represent the phrases used by his opponents. Paul's faithfulness in refuting false gospels laid a significant foundation for the early Church as well as the faith of believers today.

THE BOOK OF 2 TIMOTHY IN HISTORY

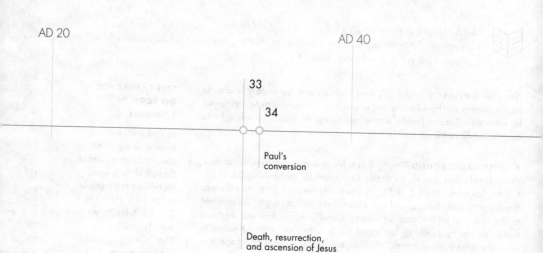

AD 20

AD 40

33

34

Paul's
conversion

Death, resurrection,
and ascension of Jesus

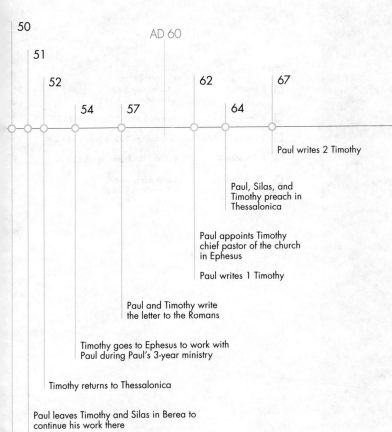

50

51

52

54   57

AD 60

62

64

67

AD 80

Paul writes 2 Timothy

Paul, Silas, and
Timothy preach in
Thessalonica

Paul appoints Timothy
chief pastor of the church
in Ephesus

Paul writes 1 Timothy

Paul and Timothy write
the letter to the Romans

Timothy goes to Ephesus to work with
Paul during Paul's 3-year ministry

Timothy returns to Thessalonica

Paul leaves Timothy and Silas in Berea to
continue his work there

Timothy and Paul are reunited in Athens

Paul and Silas come to Lystra and take Timothy
with them on their second missionary journey

READ AND UNDERSTAND 2 TIMOTHY

The Bible is a complete work in which many stories combine to tell one story. As you read the book of 2 Timothy, consider reading the additional passages to discover how the whole of Scripture works together.

GREETING

1 Paul, an apostle of Christ Jesus by God's will, for the sake of the promise of life in Christ Jesus:

² To Timothy, my dearly loved son.

Grace, mercy, and peace from God the Father and Christ Jesus our Lord.

THANKSGIVING

³ I thank God, whom I serve with a clear conscience as my ancestors did, when I constantly remember you in my prayers night and day. ⁴ Remembering your tears, I long to see you so that I may be filled with joy. ⁵ I recall your sincere faith that first lived in your grandmother Lois and in your mother Eunice and now, I am convinced, is in you also.

⁶ Therefore, I remind you to rekindle the gift of God that is in you through the laying on of my hands. ⁷ For God has not given us a spirit of fear, but one of power,ᴬ love, and sound judgment.

NOT ASHAMED OF THE GOSPEL

⁸ So don't be ashamed of the testimony about our Lord, or of me his prisoner. Instead, share in suffering for the gospel, relying on the power of God. ⁹ He has saved us and called us with a holy calling, not according to our works, but according to his own purpose and grace, which was given to us in Christ Jesus before time began. ¹⁰ This has now been made evident through the appearing of our Savior Christ Jesus, who has abolished death and has brought life and immortality to light through the gospel. ¹¹ For this gospel I was appointed a herald, apostle, and teacher,ᴮ ¹² and that is why I suffer these things. But I am not ashamed, because I know whom I have believed and am persuaded that he is able to guard what has been entrusted to meᶜ until that day.

BE LOYAL TO THE FAITH

¹³ Hold on to the pattern of sound teaching that you have heard from me, in the faith and love that are in Christ Jesus. ¹⁴ Guard the good deposit through the Holy Spirit who lives in us. ¹⁵ You know that all those in the province of Asia have deserted me, including Phygelus and Hermogenes. ¹⁶ May the Lord grant mercy to the household of Onesiphorus, because he often refreshed me and was not ashamed of my chains. ¹⁷ On the contrary, when he was in Rome, he diligently searched for me and found me. ¹⁸ May the Lord grant that he obtain mercy from him on that day. You know very well how much he ministered at Ephesus.

BE STRONG IN GRACE

2 You, therefore, my son, be strong in the grace that is in Christ Jesus. ² What you have heard from me in the presence of many witnesses, commit to faithful menᴰ who will be able to teach others also.

³ Share in suffering as a good soldier of Christ Jesus. ⁴ No one serving as a soldier gets entangled in the concerns of civilian life; he seeks to please the commanding officer. ⁵ Also, if anyone competes as an athlete, he is not

---

ᴬ1:7 Or *For the Spirit God gave us does not make us fearful, but gives us power*
ᴮ1:11 Other mss add *of the Gentiles*   ᶜ1:12 Or *guard what I have entrusted to him, or guard my deposit*   ᴰ2:2 Or *faithful people*

crowned unless he competes according to the rules. [6] The hardworking farmer ought to be the first to get a share of the crops. [7] Consider what I say, for the Lord will give you understanding in everything.

[8] Remember Jesus Christ, risen from the dead and descended from David, according to my gospel, [9] for which I suffer to the point of being bound like a criminal. But the word of God is not bound. [10] This is why I endure all things for the elect: so that they also may obtain salvation, which is in Christ Jesus, with eternal glory. [11] This saying is trustworthy:

> For if we died with him,
> we will also live with him;
> [12] if we endure, we will also reign with him;
> if we deny him, he will also deny us;
> [13] if we are faithless, he remains faithful,
> for he cannot deny himself.

AN APPROVED WORKER

[14] Remind them of these things, and charge them before God[A] not to fight about words. This is useless and leads to the ruin of those who listen. [15] Be diligent to present yourself to God as one approved, a worker who doesn't need to be ashamed, correctly teaching the word of truth. [16] Avoid irreverent and empty speech, since those who engage in it will produce even more godlessness, [17] and their teaching will spread like gangrene. Hymenaeus and Philetus are among them. [18] They have departed from the truth, saying that the resurrection has already taken place, and are ruining the faith of some. [19] Nevertheless, God's solid foundation stands firm, bearing this inscription: **The Lord knows those who are his,**[B] and let everyone who calls on the name of[C] the Lord turn away from wickedness.

[20] Now in a large house there are not only gold and silver vessels, but also those of wood and clay; some for honorable[D] use and some for dishonorable.[E] [21] So if anyone purifies himself from anything dishonorable,[F] he will be a special[G] instrument, set apart, useful to the Master, prepared for every good work.

[22] Flee from youthful passions, and pursue righteousness, faith, love, and peace, along with those who call on the Lord from a pure heart. [23] But reject foolish and ignorant disputes, because you know that they breed quarrels. [24] The Lord's servant must not quarrel, but must be gentle to everyone, able to teach,[H] and patient, [25] instructing his opponents with gentleness. Perhaps God will grant them repentance leading them to the knowledge of the truth. [26] Then they may come to their senses and escape the trap of the devil, who has taken them captive to do his will.

DIFFICULT TIMES AHEAD

3 But know this: Hard times will come in the last days. [2] For people will be lovers of self, lovers of money, boastful, proud, demeaning, disobedient to parents, ungrateful, unholy, [3] unloving, irreconcilable, slanderers, without self-control, brutal, without love for what is good, [4] traitors, reckless,

---

[A]2:14 Other mss read *before the Lord* [B]2:19 Nm 16:5 [C]2:19 Lit *everyone who names the name of* [D]2:20 Or *special* [E]2:20 Or *ordinary* [F]2:21 Lit *from these* [G]2:21 Or *an honorable* [H]2:24 Or *everyone, skillful in teaching*

ALWAYS BE PREPARED

2 TIMOTHY 3; PSALM 19:7-11

I hate feeling unprepared. I am not completely Type A, but in the category of preparedness, I absolutely am.

If I'm cooking dinner for people, I have, on occasion, created a timeline to tell myself when to put the chicken in the oven, when to cook the pasta, and when to heat the rolls, so that everything is the appropriate temperature when guests arrive.

Before a first date, I take a really long time to get ready, and then I clean my entire apartment. I know we won't step foot inside, but my imagination convinces me otherwise. *What if he asks to use my bathroom when he comes to pick me up? What if there is a national emergency and he needs to watch my TV?*

It's over-the-top weird, I know. But I feel better about life if I'm prepared for it.

Considering my need to over-prepare, it's ironic how often I neglect the ultimate preparation guide—the Bible.

Paul offered instruction on a variety of topics in his two letters to Timothy. He warned him about false teachers, and he guided him on how to handle quarrels within the church community. Paul's advice was wise and consistent, and it all seems to lead up to these crucial verses in 2 Timothy 3:16-17:

"All Scripture is inspired by God and is profitable for teaching, for rebuking, for correcting, for training in righteousness, so that the man of God may be complete, equipped for every good work."

Here Paul makes one of the most critical claims of Christianity: Scripture is God-breathed. Yes, human beings wrote down the words, but they were inspired by the Holy Spirit to write them. Scripture can be trusted and its instruction relied upon to equip us "for every good work."

More often than not, I rely on my worldly ways of preparation over the God-breathed book sitting on my bedside table. I don't always treasure Scripture as the breath of God, depending on it like I do air in my lungs. What would change if I did? How can I be equipped for kingdom work and everyday life if I don't?

Psalm 19 says, "The ordinances of the LORD are reliable and altogether righteous. They are more desirable than gold—than an abundance of pure gold; and sweeter than honey dripping from a honeycomb" (Ps 19:9-10).

May we treasure it, savor it, and cling to it like our life depends on it—because, truly, it does.

conceited, lovers of pleasure rather than lovers of God, ⁵ holding to the form of godliness but denying its power. Avoid these people.

⁶ For among them are those who worm their way into households and deceive gullible women overwhelmed by sins and led astray by a variety of passions, ⁷ always learning and never able to come to a knowledge of the truth. ⁸ Just as Jannes and Jambres resisted Moses, so these also resist the truth. They are men who are corrupt in mind and worthless in regard to the faith. ⁹ But they will not make further progress, for their foolishness will be clear to all, as was the foolishness of Jannes and Jambres.

STRUGGLES IN THE CHRISTIAN LIFE

¹⁰ But you have followed my teaching, conduct, purpose, faith, patience, love, and endurance, ¹¹ along with the persecutions and sufferings that came to me in Antioch, Iconium, and Lystra. What persecutions I endured — and yet the Lord rescued me from them all. ¹² In fact, all who want to live a godly life in Christ Jesus will be persecuted. ¹³ Evil people and impostors will become worse, deceiving and being deceived. ¹⁴ But as for you, continue in what you have learned and firmly believed. You know those who taught you, ¹⁵ and you know that from infancy you have known the sacred Scriptures, which are able to give you wisdom for salvation through faith in Christ Jesus. ¹⁶ All Scripture is inspired by God^A and is profitable for teaching, for rebuking, for correcting, for training in righteousness, ¹⁷ so that the man of God may be complete, equipped for every good work.

FULFILL YOUR MINISTRY

4 I solemnly charge you before God and Christ Jesus, who is going to judge the living and the dead, and because of his appearing and his kingdom: ² Preach the word; be ready in season and out of season; rebuke, correct, and encourage with great patience and teaching. ³ For the time will come when people will not tolerate sound doctrine, but according to their own desires, will multiply teachers for themselves because they have an itch to hear what they want to hear. ⁴ They will turn away from hearing the truth and will turn aside to myths. ⁵ But as for you, exercise self-control in everything, endure hardship, do the work of an evangelist, fulfill your ministry.

⁶ For I am already being poured out as a drink offering, and the time for my departure is close. ⁷ I have fought the good fight, I have finished the race, I have kept the faith. ⁸ There is reserved for me the crown of righteousness, which the Lord, the righteous Judge, will give me on that day, and not only to me, but to all those who have loved his appearing.^B

FINAL INSTRUCTIONS

⁹ Make every effort to come to me soon, ¹⁰ because Demas has deserted me, since he loved this present world, and has gone to Thessalonica. Crescens has gone to Galatia, Titus to Dalmatia. ¹¹ Only Luke is with me. Bring Mark with you, for he is useful to me in the ministry. ¹² I have sent Tychicus to Ephesus. ¹³ When you come, bring the cloak I left in Troas with Carpus, as well as the scrolls, especially the parchments. ¹⁴ Alexander the coppersmith did

---

^A 3:16 Lit *breathed out by God*   ^B 4:8 Or *have longed for his appearing* great harm to me. The Lord will repay him according to his works. [15] Watch out for him yourself because he strongly opposed our words.

[16] At my first defense, no one stood by me, but everyone deserted me. May it not be counted against them. [17] But the Lord stood with me and strengthened me, so that I might fully preach the word and all the Gentiles might hear it. So I was rescued from the lion's mouth. [18] The Lord will rescue me from every evil work and will bring me safely into his heavenly kingdom. To him be the glory forever and ever! Amen.

BENEDICTION

[19] Greet Prisca and Aquila, and the household of Onesiphorus. [20] Erastus has remained at Corinth; I left Trophimus sick at Miletus. [21] Make every effort to come before winter. Eubulus greets you, as do Pudens, Linus, Claudia, and all the brothers and sisters.

[22] The Lord be with your spirit. Grace be with you all.

not by
WORKS of
RIGHTEOUSNESS
but
according
TO HIS
Mercy

titus

 He saved us — not by works of righteousness that we had done, but according to his mercy — through the washing of regeneration and renewal by the Holy Spirit. **3:5**

ON THE TIMELINE Paul most likely wrote this letter after the time covered by Luke in the book of Acts (after AD 62). While Acts closes with Paul in prison, it is believed Paul was then released and continued his work around the Mediterranean, perhaps even reaching Spain (Rm 15:22-29). Titus was written during this period of further mission work, likely around AD 63.

A LITTLE BACKGROUND Titus was a Gentile companion of Paul (Gl 2:3) who Paul called "my true son in our common faith" (Ti 1:4). Titus accompanied the apostle and Barnabas to Jerusalem (Gl 2:1), probably on the famine relief visit (Ac 11:28-30). Titus seems to have been a capable person, entrusted with the delicate task of delivering Paul's severe letter to Corinth (2Co 2:1-4) and correcting problems within the church there (2Co 7:13-15). Titus's genuine concern for and evenhanded dealing with the Corinthians (2Co 8:16-17; 12:18) no doubt contributed to his success, which he reported in person to Paul, who anxiously awaited word in Macedonia (2Co 2:13; 7:5-6,13-15).

MESSAGE & PURPOSE Just as in the first letter to Timothy, Paul warned Titus against false teachers on Crete and issued instructions to various groups regarding proper Christian behavior. These false teachers enjoyed controversies and disputes (Ti 1:10; 3:9-10) and were deceptive (Ti 1:10), detestable, disobedient, and worthless (Ti 1:15-16). They also hoped for profit from their teaching (Ti 1:11). Paul viewed appointing sound leadership in Crete vital to the future of the gospel there.

GIVE THANKS FOR THE BOOK OF TITUS

Titus is a personal correspondence from an apostle to a pastor and church he loves. False teachers appeared to teach that what Christians did in their personal lives had little to do with their faith, so long as they kept certain religious rules (Ti 1:10-16). In this letter, Paul fought for their spiritual health and maturity by making the connection between faith and conduct, guiding new believers in how to live as followers of Christ. The book of Titus helps us navigate the temptation we all face to live in ways that contradict the faith we profess.

THE BOOK OF TITUS IN HISTORY

AD 50   AD 60   AD 70

49   56   62   64   67
                                                                       (approx)

                               While ministering in   Paul's martyrdom
                               Ephesus, Paul sends   in Rome
                               Titus to mediate the
                               conflict between   Major persecution
                               Paul and the church   of Christians in Rome
                               at Corinth

Paul takes Titus and   AD 62-64
Barnabas from Antioch
to Jerusalem for the   Paul writes
Jerusalem Council   1 Timothy
                                              and Titus

                                              Paul
                                              commissions
                                              Titus to train
                                              leaders for
                                              the young
                                              Christian
                                              congregations
                                              on Crete

READ AND UNDERSTAND TITUS

The Bible is a complete work in which many stories combine to tell one story. As you read the book of Titus, consider reading the additional passages to discover how the whole of Scripture works together.

GREETING

1 Paul, a servant of God and an apostle of Jesus Christ, for[A] the faith of God's elect and their knowledge of the truth that leads[B] to godliness, [2] in the hope of eternal life that God, who cannot lie, promised before time began. [3] In his own time he has revealed his word in the preaching with which I was entrusted by the command of God our Savior:

[4] To Titus, my true son in our common faith.

Grace and peace from God the Father and Christ Jesus our Savior.

TITUS'S MINISTRY IN CRETE

[5] The reason I left you in Crete was to set right what was left undone and, as I directed you, to appoint elders in every town. [6] An elder must be blameless: the husband of one wife, with faithful[C] children who are not accused of wildness or rebellion. [7] As an overseer of God's household, he must be blameless: not arrogant, not hot-tempered, not an excessive drinker, not a bully, not greedy for money, [8] but hospitable, loving what is good, sensible, righteous, holy, self-controlled, [9] holding to the faithful message as taught, so that he will be able both to encourage with sound teaching and to refute those who contradict it.

[10] For there are many rebellious people, full of empty talk and deception, especially those from the circumcision party. [11] It is necessary to silence them; they are ruining entire households by teaching what they shouldn't in order to get money dishonestly. [12] One of their very own prophets said, "Cretans are always liars, evil beasts, lazy gluttons." [13] This testimony is true. For this reason, rebuke them sharply, so that they may be sound in the faith [14] and may not pay attention to Jewish myths and the commands of people who reject the truth.

[15] To the pure, everything is pure, but to those who are defiled and unbelieving nothing is pure; in fact, both their mind and conscience are defiled. [16] They claim to know God, but they deny him by their works. They are detestable, disobedient, and unfit for any good work.

SOUND TEACHING AND CHRISTIAN LIVING

2 But you are to proclaim things consistent with sound teaching. [2] Older men are to be self-controlled, worthy of respect, sensible, and sound in faith, love, and endurance. [3] In the same way, older women are to be reverent in behavior, not slanderers, not slaves to excessive drinking. They are to teach what is good, [4] so that they may encourage the young women to love their husbands and to love their children, [5] to be self-controlled, pure, workers at home, kind, and in submission to their husbands, so that God's word will not be slandered.

[6] In the same way, encourage the young men to be self-controlled [7] in everything. Make yourself an example of good works with integrity and dignity[D] in your teaching. [8] Your message is to be sound beyond reproach, so that any opponent will be ashamed, because he doesn't have anything bad to say about us.

[9] Slaves are to submit to their masters in everything, and to be well-pleasing, not talking back [10] or stealing, but demonstrating utter faithfulness, so that they may adorn the teaching of God our Savior in everything.

[A]1:1 Or *according to*   [B]1:1 Or *corresponds*   [C]1:6 Or *believing*   [D]2:7 Other mss add *and incorruptibility*

WOMEN TEACHING WOMEN

TITUS 2; 1 TIMOTHY 5:1-2

"I don't love my husband."

I still consider it miraculous that I managed to get those words past the lump in my throat. After the birth of my second child, I was blindsided by a tidal wave of postpartum depression. With my mind in a hormonal fog, I couldn't make sense of my relationships or my roles as wife and mother. Of course I loved my husband then, and I love him today, but the truth eluded me in that season. On my own, I couldn't get any of my ducks to line up in a row.

I was gathered with a group of moms at my church when the levy finally broke. As we circled up to pray, I ripped off the Band-Aid and let the hurt and confusion and anxiety gush. In awkward words said through hot tears, I told them I didn't know how to be the woman God called me to be.

And you know what? They didn't run. They circled around me to pray and give comfort, and they continued to walk beside me, speaking God's truth to me as I learned to love my family well.

I'm perpetually shocked that being Christlike doesn't come more naturally. The blueprint for the Christian life isn't imprinted into our DNA, but **God has a game plan for showing us how to live as women of the gospel.**

"In the same way, older women are to be reverent in behavior . . . They are to teach what is good, so they may encourage the young women to love their husbands and to love their children, to be self-controlled, pure, homemakers, kind, and in submission to their husbands, so that God's word will not be slandered" (Ti 2:3-5).

In that season of postpartum depression, this passage was like a lifeline in my struggles.

Loving my husband
Loving my children
Being self-controlled
Having pure thoughts
Caring for my home
Being kind and submissive . . .

These aren't things we inherently know. According to God's Word, these virtues must be taught. And who should be our teachers? Other women! Women who've walked the path of faith ahead of us and can turn and say, "Follow me as I follow Jesus."

And here's the other side of that coin: other women need us. No matter how many candles we will blow out at our next birthday, we are younger than someone and we are older than someone. That puts us each in the perfect position to learn from the example of older Christian women and to intentionally disciple the generations behind us.

Let's not withhold the hard-won wisdom given to us by our Father. And may we always seek encouragement from those who've gone before us.

¹¹ For the grace of God has appeared, bringing salvation[A] for all people, ¹² instructing us to deny godlessness and worldly lusts and to live in a sensible, righteous, and godly way in the present age, ¹³ while we wait for the blessed hope, the appearing of the glory of our great God and Savior, Jesus Christ. ¹⁴ He gave himself for us to redeem us from all lawlessness and to cleanse for himself a people for his own possession, eager to do good works.

¹⁵ Proclaim these things; encourage and rebuke with all authority. Let no one disregard[B] you.

CHRISTIAN LIVING AMONG OUTSIDERS

3 Remind them to submit to rulers and authorities, to obey, to be ready for every good work, ² to slander no one, to avoid fighting, and to be kind, always showing gentleness to all people. ³ For we too were once foolish, disobedient, deceived, enslaved by various passions and pleasures, living in malice and envy, hateful, detesting one another.

⁴ But when the kindness of God our Savior and his love for mankind appeared, ⁵ he saved us — not by works of righteousness that we had done, but according to his mercy — through the washing of regeneration and renewal by the Holy Spirit. ⁶ He poured out his Spirit on us abundantly through Jesus Christ our Savior ⁷ so that, having been justified by his grace, we may become heirs with the hope of eternal life. ⁸ This saying is trustworthy. I want you to insist on these things, so that those who have believed God might be careful to devote themselves to good works. These are good and profitable for everyone. ⁹ But avoid foolish debates, genealogies, quarrels, and disputes about the law, because they are unprofitable and worthless. ¹⁰ Reject a divisive person after a first and second warning. ¹¹ For you know that such a person has gone astray and is sinning; he is self-condemned.

FINAL INSTRUCTIONS AND CLOSING

¹² When I send Artemas or Tychicus to you, make every effort to come to me in Nicopolis, because I have decided to spend the winter there. ¹³ Diligently help Zenas the lawyer and Apollos on their journey, so that they will lack nothing.

¹⁴ Let our people learn to devote themselves to good works for pressing needs, so that they will not be unfruitful. ¹⁵ All those who are with me send you greetings. Greet those who love us in the faith. Grace be with all of you.

[A] 2:11 Or *appeared with saving power* [B] 2:15 Or *despise*

THE WASHING OF REGENERATION

TITUS 3:1-7; JOHN 3:6-8; ROMANS 8:22-25

When my kids play outside, they get super dirty. We have a wooded area behind our house with a creek and mud and lots of critters. By the time they finally tromp back to the house from an adventure, a good bit of that mud and a disconcerting number of critters come right home with them. (Once my son casually mentioned to me that his pocket was full of worms.)

Straight to the bath or shower they go. And if there's one thing I've learned about parenting muddy children, it's this: no matter how hard they try to do it on their own, they can't get themselves clean like I can.

When they've been washed clean, all wrapped up in a fluffy towel with wet eyelashes and sweet-smelling skin, I can forget about the worms and the bugs and the mud—they are like new. We all feel better.

Think of being born again like our heavenly Father bringing us in from the woods and rinsing away our filth like only He can. He washes us clean. Our eyelashes are wet and our skin smells sweet. We are like new.

"But when the kindness of God our Savior and his love for mankind appeared, he saved us—not by works of righteousness that we had done, but according to his mercy—through the washing of regeneration and renewal by the Holy Spirit."

TITUS 3:4-5

What Paul shows us in this passage is the contrast between our dirty, wandering, worms-in-our-pockets human hearts, and our washed and renewed selves through the Holy Spirit and Jesus Christ. The word he uses is "regeneration." In Latin it means to "create again," and in Greek it means, "born again." The washing of regeneration Paul describes is a complete cleaning in which our filth becomes a distant memory and we, as believers, are a new creation (2Co 5:17).

This newness—this born-again freshness that we as believers often forget—is a foreshadowing, a glimpse, of what is to come. Like Paul says in Romans 8, we "have the Spirit as the firstfruits" (v. 23).

That image of my kids all squeaky clean after their baths? And the one of you, wrapped in the fresh towel of God's mercy? Close your eyes and imagine the promised regeneration of the whole world—a new heaven and a new earth!

Only God can do this.
He washed away our filth at our salvation.
He restores us with each new day.
And He will make everything new for His glory.

Lord, if we are in Christ, we are a new creation. Help us find our identities here. Make us clean and new and Yours. Amen.

I APPEAL

INSTEAD

ON THE

basis

of

Love

philemon

 For this reason, although I have great boldness in Christ to command you to do what is right, I appeal to you, instead, on the basis of love. **VERSES 8-9**

ON THE TIMELINE Paul's letter to Philemon was written during his imprisonment in Rome in AD 60–62. Philemon was written around the same time as Ephesians, Philippians, and Colossians, after all three of Paul's missionary journeys.

A LITTLE BACKGROUND Philemon is Paul's only letter of a private nature. It concerns a runaway slave, Onesimus, who had robbed his master, Philemon, and escaped from Colossae to Rome (Phm 15,18). Perhaps attracted by the anonymity of a large, distant city, Onesimus traveled to Rome seeking a life of freedom. While in Rome, he crossed paths with Paul and became a Christian (Phm 10,16).

Paul wrote to Philemon about Onesimus and sent both the letter and Onesimus back to Colossae. In comparison to Paul's other letters, Philemon is little more than a postcard, but it comes from the tender heart of one friend writing to another, rather than an apostle exercising his authority.

MESSAGE & PURPOSE This letter has served as an inspiration for the liberation of slaves. Paul's clear preference was to keep Onesimus with him (Phm 13), but he recognized that Onesimus was legally bound to Philemon. Paul decided to send Onesimus back (Phm 12) so Philemon could either reinstate him as a slave who was now also his Christian brother (Phm 15-16), or else set him free for further service to Paul back in Rome (Phm 13,20-21). Onesimus returned to Philemon with this letter, knowing that Paul was confident of Philemon's "obedience" (Phm 21) but also knowing that forgiveness, reinstatement, and emancipation were not guaranteed.

GIVE THANKS FOR THE BOOK OF PHILEMON

Although it is the shortest and most personal of Paul's letters, Philemon captures the heart of the gospel (Phm 16-19). When we come to God in repentance and faith, He gives us a new status and welcomes us as if we were Christ. Christ assumed personal responsibility for the full repayment of our debt to God.

A BRIEF HISTORICAL OVERVIEW
OF SLAVERY IN THE BIBLICAL ERA

1500 BC   1300 BC   400 BC   200 B

1445

500

1600

Hebrew laws contain
provisions for slaves
and slavery

Egyptians make
slaves of the
Israelites

Economies of the
Greek city-states are
dependent on slavery

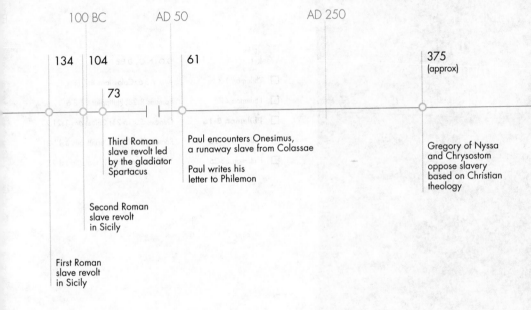

100 BC   AD 50   AD 250

134 104   61   375
                                                (approx)

        73

Third Roman
slave revolt led
by the gladiator
Spartacus

Paul encounters Onesimus,
a runaway slave from Colassae

Paul writes his
letter to Philemon

Gregory of Nyssa
and Chrysostom
oppose slavery
based on Christian
theology

Second Roman
slave revolt
in Sicily

First Roman
slave revolt
in Sicily

READ AND UNDERSTAND PHILEMON

The Bible is a complete work in which many stories combine to tell one story. As you read the book of Philemon, consider reading the additional passages to discover how the whole of Scripture works together.

GREETING

Paul, a prisoner of Christ Jesus, and Timothy our brother:

To Philemon our dear friend and coworker, ² to Apphia our sister,^ to Archippus our fellow soldier, and to the church that meets in your home.

³ Grace to you and peace from God our Father and the Lord Jesus Christ.

PHILEMON'S LOVE AND FAITH

⁴ I always thank my God when I mention you in my prayers, ⁵ because I hear of your love for all the saints and the faith that you have in the Lord Jesus. ⁶ I pray that your participation in the faith may become effective through knowing every good thing that is in us^B for the glory of Christ. ⁷ For I have great joy and encouragement from your love, because the hearts of the saints have been refreshed through you, brother.

AN APPEAL FOR ONESIMUS

⁸ For this reason, although I have great boldness in Christ to command you to do what is right, ⁹ I appeal to you, instead, on the basis of love. I, Paul, as an elderly man^C and now also as a prisoner of Christ Jesus, ¹⁰ appeal to you for my son, Onesimus.^D I became his father while I was in chains. ¹¹ Once he was useless to you, but now he is useful both to you and to me. ¹² I am sending him back to you — I am sending my very own heart.^E,F ¹³ I wanted to keep him with me, so that in my imprisonment for the gospel he might serve me in your place. ¹⁴ But I didn't want to do anything without your consent, so that your good deed might not be out of obligation, but of your own free will. ¹⁵ For perhaps this is why he was separated from you for a brief time, so that you might get him back permanently, ¹⁶ no longer as a slave, but more than a slave — as a dearly loved brother. He is especially so to me, but how much more to you, both in the flesh and in the Lord.

¹⁷ So if you consider me a partner, welcome him as you would me. ¹⁸ And if he has wronged you in any way, or owes you anything, charge that to my account. ¹⁹ I, Paul, write this with my own hand: I will repay it — not to mention to you that you owe me even your very self. ²⁰ Yes, brother, may I benefit from you in the Lord; refresh my heart in Christ. ²¹ Since I am confident of your obedience, I am writing to you, knowing that you will do even more than I say. ²² Meanwhile, also prepare a guest room for me, since I hope that through your prayers I will be restored to you.

FINAL GREETINGS

²³ Epaphras, my fellow prisoner in Christ Jesus, sends you greetings, and so do ²⁴ Mark, Aristarchus, Demas, and Luke, my coworkers.

²⁵ The grace of the Lord^G Jesus Christ be with your spirit.

---

^2 Other mss read *our beloved*   ^B6 Other mss read *in you*   ^C9 Or *an ambassador*   ^D10 In Gk, *Onesimus* means *"useful"*   ^E12 Other mss read *him back. Receive him, my own heart.*   ^F12 Lit *you — that is, my own heart*
^G25 Other mss read *our Lord*

ON THE BASIS OF LOVE

PHILEMON 8-16; COLOSSIANS 1:21-23

Relationships are complicated. Think of one in your own life that is fractured in some way by pride, stubbornness, or even a sense of injustice. What could restore peace?

The theme of Philemon is reconciliation: the reconciliation of a runaway slave to God and then to his former master who had become his brother in Christ.

Onesimus was a slave in Philemon's household in the city of Colossae. He had a tough life, but when he ran away to Rome, he made it even tougher. If anyone tries to tell you slavery in first-century Rome wasn't that bad, don't believe them. In many cases, it was horrifying. Though some slaves may have had kind masters and their servitude more or less resembled a job, many were treated as property with limited rights and protection.

Somewhere between his escape and this letter, Onesimus met Paul. Knowing Paul had a reputation for helping people in trouble, Onesimus most likely sought him out.

Through that relationship, Christ took hold of Onesimus. Instead of fearing what might happen if he was found, this runaway slave trusted Christ's work in his life, which eventually led to his desire to be reconciled to Philemon, who was now his brother in Christ.

Complicated, right? We don't know whose idea it was for Onesimus to return to Philemon, only that both Onesimus and Paul believed it was the right thing to do.

What would have driven someone like Onesimus to be reconciled to Philemon? Philemon 8-9 tells us:

_____

"For this reason, although I have great boldness in Christ to command you to do what is right, I appeal to you, instead, on the basis of love."

_____

The basis for any real reconciliation is love—a desire to be joined together in Christ, not separated by our sins against one another.

Paul appeals to love because love doesn't need to understand everything in order to seek peace. When a relationship gets complicated by some cause for division, it can be very disorienting. The truth is, we only see in part (1Co 13:12). The good news, however, is that God is weaving our tapestries, and our stories aren't finished until God says they are.

Perhaps you are where you are so that you might be reconciled to someone you've fled, or so that you might forgive someone who has wronged you. Maybe you're about to take in a spiritual fugitive. Here's what Paul's letter to Philemon promises: **the work of Christ is stronger than our pasts.**

Embrace the work of Jesus.

let us run
with endurance
the race
that lies before us

hebrews

 Let us run with endurance the race that lies before us, keeping our eyes on Jesus, the source and perfecter of our faith. For the joy that lay before him, he endured the cross, despising the shame, and sat down at the right hand of the throne of God. **12:1-2**

ON THE TIMELINE The book of Hebrews was written before the fall of Jerusalem in AD 70. The destruction of the temple would have been mentioned if it had already occurred, because it would have strengthened the letter's argument about Christ's sacrifice bringing an end to the temple sacrificial system. Hebrews was most likely written during the persecution under Nero (AD 64–68), perhaps just before the destruction of the temple.

A LITTLE BACKGROUND The text of Hebrews does not identify its author. We know the author was a second generation Christian because he said he received the confirmed message of Christ from "those who heard" Jesus Himself (Heb 2:3). Scholars have proposed Luke, Clement of Rome, Barnabas, Apollos, Timothy, Philip, Peter, Silas, Jude, and Aristion as possible authors.

MESSAGE & PURPOSE The author of Hebrews wanted to exalt Jesus Christ, a desire indicated in the consistent and repetitive usage of the Greek word *kreitton*, which means "more excellent." This word is the common thread that binds together the complex and subtle theological arguments of the book. Specifically, the author described the superiority of the new covenant to the old covenant in order to teach or remind the readers that Jesus Christ is the fulfillment of the law and of God's promises in the Old Testament.

GIVE THANKS FOR THE BOOK OF HEBREWS

More than any other book in the New Testament, Hebrews ties OT history and practices to the life and ministry of Jesus. Just as Jesus Christ taught that the OT was fulfilled in Himself (Mt 5:17-18; Lk 24:27), so the author of Hebrews taught that the old covenant was brought to completion in the new covenant (Heb 7:20–8:13). Hebrews also shows that because the old covenant was fulfilled in the new covenant, the new covenant is actually "better" (Heb 7:22). The new covenant was made superior by the ministry of Jesus Christ.

THE BOOK OF HEBREWS IN HISTORY

1600 BC

1400 BC

1000 BC

1446

1445

2046
(approx)

1406

1050

970

967

Abraham
offers Isaac
in obedience
to God

Conquest
of Canaan

1050-
970 BC
David is king
of Israel

Solomon
builds temple
in Jerusalem

Tabernacle
built and
dedicated

Israel's exodus
from Egypt

800 BC   550 BC   400 BC   AD 50   AD 100

          586   33

                    515   67-68

                              457   70

                              Worship   Temple in
                              reestablished   Jerusalem
                              in Jerusalem   destroyed by
                                                           the Romans

                    Temple
                    reconstructed
                    in Jerusalem
                    after Babylonian   AD 67-68
                    exile   Hebrews written

          Temple destroyed by   Jesus' death, resurrection,
          Nebuchadnezzar   and ascension in Jerusalem

READ AND UNDERSTAND HEBREWS

The Bible is a complete work in which many stories combine to tell one story. As you read the book of Hebrews, consider reading the additional passages to discover how the whole of Scripture works together.

Week 1	GOING DEEPER
☐ **Hebrews 1**	2 Samuel 7:12-15; 2 Corinthians 4:4-6
☐ Hebrews 2	Genesis 12:1-3; Psalm 8
☐ Hebrews 3:1-6	John 3:16-21; Romans 11:1-6
☐ Hebrews 3:7–4:13	Psalm 95:7-11; 1 Peter 1:3-5
☐ **Hebrews 4:14–5:10**	Psalm 110; Matthew 4:1-11

Week 2	GOING DEEPER
☐ Hebrews 5:11–6:12	Acts 8:14-17; Philippians 3:12-16
☐ Hebrews 6:13–7:28	Genesis 22:16-18; Romans 8:28-30
☐ Hebrews 8	Jeremiah 31:31-34; Zechariah 8:4-8
☐ Hebrews 9	Leviticus 16:6-19; 2 Timothy 1:8-10
☐ **Hebrews 10:1-18**	Psalm 40; 1 Peter 2:24

Week 3	GOING DEEPER
☐ Hebrews 10:19-39	Deuteronomy 32:35-36; Matthew 27:50-54
☐ Hebrews 11	Psalm 33:6-7; Luke 13:33-35
☐ **Hebrews 12:1-17**	Romans 12:18-21; 1 Timothy 2:5-6
☐ Hebrews 12:18-29	Genesis 4:8-13; Isaiah 62:6-12
☐ Hebrews 13	Joshua 1:5-9; Matthew 25:34-40

THE NATURE OF THE SON

1 Long ago God spoke to the fathers by the prophets at different times and in different ways. [2] In these last days, he has spoken to us by his Son. God has appointed him heir of all things and made the universe[A] through him. [3] The Son is the radiance[B] of God's glory and the exact expression[C] of his nature, sustaining all things by his powerful word. After making purification for sins,[D] he sat down at the right hand of the Majesty on high.[E] [4] So he became superior to the angels, just as the name he inherited is more excellent than theirs.

THE SON SUPERIOR TO ANGELS

[5] For to which of the angels did he ever say,

> You are my Son;
> today I have become your Father,[F,G]

or again,

> I will be his Father,
> and he will be my Son?[H]

[6] Again, when he[I] brings his firstborn into the world, he says,

> And let all God's angels worship him.[J]

[7] And about the angels he says:

> He makes his angels winds,[K]
> and his servants[L] a fiery flame,[M]

[8] but to[N] the Son:

> Your throne, O God,
> is forever and ever,
> and the scepter of your kingdom
> is a scepter of justice.
> [9] You have loved righteousness
> and hated lawlessness;
> this is why God, your God,
> has anointed you
> with the oil of joy
> beyond your companions.[O,P]

[10] And:

> In the beginning, Lord,
> you established the earth,
> and the heavens are the works of your hands;
> [11] they will perish, but you remain.
> They will all wear out like clothing;
> [12] you will roll them up like a cloak,[Q]
> and they will be changed like clothing.
> But you are the same,
> and your years will never end.[R]

[A] 1:2 Lit *ages*   [B] 1:3 Or *reflection*   [C] 1:3 Or *representation, or copy, or reproduction*   [D] 1:3 Other mss read *for our sins by himself*   [E] 1:3 Or *he sat down on high at the right hand of the Majesty*   [F] 1:5 Or *have begotten you*   [G] 1:5 Ps 2:7   [H] 1:5 2Sm 7:14; 1Ch 17:13   [I] 1:6 Or *When he again*   [J] 1:6 Dt 32:43 LXX; Ps 97:7   [K] 1:7 Or *spirits*   [L] 1:7 Or *ministers*   [M] 1:7 Ps 104:4   [N] 1:8 Or *about*   [O] 1:9 Or *associates*   [P] 1:8-9 Ps 45:6-7   [Q] 1:12 Other mss omit *like a cloak*   [R] 1:10-12 Ps 102:25-27

LOOK TO JESUS

I've lived my entire life in the Bible Belt—that big chunk of the southern United States where conservative evangelical Protestantism is more common than not. Having called Nashville home for well over a decade, I'm convinced this sweet Southern city is the Bible Belt buckle. I sometimes count the churches along my commute for fun; there are over twenty churches on one particular ten-mile stretch of road. That's a lot of steeples, y'all. (We say "y'all" in the Bible Belt.)

The first-century Hebrews had the opposite experience. They spent their lives following the Old Testament prophecy and law, until Jesus came and turned everything upside down—or right-side up, depending on your perspective.

Though the gospel is good news for all, believing was not easy for the Hebrews. Based on the tone of this letter that bears their name, it seems these new Christians may have been worried about what they'd gotten themselves into.

The author of Hebrews wrote this letter soon after the death and resurrection of Jesus, probably between AD 64 and 68. But his words are not just for the Hebrews; they are also for us.

Some of you are like me; you've been around Christianity all your life. You're familiar with the term "cultural Christian" and maybe you've even played the part, going through the motions without engaging the heart. Following Jesus is a lifelong journey, filled with glorious mountaintops and low, dark valleys. But do you ever get tired?

Do you ever grow weary and forget where you're going or why you started traveling to begin with?

And you who are new to the faith, who have recently met Jesus, do you feel your world turning upside down? Do you sometimes wonder what you've gotten yourself into?

There were the Hebrews, clinging to belief as they received this letter. And here we are, some two thousand years later, clinging just the same. The message of the letter shines through in the opening verses, which point to the supremacy of Christ over all things. He upholds the universe. He atones for our sins. He is greater than all heavenly beings. When we forget where we're going, we look to Him.

We look to Jesus.

The Old Testament prophecies were important and necessary, but Jesus is their real-life fulfillment.

The law is just and good, but Jesus is far better.

The old covenant dealt with the works of our hands, but Jesus broke through to our hearts.

Jesus is it. He is the One the Hebrews had been waiting for. He is the One we've been waiting for. He is the very image of God made man, and the gospel He brings is an exact representation of the heart of God.

Jesus is highest. Jesus is best. Jesus is God's last, perfect, complete Word. Let's look to Him.

¹³ Now to which of the angels has he ever said:

> Sit at my right hand
> until I make your enemies your footstool?^A

¹⁴ Are they not all ministering spirits sent out to serve those who are going to inherit salvation?

WARNING AGAINST NEGLECT

2 For this reason, we must pay attention all the more to what we have heard, so that we will not drift away. ² For if the message spoken through angels was legally binding^B and every transgression and disobedience received a just punishment, ³ how will we escape if we neglect such a great salvation? This salvation had its beginning when it was spoken of by the Lord, and it was confirmed to us by those who heard him. ⁴ At the same time, God also testified by signs and wonders, various miracles, and distributions of gifts from the Holy Spirit according to his will.

JESUS AND HUMANITY

⁵ For he has not subjected to angels the world to come that we are talking about. ⁶ But someone somewhere has testified:

> What is man that you remember him,
> or the son of man that you care for him?
> ⁷ You made him lower than the angels
> for a short time;
> you crowned him with glory and honor^C
> ⁸ and subjected everything under his feet.^D

For in **subjecting everything** to him, he left nothing that is not subject to him. As it is, we do not yet see **everything subjected** to him. ⁹ But we do see Jesus — **made lower than the angels for a short time** so that by God's grace he might taste death for everyone — **crowned with glory and honor** because he suffered death.

¹⁰ For in bringing many sons and daughters to glory, it was entirely appropriate that God — for whom and through whom all things exist — should make the source^E of their salvation perfect through sufferings. ¹¹ For the one who sanctifies and those who are sanctified all have one Father.^F That is why Jesus is not ashamed to call them brothers and sisters, ¹² saying:

> I will proclaim your name to my brothers and sisters;
> I will sing hymns to you in the congregation.^G

¹³ Again, **I will trust in him.**^H And again, **Here I am with the children God gave me.**^I

¹⁴ Now since the children have flesh and blood in common, Jesus also shared in these, so that through his death he might destroy the one holding the power of death — that is, the devil — ¹⁵ and free those who were held in slavery all their lives by the fear of death. ¹⁶ For it is clear that he does not reach out to help angels, but to help Abraham's offspring. ¹⁷ Therefore, he had to be like his brothers and sisters in every way, so that he could become

---

^A 1:13 Ps 110:1　^B 2:2 Or *valid, or reliable*　^C 2:7 Other mss add *and set him over the works of your hands*　^D 2:6-8 Ps 8:5-7 LXX　^E 2:10 Or *pioneer, or leader*　^F 2:11 Or *father, or origin;* lit *all are of one*　^G 2:12 Ps 22:22　^H 2:13 2Sm 22:3 LXX; Is 8:17 LXX; 12:2 LXX　^I 2:13 Is 8:18 LXX a merciful and faithful high priest in matters[A] pertaining to God, to make atonement[B] for the sins of the people. [18] For since he himself has suffered when he was tempted, he is able to help those who are tempted.

OUR APOSTLE AND HIGH PRIEST

3 Therefore, holy brothers and sisters, who share in a heavenly calling, consider Jesus, the apostle and high priest of our confession. [2] He was faithful to the one who appointed him, just as Moses was in all God's household. [3] For Jesus is considered worthy of more glory than Moses, just as the builder has more honor than the house. [4] Now every house is built by someone, but the one who built everything is God. [5] Moses was faithful as a servant in all God's household, as a testimony to what would be said in the future. [6] But Christ was faithful as a Son over his household. And we are that household if we hold on to our confidence and the hope in which we boast.[C]

WARNING AGAINST UNBELIEF

[7] Therefore, as the Holy Spirit says:

Today, if you hear his voice,
[8]   do not harden your hearts as in the rebellion,
  on the day of testing in the wilderness,
[9]   where your fathers tested me, tried me,
  and saw my works [10] for forty years.
  Therefore I was provoked to anger with that generation
  and said, "They always go astray in their hearts,
  and they have not known my ways."
[11]   So I swore in my anger,
  "They will not enter my rest."[D]

[12] Watch out, brothers and sisters, so that there won't be in any of you an evil, unbelieving heart that turns away from the living God. [13] But encourage each other daily, while it is still called **today,** so that none of you is hardened by sin's deception. [14] For we have become participants in Christ if we hold firmly until the end the reality[E] that we had at the start. [15] As it is said:

Today, if you hear his voice,
  do not harden your hearts as in the rebellion.[F]

[16] For who heard and rebelled? Wasn't it all who came out of Egypt under Moses? [17] With whom was God angry for forty years? Wasn't it with those who sinned, whose bodies fell in the wilderness? [18] And to whom did he swear that they would not enter his rest, if not to those who disobeyed? [19] So we see that they were unable to enter because of unbelief.

THE PROMISED REST

4 Therefore, since the promise to enter his rest remains, let us beware[G] that none of you be found to have fallen short.[H] [2] For we also have received the good news just as they did. But the message they heard did not benefit them, since they were not united with those who heard it in

---

[A] 2:17 Lit things   [B] 2:17 Or propitiation   [C] 3:6 Other mss add firm to the end
[D] 3:7-11 Ps 95:7-11   [E] 3:14 Or confidence   [F] 3:15 Ps 95:7-8   [G] 4:1 Lit fear
[H] 4:1 Or that any of you might seem to have missed it

THE THRONE OF GRACE

HEBREWS 4:14–5:10; MATTHEW 4:1-11; JOHN 1:14

The thing that surprised me most about the ICU wing of the hospital, in the weeks and months when my father was ill, was the camaraderie of the place. In the elevator and the hallway, at the coffee kiosk or the information desk, there was an unspoken understanding extended from one person to the next. The waiting room is its own world, and the people there get it. They're waiting, hoping, praying for someone they love, just like you. They have empathy for the battle you're fighting because they're fighting it, too.

I won't speak for you, but I personally tend to imagine Jesus' obedience to the Father came easily. I try to read these verses in Hebrews with an open heart, but I end up playing the God card in my skeptical mind. *Of course He didn't give into temptation,* I think. *He was God. How could He?*

But whether or not I fully comprehend it, Scripture clearly tells us otherwise.

Jesus' obedience came with tears. It came with desperate prayers and cries for relief. "Although he was the Son, he learned obedience from what he suffered" (Heb 5:8).

Learning implies coming to know something that was not known before. It implies practice. It implies process. Jesus did not retrieve instant obedience simply by virtue of being God's Son or calling on the boundless power at His disposal. What did He do instead? He lived it out.

"The Word became flesh and dwelt among us."

JOHN 1:14

You know the special bond you feel with someone who has walked the same road as you, experienced the same disappointment, and suffered in the same way you've suffered? It can make you feel safe, at ease, willing to be open and vulnerable, and be yourself because they get it. They've been there, too.

Jesus knows the battle you're fighting. He doesn't simply know you're fighting it; He knows it because He's fought it, too. He fought it before you and for you (Heb 4:15; 5:2). And He is the very One who sits at the throne of grace as your High Priest, your unfettered access to the Father. You can come to Him as your full self today—not your half self, your filtered and edited self, the cleaned up version you want the outside world to see.

Daughter of the Most High Priest, your tears, fears, and weakness are welcome at the throne of grace. This is not enemy territory where you have to be tough or keep up your guard. This is the place where your deepest struggles are known—where *you* are deeply known. Come to the throne room today. Jesus Christ is your Advocate, your Comrade, your Brother—and He sits ready to receive you even now.

faith.[A] [3] For we who have believed enter the rest, in keeping with what[B] he has said,

> So I swore in my anger,
> "They will not enter my rest,"[C]

even though his works have been finished since the foundation of the world. [4] For somewhere he has spoken about the seventh day in this way: **And on the seventh day God rested from all his works.**[D] [5] Again, in that passage he says, **They will never enter my rest.**[E] [6] Therefore, since it remains for some to enter it, and those who formerly received the good news did not enter because of disobedience, [7] he again specifies a certain day — **today.** He specified this speaking through David after such a long time:

> Today, if you hear his voice,
> do not harden your hearts.[F]

[8] For if Joshua had given them rest, God would not have spoken later about another day. [9] Therefore, a Sabbath rest remains for God's people. [10] For the person who has entered his rest has rested from his own works, just as God did from his. [11] Let us then make every effort to enter that rest, so that no one will fall into the same pattern of disobedience.

[12] For the word of God is living and effective and sharper than any double-edged sword, penetrating as far as the separation of soul and spirit, joints and marrow. It is able to judge the thoughts and intentions of the heart. [13] No creature is hidden from him, but all things are naked and exposed to the eyes of him to whom we must give an account.

OUR GREAT HIGH PRIEST

[14] Therefore, since we have a great high priest who has passed through the heavens — Jesus the Son of God — let us hold fast to our confession. [15] For we do not have a high priest who is unable to sympathize with our weaknesses, but one who has been tempted in every way as we are, yet without sin. [16] Therefore, let us approach the throne of grace with boldness, so that we may receive mercy and find grace to help us in time of need.

CHRIST, A HIGH PRIEST

5 For every high priest taken from among men is appointed in matters pertaining to God for the people, to offer both gifts and sacrifices for sins. [2] He is able to deal gently with those who are ignorant and are going astray, since he is also clothed with weakness. [3] Because of this, he must make an offering for his own sins as well as for the people. [4] No one takes this honor on himself; instead, a person is called by God, just as Aaron was. [5] In the same way, Christ did not exalt himself to become a high priest, but God who said to him,

> You are my Son;
> today I have become your Father,[G,H]

[6] also says in another place,

> You are a priest forever
> according to the order of Melchizedek.[I]

[A]4:2 Other mss read *since it was not united by faith in those who heard*   [B]4:3 Or *rest, just as*   [C]4:3 Ps 95:11   [D]4:4 Gn 2:2   [E]4:5 Ps 95:11   [F]4:7 Ps 95:7-8   [G]5:5 Lit *I have begotten you*   [H]5:5 Ps 2:7   [I]5:6 Gn 14:18-20; Ps 110:4

[7] During his earthly life,[A] he offered prayers and appeals with loud cries and tears to the one who was able to save him from death, and he was heard because of his reverence. [8] Although he was the Son, he learned obedience from what he suffered. [9] After he was perfected, he became the source of eternal salvation for all who obey him, [10] and he was declared by God a high priest according to the order of Melchizedek.

THE PROBLEM OF IMMATURITY

[11] We have a great deal to say about this, and it is difficult to explain, since you have become too lazy to understand. [12] Although by this time you ought to be teachers, you need someone to teach you the basic principles of God's revelation again. You need milk, not solid food. [13] Now everyone who lives on milk is inexperienced with the message about righteousness, because he is an infant. [14] But solid food is for the mature — for those whose senses have been trained to distinguish between good and evil.

WARNING AGAINST FALLING AWAY

6 Therefore, let us leave the elementary teaching about Christ and go on to maturity, not laying again a foundation of repentance from dead works, faith in God, [2] teaching about ritual washings,[B] laying on of hands, the resurrection of the dead, and eternal judgment. [3] And we will do this if God permits.

[4] For it is impossible to renew to repentance those who were once enlightened, who tasted the heavenly gift, who shared in the Holy Spirit, [5] who tasted God's good word and the powers of the coming age, [6] and who have fallen away. This is because,[C] to their own harm, they are recrucifying the Son of God and holding him up to contempt. [7] For the ground that drinks the rain that often falls on it and that produces vegetation useful to those for whom it is cultivated receives a blessing from God. [8] But if it produces thorns and thistles, it is worthless and about to be cursed, and at the end will be burned.

[9] Even though we are speaking this way, dearly loved friends, in your case we are confident of things that are better and that pertain to salvation. [10] For God is not unjust; he will not forget your work and the love[D] you demonstrated for his name by serving the saints — and by continuing to serve them. [11] Now we desire each of you to demonstrate the same diligence for the full assurance of your hope until the end, [12] so that you won't become lazy but will be imitators of those who inherit the promises through faith and perseverance.

INHERITING THE PROMISE

[13] For when God made a promise to Abraham, since he had no one greater to swear by, he swore by himself: [14] **I will indeed bless you, and I will greatly multiply you.**[E] [15] And so, after waiting patiently, Abraham obtained the promise. [16] For people swear by something greater than themselves, and for them a confirming oath ends every dispute. [17] Because God wanted to show his unchangeable purpose even more clearly to the heirs of the promise, he guaranteed it with an oath, [18] so that through two unchangeable things, in

---

A 5:7 Lit *In the days of his flesh*   B 6:2 Or *about baptisms*   C 6:6 Or *while*
D 6:10 Other mss read *labor of love*   E 6:14 Gn 22:17

which it is impossible for God to lie, we who have fled for refuge might have strong encouragement to seize the hope set before us. [19] We have this hope as an anchor for the soul, firm and secure. It enters the inner sanctuary behind the curtain. [20] Jesus has entered there on our behalf as a forerunner, because he has become a high priest forever according to the order of Melchizedek.

THE GREATNESS OF MELCHIZEDEK

7 For this Melchizedek, king of Salem, priest of God Most High, met Abraham and blessed him as he returned from defeating the kings, [2] and Abraham gave him a tenth of everything. First, his name means king of righteousness, then also, king of Salem, meaning king of peace. [3] Without father, mother, or genealogy, having neither beginning of days nor end of life, but resembling the Son of God, he remains a priest forever.

[4] Now consider how great this man was: even Abraham the patriarch gave a tenth of the plunder to him. [5] The sons of Levi who receive the priestly office have a command according to the law to collect a tenth from the people — that is, from their brothers and sisters — though they have also descended from Abraham. [6] But one without this[A] lineage collected a tenth from Abraham and blessed the one who had the promises. [7] Without a doubt, the inferior is blessed by the superior. [8] In the one case, men who will die receive a tenth, but in the other case, Scripture testifies that he lives. [9] And in a sense Levi himself, who receives a tenth, has paid a tenth through Abraham, [10] for he was still within his ancestor[B] when Melchizedek met him.

A SUPERIOR PRIESTHOOD

[11] Now if perfection came through the Levitical priesthood (for on the basis of it the people received the law), what further need was there for another priest to appear, said to be according to the order of Melchizedek and not according to the order of Aaron? [12] For when there is a change of the priesthood, there must be a change of law as well. [13] For the one these things are spoken about belonged to a different tribe. No one from it has served at the altar. [14] Now it is evident that our Lord came from Judah, and Moses said nothing about that tribe concerning priests.

[15] And this becomes clearer if another priest like Melchizedek appears, [16] who did not become a priest based on a legal regulation about physical[C] descent but based on the power of an indestructible life. [17] For it has been testified:

You are a priest forever
according to the order of Melchizedek.[D]

[18] So the previous command is annulled because it was weak and unprofitable [19] (for the law perfected nothing), but a better hope is introduced, through which we draw near to God.

[20] None of this happened without an oath. For others became priests without an oath, [21] but he became a priest with an oath made by the one who said to him:

The Lord has sworn
and will not change his mind,
"You are a priest forever."[D]

[A]7:6 Lit their   [B]7:10 Lit still in his father's loins   [C]7:16 Or fleshly
[D]7:17,21 Ps 110:4

[22] Because of this oath, Jesus has also become the guarantee of a better covenant.

[23] Now many have become Levitical priests, since they are prevented by death from remaining in office. [24] But because he remains forever, he holds his priesthood permanently. [25] Therefore, he is able to save completely those who come to God through him, since he always lives to intercede for them.

[26] For this is the kind of high priest we need: holy, innocent, undefiled, separated from sinners, and exalted above the heavens. [27] He doesn't need to offer sacrifices every day, as high priests do — first for their own sins, then for those of the people. He did this once for all time when he offered himself. [28] For the law appoints as high priests men who are weak, but the promise of the oath, which came after the law, appoints a Son, who has been perfected forever.

A HEAVENLY PRIESTHOOD

8 Now the main point of what is being said is this: We have this kind of high priest, who sat down at the right hand of the throne of the Majesty in the heavens, [2] a minister of the sanctuary and the true tabernacle that was set up by the Lord and not man. [3] For every high priest is appointed to offer gifts and sacrifices; therefore, it was necessary for this priest also to have something to offer. [4] Now if he were on earth, he wouldn't be a priest, since there are those[A] offering the gifts prescribed by the law. [5] These serve as a copy and shadow of the heavenly things, as Moses was warned when he was about to complete the tabernacle. For God said, **Be careful that you make everything according to the pattern that was shown to you on the mountain.**[B] [6] But Jesus has now obtained a superior ministry, and to that degree he is the mediator of a better covenant, which has been established on better promises.

A SUPERIOR COVENANT

[7] For if that first covenant had been faultless, there would have been no occasion for a second one. [8] But finding fault with his people,[C] he says:[D]

> See, the days are coming, says the Lord,
>> when I will make a new covenant
>> with the house of Israel
>> and with the house of Judah —
> [9] not like the covenant
>> that I made with their ancestors
>> on the day I took them by the hand
>> to lead them out of the land of Egypt.
> I showed no concern for them, says the Lord,
>> because they did not continue in my covenant.
> [10] For this is the covenant
>> that I will make with the house of Israel
>> after those days, says the Lord:
> I will put my laws into their minds
>> and write them on their hearts.

[A]8:4 Other mss read *priests* [B]8:5 Ex 25:40 [C]8:8 Lit *with them* [D]8:8 Other mss read *finding fault, he says to them*

> I will be their God,
> and they will be my people.
> ¹¹ And each person will not teach his fellow citizen,^A
> and each his brother or sister, saying, "Know the Lord,"
> because they will all know me,
> from the least to the greatest of them.
> ¹² For I will forgive their wrongdoing,
> and I will never again remember their sins.^B,C

¹³ By saying **a new covenant**, he has declared that the first is obsolete. And what is obsolete and growing old is about to pass away.

OLD COVENANT MINISTRY

9 Now the first covenant also had regulations for ministry and an earthly sanctuary. ² For a tabernacle was set up, and in the first room, which is called the holy place, were the lampstand, the table, and the presentation loaves. ³ Behind the second curtain was a tent called the most holy place. ⁴ It had the gold altar of incense and the ark of the covenant, covered with gold on all sides, in which was a gold jar containing the manna, Aaron's staff that budded, and the tablets of the covenant. ⁵ The cherubim of glory were above the ark overshadowing the mercy seat. It is not possible to speak about these things in detail right now.

⁶ With these things prepared like this, the priests enter the first room repeatedly, performing their ministry. ⁷ But the high priest alone enters the second room, and he does that only once a year, and never without blood, which he offers for himself and for the sins the people had committed in ignorance. ⁸ The Holy Spirit was making it clear that the way into the most holy place had not yet been disclosed while the first tabernacle was still standing. ⁹ This is a symbol for the present time, during which gifts and sacrifices are offered that cannot perfect the worshiper's conscience. ¹⁰ They are physical regulations and only deal with food, drink, and various washings imposed until the time of the new order.

NEW COVENANT MINISTRY

¹¹ But Christ has appeared as a high priest of the good things that have come.^D In the greater and more perfect tabernacle not made with hands (that is, not of this creation), ¹² he entered the most holy place once for all time, not by the blood of goats and calves, but by his own blood, having obtained eternal redemption. ¹³ For if the blood of goats and bulls and the ashes of a young cow, sprinkling those who are defiled, sanctify for the purification of the flesh, ¹⁴ how much more will the blood of Christ, who through the eternal Spirit offered himself without blemish to God, cleanse our^E consciences from dead works so that we can serve the living God?

¹⁵ Therefore, he is the mediator of a new covenant,^F so that those who are called might receive the promise of the eternal inheritance, because a death has taken place for redemption from the transgressions committed under

---

^A 8:11 Other mss read *neighbor* ^B 8:12 Other mss add *and their lawless deeds*
^C 8:8-12 Jr 31:31-34 ^D 9:11 Other mss read *that are to come* ^E 9:14 Other mss read *your* ^F 9:15 The Gk word used here can be translated covenant, will, or testament, also in vv. 16,17,18.

the first covenant. ¹⁶ Where a will exists, the death of the one who made it must be established. ¹⁷ For a will is valid only when people die, since it is never in effect while the one who made it is living. ¹⁸ That is why even the first covenant was inaugurated with blood. ¹⁹ For when every command had been proclaimed by Moses to all the people according to the law, he took the blood of calves and goats,ᴬ along with water, scarlet wool, and hyssop, and sprinkled the scroll itself and all the people, ²⁰ saying, **This is the blood of the covenant that God has ordained for you.**ᴮ ²¹ In the same way, he sprinkled the tabernacle and all the articles of worship with blood. ²² According to the law almost everything is purified with blood, and without the shedding of blood there is no forgiveness.

²³ Therefore, it was necessary for the copies of the things in the heavens to be purified with these sacrifices, but the heavenly things themselves to be purified with better sacrifices than these. ²⁴ For Christ did not enter a sanctuary made with hands (only a modelᶜ of the true one) but into heaven itself, so that he might now appear in the presence of God for us. ²⁵ He did not do this to offer himself many times, as the high priest enters the sanctuary yearly with the blood of another. ²⁶ Otherwise, he would have had to suffer many times since the foundation of the world. But now he has appeared one time, at the end of the ages, for the removal of sin by the sacrifice of himself. ²⁷ And just as it is appointed for people to die once — and after this, judgment — ²⁸ so also Christ, having been offered once to bear the sins of many, will appear a second time, not to bear sin, butᴰ to bring salvation to those who are waiting for him.

THE PERFECT SACRIFICE

10 Since the law has only a shadow of the good things to come, and not the reality itself of those things, it can never perfect the worshipers by the same sacrifices they continually offer year after year. ² Otherwise, wouldn't they have stopped being offered, since the worshipers, purified once and for all, would no longer have any consciousness of sins? ³ But in the sacrifices there is a reminder of sins year after year. ⁴ For it is impossible for the blood of bulls and goats to take away sins.

⁵ Therefore, as he was coming into the world, he said:

**You did not desire sacrifice and offering,
but you prepared a body for me.**
⁶ **You did not delight
in whole burnt offerings and sin offerings.**
⁷ **Then I said, "See —
it is written about me
in the scroll —
I have come to do your will, O God."**ᴱ

⁸ After he says above, **You did not desire or delight in sacrifices and offerings, whole burnt offerings and sin offerings** (which are offered according to the law), ⁹ he then says, **See, I have come to do your will.**ᶠ He takes away the first to establish the second. ¹⁰ By this will, we have been sanctified through the offering of the body of Jesus Christ once for all time.

ᴬ9:19 Some mss omit *and goats* ᴮ9:20 Ex 24:8 ᶜ9:24 Or *antitype,* or *figure*
ᴰ9:28 Lit *time, apart from sin,* ᴱ10:5-7 Ps 40:6-8 ᶠ10:9 Other mss add *God*

HE IS ENOUGH

HEBREWS 10:1-18; PSALM 40; 1 PETER 2:24

It's hard to be told you're not enough.

I remember being cut from the Junior Varsity basketball team. I absolutely remember not being cast as Maria in our school's production of *West Side Story* after singing and dancing my heart out on that enormous, empty stage. I remember being rejected by that boy when I was sixteen, not getting that scholarship for college, and spending way too many anxious nights telling myself I'm not a good mom.

Rejection is hard. Nobody wants to hear her best efforts can't possibly make the cut. It's hard enough when you're trying to earn the approval of your peers, but it's quite another thing when you're endeavoring to win the eternal approval of the One who made you.

We may no longer offer animal sacrifices to right ourselves in God's eyes, but that doesn't mean we don't throw other things at the altar to make a show of faith or to take a pass at redemption. We tithe and dig wells and adopt orphans. We read and write books, we "buy one, give one" and shop with a purpose. We make legitimate and worthy sacrifices from genuine hearts of compassion and love for the benefit of others and not ourselves.

We try. We do the right thing with the wrong heart. We do the right thing with a right heart. We sing and dance and hope our Father notices. And it's absolutely not enough.

Nothing we do can garner acceptance or atone for sins.

Our sacrifices are not sufficient, however genuine they may be. No matter how much we "act justly" and "love faithfulness" and "walk humbly" (Mc 6:8), our "blood of bulls and goats" (Heb 10:4) can never be good enough to do what the shed blood of the Lamb of God accomplished on our behalf.

You see, God always knew that a greater sacrifice would have to be made. And once and for all, it was.

"For it is impossible for the blood of bulls and goats to take away sins. Therefore, as he was coming into the world, he said: You did not desire sacrifice and offering, but you prepared a body for me. You did not delight in whole burnt offerings and sin offerings."

HEBREWS 10:4-6

Friends, you and I are not enough—and that is okay. Know that. Hear and acknowledge and embrace that.

Hear also that the blood of the spotless Lamb of God has been shed on your behalf, and it is enough.

In glorious light of the all-sufficient sacrifice of Jesus, let's lay our striving down. May any good thing we offer simply flow from the joy of a heart that is eternally redeemed and forever thankful.

[11] Every priest stands day after day ministering and offering the same sacrifices time after time, which can never take away sins. [12] But this man, after offering one sacrifice for sins forever, sat down at the right hand of God.[A] [13] He is now waiting until his enemies are made his footstool. [14] For by one offering he has perfected forever those who are sanctified. [15] The Holy Spirit also testifies to us about this. For after he says:

[16] This is the covenant I will make with them
after those days,

the Lord says,

I will put my laws on their hearts
and write them on their minds,

[17] and I will never again remember
their sins and their lawless acts. [B]

[18] Now where there is forgiveness of these, there is no longer an offering for sin.

EXHORTATIONS TO GODLINESS

[19] Therefore, brothers and sisters, since we have boldness to enter the sanctuary through the blood of Jesus — [20] he has inaugurated[C] for us a new and living way through the curtain (that is, through his flesh) — [21] and since we have a great high priest over the house of God, [22] let us draw near with a true heart in full assurance of faith, with our hearts sprinkled clean from an evil conscience and our bodies washed in pure water. [23] Let us hold on to the confession of our hope without wavering, since he who promised is faithful. [24] And let us watch out for one another to provoke love and good works, [25] not neglecting to gather together, as some are in the habit of doing, but encouraging each other, and all the more as you see the day approaching.

WARNING AGAINST DELIBERATE SIN

[26] For if we deliberately go on sinning after receiving the knowledge of the truth, there no longer remains a sacrifice for sins, [27] but a terrifying expectation of judgment and the fury of a fire about to consume the adversaries. [28] Anyone who disregarded the law of Moses died without mercy, based on the testimony of two or three witnesses. [29] How much worse punishment do you think one will deserve who has trampled on the Son of God, who has regarded as profane[D] the blood of the covenant by which he was sanctified, and who has insulted the Spirit of grace? [30] For we know the one who has said,

Vengeance belongs to me; I will repay,[E,F]

and again,

The Lord will judge his people. [G]

[31] It is a terrifying thing to fall into the hands of the living God.

[32] Remember the earlier days when, after you had been enlightened, you endured a hard struggle with sufferings. [33] Sometimes you were publicly exposed to taunts and afflictions, and at other times you were companions of those who were treated that way. [34] For you sympathized with the prisoners[H] and accepted with joy the confiscation of your possessions, because

---

[A]10:12 Or offering one sacrifice for sins, sat down forever at the right hand of God [B]10:16-17 Jr 31:33-34 [C]10:20 Or opened [D]10:29 Or ordinary [E]10:30 Other mss add says the Lord [F]10:30 Dt 32:35 [G]10:30 Dt 32:36 [H]10:34 Other mss read sympathized with my imprisonment you know that you yourselves have a better and enduring possession.[A] [35] So don't throw away your confidence, which has a great reward. [36] For you need endurance, so that after you have done God's will, you may receive what was promised.

[37]   For yet in **a very little while,**
        the Coming One will come and not delay.

[38]   **But my righteous one[B] will live by faith;**
        and if he draws back,
        I have no pleasure[C] in him.[D]

[39] But we are not those who draw back and are destroyed, but those who have faith and are saved.

LIVING BY FAITH

11 Now faith is the reality[E] of what is hoped for, the proof[F] of what is not seen. [2] For by it our ancestors won God's approval.

[3] By faith we understand that the universe was[G] created by the word of God, so that what is seen was made from things that are not visible.[H]

[4] By faith Abel offered to God a better sacrifice than Cain did. By faith he was approved as a righteous man, because God approved his gifts, and even though he is dead, he still speaks through his faith.

[5] By faith Enoch was taken away, and so he did not experience death. **He was not to be found because God took him away.**[I] For before he was taken away, he was approved as one who pleased God. [6] Now without faith it is impossible to please God, since the one who draws near to him must believe that he exists and that he rewards those who seek him.

[7] By faith Noah, after he was warned about what was not yet seen and motivated by godly fear, built an ark to deliver his family. By faith he condemned the world and became an heir of the righteousness that comes by faith.

[8] By faith Abraham, when he was called, obeyed and set out for a place that he was going to receive as an inheritance. He went out, even though he did not know where he was going. [9] By faith he stayed as a foreigner in the land of promise, living in tents as did Isaac and Jacob, coheirs of the same promise. [10] For he was looking forward to the city that has foundations, whose architect and builder is God.

[11] By faith even Sarah herself, when she was unable to have children, received power to conceive offspring, even though she was past the age, since she[J] considered that the one who had promised was faithful. [12] Therefore, from one man — in fact, from one as good as dead — came offspring as numerous as the stars of the sky and as innumerable as the grains of sand along the seashore.

[13] These all died in faith, although they had not received the things that were promised. But they saw them from a distance, greeted them, and confessed that they were foreigners and temporary residents on the earth. [14] Now

---

[A]10:34 Other mss add *in heaven*   [B]10:38 Other mss read *the righteous one*
[C]10:38 Lit *my soul has no pleasure*   [D]10:37-38 Is 26:20 LXX; Hab 2:3-4
[E]11:1 Or *assurance*   [F]11:1 Or *conviction*   [G]11:3 Or *the worlds were,* or *the ages were*   [H]11:3 Or *so that what is seen was made out of what was not visible*
[I]11:5 Gn 5:21-24   [J]11:11 Or *By faith Abraham, even though he was past age — and Sarah herself was barren — received the ability to procreate since he*

those who say such things make it clear that they are seeking a homeland. ¹⁵ If they were thinking about where they came from, they would have had an opportunity to return. ¹⁶ But they now desire a better place — a heavenly one. Therefore, God is not ashamed to be called their God, for he has prepared a city for them.

¹⁷ By faith Abraham, when he was tested, offered up Isaac. He received the promises and yet he was offering his one and only son, ¹⁸ the one to whom it had been said, **Your offspring**ᴬ **will be traced through Isaac.**ᴮ ¹⁹ He considered God to be able even to raise someone from the dead; therefore, he received him back, figuratively speaking.ᶜ

²⁰ By faith Isaac blessed Jacob and Esau concerning things to come. ²¹ By faith Jacob, when he was dying, blessed each of the sons of Joseph, and **he worshiped, leaning on the top of his staff.**ᴰ ²² By faith Joseph, as he was nearing the end of his life, mentionedᴱ the exodus of the Israelites and gave instructions concerning his bones.

²³ By faith Moses, after he was born, was hidden by his parents for three months, because they saw that the child was beautiful, and they didn't fear the king's edict. ²⁴ By faith Moses, when he had grown up, refused to be called the son of Pharaoh's daughter ²⁵ and chose to suffer with the people of God rather than to enjoy the fleeting pleasure of sin. ²⁶ For he considered reproach for the sake of Christ to be greater wealth than the treasures of Egypt, since he was looking ahead to the reward.

²⁷ By faith he left Egypt behind, not being afraid of the king's anger, for Moses persevered as one who sees him who is invisible. ²⁸ By faith he instituted the Passover and the sprinkling of the blood, so that the destroyer of the firstborn might not touch the Israelites. ²⁹ By faith they crossed the Red Sea as though they were on dry land. When the Egyptians attempted to do this, they were drowned.

³⁰ By faith the walls of Jericho fell down after being marched around by the Israelites for seven days. ³¹ By faith Rahab the prostitute welcomed the spies in peace and didn't perish with those who disobeyed.

³² And what more can I say? Time is too short for me to tell about Gideon, Barak, Samson, Jephthah, David, Samuel, and the prophets, ³³ who by faith conquered kingdoms, administered justice, obtained promises, shut the mouths of lions, ³⁴ quenched the raging of fire, escaped the edge of the sword, gained strength in weakness, became mighty in battle, and put foreign armies to flight. ³⁵ Women received their dead, raised to life again. Other people were tortured, not accepting release, so that they might gain a better resurrection. ³⁶ Others experienced mockings and scourgings, as well as bonds and imprisonment. ³⁷ They were stoned,ᶠ they were sawed in two, they died by the sword, they wandered about in sheepskins, in goatskins, destitute, afflicted, and mistreated. ³⁸ The world was not worthy of them. They wandered in deserts and on mountains, hiding in caves and holes in the ground.

³⁹ All these were approved through their faith, but they did not receive what was promised, ⁴⁰ since God had provided something better for us, so that they would not be made perfect without us.

ᴬ11:18 Lit *seed*　ᴮ11:18 Gn 21:12　ᶜ11:19 Or *back, as a foreshadowing,* or *as a type*　ᴰ11:21 Gn 47:31　ᴱ11:22 Or *remembered*　ᶠ11:37 Other mss add *they were tempted,*

THE CALL TO ENDURANCE

12 Therefore, since we also have such a large cloud of witnesses surrounding us, let us lay aside every hindrance and the sin that so easily ensnares us. Let us run with endurance the race that lies before us, ² keeping our eyes on Jesus, ᴬ the source and perfecter ᴮ of our faith. For the joy that lay before him, ᶜ he endured the cross, despising the shame, and sat down at the right hand of the throne of God.

FATHERLY DISCIPLINE

³ For consider him who endured such hostility from sinners against himself, so that you won't grow weary and give up. ⁴ In struggling against sin, you have not yet resisted to the point of shedding your blood. ⁵ And you have forgotten the exhortation that addresses you as sons:

My son, do not take the Lord's discipline lightly
or lose heart when you are reproved by him,
⁶ for the Lord disciplines the one he loves
and punishes every son he receives. ᴰ

⁷ Endure suffering as discipline: God is dealing with you as sons. For what son is there that a father does not discipline? ⁸ But if you are without discipline — which all receive ᴱ — then you are illegitimate children and not sons. ⁹ Furthermore, we had human fathers discipline us, and we respected them. Shouldn't we submit even more to the Father of spirits and live? ¹⁰ For they disciplined us for a short time based on what seemed good to them, but he does it for our benefit, so that we can share his holiness. ¹¹ No discipline seems enjoyable at the time, but painful. Later on, however, it yields the peaceful fruit of righteousness to those who have been trained by it.

¹² Therefore, strengthen your tired hands and weakened knees, ¹³ and make straight paths for your feet, so that what is lame may not be dislocated ᶠ but healed instead.

WARNING AGAINST REJECTING GOD'S GRACE

¹⁴ Pursue peace with everyone, and holiness — without it no one will see the Lord. ¹⁵ Make sure that no one falls short of the grace of God and that no root of bitterness springs up, causing trouble and defiling many. ¹⁶ And make sure that there isn't any immoral ᴳ or irreverent person like Esau, who sold his birthright in exchange for a single meal. ¹⁷ For you know that later, when he wanted to inherit the blessing, he was rejected, even though he sought it with tears, because he didn't find any opportunity for repentance.

¹⁸ For you have not come to what could be touched, to a blazing fire, to darkness, gloom, and storm, ¹⁹ to the blast of a trumpet, and the sound of words. Those who heard it begged that not another word be spoken to them, ²⁰ for they could not bear what was commanded: **If even an animal touches the mountain, it must be stoned.** ᴴ ²¹ The appearance was so terrifying that Moses said, **I am trembling with fear.** ᴵ ²² Instead, you have come to

---

ᴬ 12:2 Or *us, looking to Jesus*   ᴮ 12:2 Or *the founder and completer,* or *pioneer and perfecter*   ᶜ 12:2 Or *who instead of the joy lying before him*   ᴰ 12:6 Pr 3:11-12   ᴱ 12:8 Lit *discipline, of which all have become participants*   ᶠ 12:13 Or *so that the lame will not be turned aside*   ᴳ 12:16 Or *sexually immoral* ᴴ 12:20 Ex 19:12   ᴵ 12:21 Dt 9:19

RUN WITH ENDURANCE

HEBREWS 12:1-17; PSALM 119:105; JOHN 6:66-69

Have you ever played "Shakespeare or the Bible"? You try to guess if a quote came from Scripture or Shakespeare. Sometimes it's hard to tell. Take a shot:

"He . . . protected him as the pupil of his eye."

"It is a wise father that knows his own child."

The first quote is from Deuteronomy 32:10, and the second is from Shakespeare's *The Merchant of Venice.*

Sometimes it can be tricky, separating Scripture from other inspirational or wise words. And some Scripture can feel so familiar that we're inclined to gloss over it like we would a motivational poster. So when we come to familiar passages like Hebrews 12:1, it's easy to picture a cliché shot of a runner, crossing the finish line beneath a banner emblazoned with, "RUN WITH ENDURANCE."

It's tempting to reduce the Bible to helpful maxims and cheery consolations. But the words of Scripture are unique and set apart from all other words: they are God's words. There's a stark contrast between Scripture and any human literary achievement. While Confucius or Aesop may offer us some quotable phrases, their best wisdom cannot compare to the profound beauty, comfort, and truth of God's Word. Who else can offer what He can? He alone has "the words of eternal life" (Jn 6:68).

God's Word is life. It is life because it doesn't drive us to ourselves, but to Christ, who is "the resurrection and the life" (Jn 11:25). When we read the words, "run with endurance the race that lies before us" (Heb 12:1), we aren't called to think of our own feet, knees, and hips. Our feet get sore, our knees get wobbly, and our hips are prone to give out.

Jesus knows we can't run the exhausting race of life in our own strength. Instead, He presses us to simply look to Him. In His terrible, awesome holiness, and in His sweet and refreshing encouragement, He bids us to look to Him (Heb 12:2).

What a gorgeous, blessed relief! The race is hard! So many mornings I don't even want to put on shoes and try to walk it. I can't win this race. I will never be fast enough or strong enough. Even the power of positive thinking is not sufficient to get me through.

Jesus is the source and the perfecter of our faith. He has already endured and now sits at the right hand of God. The race is already won by Christ, whose life-giving Word sustains us and lights the way before us (Ps 119:105).

While Scripture is an awesome literary text, it's far more than that. Buddha withers, and Shakespeare fades, "but the word of our God remains forever" (Is 40:8). May His living and active Word dwell in us richly, that we may live in His light (Heb 4:12; Col 3:16).

Mount Zion, to the city of the living God (the heavenly Jerusalem), to myriads of angels, a festive gathering, 23 to the assembly of the firstborn whose names have been written[A] in heaven, to a Judge, who is God of all, to the spirits of righteous people made perfect, 24 and to Jesus, the mediator of a new covenant, and to the sprinkled blood, which says better things than the blood of Abel.

25 See to it that you do not reject the one who speaks. For if they did not escape when they rejected him who warned them on earth, even less will we if we turn away from him who warns us from heaven. 26 His voice shook the earth at that time, but now he has promised, **Yet once more I will shake not only the earth but also the heavens.** [B] 27 This expression, "Yet once more," indicates the removal of what can be shaken — that is, created things — so that what is not shaken might remain. 28 Therefore, since we are receiving a kingdom that cannot be shaken, let us be thankful. By it, we may serve God acceptably, with reverence and awe, 29 for our God is a consuming fire.

FINAL EXHORTATIONS

13 Let brotherly love continue. 2 Don't neglect to show hospitality, for by doing this some have welcomed angels as guests without knowing it. 3 Remember those in prison, as though you were in prison with them, and the mistreated,[C] as though you yourselves were suffering bodily.[D] 4 Marriage is to be honored by all and the marriage bed kept undefiled, because God will judge the sexually immoral and adulterers. 5 Keep your life free from the love of money. Be satisfied with what you have, for he himself has said, **I will never leave you or abandon you.** [E] 6 Therefore, we may boldly say,

> The Lord is my helper;
> I will not be afraid.
> What can man do to me?[F]

7 Remember your leaders who have spoken God's word to you. As you carefully observe the outcome of their lives, imitate their faith. 8 Jesus Christ is the same yesterday, today, and forever. 9 Don't be led astray by various kinds of strange teachings; for it is good for the heart to be established by grace and not by food regulations, since those who observe them have not benefited. 10 We have an altar from which those who worship at the tabernacle do not have a right to eat. 11 For the bodies of those animals whose blood is brought into the most holy place by the high priest as a sin offering are burned outside the camp. 12 Therefore, Jesus also suffered outside the gate, so that he might sanctify[G] the people by his own blood. 13 Let us then go to him outside the camp, bearing his disgrace. 14 For we do not have an enduring city here; instead, we seek the one to come. 15 Therefore, through him let us continually offer up to God a sacrifice of praise, that is, the fruit of lips that confess his name. 16 Don't neglect to do what is good and to share, for God is pleased with such sacrifices. 17 Obey your leaders[H] and submit to them, since they keep watch over your souls as those who will give an account, so that

---

[A]12:23 Or registered [B]12:26 Hg 2:6 [C]13:3 Or tortured [D]13:3 Or mistreated, since you are also in a body [E]13:5 Dt 31:6 [F]13:6 Ps 118:6 [G]13:12 Or set apart, or consecrate [H]13:17 Or rulers they can do this with joy and not with grief, for that would be unprofitable for you. ¹⁸ Pray for us, for we are convinced that we have a clear conscience, wanting to conduct ourselves honorably in everything. ¹⁹ And I urge you all the more to pray ᴬ that I may be restored to you very soon.

BENEDICTION AND FAREWELL

²⁰ Now may the God of peace, who brought up from the dead our Lord Jesus — the great Shepherd of the sheep — through the blood of the everlasting covenant, ²¹ equip ᴮ you with everything good to do his will, working in us what is pleasing in his sight, through Jesus Christ, to whom be glory forever and ever. ᶜ Amen.

²² Brothers and sisters, I urge you to receive this message of exhortation, for I have written to you briefly. ²³ Be aware that our brother Timothy has been released. If he comes soon enough, he will be with me when I see you. ²⁴ Greet all your leaders and all the saints. Those who are from Italy send you greetings. ²⁵ Grace be with you all.

ᴬ 13:19 Lit *to do this*   ᴮ 13:21 Or *perfect*   ᶜ 13:21 Other mss omit *and ever*

The

TESTING

OF YOUR

Faith

PRODUCES

ENDURANCE

james

 Consider it a great joy, my brothers and sisters, whenever you experience various trials, because you know that the testing of your faith produces endurance. And let endurance have its full effect, so that you may be mature and complete, lacking nothing. **1:2-4**

ON THE TIMELINE There is no information in James's letter to suggest a specific date, but scholars presume the writing took place between AD 48–52, ten or more years before James' death in AD 62 or 66.

A LITTLE BACKGROUND James, the brother of Jesus, is most likely the author of this epistle (Mt 13:55; Mk 6:3; Gl 1:19). Though he was not a follower of Christ during Christ's earthly ministry (Jn 7:3-5), a post-resurrection appearance convinced James that Jesus was indeed the Christ (Ac 1:14; 1Co 15:7). James later led the Jerusalem church (Gl 2:9,12) and exercised great influence there (Ac 1:14; 21:18; 1Co 15:7; Gl 2:9,12).

MESSAGE & PURPOSE As a general epistle, James was written to a broad audience rather than a specific group of people. James focuses on themes of wisdom, faith, and moral and ethical conduct. The author highlights wisdom as valuable for proper speech in worship (Jms 3:7-12), for determining who ought to teach (Jms 1:19-27; 3:1-8), and for avoiding internal conflicts within congregations (Jms 3:13-18; 4:1-12). He presents the importance of faith in action (Jms 1:19-27; 2:14-26), stating that faith which does not express itself in good works is useless (Jms 2:20). The epistle also deals with ethics and social justice (Jms 2:1-13; 4:1-12; 5:1-12).

GIVE THANKS FOR THE BOOK OF JAMES

James continually called for obedience to the law of God, showing believers that their obedience to God's moral standards was an indication of a living faith. Some choose to oversimplify the distinctions between the Old Testament and the New Testament by saying that the OT is grounded in works and the NT is grounded in faith. James brings both testaments together to show that faith and works are integrally related in both the old and new covenants.

ECHOES OF JESUS IN JAMES

The book of James is unlike any other book in the New Testament. While it reads like a letter, it often adopts the stark style of Proverbs, the rhetorical strength of an Old Testament prophet, and the structure of a sermon. Perhaps most notably is how the book of James mirrors Jesus' Sermon on the Mount, which would have been very familiar to James, the brother of Jesus.

SERMON ON THE MOUNT IN MATTHEW	JESUS' TEACHING	JAMES
5:3	Those who don't amount to much by the world's standards should be glad, for God has honored them.	1:9
5:3-4	When you humble yourself and realize your dependence on God, He will lift you up.	4:10
5:7; 6:14	Be merciful to others, as God is merciful to you.	2:13
5:9	Blessed are the peacemakers; they plant in peace and reap a harvest of goodness.	3:17-18
5:11-12	Whenever trouble comes, be joyful.	1:2
5:12	Be patient in suffering, as God's prophets were patient.	5:10
5:22	Watch out for your anger; it can be dangerous.	1:20
5:33-37	Be honest in your speech; just say a simple yes or no so that you will not sin.	5:12
6:19	Treasures on earth will only rot away and be eaten by moths. Store up eternal treasures in heaven.	5:2-3
6:24	Friendship with the world makes you an enemy of God.	4:4
7:1-2	Don't speak evil against each other. If you do, you are criticizing God's law.	4:11
7:7-12	Ask God and He will answer.	1:5; 5:15
7:21-23	Your faith must express itself in your actions.	2:14-16

READ AND UNDERSTAND JAMES

The Bible is a complete work in which many stories combine to tell one story. As you read the book of James, consider reading the additional passages to discover how the whole of Scripture works together.

GREETING

1 James, a servant of God and of the Lord Jesus Christ:
To the twelve tribes dispersed abroad.[A]
Greetings.

TRIALS AND MATURITY

[2] Consider it a great joy, my brothers and sisters, whenever you experience various trials, [3] because you know that the testing of your faith produces endurance. [4] And let endurance have its full effect, so that you may be mature and complete, lacking nothing.

[5] Now if any of you lacks wisdom, he should ask God — who gives to all generously and ungrudgingly — and it will be given to him. [6] But let him ask in faith without doubting. For the doubter is like the surging sea, driven and tossed by the wind. [7] That person should not expect to receive anything from the Lord, [8] being double-minded and unstable in all his ways.[C]

[9] Let the brother of humble circumstances boast in his exaltation, [10] but let the rich boast in his humiliation because he will pass away like a flower of the field. [11] For the sun rises and, together with the scorching wind, dries up the grass; its flower falls off, and its beautiful appearance perishes. In the same way, the rich person will wither away while pursuing his activities.

[12] Blessed is the one who endures trials, because when he has stood the test he will receive the crown of life that God[D] has promised to those who love him.

[13] No one undergoing a trial should say, "I am being tempted by God," since God is not tempted by evil, and he himself doesn't tempt anyone. [14] But each person is tempted when he is drawn away and enticed by his own evil desire. [15] Then after desire has conceived, it gives birth to sin, and when sin is fully grown, it gives birth to death.

[16] Don't be deceived, my dear brothers and sisters. [17] Every good and perfect gift is from above, coming down from the Father of lights, who does not change like shifting shadows. [18] By his own choice, he gave us birth by the word of truth so that we would be a kind of firstfruits of his creatures.

HEARING AND DOING THE WORD

[19] My dear brothers and sisters, understand this: Everyone should be quick to listen, slow to speak, and slow to anger, [20] for human anger does not accomplish God's righteousness. [21] Therefore, ridding yourselves of all moral filth and the evil that is so prevalent,[E] humbly receive the implanted word, which is able to save your souls.

[22] But be doers of the word and not hearers only, deceiving yourselves. [23] Because if anyone is a hearer of the word and not a doer, he is like someone looking at his own face[F] in a mirror. [24] For he looks at himself, goes away, and immediately forgets what kind of person he was. [25] But the one who looks intently into the perfect law of freedom and perseveres in it, and is not a forgetful hearer but a doer who works — this person will be blessed in what he does.

[A] 1:1 Gk diaspora ; Jewish people scattered throughout Gentile lands [B] 1:6 Or without divided loyalties [C] 1:8 Or in all his conduct [D] 1:12 Other mss read that the Lord [E] 1:21 Or the abundance of evil [F] 1:23 Or at his natural face

REJOICE IN SUFFERING?

JAMES 1; JEREMIAH 31:7-14

Have you ever noticed how in times of pain or trial, we comfort our friends, loved ones, and even ourselves with words like:

"You're going to make it through this."
"Tomorrow will be better."
"What can I do to ease your pain?"

Our endgame is an end to suffering. We pray for the bad times to go away. We beg that they would never come at all. A whole industry of Mylar balloons and teddy bears exists bearing the sentiment, "Get Well Soon!" We ask the Lord to remove our thorns, to help us endure our hardships, and to bring us through suffering as unscathed as possible.

But James had an entirely different take on trials.

"Consider it a great joy, my brothers and sisters, whenever you experience various trials."

JAMES 1:2

Don't get over them. Don't rush through them or past them. **Rejoice in them.**

James tells us not to be so hasty to escape the faith-testing valleys because those valleys contain the fertile soil needed to produce steadfastness. And steadfastness—being immovable, unable to be shaken, deeply rooted—is perhaps the true "wellness" we should be seeking.

As Christians, we eagerly say we want to be like Christ. (The term "Christian," after all, means "little Christ.") But many of us are really only asking for the good stuff. "Lord, make us loving

and patient and joyful!" we sing in chorus and with enthusiasm.

But while Jesus was indeed all of those things, He was also described by the prophet Isaiah as "a man of suffering who knew what sickness was" (Is 53:3). Christ Himself learned obedience through His suffering (Heb 5:8). And friends, it's from those dark yet fertile valleys that steadfastness begins to spring forth—first sprouting from faith, then budding into love, and flowering into patience and joy.

Today, or tomorrow, or whenever you find yourself in a place of trial—do not minimize it or rush through it. Instead, give thanks to the Lord. Pray for endurance and steadfastness from the One who has already endured and proven Himself steadfast.

As backwards as it may feel, this difficult trial or painful suffering is a time to thank the Lord. This is the time to rejoice!

We do not rejoice because bad things happen or because this poor, fallen world is full of death, injustice, and sorrow. No, we rejoice because the sovereign Lord calls us His own. He loves us enough to descend with us into the dark yet mysteriously fertile valleys, to produce in us a steadfastness which cannot be shaken.

Thanks be to God.

"Blessed is the one who endures trials, because when he has stood the test he will receive the crown of life that God has promised to those who love him."

JAMES 1:12

---

²⁶ If anyone^A thinks he is religious without controlling his tongue, his religion is useless and he deceives himself. ²⁷ Pure and undefiled religion before God the Father is this: to look after orphans and widows in their distress and to keep oneself unstained from the world.

THE SIN OF FAVORITISM

2 My brothers and sisters, do not show favoritism as you hold on to the faith in our glorious Lord Jesus Christ. ² For if someone comes into your meeting wearing a gold ring and dressed in fine clothes, and a poor person dressed in filthy clothes also comes in, ³ if you look with favor on the one wearing the fine clothes and say, "Sit here in a good place," and yet you say to the poor person, "Stand over there," or "Sit here on the floor by my footstool," ⁴ haven't you made distinctions among yourselves and become judges with evil thoughts?

⁵ Listen, my dear brothers and sisters: Didn't God choose the poor in this world to be rich in faith and heirs of the kingdom that he has promised to those who love him? ⁶ Yet you have dishonored the poor. Don't the rich oppress you and drag you into court? ⁷ Don't they blaspheme the good name that was invoked over you?

⁸ Indeed, if you fulfill the royal law prescribed in the Scripture, **Love your neighbor as yourself,**^B you are doing well. ⁹ If, however, you show favoritism, you commit sin and are convicted by the law as transgressors. ¹⁰ For whoever keeps the entire law, and yet stumbles at one point, is guilty of breaking it all. ¹¹ For he who said, **Do not commit adultery,**^C also said, **Do not murder.**^D So if you do not commit adultery, but you murder, you are a lawbreaker.

¹² Speak and act as those who are to be judged by the law of freedom. ¹³ For judgment is without mercy to the one who has not shown mercy. Mercy triumphs over judgment.

FAITH AND WORKS

¹⁴ What good is it, my brothers and sisters, if someone claims to have faith but does not have works? Can such faith save him?

¹⁵ If a brother or sister is without clothes and lacks daily food ¹⁶ and one of you says to them, "Go in peace, stay warm, and be well fed," but you don't give them what the body needs, what good is it? ¹⁷ In the same way faith, if it doesn't have works, is dead by itself.

¹⁸ But someone will say, "You have faith, and I have works."^E Show me your faith without works, and I will show you faith by my works. ¹⁹ You believe that God is one. Good! Even the demons believe — and they shudder.

²⁰ Senseless person! Are you willing to learn that faith without works is useless? ²¹ Wasn't Abraham our father justified by works in offering Isaac his son on the altar? ²² You see that faith was active together with his works, and by works, faith was made complete, ²³ and the Scripture was fulfilled that says, **Abraham believed God, and it was credited to him as righteousness,**^F and he was called God's friend. ²⁴ You see that a person is justified by works and not by faith alone. ²⁵ In the same way, wasn't Rahab the prostitute also justified by works

---

^A 1:26 Other mss add *among you*   ^B 2:8 Lv 19:18   ^C 2:11 Ex 20:14; Dt 5:18
^D 2:11 Ex 20:13; Dt 5:17   ^E 2:18 The quotation may end here or after v. 18b or v. 19.   ^F 2:23 Gn 15:6

in receiving the messengers and sending them out by a different route? ²⁶ For just as the body without the spirit is dead, so also faith without works is dead.

CONTROLLING THE TONGUE

3 Not many should become teachers, my brothers,ᴬ because you know that we will receive a stricter judgment. ² For we all stumble in many ways. If anyone does not stumble in what he says, he is mature, able also to control the whole body. ³ Now if we put bits into the mouths of horses so that they obey us, we direct their whole bodies. ⁴ And consider ships: Though very large and driven by fierce winds, they are guided by a very small rudder wherever the will of the pilot directs. ⁵ So too, though the tongue is a small part of the body, it boasts great things. Consider how a small fire sets ablaze a large forest. ⁶ And the tongue is a fire. The tongue, a world of unrighteousness, is placedᴮ among our members. It stains the whole body, sets the course of life on fire, and is itself set on fire by hell. ⁷ Every kind of animal, bird, reptile, and fish is tamed and has been tamed by humankind, ⁸ but no one can tame the tongue. It is a restless evil, full of deadly poison. ⁹ With the tongue we bless our Lord and Father, and with it we curse people who are made in God's likeness. ¹⁰ Blessing and cursing come out of the same mouth. My brothers and sisters, these things should not be this way. ¹¹ Does a spring pour out sweet and bitter water from the same opening? ¹² Can a fig tree produce olives, my brothers and sisters, or a grapevine produce figs? Neither can a saltwater spring yield fresh water.

THE WISDOM FROM ABOVE

¹³ Who among you is wise and understanding? By his good conduct he should show that his works are done in the gentleness that comes from wisdom. ¹⁴ But if you have bitter envy and selfish ambition in your heart, don't boast and deny the truth. ¹⁵ Such wisdom does not come down from above but is earthly, unspiritual, demonic. ¹⁶ For where there is envy and selfish ambition, there is disorder and every evil practice. ¹⁷ But the wisdom from above is first pure, then peace-loving, gentle, compliant, full of mercy and good fruits, unwavering, without pretense. ¹⁸ And the fruit of righteousness is sown in peace by those who cultivate peace.

PROUD OR HUMBLE

4 What is the source of wars and fights among you? Don't they come from your passions that wage war within you?ᶜ ² You desire and do not have. You murder and covet and cannot obtain. You fight and wage war.ᴰ You do not have because you do not ask. ³ You ask and don't receive because you ask with wrong motives, so that you may spend it on your pleasures.

⁴ You adulterous people!ᴱ Don't you know that friendship with the world is hostility toward God? So whoever wants to be the friend of the world becomes the enemy of God. ⁵ Or do you think it's without reason that the Scripture says: The spirit he made to dwell in us envies intensely?ᶠ

ᴬ3:1 Or brothers and sisters ᴮ3:6 Or places itself, or appoints itself ᶜ4:1 Or war in your members ᴰ4:2 Or You desire and do not have, so you murder. You covet and cannot obtain, so you fight and wage war. ᴱ4:4 Lit Adulteresses ᶠ4:5 Or Scripture says: He jealously yearns for the spirit he made to live in us?, or Scripture says: The Spirit he made to dwell in us longs jealously?

HOW GREAT A FOREST

JAMES 3; PSALM 12; GALATIANS 5:16-25

The idea of "controlling the tongue" is not just religious-speak to me. It is not just a heading in my Bible or a topic that generates good, honest conversation at Bible study. It is one of the most sincere prayers of my heart and one of the darkest manifestations of my sin.

Especially since becoming a mother, I've realized my words have the power to give life and hope or to steal them away. I'll never forget the look in my young daughter's eyes the first time I tossed sharp, careless words at her like a grenade and saw her wince at the explosion. I surrendered my tongue and its words to the Lord that day, and I've surrendered them countless times since.

In James 3, James describes the tongue as the epitome of hypocrisy. "With the tongue we bless our Lord and Father, and with it we curse people who are made in God's likeness" (Jms 3:9). And here's the kicker: we are all guilty of this—every one of us, in every phase of life.

James does not give us a tidy "how-to" at the end of this passage, no foolproof answer for ending this struggle which takes place in each of us. Instead, he provides one analogy after the other, illustrating the way our words can bring life and direction, or death and destruction.

"So too, though the tongue is a small part of the body, it boasts great things. Consider how a small fire sets ablaze a large forest."

JAMES 3:5

Our words have more power than we usually care to acknowledge. If we knew—really knew—the weight our words carry in each person who receives them, how would that change what we say? Would the flames of hypocrisy overcome us if we could see the fires we spark?

This forthright passage from James should bring us to our knees. Our struggle to control our tongues and rein in our thoughts should cause us to plead to the Father for wisdom, as James encourages us to do in the first chapter of his letter.

"Now if any of you lacks wisdom, he should ask God—who gives to all generously and ungrudgingly—and it will be given to him."

JAMES 1:5

Praise God that He hears us!

Just as grace pours into the darkest parts of our hearts, igniting the hope of the gospel, so does His grace pour over the fires we start with our words. The hope of Jesus and the forgiveness of the Father extend to this place, too. As a woman who's flung more sparks than I care to admit, I am so incredibly thankful.

⁶ But he gives greater grace. Therefore he says:

God resists the proud,
but gives grace to the humble.ᴬ

⁷ Therefore, submit to God. Resist the devil, and he will flee from you. ⁸ Draw near to God, and he will draw near to you. Cleanse your hands, sinners, and purify your hearts, you double-minded. ⁹ Be miserable and mourn and weep. Let your laughter be turned to mourning and your joy to gloom. ¹⁰ Humble yourselves before the Lord, and he will exalt you.

¹¹ Don't criticize one another, brothers and sisters. Anyone who defames or judges a fellow believerᴮ defames and judges the law. If you judge the law, you are not a doer of the law but a judge. ¹² There is one lawgiver and judgeᶜ who is able to save and to destroy. But who are you to judge your neighbor?

OUR WILL AND GOD'S WILL

¹³ Come now, you who say, "Today or tomorrow we will travel to such and such a city and spend a year there and do business and make a profit." ¹⁴ Yet you do not know what tomorrow will bring — what your life will be! For you are like vapor that appears for a little while, then vanishes.

¹⁵ Instead, you should say, "If the Lord wills, we will live and do this or that." ¹⁶ But as it is, you boast in your arrogance. All such boasting is evil. ¹⁷ So it is sin to know the good and yet not do it.

WARNING TO THE RICH

5 Come now, you rich people, weep and wail over the miseries that are coming on you. ² Your wealth has rotted and your clothes are moth-eaten. ³ Your gold and silver are corroded, and their corrosion will be a witness against you and will eat your flesh like fire. You have stored up treasure in the last days. ⁴ Look! The pay that you withheld from the workers who mowed your fields cries out, and the outcry of the harvesters has reached the ears of the Lord of Hosts.ᴰ ⁵ You have lived luxuriously on the earth and have indulged yourselves. You have fattened your hearts in a day of slaughter. ⁶ You have condemned, you have murdered the righteous, who does not resist you.

WAITING FOR THE LORD

⁷ Therefore, brothers and sisters, be patient until the Lord's coming. See how the farmer waits for the precious fruit of the earth and is patient with it until it receives the early and the late rains. ⁸ You also must be patient. Strengthen your hearts, because the Lord's coming is near.

⁹ Brothers and sisters, do not complain about one another, so that you will not be judged. Look, the judge stands at the door!

¹⁰ Brothers and sisters, take the prophets who spoke in the Lord's name as an example of suffering and patience. ¹¹ See, we count as blessed those who have endured.ᴱ You have heard of Job's endurance and have seen the outcome that the Lord brought about — the Lord is compassionate and merciful.

ᴬ 4:6 Pr 3:34 ᴮ 4:11 Or *his brother or sister* ᶜ 4:12 Other mss omit *and judge*
ᴰ 5:4 Gk *Sabaoth*; or *the Lord of Armies* ᴱ 5:11 Or *persevered*

TRUTHFUL SPEECH

¹² Above all, my brothers and sisters, do not swear, either by heaven or by earth or with any other oath. But let your "yes" mean "yes," and your "no" mean "no," so that you won't fall under judgment.ᴬ

EFFECTIVE PRAYER

¹³ Is anyone among you suffering? He should pray. Is anyone cheerful? He should sing praises. ¹⁴ Is anyone among you sick? He should call for the elders of the church, and they are to pray over him, anointing him with oil in the name of the Lord. ¹⁵ The prayer of faith will save the sick person, and the Lord will raise him up; if he has committed sins, he will be forgiven. ¹⁶ Therefore, confess your sins to one another and pray for one another, so that you may be healed. The prayer of a righteous person is very powerful in its effect. ¹⁷ Elijah was a human being as we are, and he prayed earnestly that it would not rain, and for three years and six months it did not rain on the land. ¹⁸ Then he prayed again, and the sky gave rain and the land produced its fruit.

¹⁹ My brothers and sisters, if any among you strays from the truth, and someone turns him back, ²⁰ let that person know that whoever turns a sinner from the error of his way will save his soul from death and cover a multitude of sins.

ᴬ5:12 Other mss read *fall into hypocrisy*

imperishable,
undefiled,
and unfading

1 peter

Blessed be the God and Father of our Lord Jesus Christ. Because of his great mercy he has given us new birth into a living hope through the resurrection of Jesus Christ from the dead and into an inheritance that is imperishable, undefiled, and unfading, kept in heaven for you. **1:3-4**

ON THE TIMELINE First Peter was likely written between AD 62–64, during the persecution of Christians under Nero's reign.

A LITTLE BACKGROUND The author of 1 Peter identified himself as "Peter, an apostle of Jesus Christ" (1Pt 1:1). He viewed himself as a divinely ordained, directly commissioned, authoritative representative of the Lord Jesus Himself. Several statements in the letter indicate that the Peter who plays a prominent role in the Gospels is the author. For example, he called himself an "elder and witness" to Christ's sufferings (1Pt 5:1).

The recipients of 1 Peter are identified in 1 Peter 1:1. Peter wrote to "those chosen, living as exiles dispersed abroad in Pontus, Galatia, Cappadocia, Asia, and Bithynia." These were Roman provinces located in the northern part of what is now modern Turkey, unless "Galatia" includes the Galatia in the southern region of Asia Minor. These people were likely persecuted Gentile Christians. They had earlier been involved in idolatry (1Pt 4:3), were ignorant (1Pt 1:14) and living a life of emptiness (1Pt 1:18) before they came to Christ, and formerly were "not a people" but now were "God's people" (1Pt 2:9-10).

MESSAGE & PURPOSE Peter wrote to encourage suffering believers in Asia Minor to stand firm for Christ in the midst of persecution. He did so by focusing on their spiritual privileges and the place where their rights and privileges truly lay: the next life. Believers in Jesus are "exiles" (1Pt 1:1; 2:11) and "strangers" (1Pt 2:11) in this world.

GIVE THANKS FOR THE BOOK OF 1 PETER

Peter's message of encouragement in the face of suffering continues to speak to believers today. First Peter reminds us of our heavenly hope and eternal inheritance. We are called to a life of love and holiness, glorifying God and imitating Christ in our daily lives.

THE BOOK OF 1 PETER IN HISTORY

AD 20

29

32

62-64

1
(approx)

33 37

66

Simon
Peter born
in Galilee

AD 60

Peter's
martyrdom
in Rome

Paul meets with
Peter and James
on his first visit to
Jerusalem following
his conversion

AD 62-64
1 Peter written

Peter denies Jesus three times after
vowing to die with Him

Jesus recommissions Peter after
His resurrection

Peter's confession that Jesus is
the Messiah

Peter, James, and John witness Jesus'
transfiguration

Peter's brother, Andrew, introduces him to Jesus

Jesus calls Peter to be the second of His 12 disciples

Jesus calls Simon Peter a name that means "rock"

READ AND UNDERSTAND 1 PETER

The Bible is a complete work in which many stories combine to tell one story. As you read the book of 1 Peter, consider reading the additional passages to discover how the whole of Scripture works together.

GREETING

1 Peter, an apostle of Jesus Christ:

To those chosen, living as exiles dispersed abroad[A] in Pontus, Galatia, Cappadocia, Asia, and Bithynia, chosen [2] according to the foreknowledge of God the Father, through the sanctifying work of the Spirit, to be obedient and to be sprinkled with the blood of Jesus Christ.

May grace and peace be multiplied to you.

A LIVING HOPE

[3] Blessed be the God and Father of our Lord Jesus Christ. Because of his great mercy he has given us new birth into a living hope through the resurrection of Jesus Christ from the dead [4] and into an inheritance that is imperishable, undefiled, and unfading, kept in heaven for you. [5] You are being guarded by God's power through faith for a salvation that is ready to be revealed in the last time. [6] You rejoice in this,[B] even though now for a short time, if necessary, you suffer grief in various trials [7] so that the proven character of your faith — more valuable than gold which, though perishable, is refined by fire — may result in praise, glory, and honor at the revelation of Jesus Christ. [8] Though you have not seen him, you love him; though not seeing him now, you believe in him, and you rejoice with inexpressible and glorious joy, [9] because you are receiving the goal of your faith, the salvation of your souls.

[10] Concerning this salvation, the prophets, who prophesied about the grace that would come to you, searched and carefully investigated. [11] They inquired into what time or what circumstances the Spirit of Christ within them was indicating when he testified in advance to the sufferings of Christ and the glories that would follow.[C] [12] It was revealed to them that they were not serving themselves but you. These things have now been announced to you through those who preached the gospel to you by the Holy Spirit sent from heaven — angels long to catch a glimpse of these things.

A CALL TO HOLY LIVING

[13] Therefore, with your minds ready for action, be sober-minded and set your hope completely on the grace to be brought to you at the revelation of Jesus Christ. [14] As obedient children, do not be conformed to the desires of your former ignorance. [15] But as the one who called you is holy, you also are to be holy in all your conduct; [16] for it is written, **Be holy, because I am holy.**[D] [17] If you appeal to the Father who judges impartially according to each one's work, you are to conduct yourselves in reverence during your time living as strangers. [18] For you know that you were redeemed from your empty way of life inherited from your fathers, not with perishable things like silver or gold, [19] but with the precious blood of Christ, like that of an unblemished and spotless lamb. [20] He was foreknown before the foundation of the world but was revealed in these last times for you. [21] Through him you believe in God, who raised him from the dead and gave him glory, so that your faith and hope are in God.

[A] 1:1 Gk *diaspora*; Jewish people scattered throughout Gentile lands
[B] 1:6 Or *In this fact rejoice*   [C] 1:11 Or *the glories after that*   [D] 1:16 Lv 11:44-45; 19:2; 20:7

A LIVING HOPE

1 PETER 1:1-12; ROMANS 8:14-17; 1 CORINTHIANS 13:12

If you or I sat down to make a list of all of the sure bets in our lives—all the things we absolutely, positively know will not change—it would likely be a pretty short list. It's also likely that some of those things are not nearly as sure as we think they are. In fact, if there's one thing any of our lives to date have taught us, it's that life is fragile. Volatile. Uncertain.

Just about everything we do carries some degree of risk. From our responsible efforts to plan for retirement, to starting the car in the morning, to assuming a positive pregnancy test promises a healthy newborn baby nine months down the road—there's no guarantee anything will turn out how we expect.

Peter knew life was uncertain, too. When he wrote to the persecuted Gentile Christians, he didn't focus on what was shaky. Instead, he told them what he knew beyond a shadow of a doubt. Peter described their (our!) inheritance as co-heirs with Christ as "imperishable, undefiled, and unfading" (1Pt 1:4).

It's not going anywhere.

This inheritance of "living hope" is more than wishful thinking (1Pt 1:3). It's different than hoping our team wins the championship or that the paint color we picked for the kitchen doesn't dry too dark. **Hope is a confident expectation of future blessing based on facts and promises.**

And that future blessing we wait for with confident expectation? It is a perfect, face-to-face union with the Maker and Lover of our souls—secured for us by Christ's sacrifice and culminating in our one-day arrival in glory.

"For now we see only a reflection as in a mirror, but then face to face. Now I know in part, but then I will know fully, as I am fully known."

1 CORINTHIANS 13:12

It's true that there are very few sure bets in our lives on earth. There's no guarantee that our husbands will make it safely home from work or that our children will ever be truly safe at school. Chances are, next week will bear little resemblance to the way we've carefully outlined it in our planners. Planning and precautionary measures are all well and good, but they do not save us.

When it comes to true certainty, our only living hope is a shared inheritance with Christ. It is the salvation of our souls and the eternal hope that is ours through faith in Jesus.

Imperishable. Undefiled. Unfading.

You can bet your life on it.

[22] Since you have purified yourselves by your obedience to the truth,[A] so that you show sincere brotherly love for each other, from a pure[B] heart love one another constantly,[C] [23] because you have been born again — not of perishable seed but of imperishable — through the living and enduring word of God. [24] For

All flesh is like grass,
and all its glory like a flower of the grass.
The grass withers, and the flower falls,
[25]   but the word of the Lord endures forever.[D]

And this word is the gospel that was proclaimed to you.

THE LIVING STONE AND A HOLY PEOPLE

2 Therefore, rid yourselves of all malice, all deceit, hypocrisy, envy, and all slander. [2] Like newborn infants, desire the pure milk of the word,[E] so that you may grow up into your salvation,[F] [3] **if you have tasted that the Lord is good.**[G] [4] As you come to him, a living stone — rejected by people but chosen and honored by[H] God — [5] you yourselves, as living stones, a spiritual house, are being built to be a holy priesthood[I] to offer spiritual sacrifices acceptable to God through Jesus Christ. [6] For it stands in Scripture:

See, I lay a stone in Zion,
a chosen and honored[J] cornerstone,
and the one who believes in him
will never be put to shame.[K]

[7] So honor will come to you who believe; but for the unbelieving,

The stone that the builders rejected —
this one has become the cornerstone,[L]

[8] and

A stone to stumble over,
and a rock to trip over.[M]

They stumble because they disobey the word; they were destined for this.

[9] But you are **a chosen race,**[N,O] **a royal priesthood,**[P] **a holy nation,**[Q] a **people for his possession,**[R] **so that you may proclaim the praises**[S,T] of the one who called you out of darkness into his marvelous light. [10] Once you were not a people, but now you are God's people; you had not received mercy, but now you have received mercy.

A CALL TO GOOD WORKS

[11] Dear friends, I urge you as strangers and exiles to abstain from sinful desires that wage war against the soul. [12] Conduct yourselves honorably among the Gentiles,[U] so that when they slander you as evildoers, they will observe your good works and will glorify God on the day he visits.

[A]1:22 Other mss add *through the Spirit*   [B]1:22 Other mss omit *pure*   [C]1:22 Or *fervently*   [D]1:24-25 Is 40:6-8   [E]2:2 Or *desire pure spiritual milk*   [F]2:2 Other mss omit *for your salvation*   [G]2:3 Ps 34:8   [H]2:4 Or *precious to*   [I]2:5 Or *you yourselves, as living stones, are being built into a spiritual house for a holy priesthood*   [J]2:6 Or *precious*   [K]2:6 Is 28:16 LXX   [L]2:7 Ps 118:22   [M]2:8 Is 8:14   [N]2:9 Or *generation, or nation*   [O]2:9 Dt 7:6; 10:15; Is 43:20 LXX   [P]2:9 Ex 19:6; 23:22 LXX; Is 61:6   [Q]2:9 Ex 19:6; 23:22 LXX   [R]2:9 Ex 19:5; 23:22 LXX; Dt 4:20; 7:6; Is 43:21 LXX   [S]2:9 Or *the mighty deeds*   [T]2:9 Is 42:12; 43:21   [U]2:12 Or *among the nations, or among the pagans*

¹³ Submit to every human authority because of the Lord, whether to the emperorᴬ as the supreme authority ¹⁴ or to governors as those sent out by him to punish those who do what is evil and to praise those who do what is good. ¹⁵ For it is God's will that you silence the ignorance of foolish people by doing good. ¹⁶ Submit as free people, not using your freedom as a cover-up for evil, but as God's slaves. ¹⁷ Honor everyone. Love the brothers and sisters. Fear God. Honor the emperor.

SUBMISSION OF SLAVES TO MASTERS

¹⁸ Household slaves, submit to your masters with all reverence not only to the good and gentle ones but also to the cruel. ¹⁹ For it brings favor if, because of a consciousness of God, someone endures grief from suffering unjustly. ²⁰ For what credit is there if when you do wrong and are beaten, you endure it? But when you do what is good and suffer, if you endure it, this brings favor with God.

²¹ For you were called to this, because Christ also suffered for you, leaving you an example, that you should follow in his steps. ²² He did not commit sin, **and no deceit was found in his mouth;**ᴮ ²³ when he was insulted, he did not insult in return; when he suffered, he did not threaten but entrusted himself to the one who judges justly. ²⁴ He himself bore our sins in his body on the tree; so that, having died to sins, we might live for righteousness. **By his wounds**ᶜ **you have been healed.** ²⁵ For you **were like sheep going astray,**ᴰ but you have now returned to the Shepherd and Overseerᴱ of your souls.

WIVES AND HUSBANDS

3 In the same way, wives, submit yourselves to your own husbands so that, even if some disobey the word, they may be won over without a word by the way their wives live ² when they observe your pure, reverent lives. ³ Don't let your beauty consist of outward things like elaborate hairstyles and wearing gold jewelry or fine clothes, ⁴ but rather what is inside the heartᶠ — the imperishable quality of a gentle and quiet spirit, which is of great worth in God's sight. ⁵ For in the past, the holy women who put their hope in God also adorned themselves in this way, submitting to their own husbands, ⁶ just as Sarah obeyed Abraham, calling him lord. You have become her children when you do what is good and do not fear any intimidation.

⁷ Husbands, in the same way, live with your wives in an understanding way, as with a weaker partner, showing them honor as coheirs of the grace of life, so that your prayers will not be hindered.

DO NO EVIL

⁸ Finally, all of you be like-minded and sympathetic, love one another, and be compassionate and humble,ᴳ ⁹ not paying back evil for evil or insult for insult but, on the contrary, giving a blessing, since you were called for this, so that you may inherit a blessing.

¹⁰   For **the one who wants to love life**
        and to see good days,

ᴬ2:13 Or *king*   ᴮ2:22 Is 53:9   ᶜ2:24 Is 53:5   ᴰ2:25 Is 53:6   ᴱ2:25 Or *Guardian*   ᶠ3:4 Or *rather, the hidden person of the heart*   ᴳ3:8 Other mss read *courteous*

> let him keep his tongue from evil
> and his lips from speaking deceit,
> ¹¹ and let him turn away from evil
> and do what is good.
> Let him seek peace and pursue it,
> ¹² because the eyes of the Lord are on the righteous
> and his ears are open to their prayer.
> But the face of the Lord is against
> those who do what is evil.^A

UNDESERVED SUFFERING

¹³ Who then will harm you if you are devoted to what is good? ¹⁴ But even if you should suffer for righteousness, you are blessed. **Do not fear what they fear**^B **or be intimidated,**^C ¹⁵ but in your hearts regard^D Christ^E the Lord as holy, ready at any time to give a defense to anyone who asks you for a reason for the hope that is in you. ¹⁶ Yet do this with gentleness and respect, keeping a clear conscience, so that when you are accused,^F those who disparage your good conduct in Christ will be put to shame. ¹⁷ For it is better to suffer for doing good, if that should be God's will, than for doing evil.

¹⁸ For Christ also suffered for sins once for all, the righteous for the unrighteous, that he might bring you to God. He was put to death in the flesh^G but made alive by the Spirit,^H ¹⁹ in which^I he also went and made proclamation to the spirits in prison ²⁰ who in the past were disobedient, when God patiently waited in the days of Noah while the ark was being prepared. In it a few — that is, eight people^J — were saved through water. ²¹ Baptism, which corresponds to this, now saves you (not as the removal of dirt from the body, but the pledge^K of a good conscience toward God) through the resurrection of Jesus Christ, ²² who has gone into heaven and is at the right hand of God with angels, authorities, and powers subject to him.

FOLLOWING CHRIST

4 Therefore, since Christ suffered^L in the flesh, arm yourselves also with the same understanding^M — because the one who suffers in the flesh is finished with sin^N — ² in order to live the remaining time in the flesh no longer for human desires, but for God's will. ³ For there has already been enough time spent in doing what the Gentiles choose to do: carrying on in unrestrained behavior, evil desires, drunkenness, orgies, carousing, and lawless idolatry. ⁴ They are surprised that you don't join them in the same flood of wild living — and they slander^O you. ⁵ They will give an account to the one who stands ready to judge the living and the dead. ⁶ For this reason the gospel was also preached to those who are now dead,^P so that, although

---

^A3:10-12 Ps 34:12-16   ^B3:14 Or *Do not fear them*   ^C3:14 Is 8:12   ^D3:15 Or *sanctify*, or *set apart*   ^E3:15 Other mss read *set God*   ^F3:16 Other mss read *when they speak against you as evildoers*   ^G3:18 Or *by the flesh*, or *in the fleshly realm*   ^H3:18 Or *in the spirit*, or *in the Spirit*, or *in the spiritual realm*   ^I3:19 Or *by whom*, or *in whom*, or *at that time*   ^J3:20 Or *souls*   ^K3:21 Or *the appeal*   ^L4:1 Other mss read *suffered for us*   ^M4:1 Or *perspective*, or *attitude*   ^N4:1 Or *the one who suffered in the flesh has finished with sin*   ^O4:4 Or *blaspheme*   ^P4:6 Or *those who are dead*

THE TIME IS NOW

1 PETER 4:1-11; ROMANS 6:11

There is no more time to waste.

You and I stand today on the timeline of our lives. Behind us lies our past, a unique combination of joys and wreckage. Some memories are tied to our belt for safekeeping and others we try desperately to leave behind. Each of our paths looks different, but there is much we have in common. Too much time wasted on guilt and bitterness. Too much time wasted in sin. Too much time spent running when we should be resting, or sitting when we should be serving. Too many days spent insisting on our own way. Too few prayers spoken. Too many lies believed.

Looking back at it all, it's clear: there is no more time to waste.

Chapter 4 of 1 Peter begins the way chapter 3 ends, with Peter pointing to the cross and the blameless, suffering Savior. I imagine us standing there with Peter, gazing into the sky and remembering the image of Christ crucified, feeling the certainty course through our veins that this—this changes everything. Then Peter turns, locks his eyes with ours and says simply: *Make the rest of your life about this.*

Sisters in Christ, it is time to stand in the grace of our Savior and reclaim our lives for His glory. It is time to be self-controlled and clear-minded so we can pray. It is time to keep on loving where

others have stopped, to let our love for one another grow deep enough to drown sin and hurt and hate. It is time to be generous without complaining, gracious without resentment. It is time to recognize our gifts and use them, to serve in the way God has equipped us. It is time to rejoice in our suffering because we are sharing in suffering with Christ. **It is time to honor God in all we do, to do it all by His grace and for His glory.**

Hear me, friends: This is not another to-do list. This is not another plate to spin or another mark on the wall to which we will never measure up. This is our life—our real, right-now life—in Christ.

Our God does not simply point to our sordid past and say, *Don't live that way anymore.* No, our God cups our face in His nail-scarred hands and says, *My child, you don't have to live that way anymore. You are free.*

We are free to walk today in a life that is alive in Christ. We are free to love, to serve, to forgive and be forgiven. We are free to glorify our Father and not ourselves because it was always His glory to begin with.

This changes everything. This is what matters. May we walk boldly today and every day, free in the knowledge of the gospel of Jesus Christ.

they might be judged in the flesh according to human standards, they might live in the spirit according to God's standards.

END-TIME ETHICS

[7] The end of all things is near; therefore, be alert and sober-minded for prayer. [8] Above all, maintain constant love for one another, since **love covers a multitude of sins.**[A] [9] Be hospitable to one another without complaining. [10] Just as each one has received a gift, use it to serve others, as good stewards of the varied grace of God. [11] If anyone speaks, let it be as one who speaks God's words; if anyone serves, let it be from the strength God provides, so that God may be glorified through Jesus Christ in everything. To him be the glory and the power forever and ever. Amen.

CHRISTIAN SUFFERING

[12] Dear friends, don't be surprised when the fiery ordeal comes among you to test you as if something unusual were happening to you. [13] Instead, rejoice as you share in the sufferings of Christ, so that you may also rejoice with great joy when his glory is revealed. [14] If you are ridiculed for the name of Christ, you are blessed, because the Spirit of glory and of God[B] rests on you. [15] Let none of you suffer as a murderer, a thief, an evildoer, or a meddler.[C] [16] But if anyone suffers as a Christian, let him not be ashamed but let him glorify God in having that name.[D] [17] For the time has come for judgment to begin with God's household, and if it begins with us, what will the outcome be for those who disobey the gospel of God?

[18]   And **if a righteous person is saved with difficulty,**
       what will become of the ungodly and the sinner?[E]

[19] So then, let those who suffer according to God's will entrust themselves to a faithful Creator while doing what is good.

ABOUT THE ELDERS

5 I exhort the elders among you as a fellow elder and witness to the sufferings of Christ, as well as one who shares in the glory about to be revealed: [2] Shepherd God's flock among you, not overseeing[F] out of compulsion but willingly, as God would have you;[G] not out of greed for money but eagerly; [3] not lording it over those entrusted to you, but being examples to the flock. [4] And when the chief Shepherd appears, you will receive the unfading crown of glory. [5] In the same way, you who are younger, be subject to the elders. All of you clothe yourselves with[H] humility toward one another, because

       God resists the proud
       but gives grace to the humble.[I]

CONCLUSION

[6] Humble yourselves, therefore, under the mighty hand of God, so that he may exalt you at the proper time, [7] casting all your cares on him, because he cares about you. [8] Be sober-minded, be alert. Your adversary the devil is prowling

---

OUR ONLY SURE FOOTING

1 PETER 5:8-14; MATTHEW 7:24-25

"It's all up to you now."

This is one of my favorite lies to believe.

I grew up in the church. I was raised with the name of Jesus on my lips long before I understood why. My own children, though small, have that same seed-like faith. "All of us in this room are smart," my young son said to me once (after I assured him that yes, Mama thinks he is such a smart boy). "But Jesus is the most smart," he said proudly.

Like my son, I've known that Jesus was "the most smart" since I was five years old. And I know that Christ in me is my living hope (1Pt 1:3-4).

Still, I often find myself drowning in worry that I will fail—fail in my faith, fail in my work, fail my family and my friends and pretty much anyone who counts on me for anything at all. I worry that I'm not enough; that somehow the gospel does not apply to me in whatever situation consumes me at the moment.

"It's up to you. Don't mess this up."

The lie is like quicksand and my feet are swallowed fast. Maybe you know that feeling of panic too? Let's quiet the lie a moment and listen to the Word of God.

"I have written to you briefly . . . to encourage you and to testify that this is the true grace of God. Stand firm in it!"

1 PETER 5:12

What is Peter's "this"?

It is the imperishable hope.
It is the call to be holy and set apart.
It is the reality that we are "a royal priesthood," coheirs with Christ Himself (1Pt 29).
It is the call to humility and submission.
It is the suffering we are sure to face (and some of us are enduring even now).
It is the freedom to rejoice, no matter what.
It is the whole of the gospel—all which is true of us and for us in Jesus.

This is the grace of God, and we can stand firm in it.

Not on the rocky terrain of our own efforts. Not in the quicksand of the world's lies. We stand on grace established, imparted, and secured by the righteousness of Jesus.

He is our only sure footing.

Whether you feel stuck in the thick mire of doubt or timidly perched on top of the world, grace is yours today. Let's stand, shaky knees and all, on the assurance that all we've read in this first letter from Peter is true.

around like a roaring lion, looking for anyone he can devour. [9] Resist him, firm in the faith, knowing that the same kind of sufferings are being experienced by your fellow believers throughout the world.

[10] The God of all grace, who called you to his eternal glory in Christ,[A] will himself restore, establish, strengthen, and support you after you have suffered a little while.[B] [11] To him be dominion[C] forever.[D] Amen.

[12] Through Silvanus,[E] a faithful brother (as I consider him), I have written to you briefly in order to encourage you and to testify that this is the true grace of God. Stand firm in it! [13] She who is in Babylon, chosen together with you, sends you greetings, as does Mark, my son. [14] Greet one another with a kiss of love. Peace to all of you who are in Christ.[F]

[A] 5:10 Other mss read *in Christ Jesus* [B] 5:10 Or *to a small extent* [C] 5:11 Some mss read *dominion and glory*; other mss read *glory and dominion* [D] 5:11 Other mss read *forever and ever* [E] 5:12 Or *Silas*; Ac 15:22-32; 16:19-40; 17:1-16 [F] 5:14 Other mss read *Christ Jesus. Amen.*

His divine power has given
us everything required
for life and godliness

2 peter

 His divine power has given us everything required for life and godliness through the knowledge of him who called us by his own glory and goodness. **1:3**

ON THE TIMELINE Second Peter was written just before Peter's death, as indicated by his mention in 1:14 that his death was near. Peter likely wrote the letter from Rome, where church tradition places the apostle in his latter days. Peter's martyrdom occurred at about AD 67, during Nero's reign.

A LITTLE BACKGROUND The author of 2 Peter plainly identified himself as the Apostle Peter (2Pt 1:1). He called himself "Simeon Peter" (2Pt 1:1), a name only used of the apostle one other time in Scripture, in Acts 15:14. The Semitic spelling of the name lends a sense of authenticity to Peter's letter, and it would have been natural for Peter, as a Jew, to use this original form of his name. Peter designated himself as "a servant and an apostle of Jesus Christ" (2Pt 1:1). He saw himself as a servant submitted to Christ's lordship and as a divinely ordained, directly commissioned, authoritative representative of the Lord Jesus Himself.

Unlike 1 Peter, 2 Peter does not mention specific recipients or an exact destination. The apostle referred to his epistle as the "second letter" he had written to his readers (2Pt 3:1).

MESSAGE & PURPOSE Peter cautioned believers to beware of false teachers with their heretical doctrines and immoral lifestyles. Peter was so concerned about the temptations of sin that he wrote this second letter as an immediate follow-up to the first. Peter also warned against denials of Christ's return and His accompanying judgment. He urged his readers to make every effort to grow in the knowledge and practice of the Christian faith.

GIVE THANKS FOR THE BOOK OF 2 PETER

The Word of God is preeminent in this short letter. Second Peter gives Scripture center stage in chapter 1 by emphasizing knowledge (2Pt 1:3,5-6, 8,12,20-21) and its divine origin; in chapter 2 by showing its historicity (2Pt 2:4-8); and in chapter 3 by indicating Paul's letters are equal with "the rest of the Scriptures" (2Pt 3:15-16). Peter made strong connections with the Old Testament and challenged his audience to live authentic Christian lives, insisting on the importance of Scripture for guiding and preserving our faith.

THE BOOK OF 2 PETER IN HISTORY

AD 35

AD 55

33

40

49

66

Peter bears witness to and baptizes Cornelius and his family at Caesarea Maritima

Peter, James, John, Paul, Barnabas, and Titus meet at the Jerusalem council to address the question of whether Gentiles had to be circumcised to become Christians

2 Peter written

Peter's martyrdom in Rome

Following His resurrection, Jesus appears to Peter and recommissions him

3000 people respond to Peter's sermon at Pentecost

READ AND UNDERSTAND 2 PETER

The Bible is a complete work in which many stories combine to tell one story. As you read the book of 2 Peter, consider reading the additional passages to discover how the whole of Scripture works together.

GREETING

1 Simeon[A] Peter, a servant and an apostle of Jesus Christ:

To those who have received a faith equal to ours through the righteousness of our God and Savior Jesus Christ.

[2] May grace and peace be multiplied to you through the knowledge of God and of Jesus our Lord.

GROWTH IN THE FAITH

[3] His[B] divine power has given us everything required for life and godliness through the knowledge of him who called us by[C] his own glory and goodness. [4] By these he has given us very great and precious promises, so that through them you may share in the divine nature, escaping the corruption that is in the world because of evil desire. [5] For this very reason, make every effort to supplement your faith with goodness, goodness with knowledge, [6] knowledge with self-control, self-control with endurance, endurance with godliness, [7] godliness with brotherly affection, and brotherly affection with love. [8] For if you possess these qualities in increasing measure, they will keep you from being useless or unfruitful in the knowledge of our Lord Jesus Christ. [9] The person who lacks these things is blind and shortsighted and has forgotten the cleansing from his past sins. [10] Therefore, brothers and sisters, make every effort to confirm your calling and election, because if you do these things you will never stumble. [11] For in this way, entry into the eternal kingdom of our Lord and Savior Jesus Christ will be richly provided for you.

[12] Therefore I will always remind you about these things, even though you know them and are established in the truth you now have. [13] I think it is right, as long as I am in this bodily tent, to wake you up with a reminder, [14] since I know that I will soon lay aside my tent, as our Lord Jesus Christ has indeed made clear to me. [15] And I will also make every effort so that you are able to recall these things at any time after my departure.[D]

THE TRUSTWORTHY PROPHETIC WORD

[16] For we did not follow cleverly contrived myths when we made known to you the power and coming of our Lord Jesus Christ; instead, we were eyewitnesses of his majesty. [17] For he received honor and glory from God the Father when the voice came to him from the Majestic Glory, saying "This is my beloved Son,[E] with whom I am well-pleased! " [18] We ourselves heard this voice when it came from heaven while we were with him on the holy mountain. [19] We also have the prophetic word strongly confirmed, and you will do well to pay attention to it, as to a lamp shining in a dark place, until the day dawns and the morning star rises in your hearts. [20] Above all, you know this: No prophecy of Scripture comes from the prophet's own interpretation, [21] because no prophecy ever came by the will of man; instead, men spoke from God as they were carried along by the Holy Spirit.

WE HAVE EVERYTHING REQUIRED

2 PETER 1:1-15; 2 CHRONICLES 16:9; EPHESIANS 3:20-21

My intent that bright summer's day was to surprise my husband with a freshly mowed lawn. I knew he'd be thrilled, so I could hardly wait to get started. Plus, I'd get some time in the sun and the chance to use our brand-new, self-propelled lawnmower.

But within minutes, our "this will make mowing so much easier" machine became increasingly difficult to push. Making even a single pass across our front lawn meant exerting every ounce of energy I could muster.

I was utterly exhausted and convinced something was dreadfully wrong with me. So I ditched the surprise idea and headed for the house to call my man.

My husband listened patiently as I recounted the details of what had unfolded. But as I started down my list of possible what-ifs related to such extreme physical weakness, he interrupted. With unwavering calmness he simply asked, "Were you holding down the self-propelled bar?"

Unbelievable! I had mowed our entire front yard in the power of my own strength when help was available all along.

It was a humbling (and exhausting) lesson, to say the least. But our God is so gracious. He used even that silly mistake to help me understand a bit more about what it means to be a follower of Christ. Hear this promise from 2 Peter 1:3:

"His divine power has given us everything required for life and godliness through the knowledge of him who called us by his own glory and goodness."

Did you catch that? Everything you and I need for today—it's already ours! **We don't have to muster up the strength to live the Christian life in our own power.** The Spirit of God, who raised Jesus from the dead, lives in us (Rm 8:11), giving us access to His resurrection power.

What does that mean in the rubber-meets-the-road reality of our lives today? It means there's more—so much more—that is ours in Christ. More than we could "ask or think" (Eph 3:20). More strength. More freedom. More joy. More hope. More power. More fruitfulness. More. It's ours because Jesus lives within us right now (Gl 2:20).

Even mundane realities like dishes, spilled milk, car-pooling, financial setbacks, strained family relationships, disappointments, and fears—they are simply the platform from which our God can display His mighty grace toward us.

"For the eyes of the LORD roam throughout the earth to show himself strong for those who are wholeheartedly devoted to him."

2 CHRONICLES 16:9

Without God's help, we are left to trudge through life in our own strength. What an exhausting way to live! But, thanks be to God, we don't have to mow the lawn or face even one day in the power of our own strength. He's already given us everything we need to live for Him.

THE JUDGMENT OF FALSE TEACHERS

2 There were indeed false prophets among the people, just as there will be false teachers among you. They will bring in destructive heresies, even denying the Master who bought them, and will bring swift destruction on themselves. ² Many will follow their depraved ways, and the way of truth will be maligned because of them. ³ They will exploit you in their greed with made-up stories. Their condemnation, pronounced long ago, is not idle, and their destruction does not sleep.

⁴ For if God didn't spare the angels who sinned but cast them into hell ᴬ and delivered them in chains ᴮ of utter darkness to be kept for judgment; ⁵ and if he didn't spare the ancient world, but protected Noah, a preacher of righteousness, and seven others, ᶜ when he brought the flood on the world of the ungodly; ⁶ and if he reduced the cities of Sodom and Gomorrah to ashes and condemned them to extinction, ᴰ making them an example of what is coming to the ungodly; ᴱ ⁷ and if he rescued righteous Lot, distressed by the depraved behavior of the immoral ⁸ (for as that righteous man lived among them day by day, his righteous soul was tormented by the lawless deeds he saw and heard) — ⁹ then the Lord knows how to rescue the godly from trials and to keep the unrighteous under punishment for the day of judgment, ¹⁰ especially those who follow the polluting desires of the flesh and despise authority.

Bold, arrogant people! They are not afraid to slander the glorious ones; ¹¹ however, angels, who are greater in might and power, do not bring a slanderous charge against them before the Lord. ᶠ ¹² But these people, like irrational animals — creatures of instinct born to be caught and destroyed — slander what they do not understand, and in their destruction they too will be destroyed. ¹³ They will be paid back with harm for the harm they have done. They consider it a pleasure to carouse in broad daylight. They are spots and blemishes, delighting in their deceptions ᴳ while they feast with you. ¹⁴ They have eyes full of adultery that never stop looking for sin. They seduce unstable people and have hearts trained in greed. Children under a curse! ¹⁵ They have gone astray by abandoning the straight path and have followed the path of Balaam, the son of Bosor, ᴴ who loved the wages of wickedness ¹⁶ but received a rebuke for his lawlessness: A speechless donkey spoke with a human voice and restrained the prophet's madness.

¹⁷ These people are springs without water, mists driven by a storm. The gloom of darkness has been reserved for them. ¹⁸ For by uttering boastful, empty words, they seduce, with fleshly desires and debauchery, people who have barely escaped ᴵ from those who live in error. ¹⁹ They promise them freedom, but they themselves are slaves of corruption, since people are enslaved to whatever defeats them. ²⁰ For if, having escaped the world's impurity through the knowledge of the Lord ᴶ and Savior Jesus Christ, they are again entangled in these things and defeated, the last state is worse for

---

ᴬ2:4 Gk *Tartarus*   ᴮ2:4 Other mss read *in pits*   ᶜ2:5 Lit *Noah, the eighth, a preacher of righteousness*   ᴰ2:6 Other mss omit *to extinction*   ᴱ2:6 Other mss read *an example of what is going to happen to the ungodly*   ᶠ2:11 Other mss read *them from the Lord*   ᴳ2:13 Other mss read *delighting in the love feasts*   ᴴ2:15 Other mss read *Beor*   ᴵ2:18 Or *people who are actually escaping*   ᴶ2:20 Other mss read *our Lord* them than the first. [21] For it would have been better for them not to have known the way of righteousness than, after knowing it, to turn back from the holy command delivered to them. [22] It has happened to them according to the true proverb: **A dog returns to its own vomit,**[A] and, "A washed sow returns to wallowing in the mud."

THE DAY OF THE LORD

3 Dear friends, this is now the second letter I have written to you; in both letters, I want to stir up your sincere understanding by way of reminder, [2] so that you recall the words previously spoken by the holy prophets and the command of our Lord and Savior given through your apostles. [3] Above all, be aware of this: Scoffers will come in the last days scoffing and following their own evil desires, [4] saying, "Where is his 'coming' that he promised? Ever since our ancestors fell asleep, all things continue as they have been since the beginning of creation." [5] They deliberately overlook this: By the word of God the heavens came into being long ago and the earth was brought about from water and through water. [6] Through these the world of that time perished when it was flooded. [7] By the same word, the present heavens and earth are stored up for fire, being kept for the day of judgment and destruction of the ungodly.

[8] Dear friends, don't overlook this one fact: With the Lord one day is like a thousand years, and a thousand years like one day. [9] The Lord does not delay his promise, as some understand delay, but is patient with you, not wanting any to perish but all to come to repentance.

[10] But the day of the Lord will come like a thief;[B] on that day the heavens will pass away with a loud noise, the elements will burn and be dissolved, and the earth and the works on it will be disclosed.[C,D] [11] Since all these things are to be dissolved in this way, it is clear what sort of people you should be in holy conduct and godliness [12] as you wait for the day of God and hasten its coming.[E] Because of that day, the heavens will be dissolved with fire and the elements will melt with heat. [13] But based on his promise, we wait for new heavens and a new earth, where righteousness dwells.

CONCLUSION

[14] Therefore, dear friends, while you wait for these things, make every effort to be found without spot or blemish in his sight, at peace. [15] Also, regard the patience of our Lord as salvation, just as our dear brother Paul has written to you according to the wisdom given to him. [16] He speaks about these things in all his letters. There are some matters that are hard to understand. The untaught and unstable will twist them to their own destruction, as they also do with the rest of the Scriptures.

[17] Therefore, dear friends, since you know this in advance, be on your guard, so that you are not led away by the error of lawless people and fall from your own stable position. [18] But grow in the grace and knowledge of our Lord and Savior Jesus Christ. To him be the glory both now and to the day of eternity.[F]

[A]2:22 Pr 26:11 [B]3:10 Other mss add *in the night* [C]3:10 Other mss read *will be burned up* [D]3:10 Some Syriac and Coptic mss read *will not be found* [E]3:12 Or *and speed the coming* [F]3:18 Other mss add *Amen.*

IF WE CONFESS OUR SINS, HE IS FAITHFUL AND RIGHTEOUS TO FORGIVE US

1 john

 If we confess our sins, he is faithful and righteous to forgive us our sins and to cleanse us from all unrighteousness. **1:9**

ON THE TIMELINE Second-century sources reported that around AD 70, the year the Romans destroyed Jerusalem and the temple, John left Jerusalem where he was a church leader and relocated to Ephesus. He continued his pastoral work in that region and lived until nearly AD 100. Ephesus is likely the place where John wrote the three New Testament letters that bear his name. They could have been composed at any time in the last quarter of the first century.

A LITTLE BACKGROUND Ancient manuscripts are unanimous in naming John as the author of 1 John. The son of Zebedee, John was "the beloved disciple" who was also the author of the Fourth Gospel. The style and vocabulary of 1, 2, and 3 John are so strikingly similar to that of John's Gospel, it makes sense that they would come from the same person.

MESSAGE & PURPOSE First John was written to help early Christians confirm their faith and avoid destructive beliefs and behaviors. John gives four purpose statements:

1. He wrote to promote his readers' fellowship and joy. "We are writing these things so that our joy may be complete" (1Jn 1:4).
2. He wrote to help readers avoid the pitfalls of sin, yet find forgiveness when they stumbled. "My little children, I am writing you these things so that you may not sin" (1Jn 2:1).
3. He wrote to protect believers from false teachers. "I have written these things to you concerning those who are trying to deceive you" (1Jn 2:26).
4. He wrote so they might know they had eternal life. "I have written these things to you who believe in the name of the Son of God so that you may know that you have eternal life" (1Jn 5:13).

The last purpose statement governs the other three and brings them together in a unifying theme.

GIVE THANKS FOR THE BOOK OF 1 JOHN

First John maps out the three main components of saving knowledge of God: faith in Jesus Christ, obedient response to God's commands, and love for God and others from the heart. This epistle shows how Jesus expects His followers to honor Him in practical church life and wherever God calls His people to go and serve.

THE BOOK OF 1 JOHN IN HISTORY

AD 25

AD 50

AD 75

29

66

32

70

33

100

8
(approx)

80
(approx)

John the
apostle, son
of Zebedee,
is born

As He dies, Jesus gives care
of His mother, Mary, to John

1 John
written

John bears witness to Jesus'
acts in Jerusalem

AD 70-100
John is the spiritual leader
of the church at Ephesus

Peter, James, and John witness
Jesus' transfiguration

Jesus calls John to be His disciple

John leaves Jerusalem
for Ephesus

READ AND UNDERSTAND 1 JOHN

The Bible is a complete work in which many stories combine to tell one story. As you read the book of 1 John, consider reading the additional passages to discover how the whole of Scripture works together.

PROLOGUE: OUR DECLARATION

1 What was from the beginning, what we have heard, what we have seen with our eyes, what we have observed and have touched with our hands, concerning the word of life — ² that life was revealed, and we have seen it and we testify and declare to you the eternal life that was with the Father and was revealed to us — ³ what we have seen and heard we also declare to you, so that you may also have fellowship with us; and indeed our fellowship is with the Father and with his Son Jesus Christ. ⁴ We are writing these things^A so that our^B joy may be complete.

FELLOWSHIP WITH GOD

⁵ This is the message we have heard from him and declare to you: God is light, and there is absolutely no darkness in him. ⁶ If we say, "We have fellowship with him," and yet we walk in darkness, we are lying and are not practicing the truth. ⁷ If we walk in the light as he himself is in the light, we have fellowship with one another, and the blood of Jesus his Son cleanses us from all sin. ⁸ If we say, "We have no sin," we are deceiving ourselves, and the truth is not in us. ⁹ If we confess our sins, he is faithful and righteous to forgive us our sins and to cleanse us from all unrighteousness. ¹⁰ If we say, "We have not sinned," we make him a liar, and his word is not in us.

2 My little children, I am writing you these things so that you may not sin. But if anyone does sin, we have an advocate with the Father — Jesus Christ the righteous one. ² He himself is the atoning sacrifice^C for our sins, and not only for ours, but also for those of the whole world.

GOD'S COMMANDS

³ This is how we know that we know him: if we keep his commands. ⁴ The one who says, "I have come to know him," and yet doesn't keep his commands, is a liar, and the truth is not in him. ⁵ But whoever keeps his word, truly in him the love of God is made complete. This is how we know we are in him: ⁶ The one who says he remains in him should walk just as he walked.

⁷ Dear friends, I am not writing you a new command but an old command that you have had from the beginning. The old command is the word you have heard. ⁸ Yet I am writing you a new command, which is true in him and in you, because the darkness is passing away and the true light is already shining. ⁹ The one who says he is in the light but hates his brother or sister is in the darkness until now. ¹⁰ The one who loves his brother or sister remains in the light, and there is no cause for stumbling in him.^D ¹¹ But the one who hates his brother or sister is in the darkness, walks in the darkness, and doesn't know where he's going, because the darkness has blinded his eyes.

REASONS FOR WRITING

¹² I am writing to you, little children,
since your sins have been forgiven
on account of his name.
¹³ I am writing to you, fathers,
because you have come to know

---

^A 1:4 Other mss add *to you*   ^B 1:4 Other mss read *your*   ^C 2:2 Or *the propitiation*
^D 2:10 Or *it*

CONFESSION BRINGS FREEDOM

1 JOHN 1:1-10; PSALM 16:11

Sometimes I'm overwhelmed by fear of confessing my sin. Other times, I'm reminded of God's goodness to me when I've laid my sins before Him in the past. And then there are the times when the idea of "confession" conjures up an image of Fraulein Maria in *The Sound of Music*, walking into the Reverend Mother's office like a dog with its tail between its legs (and the rest of my day is then spent trying to get "Do-Re-Me" out of my head).

In other words, I've not always been able to see God's command to confess as an extension of His goodness. There was a season when I lived in constant fear that my sinful actions would be uncovered. Concealing my secret sin from the world was exhausting.

My life looked a lot like what John was describing in the first chapter of his first letter: I claimed fellowship with Jesus, yet I was walking in darkness (1Jn 1:6). I'd flip-flop between hiding my sin at all costs, and convincing myself that maybe I wasn't actually sinning (1Jn 1:8). Flip. Flop. Repeat.

But our Lord doesn't leave us in our sin.
In His goodness and mercy, He uses confession and repentance as a bridge to draw us back into relationship with Him.

He began stirring my heart, leading me to confess my sin and find freedom. I kept putting it off, hiding my sin even deeper, making excuses, and justifying my behavior. I refused to confess my sin and walk in the light, rejecting fellowship with Him and others (1Jn 1:7).

But God intervened.

At a weekend retreat with over a hundred other girls, I listened as one of my peers confessed her sin to the entire group. Her courage gave me my own, and I found myself broken, confessing my deepest, darkest sin to a few friends, and to the Lord. As I sought His forgiveness, the Lord immediately began to heal and restore my heart.

For most of my life, my Type A, perfectionist mentality hated the idea of admitting my faults. But God's work in my heart at that retreat changed me. I still struggle, but He changed me. The Lord offered me freedom in exchange for my sin and shame. He offered me peace and joy in His presence (Ps 16:11).

Confession really does bring freedom.
Not because of anything we do, but because "we have an advocate with the Father—Jesus Christ, the righteous one" (1Jn 2:1).

On the cross, Jesus provided a way to cover our sin with His righteousness, restoring our relationship with Him once and for always. His sacrifice gives us great hope for eternity but also freedom for today. Let us confess our sins to Him, today and every day, so that we may find true freedom and "that our joy may be complete" (1Jn 1:4).

the one who is from the beginning.
I am writing to you, young men,
because you have conquered the evil one.
[14] I have written to you, children,
because you have come to know the Father.
I have written to you, fathers,
because you have come to know
the one who is from the beginning.
I have written to you, young men,
because you are strong,
God's word remains in you,
and you have conquered the evil one.

A WARNING ABOUT THE WORLD

[15] Do not love the world or the things in the world. If anyone loves the world, the love of the Father is not in him. [16] For everything in the world — the lust of the flesh, the lust of the eyes, and the pride in one's possessions — is not from the Father, but is from the world. [17] And the world with its lust is passing away, but the one who does the will of God remains forever.

THE LAST HOUR

[18] Children, it is the last hour. And as you have heard that antichrist is coming, even now many antichrists have come. By this we know that it is the last hour. [19] They went out from us, but they did not belong to us; for if they had belonged to us, they would have remained with us. However, they went out so that it might be made clear that none of them belongs to us.

[20] But you have an anointing from the Holy One, and all of you know the truth.[A] [21] I have not written to you because you don't know the truth, but because you do know it, and because no lie comes from the truth. [22] Who is the liar, if not the one who denies that Jesus is the Christ? This one is the antichrist: the one who denies the Father and the Son. [23] No one who denies the Son has the Father; he who confesses the Son has the Father as well.

REMAINING WITH GOD

[24] What you have heard from the beginning is to remain in you. If what you have heard from the beginning remains in you, then you will remain in the Son and in the Father. [25] And this is the promise that he himself made to us: eternal life.

[26] I have written these things to you concerning those who are trying to deceive you. [27] As for you, the anointing you received from him remains in you, and you don't need anyone to teach you. Instead, his anointing teaches you about all things and is true and is not a lie; just as it has taught you,[B] remain in him.

GOD'S CHILDREN

[28] So now, little children, remain in him so that when he appears we may have confidence and not be ashamed before him at his coming. [29] If you know that he is righteous, you know this as well: Everyone who does what is right

A2:20 Other mss read *and you know all things*   B2:27 Or *as he has taught you*

PROMISES THAT WILL REMAIN

1 JOHN 2:15-27

Over coffee and croissants overseas, I listened to my new European friends talk about the U.S. Together, we laughed over the stereotypes of Americans, but quietly, my little heart protested. After all, the people I love most and hold dearest are among those Americans. I'm one of those Americans. The thread that tied me to my family and friends at home is strong, and despite our national foibles, the States are my home.

When I read this passage in 1 John, I immediately shrink back and mildly peep: *But I love this world! It's where all my favorites live!* I'm crazy for the mess of small-town fall festivals, the scent of fresh new dresses from fancy stores, and the secret glee that comes from winning at a game of cards. I love the world! I am neck-deep in TV shows and baby clothes. What does John mean, "Do not love the world or the things in the world" (1Jn 2:15)?

The world, intrinsically speaking, is good. God Himself declared it good (Gn 1:31). So **John isn't questioning the beauty of a sunset, but rather the things of this world that pull our affections away from God.** "For everything in the world . . . is not from the Father, but is from the world" (1Jn 2:16). He goes on to list three categories belonging to the world, according to the inclinations of our hearts:

The lust of the flesh. Do we indulge our bodies with food, drink, touch, and comfort? Are we seeking luxury over knowing Christ?

The lust of the eyes. Do our minds crave worldly extravagance and grandeur? Do our ears strain for applause and accolades?

The pride in one's possessions. Do our eyes rove for treasure, possessions, and delights? Do we covet the trinkets of the world?

My answer to all these questions is "Yes"—a thousand times, "Yes!" Gimme those tacos, massage my feet, get me a robot butler, and bring down the house with your applause. We're all enticed by the comforts of this world. But John is teaching us that all these delights belong to the world, and the world is passing away. We shouldn't tie ourselves to a ship that's sinking.

Instead, we should tie ourselves to the Anchor who is pulling us heavenward. We should reserve our deepest affections for God, rather than throw them away on ice cream cones and iPhones. The world seems so readily available, and come Easter Sunday, it's easy enough to find ourselves distracted, singing enthusiastically over a pretty new dress, rather than genuinely praising the risen Christ.

But the love of the Lord is infinite and lasts forever. The Spirit's peace never fails us. And while this world and its trappings are passing away, our hope in Christ's promises is secure. He is our real treasure, and our very great reward.

3 has been born of him. ¹ See what great love ᴬ the Father has given us that we should be called God's children — and we are! The reason the world does not know us is that it didn't know him. ² Dear friends, we are God's children now, and what we will be has not yet been revealed. We know that when he appears, ᴮ we will be like him because we will see him as he is. ³ And everyone who has this hope in him purifies himself just as he is pure.

⁴ Everyone who commits sin practices lawlessness; and sin is lawlessness. ⁵ You know that he was revealed so that he might take away sins, ᶜ and there is no sin in him. ⁶ Everyone who remains in him does not sin; ᴰ everyone who sins ᴱ has not seen him or known him.

⁷ Children, let no one deceive you. The one who does what is right is righteous, just as he is righteous. ⁸ The one who commits ᶠ sin is of the devil, for the devil has sinned from the beginning. The Son of God was revealed for this purpose: to destroy the devil's works. ⁹ Everyone who has been born of God does not sin, ᴳ because his seed remains in him; he is not able to sin, ᴴ because he has been born of God. ¹⁰ This is how God's children and the devil's children become obvious. Whoever does not do what is right is not of God, especially the one who does not love his brother or sister.

LOVE IN ACTION

¹¹ For this is the message you have heard from the beginning: We should love one another, ¹² unlike Cain, who was of the evil one and murdered his brother. And why did he murder him? Because his deeds were evil, and his brother's were righteous.

¹³ Do not be surprised, brothers and sisters, if the world hates you. ¹⁴ We know that we have passed from death to life because we love our brothers and sisters. The one who does not love remains in death. ¹⁵ Everyone who hates his brother or sister is a murderer, and you know that no murderer has eternal life residing in him. ¹⁶ This is how we have come to know love: He laid down his life for us. We should also lay down our lives for our brothers and sisters. ¹⁷ If anyone has this world's goods and sees a fellow believer ᴵ in need but withholds compassion from him — how does God's love reside in him? ¹⁸ Little children, let us not love in word or speech, but in action and in truth.

¹⁹ This is how we will know that we belong to the truth and will reassure our hearts before him ²⁰ whenever our hearts condemn us; for God is greater than our hearts, and he knows all things.

²¹ Dear friends, if our hearts don't condemn us, we have confidence before God ²² and receive whatever we ask from him because we keep his commands and do what is pleasing in his sight. ²³ Now this is his command: that we believe in the name of his Son Jesus Christ, and love one another as he commanded us. ²⁴ The one who keeps his commands remains in him, and he in him. And the way we know that he remains in us is from the Spirit he has given us.

ᴬ3:1 Or *what sort of love*   ᴮ3:2 Or *when it appears*   ᶜ3:5 Other mss read *our sins*   ᴰ3:6 Or *not keep on sinning*   ᴱ3:6 Or *who keeps on sinning*   ᶠ3:8 Or *practices*   ᴳ3:9 Or *not practice sin*   ᴴ3:9 Or *to keep on sinning*   ᴵ3:17 Lit *sees his brother or sister*

THE SPIRIT OF TRUTH AND THE SPIRIT OF ERROR

4 Dear friends, do not believe every spirit, but test the spirits to see if they are from God, because many false prophets have gone out into the world. ² This is how you know the Spirit of God: Every spirit that confesses that Jesus Christ has come in the flesh is from God, ³ but every spirit that does not confess Jesus[A] is not from God. This is the spirit of the antichrist, which you have heard is coming; even now it is already in the world.

⁴ You are from God, little children, and you have conquered them, because the one who is in you is greater than the one who is in the world. ⁵ They are from the world. Therefore what they say is from the world, and the world listens to them. ⁶ We are from God. Anyone who knows God listens to us; anyone who is not from God does not listen to us. This is how we know the Spirit of truth and the spirit of deception.

KNOWING GOD THROUGH LOVE

⁷ Dear friends, let us love one another, because love is from God, and everyone who loves has been born of God and knows God. ⁸ The one who does not love does not know God, because God is love. ⁹ God's love was revealed among us[B] in this way: God sent his one and only Son into the world so that we might live through him. ¹⁰ Love consists in this: not that we loved God, but that he loved us and sent his Son to be the atoning sacrifice[C] for our sins. ¹¹ Dear friends, if God loved us in this way, we also must love one another. ¹² No one has ever seen God. If we love one another, God remains in[D] us and his love is made complete in us. ¹³ This is how we know that we remain in him and he in us: He has given us of his Spirit. ¹⁴ And we have seen and we testify that the Father has sent his Son as the world's Savior. ¹⁵ Whoever confesses that Jesus is the Son of God — God remains in him and he in God. ¹⁶ And we have come to know and to believe the love that God has for us.

God is love, and the one who remains in love remains in God, and God remains in him. ¹⁷ In this, love is made complete with us so that we may have confidence in the day of judgment, because as he is, so also are we in this world. ¹⁸ There is no fear in love; instead, perfect love drives out fear, because fear involves punishment.[E] So the one who fears is not complete in love. ¹⁹ We love[F] because he first loved us. ²⁰ If anyone says, "I love God," and yet hates his brother or sister, he is a liar. For the person who does not love his brother or sister whom he has seen cannot love God whom he has not seen.[G] ²¹ And we have this command from him: The one who loves God must also love his brother and sister.

5 Everyone who believes that Jesus is the Christ has been born of God, and everyone who loves the Father[H] also loves the one born of him. ² This is how we know that we love God's children: when we love God and obey[I] his commands. ³ For this is what love for God is: to keep his commands. And his commands are not a burden, ⁴ because everyone who has

---

[A]4:3 Other mss read *confess that Jesus has come in the flesh*   [B]4:9 Or *in us*
[C]4:10 Or *the propitiation*   [D]4:12 Or *remains among*   [E]4:18 Or *fear has its own punishment* or *torment*   [F]4:19 Other mss add *him*   [G]4:20 Other mss read *has seen, how is he able to love . . . seen?* (as a question)   [H]5:1 Or *loves the one who has given birth*   [I]5:2 Other mss read *keep*

been born of God conquers the world. This is the victory that has conquered the world: our faith.

THE CERTAINTY OF GOD'S TESTIMONY

[5] Who is the one who conquers the world but the one who believes that Jesus is the Son of God? [6] Jesus Christ — he is the one who came by water and blood, not by water only, but by water and by blood. And the Spirit is the one who testifies, because the Spirit is the truth. [7] For there are three that testify:[A] [8] the Spirit, the water, and the blood — and these three are in agreement. [9] If we accept human testimony, God's testimony is greater, because it is God's testimony that he has given about his Son. [10] The one who believes in the Son of God has this testimony within himself. The one who does not believe God has made him a liar, because he has not believed in the testimony God has given about his Son. [11] And this is the testimony: God has given us eternal life, and this life is in his Son. [12] The one who has the Son has life. The one who does not have the Son of God does not have life. [13] I have written these things to you who believe in the name of the Son of God so that you may know that you have eternal life.

EFFECTIVE PRAYER

[14] This is the confidence we have before him: If we ask anything according to his will, he hears us. [15] And if we know that he hears whatever we ask, we know that we have what we have asked of him.

[16] If anyone sees a fellow believer[B] committing a sin that doesn't lead to death, he should ask, and God will give life to him — to those who commit sin that doesn't lead to death. There is sin[C] that leads to death. I am not saying he should pray about that. [17] All unrighteousness is sin, and there is sin that doesn't lead to death.

CONCLUSION

[18] We know that everyone who has been born of God does not sin, but the one who is born of God keeps him,[D] and the evil one does not touch him. [19] We know that we are of God, and the whole world is under the sway of the evil one. [20] And we know that the Son of God has come and has given us understanding so that we may know the true one.[E] We are in the true one — that is, in his Son Jesus Christ. He is the true God and eternal life.

[21] Little children, guard yourselves from idols.

[A]5:7-8 A few late Gk mss and some late Vg mss add *testify in heaven: the Father, the Word, and the Holy Spirit, and these three are one.* [8]*And there are three who bear witness on earth:* [B]5:16 Lit *sees his brother or sister* [C]5:16 Or *is a sin* [D]5:18 Other mss read *himself* [E]5:20 Other mss read *the true God*

2 john

This is love: that we walk according to his commands. This is the command as you have heard it from the beginning: that you walk in love. **VERSE 6**

ON THE TIMELINE Second-century sources reported that around AD 70, the year the Romans destroyed Jerusalem and the temple, John left Jerusalem where he was a church leader and relocated to Ephesus. He continued his pastoral work in that region and lived until nearly AD 100. Ephesus is likely the place where John wrote the three New Testament letters that bear his name. They could have been composed at any time in the last quarter of the first century.

A LITTLE BACKGROUND "The elder" (2Jn 1) is a title that the Apostle John applied to himself late in life. (The Apostle Peter referred to himself the same way in 1 Peter 5:1.) No one other than the Apostle John was ever suggested by the early Church as the writer of 1 John. Since there are so many similarities between 1 and 2 John, it is generally accepted that John also wrote the second letter.

MESSAGE & PURPOSE Like Jesus, who wept over Jerusalem (Lk 19:41), and Paul, who wrote of "the daily pressure" of his "concern for all the churches" (2Co 11:28), John was concerned about his congregation. Would they neglect to embody God's love for one another? Would they fall prey to false teachers? Second John was written with pastoral love and concern for the fledgling church.

John's message is clear: walk in the truth, obey God's commandments, love one another, and guard the teachings of Christ. John also confirmed the spiritual safety of the believing community with a beginning and ending reference to their election by God (2Jn 1,13).

GIVE THANKS FOR THE BOOK OF 2 JOHN

It is easy for congregations to get off track. John encourages believers to stay the course by responding to one another with love, exhorting them to partner this love with the truth of the gospel. Second John heartens believers for steadfastness in Christ and hope to "receive a full reward" (2Jn 8).

THE BOOK OF 2 JOHN IN HISTORY

AD 60

AD 70

AD 80

AD 90

61

Paul writes
the letter
to the
Ephesians

66

John leaves Jerusalem
for Ephesus

70

John's
Gospel
written

82
(approx)

John's first letter sent to
the churches in Asia Minor

2 John written

84

3 John written

95

John exiled
to Patmos
where
he writes
Revelation

READ AND UNDERSTAND 2 JOHN

The Bible is a complete work in which many stories combine to tell one story. As you read the book of 2 John, consider reading the additional passages to discover how the whole of Scripture works together.

GREETING

The elder:

To the elect lady and her children, whom I love in the truth — and not only I, but also all who know the truth — [2] because of the truth that remains in us and will be with us forever.

[3] Grace, mercy, and peace will be with us from God the Father and from Jesus Christ, the Son of the Father, in truth and love.

TRUTH AND DECEPTION

[4] I was very glad to find some of your children walking in truth, in keeping with a command we have received from the Father. [5] So now I ask you, dear lady — not as if I were writing you a new command, but one we have had from the beginning — that we love one another. [6] This is love: that we walk according to his commands. This is the command as you have heard it from the beginning: that you walk in love. [A]

[7] Many deceivers have gone out into the world; they do not confess the coming of Jesus Christ in the flesh. This is the deceiver and the antichrist. [8] Watch yourselves so you don't lose what we [B] have worked for, but that you may receive a full reward. [9] Anyone who does not remain in Christ's teaching but goes beyond it does not have God. The one who remains in that teaching, this one has both the Father and the Son. [10] If anyone comes to you and does not bring this teaching, do not receive him into your home, and don't greet him; [11] for the one who greets him shares in his evil works.

FAREWELL

[12] Though I have many things to write to you, I don't want to use paper and ink. Instead, I hope to come to you and talk face to face so that our joy may be complete.

[13] The children of your elect sister send you greetings.

[A] 6 Or in it [B] 8 Other mss read you

WALK IN LOVE

2 JOHN 4-6; DEUTERONOMY 10:12

To mark the twentieth anniversary of my coming to Christ, I decided to walk twenty miles in a single day. That may be an unusual idea, but at the time I thought it was a good one.

The first few steps were easy-peasy. "I could go on like this all day!" I told myself. (Warning: never brag about your endurance in mile one of a twenty-mile walk.)

The first half of the journey passed quickly and painlessly, but somewhere around the eleven-mile mark everything started to hurt. A quick assessment revealed blisters the size of golf balls on both feet. The walking that had once come so easily suddenly felt impossible. Around mile fifteen, I waved the white flag and lay down in some grass along the trail.

"I'm just going to lie here . . . forever," I vowed. Five miles short of my goal, I didn't have the oomph to go on. No pain relievers, pep talks, or promise of victory could coerce my feet to take another step.

But love could.

My family and friends showed up in sneakers and promised to walk the final miles beside me. Bolstered by love, I stood up and took a step. For the remaining five miles, their love carried me. When nothing else could, love kept me moving toward the goal.

Walking with God is a common theme in Scripture (Gn 5:24; 2Co 5:7; Gl 5:16). Describing our faith as a walk acknowledges that following Christ isn't a sprint that's run quickly. It isn't a mountain climb, steadily moving toward the summit. It's a walk—a daily decision to put one foot in front of the other by believing His promises and living according to His Word.

Jesus' "beloved apostle" John described it this way:

"This is love: that we walk according to his commands. This is the command as you have heard it from the beginning: that you walk in love."

2 JOHN 6

John reminded his readers that this walking in love business is not a new idea. Since the wilderness, God has required His people to obey, one step at a time (Dt 10:12). It may sound easy, but the Israelites proved that day after day, year after year, walking by faith can be difficult. Our lives reveal the same reality. We need God's help.

The law isn't enough to keep us on the straight and narrow (Rm 8:3). And our own fickle affections for Christ can't keep us trudging. It is Christ's love, demonstrated on the cross, which makes it possible for us to walk by faith, not by sight (2Co 5:7). It is His love that created a way for us to be right with God, and it is His love that compels us to keep walking out our faith—one step at a time.

I HAVE NO GREATER JOY THAN THIS: TO HEAR THAT MY CHILDREN ARE WALKING IN TRUTH

3 john

I have no greater joy than this: to hear that my children are walking in truth. **VERSE 4**

ON THE TIMELINE Second-century sources reported that around AD 70, the year the Romans destroyed Jerusalem and the temple, John left Jerusalem where he was a church leader and relocated to Ephesus. He continued his pastoral work in that region and lived until nearly AD 100. Ephesus is likely the place where John wrote the three New Testament letters that bear his name. They could have been composed at any time in the last quarter of the first century.

A LITTLE BACKGROUND Second and 3 John are often described as "twin epistles." There are some significant similarities between the two letters that are worth noting.

In both epistles:
1. The author described himself as "the elder" (2Jn 1; 3Jn 1).
2. The recipients were those whom he loved "in the truth" (2Jn 1; 3Jn 1).
3. The recipients were a cause for great rejoicing by John (2Jn 4; 3Jn 3).
4. The recipients were "walking in the truth" (2Jn 4; 3Jn 3), and the elder had received good reports about them (2Jn 4; 3Jn 3,5).
5. The letters contain a warning (2Jn 8; 3Jn 9-11).
6. The elder desired to see the recipients face-to-face (2Jn 12; 3Jn 14).
7. The elder delivered greetings from others (2Jn 13; 3Jn 14).

MESSAGE & PURPOSE Third John is a personal letter that revolves around three individuals: Gaius, the recipient of the letter; Diotrephes, the one causing trouble; and Demetrius, who was probably the bearer of the letter. The purpose was to give a word of exhortation to Gaius and encourage him not to imitate the bad example of Diotrephes. Instead, Gaius was to continue the good work he was doing in receiving and supporting the traveling teachers or missionaries.

GIVE THANKS FOR THE BOOK OF 3 JOHN

This brief letter underscores central Christian convictions and testifies to the God-centeredness of the Christian faith (3Jn 7,11). Jesus and the Spirit are not mentioned specifically (unless "the truth itself" in 3Jn 12 refers to Jesus; see Jn 14:6; 1Jn 5:20). But in the writer's view, Jesus and the Spirit were undoubtedly included in the reference to "God" whose "truth" this letter appeals to so frequently (3Jn 1, 3-4, 8, 12).

THE BOOK OF 3 JOHN IN HISTORY

AD 60

61

Paul writes
the letter
to the
Ephesians

66

John leaves Jerusalem
for Ephesus

AD 70

John's
Gospel
written

AD 80

John's first letter sent to
the churches in Asia Minor

82
(approx)

84

2 John written

3 John written

AD 90

95

John exiled
to Patmos
where
he writes
Revelation

READ AND UNDERSTAND 3 JOHN

The Bible is a complete work in which many stories combine to tell one story. As you read the book of 3 John, consider reading the additional passages to discover how the whole of Scripture works together.

GREETING

The elder:
To my dear friend Gaius, whom I love in the truth.

[2] Dear friend, I pray that you are prospering in every way and are in good health, just as your whole life is going well. [A] [3] For I was very glad when fellow believers came and testified to your fidelity to the truth — how you are walking in truth. [4] I have no greater joy than this: to hear that my children are walking in truth.

GAIUS COMMENDED

[5] Dear friend, you are acting faithfully in whatever you do for the brothers and sisters, especially when they are strangers. [6] They have testified to your love before the church. You will do well to send them on their journey in a manner worthy of God, [7] since they set out for the sake of the Name, accepting nothing from pagans. [B] [8] Therefore, we ought to support such people so that we can be coworkers with the truth.

DIOTREPHES AND DEMETRIUS

[9] I wrote something to the church, but Diotrephes, who loves to have first place among them, does not receive our authority. [10] This is why, if I come, I will remind him of the works he is doing, slandering us with malicious words. And he is not satisfied with that! He not only refuses to welcome fellow believers, but he even stops those who want to do so and expels them from the church.

[11] Dear friend, do not imitate what is evil, but what is good. The one who does good is of God; the one who does evil has not seen God. [12] Everyone speaks well of Demetrius — even the truth itself. And we also speak well of him, and you know that our testimony is true.

FAREWELL

[13] I have many things to write you, but I don't want to write to you with pen and ink. [14] I hope to see you soon, and we will talk face to face.

[15] Peace to you. The friends send you greetings. Greet the friends by name.

[A]2 Or as your soul prospers   [B]7 Or Gentiles

FAITH IS AN HEIRLOOM

3 JOHN 1-4; MATTHEW 28:19-20; 1 CORINTHIANS 4:14-16

Let's lift the baby blanket veil and get real about parenthood for a moment, shall we?

I have a lot to learn but I do know this: parenthood is hard! It is physically demanding. The work required to bring each little human into the world alone is enough to make an Olympic athlete weak at the knees. Then there are the years of sleepless nights—first to care for a newborn, then to wait up for a teenager.

But the physical demands are nothing compared to the emotional toll. There's worry, and stress, and more worry. There are a million dangers lurking around every corner and a zillion ways to mess it all up.

The stakes of parenting are sky high. But like other profound and demanding relationships in life, the rewards outweigh the challenges. This is what I think of when I read these words from 3 John 4:

"I have no greater joy than this: to hear that my children are walking in truth."

Since John wrote this to his friend Gaius, rather than a biological son, we can know they apply to more than the children who share our DNA. Gaius was John's spiritual son. He may not have changed his diapers or held his hands while Gaius learned to walk, but John felt a responsibility to help Gaius grow in the faith. Judging from the tone of this letter, that's a task that wasn't always easy or carefree.

Though you're likely to hear this verse at baby dedications, John's inspiring words are about more than just raising good kids. They're about passing the torch of faith, discipling the next generation, blasting a beacon of truth for those who will come behind us. They're about discipleship; the mission Christ gave all of His followers.

"Go, therefore, and make disciples of all nations, baptizing them in the name of the Father and of the Son and of the Holy Spirit, teaching them to observe everything I have commanded you. And remember, I am with you always, to the end of the age."

MATTHEW 28:19-20

One of the ways we fulfill this commission is by passing the torch of faith from one generation to the next. It's a message we hear throughout Scripture, that faith is an heirloom.

Sure, carrying the banner of truth high enough for the next generation to see has its challenges. Much like in parenthood, there isn't a comprehensive manual and there is no one-size-fits-all discipleship model. But place those challenges and efforts on one side of the scale and the rewards on the other, and you'll see the investment is worth it.

There is no greater joy than to point the next generation to the gospel of Jesus.

glory
majesty
power and
authority

jude

Now to him who is able to protect you from stumbling and to make you stand in the presence of his glory, without blemish and with great joy, to the only God our Savior, through Jesus Christ our Lord, be glory, majesty, power, and authority before all time, now and forever. Amen. **VERSES 24-25**

ON THE TIMELINE Jude is difficult to date with precision. If Jude the brother of Jesus was the author, which many scholars believe to be true, the letter must be dated sometime within his lifetime. Any date for the letter's writing must also allow time for false teachings to have developed. Jude may be reasonably dated somewhere between AD 65–80. Nothing in the letter points to a date of writing beyond this time.

A LITTLE BACKGROUND Jude called himself "a servant of Jesus Christ and a brother of James" (Jd 1). This James to whom Jude referred cannot be James the son of Zebedee because he was martyred at an early date (Ac 12:1-2). The James whom Jude named was the well-known leader of the Jerusalem church (Ac 15:13-21; Gl 2:9), and the brother of Jesus (Mk 6:3). If Jude was a brother of James, then he was also a brother of Jesus, a fact Jude humbly downplayed when he labeled himself as Christ's servant rather than His brother.

MESSAGE & PURPOSE Jude originally meant to write a letter about salvation to his friends, but he changed his plans when he heard that false teachers had infiltrated the church (Jd 3-4). Because of their influence, Jude wrote a letter urging his readers to contend for the faith (Jd 3). Jude reminded his audience that they shared a common salvation, and he alerted them to the need for vigilance in protecting the Church from heresy.

GIVE THANKS FOR THE BOOK OF JUDE

As one of the shortest of the General Epistles, New Testament scholars have often overlooked Jude's letter. Its message, however, is relevant to believers of every era. Jude sought to protect Christian truth. He strongly opposed heretics who threatened the faith and called his readers to be just as passionate in their defense of the gospel. The book of Jude bears a strong resemblance in content to 2 Peter, which also deals firmly with false teachers who were infiltrating the Church.

THE BOOK OF JUDE IN HISTORY

AD 1   AD 20   AD 40   AD 60   AD 180

5
(approx)

33

50

5 BC

44

66

Birth of
Jesus*

Letter of Jude
written

Muratorian
Canon
includes
Jude as
Scripture

Letter of James written

Birth of Jude

James
becomes
leader
of the
church at
Jerusalem

Death,
resurrection,
and ascension
of Jesus

Pentecost

* Herod killed all boys two years old and younger in Bethlehem because
the star had appeared to the wise men approximately two years prior,
presumably at the moment of Jesus' birth. Since Herod died in 4 BC and
since Jesus was born roughly two years before Herod ordered the massacre
of the Bethlehem boys, it seems that Jesus was born in 5 BC or 6 BC.

READ AND UNDERSTAND JUDE

The Bible is a complete work in which many stories combine to tell one story. As you read the book of Jude, consider reading the additional passages to discover how the whole of Scripture works together.

GREETING

J ude, a servant of Jesus Christ and a brother of James:
To those who are the called, loved^A by God the Father and kept for Jesus Christ.
[2] May mercy, peace, and love be multiplied to you.

JUDE'S PURPOSE IN WRITING

[3] Dear friends, although I was eager to write you about the salvation we share, I found it necessary to write, appealing to you to contend for the faith that was delivered to the saints once for all. [4] For some people, who were designated for this judgment long ago,^B have come in by stealth; they are ungodly, turning the grace of our God into sensuality and denying Jesus Christ, our only Master and Lord.

APOSTATES: PAST AND PRESENT

[5] Now I want to remind you, although you came to know all these things once and for all, that Jesus^C saved a people out of Egypt and later destroyed those who did not believe; [6] and the angels who did not keep their own position but abandoned their proper dwelling, he has kept in eternal chains in deep darkness for the judgment on the great day. [7] Likewise, Sodom and Gomorrah and the surrounding towns committed sexual immorality and perversions,^D and serve as an example by undergoing the punishment of eternal fire.

[8] In the same way these people — relying on their dreams — defile their flesh, reject authority, and slander glorious ones. [9] Yet when Michael the archangel was disputing with the devil in an argument about Moses's body, he did not dare utter a slanderous condemnation against him but said, "The Lord rebuke you!" [10] But these people blaspheme anything they do not understand. And what they do understand by instinct — like irrational animals — by these things they are destroyed. [11] Woe to them! For they have gone the way of Cain, have plunged into Balaam's error for profit, and have perished in Korah's rebellion.

THE APOSTATES' DOOM

[12] These people are dangerous reefs^E at your love feasts as they eat with you without reverence. They are shepherds who only look after themselves. They are waterless clouds carried along by winds; trees in late autumn — fruitless, twice dead and uprooted. [13] They are wild waves of the sea, foaming up their shameful deeds; wandering stars for whom the blackness of darkness is reserved forever.

[14] It was about these that Enoch, in the seventh generation from Adam, prophesied: "Look! The Lord comes with tens of thousands of his holy ones [15] to execute judgment on all and to convict all the ungodly concerning all the ungodly acts that they have done in an ungodly way, and concerning all the harsh things ungodly sinners have said against him." [16] These people are discontented grumblers, living according to their desires; their mouths utter arrogant words, flattering people for their own advantage.

---

^A1 Other mss read *sanctified*   ^B4 Or *whose judgment was written about long ago*
^C5 Other mss read *the Lord,* or *God*   ^D7 Or *and went after other flesh*
^E12 Other mss read *are like blemishes*

NOW AND FOREVER

JUDE 17-25; MATTHEW 13:24-30

Do you ever wonder if we live in the "worst" time in history? In the twenty-first century, evil certainly runs rampant: slavery, genocide, hate crimes, the devaluing of human life. Jesus warned us that as the time drew near for Him to come again, morality would unravel.

But as the book of Jude reminds us, first century AD was no golden age either.

Jude, the half brother of Jesus, lived through the rise of a corrupt Roman government and the destruction of the Jewish temple. He witnessed crucifixions, extortion, and false teachings about Jesus and salvation. Yet in Jude 5-7 and 14-15, Jude reminds his readers that even the moral upheaval of his day was nothing new. The state of the world was no better in Enoch's days, when evil was running so rampant that God flooded the earth two generations later (Gn 5:21; 6–7). And it was certainly no peachier in the heyday of Sodom and Gomorrah (Gn 19).

Remember the parable Jesus told about the wheat and the weeds (Mt 13:24-30)? A farmer's enemy planted weed seeds in a field of good wheat. Rather than have his workers damage his crop by pulling the weeds mid-season, the farmer instructed them to let the weeds and wheat grow together. At harvest time they would gather the weeds for the burn pile, and then they'd harvest the good grain.

Jesus was warning us that darkness will keep on growing until He comes again. But, praise God, the good will also keep on growing, right alongside the evil. The seedpods of wickedness are filling out, ripening, and getting ready to fall. But in the same field grows a harvest of righteous sons and daughters of God, whose love, faith, and good deeds are filling out, ripening, and getting ready to spread. Evil may seem to outnumber the good, but it will never overpower good's growth.

With that picture in mind, take a moment to savor the words of Jude 24-25. Go on, I'll wait here.

It's precisely the pandemic of evil that makes good shine brighter. God's ability to protect us, hold us up, cleanse us from sin, and fill us with joy stands in stark contrast to the darkness around us. In his closing benediction, Jude reminds us that evil was no match for God in the time of Enoch, nor the time of Sodom and Gomorrah, nor the time of Jesus' murder. **God's glory, majesty, power, and authority prevails over evil—any day, any year, any age.**

I can't think of anything more reassuring in our current time in history.

As we watch evil grow in the field, getting ready for a harvest of judgment, let's not forget to thank Him for His protection from stumbling, and to marvel at how He has chosen us to belong to a great harvest of righteousness.

[17] But you, dear friends, remember what was predicted by the apostles of our Lord Jesus Christ. [18] They told you, "In the end time there will be scoffers living according to their own ungodly desires." [19] These people create divisions and are worldly, not having the Spirit.

EXHORTATION AND BENEDICTION

[20] But you, dear friends, as you build yourselves up in your most holy faith, praying in the Holy Spirit, [21] keep yourselves in the love of God, waiting expectantly for the mercy of our Lord Jesus Christ for eternal life. [22] Have mercy on those who waver; [23] save others by snatching them from the fire; have mercy on others but with fear, hating even the garment defiled by the flesh.

[24] Now to him who is able to protect you from stumbling and to make you stand in the presence of his glory, without blemish and with great joy, [25] to the only God our Savior, through Jesus Christ our Lord, [A] be glory, majesty, power, and authority before all time, [B] now and forever. Amen.

[A]25 Other mss omit *through Jesus Christ our Lord*   [B]25 Other mss omit *before all time*

revelation

 Then he said to me, "It is done! I am the Alpha and the Omega, the beginning and the end." **21:6**

ON THE TIMELINE In light of the many possible dates for the writing of the book of Revelation, many scholars allow a window of thirty years, estimating it was written between the late 60s and the mid-90s of the first century AD. Substantial historical evidence shows that some of the churches were persecuted intensely by Nero in the late 60s. But the reference in Revelation 17:9-10 to seven kings, five of whom have fallen, supports a date in the mid-90s, during the reign of Domitian. Further evidence for this date is the tradition that John the apostle was exiled to Patmos during a period of intensifying local persecution of Christians by the Emperor Domitian (ruled AD 81–96).

A LITTLE BACKGROUND The author of Revelation is traditionally believed to be the Apostle John, who wrote the Fourth Gospel and the three letters of 1, 2, and 3 John (Rv 1:4,9). The initial audience was a group of seven local churches in southwest Asia Minor (Rv 1:11; 2–3). Some of these congregations were experiencing persecution (Rv 2:9-10,13), probably under the Roman emperor Domitian. Others had doctrinal and practical problems (Rv 2:6,13-15,20-23). Underlying these surface problems was the backdrop of unseen but powerful spiritual warfare (Rv 2:10,14,24; 3:9).

MESSAGE & PURPOSE The book of Revelation focuses on events at the end of the age (eschatology) more so than any other book in the Bible. However, it also focuses on practical choices that believers and unbelievers must make in the course of their lives—choices that have far-reaching consequences at the end.

The resurrected, glorified Son of Man (Jesus Christ) revealed Himself to the Apostle John with a twofold purpose: to exhort and encourage seven of the churches in Asia Minor (Rv 2–3), and to reveal to John a series of visions setting forth events related to the end times (Rv 4–22).

GIVE THANKS FOR THE BOOK OF REVELATION

The book of Revelation provides an almost complete overview of theology. Much is said in this book about Christ, mankind and sin, the people of God, holy angels, and Satan and the demons. Revelation also includes important material on God's power and the Trinity, plus aspects of the work of the Holy Spirit and the nature of Scripture.

HINTS AT ETERNITY

We don't know everything about eternity—far from it. In fact, God's Word shares more about the promise of eternity than what it will actually be like. Most of the brief descriptions of eternity would more accurately be called hints, since they use images from present experience to describe what we cannot fully grasp until we see it for ourselves.

These references are a few "hints" at what this free gift from God will be like for those who have accepted Christ's gift of eternal life.

HINT	REFERENCE
Jesus has gone away to prepare a place for us, and He will come back to get us.	JOHN 14:2-3
We will not be limited by physical properties.	JOHN 20:19,26
It will be like nothing we have seen, heard, or imagined.	1 CORINTHIANS 2:9
We will see face to face and know fully.	1 CORINTHIANS 13:12
We will have new bodies.	1 CORINTHIANS 15:35-49
We will all be changed.	1 CORINTHIANS 15:51-52
The dead in Christ will rise first, and we will always be with Jesus.	1 THESSALONIANS 4:16-17
We will be like Christ, and we will see Him.	1 JOHN 3:2
There will be a new heaven and a new earth.	REVELATION 21:1
God will dwell with humanity.	REVELATION 21:4
There will be no tears, death, grief, crying, or pain.	REVELATION 21:4

READ AND UNDERSTAND REVELATION

The Bible is a complete work in which many stories combine to tell one story. As you read the book of Revelations, consider reading the additional passages to discover how the whole of Scripture works together.

PROLOGUE

1 The revelation of[A] Jesus Christ that God gave him to show his servants what must soon take place. He made it known by sending his angel to his servant John, [2] who testified to the word of God and to the testimony[B] of Jesus Christ, whatever he saw.[C] [3] Blessed is the one who reads aloud the words of this prophecy, and blessed are those who hear the words of this prophecy and keep[D] what is written in it, because the time is near.

[4] John: To the seven churches in Asia. Grace and peace to you from[E] the one who is, who was, and who is to come, and from the seven spirits[F] before his throne, [5] and from Jesus Christ, the faithful witness, the firstborn from the dead and the ruler of the kings of the earth.

To him who loves us and has set us free[G] from our sins by his blood, [6] and made us a kingdom, [H] priests[I] to his God and Father — to him be glory and dominion forever and ever. Amen.

[7] **Look, he is coming with the clouds,**
and **every eye will see him,**
even **those who pierced him.**
And all the tribes[J] **of the earth**[K]
will mourn over him.[L,M]
So it is to be. Amen.

[8] "I am the Alpha and the Omega," says the Lord God, "the one who is, who was, and who is to come, the Almighty."

JOHN'S VISION OF THE RISEN LORD

[9] I, John, your brother and partner in the affliction, kingdom, and endurance that are in Jesus, was on the island called Patmos because of the word of God and the testimony of Jesus. [10] I was in the Spirit[N] on the Lord's day, and I heard a loud voice behind me like a trumpet [11] saying, "Write on a scroll[O] what you see and send it to the seven churches: Ephesus, Smyrna, Pergamum, Thyatira, Sardis, Philadelphia, and Laodicea."

[12] Then I turned to see whose voice it was that spoke to me. When I turned I saw seven golden lampstands, [13] and among the lampstands was one like the Son of Man,[P] dressed in a robe and with a golden sash wrapped around his chest. [14] The hair of his head was white as wool — white as snow — and his eyes like a fiery flame. [15] His feet were like fine bronze as it is fired in a furnace, and his voice like the sound of cascading[Q] waters. [16] He had seven stars in his right hand; a sharp double-edged sword came from his mouth, and his face was shining like the sun at full strength.

[17] When I saw him, I fell at his feet like a dead man. He laid his right hand on me and said, "Don't be afraid. I am the First and the Last, [18] and the Living One. I was dead, but look — I am alive forever and ever, and I hold the keys of death

---

[A]1:1 Or *Revelation of,* or *A revelation of*   [B]1:2 Or *witness*   [C]1:2 Or *as many as he saw*   [D]1:3 Or *follow,* or *obey*   [E]1:4 Other mss add *God*   [F]1:4 Or *the sevenfold Spirit*   [G]1:5 Other mss read *has washed us*   [H]1:6 Other mss read *kings and*   [I]1:6 Or *made us into* (or *to be*) *a kingdom of priests*; Ex 19:6   [J]1:7 Or *peoples*   [K]1:7 Gn 12:3; 28:14; Zch 14:17   [L]1:7 Or *will wail because of him*   [M]1:7 Dn 7:13; Zch 12:10   [N]1:10 Or *in spirit*; lit *I became in the Spirit*   [O]1:11 Or *book*   [P]1:13 Or *like a son of man*   [Q]1:15 Lit *many* and Hades. [19] Therefore write what you have seen, what is, and what will take place after this. [20] The mystery of the seven stars you saw in my right hand and of the seven golden lampstands is this: The seven stars are the angels[A] of the seven churches, and the seven lampstands[B] are the seven churches.

THE LETTERS TO THE SEVEN CHURCHES

THE LETTER TO EPHESUS

2 "Write to the angel[C] of the church in Ephesus: Thus says the one who holds the seven stars in his right hand and who walks among the seven golden lampstands: [2] I know your works, your labor, and your endurance, and that you cannot tolerate evil people. You have tested those who call themselves apostles and are not, and you have found them to be liars. [3] I know that you have persevered and endured hardships for the sake of my name, and have not grown weary. [4] But I have this against you: You have abandoned the love you had at first. [5] Remember then how far you have fallen; repent, and do the works you did at first. Otherwise, I will come to you[D] and remove your lampstand from its place, unless you repent. [6] Yet you do have this: You hate the practices of the Nicolaitans, which I also hate.

[7] "Let anyone who has ears to hear listen to what the Spirit says to the churches. To the one who conquers, I will give the right to eat from the tree of life, which is in[E] the paradise of God.

THE LETTER TO SMYRNA

[8] "Write to the angel of the church in Smyrna: Thus says the First and the Last, the one who was dead and came to life: [9] I know your[F] affliction and poverty, but you are rich. I know the slander of those who say they are Jews and are not, but are a synagogue of Satan. [10] Don't be afraid of what you are about to suffer. Look, the devil is about to throw some of you into prison to test you, and you will experience affliction for ten days. Be faithful to the point of death, and I will give you the crown[G] of life.

[11] "Let anyone who has ears to hear listen to what the Spirit says to the churches. The one who conquers will never be harmed by the second death.

THE LETTER TO PERGAMUM

[12] "Write to the angel of the church in Pergamum: Thus says the one who has the sharp, double-edged sword: [13] I know[H] where you live — where Satan's throne is. Yet you are holding on to my name and did not deny your faith in me,[I] even in the days of Antipas, my faithful witness who was put to death among you, where Satan lives. [14] But I have a few things against you. You have some there who hold to the teaching of Balaam, who taught Balak to place a stumbling block[J] in front of the Israelites: to eat meat sacrificed to idols and to commit sexual immorality. [15] In the same way, you also have those who hold to the teaching of the Nicolaitans.[K] [16] So

---

[A] 1:20 Or *messengers*   [B] 1:20 Other mss add *that you saw*   [C] 2:1 Or *messenger,* also in vv. 8,12,18   [D] 2:5 Other mss add *quickly*   [E] 2:7 Other mss read *in the midst of*   [F] 2:9 Other mss add *works and*   [G] 2:10 Or *wreath*   [H] 2:13 Other mss add *your works and*   [I] 2:13 Or *deny my faith*   [J] 2:14 Or *to place a trap*   [K] 2:15 Other mss add *which I hate* repent! Otherwise, I will come to you quickly and fight against them with the sword of my mouth.

[17] "Let anyone who has ears to hear listen to what the Spirit says to the churches. To the one who conquers, I will give some of the hidden manna.[A] I will also give him a white stone, and on the stone a new name is inscribed that no one knows except the one who receives it.

THE LETTER TO THYATIRA

[18] "Write to the angel of the church in Thyatira: Thus says the Son of God, the one whose eyes are like a fiery flame and whose feet are like fine bronze: [19] I know your works — your love, faithfulness,[B] service, and endurance. I know that your last works are greater than the first. [20] But I have this against you: You tolerate the woman Jezebel, who calls herself a prophetess and teaches and deceives my servants to commit sexual immorality and to eat meat sacrificed to idols. [21] I gave her time to repent, but she does not want to repent of her sexual immorality. [22] Look, I will throw her into a sickbed and those who commit adultery with her into great affliction. Unless they repent of her[C] works, [23] I will strike her children dead.[D] Then all the churches will know that I am the one who examines minds and hearts, and I will give to each of you according to your works. [24] I say to the rest of you in Thyatira, who do not hold this teaching, who haven't known "the so-called secrets[E] of Satan" — as they say — I am not putting any other burden on you. [25] Only hold on to what you have until I come. [26] The one who conquers and who keeps my works to the end: I will give him authority over the nations —

[27]   **and he will rule[F] them with an iron scepter;**

    he will shatter them like pottery[G] —

[28] just as I have received this from my Father. I will also give him the morning star.

[29] "Let anyone who has ears to hear listen to what the Spirit says to the churches.

THE LETTER TO SARDIS

3 "Write to the angel[H] of the church in Sardis: Thus says the one who has the seven spirits of God and the seven stars: I know your works; you have a reputation[I] for being alive, but you are dead. [2] Be alert and strengthen[J] what remains, which is about to die,[K] for I have not found your works complete before my God. [3] Remember, then, what you have received and heard; keep it, and repent. If you are not alert, I will come[L] like a thief, and you have no idea at what hour I will come upon you. [4] But you have a few people[M] in Sardis who have not defiled[N] their clothes, and they will walk with me in white, because they are worthy.

[5] "In the same way, the one who conquers will be dressed in white clothes, and I will never erase his name from the book of life but will acknowledge his name before my Father and before his angels.

[A]2:17 Other mss add *to eat*   [B]2:19 Or *faith*   [C]2:22 Other mss read *their*   [D]2:23 Or *with a plague*   [E]2:24 Or *the secret things*   [F]2:27 Or *shepherd*   [G]2:27 Ps 2:9   [H]3:1 Or *messenger,* also in vv. 7, 14   [I]3:1 Or *have a name*   [J]3:2 Other mss read *guard*   [K]3:2 Or *strengthen who remain, who are about to die*   [L]3:3 Other mss add *upon you*   [M]3:4 Lit *few names*   [N]3:4 Or *soiled*

[6] "Let anyone who has ears to hear listen to what the Spirit says to the churches.

THE LETTER TO PHILADELPHIA

[7] "Write to the angel of the church in Philadelphia: Thus says the Holy One, the true one, the one who has the key of David, who opens and no one will close, and who closes and no one opens: [8] I know your works. Look, I have placed before you an open door that no one can close because you have but little power; yet you have kept my word and have not denied my name. [9] Note this: I will make those from the synagogue of Satan, who claim to be Jews and are not, but are lying — I will make them come and bow down at your feet, and they will know that I have loved you. [10] Because you have kept my command to endure, I will also keep you from the hour of testing that is going to come on the whole world to test those who live on the earth. [11] I am coming soon. Hold on to what you have, so that no one takes your crown.

[12] "The one who conquers I will make a pillar in the temple of my God, and he will never go out again. I will write on him the name of my God and the name of the city of my God — the new Jerusalem, which comes down out of heaven from my God — and my new name.

[13] "Let anyone who has ears to hear listen to what the Spirit says to the churches.

THE LETTER TO LAODICEA

[14] "Write to the angel of the church in Laodicea: Thus says the Amen, the faithful and true witness, the originator[A] of God's creation: [15] I know your works, that you are neither cold nor hot. I wish that you were cold or hot. [16] So, because you are lukewarm, and neither hot nor cold, I am going to vomit[B] you out of my mouth. [17] For you say, 'I'm rich; I have become wealthy and need nothing,' and you don't realize that you are wretched, pitiful, poor, blind, and naked. [18] I advise you to buy from me gold refined in the fire so that you may be rich, white clothes so that you may be dressed and your shameful nakedness not be exposed, and ointment to spread on your eyes so that you may see. [19] As many as I love, I rebuke and discipline. So be zealous and repent. [20] See! I stand at the door and knock. If anyone hears my voice and opens the door, I will come in to him and eat with him, and he with me.

[21] "To the one who conquers I will give the right to sit with me on my throne, just as I also conquered and sat down with my Father on his throne.

[22] "Let anyone who has ears to hear listen to what the Spirit says to the churches."

THE THRONE ROOM OF HEAVEN

4 After this I looked, and there in heaven was an open door. The first voice that I had heard speaking to me like a trumpet said, "Come up here, and I will show you what must take place after this."

[2] Immediately I was in the Spirit, and there was a throne in heaven and someone was seated on it. [3] The one seated[C] there had the appearance of

---

[A] 3:14 Or *beginning of God's creation*, or *ruler of God's creation*   [B] 3:16 Or *spit*
[C] 4:3 Other mss omit *The one seated*

HOLY, HOLY, HOLY

REVELATION 4–5; ISAIAH 6:1-6; EZEKIEL 1:26-28

When I think about heaven, I ask all the wrong questions.

Will we have homes? Will we recognize our friends and families? Will there be laughter and animals and all our favorite foods? Will we walk or fly or sort of float around all astronaut-like?

We all do this, right? We think about the life to come in terms of what we know about the life we have now. As human beings, it can be hard not to. This life is what we know.

When we come to Revelation 4–5, the picture we're given of Jesus takes us beyond what we know in this life. Take a minute and read those chapters. Let the imagery sink in.

Here we find a scene set in a sea of glass. Winged creatures singing, "Holy, holy, holy, Lord God, the Almighty, who was, who is, and who is to come" (Rv 4:8), surround a throne. On that throne sits the Lamb of God, slain but risen, and around His throne sit twenty-four elders, representing the twelve tribes of Israel and the twelve apostles, who rise to cast their crowns at Jesus' feet as they sing:

"Our Lord and God, you are worthy to receive glory and honor and power, because you have created all things, and by your will they exist and were created."

REVELATION 4:11

This is the Jesus we worship—the One we pray to over coffee in the morning, the one we cry out to when it seems like our worlds are falling apart. How should we respond to the imagery we read in these verses? Well, for those who do not see through a glass darkly as we do, but rather see face-to-face—they worship (1Co 13:12). The elders in Jesus' throne room happily lay the best things they have at His feet as the angels themselves sing of His mercy and love. The imagery is both vivid and mysterious at the same time.

Though our living rooms and coffee shops hardly feel like the throne room of heaven, the One we pray to is the same Jesus—yesterday, today, and forever (Heb 13:8). And the mercy and grace the angels sing of is the same mercy and grace that will one day bring those who believe into that same glorious realm.

So as you read these chapters, and the rest of this book, let the revelation of Christ's eternal glory anchor your hope in Him today and train your heart for an eternity of worshipful joy.

jasper and carnelian stone. A rainbow that had the appearance of an emerald surrounded the throne.

⁴ Around the throne were twenty-four thrones, and on the thrones sat twenty-four elders dressed in white clothes, with golden crowns on their heads.

⁵ Flashes of lightning and rumblings and peals of thunder came from the throne. Seven fiery torches were burning before the throne, which are the seven spirits of God. ⁶ Something like a sea of glass, similar to crystal, was also before the throne.

Four living creatures covered with eyes in front and in back were around the throne on each side. ⁷ The first living creature was like a lion; the second living creature was like an ox; the third living creature had a face like a man; and the fourth living creature was like a flying eagle. ⁸ Each of the four living creatures had six wings; they were covered with eyes around and inside. Day and night they never stop,ᴬ saying,

> Holy, holy, holy,
> Lord God, the Almighty,
> who was, who is, and who is to come.

⁹ Whenever the living creatures give glory, honor, and thanks to the one seated on the throne, the one who lives forever and ever, ¹⁰ the twenty-four elders fall down before the one seated on the throne and worship the one who lives forever and ever. They cast their crowns before the throne and say,

¹¹ Our Lord and God,ᴮ
> you are worthy to receive
> glory and honor and power,
> because you have created all things,
> and by your will
> they exist and were created.

THE LAMB TAKES THE SCROLL

5 Then I saw in the right hand of the one seated on the throne a scroll with writing on both sides, sealed with seven seals. ² I also saw a mighty angel proclaiming with a loud voice, "Who is worthy to open the scroll and break its seals?" ³ But no one in heaven or on earth or under the earth was able to open the scroll or even to look in it. ⁴ I wept and wept because no one was found worthy to openᶜ the scroll or even to look in it. ⁵ Then one of the elders said to me, "Do not weep. Look, the Lion from the tribe of Judah, the Root of David, has conquered so that he is able to open the scroll andᴰ its seven seals."

⁶ Then I saw one like a slaughtered lamb standing in the midst of the throne and the four living creatures and among the elders. He had seven horns and seven eyes, which are the seven spirits of God sent into all the earth. ⁷ He went and took the scroll out of the right hand of the one seated on the throne.

THE LAMB IS WORTHY

⁸ When he took the scroll, the four living creatures and the twenty-four elders fell down before the Lamb. Each one had a harp and golden bowls filled with incense, which are the prayers of the saints. ⁹ And they sang a new song:

ᴬ4:8 Or rest   ᴮ4:11 Some mss add *the Holy One*; other mss read *Lord*
ᶜ5:4 Other mss add *and read*   ᴰ5:5 Other mss add *loose*

You are worthy to take the scroll
and to open its seals,
because you were slaughtered,
and you purchased[A] people[B]
for God by your blood
from every tribe and language
and people and nation.
10 You made them a kingdom[C]
and priests to our God,
and they will reign on the earth.

¹¹ Then I looked and heard the voice of many angels around the throne, and also of the living creatures and of the elders. Their number was countless thousands, plus thousands of thousands. ¹² They said with a loud voice,

Worthy is the Lamb who was slaughtered
to receive power and riches
and wisdom and strength
and honor and glory and blessing!

¹³ I heard every creature in heaven, on earth, under the earth, on the sea, and everything in them say,

Blessing and honor and glory and power
be to the one seated on the throne,
and to the Lamb, forever and ever!

¹⁴ The four living creatures said, "Amen," and the elders fell down and worshiped.

THE FIRST SEAL ON THE SCROLL

6 Then I saw the Lamb open one of the seven[D] seals, and I heard one of the four living creatures say with a voice like thunder, "Come!" ² I looked, and there was a white horse. Its rider held a bow; a crown was given to him, and he went out as a conqueror in order to conquer.[E]

THE SECOND SEAL

³ When he opened the second seal, I heard the second living creature say, "Come!" ⁴ Then another horse went out, a fiery red one, and its rider was allowed to take peace from the earth, so that people would slaughter one another. And a large sword was given to him.

THE THIRD SEAL

⁵ When he opened the third seal, I heard the third living creature say, "Come!" And I looked, and there was a black horse. Its rider held a set of scales in his hand. ⁶ Then I heard something like a voice among the four living creatures say, "A quart of wheat for a denarius,[F] and three quarts of barley for a denarius, but do not harm the oil and the wine."

[A]5:9 Or *redeemed*   [B]5:9 Other mss read *us*   [C]5:10 Other mss read *them kings*
[D]6:1 Other mss omit *seven*   [E]6:2 Or *went out conquering and in order to conquer*
[F]6:6 A denarius = one day's wage

THE FOURTH SEAL

⁷ When he opened the fourth seal, I heard the voice of the fourth living creature say, "Come!" ⁸ And I looked, and there was a pale green^A horse. Its rider was named Death, and Hades was following after him. They were^B given authority over a fourth of the earth, to kill by the sword, by famine, by plague, and by the wild animals of the earth.

THE FIFTH SEAL

⁹ When he opened the fifth seal, I saw under the altar the souls of those who had been slaughtered because of the word of God and the testimony they had given.^C ¹⁰ They cried out with a loud voice: "Lord,^D the one who is holy and true, how long until you judge those who live on the earth and avenge our blood?" ¹¹ So they were each given a white robe, and they were told to rest a little while longer until the number would be completed of their fellow servants and their brothers and sisters, who were going to be killed just as they had been.

THE SIXTH SEAL

¹² Then I saw him open^E the sixth seal. A violent earthquake occurred; the sun turned black like sackcloth made of hair; the entire moon^F became like blood; ¹³ the stars^G of heaven fell to the earth as a fig tree drops its unripe figs when shaken by a high wind; ¹⁴ the sky was split apart like a scroll being rolled up; and every mountain and island was moved from its place.

¹⁵ Then the kings of the earth, the nobles, the generals, the rich, the powerful, and every slave and free person hid in the caves and among the rocks of the mountains. ¹⁶ And they said to the mountains and to the rocks, "Fall on us and hide us from the face of the one seated on the throne and from the wrath of the Lamb, ¹⁷ because the great day of their^H wrath has come! And who is able to stand?"

THE SEALED OF ISRAEL

7 After this I saw four angels standing at the four corners of the earth, restraining the four winds of the earth so that no wind could blow on the earth or on the sea or on any tree. ² Then I saw another angel rising up from the east, who had the seal of the living God. He cried out in a loud voice to the four angels who were allowed to harm the earth and the sea: ³ "Don't harm the earth or the sea or the trees until we seal the servants of our God on their foreheads." ⁴ And I heard the number of the sealed:

144,000 sealed from every tribe of the Israelites:

⁵ 12,000 sealed from the tribe of Judah,
12,000^I from the tribe of Reuben,
12,000 from the tribe of Gad,
⁶ 12,000 from the tribe of Asher,
12,000 from the tribe of Naphtali,
12,000 from the tribe of Manasseh,

---

^A 6:8 Or *a greenish gray* ^B 6:8 Other mss read *He was* ^C 6:9 Other mss add *about the Lamb* ^D 6:10 Or *"Master* ^E 6:12 Or *I saw when he opened* ^F 6:12 Or *the full moon* ^G 6:13 Perhaps *meteors* ^H 6:17 Other mss read *his* ^I 7:5-8 Other mss add *sealed* after each number

THE HERO OF EVERY STORY

REVELATION 6–7; JOHN 1:35-36

Do you remember "Where's Waldo?" As a child I was crazy about those giant picture books, crammed full of illustrations of tiny people designed to camouflage Waldo, the hero of each page. I can picture Waldo now, clad in a red-and-white-striped shirt, pom-pom-topped stocking cap and bottle cap glasses. I couldn't really enjoy the rest of the picture until I found Waldo, but once I spotted him, the lens of my little eyes would widen and I could take in the entire scene.

The Bible works the same way. It takes practice to see that Jesus is the Hero of every story and the gospel is the plot of every narrative. But when we do, it's a game-changer.

Look at Revelation 7. I'll shoot straight; there's some imagery here that's a little tough to process, but don't let your eyes focus there. **Look for the Hero. Look for Jesus. Look for the gospel.**

Like a page out of my favorite childhood books, there's a lot going on here. There are four angels at the four corners of the earth, another angel carrying God's seal, 144,000 Israelites, a multitude from every nation dressed in white robes, and angels, elders, and living creatures encircling the throne (Rv 7:1-2, 4-9, 11).

At first glance, the scene feels chaotic. I can't focus in one place, can't figure out what it all means. So, I train my eyes to look for the Hero.

"Salvation belongs to our God, who is seated on the throne, and to the Lamb!"

REVELATION 7:10

Bingo! In the middle of this hard-to-process scene, I lock eyes with a familiar face: Jesus, the Lamb seated on the throne (Jn 1:9, 36; Heb 8:1). Salvation belongs to Him alone.

The 144,000 aren't the point, nor are the creatures around the throne or all the believers clad in white. The gospel is the point. Salvation comes through Christ alone. Even in heaven, in the throne room of God, this is the sermon being preached. With the gospel in the foreground, the backstory suddenly makes sense.

Because of Jesus' sacrifice on the cross on our behalf, because of the gospel, this happens:

"These are the ones coming out of the great tribulation. They washed their robes and made them white in the blood of the Lamb."

REVELATION 7:14

Our rags, polluted by our sin, have been bleached pure by Christ's sacrifice (Is 1:18; 64:6). Though we were cast out of God's presence by our rebellion, we are welcome in the throne room, reconciled through Christ (Is 59:2; 2Co 5:18).

If we look, we find Him in every word. He's been there, in every scene, every story. Jesus, our Hero, is seated on the throne so that we might approach Him there with confidence, both now and forevermore.

⁷   12,000 from the tribe of Simeon,
     12,000 from the tribe of Levi,
     12,000 from the tribe of Issachar,
⁸   12,000 from the tribe of Zebulun,
     12,000 from the tribe of Joseph,
     12,000 sealed from the tribe of Benjamin.

A MULTITUDE FROM THE GREAT TRIBULATION

⁹ After this I looked, and there was a vast multitude from every nation, tribe, people, and language, which no one could number, standing before the throne and before the Lamb. They were clothed in white robes with palm branches in their hands. ¹⁰ And they cried out in a loud voice:

Salvation belongs to our God,
    who is seated on the throne,
    and to the Lamb!

¹¹ All the angels stood around the throne, and along with the elders and the four living creatures they fell facedown before the throne and worshiped God, ¹² saying,

Amen! Blessing and glory and wisdom
    and thanksgiving and honor
    and power and strength
    be to our God forever and ever. Amen.

¹³ Then one of the elders asked me, "Who are these people in white robes, and where did they come from?"

¹⁴ I said to him, "Sir,ᴬ you know."

Then he told me: These are the ones coming out of the great tribulation. They washed their robes and made them white in the blood of the Lamb.

¹⁵   For this reason they are before the throne of God,
      and they serve him day and night in his temple.
      The one seated on the throne will shelterᴮ them:
¹⁶   They will no longer hunger;
      they will no longer thirst;
      the sun will no longer strike them,
      nor will any scorching heat.
¹⁷   For the Lamb who is at the center of the throne
      will shepherd them;
      he will guide them to springs of the waters of life,
      and God will wipe away every tear from their eyes.

THE SEVENTH SEAL

8 When he opened the seventh seal, there was silence in heaven for about half an hour. ² Then I saw the seven angels who stand in the presence of God; seven trumpets were given to them. ³ Another angel, with a golden incense burner, came and stood at the altar. He was given a large amount of incense to offer with the prayers of all the saints on the golden altar in front of the throne. ⁴ The smoke of the incense, with the prayers of the saints, went up in the presence of God from the angel's hand. ⁵ The angel took the incense

---

ᴬ7:14 Or "My lord   ᴮ7:15 Or will spread his tent over

burner, filled it with fire from the altar, and hurled it to the earth; there were peals of thunder, rumblings, flashes of lightning, and an earthquake.

THE SEVEN TRUMPETS

⁶ And the seven angels who had the seven trumpets prepared to blow them.

THE FIRST TRUMPET

⁷ The first angel blew his trumpet, and hail and fire, mixed with blood, were hurled to the earth. So a third of the earth was burned up, a third of the trees were burned up, and all the green grass was burned up.

THE SECOND TRUMPET

⁸ The second angel blew his trumpet, and something like a great mountain ablaze with fire was hurled into the sea. So a third of the sea became blood, ⁹ a third of the living creatures in the sea died, and a third of the ships were destroyed.

THE THIRD TRUMPET

¹⁰ The third angel blew his trumpet, and a great star, blazing like a torch, fell from heaven. It fell on a third of the rivers and springs of water. ¹¹ The name of the star is Wormwood, and a third of the waters became wormwood. So, many of the people died from the waters, because they had been made bitter.

THE FOURTH TRUMPET

¹² The fourth angel blew his trumpet, and a third of the sun was struck, a third of the moon, and a third of the stars, so that a third of them were darkened. A third of the day was without light and also a third of the night.

¹³ I looked and heard an eagleᴬ flying high overhead, crying out in a loud voice, "Woe! Woe! Woe to those who live on the earth, because of the remaining trumpet blasts that the three angels are about to sound!"

THE FIFTH TRUMPET

9 The fifth angel blew his trumpet, and I saw a star that had fallen from heaven to earth. The key for the shaft to the abyss was given to him. ² He opened the shaft to the abyss, and smoke came up out of the shaft like smoke from a greatᴮ furnace so that the sun and the air were darkened by the smoke from the shaft. ³ Then locusts came out of the smoke on to the earth, and powerᶜ was given to them like the power that scorpions have on the earth. ⁴ They were told not to harm the grass of the earth, or any green plant, or any tree, but only those people who do not have God's seal on their foreheads. ⁵ They were not permitted to kill them but were to torment them for five months; their torment is like the torment caused by a scorpion when it stings someone. ⁶ In those days people will seek death and will not find it; they will long to die, but death will flee from them.

⁷ The appearance of the locusts was like horses prepared for battle. Something like golden crowns was on their heads; their faces were like human faces; ⁸ they had hair like women's hair; their teeth were like lions' teeth;

ᴬ8:13 Other mss read *angel*   ᴮ9:2 Other mss omit *great*   ᶜ9:3 Or *authority*, also in v. 10

[9] they had chests like iron breastplates; the sound of their wings was like the sound of many chariots with horses rushing into battle; [10] and they had tails with stingers like scorpions, so that with their tails they had the power to harm people for five months. [11] They had as their king^A the angel of the abyss; his name in Hebrew is Abaddon,^B and in Greek he has the name Apollyon.^C

[12] The first woe has passed. There are still two more woes to come after this.

THE SIXTH TRUMPET

[13] The sixth angel blew his trumpet. From the four^D horns of the golden altar that is before God, I heard a voice [14] say to the sixth angel who had the trumpet, "Release the four angels bound at the great river Euphrates." [15] So the four angels who were prepared for the hour, day, month, and year were released to kill a third of the human race. [16] The number of mounted troops was two hundred million;^E I heard their number. [17] This is how I saw the horses and their riders in the vision: They had breastplates that were fiery red, hyacinth blue, and sulfur yellow. The heads of the horses were like the heads of lions, and from their mouths came fire, smoke, and sulfur. [18] A third of the human race was killed by these three plagues — by the fire, the smoke, and the sulfur that came from their mouths. [19] For the power of the horses is in their mouths and in their tails, because their tails, which resemble snakes, have heads that inflict injury.

[20] The rest of the people, who were not killed by these plagues, did not repent of the works of their hands to stop worshiping demons and idols of gold, silver, bronze, stone, and wood, which cannot see, hear, or walk. [21] And they did not repent of their murders, their sorceries, their sexual immorality, or their thefts.

THE MIGHTY ANGEL AND THE SMALL SCROLL

10 Then I saw another mighty angel coming down from heaven, wrapped in a cloud, with a rainbow over his head.^F His face was like the sun, his legs^G were like pillars of fire, [2] and he held a little scroll opened in his hand. He put his right foot on the sea, his left on the land, [3] and he called out with a loud voice like a roaring lion. When he cried out, the seven thunders raised their voices. [4] And when the seven thunders spoke, I was about to write, but I heard a voice from heaven, saying, "Seal up what the seven thunders said, and do not write it down!"

[5] Then the angel that I had seen standing on the sea and on the land raised his right hand to heaven. [6] He swore by the one who lives forever and ever, who created heaven and what is in it, the earth and what is in it, and the sea and what is in it: "There will no longer be a delay, [7] but in the days when the seventh angel will blow his trumpet, then the mystery of God will be completed, as he announced to his servants the prophets."

[8] Then the voice that I heard from heaven spoke to me again and said, "Go, take the scroll that lies open in the hand of the angel who is standing on the sea and on the land."

---

^A 9:11 Or *as king over them*   ^B 9:11 Or *Destruction*   ^C 9:11 Or *Destroyer*
^D 9:13 Other mss omit *four*   ^E 9:16 Other mss read *a hundred million*   ^F 10:1 Or *a halo on his head*   ^G 10:1 Or *feet*

⁹ So I went to the angel and asked him to give me the little scroll. He said to me, "Take and eat it; it will be bitter in your stomach, but it will be as sweet as honey in your mouth."

¹⁰ Then I took the little scroll from the angel's hand and ate it. It was as sweet as honey in my mouth, but when I ate it, my stomach became bitter. ¹¹ And they said to me, "You must prophesy again about^A many peoples, nations, languages, and kings."

THE TWO WITNESSES

11 Then I was given a measuring reed like a rod,^B with these words: "Go^C and measure the temple of God and the altar, and count those who worship there. ² But exclude the courtyard outside the temple. Don't measure it, because it is given to the nations,^D and they will trample the holy city for forty-two months. ³ I will grant^E my two witnesses authority to prophesy for 1,260 days, dressed in sackcloth." ⁴ These are the two olive trees and the two lampstands that stand before the Lord^F of the earth. ⁵ If anyone wants to harm them, fire comes from their mouths and consumes their enemies; if anyone wants to harm them, he must be killed in this way. ⁶ They have authority to close up the sky so that it does not rain during the days of their prophecy. They also have power over the waters to turn them into blood and to strike the earth with every plague whenever they want.

THE WITNESSES MARTYRED

⁷ When they finish their testimony, the beast that comes up out of the abyss will make war on them, conquer them, and kill them. ⁸ Their dead bodies^G will lie in the main street^H of the great city, which figuratively^I is called Sodom and Egypt, where also their Lord was crucified. ⁹ And some of^J the peoples, tribes, languages, and nations will view their bodies for three and a half days and not permit their bodies to be put into a tomb. ¹⁰ Those who live on the earth will gloat over them and celebrate and send gifts to one another because these two prophets had tormented those who live on the earth.

THE WITNESSES RESURRECTED

¹¹ But after three and a half days, the breath^K of life from God entered them, and they stood on their feet. Great fear fell on those who saw them. ¹² Then they heard^L a loud voice from heaven saying to them, "Come up here." They went up to heaven in a cloud, while their enemies watched them. ¹³ At that moment a violent earthquake took place, a tenth of the city fell, and seven thousand people were killed in the earthquake. The survivors were terrified and gave glory to the God of heaven.

¹⁴ The second woe has passed. Take note: The third woe is coming soon!

---

^A10:11 Or prophesy again against   ^B11:1 Other mss add and the angel stood up
^C11:1 Lit "Arise   ^D11:2 Or Gentiles   ^E11:3 Or I will give to   ^F11:4 Other mss
read God   ^G11:8 Or Their corpse   ^H11:8 Or lie on the broad street
^I11:8 Or spiritually   ^J11:9 Lit And from   ^K11:11 Or spirit   ^L11:12 Other mss read
Then I heard

THE SEVENTH TRUMPET

[15] The seventh angel blew his trumpet, and there were loud voices in heaven saying,

> The kingdom of the world has become the kingdom
> of our Lord and of his Christ,
> and he will reign forever and ever.

[16] The twenty-four elders, who were seated before God on their thrones, fell facedown and worshiped God, [17] saying,

> We give you thanks, Lord God, the Almighty,
> who is and who was,[A]
> because you have taken your great power
> and have begun to reign.
> [18] The nations were angry,
> but your wrath has come.
> The time has come
> for the dead to be judged
> and to give the reward
> to your servants the prophets,
> to the saints, and to those who fear your name,
> both small and great,
> and the time has come to destroy
> those who destroy the earth.

[19] Then the temple of God in heaven was opened, and the ark of his covenant[B] appeared in his temple. There were flashes of lightning, rumblings and peals of thunder, an earthquake,[C] and severe hail.

THE WOMAN, THE CHILD, AND THE DRAGON

12 A great sign[D] appeared in heaven: a woman clothed with the sun, with the moon under her feet and a crown of twelve stars on her head. [2] She was pregnant and cried out in labor and agony as she was about to give birth. [3] Then another sign[E] appeared in heaven: There was a great fiery red dragon having seven heads and ten horns, and on its heads were seven crowns.[F] [4] Its tail swept away a third of the stars in heaven and hurled them to the earth. And the dragon stood in front of the woman who was about to give birth, so that when she did give birth it might devour her child. [5] She gave birth to a Son, a male who is going to rule[G] all nations with an iron rod. Her child was caught up to God and to his throne. [6] The woman fled into the wilderness, where she had a place prepared by God, to be nourished there[H] for 1,260 days.

THE DRAGON THROWN OUT OF HEAVEN

[7] Then war broke out in heaven: Michael and his angels fought against the dragon. The dragon and his angels also fought, [8] but he could not prevail, and there was no place for them in heaven any longer. [9] So the great dragon was thrown out — the ancient serpent, who is called the devil and Satan,

---

[A]11:17 Other mss add *and who is to come* [B]11:19 Other mss read *ark of the covenant of the Lord* [C]11:19 Other mss omit *an earthquake* [D]12:1 Or *great symbolic display*; see Rv 12:3 [E]12:3 Or *another symbolic display* [F]12:3 Or *diadems* [G]12:5 Or *shepherd* [H]12:6 Or *God, that they might feed her there* the one who deceives the whole world. He was thrown to earth, and his angels with him. ¹⁰ Then I heard a loud voice in heaven say,

> The salvation and the power
> and the kingdom of our God
> and the authority of his Christ
> have now come,
> because the accuser of our brothers and sisters,
> who accuses them
> before our God day and night,
> has been thrown down.

¹¹ They conquered him
> by the blood of the Lamb
> and by the word of their testimony;
> for they did not love their lives
> to the point of death.

¹² Therefore rejoice, you heavens,
> and you who dwell in them!
> Woe to the earth and the sea,
> because the devil has come down to you
> with great fury,
> because he knows his time is short.

THE WOMAN PERSECUTED

¹³ When the dragon saw that he had been thrown down to the earth, he persecuted^A the woman who had given birth to the male child. ¹⁴ The woman was given two wings of a great eagle, so that she could fly from the serpent's presence to her place in the wilderness, where she was nourished for a time, times, and half a time. ¹⁵ From his mouth the serpent spewed water like a river flowing after the woman, to sweep her away with a flood. ¹⁶ But the earth helped the woman. The earth opened its mouth and swallowed up the river that the dragon had spewed from his mouth. ¹⁷ So the dragon was furious with the woman and went off to wage war against the rest of her offspring^B — those who keep the commands of God and hold firmly to the testimony about Jesus.

THE BEAST FROM THE SEA

¹⁸ The dragon^C stood on the sand of the sea.^D

13 And I saw a beast coming up out of the sea. It had ten horns and seven heads. On its horns were ten crowns,^E and on its heads were blasphemous names.^F ² The beast I saw was like a leopard, its feet were like a bear's, and its mouth was like a lion's mouth. The dragon gave the beast his power, his throne, and great authority. ³ One of its heads appeared to be fatally wounded, but its fatal wound was healed.

The whole earth was amazed and followed the beast. ⁴ They worshiped the dragon because he gave authority to the beast. And they worshiped the beast, saying, "Who is like the beast? Who is able to wage war against it?"

---

^A 12:13 Or *pursued* ^B 12:17 Or *seed* ^C 12:18 Or *he*; other mss read *I*
^D 12:18 Some translations put Rv 12:18 either in Rv 12:17 or Rv 13:1. ^E 13:1 Or
diadems ^F 13:1 Other mss read *heads was a blasphemous name*

[5] The beast was given a mouth to utter boasts and blasphemies. It was allowed to exercise authority[A,B] for forty-two months. [6] It began to speak[C] blasphemies against God: to blaspheme his name and his dwelling — those who dwell in heaven. [7] And it was permitted to wage war against the saints and to conquer them. It was also given authority over every tribe, people, language, and nation. [8] All those who live on the earth will worship it, everyone whose name was not written from the foundation of the world in the book[D] of life of the Lamb who was slaughtered.[E]

[9] If anyone has ears to hear, let him listen.

[10]   If anyone is to be taken captive,
      into captivity he goes.
      If anyone is to be killed[F] with a sword,
      with a sword he will be killed.

This calls for endurance[G] and faithfulness from the saints.

THE BEAST FROM THE EARTH

[11] Then I saw another beast coming up out of the earth; it had two horns like a lamb,[H] but it spoke like a dragon. [12] It exercises all the authority of the first beast on its behalf and compels the earth and those who live on it to worship the first beast, whose fatal wound was healed. [13] It also performs great signs, even causing fire to come down from heaven to earth in front of people. [14] It deceives those who live on the earth because of the signs that it is permitted to perform in the presence of the beast, telling those who live on the earth to make an image[I] of the beast who was wounded by the sword and yet lived. [15] It was permitted to give breath[J] to the image of the beast, so that the image of the beast could both speak and cause whoever would not worship the image of the beast to be killed. [16] And it makes everyone — small and great, rich and poor, free and slave — to receive a mark on his right hand or on his forehead, [17] so that no one can buy or sell unless he has the mark: the beast's name or the number of its name.

[18] This calls for wisdom:[K] Let the one who has understanding calculate[L] the number of the beast, because it is the number of a person. Its number is 666.[M]

THE LAMB AND THE 144,000

14 Then I looked, and there was the Lamb, standing on Mount Zion, and with him were 144,000 who had his name and his Father's name written on their foreheads. [2] I heard a sound[N] from heaven like the sound of cascading waters and like the rumbling of loud thunder. The sound I heard was like harpists playing on their harps. [3] They sang[O] a new song before the throne and before the four living creatures and the elders, but no one could learn the song except the 144,000 who had been redeemed from the earth. [4] These are the ones who have not defiled

---

[A] 13:5 Other mss read to wage war   [B] 13:5 Or to rule   [C] 13:6 Or He opened his mouth in   [D] 13:8 Or scroll   [E] 13:8 Or written in the book of life of the Lamb who was slaughtered from the foundation of the world   [F] 13:10 Other mss read anyone kills   [G] 13:10 Or Here is the perseverance   [H] 13:11 Or ram   [I] 13:14 Or a statue, or a likeness   [J] 13:15 Or a spirit, or life   [K] 13:18 Or Here is wisdom   [L] 13:18 Or count, or figure out   [M] 13:18 Other Gk mss read 616   [N] 14:2 Or voice   [O] 14:3 Other mss add as it were themselves with women, since they remained virgins. These are the ones who follow the Lamb wherever he goes. They were redeemed ᴬ from humanity as the firstfruits for God and the Lamb. ⁵ No lie was found in their mouths; they are blameless.

THE PROCLAMATION OF THREE ANGELS

⁶ Then I saw another angel flying high overhead, with the eternal gospel to announce to the inhabitants of the earth — to every nation, tribe, language, and people. ⁷ He spoke with a loud voice: "Fear God and give him glory, because the hour of his judgment has come. Worship the one who made heaven and earth, the sea and the springs of water."

⁸ And another, a second angel, followed, saying, "It has fallen, Babylon the Great has fallen. ᴮ She made all the nations drink the wine of her sexual immorality, ᶜ which brings wrath."

⁹ And another, a third angel, followed them and spoke with a loud voice: "If anyone worships the beast and its image and receives a mark on his forehead or on his hand, ¹⁰ he will also drink the wine of God's wrath, which is poured full strength into the cup of his anger. He will be tormented with fire and sulfur in the sight of the holy angels and in the sight of the Lamb, ¹¹ and the smoke of their torment will go up forever and ever. There is no rest ᴰ day or night for those who worship the beast and its image, or anyone who receives the mark of its name. ¹² This calls for endurance from the saints, who keep God's commands and their faith in Jesus." ᴱ

¹³ Then I heard a voice from heaven saying, "Write: Blessed are the dead who die in the Lord from now on."

"Yes," says the Spirit, "so they will rest from their labors, since their works follow them."

REAPING THE EARTH'S HARVEST

¹⁴ Then I looked, and there was a white cloud, and one like the Son of Man ᶠ was seated on the cloud, with a golden crown on his head and a sharp sickle in his hand. ¹⁵ Another angel came out of the temple, crying out in a loud voice to the one who was seated on the cloud, "Use your sickle and reap, for the time to reap has come, since the harvest of the earth is ripe." ¹⁶ So the one seated on the cloud swung his sickle over the earth, and the earth was harvested.

¹⁷ Then another angel who also had a sharp sickle came out of the temple in heaven. ¹⁸ Yet another angel, who had authority over fire, came from the altar, and he called with a loud voice to the one who had the sharp sickle, "Use your sharp sickle and gather the clusters of grapes from the vineyard of the earth, because its grapes have ripened." ¹⁹ So the angel swung his sickle at the earth and gathered the grapes from the vineyard of the earth, and he threw them into the great winepress of God's wrath. ²⁰ Then the press was trampled outside the city, and blood flowed out of the press up to the horses' bridles for about 180 miles. ᴳ

ᴬ14:4 Other mss add *by Jesus*   ᴮ14:8 Other mss omit the second *has fallen*
ᶜ14:8 Or *wine of her passionate immorality*   ᴰ14:11 Or *They have no rest*
ᴱ14:12 Or *and the faith of Jesus*, or *and faithfulness to Jesus*   ᶠ14:14 Or *like a son of man*   ᴳ14:20 Lit *1,600 stadia*

PREPARATION FOR THE BOWL JUDGMENTS

15 Then I saw another great and awe-inspiring sign[A] in heaven: seven angels with the seven last plagues; for with them God's wrath will be completed. [2] I also saw something like a sea of glass mixed with fire, and those who had won the victory over the beast, its image,[B] and the number of its name, were standing on the sea of glass with harps from God. [3] They sang the song of God's servant Moses and the song of the Lamb:

Great and awe-inspiring are your works,
Lord God, the Almighty;
just and true are your ways,
King of the nations.[C]
[4] Lord, who will not fear
and glorify your name?
For you alone are holy.
All the nations will come
and worship before you
because your righteous acts
have been revealed.

[5] After this I looked, and the heavenly temple — the tabernacle of testimony — was opened. [6] Out of the temple came the seven angels with the seven plagues, dressed in pure, bright linen, with golden sashes wrapped around their chests. [7] One of the four living creatures gave the seven angels seven golden bowls filled with the wrath of God who lives forever and ever. [8] Then the temple was filled with smoke from the glory of God and from his power, and no one could enter the temple until the seven plagues of the seven angels were completed.

THE FIRST BOWL

16 Then I heard a loud voice from the temple saying to the seven angels, "Go and pour out the seven[D] bowls of God's wrath on the earth." [2] The first went and poured out his bowl on the earth, and severely painful sores broke out on the people who had the mark of the beast and who worshiped its image.

THE SECOND BOWL

[3] The second[E] poured out his bowl into the sea. It turned to blood like that of a dead person, and all life in the sea died.

THE THIRD BOWL

[4] The third[E] poured out his bowl into the rivers and the springs of water, and they became blood. [5] I heard the angel of the waters say,

You are just,
the Holy One, who is and who was,
because you have passed judgment on these things.
[6] Because they poured out

[A]15:1 Or *and awesome symbolic display*   [B]15:2 Other mss add *his mark*
[C]15:3 Other mss read *ages*   [D]16:1 Other mss omit *seven*   [E]16:3,4 Other mss add *angel*

the blood of the saints and the prophets,
you have given them blood to drink;
they deserve it!
⁷ I heard the altar say,
Yes, Lord God, the Almighty,
true and just are your judgments.

THE FOURTH BOWL

⁸ The fourth⁴ poured out his bowl on the sun. It was allowed to scorch people with fire, ⁹ and people were scorched by the intense heat. So they blasphemed the name of God, who has the power⁸ over these plagues, and they did not repent and give him glory.

THE FIFTH BOWL

¹⁰ The fifth⁴ poured out his bowl on the throne of the beast, and its kingdom was plunged into darkness. People⁶ gnawed their tongues because of their pain ¹¹ and blasphemed the God of heaven because of their pains and their sores, but they did not repent of their works.

THE SIXTH BOWL

¹² The sixth⁴ poured out his bowl on the great river Euphrates, and its water was dried up to prepare the way for the kings from the east. ¹³ Then I saw three unclean spirits like frogs coming from the dragon's mouth, from the beast's mouth, and from the mouth of the false prophet. ¹⁴ For they are demonic spirits performing signs, who travel to the kings of the whole world to assemble them for the battle on the great day of God, the Almighty. ¹⁵ "Look, I am coming like a thief. Blessed is the one who is alert and remains clothed⁰ so that he may not go around naked and people see his shame." ¹⁶ So they assembled the kings at the place called in Hebrew, Armageddon.ᴱ

THE SEVENTH BOWL

¹⁷ Then the seventh⁴ poured out his bowl into the air,ᶠ and a loud voice came out of the templeᴳ from the throne, saying, "It is done!" ¹⁸ There were flashes of lightning, rumblings, and peals of thunder. And a severe earthquake occurred like no other since people have been on the earth, so great was the quake. ¹⁹ The great city split into three parts, and the cities of the nationsᴴ fell. Babylon the Great was remembered in God's presence; he gave her the cup filled with the wine of his fierce anger. ²⁰ Every island fled, and the mountains disappeared. ²¹ Enormous hailstones, each weighing about a hundred pounds,ᴵ fell from the sky on people, and they blasphemed God for the plague of hail because that plague was extremely severe.

ᴬ16:8,10,12,17 Other mss add *angel* ᴮ16:9 Or *authority* ᶜ16:10 Lit *They*
ᴰ16:15 Or *and guards his clothes* ᴱ16:16 Some mss read *Armagedon*; other
mss read *Harmegedon*; other mss read *Mageddon*; other mss read *Magedon*
ᶠ16:17 Or *bowl on the air* ᴳ16:17 Other mss add *of heaven* ᴴ16:19 Or *the
Gentile cities* ᴵ16:21 Lit *about a talent*; talents varied in weight upwards from
75 pounds

THE WOMAN AND THE SCARLET BEAST

17 Then one of the seven angels who had the seven bowls came and spoke with me: "Come, I will show you the judgment of the notorious prostitute[A] who is seated on many[B] waters. [2] The kings of the earth committed sexual immorality with her, and those who live on the earth became drunk on the wine of her sexual immorality." [3] Then he carried me away in the Spirit[C] to a wilderness.

I saw a woman sitting on a scarlet beast that was covered[D] with blasphemous names and had seven heads and ten horns. [4] The woman was dressed in purple and scarlet, adorned with gold, jewels, and pearls. She had a golden cup in her hand filled with everything detestable and with the impurities of her[E] prostitution. [5] On her forehead was written a name, a mystery: BABYLON THE GREAT, THE MOTHER OF PROSTITUTES AND OF THE DETESTABLE THINGS OF THE EARTH. [6] Then I saw that the woman was drunk with the blood of the saints and with the blood of the witnesses to Jesus. When I saw her, I was greatly astonished.

THE MEANING OF THE WOMAN AND OF THE BEAST

[7] Then the angel said to me, "Why are you astonished? I will explain to you the mystery of the woman and of the beast, with the seven heads and the ten horns, that carries her. [8] The beast that you saw was, and is not, and is about to come up from the abyss and go to destruction. Those who live on the earth whose names have not been written in the book of life from the foundation of the world will be astonished when they see the beast that was, and is not, and is to come. [9] This calls for a mind that has wisdom.[F]

"The seven heads are seven mountains on which the woman is seated. They are also seven kings: [10] Five have fallen, one is, the other has not yet come, and when he comes, he must remain for only a little while. [11] The beast that was and is not, is itself an eighth king, but it belongs to the seven and is going to destruction. [12] The ten horns you saw are ten kings who have not yet received a kingdom, but they will receive authority as kings with the beast for one hour. [13] These have one purpose, and they give their power and authority to the beast. [14] These will make war against the Lamb, but the Lamb will conquer them because he is Lord of lords and King of kings. Those with him are called, chosen, and faithful."

[15] He also said to me, "The waters you saw, where the prostitute was seated, are peoples, multitudes, nations, and languages. [16] The ten horns you saw, and the beast, will hate the prostitute. They will make her desolate and naked, devour her flesh, and burn her up with fire. [17] For God has put it into their hearts to carry out his plan by having one purpose and to give their kingdom[G] to the beast until the words of God are fulfilled. [18] And the woman you saw is the great city that has royal power over the kings of the earth."

THE FALL OF BABYLON THE GREAT

18 After this I saw another angel with great authority coming down from heaven, and the earth was illuminated by his splendor. [2] He called out in a mighty voice:

[A] 17:1 Traditionally translated *the great whore*   [B] 17:1 Or *by many*   [C] 17:3 Or *in spirit*   [D] 17:3 Or *was filled*   [E] 17:4 Other mss read *earth's*   [F] 17:9 Or *Here is the mind of wisdom*   [G] 17:17 Or *sovereignty*

It has fallen,[A]
Babylon the Great has fallen!
She has become a home for demons,
a haunt for every unclean spirit,
a haunt for every unclean bird,
and a haunt[B] for every unclean and despicable beast.[C]

3 For all the nations have drunk[D]
the wine of her sexual immorality,
which brings wrath.
The kings of the earth
have committed sexual immorality with her,
and the merchants of the earth
have grown wealthy from her sensuality and excess.

4 Then I heard another voice from heaven:
Come out of her, my people,
so that you will not share in her sins
or receive any of her plagues.

5 For her sins are piled up[E] to heaven,
and God has remembered her crimes.

6 Pay her back the way she also paid,
and double it according to her works.
In the cup in which she mixed,
mix a double portion for her.

7 As much as she glorified herself and indulged her sensual
and excessive ways,
give her that much torment and grief.
For she says in her heart,
"I sit as a queen;
I am not a widow,
and I will never see grief."

8 For this reason her plagues will come
in just one day —
death and grief and famine.
She will be burned up with fire,
because the Lord God who judges her is mighty.

THE WORLD MOURNS BABYLON'S FALL

9 The kings of the earth who have committed sexual immorality and shared her sensual and excessive ways will weep and mourn over her when they see the smoke from her burning. 10 They will stand far off in fear of her torment, saying,

Woe, woe, the great city,
Babylon, the mighty city!
For in a single hour
your judgment has come.

[A]18:2 Other mss omit *It has fallen* [B]18:2 Or *prison* [C]18:2 Other mss omit the words *and a haunt for every unclean beast*. The words *and despicable* then refer to the *bird* of the previous line. [D]18:3 Some mss read *collapsed*; other mss read *fallen* [E]18:5 Or *sins have reached up*

¹¹ The merchants of the earth will weep and mourn over her, because no one buys their cargo any longer — ¹² cargo of gold, silver, jewels, and pearls; fine linen, purple, silk, and scarlet; all kinds of fragrant wood products; objects of ivory; objects of expensive wood, brass, ^ iron, and marble; ¹³ cinnamon, spice, ᴮ incense, myrrh, ᶜ and frankincense; wine, olive oil, fine flour, and grain; cattle and sheep; horses and carriages; and slaves — human lives.

14   The fruit you craved has left you.
        All your splendid and glamorous things are gone;
        they will never find them again.

¹⁵ The merchants of these things, who became rich from her, will stand far off in fear of her torment, weeping and mourning, ¹⁶ saying,

        Woe, woe, the great city,
        dressed in fine linen, purple, and scarlet,
        adorned with gold, jewels, and pearls;
17   for in a single hour
        such fabulous wealth was destroyed!

And every shipmaster, seafarer, the sailors, and all who do business by sea, stood far off ¹⁸ as they watched the smoke from her burning and kept crying out: "Who was like the great city?" ¹⁹ They threw dust on their heads and kept crying out, weeping, and mourning,

        Woe, woe, the great city,
        where all those who have ships on the sea
        became rich from her wealth;
        for in a single hour she was destroyed.
20   Rejoice over her, heaven,
        and you saints, apostles, and prophets,
        because God has pronounced on her the judgment she passed
          on you!

THE FINALITY OF BABYLON'S FALL

²¹ Then a mighty angel picked up a stone like a large millstone and threw it into the sea, saying,

        In this way, Babylon the great city
        will be thrown down violently
        and never be found again.
22   The sound of harpists, musicians,
        flutists, and trumpeters
        will never be heard in you again;
        no craftsman of any trade
        will ever be found in you again;
        the sound of a mill
        will never be heard in you again;
23   the light of a lamp
        will never shine in you again;

---

and the voice of a groom and bride
will never be heard in you again.
All this will happen
because your merchants
were the nobility of the earth,
because all the nations were deceived
by your sorcery.

²⁴ In her was found the blood of prophets and saints,
and of all those slaughtered on the earth.

CELEBRATION IN HEAVEN

19 After this I heard something like the loud voice of a vast multitude
in heaven, saying,

Hallelujah!
Salvation, glory, and power belong to our God,
² because his judgments are true^A and righteous,
because he has judged the notorious prostitute
who corrupted the earth with her sexual immorality;
and he has avenged the blood of his servants
that was on her hands.

³ A second time they said,

Hallelujah!
Her smoke ascends forever and ever!

⁴ Then the twenty-four elders and the four living creatures fell down and
worshiped God, who is seated on the throne, saying,

Amen! Hallelujah!

⁵ A voice came from the throne, saying,

Praise our God,
all his servants, and the ones who fear him,
both small and great!

⁶ Then I heard something like the voice of a vast multitude, like the sound of
cascading waters, and like the rumbling of loud thunder, saying,

Hallelujah, because our Lord God, the Almighty,
reigns!
⁷ Let us be glad, rejoice, and give him glory,
because the marriage of the Lamb has come,
and his bride has prepared herself.
⁸ She was given fine linen to wear, bright and pure.

For the fine linen represents the righteous acts of the saints.

⁹ Then he^B said to me, "Write: Blessed are those invited to the marriage
feast of the Lamb!" He also said to me, "These words of God are true." ¹⁰ Then
I fell at his feet to worship him, but he said to me, "Don't do that! I am a fellow servant with you and your brothers and sisters who hold firmly to the
testimony of Jesus. Worship God, because the testimony of Jesus is the spir-
it^C of prophecy."

---

^A19:2 Valid; Jn 8:16; 19:35 ^B19:9 Probably an angel; Rv 17:1; 22:8-9
^C19:10 Or *the Spirit*

KING OF KINGS

REVELATION 18–19; PSALM 113

The summer after I graduated from college, my family and I visited Israel. While we were there, we toured Mount Megiddo. The valley of Mount Megiddo is where some believe the battle of Armageddon—the battle detailed in Revelation 19—will take place.

I was sick with a cold during this part of the tour, and because of this—and the fact that our tour guide spoke at warp speed—I remember not fully understanding where we were or the significance of this particular place. In fact, there's a picture of me standing on top of Mount Megiddo with watery eyes and a runny nose, shrugging my shoulders as if to say, "I don't know what this place is or what we're doing here."

Sometimes when I read Revelation, I shrug my shoulders and think, I'm not sure what's happening here. I get bogged down in the details and imagery, trying to imagine all of these events actually happening. I feel overwhelmed and sometimes afraid.

But when I read Revelation 19, its description of the heavens opening and Jesus bursting forth is comforting to me. I see a part of my own redemption story. I see, on a larger and grander scale, what Jesus did in my own heart, in my own lifetime.

Jesus' arrival in Revelation 19:11 is the climax of the book. All events have been mounting to His arrival, to the King of kings and Lord of lords leading the charge in the battle against the beast and the false prophet, Satan's pawns.

> "Then I saw heaven opened, and there was a white horse. Its rider is called Faithful and True, and he judges and makes war with justice."
>
> REVELATION 19:11

Jesus was the climax of my own story too. He came to me in the middle of my sin, in the middle of a battle between good and evil, when I needed a King to win the battle for me. His death was my victory. His blood made me clean. His sacrifice saved me. That's not something I shrug my shoulders at. That's something I know with everything in me. I am a new person because of Jesus (2Co 5:17).

But the newness doesn't stop with me. God says, "Look! I am making everything new" (Rv 21:5). **In Revelation, we are promised that the transformation we've experienced in our own lives will happen for the entire world.** Our King of kings will cast out evil with one fell swoop of His sword (Rv 19:15), and a new kingdom will be established. It will be the eternal kingdom where "God's dwelling is with humanity . . . they will be his peoples, and God himself will be with them and will be their God" (Rv 21:3).

Friends, we can take comfort when we read this book. The King we serve is good and His victory is sure. Let's worship Him for what He has done today and what He will do for eternity.

THE RIDER ON A WHITE HORSE

¹¹ Then I saw heaven opened, and there was a white horse. Its rider is called Faithful and True, and he judges and makes war with justice. ¹² His eyes were like a fiery flame, and many crowns ^ were on his head. He had a name written that no one knows except himself. ¹³ He wore a robe dipped in blood, and his name is called the Word of God. ¹⁴ The armies that were in heaven followed him on white horses, wearing pure white linen. ¹⁵ A sharp ᴮ sword came from his mouth, so that he might strike the nations with it. He will rule ᶜ them with an iron rod. He will also trample the winepress of the fierce anger of God, the Almighty. ¹⁶ And he has a name written on his robe and on his thigh: KING OF KINGS AND LORD OF LORDS.

THE BEAST AND ITS ARMIES DEFEATED

¹⁷ Then I saw an angel standing in the sun, and he called out in a loud voice, saying to all the birds flying high overhead, "Come, gather together for the great supper of God, ¹⁸ so that you may eat the flesh of kings, the flesh of military commanders, the flesh of the mighty, the flesh of horses and of their riders, and the flesh of everyone, both free and slave, small and great."

¹⁹ Then I saw the beast, the kings of the earth, and their armies gathered together to wage war against the rider on the horse and against his army. ²⁰ But the beast was taken prisoner, and along with it the false prophet, who had performed the signs in its presence. He deceived those who accepted the mark of the beast and those who worshiped its image with these signs. Both of them were thrown alive into the lake of fire that burns with sulfur. ²¹ The rest were killed with the sword that came from the mouth of the rider on the horse, and all the birds ate their fill of their flesh.

SATAN BOUND

20 Then I saw an angel coming down from heaven holding the key to the abyss and a great chain in his hand. ² He seized the dragon, that ancient serpent who is the devil and Satan, ᴰ and bound him for a thousand years. ³ He threw him into the abyss, closed it, and put a seal on it so that he would no longer deceive the nations until the thousand years were completed. After that, he must be released for a short time.

THE SAINTS REIGN WITH CHRIST

⁴ Then I saw thrones, and people seated on them who were given authority to judge. I also saw the souls of those who had been beheaded because of their testimony about Jesus and because of the word of God, who had not worshiped the beast or his image, and who had not accepted the mark on their foreheads or their hands. They came to life and reigned with Christ for a thousand years. ⁵ The rest of the dead did not come to life until the thousand years were completed.

This is the first resurrection. ⁶ Blessed and holy is the one who shares in the first resurrection! The second death has no power ᴱ over them, but they will be priests of God and of Christ, and they will reign with him for a thousand years.

---

^19:12 Or *diadems* ᴮ19:15 Other mss add *double-edged* ᶜ19:15 Or *shepherd* ᴰ20:2 Other mss add *who deceives the whole world* ᴱ20:6 Or *authority*

SATANIC REBELLION CRUSHED

⁷ When the thousand years are completed, Satan will be released from his prison ⁸ and will go out to deceive the nations at the four corners of the earth, Gog and Magog, to gather them for battle. Their number is like the sand of the sea. ⁹ They came up across the breadth of the earth and surrounded the encampment of the saints, the beloved city. Then fire came down from heaven ᴬ and consumed them. ¹⁰ The devil who deceived them was thrown into the lake of fire and sulfur where the beast and the false prophet are, and they will be tormented day and night forever and ever.

THE GREAT WHITE THRONE JUDGMENT

¹¹ Then I saw a great white throne and one seated on it. Earth and heaven fled from his presence, and no place was found for them. ¹² I also saw the dead, the great and the small, standing before the throne, and books were opened. Another book was opened, which is the book of life, and the dead were judged according to their works by what was written in the books. ¹³ Then the sea gave up the dead that were in it, and death and Hades gave up the dead that were in them; each one was judged according to their works. ¹⁴ Death and Hades were thrown into the lake of fire. This is the second death, the lake of fire. ᴮ ¹⁵ And anyone whose name was not found written in the book of life was thrown into the lake of fire.

THE NEW CREATION

21 Then I saw a new heaven and a new earth; for the first heaven and the first earth had passed away, and the sea was no more. ² I also saw the holy city, the new Jerusalem, coming down out of heaven from God, prepared like a bride adorned for her husband.

³ Then I heard a loud voice from the throne: ᶜ Look, God's dwelling ᴰ is with humanity, and he will live with them. They will be his peoples, ᴱ and God himself will be with them and will be their God. ᶠ ⁴ He will wipe away every tear from their eyes. Death will be no more; grief, crying, and pain will be no more, because the previous things ᴳ have passed away.

⁵ Then the one seated on the throne said, "Look, I am making everything new." He also said, "Write, because these words ᴴ are faithful and true." ⁶ Then he said to me, "It is done! I am the Alpha and the Omega, the beginning and the end. I will freely give to the thirsty from the spring of the water of life. ⁷ The one who conquers will inherit these things, and I will be his God, and he will be my son. ⁸ But the cowards, faithless, ᴵ detestable, murderers, sexually immoral, sorcerers, idolaters, and all liars — their share will be in the lake that burns with fire and sulfur, which is the second death."

THE NEW JERUSALEM

⁹ Then one of the seven angels, who had held the seven bowls filled with the seven last plagues, came and spoke with me: "Come, I will show you

---

ᴬ20:9 Other mss add *from God*   ᴮ20:14 Other mss omit *the lake of fire*
ᶜ21:3 Other mss read *from heaven*   ᴰ21:3 Or *tent,* or *tabernacle*   ᴱ21:3 Other mss read *people*   ᶠ21:3 Other mss omit *and will be their God*   ᴳ21:4 Or *the first things*   ᴴ21:5 Other mss add *of God*   ᴵ21:8 Other mss add *the sinful,*

FROM BEGINNING TO END

REVELATION 21; 1 CORINTHIANS 15:42-49; COLOSSIANS 3:1-4

We all have a story. Every day another page is penned as we live and move and breathe. Sometimes it reads like an adventure, other times like a mystery or even an epic drama. But woven through every turn of events and every twist in the plot is a love story that holds it all together.

Like beautifully written books by the same author, the pages of our lives are unique yet strangely similar. All trace back to a garden and point forward to eternity. **While the details of our days on earth are still unfolding, the ending has been set in heaven since the very beginning.** And for those who are in Christ, the conclusion is infinitely more compelling than anything we could dream up.

The book of Revelation is a glimpse at the last chapter of humanity's story as we know it. And Revelation 21 is the ending we have longed for since the garden of Eden, a destiny beyond anything this world can offer. As the divine canon of Scripture comes to a close, its pages burst with the hope of redemption.

"Then the one seated on the throne said, 'Look, I am making everything new.' He also said, 'Write, because these words are faithful and true.' Then he said to me, 'It is done! I am the Alpha and the Omega, the beginning and the end. I will freely give to the thirsty from the spring of the water of life.'"

REVELATION 21:5-6

Our stories all begin this way; every pursuit in this world leaves us thirsty and unsatisfied. Our souls remain restless until we run to the well that never runs dry. Yet, we've been invited to drink deeply of God's grace and find life everlasting in the presence of Jesus. His glory satisfies our deepest longing. His mercy makes us new.

Our stories can end with satisfaction, wholeness, and redemption because of Christ alone.

In the only story written before time began, the author is both Creator and Hero. He closes the final pages of His revelation like an epic drama, describing what is to come. But merely knowing the end of the story isn't the point. It's about knowing the One who has written His grace into every chapter and left evidence of His love on every page.

He is the story. His fingerprints are on every page, His faithfulness is unwavering from beginning to end. Our Savior is restoring what sin has broken, replenishing what the enemy has stolen, and renewing what we have wasted. His victory is the hope of our eternity.

Though the days still unfold before us, the story is complete. For everyone who calls upon the name of Jesus, the end is just the beginning.

the bride, the wife of the Lamb." [10] He then carried me away in the Spirit[A] to a great, high mountain and showed me the holy city, Jerusalem, coming down out of heaven from God, [11] arrayed with God's glory. Her radiance was like a precious jewel, like a jasper stone, clear as crystal. [12] The city had a massive high wall, with twelve gates. Twelve angels were at the gates; the names of the twelve tribes of Israel's sons were inscribed on the gates. [13] There were three gates on the east, three gates on the north, three gates on the south, and three gates on the west. [14] The city wall had twelve foundations, and the twelve names of the twelve apostles of the Lamb were on the foundations.

[15] The one who spoke with me had a golden measuring rod to measure the city, its gates, and its wall. [16] The city is laid out in a square; its length and width are the same. He measured the city with the rod at 12,000 *stadia*.[B] Its length, width, and height are equal. [17] Then he measured its wall, 144 cubits according to human measurement, which the angel used. [18] The building material of its wall was jasper, and the city was pure gold clear as glass. [19] The foundations of the city wall were adorned with every kind of jewel: the first foundation is jasper, the second sapphire, the third chalcedony, the fourth emerald, [20] the fifth sardonyx, the sixth carnelian, the seventh chrysolite, the eighth beryl, the ninth topaz, the tenth chrysoprase, the eleventh jacinth, the twelfth amethyst. [21] The twelve gates are twelve pearls; each individual gate was made of a single pearl. The main street[C] of the city was pure gold, transparent as glass.

[22] I did not see a temple in it, because the Lord God the Almighty and the Lamb are its temple. [23] The city does not need the sun or the moon to shine on it, because the glory of God illuminates it, and its lamp is the Lamb. [24] The nations[D] will walk by its light, and the kings of the earth will bring their glory into it.[E] [25] Its gates will never close by day because it will never be night there. [26] They will bring the glory and honor of the nations into it.[F] [27] Nothing unclean will ever enter it, nor anyone who does what is detestable or false, but only those written in the Lamb's book of life.

THE SOURCE OF LIFE

22 Then he showed me the river[G] of the water of life, clear as crystal, flowing from the throne of God and of the Lamb [2] down the middle of the city's main street. The tree of life was on each side of the river, bearing twelve kinds of fruit, producing its fruit every month. The leaves of the tree are for healing the nations, [3] and there will no longer be any curse. The throne of God and of the Lamb will be in the city, and his servants will worship him. [4] They will see his face, and his name will be on their foreheads. [5] Night will be no more; people will not need the light of a lamp or the light of the sun, because the Lord God will give them light, and they will reign forever and ever.

[A]21:10 Or *in spirit* [B]21:16 A *stadion* (sg) = about 600 feet; 12,000 *stadia* = 1,400 miles. [C]21:21 Or *The public square* [D]21:24 Other mss add *of those who are saved* [E]21:24 Other mss read *will bring to him the nations' glory and honor* [F]21:26 Other mss add *in order that they might go in* [G]22:1 Other mss read *pure river*

THE TIME IS NEAR

⁶ Then he said to me, "These words are faithful^A and true. The Lord, the God of the spirits of the prophets, ^B has sent his angel to show his servants what must soon take place."

⁷ "Look, I am coming soon! Blessed is the one who keeps the words of the prophecy of this book."

⁸ I, John, am the one who heard and saw these things. When I heard and saw them, I fell down to worship at the feet of the angel who had shown them to me. ⁹ But he said to me, "Don't do that! I am a fellow servant with you, your brothers the prophets, and those who keep the words of this book. Worship God!"

¹⁰ Then he said to me, "Don't seal up the words of the prophecy of this book, because the time is near. ¹¹ Let the unrighteous go on in unrighteousness; let the filthy still be filthy; let the righteous go on in righteousness; let the holy still be holy."

¹² "Look, I am coming soon, and my reward is with me to repay each person according to his work. ¹³ I am the Alpha and the Omega, the first and the last, the beginning and the end.

¹⁴ "Blessed are those who wash their robes,^C so that they may have the right to the tree of life and may enter the city by the gates. ¹⁵ Outside are the dogs, the sorcerers, the sexually immoral, the murderers, the idolaters, and everyone who loves and practices falsehood.

¹⁶ "I, Jesus, have sent my angel to attest these things to you for the churches. I am the Root and descendant of David, the bright morning star."

¹⁷ Both the Spirit and the bride say, "Come!" Let anyone who hears, say, "Come!" Let the one who is thirsty come. Let the one who desires take the water of life freely.

¹⁸ I testify to everyone who hears the words of the prophecy of this book: If anyone adds to them, God will add to him the plagues that are written in this book. ¹⁹ And if anyone takes away from the words of the book of this prophecy, God will take away his share of the tree of life and the holy city, which are written about in this book.

²⁰ He who testifies about these things says, "Yes, I am coming soon." Amen! Come, Lord Jesus!

²¹ The grace of the Lord Jesus^D be with everyone.^E Amen.^F

---

^A 22:6 Or *trustworthy*   ^B 22:6 Other mss read *God of the holy prophets*
^C 22:14 Other mss read *who keep his commands*   ^D 22:21 Other mss add *Christ*
^E 22:21 Other mss read *with all the saints*   ^F 22:21 Other mss omit *Amen.*

KEY VERSES

BOOK	REF	VERSE
Genesis	1:31	God saw all that he had made, and it was very good indeed.
Exodus	20:2	I am the LORD your God, who brought you out of the land of Egypt, out of the place of slavery.
Leviticus	20:26	You are to be holy to me because I, the LORD, am holy, and I have set you apart from the nations to be mine.
Numbers	14:18	The LORD is slow to anger and abounding in faithful love, forgiving iniquity and rebellion. But he will not leave the guilty unpunished, bringing the consequences of the fathers' iniquity on the children to the third and fourth generation.
Deuteronomy	7:9	Know that the LORD your God is God, the faithful God who keeps his gracious covenant loyalty for a thousand generations with those who love him and keep his commands.
Joshua	1:9	Haven't I commanded you: be strong and courageous? Do not be afraid or discouraged, for the LORD your God is with you wherever you go.
Judges	21:25	In those days there was no king in Israel; everyone did whatever seemed right to him.
Ruth	4:14	The women said to Naomi, "Blessed be the LORD, who has not left you without a family redeemer today. May his name become well known in Israel."
1 Samuel	8:7	But the LORD told him, "Listen to the people and everything they say to you. They have not rejected you; they have rejected me as their king."
2 Samuel	7:11	The LORD declares to you: The LORD himself will make a house for you.
1 Kings	18:39	When all the people saw it, they fell facedown and said, "The LORD, he is God! The LORD, he is God!"
2 Kings	8:19	For the sake of his servant David, the LORD was unwilling to destroy Judah.
1 Chronicles	29:11	Yours, LORD, is the greatness and the power and the glory and the splendor and the majesty, for everything in the heavens and on earth belongs to you. Yours, LORD, is the kingdom, and you are exalted as head over all.
2 Chronicles	7:13-14	If I shut the sky so there is no rain, or if I command the grasshopper to consume the land, or if I send pestilence on my people, and my people, who bear my name, humble themselves, pray and seek my face, and turn from their evil ways, then I will hear from heaven, forgive their sin, and heal their land.
Ezra	3:11	They sang with praise and thanksgiving to the LORD: "For he is good; his faithful love to Israel endures forever." Then all the people gave a great shout of praise to the LORD because the foundation of the LORD's house had been laid.
Nehemiah	2:17	So I said to them, "You see the trouble we are in. Jerusalem lies in ruins and its gates have been burned. Come, let's rebuild Jerusalem's wall, so that we will no longer be a disgrace."
Esther	4:14	If you keep silent at this time, relief and deliverance will come to the Jewish people from another place, but you and your father's family will be destroyed. Who knows, perhaps you have come to your royal position for such a time as this.
Job	19:25	But I know that my Redeemer lives, and at the end he will stand on the dust.
Psalm	116:5-6	The LORD is gracious and righteous; our God is compassionate. The LORD guards the inexperienced; I was helpless, and he saved me.
Proverbs	1:7	The fear of the LORD is the beginning of knowledge; fools despise wisdom and discipline.
Ecclesiastes	12:13b	When all has been heard, the conclusion of the matter is this: fear God and keep his commands, because this is for all humanity.
Song of Songs	8:7	A huge torrent cannot extinguish love; rivers cannot sweep it away. If a man were to give all his wealth for love, it would be utterly scorned.

PENTATEUCH

HISTORICAL

WISDOM & POETRY

2201

Isaiah	43:1	Now this is what the LORD says — the one who created you, Jacob, and the one who formed you, Israel — "Do not fear, for I have redeemed you; I have called you by your name; you are mine."
Jeremiah	31:33	"Instead, this is the covenant I will make with the house of Israel after those days" —the LORD's declaration. "I will put my teaching within them and write it on their hearts. I will be their God, and they will be my people."
Lamentations	3:22-23	Because of the LORD's faithful love we do not perish, for his mercies never end. They are new every morning; great is your faithfulness!
Ezekiel	36:26	I will give you a new heart and put a new spirit within you; I will remove your heart of stone and give you a heart of flesh.
Daniel	4:34b	For his dominion is an everlasting dominion, and his kingdom is from generation to generation.
Hosea	6:6	For I desire faithful love and not sacrifice, the knowledge of God rather than burnt offerings.
Joel	2:13	Tear your hearts, not just your clothes, and return to the LORD your God. For he is gracious and compassionate, slow to anger, abounding in faithful love, and he relents from sending disaster.
Amos	5:24	But let justice flow like water, and righteousness, like an unfailing stream.
Obadiah	v. 21	Saviors will ascend Mount Zion to rule over the hill country of Esau, but the kingdom will be the LORD's.
Jonah	4:2	I knew that you are a gracious and compassionate God, slow to anger, abounding in faithful love, and one who relents from sending disaster.
Micah	6:8	Mankind, he has told each of you what is good and what it is the LORD requires of you: to act justly, to love faithfulness, and to walk humbly with your God.
Nahum	1:7	The LORD is good, a stronghold in a day of distress; he cares for those who take refuge in him.
Habakkuk	3:18-19	Yet I will celebrate in the LORD; I will rejoice in the God of my salvation! The LORD my Lord is my strength; he makes my feet like those of a deer and enables me to walk on mountain heights!
Zephaniah	3:17	The LORD your God is among you, a warrior who saves. He will rejoice over you with gladness. He will be quiet in his love. He will delight in you with singing.
Haggai	2:9	"The final glory of this house will be greater than the first," says the LORD of Armies. "I will provide peace in this place" —this is the declaration of the LORD of Armies.
Zechariah	13:9	I will put this third through the fire; I will refine them as silver is refined and test them as gold is tested. They will call on my name, and I will answer them. I will say: They are my people, and they will say: The LORD is our God.
Malachi	4:2	But for you who fear my name, the sun of righteousness will rise with healing in its wings, and you will go out and playfully jump like calves from the stall.
Matthew	4:17	From then on Jesus began to preach, "Repent, because the kingdom of heaven has come near."
Mark	10:45	For even the Son of Man did not come to be served, but to serve, and to give his life as a ransom for many.
Luke	19:10	For the Son of Man has come to seek and to save the lost.
John	1:1	In the beginning was the Word, and the Word was with God, and the Word was God.
Acts	1:8	But you will receive power when the Holy Spirit has come on you, and you will be my witnesses in Jerusalem, in all Judea and Samaria, and to the end of the earth.

CHURCH HISTORY

Romans	3:23-24	For all have sinned and fall short of the glory of God. They are justified freely by his grace through the redemption that is in Christ Jesus.
1 Corinthians	1:9	God is faithful; you were called by him into fellowship with his Son, Jesus Christ our Lord.
2 Corinthians	12:9	But he said to me, "My grace is sufficient for you, for my power is perfected in weakness." Therefore, I will most gladly boast all the more about my weaknesses, so that Christ's power may reside in me.
Galatians	2:21	I do not set aside the grace of God; for if righteousness comes through the law, then Christ died for nothing.
Ephesians	2:8-9	For you are saved by grace through faith, and this is not from yourselves; it is God's gift—not from works, so that no one can boast.
Philippians	1:21	For me, to live is Christ and to die is gain.
Colossians	1:17	He is before all things, and by him all things hold together.
1 Thessalonians	5:16-18	Rejoice always, pray constantly, give thanks in everything; for this is God's will for you in Christ Jesus.
2 Thessalonians	3:5	May the Lord direct your hearts to God's love and Christ's endurance.
1 Timothy	1:15	This saying is trustworthy and deserving of full acceptance: "Christ Jesus came into the world to save sinners"—and I am the worst of them.
2 Timothy	3:16-17	All Scripture is inspired by God and is profitable for teaching, for rebuking, for correcting, for training in righteousness, so that the man of God may be complete, equipped for every good work.
Titus	3:5	He saved us—not by works of righteousness that we had done, but according to his mercy—through the washing of regeneration and renewal by the Holy Spirit.
Philemon	vv. 8-9	For this reason, although I have great boldness in Christ to command you to do what is right, I appeal to you, instead, on the basis of love.
Hebrews	12:1-2	Let us run with endurance the race that lies before us, keeping our eyes on Jesus, the source and perfecter of our faith. For the joy that lay before him, he endured the cross, despising the shame, and sat down at the right hand of the throne of God.

James	1:2-4	Consider it a great joy, my brothers and sisters, whenever you experience various trials, because you know that the testing of your faith produces endurance. And let endurance have its full effect, so that you may be mature and complete, lacking nothing.
1 Peter	1:3-4	Blessed be the God and Father of our Lord Jesus Christ. Because of his great mercy he has given us new birth into a living hope through the resurrection of Jesus Christ from the dead and into an inheritance that is imperishable, undefiled, and unfading, kept in heaven for you.
2 Peter	1:3	His divine power has given us everything required for life and godliness through the knowledge of him who called us by his own glory and goodness.
1 John	1:9	If we confess our sins, he is faithful and righteous to forgive us our sins and to cleanse us from all unrighteousness.
2 John	v. 6	This is love: that we walk according to his commands. This is the command as you have heard it from the beginning: that you walk in love.
3 John	v. 4	I have no greater joy than this: to hear that my children are walking in truth.
Jude	vv. 24-25	Now to him who is able to protect you from stumbling and to make you stand in the presence of his glory, without blemish and with great joy, to the only God our Savior, through Jesus Christ our Lord, be glory, majesty, power, and authority before all time, now and forever. Amen.
Revelation	21:6	Then he said to me, "It is done! I am the Alpha and the Omega, the beginning and the end."

GENRE GUIDE

The Bible is one work made up of many books. Genres, or literary styles, vary throughout the Old and New Testaments. Knowing the type of literature we're reading helps us understand how to read it, keeping in mind the context, meaning, and intent of the original text.

The color of each book in the *She Reads Truth Bible* indicates that book's genre. This guide matches each color to its genre and offers a basic framework for approaching the various literary styles.

OLD TESTAMENT

▣ PENTATEUCH

The Pentateuch presents the individual laws given to Israel as well as the Law as a whole, or the standard by which God's people were to live and worship under the old covenant.

Read the Pentateuch understanding that today, we are under the new covenant. The Law is not void; rather, it is fulfilled in Christ.

▣ HISTORICAL

The Historical Books present the true account of Israel, from the settlement of the promised land through the destruction of Jerusalem.

Read the Historical Books understanding that these are stories of imperfect people with imperfect actions, collectively pointing us to the greater story of the gospel of Christ.

▣ WISDOM & POETRY

The books of Wisdom Literature present common sense sayings and philosophical reflections, while the Poetic Books are lyrical writings of prayer and worship that often use metaphor and repetition.

Read books of wisdom as a collection with a unified message rather than precise statements. Read books of poetry understanding they are words spoken to and about God, yet also inspired by God.

▣ MAJOR PROPHETS

The Major Prophets present longer messages from God to the people living in the time of the prophet.

Read the Major Prophets understanding the historical context in which they were written and keeping in mind the big picture of God's faithful covenant to an unfaithful people.

▣ MINOR PROPHETS

The Minor Prophets present shorter messages from God to the people living in the time of the prophet.

Read the Minor Prophets understanding the historical context in which they were written and keeping in mind the big picture of God's faithful covenant to an unfaithful people.

NEW TESTAMENT

■ GOSPELS

The Gospels present the life and teachings of Jesus Christ and contain narratives (stories), parables (illustrations), and exhortations (sayings).

Read the Gospels understanding they are the good news of the life, death, and resurrection of Jesus Christ.

■ CHURCH HISTORY

The book of Acts gives the history of the early Church, from Jesus' ascension to Paul's ministry at Rome.

Read Acts to learn more about Paul and Peter and the work of the Holy Spirit to spread the message of our resurrected Savior and Lord.

■ PAULINE EPISTLES

The Pauline Epistles are letters written by the Apostle Paul to leaders and members of the early Church.

Read the Pauline Epistles understanding the historical and spiritual context in which they were written, making sure to read each letter as a whole for the most complete understanding.

■ GENERAL EPISTLES

The General Epistles are letters written in response to specific needs or circumstances.

Read the General Epistles understanding the historical and spiritual context in which they were written, making sure to read each letter as a whole for the most complete understanding.

■ APOCALYPTIC

The book of Revelation is a combination of prophecy, apocalyptic literature, and letter written by the Apostle John based on revelations from God.

Read this complex book with humility, understanding that it, too, points to the gospel and reveals Jesus Christ as King of kings, the Alpha and the Omega.

THE APOSTLES' CREED

WE BELIEVE IN GOD, THE FATHER ALMIGHTY,

THE CREATOR OF HEAVEN AND EARTH, AND IN

JESUS CHRIST, HIS ONLY SON, OUR LORD: WHO

WAS CONCEIVED OF THE HOLY SPIRIT, BORN OF

THE VIRGIN MARY, SUFFERED UNDER PONTIUS

PILATE, WAS CRUCIFIED, DIED, AND WAS BURIED.

HE DESCENDED INTO HELL. ON THE THIRD DAY

HE ROSE AGAIN FROM THE DEAD. HE ASCENDED

INTO HEAVEN AND NOW SITS AT THE RIGHT HAND

OF GOD THE FATHER ALMIGHTY; FROM WHENCE

HE SHALL COME TO JUDGE THE LIVING AND THE

DEAD. WE BELIEVE IN THE HOLY SPIRIT; THE ONE

HOLY CHURCH—BOTH VISIBLE AND INVISIBLE; THE

COMMUNION OF SAINTS; THE FORGIVENESS OF

SINS; THE RESURRECTION OF THE BODY; AND THE

LIFE EVERLASTING. AMEN.

THE BIBLE IN A YEAR

Compiled by the late Rev. Robert Murray M'Cheyne, M.A.

JANUARY

This is my beloved Son, with whom I am well-pleased. Listen to him! Matthew 17:5

DATE	READING			
☐ 1	Genesis 1	Matthew 1	Ezra 1	Acts 1
☐ 2	Genesis 2	Matthew 2	Ezra 2	Acts 2
☐ 3	Genesis 3	Matthew 3	Ezra 3	Acts 3
☐ 4	Genesis 4	Matthew 4	Ezra 4	Acts 4
☐ 5	Genesis 5	Matthew 5	Ezra 5	Acts 5
☐ 6	Genesis 6	Matthew 6	Ezra 6	Acts 6
☐ 7	Genesis 7	Matthew 7	Ezra 7	Acts 7
☐ 8	Genesis 8	Matthew 8	Ezra 8	Acts 8
☐ 9	Genesis 9-10	Matthew 9	Ezra 9	Acts 9
☐ 10	Genesis 11	Matthew 10	Ezra 10	Acts 10
☐ 11	Genesis 12	Matthew 11	Nehemiah 1	Acts 11
☐ 12	Genesis 13	Matthew 12	Nehemiah 2	Acts 12
☐ 13	Genesis 14	Matthew 13	Nehemiah 3	Acts 13
☐ 14	Genesis 15	Matthew 14	Nehemiah 4	Acts 14
☐ 15	Genesis 16	Matthew 15	Nehemiah 5	Acts 15
☐ 16	Genesis 17	Matthew 16	Nehemiah 6	Acts 16
☐ 17	Genesis 18	Matthew 17	Nehemiah 7	Acts 17
☐ 18	Genesis 19	Matthew 18	Nehemiah 8	Acts 18
☐ 19	Genesis 20	Matthew 19	Nehemiah 9	Acts 19
☐ 20	Genesis 21	Matthew 20	Nehemiah 10	Acts 20
☐ 21	Genesis 22	Matthew 21	Nehemiah 11	Acts 21
☐ 22	Genesis 23	Matthew 22	Nehemiah 12	Acts 22
☐ 23	Genesis 24	Matthew 23	Nehemiah 13	Acts 23
☐ 24	Genesis 25	Matthew 24	Esther 1	Acts 24
☐ 25	Genesis 26	Matthew 25	Esther 2	Acts 25
☐ 26	Genesis 27	Matthew 26	Esther 3	Acts 26
☐ 27	Genesis 28	Matthew 27	Esther 4	Acts 27
☐ 28	Genesis 29	Matthew 28	Esther 5	Acts 28
☐ 29	Genesis 30	Mark 1	Esther 6	Romans 1
☐ 30	Genesis 31	Mark 2	Esther 7	Romans 2
☐ 31	Genesis 32	Mark 3	Esther 8	Romans 3

FEBRUARY

I have treasured the words from his mouth more than my daily food. Job 23:12

DATE	READING			
☐ 1	Genesis 33	Mark 4	Esther 9-10	Romans 4
☐ 2	Genesis 34	Mark 5	Job 1	Romans 5
☐ 3	Genesis 35-36	Mark 6	Job 2	Romans 6
☐ 4	Genesis 37	Mark 7	Job 3	Romans 7
☐ 5	Genesis 38	Mark 8	Job 4	Romans 8
☐ 6	Genesis 39	Mark 9	Job 5	Romans 9
☐ 7	Genesis 40	Mark 10	Job 6	Romans 10
☐ 8	Genesis 41	Mark 11	Job 7	Romans 11
☐ 9	Genesis 42	Mark 12	Job 8	Romans 12

☐	10	Genesis 43	Mark 13	Job 9	Romans 13
☐	11	Genesis 44	Mark 14	Job 10	Romans 14
☐	12	Genesis 45	Mark 15	Job 11	Romans 15
☐	13	Genesis 46	Mark 16	Job 12	Romans 16
☐	14	Genesis 47	Luke 1:1-38	Job 13	1 Corinthians 1
☐	15	Genesis 48	Luke 1:39-80	Job 14	1 Corinthians 2
☐	16	Genesis 49	Luke 2	Job 15	1 Corinthians 3
☐	17	Genesis 50	Luke 3	Job 16-17	1 Corinthians 4
☐	18	Exodus 1	Luke 4	Job 18	1 Corinthians 5
☐	19	Exodus 2	Luke 5	Job 19	1 Corinthians 6
☐	20	Exodus 3	Luke 6	Job 20	1 Corinthians 7
☐	21	Exodus 4	Luke 7	Job 21	1 Corinthians 8
☐	22	Exodus 5	Luke 8	Job 22	1 Corinthians 9
☐	23	Exodus 6	Luke 9	Job 23	1 Corinthians 10
☐	24	Exodus 7	Luke 10	Job 24	1 Corinthians 11
☐	25	Exodus 8	Luke 11	Job 25-26	1 Corinthians 12
☐	26	Exodus 9	Luke 12	Job 27	1 Corinthians 13
☐	27	Exodus 10	Luke 13	Job 28	1 Corinthians 14
☐	28	Exodus 11-12:21	Luke 14	Job 29	1 Corinthians 15

MARCH

Mary was treasuring up all these things in her heart and meditating on them. Luke 2:19

DATE		READING			
☐	1	Exodus 12:22ff*	Luke 15	Job 30	1 Corinthians 16
☐	2	Exodus 13	Luke 16	Job 31	2 Corinthians 1
☐	3	Exodus 14	Luke 17	Job 32	2 Corinthians 2
☐	4	Exodus 15	Luke 18	Job 33	2 Corinthians 3
☐	5	Exodus 16	Luke 19	Job 34	2 Corinthians 4
☐	6	Exodus 17	Luke 20	Job 35	2 Corinthians 5
☐	7	Exodus 18	Luke 21	Job 36	2 Corinthians 6
☐	8	Exodus 19	Luke 22	Job 37	2 Corinthians 7
☐	9	Exodus 20	Luke 23	Job 38	2 Corinthians 8
☐	10	Exodus 21	Luke 24	Job 39	2 Corinthians 9
☐	11	Exodus 22	John 1	Job 40	2 Corinthians 10
☐	12	Exodus 23	John 2	Job 41	2 Corinthians 11
☐	13	Exodus 24	John 3	Job 42	2 Corinthians 12
☐	14	Exodus 25	John 4	Proverbs 1	2 Corinthians 13
☐	15	Exodus 26	John 5	Proverbs 2	Galatians 1
☐	16	Exodus 27	John 6	Proverbs 3	Galatians 2
☐	17	Exodus 28	John 7	Proverbs 4	Galatians 3
☐	18	Exodus 29	John 8	Proverbs 5	Galatians 4
☐	19	Exodus 30	John 9	Proverbs 6	Galatians 5
☐	20	Exodus 31	John 10	Proverbs 7	Galatians 6
☐	21	Exodus 32	John 11	Proverbs 8	Ephesians 1
☐	22	Exodus 33	John 12	Proverbs 9	Ephesians 2
☐	23	Exodus 34	John 13	Proverbs 10	Ephesians 3
☐	24	Exodus 35	John 14	Proverbs 11	Ephesians 4
☐	25	Exodus 36	John 15	Proverbs 12	Ephesians 5
☐	26	Exodus 37	John 16	Proverbs 13	Ephesians 6
☐	27	Exodus 38	John 17	Proverbs 14	Philippians 1
☐	28	Exodus 39	John 18	Proverbs 15	Philippians 2
☐	29	Exodus 40	John 19	Proverbs 16	Philippians 3
☐	30	Leviticus 1	John 20	Proverbs 17	Philippians 4
☐	31	Leviticus 2-3	John 21	Proverbs 18	Colossians 1

* The abbreviation "ff" stands for "and following." Read through the end of the indicated chapter.

APRIL

Send your light and your truth; let them lead me. Psalm 43:3

MAY

From infancy you have known the sacred Scriptures. 2 Timothy 3:15

☐	17	Numbers 26	Psalm 69	Isaiah 16	1 Peter 4
☐	18	Numbers 27	Psalms 70-71	Isaiah 17-18	1 Peter 5
☐	19	Numbers 28	Psalm 72	Isaiah 19-20	2 Peter 1
☐	20	Numbers 29	Psalm 73	Isaiah 21	2 Peter 2
☐	21	Numbers 30	Psalm 74	Isaiah 22	2 Peter 3
☐	22	Numbers 31	Psalms 75-76	Isaiah 23	1 John 1
☐	23	Numbers 32	Psalm 77	Isaiah 24	1 John 2
☐	24	Numbers 33	Psalm 78	Isaiah 25	1 John 3
☐	25	Numbers 34	Psalm 79	Isaiah 26	1 John 4
☐	26	Numbers 35	Psalm 80	Isaiah 27	1 John 5
☐	27	Numbers 36	Psalm 81	Isaiah 28	2 John
☐	28	Deuteronomy 1	Psalms 82-83	Isaiah 29	3 John
☐	29	Deuteronomy 2	Psalm 84	Isaiah 30	Jude
☐	30	Deuteronomy 3	Psalm 85	Isaiah 31	Revelation 1
☐	31	Deuteronomy 4	Psalms 86-87	Isaiah 32	Revelation 2

JUNE

Blessed is the one who reads aloud the words of this prophecy, and blessed are those who hear the words of this prophecy and keep what is written in it. Revelation 1:3

DATE		READING			
☐	1	Deuteronomy 5	Psalm 88	Isaiah 33	Revelation 3
☐	2	Deuteronomy 6	Psalm 89	Isaiah 34	Revelation 4
☐	3	Deuteronomy 7	Psalm 90	Isaiah 35	Revelation 5
☐	4	Deuteronomy 8	Psalm 91	Isaiah 36	Revelation 6
☐	5	Deuteronomy 9	Psalms 92-93	Isaiah 37	Revelation 7
☐	6	Deuteronomy 10	Psalm 94	Isaiah 38	Revelation 8
☐	7	Deuteronomy 11	Psalms 95-96	Isaiah 39	Revelation 9
☐	8	Deuteronomy 12	Psalms 97-98	Isaiah 40	Revelation 10
☐	9	Deuteronomy 13-14	Psalms 99-101	Isaiah 41	Revelation 11
☐	10	Deuteronomy 15	Psalm 102	Isaiah 42	Revelation 12
☐	11	Deuteronomy 16	Psalm 103	Isaiah 43	Revelation 13
☐	12	Deuteronomy 17	Psalm 104	Isaiah 44	Revelation 14
☐	13	Deuteronomy 18	Psalm 105	Isaiah 45	Revelation 15
☐	14	Deuteronomy 19	Psalm 106	Isaiah 46	Revelation 16
☐	15	Deuteronomy 20	Psalm 107	Isaiah 47	Revelation 17
☐	16	Deuteronomy 21	Psalms 108-109	Isaiah 48	Revelation 18
☐	17	Deuteronomy 22	Psalms 110-111	Isaiah 49	Revelation 19
☐	18	Deuteronomy 23	Psalms 112-113	Isaiah 50	Revelation 20
☐	19	Deuteronomy 24	Psalms 114-115	Isaiah 51	Revelation 21
☐	20	Deuteronomy 25	Psalm 116	Isaiah 52	Revelation 22
☐	21	Deuteronomy 26	Psalms 117-118	Isaiah 53	Matthew 1
☐	22	Deuteronomy 27-28:19	Psalm 119:1-24	Isaiah 54	Matthew 2
☐	23	Deuteronomy 28:20ff	Psalm 119:25-48	Isaiah 55	Matthew 3
☐	24	Deuteronomy 29	Psalm 119:49-72	Isaiah 56	Matthew 4
☐	25	Deuteronomy 30	Psalm 119:73-96	Isaiah 57	Matthew 5
☐	26	Deuteronomy 31	Psalm 119:97-120	Isaiah 58	Matthew 6
☐	27	Deuteronomy 32	Psalm 119:121-144	Isaiah 59	Matthew 7
☐	28	Deuteronomy 33-34	Psalm 119:145-176	Isaiah 60	Matthew 8
☐	29	Joshua 1	Psalms 120-122	Isaiah 61	Matthew 9
☐	30	Joshua 2	Psalms 123-125	Isaiah 62	Matthew 10

JULY

They received the word with eagerness and examined the Scriptures daily to see if these things were so. Acts 17:11

DATE	READING			
☐ 1	Joshua 3	Psalms 126-128	Isaiah 63	Matthew 11
☐ 2	Joshua 4	Psalms 129-131	Isaiah 64	Matthew 12
☐ 3	Joshua 5-6:5	Psalms 132-134	Isaiah 65	Matthew 13
☐ 4	Joshua 6:6ff	Psalms 135-136	Isaiah 66	Matthew 14
☐ 5	Joshua 7	Psalms 137-138	Jeremiah 1	Matthew 15
☐ 6	Joshua 8	Psalm 139	Jeremiah 2	Matthew 16
☐ 7	Joshua 9	Psalms 140-141	Jeremiah 3	Matthew 17
☐ 8	Joshua 10	Psalms 142-143	Jeremiah 4	Matthew 18
☐ 9	Joshua 11	Psalm 144	Jeremiah 5	Matthew 19
☐ 10	Joshua 12-13	Psalm 145	Jeremiah 6	Matthew 20
☐ 11	Joshua 14-15	Psalms 146-147	Jeremiah 7	Matthew 21
☐ 12	Joshua 16-17	Psalms 148	Jeremiah 8	Matthew 22
☐ 13	Joshua 18-19	Psalms 149-150	Jeremiah 9	Matthew 23
☐ 14	Joshua 20-21	Acts 1	Jeremiah 10	Matthew 24
☐ 15	Joshua 22	Acts 2	Jeremiah 11	Matthew 25
☐ 16	Joshua 23	Acts 3	Jeremiah 12	Matthew 26
☐ 17	Joshua 24	Acts 4	Jeremiah 13	Matthew 27
☐ 18	Judges 1	Acts 5	Jeremiah 14	Matthew 28
☐ 19	Judges 2	Acts 6	Jeremiah 15	Mark 1
☐ 20	Judges 3	Acts 7	Jeremiah 16	Mark 2
☐ 21	Judges 4	Acts 8	Jeremiah 17	Mark 3
☐ 22	Judges 5	Acts 9	Jeremiah 18	Mark 4
☐ 23	Judges 6	Acts 10	Jeremiah 19	Mark 5
☐ 24	Judges 7	Acts 11	Jeremiah 20	Mark 6
☐ 25	Judges 8	Acts 12	Jeremiah 21	Mark 7
☐ 26	Judges 9	Acts 13	Jeremiah 22	Mark 8
☐ 27	Judges 10-11:11	Acts 14	Jeremiah 23	Mark 9
☐ 28	Judges 11:12ff	Acts 15	Jeremiah 24	Mark 10
☐ 29	Judges 12	Acts 16	Jeremiah 25	Mark 11
☐ 30	Judges 13	Acts 17	Jeremiah 26	Mark 12
☐ 31	Judges 14	Acts 18	Jeremiah 27	Mark 13

AUGUST

Speak, for your servant is listening. 1 Samuel 3:10

DATE	READING			
☐ 1	Judges 15	Acts 19	Jeremiah 28	Mark 14
☐ 2	Judges 16	Acts 20	Jeremiah 29	Mark 15
☐ 3	Judges 17	Acts 21	Jeremiah 30-31	Mark 16
☐ 4	Judges 18	Acts 22	Jeremiah 32	Psalms 1-2
☐ 5	Judges 19	Acts 23	Jeremiah 33	Psalms 3-4
☐ 6	Judges 20	Acts 24	Jeremiah 34	Psalms 5-6
☐ 7	Judges 21	Acts 25	Jeremiah 35	Psalms 7-8
☐ 8	Ruth 1	Acts 26	Jeremiah 36	Psalm 9
☐ 9	Ruth 2	Acts 27	Jeremiah 37	Psalm 10
☐ 10	Ruth 3-4	Acts 28	Jeremiah 38	Psalms 11-12
☐ 11	1 Samuel 1	Romans 1	Jeremiah 39	Psalms 13-14
☐ 12	1 Samuel 2	Romans 2	Jeremiah 40	Psalms 15-16
☐ 13	1 Samuel 3	Romans 3	Jeremiah 41	Psalm 17

☐	14	1 Samuel 4	Romans 4	Jeremiah 42	Psalm 18
☐	15	1 Samuel 5-6	Romans 5	Jeremiah 43	Psalm 19
☐	16	1 Samuel 7-8	Romans 6	Jeremiah 44-45	Psalms 20-21
☐	17	1 Samuel 9	Romans 7	Jeremiah 46	Psalm 22
☐	18	1 Samuel 10	Romans 8	Jeremiah 47	Psalms 23-24
☐	19	1 Samuel 11	Romans 9	Jeremiah 48	Psalm 25
☐	20	1 Samuel 12	Romans 10	Jeremiah 49	Psalms 26-27
☐	21	1 Samuel 13	Romans 11	Jeremiah 50	Psalms 28-29
☐	22	1 Samuel 14	Romans 12	Jeremiah 51	Psalm 30
☐	23	1 Samuel 15	Romans 13	Jeremiah 52	Psalm 31
☐	24	1 Samuel 16	Romans 14	Lamentations 1	Psalm 32
☐	25	1 Samuel 17	Romans 15	Lamentations 2	Psalm 33
☐	26	1 Samuel 18	Romans 16	Lamentations 3	Psalm 34
☐	27	1 Samuel 19	1 Corinthians 1	Lamentations 4	Psalm 35
☐	28	1 Samuel 20	1 Corinthians 2	Lamentations 5	Psalm 36
☐	29	1 Samuel 21-22	1 Corinthians 3	Ezekiel 1	Psalm 37
☐	30	1 Samuel 23	1 Corinthians 4	Ezekiel 2	Psalm 38
☐	31	1 Samuel 24	1 Corinthians 5	Ezekiel 3	Psalm 39

SEPTEMBER

The instruction of the LORD is perfect, renewing one's life. Psalm 19:7

DATE		READING			
☐	1	1 Samuel 25	1 Corinthians 6	Ezekiel 4	Psalms 40-41
☐	2	1 Samuel 26	1 Corinthians 7	Ezekiel 5	Psalms 42-43
☐	3	1 Samuel 27	1 Corinthians 8	Ezekiel 6	Psalm 44
☐	4	1 Samuel 28	1 Corinthians 9	Ezekiel 7	Psalm 45
☐	5	1 Samuel 29-30	1 Corinthians 10	Ezekiel 8	Psalms 46-47
☐	6	1 Samuel 31	1 Corinthians 11	Ezekiel 9	Psalm 48
☐	7	2 Samuel 1	1 Corinthians 12	Ezekiel 10	Psalm 49
☐	8	2 Samuel 2	1 Corinthians 13	Ezekiel 11	Psalm 50
☐	9	2 Samuel 3	1 Corinthians 14	Ezekiel 12	Psalm 51
☐	10	2 Samuel 4-5	1 Corinthians 15	Ezekiel 13	Psalms 52-54
☐	11	2 Samuel 6	1 Corinthians 16	Ezekiel 14	Psalm 55
☐	12	2 Samuel 7	2 Corinthians 1	Ezekiel 15	Psalms 56-57
☐	13	2 Samuel 8-9	2 Corinthians 2	Ezekiel 16	Psalms 58-59
☐	14	2 Samuel 10	2 Corinthians 3	Ezekiel 17	Psalms 60-61
☐	15	2 Samuel 11	2 Corinthians 4	Ezekiel 18	Psalms 62-63
☐	16	2 Samuel 12	2 Corinthians 5	Ezekiel 19	Psalms 64-65
☐	17	2 Samuel 13	2 Corinthians 6	Ezekiel 20	Psalms 66-67
☐	18	2 Samuel 14	2 Corinthians 7	Ezekiel 21	Psalm 68
☐	19	2 Samuel 15	2 Corinthians 8	Ezekiel 22	Psalm 69
☐	20	2 Samuel 16	2 Corinthians 9	Ezekiel 23	Psalms 70-71
☐	21	2 Samuel 17	2 Corinthians 10	Ezekiel 24	Psalm 72
☐	22	2 Samuel 18	2 Corinthians 11	Ezekiel 25	Psalm 73
☐	23	2 Samuel 19	2 Corinthians 12	Ezekiel 26	Psalm 74
☐	24	2 Samuel 20	2 Corinthians 13	Ezekiel 27	Psalms 75-76
☐	25	2 Samuel 21	Galatians 1	Ezekiel 28	Psalm 77
☐	26	2 Samuel 22	Galatians 2	Ezekiel 29	Psalm 78:1-37
☐	27	2 Samuel 23	Galatians 3	Ezekiel 30	Psalm 78:38ff
☐	28	2 Samuel 24	Galatians 4	Ezekiel 31	Psalm 79
☐	29	1 Kings 1	Galatians 5	Ezekiel 32	Psalm 80
☐	30	1 Kings 2	Galatians 6	Ezekiel 33	Psalms 81-82

OCTOBER

How I love your instruction! It is my meditation all day long. Psalm 119:97

DATE	READING			
☐ 1	1 Kings 3	Ephesians 1	Ezekiel 34	Psalms 83-84
☐ 2	1 Kings 4-5	Ephesians 2	Ezekiel 35	Psalm 85
☐ 3	1 Kings 6	Ephesians 3	Ezekiel 36	Psalm 86
☐ 4	1 Kings 7	Ephesians 4	Ezekiel 37	Psalms 87-88
☐ 5	1 Kings 8	Ephesians 5	Ezekiel 38	Psalm 89
☐ 6	1 Kings 9	Ephesians 6	Ezekiel 39	Psalm 90
☐ 7	1 Kings 10	Philippians 1	Ezekiel 40	Psalm 91
☐ 8	1 Kings 11	Philippians 2	Ezekiel 41	Psalms 92-93
☐ 9	1 Kings 12	Philippians 3	Ezekiel 42	Psalm 94
☐ 10	1 Kings 13	Philippians 4	Ezekiel 43	Psalms 95-96
☐ 11	1 Kings 14	Colossians 1	Ezekiel 44	Psalms 97-98
☐ 12	1 Kings 15	Colossians 2	Ezekiel 45	Psalms 99-101
☐ 13	1 Kings 16	Colossians 3	Ezekiel 46	Psalm 102
☐ 14	1 Kings 17	Colossians 4	Ezekiel 47	Psalm 103
☐ 15	1 Kings 18	1 Thessalonians 1	Ezekiel 48	Psalm 104
☐ 16	1 Kings 19	1 Thessalonians 2	Daniel 1	Psalm 105
☐ 17	1 Kings 20	1 Thessalonians 3	Daniel 2	Psalm 106
☐ 18	1 Kings 21	1 Thessalonians 4	Daniel 3	Psalm 107
☐ 19	1 Kings 22	1 Thessalonians 5	Daniel 4	Psalms 108-109
☐ 20	2 Kings 1	2 Thessalonians 1	Daniel 5	Psalms 110-111
☐ 21	2 Kings 2	2 Thessalonians 2	Daniel 6	Psalms 112-113
☐ 22	2 Kings 3	2 Thessalonians 3	Daniel 7	Psalms 114-115
☐ 23	2 Kings 4	1 Timothy 1	Daniel 8	Psalm 116
☐ 24	2 Kings 5	1 Timothy 2	Daniel 9	Psalms 117-118
☐ 25	2 Kings 6	1 Timothy 3	Daniel 10	Psalm 119:1-24
☐ 26	2 Kings 7	1 Timothy 4	Daniel 11	Psalm 119:25-48
☐ 27	2 Kings 8	1 Timothy 5	Daniel 12	Psalm 119:49-72
☐ 28	2 Kings 9	1 Timothy 6	Hosea 1	Psalm 119:73-96
☐ 29	2 Kings 10	2 Timothy 1	Hosea 2	Psalm 119:97-120
☐ 30	2 Kings 11-12	2 Timothy 2	Hosea 3-4	Psalm 119:121-144
☐ 31	2 Kings 13	2 Timothy 3	Hosea 5-6	Psalm 119:145-176

NOVEMBER

Like newborn infants, desire the pure milk of the word, so that you may grow up into your salvation.
1 Peter 2:2

DATE	READING			
☐ 1	2 Kings 14	2 Timothy 4	Hosea 7	Psalms 120-122
☐ 2	2 Kings 15	Titus 1	Hosea 8	Psalms 123-125
☐ 3	2 Kings 16	Titus 2	Hosea 9	Psalms 126-128
☐ 4	2 Kings 17	Titus 3	Hosea 10	Psalms 129-131
☐ 5	2 Kings 18	Philemon	Hosea 11	Psalms 132-134
☐ 6	2 Kings 19	Hebrews 1	Hosea 12	Psalms 135-136
☐ 7	2 Kings 20	Hebrews 2	Hosea 13	Psalms 137-138
☐ 8	2 Kings 21	Hebrews 3	Hosea 14	Psalm 139
☐ 9	2 Kings 22	Hebrews 4	Joel 1	Psalms 140-141
☐ 10	2 Kings 23	Hebrews 5	Joel 2	Psalm 142
☐ 11	2 Kings 24	Hebrews 6	Joel 3	Psalm 143

☐	12	2 Kings 25	Hebrews 7	Amos 1	Psalm 144
☐	13	1 Chronicles 1-2	Hebrews 8	Amos 2	Psalm 145
☐	14	1 Chronicles 3-4	Hebrews 9	Amos 3	Psalms 146-147
☐	15	1 Chronicles 5-6	Hebrews 10	Amos 4	Psalms 148-150
☐	16	1 Chronicles 7-8	Hebrews 11	Amos 5	Luke 1:1-38
☐	17	1 Chronicles 9-10	Hebrews 12	Amos 6	Luke 1:39ff
☐	18	1 Chronicles 11-12	Hebrews 13	Amos 7	Luke 2
☐	19	1 Chronicles 13-14	James 1	Amos 8	Luke 3
☐	20	1 Chronicles 15	James 2	Amos 9	Luke 4
☐	21	1 Chronicles 16	James 3	Obadiah	Luke 5
☐	22	1 Chronicles 17	James 4	Jonah 1	Luke 6
☐	23	1 Chronicles 18	James 5	Jonah 2	Luke 7
☐	24	1 Chronicles 19-20	1 Peter 1	Jonah 3	Luke 8
☐	25	1 Chronicles 21	1 Peter 2	Jonah 4	Luke 9
☐	26	1 Chronicles 22	1 Peter 3	Micah 1	Luke 10
☐	27	1 Chronicles 23	1 Peter 4	Micah 2	Luke 11
☐	28	1 Chronicles 24-25	1 Peter 5	Micah 3	Luke 12
☐	29	1 Chronicles 26-27	2 Peter 1	Micah 4	Luke 13
☐	30	1 Chronicles 28	2 Peter 2	Micah 5	Luke 14

DECEMBER

The instruction of his God is in his heart; his steps do not falter. Psalm 37:31

	DATE	READING			
☐	1	1 Chronicles 29	2 Peter 3	Micah 6	Luke 15
☐	2	2 Chronicles 1	1 John 1	Micah 7	Luke 16
☐	3	2 Chronicles 2	1 John 2	Nahum 1	Luke 17
☐	4	2 Chronicles 3-4	1 John 3	Nahum 2	Luke 18
☐	5	2 Chronicles 5-6:11	1 John 4	Nahum 3	Luke 19
☐	6	2 Chronicles 6:12ff	1 John 5	Habakkuk 1	Luke 20
☐	7	2 Chronicles 7	2 John	Habakkuk 2	Luke 21
☐	8	2 Chronicles 8	3 John	Habakkuk 3	Luke 22
☐	9	2 Chronicles 9	Jude	Zephaniah 1	Luke 23
☐	10	2 Chronicles 10	Revelation 1	Zephaniah 2	Luke 24
☐	11	2 Chronicles 11-12	Revelation 2	Zephaniah 3	John 1
☐	12	2 Chronicles 13	Revelation 3	Haggai 1	John 2
☐	13	2 Chronicles 14-15	Revelation 4	Haggai 2	John 3
☐	14	2 Chronicles 16	Revelation 5	Zechariah 1	John 4
☐	15	2 Chronicles 17	Revelation 6	Zechariah 2	John 5
☐	16	2 Chronicles 18	Revelation 7	Zechariah 3	John 6
☐	17	2 Chronicles 19-20	Revelation 8	Zechariah 4	John 7
☐	18	2 Chronicles 21	Revelation 9	Zechariah 5	John 8
☐	19	2 Chronicles 22-23	Revelation 10	Zechariah 6	John 9
☐	20	2 Chronicles 24	Revelation 11	Zechariah 7	John 10
☐	21	2 Chronicles 25	Revelation 12	Zechariah 8	John 11
☐	22	2 Chronicles 26	Revelation 13	Zechariah 9	John 12
☐	23	2 Chronicles 27-28	Revelation 14	Zechariah 10	John 13
☐	24	2 Chronicles 29	Revelation 15	Zechariah 11	John 14
☐	25	2 Chronicles 30	Revelation 16	Zechariah 12:1-13:1	John 15
☐	26	2 Chronicles 31	Revelation 17	Zechariah 13:2ff	John 16
☐	27	2 Chronicles 32	Revelation 18	Zechariah 14	John 17
☐	28	2 Chronicles 33	Revelation 19	Malachi 1	John 18
☐	29	2 Chronicles 34	Revelation 20	Malachi 2	John 19
☐	30	2 Chronicles 35	Revelation 21	Malachi 3	John 20
☐	31	2 Chronicles 36	Revelation 22	Malachi 4	John 21

TOPICAL INDEX

2216

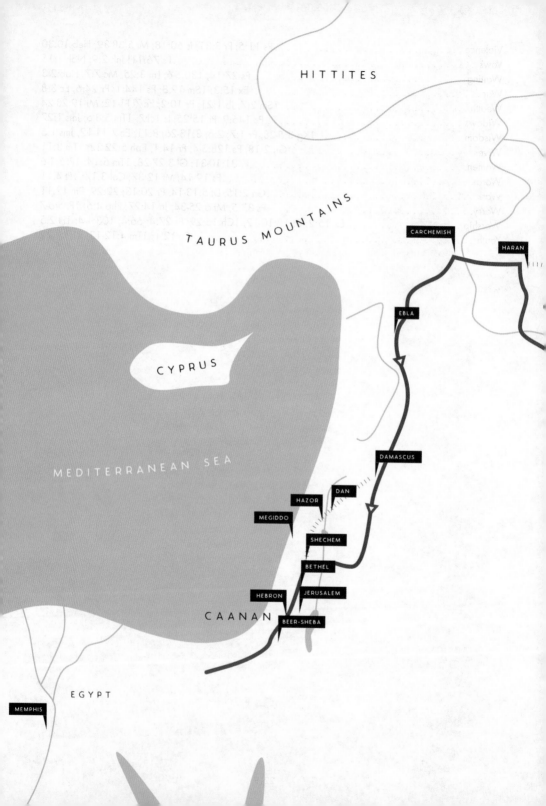

MT. ARARAT ▲

URARTU MOUNTAINS

CASPIAN SEA

ELBURZ MOUNTAINS

TIGRIS RIVER

NINEVEH

ASSHUR

ZAGROS MOUNTAINS

EUPHRATES RIVER

BABYLON

YAMUTBAL

SUSA

ELAM

UR

ABRAHAM'S MIGRATION
TO CANAAN

ABRAHAM'S MIGRATION ROUTE ▬▬

ABRAHAM'S ALTERNATIVE MIGRATION ROUTE | | | | |

MEDITERRANEAN SEA

ABILENE

SIDON

DAMASCUS

ITUREA

CAESAREA PHILIPPI

TYRE

PHOENICIA

BATANEA

TRACHONITIS

CAPERNAUM

GALILEE

SEA OF GALILEE

NAZARETH

AURANITIS

CAESAREA MARITIMA

JORDAN RIVER

SAMARIA

DECAPOLIS

PEREA

EMMAUS

JUDEA

JERUSALEM

BETHANY

GAZA

DEAD SEA

IDUMEA

BEER-SHEBA

ISRAEL IN JESUS' TIME

FIRST PROCURATORSHIP

TERRITORY OF ANTIPAS

SYRIAN TERRITORY

TERRITORY OF PHILLIP

MAJOR ROADS

OTHER ROADS

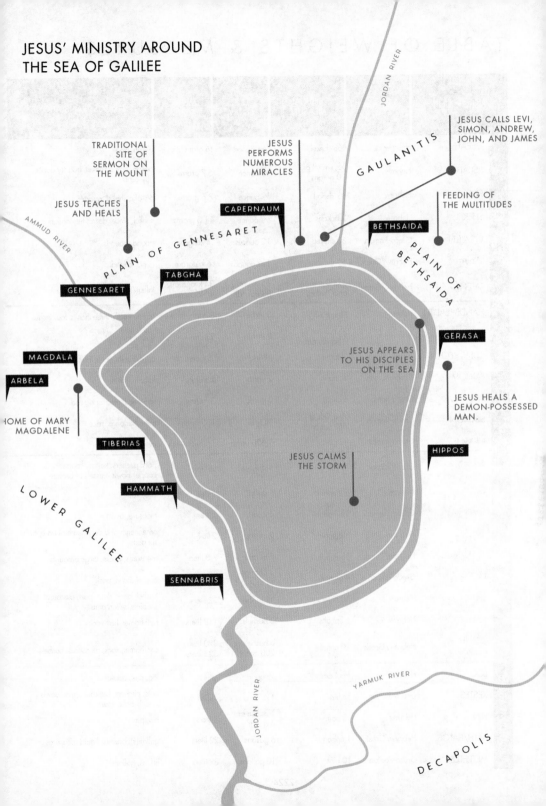

JESUS' MINISTRY AROUND
THE SEA OF GALILEE

JORDAN RIVER

TRADITIONAL
SITE OF
SERMON ON
THE MOUNT

JESUS
PERFORMS
NUMEROUS
MIRACLES

JESUS CALLS LEVI,
SIMON, ANDREW,
JOHN, AND JAMES

GAULANITIS

JESUS TEACHES
AND HEALS

CAPERNAUM

FEEDING OF
THE MULTITUDES

AMMUD RIVER

BETHSAIDA

PLAIN OF GENNESARET

PLAIN OF
BETHSAIDA

TABGHA

GENNESARET

GERASA

MAGDALA

JESUS APPEARS
TO HIS DISCIPLES
ON THE SEA

ARBELA

JESUS HEALS A
DEMON-POSSESSED
MAN.

HOME OF MARY
MAGDALENE

TIBERIAS

JESUS CALMS
THE STORM

HIPPOS

HAMMATH

LOWER GALILEE

SENNABRIS

JORDAN RIVER

YARMUK RIVER

DECAPOLIS

TABLE OF WEIGHTS & MEASURES

	BIBLICAL UNIT	LANGUAGE	BIBLICAL MEASURE	U.S. EQUIV.	METRIC EQUIV.	VARIOUS TRANSLATIONS
WEIGHT	GERAH	Hebrew	1/20 shekel	1/50 ounce	.6 gram	gerah, oboli
	BEKAH	Hebrew	1/2 shekel or 10 gerahs	1/5 ounce	5.7 grams	bekah, half a shekel, quarter ounce, fifty cents
	PIM	Hebrew	2/3 shekel	1/3 ounce	7.6 grams	2/3 of a shekel, quarter
	SHEKEL	Hebrew	2 bekahs	2/5 ounce	11.5 grams	shekel, piece, dollar, fifty dollars
	LITRA (LB)	Greco-Roman	30 shekels	12 ounces	.4 kilogram	pound, pounds
	MINA	Hebrew/Greek	50 shekels	1¼ pounds	.6 kilogram	mina, pound
	TALENT	Hebrew/Greek	3,000 shekels or 60 minas	75 pounds/ 88 pounds	34 kilograms/ 40 kilograms	talent/talents, 100 pounds
LENGTH	HANDBREADTH	Hebrew	1/6 cubit or 1/3 span	3 inches	8 cm	handbreadth, three inches, four inches
	SPAN	Hebrew	1/2 cubit or 3 handbreaths	9 inches	23 cm	span
	CUBIT/PECHYS	Hebrew/Greek	2 spans	18 inches	.5 meter	cubit/cubits, yard, half a yard, foot
	FATHOM	Greco-Roman	4 cubits	2 yards	2 meters	fathom, six feet
	KALAMOS	Greco-Roman	6 cubits	3 yards	3 meters	rod, reed, measuring rod
	STADION	Greco-Roman	1/8 milion or 400 cubits	1/8 mile	185 meters	miles, furlongs, race
	MILION	Greco-Roman	8 stadia	1,620 yards	1.5 kilometers	mile
DRY MEASURE	XESTES	Greco-Roman	1/2 cab	1⅙ pints	.5 liter	pots, pitchers, kettles, copper pots, copper bowls, vessels of bronze
	CAB	Hebrew	1/18 ephah	1 quart	1 liter	cab, kab
	CHOINIX	Greco-Roman	1/18 ephah	1 quart	1 liter	measure, quart
	OMER	Hebrew	1/10 ephah	2 quarts	2 liters	omer, tenth of a deal, tenth of an ephah, six pints
	SEAH/SATON	Hebrew/Greek	1/3 ephah	7 quarts	7.3 liters	measures, pecks, large amounts
	MODIOS	Greco-Roman	4 omers	1 peck or ¼ bushel	9 liters	bushel, bowl, peck
	EPHAH (BATH)	Hebrew	10 omers	3/5 bushel	22 liters	bushel, peck, deal, part, measure, six pints, seven pints
	LETHEK	Hebrew	5 ephahs	3 bushels	110 liters	half homer, half sack
	KOR (HOMER)/ KOROS	Hebrew/Greek	10 ephahs	6 bushels or 200 quarts	220 liters/ 525 liters	cor, homer, sack, measures, bushels
LIQUID MEASURE	LOG	Hebrew	1/72 bath	1/3 quart	.3 liter	log, pint, cotulus
	XESTES	Greco-Roman	1/8 hin	1⅙ pints	.5 liter	pots, pitchers, kettles, copper bowls, vessels of bronze
	HIN	Hebrew	1/6 bath	1 gallon or 4 quarts	4 liters	hin, pints
	BATH/BATOS	Hebrew/Greek	1 ephah	6 gallons	22 liters	gallon(s), barrels, liquid measures
	METRETES	Greco-Roman	10 hins	10 gallons	39 liters	firkins, gallons

CONTRIBUTORS

EDITORIAL STAFF

Raechel Myers, General Editor
Amanda Bible Williams, General Editor

Trevin Wax, PhD., Publisher
Melissa Fuller, Managing Editor

Theological Oversight:
Russ Ramsey, MDiv., ThM.
Doug Powell, M.A., Christian Apologetics
Steve Bond, PhD.
Nate Shurden, MDiv.

Reading Plans and Key Verses:
Russ Ramsey, MDiv., ThM.
George Grant, MDiv., PhD.
Nate Shurden, MDiv.

DESIGN STAFF

Ryan Myers, Creative Director
Amanda Barnhart, Art Director
Katie B. DeSouza, Project Manager

Charts:
Amanda Barnhart

Timelines:
Katie B. DeSouza and Kelsea Allen

Maps:
Caleb Faires: 148, 402, 452, 1636, 1694, 1844-1845, 1900, 1954, 1972, 1986, 1998, 2010
Ryan Myers: 84, 192, 310, 496, 548, 702, 722, 752-753, 2220-2221, 2222, 2223

Key Verse Art:
Kaydi Bishop: 2040, 2052
Nick Fredrickson: 700, 720, 750, 2148
Melissa Giglio: 390, 2114, 2128
Patrick Laurent: 1492, 1602
Dan Lee: 1100, 1220, 1332, 1354, 1434, 1524, 1580
Emily Lex: 1466, 2102, 2160
Fred Rodriguez: 400, 450, 494, 546, 594, 644, 1624
Carrie Shryock: 388, 1542, 1970, 1984, 1996, 2008
Christopher Vinca: 2, 82, 146, 190, 252, 350, 1504, 2168
Megan Wells: 1558, 1592
Jen Wick: 830, 2136, 2154
Cymone Wilder: 308, 1466, 1532, 1568, 1842, 2020, 2040, 2052, 2078, 2102, 2114, 2128, 2160
Eva Winters: 770, 1000, 1064, 1082, 1898, 1926, 1952, 2020, 2032, 2062, 2070
Chris Wright: 1634, 1692, 1730, 1792

DEVOTIONAL CONTENT STAFF

Raechel Myers, General Editor
Amanda Bible Williams, General Editor
Melissa Fuller, Managing Editor
Erin Davis, Project Manager, Editor
Kara Gause, Editor
Russ Ramsey, Editor

Devotional Writers:

Ali Claxton: 216, 386, 829, 873, 965, 1071, 1359, 1620, 1727, 1758, 2198

Jess Connolly: 729, 1703

Erin Davis: 18, 72, 104, 177, 257, 313, 427, 440, 463, 534, 541, 686, 727, 866, 1017, 1080, 1088, 1106, 1529, 1618, 1722, 1776, 1785, 1788, 1802, 1825, 1840, 1849, 1884, 1932, 1948, 1967, 1990, 2067, 2153, 2159, 2180

Annie Downs: 88

Debbie Eaton: 2013

Rebecca Faires: 22, 101, 231, 303, 393, 399, 456, 504, 607, 630, 756, 759, 763, 855, 942, 1061, 1097, 1196, 1287, 1338, 1444, 1484, 1514, 1537, 1539, 1563, 1588, 1598, 1612, 1668, 1763, 1980, 2001, 2038, 2099, 2143

Melissa Fuller: 341, 414, 562, 642, 845, 1282, 1640, 1852, 1916, 2141

Carrie Gaul: 1697, 1905, 2133

Betsy Gomez: 1598

Liz Curtis Higgs: 530

Ellie Holcomb: 2016

Andrea Lucado: 125, 267, 395, 659, 837, 989, 1125, 1412, 1687, 1805, 1874, 2048, 2059, 2195

Jill McDaniel: 708, 842, 1006, 1920

Jessie Minassian: 42, 171, 1477, 1859, 2165

Raechel Myers: 9, 11, 33, 49, 114, 378, 725, 748, 860, 977, 1056, 1071, 1175, 1345, 1440, 1456, 1479, 1499, 1576, 1648, 1673, 2026, 2069, 2076, 2094, 2107, 2119, 2176

Kaitlin Wernet: 326 554, 677, 775, 869, 907, 1263, 1554, 1713, 1738, 1798, 2046

Amanda Bible Williams: 319, 405, 541, 767, 797, 893, 898, 983, 1006, 1071, 1271, 1447, 1620, 1631, 1673, 1814, 1829, 1837, 1912, 1961, 1976, 1994, 2005, 2029, 2076, 2084, 2087, 2110, 2123, 2125, 2176

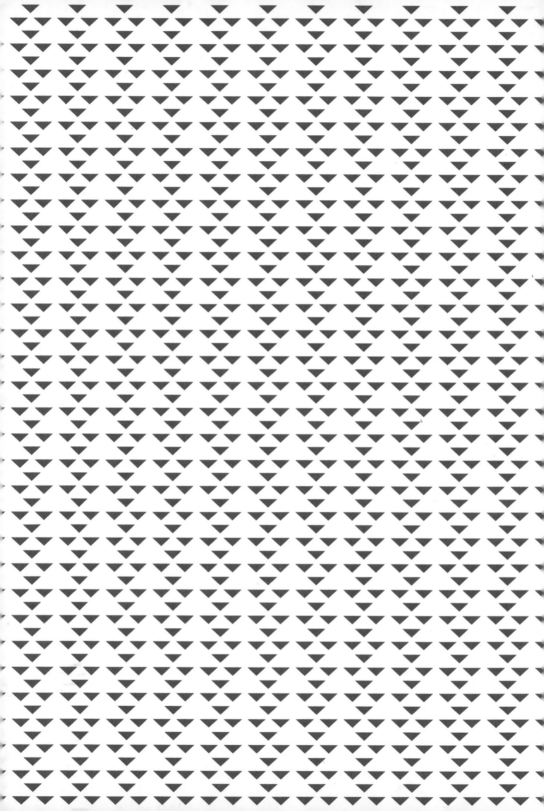